This edition first published in the USA in 1995 by Motorbooks International Publishers & Wholesalers, PO Box 2, 729 Prospect Avenue, Osceola, WI 54020 USA

© Peter Higham and Guinness Publishing 1995

Previously published by Guinness Publishing Ltd, 33 London Road, Enfield, Middlesex, UK

Library of Congress Cataloging in Publication Data Available

ISBN 0-7603-0152-2

Printed and bound in Great Britain

All photographs courtesy of **Autosport Photographic** bar the following:
pp 9, 207, 284, 380 **Alfa Romeo**; pp 193, 196, 198, 205, 382, 406, 421, 467, 481, 507 **Daimler-Benz Archive**;
p 315 **Galmer Engineering**; p 333 **Jeff Hutchinson**; p 336 **Bryn Williams**

THE GUINNESS GUIDE
TO
INTERNATIONAL MOTOR RACING

A Complete Reference
from Formula One
to Touring Cars

Peter Higham

Motorbooks International
Publishers & Wholesalers ®

Damon Hill leads Michael Schumacher during the 1994 British Grand Prix

RULES

CARS

1950-51 4500 cc normally aspirated and 1500 cc supercharged maximum engine capacity

1952-53 World Championship races were for Formula Two as there were not enough competitive F1 cars at the time. 2000 cc normally aspirated and 500 cc supercharged maximum engine capacity

1954-57 2500 cc normally aspirated and 750 cc supercharged maximum engine capacity

1958-60 Maximum engine capacity unchanged, commercial fuel compulsory

1961-65 1300 cc minimum and 1500 cc maximum engine capacity. No supercharged engines. Commercial fuel remained compulsory. 450 kg minimum dry weight. Oil could not be replaced during the race. Roll-over bar compulsory. Bodywork not allowed to enclose the wheels

1966-68 3000 cc normally aspirated and 1500 cc supercharged or turbocharged maximum engine capacity. 500 kg minimum dry weight

1969-71 Maximum engine capacity unchanged. 530 kg minimum dry weight

1972 Maximum engine capacity unchanged. Maximum of 12 cylinders. 550 kg minimum dry weight

1973-82 Maximum engine capacity unchanged. 575 kg minimum dry weight

1983-85 Maximum engine capacity unchanged. 575 kg minimum dry weight. Flat underside to the car mandatory

1986 1500 cc supercharged or turbocharged maximum engine capacity. 575 kg minimum dry weight

1987-88 3500 cc normally aspirated and 1500 cc supercharged or turbocharged maximum engine capacity

1989-94 3500 cc normally aspirated maximum engine capacity

1994 3500 cc normally aspirated maximum engine capacity. Revised aerodynamic and airbox rules introduced during season to improve safety. Underside of car had a 10 cm stepped flat bottom from German GP

RACE DISTANCES

1950-57 Over 300 kms or three hours

1958-65 Minimum between 300 and 500 kms or two hours

1966-70 Minimum between 300 and 400 kms

1971 to date Maximum of 325 kms

POINTS

1950-57 8-6-4-3-2 points awarded to the top five finishers plus one extra point awarded for fastest lap. Drivers were allowed to share cars, the points being divided accordingly

1958-59 8-6-4-3-2 points awarded to the top five finishers plus one extra point awarded for fastest lap. No shared drives allowed

1960 8-6-4-3-2-1 points awarded to the top six finishers, no extra point for fastest lap

1961-90 9-6-4-3-2-1 points awarded to the top six finishers

1991 to date 10-6-4-3-2-1 points awarded to the top six finishers

WHAT IS A GRAND PRIX START?

Those who may be worried about whether Alain Prost has started 199 or 200 Grands Prix are questioning when a driver should be credited with starting a Grand Prix.

Various sources have various definitions, resulting in minor but annoying discrepancies in the number of events competed in by Jarier, Laffite and the aforementioned Prost, to name but three. For the record I have credited a driver as starting by the following definition:

A driver who was on the grid (or in the pits prior to making a delayed entrance) when the original signal to start was given, or who joined at any subsequent restart.

The only exception relates to cars being used to make a Grand Prix movie (See Grand Prix racing and Hollywood below).

Therefore, if a driver was eliminated in a startline shunt which stopped the event and prevented him from taking the restart, he is still credited with starting that Grand Prix. This means that Mike Thackwell, who was prevented from taking the restart of the Canadian GP in 1980, did start and is therefore the youngest driver to participate in a World Championship Grand Prix. Also, Niki Lauda did race at the Nürburgring in 1976, albeit with near-fatal consequences.

The fields in some races - namely the 1958 Moroccan and 1957-58, 1966-67 and 1969 German Grands Prix - were bolstered by adding a concurrent F2 event. Although the F2 drivers did not qualify for the overall results, they are credited as having started the Grand Prix.

Finally, if a driver fails to complete the warm-up or parade lap he has not started the event. This happened to Alain Prost at the 1991 San Marino GP, hence the confusion over his number of starts.

INDIANAPOLIS 500

The Indy 500 was a round of the World Championship from 1950 to 1960. Its inclusion, however, had little effect other than to confuse. Only Alberto Ascari of the top European drivers raced at the Brickyard, failing to finish the 1952 race. I have included the top six results from the World Championship years of the Indy 500 as well as its drivers in the year-end series positions to provide the full Championship story. However, to avoid distorting the Grand Prix records I have omitted it from the records section, and from the driver summary at the conclusion of each year.

SHARED DRIVES

If a driver is classified twice in a race, the better result is given in the Drivers' Records table unless he has been classified twice in the top six in that event or if it was achieved in different types of cars where both are registered.

Those driving camera cars for films but not competing in the race are not credited with a GP start.

A brief explanation of the race results tables is perhaps necessary. The first column refers to the position in which the driver finished the race, the second is his or her name, the third is the car, the fourth the number of laps completed. The final column is time or, if applicable, the reason why the driver did not finish the race. Race times are only given for drivers finishing on the lead lap.

WORLD CHAMPIONS

	Drivers' Championship			Constructors' Cup
year	driver	nat	car	constructor
1950	Giuseppe Farina	I	Alfa Romeo 158/Alfa Romeo 159	-
1951	Juan Manuel Fangio	RA	Alfa Romeo 159	-
1952	Alberto Ascari	I	Ferrari 500	-
1953	Alberto Ascari	I	Ferrari 500	-
1954	Juan Manuel Fangio	RA	Maserati 250F/Mercedes-Benz W196	-
1955	Juan Manuel Fangio	RA	Mercedes-Benz W196	-
1956	Juan Manuel Fangio	RA	Lancia-Ferrari D50	-
1957	Juan Manuel Fangio	RA	Maserati 250F	-
1958	Mike Hawthorn	GB	Ferrari Dino 246	Vanwall
1959	Jack Brabham	AUS	Cooper T51-Climax	Cooper-Climax
1960	Jack Brabham	AUS	Cooper T53-Climax	Cooper-Climax
1961	Phil Hill	USA	Ferrari Dino 156	Ferrari
1962	Graham Hill	GB	BRM P57	BRM
1963	Jim Clark	GB	Lotus 25-Climax	Lotus-Climax
1964	John Surtees	GB	Ferrari 158	Ferrari
1965	Jim Clark	GB	Lotus 33-Climax	Lotus-Climax
1966	Jack Brabham	AUS	Brabham BT19-Repco/Brabham BT20-Repco	Brabham-Repco
1967	Denny Hulme	NZ	Brabham BT20-Repco/Brabham BT24-Repco	Brabham-Repco
1968	Graham Hill	GB	Lotus 49-Ford/Lotus 49B-Ford	Lotus-Ford
1969	Jackie Stewart	GB	Matra MS10-Ford/Matra MS80-Ford	Matra-Ford
1970	Jochen Rindt	A	Lotus 49C-Ford/Lotus 72-Ford	Lotus-Ford
1971	Jackie Stewart	GB	Tyrrell 001-Ford/Tyrrell 003-Ford	Tyrrell-Ford
1972	Emerson Fittipaldi	BR	Lotus 72-Ford	Lotus-Ford
1973	Jackie Stewart	GB	Tyrrell 005-Ford/Tyrrell 006-Ford	Lotus-Ford
1974	Emerson Fittipaldi	BR	McLaren M23-Ford	McLaren-Ford
1975	Niki Lauda	A	Ferrari 312T	Ferrari
1976	James Hunt	GB	McLaren M23-Ford	Ferrari
1977	Niki Lauda	A	Ferrari 312T2	Ferrari
1978	Mario Andretti	USA	Lotus 78-Ford/Lotus 79-Ford	Lotus-Ford
1979	Jody Scheckter	ZA	Ferrari 312T3/Ferrari 312T4	Ferrari
1980	Alan Jones	AUS	Williams FW07B-Ford	Williams-Ford
1981	Nelson Piquet	BR	Brabham BT49C-Ford	Williams-Ford
1982	Keke Rosberg	SF	Williams FW07C-Ford/Williams FW08-Ford	Ferrari
1983	Nelson Piquet	BR	Brabham BT52-BMW/Brabham BT52B-BMW	Ferrari
1984	Niki Lauda	A	McLaren MP4/2-TAG Porsche	McLaren-TAG
1985	Alain Prost	F	McLaren MP4/2B-TAG Porsche	McLaren-TAG
1986	Alain Prost	F	McLaren MP4/2C-TAG Porsche	Williams-Honda
1987	Nelson Piquet	BR	Williams FW11B-Honda	Williams-Honda
1988	Ayrton Senna	BR	McLaren MP4/4-Honda	McLaren-Honda
1989	Alain Prost	F	McLaren MP4/5-Honda	McLaren-Honda
1990	Ayrton Senna	BR	McLaren MP4/5B-Honda	McLaren-Honda
1991	Ayrton Senna	BR	McLaren MP4/6-Honda	McLaren-Honda
1992	Nigel Mansell	GB	Williams FW14B-Renault	Williams-Renault
1993	Alain Prost	F	Williams FW15C-Renault	Williams-Renault
1994	Michael Schumacher	D	Benetton B194-Ford	Williams-Renault

1950

The inaugural drivers' World Championship was dominated by the works Alfa Romeos of Giuseppe Farina and Juan Manuel Fangio. Each scored three Grand Prix wins, with Farina clinching the title at the final race. Veteran Italian Luigi Fagioli completed a championship clean sweep for the marque, finishing second on four occasions.

They relied once more on the supercharged 158 "Alfetta", a pre-war voiturette or Formula Two car, which had been virtually unbeatable since World War Two. A modified version, dubbed 159, was introduced for Farina at the Italian GP. However, the search for ever-increasing performance from its engine resulted in the 158 having poor fuel efficiency. To take advantage of Alfa's consequent pit stops Ferrari decided to build a 4.5-litre normally aspirated engine, which it was thought would be slightly less powerful but would use less fuel. The theory had been shown to have foundation at Spa when, during the Alfa Romeo pit stops, the slow but reliable Lago-Talbot of Raymond Sommer briefly snatched the lead.

In its final form the new Ferrari 375 appeared at Monza, Alberto Ascari finishing second in Dorino Serafini's car after his own had retired. Alfa Romeo would face a serious challenge in 1951.

British Grand Prix

13 May 1950. Silverstone. 70 laps of a 2.889-mile circuit = 202.230 miles. Warm, dry and sunny. World Championship round 1. Also known as the European Grand Prix

1 Giuseppe Farina	Alfa Romeo 158	70	2h13m23.6
2 Luigi Fagioli	Alfa Romeo 158	70	2h13m26.2
3 Reg Parnell	Alfa Romeo 158	70	2h14m15.6
4 Yves Giraud-Cabantous	Lago-Talbot T26C-DA	68	
5 Louis Rosier	Lago-Talbot T26C	68	
6 Bob Gerard	ERA B-type	67	

Winner's average speed: 90.950 mph. Starting grid front row: Farina, 1m50.8 (pole), Fagioli, 1m51.0, Fangio, 1m51.0 and Parnell, 1m52.2. Fastest lap: Farina, 1m50.6. Leaders: Farina, laps 1–9, 16–37, 39–70; Fagioli, 10–14, 38; Fangio, 15

Grand Prix de Monaco

21 May 1950. Monte Carlo. 100 laps of a 1.976-mile circuit = 197.600 miles. Cool, dry and sunny. World Championship round 2

1 Juan Manuel Fangio	Alfa Romeo 158	100	3h13m18.7
2 Alberto Ascari	Ferrari 125	99	
3 Louis Chiron	Maserati 4CLT/48	98	
4 Raymond Sommer	Ferrari 125	97	
5 "B Bira"	Maserati 4CLT/48	95	
6 Bob Gerard	ERA A-type	94	

Winner's average speed: 61.331 mph. Starting grid front row: Fangio, 1m50.2 (pole), Farina, 1m52.8 and Gonzalez, 1m53.7. Fastest lap: Fangio, 1m51.0. Leaders: Fangio, laps 1–100

1950 DRIVERS' RECORDS

(excluding Indianapolis)

Driver	Car	British GP	Monaco GP	Swiss GP	Belgian GP	French GP	Italian GP
Alberto Ascari	Ferrari 125	-	2	R	-	-	-
	Ferrari 275	-	-	-	5	DNS	-
	Ferrari 375	-	-	-	-	-	2
Clemente Biondetti	Ferrari 166I-Jaguar	-	-	-	-	-	R
"B Bira"	Maserati 4CLT/48	R	5	4	-	-	R
Felice Bonetto	Maserati 4CLT/50-Milano	DNS	-	5	-	R	DNS
Antonio Branca	Maserati 4CL	-	-	11	10	-	-
Eugène Chaboud	Lago-Talbot T26C	-	-	-	R	DNS	-
	Lago-Talbot T26C-DA	-	-	-	-	5	-
Louis Chiron	Maserati 4CLT/48	R	3	9	-	R	R
Johnny Claes	Lago-Talbot T26C	11	7	10	8	R	R
Gianfranco Comotti	Maserati 4CLT/50-Milano	-	-	-	-	-	R
Geoffrey Crossley	Alta GP	R	-	-	9	-	-
Philippe Étancelin	Lago-Talbot T26C	8	R	R	-	-	5
	Lago-Talbot T26C-DA	-	-	-	R	5	-
Luigi Fagioli	Alfa Romeo 158	2	R	2	2	2	3
Juan Manuel Fangio	Alfa Romeo 158	R	1PF	RP	1	1PF	RPF
Giuseppe Farina	Alfa Romeo 158	1PF	R	1F	4PF	7	-
	Alfa Romeo 159	-	-	-	-	-	1
Joe Fry	Maserati 4CL	10	-	-	-	-	-
Bob Gerard	ERA B-type	6	-	-	-	-	-
	ERA A-type	-	6	-	-	-	-
Yves Giraud-Cabantous	Lago-Talbot T26C-DA	4	-	R	R	8	-
José Froilan Gonzalez	Maserati 4CLT/48	-	R	-	R	-	-
Emanuel de Graffenried	Maserati 4CLT/48	R	R	6	-	-	6
David Hampshire	Maserati 4CLT/48	9	-	-	R	-	-
Cuth Harrison	ERA C-type	7	R	-	-	-	R
Leslie Johnson	ERA E-type	R	-	-	-	-	-
Joe Kelly	Alta GP	NC	-	-	-	-	-
"Pierre Levegh"	Lago-Talbot T26C	-	-	7	R	R	-
Henri Louveau	Lago-Talbot T26C-GS	-	-	-	-	R	-
Guy Mairesse	Lago-Talbot T26C	-	-	-	-	R	-
Robert Manzon	Simca-Gordini 15	-	R	-	4	R	/Cont'd

Indianapolis 500

30 May 1950. Indianapolis. 138 laps of a 2.500-mile circuit = 345.000 miles. Race scheduled for 200 laps but stopped due to rain. Warm and dry at the start, heavy rain later. World Championship round 3

1 Johnnie Parsons	Kurtis-Offenhauser	138	2h46m55.97
2 Bill Holland	Deidt-Offenhauser	137	
3 Mauri Rose	Deidt-Offenhauser	137	
4 Cecil Green	Kurtis KK3000-Offenhauser	137	
5 Joie Chitwood/ Tony Bettenhausen	Kurtis KK2000-Offenhauser	136	
6 Lee Wallard	Moore-Offenhauser	136	

Winner's average speed: 124.002 mph. Starting grid front row: Faulkner, 134.33 mph (pole), Agabashian, 132.792 mph and Rose, 132.319 mph. Fastest lap in the lead: Parsons

Grand Prix de Suisse

4 June 1950. Bremgarten. 42 laps of a 4.524-mile circuit = 190.008 miles. Warm, dry and sunny. World Championship round 4

Farina wins the 1950 British GP / Photo: Alfa Romeo

1 Giuseppe Farina	Alfa Romeo 158	42	2h02m53.7
2 Luigi Fagioli	Alfa Romeo 158	42	2h02m54.1
3 Louis Rosier	Lago-Talbot T26C-DA	41	
4 "B Bira"	Maserati 4CLT/48	40	
5 Felice Bonetto	Maserati 4CLT/50-Milano	40	
6 Emanuel de Graffenried	Maserati 4CLT/48	40	

Winner's average speed: 92.766 mph. Starting grid front row: Fangio, 2m42.1 (pole), Farina, 2m42.8 and Fagioli, 2m45.2. Fastest lap: Farina, 2m41.6. Leaders: Fangio, laps 1-6, 21-22; Farina, 7-20, 24-42; Fagioli, 23

Grand Prix de Belgique

18 June 1950. Spa-Francorchamps. 35 laps of a 8.774-mile circuit = 307.090 miles. Warm, dry and sunny. World Championship round 5

1 Juan Manuel Fangio	Alfa Romeo 158	35	2h47m26.0
2 Luigi Fagioli	Alfa Romeo 158	35	2h47m40.0
3 Louis Rosier	Lago-Talbot T26C-DA	35	2h49m45.0
4 Giuseppe Farina	Alfa Romeo 158	35	2h51m31.0
5 Alberto Ascari	Ferrari 275	34	
6 Luigi Villoresi	Ferrari 125	33	

Winner's average speed: 110.046 mph. Starting grid front row: Farina, 4m37 (pole), Fangio, 4m37 and Fagioli, 4m41. Fastest lap: Farina, 4m34.1. Leaders: Fangio, laps 1-6, 20-35; Farina, 7-11, 18-19; Fagioli, 12; Sommer, 13-17

Grand Prix de l'Automobile Club de France

2 July 1950. Reims. 64 laps of a 4.856-mile circuit = 310.784 miles. Hot, dry and sunny. World Championship round 6

1 Juan Manuel Fangio	Alfa Romeo 158	64	2h57m52.8
2 Luigi Fagioli	Alfa Romeo 158	64	2h58m18.5
3 Peter Whitehead	Ferrari 125	61	
4 Robert Manzon	Simca-Gordini 15	61	

1950 DRIVERS' RECORDS cont'd/ (excluding Indianapolis)

Driver	Car	British GP	Monaco GP	Swiss GP	Belgian GP	French GP	Italian GP
Eugène Martin	Lago-Talbot T26C-DA	R	-	R	-	-	-
David Murray	Maserati 4CLT/48	R	-	-	-	-	R
Nello Pagani	Maserati 4CLT/48	-	-	7	-	-	-
Reg Parnell	Alfa Romeo 158	3	-	-	-	-	-
	Maserati 4CLT/48	-	-	-	-	R	-
Alfredo Piàn	Maserati 4CLT/48	-	DNS	-	-	-	-
Paul Pietsch	Maserati 4CLT/48	-	-	-	-	-	R
Charles Pozzi	Lago-Talbot T26C	-	-	-	-	6	-
Franco Rol	Maserati 4CLT/48	-	R	-	-	R	R
Tony Rolt	ERA E-type	R	-	-	-	-	-
Louis Rosier	Lago-Talbot T26C	5	R	-	-	6	4
	Lago-Talbot T26C-DA	-	-	3	3	R	-
Consalvo Sanesi	Alfa Romeo 158	-	-	-	-	-	R
Harry Schell	Cooper T12-JAP	-	R	-	-	-	-
	Lago-Talbot T26C	-	-	8	-	-	-
Dorino Serafini	Ferrari 375	-	-	-	-	-	2
Brian Shawe-Taylor	Maserati 4CL	10	-	-	-	-	-
Raymond Sommer	Ferrari 125	-	4	-	-	-	-
	Ferrari 166/F2/50	-	-	R	-	-	-
	Lago-Talbot T26C	-	-	-	R	-	R
	Lago-Talbot T26C-GS	-	-	-	-	R	-
Piero Taruffi	Alfa Romeo 158	-	-	-	-	-	R
Maurice Trintignant	Simca-Gordini 15	-	R	-	-	-	R
Luigi Villoresi	Ferrari 125	-	R	R	6	-	-
	Ferrari 275	-	-	-	DNS	-	
Peter Walker	ERA E-type	R	-	-	-	-	-
Peter Whitehead	Ferrari 125	-	DNS	-	-	3	7

SHARED DRIVES - **British GP:** Joe Fry/Brian Shawe-Taylor (Maserati 4CL) 10; Peter Walker/Tony Rolt (ERA E-type) R. **French GP:** Philippe Étancelin/Eugène Chaboud (Lago-Talbot T26C-DA) 5; Charles Pozzi/Louis Rosier (Lago-Talbot T26C) 6. **Italian GP:** Dorino Serafini/Alberto Ascari (Ferrari 375) 2; Piero Taruffi/Juan Manuel Fangio (Alfa Romeo 158) R

5	Philippe Étancelin/		
	Eugène Chaboud	Lago-Talbot T26C-DA	59
6	Charles Pozzi/		
	Louis Rosier	Lago-Talbot T26C	56

Winner's average speed: 104.829 mph. Starting grid front row:
Fangio, 2m30.6 (pole), Farina, 2m32.5 and Fagioli, 2m34.7. Fastest
lap: Fangio, 2m35.6. Leaders: Farina, laps 1-16; Fangio, 17-64

Gran Premio d'Italia

3 September 1950. Monza. 80 laps of a 3.915-mile circuit =
313.200 miles. Warm, dry and sunny, turning overcast.
World Championship round 7

1	Giuseppe Farina	Alfa Romeo 159	80	2h51m17.4
2	Dorino Serafini/			
	Alberto Ascari	Ferrari 375	80	2h52m36.0
3	Luigi Fagioli	Alfa Romeo 158	80	2h52m53.0
4	Louis Rosier	Lago-Talbot T26C	75	
5	Philippe Étancelin	Lago-Talbot T26C	75	
6	Emanuel de			
	Graffenried	Maserati 4CLT/48	72	

Winner's average speed: 109.709 mph. Starting grid front row:
Fangio, 1m58.6 (pole), Ascari, 1m58.8, Farina, 2m00.2 and
Sanesi, 2m00.4. Fastest lap: Fangio, 2m00.0. Leaders: Farina, laps
1-13, 16-80; Ascari, 14-15

1950 FINAL CHAMPIONSHIP POSITIONS

Drivers

1	Giuseppe Farina	30	9=	Louis Chiron	4		Dorino Serafini	3
2	Juan Manuel Fangio	27		Reg Parnell	4		Raymond Sommer	3
3	Luigi Fagioli	24 (28)*		Mauri Rose	4	19	Felice Bonetto	2
4	Louis Rosier	13		Peter Whitehead	4	20=	Tony Bettenhausen	1
5	Alberto Ascari	11	13=	Philippe Étancelin	3		Eugène Chaboud	1
6	Johnnie Parsons	9		Yves Giraud-Cabantous	3		Joie Chitwood	1
7	Bill Holland	6		Cecil Green	3		*Best four results count	
8	"B Bira"	5		Robert Manzon	3			

1951

By 1951 Juan Manuel Fangio was the quickest
Alfa Romeo driver, invariably qualifying ahead of
Giuseppe Farina, and his three Grand Prix victories (one of which was shared with Luigi Fagioli)
were enough to win the World Championship.
The Alfa Romeo 159 was now so developed that
it achieved just 1.6 mpg, requiring two or more
fuel stops to complete a Grand Prix.

A strong challenge had been expected from
Ferrari, but it was not until the second half of
the season that it fully materialized. José Froilan
Gonzalez, the "Pampas Bull", scored Ferrari's
first Grand Prix win at Silverstone, with team
leader Alberto Ascari winning the subsequent
German and Italian races.

These were the first defeats inflicted on Alfa
Romeo for five years and brought the Ferrari
drivers into championship contention - although
their incorrect tyre choice for the final Grand
Prix handed Fangio victory and his first crown.
But with their rivals gaining in competitiveness,
Alfa Romeo decided to withdraw from Grand
Prix racing rather than build the totally new car
they would need to stay ahead, and the marque
would not return until 1979.

A much vaunted new challenger from Britain, the
supercharged V16 BRM, appeared for its home
Grand Prix. It was the most advanced car of the
time, and should have been able to compete with
the Italians. Although Reg Parnell finished fifth at
Silverstone, it was a disappointment, and the
team rarely mounted a concerted challenge. Its
failure would in part lead to the championship
organizers dropping Formula One in favour of
Formula Two for the following season.

Grand Prix de Suisse

27 May 1951. Bremgarten. 42 laps of a 4.524-mile circuit =
190.008 miles. Heavy rain. World Championship round 1

1	Juan Manuel Fangio	Alfa Romeo 159	42	2h07m53.64
2	Piero Taruffi	Ferrari 375	42	2h08m48.88
3	Giuseppe Farina	Alfa Romeo 159	42	2h09m12.95
4	Consalvo Sanesi	Alfa Romeo 159	41	
5	Emanuel de			
	Graffenried	Alfa Romeo 159	40	
6	Alberto Ascari	Ferrari 375	40	

Winner's average speed: 89.140 mph. Starting grid front row:
Fangio, 2m35.9 (pole), Farina, 2m37.8 and Villoresi, 2m39.3.
Fastest lap: Fangio, 2m51.1. Leaders: Fangio, laps 1-23, 29-42;
Farina, 24-28

Indianapolis 500

29 May 1951. Indianapolis. 200 laps of a 2.500-mile circuit
= 500.000 miles. Hot, dry and sunny. World Championship
round 2

1	Lee Wallard	Kurtis-Offenhauser	200	3h57m38.05
2	Mike Nazaruk	Kurtis-Offenhauser	200	3h59m25.31
3	Jack McGrath/	Kurtis KK3000-		
	Manuel Ayulo	Offenhauser	200	4h00m29.42
4	Andy Linden	Sherman-Offenhauser	200	4h02m18.06
5	Bobby Ball	Schroeder-		
		Offenhauser	200	4h02m30.27
6	Henry Banks	Moore-Offenhauser	200	4h03m18.02

Winner's average speed: 126.244 mph. Starting grid front row:
Nalon, 136.498 mph (pole), Wallard, 135.039 mph and McGrath,
134.303 mph. Fastest lap in the lead: Wallard, 1m07.26

*1951 World Champion Juan Manuel Fangio at the
British Grand Prix. He finished second to Gonzalez*

1951 DRIVERS' RECORDS

(excluding Indianapolis)

Driver	Car	Swiss GP	Belgian GP	French GP	British GP	German GP	Italian GP	Spanish GP
George Abecassis	HWM 51-Alta	R	-	-	-	-	-	-
Alberto Ascari	Ferrari 375	6	2	2	R	1^P	1	4^P
"B Bira"	Maserati 4CLT/48-OSCA	-	-	-	-	-	-	R
Felice Bonetto	Alfa Romeo 159	-	-	-	4	R	3	5
Antonio Branca	Maserati 4CLT/48	-	-	-	-	R	-	-
Eugène Chaboud	Lago-Talbot T26C-GS	-	-	8	-	-	-	-
Louis Chiron	Maserati 4CLT/48	7	-	-	-	-	-	-
	Lago-Talbot T26C	-	R	6	R	-	R	R
	Lago-Talbot T26C-DA	-	-	-	-	R	-	-
Johnny Claes	Lago-Talbot T26C-DA	13	7	R	13	11	R	R
Philippe Étancelin	Lago-Talbot T26C-DA	10	R	R	-	R	-	8
Luigi Fagioli	Alfa Romeo 159	-	-	1	-	-	-	-
Juan Manuel Fangio	Alfa Romeo 159	1^{PF}	9^{PF}	1^{PF}	2	2^F	R^P	1^F
Giuseppe Farina	Alfa Romeo 159	3	1	5	R^F	R	3^F	3
Rudolf Fischer	Ferrari 212	11	-	-	-	6	DNS	-
Philip Fotheringham-Parker	Maserati 4CL	-	-	-	R	-	-	-
Bob Gerard	ERA B-type	-	-	-	11	-	-	-
Yves Giraud-Cabantous	Lago-Talbot T26C	R	5	7	-	R	8	R
Chico Godia-Sales	Maserati 4CLT/48	-	-	-	-	-	-	10
José Froilan Gonzalez	Lago-Talbot T26C-GS	R	-	-	-	-	-	-
	Ferrari 375	-	-	2	1^P	3	2	2
Aldo Gordini	Simca-Gordini 11	-	-	R	-	-	-	-
Emanuel de Graffenried	Alfa Romeo 159	5	-	-	-	-	R	6
	Maserati 4CLT/48	-	-	R	-	R	-	-
Georges Grignard	Lago-Talbot T26C-DA	-	-	-	-	-	-	R
Duncan Hamilton	Lago-Talbot T26C	-	-	-	12	R	-	-
Peter Hirt	Veritas Meteor	R	-	-	-	-	-	-
John James	Maserati 4CLT/48	-	-	-	R	-	-	-
Juan Jover	Maserati 4CLT/48	-	-	-	-	-	-	DNS
Joe Kelly	Alta GP	-	-	-	NC	-	-	-
Chico Landi	Ferrari 375	-	-	-	-	-	R	-
"Pierre Levegh"	Lago-Talbot T26C	-	8	-	-	9	R	-
Henri Louveau	Lago-Talbot T26C	R	-	-	-	-	-	-
Guy Mairesse	Lago-Talbot T26C	14	-	9	-	-	-	-
Robert Manzon	Simca-Gordini 15	-	-	R	-	7	R	9
Onofre Marimón	Maserati 4CLT/50-Milano	-	-	R	-	-	-	-
Stirling Moss	HWM 51-Alta	8	-	-	-	-	-	-
David Murray	Maserati 4CLT/48	-	-	-	R	DNS	-	-
Reg Parnell	Ferrari 375	-	-	4	-	-	-	-
	BRM P15	-	-	-	5	-	DNS	-
Paul Pietsch	Alfa Romeo 159	-	-	-	-	R	-	-
André Pilette	Lago-Talbot T26C	-	6	-	-	-	-	-
Ken Richardson	BRM P15	-	-	-	-	-	DNS	-
Franco Rol	OSCA 4500G	-	-	-	-	-	9	-
Louis Rosier	Lago-Talbot T26C-DA	9	4	R	10	8	7	7
Consalvo Sanesi	Alfa Romeo 159	4	R	10	6	-	-	-
Harry Schell	Maserati 4CLT/48	12	-	R	-	-	-	-
Brian Shawe-Taylor	ERA B-type	-	-	-	8	-	-	-
André Simon	Simca-Gordini 15	-	-	R	-	R	6	R
Jacques Swaters	Lago-Talbot T26C	-	-	-	-	10	R	-
Piero Taruffi	Ferrari 375	2	R	-	-	5	5	R
Maurice Trintignant	Simca-Gordini 15	-	-	R	-	R	R	R
Luigi Villoresi	Ferrari 375	R	3	3	3	4	4	R
Peter Walker	BRM P15	-	-	-	7	-	-	-
Peter Whitehead	Ferrari 125	R	-	R	-	-	R	-
	Ferrari 375	-	-	-	9	-	-	-

SHARED DRIVES - **French GP:** Luigi Fagioli/Juan Manuel Fangio (Alfa Romeo 159) 1; José Froilan Gonzalez/Alberto Ascari (Ferrari 375) 2; Juan Manuel Fangio/Luigi Fagioli (Alfa Romeo 159) 11. **Italian GP:** Felice Bonetto/Giuseppe Farina (Alfa Romeo 159) 3

Grand Prix de Belgique

17 June 1951. Spa-Francorchamps. 36 laps of a 8.774-mile circuit = 315.864 miles. Warm, dry and sunny. World Championship round 3

1	Giuseppe Farina	Alfa Romeo 159	36	2h45m46.2
2	Alberto Ascari	Ferrari 375	36	2h48m37.2
3	Luigi Villoresi	Ferrari 375	36	2h50m08.1
4	Louis Rosier	Lago-Talbot T26C-DA	34	
5	Yves Giraud-Cabantous	Lago-Talbot T26C	34	
6	André Pilette	Lago-Talbot T26C	33	

Winner's average speed: 114.326 mph. Starting grid front row: Fangio, 4m25 (pole), Farina, 4m28 and Villoresi, 4m29. Fastest lap: Fangio, 4m22.1. Leaders: Villoresi, laps 1-2; Farina, 3-14, 16-36; Fangio, 15

Grand Prix de l'Automobile Club de France

1 July 1951. Reims. 77 laps of a 4.856-mile circuit = 373.912 miles. Hot, dry and sunny. World Championship round 4. Also known as the European Grand Prix

1 Luigi Fagioli/			
Juan Manuel Fangio	Alfa Romeo 159	77	3h22m11.0
2 José Froilan Gonzalez/			
Alberto Ascari	Ferrari 375	77	3h23m09.2
3 Luigi Villoresi	Ferrari 375	74	
4 Reg Parnell	Ferrari 375	73	
5 Giuseppe Farina	Alfa Romeo 159	73	
6 Louis Chiron	Lago-Talbot T26C	71	

Winner's average speed: 110.962 mph. Starting grid front row: Fangio, 2m25.7 (pole), Farina, 2m27.4 and Ascari, 2m28.1. Fastest lap: Fangio, 2m27.8. Leaders: Ascari, laps 1-8, 45-50#; Fangio, 9, 51-77*; Farina, 10-44 (#in Gonzalez's car; *in Fagioli's car)

British Grand Prix

14 July 1951. Silverstone. 90 laps of a 2.889-mile circuit = 260.010 miles. Warm, dry and sunny. World Championship round 5

1 José Froilan Gonzalez	Ferrari 375	90	2h42m18.2
2 Juan Manuel Fangio	Alfa Romeo 159	90	2h43m09.2
3 Luigi Villoresi	Ferrari 375	88	
4 Felice Bonetto	Alfa Romeo 159	87	
5 Reg Parnell	BRM P15	85	
6 Consalvo Sanesi	Alfa Romeo 159	84	

Winner's average speed: 96.107 mph. Starting grid front row: Gonzalez, 1m43.4 (pole), Fangio, 1m44.4, Farina, 1m45.0 and Ascari, 1m45.4. Fastest lap: Farina, 1m44.0. Leaders: Bonetto, lap 1; Gonzalez, laps 2-9, 39-47, 49-90; Fangio, 10-38, 48

Grosser Preis von Deutschland

29 July 1951. Nürburgring. 20 laps of a 14.167-mile circuit = 283.340 miles. Warm, dry and sunny. World Championship round 6

1 Alberto Ascari	Ferrari 375	20	3h23m03.3
2 Juan Manuel Fangio	Alfa Romeo 159	20	3h23m33.8
3 José Froilan Gonzalez	Ferrari 375	20	3h27m42.3
4 Luigi Villoresi	Ferrari 375	20	3h28m53.5
5 Piero Taruffi	Ferrari 375	20	3h30m52.4
6 Rudolf Fischer	Ferrari 212	19	

Winner's average speed: 83.723 mph. Starting grid front row: Ascari, 9m55.8 (pole), Gonzalez, 9m57.5, Fangio, 9m59.0 and Farina, 10m01.0. Fastest lap: Fangio, 9m55.8. Leaders: Fangio, laps 1-4, 11-14; Ascari, 5-9, 15-20; Gonzalez, 10

Gran Premio d'Italia

16 September 1951. Monza. 80 laps of a 3.915-mile circuit = 313.200 miles. Hot, dry and sunny. World Championship round 7

1 Alberto Ascari	Ferrari 375	80	2h42m39.3
2 José Froilan Gonzalez	Ferrari 375	80	2h43m23.9
3 Felice Bonetto/			
Giuseppe Farina	Alfa Romeo 159	79	
4 Luigi Villoresi	Ferrari 375	79	
5 Piero Taruffi	Ferrari 375	78	
6 André Simon	Simca-Gordini 15	74	

Winner's average speed: 115.533 mph. Starting grid front row: Fangio, 1m53.2 (pole), Farina, 1m53.9, Ascari, 1m55.1 and Gonzalez, 1m55.9. Fastest lap: Farina, 1m56.5. Leaders: Fangio, laps 1-3, 8-13; Ascari, 4-7, 14-90

Gran Premio de España

28 October 1951. Pedralbes. 70 laps of a 3.925-mile circuit = 274.750 miles. Hot, dry and sunny. World Championship round 8

1 Juan Manuel Fangio	Alfa Romeo 159	70	2h46m54.10
2 José Froilan Gonzalez	Ferrari 375	70	2h47m48.38
3 Giuseppe Farina	Alfa Romeo 159	70	2h48m39.64
4 Alberto Ascari	Ferrari 375	68	
5 Felice Bonetto	Alfa Romeo 159	68	
6 Emanuel de			
Graffenried	Alfa Romeo 159	66	

Winner's average speed: 98.771 mph. Starting grid front row: Ascari, 2m10.59 (pole), Fangio, 2m12.27, Gonzalez, 2m14.01 and Farina, 2m14.94. Fastest lap: Fangio, 2m16.93. Leaders: Ascari, laps 1-3; Fangio, 4-70

1951 FINAL CHAMPIONSHIP POSITIONS

Drivers

1	Juan Manuel Fangio	31 (37)*	8	Felice Bonetto	7	15=	Manuel Ayulo	2	
2	Alberto Ascari	25 (28)*	9	Mike Nazaruk	6		Bobby Ball	2	
3	José Froilan Gonzalez	24 (27)*	10	Reg Parnell	5		Yves Giraud-Cabantous	2	
4	Giuseppe Farina	19 (22)*	11	Luigi Fagioli	4		Emanuel de Graffenried	2	
5	Luigi Villoresi	15 (18)*	12=	Andy Linden	3		Jack McGrath	2	
6	Piero Taruffi	10		Louis Rosier	3		*Best four results count		
7	Lee Wallard	9		Consalvo Sanesi	3				

1952

Rather than build the new car required to beat Ferrari in 1952, Alfa Romeo withdrew from Formula One. With the BRM project continuing to disappoint, World Championship promoters switched their races for the next two years to Formula Two.

These years proved to be a Ferrari benefit, particularly for their team leader, Alberto Ascari. He elected to miss the opening round of the 1952 championship in Switzerland, instead racing unsuccessfully at Indianapolis. In his absence team-mate Piero Taruffi won, thereafter Ascari was unbeatable, winning the next nine Grands Prix in succession until the 1953 French GP.

Maserati had introduced the new A6GCM and signed reigning World Champion Juan Manuel Fangio to lead their attack. However, Fangio crashed at Monza during a pre-season race, breaking his neck. With the Argentinian out for the year, Maserati only became competitive when a modified engine was introduced towards the end of the season, José Froilan Gonzalez leading for 36 laps in Italy.

Mike Hawthorn emerged as a star of the future after a series of fine performances in his private Cooper-Bristol, while Stirling Moss raced for various British marques but without success.

Grand Prix de Suisse

18 May 1952. Bremgarten. 62 laps of a 4.524-mile circuit = 280.488 miles. Warm and dry. World Championship round 1

1 Piero Taruffi	Ferrari 500	62	3h01m46.1
2 Rudolf Fischer	Ferrari 500	62	3h04m23.3
3 Jean Behra	Gordini 16	61	
4 Ken Wharton	Frazer-Nash FN48-Bristol	60	
5 Alan Brown	Cooper T20-Bristol	59	
6 Emanuel de Graffenried	Maserati 4CLT/48-Platé	58	

Winner's average speed: 92.586 mph. Starting grid front row: Farina, 2m47.5 (pole), Taruffi, 2m50.1 and Manzon, 2m52.1. Fastest lap: Taruffi, 2m49.1. Leaders: Farina, laps 1-16; Taruffi, 17-62

Indianapolis 500

30 May 1952. Indianapolis. 200 laps of a 2.500-mile circuit = 500.000 miles. Warm, dry and sunny. World Championship round 2

1 Troy Ruttman	Kuzma-Offenhauser	200	3h52m41.88
2 Jim Rathmann	Kurtis KK3000-Offenhauser	200	3h56m44.24
3 Sam Hanks	Kurtis KK3000-Offenhauser	200	3h58m53.48
4 Duane Carter	Lesovsky-Offenhauser	200	3h59m30.21
5 Art Cross	Kurtis KK4000-Offenhauser	200	4h01m22.08
6 Jimmy Bryan	Kurtis KK3000-Offenhauser	200	4h02m06.23

Winner's average speed: 128.922 mph. Starting grid front row: Agabashian, 138.010 mph (pole), Linden, 137.002 mph and McGrath, 136.664 mph. Fastest lap in the lead: Vukovich, 1m06.60

Grand Prix de Belgique

22 June 1952. Spa-Francorchamps. 36 laps of a 8.774-mile circuit = 315.864 miles. Heavy rain. World Championship round 3. Also known as the European Grand Prix

1 Alberto Ascari	Ferrari 500	36	3h03m46.3
2 Giuseppe Farina	Ferrari 500	36	3h05m41.5
3 Robert Manzon	Gordini 16	36	3h08m14.7
4 Mike Hawthorn	Cooper T20-Bristol	35	
5 Paul Frère	HWM 51/52-Alta	34	
6 Alan Brown	Cooper T20-Bristol	34	

Winner's average speed: 103.127 mph. Starting grid front row: Ascari, 4m37 (pole), Farina, 4m40 and Taruffi, 4m46. Fastest lap: Ascari, 4m54. Leaders: Behra, lap 1; Ascari, laps 2-36

Grand Prix de l'Automobile Club de France

6 July 1952. Rouen-les-Essarts. 3 hours. 76 laps of a 3.169-mile circuit = 240.844 miles. Overcast and dry at the start, rain later. World Championship round 4

1 Alberto Ascari	Ferrari 500	76	3h00m00.0
2 Giuseppe Farina	Ferrari 500	76	
3 Piero Taruffi	Ferrari 500	75	
4 Robert Manzon	Gordini 16	74	
5 Maurice Trintignant	Simca-Gordini 15	72	
6 Peter Collins	HWM 52-Alta	70	

Winner's average speed: 80.281 mph. Starting grid front row: Ascari, 2m14.8 (pole), Farina, 2m16.2 and Taruffi, 2m17.1. Fastest lap: Ascari, 2m17.3. Leaders: Ascari, laps 1-76

British Grand Prix

19 July 1952. Silverstone. 85 laps of a 2.927-mile circuit = 248.795 miles. Overcast and dry. World Championship round 5

1 Alberto Ascari	Ferrari 500	85	2h44m11.0
2 Piero Taruffi	Ferrari 500	84	
3 Mike Hawthorn	Cooper T20-Bristol	83	
4 Dennis Poore	Connaught A-Lea-Francis	83	
5 Eric Thompson	Connaught A-Lea-Francis	82	
6 Giuseppe Farina	Ferrari 500	82	

Winner's average speed: 90.921 mph. Starting grid front row: Farina, 1m50 (pole), Ascari, 1m50, Taruffi, 1m53 and Manzon, 1m55. Fastest lap: Ascari, 1m52. Leaders: Ascari, laps 1-85

Grosser Preis von Deutschland

3 August 1952. Nürburgring. 18 laps of a 14.167-mile circuit = 255.006 miles. Warm, dry and sunny. World Championship round 6

1 Alberto Ascari	Ferrari 500	18	3h06m13.3
2 Giuseppe Farina	Ferrari 500	18	3h06m27.4
3 Rudolf Fischer	Ferrari 500	18	3h13m23.4
4 Piero Taruffi	Ferrari 500	17	
5 Jean Behra	Gordini 16	17	
6 Roger Laurent	Ferrari 500	16	

Winner's average speed: 82.162 mph. Starting grid front row: Ascari, 10m04.4 (pole), Farina, 10m07.3, Trintignant, 10m19.1 and Manzon, 10m25.3. Fastest lap: Ascari, 10m05.1. Leaders: Ascari, laps 1-18

Grote Prijs van Nederland

17 August 1952. Zandvoort. 90 laps of a 2.605-mile circuit = 234.450 miles. Cool, overcast and wet. World Championship round 7

1 Alberto Ascari	Ferrari 500	90	2h53m28.5
2 Giuseppe Farina	Ferrari 500	90	2h54m08.6
3 Luigi Villoresi	Ferrari 500	90	2h55m02.9
4 Mike Hawthorn	Cooper T20-Bristol	88	
5 Robert Manzon	Gordini 16	87	
6 Maurice Trintignant	Gordini 16	87	

Winner's average speed: 81.089 mph. Starting grid front row: Ascari, 1m46.5 (pole), Farina, 1m48.6 and Hawthorn, 1m51.6. Fastest lap: Ascari, 1m49.8. Leaders: Ascari, laps 1-90

Gran Premio d'Italia

7 September 1952. Monza. 80 laps of a 3.915-mile circuit = 313.200 miles. Warm, dry and sunny. World Championship round 8

1 Alberto Ascari	Ferrari 500	80	2h50m45.6
2 José Froilan Gonzalez	Maserati A6GCM	80	2h51m47.4
3 Luigi Villoresi	Ferrari 500	80	2h52m49.8
4 Giuseppe Farina	Ferrari 500	80	2h52m57.0
5 Felice Bonetto	Maserati A6GCM	79	
6 André Simon	Ferrari 500	79	

Winner's average speed: 110.049 mph. Starting grid front row: Ascari, 2m05.1 (pole), Villoresi, 2m06.6, Farina, 2m07.0 and Trintignant, 2m07.2. Fastest lap: Ascari and Gonzalez, 2m06.1. Leaders: Gonzalez, laps 1-36; Ascari, 37-80

1952 FINAL CHAMPIONSHIP POSITIONS

Drivers

1	Alberto Ascari	36 (53.5)*	9	José Froilan Gonzalez	6.5	16=	Felice Bonetto	2
2	Giuseppe Farina	24 (27)*	10=	Jean Behra	6		Alan Brown	2
3	Piero Taruffi	22		Jim Rathmann	6		Art Cross	2
4=	Rudolf Fischer	10	12	Sam Hanks	4		Paul Frère	2
	Mike Hawthorn	10	13=	Duane Carter	3		Eric Thompson	2
6	Robert Manzon	9		Dennis Poore	3		Maurice Trintignant	2
7=	Troy Ruttman	8		Ken Wharton	3	22	Bill Vukovich	1
	Luigi Villoresi	8					*Best four results count	

		Swiss GP	Belgian GP	French GP	British GP	German GP	Dutch GP	Italian GP
1952 DRIVERS' RECORDS								
(excluding Indianapolis)								
Driver	**Car**							
George Abecassis	HWM 52-Alta	R	-	-	-	-	-	-
Alberto Ascari	Ferrari 500	-	1PF	1PF	1F	1PF	1PF	1PF
Bill Aston	Aston NB41-Butterworth	-	-	-	DNS	R	-	DNQ
Marcel Balsa	BMW Special	-	-	-	-	R	-	-
Elie Bayol	OSCA 20	-	-	-	-	-	-	R
Jean Behra	Gordini 16	3	R	7	-	5	R	R
Gino Bianco	Maserati A6GCM	-	-	-	18	R	R	R
"B Bira"	Simca-Gordini 15	R	10	-	-	-	-	-
	Gordini 16	-	-	R	11	-	-	-
Felice Bonetto	Maserati A6GCM	-	-	-	-	DSQ	-	5
Eric Brandon	Cooper T20-Bristol	8	9	-	20	-	-	13
Alan Brown	Cooper T20-Bristol	5	6	-	22	-	-	15
Adolf Brudes	Veritas RS-BMW	-	-	-	-	R	-	-
Heitel Cantoni	Maserati A6GCM	-	-	-	R	R	-	11
Piero Carini	Ferrari 166/F2	-	-	R	-	R	-	-
Johnny Claes	Simca-Gordini 16S	-	8	-	-	-	-	-
	Simca-Gordini 15	-	-	R	15	-	-	DNQ
	HWM 52-Alta	-	-	-	-	R	-	-
Peter Collins	HWM 52-Alta	R	R	6	R	DNS	-	DNQ
Gianfranco Comotti	Ferrari 166/F2	-	-	12	-	-	-	-
Alberto Crespo	Maserati 4CLT/48-Platé	-	-	-	-	-	-	DNQ
Tony Crook	Frazer-Nash 421-BMW	-	-	-	21	-	-	-
Ken Downing	Connaught A-Lea-Francis	-	-	-	9	-	R	-
Piero Dusio	Cisitalia D46-BPM	-	-	-	-	-	-	DNQ
Philippe Étancelin	Maserati A6GCM	-	-	8	-	-	-	-
Giuseppe Farina	Ferrari 500	RP	2	2	6P	2	2	4
Ludwig Fischer	AFM 1-BMW	-	-	-	-	DNS	-	-
Rudolf Fischer	Ferrari 500	2	-	-	14	3	-	R
	Ferrari 212	-	-	11	-	-	-	-
Jan Flinterman	Maserati A6GCM	-	-	-	-	-	9	-
Paul Frère	HWM 51/52-Alta	-	5	-	-	R	-	-
	Simca-Gordini 15	-	-	-	-	-	R	-
Tony Gaze	HWM 52-Alta	-	15	-	-	-	-	-
	HWM 51/52-Alta	-	-	-	R	R	-	DNQ
Yves Giraud-Cabantous	HWM 52-Alta	-	-	10	-	-	-	-
José Froilan Gonzalez	Maserati A6GCM	-	-	-	-	-	-	2F
Emanuel de Graffenried	Maserati 4CLT/48-Platé	6	-	R	19	-	-	DNQ
Duncan Hamilton	HWM 51/52-Alta	-	-	-	R	-	-	-
	HWM 52-Alta	-	-	-	-	-	7	-
Mike Hawthorn	Cooper T20-Bristol	-	4	R	3	-	4	NC
Willi Heeks	AFM 8-BMW	-	-	-	-	R	-	-
Theo Helfrich	Veritas RS-BMW	-	-	-	-	R	-	-
Peter Hirt	Ferrari 212	7	-	11	R	-	-	-
Hans Klenk	Veritas Meteor	-	-	-	-	R	-	-
Ernst Klodwig	Heck-BMW	-	-	-	-	R	-	-
Willi Krakau	AFM 7-BMW	-	-	-	-	DNS	-	-
Rudolf Krause	Greifzu-BMW	-	-	-	-	R	-	-
Chico Landi	Maserati A6GCM	-	-	-	-	-	9	8
Roger Laurent	HWM 52-Alta	-	12	-	-	-	-	-
	Ferrari 500	-	-	-	-	6	-	-
Arthur Legat	Veritas Meteor	-	13	-	-	-	-	-
Dries van der Lof	HWM 52-Alta	-	-	-	-	-	NC	-
Lance Macklin	HWM 52-Alta	R	11	9	13	-	8	DNQ
Robert Manzon	Gordini 16	R	3	4	R	R	5	14
Kenneth McAlpine	Connaught A-Lea-Francis	-	-	-	16	-	-	R
Harry Merkel	BMW Eigenbau	-	-	-	-	DNS	-	-
Robin Montgomerie-Charrington	Aston NB41-Butterworth	-	R	-	-	-	-	-
Stirling Moss	HWM 52-Alta	R	-	-	-	-	-	-
	ERA G-type-Bristol	-	R	-	R	-	R	-
	Connaught A-Lea-Francis	-	-	-	-	-	-	R
David Murray	Cooper T20-Bristol	-	-	R	-	-	-	-
Bernd Nacke	BMW Eigenbau	-	-	-	-	R	-	-
Helmut Niedermayr	AFM 6-BMW	-	-	-	-	R	-	-
Robert O'Brien	Simca-Gordini 15	-	14	-	-	-	-	-
Reg Parnell	Cooper T20-Bristol	-	-	-	7	-	-	-
Josef Peters	Veritas RS-BMW	-	-	-	-	R	-	-
Paul Pietsch	Veritas Meteor	-	-	-	-	R	-	-

1952 DRIVERS' RECORDS cont'd/
(excluding Indianapolis)

Driver	Car	Swiss GP	Belgian GP	French GP	British GP	German GP	Dutch GP	Italian GP
Dennis Poore	Connaught A-Lea-Francis	-	-	-	4	-	-	12
Fritz Riess	Veritas RS-BMW	-	-	-	-	7	-	-
Franco Rol	Maserati A6GCM	-	-	-	-	-	-	R
Louis Rosier	Ferrari 500	R	R	R	-	-	-	10
Roy Salvadori	Ferrari 500	-	-	-	8	-	-	-
Harry Schell	Maserati 4CLT/48-Platé	R	-	R	17	-	-	-
Rudolf Schoeller	Ferrari 212	-	-	-	-	R	-	-
André Simon	Ferrari 500	R	-	-	-	-	-	6
Hans Stuck	AFM-Küchen	R	-	-	-	-	-	-
	Ferrari 212	-	-	-	-	-	-	DNQ
Piero Taruffi	Ferrari 500	1F	R	3	2	4	-	7
Max de Terra	Simca-Gordini 11	R	-	-	-	-	-	-
Eric Thompson	Connaught A-Lea-Francis	-	-	-	5	-	-	-
Charles de Tornaco	Ferrari 500	-	7	-	-	-	R	DNQ
Maurice Trintignant	Ferrari 166/F2	DNS	-	-	-	-	-	-
	Simca-Gordini 15	-	-	5	-	-	-	-
	Gordini 16	-	-	-	R	R	6	R
Toni Ulmen	Veritas Meteor	R	-	-	-	-	-	-
	Veritas Meteor-BMW	-	-	-	-	R	-	-
Luigi Villoresi	Ferrari 500	-	-	-	-	-	3	3
Ken Wharton	Frazer-Nash FN48-Bristol	4	R	-	-	-	-	-
	Frazer-Nash 421-Bristol	-	-	-	-	-	R	-
	Cooper T20-Bristol	-	-	-	-	-	-	9
Graham Whitehead	Alta F2	-	-	-	12	-	-	-
Peter Whitehead	Alta F2	-	-	R	-	-	-	-
	Ferrari 125/F2	-	-	-	10	-	-	DNQ

SHARED DRIVES - Swiss GP: André Simon/Giuseppe Farina (Ferrari 500) R. **French GP:** Rudolf Fischer/Peter Hirt (Ferrari 212 (52)) 11; Emanuel de Graffenried/Harry Schell (Maserati 4CLT/48-Platé) R. **Dutch GP:** Chico Landi/Jan Flinterman (Maserati A6GCM) 9

1953

Alberto Ascari remained the man to beat, winning the first three Grands Prix of the season. He was finally beaten (after a record nine successive victories since the 1952 Belgian GP) into fourth position in the dramatic French GP. Here his new team-mate Mike Hawthorn recorded his first Grand Prix win by overtaking Juan Manuel Fangio at the last corner after a breathtaking wheel-to-wheel duel for the lead.

Ascari won twice more on the way to his second championship, while Giuseppe Farina had also won for Ferrari, so at the last race, the Italian GP, Maserati was still looking for its first win.

It proved to be another classic slip-streaming battle, with Ascari, Farina, Fangio and Onofre Marimón (Fangio's protégé and team-mate) battling for the lead. Marimón was delayed in the pits on lap 46, but the battle for the lead continued until the last corner of the race. Farina challenged Ferrari team-mate Ascari, who spun, colliding with Marimón's lapped car in the process. Farina took to the grass in avoidance, allowing Fangio through to score Maserati's first Grand Prix victory.

Gran Premio de la Republica Argentina

18 January 1953. Buenos Aires. 97 laps of a 2.431-mile circuit = 235.807 miles. Race scheduled for three hours. Hot, dry and sunny. World Championship round 1

1 Alberto Ascari	Ferrari 500	97	3h01m04.6
2 Luigi Villoresi	Ferrari 500	96	
3 José Froilan Gonzalez	Maserati A6GCM	96	
4 Mike Hawthorn	Ferrari 500	96	
5 Oscar Galvez	Maserati A6GCM	96	
6 Jean Behra	Gordini 16	94	

Winner's average speed: 78.135 mph. Starting grid front row: Ascari, 1m55.4 (pole), Fangio, 1m56.1, Villoresi, 1m56.5 and Farina, 1m57.1. Fastest lap: Ascari, 1m48.4. Leaders: Ascari, laps 1-97

Indianapolis 500

30 May 1953. Indianapolis. 200 laps of a 2.500-mile circuit = 500.000 miles. Very hot, dry and sunny. World Championship round 2

1 Bill Vukovich	Kurtis KK500A-Offenhauser	200	3h53m01.69
2 Art Cross	Kurtis KK4000-Offenhauser	200	3h56m32.56
3 Sam Hanks/Duane Carter	Kurtis KK4000-Offenhauser	200	3h57m13.24
4 Fred Agabashian/Paul Russo	Kurtis KK500B-Offenhauser	200	3h57m40.91
5 Jack McGrath	Kurtis KK4000-Offenhauser	200	4h00m51.33
6 Jimmy Daywalt	Kurtis KK3000-Offenhauser	200	4h01m11.88

Winner's average speed: 128.740 mph. Starting grid front row: Vukovich, 138.392 mph (pole), Agabashian, 137.546 mph and McGrath, 136.602 mph. Fastest lap in the lead: Vukovich, 1m06.24

Grote Prijs van Nederland

7 June 1953. Zandvoort. 90 laps of a 2.605-mile circuit = 234.450 miles. Warm, dry and sunny. World Championship round 3

1 Alberto Ascari	Ferrari 500	90	2h53m35.8
2 Giuseppe Farina	Ferrari 500	90	2h53m46.2

3 Felice Bonetto/
José Froilan Gonzalez Maserati A6SSG 89
4 Mike Hawthorn Ferrari 500 89
5 Emanuel de
Graffenried Maserati A6SSG 88
6 Maurice Trintignant Gordini 16 87

Winner's average speed: 81.033 mph. Starting grid front row:
Ascari, 1m51.1 (pole), Fangio, 1m52.7 and Farina, 1m53.0.
Fastest lap: Villoresi, 1m52.8. Leaders: Ascari, laps 1-90

Grand Prix de Belgique

21 June 1953. Spa-Francorchamps. 36 laps of a 8.774-mile
circuit = 315.864 miles. Hot, dry and sunny. World
Championship round 4

1 Alberto Ascari Ferrari 500 36 2h48m30.3
2 Luigi Villoresi Ferrari 500 36 2h51m18.5
3 Onofre Marimón Maserati A6SSG 35
4 Emanuel de
Graffenried Maserati A6SSG 35
5 Maurice Trintignant Gordini 16 35

6 Mike Hawthorn Ferrari 500 35

Winner's average speed: 112.470 mph. Starting grid front row:
Fangio, 4m30 (pole), Ascari, 4m32 and Gonzalez 4m32. Fastest
lap: Gonzalez, 4m34. Leaders: Gonzalez, laps 1-11; Fangio,
12-13; Ascari, 14-36

Grand Prix de l'Automobile Club de France

5 July 1953. Reims. 60 laps of a 5.187-mile circuit = 311.220
miles. Hot, dry and sunny. World Championship round 5

1 Mike Hawthorn Ferrari 500 60 2h44m18.6
2 Juan Manuel Fangio Maserati A6SSG 60 2h44m19.6
3 José Froilan Gonzalez Maserati A6SSG 60 2h44m20.0
4 Alberto Ascari Ferrari 500 60 2h44m23.2
5 Giuseppe Farina Ferrari 500 60 2h45m26.2
6 Luigi Villoresi Ferrari 500 60 2h45m34.5

Winner's average speed: 113.646 mph. Starting grid front row:
Ascari, 2m41.2 (pole), Bonetto, 2m41.5 and Villoresi, 2m41.9.
Fastest lap: Fangio, 2m41.1. Leaders: Fangio, laps 1-29;
Fangio, 30-31, 35-36, 39-41, 45-47, 49-53, 55-56; Hawthorn,
32-34, 37-38, 42-44, 48, 54, 57-60

1953 DRIVERS' RECORDS

(excluding Indianapolis)

Driver	Car	Argentinian GP	Dutch GP	Belgian GP	French GP	British GP	German GP	Swiss GP	Italian GP
Kurt Adolff	Ferrari 166C	-	-	-	-	-	R	-	-
Alberto Ascari	Ferrari 500	1PF	1P	1	4P	1PF	8PF	1F	RP
John Barber	Cooper T23-Bristol	8	-	-	-	-	-	-	-
Edgar Barth	EMW-BMW	-	-	-	-	-	R	-	-
Erwin Bauer	Veritas RS	-	-	-	-	-	R	-	-
Elie Bayol	OSCA 20	-	-	R	-	-	-	DNS	R
Günther Bechem	AFM 2-BMW	-	-	-	-	-	R	-	-
Jean Behra	Gordini 16	6	-	R	10	R	R	R	-
Georges Berger	Simca-Gordini 15	-	R	-	-	-	-	-	-
"B Bira"	Connaught A-Lea-Francis	-	-	-	R	7	R	-	-
	Maserati A6SSG	-	-	-	-	-	-	-	11
Pablo Birger	Simca-Gordini 15	R	-	-	-	-	-	-	-
Felice Bonetto	Maserati A6GCM	R	-	-	-	-	-	-	-
	Maserati A6SSG	-	3	-	R	6	4	4	R
Alan Brown	Cooper T20-Bristol	9	-	-	-	-	R	-	-
	Cooper T23-Bristol	-	-	-	-	R	-	-	12
Piero Carini	Ferrari 553	-	-	-	-	-	-	-	R
Louis Chiron	OSCA 20	-	-	-	NC	DNS	-	DNS	10
Johnny Claes	Connaught A-Lea-Francis	-	NC	-	12	-	R	-	R
	Maserati A6SSG	-	-	R	-	-	-	-	-
Peter Collins	HWM 53-Alta	-	8	R	13	R	-	-	-
Tony Crook	Cooper T24-Alta	-	-	-	-	R	-	-	-
Jack Fairman	HWM 52/53-Alta	-	-	-	-	R	-	-	-
	Connaught A-Lea-Francis	-	-	-	-	-	-	-	NC
Juan Manuel Fangio	Maserati A6GCM	R	-	-	-	-	-	-	-
	Maserati A6SSG	-	R	RP	2F	2	2	4P	1F
Giuseppe Farina	Ferrari 500	R	2	R	5	3	1	2	2
John Fitch	HWM 52/53-Alta	-	-	-	-	-	-	-	R
Theo Fitzau	AFM 7-BMW	-	-	-	-	-	R	-	-
Paul Frère	HWM 53-Alta	-	-	10	-	-	R	-	-
Oscar Galvez	Maserati A6GCM	5	-	-	-	-	-	-	-
Bob Gerard	Cooper T23-Bristol	-	-	-	11	R	-	-	-
Yves Giraud-Cabantous	HWM 53-Alta	-	-	-	14	-	-	-	15
Helmut Glöckler	Cooper T23-Bristol	-	-	-	-	-	DNS	-	-
José Froilan Gonzalez	Maserati A6GCM	3	-	-	-	-	-	-	-
	Maserati A6SSG	-	3	RF	3	4F	-	-	-
Emanuel de Graffenried	Maserati A6SSG	-	5	4	7	R	5	R	R
Duncan Hamilton	HWM 53-Alta	-	-	-	-	R	-	-	-
Mike Hawthorn	Ferrari 500	4	4	6	1	5	3	3	4
Willi Heeks	Veritas Meteor	-	-	-	-	-	R	-	-
Theo Helfrich	Veritas RS	-	-	-	-	-	12	-	-
Hans Herrmann	Veritas Meteor	-	-	-	-	-	9	-	-
Peter Hirt	Ferrari 500	-	-	-	-	-	-	R	-
Otto Karch	Veritas RS	-	-	-	-	-	R	-	-

/Cont'd

British Grand Prix

18 July 1953. Silverstone. 90 laps of a 2.927-mile circuit = 263.430 miles. Overcast with occasional rain. World Championship round 6

1 Alberto Ascari	Ferrari 500	90	2h50m00.0
2 Juan Manuel Fangio	Maserati A6SSG	90	2h51m00.0
3 Giuseppe Farina	Ferrari 500	88	
4 José Froilan Gonzalez	Maserati A6SSG	88	
5 Mike Hawthorn	Ferrari 500	87	
6 Felice Bonetto	Maserati A6SSG	82	

Winner's average speed: 92.975 mph. Starting grid front row: Ascari, 1m48 (pole), Gonzalez, 1m49, Hawthorn, 1m49 and Fangio, 1m50. Fastest lap: Ascari and Gonzalez, 1m50. Leaders: Ascari, laps 1-90.

Grosser Preis von Deutschland

2 August 1953. Nürburgring. 18 laps of a 14.167-mile circuit = 255.006 miles. Warm, dry and sunny. World Championship round 7

1 Giuseppe Farina	Ferrari 500	18	3h02m25.0
2 Juan Manuel Fangio	Maserati A6SSG	18	3h03m29.0
3 Mike Hawthorn	Ferrari 500	18	3h04m08.6
4 Felice Bonetto	Maserati A6SSG	18	3h11m13.6
5 Emanuel de Graffenried	Maserati A6SSG	17	
6 Stirling Moss	Cooper T24-Alta	17	

Winner's average speed: 83.876 mph. Starting grid front row: Ascari, 9m59.8 (pole), Fangio, 10m03.7, Farina, 10m04.1 and Hawthorn, 10m12.6. Fastest lap: Ascari, 9m56.0. Leaders: Ascari, laps 1-4; Hawthorn, 5-7; Farina, 8-18

Grand Prix de Suisse

23 August 1953. Bremgarten. 65 laps of a 4.524-mile circuit = 294.060 miles. Warm, dry and sunny. World Championship round 8

1 Alberto Ascari	Ferrari 500	65	3h01m34.40
2 Giuseppe Farina	Ferrari 500	65	3h02m47.33
3 Mike Hawthorn	Ferrari 500	65	3h03m10.36
4 Juan Manuel Fangio/ Felice Bonetto	Maserati A6SSG	64	
5 Hermann Lang	Maserati A6SSG	62	
6 Luigi Villoresi	Ferrari 500	62	

Winner's average speed: 97.171 mph. Starting grid front row: Fangio, 2m40.1 (pole), Ascari, 2m40.7 and Farina, 2m42.6. Fastest lap: Ascari, 2m41.3. Leaders: Ascari, laps 1-40, 54-65; Farina, 41-53

1953 DRIVERS' RECORDS cont'd/ (excluding Indianapolis)

Driver	Car	Argentinian GP	Dutch GP	Belgian GP	French GP	British GP	German GP	Swiss GP	Italian GP
Ernst Klodwig	Heck-BMW	-	-	-	-	-	15	-	-
Rudolf Krause	BMW Eigenbau	-	-	-	-	-	14	-	-
Chico Landi	Maserati A6SSG	-	-	-	-	-	-	R	R
Hermann Lang	Maserati A6SSG	-	-	-	-	-	-	5	-
Arthur Legat	Veritas Meteor	-	-	R	-	-	-	-	-
Ernst Loof	Veritas Meteor	-	-	-	-	-	R	-	-
Lance Macklin	HWM 53-Alta	-	R	R	R	R	-	R	R
Umberto Maglioli	Ferrari 553	-	-	-	-	-	-	-	8
Sergio Mantovani	Maserati A6SSG	-	-	-	-	-	-	-	7
Robert Manzon	Gordini 16	R	-	-	-	-	-	-	-
Onofre Marimón	Maserati A6SSG	-	-	3	9	R	R	R	-
	Maserati A6GCM	-	-	-	-	-	-	-	R
Kenneth McAlpine	Connaught A-Lea-Francis	-	R	-	-	R	13	-	NC
Carlos Menditéguy	Gordini 16	R	-	-	-	-	-	-	-
Roberto Mieres	Gordini 16	-	R	-	R	-	-	-	6
Stirling Moss	Connaught A-Lea-Francis	-	9	-	-	-	-	-	-
	Cooper T24-Alta	-	-	-	-	R	6	-	13
Luigi Musso	Maserati A6SSG	-	-	-	-	-	-	-	7
Rodney Nuckey	Cooper T23-Bristol	-	-	-	-	-	11	-	-
André Pilette	Connaught A-Lea-Francis	-	-	11	-	-	-	-	-
Tony Rolt	Connaught A-Lea-Francis	-	-	-	-	R	-	-	-
Louis Rosier	Ferrari 500	-	7	8	10	10	R	-	16
Roy Salvadori	Connaught A-Lea-Francis	-	R	-	R	R	R	-	R
Harry Schell	Gordini 16	7	R	7	R	R	R	-	9
Albert Scherrer	HWM 53-Alta	-	-	-	-	-	-	8	-
Adolfo Schwelm Cruz	Cooper T20-Bristol	R	-	-	-	-	-	-	-
Wolfgang Seidel	Veritas RS	-	-	-	-	-	16	-	-
Ian Stewart	Connaught A-Lea-Francis	-	-	-	-	R	-	-	-
Jimmy Stewart	Cooper T20-Bristol	-	-	-	-	R	-	-	-
Hans Stuck	AFM 4-Küchen	-	-	-	-	-	R	-	14
Jacques Swaters	Ferrari 500	-	-	DNS	-	-	7	R	-
Max de Terra	Ferrari 166C	-	-	-	-	-	-	9	-
Charles de Tornaco	Ferrari 500	-	-	DNS	-	-	-	-	-
Maurice Trintignant	Gordini 16	7	6	5	R	R	R	R	5
Luigi Villoresi	Ferrari 500	2	R^F	2	6	R	8	6	3
Fred Wacker	Gordini 16	-	DNS	9	-	-	-	DNS	-
Ken Wharton	Cooper T23-Bristol	-	R	-	-	R	8	7	NC
Peter Whitehead	Cooper T24-Alta	-	-	-	9	-	-	-	-

SHARED DRIVES - Argentinian GP: Maurice Trintignant/Harry Schell (Gordini 16) 7. **Dutch GP:** Felice Bonetto/José Froilan Gonzalez (Maserati A6SSG) 3. **Belgian GP:** Johnny Claes/Juan Manuel Fangio (Maserati A6SSG) R. **German GP:** Alberto Ascari/Luigi Villoresi (Ferrari 500) 8; Luigi Villoresi/Alberto Ascari (Ferrari 500) R. **Swiss GP:** Juan Manuel Fangio/Felice Bonetto (Maserati A6SSG) 4; Felice Bonetto/Juan Manuel Fangio (Maserati A6SSG) R. **Italian GP:** Sergio Mantovani/Luigi Musso (Maserati A6SSG) 7

Gran Premio d'Italia

13 September 1953. Monza. 80 laps of a 3.915-mile circuit = 313.200 miles. Warm, dry and sunny. World Championship round 9

1 Juan Manuel Fangio	Maserati A6SSG	80	2h49m45.9
2 Giuseppe Farina	Ferrari 500	80	2h49m47.3
3 Luigi Villoresi	Ferrari 500	79	
4 Mike Hawthorn	Ferrari 500	79	
5 Maurice Trintignant	Gordini 16	79	
6 Roberto Mieres	Gordini 16	77	

Winner's average speed: 110.694 mph. Starting grid front row: Ascari, 2m02.7 (pole), Fangio, 2m03.2 and Farina, 2m03.9. Fastest lap: Fangio, 2m04.6. Leaders: Ascari, laps 1-6, 9, 14-24, 29-33, 36-40, 42-45, 47-49, 53-79; Fangio, 7-8, 11, 25, 27-28, 34-35, 41, 50-52, 80; Farina, 10, 12-13, 26, 46

1953 FINAL CHAMPIONSHIP POSITIONS

Drivers

1	Alberto Ascari	34.5 (47)*	8	Emanuel de Graffenried	7		Sam Hanks	2
2	Juan Manuel Fangio	27.5 (29)*	9	Felice Bonetto	6.5		Hermann Lang	2
3	Giuseppe Farina	26 (32)*	10	Art Cross	6		Jack McGrath	2
4	Mike Hawthorn	19 (27)*	11=	Onofre Marimón	4	18=	Fred Agabashian	1.5
5	Luigi Villoresi	17		Maurice Trintignant	4		Paul Russo	1.5
6	José Froilan Gonzalez	13.5 (14.5)*	13=	Duane Carter	2		*Best four results count	
7	Bill Vukovich	9		Oscar Galvez	2			

1954

After two Ferrari-dominated F2 years, the new Formula One introduced for 1954 attracted both Mercedes-Benz, renowned for their pre-war successes, and Lancia to the championship. Juan Manuel Fangio signed to lead the former, while Alberto Ascari moved to Lancia.

Neither marque was ready for the opening rounds in Argentina and Belgium, where Fangio won on guest appearances in a works Maserati 250F. The Mercedes-Benz W196 made its debut at Reims, complete with all-enveloping streamlined bodywork. The newcomers dominated the

1954 DRIVERS' RECORDS

(excluding Indianapolis)

Driver	Car	Argentinian GP	Belgian GP	French GP	British GP	German GP	Swiss GP	Italian GP	Spanish GP
Alberto Ascari	Maserati 250F	-	-	R	R^F	-	-	-	-
	Ferrari 625 (555)	-	-	-	-	-	-	R	-
	Lancia D50	-	-	-	-	-	-	-	R^PF
Elie Bayol	Gordini 16	5	-	-	-	-	-	-	-
Don Beauman	Connaught A-Lea-Francis	-	-	-	11	-	-	-	-
Jean Behra	Gordini 16	R	R	6	R^F	10	R	R	R
Georges Berger	Gordini 16	-	-	R	-	-	-	-	-
"B Bira"	Maserati 250F	7	6	4	R	R	-	-	9
Eric Brandon	Cooper T23-Bristol	-	-	R	-	-	-	-	-
Alan Brown	Cooper T23-Bristol	-	-	-	DNS	-	-	-	-
Clemar Bucci	Gordini 16	-	-	-	R	R	R	R	-
Peter Collins	Vanwall Special	-	-	-	R	-	-	7	DNS
Jorge Daponte	Maserati 250F	R	-	-	-	-	-	11	-
Juan Manuel Fangio	Maserati 250F	1	1^PF	-	-	-	-	-	-
	Mercedes-Benz W196	-	-	1^P	4^PF	1^P	1^F	1^P	3
Giuseppe Farina	Ferrari 625	2^P	-	-	-	-	-	-	-
	Ferrari 553 Squalo	-	R	-	-	-	-	-	-
Ron Flockhart	Maserati 250F	-	-	-	R	-	-	-	-
Paul Frère	Gordini 16	-	R	7	-	R	-	-	-
Bob Gerard	Cooper T23-Bristol	-	-	-	10	-	-	-	-
Chico Godia-Sales	Maserati 250F	-	-	-	-	-	-	-	6
José Froilan Gonzalez	Ferrari 625	3^F	4	-	-	-	-	3^F	-
	Ferrari 553 Squalo	-	R	R	-	-	-	R	-
	Ferrari 625 (555)	-	-	-	1^F	-	-	-	-
	Ferrari 625 (735/555)	-	-	-	-	2	2^P	-	-
Horace Gould	Cooper T23-Bristol	-	-	-	15	-	-	-	-
Emanuel de Graffenried	Maserati 250F	8	R*	-	-	-	-	-	R
Mike Hawthorn	Ferrari 625	DSQ	4	-	-	-	-	-	-
	Ferrari 553 Squalo	-	-	R	-	-	-	-	1
	Ferrari 625 (555)	-	-	-	2^F	-	-	2	-
	Ferrari 625 (735/555)	-	-	-	-	2	R	-	-
Theo Helfrich	Klenk Meteor-BMW	-	-	-	-	R	-	-	-
Hans Herrmann	Mercedes-Benz W196	-	-	R^F	-	R	3	4	R
Karl Kling	Mercedes-Benz W196	-	-	2	7	4^F	R	R	5
Hermann Lang	Mercedes-Benz W196	-	-	-	-	R	-	-	-

*Camera car for the film *The Racer*, not competing in the Grand Prix

/Cont'd

race, with Fangio and team-mate Karl Kling lapping the field.

With Lancia still delayed (also forcing Ascari into a Maserati), Mercedes appeared unbeatable, although the wide bodywork caused even Fangio difficulty judging corners and, at Silverstone, he could only finish fourth in a car

....

Fangio's dented Mercedes at Silverstone during the 1954 British Grand Prix

dented on more than one occasion by oil drums marking the course. José Froilan Gonzalez repeated his 1951 win for a Ferrari team unable to satisfactorily develop its new F1 cars.

With conventional bodywork Fangio won the German, Swiss and Italian GPs, securing his second World Championship. The Lancia D50 at last made its debut at the final race in Spain. Ascari put it on pole, led in the early laps and set the fastest lap, but Mike Hawthorn won after the Lancia suffered clutch problems. Sadly, Fangio's win at the Nürburgring was marred by the death in practice of his friend Onofre Marimón.

Gran Premio de la Republica Argentina

17 January 1954. Buenos Aires. 87 laps of a 2.431-mile circuit = 211.497 miles. Race scheduled for three hours. Dry and overcast at the start, heavy rain later. World Championship round 1

1 Juan Manuel Fangio	Maserati 250F	87	3h00m55.8
2 Giuseppe Farina	Ferrari 625	87	3h02m14.8
3 José Froilan Gonzalez	Ferrari 625	87	3h02m56.8

1954 DRIVERS' RECORDS cont'd/ (excluding Indianapolis)

Driver	Car	Argentinian GP	Belgian GP	French GP	British GP	German GP	Swiss GP	Italian GP	Spanish GP
Roger Loyer	Gordini 16	R	-	-	-	-	-	-	-
Lance Macklin	HWM 54-Alta	-	-	R	-	-	-	-	-
Umberto Maglioli	Ferrari 625	9	-	-	-	-	-	3	-
	Ferrari 553 Squalo	-	-	-	-	-	7	-	-
Sergio Mantovani	Maserati 250F	-	7	DNS	-	5	9	9	R
Robert Manzon	Ferrari 625	-	-	3	R	9	-	R	R
	Ferrari 553 Squalo	-	-	-	-	-	DNS	-	-
Onofre Marimón	Maserati 250F	R	R	R	3F	DNS	-	-	-
Leslie Marr	Connaught A-Lea-Francis	-	-	-	13	-	-	-	-
Carlos Menditéguy	Maserati 250F	DNS	-	-	-	-	-	-	-
Roberto Mieres	Maserati 250F	R	R	R	6	R	4	R	4
Stirling Moss	Maserati 250F	-	3	-	RF	R	R	10	R
Luigi Musso	Maserati 250F	DNS	-	-	-	-	-	R	2
Reg Parnell	Ferrari 625	-	-	-	R	-	-	-	-
André Pilette	Gordini 16	-	5	-	9	R	-	-	-
Jacques Pollet	Gordini 16	-	-	R	-	-	-	-	R
John Riseley-Prichard	Connaught A-Lea-Francis	-	-	-	R	-	-	-	-
Giovanni de Riu	Maserati 250F	-	-	-	-	-	-	DNS	-
Louis Rosier	Ferrari 625	R	-	R	R	8	-	-	-
	Maserati 250F	-	-	-	-	-	-	8	7
Roy Salvadori	Maserati 250F	-	-	R	R	-	-	-	-
Harry Schell	Maserati 250F	6	-	R	12	7	R	-	R
Jacques Swaters	Ferrari 625	-	R	-	-	-	8	-	R
Piero Taruffi	Ferrari 625	-	-	-	-	6	-	-	-
Leslie Thorne	Connaught A-Lea-Francis	-	-	-	14	-	-	-	-
Maurice Trintignant	Ferrari 625	4	2	R	-	3	-	-	-
	Ferrari 625 (555)	-	-	-	5	-	-	5	-
	Ferrari 625 (735/555)	-	-	-	-	-	R	-	-
	Ferrari 553 Squalo	-	-	-	-	-	-	-	R
Luigi Villoresi	Maserati 250F	-	-	5	R	DNS	-	R	-
	Lancia D50	-	-	-	-	-	-	-	R
Ottorino Volonterio	Maserati 250F	-	-	-	-	-	-	-	R
Fred Wacker	Gordini 16	-	-	-	-	-	R	6	-
Ken Wharton	Maserati 250F	-	-	R	8	DNS	6	-	8
Peter Whitehead	Cooper T24-Alta	-	-	-	R	-	-	-	-
Bill Whitehouse	Connaught A-Lea-Francis	-	-	-	R	-	-	-	-

SHARED DRIVES - **Belgian GP:** Mike Hawthorn/José Froilan Gonzalez (Ferrari 625) 4. **British GP:** "B Bira"/Ron Flockhart (Maserati 250F) R; Luigi Villoresi/Alberto Ascari (Maserati 250F) R. **German GP:** José Froilan Gonzalez/Mike Hawthorn (Ferrari 625 (735/555)) 2. **Italian GP:** Umberto Maglioli/José Froilan Gonzalez (Ferrari 625) 3. **Spanish GP:** Emanuel de Graffenried/Ottorino Volonterio (Maserati 250F) R.

World Championship Grand Prix Racing

4 Maurice Trintignant	Ferrari 625	86
5 Elie Bayol	Gordini 16 (54)	85
6 Harry Schell	Maserati 250F	84

Winner's average speed: 70.137 mph. Starting grid front row: Farina, 1m44.8 (pole), Gonzalez, 1m44.9, Fangio, 1m45.6 and Hawthorn, 1m47.0. Fastest lap: Gonzalez, 1m48.2. Leaders: Farina, laps 1-14; Gonzalez, 15-32, ?-? (Gonzalez led during a heavy rain storm - exact laps not known); Hawthorn, 33-34; Fangio, 35-?, ?-87

Indianapolis 500

31 May 1954. Indianapolis. 200 laps of a 2.500-mile circuit = 500.000 miles. Very hot, dry and sunny. World Championship round 2

1 Bill Vukovich	Kurtis KK500A-Offenhauser	200	3h49m17.27
2 Jimmy Bryan	Kuzma-Offenhauser	200	3h50m27.26
3 Jack McGrath	Kurtis KK500C-Offenhauser	200	3h50m36.97
4 Troy Ruttman/ Duane Carter	Kurtis KK500A-Offenhauser	200	3h52m09.90
5 Mike Nazaruk	Kurtis KK500C-Offenhauser	200	3h52m41.85
6 Fred Agabashian	Kurtis KK500C-Offenhauser	200	3h53m04.83

Winner's average speed: 130.840 mph. Starting grid front row: McGrath, 141.033 mph (pole), Daywalt, 139.789 mph and Bryan, 139.665 mph. Fastest lap in the lead: McGrath, 1m04.04

Grand Prix de Belgique

20 June 1954. Spa-Francorchamps. 36 laps of a 8.774-mile circuit = 315.864 miles. Warm, dry and sunny. World Championship round 3

1 Juan Manuel Fangio	Maserati 250F	36	2h44m42.4
2 Maurice Trintignant	Ferrari 625	36	2h45m06.6
3 Stirling Moss	Maserati 250F	35	
4 Mike Hawthorn/ José Froilan Gonzalez	Ferrari 625	35	
5 André Pilette	Gordini 16 (54)	35	
6 "B Bira"	Maserati 250F	35	

Winner's average speed: 115.064 mph. Starting grid front row: Fangio, 4m22.1 (pole), Gonzalez, 4m23.6 and Farina, 4m26.0. Fastest lap: Fangio, 4m25.5. Leaders: Farina, laps 1-2, 11-13; Fangio, 3-10, 14-36

Grand Prix de l'Automobile Club de France

4 July 1954. Reims. 61 laps of a 5.187-mile circuit = 316.407 miles. Overcast and dry at the start, rain later. World Championship round 4

1 Juan Manuel Fangio	Mercedes-Benz W196	61	2h42m47.9
2 Karl Kling	Mercedes-Benz W196	61	2h42m48.0
3 Robert Manzon	Ferrari 625	60	
4 "B Bira"	Maserati 250F	60	
5 Luigi Villoresi	Maserati 250F	58	
6 Jean Behra	Gordini 16 (54)	56	

Winner's average speed: 116.613 mph. Starting grid front row: Fangio, 2m29.4 (pole), Kling, 2m30.4 and Ascari, 2m30.5. Fastest lap: Herrmann, 2m32.9. Leaders: Kling, laps 1-2, 29-33, 38, 54-57, 60; Fangio, 3-28, 34-37, 39-53, 58-59, 61

British Grand Prix

17 July 1954. Silverstone. 90 laps of a 2.927-mile circuit = 263.430 miles. Cold and wet. World Championship round 5

1 José Froilan Gonzalez	Ferrari 625 (555)	90	2h56m14.0
2 Mike Hawthorn	Ferrari 625 (555)	90	2h57m24.0
3 Onofre Marimón	Maserati 250F	89	
4 Juan Manuel Fangio	Mercedes-Benz W196	89	
5 Maurice Trintignant	Ferrari 625 (555)	87	
6 Roberto Mieres	Maserati 250F	87	

Winner's average speed: 89.687 mph. Starting grid front row: Fangio, 1m45 (pole), Gonzalez, 1m46, Hawthorn, 1m46 and Moss, 1m47. Fastest lap: Ascari, Behra, Fangio, Gonzalez, Hawthorn, Marimón and Moss, all 1m50. Leaders: Gonzalez, laps 1-90

Grosser Preis von Deutschland

1 August 1954. Nürburgring. 22 laps of a 14.167-mile circuit = 311.674 miles. Warm, dry and sunny. World Championship round 6. Also known as the European Grand Prix

1 Juan Manuel Fangio	Mercedes-Benz W196	22	3h45m45.8
2 José Froilan Gonzalez/ Mike Hawthorn	Ferrari 625 (735/555)	22	3h47m22.3
3 Maurice Trintignant	Ferrari 625	22	3h50m54.4
4 Karl Kling	Mercedes-Benz W196	22	3h51m52.3
5 Sergio Mantovani	Maserati 250F	22	3h54m36.3
6 Piero Taruffi	Ferrari 625	21	

Winner's average speed: 82.832 mph. Starting grid front row: Fangio, 9m50.1 (pole), Hawthorn, 9m53.3 and Moss, 10m00.7. Fastest lap: Kling, 9m55.1. Leaders: Fangio, laps 1-14, 17-22; Kling, 15-16

Grand Prix de Suisse

22 August 1954. Bremgarten. 66 laps of a 4.524-mile circuit = 298.584 miles. Damp and dull at the start, drying. World Championship round 7

1 Juan Manuel Fangio	Mercedes-Benz W196	66	3h00m34.5
2 José Froilan Gonzalez	Ferrari 625 (735/555)	66	3h01m32.3
3 Hans Herrmann	Mercedes-Benz W196	65	
4 Roberto Mieres	Maserati 250F	64	
5 Sergio Mantovani	Maserati 250F	64	
6 Ken Wharton	Maserati 250F	64	

Winner's average speed: 99.211 mph. Starting grid front row: Gonzalez, 2m39.5 (pole), Fangio, 2m39.7 and Moss, 2m41.4. Fastest lap: Fangio, 2m39.7. Leaders: Fangio, laps 1-66

Gran Premio d'Italia

5 September 1954. Monza. 80 laps of a 3.915-mile circuit = 313.200 miles. Warm, dry and sunny. World Championship round 8

1 Juan Manuel Fangio	Mercedes-Benz W196	80	2h47m47.9
2 Mike Hawthorn	Ferrari 625 (555)	79	
3 Umberto Maglioli/ José Froilan Gonzalez	Ferrari 625	78	
4 Hans Herrmann	Mercedes-Benz W196	77	
5 Maurice Trintignant	Ferrari 625 (555)	75	
6 Fred Wacker	Gordini 16 (54)	75	

Winner's average speed: 111.992 mph. Starting grid front row: Fangio, 1m59.0 (pole), Ascari, 1m59.2 and Moss, 1m59.3. Fastest lap: Gonzalez, 2m00.8. Leaders: Kling, laps 1-3; Fangio, 4-5, 23, 68-80; Ascari, 6-22, 24-44, 46-48; Moss, 45, 49-67

Gran Premio de Espana

24 October 1954. Pedralbes. 80 laps of a 3.936-mile circuit = 314.880 miles. Warm, dry and sunny. World Championship round 9

1 Mike Hawthorn	Ferrari 553 Squalo	80	3h13m52.1
2 Luigi Musso	Maserati 250F	80	3h15m05.3
3 Juan Manuel Fangio	Mercedes-Benz W196	79	
4 Roberto Mieres	Maserati 250F	79	
5 Karl Kling	Mercedes-Benz W196	79	
6 Chico Godia-Sales	Maserati 250F	76	

Winner's average speed: 97.452 mph. Starting grid front row: Ascari, 2m18.1 (pole), Fangio, 2m19.1, Hawthorn, 2m20.6 and Schell, 2m20.6. Fastest lap: Ascari, 2m20.4. Leaders: Schell, laps 1-2, 10, 13, 15-17, 19, 21, 23; Ascari, 3-9; Trintignant, 11-12, 14, 18, 20; Hawthorn, 22, 24-80

1954 FINAL CHAMPIONSHIP POSITIONS

Drivers

1	Juan Manuel Fangio	42 (57.14)*		Roberto Mieres	6		Umberto Maglioli	2
2	José Froilan Gonzalez	25.14 (26.64)*		Luigi Musso	6		Mike Nazaruk	2
3	Mike Hawthorn	24.64	12	Jack McGrath	5		André Pilette	2
4	Maurice Trintignant	17	13=	Onofre Marimón	4.14		Luigi Villoresi	2
5	Karl Kling	12		Stirling Moss	4.14	23=	Duane Carter	1.5
6=	Hans Herrmann	8	15=	Sergio Mantovani	4		Troy Ruttman	1.5
	Bill Vukovich	8		Robert Manzon	4	25	Alberto Ascari	1.14
8=	Jimmy Bryan	6	17	"B Bira"	3	26	Jean Behra	0.14
	Giuseppe Farina	6	18=	Elie Bayol	2		*Best five results count	

1955

The 1955 season was dominated by two tragedies, one of which brought the whole sport into question. First, Alberto Ascari survived crashing his Lancia into the harbour at Monaco, only to die four days later while testing a sports car at Monza. But what followed was the worst accident to afflict motor racing, and although not in a Grand Prix, its repercussions were felt in all branches of the sport. During the Le Mans 24 hour race, a collision on the pit straight launched the Mercedes of "Pierre Levegh" into the crowd; it burst into flames, killing "Levegh" and over 80 spectators. The French, German, Swiss and Spanish GPs were all cancelled, only the British and Italian races remaining after the disaster.

The accident eventually led to the withdrawal of Mercedes from racing at the end of the year, while to this day the sport remains outlawed in Switzerland. Following the death of Ascari, Lancia decided to stop Grand Prix racing immediately, its cars and designer Vittorio Jano being re-employed by Ferrari. The resulting Lancia-Ferrari would eventually solve the problems Ferrari had been experiencing since the end of the F2 years.

With Stirling Moss joining Fangio at Mercedes, the Argentinian won all but two Grands Prix to successfully defend his championship title. At Aintree, Moss scored his first Grand Prix victory, Fangio shadowing him across the line with Karl Kling and Piero Taruffi completing a 1-2-3-4 for the marque.

Mercedes' only defeat came at Monaco, back on the World Championship calendar for the first time since 1950. Maurice Trintignant scored his first Grand Prix win when Fangio, Moss, Ascari and Roberto Mieres all retired ahead of him.

Gran Premio de la Republica Argentina

16 January 1955. Buenos Aires. 96 laps of a 2.431-mile circuit = 233.376 miles. Race scheduled for three hours. Extreme heat, dry and sunny. World Championship round 1

1	Juan Manuel Fangio	Mercedes-Benz W196	96	3h00m38.6
2	José Froilan Gonzalez/ Maurice Trintignant/ Giuseppe Farina	Ferrari 625 (555)	96	3h02m08.2
3	Giuseppe Farina/ Umberto Maglioli/ Maurice Trintignant	Ferrari 625 (555)	94	
4	Hans Herrmann/Karl Kling/Stirling Moss	Mercedes-Benz W196	94	
5	Roberto Mieres	Maserati 250F	91	

6	Harry Schell/ Jean Behra	Maserati 250F	88

Winner's average speed: 77.515 mph. Starting grid front row: Gonzalez, 1m43.1 (pole), Ascari, 1m43.2, Fangio, 1m43.6 and Behra, 1m43.8. Fastest lap: Fangio, 1m48.3. Leaders: Fangio, laps 1-2, 26-34, 43-96; Ascari, 3-5, 11-21; Gonzalez, 6-10, 22-25; Schell, 35-40; Mieres, 41-42

Grand Prix de Monaco

22 May 1955. Monte Carlo. 100 laps of a 1.954-mile circuit = 195.400 miles. Hot, dry and sunny. World Championship round 2. Also known as the European Grand Prix

1	Maurice Trintignant	Ferrari 625 (555)	100	2h58m09.8
2	Eugenio Castellotti	Lancia D50	100	2h58m30.0
3	Jean Behra/ Cesare Perdisa	Maserati 250F	99	
4	Giuseppe Farina	Ferrari 625 (555)	99	
5	Luigi Villoresi	Lancia D50	99	
6	Louis Chiron	Lancia D50	95	

Winner's average speed: 65.805 mph. Starting grid front row: Fangio, 1m41.1 (pole), Ascari, 1m41.1 and Moss, 1m41.2. Fastest lap: Fangio, 1m42.4. Leaders: Fangio, laps 1-49; Moss, 50-80; Trintignant, 81-100

Stirling Moss on the way to his first Grand Prix victory at Aintree in 1955

Indianapolis 500

30 May 1955. Indianapolis. 200 laps of a 2.500-mile circuit = 500.000 miles. Cool, dry and windy. World Championship round 3

1	Bob Sweikert	Kurtis KK500C-Offenhauser	200	3h53m59.13
2	Tony Bettenhausen/ Paul Russo	Kurtis KK500C-Offenhauser	200	3h56m43.11
3	Jimmy Davies	Kurtis KK500B-Offenhauser	200	3h57m31.89
4	Johnny Thomson	Kuzma-Offenhauser	200	3h57m38.44
5	Walt Faulkner/ Bill Homeier	Kurtis KK500C-Offenhauser	200	3h59m16.66
6	Andy Linden	Kurtis KK4000-Offenhauser	200	3h59m57.47

Winner's average speed: 128.209 mph. Starting grid front row: Hoyt, 140.045 mph (pole), Bettenhausen, 139.985 mph and McGrath, 142.580 mph. Fastest lap in the lead: Vukovich, 1m03.67

1955 DRIVERS' RECORDS

(excluding Indianapolis)

Driver	Car	Argentinian GP	Monaco GP	Belgian GP	Dutch GP	British GP	Italian GP
Alberto Ascari	Lancia D50	R	R	-	-	-	-
Elie Bayol	Gordini 16	R	R	-	-	-	-
Jean Behra	Maserati 250F	6	3	5	6	R	4
Pablo Birger	Gordini 16	R	-	-	-	-	-
Jack Brabham	Cooper T40-Bristol	-	-	-	-	R	-
Clemar Bucci	Maserati 250F	R	-	-	-	-	-
Eugenio Castellotti	Lancia D50	R	2	R^P	-	-	-
	Ferrari 555 Supersqualo	-	-	-	5	-	3
	Ferrari 625 (555)	-	-	-	-	6	-
Louis Chiron	Lancia D50	-	6	-	-	-	-
Johnny Claes	Maserati 250F	-	-	DNS	-	-	-
	Ferrari 625	-	-	-	11	-	-
Peter Collins	Maserati 250F	-	-	-	-	R	R
Jack Fairman	Connaught B-Alta	-	-	-	-	DNS	-
Juan Manuel Fangio	Mercedes-Benz W196	1^F	R^{PF}	1^F	1^P	2	1^P
Giuseppe Farina	Ferrari 625 (555)	2+3	4	-	-	-	-
	Ferrari 555 Supersqualo	-	-	3	-	-	-
	Lancia-Ferrari D50	-	-	-	-	-	DNS
John Fitch	Maserati 250F	-	-	-	-	-	9
Paul Frère	Ferrari 555 Supersqualo	-	8	4	-	-	-
José Froilan Gonzalez	Ferrari 625 (555)	2^P	-	-	-	-	-
Horace Gould	Maserati 250F	-	-	-	R	R	R
Mike Hawthorn	Vanwall VW1	-	R	R	-	-	-
	Ferrari 555 Supersqualo	-	-	-	7	-	R
	Ferrari 625 (555)	-	-	-	-	6	-
Hans Herrmann	Mercedes-Benz W196	4	-	-	-	-	-
Jesus Iglesias	Gordini 16	R	-	-	-	-	-
Karl Kling	Mercedes-Benz W196	4	-	R	R	3	R
Jean Lucas	Gordini 32	-	-	-	-	-	R
Lance Macklin	Maserati 250F	-	DNQ	-	-	8	-
Umberto Maglioli	Ferrari 625 (555)	3	-	-	-	-	-
	Ferrari 555 Supersqualo	-	-	-	-	-	6
Sergio Mantovani	Maserati 250F	7	-	-	-	-	-
Robert Manzon	Gordini 16	-	R	-	R	R	-
Leslie Marr	Connaught B-Alta	-	-	-	R	-	-

/Cont'd

Grand Prix de Belgique

5 June 1955. Spa-Francorchamps. 36 laps of a 8.774-mile circuit = 315.864 miles. Warm, dry and sunny. World Championship round 4

1 Juan Manuel Fangio	Mercedes-Benz W196	36	2h39m29.0
2 Stirling Moss	Mercedes-Benz W196	36	2h39m37.1
3 Giuseppe Farina	Ferrari 555 Supersqualo	36	2h41m09.5
4 Paul Frère	Ferrari 555 Supersqualo	36	2h42m54.5
5 Roberto Mieres/			
Jean Behra	Maserati 250F	35	
6 Maurice Trintignant	Ferrari 555 Supersqualo	35	

Winner's average speed: 118.833 mph. Starting grid front row: Castellotti, 4m18.1 (pole), Fangio, 4m18.6 and Moss, 4m19.2. Fastest lap: Fangio, 4m20.6. Leaders: Fangio, laps 1-36

Grote Prijs van Nederland

19 June 1955. Zandvoort. 100 laps of a 2.605-mile circuit = 260.500 miles. Cool, dry and overcast at the start, light rain later. World Championship round 5

1 Juan Manuel Fangio	Mercedes-Benz W196	100	2h54m23.8
2 Stirling Moss	Mercedes-Benz W196	100	2h54m24.1
3 Luigi Musso	Maserati 250F	100	2h55m20.9
4 Roberto Mieres	Maserati 250F	99	
5 Eugenio Castellotti	Ferrari 555 Supersqualo	97	
6 Jean Behra	Maserati 250F	97	

Winner's average speed: 89.623 mph. Starting grid front row: Fangio, 1m40.0 (pole), Moss, 1m40.4 and Kling, 1m41.1. Fastest lap: Mieres, 1m40.9. Leaders: Fangio, laps 1-100

British Grand Prix

16 July 1955. Aintree. 90 laps of a 3.000-mile circuit = 270.000 miles. Hot, dry and sunny. World Championship round 6

1 Stirling Moss	Mercedes-Benz W196	90	3h07m21.2
2 Juan Manuel Fangio	Mercedes-Benz W196	90	3h07m21.4
3 Karl Kling	Mercedes-Benz W196	90	3h08m33.0
4 Piero Taruffi	Mercedes-Benz W196	89	
5 Luigi Musso	Maserati 250F	89	
6 Mike Hawthorn/			
Eugenio Castellotti	Ferrari 625 (555)	87	

Winner's average speed: 86.468 mph. Starting grid front row: Moss, 2m00.4 (pole), Fangio, 2m00.6 and Behra, 2m01.4. Fastest lap: Moss, 2m00.4. Leaders: Fangio, laps 1-2, 18-25; Moss, 3-17, 26-90

Gran Premio d'Italia

11 September 1955. Monza. 50 laps of a 6.214-mile circuit = 310.700 miles. Warm, dry and sunny. World Championship round 7

1 Juan Manuel Fangio	Mercedes-Benz W196	50	2h25m04.4
2 Piero Taruffi	Mercedes-Benz W196	50	2h25m05.1
3 Eugenio Castellotti	Ferrari 555 Supersqualo	50	2h25m50.6
4 Jean Behra	Maserati 250F	50	2h29m01.9
5 Carlos Menditéguy	Maserati 250F	49	
6 Umberto Maglioli	Ferrari 555 Supersqualo	49	

Winner's average speed: 128.494 mph. Starting grid front row: Fangio, 2m46.5 (pole), Moss, 2m46.8 and Kling, 2m48.3. Fastest lap: Moss, 2m46.9. Leaders: Fangio, laps 1-7, 9-50; Moss, 8

1955 DRIVERS' RECORDS cont'd/
(excluding Indianapolis)

Driver	Car	Argentinian GP	Monaco GP	Belgian GP	Dutch GP	British GP	Italian GP
Kenneth McAlpine	Connaught B-Alta	-	-	-	-	R	-
Carlos Menditéguy	Maserati 250F	R	-	-	-	-	5
Roberto Mieres	Maserati 250F	5	R	5	4F	R	7
Stirling Moss	Mercedes-Benz W196	4	9	2	2	1PF	RF
Luigi Musso	Maserati 250F	7	R	7	3	5	R
Cesare Perdisa	Maserati 250F	-	3	8	-	-	-
Luigi Piotti	Maserati 4CLT/48-Anzani	-	-	-	-	-	DNS
Jacques Pollet	Gordini 16	-	7	-	10	-	R
Tony Rolt	Connaught B-Alta	-	-	-	-	R	-
Louis Rosier	Maserati 250F	-	R	9	9	-	-
Roy Salvadori	Maserati 250F	-	-	-	-	R	-
Harry Schell	Maserati 250F	6	-	-	-	-	-
	Ferrari 555 Supersqualo	-	R	-	-	-	-
	Vanwall VW2	-	-	-	-	R	R
	Vanwall VW3	-	-	-	-	9	-
Hermanos da Silva Ramos	Gordini 16	-	-	-	8	R	R
André Simon	Mercedes-Benz W196	-	R	-	-	-	-
	Maserati 250F	-	-	-	-	R	-
Mike Sparken	Gordini 16	-	-	-	-	7	-
Piero Taruffi	Ferrari 555 Supersqualo	-	8	-	-	-	-
	Mercedes-Benz W196	-	-	-	-	4	2
Maurice Trintignant	Ferrari 625 (555)	2+3	1	-	-	R	-
	Ferrari 555 Supersqualo	-	-	6	R	-	8
Alberto Uria	Maserati 250F	R	-	-	-	-	-
Luigi Villoresi	Lancia D50	R	5	-	-	-	-
	Lancia-Ferrari D50	-	-	-	-	-	DNS
Peter Walker	Maserati 250F	-	-	-	R	-	-
	Connaught B-Alta	-	-	-	R	-	-
Ken Wharton	Vanwall VW3	-	-	-	-	9	-
	Vanwall VW4	-	-	-	-	-	R
Ted Whiteaway	HWM 54-Alta	-	DNQ	-	-	-	-

SHARED DRIVES - Argentinian GP: José Froilan Gonzalez/Maurice Trintignant/Giuseppe Farina (Ferrari 625 (555)) 2; Giuseppe Farina/ Umberto Maglioli/Maurice Trintignant (Ferrari 625 (555)) 3; Hans Herrman/Karl Kling/Stirling Moss (Mercedes-Benz W196) 4; Harry Schell/Jean Behra (Maserati 250F) 6; Luigi Musso/Sergio Mantovani/Harry Schell (Maserati 250F) 7; Clemar Bucci/Harry Schell/Carlos Menditéguy (Maserati 250F) R; Sergio Mantovani/Luigi Musso/Jean Behra (Maserati 250F) R; Eugenio Castellotti/Luigi Villoresi (Lancia D50) R. **Monaco GP:** Jean Behra/Cesare Perdisa (Maserati 250F) 3; Piero Taruffi/Paul Frère (Ferrari 555 Supersqualo) 8. **Belgian GP:** Roberto Mieres/Jean Behra (Maserati 250F) 5; Cesare Perdisa/Jean Behra (Maserati 250F) R. **British GP:** Mike Hawthorn/Eugenio Castellotti (Ferrari 625 (555)) 6; Ken Wharton/Harry Schell (Vanwall VW3) 9; Tony Rolt/Peter Walker (Connaught B-Alta) R

1955 FINAL CHAMPIONSHIP POSITIONS

Drivers

1	Juan Manuel Fangio	40 (41)*	9=	Jean Behra	6		Carlos Menditéguy	2
2	Stirling Moss	23		Luigi Musso	6		Cesare Perdisa	2
3	Eugenio Castellotti	12	11	Karl Kling	5		Luigi Villoresi	2
4	Maurice Trintignant	11.33	12	Jimmy Davies	4	21	Umberto Maglioli	1.33
5	Giuseppe Farina	10.33	13=	Tony Bettenhausen	3	22=	Walt Faulkner	1
6	Piero Taruffi	9		Paul Frère	3		Hans Herrmann	1
7	Bob Sweikert	8		Paul Russo	3		Bill Homeier	1
8	Roberto Mieres	7		Johnny Thomson	3		Bill Vukovich	1
			17=	José Froilan Gonzalez	2		*Best five results count	

1956

With Mercedes-Benz withdrawing from F1 at the end of the previous season, Juan Manuel Fangio and Stirling Moss signed for Ferrari and Maserati respectively. BRM, now owned by the Owen Racing Organisation, returned with Mike Hawthorn as lead driver, while Bugatti made a one-off, final and unsuccessful, appearance at the French GP.

Although Fangio and Moss once more finished first and second in the championship, consecutive wins in Belgium and France for Peter Collins,

Fangio's Lancia-Ferrari team-mate, almost gave the young Englishman the title. With 13 laps of the final race to go, and while chasing Moss's Maserati for a win which would make him champion, he gave his car to Fangio (who had retired his machine earlier) - handing a third successive World Championship to the Argentinian.

The British challengers, Vanwall and BRM, both showed promise - particularly in qualifying for the French and British GPs, and in the early laps at Silverstone when Hawthorn led for BRM.

Podium finishes, however, were not forthcoming; the best finish for a British car being Ron Flockhart's third in Italy for Connaught. Jean Behra proved a consistent Maserati team-mate for Moss finishing fourth in the championship.

Gran Premio de la Republica Argentina

22 January 1956. Buenos Aires. 98 laps of a 2.431-mile circuit = 238.238 miles. Warm, dry and overcast. World Championship round 1

1 Luigi Musso/			
Juan Manuel Fangio	Lancia-Ferrari D50	98	3h00m03.7
2 Jean Behra	Maserati 250F	98	3h00m28.1
3 Mike Hawthorn	Maserati 250F	96	
4 Chico Landi/			
Gerino Gerini	Maserati 250F	92	
5 Olivier Gendebien	Lancia-Ferrari D50	91	
6 Alberto Uria/			
Oscar Gonzalez	Maserati 250F	88	

Winner's average speed: 79.385 mph. Starting grid front row: Fangio, 1m42.5 (pole), Castellotti, 1m44.7, Musso, 1m44.7 and Behra, 1m45.1. Fastest lap: Fangio, 1m45.3. Leaders: Gonzalez, laps 1-3; Menditéguy, 4-42; Moss, 43-66; Fangio, 67-98* (*in Musso's car)

Grand Prix de Monaco

13 May 1956. Monte Carlo. 100 laps of a 1.954-mile circuit = 195.400 miles. Warm, dry and sunny. World Championship round 2

1 Stirling Moss	Maserati 250F	100	3h00m32.9
2 Peter Collins/			
Juan Manuel Fangio	Lancia-Ferrari D50	100	3h00m39.0
3 Jean Behra	Maserati 250F	99	
4 Juan Manuel Fangio/			
Eugenio Castellotti	Lancia-Ferrari D50	94	
5 Hermanos			
da Silva Ramos	Gordini 16 (54)	93	
6 Elie Bayol/			
André Pilette	Gordini 32	88	

Winner's average speed: 64.936 mph. Starting grid front row: Fangio, 1m44.0 (pole), Moss, 1m44.6 and Castellotti, 1m44.9. Fastest lap: Fangio, 1m44.4. Leaders: Moss, laps 1-100

1956 DRIVERS' RECORDS

(excluding Indianapolis)

Driver	Car	Argentinian GP	Monaco GP	Belgian GP	French GP	British GP	German GP	Italian GP
Elie Bayol	Gordini 32	-	6	-	-	-	-	-
Jean Behra	Maserati 250F	2	3	7	3	3	3	R
Jo Bonnier	Maserati 250F	-	-	-	-	-	R	-
Jack Brabham	Maserati 250F	-	-	-	-	R	-	-
Tony Brooks	BRM P25	-	DNS	-	-	R	-	-
Eugenio Castellotti	Lancia-Ferrari D50	R	4	R	2	10	R	8
Colin Chapman	Vanwall VW3	-	-	-	DNS	-	-	-
Louis Chiron	Maserati 250F	-	DNQ	-	-	-	-	-
Peter Collins	Ferrari 555 Supersqualo	R	-	-	-	-	-	-
	Lancia-Ferrari D50	-	2	1	1	2	R	2
Paul Emery	Emeryson-Alta	-	-	-	-	R	-	-
Jack Fairman	Connaught B-Alta	-	-	-	-	4	-	5
Juan Manuel Fangio	Lancia-Ferrari D50	1PF	2PF+4	RP	4PF	1	1PF	2P
Ron Flockhart	BRM P25	-	-	-	-	R	-	-
	Connaught B-Alta	-	-	-	-	-	-	3
Paul Frère	Lancia-Ferrari D50	-	-	2	-	-	-	-
Olivier Gendebien	Lancia-Ferrari D50	5	-	-	R	-	-	-
Bob Gerard	Cooper T23-Bristol	-	-	-	-	11	-	-
Gerino Gerini	Maserati 250F	4	-	-	-	-	-	10
Chico Godia-Sales	Maserati 250F	-	-	R	7	8	4	4
José Froilan Gonzalez	Maserati 250F	R	-	-	-	-	-	-
	Vanwall VW1	-	-	-	-	R	-	-
Oscar Gonzalez	Maserati 250F	6	-	-	-	-	-	-
Horace Gould	Maserati 250F	-	8	R	-	5	R	-
Emanuel de Graffenried	Maserati 250F	-	-	-	-	-	-	7
Bruce Halford	Maserati 250F	-	-	-	-	R	DSQ	R
Mike Hawthorn	Maserati 250F	3	-	DNS	-	-	-	-
	BRM P25	-	DNS	-	-	R	-	-
	Vanwall VW2	-	-	-	10	-	-	-
Chico Landi	Maserati 250F	4	-	-	-	-	-	-
Les Leston	Connaught B-Alta	-	-	-	-	-	-	R
Umberto Maglioli	Maserati 250F	-	-	-	-	R	R	R
Robert Manzon	Gordini 16	-	R	-	-	-	-	-
	Gordini 32	-	-	-	9	9	R	R
Carlos Menditéguy	Maserati 250F	R	-	-	-	-	-	-
André Milhoux	Gordini 32	-	-	-	-	-	R	-
Stirling Moss	Maserati 250F	R	1	3F	5	RPF	2	1F
Luigi Musso	Lancia-Ferrari D50	1	R	-	-	-	R	R
Cesare Perdisa	Maserati 250F	-	7	3	5	7	DNS	-
André Pilette	Gordini 32	-	6	-	-	-	DNS	-
	Lancia-Ferrari D50	-	-	6	-	-	-	-
	Gordini 16	-	-	-	11	-	-	-

/Cont'd

Indianapolis 500

30 May 1956. Indianapolis. 200 laps of a 2.500-mile circuit = 500.000 miles. Warm, dry and overcast. World Championship round 3

1 Pat Flaherty	Watson-Offenhauser	200	3h53m28.84
2 Sam Hanks	Kurtis KK500C-Offenhauser	200	3h53m49.30
3 Don Freeland	Phillips-Offenhauser	200	3h54m59.07
4 Johnnie Parsons	Kuzma-Offenhauser	200	3h56m54.48
5 Dick Rathmann	Kurtis KK500C-Offenhauser	200	3h57m50.65
6 Bob Sweikert	Kuzma-Offenhauser	200	3h59m03.83

Winner's average speed: 128.490 mph. Starting grid front row: Flaherty, 145.596 mph (pole), J Rathmann, 145.120 mph and O'Connor, 144.980 mph. Fastest lap in the lead: Russo, 1m02.32

Grand Prix de Belgique

3 June 1956. Spa-Francorchamps. 36 laps of a 8.774-mile circuit = 315.864 miles. Wet and overcast, drying later. World Championship round 4

1 Peter Collins	Lancia-Ferrari D50	36	2h40m00.3
2 Paul Frère	Lancia-Ferrari D50	36	2h41m51.6
3 Cesare Perdisa/ Stirling Moss	Maserati 250F	36	2h43m16.9
4 Harry Schell	Vanwall VW1	35	
5 Luigi Villoresi	Maserati 250F	34	
6 André Pilette	Lancia-Ferrari D50	33	

Winner's average speed: 118.445 mph. Starting grid front row: Fangio, 4m09.8 (pole), Moss, 4m14.7 and Collins, 4m15.3. Fastest lap: Moss, 4m14.7. Leaders: Moss, laps 1-4; Fangio, 5-23; Collins, 24-36

Grand Prix de l'Automobile Club de France

1 July 1956. Reims. 61 laps of a 5.187-mile circuit = 316.407 miles. Warm, dry and overcast. World Championship round 5

1 Peter Collins	Lancia-Ferrari D50	61	2h34m23.4
2. Eugenio Castellotti	Lancia-Ferrari D50	61	2h34m23.7
3 Jean Behra	Maserati 250F	61	2h35m53.3
4 Juan Manuel Fangio	Lancia-Ferrari D50	61	2h35m58.5
5 Cesare Perdisa/ Stirling Moss	Maserati 250F	59	
6 Louis Rosier	Maserati 250F	58	

Winner's average speed: 122.964 mph. Starting grid front row: Fangio, 2m23.3 (pole), Castellotti, 2m24.6 and Collins, 2m24.9. Fastest lap: Fangio, 2m25.8. Leaders: Collins, laps 1, 47-48, 50-61; Castellotti, 2-3, 39-46, 49; Fangio, 4-38

British Grand Prix

14 July 1956. Silverstone. 101 laps of a 2.927-mile circuit = 295.627 miles. Warm, dry and overcast. World Championship round 6

1 Juan Manuel Fangio	Lancia-Ferrari D50	101	2h59m47.0
2 Alfonso de Portago/ Peter Collins	Lancia-Ferrari D50	100	
3 Jean Behra	Maserati 250F	99	
4 Jack Fairman	Connaught B-Alta	98	
5 Horace Gould	Maserati 250F	97	
6 Luigi Villoresi	Maserati 250F	96	

Winner's average speed: 98.661 mph. Starting grid front row: Moss, 1m41 (pole), Fangio, 1m42, Hawthorn, 1m43 and Collins, 1m43. Fastest lap: Moss, 1m43.2. Leaders: Hawthorn, laps 1-15; Moss, 16-68; Fangio, 69-101

1956 DRIVERS' RECORDS cont'd/ (excluding Indianapolis)		Argentinian GP	Monaco GP	Belgian GP	French GP	British GP	German GP	Italian GP
Driver	**Car**							
Luigi Piotti	Maserati 250F	R	-	-	-	-	R	6
Alfonso de Portago	Lancia-Ferrari D50	-	-	-	R	2	R	R
Louis Rosier	Maserati 250F	-	R	8	6	R	5	-
Roy Salvadori	Maserati 250F	-	-	-	-	R	R	11
Giorgio Scarlatti	Ferrari 500	-	DNQ	-	-	-	R	-
Harry Schell	Vanwall VW1	-	R	4	R	-	-	-
	Vanwall VW2	-	-	-	10	R	-	R
	Maserati 250F	-	-	-	-	-	R	-
Archie Scott-Brown	Connaught B-Alta	-	-	-	-	R	-	-
Piero Scotti	Connaught B-Alta	-	-	R	-	-	-	-
Hermanos da Silva Ramos	Gordini 16	-	5	-	-	-	-	-
	Gordini 32	-	-	-	8	R	-	R
André Simon	Maserati 250F	-	-	-	R	-	-	-
	Gordini 16	-	-	-	-	-	-	9
Piero Taruffi	Maserati 250F	-	-	-	R	-	-	-
	Vanwall VW1	-	-	-	-	-	-	R
Desmond Titterington	Connaught B-Alta	-	-	-	-	R	-	-
Maurice Trintignant	Vanwall VW2	-	R	R	-	-	-	-
	Bugatti T251	-	-	-	R	-	-	-
	Vanwall VW4	-	-	-	-	R	-	R
Wolfgang von Trips	Lancia-Ferrari D50	-	-	-	-	-	-	DNS
Alberto Uria	Maserati 250F	6	-	-	-	-	-	-
Luigi Villoresi	Maserati 250F	-	-	5	R	6	R	R
Ottorino Volonterio	Maserati 250F	-	-	-	-	-	NC	-

SHARED DRIVES - **Argentinian GP:** Luigi Musso/Juan Manuel Fangio (Lancia-Ferrari D50) 1; Chico Landi/Gerino Gerini (Maserati 250F) 4; Alberto Uria/Oscar Gonzalez (Maserati 250F) 6; Juan Manuel Fangio/Luigi Musso (Lancia-Ferrari D50) R. **Monaco GP:** Peter Collins/Juan Manuel Fangio (Lancia-Ferrari D50) 2; Juan Manuel Fangio/Eugenio Castellotti (Lancia-Ferrari D50) 4; Elie Bayol/André Pilette (Gordini 32) 6. **Belgian GP:** Cesare Perdisa/Stirling Moss (Maserati 250F) 3. **French GP:** Cesare Perdisa/Stirling Moss (Maserati 250F) 5; Mike Hawthorn/Harry Schell (Vanwall VW2) 10. **British GP:** Alfonso de Portago/Peter Collins (Lancia-Ferrari D50) 2; Eugenio Castellotti/Alfonso de Portago (Lancia-Ferrari D50) 10. **German GP:** Alfonso de Portago/Peter Collins (Lancia-Ferrari D50) R; Luigi Musso/Eugenio Castellotti (Lancia-Ferrari D50) R. **Italian GP:** Peter Collins/Juan Manuel Fangio (Lancia-Ferrari D50) 2; Juan Manuel Fangio/Eugenio Castellotti (Lancia-Ferrari D50) 8; Umberto Maglioli/Jean Behra (Maserati 250F) R; Luigi Villoresi/Jo Bonnier (Maserati 250F) R

Grosser Preis von Deutschland

5 August 1956. Nürburgring. 22 laps of a 14.167-mile circuit = 311.674 miles. Warm, dry and sunny. World Championship round 7

1 Juan Manuel Fangio	Lancia-Ferrari D50	22	3h38m43.7
2 Stirling Moss	Maserati 250F	22	3h39m30.1
3 Jean Behra	Maserati 250F	22	3h46m22.0
4 Chico Godia-Sales	Maserati 250F	20	
5 Louis Rosier	Maserati 250F	19	

No other finishers. Bruce Halford (Maserati 250F) finished fourth on the road but was disqualified for receiving outside assistance and subsequently ignoring black flag. Winner's average speed: 85.496 mph. Starting grid front row: Fangio, 9m51.2 (pole), Collins, 9m51.5, Castellotti, 9m54.4 and Moss, 10m03.4. Fastest lap: Fangio, 9m41.6. Leaders: Fangio, laps 1-22

Gran Premio d'Italia

2 September 1956. Monza. 50 laps of a 6.214-mile circuit = 310.700 miles. Warm, with rain showers. World Championship round 8. Also known as the European Grand Prix

1 Stirling Moss	Maserati 250F	50	2h23m41.3
2 Peter Collins/			
Juan Manuel Fangio	Lancia-Ferrari D50	50	2h23m47.0
3 Ron Flockhart	Connaught B-Alta	49	
4 Chico Godia-Sales	Maserati 250F	49	
5 Jack Fairman	Connaught B-Alta	47	
6 Luigi Piotti	Maserati 250F	47	

Winner's average speed: 129.733 mph. Starting grid front row: Fangio, 2m42.6 (pole), Castellotti, 2m43.4 and Musso, 2m43.7. Fastest lap: Moss, 2m45.5. Leaders: Castellotti, laps 1-4; Moss, 5-10, 12-45, 48-50; Schell, 11; Musso, 46-47

1956 FINAL CHAMPIONSHIP POSITIONS

Drivers

1	Juan Manuel Fangio	30 (34.5)*	10	Jack Fairman	5	19= Olivier Gendebien	2
2	Stirling Moss	27 (28)*	11=	Ron Flockhart	4	Horace Gould	2
3	Peter Collins	25		Don Freeland	4	Dick Rathmann	2
4	Jean Behra	22		Mike Hawthorn	4	Louis Rosier	2
5	Pat Flaherty	8		Luigi Musso	4	Hermanos da Silva Ramos	2
6	Eugenio Castellotti	7.5	15=	Johnnie Parsons	3	Luigi Villoresi	2
7=	Paul Frère	6		Cesare Perdisa	3	25= Gerino Gerini	1.5
	Chico Godia-Sales	6		Alfonso de Portago	3	Chico Landi	1.5
	Sam Hanks	6		Harry Schell	3	27 Paul Russo	1

*Best five results count

1957

Juan Manuel Fangio moved to Maserati for his final full season of Grand Prix racing. The 250F was modified, but although work had begun on a new V12 engine, it was only raced once, by Jean Behra at the end of the year. Mike Hawthorn replaced the "maestro" at Ferrari, and Stirling Moss moved to Tony Vandervell's improving Vanwall marque.

Fangio scores the greatest win of his career at the 1957 German Grand Prix

Fangio started with a hat-trick of wins (disregarding Indianapolis) before Vanwall came good at the British GP. Having retired his own car, Moss took over from an ill Tony Brooks to record the first win for a British car in a World Championship Grand Prix.

The following race at the Nürburgring proved the ideal stage for one of Fangio's greatest drives, which would also secure his fifth world title. Delayed by a lengthy pit stop, the Argentinian rejoined almost a minute behind the Lancia-Ferraris of Hawthorn and Peter Collins. Over the last ten 14-mile laps, Fangio repeatedly beat the old lap record as he closed in on the leaders. On the penultimate circuit he passed both Ferraris and although Hawthorn fought back, the champion was not to be denied victory.

Stirling Moss rounded off the season with two further wins for Vanwall. The first of these, the Pescara GP, was on the longest circuit ever used in the World Championship - it having been elevated in status due to the cancellation of the Belgian, Dutch and Spanish GPs. For the third successive season, Moss finished second to Fangio in the final championship table. With Fangio not contesting the whole series next year, Moss would start as favourite to become World Champion for the first time.

Gran Premio de la Republica Argentina

13 January 1957. Buenos Aires. 100 laps of a 2.431-mile circuit = 243.100 miles. Race scheduled for three hours. Hot, dry and sunny. World Championship round 1

1 Juan Manuel Fangio	Maserati 250F	100	3h00m55.9
2 Jean Behra	Maserati 250F	100	3h01m14.2
3 Carlos Menditéguy	Maserati 250F	99	
4 Harry Schell	Maserati 250F	98	
5 José Froilan Gonzalez/			
Alfonso de Portago	Lancia-Ferrari D50	98	
6 Cesare Perdisa/			
Peter Collins/			
Wolfgang von Trips	Lancia-Ferrari D50	98	

1957 DRIVERS' RECORDS

(excluding Indianapolis)

Driver	Car	Argentinian GP	Monaco GP	French GP	British GP	German GP	Pescara GP	Italian GP
Edgar Barth	Porsche 550RS	-	-	-	-	F2	-	-
Carel Godin de Beaufort	Porsche 550RS	-	-	-	-	F2	-	-
Jean Behra	Maserati 250F	2	-	6	R	6	R	-
	Maserati 250F (V12)	-	-	-	-	-	-	R
Jo Bonnier	Maserati 250F	7	-	-	R	-	R	R
Jack Brabham	Cooper T43-Climax	-	6	7	R	F2	7	-
Tony Brooks	Vanwall VW7	-	2	-	-	-	R	-
	Vanwall VW4	-	-	-	1	-	-	-
	Vanwall VW1	-	-	-	R	9	-	-
	Vanwall VW6	-	-	-	-	-	-	7[F]
Ivor Bueb	Connaught B-Alta	-	R	-	-	-	-	-
	Maserati 250F	-	-	-	8	-	-	-
Eugenio Castellotti	Lancia-Ferrari D50	R	-	-	-	-	-	-
Peter Collins	Lancia-Ferrari D50	6	R	3	4	3	-	R
Paul England	Cooper T41-Climax	-	-	-	-	F2	-	-
Jack Fairman	BRM P25	-	-	-	R	-	-	-
Juan Manuel Fangio	Maserati 250F	1	1[PF]	1[P]	R	1[PF]	2[P]	2
Ron Flockhart	BRM P25	-	R	R	-	-	-	-
Bob Gerard	Cooper T43-Bristol	-	-	-	6	-	-	-
Dick Gibson	Cooper T43-Climax	-	-	-	-	F2	-	-
Chico Godia-Sales	Maserati 250F	-	-	-	-	R	R	9
José Froilan Gonzalez	Lancia-Ferrari D50	5	-	-	-	-	-	-
Horace Gould	Maserati 250F	-	R	R	DNS	R	R	10
Masten Gregory	Maserati 250F	-	3	-	-	8	4	4
Bruce Halford	Maserati 250F	-	-	-	-	11	R	R
Mike Hawthorn	Lancia-Ferrari D50	R	R	4	3	2	-	6
Hans Herrmann	Maserati 250F	-	DNQ	-	-	R	-	-
Les Leston	Cooper T43-Climax	-	DNQ	-	-	-	-	-
	BRM P25	-	-	-	R	-	-	-
Stuart Lewis-Evans	Connaught B-Alta	-	4	-	-	-	-	-
	Vanwall VW4	-	-	R	-	R	-	-
	Vanwall VW5	-	-	-	7	-	-	-
	Vanwall VW1	-	-	-	-	-	5	-
	Vanwall VW7	-	-	-	-	-	-	R[P]
Mike MacDowel	Cooper T43-Climax	-	-	7	-	-	-	-
Herbert MacKay-Fraser	BRM P25	-	-	R	-	-	-	-
Umberto Maglioli	Porsche 550RS	-	-	-	-	F2	-	-
Tony Marsh	Cooper T43-Climax	-	-	-	-	F2	-	-
Carlos Menditéguy	Maserati 250F	3	R	R	R	-	-	-
Stirling Moss	Maserati 250F	8[PF]	-	-	-	-	-	-
	Vanwall VW3	-	R	-	-	-	-	-
	Vanwall VW1	-	-	-	R[P]	-	-	-
	Vanwall VW4	-	-	-	1[F]	-	-	-
	Vanwall VW5	-	-	-	-	5	1[F]	1
Luigi Musso	Lancia-Ferrari D50	R	-	2[F]	2	4	R	8
Brian Naylor	Cooper T43-Climax	-	-	-	-	F2	-	-
Cesare Perdisa	Lancia-Ferrari D50	6	-	-	-	-	-	-
Luigi Piotti	Maserati 250F	10	DNQ	-	-	-	R	R
Alfonso de Portago	Lancia-Ferrari D50	5	-	-	-	-	-	-
Roy Salvadori	BRM P25	-	DNQ	-	-	-	-	-
	Vanwall VW1	-	-	R	-	-	-	-
	Cooper T43-Climax	-	-	-	5	F2	R	-
Giorgio Scarlatti	Maserati 250F	-	R	-	-	10	6	5
Harry Schell	Maserati 250F	4	R	5	R	7	3	5
André Simon	Maserati 250F	-	DNQ	-	-	-	-	11
Alessandro de Tomaso	Ferrari 625	9	-	-	-	-	-	-
Maurice Trintignant	Lancia-Ferrari D50	-	5	R	4	-	-	-
Wolfgang von Trips	Lancia-Ferrari D50	6	R	-	-	-	-	3
Ottorino Volonterio	Maserati 250F	-	-	-	-	-	-	11

SHARED DRIVES - Argentinian GP: José Froilan Gonzalez/Alfonso de Portago (Lancia-Ferrari D50) 5; Cesare Perdisa/Peter Collins/Wolfgang von Trips (Lancia-Ferrari D50) 6. **Monaco GP:** Wolfgang von Trips/Mike Hawthorn (Lancia-Ferrari D50) R; Giorgio Scarlatti/Harry Schell (Maserati 250F) R. **French GP:** Mike MacDowel/Jack Brabham (Cooper T43-Climax) 7. **British GP:** Tony Brooks/Stirling Moss (Vanwall VW4) 1; Maurice Trintignant/Peter Collins (Lancia-Ferrari D50) 4; Stirling Moss/Tony Brooks (Vanwall VW1) R. **Italian GP:** Giorgio Scarlatti/Harry Schell (Maserati 250F) 5; André Simon/Ottorino Volonterio (Maserati 250F) 11

World Championship Grand Prix Racing

Winner's average speed: 80.616 mph. Starting grid front row: Moss, 1m42.6 (pole), Fangio, 1m43.7, Behra, 1m44.0 and Castellotti, 1m44.2. Fastest lap: Moss, 1m44.7. Leaders: Behra, laps 1-2, 9-12, 81, 84; Castellotti, 3-8; Collins, 13-25; Fangio, 26-80, 82-83, 85-100

Grand Prix de Monaco

19 May 1957. Monte Carlo. 105 laps of a 1.954-mile circuit = 205.170 miles. Warm, dry and sunny. World Championship round 2

1 Juan Manuel Fangio	Maserati 250F	105	3h10m12.8
2 Tony Brooks	Vanwall VW7	105	3h10m38.0
3 Masten Gregory	Maserati 250F	103	
4 Stuart Lewis-Evans	Connaught B-Alta	102	
5 Maurice Trintignant	Lancia-Ferrari D50	100	
6 Jack Brabham	Cooper T43-Climax	100	

Winner's average speed: 64.718 mph. Starting grid front row: Fangio, 1m42.7 (pole), Collins, 1m43.3 and Moss, 1m43.6. Fastest lap: Fangio, 1m45.6. Leaders: Moss, laps 1-4; Fangio, 5-105

Indianapolis 500

30 May 1957. Indianapolis. 200 laps of a 2.500-mile circuit = 500.000 miles. Warm, dry and overcast. World Championship round 3

1 Sam Hanks	Epperly-Offenhauser	200	3h41m14.25
2 Jim Rathmann	Epperly-Offenhauser	200	3h41m35.75
3 Jimmy Bryan	Kuzma-Offenhauser	200	3h43m28.25
4 Paul Russo	Kurtis-Novi	200	3h44m11.10
5 Andy Linden	Kurtis KK500G-Offenhauser	200	3h44m28.55
6 Johnny Boyd	Kurtis KK500G-Offenhauser	200	3h45m49.55

Winner's average speed: 135.601 mph. Starting grid front row: O'Connor, 143.948 mph (pole), Sachs, 143.822 mph and Ruttman, 142.772 mph. Fastest lap in the lead: J Rathmann, 1m02.75

Grand Prix de l'Automobile Club de France

7 July 1957. Rouen-les-Essarts. 77 laps of a 4.065-mile circuit = 313.005 miles. Very hot, dry and sunny. World Championship round 4

1 Juan Manuel Fangio	Maserati 250F	77	3h07m46.4
2 Luigi Musso	Lancia-Ferrari D50	77	3h08m37.2
3 Peter Collins	Lancia-Ferrari D50	77	3h09m52.4
4 Mike Hawthorn	Lancia-Ferrari D50	76	
5 Harry Schell	Maserati 250F	70	
6 Jean Behra*	Maserati 250F	69	

*Penalized one lap for completing final lap in over 7m30, a local rule. Winner's average speed: 100.016 mph. Starting grid front row: Fangio, 2m21.5 (pole), Behra, 2m22.6 and Musso, 2m22.7. Fastest lap: Musso, 2m22.5. Leaders: Musso, laps 1-3; Fangio, 4-77

British Grand Prix

20 July 1957. Aintree. 90 laps of a 3.000-mile circuit = 270.000 miles. Warm, dry and overcast. World Championship round 5. Also known as the European Grand Prix

1 Tony Brooks/ Stirling Moss	Vanwall VW4	90	3h06m37.8

2 Luigi Musso	Lancia-Ferrari D50	90	3h07m03.4
3 Mike Hawthorn	Lancia-Ferrari D50	90	3h07m20.6
4 Maurice Trintignant/ Peter Collins	Lancia-Ferrari D50	88	
5 Roy Salvadori	Cooper T43-Climax	85	
6 Bob Gerard	Cooper T43-Bristol	82	

Winner's average speed: 86.803 mph. Starting grid front row: Moss, 2m00.2 (pole), Behra, 2m00.4 and Brooks, 2m00.4. Fastest lap: Moss, 1m59.2. Leaders: Moss, laps 1-22, 70-90*; Behra, 23-69 (*in Brooks' car)

Grosser Preis von Deutschland

4 August 1957. Nürburgring. 22 laps of a 14.167-mile circuit = 311.674 miles. Hot, dry and sunny. World Championship round 6

1 Juan Manuel Fangio	Maserati 250F	22	3h30m38.3
2 Mike Hawthorn	Lancia-Ferrari D50	22	3h30m41.9
3 Peter Collins	Lancia-Ferrari D50	22	3h31m13.9
4 Luigi Musso	Lancia-Ferrari D50	22	3h34m15.9
5 Stirling Moss	Vanwall VW5	22	3h35m15.8
6 Jean Behra	Maserati 250F	22	3h35m16.8

Winner's average speed: 88.780 mph. Starting grid front row: Fangio, 9m25.6 (pole), Hawthorn, 9m28.4, Behra, 9m30.5 and Collins, 9m34.7. Fastest lap: Fangio, 9m17.4. Leaders: Hawthorn, laps 1-2, 15-20; Fangio, 3-11, 21-22; Collins, 12-14

Gran Premio di Pescara

18 August 1957. Pescara. 18 laps of a 16.032-mile circuit = 288.576 miles. Very hot, dry and sunny. World Championship round 7

1 Stirling Moss	Vanwall VW5	18	2h59m22.7
2 Juan Manuel Fangio	Maserati 250F	18	3h02m36.6
3 Harry Schell	Maserati 250F	18	3h06m09.5
4 Masten Gregory	Maserati 250F	18	3h07m39.2
5 Stuart Lewis-Evans	Vanwall VW1	17	
6 Giorgio Scarlotti	Maserati 250F	17	

Winner's average speed: 96.525 mph. Starting grid front row: Fangio, 9m44.6 (pole), Moss, 9m54.7 and Musso, 10m00.0. Fastest lap: Moss, 9m44.6. Leaders: Musso, lap 1; Moss, laps 2-18

Gran Premio d'Italia

8 September 1957. Monza. 87 laps of a 3.573-mile circuit = 310.851 miles. Hot, dry and sunny. World Championship round 8

1 Stirling Moss	Vanwall VW5	87	2h35m03.9
2 Juan Manuel Fangio	Maserati 250F	87	2h35m45.1
3 Wolfgang von Trips	Lancia-Ferrari D50	85	
4 Masten Gregory	Maserati 250F	84	
5 Giorgio Scarlatti/ Harry Schell	Maserati 250F	84	
6 Mike Hawthorn	Lancia-Ferrari D50	83	

Winner's average speed: 120.279 mph. Starting grid front row: Lewis-Evans, 1m42.4 (pole), Moss, 1m42.7, Brooks, 1m42.9 and Fangio, 1m43.1. Fastest lap: Brooks, 1m43.7. Leaders: Moss, laps 1-3, 5, 11, 21-87; Behra, 4, 6; Fangio, 7-10; Brooks, 12-15; Lewis-Evans, 16-20

1957 FINAL CHAMPIONSHIP POSITIONS

Drivers

1	Juan Manuel Fangio	40 (46)*		Sam Hanks	8	17	Paul Russo	3
2	Stirling Moss	25	10	Jim Rathmann	7	18=	Andy Linden	2
3	Luigi Musso	16	11	Jean Behra	6		Roy Salvadori	2
4	Mike Hawthorn	13	12=	Stuart Lewis-Evans	5	20=	José Froilan Gonzalez	1
5	Tony Brooks	11		Maurice Trintignant	5		Alfonso de Portago	1
6=	Masten Gregory	10	14=	Jimmy Bryan	4		Giorgio Scarlatti	1
	Harry Schell	10		Carlos Menditéguy	4		*Best five results count	
8=	Peter Collins	8		Wolfgang von Trips	4			

1958

Formula One's governing body, the CSI, announced a number of changes for the new season. Races were limited to 300 kms or two hours; points would now only be awarded to drivers who drove the complete distance and did not share their car; and commercial fuel was made obligatory. Aviation fuel, which was permissible, became standard.

This season is often regarded as having one of the more unjust World Championship results: Mike Hawthorn became champion yet won only once,

Mike Hawthorn, Britain's first World Champion, pictured at the 1958 Belgian Grand Prix

while Stirling Moss took four victories but ended the year second again. Sadly Hawthorn, who retired from racing immediately after clinching the championship at the final event, was to die in a road accident outside Guildford within months of his greatest triumph.

Vanwall and BRM both missed the start of the season while struggling to comply with the new fuel restrictions. While waiting for Vanwall, Moss won in Argentina in a Cooper-Climax entered by Rob Walker, surprising the Ferrari team by not stopping to refuel.

With Vanwall ready for Monaco, the season developed into a battle between the British Racing Green cars of Moss and Brooks and the Ferraris of Hawthorn and Peter Collins. Mid-season the Italian marque dominated, Hawthorn winning in France (Fangio's final Grand Prix) and Collins in Britain. It was to be the latter's final victory; two weeks later the flamboyant Collins was fatally injured in a crash at the Nürburgring's Pflanzgarten corner during the German GP.

Vanwall won the final four Grands Prix to secure the inaugural constructors' title, but Hawthorn had done just enough to become Britain's first World Champion, albeit for Ferrari.

Gran Premio de la Republica Argentina

19 January 1958. Buenos Aires. 80 laps of a 2.431-mile circuit = 194.480 miles. Warm, dry and sunny. World Championship round 1

1 Stirling Moss	Cooper T43-Climax	80	2h19m33.7
2 Luigi Musso	Ferrari Dino 246	80	2h19m36.4
3 Mike Hawthorn	Ferrari Dino 246	80	2h19m46.3
4 Juan Manuel Fangio	Maserati 250F	80	2h20m26.7
5 Jean Behra	Maserati 250F	78	

6 Harry Schell	Maserati 250F	77

Winner's average speed: 83.610 mph. Starting grid front row: Fangio, 1m42.0 (pole), Hawthorn, 1m42.6, Collins, 1m42.6 and Behra, 1m42.7. Fastest lap: Fangio, 1m41.8. Leaders: Behra, lap 1; Hawthorn, laps 2-9; Fangio, 10-34; Moss, 35-80

Grand Prix de Monaco

18 May 1958. Monte Carlo. 100 laps of a 1.954-mile circuit = 195.400 miles. Hot, dry and sunny. World Championship round 2

1 Maurice Trintignant	Cooper T45-Climax	100	2h52m27.9
2 Luigi Musso	Ferrari Dino 246	100	2h52m48.2
3 Peter Collins	Ferrari Dino 246	100	2h53m06.7
4 Jack Brabham	Cooper T45-Climax	97	
5 Harry Schell	BRM P25 (58)	91	
6 Cliff Allison	Lotus 12-Climax	87	

Winner's average speed: 67.979 mph. Starting grid front row: Brooks, 1m39.8 (pole), Behra, 1m40.8 and Brabham, 1m41.0. Fastest lap: Hawthorn, 1m40.6. Leaders: Behra, laps 1-27; Hawthorn, 28-32, 39-47; Moss, 33-38; Trintignant, 48-100

Grote Prijs van Nederland

25 May 1958. Zandvoort. 75 laps of a 2.605-mile circuit = 195.375 miles. Windy, dry and overcast. World Championship round 3

1 Stirling Moss	Vanwall VW10	75	2h04m49.2
2 Harry Schell	BRM P25 (58)	75	2h05m37.1
3 Jean Behra	BRM P25 (58)	75	2h06m31.5
4 Roy Salvadori	Cooper T45-Climax	74	
5 Mike Hawthorn	Ferrari Dino 246	74	
6 Cliff Allison	Lotus 12-Climax	73	

Winner's average speed: 93.915 mph. Starting grid front row: Lewis-Evans, 1m37.1 (pole), Moss, 1m38.0 and Brooks, 1m38.1. Fastest lap: Moss, 1m38.5. Leaders: Moss, laps 1-75

Indianapolis 500

30 May 1958. Indianapolis. 200 laps of a 2.500-mile circuit = 500.000 miles. Warm, dry and sunny. World Championship round 4

1 Jimmy Bryan	Epperly-Offenhauser	200	3h44m13.80
2 George Amick	Epperly-Offenhauser	200	3h44m41.45
3 Johnny Boyd	Kurtis KK500G-Offenhauser	200	3h45m23.75
4 Tony Bettenhausen	Epperly-Offenhauser	200	3h45m45.60
5 Jim Rathmann	Epperly-Offenhauser	200	3h45m49.45
6 Jimmy Reece	Watson-Offenhauser	200	3h46m30.75

Winner's average speed: 133.791 mph. Starting grid front row: D Rathmann, 145.974 mph (pole), Elisian, 145.926 mph and Reece, 145.513 mph. Fastest lap in the lead: Bettenhausen, 1m02.37

Grand Prix de Belgique

15 June 1958. Spa-Francorchamps. 24 laps of a 8.761-mile circuit = 210.264 miles. Very hot, dry and sunny. World Championship round 5. Also known as the European Grand Prix

1 Tony Brooks	Vanwall VW5	24	1h37m06.3
2 Mike Hawthorn	Ferrari Dino 246	24	1h37m07.0
3 Stuart Lewis-Evans	Vanwall VW4	24	1h40m07.2
4 Cliff Allison	Lotus 12-Climax	24	1h41m21.8
5 Harry Schell	BRM P25 (58)	23	
6 Olivier Gendebien	Ferrari Dino 246	23	

Winner's average speed: 129.920 mph. Starting grid front row: Hawthorn, 3m57.1 (pole), Musso, 3m57.5 and Moss, 3m57.6. Fastest lap: Hawthorn, 3m58.3. Leaders: Brooks, laps 1, 3; Collins, 2, 4-24

1958 DRIVERS' RECORDS

(excluding Indianapolis)

Driver	Car	Argentinian GP	Monaco GP	Dutch GP	Belgian GP	French GP	British GP	German GP	Portuguese GP	Italian GP	Moroccan GP
Cliff Allison	Lotus 12-Climax	-	6	6	4	R	R	-	-	7	10
	Lotus 16-Climax	-	-	-	-	-	-	5	-	-	-
	Maserati 250F	-	-	-	-	-	-	-	R	-	-
Edgar Barth	Porsche RSK	-	-	-	-	-	-	F2	-	-	-
Carel Godin de Beaufort	Porsche RSK	-	-	11	-	-	-	-	-	-	-
	Porsche 550RS	-	-	-	-	-	-	F2	-	-	-
Jean Behra	Maserati 250F	5	-	-	-	-	-	-	-	-	-
	BRM P25	-	R	3	R	R	R	R	4	R	R
Jo Bonnier	Maserati 250F	-	R	10	9	8	R	R	R	-	-
	BRM P25	-	-	-	-	-	-	-	-	R	4
Jack Brabham	Cooper T45-Climax	-	4	8	R	6	6	F2	7	R	F2
Tommy Bridger	Cooper T45-Climax	-	-	-	-	-	-	-	-	-	F2
Tony Brooks	Vanwall VW10	-	R^P	-	-	-	-	-	-	-	R
	Vanwall VW7	-	-	R	-	-	-	-	-	-	-
	Vanwall VW5	-	-	-	1	R	7	-	R	1	-
	Vanwall VW9	-	-	-	-	R	-	-	-	-	-
	Vanwall VW4	-	-	-	-	-	-	1	-	-	-
Ivor Bueb	Connaught B-Alta	-	-	-	-	-	R	-	-	-	-
	Lotus 12-Climax	-	-	-	-	-	-	F2	-	-	-
Ian Burgess	Cooper T45-Climax	-	-	-	-	-	R	-	-	-	-
	Cooper T43-Climax	-	-	-	-	-	-	F2	-	-	-
Giulio Cabianca	OSCA	-	DNQ	-	-	-	-	-	-	-	-
	Maserati 250F	-	-	-	-	-	-	-	-	R	-
Robert la Caze	Cooper T45-Climax	-	-	-	-	-	-	-	-	-	F2
Peter Collins	Ferrari Dino 246	R	3	R	R	5	1	R	-	-	-
Bernie Ecclestone	Connaught B-Alta	-	-	-	-	-	DNS	-	-	-	-
Paul Emery	Connaught B-Alta	-	DNQ	-	-	-	-	-	-	-	-
Jack Fairman	Connaught B-Alta	-	-	-	-	-	R	-	-	-	-
	Cooper T45-Climax	-	-	-	-	-	-	-	-	-	8
Juan Manuel Fangio	Maserati 250F	4^{PF}	-	-	-	4	-	-	-	-	-
Maria Teresa de Filippis	Maserati 250F	-	DNQ	-	10	-	-	-	R	R	-
Ron Flockhart	BRM P25	-	DNQ	-	-	-	-	-	-	-	R
	Cooper T43-Climax	-	DNQ	-	-	-	-	-	-	-	-
Olivier Gendebien	Ferrari Dino 246	-	-	-	6	-	-	-	R	R	-
Gerino Gerini	Maserati 250F	-	DNQ	-	-	9	R	-	-	R	11
Dick Gibson	Cooper T43-Climax	-	-	-	-	-	-	F2	-	-	-
Chico Godia-Sales	Maserati 250F	8	DNQ	-	R	R	-	-	-	-	-
Christian Goethals	Cooper T43-Climax	-	-	-	-	-	-	F2	-	-	-
Horace Gould	Maserati 250F	9	DNQ	-	-	-	-	-	-	-	-
Masten Gregory	Maserati 250F	-	-	R	R	-	-	-	-	4	6
André Guelfi	Cooper T45-Climax	-	-	-	-	-	-	-	-	-	F2

/Cont'd

Grand Prix de l'Automobile Club de France

6 July 1958. Reims. 50 laps of a 5.187-mile circuit = 259.350 miles. Warm, dry and sunny. World Championship round 6

1 Mike Hawthorn	Ferrari Dino 246	50	2h03m21.3
2 Stirling Moss	Vanwall VW10	50	2h03m45.9
3 Wolfgang von Trips	Ferrari Dino 246	50	2h04m21.0
4 Juan Manuel Fangio	Maserati 250F	50	2h05m51.9
5 Peter Collins	Ferrari Dino 246	50	2h08m46.2
6 Jack Brabham	Cooper T45-Climax	49	

Winner's average speed: 126.148 mph. Starting grid front row: Hawthorn, 2m21.7 (pole), Musso, 2m22.4 and Schell, 2m23.1. Fastest lap: Hawthorn, 2m24.9. Leaders: Hawthorn, laps 1-50.

British Grand Prix

19 July 1958. Silverstone. 75 laps of a 2.927-mile circuit = 219.525 miles. Warm, dry and sunny. World Championship round 7

1 Peter Collins	Ferrari Dino 246	75	2h09m04.2
2 Mike Hawthorn	Ferrari Dino 246	75	2h09m28.4
3 Roy Salvadori	Cooper T45-Climax	75	2h09m54.8
4 Stuart Lewis-Evans	Vanwall VW9	75	2h09m55.0
5 Harry Schell	BRM P25 (58)	75	2h10m19.0
6 Jack Brabham	Cooper T45-Climax	75	2h10m27.4

Winner's average speed: 102.049 mph. Starting grid front row: Moss, 1m39.4 (pole), Schell, 1m39.8, Salvadori, 1m40.0 and Hawthorn, 1m40.4. Fastest lap: Hawthorn, 1m40.8. Leaders: Collins, laps 1-75.

Grosser Preis von Deutschland

3 August 1958. Nürburgring. 15 laps of a 14.167-mile circuit = 212.505 miles. Warm, dry and overcast. World Championship round 8

1 Tony Brooks	Vanwall VW4	15	2h21m15.0
2 Roy Salvadori	Cooper T45-Climax	15	2h24m44.7
3 Maurice Trintignant	Cooper T45-Climax	15	2h26m26.2
4 Wolfgang von Trips	Ferrari Dino 246	15	2h27m31.3
5 Cliff Allison*	Lotus 16-Climax	13	

*Allison finished tenth on the road behind cars in the concurrent F2 race, he was not awarded points. No other F1 finishers. Winner's average speed: 90.268 mph. Starting grid front row: Hawthorn, 9m14.0 (pole), Brooks, 9m15.0, Moss, 9m19.1 and Collins, 9m21.9. Fastest lap: Moss, 9m09.2. Leaders: Moss, laps 1-3; Hawthorn, 4; Collins, 5-10; Brooks, 11-15.

1958 DRIVERS' RECORDS cont'd/
(excluding Indianapolis)

Driver	Car	Argentinian GP	Monaco GP	Dutch GP	Belgian GP	French GP	British GP	German GP	Portuguese GP	Italian GP	Moroccan GP
Mike Hawthorn	Ferrari Dino 246	3	R^{F}	5	2^{PF}	1^{PF}	2^{F}	R^{P}	2^{F}	2	2^{P}
Hans Herrmann	Maserati 250F	-	-	-	-	-	-	R	-	R	9
Graham Hill	Lotus 12-Climax	-	R	R	R	-	-	-	-	-	-
	Lotus 16-Climax	-	-	-	-	R	R	F2	R	6	12
Phil Hill	Maserati 250F	-	-	-	-	7	-	-	-	-	-
	Ferrari Dino 156	-	-	-	-	-	-	F2	-	-	-
	Ferrari Dino 246	-	-	-	-	-	-	-	-	3^{F}	3
Ken Kavanagh	Maserati 250F	-	DNQ	-	DNS	-	-	-	-	-	-
Bruce Kessler	Connaught B-Alta	-	DNQ	-	-	-	-	-	-	-	-
Stuart Lewis-Evans	Vanwall VW5	-	R	R^{P}	-	-	-	-	-	-	-
	Vanwall VW4	-	-	-	3	-	-	-	-	-	R
	Vanwall VW9	-	-	-	-	R	4	-	-	-	-
	Vanwall VW6	-	-	-	-	-	-	-	3	R	-
Tony Marsh	Cooper T45-Climax	-	-	-	-	-	-	F2	-	-	-
Bruce McLaren	Cooper T45-Climax	-	-	-	-	-	-	F2	-	-	F2
Carlos Menditéguy	Maserati 250F	7	-	-	-	-	-	-	-	-	-
Stirling Moss	Cooper T43-Climax	1	-	-	-	-	-	-	-	-	-
	Vanwall VW7	-	R	-	-	-	-	-	-	-	-
	Vanwall VW10	-	-	1^{F}	R	2	R^{P}	R^{F}	1^{P}	R^{P}	-
	Vanwall VW5	-	-	-	-	-	-	-	-	-	1^{F}
Luigi Musso	Ferrari Dino 246	2	2	7	R	R	-	-	-	-	-
Brian Naylor	Cooper T45-Climax	-	-	-	-	-	-	F2	-	-	-
François Picard	Cooper T43-Climax	-	-	-	-	-	-	-	-	-	F2
Luigi Piotti	OSCA	-	DNQ	-	-	-	-	-	-	-	-
Troy Ruttman	Maserati 250F	-	-	-	-	10	-	DNS	-	-	-
Roy Salvadori	Cooper T45-Climax	-	R	4	8	11	3	2	9	5	7
Giorgio Scarlatti	Maserati 250F	-	R	R	-	-	-	-	-	-	-
Harry Schell	Maserati 250F	6	-	-	-	-	-	-	-	-	-
	BRM P25	-	5	2	5	R	5	R	6	R	5
Wolfgang Seidel	Maserati 250F	-	-	-	R	-	-	-	-	-	R
	Cooper T43-Climax	-	-	-	-	-	-	F2	-	-	-
Carroll Shelby	Maserati 250F	-	-	-	R	9	-	-	R	4	-
Alan Stacey	Lotus 16-Climax	-	-	-	-	-	R	-	-	-	-
André Testut	Maserati 250F	-	DNQ	-	-	-	-	-	-	-	-
Maurice Trintignant	Cooper T45-Climax	-	1	9	-	-	-	3	8	R	R
	Maserati 250F	-	-	-	7	-	-	-	-	-	-
	BRM P25	-	-	-	-	R	-	-	-	-	-
	Cooper T43-Climax	-	-	-	-	-	8	-	-	-	-
Wolfgang von Trips	Ferrari Dino 246	-	R	-	-	3	R	4	5	R	-

SHARED DRIVES - French GP: Stuart Lewis-Evans/Tony Brooks (Vanwall VW9) R. **Italian GP:** Masten Gregory/Carroll Shelby (Maserati 250F) 4

Grande Premio de Portugal

24 August 1958. Oporto. 50 laps of a 4.603-mile circuit = 230.150 miles. Damp and overcast at the start, drying. World Championship round 9

1	Stirling Moss	Vanwall VW10	50	2h11m27.80
2	Mike Hawthorn	Ferrari Dino 246	50	2h16m40.55
3	Stuart Lewis-Evans	Vanwall VW6	49	
4	Jean Behra	BRM P25 (58)	49	
5	Wolfgang von Trips	Ferrari Dino 246	49	
6	Harry Schell	BRM P25 (58)	49	

Winner's average speed: 105.041 mph. Starting grid front row: Moss, 2m34.21 (pole), Hawthorn, 2m34.26 and Lewis-Evans, 2m34.60. Fastest lap: Hawthorn, 2m32.37. Leaders: Moss, laps 1, 8-50; Hawthorn, 2-7

Gran Premio d'Italia

7 September 1958. Monza. 70 laps of a 3.573-mile circuit = 250.110 miles. Hot, dry and sunny. World Championship round 10

1	Tony Brooks	Vanwall VW5	70	2h03m47.8
2	Mike Hawthorn	Ferrari Dino 246	70	2h04m12.0
3	Phil Hill	Ferrari Dino 246	70	2h04m16.1
4*	Masten Gregory/ Carroll Shelby	Maserati 250F	69	
5	Roy Salvadori	Cooper T45-Climax	62	
6	Graham Hill	Lotus 16-Climax	62	

Winner's average speed: 121.220 mph. Starting grid front row: Moss, 1m40.5 (pole), Brooks, 1m41.4, Hawthorn, 1m41.8 and Lewis-Evans, 1m42.4. Fastest lap: P Hill, 1m42.9. Leaders: P Hill, laps 1-4, 35-37; Hawthorn, 5-6, 9, 15-34, 38-60; Moss, 7-8, 10-14; Brooks, 61-70. *No points awarded to drivers of shared cars

Grand Prix du Maroc

19 October 1958. Ain Diab. 53 laps of a 4.724-mile circuit = 250.372 miles. Warm, dry and sunny. World Championship round 11

1	Stirling Moss	Vanwall VW5	53	2h09m15.0
2	Mike Hawthorn	Ferrari Dino 246	53	2h10m39.8
3	Phil Hill	Ferrari Dino 246	53	2h10m40.6
4	Jo Bonnier	BRM P25 (58)	53	2h11m01.8
5	Harry Schell	BRM P25 (58)	53	2h11m48.8
6	Masten Gregory	Maserati 250F	52	

Winner's average speed: 116.227 mph. Starting grid front row: Hawthorn, 2m23.1 (pole), Moss, 2m23.2 and Lewis-Evans, 2m23.7. Fastest lap: Moss, 2m22.5. Leaders: Moss, laps 1-53

1958 FINAL CHAMPIONSHIP POSITIONS

Drivers

1	Mike Hawthorn	42 (49)*		Wolfgang von Trips	9
2	Stirling Moss	41	13	Jimmy Bryan	8
3	Tony Brooks	24	14	Juan Manuel Fangio	7
4	Roy Salvadori	15	15	George Amick	6
5=	Peter Collins	14	16=	Tony Bettenhausen	4
	Harry Schell	14		Johnny Boyd	4
7=	Luigi Musso	12	18=	Cliff Allison	3
	Maurice Trintignant	12		Jo Bonnier	3
9	Stuart Lewis-Evans	11		Jack Brabham	3
10=	Jean Behra	9	21	Jim Rathmann	2
	Phil Hill	9		*Best six results count	

Manufacturers

1	Vanwall	48 (57)*
2	Ferrari	40 (57)*
3	Cooper-Climax	31
4	BRM	18
5	Maserati	6
6	Lotus-Climax	6

*Best six results count. No points awarded for Indianapolis 500, points only awarded to first car to finish for each manufacturer

1959

The shock announcement that reigning constructors' champion Vanwall was to withdraw from Formula One due to Tony Vandervell's ill-health thrust Cooper to the fore as Britain's leading team. With its ground-breaking rear-engine design, Cooper rose to the challenge, winning five of the eight Championship Grands Prix, the Constructors' Cup, and giving Jack Brabham his first World Championship.

Due to lack of finance the Argentinian GP was cancelled, so the season opened at Monaco with Brabham's first win. Three weeks later at Zandvoort, nine years after the first BRM made its highly publicized debut, the marque finally won a Grand Prix. Jo Bonnier started from pole and triumphed when Stirling Moss's gearbox broke in the closing laps.

Having won easily at Reims, the Ferrari team was forced to miss the British GP due to a strike in Italy, where Brabham triumphed again. The German GP had been moved to Avus, but the meeting was marred by tragedy. In the supporting Sports Car race, Jean Behra was killed on the fearsomely banked North Curve. In the Grand Prix Ferrari

1959 DRIVERS' RECORDS

(excluding Indianapolis)

Driver	Car	Monaco GP	Dutch GP	French GP	British GP	German GP	Portuguese GP	Italian GP	United States GP
Cliff Allison	Ferrari Dino 156	R	-	-	-	-	-	-	-
	Ferrari Dino 246	-	9	-	-	R	-	5	R
Peter Ashdown	Cooper T45-Climax	-	-	-	12	-	-	-	-
Astrubel Bayardo	Maserati 250F	-	-	DNQ	-	-	-	-	-
Carel Godin de Beaufort	Porsche RSK	-	10	-	-	-	-	-	-
	Maserati 250F	-	-	9	-	-	-	-	-
Jean Behra	Ferrari Dino 246	R	5	R	-	-	-	-	-
	Behra-Porsche	-	-	-	-	DNS	-	-	-
Lucien Bianchi	Cooper T51-Climax	DNQ	-	-	-	-	-	-	-
Harry Blanchard	Porsche RSK	-	-	-	-	-	-	-	7
Jo Bonnier	BRM P25	R	1^P	R	R	5	R	8	-
Jack Brabham	Cooper T51-Climax	1^F	2	3	1^P	R	R	-	4
	Cooper T45-Climax	-	-	-	-	-	-	3	-
Chris Bristow	Cooper T51-Borgward	-	-	-	10	-	-	-	-
Tony Brooks	Ferrari Dino 246	2	R	1^P	-	1^PF	9	R	3
	Vanwall VW5	-	-	-	-	R	-	-	-
Ivor Bueb	Cooper T51-Climax	DNQ	-	-	-	-	-	-	-
	Cooper T51-Borgward	-	-	-	13	-	-	-	-
Ian Burgess	Cooper T51-Maserati	-	-	R	R	6	-	14	-
Giulio Cabianca	Maserati 250F	-	-	-	-	-	-	15	-
Mario Araujo de Cabral	Cooper T51-Maserati	-	-	-	-	-	10	-	-
Phil Cade	Maserati 250F	-	-	-	-	-	-	-	DNS
Alain de Chagny	Cooper T51-Climax	DNQ	-	-	-	-	-	-	-
George Constantine	Cooper T45-Climax	-	-	-	-	-	-	-	R
Colin Davis	Cooper T51-Maserati	-	-	R	-	-	-	11	-
Jack Fairman	Cooper T43-Climax	-	-	-	R	-	-	-	-
	Cooper T45-Maserati	-	-	-	-	-	-	R	-
Maria Teresa de Filippis	Behra-Porsche	DNQ	-	-	-	-	-	-	-
Ron Flockhart	BRM P25	R	-	6	R	-	7	13	-
Olivier Gendebien	Ferrari Dino 246	-	-	4	-	-	-	6	-
Keith Greene	Cooper T43-Climax	-	-	-	DNQ	-	-	-	-
Masten Gregory	Cooper T45-Climax	R	-	-	-	-	-	-	-
	Cooper T51-Climax	-	3	R	7	R	2	-	-
Dan Gurney	Ferrari Dino 246	-	-	R	-	2	3	4	/Cont'd

dominated again, Tony Brooks leading impressive newcomer Dan Gurney, in his second race, and Phil Hill to a 1-2-3.

By winning the next two Grands Prix, Moss made it a three-way championship finale at Sebring, the first F1 race in the United States. However, both he and fellow contender Brooks retired early, confirming Brabham as champion. The Australian ran out of fuel in the closing laps, allowing teammate Bruce McLaren to become the youngest ever winner of a Grand Prix. The exhausted Brabham pushed his car across the line to finish fourth.

Grand Prix de Monaco

10 May 1959. Monte Carlo. 100 laps of a 1.954-mile circuit = 195.400 miles. Hot, dry and sunny. World Championship round 1

1 Jack Brabham	Cooper T51-Climax	100	2h55m51.3	
2 Tony Brooks	Ferrari Dino 246	100	2h56m11.7	
3 Maurice Trintignant	Cooper T51-Climax	98		
4 Phil Hill	Ferrari Dino 246	97		
5 Bruce McLaren	Cooper T51-Climax	96		
6 Roy Salvadori	Cooper T45-Maserati	83	transmission	

Winner's average speed: 66.669 mph. Starting grid front row: Moss, 1m39.6 (pole), Behra, 1m40.0 and Brabham, 1m40.1. Fastest lap: Brabham, 1m40.4. Leaders: Behra, laps 1-21; Moss, 22-81; Brabham, 82-100

Indianapolis 500

30 May 1959. Indianapolis. 200 laps of a 2.500-mile circuit = 500.000 miles. Warm, dry and overcast. World Championship round 2

1 Rodger Ward	Watson-Offenhauser	200	3h40m49.20
2 Jim Rathmann	Watson-Offenhauser	200	3h41m12.47
3 Johnny Thomson	Lesovsky-Offenhauser	200	3h41m39.85
4 Tony Bettenhausen	Epperly-Offenhauser	200	3h42m36.25
5 Paul Goldsmith	Epperly-Offenhauser	200	3h42m55.60
6 Johnny Boyd	Epperly-Offenhauser	200	3h44m06.23

Winner's average speed: 135.857 mph. Starting grid front row: Thomson, 145.908 mph (pole), Sachs, 145.425 mph and J Rathmann, 144.433 mph. Fastest lap in the lead: Thomson, 1m01.89

Grote Prijs van Nederland

31 May 1959. Zandvoort. 75 laps of a 2.605-mile circuit = 195.375 miles. Warm, dry and sunny. World Championship round 3

1 Jo Bonnier	BRM P25 (59)	75	2h05m26.8
2 Jack Brabham	Cooper T51-Climax	75	2h05m41.0
3 Masten Gregory	Cooper T51-Climax	75	2h06m49.8
4 Innes Ireland	Lotus 16-Climax	74	
5 Jean Behra	Ferrari Dino 246	74	
6 Phil Hill	Ferrari Dino 246	73	

Winner's average speed: 93.446 mph. Starting grid front row: Bonnier, 1m36.0 (pole), Brabham, 1m36.0 and Moss 1m36.2. Fastest lap: Moss, 1m36.6. Leaders: Bonnier, laps 1, 12-29, 34-59, 63-75; Gregory, 2-11; Brabham, 30-33; Moss, 60-62

1959 DRIVERS' RECORDS cont'd/ (excluding Indianapolis)

Driver	Car	Monaco GP	Dutch GP	French GP	British GP	German GP	Portuguese GP	Italian GP	United States GP
Bruce Halford	Lotus 16-Climax	R	-	-	-	-	-	-	-
Hans Herrmann	Cooper T51-Maserati	-	-	-	R	-	-	-	-
	BRM P25	-	-	-	-	R	-	-	-
Graham Hill	Lotus 16-Climax	R	7	R	9	R	R	R	-
Phil Hill	Ferrari Dino 246	4	6	2	-	3	R	2F	R
Innes Ireland	Lotus 16-Climax	-	4	R	-	R	R	R	5
Pete Lovely	Lotus 16-Climax	DNQ	-	-	-	-	-	-	-
Jean Lucienbonnet	Cooper T45-Climax	DNQ	-	-	-	-	-	-	-
Bruce McLaren	Cooper T51-Climax	5	-	-	-	-	-	R	-
	Cooper T45-Climax	-	-	5	3F	R	R	-	1
Bill Moss	Cooper T51-Climax	-	-	-	DNQ	-	-	-	-
Stirling Moss	Cooper T51-Climax	RP	RF	-	-	R	1PF	1P	RP
	BRM P25	-	-	RF	2F	-	-	-	-
Brian Naylor	JBW-Maserati	-	-	-	R	-	-	-	-
Fritz d'Orey	Maserati 250F	-	-	10	R	-	-	-	-
	Tec-Mec F415-Maserati	-	-	-	-	-	-	-	R
Michael Parkes	Fry-Climax	-	-	-	DNQ	-	-	-	-
Tim Parnell	Cooper T45-Climax	-	-	-	DNQ	-	-	-	-
David Piper	Lotus 16-Climax	-	-	-	R	-	-	-	-
Bob Said	Connaught C-Alta	-	-	-	-	-	-	-	R
Roy Salvadori	Cooper T45-Maserati	6	-	R	-	-	-	-	R
	Aston Martin DBR4/250	-	R	-	6	-	6	R	-
Giorgio Scarlatti	Maserati 250F	DNQ	-	8	-	-	-	-	-
	Cooper T51-Climax	-	-	-	-	-	-	12	-
Harry Schell	BRM P25	R	R	7	4	7	5	7	-
	Cooper T51-Climax	-	-	-	-	-	-	-	R
Carroll Shelby	Aston Martin DBR4/250	-	R	-	R	-	8	10	-
Alan Stacey	Lotus 16-Climax	-	-	-	8	-	-	-	R
Henry Taylor	Cooper T51-Climax	-	-	-	11	-	-	-	-
Mike Taylor	Cooper T45-Climax	-	-	-	R	-	-	-	-
Trevor Taylor	Cooper T51-Climax	-	-	-	DNQ	-	-	-	-
André Testut	Maserati 250F	DNQ	-	-	-	-	-	-	-
Alessandro de Tomaso	Cooper T43-OSCA	-	-	-	-	-	-	-	R
Maurice Trintignant	Cooper T51-Climax	3	8	11	5	4	4	9	2F
Wolfgang von Trips	Porsche 718	R	-	-	-	DNS	-	-	-
	Ferrari Dino 246	-	-	-	-	-	-	-	6
Rodger Ward	Kurtis-Offenhauser	-	-	-	-	-	-	-	R

World Championship Grand Prix Racing

Grand Prix de l'Automobile Club de France

5 July 1959. Reims. 50 laps of a 5.187-mile circuit = 259.350 miles. Very hot, dry and sunny. World Championship round 4. Also known as the European Grand Prix

1 Tony Brooks	Ferrari Dino 246	50	2h01m26.5
2 Phil Hill	Ferrari Dino 246	50	2h01m54.0
3 Jack Brabham	Cooper T51-Climax	50	2h03m04.2
4 Olivier Gendebien	Ferrari Dino 246	50	2h03m14.0
5 Bruce McLaren	Cooper T45-Climax	50	2h03m14.2
6 Ron Flockhart	BRM P25 (59)	50	2h03m32.2

Winner's average speed: 128.136 mph. Starting grid front row: Brooks, 2m19.4 (pole), Brabham, 2m19.7 and P Hill, 2m19.8. Fastest lap: Moss, 2m22.8. Leaders: Brooks, laps 1-50

British Grand Prix

18 July 1959. Aintree. 75 laps of a 3.000-mile circuit = 225.000 miles. Warm, dry and sunny. World Championship round 5

1 Jack Brabham	Cooper T51-Climax	75	2h30m11.6
2 Stirling Moss	BRM P25 (58)	75	2h30m33.8
3 Bruce McLaren	Cooper T45-Climax	75	2h30m34.0
4 Harry Schell	BRM P25 (59)	74	
5 Maurice Trintignant	Cooper T51-Climax	74	
6 Roy Salvadori	Aston Martin DBR4/250	74	

Winner's average speed: 89.884 mph. Starting grid front row: Brabham, 1m58.0 (pole), Salvadori, 1m58.0 and Schell, 1m59.2. Fastest lap: Moss and McLaren, 1m57.0. Leaders: Brabham, laps 1-75

Grosser Preis von Deutschland

2 August 1959. Avus. 2 heats of 30 laps each, 60 laps of a 5.157-mile circuit = 309.420 miles. Warm, dry and overcast. World Championship round 6

1 Tony Brooks	Ferrari Dino 246	60	2h09m31.6
2 Dan Gurney	Ferrari Dino 246	60	2h09m33.2
3 Phil Hill	Ferrari Dino 246	60	2h10m36.7
4 Maurice Trintignant	Cooper T51-Climax	59	
5 Jo Bonnier	BRM P25 (59)	58	
6 Ian Burgess	Cooper T51-Maserati	56	

Winner's average speed: 143.331 mph. Starting grid front row: Brooks, 2m05.9 (pole), Moss, 2m06.8, Gurney, 2m07.2 and Brabham, 2m07.4. Fastest lap: Brooks, 2m04.5. Leaders: Heat 1: Brooks, laps 1-2, 5-13, 15, 18-22, 24-30; Gregory, 3-4, 23; Gurney, 14, 16-17. Heat 2: P Hill, laps 1, 6, 8-9, 15, 18-19; Brooks, 2-5, 7, 10, 12, 16-17, 22-30; Gurney, 11, 13-14, 20-21. Heat 2 overall lead: Brooks, all laps bar Gurney, 11, 13-14, 20-21

Grande Premio de Portugal

23 August 1959. Monsanto. 62 laps of a 3.380-mile circuit = 209.560 miles. Hot, dry and sunny. World Championship round 7

1 Stirling Moss	Cooper T51-Climax	62	2h11m55.41
2 Masten Gregory	Cooper T51-Climax	61	
3 Dan Gurney	Ferrari Dino 246	61	
4 Maurice Trintignant	Cooper T51-Climax	60	
5 Harry Schell	BRM P25 (59)	59	
6 Roy Salvadori	Aston Martin DBR4/250	59	

Winner's average speed: 95.310 mph. Starting grid front row: Moss, 2m02.89 (pole), Brabham, 2m04.95 and Gregory, 2m06.33. Fastest lap: Moss, 2m05.07. Leaders: Moss, laps 1-62

Gran Premio d'Italia

13 September 1959. Monza. 72 laps of a 3.573-mile circuit = 257.256 miles. Warm, dry and sunny. World Championship round 8

1 Stirling Moss	Cooper T51-Climax	72	2h04m05.4
2 Phil Hill	Ferrari Dino 246	72	2h04m52.1
3 Jack Brabham	Cooper T45-Climax	72	2h05m17.9
4 Dan Gurney	Ferrari Dino 246	72	2h05m25.0
5 Cliff Allison	Ferrari Dino 246	71	
6 Olivier Gendebien	Ferrari Dino 246	71	

Winner's average speed: 124.388 mph. Starting grid front row: Moss, 1m39.7 (pole), Brooks, 1m39.8 and Brabham, 1m40.2. Fastest lap: P Hill, 1m40.4. Leaders: Moss, laps 1, 4, 15, 33-72; P Hill, 2-3, 5-14, 16-32

United States Grand Prix

12 December 1959. Sebring. 42 laps of a 5.200-mile circuit = 218.400 miles. Warm, dry and sunny. World Championship round 9

1 Bruce McLaren	Cooper T45-Climax	42	2h12m35.7
2 Maurice Trintignant	Cooper T51-Climax	42	2h12m36.3
3 Tony Brooks	Ferrari Dino 246	42	2h15m36.6
4 Jack Brabham	Cooper T51-Climax	42	2h17m33.0
5 Innes Ireland	Lotus 16-Climax	39	
6 Wolfgang von Trips	Ferrari Dino 246	38	

Winner's average speed: 98.827 mph. Starting grid front row: Moss, 3m00.0 (pole), Brabham, 3m03.0 and Schell, 3m05.2. Fastest lap: Trintignant, 3m05.0. Leaders: Moss, laps 1-5; Brabham, 6-41; McLaren, 42

1959 FINAL CHAMPIONSHIP POSITIONS

Drivers				Manufacturers	
1 Jack Brabham	31 (34)*	11 Jim Rathmann	6	1 Cooper-Climax	40 (53)*
2 Tony Brooks	27	12= Innes Ireland	5	2 Ferrari	32 (38)*
3 Stirling Moss	25.5	Harry Schell	5	3 BRM	18
4 Phil Hill	20	Johnny Thomson	5	4 Lotus-Climax	5
5 Maurice Trintignant	19	15= Tony Bettenhausen	3		
6 Bruce McLaren	16.5	Olivier Gendebien	3	*Best five results count. No points	
7 Dan Gurney	13	17= Cliff Allison	2	awarded for Indianapolis 500,	
8= Jo Bonnier	10	Jean Behra	2	points only awarded to first car	
Masten Gregory	10	Paul Goldsmith	2	to finish for each manufacturer	
10 Rodger Ward	8	*Best five results count			

1960

Following Cooper's victorious 1959 campaign, it became obvious that moving the engine behind the driver, which saved weight and allowed improved frontal aerodynamics, was the future for F1 design. Even Ferrari experimented with the rear-engined 246P.

Bruce McLaren and Cooper backed up their Sebring victory by winning the opening round at Buenos Aires, but Innes Ireland showed the promise of the new rear-engined Lotus 18 by leading the opening lap before he spun. Impressed, Stirling Moss and team owner Rob

34

Walker replaced their Cooper with a new Lotus and promptly won at Monaco.

After Jack Brabham triumphed at the Dutch GP for Cooper (where Jim Clark made his Championship debut), the F1 teams travelled to Spa for the tragic Belgian GP. In practice, Stirling Moss suffered serious leg, back and facial injuries after crashing at Burneville, while Mike Taylor broke his collar bone in a separate incident. Worse was to come; Chris Bristow and Alan Stacey were both killed during the race. Brabham won again, but like Michael Schumacher's victory at Imola in 1994, the result meant little.

Three more consecutive victories secured Brabham's second successive World Championship. Then, at the penultimate round, the Monza organizers decided to use the banking, which prompted a boycott by the British teams and a 1-2-3 for Ferrari. Conversely, with the title already decided, Ferrari missed the United States GP which Moss won in only his second race since returning from injury.

Gran Premio de la Republica Argentina

7 February 1960. Buenos Aires. 80 laps of a 2.431-mile circuit = 194.480 miles. Very hot, dry and sunny. World Championship round 1

1 Bruce McLaren	Cooper T45-Climax	80	2h17m49.5
2 Cliff Allison	Ferrari Dino 246	80	2h18m15.8
3 Maurice Trintignant/			
Stirling Moss*	Cooper T51-Climax	80	2h18m26.4
4 Carlos Menditéguy	Cooper T51-Maserati	80	2h18m42.8
5 Wolfgang von Trips	Ferrari Dino 246	79	
6 Innes Ireland	Lotus 18-Climax	79	

Winner's average speed: 84.664 mph. Starting grid front row: Moss, 1m36.9 (pole), Ireland, 1m38.5, G Hill, 1m38.9 and Bonnier, 1m38.9. Fastest lap: Moss, 1m38.9. Leaders: Ireland, lap 1; Bonnier, laps 2-15, 21-36, 41-67; Moss, 16-20, 37-40; McLaren, 68-90. *No points awarded to drivers of shared cars

Grand Prix de Monaco

29 May 1960. Monte Carlo. 100 laps of a 1.954-mile circuit = 195.400 miles. Dry at the start, rain later. World Championship round 2

1 Stirling Moss	Lotus 18-Climax	100	2h53m45.5
2 Bruce McLaren	Cooper T53-Climax	100	2h54m37.6
3 Phil Hill	Ferrari Dino 246	100	2h54m47.4
4 Tony Brooks	Cooper T51-Climax	99	
5 Jo Bonnier	BRM P48	83	
6 Richie Ginther	Ferrari Dino 246P	70	

Winner's average speed: 67.473 mph. Starting grid front row: Moss, 1m36.3 (pole), Brabham, 1m37.3 and Brooks, 1m37.7. Fastest lap: McLaren, 1m36.2. Leaders: Bonnier, laps 1-16, 61-67; Moss, 17-33, 41-60, 68-100; Brabham, 34-40

Indianapolis 500

30 May 1960. Indianapolis. 200 laps of a 2.500-mile circuit = 500.000 miles. Warm, dry and overcast. World Championship round 3

1 Jim Rathmann	Watson-Offenhauser	200	3h36m11.36
2 Rodger Ward	Watson-Offenhauser	200	3h36m24.03
3 Paul Goldsmith	Epperly-Offenhauser	200	3h39m18.58
4 Don Branson	Phillips-Offenhauser	200	3h39m19.28
5 Johnny Thomson	Lesovsky-Offenhauser	200	3h39m22.65
6 Eddie Johnson	Trevis-Offenhauser	200	3h40m21.88

Winner's average speed: 138.767 mph. Starting grid front row: Sachs, 146.592 mph (pole), J Rathmann, 146.371 mph and Ward, 145.560 mph. Fastest lap in the lead: J Rathmann, 1m01.59

Grote Prijs van Nederland

6 June 1960. Zandvoort. 75 laps of a 2.605-mile circuit = 195.375 miles. Warm, dry and sunny. World Championship round 4

1 Jack Brabham	Cooper T53-Climax	75	2h01m47.2
2 Innes Ireland	Lotus 18-Climax	75	2h02m11.2
3 Graham Hill	BRM P48	75	2h02m43.8
4 Stirling Moss	Lotus 18-Climax	75	2h02m44.9
5 Wolfgang von Trips	Ferrari Dino 246	74	
6 Richie Ginther	Ferrari Dino 246	74	

Winner's average speed: 96.254 mph. Starting grid front row: Moss, 1m33.2 (pole), Brabham, 1m33.4 and Ireland, 1m33.9. Fastest lap: Moss, 1m33.8. Leaders: Brabham, laps 1-75

Jack Brabham leads the 1960 Dutch Grand Prix at Zandvoort: his first win of the season

Grand Prix de Belgique

19 June 1960. Spa-Francorchamps. 36 laps of a 8.761-mile circuit = 315.396 miles. Warm, dry and sunny. World Championship round 5

1 Jack Brabham	Cooper T53-Climax	36	2h21m37.3
2 Bruce McLaren	Cooper T53-Climax	36	2h22m40.6
3 Olivier Gendebien	Cooper T51-Climax	35	
4 Phil Hill	Ferrari Dino 246	35	
5 Jim Clark	Lotus 18-Climax	34	
6 Lucien Bianchi	Cooper T45-Climax	28	

Winner's average speed: 133.622 mph. Starting grid front row: Brabham, 3m50.0 (pole), Brooks, 3m52.5 and P Hill, 3m53.3. Fastest lap: Brabham, P Hill and Ireland, 3m51.9. Leaders: Brabham, laps 1-36

Grand Prix de l'Automobile Club de France

3 July 1960. Reims. 50 laps of a 5.187-mile circuit = 259.350 miles. Warm, dry and overcast. World Championship round 6

1 Jack Brabham	Cooper T53-Climax	50	1h57m24.9
2 Olivier Gendebien	Cooper T51-Climax	50	1h58m13.2
3 Bruce McLaren	Cooper T53-Climax	50	1h58m16.8
4 Henry Taylor	Cooper T51-Climax	49	
5 Jim Clark	Lotus 18-Climax	49	
6 Ron Flockhart	Lotus 18-Climax	49	

Winner's average speed: 132.530 mph. Starting grid front row: Brabham, 2m16.8 (pole), P Hill, 2m18.2 and G Hill, 2m18.4. Fastest lap: Brabham, 2m17.5. Leaders: Brabham, laps 1-3, 5, 7, 9-10, 12, 14, 18-50; P Hill, 4, 6, 8, 11, 13, 15-17

British Grand Prix

16 July 1960. Silverstone. 77 laps of a 2.927-mile circuit = 225.379 miles. Warm, dry and overcast. World Championship round 7

1	Jack Brabham	Cooper T53-Climax	77	2h04m24.6
2	John Surtees	Lotus 18-Climax	77	2h05m14.2
3	Innes Ireland	Lotus 18-Climax	77	2h05m54.2
4	Bruce McLaren	Cooper T53-Climax	76	
5	Tony Brooks	Cooper T51-Climax	76	
6	Wolfgang von Trips	Ferrari Dino 246	75	

Winner's average speed: 108.695 mph. Starting grid front row: Brabham, 1m34.6 (pole), G Hill, 1m35.6, McLaren, 1m36.0 and Bonnier, 1m36.2. Fastest lap: G Hill, 1m34.4. Leaders: Brabham, laps 1-54, 72-77; G Hill, 55-71

Grande Premio de Portugal

14 August 1960. Oporto. 55 laps of a 4.602-mile circuit = 253.110 miles. Hot, dry and sunny. World Championship round 8

1	Jack Brabham	Cooper T53-Climax	55	2h19m00.03
2	Bruce McLaren	Cooper T53-Climax	55	2h19m58.00
3	Jim Clark	Lotus 18-Climax	55	2h20m53.26
4	Wolfgang von Trips	Ferrari Dino 246	55	2h20m58.84
5	Tony Brooks	Cooper T51-Climax	49	
6	Innes Ireland	Lotus 18-Climax	48	

Moss (Lotus 18-Climax) finished fifth on the road but was disqualified for driving in the wrong direction after a spin. Winner's average speed: 109.256 mph. Starting grid front row: Surtees, 2m25.56 (pole), Gurney, 2m25.63 and Brabham, 2m26.05. Fastest lap: Surtees, 2m27.53. Leaders: Gurney, laps 1-10; Surtees, 11-35; Brabham, 36-55

Gran Premio d'Italia

4 September 1960. Monza. 50 laps of a 6.214-mile circuit = 310.700 miles. Warm, dry and overcast. World Championship round 9. Also known as the European Grand Prix

1	Phil Hill	Ferrari Dino 246	50	2h21m09.2
2	Richie Ginther	Ferrari Dino 246	50	2h23m36.8
3	Willy Mairesse	Ferrari Dino 246	49	
4	Giulio Cabianca	Cooper T51-Ferrari	48	
5	Wolfgang von Trips	Ferrari Dino 156P	48	
6	Hans Herrmann	Porsche 718	47	

Winner's average speed: 132.069 mph. Starting grid front row: P Hill, 2m41.4 (pole), Ginther, 2m43.3 and Mairesse, 2m43.9. Fastest lap: P Hill, 2m43.6. Leaders: Ginther, laps 1-16, 18-25; P Hill, 17, 26-50

United States Grand Prix

20 November 1960. Riverside. 75 laps of a 3.275-mile circuit = 245.625 miles. Warm, dry and sunny. World Championship round 10

1	Stirling Moss	Lotus 18-Climax	75	2h28m52.2
2	Innes Ireland	Lotus 18-Climax	75	2h29m30.2
3	Bruce McLaren	Cooper T53-Climax	75	2h30m14.2
4	Jack Brabham	Cooper T53-Climax	74	
5	Jo Bonnier	BRM P48	74	
6	Phil Hill	Cooper T51-Climax	74	

Winner's average speed: 98.996 mph. Starting grid front row: Moss, 1m54.4 (pole), Brabham, 1m55.0 and Gurney, 1m55.2. Fastest lap: Brabham, 1m56.2. Leaders: Brabham, laps 1-4; Moss, 5-75

1960 FINAL CHAMPIONSHIP POSITIONS

Drivers

1	Jack Brabham	43
2	Bruce McLaren	34 (37)*
3	Stirling Moss	19
4	Innes Ireland	18
5	Phil Hill	16
6=	Olivier Gendebien	10
	Wolfgang von Trips	10
8=	Jim Clark	8
	Richie Ginther	8
	Jim Rathmann	8
11	Tony Brooks	7
12=	Cliff Allison	6
	John Surtees	6
	Rodger Ward	6

15=	Jo Bonnier	4
	Paul Goldsmith	4
	Graham Hill	4
	Willy Mairesse	4
19=	Don Branson	3
	Giulio Cabianca	3
	Carlos Mendítéguy	3
	Henry Taylor	3
23	Johnny Thomson	2
24=	Lucien Bianchi	1
	Ron Flockhart	1
	Hans Herrmann	1
	Eddie Johnson	1
	*Best six results count	

Manufacturers

1	Cooper-Climax	48 (58)*
2	Lotus-Climax	34 (37)*
3	Ferrari	26 (27)*
4	BRM	8
5=	Cooper-Maserati	3
	Cooper-Ferrari	3

*Best six results count. No points awarded for Indianapolis 500, points only awarded to first car to finish for each manufacturer

1960 DRIVERS' RECORDS

(excluding Indianapolis)

Driver	Car	Argentinian GP	Monaco GP	Dutch GP	Belgian GP	French GP	British GP	Portuguese GP	Italian GP	United States GP
Cliff Allison	Ferrari Dino 246	2	DNQ	-	-	-	-	-	-	-
Edgar Barth	Porsche 718	-	-	-	-	-	-	-	7	-
Carel Godin de Beaufort	Cooper T51-Climax	-	-	8	-	-	-	-	-	-
Lucien Bianchi	Cooper T45-Climax	-	-	-	6	R	R	-	-	-
Jo Bonnier	BRM P25	7	-	-	-	-	-	-	-	-
	BRM P48	-	5	R	R	R	R	R	-	5
Roberto Bonomi	Cooper T51-Maserati	11	-	-	-	-	-	-	-	-
Jack Brabham	Cooper T51-Climax	R	-	-	-	-	-	-	-	-
	Cooper T53-Climax	-	DSQ	1	1PF	1PF	1P	1	-	4F
Chris Bristow	Cooper T51-Climax	-	R	R	R	-	-	-	-	-
Tony Brooks	Cooper T51-Climax	-	4	R	R	-	5	5	-	R
	Vanwall VW11	-	-	-	-	R	-	-	-	-
Ian Burgess	Cooper T51-Maserati	-	DNQ	-	-	10	R	-	-	R
Giulio Cabianca	Cooper T51-Ferrari	-	-	-	-	-	-	-	4	-
Mario Araujo de Cabral	Cooper T51-Maserati	-	-	-	-	-	-	R	-	-
Ettore Chimeri	Maserati 250F	R	-	-	-	-	-	-	-	-

/Cont'd

1960 DRIVERS' RECORDS cont'd/ (excluding Indianapolis)

Driver	Car	Argentinian GP	Monaco GP	Dutch GP	Belgian GP	French GP	British GP	Portuguese GP	Italian GP	United States GP
Jim Clark	Lotus 18-Climax	-	-	R	5	5	16	3	-	16
Antonio Creus	Maserati 250F	R	-	-	-	-	-	-	-	-
Chuck Daigh	Scarab	-	DNQ	DNS	R	DNS	-	-	-	10
	Cooper T51-Climax	-	-	-	-	-	R	-	-	-
Bob Drake	Maserati 250F	-	-	-	-	-	-	-	-	13
Piero Drogo	Cooper T43-Climax	-	-	-	-	-	-	-	8	-
Nasif Estefano	Maserati 250F	14	-	-	-	-	-	-	-	-
Jack Fairman	Cooper T51-Climax	-	-	-	-	-	R	-	-	-
Ron Flockhart	Lotus 18-Climax	-	-	-	-	6	-	-	-	-
	Cooper T51-Climax	-	-	-	-	-	-	-	-	R
Fred Gamble	Behra-Porsche	-	-	-	-	-	-	-	10	-
Olivier Gendebien	Cooper T51-Climax	-	-	-	3	2	9	7	-	12
Richie Ginther	Ferrari Dino 246P	-	6	-	-	-	-	-	-	-
	Ferrari Dino 246	-	-	6	-	-	-	-	2	-
	Scarab	-	-	-	-	DNS	-	-	-	-
José Froilan Gonzalez	Ferrari Dino 246	10	-	-	-	-	-	-	-	-
Horace Gould	Maserati 250F	-	-	-	-	-	-	-	DNS	-
Keith Greene	Cooper T45-Maserati	-	-	-	-	-	R	-	-	-
Masten Gregory	Behra-Porsche	12	-	-	-	-	-	-	-	-
	Cooper T51-Maserati	-	DNQ	DNS	-	9	14	R	-	-
Dan Gurney	BRM P48	-	NC	R	R	R	10	R	-	R
Bruce Halford	Cooper T45-Climax	-	DNQ	-	-	-	-	-	-	-
	Cooper T51-Climax	-	-	-	-	8	-	-	-	-
Jim Hall	Lotus 18-Climax	-	-	-	-	-	-	-	-	7
Hans Herrmann	Porsche 718	-	-	-	-	-	-	-	6	-
Graham Hill	BRM P25	R	-	-	-	-	-	-	-	-
	BRM P48	-	7	3	R	R	R^F	R	-	R
Phil Hill	Ferrari Dino 246	8	3	R	4^F	12	7	R	1^{PF}	-
	Cooper T51-Climax	-	-	-	-	-	-	-	-	6
Innes Ireland	Lotus 18-Climax	6	9	2	R^F	7	3	6	-	2
Pete Lovely	Cooper T51-Ferrari	-	-	-	-	-	-	-	-	11
Willy Mairesse	Ferrari Dino 246	-	-	-	R	R	-	-	3	-
Bruce McLaren	Cooper T45-Climax	1	-	-	-	-	-	-	-	-
	Cooper T53-Climax	-	2^F	R	2	3	4	2	-	3
Carlos Menditéguy	Cooper T51-Maserati	4	-	-	-	-	-	-	-	-
Stirling Moss	Cooper T51-Climax	3^{PF}	-	-	-	-	-	-	-	-
	Lotus 18-Climax	-	1^P	4^{PF}	DNS	-	-	DSQ	-	1^P
Gino Munaron	Maserati 250F	13	-	-	-	-	-	-	-	-
	Cooper T51-Ferrari	-	-	-	-	R	15	-	R	-
Brian Naylor	JBW-Maserati	-	DNQ	-	-	-	13	-	R	R
Arthur Owen	Cooper T45-Climax	-	-	-	-	-	-	-	R	-
David Piper	Lotus 16-Climax	-	-	-	-	DNS	12	-	-	-
Lance Reventlow	Scarab	-	DNQ	DNS	R	-	-	-	-	-
	Cooper T51-Climax	-	-	-	-	-	DNS	-	-	-
Alberto Rodriguez Larreta	Lotus 16-Climax	9	-	-	-	-	-	-	-	-
Roy Salvadori	Cooper T51-Climax	-	R	-	-	-	-	-	-	8
	Aston Martin DBR4/250	-	-	DNS	-	-	-	-	-	-
	Aston Martin DBR5/250	-	-	-	-	-	R	-	-	-
Giorgio Scarlatti	Maserati 250F	R	-	-	-	-	-	-	-	-
	Cooper T51-Ferrari	-	DNQ	-	-	-	-	-	-	-
	Cooper T51-Maserati	-	-	-	-	-	-	-	R	-
Harry Schell	Cooper T51-Climax	R	-	-	-	-	-	-	-	-
Wolfgang Seidel	Cooper T45-Climax	-	-	-	-	-	-	-	9	-
Alan Stacey	Lotus 16-Climax	R	-	-	-	-	-	-	-	-
	Lotus 18-Climax	-	R	R	R	-	-	-	-	-
John Surtees	Lotus 18-Climax	-	R	-	-	-	2	R^{PF}	-	R
Henry Taylor	Cooper T51-Climax	-	-	7	-	4	8	DNS	-	14
Mike Taylor	Lotus 18-Climax	-	-	-	DNS	-	-	-	-	-
Alfonso Thiele	Cooper T51-Maserati	-	-	-	-	-	-	-	R	-
Maurice Trintignant	Cooper T51-Climax	3	-	-	-	-	-	-	-	-
	Cooper T51-Maserati	-	R	R	-	R	-	-	-	15
	Aston Martin DBR5/250	-	-	-	-	-	11	-	-	-
Wolfgang von Trips	Ferrari Dino 246	5	8	5	R	11	6	4	-	-
	Ferrari Dino 156P	-	-	-	-	-	-	-	5	-
	Cooper T51-Maserati	-	-	-	-	-	-	-	-	9
Vic Wilson	Cooper T43-Climax	-	-	-	-	-	-	-	R	-

SHARED DRIVES - Argentinian GP: Maurice Trintignant/Stirling Moss (Cooper T51-Climax) 3

1961

At the start of the year a new Formula One for 1.5-litre cars was introduced - much to the annoyance of the British teams, which struggled to find suitable engines and had to make do with underpowered 4-cylinder units before the purpose-built V8 Climax and BRM were ready. Ferrari, however, was ready with its famous "shark-nose" 156, and was the overwhelming championship favourite.

Stirling Moss conjured up his greatest win at Monaco to hold off the Ferraris in his Rob Walker-entered Lotus, but it was a short-lived triumph, the Italian marque winning the next four events. Even when the works cars retired in France, Giancarlo Baghetti, making his Grand Prix debut in a private Ferrari, won after a slip-streaming duel with Dan Gurney.

A correct tyre choice in the wet/dry German GP gave Moss a second win, but it was the Ferraris of Wolfgang von Trips and Phil Hill which led the championship before the penultimate round at Monza. Early in the race, von Trips collided with Jim Clark's Lotus at Parabolica, launching the Ferrari into the crowd, killing von Trips and fourteen spectators.

The Italian tragedy gave the title to Hill, but Ferrari missed the final race in America. At Watkins Glen, Innes Ireland spun early on but recovered to score Team Lotus's first Grand Prix win, the previous successes for the marque having come via Rob Walker's private team.

Grand Prix de Monaco

14 May 1961. Monte Carlo. 100 laps of a 1.954-mile circuit = 195.400 miles. Warm, dry and hazy. World Championship round 1

1 Stirling Moss	Lotus 18-Climax	100	2h45m50.1
2 Richie Ginther	Ferrari 156	100	2h45m53.7
3 Phil Hill	Ferrari 156	100	2h46m31.4
4 Wolfgang von Trips	Ferrari 156	98	electrics
5 Dan Gurney	Porsche 718	98	

1961 DRIVERS' RECORDS

Driver	Car	Monaco GP	Dutch GP	Belgian GP	French GP	British GP	German GP	Italian GP	United States GP
Cliff Allison	Lotus 18-Climax	8	-	-	-	-	-	-	-
	Lotus 18/21-Climax	-	-	DNQ	-	-	-	-	-
Gerry Ashmore	Lotus 18-Climax	-	-	-	-	R	16	R	-
Giancarlo Baghetti	Ferrari Dino 156	-	-	-	1	R	-	R^F	-
Lorenzo Bandini	Cooper T53-Maserati	-	-	R	-	12	R	8	-
Carel Godin de Beaufort	Porsche 718	-	14	11	R	16	14	7	-
Lucien Bianchi	Emeryson 1961-Maserati	DNQ	-	-	-	-	-	-	-
	Lotus 18-Climax	-	-	R	-	-	-	-	-
	Lotus 18/21-Climax	-	-	-	R	R	-	-	-
Jo Bonnier	Porsche 787	12	11	-	-	-	-	-	-
	Porsche 718	-	-	7	7	5	R	R	6
Jack Brabham	Cooper T55-Climax	R	6	R	R	4	-	-	-
	Cooper T58-Climax	-	-	-	-	-	R	R	R^{PF}
Tony Brooks	BRM P48/57-Climax	13	9	13	R	9^F	R	5	3
Ian Burgess	Lotus 18-Climax	-	DNQ	DNQ	14	14	-	-	-
	Cooper T53-Climax	-	-	-	-	-	12	-	-
Roberto Bussinello	de Tomaso F1/004-Alfa Romeo	-	-	-	-	-	-	R	-
Jim Clark	Lotus 21-Climax	10	3^F	12	3	R	4	R	7
Bernard Collomb	Cooper T53-Climax	-	-	-	R	-	R	-	-
Jack Fairman	Ferguson P99-Climax	-	-	-	-	DSQ	-	-	-
	Cooper T45-Climax	-	-	-	-	-	-	R	-
Olivier Gendebien	Emeryson 1961-Maserati	DNQ	-	-	-	-	-	-	-
	Ferrari Dino 156	-	-	4	-	-	-	-	-
	Lotus 18/21-Climax	-	-	-	-	-	-	-	11
Richie Ginther	Ferrari Dino 156	2^F	5	3^F	15	3	8	R	-
Keith Greene	Gilby 1961-Climax	-	-	-	-	15	-	-	-
Masten Gregory	Cooper T53-Climax	DNQ	DNQ	10	12	11	-	-	-
	Lotus 18/21-Climax	-	-	-	-	-	-	R	11
Dan Gurney	Porsche 718	5	-	6	2	7	7	2	2
	Porsche 787	-	10	-	-	-	-	-	-
Jim Hall	Lotus 18/21-Climax	-	-	-	-	-	-	-	R
Walt Hansgen	Cooper T53-Climax	-	-	-	-	-	-	-	R
Hans Herrmann	Porsche 718	9	15	-	-	-	13	-	-
Graham Hill	BRM P48/57-Climax	R	8	R	6	R	R	R	5
Phil Hill	Ferrari Dino 156	3	2^P	1^P	9^{PF}	2^P	3^{PF}	1	-
Innes Ireland	Lotus 21-Climax	DNS	-	R	4	10	R	-	1
	Lotus 18/21-Climax	-	-	-	-	-	-	R	-
Jackie Lewis	Cooper T53-Climax	-	-	9	R	R	9	4	-
Roberto Lippi	de Tomaso F1/002-OSCA	-	-	-	-	-	-	R	-
Tony Maggs	Lotus 18-Climax	-	-	-	-	13	11	-	-

/Cont'd

6 Bruce McLaren   Cooper T55-Climax   95

Winner's average speed: 70.697 mph. Starting grid front row: Moss, 1m39.1 (pole), Ginther, 1m39.3 and Clark, 1m39.6. Fastest lap: Ginther and Moss, 1m36.3. Leaders: Ginther, laps 1-13; Moss, 14-100

Grote Prijs van Nederland

22 May 1961. Zandvoort. 75 laps of a 2.605-mile circuit = 195.375 miles. Windy, dry and sunny. World Championship round 2

1 Wolfgang von Trips   Ferrari 156   75   2h01m52.1
2 Phil Hill   Ferrari 156   75   2h01m53.0
3 Jim Clark   Lotus 21-Climax   75   2h02m05.2
4 Stirling Moss   Lotus 18-Climax   75   2h02m14.3
5 Richie Ginther   Ferrari 156   75   2h02m14.4
6 Jack Brabham   Cooper T55-Climax   75   2h03m12.2

Winner's average speed: 96.190 mph. Starting grid front row: P Hill, 1m35.7 (pole), von Trips, 1m35.7 and Ginther, 1m35.9. Fastest lap: Clark, 1m35.5. Leaders: von Trips, laps 1-75

Grand Prix de Belgique

18 June 1961. Spa-Francorchamps. 30 laps of a 8.761-mile circuit = 262.830 miles. Warm, dry and overcast. World Championship round 3

1 Phil Hill   Ferrari 156   30   2h03m03.8
2 Wolfgang von Trips   Ferrari 156   30   2h03m04.5
3 Richie Ginther   Ferrari 156   30   2h03m23.3
4 Olivier Gendebien   Ferrari 156   30   2h03m49.4
5 John Surtees   Cooper T53-Climax   30   2h04m30.6
6 Dan Gurney   Porsche 718   30   2h04m34.8

Winner's average speed: 128.144 mph. Starting grid front row: P Hill, 3m59.3 (pole), von Trips, 4m00.1 and Gendebien, 4m03.0. Fastest lap: Ginther, 3m59.8. Leaders: P Hill, laps 1, 3-5, 8, 11-13, 15, 17-18, 21-23, 25-30; Gendebien, 2, 6-7; von Trips, 9-10, 14, 16, 19-20, 24

Grand Prix de l'Automobile Club de France

2 July 1961. Reims. 52 laps of a 5.187-mile circuit = 269.724 miles. Very hot, dry and sunny. World Championship round 4

1 Giancarlo Baghetti   Ferrari 156   52   2h14m17.5
2 Dan Gurney   Porsche 718   52   2h14m17.6
3 Jim Clark   Lotus 21-Climax   52   2h15m18.6
4 Innes Ireland   Lotus 21-Climax   52   2h15m27.6
5 Bruce McLaren   Cooper T55-Climax   52   2h15m59.3
6 Graham Hill   BRM P48/57-Climax   52   2h15m59.4

Winner's average speed: 120.510 mph. Starting grid front row: P Hill, 2m24.9 (pole), von Trips, 2m26.4 and Ginther, 2m26.8. Fastest lap: P Hill, 2m27.1. Leaders: P Hill, laps 1-12, 18-37; von Trips, 13-17; Ginther, 38-40; Baghetti, 41-43, 45, 47, 50, 52; Bonnier, 44; Gurney, 46, 48-49, 51

British Grand Prix

15 July 1961. Aintree. 75 laps of a 3.000-mile circuit = 225.000 miles. Cool, wet and overcast at the start, drying later. World Championship round 5

1 Wolfgang von Trips   Ferrari 156   75   2h40m53.6
2 Phil Hill   Ferrari 156   75   2h41m39.6
3 Richie Ginther   Ferrari 156   75   2h41m40.4
4 Jack Brabham   Cooper T55-Climax   75   2h42m02.2

1961 DRIVERS' RECORDS cont'd/

Driver	Car	Monaco GP	Dutch GP	Belgian GP	French GP	British GP	German GP	Italian GP	United States GP
Willy Mairesse	Lotus 18-Climax	-	-	R	-	-	-	-	-
	Lotus 21-Climax	-	-	-	R	-	-	-	-
	Ferrari Dino 156	-	-	-	-	-	R	-	-
Tony Marsh	Lotus 18-Climax	-	-	DNQ	-	R	15	-	-
Michel May	Lotus 18-Climax	R	-	-	11	-	DNQ	-	-
Bruce McLaren	Cooper T55-Climax	6	12	R	5	8	6	3	4
Stirling Moss	Lotus 18-Climax	1PF	4	-	-	-	-	-	-
	Lotus 18/21-Climax	-	-	8	R	R	1	-	R
	Ferguson P99-Climax	-	-	-	DSQ	-	-	-	-
	Lotus 21-Climax	-	-	-	-	-	-	R	-
Massimo Natili	Cooper T51-Maserati	-	-	-	-	R	-	-	-
Brian Naylor	JBW 1960-Climax	-	-	-	-	-	-	R	-
Tim Parnell	Lotus 18-Climax	-	-	-	-	R	-	10	-
Roger Penske	Cooper T53-Climax	-	-	-	-	-	-	-	8
André Pilette	Emeryson 1961-Climax	-	-	-	-	-	-	DNQ	-
Renato Pirocchi	Cooper T51-Maserati	-	-	-	-	-	-	12	-
Ricardo Rodriguez	Ferrari Dino 156	-	-	-	-	-	-	R	-
Lloyd Ruby	Lotus 18-Climax	-	-	-	-	-	-	-	R
Peter Ryan	Lotus 18/21-Climax	-	-	-	-	-	-	-	9
Roy Salvadori	Cooper T53-Climax	-	-	8	6	10	6	R	-
Giorgio Scarlatti	de Tomaso F1/001-OSCA	-	-	R	-	-	-	-	-
Wolfgang Seidel	Lotus 18-Climax	-	-	DNQ	-	17	R	R	-
Hap Sharp	Cooper T53-Climax	-	-	-	-	-	-	-	10
Gaetano Starrabba	Lotus 18-Maserati	-	-	-	-	-	-	R	-
John Surtees	Cooper T53-Climax	11	7	5	R	R	5	R	R
Henry Taylor	Lotus 18-Climax	DNQ	-	-	-	-	-	-	-
	Lotus 18/21-Climax	-	-	-	10	R	-	11	-
Trevor Taylor	Lotus 18-Climax	-	13	-	-	-	-	-	-
Maurice Trintignant	Cooper T51-Maserati	7	-	R	13	-	R	9	-
Wolfgang von Trips	Ferrari Dino 156	4	1	2	R	1	2	RP	-
Nino Vaccarella	de Tomaso F1/003-Alfa Romeo	-	-	-	-	-	-	R	-

SHARED DRIVES - British GP: Jack Fairman/Stirling Moss (Ferguson P99-Climax) DSQ. **United States GP:** Olivier Gendebien/Masten Gregory (Lotus 18/21-Climax) 11

5 Jo Bonnier	Porsche 718	75	2h42m09.8
6 Roy Salvadori	Cooper T53-Climax	75	2h42m19.8

Winner's average speed: 83.907 mph. Starting grid front row: P Hill, 1m58.8 (pole), Ginther, 1m58.8 and Bonnier, 1m58.8. Fastest lap: Brooks, 1m57.8. Leaders: P Hill, laps 1-6; von Trips, 7-75

Grosser Preis von Deutschland

6 August 1961. Nürburgring. 15 laps of a 14.167-mile circuit = 212.505 miles. Showers. World Championship round 6. Also known as the European Grand Prix

1 Stirling Moss	Lotus 18/21-Climax	15	2h18m12.4
2 Wolfgang von Trips	Ferrari 156	15	2h18m33.8
3 Phil Hill	Ferrari 156	15	2h18m34.9
4 Jim Clark	Lotus 21-Climax	15	2h19m29.5
5 John Surtees	Cooper T53-Climax	15	2h20m05.5
6 Bruce McLaren	Cooper T55-Climax	15	2h20m35.8

Winner's average speed: 92.255 mph. Starting grid front row: P Hill, 8m55.2 (pole), Brabham, 9m01.4, Moss, 9m01.7 and Bonnier, 9m04.8. Fastest lap: P Hill, 8m57.8. Leaders: Moss, laps 1-15

Gran Premio d'Italia

10 September 1961. Monza. 43 laps of a 6.214-mile circuit = 267.202 miles. Very hot, dry and sunny. World Championship round 7

1 Phil Hill	Ferrari 156	43	2h03m13.0
2 Dan Gurney	Porsche 718	43	2h03m44.2
3 Bruce McLaren	Cooper T55-Climax	43	2h05m41.4
4 Jackie Lewis	Cooper T53-Climax	43	2h05m53.4
5 Tony Brooks	BRM P48/57-Climax	43	2h05m53.5
6 Roy Salvadori	Cooper T53-Climax	42	

Winner's average speed: 130.107 mph. Starting grid front row: von Trips, 2m46.3 (pole) and R Rodriguez, 2m46.4. Fastest lap: Baghetti, 2m48.4. Leaders: P Hill, laps 1-3, 5, 7, 10, 14-43; Ginther, 4, 6, 8-9, 11-13

United States Grand Prix

8 October 1961. Watkins Glen. 100 laps of a 2.350-mile circuit = 235.000 miles. Warm, dry and sunny. World Championship round 8

1 Innes Ireland	Lotus 21-Climax	100	2h13m45.8
2 Dan Gurney	Porsche 718	100	2h13m50.1
3 Tony Brooks	BRM P48/57-Climax	100	2h14m33.6
4 Bruce McLaren	Cooper T55-Climax	100	2h14m43.8
5 Graham Hill	BRM P48/57-Climax	99	
6 Jo Bonnier	Porsche 718	98	

Winner's average speed: 105.410 mph. Starting grid front row: Brabham, 1m17.0 (pole) and G Hill, 1m18.1. Fastest lap: Brabham, 1m18.2. Leaders: Moss, laps 1-5, 16, 24-25, 34-35, 39-58; Brabham, 6-15, 17-23, 26-33, 36-38; Ireland, 59-100

1961 FINAL CHAMPIONSHIP POSITIONS

Drivers

1	Phil Hill	34 (38)*	10	Tony Brooks	6
2	Wolfgang von Trips	33	11=	Jack Brabham	4
3=	Dan Gurney	21		John Surtees	4
	Stirling Moss	21	13=	Jo Bonnier	3
5	Richie Ginther	16		Olivier Gendebien	3
6	Innes Ireland	12		Graham Hill	3
7=	Jim Clark	11		Jackie Lewis	3
	Bruce McLaren	11	17	Roy Salvadori	2
9	Giancarlo Baghetti	9		*Best five results count	

Manufacturers

1	Ferrari	40 (52)*
2	Lotus-Climax	32
3	Porsche	22 (23)*
4	Cooper-Climax	14 (18)*
5	BRM-Climax	7

*Best five results count. Points only awarded to first car to finish for each manufacturer

1962

Having dominated the first year of the 1.5-litre formula, Ferrari was rocked by the departure of team manager Romolo Tavoni and some of the engineering staff. The V8 BRM and Climax engines were now widely available and the Italian marque had let its advantage slip.

Before the championship started, Stirling Moss was seriously injured at Goodwood and announced his retirement from international motor racing. In his absence, Grand Prix racing was a two-way fight between a new generation of British drivers: Graham Hill, now with BRM, and Lotus's Jim Clark.

The season opened at Zandvoort, with the debut of the sensational new Lotus 25 in Clark's hands. The 25 featured revolutionary monocoque chassis construction, which was lighter and more rigid than the conventional space-frame. However, early teething troubles cost Clark vital points, clutch problems hampering his first two races.

Hill won in Holland, but lost out to Bruce McLaren in the final laps of the Monaco GP. It all came right for Clark at the Belgian GP, where he scored his first Grand Prix victory. Dan Gurney made up for his narrow defeat in the 1961 French GP by winning this year's event - the only win for Porsche as a car constructor.

Another Clark win at Aintree was followed by the best race of the year, the wet German GP. The first three cars, led by Hill, were separated by under five seconds at the finish, while Clark, who had stalled at the start, stormed through the field to finish fourth.

A win apiece for the two championship protagonists at Monza and Watkins Glen set up a tense finale for the new South African GP at East London. From their front row positions, Clark led Hill off the line. He opened up a convincing lead and appeared to have won both the race and the series, until failing oil pressure forced him to retire, giving Hill his first World title.

Grote Prijs van Nederland

20 May 1962. Zandvoort. 80 laps of a 2.605-mile circuit = 208.400 miles. Warm, dry and sunny. World Championship round 1. Also known as the European Grand Prix

1 Graham Hill	BRM P57	80	2h11m02.1
2 Trevor Taylor	Lotus 24-Climax	80	2h11m29.3
3 Phil Hill	Ferrari 156	80	2h12m23.2
4 Giancarlo Baghetti	Ferrari 156	79	
5 Tony Maggs	Cooper T55-Climax	78	
6 Carel de Beaufort	Porsche 718	76	

Winner's average speed: 95.425 mph. Starting grid front row: Surtees, 1m32.5 (pole), G Hill, 1m32.6 and Clark, 1m33.2. Fastest lap: McLaren, 1m34.4. Leaders: Clark, laps 1-11; G Hill, 12-54, 56-80; P Hill, 55

1962 DRIVERS' RECORDS

Driver	Car	Dutch GP	Monaco GP	Belgian GP	French GP	British GP	German GP	Italian GP	United States GP	South African GP
Gerry Ashmore	Lotus 18/21-Climax	-	-	-	-	-	-	DNQ	-	-
Giancarlo Baghetti	Ferrari 156	4	-	R	-	-	10	5	-	-
Lorenzo Bandini	Ferrari 156	-	3	-	-	-	R	8	-	-
Carel Godin de Beaufort	Porsche 718	6	DNQ	7	6	14	13	10	R	11
Lucien Bianchi	Lotus 18/21-Climax	-	-	9	-	-	-	-	-	-
	ENB 1962-Maserati	-	-	-	-	-	16	-	-	-
Jo Bonnier	Porsche 804	7	-	-	R	R	7	6	13	-
	Porsche 718	-	5	-	-	-	-	-	-	-
Jack Brabham	Lotus 24-Climax	R	8	6	R	5	-	-	-	-
	Brabham BT3-Climax	-	-	-	-	-	R	-	4	4
Ian Burgess	Cooper T59-Climax	-	-	-	-	12	11	DNQ	-	-
John Campbell-Jones	Lotus 18-Climax	-	-	11	-	-	-	-	-	-
Jay Chamberlain	Lotus 18-Climax	-	-	-	-	15	DNQ	DNQ	-	-
Jim Clark	Lotus 25-Climax	9	R^{PF}	1^{F}	R^{P}	1^{PF}	4	R^{P}	1^{PF}	R^{PF}
Bernard Collomb	Cooper T53-Climax	-	-	-	-	-	R	-	-	-
Nasif Estefano	de Tomaso F1/801	-	-	-	-	-	-	DNQ	-	-
Richie Ginther	BRM P48/57	R	R	-	-	-	-	-	-	-
	BRM P57	-	-	R	3	13	8	2	R	7
Keith Greene	Gilby 1962-BRM	-	-	-	-	-	R	DNQ	-	-
Masten Gregory	Lotus 18/21-Climax	R	-	-	-	-	-	-	-	-
	Lotus 24-BRM	-	DNQ	R	R	-	-	12	6	-
	Lotus 24-Climax	-	-	-	-	7	-	-	-	-
Dan Gurney	Porsche 804	R	R	-	1	9	3^{P}	13	5	-
	Lotus 24-BRM	-	-	DNS	-	-	-	-	-	-
Jim Hall	Lotus 21-Climax	-	-	-	-	-	-	DNS	-	-
Mike Harris	Cooper T53-Alfa Romeo	-	-	-	-	-	-	-	-	R
Graham Hill	BRM P57	1	6	2^{P}	9^{F}	4	1^{F}	1^{F}	2	1
Phil Hill	Ferrari 156	3	2	3	-	R	R	11	-	-
Innes Ireland	Lotus 24-Climax	R	R	R	R	16	-	R	8	5
Bruce Johnstone	BRM P48/57	-	-	-	-	-	-	-	-	9
Neville Lederle	Lotus 21-Climax	-	-	-	-	-	-	-	-	6
Jackie Lewis	Cooper T53-Climax	8	-	-	R	10	R	-	-	-
	BRM P48/57	-	DNQ	-	-	-	-	-	-	-
Roberto Lippi	de Tomaso F1/002-OSCA	-	-	-	-	-	-	DNQ	-	-
John Love	Cooper T55-Climax	-	-	-	-	-	-	-	-	8
Tony Maggs	Cooper T55-Climax	5	R	-	-	-	9	-	-	-
	Cooper T60-Climax	-	-	R	2	6	-	7	7	3
Willy Mairesse	Ferrari 156	-	7	R	-	-	-	4	-	-
Timmy Mayer	Cooper T53-Climax	-	-	-	-	-	-	-	R	-
Bruce McLaren	Cooper T60-Climax	R^{F}	1	R	4	3	5	3	3	2
Roger Penske	Lotus 24-Climax	-	-	-	-	-	-	-	9	-
Ernest Pieterse	Lotus 21-Climax	-	-	-	-	-	-	-	-	10
Ben Pon	Porsche 787	R	-	-	-	-	-	-	-	-
Ernesto Prinoth	Lotus 18-Climax	-	-	-	-	-	-	DNQ	-	-
Ricardo Rodriguez	Ferrari 156	R	DNP	4	-	-	6	14	-	-
Roy Salvadori	Lola Mk4-Climax	R	R	-	R	R	R	R	DNS	R
Heinz Schiller	Lotus 24-BRM	-	-	-	-	-	R	-	-	-
Rob Schroeder	Lotus 24-Climax	-	-	-	-	-	-	-	10	-
Wolfgang Seidel	Emeryson 1961-Climax	10	-	-	-	-	-	-	-	-
	Lotus 24-BRM	-	-	-	-	R	DNQ	-	-	-
Günther Seifert	Lotus 24-BRM	-	-	-	-	-	DNQ	-	-	-
Doug Serrurier	LDS Mk1-Alfa Romeo	-	-	-	-	-	-	-	-	R
Tony Settember	Emeryson 1961-Climax	-	-	-	-	11	-	R	-	-
Hap Sharp	Cooper T53-Climax	-	-	-	-	-	-	-	11	-
Tony Shelly	Lotus 18/21-Climax	-	-	-	-	R	DNQ	-	-	-
	Lotus 24-BRM	-	-	-	-	-	-	DNQ	-	-
Jo Siffert	Lotus 21-Climax	-	DNQ	10	-	-	12	-	-	-
	Lotus 24-BRM	-	-	-	R	-	-	DNQ	-	-
John Surtees	Lola Mk4-Climax	R^{P}	4	5	5	2	2	-	R	R
	Lola Mk4A-Climax	-	-	-	-	-	-	R	-	-
Trevor Taylor	Lotus 24-Climax	2	R	R	-	8	R	-	-	-
	Lotus 25-Climax	-	-	-	8	-	-	R	12	R
Maurice Trintignant	Lotus 24-Climax	-	R	8	7	-	R	R	-	-
Nino Vaccarella	Lotus 18/21-Climax	-	DNQ	-	-	-	-	-	-	-
	Porsche 718	-	-	-	-	-	-	15	-	-
	Lotus 24-Climax	-	-	-	-	-	-	9	-	-
Heini Walter	Porsche 718	-	-	-	-	-	14	-	-	-

Grand Prix de Monaco

3 June 1962. Monte Carlo. 100 laps of a 1.954-mile circuit = 195.400 miles. Dry and overcast. World Championship round 2

1 Bruce McLaren	Cooper T60-Climax	100	2h46m29.7
2 Phil Hill	Ferrari 156	100	2h46m31.0
3 Lorenzo Bandini	Ferrari 156	100	2h47m53.8
4 John Surtees	Lola Mk4-Climax	99	
5 Jo Bonnier	Porsche 718	93	
6 Graham Hill	BRM P57	92	engine

Winner's average speed: 70.417 mph. Starting grid front row: Clark, 1m35.4 (pole), G Hill, 1m35.8 and McLaren, 1m36.4. Fastest lap: Clark, 1m35.5. Leaders: McLaren, laps 1-6, 93-100; G Hill, 7-92

Grand Prix de Belgique

17 June 1962. Spa-Francorchamps. 32 laps of a 8.761-mile circuit = 280.352 miles. Warm, dry and sunny. World Championship round 3

1 Jim Clark	Lotus 25-Climax	32	2h07m32.3
2 Graham Hill	BRM P57	32	2h08m16.4
3 Phil Hill	Ferrari 156	32	2h09m38.8
4 Ricardo Rodriguez	Ferrari 156	32	2h09m38.9
5 John Surtees	Lola Mk4-Climax	31	
6 Jack Brabham	Lotus 24-Climax	30	

Winner's average speed: 131.891 mph. Starting grid front row: G Hill, 3m57.0 (pole), McLaren, 3m58.8 and T Taylor, 3m59.3. Fastest lap: Clark, 3m55.6. Leaders: G Hill, lap 1; T Taylor, laps 2-3, 5, 8; Mairesse, 4, 6-7; Clark, 9-32

Grand Prix de l'Automobile Club de France

8 July 1962. Rouen-les-Essarts. 54 laps of a 4.065-mile circuit = 219.510 miles. Warm, dry and sunny. World Championship round 4

1 Dan Gurney	Porsche 804	54	2h07m35.5
2 Tony Maggs	Cooper T60-Climax	53	
3 Richie Ginther	BRM P57	52	
4 Bruce McLaren	Cooper T60-Climax	51	
5 John Surtees	Lola Mk4-Climax	51	
6 Carel de Beaufort	Porsche 718	51	

Winner's average speed: 103.225 mph. Starting grid front row: Clark, 2m14.8 (pole), G Hill, 2m15.0 and McLaren, 2m15.4. Fastest lap: G Hill, 2m16.9. Leaders: G Hill, laps 1-29, 33-41; Clark, 30-32; Gurney, 42-54

British Grand Prix

21 July 1962. Aintree. 75 laps of a 3.000-mile circuit = 225.000 miles. Warm, dry and sunny. World Championship round 5

1 Jim Clark	Lotus 25-Climax	75	2h26m20.8
2 John Surtees	Lola Mk4-Climax	75	2h27m10.0
3 Bruce McLaren	Cooper T60-Climax	75	2h28m05.6
4 Graham Hill	BRM P57	75	2h28m17.6
5 Jack Brabham	Lotus 24-Climax	74	
6 Tony Maggs	Cooper T60-Climax	74	

Winner's average speed: 92.247 mph. Starting grid front row: Clark, 1m53.6 (pole), Surtees, 1m54.2 and Ireland, 1m54.4. Fastest lap: Clark, 1m55.0. Leaders: Clark, laps 1-75

Grosser Preis von Deutschland

5 August 1962. Nürburgring. 15 laps of a 14.167-mile circuit = 212.505 miles. Heavy rain. World Championship round 6

1 Graham Hill	BRM P57	15	2h38m45.3
2 John Surtees	Lola Mk4-Climax	15	2h38m47.8
3 Dan Gurney	Porsche 804	15	2h38m49.7
4 Jim Clark	Lotus 25-Climax	15	2h39m27.4
5 Bruce McLaren	Cooper T60-Climax	15	2h40m04.9
6 Ricardo Rodriguez	Ferrari 156	15	2h40m09.1

Winner's average speed: 80.314 mph. Starting grid front row: Gurney, 8m47.2 (pole), G Hill, 8m50.2, Clark, 8m51.2 and Surtees, 8m57.5. Fastest lap: G Hill, 10m12.2. Leaders: Gurney, laps 1-2; G Hill, 3-15

Gran Premio d'Italia

16 September 1962. Monza. 86 laps of a 3.573-mile circuit = 307.278 miles. Dry and overcast at the start, light rain later. World Championship round 7

1 Graham Hill	BRM P57	86	2h29m08.4
2 Richie Ginther	BRM P57	86	2h29m38.2
3 Bruce McLaren	Cooper T60-Climax	86	2h30m06.2
4 Willy Mairesse	Ferrari 156	86	2h30m06.6
5 Giancarlo Baghetti	Ferrari 156	86	2h30m39.7
6 Jo Bonnier	Porsche 804	85	

Winner's average speed: 123.620 mph. Starting grid front row: Clark, 1m40.35 (pole) and G Hill, 1m40.38. Fastest lap: G Hill, 1m42.3. Leaders: G Hill, laps 1-86

United States Grand Prix

7 October 1962. Watkins Glen. 100 laps of a 2.350-mile circuit = 235.000 miles. Dry and overcast. World Championship round 8

1 Jim Clark	Lotus 25-Climax	100	2h07m13.0
2 Graham Hill	BRM P57	100	2h07m22.2
3 Bruce McLaren	Cooper T60-Climax	99	
4 Jack Brabham	Brabham BT3-Climax	99	
5 Dan Gurney	Porsche 804	99	
6 Masten Gregory	Lotus 24-BRM	99	

Winner's average speed: 110.835 mph. Starting grid front row: Clark, 1m15.8 (pole) and Ginther, 1m16.6. Fastest lap: Clark, 1m15.0. Leaders: Clark, laps 1-11, 19-100; G Hill, 12-18

South African Grand Prix

29 December 1962. East London. 82 laps of a 2.436-mile circuit = 199.752 miles. Dry and windy. World Championship round 9

1 Graham Hill	BRM P57	82	2h08m03.3
2 Bruce McLaren	Cooper T60-Climax	82	2h08m53.1
3 Tony Maggs	Cooper T60-Climax	82	2h08m53.6
4 Jack Brabham	Brabham BT3-Climax	82	2h08m57.1
5 Innes Ireland	Lotus 24-Climax	81	
6 Neville Lederle	Lotus 21-Climax	78	

Winner's average speed: 93.594 mph. Starting grid front row: Clark, 1m29.3 (pole) and G Hill, 1m29.6. Fastest lap: Clark, 1m31.0. Leaders: Clark, laps 1-61; G Hill, 62-82

1962 FINAL CHAMPIONSHIP POSITIONS

Drivers

1	Graham Hill	42 (52)*
2	Jim Clark	30
3	Bruce McLaren	27 (32)*
4	John Surtees	19
5	Dan Gurney	15
6	Phil Hill	14
7	Tony Maggs	13
8	Richie Ginther	10
9	Jack Brabham	9
10	Trevor Taylor	6
11	Giancarlo Baghetti	5
12=	Lorenzo Bandini	4
	Ricardo Rodriguez	4
14=	Jo Bonnier	3
	Willy Mairesse	3
16=	Carel Godin de Beaufort	2
	Innes Ireland	2
18=	Masten Gregory	1
	Neville Lederle	1

*Best five results count

Manufacturers

1	BRM	42 (56)*
2	Lotus-Climax	36 (38)*
3	Cooper-Climax	29 (37)*
4	Lola-Climax	19
5=	Ferrari	18
	Porsche	18 (19)*
7	Brabham-Climax	6
8	Lotus-BRM	1

*Best five results count. Points only awarded to first car to finish for each manufacturer

1963

Having come so close to the title in 1962, Jim Clark in the Lotus 25 now dominated. He won seven races, and only lost the remaining three due to mechanical failures. Both Ferrari and BRM had built semi-monocoque cars to challenge the Lotus, but neither proved a match.

After failing to win a race in 1962, Ferrari signed John Surtees to lead their challenge, while BRM retained Graham Hill. Former Ferrari drivers Phil Hill and Giancarlo Baghetti moved to the new but chaotic ATS team.

At the opening round Clark retired (although he was still classified as a finisher), leaving Graham Hill to record the first of his five wins around the streets of Monaco.

Having won the next four races, engine problems slowed Clark at the Nürburgring, Surtees giving Ferrari its first win in two years.

The Italian GP followed and once again the organizers wanted to use Monza's combined road and banked course, but after initial practice, the banking was abandoned. Clark duly triumphed, clinching his first championship.

Graham Hill won the United States GP after Clark was left on the grid with electrical problems; the Scotsman then charged through the field to finish third.

The final race of the year in South Africa gave the irrepressible Clark his seventh victory in ten rounds, a record for wins in a single season that lasted until the championship was expanded to 16 races.

It also meant that British drivers had won every race - Scotland seven, England three. But for retirements in the final 1962 and 1964 races Clark would have matched Fangio's record of four consequetive World Championships between 1962-65.

Grand Prix de Monaco

26 May 1963. Monte Carlo. 100 laps of a 1.954-mile circuit = 195.400 miles. Warm, dry and sunny. World Championship round 1. Also known as the European Grand Prix

1 Graham Hill	BRM P57	100	2h41m49.7
2 Richie Ginther	BRM P57	100	2h41m54.3
3 Bruce McLaren	Cooper T66-Climax	100	2h42m02.5
4 John Surtees	Ferrari 156	100	2h42m03.8
5 Tony Maggs	Cooper T66-Climax	98	
6 Trevor Taylor	Lotus 25-Climax	98	

Winner's average speed: 72.447 mph. Starting grid front row: Clark, 1m34.3 (pole) and G Hill, 1m35.0. Fastest lap: Surtees, 1m34.5. Leaders: G Hill, laps 1-17, 79-100; Clark, 18-78

Grand Prix de Belgique

9 June 1963. Spa-Francorchamps. 32 laps of a 8.761-mile circuit = 280.352 miles. Wet and overcast. World Championship round 2

| 1 Jim Clark | Lotus 25-Climax | 32 | 2h27m47.6 |
| 2 Bruce McLaren | Cooper T66-Climax | 32 | 2h32m41.6 |

3 Dan Gurney	Brabham BT7-Climax	31	
4 Richie Ginther	BRM P57	31	
5 Jo Bonnier	Cooper T60-Climax	30	
6 Carel de Beaufort	Porsche 718	30	

Winner's average speed: 113.815 mph. Starting grid front row: G Hill, 3m54.1 (pole), Gurney, 3m55.0 and Mairesse, 3m55.3. Fastest lap: Clark, 3m58.1. Leaders: Clark, laps 1-32

Grote Prijs van Nederland

23 June 1963. Zandvoort. 80 laps of a 2.605-mile circuit = 208.400 miles. Warm, dry and sunny. World Championship round 3

1 Jim Clark	Lotus 25-Climax	80	2h08m13.07
2 Dan Gurney	Brabham BT7-Climax	79	
3 John Surtees	Ferrari 156	79	
4 Innes Ireland	BRP 1-BRM	79	
5 Richie Ginther	BRM P57	79	
6 Ludovico Scarfiotti	Ferrari 156	78	

Winner's average speed: 97.522 mph. Starting grid front row: Clark, 1m31.6 (pole), G Hill, 1m32.2 and McLaren, 1m32.3. Fastest lap: Clark, 1m33.7. Leaders: Clark, laps 1-80

Grand Prix de l'Automobile Club de France

30 June 1963. Reims. 53 laps of a 5.187-mile circuit = 274.911 miles. Occasional rain. World Championship round 4

1 Jim Clark	Lotus 25-Climax	53	2h10m54.3
2 Tony Maggs	Cooper T66-Climax	53	2h11m59.2
3 Graham Hill*	BRM P61	53	2h13m08.2
4 Jack Brabham	Brabham BT7-Climax	53	2h13m09.5
5 Dan Gurney	Brabham BT7-Climax	53	2h13m27.7
6 Jo Siffert	Lotus 24-BRM	52	

*Hill penalized one minute for being pushed at start, no points awarded. Winner's average speed: 126.005 mph. Starting grid front row: Clark, 2m20.2 (pole), G Hill, 2m20.9 and Gurney, 2m21.7. Fastest lap: Clark, 2m21.6. Leaders: Clark, laps 1-53

British Grand Prix

20 July 1963. Silverstone. 82 laps of a 2.927-mile circuit = 240.014 miles. Warm, dry and sunny. World Championship round 5

1 Jim Clark	Lotus 25-Climax	82	2h14m09.6
2 John Surtees	Ferrari 156	82	2h14m35.4
3 Graham Hill	BRM P57	82	2h14m47.2
4 Richie Ginther	BRM P57	81	
5 Lorenzo Bandini	BRM P57	81	
6 Jim Hall	Lotus 24-BRM	80	

Winner's average speed: 107.341 mph. Starting grid front row: Clark, 1m34.4 (pole), Gurney, 1m34.6, G Hill, 1m34.8 and Brabham, 1m35.0. Fastest lap: Surtees, 1m36.0. Leaders: Brabham, laps 1-3; Clark, 4-82

Grosser Preis von Deutschland

4 August 1963. Nürburgring. 15 laps of a 14.167-mile circuit = 212.505 miles. Warm, dry and sunny. World Championship round 6

1 John Surtees	Ferrari 156	15	2h13m06.8
2 Jim Clark	Lotus 25-Climax	15	2h14m24.3
3 Richie Ginther	BRM P57	15	2h15m51.7
4 Gerhard Mitter	Porsche 718	15	2h21m18.3
5 Jim Hall	Lotus 24-BRM	14	
6 Jo Bonnier	Cooper T66-Climax	14	

Winner's average speed: 95.785 mph. Starting grid front row: Clark, 8m45.8 (pole), Surtees, 8m46.7, Bandini, 8m54.3 and G Hill, 8m57.2. Fastest lap: Surtees, 8m47.0. Leaders: Ginther, lap 1; Surtees, laps 2-3, 5-15; Clark, 4

World Championship Grand Prix Racing

1963 DRIVERS' RECORDS

Driver	Car	Monaco GP	Belgian GP	Dutch GP	French GP	British GP	German GP	Italian GP	United States GP	Mexican GP	South African GP
Chris Amon	Lola Mk4A-Climax	DNS	R	R	7	7	R	DNS	-	-	-
	Lotus 24-BRM	-	-	-	-	-	-	-	-	R	-
Bob Anderson	Lola Mk4-Climax	-	-	-	-	12	-	12	-	-	-
Peter Arundell	Lotus 25-Climax	-	-	-	DNS	-	-	-	-	-	-
Giancarlo Baghetti	ATS 100	-	R	R	-	-	-	15	R	R	-
Lorenzo Bandini	BRM P57	-	-	-	10	5	R	-	-	-	-
	Ferrari 156	-	-	-	-	-	-	R	5	R	5
Carel Godin de Beaufort	Porsche 718	-	6	9	-	10	R	DNQ	6	10	10
Lucien Bianchi	Lola Mk4-Climax	-	R	-	-	-	-	-	-	-	-
Trevor Blokdyk	Cooper T51-Maserati	-	-	-	-	-	-	-	-	-	12
Jo Bonnier	Cooper T60-Climax	7	5	11	NC	-	-	-	-	-	-
	Cooper T66-Climax	-	-	-	-	R	6	7	8	5	6
Jack Brabham	Lotus 25-Climax	9	-	-	-	-	-	-	-	-	-
	Brabham BT3-Climax	-	R	-	-	-	-	5	-	-	-
	Brabham BT7-Climax	-	-	R	4	R	7	-	4	2	13
Tino Brambilla	Cooper T53-Maserati	-	-	-	-	-	-	DNQ	-	-	-
Peter Broeker	Stebro 4-Ford	-	-	-	-	-	-	-	7	-	-
Ian Burgess	Scirocco 02-BRM	-	-	-	-	R	R	-	-	-	-
Mario Araujo de Cabral	Cooper T60-Climax	-	-	-	-	-	R	DNQ	-	-	-
John Campbell-Jones	Lola Mk4-Climax	-	-	-	-	13	-	-	-	-	-
Jim Clark	Lotus 25-Climax	8^P	1^F	1^{PF}	1^{PF}	1^P	2^P	1^F	3^F	1^{PF}	1^P
Bernard Collomb	Lotus 24-Climax	DNQ	-	-	-	-	10	-	-	-	-
Frank Dochnal	Cooper T53-Climax	-	-	-	-	-	-	-	-	DNS	-
Paddy Driver	Lotus 24-BRM	-	-	-	-	-	-	-	-	-	DNS
Nasif Estefano	de Tomaso F1/801	-	-	-	DNP	-	-	-	-	-	-
Richie Ginther	BRM P57	2	4	5	R	4	3	2	2	3	R
Masten Gregory	Lotus 24-BRM	-	-	-	R	11	-	R	-	-	-
	Lola Mk4A-Climax	-	-	-	-	-	-	-	R	R	-
Dan Gurney	Brabham BT7-Climax	R	3	2	5	R	R	14	R	6	2^F
Mike Hailwood	Lotus 24-Climax	-	-	-	-	8	-	-	-	-	-
	Lola Mk4-Climax	-	-	-	-	-	-	10	-	-	-
Jim Hall	Lotus 24-BRM	R	R	8	11	6	5	8	10	8	-
Graham Hill	BRM P57	1	R^P	R	-	3	R	-	1^P	4	3
	BRM P61	-	-	-	3	-	-	16	-	-	-
Phil Hill	ATS 100	-	R	R	-	-	-	11	R	R	-
	Lotus 24-BRM	-	-	-	NC	-	-	-	-	-	-
Innes Ireland	Lotus 24-BRM	R	-	-	-	-	R	-	-	-	-
	BRP 1-BRM	-	R	4	9	R	-	4	-	-	-
Piet de Klerk	Alfa Special	-	-	-	-	-	-	-	-	-	R
Kurt Kuhnke	Lotus 18-Borgward	-	-	-	-	-	DNQ	-	-	-	-
Roberto Lippi	de Tomaso F1/002-Ferrari	-	-	-	-	-	-	DNQ	-	-	-
John Love	Cooper T55-Climax	-	-	-	-	-	-	-	-	-	9
Tony Maggs	Cooper T66-Climax	5	7	R	2	9	R	6	R	R	7
Willy Mairesse	Ferrari 156	R	R	-	-	-	R	-	-	-	-
Bruce McLaren	Cooper T66-Climax	3	2	R	12	R	R	3	11	R	4
Gerhard Mitter	Porsche 718	-	-	R	-	-	4	-	-	-	-
Brausch Niemann	Lotus 22-Ford	-	-	-	-	-	-	-	-	-	14
Tim Parnell	Lotus 18/21-Climax	-	-	-	-	-	DNQ	-	-	-	-
Ernest Pieterse	Lotus 21-Climax	-	-	-	-	-	-	-	-	-	R
André Pilette	Lotus 18/21-Climax	-	-	-	-	-	DNQ	DNQ	-	-	-
David Prophet	Brabham BT6-Ford	-	-	-	-	-	-	-	-	-	R
Ian Raby	Gilby 1962-BRM	-	-	-	-	R	DNQ	DNQ	-	-	-
Pedro Rodriguez	Lotus 25-Climax	-	-	-	-	-	-	-	R	R	-
Ludovico Scarfiotti	Ferrari 156	-	-	6	DNS	-	-	-	-	-	-
Doug Serrurier	LDS Mk1-Alfa Romeo	-	-	-	-	-	-	-	-	-	11
Tony Settember	Scirocco 01-BRM	-	8	-	R	R	R	DNQ	-	-	-
Hap Sharp	Lotus 24-BRM	-	-	-	-	-	-	-	R	7	-
Jo Siffert	Lotus 24-BRM	R	R	7	6	R	9	R	R	9	-
Moises Solana	BRM P57	-	-	-	-	-	-	-	-	11	-
Mike Spence	Lotus 25-Climax	-	-	-	-	-	-	13	-	-	-
John Surtees	Ferrari6 156	4^F	R	3	R	2^F	1^F	R^P	9	R	R
Trevor Taylor	Lotus 25-Climax	6	R	10	13	R	8	-	R	R	8
Sam Tingle	LDS Mk1-Alfa Romeo	-	-	-	-	-	-	-	-	-	R
Maurice Trintignant	Lola Mk4A-Climax	R	-	-	-	-	-	-	-	-	-
	Lotus 24-Climax	-	-	-	8	-	-	-	-	-	-
	BRM P57	-	-	-	-	-	-	9	-	-	-
Rodger Ward	Lotus 24-BRM	-	-	-	-	-	-	-	R	-	-

Gran Premio d'Italia

8 September 1963. Monza. 86 laps of a 3.573-mile circuit = 307.278 miles. Warm, dry and sunny. World Championship round 7

1 Jim Clark	Lotus 25-Climax	86	2h24m19.6
2 Richie Ginther	BRM P57	86	2h25m54.6
3 Bruce McLaren	Cooper T66-Climax	85	
4 Innes Ireland	BRP 1-BRM	84	engine
5 Jack Brabham	Brabham BT3-Climax	84	
6 Tony Maggs	Cooper T66-Climax	84	

Winner's average speed: 127.743 mph. Starting grid front row: Surtees, 1m37.3 (pole) and G Hill, 1m38.5. Fastest lap: Clark, 1m38.9. Leaders: G Hill, laps 1-3, 24-26, 29-30, 32, 34-35, 37, 39-41; Surtees, 4-16; Clark, 17-23, 28, 36, 42-45, 48-51, 53-54, 56-86; Gurney, 27, 31, 33, 38, 46-47, 52, 55

United States Grand Prix

6 October 1963. Watkins Glen. 110 laps of a 2.350-mile circuit = 258.500 miles. Hot, dry and sunny. World Championship round 8

1 Graham Hill	BRM P57	110	2h19m22.1
2 Richie Ginther	BRM P57	110	2h19m56.4
3 Jim Clark	Lotus 25-Climax	109	
4 Jack Brabham	Brabham BT7-Climax	108	
5 Lorenzo Bandini	Ferrari 156	106	
6 Carel de Beaufort	Porsche 718	99	

Winner's average speed: 111.288 mph. Starting grid front row: G Hill, 1m13.4 (pole) and Clark, 1m13.5. Fastest lap: Clark, 1m14.5. Leaders: G Hill, laps 1-6, 32, 35, 83-110; Surtees, 7-31, 33-34, 36-82

Gran Premio de Mexico

27 October 1963. Mexico City. 65 laps of a 3.107-mile circuit = 201.955 miles. Dry and overcast. World Championship round 9

1 Jim Clark	Lotus 25-Climax	65	2h09m52.1
2 Jack Brabham	Brabham BT7-Climax	65	2h11m33.2
3 Richie Ginther	BRM P57	65	2h11m46.8
4 Graham Hill	BRM P57	64	
5 Jo Bonnier	Cooper T66-Climax	62	
6 Dan Gurney	Brabham BT7-Climax	62	

Winner's average speed: 93.305 mph. Starting grid front row: Clark, 1m58.8 (pole) and Surtees, 2m00.5. Fastest lap: Clark, 1m58.1. Leaders: Clark, laps 1-65

South African Grand Prix

28 December 1963. East London. 85 laps of a 2.436-mile circuit = 207.060 miles. Hot, dry and windy. World Championship round 10

1 Jim Clark	Lotus 25-Climax	85	2h10m36.9
2 Dan Gurney	Brabham BT7-Climax	85	2h11m43.7
3 Graham Hill	BRM P57	84	
4 Bruce McLaren	Cooper T66-Climax	84	
5 Lorenzo Bandini	Ferrari 156	84	
6 Jo Bonnier	Cooper T66-Climax	83	

Winner's average speed: 95.116 mph. Starting grid front row: Clark, 1m28.9 (pole), Brabham, 1m29.0 and Gurney, 1m29.1. Fastest lap: Gurney, 1m29.1. Leaders: Clark, laps 1-85

1963 FINAL CHAMPIONSHIP POSITIONS

Drivers						Manufacturers		
1	Jim Clark	54 (73)*		12=	Jim Hall	3	1 Lotus-Climax	54 (74)*
2=	Richie Ginther	29 (34)*			Gerhard Mitter	3	2 BRM	36 (45)*
	Graham Hill	29		14	Carel Godin de Beaufort	2	3 Brabham-Climax	28 (30)*
4	John Surtees	22		15=	Ludovico Scarfiotti	1	4 Ferrari	26
5	Dan Gurney	19			Jo Siffert	1	5 Cooper-Climax	25 (26)*
6	Bruce McLaren	17			Trevor Taylor	1	6 BRP-BRM	6
7	Jack Brabham	14				*Best six results count	7 Porsche	5
8	Tony Maggs	9					8 Lotus-BRM	4
9=	Lorenzo Bandini	6					*Best six results count. Points	
	Jo Bonnier	6					only awarded to first car to	
	Innes Ireland	6					finish for each manufacturer	

1964

In 1964 John Surtees became the only man to win world titles both on bikes and in cars. The feat came after an epic three-way title decider in Mexico City reminiscent of a far-fetched Hollywood script.

Having led that race comfortably from the start, and in a position to be champion, Jim Clark's

John Surtees pictured during the 1964 Dutch Grand Prix at Zandvoort where he finished second to Jim Clark

engine failed on the very last lap. Graham Hill, leader of the championship after the penultimate round, had earlier been delayed in a collision with Lorenzo Bandini's Ferrari, but now Clark's demise briefly put him in line for the title. However, Bandini then slowed, giving his team-mate Surtees second position in the race and the points he required to become World Champion.

Clark had led the series after three early wins. But in the second half of the season Ferrari came to the fore, Surtees winning twice and Bandini scoring his only Grand Prix victory in a race of attrition on the bumpy Zeltweg circuit in Austria.

Seemingly set for a successful defence of his title after five rounds, Clark's season was blighted by poor reliability, a failing which would cost him the championship on that final lap in Mexico.

1964 DRIVERS' RECORDS

Driver	Car	Monaco GP	Dutch GP	Belgian GP	French GP	British GP	German GP	Austrian GP	Italian GP	United States GP	Mexican GP
Chris Amon	Lotus 25-BRM	DNQ	5	R	10	R	11	-	-	R	R
	Lotus 25-Climax	-	-	-	-	-	-	R	-	-	-
Bob Anderson	Brabham BT11-Climax	7	6	DNS	12	7	R	3	11	-	-
Peter Arundell	Lotus 25-Climax	3	3	9	4	-	-	-	-	-	-
Richard Attwood	BRM P67	-	-	-	-	DNS	-	-	-	-	-
Giancarlo Baghetti	BRM P57	-	10	8	-	12	R	7	8	-	-
Lorenzo Bandini	Ferrari 156	10	-	-	-	5	3	1	-	-	-
	Ferrari 158	-	R	R	9	-	-	-	3	-	-
	Ferrari 1512	-	-	-	-	-	-	-	-	R	3
Edgar Barth	Cooper T66-Climax	-	-	-	-	-	R	-	-	-	-
Carel Godin de Beaufort	Porsche 718	-	R	-	-	-	DNS	-	-	-	-
Jo Bonnier	Cooper T66-Climax	5	-	-	-	-	-	-	-	-	-
	Brabham BT11-BRM	-	9	R	-	R	R	-	-	-	-
	Brabham BT7-Climax	-	-	-	-	-	-	6	12	R	R
Jack Brabham	Brabham BT7-Climax	R	R	3	3F	4	12	-	-	-	-
	Brabham BT11-Climax	-	-	-	-	-	-	9	14	R	R
Ronnie Bucknum	Honda RA271	-	-	-	-	-	13	-	R	R	-
Mario Araujo de Cabral	ATS 100	-	-	-	-	-	-	-	R	-	-
Jim Clark	Lotus 25-Climax	4P	1F	1	RP	1PF	-	-	R	RPF	-
	Lotus 33-Climax	-	-	-	-	-	R	R	-	7	5PF
Bernard Collomb	Lotus 24-Climax	DNQ	-	-	-	-	-	-	-	-	-
Frank Gardner	Brabham BT10-Ford	-	-	-	-	R	-	-	-	-	-
Richie Ginther	BRM P261	2	11	4	5	8	7	2	4	4	8
Dan Gurney	Brabham BT7-Climax	R	RP	6PF	1	13	10	RF	10	R	1
Mike Hailwood	Lotus 25-BRM	6	12	-	8	R	R	8	R	8	R
Walt Hansgen	Lotus 33-Climax	-	-	-	-	-	-	-	-	5	-
Graham Hill	BRM P261	1F	4	5	2	2	2	RP	R	1	11
Phil Hill	Cooper T73-Climax	9	8	R	7	6	R	-	-	R	9
	Cooper T66-Climax	-	-	-	-	-	-	R	-	-	-

/Cont'd

Grand Prix de Monaco

10 May 1964. Monte Carlo. 100 laps of a 1.954-mile circuit = 195.400 miles. Hot, dry and sunny. World Championship round 1

1 Graham Hill	BRM P261	100	2h41m19.5
2 Richie Ginther	BRM P261	99	
3 Peter Arundell	Lotus 25-Climax	97	
4 Jim Clark	Lotus 25-Climax	96	engine
5 Jo Bonnier	Cooper T66-Climax	96	
6 Mike Hailwood	Lotus 25-BRM	96	

Winner's average speed: 72.673 mph. Starting grid front row: Clark, 1m34.0 (pole) and Brabham, 1m34.1. Fastest lap: G Hill, 1m33.9. Leaders: Clark, laps 1-36; Gurney, 37-52; G Hill, 53-100

Grote Prijs van Nederland

24 May 1964. Zandvoort. 80 laps of a 2.605-mile circuit = 208.400 miles. Hot, dry and sunny. World Championship round 2

1 Jim Clark	Lotus 25-Climax	80	2h07m35.4
2 John Surtees	Ferrari 158	80	2h08m29.0
3 Peter Arundell	Lotus 25-Climax	79	
4 Graham Hill	BRM P261	79	
5 Chris Amon	Lotus 25-BRM	79	
6 Bob Anderson	Brabham BT11-Climax	78	

Winner's average speed: 98.001 mph. Starting grid front row: Gurney, 1m31.2 (pole), Clark, 1m31.3 and G Hill, 1m31.4. Fastest lap: Clark, 1m32.8. Leaders: Clark, laps 1-80

Grand Prix de Belgique

14 June 1964. Spa-Francorchamps. 32 laps of a 8.761-mile circuit = 280.352 miles. Dry and overcast. World Championship round 3

1 Jim Clark	Lotus 25-Climax	32	2h06m40.5
2 Bruce McLaren	Cooper T73-Climax	32	2h06m43.9
3 Jack Brabham	Brabham BT7-Climax	32	2h07m28.6
4 Richie Ginther	BRM P261	32	2h08m39.1
5 Graham Hill	BRM P261	31	fuel pump
6 Dan Gurney	Brabham BT7-Climax	31	out of fuel

Winner's average speed: 132.790 mph. Starting grid front row: Gurney, 3m50.9 (pole), G Hill, 3m52.7 and Brabham, 3m52.8. Fastest lap: Gurney, 3m49.2. Leaders: Gurney, laps 1-2, 4-29; Surtees, 3; G Hill, 30-31; Clark, 32

Grand Prix de l'Automobile Club de France

28 June 1964. Rouen-les-Essarts. 57 laps of a 4.065-mile circuit = 231.705 miles. Dry and overcast. World Championship round 4

1 Dan Gurney	Brabham BT7-Climax	57	2h07m49.1
2 Graham Hill	BRM P261	57	2h08m13.2
3 Jack Brabham	Brabham BT7-Climax	57	2h08m14.0
4 Peter Arundell	Lotus 25-Climax	57	2h08m59.7
5 Richie Ginther	BRM P261	57	2h10m01.2
6 Bruce McLaren	Cooper T73-Climax	56	

Winner's average speed: 108.766 mph. Starting grid front row: Clark, 2m09.6 (pole), Gurney, 2m10.1 and Surtees, 2m11.1. Fastest lap: Brabham, 2m11.4. Leaders: Clark, laps 1-30; Gurney, 31-57

British Grand Prix

11 July 1964. Brands Hatch. 80 laps of a 2.650-mile circuit = 212.000 miles. Dry and overcast. World Championship round 5. Also known as the European Grand Prix

1 Jim Clark	Lotus 25-Climax	80	2h15m07.0
2 Graham Hill	BRM P261	80	2h15m09.8
3 John Surtees	Ferrari 158	80	2h16m27.6
4 Jack Brabham	Brabham BT7-Climax	79	

1964 DRIVERS' RECORDS cont'd/

Driver	Car	Monaco GP	Dutch GP	Belgian GP	French GP	British GP	German GP	Austrian GP	Italian GP	United States GP	Mexican GP
Innes Ireland	Lotus 24-BRM	DNS	-	-	-	-	-	-	-	-	-
	BRP 1-BRM	-	-	10	R	-	-	-	-	-	-
	BRP 2-BRM	-	-	-	-	10	-	5	5	R	12
John Love	Cooper T73-Climax	-	-	-	-	-	-	-	DNQ	-	-
Tony Maggs	BRM P57	-	DNS	DNS	-	R	6	4	-	-	-
Bruce McLaren	Cooper T66-Climax	R	-	-	-	-	-	-	-	-	-
	Cooper T73-Climax	-	7	2	6	R	R	R	2	R	7
Gerhard Mitter	Lotus 25-Climax	-	-	-	-	-	9	-	-	-	-
André Pilette	Scirocco 02-Climax	-	-	R	-	-	DNQ	-	-	-	-
Ian Raby	Brabham BT3-BRM	-	-	-	-	R	-	-	DNQ	-	-
Peter Revson	Lotus 24-BRM	DNQ	-	DSQ	-	R	14	-	13	-	-
	Lotus 25-BRM	-	-	-	DNS	-	-	-	-	-	-
Jochen Rindt	Brabham BT11-BRM	-	-	-	-	-	-	R	-	-	-
Pedro Rodriguez	Ferrari 156	-	-	-	-	-	-	-	-	-	6
Jean-Claude Rudaz	Cooper T60-Climax	-	-	-	-	-	-	-	DNS	-	-
"Geki" Russo	Brabham BT11-BRM	-	-	-	-	-	-	-	DNQ	-	-
Ludovico Scarfiotti	Ferrari 156	-	-	-	-	-	-	-	9	-	-
Hap Sharp	Brabham BT11-BRM	-	-	-	-	-	-	-	-	NC	13
Jo Siffert	Lotus 24-BRM	8	-	-	-	-	-	-	-	-	-
	Brabham BT11-BRM	-	13	R	R	11	4	R	7	3	R
Moises Solana	Lotus 33-Climax	-	-	-	-	-	-	-	-	-	10
Mike Spence	Lotus 25-Climax	-	-	-	-	-	9	-	-	R	4
	Lotus 33-Climax	-	-	-	-	-	8	R	6	7	-
John Surtees	Ferrari 158	R	2	R	R	3	1[PF]	R	1[PF]	2	2
John Taylor	Cooper T71/73-Ford	-	-	-	-	14	-	-	-	-	-
Trevor Taylor	BRP 1-BRM	R	-	-	-	-	R	-	DNQ	-	-
	BRP 2-BRM	-	-	7	R	-	-	-	-	6	R
	Lotus 24-BRM	-	-	-	-	R	-	-	-	-	-
Maurice Trintignant	BRM P57	R	-	11	DNQ	5	-	R	-	-	-

SHARED DRIVES - United States GP: Mike Spence/Jim Clark (Lotus 33-Climax) 7; Jim Clark/Mike Spence (Lotus 25-Climax) R

| 5 Lorenzo Bandini | Ferrari 156 | 78 |
| 6 Phil Hill | Cooper T73-Climax | 78 |

Winner's average speed: 94.141 mph. Starting grid front row: Clark, 1m38.1 (pole), G Hill, 1m38.3 and Gurney, 1m38.4. Fastest lap: Clark, 1m38.8. Leaders: Clark, laps 1-80.

Grosser Preis von Deutschland

2 August 1964. Nürburgring. 15 laps of a 14.167-mile circuit = 212.505 miles. Dry and overcast. World Championship round 6

1 John Surtees	Ferrari 158	15	2h12m04.8
2 Graham Hill	BRM P261	15	2h13m20.4
3 Lorenzo Bandini	Ferrari 156	15	2h16m57.6
4 Jo Siffert	Brabham BT11-BRM	15	2h17m27.9
5 Maurice Trintignant	BRM P57	14	battery
6 Tony Maggs	BRM P57	14	

Winner's average speed: 96.535 mph. Starting grid front row: Surtees, 8m38.4 (pole), Clark, 8m38.8, Gurney, 8m39.3 and Bandini, 8m42.6. Fastest lap: Surtees, 8m39.0. Leaders: Clark, lap 1; Surtees, laps 2-3, 5-15; Gurney, 4

Grosser Preis von Österreich

23 August 1964. Zeltweg. 105 laps of a 1.988-mile circuit = 208.740 miles. Dry and overcast. World Championship round 7

1 Lorenzo Bandini	Ferrari 156	105	2h06m18.23
2 Richie Ginther	BRM P261	105	2h06m24.41
3 Bob Anderson	Brabham BT11-Climax	102	
4 Tony Maggs	BRM P57	102	
5 Innes Ireland	BRP 2-BRM	102	
6 Jo Bonnier	Brabham BT7-Climax	101	

Winner's average speed: 99.161 mph. Starting grid front row: G Hill, 1m09.84 (pole), Surtees, 1m10.12, Clark, 1m10.21 and Gurney, 1m10.40. Fastest lap: Gurney, 1m10.56. Leaders: Gurney, laps 1, 8-46; Surtees, 2-7; Bandini, 47-105.

Gran Premio d'Italia

6 September 1964. Monza. 78 laps of a 3.573-mile circuit = 278.694 miles. Dry and overcast. World Championship round 8

1 John Surtees	Ferrari 158	78	2h10m51.8
2 Bruce McLaren	Cooper T73-Climax	78	2h11m57.8
3 Lorenzo Bandini	Ferrari 158	77	
4 Richie Ginther	BRM P261	77	
5 Innes Ireland	BRP 2-BRM	77	
6 Mike Spence	Lotus 33-Climax	77	

Winner's average speed: 127.779 mph. Starting grid front row: Surtees, 1m37.4 (pole), Gurney, 1m38.2 and G Hill, 1m38.7. Fastest lap: Surtees, 1m38.8. Leaders: Gurney, laps 1, 6-7, 10, 12-14, 16, 22, 25-26, 29, 32, 37-38, 45, 47-48, 50-52, 55; Surtees, 2-5, 8-9, 11, 15, 17-21, 23-24, 27-28, 30-31, 33-36, 39-44, 46, 49, 53-54, 56-78

United States Grand Prix

4 October 1964. Watkins Glen. 110 laps of a 2.350-mile circuit = 258.500 miles. Warm, dry and sunny. World Championship round 9

1 Graham Hill	BRM P261	110	2h16m38.0
2 John Surtees	Ferrari 158	110	2h17m08.5
3 Jo Siffert	Brabham BT11-BRM	109	
4 Richie Ginther	BRM P261	107	
5 Walt Hansgen	Lotus 33-Climax	107	
6 Trevor Taylor	BRP 2-BRM	106	

Winner's average speed: 113.515 mph. Starting grid front row: Clark, 1m12.65 (pole) and Surtees, 1m12.78. Fastest lap: Clark, 1m12.7. Leaders: Surtees, laps 1-12, 44; Clark, 13-43; G Hill, 45-110

25 October 1964. Mexico City. 65 laps of a 3.107-mile circuit = 201.955 miles. Warm, dry and sunny. World Championship round 10

1 Dan Gurney	Brabham BT7-Climax	65	2h09m50.32
2 John Surtees	Ferrari 158	65	2h10m59.26
3 Lorenzo Bandini	Ferrari 1512	65	2h10m59.95
4 Mike Spence	Lotus 25-Climax	65	2h11m12.18
5 Jim Clark	Lotus 33-Climax	64	engine
6 Pedro Rodriguez	Ferrari 156	64	

Winner's average speed: 93.326 mph. Starting grid front row: Clark, 1m57.24 (pole) and Gurney, 1m58.10. Fastest lap: Clark, 1m58.37. Leaders: Clark, laps 1-63; Gurney, 64-65

1964 FINAL CHAMPIONSHIP POSITIONS

Drivers						Manufacturers		
1	John Surtees	40	12=	Innes Ireland	4	1	Ferrari	45 (49)*
2	Graham Hill	39 (41)*		Tony Maggs	4	2	BRM	42 (51)*
3	Jim Clark	32		Mike Spence	4	3	Lotus-Climax	37 (40)*
4=	Lorenzo Bandini	23	15	Jo Bonnier	3	4	Brabham-Climax	30
	Richie Ginther	23	16=	Chris Amon	2	5	Cooper-Climax	16
6	Dan Gurney	19		Walt Hansgen	2	6	Brabham-BRM	7
7	Bruce McLaren	13		Maurice Trintignant	2	7	BRP-BRM	5
8=	Peter Arundell	11	19=	Mike Hailwood	1	8	Lotus-BRM	3
	Jack Brabham	11		Phil Hill	1		*Best six results count. Points	
10	Jo Siffert	7		Pedro Rodriguez	1		only awarded to first car to	
11	Bob Anderson	5		Trevor Taylor	1		finish for each manufacturer	
				*Best six results count				

1965

Jim Clark, the man to beat for all but the first year of the 1.5-litre Formula One, fittingly became World Champion for a second time in the final year of the formula. Not only did he win six times (including both the British and Belgian races for a fourth successive year), but he also won the Indianapolis 500 at the third attempt.

Once again British drivers dominated the series, Graham Hill completing a hat-trick of wins both in Monte Carlo (which Clark missed due to Indy) and at Watkins Glen. The Italian GP was again the closest race of the year, with the lead changing hands a record 42 times between four drivers, before Hill's team-mate Jackie Stewart scored his maiden Grand Prix victory.

Richie Ginther won the closing Grand Prix of the formula, held in Mexico City - not only his sole win, but also a first for Honda and for Goodyear tyres.

South African Grand Prix

1 January 1965. East London. 85 laps of a 2.436-mile circuit = 207.060 miles. Dry and overcast. World Championship round 1

1 Jim Clark	Lotus 33-Climax	85	2h06m46.0
2 John Surtees	Ferrari 158	85	2h07m15.0
3 Graham Hill	BRM P261	85	2h07m17.8
4 Mike Spence	Lotus 33-Climax	85	2h07m40.4
5 Bruce McLaren	Cooper T73-Climax	84	
6 Jackie Stewart	BRM P261	83	

Winner's average speed: 98.004 mph. Starting grid front row: Clark, 1m27.2 (pole), Surtees, 1m28.1 and Brabham, 1m28.3. Fastest lap: Clark, 1m27.6. Leaders: Clark, laps 1-85.

Grand Prix de Monaco

30 May 1965. Monte Carlo. 100 laps of a 1.954-mile circuit = 195.400 miles. Dry and overcast. World Championship round 2

1 Graham Hill	BRM P261	100	2h37m39.6
2 Lorenzo Bandini	Ferrari 1512	100	2h38m43.6
3 Jackie Stewart	BRM P261	100	2h39m21.5
4 John Surtees	Ferrari 158	99	out of fuel
5 Bruce McLaren	Cooper T77-Climax	98	
6 Jo Siffert	Brabham BT11-BRM	98	

Winner's average speed: 74.363 mph. Starting grid front row: G Hill, 1m32.5 (pole) and Brabham, 1m32.8. Fastest lap: G Hill, 1m31.7. Leaders: G Hill, laps 1-24, 65-100; Stewart, 25-29; Bandini, 30-33, 43-64; Brabham, 34-42

Grand Prix de Belgique

13 June 1965. Spa-Francorchamps. 32 laps of a 8.761-mile circuit = 280.352 miles. Heavy rain. World Championship round 3. Also known as the European Grand Prix

1 Jim Clark	Lotus 33-Climax	32	2h23m34.8
2 Jackie Stewart	BRM P261	32	2h24m19.6
3 Bruce McLaren	Cooper T77-Climax	31	
4 Jack Brabham	Brabham BT11-Climax	31	
5 Graham Hill	BRM P261	31	
6 Richie Ginther	Honda RA272	31	

Winner's average speed: 117.155 mph. Starting grid front row: G Hill, 3m45.4 (pole), Clark, 3m47.5 and Stewart, 3m48.8. Fastest lap: Clark, 4m12.9. Leaders: Clark, laps 1-32

Mike Spence, team owner Colin Chapman and Jim Clark (left to right) of Team Lotus confer at Spa

Grand Prix de l'Automobile Club de France

27 June 1965. Clermont-Ferrand. 40 laps of a 5.005-mile circuit = 200.200 miles. Warm, dry and sunny. World Championship round 4

1 Jim Clark	Lotus 25-Climax	40	2h14m38.4
2 Jackie Stewart	BRM P261	40	2h15m04.7
3 John Surtees	Ferrari 158	40	2h17m11.9
4 Denny Hulme	Brabham BT11-Climax	40	2h17m31.5
5 Graham Hill	BRM P261	39	
6 Jo Siffert	Brabham BT11-BRM	39	

1965 DRIVERS' RECORDS

Driver	Car	South African GP	Monaco GP	Belgian GP	French GP	British GP	Dutch GP	German GP	Italian GP	United States GP	Mexican GP
Chris Amon	Lotus 25-BRM	-	-	-	R	-	-	R	-	-	-
	Brabham BT3-BRM	-	-	-	-	DNS	-	-	-	-	-
Bob Anderson	Brabham BT11-Climax	NC	9	DNS	9	R	R	DNS	-	-	-
Richard Attwood	Lotus 25-BRM	-	R	14	-	13	12	R	6	10	6
Giancarlo Baghetti	Brabham BT7-Climax	-	-	-	-	-	-	-	R	-	-
Lorenzo Bandini	Ferrari 1512	15	2	9	8	-	-	-	4	4	8
	Ferrari 158	-	-	-	-	R	9	6	-	-	-
Giorgio Bassi	BRM P57	-	-	-	-	-	-	-	R	-	-
Lucien Bianchi	BRM P57	-	-	12	-	-	-	-	-	-	-
Trevor Blokdyk	Cooper T59-Ford	DNQ	-	-	-	-	-	-	-	-	-
Bob Bondurant	Ferrari 158	-	-	-	-	-	-	-	-	9	-
	Lotus 33-BRM	-	-	-	-	-	-	-	-	-	R
Jo Bonnier	Brabham BT7-Climax	R	7	R	R	7	R	7	7	8	-
	Brabham BT11-Climax	-	-	-	-	-	-	-	-	-	R
Jack Brabham	Brabham BT11-Climax	8	R	4	-	DNS	-	5	-	3	R
Ronnie Bucknum	Honda RA272	-	R	R	R	-	-	-	R	13	5
Roberto Bussinello	BRM P57	-	-	-	-	-	-	DNQ	13	-	-
Dave Charlton	Lotus 20-Ford	NPQ	-	-	-	-	-	-	-	-	-
Jim Clark	Lotus 33-Climax	1PF	-	1F	-	1P	1F	1PF	10PF	R	RP
	Lotus 25-Climax	-	-	-	1PF	-	-	-	-	-	-
Frank Gardner	Brabham BT11-BRM	12	R	R	-	8	11	R	R	-	-
Richie Ginther	Honda RA272	-	R	6	R	R	6	-	14	7	1
Masten Gregory	BRM P57	-	-	R	-	12	-	8	R	-	-
Brian Gubby	Lotus 24-Climax	-	-	-	DNQ	-	-	-	-	-	-
Dan Gurney	Brabham BT11-Climax	R	-	10	R	6	3	3	3	2	2F
Mike Hailwood	Lotus 25-BRM	-	R	-	-	-	-	-	-	-	-
Paul Hawkins	Brabham BT10-Ford	9	-	-	-	-	-	-	-	-	-
	Lotus 33-Climax	-	10	-	-	-	-	R	-	-	-
Graham Hill	BRM P261	3	1PF	5P	5	2F	4P	2	2	1PF	R
Denny Hulme	Brabham BT7-Climax	-	8	-	-	R	-	R	-	-	-
	Brabham BT11-Climax	-	-	-	4	-	5	-	R	-	-
Innes Ireland	Lotus 25-BRM	-	-	13	R	R	10	-	-	-	-
	Lotus 33-BRM	-	-	-	-	-	-	-	9	R	DNS
Piet de Klerk	Alfa Special	10	-	-	-	-	-	-	-	-	-
Neville Lederle	Lotus 21-Climax	DNQ	-	-	-	-	-	-	-	-	-
John Love	Cooper T55-Climax	R	-	-	-	-	-	-	-	-	-
Willy Mairesse	BRM P57	-	-	DNS	-	-	-	-	-	-	-
Tony Maggs	Lotus 25-BRM	11	-	-	-	-	-	-	-	-	-
Bruce McLaren	Cooper T73-Climax	5	-	-	-	-	-	-	-	-	-
	Cooper T77-Climax	-	5	3	R	10	R	R	5	R	R
Gerhard Mitter	Lotus 25-Climax	-	-	-	-	-	-	R	-	-	-
Brausch Niemann	Lotus 22-Ford	DNQ	-	-	-	-	-	-	-	-	-
Ernest Pieterse	Lotus 21-Climax	DNQ	-	-	-	-	-	-	-	-	-
Jackie Pretorius	LDS Mk1-Alfa Romeo	NPQ	-	-	-	-	-	-	-	-	-
David Prophet	Brabham BT10-Ford	14	-	-	-	-	-	-	-	-	-
Clive Puzey	Lotus 18/21-Climax	NPQ	-	-	-	-	-	-	-	-	-
Ian Raby	Brabham BT3-BRM	-	-	-	-	11	-	DNQ	-	-	-
John Rhodes	Cooper T60-Climax	-	-	-	-	R	-	-	-	-	-
Jochen Rindt	Cooper T73-Climax	R	-	-	-	-	-	-	8	-	-
	Cooper T77-Climax	-	DNQ	11	R	14	R	4	-	6	R
Pedro Rodriguez	Ferrari 1512	-	-	-	-	-	-	-	-	5	7
Alan Rollinson	Cooper T71/73-Ford	-	-	-	-	DNQ	-	-	-	-	-
"Geki" Russo	Lotus 25-Climax	-	-	-	-	-	-	-	R	-	-
Ludovico Scarfiotti	Ferrari 1512	-	-	-	-	-	-	-	-	-	DNS
Doug Serrurier	LDS Mk2-Climax	DNQ	-	-	-	-	-	-	-	-	-
Jo Siffert	Brabham BT11-BRM	7	6	8	6	9	13	R	R	11	4
Moises Solana	Lotus 25-Climax	-	-	-	-	-	-	-	-	12	R
Mike Spence	Lotus 33-Climax	4	-	7	7	4	-	R	11	R	3
	Lotus 25-Climax	-	-	-	-	-	8	-	-	-	-
Jackie Stewart	BRM P261	6	3	2	2	5	2	R	1	R	R
John Surtees	Ferrari 158	2	4	R	3	-	-	-	-	-	-
	Ferrari 1512	-	-	-	-	3	7	R	R	-	-
Sam Tingle	LDS Mk1-Alfa Romeo	13	-	-	-	-	-	-	-	-	-
Nino Vaccarella	Ferrari 158	-	-	-	-	-	-	-	12	-	-

World Championship Grand Prix Racing

Winner's average speed: 89.216 mph. Starting grid front row:
Clark, 3m18.3 (pole), Stewart, 3m18.8 and Bandini, 3m19.1.
Fastest lap: Clark, 3m18.9. Leaders: Clark, laps 1-40

British Grand Prix

10 July 1965. Silverstone. 80 laps of a 2.927-mile circuit = 234.160 miles. Dry and overcast. World Championship round 5

1 Jim Clark	Lotus 33-Climax	80	2h05m25.4
2 Graham Hill	BRM P261	80	2h05m28.6
3 John Surtees	Ferrari 1512	80	2h05m53.0
4 Mike Spence	Lotus 33-Climax	80	2h06m05.0
5 Jackie Stewart	BRM P261	80	2h06m40.0
6 Dan Gurney	Brabham BT11-Climax	79	

Winner's average speed: 112.017 mph. Starting grid front row:
Clark, 1m30.8 (pole), G Hill, 1m31.0, Ginther, 1m31.3 and Stewart,
1m31.3. Fastest lap: Clark, 1m32.2. Leaders: Clark, laps 1-80

Grote Prijs van Nederland

18 July 1965. Zandvoort. 80 laps of a 2.605-mile circuit = 208.400 miles. Dry and overcast. World Championship round 6

1 Jim Clark	Lotus 33-Climax	80	2h03m59.1
2 Jackie Stewart	BRM P261	80	2h04m07.1
3 Dan Gurney	Brabham BT11-Climax	80	2h04m12.1
4 Graham Hill	BRM P261	80	2h04m44.2
5 Denny Hulme	Brabham BT11-Climax	79	
6 Richie Ginther	Honda RA272	79	

Winner's average speed: 100.851 mph. Starting grid front row:
G Hill, 1m30.7 (pole), Clark, 1m31.0 and Ginther, 1m31.0. Fastest
lap: Clark, 1m30.6. Leaders: Ginther, laps 1-2; G Hill, 3-5; Clark, 6-80

Grosser Preis von Deutschland

1 August 1965. Nürburgring. 15 laps of a 14.167-mile circuit = 212.505 miles. Dry and overcast. World Championship round 7

1 Jim Clark	Lotus 33-Climax	15	2h07m52.4
2 Graham Hill	BRM P261	15	2h08m08.3
3 Dan Gurney	Brabham BT11-Climax	15	2h08m13.8
4 Jochen Rindt	Cooper T77-Climax	15	2h11m22.0
5 Jack Brabham	Brabham BT11-Climax	15	2h12m33.6
6 Lorenzo Bandini	Ferrari 158	15	2h13m01.0

Winner's average speed: 99.710 mph. Starting grid front row:
Clark, 8m22.7 (pole), Stewart, 8m26.1, G Hill, 8m26.8 and Surtees,
8m27.8. Fastest lap: Clark, 8m24.1. Leaders: Clark, laps 1-15

Gran Premio d'Italia

12 September 1965. Monza. 76 laps of a 3.573-mile circuit = 271.548 miles. Warm, dry and sunny. World Championship round 8

1 Jackie Stewart	BRM P261	76	2h04m52.8
2 Graham Hill	BRM P261	76	2h04m56.1
3 Dan Gurney	Brabham BT11-Climax	76	2h05m09.3
4 Lorenzo Bandini	Ferrari 1512	76	2h06m08.7
5 Bruce McLaren	Cooper T77-Climax	75	
6 Richard Attwood	Lotus 25-BRM	75	

Winner's average speed: 130.468 mph. Starting grid front row:
Clark, 1m35.9 (pole), Surtees, 1m36.1 and Stewart, 1m36.6.
Fastest lap: Clark, 1m36.4. Leaders: Clark, 1-2, 4, 6-7, 18, 21-24,
27, 33-35, 38, 44, 46, 51, 53-54, 57; G Hill, 3, 25-26, 28, 40, 43,
45, 50, 55-56, 64, 70-71, 73-74; Stewart, 5, 8-10, 12, 14, 17,
19-20, 29-32, 36-37, 39, 41-42, 47-49, 52, 58-63, 65-69, 72, 75-76;
Surtees, 11, 13, 15-16

United States Grand Prix

3 October 1965. Watkins Glen. 110 laps of a 2.350-mile circuit = 258.500 miles. Windy and occasional rain. World Championship round 9

1 Graham Hill	BRM P261	110	2h20m36.1
2 Dan Gurney	Brabham BT11-Climax	110	2h20m48.6
3 Jack Brabham	Brabham BT11-Climax	110	2h21m33.6
4 Lorenzo Bandini	Ferrari 1512	109	
5 Pedro Rodriguez	Ferrari 1512	109	
6 Jochen Rindt	Cooper T77-Climax	108	

Winner's average speed: 110.312 mph. Starting grid front row:
G Hill, 1m11.25 (pole) and Clark, 1m11.35. Fastest lap: G Hill,
1m11.9. Leaders: G Hill, laps 1, 5-10, 12-110; Clark, 2-4, 11

Gran Premio de Mexico

24 October 1965. Mexico City. 65 laps of a 3.107-mile circuit = 201.955 miles. Warm, dry and sunny. World Championship round 10

1 Richie Ginther	Honda RA272	65	2h08m32.10
2 Dan Gurney	Brabham BT11-Climax	65	2h08m34.99
3 Mike Spence	Lotus 33-Climax	65	2h09m32.25
4 Jo Siffert	Brabham BT11-BRM	65	2h10m26.52
5 Ronnie Bucknum	Honda RA272	64	
6 Richard Attwood	Lotus 25-BRM	64	

Winner's average speed: 94.272 mph. Starting grid front row:
Clark, 1m56.17 (pole) and Gurney, 1m56.24. Fastest lap: Gurney,
1m55.84. Leaders: Ginther, laps 1-65

1965 FINAL CHAMPIONSHIP POSITIONS

Drivers						Manufacturers	
1 Jim Clark	54		11= Denny Hulme	5		1 Lotus-Climax	54 (58)*
2 Graham Hill	40 (47)*		Jo Siffert	5		2 BRM	45 (61)*
3 Jackie Stewart	33 (34)*		13 Jochen Rindt	4		3 Brabham-Climax	27 (31)*
4 Dan Gurney	25		14= Richard Attwood	2		4 Ferrari	26 (27)*
5 John Surtees	17		Ronnie Bucknum	2		5 Cooper-Climax	14
6 Lorenzo Bandini	13		Pedro Rodriguez	2		6 Honda	11
7 Richie Ginther	11		*Best six results count			7 Brabham-BRM	5
8= Bruce McLaren	10					8 Lotus-BRM	2
Mike Spence	10					*Best six results count. Points	
10 Jack Brabham	9					only awarded to first car to	
						finish for each manufacturer	

1966

Despite having been announced in 1963, the introduction of new 3-litre engine capacity rules, often referred to as "the return to power", found many teams far from ready. As with the last major change of rules in 1961, though, Ferrari was prepared and so was favourite. Having won in

Belgium, however, the Italians lost their impetus when internal politics forced their leading driver, John Surtees, to leave and join Cooper.

Jack Brabham became the first man to win the World Championship in a car of his own name with four successive victories. His team exclusively used the new Holden/Repco engine, based on an aluminium stock block Oldsmobile, which although not as powerful as other 3-litre units was reliable and quick enough.

Coventry-Climax had withdrawn from F1 by the end of 1965, leaving the British teams looking for alternative power sources. Aside from Brabham, Cooper arranged to use V12 Maserati engines which had been raced nine years previously, Bruce McLaren's new team experimented unsuccessfully with V8s from both Ford (their Indy engine) and Serenissima, while others bored out old engines to 2-litre capacity as a stop-gap. It was with such a BRM that Jackie Stewart won at Monaco.

BRM eventually introduced the unreliable and complicated H16 unit, which was essentially two 1500 cc V8s mated together. The only win for the engine was in the US GP and then not for the team. It powered Jim Clark's Lotus 43 to his only win of the year.

Grand Prix de Monaco

22 May 1966. Monte Carlo. 100 laps of a 1.954-mile circuit = 195.400 miles. Warm, dry and hazy. World Championship round 1

1 Jackie Stewart	BRM P261	100	2h33m10.6
2 Lorenzo Bandini	Ferrari 158/246	100	2h33m50.7
3 Graham Hill	BRM P261	99	
4 Bob Bondurant	BRM P261	95	

No other finishers. Winner's average speed: 76.539 mph. Starting grid front row: Clark, 1m29.9 (pole) and Surtees, 1m30.1. Fastest lap: Bandini, 1m29.8. Leaders: Surtees, laps 1-14; Stewart, 15-100

Grand Prix de Belgique

12 June 1966. Spa-Francorchamps. 28 laps of a 8.761-mile circuit = 245.308 miles. Wet and overcast. World Championship round 2

1 John Surtees	Ferrari 312	28	2h09m11.3
2 Jochen Rindt	Cooper T81-Maserati	28	2h09m53.4
3 Lorenzo Bandini	Ferrari 158/246	27	
4 Jack Brabham	Brabham BT19-Repco	26	
5 Richie Ginther	Cooper T81-Maserati	25	

No other finishers. Winner's average speed: 113.930 mph. Starting grid front row: Surtees, 3m38.0 (pole), Rindt, 3m41.2 and Stewart, 3m41.5. Fastest lap: Surtees, 4m18.7. Leaders: Surtees, laps 1, 3, 24-28; Bandini, 2; Rindt, 4-23

Grand Prix de l'Automobile Club de France

3 July 1966. Reims. 48 laps of a 5.187-mile circuit = 248.976 miles. Very hot, dry and sunny. World Championship round 3. Also known as the European Grand Prix

1 Jack Brabham	Brabham BT19-Repco	48	1h48m31.3
2 Michael Parkes	Ferrari 312	48	1h48m40.8
3 Denny Hulme	Brabham BT20-Repco	46	
4 Jochen Rindt	Cooper T81-Maserati	46	
5 Dan Gurney	Eagle AAR101-Climax	45	
6 John Taylor	Brabham BT11-BRM	45	

Winner's average speed: 137.655 mph. Starting grid front row: Bandini, 2m07.8 (pole), Surtees, 2m08.4 and Parkes, 2m09.1. Fastest lap: Bandini, 2m11.3. Leaders: Bandini, laps 1-31; Brabham, 32-48

British Grand Prix

16 July 1966. Brands Hatch. 80 laps of a 2.650-mile circuit = 212.000 miles. Overcast and light rain at the start, drying later. World Championship round 4

1 Jack Brabham	Brabham BT19-Repco	80	2h13m13.4
2 Denny Hulme	Brabham BT20-Repco	80	2h13m23.0
3 Graham Hill	BRM P261	79	
4 Jim Clark	Lotus 33-Climax	79	
5 Jochen Rindt	Cooper T81-Maserati	79	
6 Bruce McLaren	McLaren M2B-Serenissima	78	

Winner's average speed: 95.479 mph. Starting grid front row: Brabham, 1m34.5 (pole), Hulme, 1m34.8 and Gurney, 1m35.8. Fastest lap: Brabham, 1m37.0. Leaders: Brabham, laps 1-80

Grote Prijs van Nederland

24 July 1966. Zandvoort. 90 laps of a 2.605-mile circuit = 234.450 miles. Warm, dry and sunny. World Championship round 5

1 Jack Brabham	Brabham BT19-Repco	90	2h20m32.5
2 Graham Hill	BRM P261	89	
3 Jim Clark	Lotus 33-Climax	88	
4 Jackie Stewart	BRM P261	88	
5 Mike Spence	Lotus 33-BRM	87	
6 Lorenzo Bandini	Ferrari 312	87	

Winner's average speed: 100.091 mph. Starting grid front row: Brabham, 1m28.1 (pole), Hulme, 1m28.7 and Clark, 1m28.7. Fastest lap: Hulme, 1m30.6. Leaders: Brabham, laps 1-26, 76-90; Clark, 27-75

Grosser Preis von Deutschland

7 August 1966. Nürburgring. 15 laps of a 14.167-mile circuit = 212.505 miles. Wet and overcast. World Championship round 6

1 Jack Brabham	Brabham BT19-Repco	15	2h27m03.0
2 John Surtees	Cooper T81-Maserati	15	2h27m47.4
3 Jochen Rindt	Cooper T81-Maserati	15	2h29m35.6
4 Graham Hill	BRM P261	15	2h33m44.4
5 Jackie Stewart	BRM P261	15	2h35m31.9
6 Lorenzo Bandini	Ferrari 312	15	2h37m59.4

Winner's average speed: 86.707 mph. Starting grid front row: Clark, 8m16.5 (pole), Surtees, 8m18.0, Stewart, 8m18.8 and Scarfiotti, 8m20.2. Fastest lap: Surtees, 8m49.0. Leaders: Brabham, laps 1-15

Gran Premio d'Italia

4 September 1966. Monza. 68 laps of a 3.573-mile circuit = 242.964 miles. Warm, dry and sunny. World Championship round 7

1 Ludovico Scarfiotti	Ferrari 312	68	1h47m14.8
2 Michael Parkes	Ferrari 312	68	1h47m20.6
3 Denny Hulme	Brabham BT20-Repco	68	1h47m20.9
4 Jochen Rindt	Cooper T81-Maserati	67	
5 Mike Spence	Lotus 33-BRM	67	
6 Bob Anderson	Brabham BT11-Climax	66	

Winner's average speed: 135.928 mph. Starting grid front row: Parkes, 1m31.3 (pole), Scarfiotti, 1m31.6 and Clark, 1m31.8. Fastest lap: Scarfiotti, 1m32.4. Leaders: Bandini, lap 1; Parkes, laps 2, 8-12, 27; Surtees, 3; Brabham, 4-7; Scarfiotti, 13-26, 28-68

United States Grand Prix

2 October 1966. Watkins Glen. 108 laps of a 2.350-mile circuit = 253.800 miles. Cool and dry. World Championship round 8

1 Jim Clark	Lotus 43-BRM	108	2h09m40.1
2 Jochen Rindt*	Cooper T81-Maserati	107	
3 John Surtees	Cooper T81-Maserati	107	
4 Jo Siffert	Cooper T81-Maserati	105	
5 Bruce McLaren	McLaren M2B-Ford	105	
6 Peter Arundell	Lotus 33-Climax	101	

*Rindt penalized one lap for completing his final lap in over twice the time of the fastest lap of the race winner, a local rule. Winner's average speed: 117.438 mph. Starting grid front row: Brabham, 1m08.42 (pole) and Clark, 1m08.53. Fastest lap: Surtees, 1m09.67. Leaders: Bandini, laps 1-9, 20-34; Brabham, 10-19, 35-55; Clark, 56-108

1966 DRIVERS' RECORDS

Driver	Car	Monaco GP	Belgian GP	French GP	British GP	Dutch GP	German GP	Italian GP	United States GP	Mexican GP
Kurt Ahrens Jr	Brabham BT18-Ford	-	-	-	-	-	F2	-	-	-
Chris Amon	Cooper T81-Maserati	-	-	8	-	-	-	-	-	-
	Brabham BT11-BRM	-	-	-	-	-	-	DNQ	-	-
Bob Anderson	Brabham BT11-Climax	R	-	7	NC	R	R	6	-	-
Peter Arundell	Lotus 43-BRM	-	DNS	R	-	-	-	-	-	-
	Lotus 33-BRM	-	-	-	R	R	8	8	-	7
	Lotus 33-Climax	-	-	-	-	-	-	-	6	-
Giancarlo Baghetti	Ferrari 158/246	-	-	-	-	-	-	NC	-	-
Lorenzo Bandini	Ferrari 158/246	2F	3	-	-	-	-	-	-	-
	Ferrari 312	-	-	NCPF	-	6	6	R	R	-
Jean-Pierre Beltoise	Matra MS5-Ford	-	-	-	-	-	F2	-	-	-
Bob Bondurant	BRM P261	4	R	-	9	-	R	7	-	-
	Eagle AAR101-Climax	-	-	-	-	-	-	-	R	-
	Eagle AAR102-Weslake	-	-	-	-	-	-	-	-	R
Jo Bonnier	Cooper T81-Maserati	NC	R	-	-	7	R	R	NC	6
	Brabham BT11-Climax	-	-	NC	-	-	-	-	-	-
	Brabham BT7-Climax	-	-	-	R	-	-	-	-	-
Jack Brabham	Brabham BT19-Repco	R	4	1	1PF	1P	1	R	-	-
	Brabham BT20-Repco	-	-	-	-	-	-	-	RP	2
Ronnie Bucknum	Honda RA273	-	-	-	-	-	-	-	R	8
Jim Clark	Lotus 33-Climax	RP	R	DNS	4	3	RP	-	-	-
	Lotus 43-BRM	-	-	-	-	-	-	R	1	R
Piers Courage	Lotus 44-Ford	-	-	-	-	-	F2	-	-	-
Richie Ginther	Cooper T81-Maserati	R	5	-	-	-	-	-	-	-
	Honda RA273	-	-	-	-	-	-	R	NC	4F
Dan Gurney	Eagle AAR101-Climax	-	NC	5	R	R	7	-	-	5
	Eagle AAR102-Weslake	-	-	-	-	-	-	R	R	-
Hubert Hahne	Matra MS5-BRM	-	-	-	-	-	F2	-	-	-
Hans Herrmann	Brabham BT18-Ford	-	-	-	-	-	F2	-	-	-
Graham Hill	BRM P261	3	R	R	3	2	4	-	-	-
	BRM P83	-	-	-	-	-	-	R	R	R
Phil Hill	Lotus 25-Climax	DNS*	-	-	-	-	-	-	-	-
	McLaren M3A-Ford	-	R*	-	-	-	-	-	-	-
	Eagle AAR101-Climax	-	-	-	-	-	-	DNQ	-	-
Denny Hulme	Brabham BT11-Climax	R	R	-	-	-	-	-	-	-
	Brabham BT20-Repco	-	-	3	2	RF	R	3	R	3
Jacky Ickx	Matra MS5-Ford	-	-	-	-	-	F2	-	-	-
Innes Ireland	BRM P261	-	-	-	-	-	-	-	R	R
Chris Irwin	Brabham BT11-Climax	-	-	-	7	-	-	-	-	-
Chris Lawrence	Cooper T73-Ferrari	-	-	-	11	-	R	-	-	-
Guy Ligier	Cooper T81-Maserati	NC	NC	NC	10	9	DNS	-	-	-
Bruce McLaren	McLaren M2B-Ford	R	-	-	-	-	-	-	5	R
	McLaren M2B-Serenissima	-	DNS	-	6	DNS	-	-	-	-
Michael Parkes	Ferrari 312	-	-	2	-	R	R	2P	-	-
Alan Rees	Brabham BT18-Ford	-	-	-	-	-	F2	-	-	-
Jochen Rindt	Cooper T81-Maserati	R	2	4	5	R	3	4	2	R
Pedro Rodriguez	Lotus 33-Climax	-	-	R	-	-	-	-	-	R
	Lotus 44-Ford	-	-	-	-	-	F2	-	-	-
	Lotus 33-BRM	-	-	-	-	-	-	-	R	-
"Geki" Russo	Lotus 33-Climax	-	-	-	-	-	-	9	-	-
Ludovico Scarfiotti	Ferrari 158/246	-	-	-	-	-	R	-	-	-
	Ferrari 312	-	-	-	-	-	-	1F	-	-
Jo Schlesser	Matra MS5-Ford	-	-	-	-	-	F2	-	-	-
Jo Siffert	Brabham BT11-BRM	R	-	-	-	-	-	-	-	-
	Cooper T81-Maserati	-	R	R	NC	R	-	R	4	R
Moises Solana	Cooper T81-Maserati	-	-	-	-	-	-	-	-	R
Mike Spence	Lotus 33-BRM	R	R	R	R	5	R	5	-	-
	Lotus 25-BRM	-	-	-	-	-	-	-	R	DNS
Jackie Stewart	BRM P261	1	R	-	R	4	5	-	-	-
	BRM P83	-	-	-	-	-	-	R	R	R
John Surtees	Ferrari 312	R	1PF	-	-	-	-	-	-	-
	Cooper T81-Maserati	-	-	R	R	R	2F	R	3F	1P
John Taylor	Brabham BT11-BRM	-	-	6	8	8	R	-	-	-
Trevor Taylor	Shannon SH1-Climax	-	-	-	R	-	-	-	-	-
Vic Wilson	BRM P261	-	DNS	-	-	-	-	-	-	-

*Camera car for the film *Grand Prix*, not competing in the race

Gran Premio de Mexico

23 October 1966. Mexico City. 65 laps of a 3.107-mile circuit = 201.955 miles. Warm, dry and sunny. World Championship round 9

1 John Surtees	Cooper T81-Maserati	65	2h06m35.34
2 Jack Brabham	Brabham BT20-Repco	65	2h06m43.22
3 Denny Hulme	Brabham BT20-Repco	64	
4 Richie Ginther	Honda RA273	64	
5 Dan Gurney	Eagle AAR101-Climax	64	
6 Jo Bonnier	Cooper T81-Maserati	63	

Winner's average speed: 95.722 mph. Starting grid front row: Surtees, 1m53.18 (pole) and Clark, 1m53.50. Fastest lap: Ginther, 1m53.75. Leaders: Ginther, lap 1; Brabham, laps 2-5; Surtees, 6-65

1966 FINAL CHAMPIONSHIP POSITIONS

Drivers

1	Jack Brabham	42 (45)*	14=	Bob Bondurant	3	3	Cooper-Maserati	30 (35)*
2	John Surtees	28		Bruce McLaren	3	4	BRM	22
3	Jochen Rindt	22 (24)*		Jo Siffert	3	5	Lotus-BRM	13
4	Denny Hulme	18	17=	Bob Anderson	1	6	Lotus-Climax	8
5	Graham Hill	17		Peter Arundell	1	7	Eagle-Climax	4
6	Jim Clark	16		Jo Bonnier	1	8	Honda	3
7	Jackie Stewart	14		John Taylor	1	9	McLaren-Ford	2
8=	Lorenzo Bandini	12		*Best five results count		10=	Brabham-BRM	1
	Michael Parkes	12					McLaren-Serenissima	1
10	Ludovico Scarfiotti	9					Brabham-Climax	1
11	Richie Ginther	5	**Manufacturers**				*Best five results count. Points	
12=	Dan Gurney	4	1	Brabham-Repco	42 (49)*		only awarded to first car to	
	Mike Spence	4	2	Ferrari	31 (32)*		finish for each manufacturer	

1967

Lotus signed Graham Hill to partner Jim Clark, as well as an exclusive deal to use the new Ford DFV engine which had been designed and built by Cosworth Engineering and financed by the Ford motor company. It would become the most successful F1 engine of all time, and Clark gave it a stunning debut win at Zandvoort.

The late introduction of the new engine and some initial reliability problems meant that, despite his four wins, Clark could not prevent the Brabham team repeating its championship success. This time, however, Denny Hulme beat his boss to the title.

Denny Hulme on his way to second place at Silverstone

The Kyalami circuit, hosting the South African GP for the first time, opened the season and almost produced a shock win for Rhodesian John Love. Driving an old four cylinder Cooper-Climax, Love only lost the lead to Pedro Rodriguez when he refuelled six laps from the flag. At Spa, Dan Gurney gave his Eagle concern its only Grand Prix win when Clark and Jackie Stewart were delayed.

The Italian GP was a classic example of Jim Clark virtuosity. In an incredible display, he regained a whole lap lost by an early unscheduled pit stop and retook the lead - only to run low on fuel on the very last lap.

For Ferrari it had been a year of tragedy, Lorenzo Bandini dying after crashing in flames at Monaco's chicane, and Englishman Michael Parkes injured at Spa. This put the young New Zealander, Chris

Amon into the spotlight as team leader, but his mature performances never quite yielded a Grand Prix victory. Another youngster to impress was Jacky Ickx, who, while competing in the F2 class of the German GP, ran fourth among the F1 cars only to retire.

South African Grand Prix

2 January 1967. Kyalami. 80 laps of a 2.544-mile circuit = 203.520 miles. Hot, dry and sunny. World Championship round 1

1 Pedro Rodriguez	Cooper T81-Maserati	80	2h05m45.9
2 John Love	Cooper T79-Climax	80	2h06m12.3
3 John Surtees	Honda RA273	79	
4 Denny Hulme	Brabham BT20-Repco	78	
5 Bob Anderson	Brabham BT11-Climax	78	
6 Jack Brabham	Brabham BT20-Repco	76	

Winner's average speed: 97.095 mph. Starting grid front row: Brabham, 1m28.3 (pole) and Hulme, 1m28.9. Fastest lap: Hulme, 1m29.9. Leaders: Hulme, laps 1-60; Love, 61-73; Rodriguez, 74-80

Grand Prix de Monaco

7 May 1967. Monte Carlo. 100 laps of a 1.954-mile circuit = 195.400 miles. Warm, dry and sunny. World Championship round 2

1 Denny Hulme	Brabham BT20-Repco	100	2h34m34.3
2 Graham Hill	Lotus 33-BRM	99	
3 Chris Amon	Ferrari 312	98	
4 Bruce McLaren	McLaren M4B-BRM	97	
5 Pedro Rodriguez	Cooper T81-Maserati	96	
6 Mike Spence	BRM P83	96	

Winner's average speed: 75.848 mph. Starting grid front row: Brabham, 1m27.6 (pole) and Bandini, 1m28.3. Fastest lap: Clark, 1m29.5. Leaders: Bandini, lap 1; Hulme, laps 2-5, 15-100; Stewart, 6-14

Grote Prijs van Nederland

4 June 1967. Zandvoort. 90 laps of a 2.605-mile circuit = 234.450 miles. Dry and overcast. World Championship round 3

1 Jim Clark	Lotus 49-Ford	90	2h14m45.1
2 Jack Brabham	Brabham BT19-Repco	90	2h15m08.7
3 Denny Hulme	Brabham BT20-Repco	90	2h15m10.8
4 Chris Amon	Ferrari 312	90	2h15m12.4
5 Michael Parkes	Ferrari 312	89	
6 Ludovico Scarfiotti	Ferrari 312	89	

1967 DRIVERS' RECORDS

Driver	Car	South African GP	Monaco GP	Dutch GP	Belgian GP	French GP	British GP	German GP	Canadian GP	Italian GP	United States GP	Mexican GP
Kurt Ahrens Jr	Protos-Cosworth	-	-	-	-	-	-	F2	-	-	-	-
Chris Amon	Ferrari 312	-	3	4	3	R	3	3	6	7	R	9
Bob Anderson	Brabham BT11-Climax	5	DNQ	9	8	R	R	-	-	-	-	-
Richard Attwood	Cooper T81B-Maserati	-	-	-	-	-	-	-	10	-	-	-
Giancarlo Baghetti	Lotus 49-Ford	-	-	-	-	-	-	-	-	R	-	-
Lorenzo Bandini	Ferrari 312	-	R	-	-	-	-	-	-	-	-	-
Jean-Pierre Beltoise	Matra MS5-Ford	-	DNQ	-	-	-	-	-	-	-	-	-
	Matra MS7-Cosworth	-	-	-	-	-	-	-	-	-	7	7
Jo Bonnier	Cooper T81-Maserati	R	-	-	R	-	R	5	8	R	6	10
Luki Botha	Brabham BT11-Climax	NC	-	-	-	-	-	-	-	-	-	-
Jack Brabham	Brabham BT20-Repco	6P	-	-	-	-	-	-	-	-	-	-
	Brabham BT19-Repco	-	RP	2	-	-	-	-	-	-	-	-
	Brabham BT24-Repco	-	-	-	R	1	4	2	1	2	5	2
Dave Charlton	Brabham BT11-Climax	NC	-	-	-	-	-	-	-	-	-	-
Jim Clark	Lotus 43-BRM	R	-	-	-	-	-	-	-	-	-	-
	Lotus 33-Climax	-	RF	-	-	-	-	-	-	-	-	-
	Lotus 49-Ford	-	-	1F	6P	R	1P	RP	RPF	3PF	1	1PF
Piers Courage	Lotus 25-BRM	R	-	-	-	-	-	-	-	-	-	-
	BRM P261	-	R	-	-	-	DNS	-	-	-	-	-
Mike Fisher	Lotus 33-BRM	-	-	-	-	-	-	-	-	11	-	DNS
Richie Ginther	Eagle AAR102-Weslake	-	DNQ	-	-	-	-	-	-	-	-	-
Dan Gurney	Eagle AAR101-Climax	R	-	-	-	-	-	-	-	-	-	-
	Eagle AAR103-Weslake	-	R	-	-	-	-	-	3	-	-	-
	Eagle AAR104-Weslake	-	-	R	1F	R	R	RF	-	R	R	R
Hubert Hahne	Lola T100-BMW	-	-	-	-	-	-	R	-	-	-	-
Brian Hart	Protos-Cosworth	-	-	-	-	-	-	F2	-	-	-	-
Graham Hill	Lotus 43-BRM	R	-	-	-	-	-	-	-	-	-	-
	Lotus 33-BRM	-	2	-	-	-	-	-	-	-	-	-
	Lotus 49-Ford	-	RP	R	RPF	R	R	4	R	-	2PF	R
David Hobbs	BRM P261	-	-	-	-	-	8	-	9	-	-	-
	Lola T100-BMW	-	-	-	-	-	-	F2	-	-	-	-
Denny Hulme	Brabham BT20-Repco	4F	1	3	-	-	-	-	-	-	-	-
	Brabham BT19-Repco	-	-	-	R	-	-	-	-	-	-	-
	Brabham BT24-Repco	-	-	-	-	2	2F	1	2	R	3	3
Jacky Ickx	Matra MS5-Cosworth	-	-	-	-	-	-	F2	-	-	-	-
	Cooper T81B-Maserati	-	-	-	-	-	-	-	-	6	-	-
	Cooper T86-Maserati	-	-	-	-	-	-	-	-	-	R	-
Chris Irwin	Lotus 33-BRM	-	-	7	-	-	-	-	-	-	-	-
	BRM P261	-	-	-	R	-	7	-	-	-	-	-
	BRM P83	-	-	-	5	-	7	7	R	R	R	R
Tom Jones	Cooper T82-Climax	-	-	-	-	-	-	-	DNQ	-	-	-
Guy Ligier	Cooper T81-Maserati	-	-	-	10	NC	-	-	-	-	-	-
	Brabham BT20-Repco	-	-	-	-	10	6	-	-	R	R	11
John Love	Cooper T79-Climax	2	-	-	-	-	-	-	-	-	-	-
Bruce McLaren	McLaren M4B-BRM	-	4	R	-	-	-	-	-	-	-	-
	Eagle AAR102-Weslake	-	-	-	R	R	R	-	-	-	-	-
	McLaren M5A-BRM	-	-	-	-	-	-	-	7	R	R	13
Gerhard Mitter	Brabham BT23-Cosworth	-	-	-	-	-	-	F2	-	-	-	-
Silvio Moser	Cooper T77-ATS	-	-	-	-	-	R	-	-	-	-	-
Jackie Oliver	Lotus 48-Cosworth	-	-	-	-	-	-	F2	-	-	-	-
Michael Parkes	Ferrari 312	-	-	5	R	-	-	-	-	-	-	-
Al Pease	Eagle AAR101-Climax	-	-	-	-	-	-	-	NC	-	-	-
Alan Rees	Cooper T81-Maserati	-	-	-	-	-	9	-	-	-	-	-
	Brabham BT23-Cosworth	-	-	-	-	-	-	F2	-	-	-	-
Jochen Rindt	Cooper T81-Maserati	R	-	-	-	-	-	-	R	4	-	-
	Cooper T81B-Maserati	-	R	R	4	R	-	-	-	-	R	-
	Cooper T86-Maserati	-	-	-	-	-	R	R	-	-	-	-
Pedro Rodriguez	Cooper T81-Maserati	1	5	R	9	6	5	8	-	-	-	-
	Cooper T81B-Maserati	-	-	-	-	-	-	-	-	-	-	6
Ludovico Scarfiotti	Ferrari 312	-	-	6	NC	-	-	-	-	-	-	-
	Eagle AAR103-Weslake	-	-	-	-	-	-	-	-	R	-	-
Jo Schlesser	Matra MS5-Cosworth	-	-	-	-	-	-	F2	-	-	-	-
Johnny Servoz-Gavin	Matra MS5-Ford	-	R	-	-	-	-	-	-	-	-	-
Jo Siffert	Cooper T81-Maserati	R	R	10	7	4	R	NC	DNS	R	4	12
Moises Solana	Lotus 49-Ford	-	-	-	-	-	-	-	-	-	R	R
Mike Spence	BRM P83	R	6	8	5	R	R	R	5	5	R	5

/Cont'd

1967 DRIVERS' RECORDS cont'd/ Driver	Car	South African GP	Monaco GP	Dutch GP	Belgian GP	French GP	British GP	German GP	Canadian GP	Italian GP	United States GP	Mexican GP
Jackie Stewart	BRM P83	R	-	R	2	-	R	R	R	R	R	R
	BRM P261	-	R	-	-	3	-	-	-	-	-	-
John Surtees	Honda RA273	3	R	R	R	-	6	4	-	-	-	-
	Honda RA300	-	-	-	-	-	-	-	-	1	R	4
Sam Tingle	LDS Mk3-Climax	R	-	-	-	-	-	-	-	-	-	-
Eppie Wietzes	Lotus 49-Ford	-	-	-	-	-	-	-	R	-	-	-
Jonathan Williams	Ferrari 312	-	-	-	-	-	-	-	-	-	8	-

Winner's average speed: 104.392 mph. Starting grid front row: Hill, 1m24.60 (pole), Gurney, 1m25.1 and Brabham, 1m25.6. Fastest lap: Clark, 1m28.08. Leaders: Hill, laps 1-10; Brabham, 11-15; Clark, 16-90.

Grand Prix de Belgique

18 June 1967. Spa-Francorchamps. 28 laps of a 8.761-mile circuit = 245.308 miles. Warm, dry and sunny. World Championship round 4

1	Dan Gurney	Eagle AAR104-Weslake	28	1h40m49.45
2	Jackie Stewart	BRM P83	28	1h41m52.40
3	Chris Amon	Ferrari 312	28	1h42m29.40
4	Jochen Rindt	Cooper T81B-Maserati	28	1h43m03.30
5	Mike Spence	BRM P83	27	
6	Jim Clark	Lotus 49-Ford	27	

Winner's average speed: 145.982 mph. Starting grid front row: Clark, 3m28.1 (pole), Gurney, 3m31.2 and Hill, 3m32.9. Fastest lap: Gurney, 3m31.9. Leaders: Clark, laps 1-12; Stewart, 13-20; Gurney, 21-28

Grand Prix de l'Automobile Club de France

2 July 1967. Le Mans-Bugatti. 80 laps of a 2.748-mile circuit = 219.840 miles. Warm, dry and sunny. World Championship round 5

1	Jack Brabham	Brabham BT24-Repco	80	2h13m21.3
2	Denny Hulme	Brabham BT24-Repco	80	2h14m10.8
3	Jackie Stewart	BRM P261	79	
4	Jo Siffert	Cooper T81-Maserati	77	
5	Chris Irwin	BRM P83	76	engine
6	Pedro Rodriguez	Cooper T81-Maserati	76	

Winner's average speed: 98.912 mph. Starting grid front row: Hill, 1m36.2 (pole), Brabham, 1m36.3 and Gurney, 1m37.0. Fastest lap: Hill, 1m36.7. Leaders: Hill, laps 1, 11-13; Brabham, 2-4, 24-80; Clark, 5-10, 14-23

British Grand Prix

15 July 1967. Silverstone. 80 laps of a 2.927-mile circuit = 234.160 miles. Warm, dry and sunny. World Championship round 6

1	Jim Clark	Lotus 49-Ford	80	1h59m25.6
2	Denny Hulme	Brabham BT24-Repco	80	1h59m38.4
3	Chris Amon	Ferrari 312	80	1h59m42.2
4	Jack Brabham	Brabham BT24-Repco	80	1h59m47.4
5	Pedro Rodriguez	Cooper T81-Maserati	79	
6	John Surtees	Honda RA273	78	

Winner's average speed: 117.642 mph. Starting grid front row: Clark, 1m25.3 (pole), Hill, 1m26.0, Brabham, 1m26.2 and Hulme, 1m26.3. Fastest lap: Hulme, 1m27.0. Leaders: Clark, laps 1-25, 55-80; Hill, 26-54

Grosser Preis von Deutschland

6 August 1967. Nürburgring. 15 laps of a 14.189-mile circuit = 212.835 miles. Warm, dry and sunny. World Championship round 7

1	Denny Hulme	Brabham BT24-Repco	15	2h05m55.7
2	Jack Brabham	Brabham BT24-Repco	15	2h06m34.2
3	Chris Amon	Ferrari 312	15	2h06m34.7
4	John Surtees	Honda RA273	15	2h08m21.4
5	Jo Bonnier	Cooper T81-Maserati	15	2h14m37.8
6	Guy Ligier	Brabham BT20-Repco	14	

Winner's average speed: 101.408 mph. Starting grid front row: Clark, 8m04.1 (pole), Hulme, 8m13.5, Stewart, 8m15.2 and Gurney, 8m16.9. Fastest lap: Gurney, 8m15.1. Leaders: Clark, laps 1-3; Gurney, 4-12; Hulme, 13-15

Canadian Grand Prix

27 August 1967. Mosport Park. 90 laps of a 2.459-mile circuit = 221.310 miles. Wet. World Championship round 8

1	Jack Brabham	Brabham BT24-Repco	90	2h40m40.0
2	Denny Hulme	Brabham BT24-Repco	90	2h41m41.9
3	Dan Gurney	Eagle AAR103-Weslake	89	
4	Graham Hill	Lotus 49-Ford	88	
5	Mike Spence	BRM P83	87	
6	Chris Amon	Ferrari 312	87	

Winner's average speed: 82.647 mph. Starting grid front row: Clark, 1m22.4 (pole), Hill, 1m22.7 and Hulme, 1m23.2. Fastest lap: Clark, 1m23.1. Leaders: Clark, laps 1-3, 58-67; Hulme, 4-57; Brabham, 68-90

Gran Premio d'Italia

10 September 1967. Monza. 68 laps of a 3.573-mile circuit = 242.964 miles. Warm, dry and sunny. World Championship round 9. Also known as the European Grand Prix

1	John Surtees	Honda RA300	68	1h43m45.0
2	Jack Brabham	Brabham BT24-Repco	68	1h43m45.2
3	Jim Clark	Lotus 49-Ford	68	1h44m08.1
4	Jochen Rindt	Cooper T81-Maserati	68	1h44m41.6
5	Mike Spence	BRM P83	67	
6	Jacky Ickx	Cooper T81B-Maserati	66	

Winner's average speed: 140.509 mph. Starting grid front row: Clark, 1m28.50 (pole), Brabham, 1m28.80 and McLaren, 1m29.31. Fastest lap: Clark, 1m28.5. Leaders: Gurney, laps 1-2; Clark, 3-9, 11-12, 61-67; Hulme, 10, 13-15, 17, 24-27; Brabham, 16, 59-60; Hill, 18-23, 28-58; Surtees, 68

United States Grand Prix

1 October 1967. Watkins Glen. 108 laps of a 2.350-mile circuit = 253.800 miles. Warm, dry and sunny. World Championship round 10

1	Jim Clark	Lotus 49-Ford	108	2h03m13.2
2	Graham Hill	Lotus 49-Ford	108	2h03m19.5
3	Denny Hulme	Brabham BT24-Repco	107	
4	Jo Siffert	Cooper T81-Maserati	106	
5	Jack Brabham	Brabham BT24-Repco	104	
6	Jo Bonnier	Cooper T81-Maserati	101	

Winner's average speed: 123.584 mph. Starting grid front row: Hill, 1m05.48 (pole) and Clark, 1m06.07. Fastest lap: Hill, 1m06.00. Leaders: Hill, laps 1-40; Clark, 41-108

World Championship Grand Prix Racing

Gran Premio de Mexico

22 October 1967. Mexico City. 65 laps of a 3.107-mile circuit = 201.955 miles. Warm, dry and sunny. World Championship round 11

1	Jim Clark	Lotus 49-Ford	65	1h59m28.70
2	Jack Brabham	Brabham BT24-Repco	65	2h00m54.06
3	Denny Hulme	Brabham BT24-Repco	64	
4	John Surtees	Honda RA300	64	
5	Mike Spence	BRM P83	63	
6	Pedro Rodriguez	Cooper T81B-Maserati	63	

Winner's average speed: 101.418 mph. Starting grid front row: Clark, 1m47.56 (pole) and Amon, 1m48.04. Fastest lap: Clark, 1m48.13. Leaders: Hill, laps 1-2; Clark, 3-65

1967 FINAL CHAMPIONSHIP POSITIONS

Drivers

1	Denny Hulme	51
2	Jack Brabham	46 (48)*
3	Jim Clark	41
4=	Chris Amon	20
	John Surtees	20
6=	Graham Hill	15
	Pedro Rodriguez	15
8	Dan Gurney	13
9	Jackie Stewart	10
10	Mike Spence	9
11=	John Love	6
	Jochen Rindt	6
	Jo Siffert	6
14=	Jo Bonnier	3
	Bruce McLaren	3

16=	Bob Anderson	2
	Chris Irwin	2
	Michael Parkes	2
19=	Jacky Ickx	1
	Guy Ligier	1
	Ludovico Scarfiotti	1

*Sum of best five results from the first six races and best four results from final five races

Manufacturers

1	Brabham-Repco	63 (67)*
2	Lotus-Ford	44
3	Cooper-Maserati	28
4=	Ferrari	20
	Honda	20
6	BRM	17
7	Eagle-Weslake	13
8=	Cooper-Climax	6
	Lotus-BRM	6
10	McLaren-BRM	3
11	Brabham-Climax	2

*Sum of best five results from the first six races and best four results from final five races. Points only awarded to first car to finish for each manufacturer

1968

On 7 April 1968, Jim Clark crashed during the Deutschland Trophäe F2 race at Hockenheim. The cause is still something of a mystery, but the man who had set the pace in Formula One for six years was dead. Motor racing was sent into a state of shock, and the added deaths of Ludovico Scarfiotti in a hill climb, Mike Spence during practice at Indianapolis, and Jo Schlesser at the French GP further compounded a black year for the sport.

The responsibility for lifting the Lotus team after Hockenheim was grasped by Graham Hill, who won the next two Grands Prix and would eventually become World Champion for a second time. Lotus also gave Mario Andretti his first chance in F1 at Watkins Glen and the young Indycar star responded by putting his car on pole for his debut.

The Ford Cosworth DFV was now widely available, and there were first wins for both McLaren and the Ken Tyrrell-run Matra team using the engine. In addition Jo Siffert, driving for Rob Walker, and Jacky Ickx each scored their first Grand Prix victory.

Technically, the most visible development was the introduction of aerodynamic wings, improving downforce and therefore increasing cornering speeds.

So often the innovators, Team Lotus brought Indianapolis-style commercial sponsorship to Grand Prix racing in 1968, repainting its cars red and white in deference to Gold Leaf cigarettes.

South African Grand Prix

1 January 1968. Kyalami. 80 laps of a 2.550-mile circuit = 204.000 miles. Very hot, dry and sunny. World Championship round 1

1	Jim Clark	Lotus 49-Ford	80	1h53m56.6
2	Graham Hill	Lotus 49-Ford	80	1h54m21.9
3	Jochen Rindt	Brabham BT24-Repco	80	1h54m27.0
4	Chris Amon	Ferrari 312	78	
5	Denny Hulme	McLaren M5A-BRM	78	
6	Jean-Pierre Beltoise	Matra MS7-Cosworth	77	

Winner's average speed: 107.422 mph. Starting grid front row: Clark, 1m21.6 (pole), Hill, 1m22.6 and Stewart, 1m22.7. Fastest lap: Clark, 1m23.7. Leaders: Stewart, lap 1; Clark, laps 2-80

Gran Premio de Espana

12 May 1968. Jarama. 90 laps of a 2.115-mile circuit = 190.350 miles. Hot, dry and sunny. World Championship round 2

1	Graham Hill	Lotus 49-Ford	90	2h15m20.1
2	Denny Hulme	McLaren M7A-Ford	90	2h15m36.0
3	Brian Redman	Cooper T86B-BRM	89	
4	Ludovico Scarfiotti	Cooper T86B-BRM	89	
5	Jean-Pierre Beltoise	Matra MS10-Ford	81	

No other finishers. Winner's average speed: 84.407 mph. Starting grid front row: Amon, 1m27.9 (pole), Rodriguez, 1m28.1 and Hulme, 1m28.3. Fastest lap: Beltoise, 1m28.3. Leaders: Rodriguez, laps 1-11; Beltoise, 12-15; Amon, 16-57; Hill, 58-90

Grand Prix de Monaco

26 May 1968. Monte Carlo. 80 laps of a 1.954-mile circuit = 156.320 miles. Warm, dry and sunny. World Championship round 3

1	Graham Hill	Lotus 49B-Ford	80	2h00m32.3
2	Richard Attwood	BRM P126	80	2h00m34.5
3	Lucien Bianchi	Cooper T86B-BRM	76	
4	Ludovico Scarfiotti	Cooper T86B-BRM	76	
5	Denny Hulme	McLaren M7A-Ford	73	

No other finishers. Winner's average speed: 77.811 mph. Starting grid front row: Hill, 1m28.2 (pole) and Servoz-Gavin, 1m28.8. Fastest lap: Attwood, 1m28.1. Leaders: Servoz-Gavin, laps 1-3; Hill, 4-80

Grand Prix de Belgique

9 June 1968. Spa-Francorchamps. 28 laps of a 8.761-mile circuit = 245.308 miles. Dry and overcast. World Championship round 4

1	Bruce McLaren	McLaren M7A-Ford	28	1h40m02.1
2	Pedro Rodriguez	BRM P133	28	1h40m14.2
3	Jacky Ickx	Ferrari 312	28	1h40m41.7
4	Jackie Stewart*	Matra MS10-Ford	27	

1968 DRIVERS' RECORDS

Driver	Car	South African GP	Spanish GP	Monaco GP	Belgian GP	Dutch GP	French GP	British GP	German GP	Italian GP	Canadian GP	United States GP	Mexican GP
Andrea de Adamich	Ferrari 312	R	-	-	-	-	-	-	-	-	-	-	-
Kurt Ahrens Jr	Brabham BT24-Repco	-	-	-	-	-	-	-	12	-	-	-	-
Chris Amon	Ferrari 312	4	R^P	-	R^P	6^P	10	2	R	R	R	R	R
Mario Andretti	Lotus 49B-Ford	-	-	-	-	-	-	-	-	DNS	-	R^P	-
Richard Attwood	BRM P126	-	-	2^F	R	7	7	R	14	-	-	-	-
Derek Bell	Ferrari 312	-	-	-	-	-	-	-	-	R	-	R	-
Jean-Pierre Beltoise	Matra MS7-Cosworth	6	-	-	-	-	-	-	-	-	-	-	-
	Matra MS10-Ford	-	5^F	-	-	-	-	-	-	-	-	-	-
	Matra MS11	-	-	R	8	2^F	9	R	R	5	R	R	R
Lucien Bianchi	Cooper T86B-BRM	-	-	3	6	R	-	-	R	-	NC	R	R
Jo Bonnier	Cooper T81-Maserati	R	-	-	-	-	-	-	-	-	-	-	-
	McLaren M5A-BRM	-	-	DNQ	R	8	-	R	-	6	R	NC	-
	Honda RA301	-	-	-	-	-	-	-	-	-	-	-	5
Jack Brabham	Brabham BT24-Repco	R	-	-	-	-	-	-	-	-	-	-	-
	Brabham BT26-Repco	-	DNS	R	R	R	R	R	5	R	R	R	10
Bill Brack	Lotus 49B-Ford	-	-	-	-	-	-	-	-	-	R	-	-
Dave Charlton	Brabham BT11-Repco	R	-	-	-	-	-	-	-	-	-	-	-
Jim Clark	Lotus 49-Ford	1^{PF}	-	-	-	-	-	-	-	-	-	-	-
Piers Courage	BRM P126	-	R	R	R	R	6	8	8	4	R	7	R
Vic Elford	Cooper T86B-BRM	-	-	-	-	-	4	R	R	R	5	R	8
Frank Gardner	BRM P261	-	-	-	-	-	-	-	-	DNQ	-	-	-
Dan Gurney	Eagle AAR104-Weslake	R	-	R	-	-	-	R	9	R	-	-	-
	Brabham BT24-Repco	-	-	-	-	R	-	-	-	-	-	-	-
	McLaren M7A-Ford	-	-	-	-	-	-	-	-	-	R	4	R
Hubert Hahne	Lola T100-BMW	-	-	-	-	-	-	-	10	-	-	-	-
Graham Hill	Lotus 49-Ford	2	1	-	-	-	-	-	-	-	-	-	-
	Lotus 49B-Ford	-	-	1^P	R	9	R	R^P	2	R	4	2	1
David Hobbs	Honda RA301	-	-	-	-	-	-	-	-	R	-	-	-
Denny Hulme	McLaren M5A-BRM	5	-	-	-	-	-	-	-	-	-	-	-
	McLaren M7A-Ford	-	2	5	R	R	5	4	7	1	1	R	R
Jacky Ickx	Ferrari 312	R	R	-	3	4	1	3	4^P	3	DNS	-	R
John Love	Brabham BT20-Repco	9	-	-	-	-	-	-	-	-	-	-	-
Bruce McLaren	McLaren M7A-Ford	-	R	R	1	R	8	7	13	R	2	6	2
Silvio Moser	Brabham BT20-Repco	-	-	DNQ	-	5	-	NC	DNQ	DNQ	-	-	-
Jackie Oliver	Lotus 49-Ford	-	-	R	-	-	-	R	-	-	-	-	-
	Lotus 49B-Ford	-	-	-	5	NC	DNS	-	11	R^F	R	DNS	3
Al Pease	Eagle AAR101-Climax	-	-	-	-	-	-	-	-	-	DNS	-	-
Henri Pescarolo	Matra MS11	-	-	-	-	-	-	-	-	-	R	DNS	9
Jackie Pretorius	Brabham BT7-Climax	NC	-	-	-	-	-	-	-	-	-	-	-
Brian Redman	Cooper T81B-Maserati	R	-	-	-	-	-	-	-	-	-	-	-
	Cooper T86B-BRM	-	3	-	R	-	-	-	-	-	-	-	-
Jochen Rindt	Brabham BT24-Repco	3	R	R	-	-	-	-	-	-	-	-	-
	Brabham BT26-Repco	-	-	-	R	R	R^P	R	3	R	R^P	R	R
Pedro Rodriguez	BRM P126	R	-	-	-	-	-	-	-	-	-	-	-
	BRM P133	-	R	R	2	3	12^F	R	6	-	3	R	4
	BRM P138	-	-	-	-	-	-	-	-	R	-	-	-
Basil van Rooyen	Cooper T75-Climax	R	-	-	-	-	-	-	-	-	-	-	-
Ludovico Scarfiotti	Cooper T86-Maserati	R	-	-	-	-	-	-	-	-	-	-	-
	Cooper T86B-BRM	-	4	4	-	-	-	-	-	-	-	-	-
Jo Schlesser	Honda RA302	-	-	-	-	-	R	-	-	-	-	-	-
Johnny Servoz-Gavin	Matra MS10-Ford	-	-	R	-	-	-	-	-	2	R	-	11
	Cooper T86B-BRM	-	-	-	-	-	R	-	-	-	-	-	-
Jo Siffert	Cooper T81-Maserati	7	-	-	-	-	-	-	-	-	-	-	-
	Lotus 49-Ford	-	R	R	7	R	11	-	-	-	-	-	-
	Lotus 49B-Ford	-	-	-	-	-	-	1^F	R	R	R^F	5	6^{PF}
Moises Solana	Lotus 49B-Ford	-	-	-	-	-	-	-	-	-	-	-	R
Mike Spence	BRM P83	R	-	-	-	-	-	-	-	-	-	-	-
Jackie Stewart	Matra MS9-Ford	R	-	-	-	-	-	-	-	-	-	-	-
	Matra MS10-Ford	-	-	-	4	1	3	6	1^F	R	6	1^F	7
John Surtees	Honda RA300	8	-	-	-	-	-	-	-	-	-	-	-
	Honda RA301	-	R	R	R^F	R	2	5	R	R^P	R	3	R
Sam Tingle	LDS Mk5-Repco	R	-	-	-	-	-	-	-	-	-	-	-
Bobby Unser	BRM P126	-	-	-	-	-	-	-	-	DNS	-	-	-
	BRM P138	-	-	-	-	-	-	-	-	-	-	R	-
Robin Widdows	Cooper T86B-BRM	-	-	-	-	-	-	R	-	-	-	-	-

World Championship Grand Prix Racing

5 Jackie Oliver	Lotus 49B-Ford	26	driveshaft
6 Lucien Bianchi	Cooper T86B-BRM	26	

*Stewart penalized one lap for completing his final lap in over twice the time of the race winner's fastest lap, a local rule. Winner's average speed: 147.133 mph. Starting grid front row: Amon, 3m28.6 (pole), Stewart, 3m32.3 and Ickx, 3m34.3. Fastest lap: Surtees, 3m30.5. Leaders: Amon, lap 1; Surtees, laps 2-10; Hulme, 11, 15; Stewart, 12-14, 16-27; McLaren, 28

Grote Prijs van Nederland

23 June 1968. Zandvoort. 90 laps of a 2.605-mile circuit = 234.450 miles. Heavy showers. World Championship round 5

1 Jackie Stewart	Matra MS10-Ford	90	2h46m11.26
2 Jean-Pierre Beltoise	Matra MS11	90	2h47m45.19
3 Pedro Rodriguez	BRM P133	89	
4 Jacky Ickx	Ferrari 312	88	
5 Silvio Moser	Brabham BT20-Repco	87	
6 Chris Amon	Ferrari 312	85	

Winner's average speed: 84.645 mph. Starting grid front row: Amon, 1m23.54 (pole), Rindt, 1m23.70 and Hill, 1m23.84. Fastest lap: Beltoise, 1m45.91. Leaders: Hill, laps 1-3; Stewart, 4-90

Grand Prix de France

7 July 1968. Rouen-les-Essarts. 60 laps of a 4.065-mile circuit = 243.900 miles. Wet. World Championship round 6

1 Jacky Ickx	Ferrari 312	60	2h25m40.9
2 John Surtees	Honda RA301	60	2h27m39.5
3 Jackie Stewart	Matra MS10-Ford	59	
4 Vic Elford	Cooper T86B-BRM	58	
5 Denny Hulme	McLaren M7A-Ford	58	
6 Piers Courage	BRM P126	57	

Winner's average speed: 100.452 mph. Starting grid front row: Rindt, 1m56.1 (pole), Stewart, 1m57.3 and Ickx, 1m57.7. Fastest lap: Rodriguez, 2m11.5. Leaders: Ickx, laps 1-18, 20-60; Rodriguez, 19

British Grand Prix

20 July 1968. Brands Hatch. 80 laps of a 2.650-mile circuit = 212.000 miles. Warm, dry and sunny. World Championship round 7

1 Jo Siffert	Lotus 49B-Ford	80	2h01m20.3
2 Chris Amon	Ferrari 312	80	2h01m24.7
3 Jacky Ickx	Ferrari 312	79	
4 Denny Hulme	McLaren M7A-Ford	79	
5 John Surtees	Honda RA301	78	
6 Jackie Stewart	Matra MS10-Ford	78	

Winner's average speed: 104.831 mph. Starting grid front row: Hill, 1m28.9 (pole), Oliver, 1m29.4 and Amon, 1m29.5. Fastest lap: Siffert, 1m29.7. Leaders: Oliver, laps 1-3, 27-43; Hill, 4-26; Siffert, 44-80

Grosser Preis von Deutschland

4 August 1968. Nürburgring. 14 laps of a 14.189-mile circuit = 198.646 miles. Very wet and foggy. World Championship round 8. Also known as the European Grand Prix

1 Jackie Stewart	Matra MS10-Ford	14	2h19m03.2
2 Graham Hill	Lotus 49B-Ford	14	2h23m06.4
3 Jochen Rindt	Brabham BT26-Repco	14	2h23m12.6
4 Jacky Ickx	Ferrari 312	14	2h24m58.4
5 Jack Brabham	Brabham BT26-Repco	14	2h25m24.3
6 Pedro Rodriguez	BRM P133	14	2h25m28.2

Winner's average speed: 85.714 mph. Starting grid front row: Ickx, 9m04.0 (pole), Amon, 9m14.9 and Rindt, 9m31.9. Fastest lap: Stewart, 9m36.0. Leaders: Stewart, laps 1-14

Gran Premio d'Italia

8 September 1968. Monza. 68 laps of a 3.573-mile circuit = 242.964 miles. Hot, dry and sunny. World Championship round 9

1 Denny Hulme	McLaren M7A-Ford	68	1h40m14.8
2 Johnny Servoz-Gavin	Matra MS10-Ford	68	1h41m43.2
3 Jacky Ickx	Ferrari 312	68	1h41m43.4
4 Piers Courage	BRM P126	67	
5 Jean-Pierre Beltoise	Matra MS11	66	
6 Jo Bonnier	McLaren M5A-BRM	64	

Winner's average speed: 145.420 mph. Starting grid front row: Surtees, 1m26.07 (pole), McLaren, 1m26.11 and Amon, 1m26.21. Fastest lap: McLaren, 1m26.5. Leaders: McLaren, laps 1-6, 8-12, 14; Surtees, 7; Stewart, 13, 17-18, 27, 30, 33, 40; Siffert, 15-16; Hulme, 19-26, 28-29, 31-32, 34-39, 41-68

Grand Prix du Canada

22 September 1968. St Jovite. 90 laps of a 2.650-mile circuit = 238.500 miles. Warm, dry and sunny. World Championship round 10

1 Denny Hulme	McLaren M7A-Ford	90	2h27m11.2
2 Bruce McLaren	McLaren M7A-Ford	89	
3 Pedro Rodriguez	BRM P133	88	
4 Graham Hill	Lotus 49B-Ford	86	
5 Vic Elford	Cooper T86B-BRM	86	
6 Jackie Stewart	Matra MS10-Ford	83	

Winner's average speed: 97.223 mph. Starting grid front row: Rindt, 1m33.8 (pole), Amon, 1m33.8 and Siffert, 1m34.5. Fastest lap: Siffert, 1m35.1. Leaders: Amon, laps 1-72; Hulme, 73-90

United States Grand Prix

6 October 1968. Watkins Glen. 108 laps of a 2.350-mile circuit = 253.800 miles. Dry and overcast. World Championship round 11

1 Jackie Stewart	Matra MS10-Ford	108	1h59m20.29
2 Graham Hill	Lotus 49B-Ford	108	1h59m44.97
3 John Surtees	Honda RA301	107	
4 Dan Gurney	McLaren M7A-Ford	107	
5 Jo Siffert	Lotus 49B-Ford	105	
6 Bruce McLaren	McLaren M7A-Ford	103	

Winner's average speed: 127.604 mph. Starting grid front row: Andretti, 1m04.20 (pole) and Stewart, 1m04.27. Fastest lap: Stewart, 1m05.22. Leaders: Stewart, laps 1-108

Graham Hill's Lotus, complete with high rear wing, approaches Druids Hill Bend during the British Grand Prix

Gran Premio de Mexico

3 November 1968. Mexico City. 65 laps of a 3.107-mile circuit = 201.955 miles. Warm, dry and sunny. World Championship round 12

1 Graham Hill	Lotus 49B-Ford	65	1h56m43.95
2 Bruce McLaren	McLaren M7A-Ford	65	1h58m03.27
3 Jackie Oliver	Lotus 49B-Ford	65	1h58m24.60
4 Pedro Rodriguez	BRM P133	65	1h58m25.04
5 Jo Bonnier	Honda RA301	64	
6 Jo Siffert	Lotus 49B-Ford	64	

Winner's average speed: 103.804 mph. Starting grid front row: Siffert, 1m45.22 (pole) and Amon, 1m45.62. Fastest lap: Siffert, 1m44.23. Leaders: Hill, laps 1-4, 9-21, 25-65; Stewart, 5-8; Siffert, 22-24

1968 FINAL CHAMPIONSHIP POSITIONS

Drivers						Manufacturers		
1	Graham Hill	48		13=	Richard Attwood	6	1 Lotus-Ford	62
2	Jackie Stewart	36			Jackie Oliver	6	2 McLaren-Ford	49
3	Denny Hulme	33			Ludovico Scarfiotti	6	3 Matra-Ford	45
4	Jacky Ickx	27			Johnny Servoz-Gavin	6	4 Ferrari	32
5	Bruce McLaren	22		17=	Lucien Bianchi	5	5 BRM	28
6	Pedro Rodriguez	18			Vic Elford	5	6= Cooper-BRM	14
7=	Jo Siffert	12		19=	Piers Courage	4	Honda	14
	John Surtees	12			Brian Redman	4	8 Brabham-Repco	10
9	Jean-Pierre Beltoise	11		21=	Jo Bonnier	3	9 Matra	8
10	Chris Amon	10			Dan Gurney	3	10 McLaren-BRM	3
11	Jim Clark	9		23=	Jack Brabham	2	Points only awarded to first car
12	Jochen Rindt	8			Silvio Moser	2	to finish for each manufacturer

1969

Jackie Stewart had won three Grands Prix in Ken Tyrrell's Matra-Ford during the previous year, and it was no surprise when the combination dominated the 1969 series.

The Spanish GP at Barcelona's Montjuich Park brought to a head safety concerns regarding the high aerodynamic wings. Both works Lotus 49s, driven by Graham Hill and Jochen Rindt, crashed heavily after their wings collapsed due to the downforce they were generating.

Jackie Stewart secured the first of his three world titles for Ken Tyrrell in the Matra MS80-Ford

An emergency meeting of the CSI at Monaco banned unrestricted wings with immediate effect. The teams argued that this would make the cars more dangerous as they had been designed around these wings, so that simply removing them would make the cars unstable. Shades of 1994...

Graham Hill won at Monaco for the fifth time, a record which would stand until Ayrton Senna's sixth victory in 1993. As so often before the introduction of its chicanes, Monza provided the best race of the year, Jackie Stewart winning a four-car slip-streaming battle to clinch the World Championship.

Four-wheel-drive was seen as the next logical step in Formula One design, and both Matra and Lotus introduced new cars at the Dutch GP, with the McLaren version joining the grid for the British GP. The first such Grand Prix car had in fact been the Ferguson P99, and Matra's system was developed by Ferguson. Four-wheel-drive, however, proved to be an expensive distraction.

With Ferrari and BRM both uncompetitive and Matra taking a sabbatical from engine supply, the Ford DFV won every round of the championship.

South African Grand Prix

1 March 1969. Kyalami. 80 laps of a 2.550-mile circuit = 204.000 miles. Hot, dry and sunny. World Championship round 1

1 Jackie Stewart	Matra MS10-Ford	80	1h50m39.1
2 Graham Hill	Lotus 49B-Ford	80	1h50m57.9
3 Denny Hulme	McLaren M7A-Ford	80	1h51m10.9
4 Jo Siffert	Lotus 49B-Ford	80	1h51m28.3
5 Bruce McLaren	McLaren M7A-Ford	79	
6 Jean-Pierre Beltoise	Matra MS10-Ford	78	

Winner's average speed: 110.617 mph. Starting grid front row: Brabham, 1m20.0 (pole), Rindt, 1m20.2 and Hulme, 1m20.3. Fastest lap: Stewart, 1m21.6. Leaders: Stewart, laps 1-80

Gran Premio de Espana

4 May 1969. Montjuich Park. 90 laps of a 2.355-mile circuit = 211.950 miles. Warm, dry and sunny. World Championship round 2

1 Jackie Stewart	Matra MS80-Ford	90	2h16m53.99
2 Bruce McLaren	McLaren M7C-Ford	88	
3 Jean-Pierre Beltoise	Matra MS80-Ford	87	
4 Denny Hulme	McLaren M7A-Ford	87	
5 John Surtees	BRM P138	84	
6 Jacky Ickx	Brabham BT26-Ford	83	suspension

Winner's average speed: 92.893 mph. Starting grid front row: Rindt, 1m25.7 (pole), Amon, 1m26.2 and Hill, 1m26.6. Fastest lap: Rindt, 1m28.3. Leaders: Rindt, laps 1-19; Amon, 20-56; Stewart, 57-90

Grand Prix de Monaco

18 May 1969. Monte Carlo. 80 laps of a 1.954-mile circuit = 156.320 miles. Warm, dry and overcast. World Championship round 3

1 Graham Hill	Lotus 49B-Ford	80	1h56m59.4
2 Piers Courage	Brabham BT26-Ford	80	1h57m16.7
3 Jo Siffert	Lotus 49B-Ford	80	1h57m34.0
4 Richard Attwood	Lotus 49-Ford	80	1h57m52.3
5 Bruce McLaren	McLaren M7C-Ford	79	
6 Denny Hulme	McLaren M7A-Ford	78	

Winner's average speed: 80.171 mph. Starting grid front row: Stewart, 1m24.6 (pole) and Amon, 1m25.0. Fastest lap: Stewart, 1m25.1. Leaders: Stewart, laps 1-22; Hill, 23-80

Grote Prijs van Nederland

21 June 1969. Zandvoort. 90 laps of a 2.605-mile circuit = 234.450 miles. Warm, dry and sunny. World Championship round 4

1 Jackie Stewart	Matra MS80-Ford	90	2h06m42.08
2 Jo Siffert	Lotus 49B-Ford	90	2h07m06.60
3 Chris Amon	Ferrari 312	90	2h07m12.59
4 Denny Hulme	McLaren M7A-Ford	90	2h07m19.24
5 Jacky Ickx	Brabham BT26-Ford	90	2h07m19.75
6 Jack Brabham	Brabham BT26-Ford	90	2h07m52.89

Winner's average speed: 111.025 mph. Starting grid front row: Rindt, 1m20.85 (pole), Stewart, 1m21.14 and Hill, 1m22.01. Fastest lap: Stewart, 1m22.94. Leaders: Hill, laps 1-2; Rindt, 3-16; Stewart, 17-90

Grand Prix de France

6 July 1969. Clermont-Ferrand. 38 laps of a 5.005-mile circuit = 190.190 miles. Warm, dry and sunny. World Championship round 5

1	Jackie Stewart	Matra MS80-Ford	38	1h56m47.4
2	Jean-Pierre Beltoise	Matra MS80-Ford	38	1h57m44.5
3	Jacky Ickx	Brabham BT26-Ford	38	1h57m44.7
4	Bruce McLaren	McLaren M7C-Ford	37	
5	Vic Elford	McLaren M7A/M7B-Ford	37	
6	Graham Hill	Lotus 49B-Ford	37	

Winner's average speed: 97.709 mph. Starting grid front row: Stewart, 3m00.6 (pole) and Hulme, 3m02.4. Fastest lap: Stewart, 3m02.7. Leaders: Stewart, laps 1-38

1969 DRIVERS' RECORDS

Driver	Car	South African GP	Spanish GP	Monaco GP	Dutch GP	French GP	British GP	German GP	Italian GP	Canadian GP	United States GP	Mexican GP
Kurt Ahrens Jr	Brabham BT30-Cosworth	-	-	-	-	-	-	F2	-	-	-	-
Chris Amon	Ferrari 312	R	R	R	3	10	R	-	-	-	-	-
Mario Andretti	Lotus 49B-Ford	R	-	-	-	-	-	-	-	-	-	-
	Lotus 63-Ford	-	-	-	-	-	-	R	-	R	-	-
Richard Attwood	Lotus 49-Ford	-	-	4	-	-	-	-	-	-	-	-
	Brabham BT30-Cosworth	-	-	-	-	-	-	F2	-	-	-	-
Derek Bell	McLaren M9A-Ford	-	-	-	-	-	R	-	-	-	-	-
Jean-Pierre Beltoise	Matra MS10-Ford	6	-	-	-	-	-	-	-	-	-	-
	Matra MS80-Ford	-	3	R	8	2	-	6	3F	4	R	5
	Matra MS84-Ford	-	-	-	-	-	9	-	-	-	-	-
Jo Bonnier	Lotus 63-Ford	-	-	-	-	-	R	-	-	-	-	-
	Lotus 49B-Ford	-	-	-	-	-	-	R	-	-	-	-
Jack Brabham	Brabham BT26-Ford	RP	R	R	6	-	-	-	R	2F	4	3P
Bill Brack	BRM P138	-	-	-	-	-	-	-	-	NC	-	-
Tino Brambilla	Ferrari 312	-	-	-	-	-	-	-	DNS	-	-	-
François Cevert	Tecno 306-Cosworth	-	-	-	-	-	-	F2	-	-	-	-
John Cordts	Brabham BT23B-Ford	-	-	-	-	-	-	-	-	R	-	-
Piers Courage	Brabham BT26-Ford	-	R	2	R	R	5	R	5	R	2	10
George Eaton	BRM P138	-	-	-	-	-	-	-	-	-	R	-
	BRM P139	-	-	-	-	-	-	-	-	-	-	R
Vic Elford	Cooper T86B-Maserati	-	-	7	-	-	-	-	-	-	-	-
	McLaren M7A/M7B-Ford	-	-	-	10	5	6	R	-	-	-	-
Graham Hill	Lotus 49B-Ford	2	R	1	7	6	7	4	9	R	R	-
Denny Hulme	McLaren M7A-Ford	3	4	6	4	8	R	R	7	R	R	1
Jacky Ickx	Brabham BT26-Ford	R	6	R	5	3	2	1PF	10	1PF	R	2F
Piet de Klerk	Brabham BT20-Repco	R	-	-	-	-	-	-	-	-	-	-
John Love	Lotus 49-Ford	R	-	-	-	-	-	-	-	-	-	-
Pete Lovely	Lotus 49B-Ford	-	-	-	-	-	-	-	-	7	R	9
Bruce McLaren	McLaren M7A-Ford	5	-	-	-	-	-	-	-	-	-	-
	McLaren M7C-Ford	-	2	5	R	4	3	3	4	5	DNS	DNS
John Miles	Lotus 63-Ford	-	-	-	-	R	10	-	R	R	-	R
Silvio Moser	Brabham BT24-Ford	-	-	R	R	7	-	-	R	R	6	11
Jackie Oliver	BRM P133	7	R	R	R	-	R	-	-	-	-	-
	BRM P138	-	-	-	-	-	-	R	-	-	-	-
	BRM P139	-	-	-	-	-	-	-	R	R	R	6
Al Pease	Eagle AAR101-Climax	-	-	-	-	-	-	-	-	R	-	-
Xavier Perrot	Brabham BT23C-Cosworth	-	-	-	-	-	-	F2	-	-	-	-
Henri Pescarolo	Matra MS7-Cosworth	-	-	-	-	-	-	F2	-	-	-	-
Jochen Rindt	Lotus 49B-Ford	R	RPF	-	RP	R	4P	R	2P	3	1PF	R
Pedro Rodriguez	BRM P126	R	7	R	-	-	-	-	-	-	-	-
	Ferrari 312	-	-	-	-	-	R	-	6	R	5	7
Basil van Rooyen	McLaren M7A-Ford	R	-	-	-	-	-	-	-	-	-	-
Johnny Servoz-Gavin	Matra MS7-Cosworth	-	-	-	-	-	-	F2	-	-	-	-
	Matra MS84-Ford	-	-	-	-	-	-	-	-	6	7	8
Jo Siffert	Lotus 49B-Ford	4	R	3	2	9	8	5	8	R	R	R
Jackie Stewart	Matra MS10-Ford	1F	-	-	-	-	-	-	-	-	-	-
	Matra MS80-Ford	-	1	RPF	1F	1PF	1F	2	1	R	R	4
Rolf Stommelen	Lotus 59B-Cosworth	-	-	-	-	-	-	F2	-	-	-	-
John Surtees	BRM P138	R	5	R	9	-	-	-	-	-	-	-
	BRM P139	-	-	-	-	-	R	DNS	11	R	3	R
Sam Tingle	Brabham BT24-Repco	8	-	-	-	-	-	-	-	-	-	-
Peter Westbury	Brabham BT30-Cosworth	-	-	-	-	-	-	F2	-	-	-	-

British Grand Prix

19 July 1969. Silverstone. 84 laps of a 2.927-mile circuit = 245.868 miles. Dry and overcast. World Championship round 6

1 Jackie Stewart	Matra MS80-Ford	84	1h55m55.6
2 Jacky Ickx	Brabham BT26-Ford	83	
3 Bruce McLaren	McLaren M7C-Ford	83	
4 Jochen Rindt	Lotus 49B-Ford	83	
5 Piers Courage	Brabham BT26-Ford	83	
6 Vic Elford	McLaren M7A/M7B-Ford	82	

Winner's average speed: 127.254 mph. Starting grid front row: Rindt, 1m20.8 (pole), Stewart, 1m21.2 and Hulme, 1m21.5. Fastest lap: Stewart, 1m21.3. Leaders: Rindt, laps 1-5, 16-61; Stewart, 6-15, 62-84

Grosser Preis von Deutschland

3 August 1969. Nürburgring. 14 laps of a 14.189-mile circuit = 198.646 miles. Warm, dry and sunny. World Championship round 7

1 Jacky Ickx	Brabham BT26-Ford	14	1h49m55.4
2 Jackie Stewart	Matra MS80-Ford	14	1h50m53.1
3 Bruce McLaren	McLaren M7C-Ford	14	1h53m17.0
4 Graham Hill	Lotus 49B-Ford	14	1h53m54.2
5 Jo Siffert	Lotus 49B-Ford	12	accident
6 Jean-Pierre Beltoise	Matra MS80-Ford	12	upright

Winner's average speed: 108.428 mph. Starting grid front row: Ickx, 7m42.1 (pole), Stewart, 7m42.4 and Rindt, 7m48.0. Fastest lap: Ickx, 7m43.8. Leaders: Stewart, laps 1-6; Ickx, 7-14

Gran Premio d'Italia

7 September 1969. Monza. 68 laps of a 3.573-mile circuit = 242.964 miles. Warm, dry and sunny. World Championship round 8

1 Jackie Stewart	Matra MS80-Ford	68	1h39m11.26
2 Jochen Rindt	Lotus 49B-Ford	68	1h39m11.34
3 Jean-Pierre Beltoise	Matra MS80-Ford	68	1h39m11.43
4 Bruce McLaren	McLaren M7C-Ford	68	1h39m11.45
5 Piers Courage	Brabham BT26-Ford	68	1h39m44.70
6 Pedro Rodriguez	Ferrari 312	66	

Winner's average speed: 146.972 mph. Starting grid front row: Rindt, 1m25.48 (pole) and Hulme, 1m25.69. Fastest lap: Beltoise, 1m25.2. Leaders: Stewart, laps 1-6, 9-17, 19-24, 28-30, 33, 35-36, 38-68; Rindt, 7, 25-27, 31, 34, 37; Hulme, 8; Courage, 18, 32

Canadian Grand Prix

20 September 1969. Mosport Park. 90 laps of a 2.459-mile circuit = 221.310 miles. Warm, dry and sunny. World Championship round 9

1 Jacky Ickx	Brabham BT26-Ford	90	1h59m25.7
2 Jack Brabham	Brabham BT26-Ford	90	2h00m11.9
3 Jochen Rindt	Lotus 49B-Ford	90	2h00m17.7
4 Jean-Pierre Beltoise	Matra MS80-Ford	89	
5 Bruce McLaren	McLaren M7C-Ford	87	
6 Johnny Servoz-Gavin	Matra MS84-Ford	84	

Winner's average speed: 111.185 mph. Starting grid front row: Ickx, 1m17.4 (pole), Beltoise, 1m17.9 and Rindt, 1m17.9. Fastest lap: Ickx and Brabham, 1m18.1. Leaders: Rindt, laps 1-5; Stewart, 6-32; Ickx, 33-90

United States Grand Prix

5 October 1969. Watkins Glen. 108 laps of a 2.350-mile circuit = 253.800 miles. Hot, dry and sunny. World Championship round 10

1 Jochen Rindt	Lotus 49B-Ford	108	1h57m56.84
2 Piers Courage	Brabham BT26-Ford	108	1h58m43.83
3 John Surtees	BRM P139	106	
4 Jack Brabham	Brabham BT26-Ford	106	
5 Pedro Rodriguez	Ferrari 312	101	
6 Silvio Moser	Brabham BT24-Ford	98	

Winner's average speed: 129.108 mph. Starting grid front row: Rindt, 1m03.62 (pole) and Hulme, 1m03.65. Fastest lap: Rindt, 1m04.34. Leaders: Rindt, laps 1-11, 21-108; Stewart, 12-20

Gran Premio de Mexico

19 October 1969. Mexico City. 65 laps of a 3.107-mile circuit = 201.955 miles. Warm, dry and sunny. World Championship round 11

1 Denny Hulme	McLaren M7A-Ford	65	1h54m08.80
2 Jacky Ickx	Brabham BT26-Ford	65	1h54m11.36
3 Jack Brabham	Brabham BT26-Ford	65	1h54m47.28
4 Jackie Stewart	Matra MS80-Ford	65	1h54m55.84
5 Jean-Pierre Beltoise	Matra MS80-Ford	65	1h55m47.32
6 Jackie Oliver	BRM P139	63	

Winner's average speed: 106.156 mph. Starting grid front row: Brabham, 1m42.90 (pole) and Ickx, 1m43.60. Fastest lap: Ickx, 1m43.05. Leaders: Stewart, laps 1-5; Ickx, 6-9; Hulme, 10-65

1969 FINAL CHAMPIONSHIP POSITIONS

Drivers						Manufacturers		
1	Jackie Stewart	63	10	Jack Brabham	14	1	Matra-Ford	66
2	Jacky Ickx	37	11	John Surtees	6	2	Brabham-Ford	49 (51)*
3	Bruce McLaren	26	12	Chris Amon	4	3	Lotus-Ford	47
4	Jochen Rindt	22	13=	Richard Attwood	3	4	McLaren-Ford	38 (40)*
5	Jean-Pierre Beltoise	21		Vic Elford	3	5=	BRM	7
6	Denny Hulme	20		Pedro Rodriguez	3		Ferrari	7
7	Graham Hill	19	16=	Silvio Moser	1			
8	Piers Courage	16		Jackie Oliver	1			
9	Jo Siffert	15		Johnny Servoz-Gavin	1			

*Sum of best five results from the first six races and best four results from final five races. Points only awarded to first car to finish for each manufacturer

1970

For the only time, Formula One had a posthumous World Champion; overwhelming series leader Jochen Rindt died after crashing his Lotus 72 at Parabolica in practice for the Italian GP. To complete another tragic year, Piers Courage, Rindt's great friend, died in the Dutch GP and Bruce McLaren was killed in private testing at Goodwood.

When Emerson Fittipaldi, the young replacement at Lotus, won the United States GP (in only his fourth start), Rindt's points score could not be overcome by his closest challenger, Jacky Ickx. In addition to Fittipaldi, Clay Regazzoni also scored a victory in his first year of Grand Prix racing driving for Ferrari.

A new marque, March arrived in Formula One amid much hype and publicity. In addition to works entries, Ken Tyrrell bought a March 701 for Jackie Stewart, in which he won in Spain. Meanwhile, in total secrecy the team became a constructor in its own right. Stewart qualified the Tyrrell 001 on pole for its first Grand Prix, the Canadian.

Ford had been unbeaten in 1969 but faced a sterner challenge this year. Rodriguez's BRM won at Spa, and Ferrari returned to form, powering Ickx's late-season charge.

Having started the season with a victory, three-time World Champion Jack Brabham ended it retiring from the sport; designer Ron Tauranac assuming sole leadership of the team.

South African Grand Prix

7 March 1970. Kyalami. 80 laps of a 2.550-mile circuit = 204.000 miles. Very hot, dry and sunny. World Championship round 1

1 Jack Brabham	Brabham BT33-Ford	80	1h49m34.6
2 Denny Hulme	McLaren M14A-Ford	80	1h49m42.7
3 Jackie Stewart	March 701-Ford	80	1h49m51.7
4 Jean-Pierre Beltoise	Matra-Simca MS120	80	1h50m47.7
5 John Miles	Lotus 49C-Ford	79	
6 Graham Hill	Lotus 49C-Ford	79	

Winner's average speed: 111.703 mph. Starting grid front row: Stewart, 1m19.3 (pole), Amon, 1m19.3 and Brabham, 1m19.6. Fastest lap: Surtees and Brabham, 1m20.8. Leaders: Stewart, laps 1-19; Brabham, 20-80

Gran Premio de Espana

19 April 1970. Jarama. 90 laps of a 2.115-mile circuit = 190.350 miles. Very hot, dry and sunny. World Championship round 2

1 Jackie Stewart	March 701-Ford	90	2h10m58.2
2 Bruce McLaren	McLaren M14A-Ford	89	
3 Mario Andretti	March 701-Ford	89	
4 Graham Hill	Lotus 49C-Ford	89	
5 Johnny Servoz-Gavin	March 701-Ford	88	

No other finishers. Winner's average speed: 87.220 mph. Starting grid front row: Brabham, 1m23.9 (pole), Hulme, 1m24.1 and Stewart, 1m24.2. Fastest lap: Brabham, 1m24.3. Leaders: Stewart, laps 1-90

Grand Prix de Monaco

10 May 1970. Monte Carlo. 80 laps of a 1.954-mile circuit = 156.320 miles. Warm, dry and sunny. World Championship round 3

1 Jochen Rindt	Lotus 49C-Ford	80	1h54m36.6
2 Jack Brabham	Brabham BT33-Ford	80	1h54m59.7
3 Henri Pescarolo	Matra-Simca MS120	80	1h55m28.0
4 Denny Hulme	McLaren M14A-Ford	80	1h56m04.9
5 Graham Hill	Lotus 49C-Ford	79	
6 Pedro Rodriguez	BRM P153	78	

Winner's average speed: 81.836 mph. Starting grid front row: Stewart, 1m24.0 (pole) and Amon, 1m24.6. Fastest lap: Rindt, 1m23.2. Leaders: Stewart, laps 1-27; Brabham, 28-79; Rindt, 80

Grand Prix de Belgique

7 June 1970. Spa-Francorchamps. 28 laps of a 8.761-mile circuit = 245.308 miles. Warm, dry and sunny. World Championship round 4

1 Pedro Rodriguez	BRM P153	28	1h38m09.9
2 Chris Amon	March 701-Ford	28	1h38m11.0
3 Jean-Pierre Beltoise	Matra-Simca MS120	28	1h39m53.6
4 Ignazio Giunti	Ferrari 312B	28	1h40m48.4
5 Rolf Stommelen	Brabham BT33-Ford	28	1h41m41.7
6 Henri Pescarolo	Matra-Simca MS120	27	out of fuel

Winner's average speed: 149.936 mph. Starting grid front row: Stewart, 3m28.0 (pole), Rindt, 3m30.1 and Amon, 3m30.3. Fastest lap: Amon, 3m27.4. Leaders: Amon, laps 1, 3-4; Stewart, 2; Rodriguez, 5-28

Grote Prijs van Nederland

21 June 1970. Zandvoort. 80 laps of a 2.605-mile circuit = 208.400 miles. Dry and overcast. World Championship round 5

1 Jochen Rindt	Lotus 72-Ford	80	1h50m43.41
2 Jackie Stewart	March 701-Ford	80	1h51m13.41
3 Jacky Ickx	Ferrari 312B	79	
4 Clay Regazzoni	Ferrari 312B	79	
5 Jean-Pierre Beltoise	Matra-Simca MS120	79	
6 John Surtees	McLaren M7C-Ford	79	

Winner's average speed: 112.930 mph. Starting grid front row: Rindt, 1m18.50 (pole), Stewart, 1m18.73 and Ickx, 1m18.93. Fastest lap: Ickx, 1m19.23. Leaders: Ickx, laps 1-2; Rindt, 3-80

Grand Prix de France

5 July 1970. Clermont-Ferrand. 38 laps of a 5.005-mile circuit = 190.190 miles. Warm, dry and sunny. World Championship round 6

1 Jochen Rindt	Lotus 72-Ford	38	1h55m57.00
2 Chris Amon	March 701-Ford	38	1h56m04.61
3 Jack Brabham	Brabham BT33-Ford	38	1h56m41.83
4 Denny Hulme	McLaren M14D-Ford	38	1h56m42.66
5 Henri Pescarolo	Matra-Simca MS120	38	1h57m16.42
6 Dan Gurney	McLaren M14A-Ford	38	1h57m16.65

Winner's average speed: 98.417 mph. Starting grid front row: Ickx, 2m58.22 (pole) and Beltoise, 2m58.70. Fastest lap: Brabham, 3m00.75. Leaders: Ickx, laps 1-14; Beltoise, 15-25; Rindt, 26-38

British Grand Prix

18 July 1970. Brands Hatch. 80 laps of a 2.650-mile circuit = 212.000 miles. Warm, dry and sunny. World Championship round 7

1 Jochen Rindt	Lotus 72-Ford	80	1h57m02.0
2 Jack Brabham	Brabham BT33-Ford	80	1h57m34.9
3 Denny Hulme	McLaren M14D-Ford	80	1h57m56.4
4 Clay Regazzoni	Ferrari 312B	80	1h57m56.8
5 Chris Amon	March 701-Ford	79	
6 Graham Hill	Lotus 49C-Ford	79	

Winner's average speed: 108.687 mph. Starting grid front row: Rindt, 1m24.8 (pole), Brabham, 1m24.8 and Ickx, 1m25.1. Fastest lap: Brabham, 1m25.9. Leaders: Ickx, laps 1-6; Rindt, 7-68, 80; Brabham, 69-79

Grosser Preis von Deutschland

2 August 1970. Hockenheim. 50 laps of a 4.219-mile circuit = 210.950 miles. Hot, dry and sunny. World Championship round 8

1 Jochen Rindt	Lotus 72-Ford	50	1h42m00.3
2 Jacky Ickx	Ferrari 312B	50	1h42m01.0
3 Denny Hulme	McLaren M14A-Ford	50	1h43m22.1
4 Emerson Fittipaldi	Lotus 49C-Ford	50	1h43m55.4
5 Rolf Stommelen	Brabham BT33-Ford	49	
6 Henri Pescarolo	Matra-Simca MS120	49	

Winner's average speed: 124.082 mph. Starting grid front row: Ickx, 1m59.5 (pole) and Rindt, 1m59.7. Fastest lap: Ickx, 2m00.5. Leaders: Ickx, laps 1-6, 10-17, 26-31, 36-43, 45-46, 48; Rindt, 7-9, 18-21, 24-25, 32-35, 44, 47, 49-50; Regazzoni, 22-23

1970 DRIVERS' RECORDS

Driver	Car	South African GP	Spanish GP	Monaco GP	Belgian GP	Dutch GP	French GP	British GP	German GP	Austrian GP	Italian GP	Canadian GP	United States GP	Mexican GP
Andrea de Adamich	McLaren M7D-Alfa Romeo	-	DNQ	DNQ	-	-	NC	DNS	-	-	-	-	-	-
	McLaren M14D-Alfa Romeo	-	-	-	DNQ	-	-	-	DNQ	12	8	R	DNQ	-
Chris Amon	March 701-Ford	R	R	R	2^{F}	R	2	5	R	8	7	3	5	4
Mario Andretti	March 701-Ford	R	3	-	-	-	-	R	R	R	-	-	-	-
Derek Bell	Brabham BT26-Ford	-	-	-	R	-	-	-	-	-	-	-	-	-
	Surtees TS7-Ford	-	-	-	-	-	-	-	-	-	-	-	6	-
Jean-Pierre Beltoise	Matra-Simca MS120	4	R	R	3	5	13	R	R	6	3	8	R	5
Jo Bonnier	McLaren M7C-Ford	-	-	-	-	-	-	-	-	DNQ	-	-	R	-
Jack Brabham	Brabham BT33-Ford	1^{F}	R^{PF}	2	R	11	3^{F}	2^{F}	R	13	R	R	10	R
François Cevert	March 701-Ford	-	-	-	-	R	11	7	7	R	6	9	R	R
Dave Charlton	Lotus 49C-Ford	12	-	-	-	-	-	-	-	-	-	-	-	-
Piers Courage	de Tomaso 505/38-Ford	R	DNS	NC	R	R	-	-	-	-	-	-	-	-
George Eaton	BRM P139	R	-	-	-	-	-	-	-	-	-	-	-	-
	BRM P153	-	DNQ	DNQ	-	R	12	R	-	11	R	10	R	-
Emerson Fittipaldi	Lotus 49C-Ford	-	-	-	-	-	-	8	4	15	-	-	-	-
	Lotus 72-Ford	-	-	-	-	-	-	-	-	-	DNQ	-	1	R
Nanni Galli	McLaren M7D-Alfa Romeo	-	-	-	-	-	-	-	-	DNQ	-	-	-	-
Peter Gethin	McLaren M14A-Ford	-	-	-	-	-	R	-	R	10	9	6	14	R
Ignazio Giunti	Ferrari 312B	-	-	-	4	-	14	-	-	7	R	-	-	-
Dan Gurney	McLaren M14A-Ford	-	-	-	-	R	6	R	-	-	-	-	-	-
Hubert Hahne	March 701-Ford	-	-	-	-	-	-	-	DNQ	-	-	-	-	-
Graham Hill	Lotus 49C-Ford	6	4	5	R	NC	10	6	R	-	-	-	-	-
	Lotus 72-Ford	-	-	-	-	-	-	-	-	-	DNS	NC	R	R
Denny Hulme	McLaren M14A-Ford	2	R	4	-	-	-	-	3	R	4	R	7	3
	McLaren M14D-Ford	-	-	-	-	-	4	3	-	-	-	-	-	-
Gus Hutchison	Brabham BT26-Ford	-	-	-	-	-	-	-	-	-	-	-	R	-
Jacky Ickx	Ferrari 312B	R	R	R	8	3^{F}	R^{P}	R	2^{PF}	1^{F}	R^{P}	1	4^{PF}	1^{F}
Piet de Klerk	Brabham BT26-Ford	11	-	-	-	-	-	-	-	-	-	-	-	-
John Love	Lotus 49-Ford	8	-	-	-	-	-	-	-	-	-	-	-	-
Pete Lovely	Lotus 49B-Ford	-	-	-	-	DNQ	DNQ	NC	-	-	-	-	DNQ	-
Bruce McLaren	McLaren M14A-Ford	R	2	R	-	-	-	-	-	-	-	-	-	-
John Miles	Lotus 49C-Ford	5	-	-	-	-	-	-	-	-	-	-	-	-
	Lotus 72-Ford	-	DNQ	DNQ	R	7	8	R	R	R	DNS	-	-	-
Silvio Moser	Bellasi F170-Ford	-	-	-	-	DNQ	DNQ	-	DNQ	R	DNQ	-	-	-
Jackie Oliver	BRM P153	R	R	R	R	R	R	R	R	5	R	NC	R	7
Henri Pescarolo	Matra-Simca MS120	7	R	3	6	8	5	R	6	14	R	7	8	9
Ronnie Peterson	March 701-Ford	-	-	7	NC	9	R	9	R	-	R	NC	11	-
Brian Redman	Lotus 49C-Ford	DNS	-	-	-	-	-	-	-	-	-	-	-	-
	de Tomaso 505/38-Ford	-	-	-	-	-	-	DNS	DNQ	-	-	-	-	-
Clay Regazzoni	Ferrari 312B	-	-	-	-	4	-	4	R	2^{F}	1^{F}	2^{F}	13	2^{P}
Jochen Rindt	Lotus 49C-Ford	13	-	1^{F}	R	-	-	-	-	-	-	-	-	-
	Lotus 72-Ford	-	R	-	1^{P}	1	1^{P}	1	R^{P}	DNS	-	-	-	-
Pedro Rodriguez	BRM P153	9	R	6	1	10	R	R	R	4	R	4	2	6
Tim Schenken	de Tomaso 505/38-Ford	-	-	-	-	-	-	-	-	R	R	NC	R	-
Johnny Servoz-Gavin	March 701-Ford	R	5	DNQ	-	-	-	-	-	-	-	-	-	-
Jo Siffert	March 701-Ford	10	DNQ	8	7	R	R	R	8	9	R	8	9	R
Alex Soler-Roig	Lotus 49C-Ford	-	DNQ	-	-	-	DNQ	-	-	-	-	-	-	-
	Lotus 72-Ford	-	-	-	DNQ	-	-	-	-	-	-	-	-	-
Jackie Stewart	March 701-Ford	3^{P}	1	R^{P}	R^{P}	2	9	R	R	R	2	-	-	-
	Tyrrell 001-Ford	-	-	-	-	-	-	-	-	-	-	R^{P}	R	R
Rolf Stommelen	Brabham BT33-Ford	R	R	DNQ	5	DNQ	7	DNS	5	3	5	R	12	R
John Surtees	McLaren M7C-Ford	R^{F}	R	R	-	6	-	-	-	-	-	-	-	-
	Surtees TS7-Ford	-	-	-	-	-	-	R	9	R	R	5	R	8
Peter Westbury	BRM P153	-	-	-	-	-	-	-	-	-	-	-	DNQ	-
Reine Wisell	Lotus 72-Ford	-	-	-	-	-	-	-	-	-	-	-	3	NC

Grosser Preis von Österreich

16 August 1970. Österreichring. 60 laps of a 3.673-mile circuit = 220.380 miles. Warm, dry and sunny. World Championship round 9

1	Jacky Ickx	Ferrari 312B	60	1h42m17.32
2	Clay Regazzoni	Ferrari 312B	60	1h42m17.93
3	Rolf Stommelen	Brabham BT33-Ford	60	1h43m45.20
4	Pedro Rodriguez	BRM P153	59	
5	Jackie Oliver	BRM P153	59	
6	Jean-Pierre Beltoise	Matra-Simca MS120	59	

Winner's average speed: 129.269 mph. Starting grid front row: Rindt, 1m39.23 (pole) and Regazzoni, 1m39.70. Fastest lap: Ickx and Regazzoni, 1m40.4. Leaders: Regazzoni, lap 1; Ickx, laps 2-60

Gran Premio d'Italia

6 September 1970. Monza. 68 laps of a 3.573-mile circuit = 242.964 miles. Hot, dry and sunny. World Championship round 10

1 Clay Regazzoni	Ferrari 312B	68	1h39m06.88
2 Jackie Stewart	March 701-Ford	68	1h39m12.61
3 Jean-Pierre Beltoise	Matra-Simca MS120	68	1h39m12.68
4 Denny Hulme	McLaren M14A-Ford	68	1h39m13.03
5 Rolf Stommelen	Brabham BT33-Ford	68	1h39m13.29
6 François Cevert	March 701-Ford	68	1h40m10.34

Winner's average speed: 147.081 mph. Starting grid front row: Ickx, 1m24.14 (pole) and Rodriguez, 1m24.36. Fastest lap: Regazzoni, 1m25.2. Leaders: Ickx, laps 1-3, 19-20; Rodriguez, 4, 7-8; Stewart, 5-6, 9, 11, 14-17, 26, 31, 35, 37, 42-43, 51, 53; Regazzoni, 10, 12, 32-34, 36, 38-41, 44-50, 52, 54-68; Oliver, 13, 18, 21-25, 27-28, 30; Hulme, 29

Jochen Rindt in the winning Lotus 72 at Silverstone. He became the sport's only posthumous World Champion
....

Grand Prix du Canada

20 September 1970. St Jovite. 90 laps of a 2.650-mile circuit = 238.500 miles. Warm, dry and sunny. World Championship round 11

1 Jacky Ickx	Ferrari 312B	90	2h21m18.4
2 Clay Regazzoni	Ferrari 312B	90	2h21m33.2
3 Chris Amon	March 701-Ford	90	2h22m16.3

4 Pedro Rodriguez	BRM P153	89
5 John Surtees	Surtees TS7-Ford	89
6 Peter Gethin	McLaren M14A-Ford	88

Winner's average speed: 101.269 mph. Starting grid front row: Stewart, 1m31.5 (pole) and Ickx, 1m31.6. Fastest lap: Regazzoni, 1m32.2. Leaders: Stewart, laps 1-31; Ickx, 32-90

United States Grand Prix

4 October 1970. Watkins Glen. 108 laps of a 2.350-mile circuit = 253.800 miles. Cool, dry and cloudy. World Championship round 12

1 Emerson Fittipaldi	Lotus 72-Ford	108	1h57m32.79
2 Pedro Rodriguez	BRM P153	108	1h58m09.18
3 Reine Wisell	Lotus 72-Ford	108	1h58m17.96
4 Jacky Ickx	Ferrari 312B	107	
5 Chris Amon	March 701-Ford	107	
6 Derek Bell	Surtees TS7-Ford	107	

Winner's average speed: 129.549 mph. Starting grid front row: Ickx, 1m03.07 (pole) and Stewart, 1m03.62. Fastest lap: Ickx, 1m02.74. Leaders: Stewart, laps 1-82; Rodriguez, 83-100; Fittipaldi, 101-108

Gran Premio de Mexico

25 October 1970. Mexico City. 65 laps of a 3.107-mile circuit = 201.955 miles. Warm, dry and sunny. World Championship round 13

1 Jacky Ickx	Ferrari 312B	65	1h53m28.36
2 Clay Regazzoni	Ferrari 312B	65	1h54m13.82
3 Denny Hulme	McLaren M14A-Ford	65	1h54m14.33
4 Chris Amon	March 701-Ford	65	1h54m15.41
5 Jean-Pierre Beltoise	Matra-Simca MS120	65	1h54m18.47
6 Pedro Rodriguez	BRM P153	65	1h54m53.12

Winner's average speed: 106.786 mph. Starting grid front row: Regazzoni, 1m41.86 (pole) and Stewart, 1m41.88. Fastest lap: Ickx, 1m43.11. Leaders: Regazzoni, lap 1; Ickx, laps 2-65

1970 FINAL CHAMPIONSHIP POSITIONS

Drivers

1	Jochen Rindt	45
2	Jacky Ickx	40
3	Clay Regazzoni	33
4	Denny Hulme	27
5=	Jack Brabham	25
	Jackie Stewart	25
7=	Chris Amon	23
	Pedro Rodriguez	23
9	Jean-Pierre Beltoise	16
10	Emerson Fittipaldi	12
11	Rolf Stommelen	10
12	Henri Pescarolo	8
13	Graham Hill	7

14	Bruce McLaren	6
15=	Mario Andretti	4
	Reine Wisell	4
17=	Ignazio Giunti	3
	John Surtees	3
19=	John Miles	2
	Jackie Oliver	2
	Johnny Servoz-Gavin	2
22=	Derek Bell	1
	François Cevert	1
	Peter Gethin	1
	Dan Gurney	1

Manufacturers

1	Lotus-Ford	59
2	Ferrari	52 (55)*
3	March-Ford	48
4=	Brabham-Ford	35
	McLaren-Ford	35
6=	BRM	23
	Matra-Simca	23
8	Surtees-Ford	3

*Sum of best six results from the first seven races and best five results from the final six races. Points only awarded to first car to finish for each manufacturer

1971

In its first full year as a constructor, Tyrrell gave Jackie Stewart a car that was both quick and reliable. The Scotsman dominated in a way reminiscent of his fellow countryman, Jim Clark. Adding to the Tyrrell success, Stewart's charismatic young team-mate François Cevert scored his first victory at the end of the year.

A strong challenge had been expected from Ferrari, as it had a power advantage over its Ford Cosworth rivals. Race wins did materialize, including Mario Andretti's inherited victory in South Africa, but the marque failed to sustain a year-long championship challenge.

Having moved to the works March team, Ronnie Peterson ended his second year in the World Championship as runner-up. Although he did not win a race, he finished second on four occasions and also won the European Formula Two Trophy for the team.

BRM scored successive victories in late summer: Jo Siffert in Austria, despite a last lap puncture, and Peter Gethin in Italy. The latter was the closest and fastest Grand Prix victory of all time - the first five cars were separated by just 0.61 seconds, at an average speed of over 150 mph. However, tragedy dogged the team; two of its drivers, Siffert and Pedro Rodriguez, died while competing outside the championship.

Major technical developments included the introduction of slick tyres (without tread) and airboxes, which by increasing the air pressure into the engine improved the power output. In addition, Lotus experimented with the Pratt & Whitney gas turbine engine. But while slick tyres and airboxes proved successful, gas turbines did not catch on.

South African Grand Prix

6 March 1971. Kyalami. 79 laps of a 2.550-mile circuit = 201.450 miles. Hot, dry and sunny. World Championship round 1

1 Mario Andretti	Ferrari 312B	79	1h47m35.5
2 Jackie Stewart	Tyrrell 001-Ford	79	1h47m56.4
3 Clay Regazzoni	Ferrari 312B	79	1h48m06.9
4 Reine Wisell	Lotus 72C-Ford	79	1h48m44.9
5 Chris Amon	Matra-Simca MS120B	78	
6 Denny Hulme	McLaren M19A-Ford	78	

Winner's average speed: 112.341 mph. Starting grid front row: Stewart, 1m17.8 (pole), Amon, 1m18.4 and Regazzoni, 1m18.7. Fastest lap: Andretti, 1m20.3. Leaders: Regazzoni, laps 1-16; Hulme, 17-75; Andretti, 76-79

Gran Premio de Espana

18 April 1971. Montjuich Park. 75 laps of a 2.355-mile circuit = 176.625 miles. Hot, dry and sunny. World Championship round 2

1 Jackie Stewart	Tyrrell 003-Ford	75	1h49m03.4
2 Jacky Ickx	Ferrari 312B	75	1h49m06.8
3 Chris Amon	Matra-Simca MS120B	75	1h50m01.5
4 Pedro Rodriguez	BRM P160	75	1h50m21.3
5 Denny Hulme	McLaren M19A-Ford	75	1h50m30.4
6 Jean-Pierre Beltoise	Matra-Simca MS120B	74	

Winner's average speed: 97.174 mph. Starting grid front row: Ickx, 1m25.9 (pole), Regazzoni, 1m26.0 and Amon, 1m26.0. Fastest lap: Ickx, 1m25.1. Leaders: Ickx, laps 1-5; Stewart, 6-75

Grand Prix de Monaco

23 May 1971. Monte Carlo. 80 laps of a 1.954-mile circuit = 156.320 miles. Dry and overcast. World Championship round 3

1 Jackie Stewart	Tyrrell 003-Ford	80	1h52m21.3
2 Ronnie Peterson	March 711-Ford	80	1h52m46.9
3 Jacky Ickx	Ferrari 312B2	80	1h53m14.6
4 Denny Hulme	McLaren M19A-Ford	80	1h53m28.0
5 Emerson Fittipaldi	Lotus 72D-Ford	79	
6 Rolf Stommelen	Surtees TS9-Ford	79	

Winner's average speed: 83.478 mph. Starting grid front row: Stewart, 1m23.2 (pole) and Ickx, 1m24.4. Fastest lap: Stewart, 1m22.2. Leaders: Stewart, laps 1-80

Grote Prijs van Nederland

20 June 1971. Zandvoort. 70 laps of a 2.605-mile circuit = 182.350 miles. Wet. World Championship round 4

1 Jacky Ickx	Ferrari 312B2	70	1h56m20.09
2 Pedro Rodriguez	BRM P160	70	1h56m28.08
3 Clay Regazzoni	Ferrari 312B2	69	
4 Ronnie Peterson	March 711-Ford	68	
5 John Surtees	Surtees TS9-Ford	68	
6 Jo Siffert	BRM P160	68	

Winner's average speed: 94.047 mph. Starting grid front row: Ickx, 1m17.42 (pole), Rodriguez, 1m17.46 and Stewart, 1m17.64. Fastest lap: Ickx, 1m34.95. Leaders: Ickx, laps 1-8, 30, 32-70; Rodriguez, 9-29, 31

Grand Prix de France

4 July 1971. Paul Ricard. 55 laps of a 3.610-mile circuit = 198.550 miles. Hot, dry and sunny. World Championship round 5

1 Jackie Stewart	Tyrrell 003-Ford	55	1h46m41.68
2 François Cevert	Tyrrell 002-Ford	55	1h47m09.80
3 Emerson Fittipaldi	Lotus 72D-Ford	55	1h47m15.75
4 Jo Siffert	BRM P160	55	1h47m18.85
5 Chris Amon	Matra-Simca MS120B	55	1h47m22.76
6 Reine Wisell	Lotus 72D-Ford	55	1h47m57.66

Winner's average speed: 111.655 mph. Starting grid front row: Stewart, 1m50.71 (pole), Regazzoni, 1m51.53 and Ickx, 1m51.88. Fastest lap: Stewart, 1m54.09. Leaders: Stewart, laps 1-55

Woolmark British Grand Prix

17 July 1971. Silverstone. 68 laps of a 2.927-mile circuit = 199.036 miles. Warm, dry and sunny. World Championship round 6

1 Jackie Stewart	Tyrrell 003-Ford	68	1h31m31.5
2 Ronnie Peterson	March 711-Ford	68	1h32m07.6
3 Emerson Fittipaldi	Lotus 72D-Ford	68	1h32m22.0
4 Henri Pescarolo	March 711-Ford	67	
5 Rolf Stommelen	Surtees TS9-Ford	67	
6 John Surtees	Surtees TS9-Ford	67	

Winner's average speed: 130.480 mph. Starting grid front row: Regazzoni, 1m18.1 (pole), Stewart, 1m18.1 and Siffert, 1m18.2. Fastest lap: Stewart, 1m19.9. Leaders: Regazzoni, laps 1-3; Stewart, 4-68

Grosser Preis von Deutschland

1 August 1971. Nürburgring. 12 laps of a 14.189-mile circuit = 170.268 miles. Warm, dry and sunny. World Championship round 7

1 Jackie Stewart	Tyrrell 003-Ford	12	1h29m15.7
2 François Cevert	Tyrrell 002-Ford	12	1h29m45.8
3 Clay Regazzoni	Ferrari 312B2	12	1h29m52.8
4 Mario Andretti	Ferrari 312B2	12	1h31m20.7
5 Ronnie Peterson	March 711-Ford	12	1h31m44.8
6 Tim Schenken	Brabham BT33-Ford	12	1h32m14.3

Winner's average speed: 114.451 mph. Starting grid front row: Stewart, 7m19.0 (pole) and Ickx, 7m19.2. Fastest lap: Cevert, 7m20.1. Leaders: Stewart, laps 1-12

Grosser Preis von Österreich

15 August 1971. Österreichring. 54 laps of a 3.673-mile circuit = 198.342 miles. Warm, dry and sunny. World Championship round 8

1 Jo Siffert	BRM P160	54	1h30m23.91
2 Emerson Fittipaldi	Lotus 72D-Ford	54	1h30m28.03
3 Tim Schenken	Brabham BT33-Ford	54	1h30m43.68
4 Reine Wisell	Lotus 72D-Ford	54	1h30m55.78
5 Graham Hill	Brabham BT34-Ford	54	1h31m12.34
6 Henri Pescarolo	March 711-Ford	54	1h31m48.42

Winner's average speed: 131.645 mph. Starting grid front row: Siffert, 1m37.44 (pole) and Stewart, 1m37.65. Fastest lap: Siffert, 1m38.47. Leaders: Siffert, laps 1-54

Gran Premio d'Italia

5 September 1971. Monza. 55 laps of a 3.573-mile circuit = 196.515 miles. Hot, dry and sunny. World Championship round 9

1 Peter Gethin	BRM P160	55	1h18m12.60
2 Ronnie Peterson	March 711-Ford	55	1h18m12.61
3 François Cevert	Tyrrell 002-Ford	55	1h18m12.69
4 Mike Hailwood	Surtees TS9-Ford	55	1h18m12.78
5 Howden Ganley	BRM P160	55	1h18m13.21
6 Chris Amon	Matra-Simca MS120B	55	1h18m44.96

Winner's average speed: 150.759 mph. Starting grid front row: Amon, 1m22.40 (pole) and Ickx, 1m22.82. Fastest lap: Pescarolo, 1m23.80. Leaders: Regazzoni, laps 1-3, 9; Peterson, 4-7, 10-14, 17-22, 24, 26, 33, 47-50, 54; Stewart, 8; Cevert, 15-16, 23, 31-32, 34, 36; Hailwood, 25, 27, 35, 42, 51; Siffert, 28-30; Amon, 37-41, 43-46; Gethin, 52-53, 55

Canadian Grand Prix

19 September 1971. Mosport Park. 64 laps of a 2.459-mile circuit = 157.376 miles. Scheduled for 80 laps but stopped due to rain. Wet. World Championship round 10

1 Jackie Stewart	Tyrrell 003-Ford	64	1h55m12.9
2 Ronnie Peterson	March 711-Ford	64	1h55m51.2
3 Mark Donohue	McLaren M19A-Ford	64	1h56m48.7
4 Denny Hulme	McLaren M19A-Ford	63	
5 Reine Wisell	Lotus 72D-Ford	63	
6 François Cevert	Tyrrell 002-Ford	62	

Winner's average speed: 81.956 mph. Starting grid front row: Stewart, 1m15.3 (pole), Siffert, 1m15.5 and Cevert, 1m15.7. Fastest lap: Hulme, 1m43.5. Leaders: Stewart, laps 1-17, 31-64; Peterson, 18-30

United States Grand Prix

3 October 1971. Watkins Glen. 59 laps of a 3.377-mile circuit = 199.243 miles. Warm, dry and sunny. World Championship round 11

1 François Cevert	Tyrrell 002-Ford	59	1h43m51.991
2 Jo Siffert	BRM P160	59	1h44m32.053
3 Ronnie Peterson	March 711-Ford	59	1h44m36.061
4 Howden Ganley	BRM P160	59	1h44m48.740
5 Jackie Stewart	Tyrrell 003-Ford	59	1h44m51.994
6 Clay Regazzoni	Ferrari 312B2	59	1h45m08.417

Winner's average speed: 115.096 mph. Starting grid front row: Stewart, 1m42.642 (pole), Fittipaldi, 1m42.659 and Hulme, 1m42.925. Fastest lap: Ickx, 1m43.47. Leaders: Stewart, laps 1-13; Cevert, 14-59

1971 FINAL CHAMPIONSHIP POSITIONS

Drivers

1	Jackie Stewart	62
2	Ronnie Peterson	33
3	François Cevert	26
4=	Jacky Ickx	19
	Jo Siffert	19
6	Emerson Fittipaldi	16
7	Clay Regazzoni	13
8	Mario Andretti	12
9=	Chris Amon	9
	Peter Gethin	9
	Denny Hulme	9
	Pedro Rodriguez	9
	Reine Wisell	9
14=	Howden Ganley	5
	Tim Schenken	5
16=	Mark Donohue	4
	Henri Pescarolo	4
18=	Mike Hailwood	3
	Rolf Stommelen	3
	John Surtees	3
21	Graham Hill	2
22	Jean-Pierre Beltoise	1

Manufacturers

1	Tyrrell-Ford	73
2	BRM	36
3=	Ferrari	33
	March-Ford	33 (34)*
5	Lotus-Ford	21
6	McLaren-Ford	10
7	Matra-Simca	9
8	Surtees-Ford	8
9	Brabham-Ford	5

*Sum of best five results from the first six races and best four results from the final five races. Points only awarded to first car to finish for each manufacturer

1971 DRIVERS' RECORDS

Driver	Car	South African GP	Spanish GP	Monaco GP	Dutch GP	French GP	British GP	German GP	Austrian GP	Italian GP	Canadian GP	United States GP
Andrea de Adamich	March 711-Alfa Romeo	13	R	-	-	R	NC	R	-	R	-	11
Chris Amon	Matra-Simca MS120B	5	3	R	R	5	R	R	-	6P	10	12
Mario Andretti	Ferrari 312B	1F	R	DNQ	R	-	-	-	-	-	-	-
	Ferrari 312B2	-	-	-	-	-	-	4	-	-	13	DNS
Skip Barber	March 711-Ford	-	-	DNQ	NC	-	-	-	-	-	R	NC
Derek Bell	Surtees TS9-Ford	-	-	-	-	-	R	-	-	-	-	-
Jean-Pierre Beltoise	Matra-Simca MS120B	-	6	R	9	7	7	-	-	-	R	8
Mike Beuttler	March 711-Ford	-	-	-	-	R	DSQ	NC	R	NC	-	-
Jo Bonnier	McLaren M7C-Ford	R	-	-	-	-	DNQ	DNS	10	-	16	
John Cannon	BRM P153	-	-	-	-	-	-	-	-	-	14	
François Cevert	Tyrrell 002-Ford	R	7	R	R	2	10	2F	R	3	6	1
Dave Charlton	Brabham BT33-Ford	R	-	-	-	-	-	-	-	-	-	-
	Lotus 72D-Ford	-	-	DNP	-	R	-	-	-	-	-	
Chris Craft	Brabham BT33-Ford	-	-	-	-	-	-	-	-	DNS	R	
Mark Donohue	McLaren M19A-Ford	-	-	-	-	-	-	-	-	3	DNS	
George Eaton	BRM P160	-	-	-	-	-	-	-	-	15	-	
Vic Elford	BRM P160	-	-	-	-	-	11	-	-	-	-	
Emerson Fittipaldi	Lotus 72C-Ford	R	R	-	-	-	-	-	-	-	-	-
	Lotus 72D-Ford	-	-	5	-	3	3	R	2	-	7	NC
	Lotus 56B-Pratt & Whitney	-	-	-	-	-	-	-	8	-	-	
Nanni Galli	March 711-Alfa Romeo	-	-	DNQ	R	-	-	12	12	-	-	-
	March 711-Ford	-	-	-	DNS	11	-	-	R	NC	R	
Howden Ganley	BRM P153	R	10	DNQ	7	10	8	R	-	-	-	-
	BRM P160	-	-	-	-	-	-	R	5	DNS	4	
Peter Gethin	McLaren M14A-Ford	R	8	R	-	-	-	-	-	-	-	-
	McLaren M19A-Ford	-	-	NC	9	R	R	-	-	-	-	
	BRM P160	-	-	-	-	-	-	10	1	14	9	
Mike Hailwood	Surtees TS9-Ford	-	-	-	-	-	-	-	4	-	15	/Cont'd

1971 DRIVERS' RECORDS cont'd/

Driver	Car	South African GP	Spanish GP	Monaco GP	Dutch GP	French GP	British GP	German GP	Austrian GP	Italian GP	Canadian GP	United States GP
Graham Hill	Brabham BT33-Ford	9	-	-	-	-	-	-	-	-	-	-
	Brabham BT34-Ford	-	R	R	10	R	R	9	5	R	R	7
David Hobbs	McLaren M19A-Ford	-	-	-	-	-	-	-	-	-	-	10
Denny Hulme	McLaren M19A-Ford	6	5	4	12	R	R	R	R	-	4F	R
Jacky Ickx	Ferrari 312B	8	2PF	-	-	-	-	-	-	R	-	RF
	Ferrari 312B2	-	-	3	1PF	R	R	R	R	-	8	-
Jean-Pierre Jarier	March 701-Ford	-	-	-	-	-	-	-	-	NC	-	-
Niki Lauda	March 711-Ford	-	-	-	-	-	-	-	R	-	-	-
Gijs van Lennep	Surtees TS7-Ford	-	-	-	8	-	-	-	-	-	-	-
	Surtees TS9-Ford	-	-	-	-	-	-	-	-	-	-	DNS
John Love	March 701-Ford	R	-	-	-	-	-	-	-	-	-	-
Pete Lovely	Lotus 69-Ford	-	-	-	-	-	-	-	-	-	NC	NC
Helmut Marko	McLaren M7C-Ford	-	-	-	-	-	-	DNQ	-	-	-	-
	BRM P153	-	-	-	-	-	-	-	11	R	12	-
	BRM P160	-	-	-	-	-	-	-	-	-	-	13
Jean Max	March 701-Ford	-	-	-	-	NC	-	-	-	-	-	-
François Mazet	March 701-Ford	-	-	-	-	13	-	-	-	-	-	-
Silvio Moser	Bellasi F170-Ford	-	-	-	-	-	-	-	-	R	-	-
Jackie Oliver	McLaren M14A-Ford	-	-	-	-	-	R	-	-	7	-	-
	McLaren M19A-Ford	-	-	-	-	-	-	-	9	-	-	-
Henri Pescarolo	March 701-Ford	11	-	-	-	-	-	-	-	-	-	-
	March 711-Ford	-	R	8	NC	R	4	R	6	RF	DNS	R
Ronnie Peterson	March 711-Ford	10	R	2	4	-	2	5	8	2	2	3
	March 711-Alfa Romeo	-	-	-	-	R	-	-	-	-	-	-
Sam Posey	Surtees TS9-Ford	-	-	-	-	-	-	-	-	-	-	R
Jackie Pretorius	Brabham BT26-Ford	R	-	-	-	-	-	-	-	-	-	-
Brian Redman	Surtees TS7-Ford	7	-	-	-	-	-	-	-	-	-	-
Clay Regazzoni	Ferrari 312B	3	R	-	-	-	-	-	-	-	-	-
	Ferrari 312B2	-	-	R	3	R	RP	3	R	R	R	6
Peter Revson	Tyrrell 001-Ford	-	-	-	-	-	-	-	-	-	-	R
Pedro Rodriguez	BRM P160	R	4	9	2	R	-	-	-	-	-	-
Tim Schenken	Brabham BT33-Ford	-	9	10	R	12	12	6	3	R	R	R
Jo Siffert	BRM P153	R	-	-	-	-	-	-	-	-	-	-
	BRM P160	-	R	R	6	4	9	R	1PF	9	9	2
Alex Soler-Roig	March 711-Ford	R	R	DNQ	R	R	-	-	-	-	-	-
Jackie Stewart	Tyrrell 001-Ford	2P	-	-	-	-	-	-	-	-	-	-
	Tyrrell 003-Ford	-	1	1PF	11	1PF	1F	1P	R	R	1P	5P
Rolf Stommelen	Surtees TS7-Ford	12	-	-	-	-	-	-	-	-	-	-
	Surtees TS9-Ford	-	R	6	DSQ	11	5	10	7	DNS	R	-
John Surtees	Surtees TS9-Ford	R	NC	7	5	8	6	7	R	R	11	17
Dave Walker	Lotus 56B-Pratt & Whitney	-	-	-	R	-	-	-	-	-	-	-
Reine Wisell	Lotus 72C-Ford	4	NC	R	-	-	-	-	-	-	-	-
	Lotus 72D-Ford	-	-	-	DSQ	6	-	8	4	-	5	R
	Lotus 56B-Pratt & Whitney	-	-	-	-	-	NC	-	-	-	-	-

1972

Just two years after his Grand Prix debut, Emerson Fittipaldi became, at 25, the youngest World Champion to date. Driving the three-year-old Lotus 72, the Brazilian dominated the European races and secured the title with two events to go.

Jackie Stewart, the reigning champion, was his closest challenger, despite missing the Belgian GP with a stomach ulcer. Equipped with a new Tyrrell, Stewart returned to form, winning the final two Grands Prix.

Jean-Pierre Beltoise scored the only Grand Prix win of his career, dominating the Monaco GP, which was one of the wettest races on record. This proved to be the last victory for the once great BRM marque.

Bernie Ecclestone, a successful businessman who had occasionally entered ex-works Connaughts in 1958, bought the Brabham team from Ron Tauranac. On his Grand Prix debut for the team, Carlos Reutemann qualified on pole for his home Argentinian GP, and won the non-championship Brazilian race.

Jody Scheckter also made an impressive start in the formula, driving for the Yardley-McLaren team at the final round. He qualified fourth and ran third before spinning.

Ronnie Peterson and Niki Lauda both had disastrous years in the unconventional March 721X before it was replaced. Chris Amon showed promise in the new Matra but, as ever, scored no victories.

In the fight for pole position, the two rival tyre companies, Firestone and Goodyear, introduced qualifying tyres. These were made of a super-soft compound of rubber which gave improved performance but only lasted for a few laps.

Gran Premio de la Republica Argentina

23 January 1972. Buenos Aires. 95 laps of a 2.079-mile circuit = 197.505 miles. Very hot, dry and sunny. World Championship round 1

1 Jackie Stewart	Tyrrell 003-Ford	95	1h57m58.82
2 Denny Hulme	McLaren M19A-Ford	95	1h58m24.78
3 Jacky Ickx	Ferrari 312B2	95	1h58m58.21
4 Clay Regazzoni	Ferrari 312B2	95	1h59m05.54
5 Tim Schenken	Surtees TS9B-Ford	95	1h59m07.93
6 Ronnie Peterson	March 721-Ford	94	

Winner's average speed: 100.443 mph. Starting grid front row: Reutemann, 1m12.46 (pole) and Stewart, 1m12.68. Fastest lap: Stewart, 1m13.66. Leaders: Stewart, laps 1-95

South African Grand Prix

4 March 1972. Kyalami. 79 laps of a 2.550-mile circuit = 201.450 miles. Hot, dry and sunny. World Championship round 2

1 Denny Hulme	McLaren M19A-Ford	79	1h45m49.1
2 Emerson Fittipaldi	Lotus 72D-Ford	79	1h46m03.2
3 Peter Revson	McLaren M19A-Ford	79	1h46m14.9
4 Mario Andretti	Ferrari 312B2	79	1h46m27.6
5 Ronnie Peterson	March 721-Ford	79	1h46m38.1
6 Graham Hill	Brabham BT33-Ford	78	

Winner's average speed: 114.224 mph. Starting grid front row: Stewart, 1m17.0 (pole), Regazzoni, 1m17.3 and Fittipaldi, 1m17.4. Fastest lap: Hailwood, 1m18.9. Leaders: Hulme, laps 1, 57-79; Stewart, 2-44; Fittipaldi, 45-56

Gran Premio de Espana

1 May 1972. Jarama. 90 laps of a 2.115-mile circuit = 190.350 miles. Cold and windy with showers. World Championship round 3

1972 DRIVERS' RECORDS

Driver	Car	Argentinian GP	South African GP	Spanish GP	Monaco GP	Belgian GP	French GP	British GP	German GP	Austrian GP	Italian GP	Canadian GP	United States GP
Andrea de Adamich	Surtees TS9B-Ford	R	NC	4	7	R	14	R	13	14	R	R	R
Chris Amon	Matra-Simca MS120C	DNS	15	R	6	6F	-	4	-	-	-	-	-
	Matra-Simca MS120D	-	-	-	-	-	3PF	-	15	5	R	6	15
Mario Andretti	Ferrari 312B2	R	4	R	-	-	-	-	-	-	7	-	6
Skip Barber	March 711-Ford	-	-	-	-	-	-	-	-	-	-	NC	16
Derek Bell	Tecno PA123	-	-	-	-	-	DNS	-	R	-	DNQ	DNS	R
Jean-Pierre Beltoise	BRM P160B	-	R	R	1F	R	15	-	-	-	-	-	-
	BRM P160C	-	-	-	-	-	-	11	9	8	-	-	-
	BRM P180	-	-	-	-	-	-	-	-	-	8	R	R
Mike Beuttler	March 721G-Ford	-	-	DNQ	13	R	R	13	8	R	10	NC	13
Bill Brack	BRM P180	-	-	-	-	-	-	-	-	-	-	R	-
François Cevert	Tyrrell 002-Ford	R	9	R	NC	2	4	R	10	9	R	-	-
	Tyrrell 006-Ford	-	-	-	-	-	-	-	-	-	-	R	2
Dave Charlton	Lotus 72D-Ford	-	R	-	-	-	DNQ	R	R	-	-	-	-
Patrick Depailler	Tyrrell 004-Ford	-	-	-	-	-	NC	-	-	-	-	-	7
William Ferguson	Brabham BT33-Ford	-	DNS	-	-	-	-	-	-	-	-	-	-
Emerson Fittipaldi	Lotus 72D-Ford	R	2	1	3P	1P	2	1	R	1P	1	R	R
Wilson Fittipaldi	Brabham BT33-Ford	-	-	-	7	9	-	-	-	-	-	-	-
	Brabham BT34-Ford	-	-	-	-	R	8	12	7	R	R	R	R
Nanni Galli	Tecno PA123	-	-	-	-	R	-	R	-	NC	R	-	-
	Ferrari 312B2	-	-	-	-	-	13	-	-	-	-	-	-
Howden Ganley	BRM P160B	9	NC	R	-	8	DNS	-	-	-	-	-	-
	BRM P180	-	-	-	R	-	-	-	-	-	-	-	-
	BRM P160C	-	-	-	-	-	-	-	4	6	11	10	R
Peter Gethin	BRM P160B	R	NC	-	R	R	DNS	R	-	-	-	-	-
	BRM P180	-	-	R	-	-	-	-	-	-	-	-	-
	BRM P160C	-	-	-	-	-	-	-	-	13	6	R	R
Mike Hailwood	Surtees TS9B-Ford	-	RF	R	R	4	6	R	R	4	2	-	17
Graham Hill	Brabham BT33-Ford	R	6	-	-	-	-	-	-	-	-	-	-
	Brabham BT37-Ford	-	-	10	12	R	10	R	6	R	5	8	11
Denny Hulme	McLaren M19A-Ford	2	1	R	-	-	-	-	-	-	-	-	-
	McLaren M19C-Ford	-	-	-	15	3	7	5	R	2F	3	3	3
Jacky Ickx	Ferrari 312B2	3	8	2PF	2	R	11	RP	1PF	R	RPF	12	5
Niki Lauda	March 721-Ford	11	7	-	-	-	-	-	-	-	-	-	-
	March 721X-Ford	-	-	R	16	12	-	-	-	-	-	-	-
	March 721G-Ford	-	-	-	-	-	R	9	R	10	13	DSQ	NC
John Love	Surtees TS9-Ford	-	16	-	-	-	-	-	-	-	-	-	-
Helmut Marko	BRM P153	10	14	-	-	-	-	-	-	-	-	-	-
	BRM P153B	-	-	-	8	10	-	-	-	-	-	-	-
	BRM P160B	-	-	-	-	-	R	-	-	-	-	-	-
Arturo Merzario	Ferrari 312B2	-	-	-	-	-	6	12	-	-	-	-	-
François Migault	Connew PC1-Ford	-	-	-	-	-	DNS	-	R	-	-	-	-
Jackie Oliver	BRM P160B	-	-	-	-	-	R	-	-	-	-	-	-

/Cont'd

1 Emerson Fittipaldi	Lotus 72D-Ford	90	2h03m41.23
2 Jacky Ickx	Ferrari 312B2	90	2h04m00.15
3 Clay Regazzoni	Ferrari 312B2	89	
4 Andrea de Adamich	Surtees TS9B-Ford	89	
5 Peter Revson	McLaren M19A-Ford	89	
6 Carlos Pace	March 711-Ford	89	

Winner's average speed: 92.355 mph. Starting grid front row: Ickx, 1m18.43 (pole), Hulme, 1m19.18 and E Fittipaldi, 1m19.26. Fastest lap: Ickx, 1m21.01. Leaders: Hulme, laps 1-4; Stewart, 5-8; Fittipaldi, 9-90

Grand Prix de Monaco

14 May 1972. Monte Carlo. 80 laps of a 1.954-mile circuit = 156.320 miles. Very wet. World Championship round 4

1 Jean-Pierre Beltoise	BRM P160B	80	2h26m54.7
2 Jacky Ickx	Ferrari 312B2	80	2h27m32.9
3 Emerson Fittipaldi	Lotus 72D-Ford	79	
4 Jackie Stewart	Tyrrell 004-Ford	78	
5 Brian Redman	McLaren M19A-Ford	77	
6 Chris Amon	Matra-Simca MS120C	77	

Winner's average speed: 63.842 mph. Starting grid front row: E Fittipaldi, 1m21.4 (pole) and Ickx, 1m21.6. Fastest lap: Beltoise, 1m40.0. Leaders: Beltoise, laps 1-80

Grand Prix de Belgique

4 June 1972. Nivelles. 85 laps of a 2.314-mile circuit = 196.690 miles. Warm, dry and sunny. World Championship round 5

1 Emerson Fittipaldi	Lotus 72D-Ford	85	1h44m06.7
2 François Cevert	Tyrrell 002-Ford	85	1h44m33.3
3 Denny Hulme	McLaren M19C-Ford	85	1h45m04.8
4 Mike Hailwood	Surtees TS9B-Ford	85	1h45m18.7
5 Carlos Pace	March 711-Ford	84	

6 Chris Amon	Matra-Simca MS120C	84	

Winner's average speed: 113.353 mph. Starting grid front row: E Fittipaldi, 1m11.43 (pole), Regazzoni, 1m11.58 and Hulme, 1m11.80. Fastest lap: Amon, 1m12.12. Leaders: Regazzoni, laps 1-8; E Fittipaldi, 9-85

Grand Prix de France

2 July 1972. Clermont-Ferrand. 38 laps of a 5.005-mile circuit = 190.190 miles. Warm, dry and sunny. World Championship round 6

1 Jackie Stewart	Tyrrell 003-Ford	38	1h52m21.5
2 Emerson Fittipaldi	Lotus 72D-Ford	38	1h52m49.2
3 Chris Amon	Matra-Simca MS120D	38	1h52m53.4
4 François Cevert	Tyrrell 002-Ford	38	1h53m10.8
5 Ronnie Peterson	March 721G-Ford	38	1h53m18.3
6 Mike Hailwood	Surtees TS9B-Ford	38	1h53m57.6

Winner's average speed: 101.563 mph. Starting grid front row: Amon, 2m53.4 (pole) and Hulme, 2m54.2. Fastest lap: Amon, 2m53.9. Leaders: Amon, laps 1-19; Stewart, 20-38

John Player British Grand Prix

15 July 1972. Brands Hatch. 76 laps of a 2.650-mile circuit = 201.400 miles. Warm, dry and sunny. World Championship round 7. Also known as the European Grand Prix

1 Emerson Fittipaldi	Lotus 72D-Ford	76	1h47m50.2
2 Jackie Stewart	Tyrrell 003-Ford	76	1h47m54.3
3 Peter Revson	McLaren M19A-Ford	76	1h49m02.7
4 Chris Amon	Matra-Simca MS120C	75	
5 Denny Hulme	McLaren M19C-Ford	75	
6 Arturo Merzario	Ferrari 312B2	75	

Winner's average speed: 112.058 mph. Starting grid front row: Ickx, 1m22.2 (pole) and E Fittipaldi, 1m22.6. Fastest lap: Stewart, 1m24.0. Leaders: Ickx, laps 1-48; E Fittipaldi, 49-76

1972 DRIVERS' RECORDS cont'd/

Driver	Car	Argentinian GP	South African GP	Spanish GP	Monaco GP	Belgian GP	French GP	British GP	German GP	Austrian GP	Italian GP	Canadian GP	United States GP
Carlos Pace	March 711-Ford	-	17	6	17	5	R	R	NC	NC	R	9	R
Henri Pescarolo	March 721-Ford	8	11	11	R	NC	DNS	-	R	DNS	DNQ	13	14
	Williams FX3-Ford	-	-	-	-	-	-	R	-	-	-	-	-
Ronnie Peterson	March 721-Ford	6	5	-	-	-	-	-	-	-	-	-	-
	March 721X-Ford	-	-	R	11	9	-	-	-	-	-	-	-
	March 721G-Ford	-	-	-	-	-	5	7	3	12	9	DSQ	4
Sam Posey	Surtees TS9B-Ford	-	-	-	-	-	-	-	-	-	-	-	12
Brian Redman	McLaren M19A-Ford	-	-	-	5	-	9	-	5	-	-	-	-
	BRM P180	-	-	-	-	-	-	-	-	-	-	-	R
Clay Regazzoni	Ferrari 312B2	4	12	3	R	R	-	-	2	R	R	5	8
Carlos Reutemann	Brabham BT34-Ford	7P	R	-	-	-	-	-	-	-	-	-	-
	Brabham BT37-Ford	-	-	-	-	13	12	8	R	R	R	4	R
Peter Revson	McLaren M19A-Ford	R	3	5	-	7	-	3	-	-	-	-	-
	McLaren M19C-Ford	-	-	-	-	-	-	-	-	3	4	2P	18
Jody Scheckter	McLaren M19A-Ford	-	-	-	-	-	-	-	-	-	-	-	9
Tim Schenken	Surtees TS9B-Ford	5	R	8	R	R	17	R	14	11	R	7	-
	Surtees TS14-Ford	-	-	-	-	-	-	-	-	-	-	-	R
Vern Schuppan	BRM P153B	-	-	-	-	DNS	-	-	-	-	-	-	-
Alex Soler-Roig	BRM P160B	R	-	R	-	-	-	-	-	-	-	-	-
Jackie Stewart	Tyrrell 003-Ford	1F	RP	R	-	-	1	2F	11	-	-	-	-
	Tyrrell 004-Ford	-	-	-	4	-	-	-	-	-	-	-	-
	Tyrrell 005-Ford	-	-	-	-	-	-	-	-	7	R	1F	1PF
Rolf Stommelen	Eifelland 21-Ford	-	13	R	10	11	16	10	R	NC	-	-	-
John Surtees	Surtees TS14-Ford	-	-	-	-	-	-	-	-	-	R	-	DNS
Dave Walker	Lotus 72D-Ford	DSQ	10	9	14	14	18	R	R	R	-	-	R
Reine Wisell	BRM P153	R	-	-	-	-	-	-	-	-	-	-	-
	BRM P160B	-	-	R	R	-	R	-	-	-	-	-	-
	BRM P160C	-	-	-	-	-	-	-	-	R	-	12	-
	Lotus 72D-Ford	-	-	-	-	-	-	-	-	-	-	R	10

World Championship Grand Prix Racing

Grosser Preis von Deutschland

30 July 1972. Nürburgring. 14 laps of a 14.189-mile circuit = 198.646 miles. Warm, dry and sunny. World Championship round 8

1 Jacky Ickx	Ferrari 312B2	14	1h42m12.3
2 Clay Regazzoni	Ferrari 312B2	14	1h43m00.6
3 Ronnie Peterson	March 721G-Ford	14	1h43m19.0
4 Howden Ganley	BRM P160C	14	1h44m32.5
5 Brian Redman	McLaren M19A-Ford	14	1h44m48.0
6 Graham Hill	Brabham BT37-Ford	14	1h45m11.9

Winner's average speed: 116.616 mph. Starting grid front row: Ickx, 7m07.0 (pole) and Stewart, 7m08.7. Fastest lap: Ickx, 7m13.6. Leaders: Ickx, laps 1-14

....

The Lotus-Ford of Emerson Fittipaldi, at 25 the youngest World Champion to date

Grosser Preis von Österreich

13 August 1972. Österreichring. 54 laps of a 3.673-mile circuit = 198.342 miles. Very hot, dry and sunny. World Championship round 9

1 Emerson Fittipaldi	Lotus 72D-Ford	54	1h29m16.66
2 Denny Hulme	McLaren M19C-Ford	54	1h29m17.84
3 Peter Revson	McLaren M19C-Ford	54	1h29m53.19
4 Mike Hailwood	Surtees TS9B-Ford	54	1h30m01.42
5 Chris Amon	Matra-Simca MS120D	54	1h30m02.30
6 Howden Ganley	BRM P160C	54	1h30m17.85

Winner's average speed: 133.298 mph. Starting grid front row: E Fittipaldi, 1m35.97 (pole) and Regazzoni, 1m36.04. Fastest lap: Hulme, 1m38.32. Leaders: Stewart, laps 1-23; E Fittipaldi, 24-54

Gran Premio d'Italia

10 September 1972. Monza. 55 laps of a 3.588-mile circuit = 197.340 miles. Dry and overcast. World Championship round 10

1 Emerson Fittipaldi	Lotus 72D-Ford	55	1h29m58.4
2 Mike Hailwood	Surtees TS9B-Ford	55	1h30m12.9
3 Denny Hulme	McLaren M19C-Ford	55	1h30m22.2
4 Peter Revson	McLaren M19C-Ford	55	1h30m34.1
5 Graham Hill	Brabham BT37-Ford	55	1h31m04.0
6 Peter Gethin	BRM P160C	55	1h31m20.3

Winner's average speed: 131.599 mph. Starting grid front row: Ickx, 1m35.65 (pole) and Amon, 1m35.69. Fastest lap: Ickx, 1m36.3. Leaders: Ickx, laps 1-13, 17-45; Regazzoni, 14-16; E Fittipaldi, 46-55

Canadian Grand Prix

24 September 1972. Mosport Park. 80 laps of a 2.459-mile circuit = 196.720 miles. Dry and misty. World Championship round 11

1 Jackie Stewart	Tyrrell 005-Ford	80	1h43m16.9
2 Peter Revson	McLaren M19C-Ford	80	1h44m05.1
3 Denny Hulme	McLaren M19C-Ford	80	1h44m11.5
4 Carlos Reutemann	Brabham BT37-Ford	80	1h44m17.6
5 Clay Regazzoni	Ferrari 312B2	80	1h44m23.8
6 Chris Amon	Matra-Simca MS120D	79	

Winner's average speed: 114.282 mph. Starting grid front row: Revson, 1m13.6 (pole), Hulme, 1m13.9 and Peterson, 1m14.0. Fastest lap: Stewart, 1m15.7. Leaders: Peterson, laps 1-3; Stewart, 4-80

United States Grand Prix

8 October 1972. Watkins Glen. 59 laps of a 3.377-mile circuit = 199.243 miles. Cool and dry at start, some rain later. World Championship round 12

1 Jackie Stewart	Tyrrell 005-Ford	59	1h41m45.354
2 François Cevert	Tyrrell 006-Ford	59	1h42m17.622
3 Denny Hulme	McLaren M19C-Ford	59	1h42m22.882
4 Ronnie Peterson	March 721G-Ford	59	1h43m07.870
5 Jacky Ickx	Ferrari 312B2	59	1h43m08.473
6 Mario Andretti	Ferrari 312B2	58	

Winner's average speed: 117.483 mph. Starting grid front row: Stewart, 1m40.481 (pole), Revson, 1m40.527 and Hulme, 1m41.084. Fastest lap: Stewart, 1m41.644. Leaders: Stewart, laps 1-59

1972 FINAL CHAMPIONSHIP POSITIONS

Drivers

1	Emerson Fittipaldi	61		Graham Hill	4	3	McLaren-Ford	47 (49)*
2	Jackie Stewart	45		Brian Redman	4	4	Ferrari	33
3	Denny Hulme	39	16=	Andrea de Adamich	3	5	Surtees-Ford	18
4	Jacky Ickx	27		Carlos Pace	3	6	March-Ford	15
5	Peter Revson	23		Carlos Reutemann	3	7	BRM	14
6=	François Cevert	15	19	Tim Schenken	2	8	Matra-Simca	12
	Clay Regazzoni	15	20=	Peter Gethin	1	9	Brabham-Ford	7
8	Mike Hailwood	13		Arturo Merzario	1		*Sum of best five results from	
9=	Chris Amon	12					the first six races and best five	
	Ronnie Peterson	12	**Manufacturers**				results from the final six races.	
11	Jean-Pierre Beltoise	9	1	Lotus-Ford	61		Points only awarded to first car	
12=	Mario Andretti	4	2	Tyrrell-Ford	51		to finish for each manufacturer	
	Howden Ganley	4						

1973

A classic contest between the Tyrrell and JPS-Lotus teams dominated 1973, with Jackie Stewart becoming champion for the third time in his final year of Grand Prix racing. For his team, however, the year had a tragic twist. The man Ken Tyrrell had groomed to replace Stewart as team leader,

François Cevert, was killed during practice for the United States GP.

Lotus retained the constructors' title, Emerson Fittipaldi and Ronnie Peterson scoring seven victories for the team. For Peterson, who had not won a race before, the start to his first year with Lotus proved very frustrating. The final slice of bad luck, a puncture in the closing laps of the Swedish GP, robbed him of a famous home victory.

However, that elusive first success did come at the next race in France. The surprise leader, Jody Scheckter, was eliminated by Fittipaldi, leaving Peterson to cruise to the first of four wins. Scheckter was a true star in the making, but his inexperience showed at Silverstone where in the early laps he spun at Woodcote in front of the field, causing a multi-car pile-up.

Niki Lauda had an impressive second year in Grand Prix racing, and his performances in an increasingly uncompetitive BRM were enough to attract interest from Ferrari for the following season.

Two acts of selfless heroism earned recognition from the British monarchy. In South Africa, braving flames that had engulfed the car, Mike Hailwood rescued an unconscious Clay Regazzoni from his crashed BRM. At Zandvoort, however, David Purley's similar attempt to save Roger Williamson from his overturned and burning car was sadly unsuccessful. Both Hailwood and Purley received the George Medal. Williamson was the first in a talented generation of British drivers to meet with tragic deaths over the next four years. These accidents hastened an urgent and largely fruitful review of safety, with special emphasis placed on reducing the chance of fire after an accident.

Gran Premio de la Republica Argentina

28 January 1973. Buenos Aires. 96 laps of a 2.079-mile circuit = 199.584 miles. Hot, dry and sunny. World Championship round 1

1 Emerson Fittipaldi	Lotus 72D-Ford	96	1h56m18.22
2 François Cevert	Tyrrell 006-Ford	96	1h56m22.91
3 Jackie Stewart	Tyrrell 005-Ford	96	1h56m51.41
4 Jacky Ickx	Ferrari 312B2	96	1h57m00.79
5 Denny Hulme	McLaren M19C-Ford	95	
6 Wilson Fittipaldi	Brabham BT37-Ford	95	

Winner's average speed: 102.964 mph. Starting grid front row: Regazzoni, 1m10.54 (pole) and E Fittipaldi, 1m10.84. Fastest lap: E Fittipaldi, 1m11.22. Leaders: Regazzoni, laps 1-28; Cevert, 29-85; E Fittipaldi, 86-96

Grande Premio do Brasil

11 February 1973. Interlagos. 40 laps of a 4.946-mile circuit = 197.840 miles. Very hot, dry and sunny. World Championship round 2

1 Emerson Fittipaldi	Lotus 72D-Ford	40	1h43m55.6
2 Jackie Stewart	Tyrrell 005-Ford	40	1h44m09.1
3 Denny Hulme	McLaren M19C-Ford	40	1h45m42.0
4 Arturo Merzario	Ferrari 312B2	39	
5 Jacky Ickx	Ferrari 312B2	39	
6 Clay Regazzoni	BRM P160D	39	

Winner's average speed: 114.219 mph. Starting grid front row: Peterson, 2m30.5 (pole) and E Fittipaldi, 2m30.7 and Ickx, 2m32.0. Fastest lap: E Fittipaldi and Hulme, 2m35.0. Leaders: E Fittipaldi, laps 1-40

South African Grand Prix

3 March 1973. Kyalami. 79 laps of a 2.550-mile circuit = 201.450 miles. Dry and heavy cloud. World Championship round 3

1 Jackie Stewart	Tyrrell 006-Ford	79	1h43m11.07
2 Peter Revson	McLaren M19C-Ford	79	1h43m35.62
3 Emerson Fittipaldi	Lotus 72D-Ford	79	1h43m36.13
4 Arturo Merzario	Ferrari 312B2	78	
5 Denny Hulme	McLaren M23-Ford	77	
6 George Follmer	Shadow DN1A-Ford	77	

Winner's average speed: 117.140 mph. Starting grid front row: Hulme, 1m16.28 (pole), E Fittipaldi, 1m16.41 and Scheckter, 1m16.43. Fastest lap: E Fittipaldi, 1m17.10. Leaders: Hulme, laps 1-4; Scheckter, 5-6; Stewart, 7-79

Gran Premio de Espana

29 April 1973. Montjuich Park. 75 laps of a 2.355-mile circuit = 176.625 miles. Warm, dry and sunny. World Championship round 4

1 Emerson Fittipaldi	Lotus 72D-Ford	75	1h48m18.7
2 François Cevert	Tyrrell 006-Ford	75	1h49m01.4
3 George Follmer	Shadow DN1A-Ford	75	1h49m31.8
4 Peter Revson	McLaren M23-Ford	74	
5 Jean-Pierre Beltoise	BRM P160E	74	
6 Denny Hulme	McLaren M23-Ford	74	

Winner's average speed: 97.843 mph. Starting grid front row: Peterson, 1m21.8 (pole) and Hulme, 1m22.5. Fastest lap: Peterson, 1m23.8. Leaders: Peterson, laps 1-56; E Fittipaldi, 57-75

Grand Prix de Belgique

20 May 1973. Zolder. 70 laps of a 2.622-mile circuit = 183.540 miles. Warm, dry and sunny. World Championship round 5. Also known as the European Grand Prix

1 Jackie Stewart	Tyrrell 006-Ford	70	1h42m13.43
2 François Cevert	Tyrrell 006-Ford	70	1h42m45.27
3 Emerson Fittipaldi	Lotus 72D-Ford	70	1h44m16.22
4 Andrea de Adamich	Brabham BT37-Ford	69	
5 Niki Lauda	BRM P160E	69	
6 Chris Amon	Tecno PA123	67	

Winner's average speed: 107.728 mph. Starting grid front row: Peterson, 1m22.46 (pole) and Hulme, 1m23.0. Fastest lap: Cevert, 1m25.42. Leaders: Peterson, lap 1; Cevert, laps 2-19; E Fittipaldi, 20-24; Stewart, 25-70

Grand Prix de Monaco

3 June 1973. Monte Carlo. 78 laps of a 2.037-mile circuit = 158.886 miles. Warm, dry and sunny. World Championship round 6

1 Jackie Stewart	Tyrrell 006-Ford	78	1h57m44.3
2 Emerson Fittipaldi	Lotus 72D-Ford	78	1h57m45.6
3 Ronnie Peterson	Lotus 72D-Ford	77	
4 François Cevert	Tyrrell 006-Ford	77	
5 Peter Revson	McLaren M23-Ford	76	
6 Denny Hulme	McLaren M23-Ford	76	

Winner's average speed: 80.969 mph. Starting grid front row: Stewart, 1m27.5 (pole) and Peterson, 1m27.7. Fastest lap: E Fittipaldi, 1m28.1. Leaders: Cevert, lap 1; Peterson, 2-7; Stewart, 8-78

Hitachi Sveriges Grand Prix

17 June 1973. Anderstorp. 80 laps of a 2.497-mile circuit = 199.760 miles. Warm, dry and sunny. World Championship round 7

1 Denny Hulme	McLaren M23-Ford	80	1h56m46.049
2 Ronnie Peterson	Lotus 72D-Ford	80	1h56m50.088
3 François Cevert	Tyrrell 006-Ford	80	1h57m04.117
4 Carlos Reutemann	Brabham BT42-Ford	80	1h57m00.716
5 Jackie Stewart	Tyrrell 006-Ford	80	1h57m12.047
6 Jacky Ickx	Ferrari 312B3	79	

Winner's average speed: 102.645 mph. Starting grid front row: Peterson, 1m23.810 (pole) and Cevert, 1m23.899. Fastest lap: Hulme, 1m26.146. Leaders: Peterson, laps 1-78; Hulme, 79-80

World Championship Grand Prix Racing

1973 DRIVERS' RECORDS

Driver	Car	Argentinian GP	Brazilian GP	South African GP	Spanish GP	Belgian GP	Monaco GP	Swedish GP	French GP	British GP	Dutch GP	German GP	Austrian GP	Italian GP	Canadian GP	United States GP
Andrea de Adamich	Surtees TS9B-Ford	-	-	8	-	-	-	-	-	-	-	-	-	-	-	-
	Brabham BT37-Ford	-	-	-	R	4	7	-	R	-	-	-	-	-	-	-
	Brabham BT42-Ford	-	-	-	-	-	-	-	-	R	-	-	-	-	-	-
Chris Amon	Tecno PA123	-	-	-	-	6	R	-	-	R	R	-	DNS	-	-	-
	Tyrrell 005-Ford	-	-	-	-	-	-	-	-	-	-	-	-	-	10	DNS
Tom Belso	Williams IR01-Ford	-	-	-	-	-	-	DNS	-	-	-	-	-	-	-	-
Jean-Pierre Beltoise	BRM P160C	R	-	-	-	-	-	-	-	-	-	-	-	-	-	-
	BRM P160D	-	R	R	-	-	-	-	-	-	-	-	-	-	-	-
	BRM P160E	-	-	-	5	R	R	R	11	R	5	R	5	13	4	9
Mike Beuttler	March 721G-Ford	10	R	NC	-	-	-	-	-	-	-	-	-	-	-	-
	March 731-Ford	-	-	-	7	11	R	8	-	11	R	16	R	R	R	10
Luis-Pereira Bueno	Surtees TS9B-Ford	-	12	-	-	-	-	-	-	-	-	-	-	-	-	-
François Cevert	Tyrrell 006-Ford	2	10	-	2	2F	4	3	2	5	2	2	R	5	R	DNS
	Tyrrell 005-Ford	-	-	NC	-	-	-	-	-	-	-	-	-	-	-	-
Dave Charlton	Lotus 72D-Ford	-	-	R	-	-	-	-	-	-	-	-	-	-	-	-
Emerson Fittipaldi	Lotus 72D-Ford	1F	1F	3F	1	3	2F	12	R	R	R	6	RP	2	2F	6
Wilson Fittipaldi	Brabham BT37-Ford	6	R	R	-	-	-	-	-	-	-	-	-	-	-	-
	Brabham BT42-Ford	-	-	-	10	R	11	R	16	R	R	5	R	R	11	NC
George Follmer	Shadow DN1A-Ford	-	-	6	3	R	DNS	14	R	R	10	R	R	10	17	14
Nanni Galli	Williams FX3B-Ford	R	9	-	-	-	-	-	-	-	-	-	-	-	-	-
	Williams IR01-Ford	-	-	-	11	R	R	-	-	-	-	-	-	-	-	-
Howden Ganley	Williams FX3B-Ford	NC	7	10	-	-	-	-	-	-	-	-	-	-	-	-
	Williams IR02-Ford	-	-	-	R	R	R	11	14	9	9	DNS	-	-	-	-
	Williams IR03-Ford	-	-	-	-	-	-	-	-	-	-	-	NC	R	6	12
Peter Gethin	BRM P160E	-	-	-	-	-	-	-	-	-	-	-	-	-	R	-
Mike Hailwood	Surtees TS14A-Ford	R	R	R	R	R	8	R	R	R	R	14	10	7	9	R
Graham Hill	Shadow DN1A-Ford	-	-	-	R	9	R	R	10	R	NC	13	R	14	16	13
Denny Hulme	McLaren M19C-Ford	5	3F	-	-	-	-	-	-	-	-	-	-	-	-	-
	McLaren M23-Ford	-	-	5P	6	7	6	1F	8F	3	R	12	8	15	13	4
James Hunt	March 731-Ford	-	-	-	-	-	9	-	6	4F	3	-	R	DNS	7	2F
Jacky Ickx	Ferrari 312B2	4	5	R	-	-	-	-	-	-	-	-	-	-	-	-
	Ferrari 312B3	-	-	-	12	R	R	6	5	8	-	-	-	-	-	-
	McLaren M23-Ford	-	-	-	-	-	-	-	-	-	-	3	-	-	-	-
	Ferrari 312B3S	-	-	-	-	-	-	-	-	-	-	-	-	8	-	-
	Williams IR01-Ford	-	-	-	-	-	-	-	-	-	-	-	-	-	-	7
Jean-Pierre Jarier	March 721G-Ford	R	R	NC	-	-	-	-	-	-	-	-	-	-	-	-
	March 731-Ford	-	-	-	-	R	R	R	R	-	-	-	R	-	NC	11
Eddie Keizan	Tyrrell 004-Ford	-	-	NC	-	-	-	-	-	-	-	-	-	-	-	-
Niki Lauda	BRM P160C	R	8	-	-	-	-	-	-	-	-	-	-	-	-	-
	BRM P160D	-	-	R	-	-	-	-	-	-	-	-	-	-	-	-
	BRM P160E	-	-	-	R	5	R	13	9	12	R	R	DNS	R	R	R
Gijs van Lennep	Williams IR01-Ford	-	-	-	-	-	-	-	-	-	6	-	9	R	-	-
Jochen Mass	Surtees TS14A-Ford	-	-	-	-	-	-	-	-	R	-	7	-	-	-	R
Graham McRae	Williams IR01-Ford	-	-	-	-	-	-	-	-	R	-	-	-	-	-	-
Arturo Merzario	Ferrari 312B2	9	4	4	-	-	-	-	-	-	-	-	-	-	-	-
	Ferrari 312B3	-	-	-	-	-	R	-	7	-	-	-	-	-	-	-
	Ferrari 312B3S	-	-	-	-	-	-	-	-	-	-	-	7	R	15	16
Jackie Oliver	Shadow DN1A-Ford	-	-	R	R	R	10	R	R	R	R	8	R	11	3	15
Rikky von Opel	Ensign N173-Ford	-	-	-	-	-	-	-	15	13	DNS	-	R	R	NC	R
Carlos Pace	Surtees TS14A-Ford	R	R	R	R	8	R	10	13	R	7	4F	3F	R	18	R
Henri Pescarolo	March 731-Ford	-	-	-	8	-	-	-	-	-	-	-	-	-	-	-
	Williams IR01-Ford	-	-	-	-	-	-	-	R	-	-	10	-	-	-	-
Ronnie Peterson	Lotus 72D-Ford	R	RP	11	RPF	RP	3	2P	1	2P	11PF	R	1	1P	RP	1P
Jackie Pretorius	Williams FX3B-Ford	-	-	R	-	-	-	-	-	-	-	-	-	-	-	-
David Purley	March 731-Ford	-	-	-	-	-	R	-	-	DNS	R	15	-	9	-	-
Brian Redman	Shadow DN1A-Ford	-	-	-	-	-	-	-	-	-	-	-	-	-	-	DSQ
Clay Regazzoni	BRM P160C	7P	-	-	-	-	-	-	-	-	-	-	-	-	-	-
	BRM P160D	-	6	R	-	-	-	-	-	-	-	-	-	-	-	-
	BRM P160E	-	-	-	9	10	R	9	12	7	8	R	6	R	-	8
Carlos Reutemann	Brabham BT37-Ford	R	11	7	-	-	-	-	-	-	-	-	-	-	-	-
	Brabham BT42-Ford	-	-	-	R	R	R	4	3	6	R	R	4	6	8	3
Peter Revson	McLaren M19C-Ford	8	R	2	-	-	-	-	-	-	-	-	-	-	-	-
	McLaren M23-Ford	-	-	-	4	R	5	7	-	1	4	9	R	3	1	5
Jody Scheckter	McLaren M19C-Ford	-	-	9	-	-	-	-	-	-	-	-	-	-	-	-
	McLaren M23-Ford	-	-	-	-	-	-	-	R	R	-	-	-	-	R	R/Cont'd

Driver	Car	Argentinian GP	Brazilian GP	South African GP	Spanish GP	Belgian GP	Monaco GP	Swedish GP	French GP	British GP	Dutch GP	German GP	Austrian GP	Italian GP	Canadian GP	United States GP
Tim Schenken	Williams IR01-Ford	-	-	-	-	-	-	-	-	-	-	-	-	-	14	-
Jackie Stewart	Tyrrell 005-Ford	3	2	-	-	-	-	-	-	-	-	-	-	-	-	-
	Tyrrell 006-Ford	-	-	1	R	1	1^P	5	4^P	10	1	1^P	2	4^F	5	DNS
Rolf Stommelen	Brabham BT42-Ford	-	-	-	-	-	-	-	-	-	-	11	R	12	12	-
John Watson	Brabham BT37-Ford	-	-	-	-	-	-	-	-	R	-	-	-	-	-	-
	Brabham BT42-Ford	-	-	-	-	-	-	-	-	-	-	-	-	-	-	R
Roger Williamson	March 731-Ford	-	-	-	-	-	-	-	-	R	R	-	-	-	-	-
Reine Wisell	March 731-Ford	-	-	-	-	-	DNS	R	-	-	-	-	-	-	-	-

Grand Prix de France

1 July 1973. Paul Ricard. 54 laps of a 3.610-mile circuit = 194.940 miles. Very hot, dry and sunny. World Championship round 8

1 Ronnie Peterson — Lotus 72D-Ford — 54 1h41m36.52
2 François Cevert — Tyrrell 006-Ford — 54 1h42m17.44
3 Carlos Reutemann — Brabham BT42-Ford — 54 1h42m23.00
4 Jackie Stewart — Tyrrell 006-Ford — 54 1h42m23.40
5 Jacky Ickx — Ferrari 312B3 — 54 1h42m25.42
6 James Hunt — March 731-Ford — 54 1h42m59.06

Winner's average speed: 115.112 mph. Starting grid front row: Stewart, 1m48.37 (pole), Scheckter, 1m49.18 and E Fittipaldi, 1m49.36. Fastest lap: Hulme, 1m50.99. Leaders: Scheckter, laps 1-41; Peterson, 42-54.

John Player British Grand Prix

14 July 1973. Silverstone. 67 laps of a 2.927-mile circuit = 196.109 miles. Race stopped on lap 2 due to multiple accident. Restarted over original distance. Dry and overcast. World Championship round 9

1 Peter Revson — McLaren M23-Ford — 67 1h29m18.5
2 Ronnie Peterson — Lotus 72D-Ford — 67 1h29m21.3
3 Denny Hulme — McLaren M23-Ford — 67 1h29m21.5
4 James Hunt — March 731-Ford — 67 1h29m21.9
5 Carlos Reutemann — Tyrrell 006-Ford — 67 1h29m55.1
6 Carlos Reutemann — Brabham BT42-Ford — 67 1h30m03.2

Winner's average speed: 131.752 mph. Starting grid front row: Peterson, 1m16.3 (pole), Hulme, 1m16.5 and Revson, 1m16.5. Fastest lap: Hunt, 1m18.6. Leaders: Peterson, laps 1-38; Revson, 39-67.

Grote Prijs van Nederland

29 July 1973. Zandvoort. 72 laps of a 2.626-mile circuit = 189.072 miles. Dry and overcast. World Championship round 10

1 Jackie Stewart — Tyrrell 006-Ford — 72 1h39m12.45
2 François Cevert — Tyrrell 006-Ford — 72 1h39m28.28
3 James Hunt — March 731-Ford — 72 1h40m15.46
4 Peter Revson — McLaren M23-Ford — 72 1h40m21.58
5 Jean-Pierre Beltoise — BRM P160E — 72 1h40m25.82
6 Gijs van Lennep — Williams IR01-Ford — 70

Winner's average speed: 114.349 mph. Starting grid front row: Peterson, 1m19.47 (pole), Stewart, 1m19.97 and Cevert, 1m20.12. Fastest lap: Peterson, 1m20.31. Leaders: Peterson, laps 1-63; Stewart, 64-72.

Grosser Preis von Deutschland

5 August 1973. Nürburgring. 14 laps of a 14.189-mile circuit = 198.646 miles. Warm, dry and sunny. World Championship round 11

1 Jackie Stewart — Tyrrell 006-Ford — 14 1h42m03.0
2 François Cevert — Tyrrell 006-Ford — 14 1h42m04.6

3 Jacky Ickx — McLaren M23-Ford — 14 1h42m44.2
4 Carlos Pace — Surtees TS14A-Ford — 14 1h42m56.8
5 Wilson Fittipaldi — Brabham BT42-Ford — 14 1h43m22.9
6 Emerson Fittipaldi — Lotus 72D-Ford — 14 1h43m27.3

Winner's average speed: 116.793 mph. Starting grid front row: Stewart, 7m07.8 (pole) and Peterson, 7m08.3. Fastest lap: Pace, 7m11.4. Leaders: Stewart, laps 1-14

Grosser Preis von Österreich

19 August 1973. Österreichring. 54 laps of a 3.673-mile circuit = 198.342 miles. Very hot, dry and sunny. World Championship round 12

1 Ronnie Peterson — Lotus 72D-Ford — 54 1h28m48.78
2 Jackie Stewart — Tyrrell 006-Ford — 54 1h28m57.79
3 Carlos Pace — Surtees TS14A-Ford — 54 1h29m35.42
4 Carlos Reutemann — Brabham BT42-Ford — 54 1h29m36.69
5 Jean-Pierre Beltoise — BRM P160E — 54 1h30m10.38
6 Clay Regazzoni — BRM P160E — 54 1h30m27.18

Winner's average speed: 133.995 mph. Starting grid front row: E Fittipaldi, 1m34.98 (pole) and Peterson, 1m35.37. Fastest lap: Pace, 1m37.29. Leaders: Peterson, laps 1-16, 49-54; E Fittipaldi, 17-48.

Gran Premio d'Italia

9 September 1973. Monza. 55 laps of a 3.588-mile circuit = 197.340 miles. Hot, dry and sunny. World Championship round 13

1 Ronnie Peterson — Lotus 72D-Ford — 55 1h29m17.0
2 Emerson Fittipaldi — Lotus 72D-Ford — 55 1h29m17.8
3 Peter Revson — McLaren M23-Ford — 55 1h29m45.8
4 Jackie Stewart — Tyrrell 006-Ford — 55 1h29m50.2
5 François Cevert — Tyrrell 006-Ford — 55 1h30m03.2
6 Carlos Reutemann — Brabham BT42-Ford — 55 1h30m16.8

Winner's average speed: 132.616 mph. Starting grid front row: Peterson, 1m34.80 (pole) and Revson, 1m35.29. Fastest lap: Stewart, 1m35.3. Leaders: Peterson, laps 1-55

Canadian Grand Prix

23 September 1973. Mosport Park. 80 laps of a 2.459-mile circuit = 196.720 miles. Wet at the start, drying later. World Championship round 14

1 Peter Revson — McLaren M23-Ford — 80 1h59m04.083
2 Emerson Fittipaldi — Lotus 72D-Ford — 80 1h59m36.817
3 Jackie Oliver — Shadow DN1A-Ford — 80 1h59m38.588
4 Jean-Pierre Beltoise — BRM P160E — 80 1h59m40.597
5 Jackie Stewart — Tyrrell 006-Ford — 79
6 Howden Ganley — Williams IR03-Ford — 79

Winner's average speed: 99.130 mph. Starting grid front row: Peterson, 1m13.697 (pole) and Revson, 1m14.737. Fastest lap: E Fittipaldi, 1m15.496. Leaders: Peterson, laps 1-2; Lauda, 3-19; E Fittipaldi, 20-32; Stewart, 33; Beltoise, 34-39; Oliver, 40-46; Revson, 47-80.

United States Grand Prix

7 October 1973. Watkins Glen. 59 laps of a 3.377-mile circuit = 199.243 miles. Cool and dry. World Championship round 15

1 Ronnie Peterson	Lotus 72D-Ford	59	1h41m15.779
2 James Hunt	March 731-Ford	59	1h41m16.467
3 Carlos Reutemann	Brabham BT42-Ford	59	1h41m38.729
4 Denny Hulme	McLaren M23-Ford	59	1h42m06.025
5 Peter Revson	McLaren M23-Ford	59	1h42m36.166
6 Emerson Fittipaldi	Lotus 72D-Ford	59	1h43m03.744

Winner's average speed: 118.055 mph. Starting grid front row: Peterson, 1m39.657 (pole) and Reutemann, 1m40.013. Fastest lap: Hunt, 1m41.652. Leaders: Peterson, laps 1-59

1973 FINAL CHAMPIONSHIP POSITIONS

Drivers

1	Jackie Stewart	71		
2	Emerson Fittipaldi	55		
3	Ronnie Peterson	52		
4	François Cevert	47		
5	Peter Revson	38		
6	Denny Hulme	26		
7	Carlos Reutemann	16		
8	James Hunt	14		
9	Jacky Ickx	12		
10	Jean-Pierre Beltoise	9		
11	Carlos Pace	7		
12	Arturo Merzario	6		
13	George Follmer	5		
14	Jackie Oliver	4		
15=	Andrea de Adamich	3		
	Wilson Fittipaldi	3		
17=	Niki Lauda	2		
	Clay Regazzoni	2		
19=	Chris Amon	1		
	Howden Ganley	1		
	Gijs van Lennep	1		

Manufacturers

1	Lotus-Ford	92 (96)*
2	Tyrrell-Ford	82 (86)*
3	McLaren-Ford	58
4	Brabham-Ford	22
5	March-Ford	14
6=	BRM	12
	Ferrari	12
8	Shadow-Ford	9
9	Surtees-Ford	7
10	Williams-Ford	2
11	Tecno	1

*Sum of best seven results from the first eight races and best six results from the final seven races. Points only awarded to first car to finish for each manufacturer

1974

Jackie Stewart's retirement from the sport heralded a major reshuffle of drivers among the teams. Tyrrell hired the relatively inexperienced Jody Scheckter and Patrick Depailler; Emerson Fittipaldi moved to the Texaco/Marlboro-sponsored McLaren team; Ferrari re-signed Clay Regazzoni in addition to the promising Niki Lauda from BRM, while Jacky Ickx replaced Fittipaldi at Lotus.

It was a great season for the World Championship, culminating in a three-way finale in America. With two wins, Scheckter had only an outside chance of becoming champion, but Fittipaldi and Regazzoni entered the race equal on points. With the Ferrari delayed by faulty shock absorbers, Fittipaldi's conservative race to fourth was enough to give him a second World Championship.

In fact, Niki Lauda had been the fastest driver of the year, but a number of retirements while leading cost him the series.

Young Argentinian Carlos Reutemann won the first three Grands Prix of his career in a Gordon Murray-designed Brabham BT44. But despite his best efforts, and those of a partisan crowd, Reutemann never won his home race. In 1974 he ran out of fuel two laps from victory.

Lotus introduced the disappointing 76, but Peterson was brilliant in the aging Lotus 72, scoring three wins for the team.

Gran Premio de la Republica Argentina

13 January 1974. Buenos Aires. 53 laps of a 3.709-mile circuit = 196.577 miles. Hot, dry and sunny. World Championship round 1

1 Denny Hulme	McLaren M23-Ford	53	1h41m02.01
2 Niki Lauda	Ferrari 312B3	53	1h41m11.28
3 Clay Regazzoni	Ferrari 312B3	53	1h41m22.42
4 Mike Hailwood	McLaren M23-Ford	53	1h41m33.80
5 Jean-Pierre Beltoise	BRM P160E	53	1h41m53.85
6 Patrick Depailler	Tyrrell 005-Ford	53	1h42m54.49

Winner's average speed: 116.740 mph. Starting grid front row: Peterson, 1m50.78 (pole) and Regazzoni, 1m50.96. Fastest lap: Regazzoni, 1m52.10. Leaders: Peterson, laps 1-2; Reutemann, 3-51; Hulme, 52-53

Grande Premio do Brasil

27 January 1974. Interlagos. 32 laps of a 4.946-mile circuit = 158.272 miles. Race scheduled for 40 laps, stopped due to rain. Heavy clouds. World Championship round 2

1 Emerson Fittipaldi	McLaren M23-Ford	32	1h24m37.06
2 Clay Regazzoni	Ferrari 312B3	32	1h24m50.63
3 Jacky Ickx	Lotus 72D-Ford	31	
4 Carlos Pace	Surtees TS16/2-Ford	31	
5 Mike Hailwood	McLaren M23-Ford	31	
6 Ronnie Peterson	Lotus 72D-Ford	31	

Winner's average speed: 112.226 mph. Starting grid front row: Fittipaldi, 2m32.97 (pole) and Reutemann, 2m33.21. Fastest lap: Regazzoni, 2m36.05. Leaders: Reutemann, laps 1-3; Peterson, 4-15; Fittipaldi, 16-32

Lucky Strike South African Grand Prix

30 March 1974. Kyalami. 78 laps of a 2.550-mile circuit = 198.900 miles. Warm, dry and sunny. World Championship round 3

1 Carlos Reutemann	Brabham BT44-Ford	78	1h42m40.96
2 Jean-Pierre Beltoise	BRM P201	78	1h43m14.90
3 Mike Hailwood	McLaren M23-Ford	78	1h43m23.12
4 Patrick Depailler	Tyrrell 005-Ford	78	1h43m25.15
5 Hans-Joachim Stuck	March 741-Ford	78	1h43m27.19
6 Arturo Merzario	Williams FW02-Ford	78	1h43m37.00

Winner's average speed: 116.222 mph. Starting grid front row: Lauda, 1m16.58 (pole) and Pace, 1m16.63. Fastest lap: Reutemann, 1m18.16. Leaders: Lauda, laps 1-8; Reutemann, 9-78

Gran Premio de Espana

28 April 1974. Jarama. 84 laps of a 2.115-mile circuit = 177.660 miles. Race scheduled for 90 laps, stopped after two hours. Wet at the start, drying later. World Championship round 4

1 Niki Lauda	Ferrari 312B3	84	2h00m29.56
2 Clay Regazzoni	Ferrari 312B3	84	2h01m05.17
3 Emerson Fittipaldi	McLaren M23-Ford	83	
4 Hans-Joachim Stuck	March 741-Ford	82	
5 Jody Scheckter	Tyrrell 007-Ford	82	
6 Denny Hulme	McLaren M23-Ford	82	

Winner's average speed: 88.484 mph. Starting grid front row: Lauda, 1m18.44 (pole) and Peterson, 1m18.47. Fastest lap: Lauda, 1m20.83. Leaders: Peterson, laps 1-20; Lauda, 21-23, 25-84; Ickx, 24

Bang & Olufsen Grand Prix de Belgique

12 May 1974. Nivelles. 85 laps of a 2.314-mile circuit = 196.690 miles. Warm, dry and sunny. World Championship round 5

1 Emerson Fittipaldi	McLaren M23-Ford	85	1h44m20.57
2 Niki Lauda	Ferrari 312B3	85	1h44m20.92
3 Jody Scheckter	Tyrrell 007-Ford	85	1h45m06.18
4 Clay Regazzoni	Ferrari 312B3	85	1h45m12.59
5 Jean-Pierre Beltoise	BRM P201	85	1h45m28.62
6 Denny Hulme	McLaren M23-Ford	85	1h45m31.11

Winner's average speed: 113.102 mph. Starting grid front row: Regazzoni, 1m09.82 (pole) and Scheckter, 1m10.86. Fastest lap: Hulme, 1m11.31. Leaders: Regazzoni, laps 1-38; Fittipaldi, 39-85

Grand Prix de Monaco

26 May 1974. Monte Carlo. 78 laps of a 2.037-mile circuit = 158.886 miles. Warm, dry and sunny. World Championship round 6

1 Ronnie Peterson	Lotus 72E-Ford	78	1h58m03.7
2 Jody Scheckter	Tyrrell 007-Ford	78	1h58m32.5
3 Jean-Pierre Jarier	Shadow DN3A-Ford	78	1h58m52.6
4 Clay Regazzoni	Ferrari 312B3	78	1h59m06.8
5 Emerson Fittipaldi	McLaren M23-Ford	77	
6 John Watson	Brabham BT42-Ford	77	

Winner's average speed: 80.747 mph. Starting grid front row: Lauda, 1m26.3 (pole) and Regazzoni, 1m26.6. Fastest lap: Peterson, 1m27.9. Leaders: Regazzoni, laps 1-20; Lauda, 21-32; Peterson, 33-78

Texaco Sveriges Grand Prix

9 June 1974. Anderstorp. 80 laps of a 2.497-mile circuit = 199.760 miles. Warm, dry and sunny. World Championship round 7

1 Jody Scheckter	Tyrrell 007-Ford	80	1h58m31.391
2 Patrick Depailler	Tyrrell 007-Ford	80	1h58m31.771
3 James Hunt	Hesketh 308-Ford	80	1h58m34.716
4 Emerson Fittipaldi	McLaren M23-Ford	80	1h59m24.898
5 Jean-Pierre Jarier	Shadow DN3A-Ford	80	1h59m47.794
6 Graham Hill	Lola T370-Ford	79	

Winner's average speed: 101.125 mph. Starting grid front row: Depailler, 1m24.758 (pole) and Scheckter, 1m25.076. Fastest lap: Depailler, 1m27.262. Leaders: Scheckter, laps 1-80

Grote Prijs van Nederland

23 June 1974. Zandvoort. 75 laps of a 2.626-mile circuit = 196.950 miles. Warm, dry and sunny. World Championship round 8

1 Niki Lauda	Ferrari 312B3	75	1h43m00.35
2 Clay Regazzoni	Ferrari 312B3	75	1h43m08.60
3 Emerson Fittipaldi	McLaren M23-Ford	75	1h43m30.62
4 Mike Hailwood	McLaren M23-Ford	75	1h43m31.64
5 Jody Scheckter	Tyrrell 007-Ford	75	1h43m34.63
6 Patrick Depailler	Tyrrell 007-Ford	75	1h43m51.86

Winner's average speed: 114.722 mph. Starting grid front row: Lauda, 1m18.31 (pole) and Regazzoni, 1m18.91. Fastest lap: Peterson, 1m21.44. Leaders: Lauda, laps 1-75

Grand Prix de France

7 July 1974. Dijon-Prenois. 80 laps of a 2.044-mile circuit = 163.520 miles. Warm, dry and sunny. World Championship round 9

1 Ronnie Peterson	Lotus 72E-Ford	80	1h21m55.02
2 Niki Lauda	Ferrari 312B3	80	1h22m15.38
3 Clay Regazzoni	Ferrari 312B3	80	1h22m22.86
4 Jody Scheckter	Tyrrell 007-Ford	80	1h22m23.13
5 Jacky Ickx	Lotus 72E-Ford	80	1h22m32.56
6 Denny Hulme	McLaren M23-Ford	80	1h22m33.16

Winner's average speed: 119.770 mph. Starting grid front row: Lauda, 58.79s (pole) and Peterson, 59.08s. Fastest lap: Scheckter, 1m00.0. Leaders: Lauda, laps 1-16; Peterson, 17-80

John Player British Grand Prix

20 July 1974. Brands Hatch. 75 laps of a 2.650-mile circuit = 198.750 miles. Warm, dry and sunny. World Championship round 10

1 Jody Scheckter	Tyrrell 007-Ford	75	1h43m02.2
2 Emerson Fittipaldi	McLaren M23-Ford	75	1h43m17.5
3 Jacky Ickx	Lotus 72E-Ford	75	1h44m03.7
4 Clay Regazzoni	Ferrari 312B3	75	1h44m09.4
5 Niki Lauda*	Ferrari 312B3	74	
6 Carlos Reutemann	Brabham BT44-Ford	74	

*Lauda did not complete 74 laps due to being blocked in the pits and he was originally classified ninth until Ferrari successfully protested. Winner's average speed: 115.735 mph. Starting grid front row: Lauda, 1m19.7 (pole) and Peterson, 1m19.7. Fastest lap: Lauda, 1m21.1. Leaders: Lauda, laps 1-69; Scheckter, 70-75

Grosser Preis von Deutschland

4 August 1974. Nürburgring. 14 laps of a 14.189-mile circuit = 198.646 miles. Overcast with showers. World Championship round 11. Also known as the European Grand Prix

1 Clay Regazzoni	Ferrari 312B3	14	1h41m35.0
2 Jody Scheckter	Tyrrell 007-Ford	14	1h42m25.7
3 Carlos Reutemann	Brabham BT44-Ford	14	1h42m58.2
4 Ronnie Peterson	Lotus 76-Ford	14	1h42m59.2
5 Jacky Ickx	Lotus 72E-Ford	14	1h43m00.0
6 Tom Pryce	Shadow DN3A-Ford	14	1h43m53.1

Winner's average speed: 117.330 mph. Starting grid front row: Lauda, 7m00.8 (pole) and Regazzoni, 7m01.1. Fastest lap: Scheckter, 7m11.1. Leaders: Regazzoni, laps 1-14

Memphis Grosser Preis von Österreich

18 August 1974. Österreichring. 54 laps of a 3.673-mile circuit = 198.342 miles. Very hot, dry and sunny. World Championship round 12

1 Carlos Reutemann	Brabham BT44-Ford	54	1h28m44.72
2 Denny Hulme	McLaren M23-Ford	54	1h29m27.64
3 James Hunt	Hesketh 308-Ford	54	1h29m46.26
4 John Watson	Brabham BT44-Ford	54	1h29m54.11
5 Clay Regazzoni	Ferrari 312B3	54	1h29m57.80
6 Vittorio Brambilla	March 741-Ford	54	1h29m58.54

Winner's average speed: 134.097 mph. Starting grid front row: Lauda, 1m35.40 (pole) and Reutemann, 1m35.56. Fastest lap: Regazzoni, 1m37.22. Leaders: Reutemann, laps 1-54

Gran Premio d'Italia

8 September 1974. Monza. 52 laps of a 3.592-mile circuit = 186.784 miles. Very hot, dry and sunny. World Championship round 13

1 Ronnie Peterson	Lotus 72E-Ford	52	1h22m56.6
2 Emerson Fittipaldi	McLaren M23-Ford	52	1h22m57.4
3 Jody Scheckter	Tyrrell 007-Ford	52	1h23m21.3
4 Arturo Merzario	Williams FW03-Ford	52	1h24m24.3

5 Carlos Pace	Brabham BT44-Ford	51
6 Denny Hulme	McLaren M23-Ford	51

Winner's average speed: 135.117 mph. Starting grid front row: Lauda, 1m33.16 (pole) and Reutemann, 1m33.27. Fastest lap: Pace, 1m34.2. Leaders: Lauda, laps 1-29; Regazzoni, 30-40; Peterson, 41-52

Labatt's 50 Canadian Grand Prix

22 September 1974. Mosport Park. 80 laps of a 2.459-mile circuit = 196.720 miles. Cool and dry. World Championship round 14

1 Emerson Fittipaldi	McLaren M23-Ford	80	1h40m26.136
2 Clay Regazzoni	Ferrari 312B3	80	1h40m39.170
3 Ronnie Peterson	Lotus 72E-Ford	80	1h40m40.630
4 James Hunt	Hesketh 308-Ford	80	1h40m41.805
5 Patrick Depailler	Tyrrell 007-Ford	80	1h41m21.458
6 Denny Hulme	McLaren M23-Ford	79	

Winner's average speed: 117.520 mph. Starting grid front row: Fittipaldi, 1m13.188 (pole) and Lauda, 1m13.230. Fastest lap: Lauda, 1m13.659. Leaders: Lauda, laps 1-67; Fittipaldi, 68-80

United States Grand Prix

6 October 1974. Watkins Glen. 59 laps of a 3.377-mile circuit = 199.243 miles. Warm, dry and sunny. World Championship round 15

1 Carlos Reutemann	Brabham BT44-Ford	59	1h40m21.439
2 Carlos Pace	Brabham BT44-Ford	59	1h40m32.174
3 James Hunt	Hesketh 308-Ford	59	1h41m31.823
4 Emerson Fittipaldi	McLaren M23-Ford	59	1h41m39.192
5 John Watson	Brabham BT44-Ford	59	1h41m47.243
6 Patrick Depailler	Tyrrell 007-Ford	59	1h41m48.945

Winner's average speed: 119.120 mph. Starting grid front row: Reutemann, 1m38.978 (pole) and Hunt, 1m38.995. Fastest lap: Pace, 1m40.608. Leaders: Reutemann, laps 1-59

1974 DRIVERS' RECORDS

Driver	Car	Argentinian GP	Brazilian GP	South African GP	Spanish GP	Belgian GP	Monaco GP	Swedish GP	Dutch GP	French GP	British GP	German GP	Austrian GP	Italian GP	Canadian GP	United States GP
Chris Amon	Amon AF101-Ford	-	-	-	R	-	DNS	-	-	-	-	DNQ	-	DNQ	-	-
	BRM P201	-	-	-	-	-	-	-	-	-	-	-	-	-	NC	9
Mario Andretti	Parnelli VPJ4-Ford	-	-	-	-	-	-	-	-	-	-	-	-	-	7	DSQ
Ian Ashley	Token RJ02-Ford	-	-	-	-	-	-	-	-	-	-	DSQ	NC	-	-	-
	Brabham BT42-Ford	-	-	-	-	-	-	-	-	-	-	-	-	-	DNQ	DNQ
Derek Bell	Surtees TS16/3-Ford	-	-	-	-	-	-	-	-	-	DNQ	11	DNQ	DNQ	DNQ	-
Tom Belso	Williams FW01-Ford	-	-	-	R	-	-	-	-	-	-	-	-	-	-	-
	Williams FW02-Ford	-	-	-	DNQ	-	-	8	-	-	DNQ	-	-	-	-	-
Jean-Pierre Beltoise	BRM P160E	5	10	-	-	-	-	-	-	-	-	-	-	-	-	-
	BRM P201	-	-	2	R	5	R	R	R	10	12	R	R	R	NC	DNP
Vittorio Brambilla	March 741-Ford	-	-	10	DNS	9	R	10	10	11	R	13	6	R	DNQ	R
Dave Charlton	McLaren M23-Ford	-	-	19	-	-	-	-	-	-	-	-	-	-	-	-
Patrick Depailler	Tyrrell 005-Ford	6	8	4	-	-	-	-	-	-	-	-	-	-	-	-
	Tyrrell 006-Ford	-	-	-	8	-	9	-	-	8	-	-	-	-	-	-
	Tyrrell 007-Ford	-	-	-	-	R	-	2PF	6	-	R	R	R	11	5	6
José Dolhem	Surtees TS16/3-Ford	-	-	-	-	-	-	-	DNQ	-	-	-	DNQ	-	R
Mark Donohue	Penske PC1-Ford	-	-	-	-	-	-	-	-	-	-	-	-	-	12	R
Paddy Driver	Lotus 72-Ford	-	-	R	-	-	-	-	-	-	-	-	-	-	-	-
Guy Edwards	Lola T370-Ford	11	R	-	DNQ	12	8	7	R	15	-	DNQ	-	-	-	-
Carlo Facetti	Brabham BT42-Ford	-	-	-	-	-	-	-	-	-	-	-	-	DNQ	-	-
Emerson Fittipaldi	McLaren M23-Ford	10	1P	7	3	1	5	4	3	R	2	R	R	2	1P	4
Howden Ganley	March 741-Ford	8	R	-	-	-	-	-	-	-	-	-	-	-	-	-
	Maki F101-Ford	-	-	-	-	-	-	-	-	-	DNQ	DNQ	-	-	-	-
Peter Gethin	Lola T370-Ford	-	-	-	-	-	-	-	-	-	R	-	-	-	-	-
Mike Hailwood	McLaren M23-Ford	4	5	3	9	7	R	R	4	7	R	R	-	-	-	-
Graham Hill	Lola T370-Ford	R	11	12	R	8	7	6	R	13	13	9	NC	8	14	8
David Hobbs	McLaren M23-Ford	-	-	-	-	-	-	-	-	-	-	-	7	9	-	-
Denny Hulme	McLaren M23-Ford	1	12	9	6	6F	R	R	R	6	7	R	2	6	6	R
James Hunt	March 731-Ford	R	9	-	-	-	-	-	-	-	-	-	-	-	-	-
	Hesketh 308-Ford	-	-	R	10	R	R	3	R	R	R	R	3	R	4	3
Jacky Ickx	Lotus 72D-Ford	R	3	-	-	-	-	-	-	-	-	-	-	-	-	-
	Lotus 76-Ford	-	-	R	R	R	-	-	-	-	-	-	R	R	-	-
	Lotus 72E-Ford	-	-	-	-	-	R	R	11	5	3	5	-	-	13	R
Jean-Pierre Jabouille	Williams FW01-Ford	-	-	-	-	-	-	-	-	DNQ	-	-	-	-	-	-
	Surtees TS16/3-Ford	-	-	-	-	-	-	-	-	-	-	-	DNQ	-	-	-
Jean-Pierre Jarier	Shadow DN1A-Ford	R	R	-	-	-	-	-	-	-	-	-	-	-	-	-
	Shadow DN3A-Ford	-	-	-	NC	13	3	5	R	12	R	8	8	R	R	10
Eddie Keizan	Tyrrell 004-Ford	-	-	14	-	-	-	-	-	-	-	-	-	-	-	-
Leo Kinnunen	Surtees TS16/1-Ford	-	-	-	-	DNQ	-	R	-	DNQ	DNQ	-	DNQ	DNQ	-	-
Helmuth Koinigg	Brabham BT42-Ford	-	-	-	-	-	-	-	-	-	-	-	DNQ	-	-	-
	Surtees TS16/3-Ford	-	-	-	-	-	-	-	-	-	-	-	-	-	10	R
Jacques Laffite	Williams FW02-Ford	-	-	-	-	-	-	-	-	-	-	R	NC	R	15	R
Gérard Larrousse	Brabham BT42-Ford	-	-	-	-	-	R	-	-	DNQ	-	-	-	-	-	-
Niki Lauda	Ferrari 312B3	2	R	16P	1PF	R	2RP	R	1P	2P	5PF	RP	RP	RP	RF	R
Gijs van Lennep	Williams FW02-Ford	-	-	-	-	-	14	-	-	-	-	-	-	-	-	-
	Williams FW01-Ford	-	-	-	-	-	-	-	DNQ	-	-	-	-	-	-	-/Cont'd

1974 FINAL CHAMPIONSHIP POSITIONS

Drivers

1	Emerson Fittipaldi	55
2	Clay Regazzoni	52
3	Jody Scheckter	45
4	Niki Lauda	38
5	Ronnie Peterson	35
6	Carlos Reutemann	32
7	Denny Hulme	20
8	James Hunt	15
9	Patrick Depailler	14
10=	Mike Hailwood	12
	Jacky Ickx	12
12	Carlos Pace	11
13	Jean-Pierre Beltoise	10
14=	Jean-Pierre Jarier	6
	John Watson	6
16	Hans-Joachim Stuck	5
17	Arturo Merzario	4
18=	Vittorio Brambilla	1
	Graham Hill	1
	Tom Pryce	1

Manufacturers

1	McLaren-Ford	73 (75)*
2	Ferrari	65
3	Tyrrell-Ford	52
4	Lotus-Ford	42
5	Brabham-Ford	35
6	Hesketh-Ford	15
7	BRM	10
8	Shadow-Ford	7
9	March-Ford	6
10	Williams-Ford	4
11	Surtees-Ford	3
12	Lola-Ford	1

*Sum of best seven results from the first eight races and best six results from the final seven races. Points only awarded to first car to finish for each manufacturer

1974 DRIVERS' RECORDS cont'd/

Driver	Car	Argentinian GP	Brazilian GP	South African GP	Spanish GP	Belgian GP	Monaco GP	Swedish GP	Dutch GP	French GP	British GP	German GP	Austrian GP	Italian GP	Canadian GP	United States GP
Lella Lombardi	Brabham BT42-Ford	-	-	-	-	-	-	-	-	-	DNQ	-	-	-	-	-
Jochen Mass	Surtees TS16/2-Ford	R	17	R	R	R	DNS	R	R	-	-	-	-	-	-	-
	Surtees TS16/3-Ford	-	-	-	-	-	-	-	-	R	14	R	-	-	-	-
	McLaren M23-Ford	-	-	-	-	-	-	-	-	-	-	-	-	-	16	7
Arturo Merzario	Williams FW01-Ford	R	R	-	-	-	-	-	-	-	-	-	-	-	-	-
	Williams FW02-Ford	-	-	6	-	-	-	DNS	R	9	-	-	-	-	-	-
	Williams FW03-Ford	-	-	-	R	R	R	-	-	-	R	R	R	4	R	R
François Migault	BRM P160E	R	16	15	R	16	R	-	-	14	NC	DNQ	-	-	-	-
	BRM P201	-	-	-	-	-	-	R	-	-	-	-	-	R	-	-
John Nicholson	Lyncar 006-Ford	-	-	-	-	-	-	-	-	-	DNQ	-	-	-	-	-
Rikky von Opel	Ensign N174-Ford	DNS	-	-	-	-	-	-	-	-	-	-	-	-	-	-
	Brabham BT44-Ford	-	-	-	R	R	DNQ	9	9	DNQ	-	-	-	-	-	-
Carlos Pace	Surtees TS16/2-Ford	R	4	11	13	R	R	R	-	-	-	-	-	-	-	-
	Brabham BT42-Ford	-	-	-	-	-	-	-	-	DNQ	-	-	-	-	-	-
	Brabham BT44-Ford	-	-	-	-	-	-	-	-	-	9	12	R	5F	8	2F
Larry Perkins	Amon AF101-Ford	-	-	-	-	-	-	-	-	-	DNQ	-	-	-	-	-
Henri Pescarolo	BRM P160E	9	14	18	12	R	R	-	R	-	-	-	-	-	-	-
	BRM P201	-	-	-	-	-	-	R	-	R	R	10	-	R	-	-
Ronnie Peterson	Lotus 72D-Ford	13P	6	-	-	-	-	-	-	-	-	-	-	-	-	-
	Lotus 76-Ford	-	-	R	R	R	-	-	-	-	-	-	4	-	-	-
	Lotus 72E-Ford	-	-	-	-	-	1F	R	8F	1	10	-	R	1	3	R
Teddy Pilette	Brabham BT42-Ford	-	-	-	-	17	-	-	-	-	-	-	-	-	-	-
Tom Pryce	Token RJ02-Ford	-	-	-	-	R	-	-	-	-	-	-	-	-	-	-
	Shadow DN3A-Ford	-	-	-	-	-	-	-	R	R	8	6	R	10	R	NC
David Purley	Token RJ02-Ford	-	-	-	-	-	-	-	-	-	DNQ	-	-	-	-	-
Dieter Quester	Surtees TS16/3-Ford	-	-	-	-	-	-	-	-	-	-	-	9	-	-	-
Brian Redman	Shadow DN3A-Ford	-	-	-	7	18	R	-	-	-	-	-	-	-	-	-
Clay Regazzoni	Ferrari 312B3	3F	2F	R	2	4P	4	R	2	3	4	1	5F	R	2	11
Carlos Reutemann	Brabham BT44-Ford	7	7	1F	R	R	R	R	12	R	6	3	1	R	9	1P
Peter Revson	Shadow DN3A-Ford	R	R	-	-	-	-	-	-	-	-	-	-	-	-	-
Richard Robarts	Brabham BT44-Ford	R	15	17	-	-	-	-	-	-	-	-	-	-	-	-
	Williams FW02-Ford	-	-	-	-	-	-	DNS	-	-	-	-	-	-	-	-
Bertil Roos	Shadow DN3A-Ford	-	-	-	-	-	-	R	-	-	-	-	-	-	-	-
Ian Scheckter	Lotus 72-Ford	-	-	13	-	-	-	-	-	-	-	-	-	-	-	-
	Hesketh 308-Ford	-	-	-	-	-	-	-	-	-	-	-	DNQ	-	-	-
Jody Scheckter	Tyrrell 006-Ford	R	13	8	-	-	-	-	-	-	-	-	-	-	-	-
	Tyrrell 007-Ford	-	-	-	5	3	2	1	5	4F	1	2F	R	3	R	R
Tim Schenken	Trojan T103-Ford	-	-	-	14	10	R	-	DNQ	-	R	DNQ	10	R	-	-
	Lotus 76-Ford	-	-	-	-	-	-	-	-	-	-	-	-	-	-	DSQ
Vern Schuppan	Ensign N174-Ford	-	-	-	-	-	15	R	-	R	DNQ	DNQ	R	-	-	-
	Ensign N173-Ford	-	-	-	-	-	-	-	DSQ	-	-	-	-	-	-	-
Rolf Stommelen	Lola T370-Ford	-	-	-	-	-	-	-	-	-	-	-	R	R	11	12
Hans-Joachim Stuck	March 741-Ford	R	R	5	4	R	R	-	R	DNQ	R	7	R	R	R	DNQ
John Watson	Brabham BT42-Ford	12	R	R	11	11	6	11	7	16	11	-	-	-	-	-
	Brabham BT44-Ford	-	-	-	-	-	-	-	-	-	-	R	4	7	R	5
Eppie Wietzes	Brabham BT42-Ford	-	-	-	-	-	-	-	-	-	-	-	-	-	R	-
Mike Wilds	March 731-Ford	-	-	-	-	-	-	-	-	-	-	DNQ	-	-	-	-
	Ensign N174-Ford	-	-	-	-	-	-	-	-	-	-	-	DNQ	DNQ	DNQ	NC
Reine Wisell	March 741-Ford	-	-	-	-	-	-	R	-	-	-	-	-	-	-	-

1975

Niki Lauda had promised to dominate Grand Prix racing in 1974, only to be thwarted by mechanical failures. This year he made no mistake, Ferrari winning its first World Championship since 1964. To improve weight distribution, designer Mauro Forghieri introduced the 312T with transverse gearbox (hence the "T" designation), and the combination of Lauda and Ferrari proved irresistible.

The Marlboro-McLaren team won three times, two of the victories coming in shortened races. The British GP was stopped with Emerson Fittipaldi ahead when a downpour sent 12 cars sliding into the barriers. Of the top six only two were still running at the flag!

Fittipaldi's team-mate Jochen Mass scored the only Grand Prix win of his career in the tragic Spanish GP at the end of April. Practice had been disrupted by the Grand Prix Drivers' Association protests that the circuit, and particularly its barriers, were unsafe. Their fears were realized when race leader Rolf Stommelen crashed over the barrier, killing four people.

Reduced points were awarded in Spain, and also in the wet Austrian GP, where Vittorio Brambilla celebrated his only victory by crashing over the finish line! Sadly, Mark Donohue died in practice there, after a puncture while at high speed caused him to crash.

James Hunt's Hesketh beat Lauda in a tremendous Dutch GP, but the financial burden of running a team without major sponsorship forced Lord Hesketh to quit the team at the end of the year. The Hesketh marque continued in Grand Prix racing but it would never be a force again.

Brabham continued its improving form with both Carlos Reutemann and Carlos Pace winning races for the Martini-sponsored team. For Pace the Brazilian GP was to be his only victory. Jean-Pierre Jarier showed sensational early season form for Shadow, and would have won in Brazil but for mechanical failure. Although team-mate Tom Pryce was on pole in Britain, promise did not translate into results.

The year ended in tragedy. Graham Hill had run an Embassy-sponsored team for two seasons and in May he announced his retirement from the cockpit to concentrate on management of the concern. He had possibly the best young driver of the time in Tony Brise. But in November, returning from testing at Circuit Paul Ricard, a light plane flown by Hill crashed in fog near Elstree airfield. Both Hill and Brise were killed, along with designer Andy Smallman and some of the mechanics, and the team was wound up.

Gran Premio de la Republica Argentina

12 January 1975. Buenos Aires. 53 laps of a 3.709-mile circuit = 196.577 miles. Hot, dry and sunny. World Championship round 1

1 Emerson Fittipaldi	McLaren M23-Ford	53	1h39m26.29
2 James Hunt	Hesketh 308-Ford	53	1h39m32.20
3 Carlos Reutemann	Brabham BT44B-Ford	53	1h39m43.35
4 Clay Regazzoni	Ferrari 312B3	53	1h40m02.08
5 Patrick Depailler	Tyrrell 007-Ford	53	1h40m20.54
6 Niki Lauda	Ferrari 312B3	53	1h40m45.94

Winner's average speed: 118.577 mph. Starting grid front row: Jarier, 1m49.21 (pole) and Pace, 1m49.64 - Jarier did not start. Fastest lap: Hunt, 1m50.91. Leaders: Reutemann, laps 1-25; Hunt, 26-34; E Fittipaldi, 35-53

Grande Premio do Brasil

26 January 1975. Interlagos. 40 laps of a 4.946-mile circuit = 197.840 miles. Very hot, dry and sunny. World Championship round 2

1 Carlos Pace	Brabham BT44B-Ford	40	1h44m41.17
2 Emerson Fittipaldi	McLaren M23-Ford	40	1h44m46.96
3 Jochen Mass	McLaren M23-Ford	40	1h45m17.83
4 Clay Regazzoni	Ferrari 312B3	40	1h45m24.45
5 Niki Lauda	Ferrari 312B3	40	1h45m43.05
6 James Hunt	Hesketh 308-Ford	40	1h45m46.29

Winner's average speed: 113.390 mph. Starting grid front row: Jarier, 2m29.88 (pole) and E Fittipaldi, 2m30.68. Fastest lap: Jarier, 2m34.16. Leaders: Reutemann, laps 1-4; Jarier, 5-32; Pace, 33-40

Lucky Strike South African Grand Prix

1 March 1975. Kyalami. 78 laps of a 2.550-mile circuit = 198.900 miles. Warm, dry and overcast. World Championship round 3

1 Jody Scheckter	Tyrrell 007-Ford	78	1h43m16.90
2 Carlos Reutemann	Brabham BT44B-Ford	78	1h43m20.64
3 Patrick Depailler	Tyrrell 007-Ford	78	1h43m33.82
4 Carlos Pace	Brabham BT44B-Ford	78	1h43m34.21
5 Niki Lauda	Ferrari 312T	78	1h43m45.54
6 Jochen Mass	McLaren M23-Ford	78	1h44m20.24

Winner's average speed: 115.548 mph. Starting grid front row: Pace, 1m16.41 (pole) and Reutemann, 1m16.48. Fastest lap: Pace, 1m17.20. Leaders: Pace, laps 1-2; J Scheckter, 3-78

Gran Premio de Espana

27 April 1975. Montjuich Park. 29 laps of a 2.355-mile circuit = 68.295 miles. Race scheduled for 75 laps but stopped due to serious accident; half-points awarded as under 60% of the race had been completed. Warm, dry and sunny. World Championship round 4

1 Jochen Mass	McLaren M23-Ford	29	42m53.7
2 Jacky Ickx	Lotus 72E-Ford	29	42m54.8
3 Carlos Reutemann	Brabham BT44B-Ford	28	
4 Jean-Pierre Jarier*	Shadow DN5A-Ford	28	
5 Vittorio Brambilla	March 751-Ford	28	
6 Lella Lombardi	March 751-Ford	27	

*Jarier was penalized one lap for passing another car while caution flags were being shown. Winner's average speed: 95.529 mph. Starting grid front row: Lauda, 1m23.4 (pole) and Regazzoni, 1m23.5. Fastest lap: Andretti, 1m25.10. Leaders: Hunt, laps 1-6; Andretti, 7-16; Stommelen, 17-21, 23-25; Pace, 22; Mass, 26-27, 29; Ickx, 28

Grand Prix de Monaco

11 May 1975. Monte Carlo. 75 laps of a 2.037-mile circuit = 152.775 miles. Scheduled for 78 laps but stopped under championship rules after two hours because rain had slowed the race. Rain at the start, eventually drying. World Championship round 5

1 Niki Lauda	Ferrari 312T	75	2h01m21.31
2 Emerson Fittipaldi	McLaren M23-Ford	75	2h01m24.09
3 Carlos Pace	Brabham BT44B-Ford	75	2h01m39.12
4 Ronnie Peterson	Lotus 72E-Ford	75	2h01m59.76

5 Patrick Depailler	Tyrrell 007-Ford	75	2h02m02.17
6 Jochen Mass	McLaren M23-Ford	75	2h02m03.38

Winner's average speed: 75.534 mph. Starting grid front row: Lauda, 1m26.40 (pole) and Pryce, 1m27.09. Fastest lap: Depailler, 1m28.67. Leaders: Lauda, laps 1-23, 25-75; Peterson, 24

Grand Prix de Belgique

25 May 1975. Zolder. 70 laps of a 2.648-mile circuit = 185.360 miles. Dry and overcast. World Championship round 6

1 Niki Lauda	Ferrari 312T	70	1h43m53.98
2 Jody Scheckter	Tyrrell 007-Ford	70	1h44m13.20
3 Carlos Reutemann	Brabham BT44B-Ford	70	1h44m35.80
4 Patrick Depailler	Tyrrell 007-Ford	70	1h44m54.06
5 Clay Regazzoni	Ferrari 312T	70	1h44m57.84
6 Tom Pryce	Shadow DN5A-Ford	70	1h45m22.43

Winner's average speed: 107.042 mph. Starting grid front row: Lauda, 1m25.43 (pole) and Pace, 1m25.47. Fastest lap: Regazzoni, 1m26.76. Leaders: Pace, laps 1-3; Brambilla, 4-5; Lauda, 6-70

Polar Sveriges Grand Prix

8 June 1975. Anderstorp. 80 laps of a 2.497-mile circuit = 199.760 miles. Warm, dry and sunny. World Championship round 7

1 Niki Lauda	Ferrari 312T	80	1h59m18.319
2 Carlos Reutemann	Brabham BT44B-Ford	80	1h59m24.607
3 Clay Regazzoni	Ferrari 312T	80	1h59m47.414
4 Mario Andretti	Parnelli VPJ4-Ford	80	2h00m02.699
5 Mark Donohue	Penske PC1-Ford	80	2h00m49.082
6 Tony Brise	Hill GH1-Ford	79	

Winner's average speed: 100.462 mph. Starting grid front row: Brambilla, 1m24.630 (pole) and Depailler, 1m25.010. Fastest lap: Lauda, 1m28.267. Leaders: Brambilla, laps 1-15; Reutemann, 16-69; Lauda, 70-80

Grote Prijs van Nederland

22 June 1975. Zandvoort. 75 laps of a 2.626-mile circuit = 196.950 miles. Rain at the start, drying later. World Championship round 8

1 James Hunt	Hesketh 308-Ford	75	1h46m57.40
2 Niki Lauda	Ferrari 312T	75	1h46m58.46
3 Clay Regazzoni	Ferrari 312T	75	1h47m52.46
4 Carlos Reutemann	Brabham BT44B-Ford	74	
5 Carlos Pace	Brabham BT44B-Ford	74	
6 Tom Pryce	Shadow DN5A-Ford	74	

Winner's average speed: 110.484 mph. Starting grid front row: Lauda, 1m20.29 (pole) and Regazzoni, 1m20.57. Fastest lap: Lauda, 1m21.54. Leaders: Lauda, laps 1-12; Regazzoni, 13-14; Hunt, 15-75

Grand Prix de France

6 July 1975. Paul Ricard. 54 laps of a 3.610-mile circuit = 194.940 miles. Hot, dry and sunny. World Championship round 9

1 Niki Lauda	Ferrari 312T	54	1h40m18.84
2 James Hunt	Hesketh 308-Ford	54	1h40m20.43
3 Jochen Mass	McLaren M23-Ford	54	1h40m21.15
4 Emerson Fittipaldi	McLaren M23-Ford	54	1h40m58.61
5 Mario Andretti	Parnelli VPJ4-Ford	54	1h41m20.92
6 Patrick Depailler	Tyrrell 007-Ford	54	1h41m26.24

Winner's average speed: 116.598 mph. Starting grid front row: Lauda, 1m47.82 (pole) and J Scheckter, 1m48.22. Fastest lap: Mass, 1m50.6. Leaders: Lauda, laps 1-54

John Player British Grand Prix

19 July 1975. Silverstone. 56 laps of a 2.932-mile circuit = 164.192 miles. Race scheduled for 67 laps but stopped due to numerous accidents in the heavy rain. Showers. World Championship round 10

1 Emerson Fittipaldi	McLaren M23-Ford	56	1h22m05.0
2 Carlos Pace	Brabham BT44B-Ford	55	accident
3 Jody Scheckter	Tyrrell 007-Ford	55	accident
4 James Hunt	Hesketh 308-Ford	55	accident
5 Mark Donohue	March 751-Ford	55	accident
6 Vittorio Brambilla	March 751-Ford	55	

Winner's average speed: 120.019 mph. Starting grid front row: Pryce, 1m19.36 (pole) and Pace, 1m19.50. Fastest lap: Regazzoni, 1m20.9. Leaders: Pace, laps 1-12, 22-26; Regazzoni, 13-18; Pryce, 19-20; J Scheckter, 21, 27-32; Jarier, 33-34; Hunt, 35-42; E Fittipaldi, 43-56

Grosser Preis von Deutschland

3 August 1975. Nürburgring. 14 laps of a 14.189-mile circuit = 198.646 miles. Warm, dry and sunny. World Championship round 11

1 Carlos Reutemann	Brabham BT44B-Ford	14	1h41m14.1
2 Jacques Laffite	Williams FW04-Ford	14	1h42m51.8
3 Niki Lauda	Ferrari 312T	14	1h43m37.4
4 Tom Pryce	Shadow DN5A-Ford	14	1h44m45.5
5 Alan Jones	Hill GH1-Ford	14	1h45m04.4
6 Gijs van Lennep	Ensign N175-Ford	14	1h46m19.6

Winner's average speed: 117.734 mph. Starting grid front row: Lauda, 6m58.6 (pole) and Pace, 7m00.0. Fastest lap: Regazzoni, 7m06.4. Leaders: Lauda, laps 1-9; Reutemann, 10-14

Grosser Preis von Österreich

17 August 1975. Österreichring. 29 laps of a 3.673-mile circuit = 106.517 miles. Race scheduled for 54 laps but stopped due to rain; half-points awarded as under 60% of the race had been completed. Very wet. World Championship round 12. Also known as the European Grand Prix

1 Vittorio Brambilla	March 751-Ford	29	57m56.69
2 James Hunt	Hesketh 308-Ford	29	58m23.72
3 Tom Pryce	Shadow DN5A-Ford	29	58m31.54
4 Jochen Mass	McLaren M23-Ford	29	59m09.35
5 Ronnie Peterson	Lotus 72E-Ford	29	59m20.02
6 Niki Lauda	Ferrari 312T	29	59m26.97

Winner's average speed: 110.295 mph. Starting grid front row: Lauda, 1m34.85 (pole) and Hunt, 1m34.97. Fastest lap: Brambilla, 1m53.90. Leaders: Lauda, laps 1-14; Hunt, 15-18; Brambilla, 19-29

Gran Premio d'Italia

7 September 1975. Monza. 52 laps of a 3.592-mile circuit = 186.784 miles. Dry and overcast. World Championship round 13

1 Clay Regazzoni	Ferrari 312T	52	1h22m42.6
2 Emerson Fittipaldi	McLaren M23-Ford	52	1h22m59.2
3 Niki Lauda	Ferrari 312T	52	1h23m05.8
4 Carlos Reutemann	Brabham BT44B-Ford	52	1h23m37.7
5 James Hunt	Hesketh 308C-Ford	52	1h23m39.7
6 Tom Pryce	Shadow DN5A-Ford	52	1h23m58.5

Winner's average speed: 135.498 mph. Starting grid front row: Lauda, 1m32.24 (pole) and Regazzoni, 1m32.75. Fastest lap: Regazzoni, 1m33.1. Leaders: Regazzoni, laps 1-52

United States Grand Prix

5 October 1975. Watkins Glen. 59 laps of a 3.377-mile circuit = 199.243 miles. Cool and dry. World Championship round 14

1 Niki Lauda	Ferrari 312T	59	1h42m58.175
2 Emerson Fittipaldi	McLaren M23-Ford	59	1h43m03.118
3 Jochen Mass	McLaren M23-Ford	59	1h43m45.812
4 James Hunt	Hesketh 308C-Ford	59	1h43m47.650
5 Ronnie Peterson	Lotus 72E-Ford	59	1h43m48.161
6 Jody Scheckter	Tyrrell 007-Ford	59	1h43m48.496

Winner's average speed: 116.098 mph. Starting grid front row: Lauda, 1m42.003 (pole) and E Fittipaldi, 1m42.360. Fastest lap: E Fittipaldi, 1m43.374. Leaders: Lauda, laps 1-59

1975 FINAL CHAMPIONSHIP POSITIONS

Drivers

1	Niki Lauda	64.5
2	Emerson Fittipaldi	45
3	Carlos Reutemann	37
4	James Hunt	33
5	Clay Regazzoni	25
6	Carlos Pace	24
7=	Jochen Mass	20
	Jody Scheckter	20
9	Patrick Depailler	12
10	Tom Pryce	8
11	Vittorio Brambilla	6.5
12=	Jacques Laffite	6
	Ronnie Peterson	6
14	Mario Andretti	5
15	Mark Donohue	4
16	Jacky Ickx	3
17	Alan Jones	2
18	Jean-Pierre Jarier	1.5
19=	Tony Brise	1
	Gijs van Lennep	1
21	Lella Lombardi	0.5

Manufacturers

1	Ferrari	72.5
2	Brabham-Ford	54 (56)*
3	McLaren-Ford	53
4	Hesketh-Ford	33
5	Tyrrell-Ford	25
6	Shadow-Ford	9.5
7	Lotus-Ford	9
8	March-Ford	7.5
9	Williams-Ford	6
10	Parnelli-Ford	5
11	Hill-Ford	3
12	Penske-Ford	2
13	Ensign-Ford	1

*Sum of best seven results from the first eight races and best five results from the final six races. Points only awarded to first car to finish for each manufacturer

1975 DRIVERS' RECORDS

Driver	Car	Argentinian GP	Brazilian GP	South African GP	Spanish GP	Monaco GP	Belgian GP	Swedish GP	Dutch GP	French GP	British GP	German GP	Austrian GP	Italian GP	United States GP
Chris Amon	Ensign N175-Ford	-	-	-	-	-	-	-	-	-	-	-	12	12	-
Mario Andretti	Parnelli VPJ4-Ford	R	7	17	R^F	R	-	4	-	5	12	R	R	R	R
Ian Ashley	Williams FW03-Ford	-	-	-	-	-	-	-	-	-	-	DNS	-	-	-
Vittorio Brambilla	March 741-Ford	9	R	-	-	-	-	-	-	-	-	-	-	-	-
	March 751-Ford	-	-	R	5	R	R	RP	R	R	6	R	1^F	R	7
Tony Brise	Williams FW03-Ford	-	-	-	7	-	-	-	-	-	-	-	-	-	-
	Hill GH1-Ford	-	-	-	-	-	R	6	7	7	15	R	15	R	R
Dave Charlton	McLaren M23-Ford	-	-	14	-	-	-	-	-	-	-	-	-	-	-
Jim Crawford	Lotus 72E-Ford	-	-	-	-	-	-	-	-	-	R	-	13	-	-
Patrick Depailler	Tyrrell 007-Ford	5	R	3	R	5^F	4	12	9	6	9	9	11	7	R
Mark Donohue	Penske PC1-Ford	7	R	8	R	R	11	5	8	R	-	-	-	-	-
	March 751-Ford	-	-	-	-	-	-	-	-	-	5	R	DNS	-	-
Harald Ertl	Hesketh 308-Ford	-	-	-	-	-	-	-	-	-	-	8	R	9	-
Bob Evans	Stanley BRM P201	-	-	15	R	DNQ	9	13	R	17	-	-	R	R	-
Emerson Fittipaldi	McLaren M23-Ford	1	2	NC	DNS	2	7	8	R	4	1	R	9	2	2^F
Wilson Fittipaldi	Fittipaldi FD01-Ford	R	-	-	-	-	-	-	-	-	-	-	-	-	-
	Fittipaldi FD02-Ford	-	13	DNQ	R	DNQ	12	17	-	-	-	-	-	-	-
	Fittipaldi FD03-Ford	-	-	-	-	-	-	-	11	R	R	R	DNS	-	10
Hiroshi Fushida	Maki F101C-Ford	-	-	-	-	-	-	-	DNS	-	DNQ	-	-	-	-
Brian Henton	Lotus 72E-Ford	-	-	-	-	-	-	-	-	16	-	DNS	-	NC
Graham Hill	Lola T370-Ford	10	12	DNQ	-	-	-	-	-	-	-	-	-	-	-
	Hill GH1-Ford	-	-	-	-	DNQ	-	-	-	-	-	-	-	-	-
James Hunt	Hesketh 308-Ford	2^F	6	R	R	R	R	R	1	2	4	R	2	-	-
	Hesketh 308C-Ford	-	-	-	-	-	-	-	-	-	-	-	-	5	4
Jacky Ickx	Lotus 72E-Ford	8	9	12	2	8	R	15	R	R	-	-	-	-	-
Jean-Pierre Jabouille	Tyrrell 007-Ford	-	-	-	-	-	-	-	-	12	-	-	-	-	-
Jean-Pierre Jarier	Shadow DN5A-Ford	DNS^P	R^{PF}	R	4	R	R	R	R	8	14	R	-	-	R
	Shadow DN7A-Matra	-	-	-	-	-	-	-	-	-	-	R	R	-	-
Alan Jones	Hesketh 308-Ford	-	-	-	R	R	R	11	-	-	-	-	-	-	-
	Hill GH1-Ford	-	-	-	-	-	-	-	13	16	10	5	-	-	-
Eddie Keizan	Lotus 72E-Ford	-	-	13	-	-	-	-	-	-	-	-	-	-	-
Jacques Laffite	Williams FW02-Ford	R	11	NC	-	-	-	-	-	-	-	-	-	-	-
	Williams FW04-Ford	-	-	-	-	DNQ	R	-	R	11	R	2	R	R	DNS
Niki Lauda	Ferrari 312B3	6	5	-	-	-	-	-	-	-	-	-	-	-	-
	Ferrari 312T	-	-	5	R^P	1^P	1^P	1F	2^{PF}	1^P	8	3^P	6^P	3^P	1^P
Michel Leclère	Tyrrell 007-Ford	-	-	-	-	-	-	-	-	-	-	-	-	-	R
Gijs van Lennep	Ensign N174-Ford	-	-	-	-	-	-	10	-	-	-	-	-	-	-
	Ensign N175-Ford	-	-	-	-	-	-	-	15	-	6	-	-	-	-
Lella Lombardi	March 741-Ford	-	-	R	-	-	-	-	-	-	-	-	-	-	-
	March 751-Ford	-	-	-	6	DNQ	R	R	14	18	R	7	17	R	-
	Williams FW04-Ford	-	-	-	-	-	-	-	-	-	-	-	-	-	DNS
Brett Lunger	Hesketh 308-Ford	-	-	-	-	-	-	-	-	-	-	13	10	R
Damien Magee	Williams FW03-Ford	-	-	-	-	-	14	-	-	-	-	-	-	-	-
Jochen Mass	McLaren M23-Ford	14	3	6	1	6	R	R	R	3^F	7	R	4	R	3
Arturo Merzario	Williams FW03-Ford	NC	R	R	-	DNQ	R	-	-	-	-	-	-	-	-
	Williams FW04-Ford	-	-	-	R	-	-	-	-	-	-	-	-	-	-
	Fittipaldi FD03-Ford	-	-	-	-	-	-	-	-	-	-	-	-	11	-

/Cont'd

1975 DRIVERS' RECORDS cont'd/

Driver	Car	Argentinian GP	Brazilian GP	South African GP	Spanish GP	Monaco GP	Belgian GP	Swedish GP	Dutch GP	French GP	British GP	German GP	Austrian GP	Italian GP	United States GP
François Migault	Hill GH1-Ford	-	-	-	NC	-	R	-	-	-	-	-	-	-	-
	Williams FW03-Ford	-	-	-	-	-	-	-	-	DNS	-	-	-	-	-
Dave Morgan	Surtees TS16/4-Ford	-	-	-	-	-	-	-	-	-	R	-	-	-	-
John Nicholson	Lyncar 009-Ford	-	-	-	-	-	-	-	-	-	17	-	-	-	-
Carlos Pace	Brabham BT44B-Ford	R	1	4PF	R	3	8	R	5	R	2	R	R	R	R
Torsten Palm	Hesketh 308-Ford	-	-	-	-	DNQ	-	10	-	-	-	-	-	-	-
Henri Pescarolo	Surtees TS16/4-Ford	-	-	-	-	DNP	-	-	-	-	-	-	-	-	-
Ronnie Peterson	Lotus 72E-Ford	R	15	10	R	4	R	9	15	10	R	R	5	R	5
Tom Pryce	Shadow DN3B-Ford	12	R	-	-	-	-	-	-	-	-	-	-	-	-
	Shadow DN5A-Ford	-	-	9	R	R	6	R	6	R	RP	4	3	6	NC
Clay Regazzoni	Ferrari 312B3	4	4	-	-	-	-	-	-	-	-	-	-	-	-
	Ferrari 312T	-	-	16	NC	R	5F	3	3	R	13F	RF	7	1F	R
Carlos Reutemann	Brabham BT44B-Ford	3	8	2	3	9	3	2	4	14	R	1	14	4	R
Ian Scheckter	Tyrrell 007-Ford	-	-	R	-	-	-	-	-	-	-	-	-	-	-
	Williams FW04-Ford	-	-	-	-	-	-	-	R	-	-	-	-	-	-
	Williams FW03-Ford	-	-	-	-	-	-	12	-	-	-	-	-	-	-
Jody Scheckter	Tyrrell 007-Ford	11	R	1	R	7	2	7	16	9	3	R	8	8	6
Vern Schuppan	Hill GH1-Ford	-	-	-	-	-	-	R	-	-	-	-	-	-	-
Rolf Stommelen	Lola T370-Ford	13	14	-	-	-	-	-	-	-	-	-	-	-	-
	Lola T371-Ford	-	-	7	-	-	-	-	-	-	-	-	-	-	-
	Hill GH1-Ford	-	-	-	R	-	-	-	-	-	-	-	16	R	-
Hans-Joachim Stuck	March 751-Ford	-	-	-	-	-	-	-	-	-	R	R	R	R	8
Tony Trimmer	Maki F101C-Ford	-	-	-	-	-	-	-	-	-	-	DNQ	DNQ	DNQ	-
Guy Tunmer	Lotus 72E-Ford	-	-	11	-	-	-	-	-	-	-	-	-	-	-
Joseph Vonlanthen	Williams FW03-Ford	-	-	-	-	-	-	-	-	-	-	-	R	-	-
John Watson	Surtees TS16/4-Ford	DSQ	10	R	8	R	10	16	R	13	11	-	10	-	-
	Lotus 72E-Ford	-	-	-	-	-	-	-	-	-	-	R	-	-	-
	Penske PC1-Ford	-	-	-	-	-	-	-	-	-	-	-	-	-	9
Mike Wilds	Stanley BRM P201	R	R	-	-	-	-	-	-	-	-	-	-	-	-
Roelof Wunderink	Ensign N174-Ford	-	-	-	R	DNQ	-	-	-	-	-	-	NC	DNQ	-
	Ensign N175-Ford	-	-	-	-	-	-	-	-	-	-	DNQ	-	-	R
Renzo Zorzi	Williams FW03-Ford	-	-	-	-	-	-	-	-	-	-	-	-	14	-

1976

Niki Lauda continued his World Championship-winning form in the early races of 1976 and by mid-season a second title seemed assured. Then, on the second lap of the German GP, he crashed heavily at Bergwerk and his car burst into flames. Severely injured and badly burnt, he was given the last rites in hospital. However, against all expectations he recovered, though badly scarred, and within five weeks was racing again at the Italian GP.

Before the accident, it had been an acrimonious season of disqualifications and appeals. James Hunt was a thorn in Ferrari's side and in Spain he controversially ended a run of five Ferrari victories. His McLaren had been disqualified from that win on a technicality but was later reinstated. Then Hunt won in Britain, before race officials ruled that he should not have participated in the restarted race.

By Lauda's return, Hunt had closed the gap and at the last round in Japan it was between these two. In appallingly wet and dangerous conditions Lauda withdrew, believing life to be more important than another championship. Even then, Hunt appeared to have lost the title in the confusing final laps, only to learn that he had finished third, as required to take Lauda's crown.

Hunt's opportunity at McLaren had come when Emerson Fittipaldi decided to race for the family team, a decision which prematurely halted his career as a top-flight F1 driver. Fittipaldi's form since his comeback in Indycars shows that his talent remained, despite five mediocre seasons.

Tyrrell introduced the radical six-wheel P34. Although it finished first and second in Sweden, it did not win again and was replaced by a conventional car after two seasons.

Obscured by the understandable attention focused on the championship finale, Mario Andretti returned Lotus to winning ways in Japan, while in Austria John Watson scored Penske's first and only win in the formula. It was a victory that cost Watson his beard, the result of a bet with team owner Roger Penske!

Grande Prémio do Brasil

25 January 1976. Interlagos. 40 laps of a 4.946-mile circuit = 197.840 miles. Very hot, dry and sunny. World Championship round 1

1 Niki Lauda	Ferrari 312T	40	1h45m16.78
2 Patrick Depailler	Tyrrell 007-Ford	40	1h45m38.25
3 Tom Pryce	Shadow DN5B-Ford	40	1h45m40.62
4 Hans-Joachim Stuck	March 761-Ford	40	1h46m44.95
5 Jody Scheckter	Tyrrell 007-Ford	40	1h47m13.24
6 Jochen Mass	McLaren M23-Ford	40	1h47m15.05

Winner's average speed: 112.751 mph. Starting grid front row: Hunt, 2m32.50 (pole) and Lauda, 2m32.52. Fastest lap: Jarier, 2m35.07. Leaders: Regazzoni, laps 1-8; Lauda, 9-40.

Citizen Grand Prix of South Africa

6 March 1976. Kyalami. 78 laps of a 2.550-mile circuit = 198.900 miles. Warm, dry and sunny. World Championship round 2

1 Niki Lauda	Ferrari 312T	78	1h42m18.4
2 James Hunt	McLaren M23-Ford	78	1h42m19.7
3 Jochen Mass	McLaren M23-Ford	78	1h43m04.3
4 Jody Scheckter	Tyrrell 007-Ford	78	1h43m26.8
5 John Watson	Penske PC3-Ford	77	
6 Mario Andretti	Parnelli VPJ4B-Ford	77	

Winner's average speed: 116.649 mph. Starting grid front row: Hunt, 1m16.10 (pole) and Lauda, 1m16.20. Fastest lap: Lauda, 1m17.97. Leaders: Lauda, laps 1-78.

....
James Hunt clinched the Championship for McLaren in the last race of the year at Fuji

United States Grand Prix West

28 March 1976. Long Beach. 80 laps of a 2.020-mile circuit = 161.600 miles. Warm, dry and sunny. World Championship round 3

1 Clay Regazzoni	Ferrari 312T	80	1h53m18.471
2 Niki Lauda	Ferrari 312T	80	1h54m00.885
3 Patrick Depailler	Tyrrell 007-Ford	80	1h54m08.443
4 Jacques Laffite	Ligier JS5-Matra	80	1h54m31.299
5 Jochen Mass	McLaren M23-Ford	80	1h54m40.763
6 Emerson Fittipaldi	Fittipaldi FD04-Ford	79	

Winner's average speed: 85.572 mph. Starting grid front row: Regazzoni, 1m23.099 (pole) and Depailler, 1m23.292. Fastest lap: Regazzoni, 1m23.076. Leaders: Regazzoni, laps 1-80.

Gran Premio de Espana

2 May 1976. Jarama. 75 laps of a 2.115-mile circuit = 158.625 miles. Warm, dry and sunny. World Championship round 4

1 James Hunt*	McLaren M23-Ford	75	1h42m20.43
2 Niki Lauda	Ferrari 312T2	75	1h42m51.40
3 Gunnar Nilsson	Lotus 77-Ford	75	1h43m08.45
4 Carlos Reutemann	Brabham BT45-Alfa Romeo	74	
5 Chris Amon	Ensign N176-Ford	74	
6 Carlos Pace	Brabham BT45-Alfa Romeo	74	

*Hunt was originally disqualified because his car was found to be too wide but was later reinstated. Winner's average speed: 93.016 mph. Starting grid front row: Hunt, 1m18.52 (pole) and Lauda, 1m18.84. Fastest lap: Mass, 1m20.93. Leaders: Lauda, laps 1-31; Hunt, 32-75.

Grand Prix de Belgique

16 May 1976. Zolder. 70 laps of a 2.648-mile circuit = 185.360 miles. Warm, dry and sunny. World Championship round 5

1 Niki Lauda	Ferrari 312T2	70	1h42m53.23
2 Clay Regazzoni	Ferrari 312T2	70	1h42m56.69
3 Jacques Laffite	Ligier JS5-Matra	70	1h43m28.61

4 Jody Scheckter	Tyrrell P34-Ford	70	1h44m24.31
5 Alan Jones	Surtees TS19-Ford	69	
6 Jochen Mass	McLaren M23-Ford	69	

Winner's average speed: 108.095 mph. Starting grid front row: Lauda, 1m26.55 (pole) and Regazzoni, 1m26.60. Fastest lap: Lauda, 1m25.98. Leaders: Lauda, laps 1-70.

Grand Prix de Monaco

30 May 1976. Monte Carlo. 78 laps of a 2.058-mile circuit = 160.524 miles. Warm, dry and mainly sunny. World Championship round 6

1 Niki Lauda	Ferrari 312T2	78	1h59m51.47
2 Jody Scheckter	Tyrrell P34-Ford	78	2h00m02.60
3 Patrick Depailler	Tyrrell P34-Ford	78	2h00m56.31
4 Hans-Joachim Stuck	March 761-Ford	77	
5 Jochen Mass	McLaren M23-Ford	77	
6 Emerson Fittipaldi	Fittipaldi FD04-Ford	77	

Winner's average speed: 80.357 mph. Starting grid front row: Lauda, 1m29.65 (pole) and Regazzoni, 1m29.91. Fastest lap: Regazzoni, 1m30.28. Leaders: Lauda, laps 1-78.

Gislaved Sveriges Grand Prix

13 June 1976. Anderstorp. 72 laps of a 2.497-mile circuit = 179.784 miles. Dry and overcast. World Championship round 7

1 Jody Scheckter	Tyrrell P34-Ford	72	1h46m53.729
2 Patrick Depailler	Tyrrell P34-Ford	72	1h47m13.495
3 Niki Lauda	Ferrari 312T2	72	1h47m27.595
4 Jacques Laffite	Ligier JS5-Matra	72	1h47m49.548
5 James Hunt	McLaren M23-Ford	72	1h47m53.212
6 Clay Regazzoni	Ferrari 312T2	72	1h47m54.095

Winner's average speed: 100.912 mph. Starting grid front row: Scheckter, 1m25.659 (pole) and Andretti, 1m26.008. Fastest lap: Andretti, 1m28.002. Leaders: Andretti, laps 1-45; Scheckter, 46-72.

Grand Prix de France

4 July 1976. Paul Ricard. 54 laps of a 3.610-mile circuit = 194.940 miles. Hot, dry and sunny. World Championship round 8

1 James Hunt	McLaren M23-Ford	54	1h40m58.60
2 Patrick Depailler	Tyrrell P34-Ford	54	1h41m11.30
3 John Watson*	Penske PC4-Ford	54	1h41m22.15
4 Carlos Pace	Brabham BT45-Alfa Romeo	54	1h41m23.42
5 Mario Andretti	Lotus 77-Ford	54	1h41m42.52
6 Jody Scheckter	Tyrrell P34-Ford	54	1h41m53.67

*Watson was originally disqualified because of the height of his car's rear wing but was later reinstated. Winner's average speed: 115.833 mph. Starting grid front row: Hunt, 1m47.89 (pole) and Lauda, 1m48.17. Fastest lap: Lauda, 1m51.0. Leaders: Lauda, laps 1-8; Hunt, 9-54.

John Player British Grand Prix

18 July 1976. Brands Hatch. 76 laps of a 2.614-mile circuit = 198.634 miles. Race stopped after 1st corner accident. Restarted over original distance. Warm, dry and sunny. World Championship round 9

1 Niki Lauda	Ferrari 312T2	76	1h44m19.66
2 Jody Scheckter	Tyrrell P34-Ford	76	1h44m35.84
3 John Watson	Penske PC4-Ford	75	
4 Tom Pryce	Shadow DN5B-Ford	75	
5 Alan Jones	Surtees TS19-Ford	75	
6 Emerson Fittipaldi	Fittipaldi FD04-Ford	74	

Hunt (McLaren M23-Ford) finished first on the road but was disqualified for illegally taking the restart of the race. Winner's average speed: 114.236 mph. Starting grid front row: Lauda, 1m19.35 (pole) and Hunt, 1m19.41. Fastest lap: Lauda, 1m19.91 (Hunt, 1m19.82, originally set fastest lap). Leaders: Lauda, laps 1-76 (Hunt led laps 45-76 on the road).

Grosser Preis von Deutschland

1 August 1976. Nürburgring. 14 laps of a 14.189-mile circuit = 198.646 miles. Race stopped on lap 2 due to Lauda's accident. Restarted over original distance. Rain at the start, drying later. World Championship round 10

1 James Hunt	McLaren M23-Ford	14	1h41m42.7
2 Jody Scheckter	Tyrrell P34-Ford	14	1h42m10.4
3 Jochen Mass	McLaren M23-Ford	14	1h42m35.1
4 Carlos Pace	Brabham BT45-Alfa Romeo	14	1h42m36.9
5 Gunnar Nilsson	Lotus 77-Ford	14	1h43m40.0
6 Rolf Stommelen	Brabham BT45-Alfa Romeo	14	1h44m13.0

Winner's average speed: 117.182 mph. Starting grid front row: Hunt, 7m06.5 (pole) and Lauda, 7m07.4. Fastest lap: Scheckter, 7m10.8. Leaders: Hunt, laps 1-14 (Peterson had led lap 1 and Mass lap 2 before race stopped)

Raiffeisen Grosser Preis von Österreich

15 August 1976. Österreichring. 54 laps of a 3.672-mile circuit = 198.288 miles. Warm, dry and mainly sunny. World Championship round 11

1 John Watson	Penske PC4-Ford	54	1h30m07.86
2 Jacques Laffite	Ligier JS5-Matra	54	1h30m18.65
3 Gunnar Nilsson	Lotus 77-Ford	54	1h30m19.84
4 James Hunt	McLaren M23-Ford	54	1h30m20.30
5 Mario Andretti	Lotus 77-Ford	54	1h30m29.35
6 Ronnie Peterson	March 761-Ford	54	1h30m42.20

Winner's average speed: 132.000 mph. Starting grid front row: Hunt, 1m35.02 (pole) and Watson, 1m35.84. Fastest lap: Hunt, 1m35.91. Leaders: Watson, laps 1-2, 12-54; Peterson, 3-9, 11; Scheckter, 10

Grote Prijs van Nederland

29 August 1976. Zandvoort. 75 laps of a 2.626-mile circuit = 196.950 miles. Warm, dry and sunny. World Championship round 12. Also known as the European Grand Prix

1 James Hunt	McLaren M23-Ford	75	1h44m52.09
2 Clay Regazzoni	Ferrari 312T2	75	1h44m53.01
3 Mario Andretti	Lotus 77-Ford	75	1h44m54.18
4 Tom Pryce	Shadow DN8A-Ford	75	1h44m59.03
5 Jody Scheckter	Tyrrell P34-Ford	75	1h45m14.55
6 Vittorio Brambilla	March 761-Ford	75	1h45m37.12

Winner's average speed: 112.684 mph. Starting grid front row: Peterson, 1m21.31 (pole) and Hunt, 1m21.39. Fastest lap: Regazzoni, 1m22.59. Leaders: Peterson, laps 1-11; Hunt, 12-75

Gran Premio d'Italia

12 September 1976. Monza. 52 laps of a 3.604-mile circuit = 187.408 miles. Warm, dry and sunny. World Championship round 13

1 Ronnie Peterson	March 761-Ford	52	1h30m35.6
2 Clay Regazzoni	Ferrari 312T2	52	1h30m37.9
3 Jacques Laffite	Ligier JS5-Matra	52	1h30m38.6
4 Niki Lauda	Ferrari 312T2	52	1h30m55.0
5 Jody Scheckter	Tyrrell P34-Ford	52	1h30m55.1
6 Patrick Depailler	Tyrrell P34-Ford	52	1h31m11.3

Winner's average speed: 124.117 mph. Starting grid front row: Laffite, 1m41.35 (pole) and Scheckter, 1m41.38. Fastest lap: Peterson, 1m41.3. Leaders: Scheckter, laps 1-10; Peterson, 11-52

Labatt's 50 Canadian Grand Prix

3 October 1976. Mosport Park. 80 laps of a 2.459-mile circuit = 196.720 miles. Warm, dry and sunny. World Championship round 14

1 James Hunt	McLaren M23-Ford	80	1h40m09.626
2 Patrick Depailler	Tyrrell P34-Ford	80	1h40m15.957
3 Mario Andretti	Lotus 77-Ford	80	1h40m19.992
4 Jody Scheckter	Tyrrell P34-Ford	80	1h40m29.371
5 Jochen Mass	McLaren M23-Ford	80	1h40m51.437
6 Clay Regazzoni	Ferrari 312T2	80	1h40m55.882

Winner's average speed: 117.843 mph. Starting grid front row: Hunt, 1m12.389 (pole) and Peterson, 1m12.783. Fastest lap: Depailler, 1m13.817. Leaders: Peterson, laps 1-8; Hunt, 9-80

United States Grand Prix

10 October 1976. Watkins Glen. 59 laps of a 3.377-mile circuit = 199.243 miles. Cool and dry. World Championship round 15

1 James Hunt	McLaren M23-Ford	59	1h42m40.741
2 Jody Scheckter	Tyrrell P34-Ford	59	1h42m48.771
3 Niki Lauda	Ferrari 312T2	59	1h43m43.065
4 Jochen Mass	McLaren M23-Ford	59	1h43m43.199
5 Hans-Joachim Stuck	March 761-Ford	59	1h43m48.719
6 John Watson	Penske PC4-Ford	59	1h43m48.931

Winner's average speed: 116.427 mph. Starting grid front row: Hunt, 1m43.622 (pole) and Scheckter, 1m43.870. Fastest lap: Hunt, 1m42.851. Leaders: Scheckter, laps 1-36, 41-45; Hunt, 37-40, 46-59

Japanese Grand Prix

24 October 1976. Fuji. 73 laps of a 2.709-mile circuit = 197.757 miles. Very wet and misty. World Championship round 16

1 Mario Andretti	Lotus 77-Ford	73	1h43m58.86
2 Patrick Depailler	Tyrrell P34-Ford	72	
3 James Hunt	McLaren M23-Ford	72	
4 Alan Jones	Surtees TS19-Ford	72	
5 Clay Regazzoni	Ferrari 312T2	72	
6 Gunnar Nilsson	Lotus 77-Ford	72	

Winner's average speed: 114.111 mph. Starting grid front row: Andretti, 1m12.77 (pole) and Hunt, 1m12.80. Fastest lap: Hasemi, 1m18.23. Leaders: Hunt, laps 1-61; Depailler, 62-63; Andretti, 64-73

1976 FINAL CHAMPIONSHIP POSITIONS

Drivers

1	James Hunt	69	14=	Alan Jones	7	5= Penske-Ford	20
2	Niki Lauda	68		Carlos Pace	7	Ligier-Matra	20
3	Jody Scheckter	49	16=	Emerson Fittipaldi	3	7 March-Ford	19
4	Patrick Depailler	39		Carlos Reutemann	3	8 Shadow-Ford	10
5	Clay Regazzoni	31	18	Chris Amon	2	9 Brabham-Alfa Romeo	9
6	Mario Andretti	22	19=	Vittorio Brambilla	1	10 Surtees-Ford	7
7=	Jacques Laffite	20		Rolf Stommelen	1	11 Fittipaldi-Ford	3
	John Watson	20				12 Ensign-Ford	2
9	Jochen Mass	19				13 Parnelli-Ford	1
10	Gunnar Nilsson	11	**Manufacturers**				
11=	Ronnie Peterson	10	1	Ferrari	83		
	Tom Pryce	10	2	McLaren-Ford	74 (75)*		
13	Hans-Joachim Stuck	8	3	Tyrrell-Ford	71		
			4	Lotus-Ford	29		

*Sum of best seven results from the first eight races and best seven results from the final eight races. Points only awarded to first car to finish for each manufacturer

1976 DRIVERS' RECORDS

Driver	Car	Brazilian GP	South African GP	Long Beach GP	Spanish GP	Belgian GP	Monaco GP	Swedish GP	French GP	British GP	German GP	Austrian GP	Dutch GP	Italian GP	Canadian GP	United States GP	Japanese GP
Chris Amon	Ensign N174-Ford	-	14	8	-	-	-	-	-	-	-	-	-	-	-	-	-
	Ensign N176-Ford	-	-	-	5	R	13	R	-	R	R	-	-	-	-	-	-
	Williams FW05-Ford	-	-	-	-	-	-	-	-	-	-	-	-	-	DNS	-	-
Conny Andersson	Surtees TS19-Ford	-	-	-	-	-	-	-	-	-	-	-	R	-	-	-	-
Mario Andretti	Lotus 77-Ford	R	-	-	R	R	-	R^F	5	R	12	5	3	R	3	R	1^P
	Parnelli VPJ4B-Ford	-	6	R	-	-	-	-	-	-	-	-	-	-	-	-	-
Ian Ashley	Stanley BRM P201B	R	-	-	-	-	-	-	-	-	-	-	-	-	-	-	-
Hans Binder	Ensign N176-Ford	-	-	-	-	-	-	-	-	-	-	R	-	-	-	-	-
	Williams FW05-Ford	-	-	-	-	-	-	-	-	-	-	-	-	-	-	-	R
Vittorio Brambilla	March 761-Ford	R	8	R	R	R	R	10	R	R	R	R	6	7	14	R	R
Warwick Brown	Williams FW05-Ford	-	-	-	-	-	-	-	-	-	-	-	-	-	-	14	-
Patrick Depailler	Tyrrell 007-Ford	2	9	3	-	-	-	-	-	-	-	-	-	-	-	-	-
	Tyrrell P34-Ford	-	-	-	R	R	3	2	2	R	R	R	7	6	2^F	R	2
Guy Edwards	Hesketh 308D-Ford	-	-	-	-	DNQ	-	-	17	R	15	-	-	DNS	20	-	-
Harald Ertl	Hesketh 308D-Ford	-	15	DNQ	DNQ	R	DNQ	R	R	7	R	8	R	16	DNS	13	8
Bob Evans	Lotus 77-Ford	-	10	DNQ	-	-	-	-	-	-	-	-	-	-	-	-	-
	Brabham BT44B-Ford	-	-	-	-	-	-	-	-	R	-	-	-	-	-	-	-
Emerson Fittipaldi	Fittipaldi FD04-Ford	13	17	6	R	DNQ	6	R	R	6	13	R	R	15	R	9	R
Divina Galica	Surtees TS16/4-Ford	-	-	-	-	-	-	-	DNQ	-	-	-	-	-	-	-	-
Masahiro Hasemi	Kojima KE007-Ford	-	-	-	-	-	-	-	-	-	-	-	-	-	-	-	11^F
Boy Hayje	Penske PC3-Ford	-	-	-	-	-	-	-	-	-	-	-	R	-	-	-	-
Ingo Hoffman	Fittipaldi FD03-Ford	11	-	-	-	-	-	-	-	-	-	-	-	-	-	-	-
	Fittipaldi FD04-Ford	-	-	DNQ	DNQ	-	-	-	DNQ	-	-	-	-	-	-	-	-
Kazuyoshi Hoshino	Tyrrell 007-Ford	-	-	-	-	-	-	-	-	-	-	-	-	-	-	-	R
James Hunt	McLaren M23-Ford	R^P	2^P	R	1^P	R	R	5	1^P	DSQ	1^P	4^{PF}	1	R	1^P	1^{PF}	3
Jacky Ickx	Williams FW05-Ford	8	16	DNQ	7	DNQ	DNQ	-	10	DNQ	-	-	-	-	-	-	-
	Ensign N176-Ford	-	-	-	-	-	-	-	-	-	-	-	R	10	13	R	-
Jean-Pierre Jarier	Shadow DN5B-Ford	R^F	R	7	R	9	8	12	12	9	11	R	10	19	18	10	10
Alan Jones	Surtees TS19-Ford	-	-	NC	9	5	R	13	R	5	10	R	8	12	16	8	4
Loris Kessel	Brabham BT44B-Ford	-	-	-	DNQ	12	-	R	DNQ	-	-	NC	-	-	-	-	-
	Williams FW03-Ford	-	-	-	-	-	-	-	-	-	-	-	-	DNP	-	-	-
Masami Kuwashima	Williams FW05-Ford	-	-	-	-	-	-	-	-	-	-	-	-	-	-	-	DNS
Jacques Laffite	Ligier JS5-Matra	R	R	4	12	3	12	4	14	R	R	2	R	3^P	R	R	7
Niki Lauda	Ferrari 312T	1	1^F	2	-	-	-	-	-	-	-	-	-	-	-	-	-
	Ferrari 312T2	-	-	-	2	1^{PF}	1^P	3	R^F	1^{PF}	R	-	-	4	8	3	R
Michel Leclère	Williams FW05-Ford	-	13	DNQ	10	11	11	R	13	-	-	-	-	-	-	-	-
Lella Lombardi	March 761-Ford	14	-	-	-	-	-	-	-	-	-	-	-	-	-	-	-
	Brabham BT44B-Ford	-	-	-	-	-	-	-	DNQ	DNQ	12	-	-	-	-	-	-
Brett Lunger	Surtees TS19-Ford	-	11	DNQ	DNQ	R	-	15	16	R	R	10	-	14	15	11	-
Damien Magee	Brabham BT44B-Ford	-	-	-	-	-	-	DNQ	-	-	-	-	-	-	-	-	-
Jochen Mass	McLaren M23-Ford	6	3	5	R^F	6	5	11	15	R	3	7	-	-	5	4	R
	McLaren M26-Ford	-	-	-	-	-	-	-	-	-	-	-	9	R	-	-	-
Arturo Merzario	March 761-Ford	-	-	DNQ	R	R	DNQ	14	9	R	-	-	-	-	-	-	-
	Williams FW05-Ford	-	-	-	-	-	-	-	-	-	R	R	R	DNS	R	R	R
Jac Nelleman	Brabham BT44B-Ford	-	-	-	-	-	DNQ	-	-	-	-	-	-	-	-	-	-
Patrick Neve	Brabham BT44B-Ford	-	-	-	-	R	-	-	-	-	-	-	-	-	-	-	-
	Ensign N176-Ford	-	-	-	-	-	-	-	18	-	-	-	-	-	-	-	-
Gunnar Nilsson	Lotus 77-Ford	-	R	R	3	R	R	R	R	R	5	3	R	13	12	R	6
Karl Oppitzhauser	March 761-Ford	-	-	-	-	-	-	-	-	-	DNP	-	-	-	-	-	-
Carlos Pace	Brabham BT45-Alfa Romeo	10	R	9	6	R	9	8	4	8	4	R	R	R	7	R	R
Larry Perkins	Boro-Ensign N175-Ford	-	-	-	13	8	DNQ	R	-	-	-	-	R	R	-	-	-
	Brabham BT45-Alfa Romeo	-	-	-	-	-	-	-	-	-	-	-	-	-	17	R	R
Henri Pescarolo	Surtees TS19-Ford	-	-	-	-	-	DNQ	-	R	R	DNQ	9	11	17	19	NC	-
Alessandro Pesenti-Rossi	Tyrrell 007-Ford	-	-	-	-	-	-	-	-	-	-	14	11	DNQ	18	-	-
Ronnie Peterson	Lotus 77-Ford	R	-	-	-	-	-	-	-	-	-	-	-	-	-	-	-
	March 761-Ford	-	R	10	R	R	R	7	19	R	R	6	R^P	1^F	9	R	R
Tom Pryce	Shadow DN5B-Ford	3	7	R	8	10	7	9	8	4	8	R	-	-	-	-	-
	Shadow DN8A-Ford	-	-	-	-	-	-	-	-	-	-	-	4	8	11	R	R
Clay Regazzoni	Ferrari 312T	7	R	1^{PF}	-	-	-	-	-	-	-	-	-	-	-	-	-
	Ferrari 312T2	-	-	-	11	2	14^F	6	R	R	9	-	2^F	2	6	7	5
Carlos Reutemann	Brabham BT45-Alfa Romeo	12	R	R	4	R	R	R	11	R	R	R	R	-	-	-	-
	Ferrari 312T2	-	-	-	-	-	-	-	-	-	-	-	-	9	-	-	-/Cont'd

1976 DRIVERS' RECORDS cont'd/

Driver	Car	Brazilian GP	South African GP	Long Beach GP	Spanish GP	Belgian GP	Monaco GP	Swedish GP	French GP	British GP	German GP	Austrian GP	Dutch GP	Italian GP	Canadian GP	United States GP	Japanese GP
Alex Ribeiro	Hesketh 308D-Ford	-	-	-	-	-	-	-	-	-	-	-	-	-	-	12	-
Ian Scheckter	Tyrrell 007-Ford	-	R	-	-	-	-	-	-	-	-	-	-	-	-	-	-
Jody Scheckter	Tyrrell 007-Ford	5	4	R	R	-	-	-	-	-	-	-	-	-	-	-	-
	Tyrrell P34-Ford	-	-	-	-	4	2	1^P	6	2	2F	R	5	5	4	2	R
Rolf Stommelen	Brabham BT45-																
	Alfa Romeo	-	-	-	-	-	-	-	-	-	6	-	-	R	-	-	-
	Hesketh 308D-Ford	-	-	-	-	-	-	-	-	-	-	-	12	-	-	-	-
Hans-Joachim Stuck	March 761-Ford	4	12	R	R	R	4	R	7	R	R	R	R	R	R	5	R
Otto Stuppacher	Tyrrell 007-Ford	-	-	-	-	-	-	-	-	-	-	DNP	-	DNS	DNQ	DNQ	-
Noritake Takahara	Surtees TS19-Ford	-	-	-	-	-	-	-	-	-	-	-	-	-	-	-	9
Tony Trimmer	Maki F102A-Ford	-	-	-	-	-	-	-	-	-	-	-	-	-	-	-	DNQ
Emilio de Villota	Brabham BT44B-Ford	-	-	-	DNQ	-	-	-	-	-	-	-	-	-	-	-	-
John Watson	Penske PC3-Ford	R	5	NC	R	7	10	-	-	-	-	-	-	-	-	-	-
	Penske PC4-Ford	-	-	-	-	-	-	R	3	3	7	1	R	11	10	6	R
Mike Wilds	Shadow DN3B-Ford	-	-	-	-	-	-	-	DNQ	-	-	-	-	-	-	-	-
Emilio Zapico	Williams FW04-Ford	-	-	-	DNQ	-	-	-	-	-	-	-	-	-	-	-	-
Renzo Zorzi	Williams FW04-Ford	9	-	-	-	-	-	-	-	-	-	-	-	-	-	-	-

1977

Mario Andretti's 1976 Japanese GP win signalled a resurgence for John Player Team Lotus. For the coming season Colin Chapman's design team introduced the Lotus 78 "wing car", a concept that would change the sport. It used the bodywork either side of the cockpit to channel air under the car and create downforce which radically boosted cornering speeds. These sidepods were sealed by sliding "skirts" which extended from the bottom of the bodywork to the track surface.

"Ground effect", as it was also known, was not a new idea but Lotus made it work. Engine failures mid-season robbed Andretti of vital points and the championship, but he won four times, while team-mate Gunnar Nilsson scored his first victory in the wet Belgian GP.

The first race of the season threw up a surprise, Jody Scheckter giving the new Wolf marque a victory on its debut. He had two more wins, including the 100th victory for a Ford Cosworth DFV engine at Monaco.

Two tragic events dominated the sport in the spring. Tom Pryce and a marshal died in a freak accident during the South African GP. Cresting the brow on the main straight, Pryce was unable to avoid the inexperienced marshal who was crossing the track to a retired car, and both died instantly. Within weeks, Carlos Pace was killed in an air crash.

Niki Lauda produced a typically consistent season in which he convincingly won his second World Championship. However, his relationship with the Ferrari team was strained throughout the year, and before the Italian GP he announced that he was leaving. When Ermanno Cuoghi, his chief mechanic and close ally, was sacked, Lauda walked out.

His place was taken by Gilles Villeneuve, who had made a stunning debut at the British GP in a third McLaren. The Canadian's Ferrari career did not start well as he had a huge accident in Japan. After barrel-rolling wildly, Villeneuve's Ferrari landed in a prohibited area, killing a marshal and a photographer.

Renault, returning to Grand Prix racing after an absence of almost 70 years, introduced the first turbocharged Formula One engine at the British GP; although originally fragile, it started a revolution which would see a complete grid of turbocharged engines within seven years.

James Hunt had a disappointing start to the defence of his championship. He did win three times in the second half of the season, however, including the British GP, after the ever-unlucky John Watson had retired while leading.

Gran Premio de la Republica Argentina

9 January 1977. Buenos Aires. 53 laps of a 3.709-mile circuit = 196.577 miles. Very hot, dry and sunny. World Championship round 1

1 Jody Scheckter	Wolf WR1-Ford	53	1h40m11.19
2 Carlos Pace	Brabham BT45-		
	Alfa Romeo	53	1h40m54.43
3 Carlos Reutemann	Ferrari 312T2	53	1h40m57.21
4 Emerson Fittipaldi	Fittipaldi FD04-Ford	53	1h41m06.67
5 Mario Andretti	Lotus 78-Ford	51	wheel bearing
6 Clay Regazzoni	Ensign N177-Ford	51	

Winner's average speed: 117.727 mph. Starting grid front row: Hunt, 1m48.68 (pole) and Watson, 1m48.96. Fastest lap: Hunt, 1m51.06. Leaders: Watson, laps 1-10, 32-34; Hunt, 11-31; Pace, 35-47; J Scheckter, 48-53

Grande Premio do Brasil

23 January 1977. Interlagos. 40 laps of a 4.946-mile circuit = 197.840 miles. Very hot, dry and sunny. World Championship round 2

1 Carlos Reutemann	Ferrari 312T2	40	1h45m07.72
2 James Hunt	McLaren M23-Ford	40	1h45m18.43
3 Niki Lauda	Ferrari 312T2	40	1h46m55.23
4 Emerson Fittipaldi	Fittipaldi FD04-Ford	39	
5 Gunnar Nilsson	Lotus 78-Ford	39	
6 Renzo Zorzi	Shadow DN5B-Ford	39	

Winner's average speed: 112.913 mph. Starting grid front row: Hunt, 2m30.11 (pole) and Reutemann, 2m30.18. Fastest lap: Hunt, 2m34.55. Leaders: Pace, laps 1-6; Hunt, 7-22; Reutemann, 23-40

Citizen South African Grand Prix

5 March 1977. Kyalami. 78 laps of a 2.550-mile circuit = 198.900 miles. Dry and overcast. World Championship round 3

1 Niki Lauda	Ferrari 312T2	78	1h42m21.6
2 Jody Scheckter	Wolf WR1-Ford	78	1h42m26.8
3 Patrick Depailler	Tyrrell P34-Ford	78	1h42m27.3
4 James Hunt	McLaren M23-Ford	78	1h42m31.1
5 Jochen Mass	McLaren M23-Ford	78	1h42m41.5

| 6 John Watson | Brabham BT45-Alfa Romeo | 78 | 1h42m41.8 |

Winner's average speed: 116.589 mph. Starting grid front row: Hunt, 1m15.96 (pole) and Pace, 1m16.01. Fastest lap: Watson, 1m17.63. Leaders: Hunt, laps 1-6; Lauda, 7-78

United States Grand Prix West

3 April 1977. Long Beach. 80 laps of a 2.020-mile circuit = 161.600 miles. Warm, dry and sunny. World Championship round 4

1 Mario Andretti	Lotus 78-Ford	80	1h51m35.470
2 Niki Lauda	Ferrari 312T2	80	1h51m36.243
3 Jody Scheckter	Wolf WR1-Ford	80	1h51m40.327
4 Patrick Depailler	Tyrrell P34-Ford	80	1h52m49.957
5 Emerson Fittipaldi	Fittipaldi FD04-Ford	80	1h52m56.378
6 Jean-Pierre Jarier	Penske PC4-Ford	79	

Winner's average speed: 86.889 mph. Starting grid front row: Lauda, 1m21.630 (pole) and Andretti, 1m21.868. Fastest lap: Lauda, 1m22.753. Leaders: J Scheckter, laps 1-76; Andretti, 77-80

1977 DRIVERS' RECORDS

Driver	Car	Argentinian GP	Brazilian GP	South African GP	Long Beach GP	Spanish GP	Monaco GP	Belgian GP	Swedish GP	French GP	British GP	German GP	Austrian GP	Dutch GP	Italian GP	United States GP	Canadian GP	Japanese GP
Conny Andersson	Stanley BRM P207	-	-	-	-	DNQ	-	DNQ	DNQ	DNQ	-	-	-	-	-	-	-	-
Mario Andretti	Lotus 78-Ford	5	R	R	1	1P	5	RP	6PF	1PF	14	R	R	RP	1F	2	9PF	RP
Ian Ashley	Hesketh 308E-Ford	-	-	-	-	-	-	-	-	-	-	DNQ	DNQ	DNQ	17	DNS	-	
Hans Binder	Surtees TS19-Ford	R	R	11	11	9	R	-	-	-	-	-	-	-	-	11	R	R
	Penske PC4-Ford	-	-	-	-	-	-	-	-	-	-	-	12	8	DNQ	-	-	-
Michael Bleekemolen	March 761-Ford	-	-	-	-	-	-	-	-	-	-	-	-	DNQ	-	-	-	-
Vittorio Brambilla	Surtees TS19-Ford	7	R	7	R	R	8	4	R	13	8	5	15	12	R	19	6	8
Patrick Depailler	Tyrrell P34-Ford	R	R	3	4	R	R	8	4	R	R	R	13	R	R	14	2	3
Bernard de Dryver	March 761-Ford	-	-	-	-	-	DNQ	-	-	-	-	-	-	-	-	-	-	-
Guy Edwards	Stanley BRM P207	-	-	-	-	-	-	-	-	NPQ	-	-	-	-	-	-	-	-
Harald Ertl	Hesketh 308E-Ford	-	-	-	-	R	DNQ	9	16	DNQ	-	-	-	-	-	-	-	-
Emerson Fittipaldi	Fittipaldi FD04-Ford	4	4	10	5	14	R	-	18	-	-	-	-	-	-	-	-	-
	Fittipaldi F5-Ford	-	-	-	-	-	-	R	-	11	R	DNQ	11	4	DNQ	13	R	-
Giorgio Francia	Brabham BT45B-Alfa Romeo	-	-	-	-	-	-	-	-	-	-	-	-	DNQ	-	-	-	-
Bruno Giacomelli	McLaren M23-Ford	-	-	-	-	-	-	-	-	-	-	-	-	-	R	-	-	-
Boy Hayje	March 761-Ford	-	-	R	-	DNQ	DNQ	15	DNQ	-	-	-	-	DNQ	-	-	-	-
Brian Henton	March 761B-Ford	-	-	-	10	-	-	-	-	-	-	-	-	-	-	-	-	-
	March 761-Ford	-	-	-	-	DNQ	-	-	-	DNQ	-	DNQ	-	-	-	-	-	-
	Boro-Ensign N175-Ford	-	-	-	-	-	-	-	-	-	-	-	-	DSQ	DNQ	-	-	-
Hans Heyer	Penske PC4-Ford	-	-	-	-	-	-	-	-	-	R	-	-	-	-	-	-	-
Ingo Hoffman	Fittipaldi FD04-Ford	R	7	-	-	-	-	-	-	-	-	-	-	-	-	-	-	-
Kazuyoshi Hoshino	Kojima KE009-Ford	-	-	-	-	-	-	-	-	-	-	-	-	-	-	-	-	11
James Hunt	McLaren M23-Ford	RPF	2PF	4P	7	-	R	-	-	-	-	-	-	-	-	-	-	-
	McLaren M26-Ford	-	-	-	-	R	-	7	12	3	1PF	R	R	R	RP	1P	R	1
Jacky Ickx	Ensign N177-Ford	-	-	-	-	-	10	-	-	-	-	-	-	-	-	-	-	-
Jean-Pierre Jabouille	Renault RS01	-	-	-	-	-	-	-	-	-	R	-	-	R	R	R	DNQ	-
Jean-Pierre Jarier	Penske PC4-Ford	-	-	-	6	DNQ	11	11	8	R	9	R	14	R	R	-	-	-
	Shadow DN8A-Ford	-	-	-	-	-	-	-	-	-	-	-	-	-	-	9	-	-
	Ligier JS7-Matra	-	-	-	-	-	-	-	-	-	-	-	-	-	-	-	-	R
Alan Jones	Shadow DN8A-Ford	-	-	-	R	R	6	5	17	R	7	R	1	R	3	R	4	4
Rupert Keegan	Hesketh 308E-Ford	-	-	-	-	R	12	R	13	10	R	R	7	R	9	8	R	-
Loris Kessel	Williams FW03-Ford	-	-	-	-	-	-	-	-	-	-	-	-	DNQ	-	-	-	-
Mikko Kozarowitsky	March 761-Ford	-	-	-	-	-	-	DNQ	-	NPQ	-	-	-	-	-	-	-	-
Jacques Laffite	Ligier JS7-Matra	R	R	R	9	7F	7	R	1	8	6	R	R	2	8	7	R	5
Niki Lauda	Ferrari 312T2	R	3	1	2PF	DNS	2	2	R	5	2	1F	2P	1F	2	4	-	-
Lamberto Leoni	Surtees TS19-Ford	-	-	-	-	-	-	-	-	-	-	-	-	-	DNQ	-	-	-
Brett Lunger	March 761-Ford	-	-	14	R	10	-	-	-	-	-	-	-	-	-	-	-	-
	McLaren M23-Ford	-	-	-	-	-	DNS	11	DNQ	13	R	10	9	R	10	11	-	-
Jochen Mass	McLaren M23-Ford	R	R	5	R	4	4	R	2	9	-	-	-	-	-	-	-	-
	McLaren M26-Ford	-	-	-	-	-	-	-	-	-	4	R	6	R	4	R	3	R
Brian McGuire	McGuire BM1-Ford	-	-	-	-	-	-	-	NPQ	-	-	-	-	-	-	-	-	-
Arturo Merzario	March 761B-Ford	-	-	-	-	R	DNQ	14	-	R	R	DNQ	-	DNQ	DNP	-	-	-
	Shadow DN8A-Ford	-	-	-	-	-	-	-	-	-	-	-	R	-	-	-	-	-

/Cont'd

Gran Premio de Espana

8 May 1977. Jarama. 75 laps of a 2.115-mile circuit = 158.625 miles. Warm, dry and sunny. World Championship round 5

1 Mario Andretti	Lotus 78-Ford	75	1h42m52.22
2 Carlos Reutemann	Ferrari 312T2	75	1h43m08.07
3 Jody Scheckter	Wolf WR2-Ford	75	1h43m16.73
4 Jochen Mass	McLaren M23-Ford	75	1h43m17.09
5 Gunnar Nilsson	Lotus 78-Ford	75	1h43m58.05
6 Hans-Joachim Stuck	Brabham BT45B-Alfa Romeo	74	

Winner's average speed: 92.537 mph. Starting grid front row: Andretti, 1m18.70 (pole) and Laffite, 1m19.42. Fastest lap: Laffite, 1m20.81. Leaders: Andretti, laps 1-75

Grand Prix de Monaco

22 May 1977. Monte Carlo. 76 laps of a 2.058-mile circuit = 156.408 miles. Warm, dry and sunny. World Championship round 6

1 Jody Scheckter	Wolf WR1-Ford	76	1h57m52.77
2 Niki Lauda	Ferrari 312T2	76	1h57m53.66
3 Carlos Reutemann	Ferrari 312T2	76	1h58m25.57
4 Jochen Mass	McLaren M23-Ford	76	1h58m27.37
5 Mario Andretti	Lotus 78-Ford	76	1h58m28.32
6 Alan Jones	Shadow DN8A-Ford	76	1h58m29.38

Winner's average speed: 79.611 mph. Starting grid front row: Watson, 1m29.86 (pole) and J Scheckter, 1m30.27. Fastest lap: J Scheckter, 1m31.07. Leaders: J Scheckter, laps 1-76

Grand Prix de Belgique

5 June 1977. Zolder. 70 laps of a 2.648-mile circuit = 185.360 miles. Cold and wet. World Championship round 7

1 Gunnar Nilsson	Lotus 78-Ford	70	1h55m05.71
2 Niki Lauda	Ferrari 312T2	70	1h55m19.90
3 Ronnie Peterson	Tyrrell P34-Ford	70	1h55m25.66
4 Vittorio Brambilla	Surtees TS19-Ford	70	1h55m30.69
5 Alan Jones	Shadow DN8A-Ford	70	1h56m21.18
6 Hans-Joachim Stuck	Brabham BT45B-Alfa Romeo	69	

1977 DRIVERS' RECORDS cont'd/

Driver	Car	Argentinian GP	Brazilian GP	South African GP	Long Beach GP	Spanish GP	Monaco GP	Belgian GP	Swedish GP	French GP	British GP	German GP	Austrian GP	Dutch GP	Italian GP	United States GP	Canadian GP	Japanese GP
Patrick Neve	March 761-Ford	-	-	-	-	12	-	10	15	DNQ	10	DNQ	9	DNQ	7	18	R	-
Gunnar Nilsson	Lotus 78-Ford	DNS	5	12	8	5	R	1F	19	4	3	R	R	R	R	R	R	R
Jackie Oliver	Shadow DN8A-Ford	-	-	-	-	-	-	-	9	-	-	-	-	-	-	-	-	-
Danny Ongais	Penske PC4-Ford	-	-	-	-	-	-	-	-	-	-	-	-	-	-	R	7	-
Carlos Pace	Brabham BT45-Alfa Romeo	2	R	-	-	-	-	-	-	-	-	-	-	-	-	-	-	-
	Brabham BT45B-Alfa Romeo	-	-	13	-	-	-	-	-	-	-	-	-	-	-	-	-	-
Riccardo Patrese	Shadow DN8A-Ford	-	-	-	-	-	9	R	-	R	R	10	-	13	R	-	10	6
Larry Perkins	Stanley BRM P207	-	R	-	-	-	-	-	-	-	-	-	-	-	-	-	-	-
	Stanley BRM P201B/204	-	-	15	-	-	-	-	-	-	-	-	-	-	-	-	-	-
	Surtees TS19-Ford	-	-	-	-	-	-	12	DNQ	DNQ	-	-	-	-	-	-	-	-
Ronnie Peterson	Tyrrell P34-Ford	R	R	R	R	8	R	3	R	12	R	9	5	R	6	16F	R	R
Teddy Pilette	Stanley BRM P207	-	-	-	-	-	-	-	-	-	-	DNQ	-	DNQ	DNQ	-	-	-
Tom Pryce	Shadow DN8A-Ford	R	R	R	-	-	-	-	-	-	-	-	-	-	-	-	-	-
David Purley	Lec CRP1-Ford	-	-	-	-	DNQ	-	13	14	R	NPQ	-	-	-	-	-	-	-
Hector Rebaque	Hesketh 308E-Ford	-	-	-	-	-	-	DNQ	DNQ	DNQ	-	R	DNQ	DNQ	-	-	-	-
Clay Regazzoni	Ensign N177-Ford	6	R	9	R	R	DNQ	R	7	7	DNQ	R	R	R	5	5	R	R
Carlos Reutemann	Ferrari 312T2	3	1	8	R	2	3	R	3	6	15	4	4	6	R	6	R	2
Alex Ribeiro	March 761B-Ford	R	R	R	R	DNQ	DNQ	DNQ	DNQ	DNQ	DNQ	8	DNQ	11	DNQ	15	8	12
Ian Scheckter	March 761B-Ford	R	R	-	-	11	DNQ	R	R	NC	R	R	R	-	-	-	-	-
	March 771-Ford	-	-	-	-	-	-	-	-	-	-	-	-	10	R	R	R	-
Jody Scheckter	Wolf WR1-Ford	1	R	2	3	1F	R	-	R	-	R	-	-	-	R	-	1	-
	Wolf WR2-Ford	-	-	-	-	3	-	-	-	-	-	2P	-	3	-	3	-	-
	Wolf WR3-Ford	-	-	-	-	-	-	R	-	R	-	-	R	-	-	-	-	10F
Vern Schuppan	Surtees TS19-Ford	-	-	-	-	-	-	-	-	-	12	7	16	DNQ	-	-	-	-
Hans-Joachim Stuck	March 761B-Ford	-	-	-	R	-	-	-	-	-	-	-	-	-	-	-	-	-
	Brabham BT45B-Alfa Romeo	-	-	-	R	6	R	6	10	R	5	3	3	7	R	R	R	7
Andy Sutcliffe	March 761-Ford	-	-	-	-	-	-	-	-	-	NPQ	-	-	-	-	-	-	-
Noritake Takahara	Kojima KE009-Ford	-	-	-	-	-	-	-	-	-	-	-	-	-	-	-	-	R
Kunimitsu Takahashi	Tyrrell 007-Ford	-	-	-	-	-	-	-	-	-	-	-	-	-	-	-	-	9
Patrick Tambay	Surtees TS19-Ford	-	-	-	-	-	-	-	DNQ	-	-	-	-	-	-	-	-	-
	Ensign N177-Ford	-	-	-	-	-	-	-	-	R	6	R	5	R	DNQ	5	R
Tony Trimmer	Surtees TS19-Ford	-	-	-	-	-	-	-	-	NPQ	-	-	-	-	-	-	-	-
Gilles Villeneuve	McLaren M23-Ford	-	-	-	-	-	-	-	-	11	-	-	-	-	-	-	-
	Ferrari 312T2	-	-	-	-	-	-	-	-	-	-	-	-	-	-	12	R
Emilio de Villota	McLaren M23-Ford	-	-	-	-	13	-	DNQ	DNQ	-	DNQ	DNQ	17	-	DNQ	-	-	-
John Watson	Brabham BT45-Alfa Romeo	R	R	6F	-	-	-	-	-	-	-	-	-	-	-	-	-	-
	Brabham BT45B-Alfa Romeo	-	-	-	DSQ	R	RP	R	5	2	R	R	8F	R	R	12	R	R
Renzo Zorzi	Shadow DN5B-Ford	R	6	-	-	-	-	-	-	-	-	-	-	-	-	-	-	-
	Shadow DN8A-Ford	-	-	R	R	R	-	-	-	-	-	-	-	-	-	-	-	-

Winner's average speed: 96.630 mph. Starting grid front row: Andretti, 1m24.64 (pole) and Watson, 1m26.18. Fastest lap: Nilsson, 1m27.36. Leaders: J Scheckter, laps 1-16; Mass, 17-18; Brambilla, 19-22; Lauda, 23-49; Nilsson, 50-70

Gislaved Sveriges Grand Prix

19 June 1977. Anderstorp. 72 laps of a 2.497-mile circuit = 179.784 miles. Warm, dry and sunny. World Championship round 8

1	Jacques Laffite	Ligier JS7-Matra	72	1h46m55.520
2	Jochen Mass	McLaren M23-Ford	72	1h47m03.969
3	Carlos Reutemann	Ferrari 312T2	72	1h47m09.889
4	Patrick Depailler	Tyrrell P34-Ford	72	1h47m11.828
5	John Watson	Brabham BT45B-Alfa Romeo	72	1h47m14.255
6	Mario Andretti	Lotus 78-Ford	72	1h47m20.797

Winner's average speed: 100.884 mph. Starting grid front row: Andretti, 1m25.404 (pole) and Watson, 1m25.545. Fastest lap: Andretti, 1m27.607. Leaders: Watson, lap 1; Andretti, laps 2-69; Laffite, 70-72

Niki Lauda leads James Hunt during the Monaco Grand Prix, on his way to claiming his second World title

Grand Prix de France

3 July 1977. Dijon-Prenois. 80 laps of a 2.361-mile circuit = 188.880 miles. Hot, dry and sunny. World Championship round 9

1	Mario Andretti	Lotus 78-Ford	80	1h39m40.13
2	John Watson	Brabham BT45B-Alfa Romeo	80	1h39m41.68
3	James Hunt	McLaren M26-Ford	80	1h40m14.00
4	Gunnar Nilsson	Lotus 78-Ford	80	1h40m51.21
5	Niki Lauda	Ferrari 312T2	80	1h40m54.58
6	Carlos Reutemann	Ferrari 312T2	79	

Winner's average speed: 113.705 mph. Starting grid front row: Andretti, 1m12.21 (pole) and Hunt, 1m12.73. Fastest lap: Andretti, 1m13.75. Leaders: Hunt, laps 1-4; Watson, 5-79; Andretti, 80

John Player British Grand Prix

16 July 1977. Silverstone. 68 laps of a 2.932-mile circuit = 199.376 miles. Warm, dry and sunny. World Championship round 10. Also known as European Grand Prix

1	James Hunt	McLaren M26-Ford	68	1h31m46.06
2	Niki Lauda	Ferrari 312T2	68	1h32m04.37
3	Gunnar Nilsson	Lotus 78-Ford	68	1h32m05.63
4	Jochen Mass	McLaren M26-Ford	68	1h32m33.82
5	Hans-Joachim Stuck	Brabham BT45B-Alfa Romeo	68	1h32m57.79
6	Jacques Laffite	Ligier JS7-Matra	67	

Winner's average speed: 130.357 mph. Starting grid front row: Hunt, 1m18.49 (pole) and Watson, 1m18.77. Fastest lap: Hunt, 1m19.60. Leaders: Watson, laps 1-49; Hunt, 50-68

Grosser Preis von Deutschland

31 July 1977. Hockenheim. 47 laps of a 4.219-mile circuit = 198.293 miles. Warm, dry and sunny. World Championship round 11

1	Niki Lauda	Ferrari 312T2	47	1h31m48.62
2	Jody Scheckter	Wolf WR2-Ford	47	1h32m02.95
3	Hans-Joachim Stuck	Brabham BT45B-Alfa Romeo	47	1h32m09.52
4	Carlos Reutemann	Ferrari 312T2	47	1h32m48.89
5	Vittorio Brambilla	Surtees TS19-Ford	47	1h33m15.99
6	Patrick Tambay	Ensign N177-Ford	47	1h33m18.43

Winner's average speed: 129.589 mph. Starting grid front row: J Scheckter, 1m53.07 (pole) and Watson, 1m53.34. Fastest lap: Lauda, 1m55.99. Leaders: J Scheckter, laps 1-12; Lauda, 13-47

Gröbel Möbel Grosser Preis von Österreich

14 August 1977. Österreichring. 54 laps of a 3.692-mile circuit = 199.368 miles. Damp at the start, drying later. World Championship round 12

1	Alan Jones	Shadow DN8A-Ford	54	1h37m16.49
2	Niki Lauda	Ferrari 312T2	54	1h37m36.62
3	Hans-Joachim Stuck	Brabham BT45B-Alfa Romeo	54	1h37m50.99
4	Carlos Reutemann	Ferrari 312T2	54	1h37m51.24
5	Ronnie Peterson	Tyrrell P34-Ford	54	1h38m18.58
6	Jochen Mass	McLaren M26-Ford	53	

Winner's average speed: 122.972 mph. Starting grid front row: Lauda, 1m39.32 (pole) and Hunt, 1m39.45. Fastest lap: Watson, 1m40.96. Leaders: Andretti, laps 1-11; Hunt, 12-43; Jones, 44-54

Grote Prijs van Nederland

28 August 1977. Zandvoort. 75 laps of a 2.626-mile circuit = 196.950 miles. Warm, dry and sunny. World Championship round 13

1	Niki Lauda	Ferrari 312T2	75	1h41m45.93
2	Jacques Laffite	Ligier JS7-Matra	75	1h41m47.82
3	Jody Scheckter	Wolf WR2-Ford	74	
4	Emerson Fittipaldi	Fittipaldi F5-Ford	74	
5	Patrick Tambay	Ensign N177-Ford	73	out of fuel
6	Carlos Reutemann	Ferrari 312T2	73	

Winner's average speed: 116.120 mph. Starting grid front row: Andretti, 1m18.65 (pole) and Laffite, 1m19.27. Fastest lap: Lauda, 1m19.99. Leaders: Hunt, laps 1-5; Laffite, 6-19; Lauda, 20-75

Gran Premio d'Italia

11 September 1977. Monza. 52 laps of a 3.604-mile circuit = 187.408 miles. Warm, dry and sunny. World Championship round 14

1	Mario Andretti	Lotus 78-Ford	52	1h27m50.30
2	Niki Lauda	Ferrari 312T2	52	1h28m07.26
3	Alan Jones	Shadow DN8A-Ford	52	1h28m13.93
4	Jochen Mass	McLaren M26-Ford	52	1h28m18.78
5	Clay Regazzoni	Ensign N177-Ford	52	1h28m21.41
6	Ronnie Peterson	Tyrrell P34-Ford	52	1h29m09.52

Winner's average speed: 128.010 mph. Starting grid front row: Hunt, 1m38.08 (pole) and Reutemann, 1m38.15. Fastest lap: Andretti, 1m39.10. Leaders: J Scheckter, laps 1-9; Andretti, 10-52

United States Grand Prix

2 October 1977. Watkins Glen. 59 laps of a 3.377-mile circuit = 199.243 miles. Cold and wet. World Championship round 15

1	James Hunt	McLaren M26-Ford	59	1h58m23.267
2	Mario Andretti	Lotus 78-Ford	59	1h58m25.293
3	Jody Scheckter	Wolf WR2-Ford	59	1h59m42.146
4	Niki Lauda	Ferrari 312T2	59	2h00m03.882
5	Clay Regazzoni	Ensign N177-Ford	59	2h00m11.405
6	Carlos Reutemann	Ferrari 312T2	58	

Winner's average speed: 100.978 mph. Starting grid front row: Hunt, 1m40.863 (pole) and Stuck, 1m41.138. Fastest lap: Peterson, 1m51.854. Leaders: Stuck, laps 1-14; Hunt, 15-59

Andretti, 1m13.299. Leaders: Andretti, laps 1-60, 62-78; Hunt, 61; J Scheckter, 79-80

Labatt's 50 Canadian Grand Prix

9 October 1977. Mosport Park. 80 laps of a 2.459-mile circuit = 196.720 miles. Dry and overcast. World Championship round 16

1 Jody Scheckter	Wolf WR1-Ford	80	1h40m00.00
2 Patrick Depailler	Tyrrell P34-Ford	80	1h40m06.77
3 Jochen Mass	McLaren M26-Ford	80	1h40m15.76
4 Alan Jones	Shadow DN8A-Ford	80	1h40m46.69
5 Patrick Tambay	Ensign N177-Ford	80	1h41m03.26
6 Vittorio Brambilla	Surtees TS19-Ford	78	accident

Winner's average speed: 118.032 mph. Starting grid front row: Andretti, 1m11.385 (pole) and Hunt, 1m11.942. Fastest lap:

Japanese Grand Prix

23 October 1977. Fuji. 73 laps of a 2.709-mile circuit = 197.757 miles. Warm, dry and sunny. World Championship round 17

1 James Hunt	McLaren M26-Ford	73	1h31m51.68
2 Carlos Reutemann	Ferrari 312T2	73	1h32m54.13
3 Patrick Depailler	Tyrrell P34-Ford	73	1h32m58.07
4 Alan Jones	Shadow DN8A-Ford	73	1h32m58.29
5 Jacques Laffite	Ligier JS7-Matra	72	out of fuel
6 Riccardo Patrese	Shadow DN8A-Ford	72	

Winner's average speed: 129.167 mph. Starting grid front row: Andretti, 1m12.23 (pole) and Hunt, 1m12.39. Fastest lap: J Scheckter, 1m14.3. Leaders: Hunt, laps 1-73

1977 FINAL CHAMPIONSHIP POSITIONS

Drivers

1	Niki Lauda	72	15= Vittorio Brambilla	6		4	Wolf-Ford	55
2	Jody Scheckter	55	Carlos Pace	6		5=	Brabham-Alfa Romeo	27
3	Mario Andretti	47	17= Clay Regazzoni	5			Tyrrell-Ford	27
4	Carlos Reutemann	42	Patrick Tambay	5		7	Shadow-Ford	23
5	James Hunt	40	19= Jean-Pierre Jarier	1		8	Ligier-Matra	18
6	Jochen Mass	25	Riccardo Patrese	1		9	Fittipaldi-Ford	11
7	Alan Jones	22	Renzo Zorzi	1		10	Ensign-Ford	10
8=	Patrick Depailler	20				11	Surtees-Ford	6
	Gunnar Nilsson	20				12	Penske-Ford	1
10	Jacques Laffite	18					*Sum of best eight results from	
11	Hans-Joachim Stuck	12	**Manufacturers**				the first nine races and best seven	
12	Emerson Fittipaldi	11	1 Ferrari	95 (97)*			results from the final eight races.	
13	John Watson	9	2 Lotus-Ford	62			Points only awarded to first car	
14	Ronnie Peterson	7	3 McLaren-Ford	60			to finish for each manufacturer	

1978

Mario Andretti was finally rewarded for his patient development work at Lotus with a car in which he could dominate the World Championship. He and Ronnie Peterson scored a victory apiece in the old Lotus 78, before the 79 model was introduced.

This second-generation "wing car" was the significant advantage for which all teams strive. Andretti won another five races while Peterson added the wet Austrian GP. After a disastrous year at Tyrrell, Peterson had been happy to re-sign with Lotus as number two driver, and although often quicker than the American, he respected his contract which stipulated that he followed Andretti.

However, the year of celebration for Lotus turned sour at the start of the Italian GP. In his back-up Lotus 78 Peterson was involved in a multi-car startline accident. Although his injuries were originally not believed to be life-threatening, he died a day later. The fastest driver of his generation, he was destined never to be World Champion.

Former Lotus driver Gunnar Nilsson had left to join the new Arrows team. Sadly, his year became a fight against cancer, a fight which he ultimately lost. He died shortly after Peterson, a double blow for Swedish motor racing.

Arrows did make an impression though, Riccardo Patrese leading the team's second-ever race and finishing second in Sweden. However, the Italian

was unjustly accused of causing the Monza accident and missed the US GP when other drivers refused to race with him. The original Arrows FA1 was banned mid-season by the London High Court, who ruled that it infringed the copyright of Shadow Cars, from which key members of Arrows had defected. A new model, the A1, was built, like its predecessor in record time. Seventeen years after their debut, Arrows are still waiting for their first victory.

Niki Lauda joined Brabham-Alfa Romeo and won two controversial races. In Sweden he drove the infamous "fan-car", which used a huge fan allegedly to generate downforce. Although the team claimed it was for cooling, the governing body believed it to be a moveable aerodynamic aid and thus illegal. After Sweden the "fan-car" was banned but the result stood. His second win came in the gloom at Monza, where he inherited victory after both Andretti and Villeneuve were penalized for jumping the start.

Patrick Depailler had lost the South African GP to Peterson on the last lap, but finally won his first Grand Prix at Monaco after John Watson had retired. Meanwhile Ferrari was the closest challenger to Lotus, Carlos Reutemann finishing third in the championship and Gilles Villeneuve scoring a popular home win in Canada, after Peterson's replacement at Lotus, Jean-Pierre Jarier, had retired from the lead.

World Championship Grand Prix Racing

Gran Premio de la Republica Argentina

15 January 1978. Buenos Aires. 52 laps of a 3.709-mile circuit = 192.868 miles. Race scheduled for 53 laps but stopped early. Hot, dry and sunny. World Championship round 1

1	Mario Andretti	Lotus 78-Ford	52	1h37m04.47
2	Niki Lauda	Brabham BT45C-Alfa Romeo	52	1h37m17.68
3	Patrick Depailler	Tyrrell 008-Ford	52	1h37m18.11
4	James Hunt	McLaren M26-Ford	52	1h37m20.52
5	Ronnie Peterson	Lotus 78-Ford	52	1h38m19.32
6	Patrick Tambay	McLaren M26-Ford	52	1h38m24.37

Winner's average speed: 119.208 mph. Starting grid front row: Andretti, 1m47.75 (pole) and Reutemann,1m47.84. Fastest lap: Hunt, 1m50.58. Leaders: Andretti, laps 1-52

Grande Premio do Brasil

29 January 1978. Rio de Janeiro. 63 laps of a 3.126-mile circuit = 196.938 miles. Very hot, dry and sunny. World Championship round 2

1	Carlos Reutemann	Ferrari 312T2	63	1h49m59.86
2	Emerson Fittipaldi	Fittipaldi F5A-Ford	63	1h50m48.99
3	Niki Lauda	Brabham BT45C-Alfa Romeo	63	1h50m56.88
4	Mario Andretti	Lotus 78-Ford	63	1h51m32.98
5	Clay Regazzoni	Shadow DN8A-Ford	62	
6	Didier Pironi	Tyrrell 008-Ford	62	

Winner's average speed: 107.423 mph. Starting grid front row: Peterson, 1m40.45 (pole) and Hunt, 1m40.53. Fastest lap: Reutemann, 1m43.07. Leaders: Reutemann, laps 1-63

1978 DRIVERS' RECORDS

Driver	Car	Argentinian GP	Brazilian GP	South African GP	Long Beach GP	Monaco GP	Belgian GP	Spanish GP	Swedish GP	French GP	British GP	German GP	Austrian GP	Dutch GP	Italian GP	United States GP	Canadian GP
Mario Andretti	Lotus 78-Ford	1P	4	7F	2	11	-	-	-	-	-	-	-	-	-	-	-
	Lotus 79-Ford	-	-	-	-	-	1P	1PF	RP	1	R	1P	R	1P	6PF	RP	10
René Arnoux	Martini MK23-Ford	-	-	DNQ	-	NPQ	9	-	-	14	-	NPQ	9	R	-	-	-
	Surtees TS20-Ford	-	-	-	-	-	-	-	-	-	-	-	-	-	-	9	R
Hans Binder	ATS HS1-Ford	-	-	-	-	-	-	-	-	-	-	-	-	-	-	-	-
Michael Bleekemolen	ATS HS1-Ford	-	-	-	-	-	-	-	-	-	-	-	-	DNQ	DNQ	R	DNQ
Vittorio Brambilla	Surtees TS19-Ford	18	DNQ	12	R	-	-	-	-	-	-	-	-	-	-	-	-
	Surtees TS20-Ford	-	-	-	-	-	DNQ	13	7	R	17	9	R	6	DSQ	R	-
Eddie Cheever	Theodore TR1-Ford	DNQ	DNQ	-	-	-	-	-	-	-	-	-	-	-	-	-	-
	Hesketh 308E-Ford	-	-	R	-	-	-	-	-	-	-	-	-	-	-	-	-
Alberto Colombo	ATS HS1-Ford	-	-	-	-	-	DNQ	DNQ	-	-	-	-	-	-	-	-	-
	Merzario A1-Ford	-	-	-	-	-	-	-	-	-	-	-	-	-	NPQ	-	-
Derek Daly	Hesketh 308E-Ford	-	-	-	NPQ	NPQ	DNQ	-	-	-	-	-	-	-	-	-	-
	Ensign N177-Ford	-	-	-	-	-	-	-	-	DNQ	R	-	DSQ	R	10	8	6
Patrick Depailler	Tyrrell 008-Ford	3	R	2	3	1	R	R	R	R	4	R	2	R	11	R	5
Harald Ertl	Ensign N177-Ford	-	-	-	-	-	-	-	-	-	11	R	NPQ	-	-	-	-
	ATS HS1-Ford	-	-	-	-	-	-	-	-	-	-	-	-	-	DNQ	-	-
Emerson Fittipaldi	Fittipaldi F5A-Ford	9	2	R	8	9	R	R	6	R	R	4	4	5	8	5	R
Beppe Gabbiani	Surtees TS20-Ford	-	-	-	-	-	-	-	-	-	-	-	-	-	-	DNQ	-
	Surtees TS19-Ford	-	-	-	-	-	-	-	-	-	-	-	-	-	-	-	DNQ
Divina Galica	Hesketh 308E-Ford	DNQ	DNQ	-	-	-	-	-	-	-	-	-	-	-	-	-	-
Bruno Giacomelli	McLaren M26-Ford	-	-	-	-	-	8	-	-	R	7	-	-	R	14	-	-
"Gimax"	Surtees TS20-Ford	-	-	-	-	-	-	-	-	-	-	-	-	-	DNQ	-	-
James Hunt	McLaren M26-Ford	4F	R	R	R	R	R	6	8	3	R	DSQ	R	10	R	7	R
Jacky Ickx	Ensign N177-Ford	-	-	-	-	R	12	R	DNQ	-	-	-	-	-	-	-	-
Jean-Pierre Jabouille	Renault RS01	-	-	R	R	10	NC	13	R	R	R	R	R	R	R	4	12
Jean-Pierre Jarier	ATS HS1-Ford	12	DNS	8	11	DNQ	-	-	-	-	-	DNQ	-	-	-	-	-
	Lotus 79-Ford	-	-	-	-	-	-	-	-	-	-	-	-	-	-	15F	RP
Alan Jones	Williams FW06-Ford	R	11	4	7F	R	10	8	R	5	R	R	R	R	13	2	9F
Rupert Keegan	Surtees TS19-Ford	R	R	R	DNS	R	-	-	-	-	-	-	-	-	-	-	-
	Surtees TS20-Ford	-	-	-	-	-	DNQ	11	DNQ	R	DNQ	DNQ	DNQ	DNS	-	-	-
Jacques Laffite	Ligier JS7-Matra	16	9	-	5	-	-	-	-	-	-	-	-	-	-	-	-
	Ligier JS7/9-Matra	-	-	5	-	-	-	5	-	7	10	-	-	-	-	-	-
	Ligier JS9-Matra	-	-	-	-	R	-	3	7	-	-	3	5	8	4	11	R
Niki Lauda	Brabham BT45C-Alfa Romeo	2	3	-	-	-	-	-	-	-	-	-	-	-	-	-	-
	Brabham BT46-Alfa Romeo	-	-	RP	R	2F	R	R	-	R	2F	R	R	3F	1	R	R
	Brabham BT46B-Alfa Romeo	-	-	-	-	-	-	-	1F	-	-	-	-	-	-	-	-
Geoff Lees	Ensign N175-Ford	-	-	-	-	-	-	-	-	-	-	DNQ	-	-	-	-	-
Lamberto Leoni	Ensign N177-Ford	R	DNS	DNQ	DNQ	-	-	-	-	-	-	-	-	-	-	-	-
Brett Lunger	McLaren M23-Ford	13	R	11	DNQ	-	-	-	-	-	-	-	-	-	-	-	-
	McLaren M26-Ford	-	-	-	-	NPQ	7	DNQ	DNQ	R	8	NPQ	8	R	R	-	-
	Ensign N177-Ford	-	-	-	-	-	-	-	-	-	-	-	-	-	-	13	-
Jochen Mass	ATS HS1-Ford	11	7	R	R	DNQ	11	9	13	13	NC	R	DNQ	DNQ	-	-	-
Arturo Merzario	Merzario A1-Ford	R	DNQ	R	R	NPQ	NPQ	DNQ	NC	DNQ	R	DNQ	DNQ	R	R	R	DNQ

/Cont'd

Citizen South African Grand Prix

4 March 1978. Kyalami. 78 laps of a 2.550-mile circuit = 198.900 miles. Hot, dry and sunny. World Championship round 3

1 Ronnie Peterson	Lotus 78-Ford	78	1h42m15.767
2 Patrick Depailler	Tyrrell 008-Ford	78	1h42m16.233
3 John Watson	Brabham BT46-Alfa Romeo	78	1h42m20.209
4 Alan Jones	Williams FW06-Ford	78	1h42m54.753
5 Jacques Laffite	Ligier JS7/9-Matra	78	1h43m24.985
6 Didier Pironi	Tyrrell 008-Ford	77	

Winner's average speed: 116.699 mph. Starting grid front row: Lauda, 1m14.65 (pole) and Andretti, 1m14.90. Fastest lap: Andretti, 1m17.09. Leaders: Andretti, laps 1-20; Scheckter, 21-26; Patrese, 27-63; Depailler, 64-77; Peterson, 78

United States Grand Prix West

2 April 1978. Long Beach. 80.5 laps of a 2.020-mile circuit = 162.610 miles. Warm, dry and sunny. World Championship round 4

1 Carlos Reutemann	Ferrari 312T3	80	1h52m01.301
2 Mario Andretti	Lotus 78-Ford	80	1h52m12.362
3 Patrick Depailler	Tyrrell 008-Ford	80	1h52m30.252
4 Ronnie Peterson	Lotus 78-Ford	80	1h52m46.904
5 Jacques Laffite	Ligier JS7-Matra	80	1h53m24.185
6 Riccardo Patrese	Arrows FA1-Ford	79	

Winner's average speed: 87.096 mph. Starting grid front row: Reutemann, 1m20.636 (pole) and Villeneuve, 1m20.836. Fastest lap: Jones, 1m22.215. Leaders: Villeneuve, laps 1-38; Reutemann, 39-80

Grand Prix de Monaco

7 May 1978. Monte Carlo. 75 laps of a 2.058-mile circuit = 154.350 miles. Warm, dry and sunny. World Championship round 5

1 Patrick Depailler	Tyrrell 008-Ford	75	1h55m14.66
2 Niki Lauda	Brabham BT46-Alfa Romeo	75	1h55m37.11
3 Jody Scheckter	Wolf WR1-Ford	75	1h55m46.95
4 John Watson	Brabham BT46-Alfa Romeo	75	1h55m48.19
5 Didier Pironi	Tyrrell 008-Ford	75	1h56m22.72
6 Riccardo Patrese	Arrows FA1-Ford	75	1h56m23.43

1978 DRIVERS' RECORDS cont'd/

Driver	Car	Argentinian GP	Brazilian GP	South African GP	Long Beach GP	Monaco GP	Belgian GP	Spanish GP	Swedish GP	French GP	British GP	German GP	Austrian GP	Dutch GP	Italian GP	United States GP	Canadian GP
Danny Ongais	Ensign N177-Ford	R	R	-	-	-	-	-	-	-	-	-	-	-	-	-	-
	Shadow DN9A-Ford	-	-	-	NPQ	-	-	-	-	-	-	-	-	-	NPQ	-	-
Riccardo Patrese	Arrows FA1-Ford	-	10	R	6	6	R	R	2	8	R	9	-	-	-	-	-
	Arrows A1-Ford	-	-	-	-	-	-	-	-	-	-	-	R	R	R	-	4
Ronnie Peterson	Lotus 78-Ford	5	R^P	1	4	R	2^F	-	-	-	-	-	-	-	-	-	-
	Lotus 79-Ford	-	-	-	-	-	-	2	3	2	R^P	R^F	1^PF	2	-	R	-
Nelson Piquet	Ensign N177-Ford	-	-	-	-	-	-	-	-	-	-	R	-	-	-	-	-
	McLaren M23-Ford	-	-	-	-	-	-	-	-	-	-	-	R	R	9	-	-
	Brabham BT46-Alfa Romeo	-	-	-	-	-	-	-	-	-	-	-	-	-	-	-	11
Didier Pironi	Tyrrell 008-Ford	14	6	6	R	5	6	12	R	10	R	5	R	R	R	10	7
Bobby Rahal	Wolf WR5-Ford	-	-	-	-	-	-	-	-	-	-	-	-	-	-	12	-
	Wolf WR1-Ford	-	-	-	-	-	-	-	-	-	-	-	-	-	-	-	R
Hector Rebaque	Lotus 78-Ford	DNQ	R	10	NPQ	NPQ	NPQ	R	12	DNQ	R	6	R	11	DNQ	R	DNQ
Clay Regazzoni	Shadow DN8A-Ford	15	5	DNQ	10	-	-	-	-	-	-	-	-	-	-	-	-
	Shadow DN9A-Ford	-	-	-	-	DNQ	R	15	5	R	R	DNQ	NC	DNQ	NC	14	DNQ
Carlos Reutemann	Ferrari 312T2	7	1^F	-	-	-	-	-	-	-	-	-	-	-	-	-	-
	Ferrari 312T3	-	-	R	1^P	8^P	3	R	10	18^F	1	R	DSQ	7	3	1	3
Keke Rosberg	Theodore TR1-Ford	-	-	R	NPQ	NPQ	DNQ	NPQ	-	-	-	-	-	-	-	-	-
	ATS HS1-Ford	-	-	-	-	-	-	-	15	16	R	-	-	-	-	-	-
	Wolf WR3-Ford	-	-	-	-	-	-	-	-	-	-	10	NC	-	-	-	-
	Wolf WR4-Ford	-	-	-	-	-	-	-	-	-	-	-	-	R	NPQ	-	-
	ATS D1-Ford	-	-	-	-	-	-	-	-	-	-	-	-	-	-	R	NC
Jody Scheckter	Wolf WR4-Ford	10	-	-	-	-	-	-	-	-	-	-	-	-	-	-	-
	Wolf WR1-Ford	-	R	R	-	3	-	-	-	-	-	-	-	-	-	-	-
	Wolf WR3-Ford	-	-	-	R	-	-	-	-	-	-	-	-	-	-	-	-
	Wolf WR5-Ford	-	-	-	-	-	R	4	R	6	R	2	R	-	-	-	-
	Wolf WR6-Ford	-	-	-	-	-	-	-	-	-	-	-	-	12	12	3	2
Rolf Stommelen	Arrows FA1-Ford	-	-	9	9	R	R	14	14	15	DNQ	DSQ	-	-	-	-	-
	Arrows A1-Ford	-	-	-	-	-	-	-	-	-	-	-	DNQ	NPQ	NPQ	16	DNQ
Hans-Joachim Stuck	Shadow DN8A-Ford	17	R	DNQ	-	-	-	-	-	-	-	-	-	-	-	-	-
	Shadow DN9A-Ford	-	-	-	DNS	R	R	R	11	11	5	R	R	R	R	R	R
Patrick Tambay	McLaren M26-Ford	6	R	R	12	7	-	R	4	9	6	R	R	9	5	6	8
Tony Trimmer	McLaren M23-Ford	-	-	-	-	-	-	-	-	-	-	DNQ	-	-	-	-	-
Gilles Villeneuve	Ferrari 312T2	8	R	-	-	-	-	-	-	-	-	-	-	-	-	-	-
	Ferrari 312T3	-	-	R	R	R	4	10	9	12	R	8	3	6	7	R	1
Emilio de Villota	McLaren M25-Ford	-	-	-	-	-	-	DNQ	-	-	-	-	-	-	-	-	-
John Watson	Brabham BT45C-Alfa Romeo	R	8	-	-	-	-	-	-	-	-	-	-	-	-	-	-
	Brabham BT46-Alfa Romeo	-	-	3	R	4	R	5	-	4^P	3	7	7	4	2	R	R
	Brabham BT46B-Alfa Romeo	-	-	-	-	-	-	-	R	-	-	-	-	-	-	-	-

World Championship Grand Prix Racing

Winner's average speed: 80.360 mph. Starting grid front row: Reutemann, 1m28.34 (pole) and Watson, 1m28.83. Fastest lap: Lauda, 1m28.65. Leaders: Watson, laps 1-37; Depailler, 38-75

Grand Prix de Belgique

21 May 1978. Zolder. 70 laps of a 2.648-mile circuit = 185.360 miles. Dry and overcast. World Championship round 6

1 Mario Andretti	Lotus 79-Ford	70	1h39m52.02
2 Ronnie Peterson	Lotus 78-Ford	70	1h40m01.92
3 Carlos Reutemann	Ferrari 312T3	70	1h40m16.36
4 Gilles Villeneuve	Ferrari 312T3	70	1h40m39.06
5 Jacques Laffite	Ligier JS7/9-Matra	69	accident
6 Didier Pironi	Tyrrell 008-Ford	69	

Winner's average speed: 111.364 mph. Starting grid front row: Andretti, 1m20.90 (pole) and Reutemann, 1m21.69. Fastest lap: Peterson, 1m23.13. Leaders: Andretti, laps 1-70

Gran Premio de Espana

4 June 1978. Jarama. 75 laps of a 2.115-mile circuit = 158.625 miles. Warm, dry and sunny. World Championship round 7

1 Mario Andretti	Lotus 79-Ford	75	1h41m47.06
2 Ronnie Peterson	Lotus 79-Ford	75	1h42m06.62
3 Jacques Laffite	Ligier JS9-Matra	75	1h42m24.30
4 Jody Scheckter	Wolf WR5-Ford	75	1h42m47.12
5 John Watson	Brabham BT46-Alfa Romeo	75	1h42m52.98
6 James Hunt	McLaren M26-Ford	74	

Winner's average speed: 93.524 mph. Starting grid front row: Andretti, 1m16.39 (pole) and Peterson, 1m16.68. Fastest lap: Andretti, 1m20.06. Leaders: Hunt, laps 1-5; Andretti, 6-75

Sveriges Grand Prix

17 June 1978. Anderstorp. 70 laps of a 2.505-mile circuit = 175.350 miles. Warm, dry and sunny. World Championship round 8

1 Niki Lauda	Brabham BT46B-Alfa Romeo	70	1h41m00.606
2 Riccardo Patrese	Arrows FA1-Ford	70	1h41m34.625
3 Ronnie Peterson	Lotus 79-Ford	70	1h41m34.711
4 Patrick Tambay	McLaren M26-Ford	69	
5 Clay Regazzoni	Shadow DN9A-Ford	69	
6 Emerson Fittipaldi	Fittipaldi F5A-Ford	69	

Winner's average speed: 104.158 mph. Starting grid front row: Andretti, 1m22.058 (pole) and Watson, 1m22.737. Fastest lap: Lauda, 1m24.836. Leaders: Andretti, laps 1-38; Lauda, 39-70

Grand Prix de France

2 July 1978. Paul Ricard. 54 laps of a 3.610-mile circuit = 194.940 miles. Hot, dry and sunny. World Championship round 9

1 Mario Andretti	Lotus 79-Ford	54	1h38m51.92
2 Ronnie Peterson	Lotus 79-Ford	54	1h38m54.85
3 James Hunt	McLaren M26-Ford	54	1h39m11.72
4 John Watson	Brabham BT46-Alfa Romeo	54	1h39m28.80
5 Alan Jones	Williams FW06-Ford	54	1h39m33.73
6 Jody Scheckter	Wolf WR5-Ford	54	1h39m46.45

Winner's average speed: 118.306 mph. Starting grid front row: Watson, 1m44.41 (pole) and Andretti, 1m44.46. Fastest lap: Reutemann, 1m48.56. Leaders: Andretti, laps 1-54

John Player British Grand Prix

16 July 1978. Brands Hatch. 76 laps of a 2.614-mile circuit = 198.664 miles. Warm, dry and sunny. World Championship round 10

1 Carlos Reutemann	Ferrari 312T3	76	1h42m12.39
2 Niki Lauda	Brabham BT46-Alfa Romeo	76	1h42m13.62
3 John Watson	Brabham BT46-Alfa Romeo	76	1h42m49.64
4 Patrick Depailler	Tyrrell 008-Ford	76	1h43m25.66
5 Hans-Joachim Stuck	Shadow DN9A-Ford	75	
6 Patrick Tambay	McLaren M26-Ford	75	

Winner's average speed: 116.607 mph. Starting grid front row: Peterson, 1m16.80 (pole) and Andretti, 1m17.06. Fastest lap: Lauda, 1m18.60. Leaders: Andretti, laps 1-23; Scheckter, 24-33; Lauda, 34-59; Reutemann, 60-76

Grosser Preis von Deutschland

30 July 1978. Hockenheim. 45 laps of a 4.219-mile circuit = 189.855 miles. Very hot, dry and sunny. World Championship round 11

1 Mario Andretti	Lotus 79-Ford	45	1h28m00.90
2 Jody Scheckter	Wolf WR5-Ford	45	1h28m16.25
3 Jacques Laffite	Ligier JS9-Matra	45	1h28m28.91
4 Emerson Fittipaldi	Fittipaldi F5A-Ford	45	1h28m37.78
5 Didier Pironi	Tyrrell 008-Ford	45	1h28m58.16
6 Hector Rebaque	Lotus 78-Ford	45	1h29m38.76

Winner's average speed: 129.425 mph. Starting grid front row: Andretti, 1m51.90 (pole) and Peterson, 1m51.99. Fastest lap: Peterson, 1m55.62. Leaders: Peterson, laps 1-4; Andretti, 5-45

Grosser Preis von Österreich

13 August 1978. Österreichring. 54 laps of a 3.692-mile circuit = 199.368 miles. Race stopped after seven laps due to heavy rain, restarted over remaining 47 laps. Wet. World Championship round 12

1 Ronnie Peterson	Lotus 79-Ford	54	1h41m21.57
2 Patrick Depailler	Tyrrell 008-Ford	54	1h42m09.01
3 Gilles Villeneuve	Ferrari 312T3	54	1h43m01.33
4 Emerson Fittipaldi	Fittipaldi F5A-Ford	53	
5 Jacques Laffite	Ligier JS9-Matra	53	
6 Vittorio Brambilla	Surtees TS20-Ford	53	

Winner's average speed: 118.016 mph. Starting grid front row: Peterson, 1m37.71 (pole) and Andretti, 1m37.76. Fastest lap: Peterson, 1m43.12. Leaders: Peterson, laps 1-18, 29-54; Reutemann, 19-22; Villeneuve, 23-28

The story of 1978: Mario Andretti leads Ronnie Peterson in a dominant Lotus victory at Paul Ricard

Grote Prijs van Nederland

27 August 1978. Zandvoort. 75 laps of a 2.626-mile circuit = 196.950 miles. Dry but windy. World Championship round 13

1 Mario Andretti	Lotus 79-Ford	75	1h41m04.23
2 Ronnie Peterson	Lotus 79-Ford	75	1h41m04.55
3 Niki Lauda	Brabham BT46-Alfa Romeo	75	1h41m16.44

4	John Watson	Brabham BT46-Alfa Romeo	75	1h41m25.15
5	Emerson Fittipaldi	Fittipaldi F5A-Ford	75	1h41m25.73
6	Gilles Villeneuve	Ferrari 312T3	75	1h41m50.18

Winner's average speed: 116.918 mph. Starting grid front row: Andretti, 1m16.36 (pole) and Peterson, 1m16.97. Fastest lap: Lauda, 1m19.57. Leaders: Andretti, laps 1-75

Gran Premio d'Italia

10 September 1978. Monza. 40 laps of a 3.604-mile circuit = 144.160 miles. Race stopped after multiple startline accident in which Ronnie Peterson suffered fatal injuries, scheduled for 54 laps. Warm, dry and sunny. World Championship round 14

1	Niki Lauda	Brabham BT46-Alfa Romeo	40	1h07m04.54
2	John Watson	Brabham BT46-Alfa Romeo	40	1h07m06.02
3	Carlos Reutemann	Ferrari 312T3	40	1h07m25.01
4	Jacques Laffite	Ligier JS9-Matra	40	1h07m42.07
5	Patrick Tambay	McLaren M26-Ford	40	1h07m44.93
6	Mario Andretti*	Lotus 79-Ford	40	1h07m50.87

*Andretti and Villeneuve (Ferrari 312T3) finished first and second on the road but were penalized 60 seconds for jumping the start. Winner's average speed: 128.949 mph. Starting grid front row: Andretti, 1m37.520 (pole) and Villeneuve, 1m37.866. Fastest lap: Andretti, 1m38.23. Leaders: Jabouille, laps 1-5; Lauda, 6-40 (Villeneuve led laps 1-34 and Andretti laps 35-40 on the road)

United States Grand Prix

1 October 1978. Watkins Glen. 59 laps of a 3.377-mile circuit = 199.243 miles. Dry and overcast. World Championship round 15

1	Carlos Reutemann	Ferrari 312T3	59	1h40m48.800
2	Alan Jones	Williams FW06-Ford	59	1h41m08.539
3	Jody Scheckter	Wolf WR6-Ford	59	1h41m34.501
4	Jean-Pierre Jabouille	Renault RS01	59	1h42m13.807
5	Emerson Fittipaldi	Fittipaldi F5A-Ford	59	1h42m16.889
6	Patrick Tambay	McLaren M26-Ford	59	1h42m30.010

Winner's average speed: 118.581 mph. Starting grid front row: Andretti, 1m38.114 (pole) and Reutemann, 1m39.179. Fastest lap: Jarier, 1m39.557. Leaders: Andretti, laps 1-2; Reutemann, 3-59

Grand Prix du Canada

8 October 1978. Montreal. 70 laps of a 2.796-mile circuit = 195.720 miles. Cool and dry. World Championship round 16

1	Gilles Villeneuve	Ferrari 312T3	70	1h57m49.196
2	Jody Scheckter	Wolf WR6-Ford	70	1h58m02.568
3	Carlos Reutemann	Ferrari 312T3	70	1h58m08.604
4	Riccardo Patrese	Arrows A1-Ford	70	1h58m13.863
5	Patrick Depailler	Tyrrell 008-Ford	70	1h58m17.754
6	Derek Daly	Ensign N177-Ford	70	1h58m43.672

Winner's average speed: 99.671 mph. Starting grid front row: Jarier, 1m38.015 (pole) and Scheckter, 1m38.026. Fastest lap: Jones, 1m38.072. Leaders: Jarier, laps 1-49; Villeneuve, 50-70

1978 FINAL CHAMPIONSHIP POSITIONS

Drivers

1	Mario Andretti	64
2	Ronnie Peterson	51
3	Carlos Reutemann	48
4	Niki Lauda	44
5	Patrick Depailler	34
6	John Watson	25
7	Jody Scheckter	24
8	Jacques Laffite	19
9=	Emerson Fittipaldi	17
	Gilles Villeneuve	17
11=	Alan Jones	11
	Riccardo Patrese	11
13=	James Hunt	8
	Patrick Tambay	8

15	Didier Pironi	7
16	Clay Regazzoni	4
17	Jean-Pierre Jabouille	3
18	Hans-Joachim Stuck	2
19=	Vittorio Brambilla	1
	Derek Daly	1
	Hector Rebaque	1

Manufacturers

1	Lotus-Ford	86
2	Ferrari	58
3	Brabham-Alfa Romeo	53

4	Tyrrell-Ford	38
5	Wolf-Ford	24
6	Ligier-Matra	19
7	Fittipaldi-Ford	17
8	McLaren-Ford	15
9=	Arrows-Ford	11
	Williams-Ford	11
11	Shadow-Ford	6
12	Renault	3
13=	Ensign-Ford	1
	Surtees-Ford	1

Points only awarded to first car to finish for each manufacturer

1979

Not surprisingly, the pit lane at the first Grand Prix of the season was full of Lotus 79 imitators. Early in the year the Ligier JS11 was the best adaptation of ground effect principles. Jacques Laffite dominated the first two races and Patrick Depailler, whose season was cruelly cut short by a hang-gliding accident, added a further victory for the team. However, Ligier was unable to sustain its challenge.

Although Carlos Reutemann and Mario Andretti used the Lotus 79 to finish in the points early on, it was no longer the quickest car. Its replacement, the Lotus 80, finished third in Spain but this was false promise and the car was dropped. The team would not win again until 1982.

Jody Scheckter, after a fallow year at Wolf, moved to Ferrari and formed a successful partnership with Gilles Villeneuve. The French-Canadian was quicker over a single lap but Scheckter was more consistent. Early Villeneuve wins gave way to Scheckter victories as the season progressed. Fittingly, Scheckter won at Monza and clinched the title. Villeneuve completed the Italian crowd's delirium by finishing second.

The dominant car in the second half of the season, however, was the new Williams FW07, in which Clay Regazzoni scored the team's first victory at the British GP. Alan Jones won four races after mid-season, but with an aggregate of four results from each half of the season counting towards a driver's points tally, neither he nor Williams could be champions.

At Dijon, Jean-Pierre Jabouille scored the first win for Renault and for a turbocharged engine. The race is best remembered for the exuberant, wheel-to-wheel battle for second position in the closing laps, in which René Arnoux and Villeneuve repeatedly passed and re-passed each other, their cars often touching, until Villeneuve eventually won the position.

Brabham had a frustrating final year with 12-cylinder Alfa Romeo engines. At the Canadian GP the team reverted to Ford power by introducing the BT49. Team leader Niki Lauda controversially retired from the sport at that race (although he would return in 1982), but young Brazilian Nelson Piquet was immediately on the pace in the BT49, qualifying on the front row for the final race of the year.

Gran Premio de la Republica Argentina

21 January 1979. Buenos Aires. 53 laps of a 3.709-mile circuit = 196.577 miles. Race stopped by first lap accident. Restarted over original distance. Very hot, dry and sunny. World Championship round 1

1 Jacques Laffite	Ligier JS11-Ford	53	1h36m03.21
2 Carlos Reutemann	Lotus 79-Ford	53	1h36m18.15
3 John Watson	McLaren M28-Ford	53	1h37m32.02
4 Patrick Depailler	Ligier JS11-Ford	53	1h37m44.93
5 Mario Andretti	Lotus 79-Ford	52	
6 Emerson Fittipaldi	Fittipaldi F5A-Ford	52	

Winner's average speed: 122.792 mph. Starting grid front row: Laffite, 1m44.20 (pole) and Depailler, 1m45.24. Fastest lap: Laffite, 1m46.91. Leaders: Depailler, laps 1-10; Laffite, 11-53

Grande Premio do Brasil

4 February 1979. Interlagos. 40 laps of a 4.946-mile circuit = 197.840 miles. Very hot, dry and sunny. World Championship round 2

1 Jacques Laffite	Ligier JS11-Ford	40	1h40m09.64
2 Patrick Depailler	Ligier JS11-Ford	40	1h40m14.92
3 Carlos Reutemann	Lotus 79-Ford	40	1h40m53.78
4 Didier Pironi	Tyrrell 009-Ford	40	1h41m35.52
5 Gilles Villeneuve	Ferrari 312T3	39	
6 Jody Scheckter	Ferrari 312T3	39	

Winner's average speed: 118.514 mph. Starting grid front row: Laffite, 2m23.07 (pole) and Depailler, 2m23.99. Fastest lap: Laffite, 2m28.76. Leaders: Laffite, laps 1-40

Simba South African Grand Prix

3 March 1979. Kyalami. 78 laps of a 2.550-mile circuit = 198.900 miles. Race stopped after two laps due to heavy rain, restarted over 76 laps. Occasional heavy rain. World Championship round 3

1 Gilles Villeneuve	Ferrari 312T4	78	1h41m49.96
2 Jody Scheckter	Ferrari 312T4	78	1h41m53.38
3 Jean-Pierre Jarier	Tyrrell 009-Ford	78	1h42m12.07
4 Mario Andretti	Lotus 79-Ford	78	1h42m17.84
5 Carlos Reutemann	Lotus 79-Ford	78	1h42m56.93
6 Niki Lauda	Brabham BT48-Alfa Romeo	77	

1979 DRIVERS' RECORDS

Driver	Car	Argentinian GP	Brazilian GP	South African GP	Long Beach GP	Spanish GP	Belgian GP	Monaco GP	French GP	British GP	German GP	Austrian GP	Dutch GP	Italian GP	Canadian GP	United States GP
Mario Andretti	Lotus 79-Ford	5	R	4	4	-	R	-	-	R	R	R	R	5	10	R
	Lotus 80-Ford	-	-	-	-	3	-	R	R	-	-	-	-	-	-	-
Elio de Angelis	Shadow DN9B-Ford	7	12	R	7	R	R	DNQ	16	12	11	R	R	R	R	4
René Arnoux	Renault RS01	R	R	R	DNS	9	R	-	-	-	-	-	-	-	-	-
	Renault RE10	-	-	-	-	-	-	R	3F	2	R	6PF	RP	R	R	2
Vittorio Brambilla	Alfa Romeo 177	-	-	-	-	-	-	-	-	-	-	-	-	12	-	-
	Alfa Romeo 179	-	-	-	-	-	-	-	-	-	-	-	-	-	R	DNQ
Gianfranco Brancatelli	Kauhsen WK004-Ford	-	-	-	-	DNQ	-	-	-	-	-	-	-	-	-	-
	Kauhsen WK005-Ford	-	-	-	-	-	DNQ	-	-	-	-	-	-	-	-	-
	Merzario A2-Ford	-	-	-	-	-	-	NPQ	-	-	-	-	-	-	-	-
Derek Daly	Ensign N177-Ford	11	13	-	-	DNQ	DNQ	-	-	-	-	-	-	-	-	-
	Ensign N179-Ford	-	-	DNQ	R	-	-	DNQ	-	-	-	-	-	-	-	-
	Tyrrell 009-Ford	-	-	-	-	-	-	-	-	-	-	8	-	-	R	R
Patrick Depailler	Ligier JS11-Ford	4	2	R	5	1	R	5F	-	-	-	-	-	-	-	-
Emerson Fittipaldi	Fittipaldi F5A-Ford	6	11	-	R	11	9	R	R	R	-	-	-	-	-	-
	Fittipaldi F6-Ford	-	-	13	-	-	-	-	-	-	-	-	-	-	-	-
	Fittipaldi F6A-Ford	-	-	-	-	-	-	-	-	-	R	R	R	8	8	7
Patrick Gaillard	Ensign N179-Ford	-	-	-	-	-	-	-	DNQ	13	DNQ	R	DNQ	-	-	-
Bruno Giacomelli	Alfa Romeo 177	-	-	-	-	-	R	-	17	-	-	-	-	-	-	-
	Alfa Romeo 179	-	-	-	-	-	-	-	-	-	-	-	-	R	DNP	R
James Hunt	Wolf WR7-Ford	R	R	8	-	R	-	R	-	-	-	-	-	-	-	-
	Wolf WR8-Ford	-	-	-	R	-	R	-	-	-	-	-	-	-	-	-
Jacky Ickx	Ligier JS11-Ford	-	-	-	-	-	-	-	R	6	R	R	5	R	R	R
Jean-Pierre Jabouille	Renault RS01	R	10	RP	DNS	-	-	-	-	-	-	-	-	-	-	-
	Renault RE10	-	-	-	-	R	R	NC	1P	R	RP	R	R	14P	R	R
Jean-Pierre Jarier	Tyrrell 009-Ford	R	DNS	3	6	5	11	R	5	3	-	-	R	6	R	R
Alan Jones	Williams FW06-Ford	9	R	R	3	-	-	-	-	-	-	-	-	-	-	-
	Williams FW07-Ford	-	-	-	-	R	R	R	4	RP	1	1	1	9	1PF	RP
Jacques Laffite	Ligier JS11-Ford	1PF	1PF	R	R	RP	2P	R	8	R	3	3	3	R	R	R
Jan Lammers	Shadow DN9B-Ford	R	14	R	R	12	10	DNQ	18	11	10	R	R	DNQ	9	DNQ
Niki Lauda	Brabham BT48-Alfa Romeo	R	R	6	R	R	R	R	R	R	R	R	R	4	-	-
	Brabham BT49-Ford	-	-	-	-	-	-	-	-	-	-	-	-	-	DNP	-
Geoff Lees	Tyrrell 009-Ford	-	-	-	-	-	-	-	-	-	7	-	-	-	-	-
Jochen Mass	Arrows A1-Ford	8	7	12	9	8	R	6	-	-	-	-	-	-	-	-
	Arrows A2-Ford	-	-	-	-	-	-	-	15	R	6	R	6	R	DNQ	DNQ

/Cont'd

Winner's average speed: 117.192 mph. Starting grid front row: Jabouille, 1m11.80 (pole) and Scheckter, 1m12.04. Fastest lap: Villeneuve, 1m14.412. Leaders: Jabouille, lap 1; Villeneuve, laps 2-14, 53-78; Scheckter, 15-52

Lubri Lon United States Grand Prix West

8 April 1979. Long Beach. 80.5 laps of a 2.020-mile circuit = 162.610 miles. Warm, dry and sunny. World Championship round 4

1	Gilles Villeneuve	Ferrari 312T4	80	1h50m25.40
2	Jody Scheckter	Ferrari 312T4	80	1h50m54.78
3	Alan Jones	Williams FW06-Ford	80	1h51m25.09
4	Mario Andretti	Lotus 79-Ford	80	1h51m29.73
5	Patrick Depailler	Ligier JS11-Ford	80	1h51m48.92
6	Jean-Pierre Jarier	Tyrrell 009-Ford	79	

Winner's average speed: 88.356 mph. Starting grid front row: Villeneuve, 1m18.825 (pole) and Reutemann, 1m18.886 - Reutemann started from pit lane. Fastest lap: Villeneuve, 1m21.200. Leaders: Villeneuve, laps 1-80

Gran Premio de Espana

29 April 1979. Jarama. 75 laps of a 2.115-mile circuit = 158.625 miles. Cool and dry. World Championship round 5

1	Patrick Depailler	Ligier JS11-Ford	75	1h39m11.84
2	Carlos Reutemann	Lotus 79-Ford	75	1h39m32.78
3	Mario Andretti	Lotus 80-Ford	75	1h39m39.15
4	Jody Scheckter	Ferrari 312T4	75	1h39m40.52
5	Jean-Pierre Jarier	Tyrrell 009-Ford	75	1h39m42.23
6	Didier Pironi	Tyrrell 009-Ford	75	1h40m00.27

Winner's average speed: 95.963 mph. Starting grid front row: Laffite, 1m14.50 (pole) and Depailler, 1m14.79. Fastest lap: Villeneuve, 1m16.44. Leaders: Depailler, laps 1-75

Grand Prix de Belgique

13 May 1979. Zolder. 70 laps of a 2.648-mile circuit = 185.360 miles. Hot, dry and sunny. World Championship round 6

1	Jody Scheckter	Ferrari 312T4	70	1h39m59.53
2	Jacques Laffite	Ligier JS11-Ford	70	1h40m14.89
3	Didier Pironi	Tyrrell 009-Ford	70	1h40m34.70
4	Carlos Reutemann	Lotus 79-Ford	70	1h40m46.02
5	Riccardo Patrese	Arrows A1-Ford	70	1h41m03.84
6	John Watson	McLaren M28B-Ford	70	1h41m05.38

Winner's average speed: 111.225 mph. Starting grid front row: Laffite, 1m21.13 (pole) and Depailler, 1m21.20. Fastest lap: Villeneuve, 1m23.09. Leaders: Depailler, laps 1-18, 40-46; Laffite, 19-23, 47-53; Jones, 24-39; Scheckter, 54-70

Grand Prix de Monaco

27 May 1979. Monte Carlo. 76 laps of a 2.058-mile circuit = 156.408 miles. Warm, dry and sunny. World Championship round 7

1	Jody Scheckter	Ferrari 312T4	76	1h55m22.48
2	Clay Regazzoni	Williams FW07-Ford	76	1h55m22.92

1979 DRIVERS' RECORDS cont'd/

Driver	Car	Argentinian GP	Brazilian GP	South African GP	Long Beach GP	Spanish GP	Belgian GP	Monaco GP	French GP	British GP	German GP	Austrian GP	Dutch GP	Italian GP	Canadian GP	United States GP
Arturo Merzario	Merzario A1B-Ford	R	DNQ	DNQ	R	-	-	-	-	-	-	-	-	-	-	-
	Merzario A2-Ford	-	-	-	-	DNQ	DNQ	-	DNQ	DNQ	DNQ	DNQ	DNQ	DNQ	DNQ	DNQ
Riccardo Patrese	Arrows A1-Ford	DNS	9	11	R	10	5	R	-	-	-	-	-	-	R	-
	Arrows A2-Ford	-	-	-	-	-	-	-	14	R	R	R	R	13	-	R
Nelson Piquet	Brabham BT46-Alfa Romeo	R	-	-	-	-	-	-	-	-	-	-	-	-	-	-
	Brabham BT48-Alfa Romeo	-	R	7	8	R	R	R	R	R	12	R	4	R	-	-
	Brabham BT49-Ford	-	-	-	-	-	-	-	-	-	-	-	-	-	R	R[F]
Didier Pironi	Tyrrell 009-Ford	R	4	R	DSQ	6	3	R	R	10	9	7	R	10	5	3
Hector Rebaque	Lotus 79-Ford	R	DNQ	R	R	R	R	-	12	9	R	DNQ	7	-	-	-
	Rebaque HR100-Ford	-	-	-	-	-	-	-	-	-	-	-	-	DNQ	R	DNQ
Clay Regazzoni	Williams FW06-Ford	10	15	9	R	-	-	-	-	-	-	-	-	-	-	-
	Williams FW07-Ford	-	-	-	-	R	R	2	6	1[F]	2	5	R	3[F]	3	R
Carlos Reutemann	Lotus 79-Ford	2	3	5	R	2	4	3	13	8	R	R	R	7	R	R
Alex Ribeiro	Fittipaldi F6A-Ford	-	-	-	-	-	-	-	-	-	-	-	-	-	DNQ	DNQ
Keke Rosberg	Wolf WR8-Ford	-	-	-	-	-	-	-	9	-	R	-	-	R	-	-
	Wolf WR7-Ford	-	-	-	-	-	-	-	-	R	-	-	-	-	-	-
	Wolf WR9-Ford	-	-	-	-	-	-	-	-	-	-	R	R	-	DNQ	-
	Wolf WR8/9-Ford	-	-	-	-	-	-	-	-	-	-	-	-	-	-	R
Jody Scheckter	Ferrari 312T3	R	6	-	-	-	-	-	-	-	-	-	-	-	-	-
	Ferrari 312T4	-	-	2	2	4	1	1[P]	7	5	4	4	2	1	4	R
Hans-Joachim Stuck	ATS D2-Ford	DNQ	R	R	DSQ	14	8	R	DNS	DNQ	R	-	-	-	-	-
	ATS D3-Ford	-	-	-	-	-	-	-	-	-	-	R	R	11	R	5
Marc Surer	Ensign N179-Ford	-	-	-	-	-	-	-	-	-	-	-	-	DNQ	DNQ	R
Patrick Tambay	McLaren M28-Ford	R	-	10	R	13	-	-	-	-	-	-	-	-	-	-
	McLaren M26-Ford	-	R	-	-	-	-	-	-	-	-	-	-	-	-	-
	McLaren M28B-Ford	-	-	-	-	-	DNQ	-	-	-	-	-	-	-	-	-
	McLaren M28C-Ford	-	-	-	-	-	-	-	10	7	-	-	-	-	-	-
	McLaren M29-Ford	-	-	-	-	-	-	-	-	-	R	10	R	R	R	R
Gilles Villeneuve	Ferrari 312T3	R	5	-	-	-	-	-	-	-	-	-	-	-	-	-
	Ferrari 312T4	-	-	1[F]	1[PF]	7[F]	7[F]	R	2	14	8[F]	2	R[F]	2	2	1
John Watson	McLaren M28-Ford	3	8	R	R	-	-	-	-	-	-	-	-	-	-	-
	McLaren M28B-Ford	-	-	-	-	R	6	-	-	-	-	-	-	-	-	-
	McLaren M28C-Ford	-	-	-	-	-	-	4	11	-	-	-	-	-	-	-
	McLaren M29-Ford	-	-	-	-	-	-	-	-	4	5	9	R	R	6	6
Ricardo Zunino	Brabham BT49-Ford	-	-	-	-	-	-	-	-	-	-	-	-	-	7	R

*Jody Scheckter, seen here at Zolder, led Ferrari to the
1979 World Championship*
....

3 Carlos Reutemann	Lotus 79-Ford	76	1h55m31.05
4 John Watson	McLaren M28C-Ford	76	1h56m03.79
5 Patrick Depailler	Ligier JS11-Ford	74	engine
6 Jochen Mass	Arrows A1-Ford	69	

Winner's average speed: 81.339 mph. Starting grid front row:
Scheckter, 1m26.45 (pole) and Villeneuve, 1m26.52. Fastest lap:
Depailler, 1m28.82. Leaders: Scheckter, laps 1-76

Grand Prix de France

1 July 1979. Dijon-Prenois. 80 laps of a 2.361-mile circuit =
188.880 miles. Dry and overcast. World Championship
round 8

1 Jean-Pierre Jabouille	Renault RE10	80	1h35m20.42
2 Gilles Villeneuve	Ferrari 312T4	80	1h35m35.01
3 René Arnoux	Renault RE10	80	1h35m35.25
4 Alan Jones	Williams FW07-Ford	80	1h35m57.03
5 Jean-Pierre Jarier	Tyrrell 009-Ford	80	1h36m24.93
6 Clay Regazzoni	Williams FW07-Ford	80	1h36m25.93

Winner's average speed: 118.867 mph. Starting grid front row:
Jabouille, 1m07.19 (pole) and Arnoux, 1m07.45. Fastest lap:
Arnoux, 1m09.16. Leaders: Villeneuve, laps 1-46; Jabouille, 47-80

Marlboro British Grand Prix

14 July 1979. Silverstone. 68 laps of a 2.932-mile circuit =
199.376 miles. Warm, dry and sunny. World Championship
round 9

1 Clay Regazzoni	Williams FW07-Ford	68	1h26m11.17
2 René Arnoux	Renault RE10	68	1h26m35.45
3 Jean-Pierre Jarier	Tyrrell 009-Ford	67	
4 John Watson	McLaren M29-Ford	67	
5 Jody Scheckter	Ferrari 312T4	67	
6 Jacky Ickx	Ligier JS11-Ford	67	

Winner's average speed: 138.799 mph. Starting grid front row:
Jones, 1m11.88 (pole) and Jabouille, 1m12.48. Fastest lap:
Regazzoni, 1m14.40. Leaders: Jones, laps 1-38; Regazzoni, 39-68

Grosser Preis von Deutschland

29 July 1979. Hockenheim. 45 laps of a 4.219-mile circuit =
189.855 miles. Very hot, dry and sunny. World
Championship round 10

1 Alan Jones	Williams FW07-Ford	45	1h24m48.83
2 Clay Regazzoni	Williams FW07-Ford	45	1h24m51.74
3 Jacques Laffite	Ligier JS11-Ford	45	1h25m07.22
4 Jody Scheckter	Ferrari 312T4	45	1h25m20.03
5 John Watson	McLaren M29-Ford	45	1h26m26.63
6 Jochen Mass	Arrows A2-Ford	44	

Winner's average speed: 134.309 mph. Starting grid front row:
Jabouille, 1m48.48 (pole) and Jones, 1m48.75. Fastest lap:
Villeneuve, 1m51.89. Leaders: Jones, laps 1-45

Grosser Preis von Österreich

12 August 1979. Österreichring. 54 laps of a 3.692-mile
circuit = 199.368 miles. Warm, dry and sunny. World
Championship round 11

1 Alan Jones	Williams FW07-Ford	54	1h27m38.01
2 Gilles Villeneuve	Ferrari 312T4	54	1h28m14.06
3 Jacques Laffite	Ligier JS11-Ford	54	1h28m24.78
4 Jody Scheckter	Ferrari 312T4	54	1h28m25.22
5 Clay Regazzoni	Williams FW07-Ford	54	1h28m26.93
6 René Arnoux	Renault RE10	53	

Winner's average speed: 136.501 mph. Starting grid front row:
Arnoux, 1m34.07 (pole) and Jones, 1m34.28. Fastest lap:
Arnoux, 1m35.77. Leaders: Villeneuve, laps 1-3; Jones, 4-54

Grote Prijs van Nederland

26 August 1979. Zandvoort. 75 laps of a 2.626-mile circuit
= 196.950 miles. Dry and overcast. World Championship
round 12

1 Alan Jones	Williams FW07-Ford	75	1h41m19.775
2 Jody Scheckter	Ferrari 312T4	75	1h41m41.558
3 Jacques Laffite	Ligier JS11-Ford	75	1h42m23.028
4 Nelson Piquet	Brabham BT48-		
	Alfa Romeo	74	
5 Jacky Ickx	Ligier JS11-Ford	74	
6 Jochen Mass	Arrows A2-Ford	73	

Winner's average speed: 116.619 mph. Starting grid front row:
Arnoux, 1m15.461 (pole) and Jones, 1m15.646. Fastest lap:
Villeneuve, 1m19.438. Leaders: Jones, laps 1-10, 47-75;
Villeneuve, 11-46

Gran Premio d'Italia

9 September 1979. Monza. 50 laps of a 3.604-mile circuit =
180.200 miles. Warm, dry and sunny. World Championship
round 13

1 Jody Scheckter	Ferrari 312T4	50	1h22m00.22
2 Gilles Villeneuve	Ferrari 312T4	50	1h22m00.68
3 Clay Regazzoni	Williams FW07-Ford	50	1h22m05.00
4 Niki Lauda	Brabham BT48-		
	Alfa Romeo	50	1h22m54.62
5 Mario Andretti	Lotus 79-Ford	50	1h22m59.92
6 Jean-Pierre Jarier	Tyrrell 009-Ford	50	1h23m01.77

Winner's average speed: 131.844 mph. Starting grid front row:
Jabouille, 1m34.580 (pole) and Arnoux, 1m34.704. Fastest lap:
Regazzoni, 1m35.60. Leaders: Scheckter, laps 1, 13-50; Arnoux, 2-12

Grand Prix du Canada

30 September 1979. Montreal. 72 laps of a 2.740-mile
circuit = 197.280 miles. Warm, dry and sunny. World
Championship round 14

1 Alan Jones	Williams FW07-Ford	72	1h52m06.892
2 Gilles Villeneuve	Ferrari 312T4	72	1h52m07.972
3 Clay Regazzoni	Williams FW07-Ford	72	1h53m20.548
4 Jody Scheckter	Ferrari 312T4	71	
5 Didier Pironi	Tyrrell 009-Ford	71	
6 John Watson	McLaren M29-Ford	70	

Winner's average speed: 105.577 mph. Starting grid front row:
Jones, 1m29.892 (pole) and Villeneuve, 1m30.554. Fastest lap:
Jones, 1m31.272. Leaders: Villeneuve, laps 1-50; Jones, 51-72

Toyota Grand Prix of the United States

7 October 1979. Watkins Glen. 59 laps of a 3.377-mile
circuit = 199.243 miles. Cold and wet. World
Championship round 15

1 Gilles Villeneuve	Ferrari 312T4	59	1h52m17.734
2 René Arnoux	Renault RE10	59	1h53m06.521
3 Didier Pironi	Tyrrell 009-Ford	59	1h53m10.933
4 Elio de Angelis	Shadow DN9B-Ford	59	1h53m48.246
5 Hans-Joachim Stuck	ATS D3-Ford	59	1h53m58.993
6 John Watson	McLaren M29-Ford	58	

Winner's average speed: 106.456 mph. Starting grid front row:
Jones, 1m36.615 (pole) and Piquet, 1m36.914. Fastest lap: Piquet,
1m40.054. Leaders: Villeneuve, laps 1-31, 37-59; Jones, 32-36

1979 FINAL CHAMPIONSHIP POSITIONS

Drivers					Manufacturers	
1	Jody Scheckter	51 (60)*	15=	Elio de Angelis	3	1	Ferrari	113
2	Gilles Villeneuve	47 (53)*		Jacky Ickx	3	2	Williams-Ford	75
3	Alan Jones	40 (43)*		Jochen Mass	3	3	Ligier-Ford	61
4	Jacques Laffite	36		Nelson Piquet	3	4	Lotus-Ford	39
5	Clay Regazzoni	29 (32)*	19=	Riccardo Patrese	2	5	Tyrrell-Ford	28
6=	Patrick Depailler	20 (22)*		Hans-Joachim Stuck	2	6	Renault	26
	Carlos Reutemann	20 (25)*	21	Emerson Fittipaldi	1	7	McLaren-Ford	15
8	René Arnoux	17		*Sum of best four results		8	Brabham-Alfa Romeo	7
9	John Watson	15		from the first seven races		9	Arrows-Ford	5
10=	Mario Andretti	14		and best four results from		10	Shadow-Ford	3
	Jean-Pierre Jarier	14		the final eight races		11	ATS-Ford	2
	Didier Pironi	14				12	Fittipaldi-Ford	1
13	Jean-Pierre Jabouille	9					Results for all cars entered by FOCA	
14	Niki Lauda	4					recognised constructors count	

1980

Having been the pacesetters for the last six months, the Williams team modified its cars and signed Carlos Reutemann to join Alan Jones. Once again Jones and the FW07 proved to be the class act, and after a strong challenge from the revitalized Brabham team, the Australian gave Williams its first World Championship title.

Alan Jones leads championship rival Nelson Piquet during the British Grand Prix at Brands Hatch

Nelson Piquet emerged as a serious championship contender in only his second full season with Brabham. He took the series lead by winning the Italian GP, held at Imola for the only time. However, an engine failure in the penultimate race halted that challenge and confirmed Jones's title.

Along with Piquet, other young drivers made their mark in 1980. Didier Pironi, in his only season with Ligier, won in Belgium, crashed at Monaco while leading and impressed in Britain. Renault's René Arnoux won twice early in the year, but their turbocharged engine was still unreliable.

European F3 Champion Alain Prost signed for McLaren, and promptly outshone his more experienced team leader John Watson with points finishes in his first two Grands Prix.

However, for Gilles Villeneuve it was a frustrating if spectacular season. The new Ferrari 312T5 was a retrograde step, and its Michelin tyres wore at an unacceptable rate. His team mate Jody Scheckter announced his retirement from the sport at the end of the year, but by then the team was already looking to 1981 and a new turbocharged engine was being tested.

Patrick Depailler was still recovering from his hang-gliding accident but moved to Alfa Romeo. Sadly, just as the team appeared to be making progress under his guidance, Depailler was killed testing at Hockenheim. Clay Regazzoni was also seriously injured when his Ensign crashed into a retired car at Long Beach.

Off the track, politics raged between FISA and the Formula One Constructors Association (FOCA) in a conflict which almost destroyed Formula One. The Spanish GP lost its championship status when FISA-aligned teams (Alfa Romeo, Ferrari and Renault) withdrew, while the French GP was only run after crisis talks prevented its cancellation.

Gran Premio de la Republica Argentina

13 January 1980. Buenos Aires. 53 laps of a 3.709-mile circuit = 196.577 miles. Very hot, dry and sunny. World Championship round 1

1	Alan Jones	Williams FW07-Ford	53	1h43m24.38
2	Nelson Piquet	Brabham BT49-Ford	53	1h43m48.97
3	Keke Rosberg	Fittipaldi F7-Ford	53	1h44m43.02
4	Derek Daly	Tyrrell 009-Ford	53	1h44m47.86
5	Bruno Giacomelli	Alfa Romeo 179B	52	
6	Alain Prost	McLaren M29-Ford	52	

Winner's average speed: 114.061 mph. Starting grid front row: Jones, 1m44.17 (pole) and Laffite, 1m44.44. Fastest lap: Jones, 1m50.45. Leaders: Jones, laps 1-17, 30-53; Laffite, 18-29

Grande Premio do Brasil

27 January 1980. Interlagos. 40 laps of a 4.893-mile circuit = 195.720 miles. Very hot, dry and sunny. World Championship round 2

1	René Arnoux	Renault RE20	40	1h40m01.33
2	Elio de Angelis	Lotus 81-Ford	40	1h40m23.19
3	Alan Jones	Williams FW07B-Ford	40	1h41m07.44
4	Didier Pironi	Ligier JS11/15-Ford	40	1h41m41.46
5	Alain Prost	McLaren M29B-Ford	40	1h42m26.74
6	Riccardo Patrese	Arrows A3-Ford	39	

Winner's average speed: 117.406 mph. Starting grid front row: Jabouille, 2m21.40 (pole) and Pironi, 2m21.65. Fastest lap: Arnoux, 2m27.311. Leaders: Villeneuve, lap 1; Jabouille, laps 2-24; Arnoux, 25-40

Nashua Grand Prix of South Africa

1 March 1980. Kyalami. 78 laps of a 2.550-mile circuit = 198.900 miles. Warm, dry and sunny. World Championship round 3

1980 DRIVERS' RECORDS

Driver	Car	Argentinian GP	Brazilian GP	South African GP	Long Beach GP	Belgian GP	Monaco GP	French GP	British GP	German GP	Austrian GP	Dutch GP	Italian GP	Canadian GP	United States GP
Mario Andretti	Lotus 81-Ford	R	R	12	R	R	7	R	R	7	R	8	R	R	6
Elio de Angelis	Lotus 81-Ford	R	2	R	R	10	9	R	R	16	6	R	4	10	4
René Arnoux	Renault RE20	R	1^F	1^F	9	4	R	5	NC	R	9^{PF}	2^{PF}	10^P	R	7
Vittorio Brambilla	Alfa Romeo 179B	-	-	-	-	-	-	-	-	-	-	R	R	-	-
Andrea de Cesaris	Alfa Romeo 179B	-	-	-	-	-	-	-	-	-	-	-	-	R	R
Eddie Cheever	Osella FA1-Ford	DNQ	DNQ	R	R	DNQ	DNQ	R	R	R	R	R	-	-	-
	Osella FA1B-Ford	-	-	-	-	-	-	-	-	-	-	-	12	R	R
Kevin Cogan	Williams FW07B-Ford	-	-	-	-	-	-	-	-	-	-	-	-	DNQ	-
Derek Daly	Tyrrell 009-Ford	4	14	-	-	-	-	-	-	-	-	-	-	-	-
	Tyrrell 010-Ford	-	-	R	8	9	R	11	4	10	R	R	R	R	R
Patrick Depailler	Alfa Romeo 179B	R	R	R	R	R	R	R	R	R	-	-	-	-	-
Harald Ertl	ATS D4-Ford	-	-	-	-	-	-	-	-	DNQ	-	-	-	-	-
Emerson Fittipaldi	Fittipaldi F7-Ford	NC	15	8	3	R	6	13	-	-	-	-	-	-	-
	Fittipaldi F8-Ford	-	-	-	-	-	-	-	12	R	11	R	R	R	R
Bruno Giacomelli	Alfa Romeo 179B	5	13	R	R	R	R	R	5	R	R	R	R	R	R^P
Jean-Pierre Jabouille	Renault RE20	R	R^P	R^P	10	R	R	R	R	R	1	R	R	R	-
Jean-Pierre Jarier	Tyrrell 009-Ford	R	12	-	-	-	-	-	-	-	-	-	-	-	-
	Tyrrell 010-Ford	-	-	7	R	5	R	14	5	15	R	5	R	7	NC
Stefan Johansson	Shadow DN11A-Ford	DNQ	DNQ	-	-	-	-	-	-	-	-	-	-	-	-
Alan Jones	Williams FW07-Ford	1^{PF}	-	-	-	-	-	-	-	-	-	-	-	-	-
	Williams FW07B-Ford	-	3	R	R	2^P	R	1^F	1	3^{PF}	2	11	2^F	1	1^F
Rupert Keegan	Williams FW07-Ford	-	-	-	-	-	-	-	11	-	-	-	-	-	-
	Williams FW07B-Ford	-	-	-	-	-	-	-	-	-	DNQ	15	DNQ	11	DNQ	9
David Kennedy	Shadow DN11A-Ford	DNQ	DNQ	DNQ	DNQ	DNQ	DNQ	-	-	-	-	-	-	-	-
	Shadow DN12A-Ford	-	-	-	-	-	-	-	DNQ	-	-	-	-	-	-
Jacques Laffite	Ligier JS11/15-Ford	R	R	2	R	11^F	2	3^P	R	1	4	3	9	8	5
Jan Lammers	ATS D3-Ford	DNQ	DNQ	DNQ	-	-	-	-	-	-	-	-	-	-	-
	ATS D4-Ford	-	-	-	R	R	10	-	-	-	-	-	-	-	-
	Ensign N180-Ford	-	-	-	-	-	-	DNQ	DNQ	14	DNQ	DNQ	DNQ	12	R

/Cont'd

1 René Arnoux — Renault RE20 — 78 — 1h36m52.54
2 Jacques Laffite — Ligier JS11/15-Ford — 78 — 1h37m26.61
3 Didier Pironi — Ligier JS11/15-Ford — 78 — 1h37m45.03
4 Nelson Piquet — Brabham BT49-Ford — 78 — 1h37m53.56
5 Carlos Reutemann — Williams FW07B-Ford — 77
6 Jochen Mass — Arrows A3-Ford — 77

Winner's average speed: 123.189 mph. Starting grid front row: Jabouille, 1m10.00 (pole) and Arnoux, 1m10.21. Fastest lap: Arnoux, 1m13.15. Leaders: Jabouille, laps 1-61; Arnoux, 62-78.

Toyota Grand Prix of Long Beach

30 March 1980. Long Beach. 80.5 laps of a 2.020-mile circuit = 162.610 miles. Warm, dry and sunny. World Championship round 4

1 Nelson Piquet — Brabham BT49-Ford — 81 — 1h50m18.550
2 Riccardo Patrese — Arrows A3-Ford — 81 — 1h51m07.762
3 Emerson Fittipaldi — Fittipaldi F7-Ford — 81 — 1h51m37.113
4 John Watson — McLaren M29C-Ford — 80
5 Jody Scheckter — Ferrari 312T5 — 80
6 Didier Pironi — Ligier JS11/15-Ford — 80

Winner's average speed: 88.448 mph. Starting grid front row: Piquet, 1m17.694 (pole) and Arnoux, 1m18.689. Fastest lap: Piquet, 1m19.830. Leaders: Piquet, laps 1-80.

Grand Prix de Belgique

4 May 1980. Zolder. 72 laps of a 2.648-mile circuit = 190.656 miles. Dry and windy. World Championship round 5

1 Didier Pironi — Ligier JS11/15-Ford — 72 — 1h38m46.51
2 Alan Jones — Williams FW07B-Ford — 72 — 1h39m33.88
3 Carlos Reutemann — Williams FW07B-Ford — 72 — 1h40m10.63
4 René Arnoux — Renault RE20 — 71
5 Jean-Pierre Jarier — Tyrrell 010-Ford — 71
6 Gilles Villeneuve — Ferrari 312T5 — 71

Winner's average speed: 115.812 mph. Starting grid front row: Jones, 1m19.12 (pole) and Pironi, 1m19.35. Fastest lap: Laffite, 1m20.88. Leaders: Pironi, laps 1-72

Grand Prix de Monaco

18 May 1980. Monte Carlo. 76 laps of a 2.058-mile circuit = 156.408 miles. Occasional rain and overcast. World Championship round 6

1 Carlos Reutemann — Williams FW07B-Ford — 76 — 1h55m34.365
2 Jacques Laffite — Ligier JS11/15-Ford — 76 — 1h56m47.994
3 Nelson Piquet — Brabham BT49-Ford — 76 — 1h56m52.091
4 Jochen Mass — Arrows A3-Ford — 75
5 Gilles Villeneuve — Ferrari 312T5 — 75
6 Emerson Fittipaldi — Fittipaldi F7-Ford — 74

Winner's average speed: 81.200 mph. Starting grid front row: Pironi, 1m24.813 (pole) and Reutemann, 1m24.882. Fastest lap: Patrese, 1m26.058 (in doubt as it was raining when time was set). Leaders: Pironi, laps 1-54; Reutemann, 55-76

Grand Prix de France

29 June 1980. Paul Ricard. 54 laps of a 3.610-mile circuit = 194.940 miles. Warm, dry and windy. World Championship round 7

1 Alan Jones — Williams FW07B-Ford — 54 — 1h32m43.42
2 Didier Pironi — Ligier JS11/15-Ford — 54 — 1h32m47.94
3 Jacques Laffite — Ligier JS11/15-Ford — 54 — 1h33m13.68
4 Nelson Piquet — Brabham BT49-Ford — 54 — 1h33m58.30
5 René Arnoux — Renault RE20 — 54 — 1h33m59.57
6 Carlos Reutemann — Williams FW07B-Ford — 54 — 1h34m00.16

Winner's average speed: 126.143 mph. Starting grid front row: Laffite, 1m38.88 (pole) and Arnoux, 1m39.49. Fastest lap: Jones, 1m41.45. Leaders: Laffite, laps 1-34; Jones, 35-54

1980 DRIVERS' RECORDS cont'd/

Driver	Car	Argentinian GP	Brazilian GP	South African GP	Long Beach GP	Belgian GP	Monaco GP	French GP	British GP	German GP	Austrian GP	Dutch GP	Italian GP	Canadian GP	United States GP
Geoff Lees	Shadow DN11A-Ford	-	-	R	DNQ	-	-	-	-	-	-	-	-	-	-
	Shadow DN12A-Ford	-	-	-	-	DNQ	DNQ	DNQ	-	-	-	-	-	-	-
	Ensign N180-Ford	-	-	-	-	-	-	-	-	-	-	R	DNQ	-	-
	Williams FW07B-Ford	-	-	-	-	-	-	-	-	-	-	-	-	-	DNQ
Nigel Mansell	Lotus 81B-Ford	-	-	-	-	-	-	-	-	-	R	R	-	-	-
	Lotus 81-Ford	-	-	-	-	-	-	-	-	-	-	-	DNQ	-	-
Jochen Mass	Arrows A3-Ford	R	10	6	7	R	4	10	13	8	DNP	DNP	-	11	R
Tiff Needell	Ensign N180-Ford	-	-	-	-	R	DNQ	-	-	-	-	-	-	-	-
Riccardo Patrese	Arrows A3-Ford	R	6	R	2	R	8^F	9	9	9	14	R	R	R	R
Nelson Piquet	Brabham BT49-Ford	2	R	4	1^{PF}	R	3	4	2	4	5	1	1	R^P	R
Didier Pironi	Ligier JS11/15-Ford	R	4	3	6	1	R^P	2	R^{PF}	R	R	R	6	3^F	3
Alain Prost	McLaren M29B-Ford	6	5	-	-	-	-	-	-	-	-	-	-	-	-
	McLaren M29C-Ford	-	-	DNS	-	R	R	R	6	11	7	-	-	-	-
	McLaren M30-Ford	-	-	-	-	-	-	-	-	-	-	6	7	R	DNS
Hector Rebaque	Brabham BT49-Ford	-	-	-	-	-	-	-	7	R	10	R	R	6	R
Clay Regazzoni	Ensign N180-Ford	NC	R	9	R	-	-	-	-	-	-	-	-	-	-
Carlos Reutemann	Williams FW07B-Ford	R	R	5	R	3	1	6	3	2	3	4	3	2	2
Keke Rosberg	Fittipaldi F7-Ford	3	9	R	R	7	DNQ	R	DNQ	-	-	-	-	-	-
	Fittipaldi F8-Ford	-	-	-	-	-	-	-	-	R	16	DNQ	5	9	10
Jody Scheckter	Ferrari 312T5	R	R	R	5	8	R	12	10	13	13	9	8	DNQ	11
Stephen South	McLaren M29C-Ford	-	-	-	DNQ	-	-	-	-	-	-	-	-	-	-
Marc Surer	ATS D3-Ford	R	7	-	-	-	-	-	-	-	-	-	-	-	-
	ATS D4-Ford	-	-	DNQ	-	-	-	R	R	12	12	10	R	DNQ	8
Mike Thackwell	Arrows A3-Ford	-	-	-	-	-	-	-	-	-	-	-	-	DNQ	-
	Tyrrell 010-Ford	-	-	-	-	-	-	-	-	-	-	-	-	R	DNQ
Gilles Villeneuve	Ferrari 312T5	R	16	R	R	6	5	8	R	6	8	7	R	5	R
John Watson	McLaren M29B-Ford	R	11	11	-	-	-	-	-	-	-	-	-	-	-
	McLaren M29C-Ford	-	-	-	4	NC	DNQ	7	8	R	R	R	R	4	NC
Desiré Wilson	Williams FW07-Ford	-	-	-	-	-	-	-	DNQ	-	-	-	-	-	-
Manfred Winkelhock	Arrows A3-Ford	-	-	-	-	-	-	-	-	-	-	-	DNQ	-	-
Ricardo Zunino	Brabham BT49-Ford	7	8	10	R	R	DNQ	R	-	-	-	-	-	-	-

Marlboro British Grand Prix

13 July 1980. Brands Hatch. 76 laps of a 2.614-mile circuit = 198.664 miles. Dry and overcast. World Championship round 8

1	Alan Jones	Williams FW07B-Ford	76 1h34m49.228
2	Nelson Piquet	Brabham BT49-Ford	76 1h35m00.235
3	Carlos Reutemann	Williams FW07B-Ford	76 1h35m02.513
4	Derek Daly	Tyrrell 010-Ford	75
5	Jean-Pierre Jarier	Tyrrell 010-Ford	75
6	Alain Prost	McLaren M29C-Ford	75

Winner's average speed: 125.690 mph. Starting grid front row: Pironi, 1m11.004 (pole) and Laffite, 1m11.395. Fastest lap: Pironi, 1m12.368. Leaders: Pironi, laps 1-18; Laffite, 19-30; Jones, 31-76

Grosser Preis von Deutschland

10 August 1980. Hockenheim. 45 laps of a 4.219-mile circuit = 189.855 miles. Dry and overcast. World Championship round 9

1	Jacques Laffite	Ligier JS11/15-Ford	45 1h22m59.73
2	Carlos Reutemann	Williams FW07B-Ford	45 1h23m02.92
3	Alan Jones	Williams FW07B-Ford	45 1h23m43.26
4	Nelson Piquet	Brabham BT49-Ford	45 1h23m44.21
5	Bruno Giacomelli	Alfa Romeo 179B	45 1h24m16.22
6	Gilles Villeneuve	Ferrari 312T5	45 1h24m28.45

Winner's average speed: 137.252 mph. Starting grid front row: Jones, 1m45.85 (pole) and Jabouille, 1m45.89. Fastest lap: Jones, 1m48.49. Leaders: Jabouille, laps 1-26; Jones, 27-40; Laffite, 41-45

Grosser Preis von Österreich

17 August 1980. Österreichring. 54 laps of a 3.692-mile circuit = 199.368 miles. Warm, dry and sunny. World Championship round 10

1	Jean-Pierre Jabouille	Renault RE20	54 1h26m15.73
2	Alan Jones	Williams FW07B-Ford	54 1h26m16.55
3	Carlos Reutemann	Williams FW07B-Ford	54 1h26m35.09
4	Jacques Laffite	Ligier JS11/15-Ford	54 1h26m57.75
5	Nelson Piquet	Brabham BT49-Ford	54 1h27m18.54
6	Elio de Angelis	Lotus 81-Ford	54 1h27m30.70

Winner's average speed: 138.671 mph. Starting grid front row: Arnoux, 1m30.27 (pole) and Jabouille, 1m31.48. Fastest lap: Arnoux, 1m32.53. Leaders: Jones, laps 1-2; Arnoux, 3-20; Jabouille, 21-54

Grote Prijs van Nederland

31 August 1980. Zandvoort. 72 laps of a 2.642-mile circuit = 190.224 miles. Warm, dry and sunny. World Championship round 11

1	Nelson Piquet	Brabham BT49-Ford	72 1h38m13.83
2	René Arnoux	Renault RE20	72 1h38m26.76
3	Jacques Laffite	Ligier JS11/15-Ford	72 1h38m27.26
4	Carlos Reutemann	Williams FW07B-Ford	72 1h38m29.12
5	Jean-Pierre Jarier	Tyrrell 010-Ford	72 1h39m13.85
6	Alain Prost	McLaren M30-Ford	72 1h39m36.45

Winner's average speed: 116.190 mph. Starting grid front row: Arnoux, 1m17.44 (pole) and Jabouille, 1m17.74. Fastest lap: Arnoux, 1m19.35. Leaders: Jones, lap 1; Arnoux, lap 2; Laffite, laps 3-12; Piquet, 13-72

Gran Premio d'Italia

14 September 1980. Imola. 60 laps of a 3.132-mile circuit = 187.920 miles. Warm, dry and sunny. World Championship round 12

1	Nelson Piquet	Brabham BT49-Ford	60 1h38m07.52
2	Alan Jones	Williams FW07B-Ford	60 1h38m36.45
3	Carlos Reutemann	Williams FW07B-Ford	60 1h39m21.19

4 Elio de Angelis	Lotus 81-Ford	59	
5 Keke Rosberg	Fittipaldi F8-Ford	59	
6 Didier Pironi	Ligier JS11/15-Ford	59	

Winner's average speed: 114.906 mph. Starting grid front row: Arnoux, 1m33.988 (pole) and Jabouille, 1m34.339. Fastest lap: Jones, 1m36.089. Leaders: Arnoux, laps 1-2; Jabouille, 3; Piquet, 4-60

Grand Prix Labatt du Canada

28 September 1980. Montreal. 70 laps of a 2.740-mile circuit = 191.800 miles. Stopped after first lap accident. Restarted over original distance. Cool and dry. World Championship round 13

1 Alan Jones	Williams FW07B-Ford	70	1h46m45.53
2 Carlos Reutemann	Williams FW07B-Ford	70	1h47m01.07
3 Didier Pironi*	Ligier JS11/15-Ford	70	1h47m04.60
4 John Watson	McLaren M29C-Ford	70	1h47m16.51
5 Gilles Villeneuve	Ferrari 312T5	70	1h47m40.76
6 Hector Rebaque	Brabham BT49-Ford	69	

*Pironi penalized 60 seconds for jumping the start. Winner's average speed: 107.794 mph. Starting grid front row: Piquet, 1m27.328 (pole) and Jones, 1m28.164. Fastest lap: Pironi, 1m28.769. Leaders: Jones, laps 1-2, 24-70; Piquet, 3-23 (Pironi led laps 44-70 on the road)

Toyota Grand Prix of the United States

5 October 1980. Watkins Glen. 59 laps of a 3.377-mile circuit = 199.243 miles. Cool and dry. World Championship round 14

1 Alan Jones	Williams FW07B-Ford	59	1h34m36.05
2 Carlos Reutemann	Williams FW07B-Ford	59	1h34m40.26
3 Didier Pironi	Ligier JS11/15-Ford	59	1h34m48.62
4 Elio de Angelis	Lotus 81-Ford	59	1h35m05.74
5 Jacques Laffite	Ligier JS11/15-Ford	58	
6 Mario Andretti	Lotus 81-Ford	58	

Winner's average speed: 126.369 mph. Starting grid front row: Giacomelli, 1m33.291 (pole) and Piquet, 1m34.080. Fastest lap: Jones, 1m34.068. Leaders: Giacomelli, laps 1-31; Jones, 32-59

1980 FINAL CHAMPIONSHIP POSITIONS

Drivers						Manufacturers		
1	Alan Jones	67 (71)*	15=	Emerson Fittipaldi	5	1	Williams-Ford	120
2	Nelson Piquet	54		Alain Prost	5	2	Ligier-Ford	66
3	Carlos Reutemann	42 (49)*	17=	Bruno Giacomelli	4	3	Brabham-Ford	55
4	Jacques Laffite	34		Jochen Mass	4	4	Renault	38
5	Didier Pironi	32	19	Jody Scheckter	2	5	Lotus-Ford	14
6	René Arnoux	29	20=	Mario Andretti	1	6	Tyrrell-Ford	12
7	Elio de Angelis	13		Hector Rebaque	1	7=	Arrows-Ford	11
8	Jean-Pierre Jabouille	9		*Sum of best five results			Fittipaldi-Ford	11
9	Riccardo Patrese	7		from the first seven races			McLaren-Ford	11
10=	Derek Daly	6		and best five results from		10	Ferrari	8
	Jean-Pierre Jarier	6		the final seven races		11	Alfa Romeo	4
	Keke Rosberg	6					Results for all cars entered	
	Gilles Villeneuve	6					by FOCA recognised	
	John Watson	6					constructors count	

1981

After a tortuous winter of politics, the FISA/FOCA "war" was finally resolved and the season opened at Long Beach. To reduce downforce and therefore cornering speeds, sliding skirts were banned. A minimum sidepod ground clearance of 6 cm was now stipulated. But the old order appeared unchanged, with Alan Jones winning in Southern California for Williams.

....
Three victories gave Nelson Piquet his first World Championship for Brabham

The new ground clearance rule could only be measured in the pits, so systems to lower the cars while in motion were introduced by some teams. After protests, FISA pronounced the concept legal, so everyone had to follow suit.

On the track, Brabham and Williams again disputed the championship. Carlos Reutemann defied Williams' team orders to beat Jones in Brazil, and the Argentinian led the champion-

ship for much of the year. However, he was strangely lacklustre at the final race, allowing Nelson Piquet to snatch the title for Brabham. Alan Jones announced his (albeit temporary) retirement from the sport, and won his final race for Williams at Las Vegas.

Gilles Villeneuve, now with a turbocharged Ferrari, was again in the news. After winning in Monte Carlo, he narrowly held off four quicker cars for almost the entire Spanish GP to score an incredible victory: 1.24 seconds separated the top five at the finish! The Ferrari had a powerful engine but a truly awful chassis.

The originators of the turbo, Renault, signed Alain Prost from McLaren, and he starred, winning three times. Mechanical failures, however, again restricted its championship challenge.

The newly restructured McLaren International team introduced the carbon fibre monocoque to Grand Prix racing in the John Barnard-designed MP4/1. Backed by a patriotic home crowd, John Watson won the British GP in the car, his first victory for five years. Lotus also used a composite chassis, for greater rigidity at less weight, but the team was adversely preoccupied with the controversial twin-chassis Lotus 88 concept, which FISA never allowed to race.

1981 DRIVERS' RECORDS

Driver	Car	Long Beach GP	Brazilian GP	Argentinian GP	San Marino GP	Belgian GP	Monaco GP	Spanish GP	French GP	British GP	German GP	Austrian GP	Dutch GP	Italian GP	Canadian GP	Las Vegas GP
Michele Alboreto	Tyrrell 010-Ford	-	-	-	R	12	R	DNQ	16	R	DNQ	R	-	-	-	-
	Tyrrell 011-Ford	-	-	-	-	-	-	-	-	-	-	-	9	R	11	R
Mario Andretti	Alfa Romeo 179C	4	R	8	R	10	R	8	-	R	9	R	R	R	7	R
	Alfa Romeo 179B	-	-	-	-	-	-	-	8	-	-	-	-	-	-	-
Elio de Angelis	Lotus 81-Ford	R	5	6	-	5	-	-	-	-	-	-	-	-	-	-
	Lotus 87-Ford	-	-	-	-	-	R	5	6	R	7	7	5	4	6	R
René Arnoux	Renault RE20B	8	R	5	8	-	R	-	-	-	-	-	-	-	-	-
	Renault RE30	-	-	-	-	DNQ	-	9	4^P	9^{PF}	13	2^P	R	R^P	R	R
Slim Borgudd	ATS D4-Ford	-	-	-	13	-	-	-	-	-	-	-	-	-	-	-
	ATS HGS1-Ford	-	-	-	-	DNQ	NPQ	DNQ	DNQ	6	R	R	10	R	R	DNQ
Andrea de Cesaris	McLaren M29F-Ford	R	R	11	6	R	-	-	-	-	-	-	-	-	-	-
	McLaren MP4/1-Ford	-	-	-	-	-	R	R	11	R	R	8	DNS	7	R	12
Eddie Cheever	Tyrrell 010-Ford	5	NC	R	R	6	5	NC	13	4	-	-	-	-	-	-
	Tyrrell 011-Ford	-	-	-	-	-	-	-	-	-	5	DNQ	R	R	R	R
Kevin Cogan	Tyrrell 010-Ford	DNQ	-	-	-	-	-	-	-	-	-	-	-	-	-	-
Derek Daly	March 811-Ford	DNQ	DNP	DNQ	DNQ	DNQ	NPQ	16	R	7	R	11	R	R	8	DNQ
Giorgio Francia	Osella FA1B-Ford	-	-	-	-	-	-	DNQ	-	-	-	-	-	-	-	-
Beppe Gabbiani	Osella FA1B-Ford	R	DNQ	DNQ	R	R	DNQ	DNQ	DNQ	DNQ	DNQ	DNQ	DNQ	DNQ	DNQ	DNQ
Piercarlo Ghinzani	Osella FA1B-Ford	-	-	-	-	13	DNQ	-	-	-	-	-	-	-	-	-
Bruno Giacomelli	Alfa Romeo 179C	R	R	10	R	9	R	10	-	R	15	R	R	8	4	3
	Alfa Romeo 179B	-	-	-	-	-	-	-	15	-	-	-	-	-	-	-
Miguel Angel Guerra	Osella FA1B-Ford	DNQ	DNQ	DNQ	R	-	-	-	-	-	-	-	-	-	-	-
Brian Henton	Toleman TG181-Hart	-	-	-	DNQ	DNQ	NPQ	DNQ	DNQ	DNQ	DNQ	DNQ	DNQ	10	DNQ	DNQ
Jean-Pierre Jabouille	Ligier JS17-Matra	-	DNQ	DNQ	NC	R	DNQ	R	-	-	-	-	-	-	-	-
Jean-Pierre Jarier	Ligier JS17-Matra	R	7	-	-	-	-	-	-	-	-	-	-	-	-	-
	Osella FA1B-Ford	-	-	-	-	-	-	-	-	8	8	10	R	-	-	-
	Osella FA1C-Ford	-	-	-	-	-	-	-	-	-	-	-	-	9	R	R
Alan Jones	Williams FW07C-Ford	1^F	2	4	12	R	2^F	7^F	17	R	11^F	4	3^F	2	R	1
Jacques Laffite	Ligier JS17-Matra	R	6	R	R	2	3	2^P	R	3	3	1^F	R	R	1	6
Jan Lammers	ATS D4-Ford	R	DNQ	12	DNQ	-	-	-	-	-	-	-	-	-	-	-
Nigel Mansell	Lotus 81-Ford	R	11	R	-	3	-	-	-	-	-	-	-	-	-	-
	Lotus 87-Ford	-	-	-	-	-	R	R	6	7	DNQ	R	R	R	R	4
Riccardo Patrese	Arrows A3-Ford	R^P	3	7	2	R	R	R	14	10	R	R	R	R	R	11
Nelson Piquet	Brabham BT49C-Ford	3	12^P	1^{PF}	1	R	R^P	R	3	R	1	3	2	6	5^P	5
Didier Pironi	Ferrari 126CK	R	R	R	5	8	4	15	5	R	R	9	R	5	R	9^F
Alain Prost	Renault RE20B	R	R	3	R	-	-	-	-	-	-	-	-	-	-	-
	Renault RE30	-	-	-	-	R	R	R	1^F	R	2^P	R	1^P	1	R	2
Hector Rebaque	Brabham BT49C-Ford	R	R	R	4	R	DNQ	R	9	5	4	R	4	R	R	R
Carlos Reutemann	Williams FW07C-Ford	2	1	2	3	1^{PF}	R	4	10	2	R	5	R	3^F	10	8^P
Keke Rosberg	Fittipaldi F8C-Ford	R	9	R	R	R	DNQ	12	R	DNQ	R	DNQ	-	DNQ	DNQ	DNQ	10
Eliseo Salazar	March 811-Ford	DNQ	DNQ	DNQ	R	DNQ	NPQ	-	-	-	-	-	-	-	-	-
	Ensign N180B-Ford	-	-	-	-	-	-	14	R	DNQ	NC	R	6	R	R	R
Chico Serra	Fittipaldi F8C-Ford	7	R	R	DNQ	R	DNQ	11	DNS	DNQ	DNQ	-	DNQ	DNQ	DNQ	DNQ
Siegfried Stohr	Arrows A3-Ford	DNQ	R	9	DNQ	R	R	R	DNQ	R	12	R	7	DNQ	-	-
Marc Surer	Ensign N180B-Ford	R	4^F	R	9	11	6	-	-	-	-	-	-	-	-	-
	Theodore TY01-Ford	-	-	-	-	-	-	-	12	11	14	DNS	8	DNQ	9	R
Patrick Tambay	Theodore TY01-Ford	6	10	R	11	DNQ	7	13	-	-	-	-	-	-	-	-
	Ligier JS17-Matra	-	-	-	-	-	-	-	R	R	R	R	R	R	R	R
Gilles Villeneuve	Ferrari 126CK	R	R	R	7^{PF}	4	1	1	R	R	R	10	R	R	3	R
Jacques Villeneuve	Arrows A3-Ford	-	-	-	-	-	-	-	-	-	-	-	-	-	DNQ	DNQ
Emilio de Villota	Williams FW07-Ford	-	-	-	-	-	-	DNP	-	-	-	-	-	-	-	-
Derek Warwick	Toleman TG181-Hart	-	-	-	DNQ	DNQ	NPQ	DNQ	DNQ	DNQ	DNQ	DNQ	DNQ	DNQ	DNQ	R
John Watson	McLaren M29F-Ford	R	8	-	-	-	-	-	-	-	-	-	-	-	-	-
	McLaren MP4/1-Ford	-	-	R	10	7	R	3	2	1	6	6	R	R	2^F	7
Ricardo Zunino	Tyrrell 010-Ford	-	13	13	-	-	-	-	-	-	-	-	-	-	-	-

Toyota Grand Prix of the United States West

15 March 1981. Long Beach. 80.5 laps of a 2.020-mile circuit = 162.610 miles. Warm, dry and sunny. World Championship round 1

1 Alan Jones	Williams FW07C-Ford	80	1h50m41.33
2 Carlos Reutemann	Williams FW07C-Ford	80	1h50m50.52
3 Nelson Piquet	Brabham BT49C-Ford	80	1h51m16.25
4 Mario Andretti	Alfa Romeo 179C	80	1h51m30.64
5 Eddie Cheever	Tyrrell 010-Ford	80	1h51m48.03
6 Patrick Tambay	Theodore TY01-Ford	79	

Winner's average speed: 88.144 mph. Starting grid front row: Patrese, 1m19.39 (pole) and Jones, 1m19.40. Fastest lap: Jones, 1m20.901. Leaders: Patrese, laps 1-24; Reutemann, 25-31; Jones, 32-80

Grande Premio do Brasil

29 March 1981. Rio de Janeiro. 62 laps of a 3.126-mile circuit = 193.812 miles. Race scheduled for 63 laps but stopped due to the two hour rule. Wet. World Championship round 2

1 Carlos Reutemann	Williams FW07C-Ford	62	2h00m23.66
2 Alan Jones	Williams FW07C-Ford	62	2h00m28.10
3 Riccardo Patrese	Arrows A3-Ford	62	2h01m26.74

4 Marc Surer	Ensign N180B-Ford	62	2h01m40.69
5 Elio de Angelis	Lotus 81-Ford	62	2h01m50.08
6 Jacques Laffite	Ligier JS17-Matra	62	2h01m50.49

Winner's average speed: 96.589 mph. Starting grid front row: Piquet, 1m35.079 (pole) and Reutemann, 1m35.390. Fastest lap: Surer, 1m54.302. Leaders: Reutemann, laps 1-62.

Gran Premio de la Republica Argentina

12 April 1981. Buenos Aires. 53 laps of a 3.709-mile circuit = 196.577 miles. Hot, dry and sunny. World Championship round 3

1 Nelson Piquet	Brabham BT49C-Ford	53	1h34m32.74
2 Carlos Reutemann	Williams FW07C-Ford	53	1h34m59.35
3 Alain Prost	Renault RE20B	53	1h35m22.72
4 Alan Jones	Williams FW07C-Ford	53	1h35m40.62
5 René Arnoux	Renault RE20B	53	1h36m04.59
6 Elio de Angelis	Lotus 81-Ford	52	

Winner's average speed: 124.751 mph. Starting grid front row: Piquet, 1m42.665 (pole) and Prost, 1m42.981. Fastest lap: Piquet, 1m45.287. Leaders: Piquet, laps 1-53.

Gran Premio di San Marino

3 May 1981. Imola. 60 laps of a 3.132-mile circuit = 187.920 miles. Cool and wet. World Championship round 4

1 Nelson Piquet	Brabham BT49C-Ford	60	1h51m23.97
2 Riccardo Patrese	Arrows A3-Ford	60	1h51m28.55
3 Carlos Reutemann	Williams FW07C-Ford	60	1h51m30.31
4 Hector Rebaque	Brabham BT49C-Ford	60	1h51m46.86
5 Didier Pironi	Ferrari 126CK	60	1h51m49.84
6 Andrea de Cesaris	McLaren M29F-Ford	60	1h52m30.58

Winner's average speed: 101.214 mph. Starting grid front row: Villeneuve, 1m34.523 (pole) and Reutemann, 1m35.229. Fastest lap: Villeneuve, 1m48.064. Leaders: Villeneuve, laps 1-14; Pironi, 15-46; Piquet, 47-60.

Grand Prix de Belgique

17 May 1981. Zolder. 54 laps of a 2.648-mile circuit = 142.992 miles. Scheduled for 70 laps but stopped due to rain). Warm, dry and sunny, rain later. World Championship round 5

1 Carlos Reutemann	Williams FW07C-Ford	54	1h16m31.61
2 Jacques Laffite	Ligier JS17-Matra	54	1h17m07.67
3 Nigel Mansell	Lotus 81-Ford	54	1h17m15.30
4 Gilles Villeneuve	Ferrari 126CK	54	1h17m19.25
5 Elio de Angelis	Lotus 81-Ford	54	1h17m20.81
6 Eddie Cheever	Tyrrell 010-Ford	54	1h17m24.12

Winner's average speed: 112.111 mph. Starting grid front row: Reutemann, 1m22.28 (pole) and Piquet, 1m23.13. Fastest lap: Reutemann, 1m23.30. Leaders: Pironi, laps 1-12; Jones, 13-19; Reutemann, 20-54.

Grand Prix de Monaco

31 May 1981. Monte Carlo. 76 laps of a 2.058-mile circuit = 156.408 miles. Warm, dry and sunny. World Championship round 6

1 Gilles Villeneuve	Ferrari 126CK	76	1h54m23.38
2 Alan Jones	Williams FW07C-Ford	76	1h55m03.29
3 Jacques Laffite	Ligier JS17-Matra	76	1h55m52.62
4 Didier Pironi	Ferrari 126CK	75	
5 Eddie Cheever	Tyrrell 010-Ford	74	
6 Marc Surer	Ensign N180B-Ford	74	

Winner's average speed: 82.040 mph. Starting grid front row: Piquet, 1m25.710 (pole) and Villeneuve, 1m25.788. Fastest lap: Jones, 1m27.470. Leaders: Piquet, laps 1-53; Jones, 54-72; Villeneuve, 73-76.

Gran Premio de Espana

21 June 1981. Jarama. 80 laps of a 2.115-mile circuit = 169.200 miles. Hor, dry and sunny. World Championship round 7

1 Gilles Villeneuve	Ferrari 126CK	80	1h46m35.01
2 Jacques Laffite	Ligier JS17-Matra	80	1h46m35.23
3 John Watson	McLaren MP4/1-Ford	80	1h46m35.59
4 Carlos Reutemann	Williams FW07C-Ford	80	1h46m36.02
5 Elio de Angelis	Lotus 87-Ford	80	1h46m36.25
6 Nigel Mansell	Lotus 87-Ford	80	1h47m03.59

Winner's average speed: 95.267 mph. Starting grid front row: Laffite, 1m13.754 (pole) and Jones, 1m14.024. Fastest lap: Jones, 1m17.818. Leaders: Jones, laps 1-13; Villeneuve, 14-80.

Grand Prix de France

5 July 1981. Dijon-Prenois. 80 laps of a 2.361-mile circuit = 188.880 miles. Cool and dry, rain after 58 laps when race was stopped, track surface drying when race was restarted. World Championship round 8

1 Alain Prost	Renault RE30	80	1h35m48.13
2 John Watson	McLaren MP4/1-Ford	80	1h35m50.42
3 Nelson Piquet	Brabham BT49C-Ford	80	1h36m12.35
4 René Arnoux	Renault RE30	80	1h36m30.43
5 Didier Pironi	Ferrari 126CK	79	
6 Elio de Angelis	Lotus 87-Ford	79	

Winner's average speed: 118.294 mph. Starting grid front row: Arnoux, 1m05.95 (pole) and Watson, 1m06.36. Fastest lap: Prost, 1m09.14. Leaders: Piquet, laps 1-58; Prost, 59-80

Marlboro British Grand Prix

18 July 1981. Silverstone. 68 laps of a 2.932-mile circuit = 199.376 miles. Warm, dry and sunny. World Championship round 9

1 John Watson	McLaren MP4/1-Ford	68	1h26m54.80
2 Carlos Reutemann	Williams FW07C-Ford	68	1h27m35.45
3 Jacques Laffite	Ligier JS17-Matra	67	
4 Eddie Cheever	Tyrrell 010-Ford	67	
5 Hector Rebaque	Brabham BT49C-Ford	67	
6 Slim Borgudd	ATS HGS1-Ford	67	

Winner's average speed: 137.638 mph. Starting grid front row: Arnoux, 1m11.000 (pole) and Prost, 1m11.046. Fastest lap: Arnoux, 1m15.067. Leaders: Prost, laps 1-16; Arnoux, 17-60; Watson, 61-68

Grosser Preis von Deutschland

2 August 1981. Hockenheim. 45 laps of a 4.219-mile circuit = 189.855 miles. Hot, dry and sunny. World Championship round 10

1 Nelson Piquet	Brabham BT49C-Ford	45	1h25m55.60
2 Alain Prost	Renault RE30	45	1h26m07.12
3 Jacques Laffite	Ligier JS17-Matra	45	1h27m00.20
4 Hector Rebaque	Brabham BT49C-Ford	45	1h27m35.29
5 Eddie Cheever	Tyrrell 011-Ford	45	1h27m46.12
6 John Watson	McLaren MP4/1-Ford	44	

Winner's average speed: 132.570 mph. Starting grid front row: Prost, 1m47.50 (pole) and Arnoux, 1m47.96. Fastest lap: Jones, 1m52.42. Leaders: Prost, laps 1-20; Jones, 21-38; Piquet, 39-45

Grosser Preis von Österreich

16 August 1981. Österreichring. 53 laps of a 3.692-mile circuit = 195.676 miles. Hot, dry and sunny. World Championship round 11

1 Jacques Laffite	Ligier JS17-Matra	53	1h27m36.47
2 René Arnoux	Renault RE30	53	1h27m41.64
3 Nelson Piquet	Brabham BT49C-Ford	53	1h27m43.81
4 Alan Jones	Williams FW07C-Ford	53	1h27m48.51
5 Carlos Reutemann	Williams FW07C-Ford	53	1h28m08.32
6 John Watson	McLaren MP4/1-Ford	53	1h29m07.61

Winner's average speed: 134.013 mph. Starting grid front row: Arnoux, 1m32.018 (pole) and Prost, 1m32.321. Fastest lap: Laffite, 1m37.62. Leaders: Villeneuve, lap 1; Prost, laps 2-26; Arnoux, 27-38; Laffite, 39-53

Grote Prijs van Nederland

30 August 1981. Zandvoort. 72 laps of a 2.642-mile circuit = 190.224 miles. Warm, dry and sunny. World Championship round 12

1 Alain Prost	Renault RE30	72	1h40m22.43
2 Nelson Piquet	Brabham BT49C-Ford	72	1h40m30.67
3 Alan Jones	Williams FW07C-Ford	72	1h40m57.93
4 Hector Rebaque	Brabham BT49C-Ford	71	
5 Elio de Angelis	Lotus 87-Ford	71	
6 Eliseo Salazar	Ensign N180B-Ford	70	

Winner's average speed: 113.709 mph. Starting grid front row: Prost, 1m18.176 (pole) and Arnoux, 1m18.255. Fastest lap: Jones, 1m21.83. Leaders: Prost, laps 1-22, 24-72; Jones, 23

Gran Premio d'Italia

13 September 1981. Monza. 52 laps of a 3.604-mile circuit = 187.408 miles. Warm, occasional rain. World Championship round 13

1 Alain Prost	Renault RE30	52	1h26m33.897
2 Alan Jones	Williams FW07C-Ford	52	1h26m56.072
3 Carlos Reutemann	Williams FW07C-Ford	52	1h27m24.484
4 Elio de Angelis	Lotus 87-Ford	52	1h28m06.799
5 Didier Pironi	Ferrari 126CK	52	1h28m08.419
6 Nelson Piquet	Brabham BT49C-Ford	51	engine

Winner's average speed: 129.893 mph. Starting grid front row: Arnoux, 1m33.467 (pole) and Reutemann, 1m34.140. Fastest lap: Reutemann, 1m37.528. Leaders: Prost, laps 1-52

Grand Prix Labatt du Canada

27 September 1981. Montreal. 63 laps of a 2.740-mile circuit = 172.620 miles. Scheduled for 70 laps but stopped due to two hour rule. Wet. World Championship round 14

1 Jacques Laffite	Ligier JS17-Matra	63	2h01m25.205
2 John Watson	McLaren MP4/1-Ford	63	2h01m31.438
3 Gilles Villeneuve	Ferrari 126CK	63	2h03m15.480
4 Bruno Giacomelli	Alfa Romeo 179C	62	
5 Nelson Piquet	Brabham BT49C-Ford	62	
6 Elio de Angelis	Lotus 87-Ford	62	

Winner's average speed: 85.301 mph. Starting grid front row: Piquet, 1m29.211 (pole) and Reutemann, 1m29.359. Fastest lap: Watson, 1m49.475. Leaders: Jones, laps 1-6; Prost, 7-12; Laffite, 13-63

Caesars Palace Grand Prix

17 October 1981. Caesars Palace, Las Vegas. 75 laps of a 2.268-mile circuit = 170.100 miles. Dry, hot and sunny. World Championship round 15

1 Alan Jones	Williams FW07C-Ford	75	1h44m09.077
2 Alain Prost	Renault RE30	75	1h44m29.125
3 Bruno Giacomelli	Alfa Romeo 179C	75	1h44m29.505
4 Nigel Mansell	Lotus 87-Ford	75	1h44m56.550
5 Nelson Piquet	Brabham BT49C-Ford	75	1h45m25.515
6 Jacques Laffite	Ligier JS17-Matra	75	1h45m27.252

Winner's average speed: 97.992 mph. Starting grid front row: Reutemann, 1m17.821 (pole) and Jones, 1m17.995. Fastest lap: Pironi, 1m20.156. Leaders: Jones, laps 1-75

1981 FINAL CHAMPIONSHIP POSITIONS

Drivers						Manufacturers	
1	Nelson Piquet	50	14	Nigel Mansell	8	1 Williams-Ford	95
2	Carlos Reutemann	49	15	Bruno Giacomelli	7	2 Brabham-Ford	61
3	Alan Jones	46	16	Marc Surer	4	3 Renault	54
4	Jacques Laffite	44	17	Mario Andretti	3	4 Ligier-Matra	44
5	Alain Prost	43	18=	Slim Borgudd	1	5 Ferrari	34
6	John Watson	27		Andrea de Cesaris	1	6 McLaren-Ford	28
7	Gilles Villeneuve	25		Eliseo Salazar	1	7 Lotus-Ford	22
8	Elio de Angelis	14		Patrick Tambay	1	8= Alfa Romeo	10
9=	René Arnoux	11				Arrows-Ford	10
	Hector Rebaque	11				Tyrrell-Ford	10
11=	Eddie Cheever	10				11 Ensign-Ford	5
	Riccardo Patrese	10				12= ATS-Ford	1
13	Didier Pironi	9				Theodore-Ford	1

1982

The current generation of Grand Prix cars continued to produce more and more downforce. To maintain the optimum attitude of the car and its aerodynamics to the track, the cars ran rock hard springs with virtually no suspension movement. Combined with cornering forces of up to four times gravity, these cars were the most physically demanding of all time, causing drivers neck and back injuries.

The early races were marred, first by controversy and then by tragedy. As turbocharged engines became increasingly powerful, the Ford-powered teams introduced "water cooled brakes" to allow their cars to race under the minimum weight of 580 kg. Teams were allowed to replenish cooling fluids after a race before cars were weighed, so designers introduced large containers which were empty during competition but filled with water before scrutiny. FISA ruled that the systems had nothing to do with cooling and disqualified the first two cars from the Brazilian GP for being underweight. The rules were clarified by FISA in Belgium and the system remained outlawed.

The FOCA teams (apart from Tyrrell, who had commitments to a new sponsor) withdrew from the San Marino GP, leaving Didier Pironi to beat Gilles Villeneuve in a controversial Ferrari one–two. Villeneuve felt that Pironi had disobeyed team orders to steal the race, and a feud began between the two formerly close drivers.

However, this dispute was overshadowed by the accident which befell Villeneuve ten minutes before the end of final practice for the Belgian GP. On a flying lap to make the most of his last set of qualifying tyres, his car clipped a slow-moving March, launching the Ferrari into a terrifying roll that inflicted injuries from which Villeneuve would die. The Canadian GP was also marred by the death of rookie Ricardo Paletti in a startline accident.

Pironi withdrew from the Belgian race but returned to take control of the 1982 World Championship. However, a severe accident in a wet practice session at Hockenheim caused injuries which ended his career. Villeneuve's replacement Patrick Tambay lifted the team by winning the race, but this was a terrible year for Ferrari, having begun with such promise. The Constructors' Cup was small consolation.

With series leader Pironi absent, consistent new Williams driver Keke Rosberg took the World Championship despite winning only once. John Watson won in Belgium and from the ninth row in Detroit, but lost the title at the final round. His new McLaren team-mate was none other than Niki Lauda: the Austrian won the third race of his return and added the British GP as well.

Brabham alternated between the Ford powered BT49 and the new BT50 with the exclusive BMW turbo. Riccardo Patrese won a bizarre Monaco GP in the BT49 after Alain Prost, Andrea de Cesaris, Derek Daly and Pironi had all retired in the closing laps when placed to win. Patrese had also spun in the light rain but was restarted. Nelson Piquet used the turbo BMW to win in Canada a week after failing to qualify in Detroit while the Brabham team also reintroduced refuelling in Grands Prix, as over a full race distance it gave a tactical advantage.

Two former World Champion teams also won a Grand Prix in 1982. Michele Alboreto found success in Las Vegas for Tyrrell, while Elio de Angelis held off Rosberg in Austria by 0.05 seconds to score the last victory for Lotus before team founder Colin Chapman died in December.

Quindrink-Pointerware Grand Prix of South Africa

23 January 1982. Kyalami. 77 laps of a 2.550-mile circuit = 196.350 miles. Hot, dry and sunny. World Championship round 1

1 Alain Prost	Renault RE30B	77	1h32m08.401
2 Carlos Reutemann	Williams FW07C-Ford	77	1h32m23.347
3 René Arnoux	Renault RE30B	77	1h32m36.301
4 Niki Lauda	McLaren MP4/1B-Ford	77	1h32m40.514
5 Keke Rosberg	Williams FW07C-Ford	77	1h32m54.540
6 John Watson	McLaren MP4/1B-Ford	77	1h32m59.394

Winner's average speed: 127.860 mph. Starting grid front row: Arnoux, 1m06.351 (pole) and Piquet, 1m06.625. Fastest lap: Prost, 1m08.278. Leaders: Arnoux, laps 1-13, 41-67; Prost, 14-40, 68-77

Grande Premio do Brasil

21 March 1982. Rio de Janeiro. 63 laps of a 3.126-mile circuit = 196.938 miles. Hot, dry and sunny. World Championship round 2

1 Alain Prost	Renault RE30B	63	1h44m33.134
2 John Watson	McLaren MP4/1B-Ford	63	1h44m36.124
3 Nigel Mansell	Lotus 91-Ford	63	1h45m09.993
4 Michele Alboreto	Tyrrell 011-Ford	63	1h45m23.895
5 Manfred Winkelhock	ATS D5-Ford	62	

1982 DRIVERS' RECORDS

Driver	Car	South African GP	Brazilian GP	Long Beach GP	San Marino GP	Belgian GP	Monaco GP	Detroit GP	Canadian GP	Dutch GP	British GP	French GP	German GP	Austrian GP	Swiss GP	Italian GP	Las Vegas GP
Michele Alboreto	Tyrrell 011-Ford	7	4	4	3	R	10	R	R	7	NC	6	4	R	7	5	1F
Mario Andretti	Williams FW07C-Ford	-	-	R	-	-	-	-	-	-	-	-	-	-	-	-	-
	Ferrari 126C2	-	-	-	-	-	-	-	-	-	-	-	-	-	-	3P	R
Elio de Angelis	Lotus 87B-Ford	8	-	-	-	-	-	-	-	-	-	-	-	-	-	-	-
	Lotus 91-Ford	-	R	5	-	4	5	R	4	R	4	R	R	1	6	R	R
René Arnoux	Renault RE30B	3P	R	R	RP	R	RP	10	R	RP	R	1P	2	R	16	1F	R
Mauro Baldi	Arrows A4-Ford	DNQ	10	DNQ	-	R	DNQ	R	8	6	9	R	R	6	DNQ	-	11
	Arrows A5-Ford	-	-	-	-	-	-	-	-	-	-	-	-	-	-	12	-
Raul Boesel	March 821-Ford	15	R	9	-	8	NPQ	R	R	R	DNQ	DNQ	R	DNQ	R	DNQ	13
Slim Borgudd	Tyrrell 011-Ford	16	7	10	-	-	-	-	-	-	-	-	-	-	-	-	-
Tommy Byrne	Theodore TY02-Ford	-	-	-	-	-	-	-	-	-	-	-	DNQ	R	DNQ	DNQ	R
Andrea de Cesaris	Alfa Romeo 179D	13	-	-	-	-	-	-	-	-	-	-	-	-	-	-	-
	Alfa Romeo 182	-	R	RP	R	R	3	R	6	R	R	R	R	R	10	10	9
Eddie Cheever	Ligier JS17-Matra	R	R	R	-	3	-	2	10	-	R	-	-	-	-	-	-
	Ligier JS19-Matra	-	-	-	-	-	R	-	-	DNQ	-	16	R	R	NC	6	3
Derek Daly	Theodore TY01-Ford	14	-	-	-	-	-	-	-	-	-	-	-	-	-	-	-
	Theodore TY02-Ford	-	R	R	-	-	-	-	-	-	-	-	-	-	-	-	-
	Williams FW08-Ford	-	-	-	-	R	6	5	7	5	5	7	R	R	9	R	6
Teo Fabi	Toleman TG181B-Hart	DNQ	DNQ	-	-	-	-	-	-	-	-	-	-	-	-	-	-
	Toleman TG181C-Hart	-	-	DNQ	NC	R	NPQ	-	-	DNQ	R	R	DNP	R	R	R	DNQ
Bruno Giacomelli	Alfa Romeo 179D	11	-	-	-	-	-	-	-	-	-	-	-	-	-	-	-
	Alfa Romeo 182	-	R	R	R	R	R	R	R	11	7	9	5	R	12	R	10
Roberto Guerrero	Ensign N180B-Ford	DNP	-	-	-	-	-	-	-	-	-	-	-	-	-	-	-
	Ensign N181-Ford	-	DNQ	R	-	DNQ	DNQ	R	R	DNQ	R	DNQ	8	R	R	NC	DNS
Brian Henton	Arrows A4-Ford	DNQ	DNQ	R	-	-	-	-	-	-	-	-	-	-	-	-	-
	Tyrrell 011-Ford	-	-	-	R	R	8	9	NC	R	8F	10	7	R	11	R	8
Jean-Pierre Jarier	Osella FA1C-Ford	R	9	R	4	R	DNQ	R	R	14	R	R	R	DNQ	R	R	DNS
Rupert Keegan	March 821-Ford	-	-	-	-	-	-	-	-	-	-	DNQ	R	R	DNQ	12	
Jacques Laffite	Ligier JS17-Matra	R	R	R	-	9	-	6	R	R	-	-	-	-	-	-	-
	Ligier JS19-Matra	-	-	-	-	-	R	-	-	-	R	14	R	3	R	R	R

/Cont'd

6 Didier Pironi   Ferrari 126C2   62

Nelson Piquet (Brabham BT49D-Ford) and Keke Rosberg (Williams FW07C-Ford) finished first and second on the road but were disqualified due to their cars being under the weight limit. Winner's average speed: 113.018 mph. Starting grid front row: Prost, 1m28.808 (pole) and Villeneuve, 1m29.173. Fastest lap: Prost, 1m37.016 (Piquet, 1m36.582 and Rosberg, 1m36.984 were disqualified). Leaders: Villeneuve, laps 1-29; Patrese, 30-32; Prost, 33-63 (Piquet led laps 30-63 with Rosberg second on the road)

Toyota Grand Prix of Long Beach

4 April 1982. Long Beach. 75.5 laps of a 2.130-mile circuit = 160.815 miles. Hot, dry and sunny. World Championship round 3

1 Niki Lauda   McLaren MP4/1B-Ford   75 1h58m25.318
2 Keke Rosberg   Williams FW07C-Ford   75 1h58m39.978
3 Riccardo Patrese Brabham BT49D-Ford   75 1h59m44.461
4 Michele Alboreto Tyrrell 011-Ford   75 1h59m46.265
5 Elio de Angelis   Lotus 91-Ford   74
6 John Watson   McLaren MP4/1B-Ford   74

Villeneuve (Ferrari 126C2) finished third on the road but was disqualified for illegal rear wing. Winner's average speed: 81.479 mph. Starting grid front row: de Cesaris, 1m27.316 (pole) and Lauda, 1m27.436. Fastest lap: Lauda, 1m30.831. Leaders: de Cesaris, laps 1-14; Lauda, 15-75.

Gran Premio di San Marino

25 April 1982. Imola. 60 laps of a 3.132-mile circuit = 187.920 miles. Warm, dry and sunny. World Championship round 4

1 Didier Pironi   Ferrari 126C2   60 1h36m38.887
2 Gilles Villeneuve Ferrari 126C2   60 1h36m39.253

3 Michele Alboreto   Tyrrell 011-Ford   60 1h37m46.571
4 Jean-Pierre Jarier Osella FA1C-Ford   59
5 Eliseo Salazar   ATS D5-Ford   57

Winkelhock (ATS D5-Ford) finished sixth on the road but was disqualified due to his car being under the weight limit. No other finishers. Winner's average speed: 116.662 mph. Starting grid front row: Arnoux, 1m29.765 (pole) and Prost, 1m30.249. Fastest lap: Pironi, 1m35.036. Leaders: Arnoux, laps 1-26, 31-44; Villeneuve, 27-30, 45, 49-52, 59; Pironi, 46-48, 53-58, 60

Grand Prix de Belgique

9 May 1982. Zolder. 70 laps of a 2.648-mile circuit = 185.360 miles. Warm and dry. World Championship round 5

1 John Watson   McLaren MP4/1B-Ford   70 1h35m41.995
2 Keke Rosberg   Williams FW08-Ford   70 1h35m49.263
3 Eddie Cheever   Ligier JS17-Matra   69
4 Elio de Angelis   Lotus 91-Ford   68
5 Nelson Piquet   Brabham BT50-BMW   67
6 Chico Serra   Fittipaldi F8D-Ford   67

Lauda (McLaren MP4/1B-Ford) finished third on the road but was disqualified due to his car being under the weight limit. Winner's average speed: 116.213 mph. Starting grid front row: Prost, 1m15.701 (pole) and Arnoux, 1m15.730. Fastest lap: Watson, 1m20.214. Leaders: Arnoux, laps 1-4; Rosberg, 5-68; Watson, 69-70

Grand Prix de Monaco

23 May 1982. Monte Carlo. 76 laps of a 2.058-mile circuit = 156.408 miles. Warm and dry, rain in closing laps. World Championship round 6

1 Riccardo Patrese   Brabham BT49D-Ford   76 1h54m11.259
2 Didier Pironi   Ferrari 126C2   75 electrics

1982 DRIVERS' RECORDS cont'd/

Driver	Car	South African GP	Brazilian GP	Long Beach GP	San Marino GP	Belgian GP	Monaco GP	Detroit GP	Canadian GP	Dutch GP	British GP	French GP	German GP	Austrian GP	Swiss GP	Italian GP	Las Vegas GP
Jan Lammers	Theodore TY02-Ford	-	-	-	-	DNQ	DNQ	DNQ	-	R	DNQ	DNQ	-	-	-	-	-
Niki Lauda	McLaren MP4/1B-Ford	4	R	1F	-	DSQ	R	R	R	4	1	8	DNS	5	3	R	R
Geoff Lees	Theodore TY02-Ford	-	-	-	-	-	-	R	-	-	-	-	-	-	-	-	-
	Lotus 91-Ford	-	-	-	-	-	-	-	-	-	-	12	-	-	-	-	-
Nigel Mansell	Lotus 87B-Ford	R	-	-	-	-	-	-	-	-	-	-	-	-	-	-	-
	Lotus 91-Ford	-	3	7	-	R	4	R	R	-	R	-	9	R	8	7	R
Jochen Mass	March 821-Ford	12	8	8	-	R	DNQ	7	11	R	10	R	-	-	-	-	-
Roberto Moreno	Lotus 91-Ford	-	-	-	-	-	-	-	DNQ	-	-	-	-	-	-	-	-
Ricardo Paletti	Osella FA1C-Ford	DNQ	NPQ	DNQ	R	NPQ	NPQ	DNS	R	-	-	-	-	-	-	-	-
Riccardo Patrese	Brabham BT50-BMW	R	-	-	-	R	-	-	-	15	R	RF	R	R	5	R	R
	Brabham BT49D-Ford	-	R	3	-	-	1F	R	2	-	-	-	-	-	-	-	-
Nelson Piquet	Brabham BT50-BMW	R	-	-	-	5	R	DNQ	1	2	R	R	RF	RPF	4	R	R
	Brabham BT49D-Ford	-	DSQ	R	-	-	-	-	-	-	-	-	-	-	-	-	-
Didier Pironi	Ferrari 126C2	18	6	R	1F	DNS	2	3	9PF	1	2	3	DNSP	-	-	-	-
Alain Prost	Renault RE30B	1F	1PF	R	R	RP	7	NCPF	R	R	6	2	R	8	2PF	R	4P
Carlos Reutemann	Williams FW07C-Ford	2	R	-	-	-	-	-	-	-	-	-	-	-	-	-	-
Keke Rosberg	Williams FW07C-Ford	5	DSQ	2	-	-	-	-	-	-	-	-	-	-	-	-	-
	Williams FW08-Ford	-	-	-	-	2	R	4	R	3	RP	5	3	2	1	8	5
Eliseo Salazar	ATS D5-Ford	9	R	R	5	R	R	R	R	13	DNQ	R	R	DNQ	14	9	DNQ
Chico Serra	Fittipaldi F8D-Ford	17	R	DNQ	-	6	NPQ	11	DNQ	R	R	-	-	-	-	-	-
	Fittipaldi F9-Ford	-	-	-	-	-	-	-	-	-	-	DNQ	11	7	DNQ	11	DNQ
Marc Surer	Arrows A4-Ford	-	-	-	-	7	9	8	5	10	R	13	6	R	-	R	-
	Arrows A5-Ford	-	-	-	-	-	-	-	-	-	-	-	-	-	15	-	7
Patrick Tambay	Arrows A4-Ford	DNP	-	-	-	-	-	-	-	-	-	-	-	-	-	-	-
	Ferrari 126C2	-	-	-	-	-	-	-	-	8	3	4	1	4	DNS	2	DNS
Gilles Villeneuve	Ferrari 126C2	R	R	DSQ	2	DNS	-	-	-	-	-	-	-	-	-	-	-
Emilio de Villota	March 821-Ford	-	-	-	-	NPQ	NPQ	DNQ	DNQ	NPQ	-	-	-	-	-	-	-
Derek Warwick	Toleman TG181B-Hart	R	DNQ	-	-	-	-	-	-	-	-	-	-	-	-	-	-
	Toleman TG181C-Hart	-	-	NPQ	DNS	R	DNQ	-	-	RF	R	15	10	R	R	-	-
	Toleman TG183-Hart	-	-	-	-	-	-	-	-	-	-	-	-	-	-	R	R
John Watson	McLaren MP4/1B-Ford	6	2	6	-	1F	R	1	3	9	R	R	R	R	13	4	2
Manfred Winkelhock	ATS D5-Ford	10	5	R	DSQ	R	R	R	DNQ	12	DNQ	11	R	R	R	DNQ	NC

World Championship Grand Prix Racing

3 Andrea de Cesaris	Alfa Romeo 182	75	out of fuel
4 Nigel Mansell	Lotus 91-Ford	75	
5 Elio de Angelis	Lotus 91-Ford	75	
6 Derek Daly	Williams FW08-Ford	74	accident

Winner's average speed: 82.185 mph. Starting grid front row: Arnoux, 1m23.281 (pole) and Patrese, 1m23.791. Fastest lap: Patrese, 1m26.354. Leaders: Arnoux, laps 1-14; Prost, 15-73; Patrese, 74, 76; Pironi, 75

Detroit Grand Prix

6 June 1982. Detroit. 62 laps of a 2.493-mile circuit = 154.566 miles. Race stopped after six laps due to accident; restart scheduled for 64 laps but stopped after two hours. Warm, dry and sunny. World Championship round 7

1 John Watson	McLaren MP4/1B-Ford	62	1h58m41.043
2 Eddie Cheever	Ligier JS17-Matra	62	1h58m56.769
3 Didier Pironi	Ferrari 126C2	62	1h59m09.120
4 Keke Rosberg	Williams FW08-Ford	62	1h59m53.019
5 Derek Daly	Williams FW08-Ford	62	2h00m04.800
6 Jacques Laffite	Ligier JS17-Matra	61	

Winner's average speed: 78.140 mph. Starting grid front row: Prost, 1m48.537 (pole) and de Cesaris, 1m48.872. Fastest lap: Prost, 1m50.438. Leaders: Prost, laps 1-22; Rosberg, 23-36; Watson, 37-62

Grand Prix Labatt du Canada

13 June 1982. Montreal. 70 laps of a 2.740-mile circuit = 191.800 miles. Race stopped after startline accident, restarted over original distance. Cold but dry. World Championship round 8

1 Nelson Piquet	Brabham BT50-BMW	70	1h46m39.577
2 Riccardo Patrese	Brabham BT49D-Ford	70	1h46m53.376
3 John Watson	McLaren MP4/1B-Ford	70	1h47m41.413
4 Elio de Angelis	Lotus 91-Ford	69	
5 Marc Surer	Arrows A4-Ford	69	
6 Andrea de Cesaris	Alfa Romeo 182	68	out of fuel

Winner's average speed: 107.895 mph. Starting grid front row: Pironi, 1m27.509 (pole) and Arnoux, 1m27.895. Fastest lap: Pironi, 1m28.323. Leaders: Pironi, lap 1; Arnoux, laps 2-8; Piquet, 9-70

Grote Prijs van Nederland

3 July 1982. Zandvoort. 72 laps of a 2.642-mile circuit = 190.224 miles. Warm, dry and sunny. World Championship round 9

1 Didier Pironi	Ferrari 126C2	72	1h38m03.254
2 Nelson Piquet	Brabham BT50-BMW	72	1h38m24.903
3 Keke Rosberg	Williams FW08-Ford	72	1h38m25.619
4 Niki Lauda	McLaren MP4/1B-Ford	72	1h39m26.974
5 Derek Daly	Williams FW08-Ford	71	
6 Mauro Baldi	Arrows A4-Ford	71	

Keke Rosberg recorded his first Grand Prix victory at the Swiss GP on the way to the 1982 World Championship

Winner's average speed: 116.399 mph. Starting grid front row: Arnoux, 1m14.233 (pole) and Prost, 1m14.660. Fastest lap: Warwick, 1m19.780. Leaders: Prost, laps 1-4; Pironi, 5-72

Marlboro British Grand Prix

18 July 1982. Brands Hatch. 76 laps of a 2.614-mile circuit = 198.664 miles. Hot, dry and sunny. World Championship round 10

1 Niki Lauda	McLaren MP4/1B-Ford	76	1h35m33.812
2 Didier Pironi	Ferrari 126C2	76	1h35m59.538
3 Patrick Tambay	Ferrari 126C2	76	1h36m12.248
4 Elio de Angelis	Lotus 91-Ford	76	1h36m15.054
5 Derek Daly	Williams FW08-Ford	76	1h36m15.242
6 Alain Prost	Renault RE30B	76	1h36m15.448

Winner's average speed: 124.713 mph. Starting grid front row: Rosberg, 1m09.540 (pole) and Patrese, 1m09.627 - Rosberg started from the back of the grid. Fastest lap: Henton, 1m13.028. Leaders: Piquet, laps 1-9; Lauda, 10-76

Grand Prix de France

25 July 1982. Paul Ricard. 54 laps of a 3.610-mile circuit = 194.940 miles. Hot, dry and sunny. World Championship round 11

1 René Arnoux	Renault RE30B	54	1h33m33.217
2 Alain Prost	Renault RE30B	54	1h33m50.525
3 Didier Pironi	Ferrari 126C2	54	1h34m15.345
4 Patrick Tambay	Ferrari 126C2	54	1h34m49.458
5 Keke Rosberg	Williams FW08-Ford	54	1h35m04.211
6 Michele Alboreto	Tyrrell 011-Ford	54	1h35m05.556

Winner's average speed: 125.023 mph. Starting grid front row: Arnoux, 1m34.406 (pole) and Prost, 1m34.688. Fastest lap: Patrese, 1m40.075. Leaders: Arnoux, laps 1-2, 24-54; Patrese, 3-7; Piquet, 8-23

Grosser Preis von Deutschland

8 August 1982. Hockenheim. 45 laps of a 4.224-mile circuit = 190.080 miles. Hot, dry and sunny. World Championship round 12

1 Patrick Tambay	Ferrari 126C2	45	1h27m25.178
2 René Arnoux	Renault RE30B	45	1h27m41.557
3 Keke Rosberg	Williams FW08-Ford	44	
4 Michele Alboreto	Tyrrell 011-Ford	44	
5 Bruno Giacomelli	Alfa Romeo 182	44	
6 Marc Surer	Arrows A4-Ford	44	

Winner's average speed: 130.448 mph. Starting grid front row: Pironi, 1m47.947 (pole) and Prost, 1m48.890 - Pironi did not start. Fastest lap: Piquet, 1m54.035. Leaders: Arnoux, lap 1; Piquet, laps 2-18; Tambay, 19-45

Grosser Preis von Österreich

15 August 1982. Österreichring. 53 laps of a 3.692-mile circuit = 195.676 miles. Hot, dry and sunny. World Championship round 13

1 Elio de Angelis	Lotus 91-Ford	53	1h25m02.212
2 Keke Rosberg	Williams FW08-Ford	53	1h25m02.262
3 Jacques Laffite	Ligier JS19-Matra	52	
4 Patrick Tambay	Ferrari 126C2	52	
5 Niki Lauda	McLaren MP4/1B-Ford	52	
6 Mauro Baldi	Arrows A4-Ford	52	

Winner's average speed: 138.064 mph. Starting grid front row: Piquet, 1m27.612 (pole) and Patrese, 1m27.971. Fastest lap: Piquet, 1m33.699. Leaders: Piquet, lap 1; Patrese, laps 2-27; Prost, 28-48; de Angelis, 49-53

Grand Prix de Suisse

29 August 1982. Dijon-Prenois, France. 80 laps of a 2.361-mile circuit = 188.880 miles. Hot, dry and sunny. World Championship round 14

1 Keke Rosberg	Williams FW08-Ford	80	1h32m41.087

2 Alain Prost	Renault RE30B	80	1h32m45.529
3 Niki Lauda	McLaren MP4/1B-Ford	80	1h33m41.430
4 Nelson Piquet	Brabham BT50-BMW	79	
5 Riccardo Patrese	Brabham BT50-BMW	79	
6 Elio de Angelis	Lotus 91-Ford	79	

Winner's average speed: 122.272 mph. Starting grid front row: Prost, 1m01.380 (pole) and Arnoux, 1m01.740. Fastest lap: Prost, 1m07.477. Leaders: Arnoux, lap 1; Prost, laps 2-78; Rosberg, 79-80

Gran Premio d'Italia

12 September 1982. Monza. 52 laps of a 3.604-mile circuit = 187.408 miles. Hot, dry and sunny. World Championship round 15

1 René Arnoux	Renault RE30B	52	1h22m25.734
2 Patrick Tambay	Ferrari 126C2	52	1h22m39.798
3 Mario Andretti	Ferrari 126C2	52	1h23m14.186
4 John Watson	McLaren MP4/1B-Ford	52	1h23m53.579
5 Michele Alboreto	Tyrrell 011-Ford	51	

6 Eddie Cheever	Ligier JS19-Matra	51	

Winner's average speed: 136.411 mph. Starting grid front row: Andretti, 1m28.473 (pole) and Piquet, 1m28.508. Fastest lap: Arnoux, 1m33.619. Leaders: Arnoux, laps 1-52

Caesars Palace Grand Prix

25 September 1982. Caesars Palace, Las Vegas. 75 laps of a 2.268-mile circuit = 170.100 miles. Hot, dry and sunny. World Championship round 16

1 Michele Alboreto	Tyrrell 011-Ford	75	1h41m56.888
2 John Watson	McLaren MP4/1B-Ford	75	1h42m24.180
3 Eddie Cheever	Ligier JS19-Matra	75	1h42m53.338
4 Alain Prost	Renault RE30B	75	1h43m05.536
5 Keke Rosberg	Williams FW08-Ford	75	1h43m08.263
6 Derek Daly	Williams FW08-Ford	74	

Winner's average speed: 100.110 mph. Starting grid front row: Prost, 1m16.356 (pole) and Arnoux, 1m16.786. Fastest lap: Alboreto, 1m19.639. Leaders: Prost, laps 1, 15-51; Arnoux, 2-14; Alboreto, 52-75.

1982 FINAL CHAMPIONSHIP POSITIONS

Drivers						Manufacturers		
1	Keke Rosberg	44	14	Nigel Mansell	7	1	Ferrari	74
2=	Didier Pironi	39	15=	Carlos Reutemann	6	2	McLaren-Ford	69
	John Watson	39		Gilles Villeneuve	6	3	Renault	62
4	Alain Prost	34	17=	Andrea de Cesaris	5	4	Williams-Ford	58
5	Niki Lauda	30		Jacques Laffite	5	5	Brabham-BMW/Ford	41
6	René Arnoux	28	19	Mario Andretti	4	6	Lotus-Ford	30
7=	Michele Alboreto	25	20=	Jean-Pierre Jarier	3	7	Tyrrell-Ford	25
	Patrick Tambay	25		Marc Surer	3	8	Ligier-Matra	20
9	Elio de Angelis	23	22=	Mauro Baldi	2	9	Alfa Romeo	7
10	Riccardo Patrese	21		Bruno Giacomelli	2	10	Arrows-Ford	5
11	Nelson Piquet	20		Eliseo Salazar	2	11	ATS-Ford	4
12	Eddie Cheever	15		Manfred Winkelhock	2	12	Osella-Ford	3
13	Derek Daly	8	26	Chico Serra	1	13	Fittipaldi-Ford	1

1983

In 1983 Grand Prix racing enjoyed a season free from the controversy and tragedy which had marred 1982. It was a year of change - new rules stipulated that the underside of the car between the two axles had to be flat, rendering the "wing car" dead. Teams partially compensated for the reduction in downforce by using larger wings, but the cars were now less painful to drive.

A turbocharged engine won the World Championship for the first time, but it was not the pioneer, Renault, which would benefit. Alain Prost led the series for most of the season, but lost out to Nelson Piquet's Brabham-BMW at the final race. At one stage the Renault team leader had held an apparently secure 14-point lead, but a run of late-season success gave Brabham the title.

The turbo revolution continued, with Alfa Romeo, Porsche - financed by Techniques d'Avant Garde (for McLaren) - and Honda (for Spirit and then Williams) introducing new engines, and both BMW and Renault supplying second teams. In a year dominated by turbos, John Watson (from 22nd position on the grid at Long Beach!), Keke Rosberg and Michele Alboreto scored the last victories for the Ford DFV, all on temporary street circuits.

The Belgian GP returned to a superbly modified Spa-Francorchamps circuit for the first time since 1970. Andrea de Cesaris dominated the race before his Alfa Romeo engine failed, leaving Prost to take victory.

René Arnoux joined Patrick Tambay at Ferrari, and after a slow start to the year, won in Canada and Germany to join the championship race. When Piquet and Prost collided while battling for victory in Holland, Arnoux inherited the win and appeared able to overhaul Prost's points lead. His chances evaporated in the penultimate round, however, when he was delayed by a spin.

Mid-race pit stops for fuel, reintroduced by Brabham in 1982, proved a tactical advantage and were adopted by the rest of the field.

Grande Premio do Brasil

13 March 1983. Rio de Janeiro. 63 laps of a 3.126-mile circuit = 196.938 miles. Hot, dry and sunny. World Championship round 1

1 Nelson Piquet	Brabham BT52-BMW	63	1h48m27.731
2 not awarded*			
3 Niki Lauda	McLaren MP4/1C-Ford	63	1h49m19.614
4 Jacques Laffite	Williams FW08C-Ford	63	1h49m41.682
5 Patrick Tambay	Ferrari 126C2B	63	1h49m45.848
6 Marc Surer	Arrows A6-Ford	63	1h49m45.938

*Rosberg (Williams FW08C-Ford) finished second but was disqualified for a push start during a pit stop - other competitors were not elevated. Winner's average speed: 108.944 mph. Starting grid front row: Rosberg, 1m34.526 (pole) and Prost, 1m34.672. Fastest lap: Piquet, 1m39.829. Leaders: Rosberg, laps 1-6; Piquet, 7-63

Toyota Grand Prix of Long Beach

27 March 1983. Long Beach. 75 laps of a 2.035-mile circuit = 152.625 miles. Hot, dry and sunny. World Championship round 2

1 John Watson	McLaren MP4/1C-Ford	75	1h53m34.889
2 Niki Lauda	McLaren MP4/1C-Ford	75	1h54m02.882
3 René Arnoux	Ferrari 126C2B	75	1h54m48.527
4 Jacques Laffite	Williams FW08C-Ford	74	
5 Marc Surer	Arrows A6-Ford	74	
6 Johnny Cecotto	Theodore N183-Ford	74	

Winner's average speed: 80.625 mph. Starting grid front row: Tambay, 1m26.117 (pole) and Arnoux, 1m26.935. Fastest lap: Lauda, 1m28.330. Leaders: Tambay, laps 1-25; Laffite, 26-44; Watson, 45-75

Grand Prix de France

17 April 1983. Paul Ricard. 54 laps of a 3.610-mile circuit = 194.940 miles. Cool and dry. World Championship round 3

1 Alain Prost	Renault RE40	54	1h34m13.913
2 Nelson Piquet	Brabham BT52-BMW	54	1h34m43.633
3 Eddie Cheever	Renault RE40	54	1h34m54.145
4 Patrick Tambay	Ferrari 126C2B	54	1h35m20.793
5 Keke Rosberg	Williams FW08C-Ford	53	
6 Jacques Laffite	Williams FW08C-Ford	53	

Winner's average speed: 124.124 mph. Starting grid front row: Prost, 1m36.672 (pole) and Cheever, 1m38.980. Fastest lap: Prost, 1m42.695. Leaders: Prost, laps 1-29, 33-54; Piquet, 30-32

Gran Premio di San Marino

1 May 1983. Imola. 60 laps of a 3.132-mile circuit = 187.920 miles. Warm, dry and sunny. World Championship round 4

1 Patrick Tambay	Ferrari 126C2B	60	1h37m52.460
2 Alain Prost	Renault RE40	60	1h38m41.241
3 René Arnoux	Ferrari 126C2B	59	
4 Keke Rosberg	Williams FW08C-Ford	59	
5 John Watson	McLaren MP4/1C-Ford	59	
6 Marc Surer	Arrows A6-Ford	59	

Winner's average speed: 115.201 mph. Starting grid front row: Arnoux, 1m31.238 (pole) and Piquet, 1m31.964. Fastest lap: Patrese, 1m34.437. Leaders: Arnoux, laps 1-5; Patrese, 6-34; Tambay, 35-60

Grand Prix de Monaco

15 May 1983. Monte Carlo. 76 laps of a 2.058-mile circuit = 156.408 miles. Warm and damp at the start, drying later. World Championship round 5

1 Keke Rosberg	Williams FW08C-Ford	76	1h56m38.121
2 Nelson Piquet	Brabham BT52-BMW	76	1h56m56.596
3 Alain Prost	Renault RE40	76	1h57m09.487
4 Patrick Tambay	Ferrari 126C2B	76	1h57m42.418
5 Danny Sullivan	Tyrrell 011-Ford	74	
6 Mauro Baldi	Alfa Romeo 183T	74	

Winner's average speed: 80.460 mph. Starting grid front row: Prost, 1m24.840 (pole) and Arnoux, 1m25.182. Fastest lap: Piquet, 1m27.283. Leaders: Prost, lap 1; Rosberg, laps 2-76

Grand Prix de Belgique

22 May 1983. Spa-Francorchamps. 40 laps plus 0.407 miles (start and finish at different places on circuit) of a 4.318-mile circuit = 173.127 miles. Warm, dry and sunny. World Championship round 6

1 Alain Prost	Renault RE40	40	1h27m11.502
2 Patrick Tambay	Ferrari 126C2B	40	1h27m34.684
3 Eddie Cheever	Renault RE40	40	1h27m51.371
4 Nelson Piquet	Brabham BT52-BMW	40	1h27m53.797
5 Keke Rosberg	Williams FW08C-Ford	40	1h28m01.982
6 Jacques Laffite	Williams FW08C-Ford	40	1h28m44.609

Winner's average speed: 119.136 mph. Starting grid front row: Prost, 2m04.615 (pole) and Tambay, 2m04.626. Fastest lap: de Cesaris, 2m07.493. Leaders: de Cesaris, laps 1-18; Prost, 19-22, 24-40; Piquet, 23

Detroit Grand Prix

5 June 1983. Detroit. 60 laps of a 2.500-mile circuit = 150.000 miles. Warm, dry and sunny. World Championship round 7

1 Michele Alboreto	Tyrrell 011-Ford	60	1h50m53.669
2 Keke Rosberg	Williams FW08C-Ford	60	1h51m01.371
3 John Watson	McLaren MP4/1C-Ford	60	1h51m02.952
4 Nelson Piquet	Brabham BT52-BMW	60	1h52m05.854
5 Jacques Laffite	Williams FW08C-Ford	60	1h52m26.272
6 Nigel Mansell	Lotus 92-Ford	59	

Winner's average speed: 81.158 mph. Starting grid front row: Arnoux, 1m44.734 (pole) and Piquet, 1m44.933. Fastest lap: Watson, 1m47.668. Leaders: Piquet, laps 1-9, 32-50; Arnoux, 10-31; Alboreto, 51-60

Grand Prix Labatt du Canada

12 June 1983. Montreal. 70 laps of a 2.740-mile circuit = 191.800 miles. Hot, dry and sunny. World Championship round 8

1 René Arnoux	Ferrari 126C2B	70	1h48m31.838
2 Eddie Cheever	Renault RE40	70	1h49m13.867
3 Patrick Tambay	Ferrari 126C2B	70	1h49m24.448
4 Keke Rosberg	Williams FW08C-Ford	70	1h49m48.886
5 Alain Prost	Renault RE40	69	
6 John Watson	McLaren MP4/1C-Ford	69	

Winner's average speed: 106.035 mph. Starting grid front row: Arnoux, 1m28.729 (pole) and Prost, 1m28.830. Fastest lap: Tambay, 1m30.851. Leaders: Arnoux, laps 1-35, 39-70; Patrese, 36-38

....

Late season domination gave Nelson Piquet his second World Championship for Brabham

Marlboro British Grand Prix

16 July 1983. Silverstone. 67 laps of a 2.932-mile circuit = 196.444 miles. Hot, dry and sunny. World Championship round 9

1 Alain Prost	Renault RE40	67	1h24m39.780
2 Nelson Piquet	Brabham BT52B-BMW	67	1h24m58.941
3 Patrick Tambay	Ferrari 126C3	67	1h25m06.026
4 Nigel Mansell	Lotus 94T-Renault	67	1h25m18.732
5 René Arnoux	Ferrari 126C3	67	1h25m38.654
6 Niki Lauda	McLaren MP4/1C-Ford	66	

Winner's average speed: 139.218 mph. Starting grid front row: Arnoux, 1m09.462 (pole) and Tambay, 1m10.104. Fastest lap: Prost, 1m14.212. Leaders: Tambay, laps 1-19; Prost, 20-36, 42-67; Piquet, 37-41

Grosser Preis von Deutschland

7 August 1983. Hockenheim. 45 laps of a 4.224-mile circuit = 190.080 miles. Warm, dry and sunny. World Championship round 10

1 René Arnoux	Ferrari 126C3	45	1h27m10.319
2 Andrea de Cesaris	Alfa Romeo 183T	45	1h28m20.971
3 Riccardo Patrese	Brabham BT52B-BMW	45	1h28m54.412
4 Alain Prost	Renault RE40	45	1h29m11.069
5 John Watson	McLaren MP4/1C-Ford	44	
6 Jacques Laffite	Williams FW08C-Ford	44	

Lauda (McLaren MP4/1C-Ford) finished fifth on the road but was disqualified for driving in the wrong direction. Winner's average speed: 130.819 mph. Starting grid front row: Tambay, 1m49.328 (pole) and Arnoux, 1m49.435. Fastest lap: Arnoux, 1m53.938. Leaders: Tambay, lap 1; Arnoux, laps 2-23, 31-45; Piquet, 24-30

Grosser Preis von Österreich

14 August 1983. Österreichring. 53 laps of a 3.692-mile circuit = 195.676 miles. Hot, dry and sunny. World Championship round 11

1 Alain Prost	Renault RE40	53	1h24m32.745
2 René Arnoux	Ferrari 126C3	53	1h24m39.580
3 Nelson Piquet	Brabham BT52B-BMW	53	1h25m00.404
4 Eddie Cheever	Renault RE40	53	1h25m01.140
5 Nigel Mansell	Lotus 94T-Renault	52	
6 Niki Lauda	McLaren MP4/1C-Ford	51	

Winner's average speed: 138.866 mph. Starting grid front row: Tambay, 1m29.871 (pole) and Arnoux, 1m29.935. Fastest lap: Prost, 1m33.961. Leaders: Tambay, laps 1-21; Arnoux, 22-27, 38-47; Piquet, 28-37; Prost, 48-53

1983 DRIVERS' RECORDS

Driver	Car	Brazilian GP	Long Beach GP	French GP	San Marino GP	Monaco GP	Belgian GP	Detroit GP	Canadian GP	British GP	German GP	Austrian GP	Dutch GP	Italian GP	European GP	South African GP
Kenneth Acheson	RAM-March 01-Ford	-	-	-	-	-	-	-	-	DNQ	DNQ	DNQ	DNQ	DNQ	DNQ	12
Michele Alboreto	Tyrrell 011-Ford	R	9	8	R	R	14	1	8	13	R	R	-	-	-	-
	Tyrrell 012-Ford	-	-	-	-	-	-	-	-	-	-	-	6	R	R	R
Elio de Angelis	Lotus 92-Ford	DSQ	-	-	-	-	-	-	-	-	-	-	-	-	-	-
	Lotus 93T-Renault	-	R	R	R	R	9	R	R	-	-	-	-	-	-	-
	Lotus 94T-Renault	-	-	-	-	-	-	-	-	R	R	R	R	5	R^P	R
René Arnoux	Ferrari 126C2B	10	3	7	3^P	R	R	R^P	1^P	-	-	-	-	-	-	-
	Ferrari 126C3	-	-	-	-	-	-	-	-	5^P	1^F	2	1^F	2	9	R
Mauro Baldi	Alfa Romeo 183T	R	R	R	10	6	R	12	10	7	R	5	R	5	R	R
Raul Boesel	Ligier JS21-Ford	R	7	R	9	R	13	10	R	R	R	DNQ	10	DNQ	15	NC
Thierry Boutsen	Arrows A6-Ford	-	-	-	-	R	7	7	R	15	9	13	14	R	11	9
Johnny Cecotto	Theodore N183-Ford	14	6	11	R	NPQ	10	R	R	DNQ	11	DNQ	DNQ	12	-	-
Andrea de Cesaris	Alfa Romeo 183T	DNQ	R	12	R	R	R^F	R	R	8	2	R	R	R	4	2
Eddie Cheever	Renault RE30C	R	R	-	-	-	-	-	-	-	-	-	-	-	-	-
	Renault RE40	-	-	3	R	R	3	R	2	R	R	4	R	3	10	6
Corrado Fabi	Osella FA1D-Ford	R	DNQ	R	R	DNQ	R	DNQ	R	-	-	-	-	-	-	-
	Osella FA1E-Alfa Romeo	-	-	-	-	-	-	-	-	-	DNQ	DNQ	10	11	R	DNQ	R
Piercarlo Ghinzani	Osella FA1D-Ford	DNQ	DNQ	DNQ	-	-	-	-	-	-	-	-	-	-	-	-
	Osella FA1E-Alfa Romeo	-	-	-	DNQ	DNQ	DNQ	R	DNQ	R	R	11	DNQ	R	R	R
Bruno Giacomelli	Toleman TG183B-Hart	R	R	13	R	DNQ	8	9	R	R	R	R	13	7	6	R
Roberto Guerrero	Theodore N183-Ford	NC	R	R	R	NPQ	R	NC	R	16	R	R	12	13	12	-
Jean-Pierre Jarier	Ligier JS21-Ford	R	R	9	R	R	R	R	Lauda	10	8	7	R	9	DNS	10
Stefan Johansson	Spirit 201-Honda	-	-	-	-	-	-	-	-	R	R	12	7	R	14	-
Alan Jones	Arrows A6-Ford	-	R	-	-	-	-	-	-	-	-	-	-	-	-	-
Jacques Laffite	Williams FW08C-Ford	4	4	6	7	R	6	5	R	12	6	R	R	DNQ	DNQ	-
	Williams FW09-Honda	-	-	-	-	-	-	-	-	-	-	-	-	-	-	R
Niki Lauda	McLaren MP4/1C-Ford	3	2^F	R	R	DNQ	R	R	R	6	DSQ	6	-	-	-	-
	McLaren MP4/E-TAG Porsche	-	-	-	-	-	-	-	-	-	-	-	R	R	R	11
Nigel Mansell	Lotus 92-Ford	12	12	R	12	R	R	6	R	-	-	-	-	-	-	-
	Lotus 94T-Renault	-	-	-	-	-	-	-	-	4	-	5	R	8	3^F	NC
	Lotus 93T-Renault	-	-	-	-	-	-	-	-	-	R	-	-	-	-	-
Jonathan Palmer	Williams FW08C-Ford	-	-	-	-	-	-	-	-	-	-	-	-	-	13	-
Riccardo Patrese	Brabham BT52-BMW	R	10	R	R^F	R	R	R	R	-	-	-	-	-	-	-
	Brabham BT52B-BMW	-	-	-	-	-	-	-	-	R	3	R	9	R^P	7	1
Nelson Piquet	Brabham BT52-BMW	1^F	R	2	R	2^F	4	4	R	-	-	-	-	-	-	-
	Brabham BT52B-BMW	-	-	-	-	-	-	-	-	2	13	3	R^P	1^F	1	3^F
Alain Prost	Renault RE30C	7	-	-	-	-	-	-	-	-	-	-	-	-	-	-
	Renault RE40	-	11	1^{PF}	2	3^P	1^P	8	5	1^F	4	1^F	R	R	2	R
Keke Rosberg	Williams FW08C-Ford	DSQ^P	R	5	4	1	5	2	4	11	10	8	R	11	R	-
	Williams FW09-Honda	-	-	-	-	-	-	-	-	-	-	-	-	-	-	5
Eliseo Salazar	RAM-March 01-Ford	15	R	DNQ	DNQ	DNQ	DNQ	-	-	-	-	-	-	-	-	-
Jean-Louis Schlesser	RAM-March 01-Ford	-	-	DNQ	-	-	-	-	-	-	-	-	-	-	-	-
Chico Serra	Arrows A6-Ford	9	-	R	8	7	-	-	-	-	-	-	-	-	-	-
Danny Sullivan	Tyrrell 011-Ford	11	8	R	R	5	12	R	DSQ	14	12	R	R	R	-	-
	Tyrrell 012-Ford	-	-	-	-	-	-	-	-	-	-	-	-	-	R	7
Marc Surer	Arrows A6-Ford	6	5	10	6	R	11	11	R	17	7	R	8	10	R	8
Patrick Tambay	Ferrari 126C2B	5	R^P	4	1	4	2	R	3^F	-	-	-	-	-	-	-
	Ferrari 126C3	-	-	-	-	-	-	-	-	3	R^P	R^P	2	4	R	R^P
Jacques Villeneuve	RAM-March 01-Ford	-	-	-	-	-	-	-	DNQ	-	-	-	-	-	-	-
Derek Warwick	Toleman TG183B-Hart	8	R	R	R	R	7	R	R	R	R	R	4	6	5	4
John Watson	McLaren MP4/1C-Ford	R	1	R	5	DNQ	R	3^F	6	9	5	9	3	-	-	-
	McLaren MP4/1E-TAG Porsche	-	-	-	-	-	-	-	-	-	-	-	-	R	R	R
Manfred Winkelhock	ATS D6-BMW	16	R	R	11	R	R	R	9	R	DNQ	R	R	R	8	R

Grote Prijs van Nederland

28 August 1983. Zandvoort. 72 laps of a 2.642-mile circuit = 190.224 miles. Cool and dry. World Championship round 12

1	René Arnoux	Ferrari 126C3	72 1h38m41.950
2	Patrick Tambay	Ferrari 126C3	72 1h39m02.789
3	John Watson	McLaren MP4/1C-Ford	72 1h39m25.691
4	Derek Warwick	Toleman TG183B-Hart	72 1h39m58.789
5	Mauro Baldi	Alfa Romeo 183T	72 1h40m06.242
6	Michele Alboreto	Tyrrell 012-Ford	71

Winner's average speed: 115.639 mph. Starting grid front row: Piquet, 1m15.630 (pole) and Tambay, 1m16.370. Fastest lap: Arnoux, 1m19.863. Leaders: Piquet, laps 1-41; Arnoux, 42-72

Gran Premio d'Italia

11 September 1983. Monza. 52 laps of a 3.604-mile circuit = 187.408 miles. Warm, dry and sunny. World Championship round 13

1	Nelson Piquet	Brabham BT52B-BMW	52 1h23m10.880
2	René Arnoux	Ferrari 126C3	52 1h23m21.092
3	Eddie Cheever	Renault RE40	52 1h23m29.492
4	Patrick Tambay	Ferrari 126C3	52 1h23m39.903
5	Elio de Angelis	Lotus 94T-Renault	52 1h24m04.560
6	Derek Warwick	Toleman TG183B-Hart	52 1h24m24.228

Winner's average speed: 135.177 mph. Starting grid front row: Patrese, 1m29.122 (pole) and Tambay, 1m29.650. Fastest lap: Piquet, 1m34.431. Leaders: Patrese, laps 1-3; Piquet, 4-52

John Player Grand Prix of Europe

25 September 1983. Brands Hatch. 76 laps of a 2.614-mile circuit = 198.664 miles. Hot, dry and sunny. World Championship round 14

1	Nelson Piquet	Brabham BT52B-BMW	76 1h36m45.865
2	Alain Prost	Renault RE40	76 1h36m52.436
3	Nigel Mansell	Lotus 94T-Renault	76 1h37m16.180
4	Andrea de Cesaris	Alfa Romeo 183T	76 1h37m20.261
5	Derek Warwick	Toleman TG183B-Hart	76 1h37m30.780
6	Bruno Giacomelli	Toleman TG183B-Hart	76 1h37m38.055

Winner's average speed: 123.165 mph. Starting grid front row: de Angelis, 1m12.092 (pole) and Patrese, 1m12.458. Fastest lap: Mansell, 1m14.342. Leaders: Patrese, laps 1-10; Piquet, 11-76

Southern Sun Hotels Grand Prix of South Africa

15 October 1983. Kyalami. 77 laps of a 2.550-mile circuit = 196.350 miles. Hot, dry and sunny. World Championship round 15

1	Riccardo Patrese	Brabham BT52B-BMW	77 1h33m25.708
2	Andrea de Cesaris	Alfa Romeo 183T	77 1h33m35.027
3	Nelson Piquet	Brabham BT52B-BMW	77 1h33m47.677
4	Derek Warwick	Toleman TG183B-Hart	76
5	Keke Rosberg	Williams FW09-Honda	76
6	Eddie Cheever	Renault RE40	76

Winner's average speed: 126.096 mph. Starting grid front row: Tambay, 1m06.554 (pole) and Piquet, 1m06.792. Fastest lap: Piquet, 1m09.948. Leaders: Piquet, laps 1-59; Patrese, 60-77

1983 FINAL CHAMPIONSHIP POSITIONS

Drivers						Manufacturers		
1	Nelson Piquet	59		12=	Michele Alboreto	10	1	Ferrari	89
2	Alain Prost	57			Nigel Mansell	10	2	Renault	79
3	René Arnoux	49		14	Derek Warwick	9	3	Brabham-BMW	72
4	Patrick Tambay	40		15	Marc Surer	4	4	Williams-Ford/Honda	38
5	Keke Rosberg	27		16	Mauro Baldi	3	5	McLaren-Ford/Porsche	34
6=	Eddie Cheever	22		17=	Elio de Angelis	2	6	Alfa Romeo	18
	John Watson	22			Danny Sullivan	2	7=	Tyrrell-Ford	12
8	Andrea de Cesaris	15		19=	Johnny Cecotto	1		Lotus-Renault/Ford	12
9	Riccardo Patrese	13			Bruno Giacomelli	1	9	Toleman-Hart	10
10	Niki Lauda	12					10	Arrows-Ford	4
11	Jacques Laffite	11					11	Theodore-Ford	1

1984

Having lost the 1983 World Championship, Alain Prost joined Niki Lauda in the new John Barnard-designed McLaren MP4/2-TAG Porsche, replacing John Watson. Prost scored the first of seven wins on his return to the team in Brazil, but it was still not enough to become France's first World Champion. Lauda, although only winning five times, clinched a third world title by just half a point at the final Grand Prix in Portugal.

Although Nelson Piquet's Brabham-BMW was often as quick as the McLarens, poor reliability limited him to just two wins, both in North America.

In Brazil, Derek Warwick almost won his first race for Renault, and team-mate Patrick Tambay led in France, but neither were ultimately successful. Ferrari hired Michele Alboreto, the first Italian to drive for the marque since 1973, and he scored the team's only win, defeating Warwick in Belgium.

The Toleman-Hart team replaced the departing Warwick with the reigning British F3 Champion,

Ayrton Senna. At Imola a dispute between the team and tyre supplier resulted in his failure to qualify, but the Brazilian's performance for the remainder of the year marked him as a future World Champion.

The McLaren-Porsche turbos of Niki Lauda and Alain Prost dominated in 1984, winning the last seven races

Senna almost won his first Grand Prix in torrential rain at Monaco. The race was stopped early (half points being awarded) as the Brazilian closed in on race leader Prost. Nigel Mansell, in his fourth season at Lotus, was also denied victory at Monte Carlo when he crashed while leading. It was Mansell's Lotus team-mate Elio de Angelis who provided the most consistent challenge to the McLarens: leading in Germany and scoring 11 points finishes to finish third in the series.

All bar Tyrrell now used turbos, but controversy surrounded the normally aspirated Ford-powered team. Having achieved two podium finishes, Stefan Bellof's third at Monaco and Martin Brundle's second in Detroit, FISA took fuel samples from the team at the latter race and found them to be illegal. The team was excluded from the series with all its 1984 results overturned.

Fuel stops were outlawed and fuel capacity reduced. This often led to cars grinding to an embarrassing halt in the closing laps of Grands Prix, having used the last of their precious 220 litres of fuel.

Grande Premio do Brasil

25 March 1984. Rio de Janeiro. 61 laps of a 3.126-mile circuit = 190.686 miles. Hot, dry and sunny. World Championship round 1

1 Alain Prost	McLaren MP4/2-		
	TAG Porsche	61 1h42m34.492	
2 Keke Rosberg	Williams FW09-Honda	61 1h43m15.006	
3 Elio de Angelis	Lotus 95T-Renault	61 1h43m33.620	
4 Eddie Cheever	Alfa Romeo 184T	60	
5 Patrick Tambay	Renault RE50	59	out of fuel
6 Thierry Boutsen	Arrows A6-Ford	59	

Brundle (Tyrrell 012-Ford) finished fifth on the road but was disqualified for using illegal fuel at the Detroit GP. Winner's average speed: 111.540 mph. Starting grid front row: de Angelis, 1m28.392 (pole) and Alboreto, 1m28.898. Fastest lap: Prost, 1m36.499. Leaders: Alboreto, laps 1-11; Lauda, 12-37; Prost, 38, 51-61; Warwick, 39-50

National Panasonic Grand Prix of South Africa

7 April 1984. Kyalami. 75 laps of a 2.550-mile circuit = 191.250 miles. Hot, dry and sunny. World Championship round 2

1 Niki Lauda	McLaren MP4/2-		
	TAG Porsche	75 1h29m23.430	
2 Alain Prost	McLaren MP4/2-		
	TAG Porsche	75 1h30m29.380	
3 Derek Warwick	Renault RE50	74	
4 Riccardo Patrese	Alfa Romeo 184T	73	
5 Andrea de Cesaris	Ligier JS23-Renault	73	
6 Ayrton Senna	Toleman TG183B-Hart	72	

Winner's average speed: 128.369 mph. Starting grid front row: Piquet, 1m04.871 (pole) and Rosberg, 1m05.058. Fastest lap: Tambay, 1m08.877. Leaders: Rosberg, lap 1; Piquet, laps 2-20; Lauda, 21-75

Grand Prix de Belgique

29 April 1984. Zolder. 70 laps of a 2.648-mile circuit = 185.360 miles. Warm, dry and sunny. World Championship round 3

1 Michele Alboreto	Ferrari 126C4	70 1h36m32.048	
2 Derek Warwick	Renault RE50	70 1h37m14.434	
3 René Arnoux	Ferrari 126C4	70 1h37m41.851	
4 Keke Rosberg	Williams FW09-Honda	69	out of fuel
5 Elio de Angelis	Lotus 95T-Renault	69	
6 Ayrton Senna	Toleman TG183B-Hart	68	

Bellof (Tyrrell 012-Ford) finished sixth on the road but was disqualified for using illegal fuel at the Detroit GP. Winner's

average speed: 115.209 mph. Starting grid front row: Alboreto, 1m14.846 (pole) and Arnoux, 1m15.398. Fastest lap: Arnoux, 1m19.294. Leaders: Alboreto, laps 1-70

Gran Premio di San Marino

6 May 1984. Imola. 60 laps of a 3.132-mile circuit = 187.920 miles. Warm, dry and sunny. World Championship round 4

1 Alain Prost	McLaren MP4/2-		
	TAG Porsche	60 1h36m53.679	
2 René Arnoux	Ferrari 126C4	60 1h37m07.095	
3 Elio de Angelis	Lotus 95T-Renault	59	out of fuel
4 Derek Warwick	Renault RE50	59	
5 Thierry Boutsen	Arrows A6-Ford	59	
6 Andrea de Cesaris	Ligier JS23-Renault	58	out of fuel

Bellof (Tyrrell 012-Ford) finished fifth on the road but was disqualified for using illegal fuel at the Detroit GP. Winner's average speed: 116.366 mph. Starting grid front row: Piquet, 1m28.517 (pole) and Prost, 1m28.628. Fastest lap: Piquet, 1m33.275. Leaders: Prost, laps 1-60

Grand Prix de France

20 May 1984. Dijon-Prenois. 79 laps of a 2.361-mile circuit = 186.519 miles. Warm, dry and sunny. World Championship round 5

1 Niki Lauda	McLaren MP4/2-		
	TAG Porsche	79 1h31m11.951	
2 Patrick Tambay	Renault RE50	79 1h31m19.105	
3 Nigel Mansell	Lotus 95T-Renault	79 1h31m35.920	
4 René Arnoux	Ferrari 126C4	79 1h31m55.657	
5 Elio de Angelis	Lotus 95T-Renault	79 1h32m18.076	
6 Keke Rosberg	Williams FW09-Honda	78	

Winner's average speed: 122.711 mph. Starting grid front row: Tambay, 1m02.200 (pole) and de Angelis, 1m02.336. Fastest lap: Prost, 1m05.257. Leaders: Tambay, laps 1-40, 55-61; Lauda, 41-54, 62-79

Grand Prix de Monaco

3 June 1984. Monte Carlo. 31 laps of a 2.058-mile circuit = 63.798 miles. Race scheduled for 78 laps but stopped due to wet conditions, half points awarded as under 60% of race distance was completed. Cool and very wet. World Championship round 6

1 Alain Prost	McLaren MP4/2-		
	TAG Porsche	31 1h01m07.740	
2 Ayrton Senna	Toleman TG184-Hart	31 1h01m15.186	
3 René Arnoux	Ferrari 126C4	31 1h01m36.817	
4 Keke Rosberg	Williams FW09-Honda	31 1h01m42.986	
5 Elio de Angelis	Lotus 95T-Renault	31 1h01m52.179	
6 Michele Alboreto	Ferrari 126C4	30	

Bellof (Tyrrell 012-Ford) finished third on the road but was disqualified for using illegal fuel at the Detroit GP. Winner's average speed: 62.620 mph. Starting grid front row: Prost, 1m22.661 (pole) and Mansell, 1m22.752. Fastest lap: Senna, 1m54.334. Leaders: Prost, laps 1-10, 16-31; Mansell, 11-15

Grand Prix Labatt du Canada

17 June 1984. Montreal. 70 laps of a 2.740-mile circuit = 191.800 miles. Hot, dry and sunny. World Championship round 7

1 Nelson Piquet	Brabham BT53-BMW	70 1h46m23.748	
2 Niki Lauda	McLaren MP4/2-		
	TAG Porsche	70 1h46m26.360	
3 Alain Prost	McLaren MP4/2-		
	TAG Porsche	70 1h47m51.780	
4 Elio de Angelis	Lotus 95T-Renault	69	
5 René Arnoux	Ferrari 126C4	68	
6 Nigel Mansell	Lotus 95T-Renault	68	

Winner's average speed: 108.162 mph. Starting grid front row: Piquet, 1m25.442 (pole) and Prost, 1m26.198. Fastest lap: Piquet, 1m28.763. Leaders: Piquet, laps 1-70

Detroit Grand Prix

24 June 1984. Detroit. 63 laps of a 2.500-mile circuit = 157.500 miles. Race stopped by accident on lap1, restarted over original distance. Hot, dry and sunny. World Championship round 8

1	Nelson Piquet	Brabham BT53-BMW	63	1h55m41.842
2	Elio de Angelis	Lotus 95T-Renault	63	1h56m14.480
3	Teo Fabi	Brabham BT53-BMW	63	1h57m08.370
4	Alain Prost	McLaren MP4/2-TAG Porsche	63	1h57m37.100
5	Jacques Laffite	Williams FW09-Honda	62	

No other finishers. Brundle (Tyrrell 012-Ford) finished second but was disqualified for using illegal fuel. Winner's average speed: 81.679 mph. Starting grid front row: Piquet, 1m40.980 (pole) and Prost, 1m41.640. Fastest lap: Warwick, 1m46.221. Leaders: Piquet, laps 1-63

Dallas Grand Prix

8 July 1984. Fair Park. 67 laps of a 2.424-mile circuit = 162.408 miles. Race scheduled for 78 laps but stopped due to two hour rule. Very hot, dry and sunny. World Championship round 9

1	Keke Rosberg	Williams FW09-Honda	67	2h01m22.617
2	René Arnoux	Ferrari 126C4	67	2h01m45.081
3	Elio de Angelis	Lotus 95T-Renault	66	
4	Jacques Laffite	Williams FW09-Honda	65	
5	Piercarlo Ghinzani	Osella FA1F-Alfa Romeo	65	
6	Nigel Mansell	Lotus 95T-Renault	64	gearbox

Winner's average speed: 80.283 mph. Starting grid front row: Mansell, 1m37.041 (pole) and de Angelis, 1m37.635. Fastest lap: Lauda, 1m45.353. Leaders: Mansell, laps 1-35; Rosberg, 36-48, 57-67; Prost, 49-56.

1984 DRIVERS' RECORDS

Driver	Car	Brazilian GP	South African GP	Belgian GP	San Marino GP	French GP	Monaco GP	Canadian GP	Detroit GP	Dallas GP	British GP	German GP	Austrian GP	Dutch GP	Italian GP	European GP	Portuguese GP
Michele Alboreto	Ferrari 126C4	R	11	1P	R	R	6	R	R	R	5	R	3	R	2	2F	4
Philippe Alliot	RAM 02-Hart	R	R	DNQ	R	R	DNQ	10	R	DNS	R	R	11	10	R	R	R
Elio de Angelis	Lotus 95T-Renault	3P	7	5	3	5	5	4	2	3	4	R	R	4	R	R	5
René Arnoux	Ferrari 126C4	R	R	3F	2	4	3	5	R	2	6	6	7	11F	R	5	9
Mauro Baldi	Spirit 101B-Hart	R	8	R	8	R	DNQ	-	-	-	-	-	-	-	-	8	15
Stefan Bellof	Tyrrell 012-Ford	R	R	DSQ	DSQ	R	DSQ	R	R	R	DSQ	-	DNQ	DSQ	-	-	-
Gerhard Berger	ATS D7-BMW	-	-	-	-	-	-	-	-	-	-	-	12	-	6	R	13
Thierry Boutsen	Arrows A6-Ford	6	12	-	5	-	-	-	-	-	-	-	-	-	-	-	-
	Arrows A7-BMW	-	-	R	-	11	DNQ	R	R	R	R	R	5	R	10	9	R
Martin Brundle	Tyrrell 012-Ford	DSQ	DSQ	R	DSQ	DSQ	DNQ	DSQ	DSQ	DNQ	-	-	-	-	-	-	-
Johnny Cecotto	Toleman TG183B-Hart	R	R	R	NC	-	-	-	-	-	-	-	-	-	-	-	-
	Toleman TG184-Hart	-	-	-	-	R	R	9	R	R	DNP	-	-	-	-	-	-
Andrea de Cesaris	Ligier JS23-Renault	R	5	R	6	10	R	R	R	R	10	7	R	R	R	-	-
	Ligier JS23B-Renault	-	-	-	-	-	-	-	-	-	-	-	-	-	-	7	12
Eddie Cheever	Alfa Romeo 184T	4	R	R	7	R	DNQ	11	R	R	R	R	R	13	9	R	17
Corrado Fabi	Brabham BT53-BMW	-	-	-	-	-	R	R	-	7	-	-	-	-	-	-	-
Teo Fabi	Brabham BT53-BMW	R	R	R	R	9	-	-	3	-	R	R	4	5	R	R	-
Jo Gartner	Osella FA1E-Alfa Romeo	-	-	-	R	-	-	-	-	-	-	-	-	-	-	-	-
	Osella FA1F-Alfa Romeo	-	-	-	-	-	-	-	-	-	R	R	R	12	5	R	16
Piercarlo Ghinzani	Osella FA1F-Alfa Romeo	R	DNS	R	DNQ	12	7	R	R	5	9	R	R	R	7	R	R
François Hesnault	Ligier JS23-Renault	R	10	R	R	DNS	R	R	R	R	R	8	8	7	R	10	R
Stefan Johansson	Tyrrell 012-Ford	-	-	-	-	-	-	-	-	-	R	DSQ	DNQ	DSQ	-	-	-
	Toleman TG184-Hart	-	-	-	-	-	-	-	-	-	-	-	-	-	4	R	11
Jacques Laffite	Williams FW09-Honda	R	R	R	R	8	8	R	5	4	-	-	-	-	-	-	-
	Williams FW09B-Honda	-	-	-	-	-	-	-	-	-	R	R	R	R	R	R	14
Niki Lauda	McLaren MP4/2-TAG Porsche	R	1	R	R	1	R	2	RF	1F	2	1F	2	1F	2	4	2F
Nigel Mansell	Lotus 95T-Renault	R	R	R	R	3	R	6	6P	R	4	R	3	R	R	R	R
Pierluigi Martini	Toleman TG184-Hart	-	-	-	-	-	-	-	-	-	-	-	-	-	DNQ	-	-
Jonathan Palmer	RAM 01-Hart	8	R	-	-	-	-	-	-	-	-	-	-	-	-	-	-
	RAM 02-Hart	-	-	10	9	13	DNQ	-	R	R	R	R	9	9	R	R	R
Riccardo Patrese	Alfa Romeo 184T	R	4	R	R	R	R	R	R	R	12	R	10	R	3	6	8
Nelson Piquet	Brabham BT53-BMW	R	RP	9	RPF	R	R	1PF	1P	R	7P	R	2P	R	RP	3PF	6P
Alain Prost	McLaren MP4/2-TAG Porsche	1F	2	R	1	7F	1P	3	4	R	R	1PF	R	1P	R	1	1
Keke Rosberg	Williams FW09-Honda	2	R	4	R	6	4	R	R	1	-	-	-	-	-	-	-
	Williams FW09B-Honda	-	-	-	-	-	-	-	-	-	R	R	R	8	R	R	R
Huub Rothengatter	Spirit 101B-Hart	-	-	-	-	-	-	NC	-	R	NC	9	NC	R	8	-	-
	Spirit 101C-Ford	-	-	-	-	-	-	-	DNQ	-	-	-	-	-	-	-	-
Ayrton Senna	Toleman TG183B-Hart	R	6	6	DNQ	-	-	-	-	-	-	-	-	-	-	-	-
	Toleman TG184-Hart	-	-	-	-	R	2F	7	R	R	3	R	R	R	-	R	3
Philippe Streiff	Renault RE50	-	-	-	-	-	-	-	-	-	-	-	-	-	-	-	R
Marc Surer	Arrows A6-Ford	7	9	8	-	R	DNQ	R	R	-	-	-	-	-	-	-	-
	Arrows A7-BMW	-	-	-	R	-	-	-	-	R	11	R	6	R	R	R	R
Patrick Tambay	Renault RE50	5	RF	7	R	2P	R	DNP	R	R	8	5	R	6	R	R	7
Mike Thackwell	RAM 02-Hart	-	-	-	-	-	-	R	-	-	-	-	-	-	-	-	-
	Tyrrell 012-Ford	-	-	-	-	-	-	-	-	-	-	DNQ	-	-	-	-	-
Derek Warwick	Renault RE50	R	3	2	4	R	R	RF	R	2	3	R	R	R	11	R	
Manfred Winkelhock	ATS D7-BMW	DNQ	R	R	R	R	R	8	R	8	R	R	DNS	R	DNS	-	-
	Brabham BT53-BMW	-	-	-	-	-	-	-	-	-	-	-	-	-	-	-	10

John Player Special British Grand Prix

22 July 1984. Brands Hatch. 71 laps of a 2.614-mile circuit = 185.594 miles. Race scheduled for 75 laps, stopped after 11 laps due to accident. Restarted over 60 laps. Hot, dry and sunny. World Championship round 10

1	Niki Lauda	McLaren MP4/2-TAG Porsche	71 1h29m28.532
2	Derek Warwick	Renault RE50	71 1h30m10.655
3	Ayrton Senna	Toleman TG184-Hart	71 1h30m31.860
4	Elio de Angelis	Lotus 95T-Renault	70
5	Michele Alboreto	Ferrari 126C4	70
6	René Arnoux	Ferrari 126C4	70

Winner's average speed: 124.436 mph. Starting grid front row: Piquet, 1m10.869 (pole) and Prost, 1m11.076. Fastest lap: Lauda, 1m13.191. Leaders: Piquet, laps 1-11; Prost, 12-37; Lauda, 38-71

Grosser Preis von Deutschland

5 August 1984. Hockenheim. 44 laps of a 4.224-mile circuit = 185.856 miles. Warm, dry and sunny. World Championship round 11

1	Alain Prost	McLaren MP4/2-TAG Porsche	44 1h24m43.210
2	Niki Lauda	McLaren MP4/2-TAG Porsche	44 1h24m46.359
3	Derek Warwick	Renault RE50	44 1h25m19.633
4	Nigel Mansell	Lotus 95T-Renault	44 1h25m34.873
5	Patrick Tambay	Renault RE50	44 1h25m55.159
6	René Arnoux	Ferrari 126C4	43

Winner's average speed: 131.613 mph. Starting grid front row: Prost, 1m47.012 (pole) and de Angelis, 1m47.065. Fastest lap: Prost, 1m53.538. Leaders: de Angelis, laps 1-7; Piquet, 8-21; Prost, 22-44

Grosser Preis von Österreich

19 August 1984. Österreichring. 51 laps of a 3.692-mile circuit = 188.292 miles. Warm, dry and sunny. World Championship round 12

1	Niki Lauda	McLaren MP4/2-TAG Porsche	51 1h21m12.851
2	Nelson Piquet	Brabham BT53-BMW	51 1h21m36.376
3	Michele Alboreto	Ferrari 126C4	51 1h22m01.849
4	Teo Fabi	Brabham BT53-BMW	51 1h22m09.163
5	Thierry Boutsen	Arrows A7-BMW	50
6	Marc Surer	Arrows A7-BMW	50

Winner's average speed: 139.108 mph. Starting grid front row: Piquet, 1m26.173 (pole) and Prost, 1m26.203. Fastest lap: Lauda, 1m32.882. Leaders: Piquet, laps 1-39; Lauda, 40-51

Grote Prijs van Nederland

26 August 1984. Zandvoort. 71 laps of a 2.642-mile circuit = 187.582 miles. Warm, dry and sunny. World Championship round 13

1	Alain Prost	McLaren MP4/2-TAG Porsche	71 1h37m21.468
2	Niki Lauda	McLaren MP4/2-TAG Porsche	71 1h37m31.751

3	Nigel Mansell	Lotus 95T-Renault	71 1h38m41.012
4	Elio de Angelis	Lotus 95T-Renault	70
5	Teo Fabi	Brabham BT53-BMW	70
6	Patrick Tambay	Renault RE50	70

Winner's average speed: 115.604 mph. Starting grid front row: Prost, 1m13.567 (pole) and Piquet, 1m13.872. Fastest lap: Arnoux, 1m19.465. Leaders: Piquet, laps 1-10; Prost, 11-71

Gran Premio d'Italia

9 September 1984. Monza. 51 laps of a 3.604-mile circuit = 183.804 miles. Hot, dry and sunny. World Championship round 14

1	Niki Lauda	McLaren MP4/2-TAG Porsche	51 1h20m29.065
2	Michele Alboreto	Ferrari 126C4	51 1h20m53.314
3	Riccardo Patrese	Alfa Romeo 184T	50
4	Stefan Johansson	Toleman TG184-Hart	49
5	Jo Gartner*	Osella FA1F-Alfa Romeo	49
6	Gerhard Berger*	ATS D7-BMW	49

*Not entered in the World Championship, no points awarded.
Winner's average speed: 137.019 mph. Starting grid front row: Piquet, 1m26.584 (pole) and Prost, 1m26.671. Fastest lap: Lauda, 1m31.912. Leaders: Piquet, laps 1-15; Tambay, 16-42; Lauda, 43-51

Grosser Preis von Europa

7 October 1984. Nürburgring. 67 laps of a 2.822-mile circuit = 189.074 miles. Cold and dry. World Championship round 15

1	Alain Prost	McLaren MP4/2-TAG Porsche	67 1h35m13.284
2	Michele Alboreto	Ferrari 126C4	67 1h35m37.195
3	Nelson Piquet	Brabham BT53-BMW	67 1h35m38.206
4	Niki Lauda	McLaren MP4/2-TAG Porsche	67 1h35m56.370
5	René Arnoux	Ferrari 126C4	67 1h36m14.714
6	Riccardo Patrese	Alfa Romeo 184T	66

Winner's average speed: 119.138 mph. Starting grid front row: Piquet, 1m18.871 (pole) and Prost, 1m19.175. Fastest lap: Piquet and Alboreto, 1m23.146. Leaders: Prost, laps 1-67

Grande Premio de Portugal

21 October 1984. Estoril. 70 laps of a 2.703-mile circuit = 189.210 miles. Hot, dry and sunny. World Championship round 16

1	Alain Prost	McLaren MP4/2-TAG Porsche	70 1h41m11.753
2	Niki Lauda	McLaren MP4/2-TAG Porsche	70 1h41m25.178
3	Ayrton Senna	Toleman TG184-Hart	70 1h41m31.795
4	Michele Alboreto	Ferrari 126C4	70 1h41m32.070
5	Elio de Angelis	Lotus 95T-Renault	70 1h42m43.922
6	Nelson Piquet	Brabham BT53-BMW	69

Winner's average speed: 112.184 mph. Starting grid front row: Piquet, 1m21.703 (pole) and Prost, 1m21.774. Fastest lap: Lauda, 1m22.996. Leaders: Rosberg, laps 1-8; Prost, 9-70

1984 FINAL CHAMPIONSHIP POSITIONS

Drivers

1	Niki Lauda	72
2	Alain Prost	71.5
3	Elio de Angelis	34
4	Michele Alboreto	30.5
5	Nelson Piquet	29
6	René Arnoux	27
7	Derek Warwick	23
8	Keke Rosberg	20.5
9=	Nigel Mansell	13
	Ayrton Senna	13
11	Patrick Tambay	11
12	Teo Fabi	9
13	Riccardo Patrese	8
14=	Thierry Boutsen	5
	Jacques Laffite	5
16=	Andrea de Cesaris	3
	Eddie Cheever	3
	Stefan Johansson	3
19	Piercarlo Ghinzani	2
20	Marc Surer	1

Manufacturers

1	McLaren-TAG Porsche	143.5
2	Ferrari	57.5
3	Lotus-Renault	47
4	Brabham-BMW	38
5	Renault	34
6	Williams-Honda	25.5
7	Toleman-Hart	16
8	Alfa Romeo	11
9	Arrows-Ford/BMW	11
10	Ligier-Renault	3
11	Osella-Alfa Romeo	2

1985

Alain Prost became the first Frenchman to win the World Championship after coming so close to the title in the previous two seasons. Niki Lauda won just once - by less than 0.3 seconds from Prost at Zandvoort - and announced his final retirement from the sport.

Prost's closest challenger was Michele Alboreto, although by the 14th round the championship was decided. A win in Canada gave Alboreto the series lead, but on the quick circuits that followed Prost re-established his supremacy, beating the Italian by more than a lap at Silverstone. A run of three retirements finally ended Alboreto's hopes.

Alboreto's Ferrari team-mate, René Arnoux, was replaced by the highly-rated but under-used Stefan Johansson after Brazil. Johansson almost won at Imola only to run out of fuel while leading, but his race performances were often hampered by poor grid positions.

Ayrton Senna moved to Lotus and proved to be the quickest driver in Formula One. He scored a tremendous first Grand Prix win in the wet

1985 DRIVERS' RECORDS

Driver	Car	Brazilian GP	Portuguese GP	San Marino GP	Monaco GP	Canadian GP	Detroit GP	French GP	British GP	German GP	Austrian GP	Dutch GP	Italian GP	Belgian GP	European GP	South African GP	Australian GP
Kenneth Acheson	RAM 03-Hart	-	-	-	-	-	-	-	-	-	R	DNQ	R	-	-	-	-
Michele Alboreto	Ferrari 156/85	2[P]	2	R[F]	2[F]	1	3	R	2	1	3	4	13	R	R	R	R
Philippe Alliot	RAM 03-Hart	9	R	R	DNQ	R	R	R	R	R	R	R	R	R	R	-	-
Elio de Angelis	Lotus 97T-Renault	3	4	1	3	5[P]	5	5	NC	R	5	5	6	R	5	R	DSQ
René Arnoux	Ferrari 156/85	4	-	-	-	-	-	-	-	-	-	-	-	-	-	-	-
Mauro Baldi	Spirit 101D-Hart	R	R	R	-	-	-	-	-	-	-	-	-	-	-	-	-
Stefan Bellof	Tyrrell 012-Ford	-	6	R	DNQ	11	4	13	11	-	-	-	-	-	-	-	-
	Tyrrell 014-Renault	-	-	-	-	-	-	-	-	8	7	R	-	-	-	-	-
Gerhard Berger	Arrows A8-BMW	R	R	R	R	13	11	R	8	7	R	9	R	7	10	5	6
Thierry Boutsen	Arrows A8-BMW	11	R	2	9	9	7	9	R	4	8	R	9	10	6	6	R
Martin Brundle	Tyrrell 012-Ford	8	R	9	10	12	R	-	-	10	DNQ	-	-	-	-	-	-
	Tyrrell 014-Renault	-	-	-	-	-	-	R	7	-	-	7	8	13	R	7	NC
Ivan Capelli	Tyrrell 014-Renault	-	-	-	-	-	-	-	-	-	-	-	-	-	R	-	4
Andrea de Cesaris	Ligier JS25-Renault	R	R	R	4	14	10	R	R	R	R	R	-	-	-	-	-
Eddie Cheever	Alfa Romeo 185T	R	R	R	R	17	9	10	-	-	-	-	-	-	-	-	-
	Alfa Romeo 184TB	-	-	-	-	-	-	-	-	R	R	R	R	R	11	R	R
Christian Danner	Zakspeed 841	-	-	-	-	-	-	-	-	-	-	-	-	R	R	-	-
Teo Fabi	Toleman TG185-Hart	-	-	R	R	R	14	R	R	R[P]	R	R	12	R	R	R	R
Piercarlo Ghinzani	Osella FA1G-Alfa Romeo	12	-	NC	DNQ	R	R	15	R	-	-	-	-	-	-	-	-
	Osella FA1F-Alfa Romeo	-	9	-	-	-	-	-	-	-	-	-	-	-	-	-	-
	Toleman TG185-Hart	-	-	-	-	-	-	-	-	R	R	R	R	R	R	R	R
François Hesnault	Brabham BT54-BMW	R	R	R	DNQ	-	-	-	-	-	-	-	-	-	-	-	-
	Renault RE60	-	-	-	-	-	-	-	-	R	-	-	-	-	-	-	-
Stefan Johansson	Tyrrell 012-Ford	7	-	-	-	-	-	-	-	-	-	-	-	-	-	-	-
	Ferrari 156/85	-	8	6	R	2	2	4	R	9	4	R	5	R	R	4	R
Alan Jones	Lola THL1-Hart	-	-	-	-	-	-	-	-	-	-	-	R	-	R	DNS	R
Jacques Laffite	Ligier JS25-Renault	6	R	R	6	8	12	R	3	3	R	R	R	11	R[F]	-	2
Niki Lauda	McLaren MP4/2B-TAG Porsche	R	R	4	R	R	R	R	R	5[F]	R	1	R	DNP	-	R	R
Nigel Mansell	Williams FW10-Honda	R	5	5	7	6	R	DNS	R	6	R	6	11[F]	2	1	1[P]	R
Pierluigi Martini	Minardi M185-Ford	R	R	-	-	-	-	-	-	-	-	-	-	-	-	-	-
	Minardi M185-Motori Moderni	-	-	R	DNQ	R	R	R	R	11	R	R	R	12	R	R	8
Jonathan Palmer	Zakspeed 841	-	R	DNS	11	-	-	R	R	R	R	R	-	-	-	-	-
Riccardo Patrese	Alfa Romeo 185T	R	R	R	R	10	R	11	9	-	-	-	-	-	-	-	-
	Alfa Romeo 184TB	-	-	-	-	-	-	-	-	R	R	R	R	R	9	R	R
Nelson Piquet	Brabham BT54-BMW	R	R	8	R	R	6	1	4	R	R	8[P]	2	5	R	R	R
Alain Prost	McLaren MP4/2B-TAG Porsche	1[F]	R	DSQ	1	3	R	3	1[F]	2	1[PF]	2[F]	1	3[PF]	4	3	R
Keke Rosberg	Williams FW10-Honda	R	R	R	8	4	1	2[PF]	R[P]	12	R	R	R	4	3	2[F]	1[F]
Huub Rothengatter	Osella FA1G-Alfa Romeo	-	-	-	-	-	-	-	-	R	9	NC	R	R	R	R	R
Ayrton Senna	Lotus 97T-Renault	R	1[PF]	7[P]	R[P]	16[F]	R[PF]	R	10	R	2	3	3[P]	1	2[P]	R	R[P]
Philippe Streiff	Ligier JS25-Renault	-	-	-	-	-	-	-	-	-	-	-	10	9	8	-	3
	Tyrrell 014-Renault	-	-	-	-	-	-	-	-	-	-	-	-	-	-	R	-
Marc Surer	Brabham BT54-BMW	-	-	-	-	15	8	8	6	R	R	6	10	4	8	R	R
Patrick Tambay	Renault RE60	5	3	3	R	7	R	-	-	-	-	-	-	-	-	-	-
	Renault RE60B	-	-	-	-	-	-	6	R	R	10	R	7	R	12	-	R
Derek Warwick	Renault RE60	10	7	10	5	R	R	7	-	-	-	-	-	-	-	-	-
	Renault RE60B	-	-	-	-	-	-	-	5	R	R	R	R	6	R	-	R
John Watson	McLaren MP4/2B-TAG Porsche	-	-	-	-	-	-	-	-	-	-	-	-	-	7	-	-
Manfred Winkelhock	RAM 03-Hart	13	NC	R	DNQ	R	R	12	R	R	-	-	-	-	-	-	-

Portuguese GP, but for most of the season he was unlucky, although a second victory followed at Spa in September. The meeting had started in June, but after first-qualifying the Grand Prix was postponed when the newly laid track surface broke up - the resulting loose chippings rendering Spa's fast corners highly dangerous.

Lotus team-mate Elio de Angelis managed one win (San Marino, after Prost's McLaren had been disqualified) and a pole, but after six years he signed for Brabham at the end of the season. In its continuing search for Grand Prix success, Pirelli supplied tyres to Brabham, while in his final year with the team Nelson Piquet won in France but otherwise did not figure strongly.

Williams-Honda was the quickest combination at the end of the season with three successive victories. At Brands Hatch Nigel Mansell finally won his first Grand Prix, after more than seventy unsuccessful attempts. He followed it up with victory in the South African GP, a race which some teams boycotted for political reasons. Keke Rosberg completed the Williams hat-trick at the final round, held for the first time in Australia.

After nine seasons the Renault team withdrew from racing, but would continue to supply Lotus, Ligier and Tyrrell with turbocharged engines. The Toleman team was bought by its sponsor Benetton, after a troubled year which had been delayed while the team tried to secure a tyre contract. For the coming season the cars would be known as Benettons.

John Player Special Grande Premio do Brasil

7 April 1985. Rio de Janeiro. 61 laps of a 3.126-mile circuit = 190.686 miles. Hot, dry and sunny. World Championship round 1

1 Alain Prost	McLaren MP4/2B-TAG Porsche	61 1h41m26.115
2 Michele Alboreto	Ferrari 156/85	61 1h41m29.374
3 Elio de Angelis	Lotus 97T-Renault	60
4 René Arnoux	Ferrari 156/85	59
5 Patrick Tambay	Renault RE60	59
6 Jacques Laffite	Ligier JS25-Renault	59

Winner's average speed: 112.793 mph. Starting grid front row: Alboreto, 1m27.768 (pole) and Rosberg, 1m27.864. Fastest lap: Prost, 1m36.702. Leaders: Rosberg, laps 1-9; Alboreto, 10-18; Prost, 19-61.

Grande Premio de Portugal

21 April 1985. Estoril. 67 laps of a 2.703-mile circuit = 181.101 miles. Race scheduled for 69 laps, stopped due to two hour rule. Cold and very wet. World Championship round 2

1 Ayrton Senna	Lotus 97T-Renault	67 2h00m28.006
2 Michele Alboreto	Ferrari 156/85	67 2h01m30.984
3 Patrick Tambay	Renault RE60	66
4 Elio de Angelis	Lotus 97T-Renault	66
5 Nigel Mansell	Williams FW10-Honda	65
6 Stefan Bellof	Tyrrell 012-Ford	65

Winner's average speed: 90.200 mph. Starting grid front row: Senna, 1m21.007 (pole) and Prost, 1m21.420. Fastest lap: Senna, 1m44.121. Leaders: Senna, laps 1-67

Gran Premio di San Marino

5 May 1985. Imola. 60 laps of a 3.132-mile circuit = 187.920 miles. Warm, dry and sunny. World Championship round 3

1 Elio de Angelis	Lotus 97T-Renault	60 1h34m35.955
2 Thierry Boutsen	Arrows A8-BMW	59
3 Patrick Tambay	Renault RE60	59
4 Niki Lauda	McLaren MP4/2B-TAG Porsche	59
5 Nigel Mansell	Williams FW10-Honda	58
6 Stefan Johansson	Ferrari 156/85	57 out of fuel

Prost (McLaren MP4/2B-TAG Porsche) finished first on the road but was disqualified as his car was under the weight limit. Winner's average speed: 119.189 mph. Starting grid front row: Senna, 1m27.327 (pole) and Rosberg, 1m27.354. Fastest lap: Alboreto, 1m30.961. Leaders: Senna, laps 1-56; Johansson, 57; de Angelis, 58-60 (Prost led laps 58-60 on the road)

Grand Prix de Monaco

19 May 1985. Monte Carlo. 78 laps of a 2.058-mile circuit = 160.524 miles. Cool and dry, light rain later. World Championship round 4

1 Alain Prost	McLaren MP4/2B-TAG Porsche	78 1h51m58.034
2 Michele Alboreto	Ferrari 156/85	78 1h52m05.575
3 Elio de Angelis	Lotus 97T-Renault	78 1h53m25.205
4 Andrea de Cesaris	Ligier JS25-Renault	77
5 Derek Warwick	Renault RE60	77
6 Jacques Laffite	Ligier JS25-Renault	77

Winner's average speed: 86.020 mph. Starting grid front row: Senna, 1m20.450 (pole) and Mansell, 1m20.536. Fastest lap: Alboreto, 1m22.637. Leaders: Senna, laps 1-13; Alboreto, 14-17, 24-31; Prost, 18-23, 32-78

Grand Prix de Belgique

2 June 1985 (race postponed until 15 September due to unsafe track conditions). Spa-Francorchamps

RACE POSTPONED

Starting grid front row (after one qualifying session): Alboreto, 1m56.046 (pole) and de Angelis, 1m56.277

Grand Prix Labatt du Canada

16 June 1985. Montreal. 70 laps of a 2.740-mile circuit = 191.800 miles. Cool and dry. World Championship round 5

1 Michele Alboreto	Ferrari 156/85	70 1h46m01.813
2 Stefan Johansson	Ferrari 156/85	70 1h46m03.770
3 Alain Prost	McLaren MP4/2B-TAG Porsche	70 1h46m06.154
4 Keke Rosberg	Williams FW10-Honda	70 1h46m29.634
5 Elio de Angelis	Lotus 97T-Renault	70 1h46m45.162
6 Nigel Mansell	Williams FW10-Honda	70 1h47m19.691

Winner's average speed: 108.535 mph. Starting grid front row: de Angelis, 1m24.567 (pole) and Senna, 1m24.816. Fastest lap: Senna, 1m27.445. Leaders: de Angelis, laps 1-15; Alboreto, 16-70

Detroit Grand Prix

23 June 1985. Detroit. 63 laps of a 2.500-mile circuit = 157.500 miles. Hot, dry and sunny. World Championship round 6

1 Keke Rosberg	Williams FW10-Honda	63 1h55m39.851
2 Stefan Johansson	Ferrari 156/85	63 1h56m37.400
3 Michele Alboreto	Ferrari 156/85	63 1h56m43.021
4 Stefan Bellof	Tyrrell 012-Ford	63 1h56m46.076
5 Elio de Angelis	Lotus 97T-Renault	63 1h57m06.817
6 Nelson Piquet	Brabham BT54-BMW	62

Winner's average speed: 81.702 mph. Starting grid front row: Senna, 1m42.051 (pole) and Mansell, 1m43.249. Fastest lap: Senna, 1m45.612. Leaders: Senna, laps 1-7; Rosberg, 8-63

Grand Prix de France

7 July 1985. Paul Ricard. 53 laps of a 3.610-mile circuit = 191.330 miles. Hot, dry and sunny. World Championship round 7

1 Nelson Piquet	Brabham BT54-BMW	53 1h31m46.266
2 Keke Rosberg	Williams FW10-Honda	53 1h31m52.926
3 Alain Prost	McLaren MP4/2B-TAG Porsche	53 1h31m55.551
4 Stefan Johansson	Ferrari 156/85	53 1h32m39.757
5 Elio de Angelis	Lotus 97T-Renault	53 1h32m39.956
6 Patrick Tambay	Renault RE60B	53 1h33m01.433

Winner's average speed: 125.092 mph. Starting grid front row: Rosberg, 1m32.462 (pole) and Senna, 1m32.835. Fastest lap: Rosberg, 1m39.914. Leaders: Rosberg, laps 1-10; Piquet, 11-53.

Marlboro British Grand Prix

21 July 1985. Silverstone. 65 laps of a 2.932-mile circuit = 190.580 miles. Race scheduled for 66 laps but stopped early in error. Warm, dry and sunny. World Championship round 8

1 Alain Prost	McLaren MP4/2B-TAG Porsche	65 1h18m10.436
2 Michele Alboreto	Ferrari 156/85	64
3 Jacques Laffite	Ligier JS25-Renault	64
4 Nelson Piquet	Brabham BT54-BMW	64
5 Derek Warwick	Renault RE60B	64
6 Marc Surer	Brabham BT54-BMW	63

Winner's average speed: 146.274 mph. Starting grid front row: Rosberg, 1m05.591 (pole) and Piquet, 1m06.249. Fastest lap: Prost, 1m09.886. Leaders: Senna, laps 1-57, 59; Prost, 58, 60-65

Grosser Preis von Deutschland

4 August 1985. Nürburgring. 67 laps of a 2.822-mile circuit = 189.074 miles. Cool and dry. World Championship round 9

1 Michele Alboreto	Ferrari 156/85	67 1h35m31.337
2 Alain Prost	McLaren MP4/2B-TAG Porsche	67 1h35m42.998
3 Jacques Laffite	Ligier JS25-Renault	67 1h36m22.491
4 Thierry Boutsen	Arrows A8-BMW	67 1h36m26.616
5 Niki Lauda	McLaren MP4/2B-TAG Porsche	67 1h36m45.309
6 Nigel Mansell	Williams FW10-Honda	67 1h36m48.157

Winner's average speed: 118.762 mph. Starting grid front row: Fabi, 1m17.429 (pole) and Johansson, 1m18.616. Fastest lap: Lauda, 1m22.806. Leaders: Rosberg, laps 1-15, 27-44; Senna, 16-26; Alboreto, 45-67

Alain Prost became the first Frenchman to win the World Championship

Grosser Preis von Österreich

18 August 1985. Österreichring. 52 laps of a 3.692-mile circuit = 191.984 miles. Race stopped by accident on lap 1. Restarted over original distance. Warm, dry and sunny. World Championship round 10

1 Alain Prost	McLaren MP4/2B-TAG Porsche	52 1h20m12.583
2 Ayrton Senna	Lotus 97T-Renault	52 1h20m42.585
3 Michele Alboreto	Ferrari 156/85	52 1h20m46.939
4 Stefan Johansson	Ferrari 156/85	52 1h20m51.656
5 Elio de Angelis	Lotus 97T-Renault	52 1h21m34.675
6 Marc Surer	Brabham BT54-BMW	51

Winner's average speed: 143.612 mph. Starting grid front row: Prost, 1m25.490 (pole) and Mansell, 1m26.052. Fastest lap: Prost, 1m29.241. Leaders: Prost, laps 1-26, 40-52; Lauda, 27-39

Grote Prijs van Nederland

25 August 1985. Zandvoort. 70 laps of a 2.642-mile circuit = 184.940 miles. Cool and dry. World Championship round 11

1 Niki Lauda	McLaren MP4/2B-TAG Porsche	70 1h32m29.263
2 Alain Prost	McLaren MP4/2B-TAG Porsche	70 1h32m29.495
3 Ayrton Senna	Lotus 97T-Renault	70 1h33m17.754
4 Michele Alboreto	Ferrari 156/85	70 1h33m18.100
5 Elio de Angelis	Lotus 97T-Renault	69
6 Nigel Mansell	Williams FW10-Honda	69

Winner's average speed: 119.977 mph. Starting grid front row: Piquet, 1m11.074 (pole) and Rosberg, 1m11.647. Fastest lap: Prost, 1m16.538. Leaders: Rosberg, laps 1-19; Prost, 20-33; Lauda, 34-70

Gran Premio d'Italia

8 September 1985. Monza. 51 laps of a 3.604-mile circuit = 183.804 miles. Hot, dry and sunny. World Championship round 12

1 Alain Prost	McLaren MP4/2B-TAG Porsche	51 1h17m59.451
2 Nelson Piquet	Brabham BT54-BMW	51 1h18m51.086
3 Ayrton Senna	Lotus 97T-Renault	51 1h18m59.841
4 Marc Surer	Brabham BT54-BMW	51 1h19m00.060
5 Stefan Johansson	Ferrari 156/85	50
6 Elio de Angelis	Lotus 97T-Renault	50

Winner's average speed: 141.400 mph. Starting grid front row: Senna, 1m25.084 (pole) and Rosberg, 1m25.230. Fastest lap: Mansell, 1m28.283. Leaders: Rosberg, laps 1-27, 40-44; Prost, 28-39, 45-51

Grand Prix de Belgique

15 September 1985 (race had been scheduled for 2 June but that meeting was abandoned due to unsafe track conditions). Spa-Francorchamps. 43 laps of a 4.318-mile circuit = 185.674 miles. Cool and wet, drying later. World Championship round 13

1 Ayrton Senna	Lotus 97T-Renault	43 1h34m19.893
2 Nigel Mansell	Williams FW10-Honda	43 1h34m48.315
3 Alain Prost	McLaren MP4/2B-TAG Porsche	43 1h35m15.002
4 Keke Rosberg	Williams FW10-Honda	43 1h35m35.183
5 Nelson Piquet	Brabham BT54-BMW	42
6 Derek Warwick	Renault RE60B	42

Winner's average speed: 118.096 mph. Starting grid front row: Prost, 1m55.306 (pole) and Senna, 1m55.403. Fastest lap: Prost, 2m01.730. Leaders: Senna, laps 1-8, 10-43; de Angelis, 9

Shell Oils Grand Prix of Europe

6 October 1985. Brands Hatch. 75 laps of a 2.614-mile circuit = 196.050 miles. Warm, dry and sunny. World Championship round 14

1 Nigel Mansell	Williams FW10-Honda	75 1h32m58.109
2 Ayrton Senna	Lotus 97T-Renault	75 1h33m19.505
3 Keke Rosberg	Williams FW10-Honda	75 1h33m56.642
4 Alain Prost	McLaren MP4/2B-TAG Porsche	75 1h34m04.230
5 Elio de Angelis	Lotus 97T-Renault	74
6 Thierry Boutsen	Arrows A8-BMW	73

Winner's average speed: 126.507 mph. Starting grid front row: Senna, 1m07.169 (pole) and Piquet, 1m07.482. Fastest lap: Laffite, 1m11.526. Leaders: Senna, laps 1-8; Mansell, 9-75

Southern Hotels Grand Prix of South Africa

19 October 1985. Kyalami. 75 laps of a 2.550-mile circuit = 191.250 miles. Hot, dry and sunny. World Championship round 15

1 Nigel Mansell	Williams FW10-Honda	75	1h28m22.866
2 Keke Rosberg	Williams FW10-Honda	75	1h28m30.438
3 Alain Prost	McLaren MP4/2B-TAG Porsche	75	1h30m14.660
4 Stefan Johansson	Ferrari 156/85	74	
5 Gerhard Berger	Arrows A8-BMW	74	
6 Thierry Boutsen	Arrows A8-BMW	74	

Winner's average speed: 129.835 mph. Starting grid front row: Mansell, 1m02.366 (pole) and Piquet, 1m02.490. Fastest lap: Rosberg, 1m08.149. Leaders: Mansell, laps 1-75

Mitsubishi Australian Grand Prix

3 November 1985. Adelaide. 82 laps of a 2.347-mile circuit = 192.454 miles. Hot, dry and sunny. World Championship round 16

1 Keke Rosberg	Williams FW10-Honda	82	2h00m40.473
2 Jacques Laffite	Ligier JS25-Renault	82	2h01m26.603
3 Philippe Streiff	Ligier JS25-Renault	82	2h02m09.009
4 Ivan Capelli	Tyrrell 014-Renault	81	
5 Stefan Johansson	Ferrari 156/85	81	
6 Gerhard Berger	Arrows A8-BMW	81	

Winner's average speed: 95.689 mph. Starting grid front row: Senna, 1m19.843 (pole) and Mansell, 1m20.537. Fastest lap: Rosberg, 1m23.758. Leaders: Rosberg, laps 1-42, 45-53, 62-82; Senna, 43-44, 54-55, 58-61; Lauda, 56-57

1985 FINAL CHAMPIONSHIP POSITIONS

Drivers					Manufacturers		
1	Alain Prost	73 (76)*	11=	Thierry Boutsen 11	1	McLaren-TAG Porsche	90
2	Michele Alboreto	53		Patrick Tambay 11	2	Ferrari	82
3	Keke Rosberg	40	13=	Marc Surer 5	3=	Lotus-Renault	71
4	Ayrton Senna	38		Derek Warwick 5		Williams-Honda	71
5	Elio de Angelis	33	15=	Stefan Bellof 4	5	Brabham-BMW	26
6	Nigel Mansell	31		Philippe Streiff 4	6	Ligier-Renault	23
7	Stefan Johansson	26	17=	René Arnoux 3	7	Renault	16
8	Nelson Piquet	21		Gerhard Berger 3	8	Arrows-BMW	14
9	Jacques Laffite	16		Ivan Capelli 3	9	Tyrrell-Ford/Renault	7
10	Niki Lauda	14		Andrea de Cesaris 3			
				*Best 11 results count			

1986

Alain Prost successfully defended his World Championship (the first man to do so since 1960) in a classic three-way title fight at the final round in Adelaide. Prost appeared to have little chance against the powerful Williams-Hondas of Nigel Mansell and the pre-season favourite Nelson Piquet. However, with just 18 laps remaining and the title in his grasp, Mansell suffered a spectacular 180 mph puncture, ending his hopes. Piquet was then forced to change tyres, handing the race and championship to a surprised but ecstatic Prost.

Mansell had been the revelation of the season, driving with new found maturity and speed, and a first World Championship would have been just reward for a year in which he overshadowed his more illustrious team-mate.

However, as the Williams team-mates fought a tense battle for supremacy, Prost won four times and finished in the points on all bar three occasions. His McLaren was at times no match for the Williams (he was a lapped third at Brands), but its driver more than compensated over the full season.

Ayrton Senna was the fourth major title protagonist. At Spain's new venue in Jerez, he beat Mansell by half a car length in a dash to the finish line. Another victory in Detroit kept him in the championship until the end of the European season. Senna was on pole and led at half of the Grands Prix, but ultimately his Lotus-Renault could not match his pace.

Gerhard Berger scored a first victory in Mexico after several impressive performances in the powerful Benetton-BMW. While the Goodyear runners all made tyre stops, Berger ran non-stop to give Pirelli a rare success.

This was also the year of the low-line Brabham BT55. In order to reduce frontal area and lower the centre of gravity, the BMW engine lay almost flat in the chassis and was mated to a new compact, seven-speed Weismann gearbox. However, the car suffered gearbox and overheating problems and failed to impress. Sadly, Elio de Angelis, one of Grand Prix racing's gentlemen, was killed in May while testing a BT55 at Circuit Paul Ricard.

Two established Grand Prix stars ended their F1 careers, but would be seen again in other formulae. Jacques Laffite was forced to quit after he was injured in a startline accident at Brands Hatch - the very race in which the popular Frenchman equalled Graham Hill's long standing record for Grands Prix started. Keke Rosberg announced his retirement after a disappointing season as Prost's team-mate at McLaren.

Grande Premio do Brasil

23 March 1986. Rio de Janeiro. 61 laps of a 3.126-mile circuit = 190.686 miles. Hot, dry and sunny. World Championship round 1

1 Nelson Piquet	Williams FW11-Honda	61	1h39m32.583
2 Ayrton Senna	Lotus 98T-Renault	61	1h40m07.410
3 Jacques Laffite	Ligier JS27-Renault	61	1h40m32.342
4 René Arnoux	Ligier JS27-Renault	61	1h41m01.012
5 Martin Brundle	Tyrrell 014-Renault	60	
6 Gerhard Berger	Benetton B186-BMW	59	

Winner's average speed: 114.937 mph. Starting grid front row: Senna, 1m25.501 (pole) and Piquet, 1m26.266. Fastest lap: Piquet, 1m33.546. Leaders: Senna, laps 1-2, 19, 41; Piquet, 3-18, 27-40, 42-61; Prost, 20-26

Gran Premio Tio Pepe de Espana

13 April 1986. Jerez. 72 laps of a 2.621-mile circuit =
188.705 miles. Warm, dry and sunny. World Championship
round 2

1 Ayrton Senna	Lotus 98T-Renault	72	1h48m47.735
2 Nigel Mansell	Williams FW11-Honda	72	1h48m47.749
3 Alain Prost	McLaren MP4/2C- TAG Porsche	72	1h49m09.287
4 Keke Rosberg	McLaren MP4/2C- TAG Porsche	71	
5 Teo Fabi	Benetton B186-BMW	71	
6 Gerhard Berger	Benetton B186-BMW	71	

Winner's average speed: 104.069 mph. Starting grid front row:
Senna, 1m21.605 (pole) and Piquet, 1m22.431. Fastest lap: Mansell,
1m27.176. Leaders: Senna, laps 1-39, 63-72; Mansell, 40-62

Gran Premio di San Marino

27 April 1986. Imola. 60 laps of a 3.132-mile circuit =
187.920 miles. Warm, dry and sunny. World Championship
round 3

1 Alain Prost	McLaren MP4/2C- TAG Porsche	60	1h32m28.408
2 Nelson Piquet	Williams FW11-Honda	60	1h32m36.053
3 Gerhard Berger	Benetton B186-BMW	59	
4 Stefan Johansson	Ferrari F186	59	
5 Keke Rosberg	McLaren MP4/2C- TAG Porsche	58	out of fuel
6 Riccardo Patrese	Brabham BT55-BMW	58	out of fuel

Winner's average speed: 121.929 mph. Starting grid front row:
Senna, 1m25.050 (pole) and Piquet, 1m25.569. Fastest lap: Piquet,
1m28.667. Leaders: Piquet, laps 1-28; Rosberg, 29-33; Prost, 34-60

Grand Prix de Monaco

11 May 1986. Monte Carlo. 78 laps of a 2.068-mile circuit =
161.304 miles. Warm, dry and sunny. World Championship
round 4

1 Alain Prost	McLaren MP4/2C- TAG Porsche	78	1h55m41.060
2 Keke Rosberg	McLaren MP4/2C- TAG Porsche	78	1h56m06.082
3 Ayrton Senna	Lotus 98T-Renault	78	1h56m34.706
4 Nigel Mansell	Williams FW11-Honda	78	1h56m52.462
5 René Arnoux	Ligier JS27-Renault	77	
6 Jacques Laffite	Ligier JS27-Renault	77	

Winner's average speed: 83.661 mph. Starting grid front row:
Prost, 1m22.627 (pole) and Mansell, 1m23.047. Fastest lap:
Prost, 1m26.607. Leaders: Prost, laps 1-34, 42-78; Senna, 35-41

Grand Prix de Belgique

25 May 1986. Spa-Francorchamps. 43 laps of a 4.312-mile
circuit = 185.416 miles. Hot, dry and sunny. World
Championship round 5

1 Nigel Mansell	Williams FW11-Honda	43	1h27m57.925
2 Ayrton Senna	Lotus 98T-Renault	43	1h28m17.752
3 Stefan Johansson	Ferrari F186	43	1h28m24.517
4 Michele Alboreto	Ferrari F186	43	1h28m27.559
5 Jacques Laffite	Ligier JS27-Renault	43	1h29m08.615
6 Alain Prost	McLaren MP4/2C- TAG Porsche	43	1h30m15.697

Winner's average speed: 126.470 mph. Starting grid front row:
Piquet, 1m54.331 (pole) and Berger, 1m54.468. Fastest lap:
Prost, 1m59.282. Leaders: Piquet, laps 1-16; Senna, 17-21;
Johansson, 22-23; Mansell, 24-43

Grand Prix Labatt du Canada

15 June 1986. Montreal. 69 laps of a 2.740-mile circuit =
189.060 miles. Hot and dry. World Championship round 6

1 Nigel Mansell	Williams FW11-Honda	69	1h42m26.415
2 Alain Prost	McLaren MP4/2C- TAG Porsche	69	1h42m47.074
3 Nelson Piquet	Williams FW11-Honda	69	1h43m02.677
4 Keke Rosberg	McLaren MP4/2C- TAG Porsche	69	1h44m02.088
5 Ayrton Senna	Lotus 98T-Renault	68	
6 René Arnoux	Ligier JS27-Renault	68	

Winner's average speed: 110.734 mph. Starting grid front row:
Mansell, 1m24.118 (pole) and Senna, 1m24.188. Fastest lap:
Piquet, 1m25.443. Leaders: Mansell, laps 1-16, 22-30, 32-69;
Rosberg, 17-21; Prost, 31

Detroit Grand Prix

22 June 1986. Detroit. 63 laps of a 2.500-mile circuit =
157.500 miles. Hot, dry and windy. World Championship
round 7

1 Ayrton Senna	Lotus 98T-Renault	63	1h51m12.847
2 Jacques Laffite	Ligier JS27-Renault	63	1h51m43.864
3 Alain Prost	McLaren MP4/2C- TAG Porsche	63	1h51m44.671
4 Michele Alboreto	Ferrari F186	63	1h52m43.783
5 Nigel Mansell	Williams FW11-Honda	62	
6 Riccardo Patrese	Brabham BT55-BMW	62	

Winner's average speed: 84.971 mph. Starting grid front row:
Senna, 1m38.301 (pole) and Mansell, 1m38.839. Fastest lap:
Piquet, 1m41.233. Leaders: Senna, laps 1-2, 8-14, 40-63; Mansell,
3-7; Arnoux, 15-17; Laffite, 18-30; Piquet, 31-39

Grand Prix de France

6 July 1986. Paul Ricard. 80 laps of a 2.369-mile circuit =
189.520 miles. Warm, dry and sunny. World Championship
round 8

1 Nigel Mansell	Williams FW11-Honda	80	1h37m19.272
2 Alain Prost	McLaren MP4/2C- TAG Porsche	80	1h37m36.400
3 Nelson Piquet	Williams FW11-Honda	80	1h37m56.817
4 Keke Rosberg	McLaren MP4/2C- TAG Porsche	80	1h38m07.975
5 René Arnoux	Ligier JS27-Renault	79	
6 Jacques Laffite	Ligier JS27-Renault	79	

Winner's average speed: 116.842 mph. Starting grid front row:
Senna, 1m06.526 (pole) and Mansell, 1m06.755. Fastest lap:
Mansell, 1m09.993. Leaders: Mansell, laps 1-25, 37-53, 59-80;
Prost, 26-36, 54-58

Shell Oils British Grand Prix

13 July 1986. Brands Hatch. 75 laps of a 2.614-mile circuit =
196.020 miles. Race stopped due to accident on lap 1.
Restarted over original distance. Warm, dry and sunny.
World Championship round 9

1 Nigel Mansell	Williams FW11-Honda	75	1h30m38.471
2 Nelson Piquet	Williams FW11-Honda	75	1h30m44.045
3 Alain Prost	McLaren MP4/2C- TAG Porsche	74	
4 René Arnoux	Ligier JS27-Renault	73	
5 Martin Brundle	Tyrrell 015-Renault	72	
6 Philippe Streiff	Tyrrell 015-Renault	72	

Winner's average speed: 129.756 mph. Starting grid front row:
Piquet, 1m06.961 (pole) and Mansell, 1m07.399. Fastest lap:
Mansell, 1m09.593. Leaders: Piquet, laps 1-22; Mansell, 23-75

Grosser Preis von Deutschland

27 July 1986. Hockenheim. 44 laps of a 4.224-mile circuit =
185.838 miles. Hot, dry and sunny. World Championship
round 10

1 Nelson Piquet	Williams FW11-Honda	44	1h22m08.263
2 Ayrton Senna	Lotus 98T-Renault	44	1h22m23.700
3 Nigel Mansell	Williams FW11-Honda	44	1h22m52.843
4 René Arnoux	Ligier JS27-Renault	44	1h23m23.439
5 Keke Rosberg	McLaren MP4/2C- TAG Porsche	43	out of fuel

1986 DRIVERS' RECORDS

Driver	Car	Brazilian GP	Spanish GP	San Marino GP	Monaco GP	Belgian GP	Canadian GP	Detroit GP	French GP	British GP	German GP	Hungarian GP	Austrian GP	Italian GP	Portuguese GP	Mexican GP	Australian GP
Michele Alboreto	Ferrari F186	R	R	10	R	4	8	4	8	R	R	R	2	R	5	R	R
Philippe Alliot	Ligier JS27-Renault	-	-	-	-	-	-	-	-	-	R	9	R	R	R	6	8
Elio de Angelis	Brabham BT55-BMW	8	R	R	R	R	-	-	-	-	-	-	-	-	-	-	-
René Arnoux	Ligier JS27-Renault	4	R	R	5	R	6	R	5	4	4	R	10	R	7	15	7
Allen Berg	Osella FA1F-Alfa Romeo	-	-	-	-	-	-	R	-	-	12	R	R	-	13	16	NC
	Osella FA1G-Alfa Romeo	-	-	-	-	-	-	R	-	-	-	-	-	-	-	-	-
	Osella FA1H-Alfa Romeo	-	-	-	-	-	-	-	R	-	-	-	-	-	-	-	-
Gerhard Berger	Benetton B186-BMW	6	6	3	R	10	R	R	R	R	10[F]	R	7[F]	5	R	1	R
Thierry Boutsen	Arrows A8-BMW	R	7	7	8	R	R	R	NC	NC	-	R	-	7	10	7	R
	Arrows A9-BMW	-	-	-	-	-	-	-	-	-	R	-	R	-	-	-	-
Martin Brundle	Tyrrell 014-Renault	5	R	8	-	-	-	-	-	-	-	-	-	-	-	-	-
	Tyrrell 015-Renault	-	-	-	R	R	9	R	10	5	R	6	R	10	R	11	4
Alex Caffi	Osella FA1F-Alfa Romeo	-	-	-	-	-	-	-	-	-	-	-	-	-	NC	-	-
Ivan Capelli	AGS JH21C-Motori Moderni	-	-	-	-	-	-	-	-	-	-	-	-	R	R	-	-
Andrea de Cesaris	Minardi M185B-Motori Moderni	R	R	R	DNQ	R	R	R	R	R	R	R	-	-	-	-	-
	Minardi M186-Motori Moderni	-	-	-	-	-	-	-	-	-	-	R	-	R	R	8	R
Eddie Cheever	Lola THL2-Ford	-	-	-	-	-	-	R	-	-	-	-	-	-	-	-	-
Christian Danner	Osella FA1F-Alfa Romeo	R	R	R	DNQ	R	R	-	-	-	-	-	-	-	-	-	-
	Arrows A8-BMW	-	-	-	-	-	R	11	R	R	-	6	8	11	9	R	
	Arrows A9-BMW	-	-	-	-	-	-	-	-	-	R	-	-	-	-	-	-
Johnny Dumfries	Lotus 98T-Renault	9	R	R	DNQ	R	R	7	R	7	R	5	R	R	9	R	6
Teo Fabi	Benetton B186-BMW	10	5	R	R	7	R	R	R	R	R	R	R[P]	R[PF]	8	R	10
Piercarlo Ghinzani	Osella FA1G-Alfa Romeo	R	R	R	DNQ	R	R	R	-	R	R	R	11	R	R	R	R
	Osella FA1H-Alfa Romeo	-	-	-	-	-	-	-	R	-	-	-	-	-	-	-	-
Stefan Johansson	Ferrari F186	R	R	4	10	3	R	R	R	R	11	4	3	3	6	12	3
Alan Jones	Lola THL1-Hart	R	R	-	-	-	-	-	-	-	-	-	-	-	-	-	-
	Lola THL2-Ford	-	-	-	R	R	11	10	R	R	R	9	R	4	6	R	R
Jacques Laffite	Ligier JS27-Renault	3	R	R	6	5	7	2	6	R	-	-	-	-	-	-	-
Nigel Mansell	Williams FW11-Honda	R	2[F]	R	4	1	1[P]	5	1[F]	1[F]	3	3	R	2	1[F]	5	R[P]
Alessandro Nannini	Minardi M185B-Motori Moderni	R	DNS	R	DNQ	R	R	R	R	R	R	R	-	R	R	14	R
	Minardi M186-Motori Moderni	-	-	-	-	-	-	-	-	-	-	-	R	-	-	-	-
Jonathan Palmer	Zakspeed 861	R	R	R	12	13	R	8	R	9	R	10	R	R	12	10	9
Riccardo Patrese	Brabham BT55-BMW	R	R	6	R	8	R	6	7	-	R	R	R	R	R	13	R
	Brabham BT54-BMW	-	-	-	-	-	-	-	-	R	-	-	-	-	-	-	-
Nelson Piquet	Williams FW11-Honda	1[F]	R	2[F]	7	R[P]	3[F]	R[F]	3	2[P]	1	1[F]	R	1	3	4[F]	2[F]
Alain Prost	McLaren MP4/2C-TAG Porsche	R	3	1	1[PF]	6[F]	2	3	2	3	6	R	1	R	2	2	1
Keke Rosberg	McLaren MP4/2C-TAG Porsche	R	4	5	2	R	4	R	4	R	5[P]	R	9	4	R	R	R
Huub Rothengatter	Zakspeed 861	-	-	R	DNQ	R	12	DNS	R	R	R	R	R	8	R	DNS	R
Ayrton Senna	Lotus 98T-Renault	2[P]	1[P]	R[P]	3	2	5	1[P]	R[P]	R	2	2[P]	R	R	4[P]	3[P]	R
Philippe Streiff	Tyrrell 014-Renault	7	R	R	-	-	11	-	-	-	-	-	-	-	-	-	-
	Tyrrell 015-Renault	-	-	-	11	12	-	9	R	6	R	8	R	9	R	R	5
Marc Surer	Arrows A8-BMW	R	R	9	9	9	-	-	-	-	-	-	-	-	-	-	-
Patrick Tambay	Lola THL1-Hart	R	8	R	-	-	-	-	-	-	-	-	-	-	-	-	-
	Lola THL2-Ford	-	-	-	R	R	DNS	-	R	R	8	7	5	R	NC	R	NC
Derek Warwick	Brabham BT55-BMW	-	-	-	-	-	R	10	9	8	7	R	DNS	R	R	R	R

6 Alain Prost	McLaren MP4/2C-TAG Porsche	43	out of fuel

Winner's average speed: 135.751 mph. Starting grid front row: Rosberg, 1m42.013 (pole) and Prost, 1m42.166. Fastest lap: Berger, 1m46.604. Leaders: Senna, lap 1; Rosberg, laps 2-5, 15-19, 28-38; Piquet, 6-14, 21-27, 39-44; Prost, 20

Magyar Nagydij (Hungarian Grand Prix)

10 August 1986. Hungaroring. 76 laps of a 2.494-mile circuit = 189.544 miles. Race scheduled for 77 laps, stopped due to two hour rule. Hot, dry and sunny. World Championship round 11

1 Nelson Piquet	Williams FW11-Honda	76 2h00m34.508
2 Ayrton Senna	Lotus 98T-Renault	76 2h00m52.181
3 Nigel Mansell	Williams FW11-Honda	75
4 Stefan Johansson	Ferrari F186	75
5 Johnny Dumfries	Lotus 98T-Renault	74
6 Martin Brundle	Tyrrell 015-Renault	74

Winner's average speed: 94.320 mph. Starting grid front row: Senna, 1m29.450 (pole) and Piquet, 1m29.785. Fastest lap: Piquet, 1m31.001. Leaders: Senna, laps 1-11, 36-56; Piquet, 12-35, 57-76

Grosser Preis von Österreich

17 August 1986. Österreichring. 52 laps of a 3.692-mile circuit = 191.984 miles. Hot, dry and sunny. World Championship round 12

1 Alain Prost	McLaren MP4/2C-TAG Porsche	52 1h21m22.531
2 Michele Alboreto	Ferrari F186	51
3 Stefan Johansson	Ferrari F186	50
4 Alan Jones	Lola THL2-Ford	50
5 Patrick Tambay	Lola THL2-Ford	50
6 Christian Danner	Arrows A8-BMW	49

Winner's average speed: 141.554 mph. Starting grid front row: Fabi, 1m23.549 (pole) and Berger, 1m23.743. Fastest lap: Berger, 1m29.444. Leaders: Berger, laps 1-25; Mansell, 26-28; Prost, 29-52

Gran Premio d'Italia

7 September 1986. Monza. 51 laps of a 3.604-mile circuit = 183.799 miles. Hot, dry and sunny. World Championship round 13

1 Nelson Piquet	Williams FW11-Honda	51 1h17m42.889
2 Nigel Mansell	Williams FW11-Honda	51 1h17m52.717
3 Stefan Johansson	Ferrari F186	51 1h18m05.804
4 Keke Rosberg	McLaren MP4/2C-TAG Porsche	51 1h18m36.698
5 Gerhard Berger	Benetton B186-BMW	50
6 Alan Jones	Lola THL2-Ford	49

Winner's average speed: 141.903 mph. Starting grid front row: Fabi, 1m24.078 (pole) and Prost, 1m24.514 - Fabi started from the back of the grid, Prost from the pit lane. Fastest lap: Fabi, 1m28.099. Leaders: Berger, laps 1-6, 25-26; Mansell, 7-24, 27-37; Piquet, 38-51

Grande Premio de Portugal

21 September 1986. Estoril. 70 laps of a 2.703-mile circuit = 189.210 miles. Hot, dry and sunny. World Championship round 14

1 Nigel Mansell	Williams FW11-Honda	70 1h37m21.900
2 Alain Prost	McLaren MP4/2C-TAG Porsche	70 1h37m40.672
3 Nelson Piquet	Williams FW11-Honda	70 1h38m11.174
4 Ayrton Senna	Lotus 98T-Renault	69
5 Michele Alboreto	Ferrari F186	69
6 Stefan Johansson	Ferrari F186	69

Winner's average speed: 116.598 mph. Starting grid front row: Senna, 1m16.673 (pole) and Mansell, 1m17.489. Fastest lap: Mansell, 1m20.943. Leaders: Mansell, laps 1-70

Gran Premio de Mexico

12 October 1986. Mexico City. 68 laps of a 2.747-mile circuit = 186.796 miles. Hot, dry and humid. World Championship round 15

1 Gerhard Berger	Benetton B186-BMW	68 1h33m18.700
2 Alain Prost	McLaren MP4/2C-TAG Porsche	68 1h33m44.138
3 Ayrton Senna	Lotus 98T-Renault	68 1h34m11.213
4 Nelson Piquet	Williams FW11-Honda	67
5 Nigel Mansell	Williams FW11-Honda	67
6 Philippe Alliot	Ligier JS27-Renault	67

Winner's average speed: 120.111 mph. Starting grid front row: Senna, 1m16.990 (pole) and Piquet, 1m17.279. Fastest lap: Piquet, 1m19.360. Leaders: Piquet, laps 1-31; Senna, 32-35; Berger, 36-68

Foster's Australian Grand Prix

26 October 1986. Adelaide. 82 laps of a 2.347-mile circuit = 192.454 miles. Warm, dry and sunny. World Championship round 16

1 Alain Prost	McLaren MP4/2C-TAG Porsche	82 1h54m20.388	
2 Nelson Piquet	Williams FW11-Honda	82 1h54m24.593	
3 Stefan Johansson	Ferrari F186	81	
4 Martin Brundle	Tyrrell 015-Renault	81	
5 Philippe Streiff	Tyrrell 015-Renault	80	out of fuel
6 Johnny Dumfries	Lotus 98T-Renault	80	

Winner's average speed: 100.991 mph. Starting grid front row: Mansell, 1m18.403 (pole) and Piquet, 1m18.714. Fastest lap: Piquet, 1m20.787. Leaders: Piquet, laps 1-6, 63-64; Rosberg, 7-62; Prost, 65-82

1986 FINAL CHAMPIONSHIP POSITIONS

Drivers						Manufacturers	
1	Alain Prost	72 (74)*	11	Martin Brundle	8	1 Williams-Honda	135
2	Nigel Mansell	70 (72)*	12	Alan Jones	4	2 McLaren-TAG Porsche	87
3	Nelson Piquet	69	13	Johnny Dumfries	3	3 Lotus-Renault	57
4	Ayrton Senna	55	13	Philippe Streiff	3	4 Ferrari	33
5	Stefan Johansson	23	15=	Teo Fabi	2	5 Ligier-Renault	29
6	Keke Rosberg	22		Riccardo Patrese	2	6 Benetton-BMW	19
7	Gerhard Berger	17		Patrick Tambay	2	7= Tyrrell-Renault	6
8=	Michele Alboreto	14	18=	Philippe Alliot	1	Lola-Ford	6
	René Arnoux	14		Christian Danner	1	9 Brabham-BMW	2
	Jacques Laffite	14		*Best 11 results count		10 Arrows-BMW	1

1987

For the second successive season, Nigel Mansell failed to win the World Championship, again in dramatic fashion. He recorded more wins (six) and more pole positions (eight) than any of his rivals, an accurate reflection of his dominance. However, Nelson Piquet finished in the points more often, so when Mansell was injured in a spectacular practice accident in Japan, a third World Championship was confirmed for the Brazilian.

The year had started badly for Piquet, with a huge practice accident at Tamburello preventing him from starting at Imola. However, a run of podium finishes plus lucky wins in Germany and Hungary followed by a more convincing display at Monza gave him an unassailable lead.

In retrospect, the highlight for Mansell came at Silverstone where he came from 28 seconds behind Piquet to snatch a famous victory from his team-mate with a breathtaking manoeuvre into Stowe.

McLaren used the TAG Porsche engine for a final season, but suffered as development of the unit slowed. Alain Prost was still able to win three times, including a brilliant victory in Portugal to score his record-breaking 28th Grand Prix success.

Gerhard Berger, in his first year with Ferrari, almost won at Estoril, spinning out of the lead three laps from the finish while under pressure from Prost. But Berger fulfilled his promise by winning the final two Grands Prix of the year, raising hopes of a championship challenge in 1988.

Ayrton Senna scored the first victories for the Lotus active (computer controlled) suspension system in Monaco and Detroit, but the team was unable to give him consistently competitive machinery, despite having switched to Honda power. Senna announced he would be moving to McLaren at the end of the year, and Lotus has not won since.

The Austrian GP was held at the magnificent Österreichring for the last time. After two start-line accidents had forced the race to be stopped, questions over the narrowness of the starting straight and the circuit's distance from a major city, meant that a classic venue was lost to Grand Prix racing in 1988.

Grande Premio do Brasil

12 April 1987. Rio de Janeiro. 61 laps of a 3.126-mile circuit = 190.686 miles. Hot and dry. World Championship round 1

1 Alain Prost	McLaren MP4/3-TAG Porsche	61 1h39m45.141
2 Nelson Piquet	Williams FW11B-Honda	61 1h40m25.688
3 Stefan Johansson	McLaren MP4/3-TAG Porsche	61 1h40m41.899
4 Gerhard Berger	Ferrari F187	61 1h41m24.376
5 Thierry Boutsen	Benetton B187-Ford	60
6 Nigel Mansell	Williams FW11B-Honda	60

Winner's average speed: 114.696 mph. Starting grid front row: Mansell, 1m26.128 (pole) and Piquet, 1m26.567. Fastest lap: Piquet, 1m33.861. Leaders: Piquet, laps 1-7, 17-20; Senna, 8-12; Prost, 13-16, 21-61

Gran Premio di San Marino

3 May 1987. Imola. 59 laps of a 3.132-mile circuit = 184.788 miles. Warm and dry. World Championship round 2

1 Nigel Mansell	Williams FW11B-Honda	59 1h31m24.076
2 Ayrton Senna	Lotus 99T-Honda	59 1h31m51.621
3 Michele Alboreto	Ferrari F187	59 1h32m03.220
4 Stefan Johansson	McLaren MP4/3-TAG Porsche	59 1h32m24.664
5 Martin Brundle	Zakspeed 871	57
6 Satoru Nakajima	Lotus 99T-Honda	57

Winner's average speed: 121.303 mph. Starting grid front row: Senna, 1m25.826 (pole) and Mansell, 1m25.946. Fastest lap: Fabi, 1m29.246. Leaders: Senna, laps 1, 25-26; Mansell, 2-21, 27-59; Alboreto, 22-24

Grand Prix de Belgique

17 May 1987. Spa-Francorchamps. 43 laps of a 4.312-mile circuit = 185.416 miles. Race stopped after one lap, restarted over original distance. Cool, dry and cloudy. World Championship round 3

| 1 Alain Prost | McLaren MP4/3-TAG Porsche | 43 1h27m03.217 |
| 2 Stefan Johansson | McLaren MP4/3-TAG Porsche | 43 1h27m27.981 |

1987 DRIVERS' RECORDS

Driver	Car	Brazilian GP	San Marino GP	Belgian GP	Monaco GP	Detroit GP	French GP	British GP	German GP	Hungarian GP	Austrian GP	Italian GP	Portuguese GP	Spanish GP	Mexican GP	Japanese GP	Australian GP
Michele Alboreto	Ferrari F187	8	3	R	3	R	R	R	R	R	R	R	R	15	R	4	2
Philippe Alliot	Lola LC87-Ford	-	10	8	R	R	R	R	6	R	12	R	R	6	6	R	R
René Arnoux	Ligier JS29B-Megatron BMW	-	DNS	6	11	10	-	-	-	-	-	-	-	-	-	-	-
	Ligier JS29C-Megatron BMW	-	-	-	-	-	R	R	R	R	10	10	R	R	R	R	R
Gerhard Berger	Ferrari F187	4	R	R	4	4	R	R	R	R	R	4	2PF	RF	R	1P	1PF
Thierry Boutsen	Benetton B187-Ford	5	R	R	R	R	R	7	R	4	4	5	14	16	R	5	3
Martin Brundle	Zakspeed 861	R	-	-	-	R	-	-	-	-	-	-	-	-	-	-	-
	Zakspeed 871	-	5	R	7	-	R	NC	NC	R	DSQ	R	R	11	R	R	R
Alex Caffi	Osella FA1I-Alfa Romeo	R	12	R	R	R	R	R	R	R	R	R	R	DNQ	R	R	DNQ
Adrian Campos	Minardi M187-Motori Moderni	R	R	R	DNS	R	R	R	R	R	R	R	R	14	R	R	R
Ivan Capelli	March 87P-Ford	DNS	-	-	-	-	-	-	-	-	-	-	-	-	-	-	-
	March 871-Ford	-	R	R	6	R	R	R	R	10	11	13	9	12	R	R	R
Andrea de Cesaris	Brabham BT56-BMW	R	R	3	R	R	R	R	R	R	R	R	R	R	R	R	8
Eddie Cheever	Arrows A10-Megatron BMW	R	R	4	R	6	R	R	R	8	R	R	6	8	4	9	R
Yannick Dalmas	Lola LC87-Ford	-	-	-	-	-	-	-	-	-	-	-	-	-	9	14	5
Christian Danner	Zakspeed 861	9	7	-	-	-	-	-	-	-	-	-	-	-	-	-	-
	Zakspeed 871	-	-	R	DNQ	8	R	R	R	R	9	9	R	R	R	R	7
Teo Fabi	Benetton B187-Ford	R	RF	R	8	R	5	6	R	R	3	7	4	R	5	R	R
Pascal Fabre	AGS JH22-Ford	12	13	10	13	12	9	9	R	13	NC	DNQ	DNQ	R	DNQ	-	-
Franco Forini	Osella FA1I-Alfa Romeo	-	-	-	-	-	-	-	-	-	-	R	R	DNQ	-	-	-
Piercarlo Ghinzani	Ligier JS29B-Megatron BMW	-	R	7	12	NC	-	-	-	-	-	-	-	-	-	-	-
	Ligier JS29C-Megatron BMW	-	-	-	-	-	R	DNQ	R	12	8	8	R	R	R	13	R
Stefan Johansson	McLaren MP4/3-TAG Porsche	3	4	2	R	7	8	R	2	R	7	6	5	3	R	3	R
Nicola Larini	Coloni FC187-Ford	-	-	-	-	-	-	-	-	-	-	-	DNQ	-	R	-	-
Nigel Mansell	Williams FW11B-Honda	6P	1	RP	RP	5P	1P	1F	RPF	14P	1F	3	R	1	1P	DNS	-
Stefano Modena	Brabham BT56-BMW	-	-	-	-	-	-	-	-	-	-	-	-	-	-	-	R
Roberto Moreno	AGS JH22-Ford	-	-	-	-	-	-	-	-	-	-	-	-	-	-	R	6
Satoru Nakajima	Lotus 99T-Honda	7	6	5	10	R	NC	4	R	R	13	11	8	9	R	6	R
Alessandro Nannini	Minardi M187-Motori Moderni	R	R	R	R	R	R	R	R	11	R	16	11	R	R	R	R
Jonathan Palmer	Tyrrell 016-Ford	10	R	R	5	11	7	8	5	7	14	14	10	R	7	8	4
Riccardo Patrese	Brabham BT56-BMW	R	9	R	R	9	R	R	R	5	R	R	R	13	3	11	-
	Williams FW11B-Honda	-	-	-	-	-	-	-	-	-	-	-	-	-	-	-	9
Nelson Piquet	Williams FW11B-Honda	2F	DNS	R	2	2	2F	2P	1	1F	2P	1P	3	4P	2F	15	R
Alain Prost	McLaren MP4/3-TAG Porsche	1	R	1F	9	3	3	R	7	3	6	15	1	2	R	7F	R
Ayrton Senna	Lotus 99T-Honda	R	2P	R	1F	1F	4	3	3	2	5	2F	7	5	R	2	DSQ
Philippe Streiff	Tyrrell 016-Ford	11	8	9	R	R	6	R	4	9	R	12	12	7	8	12	R
Gabriele Tarquini	Osella FA1H-Alfa Romeo	-	R	-	-	-	-	-	-	-	-	-	-	-	-	-	-
Derek Warwick	Arrows A10-Megatron BMW	R	11	R	R	R	R	5	R	6	R	R	13	10	R	10	R

3 Andrea de Cesaris	Brabham BT56-BMW	42	out of fuel
4 Eddie Cheever	Arrows A10-Megatron BMW	42	
5 Satoru Nakajima	Lotus 99T-Honda	42	
6 René Arnoux	Ligier JS29B-Megatron BMW	41	

Winner's average speed: 127.794 mph. Starting grid front row: Mansell, 1m52.026 (pole) and Piquet, 1m53.416. Fastest lap: Prost, 1m57.153. Leaders: Piquet, laps 1-9; Prost, 10-43.

Grand Prix de Monaco

31 May 1987. Monte Carlo. 78 laps of a 2.068-mile circuit = 161.304 miles. Warm, dry and sunny. World Championship round 4

1 Ayrton Senna	Lotus 99T-Honda	78 1h57m54.085
2 Nelson Piquet	Williams FW11B-Honda	78 1h58m27.297
3 Michele Alboreto	Ferrari F187	78 1h59m06.924
4 Gerhard Berger	Ferrari F187	77
5 Jonathan Palmer	Tyrrell 016-Ford	76
6 Ivan Capelli	March 871-Ford	76

Winner's average speed: 82.088 mph. Starting grid front row: Mansell, 1m23.039 (pole) and Senna, 1m23.711. Fastest lap: Senna, 1m27.685. Leaders: Mansell, laps 1-29; Senna, 30-78.

Detroit Grand Prix

21 June 1987. Detroit. 63 laps of a 2.500-mile circuit = 157.500 miles. Warm, dry and humid. World Championship round 5

1 Ayrton Senna	Lotus 99T-Honda	63 1h50m16.358
2 Nelson Piquet	Williams FW11B-Honda	63 1h50m50.177
3 Alain Prost	McLaren MP4/3-TAG Porsche	63 1h51m01.685
4 Gerhard Berger	Ferrari F187	63 1h51m18.959
5 Nigel Mansell	Williams FW11B-Honda	62
6 Eddie Cheever	Arrows A10-Megatron BMW	60 out of fuel

Winner's average speed: 85.697 mph. Starting grid front row: Mansell, 1m39.264 (pole) and Senna, 1m40.607. Fastest lap: Senna, 1m40.464. Leaders: Mansell, laps 1-33; Senna, 34-63.

Grand Prix de France

5 July 1987. Paul Ricard. 80 laps of a 2.369-mile circuit = 189.520 miles. Hot, dry and sunny. World Championship round 6

1 Nigel Mansell	Williams FW11B-Honda	80 1h37m03.839
2 Nelson Piquet	Williams FW11B-Honda	80 1h37m11.550
3 Alain Prost	McLaren MP4/3-TAG Porsche	80 1h37m59.094
4 Ayrton Senna	Lotus 99T-Honda	79
5 Teo Fabi	Benetton B187-Ford	77 driveshaft
6 Philippe Streiff	Tyrrell 016-Ford	76

Winner's average speed: 117.152 mph. Starting grid front row: Mansell, 1m06.454 (pole) and Prost, 1m06.877. Fastest lap: Piquet, 1m09.548. Leaders: Mansell, laps 1-35, 46-80; Piquet, 36-45.

Shell Oils British Grand Prix

12 July 1987. Silverstone. 65 laps of a 2.969-mile circuit = 192.985 miles. Warm, dry and sunny. World Championship round 7

1 Nigel Mansell	Williams FW11B-Honda	65 1h19m11.780
2 Nelson Piquet	Williams FW11B-Honda	65 1h19m13.698
3 Ayrton Senna	Lotus 99T-Honda	64
4 Satoru Nakajima	Lotus 99T-Honda	63
5 Derek Warwick	Arrows A10-Megatron BMW	63
6 Teo Fabi	Benetton B187-Ford	63

Winner's average speed: 146.208 mph. Starting grid front row: Piquet, 1m07.110 (pole) and Mansell, 1m07.180. Fastest lap: Mansell, 1m09.832. Leaders: Piquet, laps 1-62; Mansell, 63-65.

Grosser Preis von Deutschland

26 July 1987. Hockenheim. 44 laps of a 4.224-mile circuit = 185.856 miles. Warm, dry and sunny. World Championship round 8

1 Nelson Piquet	Williams FW11B-Honda	44 1h21m25.091
2 Stefan Johansson	McLaren MP4/3-TAG Porsche	44 1h23m04.682
3 Ayrton Senna	Lotus 99T-Honda	43
4 Philippe Streiff	Tyrrell 016-Ford	43
5 Jonathan Palmer	Tyrrell 016-Ford	43
6 Philippe Alliot	Lola LC87-Ford	42

Winner's average speed: 136.951 mph. Starting grid front row: Mansell, 1m42.616 (pole) and Senna, 1m42.873. Fastest lap: Mansell, 1m45.716. Leaders: Senna, lap 1; Mansell, laps 2-7, 19-22; Prost, 8-18, 23-39; Piquet, 40-44.

Eleven podium finishes (including here at Monaco) gave Nelson Piquet a third World Championsip

Magyar Nagydij (Hungarian Grand Prix)

9 August 1987. Hungaroring. 76 laps of a 2.494-mile circuit = 189.544 miles. Hot, dry and sunny. World Championship round 9

1 Nelson Piquet	Williams FW11B-Honda	76 1h59m26.793
2 Ayrton Senna	Lotus 99T-Honda	76 2h00m04.520
3 Alain Prost	McLaren MP4/3-TAG Porsche	76 2h00m54.249
4 Thierry Boutsen	Benetton B187-Ford	75
5 Riccardo Patrese	Brabham BT56-BMW	75
6 Derek Warwick	Arrows A10-Megatron BMW	74

Winner's average speed: 95.211 mph. Starting grid front row: Mansell, 1m28.047 (pole) and Berger, 1m28.549. Fastest lap: Piquet, 1m30.149. Leaders: Mansell, laps 1-70; Piquet, 71-76.

Grosser Preis von Österreich

16 August 1987. Österreichring. 52 laps of a 3.692-mile circuit = 191.984 miles. Race stopped twice by startline accidents. Restarted over original distance. Hot and dry. World Championship round 10

1 Nigel Mansell	Williams FW11B-Honda	52 1h18m44.898
2 Nelson Piquet	Williams FW11B-Honda	52 1h19m40.602
3 Teo Fabi	Benetton B187-Ford	51
4 Thierry Boutsen	Benetton B187-Ford	51
5 Ayrton Senna	Lotus 99T-Honda	50
6 Alain Prost	McLaren MP4/3-TAG Porsche	50

Winner's average speed: 146.277 mph. Starting grid front row: Piquet, 1m23.357 (pole) and Mansell, 1m23.459. Fastest lap: Mansell, 1m28.318. Leaders: Piquet, laps 1-20; Mansell, 21-52.

Gran Premio d'Italia

6 September 1987. Monza. 50 laps of a 3.604-mile circuit = 180.200 miles. Hot, dry and sunny. World Championship round 11

1 Nelson Piquet	Williams FW11B-Honda	50 1h14m47.707
2 Ayrton Senna	Lotus 99T-Honda	50 1h14m49.513
3 Nigel Mansell	Williams FW11B-Honda	50 1h15m36.743
4 Gerhard Berger	Ferrari F187	50 1h15m45.686
5 Thierry Boutsen	Benetton B187-Ford	50 1h16m09.026
6 Stefan Johansson	McLaren MP4/3-TAG Porsche	50 1h16m16.494

Winner's average speed: 144.551 mph. Starting grid front row: Piquet, 1m23.460 (pole) and Mansell, 1m23.559. Fastest lap: Senna, 1m26.796. Leaders: Piquet, laps 1-23, 43-50; Senna, 24-42

Grande Premio de Portugal

20 September 1987. Estoril. 70 laps of a 2.703-mile circuit = 189.210 miles. Race stopped after 1 lap, restarted over original distance. Hot, dry and sunny. World Championship round 12

1 Alain Prost	McLaren MP4/3-TAG Porsche	70	1h37m03.906
2 Gerhard Berger	Ferrari F187	70	1h37m24.399
3 Nelson Piquet	Williams FW11B-Honda	70	1h38m07.210
4 Teo Fabi	Benetton B187-Ford	69	out of fuel
5 Stefan Johansson	McLaren MP4/3-TAG Porsche	69	
6 Eddie Cheever	Arrows A10-Megatron BMW	68	

Winner's average speed: 116.959 mph. Starting grid front row: Berger, 1m17.620 (pole) and Mansell, 1m17.951. Fastest lap: Berger, 1m19.282. Leaders: Mansell, lap 1; Berger, laps 2-33, 36-67; Alboreto, 34-35; Prost, 68-70

Gran Premio Tio Pepe de Espana

27 September 1987. Jerez. 72 laps of a 2.621-mile circuit = 188.712 miles. Hot, dry and sunny. World Championship round 13

1 Nigel Mansell	Williams FW11B-Honda	72	1h49m12.692
2 Alain Prost	McLaren MP4/3-TAG Porsche	72	1h49m34.917
3 Stefan Johansson	McLaren MP4/3-TAG Porsche	72	1h49m43.510
4 Nelson Piquet	Williams FW11B-Honda	72	1h49m44.142
5 Ayrton Senna	Lotus 99T-Honda	72	1h50m26.199
6 Philippe Alliot	Lola LC87-Ford	71	

Winner's average speed: 103.673 mph. Starting grid front row: Piquet, 1m22.461 (pole) and Mansell, 1m23.081. Fastest lap: Berger, 1m26.986. Leaders: Mansell, laps 1-72

Gran Premio de Mexico

18 October 1987. Mexico City. 63 laps of a 2.747-mile circuit = 173.061 miles. Race scheduled for 68 laps, stopped after 31 laps due to an accident. Restarted over 31 laps. Hot, dry and sunny. World Championship round 14

1 Nigel Mansell	Williams FW11B-Honda	63	1h26m24.207
2 Nelson Piquet	Williams FW11B-Honda	63	1h26m50.383
3 Riccardo Patrese	Brabham BT56-BMW	63	1h27m51.086
4 Eddie Cheever	Arrows A10-Megatron BMW	63	1h28m05.559
5 Teo Fabi	Benetton B187-Ford	61	
6 Philippe Alliot	Lola LC87-Ford	60	

Winner's average speed: 120.176 mph. Starting grid front row: Mansell, 1m18.383 (pole) and Berger, 1m18.426. Fastest lap: Piquet, 1m19.132. Leaders: Berger, laps 1, 15-20; Boutsen, 2-14; Mansell, 21-63

Fuji Television Japanese Grand Prix

1 November 1987. Suzuka. 51 laps of a 3.641-mile circuit = 185.691 miles. Cool, dry and cloudy. World Championship round 15

1 Gerhard Berger	Ferrari F187	51	1h32m58.072
2 Ayrton Senna	Lotus 99T-Honda	51	1h33m15.456
3 Stefan Johansson	McLaren MP4/3-TAG Porsche	51	1h33m15.766
4 Michele Alboreto	Ferrari F187	51	1h34m18.513
5 Thierry Boutsen	Benetton B187-Ford	51	1h34m23.648
6 Satoru Nakajima	Lotus 99T-Honda	51	1h34m34.551

Winner's average speed: 119.842 mph. Starting grid front row: Berger, 1m40.042 (pole) and Prost, 1m40.652. Fastest lap: Prost, 1m43.844. Leaders: Berger, laps 1-24, 26-51; Senna, 25

Foster's Australian Grand Prix

15 November 1987. Adelaide. 82 laps of a 2.347-mile circuit = 192.454 miles. Hot, dry and sunny. World Championship round 16

1 Gerhard Berger	Ferrari F187	82	1h52m56.144
2 Michele Alboreto	Ferrari F187	82	1h54m04.028
3 Thierry Boutsen	Benetton B187-Ford	81	
4 Jonathan Palmer	Tyrrell 016-Ford	80	
5 Yannick Dalmas*	Lola LC87-Ford	79	
6 Roberto Moreno	AGS JH22-Ford	79	

Senna (Lotus 99T-Honda) finished second on the road but was disqualified for his car having oversized brake ducts. *Not entered in World Championship, no points awarded. Winner's average speed: 102.246 mph. Starting grid front row: Berger, 1m17.267 (pole) and Prost, 1m17.967. Fastest lap: Berger, 1m20.416. Leaders: Berger, laps 1-82

1987 FINAL CHAMPIONSHIP POSITIONS

Drivers					Manufacturers	
1	Nelson Piquet	73 (76)*	14=	Andrea de Cesaris	4	1 Williams-Honda	137
2	Nigel Mansell	61		Philippe Streiff	4	2 McLaren-TAG Porsche	76
3	Ayrton Senna	57	16=	Philippe Alliot	3	3 Lotus-Honda	64
4	Alain Prost	46		Derek Warwick	3	4 Ferrari	53
5	Gerhard Berger	36	18	Martin Brundle	2	5 Benetton-Ford	28
6	Stefan Johansson	30	19=	René Arnoux	1	6= Arrows-Megatron BMW	11
7	Michele Alboreto	17		Ivan Capelli	1	Tyrrell-Ford	11
8	Thierry Boutsen	16		Roberto Moreno	1	8 Brabham-BMW	10
9	Teo Fabi	12		*Best 11 results count		9 Lola-Ford	3
10	Eddie Cheever	8				10 Zakspeed	2
11=	Satoru Nakajima	7				11= Ligier-Megatron BMW	1
	Jonathan Palmer	7				March-Ford	1
13	Riccardo Patrese	6				AGS-Ford	1

1988

No team had dominated Grand Prix racing in the way McLaren did in 1988 since the days of Ascari and Ferrari. The team won all but one Grand Prix, only losing at Monza when Ayrton Senna clashed with Jean-Louis Schlesser (standing in at Williams for an ill Nigel Mansell) while lapping him two laps from victory.

Senna joined Alain Prost at McLaren, starting a now legendary all-consuming rivalry between two of the greatest Grand Prix drivers of all time. Their battle for the World Championship was epic, finally resolved by a brilliant Senna recovery at the Japanese GP. Having stalled at the start the Brazilian raced through the field to win.

In the final year of the turbocharger in F1 before the reintroduction of normally aspirated engines, other manufacturers concentrated on developing for the future - but Honda continued to improve its current unit. The low-line McLaren MP4/4-Honda was all-conquering.

Nelson Piquet moved to Lotus-Honda but disappointed, never finishing higher than third. Honda's decision to supply McLaren and Lotus's acceptance of Satoru Nakajima as Piquet's team-mate resulted in Williams losing Honda engines. Before a new long-term partner could be found, Williams used Judd normally aspirated engines. Nigel Mansell's impressive displays at a wet Silverstone and at Jerez resulted in second place finishes, but the British driver decided to move to Ferrari for 1989.

At Monza, the first Italian Grand Prix since the death of Enzo Ferrari, Senna's misfortune handed victory to the turbocharged Ferraris of Gerhard Berger and Michele Alboreto. However, it was small consolation for the pre-season favourite who had been so comprehensively beaten by McLaren.

Apart from Mansell, there were a number of other teams and drivers making their mark in the normally aspirated ranks. Alessandro Nannini joined Thierry Boutsen at Benetton and the pair were consistent points scorers, five podium finishes giving Boutsen fourth position in the championship. Ivan Capelli also impressed in the nimble Leyton House March, finishing second in Portugal and briefly leading in Japan.

Grande Premio do Brasil

3 April 1988. Rio de Janeiro. 60 laps of a 3.126-mile circuit = 187.560 miles. Hot, dry and cloudy. World Championship round 1

1	Alain Prost	McLaren MP4/4-Honda	60	1h36m06.857
2	Gerhard Berger	Ferrari F187/88C	60	1h36m16.730
3	Nelson Piquet	Lotus 100T-Honda	60	1h37m15.438
4	Derek Warwick	Arrows A10B-Megatron BMW	60	1h37m20.205
5	Michele Alboreto	Ferrari F187/88C	60	1h37m21.413
6	Satoru Nakajima	Lotus 100T-Honda	59	

Winner's average speed: 117.086 mph. Starting grid front row: Senna, 1m28.096 (pole) and Mansell, 1m28.632 - Senna started from the pit lane. Fastest lap: Berger, 1m32.943. Leaders: Prost, laps 1-60

1988 DRIVERS' RECORDS

Driver	Car	Brazilian GP	San Marino GP	Monaco GP	Mexican GP	Canadian GP	Detroit GP	French GP	British GP	German GP	Hungarian GP	Belgian GP	Italian GP	Portuguese GP	Spanish GP	Japanese GP	Australian GP
Michele Alboreto	Ferrari F187/88C	5	18	3	4	R	R	3	17	4	R	R	2F	5	R	11	R
Philippe Alliot	Lola LC88-Ford	R	17	R	R	10	R	R	14	R	12	9	R	R	14	9	10
René Arnoux	Ligier JS31-Judd	R	DNQ	R	R	R	R	DNQ	18	17	R	R	13	10	R	17	R
Julian Bailey	Tyrrell 017-Ford	DNQ	R	DNQ	DNQ	R	9	DNQ	16	DNQ	DNQ	DNQ	12	DNQ	DNQ	14	DNQ
Gerhard Berger	Ferrari F187/88C	2F	5	2	3	R	R	4	9P	3	4	RF	1	RF	6	4	R
Thierry Boutsen	Benetton B188-Ford	7	4	8	8	3	3	R	R	6	3	DSQ	6	3	9	3	5
Martin Brundle	Williams FW12-Judd	-	-	-	-	-	-	-	-	-	-	7	-	-	-	-	-
Alex Caffi	Dallara 3087-Ford	NPQ	-	-	-	-	-	-	-	-	-	-	-	-	-	-	-
	Dallara F188-Ford	-	R	R	R	NPQ	8	12	11	15	R	8	R	7	10	R	R
Adrian Campos	Minardi M188-Ford	R	16	DNQ	DNQ	DNQ	-	-	-	-	-	-	-	-	-	-	-
Ivan Capelli	March 881-Judd	R	R	10	16	5	DNS	9	R	5	R	3	5	2	R	R	6
Andrea de Cesaris	Rial ARC1-Ford	R	R	R	R	9	4	10	R	13	R	R	R	R	R	R	8
Eddie Cheever	Arrows A10B-Megatron BMW	8	7	R	6	R	R	11	7	10	R	6	3	R	R	R	R
Yannick Dalmas	Lola LC88-Ford	R	12	7	9	DNQ	7	13	13	R	9	R	R	R	11	-	-
Piercarlo Ghinzani	Zakspeed 881	DNQ	R	R	15	14	DNQ	DNQ	DNQ	14	DNQ	R	R	DNQ	DNQ	DNQ	R
Mauricio Gugelmin	March 881-Judd	R	15	R	R	R	R	8	4	8	5	R	8	R	7	10	R
Stefan Johansson	Ligier JS31-Judd	9	DNQ	R	10	R	R	DNQ	DNQ	DNQ	R	11	DNQ	R	R	DNQ	9
Nicola Larini	Osella FA1I-Alfa Romeo	DNQ	-	-	-	-	-	-	-	-	-	-	-	-	-	-	-
	Osella FA1L-Alfa Romeo	-	DNP	9	DNQ	DNQ	R	R	19	R	NPQ	R	R	12	R	R	NPQ
Oscar Larrauri	EuroBrun ER188-Ford	DNS	DNQ	R	13	R	R	R	DNQ	16	DNQ	NPQ	NPQ	NPQ	DNQ	DNQ	R
Nigel Mansell	Williams FW12-Judd	R	R	R	R	R	R	R	2F	R	R	-	-	R	2	R	R
Pierluigi Martini	Minardi M188-Ford	-	-	-	-	-	6	15	15	DNQ	R	DNQ	R	R	13	7	R
Stefano Modena	EuroBrun ER188-Ford	R	NC	DNP	DNP	12	R	14	12	R	11	DNQ	DNQ	DNQ	13	DNQ	R
Satoru Nakajima	Lotus 100T-Honda	6	8	DNQ	R	11	DNQ	7	10	9	7	R	R	R	R	7	R
Alessandro Nannini	Benetton B188-Ford	R	6	R	7	R	R	6	3	18F	R	DSQ	9	R	3	5	R
Jonathan Palmer	Tyrrell 017-Ford	R	14	5	DNQ	6	5	R	R	11	R	12	DNQ	R	R	12	R
Riccardo Patrese	Williams FW12-Judd	R	13	6	R	R	R	R	R	8	6	R	7	R	5	6	4
Nelson Piquet	Lotus 100T-Honda	3	3	R	R	4	R	5	5	R	8	4	R	8	R	8	3
Alain Prost	McLaren MP4/4-Honda	1	2F	1	1F	2	2F	1PF	R	2	2F	2	R	1P	1F	2	1F
Pierre-Henri Raphanel	Lola LC88-Ford	-	-	-	-	-	-	-	-	-	-	-	-	-	-	-	DNQ
Luis Perez Sala	Minardi M188-Ford	R	11	R	11	13	R	NC	R	DNQ	10	DNQ	R	8	12	15	R
Jean-Louis Schlesser	Williams FW12-Judd	-	-	-	-	-	-	-	-	-	-	-	11	-	-	-	-
Bernd Schneider	Zakspeed 881	DNQ	DNQ	DNQ	R	DNQ	DNQ	R	R	DNQ	12	DNQ	R	DNQ	DNQ	R	DNQ
Ayrton Senna	McLaren MP4/4-Honda	RP	1P	RPF	2P	1PF	1P	2	1	1P	1P	1P	10P	6	4P	1PF	2P
Philippe Streiff	AGS JH23-Ford	R	10	DNS	12	R	R	R	R	R	R	R	10	R	9	8	R
Aguri Suzuki	Lola LC88-Ford	-	-	-	-	-	-	-	-	-	-	-	-	-	-	16	-
Gabriele Tarquini	Coloni FC188-Ford	R	R	R	14	8	NPQ	NPQ	NPQ	NPQ	13	NC	-	-	-	-	-
	Coloni FC188B-Ford	-	-	-	-	-	-	-	-	-	-	-	DNQ	11	NPQ	NPQ	DNQ
Derek Warwick	Arrows A10B-Megatron BMW	4	9	4	5	7	R	R	6	7	R	5	4	4	R	R	R

The McLaren-Hondas of Ayrton Senna (right) and Alain Prost head the field before the start of the San Marino GP

Gran Premio di San Marino

1 May 1988. Imola. 60 laps of a 3.132-mile circuit = 187.920 miles. Warm, dry and cloudy. World Championship round 2

1 Ayrton Senna	McLaren MP4/4-Honda	60	1h32m41.264
2 Alain Prost	McLaren MP4/4-Honda	60	1h32m43.598
3 Nelson Piquet	Lotus 100T-Honda	59	
4 Thierry Boutsen	Benetton B188-Ford	59	
5 Gerhard Berger	Ferrari F187/88C	59	
6 Alessandro Nannini	Benetton B188-Ford	59	

Winner's average speed: 121.647 mph. Starting grid front row: Senna, 1m27.148 (pole) and Prost, 1m27.919. Fastest lap: Prost, 1m29.685. Leaders: Senna, laps 1-60

Grand Prix de Monaco

15 May 1988. Monte Carlo. 78 laps of a 2.068-mile circuit = 161.304 miles. Warm, dry and cloudy. World Championship round 3

1 Alain Prost	McLaren MP4/4-Honda	78	1h57m17.077
2 Gerhard Berger	Ferrari F187/88C	78	1h57m37.530
3 Michele Alboreto	Ferrari F187/88C	78	1h57m58.306
4 Derek Warwick	Arrows A10B-Megatron BMW	77	
5 Jonathan Palmer	Tyrrell 017-Ford	77	
6 Riccardo Patrese	Williams FW12-Judd	77	

Winner's average speed: 82.519 mph. Starting grid front row: Senna, 1m23.998 (pole) and Prost, 1m25.425. Fastest lap: Senna, 1m26.321. Leaders: Senna, laps 1-66; Prost, 67-78

Gran Premio de Mexico

29 May 1988. Mexico City. 67 laps of a 2.747-mile circuit = 184.049 miles. Hot, dry and sunny. World Championship round 4

1 Alain Prost	McLaren MP4/4-Honda	67	1h30m15.737
2 Ayrton Senna	McLaren MP4/4-Honda	67	1h30m22.841
3 Gerhard Berger	Ferrari F187/88C	67	1h31m13.051
4 Michele Alboreto	Ferrari F187/88C	66	
5 Derek Warwick	Arrows A10B-Megatron BMW	66	
6 Eddie Cheever	Arrows A10B-Megatron BMW	66	

Winner's average speed: 122.343 mph. Starting grid front row: Senna, 1m17.468 (pole) and Prost, 1m18.097. Fastest lap: Prost, 1m18.608. Leaders: Prost, laps 1-67

Grand Prix du Canada

12 June 1988. Montreal. 69 laps of a 2.728-mile circuit = 188.232 miles. Hot, dry and sunny. World Championship round 5

1 Ayrton Senna	McLaren MP4/4-Honda	69	1h39m46.618
2 Alain Prost	McLaren MP4/4-Honda	69	1h39m52.552
3 Thierry Boutsen	Benetton B188-Ford	69	1h40m38.027
4 Nelson Piquet	Lotus 100T-Honda	68	
5 Ivan Capelli	March 881-Judd	68	
6 Jonathan Palmer	Tyrrell 017-Ford	67	

Winner's average speed: 113.192 mph. Starting grid front row: Senna, 1m21.681 (pole) and Prost, 1m21.863. Fastest lap: Senna, 1m24.973. Leaders: Prost, laps 1-18; Senna, 19-69

Detroit Grand Prix

19 June 1988. Detroit. 63 laps of a 2.500-mile circuit = 157.500 miles. Hot, dry and sunny. World Championship round 6

1 Ayrton Senna	McLaren MP4/4-Honda	63	1h54m56.035
2 Alain Prost	McLaren MP4/4-Honda	63	1h55m34.748
3 Thierry Boutsen	Benetton B188-Ford	62	
4 Andrea de Cesaris	Rial ARC1-Ford	62	
5 Jonathan Palmer	Tyrrell 017-Ford	62	
6 Pierluigi Martini	Minardi M188-Ford	62	

Winner's average speed: 82.221 mph. Starting grid front row: Senna, 1m40.606 (pole) and Berger, 1m41.464. Fastest lap: Prost, 1m44.836. Leaders: Senna, laps 1-63

Grand Prix de France

3 July 1988. Paul Ricard. 80 laps of a 2.369-mile circuit = 189.520 miles. Hot, dry and sunny. World Championship round 7

1 Alain Prost	McLaren MP4/4-Honda	80	1h37m37.328
2 Ayrton Senna	McLaren MP4/4-Honda	80	1h38m09.080
3 Michele Alboreto	Ferrari F187/88C	80	1h38m43.833
4 Gerhard Berger	Ferrari F187/88C	79	
5 Nelson Piquet	Lotus 100T-Honda	79	
6 Alessandro Nannini	Benetton B188-Ford	79	

Winner's average speed: 116.482 mph. Starting grid front row: Prost, 1m07.589 (pole) and Senna, 1m08.067. Fastest lap: Prost, 1m11.737. Leaders: Prost, laps 1-36, 61-80; Senna, 37-60

British Grand Prix

10 July 1988. Silverstone. 65 laps of a 2.969-mile circuit = 192.985 miles. Cool and wet. World Championship round 8

1 Ayrton Senna	McLaren MP4/4-Honda	65	1h33m16.367
2 Nigel Mansell	Williams FW12-Judd	65	1h33m39.711
3 Alessandro Nannini	Benetton B188-Ford	65	1h34m07.581
4 Mauricio Gugelmin	March 881-Judd	65	1h34m27.745
5 Nelson Piquet	Lotus 100T-Honda	65	1h34m37.202
6 Derek Warwick	Arrows A10B-Megatron BMW	64	

Winner's average speed: 124.142 mph. Starting grid front row: Berger, 1m10.133 (pole) and Alboreto, 1m10.332. Fastest lap: Mansell, 1m23.308. Leaders: Berger, laps 1-13; Senna, 14-65

Grosser Preis von Deutschland

24 July 1988. Hockenheim. 44 laps of a 4.224-mile circuit = 185.856 miles. Cool and wet. World Championship round 9

1 Ayrton Senna	McLaren MP4/4-Honda	44	1h32m54.188

2 Alain Prost	McLaren MP4/4-Honda	44 1h33m07.797
3 Gerhard Berger	Ferrari F187/88C	44 1h33m46.283
4 Michele Alboreto	Ferrari F187/88C	44 1h34m35.100
5 Ivan Capelli	March 881-Judd	44 1h34m43.794
6 Thierry Boutsen	Benetton B188-Ford	43

Winner's average speed: 120.021 mph. Starting grid front row: Senna, 1m44.596 (pole) and Prost, 1m44.873. Fastest lap: Nannini, 2m03.032. Leaders: Senna, laps 1-44

Magyar Nagydij (Hungarian Grand Prix)

7 August 1988. Hungaroring. 76 laps of a 2.494-mile circuit = 189.544 miles. Hot, dry and sunny. World Championship round 10

1 Ayrton Senna	McLaren MP4/4-Honda	76 1h57m47.081
2 Alain Prost	McLaren MP4/4-Honda	76 1h57m47.610
3 Thierry Boutsen	Benetton B188-Ford	76 1h58m18.491
4 Gerhard Berger	Ferrari F187/88C	76 1h59m15.751
5 Mauricio Gugelmin	March 881-Judd	75
6 Riccardo Patrese	Williams FW12-Judd	75

Winner's average speed: 96.554 mph. Starting grid front row: Senna, 1m27.635 (pole) and Mansell, 1m27.743. Fastest lap: Prost, 1m30.639. Leaders: Senna, laps 1-76

Grand Prix de Belgique

28 August 1988. Spa-Francorchamps. 43 laps of a 4.312-mile circuit = 185.416 miles. Warm, dry and cloudy. World Championship round 11

1 Ayrton Senna	McLaren MP4/4-Honda	43 1h28m00.549
2 Alain Prost	McLaren MP4/4-Honda	43 1h28m31.019
3 Ivan Capelli	March 881-Judd	43 1h29m16.317
4 Nelson Piquet	Lotus 100T-Honda	43 1h29m24.177
5 Derek Warwick	Arrows A10B-Megatron BMW	43 1h29m25.904
6 Eddie Cheever	Arrows A10B-Megatron BMW	42

Boutsen and Nannini (both Benetton B188-Ford) finished third and fourth on the road but were disqualified for using illegal fuel. Winner's average speed: 126.407 mph. Starting grid front row: Senna, 1m53.718 (pole) and Prost, 1m54.128. Fastest lap: Berger, 2m00.772. Leaders: Senna, laps 1-43

Gran Premio d'Italia

11 September 1988. Monza. 51 laps of a 3.604-mile circuit = 183.804 miles. Hot, dry and sunny. World Championship round 12

1 Gerhard Berger	Ferrari F187/88C	51 1h17m39.744
2 Michele Alboreto	Ferrari F187/88C	51 1h17m40.246
3 Eddie Cheever	Arrows A10B-Megatron BMW	51 1h18m15.276
4 Derek Warwick	Arrows A10B-Megatron BMW	51 1h18m15.858
5 Ivan Capelli	March 881-Judd	51 1h18m32.266
6 Thierry Boutsen	Benetton B188-Ford	51 1h18m39.622

Winner's average speed: 141.998 mph. Starting grid front row: Senna, 1m25.974 (pole) and Prost, 1m26.277. Fastest lap: Alboreto, 1m29.070. Leaders: Senna, laps 1-49; Berger, 50-51

Grande Premio de Portugal

25 September 1988. Estoril. 70 laps of a 2.703-mile circuit = 189.210 miles. Hot, dry and sunny. World Championship round 13

1 Alain Prost	McLaren MP4/4-Honda	70 1h37m40.958
2 Ivan Capelli	March 881-Judd	70 1h37m50.511
3 Thierry Boutsen	Benetton B188-Ford	70 1h38m25.577
4 Derek Warwick	Arrows A10B-Megatron BMW	70 1h38m48.377
5 Michele Alboreto	Ferrari F187/88C	70 1h38m52.842
6 Ayrton Senna	McLaren MP4/4-Honda	70 1h38m59.227

Winner's average speed: 116.219 mph. Starting grid front row: Prost, 1m17.411 (pole) and Senna, 1m17.869. Fastest lap: Berger, 1m21.961. Leaders: Senna, lap 1; Prost, laps 2-70

Gran Premio de Espana

2 October 1988. Jerez. 72 laps of a 2.621-mile circuit = 188.712 miles. Hot, dry and sunny. World Championship round 14

1 Alain Prost	McLaren MP4/4-Honda	72 1h48m43.851
2 Nigel Mansell	Williams FW12-Judd	72 1h49m10.083
3 Alessandro Nannini	Benetton B188-Ford	72 1h49m19.297
4 Ayrton Senna	McLaren MP4/4-Honda	72 1h49m30.561
5 Riccardo Patrese	Williams FW12-Judd	72 1h49m31.281
6 Gerhard Berger	Ferrari F187/88C	72 1h49m35.664

Winner's average speed: 104.131 mph. Starting grid front row: Senna, 1m24.067 (pole) and Prost, 1m24.134. Fastest lap: Prost, 1m27.845. Leaders: Prost, laps 1-72

Fuji Television Japanese Grand Prix

30 October 1988. Suzuka. 51 laps of a 3.641-mile circuit = 185.691 miles. Cool and mainly dry, some drizzle. World Championship round 15

1 Ayrton Senna	McLaren MP4/4-Honda	51 1h33m26.173
2 Alain Prost	McLaren MP4/4-Honda	51 1h33m39.536
3 Thierry Boutsen	Benetton B188-Ford	51 1h34m02.282
4 Gerhard Berger	Ferrari F187/88C	51 1h34m52.887
5 Alessandro Nannini	Benetton B188-Ford	51 1h34m56.776
6 Riccardo Patrese	Williams FW12-Judd	51 1h35m03.788

Winner's average speed: 119.241 mph. Starting grid front row: Senna, 1m41.853 (pole) and Prost, 1m42.177. Fastest lap: Senna, 1m46.326. Leaders: Prost, laps 1-15, 17-27; Capelli, 16; Senna, 28-51

Australian Grand Prix

13 November 1988. Adelaide. 82 laps of a 2.347-mile circuit = 192.454 miles. Hot, dry and cloudy. World Championship round 16

1 Alain Prost	McLaren MP4/4-Honda	82 1h53m14.676
2 Ayrton Senna	McLaren MP4/4-Honda	82 1h53m51.463
3 Nelson Piquet	Lotus 100T-Honda	82 1h54m02.222
4 Riccardo Patrese	Williams FW12-Judd	82 1h54m34.764
5 Thierry Boutsen	Benetton B188-Ford	81
6 Ivan Capelli	March 881-Judd	81

Winner's average speed: 101.967 mph. Starting grid front row: Senna, 1m17.748 (pole) and Prost, 1m17.880. Fastest lap: Prost, 1m21.216. Leaders: Prost, laps 1-13, 26-82; Berger, 14-25

1988 FINAL CHAMPIONSHIP POSITIONS

Drivers

1	Ayrton Senna	90 (94)*	
2	Alain Prost	87 (105)*	
3	Gerhard Berger	41	
4	Thierry Boutsen	27	
5	Michele Alboreto	24	
6	Nelson Piquet	22	
7=	Ivan Capelli	17	
	Derek Warwick	17	
9=	Nigel Mansell	12	
	Alessandro Nannini	12	
11	Riccardo Patrese	8	
12	Eddie Cheever	6	
13=	Mauricio Gugelmin	5	
	Jonathan Palmer	5	
15	Andrea de Cesaris	3	
16=	Pierluigi Martini	1	
	Satoru Nakajima	1	

*Best 11 results count

Manufacturers

1	McLaren-Honda	199
2	Ferrari	65
3	Benetton-Ford	39
4	Lotus-Honda	22
5=	Arrows-Megatron BMW	21
	March-Judd	21
7	Williams-Judd	20
8	Tyrrell-Ford	5
9	Rial-Ford	3
10	Minardi-Ford	1

1989

A new 3.5-litre normally aspirated engine formula was introduced in 1989, ending the turbocharger era in Formula One. McLaren-Honda remained the team to beat, with Ayrton Senna and Alain Prost continuing their stormy but successful partnership. Senna won more often (six wins to four) but Prost consistently finished in the points as his rival retired, giving the Frenchman the championship lead.

A bitter season reached its climax in a suitably controversial Japanese GP. Senna needed to win to retain hopes of keeping his World Championship crown. However, Suzuka was one of the few races in which Prost was able to dominate his normally quicker team-mate, leading narrowly for the majority of the race.

On the 47th lap, Senna made an ambitious passing manoeuvre into the chicane, Prost turned into the corner early to block Senna's advance and the cars touched. Prost stepped from his but Senna returned to the track, pitted, retook the lead and won. However, he was subsequently disqualified for not rejoining the circuit at the point at which he had left it, and Prost was declared World Champion!

Nigel Mansell and the first John Barnard-designed Ferrari made a winning debut at the Brazilian GP, but poor mechanical reliability while developing a revolutionary semi-automatic gearbox prevented an effective challenge. Mansell also won brilliantly in Hungary, from 12th on the grid on a circuit where passing is near impossible. However, he was suspended from the Spanish GP after ignoring black flags during the previous week's Portuguese GP, incurred for reversing in the pit lane.

Ferrari team-mate Gerhard Berger recovered from a fiery accident at Imola's Tamburello corner during the San Marino GP to win in Portugal. No victory could have been more popular.

Renault made a winning return to Grand Prix racing with Williams, new driver Thierry Boutsen being victorious in the wet Canadian and Australian GPs. Riccardo Patrese added six podium finishes to give Williams-Renault second place in the Constructors' Championship.

Johnny Herbert, still in pain from injuries sustained during the 1988 Brands Hatch F3000 race, made a stunning debut in Brazil for Benetton, finishing fourth ahead of team-mate Alessandro Nannini. This, however, was his highlight and, as the season wore on, unhealed injuries increasingly restricted Herbert's performance. Finally, before mid-season he was replaced by Emanuele Pirro. Nannini benefited from Senna's Japanese disqualification to record his only Grand Prix victory.

The most promising newcomer was Jean Alesi, who finished fourth (having run second) in his first race for Tyrrell at the French GP. Further points-scoring performances at Monza and Jerez marked him as a star of the future. In contrast, triple World Champion Nelson Piquet had a lacklustre season for Lotus, even failing to qualify at Spa.

Grande Premio do Brasil

26 March 1989. Rio de Janeiro. 61 laps of a 3.126-mile circuit = 190.686 miles. Very hot, dry and sunny. World Championship round 1

1 Nigel Mansell	Ferrari 640	61 1h38m58.744
2 Alain Prost	McLaren MP4/5-Honda	61 1h39m06.553
3 Mauricio Gugelmin	March 881-Judd	61 1h39m08.114
4 Johnny Herbert	Benetton B188-Ford	61 1h39m09.237
5 Derek Warwick	Arrows A11-Ford	61 1h39m16.610
6 Alessandro Nannini	Benetton B188-Ford	61 1h39m16.985

Winner's average speed: 115.592 mph. Starting grid front row: Senna, 1m25.302 (pole) and Patrese, 1m26.172. Fastest lap: Patrese, 1m32.507. Leaders: Patrese, laps 1-15, 21-22; Mansell, 16-20, 28-44, 47-61; Prost, 23-27, 45-46

Gran Premio Kronenbourg di San Marino

23 April 1989. Imola. 58 laps of a 3.132-mile circuit = 181.656 miles. Race scheduled for 61 laps, stopped after three laps due to an accident. Restarted over 55 laps. Warm, dry and sunny. World Championship round 2

1 Ayrton Senna	McLaren MP4/5-Honda	58 1h26m51.245
2 Alain Prost	McLaren MP4/5-Honda	58 1h27m31.517
3 Alessandro Nannini	Benetton B188-Ford	57
4 Thierry Boutsen	Williams FW12C-Renault	57
5 Derek Warwick	Arrows A11-Ford	57
6 Jonathan Palmer	Tyrrell 018-Ford	57

Winner's average speed: 125.490 mph. Starting grid front row: Senna, 1m26.010 (pole) and Prost, 1m26.235. Fastest lap: Prost, 1m26.795. Leaders: Senna, laps 1-58

Grand Prix de Monaco

7 May 1989. Monte Carlo. 77 laps of a 2.068-mile circuit = 159.236 miles. Warm, dry and sunny. World Championship round 3

1 Ayrton Senna	McLaren MP4/5-Honda	77 1h53m33.251
2 Alain Prost	McLaren MP4/5-Honda	77 1h54m25.780
3 Stefano Modena	Brabham BT58-Judd	76
4 Alex Caffi	Dallara F189-Ford	75
5 Michele Alboreto	Tyrrell 018-Ford	75
6 Martin Brundle	Brabham BT58-Judd	75

Winner's average speed: 84.137 mph. Starting grid front row: Senna, 1m22.308 (pole) and Prost, 1m23.456. Fastest lap: Prost, 1m25.501. Leaders: Senna, laps 1-77

Gran Premio de Mexico

28 May 1989. Mexico City. 69 laps of a 2.747-mile circuit = 189.543 miles. Race stopped after one lap due to an accident. Restarted over original distance. Hot, dry and sunny. World Championship round 4

1 Ayrton Senna	McLaren MP4/5-Honda	69 1h35m21.431
2 Riccardo Patrese	Williams FW12C-Renault	69 1h35m36.991
3 Michele Alboreto	Tyrrell 018-Ford	69 1h35m52.685
4 Alessandro Nannini	Benetton B188-Ford	69 1h36m06.926
5 Alain Prost	McLaren MP4/5-Honda	69 1h36m17.544
6 Gabriele Tarquini	AGS JH23B-Ford	68

Winner's average speed: 119.263 mph. Starting grid front row: Senna, 1m17.876 (pole) and Prost, 1m18.773. Fastest lap: Mansell, 1m20.420. Leaders: Senna, laps 1-69

Iceberg United States Grand Prix

4 June 1989. Phoenix. 75 laps of a 2.360-mile circuit = 177.000 miles. Race scheduled for 81 laps, stopped due to two hour rule. Hot, dry and sunny. World Championship round 5

1 Alain Prost	McLaren MP4/5-Honda	75 2h01m33.133
2 Riccardo Patrese	Williams FW12C-Renault	75 2h02m12.829
3 Eddie Cheever	Arrows A11-Ford	75 2h02m16.343

4 Christian Danner	Rial ARC2-Ford	74	
5 Johnny Herbert	Benetton B188-Ford	74	
6 Thierry Boutsen	Williams FW12C-Renault	74	

Winner's average speed: 87.370 mph. Starting grid front row: Senna, 1m30.108 (pole) and Prost, 1m31.517. Fastest lap: Senna, 1m33.969. Leaders: Senna, laps 1-33; Prost, 34-75

Grand Prix Molson du Canada

18 June 1989. Montreal. 69 laps of a 2.728-mile circuit = 188.232 miles. Cool and wet. World Championship round 6

1 Thierry Boutsen	Williams FW12C-Renault	69	2h01m24.073
2 Riccardo Patrese	Williams FW12C-Renault	69	2h01m54.080
3 Andrea de Cesaris	Dallara F189-Ford	69	2h03m00.722
4 Nelson Piquet	Lotus 101-Judd	69	2h03m05.557
5 René Arnoux	Ligier JS33-Ford	68	
6 Alex Caffi	Dallara F189-Ford	67	

Winner's average speed: 93.030 mph. Starting grid front row: Prost, 1m20.973 (pole) and Senna, 1m21.049. Fastest lap: Palmer, 1m31.925. Leaders: Prost, lap 1; Senna, laps 2-3, 39-66; Patrese, 4-34; Warwick, 35-38; Boutsen, 67-69

Rhône-Poulenc Grand Prix de France

9 July 1989. Paul Ricard. 80 laps of a 2.369-mile circuit = 189.520 miles. Race stopped by an accident on lap 1. Restarted over original distance. Hot, dry and sunny. World Championship round 7

1 Alain Prost	McLaren MP4/5-Honda	80	1h38m29.411

2 Nigel Mansell	Ferrari 640	80	1h39m13.428
3 Riccardo Patrese	Williams FW12C-Renault	80	1h39m36.332
4 Jean Alesi	Tyrrell 018-Ford	80	1h39m42.643
5 Stefan Johansson	Onyx ORE1-Ford	79	
6 Olivier Grouillard	Ligier JS33-Ford	79	

Winner's average speed: 115.455 mph. Starting grid front row: Prost, 1m07.203 (pole) and Senna, 1m07.228. Fastest lap: Gugelmin, 1m12.090. Leaders: Prost, laps 1-80

Shell British Grand Prix

16 July 1989. Silverstone. 64 laps of a 2.969-mile circuit = 190.016 miles. Warm, dry and sunny. World Championship round 8

1 Alain Prost	McLaren MP4/5-Honda	64	1h19m22.131
2 Nigel Mansell	Ferrari 640	64	1h19m41.500
3 Alessandro Nannini	Benetton B189-Ford	64	1h20m10.150
4 Nelson Piquet	Lotus 101-Judd	64	1h20m28.866
5 Pierluigi Martini	Minardi M189-Ford	63	
6 Luis Perez Sala	Minardi M189-Ford	63	

Winner's average speed: 143.645 mph. Starting grid front row: Senna, 1m09.099 (pole) and Prost, 1m09.266. Fastest lap: Mansell, 1m12.017. Leaders: Senna, laps 1-10; Prost, 11-64

Grosser Mobil 1 Preis von Deutschland

30 July 1989. Hockenheim. 45 laps of a 4.224-mile circuit = 190.080 miles. Warm and cloudy. World Championship round 9

1 Alain Prost	McLaren MP4/5-Honda	80	1h38m29.411

1989 DRIVERS' RECORDS

Driver	Car	Brazilian GP	San Marino GP	Monaco GP	Mexican GP	United States GP	Canadian GP	French GP	British GP	German GP	Hungarian GP	Belgian GP	Italian GP	Portuguese GP	Spanish GP	Japanese GP	Australian GP
Michele Alboreto	Tyrrell 017B-Ford	10	-	-	-	-	-	-	-	-	-	-	-	-	-	-	-
	Tyrrell 018-Ford	-	DNQ	5	3	R	R	-	-	-	-	-	-	-	-	-	-
	Lola LC89-Lamborghini	-	-	-	-	-	-	-	-	R	R	R	R	11	NPQ	DNQ	NPQ
Jean Alesi	Tyrrell 018-Ford	-	-	-	-	-	-	4	R	10	9	-	5	-	4	R	R
Philippe Alliot	Lola LC88C-Lamborghini	12	-	-	-	-	-	-	-	-	-	-	-	-	-	-	-
	Lola LC89-Lamborghini	-	R	R	NC	R	R	R	R	R	NPQ	16	R	9	6	R	R
René Arnoux	Ligier JS33-Ford	DNQ	DNQ	12	14	DNQ	5	R	DNQ	11	DNQ	R	9	13	DNQ	DNQ	R
Paolo Barilla	Minardi M189-Ford	-	-	-	-	-	-	-	-	-	-	-	-	-	-	R	-
Gerhard Berger	Ferrari 640	R	R	-	R	R	R	R	R	R	R	R	2	1F	2	R	R
Eric Bernard	Lola LC89-Lamborghini	-	-	-	-	-	-	11	R	-	-	-	-	-	-	-	-
Enrico Bertaggia	Coloni C3-Ford	-	-	-	-	-	-	-	-	-	-	NPQ	NPQ	NPQ	NPQ	NPQ	NPQ
Thierry Boutsen	Williams FW12C-Renault	R	4	10	R	6	1	R	10	R	3	4	3	-	-	-	-
	Williams FW13-Renault	-	-	-	-	-	-	-	-	-	-	-	-	R	R	3	1
Martin Brundle	Brabham BT58-Judd	R	R	6	9	R	NPQ	NPQ	R	8	12	R	6	8	R	5	R
Alex Caffi	Dallara F189-Ford	NPQ	7	4	13	R	6	R	NPQ	R	7	R	11	R	R	9	R
Ivan Capelli	March 881-Judd	R	R	-	-	-	-	-	-	-	-	-	-	-	-	-	-
	March CG891-Judd	-	-	11	R	R	R	R	R	R	R	12	R	R	R	R	R
Andrea de Cesaris	Dallara F189-Ford	13	10	13	R	8	3	DNQ	R	7	R	11	R	R	7	10	R
Eddie Cheever	Arrows A11-Ford	R	9	7	7	3	R	7	DNQ	12	5	R	DNQ	R	R	8	R
Yannick Dalmas	Lola LC88C-Lamborghini	DNQ	-	-	-	-	-	-	-	-	-	-	-	-	-	-	-
	Lola LC89-Lamborghini	-	DNS	DNQ	DNQ	DNQ	DNQ	-	-	-	-	-	-	-	-	-	-
	AGS JH23B-Ford	-	-	-	-	-	-	NPQ	NPQ	NPQ	-	-	-	-	-	-	-
	AGS JH24-Ford	-	-	-	-	-	-	-	-	-	NPQ	NPQ	NPQ	NPQ	NPQ	NPQ	NPQ
Christian Danner	Rial ARC2-Ford	14	DNQ	DNQ	12	4	8	DNQ	DNQ	DNQ	DNQ	DNQ	DNQ	DNQ	-	-	-
Martin Donnelly	Arrows A11-Ford	-	-	-	-	-	-	12	-	-	-	-	-	-	-	-	-
Gregor Foitek	EuroBrun ER188B-Judd	DNQ	NPQ	NPQ	NPQ	NPQ	NPQ	NPQ	NPQ	-	-	NPQ	-	-	-	-	-
	EuroBrun ER189-Judd	-	-	-	-	-	-	-	-	NPQ	NPQ	-	-	-	-	-	-
	Rial ARC2-Ford	-	-	-	-	-	-	-	-	-	-	-	-	-	DNQ	-	-
Bertrand Gachot	Onyx ORE1-Ford	NPQ	NPQ	NPQ	NPQ	NPQ	NPQ	13	12	DNQ	R	R	R	-	-	-	-
	Rial ARC2-Ford	-	-	-	-	-	-	-	-	-	-	-	-	-	-	DNQ	DNQ
Piercarlo Ghinzani	Osella FA1M-Ford	NPQ	NPQ	NPQ	NPQ	NPQ	NPQ	NPQ	NPQ	NPQ	R	NPQ	NPQ	NPQ	R	NPQ	R
Olivier Grouillard	Ligier JS33-Ford	9	R	R	8	DNQ	DNQ	6	7	R	DNQ	13	R	DNQ	R	R	R
Mauricio Gugelmin	March 881-Judd	3	R	-	-	-	-	-	-	-	-	-	-	-	-	-	-
	March CG891-Judd	-	-	R	DNQ	R	R	NCF	R	R	R	7	R	10	R	7	7
Johnny Herbert	Benetton B188-Ford	4	11	14	15	5	DNQ	-	-	-	-	-	-	-	-	-	-
	Tyrrell 018-Ford	-	-	-	-	-	-	-	-	-	-	R	-	DNQ	-	-	-

/Cont'd

1 Ayrton Senna	McLaren MP4/5-Honda	45 1h21m43.302
2 Alain Prost	McLaren MP4/5-Honda	45 1h22m01.453
3 Nigel Mansell	Ferrari 640	45 1h23m06.556
4 Riccardo Patrese	Williams FW12C-Renault	44
5 Nelson Piquet	Lotus 101-Judd	44
6 Derek Warwick	Arrows A11-Ford	44

Winner's average speed: 139.543 mph. Starting grid front row: Senna, 1m42.300 (pole) and Prost, 1m43.295. Fastest lap: Senna, 1m45.884. Leaders: Senna, laps 1-19, 43-45; Prost, 20-42

Pop 84 Magyar Nagydij (Hungarian Grand Prix)

13 August 1989. Hungaroring. 77 laps of a 2.466-mile circuit = 189.882 miles. Hot, dry and sunny. World Championship round 10

1 Nigel Mansell	Ferrari 640	77 1h49m38.650
2 Ayrton Senna	McLaren MP4/5-Honda	77 1h50m04.617
3 Thierry Boutsen	Williams FW12C-Renault	77 1h50m17.004
4 Alain Prost	McLaren MP4/5-Honda	77 1h50m22.827
5 Eddie Cheever	Arrows A11-Ford	77 1h50m23.756
6 Nelson Piquet	Lotus 101-Judd	77 1h50m50.689

Winner's average speed: 103.908 mph. Starting grid front row: Patrese, 1m19.726 (pole) and Senna, 1m20.039. Fastest lap: Mansell, 1m22.637. Leaders: Patrese, laps 1-52; Senna, 53-57; Mansell, 58-77

Champion Grand Prix de Belgique

27 August 1989. Spa-Francorchamps. 44 laps of a 4.312-mile circuit = 189.728 miles. Cool and wet. World Championship round 11

1 Ayrton Senna	McLaren MP4/5-Honda	44 1h40m54.196
2 Alain Prost	McLaren MP4/5-Honda	44 1h40m55.500
3 Nigel Mansell	Ferrari 640	44 1h40m56.020
4 Thierry Boutsen	Williams FW12C-Renault	44 1h41m48.614
5 Alessandro Nannini	Benetton B189-Ford	44 1h42m03.001
6 Derek Warwick	Arrows A11-Ford	44 1h42m12.512

Winner's average speed: 112.818 mph. Starting grid front row: Senna, 1m50.867 (pole) and Prost, 1m51.463. Fastest lap: Prost, 2m11.571. Leaders: Senna, laps 1-44

Coca Cola Gran Premio d'Italia

10 September 1989. Monza. 53 laps of a 3.604-mile circuit = 191.012 miles. Hot, dry and sunny. World Championship round 12

1 Alain Prost	McLaren MP4/5-Honda	53 1h19m27.550
2 Gerhard Berger	Ferrari 640	53 1h19m34.876
3 Thierry Boutsen	Williams FW12C-Renault	53 1h19m42.525
4 Riccardo Patrese	Williams FW12C-Renault	53 1h20m06.272
5 Jean Alesi	Tyrrell 018-Ford	52
6 Martin Brundle	Brabham BT58-Judd	52

Winner's average speed: 144.230 mph. Starting grid front row: Senna, 1m23.720 (pole) and Berger, 1m24.734. Fastest lap: Prost, 1m28.107. Leaders: Senna, laps 1-44; Prost, 45-53

Grande Premio de Portugal

24 September 1989. Estoril. 71 laps of a 2.703-mile circuit = 191.913 miles. Hot, dry and sunny. World Championship round 13

1 Gerhard Berger	Ferrari 640	71 1h36m48.546
2 Alain Prost	McLaren MP4/5-Honda	71 1h37m21.183

1989 DRIVERS' RECORDS cont'd

Driver	Car	Brazilian GP	San Marino GP	Monaco GP	Mexican GP	United States GP	Canadian GP	French GP	British GP	German GP	Hungarian GP	Belgian GP	Italian GP	Portuguese GP	Spanish GP	Japanese GP	Australian GP
Stefan Johansson	Onyx ORE1-Ford	NPQ	NPQ	NPQ	R	R	R	5	NPQ	R	R	8	NPQ	3	NPQ	NPQ	NPQ
Nicola Larini	Osella FA1M-Ford	R	12	NPQ	NPQ	NPQ	R	NPQ	R	NPQ	NPQ	NPQ	R	NPQ	R	R	R
Oscar Larrauri	EuroBrun ER189-Judd	-	-	-	-	-	-	-	-	-	-	-	NPQ	NPQ	NPQ	NPQ	NPQ
JJ Lehto	Onyx ORE1-Ford	-	-	-	-	-	-	-	-	-	-	-	-	NPQ	R	NPQ	R
Nigel Mansell	Ferrari 640	1	R	R	R^F	R	R	2	2^F	3	1^F	3	R	R	-	R	R
Pierluigi Martini	Minardi M188B-Ford	R	R	R	-	-	-	-	-	-	-	-	-	-	-	-	-
	Minardi M189-Ford	-	-	-	R	R	R	R	5	9	R	9	7	5	R	-	6
Stefano Modena	Brabham BT58-Judd	R	R	3	10	R	R	R	R	R	11	R	DNQ	14	R	R	8
Roberto Moreno	Coloni FC188C-Ford	DNQ	DNQ	R	DNQ	DNQ	-	-	-	-	-	-	-	-	-	-	-
	Coloni C3-Ford	-	-	-	-	-	R	DNQ	R	NPQ	NPQ	NPQ	NPQ	R	NPQ	NPQ	NPQ
Satoru Nakajima	Lotus 101-Judd	8	NC	DNQ	R	R	DNQ	R	8	R	R	DNQ	10	7	R	R	4^F
Alessandro Nannini	Benetton B188-Ford	6	3	8	4	R	R	-	-	-	-	-	-	-	-	-	-
	Benetton B189-Ford	-	-	-	-	-	-	R	3	R	R	5	R	4	R	1	2
Jonathan Palmer	Tyrrell 017B-Ford	7	-	-	-	-	-	-	-	-	-	-	-	-	-	-	-
	Tyrrell 018-Ford	-	6	9	R	9	R^F	10	R	13	14	R	6	10	R	DNQ
Riccardo Patrese	Williams FW12C-Renault	R^F	R	15	2	2	2	3	R	4	R^P	R	4	-	5	-	-
	Williams FW13-Renault	-	-	-	-	-	-	-	-	-	-	-	-	R	-	2	3
Nelson Piquet	Lotus 101-Judd	R	R	R	11	R	4	8	4	5	6	DNQ	R	R	8	4	R
Emanuele Pirro	Benetton B188-Ford	-	-	-	-	-	-	9	11	-	-	-	-	-	-	-	-
	Benetton B189-Ford	-	-	-	-	-	-	-	-	R	8	10	R	R	R	R	5
Alain Prost	McLaren MP4/5-Honda	2	2^F	2^F	5	1	R^P	1^P	1	2	4	2^F	1^F	2	3	R^F	R
Pierre-Henri Raphanel	Coloni FC188C-Ford	NPQ	NPQ	R	NPQ	NPQ	-	-	-	-	-	-	-	-	-	-	-
	Coloni C3-Ford	-	-	-	-	-	NPQ	NPQ	NPQ	NPQ	NPQ	-	-	-	-	-	-
	Rial ARC2-Ford	-	-	-	-	-	-	-	-	-	-	DNQ	DNQ	DNQ	DNQ	DNQ	DNQ
Luis Perez Sala	Minardi M188B-Ford	R	R	R	-	-	-	-	-	-	-	-	-	-	-	-	-
	Minardi M189-Ford	-	-	-	DNQ	R	R	DNQ	6	DNQ	R	15	8	12	R	R	DNQ
Bernd Schneider	Zakspeed 891-Yamaha	R	NPQ	NPQ	NPQ	NPQ	NPQ	NPQ	NPQ	NPQ	NPQ	NPQ	NPQ	NPQ	NPQ	R	NPQ
Ayrton Senna	McLaren MP4/5-Honda	11^P	1^P	1^P	1^P	R^{PF}	7	R	R^P	1^{PF}	2	1^P	R^P	R^P	1^{PF}	DSQ^P	R^P
Aguri Suzuki	Zakspeed 891-Yamaha	NPQ	NPQ	NPQ	NPQ	NPQ	NPQ	NPQ	NPQ	NPQ	NPQ	NPQ	NPQ	NPQ	NPQ	NPQ	NPQ
Gabriele Tarquini	AGS JH23B-Ford	-	8	R	6	7	R	R	NPQ	-	-	-	-	-	-	-	-
	AGS JH24-Ford	-	-	-	-	-	-	-	DNQ	-	NPQ	NPQ	NPQ	NPQ	NPQ	NPQ	NPQ
Derek Warwick	Arrows A11-Ford	5	5	R	R	R	R	-	9	6	10	6	R	R	R	9	6
Volker Weidler	Rial ARC2-Ford	NPQ	NPQ	NPQ	NPQ	NPQ	NPQ	NPQ	NPQ	DNQ	DNQ	-	-	-	-	-	-
Joachim Winkelhock	AGS JH23B-Ford	NPQ	NPQ	NPQ	NPQ	NPQ	NPQ	NPQ	-	-	-	-	-	-	-	-	-

3 Stefan Johansson	Onyx ORE1-Ford	71 1h37m43.871
4 Alessandro Nannini	Benetton B189-Ford	71 1h38m10.915
5 Pierluigi Martini	Minardi M189-Ford	70
6 Jonathan Palmer	Tyrrell 018-Ford	70

Winner's average speed: 118.943 mph. Starting grid front row: Senna, 1m15.468 (pole) and Berger, 1m16.059. Fastest lap: Berger, 1m18.986. Leaders: Berger, laps 1-23, 41-71; Mansell, 24-39; Martini, 40

Gran Premio Tio Pepe de Espana

1 October 1989. Jerez. 73 laps of a 2.621-mile circuit = 191.333 miles. Hot, dry and sunny. World Championship round 14

1 Ayrton Senna	McLaren MP4/5-Honda	73 1h47m48.264
2 Gerhard Berger	Ferrari 640	73 1h48m15.315
3 Alain Prost	McLaren MP4/5-Honda	73 1h48m42.052
4 Jean Alesi	Tyrrell 018-Ford	72
5 Riccardo Patrese	Williams FW12C-Renault	72
6 Philippe Alliot	Lola LC89-Lamborghini	72

Winner's average speed: 106.485 mph. Starting grid front row: Senna, 1m20.291 (pole) and Berger, 1m20.565. Fastest lap: Senna, 1m25.779. Leaders: Senna, laps 1-73

Fuji Television Japanese Grand Prix

22 October 1989. Suzuka. 53 laps of a 3.641-mile circuit = 192.973 miles. Warm, dry and sunny. World Championship round 15

1 Alessandro Nannini	Benetton B189-Ford	53 1h35m06.277
2 Riccardo Patrese	Williams FW13-Renault	53 1h35m18.181
3 Thierry Boutsen	Williams FW13-Renault	53 1h35m19.723
4 Nelson Piquet	Lotus 101-Judd	53 1h36m50.502
5 Martin Brundle	Brabham BT58-Judd	52
6 Derek Warwick	Arrows A11-Ford	52

Senna (McLaren MP4/5-Honda) finished first on the road but was disqualified for rejoining the circuit at the wrong place after his accident with Prost. Winner's average speed: 121.744 mph. Starting grid front row: Senna, 1m38.041 (pole) and Prost, 1m39.771. Fastest lap: Prost, 1m43.506. Leaders: Prost, laps 1-20, 24-46; Senna, 21-23; Nannini, 47-53 (Senna led laps 47-48 and 51-53 on the road but was disqualified for infringement on lap 46)

Foster's Australian Grand Prix

5 November 1989. Adelaide. 70 laps of a 2.347-mile circuit = 164.290 miles. Race scheduled for 81 laps, stopped after accident on lap 1. Restarted over original distance but stopped due to two hour rule. Cool and wet. World Championship round 16

1 Thierry Boutsen	Williams FW13-Renault	70 2h00m17.421
2 Alessandro Nannini	Benetton B189-Ford	70 2h00m46.079
3 Riccardo Patrese	Williams FW13-Renault	70 2h00m55.104
4 Satoru Nakajima	Lotus 101-Judd	70 2h00m59.752
5 Emanuele Pirro	Benetton B189-Ford	68
6 Pierluigi Martini	Minardi M189-Ford	67

Winner's average speed: 81.947 mph. Starting grid front row: Senna, 1m16.665 (pole) and Prost, 1m17.403. Fastest lap: Nakajima, 1m38.480. Leaders: Senna, laps 1-13; Boutsen, 14-70

1989 FINAL CHAMPIONSHIP POSITIONS

Drivers						Manufacturers	
1	Alain Prost	76 (81)*	16=	Martin Brundle	4	1 McLaren-Honda	141
2	Ayrton Senna	60		Alex Caffi	4	2 Williams-Renault	77
3	Riccardo Patrese	40		Andrea de Cesaris	4	3 Ferrari	59
4	Nigel Mansell	38		Mauricio Gugelmin	4	4 Benetton-Ford	39
5	Thierry Boutsen	37		Stefano Modena	4	5 Tyrrell-Ford	16
6	Alessandro Nannini	32	21=	Christian Danner	3	6 Lotus-Judd	15
7	Gerhard Berger	21		Satoru Nakajima	3	7 Arrows-Ford	13
8	Nelson Piquet	12	23=	René Arnoux	2	8= Dallara-Ford	8
9	Jean Alesi	8		Jonathan Palmer	2	Brabham-Judd	8
10	Derek Warwick	7		Emanuele Pirro	2	10= Onyx-Ford	6
11=	Michele Alboreto	6	26=	Philippe Alliot	1	Minardi-Ford	6
	Eddie Cheever	6		Olivier Grouillard	1	12 March-Judd	4
	Stefan Johansson	6		Luis Perez Sala	1	13= Rial-Ford	3
14=	Johnny Herbert	5		Gabriele Tarquini	1	Ligier-Ford	3
	Pierluigi Martini	5		*Best 11 results count		15= AGS-Ford	1
						Lola-Lamborghini	1

1990

After the bitterness of his partnership with Ayrton Senna at McLaren, Alain Prost moved to Ferrari. The championship was a case of same drivers, different teams and déjà vu. At the Japanese GP the roles of 1989 were reversed. Prost, who needed to score points to remain in the championship, made the better start. However, in an act of retribution, Senna drove his rival off the road. The championship was Senna's but without glory.

Jean Alesi continued his impressive graduation to Grand Prix racing, nearly defeating Senna in the opening Grand Prix in Phoenix, and securing another second place finish at Monaco. At one point during the season three teams (Tyrrell, Williams and Ferrari) believed that they had his services for 1991; he eventually chose Ferrari. If instead he had moved to Williams, the recent history of Grand Prix racing might be very different.

Senna and Prost overshadowed their respective team-mates, Gerhard Berger and Nigel Mansell. Berger should have won in Japan but spun out of the lead while passing the aftermath of the Senna/Prost contretemps. After failing to finish the British GP, an emotional Mansell announced he would quit the sport. However, when Williams failed to sign Alesi, Mansell was tempted out of retirement before he had even stopped racing! In Portugal, after nearly crashing into his team-mate at the start, Mansell scored his sole victory of a disappointing year.

Leyton House, which had been struggling, surprised the Grand Prix circus at Paul Ricard by nearly finishing first and second. Unfortunately for the team, Gugelmin retired and Alain Prost just caught Capelli to score Ferrari's 100th Grand Prix victory and deny Leyton House a famous win.

Williams-Renault won twice as Renault developed its V10. Meanwhile Nelson Piquet resurrected his career, winning the final two races for Benetton to finish third in the championship. With Alessandro Nannini absent through injury, Piquet was backed up in a Japanese GP one–two by his longtime protégé and friend Roberto Moreno. Nannini had had his right arm severed in a helicopter accident the previous week, and although it was successfully rejoined, his Grand Prix career was over.

Lotus, now with Lamborghini engines, suffered another frustrating year which almost ended in tragedy for promising newcomer Martin Donnelly, who was critically injured during practice at Jerez. Initial fears for his life proved ill-founded, but he too would not race at this level again. Sponsor Camel announced that it was to withdraw its support of Lotus at the end of the year, forcing the team to the brink of extinction.

1990 World Champion Ayrton Senna leads Nigel Mansell at the French Grand Prix

Iceberg United States Grand Prix

11 March 1990. Phoenix. 72 laps of a 2.360-mile circuit = 169.920 miles. Cool, dry and cloudy. World Championship round 1

1 Ayrton Senna	McLaren MP4/5B-Honda	72	1h52m32.829
2 Jean Alesi	Tyrrell 018-Ford	72	1h52m41.514
3 Thierry Boutsen	Williams FW13B-Renault	72	1h53m26.909
4 Nelson Piquet	Benetton B189B-Ford	72	1h53m41.187
5 Stefano Modena	Brabham BT58-Judd	72	1h53m42.332
6 Satoru Nakajima	Tyrrell 018-Ford	71	

Winner's average speed: 90.586 mph. Starting grid front row: Berger, 1m28.664 (pole) and Martini, 1m28.731. Fastest lap: Berger, 1m31.050. Leaders: Alesi, laps 1-34; Senna, 35-72

Grande Premio do Brasil

25 March 1990. Interlagos. 71 laps of a 2.687-mile circuit = 190.777 miles. Hot, dry and sunny. World Championship round 2

1 Alain Prost	Ferrari 641	71	1h37m21.258
2 Gerhard Berger	McLaren MP4/5B-Honda	71	1h37m34.822
3 Ayrton Senna	McLaren MP4/5B-Honda	71	1h37m58.980
4 Nigel Mansell	Ferrari 641	71	1h38m08.524
5 Thierry Boutsen	Williams FW13B-Renault	70	
6 Nelson Piquet	Benetton B189B-Ford	70	

Winner's average speed: 117.577 mph. Starting grid front row: Senna, 1m17.277 (pole) and Berger, 1m17.888. Fastest lap: Berger, 1m19.899. Leaders: Senna, laps 1-32, 35-40; Berger, 33-34; Prost, 41-71

Gran Premio di San Marino

13 May 1990. Imola. 61 laps of a 3.132-mile circuit = 191.052 miles. Warm, dry and sunny. World Championship round 3

1 Riccardo Patrese	Williams FW13B-Renault	61	1h30m55.478
2 Gerhard Berger	McLaren MP4/5B-Honda	61	1h31m00.595
3 Alessandro Nannini	Benetton B190-Ford	61	1h31m01.718
4 Alain Prost	Ferrari 641/2	61	1h31m02.321
5 Nelson Piquet	Benetton B190-Ford	61	1h31m48.590
6 Jean Alesi	Tyrrell 019-Ford	60	

Winner's average speed: 126.073 mph. Starting grid front row: Senna, 1m23.220 (pole) and Berger, 1m23.781. Fastest lap: Nannini, 1m27.156. Leaders: Senna, laps 1-3; Boutsen, 4-17; Berger, 18-50; Patrese, 51-61

Grand Prix de Monaco

27 May 1990. Monte Carlo. 78 laps of a 2.068-mile circuit = 161.304 miles. Race stopped after an accident on lap 1. Restarted over original distance. Warm, dry and sunny. World Championship round 4

1 Ayrton Senna	McLaren MP4/5B-Honda	78	1h52m46.982
2 Jean Alesi	Tyrrell 019-Ford	78	1h52m48.069
3 Gerhard Berger	McLaren MP4/5B-Honda	78	1h52m49.055
4 Thierry Boutsen	Williams FW13B-Renault	77	
5 Alex Caffi	Arrows A11B-Ford	76	
6 Eric Bernard	Lola 90-Lamborghini	76	

Winner's average speed: 85.813 mph. Starting grid front row: Senna, 1m21.314 (pole) and Prost, 1m21.776. Fastest lap: Senna, 1m24.468. Leaders: Senna, laps 1-78

Grand Prix Molson du Canada

10 June 1990. Montreal. 70 laps of a 2.728-mile circuit = 190.960 miles. Warm and cloudy, damp track, drying. World Championship round 5

1 Ayrton Senna	McLaren MP4/5B-Honda	70	1h42m56.400
2 Nelson Piquet	Benetton B190-Ford	70	1h43m06.897
3 Nigel Mansell	Ferrari 641/2	70	1h43m09.785
4 Gerhard Berger*	McLaren MP4/5B-Honda	70	1h43m11.254
5 Alain Prost	Ferrari 641/2	70	1h43m12.220
6 Derek Warwick	Lotus 102-Lamborghini	68	

*Berger penalized 60 seconds for jumping the start. Winner's average speed: 111.304 mph. Starting grid front row: Senna, 1m20.399 (pole) and Berger, 1m20.465. Fastest lap: Berger, 1m22.077. Leaders: Senna, laps 1-11, 15-70; Nannini, 12-14 (Berger led laps 15-70 on the road)

Gran Premio de Mexico

24 June 1990. Mexico City. 69 laps of a 2.747-mile circuit = 189.543 miles. Warm, dry and cloudy. World Championship round 6

1 Alain Prost	Ferrari 641/2	69	1h32m35.783
2 Nigel Mansell	Ferrari 641/2	69	1h33m01.134
3 Gerhard Berger	McLaren MP4/5B-Honda	69	1h33m01.313
4 Alessandro Nannini	Benetton B190-Ford	69	1h33m16.882
5 Thierry Boutsen	Williams FW13B-Renault	69	1h33m22.452
6 Nelson Piquet	Benetton B190-Ford	69	1h33m22.726

Winner's average speed: 122.819 mph. Starting grid front row: Berger, 1m17.227 (pole) and Patrese, 1m17.498. Fastest lap: Prost, 1m17.958. Leaders: Senna, laps 1-60; Prost, 61-69

Rhône-Poulenc Grand Prix de France

8 July 1990. Paul Ricard. 80 laps of a 2.369-mile circuit = 189.520 miles. Hot, dry and sunny. World Championship round 7

1 Alain Prost	Ferrari 641/2	80	1h33m29.606
2 Ivan Capelli	Leyton House CG901-Judd	80	1h33m38.232

3 Ayrton Senna   McLaren MP4/5B-Honda 80 1h33m41.212
4 Nelson Piquet   Benetton B190-Ford   80 1h34m10.813
5 Gerhard Berger   McLaren MP4/5B-Honda 80 1h34m11.825
6 Riccardo Patrese   Williams FW13B-Renault 80 1h34m38.957

Winner's average speed: 121.626 mph. Starting grid front row:
Mansell, 1m04.402 (pole) and Berger, 1m04.512. Fastest lap:
Mansell, 1m08.012. Leaders: Berger, laps 1-27; Senna, 28-29;
Mansell, 30-31; Patrese, 32; Capelli, 33-77; Prost, 78-80

Foster's British Grand Prix

15 July 1990. Silverstone. 64 laps of a 2.969-mile circuit =
190.016 miles. Hot, dry and sunny. World Championship
round 8

1 Alain Prost   Ferrari 641/2   64 1h18m30.999
2 Thierry Boutsen   Williams FW13B-Renault 64 1h19m10.091
3 Ayrton Senna   McLaren MP4/5B-Honda 64 1h19m14.087
4 Eric Bernard   Lola 90-Lamborghini   64 1h19m46.301
5 Nelson Piquet   Benetton B190-Ford   64 1h19m55.002
6 Aguri Suzuki   Lola 90-Lamborghini   63

Winner's average speed: 145.204 mph. Starting grid front row:
Mansell, 1m07.428 (pole) and Senna, 1m08.071. Fastest lap:
Mansell, 1m11.291. Leaders: Senna, laps 1-11; Mansell, 12-21,
28-42; Berger, 22-27; Prost, 43-64

Grosser Mobil 1 Preis von Deutschland

29 July 1990. Hockenheim. 45 laps of a 4.227-mile circuit =
190.215 miles. Hot, dry and sunny. World Championship
round 9

1 Ayrton Senna   McLaren MP4/5B-Honda 45 1h20m47.164
2 Alessandro Nannini   Benetton B190-Ford   45 1h20m53.684
3 Gerhard Berger   McLaren MP4/5B-Honda 45 1h20m55.717
4 Alain Prost   Ferrari 641/2   45 1h21m32.424
5 Riccardo Patrese   Williams FW13B-Renault 45 1h21m35.192
6 Thierry Boutsen   Williams FW13B-Renault 45 1h22m08.655

Winner's average speed: 141.270 mph. Starting grid front row:
Senna, 1m40.198 (pole) and Berger, 1m40.434. Fastest lap:
Boutsen, 1m45.602. Leaders: Senna, laps 1-17, 34-45; Nannini,
18-33

Magyar Nagydij (Hungarian Grand Prix)

12 August 1990. Hungaroring. 77 laps of a 2.466-mile
circuit = 189.882 miles. Hot, dry and sunny. World
Championship round 10

1 Thierry Boutsen   Williams FW13B-Renault 77 1h49m30.597
2 Ayrton Senna   McLaren MP4/5B-Honda 77 1h49m30.885
3 Nelson Piquet   Benetton B190-Ford   77 1h49m58.490
4 Riccardo Patrese   Williams FW13B-Renault 77 1h50m02.430
5 Derek Warwick   Lotus 102-Lamborghini 77 1h50m44.841
6 Eric Bernard   Lola 90-Lamborghini   77 1h50m54.905

Winner's average speed: 104.035 mph. Starting grid front row:
Boutsen, 1m17.919 (pole) and Patrese, 1m17.955. Fastest lap:
Patrese, 1m22.058. Leaders: Boutsen, laps 1-77

Grand Prix de Belgique

25 August 1990. Spa-Francorchamps. 44 laps of a
4.312-mile circuit = 189.728 miles. Race stopped twice by
accidents on lap 1. Restarted over original distance. Warm,
dry and cloudy. World Championship round 11

1 Ayrton Senna   McLaren MP4/5B-Honda 44 1h26m31.997
2 Alain Prost   Ferrari 641/2   44 1h26m35.547
3 Gerhard Berger   McLaren MP4/5B-Honda 44 1h27m00.459
4 Alessandro Nannini   Benetton B190-Ford   44 1h27m21.334
5 Nelson Piquet   Benetton B190-Ford   44 1h28m01.647
6 Mauricio Gugelmin   Leyton House
   CG901-Judd   44 1h28m20.848

Winner's average speed: 131.553 mph. Starting grid front row:
Senna, 1m50.365 (pole) and Berger, 1m50.948. Fastest lap: Prost,
1m55.087. Leaders: Senna, laps 1-44

Coca Cola Gran Premio d'Italia

9 September 1990. Monza. 53 laps of a 3.604-mile circuit =
191.012 miles. Hot, dry and sunny. World Championship
round 12

1 Ayrton Senna   McLaren MP4/5B-Honda 53 1h17m57.878
2 Alain Prost   Ferrari 641/2   53 1h18m03.932
3 Gerhard Berger   McLaren MP4/5B-Honda 53 1h18m05.282
4 Nigel Mansell   Ferrari 641/2   53 1h18m54.097
5 Riccardo Patrese   Williams FW13B-Renault 53 1h19m23.152
6 Satoru Nakajima   Tyrrell 019-Ford   52

Winner's average speed: 146.995 mph. Starting grid front row:
Senna, 1m22.533 (pole) and Prost, 1m22.935. Fastest lap: Senna,
1m26.254. Leaders: Senna, laps 1-53

Grande Premio de Portugal

23 September 1990. Estoril. 61 laps of a 2.703-mile circuit =
164.883 miles. Race scheduled for 71 laps, stopped due to
an accident. Hot, dry and sunny. World Championship
round 13

1 Nigel Mansell   Ferrari 641/2   61 1h22m11.014
2 Ayrton Senna   McLaren MP4/5B-Honda 61 1h22m13.822
3 Alain Prost   Ferrari 641/2   61 1h22m15.203
4 Gerhard Berger   McLaren MP4/5B-Honda 61 1h22m16.910
5 Nelson Piquet   Benetton B190-Ford   61 1h23m08.432
6 Alessandro Nannini   Benetton B190-Ford   61 1h23m09.263

Winner's average speed: 120.377 mph. Starting grid front row:
Mansell, 1m13.557 (pole) and Prost, 1m13.595. Fastest lap:
Patrese, 1m18.306. Leaders: Senna, laps 1-28, 32-49; Berger,
29-31; Mansell, 50-61

Gran Premio Tio Pepe de Espana

30 September 1990. Jerez. 73 laps of a 2.621-mile circuit =
191.333 miles. Hot, dry and sunny. World Championship
round 14

1 Alain Prost   Ferrari 641/2   73 1h48m01.461
2 Nigel Mansell   Ferrari 641/2   73 1h48m23.525
3 Alessandro Nannini   Benetton B190-Ford   73 1h48m36.335
4 Thierry Boutsen   Williams FW13B-Renault 73 1h48m44.757
5 Riccardo Patrese   Williams FW13B-Renault 73 1h48m58.991
6 Aguri Suzuki   Lola 90-Lamborghini   73 1h49m05.189

Winner's average speed: 106.268 mph. Starting grid front row:
Senna, 1m18.387 (pole) and Prost, 1m18.824. Fastest lap: Patrese,
1m24.513. Leaders: Senna, laps 1-26; Piquet, 27-28; Prost, 29-73

Fuji Television Japanese Grand Prix

21 October 1990. Suzuka. 53 laps of a 3.641-mile circuit =
192.973 miles. Hot, dry and sunny. World Championship
round 15

1 Nelson Piquet   Benetton B190-Ford   53 1h34m36.824
2 Roberto Moreno   Benetton B190-Ford   53 1h34m44.047
3 Aguri Suzuki   Lola 90-Lamborghini   53 1h34m59.293
4 Riccardo Patrese   Williams FW13B-Renault 53 1h35m13.082
5 Thierry Boutsen   Williams FW13B-Renault 53 1h35m23.708
6 Satoru Nakajima   Tyrrell 019-Ford   53 1h35m49.174

Winner's average speed: 122.375 mph. Starting grid front row:
Senna, 1m36.996 (pole) and Prost, 1m37.228. Fastest lap: Patrese,
1m44.233. Leaders: Berger, lap 1; Mansell, laps 2-26; Piquet, 27-53

Foster's Australian Grand Prix

4 November 1990. Adelaide. 81 laps of a 2.347-mile circuit
= 190.107 miles. Hot, dry and sunny. World Championship
round 16

1 Nelson Piquet   Benetton B190-Ford   81 1h49m44.570
2 Nigel Mansell   Ferrari 641/2   81 1h49m47.690
3 Alain Prost   Ferrari 641/2   81 1h50m21.829
4 Gerhard Berger   McLaren MP4/5B-Honda 81 1h50m31.432
5 Thierry Boutsen   Williams FW13B-Renault 81 1h51m35.730
6 Riccardo Patrese   Williams FW13B-Renault 80

Winner's average speed: 103.938 mph. Starting grid front row:
Senna, 1m15.671 (pole) and Berger, 1m16.244. Fastest lap:
Mansell, 1m18.203. Leaders: Senna, laps 1-61; Piquet, 62-81

1990 DRIVERS' RECORDS

Driver	Car	United States GP	Brazilian GP	San Marino GP	Monaco GP	Canadian GP	Mexican GP	French GP	British GP	German GP	Hungarian GP	Belgian GP	Italian GP	Portuguese GP	Spanish GP	Japanese GP	Australian GP
Michele Alboreto	Arrows A11B-Ford	10	R	DNQ	DNQ	R	17	10	R	R	12	13	12	9	10	R	DNQ
Jean Alesi	Tyrrell 018-Ford	2	7	-	-	-	-	-	-	-	-	-	-	-	-	-	-
	Tyrrell 019-Ford	-	-	6	2	R	7	8	11	R	8	R	8	8	R	DNS	8
Philippe Alliot	Ligier JS33B-Ford	DNQ	12	9	R	R	18	9	13	R	14	DNQ	13	R	R	10	11
Paolo Barilla	Minardi M189-Ford	R	R	-	-	-	-	-	-	-	-	-	-	-	-	-	-
	Minardi M190-Ford	-	-	11	R	DNQ	14	DNQ	12	DNQ	15	R	DNQ	DNQ	DNQ	-	-
Gerhard Berger	McLaren MP4/5B-Honda	R^PF	2^F	2	3	4^F	3^P	5	14	3	16	3	3	4	R	R	4
Eric Bernard	Lola LC89-Lamborghini	8	R	-	-	-	-	-	-	-	-	-	-	-	-	-	-
	Lola 90-Lamborghini	-	-	13	6	9	R	8	4	R	6	9	R	R	R	R	R
Thierry Boutsen	Williams FW13B-Renault	3	5	R	4	R	5	R	2	6^F	1^P	R	R	R	4	5	5
David Brabham	Brabham BT59-Judd	-	-	DNQ	R	DNQ	R	15	DNQ	R	DNQ	R	DNQ	R	DNQ	R	R
Gary Brabham	Life F190	NPQ	NPQ	-	-	-	-	-	-	-	-	-	-	-	-	-	-
Alex Caffi	Arrows A11B-Ford	-	R	DNQ	5	8	DNQ	R	7	9	9	10	9	13	-	9	DNQ
Ivan Capelli	Leyton House CG901-Judd	R	DNQ	R	R	10	DNQ	2	R	7	R	7	R	R	R	R	R
Andrea de Cesaris	Dallara F190-Ford	R	R	R	R	R	13	DSQ	R	DNQ	R	R	10	R	R	R	R
Yannick Dalmas	AGS JH24-Ford	NPQ	R	-	-	-	-	-	-	-	-	-	-	-	-	-	-
	AGS JH25-Ford	-	-	DNP	NPQ	NPQ	NPQ	17	NPQ	DNQ	DNQ	DNQ	NC	R	9	DNQ	DNQ
Martin Donnelly	Lotus 102-Lamborghini	DNS	R	8	R	R	8	12	R	R	7	12	R	R	DNS	-	-
Gregor Foitek	Brabham BT58-Judd	R	R	-	-	-	-	-	-	-	-	-	-	-	-	-	-
	Onyx ORE2-Ford	-	-	R	7	R	15	DNQ	DNQ	-	-	-	-	-	-	-	-
	Monteverdi ORE2-Ford	-	-	-	-	-	-	-	-	R	DNQ	-	-	-	-	-	-
Bertrand Gachot	Coloni C3B-Subaru	NPQ	NPQ	NPQ	NPQ	NPQ	NPQ	NPQ	NPQ	-	-	-	-	-	-	-	-
	Coloni C3B-Ford	-	-	-	-	-	-	-	-	NPQ	NPQ	DNQ	DNQ	DNQ	DNQ	DNQ	DNQ
Bruno Giacomelli	Life F190	-	-	NPQ	NPQ	NPQ	NPQ	NPQ	NPQ	NPQ	NPQ	NPQ	NPQ	-	-	-	-
	Life F190-Judd	-	-	-	-	-	-	-	-	-	-	-	-	NPQ	NPQ	-	-
Olivier Grouillard	Osella FA1M-Ford	R	R	-	-	-	-	-	-	-	-	-	-	-	-	-	-
	Osella FA1Me-Ford	-	-	R	DNQ	13	19	NPQ	DNQ	DNQ	NPQ	16	R	DNQ	R	DNQ	13
Mauricio Gugelmin	Leyton House CG901-Judd	14	DNQ	R	DNQ	DNQ	DNQ	R	DNS	R	8	6	R	12	8	R	R
Johnny Herbert	Lotus 102-Lamborghini	-	-	-	-	-	-	-	-	-	-	-	-	-	-	R	R
Stefan Johansson	Onyx ORE1-Ford	DNQ	DNQ	-	-	-	-	-	-	-	-	-	-	-	-	-	-
Claudio Langes	EuroBrun ER189-Judd	NPQ	NPQ	-	-	-	-	-	-	-	-	-	-	-	-	-	-
	EuroBrun ER189B-Judd	-	-	NPQ	NPQ	NPQ	NPQ	NPQ	NPQ	NPQ	NPQ	NPQ	NPQ	NPQ	NPQ	-	-
Nicola Larini	Ligier JS33B-Ford	R	11	10	R	R	16	14	10	10	11	14	11	10	7	7	10
JJ Lehto	Onyx ORE1-Ford	DNQ	DNQ	-	-	-	-	-	-	-	-	-	-	-	-	-	-
	Onyx ORE2-Ford	-	-	12	R	R	R	DNQ	DNQ	-	-	-	-	-	-	-	-
	Monteverdi ORE2-Ford	-	-	-	-	-	-	-	-	NC	DNQ	-	-	-	-	-	-
Nigel Mansell	Ferrari 641	R	4	-	-	-	-	-	-	-	-	-	-	-	-	-	-
	Ferrari 641/2	-	-	R	R	3	2	18^PF	R^PF	R	17	R	4	1^P	2	R	2^F
Pierluigi Martini	Minardi M189-Ford	7	9	-	-	-	-	-	-	-	-	-	-	-	-	-	-
	Minardi M190-Ford	-	-	DNS	R	R	12	R	R	R	15	R	11	R	8	9	
Stefano Modena	Brabham BT58-Judd	5	R	-	-	-	-	-	-	-	-	-	-	-	-	-	-
	Brabham BT59-Judd	-	-	R	R	7	11	13	9	R	R	17	R	R	R	R	12
Gianni Morbidelli	Dallara F190-Ford	DNQ	14	-	-	-	-	-	-	-	-	-	-	-	-	-	-
	Minardi M190-Ford	-	-	-	-	-	-	-	-	-	-	-	-	-	-	R	R
Roberto Moreno	EuroBrun ER189-Judd	13	NPQ	-	-	-	-	-	-	-	-	-	-	-	-	-	-
	EuroBrun ER189B-Judd	-	-	R	DNQ	DNQ	DNQ	NPQ	NPQ	NPQ	NPQ	NPQ	NPQ	NPQ	NPQ	-	-
	Benetton B190-Ford	-	-	-	-	-	-	-	-	-	-	-	-	-	-	2	7
Satoru Nakajima	Tyrrell 018-Ford	6	8	-	-	-	-	-	-	-	-	-	-	-	-	-	-
	Tyrrell 019-Ford	-	-	R	R	11	R	R	R	R	R	R	6	DNS	R	6	R
Alessandro Nannini	Benetton B189B-Ford	11	10	-	-	-	-	-	-	-	-	-	-	-	-	-	-
	Benetton B190-Ford	-	-	3^F	R	R	4	16	R	2	R	4	8	6	3	-	-
Riccardo Patrese	Williams FW13B-Renault	9	13	1	R	R	9	6	R	5	4^F	R	5	7^F	5^F	4^F	6
Nelson Piquet	Benetton B189B-Ford	4	6	-	-	-	-	-	-	-	-	-	-	-	-	-	-
	Benetton B190-Ford	-	-	5	R	2	6	4	5	R	3	5	7	5	R	1	1
Emanuele Pirro	Dallara F190-Ford	-	-	R	R	R	R	R	11	R	10	R	R	15	R	R	R
Alain Prost	Ferrari 641	R	1	-	-	-	-	-	-	-	-	-	-	-	-	-	-
	Ferrari 641/2	-	-	4	R	5	1^F	1	1	4	R	2^F	2	3	1	R	3
Bernd Schneider	Arrows A11-Ford	12	-	-	-	-	-	-	-	-	-	-	-	-	-	-	-
	Arrows A11B-Ford	-	-	-	-	-	-	-	-	-	-	-	-	-	DNQ	-	-
Ayrton Senna	McLaren MP4/5B-Honda	1	3^P	R^P	1^PF	1^P	20	3	3	1^P	2	1^P	1^PF	2	R^P	R^P	R^P
Aguri Suzuki	Lola LC89-Lamborghini	R	R	-	-	-	-	-	-	-	-	-	-	-	-	-	-
	Lola 90-Lamborghini	-	-	R	R	12	R	7	6	R	R	R	R	14	6	3	R
Gabriele Tarquini	AGS JH24-Ford	NPQ	NPQ	-	-	-	-	-	-	-	-	-	-	-	-	-	-
	AGS JH25-Ford	-	-	NPQ	NPQ	NPQ	NPQ	DNQ	R	NPQ	13	DNQ	DNQ	DNQ	R	DNQ	R
Derek Warwick	Lotus 102-Lamborghini	R	R	7	R	6	10	11	R	8	5	11	R	R	R	R	R

1990 FINAL CHAMPIONSHIP POSITIONS

Drivers

1	Ayrton Senna	78	10=	Ivan Capelli	6
2	Alain Prost	71 (73)*		Roberto Moreno	6
3=	Gerhard Berger	43		Aguri Suzuki	6
	Nelson Piquet	43 (44)*	13	Eric Bernard	5
5	Nigel Mansell	37	14=	Satoru Nakajima	3
6	Thierry Boutsen	34		Derek Warwick	3
7	Riccardo Patrese	23	16=	Alex Caffi	2
8	Alessandro Nannini	21		Stefano Modena	2
9	Jean Alesi	13	18	Mauricio Gugelmin	1
				*Best 11 results count	

Manufacturers

1	McLaren-Honda	121
2	Ferrari	110
3	Benetton-Ford	71
4	Williams-Renault	57
5	Tyrrell-Ford	16
6	Lola-Lamborghini	11
7	Leyton House-Judd	7
8	Lotus-Lamborghini	3
9=	Arrows-Ford	2
	Brabham-Judd	2

1991

Ayrton Senna effectively clinched his third World Championship by winning the first four races of the year. During that time Nigel Mansell and Riccardo Patrese struggled to sort out their state-of-the-art but as yet unreliable Williams-Renaults. The Brazilian sealed the series with three more victories including the wet and shortened Australian GP. Furthermore, with the championship settled, Senna pulled over at the last corner of the Japanese GP to let Gerhard Berger win his first race for McLaren.

Mansell came tantalizingly close to winning in Canada only to retire on the last corner, handing victory to Nelson Piquet's Benetton. The Williams-Renaults finally held together in Mexico, but it was Patrese who led home. It eventually came good for Mansell in France and another four wins followed, but he could not catch up with Senna in the championship.

Ferrari had a poor year which ended with team leader Alain Prost being dropped prior to the Australian GP as the team management finally reacted to his public criticism of the organization. It was the first year since his debut season in 1980 that Prost had failed to win a Grand Prix. Jean Alesi came closest to giving Ferrari a win, only to retire while leading in Belgium.

Tyrrell replaced Alesi with Stefano Modena and switched to Honda V10 power. Modena's second place in Montreal was the highlight in an otherwise disappointing year.

The 7Up-sponsored Jordan team made a major impact in its first season in Grand Prix racing. But for engine failure in the closing laps, Andrea de Cesaris might have won at Spa. Bertrand Gachot also showed promise, but was jailed prior to his home Belgian GP for spraying CS gas into the face of a London taxi driver. Eddie Jordan replaced Gachot with the young Mercedes-Benz sports car driver Michael Schumacher, and the German proved so sensational in practice that Benetton controversially signed him prior to the next race.

Lotus fought back from the brink of liquidation, with Julian Bailey and the promising F3 graduate Mika Häkkinen scoring points at Imola.

Iceberg United States Grand Prix

10 March 1991. Phoenix. 81 laps of a 2.312-mile circuit = 187.272 miles. Race scheduled for 82 laps but stopped due to the two hour rule. Warm, dry and overcast. World Championship round 1

1	Ayrton Senna	McLaren MP4/6-Honda	81 2h00m47.828
2	Alain Prost	Ferrari 642	81 2h01m04.150
3	Nelson Piquet	Benetton B190B-Ford	81 2h01m05.204
4	Stefano Modena	Tyrrell 020-Honda	81 2h01m13.237
5	Satoru Nakajima	Tyrrell 020-Honda	80
6	Aguri Suzuki	Lola L91-Ford	79

Winner's average speed: 93.018 mph. Starting grid front row: Senna, 1m21.434 (pole) and Prost, 1m22.555. Fastest lap: Alesi, 1m26.758. Leaders: Senna, laps 1-81

Grande Premio do Brasil

24 March 1991. Interlagos. 71 laps of a 2.687-mile circuit = 190.777 miles. Warm and overcast, wet in closing laps. World Championship round 2

1	Ayrton Senna	McLaren MP4/6-Honda	71 1h38m28.128
2	Riccardo Patrese	Williams FW14-Renault	71 1h38m31.119
3	Gerhard Berger	McLaren MP4/6-Honda	71 1h38m33.544
4	Alain Prost	Ferrari 642	71 1h38m47.497
5	Nelson Piquet	Benetton B190B-Ford	71 1h38m50.088
6	Jean Alesi	Ferrari 642	71 1h38m51.769

Winner's average speed: 116.246 mph. Starting grid front row: Senna, 1m16.392 (pole) and Patrese, 1m16.775. Fastest lap: Mansell, 1m20.436. Leaders: Senna, laps 1-71

Gran Premio di San Marino

28 April 1991. Imola. 61 laps of a 3.132-mile circuit = 191.052 miles. Warm and sunny, wet track, drying. World Championship round 3

1	Ayrton Senna	McLaren MP4/6-Honda	61 1h35m14.750
2	Gerhard Berger	McLaren MP4/6-Honda	61 1h35m16.425
3	JJ Lehto	Dallara F191-Judd	60
4	Pierluigi Martini	Minardi M191-Ferrari	59
5	Mika Häkkinen	Lotus 102B-Judd	58
6	Julian Bailey	Lotus 102B-Judd	58

Winner's average speed: 120.353 mph. Starting grid front row: Senna, 1m21.877 (pole) and Patrese, 1m21.957. Fastest lap: Berger, 1m26.531. Leaders: Patrese, laps 1-9; Senna, 10-61

Grand Prix de Monaco

12 May 1991. Monte Carlo. 78 laps of a 2.068-mile circuit = 161.304 miles. Warm, dry and sunny. World Championship round 4

1	Ayrton Senna	McLaren MP4/6-Honda	78 1h53m02.334
2	Nigel Mansell	Williams FW14-Renault	78 1h53m20.682
3	Jean Alesi	Ferrari 642	78 1h53m49.789
4	Roberto Moreno	Benetton B191-Ford	77
5	Alain Prost	Ferrari 642	77
6	Emanuele Pirro	Dallara F191-Judd	77

Winner's average speed: 85.619 mph. Starting grid front row: Senna, 1m20.344 (pole) and Modena, 1m20.809. Fastest lap: Prost, 1m24.368. Leaders: Senna, laps 1-78

Grand Prix Molson du Canada

2 June 1991. Montreal. 69 laps of a 2.753-mile circuit = 189.957 miles. Hot, dry and sunny. World Championship round 5

1 Nelson Piquet	Benetton B191-Ford	69	1h38m51.490
2 Stefano Modena	Tyrrell 020-Honda	69	1h39m23.322
3 Riccardo Patrese	Williams FW14-Renault	69	1h39m33.707
4 Andrea de Cesaris	Jordan 191-Ford	69	1h40m11.700
5 Bertrand Gachot	Jordan 191-Ford	69	1h40m13.841
6 Nigel Mansell	Williams FW14-Renault	68	ignition

Winner's average speed: 115.291 mph. Starting grid front row: Patrese, 1m19.837 (pole) and Mansell, 1m20.225. Fastest lap: Mansell, 1m22.385. Leaders: Mansell, laps 1-68; Piquet, 69

Gran Premio de Mexico

16 June 1991. Mexico City. 67 laps of a 2.747-mile circuit = 184.049 miles. Race scheduled for 69 laps but reduced after two false starts. Warm, dry and sunny. World Championship round 6

1 Riccardo Patrese	Williams FW14-Renault	67	1h29m52.205
2 Nigel Mansell	Williams FW14-Renault	67	1h29m53.541
3 Ayrton Senna	McLaren MP4/6-Honda	67	1h30m49.561
4 Andrea de Cesaris	Jordan 191-Ford	66	throttle
5 Roberto Moreno	Benetton B191-Ford	66	
6 Eric Bernard	Lola L91-Ford	66	

Winner's average speed: 122.877 mph. Starting grid front row: Patrese, 1m16.696 (pole) and Mansell, 1m16.978. Fastest lap: Mansell, 1m16.788. Leaders: Mansell, laps 1-14; Patrese, 15-67

Rhône-Poulenc Grand Prix de France

7 July 1991. Magny-Cours. 72 laps of a 2.654-mile circuit = 191.088 miles. Warm, dry and overcast. World Championship round 7

1 Nigel Mansell	Williams FW14-Renault	72	1h38m00.056
2 Alain Prost	Ferrari 643	72	1h38m05.059
3 Ayrton Senna	McLaren MP4/6-Honda	72	1h38m34.990
4 Jean Alesi	Ferrari 643	72	1h38m35.976
5 Riccardo Patrese	Williams FW14-Renault	71	
6 Andrea de Cesaris	Jordan 191-Ford	71	

Winner's average speed: 116.992 mph. Starting grid front row: Patrese, 1m14.559 (pole) and Prost, 1m14.789. Fastest lap: Mansell, 1m19.168. Leaders: Prost, laps 1-21, 32-54; Mansell, 22-31, 55-72

Ayrton Senna leads Gerhard Berger during the wet Australian Grand Prix

British Grand Prix

14 July 1991. Silverstone. 59 laps of a 3.247-mile circuit = 191.573 miles. Hot, dry and sunny. World Championship round 8

1 Nigel Mansell	Williams FW14-Renault	59	1h27m35.479
2 Gerhard Berger	McLaren MP4/6-Honda	59	1h28m17.772
3 Alain Prost	Ferrari 643	59	1h28m35.629
4 Ayrton Senna	McLaren MP4/6-Honda	58	out of fuel
5 Nelson Piquet	Benetton B191-Ford	58	
6 Bertrand Gachot	Jordan 191-Ford	58	

Winner's average speed: 131.227 mph. Starting grid front row: Mansell, 1m20.939 (pole) and Senna, 1m21.618. Fastest lap: Mansell, 1m26.379. Leaders: Mansell, laps 1-59

Grosser Mobil 1 Preis von Deutschland

28 July 1991. Hockenheim. 45 laps of a 4.227-mile circuit = 190.215 miles. Hot, dry and sunny. World Championship round 9

1 Nigel Mansell	Williams FW14-Renault	45	1h19m29.661
2 Riccardo Patrese	Williams FW14-Renault	45	1h19m43.440
3 Jean Alesi	Ferrari 643	45	1h19m47.279
4 Gerhard Berger	McLaren MP4/6-Honda	45	1h20m02.312
5 Andrea de Cesaris	Jordan 191-Ford	45	1h20m47.198
6 Bertrand Gachot	Jordan 191-Ford	45	1h21m10.226

Winner's average speed: 143.565 mph. Starting grid front row: Mansell, 1m37.087 (pole) and Senna, 1m37.274. Fastest lap: Patrese, 1m43.569. Leaders: Mansell, laps 1-18, 21-45; Alesi, 19-20

Magyar Nagydij (Hungarian Grand Prix)

11 August 1991. Hungaroring. 77 laps of a 2.466-mile circuit = 189.882 miles. Hot, dry and sunny. World Championship round 10

1 Ayrton Senna	McLaren MP4/6-Honda	77	1h49m12.796
2 Nigel Mansell	Williams FW14-Renault	77	1h49m17.395
3 Riccardo Patrese	Williams FW14-Renault	77	1h49m28.390
4 Gerhard Berger	McLaren MP4/6-Honda	77	1h49m34.652
5 Jean Alesi	Ferrari 643	77	1h49m44.185
6 Ivan Capelli	Leyton House CG911-Ilmor	76	

Winner's average speed: 104.318 mph. Starting grid front row: Senna, 1m16.147 (pole) and Patrese, 1m17.379. Fastest lap: Gachot, 1m21.547. Leaders: Senna, laps 1-77

Grand Prix de Belgique

25 August 1991. Spa-Francorchamps. 44 laps of a 4.312-mile circuit = 189.728 miles. Hot, dry and sunny. World Championship round 11

1 Ayrton Senna	McLaren MP4/6-Honda	44	1h27m17.669
2 Gerhard Berger	McLaren MP4/6-Honda	44	1h27m19.570
3 Nelson Piquet	Benetton B191-Ford	44	1h27m49.845
4 Roberto Moreno	Benetton B191-Ford	44	1h27m54.979
5 Riccardo Patrese	Williams FW14-Renault	44	1h28m14.856
6 Mark Blundell	Brabham BT60Y-Yamaha	44	1h28m57.704

Winner's average speed: 130.405 mph. Starting grid front row: Senna, 1m47.811 (pole) and Prost, 1m48.821. Fastest lap: Moreno, 1m55.161. Leaders: Senna, laps 1-14, 31-44; Mansell, 15-16, 18-21; Piquet, 17; Alesi, 22-30

Coca Cola Gran Premio d'Italia

8 September 1991. Monza. 53 laps of a 3.604-mile circuit = 191.012 miles. Warm, dry and hazy. World Championship round 12

1 Nigel Mansell	Williams FW14-Renault	53	1h17m54.319
2 Ayrton Senna	McLaren MP4/6-Honda	53	1h18m10.581
3 Alain Prost	Ferrari 643	53	1h18m11.148
4 Gerhard Berger	McLaren MP4/6-Honda	53	1h18m22.038
5 Michael Schumacher	Benetton B191-Ford	53	1h18m28.782
6 Nelson Piquet	Benetton B191-Ford	53	1h18m39.919

Winner's average speed: 147.107 mph. Starting grid front row: Senna, 1m21.114 (pole) and Mansell, 1m21.247. Fastest lap: Senna, 1m26.061. Leaders: Senna, laps 1-25, 27-33; Patrese, 26; Mansell, 34-53

Grande Premio de Portugal

22 September 1991. Estoril. 71 laps of a 2.703-mile circuit = 191.913 miles. Warm, dry and sunny. World Championship round 13

1 Riccardo Patrese	Williams FW14-Renault	71	1h35m42.304
2 Ayrton Senna	McLaren MP4/6-Honda	71	1h36m03.245
3 Jean Alesi	Ferrari 643	71	1h36m35.858
4 Pierluigi Martini	Minardi M191-Ferrari	71	1h36m45.802
5 Nelson Piquet	Benetton B191-Ford	71	1h36m52.337
6 Michael Schumacher	Benetton B191-Ford	71	1h36m58.886

World Championship Grand Prix Racing

1991 DRIVERS' RECORDS

Driver	Car	United States GP	Brazilian GP	San Marino GP	Monaco GP	Canadian GP	Mexican GP	French GP	British GP	German GP	Hungarian GP	Belgian GP	Italian GP	Portuguese GP	Spanish GP	Japanese GP	Australian GP
Michele Alboreto	Footwork A11C-Porsche	R	DNQ	DNQ	-	-	-	-	-	-	-	-	-	-	-	-	-
	Footwork FA12-Porsche	-	-	-	R	R	R	-	-	-	-	-	-	-	-	-	-
	Footwork FA12-Ford	-	-	-	-	-	-	R	R	DNQ	DNQ	NPQ	DNQ	15	R	DNQ	13
Jean Alesi	Ferrari 642	12[F]	6	R	3	R	R	-	-	-	-	-	-	-	-	-	-
	Ferrari 643	-	-	-	-	-	-	4	R	3	5	R	R	3	4	R	R
Julian Bailey	Lotus 102B-Judd	DNQ	DNQ	6	DNQ	-	-	-	-	-	-	-	-	-	-	-	-
Fabrizio Barbazza	AGS JH25-Ford	-	-	DNQ	DNQ	DNQ	DNQ	-	-	-	-	-	-	-	-	-	-
	AGS JH25B-Ford	-	-	-	-	-	-	DNQ	DNQ	NPQ	NPQ	NPQ	NPQ	-	-	-	-
	AGS JH27-Ford	-	-	-	-	-	-	-	-	-	-	-	-	NPQ	NPQ	-	-
Michael Bartels	Lotus 102B-Judd	-	-	-	-	-	-	-	-	DNQ	DNQ	-	DNQ	-	DNQ	-	-
Gerhard Berger	McLaren MP4/6-Honda	R	3	2[F]	R	R	R	R	2	4	4	2	4	R	R[P]	1[P]	3[F]
Eric Bernard	Lola L91-Ford	R	R	R	9	R	6	R	R	R	R	R	R	DNQ	R	DNP	-
Mark Blundell	Brabham BT59Y-Yamaha	R	R	-	-	-	-	-	-	-	-	-	-	-	-	-	-
	Brabham BT60Y-Yamaha	-	-	8	R	DNQ	R	R	R	12	R	6	12	R	R	NPQ	17
Thierry Boutsen	Ligier JS35-Lamborghini	R	10	7	7	R	8	-	-	-	-	-	-	-	-	-	-
	Ligier JS35B-Lamborghini	-	-	-	-	-	-	12	R	9	17	11	R	16	R	9	R
Martin Brundle	Brabham BT59Y-Yamaha	11	12	-	-	-	-	-	-	-	-	-	-	-	-	-	-
	Brabham BT60Y-Yamaha	-	-	11	DNQ	R	R	R	R	11	R	9	13	12	10	5	DNQ
Alex Caffi	Footwork A11C-Porsche	DNQ	DNQ	-	-	-	-	-	-	-	-	-	-	-	-	-	-
	Footwork FA12-Porsche	-	-	DNQ	DNQ	-	-	-	-	-	-	-	-	-	-	-	-
	Footwork FA12-Ford	-	-	-	-	-	-	-	-	NPQ	NPQ	DNQ	NPQ	NPQ	NPQ	10	15
Ivan Capelli	Leyton House CG911-Ilmor	R	R	R	R	R	R	R	R	R	6	R	8	17	R	-	-
Andrea de Cesaris	Jordan 191-Ford	NPQ	R	R	R	4	4	6	R	5	7	13	7	8	R	R	8
Pedro Chaves	Coloni C4-Ford	NPQ	NPQ	NPQ	NPQ	NPQ	NPQ	NPQ	NPQ	NPQ	NPQ	NPQ	NPQ	NPQ	DNP	-	-
Erik Comas	Ligier JS35-Lamborghini	DNQ	R	10	10	8	DNQ	-	-	-	-	-	-	-	-	-	-
	Ligier JS35B-Lamborghini	-	-	-	-	-	-	11	DNQ	R	10	R	11	11	R	R	18
Bertrand Gachot	Jordan 191-Ford	10	R	R	8	5	R	R	6	6	9[F]	-	-	-	-	-	-
	Lola L91-Ford	-	-	-	-	-	-	-	-	-	-	-	-	-	-	-	DNQ
Olivier Grouillard	Fomet FA1Me-Ford	NPQ	NPQ	-	-	-	-	-	-	-	-	-	-	-	-	-	-
	Fomet F1-Ford	-	-	NPQ	NPQ	NPQ	R	R	NPQ	NPQ	DNQ	10	R	NPQ	-	-	-
	AGS JH27-Ford	-	-	-	-	-	-	-	-	-	-	-	-	-	NPQ	-	-
Mauricio Gugelmin	Leyton House CG911-Ilmor	R	R	12	R	R	R	7	R	R	11	R	15	7	7	8	14
Mika Häkkinen	Lotus 102B-Judd	R	9	5	R	R	9	DNQ	12	R	14	R	14	14	R	R	19
Naoki Hattori	Coloni C4-Ford	-	-	-	-	-	-	-	-	-	-	-	-	-	-	NPQ	NPQ
Johnny Herbert	Lotus 102B-Judd	-	-	-	-	DNQ	10	10	14	-	-	7	-	R	-	R	11
Stefan Johansson	AGS JH25-Ford	DNQ	DNQ	-	-	-	-	-	-	-	-	-	-	-	-	-	-
	Footwork FA12-Porsche	-	-	-	-	R	DNQ	-	-	-	-	-	-	-	-	-	-
	Footwork FA12-Ford	-	-	-	-	-	-	-	-	DNQ	DNQ	-	-	-	-	-	-
Nicola Larini	Lamborghini 291	7	NPQ	NPQ	NPQ	NPQ	NPQ	NPQ	NPQ	R	16	DNQ	16	DNQ	DNQ	DNQ	R
JJ Lehto	Dallara F191-Judd	R	R	3	11	R	R	R	13	R	R	R	R	R	8	R	12
Nigel Mansell	Williams FW14-Renault	R	R[F]	R	2	6[F]	2[F]	1[F]	1[PF]	1[P]	2	R	1	R	1	R	2
Pierluigi Martini	Minardi M191-Ferrari	9	R	4	12	7	R	9	9	R	R	12	R	4	13	R	R
Stefano Modena	Tyrrell 020-Honda	4	R	R	R	2	11	R	7	13	12	R	R	R	16	6	10
Gianni Morbidelli	Minardi M191-Ferrari	R	8	R	R	R	7	R	11	R	13	R	9	9	14	R	-
	Ferrari 643	-	-	-	-	-	-	-	-	-	-	-	-	-	-	-	6
Roberto Moreno	Benetton B190B-Ford	R	7	-	-	-	-	-	-	-	-	-	-	-	-	-	-
	Benetton B191-Ford	-	-	R	4	R	5	R	R	8	8	4[F]	-	-	-	-	-
	Jordan 191-Ford	-	-	-	-	-	-	-	-	-	-	-	-	R	10	-	-
	Minardi M191-Ferrari	-	-	-	-	-	-	-	-	-	-	-	-	-	-	-	16
Satoru Nakajima	Tyrrell 020-Honda	5	R	R	R	10	12	R	8	R	15	R	R	13	17	R	R
Riccardo Patrese	Williams FW14-Renault	R	2	R	R	3[P]	1[P]	5[P]	R	2[F]	3	5	R	1[PF]	3[F]	3	5
Nelson Piquet	Benetton B190B-Ford	3	5	-	-	-	-	-	-	-	-	-	-	-	-	-	-
	Benetton B191-Ford	-	-	R	R	1	R	8	5	R	R	3	6	5	11	7	4
Emanuele Pirro	Dallara F191-Judd	R	11	NPQ	6	9	NPQ	NPQ	10	10	R	8	10	R	15	R	7
Eric van de Poele	Lamborghini 291	NPQ	NPQ	9	NPQ	NPQ	NPQ	NPQ	NPQ	DNQ	DNQ	DNQ	DNQ	DNQ	DNQ	DNQ	DNQ
Alain Prost	Ferrari 642	2	4	DNS	5[F]	R	R	-	-	-	-	-	-	-	-	-	-
	Ferrari 643	-	-	-	-	-	-	2	3	R	R	R	3	R	2	4	-
Michael Schumacher	Jordan 191-Ford	-	-	-	-	-	-	-	-	-	-	R	-	-	-	-	-
	Benetton B191-Ford	-	-	-	-	-	-	-	-	-	-	-	5	6	6	R	R
Ayrton Senna	McLaren MP4/6-Honda	1[P]	1[P]	1[P]	1[P]	R	3	3	4	7	1[P]	1[P]	2[PF]	2	5	2[F]	1[P]
Aguri Suzuki	Lola L91-Ford	6	DNS	R	R	R	R	R	R	R	R	DNQ	DNQ	R	DNQ	R	DNQ
Gabriele Tarquini	AGS JH25-Ford	8	R	DNQ	R	DNQ	DNQ	-	-	-	-	-	-	-	-	-	-
	AGS JH25B-Ford	-	-	-	-	-	-	DNQ	DNQ	DNQ	NPQ	NPQ	-	-	-	-	-
	AGS JH27-Ford	-	-	-	-	-	-	-	-	-	-	-	-	NPQ	DNQ	-	-
	Fomet F1-Ford	-	-	-	-	-	-	-	-	-	-	-	-	-	12	11	NPQ
Karl Wendlinger	Leyton House CG911-Ilmor	-	-	-	-	-	-	-	-	-	-	-	-	-	-	R	20
Alessandro Zanardi	Jordan 191-Ford	-	-	-	-	-	-	-	-	-	-	-	-	-	9	R	9

Winner's average speed: 120.315 mph. Starting grid front row: Patrese, 1m13.001 (pole) and Berger, 1m13.221. Fastest lap: Patrese, 1m18.350 (Mansell set a fastest lap of 1m18.179 after he had been disqualified). Leaders: Patrese, laps 1-17, 30-71; Mansell, 18-29

Gran Premio Tio Pepe de Espana

29 September 1991. Catalunya. 65 laps of a 2.950-mile circuit = 191.750 miles. Warm and overcast, damp track, drying. World Championship round 14

1 Nigel Mansell	Williams FW14-Renault	65	1h38m41.541
2 Alain Prost	Ferrari 643	65	1h38m52.872
3 Riccardo Patrese	Williams FW14-Renault	65	1h38m57.450
4 Jean Alesi	Ferrari 643	65	1h39m04.313
5 Ayrton Senna	McLaren MP4/6-Honda	65	1h39m43.943
6 Michael Schumacher	Benetton B191-Ford	65	1h40m01.009

Winner's average speed: 116.563 mph. Starting grid front row: Berger, 1m18.751 (pole) and Mansell, 1m18.970. Fastest lap: Patrese, 1m22.837. Leaders: Berger, laps 1-8, 12-20; Mansell, 9, 21-65; Patrese, 10, Senna, 11

Fuji Television Japanese Grand Prix

20 October 1991. Suzuka. 53 laps of a 3.641-mile circuit = 192.973 miles. Warm, dry and sunny. World Championship round 15

1 Gerhard Berger	McLaren MP4/6-Honda	53	1h32m10.695
2 Ayrton Senna	McLaren MP4/6-Honda	53	1h32m11.039
3 Riccardo Patrese	Williams FW14-Renault	53	1h33m07.426
4 Alain Prost	Ferrari 643	53	1h33m31.456
5 Martin Brundle	Brabham BT60Y-Yamaha	52	
6 Stefano Modena	Tyrrell 020-Honda	52	

Winner's average speed: 125.609 mph. Starting grid front row: Berger, 1m34.700 (pole) and Senna, 1m34.898. Fastest lap: Senna, 1m41.532. Leaders: Berger, laps 1-17, 53; Senna, 18-21, 24-52; Patrese, 22-23

Foster's Australian Grand Prix

3 November 1991. Adelaide. 14 laps of a 2.347-mile circuit = 32.858 miles. Race scheduled for 81 laps, reduced due to unsafe conditions; half points awarded as under 60% of the race had been completed. Very wet. World Championship round 16

1 Ayrton Senna	McLaren MP4/6-Honda	14	24m34.899
2 Nigel Mansell	Williams FW14-Renault	14	24m36.158
3 Gerhard Berger	McLaren MP4/6-Honda	14	24m40.019
4 Nelson Piquet	Benetton B191-Ford	14	25m05.002
5 Riccardo Patrese	Williams FW14-Renault	14	25m25.436
6 Gianni Morbidelli	Ferrari 643	14	25m25.968

Winner's average speed: 80.201 mph. Starting grid front row: Senna, 1m14.041 (pole) and Berger, 1m14.385. Fastest lap: Berger, 1m41.141. Leaders: Senna, laps 1-14

1991 FINAL CHAMPIONSHIP POSITIONS

Drivers						Manufacturers		
1	Ayrton Senna	96		JJ Lehto	4	1	McLaren-Honda	139
2	Nigel Mansell	72		Michael Schumacher	4	2	Williams-Renault	125
3	Riccardo Patrese	53	15=	Martin Brundle	2	3	Ferrari	55.5
4	Gerhard Berger	43		Mika Häkkinen	2	4	Benetton-Ford	38.5
5	Alain Prost	34		Satoru Nakajima	2	5	Jordan-Ford	13
6	Nelson Piquet	26.5	18=	Julian Bailey	1	6	Tyrrell-Honda	12
7	Jean Alesi	21		Eric Bernard	1	7	Minardi-Ferrari	6
8	Stefano Modena	10		Mark Blundell	1	8	Dallara-Judd	5
9	Andrea de Cesaris	9		Ivan Capelli	1	9=	Lotus-Judd	3
10	Roberto Moreno	8		Emanuele Pirro	1		Brabham-Yamaha	3
11	Pierluigi Martini	6		Aguri Suzuki	1	11	Lola-Ford	2
12=	Bertrand Gachot	4	24	Gianni Morbidelli	0.5	12	Leyon House-Ilmor	1

1992

At last it was Nigel Mansell's year; with a fully reliable Williams FW14B-Renault there was never any doubt who would be World Champion. He made a record start to the season with five successive Grand Prix victories, and added four more to clinch the title in a record-breaking season. His win at Silverstone in July sparked a patriotic crowd invasion when other cars were still running at speed. Mansell's rear wheel bowled one man over but thankfully no one was hurt.

Despite finishing second in the championship, Riccardo Patrese would not be retained at Williams for 1993. Both Ayrton Senna and Alain Prost (who had taken a year off) vied to join Mansell in what was clearly the best drive available. The Brazilian even offered to drive for free, but it was Prost who signed. Mansell, unhappy with his treatment by the team during negotiations with Prost, decided to move to Indycars in 1993 rather than defend his World Championship.

Despite being at the height of his powers, Ayrton Senna had to be content with just three wins for McLaren. When Mansell was delayed in the Monaco GP, Senna held off the Williams to equal Graham Hill's record of five victories in the principality. Gerhard Berger lived in Senna's shadow, but scored a couple of victories after his team-mate and the Williams duo had retired.

Michael Schumacher continued his outstanding introduction to Formula One with Benetton. His victory in Belgium a year after his debut, and another ten top six finishes, gave the German third in the championship. Team-mate Martin Brundle could not match Schumacher in practice but often raced well - almost winning in Canada, holding off Senna in Britain and finishing second at Monza.

Ferrari's fortunes sank yet further in 1992; Jean Alesi never finished higher than third, while former Leyton House star Ivan Capelli was sacked before the end of a disastrous year.

Mika Häkkinen and Johnny Herbert enjoyed an increasingly competitive season with Lotus, giving the team fifth place in the Constructors' Championship. Häkkinen gained the results but Herbert was normally quicker, only to retire from all bar four races.

Yellow Pages South African Grand Prix

1 March 1992. Kyalami. 72 laps of a 2.648-mile circuit = 190.656 miles. Warm, dry and overcast. World Championship round 1

1 Nigel Mansell	Williams FW14B-Renault	72	1h36m45.320
2 Riccardo Patrese	Williams FW14B-Renault	72	1h37m09.680
3 Ayrton Senna	McLaren MP4/6B-Honda	72	1h37m19.995
4 Michael Schumacher	Benetton B191B-Ford	72	1h37m33.183
5 Gerhard Berger	McLaren MP4/6B-Honda	72	1h37m58.954
6 Johnny Herbert	Lotus 102D-Ford	71	

Winner's average speed: 118.230 mph. Starting grid front row: Mansell, 1m15.486 (pole) and Senna, 1m16.227. Fastest lap: Mansell, 1m17.578. Leaders: Mansell, laps 1-72

Gran Premio de Mexico

22 March 1992. Mexico City. 69 laps of a 2.747-mile circuit = 189.543 miles. Hot, dry and sunny. World Championship round 2

1 Nigel Mansell	Williams FW14B-Renault	69	1h31m53.587
2 Riccardo Patrese	Williams FW14B-Renault	69	1h32m06.558
3 Michael Schumacher	Benetton B191B-Ford	69	1h32m15.016
4 Gerhard Berger	McLaren MP4/6B-Honda	69	1h32m26.934
5 Andrea de Cesaris	Tyrrell 020B-Ilmor	68	
6 Mika Häkkinen	Lotus 102D-Ford	68	

Winner's average speed: 123.759 mph. Starting grid front row: Mansell, 1m16.346 (pole) and Patrese, 1m16.362. Fastest lap: Berger, 1m17.711. Leaders: Mansell, laps 1-69

Grande Premio do Brasil

5 April 1992. Interlagos. 71 laps of a 2.687-mile circuit = 190.777 miles. Hot, dry and sunny. World Championship round 3

1 Nigel Mansell	Williams FW14B-Renault	71	1h36m51.856
2 Riccardo Patrese	Williams FW14B-Renault	71	1h37m21.186

3 Michael Schumacher	Benetton B191B-Ford	70	
4 Jean Alesi	Ferrari F92A	70	
5 Ivan Capelli	Ferrari F92A	70	
6 Michele Alboreto	Footwork FA13-Mugen	70	

Winner's average speed: 118.172 mph. Starting grid front row: Mansell, 1m15.703 (pole) and Patrese, 1m16.894. Fastest lap: Patrese, 1m19.490. Leaders: Patrese, laps 1-31; Mansell, 32-71

Gran Premio Tio Pepe de Espana

3 May 1992. Catalunya. 65 laps of a 2.950-mile circuit = 191.750 miles. Cool and wet. World Championship round 4

1 Nigel Mansell	Williams FW14B-Renault	65	1h56m10.674
2 Michael Schumacher	Benetton B192-Ford	65	1h56m34.588
3 Jean Alesi	Ferrari F92A	65	1h56m37.136
4 Gerhard Berger	McLaren MP4/7A-Honda	65	1h57m31.321
5 Michele Alboreto	Footwork FA13-Mugen	64	
6 Pierluigi Martini	Dallara F192-Ferrari	63	

Winner's average speed: 99.019 mph. Starting grid front row: Mansell, 1m20.190 (pole) and Schumacher, 1m21.195. Fastest lap: Mansell, 1m42.503. Leaders: Mansell, laps 1-65

Gran Premio Iceberg di San Marino

17 May 1992. Imola. 60 laps of a 3.132-mile circuit = 187.920 miles. Hot, dry and sunny. World Championship round 5

1 Nigel Mansell	Williams FW14B-Renault	60	1h28m40.927
2 Riccardo Patrese	Williams FW14B-Renault	60	1h28m50.378
3 Ayrton Senna	McLaren MP4/7A-Honda	60	1h29m29.911
4 Martin Brundle	Benetton B192-Ford	60	1h29m33.934
5 Michele Alboreto	Footwork FA13-Mugen	59	
6 Pierluigi Martini	Dallara F192-Ferrari	59	

Winner's average speed: 127.142 mph. Starting grid front row: Mansell, 1m21.842 (pole) and Patrese, 1m22.895. Fastest lap: Patrese, 1m26.100. Leaders: Mansell, laps 1-60

1992 DRIVERS' RECORDS

Driver	Car	South African GP	Mexican GP	Brazilian GP	Spanish GP	San Marino GP	Monaco GP	Canadian GP	French GP	British GP	German GP	Hungarian GP	Belgian GP	Italian GP	Portuguese GP	Japanese GP	Australian GP
Michele Alboreto	Footwork FA13-Mugen	10	13	6	5	5	7	7	7	7	9	7	R	7	6	15	R
Jean Alesi	Ferrari F92A	R	R	4	3	R	R	3	R	R	5	R	-	-	-	-	-
	Ferrari F92AT	-	-	-	-	-	-	-	-	-	-	-	R	R	R	5	4
Giovanna Amati	Brabham BT60B-Judd	DNQ	DNQ	DNQ	-	-	-	-	-	-	-	-	-	-	-	-	-
Paul Belmondo	March CG911-Ilmor	DNQ	DNQ	DNQ	12	13	DNQ	14	DNQ	DNQ	13	9	-	-	-	-	-
Gerhard Berger	McLaren MP4/6B-Honda	5	4F	-	-	-	-	-	-	-	-	-	-	-	-	-	-
	McLaren MP4/7A-Honda	-	-	R	4	R	R	1F	R	5	R	3	R	4	2	2	1
Enrico Bertaggia	Coloni C4B-Judd	DNP	-	-	-	-	-	-	-	-	-	-	-	-	-	-	-
	Andrea Moda S192-Judd	-	DNP	-	-	-	-	-	-	-	-	-	-	-	-	-	-
Thierry Boutsen	Ligier JS37-Renault	R	10	R	R	R	12	10	R	10	7	R	R	R	8	R	5
Martin Brundle	Benetton B191B-Ford	R	R	R	-	-	-	-	-	-	-	-	-	-	-	-	-
	Benetton B192-Ford	-	-	-	R	4	5	R	3	3	4	5	4	2	4	3	3
Alex Caffi	Coloni C4B-Judd	DNP	-	-	-	-	-	-	-	-	-	-	-	-	-	-	-
	Andrea Moda S192-Judd	-	DNP	-	-	-	-	-	-	-	-	-	-	-	-	-	-
Ivan Capelli	Ferrari F92A	R	R	5	10	R	R	R	R	9	R	6	R	-	-	-	-
	Ferrari F92AT	-	-	-	-	-	-	-	-	-	-	-	-	R	R	-	-
Andrea de Cesaris	Tyrrell 020B-Ilmor	R	5	R	R	14	R	5	R	R	R	8	8	6	9	4	R
Andrea Chiesa	Fondmetal GR01-Ford	DNQ	R	DNQ	R	DNQ	DNQ	DNQ	-	DNQ	DNQ	-	-	-	-	-	-
	Fondmetal GR02-Ford	-	-	-	-	-	-	-	R	-	-	-	-	-	-	-	-
Erik Comas	Ligier JS37-Renault	7	9	R	R	9	10	6	5	8	6	R	DNP	R	R	R	R
Christian Fittipaldi	Minardi M191B-Lamborghini	R	R	R	11	-	-	-	-	-	-	-	-	-	-	-	-
	Minardi M192-Lamborghini	-	-	-	-	R	8	13	DNQ	-	-	-	DNQ	DNQ	12	6	9
Bertrand Gachot	Larrousse LC92-Lamborghini	R	11	R	R	R	6	R	R	R	14	R	18	R	R	R	R
Olivier Grouillard	Tyrrell 020B-Ilmor	R	R	R	R	8	R	12	11	11	R	R	R	R	R	R	R
Mauricio Gugelmin	Jordan 192-Yamaha	11	R	R	R	7	R	R	R	R	15	10	14	R	R	R	R
Mika Häkkinen	Lotus 102D-Ford	9	6	10	R	DNQ	-	-	-	-	-	-	-	-	-	-	-
	Lotus 107-Ford	-	-	-	-	-	R	R	4	6	R	4	6	R	5	R	7

/Cont'd

Grand Prix de Monaco

31 May 1992. Monte Carlo. 78 laps of a 2.068-mile circuit = 161.304 miles. Warm, dry and sunny. World Championship round 6

1 Ayrton Senna	McLaren MP4/7A-Honda	78	1h50m59.372
2 Nigel Mansell	Williams FW14B-Renault	78	1h50m59.587
3 Riccardo Patrese	Williams FW14B-Renault	78	1h51m31.215
4 Michael Schumacher	Benetton B192-Ford	78	1h51m38.666
5 Martin Brundle	Benetton B192-Ford	78	1h52m20.719
6 Bertrand Gachot	Larrousse LC92-Lamborghini	77	

Winner's average speed: 87.200 mph. Starting grid front row: Mansell, 1m19.495 (pole) and Patrese, 1m20.368. Fastest lap: Mansell, 1m21.598. Leaders: Mansell, laps 1-70; Senna, 71-78

Grand Prix Molson du Canada

14 June 1992. Montreal. 69 laps of a 2.753-mile circuit = 189.957 miles. Hot, dry and sunny. World Championship round 7

1 Gerhard Berger	McLaren MP4/7A-Honda	69	1h37m08.299
2 Michael Schumacher	Benetton B192-Ford	69	1h37m20.700
3 Jean Alesi	Ferrari F92A	69	1h38m15.626
4 Karl Wendlinger	March CG911-Ilmor	68	
5 Andrea de Cesaris	Tyrrell 020B-Ilmor	68	
6 Erik Comas	Ligier JS37-Renault	68	

Winner's average speed: 117.332 mph. Starting grid front row: Senna, 1m19.775 (pole) and Patrese, 1m19.872. Fastest lap: Berger, 1m22.325. Leaders: Senna, laps 1-37; Berger, 38-69

Rhône-Poulenc Grand Prix de France

5 July 1992. Magny-Cours. 69 laps of a 2.641-mile circuit = 182.229 miles. Race scheduled for 72 laps, stopped after 18 laps due to rain. Restarted over 51 laps. Warm, dry and overcast, turning wet. World Championship round 8

1 Nigel Mansell	Williams FW14B-Renault	69	1h38m08.459
2 Riccardo Patrese	Williams FW14B-Renault	69	1h38m54.906
3 Martin Brundle	Benetton B192-Ford	69	1h39m21.038
4 Mika Häkkinen	Lotus 107-Ford	68	
5 Erik Comas	Ligier JS37-Renault	68	
6 Johnny Herbert	Lotus 107-Ford	68	

Winner's average speed: 111.409 mph. Starting grid front row: Mansell, 1m13.864 (pole) and Patrese, 1m14.332. Fastest lap: Mansell, 1m17.070. Leaders: Patrese, laps 1-20; Mansell, 21-69

British Grand Prix

12 July 1992. Silverstone. 59 laps of a 3.247-mile circuit = 191.573 miles. Hot, dry and sunny. World Championship round 9

1 Nigel Mansell	Williams FW14B-Renault	59	1h25m42.991
2 Riccardo Patrese	Williams FW14B-Renault	59	1h26m22.085
3 Martin Brundle	Benetton B192-Ford	59	1h26m31.386
4 Michael Schumacher	Benetton B192-Ford	59	1h26m36.258
5 Gerhard Berger	McLaren MP4/7A-Honda	59	1h26m38.786
6 Mika Häkkinen	Lotus 107-Ford	59	1h27m03.129

Winner's average speed: 134.098 mph. Starting grid front row: Mansell, 1m18.965 (pole) and Patrese, 1m20.884. Fastest lap: Mansell, 1m22.539. Leaders: Mansell, laps 1-59

Grosser Mobil 1 Preis von Deutschland

26 July 1992. Hockenheim. 45 laps of a 4.235-mile circuit = 190.575 miles. Hot, dry and sunny. World Championship round 10

1 Nigel Mansell	Williams FW14B-Renault	45	1h18m22.032
2 Ayrton Senna	McLaren MP4/7A-Honda	45	1h18m26.532
3 Michael Schumacher	Benetton B192-Ford	45	1h18m56.494
4 Martin Brundle	Benetton B192-Ford	45	1h18m58.991
5 Jean Alesi	Ferrari F92A	45	1h19m34.639
6 Erik Comas	Ligier JS37-Renault	45	1h19m58.530

Winner's average speed: 145.909 mph. Starting grid front row: Mansell, 1m37.960 (pole) and Patrese, 1m38.310. Fastest lap: Patrese, 1m41.591. Leaders: Mansell, laps 1-14, 20-45; Patrese, 15-19

1992 DRIVERS' RECORDS cont'd/

Driver	Car	United States GP	Brazilian GP	San Marino GP	Monaco GP	Canadian GP	Mexican GP	French GP	British GP	German GP	Hungarian GP	Belgian GP	Italian GP	Portuguese GP	Spanish GP	Japanese GP	Australian GP
Johnny Herbert	Lotus 102D-Ford	6	7	R	R	-	-	-	-	-	-	-	-	-	-	-	-
	Lotus 107-Ford	-	-	-	-	R	R	R	6	R	R	R	13	R	R	R	13
Damon Hill	Brabham BT60B-Judd	-	-	-	DNQ	DNQ	DNQ	DNQ	DNQ	16	DNQ	11	-	-	-	-	-
Ukyo Katayama	Larrousse LC92-Lamborghini	12	12	9	DNQ	R	NPQ	R	R	R	R	R	17	9	R	11	R
Jan Lammers	March CG911-Ilmor	-	-	-	-	-	-	-	-	-	-	-	-	-	-	R	12
Nicola Larini	Ferrari F92A	-	-	-	-	-	-	-	-	-	-	-	-	-	-	12	11
JJ Lehto	Dallara F192-Ferrari	R	8	8	R	11	9	9	9	13	10	DNQ	7	11	R	9	R
Nigel Mansell	Williams FW14B-Renault	1PF	1P	1P	1PF	1P	2PF	R	1PF	1PF	1P	2F	2P	RPF	1P	RPF	RP
Pierluigi Martini	Dallara F192-Ferrari	R	R	R	6	6	R	8	10	15	11	R	R	8	R	10	R
Perry McCarthy	Andrea Moda S192-Judd	-	-	NPQ	NPQ	NPQ	NPQ	NPQ	DNP	NPQ	NPQ	NPQ	DNQ	-	-	-	-
Stefano Modena	Jordan 192-Yamaha	DNQ	R	DNQ	R	R	R	R	R	R	DNQ	R	15	DNQ	13	7	6
Gianni Morbidelli	Minardi M191B-Lamborghini	R	R	7	R	-	-	-	-	-	-	-	-	-	-	-	-
	Minardi M192-Lamborghini	-	-	-	-	R	R	11	8	R	12	DNQ	16	R	14	14	10
Roberto Moreno	Andrea Moda S192-Judd	-	-	NPQ	NPQ	NPQ	R	NPQ	DNP	NPQ	NPQ	DNQ	DNQ	-	-	-	-
Emanuele Naspetti	March CG911-Ilmor	-	-	-	-	-	-	-	-	-	-	-	12	R	11	13	R
Riccardo Patrese	Williams FW14B-Renault	2	2	2F	R	2F	3	R	2	2	8F	RP	3	5	R	1	R
Eric van de Poele	Brabham BT60B-Judd	13	DNQ	DNQ	DNQ	DNQ	DNQ	DNQ	DNQ	DNQ	DNQ	-	-	-	-	-	-
	Fondmetal GR02-Ford	-	-	-	-	-	-	-	-	-	-	R	10	R	-	-	-
Michael Schumacher	Benetton B191B-Ford	4	3	3	-	-	-	-	-	-	-	-	-	-	-	-	-
	Benetton B192-Ford	-	-	-	2	R	4	2	R	4	3	R	1F	3	7	R	2F
Ayrton Senna	McLaren MP4/6B-Honda	3	R	-	-	-	-	-	-	-	-	-	-	-	-	-	-
	McLaren MP4/7A-Honda	-	-	R	9	3	1	RP	R	R	2	1	5	1	3F	R	R
Aguri Suzuki	Footwork FA13-Mugen	8	DNQ	R	7	10	11	DNQ	R	12	R	R	9	R	10	8	8
Gabriele Tarquini	Fondmetal GR01-Ford	R	R	R	R	R	R	-	-	-	-	-	-	-	-	-	-
	Fondmetal GR02-Ford	-	-	-	-	-	-	R	R	14	R	R	R	R	-	-	-
Karl Wendlinger	March CG911-Ilmor	R	R	R	8	12	R	R	4	R	16	R	11	10	R	-	-
Alessandro Zanardi	Minardi M192-Lamborghini	-	-	-	-	-	-	-	-	-	DNQ	R	DNQ	-	-	-	-

World Championship Grand Prix Racing

Marlboro Magyar Nagydíj (Hungarian Grand Prix)

16 August 1992. Hungaroring. 77 laps of a 2.466-mile circuit = 189.882 miles. Hot, dry and sunny. World Championship round 11

1	Ayrton Senna	McLaren MP4/7A-Honda	77 1h46m19.216
2	Nigel Mansell	Williams FW14B-Renault	77 1h46m59.355
3	Gerhard Berger	McLaren MP4/7A-Honda	77 1h47m09.998
4	Mika Häkkinen	Lotus 107-Ford	77 1h47m13.529
5	Martin Brundle	Benetton B192-Ford	77 1h47m16.714
6	Ivan Capelli	Ferrari F92A	76

Winner's average speed: 107.157 mph. Starting grid front row: Patrese, 1m15.476 (pole) and Mansell, 1m15.643. Fastest lap: Mansell, 1m18.308. Leaders: Patrese, laps 1-38; Senna, 39-77

The successful Williams team of Nigel Mansell (right) and Riccardo Patrese celebrate victory at Imola

Grand Prix de Belgique

30 August 1992. Spa-Francorchamps. 44 laps of a 4.312-mile circuit = 189.728 miles. Warm, dry and overcast, turning wet before drying again. World Championship round 12

1	Michael Schumacher	Benetton B192-Ford	44 1h36m10.721
2	Nigel Mansell	Williams FW14B-Renault	44 1h36m47.316
3	Riccardo Patrese	Williams FW14B-Renault	44 1h36m54.618
4	Martin Brundle	Benetton B192-Ford	44 1h36m56.780
5	Ayrton Senna	McLaren MP4/7A-Honda	44 1h37m19.090
6	Mika Häkkinen	Lotus 107-Ford	44 1h37m20.751

Winner's average speed: 118.360 mph. Starting grid front row: Mansell, 1m50.545 (pole) and Senna, 1m52.743. Fastest lap: Schumacher, 1m53.791. Leaders: Senna, laps 1, 7-10; Mansell, 2-3, 11-33; Patrese, 4-6; Schumacher, 34-44

Pioneer Gran Premio d'Italia

13 September 1992. Monza. 53 laps of a 3.604-mile circuit = 191.012 miles. Hot, dry and sunny. World Championship round 13

1	Ayrton Senna	McLaren MP4/7A-Honda	53 1h18m15.349
2	Martin Brundle	Benetton B192-Ford	53 1h18m32.399
3	Michael Schumacher	Benetton B192-Ford	53 1h18m39.722
4	Gerhard Berger	McLaren MP4/7A-Honda	53 1h19m40.839
5	Riccardo Patrese	Williams FW14B-Renault	53 1h19m48.507
6	Andrea de Cesaris	Tyrrell 020B-Ilmor	52

Winner's average speed: 146.448 mph. Starting grid front row: Mansell, 1m22.221 (pole) and Senna, 1m22.822. Fastest lap: Mansell, 1m26.119. Leaders: Mansell, laps 1-19; Patrese, 20-47; Senna, 48-53

SG Gigante Grande Premio de Portugal

27 September 1992. Estoril. 71 laps of a 2.703-mile circuit = 191.913 miles. Warm, dry and sunny. World Championship round 14

1	Nigel Mansell	Williams FW14B-Renault	71 1h34m46.659
2	Gerhard Berger	McLaren MP4/7A-Honda	71 1h35m24.192
3	Ayrton Senna	McLaren MP4/7A-Honda	70
4	Martin Brundle	Benetton B192-Ford	70
5	Mika Häkkinen	Lotus 107-Ford	70
6	Michele Alboreto	Footwork FA13-Mugen	70

Winner's average speed: 121.493 mph. Starting grid front row: Mansell, 1m13.041 (pole) and Patrese, 1m13.672. Fastest lap: Senna, 1m16.272. Leaders: Mansell, laps 1-71

Fuji Television Japanese Grand Prix

25 October 1992. Suzuka. 53 laps of a 3.641-mile circuit = 192.973 miles. Warm, dry and cloudy. World Championship round 15

1	Riccardo Patrese	Williams FW14B-Renault	53 1h33m09.553
2	Gerhard Berger	McLaren MP4/7A-Honda	53 1h33m23.282
3	Martin Brundle	Benetton B192-Ford	53 1h34m25.056
4	Andrea de Cesaris	Tyrrell 020B-Ilmor	52
5	Jean Alesi	Ferrari F92AT	52
6	Christian Fittipaldi	Minardi M192-Lamborghini	52

Winner's average speed: 124.286 mph. Starting grid front row: Mansell, 1m37.360 (pole) and Patrese, 1m38.219. Fastest lap: Mansell, 1m40.646. Leaders: Mansell, laps 1-35; Patrese, 36-53

Foster's Australian Grand Prix

8 November 1992. Adelaide. 81 laps of a 2.347-mile circuit = 190.107 miles. Warm, dry and overcast. World Championship round 16

1	Gerhard Berger	McLaren MP4/7A-Honda	81 1h46m54.786
2	Michael Schumacher	Benetton B192-Ford	81 1h46m55.527
3	Martin Brundle	Benetton B192-Ford	81 1h47m48.942
4	Jean Alesi	Ferrari F92AT	80
5	Thierry Boutsen	Ligier JS37-Renault	80
6	Stefano Modena	Jordan 192-Yamaha	80

Winner's average speed: 106.689 mph. Starting grid front row: Mansell, 1m13.732 (pole) and Senna, 1m14.202. Fastest lap: Schumacher, 1m16.078. Leaders: Mansell, laps 1-18; Patrese, 19-50; Berger, 51-81

1992 FINAL CHAMPIONSHIP POSITIONS

Drivers

1	Nigel Mansell	108
2	Riccardo Patrese	56
3	Michael Schumacher	53
4	Ayrton Senna	50
5	Gerhard Berger	49
6	Martin Brundle	38
7	Jean Alesi	18
8	Mika Häkkinen	11
9	Andrea de Cesaris	8
10	Michele Alboreto	6
11	Erik Comas	4
12=	Ivan Capelli	3
	Karl Wendlinger	3
14=	Thierry Boutsen	2
	Johnny Herbert	2
	Pierluigi Martini	2
17=	Christian Fittipaldi	1
	Bertrand Gachot	1
	Stefano Modena	1

Manufacturers

1	Williams-Renault	164
2	McLaren-Honda	99
3	Benetton-Ford	91
4	Ferrari	21
5	Lotus-Ford	13
6	Tyrrell-Ilmor	8
7=	Footwork-Mugen	6
	Ligier-Renault	6
9	March-Ilmor	3
10	Dallara-Ferrari	2
11=	Larrousse-Lamborghini	1
	Minardi-Lamborghini	1
	Jordan-Yamaha	1

1993

With all the criticism he received, it is easy to undervalue Alain Prost's achievement in winning the World Championship again in 1993. He returned from a year off to join the all-conquering Williams team and send World Champion Mansell stateside. In the eyes of the world, every time he extended his record number of victories it was due to the car, every failure to do so was Prost's fault. However, he won seven times, always qualified on the front row and won his fourth title by 26 points.

Highly regarded by the team and by Renault, Prost felt under pressure from the governing body and the press, and when it became obvious in Portugal that Ayrton Senna would be joining Williams for 1994, he announced his retirement from the sport, only one day before he clinched his fourth title.

Senna started the year without the Honda engines he had used for the last six years, and with the seemingly impossible task of wresting the championship away from Williams. A combination of Senna's brilliance, heavy rain in which he revelled, and a nimble McLaren-Ford gave the Brazilian victories in Brazil and at Donington, as well as the championship lead after six rounds. Senna gave the performance of his career at Donington Park, passing four cars on the opening lap and out-thinking his rivals in the treacherous conditions to win the European Grand Prix. However, Prost gathered momentum and victories thereafter, and despite driving as forcefully as he could, the title slipped away from Senna.

Williams and McLaren hired Damon Hill and Michael Andretti respectively, both drivers inexperienced at this level. After near-misses at Silverstone and Hockenheim, Hill scored the first of three successive Grand Prix victories in Hungary, but Andretti struggled. Repeated mistakes led to the American relinquishing his drive after he had finished third at Monza (following another early spin). Mika Häkkinen, who had gambled on leaving Lotus to become McLaren's test driver, replaced the Indycar Champion and immediately beat Senna in qualifying, highlighting Andretti's disappointing year.

If Michael Schumacher finished, it was always on the podium; his win in Portugal the best of nine such results. Riccardo Patrese replaced Brundle as the German's team-mate. He too failed to match Schumacher's pace and had a disappointing final season in Grand Prix racing, retiring from the formula after a record 256 races.

Jean Alesi continued to be spectacular, especially in practice. But although he led in Portugal and was normally quicker than team-mate Gerhard Berger, it was another season without a win for Ferrari.

Former Swiss sports car team Sauber entered Formula One backed by Mercedes-Benz. Early promise was not fulfilled, but with the German car giant becoming increasingly involved the potential was obvious. Under new management, Ligier finished fifth in the championship. The French team's two British drivers Martin Brundle and Mark Blundell, each earned a third place finish and enhanced their reputations.

After his frustrating partnership with Yamaha, Eddie Jordan switched to the private Hart V10 engine. Jordan's promising new driver Rubens Barrichello impressed, especially at Donington, and the potential of the team was once again evident. After a number of unsuccessful second drivers, Jordan hired Ulsterman Eddie Irvine. His debut in a damp Japanese GP resulted in a competitive sixth position - and a widely reported physical altercation with Senna, after the Jordan had repassed and blocked the McLaren while being lapped.

....

Alain Prost leads Ayrton Senna, Damon Hill, J.J. Lehto, Jean Alesi, Michael Schumacher, Riccardo Patrese and Karl Wendlinger early in the Brazilian Grand Prix

Panasonic South African Grand Prix

14 March 1993. Kyalami. 72 laps of a 2.648-mile circuit = 190.656 miles. Hot, dry and cloudy, rain in closing laps. World Championship round 1

1 Alain Prost	Williams FW15C-Renault	72	1h38m45.082	
2 Ayrton Senna	McLaren MP4/8-Ford	72	1h40m04.906	
3 Mark Blundell	Ligier JS39-Renault	71		
4 Christian Fittipaldi	Minardi M193-Ford	71		
5 JJ Lehto	Sauber C12-Ilmor	70		
6 Gerhard Berger	Ferrari F93A	69		engine

Winner's average speed: 115.840 mph. Starting grid front row: Prost, 1m15.696 (pole) and Senna, 1m15.784. Fastest lap: Prost, 1m19.492. Leaders: Senna, laps 1-23; Prost, 24-72

Grande Premio do Brasil

28 March 1993. Interlagos. 71 laps of a 2.687-mile circuit = 190.777 miles. Dry and overcast, wet in mid-race laps. World Championship round 2

1 Ayrton Senna	McLaren MP4/8-Ford	71	1h51m15.485
2 Damon Hill	Williams FW15C-Renault	71	1h51m32.110
3 Michael Schumacher	Benetton B193-Ford	71	1h52m00.921
4 Johnny Herbert	Lotus 107B-Ford	71	1h52m02.042
5 Mark Blundell	Ligier JS39-Renault	71	1h52m07.612
6 Alessandro Zanardi	Lotus 107B-Ford	70	

Winner's average speed: 102.883 mph. Starting grid front row: Prost, 1m15.866 (pole) and Hill, 1m16.859. Fastest lap: Schumacher, 1m20.024. Leaders: Prost, laps 1-29; Hill, 30-41; Senna, 42-71

Sega European Grand Prix

11 April 1993. Donington Park. 76 laps of a 2.500-mile circuit = 190.000 miles. Cool and very wet. World Championship round 3

1 Ayrton Senna	McLaren MP4/8-Ford	76 1h50m46.570
2 Damon Hill	Williams FW15C-Renault	76 1h52m09.769
3 Alain Prost	Williams FW15C-Renault	75
4 Johnny Herbert	Lotus 107B-Ford	75
5 Riccardo Patrese	Benetton B193B-Ford	74
6 Fabrizio Barbazza	Minardi M193-Ford	74

Winner's average speed: 102.910 mph. Starting front row: Prost, 1m10.458 (pole) and Hill, 1m10.762. Fastest lap: Senna, 1m18.029 (time set on a lap when he pitted). Leaders: Senna, laps 1-18, 20-34, 39-76; Prost, 19, 35-38

Gran Premio di San Marino

25 April 1993. Imola. 61 laps of a 3.132-mile circuit = 191.052 miles. Cool, damp and overcast, drying later. World Championship round 4

1 Alain Prost	Williams FW15C-Renault	61 1h33m20.413	
2 Michael Schumacher	Benetton B193B-Ford	61 1h33m52.823	
3 Martin Brundle	Ligier JS39-Renault	60	
4 JJ Lehto	Sauber C12-Ilmor	59	engine
5 Philippe Alliot	Larrousse LH93-Lamborghini	59	
6 Fabrizio Barbazza	Minardi M193-Ford	59	

Winner's average speed: 122.810 mph. Starting grid front row: Prost, 1m22.070 (pole) and Hill, 1m22.168. Fastest lap: Prost, 1m26.128. Leaders: Hill, laps 1-11; Prost, 12-61

Gran Premio de Espana

9 May 1993. Catalunya. 65 laps of a 2.950-mile circuit = 191.750 miles. Hot, dry and sunny. World Championship round 5

1 Alain Prost	Williams FW15C-Renault	65 1h32m27.685
2 Ayrton Senna	McLaren MP4/8-Ford	65 1h32m44.558
3 Michael Schumacher	Benetton B193B-Ford	65 1h32m54.810
4 Riccardo Patrese	Benetton B193B-Ford	64
5 Michael Andretti	McLaren MP4/8-Ford	64
6 Gerhard Berger	Ferrari F93A	63

Winner's average speed: 124.418 mph. Starting grid front row: Prost, 1m17.809 (pole) and Hill, 1m18.346. Fastest lap: Schumacher, 1m20.989. Leaders: Hill, laps 1-10; Prost, 11-65

Grand Prix de Monaco

23 May 1993. Monte Carlo. 78 laps of a 2.068-mile circuit = 161.304 miles. Warm, dry and cloudy. World Championship round 6

1 Ayrton Senna	McLaren MP4/8-Ford	78 1h52m10.947
2 Damon Hill	Williams FW15C-Renault	78 1h53m03.065
3 Jean Alesi	Ferrari F93A	78 1h53m14.309
4 Alain Prost	Williams FW15C-Renault	77
5 Christian Fittipaldi	Minardi M193-Ford	76
6 Martin Brundle	Ligier JS39-Renault	76

Winner's average speed: 86.272 mph. Starting front row: Prost, 1m20.557 (pole) and Schumacher, 1m21.190. Fastest lap: Prost, 1m23.604. Leaders: Prost, laps 1-11; Schumacher, 12-32; Senna, 33-78

Molson Grand Prix du Canada

13 June 1993. Montreal. 69 laps of a 2.753-mile circuit = 189.957 miles. Hot, dry and sunny. World Championship round 7

1 Alain Prost	Williams FW15C-Renault	69 1h36m41.822
2 Michael Schumacher	Benetton B193B-Ford	69 1h36m56.349
3 Damon Hill	Williams FW15C-Renault	69 1h37m34.507
4 Gerhard Berger	Ferrari F93A	68
5 Martin Brundle	Ligier JS39-Renault	68
6 Karl Wendlinger	Sauber C12-Ilmor	68

Winner's average speed: 117.867 mph. Starting grid front row: Prost, 1m18.987 (pole) and Hill, 1m19.491. Fastest lap: Schumacher, 1m21.500. Leaders: Hill, laps 1-5; Prost, 6-69

Rhône-Poulenc Grand Prix de France

4 July 1993. Magny-Cours. 72 laps of a 2.641-mile circuit = 190.152 miles. Warm, dry and cloudy. World Championship round 8

1 Alain Prost	Williams FW15C-Renault	72 1h38m35.241
2 Damon Hill	Williams FW15C-Renault	72 1h38m35.583
3 Michael Schumacher	Benetton B193B-Ford	72 1h38m56.450
4 Ayrton Senna	McLaren MP4/8-Ford	72 1h39m07.646
5 Martin Brundle	Ligier JS39-Renault	72 1h39m09.036
6 Michael Andretti	McLaren MP4/8-Ford	71

Winner's average speed: 115.726 mph. Starting grid front row: Hill, 1m14.382 (pole) and Prost, 1m14.524. Fastest lap: Schumacher, 1m19.256. Leaders: Hill, laps 1-26; Prost, 27-72

British Grand Prix

11 July 1993. Silverstone. 59 laps of a 3.247-mile circuit = 191.573 miles. Cool, dry and cloudy. World Championship round 9

1 Alain Prost	Williams FW15C-Renault	59 1h25m38.189	
2 Michael Schumacher	Benetton B193B-Ford	59 1h25m45.849	
3 Riccardo Patrese	Benetton B193B-Ford	59 1h26m55.671	
4 Johnny Herbert	Lotus 107B-Ford	59 1h26m56.596	
5 Ayrton Senna	McLaren MP4/8-Ford	58	out of fuel
6 Derek Warwick	Footwork FA14-Mugen	58	

Winner's average speed: 134.223 mph. Starting grid front row: Prost, 1m19.006 (pole) and Hill, 1m19.134. Fastest lap: Hill, 1m22.515. Leaders: Hill, laps 1-41; Prost, 42-59

Grosser Mobil 1 Preis von Deutschland

25 July 1993. Hockenheim. 45 laps of a 4.235-mile circuit = 190.575 miles. Warm, dry and sunny. World Championship round 10

1 Alain Prost	Williams FW15C-Renault	45 1h18m40.885
2 Michael Schumacher	Benetton B193B-Ford	45 1h18m57.549
3 Mark Blundell	Ligier JS39-Renault	45 1h19m40.234
4 Ayrton Senna	McLaren MP4/8-Ford	45 1h19m49.114
5 Riccardo Patrese	Benetton B193B-Ford	45 1h20m12.401
6 Gerhard Berger	Ferrari F93A	45 1h20m15.639

Winner's average speed: 145.327 mph. Starting grid front row: Prost, 1m38.748 (pole) and Hill, 1m38.905. Fastest lap: Schumacher, 1m41.859. Leaders: Hill, laps 1-7, 10-43; Prost, 8-9, 44-45

Marlboro Magyar Nagydij (Hungarian Grand Prix)

15 August 1993. Hungaroring. 77 laps of a 2.466-mile circuit = 189.882 miles. Hot, dry and sunny. World Championship round 11

1 Damon Hill	Williams FW15C-Renault	77 1h47m39.098
2 Riccardo Patrese	Benetton B193B-Ford	77 1h48m51.013
3 Gerhard Berger	Ferrari F93A	77 1h48m57.140
4 Derek Warwick	Footwork FA14-Mugen	76
5 Martin Brundle	Ligier JS39-Renault	76
6 Karl Wendlinger	Sauber C12-Ilmor	76

Winner's average speed: 105.831 mph. Starting grid front row: Prost, 1m14.631 (pole) and Hill, 1m14.835 - Prost started from the back of the grid. Fastest lap: Prost, 1m19.633. Leaders: Hill, laps 1-77

Grand Prix de Belgique

29 August 1993. Spa-Francorchamps. 44 laps of a 4.312-mile circuit = 189.728 miles. Hot, dry and sunny. World Championship round 12

1 Damon Hill	Williams FW15C-Renault	44 1h24m32.124
2 Michael Schumacher	Benetton B193B-Ford	44 1h24m35.792
3 Alain Prost	Williams FW15C-Renault	44 1h24m47.112

1993 DRIVERS' RECORDS

Driver	Car	South African GP	Brazilian GP	European GP	San Marino GP	Spanish GP	Monaco GP	Canadian GP	French GP	British GP	German GP	Hungarian GP	Belgian GP	Italian GP	Portuguese GP	Japanese GP	Australian GP
Michele Alboreto	Lola T93/30-Ferrari	R	11	11	DNQ	DNQ	R	DNQ	DNQ	DNQ	16	R	14	R	R	-	-
Jean Alesi	Ferrari F93A	R	8	R	R	R	3	R	R	9	7	R	R	2	4	R	4
Philippe Alliot	Larrousse LH93-Lamborghini	R	7	R	5	R	12	R	9	11	12	8	12	9	10	-	-
Michael Andretti	McLaren MP4/8-Ford	R	R	R	R	5	8	14	6	R	R	R	8	3	-	-	-
Marco Apicella	Jordan 193-Hart	-	-	-	-	-	-	-	-	-	-	-	-	R	-	-	-
Luca Badoer	Lola T93/30-Ferrari	R	12	DNQ	7	R	DNQ	15	R	R	R	R	13	10	14	-	-
Fabrizio Barbazza	Minardi M193-Ford	R	R	6	6	R	11	R	R	-	-	-	-	-	-	-	-
Rubens Barrichello	Jordan 193-Hart	R	R	10	R	12	9	R	7	10	R	R	R	R	13	5	11
Gerhard Berger	Ferrari F93A	6	R	R	R	6	14	4	14	R	6	3	10	R	R	R	5
Mark Blundell	Ligier JS39-Renault	3	5	R	R	7	R	R	R	7	3	7	11	R	R	7	9
Thierry Boutsen	Jordan 193-Hart	-	-	R	R	11	R	12	11	R	13	9	R	-	-	-	-
Martin Brundle	Ligier JS39-Renault	R	R	R	3	R	6	5	5	14	8	5	7	R	6	9	6
Ivan Capelli	Jordan 193-Hart	R	DNQ	-	-	-	-	-	-	-	-	-	-	-	-	-	-
Andrea de Cesaris	Tyrrell 020C-Yamaha	R	R	R	R	R	10	R	15	-	-	-	-	-	-	-	-
	Tyrrell 021-Yamaha	-	-	-	-	-	-	-	-	NC	R	11	R	13	12	R	13
Erik Comas	Larrousse LH93-Lamborghini	R	10	9	R	9	R	8	16	R	R	R	R	6	11	R	12
Christian Fittipaldi	Minardi M193-Ford	4	R	7	R	8	5	9	8	12	11	R	R	8	9	-	-
Jean-Marc Gounon	Minardi M193-Ford	-	-	-	-	-	-	-	-	-	-	-	-	-	-	R	R
Mika Häkkinen	McLaren MP4/8-Ford	-	-	-	-	-	-	-	-	-	-	-	-	-	R	3	R
Johnny Herbert	Lotus 107B-Ford	R	4	4	8	R	R	10	R	4	10	R	5	R	R	11	R
Damon Hill	Williams FW15C-Renault	R	2	2	R	R	2	3	2P	RF	15	1	1	1F	3PF	4	3F
Eddie Irvine	Jordan 193-Hart	-	-	-	-	-	-	-	-	-	-	-	-	-	-	6	R
Ukyo Katayama	Tyrrell 020C-Yamaha	R	R	R	R	R	R	17	R	13	-	-	-	-	-	-	-
	Tyrrell 021-Yamaha	-	-	-	-	-	-	-	-	-	R	10	15	14	R	R	R
Pedro Lamy	Lotus 107B-Ford	-	-	-	-	-	-	-	-	-	-	-	-	11	R	13	R
JJ Lehto	Sauber C12-Ilmor	5	R	R	4	R	R	R	7	R	8	R	R	9	-	-	-
	Sauber C12	-	-	-	-	-	-	-	-	-	-	-	-	R	7	8	R
Pierluigi Martini	Minardi M193-Ford	-	-	-	-	-	-	-	-	R	14	R	R	7	8	10	R
Emanuele Naspetti	Jordan 193-Hart	-	-	-	-	-	-	-	-	-	-	-	-	R	-	-	-
Riccardo Patrese	Benetton B193-Ford	R	R	-	-	-	-	-	-	-	-	-	-	-	-	-	-
	Benetton B193B-Ford	-	-	5	R	4	R	R	10	3	5	2	6	5	R	R	8
Alain Prost	Williams FW15C-Renault	1PF	RP	3P	1PF	1P	4PF	1P	1	1P	1P	12PF	3PF	12P	2	2PF	2
Michael Schumacher	Benetton B193-Ford	R	3F	-	-	-	-	-	-	-	-	-	-	-	-	-	-
	Benetton B193B-Ford	-	-	R	2	3F	R	2F	3F	2	2F	R	2	R	1	R	R
Ayrton Senna	McLaren MP4/8-Ford	2	1	1F	R	2	1	R	4	5	4	R	4	R	R	1	1P
Aguri Suzuki	Footwork FA13B-Mugen	R	R	-	-	-	-	-	-	-	-	-	-	-	-	-	-
	Footwork FA14-Mugen	-	-	R	9	10	R	13	12	R	R	R	R	R	R	R	7
Toshio Suzuki	Larrousse LH93-Lamborghini	-	-	-	-	-	-	-	-	-	-	-	-	-	-	12	14
Derek Warwick	Footwork FA13B-Mugen	7	9	-	-	-	-	-	-	-	-	-	-	-	-	-	-
	Footwork FA14-Mugen	-	-	R	R	13	R	16	13	6	17	4	R	R	R	14	10
Karl Wendlinger	Sauber C12-Ilmor	R	R	R	R	R	13	6	R	R	9	6	R	-	-	-	-
	Sauber C12	-	-	-	-	-	-	-	-	-	-	-	-	4	5	R	15
Alessandro Zanardi	Lotus 107B-Ford	R	6	8	R	R	7	11	R	R	R	R	DNP	-	-	-	-

4 Ayrton Senna   McLaren MP4/8-Ford   44 1h26m11.887
5 Johnny Herbert   Lotus 107B-Ford   43
6 Riccardo Patrese   Benetton B193B-Ford   43

Winner's average speed: 134.662 mph. Starting grid front row: Prost, 1m47.571 (pole) and Hill, 1m48.466. Fastest lap: Prost, 1m51.095. Leaders: Prost, laps 1-30; Hill, 31-44

Pioneer Gran Premio d'Italia

12 September 1993. Monza. 53 laps of a 3.604-mile circuit = 191.012 miles. Hot, dry and sunny. World Championship round 13

1 Damon Hill   Williams FW15C-Renault   53 1h17m07.509
2 Jean Alesi   Ferrari F93A   53 1h17m47.521
3 Michael Andretti   McLaren MP4/8-Ford   52
4 Karl Wendlinger   Sauber C12   52
5 Riccardo Patrese   Benetton B193B-Ford   52
6 Erik Comas   Larrousse LH93-Lamborghini   51

Winner's average speed: 148.595 mph. Starting grid front row: Prost, 1m21.179 (pole) and Hill, 1m21.491. Fastest lap: Hill, 1m23.575. Leaders: Prost, laps 1-48; Hill, 49-53

Grande Premio de Portugal

26 September 1993. Estoril. 71 laps of a 2.703-mile circuit = 191.913 miles. Warm, dry and sunny. World Championship round 14

1 Michael Schumacher   Benetton B193B-Ford   71 1h32m46.309
2 Alain Prost   Williams FW15C-Renault   71 1h32m47.291
3 Damon Hill   Williams FW15C-Renault   71 1h32m54.515
4 Jean Alesi   Ferrari F93A   71 1h33m53.914
5 Karl Wendlinger   Sauber C12   70
6 Martin Brundle   Ligier JS39-Renault   70

Winner's average speed: 124.119 mph. Starting grid front row: Hill, 1m11.494 (pole) and Prost, 1m11.683 - Hill started from the back of the grid. Fastest lap: Hill, 1m14.859. Leaders: Alesi, laps 1-19; Prost, 20-29; Schumacher, 30-71

Fuji Television Japanese Grand Prix

24 October 1993. Suzuka. 53 laps of a 3.641-mile circuit = 192.973 miles. Dry and clear, then cool and wet. World Championship round 15

1 Ayrton Senna	McLaren MP4/8-Ford	53 1h40m27.912
2 Alain Prost	Williams FW15C-Renault	53 1h40m39.347
3 Mika Häkkinen	McLaren MP4/8-Ford	53 1h40m54.041
4 Damon Hill	Williams FW15C-Renault	53 1h41m51.450
5 Rubens Barrichello	Jordan 193-Hart	53 1h42m03.013
6 Eddie Irvine	Jordan 193-Hart	53 1h42m14.333

Winner's average speed: 115.248 mph. Starting grid front row: Prost, 1m37.154 (pole) and Senna, 1m37.284. Fastest lap: Prost, 1m41.176. Leaders: Senna, laps 1-13, 21-53; Prost, 14-20

Foster's Australian Grand Prix

7 November 1993. Adelaide. 79 laps of a 2.347-mile circuit = 185.413 miles. Warm, dry and sunny. World Championship round 16

1 Ayrton Senna	McLaren MP4/8-Ford	79 1h43m27.476
2 Alain Prost	Williams FW15C-Renault	79 1h43m36.735
3 Damon Hill	Williams FW15C-Renault	79 1h44m01.378
4 Jean Alesi	Ferrari F93A	78
5 Gerhard Berger	Ferrari F93A	78
6 Martin Brundle	Ligier JS39-Renault	78

Winner's average speed: 107.530 mph. Starting grid front row: Senna, 1m13.371 (pole) and Prost, 1m13.807. Fastest lap: Hill, 1m15.381. Leaders: Senna, laps 1-23, 29-79; Prost, 24-28

1993 FINAL CHAMPIONSHIP POSITIONS

Drivers			Drivers			Manufacturers		
1	Alain Prost	99	12	Karl Wendlinger	7	1	Williams-Renault	168
2	Ayrton Senna	73	13	Christian Fittipaldi	5	2	McLaren-Ford	84
3	Damon Hill	69	14	JJ Lehto	5	3	Benetton-Ford	72
4	Michael Schumacher	52	15=	Mika Häkkinen	4	4	Ferrari	28
5	Riccardo Patrese	20		Derek Warwick	4	5	Ligier-Renault	23
6	Jean Alesi	16	17=	Philippe Alliot	2	6=	Lotus-Ford	12
7	Martin Brundle	13		Fabrizio Barbazza	2		Sauber-Ilmor	12
8	Gerhard Berger	12		Rubens Barrichello	2	8	Minardi-Ford	7
9	Johnny Herbert	11	20=	Erik Comas	1	9	Footwork-Mugen	4
10	Mark Blundell	10		Eddie Irvine	1	10=	Larrousse-Lamborghini	3
11	Michael Andretti	7		Alessandro Zanardi	1		Jordan-Hart	3

1994

1994 was a fearful year completely overshadowed by the death of Ayrton Senna. Seemingly indestructible and arguably the most talented driver of all time, the Brazilian was killed at Imola's dauntingly fast Tamburello corner while leading the San Marino GP. His loss, coming 24 hours after rookie Roland Ratzenberger had died in practice, shocked the whole motor racing world.

These tragedies were compounded by a series of other accidents in which drivers were injured: Karl Wendlinger, Pedro Lamy, Jean Alesi, JJ Lehto and Andrea Montermini all being sidelined in one of the sport's blackest summers.

Senna was the acknowledged master of his generation and for the new season he would also drive a Williams-Renault, currently the best car; a fourth World title seemed assured. His death refocused attention on the dangers of the sport: circuits were changed and controversial new safety measures (including revised wings, airboxes, and a 10 cm wooden step on the underside) were gradually introduced to slow the cars.

In 1968 Graham Hill had lifted the spirits of Team Lotus after Jim Clark had died; now it fell to Graham's son, Damon Hill, to lead the Williams team. By the British GP he was 37 points behind a dominant Michael Schumacher, but that race proved to be the turning point. Hill won his home race (a feat never achieved by his father) but Schumacher was excluded from the results and banned for two further races for ignoring a black flag issued for overtaking Hill on the parade lap.

Worse was to come for Benetton; Jos Verstappen in the second car was temporarily engulfed in a frightening fireball during a German Grand Prix fuel stop, rumours of cheating persisted, and Schumacher was disqualified after winning the Belgian Grand Prix due to an infringement of the new stepped flat bottom rules.

Hill won both races from which Schumacher had been banned and a dramatic victory in Japan took the Williams driver to within a point of the German before the final race in Australia. The championship, however, was decided in suitably controversial circumstances: Schumacher and Hill collided while fighting for the lead in Adelaide. But with both drivers out of the race Michael Schumacher became Germany's first World Champion.

Following the Imola tragedy Williams elevated their test driver David Coulthard to the race team. He impressed more and more as the season progressed but for the final three races his place was taken by the returning Nigel Mansell (who had also raced in France). The former World Champion qualified on pole in Australia and inherited victory when Hill and Schumacher clashed.

Gerhard Berger scored Ferrari's first victory since 1990 at Hockenheim, a race in which opening-lap accidents forced ten cars to retire. Team-mate Jean Alesi had a frustrating season and was often outpaced by Berger. However, Alesi qualified on pole at Monza only for gearbox problems to rob him of a first Grand Prix victory.

McLaren used Peugeot engines in 1994, but they proved both underpowered and unreliable. Despite this, Mika Häkkinen finished on the podium six times to clinch fourth in the World Championship. Jordan continued its progress in Formula One with both Rubens Barrichello and Eddie Irvine impressing. Barrichello benefited from changeable weather conditions in Belgium to qualify on pole, the youngest man ever to do so.

Refuelling stops during Grands Prix, banned on safety grounds in 1984, were reintroduced, placing greater emphasis on race strategy and less on overtaking skills.

....

Michael Schumacher leads the Williams duo of Damon Hill and David Coulthard in Hungary

Grande Premio do Brasil

27 March 1994. Interlagos. 71 laps of a 2.867-mile circuit = 203.557 miles. Warm, dry and overcast. World Championship round 1

1 Michael Schumacher	Benetton B194-Ford	71 1h35m38.759
2 Damon Hill	Williams FW16-Renault	70
3 Jean Alesi	Ferrari 412T1	70
4 Rubens Barrichello	Jordan 194-Hart	70
5 Ukyo Katayama	Tyrrell 022-Yamaha	69
6 Karl Wendlinger	Sauber C13-Mercedes-Benz	69

Winner's average speed: 127.694 mph. Starting grid front row: Senna, 1m15.962 (pole) and Schumacher, 1m16.290. Fastest lap: Schumacher, 1m18.455. Leaders: Senna, laps 1-21; Schumacher, 22-71

Pacific Grand Prix

17 April 1994. TI Circuit, Aida. 83 laps of a 2.314-mile circuit = 192.062 miles. Warm, dry and sunny. World Championship round 2

1 Michael Schumacher	Benetton B194-Ford	83 1h46m01.693
2 Gerhard Berger	Ferrari 412T1	83 1h47m16.993
3 Rubens Barrichello	Jordan 194-Hart	82
4 Christian Fittipaldi	Footwork FA15-Ford	82
5 Heinz-Harald Frentzen	Sauber C13-Mercedes-Benz	82
6 Erik Comas	Larrousse LH94-Ford	80

Winner's average speed: 108.685 mph. Starting grid front row: Senna, 1m10.218 (pole) and Schumacher, 1m10.440. Fastest lap: Schumacher, 1m14.023. Leaders: Schumacher, laps 1-83

Gran Premio di San Marino

1 May 1994. Imola. 58 laps of a 3.132-mile circuit = 181.656 miles. Race scheduled for 61 laps, stopped after 5 laps due to Senna's accident. Restarted over 53 laps. Hot, dry and sunny. World Championship round 3

| 1 Michael Schumacher | Benetton B194-Ford | 58 1h28m28.642 |

2 Nicola Larini	Ferrari 412T1	58 1h29m23.584
3 Mika Häkkinen	McLaren MP4/9-Peugeot	58 1h29m39.321
4 Karl Wendlinger	Sauber C13-Mercedes-Benz	58 1h29m42.300
5 Ukyo Katayama	Tyrrell 022-Yamaha	57
6 Damon Hill	Williams FW16-Renault	57

Winner's average speed: 123.188 mph. Starting grid front row: Senna, 1m21.548 (pole) and Schumacher, 1m21.885. Fastest lap: Hill, 1m24.335. Leaders (on aggregate): Senna, laps 1-5; Schumacher, 6-13, 15-58; Berger, 14 (Berger, 6-14, Häkkinen, 15-18 and Larini, 19-23 led on the road)

Grand Prix de Monaco

15 May 1994. Monte Carlo. 78 laps of a 2.068-mile circuit = 161.304 miles. Hot, dry and sunny. World Championship round 4

1 Michael Schumacher	Benetton B194-Ford	78 1h49m55.372
2 Martin Brundle	McLaren MP4/9-Peugeot	78 1h50m32.650
3 Gerhard Berger	Ferrari 412T1	78 1h51m12.196
4 Andrea de Cesaris	Jordan 194-Hart	77
5 Jean Alesi	Ferrari 412T1	77
6 Michele Alboreto	Minardi M193B-Ford	77

Winner's average speed: 88.046 mph. Starting grid front row: Schumacher, 1m18.560 (pole) and Häkkinen, 1m19.488. Fastest lap: Schumacher, 1m21.076. Leaders: Schumacher, laps 1-78

Gran Premio Marlboro de Espana

29 May 1994. Catalunya. 65 laps of a 2.950-mile circuit = 191.750 miles. Hot, dry and sunny. World Championship round 5

1 Damon Hill	Williams FW16-Renault	65 1h36m14.374
2 Michael Schumacher	Benetton B194-Ford	65 1h36m38.540
3 Mark Blundell	Tyrrell 022-Yamaha	65 1h37m41.343
4 Jean Alesi	Ferrari 412T1	64
5 Pierluigi Martini	Minardi M194-Ford	64
6 Eddie Irvine	Jordan 194-Hart	64

Winner's average speed: 119.533 mph. Starting grid front row: Schumacher, 1m21.908 (pole) and Hill, 1m22.559. Fastest lap: Schumacher, 1m25.155. Leaders: Schumacher, laps 1-22, 41-45; Häkkinen, 23-30; Hill, 31-40, 46-65

Grand Prix Molson du Canada

12 June 1994. Montreal. 69 laps of a 2.765-mile circuit = 190.785 miles. Hot, dry and cloudy. World Championship round 6

1 Michael Schumacher	Benetton B194-Ford	69 1h44m31.887
2 Damon Hill	Williams FW16-Renault	69 1h45m11.547
3 Jean Alesi	Ferrari 412T1	69 1h45m45.275
4 Gerhard Berger	Ferrari 412T1	69 1h45m47.496
5 David Coulthard	Williams FW16-Renault	68
6 JJ Lehto	Benetton B194-Ford	68

Fittipaldi (Footwork FA12-Ford) finished sixth on the road but was disqualified as his car was under the weight limit. Winner's average speed: 109.509 mph. Starting grid front row: Schumacher, 1m26.178 (pole) and Alesi, 1m26.319. Fastest lap: Schumacher, 1m28.927. Leaders: Schumacher, laps 1-69

Grand Prix de France

2 July 1994. Magny-Cours. 72 laps of a 2.641-mile circuit = 190.152 miles. Hot, dry and sunny. World Championship round 7

1 Michael Schumacher	Benetton B194-Ford	72 1h38m35.704
2 Damon Hill	Williams FW16-Renault	72 1h38m48.346
3 Gerhard Berger	Ferrari 412T1B	72 1h39m28.469
4 Heinz-Harald Frentzen	Sauber C13-Mercedes-Benz	71
5 Pierluigi Martini	Minardi M193B-Ford	70
6 Andrea de Cesaris	Sauber C13-Mercedes-Benz	70

Winner's average speed: 115.717 mph. Starting grid front row: Hill, 1m16.282 (pole) and Mansell, 1m16.359. Fastest lap: Hill, 1m19.678. Leaders: Schumacher, laps 1-37, 45-75; Hill, 38-44.

British Grand Prix

10 July 1994. Silverstone. 60 laps of a 3.210-mile circuit = 192.600 miles. Hot, dry and sunny. World Championship round 8

1 Damon Hill	Williams FW16-Renault	60	1h30m03.640
2 Jean Alesi	Ferrari 412T1B	60	1h31m11.768
3 Mika Häkkinen	McLaren MP4/9-Peugeot	60	1h31m44.299
4 Rubens Barrichello	Jordan 194-Hart	60	1h31m45.391
5 David Coulthard	Williams FW16-Renault	59	
6 Ukyo Katayama	Tyrrell 022-Yamaha	59	

Schumacher (Benetton B194-Ford) finished second on the road but was disqualified for ignoring the black flag. Winner's average speed: 128.314 mph. Starting grid front row: Hill, 1m24.960 (pole) and Schumacher, 1m24.963. Fastest lap: Hill, 1m27.100. Leaders: Hill, laps 1-15, 22-60; Berger, 16-21 (Schumacher led laps 15-17 and 22-26 on the road)

Grosser Mobil 1 Preis von Deutschland

31 July 1994. Hockenheim. 45 laps of a 4.220-mile circuit = 189.900 miles. Hot, dry and sunny. World Championship round 9

1 Gerhard Berger	Ferrari 412T1B	45	1h22m37.272
2 Olivier Panis	Ligier JS39B-Renault	45	1h23m32.051
3 Eric Bernard	Ligier JS39B-Renault	45	1h23m42.314
4 Christian Fittipaldi	Footwork FA15-Ford	45	1h23m58.881

5 Gianni Morbidelli	Footwork FA15-Ford	45	1h24m07.816
6 Erik Comas	Larrousse LH94-Ford	45	1h24m22.717

Winner's average speed: 137.906 mph. Starting grid front row: Berger, 1m43.582 (pole) and Alesi, 1m44.012. Fastest lap: Coulthard, 1m46.211. Leaders: Berger, laps 1-45

Marlboro Magyar Nagydíj (Hungarian Grand Prix)

14 August 1994. Hungaroring. 77 laps of a 2.465-mile circuit = 189.805 miles. Hot, dry and sunny. World Championship round 10

1 Michael Schumacher	Benetton B194-Ford	77	1h48m00.185
2 Damon Hill	Williams FW16B-Renault	77	1h48m21.012
3 Jos Verstappen	Benetton B194-Ford	77	1h49m10.514
4 Martin Brundle	McLaren MP4/9-Peugeot	76	
5 Mark Blundell	Tyrrell 022-Yamaha	76	
6 Olivier Panis	Ligier JS39B-Renault	76	

Winner's average speed: 105.444 mph. Starting grid front row: Schumacher, 1m18.258 (pole) and Hill, 1m18.824. Fastest lap: Schumacher, 1m20.881. Leaders: Schumacher, laps 1-16, 26-77; Hill, 17-25

Grand Prix de Belgique

28 August 1994. Spa-Francorchamps. 44 laps of a 4.350-mile circuit = 191.400 miles. Warm, dry and sunny. World Championship round 11

1 Damon Hill	Williams FW16B-Renault	44	1h28m47.170
2 Mika Häkkinen	McLaren MP4/9-Peugeot	44	1h29m38.551

1994 DRIVERS' RECORDS

Driver	Car	Brazilian GP	Pacific GP	San Marino GP	Monaco GP	Spanish GP	Canadian GP	French GP	British GP	German GP	Hungarian GP	Belgian GP	Italian GP	Portuguese GP	European GP	Japanese GP	Australian GP
Philippe Adams	Lotus 109-Mugen	-	-	-	-	-	-	-	-	-	-	-	R	-	16	-	-
Michele Alboreto	Minardi M193B-Ford	R	R	R	6	R	11	R	R	R	7	9	R	13	14	R	R
Jean Alesi	Ferrari 412T1	3	-	-	5	4	3	-	-	-	-	-	-	-	-	-	-
	Ferrari 412T1B	-	-	-	-	-	-	R	2	R	R	R	R^P	R	10	3	6
Philippe Alliot	McLaren MP4/9-Peugeot	-	-	-	-	-	-	-	-	R	-	-	-	-	-	-	-
	Larrousse LH94-Ford	-	-	-	-	-	-	-	-	-	-	R	-	-	-	-	-
Rubens Barrichello	Jordan 194-Hart	4	3	DNP	R	R	7	R	4	R	R	R^P	4	4	12	R	4
Paul Belmondo	Pacific PR01-Ilmor	DNQ	DNQ	DNQ	R	R	DNQ	DNQ	DNQ	DNQ	DNQ	DNQ	DNQ	DNQ	DNQ	DNQ	DNQ
Olivier Beretta	Larrousse LH94-Ford	R	R	R	8	DNS	R	R	14	7	9	-	-	-	-	-	-
Gerhard Berger	Ferrari 412T1	R	2	R	3	R	4	-	-	-	-	-	-	-	-	-	-
	Ferrari 412T1B	-	-	-	-	-	-	3	R	1^P	12	R	2	R^P	5	R	2
Eric Bernard	Ligier JS39B-Renault	R	10	12	R	8	13	R	13	3	10	10	7	10	-	-	-
	Lotus 109-Mugen	-	-	-	-	-	-	-	-	-	-	-	-	-	18	-	-
Mark Blundell	Tyrrell 022-Yamaha	R	R	9	R	3	10	10	R	R	5	5	R	R	13	R	R
David Brabham	Simtek S941-Ford	12	R	R	R	10	14	R	15	R	11	R	R	R	R	12	R
Martin Brundle	McLaren MP4/9-Peugeot	R	R	8	2	R	R	R	R	R	4	R	5	6	R	R	3
Andrea de Cesaris	Jordan 194-Hart	-	-	R	4	-	-	-	-	-	-	-	-	-	-	-	-
	Sauber C13-Mercedes-Benz	-	-	-	-	-	R	6	R	R	R	R	R	R	-	-	-
Erik Comas	Larrousse LH94-Ford	9	6	R	10	R	R	R	R	6	8	R	8	R	9	-	-
David Coulthard	Williams FW16-Renault	-	-	-	-	R	5	-	5	R^F	-	-	-	-	-	-	-
	Williams FW16B-Renault	-	-	-	-	-	-	-	-	-	R	4	6	2^F	-	-	-
Yannick Dalmas	Larrousse LH94-Ford	-	-	-	-	-	-	-	-	-	-	-	R	14	-	-	-
Jean-Denis Deletraz	Larrousse LH94-Ford	-	-	-	-	-	-	-	-	-	-	-	-	-	-	-	R
Christian Fittipaldi	Footwork FA15-Ford	R	4	R	R	R	DSQ	8	9	4	14	R	R	8	17	8	8
Heinz-Harald Frentzen	Sauber C13-Mercedes-Benz	R	5	7	DNP	R	R	4	7	R	R	R	R	R	6	6	7
Bertrand Gachot	Pacific PR01-Ilmor	R	DNQ	R	R	R	R	DNQ	DNQ	DNQ	DNQ	DNQ	DNQ	DNQ	DNQ	DNQ	DNQ
Jean-Marc Gounon	Simtek S941-Ford	-	-	-	-	-	-	9	16	R	R	11	R	15	-	-	-
Mika Häkkinen	McLaren MP4/9-Peugeot	R	R	3	R	R	R	R	3	R	-	2	3	3	3	7	12
Johnny Herbert	Lotus 107C-Mugen	7	7	10	R	-	-	-	-	-	-	-	-	-	-	-	-
	Lotus 109-Mugen	-	-	-	-	R	8	7	11	R	R	12	R	11	-	-	-
	Ligier JS39B-Renault	-	-	-	-	-	-	-	-	-	-	-	-	-	8	-	-
	Benetton B194-Ford	-	-	-	-	-	-	-	-	-	-	-	-	-	-	R	R

/Cont'd

3 Jos Verstappen   Benetton B194-Ford   44 1h29m57.623
4 David Coulthard   Williams FW16B-Renault   44 1h30m32.957
5 Mark Blundell   Tyrrell 022-Yamaha   43
6 Gianni Morbidelli   Footwork FA15-Ford   43

Schumacher (Benetton B194-Ford) finished first on the road but was disqualified for stepped flat bottom infringement. Winner's average speed: 129.344 mph. Starting grid front row: Barrichello, 2m21.163 (pole) and Schumacher, 2m21.494. Fastest lap: Hill, 1m57.117. Leaders: Alesi, laps 1-2; Hill, 3-11, 37-44; Coulthard, 12-13, 18-36; Barrichello, 14-17 (Schumacher led laps 1-28 and 30-44 on the road but was disqualified, Coulthard led lap 29 on the road)

Gran Premio d'Italia

11 September 1994. Monza. 53 laps of a 3.625-mile circuit = 192.125 miles. Hot, dry and sunny. World Championship round 12

1 Damon Hill   Williams FW16B-Renault   53 1h18m02.754
2 Gerhard Berger   Ferrari 412T1B   53 1h18m07.684
3 Mika Häkkinen   McLaren MP4/9-Peugeot   53 1h18m28.394
4 Rubens Barrichello   Jordan 194-Hart   53 1h18m53.388
5 Martin Brundle   McLaren MP4/9-Peugeot   53 1h19m28.329
6 David Coulthard   Williams FW16B-Renault   52

Winner's average speed: 147.702 mph. Starting grid front row: Alesi, 1m23.844 (pole) and Berger, 1m23.978. Fastest lap: Hill, 1m25.930. Leaders: Alesi, laps 1-14; Berger, 15-23; Hill, 24, 29-53; Coulthard, 25, 27-28; Häkkinen, 26

Grande Premio de Portugal

25 September 1994. Estoril. 71 laps of a 2.709-mile circuit = 192.339 miles. Warm, dry and sunny. World Championship round 13

1 Damon Hill   Williams FW16B-Renault   71 1h41m10.165
2 David Coulthard   Williams FW16B-Renault   71 1h41m10.768
3 Mika Häkkinen   McLaren MP4/9-Peugeot   71 1h41m30.358
4 Rubens Barrichello   Jordan 194-Hart   71 1h41m38.168

5 Jos Verstappen   Benetton B194-Ford   71 1h41m39.550
6 Martin Brundle   McLaren MP4/9-Peugeot   71 1h42m02.867

Winner's average speed: 114.069 mph. Starting grid front row: Berger, 1m20.608 (pole) and Hill, 1m20.766. Fastest lap: Coulthard, 1m22.446. Leaders: Berger, laps 1-7; Coulthard, 8-17, 26-27; Hill, 18, 28-71; Alesi, 19-22; Barrichello, 23-25

Gran Premio de Europa

16 October 1994. Jerez. 69 laps of a 2.751-mile circuit = 189.819 miles. Hot, dry and sunny. World Championship round 14

1 Michael Schumacher   Benetton B194-Ford   69 1h40m26.689
2 Damon Hill   Williams FW16B-Renault   69 1h40m51.378
3 Mika Häkkinen   McLaren MP4/9-Peugeot   69 1h41m36.337
4 Eddie Irvine   Jordan 194-Hart   69 1h41m45.135
5 Gerhard Berger   Ferrari 412T1B   68
6 Heinz-Harald Frentzen   Sauber C13-   68

Winner's average speed: 113.387 mph. Starting grid front row: Schumacher, 1m22.762 (pole) and Hill, 1m22.892. Fastest lap: Schumacher, 1m25.04. Leaders: Hill, laps 1-17, 33-34; Schumacher, 18-32, 35-69

Fuji Television Japanese Grand Prix

6 November 1994. Suzuka. 50 laps of a 3.641-mile circuit = 182.050 miles. Race scheduled for 53 laps, stopped after 13 laps due to heavy rain. Restarted over an additional 37 laps. Very wet. World Championship round 15

1 Damon Hill   Williams FW16B-Renault   50 1h55m53.532
2 Michael Schumacher   Benetton B194-Ford   50 1h55m56.897
3 Jean Alesi   Ferrari 412T1B   50 1h56m45.577
4 Nigel Mansell   Williams FW16B-Renault   50 1h56m49.606
5 Eddie Irvine   Jordan 194-Hart   50 1h57m35.639
6 Heinz-Harald Frentzen   Sauber C13- Mercedes-Benz   50 1h57m53.395

1994 DRIVERS' RECORDS cont'd/

Driver	Car	Brazilian GP	Pacific GP	San Marino GP	Monaco GP	Spanish GP	Canadian GP	French GP	British GP	German GP	Hungarian GP	Belgian GP	Italian GP	Portuguese GP	European GP	Japanese GP	Australian GP
Damon Hill	Williams FW16-Renault	2	R	6F	R	1	2	2PF	1PF	8	-	-	-	-	-	-	-
	Williams FW16B-Renault	-	-	-	-	-	-	-	-	-	2	1F	1F	1	2	1F	R
Taki Inoue	Simtek S941-Ford	-	-	-	-	-	-	-	-	-	-	-	-	-	R	-	-
Eddie Irvine	Jordan 194-Hart	R	-	-	-	6	R	R	DNS	R	R	13	R	7	4	5	R
Ukyo Katayama	Tyrrell 022-Yamaha	5	R	5	R	R	R	R	6	R	R	R	R	R	7	R	R
Franck Lagorce	Ligier JS39B-Renault	-	-	-	-	-	-	-	-	-	-	-	-	-	-	R	11
Pedro Lamy	Lotus 107C-Mugen	10	8	R	11	-	-	-	-	-	-	-	-	-	-	-	-
Nicola Larini	Ferrari 412T1	-	R	2	-	-	-	-	-	-	-	-	-	-	-	-	-
JJ Lehto	Benetton B194-Ford	-	-	R	7	R	6	-	-	-	-	-	9	R	-	-	-
	Sauber C13-Mercedes-Benz	-	-	-	-	-	-	-	-	-	-	-	-	-	R	-	10
Nigel Mansell	Williams FW16-Renault	-	-	-	-	-	-	R	-	-	-	-	-	-	-	-	-
	Williams FW16B-Renault	-	-	-	-	-	-	-	-	-	-	-	-	-	R	4	1P
Pierluigi Martini	Minardi M193B-Ford	8	R	R	R	5	9	5	10	R	R	8	R	12	15	R	9
Andrea Montermini	Simtek S941-Ford	-	-	-	DNQ	-	-	-	-	-	-	-	-	-	-	-	-
Gianni Morbidelli	Footwork FA15-Ford	R	R	R	R	R	R	R	R	5	R	6	R	9	11	R	R
Hideki Noda	Larrousse LH94-Ford	-	-	-	-	-	-	-	-	-	-	-	-	-	R	R	R
Olivier Panis	Ligier JS39B-Renault	11	9	11	9	7	12	R	12	2	6	7	10	DSQ	9	11	5
Roland Ratzenberger	Simtek S941-Ford	DNQ	11	DNS	-	-	-	-	-	-	-	-	-	-	-	-	-
Mika Salo	Lotus 109-Mugen	-	-	-	-	-	-	-	-	-	-	-	-	-	-	10	R
Domenico Schiattarella	Simtek S941-Ford	-	-	-	-	-	-	-	-	-	-	-	-	-	19	-	R
Michael Schumacher	Benetton B194-Ford	1F	1F	1	1PF	2PF	1PF	1	DSQ	R	1PF	DSQ	-	1PF	2P	RF
Ayrton Senna	Williams FW16-Renault	RP	RP	RP	-	-	-	-	-	-	-	-	-	-	-	-	-
Aguri Suzuki	Jordan 194-Hart	-	R	-	-	-	-	-	-	-	-	-	-	-	-	-	-
Jos Verstappen	Benetton B194-Ford	R	R	-	-	-	R	8	R	3	3	R	5	R	-	-	-
Karl Wendlinger	Sauber C13-Mercedes-Benz	6	R	4	DNP	-	-	-	-	-	-	-	-	-	-	-	-
Alessandro Zanardi	Lotus 107C-Mugen	-	-	-	-	9	R	-	-	-	-	-	-	-	-	-	-
	Lotus 109-Mugen	-	-	-	-	-	-	R	R	13	-	R	-	16	13	R	

Winner's average speed: 94.251 mph. Starting grid front row: Schumacher, 1m37.209 (pole) and Hill, 1m37.696. Fastest lap: Hill, 1m56.597. Leaders: Schumacher, laps 1-18, 36-40; Hill, 19-35, 41-50

Australian Grand Prix

13 November 1994. Adelaide. 81 laps of a 2.347 mile-circuit = 190.107 miles. Warm, dry and overcast. World Championship round 16

	Driver	Car	Laps
1	Nigel Mansell	Williams FW16B-Renault	81 1h47m51.480
2	Gerhard Berger	Ferrari 412T1B	81 1h47m53.991
3	Martin Brundle	McLaren MP4/9-Peugeot	81 1h48m43.967
4	Rubens Barrichello	Jordan 194-Hart	81 1h49m02.010
5	Olivier Panis	Ligier JS39B-Renault	80
6	Jean Alesi	Ferrari 412T1B	80

Winner's average speed: 105.754 mph. Starting grid front row: Mansell, 1m16.179 (pole) and Schumacher, 1m16.197. Fastest lap: Schumacher, 1m17.14. Leaders: Schumacher, laps 1-35; Mansell, 36-53, 64-81; Berger, 54-63

1994 FINAL CHAMPIONSHIP POSITIONS

Drivers

	Driver	Pts
1	Michael Schumacher	92
2	Damon Hill	91
3	Gerhard Berger	41
4	Mika Häkkinen	26
5	Jean Alesi	24
6	Rubens Barrichello	19
7	Martin Brundle	16
8	David Coulthard	14
9	Nigel Mansell	13
10	Jos Verstappen	10
11	Olivier Panis	9
12	Mark Blundell	8
13	Heinz-Harald Frentzen	7
14=	Christian Fittipaldi	6
	Eddie Irvine	6
	Nicola Larini	6
17	Ukyo Katayama	5
18=	Eric Bernard	4
	Andrea de Cesaris	4
	Pierluigi Martini	4
	Karl Wendlinger	4
22	Gianni Morbidelli	3
23	Erik Comas	2
24=	Michele Alboreto	1
	JJ Lehto	1

Manufacturers

		Pts
1	Williams-Renault	118
2	Benetton-Ford	103
3	Ferrari	71
4	McLaren-Peugeot	42
5	Jordan-Hart	28
6=	Ligier-Renault	13
	Tyrrell-Yamaha	13
8	Sauber-Mercedes-Benz	12
9	Footwork-Ford	9
10	Minardi-Ford	5
11	Larrousse-Ford	2

MANUFACTURERS A–Z

Notes: On a number of occasions a constructor has changed its name in deference to a major sponsor. However, in this section they can be found listed under their original names unless the team was sold AND there was a major change of personnel. For example, when Toleman was bought by its sponsor Benetton, owner Ted Toleman left the organization so in this case I have included separate entries for Toleman and for Benetton. Consequently, Arrows/Footwork and March/Leyton House are found under Arrows and March respectively, but Osella and Fondmetal or Coloni and Andrea Moda are separate listings.

AFM

ALEX VON FALKENHAUSEN MOTORENBAU

GP Debut:	1952 Swiss GP	Stuck (retired)
Last GP:	1953 Italian GP	Stuck (14th)
Principal:	Alex von Falkenhausen	
Base:	Munich (D)	

WORLD CHAMPIONSHIP RECORD

GPs Started: 4
Best result: 14th 1953 Italian GP (Stuck)
Best qualif.: 14th 1952 Swiss GP (Stuck)

AFM GRAND PRIX DRIVERS

Driver	Nat	Start 1st 2nd 3rd 4th 5th 6th PP FL Points (DNS/DNQ)
Hans Stuck	D	3 - - - - - - - - -
Günther Bechem	D	1 - - - - - - - - -
Theo Fitzau	D	1 - - - - - - - - -
Willi Heeks	D	1 - - - - - - - - -
Helmut Niedermayr	D	1 - - - - - - - - -
Ludwig Fischer	D	- (1) - - - - - - - -
Willi Krakau	D	- (1) - - - - - - - -

AFM GRAND PRIX CARS

Type	Year	Engine	Designer
1	1952	BMW 328 S6	Alex von Falkenhausen
2	1953	BMW 328 S6	Alex von Falkenhausen
4	1952	Küchen V8	Alex von Falkenhausen
6	1952	BMW 328 S6	Alex von Falkenhausen
7	1952	BMW 328 S6	Alex von Falkenhausen
8	1952	BMW 328 S6	Alex von Falkenhausen

AGS

AUTOMOBILES GONFARONAISE SPORTIVE

GP Debut:	1986 Italian GP	Capelli (retired)
Last GP:	1991 Monaco GP	Tarquini (retired)
Principal:	Henri Julien, 1970-89; Cyril de Rouvre, 1989-91 when AGS applied for receivership; Gabriele Rafanelli and Patrizio Cantu, bought assets in 1991	
Base:	Gonfaron (F), 1970-89; Le Luc-en-Provence, 1990-91	

WORLD CHAMPIONSHIP RECORD

GPs Started: 47
Points: 2
Best result: 6th 1987 Australian GP (Moreno), 1989 Mexican GP (Tarquini)
Best qualif.: 10th 1988 Canadian GP (Streiff)
Best World Championship position:
Drivers: 19th in 1987 (Moreno)
Constructors: 11th in 1987

MAJOR SPONSORS

1986-87	El Charro
1988	Bouygues
1989	Faure
1990	Ted Lapidus

AGS GRAND PRIX DRIVERS

Driver	Nat	Start 1st 2nd 3rd 4th 5th 6th PP FL Points (DNS/DNQ)
Gabriele Tarquini	I	13 (31) - - - - - 1 - - 1
Roberto Moreno	BR	2 - - - - - 1 - - 1
Philippe Streiff	F	15 (1) - - - - - - - - -

Driver	Nat	Start (DNS/DNQ)	1st	2nd	3rd	4th	5th	6th	PP	FL	Points
Pascal Fabre	F	11 (3)	-	-	-	-	-	-	-	-	-
Yannick Dalmas	F	5 (20)	-	-	-	-	-	-	-	-	-
Ivan Capelli	I	2	-	-	-	-	-	-	-	-	-
Fabrizio Barbazza	I	- (12)	-	-	-	-	-	-	-	-	-
Joachim Winkelhock	D	- (7)	-	-	-	-	-	-	-	-	-
Stefan Johansson	S	- (2)	-	-	-	-	-	-	-	-	-
Olivier Grouillard	F	- (1)	-	-	-	-	-	-	-	-	-

AGS GRAND PRIX CARS

Type	Year	Engine	Designer
JH21C	1986	Motori Moderni V6 tc	Christian Vanderpleyn
JH22	1987	Ford DFZ V8	Christian Vanderpleyn
JH23	1988	Ford DFZ V8	Christian Vanderpleyn
JH23B	1989	Ford DFR V8	Christian Vanderpleyn
JH24	1989	Ford DFR V8	Claude Galopin
JH25	1990	Ford DFR V8	Michel Costa
JH25B	1991	Ford DFR V8	Michel Costa/ Christian Vanderpleyn
JH26*	1991	Ford DFR V8	Michel Costa
JH27	1991	Ford DFR V8	Mario Tollentino

*Never built due to lack of finance

ALFA ROMEO

GP Debut:	1950 British GP	Farina (1st), Fagioli (2nd), Parnell (3rd), Fangio (retired)
Last GP:	1985 Australian GP	Patrese (retired), Cheever (retired)
Base:	Portello, near Milan (I)	
Works teams:	Alfa Corse prior to 1963; Autodelta, 1963-82; Euroracing, 1983-85 (Autodelta continued to manufacturer chassis, engines and gearboxes)	
Team Principal:	Autodelta: Carlo Chiti, 1979-84; Giovanni Tonti, 1984-85 Euroracing: Paolo Pavenello	

WORLD CHAMPIONSHIP RECORD

GPs Started: 112
Points: 214
Wins: 10 1950 British GP (Farina), Monaco GP (Fangio), Swiss GP (Farina), Belgian GP (Fangio), French GP (Fangio), Italian GP (Fangio), 1951 Swiss GP (Fangio), Belgian GP (Farina), French GP (Fagioli/Fangio) and Spanish GP (Fangio)
Pole pos.: 12 1950 British GP (Farina), Monaco GP (Fangio), Swiss GP (Fangio), Belgian GP (Farina), French GP (Fangio), Italian GP (Fangio), 1951 Swiss GP (Fangio), Belgian GP (Farina), French GP (Fangio), Italian GP (Fangio), 1980 United States GP (Giacomelli), 1982 Long Beach GP (de Cesaris)
Fastest laps: 14 1950 British GP (Farina), Monaco GP (Fangio), Swiss GP (Farina), Belgian GP (Farina), French GP (Fangio), Italian GP (Fangio), 1951 Swiss GP (Fangio), Belgian GP (Fangio), French GP (Fangio), British GP (Fangio), German GP (Fangio), Italian GP (Farina), Spanish GP (Fangio), 1983 Belgian GP (de Cesaris)
Laps/miles in the lead: 702 laps/2978 miles
World Champions:
Drivers: Twice - 1950 (Farina) and 1951 (Fangio)
Best World Championship position:
Constructors: 6th in 1983

ALFA ROMEO GRAND PRIX DRIVERS

Driver	Nat	Start (DNS/DNQ)	1st	2nd	3rd	4th	5th	6th	PP	FL	Points
Juan Manuel Fangio	RA	13	6	2	-	-	-	-	8	8	64
Giuseppe Farina	I	13	4	-	3	1	1	-	2	5	52
Luigi Fagioli	I	7	1	4	1	-	-	-	-	-	32
Andrea de Cesaris	I	32 (1)	-	2	1	1	-	1	1	1	20
Bruno Giacomelli	I	49 (1)	-	-	1	3	-	1	-		13
Riccardo Patrese	I	32	-	-	1	1	-	-	-		8
Felice Bonetto	I	4	-	-	1	1	1	-	-		7
Reg Parnell	GB	1	-	-	1	-	-	-	-		4
Eddie Cheever	USA	31 (1)	-	-	-	1	-	-	-		3
Mario Andretti	USA	15	-	-	-	1	-	-	-		3
Mauro Baldi	I	15	-	-	-	-	1	1	-	-	3

Driver	Nat	Start (DNS/DNQ)	1st	2nd	3rd	4th	5th	6th	PP	FL	Points
Consalvo Sanesi	I	5	-	-	1	-	1	-	-		3
Emanuel de Graffenried	CH	3	-	-	-	1	1	-	-		2
Patrick Depailler	F	8	-	-	-	-	-	-	-	-	-
Vittorio Brambilla	I	4 (1)	-	-	-	-	-	-	-	-	-
Piet de Klerk	ZA	2	-	-	-	-	-	-	-	-	-
Paul Pietsch	D	1	-	-	-	-	-	-	-	-	-
Piero Taruffi	I	1	-	-	-	-	-	-	-	-	-

ALFA ROMEO GRAND PRIX CARS

Type	Year	Engine	Designer
158	1950	Alfa Romeo S8 sc	Gioacchino Colombo
		Championship debut, the 158 first raced in 1938	
159	1950	Alfa Romeo S8 sc	Gioacchino Colombo
Alfa Special*	1963	Alfa Romeo Giulietta S4	Piet de Klerk
177	1979	Alfa Romeo 115-12 F12	Carlo Chiti
179	1979	Alfa Romeo 1260 V12	Carlo Chiti/Robert Choulet
179B	1980	Alfa Romeo 1260 V12	Carlo Chiti/Robert Choulet
179C	1981	Alfa Romeo 1260 V12	Carlo Chiti/Robert Choulet
179D	1982	Alfa Romeo 1260 V12	Carlo Chiti/Robert Choulet
182	1982	Alfa Romeo 1260 V12	Gérard Ducarouge
183T	1983	Alfa Romeo 890T V8 tc	Gérard Ducarouge
184T	1984	Alfa Romeo 890T V8 tc	Luigi Marmiroli/Mario Tollentino/Bruno Zava
184TB	1985	Alfa Romeo 890T V8 tc	Luigi Marmiroli/Mario Tollentino/Bruno Zava
185T	1985	Alfa Romeo 890T V8 tc	John Gentry

*A private "special" built by de Klerk for South African racing

ALTA

GP Debut:	1950 British GP	Kelly (not classified), Crossley (retired)
Last GP:	1952 British GP	G Whitehead (12th)
Principal:	Geoffrey Taylor	
Base:	Tolworth, near Kingston-upon-Thames (GB)	

WORLD CHAMPIONSHIP RECORD

GPs Started: 5
Best result: 9th 1950 Belgian GP (Crossley)
Best qualif.: 12th 1950 Belgian GP (Crossley), 1952 British GP (G Whitehead)

ALTA GRAND PRIX DRIVERS

Driver	Nat	Start (DNS/DNQ)	1st	2nd	3rd	4th	5th	6th	PP	FL	Points
Geoffrey Crossley	GB	2	-	-	-	-	-	-	-	-	-
Joe Kelly	IRL	2	-	-	-	-	-	-	-	-	-
Graham Whitehead	GB	1	-	-	-	-	-	-	-	-	-
Peter Whitehead	GB	1	-	-	-	-	-	-	-	-	-

ALTA GRAND PRIX CARS

Type	Year	Engine	Designer
GP	1950*	Alta GP S4 sc	Geoffrey Taylor
F2	1952	Alta F2 S4	Geoffrey Taylor

*Championship debut, the GP first raced in 1948

AMON

Only GP:	1974 Spanish GP	Amon (retired)
Principals:	Chris Amon and John Dalton	
Base:	Reading (GB)	

WORLD CHAMPIONSHIP RECORD

Starts: 1
Best result: No finishes
Best qualif.: 20th 1974 Monaco GP (Amon) - did not start

AMON GRAND PRIX DRIVERS

Driver	Nat	Start (DNS/DNQ)	1st	2nd	3rd	4th	5th	6th	PP	FL	Points
Chris Amon	NZ	1 (3)	-	-	-	-	-	-	-	-	-
Larry Perkins	AUS	- (1)	-	-	-	-	-	-	-	-	-

World Championship Grand Prix Racing

AMON GRAND PRIX CARS

Type	Year	Engine	Designer
AF101	1974	Ford DFV V8	Gordon Fowell

ANDREA MODA

Bought Coloni in 1991 and ran Coloni C4Bs until the Simtek-built Andrea Moda S192 was ready; also see Coloni and Simtek

Only GP:	1992 Monaco GP Moreno (retired)
Principal:	Andrea Sassetti
Base:	Constructor: Banbury (GB); Team: Perugia (I)

WORLD CHAMPIONSHIP RECORD

GPs Started: 1
Best result: No finishes
Best qualif.: 26th 1992 Monaco GP (Moreno)

ANDREA MODA GRAND PRIX DRIVERS

Driver	Nat	Start (DNS/DNQ)	1st	2nd	3rd	4th	5th	6th	PP	FL	Points
Roberto Moreno	BR	1 (9)	-	-	-	-	-	-	-	-	-
Perry McCarthy	GB	- (10)	-	-	-	-	-	-	-	-	-
Enrico Bertaggia	I	- (1)	-	-	-	-	-	-	-	-	-
Alex Caffi	I	- (1)	-	-	-	-	-	-	-	-	-

ANDREA MODA GRAND PRIX CARS

Type	Year	Engine	Designer
S192	1992	Judd GV V10	Nick Wirth

ARROWS

Officially named after major sponsor/shareholder Footwork since 1991

GP Debut:	1978 Brazilian GP Patrese (10th)
Latest GP:	1994 Australian GP Fittipaldi (8th), Morbidelli (retired)
Principals:	Jackie Oliver, 1978 to date; Watara Ohasi/Footwork, 1991 to date; Arrows founded by Franco Ambrosio, Alan Rees, Oliver, Dave Wass and Tony Southgate
Base:	Milton Keynes (GB)

WORLD CHAMPIONSHIP RECORD

GPs Started:	255
Points:	135
Best result:	2nd 1978 Swedish GP (Patrese), 1980 Long Beach GP (Patrese), 1981 San Marino GP (Patrese), 1985 San Marino GP (Boutsen)
Pole pos.:	1 1981 Long Beach GP (Patrese)
Fastest laps:	1 1980 Monaco GP (Patrese)
Laps/miles in the lead:	66 laps/155 miles

Best World Championship position:
Drivers:	7th in 1988 (Warwick)
Constructors:	4th in 1988

MAJOR SPONSORS

1978	Varig, Warsteiner
1979-80	Warsteiner
1981	Ragno, Beta
1982	Ragno
1984-85	Barclay
1986	Barclay, USF&G
1987-89	USF&G
1990-93	Footwork
1994	various

ARROWS GRAND PRIX DRIVERS

Driver	Nat	Start (DNS/DNQ)	1st	2nd	3rd	4th	5th	6th	PP	FL	Points
Derek Warwick	GB	63	-	-	-	5	5	6	-	-	31
Riccardo Patrese	I	57 (1)	-	3	1	1	1	3	1	1	30
Eddie Cheever	USA	46 (2)	-	-	2	2	1	4	-	-	20

Driver	Nat	Start (DNS/DNQ)	1st	2nd	3rd	4th	5th	6th	PP	FL	Points
Thierry Boutsen	B	57 (1)	-	1	-	1	2	3	-	-	16
Marc Surer	CH	47 (1)	-	-	-	-	2	4	-	-	8
Jochen Mass	D	24 (4)	-	-	-	1	-	4	-	-	7
Michele Alboreto	I	38 (10)	-	-	-	-	2	2	-	-	6
Christian Fittipaldi	BR	16	-	-	-	2	-	-	-	-	6
Gerhard Berger	A	16	-	-	-	-	1	1	-	-	3
Gianni Morbidelli	I	16	-	-	-	-	1	1	-	-	3
Alex Caffi	I	13 (13)	-	-	-	1	-	-	-	-	2
Mauro Baldi	I	11 (4)	-	-	-	-	2	-	-	-	2
Christian Danner	D	10	-	-	-	-	1	-	-	-	1
Aguri Suzuki	J	30 (2)	-	-	-	-	-	-	-	-	-
Rolf Stommelen	D	9 (5)	-	-	-	-	-	-	-	-	-
Siegfried Stohr	I	9 (4)	-	-	-	-	-	-	-	-	-
Chico Serra	BR	4	-	-	-	-	-	-	-	-	-
Stefan Johansson	S	1 (3)	-	-	-	-	-	-	-	-	-
Brian Henton	GB	1 (2)	-	-	-	-	-	-	-	-	-
Bernd Schneider	D	1 (1)	-	-	-	-	-	-	-	-	-
Martin Donnelly	GB	1	-	-	-	-	-	-	-	-	-
Alan Jones	AUS	1	-	-	-	-	-	-	-	-	-
Jacques Villeneuve	CDN	- (2)	-	-	-	-	-	-	-	-	-
Patrick Tambay	F	- (1)	-	-	-	-	-	-	-	-	-
Mike Thackwell	NZ	- (1)	-	-	-	-	-	-	-	-	-
Manfred Winkelhock	D	- (1)	-	-	-	-	-	-	-	-	-

ARROWS GRAND PRIX CARS

Type	Year	Engine	Designer
FA1	1978	Ford DFV V8	Tony Southgate/Dave Wass
			London High Court ruled that the FA1 was an illegal copy of the Shadow DN9
A1	1978	Ford DFV V8	Tony Southgate/Dave Wass
A2	1979	Ford DFV V8	Tony Southgate/Dave Wass
A3	1980	Ford DFV V8	Tony Southgate/Dave Wass
A4	1982	Ford DFV V8	Dave Wass
A5	1982	Ford DFV V8	Dave Wass
A6	1983	Ford DFV V8	Dave Wass
A7	1984	BMW M12/13 S4 tc	Dave Wass
A8	1985	BMW M12/13 S4 tc	Dave Wass
A9	1986	BMW M12/13 S4 tc	Dave Wass
A10	1987	Megatron BMW M12/13 S4 tc	Ross Brawn
A10B	1988	Megatron BMW M12/13 S4 tc	Ross Brawn
A11	1989	Ford DFR V8	Ross Brawn/ James Robinson
A11B	1990	Ford DFR V8	Alan Jenkins/James Robinson/Ross Brawn
A11C*	1991	Porsche V12	Alan Jenkins
FA12*	1991	Porsche V12, Ford DFR V8	Alan Jenkins
FA13*	1992	Mugen MF-351H V10	Alan Jenkins
FA13B*	1993	Mugen MF-351HB V10	Alan Jenkins
FA14*	1993	Mugen MF-351HB V10	Alan Jenkins
FA15*	1994	Ford HB V8	Alan Jenkins

*Footwork

ASTON-BUTTERWORTH

GP Debut:	1952 Belgian GP Montgomerie-Charrington (retired)
Last GP:	1952 German GP Aston (retired)
Principal:	Bill Aston

WORLD CHAMPIONSHIP RECORD

GPs Started: 2
Best result: No finishes
Best qualif.: 15th 1952 Belgian GP (Montgomerie-Charrington)

ASTON-BUTTERWORTH GRAND PRIX DRIVERS

Driver	Nat	Start (DNS/DNQ)	1st	2nd	3rd	4th	5th	6th	PP	FL	Points
Bill Aston	GB	1 (2)	-	-	-	-	-	-	-	-	-
Robin Montgomerie-Charrington	USA	1	-	-	-	-	-	-	-	-	-

ASTON-BUTTERWORTH GRAND PRIX CARS

Type	Year	Engine	Designer
NB41	1952	Butterworth F4	Bill Aston

ASTON MARTIN

GP Debut:	1959 Dutch GP	Shelby (retired), Salvadori (retired)
Last GP:	1960 British GP	Trintignant (11th), Salvadori (retired)
Principal:	David Brown	
Base:	Feltham (GB)	

WORLD CHAMPIONSHIP RECORD

GPs Started: 5
Best result: 6th 1959 British GP (Salvadori), Portuguese GP (Salvadori)
Best qualif.: 2th 1959 British GP (Salvadori)

ASTON MARTIN GRAND PRIX DRIVERS

Driver	Nat	Start (DNS/DNQ)	1st	2nd	3rd	4th	5th	6th	PP	FL	Points
Roy Salvadori	GB	5 (1)	-	-	-	-	-	2	-	-	-
Carroll Shelby	USA	4	-	-	-	-	-	-	-	-	-
Maurice Trintignant	F	1	-	-	-	-	-	-	-	-	-

ASTON MARTIN GRAND PRIX CARS

Type	Year	Engine	Designer
DBR4/250	1959	Aston Martin DBR4 S6	Ted Cutting
DBR5/250	1960	Aston Martin DBR4 S6	Ted Cutting

ATS

ATS WHEELS

GP Debut:	1978 Argentinian GP	Mass (11th), Jarier (12th)
Last GP:	1984 Portuguese GP	Berger (13th)
Principal:	Hans-Günther Schmidt	
Base:	Bicester (GB)	

WORLD CHAMPIONSHIP RECORD

GPs Started: 89
Points: 7
Best result: 5th 1979 United States GP (Stuck), 1982 Brazilian GP (Winkelhock), San Marino GP (Salazar)
Best qualif.: 4th 1980 Long Beach GP (Lammers)

Best World Championship position:
Drivers: 18th in 1981 (Borgudd)
Constructors: 11th in 1979

ATS WHEELS GRAND PRIX DRIVERS

Driver	Nat	Start (DNS/DNQ)	1st	2nd	3rd	4th	5th	6th	PP	FL	Points
Manfred Winkelhock	D	38 (7)	-	-	-	-	1	-	-	-	2
Eliseo Salazar	RCH	13 (3)	-	-	-	-	1	-	-	-	2
Hans-Joachim Stuck	D	12 (3)	-	-	-	-	1	-	-	-	2
Slim Borgudd	S	7 (5)	-	-	-	-	-	1	-	-	1
Jochen Mass	D	10 (3)	-	-	-	-	-	-	-	-	-
Marc Surer	CH	9 (2)	-	-	-	-	-	-	-	-	-
Jan Lammers	NL	5 (5)	-	-	-	-	-	-	-	-	-
Keke Rosberg	SF	5	-	-	-	-	-	-	-	-	-
Gerhard Berger	A	4	-	-	-	-	1*	-	-	-	-
Jean-Pierre Jarier	F	3 (3)	-	-	-	-	-	-	-	-	-
Michael Bleekemolen	NL	1 (3)	-	-	-	-	-	-	-	-	-
Alberto Colombo	I	- (2)	-	-	-	-	-	-	-	-	-
Harald Ertl	A	- (2)	-	-	-	-	-	-	-	-	-
Hans Binder	A	- (1)	-	-	-	-	-	-	-	-	-

*not entered in World Championship so ineligible for points

ATS WHEELS GRAND PRIX CARS

Type	Year	Engine	Designer
HS1*	1978	Ford DFV V8	Geoff Ferris/Robin Herd/John Gentry
D1	1978	Ford DFV V8	John Gentry
D2	1979	Ford DFV V8	John Gentry/Giacomo Caliri

Type	Year	Engine	Designer
D3	1979	Ford DFV V8	Nigel Stroud
D4	1980	Ford DFV V8	Gustav Brunner/Tim Wardrop
HGS1	1981	Ford DFV V8	Herve Guilpin/Tim Wardrop
D5	1982	Ford DFV V8	Herve Guilpin/Don Halliday Modified HGS1
D6	1983	BMW M12/13 S4 tc	Gustav Brunner
D7	1984	BMW M12/13 S4 tc	Gustav Brunner

*Based on the Ferris-designed Penske PC4, modified by Herd and Gentry

ATS

AUTOMOBILI TURISMO E SPORT

GP Debut:	1963 Belgian GP	P Hill (retired), Baghetti (retired)
Last GP:	1964 Italian GP	Cabral (retired)
Principals:	Carlo Chiti and Romolo Tavoni	
Base:	Bologna (I)	

WORLD CHAMPIONSHIP RECORD

GPs Started: 6
Best result: 11th 1963 Italian GP (P Hill)
Best qualif.: 13th 1963 Dutch GP (P Hill)

AUTOMOBILI TURISMO E SPORT GRAND PRIX DRIVERS

Driver	Nat	Start (DNS/DNQ)	1st	2nd	3rd	4th	5th	6th	PP	FL	Points
Giancarlo Baghetti	I	5	-	-	-	-	-	-	-	-	-
Phil Hill	USA	5	-	-	-	-	-	-	-	-	-
Mario Araujo de Cabral	P	1	-	-	-	-	-	-	-	-	-

AUTOMOBILI TURISMO E SPORT GRAND PRIX CARS

Type	Year	Engine	Designer
100	1963	ATS V8	Carlo Chiti

BELLASI

GP Debut:	1970 Austrian GP	Moser (retired)
Last GP:	1971 Italian GP	Moser (retired)
Principal:	Vittorio Bellasi	

WORLD CHAMPIONSHIP RECORD

GPs Started: 2
Best result: No finishes
Best qualif.: 21st 1970 French GP (Moser) - did not qualify. 1971 Italian GP Moser qualified 22nd but started

BELLASI GRAND PRIX DRIVERS

Driver	Nat	Starts (DNS/DNQ)	1st	2nd	3rd	4th	5th	6th	PP	FL	Points
Silvio Moser	CH	2 (4)	-	-	-	-	-	-	-	-	-

BELLASI GRAND PRIX CARS

Type	Year	Engine	Designer
F170	1970	Ford DFV V8	Vittorio Bellasi

BENETTON

Bought Toleman in 1986; also see Toleman

GP Debut:	1986 Brazilian GP	Berger (6th), Fabi (10th)
Latest GP:	1994 Australian GP	Herbert (retired), Schumacher (retired)
Principal:	Peter Collins, 1986-89; Flavio Briatore, 1990 to date	
Base:	Witney (GB)	

WORLD CHAMPIONSHIP RECORD

GPs Started: 144
Points: 500.5
Wins: 15 1986 Mexican GP (Berger), 1989 Japanese GP (Nannini), 1990 Japanese GP (Piquet),

Australian GP (Piquet), 1991 Canadian GP (Piquet), 1992 Belgian GP (Schumacher), 1993 Portuguese GP (Schumacher), 1994 Brazilian GP (Schumacher), Pacific GP (Schumacher), San Marino GP (Schumacher), Monaco GP (Schumacher), Canadian GP (Schumacher), French GP (Schumacher), Hungarian GP (Schumacher), European GP (Schumacher)

Pole pos.: 8 1986 Austrian GP (Fabi), Italian GP (Fabi), 1994 Monaco GP (Schumacher), Spanish GP (Schumacher), Canadian GP (Schumacher), Hungarian GP (Schumacher), European GP (Schumacher), Japanese GP (Schumacher)

Fastest laps: 22 1986 German GP (Berger), Austrian GP (Berger), Italian GP (Fabi), 1987 San Marino GP (Fabi), 1988 German GP (Nannini), 1990 San Marino GP (Nannini), 1991 Belgian GP (Moreno), 1992 Belgian GP (Schumacher), Australian GP (Schumacher), 1993 Brazilian GP (Schumacher), Spanish GP (Schumacher), Canadian GP (Schumacher), French GP (Schumacher), German GP (Schumacher), 1994 Brazilian GP (Schumacher), Pacific GP (Schumacher), Monaco GP (Schumacher), Spanish GP (Schumacher), Canadian GP (Schumacher), Hungarian GP (Schumacher), European GP (Schumacher), Australian GP (Schumacher)

Laps/miles in the lead: 830 laps/2283 miles

World Champions:
Drivers: Once - 1994 (Schumacher)

Best World Championship position:
Constructors: 2nd in 1994

MAJOR SPONSORS

1986-90	Benetton
1991-93	Camel, Benetton
1994	Mild Seven, Benetton

BENETTON GRAND PRIX DRIVERS

Driver	Nat	Starts (DNS/DNQ)	1st	2nd	3rd	4th	5th	6th	PP	FL	Points
Michael Schumacher	D	51	10	10	7	3	1	2	6	15	201
Nelson Piquet	BR	32	3	1	3	3	7	3	-	-	70.5
Alessandro Nannini	I	46	1	2	6	4	2	4	-	2	65
Gerhard Berger	A	16	-	1	-	1	2	-	2	17
Thierry Boutsen	B	32	-	-	6	3	4	2	-	-	43
Martin Brundle	GB	16	-	1	4	4	2	-	-	-	38
Riccardo Patrese	I	16	-	1	1	1	3	1	-	20
Teo Fabi	I	32	-	-	1	1	3	1	2	2	14
Roberto Moreno	BR	13	-	1	-	2	1	-	-	1	14
Jos Verstappen	NL	10	-	-	2	-	1	-	-	-	10
Johnny Herbert	GB	7 (1)	-	-	-	1	1	-	-	-	5
Emanuele Pirro	I	10	-	-	-	-	1	-	-	-	2
JJ Lehto	SF	6	-	-	-	-	-	1	-	-	1

BENETTON GRAND PRIX CARS

Type	Year	Engine	Designer
B186	1986	BMW M12/13 S4 tc	Rory Byrne
B187	1987	Ford TEC V6 tc	Rory Byrne
B188	1988	Ford DFR V8	Rory Byrne
B189	1989	Ford HB V8	Rory Byrne
B189B	1990	Ford HB V8	Rory Byrne
B190	1990	Ford HB V8	Rory Byrne/John Barnard
B190B	1991	Ford HB V8	Rory Byrne/John Barnard
B191	1991	Ford HB V8	John Barnard/Gordon Kimball/Ross Brawn/Rory Byrne
B191B	1992	Ford HB V8	John Barnard/Gordon Kimball/Ross Brawn/Rory Byrne
B192	1992	Ford HB V8	Ross Brawn
B193	1993	Ford HB V8	Ross Brawn
B193B	1993	Ford HB V8	Ross Brawn
B194	1994	Ford Zetec-R V8	Ross Brawn

BMW

BAYERISCHE **M**OTOREN **W**ERKE

GP Debut:	1952 German GP	Balsa (retired), Nacke (retired)
Last GP:	1953 German GP	Krause (14th)
Base:	Munich (D)	

WORLD CHAMPIONSHIP RECORD

GPs Started: 2
Best result: 14th 1953 German GP (Krause)
Best qualif.: 26th 1953 German GP (Krause)

BMW GRAND PRIX DRIVERS

Driver	Nat	Starts (DNS/DNQ)	1st	2nd	3rd	4th	5th	6th	PP	FL	Points
Marcel Balsa	F	1	-	-	-	-	-	-	-	-	-
Rudolf Krause	DDR	1	-	-	-	-	-	-	-	-	-
Bernd Nacke	D	1	-	-	-	-	-	-	-	-	-
Hubert Hahne	D	- (1)	-	-	-	-	-	-	-	-	-
Harry Merkel	D	- (1)	-	-	-	-	-	-	-	-	-
Gerhard Mitter	D	- (1)	-	-	-	-	-	-	-	-	-
Dieter Quester	A	- (1)	-	-	-	-	-	-	-	-	-

BMW GRAND PRIX CARS

Type	Year	Engine	Designer
"Eigenbau"*	1952	BMW 328 S6	Various
269/F2**	1969	BMW M20 S4	Len Terry

*"Eigenbau" meaning special in German
**F2 car

BRABHAM

GP Debut:	1962 German GP	J Brabham (retired)
Last GP:	1992 Hungarian GP	D Hill (11th)
Principals:	Jack Brabham and Ron Tauranac, 1962-70; Ron Tauranac, 1971; Bernie Ecclestone, 1972-87; no team in 1988; Joachim Luhti, 1989 until arrested on embezzlement charges; Dennis Nursey/Middlebridge Group, 1990-92	
Base:	Chessington (GB), 1962-89; Milton Keynes (GB), 1990-92	

WORLD CHAMPIONSHIP RECORD

GPs Started: 394
Points: 983
Wins: 35 1964 French GP (Gurney), Mexican GP (Gurney), 1966 French GP (Brabham), British GP (Brabham), Dutch GP (Brabham), German GP (Brabham), 1967 Monaco GP (Hulme), French GP (Brabham), German GP (Hulme), Canadian GP (Brabham), 1969 German GP (Ickx), Canadian GP (Ickx), 1970 South African GP (Brabham), 1974 South African GP (Reutemann), Austrian GP (Reutemann), United States GP (Reutemann), 1975 Brazilian GP (Pace), German GP (Reutemann), 1978 Swedish GP (Lauda), Italian GP (Lauda), 1980 Long Beach GP (Piquet), Dutch GP (Piquet), Italian GP (Piquet), 1981 Argentinian GP (Piquet), San Marino GP (Piquet), German GP (Piquet), 1982 Monaco GP (Patrese), Canadian GP (Piquet), 1983 Brazilian GP (Piquet), Italian GP (Piquet), European GP (Piquet), South African GP (Patrese), 1984 Canadian GP (Piquet), Detroit GP (Piquet), 1985 French GP (Piquet)

Pole pos.: 39 1964 Dutch GP (Gurney), Belgian GP (Gurney), 1966 British GP (Brabham), Dutch GP (Brabham), United States GP (Brabham), 1967 South African GP (Brabham), Monaco GP (Rindt), 1968 French GP (Rindt), Canadian GP (Rindt), 1969 South African GP (Brabham), German GP (Ickx), Canadian GP (Ickx), Mexican GP (Brabham), 1970 Spanish GP (Brabham), 1972 Argentinian GP (Reutemann), 1974 United States GP (Reutemann), 1975 South African GP (Pace), 1977 Monaco GP (Watson), 1978 South African GP (Lauda), French GP (Watson), 1980 Long Beach GP (Piquet), Canadian GP (Piquet), 1981 Brazilian GP (Piquet), Argentinian GP (Piquet), Monaco GP (Piquet), Canadian GP

(Piquet), 1982 Austrian GP (Piquet), 1983 Dutch GP (Piquet), Italian GP (Patrese), 1984 South African GP (Piquet), San Marino GP (Piquet), Canadian GP (Piquet), Detroit GP (Piquet), British GP (Piquet), Austrian GP (Piquet), Italian GP (Piquet), European GP (Piquet), Portuguese GP (Piquet), 1985 Dutch GP (Piquet)

Fastest laps: 42 1963 South African GP (Gurney), 1964 Belgian GP (Gurney), French GP (J Brabham), Austrian GP (Gurney), 1965 Mexican GP (Gurney), 1966 British GP (J Brabham), Dutch GP (Hulme), 1967 South African GP (Hulme), British GP (Hulme), 1969 German GP (Ickx), Canadian GP (Ickx), Canadian GP (J Brabham), Mexican GP (Ickx), 1970 South African GP (J Brabham), Spanish GP (J Brabham), French GP (J Brabham), British GP (J Brabham), 1974 South African GP (Reutemann), Italian GP (Pace), United States GP (Pace), 1975 South African GP (Pace), 1977 South African GP (Watson), Austrian GP (Watson), 1978 Monaco GP (Lauda), Swedish GP (Lauda), British GP (Lauda), Dutch GP (Lauda), 1979 United States GP (Piquet), 1980 Long Beach GP (Piquet), 1981 Argentinian GP (Piquet), 1982 Monaco GP (Patrese), French GP (Patrese), German GP (Piquet), Austrian GP (Piquet), 1983 Brazilian GP (Piquet), San Marino GP (Patrese), Monaco GP (Piquet), Italian GP (Piquet), South African GP (Piquet), 1984 San Marino GP (Piquet), Canadian GP (Piquet), European GP (Piquet)

Laps/miles in the lead: 2724 laps/8252 miles

World Champions

Drivers: Four times - 1966 (Brabham), 1967 (Hulme), 1981 (Piquet) and 1983 (Piquet)

Constructors: Twice - 1966 and 1967

MAJOR SPONSORS

1968	Caltex
1970	Auto Motor und Sport
1972	Bardahl, Esso, YPF
1973	Bardahl, Ceramica Pagnossin, Hexagon, YPF
1974	Hitachi
1975-77	Martini
1978-84	Parmalat
1985-86	Olivetti
1989	Bioptron
1992	Yamazen

BRABHAM GRAND PRIX DRIVERS

Driver	Nat	Starts (DNS/DNQ)	1st	2nd	3rd	4th	5th	6th	PP	FL	Points
Nelson Piquet	BR	106 (1)	13	9	7	8	5	3	18	12	236
Jack Brabham	AUS	80 (2)	7	9	5	9	4	2	8	7	174
Carlos Reutemann	RA	66	4	2	6	6	-	3	2	1	91
Denny Hulme	NZ	26	2	4	6	2	1	-	3		74
Dan Gurney	USA	30	2	4	4	-	1	3	2	4	63
Niki Lauda	A	29 (1)	2	3	2	1	-	1	1	4	48
Riccardo Patrese	I	61	2	1	3	-	2	2	1	3	42
Jacky Ickx	B	11	2	2	1	-	1	1	2	3	37
Carlos Pace	BR	39 (1)	1	3	1	3	2	1	1	3	45
John Watson	GB	50	-	2	2	4	3	2	2	2	40
Piers Courage	GB	10	-	2	-	2	-	-	-	-	16
Hector Rebaque	MEX	21 (1)	-	-	-	3	1	1	-	-	12
Jo Siffert	CH	20	-	-	1	2	-	2	-	-	12
Hans-Joachim Stuck	D	14	-	-	2	-	1	2	-	-	12
Rolf Stommelen	D	16 (3)	-	-	1	-	3	1	-	-	11
Teo Fabi	I	12	-	-	1	1	1	-	-	-	9
Bob Anderson	RSR	23 (4)	-	-	1	-	1	2	-	-	8
Jochen Rindt	A	13	-	-	2	-	-	-	2	-	8
Stefano Modena	I	32 (1)	-	-	1	-	1	-	-	-	6
Martin Brundle	GB	28 (4)	-	-	-	-	2	2	-	-	6
Graham Hill	GB	23	-	-	-	-	2	2	-	-	6
Marc Surer	CH	12	-	-	-	1	-	2	-	-	5
Tim Schenken	AUS	10	-	-	1	-	1	-	1	-	5
Andrea de Cesaris	I	16	-	-	1	-	-	-	-	-	4
Wilson Fittipaldi	BR	25	-	-	-	-	1	1	-	-	3
Silvio Moser	CH	9 (4)	-	-	-	1	1	-	-	-	3
Andrea de Adamich	I	5	-	-	-	1	-	-	-	-	3

Driver	Nat	Starts (DNS/DNQ)	1st	2nd	3rd	4th	5th	6th	PP	FL	Points
Jo Bonnier	S	20	-	-	-	-	-	1	-	-	1
Mark Blundell	GB	14 (2)	-	-	-	-	-	1	-	-	1
Guy Ligier	F	5	-	-	-	-	-	1	-	-	1
John Taylor	GB	4	-	-	-	-	-	1	-	-	1
Derek Warwick	GB	10 (1)	-								
David Brabham	AUS	8 (6)	-								
Ricardo Zunino	RA	8 (1)	-								
Frank Gardner	AUS	8									
Rikky von Opel	FL	4 (2)	-								
Elio de Angelis	I	4									
Loris Kessel	CH	3 (2)	-								
François Hesnault	F	3 (1)	-								
Kurt Ahrens Jr	D	3									
Dave Charlton	ZA	3									
Corrado Fabi	I	3									
Larry Perkins	AUS	3									
Richard Robarts	GB	3									
Damon Hill	GB	2 (6)	-								
Ian Raby	GB	2 (2)	-								
Gregor Foitek	CH	2									
Piet de Klerk	ZA	2									
Jackie Pretorius	ZA	2									
David Prophet	GB	2									
Hap Sharp	USA	2									
Eric van de Poele	B	1 (9)	-								
Lella Lombardi	I	1 (3)	-								
Chris Craft	GB	1 (1)	-								
Gérard Larrousse	F	1 (1)	-								
Richard Attwood	GB	1									
Giancarlo Baghetti	I	1									
Derek Bell	GB	1									
Luki Botha	ZA	1									
John Cordts	CDN	1									
Bob Evans	GB	1									
Paul Hawkins	AUS	1									
Hans Herrmann	D	1									
Gus Hutchison	USA	1									
Chris Irwin	GB	1									
John Love	RSR	1									
Patrick Neve	B	1									
Xavier Perrot	CH	1									
Teddy Pilette	B	1									
Alan Rees	GB	1									
Sam Tingle	RSR	1									
Peter Westbury	GB	1									
Eppie Wietzes	CDN	1									
Manfred Winkelhock	D	1									
Giovanna Amati	I	-	(3)								
Chris Amon	NZ	-	(2)								
Ian Ashley	GB	-	(2)								
Carlo Facetti	I	-	(1)								
William Ferguson	ZA	-	(1)								
Giorgio Francia	I	-	(1)								
Helmuth Koinigg	A	-	(1)								
Damien Magee	GB	-	(1)								
Jac Nelleman	DK	-	(1)								
"Geki" Russo	I	-	(1)								
Emilio de Villota	E	-	(1)								

BRABHAM GRAND PRIX CARS

Type	Year	Engine	Designer
BT3	1962	Climax V8, BRM V8	Ron Tauranac
BT6	1963	Ford S4	Ron Tauranac
BT7	1963	Climax V8	Ron Tauranac
BT10	1964	Ford SCA S4	Ron Tauranac
BT11	1964	Climax V8, BRM V8, Repco V8	Ron Tauranac
BT16	1966	Ford SCA S4	Ron Tauranac
BT18	1966	Ford SCA S4	Ron Tauranac
BT19	1966	Repco 620 V8	Ron Tauranac
BT20	1966	Repco 620 V8	Ron Tauranac
BT23B	1969	Ford S4	Ron Tauranac

Type	Year	Engine	Designer
BT23C	1969	Ford S4	Ron Tauranac
BT24	1967	Repco V8, Ford DFV V8	Ron Tauranac
BT26	1968	Repco 860 V8,	
		Ford DFV V8	Ron Tauranac
BT30	1969	Ford S4	Ron Tauranac
BT33	1970	Ford DFV V8	Ron Tauranac
BT34	1971	Ford DFV V8	Ron Tauranac
		Lobster-claw Brabham with twin-radiators mounted as part of front wing	
BT37	1972	Ford DFV V8	Ralph Bellamy
BT39	1972	Weslake V12	Ralph Bellamy
		Prototype Weslake-powered car, never raced	
BT42	1973	Ford DFV V8	Gordon Murray
BT44	1974	Ford DFV V8	Gordon Murray
BT44B	1975	Ford DFV V8	Gordon Murray
BT45	1976	Alfa Romeo 115-12 F12	Gordon Murray
BT45B	1977	Alfa Romeo 115-12 F12	Gordon Murray
BT45C	1978	Alfa Romeo 115-12 F12	Gordon Murray
BT46	1978	Alfa Romeo 115-12 F12	Gordon Murray
BT46B	1978	Alfa Romeo 115-12 F12	Gordon Murray
		"Fan-car", raced once (winning) but subsequently banned	
BT48	1979	Alfa Romeo 1260 V12	Gordon Murray/David North
BT49	1979	Ford DFV V8	Gordon Murray/David North
BT49B	1980	Ford DFV V8	Gordon Murray/David North
		Used Weismann gearbox, soon abandoned	
BT49C	1981	Ford DFV V8	Gordon Murray/David North
BT49D	1982	Ford DFV V8	Gordon Murray/David North
BT50	1982	BMW M12/13 S4 tc	Gordon Murray/David North
BT51	1981	BMW M12/13 S4 tc	Gordon Murray/David North
		Ground-effect car, never raced as new rules banned sliding skirts and rendered it obsolete	
BT52	1983	BMW M12/13 S4 tc	Gordon Murray/David North
BT52B	1983	BMW M12/13 S4 tc	Gordon Murray/David North
BT53	1984	BMW M12/13 S4 tc	Gordon Murray/David North
BT54	1985	BMW M12/13 S4 tc	Gordon Murray/David North
BT55	1986	BMW M12/13 S4 tc	Gordon Murray/David North
		Lowline car featuring Weismann gearbox	
BT56	1987	BMW M12/13 S4 tc	John Baldwin/ Sergio Rinland/David North
BT58	1989	Judd CV V8	Sergio Rinland/ John Baldwin
BT59	1990	Judd EV V8	Sergio Rinland
BT59Y	1991	Yamaha OX99 V12	Sergio Rinland
BT60Y	1991	Yamaha OX99 V12	Sergio Rinland
BT60B	1992	Judd GV V10	Sergio Rinland/ Tim Densham

BRM

BRITISH RACING MOTORS

GP Debut: 1951 British GP — Parnell (5th), Walker (7th)
Last GP: 1977 South African GP (15th)
Principals: Raymond Mays, 1950-51; Sir Alfred Owen, 1952-74; Jean Owen and Louis Stanley, 1974-79 (entered as Stanley-BRM from 1975); John Jordan, 1980-82 (entered as Jordan-BRM in British F1); John Mangoletsi (entered in World Sports Cars), 1992
Base: Bourne, Lincolnshire (GB)

WORLD CHAMPIONSHIP RECORD

GPs Started: 197
Points: 537.5
Wins: 17 1959 Dutch GP (Bonnier), 1962 Dutch GP (Hill), German GP (Hill), Italian GP (Hill), South African GP (Hill), 1963 Monaco GP (Hill), United States GP (Hill), 1964 Monaco GP (Hill), United States GP (Hill), 1965 Monaco GP (Hill), Italian GP (Stewart), United States GP (Hill), 1966 Monaco GP (Stewart), 1970 Belgian GP (Rodriguez), 1971 Austrian GP (Siffert), Italian GP (Gethin), 1972 Monaco GP (Beltoise)
Pole pos.: 11 1959 Dutch GP (Bonnier), 1962 Belgian GP (Hill), 1963 Belgian GP (Hill), United States GP (Hill), 1964 Austrian GP (Hill), 1965 Monaco GP (Hill), Belgian GP (Hill), Dutch GP (Hill), United States GP (Hill), 1971 Austrian GP (Siffert), 1973 Argentinian GP (Regazzoni)

Fastest laps: 15 1959 French GP (Moss), British GP (Moss), 1960 British GP (Hill), 1961 British GP (Brooks), 1962 French GP (Hill), German GP (Hill), Italian GP (Hill), 1964 Monaco GP (Hill), 1965 Monaco GP (Hill), British GP (Hill), United States GP (Hill), 1968 Monaco GP (Attwood), French GP (Rodriguez), 1971 Austrian GP (Siffert), 1972 Monaco GP (Beltoise)
Laps/miles in the lead: 1342 laps/3786 miles
World Champions
Drivers: Once - 1962 (G Hill)
Constructors: Once - 1962

BRM GRAND PRIX DRIVERS

Driver	Nat	Starts (DNS/DNQ)	1st	2nd	3rd	4th	5th	6th	PP	FL	Points
Graham Hill	GB	64	10	9	7	5	4	2	8	8	193
Jackie Stewart	GB	29	2	4	2	1	2	1	-	-	58
Pedro Rodriguez	MEX	33	1	3	2	4	-	3	-	1	50
Jean-Pierre Beltoise	F	40 (1)	1	1	-	1	5	-	-	1	28
Jo Siffert	CH	11	1	1	-	1	-	1	1	1	19
Jo Bonnier	S	17	1	-	-	1	3	-	1	-	17
Peter Gethin	GB	15 (1)	1	-	-	-	-	1	-	-	10
Richie Ginther	USA	29	-	6	3	5	2	-	-	-	67
Harry Schell	USA	16	-	1	-	1	5	1	-	-	19
Howden Ganley	NZ	19 (3)	-	-	-	2	1	1	-	-	9
Mike Spence	GB	12	-	-	-	-	4	1	-	-	9
Stirling Moss	GB	2	-	1	-	-	-	-	-	2	7.5
Jean Behra	F	9	-	-	1	1	-	-	-	-	7
Tony Brooks	GB	9 (1)	-	-	1	-	1	-	-	1	6
John Surtees	GB	9 (1)	-	-	1	-	1	-	-	-	6
Richard Attwood	GB	6 (1)	-	1	-	-	-	-	-	1	6
Piers Courage	GB	12 (1)	-	-	1	-	1	-	-	-	4
Tony Maggs	ZA	3 (2)	-	-	1	-	1	-	-	-	4
Jackie Oliver	GB	24	-	-	-	1	1	-	-	-	3
Bob Bondurant	USA	5	-	-	-	1	-	-	-	-	3
Niki Lauda	A	14 (1)	-	-	-	1	-	-	-	-	2
Clay Regazzoni	CH	14	-	-	-	-	2	1	-	-	2
Chris Irwin	GB	8	-	-	-	1	-	-	-	-	2
Maurice Trintignant	F	6 (1)	-	-	-	1	-	-	-	-	2
Lorenzo Bandini	I	3	-	-	-	1	-	-	-	-	2
Reg Parnell	GB	1 (1)	-	-	-	1	-	-	-	-	2
Henri Pescarolo	F	12	-	-	-	-	-	-	-	-	-
George Eaton	CDN	11 (2)	-	-	-	-	-	-	-	-	-
François Migault	F	10 (1)	-	-	-	-	-	-	-	-	-
Ron Flockhart	GB	9 (1)	-	-	-	-	1	-	-	-	-
Helmut Marko	A	9	-	-	-	-	-	-	-	-	-
Bob Evans	GB	8 (1)	-	-	-	-	-	-	-	-	-
Dan Gurney	USA	7	-	-	-	-	-	-	-	-	-
Giancarlo Baghetti	I	6	-	-	-	-	-	-	-	-	-
Reine Wisell	S	6	-	-	-	-	-	-	-	-	-
Masten Gregory	USA	4	-	-	-	-	-	-	-	-	-
Chris Amon	NZ	2	-	-	-	-	-	-	-	-	-
Bill Brack	CDN	2	-	-	-	-	-	-	-	-	-
David Hobbs	GB	2	-	-	-	-	-	-	-	-	-
Innes Ireland	GB	2	-	-	-	-	-	-	-	-	-
Larry Perkins	AUS	2	-	-	-	-	-	-	-	-	-
Alex Soler-Roig	E	2	-	-	-	-	-	-	-	-	-
Mike Wilds	GB	2	-	-	-	-	-	-	-	-	-
Roberto Bussinello	I	1 (1)	-	-	-	-	-	-	-	-	-
Mike Hawthorn	GB	1 (1)	-	-	-	-	-	-	-	-	-
Bobby Unser	USA	1 (1)	-	-	-	-	-	-	-	-	-
Ian Ashley	GB	1	-	-	-	-	-	-	-	-	-
Giorgio Bassi	I	1	-	-	-	-	-	-	-	-	-
Lucien Bianchi	B	1	-	-	-	-	-	-	-	-	-
John Cannon	CDN	1	-	-	-	-	-	-	-	-	-
Vic Elford	GB	1	-	-	-	-	-	-	-	-	-
Jack Fairman	GB	1	-	-	-	-	-	-	-	-	-
Hans Herrmann	D	1	-	-	-	-	-	-	-	-	-
Bruce Johnstone	ZA	1	-	-	-	-	-	-	-	-	-
Les Leston Herbert	GB	1	-	-	-	-	-	-	-	-	-
MacKay-Fraser	USA	1	-	-	-	-	-	-	-	-	-
Brian Redman	GB	1	-	-	-	-	-	-	-	-	-
Moises Solana	MEX	1	-	-	-	-	-	-	-	-	-
Peter Walker	GB	1	-	-	-	-	-	-	-	-	-

Driver	Nat	Starts (DNS/DNQ)	1st	2nd	3rd	4th	5th	6th	PP	FL	Points
Conny Andersson	S	- (4)	-	-	-	-	-	-	-	-	-
Teddy Pilette	B	- (3)	-	-	-	-	-	-	-	-	-
Guy Edwards	GB	- (1)	-	-	-	-	-	-	-	-	-
Frank Gardner	AUS	- (1)	-	-	-	-	-	-	-	-	-
Jackie Lewis	GB	- (1)	-	-	-	-	-	-	-	-	-
Ken Richardson	GB	- (1)	-	-	-	-	-	-	-	-	-
Roy Salvadori	GB	- (1)	-	-	-	-	-	-	-	-	-
Vern Schuppan	AUS	- (1)	-	-	-	-	-	-	-	-	-
Peter Westbury	GB	- (1)	-	-	-	-	-	-	-	-	-
Vic Wilson	GB	- (1)	-	-	-	-	-	-	-	-	-

BRM GRAND PRIX CARS

Type	Year	Engine	Designer
P15	1951	BRM 15 V16 sc	Peter Berthon
P25	1956	BRM 256 S4	Peter Berthon/ Stuart Tresilian
P25 (58)	1958	BRM 258 S4	Peter Berthon/ Stuart Tresilian
P25 (59)	1959	BRM 259 S4	Peter Berthon/Stuart Tresilian/Tony Rudd
P48	1960	BRM 259 S4	Tony Rudd
P48/57	1961	Climax FPF S4	Tony Rudd
P48/57 (62)	1962	BRM 56 V8	Tony Rudd
P57	1962	BRM 56 V8	Tony Rudd
P61	1963	BRM 56 V8	Tony Rudd
P261	1964	BRM 56 V8	Tony Rudd
P67**	1964	BRM 56 V8	Tony Rudd
P83	1966	BRM 75 H16	Tony Rudd
P126	1968	BRM 101 V12	Len Terry
P133	1968	BRM 101 V12	Len Terry
P138	1968	BRM P142 V12	Len Terry
P139	1969	BRM P142 V12	Len Terry
P153	1970	BRM P142 V12	Tony Southgate
P160	1971	BRM P142 V12	Tony Southgate
P153B	1972	BRM P142 V12	Tony Southgate
P160B	1972	BRM P142 V12	Tony Southgate
P160C	1972	BRM P142 V12	Tony Southgate
P180	1972	BRM P142 V12	Tony Southgate
P160D	1973	BRM P142 V12	Tony Southgate
P160E	1973	BRM P142 V12	Tony Southgate/ Mike Pilbeam
P201	1974	BRM P142 V12	Mike Pilbeam
P201*	1975	BRM P200 V12	Mike Pilbeam
P201B*	1976	BRM P200 V12	Mike Pilbeam
P207*	1977	BRM P202 V12	Len Terry
P201B/204*	1977	BRM P200 V12	Mike Pilbeam

*Stanley-BRM
**4-wheel-drive

BRP

BRITISH RACING PARTNERSHIP

GP Debut:	1963 Belgian GP	Ireland (retired)
Last GP:	1964 Mexican GP	Ireland (12th), Taylor (retired)

Principals: Alfred Moss and Ken Gregory
Base: Highgate, North London (GB)

WORLD CHAMPIONSHIP RECORD

GPs Started: 13
Points: 11
Best result: 4th 1963 Dutch GP (Ireland), Italian GP (Ireland)
Best qualif.: 7th 1963 Belgian GP (Ireland), Dutch GP (Ireland)

Best World Championship position:
Drivers: 9th in 1963 (Ireland)
Constructors: 6th in 1963

BRP GRAND PRIX DRIVERS

Driver	Nat	Starts (DNS/DNQ)	1st	2nd	3rd	4th	5th	6th	PP	FL	Points
Innes Ireland	GB	12	-	-	-	2	2	-	-	-	10
Trevor Taylor	GB	6 (1)	-	-	-	-	-	1	-	-	1

BRP GRAND PRIX CARS

Type	Year	Engine	Designer
1	1963	BRM V8	Tony Robinson
2	1964	BRM V8	Tony Robinson

BUGATTI

Only World Championship GP: 1956 French GP
Trintignant (retired)
Principal: Geneviève Bugatti (founder Ettore Bugatti had died in 1947)
Base: Molsheim (F)

WORLD CHAMPIONSHIP RECORD

GPs Started: 1
Best result: No finishes
Best qualif.: 18th 1956 French GP (Trintignant)

BUGATTI GRAND PRIX DRIVERS

Driver	Nat	Starts (DNS/DNQ)	1st	2nd	3rd	4th	5th	6th	PP	FL	Points
Maurice Trintignant	F	1	-	-	-	-	-	-	-	-	-

BUGATTI GRAND PRIX CARS

Type	Year	Engine	Designer
T251	1956	Bugatti 251 S8	Gioacchino Colombo

CISITALIA

Principals: Piero Dusio and Piero Taruffi

WORLD CHAMPIONSHIP RECORD

GPs Started: None

CISITALIA GRAND PRIX DRIVERS

Driver	Nat	Starts (DNS/DNQ)	1st	2nd	3rd	4th	5th	6th	PP	FL	Points
Piero Dusio	I	- (1)	-	-	-	-	-	-	-	-	-

CISITALIA GRAND PRIX CARS

Type	Year	Engine	Designer
D46	1952	BPM	Dante Giacosa

COLONI

Also see Andrea Moda

GP Debut:	1987 Spanish GP	Larini (retired)
Last GP:	1989 Portuguese GP	Moreno (retired)

Principal: Enzo Coloni, 1987-91; Andrea Sassetti, 1991-92 (Sassetti changed name to Andrea Moda for 1992)
Base: Perugia (I)

WORLD CHAMPIONSHIP RECORD

GPs Started: 13
Best result: 8th 1988 Canadian GP (Tarquini)
Best qualif.: 15th 1989 Portuguese GP (Moreno)

MAJOR SPONSORS

1989	Himont

COLONI GRAND PRIX DRIVERS

Driver	Nat	Starts (DNS/DNQ)	1st	2nd	3rd	4th	5th	6th	PP	FL	Points
Gabriele Tarquini	I	8 (8)	-	-	-	-	-	-	-	-	-
Roberto Moreno	BR	4 (12)	-	-	-	-	-	-	-	-	-
Pierre-Henri Raphanel	F	1 (9)	-	-	-	-	-	-	-	-	-
Nicola Larini	I	1 (1)	-	-	-	-	-	-	-	-	-
Bertrand Gachot	B	- (16)	-	-	-	-	-	-	-	-	-
Pedro Chaves	P	- (14)	-	-	-	-	-	-	-	-	-
Enrico Bertaggia	I	- (7)	-	-	-	-	-	-	-	-	-
Alex Caffi	I	- (1)	-	-	-	-	-	-	-	-	-
Naoki Hattori	J	- (2)	-	-	-	-	-	-	-	-	-

COLONI GRAND PRIX CARS

Type	Year	Engine	Designer
FC187	1987	Ford DFZ V8	Roberto Ori
FC188	1988	Ford DFZ V8	Roberto Ori
FC188B	1988	Ford DFZ V8	Roberto Ori
FC188C	1989	Ford DFR V8	Roberto Ori
C3	1989	Ford DFR V8	Christian Vanderpleyn/ Michel Costa
C3B	1990	Subaru F12, Ford DFR V8	Christian Vanderpleyn/ Paul Burgess
C4	1991	Ford DFR V8	Coloni Technical Department/ Perugia University
C4B	1992	Judd GV V10	Coloni Technical Department/ Perugia University

CONNAUGHT

GP Debut:	1952 British GP	Poore (4th), Thompson (5th), Downing (9th), McAlpine (16th)
Last GP:	1959 United States GP	Said (retired)
Principals:	Rodney Clarke, Mike Oliver and Kenneth McAlpine	
Base:	Send, Surrey (GB)	

WORLD CHAMPIONSHIP RECORD

GPs Started: 17
Points: 17
Best result: 3rd 1956 Italian GP (Flockhart)
Best qualif.: 5th 1952 British GP (Downing)

Best World Championship position:
Drivers: 10th in 1956 (Fairman)
Constructors: -

CONNAUGHT GRAND PRIX DRIVERS

Driver	Nat	Starts (DNS/DNQ)	1st	2nd	3rd	4th	5th	6th	PP	FL	Points
Jack Fairman	GB	4 (1)	-	-	-	1	1	-	-	-	5
Ron Flockhart	GB	1	-	-	1	-	-	-	-	-	4
Dennis Poore	GB	2	-	-	-	1	-	-	-	-	3
Stuart Lewis-Evans	GB	1	-	-	-	1	-	-	-	-	3
Eric Thompson	GB	1	-	-	-	-	1	-	-	-	2
Kenneth McAlpine	GB	7	-	-	-	-	-	-	-	-	-
Roy Salvadori	GB	5	-	-	-	-	-	-	-	-	-
Johnny Claes	B	4	-	-	-	-	-	-	-	-	-
"B Bira"	SM	3	-	-	-	-	-	-	-	-	-
Ivor Bueb	GB	2	-	-	-	-	-	-	-	-	-
Ken Downing	GB	2	-	-	-	-	-	-	-	-	-
Leslie Marr	GB	2	-	-	-	-	-	-	-	-	-
Stirling Moss	GB	2	-	-	-	-	-	-	-	-	-
Tony Rolt	GB	2	-	-	-	-	-	-	-	-	-
Don Beauman	GB	1	-	-	-	-	-	-	-	-	-
Les Leston	GB	1	-	-	-	-	-	-	-	-	-
André Pilette	B	1	-	-	-	-	-	-	-	-	-
John Riseley-Prichard	GB	1	-	-	-	-	-	-	-	-	-
Bob Said	USA	1	-	-	-	-	-	-	-	-	-
Archie Scott-Brown	GB	1	-	-	-	-	-	-	-	-	-
Piero Scotti	I	1	-	-	-	-	-	-	-	-	-
Ian Stewart	GB	1	-	-	-	-	-	-	-	-	-
Leslie Thorne	GB	1	-	-	-	-	-	-	-	-	-
Desmond Titterington	GB	1	-	-	-	-	-	-	-	-	-
Peter Walker	GB	1	-	-	-	-	-	-	-	-	-
Bill Whitehouse	GB	1	-	-	-	-	-	-	-	-	-
Bernie Ecclestone	GB	- (1)	-	-	-	-	-	-	-	-	-
Paul Emery	GB	- (1)	-	-	-	-	-	-	-	-	-
Bruce Kessler	USA	- (1)	-	-	-	-	-	-	-	-	-

CONNAUGHT GRAND PRIX CARS

Type	Year	Engine	Designer
A	1952	Lea-Francis S4	Rodney Clarke
B	1955	Alta GP S4	Rodney Clarke
C	1959	Alta GP S4	Rodney Clarke

CONNEW

Only GP:	1972 Austrian GP	Migault (retired)
Principal:	Peter Connew	
Base:	Romford, Essex (GB)	

WORLD CHAMPIONSHIP RECORD

GPs Started: 1
Best result: No finishes
Best qualif.: 26th 1972 Austrian GP (Migault)

MAJOR SPONSORS

1972	Darnval

CONNEW GRAND PRIX DRIVERS

Driver	Nat	Starts (DNS/DNQ)	1st	2nd	3rd	4th	5th	6th	PP	FL	Points
François Migault	F	1 (1)	-	-	-	-	-	-	-	-	-

CONNEW GRAND PRIX CARS

Type	Year	Engine	Designer
PC1	1972	Ford DFV V8	Peter Connew

COOPER

GP Debut:	1950 Monaco GP	Schell (retired)
Last GP:	1969 Monaco GP	Elford (7th)
Principals:	Charles and John Cooper, 1950 until Charles' death in 1964; John Cooper, 1965; Chipstead Motor Group (Jonathan Sieff and Roy Salvadori), 1965-69	
Base:	Surbiton, Surrey (GB), 1950-65; Byfleet (GB), 1966-69	

WORLD CHAMPIONSHIP RECORD

GPs Started: 129
Points: 494.5
Wins: 16 1958 Argentinian GP (Moss), Monaco GP (Trintignant), 1959 Monaco GP (Brabham), British GP (Brabham), Portuguese GP (Moss), Italian GP (Moss), United States GP (McLaren), 1960 Argentinian GP (McLaren), Dutch GP (Brabham), Belgian GP (Brabham), French GP (Brabham), British GP (Brabham), Portuguese GP (Brabham), 1962 Monaco GP (McLaren), 1966 Mexican GP (Surtees), 1967 South African GP (Rodriguez)
Pole pos.: 11 1959 Monaco GP (Moss), British GP (Brabham), Portuguese GP (Moss), Italian GP (Moss), United States GP (Moss), 1960 Argentinian GP (Moss), Belgian GP (Brabham), French GP (Brabham), British GP (Brabham), 1961 United States GP (Brabham), 1966 Mexican GP (Surtees)
Fastest laps: 14 1959 Monaco GP (Brabham), Dutch GP (Moss), British GP (McLaren), Portuguese GP (Moss), United States GP (Trintignant), 1960 Argentinian GP (Moss), Monaco GP (McLaren), Belgian GP (Brabham), French GP (Brabham), United States GP (Brabham), 1961 United States GP (Brabham), 1962 Dutch GP (McLaren), 1966 German GP (Surtees), United States GP (Surtees)
Laps/miles in the lead: 829 laps/2822 miles

World Champions:
Drivers: Twice - 1959 (Brabham) and 1960 (Brabham)
Constructors: Twice - 1959 and 1960

COOPER GRAND PRIX DRIVERS

Driver	Nat	Starts (DNS/DNQ)	1st	2nd	3rd	4th	5th	6th	PP	FL	Points
Jack Brabham	AUS	39	7	1	2	4	-	4	5	5	84
Bruce McLaren	NZ	64	3	7	10	4	7	3	-	3	136.5
Stirling Moss	GB	11	3	-	1	-	-	1	5	3	26
Maurice Trintignant	F	25	1	1	3	2	1	-	-	1	31
John Surtees	GB	15	1	1	1	-	2	-	1	2	23
Pedro Rodriguez	MEX	8	1	-	-	-	2	2	-	-	15
Jochen Rindt	A	28 (1)	-	2	1	5	1	1	-	-	34
Tony Maggs	ZA	19	-	2	1	-	2	2	-	-	22
Roy Salvadori	GB	22	-	1	1	1	2	3	-	-	19
Jo Bonnier	S	27	-	-	-	-	4	4	-	-	12
Masten Gregory	USA	12 (4)	-	1	1	-	-	-	-	-	10
Olivier Gendebien	B	5	-	1	1	-	-	-	-	-	10

Driver	Nat	Starts (DNS/DNQ)	1st	2nd	3rd	4th	5th	6th	PP	FL	Points
Mike Hawthorn	GB	5	-	-	1	2	-	-	-	-	10
Jo Siffert	CH	18 (1)	-	-	3	-	-	-	-	-	9
Tony Brooks	GB	6	-	-	-	1	2	-	-	-	7
Lucien Bianchi	B	10 (1)	-	1	-	-	2	-	-	-	6
John Love	RSR	4 (1)	-	1	-	-	-	-	-	-	6
Ludovico Scarfiotti	I	3	-	-	-	2	-	-	-	-	6
Vic Elford	GB	8	-	-	-	1	1	-	-	-	5
Brian Redman	GB	3	-	-	1	-	-	-	-	-	4
Jackie Lewis	GB	9	-	-	-	1	-	-	-	-	3
Henry Taylor	GB	5 (1)	-	-	-	1	-	-	-	-	3
Giulio Cabianca	I	1	-	-	-	1	-	-	-	-	3
Carlos Menditéguy	RA	1	-	-	-	1	-	-	-	-	3
Phil Hill	USA	10	-	-	-	-	-	2	-	-	2
Alan Brown	GB	8 (1)	-	-	-	1	1	-	-	-	2
Richie Ginther	USA	2	-	-	-	1	-	-	-	-	2
Jacky Ickx	B	2	-	-	-	-	-	1	-	-	1
Ian Burgess	GB	12 (2)	-	-	-	-	1	-	-	-	-
Guy Ligier	F	7 (1)	-	-	-	-	-	-	-	-	-
Ken Wharton	GB	6	-	-	-	-	-	-	-	-	-
Eric Brandon	GB	5	-	-	-	-	-	-	-	-	-
Jack Fairman	GB	5	-	-	-	-	-	-	-	-	-
Bob Gerard	GB	5	-	-	-	-	1	-	-	-	-
Lorenzo Bandini	I	4	-	-	-	-	-	-	-	-	-
Chris Bristow	GB	4	-	-	-	-	-	-	-	-	-
Mario Araujo de Cabral	P	3 (1)	-	-	-	-	-	-	-	-	-
Bernard Collomb	F	3	-	-	-	-	-	-	-	-	-
Gino Munaron	I	3	-	-	-	-	-	-	-	-	-
Harry Schell	USA	3	-	-	-	-	-	-	-	-	-
Giorgio Scarlatti	I	2 (1)	-	-	-	-	-	-	-	-	-
Colin Davis	GB	2	-	-	-	-	-	-	-	-	-
Dick Gibson	GB	2	-	-	-	-	-	-	-	-	-
Chris Lawrence	GB	2	-	-	-	-	-	-	-	-	-
Tony Marsh	GB	2	-	-	-	-	-	-	-	-	-
Brian Naylor	GB	2	-	-	-	-	-	-	-	-	-
Wolfgang Seidel	D	2	-	-	-	-	-	-	-	-	-
Hap Sharp	USA	2	-	-	-	-	-	-	-	-	-
Peter Whitehead	GB	2	-	-	-	-	-	-	-	-	-
Trevor Blokdyk	ZA	1 (1)	-	-	-	-	-	-	-	-	-
Ivor Bueb	GB	1 (1)	-	-	-	-	-	-	-	-	-
Ron Flockhart	GB	1 (1)	-	-	-	-	-	-	-	-	-
Keith Greene	GB	1 (1)	-	-	-	-	-	-	-	-	-
Bruce Halford	GB	1 (1)	-	-	-	-	-	-	-	-	-
Chris Amon	NZ	1	-	-	-	-	-	-	-	-	-
Peter Ashdown	GB	1	-	-	-	-	-	-	-	-	-
Richard Attwood	GB	1	-	-	-	-	-	-	-	-	-
John Barber	GB	1	-	-	-	-	-	-	-	-	-
Edgar Barth	DDR	1	-	-	-	-	-	-	-	-	-
Carel Godin de Beaufort	NL	1	-	-	-	-	-	-	-	-	-
Roberto Bonomi	RA	1	-	-	-	-	-	-	-	-	-
Tommy Bridger	GB	1	-	-	-	-	-	-	-	-	-
Robert la Caze	MA	1	-	-	-	-	-	-	-	-	-
George Constantine	USA	1	-	-	-	-	-	-	-	-	-
Tony Crook	GB	1	-	-	-	-	-	-	-	-	-
Chuck Daigh	USA	1	-	-	-	-	-	-	-	-	-
Piero Drogo	YV	1	-	-	-	-	-	-	-	-	-
Paul England	AUS	1	-	-	-	-	-	-	-	-	-
Christian Goethals	B	1	-	-	-	-	-	-	-	-	-
Horace Gould	GB	1	-	-	-	-	-	-	-	-	-
Andre Guelfi	F	1	-	-	-	-	-	-	-	-	-
Walt Hansgen	USA	1	-	-	-	-	-	-	-	-	-
Mike Harris	RSR	1	-	-	-	-	-	-	-	-	-
Hans Herrmann	D	1	-	-	-	-	-	-	-	-	-
Pete Lovely	USA	1	-	-	-	-	-	-	-	-	-
Timmy Mayer	USA	1	-	-	-	-	-	-	-	-	-
Mike McDowell	GB	1	-	-	-	-	-	-	-	-	-
Silvio Moser	CH	1	-	-	-	-	-	-	-	-	-
David Murray	GB	1	-	-	-	-	-	-	-	-	-
Massimo Natili	I	1	-	-	-	-	-	-	-	-	-
Rodney Nuckey	GB	1	-	-	-	-	-	-	-	-	-
Arthur Owen	GB	1	-	-	-	-	-	-	-	-	-
Reg Parnell	GB	1	-	-	-	-	-	-	-	-	-
Roger Penske	USA	1	-	-	-	-	-	-	-	-	-
François Picard	F	1	-	-	-	-	-	-	-	-	-
Renato Pirocchi	I	1	-	-	-	-	-	-	-	-	-
Alan Rees	GB	1	-	-	-	-	-	-	-	-	-
John Rhodes	GB	1	-	-	-	-	-	-	-	-	-
Basil van Rooyen	ZA	1	-	-	-	-	-	-	-	-	-
Adolfo Schwelm Cruz	RA	1	-	-	-	-	-	-	-	-	-
Johnny Servoz-Gavin	F	1	-	-	-	-	-	-	-	-	-
Moises Solana	MEX	1	-	-	-	-	-	-	-	-	-
Jimmy Stewart	GB	1	-	-	-	-	-	-	-	-	-
John Taylor	GB	1	-	-	-	-	-	-	-	-	-
Mike Taylor	GB	1	-	-	-	-	-	-	-	-	-
Alfonso Thiele	USA	1	-	-	-	-	-	-	-	-	-
Alessandro de Tomaso	RA	1	-	-	-	-	-	-	-	-	-
Wolfgang von Trips	D	1	-	-	-	-	-	-	-	-	-
Robin Widdows	GB	1	-	-	-	-	-	-	-	-	-
Vic Wilson	GB	1	-	-	-	-	-	-	-	-	-
Tino Brambilla	I	- (1)	-	-	-	-	-	-	-	-	-
Alain de Chagny	B	- (1)	-	-	-	-	-	-	-	-	-
Frank Dochnal	USA	- (1)	-	-	-	-	-	-	-	-	-
Helmut Glockler	D	- (1)	-	-	-	-	-	-	-	-	-
Tom Jones	CDN	- (1)	-	-	-	-	-	-	-	-	-
Les Leston	GB	- (1)	-	-	-	-	-	-	-	-	-
Jean Lucienbonnet	F	- (1)	-	-	-	-	-	-	-	-	-
Bill Moss	GB	- (1)	-	-	-	-	-	-	-	-	-
Tim Parnell	GB	- (1)	-	-	-	-	-	-	-	-	-
Lance Reventlow	USA	- (1)	-	-	-	-	-	-	-	-	-
Alan Rollinson	GB	- (1)	-	-	-	-	-	-	-	-	-
Jean-Claude Rudaz	CH	- (1)	-	-	-	-	-	-	-	-	-
Trevor Taylor	GB	- (1)	-	-	-	-	-	-	-	-	-

COOPER GRAND PRIX CARS

Type	Year	Engine	Designer
T12	1950	JAP twin	Owen Maddock
			F3 car
T20	1952	Bristol BS S6	Owen Maddock
T23	1953	Bristol BS S6, Bristol 401 S6 (1954)	Owen Maddock
T24	1953	Alta F2 S4, Alta GP S4 (1954)	Owen Maddock
T40	1955	Bristol 401 S6	Jack Brabham
T41	1957	Climax FWB S4	Owen Maddock
T43	1957	Climax FPF S4, Bristol 401 S6, OSCA	Owen Maddock
T45	1958	Climax FPF S4, Maserati 250S S4	Owen Maddock
T51	1959	Climax FPF S4, Maserati 250S S4, Borgward 30, Ferrari 555/F1, Ferrari 625LM S4	Owen Maddock
		Ferrari-engined cars known as the Cooper-Castellotti	
T53	1960	Climax FPF S4, Maserati 250S S4, Alfa Romeo S4	Owen Maddock
T55	1961	Climax FPF S4	Owen Maddock
T58	1961	Climax FWMV V8	Owen Maddock
T59	1962	Climax FPF S4, Ford S4	Owen Maddock
T60	1962	Climax FMWV V8	Owen Maddock
T66	1963	Climax FMWV V8	Owen Maddock
T71/73	1964	Ford S4	Eddie Strait
T73	1964	Climax FMWV V8, Ferrari 250GT V12	Eddie Strait
T75	1968	Climax S4	Eddie Strait
T77	1965	Climax FMWV V8, ATS V8	Eddie Strait
T79	1967	Climax FPF S4	Eddie Strait
		Ex-Tasman Cup car used by John Love	
T81	1966	Maserati 9/F1 V12	Derrick White
T81B	1967	Maserati 9/F1 V12	Derrick White
T86	1967	Maserati 10/F1 V12	Derrick White
T86B	1968	BRM V12, Maserati 10/F1 V12	Derrick White/ Tony Robinson
T86C	1968	Alfa Romeo T33 V8	Derrick White/ Tony Robinson
		Test vehicle for Alfa Romeo, did not race	

DALLARA

GP Debut:	1988 San Marino GP	Caffi (retired)
Last GP:	1992 Australian GP	Lehto (retired),
		Martini (retired)

Principal:	Gianpaolo Dallara
Base:	Parma (I)
Works team:	Scuderia Italia
Principal:	Beppe Lucchini
Base:	Brescia (I)

WORLD CHAMPIONSHIP RECORD

GPs Started:	78
Points:	15
Best result:	3rd 1989 Canadian GP (de Cesaris),
	1991 San Marino GP (Lehto)
Best qualif.:	3rd 1989 Hungarian GP (Caffi),
	1990 United States GP (de Cesaris)

Best World Championship position:	
Drivers:	12th in 1991 (Lehto)
Constructors:	8th in 1989 and 1991

DALLARA GRAND PRIX DRIVERS

Driver	Nat	Starts (DNS/DNQ)	1st	2nd	3rd	4th	5th	6th	PP	FL	Points
JJ Lehto	SF	31 (1)	-	-	1	-	-	-	-	-	4
Andrea de Cesaris	I	30 (2)	-	-	1	-	-	-	-	-	4
Alex Caffi	I	28 (4)	-	-	-	1	-	1	-	-	4
Pierluigi Martini	I	16	-	-	-	-	2	-	-	-	2
Emanuele Pirro	I	27 (3)	-	-	-	-	1	-	-	1
Gianni Morbidelli	I	1 (1)	-	-	-	-	-	-	-	-	-

DALLARA GRAND PRIX CARS

Type	Year	Engine	Designer
3087	1988	Ford DFV V8	Gianpaolo Dallara
F188	1988	Ford DFZ V8	Sergio Rinland
F189	1989	Ford DFR V8	Gianpaolo Dallara/
			Mario Tolentino
F190	1990	Ford DFR V8	Gianpaolo Dallara/
			Christian Vanderpleyn
F191	1991	Judd GV V10	Gianpaolo Dallara/
			Nigel Couperthwaite
F192	1992	Ferrari Tipo 036 V12	Gianpaolo Dallara

DE TOMASO

see Tomaso

EAGLE

GP Debut:	1966 Belgian GP	Gurney (not classified)
Last GP:	1969 Canadian GP	Pease (retired)

Principal:	Dan Gurney
Base:	Rye, Sussex (GB) and Santa Ana, California (USA)

WORLD CHAMPIONSHIP RECORD

GPs Started:	25
Points:	17
Wins:	1 1967 Belgian GP (Gurney)
Best qualif.:	2nd 1967 Belgian GP (Gurney), Dutch GP (Gurney)
Fastest laps:	2 1967 Belgian GP (Gurney), German GP (Gurney)
Laps/miles in the lead:	19 laps/205 miles

Best World Championship position:	
Drivers:	8th in 1967 (Gurney)
Constructors:	7th in 1966 and 1967

EAGLE GRAND PRIX DRIVERS

Driver	Nat	Starts (DNS/DNQ)	1st	2nd	3rd	4th	5th	6th	PP	FL	Points
Dan Gurney	USA	24	1	-	1	-	2	-	-	2	17
Bruce McLaren	NZ	3	-	-	-	-	-	-	-	-	-
Bob Bondurant	USA	2	-	-	-	-	-	-	-	-	-
Al Pease	CDN	2 (1)	-	-	-	-	-	-	-	-	-
Ludovico Scarfiotti	I	1	-	-	-	-	-	-	-	-	-
Richie Ginther	USA	- (1)	-	-	-	-	-	-	-	-	-
Phil Hill	USA	- (1)	-	-	-	-	-	-	-	-	-

EAGLE GRAND PRIX CARS

Type	Year	Engine	Designer
AAR101	1966	Climax FPF S4	Len Terry
AAR102	1966	Weslake 58 V12	Len Terry
AAR103	1967	Weslake 58 V12	Len Terry
AAR104	1967	Weslake 58 V12	Len Terry

EIFELLAND

GP Debut:	1972 South African GP Stommelen (13th)
Last GP:	1972 Austrian GP Stommelen (not classified)
Principal:	Günther Henerici of Eifelland Caravans

WORLD CHAMPIONSHIP RECORD

GPs Started:	8
Best result:	10th 1972 Monaco GP (Stommelen), British GP
	(Stommelen)
Best qualif.:	14th 1972 German GP (Stommelen)

MAJOR SPONSORS

1972	Eifelland Caravans

EIFELLAND GRAND PRIX DRIVERS

Driver	Nat	Starts (DNS/DNQ)	1st	2nd	3rd	4th	5th	6th	PP	FL	Points
Rolf Stommelen	D	8	-	-	-	-	-	-	-	-	-

EIFELLAND GRAND PRIX CARS

Type	Year	Engine	Designer
21	1972	Ford DFV V8	Luigi Colani
		A March 721 with radical but unsuccessful new bodywork designed by Colani	

EMERYSON

GP Debut:	1956 British GP	Emery (retired)
Last GP:	1962 Italian GP	Settember (retired)

Principal:	Paul Emery
Base:	London (GB), 1956-60; Send, Surrey (GB) (ex-Connaught factory), 1960-62

WORLD CHAMPIONSHIP RECORD

GPs Started:	4
Best result:	10th 1962 Dutch GP (Seidel)
Best qualif.:	19th 1962 British GP (Settember)

EMERYSON GRAND PRIX DRIVERS

Driver	Nat	Starts (DNS/DNQ)	1st	2nd	3rd	4th	5th	6th	PP	FL	Points
Tony Settember	USA	2	-	-	-	-	-	-	-	-	-
Paul Emery	GB	1	-	-	-	-	-	-	-	-	-
Wolfgang Seidel	D	1	-	-	-	-	-	-	-	-	-
Lucien Bianchi	B	- (1)	-	-	-	-	-	-	-	-	-
Olivier Gendebien	B	- (1)	-	-	-	-	-	-	-	-	-
André Pilette	B	- (1)	-	-	-	-	-	-	-	-	-

EMERYSON GRAND PRIX CARS

Type	Year	Engine	Designer
Mk1	1956	Alta GP S4	Paul Emery
Mk2	1961	Maserati 150S S4, Climax FPF S4	Paul Emery

EMW

EISENACHER MOTOREN WERKE

Only GP:	1953 German GP	Barth (retired)
Base:	Eisenach (DDR)

WORLD CHAMPIONSHIP RECORD

GPs Started:	1
Best result:	No finishes
Best qualif.:	24th 1953 German GP (Barth)

EMW GRAND PRIX DRIVERS

Driver	Nat	Starts (DNS/DNQ)	1st	2nd	3rd	4th	5th	6th	PP	FL	Points
Edgar Barth	DDR	1	-	-	-	-	-	-	-	-	-

EMW GRAND PRIX CARS

Type	Year	Engine	Designer
EMW	1953	BMW 328 S6	-

ENB
ECURIE NATIONALE BELGE

Only GP:	1962 German GP	Bianchi (16th)
Principal:	Jacques Swaters	
Base:	Brussels (B)	

WORLD CHAMPIONSHIP RECORD

GPs Started: 1
Best result: 16th 1962 German GP (Bianchi)
Best qualif.: 25th 1962 German GP (Bianchi)

ENB GRAND PRIX DRIVERS

Driver	Nat	Starts (DNS/DNQ)	1st	2nd	3rd	4th	5th	6th	PP	FL	Points
Lucien Bianchi	B	1	-	-	-	-	-	-	-	-	-

ENB GRAND PRIX CARS

Type	Year	Engine	Designer
1962	1962	Maserati 150S S4	Paul Emery

ENSIGN

Including Boro. Bought by Theodore in 1983; also see Theodore

GP Debut:	1973 French GP	von Opel (15th)
Last GP:	1982 Italian GP	Guerrero (not classified)
Principal:	Mo Nunn	
Base:	Walsall (GB), 1973-80; Chasetown, Staffordshire (GB), 1981-82	

WORLD CHAMPIONSHIP RECORD

GPs Started: 99
Points: 19
Best result: 4th 1981 Brazilian GP (Surer)
Best qualif.: 3rd 1976 Swedish GP (Amon)
Fastest laps: 1 1981 Brazilian GP (Surer)

Best World Championship position:
Drivers: 16th in 1981 (Surer)
Constructors: 10th in 1977

MAJOR SPONSORS

1974	Dempster, Theodore Racing
1975	HB Alarms
1976	F&S Properties, First National City, John Day Models, Norris Industries, Raiffeisenkasse, Tissot
1977	Tissot, Castrol
1978	Tissot, Interscope, Mopar
1979	Rainbow Jeans
1980	Unipart
1982	Caribu, Cafe de Colombia

ENSIGN GRAND PRIX DRIVERS

Driver	Nat	Starts (DNS/DNQ)	1st	2nd	3rd	4th	5th	6th	PP	FL	Points
Clay Regazzoni	CH	19 (2)	-	-	-	-	2	1	-	-	5
Patrick Tambay	F	7 (1)	-	-	-	-	2	1	-	-	5
Marc Surer	CH	7 (2)	-	-	-	1	-	1	-	1	4
Chris Amon	NZ	10	-	-	-	-	1	-	-	-	2
Derek Daly	IRL	9 (5)	-	-	-	-	-	1	-	-	1
Eliseo Salazar	RCH	8 (1)	-	-	-	-	-	1	-	-	1
Gijs van Lennep	NL	3	-	-	-	-	-	1	-	-	1
Roberto Guerrero	USA	8 (7)	-	-	-	-	-	-	-	-	-
Jacky Ickx	B	8 (1)	-	-	-	-	-	-	-	-	-
Rikky von Opel	FL	6 (2)	-	-	-	-	-	-	-	-	-
Larry Perkins	AUS	5 (1)	-	-	-	-	-	-	-	-	-
Vern Schuppan	AUS	5 (2)	-	-	-	-	-	-	-	-	-
Jan Lammers	NL	3 (5)	-	-	-	-	-	-	-	-	-
Roelof Wunderink	NL	3 (3)	-	-	-	-	-	-	-	-	-

Driver (continued)

Driver	Nat	Starts (DNS/DNQ)	1st	2nd	3rd	4th	5th	6th	PP	FL	Points
Harald Ertl	A	2 (1)	-	-	-	-	-	-	-	-	-
Patrick Gaillard	F	2 (3)	-	-	-	-	-	-	-	-	-
Danny Ongais	USA	2	-	-	-	-	-	-	-	-	-
Hans Binder	A	1	-	-	-	-	-	-	-	-	-
Brian Henton	GB	1 (1)	-	-	-	-	-	-	-	-	-
Geoff Lees	GB	1 (2)	-	-	-	-	-	-	-	-	-
Lamberto Leoni	I	1 (3)	-	-	-	-	-	-	-	-	-
Brett Lunger	USA	1	-	-	-	-	-	-	-	-	-
Tiff Needell	GB	1 (1)	-	-	-	-	-	-	-	-	-
Patrick Neve	B	1	-	-	-	-	-	-	-	-	-
Nelson Piquet	BR	1	-	-	-	-	-	-	-	-	-
Mike Wilds	GB	1 (3)	-	-	-	-	-	-	-	-	-

ENSIGN GRAND PRIX CARS

Type	Year	Engine	Designer
N173	1973	Ford DFV V8	Mo Nunn
N174	1974	Ford DFV V8	Mo Nunn
N175	1975	Ford DFV V8	Dave Baldwin/Mo Nunn
		Run by 1974-sponsors HB as a Boro-Ensign in 1976	
N176	1976	Ford DFV V8	Dave Baldwin/Mo Nunn
N177	1977	Ford DFV V8	Dave Baldwin/Mo Nunn
N179	1979	Ford DFV V8	Dave Baldwin/Mo Nunn/ Shahab Ahmed
N180	1980	Ford DFV V8	Ralph Bellamy/ Nigel Bennett
N180B	1981	Ford DFV V8	Ralph Bellamy/ Nigel Bennett
N181	1982	Ford DFV V8	Nigel Bennett

ERA
ENGLISH RACING AUTOMOBILES

GP Debut:	1950 British GP	Gerard (6th), Harrison (7th), Walker/Rolt (retired), Johnson (retired)
Last GP:	1952 Dutch GP	Moss (retired)
Principals:	Raymond Mays, Humphrey Cook and Peter Berthon, 1933-47; Leslie Johnson, 1947-52	
Base:	Bourne, Lincolnshire (GB), 1933-39; Dunstable (GB), 1947-52	

WORLD CHAMPIONSHIP RECORD

GPs Started: 7
Best result: 6th 1950 British GP (Gerard), Monaco GP (Gerard)
Best qualif.: 10th 1950 British GP (Walker), 1951 British GP (Gerard), 1952 Belgian GP (Moss)

ERA GRAND PRIX DRIVERS

Driver	Nat	Starts (DNS/DNQ)	1st	2nd	3rd	4th	5th	6th	PP	FL	Points
Bob Gerard	GB	3	-	-	-	-	-	2	-	-	-
Cuth Harrison	GB	3	-	-	-	-	-	-	-	-	-
Stirling Moss	GB	3	-	-	-	-	-	-	-	-	-
Leslie Johnson	GB	1	-	-	-	-	-	-	-	-	-
Tony Rolt	GB	1	-	-	-	-	-	-	-	-	-
Brian Shawe-Taylor	GB	1	-	-	-	-	-	-	-	-	-
Peter Walker	GB	1	-	-	-	-	-	-	-	-	-

ERA GRAND PRIX CARS

Type	Year	Engine	Designer
A-type	1950*	ERA S6 sc	Reid Railton/Peter Berthon
B-type	1950*	ERA S6 sc	Reid Railton/Peter Berthon
C-type	1950*	ERA S6 sc	Reid Railton/Peter Berthon
E-type	1950*	ERA S6 sc	Reid Railton/Peter Berthon
G-type	1952	Bristol BS S6	David Hodkin
		*Championship debut, the A-type first raced in 1934, B-type in 1935, C-type in 1936 and E-type in 1939	

EUROBRUN

GP Debut:	1988 Brazilian GP	Modena (retired)
Last GP:	1990 San Marino GP	Moreno (retired)
Principals:	Paolo Pavanello and Walter Brun	
Base:	Senago, near Milan (I)	

WORLD CHAMPIONSHIP RECORD

GPs Started: 14
Best result: 11th 1988 Hungarian GP (Modena)
Best qualif.: 15th 1988 Canadian GP (Modena)

EUROBRUN GRAND PRIX DRIVERS

Driver	Nat	Starts (DNS/DNQ)	1st	2nd	3rd	4th	5th	6th	PP	FL	Points
Stefano Modena	I	10 (6)	-	-	-	-	-	-	-	-	-
Oscar Larrauri	RA	7 (14)	-	-	-	-	-	-	-	-	-
Roberto Moreno	BR	2 (12)	-	-	-	-	-	-	-	-	-
Gregor Foitek	CH	- (11)	-	-	-	-	-	-	-	-	-
Claudio Langes	I	- (14)	-	-	-	-	-	-	-	-	-

EUROBRUN GRAND PRIX CARS

Type	Year	Engine	Designer
ER188	1988	Ford DFZ V8	Mario Tolentino/Bruno Zava
ER188B	1989	Judd CV V8	Mario Tolentino/ Bruno Zava/George Ryton
ER189	1989	Judd CV V8	George Ryton/Roberto Ori
ER189B	1990	Judd CV V8	George Ryton/Roberto Ori

FERGUSON

Only GP: 1961 British GP — Fairman/Moss (disqualified)
Principal: Harry Ferguson
Base: Coventry (GB)

WORLD CHAMPIONSHIP RECORD

GPs Started: 1
Best result: No finishes
Best qualif.: 20th 1961 British GP (Fairman)

FERGUSON GRAND PRIX DRIVERS

Driver	Nat	Starts (DNS/DNQ)	1st	2nd	3rd	4th	5th	6th	PP	FL	Points
Jack Fairman	GB	1	-	-	-	-	-	-	-	-	-
Stirling Moss	GB	1	-	-	-	-	-	-	-	-	-

FERGUSON GRAND PRIX CARS

Type	Year	Engine	Designer
P99	1961	Climax FPF S4	Claude Hill
			4-wheel-drive

FERRARI

GP Debut: 1950 Monaco GP — Ascari (2nd), Sommer (4th), Villoresi (retired)
Latest GP: 1994 Australian GP — Berger (2nd), Alesi (6th)
Principal: Enzo Ferrari, 1929 until his death in August 1988; Cesare Fiorio, 1989-June 1991; Piero Ferrari, June 1991-92; Luca di Montezemolo, 1992 to date
Base: Modena (I), 1929-40; Maranello (I), 1945 to date

WORLD CHAMPIONSHIP RECORD

GPs Started: 536
Points: 2754.27
Wins: 104 1951 British GP (Gonzalez), German GP (Ascari), Italian GP (Ascari), 1952 Swiss GP (Taruffi), Belgian GP (Ascari), French GP (Ascari), British GP (Ascari), German GP (Ascari), Dutch GP (Ascari), Italian GP (Ascari), 1953 Argentinian GP (Ascari), Dutch GP (Ascari), Belgian GP (Ascari), French GP (Hawthorn), British GP (Ascari), German GP (Farina), Swiss GP (Ascari), 1954 British GP (Gonzalez), Spanish GP (Hawthorn), 1955 Monaco GP (Trintignant), 1956 Argentinian GP (Musso/Fangio), Belgian GP (Collins), French GP (Collins), British GP (Fangio), German GP (Fangio), 1958 French GP (Hawthorn), British GP (Collins), 1959 French GP (Brooks), German GP (Brooks), 1960 Italian GP (Hill), 1961 Dutch GP (von Trips), Belgian GP (Hill), French GP (Baghetti), British GP (von Trips), Italian GP (Hill), 1963 German GP (Surtees), 1964 German GP (Surtees), Austrian GP (Bandini), Italian GP (Surtees), 1966 Belgian GP (Surtees), Italian GP (Scarfiotti), 1968 French GP (Ickx), 1970 Austrian GP (Ickx), Italian

GP (Regazzoni), Canadian GP (Ickx), Mexican GP (Ickx), 1971 South African GP (Andretti), Dutch GP (Ickx), 1972 German GP (Ickx), 1974 Spanish GP (Lauda), Dutch GP (Lauda), German GP (Regazzoni), 1975 Monaco GP (Lauda), Belgian GP (Lauda), Swedish GP (Lauda), French GP (Lauda), Italian GP (Regazzoni), United States GP (Lauda), 1976 Brazilian GP (Lauda), South African GP (Lauda), Long Beach GP (Regazzoni), Belgian GP (Lauda), Monaco GP (Lauda), British GP (Lauda), 1977 Brazilian GP (Reutemann), South African GP (Lauda), German GP (Lauda), Dutch GP (Lauda), 1978 Brazilian GP (Reutemann), Long Beach GP (Reutemann), British GP (Reutemann), United States GP (Reutemann), Canadian GP (Villeneuve), 1979 South African GP (Villeneuve), Long Beach GP (Villeneuve), Belgian GP (Scheckter), Monaco GP (Scheckter), Italian GP (Scheckter), United States GP (Villeneuve), 1981 Monaco GP (Villeneuve), Spanish GP (Villeneuve), 1982 San Marino GP (Pironi), Dutch GP (Pironi), German GP (Tambay), 1983 San Marino GP (Tambay), Canadian GP (Arnoux), Dutch GP (Arnoux), 1984 Belgian GP (Alboreto), 1985 Brazilian GP (Alboreto), German GP (Alboreto), 1987 Japanese GP (Berger), Australian GP (Berger), 1988 Italian GP (Berger), 1989 Brazilian GP (Mansell), Hungarian GP (Mansell), Portuguese GP (Berger), 1990 Brazilian GP (Prost), Mexican GP (Prost), French GP (Prost), British GP (Prost), Portuguese GP (Mansell), Spanish GP (Prost), 1994 German GP (Berger)
Pole pos.: 113 1951 British GP (Gonzalez), German GP (Ascari), Spanish GP (Ascari), 1952 Swiss GP (Farina), Belgian GP (Ascari), French GP (Ascari), British GP (Farina), German GP (Ascari), Dutch GP (Ascari), Italian GP (Ascari), 1953 Argentinian GP (Ascari), Dutch GP (Ascari), French GP (Ascari), British GP (Ascari), German GP (Ascari), Italian GP (Ascari), 1954 Argentinian GP (Farina), Swiss GP (Gonzalez), 1955 Argentinian GP (Gonzalez), 1956 Argentinian GP (Fangio), Monaco GP (Fangio), Belgian GP (Fangio), French GP (Fangio), German GP (Fangio), Italian GP (Fangio), 1958 Belgian GP (Hawthorn), French GP (Hawthorn), German GP (Hawthorn), Moroccan GP (Hawthorn), 1959 French GP (Brooks), German GP (Brooks), 1960 Italian GP (Hill), 1961 Dutch GP (Hill), Belgian GP (Hill), French GP (Hill), British GP (Hill), German GP (Hill), Italian GP (von Trips), 1963 Italian GP (Surtees), 1964 German GP (Surtees), Italian GP (Surtees), 1966 Belgian GP (Surtees), French GP (Bandini), Italian GP (Parkes), 1968 Spanish GP (Amon), Belgian GP (Amon), Dutch GP (Amon), German GP (Ickx), 1970 French GP (Ickx), German GP (Ickx), Italian GP (Ickx), United States GP (Ickx), Mexican GP (Regazzoni), 1971 Spanish GP (Ickx), Dutch GP (Ickx), British GP (Regazzoni), 1972 German GP (Ickx), British GP (Ickx), German GP (Ickx), Italian GP (Ickx), 1974 South African GP (Lauda), Spanish GP (Lauda), Belgian GP (Regazzoni), Monaco GP (Lauda), Dutch GP (Lauda), French GP (Lauda), British GP (Lauda), German GP (Lauda), Austrian GP (Lauda), Italian GP (Lauda), 1975 Spanish GP (Lauda), Monaco GP (Lauda), Belgian GP (Lauda), Dutch GP (Lauda), French GP (Lauda), German GP (Lauda), Austrian GP (Lauda), Italian GP (Lauda), United States GP (Lauda), 1976 Long Beach GP (Regazzoni), Belgian GP (Lauda), Monaco GP (Lauda), British GP (Lauda), 1977 Long Beach GP (Lauda), Austrian GP (Lauda), 1978 Long Beach GP (Reutemann), Monaco GP (Reutemann), 1979 Long Beach GP (Villeneuve), Monaco GP (Scheckter), 1981 San Marino GP (Villeneuve), 1982 Canadian GP (Pironi), German GP (Pironi), Italian GP (Andretti), 1983 Long Beach GP (Tambay), San Marino GP (Tambay), Detroit GP (Arnoux), Canadian GP (Arnoux), British GP (Arnoux), German GP (Tambay), Austrian GP (Tambay), South African GP (Tambay), 1984 Belgian GP (Alboreto), 1985 Brazilian GP (Alboreto), 1987 Portuguese GP (Berger), Japanese GP (Berger), Australian GP (Berger), 1988 British GP (Berger), 1990 French GP (Mansell), British GP (Mansell), Portuguese GP

(Mansell), 1994 German GP (Berger), Italian GP (Alesi), Portuguese GP (Berger)

Fastest laps: 122 1952 Swiss GP (Taruffi), Belgian GP (Ascari), French GP (Ascari), British GP (Ascari), German GP (Ascari), Dutch GP (Ascari), Italian GP (Ascari), 1953 Argentinian GP (Ascari), Dutch GP (Villoresi), French GP (Ascari), British GP (Ascari), German GP (Ascari), Swiss GP (Ascari), 1954 Argentinian GP (Gonzalez), British GP (Gonzalez), Italian GP (Hawthorn), Italian GP (Gonzalez), 1956 Argentinian GP (Fangio), Monaco GP (Fangio), French GP (Fangio), German GP (Fangio), 1957 French GP (Musso), 1958 Monaco GP (Hawthorn), Belgian GP (Hawthorn), French GP (Hawthorn), British GP (Hawthorn), Portuguese GP (Hawthorn), Italian GP (Hill), 1959 German GP (Brooks), Italian GP (Hill), 1960 Belgian GP (Hill), Italian GP (Hill), 1961 Monaco GP (Ginther), Belgian GP (Ginther), French GP (Hill), German GP (Hill), Italian GP (Baghetti), 1963 Monaco GP (Surtees), British GP (Surtees), German GP (Surtees), Italian GP (Surtees), 1966 Monaco GP (Bandini), Belgian GP (Surtees), French GP (Bandini), Italian GP (Scarfiotti), 1970 Dutch GP (Ickx), German GP (Ickx), Austrian GP (Ickx), Austrian GP (Regazzoni), Italian GP (Regazzoni), Canadian GP (Regazzoni), United States GP (Ickx), Mexican GP (Ickx), 1971 South African GP (Andretti), Spanish GP (Ickx), Dutch GP (Ickx), United States GP (Ickx), 1972 Spanish GP (Ickx), German GP (Ickx), Italian GP (Ickx), 1974 Argentinian GP (Regazzoni), Brazilian GP (Regazzoni), Spanish GP (Lauda), British GP (Lauda), Austrian GP (Regazzoni), Canadian GP (Lauda), 1975 Belgian GP (Regazzoni), Swedish GP (Lauda), Dutch GP (Lauda), British GP (Regazzoni), German GP (Regazzoni), Italian GP (Regazzoni), 1976 South African GP (Lauda), Long Beach GP (Regazzoni), Belgian GP (Lauda), Monaco GP (Regazzoni), French GP (Lauda), British GP (Lauda), Dutch GP (Regazzoni), 1977 Long Beach GP (Lauda), German GP (Lauda), Dutch GP (Lauda), 1978 Argentinian GP (Villeneuve), Brazilian GP (Reutemann), French GP (Reutemann), 1979 South African GP (Villeneuve), Long Beach GP (Villeneuve), Spanish GP (Villeneuve), Belgian GP (Villeneuve), German GP (Villeneuve), Dutch GP (Villeneuve), 1981 San Marino GP (Villeneuve), Las Vegas GP (Pironi), 1982 San Marino GP (Pironi), Canadian GP (Pironi), 1983 Canadian GP (Tambay), German GP (Arnoux), Dutch GP (Arnoux), 1984 Belgian GP (Arnoux), Dutch GP (Arnoux), European GP (Alboreto), 1985 San Marino GP (Alboreto), Monaco GP (Alboreto), 1987 Portuguese GP (Berger), Spanish GP (Berger), Australian GP (Berger), 1988 Brazilian GP (Berger), Belgian GP (Berger), Italian GP (Alboreto), Portuguese GP (Berger), 1989 Mexican GP (Mansell), British GP (Mansell), Hungarian GP (Mansell), Portuguese GP (Berger), 1990 Mexican GP (Prost), French GP (Mansell), British GP (Mansell), Belgian GP (Prost), Australian GP (Mansell), 1991 United States GP (Alesi), Monaco GP (Prost)

Laps/miles in the lead: 6961 laps/23858 miles

World Champions:

Drivers: Nine times - 1952 (Ascari), 1953 (Ascari), 1956 (Fangio), 1958 (Hawthorn), 1961 (P Hill), 1964 (Surtees), 1975 (Lauda), 1977 (Lauda) and 1979 (J Scheckter)

Constructors: Eight times - 1961, 1964, 1975, 1976, 1977, 1979, 1982 and 1983

FERRARI GRAND PRIX DRIVERS

Driver	Nat	Starts (DNS/DNQ)	1st	2nd	3rd	4th	5th	6th	PP	FL	Points
Niki Lauda	A	57 (1)	15	12	5	2	4	2	23	12	242.5
Alberto Ascari	I	26 (1)	13	4	-	2	1	1	13	11	139.5
Jacky Ickx	B	55 (1)	6	4	6	4	3	1	11	11	121
Gilles Villeneuve	CDN	66 (1)	6	5	2	2	3	3	2	8	107
Gerhard Berger	A	79	5	8	5	9	3	4	6	7	151
Alain Prost	F	30 (1)	5	5	4	4	2	-	-	3	107
Carlos Reutemann	RA	34	5	2	6	2	-	3	2	2	90
Clay Regazzoni	CH	73	4	11	8	8	4	3	4	13	169

Driver	Nat	Starts (DNS/DNQ)	1st	2nd	3rd	4th	5th	6th	PP	FL	Points
John Surtees	GB	30	4	5	4	2	-	-	4	6	88
Michele Alboreto	I	80	3	9	7	7	4	1	2	4	138.5
Mike Hawthorn	GB	35	3	9	4	5	2	3	4	6	113.64
Phil Hill	USA	31	3	5	8	2	-	1	6	6	96
René Arnoux	F	32	3	4	4	2	3	2	4	4	79
Nigel Mansell	GB	31	3	5	3	2	-	-	3	6	75
Jody Scheckter	ZA	28 (1)	3	3	-	4	2	1	1	-	62
Peter Collins	GB	20	3	3	3	1	1	1	-	-	47
Juan Manuel Fangio	RA	7	3	2	-	-	-	-	6	4	34.5
Patrick Tambay	F	21 (2)	2	3	3	5	1	-	4	1	65
José Froilan Gonzalez	RA	15	2	6	3	1	1	-	3	3	56.64
Wolfgang von Trips	D	25 (1)	2	2	2	3	4	3	1	-	56
Didier Pironi	F	25 (2)	2	2	2	1	3	1	2	3	48
Tony Brooks	GB	7	2	1	1	-	-	-	2	1	27
Giuseppe Farina	I	20 (1)	1	9	3	2	1	1	3	-	75.33
Lorenzo Bandini	I	35	1	2	5	2	3	3	1	2	56
Maurice Trintignant	F	17 (1)	1	2	2	2	3	1	-	-	33.33
Luigi Musso	I	15	1	4	-	1	-	-	-	1	32
Piero Taruffi	I	13	1	2	1	1	2	1	-	1	32
Mario Andretti	USA	12 (2)	1	-	1	2	-	1	1	1	20
Giancarlo Baghetti	I	8	1	-	-	1	1	-	-	1	14
Ludovico Scarfiotti	I	6 (2)	1	-	-	-	-	2	-	1	11
Jean Alesi	F	62	-	2	9	7	4	2	1	1	79
Stefan Johansson	S	31	-	2	4	5	2	2	-	-	49
Luigi Villoresi	I	20 (2)	-	2	6	2	-	3	-	1	43
Chris Amon	NZ	27	-	1	5	2	-	2	3	-	34
Richie Ginther	USA	10	-	2	2	-	1	2	-	2	24
Michael Parkes	GB	6	-	2	-	-	1	-	1	-	14
Eugenio Castellotti	I	11	-	1	1	1	1	1	-	-	13.5
Dan Gurney	USA	4	-	1	1	1	-	-	-	-	13
Rudolf Fischer	CH	7 (1)	-	1	1	-	-	1	-	-	10
Paul Frère	B	3	-	1	-	1	-	-	-	-	9
Olivier Gendebien	B	8	-	-	-	2	1	2	-	-	8
Cliff Allison	GB	6 (1)	-	1	-	-	1	-	-	-	8
Arturo Merzario	I	11	-	-	-	2	-	1	-	-	7
Willy Mairesse	B	10	-	1	1	-	-	-	-	-	7
Pedro Rodriguez	MEX	8	-	-	-	2	2	-	-	-	6
Nicola Larini	I	4	-	1	-	-	-	-	-	-	6
Peter Whitehead	GB	7 (2)	-	-	1	-	-	-	-	-	4
Robert Manzon	F	5 (1)	-	-	1	-	-	-	-	-	4
Ricardo Rodriguez	MEX	5 (1)	-	-	-	1	-	1	-	-	4
Alfonso de Portago	E	5	-	1	-	-	1	-	-	-	4
Umberto Maglioli	I	6	-	-	2	-	-	1	-	-	3.33
Ivan Capelli	I	14	-	-	-	1	1	-	-	-	3
Ignazio Giunti	I	4	-	-	-	1	-	-	-	-	3
Reg Parnell	GB	2	-	-	-	1	-	-	-	-	3
Dorino Serafini	I	1	-	1	-	-	-	-	-	-	3
Raymond Sommer	F	1	-	-	-	1	-	-	-	-	3
Jean Behra	F	3	-	-	-	-	1	-	-	-	2
Gianni Morbidelli	I	1	-	-	-	-	-	1	-	-	0.5
Louis Rosier	F	15	-	-	-	-	-	-	-	-	
Jacques Swaters	B	5 (1)	-	-	-	-	-	-	-	-	
Peter Hirt	CH	4	-	-	-	-	-	-	-	-	
Piero Carini	I	3	-	-	-	-	-	-	-	-	
Charles de Tornaco	B	2 (2)	-	-	-	-	-	-	-	-	
Derek Bell	GB	2	-	-	-	-	-	-	-	-	
André Simon	F	2	-	-	-	-	-	1	-	-	
Giorgio Scarlatti	I	1 (1)	-	-	-	-	-	-	-	-	
Andrea de Adamich	I	1	-	-	-	-	-	-	-	-	
Kurt Adolff	D	1	-	-	-	-	-	-	-	-	
Clemente Biondetti	I	1	-	-	-	-	-	-	-	-	
Bob Bondurant	USA	1	-	-	-	-	-	-	-	-	
Johnny Claes	B	1	-	-	-	-	-	-	-	-	
Gianfranco Comotti	I	1	-	-	-	-	-	-	-	-	
Nanni Galli	I	1	-	-	-	-	-	-	-	-	
Chico Landi	BR	1	-	-	-	-	-	-	-	-	
Roger Laurent	B	1	-	-	-	-	-	-	-	-	
Cesare Perdisa	I	1	-	-	-	-	-	1	-	-	
André Pilette	B	1	-	-	-	-	-	-	-	-	
Roy Salvadori	GB	1	-	-	-	-	-	1	-	-	
Harry Schell	USA	1	-	-	-	-	-	-	-	-	
Rudolf Schoeller	CH	1	-	-	-	-	-	-	-	-	
Max de Terra	CH	1	-	-	-	-	-	-	-	-	
Alessandro de Tomaso	RA	1	-	-	-	-	-	-	-	-	

Driver	Nat	Starts	1st	2nd	3rd	4th	5th	6th	PP	FL	Points (DNS/DNQ)
Nino Vaccarella	I	1	-	-	-	-	-	-	-	-	-
Jonathan Williams	GB	1	-	-	-	-	-	-	-	-	-
Tino Brambilla	I	- (1)	-	-	-	-	-	-	-	-	-
Hans Stuck	D	- (1)	-	-	-	-	-	-	-	-	-

FERRARI GRAND PRIX CARS

Type	Year	Engine	Designer
125	1950#	Ferrari 125/F1 V12 sc	Gioacchino Colombo
166I	1950	Jaguar XK120 S6	Aurelio Lampredi; modified by Clemente Biondetti
275	1950	Ferrari 275/F1 V12	Aurelio Lampredi
375	1950	Ferrari 375/F1 V12	Aurelio Lampredi
212	1951	Ferrari 212 S4	Aurelio Lampredi
500	1952	Ferrari 500/F2 S4	Aurelio Lampredi
166/F2	1952	Ferrari 166/F2 V12	Aurelio Lampredi
212 (52)	1952	Ferrari 166/F2 V12	Aurelio Lampredi
125/F2	1952	Ferrari 166/F2 V12	Aurelio Lampredi
166C	1953	Ferrari 166/F2 V12	Aurelio Lampredi
553	1953	Ferrari 553/F2 S4	Aurelio Lampredi
625	1954	Ferrari 625/F1 S4	Aurelio Lampredi
553 Squalo	1954	Ferrari 555/F1 S4	Aurelio Lampredi
625 (555) 625	1954	Ferrari 625/555 S4	Aurelio Lampredi
(735/555) 555	1954	Ferrari 735/555 S4	Aurelio Lampredi
Supersqualo	1955	Ferrari 555/F1 S4	Aurelio Lampredi
D50*	1955	Lancia DS50 V8	Vittorio Jano

The Lancia-Ferrari D50 was also known as Ferrari 801 in 1956

Type	Year	Engine	Designer
Dino 246	1958	Ferrari 246/F1 V6	Vittorio Jano/Carlo Chiti
Dino 156	1958	Ferrari 156/F1 V6	Vittorio Jano/Carlo Chiti
Dino 246P	1960	Ferrari 246/F1 V6	Carlo Chiti
Dino 156P	1960	Ferrari 156/F1 V6	Carlo Chiti
Dino 156	1963	Ferrari 156/F1 V6	Mauro Forghieri
158	1964	Ferrari 158/F1 V8	Mauro Forghieri
1512	1964	Ferrari 1512/F1 F12	Mauro Forghieri
158/246	1966	Ferrari 246/F1 V6	Mauro Forghieri
312	1966	Ferrari 312 V12	Mauro Forghieri
312B	1970	Ferrari 312B Boxer F12	Mauro Forghieri
312B2	1971	Ferrari 312B Boxer F12	Mauro Forghieri
312B3	1973	Ferrari 312B Boxer F12	Mauro Forghieri/Franco Rocchi
312B3S	1973	Ferrari 312B Boxer F12	Mauro Forghieri/Franco Rocchi
312T	1975	Ferrari 312B Boxer F12	Mauro Forghieri/Franco Rocchi
312T2	1976	Ferrari 312B Boxer F12	Mauro Forghieri/Franco Rocchi
312T3	1978	Ferrari 312B Boxer F12	Mauro Forghieri
312T4	1979	Ferrari 312B Boxer F12	Mauro Forghieri
312T5	1980	Ferrari 312B Boxer F12	Mauro Forghieri
126CK	1981	Ferrari 126C V6 tc	Mauro Forghieri/Antonio Tomaini
126C2	1982	Ferrari 126C V6 tc	Harvey Postlethwaite
126C2B	1983	Ferrari 126C V6 tc	Harvey Postlethwaite
126C3	1983	Ferrari 126C V6 tc	Harvey Postlethwaite
126C4	1984	Ferrari 126C V6 tc	Harvey Postlethwaite/Mauro Forghieri
156/85	1985	Ferrari 126C V6 tc	Harvey Postlethwaite/Antonio Tomaini/Ildo Renzetti
F186	1986	Ferrari F186 V6 tc	Harvey Postlethwaite
F187	1987	Ferrari Tipo 033 V6 tc	Gustav Brunner
F187/88C	1988	Ferrari Tipo 033B V6 tc	Gustav Brunner
640	1989	Ferrari Tipo 034 V12	John Barnard
641	1990	Ferrari Tipo 036 V12	John Barnard
641/2	1990	Ferrari Tipo 036 V12	John Barnard
642	1991	Ferrari Tipo 036 V12	Steve Nichols
643	1991	Ferrari Tipo 036 V12	Steve Nichols
F92A	1992	Ferrari Tipo 036 V12	Steve Nichols
F92AT	1992	Ferrari Tipo 036 V12	Steve Nichols
F93A	1993	Ferrari Tipo 036 V12	George Ryton/John Barnard
412T1	1994	Ferrari Tipo 043 V12	John Barnard
412T1B	1994	Ferrari Tipo 043 V12	John Barnard

#Championship debut, the 125 first raced in 1948
*Lancia-Ferrari.

FITTIPALDI

Bought Walter Wolf Racing in 1980; also see Wolf

GP Debut:	1975 Argentinian GP	W Fittipaldi (retired)
Last GP:	1982 Italian GP	Serra (11th)
Principal:	Wilson Fittipaldi, 1975; Wilson and Emerson Fittipaldi, 1976-82	
Base:	Sao Paulo (BR) and Reading (GB)	

WORLD CHAMPIONSHIP RECORD

GPs Started: 103
Points: 44
Best result: 2nd 1978 Brazilian GP (E Fittipaldi)
Best qualif.: 5th 1976 Brazilian GP (E Fittipaldi)

Best World Championship position:
Drivers: 9th in 1978 (E Fittipaldi)
Constructors: 7th in 1978

MAJOR SPONSORS

1975-79	Copersucar
1980	Skol Brasil

FITTIPALDI GRAND PRIX DRIVERS

Driver	Nat	Starts	1st	2nd	3rd	4th	5th	6th	PP	FL	Points (DNS/DNQ)
Emerson Fittipaldi	BR	74 (3)	-	1	1	5	3	6	-	-	37
Keke Rosberg	SF	20 (8)	-	-	1	-	1	-	-	-	6
Chico Serra	BR	14 (15)	-	-	-	-	-	1	-	-	1
Wilson Fittipaldi	BR	10 (3)	-	-	-	-	-	-	-	-	-
Ingo Hoffman	BR	3 (3)	-	-	-	-	-	-	-	-	-
Arturo Merzario	I	1	-	-	-	-	-	-	-	-	-
Alex Ribeiro	BR	- (2)	-	-	-	-	-	-	-	-	-

FITTIPALDI GRAND PRIX CARS

Type	Year	Engine	Designer
FD01	1975	Ford DFV V8	Richard Divila
FD02	1975	Ford DFV V8	Richard Divila
FD03	1975	Ford DFV V8	Richard Divila
FD04	1976	Ford DFV V8	Richard Divila
F5	1977	Ford DFV V8	David Baldwin
F5A	1978	Ford DFV V8	David Baldwin/Giacomo Caliri
F6	1979	Ford DFV V8	Ralph Bellamy
F6A	1979	Ford DFV V8	Ralph Bellamy
F7	1980	Ford DFV V8	Harvey Postlethwaite. Formerly Wolf WR7, WR8 and WR9 chassis, renamed when Fittipaldi bought Wolf
F8	1980	Ford DFV V8	Harvey Postlethwaite
F8C	1981	Ford DFV V8	Harvey Postlethwaite/Gary Thomas
F8D	1982	Ford DFV V8	Harvey Postlethwaite/Gary Thomas/Tim Wright
F9	1982	Ford DFV V8	Richard Divila/Tim Wright

FONDMETAL

Bought Osella in 1991; also see Osella

GP Debut:	1991 Mexican GP	Grouillard (retired)
Last GP:	1992 Italian GP	Tarquini (retired), van de Poele (retired)
Principal:	Gabriele Rumi	
Base:	Constructor: Bicester (GB); Team: Palosco, near Bergamo (I)	

WORLD CHAMPIONSHIP RECORD

GPs Started: 19
Best result: 10th 1991 Belgian GP (Grouillard), 1992 Belgian GP (van de Poele)
Best qualif.: 10th 1991 Mexican GP (Grouillard)

MAJOR SPONSORS

1991-92	Fondmetal Wheels

FONDMETAL GRAND PRIX DRIVERS

Driver	Nat	Starts	1st	2nd	3rd	4th	5th	6th	PP	FL	Points
		(DNS/DNQ)									
Gabriele Tarquini	I	15 (1)	-	-	-	-	-	-	-	-	-
Olivier Grouillard	F	4 (9)	-	-	-	-	-	-	-	-	-
Andrea Chiesa	CH	3 (7)	-	-	-	-	-	-	-	-	-
Eric van de Poele	B	3	-	-	-	-	-	-	-	-	-

FONDMETAL GRAND PRIX CARS

Type	Year	Engine	Designer
FA1Me*	1991	Ford DFR V8	Antonio Tomaini
			Formerly Osella FA1Me, renamed Fomet
			when Fondmetal bought Osella
F1*	1991	Ford DFR V8	Tino Belli/Riccardo
			Rosa/Tim Holloway
GR01	1992	Ford HB V8	Tino Belli/Riccardo
			Rosa/Tim Holloway
GR02	1992	Ford HB V8	Sergio Rinland
			*Fomet

FOOTWORK

See Arrows

FRAZER-NASH

GP Debut: 1952 Swiss GP — Wharton (4th)
Last GP: 1952 Dutch GP — Wharton (retired)
Base: Isleworth (GB)

WORLD CHAMPIONSHIP RECORD

GPs Started: 4
Points: 3
Best result: 4th 1952 Swiss GP (Wharton)
Best qualif.: 7th 1952 Belgian GP (Wharton), Dutch GP (Wharton)
Best World Championship position:
Drivers: 13th in 1952 (Wharton)
Constructors: -

FRAZER-NASH GRAND PRIX DRIVERS

Driver	Nat	Starts	1st	2nd	3rd	4th	5th	6th	PP	FL	Points
		(DNS/DNQ)									
Ken Wharton	GB	3	-	-	-	1	-	-	-	-	3
Tony Crook	GB	1	-	-	-	-	-	-	-	-	-

FRAZER-NASH GRAND PRIX CARS

Type	Year	Engine	Designer
FN48	1952	Bristol BS S6	HJ Aldington
421	1952	BMW 328 S6, Bristol BS S6	HJ Aldington

FRY

Principal: David Fry

WORLD CHAMPIONSHIP RECORD

GPs Started: None

FRY GRAND PRIX DRIVERS

Driver	Nat	Starts	1st	2nd	3rd	4th	5th	6th	PP	FL	Points
		(DNS/DNQ)									
Michael Parkes	GB	- (1)	-	-	-	-	-	-	-	-	-

FRY GRAND PRIX CARS

Type	Year	Engine	Designer
Fry	1959	Climax FPF S4	David Fry

GILBY

GP Debut: 1961 British GP — Greene (15th)
Last GP: 1963 British GP — Raby (retired)
Principal: Sid Greene
Base: Ongar (GB)

WORLD CHAMPIONSHIP RECORD

GPs Started: 3
Best result: 15th 1961 British GP (Greene)
Best qualif.: 19th 1962 German GP (Greene), 1963 British GP (Raby)

GILBY GRAND PRIX DRIVERS

Driver	Nat	Starts	1st	2nd	3rd	4th	5th	6th	PP	FL	Points
		(DNS/DNQ)									
Keith Greene	GB	2 (1)	-	-	-	-	-	-	-	-	-
Ian Raby	GB	1 (2)	-	-	-	-	-	-	-	-	-

GILBY GRAND PRIX CARS

Type	Year	Engine	Designer
Gilby	1961	Climax FPF S4, BRM 56 V8	Len Terry

GORDINI

GP Debut: 1950 Monaco GP — Manzon (retired), Trintignant (retired)
Last GP: 1956 Italian GP — Simon (9th), Manzon (retired), da Silva Ramos (retired)
Principal: Amédée Gordini
Base: Paris (F)

WORLD CHAMPIONSHIP RECORD

GPs Started: 40
Points: 30.14
Best result: 3rd 1952 Swiss GP (Behra), Belgian GP (Manzon)
Best qualif.: 3rd 1952 Swiss GP (Manzon), German GP (Trintignant)
Fastest laps: 1 1954 British GP (Behra)
Laps/miles in the lead: 1 lap/9 miles
Best World Championship position:
Drivers: 6th in 1952 (Manzon)
Constructors: -

GORDINI GRAND PRIX DRIVERS

Driver	Nat	Starts	1st	2nd	3rd	4th	5th	6th	PP	FL	Points
		(DNS/DNQ)									
Robert Manzon	F	23	-	-	1	2	1	-	-	-	12
Jean Behra	F	20	-	-	1	-	1	2	-	1	6.14
Maurice Trintignant	F	19	-	-	-	3	2	-	-	-	6
Hermanos da Silva Ramos	F/BR	7	-	-	-	-	1	-	-	-	2
André Pilette	B	5 (1)	-	-	-	1	1	-	-	-	2
Elie Bayol	F	4	-	-	-	-	1	1	-	-	2
Harry Schell	USA	7	-	-	-	-	-	-	-	-	-
Jacques Pollet	F	5	-	-	-	-	-	-	-	-	-
André Simon	F	5	-	-	-	-	1	-	-	-	-
"B Bira"	SM	4	-	-	-	-	-	-	-	-	-
Clemar Bucci	RA	4	-	-	-	-	-	-	-	-	-
Paul Frère	B	4	-	-	-	-	-	-	-	-	-
Johnny Claes	B	3 (1)	-	-	-	-	-	-	-	-	-
Roberto Mieres	RA	3	-	-	-	-	1	-	-	-	-
Fred Wacker	USA	3 (2)	-	-	-	-	1	-	-	-	-
Georges Berger	B	2	-	-	-	-	-	-	-	-	-
Pablo Birger	RA	2	-	-	-	-	-	-	-	-	-
Aldo Gordini	F	1	-	-	-	-	-	-	-	-	-
Jesus Iglesias	RA	1	-	-	-	-	-	-	-	-	-
Roger Loyer	F	1	-	-	-	-	-	-	-	-	-
Jean Lucas	F	1	-	-	-	-	-	-	-	-	-
Carlos Mendítéguy	RA	1	-	-	-	-	-	-	-	-	-
André Milhoux	B	1	-	-	-	-	-	-	-	-	-
Robert O'Brien	USA	1	-	-	-	-	-	-	-	-	-
Mike Sparken	USA	1	-	-	-	-	-	-	-	-	-
Max de Terra	CH	1	-	-	-	-	-	-	-	-	-

GORDINI GRAND PRIX CARS

Type	Year	Engine	Designer
11*	1951#	Simca 15C S4	Amédée Gordini
11 (52)*	1952	Simca 508S S4	Amédée Gordini
15*	1950#	Simca 15C S4 sc	Amédée Gordini
15 (52)*	1952	Gordini 18 S4	Amédée Gordini
16S*	1952	Gordini 20 S6	Amédée Gordini
16	1952	Gordini 20 S6	Amédée Gordini

World Championship Grand Prix Racing

Type	Year	Engine	Designer
16 (53)	1953	Gordini 16 S6	Amédée Gordini
16 (54)	1954	Gordini 23 S6	Amédée Gordini
32	1955	Gordini 25 S8	Amédée Gordini

*Simca-Gordini. #Championship debut, the 11 first raced in 1946 and the 15 in 1947

GREIFZU

Only GP: 1952 German GP — Krause (retired)
Principal: Paul Greifzu

WORLD CHAMPIONSHIP RECORD

GPs Started: 1
Best result: No finishes
Best qualif.: No time set

GREIFZU GRAND PRIX DRIVERS

Driver	Nat	Starts	1st	2nd	3rd	4th	5th	6th	PP	FL	Points
		(DNS/DNQ)									
Rudolf Krause	DDR	1	-	-	-	-	-	-	-	-	-

GREIFZU GRAND PRIX CARS

Type	Year	Engine	Designer
Greifzu	1952	BMW 328 S6	Paul Greifzu

HECK

Also known as Klodwig

GP Debut: 1952 German GP — Klodwig (retired)
Last GP: 1953 German GP — Klodwig (15th)
Principal: Ernst Klodwig
Base: East Berlin (DDR)

WORLD CHAMPIONSHIP RECORD

GPs Started: 2
Best result: 15th 1953 German GP (Klodwig)
Best qualif.: 32nd 1953 German GP (Klodwig)

HECK GRAND PRIX DRIVERS

Driver	Nat	Starts	1st	2nd	3rd	4th	5th	6th	PP	FL	Points
		(DNS/DNQ)									
Ernst Klodwig	DDR	2	-	-	-	-	-	-	-	-	-

HECK GRAND PRIX CARS

Type	Year	Engine	Designer
Heck	1952	BMW 328 S6	Ernst Klodwig
			Rear-engined

HESKETH

GP Debut: 1974 South African GP Hunt (retired)
Last GP: 1978 South African GP Cheever (retired)
Principal: Lord Alexander Fermor-Hesketh, 1974-75 (sold equipment to Wolf-Williams Racing); Anthony "Bubbles" Horsley, 1976-78
Base: Towcester (GB)

WORLD CHAMPIONSHIP RECORD

GPs Started: 52
Points: 48
Wins: 1 1975 Dutch GP (Hunt)
Best qualif.: 2nd 1974 United States GP (Hunt), 1975 Austrian GP (Hunt)
Fastest laps: 1 1975 Argentinian GP (Hunt)
Laps/miles in the lead: 88 laps/246 miles

Best World Championship position:
Drivers: 4th in 1975 (Hunt)
Constructors: 4th in 1975

MAJOR SPONSORS

1974-75	none
1976	Penthouse, Rizla
1977	British Air Ferries, Penthouse, Rizla, Heyco, Marlboro, Obex Oil
1978	Olympus Cameras

HESKETH GRAND PRIX DRIVERS

Driver	Nat	Starts	1st	2nd	3rd	4th	5th	6th	PP	FL	Points
		(DNS/DNQ)									
James Hunt	GB	27	1	3	3	3	1	1	-	1	48
Harald Ertl	A	17 (6)	-	-	-	-	-	-	-	-	-
Rupert Keegan	GB	12	-	-	-	-	-	-	-	-	-
Guy Edwards	GB	4 (2)	-	-	-	-	-	-	-	-	-
Alan Jones	AUS	4	-	-	-	-	-	-	-	-	-
Brett Lunger	USA	3	-	-	-	-	-	-	-	-	-
Hector Rebaque	MEX	1 (5)	-	-	-	-	-	-	-	-	-
Ian Ashley	GB	1 (4)	-	-	-	-	-	-	-	-	-
Torsten Palm	S	1 (1)	-	-	-	-	-	-	-	-	-
Eddie Cheever	USA	1	-	-	-	-	-	-	-	-	-
Alex Ribeiro	BR	1	-	-	-	-	-	-	-	-	-
Rolf Stommelen	D	1	-	-	-	-	-	-	-	-	-
Derek Daly	IRL	- (3)	-	-	-	-	-	-	-	-	-
Divina Galica	GB	- (2)	-	-	-	-	-	-	-	-	-
Ian Scheckter	ZA	- (1)	-	-	-	-	-	-	-	-	-

HESKETH GRAND PRIX CARS

Type	Year	Engine	Designer
308	1974	Ford DFV V8	Harvey Postlethwaite
308B	1975	Ford DFV V8	Harvey Postlethwaite
308C	1975	Ford DFV V8	Harvey Postlethwaite
		Renamed Williams FW05 when sold to Wolf-Williams racing	
308D	1976	Ford DFV V8	Harvey Postlethwaite
308E	1977	Ford DFV V8	Frank Dernie/Nigel Stroud

HILL

GP Debut: 1975 Spanish GP — Stommelen (retired), Migault (not classified)
Last GP: 1975 United States GP Brise (retired)
Principal: Graham Hill
Base: West London (GB)

WORLD CHAMPIONSHIP RECORD

GPs Started: 10
Points: 3
Best result: 5th 1975 German GP (Jones)
Best qualif.: 6th 1975 Italian GP (Brise)
Laps/miles in the lead: 8 laps/19 miles

Best World Championship position:
Drivers: 17th in 1975 (Jones)
Constructors: 11th in 1975

MAJOR SPONSORS

1975	Embassy

HILL GRAND PRIX DRIVERS

Driver	Nat	Starts	1st	2nd	3rd	4th	5th	6th	PP	FL	Points
		(DNS/DNQ)									
Alan Jones	AUS	4	-	-	-	1	-	-	-	-	2
Tony Brise	GB	9	-	-	-	-	1	-	-	-	1
Rolf Stommelen	D	3	-	-	-	-	-	-	-	-	-
François Migault	F	2	-	-	-	-	-	-	-	-	-
Vern Schuppan	AUS	1	-	-	-	-	-	-	-	-	-
Graham Hill	GB	- (1)	-	-	-	-	-	-	-	-	-

HILL GRAND PRIX CARS

Type	Year	Engine	Designer
GH1	1975	Ford DFV V8	Andy Smallman
		Originally Lola T371, renamed Hill GH1	
GH2	1975	Ford DFV V8	Andy Smallman
		Never raced due to closure of team in 1975	

HONDA

GP Debut: 1964 German GP — Bucknum (13th)
Last GP: 1968 Mexican GP — Bonnier (5th), Surtees (retired)
Principal: Soichiro Honda
Base: Tokyo (J), 1964; Amsterdam (NL), 1965-66; Slough (GB), 1967-68

WORLD CHAMPIONSHIP RECORD

GPs Started: 35
Points: 50
Wins: 2 1965 Mexican GP (Ginther),
1967 Italian GP (Surtees)
Pole pos.: 1 1968 Italian GP (Surtees)
Fastest laps: 2 1966 Mexican GP (Ginther),
1968 Belgian GP (Surtees)
Laps/miles in the lead: 79 laps/296 miles
Best World Championship position:
Drivers: 4th in 1967 (Surtees)
Constructors: 4th in 1967

HONDA GRAND PRIX DRIVERS

Driver	Nat	Starts	1st	2nd	3rd	4th	5th	6th	PP	FL	Points
		(DNS/DNQ)									
John Surtees	GB	21	1	1	2	2	1	1	1	1	32
Richie Ginther	USA	11	1	-	-	1	-	2	-	1	14
Ronnie Bucknum	USA	11	-	-	-	-	1	-	-	-	2
Jo Bonnier	S	1	-	-	-	-	1	-	-	-	2
David Hobbs	GB	1	-	-	-	-	-	-	-	-	-
Jo Schlesser	F	1	-	-	-	-	-	-	-	-	-

HONDA GRAND PRIX CARS

Type	Year	Engine	Designer
RA270	1963	Honda RA271 V12	Yoshio Nakamura
			Test chassis, never raced
RA271	1964	Honda RA271 V12	Yoshio Nakamura
RA272	1965	Honda RA271 V12	Yoshio Nakamura
RA273	1966	Honda RA273 V12	Yoshio Nakamura
RA300	1967	Honda RA273 V12	Eric Broadley/
			John Surtees
			Based on Lola T190 Indycar monocoque
RA301	1968	Honda RA273 V12	Eric Broadley/John
			Surtees/Nakamura/
			Derrick White. Further
			modified by Len Terry
RA302	1968	Honda RA302 V8	Yoshio Nakamura
			Air-cooled
1992 car	1992	Honda RA122E V12	-
			Design study built "after hours". Tested but
			never raced. Type number unknown

HWM

HERSHAM AND WALTON MOTORS

GP Debut: 1951 Swiss GP — Moss (8th), Abecassis (retired)
Last GP: 1954 French GP — Macklin (retired)
Principals: John Heath and George Abecassis
Base: Walton-on-Thames (GB)

WORLD CHAMPIONSHIP RECORD

GPs Started: 14
Points: 2
Best result: 5th 1952 Belgian GP (Frère)
Best qualif.: 6th 1952 Swiss GP (Collins)
Best World Championship position:
Drivers: 16th in 1952 (Frère)
Constructors: -

HWM GRAND PRIX DRIVERS

Driver	Nat	Starts	1st	2nd	3rd	4th	5th	6th	PP	FL	Points
		(DNS/DNQ)									
Paul Frère	B	4	-	-	-	1	-	-	-	2
Lance Macklin	GB	12 (1)	-	-	-	-	-	-	-	-
Peter Collins	GB	8 (2)	-	-	-	-	1	-	-	-
Tony Gaze	AUS	3 (1)	-	-	-	-	-	-	-	-
Yves Giraud-Cabantous	F	3	-	-	-	-	-	-	-	-
Duncan Hamilton	GB	3	-	-	-	-	-	-	-	-
George Abecassis	GB	2	-	-	-	-	-	-	-	-
Stirling Moss	GB	2	-	-	-	-	-	-	-	-
Johnny Claes	B	1	-	-	-	-	-	-	-	-
Jack Fairman	GB	1	-	-	-	-	-	-	-	-
John Fitch	USA	1	-	-	-	-	-	-	-	-
Roger Laurent	B	1	-	-	-	-	-	-	-	-

Driver	Nat	Starts	1st	2nd	3rd	4th	5th	6th	PP	FL	Points
		(DNS/DNQ)									
Dries van der Lof	NL	1	-	-	-	-	-	-	-	-
Albert Scherrer	CH	1	-	-	-	-	-	-	-	-
Ted Whiteaway	GB	- (1)	-	-	-	-	-	-	-	-

HWM GRAND PRIX CARS

Type	Year	Engine	Designer
51	1951	Alta F2 S4	John Heath
51/52	1952	Alta F2 S4	John Heath
52	1952	Alta F2 S4	John Heath
53	1953	Alta F2 S4	John Heath
52/53	1953	Alta F2 S4	John Heath
54	1954	Alta GP S4	John Heath

JBW

GP Debut: 1959 British GP — Naylor (retired)
Last GP: 1961 Italian GP — Naylor (retired)
Principal: Brian Naylor
Base: Stockport (GB)

WORLD CHAMPIONSHIP RECORD

GPs Started: 5
Best result: 13th 1960 British GP (Naylor)
Best qualif.: 7th 1960 Italian GP (Naylor)

JBW GRAND PRIX DRIVERS

Driver	Nat	Starts	1st	2nd	3rd	4th	5th	6th	PP	FL	Points
		(DNS/DNQ)									
Brian Naylor	GB	5 (1)	-	-	-	-	-	-	-	-

JBW GRAND PRIX CARS

Type	Year	Engine	Designer
1959	1959	Maserati 250S S4	Fred Wilkinson
1960	1961	Climax FPF S4, Maserati 150S S4	Fred Wilkinson

JORDAN

GP Debut: 1991 United States GP — Gachot (10th)
Latest GP: 1994 Australian GP — Barrichello (4th),
Irvine (retired)
Principal: Eddie Jordan
Base: Silverstone (GB)

WORLD CHAMPIONSHIP RECORD

GPs Started: 64
Points: 45
Best result: 3rd 1994 Pacific GP (Barrichello)
Pole pos.: 1 1994 Belgian GP (Barrichello)
Fastest laps: 1 1991 Hungarian GP (Gachot)
Laps/miles in the lead: 7 laps/26 miles
Best World Championship position:
Drivers: 6th in 1994 (Barrichello)
Constructors: 5th in 1991 and 1994

MAJOR SPONSORS

1991	7Up/Fuji
1992-94	Sasol

JORDAN GRAND PRIX DRIVERS

Driver	Nat	Starts	1st	2nd	3rd	4th	5th	6th	PP	FL	Points
		(DNS/DNQ)									
Rubens Barrichello	BR	31 (1)	-	-	1	5	1	-	1	-	21
Andrea de Cesaris	I	17 (1)	-	-	-	3	1	1	-	-	12
Eddie Irvine	GB	14 (1)	-	-	-	1	1	2	-	-	7
Bertrand Gachot	B	10	-	-	-	-	1	2	-	1	4
Stefano Modena	I	12 (4)	-	-	-	-	-	1	-	-	1
Mauricio Gugelmin	BR	16	-	-	-	-	-	-	-	-	-
Thierry Boutsen	B	10	-	-	-	-	-	-	-	-	-
Alessandro Zanardi	I	3	-	-	-	-	-	-	-	-	-
Roberto Moreno	BR	2	-	-	-	-	-	-	-	-	-
Ivan Capelli	I	1 (1)	-	-	-	-	-	-	-	-	-
Marco Apicella	I	1	-	-	-	-	-	-	-	-	-
Emanuele Naspetti	I	1	-	-	-	-	-	-	-	-	-
Michael Schumacher	D	1	-	-	-	-	-	-	-	-	-
Aguri Suzuki	J	1	-	-	-	-	-	-	-	-	-

JORDAN GRAND PRIX CARS

Type	Year	Engine	Designer
191	1991	Ford HB V8	Gary Anderson
192	1992	Yamaha OX99 V12	Gary Anderson
193	1993	Hart 1035 V10	Gary Anderson
194	1994	Hart 1035 V10	Gary Anderson/Steve Nichols

KAUHSEN

Principal: Willi Kauhsen

WORLD CHAMPIONSHIP RECORD

GPs Started: None
Best qualif.: 27th 1979 Spanish GP (Brancatelli)

KAUHSEN GRAND PRIX DRIVERS

Driver	Nat	Starts	1st	2nd	3rd	4th	5th	6th	PP	FL	Points
		(DNS/DNQ)									
Gianfranco Brancatelli	I	- (2)	-	-	-	-	-	-	-	-	-

KAUHSEN GRAND PRIX CARS

Type	Year	Engine	Designer
WK004	1979	Ford DFV V8	Klaus Kapitza
WK005	1979	Ford DFV V8	Klaus Kapitza

KLENK

Only GP: 1954 German GP   Helfrich (retired)
Principal: Hans Klenk
Base: Stuttgart (D)

WORLD CHAMPIONSHIP RECORD

GPs Started: 1
Best result: No finishes
Best qualif.: 21st 1954 German GP (Helfrich)

KLENK GRAND PRIX DRIVERS

Driver	Nat	Starts	1st	2nd	3rd	4th	5th	6th	PP	FL	Points
		(DNS/DNQ)									
Theo Helfrich	D	1	-	-	-	-	-	-	-	-	-

KLENK GRAND PRIX CARS

Type	Year	Engine	Designer
Meteor	1954	BMW 328 S6	Hans Klenk

KOJIMA

GP Debut: 1976 Japanese GP   Hasemi (11th)
Last GP: 1977 Japanese GP   Hoshino (11th), Takahara (retired)

Principal: Matsuhisa Kojima
Base: Kyoto (J)

WORLD CHAMPIONSHIP RECORD

GPs Started: 2
Best result: 11th 1976 Japanese GP (Hasemi), 1977 Japanese GP (Hoshino)
Best qualif.: 10th 1976 Japanese GP (Hasemi)
Fastest laps: 1 1976 Japanese GP (Hasemi)

KOJIMA GRAND PRIX DRIVERS

Driver	Nat	Starts	1st	2nd	3rd	4th	5th	6th	PP	FL	Points
		(DNS/DNQ)									
Masahiro Hasemi	J	1	-	-	-	-	-	-	-	1	-
Kazuyoshi Hoshino	J	1	-	-	-	-	-	-	-	-	-
Noritake Takahara	J	1	-	-	-	-	-	-	-	-	-

KOJIMA GRAND PRIX CARS

Type	Year	Engine	Designer
KE007	1976	Ford DFV V8	Masao Ono
KE009	1977	Ford DFV V8	Masao Ono

KURTIS

Only GP: 1959 United States GP Ward (retired)
Principal: Frank Kurtis
Base: Glendale, California (USA)

WORLD CHAMPIONSHIP RECORD

GPs Started: 1
Best result: No finishes
Best qualif.: 19th 1959 United States GP (Ward)

KURTIS GRAND PRIX DRIVERS

Driver	Nat	Starts	1st	2nd	3rd	4th	5th	6th	PP	FL	Points
		(DNS/DNQ)									
Rodger Ward	USA	1	-	-	-	-	-	-	-	-	-

KURTIS GRAND PRIX CARS

Type	Year	Engine	Designer
Roadster	1959	Offenhauser S4	Frank Kurtis

LAMBORGHINI

GP Debut: 1991 United States GP Larini (7th)
Last GP: 1991 Australian GP   Larini (retired)
Principal: Mauro Forghieri
Base: Modena (I)

WORLD CHAMPIONSHIP RECORD

GPs Started: 6
Best result: 7th 1991 United States GP (Larini)
Best qualif.: 17th 1991 United States GP (Larini)

LAMBORGHINI GRAND PRIX DRIVERS

Driver	Nat	Starts	1st	2nd	3rd	4th	5th	6th	PP	FL	Points
		(DNS/DNQ)									
Nicola Larini	I	5 (11)	-	-	-	-	-	-	-	-	-
Eric van de Poele	B	1 (15)	-	-	-	-	-	-	-	-	-

LAMBORGHINI GRAND PRIX CARS

Type	Year	Engine	Designer
291	1991	Lamborghini 3512 V12	Mauro Forghieri/Mario Tollentino/Peter Wyss

LANCIA

Cars sold to Ferrari in 1955 and renamed Lancia-Ferrari; also see Ferrari

GP Debut: 1954 Spanish GP   Ascari (retired), Villoresi (retired)
Last GP: 1955 Belgian GP   Castellotti (retired)
Principal: Vincenzo Lancia and Claudio Fogolin (founders in 1906). Gianni Lancia
Base: Turin (I)

WORLD CHAMPIONSHIP RECORD

GPs Started: 4
Points: 9
Best result: 2nd 1955 Monaco GP (Castellotti)
Pole pos.: 2 1954 Spanish GP (Ascari), 1955 Belgian GP (Castellotti)
Fastest laps: 1 1954 Spanish GP (Ascari)
Laps/miles in the lead: 21 laps/62 miles

Best World Championship position:
Drivers: 3rd in 1955 (Castellotti - his 12 points included six for Ferrari)
Constructors: -

LANCIA GRAND PRIX DRIVERS

Driver	Nat	Starts	1st	2nd	3rd	4th	5th	6th	PP	FL	Points
		(DNS/DNQ)									
Eugenio Castellotti	I	3	-	1	-	-	-	-	1	-	6
Luigi Villoresi	I	3	-	-	-	1	-	-	-	-	2
Alberto Ascari	I	3	-	-	-	-	-	-	1	1	1
Louis Chiron	MC	1	-	-	-	-	1	-	-	-	-

LANCIA GRAND PRIX CARS

Type	Year	Engine	Designer
D50	1954	Lancia DS50 V8	Vittorio Jano

LAGO-TALBOT

GP Debut:	1950 British GP	Giraud-Cabantous (4th), Rosier (5th), Étancelin (8th), Claes (11th), Martin (retired)
Last GP:	1951 Spanish GP	Rosier (7th), Étancelin (8th), Claes (retired), Grignard (retired), Giraud-Cabantous (retired), Chiron (retired)
Principal:	Antonio Lago	
Base:	Suresnes (F)	

WORLD CHAMPIONSHIP RECORD

GPs Started: 13
Points: 25
Best result: 3rd 1950 Swiss GP (Rosier), Belgian GP (Rosier)
Best qualif.: 4th 1950 Monaco GP (Étancelin), French GP (Étancelin)
Laps/miles in the lead: 5 laps/44 miles
Best World Championship position:
Drivers: 4th in 1950 (Rosier)
Constructors: -

LAGO-TALBOT GRAND PRIX DRIVERS

Driver	Nat	Starts	1st	2nd	3rd	4th	5th	6th	PP	FL	Points
		(DNS/DNQ)									
Louis Rosier	F	13	-	2	2	1	1	-	-	16
Yves Giraud-Cabantous	F	10	-	-	1	1	-	-	-	5
Philippe Étancelin	F	11	-	-	-	2	-	-	-	3
Eugène Chaboud	F	3	-	-	-	1	-	-	-	1
Johnny Claes	B	13	-	-	-	-	-	-	-	-
Louis Chiron	MC	6	-	-	-	-	1	-	-	-
"Pierre Levegh"	F	6	-	-	-	-	-	-	-	-
Guy Mairesse	F	3	-	-	-	-	-	-	-	-
Raymond Sommer	F	3	-	-	-	-	-	-	-	-
Duncan Hamilton	GB	2	-	-	-	-	-	-	-	-
Henri Louveau	F	2	-	-	-	-	-	-	-	-
Eugène Martin	F	2	-	-	-	-	-	-	-	-
Jacques Swaters	B	2	-	-	-	-	-	-	-	-
José Froilan Gonzalez	RA	1	-	-	-	-	-	-	-	-
Georges Grignard	F	1	-	-	-	-	-	-	-	-
André Pilette	B	1	-	-	-	1	-	-	-	-
Charles Pozzi	F	1	-	-	-	1	-	-	-	-
Harry Schell	USA	1	-	-	-	-	-	-	-	-

LAGO-TALBOT GRAND PRIX CARS

Type	Year	Engine	Designer
T26C	1950*	Talbot 23CV S6	Antonio Lago/Carlo Marchetti
T26C-GS	1950*	Talbot 23CV S6	Antonio Lago/Carlo Marchetti
T26C-DA	1950	Talbot 23CV S6	Antonio Lago/Carlo Marchetti

*Championship debut, the T26C first raced in 1948 and the T26C-GS in 1939

LARROUSSE

GP Debut:	1992 South African GP	Katayama (12th), Gachot (retired)
Latest GP:	1994 Australian GP	Noda (retired), Deletraz (retired)
Principal:	Gérard Larrousse	
Base:	Constructor: Bicester (GB); Team: Signes, near Circuit Paul Ricard (F)	

WORLD CHAMPIONSHIP RECORD

GPs Started: 48
Points: 6
Best result: 5th 1993 San Marino GP (Alliot)
Best qualif.: 9th 1993 French GP (Comas)
Best World Championship position:
Drivers: 17th in 1992 (Gachot), and 1993 (Alliot)
Constructors: 10th in 1993

MAJOR SPONSORS

1992	Venturi, Central Park
1993	Central Park
1994	Tourtel, Kronenbourg

LARROUSSE GRAND PRIX DRIVERS

Driver	Nat	Starts	1st	2nd	3rd	4th	5th	6th	PP	FL	Points
		(DNS/DNQ)									
Erik Comas	F	31	-	-	-	-	-	3	-	-	3
Philippe Alliot	F	15	-	-	-	1	-	-	-	-	2
Bertrand Gachot	B	16	-	-	-	-	1	-	-	-	1
Ukyo Katayama	J	14 (2)	-	-	-	-	-	-	-	-	-
Olivier Beretta	MC	9 (1)	-	-	-	-	-	-	-	-	-
Hideki Noda	J	3	-	-	-	-	-	-	-	-	-
Yannick Dalmas	F	2	-	-	-	-	-	-	-	-	-
Toshio Suzuki	J	2	-	-	-	-	-	-	-	-	-
Jean-Denis Deletraz	CH	1	-	-	-	-	-	-	-	-	-

Note: Results and records do not include those achieved in Equipe Larrousse Lolas

LARROUSSE GRAND PRIX CARS

Type	Year	Engine	Designer
LC92	1992	Lamborghini 3512 V12	Tino Belli/Tim Holloway/Robin Herd
LH93	1993	Lamborghini 3512 V12	Tino Belli/Tim Holloway/Robin Herd
LH94	1994	Ford HB V8	Tino Belli/Tim Holloway/Robin Herd

LDS

LD SERRURIER

GP Debut:	1962 South African GP	Serrurier (retired)
Last GP:	1968 South African GP	Tingle (retired)
Principal:	Doug Serrurier	

WORLD CHAMPIONSHIP RECORD

GPs Started: 5
Best result: 11th 1963 South African GP (Serrurier)
Best qualif.: 14th 1962 South African GP (Serrurier), 1967 South African GP (Tingle)

LDS GRAND PRIX DRIVERS

Driver	Nat	Starts	1st	2nd	3rd	4th	5th	6th	PP	FL	Points
		(DNS/DNQ)									
Sam Tingle	RSR	4	-	-	-	-	-	-	-	-	-
Doug Serrurier	ZA	2 (1)	-	-	-	-	-	-	-	-	-
Jackie Pretorius	ZA	- (1)	-	-	-	-	-	-	-	-	-

LDS GRAND PRIX CARS

Type	Year	Engine	Designer
Mk1	1962	Alfa Romeo	Doug Serrurier
Mk2	1965	Climax FPF S4	Doug Serrurier
Mk3	1967	Climax FPF S4	Doug Serrurier
Mk5	1968	Repco V8	Doug Serrurier

LEC

GP Debut:	1977 Belgian GP	Purley (13th)
Last GP:	1977 French GP	Purley (retired)
Principal:	David Purley	
Base:	Bognor Regis (GB)	

WORLD CHAMPIONSHIP RECORD

GPs Started: 3
Best result: 13th 1977 Belgian GP (Purley)
Best qualif.: 19th 1977 Swedish GP (Purley)

MAJOR SPONSORS

1977	Lec Refrigeration, Mopar

LEC GRAND PRIX DRIVERS

Driver	Nat	Starts	1st	2nd	3rd	4th	5th	6th	PP	FL	Points
		(DNS/DNQ)									
David Purley	GB	3 (2)	-	-	-	-	-	-	-	-	-

LEC GRAND PRIX CARS

Type	Year	Engine	Designer
CRP1	1977	Ford DFV V8	Mike Pilbeam

LEYTON HOUSE

See March

LIFE

Principal: Ernesto Vita

WORLD CHAMPIONSHIP RECORD

GPs Started: None
Best qualif.: 33rd 1990 San Marino GP (Giacomelli), Belgian GP (Giacomelli), Italian GP (Giacomelli), Spanish GP (Giacomelli)

LIFE GRAND PRIX DRIVERS

Driver	Nat	Starts (DNS/DNQ)	1st	2nd	3rd	4th	5th	6th	PP	FL	Points
Bruno Giacomelli	I	- (12)	-	-	-	-	-	-	-	-	-
Gary Brabham	AUS	- (2)	-	-	-	-	-	-	-	-	-

LIFE GRAND PRIX CARS

Type	Year	Engine	Designer
F190	1990	Life W12, Judd CV V8	Richard Divila/Gianni Marelli Designed and built by First Racing

LIGIER

GP Debut:	1976 Brazilian GP	Laffite (retired)	
Latest GP:	1994 Australian GP	Panis (5th), Lagorce (11th)	
Principal:	Guy Ligier, 1976-92; Cyril de Rouvre, 1993-94; Flavio Briatore/Benetton Formula, 1994 to date		
Base:	Vichy (F), 1976-88; Magny Cours (F), 1989 to date		

WORLD CHAMPIONSHIP RECORD

GPs Started: 293
Points: 349
Wins: 8 1977 Swedish GP (Laffite), 1979 Argentinian GP (Laffite), Brazilian GP (Laffite), Spanish GP (Depailler), 1980 Belgian GP (Pironi), German GP (Laffite), 1981 Austrian GP (Laffite), Canadian GP (Laffite)
Pole pos.: 9 1976 Italian GP (Laffite), 1979 Argentinian GP (Laffite), Brazilian GP (Laffite), Spanish GP (Laffite), Belgian GP (Laffite), 1980 Monaco GP (Pironi), French GP (Laffite), British GP (Pironi), 1981 Spanish GP (Laffite)
Fastest laps: 9 1977 Spanish GP (Laffite), 1979 Argentinian GP (Laffite), Brazilian GP (Laffite), Monaco GP (Depailler), 1980 Belgian GP (Laffite), British GP (Pironi), Canadian GP (Pironi), 1981 Austrian GP (Laffite), 1985 European GP (Laffite)
Laps/miles in the lead: 521 laps/1525 miles

Best World Championship position:
Drivers: 4th in 1979, 1980 and 1981 (all Laffite)
Constructors: 2nd in 1980

MAJOR SPONSORS

1976-80	Gitanes
1981-82	Talbot, Gitanes
1983	Gitanes
1984	LOTO, Gitanes
1985	Gitanes, Candy
1986-91	LOTO, Gitanes
1992	Gitanes Blondes, LOTO
1993 to date	Gitanes Blondes

LIGIER GRAND PRIX DRIVERS

Driver	Nat	Starts (DNS/DNQ)	1st	2nd	3rd	4th	5th	6th	PP	FL	Points
Jacques Laffite	F	132	6	9	16	4	7	8	7	6	206
Didier Pironi	F	14	1	1	3	1	-	2	2	2	32
Patrick Depailler	F	7	1	1	-	1	2	-	-	1	22

Driver	Nat	Starts (DNS/DNQ)	1st	2nd	3rd	4th	5th	6th	PP	FL	Points
René Arnoux	F	53 (10)	-	-	-	3	3	2	-	-	17
Eddie Cheever	USA	14 (1)	-	1	2	-	-	1	-	-	15
Martin Brundle	GB	16	-	-	1	-	3	3	-	-	13
Mark Blundell	GB	16	-	-	2	-	1	-	-	-	10
Olivier Panis	F	16	-	1	-	-	1	1	-	-	9
Andrea de Cesaris	I	27	-	-	-	1	1	1	-	-	6
Erik Comas	F	28 (4)	-	-	-	-	1	2	-	-	4
Eric Bernard	F	13	-	-	1	-	-	-	-	-	4
Philippe Streiff	F	4	-	-	1	-	-	-	-	-	4
Jacky Ickx	B	8	-	-	-	-	1	1	-	-	3
Thierry Boutsen	B	32	-	-	-	-	1	-	-	-	2
Philippe Alliot	F	21 (2)	-	-	-	-	-	1	-	-	1
Olivier Grouillard	F	12 (4)	-	-	-	-	1	-	-	-	1
Jean-Pierre Jarier	F	17 (1)	-	-	-	-	-	-	-	-	-
Nicola Larini	F	16	-	-	-	-	-	-	-	-	-
François Hesnault	F	15 (1)	-	-	-	-	-	-	-	-	-
Piercarlo Ghinzani	I	14 (1)	-	-	-	-	-	-	-	-	-
Raul Boesel	BR	13 (2)	-	-	-	-	-	-	-	-	-
Stefan Johansson	S	10 (6)	-	-	-	-	-	-	-	-	-
Patrick Tambay	F	8	-	-	-	-	-	-	-	-	-
Jean-Pierre Jabouille	F	3 (3)	-	-	-	-	-	-	-	-	-
Franck Lagorce	F	2	-	-	-	-	-	-	-	-	-
Johnny Herbert	GB	1	-	-	-	-	-	-	-	-	-

LIGIER GRAND PRIX CARS

Type	Year	Engine	Designer
JS5	1976	Matra MS73 V12	Gérard Ducarouge/Michel Beaujon/Paul Carillo
JS7	1977	Matra MS76 V12	Gérard Ducarouge/Michel Beaujon/Paul Carillo
JS7/9	1978	Matra MS76 V12	Gérard Ducarouge/Michel Beaujon/Paul Carillo
JS9	1978	Matra MS78 V12	Gérard Ducarouge/Michel Beaujon/Paul Carillo
JS11	1979	Ford DFV V8	Gérard Ducarouge/Michel Beaujon/Paul Carillo
JS11/15	1980	Ford DFV V8	Gérard Ducarouge/Michel Beaujon
JS17*	1981	Matra MS81 V12	Gérard Ducarouge/Michel Beaujon
JS19*	1982	Matra MS81 V12	Michel Beaujon/Jean-Pierre Jabouille
JS21	1983	Ford DFV V8	Michel Beaujon/Claude Galopin
JS23	1984	Renault EF4 V6 tc	Michel Beaujon/Claude Galopin
JS23B	1984	Renault EF4 V6 tc	Michel Beaujon/Claude Galopin
JS25	1985	Renault EF4B V6 tc	Michel Têtu/Michel Beaujon
JS27	1986	Renault EF4B/EF15 V6 tc	Michel Têtu
JS29**	1987	Alfa Romeo 415T S4 tc	Michel Têtu
JS29B	1987	Megatron BMW M12/13 S4 tc	Michel Têtu
JS29C	1987	Megatron BMW M12/13 S4 tc	Michel Têtu
JS31	1988	Judd CV V8	Michel Têtu
JS33	1989	Ford DFR V8	Michel Beaujon/Richard Divila/Ken Anderson
JS33B	1990	Ford DFR V8	Michel Beaujon/Richard Divila/Ken Anderson
JS35	1991	Lamborghini 3512 V12	Michel Beaujon/Claude Galopin/Richard Divila
JS35B	1991	Lamborghini 3512 V12	Michel Beaujon/Frank Dernie
JS37	1992	Renault RS3 V10	Frank Dernie
JS39	1993	Renault RS5 V10	Gérard Ducarouge/John Davis
JS39B	1994	Renault RS5 V10	Gérard Ducarouge/John Davis

*officially Talbot-Ligier. Note: "JS" designation refers to Jo Schlesser
**Never raced due to Alfa Romeo withdrawing after Ligier's René Arnoux publicly criticized the poor performance of their new engine

LOLA

GP Debut:	1962 Dutch GP	Salvadori (retired), Surtees (retired)
Last GP:	1993 Portuguese GP	Badoer (14th), Alboreto (retired)
Principal:	Eric Broadley	
Base:	Bromley (GB), 1956-65; Slough (GB), 1965-70; Huntingdon (GB), 1970 to date	

WORLD CHAMPIONSHIP RECORD

GPs Started: 149
Points: 43
Best result: 2nd 1962 British GP (Surtees), German GP (Surtees)
Pole pos.: 1 1962 Dutch GP (Surtees)

Best World Championship position:
Drivers: 4th in 1962 (Surtees)
Constructors: 4th in 1962

LOLA GRAND PRIX DRIVERS

Driver	Nat	Starts (DNS/DNQ)	1st	2nd	3rd	4th	5th	6th	PP	FL	Points
John Surtees	GB	9	-	2	-	1	2	-	1	-	19
Aguri Suzuki	J	28 (5)	-	-	1	-	-	3	-	-	7
Eric Bernard	F	31 (2)	-	-	-	1	-	3	-	-	6
Philippe Alliot	F	46 (1)	-	-	-	-	-	4	-	-	4
Alan Jones	AUS	19 (1)	-	-	-	1	-	1	-	-	4
Patrick Tambay	F	14 (1)	-	-	-	-	1	-	-	-	2
Graham Hill	GB	17 (1)	-	-	-	-	1	-	-	-	1
Yannick Dalmas	F	16 (7)	-	-	-	1	-	-	-	-	-
Michele Alboreto	I	14 (8)	-	-	-	-	-	-	-	-	-
Luca Badoer	I	12 (2)	-	-	-	-	-	-	-	-	-
Guy Edwards	GB	7 (2)	-	-	-	-	-	-	-	-	-
Roy Salvadori	GB	7 (1)	-	-	-	-	-	-	-	-	-
Rolf Stommelen	D	7	-	-	-	-	-	-	-	-	-
Chris Amon	NZ	5 (2)	-	-	-	-	-	-	-	-	-
Bob Anderson	RSR	2	-	-	-	-	-	-	-	-	-
Masten Gregory	USA	2	-	-	-	-	-	-	-	-	-
Hubert Hahne	D	2	-	-	-	-	-	-	-	-	-
Lucien Bianchi	B	1	-	-	-	-	-	-	-	-	-
John Campbell-Jones	GB	1	-	-	-	-	-	-	-	-	-
Eddie Cheever	USA	1	-	-	-	-	-	-	-	-	-
Peter Gethin	GB	1	-	-	-	-	-	-	-	-	-
Mike Hailwood	GB	1	-	-	-	-	-	-	-	-	-
David Hobbs	GB	1	-	-	-	-	-	-	-	-	-
Maurice Trintignant	F	1	-	-	-	-	-	-	-	-	-
Bertrand Gachot	B	- (1)	-	-	-	-	-	-	-	-	-
Pierre-Henri Raphanel	F	- (1)	-	-	-	-	-	-	-	-	-
Brian Redman	GB	- (1)	-	-	-	-	-	-	-	-	-

LOLA GRAND PRIX CARS

Type	Year	Engine	Designer
Mk4	1962	Climax FMWV V8	Eric Broadley
Mk4A	1962	Climax FMWV V8	Eric Broadley
T100	1967	BMW S4	Eric Broadley
			F2 car
T370	1974	Ford DFV V8	Andy Smallman
T371	1975	Ford DFV V8	Andy Smallman
			Renamed Hill GH1
THL1*	1985	Hart 415T S4 tc	Neil Oatley/Ross Brawn/ John Baldwin
THL2*	1986	Ford TEC V6 tc	Neil Oatley/Ross Brawn/ John Baldwin
LC87	1987	Ford DFZ V8	Eric Broadley/Ralph Bellamy
LC88	1988	Ford DFZ V8	Eric Broadley/Chris Murphy
LC88C	1989	Lamborghini 3512 V12	Eric Broadley/Chris Murphy
LC89	1989	Lamborghini 3512 V12	Eric Broadley/Chris Murphy/ Gérard Ducarouge
90	1990	Lamborghini 3512 V12	Eric Broadley/Chris Murphy/ Gérard Ducarouge
L91	1991	Ford DFR V8	Eric Broadley/Mark Williams/Bruce Ashmore
T93/30	1993	Ferrari V12	Eric Broadley

*Designed and built for Carl Haas by FORCE in Colnbrook. As Lola's North American importer, Haas named them Lolas

LOTUS

GP Debut:	1958 Monaco GP	Allison (6th), G Hill (retired)
Last GP:	1994 Australian GP	Zanardi (retired), Salo (retired)
Principal:	Colin Chapman, 1952-82; Peter Warr, 1982-90; Tony Rudd, 1990; Peter Collins and Peter Wright, 1991-94; placed in receivership, purchased by David Hunt, 1994.	
Base:	Hornsey, North London (GB), 1952-59; Cheshunt, Hertfordshire (GB), 1959-67; Wymondham, Norfolk (GB), 1967-94	

WORLD CHAMPIONSHIP RECORD

GPs Started: 491
Points: 1514
Wins: 79 1960 Monaco GP (Moss), United States GP (Moss), 1961 Monaco GP (Moss), German GP (Moss), United States GP (Ireland), 1962 Belgian GP (Clark), British GP (Clark), United States GP (Clark), 1963 Belgian GP (Clark), Dutch GP (Clark), French GP (Clark), British GP (Clark), Italian GP (Clark), Mexican GP (Clark), South African GP (Clark), 1964 Dutch GP (Clark), Belgian GP (Clark), British GP (Clark), 1965 South African GP (Clark), Belgian GP (Clark), French GP (Clark), British GP (Clark), Dutch GP (Clark), German GP (Clark), 1966 United States GP (Clark), 1967 Dutch GP (Clark), British GP (Clark), United States GP (Clark), Mexican GP (Clark), 1968 South African GP (Clark), Spanish GP (Hill), Monaco GP (Hill), British GP (Siffert), Mexican GP (Hill), 1969 Monaco GP (Hill), United States GP (Rindt), 1970 Monaco GP (Rindt), Dutch GP (Rindt), French GP (Rindt), British GP (Rindt), German GP (Rindt), United States GP (Fittipaldi), 1972 Spanish GP (Fittipaldi), Belgian GP (Fittipaldi), British GP (Fittipaldi), Austrian GP (Fittipaldi), Italian GP (Fittipaldi), 1973 Argentinian GP (Fittipaldi), Brazilian GP (Fittipaldi), Spanish GP (Fittipaldi), French GP (Peterson), Austrian GP (Peterson), Italian GP (Peterson), United States GP (Peterson), 1974 Monaco GP (Peterson), French GP (Peterson), Italian GP (Peterson), 1976 Japanese GP (Andretti), 1977 Long Beach GP (Andretti), Spanish GP (Andretti), Belgian GP (Nilsson), French GP (Andretti), Italian GP (Andretti), 1978 Argentinian GP (Andretti), South African GP (Peterson), Belgian GP (Andretti), Spanish GP (Andretti), French GP (Andretti), German GP (Andretti), Austrian GP (Peterson), Dutch GP (Andretti), 1982 Austrian GP (de Angelis), 1985 Portuguese GP (Senna), San Marino GP (de Angelis), Belgian GP (Senna), 1986 Spanish GP (Senna), Detroit GP (Senna), 1987 Monaco GP (Senna), Detroit GP (Senna)

Pole pos.: 107 1960 Monaco GP (Moss), Dutch GP (Moss), Portuguese GP (Surtees), United States GP (Moss), 1961 Monaco GP (Moss), 1962 Monaco GP (Clark), French GP (Clark), British GP (Clark), Italian GP (Clark), United States GP (Clark), South African GP (Clark), 1963 Monaco GP (Clark), Dutch GP (Clark), French GP (Clark), British GP (Clark), German GP (Clark), Mexican GP (Clark), South African GP (Clark), 1964 Monaco GP (Clark), French GP (Clark), British GP (Clark), United States GP (Clark), Mexican GP (Clark), 1965 South African GP (Clark), French GP (Clark), British GP (Clark), German GP (Clark), Italian GP (Clark), Mexican GP (Clark), 1966 Monaco GP (Clark), German GP (Clark), 1967 Dutch GP (Hill), Belgian GP (Clark), French GP (Hill), British GP (Clark), German GP (Clark), Canadian GP (Clark), Italian GP (Clark), United States GP (Hill), Mexican GP (Clark), 1968 South African GP (Clark), Monaco GP (Hill), British GP (Hill), United States GP (Andretti), Mexican GP (Siffert), 1969 Spanish GP (Rindt), Dutch GP (Rindt), British GP (Rindt), Italian GP (Rindt), United States GP (Rindt), 1970 Dutch GP (Rindt), British GP (Rindt), Austrian GP (Rindt), 1972 Monaco GP (Fittipaldi), Belgian GP (Fittipaldi), Austrian GP (Fittipaldi), 1973 Brazilian GP (Peterson), Spanish GP (Peterson), Belgian GP (Peterson), Swedish GP (Peterson), British GP (Peterson), Dutch GP (Peterson), Austrian GP (Fittipaldi),

Italian GP (Peterson), Canadian GP (Peterson), United States GP (Peterson), 1974 Argentinian GP (Peterson), 1976 Japanese GP (Andretti), 1977 Spanish GP (Andretti), Belgian GP (Andretti), Swedish GP (Andretti), French GP (Andretti), Dutch GP (Andretti), Canadian GP (Andretti), Japanese GP (Andretti), 1978 Argentinian GP (Andretti), Brazilian GP (Peterson), Belgian GP (Andretti), Spanish GP (Andretti), Swedish GP (Andretti), British GP (Peterson), German GP (Andretti), Austrian GP (Peterson), Dutch GP (Andretti), Italian GP (Andretti), United States GP (Andretti), Canadian GP (Jarier), 1983 European GP (de Angelis), 1984 Brazilian GP (de Angelis), Dallas GP (Mansell), 1985 Portuguese GP (Senna), San Marino GP (Senna), Monaco GP, Canadian GP (de Angelis), Detroit GP (Senna), Italian GP (Senna), European GP (Senna), Australian GP (Senna), 1986 Brazilian GP (Senna), Spanish GP (Senna), San Marino GP (Senna), Detroit GP (Senna), French GP (Senna), Hungarian GP (Senna), Portuguese GP (Senna), Mexican GP (Senna), 1987 San Marino GP (Senna)

Fastest laps: 71 1960 Dutch GP (Moss), Belgian GP (Ireland), Portuguese GP (Surtees), 1961 Monaco GP (Moss), Dutch GP (Clark), 1962 Monaco GP (Clark), Belgian GP (Clark), British GP (Clark), United States GP (Clark), South African GP (Clark), 1963 Belgian GP (Clark), Dutch GP (Clark), French GP (Clark), Italian GP (Clark), United States GP (Clark), Mexican GP (Clark), 1964 Dutch GP (Clark), British GP (Clark), United States GP (Clark), Mexican GP (Clark), 1965 South African GP (Clark), Belgian GP (Clark), French GP (Clark), Dutch GP (Clark), German GP (Clark), Italian GP (Clark), 1967 Monaco GP (Clark), Dutch GP (Clark), French GP (G Hill), Canadian GP (Clark), Italian GP (Clark), United States GP (G Hill), Mexican GP (Clark), 1968 South African GP (Clark), British GP (Siffert), Italian GP (Oliver), Canadian GP (Siffert), Mexican GP (Siffert), 1969 Spanish GP (Rindt), United States GP (Rindt), 1970 Monaco GP (Rindt), 1973 Argentinian GP (Fittipaldi), Brazilian GP (Fittipaldi), South African GP (Fittipaldi), Spanish GP (Peterson), Monaco GP (Fittipaldi), Dutch GP (Peterson), Canadian GP (Fittipaldi), 1974 Monaco GP (Peterson), Dutch GP (Peterson), 1976 Swedish GP (Andretti), 1977 Belgian GP (Nilsson), Swedish GP (Andretti), French GP (Andretti), Italian GP (Andretti), Canadian GP (Andretti), 1978 South African GP (Andretti), Belgian GP (Peterson), Spanish GP (Andretti), German GP (Peterson), Austrian GP (Peterson), Italian GP (Andretti), United States GP (Jarier), 1983 European GP (Mansell), 1985 Portuguese GP (Senna), Canadian GP (Senna), Detroit GP (Senna), 1987 Monaco GP (Senna), Detroit GP (Senna), Italian GP (Senna), 1989 Australian GP (Nakajima)

Laps/miles in the lead: 5498 laps/16285 miles

World Champions:

Drivers: Six times - 1963 (Clark), 1965 (Clark), 1968 (G Hill), 1970 (Rindt), 1972 (Fittipaldi) and 1978 (Andretti)

Constructors: Seven times - 1963, 1965, 1968, 1970, 1972, 1973 and 1978

MAJOR SPONSORS

1968-71	Gold Leaf
1972-77	John Player Special
1978	John Player Special, Olympus
1979	Martini
1980-81	Essex, John Player Special, Courage (British GP only)
1982-84	John Player Special
1985	John Player Special, Olympus
1986	John Player Special, deLonghi
1987	Camel, deLonghi
1988	Camel, Epson
1989	Camel, Epson, PIAA
1990	Camel
1992-93	Castrol, Hitachi
1994	Hitachi, Loctite, Miller Genuine Draft

LOTUS GRAND PRIX DRIVERS

Driver	Nat	Starts (DNS/DNQ)	1st	2nd	3rd	4th	5th	6th	PP	FL	Points
Jim Clark	GB	72 (1)	25	1	6	4	3	1	33	28	274
Mario Andretti	USA	79 (1)	11	2	3	3	6	3	17	8	147
Ronnie Peterson	S	59	9	6	3	3	3	1	13	7	144
Emerson Fittipaldi	BR	42 (1)	9	6	5	1	1	2	4	5	144
Ayrton Senna	BR	48	6	10	6	2	3	-	16	6	150
Jochen Rindt	A	19 (1)	6	1	1	1	-	-	8	3	67
Graham Hill	GB	60 (1)	4	6	-	4	1	4	5	2	89
Stirling Moss	GB	12 (1)	4	-	-	2	-	-	4	2	40
Elio de Angelis	I	90	2	2	5	10	17	6	3	-	119
Innes Ireland	GB	36 (3)	1	2	1	2	2	2	-	1	37
Gunnar Nilsson	S	31 (1)	1	-	3	1	3	1	-	1	31
Jo Siffert	CH	35 (2)	1	1	1	1	2	2	1	3	28
Nigel Mansell	GB	59 (2)	-	2	-	5	4	1	4	1	38
Nelson Piquet	BR	31 (1)	-	-	3	5	3	1	-	-	34
Carlos Reutemann	RA	15	-	2	2	1	1	-	-	-	25
Mike Spence	GB	24 (1)	-	1	3	2	1	-	-	-	18
Jacky Ickx	B	24	-	1	2	-	2	-	-	-	15
Johnny Herbert	GB	54 (1)	-	-	-	3	1	2	-	-	13
Mika Hakkinen	SF	30 (2)	-	-	-	2	2	3	-	-	13
Reine Wisell	S	14	-	-	1	2	1	1	-	-	13
Peter Arundell	GB	11 (2)	-	-	2	1	-	1	-	-	12
Satoru Nakajima	J	43 (5)	-	-	-	2	1	3	-	1	11
Trevor Taylor	GB	20	-	1	-	-	-	1	-	-	7
Jackie Oliver	GB	8 (2)	-	-	1	-	1	-	-	1	6
John Surtees	GB	4	-	1	-	-	-	-	1	1	6
Richard Attwood	GB	9	-	-	-	1	-	2	-	-	5
Derek Warwick	GB	16	-	-	-	-	1	1	-	-	3
Johnny Dumfries	GB	15 (1)	-	-	-	-	1	1	-	-	3
Jim Hall	USA	11 (1)	-	-	-	-	1	1	-	-	3
Cliff Allison	GB	9 (1)	-	-	-	1	1	2	-	-	3
Jack Brabham	AUS	6	-	-	-	-	1	1	-	-	3
John Miles	GB	12 (3)	-	-	-	-	1	-	-	-	2
Chris Amon	NZ	11 (1)	-	-	-	-	1	-	-	-	2
Walt Hansgen	USA	1	-	-	-	-	1	-	-	-	2
Alessandro Zanardi	I	21 (1)	-	-	-	-	-	1	-	-	1
Hector Rebaque	MEX	18 (9)	-	-	-	-	-	1	-	-	1
Masten Gregory	USA	11 (1)	-	-	-	-	-	1	-	-	1
Mike Hailwood	GB	11	-	-	-	-	-	1	-	-	1
Julian Bailey	GB	1 (3)	-	-	-	-	-	1	-	-	1
Neville Lederle	ZA	1 (1)	-	-	-	-	-	1	-	-	1
Ron Flockhart	GB	1	-	-	-	-	-	1	-	-	1
Martin Donnelly	GB	12 (2)	-	-	-	-	-	-	-	-	-
Dave Walker	AUS	11	-	-	-	-	-	-	-	-	-
Pedro Lamy	P	8	-	-	-	-	-	-	-	-	-
Alan Stacey	GB	7	-	-	-	-	-	-	-	-	-
Maurice Trintignant	F	7	-	-	-	-	-	-	-	-	-
Pete Lovely	USA	6 (4)	-	-	-	-	-	-	-	-	-
Dave Charlton	ZA	6 (3)	-	-	-	-	-	-	-	-	-
Pedro Rodriguez	MEX	6	-	-	-	-	-	-	-	-	-
Moises Solana	MEX	6	-	-	-	-	-	-	-	-	-
Peter Revson	USA	4 (2)	-	-	-	-	-	-	-	-	-
Wolfgang Seidel	D	4 (2)	-	-	-	-	-	-	-	-	-
Lucien Bianchi	B	4	-	-	-	-	-	-	-	-	-
Gerry Ashmore	GB	3 (1)	-	-	-	-	-	-	-	-	-
Henry Taylor	GB	3 (1)	-	-	-	-	-	-	-	-	-
Tony Maggs	ZA	3	-	-	-	-	-	-	-	-	-
Ian Burgess	GB	2 (2)	-	-	-	-	-	-	-	-	-
Brian Henton	GB	2 (1)	-	-	-	-	-	-	-	-	-
Tony Marsh	GB	2 (1)	-	-	-	-	-	-	-	-	-
Michel May	CH	2 (1)	-	-	-	-	-	-	-	-	-
Gerhard Mitter	D	2 (1)	-	-	-	-	-	-	-	-	-
Tim Parnell	GB	2 (1)	-	-	-	-	-	-	-	-	-
Ernest Pieterse	ZA	2 (1)	-	-	-	-	-	-	-	-	-
David Piper	GB	2 (1)	-	-	-	-	-	-	-	-	-
Philippe Adams	B	2	-	-	-	-	-	-	-	-	-
Jo Bonnier	S	2	-	-	-	-	-	-	-	-	-
Piers Courage	GB	2	-	-	-	-	-	-	-	-	-
Jim Crawford	GB	2	-	-	-	-	-	-	-	-	-
Mike Fisher	USA	2	-	-	-	-	-	-	-	-	-
Paul Hawkins	AUS	2	-	-	-	-	-	-	-	-	-
Jean-Pierre Jarier	F	2	-	-	-	-	-	-	1	1	-
John Love	RSR	2	-	-	-	-	-	-	-	-	-
Willy Mairesse	B	2	-	-	-	-	-	-	-	-	-

Driver	Nat	Starts (DNS/DNQ)	1st	2nd	3rd	4th	5th	6th	PP	FL	Points
"Geki" Russo	I	2	-	-	-	-	-	-	-	-	-
Mika Salo	SF	2	-	-	-	-	-	-	-	-	-
Hap Sharp	USA	2	-	-	-	-	-	-	-	-	-
Jay Chamberlain	USA	1 (2)	-	-	-	-	-	-	-	-	-
Bernard Collomb	F	1 (2)	-	-	-	-	-	-	-	-	-
Tony Shelly	NZ	1 (2)	-	-	-	-	-	-	-	-	-
Paddy Driver	ZA	1 (1)	-	-	-	-	-	-	-	-	-
Bob Evans	GB	1 (1)	-	-	-	-	-	-	-	-	-
Phil Hill	USA	1 (1)	-	-	-	-	-	-	-	-	-
Brausch Niemann	ZA	1 (1)	-	-	-	-	-	-	-	-	-
Nino Vaccarella	I	1 (1)	-	-	-	-	-	-	-	-	-
Giancarlo Baghetti	I	1	-	-	-	-	-	-	-	-	-
Eric Bernard	F	1	-	-	-	-	-	-	-	-	-
Bob Bondurant	USA	1	-	-	-	-	-	-	-	-	-
Bill Brack	CDN	1	-	-	-	-	-	-	-	-	-
Ivor Bueb	GB	1	-	-	-	-	-	-	-	-	-
John Campbell-Jones	GB	1	-	-	-	-	-	-	-	-	-
Olivier Gendebien	B	1	-	-	-	-	-	-	-	-	-
Bruce Halford	GB	1	-	-	-	-	-	-	-	-	-
Chris Irwin	GB	1	-	-	-	-	-	-	-	-	-
Eddie Keizan	ZA	1	-	-	-	-	-	-	-	-	-
Geoff Lees	GB	1	-	-	-	-	-	-	-	-	-
Roger Penske	USA	1	-	-	-	-	-	-	-	-	-
Alberto Rodriguez Larreta	RA	1	-	-	-	-	-	-	-	-	-
Lloyd Ruby	USA	1	-	-	-	-	-	-	-	-	-
Peter Ryan	CDN	1	-	-	-	-	-	-	-	-	-
Ian Scheckter	ZA	1	-	-	-	-	-	-	-	-	-
Tim Schenken	AUS	1	-	-	-	-	-	-	-	-	-
Heinz Schiller	CH	1	-	-	-	-	-	-	-	-	-
Rob Schroeder	USA	1	-	-	-	-	-	-	-	-	-
Gaetano Starrabba	I	1	-	-	-	-	-	-	-	-	-
Rolf Stommelen	D	1	-	-	-	-	-	-	-	-	-
Guy Tunmer	ZA	1	-	-	-	-	-	-	-	-	-
Rodger Ward	USA	1	-	-	-	-	-	-	-	-	-
John Watson	GB	1	-	-	-	-	-	-	-	-	-
Eppie Wietzes	CDN	1	-	-	-	-	-	-	-	-	-
Michael Bartels	D	- (4)	-	-	-	-	-	-	-	-	-
Alex Soler-Roig	E	- (3)	-	-	-	-	-	-	-	-	-
André Pilette	B	- (2)	-	-	-	-	-	-	-	-	-
Brian Gubby	GB	- (1)	-	-	-	-	-	-	-	-	-
Dan Gurney	USA	- (1)	-	-	-	-	-	-	-	-	-
Hans Herrmann	D	- (1)	-	-	-	-	-	-	-	-	-
Kurt Kuhnke	D	- (1)	-	-	-	-	-	-	-	-	-
Roberto Moreno	BR	- (1)	-	-	-	-	-	-	-	-	-
Ernesto Prinoth	I	- (1)	-	-	-	-	-	-	-	-	-
Clive Puzey	ZA	- (1)	-	-	-	-	-	-	-	-	-
Brian Redman	GB	- (1)	-	-	-	-	-	-	-	-	-
Günther Seifert	D	- (1)	-	-	-	-	-	-	-	-	-
Mike Taylor	GB	- (1)	-	-	-	-	-	-	-	-	-

LOTUS GRAND PRIX CARS

Type	Year	Engine	Designer
12	1958	Climax FPF S4	Colin Chapman
16	1958	Climax FPF S4	Colin Chapman
18	1960	Climax FPF S4, Maserati 250S S4, Borgward S4	Colin Chapman
18/21	1961	Climax FPF S4	Colin Chapman
20	1965	Ford 109E S4	Colin Chapman Formula Junior car
21	1961	Climax FPF S4	Colin Chapman
22	1963	Ford 109E S4	Colin Chapman Formula Junior car
24	1962	Climax FMWV V8, BRM 56 V8	Colin Chapman
25	1962	Climax FMWV V8, BRM 56 V8	Colin Chapman First monocoque Lotus
33	1964	Climax FMWV V8, BRM 56 V8	Len Terry/ Colin Chapman
43	1966	BRM 75 H16	Colin Chapman
44	1966	Ford SCA S4	Colin Chapman F2 car
48	1967	Ford FVA S4	Colin Chapman F2 car

Type	Year	Engine	Designer
49	1967	Ford DFV V8	Colin Chapman/ Maurice Philippe
49B	1968	Ford DFV V8	Colin Chapman/ Maurice Philippe
49C	1970	Ford DFV V8	Colin Chapman /Maurice Philippe
59B	1969	Cosworth, Pratt & Whitney turbine	Colin Chapman/ Maurice Philippe F2 car fitted with gas turbine engine raced in 1971
63	1969	Ford DFV V8	Maurice Philippe 4-wheel-drive
69	1971	Ford FVA S4	Dave Baldwin F2 car
72	1970	Ford DFV V8	Colin Chapman/ Maurice Philippe
72C	1971	Ford DFV V8	Colin Chapman/ Maurice Philippe
72D	1971	Ford DFV V8	Colin Chapman/ Maurice Philippe
72E	1974	Ford DFV V8	Colin Chapman/ Maurice Philippe
76	1974	Ford DFV V8	Colin Chapman/Ralph Bellamy
77	1976	Ford DFV V8	Geoff Aldridge/Martin Ogilvie
78	1977	Ford DFV V8	Ralph Bellamy/Martin Ogilvie/Peter Wright
79	1978	Ford DFV V8	Martin Ogilvie/Geoff Aldridge
80	1979	Ford DFV V8	Martin Ogilvie/Geoff Aldridge/Peter Wright
81	1980	Ford DFV V8	Martin Ogilvie/Peter Wright
81B	1980	Ford DFV V8	Martin Ogilvie/Peter Wright
87	1981	Ford DFV V8	Colin Chapman/Martin Ogilvie/Peter Wright
87B	1982	Ford DFV V8	Colin Chapman/Martin Ogilvie/Peter Wright
91	1982	Ford DFV V8	Colin Chapman/ Martin Ogilvie
92	1983	Ford DFV V8	Colin Chapman/ Martin Ogilvie
93T	1983	Renault EF1/ EF4B V6 tc	Colin Chapman/ Martin Ogilvie
94T	1983	Renault EF1/ EF4B V6 tc	Gérard Ducarouge/ Martin Ogilvie
94T	1983	Renault EF1/ EF4B V6 tc	Gérard Ducarouge/ Martin Ogilvie
95T	1984	Renault EF4B V6 tc	Gérard Ducarouge/ Martin Ogilvie
97T	1985	Renault EF4B/ EF15 V6 tc	Gérard Ducarouge/ Martin Ogilvie
98T	1986	Renault EF15B V6 tc	Gérard Ducarouge/ Martin Ogilvie
99T	1987	Honda RA166E V6 tc	Gérard Ducarouge/ Martin Ogilvie
100T	1988	Honda RA168E V6 tc	Gérard Ducarouge/ Martin Ogilvie
101	1989	Judd CV V8	Frank Dernie/Mike Coghlan
102	1990	Lamborghini 3512 V12	Frank Dernie
102B	1991	Judd EV V8	Frank Coppuck
102C	1991	Isuzu V12	Frank Coppuck Test chassis for new Isuzu engine, never raced
102D	1992	Ford HB V8	Frank Coppuck
107	1992	Ford HB V8	Chris Murphy
107B	1993	Ford HB V8	Chris Murphy
107C	1994	Mugen MF-351HB V10	Chris Murphy
109	1994	Mugen MF-351HB V10	Chris Murphy

LYNCAR

Only GP:	1975 British GP Nicholson (17th)
Principal:	Martin Slater
Base:	Slough (GB)

WORLD CHAMPIONSHIP RECORD

GPs Started: 1
Best result: 17th 1975 British GP (Nicholson)
Best qualif.: 26th 1975 British GP (Nicholson)

MAJOR SPONSORS

1974-75	Pinch

LYNCAR GRAND PRIX DRIVERS

Driver	Nat	Starts	1st	2nd	3rd	4th	5th	6th	PP	FL	Points
		(DNS/DNQ)									
John Nicholson	NZ	1 (1)	-	-	-	-	-	-	-	-	-

LYNCAR GRAND PRIX CARS

Type	Year	Engine	Designer
006	1974	Ford DFV V8	Martin Slater
009	1975	Ford DFV V8	Martin Slater

MAKI

Principal: Kenji Mimura

WORLD CHAMPIONSHIP RECORD

GPs Started: None
Best qualif.: 25th 1975 Dutch GP (Fushida) - did not start

MAJOR SPONSORS

1975	Citizen
1976	Hotstuff

MAKI GRAND PRIX DRIVERS

Driver	Nat	Starts	1st	2nd	3rd	4th	5th	6th	PP	FL	Points
		(DNS/DNQ)									
Tony Trimmer	GB	- (4)	-	-	-	-	-	-	-	-	-
Hiroshi Fushida	J	- (2)	-	-	-	-	-	-	-	-	-
Howden Ganley	NZ	- (2)	-	-	-	-	-	-	-	-	-

MAKI GRAND PRIX CARS

Type	Year	Engine	Designer
F101	1974	Ford DFV V8	Kenji Mimura/Masao Ono
F101C	1975	Ford DFV V8	Kenji Mimura/Masao Ono
F102A	1976	Ford DFV V8	Kenji Mimura/Masao Ono

MARCH

During 1990-91 cars were officially named after major sponsor/shareholder Leyton House, renamed March in 1992. For RAM-March see RAM

GP Debut:	1970 South African GP Stewart (3rd), Siffert (10th), Amon (retired), Andretti (retired), Servoz-Gavin (retired)
Last GP:	1992 Australian GP Lammers (12th), Naspetti (retired)
Principals:	Robin Herd, 1969-89; Akira Akagi/Leyton House, 1990-91; Ken Marrable, 1992; March was founded by Max Mosley, Alan Rees, Graham Croaker and Robin Herd in 1969
Base:	Bicester (GB)

WORLD CHAMPIONSHIP RECORD

GPs Started:	227
Points:	193
Wins:	3 1970 Spanish GP (Stewart), 1975 Austrian GP (Brambilla), 1976 Italian GP (Peterson)
Pole pos.:	5 1970 South African GP (Stewart), Monaco GP (Stewart), Belgian GP (Stewart), 1975 Swedish GP (Brambilla), 1976 Dutch GP (Peterson)
Fastest laps:	7 1970 Belgian GP (Amon), 1971 Italian GP (Pescarolo), 1973 British GP (Hunt), United States GP (Hunt), 1975 Austrian GP (Brambilla), 1976 Italian GP (Peterson), 1989 French GP (Gugelmin)

Laps/miles in the lead: 338 laps/928 miles

Best World Championship position:
Drivers: 2nd in 1971 (Peterson)
Constructors: 3rd in 1970 and 1971

MAJOR SPONSORS

1970-72	STP
1973	STP, Wheatcroft Racing
1974	Beta, Jagermeister
1975	Beta, Elf, Lavazza
1976	Beta, Duckhams, First National City, Jagermeister, John Day Models, Lavazza, Monaco Fine Arts, Ovoro, Theodore Racing
1977	Hollywood, Lexington, Rothmans, Sportsman Lager
1981	Guinness, Rizla
1982	Rizla, Rothmans
1987-91	Leyton House
1992	Uliveto

MARCH GRAND PRIX DRIVERS

Driver	Nat	Starts	1st	2nd	3rd	4th	5th	6th	PP	FL	Points
		(DNS/DNQ)									
Ronnie Peterson	S	47	1	4	2	2	3	2	1	1	55
Jackie Stewart	GB	10	1	2	1	-	-	3	-	25
Vittorio Brambilla	I	41 (2)	1	-	-	-	1	3	1	1	8.5
Ivan Capelli	I	74 (4)	-	2	1	-	3	3	-	-	25
Chris Amon	NZ	13	-	2	1	1	2	-	-	1	23
James Hunt	GB	9 (1)	-	1	1	1	-	1	-	2	14
Hans-Joachim Stuck	D	34 (2)	-	-	-	3	2	-	-	1	13
Mauricio Gugelmin	BR	58 (6)	-	-	1	1	1	1	-	1	10
Henri Pescarolo	F	19 (4)	-	-	-	1	-	1	-	1	4
Mario Andretti	USA	5	-	-	1	-	-	-	-	-	4
Karl Wendlinger	A	16	-	-	-	1	-	-	-	-	3
Carlos Pace	BR	11	-	-	-	-	1	1	-	-	3
Mark Donohue	USA	2 (1)	-	-	-	-	1	-	-	-	2
Johnny Servoz-Gavin	F	2 (1)	-	-	-	-	1	-	-	-	2
François Cevert	F	9	-	-	-	-	-	1	-	-	1
Lella Lombardi	I	11 (1)	-	-	-	-	-	1	-	-	0.5
Mike Beuttler	GB	28 (1)	-	-	-	-	-	-	-	-	-
Ian Scheckter	ZA	13 (1)	-	-	-	-	-	-	-	-	-
Niki Lauda	A	13	-	-	-	-	-	-	-	-	-
Jo Siffert	CH	12 (1)	-	-	-	-	-	-	-	-	-
Jean-Pierre Jarier	F	11	-	-	-	-	-	-	-	-	-
Raul Boesel	BR	10 (5)	-	-	-	-	-	-	-	-	-
Alex Ribeiro	BR	9 (8)	-	-	-	-	-	-	-	-	-
Arturo Merzario	I	9 (6)	-	-	-	-	-	-	-	-	-
Jochen Mass	D	9 (1)	-	-	-	-	-	-	-	-	-
Derek Daly	IRL	8 (7)	-	-	-	-	-	-	-	-	-
Patrick Neve	B	8 (3)	-	-	-	-	-	-	-	-	-
Nanni Galli	I	7 (2)	-	-	-	-	-	-	-	-	-
Andrea de Adamich	I	7	-	-	-	-	-	-	-	-	-
Paul Belmondo	F	5 (6)	-	-	-	-	-	-	-	-	-
Skip Barber	USA	5 (1)	-	-	-	-	-	-	-	-	-
Emanuele Naspetti	I	5	-	-	-	-	-	-	-	-	-
David Purley	GB	4 (1)	-	-	-	-	-	-	-	-	-
Alex Soler-Roig	E	4 (1)	-	-	-	-	-	-	-	-	-
Rupert Keegan	GB	3 (2)	-	-	-	-	-	-	-	-	-
Brett Lunger	USA	3	-	-	-	-	-	-	-	-	-
Boy Hayje	NL	2 (4)	-	-	-	-	-	-	-	-	-
Reine Wisell	S	2 (1)	-	-	-	-	-	-	-	-	-
Howden Ganley	NZ	2	-	-	-	-	-	-	-	-	-
Jan Lammers	NL	2	-	-	-	-	-	-	-	-	-
Roger Williamson	GB	2	-	-	-	-	-	-	-	-	-
Eliseo Salazar	RCH	1 (5)	-	-	-	-	-	-	-	-	-
Brian Henton	GB	1 (3)	-	-	-	-	-	-	-	-	-
John Love	RSR	1	-	-	-	-	-	-	-	-	-
Jean Max	F	1	-	-	-	-	-	-	-	-	-
François Mazet	F	1	-	-	-	-	-	-	-	-	-
Emilio de Villota	E	- (5)	-	-	-	-	-	-	-	-	-
Mikko Kozarowitsky	SF	- (2)	-	-	-	-	-	-	-	-	-
Michael Bleekemolen	NL	- (1)	-	-	-	-	-	-	-	-	-
Bernard de Dryver	B	- (1)	-	-	-	-	-	-	-	-	-
Hubert Hahne	D	- (1)	-	-	-	-	-	-	-	-	-
Karl Oppitzhauser	A	- (1)	-	-	-	-	-	-	-	-	-
Andy Sutcliffe	GB	- (1)	-	-	-	-	-	-	-	-	-
Mike Wilds	GB	- (1)	-	-	-	-	-	-	-	-	-

MARCH GRAND PRIX CARS

Type	Year	Engine	Designer
701	1970	Ford DFV V8	Robin Herd/Peter Wright
711	1971	Ford DFV V8, Alfa Romeo T33 V8	Robin Herd/Geoff Ferris/ Frank Costin
721	1972	Ford DFV V8	Robin Herd
721G	1972	Ford DFV V8	Robin Herd
721X	1972	Ford DFV V8	Robin Herd
731	1973	Ford DFV V8	Robin Herd
741	1974	Ford DFV V8	Robin Herd

Type	Year	Engine	Designer
751	1975	Ford DFV V8	Robin Herd
761	1976	Ford DFV V8	Robin Herd
761B	1977	Ford DFV V8	Robin Herd/Martin Walters
771	1977	Ford DFV V8	Robin Herd/Martin Walters
811	1981	Ford DFV V8	Robin Herd/Adrian Reynard/Alan Mertens
821	1982	Ford DFV V8	Adrian Reynard
87P	1987	Ford DFZ V8	Gordon Coppuck/Tim Holloway/Andy Brown
871	1987	Ford DFZ V8	Gordon Coppuck/Tim Holloway/Andy Brown
881	1988	Judd CV V8	Adrian Newey
CG891	1989	Judd EV V8	Adrian Newey
CG901*1990		Judd EV V8	Adrian Newey/Gustav Brunner
CG911*1991		Ilmor 2175A V10	Chris Murphy/Gustav Brunner

*Leyton House (CG911 renamed March in 1992). Note: "CG" designation refers to Cesare Garibaldi of Genoa Racing

MARTINI

GP Debut:	1978 Belgian GP — Arnoux (9th)
Last GP:	1978 Dutch GP — Arnoux (retired)
Principal:	Tico Martini
Base:	Magny-Cours (F)

WORLD CHAMPIONSHIP RECORD

GPs Started: 4
Best result: 9th 1978 Belgian GP (Arnoux), Austrian GP (Arnoux)
Best qualif.: 18th 1978 French GP (Arnoux)

MAJOR SPONSORS

1978	Silver Match, RMO, Elf

MARTINI GRAND PRIX DRIVERS

Driver	Nat	Starts	1st	2nd	3rd	4th	5th	6th	PP	FL	Points
		(DNS/DNQ)									
René Arnoux	F	4 (3)	-	-	-	-	-	-	-	-	-

MARTINI GRAND PRIX CARS

Type	Year	Engine	Designer
MK23	1978	Ford DFV V8	Tico Martini

Note: The "MK" designation stands for Martini-Knight in deference to the Knight family, who operate the racing school at Magny-Cours

MASERATI

GP Debut:	1950 British GP — Hampshire (9th), Fry/Shawe-Taylor (10th), "Bira" (retired), Murray (retired), de Graffenried (retired), Chiron (retired)
Last GP:	1960 United States GP — Drake (13th)
Principals:	Alfieri Maserati 1926-32; Ernesto Maserati, 1932-37; Adolfo Orsi, 1938-60; founded by brothers Alfieri, Bindo, Carlo, Ettore, Ernesto and Mario Maserati
Base:	Bologna (I), 1926-37; Modena (I), 1937 to date

WORLD CHAMPIONSHIP RECORD

GPs Started: 68
Points: 312.92
Wins: 9 1953 Italian GP (Fangio), 1954 Argentinian GP (Fangio), Belgian GP (Fangio), 1956 Monaco GP (Moss), Italian GP (Moss), 1957 Argentinian GP (Fangio), Monaco GP (Fangio), French GP (Fangio), German GP (Fangio)
Pole pos.: 10 1953 Belgian GP (Fangio), Swiss GP (Fangio), 1954 Belgian GP (Fangio), 1956 British GP (Moss), 1957 Argentinian GP (Moss), Monaco GP (Fangio), French GP (Fangio), German GP (Fangio), Pescara GP (Fangio), 1958 Argentinian GP (Fangio)
Fastest laps: 17 1952 Italian GP (Gonzalez), 1953 Belgian GP (Gonzalez), French GP (Fangio), British GP (Gonzalez), Italian GP (Fangio), 1954 Belgian GP (Fangio), British GP (Marimon), British GP (Moss), British GP (Ascari), 1955 Dutch GP (Mieres), 1956 Belgian GP (Moss), British GP (Moss), Italian GP (Moss), 1957 Argentinian GP (Moss), Monaco GP (Fangio), German GP (Fangio), 1958 Argentinian GP (Fangio)

Laps/miles in the lead: 832 laps/2948 miles
World Champions:
Drivers: Twice - 1954 (Fangio - including 40.14 of his 57.14 points for Mercedes-Benz) and 1957 (Fangio)
Best World Championship position:
Constructors: 5th in 1958

MASERATI GRAND PRIX DRIVERS

Driver	Nat	Starts (DNS/DNQ)	1st	2nd	3rd	4th	5th	6th	PP	FL	Points
Juan Manuel Fangio	RA	19	7	5	-	3	-	-	8	6	99
Stirling Moss	GB	14	2	1	2	-	1	-	2	5	33.14
Jean Behra	F	20	-	2	5	1	2	4	-	-	36
José Froilan Gonzalez	RA	9	-	1	3	1	-	-	-	3	21
Roberto Mieres	RA	14	-	-	-	3	2	1	-	1	13
Luigi Musso	I	9 (1)	-	1	1	-	1	-	-	-	12
Felice Bonetto	I	11 (2)	-	-	1	2	2	1	-	-	10.5
Harry Schell	USA	21	-	-	1	1	2	3	-	-	10
Masten Gregory	USA	8	-	-	1	3	-	1	-	-	10
Onofre Marimón	RA	11 (1)	-	-	2	-	-	-	-	1	8.14
"B Bira"	SM	12	-	-	-	2	1	1	-	-	8
Emanuel de Graffenried	CH	19 (1)	-	-	-	1	2	3	-	-	7
Chico Godia-Sales	E	13 (1)	-	-	-	2	-	1	-	-	6
Carlos Menditéguy	RA	8 (1)	-	-	1	-	1	-	-	-	6
Cesare Perdisa	I	6 (1)	-	-	2	-	1	-	-	-	5
Luigi Villoresi	I	8 (1)	-	-	-	2	1	-	-	-	4
Sergio Mantovani	I	7 (1)	-	-	-	-	2	-	-	-	4
Louis Chiron	MC	6 (1)	-	-	1	-	-	-	-	-	4
Mike Hawthorn	GB	1 (1)	-	-	1	-	-	-	-	-	4
Horace Gould	GB	13 (3)	-	-	-	1	-	-	-	-	2
Louis Rosier	F	10	-	-	-	1	1	-	-	-	2
Oscar Galvez	RA	1	-	-	-	1	-	-	-	-	2
Hermann Lang	D	1	-	-	-	1	-	-	-	-	2
Gerino Gerini	I	6 (1)	-	-	-	1	-	-	-	-	1.5
Chico Landi	BR	5	-	-	-	1	-	-	-	-	1.5
Giorgio Scarlatti	I	8 (1)	-	-	-	1	1	1	-	-	1
Alberto Ascari	I	2	-	-	-	-	-	-	-	1	0.14
Jo Bonnier	S	12	-	-	-	-	-	-	-	-	-
Luigi Piotti	I	6 (2)	-	-	-	-	-	-	-	-	-
Bruce Halford	GB	6	-	-	-	-	-	-	-	-	-
Roy Salvadori	GB	6	-	-	-	-	-	-	-	-	-
Hans Herrmann	D	4 (1)	-	-	-	-	-	-	-	-	-
Ken Wharton	GB	4 (1)	-	-	-	1	-	-	-	-	-
Gino Bianco	BR	4	-	-	-	-	-	-	-	-	-
Franco Rol	I	4	-	-	-	-	-	-	-	-	-
Carroll Shelby	USA	4	-	-	1	-	-	-	-	-	-
Maria Teresa de Filippis	I	3 (1)	-	-	-	-	-	-	-	-	-
David Murray	GB	3 (1)	-	-	-	-	-	-	-	-	-
André Simon	F	3 (1)	-	-	-	-	-	-	-	-	-
Antonio Branca	CH	3	-	-	-	-	-	-	-	-	-
Heitel Cantoni	U	3	-	-	-	-	-	-	-	-	-
Umberto Maglioli	I	3	-	-	-	-	-	-	-	-	-
Ottorino Volonterio	CH	3	-	-	-	-	-	-	-	-	-
Giulio Cabianca	I	2	-	-	-	-	-	-	-	-	-
Peter Collins	GB	2	-	-	-	-	-	-	-	-	-
Jorge Daponte	RA	2	-	-	-	-	-	-	-	-	-
David Hampshire	GB	2	-	-	-	-	-	-	-	-	-
Fritz d'Orey	BR	2	-	-	-	-	-	-	-	-	-
Wolfgang Seidel	D	2	-	-	-	-	-	-	-	-	-
Alberto Uria	U	2	-	-	-	-	-	1	-	-	-
Johnny Claes	B	1 (1)	-	-	-	-	-	-	-	-	-
Lance Macklin	GB	1 (1)	-	-	-	-	-	-	-	-	-
Troy Ruttman	USA	1 (1)	-	-	-	-	-	-	-	-	-
Cliff Allison	GB	1	-	-	-	-	-	-	-	-	-
Carel Godin de Beaufort	NL	1	-	-	-	-	-	-	-	-	-
Jack Brabham	AUS	1	-	-	-	-	-	-	-	-	-
Clemar Bucci	RA	1	-	-	-	-	-	-	-	-	-
Ivor Bueb	GB	1	-	-	-	-	-	-	-	-	-
Ettore Chimeri	YV	1	-	-	-	-	-	-	-	-	-
Gianfranco Comotti	I	1	-	-	-	-	-	-	-	-	-
Antonio Creus	E	1	-	-	-	-	-	-	-	-	-
Bob Drake	USA	1	-	-	-	-	-	-	-	-	-

Driver	Nat	Starts (DNS/DNQ)	1st	2nd	3rd	4th	5th	6th	PP	FL	Points
Nasif Estefano	RA	1	-	-	-	-	-	-	-	-	-
Philippe Étancelin	F	1	-	-	-	-	-	-	-	-	-
John Fitch	USA	1	-	-	-	-	-	-	-	-	-
Jan Flinterman	NL	1	-	-	-	-	-	-	-	-	-
Ron Flockhart	GB	1	-	-	-	-	-	-	-	-	-
Philip Fotheringham-Parker	GB	1	-	-	-	-	-	-	-	-	-
Joe Fry	GB	1	-	-	-	-	-	-	-	-	-
Oscar Gonzalez	U	1	-	-	-	1	-	-	-	-	-
Phil Hill	USA	1	-	-	-	-	-	-	-	-	-
John James	GB	1	-	-	-	-	-	-	-	-	-
Gino Munaron	I	1	-	-	-	-	-	-	-	-	-
Nello Pagani	I	1	-	-	-	-	-	-	-	-	-
Reg Parnell	GB	1	-	-	-	-	-	-	-	-	-
Paul Pietsch	D	1	-	-	-	-	-	-	-	-	-
Brian Shawe-Taylor	GB	1	-	-	-	-	-	-	-	-	-
Piero Taruffi	I	1	-	-	-	-	-	-	-	-	-
Maurice Trintignant	F	1	-	-	-	-	-	-	-	-	-
Peter Walker	GB	1	-	-	-	-	-	-	-	-	-
Ken Kavanagh	AUS	- (2)	-	-	-	-	-	-	-	-	-
André Testut	MC	- (2)	-	-	-	-	-	-	-	-	-
Astrubel Bayardo	U	- (1)	-	-	-	-	-	-	-	-	-
Phil Cade	USA	- (1)	-	-	-	-	-	-	-	-	-
Alberto Crespo	RA	- (1)	-	-	-	-	-	-	-	-	-
Juan Jover	E	- (1)	-	-	-	-	-	-	-	-	-
Alfredo Pian	RA	- (1)	-	-	-	-	-	-	-	-	-
Giovanni de Riu	I	- (1)	-	-	-	-	-	-	-	-	-

MASERATI GRAND PRIX CARS

Type	Year	Engine	Designer
4CL	1950	Maserati 4CL S4	Ernesto Maserati
4CLT/48	1950	Maserati 4CL S4, OSCA V12 Also known as the "San Remo" Maserati	Alberto Massimino
4CLT/48-Anzani	1955	Anzani S4	Amedeo Ruggeri
4CLT/48-Platé	1952	Maserati 4CL/Plate S4	Engine modified by Enrico Platé
4CLT/50-Milano	1950	Speluzzi S4	Engine modified by Mario Speluzzi
A6GCM	1952	Maserati A6GC S6	Alberto Massimino
A6SSG	1953	Maserati A6GC S6	Alberto Massimino/Gioacchino Colombo
250F	1954	Maserati 250/F1 S6	Gioacchino Colombo/Vittorio Bellentani
250F (V12)	1957	Maserati 250-T2 V12	Gioacchino Colombo/Vittorio Bellentani

MATRA

MECANIQUE-AVIATION-TRACTION

GP Debut: 1966 German GP — Beltoise, Hahne, Schlesser, Ickx (all raced in F2 class)

Last GP: 1972 United States GP — Amon (15th)

Principal: Michel Chassagny

Works Teams: Matra Sports and Matra International

Team Principal: Matra Sports: Jean-Luc Lagardère and Claude de Guezec

Matra International: Ken Tyrrell

Base: Velizy (F)

WORLD CHAMPIONSHIP RECORD

GPs Started: 62

Points: 184

Wins: 9 1968 Dutch GP (Stewart), German GP (Stewart), United States GP (Stewart), 1969 South African GP (Stewart), Spanish GP (Stewart), Dutch GP (Stewart), French GP (Stewart), British GP (Stewart), Italian GP (Stewart)

Pole pos.: 4 1969 Monaco GP (Stewart), French GP (Stewart), 1971 Italian GP (Amon), 1972 French GP (Amon)

Fastest laps: 12 1968 Spanish GP (Beltoise), Dutch GP (Beltoise), German GP (Stewart), United States GP (Stewart), 1969 South African GP (Stewart), Monaco GP (Stewart), Dutch GP (Stewart), French GP (Stewart), British GP (Stewart), Italian GP (Beltoise), 1972 Belgian GP (Amon), French GP (Amon)

Laps/miles in the lead: 668 laps/2249 miles

World Champions:

Drivers: Once - 1969 (Stewart)

Constructors: Once - 1969

MAJOR SPONSORS

1966-72	Elf

MATRA GRAND PRIX DRIVERS

Driver	Nat	Starts (DNS/DNQ)	1st	2nd	3rd	4th	5th	6th	PP	FL	Points
Jackie Stewart	GB	21	9	1	1	2	-	2	2	7	99
Jean-Pierre Beltoise	F	46 (1)	-	2	4	2	5	5	-	3	49
Chris Amon	NZ	21 (1)	-	-	2	1	3	4	2	2	21
Henri Pescarolo	F	16 (1)	-	-	1	-	1	2	-	-	8
Johnny Servoz-Gavin	F	9	-	1	-	-	-	1	-	-	7
Jacky Ickx	B	2	-	-	-	-	-	-	-	-	-
Jo Schlesser	F	2	-	-	-	-	-	-	-	-	-
Hubert Hahne	D	1	-	-	-	-	-	-	-	-	-

MATRA GRAND PRIX CARS

Type	Year	Engine	Designer
MS5	1966	BRM 71, Ford SCA S4	Bernard Boyer
MS7	1967	Ford FVA S4	Bernard Boyer
MS9	1968	Ford DFV V8	Bernard Boyer
MS10	1968	Ford DFV V8	Bernard Boyer
MS11	1968	Matra V12	Bernard Boyer
MS80	1969	Ford DFV V8	Bernard Boyer
MS84**	1969	Ford DFV V8	Bernard Boyer/Derek Gardner
MS120*	1970	Matra MS12 V12	Bernard Boyer
MS120B*	1971	Matra MS12 V12	Bernard Boyer
MS120C*	1972	Matra MS71 V12	Bernard Boyer
MS120D*	1972	Matra MS71 V12	Bernard Boyer

*Matra-Simca
**4-wheel-drive

McLAREN

GP Debut: 1966 Monaco GP — McLaren (retired)

Latest GP: 1994 Australian GP — Brundle (3rd), Häkkinen (12th)

Principal: Bruce McLaren, 1966 until his death in June 1970; Teddy Mayer, 1970-80; Ron Dennis and Mayer, September 1980-82; Dennis, 1982 to date

Base: Feltham (GB), 1963-64; Colnbrook (GB), 1965-81; Woking (GB), 1981 to date

WORLD CHAMPIONSHIP RECORD

GPs Started: 410

Points: 2005.5

Wins: 104 1968 Belgian GP (McLaren), Italian GP (Hulme), Canadian GP (Hulme), 1969 Mexican GP (Hulme), 1972 South African GP (Hulme), 1973 Swedish GP (Hulme), British GP (Revson), Canadian GP (Revson), 1974 Argentinian GP (Hulme), Brazilian GP (Fittipaldi), Belgian GP (Fittipaldi), Canadian GP (Fittipaldi), 1975 Argentinian GP (Fittipaldi), Spanish GP (Mass), British GP (Fittipaldi), 1976 Spanish GP (Hunt), French GP (Hunt), German GP (Hunt), Dutch GP (Hunt), Canadian GP (Hunt), United States GP (Hunt), 1977 British GP (Hunt), United States GP (Hunt), Japanese GP (Hunt), 1981 British GP (Watson), 1982 Long Beach GP (Lauda), Belgian GP (Watson), Detroit GP (Watson), British GP (Lauda), 1983 Long Beach GP (Watson), 1984 Brazilian GP (Prost), South African GP (Lauda), San Marino GP (Prost), French GP (Lauda), Monaco GP (Prost), British GP (Lauda), German GP (Prost), Austrian GP (Lauda), Dutch GP (Lauda), Italian GP (Prost), European GP (Prost), Portuguese GP (Prost), 1985 Brazilian GP (Prost), Monaco GP (Prost), British GP (Prost), Austrian GP (Prost), Dutch GP (Lauda), Italian GP (Prost), 1986 San Marino GP (Prost), Monaco GP (Prost), Austrian GP (Prost), Australian GP (Prost), 1987 Belgian GP (Prost), Portuguese GP (Prost), 1988 Brazilian GP (Prost), San Marino GP (Senna), Monaco GP (Prost), Mexican GP (Prost), Canadian GP (Senna), Detroit GP (Senna),

French GP (Prost), British GP (Senna), German GP (Senna), Hungarian GP (Senna), Belgian GP (Senna), Portuguese GP (Prost), Spanish GP (Prost), Japanese GP (Senna), Australian GP (Prost), 1989 San Marino GP (Senna), Monaco GP (Senna), Mexican GP (Senna), United States GP (Prost), French GP (Prost), British GP (Prost), German GP (Senna), Belgian GP (Senna), Italian GP (Prost), Spanish GP (Senna), 1990 United States GP (Senna), Monaco GP (Senna), Canadian GP (Senna), German GP (Senna), Belgian GP (Senna), Italian GP (Senna), 1991 United States GP (Senna), Brazilian GP (Senna), San Marino GP (Senna), Monaco GP (Senna), Hungarian GP (Senna), Belgian GP (Senna), Japanese GP (Berger), Australian GP (Senna), 1992 Monaco GP (Senna), Canadian GP (Berger), Hungarian GP (Senna), Italian GP (Senna), Australian GP (Berger), 1993 Brazilian GP (Senna), European GP (Senna), Monaco GP (Senna), Japanese GP (Senna), Australian GP (Senna)

Pole pos.: 79   1972 Canadian GP (Revson), 1973 South African GP (Hulme), 1974 Brazilian GP (Fittipaldi), Canadian GP (Fittipaldi), 1976 Brazilian GP (Hunt), South African GP (Hunt), Spanish GP (Hunt), French GP (Hunt), German GP (Hunt), Austrian GP (Hunt), Canadian GP (Hunt), United States GP (Hunt), 1977 Argentinian GP (Hunt), Brazilian GP (Hunt), South African GP (Hunt), British GP (Hunt), Italian GP (Hunt), United States GP (Hunt), 1984 Monaco GP (Prost), German GP (Prost), Dutch GP (Prost), 1985 Austrian GP (Prost), Belgian GP (Prost), 1986 Monaco GP (Prost), German GP (Rosberg), 1988 Brazilian GP (Senna), San Marino GP (Senna), Monaco GP (Senna), Mexican GP (Senna), Canadian GP (Senna), Detroit GP (Senna), French GP (Prost), German GP (Senna), Hungarian GP (Senna), Belgian GP (Senna), Italian GP (Senna), Portuguese GP (Prost), Spanish GP (Senna), Japanese GP (Senna), Australian GP (Senna), 1989 Brazilian GP (Senna), San Marino GP (Senna), Monaco GP (Senna), Mexican GP (Senna), United States GP (Senna), Canadian GP (Prost), French GP (Prost), British GP (Senna), German GP (Senna), Belgian GP (Senna), Italian GP (Senna), Portuguese GP (Senna), Spanish GP (Senna), Japanese GP (Senna), Australian GP (Senna), 1990 United States GP (Berger), Brazilian GP (Senna), San Marino GP (Senna), Monaco GP (Senna), Canadian GP (Senna), Mexican GP (Berger), German GP (Senna), Belgian GP (Senna), Italian GP (Senna), Spanish GP (Senna), Japanese GP (Senna), Australian GP (Senna), 1991 United States GP (Senna), Brazilian GP (Senna), San Marino GP (Senna), Monaco GP (Senna), Hungarian GP (Senna), Belgian GP (Senna), Italian GP (Senna), Spanish GP (Berger), Japanese GP (Berger), Australian GP (Senna), 1992 Canadian GP (Senna), 1993 Australian GP (Senna)

Fastest laps: 69   1970 South African GP (Surtees), 1971 Canadian GP (Hulme), 1972 Austrian GP (Hulme), 1973 Brazilian GP (Hulme), Swedish GP (Hulme), French GP (Hulme), 1974 Belgian GP (Hulme), 1975 French GP (Mass), United States GP (Fittipaldi), 1976 Spanish GP (Mass), Austrian GP (Hunt), United States GP (Hunt), 1977 Argentinian GP (Hunt), Brazilian GP (Hunt), British GP (Hunt), 1981 Canadian GP (Watson), 1982 Long Beach GP (Lauda), Belgian GP (Watson), 1983 Long Beach GP (Lauda), Detroit GP (Watson), 1984 Brazilian GP (Prost), French GP (Prost), Dallas GP (Lauda), British GP (Lauda), German GP (Prost), Austrian GP (Lauda), Italian GP (Lauda), Portuguese GP (Lauda), 1985 Brazilian GP (Prost), British GP (Prost), German GP (Lauda), Austrian GP (Prost), Dutch GP (Prost), Belgian GP (Prost), 1986 Monaco GP (Prost), Belgian GP (Prost), 1987 Belgian GP (Prost), Japanese GP (Prost), 1988 San Marino GP (Prost), Monaco GP (Senna), Mexican GP (Prost), Canadian GP (Senna), Detroit GP (Prost), French GP (Prost), Hungarian GP (Prost), Spanish GP (Prost), Japanese GP (Senna), Australian GP (Prost), 1989 San Marino GP (Prost), Monaco GP (Prost), United States GP (Senna), German GP (Senna), Belgian GP (Prost), Italian

GP (Prost), Spanish GP (Senna), Japanese GP (Prost), 1990 United States GP (Berger), Brazilian GP (Berger), Monaco GP (Senna), Canadian GP (Berger), Italian GP (Senna), 1991 San Marino GP (Berger), Italian GP (Senna), Japanese GP (Senna), Australian GP (Berger), 1992 Mexican GP (Berger), Canadian GP (Berger), Portuguese GP (Senna), 1993 European GP (Senna)

Laps/miles in the lead: 5625 laps/16221 miles

World Champions:

Drivers: Nine times - 1974 (Fittipaldi), 1976 (Hunt), 1984 (Lauda), 1985 (Prost), 1986 (Prost), 1988 (Senna), 1989 (Prost), 1990 (Senna) and 1991 (Senna)

Constructors: Seven times - 1974, 1984, 1985, 1988, 1989, 1990 and 1991

MAJOR SPONSORS

1972-73	Yardley
1974	Texaco, Marlboro, Yardley
1975	Marlboro, Texaco
1976-77	Marlboro
1978-79	Marlboro, Lowenbrau
1979 to date	Marlboro

MCLAREN GRAND PRIX DRIVERS

Driver	Nat	Starts (DNS/DNQ)	1st	2nd	3rd	4th	5th	6th	PP	FL	Points
Ayrton Senna	BR	96	35	12	8	5	3	1	46	12	451
Alain Prost	F	107 (2)	30	21	12	3	2	6	10	24	458.5
James Hunt	GB	49	9	2	3	3	1	1	14	5	117
Niki Lauda	A	58 (3)	8	5	2	4	2	2	-	8	128
Denny Hulme	NZ	86	6	5	10	9	7	9	1	6	174
Emerson Fittipaldi	BR	28 (1)	5	6	2	3	1	-	2	1	100
John Watson	GB	73 (2)	4	4	5	5	3	8	-	3	109
Gerhard Berger	A	48	3	7	8	9	3	-	4	7	135
Peter Revson	USA	23	2	2	4	3	3	-	1	-	61
Jochen Mass	D	49	1	1	6	6	4	5	-	2	64
Bruce McLaren	NZ	33 (4)	1	4	2	3	4	2	-	-	60
Mika Häkkinen	SF	18	-	1	6	-	-	-	-	-	30
Stefan Johansson	S	16	-	2	3	1	1	1	-	-	30
Keke Rosberg	SF	16	-	1	-	4	2	-	1	-	22
Martin Brundle	GB	16	-	1	1	1	1	1	-	-	16
Mike Hailwood	GB	11	-	-	1	2	1	-	-	-	12
Patrick Tambay	F	28 (2)	-	-	-	1	1	3	-	-	8
Michael Andretti	USA	13	-	-	1	-	1	1	-	-	7
Dan Gurney	USA	6	-	-	-	1	-	1	-	-	4
Brian Redman	GB	3	-	-	-	-	2	-	-	-	4
Mark Donohue	USA	1 (1)	-	-	1	-	-	-	-	-	4
Jacky Ickx	B	1	-	-	-	1	-	-	-	-	4
Vic Elford	GB	4	-	-	-	-	1	1	-	-	3
Andrea de Cesaris	I	14 (1)	-	-	-	-	-	1	-	-	1
Peter Gethin	GB	14	-	-	-	-	-	1	-	-	1
Jo Bonnier	S	10 (4)	-	-	-	-	-	1	-	-	1
John Surtees	GB	4	-	-	-	-	-	1	-	1	1
Brett Lunger	USA	17 (7)	-	-	-	-	-	-	-	-	-
Bruno Giacomelli	I	6	-	-	-	-	-	-	-	-	-
Jody Scheckter	ZA	6	-	-	-	-	-	-	-	-	-
Andrea de Adamich	I	4 (6)	-	-	-	-	-	-	-	-	-
David Hobbs	GB	3	-	-	-	-	-	-	-	-	-
Jackie Oliver	GB	3	-	-	-	-	-	-	-	-	-
Nelson Piquet	BR	3	-	-	-	-	-	-	-	-	-
Emilio de Villota	E	2 (6)	-	-	-	-	-	-	-	-	-
Dave Charlton	ZA	2	-	-	-	-	-	-	-	-	-
Philippe Alliot	F	1	-	-	-	-	-	-	-	-	-
Derek Bell	GB	1	-	-	-	-	-	-	-	-	-
Basil van Rooyen	ZA	1	-	-	-	-	-	-	-	-	-
Gilles Villeneuve	CDN	1	-	-	-	-	-	-	-	-	-
Nanni Galli	I	- (1)	-	-	-	-	-	-	-	-	-
Phil Hill	USA	- (1)	-	-	-	-	-	-	-	-	-
Helmut Marko	A	- (1)	-	-	-	-	-	-	-	-	-
Stephen South	GB	- (1)	-	-	-	-	-	-	-	-	-
Tony Trimmer	GB	- (1)	-	-	-	-	-	-	-	-	-

MCLAREN GRAND PRIX CARS

Type	Year	Engine	Designer
M2B	1966	Ford 406 V8, Serenissima V8	Robin Herd

Type	Year	Engine	Designer
M3A	1966	Ford 406 V8	Robin Herd
M4B	1967	BRM V8	Robin Herd
M5A	1967	BRM V12	Robin Herd
M7A	1968	Ford DFV V8	Robin Herd/
			Gordon Coppuck
M7A/M7B	1969	Ford DFV V8	Robin Herd/
			Gordon Coppuck
M7C	1969	Ford DFV V8	Robin Herd/
			Gordon Coppuck
M7D	1970	Alfa Romeo T33 V8	Robin Herd/
			Gordon Coppuck
M9A	1969	Ford DFV V8	Jo Marquart
M14A	1970	Ford DFV V8	Jo Marquart
M14D	1970	Ford DFV V8,	
		Alfa Romeo T33 V8	Jo Marquart
M19A	1971	Ford DFV V8	Ralph Bellamy
M19C	1972	Ford DFV V8	Ralph Bellamy
M23	1973	Ford DFV V8	Gordon Coppuck
M25	1978	Ford DFV V8	Gordon Coppuck
M26	1976	Ford DFV V8	Gordon Coppuck
M28	1979	Ford DFV V8	Gordon Coppuck
M28B	1979	Ford DFV V8	Gordon Coppuck
M28C	1979	Ford DFV V8	Gordon Coppuck
M29	1979	Ford DFV V8	Gordon Coppuck
M29B	1980	Ford DFV V8	Gordon Coppuck
M29C	1980	Ford DFV V8	Gordon Coppuck
M29F	1981	Ford DFV V8	Gordon Coppuck/
			John Baldwin
M30	1980	Ford DFV V8	Gordon Coppuck
MP4/1	1981	Ford DFV V8	John Barnard
MP4/1B	1982	Ford DFV V8	John Barnard
MP4/1C	1983	Ford DFV V8	John Barnard
MP4/1E	1983	TAG Porsche P01 V6 tc	John Barnard
MP4/2	1984	TAG Porsche P01 V6 tc	John Barnard
MP4/2B	1985	TAG Porsche P01 V6 tc	John Barnard
MP4/2C	1986	TAG Porsche P01 V6 tc	John Barnard
MP4/3	1987	TAG Porsche P01 V6 tc	Steve Nichols
MP4/4	1988	Honda RA168E V6 tc	Steve Nichols/
			Gordon Murray
MP4/5	1989	Honda RA101E V10	Neil Oatley
MP4/5B	1990	Honda RA101E V10	Neil Oatley
MP4/6	1991	Honda RA121E V12	Neil Oatley
MP4/6B	1992	Honda RA121E V12	Neil Oatley
MP4/7A	1992	Honda RA122E V12	Neil Oatley
MP4/8	1993	Ford HB V8	Neil Oatley
MP4/9	1994	Peugeot A4/A6 V10	Neil Oatley

MERCEDES-BENZ

GP Debut:	1954 French GP	Fangio (1st), Kling (2nd), Herrmann (retired)
Last GP:	1955 Italian GP	Fangio (1st), Taruffi (2nd), Kling (retired), Moss (retired)
Principal:	Alfred Neubauer	
Base:	Untertürkheim, Stuttgart (D)	

WORLD CHAMPIONSHIP RECORD

GPs Started: 12
Points: 139.14
Wins: 9 1954 French GP (Fangio), German GP (Fangio), Swiss GP (Fangio), Italian GP (Fangio), 1955 Argentinian GP (Fangio), Belgian GP (Fangio), Dutch GP (Fangio), British GP (Moss), Italian GP (Fangio)
Pole pos.: 8 1954 French GP (Fangio), British GP (Fangio), German GP (Fangio), Italian GP (Fangio), 1955 Monaco GP (Fangio), Dutch GP (Fangio), British GP (Moss), Italian GP (Fangio)
Fastest laps: 9 1954 French GP (Herrmann), British GP (Fangio), German GP (Kling), Swiss GP (Fangio), 1955 Argentinian GP (Fangio), Monaco GP (Fangio), Belgian GP (Fangio), British GP (Moss), Italian GP (Moss)
Laps/miles in the lead: 589 laps/2472 miles
World Champions:
Drivers: Twice - 1954 (Fangio - 17 of his 57.14 points were scored for Maserati) and 1955 (Fangio)

MERCEDES-BENZ GRAND PRIX DRIVERS

Driver	Nat	Starts	1st	2nd	3rd	4th	5th	6th	PP	FL	Points
		(DNS/DNQ)									
Juan Manuel Fangio	RA	12	8	1	1	1	-	-	7	5	81.14
Stirling Moss	GB	6	1	2	-	1	-	-	1	2	23
Karl Kling	D	11	-	1	1	2	1	-	-	1	17
Hans Herrmann	D	6	-	-	1	2	-	-	1		9
Piero Taruffi	I	2	-	1	-	1	-	-	-		9
Hermann Lang	D	1	-	-	-	-	-	-	-		-
André Simon	F	1	-	-	-	-	-	-	-		-

MERCEDES-BENZ GRAND PRIX CARS

Type	Year	Engine	Designer
W196	1954	Mercedes-Benz M196 S8	Hans Scherenberg/Ludwig Kraus/Hans Gassmann

MERZARIO

GP Debut:	1978 Argentinian GP	Merzario (retired)
Last GP:	1979 Long Beach GP	Merzario (retired)
Principal:	Arturo Merzario	
Base:	Como (I)	

WORLD CHAMPIONSHIP RECORD

GPs Started: 10
Best result: No finishes
Best qualif.: 20th 1978 Argentinian GP (Merzario)

MAJOR SPONSORS

1978-79	Flor Bath

MERZARIO GRAND PRIX DRIVERS

Driver	Nat	Starts	1st	2nd	3rd	4th	5th	6th	PP	FL	Points
		(DNS/DNQ)									
Arturo Merzario	I	10 (20)	-	-	-	-	-	-	-	-	-
Gianfranco Brancatelli	I	- (1)	-	-	-	-	-	-	-	-	-
Alberto Colombo	I	- (1)	-	-	-	-	-	-	-	-	-

MERZARIO GRAND PRIX CARS

Type	Year	Engine	Designer
A1	1978	Ford DFV V8	Arturo Merzario/ Gianfranco Palazzoli
A1B	1979	Ford DFV V8	Arturo Merzario
A2	1979	Ford DFV V8	Arturo Merzario/ Simon Hadfield
A4	1979	Ford DFV V8	Arturo Merzario/Simon Hadfield/Gianpaolo Dallara

MINARDI

GP Debut:	1985 Brazilian GP	Martini (retired)
Latest GP:	1994 Australian GP	Martini (9th), Alboreto (retired)
Principals:	Giancarlo Minardi, 1985-93; Minardi and Beppe Lucchini (of Scuderia Italia), 1994 to date	
Base:	Faenza (I)	

WORLD CHAMPIONSHIP RECORD

GPs Started: 155
Points: 26
Best result: 4th 1991 San Marino GP (Martini), Portuguese GP (Martini), 1993 South African GP (Fittipaldi)
Best qualif.: 2nd 1990 United States GP (Martini)
Laps/miles in the lead: 1 lap/3 miles
Best World Championship position:
Drivers: 11th in 1991 (Martini)
Constructors: 7th in 1991

MAJOR SPONSORS

1985-86	Simod
1987	Simod, Lois, Reporter
1988	Lois, Cimarron
1989	SCM, Lois
1990-92	SCM

1993	Beta
1994	Lucchini, Beta

MINARDI GRAND PRIX DRIVERS

Driver	Nat	Starts (DNS/DNQ)	1st	2nd	3rd	4th	5th	6th	PP	FL	Points
Pierluigi Martini	I	94 (4)	-	-	-	2	4	2	-	-	16
Christian Fittipaldi	BR	24 (3)	-	-	-	1	1	1	-	-	6
Fabrizio Barbazza	I	8	-	-	-	-	2	-	-	-	2
Luis Perez Sala	E	26 (6)	-	-	-	-	-	1	-	-	1
Michele Alboreto	I	16	-	-	-	-	-	1	-	-	1
Gianni Morbidelli	I	32 (1)	-	-	-	-	-	-	-	-	-
Alessandro Nannini	I	30 (2)	-	-	-	-	-	-	-	-	-
Adrian Campos	E	17 (4)	-	-	-	-	-	-	-	-	-
Andrea de Cesaris	I	15 (1)	-	-	-	-	-	-	-	-	-
Paolo Barilla	I	9 (6)	-	-	-	-	-	-	-	-	-
Jean-Marc Gounon	F	2	-	-	-	-	-	-	-	-	-
Roberto Moreno	BR	1	-	-	-	-	-	-	-	-	-
Alessandro Zanardi	I	1 (2)	-	-	-	-	-	-	-	-	-

MINARDI GRAND PRIX CARS

Type	Year	Engine	Designer
M185	1985	Ford DFV V8, Motori Moderni V6 tc	Giacomo Caliri
M185B	1986	Motori Moderni V6 tc	Giacomo Caliri
M186	1986	Motori Moderni V6 tc	Giacomo Caliri
M187	1987	Motori Moderni V6 tc	Giacomo Caliri
M188	1988	Ford DFZ V8	Giacomo Caliri/Aldo Costa
M188B	1989	Ford DFR V8	Giacomo Caliri/Aldo Costa
M189	1989	Ford DFR V8	Aldo Costa/ Nigel Couperthwaite
M190	1990	Ford DFR V8	Aldo Costa/ Vincenzo Emiliani
M191	1991	Ferrari Tipo 036 V12	Aldo Costa
M191B	1992	Lamborghini 3512 V12	Aldo Costa
M192	1992	Lamborghini 3512 V12	Aldo Costa
M193	1993	Ford HB V8	Aldo Costa/Gustav Brunner
M193B	1994	Ford HB V8	Aldo Costa/Gustav Brunner

MONTEVERDI

see Onyx

ONYX

Includes Monteverdi

GP Debut:	1989 Mexican GP	Johansson (retired)
Last GP:	1990 German GP	Lehto (not classified), Foitek (retired). Cars were officially renamed Monteverdi for this final race
Principal:	Mike Earle and Joe Chamberlain, 1989; Jean-Pierre van Rossem/Moneytron, 1989-90; Peter Monteverdi, 1990	
Base:	Littlehampton (GB)	

WORLD CHAMPIONSHIP RECORD

GPs Started: 17
Points: 6
Best result: 3rd 1989 Portuguese GP (Johansson)
Best qualif.:   11th 1989 French GP (Gachot)

Best World Championship position:
Drivers: 11th in 1989 (Johansson)
Constructors: 10th in 1989

MAJOR SPONSORS

1989	Moneytron
1990	Moneytron, Monteverdi

ONYX GRAND PRIX DRIVERS

Driver	Nat	Starts (DNS/DNQ)	1st	2nd	3rd	4th	5th	6th	PP	FL	Points
Stefan Johansson	S	8 (10)	-	1	-	1	-	-	-	-	6
JJ Lehto	SF	7 (7)	-	-	-	-	-	-	-	-	-
Bertrand Gachot	B	5 (7)	-	-	-	-	-	-	-	-	-
Gregor Foitek	CH	5 (3)	-	-	-	-	-	-	-	-	-

ONYX GRAND PRIX CARS

Type	Year	Engine	Designer
ORE1	1989	Ford DFR V8	Alan Jenkins/Bernie Marcus
ORE2*	1990	Ford DFR V8	Alan Jenkins/Bernie Marcus

*Officially renamed Monteverdi ORE2 for its final Grand Prix

OSCA

OFFICINE SPECIALIZATE COSTRUZIONE AUTOMOBILI (FRATELLI MASERATI)

GP Debut:	1951 Italian GP	Rol (9th)
Last GP:	1953 Italian GP	Chiron (10th), Bayol (retired)
Principal:	Ernesto Maserati, 1948-53	
Base:	San Lazzaro di Savena, near Bologna (I)	

WORLD CHAMPIONSHIP RECORD

GPs Started: 4
Best result: 9th 1951 Italian GP (Rol)
Best qualif.:   10th 1952 Italian GP (Bayol)

OSCA GRAND PRIX DRIVERS

Driver	Nat	Starts (DNS/DNQ)	1st	2nd	3rd	4th	5th	6th	PP	FL	Points
Elie Bayol	F	3 (1)	-	-	-	-	-	-	-	-	-
Louis Chiron	MC	2 (2)	-	-	-	-	-	-	-	-	-
Franco Rol	I	1	-	-	-	-	-	-	-	-	-
Giulio Cabianca	I	- (1)	-	-	-	-	-	-	-	-	-
Luigi Piotti	I	- (1)	-	-	-	-	-	-	-	-	-

OSCA GRAND PRIX CARS

Type	Year	Engine	Designer
4500G	1951	OSCA V12	Ernesto Maserati/Bindo Maserati/Ettore Maserati
20	1952	OSCA S6	Ernesto Maserati/Bindo Maserati/Ettore Maserati

OSELLA

Team sold to Fondmetal in 1991; also see Fondmetal

GP Debut:	1980 South African GP Cheever (retired)
Last GP:	1990 Australian GP Grouillard (13th)
Principal:	Enzo Osella
Base:	Volpiano, near Turin (I)

WORLD CHAMPIONSHIP RECORD

GPs Started: 132
Points: 5
Best result: 4th 1982 San Marino GP (Jarier)
Best qualif.:   8th 1990 United States GP (Grouillard)

Best World Championship position:
Drivers: 19th in 1984 (Ghinzani)
Constructors: 12th in 1984

MAJOR SPONSORS

1980-81	Denim
1982	Denim, Saima
1983-85	Kelemata
1986	Landis & Gyr
1987	Landis & Gyr, Stievani
1988	Stievani
1989-90	Fondmetal

OSELLA GRAND PRIX DRIVERS

Driver	Nat	Starts (DNS/DNQ)	1st	2nd	3rd	4th	5th	6th	PP	FL	Points
Jean-Pierre Jarier	F	20 (3)	-	-	-	1	-	-	-	-	3
Piercarlo Ghinzani	I	47 (26)	-	-	-	-	1	-	-	-	2
Nicola Larini	I	18 (14)	-	-	-	-	-	-	-	-	-
Alex Caffi	I	15 (2)	-	-	-	-	-	-	-	-	-
Eddie Cheever	USA	10 (4)	-	-	-	-	-	-	-	-	-
Olivier Grouillard	F	9 (7)	-	-	-	-	-	-	-	-	-
Corrado Fabi	I	9 (6)	-	-	-	-	-	-	-	-	-
Allen Berg	CDN	9	-	-	-	-	-	-	-	-	-

World Championship Grand Prix Racing

Driver	Nat	Starts	1st	2nd	3rd	4th	5th	6th	PP	FL	Points
		(DNS/DNQ)									
Jo Gartner	A	8	-	-	-	-	1*	-	-	-	-
Huub Rothengatter	NL	7 (1)	-	-	-	-	-	-	-	-	-
Christian Danner	D	5 (1)	-	-	-	-	-	-	-	-	-
Beppe Gabbiani	I	3 (12)	-	-	-	-	-	-	-	-	-
Ricardo Paletti	I	2 (6)	-	-	-	-	-	-	-	-	-
Franco Forini	CH	2 (1)	-	-	-	-	-	-	-	-	-
Miguel Angel Guerra	RA	1 (3)	-	-	-	-	-	-	-	-	-
Gabriele Tarquini	I	1	-	-	-	-	-	-	-	-	-
Giorgio Francia	I	- (1)	-	-	-	-	-	-	-	-	-

*not entered in World Championship so ineligible for points

OSELLA GRAND PRIX CARS

Type	Year	Engine	Designer
FA1	1980	Ford DFV V8	Enzo Osella/Giorgio Stirano
FA1B	1980	Ford DFV V8	Enzo Osella/Giorgio Stirano/Giorgio Valentini
FA1C	1981	Ford DFV V8	Enzo Osella/Giorgio Valentini/Hervé Guilpin
FA1D	1983	Ford DFV V8	Enzo Osella/Giuseppe Petrotta/Hervé Guilpin
FA1E	1983	Alfa Romeo 1260 V12	Tony Southgate
FA1F	1984	Alfa Romeo 890T V8 tc	Giuseppe Petrotta
FA1G	1985	Alfa Romeo 890T V8 tc	Giuseppe Petrotta
FA1H	1986	Alfa Romeo 890T V8 tc	Giuseppe Petrotta
FA1I	1987	Alfa Romeo 890T V8 tc	Giuseppe Petrotta
FA1L	1988	Alfa Romeo 890T V8 tc*	Antonio Tomaini
FA1M	1989	Ford DFR V8	Antonio Tomaini
FA1Me	1990**	Ford DFR V8	Antonio Tomaini

*engine officially renamed Osella
**Renamed Fomet FA1Me when company sold to Fondmetal

PACIFIC

GP Debut:	1994 Brazilian GP	Gachot (retired)
Latest GP:	1994 Canadian GP	Gachot (retired)
Principal:	Keith Wiggins, 1994 to date	
Base:	Thetford (GB)	

WORLD CHAMPIONSHIP RECORD

GPs Started: 5
Best result: no finishes
Best qualif.:   23rd 1994 Monaco GP (Gachot)

MAJOR SPONSORS

1994	Ursus

PACIFIC GRAND PRIX DRIVERS

Driver	Nat	Starts	1st	2nd	3rd	4th	5th	6th	PP	FL	Points
		(DNS/DNQ)									
Bertrand Gachot	B	5 (11)	-	-	-	-	-	-	-	-	-
Paul Belmondo	F	2 (14)	-	-	-	-	-	-	-	-	-

PACIFIC GRAND PRIX CARS

Type	Year	Engine	Designer
PR01	1994	Ilmor 2175A V10	Rory Byrne/Paul Brown
		Originally designed and built by Reynard Racing Cars	

PARNELLI

GP Debut:	1974 Canadian GP	Andretti (7th)
Last GP:	1976 Long Beach GP	Andretti (retired)
Principal:	Velco Miletich and Rufus Parnelli Jones	
Base:	Torrence (USA)	

WORLD CHAMPIONSHIP RECORD

GPs Started: 16
Points: 6
Best result: 4th 1975 Swedish GP (Andretti)
Best qualif.: 3rd 1974 United States GP (Andretti)
Fastest laps: 1 1975 Spanish GP (Andretti)
Laps/miles in the lead: 10 laps/24 miles

Best World Championship position:
Drivers: 14th in 1975 (Andretti). Andretti finished sixth in 1976 scoring one point for Parnelli and 21 for Lotus
Constructors: 10th in 1975

MAJOR SPONSORS

1974-75	Viceroy
1976	American Wheels

PARNELLI GRAND PRIX DRIVERS

Driver	Nat	Starts	1st	2nd	3rd	4th	5th	6th	PP	FL	Points
		(DNS/DNQ)									
Mario Andretti	USA	16	-	-	-	1	1	1	-	1	6

PARNELLI GRAND PRIX CARS

Type	Year	Engine	Designer
VPJ4	1974	Ford DFV V8	Maurice Philippe
VPJ4B	1976	Ford DFV V8	Maurice Philippe

PENSKE

GP Debut:	1974 Canadian GP	Donohue (12th)
Last GP:	1977 Canadian GP	Ongais (7th)
Principal:	Roger Penske	
Base:	Reading, Pennsylvania (USA) and Poole (GB)	

WORLD CHAMPIONSHIP RECORD

GPs Started: 40
Points: 23
Wins: 1 1976 Austrian GP (Watson)
Best qualif.: 2nd 1976 Austrian GP (Watson)
Laps/miles in the lead: 45 laps/165 miles

Best World Championship position:
Drivers: 7th in 1976 (Watson)
Constructors: 5th in 1976

MAJOR SPONSORS

1974-76	First National City

PENSKE GRAND PRIX DRIVERS

Driver	Nat	Starts	1st	2nd	3rd	4th	5th	6th	PP	FL	Points
		(DNS/DNQ)									
John Watson	GB	17	1	-	2	-	1	1	-	-	20
Mark Donohue	USA	11	-	-	-	-	1	-	-	-	2
Jean-Pierre Jarier	F	10 (1)	-	-	-	-	-	1	-	-	1
Hans Binder	A	2 (1)	-	-	-	-	-	-	-	-	-
Danny Ongais	USA	2	-	-	-	-	-	-	-	-	-
Boy Hayje	NL	1	-	-	-	-	-	-	-	-	-
Hans Heyer	D	1	-	-	-	-	-	-	-	-	-

PENSKE GRAND PRIX CARS

Type	Year	Engine	Designer
PC1	1974	Ford DFV V8	Geoff Ferris
PC3	1976	Ford DFV V8	Geoff Ferris
PC4	1976	Ford DFV V8	Geoff Ferris

PORSCHE

GP Debut:	1957 German GP	Barth, de Beaufort and Maglioli (all raced in F2 class)
Last GP:	1964 Dutch GP	de Beaufort (retired)
Principal:	Ferry Porsche	
Base:	Zuffenhausen, Stuttgart (D)	

WORLD CHAMPIONSHIP RECORD

GPs Started: 33
Points: 50
Wins: 1 1962 French GP (Gurney)
Pole pos.:   1 1962 German GP (Gurney)
Laps/miles in the lead: 20 laps/107 miles

Best World Championship position:
Drivers: 3rd in 1961 (Gurney)
Constructors: 3rd in 1961

PORSCHE GRAND PRIX DRIVERS

Driver	Nat	Starts	1st	2nd	3rd	4th	5th	6th	PP	FL	Points
		(DNS/DNQ)									
Dan Gurney	USA	15	1	3	1	-	2	1	1	-	36
Jo Bonnier	S	15	-	-	-	-	2	2	-	-	6

Driver	Nat	Starts	1st	2nd	3rd	4th	5th	6th	PP	FL	Points
		(DNS/DNQ)									
Carel Godin											
de Beaufort	NL	26 (3)	-	-	-	-	4	-	-		4
Gerhard Mitter	D	2	-	-	1	-	-	-			3
Hans Herrmann	D	4	-	-	-	-	1	-	-		1
Edgar Barth	DDR	3	-	-	-	-	-				-
Wolfgang von Trips	D	1 (1)	-	-	-	-	-	-			-
Harry Blanchard	USA	1	-	-	-						-
Fred Gamble	USA	1	-	-	-						-
Masten Gregory	USA	1	-	-	-						-
Umberto Maglioli	I	1	-	-	-						-
Ben Pon	NL	1	-	-	-						-
Nino Vaccarella	I	1	-	-	-						-
Heini Walter	CH	1	-	-	-						-
Jean Behra	F	- (1)	-	-	-						-
Maria Teresa											
de Filippis	I	- (1)	-	-	-						-

PORSCHE GRAND PRIX CARS

Type	Year	Engine	Designer
550RS	1957	Porsche 547 F4	Wilhelm Hild
718 RSK	1958	Porsche 547 F4	Wilhelm Hild
Behra-			
Porsche	1959	Porsche RSK F4	Valerio Colotti
718	1959	Porsche RSK F4	Wilhelm Hild/Hans
			Mezger/Helmuth Bott
787	1961	Porsche RSK F4	Wilhelm Hild
804	1962	Porsche 753 F8	Hans Honich/
			Hans Mezger
			Air cooled

PROTOS

Only GP: 1967 German GP — Hart and Ahrens (both raced in F2 class)

Principal: Ron Harris

WORLD CHAMPIONSHIP RECORD

GPs Started: 1
Best result: No finishes

PROTOS GRAND PRIX DRIVERS

Driver	Nat	Starts	1st	2nd	3rd	4th	5th	6th	PP	FL	Points
		(DNS/DNQ)									
Kurt Ahrens Jr	D	1	-	-	-	-	-	-	-	-	-
Brian Hart	GB	1	-	-	-	-	-	-	-	-	-

PROTOS GRAND PRIX CARS

Type	Year	Engine	Designer
Protos	1967	Ford FVA S4	Frank Costin/Brian Hart
			F2 car, wooden chassis

RAM

GP Debut: 1983 Brazilian GP — Salazar (15th)
Last GP: 1985 European GP — Alliot (retired)
Principal: John Macdonald and Mick Ralph
Base: Bicester (GB)

WORLD CHAMPIONSHIP RECORD

GPs Started: 31
Best result: 8th 1984 Brazilian GP (Palmer)
Best qualif.: 14th 1985 Canadian GP (Winkelhock)

MAJOR SPONSORS

1984-85	Skoal Bandit

RAM GRAND PRIX DRIVERS

Driver	Nat	Starts	1st	2nd	3rd	4th	5th	6th	PP	FL	Points
		(DNS/DNQ)									
Philippe Alliot	F	26 (4)	-	-	-	-	-	-	-	-	-
Jonathan Palmer	GB	14 (1)	-	-	-	-	-	-	-	-	-
Manfred Winkelhock	D	8 (1)	-	-	-	-	-	-	-	-	-
Kenneth Acheson	GB	3 (7)	-	-	-	-	-	-	-	-	-

Driver	Nat	Starts	1st	2nd	3rd	4th	5th	6th	PP	FL	Points
		(DNS/DNQ)									
Eliseo Salazar	RCH	2 (4)	-	-	-	-	-	-	-	-	-
Mike Thackwell	NZ	1	-	-	-	-	-	-	-	-	-
Jean-Louis Schlesser	F	- (1)	-	-	-	-	-	-	-	-	-
Jacques Villeneuve	CDN	- (1)	-	-	-	-	-	-	-	-	-

RAM GRAND PRIX CARS

Type	Year	Engine	Designer
01*	1983	Ford DFV V8	Dave Kelly
01	1984	Hart 415T S4 tc	Dave Kelly
02	1984	Hart 415T S4 tc	Dave Kelly
03	1985	Hart 415T S4 tc	Gustav Brunner/
			Sergio Rinland/Tim Feast
			*RAM-March

REBAQUE

Only GP: 1979 Canadian GP — Rebaque (retired)
Principal: Hector Rebaque
Base: Constructor: Poole (GB); Team: Leamington-Spa (GB)

WORLD CHAMPIONSHIP RECORD

GPs Started: 1
Best result: No finishes
Best qualif.: 22nd 1979 Canadian GP (Rebaque)

REBAQUE GRAND PRIX DRIVERS

Driver	Nat	Starts	1st	2nd	3rd	4th	5th	6th	PP	FL	Points
		(DNS/DNQ)									
Hector Rebaque	MEX	1 (2)	-	-	-	-	-	-	-	-	-

REBAQUE GRAND PRIX CARS

Type	Year	Engine	Designer
HR100	1979	Ford DFV V8	Geoff Ferris
			Designed and built by Penske Cars

RENAULT

GP Debut: 1977 British GP — Jabouille (retired)
Last GP: 1985 Australian GP — Warwick (retired), Tambay (retired)
Principal: François Castaing; Bernard Dudot
Base: Viry-Châtillon (F)

WORLD CHAMPIONSHIP RECORD

GPs Started: 123
Points: 312
Wins: 15 1979 French GP (Jabouille), 1980 Brazilian GP (Arnoux), South African GP (Arnoux), Austrian GP (Jabouille), 1981 French GP (Prost), Dutch GP (Prost), Italian GP (Prost), 1982 South African GP (Prost), Brazilian GP (Prost), French GP (Arnoux), Italian GP (Arnoux), 1983 French GP (Prost), Belgian GP (Prost), British GP (Prost), Austrian GP (Prost)
Pole pos.: 31 1979 South African GP (Jabouille), French GP (Jabouille), German GP (Jabouille), Austrian GP (Arnoux), Dutch GP (Arnoux), Italian GP (Jabouille), 1980 Brazilian GP (Jabouille), South African GP (Jabouille), Austrian GP (Arnoux), Dutch GP (Arnoux), Italian GP (Arnoux), 1981 French GP (Arnoux), British GP (Arnoux), German GP (Prost), Austrian GP (Arnoux), Dutch GP (Prost), Italian GP (Arnoux), 1982 South African GP (Arnoux), Brazilian GP (Prost), San Marino GP (Arnoux), Belgian GP (Prost), Monaco GP (Arnoux), Detroit GP (Prost), Dutch GP (Arnoux), French GP (Arnoux), Swiss GP (Prost), Las Vegas GP (Prost), 1983 French GP (Prost), Monaco GP (Prost), Belgian GP (Prost), 1984 French GP (Tambay)
Fastest laps: 18 1979 French GP (Arnoux), Austrian GP (Arnoux), 1980 Brazilian GP (Arnoux), South African GP (Arnoux), Austrian GP (Arnoux), Dutch GP (Arnoux), 1981 French GP (Prost), British GP (Arnoux), 1982 South African GP (Prost), Brazilian GP (Prost), Detroit GP (Prost), Swiss GP (Prost), Italian GP (Arnoux), 1983 French GP (Prost),

British GP (Prost), Austrian GP (Prost), 1984 South
African GP (Tambay), Detroit GP (Warwick)

Laps/miles in the lead: 1220 laps/3707 miles

Best World Championship position:
Drivers: 2nd in 1983 (Prost)
Constructors: 2nd in 1983

MAJOR SPONSORS

1977-85	Elf

RENAULT GRAND PRIX DRIVERS

Driver	Nat	Starts	1st	2nd	3rd	4th	5th	6th	PP	FL	Points
		(DNS/DNQ)									
Alain Prost	F	46	9	6	2	2	1	1	10	8	134
René Arnoux	F	58 (2)	4	5	2	2	2	1	14	8	85
Jean-Pierre Jabouille	F	45 (2)	2	-	-	1	-	-	6	-	21
Derek Warwick	GB	31	-	2	2	1	2	1	-	1	28
Patrick Tambay	F	30 (1)	-	1	2	-	3	2	1	1	22
Eddie Cheever	USA	15	-	1	3	1	-	1	-	-	22
François Hesnault	F	1	-	-	-	-	-	-	-	-	-
Philippe Streiff	F	1	-	-	-	-	-	-	-	-	-

RENAULT GRAND PRIX CARS

Type	Year	Engine	Designer
RS01	1977	Renault EF1 V6 tc	Andre de Cortanze/ Marcel Hubert
RE10	1979	Renault EF1 V6 tc	Michel Têtu
RE20	1980	Renault EF1 V6 tc	Michel Têtu
RE20B	1981	Renault EF1 V6 tc	Michel Têtu
RE30	1981	Renault EF1 V6 tc	Michel Têtu
RE30B	1982	Renault EF1 V6 tc	Michel Têtu
RE30C	1983	Renault EF1 V6 tc	Michel Têtu
RE40	1983	Renault EF1 V6 tc	Michel Têtu
RE50	1984	Renault EF4 V6 tc	Michel Têtu
RE60	1984	Renault EF4B V6 tc	Michel Têtu/Jean-Marc d'Adda/Bernard Touret
RE60B	1985	Renault EF15 V6 tc	Jean-Marc d'Adda/ Bernard Touret

RIAL

GP Debut: 1988 Brazilian GP   de Cesaris (retired)
Last GP: 1989 Canadian GP   Danner (8th)
Principal: Hans-Günther Schmidt
Base: Fussgoenheim (D)

WORLD CHAMPIONSHIP RECORD

GPs Started: 20
Points: 6
Best result: 4th 1988 Detroit GP (de Cesaris), 1989 United
States GP (Danner)
Best qualif.: 12th 1988 Mexican GP (de Cesaris), Canadian GP (de
Cesaris), Detroit GP (de Cesaris), French GP (de
Cesaris), Portuguese GP (de Cesaris)

Best World Championship position:
Drivers: 15th in 1988 (de Cesaris)
Constructors: 9th in 1988

MAJOR SPONSORS

1988-89	Rial Wheels

RIAL GRAND PRIX DRIVERS

Driver	Nat	Starts	1st	2nd	3rd	4th	5th	6th	PP	FL	Points
		(DNS/DNQ)									
Andrea de Cesaris	I	16	-	-	-	1	-	-	-	-	3
Christian Danner	D	4 (9)	-	-	-	1	-	-	-	-	3
Volker Weidler	D	- (10)	-	-	-	-	-	-	-	-	-
Pierre-Henri Raphanel	F	- (6)	-	-	-	-	-	-	-	-	-
Bertrand Gachot	B	- (2)	-	-	-	-	-	-	-	-	-
Gregor Foitek	CH	- (1)	-	-	-	-	-	-	-	-	-

RIAL GRAND PRIX CARS

Type	Year	Engine	Designer
ARC1	1988	Ford DFZ V8	Gustav Brunner
ARC2	1989	Ford DFR V8	Gustav Brunner/ Stefan Fober/Bob Bell

SAUBER

GP Debut: 1993 South African GP Lehto (5th),
Wendlinger (retired)
Latest GP: 1994 Australian GP   Frentzen (7th), Lehto (10th)
Principal: Peter Sauber
Base: Hinwil (CH)

WORLD CHAMPIONSHIP RECORD

GPs Started: 31
Points: 24
Best result: 4th 1993 San Marino GP (Lehto), Italian GP
(Wendlinger) 1994 San Marino GP
(Wendlinger) and French GP (Frentzen)
Best qualif.: 3rd 1994 Japanese GP (Frentzen)

Best World Championship position:
Drivers: 12th in 1993 (Wendlinger)
Constructors: 6th in 1993

MAJOR SPONSORS

1993	Mercedes-Benz, Lighthouse
1994	Mercedes-Benz, Broker, Tissot

SAUBER GRAND PRIX DRIVERS

Driver	Nat	Starts	1st	2nd	3rd	4th	5th	6th	PP	FL	Points
		(DNS/DNQ)									
Karl Wendlinger	A	19 (1)	-	-	-	2	1	3	-	-	11
Heinz-Harald Frentzen	D	15 (1)	-	-	-	1	1	2	-	-	7
JJ Lehto	SF	18	-	-	-	1	1	-	-	-	5
Andrea de Cesaris	I	9	-	-	-	-	-	1	-	-	1

SAUBER GRAND PRIX CARS

Type	Year	Engine	Designer
C12	1993	Ilmor 2175A V10, Sauber V10	Leo Ress
C13	1994	Mercedes-Benz V10	Leo Ress

SCARAB

GP Debut: 1960 Belgian GP   Daigh (retired),
Reventlow (retired)
Last GP: 1960 United States GP Daigh (10th)
Principal: Lance Reventlow
Base: Culver City (USA)

WORLD CHAMPIONSHIP RECORD

GPs Started: 2
Best result: 10th 1960 United States GP (Daigh)
Best qualif.: 16th 1960 Dutch GP (Daigh) - did not start, Belgian
GP (Reventlow)

SCARAB GRAND PRIX DRIVERS

Driver	Nat	Starts	1st	2nd	3rd	4th	5th	6th	PP	FL	Points
		(DNS/DNQ)									
Chuck Daigh	USA	2 (3)	-	-	-	-	-	-	-	-	-
Lance Reventlow	USA	1 (2)	-	-	-	-	-	-	-	-	-
Richie Ginther	USA	- (1)	-	-	-	-	-	-	-	-	-

SCARAB GRAND PRIX CARS

Type	Year	Engine	Designer
Scarab	1960	Scarab S4	Dick Troutmann/ Tom Barnes

SCIROCCO

GP Debut: 1963 Belgian GP   Settember (8th)
Last GP: 1964 Belgian GP   Pilette (retired)
Principal: Hugh Powell
Base: West London (GB)

WORLD CHAMPIONSHIP RECORD

GPs Started: 5
Best result: 8th 1963 Belgian GP (Settember)
Best qualif.: 18th 1963 British GP (Settember)

SCIROCCO GRAND PRIX DRIVERS

Driver	Nat	Starts	1st	2nd	3rd	4th	5th	6th	PP	FL	Points
		(DNS/DNQ)									
Tony Settember	USA	4 (1)	-	-	-	-	-	-	-	-	-
Ian Burgess	GB	2	-	-	-	-	-	-	-	-	-
André Pilette	B	1 (1)	-	-	-	-	-	-	-	-	-

SCIROCCO GRAND PRIX CARS

Type	Year	Engine	Designer
01	1963	BRM 56 V8	Hugh Aiden-Jones/ Paul Emery
02	1963	BRM 56 V8, Climax FMWV V8	Hugh Aiden-Jones/ Paul Emery

SHADOW

GP Debut:	1973 South African GP Follmer (6th), Oliver (retired)
Last GP:	1980 South African GP Lees (retired)
Principal:	Don Nichols
Base:	Northampton (GB)

WORLD CHAMPIONSHIP RECORD

GPs Started: 104
Points: 68.5
Wins: 1 1977 Austrian GP (Jones)
Pole pos.: 3 1975 Argentinian GP (Jarier), Brazilian GP (Jarier), British GP (Pryce)
Fastest laps: 2 1975 Brazilian GP (Jarier), 1976 Brazilian GP (Jarier)
Laps/miles in the lead: 50 laps/208 miles
Best World Championship position:
Drivers: 7th in 1977 (Jones)
Constructors: 6th in 1975

MAJOR SPONSORS

1973-75	UOP (Universal Oil Products)
1976	Benihana, Bic, Lucky Strike, Tabatip
1977	Ambrosio, Tabatip
1978	Villiger
1979	Interscope, Samson
1980	Theodore, Interlekt

SHADOW GRAND PRIX DRIVERS

Driver	Nat	Starts	1st	2nd	3rd	4th	5th	6th	PP	FL	Points
		(DNS/DNQ)									
Alan Jones	AUS	14	1	-	1	2	1	1	-	-	22
Tom Pryce	GB	41	-	-	2	3	-	4	1	-	19
Jean-Pierre Jarier	F	44 (1)	-	-	1	1	1	-	2	2	7.5
George Follmer	USA	12 (1)	-	-	1	-	-	1	-	-	5
Jackie Oliver	GB	14	-	-	1	-	-	-	-	-	4
Clay Regazzoni	CH	11 (5)	-	-	-	2	-	-	-	-	4
Hans-Joachim Stuck	D	14 (2)	-	-	-	-	1	-	-	-	2
Elio de Angelis	I	14 (1)	-	-	-	1	-	-	-	-	3
Riccardo Patrese	I	9	-	-	-	-	-	1	-	-	1
Renzo Zorzi	I	5	-	-	-	-	-	1	-	-	1
Jan Lammers	NL	12 (3)	-	-	-	-	-	-	-	-	-
Graham Hill	GB	12	-	-	-	-	-	-	-	-	-
Brian Redman	GB	4	-	-	-	-	-	-	-	-	-
Peter Revson	USA	2	-	-	-	-	-	-	-	-	-
Geoff Lees	GB	1 (4)	-	-	-	-	-	-	-	-	-
Arturo Merzario	I	1	-	-	-	-	-	-	-	-	-
Bertil Roos	S	1	-	-	-	-	-	-	-	-	-
David Kennedy	IRL	- (7)	-	-	-	-	-	-	-	-	-
Stefan Johansson	S	- (2)	-	-	-	-	-	-	-	-	-
Danny Ongais	USA	- (2)	-	-	-	-	-	-	-	-	-
Mike Wilds	GB	- (1)	-	-	-	-	-	-	-	-	-

SHADOW GRAND PRIX CARS

Type	Year	Engine	Designer
DN1A	1973	Ford DFV V8	Tony Southgate
DN3A	1974	Ford DFV V8	Tony Southgate
DN3B	1975	Ford DFV V8	Tony Southgate
DN5A	1975	Ford DFV V8	Tony Southgate
DN5B	1976	Ford DFV V8	Tony Southgate
DN7A	1975	Matra MS73 V12	Tony Southgate
DN8A	1976	Ford DFV V8	Tony Southgate/Dave Wass
DN9A	1978	Ford DFV V8	Tony Southgate/ John Baldwin
DN9B	1979	Ford DFV V8	Richard Owen/John Gentry
DN11A	1980	Ford DFV V8	John Gentry/ Richard Owen/Vic Morris
DN12A	1980	Ford DFV V8	Vic Morris/Chuck Greameger

SHANNON

Only GP:	1966 British GP Taylor (retired)
Principal:	Hugh Aiden-Jones and Paul Emery

WORLD CHAMPIONSHIP RECORD

GPs Started: 1
Best result: No finishes
Best qualif.: 18th 1966 British GP (Taylor)

SHANNON GRAND PRIX DRIVERS

Driver	Nat	Starts	1st	2nd	3rd	4th	5th	6th	PP	FL	Points
		(DNS/DNQ)									
Trevor Taylor	GB	1	-	-	-	-	-	-	-	-	-

SHANNON GRAND PRIX CARS

Type	Year	Engine	Designer
SH1	1966	Climax FPE V8	Hugh Aiden-Jones/ Paul Emery

SIMTEK

GP Debut:	1994 Brazilian GP Brabham (12th)
Latest GP:	1994 Australian GP Brabham (retired), Schiattarella (retired)
Principal:	Nick Wirth
Base:	Banbury (GB)

WORLD CHAMPIONSHIP RECORD

GPs Started: 16
Best result: 9th 1994 French GP (Gounon)
Best qualif.: 21st 1994 Belgian GP (Brabham)

MAJOR SPONSORS

1994	MTV

SIMTEK GRAND PRIX DRIVERS

Driver	Nat	Starts	1st	2nd	3rd	4th	5th	6th	PP	FL	Points
		(DNS/DNQ)									
David Brabham	AUS	16	-	-	-	-	-	-	-	-	-
Jean-Marc Gounon	F	7	-	-	-	-	-	-	-	-	-
Domenico Schiattarella	I	2	-	-	-	-	-	-	-	-	-
Roland Ratzenberger	A	1 (2)	-	-	-	-	-	-	-	-	-
Taki Inoue	J	1	-	-	-	-	-	-	-	-	-
Andrea Montermini	I	- (1)	-	-	-	-	-	-	-	-	-

SIMTEK GRAND PRIX CARS

Type	Year	Engine	Designer
S941	1994	Ford HB V8	Nick Wirth

SPIRIT

GP Debut:	1983 British GP Johansson (retired)
Last GP:	1985 San Marino GP Baldi (retired)
Principal:	John Wickham and Gordon Coppuck
Base:	Slough (GB)

WORLD CHAMPIONSHIP RECORD

GPs Started: 23
Best result: 7th 1983 Dutch GP (Johansson)
Best qualif.: 13th 1983 German GP (Johansson)

SPIRIT GRAND PRIX DRIVERS

Driver	Nat	Starts	1st	2nd	3rd	4th	5th	6th	PP	FL	Points
		(DNS/DNQ)									
Mauro Baldi	I	10 (1)	-	-	-	-	-	-	-	-	-
Huub Rothengatter	NL	7 (1)	-	-	-	-	-	-	-	-	-
Stefan Johansson	S	6	-	-	-	-	-	-	-	-	-

SPIRIT GRAND PRIX CARS

Type	Year	Engine	Designer
201*	1983	Honda RA163E V6 tc	Gordon Coppuck/
			John Baldwin
101B	1984	Hart 415T S4 tc	Gordon Coppuck
101C	1984	Ford DFV V8	Gordon Coppuck
101D	1985	Hart 415T S4 tc	Gordon Coppuck
			*Converted F2 car

STEBRO

Only GP: 1963 United States GP Broeker (7th)

WORLD CHAMPIONSHIP RECORD

GPs Started: 1
Best result: 7th 1963 United States GP (Broeker)
Best qualif.: 21st 1963 United States GP (Broeker)

STEBRO GRAND PRIX DRIVERS

Driver	Nat	Starts	1st	2nd	3rd	4th	5th	6th	PP	FL	Points
		(DNS/DNQ)									
Peter Broeker	CDN	1	-	-	-	-	-	-	-	-	-

STEBRO GRAND PRIX CARS

Type	Year	Engine	Designer
4	1963	Ford 105E S4	-

SURTEES

GP Debut:	1970 British GP	Surtees (retired)
Last GP:	1978 Canadian GP	Arnoux (retired)
Principal:	John Surtees
Base:	Edenbridge, Kent (GB)

WORLD CHAMPIONSHIP RECORD

GPs Started: 118
Points: 54
Best result: 2nd 1972 Italian GP (Hailwood)
Best qualif.: 2nd 1974 South African GP (Pace)
Fastest laps: 3 1972 South African GP (Hailwood), 1973 German GP (Pace), Austrian GP (Pace)
Laps/miles in the lead: 9 laps/28 miles

Best World Championship position:
Drivers: 8th in 1972 (Hailwood)
Constructors: 5th in 1972

MAJOR SPONSORS

1971	Brooke Bond Oxo, Rob Walker, AMS, Eifelland
1972	Brooke Bond Oxo, Rob Walker, Ceramica Pagnossin, Flame Out
1973	Brooke Bond Oxo, Rob Walker, Ceramica Pagnossin, Fina
1974	Bang & Olufsen, Fina, Memphis
1975	Matchbox, National
1976	Campari, Chesterfield, Durex, Theodore
1977	Beta, Durex
1978	Beta, Durex, British Air Ferries

SURTEES GRAND PRIX DRIVERS

Driver	Nat	Starts	1st	2nd	3rd	4th	5th	6th	PP	FL	Points
		(DNS/DNQ)									
Mike Hailwood	GB	27	-	1	-	3	-	1	-	1	16
Carlos Pace	BR	22	-	-	1	2	-	-	-	2	10
Vittorio Brambilla	I	29 (2)	-	-	-	1	1	2	-	-	7
Alan Jones	AUS	14	-	-	-	1	2	-	-	-	7
John Surtees	GB	19 (1)	-	-	-	-	2	1	-	-	5
Andrea de Adamich	I	13	-	-	-	1	-	-	-	-	3
Rolf Stommelen	D	9 (1)	-	-	-	-	1	1	-	-	3
Tim Schenken	AUS	12	-	-	-	-	1	-	-	-	2
Derek Bell	GB	3 (4)	-	-	-	-	1	-	-	-	1
Jochen Mass	D	13 (1)	-	-	-	-	-	-	-	-	-
John Watson	GB	11	-	-	-	-	-	-	-	-	-
Brett Lunger	USA	10 (2)	-	-	-	-	-	-	-	-	-
Hans Binder	A	9	-	-	-	-	-	-	-	-	-
Henri Pescarolo	F	7 (3)	-	-	-	-	-	-	-	-	-
Rupert Keegan	GB	6 (7)	-	-	-	-	-	-	-	-	-
Vern Schuppan	AUS	3 (1)	-	-	-	-	-	-	-	-	-
René Arnoux	F	2	-	-	-	-	-	-	-	-	-
Helmuth Koinigg	A	2	-	-	-	-	-	-	-	-	-
Sam Posey	USA	2	-	-	-	-	-	-	-	-	-
Leo Kinnunen	SF	1 (5)	-	-	-	-	-	-	-	-	-
Larry Perkins	AUS	1 (2)	-	-	-	-	-	-	-	-	-
José Dolhem	F	1 (2)	-	-	-	-	-	-	-	-	-
Gijs van Lennep	NL	1 (1)	-	-	-	-	-	-	-	-	-
Conny Andersson	S	1	-	-	-	-	-	-	-	-	-
Luis-Pereira Bueno	BR	1	-	-	-	-	-	-	-	-	-
John Love	RSR	1	-	-	-	-	-	-	-	-	-
Dave Morgan	GB	1	-	-	-	-	-	-	-	-	-
Dieter Quester	A	1	-	-	-	-	-	-	-	-	-
Brian Redman	GB	1	-	-	-	-	-	-	-	-	-
Noritake Takahara	J	1	-	-	-	-	-	-	-	-	-
Beppe Gabbiani	I	- (2)	-	-	-	-	-	-	-	-	-
Divina Galica	GB	- (1)	-	-	-	-	-	-	-	-	-
"Gimax"	I	- (1)	-	-	-	-	-	-	-	-	-
Jean-Pierre Jabouille	F	- (1)	-	-	-	-	-	-	-	-	-
Lamberto Leoni	I	- (1)	-	-	-	-	-	-	-	-	-
Patrick Tambay	F	- (1)	-	-	-	-	-	-	-	-	-
Tony Trimmer	GB	- (1)	-	-	-	-	-	-	-	-	-

SURTEES GRAND PRIX CARS

Type	Year	Engine	Designer
TS7	1970	Ford DFV V8	John Surtees/Peter Connew/Shahab Ahmed
TS9	1971	Ford DFV V8	John Surtees/Peter Connew/Shahab Ahmed
TS9B	1972	Ford DFV V8	John Surtees/Peter Connew/Shahab Ahmed
TS14	1972	Ford DFV V8	John Surtees
TS14A	1973	Ford DFV V8	John Surtees
TS16/1	1974	Ford DFV V8	John Surtees
TS16/2	1974	Ford DFV V8	John Surtees
TS16/3	1974	Ford DFV V8	John Surtees
TS16/4	1975	Ford DFV V8	John Surtees
TS19	1976	Ford DFV V8	John Surtees/Ken Sears
TS20	1978	Ford DFV V8	John Surtees/Ken Sears

TALBOT

see Lago-Talbot

TEC-MEC

STUDIO TECHNICA-MECCANICA

Only GP: 1959 United States GP d'Orey (retired)
Principal: Valerio Colotti
Base: Modena (I)

WORLD CHAMPIONSHIP RECORD

GPs Started: 1
Best result: No finishes
Best qualif.: 17th 1959 United States GP (d'Orey)

TEC-MEC GRAND PRIX DRIVERS

Driver	Nat	Starts	1st	2nd	3rd	4th	5th	6th	PP	FL	Points
		(DNS/DNQ)									
Fritz d'Orey	BR	1	-	-	-	-	-	-	-	-	-

TEC-MEC GRAND PRIX CARS

Type	Year	Engine	Designer
F415	1959	Maserati 250F S6	Valerio Colotti

TECNO

GP Debut:	1969 German GP Cevert (F2 class)
Last GP:	1973 Dutch GP Amon (retired)
Principal:	Luciano and Gianfranco Pederzani
Base:	Bologna (I)

WORLD CHAMPIONSHIP RECORD

GPs Started: 11
Points: 1
Best result: 6th 1973 Belgian GP (Amon)
Best qualif.: 12th 1973 Monaco GP (Amon)

Best World Championship position:
Drivers: 19th in 1973 (Amon)
Constructors: 11th in 1973

MAJOR SPONSORS

1972-73	Martini

TECNO GRAND PRIX DRIVERS

Driver	Nat	Starts (DNS/DNQ)	1st	2nd	3rd	4th	5th	6th	PP	FL	Points
Chris Amon	NZ	4 (1)	-	-	-	-	1	-	-	1
Nanni Galli	I	4	-	-	-	-	-	-	-	-
Derek Bell	GB	2 (3)	-	-	-	-	-	-	-	-
François Cevert	F	1	-	-	-	-	-	-	-	-

TECNO GRAND PRIX CARS

Type	Year	Engine	Designer
306	1969	Cosworth	Gianfranco Pederzani/ Luciano Pederzani
PA123	1972	Tecno Series P F12	Gianfranco Pederzani/ Luciano Pederzani
PA123 (73)	1973	Tecno Series P F12	Alan McCall

THEODORE

Took over Ensign in 1983; also see Ensign

GP Debut:	1978 South African GP Rosberg (retired)
Last GP:	1983 European GP Guerrero (12th)
Principal:	Teddy Yip
Base:	Woking (GB), 1978; Northampton (GB), 1981-82; Chasetown, Staffordshire (GB), 1983

WORLD CHAMPIONSHIP RECORD

GPs Started: 33
Points: 2
Best result: 6th 1981 Long Beach GP (Tambay), 1983 Long Beach GP (Cecotto)
Best qualif.: 11th 1983 Detroit GP (Guerrero)

Best World Championship position:
Drivers: 18th in 1981 (Tambay)
Constructors: 12th in 1981 and 1983

MAJOR SPONSORS

1981-82	Theodore
1983	Cafe do Colombia

THEODORE GRAND PRIX DRIVERS

Driver	Nat	Starts (DNS/DNQ)	1st	2nd	3rd	4th	5th	6th	PP	FL	Points
Johnny Cecotto	YV	9 (4)	-	-	-	-	1	-	-	1
Patrick Tambay	F	6 (1)	-	-	-	-	1	-	-	1
Roberto Guerrero	USA	13 (1)	-	-	-	-	-	-	-	-
Marc Surer	CH	6 (2)	-	-	-	-	-	-	-	-
Derek Daly	IRL	3	-	-	-	-	-	-	-	-
Tommy Byrne	IRL	2 (3)	-	-	-	-	-	-	-	-
Jan Lammers	NL	1 (5)	-	-	-	-	-	-	-	-
Keke Rosberg	SF	1 (4)	-	-	-	-	-	-	-	-
Geoff Lees	GB	1	-	-	-	-	-	-	-	-
Eddie Cheever	USA	- (2)	-	-	-	-	-	-	-	-

THEODORE GRAND PRIX CARS

Type	Year	Engine	Designer
TR1	1978	Ford DFV V8	Ron Tauranac/Len Bailey
TR2*	1981	Ford DFV V8	Vic Morris/Chuck Greameger
TY01	1981	Ford DFV V8	Tony Southgate
TY02	1982	Ford DFV V8	Tony Southgate
N183	1983	Ford DFV V8	Nigel Bennett

*Formerly Shadow DN12A, renamed Theodore TR2. Only raced in the non-championship South African GP

TOKEN

GP Debut:	1974 Belgian GP Pryce (retired)
Last GP:	1974 Austrian GP Ashley (not classified)
Principal:	Tony Vlassopoulo and Ken Grob
Base:	Woking (GB)

WORLD CHAMPIONSHIP RECORD

GPs Started: 3
Best result: No finishes
Best qualif.: 20th 1974 Belgian GP (Pryce)

MAJOR SPONSORS

1974	Harper, ShellSport

TOKEN GRAND PRIX DRIVERS

Driver	Nat	Starts (DNS/DNQ)	1st	2nd	3rd	4th	5th	6th	PP	FL	Points
Ian Ashley	GB	2	-	-	-	-	-	-	-	-
Tom Pryce	GB	1	-	-	-	-	-	-	-	-
David Purley	GB	- (1)	-	-	-	-	-	-	-	-

TOKEN GRAND PRIX CARS

Type	Year	Engine	Designer
RJ02	1974	Ford DFV V8	Ray Jessop

Commissioned and built by Rondel Racing (owned by Ron Dennis and Neil Trundle). Project sold to Token when money ran out. Renamed Safir after new owners in 1975 but only used in non-championship races

TOLEMAN

Team sold to Benetton in 1985; also see Benetton

GP Debut:	1981 Italian GP Henton (10th)
Last GP:	1985 Australian GP Fabi (retired), Ghinzani (retired)
Principal:	Ted Toleman
Base:	Witney, Oxfordshire (GB)

WORLD CHAMPIONSHIP RECORD

GPs Started: 57
Points: 26
Best result: 2nd 1984 Monaco GP (Senna)
Pole pos.: 1 1985 German GP (Fabi)
Fastest laps: 2 1982 Dutch GP (Warwick), 1984 Monaco GP (Senna)

Best World Championship position:
Drivers: 9th in 1984 (Senna)
Constructors: 7th in 1984

MAJOR SPONSORS

1981-83	Candy
1984	Segafredo
1985	Benetton

TOLEMAN GRAND PRIX DRIVERS

Driver	Nat	Starts (DNS/DNQ)	1st	2nd	3rd	4th	5th	6th	PP	FL	Points
Ayrton Senna	BR	14 (1)	-	1	2	-	-	2	-	1	13
Derek Warwick	GB	26 (15)	-	-	2	1	1	-	1	9
Stefan Johansson	S	3	-	-	-	1	-	-	-	3
Bruno Giacomelli	I	14 (1)	-	-	-	-	1	-	-	1

Driver	Nat	Starts	1st	2nd	3rd	4th	5th	6th	PP	FL	Points
		(DNS/DNQ)									
Teo Fabi	I	20 (7)	-	-	-	-	-	1	-	-	
Johnny Cecotto	YV	9 (1)	-	-	-	-	-	-	-	-	
Piercarlo Ghinzani	I	7	-	-	-	-	-	-	-	-	
Brian Henton	GB	1 (11)	-	-	-	-	-	-	-	-	
Pierluigi Martini	I	- (1)	-	-	-	-	-	-	-	-	

TOLEMAN GRAND PRIX CARS

Type	Year	Engine	Designer
TG181	1981	Hart 415T S4 tc	Rory Byrne/John Gentry
TG181B	1982	Hart 415T S4 tc	Rory Byrne/John Gentry
TG181C	1982	Hart 415T S4 tc	Rory Byrne/John Gentry
TG183	1982	Hart 415T S4 tc	Rory Byrne/John Gentry
TG183B	1983	Hart 415T S4 tc	Rory Byrne/John Gentry
TG184	1984	Hart 415T S4 tc	Rory Byrne/John Gentry
TG185	1985	Hart 415T S4 tc	Rory Byrne

DE TOMASO

GP Debut:	1961 French GP	Scarlatti (retired)	
Last GP:	1970 United States GP	Schenken (retired)	
Principal:	Alessandro de Tomaso		
Base:	Modena (I)		

WORLD CHAMPIONSHIP RECORD

GPs Started: 10
Best result: No finishes
Best qualif.: 9th 1970 Monaco GP (Courage), Dutch GP (Courage)

DE TOMASO GRAND PRIX DRIVERS

Driver	Nat	Starts	1st	2nd	3rd	4th	5th	6th	PP	FL	Points
		(DNS/DNQ)									
Piers Courage	GB	4 (1)	-	-	-	-	-	-	-	-	
Tim Schenken	AUS	4	-	-	-	-	-	-	-	-	
Roberto Lippi	I	1 (2)	-	-	-	-	-	-	-	-	
Roberto Bussinello	I	1	-	-	-	-	-	-	-	-	
Giorgio Scarlatti	I	1	-	-	-	-	-	-	-	-	
Nino Vaccarella	I	1	-	-	-	-	-	-	-	-	
Nasif Estefano	RA	- (2)	-	-	-	-	-	-	-	-	
Brian Redman	GB	- (2)	-	-	-	-	-	-	-	-	

DE TOMASO GRAND PRIX CARS

Type	Year	Engine	Designer
F1/001	1961	OSCA S4	Alessandro de Tomaso
F1/002	1961	OSCA S4, Ferrari V6	Alessandro de Tomaso
F1/003	1961	Alfa Romeo Giulietta S4	Alessandro de Tomaso
F1/004	1961	Alfa Romeo Giulietta S4	Alessandro de Tomaso
F1/801	1962	de Tomaso F8	Alberto Massimino
505/38	1970	Ford DFV V8	Gianpaolo Dallara

TROJAN

GP Debut:	1974 Spanish GP	Schenken (14th)	
Last GP:	1974 Italian GP	Schenken (retired)	
Principal:	Peter Agg		
Base:	Croydon (GB)		

WORLD CHAMPIONSHIP RECORD

GPs Started: 6
Best result: 10th 1974 Belgian GP (Schenken), Austrian GP (Schenken)
Best qualif.: 19th 1974 Austrian GP (Schenken)

MAJOR SPONSORS

1974	Suzuki, Homelite

TROJAN GRAND PRIX DRIVERS

Driver	Nat	Starts	1st	2nd	3rd	4th	5th	6th	PP	FL	Points
		(DNS/DNQ)									
Tim Schenken	AUS	6 (2)	-	-	-	-	-	-	-	-	

TROJAN GRAND PRIX CARS

Type	Year	Engine	Designer
T103	1974	Ford DFV V8	Ron Tauranac

TYRRELL

GP Debut:	1970 Canadian GP	Stewart (retired)
Latest GP:	1994 Australian GP	Katayama (retired), Blundell (retired)
Principal:	Ken Tyrrell	
Base:	Ockham, Surrey (GB)	

WORLD CHAMPIONSHIP RECORD

GPs Started: 364
Points: 699
Wins: 23 1971 Spanish GP (Stewart), Monaco GP (Stewart), French GP (Stewart), British GP (Stewart), German GP (Stewart), Canadian GP (Stewart), United States GP (Cevert), 1972 Argentinian GP (Stewart), French GP (Stewart), Canadian GP (Stewart), United States GP (Stewart), 1973 South African GP (Stewart), Belgian GP (Stewart), Monaco GP (Stewart), Dutch GP (Stewart), German GP (Stewart), 1974 Swedish GP (Scheckter), British GP (Scheckter), 1975 South African GP (Scheckter), 1976 Swedish GP (Scheckter), 1978 Monaco GP (Depailler), 1982 Las Vegas GP (Alboreto), 1983 Detroit GP (Alboreto)
Pole pos.: 14 1970 Canadian GP (Stewart), 1971 South African GP (Stewart), Monaco GP (Stewart), French GP (Stewart), German GP (Stewart), Canadian GP (Stewart), United States GP (Stewart), 1972 South African GP (Stewart), United States GP (Stewart), 1973 Monaco GP (Stewart), French GP (Stewart), German GP (Stewart), 1974 Swedish GP (Depailler), 1976 Swedish GP (Scheckter)
Fastest laps: 20 1971 Monaco GP (Stewart), French GP (Stewart), British GP (Stewart), German GP (Cevert), 1972 Argentinian GP (Stewart), British GP (Stewart), Canadian GP (Stewart), United States GP (Stewart), 1973 Belgian GP (Cevert), Italian GP (Stewart), 1974 Swedish GP (Depailler), French GP (Scheckter), German GP (Scheckter), 1975 Monaco GP (Depailler), 1976 German GP (Scheckter), Canadian GP (Depailler), 1977 United States GP (Peterson), 1982 British GP (Henton), Las Vegas GP (Alboreto), 1989 Canadian GP (Palmer)
Laps/miles in the lead: 1493 laps/4191 miles
World Champions:
Drivers: Twice - 1971 (Stewart), and 1973 (Stewart). Stewart also won the 1969 championship in a Tyrrell-run Matra
Constructors: Once - 1971

MAJOR SPONSORS

1970-76	Elf
1977-78	Elf, Citibank
1979-80	Candy
1981	Ceramica Imola, Michelob
1982	Candy, Denim
1983	Benetton
1986-87	Data General
1989	Camel
1990	Epson, PIAA
1991	Braun, Epson, PIAA
1992	Calbee, Club Angle
1993	Cabin, Calbee
1994	Mild Seven, Calbee, Club Angle, Fondmetal Wheels

TYRRELL GRAND PRIX DRIVERS

Driver	Nat	Starts	1st	2nd	3rd	4th	5th	6th	PP	FL	Points
		(DNS/DNQ)									
Jackie Stewart	GB	39 (1)	15	4	1	3	3	-	12	8	178
Jody Scheckter	ZA	45	4	7	3	4	5	2	1	3	114
Michele Alboreto	I	46 (3)	2	-	2	3	2	2	-	1	41
Patrick Depailler	F	80	1	9	7	5	4	5	1	3	119
François Cevert	F	37 (1)	1	10	2	2	2	1	-	2	88

Driver	Nat	Starts (DNS/DNQ)	1st	2nd	3rd	4th	5th	6th	PP	FL	Points
Didier Pironi	F	31	-	2	1	3	4	-	-	-	21
Jean Alesi	F	23 (1)	-	2	-	2	1	1	-	-	21
Jean-Pierre Jarier	F	26 (1)	-	-	2	-	5	2	-	-	20
Jonathan Palmer	GB	45 (3)	-	-	-	1	4	3	-	1	14
Stefano Modena	I	16	-	1	-	1	-	1	-	-	10
Eddie Cheever	USA	14 (1)	-	-	-	1	3	1	-	-	10
Martin Brundle	GB	38 (3)	-	-	-	1	2	1	-	-	8
Andrea de Cesaris	I	32	-	-	-	1	2	1	-	-	8
Mark Blundell	GB	16	-	-	1	-	2	-	-	-	8
Philippe Streiff	F	33	-	-	-	1	1	2	-	-	7
Ronnie Peterson	S	17	-	-	1	-	1	1	-	1	7
Derek Daly	IRL	17	-	-	-	2	-	-	-	-	6
Ukyo Katayama	J	32	-	-	-	-	2	1	-	-	5
Satoru Nakajima	J	31 (1)	-	-	-	-	1	3	-	-	5
Stefan Bellof	D	20 (2)	-	-	-	1	-	1	-	-	4
Ivan Capelli	I	2	-	-	-	1	-	-	-	-	3
Danny Sullivan	USA	15	-	-	-	-	1	-	-	-	2
Olivier Grouillard	F	16	-	-	-	-	-	-	-	-	-
Brian Henton	GB	13	-	-	-	-	-	-	-	1	-
Julian Bailey	GB	6 (10)	-	-	-	-	-	-	-	-	-
Stefan Johansson	S	4 (1)	-	-	-	-	-	-	-	-	-
Alessandro Pesenti-Rossi	I	3 (1)	-	-	-	-	-	-	-	-	-
Slim Borgudd	S	3	-	-	-	-	-	-	-	-	-
Eddie Keizan	ZA	2	-	-	-	-	-	-	-	-	-
Ian Scheckter	ZA	2	-	-	-	-	-	-	-	-	-
Ricardo Zunino	RA	2	-	-	-	-	-	-	-	-	-
Mike Thackwell	NZ	1 (2)	-	-	-	-	-	-	-	-	-
Chris Amon	NZ	1 (1)	-	-	-	-	-	-	-	-	-
Johnny Herbert	GB	1 (1)	-	-	-	-	-	-	-	-	-
Kazuyoshi Hoshino	J	1	-	-	-	-	-	-	-	-	-
Jean-Pierre Jabouille	F	1	-	-	-	-	-	-	-	-	-
Michel Leclère	F	1	-	-	-	-	-	-	-	-	-
Geoff Lees	GB	1	-	-	-	-	-	-	-	-	-
Peter Revson	USA	1	-	-	-	-	-	-	-	-	-
Kunimitsu Takahashi	J	1	-	-	-	-	-	-	-	-	-
Otto Stuppacher	A	- (4)	-	-	-	-	-	-	-	-	-
Kevin Cogan	USA	- (1)	-	-	-	-	-	-	-	-	-

TYRRELL GRAND PRIX CARS

Type	Year	Engine	Designer
001	1970	Ford DFV V8	Derek Gardner
002	1971	Ford DFV V8	Derek Gardner
003	1971	Ford DFV V8	Derek Gardner
004	1972	Ford DFV V8	Derek Gardner
005	1972	Ford DFV V8	Derek Gardner
006	1972	Ford DFV V8	Derek Gardner
007	1974	Ford DFV V8	Derek Gardner
P34	1976	Ford DFV V8	Derek Gardner Six-wheel car
008	1978	Ford DFV V8	Maurice Philippe
009	1979	Ford DFV V8	Maurice Philippe
010	1980	Ford DFV V8	Maurice Philippe
011	1981	Ford DFV V8	Maurice Philippe/Brian Lisles
012	1983	Ford DFY V8	Maurice Philippe/Brian Lisles
014	1985	Renault EF4B/EF15 V6 tc	Maurice Philippe/Brian Lisles
015	1986	Renault EF4B/EF15 V6 tc	Maurice Philippe/Brian Lisles
016	1987	Ford DFZ V8	Brian Lisles/Maurice Philippe
017	1988	Ford DFZ V8	Brian Lisles/Maurice Philippe/Graham Heard
017B	1989	Ford DFR V8	Brian Lisles/Graham Heard
018	1989	Ford DFR V8	Harvey Postlethwaite/Jean-Claude Migeot
019	1990	Ford DFR V8	Harvey Postlethwaite/Jean-Claude Migeot
020	1991	Honda RA101E V10	George Ryton
020B	1992	Ilmor 2175A V10	Harvey Postlethwaite/George Ryton
020C	1993	Yamaha OX10A V10	Harvey Postlethwaite/George Ryton
021	1993	Yamaha OX10A V10	Mike Coughlan
022	1994	Yamaha OX10A V10	Harvey Postlethwaite/Jean-Claude Migeot

VANWALL

GP Debut:	1954 British GP	Collins (retired)
Last GP:	1960 French GP	Brooks (retired)
Principal:	Tony Vandervell	
Base:	Acton, West London (GB)	

WORLD CHAMPIONSHIP RECORD

GPs Started: 28
Points: 108
Wins: 9 1957 British GP (Brooks/Moss), Pescara GP (Moss), Italian GP (Moss), 1958 Dutch GP (Moss), Belgian GP (Brooks), German GP (Brooks), Portuguese GP (Moss), Italian GP (Brooks), Moroccan GP (Moss)
Pole pos.: 7 1957 British GP (Moss), Italian GP (Lewis-Evans), 1958 Monaco GP (Moss), Dutch GP (Lewis-Evans), British GP (Moss), Portuguese GP (Moss), Italian GP (Moss)
Fastest laps: 6 1957 British GP (Moss), Pescara GP (Moss), Italian GP (Brooks), 1958 Dutch GP (Moss), German GP (Moss), Moroccan GP (Moss)
Laps/miles in the lead: 371 laps/1732 miles
World Champions:
Constructors: Once - 1958
Best World Championship position:
Drivers: 2nd in 1957 (Moss) and 1958 (Moss - including 8 of his 41 points in a Cooper-Climax)

VANWALL GRAND PRIX DRIVERS

Driver	Nat	Starts (DNS/DNQ)	1st	2nd	3rd	4th	5th	6th	PP	FL	Points
Stirling Moss	GB	14	6	1	-	-	1	-	4	5	57
Tony Brooks	GB	16	4	1	-	-	-	-	1	1	35
Stuart Lewis-Evans	GB	13	-	2	1	1	-	2	-	13
Harry Schell	USA	7	-	-	1	-	-	-	-	3
Maurice Trintignant	F	4	-	-	-	-	-	-	-	-
Mike Hawthorn	GB	3	-	-	-	-	-	-	-	-
Peter Collins	GB	2 (1)	-	-	-	-	-	-	-	-
Ken Wharton	GB	2	-	-	-	-	-	-	-	-
José Froilan Gonzalez	RA	1	-	-	-	-	-	-	-	-
Roy Salvadori	GB	1	-	-	-	-	-	-	-	-
Piero Taruffi	I	1	-	-	-	-	-	-	-	-
Colin Chapman	GB	- (1)	-	-	-	-	-	-	-	-

VANWALL GRAND PRIX CARS

Type	Year	Engine	Designer
Special	1954	Vanwall S4	Owen Maddock
VW1, VW2,	1955	Vanwall S4	Frank Costin/Colin Chapman
VW3, VW4			
VW5,			Frank Costin/Colin Chapman
VW6, VW7	1957	Vanwall S4	
VW9, VW10	1958	Vanwall S4	Frank Costin/Colin Chapman
VW11	1960	Vanwall S4	Frank Costin/Valerio Colotti

VERITAS

GP Debut:	1951 Swiss GP	Hirt (retired)
Last GP:	1953 German GP	Herrmann (9th), Helfrich (12th), Seidel (16th), Karch (retired), Heeks (retired), Bauer (retired), Loof (retired)
Principal:	Ernst Loof	
Base:	Messkirch (D), 1948-49; Nürburgring (D), 1950-56	

WORLD CHAMPIONSHIP RECORD

GPs Started: 6
Best result: 7th 1952 German GP (Riess)
Best qualif.: 7th 1952 German GP (Pietsch)

VERITAS GRAND PRIX DRIVERS

Driver	Nat	Starts (DNS/DNQ)	1st	2nd	3rd	4th	5th	6th	PP	FL	Points
Theo Helfrich	D	2	-	-	-	-	-	-	-	-	-
Arthur Legat	B	2	-	-	-	-	-	-	-	-	-

Driver	Nat	Starts (DNS/DNQ)	1st	2nd	3rd	4th	5th	6th	PP	FL	Points
Toni Ulmen	D	2	-	-	-	-	-	-	-	-	-
Erwin Bauer	D	1	-	-	-	-	-	-	-	-	-
Adolf Brudes	D	1	-	-	-	-	-	-	-	-	-
Willi Heeks	D	1	-	-	-	-	-	-	-	-	-
Hans Herrmann	D	1	-	-	-	-	-	-	-	-	-
Peter Hirt	CH	1	-	-	-	-	-	-	-	-	-
Oswald Karch	D	1	-	-	-	-	-	-	-	-	-
Hans Klenk	D	1	-	-	-	-	-	-	-	-	-
Ernst Loof	D	1	-	-	-	-	-	-	-	-	-
Josef Peters	D	1	-	-	-	-	-	-	-	-	-
Paul Pietsch	D	1	-	-	-	-	-	-	-	-	-
Fritz Riess	D	1	-	-	-	-	-	-	-	-	-
Wolfgang Seidel	D	1	-	-	-	-	-	-	-	-	-

VERITAS GRAND PRIX CARS

Type	Year	Engine	Designer
Meteor	1951	Veritas S6, BMW 328 S6	Ernst Loof
RS	1952	Veritas S6, BMW 328 S6	Ernst Loof

WILLIAMS

GP Debut: 1972 British GP — Pescarolo (retired)

Latest GP: 1994 Australian GP — Mansell (1st), Hill (retired)

Principal: **Frank Williams Racing Cars:** Frank Williams, 1969-74; Walter Wolf and Williams, 1975 until September 1976 when Williams left the company; **Williams Grand Prix Engineering:** Williams and Patrick Head, 1977 to date

Base: **Frank Williams Racing Cars:** Reading (GB), 1969-76 (became Walter Wolf Racing); **Williams Grand Prix Engineering:** Didcot (GB), 1977 to date

WORLD CHAMPIONSHIP RECORD

GPs Started: 322

Points: 1512.5

Wins: 78 1979 British GP (Regazzoni), German GP (Jones), Austrian GP (Jones), Dutch GP (Jones), Canadian GP (Jones), 1980 Argentinian GP (Jones), Monaco GP (Reutemann), French GP (Jones), British GP (Jones), Canadian GP (Jones), United States GP (Jones), 1981 Long Beach GP (Jones), Brazilian GP (Reutemann), Belgian GP (Reutemann), Las Vegas GP (Jones), 1982 Swiss GP (Rosberg), 1983 Monaco GP (Rosberg), 1984 Dallas GP (Rosberg), 1985 Detroit GP (Rosberg), European GP (Mansell), South African GP (Mansell), Australian GP (Rosberg), 1986 Brazilian GP (Piquet), Belgian GP (Mansell), Canadian GP (Mansell), French GP (Mansell), British GP (Mansell), German GP (Piquet), Hungarian GP (Piquet), Italian GP (Piquet), Portuguese GP (Mansell), 1987 San Marino GP (Mansell), French GP (Mansell), British GP (Mansell), German GP (Piquet), Hungarian GP (Piquet), Austrian GP (Mansell), Italian GP (Piquet), Spanish GP (Mansell), Mexican GP (Mansell), 1989 Canadian GP (Boutsen), Australian GP (Boutsen), 1990 San Marino GP (Patrese), Hungarian GP (Boutsen), 1991 Mexican GP (Patrese), French GP (Mansell), British GP (Mansell), German GP (Mansell), Italian GP (Mansell), Portuguese GP (Patrese), Spanish GP (Mansell), 1992 South African GP (Mansell), Mexican GP (Mansell), Brazilian GP (Mansell), Spanish GP (Mansell), San Marino GP (Mansell), French GP (Mansell), British GP (Mansell), German GP (Mansell), Portuguese GP (Mansell), Japanese GP (Riccardo Patrese), 1993 South African GP (Prost), San Marino GP (Prost), Spanish GP (Prost), Canadian GP (Prost), French GP (Prost), British GP (Prost), German GP (Prost), Hungarian GP (Hill), Belgian GP (Hill), Italian GP (Hill), 1994 Spanish GP (Hill), British GP (Hill), Belgian GP (Hill), Italian GP (Hill), Portuguese GP (Hill), Japanese GP (Hill), Australian GP (Mansell)

Pole pos.: 73 1979 British GP (Jones), Canadian GP (Jones), United States GP (Jones), 1980 Argentinian GP (Jones), Belgian GP (Jones), German GP (Jones), 1981 Belgian GP (Reutemann), Las Vegas GP (Reutemann), 1982 British GP (Rosberg), 1983 Brazilian GP (Rosberg), 1985 French GP (Rosberg), British GP (Rosberg), South African GP (Mansell), 1986 Belgian GP (Piquet), Canadian GP (Mansell), British GP (Piquet), Australian GP (Mansell), 1987 Brazilian GP (Mansell), Belgian GP (Mansell), Monaco GP (Mansell), Detroit GP (Mansell), French GP (Mansell), British GP (Piquet), German GP (Mansell), Hungarian GP (Mansell), Austrian GP (Piquet), Italian GP (Piquet), Spanish GP (Piquet), Mexican GP (Mansell), 1989 Hungarian GP (Patrese), 1990 Hungarian GP (Boutsen), 1991 Canadian GP (Patrese), Mexican GP (Patrese), French GP (Patrese), British GP (Mansell), German GP (Mansell), Portuguese GP (Patrese), 1992 South African GP (Mansell), Mexican GP (Mansell), Brazilian GP (Mansell), Spanish GP (Mansell), San Marino GP (Mansell), Monaco GP (Mansell), French GP (Mansell), British GP (Mansell), German GP (Mansell), Hungarian GP (Patrese), Belgian GP (Mansell), Italian GP (Mansell), Portuguese GP (Mansell), Japanese GP (Mansell), Australian GP (Mansell), 1993 South African GP (Prost), Brazilian GP (Prost), European GP (Prost), San Marino GP (Prost), Spanish GP (Prost), Monaco GP (Prost), Canadian GP (Prost), French GP (Hill), British GP (Prost), German GP (Prost), Hungarian GP (Prost), Belgian GP (Prost), Italian GP (Prost), Portuguese GP (Hill), Japanese GP (Prost), 1994 Brazilian GP (Senna), Pacific GP (Senna), San Marino GP (Senna), French GP (Hill), British GP (Hill), Australian GP (Mansell)

Fastest laps: 83 1978 Long Beach GP (Jones), Canadian GP (Jones), 1979 British GP (Regazzoni), Italian GP (Regazzoni), Canadian GP (Jones), 1980 Argentinian GP (Jones), French GP (Jones), German GP (Jones), Italian GP (Jones), United States GP (Jones), 1981 Long Beach GP (Jones), Belgian GP (Reutemann), Monaco GP (Jones), Spanish GP (Jones), German GP (Jones), Dutch GP (Jones), Italian GP (Reutemann), 1985 French GP (Rosberg), Italian GP (Mansell), South African GP (Rosberg), Australian GP (Rosberg), 1986 Brazilian GP (Piquet), Spanish GP (Mansell), San Marino GP (Piquet), Canadian GP (Piquet), Detroit GP (Piquet), French GP (Mansell), British GP (Mansell), Hungarian GP (Piquet), Portuguese GP (Mansell), Mexican GP (Piquet), Australian GP (Piquet), 1987 Brazilian GP (Piquet), French GP (Piquet), British GP (Mansell), German GP (Mansell), Hungarian GP (Piquet), Austrian GP (Mansell), Mexican GP (Piquet), 1988 British GP (Mansell), 1989 Brazilian GP (Patrese), 1990 German GP (Boutsen), Hungarian GP (Patrese), Portuguese GP (Patrese), Spanish GP (Patrese), Japanese GP (Patrese), 1991 Brazilian GP (Mansell), Canadian GP (Mansell), Mexican GP (Mansell), French GP (Mansell), British GP (Mansell), German GP (Patrese), Portuguese GP (Patrese), Spanish GP (Patrese), 1992 South African GP (Mansell), Brazilian GP (Patrese), Spanish GP (Mansell), San Marino GP (Patrese), Monaco GP (Mansell), French GP (Mansell), British GP (Mansell), German GP (Patrese), Hungarian GP (Mansell), Italian GP (Mansell), Japanese GP (Mansell), 1993 South African GP (Prost), San Marino GP (Prost), Monaco GP (Prost), British GP (Hill), Hungarian GP (Prost), Belgian GP (Prost), Italian GP (Hill), Portuguese GP (Hill), Japanese GP (Prost), Australian GP (Hill), 1994 San Marino GP (Hill), British GP (Hill), German GP (Coulthard), Belgian GP (Hill), Italian GP (Hill), Portuguese GP (Coulthard), Japanese GP (Hill)

Laps/miles in the lead: 5047 laps/14696 miles

World Champions:

Drivers: Five times - 1980 (Jones), 1982 (Rosberg), 1987 (Piquet), 1992 (Mansell) and 1993 (Prost)

Constructors: Seven times - 1980, 1981, 1986, 1987, 1992, 1993 and 1994

MAJOR SPONSORS

1972	Politoys, Motul
1973-74	Iso, Marlboro
1975	Ambrozium H7, Lavazza
1976	Walter Wolf, Mapfre
1978	Saudia Airlines
1979	Saudia Airlines, Albilad
1980	Saudia Airlines, Leyland
1981	Saudia Airlines, Leyland, TAG
1982-83	Saudia Airlines, TAG
1984	Saudia Airlines, Denim, Mobil
1985-87	Canon, ICI, Denim
1988-90	Canon, ICI, Barclay
1991-92	Canon, Labatt's, Camel
1993	Canon, Sega, Camel
1994 to date	Rothmans

WILLIAMS GRAND PRIX DRIVERS

Driver	Nat	Starts (DNS/DNQ)	1st	2nd	3rd	4th	5th	6th	PP	FL	Points
Nigel Mansell	GB	95 (2)	28	12	3	2	5	5	28	22	369
Alan Jones	AUS	60	11	7	4	4	1	-	6	13	171
Damon Hill	GB	32	9	9	3	1	-	1	4	10	160
Nelson Piquet	BR	31 (1)	7	10	4	2	-	-	6	11	145
Alain Prost	F	16	7	3	2	1	-	-	13	6	99
Keke Rosberg	SF	62	5	7	3	7	6	1	4	3	131.5
Riccardo Patrese	I	81	4	12	8	5	9	5	6	11	180
Carlos Reutemann	RA	31	3	7	6	2	2	1	2	2	104
Thierry Boutsen	B	32	3	1	4	4	4	2	1	1	71
Clay Regazzoni	CH	15	1	2	2	-	1	1	-	2	32
Jacques Laffite	F	44 (4)	-	1	-	3	2	3	-	-	22
David Coulthard	GB	8	-	1	-	1	2	1	-	2	14
Derek Daly	IRL	12	-	-	-	-	3	2	-	-	8
Arturo Merzario	I	25 (3)	-	-	-	1	-	1	-	-	4
Howden Ganley	NZ	14 (1)	-	-	-	-	-	1	-	-	1
Gijs van Lennep	NL	4 (1)	-	-	-	-	1	-	-	-	1
Michel Leclère	F	6 (1)	-								
Jacky Ickx	B	5 (4)	-								
Nanni Galli	I	5									
Rupert Keegan	GB	4 (3)	-								
Henri Pescarolo	F	3									
Ayrton Senna	BR	3	-	-	-	-	-	3	-	-	
Tom Belso	DK	2 (3)	-								
Ian Scheckter	ZA	2									
Renzo Zorzi	I	2									
Mario Andretti	USA	1									
Hans Binder	A	1									
Tony Brise	GB	1									
Warwick Brown	AUS	1									
Martin Brundle	GB	1									
Damien Magee	GB	1									
Graham McRae	NZ	1									
Jonathan Palmer	GB	1									
Jackie Pretorius	ZA	1									
Tim Schenken	AUS	1									
Jean-Louis Schlesser	F	1									
Joseph Vonlanthen	CH	1									
Loris Kessel	CH	- (2)	-								
Chris Amon	NZ	- (1)	-								
Ian Ashley	GB	- (1)	-								
Kevin Cogan	USA	- (1)	-								
Jean-Pierre Jabouille	F	- (1)	-								
Masami Kuwashima	J	- (1)	-								
Geoff Lees	GB	- (1)	-								
Lella Lombardi	I	- (1)	-								
Brian McGuire	AUS	- (1)	-								
François Migault	F	- (1)	-								
Richard Robarts	GB	- (1)	-								
Emilio de Villota	E	- (1)	-								
Desire Wilson	ZA	- (1)	-								
Emilio Zapico	E	- (1)	-								

WILLIAMS GRAND PRIX CARS

Type	Year	Engine	Designer
FX3*	1972	Ford DFV V8	Len Bailey
FX3B*	1973	Ford DFV V8	Len Bailey
IR01**	1973	Ford DFV V8	John Clarke Renamed FW01
IR02**	1973	Ford DFV V8	John Clarke Renamed FW02
IR03**	1973	Ford DFV V8	John Clarke Renamed FW03
FW01	1974	Ford DFV V8	John Clarke
FW02	1974	Ford DFV V8	John Clarke
FW03	1974	Ford DFV V8	John Clarke Sold and renamed Apollon-Ford in 1977
FW04	1975	Ford DFV V8	Ray Stokoe Sold and renamed McGuire BM1-Ford in 1977
FW05	1976	Ford DFV V8	Harvey Postlethwaite Formerly Hesketh 308C
FW06	1978	Ford DFV V8	Patrick Head
FW07	1979	Ford DFV V8	Patrick Head
FW07B	1980	Ford DFV V8	Patrick Head
FW07C	1981	Ford DFV V8	Patrick Head/Frank Dernie
FW08	1982	Ford DFV V8	Patrick Head/Frank Dernie
FW08C	1983	Ford DFV V8	Patrick Head/Frank Dernie
FW09	1983	Honda RA163E V6 tc	Patrick Head/Frank Dernie
FW09B	1984	Honda RA163E V6 tc	Patrick Head/Frank Dernie
FW10	1985	Honda RA163E V6 tc	Patrick Head/Frank Dernie
FW11	1986	Honda RA166E V6 tc	Patrick Head/Frank Dernie
FW11B	1987	Honda RA167E V6 tc	Patrick Head/Frank Dernie
FW12	1988	Judd CV V8	Patrick Head/Frank Dernie
FW12C	1989	Renault RS01 V10	Patrick Head/ Enrique Scalabroni
FW13	1989	Renault RS01 V10	Patrick Head/ Enrique Scalabroni
FW13B	1990	Renault RS02 V10	Patrick Head/ Enrique Scalabroni
FW14	1991	Renault RS03 V10	Patrick Head/Adrian Newey
FW14B	1992	Renault RS03 V10	Patrick Head/Adrian Newey
FW15C	1993	Renault RS05 V10	Patrick Head/Adrian Newey
FW16	1994	Renault RS06 V10	Patrick Head/Adrian Newey
FW16B	1994	Renault RS06 V10	Patrick Head/Adrian Newey

*officially known as Politoys.
**officially known as Iso-Marlboro

WOLF

Team sold to Fittipaldi in 1980; also see Fittipaldi

GP Debut:	1977 Argentinian GP Scheckter (1st)
Last GP:	1979 United States GP Rosberg (retired)
Principal:	Walter Wolf
Base:	Reading (GB)

WORLD CHAMPIONSHIP RECORD

GPs Started:	47
Points:	79
Wins:	3 1977 Argentinian GP (Scheckter), Monaco GP (Scheckter), Canadian GP (Scheckter)
Pole pos.:	1 1977 German GP (Scheckter)
Fastest laps:	2 1977 Monaco GP (Scheckter), Japanese GP (Scheckter)

Laps/miles in the lead: 213 laps/504 miles

Best World Championship position:

Drivers:	2nd in 1977 (Scheckter)
Constructors:	4th in 1977

MAJOR SPONSORS

1977-78	Castrol
1979	Olympus

WOLF GRAND PRIX DRIVERS

Driver	Nat	Starts (DNS/DNQ)	1st	2nd	3rd	4th	5th	6th	PP	FL	Points
Jody Scheckter	ZA	33	3	4	6	1	-	1	1	2	79
Keke Rosberg	SF	10 (2)	-	-	-	-	-	-	-	-	
James Hunt	GB	7	-	-	-	-	-	-	-	-	
Bobby Rahal	USA	2	-	-	-	-	-	-	-	-	

WOLF GRAND PRIX CARS

Type	Year	Engine	Designer
WR1, WR2,			
WR3, WR4	1977	Ford DFV V8	Harvey Postlethwaite
WR5, WR6	1978	Ford DFV V8	Harvey Postlethwaite
WR7, WR8,			
WR8/9, WR9	1979	Ford DFV V8	Harvey Postlethwaite

Renamed Fittipaldi F7 when team was sold

ZAKSPEED

GP Debut:	1985 Portuguese GP	Palmer (retired)
Last GP:	1989 Japanese GP	Schneider (retired)
Principal:	Erich Zakowski	
Base:	Niederzissen (D)	

WORLD CHAMPIONSHIP RECORD

GPs Started: 53
Points: 2
Best result: 5th 1987 San Marino GP (Brundle)
Best qualif.: 13th 1987 Mexican GP (Brundle)

Best World Championship position:
Drivers: 18th in 1987 (Brundle)
Constructors: 10th in 1987

MAJOR SPONSORS

1985-89   West

ZAKSPEED GRAND PRIX DRIVERS

Driver	Nat	Starts (DNS/DNQ)	1st	2nd	3rd	4th	5th	6th	PP	FL	Points
Martin Brundle	GB	16	-	-	-	-	1	-	-	-	2
Jonathan Palmer	GB	23 (1)	-	-	-	-	-	-	-	-	-
Christian Danner	D	17 (1)	-	-	-	-	-	-	-	-	-
Huub Rothengatter	NL	11 (3)	-	-	-	-	-	-	-	-	-
Bernd Schneider	D	8 (24)	-	-	-	-	-	-	-	-	-
Piercarlo Ghinzani	I	8 (8)	-	-	-	-	-	-	-	-	-
Aguri Suzuki	J	- (16)	-	-	-	-	-	-	-	-	-

ZAKSPEED GRAND PRIX CARS

Type	Year	Engine	Designer
841	1985	Zakspeed S4 tc	Paul Brown
861	1986	Zakspeed S4 tc	Paul Brown
871	1987	Zakspeed S4 tc	Chris Murphy/Heinz Zollinir
881	1988	Zakspeed S4 tc	Chris Murphy/Heinz Zollinir
891	1989	Yamaha OX88 V8	Gustav Brunner/ Nino Frisson/Peter Wyss

RECORDS

DRIVERS' RECORDS

MOST STARTS

Riccardo Patrese	256		Thierry Boutsen	163
Andrea de Cesaris	208		Ayrton Senna	161
Nelson Piquet	204		John Watson	152
Alain Prost	199		René Arnoux	149
Michele Alboreto	194		Carlos Reutemann	146
Nigel Mansell	185		Derek Warwick	146
Graham Hill	176		Emerson Fittipaldi	144
Jacques Laffite	176		Jean-Pierre Jarier	133
Niki Lauda	171		Eddie Cheever	132
Gerhard Berger	163		Clay Regazzoni	132

YOUNGEST DRIVERS TO START A GRAND PRIX

19 years 182 days	Mike Thackwell	Retired	1980	Canadian GP
19 years 208 days	Ricardo Rodriguez	Retired	1961	Italian GP
19 years 324 days	Chris Amon	Retired	1963	Belgian GP
20 years 53 days	Eddie Cheever	Retired	1978	South African GP
20 years 192 days	Peter Collins	Retired	1952	Swiss GP
20 years 295 days	Rubens Barrichello	Retired	1993	South African GP
20 years 301 days	Elio de Angelis	7th	1979	Argentinian GP
20 years 338 days	Bruce McLaren	F2 class	1958	German GP
21 years 43 days	Christian Fittipaldi	Retired	1992	South African GP
21 years 102 days	Fritz d'Orey	10th	1959	French GP

OLDEST DRIVERS TO START A GRAND PRIX

55 years 292 days	Louis Chiron	6th	1955	Monaco GP
55 years 190 days	Philippe Étancelin	8th	1952	French GP
54 years 232 days	Arthur Legat	R	1953	Belgian GP
53 years 21 days	Luigi Fagioli	1st	1951	French GP
52 years 292 days	Adolf Brudes	R	1952	German GP
52 years 260 days	Hans Stuck	14th	1953	Italian GP
52 years 127 days	Bill Aston	R	1952	German GP
51 years 319 days	Clemente Biondetti	R	1950	Italian GP
51 years 206 days	Marcel Balsa	R	1952	German GP
50 years 273 days	Louis Rosier	5th	1956	German GP

DID NOT START

Drivers with the greatest number of occasions in which they practised but did not start the Grand Prix, whether it be for not qualifying, mechanical failure or another reason.

Gabriele Tarquini	40		Yannick Dalmas	27
Bertrand Gachot	37		Nicola Larini	26
Piercarlo Ghinzani	35		Bernd Schneider	25
Roberto Moreno	34		Stefan Johansson	24
Arturo Merzario	29		Eric van de Poele	24

MOST WINS

Alain Prost	51		Juan Manuel Fangio	24
Ayrton Senna	41		Nelson Piquet	23
Nigel Mansell	31		Stirling Moss	16
Jackie Stewart	27		Jack Brabham	14
Jim Clark	25		Emerson Fittipaldi	14
Niki Lauda	25		Graham Hill	14

YOUNGEST DRIVERS TO WIN A GRAND PRIX

22 years 104 days	Bruce McLaren	1959	United States GP
23 years 188 days	Jacky Ickx	1968	French GP
23 years 240 days	Michael Schumacher	1992	Belgian GP
23 years 297 days	Emerson Fittipaldi	1970	United States GP
24 years 86 days	Mike Hawthorn	1953	French GP
24 years 131 days	Jody Scheckter	1974	Swedish GP
24 years 142 days	Elio de Angelis	1982	Austrian GP
24 years 208 days	Peter Collins	1956	Belgian GP
25 years 31 days	Ayrton Senna	1985	Portuguese GP
25 years 65 days	Niki Lauda	1974	Spanish GP

OLDEST DRIVERS TO WIN A GRAND PRIX

53 years 21 days	Luigi Fagioli	1951	French GP
46 years 277 days	Giuseppe Farina	1953	German GP
46 years 42 days	Juan Manuel Fangio	1957	German GP
45 years 219 days	Piero Taruffi	1952	Swiss GP
43 years 339 days	Jack Brabham	1970	South African GP
41 years 96 days	Nigel Mansell	1994	Australian GP

40 years 199 days	Maurice Trintignant	1958	Monaco GP
40 years 91 days	Graham Hill	1969	Monaco GP
39 years 312 days	Clay Regazzoni	1979	British GP
39 years 35 days	Carlos Reutemann	1981	Belgian GP

HIGHEST POINTS TOTALS

Alain Prost	798.5	Carlos Reutemann	310
Ayrton Senna	614	Gerhard Berger	306
Nelson Piquet	485.5	Graham Hill	289
Nigel Mansell	482	Emerson Fittipaldi	281
Niki Lauda	420.5	Riccardo Patrese	281
Jackie Stewart	360	Juan Manuel Fangio	278.64

YOUNGEST DRIVERS TO HAVE SCORED POINTS

20 years 123 days	Ricardo Rodriguez	4th	1962	Belgian GP
20 years 309 days	Chris Amon	5th	1964	Dutch GP
21 years 154 days	Rubens Barrichello	5th	1993	Japanese GP
21 years 195 days	Elio de Angelis	4th	1979	United States GP
21 years 253 days	Bruce McLaren	5th	1959	Monaco GP

OLDEST DRIVERS TO HAVE SCORED POINTS

53 years 248 days	Philippe Étancelin	5th	1950	Italian GP
53 years 21 days	Luigi Fagioli	1st	1951	French GP
50 years 291 days	Louis Chiron	3rd	1950	Monaco GP
50 years 274 days	Louis Rosier	5th	1956	German GP
50 years 76 days	Felice Bonetto	4th	1953	Swiss GP

HIGHEST POINTS PER START AVERAGES

Juan Manuel Fangio	5.464	Michael Schumacher	3.865
Damon Hill	4.706	Giuseppe Farina	3.858
Luigi Fagioli	4.571	Ayrton Senna	3.814
Alberto Ascari	4.537	Jim Clark	3.806
Alain Prost	4.013	Jackie Stewart	3.636

MOST POLE POSITIONS

Ayrton Senna	65	Niki Lauda	24
Jim Clark	33	Nelson Piquet	24
Alain Prost	33	Mario Andretti	18
Nigel Mansell	32	René Arnoux	18
Juan Manuel Fangio	29	Jackie Stewart	17

YOUNGEST DRIVERS TO QUALIFY ON POLE FOR A GRAND PRIX

22 years 97 days	Rubens Barrichello	1994	Belgian GP
22 years 309 days	Andrea de Cesaris	1982	Long Beach GP
23 years 216 days	Jacky Ickx	1968	German GP
24 years 238 days	Eugenio Castellotti	1955	Belgian GP
24 years 297 days	Chris Amon	1968	Spanish GP
25 years 31 days	Ayrton Senna	1985	Portuguese GP
25 years 36 days	Niki Lauda	1974	South African GP
25 years 132 days	Michael Schumacher	1994	Monaco GP
25 years 154 days	Emerson Fittipaldi	1972	Monaco GP
25 years 183 days	Elio de Angelis	1983	European GP

OLDEST DRIVERS TO QUALIFY ON POLE FOR A GRAND PRIX

47 years 80 days	Giuseppe Farina	1954	Argentinian GP
46 years 210 days	Juan Manuel Fangio	1958	Argentinian GP
44 years 17 days	Jack Brabham	1970	Spanish GP
42 years 197 days	Mario Andretti	1982	Italian GP
41 years 96 days	Nigel Mansell	1994	Australian GP
39 years 188 days	Carlos Reutemann	1981	Las Vegas GP
39 years 155 days	Graham Hill	1968	British GP
38 years 242 days	Alain Prost	1993	Japanese GP
38 years 121 days	Riccardo Patrese	1992	Hungarian GP
37 years 232 days	Keke Rosberg	1986	German GP

MOST FRONT ROW QUALIFICATIONS

Ayrton Senna	87	Nelson Piquet	44
Alain Prost	86	Graham Hill	42
Nigel Mansell	56	Jackie Stewart	42
Jim Clark	48	Jack Brabham	38
Juan Manuel Fangio	48	Stirling Moss	37

MOST FASTEST LAPS

Alain Prost	41	Ayrton Senna	19
Nigel Mansell	29	Gerhard Berger	16
Jim Clark	28	Riccardo Patrese	15
Niki Lauda	24	Clay Regazzoni	15
Juan Manuel Fangio	23	Michael Schumacher	15
Nelson Piquet	23	Jackie Stewart	15
Stirling Moss	19	Jacky Ickx	14

YOUNGEST DRIVERS TO RECORD THE FASTEST LAP

21 years 322 days	Bruce McLaren	1959	British GP
23 years 127 days	David Coulthard	1994	German GP
23 years 240 days	Michael Schumacher	1992	Belgian GP
23 years 357 days	Andrea de Cesaris	1983	Belgian GP
24 years 74 days	Ayrton Senna	1984	Monaco GP

OLDEST DRIVERS TO RECORD THE FASTEST LAP

46 years 210 days	Juan Manuel Fangio	1958	Argentinian GP
45 years 219 days	Piero Taruffi	1952	Swiss GP
44 years 321 days	Giuseppe Farina	1951	Italian GP
44 years 107 days	Jack Brabham	1970	British GP
44 years 22 days	Luigi Villoresi	1953	Dutch GP

MOST LAPS IN THE LEAD

Ayrton Senna	2981	Niki Lauda	1657
Alain Prost	2712	Nelson Piquet	1568
Nigel Mansell	2089	Juan Manuel Fangio	1353
Jim Clark	1945	Stirling Moss	1181
Jackie Stewart	1913	Graham Hill	1103

MOST MILES IN THE LEAD

Ayrton Senna	8094	Jim Clark	5211
Alain Prost	7723	Nelson Piquet	4628
Juan Manuel Fangio	5805	Niki Lauda	4593
Nigel Mansell	5767	Stirling Moss	3961
Jackie Stewart	5493	Alberto Ascari	3438

OTHER RECORDS

Most World Championships:
Five, Juan Manuel Fangio

Race with the youngest average age:
1994 Brazilian GP, 28 years 293 days

Race with the oldest average age:
1951 Belgian GP, 42 years 315 days

Widest championship-winning margin:
52 points, Nigel Mansell, 1992

Narrowest championship-winning margin:
0.5 points, Niki Lauda, 1984

Most wins in a season:
Nine, Nigel Mansell, 1992

Most successive wins at the start of the season:
Five, Nigel Mansell, 1992

Most points in a season:
108, Nigel Mansell, 1992

Most pole positions in a season:
14, Nigel Mansell, 1992

Most fastest laps in a season:
Eight, Nigel Mansell, 1992 and Michael Schumacher, 1994

Most laps/miles in the lead in a season:
692 laps/2040 miles, Nigel Mansell, 1992

Fastest race:
150.759 mph, 1971 Italian GP

Slowest race:
61.331 mph, 1950 Monaco GP

Longest circuit used:
16.032 miles, Pescara, 1957

Shortest circuit used:
1.954 miles, Monaco, 1955-72

Most lead changes in a single race:
43, 1965 Italian GP

Most races without a win:
208, Andrea de Cesaris

Longest race career without scoring a point:
34 races, Brett Lunger

ENGINE RECORDS

MOST WINS			
Ford	174	BRM	18
Ferrari	104	Alfa Romeo	12
Honda	71	Maserati	11
Renault	58	BMW	9
Climax	40	Mercedes-Benz	9
Porsche	26	Vanwall	9

MOST POLE POSITIONS			
Ford	138	Alfa Romeo	15
Ferrari	113	BMW	15
Renault	94	BRM	11
Honda	74	Maserati	11
Climax	44	Mercedes-Benz	8

HIGHEST POINTS TOTALS			
Ford	4535	BRM	607.5
Ferrari	2765.27	Porsche	455.5
Renault	1319	Maserati	393.92
Honda	1224.5	Alfa Romeo	330
Climax	866.5	BMW	207

MANUFACTURERS' RECORDS

MOST STARTS			
Ferrari	536	Ligier	293
Lotus	491	Arrows	255
McLaren	410	(including Footwork)	
Brabham	394	March	227
Tyrrell	364	(including Leyton House)	
Williams	322	BRM	197

MOST WINS			
Ferrari	104	Tyrrell	23
McLaren	104	BRM	17
Lotus	79	Cooper	16
Williams	78	Benetton	15
Brabham	35	Renault	15

MOST POINTS			
Ferrari	2754.27	Tyrrell	699
McLaren	2005.5	BRM	537.5
Lotus	1514	Benetton	500.5
Williams	1512.5	Cooper	494.5
Brabham	983	Ligier	349

HIGHEST POINTS PER START AVERAGES			
Mercedes-Benz	11.595	Vanwall	3.857
Ferrari	5.139	Cooper	3.833
McLaren	4.891	Benetton	3.476
Williams	4.697	Lotus	3.084
Maserati	4.602	Matra	2.968

MOST POLE POSITIONS			
Ferrari	113	Renault	31
Lotus	107	Tyrrell	14
McLaren	79	Alfa Romeo	12
Williams	73	BRM	11
Brabham	39	Cooper	11

MOST FASTEST LAPS			
Ferrari	122	Benetton	22
Williams	83	Tyrrell	20
Lotus	71	Renault	18
McLaren	69	Maserati	17
Brabham	42	BRM	15

MOST LAPS IN THE LEAD			
Ferrari	6961	Tyrrell	1493
McLaren	5625	BRM	1342
Lotus	5498	Renault	1220
Williams	5047	Maserati	832
Brabham	2724	Benetton	830

MOST MILES IN THE LEAD			
Ferrari	23858	Tyrrell	4191
Lotus	16285	BRM	3786
McLaren	16221	Renault	3707
Williams	14649	Alfa Romeo	2978
Brabham	8252	Maserati	2948

EARLY GRAND PRIX RACING

Manfred von Brauchitsch's Mercedes-Benz W125 at Donington in 1937

CITY TO CITY RACES 1894–1903

There had been an unsuccessful attempt to organize a motoring competition near Paris as early as 1887 but motor racing was born when 21 cars left the Porte Maillot in Paris on 22 July 1894 for the 80-mile trip to Rouen. The *Petit Journal*-organized event was a reliability trial with a first prize of 5000 francs awarded for the car which completed the course safely and at low running cost. Another stipulation was that each car should have both a driver and a mechanic; as the first driver to arrive, Count de Dion, did not have a mechanic he forfeited the spoils of victory.

Within 12 months a newly formed committee (which would become the Automobile Club de France in 1896) organized the first true race from Paris to Bordeaux and back. This set the format for the inter-city races which would dominate racing for eight years.

Each year the ACF decided upon a new destination for their Paris races. Cars had to be under 1000 kg and in order to have the largest possible engines designers built light (and fragile) chassis. On the first day's run to Bordeaux an estimated three million spectators lined the roads to watch these huge cars, some of which were capable of over 80 mph in a straight line. Unfortunately, their brakes were not as effective and a series of fearful accidents left five competitors and numerous spectators dead and the event was abandoned.

The searing heat, blinding dust and poor crowd control had turned the Paris–Madrid race into a disaster and the ACF turned to closed circuit racing for the future, albeit on courses of over 50 miles in length.

1894

Paris–Rouen

22 June 1894. 78.75 miles

1 Count de Dion*	de Dion	6h48m00
2 Lemaitre	Peugeot	6h51m30
3 Doriot	Peugeot	7h04m30
4 H Panhard	Panhard	7h21m30
5 Emile Levassor	Panhard	7h43m30
6 Kraeutler	Peugeot	7h46m30

*Ineligible for first prize as not accompanied by a mechanic.
Winner's average speed: 11.58 mph

1895

Paris–Bordeaux–Paris

11-13 June 1895. 732 miles

1 Emile Levassor*	Panhard	48h48m00
2 Rigoulot*	Peugeot	54h35m00
3 A Koechlin	Peugeot	59h48m00
4 Doriot	Peugeot	59h49m00
5 Thum	Benz	64h30m00
6 Mayade	Panhard	72h14m00

*Ineligible for first prize as their cars were two-seaters and only four-seaters were eligible. Winner's average speed: 15.00 mph

1896

Paris–Marseille–Paris

24 September-3 October 1896. 1062.5 miles

1 Mayade	Panhard	67h42m58
2 Merkel	Panhard	68h11m05
3 Viet	de Dion tricycle	71h01m05
4 d'Hostingue	Panhard	71h23m22
5 Collomb	de Dion tricycle	73h30m12
6 Berlet	Peugeot	75h29m48

Winner's average speed: 15.69 mph

1897

Paris–Dieppe

24 July 1897. 106.2 miles

1 Jamin	Bollée	4h13m33
2 Count de Dion	de Dion	4h19m34
3 Hourgières	Panhard	4h36m00
4 Fernand Charron	Panhard	4h38m31
5 Pellier	Bollée	4h43m55
6 Bertrand	de Dion	4h45m15

Winner's average speed: 25.13 mph

1898

Paris–Amsterdam–Paris

7-13 July 1898. 889.25 miles

1 Fernand Charron	Panhard	33h04m34
2 Léonce Girardot	Panhard	33h25m18
3 Etienne Giraud	Bollée	34h08m58
4 René de Knyff	Panhard	34h58m50
5 Loysel	Bollée	35h19m09
6 Adam	Panhard	35h45m57

Winner's average speed: 26.88 mph

1899

Paris–Bordeaux

24 May 1899. 351 miles

1 Fernand Charron	Panhard	11h43m20
2 René de Knyff	Panhard	11h51m26
3 Léonce Girardot	Panhard	12h32m35
4 Archambault	Panhard	12h37m45
5 Hourgières	Panhard	13h03m44
6 Antony	Mors	13h17m43

Winner's average speed: 29.94 mph

Tour de France Automobile

16-24 July 1899. 1350 miles

1 René de Knyff	Panhard	44h43m39.2
2 Léonce Girardot	Panhard	49h37m39.4
3 Count de Chasseloup-Laubat	Panhard	49h44m18.0
4 Pinson	Panhard	52h34m17.8
5 Castelnau	Bollée	53h29m07.0
6 George Heath	Panhard	58h47m26.0

Winner's average speed: 30.18 mph

1900

Paris–Toulouse–Paris

25-28 July 1900. 837.1 miles

1 Alfred Levegh	Mors	20h50m09
2 Teste	de Dion	23h54m01
3 Pinson	Panhard	22h11m01
4 Voight	Panhard	22h11m51

5 Etienne Giraud	Panhard	22h55m32
6 Antony	Mors	26h46m27

Winner's average speed: 40.18 mph

1901

Paris–Bordeaux

29 May 1901. 327.6 miles

1 Henri Fournier	Mors	6h10m44
2 Maurice Farman	Panhard	6h41m15
3 Voight	Panhard	7h15m11
4 Pinson	Panhard	7h45m51
5 Axt	Panhard	7h46m17
6 Etienne Giraud	Panhard	8h08m48

Winner's average speed: 53.02 mph

Paris–Berlin

27-29 June 1901. 687 miles

1 Henri Fournier	Mors	15h33m06
2 Léonce Girardot	Panhard	16h38m38
3 René de Knyff	Panhard	16h40m02
4 Brasier	Mors	17h14m35
5 Henri Farman	Panhard	17h46m06
6 Fernand Charron	Panhard	18h20m57

Winner's average speed: 44.18 mph

1902

Paris–Vienna

26-29 June 1902. 615.4 miles

1 Marcel Renault	Renault	15h47m43.8
2 Henri Farman	Panhard	16h00m30.2
3 Edmond	Darracq	16h10m16.2
4 Zborowski	Mercedes	16h13m29.6
5 Maurice Farman	Panhard	16h19m29.4
6 Baras	Darracq	17h04m52.0

Winner's average speed: 38.96 mph

1903

Paris–Madrid

24 May 1903. 342 miles. Race stopped at Bordeaux due to fatal accidents

1 Fernand Gabriel	Mors	5h14m31.2
2 Louis Renault	Renault	5h29m39.2
3 Jacques Salleron	Mors	5h47m01.8
4 Charles Jarrott	de Dietrich	5h52m55.0
5 Pierre de Crawhez	Panhard	5h54m11.4
6 Warden	Mercedes	5h55m30.8

Winner's average speed: 65.24 mph

GORDON BENNETT TROPHY

The promotional value of motorsport was recognized quickly and in 1899 James Gordon Bennett of the *New York Herald* European edition announced the first Coupe Internationale, now better known as the Gordon Bennett Trophy.

National teams of up to three competitors could enter with drivers and riding mechanics being members of the national motoring organization and all components being made in that country (causing Mercedes to build cars both in Germany and Austria in 1904-05 in order to gain more entries). The winners would then hold the race in the following year.

Although not well-supported at first, by 1904 six nations competed, and the Automobile Club de France was forced to organize an elimination race to decide its entries from a field of 29. The pressure for French entries finally forced the Trophy to be abandoned after the 1905 race. The ACF decided to replace it with a new event in which all manufacturers, irrespective of nationality, could enter up to three cars, and so Grand Prix racing was born.

1900

14 June 1900. Paris–Lyon. 353.35 miles

1 Fernand Charron	Panhard 40	9h09m00
2 Léonce Girardot	Panhard 40	10h36m23

No other finishers. Winner's average speed: 38.617 mph

Spectators line the route as Camille Jenatzy leads in the 1903 Gordon Bennett Trophy race

1901

29 May 1901. Paris–Bordeaux. 327.60 miles

1 Léonce Girardot	Panhard 40		8h50m59

No other finishers. Winner's average speed: 37.018 mph

1902

26 June 1902. Paris-Innsbruck (part of the Paris-Vienna race). 351.46 miles

1 Selwyn Edge	Napier 50		11h02m52.6

No other finishers. Winner's average speed: 31.812 mph

1903

2 July 1903. Athy. 3 laps of the 40-mile circuit A and 4 laps of the 51.88-mile circuit B = 327.52 miles

1 Camille Jenatzy	Mercedes 90 hp	7	6h39m00
2 René de Knyff	Panhard 70	7	6h50m40
3 Henri Farman	Panhard 70	7	6h51m44
4 Fernand Gabriel	Mors Z	7	7h11m33

No other finishers. Winner's average speed: 49.245 mph. Fastest lap: Circuit A: Foxhall Keene (Mercedes 90hp), 46m03; Circuit B: Gabriel, 1h00m19

1904

17 June 1904. Homburg. 4 laps of a 79.465-mile circuit = 317.860 miles

1 Léon Théry	Richard-Brasier	4	5h50m01.4
2 Camille Jenatzy	Mercedes 60	4	6h01m29.4
3 Henri Rougier	Turcat-Méry	4	6h47m09.8
4 Pierre de Caters	Mercedes 60	4	6h47m30.0
5 Edgar Braun	Mercedes 60	4	6h59m47.8
6 Lucien Hautvast	Pipe	4	7h02m35.0

Winner's average speed: 54.487 mph. Fastest lap: Théry, 1h26m22.2

1905

5 July 1905. Auvergne. 4 laps of a 85.350-mile circuit = 341.400 miles

1 Léon Théry	Richard-Brasier	4	7h02m42.6
2 Felice Nazzaro	Fiat	4	7h10m09.2
3 Alessandro Cagno	Fiat	4	7h21m22.6
4 Gustave Caillois	Richard-Brasier	4	7h27m06.4
5 Christian Werner	Mercedes	4	8h03m30.0
6 Arthur Duray	de Dietrich 24/28	4	8h05m00.0

Winner's average speed: 48.459 mph. Fastest lap: Vincenzo Lancia (Fiat), 1h34m57

GRAND PRIX 1906–49

RULES

1906	1000 kg maximum weight
1907	9.4 mpg fuel consumption limit
1908	1100 kg minimum weight. Cylinder bore limited to 155 mm for 4-cylinder engines and 127 mm for 6-cylinders engines
1909-11	NO GRAND PRIX RACING
1912	1750 mm minimum width
1913	800 kg minimum weight, 1100 kg maximum weight. 14 mpg fuel consumption limit
1914	4500 cc maximum engine capacity. 1100 kg maximum weight
1915-20	NO GRAND PRIX RACING
1921	3000 cc maximum engine capacity. 800 kg minimum weight
1922-24	2000 cc maximum engine capacity. 650 kg minimum weight
1925	Engine capacity and minimum weight unchanged. Riding mechanics banned but cars still required to have two seats
1926	1500 cc maximum engine capacity. 600 kg minimum weight
1927	Engine capacity unchanged. 700 kg minimum weight. Two seats no longer required
1928	550 kg minimum weight, 750 kg maximum
1929	900 kg minimum weight, commercial fuel stipulated
1930	1100 cc minimum engine capacity. 900 kg minimum weight. 30% benzole fuel allowed
1931-33	No engine or weight restrictions
1934-37	750 kg minimum weight
1938-39	4500 cc for normally aspirated and 3000 cc supercharged maximum engine capacity. 400–850 kg minimum weight depending on engine size
1945-46	No standardized rules
1947-53	The first Formula One. 4500 cc normally aspirated and 1500 cc supercharged maximum engine capacity

RACE DISTANCES

1931	Minimum race duration of ten hours
1932	Race duration between five and ten hours
1933	500 kms maximum

WORLD CHAMPIONSHIP

The first World Championship of Grand Prix racing was held in 1925 as a manufacturers' title with the Indianapolis 500 joining national Grands Prix as qualifying rounds.

year	constructors' champion	qualifying races
1925	Alfa Romeo	Indianapolis 500, Belgian GP, French GP and Italian GP
1926	Bugatti	Indianapolis 500, French GP, European GP, Spanish GP, English GP and Italian GP
1927	Delage	Indianapolis 500, French GP, Spanish GP, Italian GP and English GP

EUROPEAN CHAMPIONSHIP

In 1935 the German national authority suggested that for the first time an official champion driver should be chosen for Grand Prix racing. There had been some doubt about how the successful driver was chosen until Chris Nixon unearthed a points system which had been used in 1937 while researching the book *Racing the Silver Arrows*. Under this points were awarded as follows:

1 to 1st	5 to those who have completed 50% of race
2 to 2nd	6 to those who have completed 25% of race
3 to 3rd	7 to those who have completed less than 25% of race
4 to 4th and all those to have completed over 75% of race	8 to those who did not start

with the champion having scored the fewest points.

However, when applied to the 1939 season, this system makes Hermann Müller of Auto Union European Champion rather than Hermann Lang as previously believed.

year	driver	nat	car	qualifying rounds
1935	Rudolf Caracciola	D	Mercedes-Benz W25B	Belgian GP, German GP, Swiss GP, Italian GP and Spanish GP
1936	Bernd Rosemeyer	D	Auto Union C	Monaco GP, German GP, Swiss GP and Italian GP
1937	Rudolf Caracciola	D	Mercedes-Benz W125	Belgian GP, German GP, Monaco GP, Swiss GP and Italian GP
1938	Rudolf Caracciola	D	Mercedes-Benz W154	French GP, German GP, Swiss GP and Italian GP
1939*	Hermann Lang	D	Mercedes-Benz W163	Belgian GP, French GP, German GP and Swiss GP
or	Hermann Müller	D	Auto Union D	

*champion in doubt due to scoring inconsistency

1906

Grand Prix de l'Automobile Club de France

26-27 June 1906. Le Mans. 12 laps of a 64.120-mile circuit = 769.440 miles

1	Ferenc Szisz	Renault AK	12	12h14m07.0
2	Felice Nazzaro	Fiat 130 hp	12	12h46m26.4
3	Albert Clément	Clément-Bayard 100 hp	12	12h49m46.2
4	Jules Barillier	Brasier 105 hp	12	13h53m00.0
5	Vincenzo Lancia	Fiat 130 hp	12	14h22m11.0
6	George Heath	Panhard 130	12	14h47m45.4

Winner's average speed: 62.887 mph. Fastest lap: Paul Baras (Brasier 105hp), 52m25.4

1907

Grand Prix de l'Automobile Club de France

2 July 1907. Dieppe. 10 laps of a 47.840-mile circuit = 478.400 miles

1	Felice Nazzaro	Fiat	10	6h46m33.0
2	Ferenc Szisz	Renault AK	10	6h53m10.6
3	Paul Baras	Brasier	10	7h05m05.6
4	Fernand Gabriel	Lorraine-Dietrich	10	7h11m39.0
5	Victor Rigal	Darracq	10	7h12m36.4
6	Gustave Caillois	Darracq	10	7h15m58.6

Winner's average speed: 70.604 mph. Fastest lap: Arthur Duray (Lorraine-Dietrich), 37m59.8

1908

Grand Prix de l'Automobile Club de France

7 July 1908. Dieppe. 10 laps of a 47.840-mile circuit = 478.400 miles

1	Christian Lautenschlager	Mercedes	10	6h55m43.8
2	Victor Hémery	Benz 150 hp	10	7h04m24.0
3	René Hanriot	Benz 150 hp	10	7h05m13.0
4	Victor Rigal	Clément-Bayard	10	7h30m36.6
5	Willy Pöge	Mercedes	10	7h32m31.0
6	Carl Jörns	Opel	10	7h39m40.0

Winner's average speed: 69.045 mph. Fastest lap: Otto Salzer (Mercedes), 36m31.0

American Grand Prize

26 November 1908. Savannah. 16 laps of a 25.130-mile circuit = 402.080 miles

1	Louis Wagner	Fiat	16	6h10m31.0
2	Victor Hémery	Benz 150 hp	16	6h11m27.0
3	Felice Nazzaro	Fiat	16	6h18m47.0
4	René Hanriot	Benz 150 hp	16	6h26m12.0
5	Lucien Hautvast	Clément-Bayard	16	6h34m06.0
6	Louis Strang	Renault	16	6h43m37.0

Winner's average speed: 65.111 mph. Fastest lap: Ralph de Palma (Fiat), 21m36.0

1910

American Grand Prize

12 November 1910. Savannah. 24 laps of a 17.300-mile circuit = 415.200 miles

1	David Bruce-Brown	Benz	24	5h53m05.4
2	Victor Hémery	Benz	24	5h53m06.8
3	Bob Burman	Marquette-Buick	24	6h11m23.5
4	Ralph Mulford	Lozier	24	6h26m12.7
5	Joe Horan	Lozier 6	24	6h30m02.7
6	Ray Harroun/ Joe Dawson	Marmon	24	6h30m22.2

Winner's average speed: 70.554 mph. Fastest lap: Felice Nazzaro (Fiat), 13m42.0

1911

American Grand Prize

30 November 1911. Savannah. 24 laps of a 17.140-mile circuit = 411.360 miles

1	David Bruce-Brown	Fiat S74	24	5h31m29.1
2	Eddie Hearne	Benz	24	5h33m33.1
3	Ralph de Palma	Mercedes	24	5h34m40.8
4	Caleb Bragg	Fiat S74	24	5h51m55.3
5	Lou Disbrow	Pope-Hartford	24	6h26m44.0
6	Bill Mitchell	Abbott Detroit-Continental	24	

Winner's average speed: 74.458 mph. Fastest lap: Victor Hémery (Benz), 12m36.0

1912

Grand Prix de l'Automobile Club de France

25-26 June 1912. Dieppe. 20 laps of a 47.840-mile circuit = 956.800 miles

1	Georges Boillot	Peugeot L76	20	13h58m02.6

2 Louis Wagner	Fiat S74	20	14h11m08.4
3 Victor Rigal	Sunbeam	20	14h38m36.0
4 Dario Resta	Sunbeam	20	14h39m51.8
5 Emil Medinger	Sunbeam	20	15h59m41.4
6 Joseph Christiaens	Excelsior	20	16h23m38.8

Winner's average speed: 68.502 mph. Fastest lap: David Bruce-Brown (Fiat S74), 36m32.0

American Grand Prize

5 October 1912. Milwaukee. 52 laps of a 7.880-mile circuit = 409.760 miles

1 Caleb Bragg	Fiat S74	52	5h59m27.4
2 Erwin Bergdoll	Benz	52	6h14m58.4
3 Gil Anderson	Stutz	52	6h15m22.5
4 Barney Oldfield	Fiat S74	52	6h19m54.7
5 Ralph de Palma	Mercedes	51	accident
6 George Clark	Mercedes	51	

Winner's average speed: 68.396 mph. Fastest lap: Teddy Tetzlaff (Fiat S74), 6m07.0

1913

Grand Prix de l'Automobile Club de France

12 July 1913. Amiens. 29 laps of a 19.650-mile circuit = 569.850 miles

1 Georges Boillot	Peugeot EX3	29	7h53m56.8
2 Jules Goux	Peugeot EX3	29	7h56m22.4
3 Jean Chassagne	Sunbeam	29	8h06m20.2
4 Paul Bablot	Delage Y	29	8h16m13.6
5 Albert Guyot	Delage Y	29	8h17m58.8
6 Dario Resta	Sunbeam	29	8h21m38.4

Winner's average speed: 72.141 mph. Fastest lap: Bablot, 15m22

Christian Lautenschlager's Mercedes leads the 1914 French GP in a dominant victory for the German marque

1914

American Grand Prize

28 February 1914. Santa Monica. 48 laps of a 8.417-mile circuit = 404.016 miles

1 Eddie Pullen	Mercer	48	5h13m30.0
2 Guy Ball	Marmon	48	5h53m23.0
3 William Taylor	Alco	48	6h08m29.0
4 Ralph de Palma	Mercedes	48	6h09m08.0
5 Gil Anderson	Stutz	45	piston
6 Huntley Gordon	Mercer	41	

Winner's average speed: 77.324 mph. Fastest lap: Teddy Tetzlaff (Fiat S74), 5m49.0

Grand Prix de l'Automobile Club de France

4 July 1914. Lyon. 20 laps of a 23.380-mile circuit = 467.600 miles

1 Christian Lautenschlager	Mercedes GP	20	7h08m18.4
2 Louis Wagner	Mercedes GP	20	7h09m54.2
3 Otto Salzer	Mercedes GP	20	7h13m15.8
4 Jules Goux	Peugeot EX5	20	7h17m47.2
5 Dario Resta	Sunbeam	20	7h28m17.4
6 Dragutin Esser	Nagant	20	7h40m28.2

Winner's average speed: 65.504 mph. Fastest lap: Max Sailer (Mercedes GP), 20m06.0

1915

American Grand Prize

27 February 1915. San Francisco. 104 laps of a 3.840-mile circuit = 399.360 miles

1 Dario Resta	Peugeot EX3	104	7h07m53.0
2 Howdy Wilcox	Stutz	104	7h14m36.0
3 Hughie Hughes	Ono	104	7h21m46.0
4 Gil Anderson	Stutz	104	7h30m21.0
5 Lou Disbrow	Simplex ZIP 90 hp	104	7h31m38.0

No other finishers. Winner's average speed: 56.000 mph. Fastest lap: n/a

1916

American Grand Prize

18 November 1916. Santa Monica. 48 laps of a 8.417-mile circuit = 404.016 miles

1 Howdy Wilcox/ Johnny Aitken	Peugeot EX5	48	4h42m47.0
2 Earl Cooper	Stutz	48	4h48m59.0
3 AH Patterson	Hudson 6	48	5h09m39.0
4 Clyde Roades	Hudson 6	48	5h54m05.0
5 William Weightman/ Eddie Rickenbacher	Duesenberg	45	

No other finishers. Winner's average speed: 85.723 mph. Fastest lap: Ed Ruckstell (Mercer), time n/a

1921

Grand Prix de l'Automobile Club de France

26 July 1921. Le Mans. 30 laps of a 10.726-mile circuit = 321.780 miles

1 Jimmy Murphy	Duesenberg	30	4h07m11.4
2 Ralph de Palma	Ballot 3L	30	4h22m10.6
3 Jules Goux	Ballot 2LS	30	4h28m38.2
4 André Dubonnet	Duesenberg	30	4h30m19.2
5 André Boillot	Sunbeam	30	4h35m17.4
6 Albert Guyot	Duesenberg	30	4h38m13.0

Winner's average speed: 78.105 mph. Starting grid front row: de Palma and Emile Mathis (Mathis) – positions drawn. Fastest lap: Murphy, 7m43.0

Gran Premio d'Italia

4 September 1921. Brescia. 30 laps of a 10.750-mile circuit = 322.500 miles

1 Jules Goux	Ballot 3L	30	3h35m09.0
2 Jean Chassagne	Ballot 3L	30	3h40m52.0
3 Louis Wagner	Fiat 802	30	3h45m33.0

No other finishers. Winner's average speed: 89.937 mph. Race started in numerical order every 60 seconds, numbers drawn. Fastest lap: Pietro Bordino (Fiat 802), 6m54.2

1922

Grand Prix de l'Automobile Club de France

16 July 1922. Strasbourg. 60 laps of a 8.300-mile circuit = 498.000 miles

1 Felice Nazzaro	Fiat 804	60	6h17m17.0
2 Pierre de Vizcaya	Bugatti T30	60	7h15m09.8
3 Piero Marco	Bugatti T30	60	7h48m04.2
4 Pietro Bordino	Fiat 804	58	accident
5 Jacques Mones-Maury	Bugatti T30	57	

No other finishers. Winner's average speed: 79.198 mph. Starting grid front row: F Nazzaro – positions drawn. Fastest lap: Bordino, 5m43

Gran Premio d'Italia

3 September 1922. Monza. 80 laps of a 6.214-mile circuit = 497.120 miles

1	Pietro Bordino	Fiat 804	80	5h43m13.0
2	Felice Nazzaro	Fiat 804	80	5h51m35.0
3	Pierre de Vizcaya	Bugatti T30	76	

No other finishers. Winner's average speed: 86.905 mph. Starting grid front row: Franz Heim (Heim) and Nazzaro – positions drawn. Fastest lap: Bordino, 4m05.0

1923

Grand Prix de l'Automobile Club de France

2 June 1923. Tours. 35 laps of a 14.180-mile circuit = 496.300 miles

1	Henry Segrave	Sunbeam	35	6h35m19.6
2	Albert Divo	Sunbeam	35	6h54m25.8
3	Ernst Friedrich	Bugatti T30	35	7h00m22.4
4	Kenelm Lee Guinness	Sunbeam	35	7h02m03.0
5	André Lefebvre	Voisin Laboratoire	35	7h50m29.2

No other finishers. Winner's average speed: 75.325 mph. Starting grid front row: René Thomas (Delage 2LCV) and Lee Guinness – positions drawn. Fastest lap: Pietro Bordino (Fiat 805), 9m36

Gran Premio d'Italia

9 September 1923. Monza. 80 laps of a 6.214-mile circuit = 497.120 miles. Also known as the European Grand Prix

1	Carlo Salamano	Fiat 805	80	5h27m38.4
2	Felice Nazzaro	Fiat 805	80	5h28m02.0
3	Jimmy Murphy	Miller 122	80	5h32m51.0
4	Ferdinando Minoia	Benz RH	76	
5	Franz Horner	Benz RH	71	
6	Martin de Alsaga	Miller 122	70	

Winner's average speed: 91.037 mph. Starting grid front row: Minoia, Pietro Bordino (Fiat 805) and Eugenio Silvani (Voisin Laboratoire) – positions drawn, rolling start. Fastest lap: Bordino, 3m44

Gran Premio de Espana

28 October 1923. Sitges. 200 laps of a 1.243-mile circuit = 248.600 miles. Race scheduled for 300 laps but reduced after rain delayed start

1	Albert Divo	Sunbeam	200	2h33m50.0
2	Louis Zborowski	Miller 122	200	2h34m46.0
3	Alfonso Carreras	Elizalde 511	200	3h26m35.0
4	José dos Santos-Mora	Diatto 20S	200	
5	José Feliu	Elizalde 511	200	

No other finishers. Winner's average speed: 96.962 mph. Starting grid front row: n/a. Fastest lap: Zborowski, 45.8s

1924

Grand Prix de l'Automobile Club de France

3 August 1924. Lyon. 35 laps of a 14.380-mile circuit = 503.300 miles. Also known as the European Grand Prix

1	Giuseppe Campari	Alfa Romeo P2	35	7h05m34.8
2	Albert Divo	Delage 2LCV	35	7h06m40.2
3	Robert Benoist	Delage 2LCV	35	7h17m00.8
4	Louis Wagner	Alfa Romeo P2	35	7h25m10.8
5	Henry Segrave	Sunbeam	35	7h28m56.0
6	René Thomas	Delage 2LCV	35	7h37m27.4

Winner's average speed: 70.957 mph. Starting grid front row: Segrave and Divo – positions drawn. Fastest lap: Segrave, 11m19.0

Gran Premio de San Sebastian

25 September 1924. Lasarte. 35 laps of a 11.029-mile circuit = 386.015 miles

1	Henry Segrave	Sunbeam	35	6h01m19.0
2	Meo Costantini	Bugatti T35	35	6h02m44.0
3	André Morel	Delage 2LCV	35	6h03m47.0
4	Albert Divo	Delage 2LCV	35	6h11m11.0
5	Pierre de Vizcaya	Bugatti T35	35	6h29m09.0
6	Jean Chassagne	Bugatti T35	35	6h46m30.0

Winner's average speed: 64.101 mph. Starting grid front row: n/a. Fastest lap: Costantini, 9m13.8

Gran Premio d'Italia

19 October 1924. Monza. 80 laps of a 6.214-mile circuit = 497.120 miles

1	Antonio Ascari	Alfa Romeo P2	80	5h02m05.0
2	Louis Wagner	Alfa Romeo P2	80	5h18m05.0
3	Giuseppe Campari/ Cesare Pastore	Alfa Romeo P2	80	5h21m59.0
4	Ferdinando Minoia	Alfa Romeo P2	80	5h22m43.4
5	Jules Goux	Rolland Pilain-Schmid	80	6h10m22.0
6	Giulio Foresti	Rolland Pilain-Schmid	80	6h32m03.0

Winner's average speed: 98.738 mph. Starting grid front row: Ascari, Christian Werner (Mercedes M72/94) and Goux – positions drawn. Fastest lap: Ascari, 3m43.6

1925

Grand Prix de Belgique

28 June 1925. Spa-Francorchamps. 54 laps of a 9.310-mile circuit = 502.740 miles. Also known as the European Grand Prix

1	Antonio Ascari	Alfa Romeo P2	54	6h42m57.0
2	Giuseppe Campari	Alfa Romeo P2	54	7h04m55.0

No other finishers. Winner's average speed: 74.859 mph. Starting grid front row: René Thomas (Delage 2LCV), Ascari and Robert Benoist (Delage 2LCV) – positions drawn. Fastest lap: Ascari, 6m51.2

Grand Prix de l'Automobile Club de France

26 July 1925. Montlhéry. 80 laps of a 7.767-mile circuit = 621.360 miles

1	Robert Benoist/ Albert Divo	Delage 2LCV	80	8h54m41.2
2	Louis Wagner/ Paul Torchy	Delage 2LCV	80	9h02m27.4
3	Giulio Masetti	Sunbeam	80	9h06m15.2
4	Meo Costantini	Bugatti T35	80	9h07m38.4
5	Jules Goux	Bugatti T35	80	9h15m11.2
6	Ferdinand de Vizcaya	Bugatti T35	80	9h20m48.4

Winner's average speed: 69.726 mph. Starting grid front row: Pierre de Vizcaya (Bugatti T35), Giuseppe Campari (Alfa Romeo P2) and Henry Segrave (Sunbeam) – positions drawn, rolling start. Fastest lap: Divo, 5m48.0

Gran Premio d'Italia

6 September 1925. Monza. 80 laps of a 6.214-mile circuit = 497.120 miles

1	Gastone Brilli-Peri	Alfa Romeo P2	80	5h14m33.3
2	Giuseppe Campari/ Giovanni Minozzi	Alfa Romeo P2	80	5h33m30.2
3	Meo Costantini	Bugatti T39	80	5h44m40.9
4	Tommy Milton	Duesenberg 122	80	5h46m40.5
5	Peter de Paolo	Alfa Romeo P2	80	5h48m10.3
6	Ferdinand de Vizcaya	Bugatti T37	80	5h50m49.4

Winner's average speed: 94.823 mph. Starting grid front row: Emilio Materassi (Diatto GP), Albert Guyot (Rolland Pilain-McCollum), Campari and Alfieri Maserati (Diatto 20S) – positions drawn. Fastest lap: Peter Kreis (Duesenberg), 3m36.7

Gran Premio de San Sebastian

19 September 1925. Lasarte. 40 laps of a 11.029-mile circuit = 441.160 miles

1 Albert Divo/			
André Morel	Delage 2LCV	40	5h45m01.0
2 Robert Benoist	Delage 2LCV	40	5h55m43.0
3 René Thomas	Delage 2LCV	40	5h56m26.0
4 Pierre de Vizcaya	Bugatti T35	40	6h01m40.0
5 Ferdinand			
de Vizcaya	Bugatti T35	40	6h11m33.0

No other finishers. Winner's average speed: 76.720 mph. Starting grid front row: n/a. Fastest lap: Meo Costantini (Bugatti T35), 8m00.0

1926

Grand Prix de l'Automobile Club de France

27 June 1926. Miramas. 100 laps of a 3.107-mile circuit = 310.700 miles

1 Jules Goux	Bugatti T39A	100	4h38m43.8

No other finishers, only three cars started. Winner's average speed: 66.882 mph. Starting grid front row: Pierre de Vizcaya, Meo Costantini and Goux (all Bugatti T37A) – positions drawn. Fastest lap: Goux, 2m24

Grosser Preis von Deutschland

11 July 1926. Avus. Sports Car race. 20 laps of a 12.160-mile circuit = 243.200 miles

1 Rudolf Caracciola	Mercedes	20	2h54m17.8
2 Christian Riecken	NAG	20	2h57m33.2
3 Willy Cleer	Alfa Romeo	20	3h00m16.8
4 Pierre Clause	Bignan	20	3h02m07.4
5 Georg Klöble	NSU	20	3h07m27.0
6 Max zu			
Schaumburg-Lippe	OM	20	3h10m57.4

Winner's average speed: 83.719 mph. Starting grid front row: n/a. Fastest lap: Ferdinando Minoia (OM), time n/a

Gran Premio de Europa

18 July 1926. Lasarte. 45 laps of a 11.029-mile circuit = 496.305 miles

1 Jules Goux	Bugatti T39A	45	6h51m52.0
2 Edmond Bourlier/			
Robert Sénéchal	Delage 15S8	45	6h59m42.0
3 Meo Costantini	Bugatti T39A	45	7h28m18.0
4 André Morel/			
Edmond Bourlier/			
Louis Wagner	Delage 15S8	40	
5 Ferdinando Minoia	Bugatti T39A	40	

No other finishers. Winner's average speed: 72.301 mph. Starting grid front row: Robert Benoist (Delage 2LCV) and Goux – positions drawn. Fastest lap: Wagner, 8m53.5

Gran Premio de Espana

25 July 1926. Lasarte. 40 laps of a 11.029-mile circuit = 441.160 miles

1 Meo Costantini	Bugatti T35	40	5h35m47.0
2 Jules Goux	Bugatti T35	40	5h52m15.0
3 Louis Wagner/			
Robert Benoist	Delage 2LCV	40	5h56m57.0
4 Ferdinando Minoia	Bugatti T35	40	5h57m27.0
5 Ferry	Bugatti T35	33	

No other finishers. Winner's average speed: 78.829 mph. Starting grid front row: n/a. Fastest lap: Costantini, time n/a

English Grand Prix

7 August 1926. Brooklands. 110 laps of a 2.616-mile circuit = 287.760 miles

1 Robert Sénéchal/			
Louis Wagner	Delage 15S8	110	4h00m56.0
2 Malcolm Campbell	Bugatti T39A	110	4h10m44.0
3 Robert Benoist/			
André Dubonnet	Delage 15S8	110	4h18m08.0

No other finishers. Winner's average speed: 71.661 mph. Starting grid front row: in line across track. Fastest lap: Henry Segrave (Talbot T700), 1m49.5

Gran Premio d'Italia

5 September 1926. Monza. 60 laps of a 6.214-mile circuit = 372.840 miles

1 "Sabipa"	Bugatti T39A	60	4h20m29.0
2 Meo Costantini	Bugatti T39A	60	4h27m01.4

No other finishers. Winner's average speed: 85.880 mph. Starting grid front row: Emilio Materassi (Maserati 26), Roberto Serboli (Chiribiri 12/16) and Jules Goux (Bugatti T39A) – positions drawn. Fastest lap: Costantini, 3m47.0

1927

Grand Prix de l'Automobile Club de France

3 July 1927. Montlhéry. 48 laps of a 7.767-mile circuit = 372.816 miles

1 Robert Benoist	Delage 15S8	48	4h45m41.2
2 Edmond Bourlier	Delage 15S8	48	4h53m55.6
3 André Morel	Delage 15S8	48	5h11m31.4
4 "W Williams"/			
Jules Moriceau	Talbot T700	48	5h24m30.0

No other finishers. Winner's average speed: 78.299 mph. Starting grid front row: George Eyston (Halford), Albert Divo (Talbot T700) and Benoist – positions drawn. Fastest lap: Benoist, 5m41.0

Grosser Preis von Deutschland

17 July 1927. Nürburgring. Sports Car race. 18 laps of a 17.563-mile circuit = 316.134 miles

1 Otto Merz	Mercedes S	18	4h59m35.6
2 Christian Werner	Mercedes S	18	5h02m54.6
3 Willy Walb	Mercedes S	18	5h10m49.0
4 Elizabeth Junek	Bugatti	18	5h40m07.6
5 Hugo Urban-			
Emmerich	Talbot	18	6h00m32.0
6 Willy Cleer	Bugatti	18	6h07m11.0

Winner's average speed: 63.313 mph. Starting grid front row: n/a. Fastest lap: Werner, 15m51.6

Rudi Caracciola and his riding mechanic take the applause at the 1926 German Grand Prix

Gran Premio de Espana

31 July 1927. Lasarte. 40 laps of a 11.029-mile circuit = 441.160 miles

1 Robert Benoist	Delage 15S8	40	5h20m45.0
2 Caberto Conelli	Bugatti T39A	40	5h23m02.0
3 Edmond Bourlier	Delage 15S8	40	5h28m12.0

No other finishers. Winner's average speed: 82.524 mph. Starting grid front row: n/a. Fastest lap: Benoist, 7m33.0

Gran Premio d'Italia

4 September 1927. Monza. 60 laps of a 6.214-mile circuit = 372.840 miles. Also known as the European Grand Prix

1 Robert Benoist	Delage 15S8	60	3h26m59.7
2 Giuseppe Morandi	OM 865	60	3h49m32.5
3 Earl Cooper/			
Peter Kreis	Miller 91	60	4h02m05.7
4 Ferdinando Minoia	OM 865	60	4h02m28.5

No other finishers. Winner's average speed: 108.072 mph. Starting grid front row: Minoia, Benoist and Kreis – positions drawn. Fastest lap: Benoist, 3m57.24

English Grand Prix

1 October 1927. Brooklands. 125 laps of a 2.616-mile circuit = 327.000 miles

1 Robert Benoist	Delage 15S8	125	3h49m14.6
2 Edmond Bourlier	Delage 15S8	125	3h49m21.6
3 Albert Divo	Delage 15S8	125	3h52m20.0
4 Louis Chiron	Bugatti T39A	125	4h17m50.0
5 Emilio Materassi	Bugatti T39A	118	

No other finishers. Winner's average speed: 85.586 mph. Starting grid front row: in line across track. Fastest lap: n/a

1928

Grand Prix de l'Automobile Club de France

1 July 1928. St Gaudens. Sports Car handicap race. 10 laps of a 16.156-mile circuit = 161.560 miles

1 "W Williams"	Bugatti T35C	10	2h27m40.8
2 André Rousseau	Salmson	10	2h30m04.6
3 Edouard Brisson	Stutz	10	2h31m13.4
4 Lucien Desvaux	Lombard	10	2h31m28.4
5 Georges Casse	Salmson	10	2h38m36.0
6 Henri Stoffel	Chrysler	10	2h40m14.0

Note: time shown includes the handicap. Winner's average speed: 65.639 mph. Starting grid front row: n/a. Fastest lap: "Williams", 10m48

Grosser Preis von Deutschland

15 July 1928. Nürburgring. Sports Car race. 18 laps of a 17.563-mile circuit = 316.134 miles

1 Rudolf Caracciola/			
Christian Werner	Mercedes SS	18	4h54m24.0
2 Otto Merz	Mercedes SS	18	4h56m02.0
3 Christian Werner/			
Willy Walb	Mercedes SS	18	5h04m23.0
4 Gastone Brilli-Peri	Bugatti	18	5h05m16.0
5 Georg Kimpel/			
Adolff Rosenberger	Mercedes SS	18	5h06m29.0
6 Louis Chiron	Bugatti	18	5h17m26.0

Winner's average speed: 64.429 mph. Starting grid front row: n/a. Fastest lap: Caracciola, 15m13.2

Gran Premio de San Sebastien

25 July 1928. Lasarte. 40 laps of a 11.029-mile circuit = 441.160 miles

1 Louis Chiron	Bugatti T35C	40	5h20m30.0
2 Robert Benoist	Bugatti T35B	40	5h22m56.5
3 Marcel Lehoux	Bugatti T35C	40	5h32m35.0
4 Goffredo Zehender	Bugatti T37A	40	5h42m23.7
5 Manuel Blancas	Bugatti T35B	40	6h04m46.8
6 Torres	Bugatti T37A	29	

Winner's average speed: 82.588 mph. Starting grid front row: n/a. Fastest lap: Chiron, 6m50.6

Gran Premio de Espana

29 July 1928. Lasarte. Handicap race. 15 laps of a 11.029-mile circuit = 165.435 miles

1 Louis Chiron	Bugatti T35C	15	2h25m00.0
2 Georges Bouriano	Bugatti T35	15	2h30m14.0
3 Delemer	EHP	15	2h30m37.0
4 Christian	Lombard	15	2h35m43.0
5 Robert Laly	Ariès	15	2h35m51.0
6 Cyril de Vere	Chrysler	15	2h36m24.0

Note: time shown includes the handicap. Winner's average speed: 68.456 mph. Starting grid front row: n/a. Fastest lap: Bouriano, no time available

Gran Premio d'Italia

9 September 1928. Monza. 60 laps of a 6.214-mile circuit = 372.840 miles. Also known as the European Grand Prix

1 Louis Chiron	Bugatti T35C	60	3h45m08.6
2 Achille Varzi/			
Giuseppe Campari	Alfa Romeo P2	60	3h47m29.0
3 Tazio Nuvolari	Bugatti T35C	60	3h59m27.6
4 Guy Drouet	Bugatti T35B	60	3h59m37.8
5 Aymo Maggi	Maserati 26R	60	4h10m29.0
6 Ernesto Maserati	Maserati 26R	55	

Winner's average speed: 99.361 mph. Starting grid front row: Baconin Borzacchini (Maserati 26B), Giuliio Foresti (Bugatti T35C), Emilio Materassi (Talbot T700), "W Williams" (Bugatti T35B) and Gastone Brilli-Peri (Talbot T700). Fastest lap: Luigi Arcangeli (Talbot T700), 3m37.4

1929

Grand Prix de Monaco

14 April 1929. Monte Carlo. 100 laps of a 1.976-mile circuit = 197.600 miles

1 "W Williams"	Bugatti T35B	100	3h56m11.0
2 Georges Bouriano	Bugatti T35C	100	3h57m28.8
3 Rudolf Caracciola	Mercedes-Benz SSK	100	3h58m33.6
4 "Georges Philippe"	Bugatti T35C	99	
5 René Dreyfus	Bugatti T37A	97	
6 Philippe Étancelin	Bugatti T35C	96	

Winner's average speed: 50.198 mph. Starting grid front row: Étancelin, Christian Dauvergne (Bugatti T35C) and Marcel Lehoux (Bugatti T35B) – positions drawn. Fastest lap: "Williams", 2m15.0

Grand Prix de l'Automobile Club de France

30 June 1929. Le Mans. 37 laps of a 10.153-mile circuit = 375.661 miles

1 "W Williams"	Bugatti T35B	37	4h33m01.2
2 André Boillot	Peugeot 174S	37	4h34m20.0
3 Caberto Conelli	Bugatti T35C	37	4h34m28.0
4 Albert Divo	Bugatti T35B	37	4h41m27.4
5 Robert Sénéchal	Bugatti T35B	37	4h42m27.8
6 Robert Gauthier	Bugatti T35C	37	5h18m38.4

Winner's average speed: 82.557 mph. Starting grid front row: Raoul de Rovin (Bugatti T35B) and Jean Chassagne (Ballot RH2) – positions drawn. Fastest lap: "Williams", 7m01.0

Grosser Preis von Deutschland

14 July 1929. Nürburgring. 18 laps of a 17.563-mile circuit = 316.134 miles

1 Louis Chiron	Bugatti T35C	18	4h46m06.4
2 "Georges Philippe"	Bugatti T35C	18	4h57m52.2
3 August Momberger/			
Max Arco-Zinneberg	Mercedes-Benz SSK	18	5h00m37.8
4 Guy Bouriat	Bugatti T35C	18	5h03m28.4
5 Mario Lepori	Bugatti	18	
6 W Rosenstein/			
Adolff Rosenberger	Mercedes-Benz SSK	18	

Winner's average speed: 66.297 mph. Starting grid front row: n/a. Fastest lap: Chiron, 15m06.0

Early Grand Prix Racing

Gran Premio de Espana

25 July 1929. Lasarte. 40 laps of a 11.029-mile circuit
= 441.160 miles

1 Louis Chiron	Bugatti T35B	40	5h57m06.0
2 "Georges Philippe"/			
Guy Bouriat	Bugatti T35C	40	6h02m59.0
3 Marcel Lehoux	Bugatti T35C	40	6h04m18.0
4 René Dreyfus	Bugatti T35C	40	6h09m51.0
5 Edmond Bourlier	Bugatti T35B	40	6h19m05.0
6 Jean de Maleplane	Bugatti T35C	40	6h32m05.0

Winner's average speed: 74.124 mph. Starting grid front row:
n/a. Fastest lap: Chiron, 7m26.0

Gran Premio di Monza

15 September 1929. Monza. Final: 22 laps of a 2.796-mile
circuit = 61.512 miles

1 Achille Varzi	Alfa Romeo P2	22	31m38.4
2 Tazio Nuvolari	Talbot T700	22	33m15.0
3 August Momberger	Mercedes-Benz SS	22	34m17.2
4 Gastone Brilli-Peri	Alfa Romeo P2	22	34m18.3
5 Federico Caflisch	Mercedes-Benz SS	22	34m20.0
6 Alfieri Maserati	Maserati V4	22	34m48.2

Winner's average speed: 116.647 mph. Starting grid front row:
A Maserati, Momberger, Caflisch, Luigi Arcangeli (Talbot T700)
and Nuvolari – positions drawn. Fastest lap: A Maserati, 1m21.0

1930

Grand Prix de Monaco

6 April 1930. Monte Carlo. 100 laps of a 1.976-mile circuit
= 197.600 miles

1 René Dreyfus	Bugatti T35B	100	3h41m02.6
2 Louis Chiron	Bugatti T35C	100	3h41m24.4
3 Guy Bouriat	Bugatti T35C	100	3h49m20.4
4 Goffredo Zehender	Bugatti T35B	100	3h54m39.6
5 Michel Doré	Bugatti T37A	100	4h12m06.6
6 Hans Stuber	Bugatti T35C	94	

Winner's average speed: 53.637 mph. Starting grid front row:
Baconin Borzacchini (Maserati 26B), Bobby Bowes (Frazer Nash-
Anzani) and "W Williams" (Bugatti T35C) – positions drawn,
Bowes did not start. Fastest lap: Dreyfus, 2m07.0

Grand Prix de Belgique

20 July 1930. Spa-Francorchamps. 40 laps of a 9.236-mile
circuit = 369.440 miles. Also known as the European
Grand Prix

1 Louis Chiron	Bugatti T35C	40	5h08m34.6
2 Guy Bouriat	Bugatti T35C	40	5h09m34.0
3 Albert Divo	Bugatti T35C	40	5h13m54.0
4 Arthur Duray	Ariès	40	5h22m26.0
5 Goffredo Zehender	Imperia	40	5h25m19.0
6 Charles Montier	Montier Spéciale-Ford	40	5h30m30.0

Winner's average speed: 71.834 mph. Starting grid front row:
n/a. Fastest lap: Bouriat, 7m05.0

Gran Premio di Monza

7 September 1930. Monza. Final: 35 laps of a 4.263-mile
circuit = 149.205 miles

1 Achille Varzi	Maserati 26M	35	1h35m46.2
2 Luigi Arcangeli	Maserati 26M	35	1h35m46.4
3 Ernesto Maserati	Maserati V4	35	1h36m10.4
4 Giovanni Minozzi	Bugatti T35C	35	1h39m23.2
5 Luigi Fagioli	Maserati 26M	35	1h39m23.6
6 Philippe Étancelin	Bugatti T35C	35	1h39m49.8

Winner's average speed: 93.477 mph. Starting grid front row:
Arcangeli, Baconin Borzacchini (Alfa Romeo P2) and Fagioli –
positions decided by heat results. Fastest lap: Varzi, 2m32.6

Grand Prix de l'Automobile Club de France

21 September 1930. Pau. 25 laps of a 9.860-mile circuit
= 246.500 miles

1 Philippe Étancelin	Bugatti T35C	25	2h43m18.4
2 Tim Birkin	Bentley 4.5	25	2h46m44.6
3 Juan Zanelli	Bugatti T35B	25	2h46m58.8
4 Stanislav Czaykowski	Bugatti T35C	25	2h51m27.0
5 Jean de l'Espée	Bugatti T35C	25	2h54m28.8
6 Robert Sénéchal	Delage 15S8	25	2h56m28.6

Winner's average speed: 90.566 mph. Starting grid front row:
Marcel Lehoux (Bugatti T35B), Czaykowski and Louis Casali (La
Perle) – positions drawn. Fastest lap: "Williams", 6m10.0

Masarykuv Okruh (Czech Grand Prix)

21 September 1930. Brno. 17 laps of a 18.109-mile circuit
= 307.853 miles

1 Hermann zu			
Leiningen/Heinrich-			
Joachim von Morgen	Bugatti T35B	17	4h54m13.0
2 Ernst-Günther			
Burgaller	Bugatti T35B	17	4h57m08.9
3 Tazio Nuvolari/			
Baconin Borzacchini	Alfa Romeo P2	17	5h26m13.9
4 Jan Kubicek	Bugatti T35	17	5h33m31.9
5 Milos Bondy	Bugatti T35	17	5h38m57.3

No other finishers. Winner's average speed: 62.781 mph.
Starting grid front row: n/a. Fastest lap: Rudolf Caracciola
(Mercedes-Benz SSK), 15m27.2

Gran Premio de Espana

5 October 1930. Lasarte. 30 laps of a 11.029-mile circuit
= 330.870 miles

1 Achille Varzi	Maserati 26M	30	3h43m05.0
2 Aymo Maggi	Maserati 26M	30	4h05m03.0
3 Henri Stoffel	Peugeot 174S	30	4h08m48.0
4 René Ferrand	Peugeot 174S	30	4h10m10.0
5 Max Fourny	Bugatti T35C	30	4h13m58.0
6 Jean de Maleplane	Bugatti T35C	30	4h14m48.0

Winner's average speed: 88.990 mph. Starting grid front row:
n/a. Fastest lap: Varzi, 7m05.6

1931

Grand Prix de Monaco

19 April 1931. Monte Carlo. 100 laps of a 1.976-mile circuit
= 197.600 miles

1 Louis Chiron	Bugatti T51	100	3h39m09.2
2 Luigi Fagioli	Maserati 26M	100	3h43m04.6
3 Achille Varzi	Bugatti T51	100	3h43m13.2
4 Guy Bouriat	Bugatti T51	98	
5 Goffredo Zehender	Alfa Romeo 6C-1750	97	
6 André Boillot	Peugeot 174S	96	

Winner's average speed: 54.099 mph. Starting grid front row:
René Dreyfus (Maserati 26M), Hans Stuber (Bugatti T35C) and
Bernd Ackerl (Bugatti T37A) – positions drawn. Fastest lap:
Chiron and Fagioli, 2m07

Gran Premio d'Italia

24 May 1931. Monza. Race scheduled for ten hours. 155
laps of a 6.214-mile circuit = 963.170 miles

1 Giuseppe Campari/	Alfa Romeo 8C		
Tazio Nuvolari	"Monza"	155	10 hours
2 Ferdinando Minoia/	Alfa Romeo 8C		
Baconin Borzacchini	"Monza"	153	
3 Albert Divo/			
Guy Bouriat	Bugatti T51	152	
4 Jean-Pierre Wimille/			
Jean Gaupillat	Bugatti T51	138	
5 Boris Ivanowski/			
Henri Stoffel	Mercedes-Benz SSKL	134	

6 Francesco Pirola/
Johnny Lurani   Alfa Romeo 6C-1500   129

Winner's average speed: 96.317 mph. Starting grid front row:
Campari, Wimille and Robert Sénéchal (Delage 15S8) – positions
drawn. Fastest lap: Campari, 3m32.8

Grand Prix de l'Automobile Club de France

**21 June 1931. Montlhéry. Race scheduled for ten hours.
101 laps of a 7.767-mile circuit = 784.467 miles**

1 Achille Varzi/			
Louis Chiron	Bugatti T51	101	10 hours
2 Giuseppe Campari/			
Baconin Borzacchini	Alfa Romeo 8C "Monza"	97	
3 Clemente Biondetti/			
Luigi Parenti	Maserati 26M	94	
4 Tim Birkin/			
George Eyston	Maserati 26M	94	
5 Robert Sénéchal	Delage 15S8	91	
6 Ferdinando Minoia/			
Goffredo Zehender	Alfa Romeo 8C "Monza"	91	

Winner's average speed: 78.447 mph. Starting grid front row:
n/a. Fastest lap: Luigi Fagioli (Maserati 26M), 5m29.0

Grand Prix de Belgique

**12 July 1931. Spa-Francorchamps. Race scheduled for ten
hours. 88 laps of a 9.236-mile circuit = 812.768 miles**

1 "W Williams"/			
Caberto Conelli	Bugatti T51	88	10 hours
2 Tazio Nuvolari/			
Baconin Borzacchini	Alfa Romeo 8C "Monza"	88	
3 Ferdinando Minoia/			
Giovanni Minozzi	Alfa Romeo 6C-1750	85	
4 Tim Birkin/	Alfa Romeo 8C		
Brian Lewis	"Monza" LM	83	
5 Henri Stoffel/			
Boris Ivanowski	Mercedes-Benz SSK	81	
6 Jean Pesato/			
Pierre Félix	Alfa Romeo 6C-1750	73	

Winner's average speed: 81.277 mph. Starting grid front row:
Minoia, "Williams" and Albert Divo (Bugatti T51) – positions
drawn. Fastest lap: Louis Chiron (Bugatti T51), 6m18.6

Grosser Preis von Deutschland

**19 July 1931. Nürburgring. Formula Libre. 22 laps of a
14.167-mile circuit = 311.674 miles**

1 Rudolf Caracciola	Mercedes-Benz SSKL	22	4h38m10.0
2 Louis Chiron	Bugatti T51	22	4h39m28.0
3 Achille Varzi	Bugatti T51	22	4h42m10.0
4 Tazio Nuvolari	Alfa Romeo 8C "Monza"	22	4h43m54.0
5 Otto Merz	Mercedes-Benz SSKL	22	4h43m54.0
6 Hans Stuck	Mercedes-Benz SSKL	22	4h47m34.0

Winner's average speed: 67.227 mph. Starting grid front row:
Manfred von Brauchitsch (Mercedes-Benz SSKL), Ernst-Günther
Burgaller (Bugatti T35B) and Heinrich-Joachim von Morgen
(Bugatti T35B) – positions drawn. Fastest lap: Varzi, 11m48.0

Masarykuv Okruh (Czech Grand Prix)

**27 September 1931. Brno. 17 laps of a 18.109-mile circuit
= 307.853 miles**

1 Louis Chiron	Bugatti T51	17	4h12m07.5
2 Hans Stuck	Mercedes-Benz SSKL	17	4h26m10.4
3 Heinrich-Joachim			
von Morgen	Bugatti T35B	17	4h30m01.0
4 Georg-Kristian			
Lobkowicz	Bugatti T51	17	4h33m50.5
5 Hermann			
zu Leiningen	Bugatti T35C	17	5h00m06.7
6 Tivador Zichy	Bugatti T35C	17	5h05m43.6

Winner's average speed: 73.262 mph. Starting grid front row:
Luigi Fagioli (Maserati 26M), 15m14.4 (pole), Baconin
Borzacchini (Alfa Romeo 8C "Monza"), 15m17.3 and Achille
Varzi (Bugatti T51), 15m24.2. Fastest lap: Chiron, 14m24.8

1932

Grand Prix de Monaco

**17 April 1932. Monte Carlo. 100 laps of a 1.976-mile circuit
= 197.600 miles**

1 Tazio Nuvolari	Alfa Romeo 8C "Monza"	100	3h32m25.3
2 Rudolf Caracciola	Alfa Romeo 8C "Monza"	100	3h32m28.0
3 Luigi Fagioli	Maserati 26M	100	3h34m43.0
4 Earl Howe	Bugatti T51	98	
5 Goffredo Zehender	Alfa Romeo 8C "Monza"	96	
6 Marcel Lehoux	Bugatti T51	95	

Winner's average speed: 55.814 mph. Starting grid front row:
"W Williams" (Bugatti T51), Philippe Étancelin (Alfa Romeo 8C
"Monza") and Amedeo Ruggeri (Maserati 26M) – positions
drawn. Fastest lap: Achille Varzi (Bugatti T51), 2m02.0

Gran Premio d'Italia

**5 June 1932. Monza. Race scheduled for five hours. 83 laps
of a 6.214-mile circuit = 515.762 miles**

1 Tazio Nuvolari	Alfa Romeo Tipo-B "P3"	83	5 hours
2 Luigi Fagioli	Maserati V5	82	
3 Baconin Borzacchini/			
Attilio Marinoni/			
Rudolf Caracciola	Alfa Romeo 8C "Monza"	82	
4 Giuseppe Campari	Alfa Romeo Tipo-B "P3"	82	
5 René Dreyfus	Bugatti T51	82	
6 Albert Divo/			
Guy Bouriat	Bugatti T51	81	

Winner's average speed: 103.152 mph. Starting grid front row:
Luigi Castelbarco (Maserati 26M), Marcel Lehoux (Bugatti T51)
and Borzacchini – positions drawn. Fastest lap: Nuvolari, 3m22.6

Grand Prix de l'Automobile Club de France

**3 July 1932. Reims. Race scheduled for five hours. 92 laps
of a 4.865-mile circuit = 447.580 miles**

1 Tazio Nuvolari	Alfa Romeo Tipo-B "P3"	92	5 hours
2 Baconin Borzacchini	Alfa Romeo Tipo-B "P3"	92	
3 Rudolf Caracciola	Alfa Romeo Tipo-B "P3"	92	
4 Louis Chiron	Bugatti T51	91	
5 René Dreyfus	Bugatti T51	90	
6 "W Williams"	Bugatti T51	90	

Winner's average speed: 89.516 mph. Starting grid front row:
Max Fourny (Bugatti T35C), Philippe Étancelin (Alfa Romeo 8C
"Monza") and Jean Gaupillat (Bugatti T51) – positions drawn.
Fastest lap: Nuvolari, 3m00.0

Grosser Preis von Deutschland

**17 July 1932. Nürburgring. 25 laps of a 14.167-mile circuit
= 354.175 miles**

1 Rudolf Caracciola	Alfa Romeo Tipo-B "P3"	25	4h47m22.8
2 Tazio Nuvolari	Alfa Romeo Tipo-B "P3"	25	4h47m53.0
3 Baconin Borzacchini	Alfa Romeo Tipo-B "P3"	25	4h54m33.0
4 René Dreyfus	Bugatti T51	25	5h01m05.4

No other finishers. Winner's average speed: 73.946 mph.
Starting grid front row: n/a. Fastest lap: Nuvolari, 10m49.4

Masarykuv Okruh (Czech Grand Prix)

**4 September 1932. Brno. 17 laps of a 18.109-mile circuit
= 307.853 miles**

1 Louis Chiron	Bugatti T51	17	4h37m29.7
2 Luigi Fagioli	Maserati 8C-3000	17	4h42m30.5
3 Tazio Nuvolari	Alfa Romeo 8C "Monza"	17	5h06m20.1
4 Antonio Brivio	Alfa Romeo 8C "Monza"	17	5h08m03.0
5 V Stasny	Bugatti T35B	17	5h31m01.0

No other finishers. Winner's average speed: 66.564 mph.
Starting grid front row: n/a. Fastest lap: Chiron, 14m44.9

1933

Grand Prix de Monaco

23 April 1933. Monte Carlo. 100 laps of a 1.976-mile circuit = 197.600 miles

1 Achille Varzi	Bugatti T51	100	3h27m49.4
2 Baconin Borzacchini	Alfa Romeo 8C "Monza"	100	3h29m49.4
3 René Dreyfus	Bugatti T51	99	
4 Louis Chiron	Alfa Romeo 8C "Monza"	97	
5 Carlo Felice Trossi	Alfa Romeo 8C "Monza"	97	
6 Goffredo Zehender	Maserati 8CM	94	

Winner's average speed: 57.048 mph. Starting grid front row: Varzi, 2m02.0 (pole), Chiron, 2m03.0 and Borzacchini, 2m03.0. Fastest lap: Varzi, 1m59.0

Grand Prix de l'Automobile Club de France

11 June 1933. Montlhéry. 40 laps of a 7.767-mile circuit = 310.680 miles

1 Giuseppe Campari	Maserati 8C-3000	40	3h48m45.4
2 Philippe Étancelin	Alfa Romeo 8C "Monza"	40	3h49m37.4
3 George Eyston	Alfa Romeo 8C "Monza"	39	
4 Raymond Sommer	Alfa Romeo 8C "Monza"	39	
5 Guy Moll	Alfa Romeo 8C "Monza"	38	
6 Julio Villars	Alfa Romeo 8C "Monza"	34	

Winner's average speed: 81.487 mph. Starting grid front row: Juan Zanelli (Alfa Romeo 8C "Monza"), Pierre Félix (Alfa Romeo 8C "Monza") and Earl Howe (Bugatti T51) – positions drawn. Fastest lap: Campari, 5m23.0

Grand Prix de Belgique

9 July 1933. Spa-Francorchamps. 40 laps of a 9.236-mile circuit = 369.440 miles

1 Tazio Nuvolari	Maserati 8CM	40	4h09m11.0
2 Achille Varzi	Bugatti T51	40	4h12m26.0
3 René Dreyfus	Bugatti T51	40	4h12m59.0
4 Marcel Lehoux	Bugatti T51	40	4h13m28.0
5 Eugenio Siena	Alfa Romeo 8C "Monza"	40	4h17m10.0
6 "W Williams"	Bugatti T51	39	

Winner's average speed: 88.956 mph. Starting grid front row: Louis Chiron (Alfa Romeo 8C "Monza"), Lehoux and Guy Moll (Alfa Romeo 8C "Monza") – positions drawn. Fastest lap: Nuvolari, 6m00.0

Gran Premio d'Italia

10 September 1933. Monza. 50 laps of a 6.214-mile circuit = 310.700 miles

1 Luigi Fagioli	Alfa Romeo Tipo-B "P3"	50	2h51m41.0
2 Tazio Nuvolari	Maserati 8CM	50	2h52m21.2
3 Goffredo Zehender	Maserati 8CM	48	
4 Marcel Lehoux	Alfa Romeo 8C "Monza"	47	
5 Eugenio Siena/			
Antonio Brivio	Alfa Romeo 8C "Monza"	47	
6 Luigi Castelbarco	Alfa Romeo 8C "Monza"	47	

Winner's average speed: 108.584 mph. Starting grid front row: Robert Brunet (Bugatti T51), Jean Gaupillat (Bugatti T51), Luigi Premoli (PBM-Maserati) and Siena – positions drawn. Fastest lap: Fagioli, 3m13.2

Masarykuv Okruh (Czech Grand Prix)

17 September 1933. Brno. 17 laps of a 18.109-mile circuit = 307.853 miles

1 Louis Chiron	Alfa Romeo Tipo-B "P3"	17	4h50m22.6
2 Luigi Fagioli	Alfa Romeo Tipo-B "P3"	17	4h54m02.0
3 Jean-Pierre Wimille	Alfa Romeo 8C "Monza"	17	5h00m04.0
4 René Dreyfus	Bugatti T51	17	5h02m12.0
5 Zdenek Pohl	Bugatti T35B	16	
6 Laszlo Hartmann	Bugatti T51	16	

Winner's average speed: 63.611 mph. Starting grid front row: n/a. Fastest lap: Fagioli, 15m21.0

Gran Premio de Espana

24 September 1933. Lasarte. 30 laps of a 11.029-mile circuit = 330.870 miles

1 Louis Chiron	Alfa Romeo Tipo-B "P3"	30	3h50m57.8
2 Luigi Fagioli	Alfa Romeo Tipo-B "P3"	30	3h55m22.0
3 Marcel Lehoux	Bugatti T51	30	4h12m50.0
4 Achille Varzi	Bugatti T59	30	4h14m14.0
5 Jean-Pierre Wimille	Alfa Romeo 8C "Monza"	30	4h15m57.0
6 René Dreyfus	Bugatti T59	29	

Winner's average speed: 85.954 mph. Starting grid front row: n/a. Fastest lap: Tazio Nuvolari (Maserati 8CM), 6m41.2

1934

Grand Prix de Monaco

2 April 1934. Monte Carlo. 100 laps of a 1.976-mile circuit = 197.600 miles

1 Guy Moll	Alfa Romeo Tipo-B "P3"	100	3h31m31.4
2 Louis Chiron	Alfa Romeo Tipo-B "P3"	100	3h32m33.4
3 René Dreyfus	Bugatti T59	99	
4 Marcel Lehoux	Alfa Romeo Tipo-B "P3"	99	
5 Tazio Nuvolari	Bugatti T59	98	
6 Achille Varzi	Alfa Romeo Tipo-B "P3"	98	

Winner's average speed: 56.051 mph. Starting grid front row: Carlo Felice Trossi (Alfa Romeo Tipo-B "P3"), 1m58.0 (pole), Philippe Étancelin (Maserati 8CM), 1m59.0 and Dreyfus, 1m59.0. Fastest lap: Trossi, 2m02.0

Grand Prix de l'Automobile Club de France

1 July 1934. Montlhéry. 40 laps of a 7.767-mile circuit = 310.680 miles

1 Louis Chiron	Alfa Romeo Tipo-B "P3"	40	3h39m14.6
2 Achille Varzi	Alfa Romeo Tipo-B "P3"	40	3h42m31.9
3 Carlo Felice Trossi/			
Guy Moll	Alfa Romeo Tipo-B "P3"	40	3h43m23.8
4 Robert Benoist	Bugatti T59	36	

No other finishers. Winner's average speed: 85.023 mph. Starting grid front row: Hermann zu Leiningen (Auto Union A), Hans Stuck (Auto Union A) and Varzi – positions drawn, Leiningen did not start. Fastest lap: Chiron, 5m06.0

Grosser Preis von Deutschland

15 July 1934. Nürburgring. 25 laps of a 14.167-mile circuit = 354.175 miles

1 Hans Stuck	Auto Union A	25	4h38m19.2
2 Luigi Fagioli	Mercedes-Benz W25A	25	4h40m26.2
3 Louis Chiron	Alfa Romeo Tipo-B "P3"	25	4h46m32.8
4 Tazio Nuvolari	Maserati 8CM	25	4h55m10.2
5 Hanns Geier	Mercedes-Benz W25A	25	4h59m05.4
6 Goffredo Zehender	Maserati 8CM	25	5h14m46.8

Winner's average speed: 76.353 mph. Starting grid front row: Renato Balestrero (Alfa Romeo 8C "Monza"), Hugh Hamilton (Maserati 8CM) and Giovanni Minozzi (Alfa Romeo 8C "Monza") – positions drawn. Fastest lap: Stuck, 10m43.8

Grand Prix de Belgique

29 July 1934. Spa-Francorchamps. 40 laps of a 9.290-mile circuit = 371.600 miles

1 René Dreyfus	Bugatti T59	40	4h15m03.8
2 Antonio Brivio	Bugatti T59	40	4h16m54.8
3 Raymond Sommer	Maserati 8CM	39	
4 Robert Benoist	Bugatti T59	37	
5 Charles Montier	Montier Spéciale-Ford	30	

No other finishers. Winner's average speed: 87.414 mph. Starting grid front row: Brivio, Louis Chiron (Alfa Romeo Tipo-B "P3") and Dreyfus – positions drawn. Fastest lap: Brivio, 5m45.0

Grand Prix de Suisse

26 August 1934. Bremgarten. 70 laps of a 4.524-mile circuit = 316.680 miles

1 Hans Stuck	Auto Union A	70	3h37m57.6
2 August Momberger	Auto Union A	69	
3 René Dreyfus	Bugatti T59	69	
4 Achille Varzi/			
Carlo Felice Trossi	Alfa Romeo Tipo-B "P3"	69	
5 Louis Chiron	Alfa Romeo Tipo-B "P3"	69	
6 Luigi Fagioli	Mercedes-Benz W25A	68	

Winner's average speed: 87.176 mph. Starting grid front row: Goffredo Zehender (Maserati 4CM), Varzi and Stuck – positions drawn, Zehender did not start. Fastest lap: Stuck, 3m00.0

Gran Premio d'Italia

9 September 1934. Monza. 116 laps of a 2.690-mile circuit = 312.040 miles

1 Rudolf Caracciola/			
Luigi Fagioli	Mercedes-Benz W25A	116	4h45m47.0
2 Hans Stuck/Hermann			
zu Leiningen	Auto Union A	115	
3 Carlo Felice Trossi/			
Gianfranco Comotti	Alfa Romeo Tipo-B "P3"	114	
4 Louis Chiron	Alfa Romeo Tipo-B "P3"	113	
5 Tazio Nuvolari	Maserati 6C-34	113	
6 Gianfranco Comotti/			
Attilio Marinoni	Alfa Romeo Tipo-B "P3"	113	

Winner's average speed: 65.513 mph. Starting grid front row: Caracciola, Achille Varzi (Alfa Romeo Tipo-B "P3") and Antonio Brivio (Bugatti T59) – positions drawn, Brivio did not start. Fastest lap: Stuck, 2m13.6

Gran Premio de Espana

23 September 1934. Lasarte. 30 laps of a 11.029-mile circuit = 330.870 miles

1 Luigi Fagioli	Mercedes-Benz W25A	30	3h19m41.6
2 Rudolf Caracciola	Mercedes-Benz W25A	30	3h20m24.4
3 Tazio Nuvolari	Bugatti T59	30	3h20m48.0
4 Hermann zu Leiningen/			
Hans Stuck	Auto Union A	30	3h21m03.0
5 Achille Varzi/			
Louis Chiron	Alfa Romeo Tipo-B "P3"	30	3h21m49.0
6 Jean-Pierre Wimille	Bugatti T59	30	3h26m21.8

Winner's average speed: 99.413 mph. Starting grid front row: Stuck, Wimille and Caracciola – positions drawn. Fastest lap: Stuck, 6m20.0

Masarykuv Okruh (Czech Grand Prix)

30 September 1934. Brno. 17 laps of a 18.109-mile circuit = 307.853 miles

1 Hans Stuck	Auto Union A	17	3h53m27.9
2 Luigi Fagioli	Mercedes-Benz W25A	17	3h56m24.5
3 Tazio Nuvolari	Maserati 6C-34	17	3h57m14.1
4 Hermann zu Leiningen	Auto Union A	17	4h02m05.2
5 Achille Varzi	Alfa Romeo Tipo-B "P3"	17	4h04m08.9
6 Ernst Henne/			
Hanns Geier	Mercedes-Benz W25A	17	4h12m12.6

Winner's average speed: 79.118 mph. Starting grid front row: Louis Chiron (Alfa Romeo Tipo-B "P3"), Varzi and Laszlo Hartmann (Bugatti T51) – positions drawn. Fastest lap: Fagioli, 13m16.2

1935

Grand Prix de Monaco

22 April 1935. Monte Carlo. 100 laps of a 1.976-mile circuit = 197.600 miles

1 Luigi Fagioli	Mercedes-Benz W25B	100	3h23m49.8
2 René Dreyfus	Alfa Romeo Tipo-B "P3"	100	3h24m21.3
3 Antonio Brivio	Alfa Romeo Tipo-B "P3"	100	3h24m56.2
4 Philippe Étancelin	Maserati 6C-34	99	
5 Louis Chiron	Alfa Romeo Tipo-B "P3"	97	
6 Raymond Sommer	Alfa Romeo Tipo-B "P3"	94	

Winner's average speed: 58.166 mph. Starting grid front row: Rudolf Caracciola (Mercedes-Benz W25B), 1m56.6 (pole), Manfred von Brauchitsch (Mercedes-Benz W25B), 1m57.0 and Fagioli, 1m57.3. Fastest lap: Fagioli, 1m58.4

Grand Prix de l'Automobile Club de France

23 June 1935. Montlhéry. 40 laps of a 7.767-mile circuit = 310.680 miles

1 Rudolf Caracciola	Mercedes-Benz W25B	40	4h00m54.6
2 Manfred von Brauchitsch	Mercedes-Benz W25B	40	4h00m55.1
3 Goffredo Zehender	Maserati 6C-34	38	
4 Luigi Fagioli	Mercedes-Benz W25B	37	
5 Achille Varzi/			
Bernd Rosemeyer	Auto Union B	35	
6 Raymond Sommer	Maserati 8CM	35	

Winner's average speed: 77.377 mph. Starting grid front row: Varzi, 5m20.1 (pole), Tazio Nuvolari (Alfa Romeo Tipo-B "P3"), 5m23.6 and Hans Stuck (Auto Union B), 5m28.8. Fastest lap: Nuvolari, 5m29.1

Grand Prix de Belgique

14 July 1935. Spa-Francorchamps. 34 laps of a 9.290-mile circuit = 315.860 miles

1 Rudolf Caracciola	Mercedes-Benz W25B	34	3h12m31.0
2 Luigi Fagioli/Manfred von Brauchitsch	Mercedes-Benz W25B	34	3h14m08.0
3 Louis Chiron	Alfa Romeo Tipo-B "P3"	34	3h14m47.0
4 René Dreyfus/			
Attilio Marinoni	Alfa Romeo Tipo-B "P3"	34	3h17m54.0
5 Robert Benoist	Bugatti T59	31	
6 Piero Taruffi	Bugatti T59	31	

Winner's average speed: 98.441 mph. Starting grid front row: Marcel Lehoux (Maserati 8CM) and Dreyfus – positions drawn. Fastest lap: von Brauchitsch, 5m23

Grosser Preis von Deutschland

28 July 1935. Nürburgring. 22 laps of a 14.167-mile circuit = 311.674 miles

1 Tazio Nuvolari	Alfa Romeo Tipo-B "P3"	22	4h08m04.1
2 Hans Stuck	Auto Union B	22	4h10m18.4
3 Rudolf Caracciola	Mercedes-Benz W25B	22	4h11m13.1
4 Bernd Rosemeyer	Auto Union B	22	4h12m51.0
5 Manfred von Brauchitsch	Mercedes-Benz W25B	22	4h14m17.4
6 Luigi Fagioli	Mercedes-Benz W25B	22	4h15m58.3

Winner's average speed: 75.384 mph. Starting grid front row: Renato Balestrero (Alfa Romeo 8C "Monza"), Nuvolari and Stuck – positions drawn. Fastest lap: von Brauchitsch, 10m32.0

Grand Prix de Suisse

25 August 1935. Bremgarten. 70 laps of a 4.524-mile circuit = 316.680 miles

1 Rudolf Caracciola	Mercedes-Benz W25B	70	3h31m12.2
2 Luigi Fagioli	Mercedes-Benz W25B	70	3h31m48.1
3 Bernd Rosemeyer	Auto Union B	70	3h32m20.0
4 Achille Varzi	Auto Union B	69	
5 Tazio Nuvolari	Alfa Romeo Tipo-B "P3"	68	
6 Hermann Lang	Mercedes-Benz W25B	67	

Winner's average speed: 89.964 mph. Starting grid front row: Varzi, 2m41.8 (pole), Caracciola, 2m42.8 and Hans Stuck (Auto Union B), 2m43.6. Fastest lap: Caracciola, 2m44.4

Early Grand Prix Racing

Gran Premio d'Italia

8 September 1935. Monza. 73 laps of a 4.320-mile circuit
= 315.360 miles

1 Hans Stuck	Auto Union B	73	3h40m09.0
2 René Dreyfus/	Alfa Romeo		
Tazio Nuvolari	Tipo-C "8C-35"	73	3h41m50.0
3 Paul Pietsch/			
Bernd Rosemeyer	Auto Union B	70	
4 Attilio Marinoni	Alfa Romeo Tipo-B "P3"	68	
5 Piero Taruffi	Bugatti T59	49	

No other finishers. Winner's average speed: 85.949 mph.
Starting grid front row: Rudolf Caracciola (Mercedes-Benz
W25B), Taruffi and Giuseppe Farina (Maserati V8RI) – positions
drawn, Farina did not start. Fastest lap: Nuvolari, 2m49.8

Gran Premio de Espana

22 September 1935. Lasarte. 30 laps of a 11.029-mile
circuit = 330.870 miles

1 Rudolf Caracciola	Mercedes-Benz W25B	30	3h09m59.4
2 Luigi Fagioli	Mercedes-Benz W25B	30	3h10m42.4
3 Manfred von			
Brauchitsch	Mercedes-Benz W25B	30	3h12m14.2
4 Jean-Pierre Wimille	Bugatti T59	30	3h12m54.8
5 Bernd Rosemeyer	Auto Union B	30	3h15m51.0
6 Robert Benoist	Bugatti T59	29	

Winner's average speed: 104.491 mph. Starting grid front row:
Wimille, Rosemeyer and Achille Varzi (Auto Union B) – positions
drawn. Fastest lap: Varzi, 5m58.0

Masarykuv Okruh (Czech Grand Prix)

29 September 1935. Brno. 17 laps of a 18.109-mile circuit
= 307.853 miles

1 Bernd Rosemeyer	Auto Union B	17	3h44m10.6
2 Tazio Nuvolari	Alfa Romeo		
	Tipo-C "8C-35"	17	3h50m48.4
3 Louis Chiron	Alfa Romeo Tipo-B "P3"	17	3h50m52.2
4 Antonio Brivio	Alfa Romeo Tipo-B "P3"	17	3h52m12.0
5 Laszlo Hartmann	Maserati 8CM	15	

No other finishers. Winner's average speed: 82.396 mph.
Starting grid front row: n/a. Fastest lap: Achille Varzi (Auto
Union B), 12m49.0

Donington Grand Prix

5 October 1935. Donington Park. 120 laps of a 2.550-mile
circuit = 306.000 miles

1 Richard Shuttleworth	Alfa Romeo Tipo-B "P3"	120	4h47m12.0
2 Earl Howe	Bugatti T59	120	4h47m57.8
3 Charlie Martin	Bugatti T59	120	4h49m47.4
4 Bill Everitt/			
Gino Rovere	Maserati 6C-34	120	4h53m59.0
5 "B Bira"	ERA B-type	120	4h58m16.0
6 Roy Eccles/			
Pat Fairfield	Bugatti T59	120	4h59m33.0

Winner's average speed: 63.928 mph. Starting grid front row:
Raymond Sommer (Alfa Romeo Tip-B "P3"), 2m04.0 (pole),
Giuseppe Farina (Maserati V8RI), 2m08.4 and Percy Maclure
(Riley 2000/6), 2m14.0. Fastest lap: Farina, 2m08.4

1936

Grand Prix de Monaco

13 April 1936. Monte Carlo. 100 laps of a 1.976-mile circuit
= 197.600 miles

1 Rudolf Caracciola	Mercedes-Benz W25C	100	3h49m20.4
2 Achille Varzi	Auto Union C	100	3h51m09.5
3 Hans Stuck	Auto Union C	99	
4 Tazio Nuvolari	Alfa Romeo		
	Tipo-C "8C-35"	99	
5 Antonio Brivio/	Alfa Romeo		
Giuseppe Farina	Tipo-C "8C-35"	97	
6 Jean-Pierre Wimille	Bugatti T59	97	

Winner's average speed: 51.696 mph. Starting grid front row:
Louis Chiron (Mercedes-Benz W25C), 1m53.2 (pole), Nuvolari,
1m53.7 and Caracciola, 1m54.0. Fastest lap: Stuck, 2m07.4

Magyar Nagydij (Hungarian Grand Prix)

21 June 1936. Budapest. 50 laps of a 3.100-mile circuit
= 155.000 miles

1 Tazio Nuvolari	Alfa Romeo		
	Tipo-C "8C-35"	50	2h14m03.5
2 Bernd Rosemeyer	Auto Union C	50	2h14m17.7
3 Achille Varzi	Auto Union C	49	
4 Mario Tadini	Alfa Romeo		
	Tipo-C "8C-35"	47	
5 Hans Stuck/			
Ernst von Delius	Auto Union C	46	
6 Austin Dobson	Alfa Romeo Tipo-B "P3"	45	

Winner's average speed: 69.373 mph. Starting grid front row:
Rosemeyer and Stuck. Fastest lap: Nuvolari, 2m35.68

Grand Prix de l'Automobile Club de France

28 June 1936. Montlhéry. Sports Cars. 80 laps of a
7.767-mile circuit = 621.360 miles

1 Jean-Pierre Wimille/			
Raymond Sommer	Bugatti T57G	80	7h58m53.7
2 "Michel Paris"/			
Marcel Mongin	Delahaye 135	80	7h59m44.3
3 Robert Brunet/			
Goffredo Zehender	Delahaye 135	80	8h00m25.6
4 Laury Schell/			
René Carrière	Delahaye 135	79	
5 Albert Perrot/Dhôme	Delahaye 135	78	
6 Pierre Veyron/			
"W Williams"	Bugatti T57G	78	

Winner's average speed: 77.849 mph. Starting grid front row:
n/a. Fastest lap: René Dreyfus (Talbot), 5m36.0

Grosser Preis von Deutschland

26 July 1936. Nürburgring. 22 laps of a 14.167-mile circuit
= 311.674 miles

1 Bernd Rosemeyer	Auto Union C	22	3h48m39.6
2 Hans Stuck	Auto Union C	22	3h52m36.4
3 Antonio Brivio	Alfa Romeo		
	Tipo-C "8C-35"	22	3h57m05.0
4 Rudolf Hasse	Auto Union C	22	3h59m13.2
5 Luigi Fagioli/			
Rudolf Caracciola	Mercedes-Benz W25C	21	
6 Ernst von Delius	Auto Union C	21	

Winner's average speed: 81.783 mph. Starting grid front row:
Tazio Nuvolari (Alfa Romeo Tipo-C "8C-35"), Stuck and Jean-
Pierre Wimille (Bugatti T59) – positions drawn. Fastest lap:
Rosemeyer, 9m56.6

Grand Prix de Suisse

23 August 1936. Bremgarten. 70 laps of a 4.524-mile circuit
= 316.680 miles

1 Bernd Rosemeyer	Auto Union C	70	3h09m01.6
2 Achille Varzi	Auto Union C	70	3h09m54.2
3 Hans Stuck	Auto Union C	69	
4 Hermann Lang/			
Luigi Fagioli	Mercedes-Benz W25C	69	
5 Rudolf Hasse	Auto Union C	67	

No other finishers. Winner's average speed: 100.519 mph.
Starting grid front row: Rudolf Caracciola (Mercedes-Benz
W25C), 2m37.9 (pole), Rosemeyer, 2m39.3 and Varzi, 2m39.5.
Fastest lap: Rosemeyer, 2m34.5

Gran Premio d'Italia

13 September 1936. Monza. 72 laps of a 4.320-mile circuit = 311.040 miles

1 Bernd Rosemeyer	Auto Union C	72	3h43m25.0
2 Tazio Nuvolari	Alfa Romeo Tipo-C "8C-35"	72	3h45m30.3
3 Ernst von Delius	Auto Union C	70	
4 René Dreyfus	Alfa Romeo Tipo-C "8C-35"	70	
5 Carlo Maria Pintacuda	Alfa Romeo Tipo-C "8C-35"	68	
6 Piero Dusio	Maserati 6C-34	59	

Winner's average speed: 83.532 mph. Starting grid front row: Rosemeyer, 2m56.4 (pole), Hans Stuck (Auto Union C), 2m58.8 and Nuvolari, 3m00.6. Fastest lap: Rosemeyer, 2m59.6

Donington Grand Prix

3 October 1936. Donington Park. 120 laps of a 2.550-mile circuit = 306.000 miles

1 Hans Ruesch/ Dick Seaman	Alfa Romeo Tipo-C "8C-35"	120	4h25m22.0
2 Charlie Martin	Alfa Romeo Tipo-B "P3"	120	4h28m25.0
3 Peter Whitehead/ Peter Walker	ERA B-type	120	4h31m35.0
4 Reggie Tongue	ERA B-type	120	4h32m29.0
5 "B Bira"	Maserati 8CM	120	4h33m19.0
6 Austin Dobson	Alfa Romeo Tipo-B "P3"	120	4h35m00.0

Winner's average speed: 69.187 mph. Starting grid front row: George Cholmondley-Tapper (Maserati 8CM), Tommy Clarke (Delahaye 135), Percy Maclure (Riley 2000/6) and Reg Parnell (MG K3 Magnette) – positions drawn. Fastest lap: n/a

Manfred von Brauchitsch battles for the lead with Rudolf Caracciola at Monaco in 1937

1937

Grand Prix de l'Automobile Club de France

4 July 1937. Montlhéry. Sports Cars. 40 laps of a 7.767-mile circuit = 310.680 miles

1 Louis Chiron	Talbot T150C	40	3h46m06.1
2 Gianfranco Comotti	Talbot T150C	40	3h48m12.5
3 Albert Divo	Talbot T150C	40	3h49m48.9
4 René Carrière	Delahaye 135	39	
5 Raymond Sommer	Talbot T150C	38	
6 Eugène Chaboud/ Jean Trémoulet	Delahaye 135	33	

Winner's average speed: 82.444 mph. Starting grid front row: n/a. Fastest lap: Chiron, 5m29.7

Grand Prix de Belgique

11 July 1937. Spa-Francorchamps. 34 laps of a 9.290-mile circuit = 315.860 miles

1 Rudolf Hasse	Auto Union C	34	3h01m29.0
2 Hans Stuck	Auto Union C	34	3h02m24.0
3 Hermann Lang	Mercedes-Benz W125	34	3h04m07.0
4 Christian Kautz	Mercedes-Benz W125	34	3h04m25.0
5 Raymond Sommer	Alfa Romeo 12C-36	34	3h05m54.0

No other finishers. Winner's average speed: 104.426 mph. Starting grid front row: Manfred von Brauchitsch (Mercedes-Benz W125), Lang and Stuck – positions drawn. Fastest lap: Lang, 5m05.6

Grosser Preis von Deutschland

25 July 1937. Nürburgring. 22 laps of a 14.167-mile circuit = 311.674 miles

1 Rudolf Caracciola	Mercedes-Benz W125	22	3h46m00.1
2 Manfred von Brauchitsch	Mercedes-Benz W125	22	3h46m46.3
3 Bernd Rosemeyer	Auto Union C	22	3h47m01.4
4 Tazio Nuvolari	Alfa Romeo 12C-36	22	3h50m04.0
5 Rudolf Hasse	Auto Union C	22	3h51m25.1
6 Christian Kautz	Mercedes-Benz W125	22	3h52m10.3

Winner's average speed: 82.745 mph. Starting grid front row: Rosemeyer, 9m46.2 (pole), Hermann Lang (Mercedes-Benz W125), 9m52.2 and von Brauchitsch, 9m55.1. Fastest lap: Rosemeyer, 9m55.4

Grand Prix de Monaco

8 August 1937. Monte Carlo. 100 laps of a 1.976-mile circuit = 197.600 miles

1 Manfred von Brauchitsch	Mercedes-Benz W125	100	3h07m23.9
2 Rudolf Caracciola	Mercedes-Benz W125	100	3h08m48.2
3 Christian Kautz	Mercedes-Benz W125	98	
4 Hans Stuck/ Bernd Rosemeyer	Auto Union C	97	
5 Goffredo Zehender	Mercedes-Benz W125	97	
6 Giuseppe Farina	Alfa Romeo 12C-36	97	

Winner's average speed: 63.266 mph. Starting grid front row: Caracciola, 1m47.5 (pole), von Brauchitsch, 1m48.4 and Rosemeyer, 1m49.0. Fastest lap: Caracciola, 1m46.5

Grand Prix de Suisse

22 August 1937. Bremgarten. 50 laps of a 4.524-mile circuit = 226.200 miles

1 Rudolf Caracciola	Mercedes-Benz W125	50	2h17m39.3
2 Hermann Lang	Mercedes-Benz W125	50	2h18m28.7
3 Manfred von Brauchitsch	Mercedes-Benz W125	50	2h18m45.7
4 Hans Stuck	Auto Union C	50	2h18m50.8
5 Tazio Nuvolari/ Bernd Rosemeyer	Auto Union C	50	2h19m00.5
6 Christian Kautz	Mercedes-Benz W125	49	

Winner's average speed: 98.594 mph. Starting grid front row: Caracciola, 2m32.0 (pole), Rosemeyer, 2m32.5 and Stuck, 2m34.3. Fastest lap: Rosemeyer, 2m36.1

Gran Premio d'Italia

12 September 1937. Livorno. 50 laps of a 4.340-mile circuit = 217.000 miles

1 Rudolf Caracciola	Mercedes-Benz W125	50	2h44m54.4
2 Hermann Lang	Mercedes-Benz W125	50	2h44m54.8
3 Bernd Rosemeyer	Auto Union C	50	2h46m19.8
4 Dick Seaman	Mercedes-Benz W125	49	
5 Hermann Müller	Auto Union C	49	
6 Achille Varzi	Auto Union C	49	

Winner's average speed: 78.954 mph. Starting grid front row: Caracciola, 3m11.0 (pole), Varzi, 3m13.6 and Rosemeyer, 3m14.2. Fastest lap: Lang and Caracciola, 3m11.2

Masarykuv Okruk (Czech Grand Prix)

26 September 1937. Brno. 15 laps of a 18.109-mile circuit = 271.635 miles

1 Rudolf Caracciola	Mercedes-Benz W125	15	3h09m25.3

Early Grand Prix Racing

2 Manfred			
von Brauchitsch	Mercedes-Benz W125	15	3h10m01.7
3 Hermann Müller/			
Bernd Rosemeyer	Auto Union C	15	3h10m07.1
4 Dick Seaman	Mercedes-Benz W125	15	3h10m43.8
5 Tazio Nuvolari	Alfa Romeo 12C-36	14	
6 Antonio Brivio	Alfa Romeo 12C-36	14	

Winner's average speed: 86.041 mph. Starting grid front row: Nuvolari and Hermann Lang (Mercedes-Benz W125) – positions drawn. Fastest lap: Caracciola, 11m59.3

Donington Grand Prix

2 October 1937. Donington Park. 80 laps of a 3.125-mile circuit = 250.000 miles

1 Bernd Rosemeyer	Auto Union C	80	3h01m02.2
2 Manfred			
von Brauchitsch	Mercedes-Benz W125	80	3h01m40.0
3 Rudolf Caracciola	Mercedes-Benz W125	80	3h02m18.8
4 Hermann Müller	Auto Union C	80	3h04m50.0
5 Rudolf Hasse	Auto Union C	80	3h09m50.0
6 "B Bira"	Maserati 8CM	78	

Winner's average speed: 82.856 mph. Starting grid front row: von Brauchitsch, 2m10.4 (pole), Rosemeyer, 2m11.4, Hermann Lang (Mercedes-Benz W125), 2m14.3 and Dick Seaman (Mercedes-Benz W125), 2m15.4. Fastest lap: Rosemeyer and von Brauchitsch, 2m11.4

1938

Grand Prix de l'Automobile Club de France

3 July 1938. Reims. 64 laps of a 4.865-mile circuit = 311.360 miles

1 Manfred			
von Brauchitsch	Mercedes-Benz W154	64	3h04m38.5
2 Rudolf Caracciola	Mercedes-Benz W154	64	3h06m19.6
3 Hermann Lang	Mercedes-Benz W154	63	
4 René Carrière	Talbot T26SS	54	

No other finishers. Winner's average speed: 101.178 mph. Starting grid front row: Lang, 2m39.2 (pole) and von Brauchitsch, 2m40.7. Fastest lap: Lang, 2m45.1

Grosser Preis von Deutschland

24 July 1938. Nürburgring. 22 laps of a 14.167-mile circuit = 311.674 miles

1 Dick Seaman	Mercedes-Benz W154	22	3h51m46.2
2 Rudolf Caracciola/			
Hermann Lang	Mercedes-Benz W154	22	3h55m06.1
3 Hans Stuck	Auto Union D	22	4h00m42.3
4 Hermann Müller/			
Tazio Nuvolari	Auto Union D	22	4h01m19.1
5 René Dreyfus	Delahaye 145	21	
6 Paul Pietsch	Maserati 4CM	20	

Winner's average speed: 80.685 mph. Starting grid front row: Manfred von Brauchitsch (Mercedes-Benz W154), 9m48.4 (pole), Lang, 9m54.1 and Seaman, 10m01.2. Fastest lap: Seaman, 10m09.1

Grand Prix de Suisse

21 August 1938. Bremgarten. 50 laps of a 4.524-mile circuit = 226.200 miles

1 Rudolf Caracciola	Mercedes-Benz W154	50	2h32m07.8
2 Dick Seaman	Mercedes-Benz W154	50	2h32m33.8
3 Manfred			
von Brauchitsch	Mercedes-Benz W154	50	2h33m11.6
4 Hans Stuck	Auto Union D	48	
5 Giuseppe Farina	Alfa Romeo 312	48	
6 Piero Taruffi	Alfa Romeo 308	47	

Winner's average speed: 89.213 mph. Starting grid front row: Seaman, 2m38.8 (pole), Hermann Lang (Mercedes-Benz W154), 2m42.0 and Caracciola, 2m42.2. Fastest lap: Seaman, 2m50.8

Gran Premio d'Italia

11 September 1938. Monza. 60 laps of a 4.350-mile circuit = 261.000 miles

1 Tazio Nuvolari	Auto Union D	60	2h41m39.6
2 Giuseppe Farina	Alfa Romeo 316	58	
3 Rudolf Caracciola/			
Manfred			
von Brauchitsch	Mercedes-Benz W154	57	
4 Clemente Biondetti	Alfa Romeo 316	56	
5 Pietro Ghersi	Alfa Romeo 308	47	

No other finishers. Winner's average speed: 96.870 mph. Starting grid front row: Hermann Lang (Mercedes-Benz W154), 2m32.4 (pole), von Brauchitsch, 2m33.1, Caracciola, 2m33.3 and Hermann Müller (Auto Union D), 2m34.4. Fastest lap: Lang, 2m34.2

Donington Grand Prix

22 October 1938. Donington Park. 80 laps of a 3.125-mile circuit = 250.000 miles

1 Tazio Nuvolari	Auto Union D	80	3h06m22.0
2 Hermann Lang	Mercedes-Benz W154	80	3h08m00.0
3 Dick Seaman	Mercedes-Benz W154	79	
4 Hermann Müller	Auto Union D	79	
5 Manfred			
von Brauchitsch	Mercedes-Benz W154	79	
6 Arthur Dobson	ERA B-type	74	

Winner's average speed: 80.486 mph. Starting grid front row: Lang, 2m11.0 (pole), Nuvolari, 2m11.2, von Brauchitsch, 2m11.4 and Seaman, 2m12.2. Fastest lap: Nuvolari, 2m14.4

1939

Grand Prix de Belgique

26 June 1939. Spa-Francorchamps. 34 laps of a 9.060-mile circuit = 308.040 miles

1 Hermann Lang	Mercedes-Benz W163	34	3h20m21.1
2 Rudolf Hasse	Auto Union D	34	3h20m37.9
3 Manfred			
von Brauchitsch	Mercedes-Benz W163	34	3h22m14.0
4 Raymond Sommer	Alfa Romeo 312	32	
5 Robert Mazaud	Delahaye 135	30	
6 Louis Gérard	Delahaye 135	29	

Winner's average speed: 92.250 mph. Starting grid front row: Giuseppe Farina (Alfa Romeo 316), Lang and Hermann Müller (Auto Union D) – positions drawn. Fastest lap: Lang, 5m19.9

Grand Prix de l'Automobile Club de France

9 July 1939. Reims. 51 laps of a 4.865-mile circuit = 248.115 miles

1 Hermann Müller	Auto Union D	51	2h21m11.8
2 Georg Meïer	Auto Union D	50	
3 René le Bègue	Talbot T26C	48	
4 Philippe Étancelin	Talbot T26C	48	
5 Raymond Sommer	Alfa Romeo 308	47	
6 Hans Stuck	Auto Union D	47	

Winner's average speed: 105.434 mph. Starting grid front row: Hermann Lang (Mercedes-Benz W163), 2m27.7 (pole), Rudolf Caracciola (Mercedes-Benz W163), 2m29.6 and Tazio Nuvolari (Auto Union D), 2m29.9. Fastest lap: Lang, 2m32.2

Grosser Preis von Deutschland

23 July 1939. Nürburgring. 22 laps of a 14.167-mile circuit = 311.674 miles

1 Rudolf Caracciola	Mercedes-Benz W163	22	4h08m41.8
2 Hermann Müller	Auto Union D	22	4h09m39.6
3 Paul Pietsch	Maserati 8CTF	21	
4 René Dreyfus	Delahaye 145	20	
5 "Georges Raph"	Delahaye 145	19	
6 Robert Mazaud	Delahaye 135	19	

Winner's average speed: 75.194 mph. Starting grid front row: Hermann Lang (Mercedes-Benz W163), 9m43.1 (pole), Manfred von Brauchitsch (Mercedes-Benz W163), 9m51.0 and Caracciola, 9m56.0. Fastest lap: Caracciola, 10m24.2

Grand Prix de Suisse

20 August 1939. Bremgarten. Final: 30 laps of a 4.524-mile circuit = 135.720 miles

1 Hermann Lang	Mercedes-Benz W163	30	1h24m47.6
2 Rudolf Caracciola	Mercedes-Benz W163	30	1h24m50.7
3 Manfred			
von Brauchitsch	Mercedes-Benz W163	30	1h25m57.5
4 Hermann Müller	Auto Union D	30	1h27m01.3
5 Tazio Nuvolari	Auto Union D	30	1h27m08.6
6 Giuseppe Farina	Alfa Romeo 158	29	

Winner's average speed: 96.036 mph. Starting grid front row: Lang (pole), Caracciola and von Brauchitsch – positions based on heat results. Fastest lap: Lang, 2m38.4 (2m36 in the second qualifying heat)

Yugoslavian Grand Prix

3 September 1939. Belgrade. 50 laps of a 1.734-mile circuit = 86.700 miles

1 Tazio Nuvolari	Auto Union D	50	1h04m03.8
2 Manfred			
von Brauchitsch	Mercedes-Benz W163	50	1h04m11.4
3 Hermann Müller	Auto Union D	50	1h04m34.4

No other finishers. Winner's average speed: 81.201 mph. Starting grid front row: von Brauchitsch, 1m14.2 (pole) and Hermann Lang (Mercedes-Benz W163), 1m15.0. Fastest lap: Müller, 1m14.0

1947

Grand Prix de Suisse

8 June 1947. Bremgarten. Final: 30 laps of a 4.524-mile circuit = 135.720 miles

1 Jean-Pierre Wimille	Alfa Romeo 158	30	1h25m09.1
2 Achille Varzi	Alfa Romeo 158	30	1h25m53.8
3 Carlo Felice Trossi	Alfa Romeo 158	30	1h26m26.5
4 Raymond Sommer	Maserati 4CL	29	
5 Consalvo Sanesi	Alfa Romeo 158	29	
6 Luigi Villoresi	Maserati 4CL	29	

Winner's average speed: 95.632 mph. Starting grid front row: Wimille (pole), Varzi and Sanesi – positions based on heat results. Fastest lap: Wimille, 2m47.0

Grand Prix de Belgique

29 June 1947. Spa-Francorchamps. 35 laps of a 9.060-mile circuit = 317.100 miles. Also known as the European Grand Prix

1 Jean-Pierre Wimille	Alfa Romeo 158	35	3h18m28.6
2 Achille Varzi	Alfa Romeo 158	34	
3 Carlo Felice Trossi/			
Giovanni-Battista			
Guidotti	Alfa Romeo 158	33	
4 Bob Gerard/			
Cuth Harrison	ERA B	32	
5 Maurice Trintignant	Delage 3L	31	
6 Louis Rosier	Lago-Talbot SS	30	

Winner's average speed: 95.860 mph. Starting grid front row: Wimille, 5m12.5 (pole), Varzi and Louis Chiron (Lago-Talbot T26C). Fastest lap: Wimille, 5m18.0

Gran Premio d'Italia

7 September 1947. Milan. 100 laps of a 2.144-mile circuit = 214.400 miles

1 Carlo Felice Trossi	Alfa Romeo 158	100	3h02m52.0
2 Achille Varzi	Alfa Romeo 158	100	3h02m52.1
3 Consalvo Sanesi	Alfa Romeo 158	99	
4 Alessandro Gaboardi	Alfa Romeo 158	95	

5 Alberto Ascari	Maserati 4CLT	94
6 Henri Louveau	Delage 3L	91

Winner's average speed: 70.346 mph. Starting grid front row: Sanesi, 1m44.0 (pole), Trossi, 1m44.8 and Luigi Villoresi (Maserati 4CLT/48), 1m45.4. Fastest lap: Trossi, 1m44.0

Grand Prix de l'Automobile Club de France

21 September 1947. Lyon. 70 laps of a 4.490-mile circuit = 314.300 miles

1 Louis Chiron	Lago-Talbot T26C	70	4h03m40.7
2 Henri Louveau	Maserati 4CLT	70	4h05m18.6
3 Eugène Chaboud	Talbot T150C	69	
4 Louis Rosier	Talbot T150C	69	
5 Charles Pozzi	Delahaye 135S	67	
6 Gianfranco Comotti	Talbot T150C	62	

Winner's average speed: 77.389 mph. Starting grid front row: Louveau, 3m17.9 (pole), Chiron, 3m18.3 and Chaboud, 3m23.1. Fastest lap: Alberto Ascari (Maserati 4CLT), Luigi Villoresi (Maserati 4CLT) and "Georges Raph" (Maserati 4CL), 3m17.5

1948

Grand Prix de Monaco

16 May 1948. Monte Carlo. 100 laps of a 1.976-mile circuit = 197.600 miles

1 Giuseppe Farina	Maserati 4CLT	100	3h18m26.9
2 Louis Chiron	Lago-Talbot T26C	100	3h19m02.1
3 Emanuel			
de Graffenried	Maserati 4CL	98	
4 Maurice Trintignant	Simca-Gordini 15	98	
5 Alberto Ascari/			
Luigi Villoresi	Maserati 4CLT	97	
6 Yves Giraud-			
Cabantous	Talbot T150C	95	

Winner's average speed: 59.744 mph. Starting grid front row: Farina, 1m53.8 (pole), Jean-Pierre Wimille (Simca-Gordini 11), 1m54.2 and Villoresi, 1m54.3. Fastest lap: Farina, 1m53.9

Jean-Pierre Wimille's Alfa Romeo 158 at the 1948 Italian Grand Prix

Grand Prix de Suisse

4 July 1948. Bremgarten. 40 laps of a 4.524-mile circuit = 180.960 miles. Also known as the European Grand Prix

1 Carlo Felice Trossi	Alfa Romeo 158	40	1h59m17.3
2 Jean-Pierre Wimille	Alfa Romeo 158	40	1h59m17.5
3 Luigi Villoresi	Maserati 4CLT/48	40	2h01m54.6
4 Consalvo Sanesi	Alfa Romeo 158	39	
5 Alberto Ascari	Maserati 4CLT/48	39	
6 Louis Chiron	Lago-Talbot T26C	38	

Winner's average speed: 91.020 mph. Starting grid front row: Wimille, 2m54.2 (pole), Giuseppe Farina (Maserati 4CLT), 2m54.3 and Villoresi, 2m56.7. Fastest lap: Wimille, 2m51.0

Grand Prix de l'Automobile Club de France

18 July 1948. Reims. 64 laps of a 4.856-mile circuit = 310.784 miles

1	Jean-Pierre Wimille	Alfa Romeo 158	64	3h01m07.5
2	Consalvo Sanesi	Alfa Romeo 158	64	3h01m32.0
3	Alberto Ascari	Alfa Romeo 158	64	3h01m32.5
4	Gianfranco Comotti	Lago-Talbot T26C	62	
5	"Georges Raph"	Lago-Talbot T26C	62	
6	Louis Rosier	Lago-Talbot T26C	60	

Winner's average speed: 102.951 mph. Starting grid front row: Wimille, 2m35.2 (pole), Ascari, 2m44.7 and Sanesi, 2m51.2. Fastest lap: Wimille, 2m41.2

Gran Premio d'Italia

5 September 1948. Turin. 75 laps of a 2.980-mile circuit = 223.500 miles

1	Jean-Pierre Wimille	Alfa Romeo 158	75	3h10m42.4
2	Luigi Villoresi	Maserati 4CLT/48	74	
3	Raymond Sommer	Ferrari 125	73	
4	Alberto Ascari	Maserati 4CLT/48	72	
5	Reg Parnell	Maserati 4CLT	72	
6	Louis Rosier	Lago-Talbot T26C	70	

Winner's average speed: 70.317 mph. Starting grid front row: Wimille, 2m16.6 (pole), Carlo Felice Trossi (Alfa Romeo 158), 2m18.4, Villoresi, 2m20.0 and Sommer, 2m20.4. Fastest lap: Wimille, 2m22.4

British Grand Prix

2 October 1948. Silverstone. 65 laps of a 3.670-mile circuit = 238.550 miles

1	Luigi Villoresi	Maserati 4CLT/48	65	3h18m03.0
2	Alberto Ascari	Maserati 4CLT/48	65	3h18m17.0
3	Bob Gerard	ERA B	65	3h20m06.0
4	Louis Rosier	Lago-Talbot T26C	65	3h22m38.6
5	"B Bira"	Maserati 4CLT/48	64	
6	John Bolster/ Peter Bell	ERA B	63	

Winner's average speed: 72.270 mph. Starting grid front row: Louis Chiron (Lago-Talbot T26C), 2m56.0 (pole), Emanuel de Graffenried (Maserati 4CL), 2m57.0, Philippe Étancelin (Lago-Talbot T26C), 2m58.0, Gerard, 2m58.2 and Leslie Johnson (ERA E), 2m58.6. Fastest lap: Villoresi, 2m52.0

1949

British Grand Prix

14 May 1949. Silverstone. 100 laps of a 3.000-mile circuit = 300.000 miles

1	Emanuel de Graffenried	Maserati 4CLT/48	100	3h52m50.2
2	Bob Gerard	ERA B	100	3h53m55.4
3	Louis Rosier	Lago-Talbot T26C	99	
4	David Hampshire/ Billy Cotton	ERA B	99	
5	Philippe Étancelin	Lago-Talbot T26C	97	
6	Fred Ashmore	Maserati 4CLT/48	97	

Winner's average speed: 77.307 mph. Starting grid front row: Luigi Villoresi (Maserati 4CLT/48), 2m09.8 (pole), "B Bira" (Maserati 4CLT/48), 2m10.2, Peter Walker (ERA B), 2m13.2, de Graffenried, 2m13.6 and Gerard, 2m14.4. Fastest lap: "Bira", 2m10.4

Grand Prix de Belgique

19 June 1949. Spa-Francorchamps. 35 laps of a 9.060-mile circuit = 317.100 miles

1	Louis Rosier	Lago-Talbot T26C	35	3h15m17.7
2	Luigi Villoresi	Ferrari 125	35	3h16m06.8
3	Alberto Ascari	Ferrari 125	35	3h19m28.4
4	Peter Whitehead	Ferrari 125	35	3h20m35.6
5	Johnny Claes	Lago-Talbot T26C	34	
6	Fred Ashmore	Maserati 4CLT/48	33	

Winner's average speed: 97.422 mph. Starting grid front row: Villoresi, Juan Manuel Fangio (Maserati 4CLT/48) and Philippe Étancelin (Lago-Talbot T26C) – positions drawn. Fastest lap: Giuseppe Farina (Maserati 4CLT/48), 5m19.0

Grand Prix de Suisse

3 July 1949. Bremgarten. 40 laps of a 4.524-mile circuit = 180.960 miles

1	Alberto Ascari	Ferrari 125	40	1h59m24.6
2	Luigi Villoresi	Ferrari 125	40	2h00m21.2
3	Raymond Sommer	Lago-Talbot T26C	35	2h00m41.3
4	Philippe Étancelin	Lago-Talbot T26C	40	2h01m07.9
5	"B Bira"	Maserati 4CLT/48	35	2h01m31.3
6	Louis Rosier	Lago-Talbot T26C	35	2h01m52.9

Winner's average speed: 90.927 mph. Starting grid front row: Giuseppe Farina (Maserati 4CLT/48), 2m50.4 (pole), "Bira", 2m53.2 and Ascari, 2m54.7. Fastest lap: Farina, 2m52.2

Grand Prix de France

17 July 1949. Reims. 64 laps of a 4.856-mile circuit = 310.784 miles

1	Louis Chiron	Lago-Talbot T26C	64	3h06m33.7
2	"B Bira"	Maserati 4CLT/48	64	3h06m51.3
3	Peter Whitehead	Ferrari 125	64	3h07m22.2
4	Louis Rosier	Lago-Talbot T26C	64	3h07m30.4
5	Raymond Sommer	Lago-Talbot T26C	61	
6	Eugène Chaboud	Delahaye 135	58	

Winner's average speed: 99.951 mph. Starting grid front row: Luigi Villoresi (Ferrari 125), 2m42 (pole), Juan Manuel Fangio (Maserati 4CLT/48) and Rosier. Fastest lap: Whitehead, 2m46.2

Grand Prix de l'Automobile Club de France

7 August 1949. St Gaudens. Sports Cars. 46 laps of a 6.835-mile circuit = 314.410 miles

1	Charles Pozzi	Delahaye 135S	46	3h34m02.2
2	John Heath	Alta	45	
3	José Scaron	Simca-Gordini T8	44	
4	Louis Chiron/ Paul Vallée	Lago-Talbot Monoplace Decallée	44	
5	Henri Louveau	Delage D6S	44	
6	Auguste Veuillet	Delage D6S	43	

Winner's average speed: 88.137 mph. Starting grid front row: Raymond Sommer (Lago-Talbot T26GS), 4m0. Fastest lap: Chiron, time n/a

Gran Premio d'Italia

11 September 1949. Monza. 80 laps of a 3.915-mile circuit = 313.200 miles. Also known as the European Grand Prix

1	Alberto Ascari	Ferrari 125	80	2h58m53.6
2	Philippe Étancelin	Lago-Talbot T26C	79	
3	"B Bira"	Maserati 4CLT/48	77	
4	Emanuel de Graffenried	Maserati 4CLT/48	76	
5	Raymond Sommer	Ferrari 125	75	
6	Cuth Harrison	ERA B	75	

Winner's average speed: 105.046 mph. Starting grid front row: Ascari, 2m05.0 (pole), Luigi Villoresi (Ferrari 125), 2m05.4, Giuseppe Farina (Maserati 4CLT/48), 2m07.8 and Sommer, 2m09.8. Fastest lap: Ascari, 2m06.8

Czech Grand Prix

25 September 1949. Brno. 20 laps of a 11.060-mile circuit = 221.200 miles

1	Peter Whitehead	Ferrari 125	20	2h48m41.0
2	Philippe Étancelin	Lago-Talbot T26C	20	2h49m16.6
3	Franco Cortese	Ferrari 125	20	2h53m30.4
4	"Pierre Levegh"	Lago-Talbot T26C	19	
5	Henri Louveau	Maserati 4CLT	19	
6	Johnny Claes	Lago-Talbot T26C	19	

Winner's average speed: 78.680 mph. Starting grid front row: "B Bira" (Maserati 4CLT/48) and Giuseppe Farina (Maserati 4CLT/48) – positions drawn. Fastest lap: "Bira" and Emanuel de Graffenried (Maserati 4CLT/48), 8m03.0

Mike Thackwell leads at the start of the 1983 Donington Park F2 race

The less powerful Formula Two was first created as a supporting category to Formula One in 1948. Since the earliest days of motor racing there had been a small car class, whether it be termed "light car" or "voiturette". The World Championship was held for Formula Two in 1952-53 (see page 12–18) but it was not until 1967 that a European Championship was organized for the category.

At the time, Grand Prix drivers often used to compete in F2 but it was decided that the new European Champion should be in his formative years and on his way to Formula One. Consequently, experienced drivers were ineligible for points (see Graded Drivers right).

However, the championship gave newcomers the opportunity to compare with the likes of Jim Clark, Jackie Stewart and the formula's acknowledged master, Jochen Rindt.

The series was held for the next 17 years before, with F2 fields dwindling, it was replaced by the newly announced Formula 3000. Critics claimed that F2 had failed to foster new Grand Prix stars (no F2 champion has gone on to win the world title) and that the best prospects such as Alain Prost, Ayrton Senna and Nelson Piquet bypassed the formula by moving straight from F3 to Grand Prix racing.

GRADED DRIVERS

A driver was A-graded when they had finished in the top six in at least two Grands Prix, or in the top three in two or more World Sports Car events or a combination of these during the previous two seasons. In addition the European F2 Champion was graded for one season, and World Champions for five years. ♦ indicates a graded driver in the results below; points were awarded to the top six non-graded drivers to finish.

RULES

CARS

1948-53 2000 cc normally aspirated or 500 cc supercharged engine capacity

1957-60 1500 cc normally aspirated engine capacity

1964-66 1000 cc normally aspirated engine capacity, maximum of four cylinders

1967-71 1300-1600 cc normally aspirated engine capacity, maximum of six cylinders, engine block from a type of car of which at least 500 had been built in the last year

1972-75 2000 cc normally aspirated engine capacity, engine block and cylinder head from a type of car of which at least 1000 had been built

1976-84 2000 cc normally aspirated engine capacity, pure racing engines allowed, maximum of six cylinders

POINTS

9-6-4-3-2-1 awarded to the top six eligible finishers

EUROPEAN FORMULA TWO CHAMPIONS

year	driver	nat	team	car
1967	Jacky Ickx	B	Tyrrell Racing Organisation	Matra MS5-Ford/Matra MS7-Ford
1968	Jean-Pierre Beltoise	F	Matra Sports	Matra MS7-Ford
1969	Johnny Servoz-Gavin	F	Tyrrell Racing Organisation	Matra MS7-Ford
1970	Clay Regazzoni	CH	Tecno Racing Team	Tecno 68-Ford/Tecno 70-Ford
1971	Ronnie Peterson	S	March Engineering	March 712M-Ford
1972	Mike Hailwood	GB	Team Surtees	Surtees TS10-Ford
1973	Jean-Pierre Jarier	F	March Engineering	March 732-BMW
1974	Patrick Depailler	F	March Engineering	March 742-BMW
1975	Jacques Laffite	F	Automobiles Martini	Martini MK16-BMW
1976	Jean-Pierre Jabouille	F	Equipe Elf	Elf 2J-Renault
1977	René Arnoux	F	Automobiles Martini	Martini MK22-Renault
1978	Bruno Giacomelli	I	March Engineering	March 782-BMW
1979	Marc Surer	CH	March Engineering	March 792-BMW
1980	Brian Henton	GB	Toleman Group Motorsport	Toleman TG280-Hart/Toleman TG280B-Hart
1981	Geoff Lees	GB	Ralt Racing	Ralt RH6/81-Honda
1982	Corrado Fabi	I	March Engineering	March 822-BMW
1983	Jonathan Palmer	GB	Ralt Racing	Ralt RH6/83-Honda
1984	Mike Thackwell	NZ	Ralt Racing	Ralt RH6/84-Honda

1967

Guards 100

24 March 1967. Snetterton. 40 laps of a 2.710-mile circuit = 108.400 miles

1	Jochen Rindt♦	Brabham BT23-Ford	40	59m40.6
2	Graham Hill♦	Lotus 48-Ford	40	59m40.6
3	Alan Rees	Brabham BT23-Ford	40	1h00m23.0
4	Denny Hulme♦	Brabham BT23-Ford	40	1h00m35.8
5	Bruce McLaren♦	McLaren M4A-Ford	40	1h00m49.0
6	Jack Brabham♦	Brabham BT23-Ford	40	1h01m04.0
7	Piers Courage	McLaren M4A-Ford	39	
8	Ian Raby	Brabham BT16-Ford	32	

Winner's average speed: 108.987 mph. Pole position: Rindt, 1m28.8. Fastest lap: Stewart (Matra MS5-Ford), Rindt and Hill, 1m28.2

Wills Trophy

27 March 1967. Silverstone. 40 laps of a 2.927-mile circuit = 117.080 miles

1	Jochen Rindt♦	Brabham BT23-Ford	40	1h00m13.0
2	Alan Rees	Brabham BT23-Ford	40	1h00m29.0
3	John Surtees♦	Lola T100-Ford	40	1h00m37.0
4	Bruce McLaren♦	McLaren M4A-Ford	40	1h00m48.2
5	Jackie Stewart♦	Matra MS5-Ford	40	1h00m53.2
6	Frank Gardner	Brabham BT23-Ford	40	1h01m21.2
7	Jacky Ickx	Matra MS5-Ford	40	1h01m39.2
8	Rob Widdows	Brabham BT23-Ford	40	1h02m01.6
9	Mike Spence♦	Parnell-Ford	40	1h02m03.8
10	Philip Robinson	Alexis-Ford	36	
11	Ian Raby	Brabham BT16-Ford	34	

Winner's average speed: 116.659 mph. Pole position: Rindt, 1m29.2. Fastest lap: Graham Hill (Lotus 48-Ford) and Rindt, 1m29.2

Eifelrennen

23 April 1967. Nürburgring. 30 laps of a 4.814-mile circuit = 144.420 miles

1	Jochen Rindt♦	Brabham BT23-Ford	30	1h35m46.4
2	John Surtees♦	Lola T100-BMW	30	1h36m03.3
3	Jacky Ickx	Matra MS5-Ford	30	1h36m33.3
4	Hubert Hahne	Lola T100-BMW	30	1h37m27.8
5	Piers Courage	McLaren M4A-Ford	30	1h37m28.2
6	Bruce McLaren♦	McLaren M4A-Ford	29	
7	Chris Irwin	Lola T100-Ford	29	
8	Gerhard Mitter	Brabham BT23-Ford	28	
9	Alan Rees	Brabham BT23-Ford	28	

Winner's average speed: 90.476 mph. Pole position: Clark (Lotus 48-Ford), 2m49.6. Fastest lap: Rindt, 3m07.8

Deutschland Trophäe

9 July 1967. Hockenheim. 45 laps of a 4.206-mile circuit = 189.270 miles

1	Frank Gardner	Brabham BT23-Ford	45	1h32m48.3
2	Brian Hart	Protos-Ford	45	1h33m28.1
3	Piers Courage	McLaren M4A-Ford	45	1h33m50.3
4	Rob Widdows	Brabham BT23-Ford	43	
5	Ian Raby	Brabham BT14-Ford	42	
6	Alan Rollinson	Cooper T83-Ford	42	

Winner's average speed: 122.366 mph. Pole position: Irwin (Lola T100-Ford), 2m01.5. Fastest lap: Hart, 2m00.0

Flugplatzrennen Tulln-Langenlebarn

16 July 1967. Tulln-Langenlebarn. 50 laps of a 1.780-mile circuit = 89.000 miles

1	Jochen Rindt♦	Brabham BT23-Ford	50	54m44.40
2	Jack Brabham♦	Brabham BT23-Ford	50	54m45.80
3	Jean-Pierre Beltoise	Matra MS5-Ford	50	55m07.54
4	Frank Gardner	Brabham BT23-Ford	50	55m21.79
5	Jacky Ickx	Matra MS7-Ford	50	55m23.61
6	Graham Hill♦	Lotus 48-Ford	50	55m30.65
7	Chris Irwin	Lola T100-Ford	50	55m36.86
8	Johnny Servoz-Gavin	Matra MS5-Ford	49	
9	Piers Courage	McLaren M4A-Ford	49	

Winner's average speed: 97.552 mph. Pole position: Beltoise, 1m00.53. Fastest lap: Clark (Lotus 48-Ford), 1m04.24

Gran Premio de Madrid

23 July 1967. Jarama. 55 laps of a 2.115-mile circuit = 116.325 miles

1	Jim Clark♦	Lotus 48-Ford	55	1h25m29.1
2	Jackie Stewart♦	Matra MS7-Ford	55	1h25m37.0
3	Chris Irwin	Lola T100-Ford	55	1h26m43.2
4	Jack Brabham♦	Brabham BT23-Ford	55	1h26m53.7
5	Johnny Servoz-Gavin	Matra MS5-Ford	54	
6	Brian Redman	Lola T100-Ford	54	
7	Pedro Rodriguez♦	Protos-Ford	54	

8	Piers Courage	McLaren M4A-Ford	54
9	Rob Widdows	Brabham BT23-Ford	52
10	Robs Lamplough	Lola T62-Ford	50

Winner's average speed: 81.661 mph. Pole position: Hill (Lotus 48-Ford), 1m31.3. Fastest lap: Clark, 1m30.7

Grote Prijs van Zandvoort

30 July 1967. Zandvoort. 30 laps of a 2.605-mile circuit = 78.150 miles

1	Jacky Ickx	Matra MS5-Ford	30	44m43.2
2	Piers Courage	McLaren M4A-Ford	30	44m58.1
3	Frank Gardner	Brabham BT23-Ford	30	45m16.6
4	Jean-Pierre Beltoise	Matra MS7-Ford	30	45m44.1
5	Alan Rees	Brabham BT23-Ford	30	45m59.5
6	Brian Hart	Protos-Ford	30	46m02.0

Winner's average speed: 104.852 mph. Pole position: Ickx, 1m27.5. Fastest lap: Ickx, 1m27.9

Jochen Rindt, the "King of F2", won five races in the 1967 season for Roy Winkelmann Racing

Gran Premio del Mediterraneo

20 August 1967. Enna-Pergusa. 80 laps of a 2.983-mile circuit = 238.640 miles

1	Jackie Stewart♦	Matra MS7-Ford	80	1h40m19.2
2	Jean-Pierre Beltoise	Matra MS7-Ford	80	1h40m19.9
3	Jacky Ickx	Matra MS5-Ford	80	1h41m00.2
4	Jo Schlesser	Matra MS5-Ford	80	1h41m08.6
5	Johnny Servoz-Gavin	Matra MS5-Ford	80	1h41m13.9
6	Alan Rees	Brabham BT23-Ford	79	
7	Graham Hill♦	Lotus 48-Ford	79	
8	Brian Hart	Protos-Ford	79	

Winner's average speed: 142.727 mph. Pole position: Beltoise, 1m14.5. Fastest lap: Ickx, 1m13.3

Guards International Trophy

28 August 1967. Brands Hatch. 40 laps of a 2.650-mile circuit = 106.000 miles

1	Jochen Rindt♦	Brabham BT23-Ford	40	1h02m44.2
2	Jackie Stewart♦	Matra MS7-Ford	40	1h03m03.6
3	Jo Schlesser	Matra MS5-Ford	40	1h03m15.4
4	Frank Gardner	Brabham BT23-Ford	40	1h03m30.8
5	Jacky Ickx	Matra MS5-Ford	40	1h03m49.8
6	Jackie Oliver*	Lotus 48-Ford	40	1h04m15.0
7	Graham Hill♦	Lotus 48-Ford	40	1h04m15.4
8	Brian Redman	Lola T100-Ford	39	
9	Hubert Hahne	Lola T100-BMW	39	

*Oliver penalized one minute for jumping the start. Winner's average speed: 101.376 mph. Pole position: Surtees (Lola T100-Ford), 1m33.0. Fastest lap: Rindt, 1m33.0

Gran Premio di Roma

8 October 1967. Vallelunga. 60 laps of a 1.988-mile circuit = 119.280 miles

1	Jacky Ickx	Matra MS7-Ford	60	1h20m27.8
2	Jean-Pierre Beltoise	Matra MS7-Ford	60	1h20m52.0

Formula Two

3	Johnny Servoz-Gavin	Matra MS5-Ford	60	1h21m25.1
4	Brian Redman	Lola T100-Ford	60	1h21m49.6
5	Frank Gardner	Brabham BT23-Ford	60	1h21m55.0
6	Jean-Pierre Jaussaud	Matra MS5-Ford	60	1h22m24.1

Winner's average speed: 88.945 mph. Pole position: Ickx, 1m18.4. Fastest lap: Ickx, 1m18.7

FINAL CHAMPIONSHIP POSITIONS

Drivers

1	Jacky Ickx	41 (45)*	12=	Hubert Hahne	7
2	Frank Gardner	33		Ian Raby	7
3	Jean-Pierre Beltoise	27	14	Jackie Oliver	3
4	Piers Courage	24	15=	Gerhard Mitter	2
5	Alan Rees	23		Philip Robinson	2
6=	Chris Irwin	15	17=	Jean-Pierre Jaussaud	1
	Johnny Servoz-Gavin	15		Robs Lamplough	1
8	Jo Schlesser	13		Alan Rollinson	1
9	Brian Redman	9		♦ Graded driver ineligible	
10=	Brian Hart	8		for points.	
	Rob Widdows	8		*Best six results count	

1968

Deutschland Trophäe

7 April 1968. Hockenheim. 40 laps of a 4.206-mile circuit = 168.240 miles

1	Jean-Pierre Beltoise	Matra MS7-Ford	40	1h25m49.7
2	Henri Pescarolo	Matra MS7-Ford	40	1h25m51.8
3	Piers Courage	Brabham BT23C-Ford	40	1h26m51.9
4	Chris Lambert	Brabham BT23C-Ford	40	1h27m13.0
5	Chris Amon♦	Ferrari Dino 166	40	1h28m30.3
6	Jo Schlesser	McLaren M4A-Ford	40	1h28m30.6
7	Chris Irwin	Lola T100-Ford	40	1h29m30.7

Winner's average speed: 117.612 mph. Pole position: Beltoise, 1m59.3. Fastest lap: Pescarolo, 2m00.1

BARC Thruxton Trophy

15 April 1968. Thruxton. 54 laps of a 2.356-mile circuit = 127.224 miles

1	Jochen Rindt♦	Brabham BT23C-Ford	54	1h09m45.6
2	Jean-Pierre Beltoise	Matra MS7-Ford	54	1h09m53.0
3	Derek Bell	Brabham BT23C-Ford	54	1h10m18.8
4	Jackie Oliver	Lotus 48-Ford	53	
5	Kurt Ahrens Jr	Brabham BT23C-Ford	53	
6	Chris Williams	Lola T100-Ford	52	
7	Alan Rees	Brabham BT23C-Ford	52	

Winner's average speed: 109.424 mph. Pole position: Beltoise, 1m16.4. Fastest lap: Rindt, 1m16.0

Gran Premio de Madrid

28 April 1968. Jarama. 60 laps of a 2.115-mile circuit = 126.900 miles

1	Jean-Pierre Beltoise	Matra MS7-Ford	60	1h30m09.7
2	Jochen Rindt♦	Brabham BT23C-Ford	60	1h30m28.4
3	Kurt Ahrens Jr	Brabham BT23C-Ford	60	1h31m12.4
4	Henri Pescarolo	Matra MS7-Ford	60	1h31m14.0
5	Clay Regazzoni	Tecno 68-Ford	59	
6	Jorge de Bagration	Lola T100-Ford	57	
7	Brian Hart	Merlyn Mk12-Ford	57	

Winner's average speed: 84.464 mph. Pole position: Stewart (Matra MS7-Ford), 1m28.4 - Stewart did not start. Fastest lap: Beltoise, 1m28.2

Holts Trophy

3 June 1968. Crystal Palace. 90 laps of a 1.390-mile circuit = 125.100 miles

1	Jochen Rindt♦	Brabham BT23C-Ford	90	1h20m06.8
2	Brian Redman	Lola T100-Ford	90	1h20m37.0
3	Clay Regazzoni	Tecno 68-Ford	89	

4	Jackie Oliver	Lotus 48-Ford	89	
5	Jo Schlesser	McLaren M4A-Ford	88	accident
6	Jean-Pierre Jaussaud	Tecno 68-Ford	85	

No other finishers. Winner's average speed: 93.692 mph. Pole position: Rindt, based on heat results. Fastest lap: Rindt, 52.0s

Flugplatzrennen Tulln-Langenlebarn

14 July 1968. Tulln-Langenlebarn. 70 laps of a 1.780-mile circuit = 124.600 miles

1	Jochen Rindt♦	Brabham BT23C-Ford	70	1h15m24.63
2	Jean-Pierre Beltoise	Matra MS7-Ford	70	1h15m57.10
3	Henri Pescarolo	Matra MS7-Ford	70	1h16m17.90
4	Kurt Ahrens Jr	Brabham BT23C-Ford	70	1h16m35.80
5	Jackie Oliver	Lotus 48-Ford	70	1h17m03.20
6	Tino Brambilla	Brabham BT23C-Ford	70	1h17m22.10
7	Derek Bell	Ferrar Dino 166	69	

Winner's average speed: 99.137 mph. Pole position: Rindt, 1m03.27. Fastest lap: Rindt, 1m03.2

Grote Prijs van Zandvoort

28 July 1968. Zandvoort. 50 laps of a 2.605-mile circuit = 130.250 miles

1	Jean-Pierre Beltoise	Matra MS7-Ford	50	1h13m52.18
2	Henri Pescarolo	Matra MS7-Ford	49	
3	Richard Attwood	Tecno 68-Ford	49	
4	Silvio Moser	Tecno 68-Ford	49	
5	Eric Offenstadt	Tecno 68-Ford	49	
6	Rob Widdows	McLaren M4A-Ford	49	

Winner's average speed: 105.794 mph. Pole position: Bell (Ferrari Dino 166), 1m26.6. Fastest lap: Attwood, 1m26.84

Gran Premio del Mediterraneo

25 August 1968. Enna-Pergusa. 50 laps of a 2.983-mile circuit = 149.150 miles

1	Jochen Rindt♦	Brabham BT23C-Ford	50	1h02m40.6
2	Piers Courage	Brabham BT23C-Ford	50	1h02m40.6
3	Tino Brambilla	Brabham BT23C-Ford	50	1h02m40.6
4	Clay Regazzoni	Tecno 68-Ford	50	1h02m40.6
5	Derek Bell	Brabham BT23C-Ford	50	1h02m41.5
6	Jacky Ickx♦	Ferrari Dino 166	50	1h02m43.8
7	Brian Hart	Brabham BT23C-Ford	50	1h02m44.0
8	Henri Pescarolo	Matra MS7-Ford	50	1h02m52.4

First four cars credited with the same race time. Winner's average speed: 142.780 mph. Pole position: Pescarolo, 1m13.7. Fastest lap: Rindt, 1m12.8

Preis von Hessen und Württemberg

13 October 1968. Hockenheim. 35 laps of a 4.206-mile circuit = 147.210 miles

1	Tino Brambilla	Ferrari Dino 166	35	1h11m40.2
2	Henri Pescarolo	Matra MS7-Ford	35	1h11m40.4
3	Derek Bell	Ferrari Dino 166	35	1h11m40.6
4	Jackie Oliver	Lotus 48-Ford	35	1h11m41.3
5	David Hobbs	Lola T100-Ford	35	1h11m42.4
6	Brian Hart	Brabham BT23C-Ford	35	1h11m42.6

Winner's average speed: 123.240 mph. Pole position: Rindt (Brabham BT23C-Ford), 1m58.7. Fastest lap: T Brambilla, 1m59.0

Gran Premio di Roma

27 October 1968. Vallelunga. 80 laps of a 1.988-mile circuit = 159.040 miles

1	Tino Brambilla	Ferrari Dino 166	80	1h43m02.7
2	Andrea de Adamich	Ferrari Dino 166	80	1h43m08.1
3	Peter Gethin	Brabham BT23C-Ford	80	1h43m10.4
4	Jean-Pierre Beltoise	Matra MS7-Ford	80	1h43m51.6
5	Henri Pescarolo	Matra MS7-Ford	80	1h44m05.0
6	Derek Bell	Ferrari Dino 166	80	1h44m08.0

Winner's average speed: 92.604 mph. Pole position: T Brambilla, 1m16.4. Fastest lap: T Brambilla, 1m16.2

Drivers

1	Jean-Pierre		Brian Hart		4
	Beltoise	48	15= Chris Lambert		3
2	Henri Pescarolo	30 (31)*	Silvio Moser		3
3	Tino Brambilla	26	17= Jorge de Bagration		2
4	Derek Bell	15	David Hobbs		2
5	Jackie Oliver	14	Jean-Pierre Jaussaud	2
6=	Kurt Ahrens Jr	13	Eric Offenstadt		2
	Piers Courage	13	Chris Williams		2
	Clay Regazzoni	13	22= Chris Irwin		1
9	Brian Redman	9	Alan Rees		1
10	Andrea de Adamich	6	Rob Widdows		1
11	Jo Schlesser	5	♦ Graded driver ineligible		
12=	Richard Attwood	4	for points.		
	Peter Gethin	4	*Best six results count		

1969

Wills Trophy

7 April 1969. Thruxton. 50 laps of a 2.356-mile circuit = 117.800 miles

1	Jochen Rindt♦	Lotus 59B-Ford	50	1h02m44.6
2	Jackie Stewart♦	Matra MS7-Ford	50	1h03m14.8
3	Jean-Pierre Beltoise♦	Matra MS7-Ford	50	1h03m57.4
4	Henri Pescarolo	Matra MS7-Ford	49	
5	Johnny Servoz-Gavin	Matra MS7-Ford	49	
6	Tino Brambilla	Ferrari Dino 166	48	
7	Piers Courage♦	Brabham BT23C-Ford	48	
8	François Cevert	Tecno 69-Ford	48	
9	Enzo Corti	Brabham BT23-Ford	48	
10	Clay Regazzoni	Ferrari Dino 166	47	

Winner's average speed: 112.649 mph. Pole position: Rindt, 1m13.2. Fastest lap: Rindt, 1m14.0

Jim Clark-Rennen/Deutschland Trophäe

13 April 1969. Hockenheim. 40 laps of a 4.206-mile circuit = 168.240 miles

1	Jean-Pierre Beltoise♦	Matra MS7-Ford	40	1h21m39.6
2	Hubert Hahne	BMW T102	40	1h21m40.2
3	Piers Courage♦	Brabham BT23C-Ford	40	1h21m43.8
4	Kurt Ahrens Jr	Brabham BT30-Ford	40	1h22m01.1
5	Henri Pescarolo	Matra MS7-Ford	40	1h22m20.3*
6	Johnny Servoz-Gavin	Matra MS7-Ford	40	1h22m01.4*
7	Alan Rollinson	Lotus 59B-Ford	40	1h22m03.0*
8	Nanni Galli	Tecno 69-Ford	40	1h22m23.6

*Positions decided on points awarded for results of the two heats and not on aggregate times. Winner's average speed: 123.615 mph. Pole position: Pescarolo, 2m08.9. Fastest lap: Beltoise, 1m59.1

Eifelrennen

27 April 1969. Nürburgring. 10 laps of a 14.189-mile circuit = 141.890 miles

1	Jackie Stewart♦	Matra MS7-Ford	10	1h21m40.4
2	Jo Siffert♦	BMW T102	10	1h22m56.4
3	Jean-Pierre Beltoise♦	Matra MS7-Ford	10	1h23m11.7
4	Hubert Hahne	BMW T102	10	1h23m52.4
5	Derek Bell	Ferrari Dino 166	10	1h23m55.7
6	Johnny Servoz-Gavin	Matra MS7-Ford	10	1h24m05.3
7	François Cevert	Tecno 69-Ford	10	1h24m49.9
8	Malcolm Guthrie	Brabham BT23C-Ford	10	1h28m18.5
9	Werner Lindermann	Brabham BT23-Ford	9	

Winner's average speed: 104.237 mph. Pole position: Siffert, 9m03.8. Fastest lap: Stewart, 8m05.3

Gran Premio de Madrid

11 May 1969. Jarama. 60 laps of a 2.115-mile circuit = 126.900 miles

1	Jackie Stewart♦	Matra MS7-Ford	60	1h29m36.7
2	Jean-Pierre Beltoise♦	Matra MS7-Ford	60	1h29m37.2
3	Piers Courage♦	Brabham BT23C-Ford	60	1h29m57.2
4	Johnny Servoz-Gavin	Matra MS7-Ford	59	
5	Hubert Hahne	BMW T102	59	
6	Tino Brambilla	Ferrari Dino 166	59	
7	Peter Westbury	Brabham BT30-Ford	59	
8	Derek Bell	Ferrari Dino 166	58	
9	Nanni Galli	Tecno 69-Ford	58	

Winner's average speed: 84.983 mph. Pole position: Beltoise, 1m28.6. Fastest lap: Stewart and Beltoise, 1m28.4

Flugplatzrennen Tulln-Langenlebarn

13 July 1969. Tulln-Langenlebarn. 70 laps of a 1.780-mile circuit = 124.600 miles

1	Jochen Rindt♦	Lotus 59B-Ford	70	1h13m22.02
2	Jackie Stewart♦	Matra MS7-Ford	70	1h13m24.64
3	Graham Hill♦	Lotus 59B-Ford	70	1h13m42.12
4	Jean-Pierre Beltoise♦	Matra MS7-Ford	70	1h13m59.74
5	François Cevert	Tecno 69-Ford	70	1h14m33.40
6	Nanni Galli	Tecno 69-Ford	70	1h14m45.39
7	Hubert Hahne	BMW T102	69	
8	Xavier Perrot	Brabham BT23C-Ford	69	
9	Peter Westbury	Brabham BT30-Ford	64	engine
10	Werner Lindermann	Brabham BT23-Ford	63	

Winner's average speed: 101.899 mph. Pole position: Rindt, 1m02.1. Fastest lap: Rindt, 1m01.7

Gran Premio del Mediterraneo

24 August 1969. Enna-Pergusa. 62 laps of a 2.983-mile circuit = 184.946 miles

1	Piers Courage♦	Brabham BT30-Ford	62	1h17m58.0
2	Johnny Servoz-Gavin	Matra MS7-Ford	62	1h17m58.7
3	François Cevert	Tecno 69-Ford	62	1h17m59.3
4	Clay Regazzoni	Tecno 69-Ford	62	1h18m00.3
5	Rob Widdows	Brabham BT23C-Ford	62	1h18m28.5
6	Graham Hill♦	Lotus 59B-Ford	62	1h18m57.1
7	Alan Rollinson	Brabham BT30-Ford	62	1h18m58.6
8	Patrick Dal Bo	Pygmee MDB12-Ford	62	1h19m25.8

Winner's average speed: 142.327 mph. Pole position: Regazzoni, 1m13.5. Fastest lap: Hill, 1m12.9

Gran Premio di Roma

12 October 1969. Vallelunga. 80 laps of a 1.988-mile circuit = 159.040 miles

1	Johnny Servoz-Gavin	Matra MS7-Ford	80	1h42m43.4
2	Peter Westbury	Brabham BT30-Ford	79	
3	John Miles	Lotus 59B-Ford	79	
4	Derek Bell	Brabham BT30-Ford	78	
5	Franco Bernabei	Brabham BT23C-Ford	77	
6	John Pollock	Lotus 48-Ford	76	

Winner's average speed: 92.894 mph. Pole position: Servoz-Gavin, 1m15.49. Fastest lap: Servoz-Gavin, 1m15.7

FINAL CHAMPIONSHIP POSITIONS

Drivers

1	Johnny		11= John Miles		4
	Servoz-Gavin	37 (40)*	Alan Rollinson		4
2	Hubert Hahne	28	13= Xavier Perrot		3
3	François Cevert	21	Rob Widdows		3
4	Henri Pescarolo	13	15= Franco Bernabei		2
5=	Derek Bell	11	Enzo Corti		2
	Peter Westbury	11	Malcolm Guthrie		2
7=	Tino Brambilla	8	Werner Lindermann	2
	Nanni Galli	8	19= Patrick Dal Bo		1
9	Kurt Ahrens Jr	6	John Pollock		1
10	Clay Regazzoni	5	♦ Graded driver ineligible		
			for points.		
			*Best five results count		

Formula Two

1970

Wills Trophy

30 March 1970. Thruxton. 46 laps of a 2.356-mile circuit
= 108.376 miles

1 Jochen Rindt♦	Lotus 69-Ford	46	57m41.0
2 Jackie Stewart♦	Brabham BT30-Ford	46	57m53.4
3 Derek Bell	Brabham BT30-Ford	45	
4 Rob Widdows	Brabham BT30-Ford	45	
5 Alistair Walker	Brabham BT23C-Ford	45	
6 Jacky Ickx♦	BMW F270	44	
7 Dieter Quester	BMW T102	44	
8 Clay Regazzoni	Tecno 68-Ford	44	
9 Tommy Reid	Brabham BT30-Ford	44	

Winner's average speed: 112.729 mph. Pole position: Stewart,
1m13.6. Fastest lap: Rindt, 1m14.0

Jim Clark-Rennen/Deutschland Trophäe

12 April 1970. Hockenheim. 40 laps of a 4.206-mile circuit
= 168.240 miles

1 Clay Regazzoni	Tecno 70-Ford	40	1h22m01.3
2 Tetsu Ikuzawa	Lotus 69-Ford	40	1h22m01.6
3 Derek Bell	Brabham BT30-Ford	40	1h22m03.1
4 Hubert Hahne	BMW F270	40	1h22m16.2
5 Emerson Fittipaldi	Lotus 69-Ford	40	1h22m17.4*
6 Rolf Stommelen♦	March 702-Ford	40	1h22m16.9*
7 Peter Gaydon	Brabham BT30-Ford	40	1h23m24.0

*Positions decided on points awarded for results of the two
heats and not on aggregate times. Winner's average speed:
123.070 mph. Pole position: Rindt (Lotus 69-Ford), 1m58.0.
Fastest lap: Quester (BMW T102), 1m58.6

Gran Premio de Barcelona

26 April 1970. Montjuich Park. 45 laps of a 2.355-mile
circuit = 105.975 miles

1 Derek Bell	Brabham BT30-Ford	45	1h08m07.6
2 Henri Pescarolo	Brabham BT30-Ford	45	1h08m29.9
3 Emerson Fittipaldi	Lotus 69-Ford	44	
4 Rob Widdows	Brabham BT30-Ford	44	
5 Dieter Quester	BMW F270	44	
6 Carlos Reutemann	Brabham BT30-Ford	44	

Winner's average speed: 93.333 mph. Pole position: Pescarolo,
1m29.7. Fastest lap: Bell, 1m29.5

Grand Prix de Rouen-les-Essarts

28 June 1970. Rouen-les-Essarts. 25 laps of a 4.065-mile
circuit = 101.625 miles

1 Jo Siffert♦	BMW F270	25	51m24.3
2 Clay Regazzoni	Tecno 68-Ford	25	51m24.4
3 Emerson Fittipaldi	Lotus 69-Ford	25	51m24.5
4 Jacky Ickx♦	BMW F270	25	51m25.0
5 Tim Schenken	Brabham BT30-Ford	25	51m25.3
6 Ronnie Peterson	March 702-Ford	25	51m25.7
7 Derek Bell	Brabham BT30-Ford	25	51m26.2
8 Jack Brabham♦	Brabham BT30-Ford	25	51m26.7
9 Jochen Rindt♦	Lotus 69-Ford	25	51m35.6
10 Peter Westbury	Brabham BT30-Ford	25	51m35.8

Winner's average speed: 118.617 mph. Pole position: Regazzoni,
2m02.5. Fastest lap: Schenken, 2m00.8

Gran Premio del Mediterraneo

23 August 1970. Enna-Pergusa. 62 laps of a 3.010-mile
circuit = 186.620 miles

1 Clay Regazzoni	Tecno 70-Ford	62	1h28m03.5
2 Jacky Ickx♦	BMW F270	62	1h28m03.8
3 Jo Siffert♦	BMW F270	62	1h28m04.1
4 Peter Westbury	Brabham BT30-Ford	62	1h28m10.0
5 Emerson Fittipaldi	Lotus 69-Ford	62	1h28m18.6
6 Rolf Stommelen♦	Brabham BT30-Ford	62	1h28m28.0
7 Derek Bell	Brabham BT30-Ford	60	
8 Jean-Pierre Jabouille	Pygmee MDB15-Ford	59	

No other finishers. Winner's average speed: 127.157 mph. Pole
position: Ickx, 1m22.8. Fastest lap: Regazzoni, 1m23.5

Flugplatzrennen Tulln-Langenlebarn

13 September 1970. Tulln-Langenlebarn. 70 laps of a
1.780-mile circuit = 124.600 miles

1 Jacky Ickx♦	BMW F270	70	1h13m45.82
2 Jack Brabham♦	Brabham BT30-Ford	70	1h13m49.68
3 François Cevert	Tecno 70-Ford	70	1h14m17.33
4 Derek Bell	Brabham BT30-Ford	70	1h14m39.12
5 Ronnie Peterson	March 702-Ford	70	1h15m05.94
6 Vittorio Brambilla	Brabham BT30-Ford	69	
7 Tetsu Ikuzawa	Lotus 69-Ford	69	
8 Alistair Walker	Brabham BT30-Ford	68	

Winner's average speed: 101.351 mph. Pole position: Regazzoni
(Tecno 70-Ford), 1m01.5. Fastest lap: Cevert, 1m01.6

Gran Premio Citti di Imola

27 September 1970. Imola. 56 laps of a 3.118-mile circuit
= 174.608 miles

1 Clay Regazzoni	Tecno 70-Ford	56	1h30m50.3
2 Emerson Fittipaldi	Lotus 69-Ford	56	1h30m58.2
3 Derek Bell	Brabham BT30-Ford	56	1h31m12.3
4 Ronnie Peterson	March 702-Ford	56	1h31m12.8
5 Rolf Stommelen♦	Brabham BT30-Ford	56	1h31m21.8
6 Mike Goth	Brabham BT30-Ford	56	1h32m58.4
7 Tetsu Ikuzawa	Lotus 69-Ford	55	

Winner's average speed: 115.331 mph. Pole position: Regazzoni,
1m36.34. Fastest lap: Ickx (BMW F270), 1m35.5

Preis von Hessen und Württemberg

11 October 1970. Hockenheim. 35 laps of a 4.206-mile
circuit = 147.210 miles

1 Dieter Quester	BMW F270	35	1h16m34.4
2 Clay Regazzoni	Tecno 70-Ford	35	1h16m36.1
3 Ronnie Peterson	March 702-Ford	35	1h17m05.0
4 Emerson Fittipaldi	Lotus 69-Ford	35	1h17m05.4
5 Carlos Reutemann	Brabham BT30-Ford	35	1h18m13.9
6 Derek Bell	Brabham BT30-Ford	35	1h18m17.9

Winner's average speed: 115.348 mph. Pole position: Peterson,
2m09.0. Fastest lap: Quester, 2m08.7

FINAL CHAMPIONSHIP POSITIONS

Drivers

1 Clay Regazzoni	44	12 Tim Schenken	4
2 Derek Bell	35 (38)*	13= Vittorio Brambilla	3
3 Emerson Fittipaldi	25	Hubert Hahne	3
4= Ronnie Peterson	14	Carlos Reutemann	3
Dieter Quester	14	16= Mike Goth	3
6= François Cevert	9	Jean-Pierre Jabouille	2
Tetsu Ikuzawa	9	18= Peter Gaydon	1
Rob Widdows	9	Tommy Reid	1
9 Peter Westbury	7	♦ Graded driver ineligible	
10 Henri Pescarolo	6	for points.	
11 Alistair Walker	5	*Best six results count	

1971

Jim Clark-Rennen

4 April 1971. Hockenheim. 40 laps of a 4.219-mile circuit
= 168.760 miles

1 François Cevert	Tecno 71-Ford	40	1h27m09.8
2 Graham Hill♦	Brabham BT36-Ford	40	1h27m14.7
3 Carlos Reutemann	Brabham BT30-Ford	40	1h27m21.5
4 Wilson Fittipaldi	Lotus 69-Ford	40	1h27m31.7
5 Tim Schenken	Brabham BT36-Ford	40	1h27m34.8
6 Gerry Birrell	Lotus 69-Ford	40	1h28m36.1
7 Brian Hart	Brabham BT30-Ford	39	

Winner's average speed: 116.168 mph. Pole position: Peterson
(March 712M-Ford), 2m08.0. Fastest lap: Peterson, 2m04.2

Yellow Pages Jochen Rindt Trophy

12 April 1971. Thruxton. 50 laps of a 2.356-mile circuit = 117.800 miles

1 Graham Hill♦	Brabham BT36-Ford	50	1h02m36.2
2 Ronnie Peterson	March 712M-Ford	50	1h02m36.8
3 Derek Bell	March 712M-Ford	50	1h02m56.0
4 François Cevert	Tecno 71-Ford	50	1h03m15.6
5 Tim Schenken	Brabham BT36-Ford	50	1h03m16.0
6 Wilson Fittipaldi	Lotus 69-Ford	50	1h03m37.6
7 Alistair Walker	Brabham BT30-Ford	49	

Winner's average speed: 112.901 mph. Pole position: Peterson, 1m13.4. Fastest lap: Peterson, 1m13.4

Ronnie Peterson, Formula Two champion in 1971

Eifelrennen

2 May 1971. Nürburgring. 10 laps of a 14.189-mile circuit = 141.890 miles

1 François Cevert	Tecno 71-Ford	10	1h20m19.2
2 Emerson Fittipaldi♦	Lotus 69-Ford	10	1h20m37.0
3 Carlos Reutemann	Brabham BT30-Ford	10	1h20m42.1
4 Peter Westbury	Brabham BT36-Ford	10	1h20m48.2
5 Graham Hill♦	Brabham BT36-Ford	10	1h20m48.4
6 Niki Lauda	March 712M-Ford	10	1h21m08.8
7 Wilson Fittipaldi	Lotus 69-Ford	10	1h21m43.7
8 Helmut Marko	Lola T240-Ford	10	1h21m54.7

Winner's average speed: 105.994 mph. Pole position: Bell (March 712M-Ford), 7m59.7. Fastest lap: Peterson (March 712M-Ford), 7m57.1

Gran Premio de Madrid

16 May 1971. Jarama. 60 laps of a 2.115-mile circuit = 126.900 miles

1 Emerson Fittipaldi♦	Lotus 69-Ford	60	1h29m42.9
2 Dieter Quester	March 712M-BMW	60	1h29m57.7
3 Carlos Reutemann	Brabham BT30-Ford	60	1h30m12.3
4 John Cannon	March 712M-Ford	60	1h30m17.0
5 Jean-Pierre Jaussaud	March 712M-Ford	60	1h30m37.4
6 Wilson Fittipaldi	Lotus 69-Ford	60	1h30m42.9
7 Niki Lauda	March 712M-Ford	60	1h30m46.4

Winner's average speed: 84.885 mph. Pole position: Peterson (March 712M-Ford), 1m28.0. Fastest lap: Schenken (Brabham BT36-Ford), 1m28.2

Hilton Transport Trophy

31 May 1971. Crystal Palace. 50 laps of a 1.390-mile circuit = 69.500 miles

1 Emerson Fittipaldi♦	Lotus 69-Ford	50	42m03.0
2 Tim Schenken	Brabham BT36-Ford	50	42m07.4
3 Ronnie Peterson	March 712M-Ford	50	42m08.2
4 Jean-Pierre Jaussaud	March 712M-Ford	50	42m08.8
5 Carlos Reutemann	Brabham BT30-Ford	49	
6 Gerry Birrell	Lotus 69-Ford	49	
7 Silvio Moser	Brabham BT30-Ford	49	

Winner's average speed: 99.168 mph. Pole position: Peterson, 49.4s. Fastest lap: Schenken, Peterson, Jaussaud and E Fittipaldi, all 49.6s

Grand Prix de Rouen-les-Essarts

27 June 1971. Rouen-les-Essarts. 25 laps of a 4.065-mile circuit = 101.625 miles

1 Ronnie Peterson	March 712M-Ford	25	55m36.3
2 Dieter Quester	March 712M-BMW	25	55m42.8
3 Graham Hill♦	Brabham BT36-Ford	25	55m43.6
4 Niki Lauda	March 712M-Ford	25	56m01.1
5 François Migault	Lotus 69-Ford	25	56m41.8
6 Tim Schenken	Brabham BT36-Ford	22	
7 Carlos Pace	March 712M-Ford	22	

Reutemann and Mazet finished sixth and seventh on the road respectively but were disqualified for missing the chicane. Winner's average speed: 109.657 mph. Pole position: Peterson, 2m09.7. Fastest lap: Cevert (Tecno 71-Ford), 2m11.0

Mantorp Park Grand Prix

8 August 1971. Mantorp Park. 72 laps of a 2.543-mile circuit = 183.096 miles

1 Ronnie Peterson	March 712M-Ford	72	1h45m45.8
2 Tim Schenken	Brabham BT36-Ford	72	1h46m43.7
3 Carlos Reutemann	Brabham BT36-Ford	72	1h46m50.1
4 Wilson Fittipaldi	March 712M-Ford	72	1h47m25.2
5 John Watson	Brabham BT30-Ford	72	1h47m50.6
6 Gerry Birrell	Lotus 69-Ford	72	1h47m57.7

Winner's average speed: 103.506 mph. Pole position: Peterson, 1m38.0. Fastest lap: Peterson, 1m27.1

Flugplatzrennen Tulln-Langenlebarn

12 September 1971. Tulln-Langenlebarn. 70 laps of a 1.780-mile circuit = 124.600 miles

1 Ronnie Peterson	March 712M-Ford	70	1h24m32.26
2 Tim Schenken	Brabham BT36-Ford	70	1h24m59.91
3 Dieter Quester	March 712M-BMW	70	1h25m12.94
4 Wilson Fittipaldi	March 712M-Ford	70	1h25m44.29
5 John Watson	Brabham BT30-Ford	69	
6 Bob Wollek	Brabham BT36-Ford	69	

Winner's average speed: 88.434 mph. Pole position: Peterson, 1m00.48. Fastest lap: Schenken, 1m10.79

Grand Prix d'Albi

26 September 1971. Albi. 63 laps of a 2.090-mile circuit = 131.670 miles

1 Emerson Fittipaldi♦	Lotus 69-Ford	63	1h16m49.1
2 Carlos Reutemann	Brabham BT36-Ford	63	1h17m49.6
3 Jean-Pierre Jarier	March 712M-Ford	63	1h17m59.5
4 François Migault	March 712M-Ford	62	
5 Graham Hill♦	Brabham BT36-Ford	61	
6 Ronnie Peterson	March 712M-Ford	61	
7 Jean-Pierre Jaussaud	March 712M-Ford	58	
8 Peter Westbury	Brabham BT36-Ford	57	

Winner's average speed: 102.843 mph. Pole position: Reutemann, 1m11.0. Fastest lap: Reutemann, 1m11.7

Gran Premio di Roma

10 October 1971. Vallelunga. 70 laps of a 1.988-mile circuit = 139.160 miles

1 Ronnie Peterson	March 712M-Ford	70	1h25m47.2
2 Dieter Quester	March 712M-BMW	70	1h26m07.0
3 Carlos Reutemann	Brabham BT36-Ford	70	1h26m38.9
4 Mike Beuttler	March 712M-Ford	70	1h26m51.2
5 Gerry Birrell	Lotus 69-Ford	70	1h27m07.7
6 John Watson	Brabham BT30-Ford	70	1h27m10.0

Winner's average speed: 97.330 mph. Pole position: Emerson Fittipaldi (Lotus 69-Ford), 1m11.75. Fastest lap: E Fittipaldi, 1m12.8

Gran Premio di Madunina

17 October 1971. Vallelunga. 65 laps of a 1.988-mile circuit = 129.220 miles

1 Mike Beuttler	March 712M-Ford	65	1h19m49.1

Formula Two

2	Dieter Quester	March 712M-BMW	65	1h20m00.1
3	Jean-Pierre Jarier	March 712M-Ford	65	1h20m45.4
4	Carlos Ruesch	Brabham BT36-Ford	65	1h20m59.6
5	Vittorio Brambilla	March 712M-Ford	65	1h21m01.0
6	Silvio Moser	Brabham BT36-Ford	64	

Winner's average speed: 97.136 mph. Pole position: E Fittipaldi (Lotus 69-Ford), 1m11.68. Fastest lap: Quester and Beuttler, 1m12.5

FINAL CHAMPIONSHIP POSITIONS

Drivers

1	Ronnie Peterson	54	14=	John Watson	5
2	Carlos Reutemann	38		Peter Westbury	5
3	Dieter Quester	31	16	John Cannon	4
4	Tim Schenken	29	17	Carlos Ruesch	3
5	François Cevert	22	18=	Vittorio Brambilla	2
6	Wilson Fittipaldi	16		Silvio Moser	2
7	Mike Beuttler	12	20=	Brian Hart	1
8	Jean-Pierre Jarier	10		Helmut Marko	1
9	Jean-Pierre Jaussaud	9		Carlos Pace	1
10	Niki Lauda	8		Alistair Walker	1
11=	Gerry Birrell	7		Bob Wollek	1
	François Migault	7		♦ Graded driver ineligible	
13	Derek Bell	6		for points	

1972

Mallory Park F2

12 March 1972. Mallory Park. 100 laps of a 1.350-mile circuit = 135.000 miles

1	Dave Morgan	Brabham BT35-Ford	100	1h14m32.8
2	Niki Lauda	March 722-Ford	100	1h14m36.0
3	Carlos Reutemann	Brabham BT38-Ford	100	1h14m42.0
4	Jody Scheckter	McLaren M21-Ford	100	1h15m15.0
5	Mike Hailwood	Surtees TS10-Ford	99	
6	Xavier Perrot	March 722-Ford	99	

Winner's average speed: 108.657 mph. Pole position: Peterson (March 722-Ford), 43.4s. Fastest lap: Peterson, 43.0s

Esso Uniflo Jochen Rindt Trophy

3 April 1972. Thruxton. 50 laps of a 2.356-mile circuit = 117.800 miles

1	Ronnie Peterson♦	March 722-Ford	50	1h00m19.4
2	François Cevert♦	March 722-Ford	50	1h00m44.0
3	Niki Lauda	March 722-Ford	49	
4	Patrick Dal Bo	Pygmee MDB17-Ford	48	
5	Claudio Francisci	Brabham BT38-Ford	47	

No other finishers. Winner's average speed: 117.169 mph. Pole position: Reutemann (Brabham BT38-Ford), 1m12.6. Fastest lap: Peterson, 1m11.6

Jim Clark-Rennen

16 April 1972. Hockenheim. 40 laps of a 4.219-mile circuit = 168.760 miles

1	Jean-Pierre Jaussaud	Brabham BT38-Ford	40	1h25m24.2
2	Mike Beuttler	March 722-Ford	40	1h25m37.5
3	Bob Wollek	Brabham BT38-Ford	40	1h25m43.8
4	Xavier Perrot	March 722-Ford	40	1h28m05.3
5	Tom Belso	Brabham BT38-Ford	40	1h29m31.0
6	John Wingfield	Brabham BT36-Ford	39	

Winner's average speed: 118.562 mph. Pole position: Lauda (March 722-Ford), 2m08.0. Fastest lap: Depailler (March 722-Ford), 2m06.0

Grand Prix de Pau

7 May 1972. Pau. 70 laps of a 1.715-mile circuit = 120.050 miles

1	Peter Gethin	Chevron B20-Ford	70	1h33m40.8
2	Patrick Depailler	March 722-Ford	70	1h33m41.7
3	David Purley	March 722-Ford	68	
4	Jean-Pierre Jaussaud	Brabham BT38-Ford	66	
5	Mike Hailwood	Surtees TS10-Ford	66	

6	Reine Wisell♦	GRD 272-Ford	65	
7	Bob Wollek	Brabham BT38-Ford	64	

Winner's average speed: 76.889 mph. Pole position: Depailler, 1m16.5. Fastest lap: Gethin, 1m16.1

Greater London Trophy

29 May 1972. Crystal Palace. 50 laps of a 1.390-mile circuit = 69.500 miles

1	Jody Scheckter	McLaren M21-Ford	50	41m32.4
2	Mike Hailwood	Surtees TS10-Ford	50	41m34.6
3	Carlos Reutemann	Brabham BT38-Ford	50	41m35.8
4	Vic Elford	Chevron B20-Ford	50	41m37.0
5	François Cevert♦	March 722-Ford	50	41m44.2
6	Jean-Pierre Beltoise♦	Brabham BT38-Ford	50	42m14.0
7	Patrick Depailler	March 722-Ford	40	42m15.8
8	Jochen Mass	March 722-Ford	50	42m16.2

Winner's average speed: 100.385 mph. Pole position: Surtees (Surtees TS10-Ford), 49.0s. Fastest lap: Cevert and Scheckter, 48.6s

Jochen Rindt-Rennen/Rhein-Pokal

11 June 1972. Hockenheim. 30 laps of a 4.219-mile circuit = 126.570 miles

1	Emerson Fittipaldi♦	Lotus 69-Ford	30	1h13m39.2
2	Jean-Pierre Jaussaud	Brabham BT38-Ford	30	1h15m05.6
3	Ronnie Peterson♦	March 722-Ford	30	1h15m28.6
4	Mike Beuttler	March 722-Ford	30	1h15m59.1*
5	Xavier Perrot	March 722-Ford	30	1h15m57.8*
6	Tim Schenken♦	Brabham BT38-Ford	30	1h15m58.9*
7	Carlos Reutemann	Brabham BT38-Ford	30	1h16m33.2*
8	Dave Morgan	Brabham BT38-Ford	28	*
9	Carlos Ruesch	Surtees TS10-Ford	30	1h16m43.8*

*Positions decided on points awarded for results of the two heats and not on aggregate times. Winner's average speed: 103.107 mph. Pole position: Lauda (March 722-Ford), 2m02.9. Fastest lap: E Fittipaldi, 2m22.7

Grand Prix de Rouen-les-Essarts

25 June 1972. Rouen-les-Essarts. 30 laps of a 3.444-mile circuit = 103.320 miles

1	Emerson Fittipaldi♦	Lotus 69-Ford	30	54m20.0
2	Mike Hailwood	Surtees TS10-Ford	30	54m28.0
3	Carlos Reutemann	Brabham BT38-Ford	30	54m47.4
4	Dave Morgan	Brabham BT38-Ford	30	54m58.6
5	John Watson	Tui BH2-Ford	30	55m01.6
6	François Cevert♦	March 722-Ford	30	55m02.7
7	Graham Hill♦	Brabham BT38-Ford	30	55m37.3
8	José Dolhem	March 722-Ford	29	
9	Bob Wollek	Brabham BT38-Ford	27	

Winner's average speed: 114.096 mph. Pole position: E Fittipaldi, 1m48.1. Fastest lap: Hailwood, 1m46.8

Jochen Rindt-Rennen

9 July 1972. Österreichring. 34 laps of a 3.673-mile circuit = 124.882 miles

1	Emerson Fittipaldi♦	Lotus 69-Ford	34	59m23.51
2	Mike Hailwood	Surtees TS10-Ford	34	59m39.52
3	Carlos Reutemann	Brabham BT38-Ford	34	1h00m10.03
4	Dave Morgan	Brabham BT38-Ford	34	1h00m10.59
5	Patrick Depailler	March 722-Ford	34	1h00m11.37
6	Bob Wollek	Brabham BT38-Ford	34	1h00m29.57
7	Carlos Ruesch	Surtees TS10-Ford	34	1h00m39.40

Winner's average speed: 126.161 mph. Pole position: E Fittipaldi, 1m42.57. Fastest lap: E Fittipaldi, 1m43.8

Gran Premio Shell

23 July 1972. Imola. 56 laps of a 3.118-mile circuit = 174.608 miles

1	John Surtees♦	Surtees TS10-Ford	56	1h28m08.2
2	Bob Wollek	Brabham BT38-Ford	56	1h28m16.7
3	Niki Lauda	March 722-Ford	56	1h28m32.2
4	Andrea de Adamich	Surtees TS10-Ford	56	1h28m38.6

5	Graham Hill♦	Brabham BT38-Ford	56	1h29m26.0
6	Jody Scheckter	McLaren M21-Ford	56	1h29m48.7
7	Jean-Pierre Jaussaud	Brabham BT38-Ford	53	
8	John Watson	Tui BH2-Ford	52	

Winner's average speed: 118.866 mph. Pole position: Jaussaud, 1m32.05. Fastest lap: Gethin (Chevron B20-Ford), 1m31.9

Hitachi Mantorp Grand Prix

6 August 1972. Mantorp Park. 72 laps of a 2.543-mile circuit = 183.096 miles

1	Mike Hailwood	Surtees TS10-Ford	72	1h45m51.1
2	Jean-Pierre Jabouille	March 722-Ford	72	1h45m57.3
3	Jean-Pierre Jaussaud	Brabham BT38-Ford	72	1h46m41.4
4	Brett Lunger	March 722-Ford	72	1h47m33.4
5	Carlos Ruesch	Surtees TS10-Ford	71	
6	Carlos Reutemann	Brabham BT38-Ford	71	

Winner's average speed: 103.784 mph. Pole position: Gethin (Chevron B21-Ford), 1m25.6. Fastest lap: Gethin, 1m25.9

Gran Premio del Mediterraneo

20 August 1972. Enna-Pergusa. 64 laps of a 3.011-mile circuit = 192.704 miles

1	Henri Pescarolo♦	Brabham BT38-Ford	64	1h33m22.8
2	Patrick Depailler	March 722-Ford	64	1h33m46.2
3	Carlos Ruesch	Surtees TS10-Ford	64	1h34m10.6
4	Wilson Fittipaldi	Brabham BT38-Ford	62	
5	Hiroshi Kazato	March 722-Ford	62	
6	Carlos Reutemann	Brabham BT38-Ford	61	
7	Jean-Pierre Jaussaud	Brabham BT38-Ford	61	

Winner's average speed: 123.819 mph. Pole position: Hailwood (Surtees TS10-Ford), 1m25.7. Fastest lap: Pace (Surtees TS10-Ford), 1m25.1

Salzburger Festspielpreis

3 September 1972. Salzburgring. 60 laps of a 2.633-mile circuit = 157.980 miles

1	Mike Hailwood	Surtees TS10-Ford	60	1h13m31.76
2	Carlos Pace	Surtees TS10-Ford	60	1h13m32.94
3	Dave Morgan	Brabham BT38-Ford	60	1h13m42.78
4	Graham Hill♦	Brabham BT38-Ford	60	1h13m46.89
5	Peter Gethin	Chevron B20-Ford	60	1h14m39.38
6	Niki Lauda	March 722-Ford	60	1h14m47.21
7	Patrick Depailler	March 722-Ford	60	1h15m09.56

Winner's average speed: 128.912 mph. Pole position: Pace, 1m12.15. Fastest lap: Hailwood, 1m11.89

Grand Prix d'Albi

24 September 1972. Albi. 32 laps of a 2.090-mile circuit = 66.880 miles

1	Jean-Pierre Jaussaud	Brabham BT38-Ford	32	37m53.5
2	Patrick Depailler	March 722-Ford	32	37m53.7
3	Bob Wollek	Brabham BT38-Ford	32	38m11.4
4	Tom Belso	Brabham BT38-Ford	32	38m15.2
5	James Hunt	March 712M-Ford	32	38m18.6
6	Carlos Ruesch	Surtees TS10-Ford	32	38m30.4

Winner's average speed: 105.902 mph. Pole position: Jaussaud, 1m09.9. Fastest lap: Depailler, 1m10.1

Preis von Hessen und Württemberg

1 October 1972. Hockenheim. 32 laps of a 4.219-mile circuit = 135.008 miles

1	Tim Schenken♦	Brabham BT38-Ford	32	1h07m22.7
2	Mike Hailwood	Surtees TS10-Ford	32	1h07m40.6
3	Ronnie Peterson♦	March 722-Ford	32	1h07m42.8
4	Wilson Fittipaldi	Brabham BT38-Ford	32	1h07m43.1
5	Graham Hill♦	Brabham BT38-Ford	32	1h07m56.5
6	Tino Brambilla	March 712M-Ford	32	1h07m59.7
7	Henri Pescarolo♦	Brabham BT38-Ford	32	1h08m13.8
8	James Hunt	March 712M-Ford	32	1h08m18.1
9	Niki Lauda	March 722-Ford	32	1h08m30.3
10	Jean-Pierre Jabouille	Elf 2/A367-Ford	32	1h08m49.0

Winner's average speed: 120.224 mph. Pole position: E Fittipaldi (Lotus 69-Ford), 2m03.4. Fastest lap: E Fittipaldi, 2m05.0

FINAL CHAMPIONSHIP POSITIONS

Drivers

1	Mike Hailwood	55	15=	Patrick Dal Bo	6
2	Jean-Pierre Jaussaud	37		Carlos Pace	6
3	Patrick Depailler	27	17=	Tom Belso	5
4	Carlos Reutemann	26		James Hunt	5
5	Niki Lauda	25	19=	Andrea de Adamich	4
6	Dave Morgan	23		Tino Brambilla	4
7	Bob Wollek	17		Claudio Francisci	4
8	Jody Scheckter	15		David Purley	4
9=	Mike Beuttler	12		John Watson	4
	Peter Gethin	12	24=	Vic Elford	3
11	Carlos Ruesch	11		Hiroshi Kazato	3
12	Wilson Fittipaldi	10		Brett Lunger	3
13	Xavier Perrot	8	27	José Dolhem	2
14	Jean-Pierre Jabouille	7	28=	Jochen Mass	1
				John Wingfield	1

♦Graded driver ineligible for points

1973

Radio Luxembourg Trophy

11 March 1973. Mallory Park. 100 laps of a 1.350-mile circuit = 135.000 miles. "B" race

1	Jean-Pierre Jarier	March 732-BMW	100	1h12m09.8
2	Mike Hailwood♦	Surtees TS15-Ford	100	1h13m05.4
3	Dave McConnell	Surtees TS15-Ford	97	
4	Dave Morgan	Chevron B25-Ford	95	
5	John Lepp	Chevron B25-Ford	94	
6	Vittorio Brambilla	March 712M-Ford	94	
7	Bob Salisbury	Surtees TS15-Ford	92	

Winner's average speed: 112.245 mph. Pole position: Beltoise (March 732-BMW), 42.5s. Fastest lap: Jarier, 41.8s

Jim Clark-Rennen

8 April 1973. Hockenheim. 40 laps of a 4.219-mile circuit = 168.760 miles. "A" race

1	Jean-Pierre Jarier	March 732-BMW	40	1h22m27.0
2	Patrick Depailler	Elf 2/A367-Ford	40	1h22m46.9
3	Derek Bell	Surtees TS15-Ford	40	1h23m59.4
4	Henri Pescarolo♦	Motul M1-Ford	40	1h24m55.5
5	Wilson Fittipaldi	Brabham BT40-Ford	40	1h25m20.8
6	Colin Vandervell	March 732-BMW	40	1h25m53.4
7	Jacques Coulon	March 732-BMW	39	

Winner's average speed: 122.809 mph. Pole position: Beltoise (March 732-BMW), 2m02.8. Fastest lap: Jarier, 2m02.4

Esso Uniflo Jochen Rindt Trophy

23 April 1973. Thruxton. 50 laps of a 2.356-mile circuit = 117.800 miles. "A" race

1	Henri Pescarolo♦	Motul M1-Ford	50	1h01m45.4
2	Bob Wollek	Motul M1-Ford	50	1h02m00.2
3	Mike Beuttler	March 732-BMW	50	1h02m01.8
4	Gerry Birrell	Chevron B25-Ford	50	1h02m21.0
5	Dave Morgan	Chevron B25-Ford	50	1h02m33.0
6	Jean-Pierre Jaussaud	Motul M1-Ford	50	1h03m21.8
7	Vittorio Brambilla	March 732-BMW	49	

Winner's average speed: 114.449 mph. Pole position: Depailler (Elf 2/A367-Ford), 1m11.0. Fastest lap: Coulon (March 732-BMW), 1m11.2

Eifelrennen

29 April 1973. Nürburgring. 10 laps of a 14.189-mile circuit = 141.890 miles. "A" race

1	Reine Wisell♦	GRD 273-Ford	10	1h31m22.9
2	Tim Schenken♦	Motul M1-Ford	10	1h31m25.1
3	Patrick Depailler	Elf 2/A367-Ford	10	1h31m40.5
4	Derek Bell	Surtees TS15-Ford	10	1h32m09.0

Formula Two

5	Vittorio Brambilla	March 732-BMW	10	1h32m11.7
6	Bob Wollek	Motul M1-Ford	10	1h32m46.5
7	Richard Scott	Scott-Ford	10	1h33m48.5
8	Silvio Moser	Surtees TS10-Ford	10	1h35m49.2

Winner's average speed: 93.163 mph. Pole position: Stuck (March 732-BMW), 7m30.5. Fastest lap: Bell, 8m36.7

Grand Prix de Pau

6 May 1973. Pau. 70 laps of a 1.715-mile circuit = 120.050 miles. "B" race

1	François Cevert♦	Elf 2/A367-Ford	70	1h30m49.77
2	Jean-Pierre Jarier	March 732-BMW	70	1h31m14.44
3	Tim Schenken♦	Motul M1-Ford	70	1h31m25.70
4	Mike Beuttler	March 732-BMW	69	
5	Bob Wollek	Motul M1-Ford	69	
6	Jean-Pierre Jaussaud	Motul M1-Ford	69	
7	Roger Williamson	GRD 273-Ford	68	
8	Sten Gunnarsson	GRD 273-Ford	68	

Winner's average speed: 79.302 mph. Pole position: Jarier, 1m15.0. Fastest lap: Beltoise (March 732-BMW), 1m15.0

Swedish Gold Cup

20 May 1973. Kinnekulle. 96 laps of a 1.286-mile circuit = 123.456 miles. "B" race

1	Jochen Mass	Surtees TS15-Ford	96	1h20m49.3
2	Patrick Depailler	Elf 2/A367-Ford	96	1h21m20.4
3	Tim Schenken♦	Motul M1-Ford	96	1h21m48.8
4	Sten Gunnarsson	GRD 273-Ford	94	
5	Hakan Dahlqvist	GRD 273-Ford	93	

No other finishers. Winner's average speed: 91.651 mph. Pole position: Mass, 48.6s. Fastest lap: Mass, 49.5s

Grand Prix GB

10 June 1973. Nivelles. 56 laps of a 2.314-mile circuit = 129.584 miles. "A" race

1	Jean-Pierre Jarier	March 732-BMW	56	1h10m33.35
2	Jochen Mass	Surtees TS15-Ford	56	1h10m57.23
3	Vittorio Brambilla	March 732-BMW	56	1h11m07.65
4	Mike Beuttler	March 732-BMW	56	1h11m36.97
5	Colin Vandervell	March 732-BMW	56	1h11m37.42
6	Dave Morgan	Chevron B25-Ford	56	1h12m03.73

Winner's average speed: 110.197 mph. Pole position: Jarier, 1m14.12. Fastest lap: Mass, 1m14.17

Jochen Rindt-Rennen/Rhein-Pokal

17 June 1973. Hockenheim. 40 laps of a 4.219-mile circuit = 168.760 miles. "B" race

1	Jochen Mass	Surtees TS15-Ford	40	1h22m20.7
2	Colin Vandervell	March 732-BMW	40	1h22m31.4
3	Jacques Coulon	March 732-BMW	40	1h23m04.7
4	Vittorio Brambilla	March 732-BMW	40	1h23m54.4
5	Henri Pescarolo♦	Motul M1-Ford	40	1h24m48.4
6	Hiroshi Kazato	GRD 273-Ford	40	1h25m58.2
7	Silvio Moser	Surtees TS10-Ford	40	1h26m23.5

Winner's average speed: 122.966 mph. Pole position: Mass, 2m01.6. Fastest lap: Mass, 2m02.7

Grand Prix de Rouen-les-Essarts

24 June 1973. Rouen-les-Essarts. 30 laps of a 3.444-mile circuit = 103.320 miles. "A" race

1	Jean-Pierre Jarier	March 732-BMW	30	56m20.7
2	Jochen Mass	Surtees TS15-Ford	30	56m40.0
3	Tim Schenken♦	Motul M1-Ford	30	56m41.4
4	Jacques Coulon	March 732-BMW	30	57m03.6
5	Wilson Fittipaldi	Brabham BT40-BMW	30	57m10.6
6	Patrick Depailler	Elf 2/A367-Ford	30	57m40.9
7	Brett Lunger	Chevron B25-Ford	29	

Winner's average speed: 110.022 mph. Pole position: Jarier, 1m43.8. Fastest lap: Jarier, 1m49.3

Gran Premio della Lotteria di Monza

29 June 1973. Monza. 40 laps of a 3.573-mile circuit = 142.920 miles. "B" race

1	Roger Williamson	March 732-BMW	40	1h09m05.6
2	Patrick Depailler	Elf 2/A367-Ford	40	1h09m22.0
3	Jacques Coulon	March 732-BMW	40	1h10m25.6
4	Derek Bell	Surtees TS15-Ford	39	
5	Hiroshi Kazato	GRD 273-Ford	37	

No other finishers. Winner's average speed: 124.110 mph. Pole position: Williamson, 1m42.2. Fastest lap: Williamson, 1m41.0

Mantorp Park F2

29 July 1973. Mantorp Park. 72 laps of a 2.543-mile circuit = 183.096 miles. "A" race

1	Jean-Pierre Jarier	March 732-BMW	72	1h42m05.0
2	Jochen Mass	Surtees TS15-Ford	72	1h42m25.7
3	John Watson	Chevron B25-Ford	72	1h42m30.6
4	Patrick Depailler	Elf 2/A367-Ford	72	1h42m50.6
5	Tom Pryce	Motul M1-Ford	72	1h43m17.6
6	Jean-Pierre Jaussaud	Motul M1-Ford	72	1h43m43.1

Winner's average speed: 107.616 mph. Pole position: Depailler, 1m22.8. Fastest lap: Depailler, 1m24.0

Kannonloppet

12 August 1973. Karlskoga. 48 laps of a 1.864-mile circuit = 89.472 miles. "B" race

1	Jean-Pierre Jarier	March 732-BMW	48	59m14.4
2	Peter Gethin	Chevron B25-Ford	48	59m14.6
3	Torsten Palm	Surtees TS15-Ford	48	59m16.9
4	Tim Schenken♦	Motul M1-Ford	48	1h00m01.4
5	Ronnie Peterson♦	Lotus 74-Ford	48	1h00m10.8
6	Jacques Coulon	March 732-BMW	48	1h00m20.0
7	Colin Vandervell	March 732-BMW	47	
8	Bill Gubelmann	March 732-BMW	47	

Winner's average speed: 90.620 mph. Pole position: Gethin, 1m12.5. Fastest lap: Palm, 1m12.8

Gran Premio del Mediterraneo

26 August 1973. Enna-Pergusa. 60 laps of a 3.011-mile circuit = 180.660 miles. "A" race

1	Jean-Pierre Jarier	March 732-BMW	60	1h23m53.6
2	Vittorio Brambilla	March 732-BMW	60	1h24m22.8
3	Jochen Mass	Surtees TS15-Ford	60	1h25m07.3
4	Tim Schenken♦	Motul M1-Ford	60	1h25m47.0
5	Bob Wollek	Motul M1-Ford	60	1h25m49.2
6	Bill Gubelmann	March 732-BMW	59	
7	Ronnie Peterson♦	Lotus 74-Ford	58	
8	Gabriele Serblin	Brabham BT40-Ford	55	

Winner's average speed: 129.207 mph. Pole position: Jarier, 1m22.73. Fastest lap: Depailler (Elf 2/A367-Ford), 1m22.4

Salzburger Festspielpreis

2 September 1973. Salzburgring. 50 laps of a 2.633-mile circuit = 131.650 miles. "B" race

1	Vittorio Brambilla	March 732-BMW	50	59m47.28
2	Patrick Depailler	Elf 2/A367-Ford	50	59m49.13
3	Jacques Coulon	March 732-BMW	50	1h00m23.69
4	Carlos Pace♦	Surtees TS15-Ford	50	1h00m43.40
5	Bill Gubelmann	March 732-BMW	49	
6	Roland Binder	March 732-BMW	49	
7	Kurt Rieder	March 732-BMW	49	

Winner's average speed: 132.117 mph. Pole position: Depailler, 1m10.67. Fastest lap: Depailler, 1m10.84

Norisring-Rennen

9 September 1973. Norisring. 120 laps of a 1.429-mile circuit = 171.480 miles. "B" race

1	Tim Schenken♦	Motul M1-Ford	120	1h46m40.9
2	Tom Pryce	Motul M1-Ford	120	1h47m59.1
3	Henri Pescarolo♦	Motul M1-BMW	116	

4	Gunnar Nilsson	GRD 273-Ford	112
5	Bob Wollek	Motul M1-Ford	111

No other finishers. Winner's average speed: 96.460 mph. Pole position: Jarier (March 732-BMW), 51.2s. Fastest lap: Jarier, 51.9s

Grand Prix d'Albi

16 September 1973. Albi. 56 laps of a 2.090-mile circuit = 117.040 miles. "A" race

1	Vittorio Brambilla	March 732-BMW	56	1h04m59.2
2	Jean-Pierre Jarier	March 732-BMW	56	1h05m02.6
3	Jean-Pierre Beltoise♦	March 732-BMW	56	1h05m03.6
4	Jacques Coulon	March 732-BMW	56	1h05m29.6
5	Jean-Pierre Jabouille	Elf 2/A367-Ford	56	1h05m48.6
6	Jochen Mass	Surtees TS15-Ford	56	1h05m49.8
7	Tim Schenken♦	Motul M1-Ford	56	1h05m56.6
8	Bertil Roos	GRD 273-Ford	55	

Winner's average speed: 108.059 mph. Pole position: V Brambilla, 1m08.3. Fastest lap: Beltoise, 1m08.9

Gran Premio di Roma

14 October 1973. Vallelunga. 70 laps of a 1.988-mile circuit = 139.160 miles. "A" race

1	Jacques Coulon	March 732-BMW	70	1h24m40.0
2	Vittorio Brambilla	March 732-BMW	70	1h25m10.6
3	Jo Vonlanthen	GRD 273-Ford	67	
4	Roland Binder	March 732-BMW	63	

No other finishers. Winner's average speed: 98.617 mph. Pole position: V Brambilla, 1m11.35. Fastest lap: V Brambilla, 1m10.7

FINAL CHAMPIONSHIP POSITIONS

Drivers

1	Jean-Pierre Jarier	78	21=	Gerry Birrell	4
2	Jochen Mass	42		Hiroshi Kazato	4
3	Patrick Depailler	38		Torsten Palm	4
4	Vittorio Brambilla	35(44)*		Jo Vonlanthen	4
5	Jacques Coulon	33		John Watson	4
6	Bob Wollek	23	26=	Hakan Dahlqvist	3
7	Mike Beuttler	15		Jean-Pierre Jabouille	3
8	Derek Bell	13		John Lepp	3
9	Colin Vandervell	12	29=	Silvio Moser	2
10=	Tom Pryce	11		Richard Scott	2
	Roger Williamson	11	31=	Brett Lunger	1
12	Dave Morgan	8		Kurt Rieder	1
13=	Wilson Fittipaldi	6		Bertil Roos	1
	Peter Gethin	6		Bob Salisbury	1
	Bill Gubelmann	6		Gabriele Serblin	1
	Jean-Pierre Jaussaud	6			
	Dave McConnell	6			
	Gunnar Nilsson	6			
19=	Roland Biland	5			
	Sten Gunnarsson	5			

♦Graded driver ineligible for points.
*Best nine "A" and four "B" results count. Brambilla won at the Salzburgring, but as it was his fifth "B" race he could not count the points

1974

Gran Premio de Barcelona

24 March 1974. Montjuich Park. 54 laps of a 2.355-mile circuit = 127.170 miles

1	Hans-Joachim Stuck	March 742-BMW	54	1h18m47.68
2	Patrick Depailler	March 742-BMW	54	1h18m51.50
3	Jean-Pierre Jabouille	Elf 2/A367-BMW	54	1h19m45.65
4	Gabriele Serblin	March 742-BMW	54	1h20m02.75
5	Andy Sutcliffe	March 732-BMW	53	
6	Michel Leclère	Elf 2/A367-BMW	53	

Winner's average speed: 96.837 mph. Pole position: Stuck, 1m25.8. Fastest lap: Stuck, 1m25.58

Jim Clark-Rennen

7 April 1974. Hockenheim. 40 laps of a 4.219-mile circuit = 168.760 miles

1	Hans-Joachim Stuck	March 742-BMW	40	1h21m37.1
2	John Watson	Surtees TS15-Ford	40	1h22m38.2
3	Michel Leclère	Elf 2/A367-BMW	40	1h22m39.2
4	Patrick Depailler	March 742-BMW	40	1h22m41.2
5	Patrick Tambay	Elf 2/A367-BMW	40	1h22m56.2
6	Bertil Roos	Chevron B27-Ford	40	1h23m00.1

Winner's average speed: 124.060 mph. Pole position: Stuck, 2m00.2. Fastest lap: Stuck, 2m00.9

Grand Prix de Pau

5 May 1974. Pau. 75 laps of a 1.715-mile circuit = 128.625 miles

1	Patrick Depailler	March 742-BMW	75	1h54m33.57
2	Jacques Laffite	March 742-BMW	74	
3	Andy Sutcliffe	March 732-BMW	74	
4	Jean-Pierre Jabouille	Elf 2/A367-Ford	74	
5	Michel Leclère	Elf 2/A367-BMW	74	
6	Tim Schenken♦	Surtees TS15A-BMW	73	
7	David Purley	March 742-BMW	72	

Winner's average speed: 67.367 mph. Pole position: Depailler, 1m16.17. Fastest lap: Laffite, 1m28.06

Salzburger Festspielpreis

2 June 1974. Salzburgring. 50 laps of a 2.633-mile circuit = 131.650 miles

1	Jacques Laffite	March 742-BMW	50 1h00m33.00
2	David Purley	Chevron B27-BMW	50 1h00m37.98
3	José Dolhem	Surtees TS15-Ford	50 1h00m38.58
4	Patrick Tambay	Elf 2/A367-BMW	50 1h01m32.00
5	Maurizio Flammini	March 742-BMW	49
6	Torsten Palm	GRD 273-BMW	49

Winner's average speed: 130.454 mph. Pole position: Pryce (Chevron B27-BMW), 1m11.68. Fastest lap: Dolhem, 1m11.47

Jochen Rindt-Rennen/Rhein Pokal

9 June 1974. Hockenheim. 35 laps of a 4.219-mile circuit = 147.665 miles

1	Jean-Pierre Jabouille	Elf 2/A367-BMW	35	1h11m43.9
2	Jacques Laffite	March 742-BMW	35	1h11m56.0
3	Hans-Joachim Stuck	March 742-BMW	35	1h12m01.3
4	Tom Pryce	Chevron B27-BMW	35	1h12m22.9
5	Michel Leclère	March 742-BMW	35	1h13m21.6
6	Andy Sutcliffe	March 732/742-BMW	35	1h13m30.7

Winner's average speed: 123.514 mph. Pole position: Stuck, 2m00.1. Fastest lap: Jabouille, 2m01.2

Euro Mugello

14 July 1974. Mugello. 50 laps of a 3.259-mile circuit = 162.950 miles

1	Patrick Depailler	March 742-BMW	50	1h32m46.4
2	Jean-Pierre Paoli	March 742-BMW	50	1h33m04.2
3	Tom Pryce	Chevron B27-BMW	50	1h33m50.9
4	Jacques Coulon	March 742-BMW	50	1h34m13.2
5	Giancarlo Martini	March 742-BMW	50	1h35m41.4
6	Brian Henton	March 742-BMW	49	

Winner's average speed: 105.386 mph. Pole position: Laffite (March 742-BMW), 1m46.5. Fastest lap: Jabouille (Elf 2/A367-BMW), 1m49.8

Kannonloppet

11 August 1974. Karlskoga. 68 laps of a 1.864-mile circuit = 126.752 miles

1	Ronnie Peterson♦	March 742-BMW	68	1h23m00.4
2	Patrick Depailler	March 742-BMW	68	1h23m00.7
3	Jacques Laffite	March 742-BMW	68	1h23m19.7
4	Masami Kuwashima	March 742-BMW	68	1h23m20.0
5	Gabriele Serblin	March 742-BMW	67	
6	Alain Cudini	Elf 2/A367-BMW	67	
7	Torsten Palm	GRD 273-BMW	67	

Winner's average speed: 91.621 mph. Pole position: Depailler, 1m12.2. Fastest lap: Depailler, 1m12.1

Formula Two

Gran Premio del Mediterraneo

25 August 1974. Enna-Pergusa. 60 laps of a 3.011-mile circuit = 180.660 miles

1	Hans-Joachim Stuck	March 742-BMW	60	1h24m31.9
2	David Purley	Chevron B27-BMW	60	1h25m34.6
3	Gabriele Serblin	March 742-BMW	60	1h25m55.2
4	Michel Leclère	Elf 2/A367-BMW	59	accident
5	Duilio Truffo	March 742-BMW	58	
6	Cosimo Turizio	March 742-BMW	58	

Winner's average speed: 128.231 mph. Pole position: Stuck, 1m22.4. Fastest lap: Stuck, 1m22.6

Preis von Hessen und Württemberg

29 September 1974. Hockenheim. 40 laps of a 4.219-mile circuit = 168.760 miles

1	Patrick Depailler	March 742-BMW	40	1h23m26.4
2	Hans-Joachim Stuck	March 742-BMW	40	1h23m34.7
3	Jean-Pierre Jabouille	Elf 2/A367-BMW	40	1h23m52.5
4	Patrick Tambay	Elf 2/A367-BMW	40	1h24m38.5
5	Jacques Coulon	March 742-BMW	40	1h24m55.7
6	Alessandro Pesenti-Rossi	March 742-BMW	40	1h27m28.2

Winner's average speed: 121.352 mph. Pole position: Laffite (March 742-BMW), 2m02.1. Fastest lap: Jabouille, 2m01.2

Gran Premio di Roma

13 October 1974. Vallelunga. 70 laps of a 1.988-mile circuit = 139.160 miles

1	Patrick Depailler	March 742-BMW	70	1h22m48.59
2	Hans-Joachim Stuck	March 742-BMW	70	1h23m35.72
3	Jacques Laffite	March 742-BMW	70	1h23m37.30
4	Patrick Tambay	Elf 2/A367-BMW	70	1h24m35.83
5	Tom Pryce	Chevron B27-BMW	70	1h24m43.38
6	Tim Schenken♦	Surtees TS15A-BMW	69	
7	Alessandro Pesenti-Rossi	March 742-BMW	68	

Winner's average speed: 100.829 mph. Pole position: Depailler, 1m09.94. Fastest lap: Depailler, 1m09.79

FINAL CHAMPIONSHIP POSITIONS

Drivers

1	Patrick Depailler	54	14=	José Dolhem	4
2	Hans-Joachim Stuck	43		Masami Kuwashima	4
3	Jacques Laffite	31	16=	Alain Cudini	2
4	Jean-Pierre Jabouille	20		Maurizio Flammini	2
5	David Purley	13		Giancarlo Martini	2
6	Michel Leclère	12		Torsten Palm	2
7	Patrick Tambay	11		Alessandro Pesenti-Rossi	2
8	Gabriele Serblin	10		Duilio Truffo	2
9	Tom Pryce	9	22=	Brian Henton	1
10	Andy Sutcliffe	7		Bertil Roos	1
11=	Jean-Pierre Paoli	6		Cosimo Turizio	1
	John Watson	6	♦	Graded driver ineligible	
13	Jacques Coulon	5		for points	

1975

Grande Premio do Estoril

9 March 1975. Estoril. 50 laps of a 2.703-mile circuit = 135.150 miles

1	Jacques Laffite	Martini MK16-BMW	50	1h35m05.83
2	Jo Vonlanthen	March 742-BMW	50	1h35m36.02
3	Lamberto Leoni	March 752-BMW	50	1h35m36.40
4	Giorgio Francia	Osella FA2/75-BMW	49	
5	Duilio Truffo	March 742-BMW	49	
6	Giancarlo Martini	March 752-BMW	48	

Winner's average speed: 85.271 mph. Pole position: Leclère (March 752-BMW), 1m34.61. Fastest lap: Francia, 1m44.06

Wella European Trophy/ Jochen Rindt Trophy

31 March 1975. Thruxton. 60 laps of a 2.356-mile circuit = 141.360 miles

1	Jacques Laffite	Martini MK16-BMW	60	1h13m07.8
2	Patrick Tambay	March 752-BMW	60	1h13m51.4
3	Giancarlo Martini	March 752-BMW	59	
4	Hector Rebaque	Chevron B29-Ford	59	
5	Jean-Pierre Jabouille	Elf 2J-BMW	59	
6	Duilio Truffo	Osella FA2/75-BMW	59	

Winner's average speed: 115.980 mph. Pole position: Laffite, 1m10.1. Fastest lap: Henton (March 752-Ford) and Laffite, 1m11.0

Jacques Laffite: five wins from the first six races of the 1975 season

Jim Clark-Rennen

13 April 1975. Hockenheim. 40 laps of a 4.219-mile circuit = 168.760 miles

1	Gérard Larrousse	Elf 2/A367-BMW	40	1h22m57.9
2	Hans-Joachim Stuck♦	March 752-BMW	40	1h23m22.2
3	Brian Henton	March 752-Ford	40	1h24m01.4
4	Loris Kessel	March 742-BMW	40	1h24m38.8
5	Giorgio Francia	Osella FA2/75-BMW	40	1h24m51.2
6	Claude Bourgoignie	March 752-BMW	40	1h25m07.9
7	Alessandro Pesenti-Rossi	March 732-BMW	40	1h25m29.1

Winner's average speed: 122.047 mph. Pole position: Tambay (March 752-BMW), 2m12.3. Fastest lap: Laffite (Martini MK16-BMW), 2m01.7

Eifelrennen

26 April 1975. Nürburgring. 14 laps of a 14.189-mile circuit = 198.646 miles

1	Jacques Laffite	Martini MK16-BMW	14	1h46m24.2
2	Patrick Tambay	March 752-BMW	14	1h47m39.0
3	Harald Ertl	Chevron B27-BMW	14	1h47m06.2
4	Jean-Pierre Jabouille	Elf 2J-BMW	14	1h51m06.2
5	Sandro Cinotti	March 752-BMW	14	1h51m07.6
6	Giorgio Francia	Osella FA2/75-BMW	14	1h51m09.0

Winner's average speed: 112.015 mph. Pole position: Laffite, 7m21.7. Fastest lap: Stuck (March 752-BMW), 7m24.5

Grand Prix de Pau

19 May 1975. Pau. 73 laps of a 1.715-mile circuit = 125.195 miles

1	Jacques Laffite	Martini MK16-BMW	73	1h32m10.7
2	Jean-Pierre Jabouille	Elf 2J-BMW	73	1h32m27.2
3	Patrick Depailler♦	March 752-BMW	73	1h33m07.1
4	Gérard Larrousse	Elf 2/A367-BMW	72	
5	Michel Leclère	March 752-BMW	72	
6	Duilio Truffo	Osella FA2/75-BMW	72	
7	Claude Bourgoignie	March 752-BMW	69	

Winner's average speed: 81.491 mph. Pole position: Laffite, 1m13.61. Fastest lap: Laffite, 1m14.68

Jochen Rindt-Rennen/Rhein Pokal

8 June 1975. Hockenheim. 40 laps of a 4.219-mile circuit = 168.760 miles

1	Jacques Laffite	Martini MK16-BMW	40	1h22m51.2

2	Claude Bourgoignie	March 752-BMW	40	1h23m42.2
3	Maurizio Flammini	March 742-BMW	40	1h24m01.2
4	Loris Kessel	March 742-BMW	40	1h24m25.7
5	Giorgio Francia	Osella FA2/75-BMW	40	1h24m38.5
6	Duilio Truffo	Osella FA2/75-BMW	40	1h25m05.5

Winner's average speed: 122.211 mph. Pole position: Laffite, 2m01.1. Fastest lap: Leclère (March 752-BMW), 2m01.6.

Salzburger Festspielpreis

15 June 1975. Salzburgring. 55 laps of a 2.633-mile circuit = 144.815 miles

1	Jean-Pierre Jabouille	Elf 2J-BMW	55	1h06m23.48
2	Hans Binder	March 752-BMW	55	1h06m28.24
3	Gabriele Serblin	March 752-BMW	55	1h06m45.93
4	Claude Bourgoignie	March 752-BMW	55	1h07m01.46
5	Giorgio Francia	Osella FA2/75-BMW	55	1h07m29.87
6	Maurizio Flammini	March 742-BMW	55	1h07m29.87

Winner's average speed: 130.874 mph. Pole position: Leclère (March 752-BMW), 1m10.54. Fastest lap: Jabouille, 1m10.97.

Grand Prix de Rouen-les-Essarts

29 June 1975. Rouen-les-Essarts. 40 laps of a 3.444-mile circuit = 137.760 miles

1	Michel Leclère	March 752-BMW	40	1h13m30.48
2	Patrick Tambay	March 752-BMW	40	1h13m37.13
3	Claude Bourgoignie	March 752-BMW	40	1h14m44.42
4	Jean-Pierre Jaussaud	March 752-Ford	40	1h14m46.25
5	Bernard de Dryver	March 752-BMW	39	

No other finishers. Winner's average speed: 112.445 mph. Pole position: Jabouille (Elf 2J-BMW), 1m47.28. Fastest lap: Jaussaud, 1m48.74

Euro Mugello/Trofeo Etienne Aigner

13 July 1975. Mugello. 50 laps of a 3.259-mile circuit = 162.950 miles

1	Maurizio Flammini	March 742-BMW	50	1h34m26.2
2	Alessandro Pesenti-Rossi	March 742-BMW	50	1h34m37.1
3	"Gianfranco"	March 742-BMW	50	1h36m49.3
4	Carlo Giorgio	March 742-Ford	50	1h37m30.4
5	Duilio Truffo	Osella FA2/75-BMW	49	
6	Bernard de Dryver	March 752-BMW	49	

Winner's average speed: 103.530 mph. Pole position: Truffo, 1m48.31. Fastest lap: Truffo, 1m50.5

Gran Premio del Mediterraneo

27 July 1975. Enna-Pergusa. 60 laps of a 3.076-mile circuit = 184.560 miles

1	Jacques Laffite	Martini MK16-BMW	60	1h39m58.3
2	Gérard Larrousse	Elf 2/A367-BMW	60	1h40m03.3
3	Gabriele Serblin	March 752-BMW	60	1h41m23.2
4	Giorgio Francia	Osella FA2/75-BMW	60	1h41m44.7
5	Duilio Truffo	Osella FA2/75-BMW	60	1h41m56.3
6	Alessandro Pesenti-Rossi	March 742-BMW	60	1h42m32.1

Winner's average speed: 110.767 mph. Pole position: Tambay (March 752-BMW), 1m35.66. Fastest lap: Leclère (March 752-BMW), 1m36.4

BRDC European Trophy

31 August 1975. Silverstone. 50 laps of a 2.932-mile circuit = 146.600 miles

1	Michel Leclère	March 752-BMW	50	1h11m05.56
2	Gérard Larrousse	Elf 2J-BMW	50	1h11m12.46
3	Brian Henton	Wheatcroft R18-Ford	50	1h11m15.31
4	Patrick Tambay	March 752-BMW	50	1h12m04.12
5	Gabriele Serblin	March 752-BMW	50	1h12m13.66
6	Giancarlo Martini	March 752-BMW	50	1h12m14.77

Winner's average speed: 123.726 mph. Pole position: Leclère, 1m23.24. Fastest lap: Jabouille (Elf 2J-BMW), 1m24.15

Grand Prix Elf

14 September 1975. Zolder. 48 laps of a 2.648-mile circuit = 127.104 miles

1	Michel Leclère	March 752-BMW	48	1h12m46.82
2	Patrick Tambay	March 752-BMW	48	1h13m14.40
3	Maurizio Flammini	March 742-BMW	48	1h13m38.89
4	Hans Binder	Chevron B29-BMW	48	1h14m22.85
5	Giorgio Francia	Osella FA2/75-BMW	48	1h14m35.06
6	Ray Mallock	March 742/75B-Ford	48	1h15m05.04

Winner's average speed: 104.784 mph. Pole position: Laffite (Martini MK16-BMW), 1m28.75. Fastest lap: Larrousse (Elf 2J-BMW), 1m28.69

Grand Prix de Nogaro

28 September 1975. Nogaro. 65 laps of a 1.939-mile circuit = 126.035 miles

1	Patrick Tambay	March 752-BMW	65	1h20m44.08
2	Michel Leclère	March 752-BMW	65	1h20m52.60
3	Jean-Pierre Jabouille	Elf 2J-BMW	65	1h21m29.78
4	Jean-Pierre Jaussaud	March 752-BMW	64	
5	Alessandro Pesenti-Rossi	March 742-BMW	64	
6	Alberto Colombo	March 752-BMW	64	

Winner's average speed: 93.666 mph. Pole position: Tambay, 1m12.62. Fastest lap: Jabouille, 1m13.21

Gran Premio di Roma

12 October 1975. Vallelunga. 70 laps of a 1.988-mile circuit = 139.160 miles

1	Vittorio Brambilla	March 752-BMW	70	1h26m08.7
2	Jacques Laffite	Martini MK16-BMW	70	1h26m48.0
3	Maurizio Flammini	March 742-BMW	70	1h26m49.0
4	Alessandro Pesenti-Rossi	March 742-BMW	70	1h27m21.3
5	Giancarlo Martini	March 752-BMW	70	1h27m55.6
6	Gérard Larrousse	Elf 2J-BMW	69	

Winner's average speed: 96.925 mph. Pole position: Leclère (March 752-BMW), 1m10.23. Fastest lap: Laffite, 1m10.81

FINAL CHAMPIONSHIP POSITIONS

Drivers

1	Jacques Laffite	60		15	Giancarlo Martini	8
2=	Michel Leclère	36		16	Loris Kessel	7
	Patrick Tambay	36		17=	Jean-Pierre Jaussaud	6
4	Gérard Larrousse	26			Jo Vonlanthen	6
5	Jean-Pierre Jabouille	24		19=	Harald Ertl	4
6	Maurizio Flammini	22			"Gianfranco"	4
7=	Claude Bourgoignie	16			Lamberto Leoni	4
	Giorgio Francia	16		22=	Bernard de Dryver	3
9	Alessandro Pesenti-Rossi	13			Carlo Giorgio	3
					Hector Rebaque	3
10=	Brian Henton	10		25	Sandro Cinotti	2
	Gabriele Serblin	10		26=	Alberto Colombo	1
	Duilio Truffo	10			Ray Mallock	1
13=	Hans Binder	9		♦	Graded driver ineligible for points
	Vittorio Brambilla	9			

1976

Jim Clark-Rennen

11 April 1976. Hockenheim. 40 laps of a 4.219-mile circuit = 168.760 miles

1	Hans-Joachim Stuck ♦	March 762-BMW	40	1h21m45.6
2	René Arnoux	Martini MK16-Renault	40	1h23m03.0
3	Patrick Tambay	Martini MK19-Renault	40	1h23m15.4
4	Willi Deutsch	March 762-BMW	40	1h23m20.2
5	Roberto Marazzi	Chevron B35-BMW	40	1h23m56.7
6	Harald Ertl	March 752-BMW	40	1h24m42.9
7	Hans Heyer	Toj F201-BMW	40	1h25m12.3

Formula Two

Winner's average speed: 123.845 mph. Pole position: Stuck,
1m58.9. Fastest lap: Stuck, 1m59.8

Jochen Rindt Trophy

19 April 1976. Thruxton. 55 laps of a 2.356-mile circuit
= 129.580 miles

1	Maurizio Flammini	March 762-BMW	55	1h06m51.54
2	Alex Ribeiro	March 762-BMW	55	1h07m18.35
3	Patrick Tambay	Martini MK19-Renault	55	1h07m19.72
4	Eddie Cheever	March 762-Hart	55	1h07m29.10
5	Ingo Hoffman	March 762-Hart	54	
6	François Migault	Osella FA2/76-BMW	54	

Winner's average speed: 116.287 mph. Pole position: Flammini,
1m10.22. Fastest lap: Flammini, 1m10.73

Gran Premio di Roma

9 May 1976. Vallelunga. 65 laps of a 1.988-mile circuit
= 129.220 miles

1	Jean-Pierre Jabouille	Elf 2J-Renault	65	1h18m03.1
2	Patrick Tambay	Martini MK19-Renault	65	1h18m12.2
3	Alex Ribeiro	March 762-BMW	65	1h18m20.1
4	Michel Leclère	Elf 2J-Renault	65	1h18m27.0
5	Alessandro Pesenti-Rossi	March 762-BMW	65	1h18m41.2
6	Jean-Pierre Jaussaud	Chevron B35-Chrysler	65	1h18m58.9

Winner's average speed: 99.334 mph. Pole position:
Jabouille, 1m09.40. Fastest lap: Arnoux (Martini MK19-
Renault), 1m10.7

Salzburger Festspielpreis

23 May 1976. Salzburgring. 50 laps of a 2.635-mile circuit
= 131.750 miles

1	Michel Leclère	Elf 2J-Renault	50	1h04m28.82
2	Maurizio Flammini	March 762-BMW	50	1h04m34.43
3	Patrick Tambay	Martini MK19-Renault	50	1h04m36.42
4	René Arnoux	Martini MK19-Renault	50	1h04m40.63
5	Alex Ribeiro	March 762-BMW	50	1h04m45.78
6	Jean-Pierre Jabouille	Elf 2J-Renault	50	1h05m27.56

Winner's average speed: 122.596 mph. Pole position: Flammini,
1m24.05. Fastest lap: Arnoux, 1m14.95

Grand Prix de Pau

7 June 1976. Pau. 73 laps of a 1.715-mile circuit = 125.195
miles

1	René Arnoux	Martini MK19-Renault	73	1h32m11.58
2	Jacques Laffite♦	Chevron B35-BMW	73	1h32m54.49
3	Jean-Pierre Jabouille	Elf 2J-Renault	72	
4	Jean-Pierre Jarier♦	Chevron B35-Hart	72	
5	Giancarlo Martini	March 762-BMW	72	
6	Alex Ribeiro	March 762-BMW	71	
7	Klaus Ludwig	March 762-Hart	70	
8	Freddy Kottulinsky	Ralt RT1-BMW	69	

Winner's average speed: 81.478 mph. Pole position: Tambay
(Martini MK19-Renault), 1m13.77. Fastest lap: Laffite,
1m14.37

Rhein Pokal

20 June 1976. Hockenheim. 40 laps of a 4.219-mile circuit
= 168.760 miles

1	Hans-Joachim Stuck♦	March 762-BMW	40	1h21m27.6
2	Michel Leclère	Elf 2J-Renault	40	1h21m34.3
3	Patrick Tambay	Martini MK19-Renault	40	1h21m40.8
4	Jean-Pierre Jabouille	Elf 2J-Renault	40	1h21m43.1
5	René Arnoux	Martini MK19-Renault	40	1h21m58.9
6	Giancarlo Martini	March 762-BMW	40	1h23m05.0
7	Maurizio Flammini	March 762-BMW	40	1h23m15.4

Winner's average speed: 124.301 mph. Pole position: Stuck,
1m59.9. Fastest lap: Leclère, 2m00.7

Grand Prix de Rouen-les-Essarts

27 June 1976. Rouen-les-Essarts. 38 laps of a 3.444-mile
circuit = 130.872 miles

1	Maurizio Flammini	March 762-BMW	38	1h09m59.27
2	Jean-Pierre Jabouille	Elf 2J-Renault	38	1h10m12.81
3	Giancarlo Martini	March 762-BMW	38	1h10m29.18
4	Keke Rosberg	Toj F201-BMW	38	1h10m41.75
5	Roberto Marazzi	Chevron B35-BMW	38	1h10m54.42
6	Ingo Hoffman	March 762-Hart	38	1h11m07.80

Winner's average speed: 112.196 mph. Pole position: Ribeiro
(March 762-BMW), 1m47.19. Fastest lap: Arnoux (Martini MK19-
Renault), 1m47.552

Gran Premio Etienne Aigner

11 July 1976. Mugello. 43 laps of a 3.259-mile circuit
= 140.137 miles

1	Jean-Pierre Jabouille	Elf 2J-Renault	43	1h19m28.8
2	René Arnoux	Martini MK19-Renault	43	1h19m31.4
3	Patrick Tambay	Martini MK19-Renault	43	1h19m52.7
4	Alex Ribeiro	March 762-BMW	43	1h20m01.8
5	Giancarlo Martini	March 762-BMW	43	1h20m20.5
6	Maurizio Flammini	March 762-BMW	43	1h20m30.9

Winner's average speed: 105.790 mph. Pole position: Jabouille,
1m48.20. Fastest lap: Arnoux, 1m49.8

Gran Premio del Mediterraneo

25 July 1976. Enna-Pergusa. 60 laps of a 3.076-mile circuit
= 184.560 miles

1	René Arnoux	Martini MK19-Renault	60	1h36m12.9
2	Alex Ribeiro	March 762-BMW	60	1h36m17.4
3	Eddie Cheever	March 752/762-Hart	60	1h37m37.1
4	Jean-Pierre Jabouille	Elf 2J-Renault	60	1h38m04.7
5	Hans Binder	Chevron B35-BMW	60	1h38m06.0
6	Markus Hotz	March 762-BMW	59	

Winner's average speed: 115.092 mph. Pole position: Tambay
(Martini MK19-Renault), 1m33.16. Fastest lap: Ribeiro, 1m34.2

Grande Premio do Estoril

8 August 1976. Estoril. 50 laps of a 2.703-mile circuit
= 135.150 miles

1	René Arnoux	Martini MK19-Renault	50	1h20m19.77
2	Jean-Pierre Jabouille	Elf 2J-Renault	50	1h20m42.22
3	Alex Ribeiro	March 762-BMW	50	1h20m46.53
4	Hans Binder	Chevron B35-BMW	50	1h20m47.65
5	Eddie Cheever	March 752/762-Hart	50	1h21m17.19
6	Alberto Colombo	March 752-BMW	50	1h21m32.32

Winner's average speed: 100.947 mph. Pole position: Arnoux,
1m34.01. Fastest lap: Arnoux, 1m34.55

Grand Prix de Nogaro

19 September 1976. Nogaro. 65 laps of a 1.939-mile circuit
= 126.035 miles

1	Patrick Tambay	Martini MK19-Renault	65	1h20m12.91
2	Jacques Laffite♦	Chevron B35-Hart	65	1h20m29.24
3	Michel Leclère	Elf 2J-Renault	65	1h20m37.15
4	Hans Binder	Chevron B35-BMW	65	1h20m40.61
5	Alex Ribeiro	March 762-BMW	65	1h21m24.41
6	Klaus Ludwig	March 762-Hart	65	1h21m24.83
7	Rolf Stommelen♦	March 762-BMW	65	1h21m25.18
8	Eddie Cheever	Ralt RT1-Hart	65	1h21m31.63

Winner's average speed: 94.273 mph. Pole position: Jabouille
(Elf 2J-Renault), 1m11.84. Fastest lap: Tambay, 1m12.92

Texaco Gold Pokal

26 September 1976. Hockenheim. 40 laps of a 4.219-mile
circuit = 168.760 miles

1	Jean-Pierre Jabouille	Elf 2J-Renault	40	1h22m32.9
2	Michel Leclère	Elf 2J-Renault	40	1h22m36.5

3	René Arnoux	Martini MK19-Renault	40	1h22m38.0
4	Hans Binder	Chevron B35-BMW	40	1h23m15.6
5	Keke Rosberg	Toj F201-BMW	40	1h23m48.2
6	Jochen Mass♦	Chevron B35-BMW	40	1h23m51.8
7	Giorgio Francia	Chevron B35-BMW	40	1h24m03.9

Winner's average speed: 122.663 mph. Pole position: Jabouille, 1m58.6. Fastest lap: Arnoux, 2m00.8

FINAL CHAMPIONSHIP POSITIONS

Drivers

1	Jean-Pierre Jabouille	53		14	Ingo Hoffman	3
2	René Arnoux	52		15=	Harald Ertl	2
3	Patrick Tambay	39			Alessandro	
4	Michel Leclère	33			Pesenti-Rossi	2
5	Alex Ribeiro	31		17=	Alberto Colombo	1
6	Maurizio Flammini	26			Giorgio Francia	1
7=	Hans Binder	12			Hans Heyer	1
	Giancarlo Martini	12			Markus Hotz	1
9	Eddie Cheever	10			Jean-Pierre Jaussaud	1
10=	Roberto Marazzi	5			Freddy Kottulinsky	1
	Keke Rosberg	5			François Migault	1
12=	Willi Deutsch	4			♦ Graded driver ineligible	
	Klaus Ludwig	4			for points	

1977

Daily Express International Trophy

6 March 1977. Silverstone. 47 laps of a 2.932-mile circuit = 137.804 miles

1	René Arnoux	Martini MK22-Renault	47	1h05m45.52
2	Ray Mallock	Chevron B40-Hart	47	1h06m00.32
3	Patrick Neve	March 772P-BMW	47	1h06m03.61
4	Ingo Hoffman	Ralt RT1-BMW	47	1h06m21.43
5	Alberto Colombo	March 772-BMW	47	1h06m23.37
6	Riccardo Patrese	Chevron B35-BMW	47	1h06m25.27

Winner's average speed: 125.736 mph. Pole position: Leclère (Kauhsen-Renault), 1m21.85. Fastest lap: Neve, 1m21.85

Philips Car Radio Jochen Rindt Trophy

11 April 1977. Thruxton. 55 laps of a 2.356-mile circuit = 129.580 miles

1	Brian Henton	Boxer PR276-Hart	55	1h05m59.43
2	Eddie Cheever	Ralt RT1-BMW	55	1h06m03.27
3	Alex Ribeiro	March 772P-BMW	55	1h06m40.08
4	Alberto Colombo	March 772-BMW	55	1h06m40.20
5	Riccardo Patrese	Chevron B35-BMW	55	1h06m54.44
6	Hans Royer	Chevron B35-Hart	54	

Winner's average speed: 117.817 mph. Pole position: Ribeiro, 1m08.87. Fastest lap: Henton, 1m10.67

Jim Clark-Rennen/Martini Gold Cup

17 April 1977. Hockenheim. 40 laps of a 4.219-mile circuit = 168.760 miles

1	Jochen Mass♦	March 772P-BMW	40	1h21m20.4
2	René Arnoux	Martini MK22-Renault	40	1h21m30.4
3	Riccardo Patrese	Chevron B35-BMW	40	1h21m33.1
4	Alessandro Pesenti-Rossi	March 772-BMW	40	1h22m32.8
5	Brian Henton	Boxer PR276-Hart	40	1h22m38.7
6	Alberto Colombo	March 772-BMW	40	1h22m44.8
7	Jacques Laffite♦	Chevron B40-Hart	40	1h22m51.9
8	Keke Rosberg	Chevron B40-Hart	40	1h23m06.6

Winner's average speed: 124.485 mph. Pole position: Mass, 1m59.6. Fastest lap: Cheever (Ralt RT1-BMW), 2m00.4

Eifelrennen

1 May 1977. Nürburgring. 9 laps of a 14.189-mile circuit = 127.701 miles

1	Jochen Mass♦	March 772P-BMW	9	1h06m41.1
2	Eddie Cheever	Ralt RT1-BMW	9	1h06m54.3

3	Keke Rosberg	Chevron B40-Hart	9	1h07m00.5
4	Didier Pironi	Martini MK22-Renault	9	1h07m02.6
5	René Arnoux	Martini MK22-Renault	9	1h07m05.3
6	Bruno Giacomelli	March 772-Hart	9	1h07m19.8
7	Ingo Hoffman	Ralt RT1-BMW	9	1h07m42.6

Winner's average speed: 114.899 mph. Pole position: Patrese (Chevron B40-BMW), 7m15.3. Fastest lap: Mass, 7m20.3

Gran Premio di Roma

15 May 1977. Vallelunga. 65 laps of a 1.988-mile circuit = 129.220 miles

1	Bruno Giacomelli	March 772P-BMW	65	1h16m57.36
2	Didier Pironi	Martini MK22-Renault	65	1h17m41.88
3	Eddie Cheever	Ralt RT1-BMW	65	1h17m51.61
4	Alessandro Pesenti-Rossi	March 772-BMW	65	1h17m53.73
5	Alberto Colombo	March 772-BMW	65	1h18m04.57
6	Luciano Pavesi	Ralt RT1-Hart	64	

Winner's average speed: 100.748 mph. Pole position: Giacomelli, 1m09.02. Fastest lap: Giacomelli, 1m10.38

Grand Prix de Pau

30 May 1977. Pau. 59 laps of a 1.715-mile circuit = 101.185 miles. Race scheduled for 73 laps but stopped due to heavy rain and various accidents

1	René Arnoux	Martini MK22-Renault	59	1h14m52.52
2	Didier Pironi	Martini MK22-Renault	59	1h14m52.94
3	Riccardo Patrese	Chevron B40-BMW	59	1h15m11.06
4	Alberto Colombo	March 772-BMW	58	
5	Gaudenzio Mantova	March 762-BMW	58	
6	Ricardo Zunino	March 772-Hart	57	

Winner's average speed: 81.083 mph. Pole position: Tambay (Chevron B40-Hart), 1m13.38. Fastest lap: Pironi, 1m14.57

Gran Premio Etienne Aigner

19 June 1977. Mugello. 42 laps of a 3.259-mile circuit = 136.878 miles

1	Bruno Giacomelli	March 772P-BMW	42	1h16m36.5
2	Riccardo Patrese	Chevron B40-BMW	42	1h16m55.9
3	Alberto Colombo	March 772-BMW	42	1h17m06.5
4	Alessandro Pesenti-Rossi	March 772-BMW	42	1h17m17.6
5	Marc Surer	March 762-BMW	42	1h17m44.7
6	Bernard de Dryver	March 772-BMW	42	1h17m46.2

Winner's average speed: 107.203 mph. Pole position: Patrese, 1m47.20. Fastest lap: Pesenti-Rossi, 1m48.4

Grand Prix de Rouen-les-Essarts

26 June 1977. Rouen-les-Essarts. 38 laps of a 3.444-mile circuit = 130.872 miles

1	Eddie Cheever	Ralt RT1-BMW	38	1h08m36.19
2	Riccardo Patrese	Chevron B40-BMW	38	1h08m43.79
3	Didier Pironi	Martini MK22-Renault	38	1h08m45.74
4	Gianfranco Brancatelli	Ralt RT1-Ferrari	38	1h09m32.54
5	Ingo Hoffman	Ralt RT1-BMW	38	1h09m42.96
6	Alberto Colombo	March 772-BMW	38	1h09m59.42

Winner's average speed: 114.460 mph. Pole position: Cheever, 1m45.7. Fastest lap: Hoffman, 1m47.05

Grand Prix de Nogaro

10 July 1977. Nogaro. 65 laps of a 1.939-mile circuit = 126.035 miles

1	René Arnoux	Martini MK22-Renault	65	1h20m42.60
2	Riccardo Patrese	Chevron B40-BMW	65	1h21m10.29
3	Ingo Hoffman	Ralt RT1-BMW	65	1h21m22.13
4	Bruno Giacomelli	March 772P-BMW	65	1h21m46.37
5	Eddie Cheever	Ralt RT1-BMW	65	1h21m53.54
6	Alberto Colombo	March 772-BMW	65	1h21m58.13

Formula Two

Winner's average speed: 93.695 mph. Pole position: Arnoux, 1m12.27. Fastest lap: Patrese, 1m13.79

Gran Premio del Mediterraneo

24 July 1977. Enna-Pergusa. 60 laps of a 3.076-mile circuit = 184.560 miles

1	Keke Rosberg	Chevron B40-Hart	60	1h36m18.0
2	René Arnoux	Martini MK22-Renault	60	1h37m07.8
3	Ingo Hoffman	Ralt RT1-BMW	60	1h37m15.8
4	Didier Pironi	Martini MK22-Renault	60	1h37m52.2
5	Gaudenzio Mantova	March 762-BMW	60	1h37m59.3
6	"Gianfranco"	March 762-BMW	60	1h38m39.1

Winner's average speed: 114.991 mph. Pole position: Rosberg, 1m33.08. Fastest lap: Patrese (Chevron B40-BMW), 1m33.9

Gran Premio del Adriatico

7 August 1977. Misano. 60 laps of a 2.167-mile circuit = 130.020 miles

1	Lamberto Leoni	Chevron B40-Ferrari	60	1h13m44.8
2	Eddie Cheever	Ralt RT1-BMW	60	1h13m47.5
3	Ingo Hoffman	Ralt RT1-BMW	60	1h14m07.4
4	Alessandro Pesenti-Rossi	March 772-BMW	60	1h14m21.1
5	Didier Pironi	Martini MK22-Renault	60	1h14m30.7
6	Clay Regazzoni♦	Chevron B40-Hart	60	1h14m47.6
7	Patrick Bardinon	March 772-BMW	60	1h15m02.6

Winner's average speed: 105.784 mph. Pole position: Giacomelli (March 772P-BMW), 1m11.5. Fastest lap: Giacomelli, 1m12.3

Grande Premio do Estoril

2 October 1977. Estoril. 50 laps of a 2.703-mile circuit = 135.150 miles

1	Didier Pironi	Martini MK22-Renault	50	1h19m29.30
2	René Arnoux	Martini MK22-Renault	50	1h19m46.65
3	Eddie Cheever	Ralt RT1-BMW	50	1h19m47.22
4	Keke Rosberg	Chevron B40-Hart	50	1h19m47.52
5	Derek Daly	Chevron B40-Hart	50	1h19m55.49
6	Riccardo Patrese	Chevron B40-BMW	50	1h19m56.18

Winner's average speed: 102.015 mph. Pole position: Pironi, 1m33.05. Fastest lap: Daly, 1m34.16

BRSCC Formula 2 Trophy

30 October 1977. Donington Park. 65 laps of a 1.957-mile circuit = 127.205 miles

1	Bruno Giacomelli	March 772P/782-BMW	65	1h12m40.35
2	Keke Rosberg	Chevron B40-Hart	65	1h13m08.04
3	Didier Pironi	Martini MK22-Renault	65	1h13m25.36
4	Marc Surer	March 772P-BMW	65	1h13m28.88
5	Danny Sullivan	Boxer PR276-Hart	65	1h13m35.35
6	René Arnoux	Martini MK22-Renault	65	1h14m04.05

Winner's average speed: 105.039 mph. Pole position: Giacomelli, 1m05.00. Fastest lap: Giacomelli, 1m06.19

FINAL CHAMPIONSHIP POSITIONS

Drivers

1	René Arnoux	52	14=	Gaudenzio Mantova	4
2	Eddie Cheever	40		Patrick Neve	4
3	Didier Pironi	38		Alex Ribeiro	4
4=	Bruno Giacomelli	32	17	Gianfranco	
	Riccardo Patrese	32		Brancatelli	3
6	Keke Rosberg	25	18=	Derek Daly	2
7=	Alberto Colombo	18		Danny Sullivan	2
	Ingo Hoffman	18	20=	Patrick Bardinon	1
9	Alessandro			Bernard de Dryver	1
	Pesenti-Rossi	13		"Gianfranco"	1
10	Brian Henton	12		Luciano Pavesi	1
11	Lamberto Leoni	9		Hans Royer	1
12	Ray Mallock	6		Ricardo Zunino	1
13	Marc Surer	5		♦ Graded driver ineligible for points	

1978

Philips Car Stereo Jochen Rindt Trophy

27 March 1978. Thruxton. 55 laps of a 2.356-mile circuit = 129.580 miles

1	Bruno Giacomelli	March 782-BMW	55	1h06m13.77
2	Marc Surer	March 782-BMW	55	1h06m17.12
3	Rad Dougall	March 782-BMW	55	1h06m24.66
4	Eddie Cheever	March 782-BMW	55	1h06m25.37
5	Manfred Winkelhock	March 782-BMW	55	1h06m30.70
6	Derek Daly	Chevron B42-Hart	55	1h06m57.57

Winner's average speed: 117.392 mph. Pole position: Giacomelli, 1m09.13. Fastest lap: Giacomelli, 1m10.86

Jim Clark-Rennen

9 April 1978. Hockenheim. 40 laps of a 4.219-mile circuit = 168.760 miles

1	Bruno Giacomelli	March 782-BMW	40	1h20m22.0
2	Marc Surer	March 782-BMW	40	1h20m31.9
3	Jean-Pierre Jarier♦	March 782-BMW	40	1h20m46.6
4	Ingo Hoffman	March 782-BMW	40	1h20m52.2
5	Alberto Colombo	March 782-BMW	40	1h21m02.2
6	Alex Ribeiro	March 782-Hart	40	1h21m23.5
7	Jochen Mass♦	Chevron B42-Hart	40	1h21m56.2
8	Keke Rosberg	Chevron B42-Hart	40	1h22m00.0

Winner's average speed: 125.993 mph. Pole position: Giacomelli, 1m59.0. Fastest lap: Giacomelli and Surer, 1m59.4

Eifelrennen

30 April 1978. Nürburgring. 9 laps of a 14.189-mile circuit = 127.701 miles

1	Alex Ribeiro	March 782-Hart	9	1h06m34.2
2	Keke Rosberg	Chevron B42-Hart	9	1h06m34.3
3	Eddie Cheever	March 782-BMW	9	1h06m34.8
4	Marc Surer	March 782-BMW	9	1h06m42.2
5	Brian Henton	March 782-Hart	9	1h06m45.2
6	Ingo Hoffman	March 782-BMW	9	1h06m45.8

Winner's average speed: 115.098 mph. Pole position: Giacomelli (March 782-BMW), 7m11.5. Fastest lap: Rosberg, 7m17.3

Grand Prix de Pau

15 May 1978. Pau. 73 laps of a 1.715-mile circuit = 125.195 miles

1	Bruno Giacomelli	March 782-BMW	73	1h33m11.73
2	Eje Elgh	Chevron B42-Hart	73	1h33m33.47
3	Marc Surer	March 782-BMW	73	1h33m45.98
4	Piero Necchi	March 782-BMW	73	1h34m04.56
5	Eddie Cheever	March 782-BMW	73	1h34m25.16
6	Patrick Tambay♦	Chevron B42-Hart	72	engine
7	Roberto Marazzi	March 782-BMW	70	

Winner's average speed: 80.602 mph. Pole position: Henton (March 782-Hart), 1m13.64. Fastest lap: Giacomelli, 1m14.45

Euro Mugello

28 May 1978. Mugello. 42 laps of a 3.259-mile circuit = 136.878 miles

1	Derek Daly	Chevron B42-Hart	42	1h15m39.7
2	Marc Surer	March 782-BMW	42	1h15m40.1
3	Bruno Giacomelli	March 782-BMW	42	1h15m41.2
4	Ingo Hoffman	March 782-BMW	42	1h16m39.1
5	Alberto Colombo	March 782-BMW	42	1h16m45.3
6	Arturo Merzario♦	Chevron B42-Hart	42	1h16m48.8
7	Eddie Cheever	March 782-BMW	42	1h16m50.2

Winner's average speed: 108.545 mph. Pole position: Giacomelli, 1m45.54. Fastest lap: Cheever, 1m46.7

Gran Premio di Roma

4 June 1978. Vallelunga. 65 laps of a 1.988-mile circuit = 129.220 miles

1	Derek Daly	Chevron B42-Hart	65	1h17m12.2
2	Bruno Giacomelli	March 782-BMW	65	1h17m13.2
3	Piero Necchi	March 782-BMW	65	1h17m15.0
4	Manfred Winkelhock	March 782-BMW	65	1h17m47.4
5	Beppe Gabbiani	Chevron B42-Ferrari	65	1h17m47.7
6	Ricardo Zunino	March 782-BMW	65	1h17m48.5

Winner's average speed: 100.426 mph. Pole position:
Giacomelli, 1m08.48. Fastest lap: Giacomelli, 1m10.0

Grand Prix de Rouen-les-Essarts

18 June 1978. Rouen-les-Essarts. 38 laps of a 3.444-mile circuit = 130.872 miles

1	Bruno Giacomelli	March 782-BMW	38	1h08m43.2
2	Eddie Cheever	March 782-BMW	38	1h08m55.1
3	Marc Surer	March 782-BMW	38	1h09m27.7
4	Alberto Colombo	March 782-BMW	38	1h09m42.6
5	Ricardo Zunino	March 782-BMW	38	1h09m45.9
6	Eje Elgh	Chevron B42-Hart	38	1h09m47.4

Winner's average speed: 114.265 mph. Pole position:
Giacomelli, 1m58.79. Fastest lap: Hoffman (March 782-BMW),
1m46.31

£50,000 European Championship Trophy

25 June 1978. Donington Park. 80 laps of a 1.957-mile circuit = 156.560 miles

1	Keke Rosberg	Chevron B42-Hart	80	1h29m51.43
2	Piero Necchi	March 782-BMW	80	1h29m56.61
3	Marc Surer	March 782-BMW	80	1h30m08.88
4	Ingo Hoffman	March 782-BMW	80	1h30m15.23
5	Manfred Winkelhock	March 782-BMW	80	1h30m48.60
6	Rad Dougall	March 782-BMW	80	1h31m09.65

Winner's average speed: 104.555 mph. Pole position: Giacomelli
(March 782-BMW), 1m04.68. Fastest lap: Henton (March 782-
Hart), 1m04.91

Grand Prix de Nogaro

9 July 1978. Nogaro. 65 laps of a 1.939-mile circuit = 126.035 miles

1	Bruno Giacomelli	March 782-BMW	65	1h19m12.23
2	Marc Surer	March 782-BMW	65	1h19m28.43
3	Derek Daly	Chevron B42-Hart	65	1h19m41.43
4	Alberto Colombo	March 782-BMW	65	1h19m42.64
5	Ingo Hoffman	March 782-BMW	65	1h19m56.67
6	Geoff Lees	Chevron B42-Hart	65	1h20m05.32

Winner's average speed: 95.476 mph. Pole position: Giacomelli,
1m10.59. Fastest lap: Giacomelli, 1m12.39

Gran Premio del Mediterraneo

23 July 1978. Enna-Pergusa. 41 laps of a 3.076-mile circuit = 126.116 miles

1	Bruno Giacomelli	March 782-BMW	41	1h04m05.6
2	Eddie Cheever	March 782-BMW	41	1h04m13.3
3	Derek Daly	Chevron B42-Hart	41	1h04m19.9
4	Piercarlo Ghinzani	March 782-BMW	41	1h04m33.4
5	Ricardo Zunino	March 782-BMW	41	1h04m47.9
6	Brian Henton	March 782-Hart	41	1h05m00.4

Winner's average speed: 118.062 mph. Pole position: Daly,
1m31.34. Fastest lap: Daly, 1m31.5

Gran Premio del Adriatico

6 August 1978. Misano. 60 laps of a 2.167-mile circuit = 130.020 miles

1	Bruno Giacomelli	March 782-BMW	60	1h13m45.09
2	Marc Surer	March 782-BMW	60	1h13m53.49
3	Elio de Angelis	Chevron B42-Hart	60	1h14m16.08
4	Geoff Lees	Chevron B42-Hart	60	1h14m27.58
5	Arturo Merzario♦	Chevron B42-Hart	60	1h14m32.57
6	Eddie Cheever	March 782-BMW	60	1h14m43.18
7	Ricardo Zunino	March 782-BMW	60	1h14m50.73

Winner's average speed: 105.777 mph. Pole position: Brian Henton
(March 782-Hart), 1m11.67. Fastest lap: Giacomelli, 1m12.7

Preis von Hessen und Württemberg

24 September 1978. Hockenheim. 40 laps of a 4.219-mile circuit = 168.760 miles

1	Bruno Giacomelli	March 782-BMW	40	1h20m29.02
2	Marc Surer	March 782-BMW	40	1h20m35.39
3	Manfred Winkelhock	March 782-BMW	40	1h21m15.64
4	Stephen South	March 782-Hart	40	1h21m19.09
5	Ricardo Zunino	March 782-BMW	40	1h21m23.42
6	Eje Elgh	Chevron B42-Hart	40	1h21m24.06

Winner's average speed: 125.809 mph. Pole position: Surer,
1m58.68. Fastest lap: Derek Daly (Chevron B42-Hart), 1m59.17

FINAL CHAMPIONSHIP POSITIONS

Drivers

1	Bruno Giacomelli	78(82)*		13	Rad Dougall	5
2	Marc Surer	48(51)*		14=	Elio de Angelis	4
3	Derek Daly	27			Geoff Lees	4
4	Eddie Cheever	24		16=	Piercarlo Ghinzani	3
5	Keke Rosberg	16			Brian Henton	3
6=	Ingo Hoffman	13			Stephen South	3
	Piero Necchi	13		19	Beppe Gabbiani	2
8=	Alberto Colombo	11		20	Roberto Marazzi	1
	Alex Ribeiro	11			♦Graded driver ineligible
	Manfred Winkelhock	11			for points.
11=	Eje Elgh	8			*Best nine results count
	Ricardo Zunino	8			

1979

Marlboro/Daily Express International Trophy

25 March 1979. Silverstone. 40 laps of a 2.932-mile circuit = 117.280 miles. Race scheduled for 47 laps but stopped due to an accident

1	Eddie Cheever	Osella FA2/79-BMW	40	1h01m42.52
2	Derek Daly	March 792-BMW	40	1h01m42.85
3	Brian Henton	Ralt RT2-Hart	40	1h02m16.61
4	Bobby Rahal	Chevron B48-Hart	40	1h02m39.45
5	Stephen South	March 792-BMW	40	1h03m07.98
6	Alberto Colombo	March 782-BMW	39	

Winner's average speed: 114.033 mph. Pole position: Cheever,
1m19.81. Fastest lap: Daly, 1m30.01

Jim Clark-Rennen/Martini Gold Cup

8 April 1979. Hockenheim. 40 laps of a 4.219-mile circuit = 168.760 miles

1	Keke Rosberg	March 792-BMW	40	1h20m27.1
2	Rad Dougall	March 782-Hart	40	1h20m54.3
3	Miguel Angel Guerra	March 792-BMW	40	1h21m07.1
4	Brian Henton	Ralt RT2-Hart	40	1h21m12.4
5	Eddie Cheever	Osella FA2/79-BMW	40	1h21m28.0
6	Teo Fabi	March 792-BMW	40	1h21m28.4

Winner's average speed: 125.859 mph. Pole position: Surer (March
792-BMW), 1m56.9. Fastest lap: South (March 792-BMW), 1m59.0

Philips Car Radio Jochen Rindt Trophy

16 April 1979. Thruxton. 55 laps of a 2.356-mile circuit = 129.580 miles

1	Rad Dougall	March 782-Hart	55	1h04m10.31
2	Derek Daly	March 792-BMW	55	1h04m53.27
3	Alberto Colombo	March 782-BMW	55	1h05m02.32
4	Miguel Angel Guerra	March 792-BMW	55	1h05m07.39
5	Bobby Rahal	Chevron B48-Hart	55	1h05m19.68
6	Huub Rothengatter	Chevron B48-Hart	54	

Winner's average speed: 121.156 mph. Pole position: Dougall,
1m07.97. Fastest lap: Surer (March 792-BMW), 1m09.11

Formula Two

Eifelrennen

29 April 1979. Nürburgring. 9 laps of a 14.189-mile circuit = 127.701 miles

1	Marc Surer	March 792-BMW	9	1h12m46.7
2	Brian Henton	March 782-Hart	9	1h13m31.0
3	Manfred Winkelhock	Ralt RT1-BMW	9	1h13m47.3
4	Siegfried Stohr	Chevron B48-BMW	9	1h13m53.7
5	Huub Rothengatter	Chevron B48-Hart	9	1h13m53.9
6	Rad Dougall	March 782-Hart	9	1h14m14.1

Winner's average speed: 105.279 mph. Pole position: Rosberg (March 792-BMW), 7m06.9. Fastest lap: Winkelhock, 7m29.1

Gran Premio di Roma

13 May 1979. Vallelunga. 65 laps of a 1.988-mile circuit = 129.220 miles

1	Marc Surer	March 792-BMW	65	1h16m34.9
2	Siegfried Stohr	Chevron B48-BMW	65	1h17m09.4
3	Maurizio Flammini	March 792-BMW	65	1h17m17.5
4	Bobby Rahal	Chevron B48-Hart	65	1h17m21.5
5	Rad Dougall	March 782-Hart	65	1h17m32.8
6	Andrea de Cesaris	March 792-BMW	64	

Winner's average speed: 101.241 mph. Pole position: South (March 792-BMW), 1m08.04. Fastest lap: Henton (March 782-Hart), 1m09.5

Gran Premio Vanucci

20 May 1979. Mugello. 42 laps of a 3.259-mile circuit = 136.878 miles

1	Brian Henton	Ralt RT2-Hart	42	1h15m46.8
2	Beppe Gabbiani	March 792-BMW	42	1h15m59.8
3	Eje Elgh	March 792-BMW	42	1h16m05.0
4	Teo Fabi	March 792-BMW	42	1h16m11.7
5	Derek Warwick	March 792-Hart	42	1h16m18.5
6	Bobby Rahal	Chevron B48-Hart	42	1h16m20.6

Winner's average speed: 108.375 mph. Pole position: Henton, 1m44.74. Fastest lap: Gabbiani, 1m47.0

Grand Prix de Pau

4 June 1979. Pau. 73 laps of a 1.715-mile circuit = 125.195 miles

1	Eddie Cheever	Osella FA2/79-BMW	73	1h54m30.32
2	Siegfried Stohr	Chevron B48-BMW	73	1h54m58.40
3	Marc Surer	March 792-BMW	72	
4	Beppe Gabbiani	March 792-BMW	72	
5	Patrick Gaillard	Chevron B48-Hart	72	
6	Miguel Angel Guerra	March 792-BMW	71	

Winner's average speed: 65.601 mph. Pole position: Surer, 1m13.25. Fastest lap: Cheever, 1m31.52

Preis von Hessen und Württemberg

10 June 1979. Hockenheim. 40 laps of a 4.219-mile circuit = 168.760 miles

1	Stephen South	March 792-BMW	40	1h20m56.57
2	Derek Daly	March 792-BMW	40	1h21m09.49
3	Beppe Gabbiani	March 792-BMW	40	1h21m34.21
4	Patrick Gaillard	Chevron B48-Hart	40	1h21m58.17
5	Marc Surer	March 792-BMW	40	1h22m13.40
6	Bobby Rahal	Chevron B48-BMW	40	1h22m26.08

Winner's average speed: 125.096 mph. Pole position: South, 1m58.36. Fastest lap: Colombo (March 782-BMW), 1m59.98

Zandvoort F2

15 July 1979. Zandvoort. 50 laps of a 2.626-mile circuit = 131.300 miles

1	Eddie Cheever	Osella FA2/79-BMW	50	1h09m37.86
2	Teo Fabi	March 792-BMW	50	1h09m39.16
3	Marc Surer	March 792-BMW	50	1h09m39.87
4	Alberto Colombo	March 782-BMW	50	1h09m60.11
5	Brian Henton	Ralt RT2-Hart	50	1h09m56.07
6	Eje Elgh	March 792-BMW	50	1h10m01.90

Winner's average speed: 113.139 mph. Pole position: Henton, 1m20.21. Fastest lap: Cheever, 1m21.70

Gran Premio del Mediterraneo

29 July 1979. Enna-Pergusa. 45 laps of a 3.076-mile circuit = 138.420 miles

1	Eje Elgh	March 792-BMW	45	1h11m02.9
2	Derek Daly	March 792-BMW	45	1h11m18.8
3	Stephen South	March 792-BMW	45	1h11m23.2
4	Teo Fabi	March 792-BMW	45	1h11m38.6
5	Eddie Cheever	Osella FA2/79-BMW	45	1h11m56.2
6	Rad Dougall	Ralt RT2-Hart	45	1h12m04.7

Henton (Ralt RT2-Hart) finished first on the road but was disqualified for missing the chicane at the start. Winner's average speed: 116.895 mph. Pole position: Henton, 1m31.45. Fastest lap: South, 1m33.20

Gran Premio del Adriatico

5 August 1979. Misano. 60 laps of a 2.167-mile circuit = 130.020 miles

1	Brian Henton	Ralt RT2-Hart	60	1h14m29.0
2	Beppe Gabbiani	March 792-BMW	60	1h15m25.3
3	Marc Surer	March 792-BMW	60	1h15m31.4
4	Juan Traverso	March 792-Hart	59	
5	Siegfried Stohr	March 792-BMW	58	
6	Eddie Cheever	Osella FA2/79-BMW	58	

Winner's average speed: 104.738 mph. Pole position: Henton, 1m11.63. Fastest lap: Henton, 1m13.2

Donington Park F2

19 August 1979. Donington Park. 65 laps of a 1.957-mile circuit = 127.225 miles

1	Derek Daly	March 792-BMW	65	1h11m53.20
2	Marc Surer	March 792-BMW	65	1h11m56.10
3	Stephen South	March 792-BMW	65	1h12m28.37
4	Brian Henton	Ralt RT2-Hart	65	1h12m36.01
5	Eje Elgh	March 792-BMW	65	1h12m44.57
6	Oscar Pedersoli	March 782-BMW	65	1h12m56.29

Winner's average speed: 106.188 mph. Pole position: Daly, 1m04.05. Fastest lap: Daly, 1m05.34

FINAL CHAMPIONSHIP POSITIONS

Drivers

1	Marc Surer	38		12	Keke Rosberg	9
2	Brian Henton	36		13=	Alberto Colombo	8
3	Derek Daly	33			Miguel Angel Guerra	8
4	Eddie Cheever	32		15	Patrick Gaillard	5
5=	Rad Dougall	19		16=	Maurizio Flammini	4
	Beppe Gabbiani	19			Manfred Winkelhock	4
	Stephen South	19		18=	Juan Traverso	3
8	Siegfried Stohr	17			Huub Rothengatter	3
9	Eje Elgh	16		20	Derek Warwick	2
10	Teo Fabi	13		21=	Andrea de Cesaris	1
11	Bobby Rahal	10			Oscar Pedersoli	1

1980

P&O Ferries Jochen Rindt Trophy

7 April 1980. Thruxton. 55 laps of a 2.356-mile circuit = 129.580 miles

1	Brian Henton	Toleman TG280-Hart	55	1h04m10.56
2	Derek Warwick	Toleman TG280-Hart	55	1h04m14.25
3	Andrea de Cesaris	March 802-BMW	55	1h04m57.29
4	Chico Serra	March 802-BMW	55	1h05m20.68
5	Oscar Pedersoli	March 782-BMW	54	
6	Huub Rothengatter	Toleman TG280-Hart	54	

Winner's average speed: 121.148 mph. Pole position: Warwick, 1m07.60. Fastest lap: Henton, 1m09.04

Jim Clark-Rennen

13 April 1980. Hockenheim. 27 laps of a 4.219-mile circuit = 113.913 miles

1 Teo Fabi	March 802-BMW	27	54m28.99
2 Brian Henton	Toleman TG280-Hart	27	54m37.88
3 Alberto Colombo	March 782-BMW	27	54m43.74
4 Chico Serra	March 802-BMW	26	
5 Huub Rothengatter	Toleman TG280-Hart	26	
6 Oscar Pedersoli	March 782-BMW	26	

Winner's average speed: 125.448 mph. Pole position: Cesaris (March 802-BMW), 1m56.73. Fastest lap: Thackwell (March 802-BMW), 1m59.23

Eifelrennen

27 April 1980. Nürburgring. 9 laps of a 14.189-mile circuit = 127.701 miles

1 Teo Fabi	March 802-BMW	9	1h08m08.51
2 Brian Henton	Toleman TG280-Hart	9	1h08m42.19
3 Derek Warwick	Toleman TG280-Hart	9	1h08m45.16
4 Siegfried Stohr	Toleman TG280-Hart	9	1h09m15.33
5 Jochen Dauer	Chevron B48-BMW	9	1h09m46.38
6 Huub Rothengatter	Toleman TG280-Hart	9	1h09m53.65

Winner's average speed: 112.443 mph. Pole position: Dallest (AGS JH17-BMW), 8m56.56. Fastest lap: Thackwell (March 802-BMW), 7m23.65

Gran Premio di Roma

12 May 1980. Vallelunga. 65 laps of a 1.988-mile circuit = 129.220 miles

1 Brian Henton	Toleman TG280-Hart	65	1h15m56.1
2 Andrea de Cesaris	March 802-BMW	65	1h16m00.5
3 Derek Warwick	Toleman TG280-Hart	65	1h16m02.3
4 Mike Thackwell	March 802-BMW	65	1h16m25.9
5 Siegfried Stohr	Toleman TG280-Hart	65	1h16m45.5
6 Alberto Colombo	March 782-BMW	65	1h16m51.6

Winner's average speed: 102.103 mph. Pole position: Warwick, 1m07.69. Fastest lap: Henton, 1m09.2

Grand Prix de Pau

26 May 1980. Pau. 73 laps of a 1.715-mile circuit = 125.195 miles

1 Richard Dallest	AGS JH17-BMW	73	1h34m03.57
2 Siegfried Stohr	Toleman TG280-Hart	73	1h34m05.08
3 Brian Henton	Toleman TG280-Hart	73	1h34m38.49
4 Mike Thackwell	March 802-BMW	73	1h34m53.64
5 Miguel Angel Guerra	Minardi GM75-BMW	72	
6 Alberto Colombo	March 782-BMW	71	

Winner's average speed: 79.861 mph. Pole position: Warwick (Toleman TG280-Hart), 1m12.09. Fastest lap: Henton, 1m14.59

Marlboro Formula 2 Trophy

8 June 1980. Silverstone. 47 laps of a 2.932-mile circuit = 137.804 miles

1 Derek Warwick	Toleman TG280-Hart	47	1h03m18.66
2 Andrea de Cesaris	March 802-BMW	47	1h03m34.33
3 Mike Thackwell	March 802-BMW	47	1h03m45.49
4 Teo Fabi	March 802-BMW	47	1h04m07.89
5 Huub Rothengatter	Toleman TG280-Hart	47	1h04m11.41
6 Miguel Angel Guerra	Minardi GM75-BMW	47	1h04m29.02

Winner's average speed: 130.597 mph. Pole position: Henton (Toleman TG280-Hart), 1m18.50. Fastest lap: Henton, 1m19.11

Grand Prix de Belgique Formule 2

22 June 1980. Zolder. 50 laps of a 2.648-mile circuit = 132.400 miles

1 Huub Rothengatter	Toleman TG280-Hart	50	1h13m44.61
2 Brian Henton	Toleman TG280-Hart	50	1h14m03.63
3 Siegfried Stohr	Toleman TG280-Hart	50	1h14m04.73
4 Derek Warwick	Toleman TG280-Hart	50	1h14m35.04
5 Miguel Angel Guerra	Minardi GM75-BMW	50	1h14m36.90
6 Mike Thackwell	March 802-BMW	50	1h15m00.87

Winner's average speed: 107.725 mph. Pole position: T Fabi (March 802-BMW), 1m26.12. Fastest lap: Henton, 1m26.97

Marlboro Euro Mugello

6 July 1980. Mugello. 42 laps of a 3.259-mile circuit = 136.878 miles

1 Brian Henton	Toleman TG280B-Hart	42	1h15m22.6
2 Derek Warwick	Toleman TG280B-Hart	42	1h15m22.7
3 Teo Fabi	March 802-BMW	42	1h16m07.6
4 Miguel Angel Guerra	Minardi GM75-BMW	42	1h16m09.1
5 Andrea de Cesaris	March 802-BMW	42	1h16m17.2
6 Siegfried Stohr	Toleman TG28-Hart	42	1h16m44.3

Winner's average speed: 108.955 mph. Pole position: Warwick, 1m42.46. Fastest lap: Warwick, 1m46.5

Brian Henton, Formula Two champion in 1980

Zandvoort F2

20 July 1980. Zandvoort. 45 laps of a 2.642-mile circuit = 118.890 miles

1 Richard Dallest	AGS JH17-BMW	45	1h15m53.593
2 Derek Warwick	Toleman TG280B-Hart	45	1h15m57.238
3 Teo Fabi	March 802-BMW	45	1h16m16.347
4 Chico Serra	March 802-BMW	45	1h16m29.465
5 Nigel Mansell	Ralt RH6/80-Honda	45	1h16m48.814
6 Beppe Gabbiani	Maurer MM80-BMW	45	1h17m14.801

Winner's average speed: 93.993 mph. Pole position: Dallest, 1m37.249. Fastest lap: Henton (Toleman TG280B-Hart), 1m35.631

Gran Premio del Mediterraneo

2 August 1980. Enna-Pergusa. 45 laps of a 3.076-mile circuit = 138.420 miles

1 Siegfried Stohr	Toleman TG280-Hart	45	1h10m39.79
2 Brian Henton	Toleman TG280B-Hart	45	1h10m49.46
3 Manfred Winkelhock	March 802-BMW	45	1h11m10.26
4 Huub Rothengatter	Toleman TG280-Hart	45	1h11m15.73
5 Richard Dallest	AGS JH15-BMW	45	1h11m16.23
6 Andrea de Cesaris	March 802-BMW	45	1h11m30.87

Winner's average speed: 117.532 mph. Pole position: Stohr, 1m31.40. Fastest lap: T Fabi (March 802-BMW), 1m31.26

Gran Premio del Adriatico

10 August 1980. Misano. 60 laps of a 2.167-mile circuit = 130.020 miles

1 Andrea de Cesaris	March 802-BMW	60	1h12m39.38
2 Brian Henton	Toleman TG280B-Hart	60	1h12m40.55
3 Derek Warwick	Toleman TG280B-Hart	60	1h13m01.36
4 Huub Rothengatter	Toleman TG280-Hart	60	1h13m25.93
5 Miguel Angel Guerra	Minardi GM75-BMW	60	1h13m31.00
6 Alberto Colombo	Toleman TG280-Hart	60	1h13m48.76

Winner's average speed: 107.371 mph. Pole position: Henton, 1m10.63. Fastest lap: Henton, 1m11.22

Preis von Hessen und Württemberg

28 September 1980. Hockenheim. 30 laps of a 4.219-mile circuit = 126.570 miles

1 Teo Fabi	March 802-BMW	30	59m41.06

Formula Two

2	Nigel Mansell	Ralt RH6/80-Honda	30 1h00m01.38
3	Siegfried Stohr	Toleman TG280-Hart	30 1h00m26.26
4	Richard Dallest	AGS JH17-BMW	30 1h00m28.71
5	Alberto Colombo	Toleman TG280-Hart	30 1h01m25.77
6	Fredy Schnarwiler	March 802-BMW	30 1h01m46.91

Winner's average speed: 127.239 mph. Pole position: T Fabi.
Fastest lap: T Fabi, 1m57.09

FINAL CHAMPIONSHIP POSITIONS

Drivers

1	Brian Henton	61		10=	Alberto Colombo	9
2	Derek Warwick	42			Chico Serra	9
3	Teo Fabi	38		12	Nigel Mansell	8
4	Siegfried Stohr	29		13	Manfred Winkelhock	4
5	Andrea de Cesaris	28		14	Oscar Pedersoli	3
6	Richard Dallest	23		15	Jochen Dauer	2
7	Huub Rothengatter	21		16=	Beppe Gabbiani	1
8	Mike Thackwell	11			Fredy Schnarwiler	1
9	Miguel Angel Guerra	10				

1981

Marlboro/Daily Express International Trophy

29 March 1981. Silverstone. 47 laps of a 2.932-mile circuit = 137.804 miles

1	Mike Thackwell	Ralt RH6/81-Honda	47 1h11m44.67
2	Ricardo Paletti	March 812-BMW	47 1h12m20.86
3	Corrado Fabi	March 812-BMW	46
4	Jim Crawford	Toleman TG280-Hart	46
5	Carlo Rossi	Toleman TG280-Hart	46
6	Brian Robinson	Chevron B42-Hart	46

Winner's average speed: 115.246 mph. Pole position: Thackwell, 1m18.59. Fastest lap: Lees (Ralt RH6/81-Honda), 1m23.82

Jim Clark-Rennen

5 April 1981. Hockenheim. 30 laps of a 4.219-mile circuit = 126.570 miles

1	Stefan Johansson	Toleman T850-Hart	30 1h00m28.05
2	Manfred Winkelhock	Ralt RT2-BMW	30 1h00m29.19
3	Mike Thackwell	Ralt RH6/81-Honda	30 1h00m42.62
4	Eje Elgh	Maurer MM81-BMW	30 1h00m44.87
5	Geoff Lees	Ralt RH6/81-Honda	30 1h00m45.79
6	Carlo Rossi	Toleman TG280-Hart	30 1h00m56.00

Winner's average speed: 125.591 mph. Pole position: Lees, 1m57.14. Fastest lap: Paletti (March 812-BMW), 1m59.26

P&O Ferries Jochen Rindt Trophy

20 April 1981. Thruxton. 55 laps of a 2.356-mile circuit = 129.580 miles

1	Roberto Guerrero	Maurer MM81-BMW	55 1h04m02.40
2	Ricardo Paletti	March 812-BMW	55 1h04m43.60
3	Johnny Cecotto	Minardi FLY281-BMW	55 1h04m59.61
4	Christian Danner	March 812-BMW	55 1h06m01.69
5	Pierro Necchi	March 812-BMW	54
6	Stefan Johansson	Toleman T850-Hart	53

Winner's average speed: 121.405 mph. Pole position: Boutsen (March 812-BMW), 1m06.38. Fastest lap: Surer (March 812-BMW), 1m08.00

Eifelrennen

26 April 1981. Nürburgring. 9 laps of a 14.189-mile circuit = 127.701 miles

1	Thierry Boutsen	March 812-BMW	9 1h05m04.63
2	Eje Elgh	Maurer MM81-BMW	9 1h06m06.56
3	Corrado Fabi	March 812-BMW	9 1h06m06.81
4	Stefan Johansson	Toleman T850-Hart	9 1h06m10.26
5	Geoff Lees	Ralt RH6/81-Honda	9 1h06m37.78
6	Kenneth Acheson	Toleman T850-Hart	9 1h07m05.24

Winner's average speed: 117.738 mph. Pole position: C Fabi, 7m10.25. Fastest lap: Boutsen, 7m10.33

Gran Premio di Roma

10 May 1981. Vallelunga. 65 laps of a 1.988-mile circuit = 129.220 miles

1	Eje Elgh	Maurer MM81-BMW	65 1h16m01.14
2	Stefan Johansson	Toleman T850-Hart	65 1h16m04.42
3	Thierry Boutsen	March 812-BMW	65 1h16m07.74
4	Corrado Fabi	March 812-BMW	65 1h16m13.19
5	Geoff Lees	Ralt RH6/81-Honda	65 1h16m24.13
6	Ricardo Paletti	March 812-BMW	65 1h16m53.09

Winner's average speed: 101.990 mph. Pole position: Elgh, 1m07.79. Fastest lap: C Fabi, 1m09.06

Euro Mugello

24 May 1981. Mugello. 42 laps of a 3.259-mile circuit = 136.878 miles

1	Corrado Fabi	March 812-BMW	42 1h15m20.99
2	Geoff Lees	Ralt RH6/81-Honda	42 1h15m22.40
3	Piero Necchi	March 812-BMW	42 1h15m31.82
4	Eje Elgh	Maurer MM81-BMW	42 1h15m32.95
5	Mike Thackwell	Ralt RH6/81-Honda	42 1h15m57.14
6	Roberto Guerrero	Maurer MM81-BMW	42 1h16m08.59

Winner's average speed: 108.994 mph. Pole position: Boutsen (March 812-BMW), 1m42.82. Fastest lap: Necchi, 1m46.27

Grand Prix de Pau

8 June 1981. Pau. 73 laps of a 1.715-mile circuit = 125.195 miles

1	Geoff Lees	Ralt RH6/81-Honda	73 1h33m13.91
2	Thierry Boutsen	March 812-BMW	73 1h33m14.43
3	Piero Necchi	March 812-BMW	73 1h34m11.87
4	Carlo Rossi	Toleman TG280-Hart	72
5	Eje Elgh	Maurer MM81-BMW	72
6	Mike Thackwell	Ralt RH6/81-Honda	72

Winner's average speed: 80.570 mph. Pole position: Alboreto (Minardi FLY281-BMW), 1m13.07. Fastest lap: Lees, 1m15.00

Gran Premio del Mediterraneo

26 July 1981. Enna-Pergusa. 45 laps of a 3.076-mile circuit = 138.420 miles

1	Thierry Boutsen	March 812-BMW	45 1h10m09.82
2	Huub Rothengatter	March 812-BMW	45 1h10m13.12
3	Michele Alboreto	Minardi FLY281-BMW	45 1h10m24.58
4	Roberto Guerrero	Maurer MM81-BMW	45 1h10m28.63
5	Eje Elgh	Maurer MM81-BMW	45 1h10m37.44
6	Jo Gartner	Toleman TG280-BMW	45 1h11m18.66

Winner's average speed: 118.369 mph. Pole position: Boutsen, 1m30.92. Fastest lap: Boutsen, 1m32.05

Grand Prix de Belgique Formule 2

9 August 1981. Spa-Francorchamps. 30 laps of a 4.332-mile circuit = 129.960 miles

1	Geoff Lees	Ralt RH6/81-Honda	30 1h10m02.68
2	Thierry Boutsen	March 812-BMW	30 1h10m11.65
3	Eje Elgh	Maurer MM81-BMW	30 1h10m47.18
4	Corrado Fabi	March 812-BMW	30 1h10m48.95
5	Manfred Winkelhock	Maurer MM81-BMW	30 1h10m57.46
6	Jim Crawford	Toleman TG280-Hart	30 1h11m19.35

Winner's average speed: 111.323 mph. Pole position: Boutsen, 2m15.39. Fastest lap: Lees, 2m16.81

John Howitt Trophy

16 August 1981. Donington Park. 70 laps of a 1.957-mile circuit = 136.990 miles

1	Geoff Lees	Ralt RH6/81-Honda	70 1h16m49.82
2	Corrado Fabi	March 812-BMW	70 1h17m00.58

3	Manfred Winkelhock	Maurer MM81-BMW	70 1h17m18.58
4	Stefan Johansson	Toleman TG280B-Hart	70 1h17m41.10
5	Mike Thackwell	Ralt RH6/81-Honda	70 1h17m45.49
6	Johnny Cecotto	March 812-BMW	70 1h17m54.78

Winner's average speed: 106.998 mph. Pole position: Winkelhock, 1m02.74. Fastest lap: Lees and C Fabi, 1m05.10

Gran Premio del Adratico

6 September 1981. Misano. 60 laps of a 2.167-mile circuit = 130.020 miles

1	Michele Alboreto	Minardi FLY281-BMW	60 1h12m03.74
2	Geoff Lees	Ralt RH6/81-Honda	60 1h12m12.90
3	Mike Thackwell	Ralt RH6/81-Honda	60 1h12m54.50
4	Roberto Guerrero	Maurer MM81-BMW	60 1h12m55.01
5	Richard Dallest	AGS JH18-BMW	60 1h12m55.32
6	Johnny Cecotto	March 812-BMW	60 1h13m15.33

Winner's average speed: 108.256 mph. Pole position: Boutsen (March 812-BMW), 1m10.49. Fastest lap: Alboreto and Lees, 1m11.01

Mantorp Park F2

20 September 1981. Mantorp Park. 65 laps of a 1.942-mile circuit = 126.230 miles

1	Stefan Johansson	Toleman TG280B-Hart	65 1h20m08.8
2	Geoff Lees	Ralt RH6/81-Honda	65 1h20m15.3
3	Kenneth Acheson	Toleman T850-Hart	65 1h20m44.5
4	Thierry Boutsen	March 812-BMW	65 1h20m45.8
5	Richard Dallest	AGS JH18-BMW	65 1h21m05.3
6	Johnny Cecotto	March 812-BMW	65 1h21m20.5

Winner's average speed: 94.499 mph. Pole position: C Fabi (March 812-BMW), 1m10.09. Fastest lap: Cecotto, 1m11.69

FINAL CHAMPIONSHIP POSITIONS

Drivers

1	Geoff Lees	51	11	Piero Necchi	10
2	Thierry Boutsen	37	12	Johnny Cecotto	7
3	Stefan Johansson	31	13=	Carlo Rossi	6
4=	Eje Elgh	29		Huub Rothengatter	6
	Corrado Fabi	29	15	Kenneth Acheson	5
6	Mike Thackwell	22	16=	Jim Crawford	4
7	Roberto Guerrero	16		Richard Dallest	4
8=	Michele Alboreto	13	18	Christian Danner	3
	Ricardo Paletti	13	19=	Jo Gartner	1
10	Manfred Winkelhock	12		Brian Robinson	1

1982

Marlboro/Daily Express International Trophy

21 March 1982. Silverstone. 47 laps of a 2.932-mile circuit = 137.804 miles

1	Stefan Bellof	Maurer MM82-BMW	47 1h11m51.38
2	Satoru Nakajima	March 812-Honda	47 1h12m12.64
3	Beppe Gabbiani	Maurer MM82-BMW	47 1h12m12.76
4	Roberto del Castello	Toleman T850-BMW	47 1h12m19.06
5	Alessandro Nannini	Minardi FLY281B-BMW	47 1h12m22.86
6	Jo Gartner	March 822-BMW	47 1h12m58.08

Winner's average speed: 115.066 mph. Pole position: Johansson (Spirit 201-Honda), 1m20.61. Fastest lap: Danner (March 822-BMW), 1m29.35

Jim Clark-Rennen

4 April 1982. Hockenheim. 30 laps of a 4.224-mile circuit = 126.720 miles

1	Stefan Bellof	Maurer MM82-BMW	30 1h03m03.44
2	Thierry Boutsen	Spirit 201-Honda	30 1h03m08.23
3	Corrado Fabi	March 822-BMW	30 1h03m16.34
4	Johnny Cecotto	March 822-BMW	30 1h03m16.60

5	Beppe Gabbiani	Maurer MM82-BMW	30 1h03m28.13
6	Thierry Tassin	Toleman DS1-Hart	30 1h03m35.79

Winner's average speed: 120.565 mph. Pole position: Bellof, 2m02.05. Fastest lap: Bellof, 2m04.21

P&O Ferries Jochen Rindt Trophy

12 April 1982. Thruxton. 55 laps of a 2.356-mile circuit = 129.580 miles

1	Johnny Cecotto	March 822-BMW	55 1h03m49.22
2	Kenneth Acheson	Ralt RH6/82-Honda	55 1h04m01.00
3	Thierry Boutsen	Spirit 201-Honda	55 1h04m05.09
4	Beppe Gabbiani	Maurer MM82-BMW	55 1h04m17.21
5	Philippe Streiff	AGS JH19-BMW	55 1h04m20.26
6	Richard Dallest	March 822-BMW	55 1h04m28.37

Winner's average speed: 121.823 mph. Pole position: Johansson (Spirit 201-Honda), 1m05.33. Fastest lap: Cecotto, 1m07.37

Eifelrennen

25 April 1982. Nürburgring. 9 laps of a 14.189-mile circuit = 127.701 miles

1	Thierry Boutsen	Spirit 201-Honda	9 1h05m01.37
2	Corrado Fabi	March 822-BMW	9 1h05m01.54
3	Johnny Cecotto	March 822-BMW	9 1h05m59.35
4	Kenneth Acheson	Ralt RH6/82-Honda	9 1h06m02.15
5	Stefan Bellof	Maurer MM82-BMW	9 1h06m10.75
6	Stefan Johansson	Spirit 201-Honda	9 1h06m13.77

Winner's average speed: 117.836 mph. Pole position: Tassin (Toleman DS1-Hart), 8m21.02. Fastest lap: Bellof, 7m06.51

Euro Mugello

9 May 1982. Mugello. 42 laps of a 3.259-mile circuit = 136.878 miles

1	Corrado Fabi	March 822-BMW	42 1h14m32.79
2	Johnny Cecotto	March 822-BMW	42 1h14m36.92
3	Stefan Johansson	Spirit 201-Honda	42 1h14m42.87
4	Thierry Boutsen	Spirit 201-Honda	42 1h14m44.05
5	Jonathan Palmer	Ralt RH6/82-Honda	42 1h14m56.67
6	Kenneth Acheson	Ralt RH6/82-Honda	42 1h15m30.82

Winner's average speed: 110.169 mph. Pole position: Johansson, 1m57.87. Fastest lap: C Fabi, 1m44.21

Gran Premio di Roma

16 May 1982. Vallelunga. 65 laps of a 1.988-mile circuit = 129.220 miles

1	Corrado Fabi	March 822-BMW	65 1h15m45.40
2	Philippe Streiff	AGS JH19-BMW	65 1h15m56.23
3	Pascal Fabre	AGS JH19-BMW	65 1h16m36.31
4	Stefan Johansson	Spirit 201-Honda	64
5	Jonathan Palmer	Ralt RH6/82-Honda	64
6	Thierry Boutsen	Spirit 201-Honda	64

Winner's average speed: 102.343 mph. Pole position: Johansson, 1m07.10. Fastest lap: Bellof (Maurer MM82-BMW), 1m08.63

Grand Prix de Pau

31 May 1982. Pau. 73 laps of a 1.715-mile circuit = 125.195 miles

1	Johnny Cecotto	March 822-BMW	73 1h31m00.03
2	Thierry Boutsen	Spirit 201-Honda	73 1h31m15.93
3	Mike Thackwell	March 822-BMW	73 1h32m17.02
4	Frank Jelinski	Maurer MM82-BMW	72
5	Kenneth Acheson	Ralt RH6/82-Honda	72
6	Jonathan Palmer	Ralt RH6/82-Honda	72

Winner's average speed: 82.546 mph. Pole position: Boutsen, 1m11.23. Fastest lap: Acheson, 1m12.37

Grand Prix de Belgique Formule 2

13 June 1982. Spa-Francorchamps. 23 laps of a 4.332-mile circuit = 99.636 miles

1	Thierry Boutsen	Spirit 201-Honda	23 58m17.47

2	Johnny Cecotto	March 822-BMW	23	58m40.06
3	Mike Thackwell	March 822-BMW	23	59m05.44
4	Philippe Streiff	AGS JH19-BMW	23	59m11.00
5	Corrado Fabi	March 822-BMW	23	59m14.17
6	Jonathan Palmer	Ralt RH6/82-Honda	23	1h00m07.55

Winner's average speed: 102.557 mph. Pole position:
Johansson (Spirit 201-Honda), 2m13.10. Fastest lap: Thackwell,
2m29.48

Hockenheim F2

**20 June 1982. Hockenheim. 30 laps of a 4.224-mile circuit
= 126.720 miles**

1	Corrado Fabi	March 822-BMW	30	1h03m04.32
2	Beppe Gabbiani	Maurer MM82-BMW	30	1h03m06.92
3	Stefan Bellof	Maurer MM82-BMW	30	1h03m08.52
4	Stefan Johansson	Spirit 201-Honda	30	1h03m46.63
5	Frank Jelinski	Maurer MM82-BMW	30	1h03m49.83
6	Johnny Cecotto	March 822-BMW	30	1h03m51.26

Winner's average speed: 120.537 mph. Pole position: Boutsen
(Spirit 201-Honda), 2m02.00. Fastest lap: C Fabi, 2m04.28

*Johnny Cecotto leads Alessandro Nannini and Alain
Ferté at Hockenheim*

John Howitt Trophy

**4 July 1982. Donington Park. 70 laps of a 1.957-mile circuit
= 136.990 miles**

1	Corrado Fabi	March 822-BMW	70	1h15m42.11
2	Johnny Cecotto	March 822-BMW	70	1h15m42.70
3	Jonathan Palmer	Ralt RH6/82-Honda	70	1h15m57.70
4	Beppe Gabbiani	Maurer MM82-BMW	70	1h16m08.49
5	Philippe Streiff	AGS JH19-BMW	70	1h16m12.60
6	Stefan Bellof	Maurer MM82-BMW	70	1h16m15.95

Winner's average speed: 108.593 mph. Pole position: Palmer,
1m02.21. Fastest lap: C Fabi, 1m03.82

Mantorp Park F2

**18 July 1982. Mantorp Park. 65 laps of a 1.942-mile circuit
= 126.230 miles**

1	Johnny Cecotto	March 822-BMW	65	1h18m28.40
2	Philippe Streiff	AGS JH19-BMW	65	1h18m53.80
3	Beppe Gabbiani	Maurer MM82-BMW	65	1h18m58.10
4	Thierry Boutsen	Spirit 201-Honda	65	1h19m29.11
5	Christian Danner	March 822-BMW	65	1h19m31.80
6	Pascal Fabre	AGS JH19-BMW	64	

Winner's average speed: 96.514 mph. Pole position: C Fabi
(March 822-BMW), 1m09.40. Fastest lap: not published

Gran Premio del Mediterraneo

**1 August 1982. Enna-Pergusa. 45 laps of a 3.076-mile
circuit = 138.420 miles**

1	Thierry Boutsen	Spirit 201-Honda	45	1h09m22.15
2	Stefan Bellof	Maurer MM82-BMW	45	1h09m26.42
3	Johnny Cecotto	March 822-BMW	45	1h10m32.23
4	Philippe Streiff	AGS JH19-BMW	45	1h10m43.61
5	Frank Jelinski	Maurer MM82-BMW	45	1h10m45.07

| 6 | Christian Danner | March 822-BMW | 44 | |

Winner's average speed: 119.725 mph. Pole position: Boutsen,
1m30.44. Fastest lap: Bellof, 1m30.75

Gran Premio del Adriatico

**7 August 1982. Misano. 60 laps of a 2.167-mile circuit
= 130.020 miles**

1	Corrado Fabi	March 822-BMW	60	1h18m25.19
2	Alessandro Nannini	Minardi FLY281B-BMW	60	1h18m35.58
3	Beppe Gabbiani	Maurer MM82-BMW	60	1h18m40.28
4	Christian Danner	March 822-BMW	60	1h18m55.21
5	Stefan Bellof	Maurer MM82-BMW	60	1h18m56.33
6	Thierry Boutsen	Spirit 201-Honda	60	1h19m10.60

Winner's average speed: 99.480 mph. Pole position: C Fabi,
1m08.68. Fastest lap: Bellof, 1m10.89

FINAL CHAMPIONSHIP POSITIONS

Drivers

1	Corrado Fabi	57		12	Frank Jelinski	7
2	Johnny Cecotto	56 (57)*		13=	Christian Danner	6
3	Thierry Boutsen	50 (51)*			Satoru Nakajima	6
4	Stefan Bellof	33		15	Pascal Fabre	5
5	Beppe Gabbiani	26		16	Roberto del Castello	3
6	Philippe Streiff	22		17=	Richard Dallest	1
7	Kenneth Acheson	12			Jo Gartner	1
8	Stefan Johansson	11			Thierry Tassin	1
9	Jonathan Palmer	10			*Best nine results count	
10=	Alessandro Nannini	8				
	Mike Thackwell	8				

1983

Marlboro/Daily Express
International Trophy

**20 March 1983. Silverstone. 47 laps of a 2.932-mile circuit
= 137.804 miles**

1	Beppe Gabbiani	March 832-BMW	47	1h08m30.71
2	Mike Thackwell	Ralt RH6/83-Honda	47	1h08m57.31
3	Christian Danner	March 832-BMW	47	1h09m40.25
4	Stefan Bellof	Maurer MM83-BMW	46	throttle cable
5	Philippe Streiff	AGS JH19B-BMW	46	
6	Lamberto Leoni	March 832-BMW	46	

Winner's average speed: 120.683 mph. Pole position: Scott
(March 832-BMW), 1m16.95. Fastest lap: Bellof, 1m19.93

P&O Ferries Jochen Rindt Trophy

**4 April 1983. Thruxton. 55 laps of a 2.356-mile circuit
= 129.580 miles**

1	Beppe Gabbiani	March 832-BMW	55	1h03m54.06
2	Mike Thackwell	Ralt RH6/83-Honda	55	1h04m01.91
3	Jonathan Palmer	Ralt RH6/83-Honda	55	1h04m08.57
4	Thierry Tassin	March 832-BMW	55	1h04m24.64
5	Philippe Alliot	Martini 001-BMW	55	1h04m42.34
6	Frank Jelinski	Maurer MM82-BMW	54	

Winner's average speed: 121.669 mph. Pole position: Thackwell,
1m05.78. Fastest lap: Thackwell, 1m07.70

Jim Clark-Rennen

**10 April 1983. Hockenheim. 30 laps of a 4.224-mile circuit
= 126.720 miles**

1	Jonathan Palmer	Ralt RH6/83-Honda	30	1h02m25.22
2	Christian Danner	March 832-BMW	30	1h02m47.52
3	Mike Thackwell	Ralt RH6/83-Honda	30	1h03m15.02
4	Jo Gartner	Spirit 201-BMW	30	1h03m20.50
5	Alessandro Nannini	Minardi M283-BMW	30	1h03m53.14
6	Thierry Tassin	March 832-BMW	30	1h03m56.36

Winner's average speed: 121.795 mph. Pole position: Leoni
(March 832-BMW), 2m14.83. Fastest lap: Palmer, 2m03.76

Eifelrennen

24 April 1983. Nürburgring. 9 laps of a 12.944-mile circuit
= 116.496 miles

1	Beppe Gabbiani	March 832-BMW	9 58m46.44
2	Alessandro Nannini	Minardi FLY281B-BMW	9 58m53.41
3	Christian Danner	March 832-BMW	9 58m58.26
4	Jonathan Palmer	Ralt RH6/83-Honda	9 59m34.28
5	Alain Ferté	Maurer MM83-BMW	9 59m39.53
6	Thierry Tassin	March 832-BMW	9 59m40.64

Winner's average speed: 118.926 mph. Pole position: Danner, 6m26.19. Fastest lap: Danner, 6m28.03.

Gran Premio di Roma

8 May 1983. Vallelunga. 65 laps of a 1.988-mile circuit
= 129.220 miles

1	Beppe Gabbiani	March 832-BMW	65 1h14m59.60
2	Jonathan Palmer	Ralt RH6/83-Honda	65 1h15m09.85
3	Mike Thackwell	Ralt RH6/83-Honda	65 1h15m28.87
4	Thierry Tassin	March 832-BMW	65 1h15m29.34
5	Philippe Streiff	AGS JH19B-BMW	65 1h15m43.82
6	Guido Dacco	Toleman T850-BMW	64

Winner's average speed: 103.385 mph. Pole position: Gabbiani, 1m06.49. Fastest lap: Gabbiani, 1m08.14

Grand Prix de Pau

23 May 1983. Pau. 73 laps of a 1.715-mile circuit = 125.195 miles

1	Jo Gartner	Spirit 201-BMW	73 1h45m18.65
2	Kenneth Acheson	Maurer MM83-BMW	73 1h45m44.56
3	Jonathan Palmer	Ralt RH6/83-Honda	73 1h46m12.61
4	Thierry Tassin	March 832-BMW	73 1h46m24.58
5	Christian Danner	March 832-BMW	73 1h46m24.89
6	Rolf Biland	March 832-BMW	69

A Ferté (Maurer MM83-BMW) and Bellof (Maurer MM83-BMW) finished first and third on the road respectively but were disqualified as their cars were under the weight limit. Winner's average speed: 71.329 mph. Pole position: Bellof, 1m11.87. Fastest lap: n\a (Bellof set 1m13.12 but was subsequently disqualified)

Jarama F2

12 June 1983. Jarama. 65 laps of a 2.115-mile circuit
= 137.475 miles

1	Mike Thackwell	Ralt RH6/83-Honda	65 1h28m50.80
2	Stefan Bellof	Maurer MM83-BMW	65 1h28m53.16
3	Jonathan Palmer	Ralt RH6/83-Honda	65 1h29m06.29
4	Philippe Streiff	AGS JH19B-BMW	65 1h29m25.62
5	Alain Ferté	Maurer MM83-BMW	65 1h29m29.99
6	Enrique Mansilla	March 832-BMW	65 1h29m43.15

Winner's average speed: 92.857 mph. Pole position: Palmer, 1m16.79. Fastest lap: Thackwell, 1m20.02

Donington Park F2

25 June 1983. Donington Park. 70 laps of a 1.957-mile circuit = 136.990 miles

1	Jonathan Palmer	Ralt RH6/83-Honda	70 1h16m39.02
2	Mike Thackwell	Ralt RH6/83-Honda	70 1h16m57.39
3	Philippe Streiff	AGS JH19B-BMW	70 1h17m18.12
4	Kazuyoshi Hoshino	March 832-BMW	70 1h17m23.96
5	Christian Danner	March 832-BMW	70 1h17m35.50
6	Dave Scott	March 832-BMW	69

Winner's average speed: 107.249 mph. Pole position: Palmer, 1m00.93. Fastest lap: Thackwell, 1m04.69

Trofeo Ricardo Paletti

24 July 1983. Misano. 58 laps of a 2.167-mile circuit
= 125.686 miles

1	Jonathan Palmer	Ralt RH6/83-Honda	58 1h09m37.74
2	Pierluigi Martini	Minardi M283-BMW	58 1h10m41.61
3	Roberto del Castello	March 832-BMW	58 1h10m50.60

4	Guido Dacco	March 832-BMW	57
5	Fulvio Ballabio	AGS JH19B-BMW	57
6	Fredy Leinhard	March 832-BMW	55

Winner's average speed: 108.305 mph. Pole position: Alliot (Martini 001-BMW), 1m09.21. Fastest lap: Alliot, 1m10.95

Gran Premio del Mediterraneo

31 July 1983. Enna-Pergusa. 45 laps of a 3.076-mile circuit
= 138.420 miles

1	Jonathan Palmer	Ralt RH6/83-Honda	45 1h10m11.30
2	Philippe Streiff	AGS JH19B-BMW	45 1h10m18.07
3	Mike Thackwell	Ralt RH6/83-Honda	45 1h10m24.63
4	Beppe Gabbiani	March 832-BMW	45 1h10m45.71
5	Jo Gartner	Spirit 201-BMW	45 1h10m58.19
6	Michel Ferté	Martini 001-BMW	45 1h10m59.94

Winner's average speed: 118.327 mph. Pole position: Thackwell, 1m30.82. Fastest lap: Nannini (Minardi M283-BMW), 1m31.37.

Grand Prix de Formule 2

21 August 1983. Zolder. 46 laps of a 2.648-mile circuit
= 121.808 miles

1	Jonathan Palmer	Ralt RH6/83-Honda	46 1h06m12.03
2	Mike Thackwell	Ralt RH6/83-Honda	46 1h06m22.86
3	Philippe Streiff	AGS JH19B-BMW	46 1h06m55.98
4	Christian Danner	March 832-BMW	46 1h06m57.41
5	Philippe Alliot	Martini 001-BMW	46 1h07m06.03
6	Enrique Mansilla	March 832-BMW	46 1h07m26.92

Winner's average speed: 110.399 mph. Pole position: Palmer, 1m24.09. Fastest lap: Palmer, 1m25.09

Euro Mugello

4 September 1983. Mugello. 42 laps of a 3.259-mile circuit
= 136.878 miles

1	Jonathan Palmer	Ralt RH6/83-Honda	42 1h14m58.38
2	Mike Thackwell	Ralt RH6/83-Honda	42 1h14m58.70
3	Philippe Streiff	AGS JH19B-BMW	42 1h16m06.00
4	Alessandro Nannini	Minardi M283-BMW	42 1h16m27.42
5	Dave Scott	March 832-BMW	42 1h16m32.69
6	Fulvio Ballabio	AGS JH19B-BMW	41

Winner's average speed: 109.542 mph. Pole position: Palmer, 1m40.73. Fastest lap: Palmer, 1m45.69

FINAL CHAMPIONSHIP POSITIONS

Drivers

1	Jonathan Palmer	68(75)*	12=	Philippe Alliot	4
2	Mike Thackwell	51		Roberto del Castello	4
3	Beppe Gabbiani	39		Guido Dacco	4
4	Philippe Streiff	25		Alain Ferté	4
5	Christian Danner	21	16	Kazuyoshi Hoshino	3
6	Jo Gartner	14	17=	Fulvio Ballabio	3
7=	Alessandro Nannini	11		Dave Scott	3
	Thierry Tassin	11	19	Enrique Mansilla	2
9	Stefan Bellof	9	20=	Rolf Biland	1
10=	Kenneth Acheson	6		Michel Ferté	1
	Pierluigi Martini	6		Frank Jelinski	1
				Lamberto Leoni	1
				Fredy Lienhard	1
				*Best nine results count	

1984

Marlboro/Daily Express International Trophy

1 April 1984. Silverstone. 47 laps of a 2.932-mile circuit
= 137.804 miles

1	Mike Thackwell	Ralt RH6/84-Honda	47 1h01m04.11
2	Roberto Moreno	Ralt RH6/84-Honda	47 1h01m38.25
3	Michel Ferté	Martini 002-BMW	46
4	Thierry Tassin	March 842-BMW	46

Formula Two

5 Pascal Fabre   March 842-BMW   46
6 Emanuele Pirro   March 842-BMW   46

Winner's average speed: 135.393 mph. Pole position: Moreno, 1m14.82. Fastest lap: Thackwell, 1m16.00

Jim Clark-Rennen

8 April 1984. Hockenheim. 30 laps of a 4.224-mile circuit = 126.708 miles

1 Roberto Moreno   Ralt RH6/84-Honda   30 1h01m43.63
2 Mike Thackwell   Ralt RH6/84-Honda   30 1h01m44.16
3 Michel Ferté   Martini 002-BMW   30 1h02m16.49
4 Emanuele Pirro   March 842-BMW   30 1h02m23.55
5 Philippe Streiff   AGS JH19C-BMW   30 1h02m26.35
6 Christian Danner   March 842-BMW   30 1h02m28.37

Winner's average speed: 123.163 mph. Pole position: M Ferté, 2m00.19. Fastest lap: Thackwell, 2m01.21

P&O Ferries Jochen Rindt Trophy

23 April 1984. Thruxton. 55 laps of a 2.356-mile circuit = 129.580 miles

1 Mike Thackwell   Ralt RH6/84-Honda   55 1h03m11.78
2 Christian Danner   March 842-BMW   55 1h03m33.05
3 Philippe Streiff   AGS JH19C-BMW   55 1h04m22.51
4 Emanuele Pirro   March 842-BMW   54
5 Thierry Tassin   March 842-BMW   54
6 Didier Theys   Martini 002-BMW   54

Winner's average speed: 123.026 mph. Pole position: Thackwell, 1m05.68. Fastest lap: Thackwell, 1m07.38

Gran Premio di Roma

13 May 1984. Vallelunga. 65 laps of a 1.988-mile circuit = 129.220 miles

1 Mike Thackwell   Ralt RH6/84-Honda   65 1h15m59.41
2 Roberto Moreno   Ralt RH6/84-Honda   65 1h16m17.87
3 Christian Danner   March 842-BMW   65 1h16m37.94
4 Michel Ferté   Martini 002-BMW   64
5 Pascal Fabre   March 842-BMW   64
6 Didier Theys   Martini 002-BMW   64

Winner's average speed: 102.029 mph. Pole position: Thackwell, 1m05.69. Fastest lap: Thackwell, 1m07.38

Trofeo Banca Toscana

19 May 1984. Mugello. 42 laps of a 3.259-mile circuit = 136.878 miles

1 Mike Thackwell   Ralt RH6/84-Honda   42 1h13m38.89
2 Michel Ferté   Martini 002-BMW   42 1h14m58.89
3 Christian Danner   March 842-BMW   42 1h15m00.93
4 Emanuele Pirro   March 842-BMW   42 1h15m15.35
5 Thierry Tassin   March 842-BMW   41
6 Didier Theys   Martini 002-BMW   41

Winner's average speed: 111.512 mph. Pole position: Danner, 1m39.45. Fastest lap: Thackwell, 1m43.92

Grand Prix de Pau

11 June 1984. Pau. 73 laps of a 1.715-mile circuit = 125.195 miles

1 Mike Thackwell   Ralt RH6/84-Honda   73 1h29m39.73
2 Philippe Streiff   AGS JH19C-BMW   73 1h30m20.59
3 Roberto Moreno   Ralt RH6/84-Honda   73 1h30m23.45
4 Christian Danner   March 842-BMW   73 1h30m41.70
5 Alain Ferté   Martini 002-BMW   73 1h30m48.82
6 Pierre Petit   March 842-BMW   72

Winner's average speed: 83.778 mph. Pole position: Thackwell, 1m10.51. Fastest lap: Thackwell, 1m12.65

Hockenheim F2

24 June 1984. Hockenheim. 30 laps of a 4.224-mile circuit = 126.708 miles

1 Pascal Fabre   March 842-BMW   30 1h02m20.22
2 Thierry Tassin   March 842-BMW   30 1h02m27.14
3 Michel Ferté   Martini 002-BMW   30 1h02m28.63
4 Alessandro Nannini Minardi M283-BMW   30 1h02m29.28
5 Pierre Petit   March 842-BMW   30 1h03m10.93
6 Roberto del Castello Minardi M283-BMW   30 1h03m11.49

Winner's average speed: 121.958 mph. Pole position: Thackwell (Ralt RH6/84-Honda), 2m00.33. Fastest lap: Thackwell, 2m01.73

Gran Premio del Adriatico

22 July 1984. Misano. 58 laps of a 2.167-mile circuit = 125.686 miles

1 Mike Thackwell   Ralt RH6/84-Honda   58 1h08m15.71
2 Philippe Streiff   AGS JH19C-BMW   57
3 Pierre Petit   March 842-BMW   57
4 Thierry Tassin   March 842-BMW   57
5 Guido Dacco   March 832-BMW   57
6 Christian Danner   March 842-BMW   57

Winner's average speed: 110.474 mph. Pole position: Moreno (Ralt RH6/84-Honda), 1m08.72. Fastest lap: Moreno, 1m08.50

Gran Premio del Mediterraneo

29 July 1984. Enna-Pergusa. 45 laps of a 3.076-mile circuit = 138.420 miles

1 Mike Thackwell   Ralt RH6/84-Honda   45 1h08m55.21
2 Roberto Moreno   Ralt RH6/84-Honda   45 1h08m57.71
3 Alessandro Nannini Minardi M283-BMW   45 1h09m27.21
4 Pierre Petit   March 842-BMW   45 1h09m27.23
5 Michel Ferté   Martini 002-BMW   45 1h10m11.07
6 Emanuele Pirro   March 842-BMW   45 1h10m21.32

Winner's average speed: 120.505 mph. Pole position: Thackwell, 1m29.48. Fastest lap: Thackwell, 1m30.09

Derby Evening Telegraph Trophy

27 August 1984. Donington Park. 70 laps of a 1.957-mile circuit = 136.990 miles

1 Roberto Moreno   Ralt RH6/84-Honda   70 1h16m32.37
2 Emanuele Pirro   March 842-BMW   70 1h16m46.50
3 Christian Danner   March 842-BMW   70 1h16m47.76
4 Mike Thackwell   Ralt RH6/84-Honda   70 1h16m51.35
5 Thierry Tassin   March 842-BMW   70 1h16m59.21
6 "Pierre Chauvet"   March 842-BMW   69

Winner's average speed: 107.404 mph. Pole position: Thackwell, 1m01.06. Fastest lap: Thackwell, 1m04.37

Daily Mail Trophy

23 September 1984. Brands Hatch. 47 laps of a 2.614-mile circuit = 122.858 miles. Race stopped and restarted due to rain

1 Philippe Streiff   AGS JH19C-BMW   47 1h09m11.39
2 Michel Ferté   Martini 002-BMW   47 1h10m21.48
3 Roberto Moreno   Ralt RH6/84-Honda   47 1h10m32.38
4 Tomas Kaiser   March 842-BMW   47 1h10m34.84
5 Alessandro Nannini Minardi M283-BMW   47 1h10m51.63
6 Emanuele Pirro   March 842-BMW   46

Winner's average speed: 106.524 mph. Pole position: Moreno, 1m16.63. Fastest lap: Moreno, 1m18.57

FINAL CHAMPIONSHIP POSITIONS

Drivers

1	Mike Thackwell	69 (72)*	9	Pierre Petit	10
2	Roberto Moreno	44	10	Alessandro Nannini	9
3	Michel Ferté	29	11=	Tomas Kaiser	3
4	Philippe Streiff	27		Didier Theys	3
5	Christian Danner	23	13=	Guido Dacco	2
6=	Emanuele Pirro	18		Alain Ferté	2
	Thierry Tassin	18	15=	Roberto del Castello	1
8	Pascal Fabre	13		"Pierre Chauvet"	1
				*Best eight results count	

RECORDS

DRIVERS' RECORDS

MOST WINS

Jochen Rindt	12	Emerson Fittipaldi	6
Bruno Giacomelli	11	Brian Henton	6
Mike Thackwell	9	Jonathan Palmer	6
Jean-Pierre Jarier	7	Ronnie Peterson	6
Jacques Laffite	7	Thierry Boutsen	5
René Arnoux	6	Jean-Pierre Jabouille	5
Corrado Fabi	6	Hans-Joachim Stuck	5

HIGHEST POINTS TOTALS

Mike Thackwell	164	Thierry Boutsen	88
Brian Henton	123	Jean-Pierre Jarier	88
Patrick Depailler	119	Bebbe Gabbiani	87
Bruno Giacomelli	114	Corrado Fabi	86
Jean-Pierre Jabouille	109	Patrick Tambay	86
Eddie Cheever	106	Jonathan Palmer	85
René Arnoux	104	Derek Bell	83
Marc Surer	94	Michel Leclère	81
Jacques Laffite	91	Jean-Pierre Beltoise	75

MOST POLE POSITIONS

Bruno Giacomelli	11	Hans-Joachim Stuck	7
Ronnie Peterson	9	Patrick Tambay	6
Mike Thackwell	9	Emerson Fittibaldi	5
Thierry Boutsen	8	Jean-Pierre Jabouille	5
Brian Henton	8	Jean-Pierre Jarier	5
Jochen Rindt	8	Stefan Johansson	5
Jean-Pierre Beltoise	7	Michel Leclère	5
Patrick Depailler	7	Jonathan Palmer	5
Jacques Laffite	7		

MOST FASTEST LAPS

Mike Thackwell	16	Stefan Bellof	6
Brian Henton	12*	Jean-Pierre Jabouille	6
Jochen Rindt	11**	Jean-Pierre Beltoise	5*
Bruno Giacomelli	9*		*includes a shared
Patrick Depailler	8		fastest lap
Ronnie Peterson	7		**includes two shared
René Arnoux	6		fastest laps

YOUNGEST DRIVERS TO WIN A FORMULA TWO RACE

19 years 168 days	Eddie Cheever	1977 Rouen
19 years 364 days	Mike Thackwell	1981 Silverstone
20 years 42 days	Corrado Fabi	1981 Mugello
21 years 72 days	Andrea de Cesaris	1980 Misano

OLDEST DRIVERS TO WIN A FORMULA TWO RACE

42 years 56 days	Graham Hill	1971 Thruxton
38 years 163 days	John Surtees	1972 Imola
37 years 335 days	Vittorio Brambilla	1975 Vallelunga
35 years 281 days	Frank Gardner	1967 Hockenheim

OTHER RECORDS

Widest championship-winning margin:
36 points, Jean-Pierre Jarier, 1973

Narrowest championship-winning margin:
One point, Jean-Pierre Jabouille, 1976 and Corrado Fabi, 1982

Most wins in a season:
Eight, Bruno Giacomelli, 1978

Most successive wins:
Five, Jonathan Palmer, 1983

Most points in a season:
82, Bruno Giacomelli, 1978

Most successive points-scoring finishes:
Nine, Derek Bell, 1969-70 and Mike Thackwell, 1983-84

Driver to score points in all championship rounds in a season:
Derek Bell, 1970 (Eight races)

Narrowest race-winning margin:
The first four drivers (Rindt, Courage, Tino Brambilla and Regazzoni) were all credited with the same time for the 1968 Mediterranean GP at Enna-Pergusa. The first two drivers (Rindt and Graham Hill) were also credited with the same time at Snetterton 1967

Widest race-winning margin:
One lap. Four events have been won by over a lap: Beltoise, 1968 Zandvoort; Servoz-Gavin, 1969 Vallelunga; Depailler, 1974 Pau and Thackwell, 1984 Misano. The widest victory in terms of time is 1m26.4, Emerson Fittipaldi, 1972 Hockenheim second race

ENGINE RECORDS

MOST WINS

BMW	94	Hart	17
Ford	60	Renault	12
Honda	23	Ferrari	3

MANUFACTURERS' RECORDS

MOST WINS

March	77	Elf	8
Ralt	23	Toleman	8
Brabham	18	Chevron	6
Martini	14	Surtees	5
Lotus	10	Tecno	5
Matra	10		

TEAMS' RECORDS

MOST WINS

March Engineering	58	Tyrrell Racing	
Ralt Racing	20	Organisation	6
Automobiles Martini	14	Project 4 Racing	5
Roy Winkelmann		Rondel Racing	5
Racing	11	Team Surtees	5
Elf Switzerland	7	Tecno Racing Team	5
Toleman Group			
Motorsport	7		

INTERNATIONAL FORMULA 3000 CHAMPIONSHIP

The start of the 1987 Birmingham Super Prix with eventual winner Stefano Modena to the fore

Formula 3000 had first been proposed in 1983 as a replacement for Formula Two but it was not until 1985 that the first series was organized. F2 chassis regulations remained but 3000 cc engines were specified (hence Formula 3000).

Most competitors opted for power from the Ford Cosworth DFV which had been the mainstay of the British Grand Prix teams since the late 1960s. The championship suffered from a lack of competitors

in its first year, with only 11 cars starting at Pau, but since then F3000 has been well supported.

However, teams have always complained that the series is poorly promoted, and with costs spiralling major changes are expected for the 1996 season.

As the F2 champion failed to win the World Championship, a F3000 champion has yet to win a Grand Prix, a statistic that Alesi, Panis et al will be keen to remedy.

RULES

CARS

Single seater cars using 3000 cc racing engines. From 1986 Avon tyres were specified.

POINTS

9-6-4-3-2-1 to the top six finishers.

INTERNATIONAL FORMULA 3000 CHAMPIONS

year	driver	nat	team	car
1985	Christian Danner	D	Bob Sparshott Automotive	March 85B-Cosworth
1986	Ivan Capelli	I	Genoa Racing	March 86B-Cosworth
1987	Stefano Modena	I	Onyx Race Engineering	March 87B-Cosworth
1988	Roberto Moreno	BR	Bromley Motorsport	Reynard 88D-Cosworth
1989	Jean Alesi	F	Eddie Jordan Racing	Reynard 89D-Mugen
1990	Erik Comas	F	DAMS	Lola T90/50-Mugen
1991	Christian Fittipaldi	BR	Pacific Racing	Reynard 91D-Mugen
1992	Luca Badoer	I	Team Crypton	Reynard 92D-Cosworth
1993	Olivier Panis	F	DAMS	Reynard 93D-Cosworth
1994	Jules Boullion	F	DAMS	Reynard 94D-Cosworth

1985

Marlboro/Daily Express International Trophy

24 March 1985. Silverstone. 44 laps of a 2.932-mile circuit = 129.008 miles

1	Mike Thackwell	Ralt RB20-Cosworth	44	1h07m41.01
2	John Nielsen	Ralt RB20-Cosworth	44	1h08m13.35
3	Michel Ferté	March 85B-Cosworth	44	1h09m09.77
4	Christian Danner	March 85B-Cosworth	43	
5	Gabriele Tarquini	March 85B-Cosworth	42	
6	Roberto Moreno	Tyrrell 012-Cosworth	42	

Winner's average speed: 114.363 mph. Pole position: M Ferté, 1m17.92. Fastest lap: Nielsen, 1m27.64

Townsend Thoresen Jochen Rindt Trophy

8 April 1985. Thruxton. 54 laps of a 2.356-mile circuit = 127.224 miles

1	Emanuele Pirro	March 85B-Cosworth	54	1h05m00.83
2	Mike Thackwell	Ralt RB20-Cosworth	54	1h05m03.31
3	Michel Ferté	March 85B-Cosworth	54	1h05m14.44
4	Tomas Kaiser	March 85B-Cosworth	54	1h06m09.18
5	Gabriele Tarquini	March 85B-Cosworth	53	
6	Christian Danner	March 85B-Cosworth	53	

Winner's average speed: 117.413 mph. Pole position: Thackwell, 1m06.33. Fastest lap: Danner, 1m09.40

Estoril F3000

20 April 1985. Estoril. 47 laps of a 2.703-mile circuit = 127.041 miles

1	John Nielsen	Ralt RB20-Cosworth	47	1h12m44.424
2	Michel Ferté	March 85B-Cosworth	47	1h12m57.792
3	Gabriele Tarquini	March 85B-Cosworth	47	1h13m36.616
4	Emanuele Pirro	March 85B-Cosworth	47	1h14m14.674
5	Roberto Moreno	Tyrrell 012-Cosworth	46	
6	Olivier Grouillard	March 85B-Cosworth	46	

Winner's average speed: 104.790 mph. Pole position: Thackwell (Ralt RB20-Cosworth), 1m30.180. Fastest lap: Thackwell, 1m30.306

Mike Thackwell: winner of the first ever F3000 championship race

Eifelrennen

28 April 1985. Nürburgring. Cancelled due to snow on raceday

NO RACE

Pole position: Thackwell (Ralt RB20-Cosworth), 1m28.47

Gran Premio di Roma

12 May 1985. Vallelunga. 65 laps of a 1.988-mile circuit = 129.220 miles

1	Emanuele Pirro	March 85B-Cosworth	65	1h15m14.83
2	John Nielsen	Ralt RB20-Cosworth	65	1h15m36.66
3	Christian Danner	March 85B-Cosworth	65	1h15m37.12
4	Olivier Grouillard	March 85B-Cosworth	65	1h15m37.74
5	Philippe Streiff	AGS JH20-Cosworth	65	1h16m03.81
6	Johnny Dumfries	March 85B-Cosworth	65	1h16m15.34

Winner's average speed: 103.036 mph. Pole position: Thackwell (Ralt RB20-Cosworth), 1m05.88. Fastest lap: Pirro, 1m08.36

Grand Prix de Pau

27 May 1985. Pau. 72 laps of a 1.715-mile circuit = 123.480 miles

International Formula 3000 Championship

1	Christian Danner	March 85B-Cosworth	72	1h30m28.63
2	Emanuele Pirro	March 85B-Cosworth	72	1h31m10.38
3	Lamberto Leoni	Williams FW08C-		
		Cosworth	72	1h31m28.25
4	Olivier Grouillard	March 85B-Cosworth	72	1h31m32.13
5	Philippe Streiff	AGS JH20-Cosworth	71	

No other finishers. Winner's average speed: 81.886 mph. Pole position: Pirro, 1m12.65. Fastest lap: Danner, 1m13.26

Grand Prix de Belgique Formule 3000

2 June 1985. Spa-Francorchamps. 29 laps of a 4.318-mile circuit = 125.222 miles

1	Mike Thackwell	Ralt RB20-Cosworth	29	1h11m56.510
2	Alain Ferté	March 85B-Cosworth	29	1h12m46.546
3	Christian Danner	March 85B-Cosworth	29	1h12m55.153
4	Gabriele Tarquini	March 85B-Cosworth	29	1h12m57.814
5	Guido Dacco	March 85B-Cosworth	29	1h13m37.044
6	Juan Manuel			
	Fangio II	Lola T950-Cosworth	29	1h13m52.332

Winner's average speed: 104.434 mph. Pole position: M Ferté (March 85B-Cosworth), 2m11.195. Fastest lap: Thackwell, 2m26.769

Dijon-Prenois F3000

30 June 1985. Dijon-Prenois. 55 laps of a 2.361-mile circuit = 129.855 miles

1	Christian Danner	March 85B-Cosworth	55	1h08m54.10
2	Mike Thackwell	Ralt RB20-Cosworth	55	1h09m16.96
3	John Nielsen	Ralt RB20-Cosworth	55	1h10m04.59
4	Alain Ferté	March 85B-Cosworth	55	1h10m05.05
5	Guido Dacco	March 85B-Cosworth	54	
6	Philippe Alliot	March 85B-Cosworth	54	

Winner's average speed: 113.079 mph. Pole position: Nielsen, 1m10.21. Fastest lap: Tassin (March 85B-Cosworth), 1m13.80

Gran Premio del Mediterraneo

28 July 1985. Enna-Pergusa. 40 laps of a 3.076-mile circuit = 123.040 miles

1	Mike Thackwell	Ralt RB20-Cosworth	40	1h01m58.99
2	Emanuele Pirro	March 85B-Cosworth	40	1h01m59.62
3	Christian Danner	March 85B-Cosworth	40	1h02m20.10
4	Gabriele Tarquini	March 85B-Cosworth	40	1h02m51.85
5	Mario Hytten	March 85B-Cosworth	40	1h02m52.61
6	Guido Dacco	March 85B-Cosworth	40	1h02m53.32

Winner's average speed: 119.103 mph. Pole position: Thackwell, 1m29.52. Fastest lap: Danner, 1m31.29

Österreichring F3000

17 August 1985. Österreichring. 31 laps of a 3.692-mile circuit = 114.452 miles

1	Ivan Capelli	March 85B-Cosworth	31	53m56.114
2	John Nielsen	Ralt RB20-Cosworth	31	53m56.698
3	Lamberto Leoni	March 85B-Cosworth	31	54m12.296
4	Emanuele Pirro	March 85B-Cosworth	31	54m19.762
5	Philippe Streiff	AGS JH20-Cosworth	31	54m22.483
6	Thierry Tassin	March 85B-Cosworth	31	54m25.584

Winner's average speed: 127.322 mph. Pole position: Danner (March 85B-Cosworth), 1m39.780. Fastest lap: Thackwell (Ralt RB20-Cosworth), 1m42.244

Zandvoort F3000

24 August 1985. Zandvoort. 48 laps of a 2.642-mile circuit = 126.816 miles

1	Christian Danner	March 85B-Cosworth	48	1h15m19.023
2	Mike Thackwell	Ralt RB20-Cosworth	48	1h15m23.404
3	Philippe Streiff	AGS JH20-Cosworth	48	1h15m51.264
4	John Nielsen	Ralt RB20-Cosworth	48	1h16m14.199
5	Emanuele Pirro	March 85B-Cosworth	47	
6	Guido Dacco	March 85B-Cosworth	47	

Winner's average speed: 101.026 mph. Pole position: Danner, 1m21.450. Fastest lap: Danner, 1m23.645

Donington Park F3000

22 September 1985. Donington Park. 40 laps of a 2.500-mile circuit = 100.000 miles

1	Christian Danner	March 85B-Cosworth	40	59m17.83
2	Mario Hytten	March 85B-Cosworth	40	59m27.96
3	Ivan Capelli	March 85B-Cosworth	40	59m28.47
4	Michel Ferté	March 85B-Cosworth	40	59m35.67
5	Philippe Streiff	AGS JH20-Cosworth	40	59m41.23
6	Alain Ferté	March 85B-Cosworth	40	59m41.52

Winner's average speed: 101.185 mph. Pole position: Thackwell (Ralt RB20-Cosworth), 1m23.59. Fastest lap: Capelli, 1m27.60

FINAL CHAMPIONSHIP POSITIONS

Drivers

1	Christian			12	Olivier Grouillard	7
	Danner	51 (52)*		13	Guido Dacco	6
2	Mike Thackwell	45		14=	Tomas Kaiser	
3	Emanuele Pirro	38			Roberto Moreno	3
4	John Nielsen	34		16=	Philippe Alliot	1
5	Michel Ferté	17			Johnny Dumfries	1
6	Gabriele Tarquini	14			Juan Manuel	
7	Ivan Capelli	13			Fangio II	1
8	Philippe Streiff	12			Thierry Tassin	1
9	Alain Ferté	10			*Best eight results count	
10=	Mario Hytten	8				
	Lamberto Leoni	8				

1986

Daily Express International Trophy

13 April 1986. Silverstone. 24 laps of a 2.932-mile circuit = 70.368 miles. Race scheduled for 44 laps but abandoned when a serious accident stopped the race for the second time, aggregate of a two and a 22-lap heat, half points awarded

1	Pascal Fabre	Lola T86/50-Cosworth	24	35m33.97
2	Emanuele Pirro	March 86B-Cosworth	24	35m35.19
3	John Nielsen	Ralt RT20-Honda	24	35m50.26
4	Mike Thackwell	Lola T86/50-Cosworth	24	35m51.50
5	Tomas Kaiser	Lola T86/50-Cosworth	24	36m01.06
6	Alessandro Santin	Lola T86/50-Cosworth	24	36m01.32

Winner's average speed: 118.711 mph. Pole position: Fabre, 1m19.83. Fastest lap: Fabre, 1m26.65

Gran Premio di Roma

4 May 1986. Vallelunga. 64 laps of a 1.988-mile circuit = 127.232 miles

1	Ivan Capelli	March 86B-Cosworth	64	1h14m24.22
2	Pascal Fabre	Lola T86/50-Cosworth	64	1h14m42.88
3	Emanuele Pirro	March 86B-Cosworth	64	1h14m43.23
4	Mauricio Gugelmin	March 86B-Cosworth	64	1h14m45.77
5	Satoru Nakajima	Ralt RT20-Honda	64	1h14m46.02
6	Alessandro Santin	Lola T86/50-Cosworth	64	1h15m16.90

Winner's average speed: 102.601 mph. Pole position: Capelli, 1m07.13. Fastest lap: Capelli, 1m08.27

Grand Prix de Pau

19 May 1986. Pau. 73 laps of a 1.715-mile circuit = 125.195 miles

1	Mike Thackwell	Ralt RT20-Honda	73	1h31m17.92
2	Emanuele Pirro	March 86B-Cosworth	73	1h32m11.07
3	Michel Ferté	March 86B-Cosworth	73	1h32m31.14
4	Richard Dallest	AGS JH20B-Cosworth	72	
5	Luis Perez Sala	Ralt RT20-Cosworth	72	
6	John Jones	March 86B-Cosworth	71	

Winner's average speed: 82.276 mph. Pole position: Pirro, 1m11.83. Fastest lap: Pirro, 1m13.70

Grand Prix de Belgique Formule 3000

24 May 1986. Spa-Francorchamps. 28 laps of a 4.318-mile circuit = 120.904 miles

1	Philippe Alliot	March 86B-Cosworth	28	1h02m03.562
2	John Nielsen	Ralt RT20-Honda	28	1h02m06.078
3	Ivan Capelli	March 86B-Cosworth	28	1h02m12.390
4	Luis Perez Sala	Ralt RT20-Cosworth	28	1h02m26.430
5	Michel Ferté	March 86B-Cosworth	28	1h02m43.260
6	Pierre-Henri Raphanel	March 86B-Cosworth	28	1h02m49.760

Winner's average speed: 116.889 mph. Pole position: Alliot, 2m09.87. Fastest lap: Nielsen, 2m11.139

Trofeo Elio de Angelis

8 June 1986. Imola. 39 laps of a 3.132-mile circuit = 122.148 miles

1	Pierluigi Martini	Ralt RT20-Cosworth	39	1h05m48.56
2	Ivan Capelli	March 86B-Cosworth	39	1h05m49.37
3	Alain Ferté	March 86B-Cosworth	39	1h06m14.84
4	Gabriele Tarquini	March 85B-Cosworth	39	1h06m26.00
5	Luis Perez Sala	Ralt RT20-Cosworth	39	1h06m26.55
6	Franco Forini	March 86B-Cosworth	39	1h06m54.62

Winner's average speed: 111.365 mph. Pole position: Capelli, 1m39.25. Fastest lap: M Ferté (March 86B-Cosworth), 1m39.60

Euro Mugello

29 June 1986. Mugello. 38 laps of a 3.259-mile circuit = 123.842 miles

1	Pierluigi Martini	Ralt RT20-Cosworth	38	1h10m48.43
2	Michel Ferté	March 86B-Cosworth	38	1h10m48.85
3	Ivan Capelli	March 86B-Cosworth	38	1h10m54.34
4	Olivier Grouillard	Lola T86/50-Cosworth	38	1h10m59.80
5	Satoru Nakajima	Ralt RT20-Honda	38	1h11m12.92
6	Emanuele Pirro	March 86B-Cosworth	38	1h11m33.71

Winner's average speed: 104.940 mph. Pole position: Martini, 1m44.73. Fastest lap: Martini, 1m49.35

Gran Premio del Mediterraneo

20 July 1986. Enna-Pergusa. 40 laps of a 3.076-mile circuit = 123.040 miles

1	Luis Perez Sala	Ralt RT20-Cosworth	40	1h01m42.72
2	Pierluigi Martini	Ralt RT20-Cosworth	40	1h01m49.52
3	Pascal Fabre	Lola T86/50-Cosworth	40	1h01m50.63
4	Tomas Kaiser	Lola T86/50-Cosworth	40	1h01m55.66
5	Claudio Langes	Lola T86/50-Cosworth	40	1h01m57.17
6	John Nielsen	Ralt RT20-Honda	40	1h02m04.46

Winner's average speed: 119.627 mph. Pole position: Capelli (March 86B-Cosworth), 1m29.75. Fastest lap: Thackwell (Lola T86/50-Cosworth), 1m30.92

Österreichring F3000

16 August 1986. Österreichring. 34 laps of a 3.692-mile circuit = 125.528 miles

1	Ivan Capelli	March 86B-Cosworth	34	58m47.530
2	John Nielsen	Ralt RT20-Honda	34	58m49.688
3	Gabriele Tarquini	March 85B-Cosworth	34	59m22.944
4	Satoru Nakajima	Ralt RT20-Honda	34	59m23.120
5	Luis Perez Sala	Ralt RT20-Cosworth	34	59m27.301
6	Olivier Grouillard	Lola T86/50-Cosworth	34	59m31.762

Winner's average speed: 128.107 mph. Pole position: Nielsen, 1m40.527. Fastest lap: Nielsen, 1m42.704

Halfords Birmingham Superprix

25 August 1986. Birmingham. 24 laps of a 2.470-mile circuit = 59.280 miles. Race scheduled for 52 laps but stopped due to heavy rain, half points awarded

1	Luis Perez Sala	Ralt RT20-Cosworth	24	42m24.40
2	Pierluigi Martini	Ralt RT20-Cosworth	24	42m27.72
3	Michel Ferté	March 86B-Cosworth	24	42m29.70
4	Eliseo Salazar	Lola T86/50-Cosworth	24	42m37.63
5	Pascal Fabre	Lola T86/50-Cosworth	24	43m07.83
6	Russell Spence	March 86B-Cosworth	24	43m20.19

Winner's average speed: 83.87 mph. Pole position: Martini, 1m22.16. Fastest lap: Salazar, 1m42.62

Le Mans F3000

28 September 1986. Le Mans-Bugatti. 47 laps of a 2.635-mile circuit = 123.845 miles

1	Emanuele Pirro	March 86B-Cosworth	47	1h10m36.43
2	Michel Ferté	March 86B-Cosworth	47	1h10m42.95
3	Pierre-Henri Raphanel	March 86B-Cosworth	47	1h10m48.83
4	Ivan Capelli	March 86B-Cosworth	47	1h10m56.28
5	Luis Perez Sala	Ralt RT20-Cosworth	47	1h11m49.00
6	Claudio Langes	Lola T86/50-Cosworth	47	1h12m04.01

Winner's average speed: 105.240 mph. Pole position: Pirro, 1m27.31. Fastest lap: Pirro, 1m29.20

Jarama F3000

5 October 1986. Jarama. 58 laps of a 2.115-mile circuit = 122.670 miles. Race stopped after 43 laps and restarted over a further 15 laps

1	Pierluigi Martini	Ralt RT20-Cosworth	58	*
2	Emanuele Pirro	March 86B-Cosworth	58	1h18m05.49
3	Michel Ferté	March 86B-Cosworth	58	1h18m15.92
4	Ivan Capelli	March 86B-Cosworth	58	1h18m36.42
5	John Nielsen	Ralt RT20-Honda	58	1h18m44.42
6	Mauricio Gugelmin	March 86B-Cosworth	58	1h18m48.07

*Originally disqualified because the team worked on the car between heats, later reinstated but no time published. Winner's average speed: n/a. Pole position: Pirro, 1m18.17. Fastest lap: M Ferté, 1m19.51

FINAL CHAMPIONSHIP POSITIONS

Drivers

1	Ivan Capelli	38	13=	Alain Ferté	4
2	Pierluigi Martini	36		Olivier Grouillard	4
3	Emanuele Pirro	29		Mauricio Gugelmin	4
4	Luis Perez Sala	24.5		Tomas Kaiser	4
5	Michel Ferté	24	17=	Richard Dallest	3
6	John Nielsen	17		Claudio Langes	3
7	Pascal Fabre	15.5	19=	Eliseo Salazar	1.5
8	Mike Thackwell	10.5		Alessandro Santin	1.5
9	Philippe Alliot	9	21=	Franco Forini	1
10=	Satoru Nakajima	7		John Jones	1
	Gabriele Tarquini	7	23	Russell Spence	0.5
12	Pierre-Henri Raphanel	5			

1987

Marlboro International Trophy

12 April 1987. Silverstone. 42 laps of a 2.969-mile circuit = 124.698 miles

1	Mauricio Gugelmin	Ralt RT21-Honda	42	57m07.10
2	Michel Trollé	Lola T87/50-Cosworth	42	57m20.73
3	Roberto Moreno	Ralt RT21-Honda	42	57m21.81
4	Stefano Modena	March 87B-Cosworth	42	57m22.83
5	Pierluigi Martini	Ralt RT21-Cosworth	42	57m51.33
6	Alfonso Garcia de Vinuesa	Lola T87/50-Cosworth	42	57m55.32

Winner's average speed: 130.989 mph. Pole position: Moreno, 1m19.08. Fastest lap: Moreno, 1m20.66

Gran Premio di Roma

10 May 1987. Vallelunga. 61 laps of a 1.988-mile circuit = 121.268 miles. Race stopped after 19 laps and restarted over a further 42 laps

1	Stefano Modena	March 87B-Cosworth	61	1h10m06.20
2	Luis Perez Sala	Lola T87/50-Cosworth	61	1h10m18.53
3	Mauricio Gugelmin	Ralt RT21-Honda	61	1h10m40.72
4	Pierre-Henri Raphanel	March 87B-Cosworth	61	1h10m43.25
5	John Jones	Lola T87/50-Cosworth	61	1h11m08.83
6	Mark Blundell	Lola T86/50-Cosworth	61	1h11m12.10

Winner's average speed: 103.791 mph. Pole position: Dalmas (March 87B-Cosworth), 1m06.30. Fastest lap: Modena, 1m08.05

International Formula 3000 Championship

Spa-Francorchamps F3000

16 May 1987. Spa-Francorchamps. 16 laps of a 4.318-mile circuit = 69.088 miles. Race scheduled for 29 laps but stopped due to accident, half points awarded

1	Michel Trollé	Lola T87/50-Cosworth	16	38m57.67
2	Mark Blundell	Lola T86/50-Cosworth	16	39m00.72
3	Roberto Moreno	Ralt RT21-Honda	16	39m07.52
4	Andy Wallace	March 87B-Cosworth	16	39m10.31
5	Marco Apicella	Dallara 3087-Cosworth	16	39m25.46
6	Gary Evans	Ralt RT21-Cosworth	16	39m51.52

Winner's average speed: 106.393 mph. Pole position: Moreno, 2m23.77. Fastest lap: Sala (Lola T87/50-Cosworth), 2m15.99

Grand Prix de Pau

8 June 1987. Pau. 72 laps of a 1.715-mile circuit = 123.480 miles

1	Yannick Dalmas	March 87B-Cosworth	72	1h30m14.55
2	John Jones	Lola T87/50-Cosworth	72	1h30m24.47
3	Michel Ferté	Lola T87/50-Cosworth	72	1h30m24.80
4	Olivier Grouillard	March 87B-Cosworth	72	1h30m41.11
5	Paul Belmondo	Lola T87/50-Cosworth	72	1h30m50.10
6	Lamberto Leoni	March 87B-Cosworth	72	1h30m52.40

Winner's average speed: 82.099 mph. Pole position: Raphanel (March 87B-Cosworth), 1m11.88. Fastest lap: Moreno (Ralt RT21-Honda), 1m13.64

Donington Park F3000

28 June 1987. Donington Park. 50 laps of a 2.500-mile circuit = 125.000 miles

1	Luis Perez Sala	Lola T87/50-Cosworth	50	1h12m16.41
2	Stefano Modena	March 87B-Cosworth	50	1h12m23.08
3	Pierre-Henri Raphanel	March 87B-Cosworth	50	1h12m40.12
4	Roberto Moreno	Ralt RT21-Honda	50	1h12m45.03
5	Michel Trollé	Lola T87/50-Cosworth	50	1h13m05.07
6	Michel Ferté	Lola T87/50-Cosworth	50	1h13m07.06

Winner's average speed: 103.772 mph. Pole position: Sala, 1m23.84. Fastest lap: Dalmas (March 87B-Cosworth), 1m25.60

Gran Premio del Mediterraneo

19 July 1987. Enna-Pergusa. 41 laps of a 3.076-mile circuit = 126.116 miles

1	Roberto Moreno	Ralt RT21-Honda	41	1h03m09.90
2	Pierluigi Martini	Ralt RT20-Cosworth	41	1h03m12.15
3	Gabriele Tarquini	March 87B-Cosworth	41	1h03m12.53
4	Julian Bailey	Lola T87/50-Cosworth	41	1h03m12.93
5	Lamberto Leoni	March 87B-Cosworth	41	1h03m13.80
6	Stefano Modena	March 87B-Cosworth	41	1h03m26.16

Winner's average speed: 119.797 mph. Pole position: Gugelmin (Ralt RT21-Honda), 1m29.46. Fastest lap: Leoni, 1m30.93

Brands Hatch F3000

23 August 1987. Brands Hatch. 45 laps of a 2.614-mile circuit = 117.630 miles. Race scheduled for 48 laps but stopped due to accident

1	Julian Bailey	Lola T87/50-Cosworth	45	59m09.96
2	Mauricio Gugelmin	Ralt RT21-Honda	45	59m12.09
3	Roberto Moreno	Ralt RT21-Honda	45	59m21.91
4	Stefano Modena	March 87B-Cosworth	45	59m24.23
5	Yannick Dalmas	March 87B-Cosworth	45	59m24.66
6	Mark Blundell	Lola T86/50-Cosworth	45	59m29.22

Winner's average speed: 119.270 mph. Pole position: Moreno, 1m16.46. Fastest lap: Dalmas, 1m17.33

Halfords Birmingham Superprix

31 August 1987. Birmingham. 51 laps of a 2.470-mile circuit = 125.970 miles

1	Stefano Modena	March 87B-Cosworth	51	1h11m44.52
2	Roberto Moreno	Ralt RT21-Honda	51	1h11m55.94
3	Mauricio Gugelmin	Ralt RT21-Honda	51	1h11m57.82
4	Luis Perez Sala	Lola T87/50-Cosworth	51	1h12m00.64
5	Andy Wallace	Lola T87/50-Cosworth	51	1h12m17.29
6	Olivier Grouillard	March 87B-Cosworth	51	1h12m17.55

Winner's average speed: 105.353 mph. Pole position: Gugelmin, 1m21.77. Fastest lap: Moreno, 1m22.91

Imola F3000

13 September 1987. Imola. 40 laps of a 3.132-mile circuit = 125.280 miles

1	Stefano Modena	March 87B-Cosworth	40	1h06m13.38
2	Gabriele Tarquini	March 87B-Cosworth	40	1h06m31.96
3	Luis Perez Sala	Lola T87/50-Cosworth	40	1h06m34.07
4	Lamberto Leoni	March 87B-Judd	40	1h06m36.99
5	Roberto Moreno	Ralt RT21-Honda	40	1h06m44.46
6	Andy Wallace	Lola T87/50-Cosworth	40	1h06m48.60

Winner's average speed: 113.507 mph. Pole position: Moreno, 1m36.59. Fastest lap: Tarquini, 1m38.29

Le Mans F3000

27 September 1987. Le Mans-Bugatti. 47 laps of a 2.635-mile circuit = 123.845 miles

1	Luis Perez Sala	Lola T87/50-Cosworth	47	1h12m49.12
2	Russell Spence	March 87B-Cosworth	47	1h13m07.21
3	Michel Trollé	Lola T87/50-Cosworth	47	1h13m11.48
4	Lamberto Leoni	March 87B-Judd	47	1h13m17.92
5	Gabriele Tarquini	March 87B-Cosworth	47	1h13m26.69
6	Julian Bailey	Lola T87/50-Cosworth	47	1h13m32.71

Winner's average speed: 102.044 mph. Pole position: Sala, 1m30.35. Fastest lap: Sala

Jarama F3000

11 October 1987. Jarama. 61 laps of a 2.115-mile circuit = 129.039 miles

1	Yannick Dalmas	March 87B-Cosworth	61	1h23m21.289
2	Mauricio Gugelmin	Ralt RT21-Honda	61	1h23m35.931
3	Russell Spence	March 87B-Cosworth	61	1h23m45.770
4	Lamberto Leoni	March 87B-Judd	61	1h23m46.670
5	Luis Perez Sala	Lola T87/50-Cosworth	61	1h23m47.930
6	Stefano Modena	March 87B-Cosworth	61	1h24m13.010

Winner's average speed: 92.884 mph. Pole position: J Jones (Lola T87/50-Cosworth), 1m28.188. Fastest lap: Dalmas, 1m20.092

FINAL CHAMPIONSHIP POSITIONS

Drivers

1	Stefano Modena	40 (41)*	13	Pierre-Henri	
2	Luis Perez Sala	33		Raphanel	7
3	Roberto Moreno	30	14=	Mark Blundell	5
4	Mauricio Gugelmin	29		Michel Ferté	5
5	Yannick Dalmas	20	16	Andy Wallace	4.5
6	Michel Trollé	16.5	17	Olivier Grouillard	4
7	Julian Bailey	13	18	Paul Belmondo	2
8=	Lamberto Leoni	12	19=	Marco Apicella	1
	Gabriele Tarquini	12		Alfonso Garcia	
10	Russell Spence	10		de Vinuesa	1
11=	John Jones	8	21	Gary Evans	0.5
	Pierluigi Martini	8		*Best seven results count	

1988

Jerez F3000

17 April 1988. Jerez. 47 laps of a 2.621-mile circuit = 123.187 miles

1	Johnny Herbert	Reynard 88D-Cosworth	47	1h17m20.02
2	Mark Blundell	Lola T88/50-Cosworth	47	1h17m29.33
3	Michel Trollé	Lola T88/50-Cosworth	47	1h17m52.04
4	Fabien Giroix	Lola T88/50-Cosworth	47	1h18m28.83
5	Olivier Grouillard	Lola T88/50-Cosworth	47	1h18m30.93
6	Eric Bernard	Ralt RT22-Judd	47	1h18m37.89

Winner's average speed: 95.572 mph. Pole position: Herbert, 1m32.85. Fastest lap: Trollé, 1m37.09

Gran Premio di Roma

8 May 1988. Vallelunga. 63 laps of a 1.988-mile circuit = 125.244 miles

1	Gregor Foitek	Lola T88/50-Cosworth	63	1h13m49.83
2	Bertrand Gachot	Reynard 88D-Cosworth	63	1h13m56.02
3	Olivier Grouillard	Lola T88/50-Cosworth	63	1h13m58.41
4	Roberto Moreno	Reynard 88D-Cosworth	63	1h13m58.61
5	Mark Blundell	Lola T88/50-Cosworth	63	1h13m59.04
6	Michel Trollé	Lola T88/50-Cosworth	63	1h14m26.60

Winner's average speed: 101.782 mph. Pole position: Foitek, 1m06.52. Fastest lap: Trollé, 1m08.26

Grand Prix de Pau

23 May 1988. Pau. 72 laps of a 1.715-mile circuit = 123.480 miles

1	Roberto Moreno	Reynard 88D-Cosworth	72	1h29m01.76
2	Jean Alesi	Reynard 88D-Cosworth	72	1h29m23.79
3	Pierluigi Martini	March 88B-Judd	72	1h29m24.71
4	Eric Bernard	Ralt RT22-Judd	72	1h29m25.22
5	Marco Apicella	March 88B-Judd	72	1h29m26.30
6	Pierre-Henri Raphanel	Reynard 88D-Cosworth	72	1h29m54.24

Winner's average speed: 83.218 mph. Pole position: Moreno, 1m10.86. Fastest lap: Apicella, 1m12.72

International Trophy

5 June 1988. Silverstone. 42 laps of a 2.969-mile circuit = 124.698 miles

1	Roberto Moreno	Reynard 88D-Cosworth	42	56m33.83
2	Bertrand Gachot	Reynard 88D-Cosworth	42	56m55.62
3	Pierre-Henri Raphanel	Reynard 88D-Cosworth	42	57m04.42
4	Gregor Foitek	Lola T88/50-Cosworth	42	57m13.53
5	Jean Alesi	Reynard 88D-Cosworth	42	57m16.59
6	Marco Apicella	March 88B-Judd	42	57m16.85

Winner's average speed: 132.273 mph. Pole position: Gachot, 1m19.61. Fastest lap: Moreno, 1m19.70

Monza F3000

26 June 1988. Monza. 31 laps of a 3.604-mile circuit = 111.721 miles. Race stopped after 13 laps and restarted over a further 18 laps

1	Roberto Moreno	Reynard 88D-Cosworth	31	51m40.552
2	Marco Apicella	March 88B-Judd	31	51m58.147
3	Johnny Herbert	Reynard 88D-Cosworth	31	52m14.330
4	Gregor Foitek	Lola T88/50-Cosworth	31	52m32.430
5	Claudio Langes	Lola T88/50-Cosworth	31	52m41.410
6	Andrea Chiesa	Lola T87/50-Cosworth	31	52m46.530

Winner's average speed: 129.717 mph. Pole position: Moreno, 1m37.22. Fastest lap: Herbert, 1m38.120

Gran Premio de Mediterraneo

17 July 1988. Enna-Pergusa. 37 laps of a 3.076-mile circuit = 113.812 miles

1	Pierluigi Martini	March 88B-Judd	37	56m20.62
2	Olivier Grouillard	Lola T88/50-Cosworth	37	56m24.67
3	Michel Trollé	Lola T88/50-Cosworth	37	56m32.45
4	Claudio Langes	Lola T88/50-Cosworth	37	56m35.82
5	Pierre-Henri Raphanel	Reynard 88D-Cosworth	37	56m41.33
6	Jean Alesi	Reynard 88D-Cosworth	37	56m45.11

Winner's average speed: 121.198 mph. Pole position: Grouillard, 1m29.07. Fastest lap: Martini, 1m30.14

Brands Hatch F3000

21 August 1988. Brands Hatch. 42 laps of a 2.600-mile circuit = 109.200 miles. Race stopped after 22 laps and restarted over a further 20 laps

1	Martin Donnelly	Reynard 88D-Cosworth	42	54m14.20
2	Pierluigi Martini	March 88B-Judd	42	54m42.97
3	Mark Blundell	Lola T88/50-Cosworth	42	54m45.26
4	Paolo Barilla	Reynard 88D-Cosworth	42	54m56.15
5	Cor Euser	Reynard 88D-Cosworth	42	55m09.47
6	Volker Weidler	March 88B-Cosworth	42	55m42.35*

Bernard (Reynard 88D-Cosworth) finished sixth but was disqualified due to an illegal rear wing. *Includes one minute penalty. Winner's average speed: 120.813 mph. Pole position: Herbert (Reynard 88D-Cosworth), 1m14.77. Fastest lap: Donnelly, 1m15.88

Halfords Birmingham Superprix

29 August 1988. Birmingham. 43 laps of a 2.470-mile circuit = 106.210 miles

1	Roberto Moreno	Reynard 88D-Cosworth	43	1h00m19.78
2	Martin Donnelly	Reynard 88D-Cosworth	43	1h00m27.48
3	Pierluigi Martini	March 88B-Judd	43	1h00m41.48
4	Volker Weidler	March 88B-Cosworth	43	1h00m57.48
5	Bertrand Gachot	Reynard 88D-Cosworth	43	1h00m58.16
6	Michel Ferté	Lola T88/50-Cosworth	43	1h01m31.24

Bernard (Reynard 88D-Cosworth) finished sixth but was disqualified as his car was under the weight limit. Winner's average speed: 105.630 mph. Pole position: Grouillard (Lola T88/50-Cosworth), 1m21.81. Fastest lap: Donnelly, 1m23.33

Le Mans F3000

25 September 1988. Le Mans-Bugatti. 47 laps of a 2.635-mile circuit = 123.845 miles

1	Olivier Grouillard	Lola T88/50-Cosworth	47	1h12m15.23
2	Martin Donnelly	Reynard 88D-Cosworth	47	1h12m22.55
3	Jean-Denis Deletraz	Lola T88/50-Cosworth	47	1h12m53.22
4	Bertrand Gachot	Reynard 88D-Cosworth	47	1h12m54.02
5	Roberto Moreno	Reynard 88D-Cosworth	47	1h13m03.69
6	Pierre-Henri Raphanel	Reynard 88D-Cosworth	47	1h13m24.65

Winner's average speed: 102.842 mph. Pole position: Grouillard, 1m28.86. Fastest lap: Grouillard , 1m31.14

Zolder F3000

16 October 1988. Zolder. 49 laps of a 2.606-mile circuit = 127.694 miles

1	Olivier Grouillard	Lola T88/50-Cosworth	49	1h13m30.27
2	Mark Blundell	Lola T88/50-Cosworth	49	1h13m30.49
3	Jean-Denis Deletraz	Lola T88/50-Cosworth	49	1h14m00.16
4	Eric Bernard	Reynard 88D-Cosworth	49	1h14m00.62
5	Roberto Moreno	Reynard 88D-Cosworth	49	1h14m01.56
6	Bertrand Gachot	Reynard 88D-Cosworth	49	1h14m56.28

Winner's average speed: 104.234 mph. Pole position: Donnelly (Reynard 88D-Cosworth), 1m27.75. Fastest lap: Grouillard, 1m28.27

Dijon-Prenois F3000

23 October 1988. Dijon-Prenois. 54 laps of a 2.361-mile circuit = 127.494 miles

1	Martin Donnelly	Reynard 88D-Cosworth	54	1h04m57.03
2	Eric Bernard	Reynard 88D-Cosworth	54	1h04m58.65
3	Olivier Grouillard	Lola T88/50-Cosworth	54	1h05m05.67
4	Bertrand Gachot	Reynard 88D-Cosworth	54	1h05m07.58
5	Jean Alesi	Reynard 88D-Cosworth	54	1h05m18.89
6	Volker Weidler	March 88B-Cosworth	54	1h05m18.96

Winner's average speed: 117.776 mph. Pole position: Moreno (Reynard 88D-Cosworth), 1m07.61. Fastest lap: Blundell (Lola T88/50-Cosworth), 1m10.74

FINAL CHAMPIONSHIP POSITIONS

Drivers

1	Roberto Moreno	43	13=	Jean-Denis Deletraz	8
2	Olivier Grouillard	34		Pierre-Henri Raphanel	8
3	Martin Donnelly	30	15=	Claudio Langes	5
4	Pierluigi Martini	23		Volker Weidler	5
5	Bertrand Gachot	21	17=	Paolo Barilla	3
6	Mark Blundell	18		Fabien Giroix	3
7	Gregor Foitek	15	19	Cor Euser	2
8=	Eric Bernard	13	20=	Andrea Chiesa	1
	Johnny Herbert	13		Michel Ferté	1
10	Jean Alesi	11			
11=	Marco Apicella	9			
	Michel Trollé	9			

1989

Motoring News International Trophy

9 April 1989. Silverstone. 41 laps of a 2.969-mile circuit
= 121.729 miles

1	Thomas Danielsson	Reynard 89D-Cosworth	41	55m31.92
2	Philippe Favre	Lola T89/50-Cosworth	41	55m32.50
3	Mark Blundell	Reynard 89D-Cosworth	41	55m55.89
4	Jean Alesi	Reynard 89D-Mugen	41	55m56.57
5	Erik Comas	Lola T89/50-Mugen	41	56m03.10
6	Eric van de Poele	Lola T89/50-Cosworth	41	56m07.36

Lehto (Reynard 89D-Mugen) finished third but was disqualified
due to an illegal rev limiter. Winner's average speed: 131.523
mph. Pole position: Favre, 1m17.41. Fastest lap: Favre, 1m20.19

Gran Premio di Roma

30 April 1989. Vallelunga. 64 laps of a 1.988-mile circuit
= 127.232 miles

1	Fabrizio Giovanardi	Leyton March 89B-Judd	64	1h13m08.797
2	Andrea Chiesa	Reynard 89D-Cosworth	64	1h13m13.706
3	Eric van de Poele	Lola T89/50-Cosworth	64	1h13m24.010
4	Erik Comas	Lola T89/50-Mugen	64	1h13m28.040
5	Emanuele Naspetti	Reynard 89D-Cosworth	64	1h13m36.510
6	Alain Ferté	Reynard 89D-Cosworth	64	1h13m45.780

Donnelly (Reynard 89D-Mugen) finished first but was disqualified
as new nose-cone had not taken mandatory crash test. Winner's
average speed: 104.890 mph. Pole position: Donnelly, 1m04.97.
Fastest lap: Apicella (Reynard 89D-Judd), 1m06.772

Grand Prix de Pau

15 May 1989. Pau. 72 laps of a 1.715-mile circuit
= 123.480 miles

1	Jean Alesi	Reynard 89D-Mugen	72	1h28m51.90
2	Marco Apicella	Reynard 89D-Judd	72	1h29m00.99
3	Thomas Danielsson	Reynard 89D-Cosworth	72	1h29m26.63
4	JJ Lehto	Reynard 89D-Mugen	72	1h29m26.67
5	Alain Ferté	Reynard 89D-Cosworth	71	
6	Mark Blundell	Reynard 89D-Cosworth	70	

Winner's average speed: 83.371 mph. Pole position: Apicella,
1m10.65. Fastest lap: Apicella and Bernard (Lola T89/50-Mugen),
1m11.93

Jerez F3000

4 June 1989. Jerez. 48 laps of a 2.621-mile circuit
= 125.808 miles

1	Eric Bernard	Lola T89/50-Mugen	48	1h18m28.48
2	Erik Comas	Lola T89/50-Mugen	48	1h18m48.52
3	Marco Apicella	Reynard 89D-Judd	48	1h18m50.93
4	Eric van de Poele	Lola T89/50-Cosworth	48	1h19m10.77
5	Jean Alesi	Reynard 89D-Mugen	48	1h19m13.31
6	JJ Lehto	Reynard 89D-Mugen	48	1h19m20.00

Winner's average speed: 96.186 mph. Pole position: Bernard,
1m31.84. Fastest lap: Bernard, 1m34.79

Gran Premio del Mediterraneo

23 July 1989. Enna-Pergusa. 39 laps of a 3.076-mile circuit
= 119.964 miles

1	Andrea Chiesa	Reynard 89D-Cosworth	39	58m54.516
2	Claudio Langes	Lola T89/50-Cosworth	39	58m55.128
3	Eddie Irvine	Reynard 89D-Mugen	39	58m55.690
4	Marco Apicella	Reynard 89D-Judd	39	59m36.650
5	Gary Evans	Reynard 89D-Cosworth	39	59m57.930

No other finishers. Winner's average speed: 122.187 mph. Pole
position: Alesi (Reynard 89D-Mugen), 1m26.55. Fastest lap:
Donnelly (Reynard 89D-Mugen), 1m28.860

Brands Hatch F3000

20 August 1989. Brands Hatch. 48 laps of a 2.600-mile
circuit = 124.800 miles

1	Martin Donnelly	Reynard 89D-Mugen	48	1h02m03.76

Jean Alesi won the Formula 3000 Championship in
1989 due to scoring a greater number of wins than
Erik Comas

2	Jean Alesi	Reynard 89D-Mugen	48	1h02m17.06
3	Erik Comas	Lola T89/50-Mugen	48	1h02m20.46
4	Eric Bernard	Lola T89/50-Mugen	48	1h02m53.63
5	Gary Brabham	Leyton March 89B-Judd	48	1h03m02.56
6	Claudio Langes	Lola T89/50-Cosworth	48	1h03m04.22

Winner's average speed: 120.662 mph. Pole position: Comas,
1m14.33. Fastest lap: Bernard, 1m15.51

Halfords Birmingham Superprix

28 August 1989. Birmingham. 51 laps of a 2.470-mile
circuit = 125.970 miles

1	Jean Alesi	Reynard 89D-Mugen	51	1h11m48.98
2	Marco Apicella	Reynard 89D-Judd	51	1h11m49.42
3	Martin Donnelly	Reynard 89D-Mugen	51	1h12m26.68
4	Eric Bernard	Lola T89/50-Mugen	51	1h12m46.32
5	Mark Blundell	Reynard 89D-Cosworth	51	1h13m04.64
6	Eddie Irvine	Reynard 89D-Mugen	51	1h13m10.66

Winner's average speed: 105.243 mph. Pole position: Alesi,
1m20.66. Fastest lap: Alesi, 1m23.03

Spa-Francorchamps F3000

16 September 1989. Spa-Francorchamps. 28 laps of a
4.312-mile circuit = 120.736 miles

1	Jean Alesi	Reynard 89D-Mugen	28	1h02m40.93
2	Erik Comas	Lola T89/50-Mugen	28	1h02m57.02
3	Marco Apicella	Reynard 89D-Judd	28	1h03m17.46
4	Eric van de Poele	Lola T89/50-Mugen	28	1h03m17.65
5	JJ Lehto	Reynard 89D-Mugen	28	1h03m17.81
6	Thomas Danielsson	Reynard 89D-Cosworth	28	1h04m07.15

Winner's average speed: 115.570 mph. Pole position: Comas,
2m22.35. Fastest lap: Comas, 2m11.45

Le Mans F3000

24 September 1989. Le Mans-Bugatti. 45 laps of a
2.750-mile circuit = 123.750 miles

1	Erik Comas	Lola T89/50-Mugen	45	1h10m54.30
2	Eric van de Poele	Lola T89/50-Cosworth	45	1h11m05.68
3	Eric Bernard	Lola T89/50-Mugen	45	1h11m06.35
4	Eddie Irvine	Reynard 89D-Mugen	45	1h11m12.38
5	Stéphane Proulx	Lola T89/50-Cosworth	45	1h11m13.74
6	Jean Alesi	Reynard 89D-Mugen	45	1h11m14.46

Winner's average speed: 104.718 mph. Pole position: Bernard,
1m30.47. Fastest lap: Comas, 1m33.42

Dijon-Prenois F3000

22 October 1989. Dijon-Prenois. 54 laps of a
2.361-mile circuit = 127.494 miles

1	Erik Comas	Lola T89/50-Mugen	54	1h05m07.20
2	Eric Bernard	Lola T89/50-Mugen	54	1h05m15.42
3	Andrew Gilbert-Scott	Lola T89/50-Cosworth	54	1h05m33.24
4	Eddie Irvine	Reynard 89D-Mugen	54	1h06m03.42
5	Eric van de Poele	Lola T89/50-Cosworth	54	1h06m11.32
6	Mark Blundell	Reynard 89D-Cosworth	54	1h06m15.00

Winner's average speed: 117.470 mph. Pole position: Bernard,
1m08.96. Fastest lap: Comas, 1m10.43

FINAL CHAMPIONSHIP POSITIONS

Drivers

1	Jean Alesi	39*	12	Claudio Langes	7
2	Erik Comas	39	13=	Philippe Favre	6
3	Eric Bernard	25		JJ Lehto	6
4	Marco Apicella	23	15	Andrew	
5	Eric van de Poele	19		Gilbert-Scott	4
6	Andrea Chiesa	15	16	Alain Ferté	3
7	Thomas Danielsson	14	17=	Gary Brabham	2
8	Martin Donnelly	13		Gary Evans	2
9	Eddie Irvine	11		Emanuele Naspetti	2
10	Fabrizio Giovanardi	9		Stéphane Proulx	2
11	Mark Blundell	8		*Alesi was champion as he won more races	

1990

Donington 200 Gold Cup

22 April 1990. Donington Park. 50 laps of a 2.500-mile circuit = 125.000 miles

1	Erik Comas	Lola T90/50-Mugen	50	1h12m15.34
2	Andrea Chiesa	Lola T90/50-Mugen	50	1h12m41.20
3	John Jones	Lola T90/50-Mugen	50	1h12m42.17
4	Antonio Tamburini	Reynard 90D-Mugen	50	1h12m42.74
5	Richard Dean	Reynard 90D-Mugen	50	1h12m54.30
6	Eric van de Poele	Reynard 90D-Cosworth	50	1h13m19.01

Winner's average speed: 103.798 mph. Pole position: Montermini (Reynard 90D-Mugen), 1m20.18. Fastest lap: Proulx (Lola T90/50-Mugen), 1m22.29

International Trophy

19 May 1990. Silverstone. 41 laps of a 2.969-mile circuit = 121.729 miles

1	Allan McNish	Lola T90/50-Mugen	41	54m23.21
2	Erik Comas	Lola T90/50-Mugen	41	54m25.22
3	Marco Apicella	Reynard 90D-Mugen	41	54m34.06
4	Andrea Montermini	Reynard 90D-Mugen	41	54m51.52
5	Eric van de Poele	Reynard 90D-Cosworth	41	54m52.51
6	Eddie Irvine	Reynard 90D-Mugen	41	54m53.05

Winner's average speed: 134.293 mph. Pole position: McNish, 1m16.53. Fastest lap: McNish, 1m18.31

Grand Prix de Pau

4 June 1990. Pau. 69 laps of a 1.715-mile circuit = 118.335 miles

1	Eric van de Poele	Reynard 90D-Cosworth	69	1h24m18.72
2	Fabrizio Giovanardi	Reynard 90D-Mugen	69	1h24m39.02
3	Gianni Morbidelli	Lola T90/50-Cosworth	69	1h24m55.50
4	John Jones	Lola T90/50-Mugen	69	1h25m22.14
5	Franck Fréon	Lola T89/50-Mugen	65	accident
6	Allan McNish	Lola T90/50-Mugen	65	accident

Winner's average speed: 84.212 mph. Pole position: Comas (Lola T90/50-Mugen), 1m10.55. Fastest lap: Apicella (Reynard 90D-Mugen), 1m11.71

Jerez F3000

17 June 1990. Jerez. 48 laps of a 2.621-mile circuit = 125.803 miles

1	Erik Comas	Lola T90/50-Mugen	48	1h18m07.02
2	Marco Apicella	Reynard 90D-Mugen	48	1h18m08.29
3	Andrea Montermini	Reynard 90D-Mugen	48	1h18m38.13
4	Fabrizio Barbazza	Leyton March 90B-Cosworth	48	1h19m01.81
5	Andrea Chiesa	Lola T90/50-Mugen	48	1h19m07.40
6	Fabrizio Giovanardi	Reynard 90D-Mugen	48	1h19m09.19

Winner's average speed: 96.627 mph. Pole position: Comas, 1m30.44. Fastest lap: Apicella, 1m35.22

Monza F3000

24 June 1990. Monza. 34 laps of a 3.604-mile circuit = 122.533 miles

1	Erik Comas	Lola T90/50-Mugen	34	55m19.12
2	Eddie Irvine	Reynard 90D-Mugen	34	55m20.82
3	Gary Brabham	Lola T90/50-Cosworth	34	55m22.64
4	Gianni Morbidelli	Lola T90/50-Cosworth	34	55m23.77
5	Marco Apicella	Reynard 90D-Mugen	34	55m26.52
6	Allan McNish	Lola T90/50-Mugen	34	55m28.33

Winner's average speed: 132.902 mph. Pole position: D Hill (Lola T90/50-Cosworth), 1m34.53. Fastest lap: Hill, 1m35.66

Gran Premio del Mediterraneo

22 July 1990. Enna-Pergusa. 36 laps of a 3.076-mile circuit = 110.736 miles

1	Gianni Morbidelli	Lola T90/50-Cosworth	36	55m27.219
2	Allan McNish	Lola T90/50-Mugen	36	56m14.083
3	Gary Brabham	Lola T90/50-Cosworth	36	56m40.320
4	Eddie Irvine	Reynard 90D-Mugen	36	56m41.140
5	Heinz-Harald Frentzen	Reynard 90D-Mugen	36	56m44.740
6	Fabrizio Giovanardi	Reynard 90D-Mugen	36	57m13.850

Winner's average speed: 119.815 mph. Pole position: D Hill (Lola T90/50-Cosworth), 1m25.62. Fastest lap: Hill, 1m29.423

Hockenheim F3000

28 July 1990. Hockenheim. 29 laps of a 4.227-mile circuit = 122.580 miles

1	Eddie Irvine	Reynard 90D-Mugen	29	58m14.604
2	Marco Apicella	Reynard 90D-Mugen	29	58m19.442
3	Jean-Marc Gounon	Reynard 90D-Mugen	29	58m47.400
4	Erik Comas	Lola T90/50-Mugen	29	58m54.160
5	Karl Wendlinger	Lola T90/50-Cosworth	29	59m08.180
6	Heinz-Harald Frentzen	Reynard 90D-Mugen	29	59m09.410

Winner's average speed: 126.277 mph. Pole position: D Hill (Lola T90/50-Cosworth), 1m56.150. Fastest lap: Apicella, 1m59.397

Brands Hatch F3000

19 August 1990. Brands Hatch. 48 laps of a 2.600-mile circuit = 124.800 miles

1	Allan McNish	Lola T90/50-Mugen	48	1h09m09.68
2	Damon Hill	Lola T90/50-Cosworth	48	1h09m19.75
3	Eddie Irvine	Reynard 90D-Mugen	48	1h09m32.17
4	Pedro Chaves	Reynard 90D-Cosworth	48	1h09m45.96
5	Andrea Chiesa	Lola T90/50-Mugen	48	1h09m52.50
6	Jean-Marc Gounon	Reynard 90D-Mugen	48	1h10m03.21

Apicella (Reynard 90D-Mugen) finished third but was disqualified due to fuel illegalities. Winner's average speed: 108.277 mph. Pole position: Irvine, 1m12.70. Fastest lap: Bartels (Reynard 90D-Mugen), 1m15.56

Halfords Birmingham Superprix

27 August 1990. Birmingham. 51 laps of a 2.470-mile circuit = 125.970 miles

1	Eric van de Poele	Reynard 90D-Cosworth	51	1h11m47.02
2	Andrea Chiesa	Lola T90/50-Mugen	51	1h12m05.96
3	Didier Artzet	Reynard 90D-Cosworth	51	1h12m06.68
4	Jean-Marc Gounon	Reynard 90D-Mugen	51	1h12m07.51
5	Fabrizio Giovanardi	Reynard 90D-Mugen	51	1h12m20.81
6	Emanuele Naspetti	Reynard 90D-Mugen	51	1h12m30.47

Winner's average speed: 105.291 mph. Pole position: Apicella (Reynard 90D-Mugen), 1m20.95. Fastest lap: Apicella, 1m22.93

Le Mans F3000

23 September 1990. Le Mans-Bugatti. 45 laps of a 2.750-mile circuit = 123.750 miles

1	Erik Comas	Lola T90/50-Mugen	45	1h11m41.65
2	Andrea Montermini	Reynard 90D-Mugen	45	1h11m52.77
3	Eddie Irvine	Reynard 90D-Mugen	45	1h11m58.58
4	Jean-Marc Gounon	Reynard 90D-Mugen	45	1h11m58.79
5	Andrea Chiesa	Lola T90/50-Mugen	45	1h11m59.97
6	Paul Belmondo	Reynard 90D-Mugen	45	1h12m00.47

Winner's average speed: 103.565 mph. Pole position: Comas, 1m30.60. Fastest lap: Gache (Lola T89/50-Cosworth), 1m33.21

International Formula 3000 Championship

Grand Prix de Nogaro

7 October 1990. Nogaro. 55 laps of a 2.259-mile circuit
= 124.245 miles

1	Eric van de Poele	Reynard 90D-Cosworth	55	1h20m27.81
2	Erik Comas	Lola T90/50-Cosworth	55	1h20m38.84
3	Gianni Morbidelli	Lola T90/50-Cosworth	55	1h20m54.16
4	Antonio Tamburini	Reynard 90D-Cosworth	55	1h21m13.87
5	Marco Apicella	Reynard 90D-Mugen	55	1h21m14.28
6	Michael Bartels	Reynard 90D-Mugen	55	1h21m16.10

Winner's average speed: 92.647 mph. Pole position: Morbidelli,
1m18.61. Fastest lap: Comas, 1m20.30

FINAL CHAMPIONSHIP POSITIONS

Drivers

1	Erik Comas	51	13=	Damon Hill		6
2	Eric van de Poele	30		Antonio Tamburini		6
3	Eddie Irvine	27	15	Didier Artzet		4
4	Allan McNish	26	16=	Fabrizio Barbazza		3
5=	Marco Apicella	20		Pedro Chaves		3
	Gianni Morbidelli	20		Heinz-Harald		
7	Andrea Chiesa	18		Frentzen		3
8	Andrea Montermini	13	19=	Richard Dean		2
9	Jean-Marc Gounon	11		Franck Fréon		2
10	Fabrizio Giovanardi	10		Karl Wendlinger		2
11	Gary Brabham	8	22=	Michael Bartels		1
12	John Jones	7		Paul Belmondo		1
				Emanuele Naspetti		1

1991

Gran Premio di Roma

14 April 1991. Vallelunga. 60 laps of a 1.988-mile circuit
= 119.280 miles. Race stopped after 37 laps and restarted
over a further 23 laps

1	Alessandro Zanardi	Reynard 91D-Mugen	60	1h06m05.152
2	Christian Fittipaldi	Reynard 91D-Mugen	60	1h06m16.800
3	Antonio Tamburini	Reynard 91D-Mugen	60	1h06m20.876
4	Damon Hill	Lola T91/50-Cosworth	60	1h06m22.937
5	Giuseppe Bugatti	Reynard 91D-Mugen	60	1h06m37.009
6	Alain Menu	Reynard 91D-Cosworth	60	1h06m41.183

Winner's average speed: 108.295 mph. Pole position: Fittipaldi,
1m03.236. Fastest lap: Zanardi, 1m04.939

Grand Prix de Pau

20 May 1991. Pau. 72 laps of a 1.715-mile circuit
= 123.480 miles

1	Jean-Marc Gounon	Ralt RT23-Cosworth	72	1h26m31.24
2	Christian Fittipaldi	Reynard 91D-Mugen	72	1h26m43.39
3	Eric Hélary	Reynard 91D-Cosworth	72	1h26m48.49
4	Marco Apicella	Lola T91/50-Mugen	72	1h26m54.65
5	Fabrizio Giovanardi	Lola T91/50-Cosworth	72	1h26m55.89
6	Alain Menu	Reynard 91D-Cosworth	72	1h26m56.10

Winner's average speed: 85.630 mph. Pole position: Zanardi
(Reynard 91D-Mugen), 1m09.48. Fastest lap: Montermini (Ralt
RT23-Cosworth), 1m10.47

Jerez F3000

9 June 1991. Jerez. 48 laps of a 2.621-mile circuit
= 125.808 miles

1	Christian Fittipaldi	Reynard 91D-Mugen	48	1h18m15.69
2	Alessandro Zanardi	Reynard 91D-Mugen	48	1h18m23.44
3	Andrea Montermini	Ralt RT23-Cosworth	48	1h18m24.06
4	Antonio Tamburini	Reynard 91D-Mugen	48	1h18m24.62
5	Karl Wendlinger	Reynard 91D-Cosworth	48	1h18m29.58
6	Jean-Marc Gounon	Ralt RT23-Cosworth	48	1h18m58.02

Winner's average speed: 96.448 mph. Pole position: Fittipaldi,
1m30.38. Fastest lap: Fittipaldi, 1m35.19

Euro Mugello

23 June 1991. Mugello. 38 laps of a 3.259-mile circuit
= 123.842 miles

1	Alessandro Zanardi	Reynard 91D-Mugen	38	1h03m08.380
2	Marco Apicella	Lola T91/50-Mugen	38	1h03m14.825
3	Christian Fittipaldi	Reynard 91D-Mugen	38	1h03m29.075
4	Vincenzo Sospiri	Lola T91/50-Cosworth	38	1h03m32.985
5	Allan McNish	Lola T91/50-Mugen	38	1h03m39.145
6	Heinz-Harald			
	Frentzen	Lola T91/50-Mugen	38	1h03m40.940

Winner's average speed: 117.684 mph. Pole position: Zanardi,
1m35.096. Fastest lap: Zanardi, 1m38.367

Gran Premio del Mediterraneo

7 July 1991. Enna-Pergusa. 40 laps of a 3.076-mile circuit
= 123.040 miles

1	Emanuele Naspetti	Reynard 91D-Cosworth	40	59m34.254
2	Marco Apicella	Lola T91/50-Mugen	40	59m41.389
3	Giuseppe Bugatti	Reynard 91D-Mugen	40	59m51.130
4	Antonio Tamburini	Reynard 91D-Mugen	40	59m53.402
5	Heinz-Harald			
	Frentzen	Lola T91/50-Mugen	40	59m54.265
6	Jean-Marc Gounon	Ralt RT23-Cosworth	40	1h00m20.320*

*Includes one minute penalty for jumping the start. Winner's
average speed: 123.926 mph. Pole position: Naspetti, 1m26.086.
Fastest lap: Gounon, 1m27.786

Hockenheim F3000

27 July 1991. Hockenheim. 29 laps of a 4.227-mile circuit
= 122.583 miles

1	Emanuele Naspetti	Reynard 91D-Cosworth	29	57m19.217
2	Vincenzo Sospiri	Lola T91/50-Cosworth	29	57m22.174
3	Karl Wendlinger	Reynard 91D-Cosworth	29	57m35.040
4	Christian Fittipaldi	Reynard 91D-Mugen	29	57m43.329
5	Jean-Marc Gounon	Ralt RT23-Cosworth	29	57m47.817
6	Antonio Tamburini	Reynard 91D-Mugen	29	57m49.544

Winner's average speed: 128.311 mph. Pole position:
Montermini (Ralt RT23-Cosworth), 1m54.327. Fastest lap:
Montermini, 1m56.969

Brands Hatch Formula 3000 Trophy

18 August 1991. Brands Hatch. 48 laps of a 2.600-mile
circuit = 124.800 miles

1	Emanuele Naspetti	Reynard 91D-Cosworth	48	1h00m26.28
2	Alessandro Zanardi	Reynard 91D-Mugen	48	1h00m27.96
3	Christian Fittipaldi	Reynard 91D-Mugen	48	1h00m56.89
4	Marco Apicella	Lola T91/50-Mugen	48	1h01m04.04
5	Antonio Tamburini	Reynard 91D-Mugen	48	1h01m05.15
6	Damon Hill	Lola T91/50-Cosworth	48	1h01m08.52

Winner's average speed: 123.905 mph. Pole position: Zanardi,
1m12.44. Fastest lap: Naspetti, 1m13.86

Spa-Francorchamps F3000

24 August 1991. Spa-Francorchamps. 29 laps of a
4.312-mile circuit = 125.048 miles

1	Emanuele Naspetti	Reynard 91D-Cosworth	29	1h03m09.82
2	Alessandro Zanardi	Reynard 91D-Mugen	29	1h03m10.99
3	Laurent Aiello	Lola T91/50-Mugen	29	1h03m30.07
4	Eric Hélary	Reynard 91D-Cosworth	29	1h03m31.14
5	Heinz-Harald			
	Frentzen	Lola T91/50-Mugen	29	1h03m31.95
6	Fabrizio Giovanardi	Reynard 91D-Cosworth	29	1h03m38.95

Winner's average speed: 118.785 mph. Pole position: Aiello,
2m05.74. Fastest lap: Naspetti, 2m09.21

Le Mans F3000

22 September 1991. Le Mans-Bugatti. 45 laps of a
2.753-mile circuit = 123.885 miles

1	Antonio Tamburini	Reynard 91D-Mugen	45	1h24m09.87
2	Christian Fittipaldi	Reynard 91D-Mugen	45	1h25m05.56
3	Andrea Montermini	Ralt RT23-Cosworth	45	1h25m15.30
4	Damon Hill	Lola T91/50-Cosworth	45	1h25m48.26

5 Philippe Gache   Lola T89/50-Cosworth 44
6 Gabriel Furlan   Reynard 91D-Judd   44

Winner's average speed: 88.316 mph. Pole position: Fittipaldi,
1m30.65. Fastest lap: Tamburini, 1m49.60

Grand Prix de Nogaro

**6 October 1991. Nogaro. 55 laps of a 2.259-mile circuit
= 124.245 miles**

1 Christian Fittipaldi Reynard 91D-Mugen   55 1h14m26.15
2 Alessandro Zanardi   Reynard 91D-Mugen   55 1h14m30.37
3 Damon Hill   Reynard 91D-Cosworth 55 1h15m00.66
4 Fabrizio Giovanardi   Reynard 91D-Cosworth 55 1h15m15.49
5 Eric Hélary   Reynard 91D-Cosworth 55 1h15m20.13
6 Emanuele Naspetti   Reynard 91D-Cosworth 55 1h15m32.71

Winner's average speed: 100.149 mph. Pole position: Fittipaldi,
1m17.76. Fastest lap: Zanardi, 1m20.16

FINAL CHAMPIONSHIP POSITIONS

Drivers

1	Christian Fittipaldi	47	
2	Alessandro Zanardi	42	11= Giuseppe Bugatti	6
3	Emanuele Naspetti	37	Fabrizio Giovanardi	6
4	Antonio Tamburini	22	Karl Wendlinger	6
5	Marco Apicella	18	14 Heinz-Harald	
6	Jean-Marc Gounon	13	Frentzen	5
7	Damon Hill	11	15 Laurent Aiello	4
8=	Eric Hélary	9	16= Philippe Gache	2
	Vincenzo Sospiri	9	Allan McNish	2
			Alain Menu	2
10	Andrea Montermini	8	19 Gabriel Furlan	1

1992

BRDC International Trophy

**10 May 1992. Silverstone. 37 laps of a 3.247-mile circuit
= 120.139 miles**

1 Jordi Gene   Reynard 92D-Mugen   37   59m21.470
2 Rubens Barrichello Reynard 92D-Judd   37   59m39.169
3 Olivier Panis   Lola T92/50-Cosworth 37   59m55.192
4 Jean-Marc Gounon   Lola T92/50-Cosworth 37 1h00m01.193
5 Luca Badoer   Reynard 92D-Cosworth 37 1h00m02.677
6 Emanuele Naspetti   Reynard 92D-Cosworth 37 1h00m22.346

Winner's average speed: 121.439 mph. Pole position: Gene,
1m54.518. Fastest lap: Barrichello, 1m34.904

Grand Prix de Pau

**8 June 1992. Pau. 72 laps of a 1.715-mile circuit
= 123.480 miles**

1 Emanuele Naspetti   Reynard 92D-Cosworth 72 1h25m38.91
2 Michael Bartels   Reynard 92D-Cosworth 72 1h25m47.76
3 Rubens Barrichello Reynard 92D-Judd   72 1h25m57.02
4 Vittorio Zoboli   Reynard 92D-Cosworth 72 1h26m02.10
5 Giuseppe Bugatti   Reynard 92D-Mugen   71
6 Luca Badoer   Reynard 92D-Cosworth 71

Winner's average speed: 86.502 mph. Pole position: Montermini
(Reynard 92D-Judd), 1m08.60. Fastest lap: Naspetti, 1m09.82

Barcelona F3000

**21 June 1992. Catalunya. 43 laps of a 2.950-mile circuit
= 126.837 miles**

1 Andrea Montermini   Reynard 92D-Judd   43 1h06m51.154
2 Rubens Barrichello Reynard 92D-Judd   43 1h07m04.061
3 Jordi Gene   Reynard 92D-Mugen   43 1h07m12.181
4 Emmanuel Collard   Lola T92/50-Cosworth 43 1h07m15.825
5 Allan McNish   Reynard 92D-Mugen   43 1h07m16.310
6 Luca Badoer   Reynard 92D-Cosworth 43 1h07m16.572

Winner's average speed: 113.836 mph. Pole position:
Montermini, 1m29.565. Fastest lap: Naspetti (Reynard 92D-
Cosworth), 1m30.536

Gran Premio del Mediterraneo

**12 July 1992. Enna-Pergusa. 40 laps of a 3.076-mile circuit
= 123.040 miles**

1 Luca Badoer   Reynard 92D-Cosworth 40   58m20.958
2 Emanuele Naspetti   Reynard 92D-Cosworth 40   58m42.445
3 Andrea Montermini   Reynard 92D-Judd   40   58m44.749
4 Michael Bartels   Reynard 92D-Cosworth 40   58m54.717
5 Alessandro
   Zampedri   Reynard 92D-Cosworth 40   59m01.754
6 Jérome Policand   Lola T92/50-Cosworth 40   59m15.437

Winner's average speed: 126.521 mph. Pole position: Badoer,
1m24.708. Fastest lap: Badoer, 1m26.242

Hockenheim F3000

**25 July 1992. Hockenheim. 29 laps of a 4.235-mile circuit
= 122.815 miles**

1 Luca Badoer   Reynard 92D-Cosworth 29   56m24.640
2 Michael Bartels   Reynard 92D-Cosworth 29   56m32.508
3 Allan McNish   Reynard 92D-Mugen   29   56m35.068
4 Emanuele Naspetti   Reynard 92D-Cosworth 29   56m46.874
5 Jordi Gene   Reynard 92D-Mugen   29   56m49.284
6 Rubens Barrichello Reynard 92D-Judd   29   56m50.742

Winner's average speed: 130.630 mph. Pole position: Badoer,
1m53.483. Fastest lap: Badoer, 1m55.381

Nürburgring F3000

**23 August 1992. Nürburgring. 45 laps of a 2.822-mile
circuit = 126.990 miles**

1 Luca Badoer   Reynard 92D-Cosworth 45 1h06m10.45
2 Michael Bartels   Reynard 92D-Cosworth 45 1h06m23.66
3 Rubens Barrichello Reynard 92D-Cosworth 45 1h06m24.52
4 Emmanuel Collard   Lola T92/50-Cosworth 45 1h06m35.14
5 Laurent Aiello   Reynard 92D-Mugen   45 1h06m36.23
6 Jean-Marc Gounon   Lola T92/50-Cosworth 45 1h06m48.87

Winner's average speed: 115.142 mph. Pole position: Naspetti
(Reynard 92D-Cosworth), 1m25.72. Fastest lap: Barrichello, 1m26.98

Spa-Francorchamps F3000

**29 August 1992. Spa-Francorchamps. 25 laps of a
4.312-mile circuit = 107.800 miles. Race stopped after 3
laps and restarted over a further 22 laps**

1 Andrea Montermini   Reynard 92D-Cosworth 25   53m48.61
2 Jordi Gene   Reynard 92D-Mugen   25   54m06.21
3 Michael Bartels   Reynard 92D-Cosworth 25   54m18.66
4 David Coulthard   Reynard 92D-Judd   25   54m29.35
5 Rubens Barrichello Reynard 92D-Cosworth 25   54m29.75
6 Laurent Aiello   Reynard 92D-Mugen   25   54m30.26

Winner's average speed: 120.200 mph. Pole position:
Montermini, 2m06.78. Fastest lap: Montermini, 2m07.29

Albacete F3000

**13 September 1992. Albacete. 57 laps of a 2.236-mile
circuit = 127.452 miles**

1 Andrea Montermini   Reynard 92D-Cosworth 57 1h20m36.22
2 Luca Badoer   Reynard 92D-Cosworth 57 1h20m41.61
3 Emmanuel Collard   Lola T92/50-Cosworth 57 1h20m47.96
4 Paul Stewart   Reynard 92D-Judd   57 1h21m33.87
5 Allan McNish   Reynard 92D-Mugen   57 1h21m51.54
6 Rubens Barrichello Reynard 92D-Cosworth 57 1h21m52.63

Winner's average speed: 94.873 mph. Pole position: Badoer,
1m18.54. Fastest lap: Montermini, 1m21.94

Grand Prix de Nogaro

**11 October 1992. Nogaro. 55 laps of a 2.259-mile circuit
= 124.245 miles**

1 Luca Badoer   Reynard 92D-Cosworth 55 1h14m39.94
2 Jean-Marc Gounon   Lola T92/50-Cosworth 55 1h14m51.37
3 David Coulthard   Reynard 92D-Judd   55 1h14m52.35
4 Andrea Montermini   Reynard 92D-Cosworth 55 1h14m54.09
5 Alessandro
   Zampedri   Reynard 92D-Cosworth 55 1h15m12.67

International Formula 3000 Championship

6 Rubens Barrichello Reynard 92D-Cosworth 55 1h15m20.67

Winner's average speed: 99.841 mph. Pole position: Badoer, 1m17.69. Fastest lap: Badoer, 1m20.58

Magny-Cours F3000

18 October 1992. Magny-Cours. 47 laps of a 2.641-mile circuit = 124.127 miles

1	Jean-Marc Gounon	Lola T92/50-Cosworth	47	1h08m13.148
2	Olivier Panis	Lola T92/50-Cosworth	47	1h08m13.522
3	David Coulthard	Reynard 92D-Judd	47	1h08m14.452
4	Emmanuel Collard	Lola T92/50-Cosworth	47	1h08m20.324
5	Rubens Barrichello	Reynard 92D-Cosworth	47	1h08m21.212
6	Giampiero Simoni	Reynard 92D-Judd	47	1h08m41.368

Winner's average speed: 109.172 mph. Pole position: Badoer (Reynard 92D-Cosworth), 1m24.270. Fastest lap: Coulthard, 1m25.759

FINAL CHAMPIONSHIP POSITIONS

Drivers

1	Luca Badoer	46	10	Olivier Panis	10
2	Andrea Montermini	34	11	Allan McNish	8
3	Rubens Barrichello	27	12	Alessandro Zampedri	4
4	Michael Bartels	25	13=	Laurent Aiello	3
5	Jordi Gene	21		Paul Stewart	3
6=	Jean-Marc Gounon	19		Vittorio Zoboli	3
	Emanuele Naspetti	19	16	Giuseppe Bugatti	2
8	Emmanuel Collard	13	17=	Jérome Policand	1
9	David Coulthard	11		Giampiero Simoni	1

1993

Tom Wheatcroft Cup

3 May 1993. Donington Park. 46 laps of a 2.500-mile circuit = 115.000 miles. Race stopped after 2 laps and restarted over a further 44 laps

1	Olivier Beretta	Reynard 93D-Cosworth	46	1h03m01.35
2	Pedro Lamy	Reynard 92D-Cosworth	46	1h03m07.41
3	Olivier Panis	Reynard 93D-Cosworth	46	1h03m08.84
4	Massimiliano Papis	Reynard 93D-Cosworth	46	1h03m28.15
5	Paul Stewart	Reynard 93D-Cosworth	46	1h03m42.23
6	Giampiero Simoni	Reynard 93D-Judd	46	1h03m47.64

Winner's average speed: 109.485 mph. Pole position: Beretta, 1m19.55. Fastest lap: de Ferran (Reynard 93D-Cosworth), 1m20.97

BRDC International Trophy

9 May 1993. Silverstone. 37 laps of a 3.247-mile circuit = 120.139 miles

1	Gil de Ferran	Reynard 93D-Cosworth	37	1h00m20.32
2	David Coulthard	Reynard 93D-Cosworth	37	1h00m29.86
3	Michael Bartels	Reynard 93D-Cosworth	37	1h00m37.81
4	Franck Lagorce	Reynard 93D-Cosworth	37	1h00m38.68
5	Paul Stewart	Reynard 93D-Cosworth	37	1h00m45.20
6	Olivier Panis	Reynard 93D-Cosworth	37	1h00m47.01

Zampedri (Reynard 93D-Cosworth) finished sixth but was disqualified as his car was under the weight limit. Winner's average speed: 119.465 mph. Pole position: de Ferran, 1m33.20. Fastest lap: Coulthard, 1m35.78

Grand Prix de Pau

31 May 1993. Pau. 72 laps of a 1.715-mile circuit = 123.480 miles

1	Pedro Lamy	Reynard 92D-Cosworth	72	1h25m55.83
2	David Coulthard	Reynard 93D-Cosworth	72	1h26m31.37
3	Paul Stewart	Reynard 93D-Cosworth	72	1h26m33.66
4	Olivier Beretta	Reynard 93D-Cosworth	72	1h26m35.38
5	Massimiliano Papis	Reynard 93D-Cosworth	72	1h26m53.85
6	Vincenzo Sospiri	Reynard 93D-Judd	72	1h27m04.06

Winner's average speed: 86.219 mph. Pole position: Lamy, 1m09.28. Fastest lap: Panis (Reynard 93D-Cosworth), 1m10.07

Gran Premio del Mediterraneo

18 July 1993. Enna-Pergusa. 37 laps of a 3.076-mile circuit = 113.812 miles. Race stopped after 10 laps and restarted over a further 27 laps

1	David Coulthard	Reynard 93D-Cosworth	37	53m47.53
2	Vincenzo Sospiri	Reynard 92D-Judd	37	54m16.34
3	Jérome Policand	Reynard 92D-Judd	37	54m48.05
4	Jan Lammers	Reynard 93D-Cosworth	37	54m58.08
5	Enrico Bertaggia	Reynard 92D-Cosworth	37	55m53.42
6	Andrea Gilardi	Reynard 92D-Cosworth	37	56m02.56

Winner's average speed: 126.946 mph. Pole position: Bartels (Reynard 93D-Cosworth), 1m24.34. Fastest lap: Coulthard, 1m26.59

Hockenheim F3000

24 July 1993. Hockenheim. 26 laps of a 4.235-mile circuit = 110.110 miles. Race stopped after 2 laps and restarted over a further 24 laps

1	Olivier Panis	Reynard 93D-Cosworth	26	51m01.607
2	Pedro Lamy	Reynard 92D-Cosworth	26	51m07.422
3	Vincenzo Sospiri	Reynard 93D-Judd	26	51m27.440
4	Olivier Beretta	Reynard 93D-Cosworth	26	51m28.410
5	Paolo delle Piane	Reynard 93D-Cosworth	26	51m41.264
6	Andrea Gilardi	Reynard 92D-Cosworth	26	52m12.670

Winner's average speed: 129.473 mph. Pole position: Lamy, 1m52.922. Fastest lap: Panis, 1m55.950

Nürburgring F3000

22 August 1993. Nürburgring. 45 laps of a 2.822-mile circuit = 126.990 miles

1	Olivier Panis	Reynard 93D-Cosworth	45	1h06m52.13
2	Gil de Ferran	Reynard 93D-Cosworth	45	1h07m02.50
3	Alessandro Zampedri	Reynard 93D-Cosworth	45	1h07m08.81
4	Pedro Lamy	Reynard 92D-Cosworth	45	1h07m10.11
5	Olivier Beretta	Reynard 93D-Cosworth	45	1h07m14.98
6	Vincenzo Sospiri	Reynard 93D-Judd	45	1h07m17.78

Winner's average speed: 113.945 mph. Pole position: Panis, 1m24.03. Fastest lap: Lamy, 1m27.63

Spa-Francorchamps F3000

28 August 1993. Spa-Francorchamps. 29 laps of a 4.312-mile circuit = 125.048 miles

1	Olivier Panis	Reynard 93D-Cosworth	29	1h01m57.34
2	Gil de Ferran	Reynard 93D-Cosworth	29	1h01m58.39
3	David Coulthard	Reynard 93D-Cosworth	29	1h02m01.15
4	Pedro Lamy	Reynard 92D-Cosworth	29	1h02m10.53
5	Vincenzo Sospiri	Reynard 93D-Judd	29	1h02m18.93
6	Paul Stewart	Reynard 93D-Cosworth	29	1h02m19.91

Winner's average speed: 121.101 mph. Pole position: Panis, 2m04.026. Fastest lap: Lamy, 2m06.94

Magny-Cours F3000

3 October 1993. Magny-Cours. 47 laps of a 2.641-mile circuit = 124.127 miles

1	Franck Lagorce	Reynard 93D-Cosworth	47	1h17m20.577
2	Jules Boullion	Reynard 93D-Cosworth	47	1h18m26.430
3	Pedro Lamy	Reynard 92D-Cosworth	47	1h18m38.326
4	Nicolas Leboissetier	Reynard 93D-Cosworth	47	1h18m46.381
5	Vincenzo Sospiri	Reynard 93D-Judd	47	1h18m49.419
6	Paul Stewart	Reynard 93D-Cosworth	47	1h18m57.416

Winner's average speed: 96.293 mph. Pole position: Collard (Reynard 93D-Cosworth), 1m24.44. Fastest lap: Lagorce, 1m27.577

Grand Prix de Nogaro

10 October 1993. Nogaro. 55 laps of a 2.259-mile circuit = 124.245 miles

1	Franck Lagorce	Reynard 93D-Cosworth	55	1h14m44.597
2	Jules Boullion	Reynard 93D-Cosworth	55	1h14m45.044
3	Emmanuel Collard	Reynard 93D-Cosworth	55	1h14m45.705
4	Olivier Beretta	Reynard 93D-Cosworth	55	1h15m33.083
5	Yvan Müller	Reynard 92D-Judd	55	1h16m01.082
6	Massimiliano Papis	Reynard 93D-Cosworth	55	1h16m05.677

Winner's average speed: 99.737 mph. Pole position: Lagorce, 1m17.342. Fastest lap: Boullion, 1m20.250

FINAL CHAMPIONSHIP POSITIONS

Drivers

1	Olivier Panis	32	11=	Michael Bartels	4
2	Pedro Lamy	31		Emmanuel Collard	4
3	David Coulthard	25		Jérome Policand	4
4=	Gil de Ferran	21		Alessandro Zampedri	4
	Franck Lagorce	21	15=	Jan Lammers	3
6	Olivier Beretta	20		Nicolas Leboissetier	3
7	Vincenzo Sospiri	16	17=	Enrico Bertaggia	2
8	Jules Boullion	12		Andrea Gilardi	2
9	Paul Stewart	10		Yvan Müller	2
10	Massimiliano Papis	6		Paolo delle Piane	2
			21	Giampiero Simoni	1

1994

Autosport International Trophy

2 May 1994. Silverstone. 38 laps of a 3.247-mile circuit = 123.386 miles

1	Franck Lagorce	Reynard 94D-Cosworth	38	1h01m56.79
2	David Coulthard	Reynard 94D-Cosworth	38	1h02m00.89
3	Gil de Ferran	Reynard 94D-Judd	38	1h02m04.31
4	Vincenzo Sospiri	Reynard 94D-Cosworth	38	1h02m37.98
5	Hideki Noda	Reynard 94D-Cosworth	38	1h02m39.61
6	Didier Cottaz	Reynard 94D-Judd	38	1h02m40.65

Winner's average speed: 119.509 mph. Pole position: Lagorce, 1m33.83. Fastest lap: Lagorce, 1m37.67

Grand Prix de Pau

23 May 1994. Pau. 71 laps of a 1.715-mile circuit = 121.765 miles

1	Gil de Ferran	Reynard 94D-Judd	71	1h25m39.27
2	Vincenzo Sospiri	Reynard 94D-Cosworth	71	1h25m44.74
3	Didier Cottaz	Reynard 94D-Judd	71	1h25m51.12
4	Jules Boullion	Reynard 94D-Cosworth	71	1h25m52.83
5	Franck Lagorce	Reynard 94D-Cosworth	71	1h26m23.34
6	Guillaume Gomez	Reynard 94D-Cosworth	70	

Winner's average speed: 85.295 mph. Pole position: de Ferran, 1m09.63. Fastest lap: Sospiri, 1m11.39

Barcelona F3000

28 May 1994. Catalunya. 41 laps of a 2.950-mile circuit = 120.950 miles

1	Massimiliano Papis	Reynard 94D-Judd	41	1h05m41.393
2	Fabrizio de Simone	Reynard 94D-Judd	41	1h06m04.825
3	Vincenzo Sospiri	Reynard 94D-Cosworth	41	1h06m05.302
4	Jordi Gene	Lola T94/50-Cosworth	41	1h06m13.991
5	Franck Lagorce	Reynard 94D-Cosworth	41	1h06m15.529
6	Marc Goossens	Lola T94/50-Cosworth	41	1h06m27.295

Winner's average speed: 110.462 mph. Pole position: Papis, 1m30.889. Fastest lap: Boullion (Reynard 94D-Cosworth), 1m34.639

Gran Premio del Mediterraneo

17 July 1994. Enna-Pergusa. 41 laps of a 3.076-mile circuit = 126.116 miles

1	Gil de Ferran	Reynard 94D-Judd	41	57m41.731
2	Franck Lagorce	Reynard 94D-Cosworth	41	57m52.357
3	Hideki Noda	Reynard 94D-Cosworth	41	57m55.845
4	Massimiliano Papis	Reynard 94D-Judd	41	58m13.860
5	Jérome Policand	Reynard 94D-Cosworth	41	58m19.358
6	Christian Pescatori	Reynard 93D-Cosworth	41	58m24.122

Winner's average speed: 131.153 mph. Pole position: Lagorce, 1m24.159. Fastest lap: Pescatori, 1m25.157

Hockenheim F3000

30 July 1994. Hockenheim. 29 laps of a 4.235-mile circuit = 122.815 miles

1	Franck Lagorce	Reynard 94D-Cosworth	29	58m07.686
2	Jules Boullion	Reynard 94D-Cosworth	29	58m15.484
3	Gil de Ferran	Reynard 94D-Judd	29	58m28.089
4	Vincenzo Sospiri	Reynard 94D-Cosworth	29	58m38.724
5	Marc Goossens	Lola T94/50-Cosworth	29	58m46.652
6	Wim Eyckmans	Reynard 94D-Cosworth	29	58m55.587

Winner's average speed: 126.770 mph. Pole position: Gomez (Reynard 94D-Cosworth), 1m55.880. Fastest lap: Lagorce, 1m59.278

Spa-Francorchamps F3000

27 August 1994. Spa-Francorchamps. 27 laps of a 4.350-mile circuit = 117.450 miles

1	Jules Boullion	Reynard 94D-Cosworth	27	1h11m34.525
2	Didier Cottaz	Reynard 94D-Judd	27	1h11m51.464
3	Kenny Bräck	Reynard 94D-Judd	27	1h12m12.698
4	Guillaume Gomez	Reynard 94D-Cosworth	27	1h12m22.004
5	Gil de Ferran	Reynard 94D-Judd	27	1h12m26.967
6	Fabrizio de Simone	Reynard 94D-Judd	27	1h12m38.048

Winner's average speed: 98.456 mph. Pole position: Lagorce (Reynard 94D-Cosworth), 2m07.685. Fastest lap: Marques (Reynard 94D-Cosworth), 2m32.38

Estoril F3000

24 September 1994. Estoril. 44 laps of a 2.709-mile circuit = 119.196 miles

1	Jules Boullion	Reynard 94D-Cosworth	44	1h08m11.419
2	Vincenzo Sospiri	Reynard 94D-Cosworth	44	1h08m32.879
3	Guillaume Gomez	Reynard 94D-Cosworth	44	1h08m35.054
4	Pedro Diniz	Reynard 94D-Cosworth	44	1h08m37.572
5	Didier Cottaz	Reynard 94D-Judd	44	1h08m38.358
6	Kenny Bräck	Reynard 94D-Judd	44	1h08m40.463

Winner's average speed: 104.879 mph. Pole position: Emmanuel Clérico (Reynard 94D-Cosworth), 1m28.852. Fastest lap: Clérico, 1m31.193

Jules Boullion won the last three races of the season to snatch the 1994 title from Franck Lagorce and Gil de Ferran

Magny-Cours F3000

2 October 1994. Magny-Cours. 48 laps of a 2.641-mile circuit = 126.768 miles

1	Jules Boullion	Reynard 94D-Cosworth	48	1h10m41.298
2	Franck Lagorce	Reynard 94D-Cosworth	48	1h10m45.661
3	Guillaume Gomez	Reynard 94D-Cosworth	48	1h10m53.138
4	Tarso Marques	Reynard 94D-Cosworth	48	1h11m51.018
5	Vincenzo Sospiri	Reynard 94D-Cosworth	48	1h11m56.800
6	Massimiliano Papis	Reynard 94D-Judd	48	1h12m3.743

Winner's average speed: 107.600 mph. Pole position: Lagorce, 1m37.332. Fastest lap: Lagorce, 1m27.211

FINAL CHAMPIONSHIP POSITIONS

Drivers

1	Jules Boullion	36	11	Kenny Bräck	5
2	Franck Lagorce	34	12=	Pedro Diniz	3
3	Gil de Ferran	28		Jordi Gene	3
4	Vincenzo Sospiri	24		Marc Goossens	3
5=	Didier Cottaz	13		Tarso Marques	3
	Massimiliano Papis	13	16	Jérome Policand	2
7	Guillaume Gomez	12	17=	Wim Eyckmans	1
8	Fabrizio de Simone	7		Christian Pescatori	1
9=	David Coulthard	6			
	Hideki Noda	6			

RECORDS

DRIVERS' RECORDS

MOST WINS			
Erik Comas	6	Jules Boullion	3
Roberto Moreno	5	Ivan Capelli	3
Emanuele Naspetti	5	Martin Donnelly	3
Luca Badoer	4	Gil de Ferran	3
Christian Danner	4	Stefano Modena	3
Franck Lagorce	4	Andrea Montermini	3
Pierluigi Martini	4	Olivier Panis	3
Luis Perez Sala	4	Emanuele Pirro	3
Mike Thackwell	4	Eric van de Poele	3
Jean Alesi	3		

HIGHEST POINTS TOTALS			
Erik Comas	90	Emanuele Naspetti	59
Roberto Moreno	76	Luis Perez Sala	57.5
Marco Apicella	71	Mike Thackwell	55.5
Pierluigi Martini	67	Franck Lagorce	55
Emanuele Pirro	67	Andrea Montermini	55

MOST POLE POSITIONS			
Roberto Moreno	7	Emanuele Pirro	4
Luca Badoer	5	Eric Bernard	3
Erik Comas	5	Ivan Capelli	3
Franck Lagorce	5	Olivier Grouillard	3
Andrea Montermini	5	Damon Hill	3
Mike Thackwell	5	Alessandro Zanardi	3
Christian Fittipaldi	4		

MOST FASTEST LAPS			
Marco Apicella	7*	Eric Bernard	3*
Erik Comas	4	David Coulthard	3
Christian Danner	4	Yannick Dalmas	3
Franck Lagorce	4	Martin Donnelly	3
Andrea Montermini	4	John Nielsen	3
Roberto Moreno	4	Emanuele Pirro	3
Emanuele Naspetti	4	Alessandro Zanardi	3
Mike Thackwell	4		*includes shared
Luca Badoer	3		fastest lap

YOUNGEST DRIVERS TO WIN A FORMULA TWO RACE		
20 years 141 days	Allan McNish	1990 Silverstone
20 years 142 days	Christian Fittipaldi	1991 Jerez
21 years 72 days	Pedro Lamy	1993 Pau
21 years 157 days	Jordi Gene	1992 Silverstone
21 years 169 days	Luca Badoer	1992 Enna-Pergusa

OLDEST DRIVERS TO WIN A FORMULA TWO RACE		
31 years 302 days	Philippe Alliot	1986 Spa
30 years 45 days	Olivier Grouillard	1988 Zolder
29 years 291 days	Jean-Marc Gounon	1992 Magny-Cours
29 years 200 days	Roberto Moreno	1988 Birmingham
29 years 73 days	John Nielsen	1985 Estoril

OTHER RECORDS

Widest championship-winning margin:
21 points, Erik Comas, 1990

Narrowest championship-winning margin:
No points, Jean Alesi, 1989. Alesi won the championship as he had recorded more wins than Erik Comas

Most wins in a season:
Four, Christian Danner, 1985; Roberto Moreno, 1988; Erik Comas, 1990; Emanuele Naspetti, 1991 and Luca Badoer, 1992

Most successive wins:
Four, Emanuele Naspetti, 1991

Most points in a season:
52, Christian Danner, 1985. Only 51 counted towards the championship due to dropped scores, Erik Comas scored 51 points in 1990

Most successive points-scoring finishes:
Seven, Franck Lagorce, 1993-94

Driver to score points in all championship rounds in a season:
Never achieved

Narrowest race-winning margin:
0.22 seconds, Olivier Grouillard, 1988 Zolder

Widest race-winning margin:
1m05.853, Franck Lagorce, 1993 Magny-Cours. No race has been won by one lap or more

ENGINE RECORDS

MOST WINS			
Cosworth	73	Judd	6
Mugen	20	Honda	3

MANUFACTURERS' RECORDS

MOST WINS			
Reynard	52	March	18
Lola	19	Ralt	13

TEAMS' RECORDS

MOST WINS			
DAMS	18	GA Motorsport	5
Forti Corse	9	Luciano Pavesi Racing	5
Eddie Jordan Racing	8	Pacific Racing	5
Ralt Racing	7	Bromley Motorsport	4
Onyx Race Engineering	6	Bob Sparshott	
Team Crypton	5	Automotive	4

EUROPEAN FORMULA THREE CHAMPIONSHIP

Gerhard Berger, David Hunt and Franz Konrad in the final year of the championship

European Formula Three Championship

RULES

CARS

1975-84 2000 cc maximum engine capacity. Normally aspirated stock-block engines. Maximum of four cylinders

POINTS

1975-84 9-6-4-3-2-1 points awarded to the top six finishers

FIA EUROPEAN FORMULA THREE CHAMPIONS

year	driver	nat	team	car
1975	Larry Perkins	AUS	Team Cowangie	Ralt RT1-Ford
1976	Riccardo Patrese	I	Trivellato Racing	Chevron B34-Toyota
1977	Piercarlo Ghinzani	I	AFMP Euroracing	March 773-Toyota
1978	Jan Lammers	NL	Roger Heavens Racing	Ralt RT1-Toyota
1979	Alain Prost	F	Automobiles Martini	Martini MK27-Renault
1980	Michele Alboreto	I	Euroracing	March 803-Alfa Romeo/March 803B-Alfa Romeo
1981	Mauro Baldi	I	Euroracing	March 813-Alfa Romeo
1982	Oscar Larrauri	RA	Euroracing	Euroracing 101-Alfa Romeo
1983	Pierluigi Martini	I	Luciano Pavesi	Ralt RT3-Alfa Romeo
1984	Ivan Capelli	I	Enzo Coloni Racing	Martini MK42-Alfa Romeo

FIA FORMULA THREE EUROPEAN CUP

When the European F3 Championship was cancelled, FISA replaced it with a one-off race to decide the European Champion. The top six from each national series were invited. Run at Paul Ricard (1985), Imola (1986), Silverstone (1987), Nürburgring (1988), Misano (1989) and Le Mans (1990); it was due to be held at Donington Park in 1991 but the event was cancelled.

year	driver	nat	team	car
1985	Alex Caffi	I	Enzo Coloni Racing	Dallara 385-Alfa Romeo
1986	Stefano Modena	I	Seresina/Ferdinando Ravarotto	Reynard 863-Alfa Romeo
1987	Steve Kempton	GB	Reynard Research & Development	Reynard 873-Alfa Romeo
1988	Joachim Winkelhock	D	WTS Racing	Reynard 883-Volkswagen
1989	Gianni Morbidelli	I	Forti Corse	Dallara 389-Alfa Romeo
1990	Alessandro Zanardi	I	RC Motorsport	Dallara 390-Alfa Romeo
1991	RACE CANCELLED			

EFDA EUROPEAN FORMULA THREE EUROSERIES

An attempt by Dan Partel of the European Formula Drivers' Association to reintroduce a European F3 series. Cancelled by FISA after just one season.

year	driver	nat	team	car
1987	Dave Coyne	GB	Bross Druck Chemie	Reynard 873-Volkswagen

RACE WINNERS

1975

date	race	driver	nat	car	mph
10.05.75	Monte Carlo	Renzo Zorzi	I	GRD 374-Lancia	75.515
01.06.75	Nürburgring	Freddy Kottulinsky	S	Modus M1-BMW	104.260
08.06.75	Anderstorp	Conny Andersson	S	March 753-Toyota	92.390
29.06.75	Monza	Larry Perkins	AUS	Ralt RT1-Ford	116.799
02.08.75	Djurslandring	Terry Perkins	AUS	Ralt RT1-Ford	n/a

1976

date	race	driver	nat	car	mph
04.04.76	Nürburgring	Conny Andersson	S	March 753-Toyota	101.282
19.04.76	Zandvoort	Riccardo Patrese	I	Chevron B34-Toyota	102.642
09.05.76	Mantorp Park	Gianfranco Brancatelli	I	March 763-Toyota	101.219
23.05.76	Avus	Conny Andersson	S	March 763-Toyota	n/a*
13.06.76	Enna-Pergusa	Riccardo Patrese	I	Chevron B34-Toyota	101.092
27.06.76	Monza	Riccardo Patrese	I	Chevron B34-Toyota	112.524
25.07.76	Croix-en-Ternois	Conny Andersson	S	March 763-Toyota	76.756
22.08.76	Kassel-Calden	Riccardo Patrese	I	Chevron B34-Toyota	n/a*
04.09.76	Knutstorp	Conny Andersson	S	March 763-Toyota	78.517
03.10.76	Vallelunga	Gianfranco Brancatelli	I	March 763-Toyota	93.691

*Race decided by points awarded for results in the two heats

1977

20.03.77	Paul Ricard	Beppe Gabbiani	I	Chevron B38-Toyota	91.573
27.03.77	Nürburgring	Piercarlo Ghinzani	I	March 773-Toyota	88.897
11.04.77	Zandvoort	Anders Olofsson	S	Ralt RT1-Toyota	103.263
24.04.77	Zolder	Piercarlo Ghinzani	I	March 773-Toyota	93.748
08.05.77	Österreichring	Anders Olofsson	S	Ralt RT1-Toyota	106.234
29.05.77	Imola	Piercarlo Ghinzani	I	March 773-Toyota	101.789
12.06.77	Enna-Pergusa	Oscar Pedersoli	I	Ralt RT1-Toyota	107.930
26.06.77	Monza	Elio de Angelis	I	Ralt RT1-Toyota	113.476
24.07.77	Croix-en-Ternois	Derek Daly	IRL	Chevron B38-Toyota	77.363
07.08.77	Knutstorp	Anders Olofsson	S	Ralt RT1-Toyota	79.956
21.08.77	Kassel-Calden	Nelson Piquet	BR	Ralt RT1-Toyota	101.603
27.08.77	Donington Park	Brett Riley	NZ	March 773-Toyota	98.142
18.09.77	Jarama	Nelson Piquet	BR	Ralt RT1-Toyota	85.291
09.10.77	Vallelunga	Oscar Pedersoli	I	Ralt RT1-Toyota	94.230

1978

27.03.78	Zandvoort	Jan Lammers	NL	Ralt RT1-Toyota	104.335
02.04.78	Nürburgring	Anders Olofsson	S	Ralt RT1-Toyota	106.484
16.04.78	Österreichring	Anders Olofsson	S	Ralt RT1-Toyota	113.861
23.04.78	Zolder	Teo Fabi	I	March 783-Toyota	78.357
14.05.78	Imola	Patrick Gaillard	F	Chevron B43-Toyota	103.190
27.05.78	Nürburgring	Patrick Gaillard	F	Chevron B43-Toyota	107.655
04.06.78	Dijon-Prenois	Teo Fabi	I	March 783-Toyota	103.986
25.06.78	Monza	Jan Lammers	NL	Ralt RT1-Toyota	94.510
02.07.78	Enna-Pergusa	Michael Bleekemolen	NL	Chevron B43-Toyota	109.640
16.07.78	Magny-Cours	Jan Lammers	NL	Ralt RT1-Toyota	98.401
06.08.78	Knutstorp	Anders Olofsson	S	Ralt RT1-Toyota	79.498
13.08.78	Karlskoga	Jan Lammers	NL	Ralt RT1-Toyota	86.959
26.08.78	Donington Park	Derek Warwick	GB	Ralt RT1-Toyota	99.330
03.09.78	Kassel-Calden	Anders Olofsson	S	Ralt RT1-Toyota	102.505
17.09.78	Jarama	Alain Prost	F	Martini MK21B-Renault	86.456
08.10.78	Vallelunga	Teo Fabi	I	March 783-Toyota	95.659

1979

18.03.79	Vallelunga	Piercarlo Ghinzani	I	March 793-Alfa Romeo	95.095
15.04.79	Österreichring	Alain Prost	F	Martini MK27-Renault	116.432
22.04.79	Zolder	Alain Prost	F	Martini MK27-Renault	98.906

Alain Prost wins at Zolder in 1979, the year he took the European Formula Three Championship

01.05.79	Magny-Cours	Alain Prost	F	Martini MK27-Renault	98.542
20.05.79	Donington Park	Brett Riley	NZ	March 783/793-Triumph	80.856
04.06.79	Zandvoort	Alain Prost	F	Martini MK27-Renault	104.428
17.06.79	Enna-Pergusa	Piercarlo Ghinzani	I	March 793-Alfa Romeo	105.790
24.06.79	Monza	Mike Thackwell	NZ	March 793-Toyota	114.082
05.08.79	Knutstorp	Alain Prost	F	Martini MK27-Renault	80.125
12.08.79	Kinnekulle	Richard Dallest	F	Martini MK27-Toyota	88.822
09.09.79	Jarama	Alain Prost	F	Martini MK27-Renault	86.280
07.10.79	Kassel-Calden	Michael Korten	D	March 793-Toyota	101.264

1980

30.03.80	Nürburgring	Thierry Boutsen	B	Martini MK31-Toyota	105.972
06.04.80	Österreichring	Michele Alboreto	I	March 803-Alfa Romeo	116.658
20.04.80	Zolder	Thierry Boutsen	B	Martini MK31-Toyota	95.201
27.04.80	Magny-Cours	Thierry Boutsen	B	Martini MK31-Toyota	98.781
26.05.80	Zandvoort	Mauro Baldi	I	Martini MK31-Toyota	100.396
01.06.80	La Châtre	Michele Alboreto	I	March 803-Alfa Romeo	79.525

European Formula Three Championship

15.06.80	Mugello	Corrado Fabi	I	March 803-Alfa Romeo	101.170
29.06.80	Monza	Michele Alboreto	I	March 803-Alfa Romeo	113.443
27.07.80	Misano	Mauro Baldi	I	Martini MK31-Toyota	100.742
10.08.80	Knutstorp	Corrado Fabi	I	March 803-Alfa Romeo	77.576
07.09.80	Silverstone	Mike White	ZA	March 803B-Toyota	119.763
21.09.80	Jarama	Mauro Baldi	I	Martini MK31-Toyota	88.399
05.10.80	Kassel-Calden	Michele Alboreto	I	March 803B-Alfa Romeo	104.960
12.10.80	Zolder	Philippe Streiff	F	Martini MK31-Toyota	100.839

1981

15.03.81	Vallelunga	Mauro Baldi	I	March 813-Alfa Romeo	96.240
29.03.81	Nürburgring	Oscar Larrauri	RA	March 813-Toyota	94.370
05.04.81	Donington Park	Mike White	ZA	March 813-Alfa Romeo	100.797
19.04.81	Österreichring	Mauro Baldi	I	March 813-Alfa Romeo	119.129
26.04.81	Zolder	Mauro Baldi	I	March 813-Alfa Romeo	102.901
03.05.81	Magny-Cours	Philippe Alliot	F	Martini MK34-Alfa Romeo	101.259
24.05.81	La Châtre	Philippe Alliot	F	Martini MK34-Alfa Romeo	80.550
08.06.81	Zandvoort	Mauro Baldi	I	March 813-Alfa Romeo	102.672
21.06.81	Silverstone	Roberto Moreno	BR	Ralt RT3/81-Toyota	122.634
28.06.81	Croix-en-Ternois	Mauro Baldi	I	March 813-Alfa Romeo	77.980
19.07.81	Misano	Mauro Baldi	I	March 813-Alfa Romeo	87.162
09.08.81	Knutstorp	Mauro Baldi	I	March 813-Alfa Romeo	80.037
06.09.81	Jarama	Alain Ferté	F	Martini MK34-Alfa Romeo	89.297
20.09.81	Imola	Mauro Baldi	I	March 813-Alfa Romeo	101.749
04.10.81	Mugello	Emanuele Pirro	I	Martini MK34-Toyota	102.792

1982

14.03.82	Mugello	Oscar Larrauri	RA	Euroracing 101-Alfa Romeo	102.980
28.03.82	Nürburgring	Oscar Larrauri	RA	Euroracing 101-Alfa Romeo	98.467
04.04.82	Donington Park	James Weaver	GB	Ralt RT3/81-Toyota	100.903
18.04.82	Zolder	Oscar Larrauri	RA	Euroracing 101-Alfa Romeo	101.655
02.05.82	Magny-Cours	Alain Ferté	F	Martini MK37-Alfa Romeo	101.525
16.05.82	Österreichring	Emanuele Pirro	I	Euroracing 101-Alfa Romeo	118.335
31.05.82	Zandvoort	Oscar Larrauri	RA	Euroracing 101-Alfa Romeo	102.130
13.06.82	Silverstone	Emanuele Pirro	I	Euroracing 101-Alfa Romeo	121.741
27.06.82	Monza	Oscar Larrauri	RA	Euroracing 101-Alfa Romeo	115.625
04.07.82	Enna-Pergusa	Oscar Larrauri	RA	Euroracing 101-Alfa Romeo	111.011
18.07.82	La Châtre	Philippe Alliot	F	Martini MK37-Alfa Romeo	81.150
08.08.82	Knutstorp	Oscar Larrauri	RA	Euroracing 101-Alfa Romeo	80.131
05.09.82	Nogaro	James Weaver	GB	Ralt RT3/82-Toyota	91.950
12.09.82	Jarama	James Weaver	GB	Ralt RT3/82-Toyota	89.057
03.10.82	Kassel-Calden	Emanuele Pirro	I	Euroracing 101-Alfa Romeo	87.381

1983

13.03.83	Vallelunga	Emanuele Pirro	I	Ralt RT3/83-Alfa Romeo	96.920
17.04.83	Zolder	Emanuele Pirro	I	Ralt RT3/83-Alfa Romeo	102.348
01.05.83	Magny-Cours	John Nielsen	DK	Ralt RT3/83-Volkswagen	97.829
22.05.83	Österreichring	Tommy Byrne	IRL	Ralt RT3/83-Toyota	119.329
05.06.83	La Châtre	Roberto Ravaglia	I	Ralt RT3/83-Toyota	80.154
12.06.83	Silverstone	Martin Brundle	GB	Ralt RT3/83-Toyota	122.400
26.06.83	Monza	John Nielsen	DK	Ralt RT3/83-Volkswagen	116.290
10.07.83	Misano	Tommy Byrne	IRL	Ralt RT3/83-Toyota	101.984
31.07.83	Zandvoort	John Nielsen	DK	Ralt RT3/83-Volkswagen	101.668
07.08.83	Knutstorp	John Nielsen	DK	Ralt RT3/83-Volkswagen	80.671
04.09.83	Nogaro	Pierluigi Martini	I	Ralt RT3/83-Alfa Romeo	91.849
11.09.83	Jarama	Pierluigi Martini	I	Ralt RT3/83-Alfa Romeo	89.404
25.09.83	Imola	Pierluigi Martini	I	Ralt RT3/83-Alfa Romeo	103.857
09.10.83	Donington Park	Martin Brundle	GB	Ralt RT3/83-Toyota	93.242
23.10.83	Croix-en-Ternois	Pierluigi Martini	I	Ralt RT3/83-Alfa Romeo	79.694

1984

25.03.84	Donington Park	Johnny Dumfries	GB	Ralt RT3/83-Volkswagen	85.842
15.04.84	Zolder	John Nielsen	DK	Ralt RT3/84-Volkswagen	102.885
01.05.84	Magny-Cours	Ivan Capelli	I	Martini MK42-Alfa Romeo	102.472
13.05.84	La Châtre	Ivan Capelli	I	Martini MK42-Alfa Romeo	81.067
27.05.84	Österreichring	Gerhard Berger	A	Ralt RT3/84-Alfa Romeo	120.560
10.06.84	Silverstone	Johnny Dumfries	GB	Ralt RT3/83-Volkswagen	124.430
17.06.84	Nürburgring	Johnny Dumfries	GB	Ralt RT3/83-Volkswagen	103.697
24.06.84	Monza	Gerhard Berger	A	Ralt RT3/84-Alfa Romeo	115.723
08.07.84	Enna-Pergusa	Ivan Capelli	I	Martini MK42-Alfa Romeo	112.675
15.07.84	Mugello	Ivan Capelli	I	Martini MK42-Alfa Romeo	104.569
19.08.84	Knutstorp	Claudio Langes	I	Ralt RT3/84-Toyota	80.082
16.09.84	Nogaro	John Nielsen	DK	Ralt RT3/84-Volkswagen	94.408
21.10.84	Jarama	Johnny Dumfries	GB	Ralt RT3/83-Volkswagen	90.527

LE MANS
24 HOURS

The Schlesser/Jabouille/Cudini Sauber-Mercedes heads its team-mates during the 1989 race

RULES

Always a Sports Car race, the Le Mans 24 hours normally adopted the World Championship rules until that series was abandoned in 1992. Since then a mixture of 1990 and 1992 Group C Sports Cars, IMSA GTS (Silhouette) and roadcar-based GT cars have competed, with the organizers attempting to equalize the power-to-weight ratio of the different classes by fuel capacity and minimum weight restrictions.

1923

26-27 May. 128 laps of a 10.726-mile circuit = 1372.928 miles

1 André Lagache/René Leonard	Chenard & Walcker "Sport"	128
2 Raoul Bachmann/ Christian Dauvergne	Chenard & Walcker "Sport"	124
3 Raymond de Tornaco/Paul Gros	Bignan 11HP "Desmo"	120
4=John Duff/Frank Clement	Bentley "Sport"	112
4=Philippe de Marne/Jean Martin	Bignan 11HP "Commercial"	112
4=André Dils/Nicolas Caerels	Excelsior "Albert 1er"	112

Winner's average speed: 57.205 mph. Fastest lap: Clement, 9m39

1924

14-15 June. 120 laps of a 10.726-mile circuit = 1287.120 miles

1 John Duff/Frank Clement	Bentley "Sport"	120
2 Henri Stoffel/Edouard Brisson	Lorraine-Dietrich B3-6	119
3 Gérard de Courcelles/ André Rossignol	Lorraine-Dietrich B3-6	119
4 André Pisard/Chavée	Chenard & Walcker 2-litre	111
5 Christian Dauvergne/ Manso de Zuniga	Chenard & Walcker 2-litre	108
6 Gaston Delalande/ Georges Guignard	Rolland Pilain C23	106

Winner's average speed: 53.630 mph. Fastest lap: André Lagache (Chenard & Walcker), 9m19

1925

20-21 June. 129 laps of a 10.726-mile circuit = 1383.654 miles

1 Gérard de Courcelles/ André Rossignol	Lorraine-Dietrich B3-6	129
2 Jean Chassagne/Sammy Davis	Sunbeam "Sport" DA8206	125
3 Stalter/Edouard Brisson	Lorraine-Dietrich B3-6	124
4=Tino Danieli/Mario Danieli	OM 665S "Superba"	120
4=Giulio Foresti/Aimé Vassiaux	OM 665S "Superba"	120
6 Louis Wagner/Charles Flohot	Ariès 3-litre	119

Winner's average speed: 57.652 mph. Fastest lap: André Lagache (Chenard & Walcker), 9m10

1926

12-13 June. 147 laps of a 10.726-mile circuit = 1576.722 miles

1 Robert Bloch/André Rossignol	Lorraine-Dietrich B3-6	147
2 Gérard de Courcelles/ Marcel Mongin	Lorraine-Dietrich B3-6	146
3 Stalter/Edouard Brisson	Lorraine-Dietrich B3-6	139
4 Ferdinando Minoia/Giulio Foresti	OM 665SS "Superba"	134
5 Tino Danieli/Mario Danieli	OM 665SS "Superba"	131
6 Pierre Tabourin/Auguste Lefranc	Théo Schneider 25SP	118

Winner's average speed: 65.697 mph. Fastest lap: de Courcelles, 9m03

1927

18-19 June. 137 laps of a 10.726-mile circuit = 1469.462 miles

1 Sammy Davis/John Benjafield	Bentley "Sport"	137
2 André de Victor/J Hasley	Salmson GS	117
3 Georges Casse/André Rousseau	Salmson GS	115
4 Lucien Desvaux/Fernand Vallon	SCAP 1.5-litre	110
5 Guy Bouriat/Pierre Bussienne	EHP DS-Cime	108
6 André Marandet/ Gonzague Lecureul	SARA BDE	106

Winner's average speed: 61.228 mph. Fastest lap: Frank Clement (Bentley "Super Sport"), 8m46

1928

16-17 June. 154 laps of a 10.726-mile circuit = 1651.804 miles

1 Woolf Barnato/Bernard Rubin	Bentley 4.4	154
2 Edouard Brisson/Robert Bloch	Stutz DV "Black Hawk"	153
3 Henri Stoffel/André Rossignol	Chrysler 72	144
4 Jean Ghica Cantacuzino/ G Ghica Cantacuzino	Chrysler 72	139
5 Tim Birkin/Jean Chassagne	Bentley 4.4	135
6 Maurice Harvey/Harold Purdy	Alvis TA	132

Winner's average speed: 68.825 mph. Fastest lap: Birkin, 8m07

1929

15-16 June. 173 laps of a 10.153-mile circuit = 1756.469 miles

1 Woolf Barnato/Tim Birkin	Bentley "Speed Six"	173
2 Jack Dunfee/Glen Kidston	Bentley 4.4	166
3 John Benjafield/André d'Erlanger	Bentley 4.4	158
4 Frank Clement/Jean Chassagne	Bentley 4.4	156
5 Guy Bouriat/"Georges Philippe"	Stutz DV	152
6 Henri Stoffel/Robert Benoist	Chrysler 75	151

Winner's average speed: 73.186 mph. Fastest lap: Birkin, 7m21

1930

21-22 June. 178 laps of a 10.153-mile circuit = 1807.234 miles

1 Woolf Barnato/Glen Kidston	Bentley "Speed Six"	178
2 Frank Clement/Richard Watney	Bentley "Speed Six"	172
3 Brian Lewis/Hugh Eaton	Talbot GB-90	161
4 John Hindmarsh/Tim Rose-Richards	Talbot GB-90	159
5 Earl Howe/Leslie Callingham	Alfa Romeo 6C Sport	158
6 Kenneth Peacock/Sammy Newsome	Lea-Francis S	139

Winner's average speed: 75.301 mph. Fastest lap: Tim Birkin (Bentley 4.4), 6m48

1931

13-14 June. 183 laps of a 10.153-mile circuit = 1857.999 miles

1 Earl Howe/Tim Birkin	Alfa Romeo 8C	183
2 Boris Ivanowski/Henri Stoffel	Mercedes-Benz SSK	176
3 Tim Rose-Richards/ AC Saunders Davies	Talbot T105	172
4 Robert Trébor/Louis Balart	Lorraine-Dietrich B3-6	149
5 Augustus Bertelli/Maurice Harvey	Aston Martin LM5	139
6 Just-Emile Vernet/Fernand Vallon	Caban Spéciale-Ruby K	127

Winner's average speed: 77.417 mph. Fastest lap: Ivanowski, 7m02

1932

18-19 June. 218 laps of a 8.378-mile circuit = 1826.404 miles

1 Raymond Sommer/Luigi Chinetti	Alfa Romeo 8C	218
2 Franco Cortese/ Giovanni-Battista Guidotti	Alfa Romeo 8C	216
3 Brian Lewis/Tim Rose-Richards	Talbot T105	180
4 Odette Siko/"Sabipa"	Alfa Romeo 6C	179
5 Sammy Newsome/ Henken Widengren	Aston Martin 1.5-litre	174
6 Jean Sébilleau/Georges Delaroche	Bugatti T40	172

Winner's average speed: 76.100 mph. Fastest lap: Ferdinando Minoia (Alfa Romeo 8C), 5m41

1933

17-18 June. 233 laps of a 8.378-mile circuit = 1952.074 miles

1 Raymond Sommer/Tazio Nuvolari	Alfa Romeo 8C	233
2 Luigi Chinetti/Philippe Varent	Alfa Romeo 8C	232
3 Brian Lewis/Tim Rose-Richards	Alfa Romeo 8C	225
4 Alex van der Becke/ Kenneth Peacock	Riley 9 "Brooklands"	191
5 Pat Driscoll/Clifton Penn-Hughes	Aston Martin Ulster	188
6 Ludovic Ford/Maurice Baumer	MG Midget C	176

Winner's average speed: 81.336 mph. Fastest lap: Sommer, 5m31.4

1934

16-17 June. 213 laps of a 8.378-mile circuit = 1784.514 miles

1 Philippe Étancelin/Luigi Chinetti	Alfa Romeo 8C	213
2 Jean Sébilleau/Georges Delaroche	Riley 9 MPH Racing	200

3	Fred Dixon/Cyril Paul	Riley 9 MPH Racing	199
4	Roy Eccles/Charlie Martin	MG Magnette K3	197
5	Alex van der Becke/		
	Kenneth Peacock	Riley 9 "Brooklands"	195
6	Sammy Newsome/Percy Maclure	Riley Ulster Imp	195

Winner's average speed: 74.355 mph. Fastest lap: Étancelin, 5m41.0

1935

15-16 June. 222 laps of a 8.378-mile circuit = 1859.916 miles

1	John Hindmarsh/Luis Fontes	Lagonda Rapide	222
2	"Heldé"/Henri Stoffel	Alfa Romeo 8C	222
3	Charlie Martin/Charles Brackenbury	Aston Martin Ulster	215
4	Alex van der Becke/Cliff Richardson	Riley 9 MPH	208
5	"Michel Paris"/Marcel Mongin	Delahaye 135	207
6	Guy Don/Jean Desvignes	Alfa Romeo 6C	204

Winner's average speed: 77.497 mph. Fastest lap: Earl Howe (Alfa Romeo 8C), 5m47.9

1937

19-20 June. 244 laps of a 8.378-mile circuit = 2044.232 miles

1	Jean-Pierre Wimille/Robert Benoist	Bugatti T57G	244
2	Joseph Paul/Marcel Mongin	Delahaye 135S	236
3	René Dreyfus/Henri Stoffel	Delahaye 135S	232
4	Louis Gérard/Jacques de Valence	Delage D6	215
5	JM Skeffington/RC Murton-Neale	Aston Martin Ulster	205
6	Peter Orsich/Rudolf Sauerwein	Adler Trumpf	205

Winner's average speed: 85.176 mph. Fastest lap: Wimille, 5m13.0

1938

18-19 June. 235 laps of a 8.378-mile circuit = 1968.830 miles

1	Eugène Chaboud/Jean Trémoulet	Delahaye 135S	235
2	Gaston Serraud/		
	Yves Giraud-Cabantous	Delahaye 135S	233
3	Jean Prenant/André Morel	Lago-Talbot SS	219
4	Louis Villeneuve/René Biolay	Delahaye 135S	218
5	Charles de Cortanze/		
	Marcel Contet	Peugeot 402 DS Darl'Mat	214
6	Peter Orsich/Rudolf Sauerwein	Adler Super Trumpf	211

Winner's average speed: 82.035 mph. Fastest lap: Raymond Sommer (Alfa Romeo 8C-2900B), 5m13.8

1939

17-18 June. 248 laps of a 8.378-mile circuit = 2077.744 miles

1	Jean-Pierre Wimille/Pierre Veyron	Bugatti T57C	248
2	Louis Gérard/Georges Monneret	Delage 3L	245
3	Arthur Dobson/Charles Brackenbury	Lagonda V12	239
4	Lord Selsdon/Lord Waleran	Lagonda V12	238
5	Paul von Schaumburg-Lippe/		
	Fritz Wencher	BMW 328 "Touring"	236
6	Louis Villeneuve/René Biolay	Delahaye 135S	235

Winner's average speed: 86.573 mph. Fastest lap: Robert Mazaud (Delahaye 135S), 5m12.1

1949

25-26 June. 235 laps of a 8.378-mile circuit = 1968.830 miles

1	Luigi Chinetti/Lord Selsdon	Ferrari 166MM	235
2	Henri Louveau/Juan Jover	Delage D6S	234
3	Norbert Culpan/HJ Aldington	Frazer-Nash RLM-Bristol	224
4	Louis Gérard/Chico Godia-Sales	Delage D6S	212
5	Georges Grignard/Robert Brunet	Delahaye 135S	210
6	"Soltan" Hay/Tommy Wisdom	Bentley Corniche	210

Winner's average speed: 82.035 mph. Fastest lap: André Simon (Delahaye 175S), 5m12.5

1950

24-25 June. 256 laps of a 8.378-mile circuit = 2144.768 miles

1	Louis Rosier/Jean-Louis Rosier	Lago-Talbot T26C-GS	256
2	Pierre Meyrat/Guy Mairesse	Lago-Talbot monoplace	254
3	Sydney Allard/Tom Cole	Allard J2-Cadillac	251
4	Tony Rolt/Duncan Hamilton	Healey-Nash	250
5	George Abecassis/Lance Macklin	Aston Martin DB2	249
6	Charles Brackenbury/Reg Parnell	Aston Martin DB2	244

Winner's average speed: 89.365 mph. Fastest lap: L Rosier, 4m53.5

1951

23-24 June. 267 laps of a 8.378-mile circuit = 2236.926 miles

1	Peter Walker/Peter Whitehead	Jaguar C-type	267
2	Pierre Meyrat/Guy Mairesse	Lago-Talbot T26C-GS	258
3	Lance Macklin/Eric Thompson	Aston Martin DB2	257
4	"Pierre Levegh"/René Marchand	Lago-Talbot monoplace	256
5	George Abecassis/		
	Brian Shawe-Taylor	Aston Martin DB2	255
6	Tony Rolt/Duncan Hamilton	Healey Sport Coupé-Nash	255

Winner's average speed: 93.205 mph. Fastest lap: Stirling Moss (Jaguar C-type), 4m46.8

1952

14-15 June. 276 laps of a 8.378-mile circuit = 2312.328 miles

1	Hermann Lang/Fritz Riess	Mercedes-Benz 300SL	276
2	Theo Helfrich/Helmut Niedermayr	Mercedes-Benz 300SL	275
3	Leslie Johnson/Tommy Wisdom	Healey-Nash 4-litre	261
4	Briggs Cunningham/Bill Spear	Cunningham C4R-Chrysler	251
5	André Simon/Lucien Vincent	Ferrari 340 America	249
6	Luigi Valenzano/"Ippocampo"	Lancia Aurelia B20	247

Winner's average speed: 96.347 mph. Fastest lap: Alberto Ascari (Ferrari 250S), 4m40.5

1953

13-14 June. 302 laps of a 8.378-mile circuit = 2530.156 miles

1	Tony Rolt/Duncan Hamilton	Jaguar C-type	302
2	Peter Walker/Stirling Moss	Jaguar C-type	299
3	Phil Walters/John Fitch	Cunningham C5R-Chrysler	297
4	Peter Whitehead/Ian Stewart	Jaguar C-type	296
5	Paolo Marzotto/Giannino Marzotto	Ferrari 340MM	293
6	Maurice Trintignant/Harry Schell	Gordini T24S	292

Winner's average speed: 105.423 mph. Fastest lap: Alberto Ascari (Ferrari 375MM), 4m27.4

1954

12-13 June. 300 laps of a 8.378-mile circuit = 2513.400 miles

1	Maurice Trintignant/		
	José Froilan Gonzalez	Ferrari 375 Plus	300
2	Tony Rolt/Duncan Hamilton	Jaguar D-type	300
3	Bill Spear/Sherwood Johnston	Cunningham C4R-Chrysler	282
4	Roger Laurent/Jacques Swaters	Jaguar C-type	276
5	Briggs Cunningham/John Benett	Cunningham C4R-Chrysler	272
6	André Guelfi/Jacques Pollet	Gordini T30S	262

Winner's average speed: 104.725 mph. Fastest lap: Gonzalez, 4m16.8

1955

11-12 June. 306 laps of a 8.378-mile circuit = 2563.668 miles

1	Mike Hawthorn/Ivor Bueb	Jaguar D-type	306
2	Peter Collins/Paul Frère	Aston Martin DB3S	301
3	Johnny Claes/Jacques Swaters	Jaguar D-type	295
4	Helmuth Polensky/		
	Richard von Frankenberg	Porsche 550	283
5	Wolfgang Seidel/Olivier Gendebien	Porsche 550	275
6	Helmut Glöckler/Jaroslav Juhan	Porsche 550	272

Winner's average speed: 106.820 mph. Fastest lap: Hawthorn, 4m06.6

1956

28-29 July. 299 laps of a 8.365-mile circuit = 2501.135 miles

1	Ninian Sanderson/Ron Flockhart	Jaguar D-type	299
2	Stirling Moss/Peter Collins	Aston Martin DB3S	298
3	Maurice Trintignant/		
	Olivier Gendebien	Ferrari 625LM	292
4	Jacques Swaters/Freddy Rousselle	Jaguar D-type	283
5	Wolfgang von Trips/		
	Richard von Frankenberg	Porsche RS550A	281
6	Mike Hawthorn/Ivor Bueb	Jaguar D-type	279

Winner's average speed: 104.214 mph. Fastest lap: Hawthorn, 4m20.0

1957

22-23 June. 326 laps of a 8.365-mile circuit = 2726.990 miles

1	Ivor Bueb/Ron Flockhart	Jaguar D-type	326
2	Ninian Sanderson/John Lawrence	Jaguar D-type	318
3	Jean Lucas/"Mary"	Jaguar D-type	316
4	Paul Frère/Freddy Rousselle	Jaguar D-type	309
5	Stuart Lewis-Evans/Martino Severi	Ferrari 315S	299
6	Duncan Hamilton/Masten Gregory	Jaguar D-type	298

Winner's average speed: 113.625 mph. Fastest lap: Mike Hawthorn (Ferrari 335MM), 3m58.7

1958

21-22 June. 304 laps of a 8.365-mile circuit = 2542.960 miles

1	Olivier Gendebien/Phil Hill	Ferrari 250TR	304
2	Peter Whitehead/Graham Whitehead	Aston Martin DB3S	292
3	Jean Behra/Hans Herrmann	Porsche 718 RSK	290
4	Edgar Barth/Paul Frère	Porsche 718 RSK	289
5	Carel Godin de Beaufort/ Herbert Linge	Porsche 550A	287
6	"Beurlys"/Alain de Chagny	Ferrari 250TR	278

Winner's average speed: 105.957 mph. Fastest lap: Mike Hawthorn (Ferrari 250TR), 4m08

1959

20-21 June. 322 laps of a 8.365-mile circuit = 2693.530 miles

1	Roy Salvadori/Carroll Shelby	Aston Martin DBR1	322
2	Maurice Trintignant/Paul Frère	Aston Martin DBR1	322
3	"Beurlys"/"Eldé"	Ferrari 250GT	297
4	André Pilette/Georges Arents	Ferrari 250GT	296
5	Bob Grossman/Fernand Tavano	Ferrari 250GT California	294
6	Lino Fayen/Gino Munaron	Ferrari 250GT	293

Winner's average speed: 112.230 mph. Fastest lap: Jean Behra (Ferrari 250GT), 4m00.9

1960

25-26 June. 313 laps of a 8.365-mile circuit = 2618.245 miles

1	Olivier Gendebien/Paul Frère	Ferrari 250TR	313
2	Ricardo Rodriguez/André Pilette	Ferrari 250TR	309
3	Roy Salvadori/Jim Clark	Aston Martin DBR1	305
4	Fernand Tavano/"Loustel"	Ferrari 250GT	301
5	Georges Arents/Alan Connell	Ferrari 250GT	299
6	"Eldé"/Pierre Noblet	Ferrari 250GT	299

Winner's average speed: 109.094 mph. Fastest lap: Masten Gregory (Maserati T61), 4m04

1961

10-11 June. 332 laps of a 8.365-mile circuit = 2777.180 miles

1	Olivier Gendebien/Phil Hill	Ferrari 250TR	332
2	Willy Mairesse/Michael Parkes	Ferrari 250TR	329
3	Pierre Noblet/Jean Guichet	Ferrari 250GT	316
4	Augie Pabst/Richard Thompson	Maserati T63	310
5	Masten Gregory/Bob Holbert	Porsche RS61	308
6	Bob Grossman/André Pilette	Ferrari 250GT	308

Winner's average speed: 115.716 mph. Fastest lap: Ricardo Rodriguez (Ferrari 250TR), 3m59.09

1962

23-24 June. 330 laps of a 8.365-mile circuit = 2760.450 miles

1	Olivier Gendebien/Phil Hill	Ferrari 330LM	330
2	Jean Guichet/Pierre Noblet	Ferrari 250GTO	325
3	"Eldé"/"Beurlys"	Ferrari 250GTO	312
4	Briggs Cunningham/Roy Salvadori	Jaguar E-type	309
5	Peter Lumsden/Peter Sargent	Jaguar E-type	309
6	Bob Grossman/"Fireball" Roberts	Ferrari 250TR "Experimental"	296

Winner's average speed: 115.019 mph. Pole position: P Hill. Fastest lap: P Hill, 3m57.3

1963

15-16 June. 338 laps of a 8.365-mile circuit = 2827.370 miles

1	Ludovico Scarfiotti/Lorenzo Bandini	Ferrari 250P	338
2	"Beurlys"/ Gérard Langlois van Ophem	Ferrari 250GTO	322
3	Michael Parkes/Umberto Maglioli	Ferrari 250P	322

4	"Eldé"/Pierre Dumay	Ferrari 250GTO	321
5	Jack Sears/Mike Salmon	Ferrari 330LMB	313
6	Masten Gregory/David Piper	Ferrari 250GTO	311

Winner's average speed: 117.807 mph. Pole position: Pedro Rodriguez (Ferrari 330TR), 3m50.9. Fastest lap: John Surtees (Ferrari 250P), 3m53.3

1964

20-21 June. 348 laps of a 8.365-mile circuit = 2911.020 miles

1	Jean Guichet/Nino Vaccarella	Ferrari 275P	348
2	Jo Bonnier/Graham Hill	Ferrari 330P	343
3	John Surtees/Lorenzo Bandini	Ferrari 330P	323
4	Dan Gurney/Bob Bondurant	AC Cobra Daytona-Ford	333
5	Lucien Bianchi/"Beurlys"	Ferrari 250GTO	332
6	Innes Ireland/Tony Maggs	Ferrari 250GTO	327

Winner's average speed: 121.293 mph. Pole position: John Surtees: 3m42.0. Fastest lap: Phil Hill (Ford GT40), 3m49.2

1965

19-20 June. 347 laps of a 8.365-mile circuit = 2902.655 miles

1	Masten Gregory/Jochen Rindt	Ferrari 275LM	347
2	Pierre Dumay/Gustave Gosselin	Ferrari 275LM	341
3	Willy Mairesse/"Beurlys"	Ferrari 250GTB	338
4	Herbert Linge/Peter Nöcker	Porsche 904/6	334
5	Gerhard Koch/Anton Fischaber	Porsche 904GTS	324
6	Dieter Spoerry/Peter Boller	Ferrari 275LM	323

Winner's average speed: 120.944 mph. Pole position: Phil Hill (Ford GT40), 3m33.0. Fastest lap: P Hill, 3m37.5

1966

17-18 June. 359 laps of a 8.365-mile circuit = 3003.035 miles

1	Bruce McLaren/Chris Amon	Ford GT40 Mk2	359
2	Ken Miles/Denny Hulme	Ford GT40 Mk2	359
3	Ronnie Bucknum/Dick Hutcherson	Ford GT40 Mk2	347
4	Jo Siffert/Colin Davis	Porsche 906 Carrera 6LH	338
5	Hans Herrmann/Herbert Linge	Porsche 906 Carrera 6LH	337
6	Udo Schütz/Piet de Klerk	Porsche 906 Carrera 6LH	336

Winner's average speed: 125.126 mph. Pole position: Dan Gurney (Ford GT40 Mk2), 3m30.6. Fastest lap: Gurney, 3m30.6

The Ford GT40 Mk2 won at Le Mans at the third attempt – Chris Amon and Bruce McLaren celebrate their historic win in 1966

1967

10-11 June. 388 laps of a 8.365-mile circuit = 3245.620 miles

1	Dan Gurney/AJ Foyt Jr	Ford GT40 Mk4	388
2	Ludovico Scarfiotti/Michael Parkes	Ferrari 330P4	384
3	Willy Mairesse/"Beurlys"	Ferrari 330P4	377
4	Bruce McLaren/Mark Donohue	Ford GT40 Mk4	359
5	Jo Siffert/Hans Herrmann	Porsche 907/6	358
6	Rolf Stommelen/Jochen Neerpasch	Porsche 910/6	351

Winner's average speed: 135.234 mph. Pole position: McLaren, 3m24.4. Fastest lap: Denny Hulme (Ford GT40 Mk4) and Mario Andretti (Ford GT40 Mk4), 3m23.6

1968

28-29 September. 330 laps of a 8.369-mile circuit = 2761.770 miles

1	Pedro Rodriguez/Lucien Bianchi	Ford GT40	330
2	Dieter Spoerry/Rico Steinemann	Porsche 907/8	325

3 Rolf Stommelen/Jochen Neerpasch Porsche 908LH 324
4 Ignazio Giunti/Nanni Galli Alfa Romeo T33/2 321
5 Carlo Facetti/Spartico Dini Alfa Romeo T33/2 314
6 Mario Casoni/Giampiero Biscaldi Alfa Romeo T33/2 304
Winner's average speed: 115.074 mph. Pole position: Jo Siffert (Porsche 908LH), 3m35.4. Fastest lap: Stommelen, 3m38.1

1969
14-15 June. 371 laps of a 8.369-mile circuit = 3104.899 miles
1 Jacky Ickx/Jackie Oliver Ford GT40 371
2 Hans Herrmann/Gérard Larrousse Porsche 908LH 371
3 David Hobbs/Mike Hailwood Ford GT40 367
4 Jean-Pierre Beltoise/Piers Courage Matra-Simca MS650 367
5 Jean Guichet/Nino Vaccarella Matra-Simca MS630 358
6 Helmut Kelleners/Reinhold Jöst Ford GT40 340
Winner's average speed: 129.371 mph. Pole position: Rolf Stommelen (Porsche 917LH), 3m22.9. Fastest lap: Vic Elford (Porsche 917LH), 3m27.2

1970
13-14 June. 342 laps of a 8.369-mile circuit = 2862.198 miles
1 Hans Herrmann/Richard Attwood Porsche 917K 342
2 Gérard Larrousse/Willi Kauhsen Porsche 917LH 337
3 Rudi Lins/Helmut Marko Porsche 908/2LH 334
4 Sam Posey/Ronnie Bucknum Ferrari 512S 312
5 Hughes de Fierlandt/Alistair Walker Ferrari 512S 304
6 Guy Chasseuil/Claude Ballot-Lena Porsche 914/6 284
Winner's average speed: 119.258 mph. Pole position: Vic Elford (Porsche 917LH), 3m19.8. Fastest lap: Elford, 3m21.0

1971
12-13 June. 396 laps of a 8.369-mile circuit = 3314.124 miles
1 Helmut Marko/Gijs van Lennep Porsche 917K 396
2 Herbert Müller/Richard Attwood Porsche 917K 394
3 Sam Posey/Tony Adamowicz Ferrari 512M 365
4 Chris Craft/David Weir Ferrari 512M 354
5 Bob Grossman/Luigi Chinetti Jr Ferrari 365 GTB4 313
6 Raymond Touroul/"André Anselme" Porsche 911S 305
Note: first rolling start. Winner's average speed: 138.089 mph. Pole position: Pedro Rodriguez (Porsche 917LH), 3m13.9. Fastest lap: Jackie Oliver (Porsche 917LH), 3m18.4

1972
10-11 June. 343 laps of a 8.476-mile circuit = 2907.268 miles
1 Henri Pescarolo/Graham Hill Matra-Simca MS670 343
2 François Cevert/Howden Ganley Matra-Simca MS670 333
3 Reinhold Jöst/Michel Weber/ Mario Casoni Porsche 908LH 324
4 Andrea de Adamich/Nino Vaccarella Alfa Romeo T33TT/3 306
5 Jean-Claude Andruet/Claude Ballot-Lena/François Migault Ferrari 365 GTB4 Daytona 305
6 Sam Posey/Tony Adamowicz Ferrari 365 GTB4 Daytona 303
Winner's average speed: 121.136 mph. Pole position: Cevert, 3m42.2. Fastest lap: Gijs van Lennep (Lola T280-Ford), 3m46.9

1973
9-10 June. 355 laps of a 8.476-mile circuit = 3008.980 miles
1 Henri Pescarolo/Gérard Larrousse Matra-Simca MS670B 355
2 Arturo Merzario/Carlos Pace Ferrari 312P 349
3 Jean-Pierre Jabouille/ Jean-Pierre Jaussaud Matra-Simca MS670B 331
4 Gijs van Lennep/Herbert Müller Porsche Carrera RSR 328
5 Juan Fernandez/Bernard Chenevière/Paco Torredemer Porsche 908/3 319
6 Vic Elford/Claude Ballot-Lena Ferrari 365 GTB4 Daytona 316
Winner's average speed: 125.374 mph. Pole position: Merzario, 3m37.5. Fastest lap: François Cevert (Matra-Simca MS670B), 3m39.6

1974
15-16 June. 337 laps of a 8.476-mile circuit = 2856.412 miles
1 Henri Pescarolo/Gérard Larrousse Matra-Simca MS670B 337
2 Gijs van Lennep/Herbert Müller Porsche Carrera RSR turbo 331
3 Jean-Pierre Jabouille/François Migault Matra-Simca MS670B 324

4 Mike Hailwood/Derek Bell Mirage GR7-Ford 317
5 Cyrille Grandet/Dominique Bardini Ferrari 365 GTB4 Daytona 313
6 David Heinz/Alain Cudini Ferrari 365 GTB4 Daytona 312
Winner's average speed: 119.017 mph. Pole position: Pescarolo, 3m35.8. Fastest lap: Jean-Pierre Jarier (Matra-Simca MS680), 3m42.7

1975
14-15 June. 336 laps of a 8.476-mile circuit = 2847.936 miles
1 Jacky Ickx/Derek Bell Mirage GR8-Ford 336
2 Guy Chasseuil/Jean-Louis Lafosse Ligier JS2-Ford 335
3 Vern Schuppan/Jean-Pierre Jaussaud Mirage GR8-Ford 330
4 Reinhold Jöst/Mario Casoni/ Jürgen Barth Porsche 908/3LH 325
5 John Fitzpatrick/Gijs van Lennep/ Manfred Schurti/Toine Hezemans Porsche Carrera RSR 315
6 Nick Faure/John Cooper/"Beurlys" Porsche Carrera RSR 311
Winner's average speed: 118.664 mph. Pole position: Ickx, 3m49.4. Fastest lap: Chris Craft (Lola T380-Ford), 3m53.8

1976
12-13 June. 349 laps of a 8.476-mile circuit = 2958.124 miles
1 Jacky Ickx/Gijs van Lennep Porsche 936 349
2 Jean-Louis Lafosse/François Migault Mirage GR8-Ford 338
3 Chris Craft/Alain de Cadenet Lola T380LM-Ford 337
4 Rolf Stommelen/Manfred Schurti Porsche 935 331
5 Derek Bell/Vern Schuppan Mirage GR8-Ford 326
6 Alain Cudini/Raymond Touroul/ René Boubet Porsche Carrera RSR 314
Winner's average speed: 123.255 mph. Pole position: Jean-Pierre Jabouille (Alpine A442-Renault), 3m33.1. Fastest lap: Jabouille, 3m43.0

1977
11-12 June. 342 laps of a 8.476-mile circuit = 2898.792 miles
1 Jacky Ickx/Jürgen Barth/ Hurley Haywood Porsche 936 342
2 Vern Schuppan/Jean-Pierre Jarier Mirage GR8-Renault 331
3 Claude Ballot-Lena/Peter Gregg Porsche 935 315
4 Jean Ragnotti/Jean Rondeau Inaltéra GTP-Ford 315
5 Alain de Cadenet/Chris Craft Lola T380LM-Ford 315
6 Michel Pignard/Alfred Dufrenne/ Jacques Henry Chevron B36-Chrysler 303
Winner's average speed: 120.783 mph. Pole position: Jean-Pierre Jabouille (Alpine A442-Renault). Fastest lap: Ickx, 3m36.5

1978
10 June. 369 laps of a 8.476-mile circuit = 3127.644 miles
1 Didier Pironi/Jean-Pierre Jaussaud Alpine A442B-Renault 369
2 Bob Wollek/Jürgen Barth/ Jacky Ickx Porsche 936 364
3 Hurley Haywood/Peter Gregg/ Reinhold Jöst Porsche 936 362
4 Guy Fréquelin/Jean Ragnotti/ José Dolhem/Jean-Pierre Jabouille Alpine A442B-Renault 358
5 Brian Redman/Dick Barbour/ John Paul Porsche 935 337
6 Jim Busby/Chris Cord/Fred Knoop Porsche 935 336
Winner's average speed: 130.319 mph. Pole position: Ickx, 3m27.6. Fastest lap: Jabouille, 3m34.2

1979
9-10 June. 306 laps of a 8.467-mile circuit = 2590.902 miles
1 Klaus Ludwig/Bill Whittington/ Don Whittington Porsche 935-K3 306
2 Rolf Stommelen/Dick Barbour/ Paul Newman Porsche 935 299
3 Laurent Ferrier/François Servanin/ François Trisconi Porsche 935 292
4 Angelo Pallavicini/ Herbert Müller/Marco Vanoli Porsche 934 291
5 Bernard Darniche/Jean Ragnotti Rondeau M379-Ford 287
6 Hervé Poulain/Marcel Mignot/ Manfred Winkelhock BMW M1 Coupé 284
Winner's average speed: 107.954 mph. Pole position: Bob Wollek (Porsche 936), 3m30.07. Fastest lap: Jacky Ickx (Porsche 936), 3m36.01

Le Mans 24 Hours

1980

14-15 June. 338 laps of a 8.467-mile circuit = 2861.846 miles

1	Jean-Pierre Jaussaud/Jean Rondeau	Rondeau M379B-Ford	338
2	Jacky Ickx/Reinhold Jöst	Porsche 936/80	336
3	Jean-Michel Martin/ Philippe Martin/Gordon Spice	Rondeau M379B-Ford	329
4	Guy Fréquelin/Roger Dorchy	WM P79/80-Peugeot	318
5	John Fitzpatrick/Brian Redman/ Dick Barbour	Porsche 935-K3	317
6	Jürgen Barth/Manfred Schurti/ Eberhard Braun	Porsche 924 Carrera	316

Winner's average speed: 119.244 mph. Pole position: Fitzpatrick, 3m40.2. Fastest lap: Ickx, 3m40.6

1981

13-14 June. 354 laps of a 8.467-mile circuit = 2997.318 miles

1	Jacky Ickx/Derek Bell	Porsche 936/81	354
2	Jacky Haran/Jean-Louis Schlesser/ Philippe Streiff	Rondeau M379C-Ford	340
3	Gordon Spice/François Migault	Rondeau M379C-Ford	335
4	John Cooper/Dudley Wood/ Claude Bourgoignie	Porsche 935-K3	330
5	Claude Ballot-Lena/ Jean-Claude Andruet/Hervé Regout	Ferrari 512BB	328
6	Anny-Charlotte Verney/ Ralph Kent-Cooke/Bob Garretson	Porsche 935-K3	327

Winner's average speed: 124.888 mph. Pole position: Ickx, 3m29.44. Fastest lap: Hurley Haywood (Porsche 936/81), 3m34.0

1982

19-20 June. 359 laps of a 8.467-mile circuit = 3039.653 miles

1	Jacky Ickx/Derek Bell	Porsche 956	359
2	Jochen Mass/Vern Schuppan	Porsche 956	356
3	Hurley Haywood/Al Holbert/ Jürgen Barth	Porsche 956	340
4	John Fitzpatrick/David Hobbs	Porsche 935-K4	329
5	Dany Snobeck/François Servanin/ René Metge	Porsche 935-K3	325
6	Pierre Dieudonné/Carson Baird/ Jean-Paul Libert	Ferrari 512BB	322

Winner's average speed: 126.652 mph. Pole position: Ickx, 3m28.40. Fastest lap: Jean Ragnotti (Rondeau M382C-Ford), 3m36.9

1983

18-19 June. 370 laps of a 8.467-mile circuit = 3132.790 miles

1	Vern Schuppan/Hurley Haywood/ Al Holbert	Porsche 956	370
2	Jacky Ickx/Derek Bell	Porsche 956	370
3	Mario Andretti/Michael Andretti/ Philippe Alliot	Porsche 956	364
4	Volkert Merl/Clemens Schickentanz/ Maurizio de Narvaez	Porsche 956	361
5	John Fitzpatrick/Guy Edwards/ Rupert Keegan	Porsche 956	358
6	Klaus Ludwig/Stefan Johansson/ Bob Wollek	Porsche 956	354

Winner's average speed: 130.533 mph. Pole position: Ickx, 3m16.36. Fastest lap: Ickx, 3m29.7

1984

16-17 June. 359 laps of a 8.467-mile circuit = 3039.653 miles

1	Klaus Ludwig/Henri Pescarolo	Porsche 956	359
2	Jean Rondeau/John Paul Jr/ Preston Henn	Porsche 956	357
3	David Hobbs/Philippe Streiff/ Sarel van der Merwe	Porsche 956	350
4	Walter Brun/Bob Akin/ Leopold von Bayern	Porsche 956	339
5	Volkert Merl/Dieter Schornstein/ "John Winter"	Porsche 956	339
6	Vern Schuppan/Alan Jones/ Jean-Pierre Jarier	Porsche 956	336

Winner's average speed: 126.652 mph. Pole position: Bob Wollek (Lancia LC2), 3m17.11. Fastest lap: Alessandro Nannini (Lancia LC2), 3m28.9

1985

15-16 June. 373 laps of a 8.467-mile circuit = 3158.191 miles

1	Klaus Ludwig/Paolo Barilla/ "John Winter"	Porsche 956	373
2	Jonathan Palmer/James Weaver/ Richard Lloyd	Porsche 956GTI	370
3	Derek Bell/Hans-Joachim Stuck/ Jacky Ickx	Porsche 962	366
4	David Hobbs/Jo Gartner/Guy Edwards	Porsche 956	365
5	Sarel van der Merwe/ George Fouché/Mario Hytten	Porsche 956	360
6	Bob Wollek/Alessandro Nannini/ Lucio Cesario	Lancia LC2	359

Winner's average speed: 131.591 mph. Fastest lap: Jochen Mass (Porsche 962), 3m25.1

1986

31 May-1 June. 367 laps of a 8.406-mile circuit = 3085.002 miles

1	Hans-Joachim Stuck/Derek Bell/ Al Holbert	Porsche 962	367
2	Oscar Larrauri/Joël Gouhier/ Jesus Pareja	Porsche 962	359
3	George Follmer/John Morton/ Kemper Miller	Porsche 956	354
4	Emilio de Villota/George Fouché/ Fermin Velez	Porsche 956	348
5	Jürgen Lässig/Fulvio Ballabio/ Dudley Wood	Porsche 956	344
6	Siegfried Brunn/Ernst Schuster/ Rudi Seher	Porsche 936CJ	343

Winner's average speed: 128.542 mph. Pole position: Jochen Mass (Porsche 962), 3m15.99. Fastest lap: Klaus Ludwig/Paolo Barilla/"John Winter" (Porsche 956), 3m23.3 (ACO did not publish who was driving when time was set)

1987

13-14 June. 354 laps of a 8.410-mile circuit = 2977.140 miles

1	Derek Bell/Hans-Joachim Stuck/ Al Holbert	Porsche 962	354
2	Jürgen Lässig/Pierre Yver/ Bernard de Dryver	Porsche 962	334
3	Pierre-Henri Raphanel/ Hervé Regout/Yves Courage	Cougar C20-Porsche	331
4	George Fouché/Franz Konrad/ Wayne Taylor	Porsche 962	326
5	Eddie Cheever/Raul Boesel/ Jan Lammers	Jaguar XJR-8LM	324
6	Gordon Spice/Fermin Velez/ Philippe de Henning	Spice SE87C-Cosworth	320

Winner's average speed: 124.048 mph. Pole position: Bob Wollek (Porsche 962), 3m21.09. Fastest lap: Johnny Dumfries (Sauber C9-Mercedes-Benz), 3m25.04

1988

11-12 June. 394 laps of a 8.410-mile circuit = 3313.540 miles

1	Johnny Dumfries/Andy Wallace/ Jan Lammers	Jaguar XJR-9LM	394
2	Hans-Joachim Stuck/ Klaus Ludwig/Derek Bell	Porsche 962	394
3	Stanley Dickens/Frank Jelinski/ "John Winter"	Porsche 962	385
4	Derek Daly/Larry Perkins/ Kevin Cogan	Jaguar XJR-9LM	383
5	David Hobbs/Didier Theys/ Franz Konrad	Porsche 962	380
6	Mario Andretti/Michael Andretti/ John Andretti	Porsche 962	375

Winner's average speed: 137.732 mph. Pole position: Stuck, 3m15.64. Fastest lap: Stuck, 3m22.50

1989

10-11 June. 389 laps of a 8.410-mile circuit = 3271.490 miles

1	Jochen Mass/Manuel Reuter/ Stanley Dickens	Sauber C9/88- Mercedes-Benz	389
2	Mauro Baldi/Kenneth Acheson/ Gianfranco Brancatelli	Sauber C9/88- Mercedes-Benz	384
3	Bob Wollek/Hans-Joachim Stuck	Porsche 962	382

4 Jan Lammers/Patrick Tambay/
  Andrew Gilbert-Scott   Jaguar XJR-9LM   380
5 Jean-Louis Schlesser/   Sauber C9/88-
  Jean-Pierre Jabouille/Alain Cudini Mercedes-Benz   378
6 Henri Pescarolo/Jean-Louis Ricci/
  Claude Ballot-Lena   Porsche 962   371

Winner's average speed: 136.312 mph. Pole position: Schlesser, 3m15.04. Fastest lap: Alain Ferté (Jaguar XJR-9LM), 3m21.27

1990

16-17 June. 359 laps of a 8.450-mile circuit = 3033.550 miles

1 Martin Brundle/John Nielsen/ Price Cobb	Jaguar XJR-12	359
2 Jan Lammers/Andy Wallace/ Franz Konrad	Jaguar XJR-12	355
3 Tiff Needell/David Sears/ Anthony Reid	Porsche 962	352
4 Frank Jelinski/Derek Bell/ Hans-Joachim Stuck	Porsche 962	350
5 Masahiro Hasemi/Kazuyoshi Hoshino/ Toshio Suzuki	Nissan R89C	348
6 Geoff Lees/Hitoshi Ogawa/ Masanori Sekiya	Toyota 90CV	347

Winner's average speed: 126.398 mph. Pole position: Mark Blundell (Nissan R90CK), 3m27.02. Fastest lap: Bob Earl (Nissan R90CK), 3m40.03

1991

22-23 June. 362 laps of a 8.451-mile circuit = 3059.262 miles

1 Volker Weidler/Johnny Herbert/ Bertrand Gachot	Mazda 787B	362
2 Raul Boesel/Michel Ferté/Davy Jones	Jaguar XJR-12	360
3 Teo Fabi/Bob Wollek/ Kenneth Acheson	Jaguar XJR-12	358
4 Derek Warwick/John Nielsen/ Andy Wallace	Jaguar XJR-12	356
5 Karl Wendlinger/Michael Schumacher/Fritz Kreutzpointner	Mercedes-Benz C11	355
6 David Kennedy/Stefan Johansson/ Maurizio Sandro Sala	Mazda 787B	355

Winner's average speed: 127.593 mph. Pole position: Jean-Louis Schlesser, 3m31.250 (Mercedes-Benz C11). Fastest lap: Schumacher, 3m35.564

1992

20-21 June. 352 laps of a 8.451-mile circuit = 2974.752 miles

1 Derek Warwick/Yannick Dalmas/ Mark Blundell	Peugeot 905B	352

2 Masanori Sekiya/Pierre-Henri Raphanel/Kenneth Acheson	Toyota TS010	346
3 Mauro Baldi/Philippe Alliot/ Jean-Pierre Jabouille	Peugeot 905B	345
4 Johnny Herbert/Volker Weidler/Bertrand Gachot/Maurizio Sandro Sala	Mazda MXR01	336
5 George Fouché/Steven Andskär/ Stefan Johansson	Toyota 92CV	336
6 Bob Wollek/Henri Pescarolo/ Jean-Louis Ricci	Cougar C28S-Porsche	335

Winner's average speed: 123.869 mph. Pole position: Alliot, 3m21.209. Fastest lap: Jan Lammers (Toyota TS010), 3m32.295

1993

19-20 June. 375 laps of a 8.451-mile circuit = 3169.125 miles

1 Eric Hélary/Christophe Bouchut/ Geoff Brabham	Peugeot 905B	375
2 Thierry Boutsen/ Yannick Dalmas/Teo Fabi	Peugeot 905B	374
3 Philippe Alliot/Mauro Baldi/ Jean-Pierre Jabouille	Peugeot 905B	367
4 Eddie Irvine/Toshio Suzuki/ Masanori Sekiya	Toyota TS010	364
5 Roland Ratzenberger/ Mauro Martini/Naoki Nagasaka	Toyota 92CV	363
6 George Fouché/Eje Elgh/ Steven Andskär	Toyota 92CV	358

Winner's average speed: 132.580 mph. Pole position: Alliot, 3m24.94. Fastest lap: Irvine, 3m30.48

1994

18-19 June. 344 laps of a 8.451-mile circuit = 2907.144 miles

1 Yannick Dalmas/Hurley Haywood/ Mauro Baldi	Dauer 962LM-Porsche	344
2 Eddie Irvine/Mauro Martini/ Jeff Krosnoff	Toyota 94CV	343
3 Hans-Joachim Stuck/Danny Sullivan/ Thierry Boutsen	Dauer 962LM-Porsche	343
4 Steven Andskär/George Fouché/ Bob Wollek	Toyota 94CV	328
5 Steve Millen/Johnny O'Connell/ John Morton	Nissan 300ZX	317
6 Derek Bell/Robin Donovan/ Jürgen Lässig	Kremer K8-Porsche	316

Winner's average speed: 121.131 mph. Pole position: Alain Ferté (Cougar C32LM-Porsche), 3m51.05. Fastest lap: Boutsen, 3m52.54

RECORDS

DRIVERS' RECORDS

MOST WINS			
Jacky Ickx	6	Luigi Chinetti	3
Derek Bell	5	Hurley Haywood	3
Olivier Gendebien	4	Phil Hill	3
Henri Pescarolo	4	Al Holbert	3
Woolf Barnato	3	Klaus Ludwig	3

MANUFACTURERS' RECORDS

MOST WINS			
Porsche (including Dauer-Porsche)	13	Peugeot	2
Ferrari	9	Aston Martin	1
Jaguar	7	Chenard et Walcker	1
Alfa Romeo	4	Delahaye	1
Matra-Simca	3	Mazda	1
Bugatti	2	Mirage-Ford	1
La Lorraine	2	Lagonda	1
Mercedes-Benz (including Sauber-Mercedes-Benz)	2	Alpine-Renault	1
		Rondeau-Ford	1
		Lago-Talbot	1

OTHER RECORDS

Most starts:
  28, Henri Pescarolo

Most pole positions:
  Five, Jacky Ickx

Closest finish:
  120 metres, 1969, Jacky Ickx beat Hans Herrmann (excludes "staged" finishes)

Widest winning margin:
  217 miles in 1927

Most starters:
  60, 1950 and 1951

Fewest starters:
  17, 1930

Most finishers:
  30, 1923 (out of 33 starters) and 1951

Fewest finishers:
  Six, 1931

Furthest distance covered by winning car:
  3314 miles, 1971

Shortest distance covered by winning car:
  1287 miles, 1924

100% record:
  Woolf Barnato raced at Le Mans on three occasions, winning each time

Silk Cut Jaguar won the first of their three Teams Championships in 1987

Since 1953 World Championship Sports Car racing has had a chequered history of success and failure, boom and decline.

During the 1950s the championship attracted competition from Ferrari, Jaguar, Aston Martin, Mercedes-Benz, Cunningham, Lancia, Alfa Romeo and Maserati but by 1961 serious challenge to Ferrari (which had been champion for all but two seasons to date) had dwindled and the FIA cancelled the series.

However, as the governing body turned their attention to Grand Touring cars, the organizers of the Sebring 12 hours, Targa Florio, Nürburgring 1000 kms and Le Mans 24 hours joined forces to promote the Speed World Challenge for Sports Cars and Prototypes. It proved a success and was adopted by the FIA in 1963 and developed into a full World Championship for Makes.

Ferrari continued to dominate until Ford developed its spectacular GT40 into a race-winning force in 1965. World Championship victories for Ford followed in 1966 and under new regulations in 1968.

Porsche, destined to become the most successful Sports Car manufacturer, introduced the 917 in 1969 and withstood a renewed challenge from Ferrari to win three successive championships from 1969-71, prompting another new formula for 1972. This change brought Ferrari back to the fore but ultimately it withdrew from Sports Car racing at the end of 1973 to concentrate on Formula One.

Matra, Alfa Romeo and Renault all made brief and successful forays into Sports Car racing during the 1970s but Porsche continued to be the mainstay of the category. In 1976 and 1977 separate championships were organized for Group 5 and Group 6 cars but Sports Car racing had entered a period of decline.

A Drivers' Championship was introduced in 1981 and new Group C rules were adopted a year later, prompting new optimism and interest. Although Porsche continued to rewrite their unrivalled record with the 956 and 962 Group C cars, it faced strong challenges in the late 1980s, first from Jaguar and then from Mercedes-Benz.

To reflect the number of privateers running Porsches, a Teams' Championship replaced the manufacturers' title in 1985. After Brun Motorsport won the 1986 series for Porsche, it was dominated by TWR Jaguar and Sauber-Mercedes.

However, the introduction of new 3.5-litre engines during a transitional period from 1989-91 alienated the privateer teams which had formed the backbone of the Group C years and the Championship was abandoned after a final, under-supported year in 1992.

RULES

WORLD SPORTS CAR CHAMPIONSHIP (1953–61)

1953–55 Prototypes, Racing Sports Cars and Production Cars. No engine limit. Minimum homologation for Production Cars of 100

1956–57 Prototypes only. 2500 cc maximum engine capacity

1958–61 Prototypes only. 3000 cc maximum engine capacity

SPEED WORLD CHALLENGE (1962–63)

1962 Prototypes and Grand Touring Cars. 4000 cc maximum engine capacity for prototypes

1963 GT Prototypes and Grand Touring Cars. No engine limit

INTERNATIONAL CHAMPIONSHIP FOR MAKES (1964–71)

1964–65 Prototypes and Grand Touring Cars. No engine limit

1966–67 Group 6 (Sports-Prototypes), Group 5 (Special Touring Cars) and Group 4 (Sports Cars). Minimum homologation for Group 4 of 50. No engine limit. Two divisions: above 2000 cc and up to 2000 cc

1968–69 Groups 6 (Sports-Prototypes), 4 (Sports Cars) and 3 (Special GT). Stockblock engines only in Group 4. 3000 cc maximum engine capacity for Group 6, 5000 cc for Group 4, no engine limit for Group 3

1970–71 Groups 6 (Sports-Prototypes), 5 (Sports Cars) and 4 (Special GT). Minimum homologation for Group 5 of 25. 3000 cc maximum engine capacity for Group 6, 5000 cc for Group 5, no engine limit for Group 4

WORLD CHAMPIONSHIP FOR MAKES (1972–81)

1972–75 Groups 5 (Sports Cars) and 4 (Special GT). 3000 cc maximum engine capacity for Group 5, no engine limit for Group 4

1976–77 Group 5 (Special Production Cars) in three divisions: up to 6000 cc, 3000 cc and 2000 cc

1978–80 Group 5 (Special Production Cars) in two divisions: over and up to 2000 cc

1981 Group 5 (Special Production Cars) in three divisions: over and up to 2000 cc, and IMSA GTX

WORLD SPORTS CAR CHAMPIONSHIP (1976–77)

1976–77 Groups 6 (Sports-Prototypes) and 5 (Sports Cars). 5000 cc maximum engine capacity for stockblocks, 3000 cc for normally aspirated racing engines or 2140 cc for turbocharged racing engines in Group 6, 3000 cc for Group 5

Sports Car World Championship

WORLD ENDURANCE CHAMPIONSHIP (1982–85)

1982–84   Group C (Sports-Prototypes). No engine limit. Maximum fuel consumption of 60 litres per 100 kms

1985   Group C (Sports-Prototypes). No engine limit. Maximum fuel consumption of 51 litres per 100 kms

WORLD SPORTS-PROTOTYPE CHAMPIONSHIP (1986–90)

1986–88   1985 rules: Group C (Sports-Prototypes). No engine limit. Maximum fuel consumption of 51 litres per 100 kms

1989–90   Categories 1 (3.5-litre Sports-Prototypes) and 2 (old Group C). Category 1: 3500 cc maximum engine capacity. Normally aspirated engines. Maximum 12 cylinders. No fuel restriction

WORLD SPORTS CAR CHAMPIONSHIP (1991–92)

1991–92   Categories 1 (3.5-litre Sports-Prototypes) and 2 (old Group C). Category 1: 3500 cc maximum engine capacity. Normally aspirated engines. Maximum 12 cylinders. No fuel restriction

POINTS

WORLD SPORTS CAR CHAMPIONSHIP (1953–61)

1953–57   8–6–4–3–2–1 points awarded to the top six finishers. Best result per marque at each race counted

1958   8–6–4–3–2–1 points awarded to the top six finishers except Tourist Trophy where 4–3–2–1 points awarded to top four finishers as race was only four hours long. Best result per marque at each race counted

1959–60   8–6–4–3–2–1 points awarded to the top six finishers. Best result per marque at each race counted

1961   8–6–4–3–2–1 points awarded to the top six finishers except at races of under 1000 kms or six hours where half points were awarded. Best result per marque at each race counted

SPEED WORLD CHALLENGE (1962–63)

1962–63   10–9–8–6–5–4–3–2 points awarded to the top eight finishers plus one point to all other finishers. Best result per marque at each race counted. Marque had to compete in every round to qualify for points

INTERNATIONAL CHAMPIONSHIP FOR MAKES (1964–71)

1964–67   9–6–4–3–2–1 points awarded to the top six finishers. Best result per marque at each race counted

1968   8–6–4–3–2–1 points awarded to the top six finishers except at Zeltweg where half points were awarded. Best result per marque at each race counted

1969–71   8–6–4–3–2–1 points awarded to the top six finishers. Best result per marque at each race counted

WORLD CHAMPIONSHIP FOR MAKES (1972–81)

1972–80   20–15–12–10–8–6–4–3–2–1 points awarded to the top ten finishers. Best result per marque at each race counted

1981   Manufacturers' title: 20–15–12–10–8–6–4–3–2–1 points awarded to the top ten finishers in both over 2000 cc and under 2000 cc classes. Best result per marque at each race in each class counted.

Drivers' title: 20–19–18–17–16–15–14–13–12–11–10–9–8–6–4–3–2–1 points awarded to the top twenty finishers plus bonus points awarded as follows:

no bonus point to category 1 (Group 6 over 2000 cc)

1 bonus point to category 2 (Group 5 over 2000 cc, IMSA GTP over 2000 cc, Group C over 2000 cc, IMSA GTX over 2000 cc, IMSA AAGT)

2 bonus points to category 3 (Group 6 under 2000 cc, Group 5 under 2000 cc, Group 4 over 2000 cc, IMSA GTO, IMSA GTX under 2000 cc)

3 bonus points to category 4 (IMSA GTP under 2000 cc, Group 2 over 2000 cc, IMSA GTU, Group C under 2000 cc)

4 bonus points to category 5 (Group 4 under 2000 cc, Group 1 over 2000 cc)

5 bonus points to category 6 (Group 2 under 2000 cc, Group 1 under 2000 cc, IMSA RS)

WORLD ENDURANCE CHAMPIONSHIP (1982–85)

1982–85   20–15–12–10–8–6–4–3–2–1 points awarded to the top ten finishers. Best result per marque at each race counted. Bonus points awarded in drivers' championship as follows:

no bonus to category 1 (Group C, Group 6 over 2000 cc, Group 5 over 2000 cc, IMSA GTX over 2000 cc)

1 bonus point to category 2 (Group B over 2000 cc, Group 6 under 2000 cc, Group 5 under 2000 cc, Group 4 over 2000 cc, IMSA GTO)

2 bonus points to category 3 (IMSA GTU, Group 2 over 2000 cc, Group 3 over 2000 cc)

3 bonus points to category 4 (Group B under 2000 cc, Group 4 under 2000 cc, Group 2 under 2000 cc, Group 3 under 2000 cc)

1983–84   Both manufacturers' and drivers' titles: 20–15–12–10–8–6–4–3–2–1 points awarded to the top ten finishers. Best result per marque at each race counted

1985   Both teams' and drivers' titles: 20–15–12–10–8–6–4–3–2–1 points awarded to the top ten finishers. Best result per team at each race counted

WORLD SPORTS PROTOTYPE CHAMPIONSHIP (1986–90)

1986   20–15–12–10–8–6–4–3–2–1 points awarded to the top ten finishers. Best result per marque at each race counted

1987   20–15–12–10–8–6–4–3–2–1 points awarded to the top ten finishers. Group C2 drivers scored 2 bonus points for finishing in the top ten. Best result per marque at each race counted

1988   60–45–36–30–24–18–12–9–6–3 points awarded to the top ten finishers at 24-hour races (Le Mans); 40–30–24–20–16–12–8–6–4–2 points awarded to the top ten finishers at 800–1000 kms races (Jerez, Monza, Silverstone, Brands Hatch, Nürburgring, Spa and Fuji); 20–15–12–10–8–6–4–3–2–1 points awarded to the top ten finishers at sprint races (Jarama, Brno and Sandown Park). Drivers had to complete at least 30% of their car's total race distance to qualify for points and could only drive in one car. C2 drivers awarded bonus points for finishing in the top ten overall as follows: 6 points at 24-hour races; 4 at 800–1000 kms races; and 2 at sprint races

1989   20–15–12–10–8–6–4–3–2–1 points awarded to the top ten finishers. Drivers had to complete at least 30% of their car's total race distance to qualify for points and could only drive in one car

1990   9–6–4–3–2–1 points awarded to the top six finishers. Drivers had to complete at least 30% of their car's total race distance to qualify for points and could only drive in one car.

WORLD SPORTS CAR CHAMPIONSHIP (1991–92)

1991–92   20–15–12–10–8–6–4–3–2–1 points awarded to the top ten finishers. Drivers had to complete at least 30% of their car's total race distance to qualify for points and could only drive in one car. Car had to be entered in championship to qualify for points

WORLD CHAMPIONS

Drivers

year	champion	nat	team	car
1981	Bob Garretson	USA	Cooke-Woods Racing/ Garretson Racing/Varde Racing	Porsche 935/Porsche 935-K3/Mazda RX-3
1982	Jacky Ickx	B	Rothmans Porsche	Porsche 956
1983	Jacky Ickx	B	Rothmans Porsche	Porsche 956
1984	Stefan Bellof	D	Rothmans Porsche	Porsche 956
1985	Derek Bell/Hans-Joachim Stuck	GB/D	Rothmans Porsche	Porsche 962
1986	Derek Bell	GB	Rothmans Porsche	Porsche 962
1987	Raul Boesel	BR	Silk Cut Jaguar (TWR)	Jaguar XJR-8
1988	Martin Brundle	GB	Silk Cut Jaguar (TWR)	Jaguar XJR-9
1989	Jean-Louis Schlesser	F	Team Sauber Mercedes	Sauber C9/88-Mercedes-Benz
1990	Mauro Baldi/Jean-Louis Schlesser	I/F	Team Sauber Mercedes	Sauber C9/88-Mercedes-Benz/Mercedes-Benz C11
1991	Teo Fabi	I	Silk Cut Jaguar (TWR)	Jaguar XJR-14/Jaguar XJR-12
1992	Yannick Dalmas/Derek Warwick	F/GB	Peugeot Talbot Sport	Peugeot 905B

Manufacturers/Teams

year	championship	manufacturer/ team		year	championship	manufacturer/ team
1953	World Sports Car Championship	Ferrari		1977	World Championship for Makes	Porsche
1954	World Sports Car Championship	Ferrari			World Championship for Sports Cars	Alfa Romeo
1955	World Sports Car Championship	Mercedes-Benz		1978	World Championship for Makes	Porsche
1956	World Sports Car Championship	Ferrari		1979	World Championship for Makes	Porsche
1957	World Sports Car Championship	Ferrari		1980	World Championship for Makes	Porsche
1958	World Sports Car Championship	Ferrari		1981	World Championship for Makes	Lancia
1959	World Sports Car Championship	Aston Martin		1982	World Endurance Championship	Porsche
1960	World Sports Car Championship	Ferrari		1983	World Endurance Championship	Porsche
1961	World Sports Car Championship	Ferrari		1984	World Endurance Championship	Porsche
1962	Speed World Challenge	Ferrari		1985	World Endurance Championship for Teams	Rothmans Porsche
1963	Speed and Endurance World Challenge	Ferrari				
1964	International Championship for Makes	Ferrari		1986	World Sports-Prototype Championship for Teams	Brun Motorsport
1965	International Championship for Makes	Ferrari				
1966	International Championship for Makes	Ford		1987	World Sports-Prototype Championship for Teams	Silk Cut Jaguar (TWR)
1967	International Championship for Makes	Ferrari				
1968	International Championship for Makes	Ford		1988	World Sports-Prototype Championship for Teams	Silk Cut Jaguar (TWR)
1969	International Championship for Makes	Porsche				
1970	International Championship for Makes	Porsche		1989	World Sports-Prototype Championship for Teams	Team Sauber Mercedes
1971	International Championship for Makes	Porsche				
1972	World Championship for Makes	Ferrari		1990	World Sports-Prototype Championship for Teams	Team Sauber Mercedes
1973	World Championship for Makes	Matra-Simca				
1974	World Championship for Makes	Matra-Simca		1991	World Sports Car Championship for Teams	Silk Cut Jaguar (TWR)
1975	World Championship for Makes	Alfa Romeo				
1976	World Championship for Makes	Porsche		1992	World Sports Car Championship for Teams	Peugeot Talbot Sport
	World Championship for Sports Cars	Porsche				

1953

WORLD SPORTS CAR CHAMPIONSHIP

12 hours of Sebring

8 March 1953. Sebring. 173 laps of a 5.200-mile circuit = 899.600 miles

1 John Fitch/Phil Walters	Cunningham C4R-Chrysler	173	12h00m03
2 Reg Parnell/ George Abecassis	Aston Martin DB3	172	
3 Sherwood Johnston/ Bob Wilder	Jaguar C-type	162	
4 Bob Gegan/Harry Gray	Jaguar C-type	155	
5 Briggs Cunningham/ Bill Lloyd	OSCA	153	
6 Ed Lunken/Charles Hassan	Ferrari 166MM	153	

Winner's average speed: 74.961 mph

Mille Miglia

26 April 1953. Brescia-Rome-Brescia. 945.000 miles

1 Giannino Marzotto/ Marco Crosara	Ferrari 340MM	10h37m19
2 Juan Manuel Fangio/ Giancarlo Sala	Alfa Romeo 6C-3000 CM	10h49m03
3 Felice Bonetto/U Peruzzi	Lancia D20	11h07m40
4 Tom Cole/Mario Vandelli	Ferrari 340MM	11h20m39
5 Reg Parnell/ Louis Klementasky	Aston Martin DB3	11h32m43
6 Emilio Giletti/ Guido Bertocchi	Maserati A6GCS	11h38m42

Winner's average speed: 88.967 mph

24 heures du Mans

13-14 June 1953. Le Mans. 302 laps of a 8.378-mile circuit = 2530.156 miles

1 Tony Rolt/Duncan Hamilton	Jaguar C-type	302	24 hours
2 Peter Walker/Stirling Moss	Jaguar C-type	299	
3 Phil Walter/John Fitch	Cunningham C5R-Chrysler	297	
4 Peter Whitehead/ Ian Stewart	Jaguar C-type	296	
5 Paolo Marzotto/ Giannino Marzotto	Ferrari 340MM	293	
6 Maurice Trintignant/ Harry Schell	Gordini T24S	292	

Winner's average speed: 105.423 mph. Fastest lap: Alberto Ascari (Ferrari 375MM), 4m27.4

24 heures de Spa-Francorchamps

25-26 July 1953. Spa-Francorchamps. 260 laps of a 8.774-mile circuit = 2281.240 miles

1 Giuseppe Farina/ Mike Hawthorn	Ferrari 340MM	260	24 hours
2 Sir James Scott-Douglas/ Guy Gale	Jaguar C-type	242	
3 Hermann Roosdorp/ Toni Ulmen	Jaguar C-type	231	
4 Marc Gignoux/Claude Storez	Panhard-DB	211	
5 René Faure/Quetelart	Panhard-DB	186	
6 Bovens/Giraud	Panhard-DB	184	

Winner's average speed: 95.052 mph. Pole position: Hawthorn, 4m39. Fastest lap: Farina, time n/a

ADAC 1000 km-Rennen

30 August 1953. Nürburgring. 44 laps of a 14.167-mile circuit = 623.348 miles

1 Alberto Ascari/ Giuseppe Farina	Ferrari 340MM	44	8h20m44
2 Ian Stewart/Roy Salvadori	Jaguar C-type	44	8h35m49
3 Günther Bechem/ Theo Helfrich	Borgward H1500S44	44	8h40m03
4 Trenkel/Schlutter	Porsche 550	44	8h56m52
5 Wolfgang Seidel/ Josef Peters	Veritas Meteor	44	9h25m17
6 John Lawrence/ Jimmy Stewart	Jaguar C-type	44	9h50m58

Winner's average speed: 74.692 mph. Fastest lap: Robert Manzon (Lancia D23), time n/a

Tourist Trophy

5 September 1953. Dundrod. Overall result counted towards the World Championship. 106 laps of a 7.416-mile circuit = 786.096 miles

1 Peter Collins/ Pat Griffith	Aston Martin DB3S	106	9h37m12
2 Reg Parnell/ Eric Thompson	Aston Martin DB3S	106	9h40m35
3 Stirling Moss/Peter Walker	Jaguar C-type	103	
4 Graham Whitehead/ Tony Gaze	Aston Martin DB3	102	
5 Tom Dickson/ Desmond Titterington	Aston Martin DB3	101	
6 Ken Wharton/Ernie Robb	Frazer-Nash MkII	101	

Handicap result (which decided the Tourist Trophy): 1 Collins/ Griffith; 2 Parnell/Thompson; 3 Wharton/Robb; 4 Moss/Walker; 5 Whitehead/Gaze; 6 Dickson/Titterington. Overall winner's average speed: 81.715 mph. Fastest lap: Walker, time n/a

Carrera Panamericana

19-23 November 1953. Tuxla Gutierrez-Ciudad Juarez, Mexico. 1954.000 miles

1 Juan Manuel Fangio/ Bronzoni	Lancia D24	18h11m00
2 Piero Taruffi/Maggio	Lancia D24	18h18m51
3 Eugenio Castellotti/Luoni	Lancia D23	18h24m52
4 Guido Mancini/Serena	Ferrari	19h40m29
5 Louis Rosier	Lago-Talbot T26GS	20h11m22
6 Umberto Maglioli/Ricci	Ferrari	20h16m28

Winner's average speed: 105.150 mph

FINAL CHAMPIONSHIP POSITIONS

Manufacturers

1	Ferrari	27 (30)*	9	Porsche		3
2	Jaguar	24 (28)*	10=	Lago-Talbot		2
3	Aston Martin	16		OSCA		2
4=	Cunningham-Chrysler	12		Veritas		2
	Lancia	12	13=	Frazer Nash		1
6	Alfa Romeo	6		Gordini		1
7=	Borgward	4		Maserati		1
	Panhard-DB	4		*Best four results count		

1954

WORLD SPORTS CAR CHAMPIONSHIP

1000 km de la Ciudad de Buenos Aires

24 January 1954. Buenos Aires. 106 laps of a 5.890-mile circuit = 624.340 miles

1 Giuseppe Farina/ Umberto Maglioli	Ferrari 375MM	106	6h41m50.8
2 Harry Schell/ Alfonso de Portago	Ferrari	103	
3 Peter Collins/Pat Griffith	Aston Martin DB3S	101	
4 Sir James Scott-Douglas/ Ninian Sanderson	Jaguar C-type	101	
5 Luis Milan/Elpidio Tortone	Ferrari	99	
6 Emilio Giletti/Luigi Musso	Maserati A6GCS	97	

Winner's average speed: 93.221 mph. Fastest lap: Farina, 3m34.6

12 hours of Sebring

8 March 1954. Sebring. 168 laps of a 5.200-mile circuit = 873.600 miles

1 Stirling Moss/Bill Lloyd	OSCA MT4	167	12h04m16.7
2 Porfirio Rubirosa/			
Luigi Valenzano	Lancia D24	163	
3 Lance Macklin/	Austin Healey		
George Huntoon	100S	163	
4 James Simpson/			
George Colby	OSCA MT4	163	
5 Otto Linton/Harry Beck	OSCA	161	
6 WK Carpenter/			
John van Driel	Kieft-Bristol	158	

Winner's average speed: 72.370 mph. Fastest lap: Alberto Ascari (Lancia D24) - unofficial

Mille Miglia

1-2 May 1954. Brescia-Rome-Brescia. 998.000 miles

1 Alberto Ascari	Lancia D24	11h26m10
2 Vittorio Marzotto	Ferrari 375 Plus	12h00m01
3 Luigi Musso/A Zocco	Maserati A6GCS	12h00m10
4 Clemente Biondetti	Ferrari	12h15m36
5 Bruno Venezian/M Orlandi	Maserati A6GCS	12h27m43
6 Hans Herrmann/		
Herbert Linge	Porsche 356	12h35m44

Winner's average speed: 87.267 mph

24 heures du Mans

12-13 June 1954. Le Mans. 300 laps of a 8.378-mile circuit = 2513.400 miles

1 Maurice Trintignant/	Ferrari		
José Froilan Gonzalez	375 Plus	300	24 hours
2 Tony Rolt/Duncan Hamilton	Jaguar D-type	300	
3 Bill Spear/	Cunningham		
Sherwood Johnston	C4R-Chrysler	282	
4 Roger Laurent/			
Jacques Swaters	Jaguar C-type	276	
5 Briggs Cunningham/	Cunningham		
John Benett	C4R-Chrysler	272	
6 André Guelfi/Jacques Pollet	Gordini T30S	262	

Winner's average speed: 104.725 mph. Fastest lap: Gonzalez, 4m16.8

Tourist Trophy

11 September 1954. Dundrod. Overall result counted towards the World Championship. 94 laps of a 7.416-mile circuit = 697.104 miles

1 Mike Hawthorn/	Ferrari		
Maurice Trintignant	750 Monza	94	7h14m13
2 Juan Manuel Fangio/			
Piero Taruffi	Lancia D25	84	
3 Robert Manzon/			
Luigi Valenzano	Lancia D24	82	
4 Luigi Musso/Sergio			
Mantovani	Maserati A6GCS	79	
5 Peter Whitehead/			
Ken Wharton	Jaguar D-type	79	
6 Bob Said/Masten Gregory	Ferrari	75	

Handicap result (which decided the Tourist Trophy): 1 Laureau/ Armagnac; 2 Hawthorn/Trintignant; 3 Musso/Mantovani; 4 Taruffi/ Fangio; 5 Whitehead/Wharton; 6 Manzon/Valenzano. Overall winner's average speed: 96.326 mph. Pole position: Alberto Ascari (Lancia D25), 4m54.0. Fastest lap: Hawthorn, 4m49.0

Carrera Panamericana

19-23 November 1954. Tuxla Gutierrez-Ciudad Juarez, Mexico. 1908.000 miles

1 Umberto Maglioli	Ferrari 375 Plus	17h40m26
2 Phil Hill/Richie Ginther	Ferrari 365MM	18h04m54
3 Hans Herrmann	Porsche 550	19h32m33

4 Jaroslav Juhan	Porsche 550	19h33m09
5 Franco Cornacchia	Ferrari	19h52m06
6 Luigi Chinetti	Ferrari	20h15m18

Winner's average speed: 107.930 mph

FINAL CHAMPIONSHIP POSITIONS

Manufacturers

1	Ferrari	32 (38)*	8= Aston Martin	4
2	Lancia	20	Austin Healey	4
3	Jaguar	11	Cunningham-	
4=	Maserati	8	Chrysler	4
	OSCA	8	11 Kieft-Bristol	1
6	Gordini	6	*Best four results count	
7	Porsche	5		

1955

WORLD SPORTS CAR CHAMPIONSHIP

1000 km de la Ciudad de Buenos Aires

23 January 1955. Buenos Aires. 58 laps of a 10.560-mile circuit = 612.480 miles

1 Enrique Saenz Valiente/			
José Maria Ibanez	Ferrari 375 Plus	58	6h35m15.4
2 Najurieta/Rivero	Ferrari	58	6h40m12.1
3 Grandio/Faraoni	Maserati 300S	56	
4 Jaroslav Juhan/Chavez	Porsche 550	56	
5 Elie Bayol/Harry Schell	Gordini	54	
6 J Camano/O Camano	Ferrari	53	

Winner's average speed: 92.975 mph. Pole position: Maurice Trintignant (Ferrari). Fastest lap: José Froilan Gonzalez (Ferrari), 6m06.1

12 hours of Sebring

13 March 1955. Sebring. 182 laps of a 5.200-mile circuit = 946.400 miles

1 Mike Hawthorn/			
Phil Walters	Jaguar D-type	182	12h00m03.7
2 Phil Hill/Carroll Shelby	Ferrari		
	750S Monza	182	12h00m29.1
3 Bill Spear/			
Sherwood Johnston	Maserati 300S	180	
4 Luigi Valenzano/			
Cesare Perdisa	Maserati 300S	178	
5 Piero Taruffi/Harry Schell	Ferrari		
	750S Monza	177	
6 Stirling Moss/Lance Macklin	Austin		
	Healey 100S	176	

Winner's average speed: 78.860 mph. Fastest lap: Walters, 3m34.0

Mille Miglia

28 April-1 May 1955. Brescia-Rome-Brescia. 998.000 miles

1 Stirling Moss/	Mercedes-Benz	
Denis Jenkinson	300SLR	10h07m48
2 Juan Manuel Fangio	Mercedes-Benz	
	300SLR	10h39m33
3 Umberto Maglioli/		
G Monteferrario	Ferrari 118LM	10h52m47
4 Francesco Giardini	Maserati A6GCS	11h15m32
5 John Fitch	Mercedes-Benz	
	300SLR	11h29m31
6 Sergio Sighinolfi/G Bellei	Ferrari	11h33m27

Winner's average speed: 98.519 mph

24 heures du Mans

11-12 June 1955. Le Mans. 306 laps of a 8.378-mile circuit = 2563.668 miles

1 Mike Hawthorn/Ivor Bueb	Jaguar D-type	306	24 hours
2 Peter Collins/Paul Frère	Aston Martin		
	DB3S	301	

3 Johnny Claes/		
Jacques Swaters	Jaguar D-type	295
4 Helmuth Polensky/		
Richard von Frankenberg	Porsche 550	283
5 Wolfgang Seidel/		
Olivier Gendebien	Porsche 550	275
6 Helmut Glöckler/		
Jaroslav Juhan	Porsche 550	272

Winner's average speed: 106.820 mph. Fastest lap: Hawthorn, 4m06.6

Tourist Trophy

17 September 1955. Dundrod. 84 laps of a
7.416-mile circuit = 622.944 miles

1 Stirling Moss/John Fitch	Mercedes-Benz		
	300SLR	84	7h03m11
2 Juan Manuel Fangio/	Mercedes-Benz		
Karl Kling	300SLR	83	
3 Wolfgang von Trips/	Mercedes-Benz		
André Simon/Karl Kling	300SLR	82	
4 Peter Walker/Dennis Poore	Aston Martin		
	DB3S	81	
5 Luigi Musso/Franco			
Bordoni/Jean Behra	Maserati 300S	79	
6 Eugenio Castellotti/			
Piero Taruffi	Ferrari	79	

Winner's average speed: 88.323 mph. Pole position: Moss,
4m48. Fastest lap: Mike Hawthorn (Jaguar D-type), 4m42

Targa Florio

16 October 1955. Madonie (Piccolo). 13 laps of a
44.739-mile circuit = 581.607 miles

1 Stirling Moss/Peter Collins	Mercedes-Benz		
	300SLR	13	9h43m14.0
2 Juan Manuel Fangio/	Mercedes-Benz		
Karl Kling	300SLR	13	9h47m55.4
3 Eugenio Castellotti/	Ferrari 860		
Robert Manzon	Monza	13	9h53m20.8
4 Desmond Titterington/	Mercedes-Benz		
John Fitch	300SLR	13	9h54m53.4
5 Azzuro Manzini/			
Francesco Giardini	Maserati 300S	13	10h41m15.0
6 Giuseppe Musso/			
Giuseppe Rossi	Maserati 300S	13	10h48m53.2

Winner's average speed: 59.833 mph. Fastest lap: Moss, 43m07

FINAL CHAMPIONSHIP POSITIONS

Manufacturers

1	Mercedes-Benz	24		5	Aston Martin	9
2	Ferrari	22 (23)*		6	Porsche	6
3	Jaguar	16		7	Gordini	2
4	Maserati	13 (15)*		8	Austin Healey	1
					*Best four results count	

1956

WORLD SPORTS CAR CHAMPIONSHIP

1000 km de la Ciudad de Buenos Aires

29 January 1956. Buenos Aires. 106 laps of a
5.890-mile circuit = 624.340 miles

1 Stirling Moss/			
Carlos Menditéguy	Maserati 300S	106	6h29m37.9
2 Olivier Gendebien/Phil Hill	Ferrari 860		
	Monza	104	
3 Jean Behra/			
José Froilan Gonzalez	Maserati 300S	101	
4 Alessandro de Tomaso/			
C de Tomaso	Maserati 150S	94	
5 E Muro/J Pola	Ferrari	93	
6 Kovacs/Jaja	Mercedes-Benz	90	

Winner's average speed: 96.143 mph. Pole position: Juan
Manuel Fangio (Ferrari 375 Plus). Fastest lap: Peter Collins
(Ferrari 375 Plus), 3m26.7

12 hours of Sebring

24 March 1956. Sebring. 194 laps of a 5.200-mile circuit
= 1008.800 miles

1 Juan Manuel Fangio/	Ferrari 860		
Eugenio Castellotti	Monza	194	12 hours
2 Luigi Musso/Harry Schell	Ferrari 860		
	Monza	192	
3 Bob Sweikert/Jack Ensley	Jaguar D-type	188	
4 Roy Salvadori/Carroll Shelby	Aston Martin		
	DB3S	186	
5 Jean Behra/Piero Taruffi	Maserati 300S	186	
6 Hans Herrmann/			
Wolfgang von Trips	Porsche	182	

Winner's average speed: 84.067 mph. Fastest lap: Behra, 3m29.8

Mille Miglia

28-29 April 1956. Brescia-Rome-Brescia. 998.000 miles

1 Eugenio Castellotti	Ferrari 290MM	11h37m10
2 Peter Collins/	Ferrari 860	
Louis Klementaski	Monza	11h48m28
3 Luigi Musso	Ferrari 860	
	Monza	12h11m49
4 Juan Maunel Fangio	Ferrari 290MM	12h26m50
5 Olivier Gendebien/		
Philip Washer	Ferrari 250GT	12h29m58
6 Paul Metternich/	Mercedes-Benz	
Wittigo Einseidel	300SL	12h36m38

Winner's average speed: 85.891 mph

ADAC 1000 km-Rennen

27 May 1956. Nürburgring. 44 laps of a 14.167-mile circuit
= 623.348 miles

1 Stirling Moss/Jean Behra/			
Harry Schell/Piero Taruffi	Maserati 300S	44	7h43m54.5
2 Juan Manuel Fangio/	Ferrari 860		
Eugenio Castellotti	Monza	44	7h44m20.7
3 Phil Hill/Olivier Gendebien/			
Alfonso de Portago/	Ferrari 860		
Ken Wharton	Monza	44	7h53m55.9
4 Wolfgang von Trips/	Porsche RS		
Umberto Maglioli	Spyder	44	8h01m45.9
5 Peter Collins/Tony Brooks	Aston Martin		
	DB3S	43	
6 Hans Herrmann/	Porsche RS		
Richard von Frankenberg	Spyder	44	8h06m10.2*

*Each class leader completed the full 44-lap distance. Winner's
average speed: 80.621 mph. Pole position: Fangio, 10m03.6.
Fastest lap: Fangio, 10m05.3

Sveriges Grand Prix

12 August 1956. Kristianstad. 153 laps of a
4.062-mile circuit = 621.486 miles

1 Maurice Trintignant/Phil Hill	Ferrari 290MM	153	6h33m47.7
2 Peter Collins/			
Wolfgang von Trips	Ferrari 290MM	153	6h34m27.6
3 Mike Hawthorn/			
Duncan Hamilton/			
Alfonso de Portago	Ferrari 290MM	152	
4 Kvarnstrom/Lundgren*	Ferrari 250GT	148	
5 Borgefors/CG Hammarlund*	Ferrari 250GT	147	
6 Peter Whitehead/			
Graham Whitehead	Jaguar D-type	145	

*GT cars ineligible for points, sixth-placed Jaguar awarded
points as if it had finished fourth. Winner's average speed:
94.692 mph. Pole position: Stirling Moss (Maserati 300S),
2m23.3. Fastest lap: Collins, 2m27.1

FINAL CHAMPIONSHIP POSITIONS

Manufacturers

1	Ferrari	24 (36)*	5	Porsche	4
2	Maserati	18	6	Mercedes-Benz	2
3	Jaguar	7		*Best three results count	
4	Aston Martin	5			

1957

WORLD SPORTS CAR CHAMPIONSHIP

1000 km de la Ciudad de Buenos Aires

20 January 1957. Buenos Aires. 98 laps of a
6.300-mile circuit = 617.400 miles

1 Masten Gregory/ Cesare Perdisa/Eugenio Castellotti/Luigi Musso	Ferrari 290MM	98	6h10m29.9
2 Jean Behra/Carlos Menditéguy/Stirling Moss	Maserati 300S	98	6h11m53.4
3 Alfonso de Portago/ Wolfgang von Trips/Peter Collins/Eugenio Castellotti	Ferrari 290MM	98	6h12m59.6
4 Ninian Sanderson/ Roberto Mieres	Jaguar D-type	95	
5 Luigi Piotti/Roberto Bonomi	Maserati 300S	91	
6 Alessandro de Tomaso/ Isabel Haskell	OSCA 1.5	88	

Winner's average speed: 99.984 mph. Pole position: Juan Manuel Fangio (Maserati 450S), 3m36.1. Fastest lap: Moss, 3m36.0

12 hours of Sebring

23 March 1957. Sebring. 197 laps of a 5.200-mile circuit
= 1024.400 miles

1 Juan Manuel Fangio/ Jean Behra	Maserati 450S	197	12h00m03.4
2 Stirling Moss/Harry Schell	Maserati 300S	195	
3 Mike Hawthorn/Ivor Bueb	Jaguar D-type	193	
4 Masten Gregory/Lou Brero	Ferrari 290MM	193	
5 Walt Hansgen/Russ Boss	Jaguar D-type	188	
6 Peter Collins/ Maurice Trintignant	Ferrari 315S	187	

Winner's average speed: 85.360 mph. Fastest lap: Behra, 3m24.5

Mille Miglia

12 May 1957. Brescia-Rome-Brescia. 998.000 miles

1 Piero Taruffi	Ferrari 315S	10h27m47
2 Wolfgang von Trips	Ferrari 315S	10h30m48
3 Olivier Gendebien/ Philip Washer	Ferrari 250GT	10h35m53
4 Giorgio Scarlatti	Maserati 300S	11h00m58
5 Umberto Maglioli	Porsche RS Spyder	11h14m07
6 Camillo Luglio/Umberto Carli	Ferrari 250GT	11h26m58

Winner's average speed: 95.383 mph

ADAC 1000 km-Rennen

26 May 1957. Nürburgring. 44 laps of a 14.167-mile circuit
= 623.348 miles

1 Tony Brooks/ Noël Cunningham-Reid	Aston Martin DBR144		7h33m38.2
2 Peter Collins/ Olivier Gendebien	Ferrari 412	44	7h37m51.9
3 Mike Hawthorn/ Maurice Trintignant	Ferrari 315S	44	7h39m27.2
4 Umberto Maglioli/ Edgar Barth	Porsche RS Spyder	44	7h47m17.2
5 Juan Manuel Fangio/ Stirling Moss/Chico Godia-Sales/Horace Gould	Maserati 300S	43	
6 Roy Salvadori/Les Leston	Aston Martin DBR1	43	

Winner's average speed: 82.447 mph. Pole position: Fangio, 9m36.9. Fastest lap: Moss, 9m49.9

24 heures du Mans

22-23 June 1957. Le Mans. 326 laps of a 8.365-mile circuit
= 2726.990 miles

1 Ivor Bueb/Ron Flockhart	Jaguar D-type	326	24 hours
2 Ninian Sanderson/ John Lawrence	Jaguar D-type	318	
3 Jean Lucas/"Mary"	Jaguar D-type	316	
4 Paul Frère/Freddy Rousselle	Jaguar D-type	309	
5 Stuart Lewis-Evans/ Martino Severi	Ferrari 315S	299	
6 Duncan Hamilton/ Masten Gregory	Jaguar D-type	298	

Winner's average speed: 113.625 mph. Fastest lap: Mike Hawthorn (Ferrari 335MM), 3m58.7

Sveriges Grand Prix

11 August 1957. Kristianstad. 145 laps of a
4.062-mile circuit = 588.990 miles

1 Jean Behra/Stirling Moss	Maserati 450S	145	6h01m00.9
2 Phil Hill/Peter Collins	Ferrari 412	144	
3 Jo Bonnier/Giorgio Scarlatti/ Harry Schell/Stirling Moss	Maserati 300S	138	
4 Mike Hawthorn/Luigi Musso	Ferrari 412	134	
5 Alain de Changy/ Claude Dubois	Jaguar D-type	132	
6 Bremer/Pinoari	Ferrari	132	

Winner's average speed: 97.889 mph. Pole position: Musso, 2m17.5. Fastest lap: Behra, 2m20.9

Gran Premio di Venezuela/ Caracas 1000 kms

3 November 1957. Caracas. 101 laps of a 6.200-mile circuit
= 626.200 miles

1 Peter Collins/Phil Hill	Ferrari 412	101	6h31m55.8
2 Luigi Musso/Mike Hawthorn	Ferrari 412	100	
3 Wolfgang von Trips/ Wolfgang Seidel	Ferrari 250TR	99	
4 Maurice Trintignant/ Olivier Gendebien	Ferrari 250TR	97	
5 Huschke von Hanstein/ Edgar Barth	Porsche RS Spyder	91	
6 Marcotulli/Ettore Chimeri	Maserati 300S	91	

Winner's average speed: 95.864 mph. Pole position: Stirling Moss (Maserati 450S), 3m41.1. Fastest lap: Moss, 3m38.0

FINAL CHAMPIONSHIP POSITIONS

Manufacturers

1	Ferrari	30 (41)*	5	Porsche	7
2	Maserati	25 (28)*	6	OSCA	1
3	Jaguar	17		*Best four results count	
4	Aston Martin	8			

1958

WORLD SPORTS CAR CHAMPIONSHIP

1000 km de la Ciudad de Buenos Aires

26 January 1958. Buenos Aires. 106 laps of a
5.890-mile circuit = 624.340 miles

1 Peter Collins/Phil Hill	Ferrari 250TR	106	6h19m55.4
2 Wolfgang von Trips/ Olivier Gendebien/Mike Hawthorn/Luigi Musso	Ferrari 250TR	106	6h23m08.0
3 Stirling Moss/Jean Behra	Porsche 718 RSK	106	6h23m17.8
4 Piero Drogo/Sergio Gonzalez	Ferrari	102	
5 Roberto Mieres/Edgar Barth	Porsche RS Spyder	99	
6 Sergio Mantovani/ Gino Munaron	Ferrari	98	

Winner's average speed: 98.600 mph. Pole position: P Hill, 3m27.5. Fastest lap: P Hill, 3m25.9

Sports Car World Championship

12 hours of Sebring

22 March 1958. Sebring. 200 laps of a 5.200-mile circuit = 1040.000 miles

1 Peter Collins/Phil Hill	Ferrari 250TR	200	12 hours
2 Luigi Musso/			
Olivier Gendebien	Ferrari 250TR	199	
3 Harry Schell/	Porsche RS		
Wolfgang Seidel	Spyder	193	
4 Sam Weiss/Dave Tallakson	Lotus 11-Climax	179	
5 Bruce Kessler/Paul O'Shea/			
D Cunningham	Ferrari 250GT	179	
6 Colin Chapman/Cliff Allison	Lotus 11-Climax	179	

Winner's average speed: 86.667 mph. Pole position: Stirling Moss (Aston Martin DBR1). Fastest lap: Moss, 3m20.3

Targa Florio

11 May 1958. Madonie (Piccolo). 14 laps of a 44.739-mile circuit = 626.346 miles

1 Luigi Musso/			
Olivier Gendebien	Ferrari 250TR	14	10h37m58.1
2 Jean Behra/Giorgio Scarlatti	Porsche 718 RSK	14	10h43m37.9
3 Mike Hawthorn/			
Wolfgang von Trips	Ferrari 250TR	14	10h44m29.3
4 Peter Collins/Phil Hill	Ferrari 250TR	14	11h10m01.4
5 Giulio Cabianca/			
Franco Bordoni	OSCA	14	11h25m35.7
6 Huschke von Hanstein/			
Antonio Pucci	Porsche Carrera	14	11h34m04.6

Winner's average speed: 58.907 mph. Fastest lap: Stirling Moss (Aston Martin DBR1), 42m17.5

ADAC 1000 km-Rennen

1 June 1958. Nürburgring. 44 laps of a 14.167-mile circuit = 623.348 miles

1 Stirling Moss/Jack Brabham	Aston Martin		
	DBR1	44	7h23m33
2 Mike Hawthorn/Peter Collins	Ferrari 250TR	44	7h27m17
3 Wolfgang von Trips/			
Olivier Gendebien	Ferrari 250TR	44	7h33m15
4 Luigi Musso/Phil Hill	Ferrari 250TR	43	
5 Wolfgang Seidel/			
Gino Munaron	Ferrari 250TR	42	
6 Graham Whitehead/			
Peter Whitehead	Aston Martin DB3S	42	

Winner's average speed: 84.322 mph. Pole position: Hawthorn, 9m43.4. Fastest lap: Moss, 9m43.0

24 heures du Mans

21-22 June 1958. Le Mans. 304 laps of a 8.365-mile circuit = 2542.960 miles

1 Olivier Gendebien/Phil Hill	Ferrari 250TR	304	24 hours
2 Peter Whitehead/	Aston Martin		
Graham Whitehead	DB3S	292	
3 Jean Behra/Hans Herrmann	Porsche 718 RSK	290	
4 Edgar Barth/Paul Frère	Porsche 718 RSK	289	
5 Carel Godin de Beaufort/			
Herbert Linge	Porsche 550A	287	
6 "Beurlys"/Alain de Chagny	Ferrari 250TR	278	

Winner's average speed: 105.957 mph. Fastest lap: Mike Hawthorn (Ferrari 250TR), 4m08

Tourist Trophy

13 September 1958. Goodwood. 148 laps of a 2.400-mile circuit = 355.200 miles

1 Stirling Moss/Tony Brooks	Aston Martin		
	DBR1	148	4h01m17.0
2 Roy Salvadori/Jack Brabham	Aston Martin		
	DBR1	148	4h01m17.4
3 Carroll Shelby/	Aston Martin		
Stuart Lewis-Evans	DBR1	148	4h01m17.8

4 Jean Behra/Edgar Barth	Porsche 718 RSK	144
5 Masten Gregory/		
Innes Ireland	Jaguar D-type	143
6 Peter Blond/		
Duncan Hamilton	Jaguar D-type	142

Winner's average speed: 88.328 mph. Pole position: Moss, 1m32.0. Fastest lap: Moss, 1m32.6

FINAL CHAMPIONSHIP POSITIONS

Manufacturers

1	Ferrari	32 (38)*	4	Lotus-Climax	3
2=	Aston Martin	18	5	OSCA	2
	Porsche	18 (19)*		*Best four results count	

1959

WORLD SPORTS CAR CHAMPIONSHIP

12 hours of Sebring

21 March 1959. Sebring. 188 laps of a 5.200-mile circuit = 977.600 miles

1 Dan Gurney/Chuck Daigh/			
Phil Hill/Olivier Gendebien	Ferrari 250TR	188	12 hours
2 Jean Behra/Cliff Allison	Ferrari 250TR	187	
3 Jo Bonnier/			
Wolfgang von Trips	Porsche 718 RSK	184	
4 Bob Holbert/Don Sesslar	Porsche 718 RSK	182	
5 John Fitch/Edgar Barth	Porsche 718 RSK	181	
6 Ed Martin/Lance Reventlow	Ferrari 250TR	174	

Winner's average speed: 81.467 mph. Fastest lap: Behra, time n/a

Mike Hawthorn at the wheel for Ferrari during the Nürburgring 1000 km in 1958

Targa Florio

24 May 1959. Madonie (Piccolo). 14 laps of a 44.739-mile circuit = 626.346 miles

1 Edgar Barth/			
Wolfgang Seidel	Porsche 718 RSK	14	11h02m21.8
2 Herbert Linge/Scagliarini	Porsche RS		
	Spyder	14	11h24m20.2
3 Antonio Pucci/			
Huschke von Hanstein	Porsche 718 RSK	14	11h31m44.0
4 Paul Ernst Strähle/Herbert			
Linge/Eberhard Mahle	Porsche 718 RSK	14	11h36m00.0
5 Mennato Boffa/Piero Drogo	Maserati A6G	14	11h41m20.0
6 Colin Davis/Dario Sepe	Alfa Romeo		
	Giulietta SV	14	12h04m09.0

Winner's average speed: 56.737 mph. Fastest lap: Jo Bonnier (Porsche 718 RSK), 43m11.6

ADAC 1000 km-Rennen

7 June 1959. Nürburgring. 44 laps of a 14.167-mile circuit = 623.348 miles

1 Stirling Moss/Jack Fairman	Aston Martin		
	DBR1	44	7h33m18
2 Olivier Gendebien/Phil Hill	Ferrari 250TR	44	7h33m59
3 Tony Brooks/Jean Behra	Ferrari 250TR	44	7h36m45
4 Umberto Maglioli/			
Hans Herrmann	Porsche 718 RSK	44	7h40m57

| 5 | Dan Gurney/Cliff Allison | Ferrari 250TR | 43 |
| 6 | Walter/Heuberger | Porsche RS Spyder | 42 |

Winner's average speed: 82.508 mph. Fastest lap: Moss, 9m32

24 heures du Mans

20-21 June 1959. Le Mans. 322 laps of a 8.365-mile circuit = 2693.530 miles

1	Roy Salvadori/Carroll Shelby	Aston Martin DBR1	322	24 hours
2	Maurice Trintignant/ Paul Frère	Aston Martin DBR1	322	
3	"Beurlys"/"Eldé"	Ferrari 250GT	297	
4	André Pilette/Georges Arents	Ferrari 250GT	296	
5	Bob Grossman/ Fernand Tavano	Ferrari 250GT California	294	
6	Lino Fayen/Gino Munaron	Ferrari 250GT	293	

Winner's average speed: 112.230 mph. Fastest lap: Jean Behra (Ferrari 250GT), 4m00.9

Tourist Trophy

5 September 1959. Goodwood. 224 laps of a 2.400-mile circuit = 537.600 miles

1	Carroll Shelby/ Jack Fairman/Stirling Moss	Aston Martin DBR1	224	6h00m46.8
2	Jo Bonnier/ Wolfgang von Trips	Porsche 718 RSK	223	
3	Tony Brooks/Phil Hill/Cliff Allison/Olivier Gendebien	Ferrari 250TR	223	
4	Maurice Trintignant/ Paul Frère	Aston Martin DBR1	221	
5	Tony Brooks/Dan Gurney	Ferrari 250TR	220	
6	Peter Ashdown/A Ross	Lola-Climax	210	

Winner's average speed: 89.406 mph. Fastest lap: Brooks, 1m31.8

FINAL CHAMPIONSHIP POSITIONS

Manufacturers

1	Aston Martin	24	5=	Alfa Romeo	1
2=	Ferrari	18 (22)*		Lola-Climax	1
	Porsche	18 (21)*		*Best three results count	
4	Maserati	2			

1960

WORLD SPORTS CAR CHAMPIONSHIP

1000 km de la Ciudad de Buenos Aires

31 January 1960. Buenos Aires. 106 laps of a 5.890-mile circuit = 624.340 miles

1	Phil Hill/Cliff Allison	Ferrari 250TR	106	6h17m12.1
2	Wolfgang von Trips/ Richie Ginther	Ferrari 250TR	105	
3	Jo Bonnier/Graham Hill	Porsche 718 RSK	101	
4	Barberis/Heins	Maserati 300S	101	
5	von Döry/Oelke/ Juan Manuel Bordeu	Porsche 718 RSK	100	
6	Christian Goethals/Delfosse	Porsche 718 RSK	100	

Winner's average speed: 99.311 mph. Pole position: P Hill, 3m23.4. Fastest lap: Dan Gurney (Maserati T61), 3m22.4

12 hours of Sebring

26 March 1960. Sebring. 196 laps of a 5.200-mile circuit = 1019.200 miles

1	Olivier Gendebien/ Hans Herrmann	Porsche 718 RSK	196	12h00m02.9
2	Bob Holbert/Roy Schechter/Howard Fowler	Porsche 718 RSK	187	
3	Jack Nethercutt/Pete Lovely	Ferrari 250TR	186	
4	Ed Hugus/Augie Pabst	Ferrari 250GT	185	
5	George Reed/Alan Connell	Ferrari 250GT California	185	
6	William Sturgis/Fritz d'Orey	Ferrari 250GT	183	

Winner's average speed: 84.928 mph. Fastest lap: Stirling Moss (Maserati T61), 3m18.14

Targa Florio

8 May 1960. Madonie (Piccolo). 10 laps of a 44.739-mile circuit = 447.390 miles

1	Jo Bonnier/Hans Herrmann/ Graham Hill	Porsche RS60	10	7h33m08.4
2	Wolfgang von Trips/ Phil Hill	Ferrari Dino 246S	10	7h39m11.0
3	Olivier Gendebien/ Hans Herrmann	Porsche RS60	10	7h41m46.0
4	Willy Mairesse/Ludovico Scarfiotti/Giulio Cabianca/ Paul Frère	Ferrari Dino 246S	10	7h44m49.0
5	Carel Godin de Beaufort/ Edgar Barth	Porsche 718 RSK	10	7h59m11.6
6	Herbert Linge/ Paul Ernst Strähle	Porsche Carrera	10	8h10m06.2

Winner's average speed: 59.239 mph. Fastest lap: Bonnier, 42m26.0

ADAC 1000 km-Rennen

22 May 1960. Nürburgring. 44 laps of a 14.167-mile circuit = 623.348 miles

1	Stirling Moss/Dan Gurney	Maserati T61	44	7h31m40.5
2	Jo Bonnier/Olivier Gendebien	Porsche RS60	44	7h34m32.9
3	Cliff Allison/Willy Mairesse/Wolfgang von Trips/Phil Hill	Ferrari 250TR	44	7h35m44.1
4	Hans Herrmann/ Maurice Trintignant	Porsche RS60	44	7h37m57.7
5	Gino Munaron/ Masten Gregory	Maserati T61	43	
6	Walter/Losinger	Porsche 718 RSK	42	

Winner's average speed: 82.805 mph. Pole position: Bonnier, 9m43.6. Fastest lap: Moss, 9m37.0

24 heures du Mans

25-26 June 1960. Le Mans. 313 laps of a 8.365-mile circuit = 2618.245 miles

1	Olivier Gendebien/Paul Frère	Ferrari 250TR	313	24 hours
2	Ricardo Rodriguez/ André Pilette	Ferrari 250TR	309	
3	Roy Salvadori/Jim Clark	Aston Martin DBR1	305	
4	Fernand Tavano/"Loustel"	Ferrari 250GT	301	
5	Georges Arents/Alan Connell	Ferrari 250GT	299	
6	"Eldé"/Pierre Noblet	Ferrari 250GT	299	

Winner's average speed: 109.094 mph. Fastest lap: Masten Gregory (Maserati T61), 4m04

FINAL CHAMPIONSHIP POSITIONS

Manufacturers

1	Ferrari	22 (30)*	*Best three results count.
2	Porsche	22 (26)*	Ferrari won championship
3	Maserati	11	due to having the greater
4	Aston Martin	4	number of total points

1961

WORLD SPORTS CAR CHAMPIONSHIP

12 hours of Sebring

25 March 1961. Sebring. 210 laps of a 5.200-mile circuit = 1092.000 miles

1	Phil Hill/Olivier Gendebien	Ferrari 250TR	210	12h02m22.9
2	Willy Mairesse/Giancarlo Baghetti/Richie Ginther/ Wolfgang von Trips	Ferrari 250TR	208	
3	Pedro Rodriguez/ Ricardo Rodriguez	Ferrari 250TR	204	

4 Hap Sharp/Ronnie Hissom	Ferrari 250TR	203
5 Bob Holbert/Roger Penske	Porsche RS61	199
6 Jim Hall/	Ferrari Dino	
George Constantine	246S	199

Winner's average speed: 90.700 mph. Fastest lap: Stirling Moss (Maserati T63), 3m14.8

Targa Florio

30 April 1961. Madonie (Piccolo). 10 laps of a 44.739-mile circuit = 447.390 miles

1 Wolfgang von Trips/	Ferrari Dino		
Olivier Gendebien	246SP	10	6h57m39.4
2 Jo Bonnier/Dan Gurney	Porsche Spyder	10	7h02m03.5
3 Hans Herrmann/Edgar Barth	Porsche	10	7h14m14.0
4 Nino Vaccarella/			
Maurice Trintignant	Maserati T61	10	7h28m49.6
5 Umberto Maglioli/			
Giorgio Scarlatti	Maserati T61	10	7h40m04.2
6 Antonio Pucci/			
Paul Ernst Strähle	Porsche Carrera	10	7h48m25.8

Winner's average speed: 64.271 mph. Fastest lap: von Trips, 40m03.5

ADAC 1000 km-Rennen

28 May 1961. Nürburgring. 44 laps of a 14.167-mile circuit = 623.348 miles

1 Masten Gregory/			
Lucky Casner	Maserati T61	44	7h51m39.2
2 Pedro Rodriguez/			
Ricardo Rodriguez	Ferrari 250TR	43	
3 Wolfgang von Trips/			
Phil Hill/Olivier Gendebien/	Ferrari Dino		
Richie Ginther	246SP	43	
4 Carlo Abate/Colin Davis	Ferrari 250GT	43	
5 Willy Mairesse/			
Giancarlo Baghetti	Ferrari 250GT	43	
6 Fritz Hahnl/Helmuth Zick	Porsche Carrera	43	

Winner's average speed: 79.297 mph. Pole position: P Hill, 9m33.7. Fastest lap: P Hill, 9m15.8

24 heures du Mans

10-11 June 1961. Le Mans. 332 laps of a 8.365-mile circuit = 2777.180 miles

1 Olivier Gendebien/Phil Hill	Ferrari 250TR	332	24 hours
2 Willy Mairesse/			
Michael Parkes	Ferrari 250TR	329	
3 Pierre Noblet/Jean Guichet	Ferrari 250GT	316	
4 Augie Pabst/			
Richard Thompson	Maserati T63	310	
5 Masten Gregory/Bob Holbert	Porsche RS61	308	
6 Bob Grossman/André Pilette	Ferrari 250GT	308	

Winner's average speed: 115.716 mph. Fastest lap: Ricardo Rodriguez (Ferrari 250TR), 3m59.09

4 ore di Pescara

15 August 1961. Pescara. 22 laps of a 16.032-mile circuit = 352.704 miles. Half points awarded as race was under six hours/1000 kms in duration

1 Lorenzo Bandini/			
Giorgio Scarlatti	Ferrari 250TR	22	4 hours
2 Edgar Barth/K Orthuber	Porsche RS60	21	
3 Mennato Boffa	Maserati T60	21	
4 Georges Arents/			
George Hamill	Ferrari 250GT	21	
5 Colin Davis	OSCA	20	
6 Bettoja/"Kim"	Ferrari 250GT	20	

Winner's average speed: 88.176 mph. Pole position: Giancarlo Baghetti (Ferrari Dino 246SP). Fastest lap: Richie Ginther (Ferrari Dino 246SP), 9m55.5

1962

SPEED WORLD CHALLENGE

12 hours of Sebring

24 March 1962. Sebring. 206 laps of a 5.200-mile circuit = 1071.200 miles

1 Jo Bonnier/Lucien Bianchi	Ferrari 250TR	206	12h01m00.5
2 Phil Hill/Olivier Gendebien	Ferrari 250GTO	196	
3 Bruce Jennings/Frank Rand/			
Bill Wuesthoff	Porsche RS60	195	
4 George Hamill/			
Fabrizio Serena	Ferrari 250GT	190	
5 Bruce McLaren/	Cooper-		
Roger Penske	Maserati	190	
6 Hap Sharp/	Chaparral-		
Ronnie Hissom/Jim Hall	Chevrolet	189	

Winner's average speed: 89.142 mph. Pole position: Stirling Moss (Ferrari 250TR). Fastest lap: Pedro Rodriguez (Ferrari Dino 246SP), 3m12.4

Targa Florio

6 May 1962. Madonie (Piccolo). 10 laps of a 44.739-mile circuit = 447.390 miles

1 Willy Mairesse/Ricardo	Ferrari Dino		
Rodriguez/Olivier Gendebien	246SP	10	7h02m56.6
2 Giancarlo Baghetti/	Ferrari Dino		
Lorenzo Bandini	196SP	10	7h14m24.0
3 Jo Bonnier/Nino Vaccarella	Porsche RS62	10	7h17m20.0
4 Giorgio Scarlatti/			
Pietro Ferraro	Ferrari 250GTO	10	7h22m08.1
5 Roger de Lageneste/			
Jean Rolland	Ferrari 250GTO	10	7h44m33.0
6 Hans Herrmann/			
Herbert Linge	Porsche Abarth	10	7h45m26.0

Winner's average speed: 63.468 mph. Fastest lap: Mairesse, 40m00.3

ADAC 1000 km-Rennen

27 May 1962. Nürburgring. 44 laps of a 14.167-mile circuit = 623.348 miles

1 Olivier Gendebien/Phil Hill	Ferrari Dino		
	246SP	44	7h32m27.7
2 Willy Mairesse/			
Michael Parkes	Ferrari 330LM	44	7h35m49.2
3 Graham Hill/Hans Herrmann	Porsche RS62	44	7h42m24.6
4 Bruce McLaren/Tony Maggs	Aston Martin	42	
5 Peter Nöcker/			
Wolfgang Seidel	Ferrari 250GT	41	
6 Edgar Barth/Herbert Linge	Porsche Abarth	41	

Winner's average speed: 82.661 mph. Pole position: P Hill, 9m25.5. Fastest lap: P Hill, 9m31.9

24 heures du Mans

23-24 June 1962. Le Mans. 330 laps of a 8.365-mile circuit = 2760.450 miles

1 Olivier Gendebien/Phil Hill	Ferrari 330LM	330	24 hours
2 Jean Guichet/Pierre Noblet	Ferrari 250GTO	325	
3 "Eldé"/"Beurlys"	Ferrari 250GTO	312	
4 Briggs Cunningham/			
Roy Salvadori	Jaguar E-type	309	
5 Peter Lumsden/Peter Sargent	Jaguar E-type	309	
6 Bob Grossman/			
"Fireball" Roberts	Ferrari 250TR	"Experimental" 296	

Winner's average speed: 115.019 mph. Pole position: P Hill. Fastest lap: P Hill, 3m57.3

FINAL CHAMPIONSHIP POSITIONS

Manufacturers

1	Ferrari	39	Only manufacturers
2	Porsche	35	which competed in every
3	Alfa Romeo	25	round were eligible

1963

SPEED AND ENDURANCE WORLD CHALLENGE

12 hours of Sebring

23 March 1963. Sebring. 209 laps of a 5.200-mile circuit = 1086.800 miles

1	John Surtees/ Ludovico Scarfiotti	Ferrari 250P	209	12h01m24.2
2	Willy Mairesse/Nino Vaccarella/Lorenzo Bandini	Ferrari 250P	208	
3	Pedro Rodriguez/Graham Hill	Ferrari 330LM	207	
4	Roger Penske/Augie Pabst	Ferrari 250GTO	203	
5	Carlo Abate/ Jean-Manuel Bordeu	Ferrari 250GTO	197	
6	Innes Ireland/Richie Ginther	Ferrari 250GTO	196	

Winner's average speed: 90.390 mph. Fastest lap: Surtees, 3m11.4

Targa Florio

5 May 1963. Madonie (Piccolo). 10 laps of a 44.739-mile circuit = 447.390 miles

1	Jo Bonnier/Carlo Abate	Porsche RS62	10	6h55m45.2
2	Willy Mairesse/Ludovico Scarfiotti/Lorenzo Bandini	Ferrari Dino 196SP	10	6h55m57.0
3	Edgar Barth/Herbert Linge	Porsche 356 Carrera 2	10	7h25m19.4
4	Maurizio Grana/ Gianni Bulgari	Ferrari 250GTO	10	7h26m31.4
5	Antonio Pucci/ Paul Ernst Strähle	Porsche 356 Carrera 2	10	7h33m37.2
6	Jean Manuel Bordeu/ Giorgio Scarlatti	Ferrari 250GTO	10	7h40m16.2

Winner's average speed: 64.566 mph. Fastest lap: Mairesse, 40m04.4

ADAC 1000 km-Rennen

19 May 1963. Nürburgring. 44 laps of a 14.167-mile circuit = 623.348 miles

1	John Surtees/Willy Mairesse	Ferrari 250P	44	7h32m18.4
2	Jean Guichet/Pierre Noblet	Ferrari 250GTO	44	7h40m03.0
3	Carlo Abate/ Umberto Maglioli	Ferrari 250TR	43	
4	Edgar Barth/Herbert Linge/ Ben Pon/Heini Walter	Porsche 356 Carrera 2	43	
5	"Eldé"/ Gérard Langlois van Ophem	Ferrari 250GT Special	41	
6	David Piper/Ed Cantrell	Ferrari 250GTO	41	

Winner's average speed: 82.689 mph. Pole position: Surtees, 9m13.1. Fastest lap: Surtees, 91.8 mph

The Ferrari 330LM at the Nürburgring in 1962. Michael Parkes is the driver

24 heures du Mans

15-16 June 1963. Le Mans. 338 laps of a 8.365-mile circuit = 2827.370 miles

1	Ludovico Scarfiotti/ Lorenzo Bandini	Ferrari 250P	338	24 hours
2	"Beurlys"/ Gérard Langlois van Ophem	Ferrari 250GTO	322	
3	Michael Parkes/ Umberto Maglioli	Ferrari 250P	322	
4	"Eldé"/Pierre Dumay	Ferrari 250GTO	321	
5	Jack Sears/Mike Salmon	Ferrari 330LMB	313	
6	Masten Gregory/David Piper	Ferrari 250GTO	311	

Winner's average speed: 117.807 mph. Pole position: Rodriguez (Ferrari 330TR), 3m50.9. Fastest lap: Surtees (Ferrari 250P), 3m53.3

FINAL CHAMPIONSHIP POSITIONS

Manufacturers

1	Ferrari	39	Only manufacturers
2	Porsche	35	which competed in every
3	Jaguar	22	round were eligible
4	Alfa Romeo	10	

1964

INTERNATIONAL CHAMPIONSHIP FOR MAKES

Daytona Continental

16 February 1964. Daytona. 327 laps of a 3.810-mile circuit = 1245.870 miles

1	Phil Hill/Pedro Rodriguez	Ferrari 250GTO	327	12h40m25.8
2	David Piper/Lucien Bianchi	Ferrari 250GTO	-	
3	Bob Grossman/Walt Hansgen	Ferrari 250GTO	-	
4	Dan Gurney/Bob Johnson	AC Cobra-Ford	-	
5	Ulf Norinder/John Cannon	Ferrari 250GTO	-	
6	Edgar Barth/ Herbert Linge/Jo Bonnier	Porsche 365 Carrera 2	-	

Winner's average speed: 98.303 mph. Fastest lap: n/a

12 hours of Sebring

21 March 1964. Sebring. 214 laps of a 5.200-mile circuit = 1112.800 miles

1	Michael Parkes/ Umberto Maglioli	Ferrari 275P	214	12h02m53.4
2	Ludovico Scarfiotti/ Nino Vaccarella	Ferrari 275P	213	
3	John Surtees/ Lorenzo Bandini	Ferrari 330P	212	
4	Bob Holbert/ Dave MacDonald	AC Cobra-Ford	209	
5	Lew Spencer/Bob Bondurant	AC Cobra-Ford	205	
6	Jo Schlesser/John Morton/ Edward Butler/Phil Hill	AC Cobra-Ford	203	

Winner's average speed: 92.363 mph. Pole position: Surtees, 3m04.2 (first occasional at Sebring where pole was decided by qualifying times). Fastest lap: Surtees, 3m06.2

Targa Florio

26 April 1964. Madonie (Piccolo). 10 laps of a 44.739-mile circuit = 447.390 miles

1	Antonio Pucci/Colin Davis	Porsche 904GTS	10	7h10m53.6
2	Gianni Balzarini/ Herbert Linge	Porsche 904GTS	10	7h23m15.3
3	Roberto Bussinello/ Nino Todaro	Alfa Romeo Giulia TZ	10	7h27m07.0
4	"Kim"/Alfonso Thiele	Alfa Romeo Giulia TZ	10	7h27m38.2
5	Claudio Ferlaino/ Luigi Taramazzo	Ferrari 250GTO	10	7h28m25.0
6	Edgar Barth/ Umberto Maglioli	Porsche 908	10	7h29m16.4

Winner's average speed: 62.297 mph. Fastest lap: Davis, 41m10.8

Grand Prix de Spa-Francorchamps

17 May 1964. Spa-Francorchamps. 36 laps of a 8.761-mile circuit = 315.396 miles

1 Michael Parkes	Ferrari 250GTO	36	2h32m05.2
2 Jean Guichet	Ferrari 250GTO	36	
3 Lorenzo Bandini	Ferrari 250GTO	36	
4 David Piper	Ferrari 250GTO	36	
5 Edgar Barth	Porsche 904GTS	35	
6 Gérard Langlois van Ophem	Ferrari 250GTO	35	

Winner's average speed: 124.427 mph. Pole position: Parkes, 4m09.0. Fastest lap: Phil Hill (Ferrari 250GTO), 4m04.5

ADAC 1000 km-Rennen

31 May 1964. Nürburgring. 44 laps of a 14.167-mile circuit = 623.348 miles

1 Ludovico Scarfiotti/			
Nino Vaccarella	Ferrari 275P	44	7h08m27.0
2 Michael Parkes/Jean Guichet	Ferrari 250GTO	43	
3 Ben Pon/Gerhard Koch	Porsche 904GTS	43	
4 Lucien Bianchi/			
Gérard Langlois van Ophem	Ferrari 250GTO	43	
5 Jo Bonnier/Richie Ginther	Porsche RS62	42	
6 Herbert Müller/André Knorr	Porsche 904GTS	42	

Winner's average speed: 87.293 mph. Pole position: John Surtees (Ferrari 275P), 8m57.9. Fastest lap: Surtees, 9m09.0

24 heures du Mans

20-21 June 1964. Le Mans. 348 laps of a 8.365-mile circuit = 2911.020 miles

1 Jean Guichet/Nino Vaccarella	Ferrari 275P	348	24 hours
2 Jo Bonnier/Graham Hill	Ferrari 330P	343	
3 John Surtees/			
Lorenzo Bandini	Ferrari 330P	323	
4 Dan Gurney/Bob Bondurant	AC Cobra		
	Daytona-Ford	333	
5 Lucien Bianchi/"Beurlys"	Ferrari 250GTO	332	
6 Innes Ireland/Tony Maggs	Ferrari 250GTO	327	

Winner's average speed: 121.293 mph. Pole position: Surtees, 3m42.0. Fastest lap: Phil Hill (Ford GT40), 3m49.2

12 heures de Reims

5 July 1964. Reims. 293 laps of a 5.187-mile circuit = 1519.791 miles

1 Graham Hill/Jo Bonnier	Ferrari 250LM	293	12 hours
2 John Surtees/			
Lorenzo Bandini	Ferrari 250LM	277	
3 Michael Parkes/			
Ludovico Scarfiotti	Ferrari 250GTO	253	
4 David Piper/Tony Maggs	Ferrari 250GTO	243	
5 Nasif Estefano/	Porsche		
Andrea Vianini	904GTS	242	
6 Gerhard Koch/	Porsche		
Gerhard Mitter	904GTS	240	

Winner's average speed: 126.649 mph. Pole position: Surtees, 2m19.2. Fastest lap: G Hill, 2m19.2

Tourist Trophy

29 August 1964. Goodwood. 130 laps of a 2.400-mile circuit = 312.000 miles

1 Graham Hill	Ferrari 330P	130	3h12m43.6
2 David Piper	Ferrari 250LM	129	
3 Dan Gurney	AC Cobra-Ford	129	
4 Jack Sears	AC Cobra-Ford	127	
5 Bob Olthoff	AC Cobra-Ford	126	
6 Innes Ireland	Ferrari 250GTO	125	

Winner's average speed: 97.132 mph. Pole position: Bruce McLaren (Cooper-Oldsmobile), 1m23.2. Fastest lap: McLaren, 1m23.8

1000 km de Paris

11 October 1964. Montlhéry. 129 laps of a 4.826-mile circuit = 622.554 miles

1 Graham Hill/Jo Bonnier	Ferrari 330P	129	n/a
2 Pedro Rodriguez/Jo Schlesser	Ferrari 250GTO	127	
3 Edgar Barth/Colin Davis	Porsche RS62	126	
4 Tony Maggs/David Piper	Ferrari 250GTO	126	
5 Lucien Bianchi/			
Gérard Langlois van Ophem	Ferrari 250GTO	125	
6 Rob Slotemaker/			
David van Lennep	Porsche 904GTS	124	

Winner's average speed: 96.500 mph. Pole position: G Hill, 2m43.6. Fastest lap: Jackie Stewart, 2m45.1

FINAL CHAMPIONSHIP POSITIONS

Manufacturers

1	Ferrari	54 (74)*	4	Alfa Romeo	4
2	Porsche	22		*Best six results count	
3	AC Cobra-Ford	13			

1965

INTERNATIONAL CHAMPIONSHIP FOR MAKES

Daytona Continental

1 March 1965. Daytona. 327 laps of a 3.810-mile circuit = 1245.870 miles

1 Ken Miles/Lloyd Ruby	Ford GT40	327	12h27m09.0
2 Jo Schlesser/Harold Keck/	AC Cobra		
Bob Johnson	Daytona-Ford	322	
3 Richie Ginther/			
Bob Bondurant	Ford GT40	319	
4 Rich Muther/	AC Cobra		
John Timanus/Tom Payne	Daytona-Ford	318	
5 Charles Kolb/Roger Heftler	Porsche 904GTS	313	
6 Ed Leslie/Allen Grant	AC Cobra		
	Daytona-Ford	312	

Winner's average speed: 100.050 mph. Pole position: Pedro Rodriguez (Ferrari 330P2), 2m00.6. Fastest lap: n/a

12 hours of Sebring

27 March 1965. Sebring. 196 laps of a 5.200-mile circuit = 1019.200 miles

1 Jim Hall/Hap Sharp	Chaparral 2D-		
	Chevrolet*	196	12h01m48.9
2 Bruce McLaren/Ken Miles	Ford GT40	192	
3 David Piper/Tony Maggs	Ferrari 250LM	190	
4 Jo Schlesser/	AC Cobra		
Bob Bondurant	GT Coupé-Ford	187	
5 Lake Underwood/			
Gunther Klass	Porsche 904GTS	185	
6 Ben Pon/Joe Buzzetta	Porsche 904GTS	185	

*Sports-racing car, ineligible for points. Winner's average speed: 84.720 mph. Pole position: Hall, 2m57.6. Fastest lap: Hall, 2m59.3

1000 km di Monza/ Trofeo Filippo Caracciolo

27 April 1965. Monza. 100 laps of a 6.214-mile circuit = 621.400 miles

1 Michael Parkes/Jean Guichet	Ferrari 275P2	100	4h56m08.0
2 John Surtees/			
Ludovico Scarfiotti	Ferrari 330P2	100	4h57m59.9
3 Bruce McLaren/Ken Miles	Ford GT40	96	
4 Ben Pon/Rob Slotemaker	Porsche 904GTS	92	
5 Pierre Noblet/Mario Casoni	Iso Grifo-		
	Chevrolet	92	
6 Innes Ireland/Mike Salmon	Ferrari 250LM	91	

Winner's average speed: 125.897 mph. Pole position: Parkes, 2m46.9. Fastest lap: Surtees, 2m47.2

Through the chicane on the first lap at Monza in 1965

Tourist Trophy

2 May 1965. Oulton Park. 138 laps of a 2.761-mile circuit
= 381.018 miles

1 Denny Hulme	Brabham BT8-Climax*	138	4h03m01.4
2 David Hobbs	Lola T70-Ford*	137	
3 David Piper	Ferrari 250LM*	133	
4 Sir John Whitmore	AC Cobra-Ford	130	
5 Peter Sutcliffe	Ferrari 250LM	130	
6 Allen Grant	AC Cobra-Ford	128	

*Sports-racing car, ineligible for points. Winner's average speed:
94.069 mph. Pole position: John Surtees (Lola T70-Chevrolet),
1m36.6. Fastest lap: Bruce McLaren (McLaren-Elva-Oldsmobile),
1m39.0

Targa Florio

9 May 1965. Madonie (Piccolo). 10 laps of a
44.739-mile circuit = 447.390 miles

1 Nino Vaccarella/ Lorenzo Bandini	Ferrari 275P2	10	7h01m12.4
2 Colin Davis/Gerhard Mitter	Porsche RS62	10	7h05m34.0
3 Umberto Maglioli/ Herbert Linge	Porsche 906	10	7h06m58.0
4 Jo Bonnier/Graham Hill	Porsche RS62	10	7h10m08.0
5 Antonio Pucci/Gunther Klass	Porsche 914GTS	10	7h11m07.0
6 Hans Herrmann/Leo Cella	Fiat Abarth 1600 OT	10	7h17m23.0

Winner's average speed: 63.730 mph. Pole position: Vaccarella,
39m29.0. Fastest lap: Vaccarella, 39m21.0

Grand Prix de Spa-Francorchamps

16 May 1965. Spa-Francorchamps. 36 laps of a
8.761-mile circuit = 315.396 miles

1 Willy Mairesse	Ferrari 250LM	36	2h29m45.7
2 David Piper	Ferrari 250LM	36	2h31m43.5
3 Ben Pon	Porsche 904GTS	36	2h32m37.4
4 Peter Sutcliffe	Ferrari 250GTO	36	2h32m43.8
5 Bob Bondurant	AC Cobra GT-Ford	36	2h32m49.8
6 Mike Salmon	Ferrari 250GTO	35	

Winner's average speed: 126.359 mph. Pole position: Michael
Parkes (Ferrari 250LM), 3m59.7. Fastest lap: Parkes, 4m01.3

ADAC 1000 km-Rennen

23 May 1965. Nürburgring. 44 laps of a 14.167-mile circuit
= 623.348 miles

1 John Surtees/ Ludovico Scarfiotti	Ferrari 330P2	44	6h53m05.4
2 Michael Parkes/Jean Guichet	Ferrari 275P2	44	6h53m50.2
3 Jo Bonnier/Jochen Rindt	Porsche RS62	44	7h00m59.6
4 Lorenzo Bandini/ Nino Vaccarella	Ferrari Dino 166P Coupé	43	
5 Umberto Maglioli/ Herbert Linge	Porsche 906	43	
6 Peter Nöcker/Gunther Klass	Porsche 906	43	

Winner's average speed: 90.539 mph. Fastest lap: Surtees,
8m53.1. Fastest lap: Surtees, 8m50.5

24 heures du Mans

19-20 June 1965. Le Mans. 347 laps of a 8.365-mile circuit
= 2902.655 miles

1 Masten Gregory/ Jochen Rindt	Ferrari 275LM	347	24 hours
2 Pierre Dumay/ Gustave Gosselin	Ferrari 275LM	341	
3 Willy Mairesse/"Beurlys"	Ferrari 250GTB	338	
4 Herbert Linge/Peter Nöcker	Porsche 904/6	334	
5 Gerhard Koch/ Anton Fischaber	Porsche 904GTS	324	
6 Dieter Spoerry/Peter Boller	Ferrari 275LM	323	

Winner's average speed: 120.944 mph. Pole position: Phil Hill
(Ford GT40), 3m33.0. Fastest lap: P Hill, 3m37.5

12 heures de Reims

3-4 July 1965. Reims. 284 laps of a 5.187-mile circuit
= 1473.108 miles

1 Pedro Rodriguez/ Jean Guichet	Ferrari 365P2	284	12 hours
2 John Surtees/Michael Parkes	Ferrari 365P2	282	
3 Willy Mairesse/"Beurlys"	Ferrari 250LM	279	
4 David Piper/Richard Attwood	Ferrari 250LM	273	
5 Bob Bondurant/Jo Schlesser	AC Cobra-Ford	270	
6 Mike de Udy/Paul Hawkins	Porsche 904GTS	261	

Winner's average speed: 122.759 mph. Pole position: Rodriguez,
2m18.5. Fastest lap: Surtees, 2m17.9

FINAL CHAMPIONSHIP POSITIONS

Manufacturers				
1 Ferrari	54 (66)*	5 Iso Grifo	2
2= AC Cobra-Ford	23	6 Fiat-Abarth	1
Porsche	23 (26)*	*Best six results count	
4 Ford	22		

1966

INTERNATIONAL CHAMPIONSHIP FOR MAKES

Daytona 24 hours

5-6 February 1966. Daytona. 678 laps of a
3.810-mile circuit = 2583.180 miles

1 Ken Miles/Lloyd Ruby	Ford GT40 Mk2	678	24h00m07.6
2 Dan Gurney/Jerry Grant	Ford GT40 Mk2	670	
3 Walt Hansgen/ Mark Donohue	Ford GT40 Mk2	669	
4 Pedro Rodriguez/ Mario Andretti	Ferrari 365P2	664	
5 Bruce McLaren/Chris Amon	Ford GT40 Mk2	652	
6 Hans Herrmann/ Herbert Linge	Porsche 906 Carrera 6	623	

Winner's average speed: 107.388 mph. Pole position:
Miles/Ruby, 1m57.8. Fastest lap: Gurney, 1m57.7

12 hours of Sebring

26 March 1966. Sebring. 228 laps of a 5.200-mile circuit
= 1185.600 miles

1 Lloyd Ruby/Ken Miles	Ford GTX1	228	12h01m16.1
2 Walt Hansgen/ Mark Donohue	Ford GT40 Mk2	216	
3 Peter Revson/Skip Scott	Ford GT40	213	
4 Hans Herrmann/Joe Buzzetta/Gerhard Mitter	Porsche 906 Carrera 6	209	
5 Lorenzo Bandini/ Ludovico Scarfiotti	Ferrari Dino 206S Spyder	206	
6 Charles Vögele/Jo Siffert	Porsche 906 Carrera 6	205	

Winner's average speed: 98.626 mph. Pole position: Dan Gurney
(Ford GT40 Mk2), 2m54.6. Fastest lap: Gurney, 2m54.8

Sports Car World Championship

1000 km di Monza/ Trofeo Filippo Caracciolo

25 April 1966. Monza. 100 laps of a 6.214-mile circuit = 621.400 miles

1 John Surtees/Michael Parkes	Ferrari 330P3	100	6h05m11.6
2 Sir John Whitmore/ Masten Gregory	Ford GT40	99	
3 Herbert Müller/ Willy Mairesse	Ford GT40	98	
4 Gerhard Mitter/ Hans Herrmann	Porsche 906 Carrera 6	98	
5 Jo Siffert/Charles Vögele	Porsche 906 Carrera 6	96	
6 Guy Ligier/Henri Greder	Ford GT40	95	

Winner's average speed: 102.089 mph. Pole position: Parkes, 2m58.1. Fastest lap: Surtees, 3m26.7

Targa Florio

8 May 1966. Madonie (Piccolo). 10 laps of a 44.739-mile circuit = 447.390 miles

1 Willy Mairesse/ Herbert Müller	Porsche 906 Carrera 6	10	7h16m32.3
2 Jean Guichet/ Giancarlo Baghetti	Ferrari Dino 206S Coupé	10	7h25m02.2
3 Antonio Pucci/ Vincenzo Arena	Porsche 906 Carrera 6	10	7h34m08.0
4 Enrico Pinto/Nino Todaro	Alfa Romeo GTZ	10	7h45m24.2
5 Claude Bourillet/ Umberto Maglioli	Porsche 906 Carrera 6	10	7h51m55.0
6 Roger de Lageneste/ José Rosinski	Alpine-Renault	10	7h52m33.8

Winner's average speed: 61.492 mph. Fastest lap: Nino Vaccarella (Ferrari 330P3), 41m51.2

1000 km de Spa-Francorchamps

22 May 1966. Spa-Francorchamps. 71 laps of a 8.761-mile circuit = 622.031 miles

1 Michael Parkes/ Ludovico Scarfiotti	Ferrari 330P3	71	4h43m24.0
2 Sir John Whitmore/ Frank Gardner	Ford GT40 Mk2	70	
3 Skip Scott/Peter Revson	Ford GT40	69	
4 Peter Sutcliffe/Brian Redman	Ford GT40	68	
5 Innes Ireland/Chris Amon	Ford GT40	67	
6 Richard Attwood/ Jean Guichet	Ferrari Dino 206S Spyder	67	

Winner's average speed: 131.693 mph. Pole position: Parkes, 3m47.4. Fastest lap: Parkes, 3m46.4

ADAC 1000 km-Rennen

5 June 1966. Nürburgring. 44 laps of a 14.167-mile circuit = 623.348 miles

1 Phil Hill/Jo Bonnier	Chaparral 2D-Chevrolet	44	6h58m47.6
2 Ludovico Scarfiotti/ Lorenzo Bandini	Ferrari Dino 206S Spyder	44	6h59m29.2
3 Pedro Rodriguez/ Richie Ginther	Ferrari Dino 206S Spyder	44	7h00m02.4
4 Bob Bondurant/ Paul Hawkins	Porsche 906 Carrera 6	44	7h06m52.8
5 Guy Ligier/Jo Schlesser	Ford GT40	43	
6 Peter Sutcliffe/John Taylor	Ford GT40	43	

Winner's average speed: 89.306 mph. Pole position: John Surtees (Ferrari 330P3), 8m31.9. Fastest lap: Surtees, 8m37.0

24 heures du Mans

17-18 June 1966. Le Mans. 359 laps of a 8.365-mile circuit = 3003.035 miles

1 Bruce McLaren/Chris Amon	Ford GT40 Mk2	359	24 hours
2 Ken Miles/Denny Hulme	Ford GT40 Mk2	359	

3 Ronnie Bucknum/ Dick Hutcherson	Ford GT40 Mk2	347	
4 Jo Siffert/Colin Davis	Porsche 906 Carrera 6LH	338	
5 Hans Herrmann/ Herbert Linge	Porsche 906 Carrera 6LH	337	
6 Udo Schütz/Piet de Klerk	Porsche 906 Carrera 6LH	336	

Winner's average speed: 125.126 mph. Pole position: Dan Gurney (Ford GT40 Mk2), 3m30.6. Fastest lap: Gurney, 3m30.6

FINAL CHAMPIONSHIP POSITIONS

Manufacturers

1	Ford	39 (41)*	5	Alfa Romeo	3
2	Ferrari	33 (35)*	6	Alpine-Renault	1
3	Porsche	21 (22)*		*Best five results count	
4	Chaparral-Chevrolet	9			

1967

INTERNATIONAL CHAMPIONSHIP FOR MAKES

Daytona 24 hours

4-5 February 1967. Daytona. 666 laps of a 3.810-mile circuit = 2537.46 miles

1 Lorenzo Bandini/Chris Amon	Ferrari 330P4	666	24h00m38.3
2 Michael Parkes/ Ludovico Scarfiotti	Ferrari 330P4	663	
3 Pedro Rodriguez/ Jean Guichet	Ferrari 412P	637	
4 Hans Herrmann/Jo Siffert	Porsche 910/6	618	
5 Dieter Spoerry/ Rico Steinemann	Porsche 906 Carrera 6	608	
6 Jacky Ickx/Dick Thompson	Ford GT40 Mk2	601	

Winner's average speed: 105.681 mph. Pole position: AJ Foyt Jr (Ford GT40 Mk2), 1m55.10. Fastest lap: Phil Hill (Chaparral 2F-Chevrolet), 1m55.69

12 hours of Sebring

1 April 1967. Sebring. 238 laps of a 5.200-mile circuit = 1237.600 miles

1 Mario Andretti/ Bruce McLaren	Ford GT40 Mk4	238	12h01m37.5
2 AJ Foyt Jr/Lloyd Ruby	Ford GT40 Mk2	226	
3 Gerhard Mitter/ Scooter Patrick	Porsche 910/6	226	
4 Hans Herrmann/Jo Siffert	Porsche 910/6	223	
5 Umberto Maglioli/ Nino Vaccarella	Ford GT40	223	
6 Dieter Spoerry/ Rico Steinemann	Porsche 906 Carrera 6	218	

Winner's average speed: 102.901 mph. Pole position: Andretti, 2m48.0. Fastest lap: Mike Spence (Chaparral 2F-Chevrolet), 2m48.6

1000 km di Monza/ Trofeo Filippo Caracciolo

25 April 1967. Monza. 100 laps of a 6.214-mile circuit = 621.370 miles

1 Chris Amon/Lorenzo Bandini	Ferrari 330P4	100	5h07m43.0
2 Ludovico Scarfiotti/ Michael Parkes	Ferrari 330P4	100	5h10m59.2
3 Gerhard Mitter/Jochen Rindt	Porsche 910/6	96	
4 Herbert Müller/ Nino Vaccarella	Ferrari 412P	95	
5 Hans Herrmann/Jo Siffert	Porsche 910/6	95	
6 Jo Schlesser/Guy Ligier	Ford GT40	95	

Winner's average speed: 121.158 mph. Pole position: Mike Spence (Chaparral 2F-Chevrolet), 2m53.8. Fastest lap: Amon, 2m55.8

1000 km de Spa-Francorchamps

1 May 1967. Spa-Francorchamps. 71 laps of a 8.761-mile circuit = 622.031 miles

1 Jacky Ickx/Dick Thompson	Mirage Mk1-		
	Ford	71	5h09m46.5
2 Jo Siffert/Hans Herrmann	Porsche 910/2	70	
3 Richard Attwood/			
Lucien Bianchi	Ferrari 412P	70	
4 Paul Hawkins/Jackie Epstein	Lola T70 Mk3-		
	Chevrolet	69	
5 Michael Parkes/			
Ludovico Scarfiotti	Ferrari 330P4	69	
6 Peter Sutcliffe/Brian Redman	Ford GT40	68	

Winner's average speed: 120.481 mph. Pole position: Phil Hill (Chaparral 2F-Chevrolet), 3m35.6. Fastest lap: Mike Spence (Chaparral 2F-Chevrolet), 4m03.5

Targa Florio

14 May 1967. Madonie (Piccolo). 10 laps of a 44.739-mile circuit = 447.390 miles

1 Paul Hawkins/			
Rolf Stommelen	Porsche 910/8	10	6h37m01.0
2 Leo Cella/Giampiero Biscaldi	Porsche 910/6	10	6h37m48.2
3 Jochen Neerpasch/Vic Elford	Porsche 910/6	10	6h41m03.8
4 Vittorio Venturi/			
Jonathan Williams	Ferrari Dino 206S Spyder	10	6h52m10.2
5 Henri Greder/			
Jean-Michel Giorgi	Ford GT40	10	7h20m36.6
6 Hans Herrmann/Jo Siffert	Porsche 910/8	9	

Winner's average speed: 67.613 mph. Fastest lap: Herbert Müller (Ferrari 330P3/4), 37m09.0

ADAC 1000 km-Rennen

28 May 1967. Nürburgring. 44 laps of a 14.189-mile circuit = 624.316 miles

1 Udo Schütz/Joe Buzzetta	Porsche 910/6	44	6h54m12.9
2 Paul Hawkins/Gerhard Koch	Porsche 910/6	44	6h54m13.1
3 Jochen Neerpasch/Vic Elford	Porsche 910/6	44	6h58m32.6
4 Gerhard Mitter/			
Lucien Bianchi	Porsche 910/8	43	
5 Andrea de Adamich/Nanni			
Galli/Roberto Bussinello/			
Teodoro Zeccoli	Alfa Romeo T33	43	
6 Hans-Dieter Dechent/	Porsche 906		
Robert Huhn	Carrera 6	42	

Winner's average speed: 90.434 mph. Pole position: Mike Spence (Chaparral 2F-Chevrolet), 8m31.9. Fastest lap: Phil Hill (Chaparral 2F-Chevrolet), 8m42.1

24 heures du Mans

10-11 June 1967. Le Mans. 388 laps of a 8.365-mile circuit = 3245.620 miles

1 Dan Gurney/AJ Foyt Jr	Ford GT40 Mk4	388	24 hours
2 Ludovico Scarfiotti/			
Michael Parkes	Ferrari 330P4	384	
3 Willy Mairesse/"Beurlys"	Ferrari 330P4	377	
4 Bruce McLaren/			
Mark Donohue	Ford GT40 Mk4	359	
5 Jo Siffert/Hans Herrmann	Porsche 907/6	358	
6 Rolf Stommelen/			
Jochen Neerpasch	Porsche 910/6	351	

Winner's average speed: 135.234 mph. Pole position: McLaren, 3m24.4. Fastest lap: Denny Hulme (Ford GT40 Mk4) and Mario Andretti (Ford GT40 Mk4), 3m23.6

BOAC 6 hours

30 July 1967. Brands Hatch. 211 laps of a 2.650-mile circuit = 559.150 miles

1 Mike Spence/Phil Hill	Chaparral 2F-		
	Chevrolet	211	6h00m26.0
2 Jackie Stewart/Chris Amon	Ferrari 330P4	211	6h01m24.6
3 Jo Siffert/Bruce McLaren	Porsche 910/8	209	
4 Hans Herrmann/			
Jochen Neerpasch	Porsche 907/8	206	
5 Ludovico Scarfiotti/			
Peter Sutcliffe	Ferrari 330P4	2066	

| 6 Paul Hawkins/ | | |
| Jonathan Williams | Ferrari 330P4 | 204 |

Winner's average speed: 93.080 mph. Pole position: Denny Hulme (Lola T70-Chevrolet), 1m36.6. Fastest lap: Hulme, 1m37.2

FINAL CHAMPIONSHIP POSITIONS

Manufacturers

1	Ferrari	34 (37)*		Mirage-Ford	9
2	Porsche	32 (41)*	6	Lola-Chevrolet	3
3	Ford	22 (23)*	7	Alfa Romeo	2
4=	Chaparral-Chevrolet	9		*Best five results count

1968

INTERNATIONAL CHAMPIONSHIP FOR MAKES

Daytona 24 hours

3-4 February 1968. Daytona. 673 laps of a 3.810-mile circuit = 2564.130 miles

1 Vic Elford/Jochen Neerpasch/			
Rolf Stommelen/Jo Siffert/			
Hans Herrmann	Porsche 907/8	673	24h01m54.7
2 Jo Siffert/Hans Herrmann	Porsche 907/8	668	
3 Joe Buzzetta/Jo Schlesser	Porsche 907/8	659	
4 Jerry Titus/Ronnie Bucknum	Ford Mustang	629	
5 Udo Schütz/Nino Vaccarella	Alfa Romeo T33	617	
6 Mario Andretti/			
Lucien Bianchi	Alfa Romeo T33	609	

Winner's average speed: 106.697 mph. Pole position: Jacky Ickx (Ford GT40), 1m54.91. Fastest lap: Ickx, time n/a

12 hours of Sebring

23 March 1968. Sebring. 237 laps of a 5.200-mile circuit = 1232.400 miles

1 Hans Herrmann/Jo Siffert	Porsche 907/8	237	12h01m19.4
2 Vic Elford/Jochen Neerpasch	Porsche 907/8	227	
3 Mark Donohue/Craig Fisher	Chevrolet Camaro	221	
4 Joseph Welch/Bob Johnson/	Chevrolet		
Craig Fisher	Camaro	217	
5 Jerry Titus/Ronnie Bucknum	Ford Mustang	217	
6 Dave Morgan/Hap Sharp/	Chevrolet Corvette		
Joe Austin	Stingray	208	

Winner's average speed: 102.512 mph. Pole position: Herrmann, 2m49.4. Fastest lap: Scooter Patrick (Lola T70 Mk3-Chevrolet), 2m49.0

BOAC 6 hours

7 April 1968. Brands Hatch. 218 laps of a 2.650-mile circuit = 577.700 miles

1 Jacky Ickx/Brian Redman	Ford GT40	218	6h01m13.0
2 Ludovico Scarfiotti/			
Gerhard Mitter	Porsche 907/8	218	6h01m35.0
3 Vic Elford/Jochen Neerpasch	Porsche 907/8	216	
4 Paul Hawkins/David Hobbs	Ford GT40	210	
5 Pedro Rodriguez/			
Roy Pierpoint	Ferrari 275LM	209	
6 Jo Bonnier/Sten Axelsson	Lola T70 Mk3-		
	Chevrolet	207	

Winner's average speed: 95.959 mph. Pole position: Jo Siffert (Porsche 907/8), 1m34.6. Fastest lap: Bruce McLaren (Ford 3L), time n/a

1000 km di Monza/ Trofeo Filippo Caracciolo

25 April 1968. Monza. 100 laps of a 6.214-mile circuit = 621.370 miles

1 Paul Hawkins/David Hobbs	Ford GT40	100	5h18m03.4
2 Rolf Stommelen/			
Jochen Neerpasch	Porsche 907/8	100	5h20m15.8

3 Patrick Depailler/	Alpine A211-		
André de Cortanze	Renault	97	
4 Gerhard Koch/Rudi Lins	Porsche 910/8	95	
5 Antonio Nicodemi/			
Carlo Facetti	Porsche 910/8	94	
6 André Wicky/			
Jean-Pierre Hanrioud	Porsche 910/8	92	

Winner's average speed: 117.219 mph. Pole position: Jacky Ickx (Ford GT40), 2m57.0. Fastest lap: Ickx, 2m56.5

Targa Florio

5 May 1968. Madonie (Piccolo). 10 laps of a 44.739-mile circuit = 447.390 miles

1 Vic Elford/Umberto Maglioli	Porsche 907/8	10	6h28m47.9
2 Nanni Galli/Ignazio Giunti	Alfa Romeo T33	10	6h31m30.7
3 Mario Casoni/Lucien Bianchi	Alfa Romeo T33	10	6h37m55.1
4 Hans Herrmann/			
Jochen Neerpasch	Porsche 907/8	10	6h38m48.7
5 Teddy Pilette/			
Rob Slotemaker	Alfa Romeo T33	10	6h55m28.8
6 Giancarlo Baghetti/			
Giampiero Biscaldi	Alfa Romeo T33	10	7h00m08.5

Winner's average speed: 69.042 mph. Fastest lap: Elford, 36m2.3

ADAC 1000 km-Rennen

19 May 1968. Nürburgring. 44 laps of a 14.189-mile circuit = 624.316 miles

1 Jo Siffert/Vic Elford	Porsche 908	44	6h34m06.3
2 Hans Herrmann/			
Rolf Stommelen	Porsche 907/8	44	6h37m07.8
3 Jacky Ickx/Paul Hawkins	Ford GT40	44	6h37m57.5
4 Jochen Neerpasch/			
Joe Buzzetta	Porsche 907/8	44	6h42m22.9
5 Nanni Galli/Ignazio Giunti	Alfa Romeo T33	43	
6 David Hobbs/Brian Redman	Ford GT40	43	

Winner's average speed: 95.048 mph. Pole position: Herrmann, 8m32.8. Fastest lap: Siffert, 8m33.0

1000 km de Spa-Francorchamps

26 May 1968. Spa-Francorchamps. 70 laps of a 8.761-mile circuit = 613.270 miles

1 Jacky Ickx/Brian Redman	Ford GT40	70	5h05m19.3
2 Gerhard Mitter/Jo Schlesser	Porsche 907/8	70	
3 Hans Herrmann/Rolf			
Stommelen/Tetsu Ikuzawa	Porsche 908	69	
4 Paul Hawkins/David Hobbs	Ford GT40	67	
5 Gerhard Koch/Rudi Lins	Porsche 910/8	67	
6 Dieter Spoerry/			
Rico Steinemann	Porsche 910/8	66	

Winner's average speed: 120.516 mph. Pole position: Frank Gardner (Ford 3L), 3m36.3. Fastest lap: Schlesser, 4m00.3

Watkins Glen 6 hours

14 July 1968. Watkins Glen. 286 laps of a 2.350-mile circuit = 672.100 miles

1 Jacky Ickx/Lucien Bianchi	Ford GT40	286	6h00m27.8
2 David Hobbs/Paul Hawkins	Ford GT40	267	
3 Dick Thompson/	Howmet TX		
Ray Heppenstall	Turbine	267	
4 Werner Frank/	Porsche 906		
Ralph Tritchmann	Carrera 6	267	
5 Jim Locke/Bob Bailey	Porsche 906		
	Carrera 6	257	
6 Hans Herrmann/			
Tetsu Ikuzawa/Jo Siffert	Porsche 908	257	

Winner's average speed: 111.873 mph. Pole position: Siffert, 1m10.2. Fastest lap: Ickx, 1m11.1

Grosser Preis von Österreich

25 August 1968. Zeltweg. 157 laps of a 1.988-mile circuit = 312.116 miles. Half points awarded because of the short race distance

1 Jo Siffert	Porsche 908	157	2h55m17.74
2 Hans Herrmann/			
Kurt Ahrens Jr	Porsche 908	157	2h55m30.23
3 Paul Hawkins	Ford GT40	152	
4 Teddy Pilette	Alfa Romeo T33	152	
5 Willi Kauhsen/			
Karl von Wendt	Porsche 910/8	147	
6 Rico Steinemann/			
Dieter Spoerry	Porsche 910/8	147	

Winner's average speed: 106.831 mph. Pole position: Siffert, 1m04.86. Fastest lap: Siffert, 1m04.82

24 heures du Mans

28-29 September 1968. Le Mans. 330 laps of a 8.369-mile circuit = 2761.770 miles

1 Pedro Rodriguez/			
Lucien Bianchi	Ford GT40	330	24 hours
2 Dieter Spoerry/			
Rico Steinemann	Porsche 907/8	325	
3 Rolf Stommelen/			
Jochen Neerpasch	Porsche 908LH	324	
4 Ignazio Giunti/Nanni Galli	Alfa Romeo		
	T33/2	321	
5 Carlo Facetti/Spartico Dini	Alfa Romeo		
	T33/2	314	
6 Mario Casoni/	Alfa Romeo		
Giampiero Biscaldi	T33/2	304	

Winner's average speed: 115.074 mph. Pole position: Jo Siffert (Porsche 908LH), 3m35.4. Fastest lap: Stommelen, 3m38.1

FINAL CHAMPIONSHIP POSITIONS

Manufacturers					
1	Ford	45 (56)*		Howmet	4
2	Porsche	42 (67.5)*	7	Ferrari	2
3	Alfa Romeo	14.5	8	Lola-Chevrolet	1
4=	Alpine-Renault	4		*Best five results count	
	Chevrolet	4			

1969

INTERNATIONAL CHAMPIONSHIP FOR MAKES

Daytona 24 hours

1-2 February 1969. Daytona. 626 laps of a 3.810-mile circuit = 2385.060 miles

1 Mark Donohue/	Lola T70 Mk3B-		
Chuck Parsons	Chevrolet	626	24h01m36.3
2 Lothar Motschenbacher/	Lola T70 Mk3B-		
Ed Leslie	Chevrolet	596	
3 Joe Ward/Jerry Titus	Pontiac Firebird	591	
4 Bruce Jennings/H Weston/			
Tony Adamowicz	Porsche 911T	583	
5 B Everett/A Johnson/			
Linley Coleman	Porsche 911	581	
6 J Gunn/Bob Beatty/	Chevron B8-		
Hubert Kleinpeter	BMW	579	

Winner's average speed: 99.267 mph. Pole position: Vic Elford (Porsche 908), 1m52.2. Fastest lap: Elford, time n/a

12 hours of Sebring

22 March 1969. Sebring. 239 laps of a 5.200-mile circuit = 1242.800 miles

1 Jacky Ickx/Jackie Oliver	Ford GT40	239	12h01m25.16
2 Chris Amon/Mario Andretti	Ferrari 312P	238	
3 Rolf Stommelen/Joe			
Buzzetta/Kurt Ahrens Jr	Porsche 908/2	235	

4 Alex Soler-Roig/Rudi Lins   Porsche 907/8   233
5 Gerhard Mitter/Udo Schütz   Porsche 908/2   232
6 Ed Leslie/   Lola T70 Mk3B-
  Lothar Motschenbacher   Chevrolet   229

Winner's average speed: 103.363 mph. Pole position: Amon, 2m40.14. Fastest lap: Siffert (Porsche 908/2), time n/a

BOAC 6 hours

13 April 1969. Brands Hatch. 227 laps of a 2.650-mile circuit = 601.550 miles

1 Jo Siffert/Brian Redman   Porsche 908/2   227   6h00m08.4
2 Vic Elford/Richard Attwood   Porsche 908/2   225
3 Gerhard Mitter/Udo Schütz   Porsche 908/2   223
4 Chris Amon/Pedro Rodriguez   Ferrari 312P   223
5 David Hobbs/Mike Hailwood   Ford GT40   207
6 Hans Herrmann/
  Rolf Stommelen   Porsche 908/2   205

Winner's average speed: 100.219 mph. Pole position: Siffert, 1m28.8. Fastest lap: Siffert, time n/a

1000 km di Monza/ Trofeo Filippo Caracciolo

25 April 1969. Monza. 100 laps of a 6.214-mile circuit = 621.400 miles

1 Jo Siffert/Brian Redman   Porsche 908LH   100   4h53m41.2
2 Hans Herrmann/
  Kurt Ahrens Jr   Porsche 908LH   99
3 Gerhard Koch/
  Hans-Dieter Dechent   Porsche 907/8   92
4 Helmut Kelleners/
  Reinhold Jöst   Ford GT40   92
5 Andrea de Adamich/   Lola T70 Mk3B-
  Frank Gardner   Chevrolet   92
6 Patrick Depailler/   Alpine A220-
  Jean-Pierre Jabouille   Renault   91   accident

Winner's average speed: 126.945 mph. Pole position: Mario Andretti (Ferrari 312P), 2m48.2. Fastest lap: Pedro Rodriguez (Ferrari 312P), 2m48.1

Targa Florio

4 May 1969. Madonie (Piccolo). 10 laps of a 44.739-mile circuit = 447.390 miles

1 Gerhard Mitter/Udo Schütz   Porsche 908/2   10   6h07m45.7
2 Vic Elford/Umberto Maglioli   Porsche 908/2   10   6h10m34.0
3 Hans Herrmann/
  Rolf Stommelen   Porsche 908/2   10   6h21m26.7
4 Karl von Wendt/
  Willi Kauhsen   Porsche 908/2   10   6h35m33.5
5 Enrico Pinto/Giovanni Alberti   Alfa Romeo T33 10   6h46m35.3
6 Gerhard Koch/
  Hans-Dieter Dechent   Porsche 907/8   9

Winner's average speed: 72.991 mph. Fastest lap: Elford, 35m08.2

1000 km de Spa-Francorchamps

11 May 1969. Spa-Francorchamps. 71 laps of a 8.761-mile circuit = 622.031 miles

1 Jo Siffert/Brian Redman   Porsche 908LH   71   4h24m19.6
2 Pedro Rodriguez/
  David Piper   Ferrari 312P   71   4h27m52.1
3 Vic Elford/Kurt Ahrens Jr   Porsche 908LH   70
4 Rolf Stommelen/
  Hans Herrmann   Porsche 908LH   67
5 Jo Bonnier/Herbert Müller   Lola T70 Mk3B-
                                Chevrolet   67
6 Teddy Pilette/Rob Slotemaker Alfa Romeo T33 65

Winner's average speed: 141.196 mph. Pole position: Paul Hawkins (Lola T70 Mk3B-Chevrolet), 3m42.5. Fastest lap: Redman, 3m37.1

ADAC 1000 km-Rennen

1 June 1969. Nürburgring. 44 laps of a 14.189-mile circuit = 624.316 miles

1 Jo Siffert/Brian Redman   Porsche 908/2   44   6h11m02.3
2 Rolf Stommelen/
  Hans Herrmann   Porsche 908/2   44   6h15m04.2
3 Vic Elford/Kurt Ahrens Jr   Porsche 908/2   44   6h16m09.8
4 Richard Attwood/Rudi Lins   Porsche 908/2   43
5 Willi Kauhsen/
  Karl von Wendt   Porsche 908/2   42
6 Helmut Kelleners/
  Reinhold Jöst   Ford GT40   41

Winner's average speed: 100.957 mph. Pole position: Siffert, 8m00.2. Fastest lap: Chris Amon (Ferrari 312P), 8m03.3

24 heures du Mans

14-15 June 1969. Le Mans. 371 laps of a 8.369-mile circuit = 3104.899 miles

1 Jacky Ickx/Jackie Oliver   Ford GT40   371   24 hours
2 Hans Herrmann/
  Gérard Larrousse   Porsche 908LH   371
3 David Hobbs/Mike Hailwood   Ford GT40   367
4 Jean-Pierre Beltoise/   Matra-Simca
  Piers Courage   MS650   367
5 Jean Guichet/   Matra-Simca
  Nino Vaccarella   MS630   358
6 Helmut Kelleners/
  Reinhold Jöst   Ford GT40   340

Winner's average speed: 129.371 mph. Pole position: Rolf Stommelen (Porsche 917LH), 3m22.9. Fastest lap: Vic Elford (Porsche 917LH), 3m27.2

Watkins Glen 6 hours

13 July 1969. Watkins Glen. 291 laps of a 2.350-mile circuit = 683.850 miles

1 Jo Siffert/Brian Redman   Porsche 908/2   291   6h01m10.0
2 Vic Elford/
  Richard Attwood/Tony Dean   Porsche 908/2   291   6h02m45.2
3 Rudi Lins/Joe Buzzetta   Porsche 908/2   282
4 Johnny Servoz-Gavin/   Matra-Simca
  Pedro Rodriguez   MS650   267
5 Helmut Kelleners/
  Reinhold Jöst   Ford GT40   265
6 Dick Smothers/   Porsche 906
  Fred Baker/Lou Sell   Carrera 6   257

Winner's average speed: 113.607 mph. Pole position: Siffert, 1m08.47. Fastest lap: Elford, 1m09.13

Grosser Preis von Österreich

10 August 1969. Österreichring. 170 laps of a 3.673-mile circuit = 624.410 miles

1 Jo Siffert/Kurt Ahrens Jr   Porsche 917   170   5h23m36.98
2 Jo Bonnier/Herbert Müller   Lola T70 Mk3B-
                                Chevrolet   170   5h24m44.13
3 Richard Attwood/
  Brian Redman   Porsche 917   169
4 Masten Gregory/
  Richard Brostrom   Porsche 908/2   168
5 Rudi Lins/Gérard Larrousse   Porsche 908/2   168
6 Karl von Wendt/
  Willi Kauhsen   Porsche 908/2   166

Winner's average speed: 115.769 mph. Pole position: Jacky Ickx (Mirage M3-Ford), 1m47.6. Fastest lap: Ickx, 1m46.6

FINAL CHAMPIONSHIP POSITIONS

Manufacturers

1	Porsche	45 (76)*	6	Pontiac	4
2	Ford	25 (26)*	7	Alfa Romeo	3
3	Lola-Chevrolet	20	8=	Alpine-Renault	1
4	Ferrari	15		Chevron-BMW	1
5	Matra-Simca	6		*Best five results count	

Sports Car World Championship

1970
INTERNATIONAL CHAMPIONSHIP FOR MAKES

Daytona 24 hours

31 January-1 February 1970. Daytona. 724 laps of a
3.810-mile circuit = 2758.440 miles

1 Pedro Rodriguez/			
Leo Kinnunen	Porsche 917	724	24h00m52.1
2 Jo Siffert/Brian Redman	Porsche 917	679	
3 Mario Andretti/Jacky Ickx/			
Arturo Merzario	Ferrari 512S	676	
4 Michael Parkes/Sam Posey	Ferrari 312P	647	
5 David Piper/Tony Adamowicz	Ferrari 312P	632	
6 Jerry Thompson/	Chevrolet		
John Mahler	Corvette	608	

Winner's average speed: 114.866 mph. Pole position: Andretti,
1m51.6. Fastest lap: Siffert, time n/a

12 hours of Sebring

21 March 1970. Sebring. 248 laps of a 5.200-mile circuit
= 1289.600 miles

1 Ignazio Giunti/Nino			
Vaccarella/Mario Andretti	Ferrari 512S	248	12h01m11.2
2 Steve McQueen/Peter Revson	Porsche 908/2	248	12h01m32.3
3 Masten Gregory/	Alfa Romeo		
Toine Hezemans	T33/3	247	
4 Pedro Rodriguez/			
Leo Kinnunen/Jo Siffert	Porsche 917	244	
5 Henri Pescarolo/	Matra-Simca		
Johnny Servoz-Gavin	MS650	242	
6 Michael Parkes/			
Chuck Parsons	Ferrari 312P	240	

Winner's average speed: 107.290 mph. Pole position: Andretti,
2m33.50. Fastest lap: Kinnunen, 2m32.77

BOAC 1000 kms

12 April 1970. Brands Hatch. 235 laps of a
2.650-mile circuit = 622.750 miles

1 Pedro Rodriguez/			
Leo Kinnunen	Porsche 917	235	6h45m29.6
2 Vic Elford/Denny Hulme	Porsche 917	230	
3 Richard Attwood/			
Hans Herrmann	Porsche 917	227	
4 Gijs van Lennep/Hans Laine	Porsche 908/2	227	
5 Chris Amon/Arturo Merzario	Ferrari 512S	225	
6 Gérard Larrousse/			
Gerhard Koch	Porsche 908/2	217	

Winner's average speed: 92.147 mph. Pole position: Amon,
1m28.6. Fastest lap: Jo Siffert (Porsche 917), time n/a

1000 km di Monza/ Trofeo Filippo Caracciolo

25 April 1970. Monza. 174 laps of a 3.573-mile circuit
= 621.702 miles

1 Pedro Rodriguez/			
Leo Kinnunen	Porsche 917	174	4h18m01.7
2 Ignazio Giunti/Nino			
Vaccarella/Chris Amon	Ferrari 512S	174	4h19m27.6
3 John Surtees/Peter Schetty	Ferrari 512S	171	
4 Chris Amon/Arturo Merzario	Ferrari 512S	171	
5 Jean-Pierre Beltoise/	Matra-Simca		
Jack Brabham	MS650	169	
6 Henri Pescarolo/	Matra-Simca		
Johnny Servoz-Gavin	MS650	169	

Winner's average speed: 144.566 mph. Pole position: Jo Siffert
(Porsche 917), 1m25.21. Fastest lap: Vic Elford (Porsche 917),
1m24.80

Targa Florio

3 May 1970. Madonie (Piccolo). 11 laps of a
44.739-mile circuit = 492.129 miles

1 Jo Siffert/Brian Redman	Porsche 908/3	11	6h35m30.0
2 Pedro Rodriguez/			
Leo Kinnunen	Porsche 908/3	11	6h37m12.5
3 Nino Vaccarella/			
Ignazio Giunti	Ferrari 512S	11	6h39m05.2
4 Gijs van Lennep/Hans Laine	Porsche 908/2	11	6h44m51.7
5 Richard Attwood/			
Bjorn Waldegaard	Porsche 908/3	11	6h45m01.6
6 Herbert Müller/			
Michael Parkes	Ferrari 512S	10	

Winner's average speed: 74.659 mph. Fastest lap: Kinnunen,
33m36.0

1000 km de Spa-Francorchamps

17 May 1970. Spa-Francorchamps. 71 laps of a
8.761-mile circuit = 622.031 miles

1 Jo Siffert/Brian Redman	Porsche 917K	71	4h09m47.8
2 Jacky Ickx/John Surtees	Ferrari 512S	71	4h12m23.3
3 Vic Elford/Kurt Ahrens Jr	Porsche 917K	70	
4 Ignazio Giunti/			
Nino Vaccarella	Ferrari 512S	68	
5 Gijs van Lennep/Hans Laine	Porsche 917K	68	
6 Richard Attwood/			
Hans Herrmann	Porsche 917K	68	

Winner's average speed: 149.409 mph. Pole position: Pedro
Rodriguez (Porsche 917), 3m19.8. Fastest lap: Rodriguez, 3m16.5

ADAC 1000 km-Rennen

31 May 1970. Nürburgring. 44 laps of a 14.189-mile circuit
= 624.316 miles

1 Vic Elford/Kurt Ahrens Jr	Porsche 908/3	44	6h05m21.2
2 Hans Herrmann/			
Richard Attwood	Porsche 908/3	44	6h10m34.8
3 John Surtees/Nino Vaccarella	Ferrari 512S	43	
4 Herbert Müller/			
Michael Parkes	Ferrari 512S	42	
5 Gérard Larrousse/			
Helmut Marko	Porsche 908/2	42	
6 Rudi Lins/Willi Kauhsen	Porsche 908/2	42	

Winner's average speed: 102.528 mph. Pole position: Jo Siffert
(Porsche 908/3), 7m43.3. Fastest lap: Pedro Rodriguez (Porsche
908/3), 7m50.4

24 heures du Mans

13-14 June 1970. Le Mans. 342 laps of a 8.369-mile circuit
= 2862.198 miles

1 Hans Herrmann/			
Richard Attwood	Porsche 917K	342	24 hours
2 Gérard Larrousse/			
Willi Kauhsen	Porsche 917LH	337	
3 Rudi Lins/	Porsche		
Helmut Marko	908/2LH	334	
4 Sam Posey/Ronnie Bucknum	Ferrari 512S	312	
5 Hughes de Fierlandt/			
Alistair Walker	Ferrari 512S	304	
6 Guy Chasseuil/			
Claude Ballot-Lena	Porsche 914/6	284	

Winner's average speed: 119.258 mph. Pole position: Vic Elford
(Porsche 917LH), 3m19.8. Fastest lap: Elford, 3m21.0

Watkins Glen 6 hours

11 July 1970. Watkins Glen. 308 laps of a 2.350-mile circuit
= 723.800 miles

1 Pedro Rodriguez/			
Leo Kinnunen	Porsche 917K	308	6h00m47.7
2 Jo Siffert/Brian Redman	Porsche 917K	308	6h01m31.9

3 Mario Andretti/			
Ignazio Giunti	Ferrari 512S	305	
4 Vic Elford/Denny Hulme	Porsche 917K	302	
5 Jacky Ickx/Peter Schetty	Ferrari 512S	299	
6 Richard Attwood/			
Kurt Ahrens Jr	Porsche 917K	295	

Winner's average speed: 120.368 mph. Pole position: Siffert, 1m06.3. Fastest lap: Rodriguez, 1m04.9

Österreichring 1000 km-Rennen

11 October 1970. Österreichring. 170 laps of a 3.673-mile circuit = 624.410 miles

1 Jo Siffert/Brian Redman	Porsche 917K	170	5h08m04.67
2 Andrea de Adamich/	Alfa Romeo		
Henri Pescarolo	T33/3	168	engine
3 Gérard Larrousse/Rudi Lins	Porsche 908/2	167	
4 Vic Elford/Richard Attwood	Porsche 917K	162	
5 Reinhold Jöst/	Porsche 908/2		
Gerhold Pankl	Special	162	
6 Niki Lauda/Peter Peter	Porsche 908/2	161	

Winner's average speed: 121.608 mph. Pole position: Pedro Rodriguez (Porsche 917K), 1m40.48. Fastest lap: Jacky Ickx (Ferrari 312S), 1m40.0

FINAL CHAMPIONSHIP POSITIONS

Manufacturers

1	Porsche	63 (87)*		4	Matra-Simca	4
2	Ferrari	37 (42)*		5	Chevrolet	1
3	Alfa Romeo	10			*Best seven results count	

1971

INTERNATIONAL CHAMPIONSHIP FOR MAKES

1000 km de la Ciudad de Buenos Aires

10 January 1971. Buenos Aires. 164 laps of a 3.709-mile circuit = 608.276 miles

1 Jo Siffert/Derek Bell	Porsche 917K	164	5h25m25.94
2 Pedro Rodriguez/			
Jackie Oliver	Porsche 917K	164	
3 Nanni Galli/Rolf Stommelen	Alfa Romeo		
	T33/3	163	
4 Andrea de Adamich/	Alfa Romeo		
Henri Pescarolo	T33/3	161	
5 José Juncadella/			
Carlos Pairetti	Ferrari 512M	155	
6 Gustave Gosselin/			
Hughes de Fierlandt	Ferrari 512S	153	

Winner's average speed: 112.148 mph. Pole position: Rodriguez, 1m52.70. Fastest lap: Siffert, 1m51.53

Daytona 24 hours

30-31 January 1971. Daytona. 688 laps of a 3.810-mile circuit = 2621.280 miles

1 Pedro Rodriguez/			
Jackie Oliver	Porsche 917K	688	24h00m13.81
2 Ronnie Bucknum/			
Tony Adamowicz	Ferrari 512S	687	
3 Mark Donohue/David Hobbs	Ferrari 512M	674	
4 Tony de Lorenzo/	Chevrolet		
Don Yenko/John Mahler	Corvette	613	
5 Luigi Chinetti Jr/Nestor Veiga	Ferrari 312P	584	
6 David Heinz/Or Costanzo	Chevrolet		
	Corvette	581	

Winner's average speed: 109.203 mph. Pole position: Donohue, 1m42.42. Fastest lap: Donohue, time n/a

12 hours of Sebring

20 March 1971. Sebring. 260 laps of a 5.200-mile circuit = 1352.000 miles

1 Vic Elford/Gérard Larrousse	Porsche 917K	260	12h01m03.77
2 Nanni Galli/	Alfa Romeo		
Rolf Stommelen	T33/3	257	
3 Andrea de Adamich/Henri	Alfa Romeo		
Pescarolo/Nino Vaccarella	T33/3	248	
4 Pedro Rodriguez/			
Jackie Oliver	Porsche 917K	248	
5 Jo Siffert/Derek Bell	Porsche 917K	244	
6 Mark Donohue/David Hobbs	Ferrari 512M	243	

Winner's average speed: 112.501 mph. Pole position: Donohue, 2m31.65. Fastest lap: Siffert, 2m30.46

BOAC 1000 kms

4 April 1971. Brands Hatch. 235 laps of a 2.650-mile circuit = 622.750 miles

1 Andrea de Adamich/	Alfa Romeo		
Henri Pescarolo	T33/3	235	6h24m32.2
2 Jacky Ickx/Clay Regazzoni	Ferrari 312BP	232	
3 Jo Siffert/Derek Bell	Porsche 917K	229	
4 Herbert Müller/René Herzog	Ferrari 512M	228	
5 José Juncadella/David Hobbs	Ferrari 512M	227	
6 Reinhold Jöst/Willi Kauhsen	Porsche 917K	221	

Winner's average speed: 97.169 mph. Pole position: Regazzoni, 1m27.4. Fastest lap: Regazzoni, time n/a

1000 km di Monza/ Trofeo Filippo Caracciolo

25 April 1971. Monza. 175 laps of a 3.573-mile circuit = 625.275 miles

1 Pedro Rodriguez/			
Jackie Oliver	Porsche 917K	175	4h14m32.6
2 Jo Siffert/Derek Bell	Porsche 917K	172	
3 Andrea de Adamich/	Alfa Romeo		
Henri Pescarolo	T33/3	169	
4 Rolf Stommelen/	Alfa Romeo		
Toine Hezemans	T33/3	168	
5 Nino Vaccarella/Toine	Alfa Romeo		
Hezemans/Rolf Stommelen	T33/3	167	
6 Herbert Müller/			
René Herzog	Ferrari 512M	165	

Winner's average speed: 147.387 mph. Pole position: Vic Elford (Porsche 917K), 1m32.93. Fastest lap: Rodriguez, 1m24.0

1000 km de Spa-Francorchamps

9 May 1971. Spa-Francorchamps. 71 laps of a 8.761-mile circuit = 622.031 miles

1 Pedro Rodriguez/			
Jackie Oliver	Porsche 917K	71	4h01m09.7
2 Jo Siffert/Derek Bell	Porsche 917K	71	4h01m10.1
3 Andrea de Adamich/	Alfa Romeo		
Henri Pescarolo	T33/3	67	
4 Reinhold Jöst/Willi Kauhsen	Porsche 917K	66	
5 Claude Ballot-Lena/			
Guy Chasseuil	Porsche 908/2	60	
6 Teddy Pilette/Gustave Gosselin	Lola T70 Mk3B-		
	Chevrolet	58	

Winner's average speed: 154.759 mph. Pole position: Bell, 3m16.0. Fastest lap: Siffert, 3m14.6

Targa Florio

16 May 1971. Madonie (Piccolo). 11 laps of a 44.739-mile circuit = 492.129 miles

1 Nino Vaccarella/	Alfa Romeo		
Toine Hezemans	T33/3	11	6h35m46.2
2 Andrea de Adamich/	Alfa Romeo		
Gijs van Lennep	T33/3	11	6h36m57.9
3 Jo Bonnier/Richard Attwood	Lola T212-Ford	11	7h00m05.2
4 Bernard Cheneviére/			
Paul Keller	Porsche 911S	10	
5 Michael Parkes/			
Peter Westbury	Lola T212-Ford	10	

6 Giulio Pucci/Dieter Schmid   Porsche 911S   10

Winner's average speed: 74.608 mph. Fastest lap: Vic Elford
(Porsche 908/3), 33m45.6

ADAC 1000 km-Rennen

**30 May 1971. Nürburgring. 44 laps of a 14.189-mile circuit
= 624.316 miles**

1 Vic Elford/Gérard Larrousse	Porsche 908/3	44	5h51m49.3
2 Pedro Rodriguez/Jo Siffert	Porsche 908/3	44	5h53m33.4
3 Helmut Marko/			
Gijs van Lennep	Porsche 908/3	44	5h53m33.5
4 Andrea de Adamich/	Alfa Romeo		
Henri Pescarolo	T33/3	44	5h56m20.0
5 Toine Hezemans/	Alfa Romeo		
Nino Vaccarella	T33/3	42	
6 Reinhold Jöst/Willi Kauhsen	Porsche 917K	40	

Winner's average speed: 106.471 mph. Pole position: Jacky Ickx
(Ferrari 312PB), 7m36.1. Fastest lap: Ickx, 7m40.8

24 heures du Mans

**12-13 June 1971. Le Mans. 396 laps of a 8.369-mile circuit
= 3314.124 miles**

1 Helmut Marko/			
Gijs van Lennep	Porsche 917K	396	24 hours
2 Herbert Müller/			
Richard Attwood	Porsche 917K	394	
3 Sam Posey/Tony Adamowicz	Ferrari 512M	365	
4 Chris Craft/David Weir	Ferrari 512M	354	
5 Bob Grossman/	Ferrari 365		
Luigi Chinetti Jr	GTB4	313	
6 Raymond Touroul/			
"André Anselme"	Porsche 911S	305	

Winner's average speed: 138.089 mph. Pole position: Pedro
Rodriguez (Porsche 917LH), 3m13.9. Fastest lap: Jackie Oliver
(Porsche 917LH), 3m18.4

Österreichring 1000 km-Rennen

**27 June 1971. Österreichring. 170 laps of a
3.673-mile circuit = 624.410 miles**

1 Pedro Rodriguez/			
Richard Attwood	Porsche 917K	170	5h04m26.01
2 Toine Hezemans/	Alfa Romeo		
Nino Vaccarella	T33/3	168	
3 Rolf Stommelen/	Alfa Romeo		
Nanni Galli	T33/3	168	
4 Marsilio Pasotti/Mario Casoni	Ferrari 512M	159	
5 "Pooky"/Ennio Bonomelli	Porsche 910	140	
6 Claude Schickentanz/			
Peter Kersten	Porsche 911S	139	

Winner's average speed: 123.063 mph. Pole position: Rodriguez,
1m39.49. Fastest lap: Rodriguez, 1m39.35

Watkins Glen 6 hours

**24 July 1971. Watkins Glen. 279 laps of a 2.430-mile circuit
= 677.970 miles**

1 Andrea de Adamich/	Alfa Romeo		
Ronnie Peterson	T33/3	279	6h00m25.063
2 Jo Siffert/Gijs van Lennep	Porsche 917K	277	
3 Derek Bell/Richard Attwood	Porsche 917K	259	
4 Vic Elford/	Alfa Romeo		
Nanni Galli	T33/3	258	
5 Alain de Cadenet/			
Lothar Motschenbacher	Ferrari 512M	253	
6 John Greenwood/	Chevrolet		
Bob Johnson	Camaro	229	

Winner's average speed: 112.864 mph. Pole position: Mark
Donohue (Ferrari 512M), 1m07.740. Fastest lap: Derek Bell
(Porsche 917K), 1m08.297

FINAL CHAMPIONSHIP POSITIONS

Manufacturers

1	Porsche	63 (85)*	4=	Chevrolet	4
2	Alfa Romeo	47 (54)*		Lola-Ford	4
3	Ferrari	24 (25)*	6	Lola-Chevrolet	1
				*Best seven results count	

1972

WORLD CHAMPIONSHIP FOR MAKES

1000 km de la Ciudad de Buenos Aires

**9 January 1972. Buenos Aires. 168 laps of a
3.709-mile circuit = 623.112 miles**

1 Ronnie Peterson/			
Tim Schenken	Ferrari 312P	168	5h45m58.22
2 Clay Regazzoni/			
Brian Redman	Ferrari 312P	168	5h48m02.97
3 Giovanni Alberti/Carlo	Alfa Romeo		
Facetti/Andrea de Adamich	T33/3	162	
4 Vic Elford/Helmut Marko	Alfa Romeo		
	T33TT/3	160	
5 José Juncadella/John Hine	Chevron		
	B19-Ford	158	
6 Juan Fernandez/			
Jorge de Bagration	Porsche 908/3	157	

Winner's average speed: 108.063 mph. Pole position: Peterson,
1m58.59. Fastest lap: Reine Wisell (Lola T280-Ford), 1m58.39

6 hours of Daytona

**6 February 1972. Daytona. 194 laps of a 3.810-mile circuit
= 739.140 miles**

1 Jacky Ickx/Mario Andretti	Ferrari 312P	194	6h01m36.4
2 Ronnie Peterson/			
Tim Schenken	Ferrari 312P	192	
3 Vic Elford/Helmut Marko	Alfa Romeo		
	T33TT/3	190	
4 Clay Regazzoni/			
Brian Redman	Ferrari 312P	179	
5 Andrea de Adamich/	Alfa Romeo		
Nanni Galli	T33/3	175	
6 Hubert Kleinpeter/			
Thomas Waugh	Lola T212-Ford	166	

Winner's average speed: 122.643 mph. Pole position: Andretti,
1m49.22. Fastest lap: Redman, time n/a

12 hours of Sebring

**25 March 1972. Sebring. 259 laps of a 5.200-mile circuit
= 1346.800 miles**

1 Jacky Ickx/Mario Andretti	Ferrari 312P	259	12h04m40.0
2 Ronnie Peterson/			
Tim Schenken	Ferrari 312P	257	
3 Toine Hezemans/	Alfa Romeo		
Nino Vaccarella	T33TT/3	233	
4 David Heinz/Bob Johnson	Chevrolet		
	Corvette	221	
5 Peter Gregg/Hurley Haywood	Porsche 911S	215	
6 Jo Bonnier/Reine Wisell/			
Gérard Larrousse	Lola T280-Ford	213	

Winner's average speed: 111.511 mph. Pole position: Andretti,
2m31.44. Fastest lap: Schenken, 2m33.80

BOAC 1000 kms

**16 April 1972. Brands Hatch. 235 laps of a
2.650-mile circuit = 622.750 miles**

1 Jacky Ickx/Mario Andretti	Ferrari 312P	235	5h55m27.5
2 Ronnie Peterson/			
Tim Schenken	Ferrari 312P	234	
3 Rolf Stommelen/	Alfa Romeo		
Peter Revson	T33TT/3	233	

4 Vic Elford/	Alfa Romeo	
Andrea de Adamich	T33TT/3	231
5 Clay Regazzoni/		
Brian Redman	Ferrari 312P	220
6 Helmut Marko/Nanni Galli	Alfa Romeo	
	T33TT/3	220

Winner's average speed: 105.118 mph. Pole position: Regazzoni, 1m26.6. Fastest lap: Ickx, Peterson and Regazzoni, 1m27.4

1000 km di Monza/ Trofeo Filippo Caracciolo

25 April 1972. Monza. 174 laps of a 3.573-mile circuit = 621.702 miles

1 Jacky Ickx/Clay Regazzoni	Ferrari 312P	174	5h52m05.6
2 Reinhold Jöst/			
Gerhard Schüller	Porsche 908/3	170	
3 Ronnie Peterson/			
Tim Schenken	Ferrari 312P	165	
4 Peter Mattli/Hervé Bayard	Porsche 907	153	
5 Ugo Locatelli/"Pal Joe"	de Tomaso		
	Pantera-Ford	147	
6 Eris Tondelli/	Chevron B19-		
Mauro Formento	Ford	129	

Winner's average speed: 105.944 mph. Pole position: Peterson, 1m24.75. Fastest lap: Peterson, 1m46.1

The champion Ferrari in 1972 driven by Jacky Ickx

1000 km de Spa-Francorchamps

7 May 1972. Spa-Francorchamps. 71 laps of a 8.761-mile circuit = 622.031 miles

1 Brian Redman/			
Arturo Merzario	Ferrari 312P	71	4h17m19.1
2 Jacky Ickx/Clay Regazzoni	Ferrari 312P	70	
3 John Hine/John Bridges	Chevron B19/21-		
	Ford	66	
4 Derek Bell/Gijs van Lennep	Mirage M6-Ford	64	
5 Gérard Larrousse/			
Hughes de Fierlandt	Lola T280-Ford	64	
6 Peter Humble/Nick May	Chevron B19/21-		
	Ford	60	

Winner's average speed: 145.042 mph. Pole position: Ickx, 3m20.4. Fastest lap: Ickx, 3m20.7

Targa Florio

21 May 1972. Madonie (Piccolo). 11 laps of a 44.739-mile circuit = 492.129 miles

1 Arturo Merzario/			
Sandro Munari	Ferrari 312P	11	6h27m48.0
2 Helmut Marko/Nanni Galli	Alfa Romeo		
	T33TT/3	11	6h28m04.9
3 Andrea de Adamich/	Alfa Romeo		
Toine Hezemans	T33TT/3	11	6h46m12.2
4 Antonio Zadra/			
Enrico Pasolini	Lola T290-Ford	10	

5 Pino Pica/Gabriele Gottifredi	Porsche 911S	10
6 Günther Steckkönig/		
Giulio Pucci	Porsche 911S	9

Winner's average speed: 76.142 mph. Fastest lap: Marko, 33m41.0

ADAC 1000 km-Rennen

28 May 1972. Nürburgring. 44 laps of a 14.189-mile circuit = 624.316 miles

1 Ronnie Peterson/			
Tim Schenken	Ferrari 312P	44	6h01m40.2
2 Brian Redman/			
Arturo Merzario	Ferrari 312P	44	6h06m09.9
3 Andrea de Adamich/	Alfa Romeo		
Helmut Marko	T33TT/3	43	
4 Derek Bell/Gijs van Lennep	Mirage M6-Ford	42	
5 John Hine/John Bridges	Chevron B21-		
	Ford	41	
6 Gérard Larrousse/Jo Bonnier	Lola T290-Ford	39	

Winner's average speed: 103.572 mph. Pole position: Peterson, 7m56.1. Fastest lap: Rolf Stommelen (Alfa Romeo T33TT/3), 7m42.2

24 heures du Mans

10-11 June 1972. Le Mans. 343 laps of a 8.476-mile circuit = 2907.268 miles

1 Henri Pescarolo/Graham Hill	Matra-Simca		
	MS670	343	24 hours
2 François Cevert/	Matra-Simca		
Howden Ganley	MS670	333	
3 Reinhold Jöst/Michel Weber/			
Mario Casoni	Porsche 908LH	324	
4 Andrea de Adamich/	Alfa Romeo		
Nino Vaccarella	T33TT/3	306	
5 Jean-Claude Andruet/Claude	Ferrari 365		
Ballot-Lena/François Migault	GTB4 Daytona	305	
6 Sam Posey/Tony Adamowicz	Ferrari 365		
	GTB4 Daytona	303	

Winner's average speed: 121.136 mph. Pole position: Cevert, 3m42.2. Fastest lap: Gijs van Lennep (Lola T280-Ford), 3m46.9

Österreichring 1000 km-Rennen

25 June 1972. Österreichring. 170 laps of a 3.673-mile circuit = 624.410 miles

1 Jacky Ickx/Brian Redman	Ferrari 312P	170	4h58m46.28
2 Helmut Marko/Carlos Pace	Ferrari 312P	169	
3 Ronnie Peterson/			
Tim Schenken	Ferrari 312P	166	
4 Arturo Merzario/			
Sandro Munari	Ferrari 312P	164	
5 Rolf Stommelen/	Chevron B21-		
Toine Hezemans	BMW	164	
6 José Juncadella/	Chevron B21-		
John Bridges	Ford	158	

Winner's average speed: 125.396 mph. Pole position: Derek Bell (Mirage M6-Ford), 1m40.60. Fastest lap: Ickx, 1m41.88

Watkins Glen 6 hours

22 July 1972. Watkins Glen. 195 laps of a 3.377-mile circuit = 658.515 miles

1 Jacky Ickx/Mario Andretti	Ferrari 312P	195	6h01m11.276
2 Ronnie Peterson/			
Tim Schenken	Ferrari 312P	195	6h01m25.300
3 Derek Bell/Carlos Pace	Mirage M6-Ford	181	
4 Tony Dean/Bob Brown	Porsche 908/2	171	
5 Reinhold Jöst/Mario Casoni	Porsche 908/3	166	
6 Jean-Pierre Jarier/	Ferrari 365		
Gregg Young	GTB4 Daytona	156	

Winner's average speed: 109.392 mph. Pole position: Schenken, 1m47.387. Fastest lap: Ickx, 1m47.204

Sports Car World Championship

FINAL CHAMPIONSHIP POSITIONS

Manufacturers

1	Ferrari	160 (208)*	8	Chevrolet	14
2	Alfa Romeo	85	9	de Tomaso-Ford	12
3	Porsche	66 (71)*	10	Chevron-BMW	8
4	Lola-Ford	48	11	Ford	5
5	Chevron-Ford	45	12	Osella-Abarth	4
6	Mirage-Ford	32	13	Lola-Alfa Romeo	3
7	Matra-Simca	20		*Best eight results count	

1973

WORLD CHAMPIONSHIP FOR MAKES

Daytona 24 hours

3-4 February 1973. Daytona. 670 laps of a
3.810-mile circuit = 2552.700 miles

1 Peter Gregg/	Porsche 911		
Hurley Haywood	Carrera RS	670	24h01m11.9
2 Milt Minter/	Ferrari 365		
François Migault	GTB4 Daytona	648	
3 David Heinz/Bob McClure	Chevrolet		
	Corvette	644	
4 George Stone/Bruce			
Jennings/Mike Downs	Porsche 911S	638	
5 Luigi Chinetti Jr/Bob	Ferrari 365		
Grossman/Wilbur Shaw Jr	GTB4 Daytona	632	
6 John Fitzpatrick/			
Erwin Kremer/Paul Keller	Porsche 911S	630	

Winner's average speed: 106.274 mph. Pole position: Derek Bell
(Mirage M6-Ford), 1m45.512. Fastest lap: Mike Hailwood
(Mirage M6-Ford), 1m49.609

6 ore di Vallelunga

25 March 1973. Vallelunga. 290 laps of a 1.988-mile circuit
= 576.520 miles

1 Henri Pescarolo/Gérard	Matra-Simca		
Larrousse/François Cevert	MS670	290	6 hours
2 Tim Schenken/			
Carlos Reutemann	Ferrari 312P	289	
3 Jacky Ickx/Brian Redman	Ferrari 312P	289	
4 Carlos Pace/Arturo Merzario	Ferrari 312P	288	
5 Reinhold Jöst/Mario Casoni	Porsche 908/3	272	
6 Reine Wisell/			
Jean-Louis Lafosse	Lola T282-Ford	268	

Winner's average speed: 96.087 mph. Pole position: Cevert,
1m08.55. Fastest lap: Schenken, 1m09.7

1000 km de Dijon

15 April 1973. Dijon-Prenois. 312 laps of a
2.044-mile circuit = 637.728 miles

1 Henri Pescarolo/	Matra-Simca		
Gérard Larrousse	MS670	312	5h34m37.1
2 Jacky Ickx/Brian Redman	Ferrari 312P	311	
3 Jean-Pierre Beltoise/	Matra-Simca		
François Cevert	MS670	308	
4 Carlos Pace/Arturo Merzario	Ferrari 312P	308	
5 Mike Hailwood/	Mirage M6-		
Vern Schuppan	Ford	303	
6 Reine Wisell/			
Jean-Louis Lafosse	Lola T282-Ford	290	

Winner's average speed: 114.350 mph. Pole position: Cevert,
59.4s. Fastest lap: Cevert, 1m00.6

1000 km di Monza/ Trofeo Filippo Caracciolo

25 April 1973. Monza. 174 laps of a 3.573-mile circuit
= 621.702 miles

1 Jacky Ickx/Brian Redman	Ferrari 312P	174	4h07m34.4
2 Tim Schenken/			
Carlos Reutemann	Ferrari 312P	171	

3 Henri Pescarolo/	Matra-Simca		
Gérard Larrousse	MS670	164	
4 Giancarlo Gagliardi/"Pooky"	Lola T290-Ford	150	
5 Carlo Facetti/"Pam"	Alfa Romeo		
	T33TT/3	149	
6 Giorgio Schön/"Pal Joe"	Lola T290-		
	Abarth	145	

Winner's average speed: 150.671 mph. Pole position: François
Cevert (Matra-Simca MS670), 1m21.13. Fastest lap: Cevert, 1m21.9

1000 km de Spa-Francorchamps

6 May 1973. Spa-Francorchamps. 71 laps of a
8.761-mile circuit = 622.031 miles

1 Derek Bell/Mike Hailwood	Mirage M6-Ford	71	4h05m43.5
2 Mike Hailwood/Vern			
Schuppan/Howden Ganley	Mirage M6-Ford	69	
3 Henri Pescarolo/Gérard	Matra-Simca		
Larrousse/Chris Amon	MS670	68	
4 Arturo Merzario/Carlos Pace	Ferrari 312P	67	
5 Gijs van Lennep/	Porsche 911		
Herbert Müller	Carrera RSR	63	
6 Carlos Santos/			
Santos Mendoza	Lola T292-Ford	62	

Winner's average speed: 151.885 mph. Pole position: Jacky Ickx
(Ferrari 312PB), 3m12.7. Fastest lap: Pescarolo, 3m13.4

Targa Florio

13 May 1973. Madonie (Piccolo). 11 laps of a
44.739-mile circuit = 492.129 miles

1 Gijs van Lennep/	Porsche 911		
Herbert Müller	Carrera RSR	11	6h54m19.9
2 Sandro Munari/			
Jean-Claude Andruet	Lancia Stratos	11	7h00m30.5
3 Leo Kinnunen/Claude Haldi	Porsche 911		
	Carrera RSR	11	7h12m42.5
4 Luigi Moreschi/	Chevron		
"Frank McBoden"	B21-Ford	11	7h17m34.4
5 Silvio Moser/	Lola T290-		
Antonio Nicodemi	Abarth	11	7h25m35.5
6 Günther Steckkönig/	Porsche 911		
Giulio Pucci	Carrera RSR	11	7h27m29.9

Winner's average speed: 71.266 mph. Fastest lap: Rolf
Stommelen (Alfa Romeo T33TT/12), 34m13.1

ADAC 1000 km-Rennen

27 May 1973. Nürburgring. 44 laps of a 14.189-mile circuit
= 624.316 miles

1 Jacky Ickx/Brian Redman	Ferrari 312P	44	5h36m53.4
2 Arturo Merzario/Carlos Pace	Ferrari 312P	44	5h36m53.5
3 John Burton/John Bridges	Chevron B23-		
	Ford	40	
4 Claude Haldi/			
Bernard Chenevière	Porsche 908/3	40	
5 Gijs van Lennep/	Porsche 911		
Herbert Müller	Carrera RSR	40	
6 John Fitzpatrick/	Ford Capri		
Gerry Birrell	RS2600	39	

Winner's average speed: 111.190 mph. Pole position: François
Cevert (Matra-Simca MS670), 7m12.8. Fastest lap: Cevert, 7m20.3

24 heures du Mans

9-10 June 1973. Le Mans. 355 laps of a 8.476-mile circuit
= 3008.980 miles

1 Henri Pescarolo/	Matra-Simca		
Gérard Larrousse	MS670B	355	24 hours
2 Arturo Merzario/Carlos Pace	Ferrari 312P	349	
3 Jean-Pierre Jabouille/	Matra-Simca		
Jean-Pierre Jaussaud	MS670B	331	
4 Gijs van Lennep/	Porsche		
Herbert Müller	Carrera RSR	328	

5 Juan Fernandez/Bernard
  Cheneviére/Paco Torredemer Porsche 908/3 319
6 Vic Elford/   Ferrari 365
  Claude Ballot-Lena   GTB4 Daytona 316

Winner's average speed: 125.374 mph. Pole position: Merzario, 3m37.5. Fastest lap: François Cevert (Matra-Simca MS670B), 3m39.6

Österreichring 1000 km-Rennen

24 June 1973. Österreichring. 170 laps of a 3.673-mile circuit = 624.410 miles

1 Henri Pescarolo/   Matra-Simca
  Gérard Larrousse   MS670   170 4h48m57.80
2 Jean-Pierre Beltoise/ Matra-Simca
  François Cevert   MS670   170 4h49m44.43
3 Jacky Ickx/Brian Redman Ferrari 312P 169
4 Mike Hailwood/John Watson Mirage M6-Ford 167
5 Derek Bell/Howden Ganley Mirage M6-Ford 166
6 Arturo Merzario/Carlos Pace Ferrari 312P 164

Winner's average speed: 129.652 mph. Pole position: Cevert, 1m37.64. Fastest lap: Cevert, 1m38.30

Watkins Glen 6 hours

21 July 1973. Watkins Glen. 199 laps of a 3.377-mile circuit = 672.023 miles

1 Henri Pescarolo/   Matra-Simca
  Gérard Larrousse   MS670   199 6h00m20.938
2 Jacky Ickx/Brian Redman Ferrari 312P 197
3 Arturo Merzario/Carlos Pace Ferrari 312P 196
4 Derek Bell/Howden Ganley Mirage M6-Ford 180
5 Mike Hailwood/John Watson Mirage M6-Ford 179
6 Mark Donohue/   Porsche
  George Follmer   Carrera RSR 178

Winner's average speed: 111.895 mph. Pole position: François Cevert (Matra-Simca MS670), 1m42.273. Fastest lap: Cevert, 1m43.847

FINAL CHAMPIONSHIP POSITIONS

Manufacturers

1	Matra-Simca	124	7	Lancia	15
2	Ferrari	115 (137)*	8	Chevrolet	14
3	Porsche	82 (91)*	9	Alfa Romeo	13
4	Mirage-Ford	48	10=	BMW	6
5	Lola-Ford/Abarth	36		Ford	6
6	Chevron-Ford	30		*Best seven results count	

1974

WORLD CHAMPIONSHIP FOR MAKES

1000 km di Monza/ Trofeo Filippo Caracciolo

25 April 1974. Monza. 174 laps of a 3.585-mile circuit = 623.840 miles

1 Arturo Merzario/   Alfa Romeo
  Mario Andretti   T33TT/12   174 4h45m57.4
2 Rolf Stommelen/   Alfa Romeo
  Jacky Ickx   T33TT/12   170
3 Carlo Facetti/   Alfa Romeo
  Andrea de Adamich   T33TT/12   166
4 Mike Hailwood/Derek Bell Mirage GR7-
                            Ford   166
5 Gijs van Lennep/   Porsche 911
  Herbert Müller   Carrera RSR 165
6 Pino Pica/Giorgio Pianta Lola T280-Ford 161

Winner's average speed: 130.896 mph. Pole position: Merzario, 1m28.26. Fastest lap: Bell, 1m31.3

1000 km de Spa-Francorchamps

5 May 1974. Spa-Francorchamps. 71 laps of a 8.761-mile circuit = 622.031 miles

1 Jacky Ickx/Jean-Pierre Jarier Matra-Simca
                                 MS670C 71 4h12m15.6

2 Mike Hailwood/Derek Bell Mirage GR7-Ford 71 4h15m10.6
3 Gijs van Lennep/   Porsche 911
  Herbert Müller   Carrera RSR 66
4 John Fitzpatrick/   Porsche 911
  Jürgen Barth   Carrera RSR 62
5 Clemens Schickentanz/   Porsche 911
  Willi Kauhsen   Carrera RSR 62
6 Paul Keller/Hans Heyer   Porsche 911
                            Carrera RSR 62

Winner's average speed: 147.950 mph. Pole position: Bell, 3m23.9. Fastest lap: Ickx, 3m19.7

ADAC 1000 km-Rennen

19 May 1974. Nürburgring. 33 laps of a 14.189-mile circuit = 468.237 miles. Race reduced in length due to the oil crisis

1 Jean-Pierre Beltoise/   Matra-Simca
  Jean-Pierre Jarier   MS670C   33 4h07m24.1
2 Rolf Stommelen/   Alfa Romeo
  Carlos Reutemann   T33TT/12   32
3 Carlo Facetti/   Alfa Romeo
  Andrea de Adamich   T33TT/12   32
4 James Hunt/
  Vern Schuppan/Derek Bell Mirage GR7-Ford 32
5 Henri Pescarolo/   Matra-Simca
  Gérard Larrousse   MS670C   31
6 Gijs van Lennep/   Porsche 911
  Herbert Müller   Carrera RSR 30

Winner's average speed: 113.557 mph. Pole position: Pescarolo, 7m10.8. Fastest lap: Jarier, 7m15.9

1000 km di Imola

2 June 1974. Imola. 198 laps of a 3.144-mile circuit = 622.512 miles

1 Henri Pescarolo/   Matra-Simca
  Gérard Larrousse   MS670C   198 6h13m36.0
2 Rolf Stommelen/   Alfa Romeo
  Carlos Reutemann   T33TT/12   196
3 Carlo Facetti/   Alfa Romeo
  Andrea de Adamich   T33TT/12   189
4 Jean-Pierre Beltoise/ Matra-Simca
  Jean-Pierre Jarier   MS670C   184
5 Paul Keller/Hans Heyer Porsche 911
                          Carrera RSR 177
6 Giovanni Borri/   Porsche 911
  Giorgio Schön   Carrera RSR 173

Winner's average speed: 99.975 mph. Pole position: Beltoise, 1m40.17. Fastest lap: Larrousse, 1m40.8

24 heures du Mans

15-16 June 1974. Le Mans. 337 laps of a 8.476-mile circuit = 2856.412 miles

1 Henri Pescarolo/   Matra-Simca
  Gérard Larrousse   MS670B   337 24 hours
2 Gijs van Lennep/   Porsche Carrera
  Herbert Müller   RSR turbo   331
3 Jean-Pierre Jabouille/ Matra-Simca
  François Migault   MS670B   324
4 Mike Hailwood/Derek Bell Mirage GR7-Ford 317
5 Cyrille Grandet/"Bardini" Ferrari 365
                             GTB4 Daytona 313
6 David Heinz/Alain Cudini Ferrari 365
                            GTB4 Daytona 312

Winner's average speed: 119.017 mph. Pole position: Pescarolo, 3m35.8. Fastest lap: Jean-Pierre Jarier (Matra-Simca MS680), 3m42.7

Österreichring 1000 km-Rennen

30 June 1974. Österreichring. 170 laps of a 3.673-mile circuit = 624.410 miles

1 Henri Pescarolo/   Matra-Simca
  Gérard Larrousse   MS670C   170 4h51m20.27
2 Carlo Facetti/   Alfa Romeo
  Andrea de Adamich   T33TT/12   167

3 Jean-Pierre Beltoise/	Matra-Simca		
Jean-Pierre Jarier	MS670C	166	
4 Mike Hailwood/Derek Bell	Mirage GR7-Ford	166	
5 Jacky Ickx/Arturo Merzario	Alfa Romeo		
	T33TT/12	152	
6 Gijs van Lennep/	Porsche 911		
Herbert Müller	Carrera RSR	151	

Winner's average speed: 128.595 mph. Pole position: Pescarolo, 1m35.97. Fastest lap: Ickx, 1m35.81

Watkins Glen 6 hours

13 July 1974. Watkins Glen. 193 laps of a 3.377-mile circuit = 651.761 miles

1 Jean-Pierre Beltoise/	Matra-Simca		
Jean-Pierre Jarier	MS670C	193	6h01m33.8
2 Gijs van Lennep/	Porsche 911		
Herbert Müller	Carrera RSR	184	
3 Peter Gregg/	Porsche 911		
Hurley Haywood	Carrera RSR	176	
4 Ludwig Heimrath/Jim Cook	Porsche 911		
	Carrera RSR	172	
5 Maurice Carter/	Chevrolet		
Tony de Lorenzo	Camaro	168	
6 Jacques Bienvenue/	Porsche 911		
Marc Dancos	Carrera RSR	164	

Winner's average speed: 108.157 mph. Pole position: Gérard Larrousse (Matra-Simca MS670C), 1m43.698. Fastest lap: Beltoise, 1m44.005

1000 km du Castellet

15 August 1974. Paul Ricard. 130 laps of a 3.610-mile circuit = 469.300 miles. Race reduced in length due to the oil crisis

1 Jean-Pierre Beltoise/	Matra-Simca		
Jean-Pierre Jarier	MS670C	130	4h10m57.7
2 Henri Pescarolo/	Matra-Simca		
Gérard Larrousse	MS670C	127	
3 Jacky Ickx/Derek Bell	Mirage GR7-Ford	125	
4 Reinhold Jöst/Mario Casoni	Porsche 908/3	119	
5 Paul Blancpain/			
Knut-Holger Lehmann	Porsche 908/3	114	
6 Guy Chasseuil/	Ligier JS2-		
François Migault	Maserati	114	

Winner's average speed: 112.200 mph. Pole position: Jarier, 1m49.1. Fastest lap: Beltoise, 1m50.6

British Airways 1000 kms

29 September 1974. Brands Hatch. 235 laps of a 2.650-mile circuit = 622.750 miles

1 Jean-Pierre Beltoise/	Matra-Simca		
Jean-Pierre Jarier	MS670C	235	5h47m33.01
2 Henri Pescarolo/	Matra-Simca		
Gérard Larrousse	MS670C	235	5h47m35.80
3 Derek Bell/David Hobbs	Mirage GR7-		
	Ford	224	
4 Peter Gethin/Brian Redman	Chevron B26-		
	Hart	224	
5 Herbert Müller/	Porsche 911		
Gijs van Lennep	Carrera RSR	219	
6 Jürgen Barth/Claude Haldi	Porsche 908/3	213	

Winner's average speed: 107.510 mph. Pole position: Beltoise, 1m23.3. Fastest lap: Jarier, 1m22.6

Kyalami 9 hours

10 November 1974. Kyalami. 235 laps of a 2.550-mile circuit = 599.250 miles. Race reduced to six hours due to the oil crisis

1 Henri Pescarolo/	Matra-Simca		
Gérard Larrousse	MS670C	235	6 hours
2 Jean-Pierre Beltoise/	Matra-Simca		
Jean-Pierre Jarier	MS670C	235	

3 Derek Bell/David Hobbs	Mirage GR7-		
	Ford	229	
4 John Lepp/Guy Tunmer	Chevron B26-		
	Ford	217	
5 Jochen Mass/	Ford Capri		
Toine Hezemans	RS3100	215	
6 Rolf Stommelen/John	Porsche 911		
Fitzpatrick/Tim Schenken	Carrera RSR	214	

Winner's average speed: 99.875 mph. Pole position: Beltoise, 1m18.03. Fastest lap: Larrousse, 1m19.3

FINAL CHAMPIONSHIP POSITIONS

Manufacturers

1	Matra-Simca	140 (180)*		Ford	8
2	Mirage-Ford	81 (91)*	11=	BMW	3
3	Porsche	76 (94)*		March-Ford	3
4	Alfa Romeo	65	13	Mazda	2
5	Chevron-Ford/Hart	30	14=	Alpine-Renault	1
6	Ligier-Maserati	12		AMS-Ford	1
7	Lola-Ford	10		Ecosse-Ford	1
8=	Chevrolet	8		*Best seven results count	
	Ferrari	8			

1975

WORLD CHAMPIONSHIP FOR MAKES

Daytona 24 hours

1-2 February 1975. Daytona. 684 laps of a 3.840-mile circuit = 2626.560 miles

1 Peter Gregg/	Porsche 911		
Hurley Haywood	Carrera RS	684	24 hours
2 Michael Keyser/Bill Sprowls/	Porsche 911		
Andreas Contreras	Carrera RS	669	
3 Charlie Kemp/Carson Baird	Porsche 911		
	Carrera RS	668	
4 George Dyer/	Porsche 911		
Jacques Bienvenue	Carrera RS	665	
5 Bill Webbe/George Dickinson/			
Harry Theodoracopulos	Porsche 911		
	Carrera RS	623	
6 John Graves/John O'Steen/	Porsche 911		
Dave Helmick	Carrera RS	619	

Winner's average speed: 109.440 mph. Pole position: John Greenwood (Chevrolet Corvette), 1m55.223. Fastest lap: Greenwood, 1m57.300

1000 km di Mugello

23 March 1975. Mugello. 150 laps of a 3.259-mile circuit = 488.850 miles. Race reduced in length due to the oil crisis

1 Gérard Larrousse/	Alpine A442-		
Jean-Pierre Jabouille	Renault	150	4h47m34.7
2 Arturo Merzario/Jacky Ickx	Alfa Romeo		
	T33TT/12	149	
3 Gijs van Lennep/			
Herbert Müller	Porsche 908/3	149	
4 Henri Pescarolo/Derek Bell	Alfa Romeo		
	T33TT/12	148	
5 John Hine/Ian Grob	Chevron B31-		
	Hart	144	
6 Lella Lombardi/	Alpine A441-		
Marie-Claude Beaumont	Renault	144	

Winner's average speed: 101.993 mph. Pole position: Merzario, 1m48.83. Fastest lap: Jabouille, 1m49.8

1000 km de Dijon

6 April 1975. Dijon-Prenois. 245 laps of a 2.044-mile circuit = 500.780 miles. Race reduced in length due to the oil crisis

1 Arturo Merzario/	Alfa Romeo		
Jacques Laffite	T33TT/12	245	4h27m28.8
2 Reinhold Jöst/Mario Casoni	Porsche 908/3T	238	

3 John Hine/Ian Grob	Chevron B31-Hart	234	
4 Henri Pescarolo/Derek Bell	Alfa Romeo T33TT/12	225	
5 Toine Hezemans/ John Fitzpatrick	Porsche 911 Carrera RS	220	
6 François Migault/ Jean-Pierre Jarier	Ligier JS2-Ford	219	

Winner's average speed: 112.333 mph. Pole position: Gérard Larrousse (Alpine A442-Renault), 1m00.9. Fastest lap: Merzario, 1m01.5

1000 km di Monza/ Trofeo Filippo Caracciolo

20 April 1975. Monza. 174 laps of a 3.592-mile circuit = 625.008 miles

1 Arturo Merzario/ Jacques Laffite	Alfa Romeo T33TT/12	174	4h43m21.8
2 Reinhold Jöst/Mario Casoni	Porsche 908/3T	171	
3 Gérard Larrousse/ Jean-Pierre Jabouille	Alpine A442-Renault	170	
4 Lella Lombardi/ Marie-Claude Beaumont	Alpine A441-Renault	166	
5 Jürgen Barth/Ernst Kraus	Porsche 908/3	162	
6 Toine Hezemans/Manfred Schurti/John Fitzpatrick	Porsche 911 Carrera RS	159	

Winner's average speed: 132.341 mph. Pole position: Jochen Mass (Mirage GR7-Ford), 1m28.94. Fastest lap: Larrousse, 1m30.2

1000 km de Spa-Francorchamps

4 May 1975. Spa-Francorchamps. 54 laps of a 8.761-mile circuit = 473.094 miles. Race reduced in length due to the oil crisis

1 Henri Pescarolo/Derek Bell	Alfa Romeo T33TT/12	54	3h32m54.4
2 Jacky Ickx/Arturo Merzario	Alfa Romeo T33TT/12	53	
3 Alain Peltier/Siegfried Müller	BMW 3.0 CSL	49	
4 Claudi Haldi/Bernard Beguin	Porsche 911 Carrera RS	48	
5 Claude Ballot-Lena/ Jean-Claude Andruet	Porsche 911 Carrera RS	48	
6 Clemens Schickentanz/ Hartwig Bertrams	Porsche 911 Carrera RS	48	

Winner's average speed: 133.324 mph. Pole position: Bell, 3m20.4. Fastest lap: Ickx, 3m25.5

Coppa Florio

18 May 1975. Enna-Pergusa. 207 laps of a 3.011-mile circuit = 623.277 miles

1 Arturo Merzario/ Jochen Mass	Alfa Romeo T33TT/12	207	5h05m25.7
2 Henri Pescarolo/Derek Bell	Alfa Romeo T33TT/12	206	
3 Reinhold Jöst/Mario Casoni	Porsche 908/3T	184	
4 Hartwig Bertrams/Reine Wisell/Clemens Schickentanz	Porsche 911 Carrera RS	182	
5 Clemens Schickentanz/Hartwig Bertrams/Reine Wisell	Porsche 911 Carrera RS	178	
6 Giancarlo Gagliardi/ "Bramen"	Chevron B31-Ford	175	

Winner's average speed: 122.440 mph. Pole position: Merzario, 1m21.76. Fastest lap: Merzario, 1m24.1

ADAC 1000 km-Rennen

1 June 1975. Nürburgring. 44 laps of a 14.189-mile circuit = 624.316 miles

1 Arturo Merzario/ Jacques Laffite	Alfa Romeo T33TT/12	44	5h41m14.1
2 Tim Schenken/ Howden Ganley	Mirage GR7-Ford	44	5h41m54.0

3 Herbert Müller/Leo Kinnunen	Porsche 908/3	43	
4 Gérard Larrousse/ Jean-Pierre Jabouille	Alpine A442-Renault	43	
5 Jürgen Barth/Ernst Kraus	Porsche 908/3	42	
6 Jochen Mass/Jody Scheckter	Alfa Romeo T33TT/12	42	

Winner's average speed: 109.775 mph. Pole position: Larrousse, 7m12.1. Fastest lap: Larrousse, 7m20.8

Österreichring 1000 km-Rennen

29 June 1975. Österreichring. 103 laps of a 3.673-mile circuit = 378.319 miles. Race stopped due to rain

1 Henri Pescarolo/Derek Bell	Alfa Romeo T33TT/12	103	3h34m50.88
2 Arturo Merzario/ Vittorio Brambilla	Alfa Romeo T33TT/12	103	3h36m13.28
3 Reinhold Jöst/Mario Casoni	Porsche 908/3T	102	
4 Jürgen Barth/Ernst Kraus	Porsche 908/3	92	
5 Dave Morgan/John Lepp	March 75S-Hart	90	
6 Manfred Mohr/ Martino Finotto	Lola T294-Ferrari	87	

Winner's average speed: 105.652 mph. Pole position: Jean-Pierre Jarier (Alpine A442-Renault), 1m36.35. Fastest lap: Jody Scheckter (Alpine A442-Renault), 1m41.21

A victory photograph for the Alfa Romeo team at the Österreichring in 1975. On the left, the winning car of Derek Bell and Henri Pescarolo

Watkins Glen 6 hours

12 July 1975. Watkins Glen. 152 laps of a 3.377-mile circuit = 513.304 miles

1 Henri Pescarolo/Derek Bell	Alfa Romeo T33TT/12	152	6h01m23.900
2 Mario Andretti/ Arturo Merzario	Alfa Romeo T33TT/12	152	6h02m43.932
3 Gérard Larrousse/ Jean-Pierre Jarier	Alpine A442-Renault	149	
4 Reinhold Jöst/Mario Casoni	Porsche 908/3T	149	
5 Robert Hagestad/ Hurley Haywood	Porsche 911 Carrera RS	143	
6 Brian Redman/Sam Posey	BMW 3.0 CSL	142	

Winner's average speed: 85.220 mph. Pole position: Jody Scheckter (Alpine A442-Renault), 1m42.890. Fastest lap: Larrousse, 1m45.956

FINAL CHAMPIONSHIP POSITIONS

Manufacturers

1	Alfa Romeo	140 (155)*	7	March-Hart	12
2	Porsche	98 (118)*	8=	Ligier-Ford	10
3	Alpine-Renault	54		Lola-Ford/Ferrari	10
4	Chevron-Ford/Hart	35	10	Ferrari	4
5	BMW	18	11	Chevrolet	2
6	Mirage-Ford	15		*Best seven results count	

1976

WORLD CHAMPIONSHIP FOR MAKES

6 ore Etienne Aigner

21 March 1976. Mugello. 174 laps of a 3.259-mile circuit = 567.066 miles

1 Jacky Ickx/Jochen Mass	Porsche 935	174	6h00m53.7
2 Bob Wollek/Hans Heyer	Porsche 935	168	
3 Leo Kinnunen/Egon Evertz	Porsche 934	162	
4 Reinhold Jöst/Jürgen Barth/			
Willi Bartels	Porsche 934	161	
5 Kenneth Leim/	Porsche		
Kurt Simonsen	Carrera RS	157	
6 Rolf Stommelen/			
Tim Schenken	Porsche 934	155	

Winner's average speed: 94.277 mph. Pole position: Ickx, 1m55.28. Fastest lap: Ickx, 1m58.7

6 ore di Vallelunga/Trofeo Ignazio Giunti

4 April 1976. Vallelunga. 269 laps of a 1.988-mile circuit = 534.772 miles

1 Jacky Ickx/Jochen Mass	Porsche 935	269	6 hours
2 Harald Grohs/Sam Posey/			
Hughes de Fierlandt	BMW 3.0 CSL	253	
3 Kenneth Leim/	Porsche		
Kurt Simonsen	Carrera RS	244	
4 John Fitzpatrick/			
Tom Walkinshaw	BMW 3.0 CSL	242	
5 Giorgio Schön/Luigi			
Tommasi/Giuseppe Bianco	Porsche 934	242	
6 Michele di Gioia/	Porsche		
Vittorio Bernasconi	Carrera RS	241	

Winner's average speed: 89.129 mph. Pole position: Ickx, 1m14.7. Fastest lap: Ickx, 1m16.9

Silverstone 6 hours

9 May 1976. Silverstone. 217 laps of a 2.932-mile circuit = 636.244 miles

1 John Fitzpatrick/			
Tom Walkinshaw	BMW 3.0 CSL	217	6 hours
2 Bob Wollek/Hans Heyer	Porsche 935	217	
3 Leo Kinnunen/Egon Evertz	Porsche 934/5	215	
4 Harald Grohs/			
Hughes de Fierlandt	BMW 3.0 CSL	213	
5 Lella Lombardi/Heinz Martin	Porsche 934	205	
6 Umberto Grano/			
Martino Finotto	Ford Escort RS	199	

Winner's average speed: 106.041 mph. Pole position: Jochen Mass (Porsche 935), 1m26.85. Fastest lap: Mass, 1m28.19

ADAC 1000 km-Rennen

30 May 1976. Nürburgring. 47 laps of a 14.189-mile circuit = 666.883 miles

1 Dieter Quester/			
Albrecht Krebs	BMW 3.0 CSL	47	6h38m20.6
2 Toine Hezemans/			
Tim Schenken	Porsche 934/5	47	6h42m14.2
3 Derek Bell/Reinhardt Stenzel/			
Helmut Kelleners	Porsche 934	46	
4 Claude Haldi/Markus Hotz	Porsche 934/5	46	
5 Gijs van Lennep/			
Hartwig Bertrams	Porsche 934/5	45	
6 Helmut Bross/			
Eberhard Sindel	Porsche 934	44	

Winner's average speed: 100.448 mph. Pole position: Manfred Schurti (Porsche 935), 7m37.7. Fastest lap: Rolf Stommelen (Porsche 935), 8m02.7

Martha 1000

27 June 1976. Österreichring. 187 laps of a 3.673-mile circuit = 686.851 miles

1 Dieter Quester/			
Gunnar Nilsson	BMW 3.0 CSL	187	6h00m16.43
2 John Fitzpatrick/			
Tom Walkinshaw	BMW 3.0 CSL	186	
3 Claude Haldi/Peter Zbinden	Porsche 934	182	
4 Derek Bell/Vern Schuppan	Porsche 935	175	
5 Girolama Capra/			
Gabriele Gottifredi	Porsche 934/5	169	
6 Norbert Neumann/			
Kalli Hufstadt	BMW 2002 Ti	166	

Winner's average speed: 114.388 mph. Pole position: Jacky Ickx (Porsche 935), 1m43.96. Fastest lap: Bell, 1m49.80

Watkins Glen 6 hours

10 July 1976. Watkins Glen. 174 laps of a 3.377-mile circuit = 587.598 miles

1 Rolf Stommelen/			
Manfred Schurti	Porsche 935	174	6h00m28.60
2 Leo Kinnunen/Egon Evertz/			
Toine Hezemans	Porsche 935	173	
3 Jacky Ickx/Jochen Mass	Porsche 935	173	
4 Peter Gregg/Hurley Haywood	BMW 3.0 CSL	170	
5 Dieter Quester/Ronnie			
Peterson/Brian Redman	BMW 3.0 CSL	166	
6 John O'Steern/Dave	Porsche		
Helmick/John Graves	Carrera RS	164	

Winner's average speed: 97.804 mph. Pole position: Mass, 1m55.249. Fastest lap: Stommelen, 1m55.53

6 heures de l'Automobile Club de France

4 September 1976. Dijon-Prenois. 310 laps of a 2.044-mile circuit = 633.640 miles

1 Jacky Ickx/Jochen Mass	Porsche 935	310	6 hours
2 Bob Wollek/Hans Heyer	Porsche 935	309	
3 Rolf Stommelen/			
Manfred Schurti	Porsche 935	303	
4 Leo Kinnunen/Egon Evertz	Porsche 935	300	
5 Claude Haldi/Herbert Müller	Porsche 934/5	297	
6 Dieter Quester/Ronnie			
Peterson/Albrecht Krebs	BMW 3.0 CSL	296	

Winner's average speed: 105.607 mph. Pole position: Peterson, 1m05.23. Fastest lap: Ickx, 1m06.84

FINAL CHAMPIONSHIP POSITIONS

Manufacturers

1	Porsche	95 (122)*	5=	Lancia	3
2	BMW	85 (92)*		MG	3
3	Ford	8		*Best five results count	
4	de Tomaso-Ford	5			

1976

WORLD CHAMPIONSHIP FOR SPORTS CARS

ADAC/Goodyear 300 km-Rennen

4 April 1976. Nürburgring. 11 laps of a 14.189-mile circuit = 156.079 miles

1 Reinhold Jöst	Porsche 908/3T	11	1h44m15.8
2 Toine Hezemans	Porsche 934*	11	1h47m24.9
3 Helmut Bross	Lola T292-BMW	11	1h47m25.3
4 Helmut Kelleners	Porsche 934*	11	1h47m44.0
5 Rolf Stommelen	Porsche 936	11	1h48m06.2
6 Stanislav Sterzel	March 75S-BMW	11	1h49m13.1

*Car ineligible for points as it was not competing in the championship. Winner's average speed: 89.818 mph. Pole position: Patrick Depailler (Alpine A442-Renault), 7m16.9. Fastest lap: Stommelen, 9m11.6

4 ore di Monza/Trofeo Filippo Caracciolo

25 April 1976. Monza. 153 laps of a 3.585-mile circuit = 548.505 miles

1 Jacky Ickx/Jochen Mass	Porsche 936	153	4h00m54.4
2 Henri Pescarolo/	Alpine A442-		
Jean-Pierre Jarier	Renault	152	
3 Jürgen Barth/Horst Godel/			
Reinhold Jöst	Porsche 908/3	132	
4 "Amphicar"/	Osella PA4-		
Armando Floridia	BMW	132	
5 Danilo Tesini/"Mici"	Osella PA4-		
	BMW	130	
6 Ermano Pettiti/	Osella PA4-		
Roby Filannino	BMW	129	

Winner's average speed: 136.610 mph. Pole position: Ickx, 1m32.33. Fastest lap: Jarier, 1m29.6

500 km di Imola/Trofeo Ignazio Giunti

23 May 1976. Imola. 100 laps of a 3.144-mile circuit = 314.400 miles

1 Jacky Ickx/Jochen Mass	Porsche 936	100	2h59m57.9
2 Arturo Merzario/	Alfa Romeo		
Vittorio Brambilla	T33SC/12	96	
3 Jürgen Barth/Horst Godel/			
Reinhold Jöst	Porsche 908/3	94	
4 Ermano Pettiti/	Osella PA4-		
Roby Filannino	BMW	93	
5 "Amphicar"/	Osella PA4-		
Armando Floridia	BMW	92	
6 Ian Bracey/	Lola T290/4-		
Tony Birchenhough	Ford	91	

Winner's average speed: 104.820 mph. Pole position: Jean-Pierre Jarier (Alpine A442-Renault), 1m40.23. Fastest lap: Jarier, 1m42.3

Coppa Florio

27 June 1976. Enna-Pergusa. 102 laps of a 3.076-mile circuit = 313.752 miles

1 Jochen Mass/Rolf Stommelen	Porsche 936	102	2h57m48.9
2 Ermano Pettiti/	Osella PA4-		
Roby Filannino	BMW	92	
3 Stanislav Sterzel/"Gimax"	March 75S-BMW	92	
4 Pasquale Barberio/	Osella PA4-		
Carlo Bilotti	BMW	90	
5 Jürgen Barth/Horst Godel	Porsche 908/3	90	
6 "Amphicar"/	Osella PA4-		
Armando Floridia	BMW	89	

Winner's average speed: 105.869 mph. Pole position: Jacques Laffite (Alpine A442-Renault), 1m35.56. Fastest lap: Jean-Pierre Jarier (Alpine A442-Renault), 1m36.0

Player's 200

22 August 1976. Mosport Park. 80 laps of a 2.459-mile circuit = 196.720 miles

1 Jackie Oliver	Shadow DN4A-		
	Chevrolet*	80	1h45m57.592
2 George Follmer	McLaren M20-		
	Chevrolet*	80	1h46m05.450
3 Jacky Ickx	Porsche 936	80	1h46m43.767
4 Patrick Depailler	Alpine A442-		
	Renault	79	
5 Vern Schuppan	Mirage GR8-Ford	77	
6 Anthony Cicale	Chevron B26-		
	Ford	75	

*Car ineligible for points as it was not competing in the championship. Winner's average speed: 111.393 mph. Pole position: Oliver, 1m15.520. Fastest lap: Oliver, 1m16.240

500 km de l'Automobile Club de France

5 September 1976. Dijon-Prenois. 152 laps of a 2.044-mile circuit = 310.688 miles

1 Jacky Ickx/Jochen Mass	Porsche 936	152	2h41m23.89
2 Patrick Depailler/	Alpine A442-		
Jacques Laffite	Renault	152	2h41m49.98
3 Jean-Pierre Jabouille/	Alpine A442-		
Jean-Pierre Jarier	Renault	148	
4 Reinhold Jöst/Jürgen Barth	Porsche 908/3T	144	
5 Xavier Lapeyre/Alain Cudini	Lola T286-Ford	144	
6 Bob Wollek/Horst Godel	Porsche 908/3	140	

Winner's average speed: 115.499 mph. Pole position: Depailler, 1m00.09. Fastest lap: Mass, 1m01.18

Salzburgring Elan Trophäe

19 September 1976. Salzburgring. 70 laps of a 2.635-mile circuit = 184.450 miles

1 Jochen Mass	Porsche 936	70	1h28m25.24
2 Reinhold Jöst	Porsche 908/3T	68	
3 Dieter Quester	Osella PA4-BMW	65	
4 Jürgen Barth	Porsche 908/3	65	
5 Eugen Strähl	Sauber C5-BMW	65	
6 Giorgio Schön	Osella Abarth		
	SEO27-BMW	63	

Winner's average speed: 125.163 mph. Pole position: Vittorio Brambilla (Alfa Romeo T33SC/12), 1m22.89. Fastest lap: Brambilla, 1m13.23

FINAL CHAMPIONSHIP POSITIONS

Manufacturers

1	Porsche	100 (140)*	7	Alfa Romeo	15
2=	Alpine-Renault	47	8	Mirage-Ford	12
	Osella-BMW	47	9=	KMW-Porsche	8
4	Lola-BMW/Ford	40		McLaren-Chevrolet	8
5	March-BMW	28		Sauber-BMW	8
6	Chevron-Chrysler/		12	Rex-Ford	6
	Ford	23	13	Cheetah-BMW	2
				*Best five results count	

1977

WORLD CHAMPIONSHIP FOR MAKES

Daytona 24 hours

5–6 February 1977. Daytona. 681 laps of a 3.840-mile circuit = 2615.040 miles

1 John Graves/Hurley	Porsche		
Haywood/Dave Helmick	Carrera RSR	681	24h02m06.174
2 Martino Finotto/Carlo			
Facetti/Romeo Camathias	Porsche 935	679	
3 Reinhold Jöst/Bob Wollek/			
Albrecht Krebs	Porsche 935	670	
4 George Dyer/Brad Frisselle	Porsche		
	Carrera RSR	663	
5 Paul Newman/Elliott Forbes-	Ferrari 365		
Robinson/Milt Minter	GTB4 Daytona	631	
6 Lyn St James/John Carusso/	Chevrolet		
Emory Donaldson	Corvette	628	

Winner's average speed: 108.801 mph. Pole position: Jochen Mass (Porsche 935), 1m48.289. Fastest lap: Jacky Ickx (Porsche 935), 1m52.004

6 ore di Mugello

20 March 1977. Mugello. 161 laps of a 3.259-mile circuit = 524.699 miles

1 Rolf Stommelen/			
Manfred Schurti	Porsche 935	161	6h00m12.5
2 Martino Finotto/Carlo			
Facetti/Romeo Camathias	Porsche 935	155	
3 Vittorio Coggiola/			
Piero Monticone	Porsche 935	154	
4 Arturo Merzario/			
Giuseppe Bianco	Porsche 934	149	
5 "Amphicar"/Luigi Moreschi	Porsche		
	Carrera RSR	147	

6 Klaus Utz/Rolf Biland   Porsche
Carrera RSR   145

Winner's average speed: 87.399 mph. Pole position: Jochen Mass (Porsche 935), 2m11.2. Fastest lap: Mass, 1m57.2

Kosset 6 hours

15 May 1977. Silverstone. 230 laps of a 2.932-mile circuit = 674.360 miles

1 Jacky Ickx/Jochen Mass	Porsche 935	230	6 hours
2 Bob Wollek/John Fitzpatrick	Porsche 935	228	
3 Rolf Stommelen/ Toine Hezemans	Porsche 935	222	
4 Ronnie Peterson/ Helmut Kelleners	BMW 320i	215	
5 Franz Konrad/Peter Hähnlein	Porsche 935	214	
6 Martino Finotto/Carlo Facetti	Porsche 935	211	

Winner's average speed: 112.393 mph. Pole position: Mass, 1m25.91. Fastest lap: Mass, 1m27.28

ADAC 1000 km-Rennen

29 May 1977. Nürburgring. 44 laps of a 14.189-mile circuit = 624.316 miles

1 Toine Hezemans/Tim Schenken/Rolf Stommelen	Porsche 935	44	5h58m30.5
2 Bob Wollek/John Fitzpatrick	Porsche 935	43	
3 Marc Surer/ Manfred Winkelhock	BMW 320i	43	
4 Franz Konrad/Paul Keller	Porsche 935	42	
5 Dieter Schornstein/ Götz von Tschirnhaus	Porsche 934/5	41	
6 Manfred Schurti/ Helmut Kelleners	Porsche 935	41	

Winner's average speed: 104.486 mph. Pole position: Jochen Mass (Porsche 935), 7m31.9. Fastest lap: Wollek, 7m40.1

Watkins Glen 6 hours

9 July 1977. Watkins Glen. 173 laps of a 3.377-mile circuit = 584.221 miles

1 Jacky Ickx/Jochen Mass	Porsche 935	173	6h01m56.685
2 George Follmer/Brett Lunger	Porsche 935	170	
3 Hurley Haywood/ Bob Hagestad	Porsche Carrera RSR	169	
4 Dick Barbour/ Johnny Rutherford	Porsche Carrera RSR	166	
5 Ted Field/Danny Ongais	Porsche 934	165	
6 Peter Gregg/Claude Ballot-Lena/John Gunn	Porsche 934	163	

Winner's average speed: 96.847 mph. Pole position: Mass, 1m52.518. Fastest lap: Mass, 1m53.277

Molson Diamond 6 hours

20 August 1977. Mosport Park. 243 laps of a 2.459-mile circuit = 597.537 miles

1 Peter Gregg/Bob Wollek	Porsche 934	243	5h59m51.288
2 Ludwig Heimrath/Paul Miller	Porsche 934	240	
3 Gilles Villeneuve/ Eddie Cheever	BMW 320i	234	
4 Bob Tullius/Brian Fuerstenau	Jaguar XJS	229	
5 John Bauer/Tom Spalding/ Elliott Forbes-Robinson	Porsche 934	227	
6 Harry Bytzek/Klaus Bytzek/ Rudy Bartling	Porsche Carrera RSR	224	

Winner's average speed: 99.630 mph. Pole position: Jacky Ickx (Porsche 935), 1m20.123. Fastest lap: Ickx, 1m21.948

Brands Hatch 6 hours

25 September 1977. Brands Hatch. 103 laps of a 2.614-mile circuit = 269.242 miles

1 Jacky Ickx/Jochen Mass	Porsche 935	103	2h44m30.8
2 Manfred Schurti/Edgar Dören	Porsche 935	101	

3 Franz Konrad/Bob Wollek/ Reinhold Jöst	Porsche 935	97	
4 Bob Wollek/Nick Faure	Porsche 935	95	
5 Eberhard Sindel/ Günther Steckkönig	Porsche 935	94	
6 Claude Haldi/ Angelo Pallavicini	Porsche 934	82	

Winner's average speed: 98.181 mph. Pole position: Ickx, 1m26.25. Fastest lap: n/a

Preis von Hessen und Württemburg

8-9 October 1977. Hockenheim. 165 laps of a 4.219 mile-circuit = 696.135 miles. Aggregate of two three-hour heats

1 Bob Wollek/John Fitzpatrick	Porsche 935-K2	165	6 hours
2 Claude Ballot-Lena/ Jean-Louis Lafosse	Porsche 935	157	
3 Marc Surer/Eddie Cheever	BMW 320i	156	
4 Claude Haldi/Werner Christmann/Bob Wollek	Porsche 935	155	
5 Volkert Merl/Peter Hähnlein/ Franz Konrad	Porsche 935	151	
6 Eberhard Sindel/ Günther Steckkönig	Porsche 934	150	

Winner's average speed: 116.023 mph. Pole position: Wollek, 2m02.0. Fastest lap: Jacky Ickx (Porsche 935), 2m03.2

6 ore di Vallelunga

23 October 1977. Vallelunga. 249 laps of a 1.988-mile circuit = 495.012 miles

1 Luigi Moreschi/"Dino"	Porsche 935	249	6h00m07.1
2 "Victor"/Piero Monticone	Porsche 935	248	
3 Marco Micangeli/ Carlo Pietromarchi	de Tomaso Pantera-Ford	241	
4 Kenneth Leim/ Lella Lombardi	Porsche Carrera RSR	240	
5 Michele di Gioia/Agazzotti	Porsche Carrera RSR	238	
6 Franco Bernabei/Gianluigi Picchi/del Fante	Porsche Carrera RSR	227	

Winner's average speed: 82.475 mph. Pole position: Carlo Facetti (Porsche 935), 1m16.23. Fastest lap: Facetti, 1m17.2

FINAL CHAMPIONSHIP POSITIONS

Manufacturers

1	Porsche	140 (180)*	6	Chevrolet	7
2	BMW	49	7=	Fiat	3
3	de Tomaso-Ford	12		Lancia	3
4	Jaguar	10	9	Ford	2
5	Ferrari	8		*Best seven results count	

1977

WORLD CHAMPIONSHIP FOR SPORTS CARS

500 km de l'Automobile Club de France

17 April 1977. Dijon-Prenois. 132 laps of a 2.361-mile circuit = 311.652 miles

1 Arturo Merzario/ Jean-Pierre Jarier	Alfa Romeo T33SC/12	132	3h02m18.4
2 "Amphicar"/ Giuseppe Virgilio	Osella PA5-BMW	125	
3 Alain de Cadenet/Ernst Berg	Lola T290/4-Ford	123	
4 Giovanni Bordima/ Ermanno Pettiti	Osella PA5-BMW	122	
5 Michel Pignard/ Jean-Louis Bos/Fred Stalder	Chevron B36-Chrysler	119	
6 Sandro Plastina/Mario Luini/ Jean-Pierre Pochon	Cheetah G601-BMW	116	

Winner's average speed: 102.570 mph. Pole position: Vittorio Brambilla (Alfa Romeo T33SC/12), 1m16.21. Fastest lap: Merzario, 1m17.4

500 km di Monza/Trofeo Filippo Caracciolo

24 April 1977. Monza. 85 laps of a 3.604-mile circuit
= 306.340 miles

1 Vittorio Brambilla	Alfa Romeo		
	T33SC/12	85	2h40m06.0
2 Giorgio Francia/Artina	Osella PA5-BMW	84	
3 Danilo Tesini/"Gianfranco"	Osella PA5-BMW	81	
4 Peter Hoffmann	McLaren M8F-		
	Chevrolet	81	
5 Luigi Colzani/Gabriele Ciuti	Osella PA4-BMW	80	
6 Giorgio Schön/"Pal Joe"	Osella PA5-BMW	79	

Winner's average speed: 114.803 mph. Pole position: Brambilla, 1m42.53. Fastest lap: Arturo Merzario (Alfa Romeo T33SC/12), 1m45.8

Trofeo Ignazio Giunti/400 km di Vallelunga

29 May 1977. Vallelunga. 125 laps of a 1.988-mile circuit
= 248.500 miles

1 Vittorio Brambilla	Alfa Romeo		
	T33SC/12	125	2h36m17.2
2 Arturo Merzario	Alfa Romeo		
	T33SC/12	124	
3 Giorgio Francia	Osella PA5-		
	BMW	123	
4 Claudio Francisci	Chevron B31-		
	Ford	120	
5 "Amphicar"/Luigi Moreschi	Osella PA5-		
	BMW	119	
6 Danilo Tesini/"Gianfranco"	Osella PA5-		
	BMW	118	

Winner's average speed: 95.402 mph. Pole position: Brambilla, 1m10.8. Fastest lap: Brambilla, 1m12.2

Coppa Florio

19 June 1977. Enna-Pergusa. 100 laps of a
3.076-mile circuit = 307.600 miles

1 Arturo Merzario	Alfa Romeo		
	T33SC/12	100	2h57m40.2
2 Eugen Strähl/Peter Bernhard	Sauber C5-BMW	97	
3 Giampaolo Ceraolo/			
Pasquale Anastasio	Osella PA5-Ford	94	
4 Fabio Siliprandi/Castro	Chevron B36-		
	Ford	89	
5 Corrado Manfredini/			
Mario Casoni	Lola T294-Ford	88	
6 Adelino Zenone/De Bartoli	Osella PA4-BMW	88	

Winner's average speed: 103.878 mph. Pole position: Merzario, 1m35.7. Fastest lap: Merzario, 1m39.1

Grande Premio Costa del Sol

10 July 1977. Estoril. 89 laps of a 2.703-mile circuit
= 240.567 miles

1 Arturo Merzario	Alfa Romeo		
	T33SC/12	89	2h30m56.68
2 Vittorio Brambilla	Alfa Romeo		
	T33SC/12	89	2h30m56.79
3 Spartaco Dini/	Alfa Romeo		
Giorgio Francia	T33SC/12	86	
4 Chris Craft	Lola T296-Ford	84	
5 Eugen Strähl/Peter Bernhard	Sauber C5-BMW	82	
6 Ian Bracey/			
Tony Birchenhough	Lola T290/4-Ford	73	

Winner's average speed: 95.625 mph. Pole position: Merzario, 1m38.43. Fastest lap: Brambilla, 1m37.73

500 km du Castellet

24 July 1977. Paul Ricard. 150 laps of a 2.028-mile circuit
= 304.200 miles

1 Arturo Merzario/	Alfa Romeo		
Jean-Pierre Jarier	T33SC/12	150	3h23m14.9

2 Jorg Obermoser/	Toj SC302-		
Pierre-François Rousselot	Ford	148	
3 Jean-Pierre Jaussaud/	Chevron B31-		
Jacques Henry	Chrysler	145	
4 Tony Charnell/Robin Smith	Chevron B31-		
	Ford	144	
5 Eugen Strähl/Peter Bernhard	Sauber C5-BMW	142	
6 Georges Morand/Frederick			
Alliot/Christian Blanc	Lola T296-Ford	141	

Winner's average speed: 89.801 mph. Pole position: Vittorio Brambilla (Alfa Romeo T33SC/12), 1m15.50. Fastest lap: Brambilla, 1m17.30

250 km di Imola

4 September 1977. Imola. 50 laps of a 3.144-mile circuit
= 157.200 miles

1 Vittorio Brambilla	Alfa Romeo		
	T33SC/12	50	1h29m43.5
2 Giorgio Francia	Osella PA5-BMW	49	
3 Lella Lombardi/			
Giovanni Anzeloni	Osella PA5-BMW	47	
4 Francesco Cerulli-Irelli	AMS 277-Ford	47	
5 Renzo Zorzi/	Chevron B36-		
Giuseppe Piazzi	BMW	47	
6 Duilio Ghislotti/			
Romeo Camathias	Lola T296-BMW	46	

Winner's average speed: 105.121 mph. Pole position: Brambilla, 1m41.73. Fastest lap: Arturo Merzario (Alfa Romeo T33SC/12), 1m43.4

Salzburger Festspielpreis

18 September 1977. Salzburgring. 70 laps of a
2.635-mile circuit = 184.450 miles

1 Vittorio Brambilla	Alfa Romeo		
	T33SC/12	70	1h27m26.79
2 Arturo Merzario	Alfa Romeo		
	T33SC/12	69	
3 Spartaco Dini/	Alfa Romeo		
Giorgio Francia	T33SC/12	68	
4 Guy Edwards/Ray Mallock	Lola T296-Ford	65	
5 Herbert Müller	March 75S-BMW	64	

No other finishers. Winner's average speed: 126.557 mph. Pole position: Brambilla, 1m12.65. Fastest lap: Brambilla, 1m12.45

FINAL CHAMPIONSHIP POSITIONS

Manufacturers

1	Alfa Romeo	120 (160)*	7	AMS-Ford	15
2	Osella-BMW/Ford	73	8	McLaren-Chevrolet	13
3=	Lola-Ford/BMW	43	9	March-BMW	8
	Chevron-Chrysler/		10=	Cheetah-BMW	6
	Ford	43		Porsche	6
5	Sauber-BMW	31		*Best six results count	
6	Toj-Ford	17			

1978

WORLD CHAMPIONSHIP FOR MAKES

Daytona 24 hours

4-5 February 1978. Daytona. 680 laps of a 3.840-mile
circuit = 2611.200 miles

1 Rolf Stommelen/Toine			
Hezemans/Peter Gregg	Porsche 935	680	24h00m45.4
2 Dick Barbour/Johnny			
Rutherford/Manfred Schurti	Porsche 935	650	
3 Diego Febles/Alec Poole	Porsche		
	Carrera RSR	645	
4 Bonky Fernandez/	Porsche		
John Paul/Phil Currin	Carrera RSR	637	
5 "John Winter"/Dieter			
Schornstein/Josef Brambring	Porsche 935	635	

6 Steve Earle/Bob Akin/   Porsche
Rick Knoop   Carrera RSR   632

Winner's average speed: 108.743 mph. Pole position: Danny
Ongais (Porsche 935). Fastest lap: Stommelen, 1m51.845

6 ore di Mugello

**19 March 1978. Mugello. 176 laps of a 3.259-mile circuit
= 573.584 miles**

1	Toine Hezemans/ John Fitzpatrick/Hans Heyer	Porsche 935	176	6h01m49.4
2	Franz Konrad/Reinhold Jöst/ Volkert Merl	Porsche 935	175	
3	Dieter Quester/Derek Bell	BMW 320i	174	
4	Claude Haldi/Herbert Müller	Porsche 935	174	
5	Martino Finotto/ Carlo Facetti	Porsche 935	174	
6	Bo Emanuelsson/ Anders Olofsson	BMW 320i	174	

Winner's average speed: 95.116 mph. Pole position: Fitzpatrick,
1m55.42. Fastest lap: Hezemans, 1m56.9

4 heures de Dijon

**16 April 1978. Dijon-Prenois. 169 laps of a
2.361-mile circuit = 399.009 miles**

1	Bob Wollek/Henri Pescarolo	Porsche 935	169	4h00m55.85
2	John Fitzpatrick/Hans Heyer	Porsche 935	166	
3	Giorgio Francia/ Eddie Cheever	BMW 320i	165	
4	Bo Emanuelsson/ Ingvar Carlsson	BMW 320i	165	
5	Jean-Louis Lafosse/ Claude Ballot-Lena	Porsche 935	162	
6	Dieter Schornstein/ "John Winter"	Porsche 935	157	

Winner's average speed: 99.367 mph. Pole position: Toine
Hezemans (Porsche 935), 1m20.44. Fastest lap: Hezemans, 1m21.70

Silverstone 6 hours

**14 May 1978. Silverstone. 235 laps of a 2.932-mile circuit
= 689.020 miles**

1	Jacky Ickx/Jochen Mass	Porsche 935	235	6 hours
2	Bob Wollek/Henri Pescarolo	Porsche 935	228	
3	Harald Grohs/Eddy Joosen	BMW 320i	219	
4	Freddy Kottulinsky/ Markus Hotz	BMW 320i	219	
5	Dieter Schornstein/ "John Winter"/Bob Wollek	Porsche 935	218	
6	Franz Konrad/Volkert Merl	Porsche 935	202	

Winner's average speed: 114.837 mph. Pole position: Ickx,
1m22.38. Fastest lap: Mass, 1m23.88

ADAC 1000 km-Rennen

**28 May 1978. Nürburgring. 44 laps of a 14.189-mile circuit
= 624.316 miles. Aggregate of two 22-lap heats**

1	Klaus Ludwig/Hans Heyer/ Toine Hezemans	Porsche 935	44	5h55m46.6
2	Jacky Ickx/Manfred Schurti	Porsche 935	44	5h56m45.2
3	Bob Wollek/Henri Pescarolo	Porsche 935	44	6h01m03.2
4	Franz Konrad/Volkert Merl/ Ralf-Dieter Schreiber	Porsche 935	44	6h05m09.3
5	Reinhold Jöst/Jürgen Barth	Porsche 935	44	6h06m24.4
6	Hans-Joachim Stuck/ Markus Hottinger	BMW 320i	44	6h07m53.2

Winner's average speed: 105.288 mph. Pole position: Hezemans,
7m36.2. Fastest lap: not published

6 ore di Misano

**25 June 1978. Misano. 261 laps of a 2.167-mile circuit
= 565.587 miles**

1	Bob Wollek/Henri Pescarolo	Porsche 935	261	6h00m56.6
2	Franz Konrad/Volkert Merl	Porsche 935	255	
3	Vittorio Coggiola/ Piero Monticone	Porsche 935	257	
4	Harald Grohs/Patrick Neve	BMW 320i	255	
5	Dieter Quester/ Wolfgang Wolf	BMW 320i	246	
6	Freddy Kottulinsky/ Markus Hotz	BMW 320i	240	

Winner's average speed: 94.018 mph. Pole position: Wollek,
1m16.64. Fastest lap: John Fitzpatrick (Porsche 935), 1m18.3

Watkins Glen 6 hours

**8 July 1978. Watkins Glen. 146 laps of a 3.377-mile circuit
= 493.042 miles**

1	Toine Hezemans/John Fitzpatrick/Peter Gregg	Porsche 935	146	6h01m54.999
2	Dick Barbour/Manfred Schurti/Rolf Stommelen	Porsche 935	146	6h02m25.132
3	Hans-Joachim Stuck/ Dieter Quester	BMW 320i	138	
4	Hal Shaw Jr/Monte Shelton	Porsche 935	136	
5	Chris Cord/Jim Adams	Chevrolet Monza*	132	
6	Otis Chandler/John Thomas Jr	Porsche 935	132	

*Car ineligible for points. Winner's average speed: 81.738 mph.
Pole position: Stommelen. Fastest lap: Fitzpatrick, 1m54.700

6 ore di Vallelunga

**3 September 1978. Vallelunga. 267 laps of a
1.988-mile circuit = 530.796 miles**

1	Bob Wollek/Henri Pescarolo	Porsche 935	267	6h01m00.4
2	Toine Hezemans/Hans Heyer/John Fitzpatrick	Porsche 935	267	6h02m21.6
3	Klaus Ludwig/John Fitzpatrick/Toine Hezemans	Porsche 935	266	
4	Marc Surer/ Freddy Kottulinsky	BMW 320i	261	
5	Carlo Facetti/Piercarlo Ghinzani/Luigi Moreschi	Porsche 935	254	
6	Dieter Schornstein/ "John Winter"	Porsche 935	247	

Winner's average speed: 88.219 mph. Pole position: Jacky Ickx
(Porsche 935). Fastest lap: Ickx, 1m15.4

FINAL CHAMPIONSHIP POSITIONS

Manufacturers

1	Porsche	120 (160)*	5	Chevrolet	2
2	BMW	68 (74)*	6	Fiat	1
3=	Ferrari	3		*(Best six results count)	
	de Tomaso-Ford	3			

1979

WORLD CHAMPIONSHIP FOR MAKES

Pepsi-Cola Daytona 24 hours

**3-4 February 1979. Daytona. 684 laps of a
3.840-mile circuit = 2626.560 miles**

1	Danny Ongais/ Hurley Haywood/Ted Field	Porsche 935	684	24h00m24.87
2	John Morton/ Tony Adamowicz	Ferrari 365 GTB4 Daytona	635	
3	Rick Mears/Bruce Canepa/ Monte Shelton	Porsche 935	627	
4	Don Whittington/Jürgen Barth/Bill Whittington	Porsche 935	622	
5	Yoshimi Katayama/ Yojiro Terada/Takashi Yorino	Mazda RX-7	617	
6	Walt Bohren/Jim Downing/ Roger Manderville	Mazda RX-7	615	

Winner's average speed: 109.409 mph. Pole position: Carlo Facetti (Porsche 935), 1m46.113. Fastest lap: Bob Wollek/Jacky Ickx/Peter Gregg (Porsche 935), 1m49.477 (Daytona did not publish who was driving when time was set)

6 ore di Mugello

18 March 1979. Mugello. 138 laps of a 3.259-mile circuit = 449.742 miles

1 John Fitzpatrick/Manfred Schurti/Bob Wollek	Porsche 935	138	5h15m47.5
2 Bob Wollek/Jacky Ickx/ Manfred Schurti	Porsche 935	136	
3 Carlo Facetti/Martino Finotto	Porsche 935	136	
4 Giorgio Francia/ Lella Lombardi	Osella PA6-BMW	133	
5 Angelo Pallavicini/ Marco Vanoli	Porsche Carrera RSR	122	
6 Enzo Calderari/ Willi Spavetti	Porsche Carrera RSR	120	

Winner's average speed: 85.450 mph. Pole position: Francia, 1m52.97. Fastest lap: Facetti, 1m57.9

6 heures de Dijon

22 April 1979. Dijon-Prenois. 255 laps of a 2.361-mile circuit = 602.055 miles

1 Reinhold Jöst/Volkert Merl/ Mario Ketterer	Porsche 908/4	255	6h00m03.4
2 Jacky Ickx/Bob Wollek/ Manfred Schurti	Porsche 935	251	
3 Dieter Schornstein/ Edgar Dören	Porsche 935	239	
4 Claude Haldi/Herbert Lowe	Porsche 935	235	
5 Peter Hähnlein/Franz Gschwender/Klaus Boehm	Porsche 935	232	
6 Mario Luini/Philippe Roux/ Philippe Jeanneret	Cheetah G501-Ford	232	

Winner's average speed: 100.327 mph. Pole position: Jöst, 1m17.77. Fastest lap: Jöst, 1m18.6

Rivet Supply 6 hours

6 May 1979. Silverstone. 228 laps of a 2.932-mile circuit = 668.496 miles

1 John Fitzpatrick/Bob Wollek/ Hans Heyer	Porsche 935	228	6 hours
2 Alain de Cadenet/ François Migault	de Cadenet LM-Ford	221	
3 Dieter Schornstein/ Edgar Dören	Porsche 935	216	
4 Jean-Pierre Delauney/ Cyril Grandet	Porsche Carrera RSR	209	
5 Manfred Schurti/ John Fitzpatrick/Bob Wollek	Porsche 935	209	
6 Peter Zbinden/Eddi Kofel	Porsche 934	209	

Winner's average speed: 111.416 mph. Pole position: Jochen Mass (Porsche 936), 1m20.13. Fastest lap: Mass, 1m23.25

ADAC 1000 km-Rennen

3 June 1979. Nürburgring. 44 laps of a 14.189-mile circuit = 624.316 miles

1 Manfred Schurti/ John Fitzpatrick/Bob Wollek	Porsche 935	44	5h57m35.1
2 Klaus Ludwig/ Axel Plankenhorn	Porsche 935-K3	44	5h57m46.8
3 Henri Pescarolo/ Brian Redman	Porsche 935	43	
4 Dieter Schornstein/Edgar Dören/Götz von Tschirnhaus	Porsche 935	43	
5 Volkert Merl/Derek Bell/ Rolf Stommelen	Porsche 935	41	
6 Eckhart Schimpf/Hans-Georg Bürger/Anton Fischaber	BMW 320i	41	

Winner's average speed: 104.755 mph. Pole position: Stommelen, 7m32.2. Fastest lap: Stommelen, 7m41.9

24 heures du Mans

9-10 June 1979. Le Mans. 306 laps of a 8.467-mile circuit = 2590.902 miles

1 Klaus Ludwig/Bill Whittington/ Don Whittington	Porsche 935-K3	306	24 hours
2 Rolf Stommelen/ Dick Barbour/Paul Newman	Porsche 935	299	
3 Laurent Ferrier/François Servanin/François Trisconi	Porsche 935	292	
4 Angelo Pallavicini/Herbert Müller/Marco Vanoli	Porsche 934	291	
5 Bernard Darniche/ Jean Ragnotti	Rondeau M379-Ford	287	
6 Hervé Poulain/Marcel Mignot/ Manfred Winkelhock	BMW M1 Coupé	284	

Winner's average speed: 107.954 mph. Pole position: Bob Wollek (Porsche 936), 3m30.07. Fastest lap: Jacky Ickx (Porsche 936), 3m36.01

Coppa Florio

24 June 1979. Enna-Pergusa. 180 laps of a 3.076-mile circuit = 553.680 miles

1 Lella Lombardi/ Enrico Grimaldi	Osella PA7-BMW	180	6h01m35.6
2 Riccardo Patrese/ Carlo Facetti	Lancia Beta Monte Carlo	179	
3 Angelo Pallavicini/ Marco Vanoli	Porsche Carrera RSR	177	
4 Daniel Brillat/ Jean-Pierre Aeschlimann	Cheetah G601-BMW	176	
5 Felice Besenzoni/ Luciano del Ben	Ferrari 308 GTB	173	
6 Veninata/Cascone	Osella PA6-Ford	170	

Winner's average speed: 98.908 mph. Pole position: Patrese, 1m39.52. Fastest lap: Lombardi, 1m42.5

Watkins Glen 6 hours

7 July 1979. Watkins Glen. 175 laps of a 3.377-mile circuit = 590.975 miles

1 Don Whittington/Klaus Ludwig/Bill Whittington	Porsche 935-K3	175	6h00m10.238
2 Rolf Stommelen/Dick Barbour/Paul Newman	Porsche 935	171	
3 Rob McFarlin/Bob Akin/ Roy Woods	Porsche 935	170	
4 Elliott Forbes-Robinson/Randy Townsend/Brett Lunger	Porsche 935	169	
5 John Paul/Al Holbert	Porsche 935	167	
6 Bob Tullius/Brian Fuerstenau	Triumph TR8	162	

Winner's average speed: 98.449 mph. Pole position: Stommelen, 1m50.354. Fastest lap: Stommelen, 1m54.763

Rivet Supply 6 hours

5 August 1979. Brands Hatch. 231 laps of a 2.614-mile circuit = 603.834 miles

1 Reinhold Jöst/Volkert Merl	Porsche 908/4	231	6h00m04.1
2 Klaus Ludwig/ Axel Plankenhorn	Porsche 935-K3	229	
3 Tony Charnell/ Martin Raymond	Chevron B36-Ford	220	
4 Dieter Schornstein/ Edgar Dören	Porsche 935	218	
5 Riccardo Patrese/ Walter Rohrl	Lancia Beta Monte Carlo	214	
6 Alain de Cadenet/ François Migault	de Cadenet LM-Ford	212	

Winner's average speed: 100.605 mph. Pole position: Jöst, 1m26.67. Fastest lap: n/a

Sports Car World Championship

Trofeo Ignazio Giunti/6 ore di Vallelunga

16 September 1979. Vallelunga. 265 laps of a
1.988-mile circuit = 526.820 miles

1 Lella Lombardi/	Osella PA7-		
Giorgio Francia	BMW	265	6h00m15.15
2 Enzo Coloni/Pasquale	Osella PA6-		
Barberio/Gerardo Vatielli	BMW	261	
3 "Gero"/"Robin Hood"	Osella PA3-Ford	250	
4 Marc Surer/Laurent Ferrier	Chevron B36-		
	Chrysler	248	
5 "Torre"/"Rocca"	Osella PA7-		
	BMW	245	
6 Luigi Moreschi/"Amphicar"	Osella PA7-		
	BMW	245	

Winner's average speed: 87.742 mph. Pole position: Coloni,
1m12.65. Fastest lap: Maurizio Flammini (Chevron B36-BMW),
1m13.8

FINAL CHAMPIONSHIP POSITIONS

Manufacturers - over 2000 cc		Manufacturers - 2000 cc	
1 Porsche	140 (180)*	1 Lancia	50
2 Ferrari	30	2 BMW	32
3 de Tomaso-Ford	6	3= Ford	30
4 Triumph	4	Porsche	30
5 BMW	1	5 Fiat	20
*Best seven results count		6 Volkswagen	6
		7 Audi	2

Manufacturers - overall	
1 Porsche	

1980

WORLD CHAMPIONSHIP FOR MAKES

Daytona 24 hours

2-3 February 1980. Daytona. 715 laps of a
3.840-mile circuit = 2745.600 miles

1 Rolf Stommelen/Reinhold			
Jöst/Volkert Merl	Porsche 935	715	24h01m13.33
2 John Paul/Al Holbert/			
Preston Henn	Porsche 935-K3	682	
3 Ted Field/Danny Ongais/			
Milt Minter	Porsche 935-K3	664	
4 Maurice Carter/Craig Carter/	Chevrolet		
Murray Edwards	Camaro	636	
5 Bill Koll/Jim Cook/			
Greg Lacava	Porsche 914/6	632	
6 Tony Garcia/Alberto	Porsche		
Vadia Jr/Terry Herman	Carrera RSR	630	

Winner's average speed: 114.303 mph. Pole position: Don
Whittington (Porsche 935), 1m44.110. Fastest lap: Bill Whittington/
Don Whittington/Dale Whittington (Porsche 935), 1m47.964

Daily Mail Brands Hatch 6 hours

16 March 1980. Brands Hatch. 147 laps of a
2.614-mile circuit = 384.258 miles

1 Riccardo Patrese/	Lancia Beta		
Walter Rohrl	Monte Carlo	147	3h51m57
2 Eddie Cheever/	Lancia Beta		
Michele Alboreto	Monte Carlo	146	
3 Alain de Cadenet/	de Cadenet		
Desiré Wilson	LM-Ford	145	
4 Martino Finotto/	Lancia Beta		
Carlo Facetti	Monte Carlo	143	
5 Dudley Wood/John Cooper/			
Peter Lovett	Porsche 935-K3	139	
6 Adrian Yates-Smith/			
Barrie Williams	Porsche 911SC	135	

Winner's average speed: 99.383 mph. Pole position: Reinhold
Jöst (Porsche 908/3), 1m25.42. Fastest lap: n/a

6 ore di Mugello

13 April 1980. Mugello. 177 laps of a 3.259-mile circuit
= 576.843 miles

1 Riccardo Patrese/	Lancia Beta		
Eddie Cheever	Monte Carlo	177	6h01m07.7
2 Michele Alboreto/	Lancia Beta		
Walter Rohrl	Monte Carlo	176	
3 Mario Gallo/"Gimax"	Osella PA8-BMW	173	
4 Martino Finotto/	Lancia Beta		
Carlo Facetti	Monte Carlo	171	
5 Gerardo Vatielli/			
Paolo Giangrosso	Osella PA7-Ford	170	
6 Didier Pironi/Dieter Quester	BMW M1	167	

Winner's average speed: 95.840 mph. Pole position: Vittorio
Brambilla (Osella PA8-BMW), 1m51.77. Fastest lap: Brambilla,
1m53.8

6 ore di Monza/Trofeo Filippo Caracciolo

27 April 1980. Monza. 183 laps of a 3.604-mile circuit
= 659.532 miles

1 Alain de Cadenet/	de Cadenet		
Desiré Wilson	LM-Ford	183	6h01m08.8
2 Henri Pescarolo/Jürgen Barth	Porsche 935	183	6h01m18.7
3 Riccardo Patrese/	Lancia Beta		
Walter Rohrl	Monte Carlo	182	
4 Dieter Schornstein/			
Harald Grohs	Porsche 935	180	
5 Eddie Cheever/	Lancia Beta		
Piercarlo Ghinzani	Monte Carlo	176	
6 Ruggero Parpinelli/	Osella PA6-		
Silvano Frisori	Ford	170	

Winner's average speed: 109.570 mph. Pole position: Renzo
Zorzi (Coporferri-Ford). Fastest lap: Zorzi, 1m48.6

Silverstone 6 hours

11 May 1980. Silverstone. 234 laps of a 2.932-mile circuit
= 686.088 miles

1 Alain de Cadenet/	de Cadenet		
Desiré Wilson	LM-Ford	234*	6 hours
2 Jürgen Barth/Siegfried Brunn	Porsche 908/3	234	
3 John Paul/Brian Redman/			
John Paul Jr	Porsche 935-K3	232	
4 Michele Alboreto/	Lancia Beta		
Walter Rohrl	Monte Carlo	231	
5 Dieter Schornstein/			
Harald Grohs	Porsche 935	227	
6 Edgar Dören/Jürgen Lässig/			
Gerhard Holup	Porsche 935-K3	224	

*Includes a one lap penalty for missing the Woodcote chicane.
Winner's average speed: 114.348 mph. Pole position: John
Fitzpatrick (Porsche 935), 1m22.09. Fastest lap: Fitzpatrick, 1m25.53

ADAC 1000 km-Rennen

25 May 1980. Nürburgring. 44 laps of a 14.189-mile circuit
= 624.316 miles

1 Rolf Stommelen/Jürgen Barth	Porsche 908/4	44	5h52m15.1
2 John Fitzpatrick/Axel			
Plankenhorn/Dick Barbour	Porsche 935-K3	44	5h52m56.0
3 Hans-Joachim Stuck/			
Nelson Piquet	BMW M1	44	5h53m10.2
4 Riccardo Patrese/	Lancia Beta		
Hans Heyer	Monte Carlo	44	5h55m48.0
5 Bob Wollek/Manfred Schurti	Porsche 935-K3	44	5h56m24.9
6 Eddie Cheever/	Lancia Beta		
Piercarlo Ghinzani	Monte Carlo	43	

Winner's average speed: 106.341 mph. Pole position:
Stommelen, 7m26.0. Fastest lap: Fitzpatrick, 7m34.3

24 heures du Mans

14-15 June 1980. Le Mans. 338 laps of a 8.467-mile circuit
= 2861.846 miles

1 Jean-Pierre Jaussaud/	Rondeau		
Jean Rondeau	M379B-Ford	338	24 hours
2 Jacky Ickx/Reinhold Jöst	Porsche 936/80	336	
3 Jean-Michel Martin/Philippe	Rondeau		
Martin/Gordon Spice	M379B-Ford	329	
4 Guy Fréquelin/	WM P79/80-		
Roger Dorchy	Peugeot	318	
5 John Fitzpatrick/Brian			
Redman/Dick Barbour	Porsche 935-K3	317	
6 Jürgen Barth/Manfred	Porsche		
Schurti/Eberhard Braun	924 Carrera	316	

Winner's average speed: 119.244 mph. Pole position:
Fitzpatrick, 3m40.2. Fastest lap: Ickx, 3m40.6

Watkins Glen 6 hours

5 July 1980. Watkins Glen. 139 laps of a 3.377-mile circuit
= 469.403 miles

1 Riccardo Patrese/Hans Heyer	Lancia Beta		
	Monte Carlo	139	6h02m15.3
2 Eddie Cheever/	Lancia Beta		
Michele Alboreto	Monte Carlo	138	
3 John Fitzpatrick/			
Brian Redman	Porsche 935-K3	134	
4 Ted Field/Danny Ongais	Porsche 935-K3	133	
5 Jürgen Barth/Volkert Merl	Porsche 935-K3	133	
6 Martino Finotto/	Lancia Beta		
Piercarlo Ghinzani	Monte Carlo	133	

Winner's average speed: 77.747 mph. Pole position: Bobby
Rahal (Porsche 935-K3), 1m51.638. Fastest lap: n/a

Molson Canadian 1000

17 August 1980. Mosport Park. 245 laps of a
2.459-mile circuit = 602.455 miles

1 John Fitzpatrick/			
Brian Redman	Porsche 935-K3	245	6h00m11.807
2 John Paul/John Paul Jr	Porsche 935-K3	245	6h01m31.000
3 Ted Field/Danny Ongais/			
Bobby Rahal	Porsche 935-K3	244	
4 Hans Heyer/Walter Rohrl	Lancia Beta		
	Monte Carlo	241	
5 Rick Mears/			
Skeeter McKitterick	Porsche 935	237	
6 Bob Akin/Paul Miller/			
Kees Nierop	Porsche 935	234	

Winner's average speed: 100.354 mph. Pole position:
Fitzpatrick, 1m20.015. Fastest lap: Ongais, 1m19.96

6 ore di Vallelunga

7 September 1980. Vallelunga. 271 laps of a
1.988-mile circuit = 538.748 miles

1 Giorgio Francia/	Osella		
Roberto Marazzi	PA8-BMW	271	6h01m13.5
2 Siegfried Brunn/Derek Bell	Porsche 908/3	267	
3 Riccardo Patrese/	Lancia Beta		
Eddie Cheever	Monte Carlo	266	
4 S Frisoli/Ruggero Bardinelli	Osella PA7-		
	Ford	263	
5 Edgar Dören/Jürgen Lässig	Porsche 935	262	
6 Claudio Francisci/"Gimax"	Osella PA8-		
	BMW	262	

Winner's average speed: 89.487 mph. Pole position: Francia,
1m12.06. Fastest lap: Vittorio Brambilla (Osella PA8-BMW), 1m15.1

1000 km de Dijon

28 September 1980. Dijon-Prenois. 180 laps of a 2.361-mile
circuit = 424.980 miles . Race stopped early

1 Henri Pescarolo/Jürgen Barth	Porsche 935	180	4h25m35.23
2 Claude Haldi/Bernard Beguin	Porsche 935	178	
3 Christian Justice/	Chevron B35-		
Victor Chéli	Ford	177	

4 John Cooper/Dudley Wood	Porsche 935	173
5 Nino del Bello/René Boccard	Lola T298-	
	Simca	172
6 François Servanin/		
Laurent Ferrier	BMW M1	172

Winner's average speed: 96.009 mph. Pole position: Vittorio
Brambilla (Osella PA8-BMW), 1m18.62. Fastest lap: n/a

1981

WORLD CHAMPIONSHIP FOR MAKES

Pepsi-Cola Daytona 24 hours

31 January-1 February 1981. Daytona. 708 laps of a
3.840-mile circuit = 2718.720 miles

1 Bob Garretson/Bobby Rahal/	Porsche		
Brian Redman	935-K3	708	24h01m36.871
2 Bob Akin/Derek Bell/			
Craig Siebert	Porsche 935	695	
3 William Koll/Jeff Kline/			
Rob McFarlin	Porsche 911SC	644	
4 Frank Carney/Dick			
Davenport/Rameau Johnson	Datsun ZX	626	
5 Carlo Facetti/Martino	Lancia Beta		
Finotto/Emanuele Pirro	Monte Carlo	609	
6 Hans-Joachim Stuck/Alf			
Gebhardt/Walter Brun	BMW M1	608	

Winner's average speed: 113.153 mph. Pole position: Rolf
Stommelen (Porsche 935), 1m43.104. Fastest lap: Facetti, 1m48.14

Coca-Cola 12 hours of Sebring

21 March 1981. Sebring. 245 laps of a 5.200-mile circuit
= 1274.000 miles

1 Bruce Leven/Hurley			
Haywood/Al Holbert	Porsche 935	245	12h00m49.855
2 Roy Woods/Ralph Kent-	Porsche		
Cooke/Skeeter McKitterick	935-K3	242	
3 Marty Hinze/Milt Minter/			
Bill Whittington	Porsche 935	240	
4 Howard Meister/Rolf			
Stommelen/Harald Grohs	Porsche 935	233	
5 Chuck Kendall/	Porsche		
Pete Smith/Dennis Aase	Carrera RSR	218	
6 Gianpiero Moretti/Charles			
Mendez/Mauricio de Narvaez	Porsche 935	213	

Winner's average speed: 106.044 mph. Pole position: John
Fitzpatrick (Porsche 935), 2m28.675. Fastest lap: John Paul Jr
(Porsche 935), 2m28.65

6 ore di Mugello

12 April 1981. Mugello. 177 laps of a 3.259-mile circuit
= 576.843 miles

1 Lella Lombardi/	Osella		
Giorgio Francia	PA9-BMW	177	6h00m24.74
2 John Cooper/Dudley Wood	Porsche 935-K3	168	
3 Anton Fischaber/			
Mario Ketterer	BMW 320i	160	

Sports Car World Championship

4 Christian Bussi/
Jacques Guérin   Porsche 935   160
5 François Servanin/Laurent Ferrier/
Pierre-François Rousselot   BMW M1   160
6 Mario Benusiglio/   Osella
Luigi de Angelis   PA8-Ford   160

Alboreto/Ghinzani (Lancia Beta Monte Carlo) finished third but were disqualified as the gearbox casing had been changed during the race. Winner's average speed: 96.031 mph. Pole position: Francia, 1m52.57. Fastest lap: Alboreto, 1m56.79

1000 km di Monza/ Trofeo Filippo Caracciolo

26 April 1981. Monza. 173 laps of a 3.604-mile circuit = 623.492 miles

1 Edgar Dören/Jürgen Lässig/
Gerhard Holup   Porsche 935-K3 173   6h33m49.09
2 Lella Lombardi/   Osella
Giorgio Francia   PA9-BMW   172
3 "Gimax"/Luigi Moreschi   Osella PA9-BMW 171
4 Teo Fabi/Dieter Quester   BMW M1   170
5 Siegfried Brunn/
Eddie Jordan   Porsche 908/4   170
6 François Servanin/Laurent Ferrier/
Pierre-François Rousselot   BMW M1   167

Winner's average speed: 94.989 mph. Pole position: Carlo Facetti (Ferrari 308GTB), 1m46.69. Fastest lap: Harald Grohs (Porsche 935), 2m01.8

Los Angeles Times/ Toyota 6 hour Grand Prix of Endurance

26 April 1981. Riverside. 199 laps of a 3.250-mile circuit = 646.750 miles

1 John Fitzpatrick/Jim Busby   Porsche 935-K3 199 6h00m46.114
2 John Paul/John Paul Jr   Porsche 935   199 6h01m19.098
3 Bobby Rahal/Brian Redman   Porsche 935-K3 197
4 Bob Garretson/Roy Woods/
Ralph Kent-Cooke   Porsche 935-K3 190
5 Hurley Haywood/Bruce Leven Porsche 935   189
6 David Hobbs/Marc Surer   BMW M1C   188

Winner's average speed: 107.563 mph. Pole position: Paul Jr, 1m38.090. Fastest lap: Paul Jr, 1m40.710

Silverstone 6 hours

10 May 1981. Silverstone. 205 laps of a 2.932-mile circuit = 601.060 miles

1 Dieter Schornstein/
Harald Grohs/Walter Rohrl   Porsche 935   205   6 hours
2 Derek Bell/Steve O'Rourke/
David Hobbs   BMW M1   203
3 Siegfried Brunn/Eddie Jordan   Porsche 908/3   203
4 Lella Lombardi/   Osella
Giorgio Francia   PA9-BMW   200
5 Edgar Dören/Jürgen Lässig   Porsche 935   199
6 Bob Akin/Bobby Rahal/
Peter Lovett   Porsche 935-K3 198

Winner's average speed: 100.177 mph. Pole position: Jochen Mass (Porsche 908/80), 1m21.32. Fastest lap: Jordan, 1m26.02

ADAC 1000 km-Rennen

24 May 1981. Nürburgring. 17 laps of a 14.189-mile circuit = 241.213 miles. Race stopped early due to Herbert Müller's fatal accident, half points awarded

1 Hans-Joachim Stuck/
Nelson Piquet   BMW M1   17   2h16m50.86
2 Reinhold Jöst/Jochen Mass   Porsche 908/80   17   2h17m10.85
3 Bob Wollek   Porsche 935-K3   17   2h18m15.59

4 Hans Heyer/   Lancia Beta
Piercarlo Ghinzani   Monte Carlo   17   2h18m18.70
5 Edgar Dören/Jürgen Lässig   Porsche 935   17   2h21m05.72
6 Volkert Merl/Jürgen Barth   Porsche 908/4   16

Winner's average speed: 105.758 mph. Pole position: Manfred Winkelhock (Ford Capri), 7m31.01. Fastest lap: Mass, 7m33.53

24 heures du Mans

13-14 June 1981. Le Mans. 354 laps of a 8.467-mile circuit = 2997.318 miles

1 Jacky Ickx/Derek Bell   Porsche 936/81 354   24 hours
2 Jacky Haran/Jean-Louis
Schlesser/Philippe Streiff   Rondeau
    M379C-Ford   340
3 Gordon Spice/
François Migault   Rondeau
    M379C-Ford   335
4 John Cooper/Dudley Wood/
Claude Bourgoignie   Porsche 935-K3 330
5 Claude Ballot-Lena/Jean-Claude
Andruet/Hervé Regout   Ferrari 512BB   328
6 Anny-Charlotte Verney/Ralph
Kent-Cooke/Bob Garretson   Porsche 935-K3 327

Winner's average speed: 124.888 mph. Pole position: Ickx, 3m29.44. Fastest lap: Hurley Haywood (Porsche 936/81), 3m34.0

Coppa Florio/6 ore Enna-Pergusa

28 June 1981. Enna-Pergusa. 202 laps of a 3.076-mile circuit = 621.352 miles

1 Guy Edwards/
Emilio de Villota   Lola T600-Ford 202   6h00m51.92
2 Giorgio Francia/   Osella
Lella Lombardi   PA9-BMW   200
3 "Gimax"/Luigi Moreschi   Osella
    PA9-BMW   194
4 Edgar Dören/
Angelo Pallavicini   Porsche 934   178
5 Duilio Truffo/Fabrizio Violati Ferrari 512BB   173
6 Enrico Uncini/   Osella
Gabriele Ciuti   PA7-BMW   169

Winner's average speed: 103.310 mph. Pole position: Carlo Facetti (Ferrari 308GTB), 1m36.08. Fastest lap: de Villota, 1m38.45

Daytona 6 hours/ Champion Spark Plug Challenge

5 July 1981. Daytona. 152 laps of a 3.840-mile circuit = 583.680 miles

1 Roger Manderville/
Amos Johnson   Mazda RX-3   152 6h00m29.730
2 Jim Downing/Tom Waugh   Mazda RX-3   152 6h00m45.550
3 Jack Dunham/
Hurley Haywood   Mazda RX-3   147
4 Fred Stiff/VJ Elmore   Mazda RX-3   145
5 Chuck Ulinski/ML Speer/
Ray Ratcliff   Mazda RX-3   145
6 Jim Nealon/Bill Jobe   Mazda RX-3   145

Winner's average speed: 97.146 mph. Pole position: Hoerr, 2m14.272. Fastest lap: Downing, 2m16.620

Watkins Glen 6 hours

12 July 1981. Watkins Glen. 173 laps of a 3.377-mile circuit = 584.221 miles

1 Riccardo Patrese/
Michele Alboreto   Monte Carlo   173 6h00m28.053
2 Andrea de Cesaris/   Lancia Beta
Henri Pescarolo   Monte Carlo   171
3 Rick Mears/Johnny
Rutherford/Bob Garretson   Porsche 935-K3 168
4 John Fitzpatrick/Jim Busby   Porsche 935-K3 160
5 Preston Henn/Marty Hinze/
Dale Whittington   Porsche 935-K3 157

6 Gianpiero Moretti/
Bobby Rahal   Porsche 935   157

Winner's average speed: 97.240 mph. Pole position: Bill
Whittington (Porsche 935-K3), 1m48.583. Fastest lap:
John Paul Jr (Porsche 935), 1m52.831

24 heures de Spa-Francorchamps

**25-26 July 1981. Spa-Francorchamps. 456 laps of a
4.332-mile circuit = 1975.392 miles**

1 Pierre Dieudonné/			
Tom Walkinshaw	Mazda RX-7	456	24 hours
2 Eddy Joosen/			
Jean-Claude Andruet	BMW 530i	454	
3 Vince Woodman/			
Jonathan Buncombe	Ford Capri	453	
4 Jean Xhenceval/Daniel			
Herregods/Umberto Grano	BMW 530i	451	
5 Marc Duez/Jeff Allam/			
Chuck Nicholson/Win Percy	Mazda RX-7	445	
6 Holman Blackburn/			
Bob Akin/John Morrison	Ford Capri	435	

Winner's average speed: 82.308 mph. Pole position: Claude
Bourgoignie (Chevrolet Camaro), 2m51.25. Fastest lap:
Dieudonné/Walkinshaw, 2m54.5

Molson 1000

**16 August 1981. Mosport Park. 229 laps of a
2.459-mile circuit = 563.111 miles**

1 Rolf Stommelen/			
Harald Grohs	Porsche 935	229	6h00m43.972
2 Brian Redman/			
Eppie Wietzes	Lola T600-Chevrolet	229	6h01m06.708
3 Ted Field/Bill Whittington	Porsche 935-K3	222	
4 Preston Henn/Edgar Dören	Porsche 935-K3	219	
5 Dave Cowart/Kenper Miller	BMW M1	218	
6 John Fitzpatrick/Jim Busby	Porsche 935-K3	218	

Winner's average speed: 93.665 mph. Pole position: Stommelen,
1m18.956. Fastest lap: Bill Whittington, 1m20.657

Pabst 500 miles

**23 August 1981. Elkhart Lake. 125 laps of a
4.000-mile circuit = 500.000 miles**

1 Rolf Stommelen/			
Harald Grohs	Porsche 935	125	4h44m35.380
2 Brian Redman/Sam Posey	Lola T600-Chevrolet	125	4h45m26.000
3 Chris Cord/Jim Adams	Lola T600-Chevrolet	121	
4 Bob Garretson/Tom Gloy	Porsche 935-K3	119	
5 Gianpiero Moretti/			
Bobby Rahal	Porsche 935	118	
6 John Fitzpatrick/Jim Busby	Porsche 935-K3	118	

Winner's average speed: 105.415 mph. Pole position: Stommelen,
2m08.359. Fastest lap: John Paul Jr (Porsche 935), 2m10.25

Flying Tigers 1000

**27 September 1981. Brands Hatch. 238 laps of a
2.614-mile circuit = 622.132 miles**

1 Guy Edwards/			
Emilio de Villota	Lola T600-Ford	238	6h13m32.0
2 Bob Garretson/Bobby Rahal	Porsche 935-K3	230	
3 Derek Bell/Chris Craft	BMW M1	227	
4 John Cooper/Dudley Wood	Porsche 935-K3	226	
5 Lella Lombardi/			
Giorgio Francia	Osella PA9-BMW	226	
6 Dieter Schornstein/			
Harald Grohs	Porsche 935	221	

Winner's average speed: 99.917 mph. Pole position: Manfred
Winkelhock (Ford C100), 1m25.5. Fastest lap: n/a

FINAL CHAMPIONSHIP POSITIONS

Drivers		Manufacturers - over		
1 Bob Garretson	132	**2000 cc**		
2 Harald Grohs	116.5	1 Porsche	100 (107.5)*	
3 Derek Bell	113	2 BMW	52	
4= Giorgio Francia	101	3 Ferrari	18	
Lella Lombardi	101	4 Lancia	6	
6 Bobby Rahal	98	5 Morgan	2	
7 Edgar Dören	97.5	*Best five results count		
8 Bob Akin	89			
9 Brian Redman	85	**Manufacturers - 2000 cc**		
10 Hurley Haywood	75	1 Lancia	100 (110)*	
11= John Cooper	72.5	2 BMW	22.5	
Dudley Wood	72.5	3 Opel	6	
13 Fred Stiff	71.5	4 Ford	4	
14 Lee Mueller	63	5 Toyota	3	
15 Rolf Stommelen	60	6 Porsche	2	
16= Amos Johnson	59	7 Audi	1.5	
Roger Mandeville	59	*Best five results count		
Bill Whittington	59			
19= Michele Alboreto	58	**Manufacturers - overall**		
David Hobbs	58	1 Lancia		

1982

WORLD ENDURANCE CHAMPIONSHIP

1000 km di Monza/ Trofeo Filippo Caracciolo

**18 April 1982. Monza. 173 laps of a 3.604-mile circuit
= 623.492 miles**

1 Henri Pescarolo/Giorgio			
Francia/Jean Rondeau	Rondeau M382C-Ford	173	5h33m56.2
2 Rolf Stommelen/Ted Field	Porsche 935-K3	172	
3 Gabriele Ciuti/Mario			
Benusiglio/Giulio Piazzi	Osella PA7-BMW	167	
4 Volkert Merl/			
Dieter Schornstein	Porsche 935	167	
5 Mario Casoni/Joe Castellano/	Lancia Beta		
Mark Thatcher	Monte Carlo	163	
6 Guy Fréquelin/Roger Dorchy/	WM P82-		
Jean-Daniel Raulet	Peugeot	162	

Winner's average speed: 112.023 mph. Pole position: Riccardo
Patrese (Lancia LC1), 1m39.91. Fastest lap: Patrese, 1m44.3

Pace Petroleum 6 hours

**16 May 1982. Silverstone. 240 laps of a 2.932-mile circuit
= 703.680 miles**

1 Riccardo Patrese/			
Michele Alboreto	Lancia LC1	240	6h00m15.42
2 Jacky Ickx/Derek Bell	Porsche 956	237	
3 Jean-Michel Martin/Philippe			
Martin/Bob Wollek	Porsche 936C	231	
4 Giorgio Francia/			
Duilio Truffo	Osella PA9-BMW	228	
5 Henri Pescarolo/			
Gordon Spice	Rondeau M382C-Ford	227	
6 Ray Mallock/Mike Salmon	Nimrod NRA/C2-Aston Martin	227	

Winner's average speed: 117.196 mph. Pole position: Ickx,
1m16.91. Fastest lap: Patrese/Alboreto, 1m21.18

ADAC 1000 km-Rennen

**30 May 1982. Nürburgring. 44 laps of a 14.189-mile circuit
= 624.316 miles**

1 Riccardo Patrese/			
Michele Alboreto/Teo Fabi	Lancia LC1	44	5h54m10.83
2 Henri Pescarolo/			
Rolf Stommelen	Rondeau M382C-Ford	43	
3 Helmut Kelleners/Enzo			
Calderari/Umberto Grano	BMW M1	41	

4 Mario Ketterer/Anton		
Fischaber/Eckart Schimpf	BMW 320i	39
5 Richard Lloyd/Tony Dron/	Porsche 924	
Hans Volker	Carrera GTR	39
6 Armin Hahne/Heinz Becker	Mazda RX-7	39

Winner's average speed: 105.762 mph. Pole position: Klaus Ludwig (Ford C100), 7m16.57. Fastest lap: Manfred Winkelhock (Ford C100), 7m23.97

24 heures du Mans

19-20 June 1982. Le Mans. 359 laps of a 8.467-mile circuit = 3039.653 miles

1 Jacky Ickx/Derek Bell	Porsche 956	359	24 hours
2 Jochen Mass/Vern Schuppan	Porsche 956	356	
3 Hurley Haywood/			
Al Holbert/Jürgen Barth	Porsche 956	355	
4 John Fitzpatrick/David Hobbs	Porsche 935-K4	329	
5 Dany Snobeck/François			
Servanin/René Metge	Porsche 935-K3	325	
6 Pierre Dieudonné/Carson			
Baird/Jean-Paul Libert	Ferrari 512BB	322	

Winner's average speed: 126.652 mph. Pole position: Ickx, 3m28.40. Fastest lap: Jean Ragnotti (Rondeau M382C-Ford), 3m36.90

Trophée Diners Club/ 1000 km de Spa-Francorchamps

5 September 1982. Spa-Francorchamps. 144 laps of a 4.332-mile circuit = 623.808 miles

1 Jacky Ickx/Jochen Mass	Porsche 956	144	6h06m04.14
2 Derek Bell/Vern Schuppan	Porsche 956	141	
3 Riccardo Patrese/Teo Fabi	Lancia LC1	140	
4 Jean-Michel Martin/			
Philippe Martin	Porsche 936C	134	
5 François Migault/	Rondeau		
Gordon Spice	M382C-Ford	133	
6 Giorgio Francia/	Osella		
Luigi Moreschi	PA9-BMW	132	

Winner's average speed: 102.244 mph. Pole position: Ickx, 2m15.12. Fastest lap: Michele Alboreto (Lancia LC1), 2m21.18

Trofeo Banca Toscana

19 September 1982. Mugello. 191 laps of a 3.259-mile circuit = 622.469 miles

1 Michele Alboreto/			
Piercarlo Ghinzani	Lancia LC1	191	6h18m40.05
2 Corrado Fabi/			
Alessandro Nannini	Lancia LC1	191	6h20m12.21
3 Bob Wollek/Hans Heyer/			
Henri Pescarolo	Porsche 936C	184	
4 Giorgio Francia/	Osella		
Luigi Moreschi	PA9-BMW	175	
5 Walter Brun/Sigi Müller Jr	Sauber C6-Ford	175	
6 Dieter Schornstein/			
Volkert Merl/Bob Wollek	Porsche 935	175	

Winner's average speed: 98.630 mph. Pole position: Riccardo Patrese (Lancia LC1), 1m45.29. Fastest lap: Teo Fabi and Piercarlo Ghinzani (both Lancia LC1), 1m47.88

Fuji 6 hours

3 October 1982. Fuji. 260 laps of a 2.672-mile circuit = 694.720 miles

1 Jacky Ickx/Jochen Mass	Porsche 956	260	6h00m41.05
2 Riccardo Patrese/Teo Fabi	Lancia LC1	258	
3 Masakazu Nakamura/	March 75S-		
Kiyashi Misaki	BMW	243	
4 Naoki Nagasaka/			
Fumiyasu Sato	BMW M1	238	
5 Kaoru Hoshino/Nobuhide			
Tachi/Aguri Suzuki	Toyota Celica C	234	

6 Tom Walkinshaw/Takashi			
Yorino/Masanori Sekiya	Mazda 254i	228	

Winner's average speed: 115.567 mph. Pole position: Michele Alboreto (Lancia LC1), 1m12.39. Fastest lap: n/a

Shell Oils 1000 kms

17 October 1982. Brands Hatch. 211 laps of a 2.614-mile circuit = 551.470 miles. Race stopped due to heavy rain after nine laps. Restarted over 202 laps, aggregate result

1 Jacky Ickx/Derek Bell	Porsche 956	211	5h35m01.6
2 Riccardo Patrese/Teo Fabi	Lancia LC1	211	5h35m06.3
3 David Hobbs/			
John Fitzpatrick/Bob Wollek	Porsche 935-K4	202	
4 Jonathan Palmer/			
Desiré Wilson	Ford C100	201	
5 Marc Surer/Klaus Ludwig/			
Manfred Winkelhock	Ford C100	200	
6 John Paul Jr/Frank Jelinski	Kremer CK5-		
	Porsche	198	

Winner's average speed: 98.763 mph. Pole position: Surer, 1m27.50. Fastest lap: Ickx, 1m21.00

FINAL CHAMPIONSHIP POSITIONS

Drivers

1	Jacky Ickx	95
2	Riccardo Patrese	87
3	Derek Bell	70
4	Teo Fabi	66
5	Michele Alboreto	63
6	Henri Pescarolo	61
7	Jochen Mass	55
8	Giorgio Francia	49
9=	Vern Schuppan	30
	Rolf Stommelen	30
11	Bob Wollek	24
12=	John Fitzpatrick	22
	David Hobbs	22
	Jean-Michel Martin	22
	Philippe Martin	22
16	Piercarlo Ghinzani	21
17	Luigi Moreschi	18
18	Hans Heyer	17

19=	Corrado Fabi	16
	Volkert Merl	16
	Alessandro Nannini	16
	Dieter Schornstein	16
	Gordon Spice	16

Drivers who changed cars during a race ineligible for points

Manufacturers

1	Porsche	75
2	Rondeau-Ford	62
3	Nimrod-	
	Aston Martin	24
4	WM-Peugeot	21
5=	Ford	10
	Sauber-Ford	10
7	Lola-Ford	3

1983

WORLD ENDURANCE CHAMPIONSHIP

1000 km di Monza/ Trofeo Filippo Caracciolo

10 April 1983. Monza. 173 laps of a 3.604-mile circuit = 623.492 miles

1 Bob Wollek/Thierry Boutsen	Porsche 956	173	5h12m06.9
2 Jacky Ickx/Jochen Mass	Porsche 956	173	5h13m19.8
3 Rolf Stommelen/Hans Heyer/			
Clemens Schickentanz	Porsche 956	170	
4 Axel Plankenhorn/			
Jürgen Barth/Jürgen Lässig	Porsche 956	163	
5 John Fitzpatrick/David Hobbs	Porsche 956	161	
6 Jan Lammers/Tiff Needell/			
Richard Lloyd	Porsche 956	161	

Winner's average speed: 119.855 mph. Pole position: Piercarlo Ghinzani (Lancia LC2), 1m35.86. Fastest lap: Fitzpatrick, 1m40.4

Grand Prix International 1000 kms

8 May 1983. Silverstone. 212 laps of a 2.932-mile circuit = 621.584 miles

1 Derek Bell/Stefan Bellof	Porsche 956	212	5h02m42.93
2 Bob Wollek/Stefan Johansson	Porsche 956	212	5h03m36.14
3 Jan Lammers/Thierry Boutsen	Porsche 956	205	

4 Jürgen Lässig/Axel
Plankenhorn/Harald Grohs Porsche 956 201
5 Alan Jones/Vern Schuppan Porsche 956 201
6 Tony Dron/Richard Cleare Kremer CK5-
Porsche 197

Winner's average speed: 123.202 mph. Pole position: Bellof,
1m13.15. Fastest lap: Riccardo Patrese (Lancia LC2), 1m18.39

ADAC Bitburger 1000 km-Rennen

**29 May 1983. Nürburgring. 44 laps of a 12.944-mile circuit
= 569.536 miles. Race stopped after 26 laps due to an
accident. Restarted over 18 laps, aggregate result**

1 Jochen Mass/Jacky Ickx Porsche 956 44 5h26m34.63
2 Bob Wollek/Stefan Johansson Porsche 956 44 5h30m34.99
3 Keke Rosberg/Jan Lammers/
Jonathan Palmer Porsche 956 43
4 Hans Heyer/Axel
Plankenhorn/Jürgen Lässig Porsche 956 42
5 Oscar Larrauri/
Massimo Sigala Lancia LC1 40
6 John Fitzpatrick/David Hobbs Porsche 956 39

Winner's average speed: 104.637 mph. Pole position: Stefan
Bellof (Porsche 956), 6m11.13. Fastest lap: Bellof, 6m25.91

24 heures du Mans

**18-19 June 1983. Le Mans. 370 laps of a 8.467-mile circuit
= 3132.790 miles**

1 Vern Schuppan/
Hurley Haywood/Al Holbert Porsche 956 370 24 hours
2 Jacky Ickx/Derek Bell Porsche 956 370
3 Mario Andretti/Michael
Andretti/Philippe Alliot Porsche 956 364
4 Volkert Merl/
Clemens Schickentanz/
Maurizio de Narvaez Porsche 956 361
5 John Fitzpatrick/
Guy Edwards/Rupert Keegan Porsche 956 358
6 Klaus Ludwig/Stefan
Johansson/Bob Wollek Porsche 956 354

Winner's average speed: 130.533 mph. Pole position: Ickx,
3m16.36. Fastest lap: Ickx, 3m29.7

Trophée Diners Club/
1000 km de Spa-Francorchamps

**4 September 1983. Spa-Francorchamps. 144 laps of a
4.318-mile circuit = 621.792 miles**

1 Jacky Ickx/Jochen Mass Porsche 956 144 5h44m33.52
2 Derek Bell/Stefan Bellof Porsche 956 144 5h45m36.54
3 John Fitzpatrick/David Hobbs Porsche 956 139
4 Hans-Joachim Stuck/
Harald Grohs/Walter Brun Porsche 956 138
5 Jürgen Lässig/Axel
Plankenhorn/Hervé Regout Porsche 956 136
6 Giorgio Francia/Paolo Barilla Lancia LC2 134

Winner's average speed: 108.274 mph. Pole position: Ickx,
2m09.38. Fastest lap: Bellof, 2m14.11

Fuji 1000 kms

**2 October 1983. Fuji. 225 laps of a 2.707-mile circuit
= 609.008 miles. Race shortened**

1 Derek Bell/Stefan Bellof Porsche 956 225 4h57m06.36
2 Jacky Ickx/Jochen Mass Porsche 956 225 4h57m56.29
3 Vern Schuppan/
Naohiro Fumita Porsche 956 219
4 Henri Pescarolo/
Thierry Boutsen Porsche 956 218
5 Bob Wollek/Hans Heyer Porsche 956 209
6 Kenji Takahashi/
Clemens Schickentanz Porsche 956 203

Winner's average speed: 122.988 mph. Pole position: Bellof,
1m10.02. Fastest lap: Bellof, time n/a

Castrol 1000 kms

**10 December 1983. Kyalami. 244 laps of a
2.550-mile circuit = 622.200 miles**

1 Derek Bell/Stefan Bellof Porsche 956 244 5h44m06.33
2 Riccardo Patrese/
Alessandro Nannini Lancia LC2 240
3 Jacky Ickx/Jochen Mass Porsche 956 236
4 Dieter Schornstein/
"John Winter"/Bob Wollek Porsche 956 228
5 Jonathan Palmer/
Jan Lammers Porsche 956 225
6 Sarel van der Merwe/Tony
Martin/Graham Duxbury Porsche 956 224

Winner's average speed: 108.490 mph. Pole position: Bellof,
1m10.88. Fastest lap: Bellof, 1m15.59

FINAL CHAMPIONSHIP POSITIONS

Drivers		Manufacturers	
1 Jacky Ickx	97	1 Porsche	100 (140)*
2 Derek Bell	94	2 Lancia	32
3 Jochen Mass	82	3= March-Nissan	4
4 Stefan Bellof	75	Nimrod-	
5 Bob Wollek	64	Aston Martin	4
6 Thierry Boutsen	44	5 Sauber-BMW	3
7 Jan Lammers	43	6 Dome-Toyota	2
8= Jürgen Lässig	42	7 URD-BMW	1
Axel Plankenhorn	42	*Best five results count	
10 Vern Schuppan	40		
11 Stefan Johansson	36		
12 Hans Heyer	30	**Manufacturers -**	
13= John Fitzpatrick	29	**Group C Junior**	
David Hobbs	29	1 Alba-Giannini	75
15 Clemens			
Schickentanz	28		
16 Al Holbert	24	**Manufacturers -**	
17 Jonathan Palmer	23	**Group B**	
18 Riccardo Patrese	21	1 Porsche	82 (94)*
19= Harald Grohs	20	*Best five results count	
Hurley Haywood	20		

*The works Porsche 956s dominated in the 1983
championship*

1984

WORLD ENDURANCE CHAMPIONSHIP

1000 km di Monza/
Trofeo Filippo Caracciolo

**23 April 1984. Monza. 173 laps of a 3.604-mile circuit
= 623.492 miles**

1 Derek Bell/Stefan Bellof Porsche 956 173 5h06m15.60
2 Jacky Ickx/Jochen Mass Porsche 956 173 5h06m39.56
3 Mauro Baldi/Paolo Barilla Lancia LC2 168
4 Hans-Joachim Stuck/Harald
Grohs/Walter Brun Porsche 956 167
5 Jonathan Palmer/
Jan Lammers Porsche 956 159
6 Dieter Schornstein/
Volkert Merl Porsche 956 155

Winner's average speed: 122.146 mph. Pole position: Bellof,
1m35.85. Fastest lap: Riccardo Patrese (Lancia LC2), 1m38.00

Sports Car World Championship

Grand Prix International 1000 kms

13 May 1984. Silverstone. 212 laps of a 2.932-mile circuit = 621.584 miles

1 Jacky Ickx/Jochen Mass	Porsche 956	212	5h05m21.20
2 Klaus Ludwig/Henri Pescarolo	Porsche 956	210	
3 Rupert Keegan/Guy Edwards	Porsche 956	207	
4 Paolo Barilla/Mauro Baldi	Lancia LC2	206	
5 Jonathan Palmer/ Jan Lammers	Porsche 956	203	
6 Franz Konrad/ David Sutherland	Porsche 956	202	

Winner's average speed: 122.137 mph. Pole position: Riccardo Patrese (Lancia LC2), 1m13.84. Fastest lap: Mass, 1m16.76

24 heures du Mans

16-17 June 1984. Le Mans. 359 laps of a 8.467-mile circuit = 3039.653 miles

1 Klaus Ludwig/ Henri Pescarolo	Porsche 956	359	24 hours
2 Jean Rondeau/John Paul Jr/ Preston Henn	Porsche 956	357	
3 David Hobbs/Philippe Streiff/ Sarel van der Merwe	Porsche 956	350	
4 Walter Brun/Bob Akin/ Leopold von Bayern	Porsche 956	339	
5 Volkert Merl/Dieter Schornstein/"John Winter"	Porsche 956	339	
6 Vern Schuppan/Alan Jones/ Jean-Pierre Jarier	Porsche 956	336	

Winner's average speed: 126.652 mph. Pole position: Bob Wollek (Lancia LC2), 3m17.11. Fastest lap: Alessandro Nannini (Lancia LC2), 3m28.9

ADAC 1000 km-Rennen

15 July 1984. Nürburgring. 207 laps of a 2.822-mile circuit = 584.154 miles. Race shortened to six hours

1 Stefan Bellof/Derek Bell	Porsche 956	207	6h00m43.59
2 Thierry Boutsen/David Hobbs	Porsche 956	207	6h00m59.27
3 Alessandro Nannini/ Paolo Barilla	Lancia LC2	206	
4 Jonathan Palmer/Jan Lammers/Christian Danner	Porsche 956	205	
5 Marc Surer/ Manfred Winkelhock	Porsche 956	204	
6 Oscar Larrauri/ Massimo Sigala	Porsche 956	203	

Winner's average speed: 97.163 mph. Pole position: Stefan Bellof (Porsche 956), 1m28.68. Fastest lap: Palmer, 1m32.75

British Aerospace 1000 kms

29 July 1984. Brands Hatch. 238 laps of a 2.614-mile circuit = 622.132 miles

1 Jonathan Palmer/ Jan Lammers	Porsche 956	238	5h41m46.33
2 Jochen Mass/Henri Pescarolo	Porsche 956	236	
3 Thierry Boutsen/ Rupert Keegan/Guy Edwards	Porsche 962	234	
4 David Sutherland/Desiré Wilson/George Fouché	Porsche 956	229	
5 Stefan Bellof/Harald Grohs	Porsche 956	224	
6 David Hobbs/Guy Edwards/ Thierry Boutsen	Porsche 956	222	

Winner's average speed: 109.202 mph. Pole position: Palmer, 1m17.32. Fastest lap: Palmer and Bob Wollek (Lancia LC2), 1m21.03

Budweiser GT 1000 kms

5 August 1984. Mosport Park. 253 laps of a 2.459-mile circuit = 622.127 miles

1 Jacky Ickx/Jochen Mass	Porsche 956	253	6h00m41.41
2 David Hobbs/Rupert Keegan/ Franz Konrad	Porsche 956	245	

3 Almo Coppelli/Guido Dacco	Alba AR2- Giannini	229	
4 Stefan Bellof/Derek Bell	Porsche 956	221	
5 Pasquale Barberio/Maurizio Gellini/Gerardo Vattielli	Alba AR3-Ford	217	
6 Martino Finotto/Carlo Facetti/Alfredo Sebastiani	Alba AR2- Giannini	204	

Winner's average speed: 103.489 mph. Pole position: Bellof, 1m14.957. Fastest lap: Bellof, 1m13.874

1000 km de Spa-Francorchamps Rothmans

2 September 1984. Spa-Francorchamps. 144 laps of a 4.318-mile circuit = 621.792 miles

1 Stefan Bellof/Derek Bell	Porsche 956	144	5h53m17.19
2 Jochen Mass/Jacky Ickx	Porsche 956	144	5h54m14.90
3 Hans-Joachim Stuck/ Harald Grohs/Walter Brun	Porsche 956	142	
4 Massimo Sigala/ Oscar Larrauri	Porsche 956	141	
5 Jürgen Lässig/Hervé Regout/ Philippe Martin	Porsche 956	141	
6 Vern Schuppan/John Watson	Porsche 956	139	

Winner's average speed: 105.599 mph. Pole position: Thierry Boutsen (Porsche 956), 2m09.63. Fastest lap: Bellof, 2m15.57

1000 km di Imola

16 September 1984. Imola. 199 laps of a 3.132-mile circuit = 623.268 miles

1 Stefan Bellof/ Hans-Joachim Stuck	Porsche 956	199	5h54m56.32
2 Jonathan Palmer/ Jan Lammers	Porsche 956GTI	199	5h55m30.53
3 Jochen Mass/Henri Pescarolo/Hans Heyer	Porsche 956	197	
4 Walter Brun/George Fouché/ Leopold von Bayern	Porsche 956	195	
5 Oscar Larrauri/ Massimo Sigala	Porsche 956	193	
6 Harald Grohs/Hervé Regout/ Jürgen Lässig	Porsche 956	191	

Winner's average speed: 105.359 mph. Pole position: Riccardo Patrese (Lancia LC2), 1m37.82. Fastest lap: Pierluigi Martini (Lancia LC2), 1m37.84

Fuji 1000 kms

30 September 1984. Fuji. 226 laps of a 2.740-mile circuit = 619.240 miles

1 Stefan Bellof/John Watson	Porsche 956	226	5h30m00.37
2 Jochen Mass/Jacky Ickx	Porsche 956	226	5h30m32.67
3 Hans-Joachim Stuck/ Vern Schuppan	Porsche 956	224	
4 Stefan Johansson/ Henri Pescarolo	Porsche 956	222	
5 Manfred Winkelhock/ Mike Thackwell	Porsche 956	216	
6 Naoki Nagasaka/ Keiichi Suzuki	Lotec M1C- BMW	209	

Winner's average speed: 112.603 mph. Pole position: Bellof. Fastest lap: n/a

Kyalami 1000 kms

3 November 1984. Kyalami. 244 laps of a 2.550-mile circuit = 622.200 miles

1 Riccardo Patrese/ Alessandro Nannini	Lancia LC2	244	5h38m13.92
2 Bob Wollek/Paolo Barilla	Lancia LC2	242	
3 George Santana/Hanni van der Linde/Errol Shearsby	Nissan Skyline	202	
4 Ben Morganrood/Johann Coetzee/Willie Hapburn	Mazda RX-7	201	
5 Nicolo Bianco/Arnold Chatz	Alfa Romeo GTV6	200	

6 Paul Moni/Mick Formato Alfa Romeo
GTV6   193

Winner's average speed: 110.374 mph. Pole position: Wollek,
1m12.96. Fastest lap: Patrese/Nannini, 1m16.18

Sandown Park 1000 kms

2 December 1984. Sandown Park. 206 laps of a 2.425 mile-
circuit = 499.550 miles. Race shortened to 6 hours

1 Stefan Bellof/Derek Bell	Porsche 956	206	6h01m30.3
2 Jochen Mass/Jacky Ickx	Porsche 956	203	
3 Jonathan Palmer/			
Jan Lammers	Porsche 956GTI	202	
4 Sarel van der Merwe/			
George Fouché	Porsche 956	200	
5 Manfred Winkelhock/			
Rusty French	Porsche 956	200	
6 Colin Bond/			
Andrew Miedecke	Porsche 962	198	

Winner's average speed: 82.912 mph. Pole position: Bellof,
1m31.6. Fastest lap: Bellof, 1m34.5

FINAL CHAMPIONSHIP POSITIONS

Drivers
1 Stefan Bellof 138 (139)*
2 Jochen Mass 127 (131)*
3 Jacky Ickx 104
4= Derek Bell 91
   Henri Pescarolo 91
6= Jan Lammers 75
   Jonathan Palmer 75
8= David Hobbs 54
   Hans-Joachim Stuck 54
10 Paolo Barilla 49
11 Walter Brun 47
12 Rupert Keegan 44
13 Klaus Ludwig 39
14 Dieter Schornstein 38
15 Harald Grohs 36
16 Alessandro Nannini 35
17 George Fouché 34
18 "John Winter" 32
19= Mauro Baldi 28
    Oscar Larrauri 28
    Massimo Sigala 28
*Best eight results count

Manufacturers
1 Porsche 120 (152)*
2 Lancia 57
3 Alba-Giannini 12
4 Alba-Ford 8
5= Lotec-BMW 6
   Tiga-Ford 6
7 Rondeau-Ford 5
8= Dome-Toyota 4
   Lola-Mazda 4
10 March-Mazda 3
11 BMW 2
12= Ecosse-Ford 1
    Lola-Chevrolet 1
*Best six results count

Manufacturers - Group C2
1 Alba-Giannini 82 (90)*
*Best six results count

Manufacturers - Group B
1 BMW 100

1985
WORLD ENDURANCE CHAMPIONSHIP

6 ore di Mugello

14 April 1985. Mugello. 190 laps of a 3.259-mile circuit
= 619.210 miles

1 Jacky Ickx/Jochen Mass	Porsche 962	190	5h59m52.21
2 Marc Surer/			
Manfred Winkelhock	Porsche 962	190	6h00m22.05
3 Stefan Bellof/Thierry Boutsen	Porsche 962	189	
4 Mauro Baldi/Bob Wollek	Lancia LC2	186	
5 Klaus Ludwig/George			
Fouché/Gianni Mussati	Porsche 956	184	
6 Mike Thackwell/			
Hervé Regout/Jürgen Lässig	Porsche 956	179	

Winner's average speed: 103.239 mph. Pole position: Riccardo
Patrese (Lancia LC2), 1m39.07. Fastest lap: Patrese, 1m45.79

1000 km di Monza/ Trofeo Filippo Caracciolo

28 April 1985. Monza. 138 laps of a 3.604-mile circuit =
497.352 miles. Race stopped when a tree fell across the track

1 Manfred Winkelhock/			
Marc Surer	Porsche 962	138	4h04m41.43

2 Hans-Joachim Stuck/
Derek Bell   Porsche 956 138 4h05m13.07
3 Riccardo Patrese/
Alessandro Nannini Lancia LC2 138
4 Jochen Mass/Jacky Ickx Porsche 962 138
5 Jonathan Palmer/
Jan Lammers   Porsche 956GTI 134
6 Oscar Larrauri/
Massimo Sigala/Renzo Zorzi Porsche 956 129

Winner's average speed: 121.951 mph. Pole position: Patrese,
1m31.00. Fastest lap: n/a

Silverstone 1000 kms

12 May 1985. Silverstone. 212 laps of a 2.932-mile circuit
= 621.584 miles

1 Jochen Mass/Jacky Ickx	Porsche 962	212	4h54m03.22
2 Derek Bell/			
Hans-Joachim Stuck	Porsche 956	211	
3 Riccardo Patrese/			
Alessandro Nannini	Lancia LC2	210	
4 Manfred Winkelhock/			
Marc Surer	Porsche 962	210	
5 Jonathan Palmer/			
Jan Lammers	Porsche 956GTI	207	
6 Klaus Ludwig/Paolo Barilla/			
Paul Belmondo	Porsche 956	206	

Winner's average speed: 126.831 mph. Pole position: Patrese,
1m10.84. Fastest lap: Palmer, 1m15.96

24 heures du Mans

15-16 June 1985. Le Mans. 373 laps of a 8.467-mile circuit
= 3158.191 miles

1 Klaus Ludwig/Paolo Barilla/			
"John Winter"	Porsche 956	373	24 hours
2 Jonathan Palmer/			
James Weaver/Richard Lloyd	Porsche 956GTI	370	
3 Derek Bell/			
Hans-Joachim Stuck	Porsche 962	366	
4 David Hobbs/Jo Gartner/			
Guy Edwards	Porsche 962	365	
5 Sarel van der Merwe/George			
Fouché/Mario Hytten	Porsche 956	360	
6 Bob Wollek/Alessandro			
Nannini/Lucio Cesario	Lancia LC2	359	

Winner's average speed: 131.591 mph. Pole position: Stuck,
3m14.80. Fastest lap: Jochen Mass (Porsche 962), 3m25.10

Duschfrisch 1000 km-Rennen

14 July 1985. Hockenheim. 147 laps of a 4.224-mile circuit
= 620.928 miles

1 Derek Bell/			
Hans-Joachim Stuck	Porsche 962	147	5h23m00.68
2 Oscar Larrauri/			
Massimo Sigala	Porsche 956	147	5h23m40.59
3 Klaus Ludwig/Paolo Barilla	Porsche 956	145	
4 Bob Wollek/Mauro Baldi	Lancia LC2	145	
5 Jonathan Palmer/David Hobbs	Porsche 956GTI	143	
6 Gerhard Berger/Walter Brun	Porsche 956	142	

Winner's average speed: 115.328 mph. Pole position: Jochen
Mass (Porsche 962), 1m55.18. Fastest lap: Stefan Bellof (Porsche
956), 2m00.66

Budweiser GT 1000 kms

11 August 1985. Mosport Park. 253 laps of a
2.459-mile circuit = 622.127 miles

1 Derek Bell/			
Hans-Joachim Stuck	Porsche 962	253	5h55m41.988
2 Jochen Mass/Jacky Ickx	Porsche 962	253	5h57m06.848
3 Martin Brundle/			
Mike Thackwell/			
Jean-Louis Schlesser	Jaguar XJR-6	234	

4 Ludwig Heimrath/		
Ludwig Heimrath Jr/		
Kees Kroesemeijer	Porsche 956	234
5 Gordon Spice/Ray Bellm	Tiga GC85-Ford	231
6 Frank Jelinski/John Graham	Gebhardt 853-Ford	225

Winner's average speed: 104.941 mph. Pole position: Stuck, 1m09.775. Fastest lap: Stuck, 1m12.915

1000 km de Spa-Francorchamps

1 September 1985. Spa-Francorchamps. 122 laps of a 4.318-mile circuit = 526.796 miles. Race stopped due to Stefan Bellof's fatal accident

1 Bob Wollek/Mauro Baldi/			
Riccardo Patrese	Lancia LC2	122	5h00m23.42
2 Hans-Joachim Stuck/			
Derek Bell	Porsche 962	122	5h02m37.86
3 Klaus Ludwig/Paolo Barilla	Porsche 956	121	
4 Alessandro Nannini/Riccardo			
Patrese/Mauro Baldi	Lancia LC2	121	
5 Martin Brundle/			
Mike Thackwell	Jaguar XJR-6	120	
6 Marc Duez/"John Winter"/			
Volker Weidler	Porsche 956	120	

Winner's average speed: 105.220 mph. Pole position: Patrese, 2m05.91. Fastest lap: Jochen Mass (Porsche 962), 2m10.73

Shell Gemini 1000 kms

22 September 1985. Brands Hatch. 238 laps of a 2.614-mile circuit = 622.132 miles

1 Derek Bell/			
Hans-Joachim Stuck	Porsche 962	238	5h34m26.02
2 Jochen Mass/Jacky Ickx	Porsche 962	238	5h34m38.01
3 Bob Wollek/Andrea			
de Cesaris/Mauro Baldi	Lancia LC2	237	
4 Riccardo Patrese/			
Alessandro Nannini	Lancia LC2	233	
5 Vern Schuppan/Al Holbert	Porsche 956	224	
6 Ray Mallock/Mike Wilds/			
David Leslie	Ecosse C285-Ford	219	

Winner's average speed: 111.598 mph. Pole position: Patrese, 1m14.66. Fastest lap: de Cesaris, 1m19.11

Fuji 1000 kms

6 October 1985. Fuji. 62 laps of a 2.740-mile circuit = 169.880 miles. Race stopped after two hours due to heavy rain, half points awarded

1 Kazuyoshi Hoshino	March 85G-Nissan	62	2h01m10.79
2 Osamu Nakako	Le Mans 05C-Nissan	61	
3 Satoru Nakajima	Dome 85C-Toyota	61	
4 Naoki Nagasaka	Dome 85C-Toyota	61	
5 Masahiro Hasemi	March 85G-Nissan	60	
6 Vern Schuppan	Porsche 956	60	

Winner's average speed: 84.125 mph. Pole position: Hans-Joachim Stuck (Porsche 962), 1m15.92. Fastest lap: n/a

Selangor 800 kms

1 December 1985. Shah Alam. 217 laps of a 2.295-mile circuit = 498.015 miles

1 Jochen Mass/Jacky Ickx	Porsche 962	217	5h32m03.34
2 Mike Thackwell/			
John Nielsen/Jan Lammers	Jaguar XJR-6	217	5h33m25.73
3 Vern Schuppan/			
James Weaver	Porsche 956	208	
4 Franz Konrad/			
Andrew Miedecke	Porsche 956	205	
5 Oscar Larrauri/Massimo			
Sigala/Frank Jelinski	Porsche 956	195	

| 6 Richard Piper/Ian Harrower/ | | |
| Evan Clements | Gebhardt 843-Ford | 191 |

Winner's average speed: 89.988 mph. Pole position: Mass, 1m21.33. Fastest lap: Mass, 1m24.52

FINAL CHAMPIONSHIP POSITIONS

Drivers

1= Derek Bell	117
Hans-Joachim Stuck	117
3= Jacky Ickx	101
Jochen Mass	101
5= Klaus Ludwig	58
Bob Wollek	58
7 Paolo Barilla	52
8 Alessandro Nannini	50
9= Marc Surer	45
Manfred Winkelhock	45
11 Mike Thackwell	43
12 Jonathan Palmer	39
13 Mauro Baldi	36
14 Riccardo Patrese	34
15 Jan Lammers	31
16= Ray Bellm	30
Gordon Spice	30
18 Oscar Larrauri	29
19 James Weaver	27
20= Vern Schuppan	23
Massimo Sigala	23

Teams

1 Rothmans Porsche	107
2 Martini Lancia	58
3 Jöst Racing	50
4 Porsche Kremer Racing	43
5 Richard Lloyd Racing	31
6 Brun Motorsport	28
7= Jaguar (TWR)	20
Obermaier Racing	20
9 Spice Engineering	16
10= Fitzpatrick Porsche Team	10
Hoshino Racing	10

Drivers - C2

| 1= Ray Bellm | 130 |
| Gordon Spice | 130 |

Teams - C2

| 1 Spice Engineering | 110 |

1986

World Sports-Prototype Championship

Kouros Cup/Trofeo Filippo Caracciolo

20 April 1986. Monza. 63 laps of a 3.604-mile circuit = 227.052 miles

1 Hans-Joachim Stuck/			
Derek Bell	Porsche 962	63	1h48m40.29
2 Andrea de Cesaris/			
Alessandro Nannini	Lancia LC2	63	1h49m29.39
3 Massimo Sigala/Walter Brun	Porsche 956	61	
4 Oscar Larrauri/Jesus Pareja	Porsche 962	61	
5 Drake Olson/Thierry Boutsen	Porsche 962	61	
6 Jochen Mass/Bob Wollek	Porsche 962	61	

Winner's average speed: 125.357 mph. Pole position: de Cesaris, 1m32.32. Fastest lap: Nannini, 1m36.96

Kouros 1000 kms

5 May 1986. Silverstone. 212 laps of a 2.932-mile circuit = 621.584 miles

1 Derek Warwick/			
Eddie Cheever	Jaguar XJR-6	212	4h48m55.37
2 Derek Bell/			
Hans-Joachim Stuck	Porsche 962	210	
3 Jo Gartner/Tiff Needell	Porsche 962	207	
4 James Weaver/			
Klaus Niedzwiedz	Porsche 956GTI	206	
5 Emilio de Villota/Fermin Velez	Porsche 956	206	
6 George Follmer/John			
Morton/Paolo Barilla	Porsche 956	205	

Winner's average speed: 129.083 mph. Pole position: Andrea de Cesaris (Lancia LC2), 1m10.81. Fastest lap: de Cesaris, 1m13.95

24 heures du Mans

31 May-1 June 1986. Le Mans. 367 laps of a 8.406-mile circuit = 3085.002 miles

1 Hans-Joachim Stuck/			
Derek Bell/Al Holbert	Porsche 962	367	24 hours
2 Oscar Larrauri/Joël Gouhier/			
Jesus Pareja	Porsche 962	359	
3 George Follmer/			
John Morton/Kemper Miller	Porsche 956	354	

4 Emilio de Villota/George
  Fouché/Fermin Velez   Porsche 956   348
5 Jürgen Lässig/Fulvio Ballabio/
  Dudley Wood   Porsche 956   344
6 Siegfried Brunn/
  Ernst Schuster/Rudi Seher Porsche 936CJ 343

Winner's average speed: 128.542 mph. Pole position: Jochen Mass (Porsche 962), 3m15.99. Fastest lap: Klaus Ludwig/Paolo Barilla/"John Winter" (Porsche 956), 3m23.3 (ACO did not publish who was driving when time was set)

100 Meilen von Nürnberg

29 June 1986. Norisring. 79 laps of a 1.429-mile circuit = 112.891 miles

1 Klaus Ludwig   Porsche 956   79 1h07m00.36
2 Eddie Cheever   Jaguar XJR-6   79 1h07m08.03
3 Derek Warwick   Jaguar XJR-6   79
4 Frank Jelinski   Porsche 962   78
5 James Weaver   Porsche 962   78
6 Walter Brun   Porsche 962   78

Winner's average speed: 101.087 mph. Pole position: Hans-Joachim Stuck (Porsche 962), 46.54s. Fastest lap: Stuck, 48.28s

Shell Gemini 1000 kms

20 July 1986. Brands Hatch. 236 laps of a 2.614-mile circuit = 616.904 miles

1 Bob Wollek/Mauro Baldi Porsche 956GTI 236 5h53m44.43
2 Hans-Joachim Stuck/
  Derek Bell/Klaus Ludwig Porsche 956   232
3 Thierry Boutsen/Frank Jelinski Porsche 956 231
4 Derek Warwick/
  Jean-Louis Schlesser   Jaguar XJR-6   231
5 Paolo Barilla/"John Winter"/
  Klaus Ludwig   Porsche 956   230
6 Eddie Cheever/
  Gianfranco Brancatelli Jaguar XJR-6   230

Winner's average speed: 104.621 mph. Pole position: Stuck, 1m16.27. Fastest lap: Wollek, 1m18.68

Trofeo Silk Cut

3 August 1986. Jerez. 86 laps of a 2.621-mile circuit = 225.406 miles

1 Oscar Larrauri/Jesus Pareja Porsche 962 86 2h27m47.34
2 Walter Brun/Frank Jelinski   Porsche 956 86 2h28m23.24
3 Derek Warwick/
  Jan Lammers   Jaguar XJR-6   84
4 Fulvio Ballabio/
  Dudley Wood/Jürgen Lässig Porsche 956 82
5 Gordon Spice/Ray Bellm Spice SE86C-
                          Ford   79
6 Evan Clements/
  Ian Harrower   Gebhardt 843-
                          Ford   78

Winner's average speed: 91.508 mph. Pole position: Jelinksi, 1m33.48. Fastest lap: Larrauri, 1m38.09

ADAC Kouros 1000 km-Rennen

24 August 1986. Nürburgring. 121 laps of a 2.822-mile circuit = 341.462 miles. Race stopped after 22 laps due to heavy rain. Restarted over three hours, aggregate result

1 Mike Thackwell/
  Henri Pescarolo   Sauber C8-
                         Mercedes-Benz 121 3h42m30.02
2 Mauro Baldi/
  Klaus Niedzwiedz   Porsche 956GTI 119
3 Emilio de Villota/Fermin Velez Porsche 956 119
4 Jürgen Lässig/
  Fulvio Ballabio/Harald Grohs Porsche 956 115
5 Ray Mallock/Marc Duez Ecosse C286-
                         Rover   115
6 Walter Lechner/
  Ernst Franzmeier/Max Payne Ford   112

Winner's average speed: 92.080 mph. Pole position: Boutsen, 1m27.27. Fastest lap: Baldi, 1m34.82

1000 km de Spa-Francorchamps Kouros

15 September 1986. Spa-Francorchamps. 145 laps of a 4.318-mile circuit = 626.096 miles

1 Thierry Boutsen/Frank Jelinski Porsche 962 145 5h35m54.54
2 Derek Warwick/Jan Lammers Jaguar XJR-6 145 5h35m55.34
3 Derek Bell/
  Hans-Joachim Stuck   Porsche 962   145
4 Paolo Barilla/Klaus Ludwig Porsche 956 144
5 Eddie Cheever/
  Jean-Louis Schlesser   Jaguar XJR-6   143
6 Mike Thackwell/
  Henri Pescarolo   Sauber C8-
                         Mercedes-Benz 140

Winner's average speed: 111.833 mph. Pole position: Thierry Boutsen (Porsche 956), 2m06.87. Fastest lap: Cheever, 2m09.38

Fuji 1000 kms

6 October 1986. Fuji. 226 laps of a 2.740-mile circuit = 619.330 miles

1 Paolo Barilla/
  Piercarlo Ghinzani   Porsche 956   226 5h29m25.332
2 Frank Jelinski/Stanley Dickens Porsche 956 225
3 Eddie Cheever/
  Derek Warwick   Jaguar XJR-6   225
4 Bruno Giacomelli/
  Volker Weidler   Porsche 962   224
5 Kris Nissen/Harald Grohs/
  "John Winter"   Porsche 956   223
6 Vern Schuppan/George
  Fouché/Keiichi Suzuki Porsche 956   223

Winner's average speed: 112.803 mph. Pole position: Oscar Larrauri (Porsche 962). Fastest lap: n/a

FINAL CHAMPIONSHIP POSITIONS

Drivers		Teams	
1 Derek Bell	82*	1 Brun Motorsport	57
2 Hans-Joachim		2 Jöst Racing	48
Stuck	82	3= Rothmans Porsche	47
=3 Derek Warwick	81	Silk Cut	
4 Frank Jelinski	74	Jaguar (TWR)	47
5 Eddie Cheever	61	5 Fitzpatrick	
6= Oscar Larrauri	50	Porsche Team	30
Jesus Pareja	50	6 Kouros Sauber	29
8 Paolo Barilla	44	7 Richard Lloyd	
9 Thierry Boutsen	41	Racing	28
10 Mauro Baldi	38	8= Porsche Kremer	
11 Walter Brun	37	Racing	18
12= Fulvio Ballabio	35	Obermaier Racing	18
Jürgen Lässig	35	10 Ecurie Ecosse	8
14= Fermin Velez	34		
Emilio de Villota	34		
16 Henri Pescarolo	31		
17 Klaus Ludwig	30	Drivers - C2	
18= Mike Thackwell	29	1= Ray Bellm	105
Bob Wollek	29	Gordon Spice	105
20 Klaus Niedzwiedz	28		

*Bell was declared champion as he finished higher than Stuck at the Norisring. It was the only event at which they did not compete together. Bell finished 11th, Stuck 15th.

Teams - C2	
1 Ecurie Ecosse	70

1987

WORLD SPORTS-PROTOTYPE CHAMPIONSHIP

Gran Premio Fortuna

22 March 1987. Jarama. 109 laps of a 2.115-mile circuit = 230.579 miles

1 Jan Lammers/John Watson Jaguar XJR-8 109 2h29m56.30
2 Hans-Joachim Stuck/
  Derek Bell   Porsche 962   109 2h29m57.94
3 Eddie Cheever/Raul Boesel Jaguar XJR-8 109
4 Volker Weidler/Kris Nissen Porsche 962 106

5 Oscar Larrauri/Jesus Pareja   Porsche 962   106
6 Massimo Sigala/
  Gianfranco Brancatelli   Porsche 962   105

Winner's average speed: 92.269 mph. Pole position: Cheever, 1m14.54. Fastest lap: Stuck, 1m17.87

Jerez 1000 kms

29 March 1987. Jerez. 211 laps of a 2.621-mile circuit = 553.010 miles. Race stopped after six hours

1 Eddie Cheever/Raul Boesel   Jaguar XJR-8   211   6h01m15.46
2 Kris Nissen/Volker Weidler   Porsche 962   208
3 Hans-Joachim Stuck/
  Derek Bell   Porsche 962   205
4 Fermin Velez/Gordon Spice   Spice SE86C-
                               Ford   199
5 Ray Mallock/David Leslie   Ecosse C286-
                              Ford   199
6 Gianfranco Brancatelli/
  Massimo Sigala   Porsche 962   188

Winner's average speed: 91.847 mph. Pole position: Stuck, 1m29.19. Fastest lap: n/a

1000 km di Monza/ Trofeo Filippo Caracciolo

12 April 1987. Monza. 173 laps of a 3.604-mile circuit = 623.475 miles

1 Jan Lammers/John Watson   Jaguar XJR-8   173   5h03m55.37
2 Hans-Joachim Stuck/
  Derek Bell   Porsche 962   171
3 Frank Jelinski/Jesus Pareja/
  Oscar Larrauri*   Porsche 962   168
4 "John Winter"/Stanley
  Dickens*/Klaus Ludwig   Porsche 962   167
5 Gianfranco Brancatelli/
  Massimo Sigala   Porsche 962   165
6 Bob Wollek/Jochen Mass   Porsche 962   159

*Larrauri and Dickens drove for under 30% of the race so were ineligible for points. Winner's average speed: 123.085 mph. Pole position: Stuck, 1m32.17. Fastest lap: Lammers, 1m37.16

Autoglass 1000 kms

10 May 1987. Silverstone. 210 laps of a 2.969-mile circuit = 623.490 miles

1 Eddie Cheever/Raul Boesel   Jaguar XJR-8   210   5h03m06.22
2 Jan Lammers/John Watson   Jaguar XJR-8   210   5h03m12.36
3 Hans-Joachim Stuck/
  Derek Bell   Porsche 962   209
4 Jochen Mass/Bob Wollek   Porsche 962   202
5 Walter Brun/Uwe Schäfer   Porsche 962   200
6 Ray Mallock/David Leslie   Ecosse C286-
                              Ford   191

Winner's average speed: 123.421 mph. Pole position: Hans-Joachim Stuck (Porsche 962), 1m15.11. Fastest lap: Cheever, 1m18.12

24 heures du Mans

13-14 June 1987. Le Mans. 354 laps of a 8.410-mile circuit = 2977.140 miles

1 Derek Bell/Hans-Joachim
  Stuck/Al Holbert   Porsche 962   354   24 hours
2 Jürgen Lässig/Pierre Yver/
  Bernard de Dryver   Porsche 962   334
3 Pierre-Henri Raphanel/
  Hervé Regout/Yves Courage   Cougar C20-
                              Porsche   331
4 George Fouché/
  Franz Konrad/Wayne Taylor   Porsche 962   326
5 Eddie Cheever/Raul Boesel/   Jaguar XJR-
  Jan Lammers   8LM   324
6 Gordon Spice/Fermin Velez/   Spice SE87C-
  Philippe de Henning   Ford   320

Winner's average speed: 124.048 mph. Pole position: Bob Wollek (Porsche 962), 3m21.09. Fastest lap: Johnny Dumfries (Sauber C9-Mercedes-Benz), 3m25.04

200 Meilen von Nürnberg

28 June 1987. Norisring. 154 laps of a 1.429-mile circuit = 220.066 miles. Aggregate of two 77-lap heats

1 Mauro Baldi/
  Jonathan Palmer   Porsche 962GTI 154   2h09m39.95
2 Oscar Larrauri/Jochen Mass*   Porsche 962   151
3 "John Winter"/
  Stanley Dickens   Porsche 962   150
4 Eddie Cheever/Raul Boesel   Jaguar XJR-8   147
5 Jürgen Lässig/Pierre Yver   Porsche 962   146
6 Fermin Velez/Gordon Spice   Spice SE86C-
                              Ford   143

*Mass drove under 30% of race, ineligible for points. Winner's average speed: 101.831 mph. Pole position: Hans-Joachim Stuck (Porsche 962), 47.07s. Fastest lap: n/a

Shell Gemini 1000 kms

26 July 1987. Brands Hatch. 238 laps of a 2.614-mile circuit = 622.132 miles

1 Raul Boesel/John Nielsen   Jaguar XJR-8   238   5h33m48.51
2 Mauro Baldi/
  Johnny Dumfries   Porsche 962GTI 238   5h35m01.51
3 Jan Lammers/John Watson   Jaguar XJR-8   229
4 Hans-Joachim Stuck/
  Derek Bell   Porsche 962   228
5 Jochen Mass/Oscar Larrauri   Porsche 962   228
6 Kris Nissen/Volker Weidler   Porsche 962   225

Winner's average speed: 111.807 mph. Pole position: Lammers, 1m14.44. Fastest lap: Lammers, 1m16.44

ADAC 1000 km-Rennen

30 August 1987. Nürburgring. 221 laps of a 2.822-mile circuit = 623.662 miles

1 Eddie Cheever/Raul Boesel   Jaguar XJR-8   221   5h55m53.12
2 Derek Bell/
  Hans-Joachim Stuck   Porsche 962   218
3 Jochen Mass/Oscar Larrauri   Porsche 962   216
4 Frank Jelinski/"John
  Winter"*/Stanley Dickens   Porsche 962   212
5 Mauro Baldi/
  Jonathan Palmer   Porsche 962GTI 211
6 Hans-Peter Kaufmann/
  Franz Hunkeler/Jesus Pareja* Porsche 962   208

*"Winter" and Pareja drove for under 30% of the race so were ineligible for points. Winner's average speed: 105.145 mph. Pole position: Baldi. Fastest lap: Klaus Ludwig (Porsche 962), 1m29.51

1000 km de Spa-Francorchamps Kouros

13 September 1987. Spa-Francorchamps. 142 laps of a 4.312-mile circuit = 612.304 miles. Race stopped after 6 hours

1 Martin Brundle/Johnny
  Dumfries/Raul Boesel   Jaguar XJR-8   142   6h00m16.18
2 Jan Lammers/John Watson   Jaguar XJR-8   141
3 Jochen Mass/Oscar Larrauri   Porsche 962   140
4 Eddie Cheever/John Nielsen   Jaguar XJR-8   140
5 Hans-Joachim Stuck/
  Derek Bell/Bob Wollek   Porsche 962   139
6 Frank Jelinski/"John
  Winter"*/Stanley Dickens*   Porsche 962   138

*"Winter" and Dickens drove for under 30% of the race so were ineligible for points. Winner's average speed: 101.974 mph. Pole position: Mike Thackwell (Sauber C9-Mercedes-Benz), 2m04.04. Fastest lap: Thackwell, 2m09.30

Fuji 1000 kms

27 September 1987. Fuji. 224 laps of a 2.777-mile circuit = 622.048 miles

1 Jan Lammers/John Watson   Jaguar XJR-8   224   5h40m55.034
2 Raul Boesel/Johnny Dumfries   Jaguar XJR-8   224   5h41m52.124
3 Mauro Baldi/Mike Thackwell   Porsche 962GTI 221
4 Jochen Mass/Oscar Larrauri   Porsche 962   218

5 Frank Jelinski/Stanley
   Dickens/"John Winter"*   Porsche 962   218
6 Derek Bell/Geoff Brabham   Porsche 962   218

*"Winter" drove for under 30% of the race so was ineligible for points. Winner's average speed: 109.478 mph. Pole position: Takao Wada (Nissan 86G), 1m19.021. Fastest lap: Geoff Lees (Toyota 87C), 1m23.096

FINAL CHAMPIONSHIP POSITIONS

Drivers

1	Raul Boesel	127 (145)*	6	Porsche Kremer	
2=	Jan Lammers	102		Racing	41
	John Watson	102	7	Spice Engineering	39
4	Eddie Cheever	100	8	Primagaz Racing	
5=	Derek Bell	99 (113)*		(Courage and	
	Hans-Joachim			Obermaier)	31
	Stuck	99 (107)*	9	Ecurie Ecosse	28
7	Oscar Larrauri	69	10	Mazdaspeed	8
8=	Mauro Baldi	58	11	Rothmans Porsche	
	Jochen Mass	58		Japan	6
10=	Gordon Spice	50	12=	Cosmik/	
	Fermin Velez	50		GP Motorsport	4
12=	Frank Jelinski	40		Kelmar Racing	4
	David Leslie	40		Kouros Sauber	4
	Ray Mallock	40	15	Dauer Racing	3
15	Jesus Pareja	38	16=	From A Racing	2
16	Johnny Dumfries	35		Richard Cleare	
17	John Nielsen	32		Racing	2
18=	Kris Nissen	31	18=	Tiga Team Dana	
	Jonathan Palmer	31		Ford	1
	Volker Weidler	31		Trust Engineering	1
	*Best seven results count			URD Junior Team	1

Teams

1	Silk Cut			**Drivers - C2**	
	Jaguar (TWR)	178	1=	Gordon Spice	140 (170)*
2	Brun Motorsport	91		Fermin Velez	140 (170)*
3	Rothmans Porsche	74		*Best seven results count	
4	Jöst Racing	63			
5	Brittain Lloyd			**Teams - C2**	
	Racing	58	1	Spice Engineering	170

1988

WORLD SPORTS-PROTOTYPE CHAMPIONSHIP

Jerez 800 kms

6 March 1988. Jerez. 190 laps of a 2.621-mile circuit = 497.990 miles

1	Jean-Louis Schlesser/		Sauber C9/88-	
	Mauro Baldi/Jochen Mass		Mercedes-Benz	190 5h18m03.15
2	John Nielsen/Andy Wallace/			
	John Watson		Jaguar XJR-9	190 5h18m27.68
3	Bob Wollek/Klaus Ludwig		Porsche 962	188
4	James Weaver/Derek Bell		Porsche 962GTI	184
5	Frank Jelinski/"John Winter"		Porsche 962	183
6	Manuel Reuter/Uwe Schäfer		Porsche 962BM	183

Winner's average speed: 93.941 mph. Pole position: Schlesser, 1m28.67. Fastest lap: n/a

Jarama 360 kms

13 March 1988. Jarama. 109 laps of a 2.115-mile circuit = 230.535 miles

1	Eddie Cheever/			
	Martin Brundle		Jaguar XJR-9	109 2h30m04.979
2	Jean-Louis Schlesser/		Sauber C9/88-	
	Mauro Baldi		Mercedes-Benz	109 2h30m24.252
3	John Nielsen/John Watson		Jaguar XJR-9	107
4	Uwe Schäfer/Manuel Reuter		Porsche 962BM	107
5	Kris Nissen/Volker Weidler		Porsche 962	106
6	Oscar Larrauri/Jesus Pareja		Porsche 962	106

Winner's average speed: 92.180 mph. Pole position: Schlesser, 1m14.350. Fastest lap: Schlesser, 1m18.464

1000 km di Monza/ Trofeo Filippo Caracciolo

10 April 1988. Monza. 173 laps of a 3.604-mile circuit = 623.492 miles

1	Martin Brundle/			
	Eddie Cheever		Jaguar XJR-9	173 4h52m13.52
2	Jean-Louis Schlesser/		Sauber C9/88-	
	Mauro Baldi/Jochen Mass		Mercedes-Benz	172
3	Oscar Larrauri/			
	Massimo Sigala		Porsche 962	171
4	Frank Jelinski/"John Winter"		Porsche 962	168
5	Klaus Ludwig/Bob Wollek		Porsche 962	164
6	Volker Weidler/			
	Bruno Giacomelli		Porsche 962	164

Winner's average speed: 128.012 mph. Pole position: Schlesser, 1m31.69. Fastest lap: Schlesser, 1m35.75

Autosport 1000 kms

8 May 1988. Silverstone. 210 laps of a 2.969-mile circuit = 623.490 miles

1	Eddie Cheever/			
	Martin Brundle		Jaguar XJR-9	210 4h50m48.59
2	Jean-Louis Schlesser/		Sauber C9/88-	
	Jochen Mass		Mercedes-Benz	210 4h51m24.20
3	Mauro Baldi/		Sauber C9/88-	
	James Weaver		Mercedes-Benz	208
4	Bob Wollek/Philippe Streiff/			
	David Hobbs		Porsche 962	201
5	Frank Jelinski/Stanley			
	Dickens/"John Winter"		Porsche 962	198
6	Thorkild Thyrring/		Spice SE88C-	
	Almo Coppelli		Ford	191

Winner's average speed: 128.639 mph. Pole position: Schlesser, 1m15.02. Fastest lap: Baldi, 1m18.24

24 heures du Mans

11-12 June 1988. Le Mans. 394 laps of a 8.410-mile circuit = 3313.540 miles

1	Johnny Dumfries/		Jaguar	
	Andy Wallace/Jan Lammers		XJR-9LM	394 24h03m28.26
2	Hans-Joachim Stuck/			
	Klaus Ludwig/Derek Bell		Porsche 962	394 24h06m05.11
3	Stanley Dickens/			
	Frank Jelinski/"John Winter"		Porsche 962	385
4	Derek Daly/Larry Perkins/		Jaguar	
	Kevin Cogan		XJR-9LM	383
5	David Hobbs/Didier Theys/			
	Franz Konrad		Porsche 962	380
6	Mario Andretti/Michael			
	Andretti/John Andretti		Porsche 962	375

Winner's average speed: 137.732 mph. Pole position: Stuck, 3m15.64. Fastest lap: Stuck, 3m22.50

Grand Prix CSSR

10 July 1988. Brno. 67 laps of a 3.352-mile circuit = 224.584 miles

1	Jean-Louis Schlesser/		Sauber C9/88-	
	Jochen Mass		Mercedes-Benz	67 2h06m40.62
2	Martin Brundle/John Nielsen		Jaguar XJR-9	67 2h07m00.67
3	Jan Lammers/			
	Johnny Dumfries		Jaguar XJR-9	67
4	Mauro Baldi/James Weaver		Sauber C9/88-	
			Mercedes-Benz	67
5	Bob Wollek/"John Winter"		Porsche 962	66
6	Franz Konrad/Jürgen Barth		Porsche 962	65

Winner's average speed: 106.373 mph. Pole position: Schlesser, 1m46.44. Fastest lap: Baldi, 1m49.77

Brands Hatch 1000 kms

24 July 1988. Brands Hatch. 240 laps of a 2.600-mile circuit = 624.000 miles

1	John Nielsen/Martin Brundle/			
	Andy Wallace		Jaguar XJR-9	240 5h33m23.08

2 Klaus Ludwig/Bob Wollek   Porsche 962   239
3 Mauro Baldi/   Sauber C9/88-
Jean-Louis Schlesser   Mercedes-Benz 235
4 Gordon Spice/Ray Bellm   Spice SE88C-
                             Ford   224
5 Almo Coppelli/   Spice SE88C-
Thorkild Thyrring   Ford   224
6 Costas Los/Wayne Taylor   Spice SE87C-
                             Ford   219

Winner's average speed: 112.311 mph. Pole position: Baldi, 1m14.17. Fastest lap: Schlesser, 1m15.82

ADAC 1000 km-Rennen

3-4 September 1988. Nürburgring. 200 laps of a 2.822-mile circuit = 564.400 miles. Race stopped after 91 laps and restarted over a further 109 laps

1 Jean-Louis Schlesser/   Sauber C9/88-
Jochen Mass   Mercedes-Benz 200 5h53m00.60
2 Eddie Cheever/
Martin Brundle   Jaguar XJR-9   199
3 Bob Wollek/Paolo Barilla   Porsche 962   196
4 Frank Jelinski/"John Winter" Porsche 962 194
5 Manuel Reuter/Jesus Pareja Porsche 962   193
6 Walter Brun/Harald Huysman Porsche 962   192

Winner's average speed: 95.929 mph. Pole position: Mauro Baldi (Sauber C9/88-Mercedes-Benz), 1m24.92. Fastest lap: Schlesser, 1m28.55

1000 km de Spa-Francorchamps

18 September 1988. Spa-Francorchamps. 142 laps of a 4.312-mile circuit = 612.304 miles. Race scheduled for 145 laps, stopped after six hours

1 Mauro Baldi/   Sauber C9/88-
Stefan Johansson   Mercedes-Benz 142 6h01m34.23
2 Jan Lammers/Martin Brundle Jaguar XJR-9   142 6h01m58.79
3 Jochen Mass/   Sauber C9/88-
Jean-Louis Schlesser   Mercedes-Benz 139
4 Oscar Larrauri/Manuel Reuter Porsche 962 138
5 Thorkild Thyrring/   Spice SE88C-
Almo Coppelli   Ford   134
6 Gordon Spice/Ray Bellm   Spice SE88C-
                             Ford   132

Winner's average speed: 101.607 mph. Pole position: Baldi, 2m02.25. Fastest lap: Lammers, 2m22.12

Fuji 1000 kms

9 October 1988. Fuji. 224 laps of a 2.777-mile circuit = 622.048 miles

1 Martin Brundle/
Eddie Cheever   Jaguar XJR-9   224 5h28m05.941
2 Klaus Ludwig/Price Cobb   Porsche 962   223
3 Frank Jelinski/"John Winter" Porsche 962 221
4 Stanley Dickens/
Hideki Okada   Porsche 962   221
5 Jochen Mass/Kenneth   Sauber C9/88-
Acheson/Jean-Louis Schlesser Mercedes-Benz 220
6 Kunimitsu Takahashi/
Kazuo Mogi   Porsche 962   217

Winner's average speed: 113.755 mph. Pole position: Hideki Okada (Porsche 962), 1m18.210. Fastest lap: Ludwig, 1m21.795

Lucas Supersprint 360

20 November 1988. Sandown Park. 93 laps of a 2.425-mile circuit = 225.525 miles

1 Jean-Louis Schlesser/   Sauber C9/88-
Jochen Mass   Mercedes-Benz 93 2h30m51.35
2 Mauro Baldi/   Sauber C9/88-
Stefan Johansson   Mercedes-Benz 93 2h30m56.00
3 Eddie Cheever/
Martin Brundle   Jaguar XJR-9   93
4 Jan Lammers/
Johnny Dumfries   Jaguar XJR-9   92

5 Gordon Spice/Ray Bellm   Spice SE88C-
                             Ford   88
6 Neil Crang/Tim Lee-Davey   Porsche 962   88

Winner's average speed: 89.698 mph. Pole position: Schlesser. Fastest lap: Schlesser, 1m33.58

FINAL CHAMPIONSHIP POSITIONS

Drivers

1	Martin Brundle	240 (267)*	7	Swiss Team Salamin 38
2	Jean-Louis Schlesser	208 (259)*	8	Porsche Kremer Racing 37
3	Mauro Baldi	188 (198)*	9	Richard Lloyd Racing 28
4	Eddie Cheever	182	10	From A Racing 20
5	Jochen Mass	180	11	GP Motorsport 18
6	Klaus Ludwig	145	12	Chamberlain Engineering 16
7	"John Winter"	140 (143)*	13=	Alpha/Nova Engineering 12
8	Frank Jelinski	135		Team Davey 12
9	Bob Wollek	122	15	Kelmar Racing 9
10	Jan Lammers	118	16=	Obermaier Racing 8
11	John Nielsen	97		Rothmans Team Schuppan 8
12=	Ray Bellm	88 (94)*	18=	ADA Engineering 4
	Gordon Spice	88 (94)*		Lucky Strike Schanche 4
14	Johnny Dumfries	88		Mazdaspeed 4
15	Stanley Dickens	72		Nissan Motorsport 4
16=	Almo Coppelli	67	22	Takefuji Team Schuppan 3
	Thorkild Thyrring	67	23	Trust Engineering 2
18	Manuel Reuter	58	24	Maurer Design 1
19	Stefan Johansson	55		
20	James Weaver	54		
	*Best seven results count			

Teams

1	Silk Cut Jaguar (TWR)	357
2	AEG Sauber Mercedes	278
3	Jöst Racing	189
4	Brun Motorsport	94
5	Spice Engineering	78
6	Porsche System Engineering	75

Drivers - C2

1=	Ray Bellm	260 (300)*
	Gordon Spice	260 (300)*
	*Best seven results count	

Teams - C2

1	Spice Engineering	390

1989

World Sports-Prototype Championship

Suzuka 480 kms

9 April 1989. Suzuka. 82 laps of a 3.641-mile circuit = 298.562 miles

1 Jean-Louis Schlesser/   Sauber C9/88-
Mauro Baldi   Mercedes-Benz 82 2h48m58.453
2 Kenneth Acheson   Sauber C9/88-
                             Mercedes-Benz 82 2h49m04.634
3 Bob Wollek/Frank Jelinski Porsche 962   82
4 Toshio Suzuki/
Kazuyoshi Hoshino   Nissan R88C   81
5 John Nielsen/Andy Wallace Jaguar XJR-9   81
6 Paolo Barilla/Hitoshi Ogawa Toyota 89CV   81

Winner's average speed: 106.015 mph. Pole position: Geoff Lees (Toyota 89CV), 1m50.635. Fastest lap: Jan Lammers (Jaguar XJR-9), 1m57.549

Coupe de Dijon

21 May 1989. Dijon-Prenois. 127 laps of a 2.361-mile circuit = 299.847 miles

1 Bob Wollek/Frank Jelinski Porsche 962   127 2h42m21.903
2 Jean-Louis Schlesser/   Sauber C9/88-
Jochen Mass   Mercedes-Benz 127 2h43m00.298
3 Mauro Baldi/   Sauber C9/88-
Kenneth Acheson   Mercedes-Benz 127

4 Johnny Dumfries/Geoff Lees Toyota 88C 126
5 Derek Bell/Tiff Needell Porsche 962GTI 124
6 Pascal Fabre/ Cougar C22-
 Jean-Louis Bousquet Porsche 123

Winner's average speed: 110.805 mph. Pole position: Schlesser,
1m07.275. Fastest lap: Mauro Baldi (Sauber C9/88-Mercedes-
Benz), 1m11.739.

Trofeo Repsol

**25 June 1989. Jarama. 145 laps of a 2.115-mile circuit =
306.675 miles**

1 Jochen Mass/ Sauber C9/88-
 Jean-Louis Schlesser Mercedes-Benz 145 3h26m13.882
2 Jan Lammers/Patrick Tambay Jaguar XJR-9 144
3 Oscar Larrauri/Jesus Pareja* Porsche 962 143
4 Thorkild Thyrring/ Spice SE89C-
 Wayne Taylor Ford 143
5 Mauro Baldi/ Sauber C9/88-
 Kenneth Acheson Mercedes-Benz 143
6 John Nielsen/Andy Wallace Jaguar XJR-9 142

*Pareja drove for less than 30% of the race so was ineligible for
points. Winner's average speed: 89.239 mph. Pole position:
Baldi, 1m15.580. Fastest lap: Baldi, 1m20.970

Brands Hatch Trophy

**23 July 1989. Brands Hatch. 115 laps of a 2.600-mile circuit
= 299.000 miles**

1 Mauro Baldi/ Sauber C9/88-
 Kenneth Acheson Mercedes-Benz 115 2h41m37.754
2 Bob Wollek/Frank Jelinski Porsche 962 115 2h42m54.796
3 Jean-Louis Schlesser/ Sauber C9/88-
 Jochen Mass Mercedes-Benz 114
4 David Leslie/Brian Redman Aston Martin
 AMR1 112
5 Jan Lammers/Patrick Tambay Jaguar XJR-11 111
6 Walter Brun/Jesus Pareja Porsche 962 111

Winner's average speed: 111.003 mph. Pole position: Lammers,
1m12.927. Fastest lap: Baldi, 1m16.111

ADAC Trophäe

**20 August 1989. Nürburgring. 106 laps of a
2.822-mile circuit = 299.132 miles**

1 Jean-Louis Schlesser/ Sauber C9/88-
 Jochen Mass Mercedes-Benz 106 2h47m14.599
2 Mauro Baldi/ Sauber C9/88-
 Kenneth Acheson Mercedes-Benz 106 2h47m16.677
3 George Fouché/ Porsche
 Giovanni Lavaggi 962-CK6 104
4 Walter Brun/Jesus Pareja Porsche 962 104
5 John Nielsen/Andy Wallace Jaguar XJR-11 104
6 Oscar Larrauri/Franz Konrad Porsche 962 104

Winner's average speed: 107.316 mph. Pole position: Baldi,
1m23.125. Fastest lap: Schlesser, 1m29.281

Wheatcroft Gold Cup

**3 September 1989. Donington Park. 120 laps of a
2.500-mile circuit = 300.000 miles**

1 Jochen Mass/ Sauber C9/88-
 Jean-Louis Schlesser Mercedes-Benz 120 2h57m50.883
2 Kenneth Acheson/ Sauber C9/88-
 Mauro Baldi Mercedes-Benz 120 2h58m42.777
3 Julian Bailey/Mark Blundell Nissan R89C 120
4 Bob Wollek/Frank Jelinski Porsche 962 119
5 Oscar Larrauri/
 Harald Huysman Porsche 962 119
6 David Leslie/Michael Roe Aston Martin
 AMR1 118

Winner's average speed: 101.210 mph. Pole position: Baldi,
1m19.123. Fastest lap: Bailey, 1m24.500

Coupe de Spa

**17 September 1989. Spa-Francorchamps. 70 laps of a
4.312-mile circuit = 301.840 miles**

1 Mauro Baldi/ Sauber C9/88-
 Kenneth Acheson Mercedes-Benz 70 2h39m16.453
2 Bob Wollek/Frank Jelinski Porsche 962 70 2h41m32.434
3 Julian Bailey/Mark Blundell Nissan R89C 69
4 Oscar Larrauri/
 Roland Ratzenberger Porsche 962 68
5 Wayne Taylor/ Spice SE89C-
 Thorkild Thyrring Ford 68
6 Henri Pescarolo/
 Jean-Louis Ricci Porsche 962 68

Winner's average speed: 113.706 mph. Pole position: Baldi,
2m05.900. Fastest lap: Baldi, 2m07.863

Trofeo Hermanos Rodriguez

**29 October 1989. Mexico City. 109 laps of a
2.747-mile circuit = 299.423 miles**

1 Jean-Louis Schlesser/ Sauber C9/88-
 Jochen Mass Mercedes-Benz 109 2h51m17.986
2 Oscar Larrauri/
 Harald Huysman Porsche 962 109 2h51m54.429
3 Henri Pescarolo/Frank Jelinski Porsche 962 109
4 Derek Bell/Tiff Needell Porsche 962GTI 108
5 Andy Wallace/Alain Ferté Jaguar XJR-9 108
6 Patrick Tambay/Jan Lammers Jaguar XJR-9 108

Winner's average speed: 104.877 mph. Pole position: Mauro
Baldi (Sauber C9/88-Mercedes-Benz), 1m22.571. Fastest lap:
Schlesser, 1m25.120

FINAL CHAMPIONSHIP POSITIONS

Drivers

1	Jean-Louis		3	Brun Motorsport	66
	Schlesser	115 (127)*	4	Silk Cut	
2	Jochen Mass	107		Jaguar (TWR)	57
3	Mauro Baldi	102 (110)*	5	Nissan Motorsport	37
4	Kenneth		6	Aston Martin	26
	Acheson	97 (105)*	7	Toyota Team	
5	Frank Jelinski	84		TOM's	25
6	Bob Wollek	72	8	Porsche Kremer	
7	Oscar Larrauri	54		Racing	21
8=	Jan Lammers	30	9	Spice Engineering	19
	Patrick Tambay	30	10	Richard Lloyd	
	Andy Wallace	30		Racing	18
11	Julian Bailey	27	11	Courage	
	Mark Blundell	27		Compétition	16
13	Harald Huysman	25	12	Porsche Almeras	5
14=	Henri Pescarolo	24	13=	Chamberlain	
	Brian Redman	24		Engineering	3
16=	David Leslie	22		France Promoteam	3
	John Nielsen	22		Mazdaspeed	3
18=	Walter Brun	20	16	Obermaier Racing	1
	Jesus Pareja	20			
20=	Johnny Dumfries	19			
	Thorkild Thyrring	19	**Drivers - C2**		
	*Best six results count		1=	Nick Adams	107
				Fermin Velez	107

Teams

1	Team Sauber		**Teams - C2**		
	Mercedes	155	1	Chamberlain	
2	Jöst Racing	84		Engineering	120

1990

WORLD SPORTS-PROTOTYPE CHAMPIONSHIP

Fuji Film Cup

**8 April 1990. Suzuka. 82 laps of a 3.641-mile circuit
= 298.562 miles**

1 Jean-Louis Schlesser/ Sauber C9/88-
 Mauro Baldi Mercedes-Benz 82 2h43m45.429

2 Jochen Mass/ Sauber C9/88-
Karl Wendlinger Mercedes-Benz 82 2h44m27.762
3 Masahiro Hasemi/
Anders Olofsson Nissan R89C 81
4 Geoff Lees/Hitoshi Ogawa Toyota 90CV 81
5 Kunimitsu Takahashi/
Kazuo Mogi Porsche 962 80
6 Oscar Larrauri/
Harald Huysman Porsche 962 80

Winner's average speed: 109.392 mph. Pole position: Lees, 1m48.716. Fastest lap: Martin Brundle (Jaguar XJR-11), 1m53.732

Trofeo Filippo Caracciolo

29 April 1990. Monza. 83 laps of a 3.604-mile circuit = 299.132 miles

1 Mauro Baldi/ Mercedes-Benz
Jean-Louis Schlesser C11 83 2h17m11.736
2 Jochen Mass/ Mercedes-Benz
Karl Wendlinger C11 83 2h17m29.348
3 Martin Brundle/Alain Ferté Jaguar XJR-11 83
4 Jan Lammers/Andy Wallace Jaguar XJR-11 82
5 Bob Wollek/Frank Jelinski Porsche 962 82
6 Wayne Taylor/ Spice SE90C-
Eric van de Poele Ford 81

Winner's average speed: 130.816 mph. Pole position: Baldi, 1m29.165. Fastest lap: Mass, 1m33.426

British Empire Trophy

20 May 1990. Silverstone. 101 laps of a 2.969-mile circuit = 299.869 miles

1 Martin Brundle/Alain Ferté Jaguar XJR-11 101 2h19m39.467
2 Jan Lammers/Andy Wallace Jaguar XJR-11 100
3 Bruno Giacomelli/ Spice SE90C-
Fermin Velez Ford 100
4 Bob Wollek/Frank Jelinski Porsche 962 99
5 Bernd Schneider/ Porsche
Steven Andskär 962-CK6 98
6 Oscar Larrauri/
Harald Huysman Porsche 962BM 97

Winner's average speed: 128.830 mph. Pole position: Jean-Louis Schlesser (Mercedes-Benz C11), 1m12.073. Fastest lap: Schlesser, 1m16.649

Coupe de Spa

3 June 1990. Spa-Francorchamps. 70 laps of a 4.312-mile circuit = 301.840 miles

1 Jochen Mass/ Mercedes-Benz
Karl Wendlinger C11 70 2h42m54.880
2 Jan Lammers/Andy Wallace Jaguar XJR-11 70 2h44m25.656
3 Julian Bailey/
Kenneth Acheson Nissan R90C 70
4 Tim Harvey/Fermin Velez Spice SE90C-
Ford 69
5 Oscar Larrauri/
Harald Huysman Porsche 962BM 69
6 Steven Andskär/
Manuel Reuter Porsche 962GTI 69

Winner's average speed: 111.165 mph. Pole position: Mauro Baldi (Mercedes-Benz C11), 1m59.350. Fastest lap: Baldi, 2m06.211

Coupe de Dijon

22 July 1990. Dijon-Prenois. 127 laps of a 2.361-mile circuit = 299.847 miles

1 Jean-Louis Schlesser/ Mercedes-Benz
Mauro Baldi C11 127 2h39m03.603
2 Jochen Mass/ Mercedes-Benz
Michael Schumacher C11 127 2h39m07.448

3 Julian Bailey/Mark Blundell Nissan R90C 126
4 Jan Lammers/Andy Wallace Jaguar XJR-11 125
5 Martin Brundle/Alain Ferté Jaguar XJR-11 125
6 Wayne Taylor/Eliseo Salazar Spice SE90C-
Ford 124

Winner's average speed: 113.107 mph. Pole position: Schlesser, 1m05.527. Fastest lap: Schlesser, 1m08.973

ADAC Sportswagen Trophäe

19 August 1990. Nürburgring. 106 laps of a 2.822-mile circuit = 299.132 miles

1 Mauro Baldi/ Mercedes-Benz
Jean-Louis Schlesser C11 106 2h39m15.913
2 Jochen Mass/ Mercedes-Benz
Michael Schumacher C11 106 2h39m38.475
3 Martin Brundle/Alain Ferté Jaguar XJR-11 105
4 Jan Lammers/Andy Wallace Jaguar XJR-11 105
5 Mark Blundell Nissan R90C 103
6 Bob Wollek/Frank Jelinski Porsche 962 103

Winner's average speed: 112.692 mph. Pole position: Schlesser, 1m20.344. Fastest lap: Schlesser, 1m26.092

Shell Donington Trophy

2 September 1990. Donington Park. 120 laps of a 2.500-mile circuit = 300.000 miles

1 Jean-Louis Schlesser/ Mercedes-Benz
Mauro Baldi C11 120 2h53m40.919
2 Jochen Mass/ Mercedes-Benz
Heinz-Harald Frentzen C11 120 2h55m03.134
3 Tim Harvey/Cor Euser Spice SE90C-
Ford 118
4 Kenneth Acheson/
Gianfranco Brancatelli Nissan R90C 117
5 Eric van de Poele/ Spice SE90C-
Bruno Giacomelli Ford 117
6 Julian Bailey/Mark Blundell Nissan R90C 117

Winner's average speed: 103.638 mph. Pole position: Baldi, 1m16.952. Fastest lap: Baldi, 1m23.597

Mondial Players LTEE

23 September 1990. Montréal. 61 laps of a 2.728-mile circuit = 166.408 miles. Race scheduled for 110 laps but stopped due to an accident, half points awarded

1 Mauro Baldi/ Mercedes-Benz
Jean-Louis Schlesser C11 61 1h44m42.012
2 Mark Blundell/Julian Bailey Nissan R90C 61 1h44m48.460
3 Manuel Reuter Porsche 962GTI 61
4 Bernd Schneider Porsche 962-CK6 61
5 Kenneth Acheson Nissan R90C 61
6 Bob Wollek/Frank Jelinski Porsche 962 61

Winner's average speed: 95.363 mph. Pole position: Schlesser, 1m25.407. Fastest lap: Baldi, 1m28.725

Trofeo Hermanos Rodriguez

7 October 1990. Mexico City. 109 laps of a 2.747-mile circuit = 299.423 miles

1 Jochen Mass/ Mercedes-Benz
Michael Schumacher C11 109 2h47m54.970
2 Julian Bailey/Mark Blundell Nissan R90C 107
3 Andy Wallace/Davy Jones Jaguar XJR-11 107
4 Gianfranco Brancatelli/
Kenneth Acheson Nissan R90C 106
5 Hans-Joachim Stuck/
Jonathan Palmer Porsche 962 106
6 Bob Wollek/Frank Jelinski Porsche 962 105

Winner's average speed: 107.000 mph. Pole position: Martin Brundle (Jaguar XJR-11), 1m20.626. Fastest lap: Schumacher, 1m23.250

FINAL CHAMPIONSHIP POSITIONS

Drivers

1=	Mauro Baldi	49.5	20=	Cor Euser	4
	Jean-Louis			Masahiro Hasemi	4
	Schlesser	49.5		Davy Jones	4
3	Jochen Mass	48		Oscar Larrauri	4
4	Andy Wallace	25		Anders Olofsson	4
5=	Jan Lammers	21			
	Michael				
	Schumacher	21	**Teams**		
	Karl Wendlinger	21	1	Team Sauber	
8	Martin Brundle	19		Mercedes	67.5
9	Julian Bailey	18	2	Silk Cut	
10	Mark Blundell	16		Jaguar (TWR)	30
11	Kenneth Acheson	11	3	Nissan Motorsport	26
12	Alain Ferté	10	4	Spice Engineering	13
13=	Frank Jelinski	7.5	5	Jöst Racing	8.5
	Bob Wollek	7.5	6	Porsche Kremer	
15=	Tim Harvey	7		Racing	5.5
	Fermin Velez	7	7	Brun Motorsport	4
17=	Gianfranco		8=	Richard Lloyd	
	Brancatelli	6		Racing	3
	Heinz-Harald			Toyota Team TOM's	3
	Frentzen	6			
	Bruno Giacomelli	6			

1991

WORLD SPORTS CAR CHAMPIONSHIP

Fuji Film Cup

14 April 1991. Suzuka. 74 laps of a 3.641-mile circuit = 269.434 miles

1	Mauro Baldi/Philippe Alliot	Peugeot 905	74	2h25m01.688
2	Jean-Louis Schlesser/	Mercedes-Benz		
	Jochen Mass	C11	73	
3	Manuel Reuter/	Porsche		
	Harri Toivonen	962-CK6	72	
4	Charles Zwolsman/Cor Euser	Spice SE90C-Ford	72	
5	George Fouché/			
	Steven Andskär	Porsche 962	71	
6	David Kennedy/			
	Maurizio Sandro Sala	Mazda 787B	71	

Winner's average speed: 111.468 mph. Pole position: Derek Warwick (Jaguar XJR-14), 1m48.084. Fastest lap: Warwick, 1m50.454

The Jaguar XJR-14, to many the ultimate racing Sports Car

Trofeo Filippo Caracciolo

5 May 1991. Monza. 75 laps of a 3.604-mile circuit = 270.300 miles

1	Martin Brundle/ Derek Warwick	Jaguar XJR-14	75	2h05m42.844
2	Teo Fabi/Martin Brundle	Jaguar XJR-14	74	
3	Jean-Louis Schlesser/ Jochen Mass	C11	73	
4	Cor Euser/Charles Zwolsman	Spice SE90C-Ford	71	
5	Manuel Reuter/ Harri Toivonen	Porsche 962-CK6	71	

6	Oscar Larrauri/ Massimo Sigala	Porsche 962	69

Winner's average speed: 129.003 mph. Pole position: Fabi, 1m33.672. Fastest lap: Brundle, 1m29.182

Castrol BRDC Empire Trophy

19 May 1991. Silverstone. 83 laps of a 3.247-mile circuit = 269.501 miles

1	Derek Warwick*/Teo Fabi	Jaguar XJR-14	83	2h12m30.045
2	Karl Wendlinger/ Michael Schumacher	Mercedes-Benz C291	82	
3	Martin Brundle	Jaguar XJR-14	79	
4	Jean-Louis Schlesser/ Jochen Mass	Mercedes-Benz C11	79	
5	Cor Euser/Richard Piper	Spice SE90C-Ford	78	
6	Philippe Alliot/Mauro Baldi	Peugeot 905	78	

*Warwick not entered in car so was ineligible for points. Winner's average speed: 122.037 mph. Pole position: Fabi, 1m27.478. Fastest lap: Brundle, 1m29.372

24 heures du Mans

22-23 June 1991. Le Mans. 362 laps of a 8.451-mile circuit = 3059.262 miles

1	Volker Weidler/Johnny Herbert/Bertrand Gachot*	Mazda 787B	362	23h58m35.912
2	Raul Boesel/Michel Ferté*/ Davy Jones	Jaguar XJR-12	360	
3	Teo Fabi/Bob Wollek/ Kenneth Acheson	Jaguar XJR-12	358	
4	Derek Warwick/ John Nielsen/Andy Wallace	Jaguar XJR-12	356	
5	Karl Wendlinger/ Michael Schumacher/ Fritz Kreutzpointner	Mercedes-Benz C11	355	
6	David Kennedy/ Stefan Johansson/ Maurizio Sandro Sala	Mazda 787B	355	

*Gachot and Ferté drove insufficient distance to score points. Winner's average speed: 127.593 mph. Pole position: Jean-Louis Schlesser (Mercedes-Benz C11), 3m31.250. Fastest lap: Schumacher, 3m35.564

ADAC Sportswagon Trophäe

18 August 1991. Nürburgring. 95 laps of a 2.822-mile circuit = 268.090 miles

1	David Brabham/ Derek Warwick	Jaguar XJR-14	95	2h23m41.028
2	Teo Fabi/David Brabham	Jaguar XJR-14	95	2h23m45.937
3	Manuel Reuter/ Harri Toivonen	Porsche 962-CK6	89	
4	Jürgen Oppermann/ Otto Altenbach	Porsche 962	89	
5	Maurizio Sandro Sala/ David Kennedy	Mazda 787B	89	
6	Lionel Robert/ François Migault*	Cougar C26S-Porsche	89	

*includes a one minute penalty for overtaking another car while yellow flags were being shown. Winner's average speed: 111.950 mph. Pole position: Fabi, 1m19.519. Fastest lap: Fabi, 1m21.533

SWC Magny-Cours

15 September 1991. Magny-Cours. 101 laps of a 2.654-mile circuit = 268.054 miles

1	Yannick Dalmas/ Keke Rosberg	Peugeot 905B	101	2h31m38.258
2	Philippe Alliot/Mauro Baldi	Peugeot 905B	101	2h32m21.078
3	Teo Fabi/David Brabham	Jaguar XJR-14	99	
4	Cor Euser/ Charles Zwolsman	Spice SE90C-Ford	95	
5	David Brabham/ Derek Warwick	Jaguar XJR-14	94	
6	Manuel Reuter/ Harri Toivonen	Porsche 962-CK6	93	

Winner's average speed: 106.064 mph. Pole position: Dalmas, 1m21.821. Fastest lap: Alliot, 1m25.823

Sports Car World Championship

Trofeo Hermanos Rodriguez

6 October 1991. Mexico City. 98 laps of a 2.747-mile circuit = 269.206 miles

1	Keke Rosberg/		
	Yannick Dalmas	Peugeot 905B	98 2h29m25.811
2	Philippe Alliot/Mauro Baldi	Peugeot 905B	97
3	Bernd Schneider/		
	"John Winter"*	Porsche 962	94
4	Cor Euser/Charles Zwolsman	Spice SE90C-Ford	93
5	Derek Bell/		
	Gianpiero Moretti	Porsche 962	92
6	David Brabham/		
	Derek Warwick	Jaguar XJR-14	92

*"Winter" drove insufficient distance to score points. Winner's average speed: 108.093 mph. Pole position: Alliot, 1m19.229. Fastest lap: Michael Schumacher (Mercedes-Benz C291), 1m21.611

SWC Autopolis

27 October 1991. Autopolis. 93 laps of a 2.904-mile circuit = 270.072 miles

1	Michael Schumacher/	Mercedes-Benz	
	Karl Wendlinger	C291	93 2h26m36.699
2	Derek Warwick	Jaguar XJR-14	93 2h27m07.187
3	Teo Fabi/David Brabham	Jaguar XJR-14	93 2h28m15.860
4	Mauro Baldi/Philippe Alliot	Peugeot 905B	92
5	Jean-Louis Schlesser/	Mercedes-Benz	
	Jochen Mass	C291	92
6	Geoff Lees/Andy Wallace*	Toyota TS010	90

*Toyota not entered in championship so was ineligible for points. Winner's average speed: 110.525 mph. Pole position: Fabi, 1m27.188. Fastest lap: Yannick Dalmas (Peugeot 905B), 1m30.615

FINAL CHAMPIONSHIP POSITIONS

Drivers

1	Teo Fabi	86		18=	David Brabham	18
2	Derek Warwick	79		19=	David Kennedy	16
3=	Philippe Alliot	69			Jesus Pareja	16
	Mauro Baldi	69				
5	Cor Euser	54		**Teams**		
6	Charles Zwolsman	46		1	Silk Cut	
7=	Jochen Mass	45			Jaguar (TWR)	108
	Jean-Louis			2	Peugeot Talbot	
	Schlesser	45			Sport	79
9=	Manuel Reuter	43		3	Team Sauber	
	Michael				Mercedes	70
	Schumacher	43		4	Euro Racing	54
	Karl Wendlinger	43		5	Mazdaspeed	47
12	Harri Toivonen	41		6	Porsche Kremer	
13=	Yannick Dalmas	40			Racing	43
	Keke Rosberg	40		7	Courage	
15	Maurizio Sandro				Compétition	28
	Sala	31		8	Swiss Team Salamin	26
16=	Johnny Herbert	20		9	Brun Motorsport	22
	Volker Weidler	20		10	Konrad Motorsport	6

1992

WORLD SPORTS CAR CHAMPIONSHIP

Trofeo Filippo Caracciolo

26 April 1992. Monza. 87 laps of a 3.604-mile circuit = 313.548 miles

1	Geoff Lees/Hitoshi Ogawa	Toyota TS010	87 2h16m42.659
2	Derek Warwick/		
	Yannick Dalmas	Peugeot 905B	85
3	Bernard Thuner/	Spice SE89C-	
	Ferdinand de Lesseps	Ford	76

4	Almo Coppelli/	Gebhardt C91-	
	Frank Krämer	Ford	75
5	Luigi Taverna/	Spice SE90C-	
	Alessandro Gini	Ford	60
6	Raineri Randaccio/	Spice SE90C-	
	"Stingbrace"	Ford	46

Winner's average speed: 137.607 mph. Pole position: Dalmas, 1m26.019. Fastest lap: Mauro Baldi (Peugeot 905B), 1m29.386

Castrol BRDC Empire Trophy

10 May 1992. Silverstone. 96 laps of a 3.247-mile circuit = 311.712 miles

1	Derek Warwick/		
	Yannick Dalmas	Peugeot 905B	96 2h32m29.226
2	Maurizio Sandro Sala/		
	Johnny Herbert	Mazda MXR01	94
3	Will Hoy/	Spice SE89C-	
	Ferdinand de Lesseps	Ford	85
4	Raineri Randaccio/	Spice SE90C-	
	"Stingbrace"	Ford	76
5	Geoff Lees/Hitoshi Ogawa	Toyota TS010	55
6	Cor Euser/Charles Zwolsman	Lola T92/10-Judd	29

Winner's average speed: 122.651 mph. Pole position: Warwick, 1m24.421. Fastest lap: Warwick, 1m29.043

24 heures du Mans

20-21 June 1992. Le Mans. 352 laps of a 8.451-mile circuit = 2974.752 miles

1	Derek Warwick/Yannick		
	Dalmas/Mark Blundell	Peugeot 905B	352 24h00m54.765
2	Masanori Sekiya/Pierre-Henri		
	Raphanel/Kenneth Acheson	Toyota TS010	346
3	Mauro Baldi/Philippe Alliot/		
	Jean-Pierre Jabouille	Peugeot 905B	345
4	Johnny Herbert/Volker		
	Weidler/Bertrand Gachot/		
	Maurizio Sandro Sala	Mazda MXR01	336
5	George Fouché/Steven		
	Andskär/Stefan Johansson	Toyota 92CV	336
6	Bob Wollek/Henri Pescarolo/	Cougar C28S-	
	Jean-Louis Ricci	Porsche	335

Winner's average speed: 123.869 mph. Pole position: Alliot, 3m21.209. Fastest lap: Jan Lammers (Toyota TS010), 3m32.295

Triton Showers Trophy

19 July 1992. Donington Park. 125 laps of a 2.500-mile circuit = 312.500 miles

1	Mauro Baldi/Philippe Alliot	Peugeot 905B	125 2h54m03.868
2	Derek Warwick/		
	Yannick Dalmas	Peugeot 905B	125 2h54m04.444
3	Geoff Lees/David Brabham	Toyota TS010	125 2h54m32.016
4	Phil Andrews/	Lola T92/10-	
	Heinz-Harald Frentzen	Judd	119
5	Maurizio Sandro Sala/		
	Alex Caffi	Mazda MXR01	112
6	Ferdinand de Lesseps/	Spice SE89C-	
	Will Hoy	Ford	111

Winner's average speed: 107.719 mph. Pole position: Warwick, 1m15.285. Fastest lap: Warwick, 1m19.380

Fuji Film Cup

30 August 1992. Suzuka. 171 laps of a 3.641-mile circuit = 622.611 miles

1	Derek Warwick/		
	Yannick Dalmas	Peugeot 905B	171 5h30m09.627
2	Geoff Lees/Jan Lammers/		
	David Brabham	Toyota TS010	171
3	Mauro Baldi/Philippe Alliot	Peugeot 905B	163
4	Mauro Martini/Katsutomo		
	Kaneishi/Jeff Krosnoff	Nissan R91CK	163
5	Jesus Pareja/	Lola T92/10-	
	Hideshi Matsuda	Judd	160

6 Ferdinand de Lesseps/Nick
Adams/Masahiro Kimoto   Spice SE90C-
Ford   144

Winner's average speed: 113.147 mph. Pole position: Alliot,
1m43.957. Fastest lap: Alliot, 1m50.660

SWC Magny-Cours

18 October 1992. Magny-Cours. 118 laps of a
2.641-mile circuit = 311.638 miles

1	Philippe Alliot/Mauro Baldi	Peugeot 905B	118 2h44m19.617
2	Christophe Bouchut/		
	Eric Hélary	Peugeot 905B	116
3	Geoff Lees/Jan Lammers	Toyota TS010	114
4	Andy Wallace/		
	David Brabham	Toyota TS010	113
5	Derek Warwick/		
	Yannick Dalmas	Peugeot 905B	113
6	Alex Caffi/		
	Maurizio Sandro Sala	Mazda MXR01	107

Winner's average speed: 113.787 mph. Pole position: Alliot,
1m16.415. Fastest lap: Alliot, 1m20.346

FINAL CHAMPIONSHIP POSITIONS

Drivers

1=	Yannick Dalmas	98	16=	Kenneth Acheson	15
	Derek Warwick	98		Christophe Bouchut	15
3=	Philippe Alliot	64		Eric Hélary	15
	Mauro Baldi	64		Pierre-Henri	
5	Geoff Lees	59		Raphanel	15
6	Jan Lammers	35	20	Alex Caffi	14
7	Ferdinand				
	de Lesseps	34		**Teams**	
8	Maurizio Sandro		1	Peugeot Talbot	
	Sala	29		Sport	115
9	Johnny Herbert	25	2	Toyota Team	
10	David Brabham	22		TOM's	74
11	Hitoshi Ogawa	20	3	Mazdaspeed	39
12=	Will Hoy	18	4	Chamberlain	
	Andy Wallace	18		Engineering	34
14	Raineri Randaccio	17	5	Euro Racing	26
15	Heinz-Harald		6	Team SCI	17
	Frentzen	16			

RECORDS

DRIVERS' RECORDS

MOST WINS

Jacky Ickx	37	Jean-Louis Schlesser	15
Jochen Mass	32	Phil Hill	14
Derek Bell	21	Jo Siffert	13
Henri Pescarolo	21	Bob Wollek	12
Mauro Baldi	17	Gérard Larrousse	12
Brian Redman	16	Stirling Moss	12

MOST POLE POSITIONS

Jacky Ickx	20	Hans-Joachim Stuck	10
Jochen Mass	13	Vittorio Brambilla	9
Mauro Baldi	12	Stefan Bellof	8
Jean-Louis Schlesser	12	Pedro Rodriguez	8
Riccardo Patrese	10	Rolf Stommelen	8
Jo Siffert	10	John Surtees	8

MOST FASTEST LAPS

Jacky Ickx	25**	Phil Hill	9
Jochen Mass	13	Jo Siffert	9
Stirling Moss	12	Rolf Stommelen	9
Mauro Baldi	11	Stefan Bellof	8
Jean-Louis Schlesser	10	Vic Elford	8
John Surtees	10	*includes fastest lap shared twice	

MANUFACTURERS' RECORDS

MOST WINS

Porsche	126	Matra-Simca	15
Ferrari	63	Ford	13
Mercedes-Benz		Lancia	11
(including Sauber)	25	Aston Martin	7
Jaguar	23	Peugeot	7
Alfa Romeo	19		

MOST POLE POSITIONS

Porsche	105	Ford	14
Ferrari	50	Alfa Romeo	13
Mercedes-Benz		Jaguar	9
(including Sauber)	25	Alpine-Renault	8
Lancia	17	Peugeot	8
Matra-Simca	15		

MOST FASTEST LAPS

Porsche	104*	Lancia	15*
Ferrari	55	Matra-Simca	15
Mercedes-Benz		Maserati	11
(including Sauber)	26	Alpine-Renault	8
Alfa Romeo	16	Peugeot	7
Jaguar	15	*includes a shared fastest lap	

INTERNATIONAL GT SERIES

In an attempt to fill the void made by the cancellation of the World Sports Car Championship the private BPR Organization promoted a series of non-championship endurance races for GT cars in 1994. It has attracted a healthy field of private Porsches, Venturis, Lotuses and Ferraris, and championship status has been awarded for 1995.

RACE WINNERS

1994

date	race	driver	nat	car	mph
06.03.94	Paul Ricard	Jean-Pierre Jarier/Jesus Pareja/Bob Wollek	F/E/F	Porsche 911 turbo LM	102.056
10.04.94	Jarama	Jean-Pierre Jarier/Jesus Pareja/Dominique Dupuy	F/E/F	Porsche 911 turbo LM	83.720
30.04.94	Dijon-Prenois	Michel Ferté/Michel Neugarten	F/B	Venturi 600LM	96.211
29.05.94	Montlhéry	Jean-Claude Basso/Henri Pescarolo	F	Venturi 600LM	81.704
10.07.94	Vallelunga	Anders Olofsson/Luciano della Noce	S/I	Ferrari F40	88.069
22.07.94	Spa-Francorchamps	Michel Ferté/Michel Neugarten	F/B	Venturi 600LM	94.926
28.08.94	Suzuka	Jean-Pierre Jarier/Bob Wollek/Jesus Pareja	F/F/E	Porsche 911 turbo LM	91.950
13.11.94	Zhuhai	Bob Wollek/Jean-Pierre Jarier/Jacques Laffite	F	Porsche 911 turbo LM	78.067

INDIANAPOLIS
500

Turn 1 at the 1988 Indianapolis 500

RULES

The rules for the Indianapolis 500 are the same as those which apply to the Indycar Championship (see page 317).

1911

30 May. 200 laps of a 2.500 mile-circuit = 500.000 miles

1 Ray Harroun/			
Cyrus Patschke	Marmon Wasp	200	6h42m08.000
2 Ralph Mulford	Lozier	200	6h43m51.000
3 David			
Bruce-Brown	Fiat	200	6h52m29.000
4 Spencer Wishart/			
Dave Murphy	Mercedes	200	6h52m57.000
5 Joe Dawson/			
Cyrus Patschke	Marmon	200	6h54m34.000
6 Ralph de Palma	Simplex	200	7h02m02.000

Winner's average speed: 74.602 mph. Starting grid front row: Strang (pole), de Palma, H Endicott and Aitken – positions decided by date of entry

1912

30 May. 200 laps of a 2.500-mile circuit = 500.000 miles

1 Joe Dawson/			
Don Herr	National	200	6h21m06.000
2 Teddy Tetzlaff/			
Caleb Bragg	Fiat	200	6h31m29.000
3 Hughie Hughes	Mercer	200	6h33m09.000
4 Charles Merz/			
William Knipper	Stutz-Wisconsin	200	6h34m40.000
5 Bill Endicott/			
Harry Endicott	Schacht-Wisconsin	200	6h46m28.200
6 Len Zengel/			
William Knipper	Schacht-Wisconsin	200	6h50m28.400

Winner's average speed: 78.719 mph. Starting grid front row: Anderson, 80.93 mph (pole), Zengel, 78.85 mph, Tetzlaff, 84.24 mph and de Palma, 86.02 mph - positions decided by date of entry. Fastest qualifier: Bruce-Brown, 88.45 mph

1913

30 May. 200 laps of a 2.500-mile circuit = 500.000 miles

1 Jules Goux	Peugeot L76	200	6h35m05.000
2 Spencer Wishart/			
Ralph de Palma	Mercer	200	6h48m13.400
3 Charles Merz/			
Earl Cooper	Stutz-Wisconsin	200	6h48m49.250
4 Albert Guyot	Sunbeam	200	7h02m58.950
5 Theodore Pilette	Mercedes-Knight	200	7h20m13.000
6 Howdy Wilcox/			
Frank Fox	Pope-Hartford	200	7h23m26.550

Winner's average speed: 75.933 mph. Starting grid front row: Bragg, 87.34 mph (pole), Guyot, 80.75 mph, Liesaw, 78.02 mph and B Evans, 82.01 mph - positions drawn. Fastest qualifier: Tower, 88.23 mph

1914

30 May. 200 laps of a 2.500-mile circuit = 500.000 miles

1 René Thomas	Delage	200	6h03m45.000
2 Arthur Duray	Peugeot	200	6h10m24.000
3 Albert Guyot	Delage	200	6h14m01.000
4 Jules Goux	Peugeot	200	6h17m24.000
5 Barney Oldfield/			
Gil Anderson	Stutz	200	6h23m51.000
6 Joseph			
Christiaens	Excelsior	200	6h27m24.000

Winner's average speed: 82.474 mph. Starting grid front row: Chassagne, 88.31 mph (pole), Tetzlaff, 96.36 mph, Wilcox, 90.76 mph and Chandler, 87.54 mph - positions drawn. Fastest qualifier: Boillot, 99.86 mph

1915

31 May. 200 laps of a 2.500-mile circuit = 500.000 miles

1 Ralph de Palma	Mercedes	200	5h33m55.510
2 Dario Resta	Peugeot	200	5h37m24.940
3 Gil Anderson/			
Johnny Aitken	Stutz	200	5h42m27.580
4 Earl Cooper/			
Johnny Aitken	Stutz	200	5h46m19.360
5 Eddie O'Donnell	Duesenberg	200	6h08m13.270
6 Bob Burman	Peugeot	200	6h13m19.610

Winner's average speed: 89.840 mph. Starting grid front row: Wilcox, 98.90 mph (pole), R de Palma, 98.58 mph, Resta, 98.47 mph and E Cooper, 96.77 mph

1916

30 May. 120 laps of a 2.500-mile circuit = 300.000 miles

1 Dario Resta	Peugeot	120	3h34m17.000
2 Wilbur d'Alene	Duesenberg	120	3h36m15.000
3 Ralph Mulford	Peugeot	120	3h37m56.000
4 Joseph			
Christiaens	Sunbeam	120	3h46m36.000
5 Barney Oldfield	Delage	120	3h47m19.000
6 Pete Henderson/Eddie			
Rickenbacher	Maxwell	120	3h49m56.000

Winner's average speed: 84.001 mph. Starting grid front row: Aitken, 96.69 mph (pole), Rickenbacher, 96.44 mph, Anderson, 95.94 mph and Resta, 94.40 mph

1919

30 May. 200 laps of a 2.500-mile circuit = 500.000 miles

1 Howdy Wilcox	Peugeot	200	5h40m42.870
2 Eddie Hearne	Stutz	200	5h44m29.040
3 Jules Goux	Peugeot-Premier	200	5h49m06.180
4 Albert Guyot	Ballot	200	5h55m16.270
5 Tom Alley	Bender	200	6h05m03.920
6 Ralph de Palma	Packard	200	6h10m10.920

Winner's average speed: 88.050 mph. Starting grid front row: Thomas, 104.70 mph (pole), Wilcox, 100.01 mph, Guyot, 98.30 mph and R de Palma, 98.20 mph

1920

30 May. 200 laps of a 2.500-mile circuit = 500.000 miles

1 Gaston			
Chevrolet	Frontenac	200	5h40m16.140
2 René Thomas	Ballot	200	5h43m02.290
3 Tommy Milton	Duesenberg	200	5h46m43.380
4 Jimmy Murphy	Duesenberg	200	5h52m31.370
5 Ralph de Palma	Ballot	200	6h05m19.150
6 Eddie Hearne	Duesenberg	200	6h14m19.160

Winner's average speed: 88.166 mph. Starting grid front row: R de Palma, 99.15 mph (pole), Boyer, 96.90 mph, L Chevrolet, 96.30 mph and Chassagne, 95.45 mph

1921

30 May. 200 laps of a 2.500-mile circuit = 500.000 miles

1 Tommy Milton	Frontenac	200	5h34m44.650
2 Roscoe Sarles	Duesenberg	200	5h38m34.030
3 Percy Ford/			
Jules Ellingboe	Frontenac	200	5h52m50.300
4 Eddie Miller/			
Jimmy Murphy	Duesenberg	200	5h54m24.980
5 Ora Haibe	Sunbeam	200	5h55m58.200
6 Albert Guyot/			
Joe Boyer/			
Eddie Miller	Duesenberg	200	6h01m17.700

Winner's average speed: 89.621 mph. Starting grid front row: R de Palma, 100.75 mph (pole), Sarles, 98.35 mph, Boyer, 96.65 mph and Hearne, 96.18 mph

Indianapolis 500

1922

30 May. 200 laps of a 2.500-mile circuit = 500.000 miles

1 Jimmy Murphy	Duesenberg-Miller	200	5h17m30.790
2 Harry Hartz	Duesenberg	200	5h20m44.390
3 Eddie Hearne	Ballot	200	5h22m26.060
4 Ralph de Palma	Duesenberg	200	5h31m04.650
5 Ora Haibe/			
Jules Ellingboe	Duesenberg	200	5h31m13.450
6 Jerry Wonderlich/			
Jules Ellingboe	Duesenberg	200	5h37m52.840

Winner's average speed: 94.484 mph. Starting grid front row: Murphy, 100.50 mph (pole), Hartz, 99.97 mph and de Palma, 99.55 mph

1923

30 May. 200 laps of a 2.500-mile circuit = 500.000 miles

1 Tommy Milton/			
Howdy Wilcox	Miller	200	5h29m50.170
2 Harry Hartz	Miller	200	5h33m05.090
3 Jimmy Murphy	Miller	200	5h40m36.640
4 Eddie Hearne/			
Earl Cooper	Miller	200	5h46m14.230
5 Lora Corum	Ford T-Fronty Ford	200	6h03m16.810
6 Frank Elliott/			
Dave Lewis	Miller	200	6h04m52.870

Winner's average speed: 90.954 mph. Starting grid front row: Milton, 108.17 mph (pole), Hartz, 103.70 mph and Resta, 98.02 mph

1924

30 May. 200 laps of a 2.500-mile circuit = 500.000 miles

1 Lora Corum/			
Joe Boyer	Duesenberg	200	5h05m23.510
2 Earl Cooper	Miller	200	5h06m47.180
3 Jimmy Murphy	Miller	200	5h08m25.390
4 Harry Hartz	Miller	200	5h10m44.390
5 Bennett Hill	Miller	200	5h11m00.070
6 Peter de Paolo	Duesenberg	200	5h18m08.550

Winner's average speed: 98.234 mph. Starting grid front row: Murphy, 108.037 mph (pole), Hartz, 107.130 mph and Milton, 105.200 mph

1925

30 May. 200 laps of a 2.500-mile circuit = 500.000 miles

1 Peter de Paolo/			
Norman Batten	Duesenberg	200	4h56m39.470
2 Dave Lewis/			
Bennett Hill	Miller	200	4h57m33.150
3 "Red" Shafer/			
Wade Morton	Duesenberg	200	4h59m26.790
4 Harry Hartz	Miller	200	5h03m21.590
5 Tommy Milton	Miller	200	5h08m25.720
6 "Leon Duray"/			
Fred Comer	Miller	200	5h09m34.010

Winner's average speed: 101.127 mph. Starting grid front row: "Duray", 113.196 mph (pole), de Paolo, 113.083 mph and Hartz, 112.433 mph

1926

31 May. 160 laps of a 2.500-mile circuit = 400.000 miles

1 Frank Lockhart	Miller	160	4h10m14.950
2 Harry Hartz	Miller	158	
3 Cliff Woodbury	Miller	158	
4 Fred Comer/			
Wade Morton	Miller	155	
5 Peter de Paolo	Duesenberg	153	
6 Frank Elliott/			
"Leon Duray"	Miller	152	

Winner's average speed: 95.904 mph. Starting grid front row: Cooper, 111.735 mph (pole), Hartz, 109.542 mph and "Duray", 109.186 mph

1927

30 May. 200 laps of a 2.500-mile circuit = 500.000 miles

1 George Souders	Duesenberg	200	5h07m33.080
2 Earl de Vore/			
Zeke Meyer	Miller	200	5h19m35.950
3 Tony Gulotta/			
Peter de Paolo	Miller	200	5h22m05.880
4 Wilbur Shaw/			
Louis Meyer	Miller	200	5h22m12.050
5 Dave Evans/			
Steve Nemish	Duesenberg	200	5h30m27.710
6 Robert McDonough/			
Peter de Paolo	Cooper-Miller	200	5h31m49.340

Winner's average speed: 97.545 mph. Starting grid front row: Lockhart, 120.100 mph (pole), de Paolo, 119.510 mph and "Duray", 118.788 mph

1928

30 May. 200 laps of a 2.500-mile circuit = 500.000 miles

1 Louis Meyer	Miller	200	5h01m33.750
2 Lou Moore/			
Louis Schneider	Miller	200	5h02m17.640
3 George Souders	Miller	200	5h06m01.040
4 Ray Keech/			
Wilbur Shaw	Miller	200	5h21m28.450
5 Norman Batten/			
Zeke Meyer	Fengler-Miller	200	5h21m47.510
6 Babe Stapp/			
Ralph Hepburn	Miller	200	5h23m50.410

Winner's average speed: 99.482 mph. Starting grid front row: "Duray", 122.391 mph (pole), Woodbury, 120.418 mph and Bergere, 119.956 mph

1929

30 May. 200 laps of a 2.500-mile circuit = 500.000 miles

1 Ray Keech	Miller	200	5h07m25.420
2 Louis Meyer	Miller	200	5h13m49.210
3 Jimmy Gleason/			
Thane Houser/			
Ernest Triplett	Duesenberg	200	5h20m10.460
4 Carl Marchese	Miller	200	5h20m42.950
5 Fred Winnai/			
Lora Corum/			
Roscoe Ford	Duesenberg	200	5h37m52.050
6 "Speed" Gardner/			
Chet Gardner	Miller	200	5h39m24.270

Winner's average speed: 97.585 mph. Starting grid front row: Woodbury, 120.599 mph (pole), "Duray", 119.087 mph and Hepburn, 116.543 mph

1930

30 May. 200 laps of a 2.500-mile circuit = 500.000 miles

1 Billy Arnold	Summers-Miller	200	4h58m39.720
2 "Shorty" Cantlon/			
Herman Schurch	Stevens-Miller	200	5h05m57.180
3 Louis Schneider	Stevens-Miller	200	5h10m04.210
4 Louis Meyer	Stevens-Miller	200	5h14m57.070
5 Bill Cummings/	Stevens-		
Fred Winnai	Duesenberg	200	5h20m35.110
6 Dave Evans	Stevens-Miller	200	5h24m04.500

Winner's average speed: 100.448 mph. Starting grid front row: Arnold, 113.268 mph (pole), Meyer, 111.290 mph and Cantlon, 109.810 mph

1931

30 May. 200 laps of a 2.500-mile circuit = 500.000 miles

1 Louis Schneider	Stevens-Miller	200	5h10m27.930
2 Fred Frame	Duesenberg	200	5h11m11.120
3 Ralph Hepburn/			
Peter Kreis	Miller	200	5h18m23.350
4 Myron Stevens/			
Zeke Meyer	Stevens-Miller	200	5h18m40.090
5 Russell			
Snowberger	Snowberger-Studebaker	200	5h18m50.700

6 Jimmy Gleason/
Wilbur Shaw Duesenberg 200 5h20m29.760

Winner's average speed: 96.629 mph. Starting grid front row:
Snowberger, 112.796 mph (pole), Cummings, 112.563 mph and
Bost, 112.125 mph. Fastest qualifier: Arnold, 116.080 mph

1932

30 May. 200 laps of a 2.500-mile circuit = 500.000 miles

1 Fred Frame	Wetteroth-Miller	200	4h48m03.790
2 Howdy Wilcox II	Stevens-Miller	200	4h48m47.450
3 Cliff Bergere	Rigling-Studebaker	200	4h52m13.240
4 Bob Carey	Stevens-Miller	200	4h55m57.900
5 Russell Snowberger	Snowberger-Hupmobile	200	4h57m38.720
6 Zeke Meyer	Rigling-Studebaker	200	5h04m38.520

Winner's average speed: 104.144 mph. Starting grid front row:
Moore, 117.363 mph (pole), Arnold, 116.290 mph and
Saulpaugh, 114.369 mph

1933

30 May. 200 laps of a 2.500-mile circuit = 500.000 miles

1 Louis Meyer	Miller	200	4h48m00.750
2 Wilbur Shaw	Stevens-Miller	200	4h54m42.640
3 Lou Moore	Duesenberg-Miller	200	4h55m16.790
4 Chet Gardner	Stevens-Miller	200	4h56m29.710
5 "Stubby" Stubblefield	Rigling-Buick	200	4h57m43.820
6 Dave Evans	Rigling-Studebaker	200	4h58m43.820

Winner's average speed: 104.162 mph. Starting grid front row:
Cummings, 118.521 mph (pole), Brisko, 118.388 mph and Frame,
117.864 mph

1934

30 May. 200 laps of a 2.500-mile circuit = 500.000 miles

1 Bill Cummings	Miller	200	4h46m05.200
2 Mauri Rose	Stevens-Miller	200	4h46m32.430
3 Lou Moore/ Wilbur Shaw	Miller	200	4h52m19.630
4 "Deacon" Litz/ Babe Stapp	Miller	200	4h57m46.270
5 Joe Russo	Duesenberg	200	5h00m19.210
6 Al Miller/ Zeke Meyer	Rigling-Buick	200	5h05m18.080

Winner's average speed: 104.863 mph. Starting grid front row:
Petillo, 119.329 mph (pole), Shaw, 117.647 mph and Brisko,
116.894 mph

1935

30 May. 200 laps of a 2.500-mile circuit = 500.000 miles

1 Kelly Petillo	Wetteroth-Offenhauser	200	4h42m22.710
2 Wilbur Shaw	Shaw-Offenhauser	200	4h43m02.730
3 Bill Cummings	Miller	200	4h46m22.480
4 Floyd Roberts	Miller	200	4h50m37.050
5 Ralph Hepburn/ Gene Haustein	Miller	200	4h50m45.730
6 "Shorty" Cantlon/ Bill Winn	Stevens-Miller	200	4h56m37.070

Winner's average speed: 106.240 mph. Starting grid front row:
Mays, 120.736 mph (pole), Gordon, 119.481 mph and Roberts,
118.671 mph

1936

30 May. 200 laps of a 2.500-mile circuit = 500.000 miles

1 Louis Meyer	Stevens-Miller	200	4h35m03.390
2 Ted Horn	Wetteroth-Miller	200	4h37m20.540
3 "Doc" MacKenzie/ Kelly Petillo	Wetteroth-Offenhauser	200	4h39m10.360
4 Mauri Rose	Miller	200	4h39m39.850
5 Chet Miller	Summers-Miller	200	4h40m35.170
6 Ray Pixley	Miller	200	4h45m01.580

Winner's average speed: 109.069 mph. Starting grid front row:
Mays, 119.644 mph (pole), Stapp, 118.945 mph and Miller,
117.675 mph

1937

30 May. 30 laps of a 2.500-mile circuit = 500.000 miles

1 Wilbur Shaw	Shaw-Offenhauser	200	4h24m7.800
2 Ralph Hepburn/ Bob Swanson	Stevens-Offenhauser	200	4h24m9.960
3 Ted Horn	Wetteroth-Miller	200	4h24m28.870
4 Louis Meyer	Miller	200	4h30m55.700
5 Cliff Bergere/George Barringer	Stevens-Offenhauser	200	4h35m23.600
6 Bill Cummings/ Chet Miller	Miller-Offenhauser	200	4h40m3.030

Winner's average speed: 113.580 mph. Starting grid front row:
Cummings, 123.455 mph (pole), Shaw, 122.791 mph and
Ardinger, 121.983 mph. Fastest qualifier: Snyder, 125.287 mph

1938

30 May. 200 laps of a 2.500-mile circuit = 500.000 miles

1 Floyd Roberts	Wetteroth-Miller	200	4h15m58.400
2 Wilbur Shaw	Shaw-Offenhauser	200	4h19m33.670
3 Chet Miller	Summers-Offenhauser	200	4h20m59.510
4 Ted Horn	Wetteroth-Miller	200	4h27m22.390
5 Chet Gardner	Rigling-Offenhauser	200	4h31m57.480
6 Herb Ardinger/ Russell Snowberger/ Cliff Bergere	Miller Ford-Offenhauser	199	

Winner's average speed: 117.200 mph. Starting grid front row:
Roberts, 125.681 mph (pole), Snowberger, 124.027 mph and
Mays, 122.845 mph. Fastest qualifier: Householder, 125.769 mph

1939

30 May. 200 laps of a 2.500-mile circuit = 500.000 miles

1 Wilbur Shaw	Maserati 8CTF	200	4h20m47.390
2 Jimmy Snyder	Adams-Sparks	200	4h22m35.610
3 Cliff Bergere	Miller Ford-Offenhauser	200	4h23m51.400
4 Ted Horn	Miller	200	4h28m08.820
5 Babe Stapp	Alfa Romeo Tipo-C "8C-35"	200	4h29m42.680
6 George Barringer	Weil-Offenhauser	200	4h30m12.600

Winner's average speed: 115.035 mph. Starting grid front row:
Snyder, 130.138 mph (pole), Meyer, 130.067 mph and Shaw,
128.977 mph

1940

30 May. 200 laps of a 2.500-mile circuit = 500.000 miles

1 Wilbur Shaw	Maserati 8CTF	200	4h22m31.170
2 Rex Mays	Stevens-Winfield	200	4h23m45.310
3 Mauri Rose	Wetteroth-Offenhauser	200	4h24m08.960
4 Ted Horn	Miller	199	
5 Joël Thorne	Adams-Sparks	197	
6 Bob Swanson	Stevens-Sampson	196	

Winner's average speed: 114.277 mph. Starting grid front row: Mays,
127.850 mph (pole), Shaw, 127.065 mph and Rose, 125.624 mph

1941

30 May. 200 laps of a 2.500-mile circuit = 500.000 miles

1 Floyd Davis/ Mauri Rose	Wetteroth-Offenhauser	200	4h20m36.240
2 Rex Mays	Stevens-Winfield	200	4h22m06.190
3 Ted Horn	Adams-Sparks	200	4h23m28.390
4 Ralph Hepburn	Miller Ford-Novi	200	4h24m00.790
5 Cliff Bergere	Wetteroth-Offenhauser	200	4h24m15.100
6 Chet Miller	Miller	200	4h28m02.750

Winner's average speed: 115.117 mph. Starting grid front row: Rose,
128.691 mph (pole), Mays, 128.301 mph and Shaw, 127.836 mph

1946

30 May. 200 laps of a 2.500-mile circuit = 500.000 miles

1 George Robson	Adams-Sparks	200	4h21m26.700
2 Jimmy Jackson	Miller-Offenhauser	200	4h22m00.740
3 Ted Horn	Maserati 8CTF	200	4h33m19.600
4 Emil Andres	Maserati	200	4h35m28.650
5 Joie Chitwood/ Sam Hanks	Wetteroth-Offenhauser	200	4h36m45.300
6 Louis Durant	Alfa Romeo	200	4h45m30.880

Winner's average speed: 114.747 mph. Starting grid front row: Bergere, 126.471 mph (pole), Russo, 126.183 mph and Hanks, 124.762 mph. Fastest qualifier: Hepburn, 133.944 mph

1947

30 May. 200 laps of a 2.500-mile circuit = 500.000 miles

1 Mauri Rose	Deidt-Offenhauser	200	4h17m52.170
2 Bill Holland	Deidt-Offenhauser	200	4h18m24.290
3 Ted Horn	Maserati	200	4h20m52.550
4 Herb Ardinger/			
Cliff Bergere	Kurtis-Novi	200	4h24m32.520
5 Jimmy Jackson	Miller-Offenhauser	200	4h25m52.650
6 Rex Mays	Kurtis-Winfield	200	4h30m08.050

Winner's average speed: 116.338 mph. Starting grid front row: Horn, 126.564 mph (pole), Bergere, 124.957 mph and Rose, 124.040 mph. Fastest qualifier: Holland, 128.755 mph

1948

30 May. 200 laps of a 2.500-mile circuit = 500.000 miles

1 Mauri Rose	Deidt-Offenhauser	200	4h10m23.330
2 Bill Holland	Deidt-Offenhauser	200	4h11m47.400
3 Duke Nalon	Kurtis-Novi	200	4h14m09.780
4 Ted Horn	Maserati	200	4h14m34.470
5 Mack Hellings	Kurtis KK2000-Offenhauser	200	4h24m38.520
6 Hal Cole	Kurtis KK2000-Offenhauser	200	4h28m50.860

Winner's average speed: 119.814 mph. Starting grid front row: Mays, 130.577 mph (pole), Holland, 129.515 mph and Rose, 129.129 mph. Fastest qualifier: Nalon, 131.603 mph

1949

30 May. 200 laps of a 2.500-mile circuit = 500.000 miles

1 Bill Holland	Deidt-Offenhauser	200	4h07m15.970
2 Johnnie Parsons	Kurtis-Offenhauser	200	4h10m26.970
3 George Connor	Lesovsky-Offenhauser	200	4h10m50.780
4 Myron Fohr	Marchese-Offenhauser	200	4h12m32.650
5 Joie Chitwood	Kurtis KK2000-Offenhauser	200	4h12m36.970
6 Jimmy Jackson	Deidt-Offenhauser	200	4h14m31.000

Winner's average speed: 121.327 mph. Starting grid front row: Nalon, 132.939 mph (pole), Mays, 129.552 mph and McGrath, 128.884 mph

1950

30 May. 138 laps of a 2.500-mile circuit = 345.000 miles

1 Johnnie Parsons	Kurtis-Offenhauser	138	2h46m55.970
2 Bill Holland	Deidt-Offenhauser	137	
3 Mauri Rose	Deidt-Offenhauser	137	
4 Cecil Green	Kurtis KK3000-Offenhauser	137	
5 Joie Chitwood/Tony			
Bettenhausen	Kurtis KK2000-Offenhauser	136	
6 Lee Wallard	Moore-Offenhauser	136	

Winner's average speed: 124.002 mph. Starting grid front row: Faulkner, 134.343 mph (pole), Agabashian, 132.792 mph and Rose, 132.319 mph

1951

30 May. 200 laps of a 2.500-mile circuit = 500.000 miles

1 Lee Wallard	Kurtis-Offenhauser	200	3h57m38.050
2 Mike Nazaruk	Kurtis-Offenhauser	200	3h59m25.310
3 Manuel Ayulo/	Kurtis KK3000-		
Jack McGrath	Offenhauser	200	4h00m29.420
4 Andy Linden	Sherman-Offenhauser	200	4h02m18.060
5 Bobby Ball	Schroeder-Offenhauser	200	4h02m30.270
6 Henry Banks	Moore-Offenhauser	200	4h03m18.020

Winner's average speed: 126.244 mph. Starting grid front row: Nalon, 136.498 mph (pole), Wallard, 135.039 mph and McGrath, 134.303 mph. Fastest qualifier: Faulkner, 136.872 mph

1952

30 May. 200 laps of a 2.500-mile circuit = 500.000 miles

1 Troy Ruttman	Kuzma-Offenhauser	200	3h52m41.880
2 Jim Rathmann	Kurtis KK3000-Offenhauser	200	3h56m44.240
3 Sam Hanks	Kurtis KK3000-Offenhauser	200	3h58m53.480

4 Duane Carter	Lesovsky-Offenhauser	200	3h59m30.210
5 Art Cross	Kurtis KK4000-Offenhauser	200	4h01m22.080
6 Jimmy Bryan	Kurtis KK3000-Offenhauser	200	4h02m06.230

Winner's average speed: 128.922 mph. Starting grid front row: Agabashian, 138.010 mph (pole), Linden, 137.002 mph and McGrath, 136.664 mph. Fastest qualifier: Miller, 139.034 mph

1953

30 May. 200 laps of a 2.500-mile circuit = 500.000 miles

1 Bill Vukovich	Kurtis KK500A-Offenhauser	200	3h53m01.690
2 Art Cross	Kurtis KK4000-Offenhauser	200	3h56m32.560
3 Sam Hanks/			
Duane Carter	Kurtis KK4000-Offenhauser	200	3h57m13.240
4 Fred Agabashian/			
Paul Russo	Kurtis KK500B-Offenhauser	200	3h57m40.910
5 Jack McGrath	Kurtis KK4000-Offenhauser	200	4h00m51.330
6 Jimmy Daywalt	Kurtis KK3000-Offenhauser	200	4h01m11.880

Winner's average speed: 128.740 mph. Starting grid front row: Vukovich, 138.392 mph (pole), Agabashian, 137.546 mph and McGrath, 136.602 mph

1954

31 May. 200 laps of a 2.500-mile circuit = 500.000 miles

1 Bill Vukovich	Kurtis KK500A-Offenhauser	200	3h49m17.270
2 Jimmy Bryan	Kuzma-Offenhauser	200	3h50m27.260
3 Jack McGrath	Kurtis KK500C-Offenhauser	200	3h50m36.970
4 Troy Ruttman/			
Duane Carter	Kurtis KK500A-Offenhauser	200	3h52m09.900
5 Mike Nazaruk	Kurtis KK500C-Offenhauser	200	3h52m41.850
6 Fred Agabashian	Kurtis KK500C-Offenhauser	200	3h53m04.830

Winner's average speed: 130.840 mph. Starting grid front row: McGrath, 141.033 mph (pole), Daywalt, 139.789 mph and Bryan, 139.665 mph

1955

30 May. 200 laps of a 2.500-mile circuit = 500.000 miles

1 Bob Sweikert	Kurtis KK500D-Offenhauser	200	3h53m59.530
2 Tony Bettenhausen/			
Paul Russo	Kurtis KK500C-Offenhauser	200	3h56m43.110
3 Jimmy Davies	Kurtis KK500B-Offenhauser	200	3h57m31.890
4 Johnny Thomson	Kuzma-Offenhauser	200	3h57m38.440
5 Walt Faulkner/			
Bill Homeier	Kurtis KK500C-Offenhauser	200	3h59m16.660
6 Andy Linden	Kurtis KK4000-Offenhauser	200	3h59m57.470

Winner's average speed: 128.209 mph. Starting grid front row: Hoyt, 140.045 mph (pole), Bettenhausen, 139.985 mph and McGrath, 142.580 mph. Fastest qualifier: McGrath, speed n/a

1956

30 May. 200 laps of a 2.500-mile circuit = 500.000 miles

1 Pat Flaherty	Watson-Offenhauser	200	3h53m28.840
2 Sam Hanks	Kurtis KK500C-Offenhauser	200	3h53m49.300
3 Don Freeland	Phillips-Offenhauser	200	3h54m59.070
4 Johnnie Parsons	Kuzma-Offenhauser	200	3h56m54.480
5 Dick Rathmann	Kurtis KK500C-Offenhauser	200	3h57m50.650
6 Bob Sweikert	Kuzma-Offenhauser	200	3h59m03.830

Winner's average speed: 128.490 mph. Starting grid front row: Flaherty, 145.596 mph (pole), J Rathmann, 145.120 mph and O'Connor, 144.980 mph

1957

30 May. 200 laps of a 2.500-mile circuit = 500.000 miles

1 Sam Hanks	Epperly-Offenhauser	200	3h41m14.250
2 Jim Rathmann	Epperly-Offenhauser	200	3h41m35.750
3 Jimmy Bryan	Kuzma-Offenhauser	200	3h43m28.250
4 Paul Russo	Kurtis 500F-Novi	200	3h44m11.100
5 Andy Linden	Kurtis KK500G-Offenhauser	200	3h44m28.550
6 Johnny Boyd	Kurtis KK500G-Offenhauser	200	3h45m49.550

Winner's average speed: 135.601 mph. Starting grid front row: O'Connor, 143.948 mph (pole), Sachs, 143.822 mph and Ruttman, 142.772 mph. Fastest qualifier: Russo, 144.817 mph

1958

30 May. 200 laps of a 2.500-mile circuit = 500.000 miles

1 Jimmy Bryan	Epperly-Offenhauser	200	3h44m13.800
2 George Amick	Epperly-Offenhauser	200	3h44m41.450
3 Johnny Boyd	Kurtis KK500G-Offenhauser	200	3h45m23.750
4 Tony Bettenhausen	Epperly-Offenhauser	200	3h45m45.600
5 Jim Rathmann	Epperly-Offenhauser	200	3h45m49.450
6 Jimmy Reece	Watson-Offenhauser	200	3h46m30.750

Winner's average speed: 133.791 mph. Starting grid front row: D Rathmann, 145.974 mph (pole), Elisian, 145.926 mph and Reece, 145.513 mph

1959

30 May. 200 laps of a 2.500-mile circuit = 500.000 miles

1 Rodger Ward	Watson-Offenhauser	200	3h40m49.200
2 Jim Rathmann	Watson-Offenhauser	200	3h41m12.470
3 Johnny Thomson	Lesovsky-Offenhauser	200	3h41m39.850
4 Tony Bettenhausen	Epperly-Offenhauser	200	3h42m36.250
5 Paul Goldsmith	Epperly-Offenhauser	200	3h42m55.600
6 Johnny Boyd	Epperly-Offenhauser	200	3h44m06.230

Winner's average speed: 135.857 mph. Starting grid front row: Thomson, 145.908 mph (pole), Sachs, 145.425 mph and J Rathmann, 144.433 mph

1960

30 May. 200 laps of a 2.500-mile circuit = 500.000 miles

1 Jim Rathmann	Watson-Offenhauser	200	3h36m11.360
2 Rodger Ward	Watson-Offenhauser	200	3h36m24.030
3 Paul Goldsmith	Epperly-Offenhauser	200	3h39m18.580
4 Don Branson	Phillips-Offenhauser	200	3h39m19.280
5 Johnny Thomson	Lesovsky-Offenhauser	200	3h39m22.650
6 Eddie Johnson	Trevis-Offenhauser	200	3h40m21.880

Winner's average speed: 138.767 mph. Starting grid front row: Sachs, 146.592 mph (pole), J Rathmann, 146.371 mph and Ward, 145.560 mph. Fastest qualifier: Hurtubise, 149.056 mph

1961

30 May. 200 laps of a 2.500-mile circuit = 500.000 miles

1 AJ Foyt Jr	Watson-Offenhauser	200	3h35m37.490
2 Eddie Sachs	Ewing-Offenhauser	200	3h35m45.770
3 Rodger Ward	Watson-Offenhauser	200	3h36m32.680
4 Shorty Templeman	Watson-Offenhauser	200	3h39m10.840
5 Al Keller	Phillips-Offenhauser	200	3h40m31.940
6 Chuck Stevenson	Epperly-Offenhauser	200	3h41m00.450

Winner's average speed: 139.131 mph. Starting grid front row: Sachs, 147.481 mph (pole), Branson, 146.843 mph and Hurtubise, 146.306 mph

1962

30 May. 200 laps of a 2.500-mile circuit = 500.000 miles

1 Rodger Ward	Watson-Offenhauser	200	3h33m50.330
2 Len Sutton	Watson-Offenhauser	200	3h34m01.850
3 Eddie Sachs	Ewing-Offenhauser	200	3h34m10.260
4 Don Davis	Lesovsky-Offenhauser	200	3h34m38.460
5 Bobby Marshman	Epperly-Offenhauser	200	3h36m09.270
6 Jim McElreath	Kurtis-Offenhauser	200	3h36m22.020

Winner's average speed: 140.293 mph. Starting grid front row: Jones, 150.370 mph (pole), Ward, 149.371 mph and Marshman, 149.347 mph

1963

30 May. 200 laps of a 2.500-mile circuit = 500.000 miles

1 Parnelli Jones	Watson-Offenhauser	200	3h29m35.400
2 Jim Clark	Lotus 29-Ford	200	3h30m09.240
3 AJ Foyt Jr	Trevis-Offenhauser	200	3h30m57.340
4 Rodger Ward	Watson-Offenhauser	200	3h32m37.800
5 Don Branson	Watson-Offenhauser	200	3h32m58.110
6 Jim McElreath	Watson-Offenhauser	200	3h32m58.430

Winner's average speed: 143.137 mph. Starting grid front row: Jones, 151.153 mph (pole), Hurtubise, 150.257 mph and Branson, 150.188 mph

1964

30 May. 200 laps of a 2.500-mile circuit = 500.000 miles

1 AJ Foyt Jr	Watson-Offenhauser	200	3h23m35.830
2 Rodger Ward	Watson-Offenhauser	200	3h25m00.180
3 Lloyd Ruby	Watson-Offenhauser	200	3h27m52.310
4 Johnny White	Watson-Offenhauser	200	3h29m29.300
5 Johnny Boyd	Kuzma-Offenhauser	200	3h30m45.310
6 Bud Tingelstad	Trevis-Offenhauser	198	

Winner's average speed: 147.350 mph. Starting grid front row: Clark, 158.828 mph (pole), Marshman, 157.857 mph and Ward, 156.406 mph

1965

31 May. 200 laps of a 2.500-mile circuit = 500.000 miles

1 Jim Clark	Lotus 38-Ford	200	3h19m05.340
2 Parnelli Jones	Kuzma/Lotus 34-Ford	200	3h21m04.320
3 Mario Andretti	Brawner/Brabham-Ford	200	3h21m10.700
4 Al Miller	Lotus 29-Ford	200	3h24m39.890
5 Gordon Johncock	Watson-Offenhauser	200	3h24m53.620
6 Mick Rupp	Gerhardt-Offenhauser	198	

Winner's average speed: 150.686 mph. Starting grid front row: Foyt Jr, 161.233 mph (pole), Clark, 160.729 mph and Gurney, 158.898 mph

1966

30 May. 200 laps of a 2.500-mile circuit = 500.000 miles

1 Graham Hill	Lola T90-Ford	200	3h27m52.530	
2 Jim Clark	Lotus 38-Ford	200	3h28m33.660	
3 Jim McElreath	Brabham-Ford	200	3h28m42.420	
4 Gordon Johncock	Gerhardt-Ford	200	3h29m40.000	
5 Mel Kenyon	Gerhardt-Offenhauser	198		
6 Jackie Stewart	Lola T90-Ford	190		oil pressure

Winner's average speed: 144.317 mph. Starting grid front row: Andretti, 165.899 mph (pole), Clark, 164.114 mph and Snider, 162.521 mph

1967

30 May. 200 laps of a 2.500-mile circuit = 500.000 miles

1 AJ Foyt Jr	Coyote/Lotus 34-Ford	200	3h18m24.220
2 Al Unser	Lola T90-Ford	198	
3 Joe Leonard	Coyote/Lotus 34-Ford	197	
4 Denny Hulme	Eagle 67-Ford	197	
5 Jim McElreath	Moore-Ford	197	
6 Parnelli Jones	Granatelli turbine	196	

Winner's average speed: 151.207 mph. Starting grid front row: Andretti, 168.982 mph (pole), Gurney, 167.224 mph and Johncock, 166.559 mph

1968

30 May. 200 laps of a 2.500-mile circuit = 500.000 miles

1 Bobby Unser	Eagle 68-Drake/Offenhauser	200	3h16m13.760
2 Dan Gurney	Eagle 68-Ford/Weslake	200	3h17m07.570
3 Mel Kenyon	Gerhardt-Drake/Offenhauser	200	3h21m02.430
4 Denny Hulme	Eagle 68-Ford	200	3h21m08.710
5 Lloyd Ruby	Mongoose-Drake/Offenhauser	200	3h21m58.830
6 Ronnie Duman	Brabham-Drake/Offenhauser	199	

Winner's average speed: 152.882 mph. Starting grid front row: Leonard, 171.559 mph (pole), Hill, 171.208 mph and B Unser, 169.507 mph

1969

30 May. 200 laps of a 2.500-mile circuit = 500.000 miles

1 Mario Andretti	Brawner/Hawk III-Ford	200	3h11m14.710
2 Dan Gurney	Eagle 69-Ford/Weslake	200	3h13m07.740
3 Bobby Unser	Lola T152-Offenhauser	200	3h14m41.450

4 Mel Kenyon	Gerhardt-Offenhauser	200 3h17m08.320
5 Peter Revson	Brabham BT25-Repco	197
6 Joe Leonard	Eagle 69-Ford	193

Winner's average speed: 156.867 mph. Starting grid front row:
Foyt, 170.568 mph (pole), Andretti, 169.851 mph and B Unser,
169.683 mph

1970

30 May. 200 laps of a 2.500-mile circuit = 500.000 miles

1 Al Unser	Colt 70-Ford	200 3h12m37.040
2 Mark Donohue	Lola T153-Ford	200 3h13m09.230
3 Dan Gurney	Eagle 70-Offenhauser	200 3h15m49.250
4 Donnie Allison	Eagle 70-Ford	200 3h16m21.860
5 Jim McElreath	Coyote-Ford	200 3h17m07.950
6 Mario Andretti	McNamara T500-Ford	199

Winner's average speed: 155.749 mph. Starting grid front row:
A Unser, 170.221 mph (pole), Rutherford, 170.213 mph and
Foyt, 170.004 mph

1971

29 May. 200 laps of a 2.500-mile circuit = 500.000 miles

1 Al Unser	Colt 71-Ford	200 3h10m11.560
2 Peter Revson	McLaren M16-Offenhauser	200 3h10m34.440
3 AJ Foyt Jr	Coyote-Ford	200 3h12m13.370
4 Jim Malloy	Eagle 70-Offenhauser	200 3h14m04.650
5 Bill Vukovich Jr	Brabham BT32-Offenhauser	200 3h14m05.770
6 Donnie Allison	Coyote-Ford	199

Winner's average speed: 157.735 mph. Starting grid front row:
Revson, 178.696 mph (pole), Donohue, 177.087 mph and B
Unser, 175.816 mph

1972

27 May. 200 laps of a 2.500-mile circuit = 500.000 miles

1 Mark Donohue	McLaren M16B-	
	Offenhauser	200 3h04m05.540
2 Al Unser	Parnelli-Offenhauser	200 3h07m16.490
3 Joe Leonard	Parnelli-Offenhauser	200 3h08m17.510
4 Sam Sessions	Lola-Ford	200 3h09m22.880
5 Sam Posey	Eagle 72-Offenhauser	198
6 Lloyd Ruby	Atlanta-Foyt/Ford	196

Winner's average speed: 162.962 mph. Starting grid front row:
B Unser, 195.940 mph (pole), Revson, 192.885 mph and
Donohue, 191.408 mph

1973

**28 May. 133 laps of a 2.500-mile circuit = 332.500 miles.
Race stopped early due to rain**

1 Gordon Johncock	Eagle 73-Offenhauser	133 2h05m26.590
2 Bill Vukovich Jr	Eagle 73-Offenhauser	133 2h06m51.500
3 Roger	McLaren M16B-	
McCluskey	Offenhauser	131
4 Mel Kenyon	Eagle 73-Foyt/Ford	131
5 Gary	McLaren M16C-	
Bettenhausen	Offenhauser	130
6 Steve Krisiloff	Kingfish-Offenhauser	129

Winner's average speed: 159.036 mph. Starting grid front row:
Rutherford, 198.413 mph (pole), B Unser, 198.183 mph and
Donohue, 197.412 mph

1974

26 May. 200 laps of a 2.500-mile circuit = 500.000 miles

1 Johnny	McLaren M16C/D-	
Rutherford	Offenhauser	200 3h09m10.060
2 Bobby Unser	Eagle 74-Offenhauser	200 3h09m32.380
3 Bill Vukovich Jr	Eagle 74-Offenhauser	199
4 Gordon Johncock	Eagle 74-Offenhauser	198
5 David Hobbs	McLaren M16C/D-	
	Offenhauser	196
6 Jim McElreath	Eagle 74-Offenhauser	194

Winner's average speed: 158.589 mph. Starting grid front row:
Foyt, 191.632 mph (pole), Dallenbach, 189.683 mph and Hiss,
187.490 mph

1975

**25 May. 174 laps of a 2.500-mile circuit = 435.000 miles.
Race stopped early due to rain**

1 Bobby Unser	Eagle 75-Offenhauser	174 2h54m55.080
2 Johnny	McLaren M16E-	
Rutherford	Offenhauser	174 2h55m59.080
3 AJ Foyt Jr	Coyote-Foyt/Ford	174 2h56m43.700
4 Pancho Carter	Eagle 75-Offenhauser	169
5 Roger McCluskey	Riley-Offenhauser	167
6 Bill Vukovich Jr	Eagle 75-Offenhauser	166

Winner's average speed: 149.213 mph. Starting grid front row:
Foyt, 193.976 mph (pole), Johncock, 191.652 mph and B Unser,
191.073 mph

1976

**30 May. 102 laps of a 2.500-mile circuit = 255.000 miles.
Race stopped early due to rain**

1 Johnny	McLaren M16E-	
Rutherford	Offenhauser	102 1h42m52.480
2 AJ Foyt Jr	Coyote-Foyt/Ford	102 1h43m07.840
3 Gordon Johncock	Wildcat-DGS/Offenhauser	102 1h44m37.430
4 Wally Dallenbach	Wildcat-DGS/Offenhauser	101
5 Pancho Carter	Eagle 76-Offenhauser	101
6 Tom Sneva	McLaren M16C/D-	
	Offenhauser	101

Winner's average speed: 148.725 mph. Starting grid front row:
Rutherford, 188.957 mph (pole), Johncock, 188.531 mph and
Sneva, 186.355 mph. Fastest qualifier: Andretti, 189.404 mph

1977

29 May. 200 laps of a 2.500-mile circuit = 500.000 miles

1 AJ Foyt Jr	Coyote-Foyt/Ford	200 3h05m57.160
2 Tom Sneva	McLaren M24-Cosworth	200 3h06m25.790
3 Al Unser	Parnelli VPJ6B-Cosworth	199
4 Wally Dallenbach	Wildcat-DGS/Offenhauser	199
5 Johnny Parsons Jr	Wildcat-DGS/Offenhauser	193
6 Tom Bigelow	Watson-Offenhauser	192

Winner's average speed: 161.331 mph. Starting grid front row:
Sneva, 198.884 mph (pole), B Unser, 197.618 mph and A Unser,
195.950 mph

1978

28 May. 200 laps of a 2.500-mile circuit = 500.000 miles

1 Al Unser	Lola T500-Cosworth	200 3h05m54.990
2 Tom Sneva	Penske PC6-Cosworth	200
3 Gordon Johncock	Wildcat-DGS/Offenhauser	199
4 Steve Krisiloff	Wildcat-DGS/Offenhauser	198
5 Wally Dallenbach	McLaren M24-Cosworth	196 out of fuel
6 Bobby Unser	Eagle 78-Cosworth	195

Winner's average speed: 161.363 mph. Starting grid front row: Sneva,
202.156 mph (pole), Ongais, 200.122 mph and Mears, 200.078 mph

Al Unser celebrates victory in the 1978 race

1979

27 May. 200 laps of a 2.500-mile circuit = 500.000 miles

1 Rick Mears	Penske PC6-Cosworth	200 3h08m47.970
2 AJ Foyt Jr	Parnelli VPJ6C-Cosworth	200 3h09m33.660
3 Mike Mosley	Eagle 79-Cosworth	200 3h09m36.000
4 Danny Ongais	Parnelli VPJ6B-Cosworth	199

5 Bobby Unser   Penske PC7-Cosworth   199
6 Gordon Johncock Penske PC6-Cosworth   197

Winner's average speed: 158.899 mph. Starting grid front row: Mears, 193.736 mph (pole), Sneva, 192.998 mph and A Unser, 192.503 mph

1980

25 May. 200 laps of a 2.500-mile circuit = 500.000 miles

1 Johnny Rutherford	Chaparral 2K-Cosworth	200	3h29m59.550
2 Tom Sneva	McLaren M24-Cosworth	200	3h30m29.490
3 Gary Bettenhausen	Wildcat Mk2-DGS/ Offenhauser	200	3h30m32.900
4 Gordon Johncock	Penske PC6-Cosworth	200	3h30m33.170
5 Rick Mears	Penske PC9-Cosworth	199	
6 Pancho Carter	Penske PC7-Cosworth	199	

Winner's average speed: 142.862 mph. Starting grid front row: Rutherford, 192.256 mph (pole), Andretti, 191.012 mph and B Unser, 189.994 mph

1981

24 May. 200 laps of a 2.500-mile circuit = 500.000 miles

1 Bobby Unser	Penske PC9B-Cosworth	200	3h35m41.780
2 Mario Andretti	Wildcat Mk8-Cosworth	200	3h35m46.960
3 Vern Schuppan	McLaren M24B-Cosworth	199	
4 Kevin Cogan	Phoenix-Cosworth	197	
5 Geoff Brabham	Penske PC9-Cosworth	197	
6 Sheldon Kinser	Longhorn LR01-Cosworth	195	

Winner's average speed: 139.084 mph. Starting grid front row: B Unser, 200.546 mph (pole), Mosley, 197.141 mph and Foyt, 196.078 mph. Fastest qualifier: Sneva, 200.691 mph

1982

30 May. 200 laps of a 2.500-mile circuit = 500.000 miles

1 Gordon Johncock	Wildcat Mk8B-Cosworth	200	3h05m09.140
2 Rick Mears	Penske PC10-Cosworth	200	3h05m09.300
3 Pancho Carter	March 82C-Cosworth	199	
4 Tom Sneva	March 82C-Cosworth	197	engine
5 Al Unser	Longhorn LR03-Cosworth	197	
6 Don Whittington	March 81C-Cosworth	196	

Winner's average speed: 162.029 mph. Starting grid front row: Mears, 207.004 mph (pole), Cogan, 204.082 mph and Foyt, 203.332 mph

1983

29 May. 200 laps of a 2.500-mile circuit = 500.000 miles

1 Tom Sneva	March 83C-Cosworth	200	3h05m03.066
2 Al Unser	Penske PC11-Cosworth	200	3h05m14.240
3 Rick Mears	Penske PC11-Cosworth	200	3h05m24.928
4 Geoff Brabham	Penske PC10-Cosworth	199	
5 Kevin Cogan	March 83C-Cosworth	198	
6 Howdy Holmes	March 83C-Cosworth	198	

Winner's average speed: 162.117 mph. Starting grid front row: Fabi, 207.395 mph (pole), Mosley, 205.372 mph and Mears, 204.301 mph

1984

27 May. 200 laps of a 2.500-mile circuit = 500.000 miles

1 Rick Mears	March 84C-Cosworth	200	3h03m21.660
2 Roberto Guerrero	March 84C-Cosworth	198	
3 Al Unser	March 84C-Cosworth	198	
4 Al Holbert	March 84C-Cosworth	198	
5 Michael Andretti	March 84C-Cosworth	198	
6 AJ Foyt Jr	March 84C-Cosworth	198	

Winner's average speed: 163.612 mph. Starting grid front row: Sneva, 210.029 mph (pole), Holmes, 207.977 mph and Mears, 207.847 mph

1985

26 May. 200 laps of a 2.500-mile circuit = 500.000 miles

1 Danny Sullivan	March 85C-Cosworth	200	3h16m06.069
2 Mario Andretti	Lola T900-Cosworth	200	3h16m08.546
3 Roberto Guerrero	March 85C-Cosworth	200	
4 Al Unser	March 85C-Cosworth	199	

Al Unser Jr, pictured on right with Galmer designer Alan Mertens, followed his father as a winner of the Indianapolis 500 in 1992

5 Johnny Parsons Jr	March 85C-Cosworth	198	
6 Johnny Rutherford	March 85C-Cosworth	198	

Winner's average speed: 152.982 mph. Starting grid front row: Carter, 212.583 mph (pole), Brayton, 212.354 mph and Rahal, 211.818 mph

1986

1 June. 200 laps of a 2.500-mile circuit = 500.000 miles

1 Bobby Rahal	March 86C-Cosworth	200	2h55m43.480
2 Kevin Cogan	March 86C-Cosworth	200	2h55m44.921
3 Rick Mears	March 86C-Cosworth	200	
4 Roberto Guerrero	March 86C-Cosworth	200	
5 Al Unser Jr	Lola T86/00-Cosworth	199	
6 Michael Andretti	March 86C-Cosworth	199	

Winner's average speed: 170.722 mph. Starting grid front row: Mears, 216.828 mph (pole), Sullivan, 215.382 mph and Michael Andretti, 214.522 mph

1987

24 May. 200 laps of a 2.500-mile circuit = 500.000 miles

1 Al Unser	March 86C-Cosworth	200	3h04m59.147
2 Roberto Guerrero	March 87C-Cosworth	200	3h05m03.634
3 Fabrizio Barbazza	March 87C-Cosworth	198	
4 Al Unser Jr	March 87C-Cosworth	196	
5 Gary Bettenhausen	March 86C-Cosworth	195	
6 Dick Simon	Lola T87/00-Cosworth	193	

Winner's average speed: 162.175 mph. Starting grid front row: Mario Andretti, 215.390 mph (pole), Rahal, 213.316 mph and Mears, 211.467 mph

1988

29 May. 200 laps of a 2.500-mile circuit = 500.000 miles

1 Rick Mears	Penske PC17-Chevrolet	200	3h27m10.204
2 Emerson Fittipaldi	March 88C-Chevrolet	200	3h27m17.280
3 Al Unser	Penske PC17-Chevrolet	199	
4 Michael Andretti	March 88C-Cosworth	199	
5 Bobby Rahal	Lola T88/00-Judd	199	
6 Jim Crawford	Lola T87/00-Buick	198	

Winner's average speed: 144.809 mph. Starting grid front row: Mears, 219.198 mph (pole), Sullivan, 216.214 mph and A Unser Sr, 215.270 mph

1989

28 May. 200 laps of a 2.500-mile circuit = 500.000 miles

1 Emerson Fittipaldi	Penske PC18-Chevrolet	200	2h59m01.040
2 Al Unser Jr	Lola T89/00-Chevrolet	198	accident
3 Raul Boesel	Lola T89/00-Judd	194	
4 Mario Andretti	Lola T89/00-Chevrolet	193	
5 AJ Foyt Jr	Lola T89/00-Cosworth	193	
6 Scott Brayton	Lola T89/00-Buick	193	

Winner's average speed: 167.582 mph. Starting grid front row: Mears, 223.885 mph (pole), A Unser Sr, 223.471 mph and Fittipaldi, 222.329 mph

1990

27 May. 200 laps of a 2.500-mile circuit = 500.000 miles

1 Arie Luyendyk	Lola T90/00-Chevrolet	200	2h41m18.248
2 Bobby Rahal	Lola T90/00-Chevrolet	200	2h41m29.282
3 Emerson Fittipaldi	Penske PC19-Chevrolet	200	
4 Al Unser Jr	Lola T90/00-Chevrolet	199	
5 Rick Mears	Penske PC19-Chevrolet	198	
6 AJ Foyt Jr	Lola T90/00-Chevrolet	194	

Winner's average speed: 185.984 mph. Starting grid front row: Fittipaldi, 225.301 mph (pole), Mears, 224.215 mph and Luyendyk, 223.304 mph

1991

26 May. 200 laps of a 2.500-mile circuit = 500.000 miles

1 Rick Mears	Penske PC20-Chevrolet	200	2h50m00.791
2 Michael Andretti	Lola T91/00-Chevrolet	200	2h50m03.940
3 Arie Luyendyk	Lola T91/00-Chevrolet	199	
4 Al Unser Jr	Lola T91/00-Chevrolet	198	
5 John Andretti	Lola T91/00-Chevrolet	197	
6 Gordon Johncock	Lola T90/00-Cosworth	188	

Winner's average speed: 176.457 mph. Starting grid front row: Mears, 224.113 mph (pole), Foyt, 222.443 mph and Mario Andretti, 221.818 mph. Fastest qualifier: G Bettenhausen, 224.468 mph

1992

24 May. 200 laps of a 2.500-mile circuit = 500.000 miles

1 Al Unser Jr	Galmer G92-Chevrolet	200	3h43m04.991
2 Scott Goodyear	Lola T92/00-Chevrolet	200	3h43m05.034
3 Al Unser	Lola T92/00-Buick	200	3h43m15.226
4 Eddie Cheever	Lola T92/00-Ford	200	3h43m15.271
5 Danny Sullivan	Galmer G92-Chevrolet	199	
6 Bobby Rahal	Lola T92/00-Chevrolet	199	

Winner's average speed: 134.479 mph. Starting grid front row: Guerrero, 232.482 mph (pole), Cheever, 229.639 mph and Mario Andretti, 229.503 mph - Guerrero did not take the green flag as he had spun off during the parade laps

Rick Mears claimed a joint record fourth win in 1991

1993

30 May. 200 laps of a 2.500-mile circuit = 500.000 miles

1 Emerson Fittipaldi	Penske PC22-Chevrolet	200	3h10m49.860
2 Arie Luyendyk	Lola T93/00-Ford	200	3h10m52.722
3 Nigel Mansell	Lola T93/00-Ford	200	3h10m54.608
4 Raul Boesel	Lola T93/00-Ford	200	3h10m54.977
5 Mario Andretti	Lola T93/00-Ford	200	3h10m55.264
6 Scott Brayton	Lola T93/00-Ford	200	3h10m57.743

Winner's average speed: 157.207 mph. Starting grid front row: Luyendyk, 223.967 mph (pole), Mario Andretti, 223.414 mph and Boesel, 222.379 mph

1994

29 May. Indianapolis. 200 laps of a 2.500-mile circuit = 500.000 miles

1 Al Unser Jr	Penske PC23-Mercedes-Benz	200	3h06m29.006
2 Jacques Villeneuve	Reynard 94I-Ford	200	3h06m37.610
3 Bobby Rahal	Penske PC22-Ilmor	199	
4 Jimmy Vasser	Reynard 94I-Ford	199	
5 Robby Gordon	Lola T94/00-Ford	199	
6 Michael Andretti	Reynard 94I-Ford	198	

Winner's average speed: 160.872 mph. Starting grid front row: Unser Jr, 228.011 mph (pole), Boesel, 227.618 mph and Fittipaldi, 227.303 mph

RECORDS

DRIVERS' RECORDS

MOST WINS

AJ Foyt Jr	4	Emerson Fittipaldi	2
Rick Mears	4	Gordon Johncock	2
Al Unser	4	Tommy Milton	2
Louis Meyer	3	Al Unser Jr	2
Mauri Rose	3	Bill Vukovich	2
Johnny Rutherford	3	Rodger Ward	2
Wilbur Shaw	3	Howdy Wilcox	2
Bobby Unser	3		

MOST STARTS

AJ Foyt Jr	35	George Snider	22
Mario Andretti	29	Gary Bettenhausen	21
Al Unser	27	Cliff Bergere	20
Gordon Johncock	24	Ralph Hepburn	20
Johnny Rutherford	24		

OTHER RECORDS

Youngest winner:
22 years 81 days, Troy Ruttman, 1952

Oldest winner:
47 years 360 days, Al Unser Sr, 1987

Most pole positions:
Six, Rick Mears

Most laps led in a race:
198 laps, Billy Arnold, 1930

Least laps led by the winning driver:
Two laps, Joe Dawson, 1912

Most laps in the lead in total:
644 laps, Al Unser Sr

Most lead changes in a race:
29, 1960

Consecutive wins:
Two, Wilbur Shaw, 1939-40; Mauri Rose, 1947-48; Bill Vukovich, 1953-54; Al Unser, 1970-71

Narrowest race-winner margin:
0.043 seconds, Al Unser Jr, 1992

Widest race-winning margin:
13m08.0, Jules Goux, 1913

Fastest race:
185.984 mph, 1990

Slowest race:
74.602 mph, 1911

Rookies to have won the race:
Ray Harroun, 1911; Jules Goux, 1913; René Thomas, 1914; Frank Lockhart, 1926; George Souders, 1927; Graham Hill, 1966

Wins from pole position:
Jimmy Murphy, 1922; Tommy Milton, 1923; Billy Arnold, 1930; Floyd Roberts, 1938; Bill Vukovich, 1953; Pat Flaherty, 1956; Parnelli Jones, 1963; Al Unser, 1970; Johnny Rutherford, 1976; Rick Mears, 1979; Johnny Rutherford, 1980; Bobby Unser, 1981; Rick Mears, 1988; Rick Mears, 1991; Al Unser Jr, 1994

INDYCAR CHAMPIONSHIP

Rick Mears' Penske PC18-Chevrolet at the 1989 Long Beach Grand Prix

The Indycar Championship is the oldest racing series in the World. Inaugurated in 1916 by the American Automobile Association (AAA), the championship has been contested every year since - apart from 1917-19 and 1942-45 when it was suspended because of war.

The United States Auto Club (USAC) replaced the AAA as governing body in 1956, but during the 1970s teams grew disenchanted with USAC. In 1979 they formed their own breakaway series under the Championship Auto Racing Teams (CART) banner. USAC also ran a series that year, but it was an uncompetitive affair. It has continued to run the Indianapolis 500 but from 1980 the CART series has been the undisputed Indycar championship.

The series calls for versatility - in its time it has included paved and dirt ovals, the Pikes Peak hill climb, road courses and its centrepiece, the Indianapolis 500.

RULES

1911-12	9800 cc maximum engine capacity
1913-14	7400 cc maximum engine capacity
1915-19	4900 cc maximum engine capacity
1920-22	3000 cc maximum engine capacity
1923-25	2000 cc maximum engine capacity
1926-29	1500 cc maximum engine capacity
1930-33	6000 cc supercharged production-based engines
1934	6000 cc supercharged production-based engines. 45 gallon maximum fuel limit
1935	6000 cc supercharged production-based engines. 42.5 gallon maximum fuel limit
1936	No maximum engine capacity. 37.5 gallon maximum fuel limit
1937	As 1936, commercial pump fuel compulsory
1938-56	4500 cc normally aspirated and 3000 cc supercharged maximum engine capacity
1957-68	4200 cc normally aspirated and 2800 cc supercharged maximum engine capacity
1969-70	4200 cc normally aspirated, 2650 cc turbocharged and 5000 cc stockblock rocker arm normally aspirated maximum engine capacity
1971	4200 cc normally aspirated, 2650 cc turbocharged and 5878 cc stockblock normally aspirated maximum engine capacity
1972-78	4500 cc normally aspirated, 2650 cc turbocharged and 5878 cc stockblock normally aspirated maximum engine capacity. Turbo boost restrictions progressively introduced from 1973
1979-84	4500 cc normally aspirated, 2650 cc turbocharged and 5878 cc stockblock normally aspirated maximum engine capacity
1985 to date	2650 cc turbocharged maximum engine capacity. 5878 cc stockblock normally aspirated engines phased out, with only teams which had consistently used them in the past allowed to continue doing so

Note: From 1979, the maximum manifold intake pressure restrictions differed between the Indianapolis 500 and the other championship races, in favour of stockblock engines at Indianapolis. In addition, 3430 cc stockblock turbocharged engines have been allowed at the Indianapolis 500 since this date

\ AAA NATIONAL CHAMPIONSHIP						
year	driver	nat	car	year	driver	nat	car
1916	Dario Resta	I	Peugeot	1937	Wilbur Shaw	USA	Shaw/Stevens-Offenhauser
1920	Gaston Chevrolet	USA	Frontenac	1938	Floyd Roberts	USA	Wetteroth-Offenhauser
1921	Tommy Milton	USA	Durant-Duesenberg/	1939	Wilbur Shaw	USA	Maserati
			Frontenac/Durant-Miller	1940	Rex Mays	USA	Stevens-Winfield
1922	Jimmy Murphy	USA	Duesenberg-Miller	1941	Rex Mays	USA	Stevens-Winfield
1923	Eddie Hearne	USA	Miller	1946	Ted Horn	USA	Horn-Offenhauser/Maserati
1924	Jimmy Murphy	USA	Miller	1947	Ted Horn	USA	Horn-Offenhauser/Maserati
1925	Peter de Paolo	USA	Duesenberg	1948	Ted Horn	USA	Horn-Offenhauser/Maserati
1926	Harry Hartz	USA	Miller	1949	Johnnie Parsons	USA	Kurtis-Offenhauser
1927	Peter de Paolo	USA	Miller	1950	Henry Banks	USA	Maserati-Offenhauser/
1928	Louis Meyer	USA	Miller				Moore-Offenhauser
1929	Louis Meyer	USA	Miller	1951	Tony Bettenhausen	USA	Deidt-Offenhauser/
1930	Billy Arnold	USA	Summers-Miller				Kurtis-Offenhauser
1931	Louis Schneider	USA	Stevens-Miller	1952	Chuck Stevenson	USA	Kurtis KK4000-Offenhauser
1932	Bob Carey	USA	Stevens-Miller	1953	Sam Hanks	USA	Kurtis KK4000-Offenhauser
1933	Louis Meyer	USA	Miller	1954	Jimmy Bryan	USA	Kuzma-Offenhauser
1934	Bill Cummings	USA	Miller	1955	Bob Sweikert	USA	Kurtis KK500D-Offenhauser/
1935	Kelly Petillo	USA	Wetteroth-Offenhauser				Watson-Offenhauser
1936	Mauri Rose	USA	Miller-Offenhauser				

USAC NATIONAL CHAMPIONSHIP

year	driver	nat	team	car
1956	Jimmy Bryan	USA	Dean Van Lines	Kuzma-Offenhauser
1957	Jimmy Bryan	USA	Dean Van Lines	Kuzma-Offenhauser
1958	Tony Bettenhausen	USA	John Zink Jr*	Epperly-Offenhauser/Kurtis KK4000-Offenhauser/Watson-Offenhauser
1959	Rodger Ward	USA	Leader Cards	Watson-Offenhauser
1960	AJ Foyt Jr	USA	Bowes Seal Fast	Meskowski-Offenhauser
1961	AJ Foyt Jr	USA	Bowes Seal Fast	Watson/Trevis-Offenhauser/Meskowski-Offenhauser
1962	Rodger Ward	USA	Leader Cards	Watson-Offenhauser
1963	AJ Foyt Jr	USA	Sheraton-Thompson	Meskowski-Offenhauser/Watson/Trevis-Offenhauser
1964	AJ Foyt Jr	USA	Sheraton-Thompson	Watson-Offenhauser/Meskowski-Offenhauser
1965	Mario Andretti	USA	Dean Racing Enterprises	Hawk-Ford/Kuzma-Offenhauser
1966	Mario Andretti	USA	Dean Racing Enterprises	Hawk-Ford/Kuzma-Offenhauser
1967	AJ Foyt Jr	USA	Sheraton-Thompson	Coyote-Ford/Meskowski-Offenhauser
1968	Bobby Unser	USA	Leader Cards	Eagle 68-Ford/Eagle 68-Offenhauser/Unser-Chevrolet
1969	Mario Andretti	USA	STP Granatelli	Hawk-Ford/Kuzma-Offenhauser
1970	Al Unser	USA	Vel's Parnelli Jones	Colt 70-Ford/King-Ford
1971	Joe Leonard	USA	Vel's Parnelli Jones	Colt 71-Ford
1972	Joe Leonard	USA	Vel's Parnelli Jones	Parnelli-Offenhauser
1973	Roger McCluskey	USA	Lindsey Hopkins	McLaren M16B-Offenhauser
1974	Bobby Unser	USA	All-American Racers	Eagle 74-Offenhauser
1975	AJ Foyt Jr	USA	Gilmore-Foyt Racing	Coyote-Ford
1976	Gordon Johncock	USA	Patrick Racing	Wildcat-Offenhauser
1977	Tom Sneva	USA	Penske Racing	McLaren M24-Cosworth
1978	Tom Sneva	USA	Penske Racing	Penske PC6-Cosworth
1979	AJ Foyt Jr	USA	Gilmore-Foyt Racing	Parnelli VPJ6C-Cosworth/Coyote-Ford

*also drove for Jones & Maley and Hardwood Special

CART INDYCAR WORLD SERIES

year	driver	nat	team	car
1979	Rick Mears	USA	Penske Racing	Penske PC7-Cosworth/Penske PC6-Cosworth
1980	Johnny Rutherford	USA	Chaparral Racing	Chaparral 2K-Cosworth
1981	Rick Mears	USA	Penske Racing	Penske PC9B-Cosworth
1982	Rick Mears	USA	Penske Racing	Penske PC10-Cosworth
1983	Al Unser	USA	Penske Racing	Penske PC11-Cosworth/Penske PC10B-Cosworth
1984	Mario Andretti	USA	Newman-Haas Racing	Lola T800-Cosworth
1985	Al Unser	USA	Penske Racing	March 85C-Cosworth
1986	Bobby Rahal	USA	Truesports	March 86C-Cosworth
1987	Bobby Rahal	USA	Truesports	Lola T87/00-Cosworth
1988	Danny Sullivan	USA	Penske Racing	Penske PC17-Chevrolet
1989	Emerson Fittipaldi	BR	Patrick Racing	Penske PC17-Chevrolet/Penske PC18-Chevrolet
1990	Al Unser Jr	USA	Galles-Kraco Racing	Lola T90/00-Chevrolet
1991	Michael Andretti	USA	Newman-Haas Racing	Lola T91/00-Chevrolet
1992	Bobby Rahal	USA	Rahal-Hogan Racing	Lola T92/00-Chevrolet
1993	Nigel Mansell	GB	Newman-Haas Racing	Lola T93/00-Ford
1994	Al Unser Jr	USA	Penske Racing	Penske PC23-Ilmor/Penske PC23-Mercedes-Benz

The most successful driver in the history of the Indycar championships, AJ Foyt Jr, on his way to victory in the 1977 Indy 500

NOTE: In 1926-27 the Secretary of the AAA Contest Board Val Haresnape retrospectively announced champions for 1909-15 and 1917-19 based on all AAA races, whether they be a five-mile dash, class result or city-to-city marathon. The confusion was compounded in 1951 when historian Russ Catlin further revised the official AAA records. He published new champions for 1902-08, amended the 1909 Haresnape champion from Bert Dingley to George Robertson and gave the 1920 series to Tommy Milton rather than to original winner Gaston Chevrolet. His calculations were again based on all AAA races and not just championship events.

I do not feel that a championship awarded 49 years late can be considered genuine. However, I have included the Haresnape and Catlin revisions below, as well as all relevant race results since 1909 to complete the section on Indycars, and to explain some championship listings published elsewhere.

Indycar Championship

Haresnape-created champions				Catlin-added champions (plus revision for 1909)		
year	driver	nat	car	year	driver	nat
1909	Bert Dingley	USA	Chalmers Detroit	1902	Harry Harkness	USA
1910	Ray Harroun	USA	Marmon	1903	Barney Oldfield	USA
1911	Ralph Mulford	USA	Lozier	1904	George Heath	USA
1912	Ralph de Palma	USA	Mercedes	1905	Victor Hémery	F
1913	Earl Cooper	USA	Stutz	1906	Joe Tracy	USA
1914	Ralph de Palma	USA	Mercedes	1907	Eddie Bald	USA
1915	Earl Cooper	USA	Stutz	1908	Louis Strang	USA
1917	Earl Cooper	USA	Stutz	1909	George Robertson	USA
1918	Ralph Mulford	USA	Frontenac			
1919	Howard Wilcox	USA	Peugeot			
1920	Tommy Milton	USA	Duesenberg/Frontenac			

RACE WINNERS

AAA NATIONAL CHAMPIONSHIP
NOTE: 1909-16 and 1917-19 are races included in the AAA revisions of 1926-27 and 1951

1909

date	race	driver	nat	car	mph
12.06.09	Portland	Howard Covey	USA	Cadillac	55.757
12.06.09	Portland	Charles Arnold	USA	Pope-Hartford	57.276
12.06.09	Portland	Bert Dingley	USA	Chalmers-Detroit	58.600
18.06.09	Crown Point	Joe Matson	USA	Chalmers-Detroit	51.463
19.06.09	Crown Point	Louis Chevrolet	USA	Buick	49.288
05.07.09	Denver	Eaton McMillian	USA	Colburn	38.978
10.07.09	Santa Monica	Harris Hanshue	USA	Apperson	64.453
10.07.09	Santa Monica	Bert Dingley	USA	Chalmers-Detroit	55.429
19.08.09	Indianapolis	Bob Burman	USA	Buick	53.772
20.08.09	Indianapolis	Louis Strang	USA	Buick	64.739
21.08.09	Indianapolis	Leigh Lynch	USA	Jackson	57.983
06.09.09	Lowell	Bob Burman	USA	Buick	55.514
07.09.09	Lowell	William Knipper	USA	Chalmers-Detroit	51.500
07.09.09	Lowell	Louis Chevrolet	USA	Buick	54.200
08.09.09	Lowell	George Robertson	USA	Simplex	54.201
29.09.09	Riverhead	Ralph de Palma	USA	Fiat	62.430
29.09.09	Riverhead	Frank Lescault	USA	Palmer Singer	62.000
29.09.09	Riverhead	William Sharp	USA	Sharp Arrow	63.400
29.09.09	Riverhead	Louis Chevrolet	USA	Buick	70.300
29.09.09	Riverhead	Arthur See	USA	Maxwell	60.000
09.10.09	Philadelphia	George Robertson	USA	Simplex	55.485
24.10.09	San Leandro	Jack Fleming	USA	Pope-Hartford	76.516
30.10.09	Vanderbilt Cup (Long Island)	Harry Grant	USA	Alco	62.796
06.11.09	Los Angeles-Phoenix	Joe Nikrent	USA	Buick	24.967

1910

05.05.10	Atlanta	Ray Harroun	USA	Marmon	65.746
06.05.10	Atlanta	Bill Endicott	USA	Cole	59.500
06.05.10	Atlanta	Herb Lytle	USA	American	74.380
07.05.10	Atlanta	Tom Kincaid/Johnny Aitken	USA	National	65.788
27.05.10	Indianapolis	Tom Kincaid	USA	National	71.669
28.05.10	Indianapolis	Ray Harroun	USA	Marmon	72.058
30.05.10	Indianapolis	Ray Harroun	USA	Marmon	70.551
02.07.10	Indianapolis	Bob Burman	USA	Marquette-Buick	74.447
04.07.10	Indianapolis	Joe Dawson	USA	Marmon	73.468
26.08.10	Elgin	Dave Buick	USA	Marmon	55.206
26.08.10	Elgin	Al Livingstone	USA	National	60.852
27.08.10	Elgin	Ralph Mulford	USA	Lozier	62.770
03.09.10	Indianapolis	Eddie Hearne	USA	Benz	75.030
03.09.10	Indianapolis	Howdy Wilcox	USA	National	72.238
05.09.10	Indianapolis	Eddie Hearne	USA	Benz	78.851
05.09.10	Indianapolis	Johnny Aitken	USA	National	71.466
01.10.10	Long Island	Bill Endicott	USA	Cole	54.930
01.10.10	Long Island	Frank Gelnaw	USA	Falcar	58.443
01.10.10	Vanderbilt Cup (Long Island)	Harry Grant	USA	Alco	65.181

1911

22.02.11	Oakland	Charles Bigelow	USA	Mercer	57.143
22.02.11	Oakland	Charles Merz	USA	National	66.801
22.02.11	Oakland	Bert Dingley	USA	Pope-Hartford	65.755
28.03.11	Jacksonville	Lou Disbrow	USA	Pope-Hartford	79.558
30.05.11	Indianapolis 500	Ray Harroun/Cyrus Patschke	USA	Marmon Wasp	74.602
04.07.11	Bakersfield	Harvey Herrick	USA	National	48.596
25.08.11	Elgin	Hughie Hughes	USA	Mercer	64.824
25.08.11	Elgin	Don Herr	USA	National	65.836

Date	Location	Winner	Nat.	Car	Speed
26.08.11	Elgin	Len Zengel	USA	National	66.606
09.09.11	Cincinnati	John Jenkins	USA	Cole	54.096
09.09.11	Cincinnati	Eddie Hearne	USA	Fiat	56.684
09.10.11	Philadelphia	Erwin Bergdoll	USA	Benz	61.151
09.10.11	Philadelphia	Ralph Mulford	USA	Lozier	60.184
09.10.11	Philadelphia	Lou Disbrow	USA	National	58.311
09.10.11	Philadelphia	Hughie Hughes	USA	Mercer	57.925
14.10.11	Santa Monica	Bruce Keene	USA	Marmon	68.780
14.10.11	Santa Monica	Charles Merz	USA	National	74.425
14.10.11	Santa Monica	Louis Nikrent	USA	Buick	59.211
14.10.11	Santa Monica	Harvey Herrick	USA	National	74.629
27.11.11	Vanderbilt Cup (Savannah)	Ralph Mulford	USA	Lozier	74.076
30.11.11	American GP (Savannah)	David Bruce-Brown	USA	Fiat S74	74.548

1912

Date	Location	Winner	Nat.	Car	Speed
04.05.12	Santa Monica	George Joermann	USA	Maxwell	61.871
04.05.12	Santa Monica	Ralph de Palma	USA	Mercer	69.542
04.05.12	Santa Monica	Teddy Tetzlaff	USA	Fiat	78.721
30.05.12	Indianapolis 500	Joe Dawson/Don Herr	USA	National	78.719
05.07.12	Tacoma	Eddie Pullen	USA	Mercer	62.183
05.07.12	Tacoma	Earl Cooper	USA	Stutz	66.889
05.07.12	Tacoma	Teddy Tetzlaff	USA	Fiat	69.380
06.07.12	Tacoma	Teddy Tetzlaff	USA	Fiat	65.681
25.08.12	Columbus	Spencer Wishart	USA	Mercer	57.672
30.08.12	Elgin	Hughie Hughes	USA	Mercer	65.261
30.08.12	Elgin	Charles Merz	USA	Stutz	66.328
31.08.12	Elgin	Ralph de Palma	USA	Mercedes	68.579
31.08.12	Elgin	Ralph de Palma	USA	Mercedes	69.125
02.10.12	Vanderbilt Cup (Milwaukee)	Ralph de Palma	USA	Mercedes	68.980
03.10.12	Milwaukee	Bill Endicott	USA	Mason	55.699
03.10.12	Milwaukee	Mortimer Roberts	USA	Mason	58.799
05.11.12	Brighton Beach	Ralph Mulford	USA	Mason	58.718

1913

Date	Location	Winner	Nat.	Car	Speed
01.01.13	San Diego	George Hill	USA	Fiat	46.196
02.03.13	San Diego	Willie Carlson	USA	Benz	59.247
30.05.13	Indianapolis 500	Jules Goux	F	Peugeot L76	75.933
04.07.13	Columbus	Ralph Mulford	USA	Mason	59.465
05.07.13	Tacoma	Earl Cooper	USA	Stutz	70.571
07.07.13	Tacoma	Earl Cooper	USA	Stutz	71.275
28.07.13	Galveston	Lou Disbrow	USA	Simplex	71.443
29.07.13	Galveston	WE Ferguson	USA	Peugeot	71.443
30.07.13	Galveston	Lou Disbrow	USA	Simplex	69.098
09.08.13	Santa Monica	Earl Cooper	USA	Stutz	73.967
29.08.13	Elgin	Ralph de Palma	USA	Mercer	67.513
30.08.13	Elgin	Gil Anderson	USA	Stutz	72.383
09.09.13	Corona	Earl Cooper	USA	Stutz	75.031
09.09.13	Corona	Earl Cooper	USA	Stutz	74.177

1914

Date	Location	Winner	Nat.	Car	Speed
26.02.14	Vanderbilt Cup (Santa Monica)	Ralph de Palma	USA	Mercedes	75.000
28.02.14	American GP (Santa Monica)	Eddie Pullen	USA	Mercer	77.324
30.05.14	Indianapolis 500	René Thomas	F	Delage	82.474
03.07.14	Tacoma	Hughie Hughes	USA	Maxwell	74.285
04.07.14	Tacoma	Earl Cooper	USA	Stutz	73.321
04.07.14	Sioux City	Eddie Rickenbacher	USA	Duesenberg	78.591
30.07.14	Galveston	Ralph Mulford	USA	Peugeot	88.253
01.08.14	Galveston	Ralph Mulford	USA	Peugeot	59.900
03.08.14	Galveston	Ralph Mulford	USA	Peugeot	63.091
21.08.14	Elgin	Ralph de Palma	USA	Mercedes	74.934
22.08.14	Elgin	Ralph de Palma	USA	Mercedes	74.543
26.09.14	Kalamazoo	Bob Burman	USA	Peugeot	63.499
22.10.14	Galesburg	Ralph Mulford	USA	Duesenberg	64.580
24.10.14	Minneapolis	Tom Alley	USA	Duesenberg	65.574
26.11.14	Corona	Eddie Pullen	USA	Mercer	87.927

1915

Date	Location	Winner	Nat.	Car	Speed
09.01.15	San Diego	Earl Cooper	USA	Stutz	65.335
03.02.15	Glendale	Eddie O'Donnell	USA	Duesenberg	47.531
07.02.15	Ascot Park	Eddie O'Donnell	USA	Duesenberg	59.104
27.02.15	American GP (San Francisco)	Dario Resta	I	Peugeot EX3	56.130
06.03.15	Vanderbilt Cup (San Francisco)	Dario Resta	I	Peugeot EX3	66.400
17.03.15	Venice	Barney Oldfield	USA	Maxwell	67.143
20.03.15	Tucson	Barney Oldfield	USA	Maxwell	67.121
29.04.15	Oklahoma City	Bob Burman	USA	Peugeot	68.007
31.05.15	Indianapolis 500	Ralph de Palma	USA	Mercedes	89.840
09.06.15	Galesburg	Eddie O'Donnell	USA	Duesenberg	62.500
26.06.15	Maywood Speedway, Chicago	Dario Resta	I	Peugeot EX3	97.582
03.07.15	Sioux City	Eddie Rickenbacher	USA	Maxwell	74.705

04.07.15 Tacoma	Grover Ruckstell	USA	Mercer	84.722
05.07.15 Tacoma	Eddie Pullen	USA	Mercer	84.966
05.07.15 Omaha Speedway	Eddie Rickenbacher	USA	Maxwell	91.122
09.07.15 Burlington	Bob Burman	USA	Peugeot	47.061
07.08.15 Des Moines	Ralph Mulford	USA	Duesenberg	86.919
07.08.15 Maywood Speedway, Chicago	Dario Resta	I	Peugeot EX3	101.862
20.08.15 Elgin	Earl Cooper	USA	Stutz	74.941
21.08.15 Elgin	Gil Anderson	USA	Stutz	77.212
28.08.15 Kalamazoo	Ralph de Palma	USA	Stutz	64.155
04.09.15 Twin City	Earl Cooper	USA	Stutz	86.334
18.09.15 Narragansett Park, Providence	Eddie Rickenbacher	USA	Maxwell	67.105
09.10.15 Sheepshead Bay	Gil Anderson	USA	Stutz	102.589
02.11.15 Sheepshead Bay	Dario Resta	I	Peugeot EX3	105.395
20.11.15 Phoenix	Earl Cooper	USA	Stutz	64.390
25.11.15 San Francisco	Earl Cooper	USA	Stutz	57.417

1916

13.05.16 Sheepshead Bay	Eddie Rickenbacher	USA	Maxwell	96.240
30.05.16 Indianapolis 500	Dario Resta	I	Peugeot	84.001
10.06.16 Maywood Speedway, Chicago	Dario Resta	I	Peugeot	98.615
24.06.16 Des Moines	Ralph de Palma	USA	Mercedes	93.162
04.07.16 Twin City	Ralph de Palma	USA	Mercedes	91.075
15.07.16 Omaha Speedway	Dario Resta	I	Peugeot	99.194
05.08.16 Tacoma	Eddie Rickenbacher	USA	Maxwell	89.255
04.09.16 Cincinnati	Johnny Aitken	USA	Peugeot EX3	97.059
09.09.16 Indianapolis	Johnny Aitken	USA	Peugeot EX3	89.440
30.09.16 Sheepshead Bay	Johnny Aitken	USA	Peugeot EX3	104.846
14.10.16 Maywood Speedway, Chicago	Dario Resta	I	Peugeot	103.966
28.10.16 Sheepshead Bay	Johnny Aitken	USA	Peugeot EX3	105.956
16.11.16 Vanderbilt Cup (Santa Monica)	Dario Resta	I	Peugeot	87.155
18.11.16 American GP (Santa Monica)	Howdy Wilcox/Johnny Aitken	USA	Peugeot EX5	85.723
30.11.16 Ascot Park	Eddie Rickenbacher	USA	Duesenberg	67.538

1917

04.03.17 Ascot Park	Earl Cooper	USA	Stutz	68.363
10.05.17 Uniontown	William Taylor	USA	Newman-Stutz	89.246
30.05.17 Cincinnati	Louis Chevrolet	USA	Frontenac	102.181
16.06.17 Maywood Speedway, Chicago	Earl Cooper	USA	Stutz	103.107
04.07.17 Omaha Speedway	Ralph Mulford	USA	Hudson	101.256
14.07.17 Twin City	Earl Cooper	USA	Stutz	97.297
14.07.17 Twin City	Ira Vail	USA	Hudson	96.264
03.09.17 Tacoma	Earl Cooper	USA	Stutz	87.146
03.09.17 Maywood Speedway, Chicago	Ralph de Palma	USA	Packard 299	106.572
03.09.17 Maywood Speedway, Chicago	Louis Chevrolet	USA	Frontenac	106.210
08.09.17 Uniontown	Frank Elliott	USA	Delage-Miller	90.685
15.09.17 Narragansett Park, Providence	Ralph Mulford	USA	Frontenac	75.630
15.09.17 Narragansett Park, Providence	Tommy Milton	USA	Duesenberg	75.885
15.09.17 Narragansett Park, Providence	Tommy Milton	USA	Duesenberg	70.835
22.09.17 Sheepshead Bay	Louis Chevrolet	USA	Frontenac	110.396
13.10.17 Maywood Speedway, Chicago	Tom Alley	USA	Alley-Miller	105.556
13.10.17 Maywood Speedway, Chicago	Ralph Mulford	USA	Frontenac	105.960
13.10.17 Maywood Speedway, Chicago	Pete Henderson	USA	Roamer	109.608
29.10.17 Uniontown	Eddie Hearne	USA	Duesenberg	92.855
29.11.17 Ascot Park	Louis Chevrolet	USA	Frontenac	76.433
29.11.17 Ascot Park	Eddie Hearne	USA	Duesenberg	71.576

1918

16.05.18 Uniontown	Tommy Milton	USA	Duesenberg	101.301
16.05.18 Uniontown	Ralph Mulford	USA	Frontenac	97.484
16.05.18 Uniontown	Eddie Hearne	USA	Frontenac	96.272
16.05.18 Uniontown	Louis Chevrolet	USA	Frontenac	94.952
16.05.18 Uniontown	Ralph Mulford	USA	Frontenac	96.927
04.07.18 Tacoma	Cliff Durant	USA	Stutz	98.966
04.07.18 Tacoma	Cliff Durant	USA	Stutz	97.954
04.07.18 Tacoma	Eddie Hearne	USA	Duesenberg	94.290
18.07.18 Uniontown	Louis Chevrolet	USA	Frontenac	94.572
28.07.18 Maywood Speedway, Chicago	Ralph de Palma	USA	Packard 299	110.735
28.07.18 Maywood Speedway, Chicago	Ralph de Palma	USA	Packard 299	106.425
17.08.18 Sheepshead Bay	Ralph de Palma	USA	Packard 299	111.180
17.08.18 Sheepshead Bay	Ralph de Palma	USA	Packard 299	108.959
17.08.18 Sheepshead Bay	Ralph de Palma	USA	Packard 299	109.144
02.09.18 Uniontown	Ralph Mulford	USA	Frontenac	96.173

1919

15.03.19 Santa Monica	Cliff Durant	USA	Chevrolet	82.006
23.03.19 Ascot Park	Roscoe Sarles	USA	Duesenberg	70.848
19.05.19 Uniontown	Tommy Milton	USA	Duesenberg	96.215
30.05.19 Indianapolis 500	Howdy Wilcox	USA	Peugeot	88.050
14.06.19 Sheepshead Bay	Tommy Milton	USA	Duesenberg	112.430

14.06.19 Sheepshead Bay	Ralph Mulford	USA	Frontenac	110.137
14.06.19 Sheepshead Bay	Ralph de Palma	USA	Packard 299	113.679
04.07.19 Tacoma	Louis Chevrolet	USA	Frontenac	97.317
04.07.19 Sheepshead Bay	Gaston Chevrolet	USA	Frontenac	110.527
19.07.19 Uniontown	Tommy Milton	USA	Duesenberg	100.891
19.07.19 Uniontown	Dave Lewis	USA	Duesenberg	98.301
19.07.19 Uniontown	Ira Fetterman	USA	Peerless	99.877
19.07.19 Uniontown	Roscoe Sarles	USA	Miller	93.968
19.07.19 Uniontown	Tommy Milton	USA	Duesenberg	101.250
23.08.19 Elgin	Tommy Milton	USA	Duesenberg	73.745
01.09.19 Uniontown	Gaston Chevrolet/Joe Boyer	USA	Frontenac	93.537
20.09.19 Sheepshead Bay	Gaston Chevrolet	USA	Frontenac	108.998
12.10.19 Cincinnati	Joe Boyer	USA	Frontenac	101.818

1920

28.02.20 Beverly Hills	Jimmy Murphy	USA	Duesenberg	103.243
10.04.20 Beverly Hills*	Art Klein	USA	Peugeot	110.837
10.04.20 Beverly Hills*	Jimmy Murphy	USA	Duesenberg	110.294
10.04.20 Beverly Hills*	Tommy Milton	USA	Duesenberg	111.801
30.05.20 Indianapolis 500	Gaston Chevrolet	USA	Frontenac	88.166
19.06.20 Uniontown*	Tommy Milton	USA	Duesenberg	94.578
05.07.20 Tacoma	Tommy Milton	USA	Duesenberg	94.099
28.08.20 Elgin	Ralph de Palma	USA	Ballot	78.673
06.09.20 Uniontown*	Tommy Milton	USA	Duesenberg	96.601
02.10.20 Fresno*	Jimmy Murphy	USA	Duesenberg	96.360
25.11.20 Beverly Hills	Roscoe Sarles	USA	Duesenberg	103.199
			*non-championship race but included in AAA revisions	

1921

27.02.21 Beverly Hills	Ralph de Palma	USA	Ballot	106.509
27.02.21 Beverly Hills	Roscoe Sarles	USA	Duesenberg	107.271
27.02.21 Beverly Hills	Jimmy Murphy	USA	Duesenberg	103.806
27.02.21 Beverly Hills	Tommy Milton	USA	Durant-Duesenberg	104.287
27.02.21 Beverly Hills	Ralph de Palma	USA	Ballot	107.399
10.04.21 Beverly Hills	Ralph de Palma	USA	Ballot	106.383
10.04.21 Beverly Hills	Eddie Pullen	USA	Duesenberg	107.914
10.04.21 Beverly Hills	Joe Thomas	USA	Duesenberg	105.882
10.04.21 Beverly Hills	Jimmy Murphy	USA	Duesenberg	107.399
10.04.21 Beverly Hills	Jimmy Murphy	USA	Duesenberg	109.290
30.04.21 Fresno	Joe Thomas	USA	Duesenberg	100.409
30.05.21 Indianapolis 500	Tommy Milton	USA	Frontenac	89.621
18.06.21 Uniontown	Roscoe Sarles	USA	Duesenberg	97.755
04.07.21 Tacoma	Tommy Milton	USA	Durant-Miller	97.403
14.08.21 Santa Rosa	Eddie Hearne	USA	Duesenberg	110.674
05.09.21 Uniontown	Ira Fetterman	USA	Duesenberg	99.803
01.10.21 Fresno	Earl Cooper	USA	Duesenberg	100.784
23.10.21 Santa Rosa	Roscoe Sarles	USA	Duesenberg	110.339
24.11.21 Beverly Hills	Eddie Hearne	USA	Duesenberg	110.362
11.12.21 San Carlos	Jimmy Murphy	USA	Duesenberg	110.958

1922

05.03.22 Beverly Hills	Tommy Milton	USA	Durant-Miller	110.837
02.04.22 Beverly Hills	Pietro Bordino	I	Fiat 802	114.943
02.04.22 Beverly Hills	Tommy Milton	USA	Durant-Miller	115.237
02.04.22 Beverly Hills	Jimmy Murphy	USA	Duesenberg	114.213
02.04.22 Beverly Hills	Frank Elliott	USA	Miller	114.504
02.04.22 Beverly Hills	Tommy Milton	USA	Durant-Miller	115.311
16.04.22 San Carlos	Harry Hartz	USA	Duesenberg	111.616
27.04.22 Fresno	Jimmy Murphy	USA	Duesenberg	102.857
07.05.22 Santa Rosa	Pietro Bordino	I	Fiat 802	114.405
07.05.22 Santa Rosa	Jimmy Murphy	USA	Duesenberg-Miller	115.339
30.05.22 Indianapolis 500	Jimmy Murphy	USA	Duesenberg-Miller	94.484
17.06.22 Uniontown	Jimmy Murphy	USA	Duesenberg-Miller	102.258
04.07.22 Tacoma	Jimmy Murphy	USA	Duesenberg-Miller	97.603
06.08.22 Santa Rosa	Frank Elliott	USA	Miller	116.152
06.08.22 Santa Rosa	Frank Elliott	USA	Miller	113.208
17.09.22 Kansas City	Tommy Milton	USA	Miller	107.218
30.09.22 Fresno	Bennett Hill	USA	Miller	102.541
03.12.22 Beverly Hills	Jimmy Murphy	USA	Miller	114.606

1923

25.02.23 Beverly Hills	Jimmy Murphy	USA	Miller	115.628
26.04.23 Fresno	Jimmy Murphy	USA	Miller	103.567
30.05.23 Indianapolis 500	Tommy Milton/Howdy Wilcox	USA	Miller	90.954
04.07.23 Kansas City	Eddie Hearne	USA	Miller	106.118
04.09.23 Altoona	Eddie Hearne	USA	Miller	111.501
29.09.23 Fresno	Harry Hartz	USA	Miller	103.647
21.10.23 Kansas City	Harlan Fengler	USA	Miller	112.847
29.11.23 Beverly Hills	Bennett Hill	USA	Miller	112.430

Indycar Championship

1924

24.02.24 Beverly Hills	Harlan Fengler	USA	Miller	116.060
30.05.24 Indianapolis 500	LL Corum/Joe Boyer	USA	Duesenberg	98.234
14.06.24 Altoona	Jimmy Murphy	USA	Miller	114.548
04.07.24 Kansas City	Jimmy Murphy	USA	Miller	114.421
01.09.24 Altoona	Jimmy Murphy	USA	Miller	114.382
15.09.24 Syracuse	"Red" Shafer	USA	Duesenberg	78.658
02.10.24 Fresno	Earl Cooper	USA	Miller	105.613
25.10.24 Charlotte	Tommy Milton	USA	Miller	118.171
14.12.24 Culver City	Bennett Hill	USA	Miller	126.786

1925

01.03.25 Culver City	Tommy Milton	USA	Miller	126.886
30.04.25 Fresno	Peter de Paolo	USA	Duesenberg	104.875
11.05.25 Charlotte	Earl Cooper	USA	Miller	122.034
30.05.25 Indianapolis 500	Peter de Paolo/Norman Batten	USA	Duesenberg	101.127
13.06.25 Altoona	Peter de Paolo	USA	Duesenberg	115.605
11.07.25 Laurel	Peter de Paolo	USA	Duesenberg	123.300
07.09.25 Altoona	Robert McDonough	USA	Miller	118.196
26.10.25 Laurel	Robert McDonough	USA	Miller	126.003
31.10.25 Salem	Peter de Paolo	USA	Duesenberg	126.006
11.11.25 Charlotte	Tommy Milton	USA	Duesenberg	124.971
29.11.25 Culver City	Frank Elliott	USA	Miller	127.874

1926

22.02.26 Miami	Peter de Paolo	USA	Duesenberg	129.296
21.03.26 Culver City	Bennett Hill	USA	Miller	131.295
01.05.26 Atlantic City	Harry Hartz	USA	Miller	134.092
10.05.26 Charlotte	Earl de Vore	USA	Miller	120.088
31.05.26 Indianapolis 500	Frank Lockhart	USA	Miller	95.904
12.06.26 Altoona	Dave Lewis	USA	Miller	112.435
05.07.26 Salem	Peter de Paolo	USA	Duesenberg	128.249
05.07.26 Salem	Earl Cooper	USA	Miller	116.562
17.07.26 Atlantic City	Harry Hartz	USA	Miller	128.659
17.07.26 Atlantic City	Norman Batten	USA	Miller	120.755
17.07.26 Atlantic City	Fred Comer	USA	Miller	124.742
17.07.26 Atlantic City	Harry Hartz	USA	Miller	123.411
23.08.26 Charlotte	Earl Cooper	USA	Miller	128.848
23.08.26 Charlotte	Dave Lewis	USA	Miller	125.320
23.08.26 Charlotte	Frank Lockhart	USA	Miller	122.549
23.08.26 Charlotte	Frank Lockhart	USA	Miller	120.878
18.09.26 Altoona	Frank Lockhart	USA	Miller	116.379
02.10.26 Fresno	Bennett Hill	USA	Miller	106.257
02.10.26 Fresno	Frank Lockhart	USA	Miller	100.739
12.10.26 Salem	Bennett Hill	USA	Miller	129.977
12.10.26 Salem	"Leon Duray"	USA	Miller	130.393
12.10.26 Salem	Harry Hartz	USA	Miller	123.261
11.11.26 Charlotte	Frank Lockhart	USA	Miller	132.548
11.11.26 Charlotte	Dave Lewis	USA	Miller	127.119
11.11.26 Charlotte	Harry Hartz	USA	Miller	129.403
11.11.26 Charlotte	"Leon Duray"	USA	Miller	122.045

1927

06.03.27 Culver City	"Leon Duray"	USA	Miller	124.712
07.05.27 Atlantic City	Dave Lewis	USA	Miller	130.059
30.05.27 Indianapolis 500	George Souders	USA	Duesenberg	97.545
11.06.27 Altoona	Peter de Paolo	USA	Miller	116.565
04.07.27 Salem	Peter de Paolo	USA	Miller	124.348
05.09.27 Altoona	Frank Lockhart	USA	Miller	116.705
19.09.27 Charlotte	Frank Lockhart	USA	Miller	127.540
19.09.27 Charlotte	Peter de Paolo	USA	Miller	126.050
19.09.27 Charlotte	Babe Stapp	USA	Miller	119.915
12.10.27 Salem	Frank Lockhart	USA	Miller	125.739
12.10.27 Salem	Frank Lockhart	USA	Miller	126.701

1928

30.05.28 Indianapolis 500	Louis Meyer	USA	Miller	99.482
10.06.28 Detroit	Ray Keech	USA	Miller	77.664
04.07.28 Salem	"Leon Duray"	USA	Miller	130.751
04.07.28 Salem	Ray Keech	USA	Miller	122.742
19.08.28 Altoona	Louis Meyer	USA	Miller	116.637
01.09.28 Syracuse	Ray Keech	USA	Miller	75.314
12.10.28 Salem	Cliff Woodbury	USA	Miller	117.005

1929

30.05.29 Indianapolis 500	Ray Keech	USA	Miller	97.585
09.06.29 Detroit	Cliff Woodbury	USA	Miller	76.224
15.06.29 Altoona	Louis Meyer	USA	Miller	119.000
31.08.29 Syracuse	Wilbur Shaw	USA	Miller	81.066
02.09.29 Altoona	Louis Meyer	USA	Miller	109.476

1930

03.05.30 Langhorne	Bill Cummings	USA	Miller	77.320
30.05.30 Indianapolis 500	Billy Arnold	USA	Summers-Miller	100.448
09.06.30 Detroit	Wilbur Shaw	USA	Smith-Miller	68.256
14.06.30 Altoona	Billy Arnold	USA	Summers-Miller	111.173
22.06.30 Akron	"Shorty" Cantlon	USA	Stevens-Miller	67.771
04.07.30 Bridgeville	Wilbur Shaw	USA	Smith-Miller	66.790
01.09.30 Altoona	Billy Arnold	USA	Summers-Miller	113.261
06.09.30 Syracuse	Bill Cummings	USA	Duesenberg	83.484

1931

30.05.31 Indianapolis 500	Louis Schneider	USA	Stevens-Miller	96.629
14.06.31 Detroit	Louis Meyer	USA	Stevens-Miller	75.472
04.07.31 Altoona	Lou Moore	USA	Miller	112.853
07.09.31 Altoona	Jimmy Gleason	USA	Duesenberg	117.801
07.09.31 Altoona	"Shorty" Cantlon	USA	Stevens-Miller	114.068
07.09.31 Altoona	"Shorty" Cantlon	USA	Stevens-Miller	109.656
12.09.31 Syracuse	Lou Moore	USA	Miller	74.077

1932

30.05.32 Indianapolis 500	Fred Frame	USA	Wetteroth-Miller	104.144
05.06.32 Detroit	Bob Carey	USA	Stevens-Miller	71.625
19.06.32 Roby	"Stubby" Stubblefield	USA	Adams-Miller	76.271
02.07.32 Syracuse	Bob Carey	USA	Stevens-Miller	81.158
10.09.32 Detroit	Mauri Rose	USA	Stevens-Miller	74.457
13.11.32 Oakland	Bill Cummings	USA	Miller	90.452

1933

30.05.33 Indianapolis 500	Louis Meyer	USA	Miller	104.162
11.06.33 Detroit	Bill Cummings	USA	Miller	73.907
09.09.33 Syracuse	Bill Cummings	USA	Miller	81.874

1934

30.05.34 Indianapolis 500	Bill Cummings	USA	Miller	104.863
25.08.34 Springfield	Bill Winn	USA	Miller	77.771
09.09.34 Syracuse	"Shorty" Cantlon	USA	Weil-Miller	79.893
23.12.34 Mines Field	Kelly Petillo	USA	Stevens/Summers-Sparks	81.494

1935

30.05.35 Indianapolis 500	Kelly Petillo	USA	Wetteroth-Offenhauser	106.240
04.07.35 St Paul	Kelly Petillo	USA	Wetteroth-Offenhauser	77.270
24.08.35 Springfield	Bill Winn	USA	Duesenberg-Miller	80.393
02.09.35 Syracuse	Bill Winn	USA	Duesenberg-Miller	83.546
07.09.35 Altoona	Louis Meyer	USA	Stevens-Miller	86.559
13.10.35 Langhorne	Kelly Petillo	USA	Wetteroth-Offenhauser	91.900

1936

30.05.36 Indianapolis 500	Louis Meyer	USA	Stevens-Miller	109.069
20.06.36 Goshen	Rex Mays	USA	Stevens/Summers-Sparks	76.410
15.09.36 Syracuse	Mauri Rose	USA	Miller-Offenhauser	82.378
12.10.36 Vanderbilt Cup (Roosevelt Raceway)	Tazio Nuvolari	I	Alfa Romeo 12C-36	65.503

1937

30.05.37 Indianapolis 500	Wilbur Shaw	USA	Shaw-Offenhauser	113.580
05.07.37 Vanderbilt Cup (Roosevelt Raceway)	Bernd Rosemeyer	D	Auto Union C	82.234
12.09.37 Syracuse	Bill Winn	USA	Weil-Miller	87.491

1938

30.05.38 Indianapolis 500	Floyd Roberts	USA	Wetteroth-Miller	117.200
10.09.38 Syracuse	Jimmy Snyder	USA	Lencki-Offenhauser	84.211

1939

30.05.39 Indianapolis 500	Wilbur Shaw	USA	Maserati 8CTF	115.035
27.08.39 Milwaukee	Babe Stapp	USA	Stevens-Miller	83.663
02.09.39 Syracuse	Mauri Rose	USA	Wetteroth-Offenhauser	74.906

1940

30.05.40 Indianapolis 500	Wilbur Shaw	USA	Maserati 8CTF	114.277
24.08.40 Springfield	Rex Mays	USA	Stevens-Winfield	87.464
02.09.40 Syracuse	Rex Mays	USA	Stevens-Winfield	85.268

1941

30.05.41 Indianapolis 500	Floyd Davis/Mauri Rose	USA	Wetteroth-Offenhauser	115.117
24.08.41 Milwaukee	Rex Mays	USA	Stevens-Winfield	82.248
01.09.41 Syracuse	Rex Mays	USA	Stevens-Winfield	84.567

1946

30.05.46 Indianapolis 500	George Robson	USA	Adams-Sparks	114.747
30.06.46 Langhorne	Rex Mays	USA	Stevens-Winfield	85.144

02.09.46	Lakewood Park, Atlanta	George Connor	USA	Kurtis-Offenhauser	n\a
15.09.46	Indiana State Fair	Rex Mays	USA	Stevens-Winfield	78.888
22.09.46	Milwaukee	Rex Mays	USA	Stevens-Winfield	84.814
06.10.46	Goshen	Tony Bettenhausen	USA	Wetteroth-Offenhauser	77.644

1947

30.05.47	Indianapolis 500	Mauri Rose	USA	Deidt-Offenhauser	116.338
08.06.47	Milwaukee	Bill Holland	USA	Wetteroth-Offenhauser	87.280
22.06.47	Langhorne	Bill Holland	USA	Wetteroth-Offenhauser	87.728
04.07.47	Lakewood Park, Atlanta	Walt Ader	USA	Adams-Offenhauser	75.224
13.07.47	Bainbridge	Ted Horn	USA	Horn-Offenhauser	85.378
27.07.47	Milwaukee	Charles van Acker	USA	Stevens-Offenhauser	85.960
17.08.47	Goshen	Tony Bettenhausen	USA	Stevens-Offenhauser	80.062
24.08.47	Milwaukee	Ted Horn	USA	Horn-Offenhauser	84.336
01.09.47	Pikes Peak	Louis Unser	USA	Maserati	45.598
28.09.47	Springfield	Tony Bettenhausen	USA	Stevens-Offenhauser	92.519
02.10.47	Arlington Downs, Dallas	Ted Horn	USA	Horn-Offenhauser	85.097

1948

25.04.48	Arlington Downs, Dallas	Ted Horn	USA	Horn-Offenhauser	78.539
30.05.48	Indianapolis 500	Mauri Rose	USA	Deidt-Offenhauser	119.814
06.06.48	Milwaukee	Emil Andres	USA	Kurtis-Offenhauser	85.320
20.06.48	Langhorne	Walt Brown	USA	Kurtis-Offenhauser	89.649
15.08.48	Milwaukee	Johnny Mantz	USA	Kurtis-Offenhauser	85.327
21.08.48	Springfield	Ted Horn	USA	Horn-Offenhauser	90.520
29.08.48	Milwaukee	Tony Bettenhausen/Myron Fohr	USA	Marchese-Offenhauser	86.734
04.09.48	Du Quoin	Lee Wallard	USA	Meyer-Offenhauser	88.387
06.09.48	Lakewood Park, Atlanta	Mel Hansen	USA	Wetteroth-Offenhauser	79.278
06.09.48	Pikes Peak	Al Rogers	USA	Offenhauser	47.065
19.09.48	Springfield	Myron Fohr	USA	Marchese-Offenhauser	88.692
10.10.48	Du Quoin	Johnnie Parsons	USA	Kurtis-Offenhauser	83.571

1949

24.04.49	Arlington Downs, Dallas	Johnnie Parsons	USA	Kurtis-Offenhauser	n\a
30.05.49	Indianapolis 500	Bill Holland	USA	Deidt-Offenhauser	121.327
05.06.49	Milwaukee	Myron Fohr	USA	Marchese-Offenhauser	83.615
19.06.49	Trenton	Myron Fohr	USA	Marchese-Offenhauser	75.765
20.08.49	Springfield	Mel Hansen	USA	Lesovsky-Offenhauser	87.912
28.08.49	Milwaukee	Johnnie Parsons	USA	Kurtis-Offenhauser	85.817
03.09.49	Du Quoin	Tony Bettenhausen	USA	Kurtis-Offenhauser	90.068
05.09.49	Pikes Peak	Al Rogers	USA	Offenhauser	46.868
10.09.49	Syracuse	Johnnie Parsons	USA	Kurtis-Offenhauser	86.196
11.09.49	Detroit	Tony Bettenhausen	USA	Kurtis-Offenhauser	81.264
25.09.49	Springfield	Johnnie Parsons	USA	Kurtis-Offenhauser	91.720
16.10.49	Langhorne	Johnnie Parsons	USA	Kurtis-Offenhauser	93.623
30.10.49	Sacramento	Fred Agabashian	USA	Kurtis-Offenhauser	84.486
06.11.49	Del Mar	Jimmy Davies	USA	Ewing-Offenhauser	85.359

1950

30.05.50	Indianapolis 500	Johnnie Parsons	USA	Kurtis-Offenhauser	124.002
11.06.50	Milwaukee	Tony Bettenhausen	USA	Wetteroth-Offenhauser	85.027
25.06.50	Langhorne	Jack McGrath	USA	Kurtis KK3000-Offenhauser	88.517
19.08.50	Springfield	Paul Russo	USA	Nichels-Offenhauser	91.278
27.08.50	Milwaukee	Walt Faulkner	USA	Kurtis KK2000-Offenhauser	87.315
04.09.50	Pikes Peak	Al Rogers	USA	Coniff-Offenhauser	47.617
09.09.50	Syracuse	Jack McGrath	USA	Kurtis KK3000-Offenhauser	87.350
10.09.50	Detroit	Henry Banks	USA	Moore-Offenhauser	82.853
01.10.50	Springfield	Tony Bettenhausen	USA	Kurtis-Offenhauser	87.637
15.10.50	Sacramento	Duke Dinsmore	USA	Kurtis KK2000-Offenhauser	82.474
12.11.50	Phoenix	Jimmy Davies	USA	Ewing-Offenhauser	78.020
26.11.50	Bay Meadows	Tony Bettenhausen	USA	Kurtis-Offenhauser	86.163
10.12.50	Darlington	Johnnie Parsons	USA	Nichels-Offenhauser	104.541

1951

30.05.51	Indianapolis 500	Lee Wallard	USA	Kurtis-Offenhauser	126.244
10.06.51	Milwaukee	Tony Bettenhausen	USA	Kurtis-Offenhauser	90.041
24.06.51	Langhorne	Tony Bettenhausen	USA	Kurtis-Offenhauser	92.374
04.07.51	Darlington	Walt Faulkner	USA	Kuzma-Offenhauser	104.719
18.08.51	Springfield	Tony Bettenhausen	USA	Kurtis-Offenhauser	90.054
26.08.51	Milwaukee	Walt Faulkner	USA	Kuzma-Offenhauser	91.342
01.09.51	Du Quoin	Tony Bettenhausen	USA	Kurtis-Offenhauser	88.311
03.09.51	Du Quoin	Tony Bettenhausen	USA	Kurtis-Offenhauser	87.425
03.09.51	Pikes Peak	Al Rogers	USA	Offenhauser	47.597
08.09.51	Syracuse	Tony Bettenhausen	USA	Kurtis-Offenhauser	n/a
09.09.51	Detroit	Paul Russo	USA	Nichels-Offenhauser	83.639
23.09.51	Centennial Park, Denver	Tony Bettenhausen	USA	Kurtis-Offenhauser	86.643
21.10.51	San Jose	Tony Bettenhausen	USA	Kurtis-Offenhauser	80.645
04.11.51	Phoenix	Johnnie Parsons	USA	Kurtis KK4000-Offenhauser	84.626
11.11.51	Bay Meadows	Johnnie Parsons	USA	Kurtis KK4000-Offenhauser	87.708

1952

30.05.52 Indianapolis 500	Troy Ruttman	USA	Kuzma-Offenhauser	128.922
08.06.52 Milwaukee	Mike Nazaruk	USA	Kurtis-Offenhauser	92.255
04.07.52 Raleigh	Troy Ruttman	USA	Kuzma-Offenhauser	89.109
16.08.52 Springfield	Bill Schindler	USA	Nichels-Offenhauser	94.336
24.08.52 Milwaukee	Chuck Stevenson	USA	Kurtis KK4000-Offenhauser	81.392
30.08.52 Detroit	Bill Vukovich	USA	Kuzma-Offenhauser	81.559
01.09.52 Pikes Peak	George Hammond	USA	Kurtis-Offenhauser	47.897
01.09.52 Du Quoin	Chuck Stevenson	USA	Kurtis KK4000-Offenhauser	88.409
06.09.52 Syracuse	Jack McGrath	USA	Kurtis KK4000-Offenhauser	89.073
28.09.52 Centennial Park, Denver	Bill Vukovich	USA	Kuzma-Offenhauser	87.357
02.11.52 San Jose	Bobby Ball	USA	Kurtis KK4000-Offenhauser	n/a
11.11.52 Phoenix	Johnnie Parsons	USA	Kurtis KK4000-Offenhauser	85.878

1953

30.05.53 Indianapolis 500	Bill Vukovich	USA	Kurtis KK500A-Offenhauser	128.740
07.06.53 Milwaukee	Jack McGrath	USA	Kurtis KK4000-Offenhauser	93.634
21.06.53 Springfield	Rodger Ward	USA	Kurtis-Offenhauser	89.483
04.07.53 Detroit	Rodger Ward	USA	Kurtis-Offenhauser	82.257
22.08.53 Springfield	Sam Hanks	USA	Kurtis KK4000-Offenhauser	91.162
30.08.53 Milwaukee	Chuck Stevenson	USA	Kuzma-Offenhauser	89.580
07.09.53 Du Quoin	Sam Hanks	USA	Kurtis KK4000-Offenhauser	89.984
07.09.53 Pikes Peak	Louis Unser	USA	Kurtis-Offenhauser	48.840
12.09.53 Syracuse	Tony Bettenhausen	USA	Kurtis-Offenhauser	74.089
26.09.53 Indiana State Fair	Bob Sweikert	USA	Kuzma-Offenhauser	87.192
25.10.53 Sacramento	Jimmy Bryan	USA	Kurtis KK4000-Offenhauser	79.786
11.11.53 Phoenix	Tony Bettenhausen	USA	Kurtis-Offenhauser	83.916

1954

31.05.54 Indianapolis 500	Bill Vukovich	USA	Kurtis KK500A-Offenhauser	130.840
06.06.54 Milwaukee	Chuck Stevenson	USA	Kuzma-Offenhauser	97.527
20.06.54 Langhorne	Jimmy Bryan	USA	Kuzma-Offenhauser	97.545
05.07.54 Darlington	Manuel Ayulo	USA	Kuzma-Offenhauser	122.665
21.08.54 Springfield	Jimmy Davies	USA	Ewing-Offenhauser	92.546
29.08.54 Milwaukee	Manuel Ayulo	USA	Kuzma-Offenhauser	96.261
06.09.54 Du Quoin	Sam Hanks	USA	Kurtis-Offenhauser	88.029
06.09.54 Pikes Peak	Keith Andrews	USA	Offenhauser	50.843
11.09.54 Syracuse	Bob Sweikert	USA	Kurtis KK4000-Offenhauser	90.339
18.09.54 Indiana State Fair	Jimmy Bryan	USA	Kuzma-Offenhauser	85.395
17.10.54 Sacramento	Jimmy Bryan	USA	Kuzma-Offenhauser	86.940
07.11.54 Phoenix	Jimmy Bryan	USA	Kuzma-Offenhauser	84.524
14.11.54 Las Vegas	Jimmy Bryan	USA	Kuzma-Offenhauser	84.818

1955

30.05.55 Indianapolis 500	Bob Sweikert	USA	Kurtis KK500D-Offenhauser	128.209
05.06.55 Milwaukee	Johnny Thomson	USA	Kuzma-Offenhauser	98.844
19.06.55 Langhorne	Jimmy Bryan	USA	Kuzma-Offenhauser	95.727
20.08.55 Springfield	Jimmy Bryan	USA	Kuzma-Offenhauser	90.524
28.08.55 Milwaukee	Pat Flaherty	USA	Kurtis KK500B-Offenhauser	95.033
05.09.55 Du Quoin	Jimmy Bryan	USA	Kuzma-Offenhauser	93.530
05.09.55 Pikes Peak	Bob Finney	USA	Lincoln	51.607
10.09.55 Syracuse	Bob Sweikert	USA	Watson-Offenhauser	89.928
17.09.55 Indiana State Fair	Jimmy Bryan	USA	Kuzma-Offenhauser	83.978
16.10.55 Sacramento	Jimmy Bryan	USA	Kuzma-Offenhauser	86.207
06.11.55 Phoenix	Jimmy Bryan	USA	Kuzma-Offenhauser	83.862

USAC NATIONAL CHAMPIONSHIP

1956

30.05.56 Indianapolis 500	Pat Flaherty	USA	Watson-Offenhauser	128.490
10.06.56 Milwaukee	Pat Flaherty	USA	Watson-Offenhauser	98.847
24.06.56 Langhorne	George Amick	USA	Kuzma-Offenhauser	95.201
04.07.56 Darlington	Pat O'Connor	USA	Templeton-Offenhauser	124.066
14.07.56 Lakewood Park, Atlanta	Eddie Sachs	USA	Hillegass-Offenhauser	n\a
19.08.56 Springfield	Jimmy Bryan	USA	Kuzma-Offenhauser	88.471
26.08.56 Milwaukee	Jimmy Bryan	USA	Kuzma-Offenhauser	92.733
03.09.56 Du Quoin	Jimmy Bryan	USA	Kuzma-Offenhauser	91.706
08.09.56 Syracuse	Tony Bettenhausen	USA	Kuzma-Offenhauser	90.804
15.09.56 Indiana State Fairgrounds	Jimmy Bryan	USA	Kuzma-Offenhauser	80.727
21.10.56 Sacramento	Jud Larson	USA	Watson-Offenhauser	86.797
12.11.56 Phoenix	George Amick	USA	Lesovsky-Offenhauser	91.826

1957

30.05.57 Indianapolis 500	Sam Hanks	USA	Epperly-Offenhauser	135.601
02.06.57 Langhorne	Johnny Thomson	USA	Kuzma-Offenhauser	100.174
09.06.57 Milwaukee	Rodger Ward	USA	Lesovsky-Offenhauser	97.789
23.06.57 Detroit	Jimmy Bryan	USA	Kuzma-Offenhauser	80.232
04.07.57 Lakewood Park, Atlanta	George Amick	USA	Lesovsky-Offenhauser	89.995
17.08.57 Springfield	Rodger Ward	USA	Lesovsky-Offenhauser	96.015
25.08.57 Milwaukee	Jim Rathmann	USA	Epperly-Offenhauser	98.134

02.09.57 Du Quoin	Jud Larson	USA	Watson-Offenhauser	90.948
07.09.57 Syracuse	Elmer George	USA	Watson-Offenhauser	94.295
14.09.57 Indiana State Fairgrounds	Jud Larson	USA	Watson-Offenhauser	91.751
29.09.57 Trenton	Pat O'Connor	USA	Kuzma-Offenhauser	100.279
20.10.57 Sacramento	Rodger Ward	USA	Lesovsky-Offenhauser	90.965
11.11.57 Phoenix	Jimmy Bryan	USA	Kuzma-Offenhauser	86.001

1958

30.03.58 Trenton	Len Sutton	USA	Kuzma-Offenhauser	95.527
30.05.58 Indianapolis 500	Jimmy Bryan	USA	Epperly-Offenhauser	133.791
08.06.58 Milwaukee	Art Bisch	USA	Kuzma-Offenhauser	94.013
15.06.58 Langhorne	Eddie Sachs	USA	Kuzma-Offenhauser	91.976
04.07.58 Lakewood Park, Atlanta	Jud Larson	USA	Watson-Offenhauser	87.146
16.08.58 Springfield	Johnny Thomson	USA	Kuzma-Offenhauser	98.137
24.08.58 Milwaukee	Rodger Ward	USA	Lesovsky-Offenhauser	97.809
01.09.58 Du Quoin	Johnny Thomson	USA	Kuzma-Offenhauser	94.753
06.09.58 Syracuse	Johnny Thomson	USA	Kuzma-Offenhauser	94.953
13.09.58 Indiana State Fairgrounds	Eddie Sachs	USA	Kuzma-Offenhauser	92.142
28.09.58 Trenton	Rodger Ward	USA	Lesovsky-Offenhauser	99.368
26.10.58 Sacramento	Johnny Thomson	USA	Kuzma-Offenhauser	89.175
11.11.58 Phoenix	Jud Larson	USA	Lesovsky-Offenhauser	92.738

1959

04.04.59 Daytona	Jim Rathmann	USA	Watson-Offenhauser	170.261
19.04.59 Trenton	Tony Bettenhausen	USA	Kuzma-Offenhauser	91.161
30.05.59 Indianapolis 500	Rodger Ward	USA	Watson-Offenhauser	135.857
07.06.59 Milwaukee	Johnny Thomson	USA	Lesovsky-Offenhauser	98.609
14.06.59 Langhorne	Van Johnson	USA	Kurtis KK4000-Offenhauser	99.553
22.08.59 Springfield	Len Sutton	USA	Kuzma-Offenhauser	95.186
30.08.59 Milwaukee	Rodger Ward	USA	Watson-Offenhauser	96.317
07.09.59 Du Quoin	Rodger Ward	USA	Watson-Offenhauser	93.268
12.09.59 Syracuse	Eddie Sachs	USA	Meskowski-Offenhauser	94.121
19.09.59 Indiana State Fairgrounds	Rodger Ward	USA	Watson-Offenhauser	91.033
27.09.59 Trenton	Eddie Sachs	USA	Meskowski-Offenhauser	97.398
18.10.59 Phoenix	Tony Bettenhausen	USA	Kuzma-Offenhauser	88.458
25.10.59 Sacramento	Jim Hurtubise	USA	Kuzma-Offenhauser	86.464

1960

10.04.60 Trenton	Rodger Ward	USA	Watson-Offenhauser	95.486
30.05.60 Indianapolis 500	Jim Rathmann	USA	Watson-Offenhauser	138.767
05.06.60 Milwaukee	Rodger Ward	USA	Watson-Offenhauser	99.465
19.06.60 Langhorne	Jim Hurtubise	USA	Kuzma-Offenhauser	100.786
20.08.60 Springfield	Jim Packard	USA	Lesovsky-Offenhauser	90.909
28.08.60 Milwaukee	Len Sutton	USA	Watson-Offenhauser	100.131
05.09.60 Du Quoin	AJ Foyt Jr	USA	Meskowski-Offenhauser	93.351
10.09.60 Syracuse	Bobby Grim	USA	Meskowski-Offenhauser	93.258
17.09.60 Indiana State Fairgrounds	AJ Foyt Jr	USA	Meskowski-Offenhauser	89.286
25.09.60 Trenton	Eddie Sachs	USA	Kuzma-Offenhauser	99.223
30.10.60 Sacramento	AJ Foyt Jr	USA	Meskowski-Offenhauser	84.796
20.11.60 Phoenix	AJ Foyt Jr	USA	Meskowski-Offenhauser	89.078

1961

09.04.61 Trenton	Eddie Sachs	USA	Kuzma-Offenhauser	98.680
30.05.61 Indianapolis 500	AJ Foyt Jr	USA	Watson-Offenhauser	139.131
04.06.61 Milwaukee	Rodger Ward	USA	Watson-Offenhauser	103.860
18.06.61 Langhorne	AJ Foyt Jr	USA	Meskowski-Offenhauser	99.601
20.08.61 Milwaukee	Lloyd Ruby	USA	Watson-Offenhauser	101.638
21.08.61 Springfield	Jim Hurtubise	USA	Kuzma-Offenhauser	97.459
04.09.61 Du Quoin	AJ Foyt Jr	USA	Meskowski-Offenhauser	92.755
09.09.61 Syracuse	Rodger Ward	USA	Watson-Offenhauser	95.090
16.09.61 Indiana State Fairgrounds	AJ Foyt Jr	USA	Meskowski-Offenhauser	92.370
24.09.61 Trenton	Eddie Sachs	USA	Kuzma-Offenhauser	101.013
29.10.61 Sacramento	Rodger Ward	USA	Watson-Offenhauser	88.779
19.11.61 Phoenix	Parnelli Jones	USA	Kuzma-Offenhauser	n/a

1962

08.04.62 Trenton	AJ Foyt Jr	USA	Meskowski-Offenhauser	101.102
30.05.62 Indianapolis 500	Rodger Ward	USA	Watson-Offenhauser	140.293
10.06.62 Milwaukee	AJ Foyt Jr	USA	Watson/Trevis-Offenhauser	100.860
01.07.62 Langhorne	AJ Foyt Jr	USA	Meskowski-Offenhauser	93.187
22.07.62 Trenton	Rodger Ward	USA	Watson-Offenhauser	100.977
19.08.62 Springfield	Jim Hurtubise	USA	Kuzma-Offenhauser	92.625
19.08.62 Milwaukee	Rodger Ward	USA	Watson-Offenhauser	100.015
26.08.62 Langhorne	Don Branson	USA	Watson-Offenhauser	104.800
08.09.62 Syracuse	Rodger Ward	USA	Watson-Offenhauser	95.572
15.09.62 Indiana State Fairgrounds	Parnelli Jones	USA	Kuzma-Offenhauser	90.612
23.09.62 Trenton	Don Branson	USA	Watson-Offenhauser	102.529
28.10.62 Sacramento	AJ Foyt Jr	USA	Meskowski-Offenhauser	95.260
18.11.62 Phoenix	Bobby Marshman	USA	Meskowski-Offenhauser	92.122

1963

21.04.63 Trenton	AJ Foyt Jr	USA	Meskowski-Offenhauser	102.492
30.05.63 Indianapolis 500	Parnelli Jones	USA	Watson-Offenhauser	143.137

09.06.63	Milwaukee	Rodger Ward	USA	Watson-Offenhauser	100.585
23.06.63	Langhorne	AJ Foyt Jr	USA	Meskowski-Offenhauser	104.135
28.07.63	Trenton	AJ Foyt Jr	USA	Watson/Trevis-Offenhauser	100.403
17.08.63	Springfield	Rodger Ward	USA	Watson-Offenhauser	95.557
18.08.63	Milwaukee	Jim Clark	GB	Lotus 29-Ford	104.452
02.09.63	Du Quoin	AJ Foyt Jr	USA	Meskowski-Offenhauser	95.234
14.09.63	Indiana State Fairgrounds	Rodger Ward	USA	Watson-Offenhauser	93.545
22.09.63	Trenton	AJ Foyt Jr	USA	Watson/Trevis-Offenhauser	101.358
27.10.63	Sacramento	Rodger Ward	USA	Watson-Offenhauser	92.174
17.11.63	Phoenix	Rodger Ward	USA	Watson-Offenhauser	85.026

1964

22.03.64	Phoenix	AJ Foyt Jr	USA	Watson-Offenhauser	107.536
19.04.64	Trenton	AJ Foyt Jr	USA	Watson-Offenhauser	104.530
30.05.64	Indianapolis 500	AJ Foyt Jr	USA	Watson-Offenhauser	147.350
07.06.64	Milwaukee	AJ Foyt Jr	USA	Watson-Offenhauser	100.346
21.06.64	Langhorne	AJ Foyt Jr	USA	Meskowski-Offenhauser	102.552
19.07.64	Trenton	AJ Foyt Jr	USA	Watson-Offenhauser	105.590
22.08.64	Springfield	AJ Foyt Jr	USA	Meskowski-Offenhauser	95.238
23.08.64	Milwaukee	Parnelli Jones	USA	Lotus 34-Ford	104.751
07.09.64	Du Quoin	AJ Foyt Jr	USA	Meskowski-Offenhauser	97.800
26.09.64	Indiana State Fairgrounds	AJ Foyt Jr	USA	Meskowski-Offenhauser	89.056
27.09.64	Trenton	Parnelli Jones	USA	Lotus 34-Ford	96.415
25.10.64	Sacramento	AJ Foyt Jr	USA	Meskowski-Offenhauser	91.451
22.11.64	Phoenix	Lloyd Ruby	USA	Halibrand-Offenhauser	107.736

1965

28.03.65	Phoenix	Don Branson	USA	Watson-Offenhauser	106.456
25.04.65	Trenton	Jim McElreath	USA	Brabham-Offenhauser	97.186
31.05.65	Indianapolis 500	Jim Clark	GB	Lotus 38-Ford	150.686
06.06.65	Milwaukee	Parnelli Jones	USA	Kuzma/Lotus 34-Ford	101.747
20.06.65	Langhorne	Jim McElreath	USA	Brabham-Offenhauser	89.109
04.07.65	Pikes Peak	Al Unser	USA	Eisert/Lotus 34-Ford	57.652
18.07.65	Trenton	AJ Foyt Jr	USA	Bignotti/Lotus 34-Ford	98.361
25.07.65	Indianapolis Raceway Park	Mario Andretti	USA	Hawk-Ford	101.657
01.08.65	Atlanta	Johnny Rutherford	USA	Watson-Ford	143.807
08.08.65	Langhorne	Jim McElreath	USA	Brabham-Offenhauser	104.858
14.08.65	Milwaukee	Joe Leonard	USA	Hallibrand-Ford	97.277
21.08.65	Springfield	AJ Foyt Jr	USA	Meskowski-Offenhauser	96.174
22.08.65	Milwaukee	Gordon Johncock	USA	Gerhardt-Offenhauser	100.453
06.09.65	Du Quoin	Don Branson	USA	Watson-Offenhauser	88.792
18.09.65	Indiana State Fairgrounds	AJ Foyt Jr	USA	Meskowski-Offenhauser	84.849
26.09.65	Trenton	AJ Foyt Jr	USA	Bignotti/Lotus 34-Ford	99.953
24.10.65	Sacramento	Don Branson	USA	Watson-Offenhauser	86.320
21.11.65	Phoenix	AJ Foyt Jr	USA	Bignotti/Lotus 34-Ford	99.986

1966

20.03.66	Phoenix	Jim McElreath	USA	Brabham-Ford	98.819
24.04.66	Trenton	Rodger Ward	USA	Lola T90-Drake/Offenhauser	99.905
30.05.66	Indianapolis 500	Graham Hill	GB	Lola T90-Ford	144.317
05.06.66	Milwaukee	Mario Andretti	USA	Brawner/Brabham-Ford	95.655
12.06.66	Langhorne	Mario Andretti	USA	Brawner/Brabham-Ford	98.690
26.06.66	Atlanta	Mario Andretti	USA	Brawner/Brabham-Ford	141.362
04.07.66	Pikes Peak	Bobby Unser	USA	Unser-Chevrolet	60.081
24.07.66	Indianapolis Raceway Park	Mario Andretti	USA	Brawner/Brabham-Ford	95.373
07.08.66	Langhorne	Roger McCluskey	USA	Eagle 66-Ford	108.494
20.08.66	Springfield	Don Branson	USA	Watson-Offenhauser	95.243
27.08.66	Milwaukee	Mario Andretti	USA	Brawner/Brabham-Ford	104.060
05.09.66	Du Quoin	Bud Tingelstad	USA	Meskowski-Offenhauser	95.102
10.09.66	Indiana State Fairgrounds	Mario Andretti	USA	Kuzma-Offenhauser	96.582
25.09.66	Trenton	Mario Andretti	USA	Brawner/Brabham-Ford	105.127
23.10.66	Sacramento	Dick Atkins	USA	Watson-Offenhauser	88.568
20.11.66	Phoenix	Mario Andretti	USA	Brawner/Brabham-Ford	104.686

1967

09.04.67	Phoenix	Lloyd Ruby	USA	Mongoose-Drake/Offenhauser	86.295
23.04.67	Trenton	Mario Andretti	USA	Brawner/Hawk-Ford	109.838
30.05.67	Indianapolis 500	AJ Foyt Jr	USA	Coyote/Lotus 34-Ford	151.207
04.06.67	Milwaukee	Gordon Johncock	USA	Gerhardt-Ford	98.643
18.06.67	Langhorne	Lloyd Ruby	USA	Lotus 38-Ford	113.380
25.06.67	Pikes Peak	Wes Vandervoort	USA	Chevrolet	58.254
01.07.67	Mosport Park	Bobby Unser	USA	Eagle 67-Ford	99.609
01.07.67	Mosport Park	Bobby Unser	USA	Eagle 67-Ford	n/a
23.07.67	Indianapolis Raceway Park	Mario Andretti	USA	Brawner/Hawk-Ford	113.611
30.07.67	Langhorne	Mario Andretti	USA	Brawner/Hawk-Ford	113.184
06.08.67	St Jovite	Mario Andretti	USA	Brawner/Hawk-Ford	87.151
06.08.67	St Jovite	Mario Andretti	USA	Brawner/Hawk-Ford	92.401
19.08.67	Springfield	AJ Foyt Jr	USA	Meskowski-Offenhauser	86.326
20.08.67	Milwaukee	Mario Andretti	USA	Brawner/Hawk-Ford	105.386
04.09.67	Du Quoin	AJ Foyt Jr	USA	Meskowski-Offenhauser	93.578
09.09.67	Indiana State Fairgrounds	Mario Andretti	USA	Kuzma-Offenhauser	95.546

24.09.67 Trenton	AJ Foyt Jr	USA	Coyote-Ford	92.223
01.10.67 Sacramento	AJ Foyt Jr	USA	Meskowski-Offenhauser	87.712
22.10.67 Hanford	Gordon Johncock	USA	Gerhardt-Ford	127.523
19.11.67 Phoenix	Mario Andretti	USA	Brawner/Hawk-Ford	109.872
26.11.67 Riverside	Dan Gurney	USA	Eagle 67-Ford/Weslake	107.995

1968

17.03.68 Hanford	Gordon Johncock	USA	Gerhardt-Drake/Offenhauser	121.511
31.03.68 Stardust, Las Vegas	Bobby Unser	USA	Eagle 68-Ford	113.269
07.04.68 Phoenix	Bobby Unser	USA	Eagle 68-Drake/Offenhauser	100.938
21.04.68 Trenton	Bobby Unser	USA	Eagle 68-Drake/Offenhauser	103.397
30.05.68 Indianapolis 500	Bobby Unser	USA	Eagle 68-Drake/Offenhauser	152.882
09.06.68 Milwaukee	Lloyd Ruby	USA	Mongoose-Drake/Offenhauser	100.739
15.06.68 Mosport Park	Dan Gurney	USA	Eagle 68-Ford/Weslake	103.993
15.06.68 Mosport Park	Dan Gurney	USA	Eagle 68-Ford/Weslake	106.784
23.06.68 Langhorne	Gordon Johncock	USA	Gerhardt-Drake/Offenhauser	103.464
30.06.68 Pikes Peak	Bobby Unser	USA	Unser-Chevrolet	62.609
07.07.68 Castle Rock	AJ Foyt Jr	USA	Coyote-Ford	83.168
13.07.68 Nazareth	Al Unser	USA	Ward-Offenhauser	99.558
21.07.68 Indianapolis Raceway Park	Al Unser	USA	Lola T150-Ford	96.795
21.07.68 Indianapolis Raceway Park	Al Unser	USA	Lola T150-Ford	86.768
28.07.68 Langhorne	Al Unser	USA	Lola T150-Ford	107.651
28.07.68 Langhorne	Al Unser	USA	Lola T150-Ford	124.875
04.08.68 St Jovite	Mario Andretti	USA	Brawner/Hawk-Ford	96.492
04.08.68 St Jovite	Mario Andretti	USA	Brawner/Hawk-Ford	90.022
17.08.68 Springfield	Roger McCluskey	USA	Meskowski-Offenhauser	90.046
18.08.68 Milwaukee	Lloyd Ruby	USA	Mongoose-Drake/Offenhauser	108.735
02.09.68 Du Quoin	Mario Andretti	USA	Kuzma-Offenhauser	91.518
07.09.68 Indiana State Fairgrounds	AJ Foyt Jr	USA	Meskowski-Offenhauser	93.294
22.09.68 Trenton	Mario Andretti	USA	Brawner-Drake/Offenhauser	104.543
29.09.68 Sacramento	AJ Foyt Jr	USA	Meskowski-Offenhauser	87.118
13.10.68 Michigan	Ronnie Bucknum	USA	Eagle 68-Drake/Offenhauser	161.812
03.11.68 Hanford	AJ Foyt Jr	USA	Coyote-Ford	134.416
17.11.68 Phoenix	Gary Bettenhausen	USA	Gerhardt-Drake/Offenhauser	104.972
01.12.68 Riverside	Dan Gurney	USA	Eagle 68-Ford/Weslake	112.548

1969

30.03.69 Phoenix	George Follmer	USA	Gilbert-Chevrolet	109.866
13.04.69 Hanford	Mario Andretti	USA	Brawner/Hawk III-Ford	n/a
30.05.69 Indianapolis 500	Mario Andretti	USA	Brawner/Hawk III-Ford	156.867
08.06.69 Milwaukee	Art Pollard	USA	Gerhardt-Drake/Offenhauser	112.156
15.06.69 Langhorne	Bobby Unser	USA	Eagle 69-Drake/Offenhauser	112.425
29.06.69 Pikes Peak	Mario Andretti	USA	King-Chevrolet	58.424
06.07.69 Castle Rock	Gordon Johncock	USA	Eagle 69-Ford	84.337
12.07.69 Nazareth	Mario Andretti	USA	Kuzma-Offenhauser	105.851
19.07.69 Trenton	Mario Andretti	USA	Brawner/Hawk III-Ford	139.591
27.07.69 Indianapolis Raceway Park	Dan Gurney	USA	Eagle 69-Ford	92.275
27.07.69 Indianapolis Raceway Park	Peter Revson	USA	Brabham-Repco	94.967
17.08.69 Milwaukee	Al Unser	USA	Lola T152-Ford	106.758
18.08.69 Springfield	Mario Andretti	USA	Kuzma-Offenhauser	96.642
24.08.69 Dover Downs	Art Pollard	USA	Gerhardt-Plymouth	124.978
01.09.69 Du Quoin	Al Unser	USA	King-Ford	94.724
06.09.69 Indiana State Fairgrounds	AJ Foyt Jr	USA	Meskowski-Ford	93.609
14.09.69 Brainerd	Gordon Johncock	USA	Eagle 69-Ford	110.436
14.09.69 Brainerd	Dan Gurney	USA	Eagle 69-Ford	114.894
21.09.69 Trenton	Mario Andretti	USA	Brawner/Hawk III-Ford	134.382
28.09.69 Sacramento	Al Unser	USA	King-Ford	93.526
19.10.69 Seattle	Mario Andretti	USA	Brawner/Hawk III-Ford	85.164
19.10.69 Seattle	Al Unser	USA	Lola T152-Ford	83.486
15.11.69 Phoenix	Al Unser	USA	Lola T152-Ford	110.109
07.12.69 Riverside	Mario Andretti	USA	Brawner/Hawk III-Ford	107.786

1970

28.03.70 Phoenix	Al Unser	USA	Colt 70-Ford	n/a
04.04.70 Sears Point	Dan Gurney	USA	Eagle 70-Ford	86.972
26.04.70 Trenton	Lloyd Ruby	USA	Mongoose-Drake/Offenhauser	135.967

Mario Andretti, Indycar champion again and winner at the speedway for the only time in 1969

Date	Venue	Driver	Country	Car	Speed
30.05.70	Indianapolis 500	Al Unser	USA	Colt 70-Ford	155.749
07.06.70	Milwaukee	Joe Leonard	USA	Colt 70-Ford	108.299
16.06.70	Langhorne	Bobby Unser	USA	Eagle 70-Drake/Offenhauser	106.302
28.06.70	Castle Rock	Mario Andretti	USA	McNamara T500-Ford	84.013
04.07.70	Michigan	Gary Bettenhausen	USA	Gerhardt-Drake/Offenhauser	140.625
26.07.70	Indianapolis Raceway Park	Al Unser	USA	Colt 70-Ford	92.799
22.08.70	Springfield	Al Unser	USA	King-Ford	62.301
23.08.70	Milwaukee	Al Unser	USA	Colt 70-Ford	114.304
06.09.70	Ontario	Jim McElreath	USA	Coyote-Ford	160.106
07.09.70	Du Quoin	Al Unser	USA	King-Ford	98.155
12.09.70	Indiana State Fairgrounds	Al Unser	USA	King-Ford	97.994
19.09.70	Sedalia	Al Unser	USA	King-Ford	98.039
03.10.70	Trenton	Al Unser	USA	Colt 70-Ford	137.639
04.10.70	Sacramento	Al Unser	USA	King-Ford	93.376
21.11.70	Phoenix	Swede Savage	USA	Eagle 70-Ford	116.807

1971

Date	Venue	Driver	Country	Car	Speed
28.02.71	Rafaela (RA)	Al Unser	USA	Colt 71-Ford	166.851
28.02.71	Rafaela (RA)	Al Unser	USA	Colt 71-Ford	148.764
27.03.71	Phoenix	Al Unser	USA	Colt 71-Ford	111.565
25.04.71	Trenton	Mike Mosley	USA	Eagle 71-Ford	132.562
29.05.71	Indianapolis 500	Al Unser	USA	Colt 71-Ford	157.735
06.06.71	Milwaukee	Al Unser	USA	Colt 71-Ford	114.912
03.07.71	Pocono	Mark Donohue	USA	McLaren M16A-Drake/Offenhauser	138.650
18.07.71	Michigan	Mark Donohue	USA	McLaren M16A-Drake/Offenhauser	146.074
15.08.71	Milwaukee	Bobby Unser	USA	Eagle 71-Drake/Offenhauser	109.384
05.09.71	Ontario	Joe Leonard	USA	Colt 71-Ford	152.355
03.10.71	Trenton	Bobby Unser	USA	Eagle 71-Drake/Offenhauser	140.778
23.10.71	Phoenix	AJ Foyt Jr	USA	Coyote-Ford	110.701

1972

Date	Venue	Driver	Country	Car	Speed
18.03.72	Phoenix	Bobby Unser	USA	Eagle 72-Offenhauser	102.825
23.04.72	Trenton	Gary Bettenhausen	USA	McLaren M16B-Offenhauser	145.642
27.05.72	Indianapolis 500	Mark Donohue	USA	McLaren M16B-Offenhauser	162.962
04.06.72	Milwaukee	Bobby Unser	USA	Eagle 72-Offenhauser	109.131
16.07.72	Michigan	Joe Leonard	USA	Parnelli-Offenhauser	139.316
29.07.72	Pocono	Joe Leonard	USA	Parnelli-Offenhauser	154.781
13.08.72	Milwaukee	Joe Leonard	USA	Parnelli-Offenhauser	111.652
03.09.72	Ontario	Roger McCluskey	USA	McLaren M16B-Offenhauser	148.995
24.09.72	Trenton	Bobby Unser	USA	Eagle 72-Offenhauser	143.880
04.11.72	Phoenix	Bobby Unser	USA	Eagle 72-Offenhauser	127.618

1973

Date	Venue	Driver	Country	Car	Speed
07.04.73	Texas World Speedway	Al Unser	USA	Parnelli-Offenhauser	153.224
15.04.73	Trenton	AJ Foyt Jr	USA	Coyote-Foyt/Ford	138.359
15.04.73	Trenton	Mario Andretti	USA	Parnelli-Offenhauser	149.626
28.05.73	Indianapolis 500	Gordon Johncock	USA	Eagle 73-Offenhauser	159.036
10.06.73	Milwaukee	Bobby Unser	USA	Eagle 73-Offenhauser	113.957
01.07.73	Pocono	AJ Foyt Jr	USA	Coyote-Foyt/Ford	144.948
15.07.73	Michigan	Roger McCluskey	USA	McLaren M16B-Offenhauser	161.146
12.08.73	Milwaukee	Wally Dallenbach	USA	Eagle 73-Offenhauser	108.320
26.08.73	Ontario	Wally Dallenbach	USA	Eagle 73-Offenhauser	179.919
26.08.73	Ontario	Johnny Rutherford	USA	McLaren M16C-Offenhauser	164.162
02.09.73	Ontario	Wally Dallenbach	USA	Eagle 73-Offenhauser	157.660
16.09.73	Michigan	Bill Vukovich Jr	USA	Eagle 73-Offenhauser	134.026
16.09.73	Michigan	Johnny Rutherford	USA	McLaren M16C-Offenhauser	157.243
23.09.73	Trenton	Gordon Johncock	USA	Eagle 73-Offenhauser	135.025
06.10.73	Texas World Speedway	Gary Bettenhausen	USA	McLaren M16C-Offenhauser	181.910
03.11.73	Phoenix	Gordon Johncock	USA	Eagle 73-Offenhauser	115.015

1974

Date	Venue	Driver	Country	Car	Speed
03.03.74	Ontario	AJ Foyt Jr	USA	Coyote-Foyt/Ford	176.873
03.03.74	Ontario	Johnny Rutherford	USA	McLaren M16C/D-Offenhauser	172.673
10.03.74	Ontario	Bobby Unser	USA	Eagle 74-Offenhauser	157.017
17.03.74	Phoenix	Mike Mosley	USA	Eagle 74-Offenhauser	116.681
07.04.74	Trenton	Bobby Unser	USA	Eagle 74-Offenhauser	128.708
26.05.74	Indianapolis 500	Johnny Rutherford	USA	McLaren M16C/D-Offenhauser	158.589
09.06.74	Milwaukee	Johnny Rutherford	USA	McLaren M16C/D-Offenhauser	110.226
30.06.74	Pocono	Johnny Rutherford	USA	McLaren M16C/D-Offenhauser	156.701
21.07.74	Michigan	Bobby Unser	USA	Eagle 74-Offenhauser	141.717
11.08.74	Milwaukee	Gordon Johncock	USA	Eagle 74-Offenhauser	118.752
15.09.74	Michigan	Al Unser	USA	Eagle 74-Offenhauser	142.141
22.09.74	Trenton	AJ Foyt Jr	USA	Coyote-Foyt/Ford	135.372
22.09.74	Trenton	Bobby Unser	USA	Eagle 74-Offenhauser	156.069
02.11.74	Phoenix	Gordon Johncock	USA	Eagle 74-Offenhauser	124.202

1975

Date	Venue	Driver	Country	Car	Speed
02.03.75	Ontario	AJ Foyt Jr	USA	Coyote-Foyt/Ford	177.085
02.03.75	Ontario	Wally Dallenbach	USA	Eagle 75-Offenhauser	150.305
09.03.75	Ontario	AJ Foyt Jr	USA	Coyote-Foyt/Ford	154.344
16.03.75	Phoenix	Johnny Rutherford	USA	McLaren M16D-Offenhauser	110.971

06.04.75 Trenton	AJ Foyt Jr	USA	Coyote-Foyt/Ford	154.646
25.05.75 Indianapolis 500	Bobby Unser	USA	Eagle 75-Offenhauser	149.213
08.06.75 Milwaukee	AJ Foyt Jr	USA	Coyote-Foyt/Ford	114.042
29.06.75 Pocono	AJ Foyt Jr	USA	Coyote-Foyt/Ford	140.712
20.07.75 Michigan	AJ Foyt Jr	USA	Coyote-Foyt/Ford	158.907
17.08.75 Milwaukee	Mike Mosley	USA	Eagle 75-Offenhauser	114.393
13.09.75 Michigan	Tom Sneva	USA	McLaren M16C-Offenhauser	176.160
21.09.75 Trenton	Gordon Johncock	USA	Wildcat-Offenhauser	123.511
09.11.75 Phoenix	AJ Foyt Jr	USA	Coyote-Foyt/Ford	111.055

1976

14.03.76 Phoenix	Bobby Unser	USA	Eagle 76-Offenhauser	107.918
02.05.76 Trenton	Johnny Rutherford	USA	McLaren M16E-Offenhauser	147.499
30.05.76 Indianapolis 500	Johnny Rutherford	USA	McLaren M16E-Offenhauser	148.725
13.06.76 Milwaukee	Mike Mosley	USA	Eagle 76-Offenhauser	121.557
27.06.76 Pocono	Al Unser	USA	Parnelli VPJ6B-Cosworth	143.622
18.07.76 Michigan	Gordon Johncock	USA	Wildcat-DGS/Offenhauser	165.033
01.08.76 Texas World Speedway	AJ Foyt Jr	USA	Coyote-Foyt/Ford	172.885
15.08.76 Trenton	Gordon Johncock	USA	Wildcat-DGS/Offenhauser	135.929
22.08.76 Milwaukee	Al Unser	USA	Parnelli VPJ6B-Cosworth	121.907
05.09.76 Ontario	Bobby Unser	USA	Eagle 76-Offenhauser	143.246
18.09.76 Michigan	AJ Foyt Jr	USA	Coyote-Foyt/Ford	164.068
31.10.76 Texas World Speedway	Johnny Rutherford	USA	McLaren M16E-Offenhauser	150.313
07.11.76 Phoenix	Al Unser	USA	Parnelli VPJ6B-Cosworth	107.695

1977

06.03.77 Ontario	AJ Foyt Jr	USA	Coyote-Foyt/Ford	154.073
27.03.77 Phoenix	Johnny Rutherford	USA	McLaren M24-Cosworth	111.395
02.04.77 Texas World Speedway	Tom Sneva	USA	McLaren M24-Cosworth	157.711
30.04.77 Trenton	Wally Dallenbach	USA	Wildcat-DGS/Offenhauser	151.288
29.05.77 Indianapolis 500	AJ Foyt Jr	USA	Coyote-Foyt/Ford	161.331
12.06.77 Milwaukee	Johnny Rutherford	USA	McLaren M24-Cosworth	92.962
26.06.77 Pocono	Tom Sneva	USA	McLaren M24-Cosworth	152.131
03.07.77 Mosport Park	AJ Foyt Jr	USA	Coyote-Foyt/Ford	90.723
17.07.77 Michigan	Danny Ongais	USA	Parnelli VPJ6B-Cosworth	149.152
31.07.77 Texas World Speedway	Johnny Rutherford	USA	McLaren M24-Cosworth	164.191
21.08.77 Milwaukee	Johnny Rutherford	USA	McLaren M24-Cosworth	103.798
04.09.77 Ontario	Al Unser	USA	Parnelli VPJ6B-Cosworth	152.074
17.09.77 Michigan	Gordon Johncock	USA	Wildcat-DGS/Offenhauser	175.250
29.10.77 Phoenix	Gordon Johncock	USA	Wildcat-DGS/Offenhauser	108.596

1978

18.03.78 Phoenix	Gordon Johncock	USA	Wildcat Mk2-DGS/Offenhauser	116.757
26.03.78 Ontario	Danny Ongais	USA	Parnelli VPJ6B-Cosworth	162.810
15.04.78 Texas World Speedway	Danny Ongais	USA	Parnelli VPJ6B-Cosworth	173.594
23.04.78 Trenton	Gordon Johncock	USA	Wildcat Mk2-DGS/Offenhauser	130.988
28.05.78 Indianapolis 500	Al Unser	USA	Lola T500-Cosworth	161.363
11.06.78 Mosport Park	Danny Ongais	USA	Parnelli VPJ6B-Cosworth	87.164
18.06.78 Milwaukee	Rick Mears	USA	Penske PC6-Cosworth	120.677
25.06.78 Pocono	Al Unser	USA	Lola T500-Cosworth	142.261
16.07.78 Michigan	Johnny Rutherford	USA	McLaren M24B-Cosworth	159.941
23.07.78 Atlanta	Rick Mears	USA	Penske PC6-Cosworth	143.286
06.08.78 Texas World Speedway	AJ Foyt Jr	USA	Coyote-Foyt/Ford	159.060
20.08.78 Milwaukee	Danny Ongais	USA	Parnelli VPJ6B-Cosworth	108.385
03.09.78 Ontario	Al Unser	USA	Lola T500-Cosworth	145.158
16.09.78 Michigan	Danny Ongais	USA	Parnelli VPJ6B-Cosworth	146.246
23.09.78 Trenton	Mario Andretti	USA	Penske PC6-Cosworth	120.080
01.10.78 Silverstone (GB)	AJ Foyt Jr	USA	Coyote-Foyt/Ford	104.361
07.10.78 Brands Hatch (GB)	Rick Mears	USA	Penske PC6-Cosworth	95.789
28.10.78 Phoenix	Johnny Rutherford	USA	McLaren M24B-Cosworth	120.974

1979

25.03.79 Ontario	AJ Foyt Jr	USA	Parnelli VPJ6C-Cosworth	154.279
08.04.79 Texas World Speedway	AJ Foyt Jr	USA	Coyote-Foyt/Ford	129.575
27.05.79 Indianapolis 500	Rick Mears	USA	Penske PC6-Cosworth	158.899
10.06.79 Milwaukee	AJ Foyt Jr	USA	Parnelli VPJ6C-Cosworth	108.955
24.06.79 Pocono	AJ Foyt Jr	USA	Parnelli VPJ6C-Cosworth	134.995
29.07.79 Texas World Speedway	AJ Foyt Jr	USA	Parnelli VPJ6C-Cosworth	162.934
12.08.79 Milwaukee	Roger McCluskey	USA	Lola T500B-Cosworth	117.135

CART INDYCAR WORLD SERIES

1979

11.03.79 Phoenix	Gordon Johncock	USA	Penske PC6-Cosworth	119.389
22.04.79 Atlanta	Johnny Rutherford	USA	McLaren M24B-Cosworth	157.758
22.04.79 Atlanta	Johnny Rutherford	USA	McLaren M24B-Cosworth	163.976
27.05.79 Indianapolis 500	Rick Mears	USA	Penske PC6-Cosworth	158.899
10.06.79 Trenton	Bobby Unser	USA	Penske PC7-Cosworth	121.003
10.06.79 Trenton	Bobby Unser	USA	Penske PC7-Cosworth	147.915
15.07.79 Michigan	Gordon Johncock	USA	Penske PC6-Cosworth	170.976

15.07.79 Michigan	Bobby Unser	USA	Penske PC7-Cosworth	155.342
05.08.79 Watkins Glen	Bobby Unser	USA	Penske PC7-Cosworth	121.012
19.08.79 Trenton	Rick Mears	USA	Penske PC7-Cosworth	129.808
02.09.79 Ontario	Bobby Unser	USA	Penske PC7-Cosworth	146.795
15.09.79 Michigan	Bobby Unser	USA	Penske PC7-Cosworth	175.211
30.09.79 Atlanta	Rick Mears	USA	Penske PC7-Cosworth	182.094
20.10.79 Phoenix	Al Unser	USA	Chaparral 2K-Cosworth	123.203

1980

13.04.80 Ontario	Johnny Rutherford	USA	Chaparral 2K-Cosworth	162.016
25.05.80 Indianapolis 500	Johnny Rutherford	USA	Chaparral 2K-Cosworth	142.862
08.06.80 Milwaukee	Bobby Unser	USA	Penske PC9-Cosworth	112.773
22.06.80 Pocono	Bobby Unser	USA	Penske PC9-Cosworth	151.454
13.07.80 Mid-Ohio	Johnny Rutherford	USA	Chaparral 2K-Cosworth	86.601
19.07.80 Michigan	Johnny Rutherford	USA	Chaparral 2K-Cosworth	148.515
03.08.80 Watkins Glen	Bobby Unser	USA	Penske PC9-Cosworth	99.500
10.08.80 Milwaukee	Johnny Rutherford	USA	Chaparral 2K-Cosworth	105.063
31.08.80 Ontario	Bobby Unser	USA	Penske PC9-Cosworth	156.372
20.09.80 Michigan	Mario Andretti	USA	Penske PC9-Cosworth	167.494
26.10.80 Mexico City (MEX)	Rick Mears	USA	Penske PC9-Cosworth	116.329
08.11.80 Phoenix	Tom Sneva	USA	Phoenix-Cosworth	99.926

1981

22.03.81 Phoenix	Johnny Rutherford	USA	Chaparral 2K-Cosworth	116.681
24.05.81 Indianapolis 500*	Bobby Unser	USA	Penske PC9B-Cosworth	139.084
07.06.81 Milwaukee	Mike Mosley	USA	Eagle 81-Chevrolet	113.839
21.06.81 Pocono*	AJ Foyt Jr	USA	March 81C-Cosworth	137.196
28.06.81 Atlanta	Rick Mears	USA	Penske PC9B-Cosworth	147.224
28.06.81 Atlanta	Rick Mears	USA	Penske PC9B-Cosworth	167.196
25.07.81 Michigan	Pancho Carter	USA	Penske PC7-Cosworth	132.890
30.08.81 Riverside	Rick Mears	USA	Penske PC9B-Cosworth	113.176
05.09.81 Milwaukee	Tom Sneva	USA	March 81C-Cosworth	118.013
20.09.81 Michigan	Rick Mears	USA	Penske PC9B-Cosworth	125.957
04.10.81 Watkins Glen	Rick Mears	USA	Penske PC9B-Cosworth	108.273
18.10.81 Mexico City (MEX)	Rick Mears	USA	Penske PC9B-Cosworth	103.487
31.10.81 Phoenix	Tom Sneva	USA	March 81C-Cosworth	112.266

*Non-championship

1982

28.03.82 Phoenix	Rick Mears	USA	Penske PC10-Cosworth	118.727
01.05.82 Atlanta	Rick Mears	USA	Penske PC10-Cosworth	164.750
30.05.82 Indianapolis 500*	Gordon Johncock	USA	Wildcat Mk8B-Cosworth	162.029
13.06.82 Milwaukee	Gordon Johncock	USA	Wildcat Mk8B-Cosworth	126.978
04.07.82 Cleveland	Bobby Rahal	USA	March 82C-Cosworth	101.438
18.07.82 Michigan	Gordon Johncock	USA	Wildcat Mk8B-Cosworth	153.925
01.08.82 Milwaukee	Tom Sneva	USA	March 82C-Cosworth	109.132
15.08.82 Pocono	Rick Mears	USA	Penske PC10-Cosworth	145.879
29.08.82 Riverside	Rick Mears	USA	Penske PC10-Cosworth	111.783
19.09.82 Elkhart Lake	Hector Rebaque	MEX	March 82C-Cosworth	109.156
26.09.82 Michigan	Bobby Rahal	USA	March 82C-Cosworth	140.515
06.11.82 Phoenix	Tom Sneva	USA	March 82C-Cosworth	110.997

*Non-championship

1983

17.04.83 Atlanta	Gordon Johncock	USA	Wildcat Mk9C-Cosworth	146.133
29.05.83 Indianapolis 500	Tom Sneva	USA	March 83C-Cosworth	162.117
12.06.83 Milwaukee	Tom Sneva	USA	March 83C-Cosworth	116.104
03.07.83 Cleveland	Al Unser	USA	Penske PC11-Cosworth	108.421
17.07.83 Michigan	John Paul Jr	USA	Penske PC10-Cosworth	134.862
31.07.83 Elkhart Lake	Mario Andretti	USA	Lola T700-Cosworth	99.410
14.08.83 Pocono	Teo Fabi	I	March 83C-Cosworth	134.852
28.08.83 Riverside	Bobby Rahal	USA	March 83C-Cosworth	111.956

Johnny Rutherford won five races for Chaparral, including the Indy 500 (above), in 1980 to become champion

11.09.83 Mid-Ohio	Teo Fabi	I	March 83C-Cosworth	99.297
18.09.83 Michigan	Rick Mears	USA	Penske PC10B-Cosworth	182.325
09.10.83 Caesars Palace	Mario Andretti	USA	Lola T700-Cosworth	87.192
23.10.83 Laguna Seca	Teo Fabi	I	March 83C-Cosworth	106.943
30.10.83 Phoenix	Teo Fabi	I	March 83C-Cosworth	126.671

1984

01.04.84 Long Beach	Mario Andretti	USA	Lola T800-Cosworth	82.894
15.04.84 Phoenix	Tom Sneva	USA	March 84C-Cosworth	120.551
27.05.84 Indianapolis 500	Rick Mears	USA	March 84C-Cosworth	163.612
03.06.84 Milwaukee	Tom Sneva	USA	March 84C-Cosworth	118.030
17.06.84 Portland	Al Unser Jr	USA	March 84C-Cosworth	105.478
01.07.84 Meadowlands	Mario Andretti	USA	Lola T800-Cosworth	80.742
08.07.84 Cleveland	Danny Sullivan	USA	Lola T800-Cosworth	118.974
15.07.84 Michigan	Mario Andretti	USA	Lola T800-Cosworth	133.482
05.08.84 Elkhart Lake	Mario Andretti	USA	Lola T800-Cosworth	116.347
19.08.84 Pocono	Danny Sullivan	USA	Lola T800-Cosworth	137.303
02.09.84 Mid-Ohio	Mario Andretti	USA	Lola T800-Cosworth	100.939
09.09.84 Sanair (CDN)	Danny Sullivan	USA	Lola T800-Cosworth	111.707
22.09.84 Michigan	Mario Andretti	USA	Lola T800-Cosworth	168.523
14.10.84 Phoenix	Bobby Rahal	USA	March 84C-Cosworth	98.048
21.10.84 Laguna Seca	Bobby Rahal	USA	March 84C-Cosworth	119.105
11.11.84 Caesars Palace	Tom Sneva	USA	March 84C-Cosworth	93.702

1985

14.04.85 Long Beach	Mario Andretti	USA	Lola T900-Cosworth	87.694
26.05.85 Indianapolis 500	Danny Sullivan	USA	March 85C-Cosworth	152.982
02.06.85 Milwaukee	Mario Andretti	USA	Lola T900-Cosworth	124.162
16.06.85 Portland	Mario Andretti	USA	Lola T900-Cosworth	107.083
30.06.85 Meadowlands	Al Unser Jr	USA	Lola T900-Cosworth	90.167
07.07.85 Cleveland	Al Unser Jr	USA	Lola T900-Cosworth	124.331
28.07.85 Michigan	Emerson Fittipaldi	BR	March 85C-Cosworth	128.220
04.08.85 Elkhart Lake	Jacques Villeneuve	CDN	March 85C-Cosworth	114.066
18.08.85 Pocono	Rick Mears	USA	March 85C-Cosworth	151.676
01.09.85 Mid-Ohio	Bobby Rahal	USA	March 85C-Cosworth	107.628
08.09.85 Sanair (CDN)	Johnny Rutherford	USA	March 85C-Cosworth	89.996
22.09.85 Michigan	Bobby Rahal	USA	March 85C-Cosworth	163.657
06.10.85 Laguna Seca	Bobby Rahal	USA	March 85C-Cosworth	112.923
13.10.85 Phoenix	Al Unser	USA	March 85C-Cosworth	120.644
09.11.85 Tamiami Park	Danny Sullivan	USA	March 85C-Cosworth	95.915

1986

06.04.86 Phoenix	Kevin Cogan	USA	March 86C-Cosworth	120.346
13.04.86 Long Beach	Michael Andretti	USA	March 86C-Cosworth	80.965
01.06.86 Indianapolis 500	Bobby Rahal	USA	March 86C-Cosworth	170.722
08.06.86 Milwaukee	Michael Andretti	USA	March 86C-Cosworth	116.788
15.06.86 Portland	Mario Andretti	USA	Lola T86/00-Cosworth	107.760
29.06.86 Meadowlands	Danny Sullivan	USA	March 86C-Cosworth	92.340
06.07.86 Cleveland	Danny Sullivan	USA	March 86C-Cosworth	127.362
20.07.86 Toronto (CDN)	Bobby Rahal	USA	March 86C-Cosworth	87.414
02.08.86 Michigan	Johnny Rutherford	USA	March 86C-Cosworth	137.140
17.08.86 Pocono	Mario Andretti	USA	Lola T86/00-Cosworth	152.107
31.08.86 Mid-Ohio	Bobby Rahal	USA	March 86C-Cosworth	103.998
07.09.86 Sanair (CDN)	Bobby Rahal	USA	March 86C-Cosworth	103.157
28.09.86 Michigan	Bobby Rahal	USA	March 86C-Cosworth	181.701
04.10.86 Elkhart Lake	Emerson Fittipaldi	BR	March 86C-Cosworth	81.833
12.10.86 Laguna Seca	Bobby Rahal	USA	March 86C-Cosworth	119.693
19.10.86 Phoenix	Michael Andretti	USA	March 86C-Cosworth	134.676
09.11.86 Tamiami Park	Al Unser Jr	USA	Lola T86/00-Cosworth	106.322

1987

05.04.87 Long Beach	Mario Andretti	USA	Lola T87/00-Chevrolet	85.333
12.04.87 Phoenix	Roberto Guerrero	USA	March 87C-Cosworth	138.020
24.05.87 Indianapolis 500	Al Unser	USA	March 86C-Cosworth	162.175
31.05.87 Milwaukee	Michael Andretti	USA	March 87C-Cosworth	111.853
14.06.87 Portland	Bobby Rahal	USA	Lola T87/00-Cosworth	108.591
28.06.87 Meadowlands	Bobby Rahal	USA	Lola T87/00-Cosworth	86.032
05.07.87 Cleveland	Emerson Fittipaldi	BR	March 87C-Chevrolet	128.703
19.07.87 Toronto (CDN)	Emerson Fittipaldi	BR	March 87C-Chevrolet	95.991
02.08.87 Michigan	Michael Andretti	USA	March 87C-Chevrolet	171.493
16.08.87 Pocono	Rick Mears	USA	March 86C-Chevrolet	156.373
30.08.87 Elkhart Lake	Mario Andretti	USA	Lola T87/00-Chevrolet	120.155
06.09.87 Mid-Ohio	Roberto Guerrero	USA	March 87C-Cosworth	108.021
20.09.87 Nazareth	Michael Andretti	USA	March 87C-Cosworth	128.971
11.10.87 Laguna Seca	Bobby Rahal	USA	Lola T87/00-Cosworth	118.879
01.11.87 Tamiami Park	Michael Andretti	USA	March 87C-Cosworth	94.873

1988

10.04.88 Phoenix	Mario Andretti	USA	Lola T88/00-Chevrolet	121.993
17.04.88 Long Beach	Al Unser Jr	USA	March 88C-Chevrolet	83.655
29.05.88 Indianapolis 500	Rick Mears	USA	Penske PC17-Chevrolet	144.809
05.06.88 Milwaukee	Rick Mears	USA	Penske PC17-Chevrolet	122.819

Date	Location	Driver	Nat	Car	Speed
19.06.88	Portland	Danny Sullivan	USA	Penske PC17-Chevrolet	101.881
03.07.88	Cleveland	Mario Andretti	USA	Lola T88/00-Chevrolet	124.546
17.07.88	Toronto (CDN)	Al Unser Jr	USA	March 88C-Chevrolet	91.994
24.07.88	Meadowlands	Al Unser Jr	USA	March 88C-Chevrolet	99.352
07.08.88	Michigan	Danny Sullivan	USA	Penske PC17-Chevrolet	180.654
21.08.88	Pocono	Bobby Rahal	USA	Lola T88/00-Judd	133.713
04.09.88	Mid-Ohio	Emerson Fittipaldi	BR	Lola T87/00-Chevrolet	90.062
11.09.88	Elkhart Lake	Emerson Fittipaldi	BR	Lola T87/00-Chevrolet	122.215
25.09.88	Nazareth	Danny Sullivan	USA	Penske PC17-Chevrolet	148.526
16.10.88	Laguna Seca	Danny Sullivan	USA	Penske PC17-Chevrolet	94.090
06.11.88	Tamiami Park	Al Unser Jr	USA	March 88C-Chevrolet	101.471

1989

Date	Location	Driver	Nat	Car	Speed
09.04.89	Phoenix	Rick Mears	USA	Penske PC18-Chevrolet	126.112
16.04.89	Long Beach	Al Unser Jr	USA	Lola T89/00-Chevrolet	85.503
28.05.89	Indianapolis 500	Emerson Fittipaldi	BR	Penske PC18-Chevrolet	167.582
04.06.89	Milwaukee	Rick Mears	USA	Penske PC18-Chevrolet	130.160
18.06.89	Detroit	Emerson Fittipaldi	BR	Penske PC18-Chevrolet	76.112
25.06.89	Portland	Emerson Fittipaldi	BR	Penske PC18-Chevrolet	103.605
02.07.89	Cleveland	Emerson Fittipaldi	BR	Penske PC18-Chevrolet	128.330
16.07.89	Meadowlands	Bobby Rahal	USA	Lola T89/00-Cosworth	81.863
23.07.89	Toronto (CDN)	Michael Andretti	USA	Lola T89/00-Chevrolet	90.901
06.08.89	Michigan	Michael Andretti	USA	Lola T89/00-Chevrolet	160.210
20.08.89	Pocono	Danny Sullivan	USA	Penske PC18-Chevrolet	170.720
03.09.89	Mid-Ohio	Teo Fabi	I	March 89P-Porsche	105.395
10.09.89	Elkhart Lake	Danny Sullivan	USA	Penske PC18-Chevrolet	122.803
24.09.89	Nazareth	Emerson Fittipaldi	BR	Penske PC18-Chevrolet	134.759
15.10.89	Laguna Seca	Rick Mears	USA	Penske PC18-Chevrolet	94.174

1990

Date	Location	Driver	Nat	Car	Speed
08.04.90	Phoenix	Rick Mears	USA	Penske PC19-Chevrolet	126.291
22.04.90	Long Beach	Al Unser Jr	USA	Lola T90/00-Chevrolet	84.227
27.05.90	Indianapolis 500	Arie Luyendyk	NL	Lola T90/00-Chevrolet	185.984
03.06.90	Milwaukee	Al Unser Jr	USA	Lola T90/00-Chevrolet	133.670
17.06.90	Detroit	Michael Andretti	USA	Lola T90/00-Chevrolet	84.902
24.06.90	Portland	Michael Andretti	USA	Lola T90/00-Chevrolet	110.269
08.07.90	Cleveland	Danny Sullivan	USA	Penske PC19-Chevrolet	112.483
15.07.90	Meadowlands	Michael Andretti	USA	Lola T90/00-Chevrolet	97.291
22.07.90	Toronto (CDN)	Al Unser Jr	USA	Lola T90/00-Chevrolet	74.127
05.08.90	Michigan	Al Unser Jr	USA	Lola T90/00-Chevrolet	189.727
26.08.90	Denver	Al Unser Jr	USA	Lola T90/00-Chevrolet	71.243
02.09.90	Vancouver (CDN)	Al Unser Jr	USA	Lola T90/00-Chevrolet	77.345
16.09.90	Mid-Ohio	Michael Andretti	USA	Lola T90/00-Chevrolet	86.160
23.09.90	Elkhart Lake	Michael Andretti	USA	Lola T90/00-Chevrolet	106.192
07.10.90	Nazareth	Emerson Fittipaldi	BR	Penske PC19-Chevrolet	112.700
21.10.90	Laguna Seca	Danny Sullivan	USA	Penske PC19-Chevrolet	103.556

1991

Date	Location	Driver	Nat	Car	Speed
17.03.91	Surfers' Paradise (AUS)	John Andretti	USA	Lola T91/00-Chevrolet	81.953
14.04.91	Long Beach	Al Unser Jr	USA	Lola T91/00-Chevrolet	81.195
21.04.91	Phoenix	Arie Luyendyk	NL	Lola T91/00-Chevrolet	129.988
26.05.91	Indianapolis 500	Rick Mears	USA	Penske PC20-Chevrolet	176.457
02.06.91	Milwaukee	Michael Andretti	USA	Lola T91/00-Chevrolet	134.557
16.06.91	Detroit	Emerson Fittipaldi	BR	Penske PC20-Chevrolet	78.824
23.06.91	Portland	Michael Andretti	USA	Lola T91/00-Chevrolet	115.208
07.07.91	Cleveland	Michael Andretti	USA	Lola T91/00-Chevrolet	117.530
14.07.91	Meadowlands	Bobby Rahal	USA	Lola T91/00-Chevrolet	95.551
21.07.91	Toronto (CDN)	Michael Andretti	USA	Lola T91/00-Chevrolet	99.143
04.08.91	Michigan	Rick Mears	USA	Penske PC20-Chevrolet	167.230
25.08.91	Denver	Al Unser Jr	USA	Lola T91/00-Chevrolet	68.141
01.09.91	Vancouver (CDN)	Michael Andretti	USA	Lola T91/00-Chevrolet	93.888
15.09.91	Mid-Ohio	Michael Andretti	USA	Lola T91/00-Chevrolet	100.265
22.09.91	Elkhart Lake	Michael Andretti	USA	Lola T91/00-Chevrolet	126.205
06.10.91	Nazareth	Arie Luyendyk	NL	Lola T91/00-Chevrolet	131.310
20.10.91	Laguna Seca	Michael Andretti	USA	Lola T91/00-Chevrolet	103.604

1992

Date	Location	Driver	Nat	Car	Speed
22.03.92	Surfers' Paradise (AUS)	Emerson Fittipaldi	BR	Penske PC21-Chevrolet	77.561
05.04.92	Phoenix	Bobby Rahal	USA	Lola T92/00-Chevrolet	130.526
12.04.92	Long Beach	Danny Sullivan	USA	Galmer G92-Chevrolet	91.945
24.05.92	Indianapolis 500	Al Unser Jr	USA	Galmer G92-Chevrolet	134.479
07.06.92	Belle Isle	Bobby Rahal	USA	Lola T92/00-Chevrolet	81.989
21.06.92	Portland	Michael Andretti	USA	Lola T92/00-Ford	105.219
28.06.92	Milwaukee	Michael Andretti	USA	Lola T92/00-Ford	138.031
05.07.92	New Hampshire	Bobby Rahal	USA	Lola T92/00-Chevrolet	133.621
19.07.92	Toronto (CDN)	Michael Andretti	USA	Lola T92/00-Ford	97.898
02.08.92	Michigan	Scott Goodyear	CDN	Lola T92/00-Chevrolet	177.625
09.08.92	Cleveland	Emerson Fittipaldi	BR	Penske PC21-Chevrolet	133.292
23.08.92	Elkhart Lake	Emerson Fittipaldi	BR	Penske PC21-Chevrolet	110.656
30.08.92	Vancouver (CDN)	Michael Andretti	USA	Lola T92/00-Ford	98.796
13.09.92	Mid-Ohio	Emerson Fittipaldi	BR	Penske PC21-Chevrolet	107.864
04.10.92	Nazareth	Bobby Rahal	USA	Lola T92/00-Chevrolet	128.848
18.10.92	Laguna Seca	Michael Andretti	USA	Lola T92/00-Ford	99.996

1993

Date	Location	Driver	Nat	Car	Speed
21.03.93	Surfers' Paradise (AUS)	Nigel Mansell	GB	Lola T93/00-Ford	97.284
04.04.93	Phoenix	Mario Andretti	USA	Lola T93/00-Ford	123.847
18.04.93	Long Beach	Paul Tracy	CDN	Penske PC22-Chevrolet	93.089
30.05.93	Indianapolis 500	Emerson Fittipaldi	BR	Penske PC22-Chevrolet	157.207
06.06.93	Milwaukee	Nigel Mansell	GB	Lola T93/00-Ford	110.970
13.06.93	Belle Isle	Danny Sullivan	USA	Lola T93/00-Chevrolet	83.116
27.06.93	Portland	Emerson Fittipaldi	BR	Penske PC22-Chevrolet	96.312
11.07.93	Cleveland	Paul Tracy	CDN	Penske PC22-Chevrolet	127.913
18.07.93	Toronto (CDN)	Paul Tracy	CDN	Penske PC22-Chevrolet	96.510
01.08.93	Michigan	Nigel Mansell	GB	Lola T93/00-Ford	188.203
08.08.93	New Hampshire	Nigel Mansell	GB	Lola T93/00-Ford	130.148
22.08.93	Elkhart Lake	Paul Tracy	CDN	Penske PC22-Chevrolet	118.408
29.08.93	Vancouver (CDN)	Al Unser Jr	USA	Lola T93/00-Chevrolet	91.794
12.09.93	Mid-Ohio	Emerson Fittipaldi	BR	Penske PC22-Chevrolet	102.704
19.09.93	Nazareth	Nigel Mansell	GB	Lola T93/00-Ford	158.686
03.10.93	Laguna Seca	Paul Tracy	CDN	Penske PC22-Chevrolet	106.303

1994

Date	Location	Driver	Nat	Car	Speed
20.03.94	Surfers' Paradise (AUS)	Michael Andretti	USA	Reynard 94I-Ford	80.994
10.04.94	Phoenix	Emerson Fittipaldi	BR	Penske PC23-Ilmor	107.437
17.04.94	Long Beach	Al Unser Jr	USA	Penske PC23-Ilmor	99.283
29.05.94	Indianapolis 500	Al Unser Jr	USA	Penske PC23-Mercedes-Benz	160.872
05.06.94	Milwaukee	Al Unser Jr	USA	Penske PC23-Ilmor	118.804
12.06.94	Belle Isle	Paul Tracy	CDN	Penske PC23-Ilmor	146.985
26.06.94	Portland	Al Unser Jr	USA	Penske PC23-Ilmor	108.371
10.07.94	Cleveland	Al Unser Jr	USA	Penske PC23-Ilmor	138.026
17.07.94	Toronto (CDN)	Michael Andretti	USA	Reynard 94I-Ford	96.673
31.07.94	Michigan	Scott Goodyear	CDN	Lola T94/00-Ford	155.520
14.08.94	Mid-Ohio	Al Unser Jr	USA	Penske PC23-Ilmor	109.079
21.08.94	New Hampshire	Al Unser Jr	USA	Penske PC23-Ilmor	122.635
04.09.94	Vancouver (CDN)	Al Unser Jr	USA	Penske PC23-Ilmor	88.896
11.09.94	Elkhart Lake	Jacques Villeneuve	CDN	Reynard 94I-Ford	114.634
18.09.94	Nazareth	Paul Tracy	CDN	Penske PC23-Ilmor	131.141
10.10.94	Laguna Seca	Paul Tracy	CDN	Penske PC23-Ilmor	92.978

RECORDS

DRIVERS' RECORDS

MOST WINS (CHAMPIONSHIP RACES)

AJ Foyt Jr	66*	Al Unser Jr	27
Mario Andretti	52	Rodger Ward	26
Al Unser	39	Gordon Johncock	24*
Bobby Unser	34*		
Michael Andretti	29		
Rick Mears	29		
Johnny Rutherford	27		

*Foyt, Bobby Unser and Johncock also won a non-championship race each

MOST STARTS

Mario Andretti	407	Bobby Unser	259
AJ Foyt Jr	369	Roger McCluskey	230
Al Unser	321	Tom Sneva	206
Johnny Rutherford	315	Rick Mears	203
Gordon Johncock	262	Bobby Rahal	196

MOST POLE POSITIONS (1930-94)

Mario Andretti	66	Al Unser	27
AJ Foyt Jr	53	Johnny Rutherford	23
Bobby Unser	49	Gordon Johncock	20
Rick Mears	40	Rex Mays	19
Michael Andretti	27	Danny Sullivan	19

MOST LAPS IN THE LEAD (1946-94)

Mario Andretti	7587	Rick Mears	3506
AJ Foyt Jr	6621	Gordon Johncock	3417
Al Unser	5812	Bobby Rahal	2965
Bobby Unser	4862	Rodger Ward	2955
Michael Andretti	4460	Tony Bettenhausen	2869

Penske (Emerson Fittipaldi, Al Unser J, and Paul Tracy – left to right) dominated the 1994 series, filling the first three places on five occasions including at Milwaukee

OTHER RECORDS

Most lead changes in a race:
31, 1973 California 500 at Ontario

Most wins in a season:
Ten, AJ Foyt Jr in 1964 and Al Unser in 1970

Closest all-time finish:
0.02 seconds, 1921 Beverly Hills race 6 won by Ralph de Palma

Closest road race finish:
0.07 seconds, 1986 Portland won by Mario Andretti

Closest 500-mile race:
0.043 seconds, 1992 Indianapolis 500 won by Al Unser Jr

Most pole positions in a season:
Ten, AJ Foyt Jr

Fastest race:
1990 Michigan 500, Al Unser Jr won at 189.727 mph

Paul Radisich - winner of both Touring Car World Cups to date

TASMAN CUP

During the 1960s the Tasman Cup was a healthy winter series held jointly by the Australian and New Zealand motorsport authorities. By adopting the 2.5-litre Formula One rules of 1954-60 the organizers attracted works teams such as Cooper, Ferrari, BRM and Lotus which ran old Grand Prix engines in new chassis.

Drivers of the calibre of Graham Hill, Jackie Stewart, Jim Clark and Jochen Rindt were pitted against locals Jack Brabham, Chris Amon and Bruce McLaren, making it in reality a winter World Championship. During these years Clark won the title three times, a record matched by New Zealander Graham McRae after organizers switched to Formula 5000 rules.

However, as the Grand Prix World Championship expanded, F5000 failed to attract the European teams and the popularity of the Tasman Cup waned. Finally, in 1976 the series was abandoned in favour of separate championships in each country; the Gold Star in Australia and International Series in New Zealand.

TASMAN CUP

year	driver	nat	team	car
1964	Bruce McLaren	NZ	Bruce McLaren Motor Racing	Cooper T70-Climax
1965	Jim Clark	GB	Team Lotus	Lotus 32B-Climax
1966	Jackie Stewart	GB	Owen Racing Organisation	BRM P261
1967	Jim Clark	GB	Team Lotus	Lotus 33-Climax
1968	Jim Clark	GB	Team Lotus	Lotus 49T-Ford
1969	Chris Amon	NZ	Scuderia Ferrari	Ferrari 246T
1970	Graeme Lawrence	NZ	Graeme Lawrence	Ferrari 246T
1971	Graham McRae	NZ	Graham McRae	McLaren M10B-Chevrolet
1972	Graham McRae	NZ	Graham McRae	McRae GM1-Chevrolet
1973	Graham McRae	NZ	Graham McRae	McRae GM1-Chevrolet
1974	Peter Gethin	GB	Team VDS	Chevron B24-Chevrolet
1975	Warwick Brown	AUS	Pat Burke Racing	Lola T332-Chevrolet

1964-69 for 2500 cc single-seaters, 1970-75 F5000

RACE WINNERS

1964

date	circuit/race	driver	nat	car	mph
04.01.64	Levin	Denny Hulme	NZ	Brabham BT7A-Climax	73.370
11.01.64	New Zealand GP (Pukekohe)	Bruce McLaren	NZ	Cooper T70-Climax	87.846
18.01.64	Lady Wigram Trophy (Wigram)	Bruce McLaren	NZ	Cooper T70-Climax	94.130
25.01.64	Teretonga Park	Bruce McLaren	NZ	Cooper T70-Climax	77.040
09.02.64	Australian GP (Sandown Park)	Jack Brabham	AUS	Brabham BT7A-Climax	96.809
16.02.64	Warwick Farm	Jack Brabham	AUS	Brabham BT7A-Climax	82.370
23.02.64	Lakeside	Jack Brabham	AUS	Brabham BT7A-Climax	88.960
29.02.64	Longford	Graham Hill	GB	Brabham BT4-Climax	111.700

1965

date	circuit/race	driver	nat	car	mph
09.01.65	New Zealand GP (Pukekohe)	Graham Hill	GB	Brabham BT11A-Climax	89.512
16.01.65	Levin	Jim Clark	GB	Lotus 32B-Climax	77.180
23.01.65	Lady Wigram Trophy (Wigram)	Jim Clark	GB	Lotus 32B-Climax	95.159
30.01.65	Teretonga Park	Jim Clark	GB	Lotus 32B-Climax	84.950
14.02.65	Warwick Farm	Jim Clark	GB	Lotus 32B-Climax	84.440
21.02.65	Sandown Park	Jack Brabham	AUS	Brabham BT11A-Climax	101.180
01.03.65	Australian GP (Longford)	Bruce McLaren	NZ	Cooper T79-Climax	114.740

1966

date	circuit/race	driver	nat	car	mph
08.01.66	New Zealand GP (Pukekohe)	Graham Hill	GB	BRM P261	83.010
15.01.66	Levin	Richard Attwood	GB	BRM P261	86.897
22.01.66	Lady Wigram Trophy (Wigram)	Jackie Stewart	GB	BRM P261	95.269
29.01.66	Teretonga Park	Jackie Stewart	GB	BRM P261	90.088
13.02.66	Warwick Farm	Jim Clark	GB	Lotus 39-Climax	85.491
20.02.66	Australian GP (Lakeside)	Graham Hill	GB	BRM P261	94.838
27.02.66	Sandown Park	Jackie Stewart	GB	BRM P261	100.950
07.03.66	Longford	Jackie Stewart	GB	BRM P261	115.855

1967

date	circuit/race	driver	nat	car	mph
07.01.67	New Zealand GP (Pukekohe)	Jackie Stewart	GB	BRM P261	100.971
14.01.67	Levin	Jim Clark	GB	Lotus 33-Climax	88.482
21.01.67	Lady Wigram Trophy (Wigram)	Jim Clark	GB	Lotus 33-Climax	97.046
28.01.67	Teretonga Park	Jim Clark	GB	Lotus 33-Climax	88.947
12.02.67	Lakeside	Jim Clark	GB	Lotus 33-Climax	97.478
19.02.67	Australian GP (Warwick Farm)	Jackie Stewart	GB	BRM P261	87.677
26.02.67	Sandown Park	Jim Clark	GB	Lotus 33-Climax	101.724
05.03.67	Longford	Jack Brabham	AUS	Brabham BT23A-Repco	114.936

1968

06.01.68 New Zealand GP (Pukekohe)	Chris Amon	NZ	Ferrari 246T	102.638
13.01.68 Levin	Chris Amon	NZ	Ferrari 246T	89.520
20.01.68 Lady Wigram Trophy (Wigram)	Jim Clark	GB	Lotus 49T-Ford	102.602
27.01.68 Teretonga Park	Bruce McLaren	NZ	BRM P126	84.441
11.02.68 Surfers' Paradise	Jim Clark	GB	Lotus 49T-Ford	98.796
18.02.68 Warwick Farm	Jim Clark	GB	Lotus 49T-Ford	88.963
20.02.68 Australian GP (Sandown Park)	Jim Clark	GB	Lotus 49T-Ford	101.572
04.03.68 Longford	Piers Courage	GB	McLaren M4A-Cosworth	96.909

1969

04.01.69 New Zealand GP (Pukekohe)	Chris Amon	NZ	Ferrari 246T	105.139
11.01.69 Levin	Chris Amon	NZ	Ferrari 246T	90.455
18.01.69 Lady Wigram Trophy (Wigram)	Jochen Rindt	A	Lotus 49B-Ford	103.102
25.01.69 Teretonga Park	Piers Courage	GB	Brabham BT24-Ford	97.313
02.02.69 Australian GP (Lakeside)	Chris Amon	NZ	Ferrari 246T	100.144
09.02.69 Warwick Farm	Jochen Rindt	A	Lotus 49B-Ford	77.672
16.02.69 Sandown Park	Chris Amon	NZ	Ferrari 246T	105.784

1970

03.01.70 Levin	Graeme Lawrence	NZ	Ferrari 246T	90.305
10.01.70 New Zealand GP (Pukekohe)	Frank Matich	AUS	McLaren M10A-Chevrolet	103.810
17.01.70 Lady Wigram Trophy (Wigram)	Frank Matich	AUS	McLaren M10A-Chevrolet	101.363
24.01.70 Teretonga Park	Graham McRae	NZ	McLaren M10A-Chevrolet	94.504
07.02.70 Surfers' Paradise	Graham McRae	NZ	McLaren M10A-Chevrolet	100.709
14.02.70 Warwick Farm	Kevin Bartlett	AUS	Mildren-Waggott	90.973
21.02.70 Sandown Park	Niel Allen	AUS	McLaren M10B-Chevrolet	102.706

1971

02.01.71 Levin	Graham McRae	NZ	McLaren M10B-Chevrolet	89.786
09.01.71 New Zealand GP (Pukekohe)	Niel Allen	AUS	McLaren M10B-Chevrolet	107.883
16.01.71 Lady Wigram Trophy (Wigram)	Graham McRae	NZ	McLaren M10B-Chevrolet	104.937
24.01.71 Teretonga Park	Niel Allen	AUS	McLaren M10B-Chevrolet	97.765
14.02.71 Warwick Farm	Frank Gardner	AUS	Lola T192-Chevrolet	93.030
21.02.71 Sandown Park	Graham McRae	NZ	McLaren M10B-Chevrolet	107.140
28.02.71 Surfers' Paradise	Frank Matich	AUS	McLaren M10B-Holden	102.961

1972

08.01.72 New Zealand GP (Pukekohe)	Frank Gardner	AUS	Lola T300-Chevrolet	106.329
15.01.72 Levin	Graham McRae	NZ	McRae GM1-Chevrolet	93.381
22.01.72 Lady Wigram Trophy (Wigram)	Graham McRae	NZ	McRae GM1-Chevrolet	112.920
30.01.72 Teretonga Park	Kevin Bartlett	AUS	McLaren M10B-Chevrolet	87.941
06.02.72 Surfers' Paradise	Graham McRae	NZ	McRae GM1-Chevrolet	102.389
13.02.72 Warwick Farm	Frank Matich	AUS	Matich A50-Holden/Repco	93.606
20.02.72 Australian GP (Sandown Park)	Graham McRae	NZ	McRae GM1-Chevrolet	109.447
27.02.72 Adelaide	David Hobbs	GB	McLaren M18B-Chevrolet	100.519

1973

06.01.73 New Zealand GP (Pukekohe)	John McCormack	AUS	Elfin MR5-Holden/Repco	89.960
13.01.73 Levin	Graham McRae	NZ	McRae GM1-Chevrolet	96.200
20.01.73 Lady Wigram Trophy (Wigram)	Graham McRae	NZ	McRae GM1-Chevrolet	114.274
28.01.73 Teretonga Park	Alan Rollinson	GB	McRae GM1-Chevrolet	80.830
04.02.73 Surfers' Paradise	Frank Matich	AUS	Matich A50-Holden/Repco	102.243
11.02.73 Warwick Farm	Steve Thompson	GB	Chevron B24-Chevrolet	81.453
18.02.73 Sandown Park	Graham McRae	NZ	McRae GM1-Chevrolet	108.366
25.02.73 Adelaide	John McCormack	AUS	Elfin MR5-Holden/Repco	104.564

1974

05.01.74 Levin	Johnnie Walker	AUS	Lola T330-Holden/Repco	94.020
12.01.74 Pukekohe	Peter Gethin	GB	Chevron B24-Chevrolet	97.461
19.01.74 New Zealand GP* (Wigram)	John McCormack	AUS	Elfin MR5-Holden/Repco	114.419
26.01.74 Teretonga Park	Max Stewart	AUS	Lola T330-Chevrolet	104.104
03.02.74 Oran Park	Max Stewart	AUS	Lola T330-Chevrolet	109.995
10.02.74 Surfers' Paradise	Teddy Pilette	B	Chevron B24-Chevrolet	104.278
17.02.74 Sandown Park	Peter Gethin	GB	Chevron B24-Chevrolet	110.698
24.02.74 Adelaide	Warwick Brown	AUS	Lola T332-Chevrolet	102.978

*incorporating the Lady Wigram Trophy

1975

05.01.75 Levin	Graeme Lawrence	NZ	Lola T332-Chevrolet	96.112
12.01.75 New Zealand GP (Pukekohe)	Warwick Brown	AUS	Lola T332-Chevrolet	87.137
19.01.75 Lady Wigram Trophy (Wigram)	Graham McRae	NZ	McRae GM2-Chevrolet	115.021
26.01.75 Teretonga Park	Chris Amon	NZ	Talon MR1-Chevrolet	98.770
02.02.75 Oran Park	Warwick Brown	AUS	Lola T332-Chevrolet	97.983
09.02.75 Surfers' Paradise	Johnnie Walker	AUS	Lola T330/332-Holden/Repco	103.719
16.02.75 Adelaide	Graeme Lawrence	NZ	Lola T332-Chevrolet	106.912
23.02.75 Sandown Park	John Goss	AUS	Matich A53-Holden/Repco	110.108

CAN-AM CHALLENGE

μThe Canadian-American Challenge was a road racing championship for Group 7 sports-racing cars established in September 1966. These spectacular cars were powered by large capacity stockblock engines with Chevrolet outnumbering its rivals.

After John Surtees won the inaugural series in a Lola, McLaren Cars dominated the series winning 23 consecutive races from 1968-1970 until challenged by George Follmer's Porsche 917 in 1972. After two more seasons the series was cancelled in favour of a North American Formula 5000 Championship but was reinstated in 1977.

The new era was initially dominated by the Carl Haas Lola-Chevrolets but the series slipped into obscurity in the mid-1980s and was cancelled after the 1986 season.

Until these final poor seasons, the Can-Am Challenge had been a high-profile series, attracting the world's best drivers (six F1 World Champions - John Surtees, Denny Hulme, Phil Hill, Jackie Stewart, Alan Jones and Keke Rosberg - have won races) to race on North America's finest road courses.

CAN-AM CHALLENGE CUP

year	driver	nat	team	car
1966	John Surtees	GB	Team Surtees	Lola T70-Chevrolet
1967	Bruce McLaren	NZ	Bruce McLaren Motor Racing	McLaren M6A-Chevrolet
1968	Denny Hulme	NZ	Bruce McLaren Motor Racing	McLaren M8A-Chevrolet
1969	Bruce McLaren	NZ	Bruce McLaren Motor Racing	McLaren M8B-Chevrolet
1970	Denny Hulme	NZ	Bruce McLaren Motor Racing	McLaren M8D-Chevrolet
1971	Peter Revson	USA	Bruce McLaren Motor Racing	McLaren M8F-Chevrolet
1972	George Follmer	USA	Penske Racing	Porsche 917/10
1973	Mark Donohue	USA	Penske Racing	Porsche 917/30
1974	Jackie Oliver	GB	Shadow Racing Team	Shadow DN4A-Chevrolet
1977	Patrick Tambay	F	Haas-Hall Racing	Lola T333CS-Chevrolet
1978	Alan Jones	AUS	Haas-Hall Racing	Lola T333CS-Chevrolet
1979	Jacky Ickx	B	Carl Haas Racing	Lola T333CS-Chevrolet
1980	Patrick Tambay	F	Carl Haas Racing	Lola T530-Chevrolet
1981	Geoff Brabham	AUS	Team VDS	Lola T530-Chevrolet/VDS 001-Chevrolet
1982	Al Unser Jr	USA	Galles Racing	Frissbee GR3-Chevrolet
1983	Jacques Villeneuve	CDN	Canadian Tire	Frissbee GR3-Chevrolet
1984	Michael Roe	IRL	Don Walker	VDS 002-Chevrolet/VDS 004-Chevrolet
1985	Rick Miaskiewicz	USA	Mosquitto Autosport	Frissbee-Chevrolet
1986	Horst Kroll	USA	Kroll Racing	Frissbee KR3-Chevrolet

RACE WINNERS

1966
Ste Jovite	John Surtees	GB	Lola T70-Chevrolet
Bridgehampton	Dan Gurney	USA	Lola T70-Ford
Canadian GP (Mosport Park)	Mark Donohue	USA	Lola T70-Chevrolet
Laguna Seca	Phil Hill	USA	Chaparral 2F-Chevrolet
Riverside	John Surtees	GB	Lola T70-Chevrolet
Stardust, Las Vegas	John Surtees	GB	Lola T70-Chevrolet

1967
Elkhart Lake	Denny Hulme	NZ	McLaren M6A-Chevrolet
Bridgehampton	Denny Hulme	NZ	McLaren M6A-Chevrolet
Mosport Park	Denny Hulme	NZ	McLaren M6A-Chevrolet
Laguna Seca	Bruce McLaren	NZ	McLaren M6A-Chevrolet
Riverside	Bruce McLaren	NZ	McLaren M6A-Chevrolet
Stardust, Las Vegas	John Surtees	GB	Lola T70-Chevrolet

1968
Elkhart Lake	Denny Hulme	NZ	McLaren M8A-Chevrolet
Bridgehampton	Mark Donohue	USA	McLaren M6B-Chevrolet
Edmonton	Denny Hulme	NZ	McLaren M8A-Chevrolet
Laguna Seca	John Cannon	CDN	McLaren M1B-Chevrolet
Riverside	Bruce McLaren	NZ	McLaren M8A-Chevrolet
Stardust, Las Vegas	Denny Hulme	NZ	McLaren M8A-Chevrolet

1969
Mosport Park	Bruce McLaren	NZ	McLaren M8B-Chevrolet
Ste Jovite	Denny Hulme	NZ	McLaren M8B-Chevrolet
Watkins Glen	Bruce McLaren	NZ	McLaren M8B-Chevrolet
Edmonton	Denny Hulme	NZ	McLaren M8B-Chevrolet
Mid-Ohio	Denny Hulme	NZ	McLaren M8B-Chevrolet
Elkhart Lake	Bruce McLaren	NZ	McLaren M8B-Chevrolet
Bridgehampton	Denny Hulme	NZ	McLaren M8B-Chevrolet
Michigan	Bruce McLaren	NZ	McLaren M8B-Chevrolet

Laguna Seca	Bruce McLaren	NZ	McLaren M8B-Chevrolet
Riverside	Denny Hulme	NZ	McLaren M8B-Chevrolet
Texas World Speedway	Bruce McLaren	NZ	McLaren M8B-Chevrolet

1970
Mosport Park	Dan Gurney	USA	McLaren M8D-Chevrolet
Ste Jovite	Dan Gurney	USA	McLaren M8D-Chevrolet
Watkins Glen	Denny Hulme	NZ	McLaren M8D-Chevrolet
Edmonton	Denny Hulme	NZ	McLaren M8D-Chevrolet
Mid-Ohio	Denny Hulme	NZ	McLaren M8D-Chevrolet
Elkhart Lake	Peter Gethin	GB	McLaren M8D-Chevrolet
Road Atlanta	Tony Dean	GB	Porsche 908
Brainerd	Denny Hulme	NZ	McLaren M8D-Chevrolet
Laguna Seca	Denny Hulme	NZ	McLaren M8D-Chevrolet
Riverside	Denny Hulme	NZ	McLaren M8D-Chevrolet

1971
Mosport Park	Denny Hulme	NZ	McLaren M8F-Chevrolet
Ste Jovite	Jackie Stewart	GB	Lola T260-Chevrolet
Road Atlanta	Peter Revson	USA	McLaren M8F-Chevrolet
Watkins Glen	Peter Revson	USA	McLaren M8F-Chevrolet
Mid-Ohio	Jackie Stewart	GB	Lola T260-Chevrolet
Elkhart Lake	Peter Revson	USA	McLaren M8F-Chevrolet
Brainerd	Peter Revson	USA	McLaren M8F-Chevrolet
Edmonton	Denny Hulme	NZ	McLaren M8F-Chevrolet
Laguna Seca	Peter Revson	USA	McLaren M8F-Chevrolet
Riverside	Denny Hulme	NZ	McLaren M8F-Chevrolet

1972
Mosport Park	Denny Hulme	NZ	McLaren M20-Chevrolet
Road Atlanta	George Follmer	USA	Porsche 917/10
Watkins Glen	Denny Hulme	NZ	McLaren M20-Chevrolet
Mid-Ohio	George Follmer	USA	Porsche 917/10
Elkhart Lake	George Follmer	USA	Porsche 917/10
Brainerd	François Cevert	F	McLaren M8F-Chevrolet
Edmonton	Mark Donohue	USA	Porsche 917/10

Laguna Seca	George Follmer	USA	Porsche 917/10
Riverside	George Follmer	USA	Porsche 917/10

1973

Mosport Park	Charlie Kemp	USA	Porsche 917/10
Road Atlanta	George Follmer	USA	Porsche 917/10
Watkins Glen	Mark Donohue	USA	Porsche 917/30
Mid-Ohio	Mark Donohue	USA	Porsche 917/30
Elkhart Lake	Mark Donohue	USA	Porsche 917/30
Edmonton	Mark Donohue	USA	Porsche 917/30
Laguna Seca	Mark Donohue	USA	Porsche 917/30
Riverside	Mark Donohue	USA	Porsche 917/30

1974

Mosport Park	Jackie Oliver	GB	Shadow DN4A-Chevrolet
Road Atlanta	Jackie Oliver	GB	Shadow DN4A-Chevrolet
Watkins Glen	Jackie Oliver	GB	Shadow DN4A-Chevrolet
Mid-Ohio	Jackie Oliver	GB	Shadow DN4A-Chevrolet
Elkhart Lake	Scooter Patrick	USA	McLaren M20-Chevrolet

1975-76 - NO SERIES

1977

Ste Jovite	Tom Klausler	USA	Schkee DB1-Chevrolet
Laguna Seca	Don Breidenbach	USA	Lola T333CS-Chevrolet
Watkins Glen	Patrick Tambay	F	Lola T333CS-Chevrolet
Elkhart Lake	Peter Gethin	GB	Lola T333CS-Chevrolet
Mid-Ohio	Patrick Tambay	F	Lola T333CS-Chevrolet
Mosport Park	Patrick Tambay	F	Lola T333CS-Chevrolet
Trois Rivières	Patrick Tambay	F	Lola T333CS-Chevrolet
Sears Point	Patrick Tambay	F	Lola T333CS-Chevrolet
Riverside	Patrick Tambay	F	Lola T333CS-Chevrolet

1978

Road Atlanta	Alan Jones	AUS	Lola T333CS-Chevrolet
Charlotte	Elliott Forbes-Robinson	USA	Spyder NF10-Chevrolet
Mid-Ohio	Alan Jones	AUS	Lola T333CS-Chevrolet
Ste Jovite	George Follmer	USA	Prophet-Chevrolet
Watkins Glen	Warwick Brown	AUS	Lola T333CS-Chevrolet
Elkhart Lake	Alan Jones	AUS	Lola T333CS-Chevrolet
Mosport Park	Alan Jones	AUS	Lola T333CS-Chevrolet
Trois Rivières	Elliott Forbes-Robinson	USA	Spyder NF10-Chevrolet
Laguna Seca	Al Holbert	USA	Lola T333CS-Chevrolet
Riverside	Alan Jones	AUS	Lola T333CS-Chevrolet

1979

Road Atlanta	Keke Rosberg	SF	Spyder NF11-Chevrolet
Charlotte	Jacky Ickx	B	Lola T333CS-Chevrolet
Mosport Park	Jacky Ickx	B	Lola T333CS-Chevrolet
Mid-Ohio	Alan Jones	AUS	Lola T333CS-Chevrolet
Watkins Glen	Keke Rosberg	SF	Spyder NF11-Chevrolet
Elkhart Lake	Jacky Ickx	B	Lola T333CS-Chevrolet
Brainerd	Jacky Ickx	B	Lola T333CS-Chevrolet
Trois Rivières	Elliott Forbes-Robinson	USA	Spyder NF11-Chevrolet
Laguna Seca	Bobby Rahal	USA	Prophet-Chevrolet
Riverside	Jacky Ickx	B	Lola T333CS-Chevrolet

1980

Sears Point	Patrick Tambay	F	Lola T530-Chevrolet
Mid-Ohio	Patrick Tambay	F	Lola T530-Chevrolet
Mosport Park	Patrick Tambay	F	Lola T530-Chevrolet
Watkins Glen	Patrick Tambay	F	Lola T530-Chevrolet
Elkhart Lake	Al Holbert	USA	CAC 1-Chevrolet
Brainerd	Patrick Tambay	F	Lola T530-Chevrolet
Trois Rivières	Patrick Tambay	F	Lola T530-Chevrolet
Road Atlanta	Geoff Brabham	AUS	Lola T530-Chevrolet
Laguna Seca	Al Unser	USA	Frissbee-Chevrolet
Riverside	Al Holbert	USA	CAC 1-Chevrolet

1981

Mosport Park	Teo Fabi	I	March 817-Chevrolet
Mid-Ohio	Teo Fabi	I	March 817-Chevrolet
Watkins Glen	Al Holbert	USA	CAC 2-Chevrolet
Elkhart Lake	Geoff Brabham	AUS	Lola T530-Chevrolet
Edmonton	Geoff Brabham	AUS	VDS 001-Chevrolet
Trois Rivières	Al Holbert	USA	CAC 2-Chevrolet
Mosport Park	Teo Fabi	I	March 817-Chevrolet
Riverside	Al Holbert	USA	CAC 2-Chevrolet
Laguna Seca	Teo Fabi	I	March 817-Chevrolet
Caesars Palace, Las Vegas	Danny Sullivan	USA	Frissbee GR2-Chevrolet

1982

Road Atlanta	Al Unser Jr	USA	Frissbee GR3-Chevrolet
Mosport Park	Al Unser Jr	USA	Frissbee GR3-Chevrolet
Mid-Ohio	Al Holbert	USA	VDS 001-Chevrolet
Elkhart Lake	Al Holbert	USA	VDS 001-Chevrolet
Trois Rivières	Al Holbert	USA	VDS 001-Chevrolet
Mosport Park	Al Unser Jr	USA	Frissbee GR3-Chevrolet
Caesars Palace, Las Vegas	Danny Sullivan	USA	March 827-Chevrolet
Riverside	Al Holbert	USA	VDS 001-Chevrolet
Laguna Seca	Al Unser Jr	USA	Frissbee GR3-Chevrolet

1983

Mosport Park	Jacques Villeneuve	CDN	Frissbee GR3-Chevrolet
Lime Rock	Jim Crawford	GB	Ensign RK180B-Ford
Elkhart Lake	John Fitzpatrick	GB	Porsche 956
Trois Rivières	Jacques Villeneuve	CDN	Frissbee GR3-Chevrolet
Mosport Park	Jim Crawford	GB	Ensign RK180B-Ford
Sears Point	Jacques Villeneuve	CDN	Frissbee GR3-Chevrolet

1984

Mosport Park	Michael Roe	IRL	VDS 002-Chevrolet
Fair Park, Dallas	Michael Roe	IRL	VDS 002-Chevrolet
Brainerd	Michael Roe	IRL	VDS 002-Chevrolet
Lime Rock	Michael Roe	IRL	VDS 002-Chevrolet
Road Atlanta	Jim Crawford	GB	March 847-Chevrolet
Trois Rivières	Jim Crawford	GB	March 847-Chevrolet
Mosport Park	Michael Roe	IRL	VDS 002-Chevrolet
Sears Point	Michael Roe	IRL	VDS 002-Chevrolet
Riverside	Michael Roe	IRL	VDS 002-Chevrolet
Green Valley	Jim Crawford	GB	March 847-Chevrolet

1985

Mosport Park	Horst Kroll	USA	Frissbee-Chevrolet
Lime Rock	Rick Miaskiewicz	USA	Frissbee-Chevrolet
Mosport Park	Rick Miaskiewicz	USA	Frissbee-Chevrolet
St Louis	Rick Miaskiewicz	USA	Frissbee-Chevrolet
St Petersburg	Lou Sell	USA	March 832-Chevrolet

1986

Mosport Park	Horst Kroll	USA	Frissbee KR3-Chevrolet
Summit Point	Bill Tempero	USA	March 84C-Chevrolet
St Louis	Lou Sell	USA	March 85C-Chevrolet
Mosport Park	Paul Tracy	CDN	Frissbee KR3-Chevrolet

BMW M1 PROCAR SERIES

A series ran by BMW Motorsport in 1979-80 to promote its spectacular M1 sports car. Races normally supported Grands Prix with the top five Formula One drivers in qualifying for the GP invited to take part in works cars. Other cars were run by teams of the calibre of Sauber, Project 4 (team owner Ron Dennis would soon buy McLaren), Schnitzer and Eggenberger, thus ensuring a competitive entry.

Initial teething problems were speedily resolved and Procar quickly developed into a popular and entertaining diversion from the business of

Grand Prix racing. In 1980 *Autosport* described the championship as "quite simply the greatest one-make series to date" but BMW decided not to organize a third edition.

CHAMPIONS

year	driver	nat	team	car
1979	Niki Lauda	A	Project 4 Racing	BMW M1
1980	Nelson Piquet	BR	BMW Motorsport	BMW M1

RACE WINNERS

1979

date	circuit	driver	nat	team	mph
12.05.79	Zolder	Elio de Angelis	I	BMW Italia	94.020
26.05.79	Monte Carlo	Niki Lauda	A	Project 4 Racing	71.046
30.06.79	Dijon-Prenois	Nelson Piquet	BR	BMW Motorsport	n/a
13.07.79	Silverstone	Niki Lauda	A	Project 4 Racing	115.450
28.07.79	Hockenheim	Niki Lauda	A	Project 4 Racing	n/a
11.08.79	Österreichring	Jacques Laffite	F	BMW Motorsport	114.842
25.08.79	Zandvoort	Hans-Joachim Stuck	D	Manfred Cassani	99.497
08.09.79	Monza	Hans-Joachim Stuck	D	Manfred Cassani	112.902

1980

date	circuit	driver	nat	team	mph
26.04.80	Donington Park	Jan Lammers	NL	BMW Nederland	94.440
11.05.80	Avus	Manfred Schurti	FL	Manfred Cassani	132.730
17.05.80	Monte Carlo	Hans-Joachim Stuck	D	Project 4 Racing	69.350
22.06.80	Norisring	Hans-Joachim Stuck	D	Project 4 Racing	95.065
12.07.80	Brands Hatch	Carlos Reutemann	RA	BMW Motorsport	102.700
09.08.80	Hockenheim	Didier Pironi	F	BMW Motorsport	113.910
16.08.80	Österreichring	Nelson Piquet	BR	BMW Motorsport	114.036
31.08.80	Zandvoort	Nelson Piquet	BR	BMW Motorsport	96.853
13.09.80	Imola	Nelson Piquet	BR	BMW Motorsport	96.505

OTHER MAJOR CHAMPIONSHIPS

WORLD TOURING CAR CHAMPIONSHIP

year	driver	nat	team	car	entrant
1987	Roberto Ravaglia	I	Schnitzer	BMW M3	Ford/Texaco

EUROPEAN TOURING CAR CHAMPIONSHIP

	Drivers' Championship				Constructors' Championship
year	class	driver	nat	team	car	constructor

year	class	driver	nat	team	car	constructor
1963		Peter Nöcker	D	-	Jaguar	-
1964		Warwick Banks	GB	-	BMC	-
1965	over 1600 cc	Jacky Ickx	B	-	Ford	Ford
	1600 cc	John Whitmore	GB	-	Ford	Ford
	1000 cc	Ed Swart	NL	-	Fiat Abarth	Fiat Abarth
1966	over 1600 cc	Hubert Hahne	D	-	BMW	BMW
	1600 cc	Andrea de Adamich	I	-	Alfa Romeo Giulia GTA	Alfa Romeo
	1000 cc	Giancarlo Baghetti	I	-	Fiat Abarth	Fiat Abarth
1967	over 1600 cc	Karl von Wendt	D	-	Porsche	Porsche
	1600 cc	Andrea de Adamich	I	-	Alfa Romeo	Alfa Romeo
	1000 cc	Willi Kauhsen	D	-	Fiat Abarth	Fiat Abarth
1968	over 1600 cc	Dieter Quester	A	-	BMW 2002	BMW
	1600 cc	John Rhodes	GB	-	BMC Mini Cooper S	BMC
	1000 cc	John Handley	GB	-	BMC Mini Cooper	BMC
1969	over 1600cc	Dieter Quester	A	-	BMW	BMW
	1600 cc	Spartico Dini	I	-	Alfa Romeo	Alfa Romeo
	1000 cc	"Pam"	I	-	Fiat Abarth	Fiat Abarth
1970	Overall	Toine Hezemans	NL	Autodelta	Alfa Romeo GTAm	BMW
	over 1600 cc	Toine Hezemans	NL	Autodelta	Alfa Romeo GTAm	-
	1600 cc	Carlo Truci	I	-	Alfa Romeo GTA Junior	-
	1000 cc	Johann Abt	D	Abt Tuning	Fiat Abarth 1000	-
1971	over 2000 cc	Dieter Glemser	D	Ford Deutschland	Ford Capri RS	Ford
	2000 cc	Toine Hezemans	NL	Autodelta	Alfa Romeo GTAm	Alfa Romeo
	1300 cc	Gianluigi Picchi	I	Autodelta	Alfa Romeo GTA Junior	Alfa Romeo
1972		Jochen Mass	D	-	Ford Capri RS2600	Alfa Romeo
1973		Toine Hezemans	NL	BMW	BMW 3.0 CSL	BMW
1974		Hans Heyer	D	-	Ford Capri/Ford Escort	Ford
1975		Sigi Müller/Alain Peltier	D/B	-	BMW 3.0 CSL	BMW
1976		Pierre Dieudonné/Jean Xhenceval	B	-	BMW 3.0 CSL	BMW
1977		Dieter Quester	A	Alpina	BMW 3.0 CSL	BMW
1978		Umberto Grano	I	Luigi Racing	BMW 3.0 CSL	BMW
1979		Carlo Facetti/Martino Finotto	I	-	BMW 3.0 CSL	BMW
1980		Helmut Kelleners/Sigi Müller Jr	D	Eggenberger	BMW 320i	Audi
1981		Umberto Grano/Helmut Kelleners	I/D	Eggenberger	BMW 635 CSi	Skoda

1982	Umberto Grano/Helmut Kelleners	I/D	Eggenberger	BMW 528i	Alfa Romeo
1983	Dieter Quester	A	-	BMW 635 CSi	Alfa Romeo
1984	Tom Walkinshaw	GB	TWR	Jaguar XJS	Alfa Romeo
1985	Gianfranco Brancatelli/				
	Thomas Lindstrom	I/S	Eggenberger	Volvo 240 turbo	Alfa Romeo
1986	Roberto Ravaglia	I	Schnitzer	BMW 635 CSi	Toyota
1987	Winni Vogt	D	Linder	BMW M3	Linder/BMW*
1988	Roberto Ravaglia	I	Schnitzer	BMW M3	Eggenberger/Ford*

*Entrants championship

Roberto Ravaglia, who won the World Touring Car Championship in 1987 having claimed the European title the previous year

Jim Clark in action at Crystal Palace in 1964

Asia-Pacific Touring Car Championship

year	driver	nat	team	car
1994	Joachim Winkelhock	D	Schnitzer	BMW 318i

Touring Car World Cup

A one-off race to decided the world's best driver in the category, won on both occasions to date by Ford's Paul Radisich

year	circuit	driver	nat	team	car
1993	Monza	Paul Radisich	NZ	Andy Rouse Engineering	Ford Mondeo
1994	Donington Park	Paul Radisich	NZ	Andy Rouse Engineering	Ford Mondeo

Formula Opel Euroseries (formerly GM-Lotus Euroseries)

year	driver	nat	team	car
1988	Mika Häkkinen	SF	Dragon Motorsport	GM-Lotus
1989	Peter Kox	NL	Opel Dealer Team Holland	GM-Lotus
1990	Rubens Barrichello	BR	Draco Racing	GM-Lotus
1991	Pedro Lamy	P	Draco Racing	GM-Lotus
1992	Gareth Rees	GB	David Sears Motorsport	GM-Lotus
1993	Patrick Crinelli	I	Draco Racing	GM-Lotus
1994	Marcos Campos	BR	Draco Racing	Formula Opel

European Endurance Championship

year	driver	nat	team	car
1983	Bob Wollek	F	Jöst Racing	Porsche 956

European Championship for Grand Touring Cars

year	driver	nat	car
1972*	John Fitzpatrick	GB	Porsche 911S
1973	Claude Ballot-Lena/ Clemens Schickentanz	F/D	Porsche 911 Carrera RSR
1974	John Fitzpatrick	GB	Porsche 911 Carrera RSR
1975	Hartwig Bertrams	D	Porsche
1976	Toine Hezemans	NL	Porsche 934

*European Trophy

European 2-litre Championship of Makes

The 1975 series was cancelled when ten of the 12 qualifying races were cancelled due to financial problems. In the remaining events Chris Skeaping (March 75S-Ford) amassed the highest points total finishing 3rd and 4th but he was not crowned champion.

year	formula	driver	nat	car
1970	Group 6	Jo Bonnier	S	Lola T210-Ford
	Group 5	Ed Swart	NL	Fiat Abarth 2000S
	Group 4	Kurt Simonsen	S	Porsche 911S

1971		Helmut Marko	A	Lola T212-Ford
1972		Arturo Merzario	I	Osella Abarth 2000P
1973		Chris Craft	GB	Lola T292-Ford
1974		Alain Serpaggi	F	Alpine A441-Renault
1975	SERIES ABANDONED			

European Sports Car Championship

year	formula	driver	nat	car
1977	Class 1	Reinhold Jöst	D	Porsche 908/3
	Class 2	"Gimax"	I	Osella PA6-BMW

Renault Europa Cup

year	driver	nat	car
1981	Wolfgang Schultz	D	Renault 5 turbo
1982	Joël Gouhier	F	Renault 5 turbo
1983	Jan Lammers	NL	Renault 5 turbo
1984	Jan Lammers	NL	Renault 5 turbo
1985	Oscar Larrauri	RA	Renault Alpine V6 turbo
1986	Massimo Sigala	I	Renault Alpine V6 turbo
1987	Massimo Sigala	I	Renault Alpine V6 turbo
1988	Massimo Sigala	I	Renault Alpine V6 turbo
1989	Massimo Sigala	I	Renault 21 turbo
1990	Massimo Sigala	I	Renault 21 turbo
1992	Bernard Castagne	F	Renault Clio 16v
1993	Salvatore Pirro	I	Renault Clio 16v
1994	Bernard Castagne	F	Renault Clio 16v

Sud-Am Formula Three Championship

year	driver	nat	car
1987	Leonel Friedrich	BR	Berta Mk3-Volkswagen
1988	Juan Carlos Giacchino	RA	Dallara 387-Alfa Romeo/ Dallara 388-Alfa Romeo
1989	Gabriel Furlan	RA	Dallara 388-Alfa Romeo
1990	Christian Fittipaldi	BR	Reynard 883-Alfa Romeo
1991	Affonso Giaffone Neto	BR	Ralt RT32-Volkswagen/ Ralt RT33-Volkswagen
1992	Marcos Gueiros	BR	Ralt RT33-Mugen
1993	Fernando Croceri	RA	Ralt RT33-Mugen
1994	Gabriel Furlan	RA	Dallara 390-Fiat

Codasur Formula Two Championship

A South American single-seater formula using 1600 cc stock-block engines. Replaced by Sud-Am F3 in 1987.

year	driver	nat	car
1983	Guillermo Maldonaldo	RA	-
1984	Guillermo Maldonaldo	RA	-
1985	Guillermo Maldonaldo	RA	Berta-Volkswagen
1986	Guillermo Maldonaldo	RA	Berta-Volkswagen

RACING AROUND THE WORLD

Jim Clark, Stirling Moss and Jo Bonnier during the 1961 Monaco Grand Prix

ARGENTINA

MAJOR CHAMPIONSHIPS

Sud-Am Formula Three Championship

see page 343

Codusur Formula Two Championship

see page 343

Temporada Championship

Originally a series of non-championship Formula Libre races which began in 1947, the Temporada (meaning season) developed into a full World Championship Grand Prix and Sports Car race during the 1950s. When these were abandoned due to lack of finance the organizers experimented with championships for F2 and F3 (see below). The Argentinian GP returned to the calendar in 1971 but a proposed 1979 F3 series proved to be a shambles and was abandoned with only nine cars entered and rumours of race-fixing. Unfortunately, the Falklands War and further economic problems once more limited Argentina's international participation but an invitation Formula 3000 race was held in 1992 and the Argentinian Grand Prix has been resurrected as part of the 1995 World Championship.

year	formula	driver	nat	car
1964	F2	Silvio Moser	CH	Brabham BT10-Ford
1966	F3	Charles Crichton-Stuart	GB	Brabham BT10-Ford
1967	F3	Jean-Pierre Beltoise	F	Matra MS5-Ford
1968	F2	Andrea de Adamich	I	Ferrari Dino 166

MAJOR INTERNATIONAL RACES

ARGENTINIAN GRAND PRIX						
year	formula	circuit	winner	nat	car	mph
1953	F2 W	Buenos Aires	Alberto Ascari	I	Ferrari 500	78.135
1954	F1 W	Buenos Aires	Juan Manuel Fangio	RA	Maserati 250F	70.137
1955	F1 W	Buenos Aires	Juan Manuel Fangio	RA	Mercedes-Benz W196	77.515
1956	F1 W	Buenos Aires	Luigi Musso/ Juan Manuel Fangio	I/RA	Lancia-Ferrari D50	79.385
1957	F1 W	Buenos Aires	Juan Manuel Fangio	RA	Maserati 250F	80.616
1958	F1 W	Buenos Aires	Stirling Moss	GB	Cooper T43-Climax	83.610
1960	F1 W	Buenos Aires	Bruce McLaren	NZ	Cooper T45-Climax	84.664
1971	F1	Buenos Aires	Chris Amon	NZ	Matra-Simca MS120	97.209
1972	F1 W	Buenos Aires	Jackie Stewart	GB	Tyrrell 003-Ford	100.443
1973	F1 W	Buenos Aires	Emerson Fittipaldi	BR	Lotus 72D-Ford	102.964
1974	F1 W	Buenos Aires	Denny Hulme	NZ	McLaren M23-Ford	116.740
1975	F1 W	Buenos Aires	Emerson Fittipaldi	BR	McLaren M23-Ford	118.613
1977	F1 W	Buenos Aires	Jody Scheckter	ZA	Wolf WR1-Ford	117.727
1978	F1 W	Buenos Aires	Mario Andretti	USA	Lotus 78-Ford	119.208
1979	F1 W	Buenos Aires	Jacques Laffite	F	Ligier JS11-Ford	122.792
1980	F1 W	Buenos Aires	Alan Jones	AUS	Williams FW07-Ford	114.061
1981	F1 W	Buenos Aires	Nelson Piquet	BR	Brabham BT49C-Ford	124.751

CIRCUITS AND OTHER RACES

BUENOS AIRES

The October 17 Autodrome (celebrating the date of President Peron's accession to power) was built within the city limits and opened on March 9 1952. It boasted numerous circuit variations; not content with these, Sports Car races combined parts of the Autodrome with the public roads outside. It was renamed Municipal Autodrome at the end of Peron's era. Little used for international racing since the Falklands War, the Formula One World Championship Grand Prix returns in 1995.

Argentinian Grand Prix see above

Buenos Aires City Grand Prix

year	formula	winner	nat	car	mph
1953	FL	Giuseppe Farina	I	Ferrari	72.450
1954	FL	Maurice Trintignant	F	Ferrari	71.930
1955	FL	Juan Manuel Fangio	RA	Mercedes-Benz W196	73.320
1956*	F1	Juan Manuel Fangio	RA	Lancia-Ferrari D50	83.090
1957	F1	Juan Manuel Fangio	RA	Maserati 250F	71.669
1958	FL	Juan Manuel Fangio	RA	Maserati 250F	66.310
1960#	FL	Maurice Trintignant	F	Cooper-Climax	76.120

At Buenos Aires except *at Mendoza and #at Cordoba

Buenos Aires 1000 kms/World Sports Car race

year	formula	winner	nat	car	mph
1954	SC W	Giuseppe Farina/Umberto Maglioli	I	Ferrari 375MM	93.221
1955	SC W	Enrique Saenz Valiente/José Maria Ibanez	RA	Ferrari 375 Plus	92.975
1956	SC W	Stirling Moss/Carlos Menditéguy	GB/RA	Maserati 300S	96.143

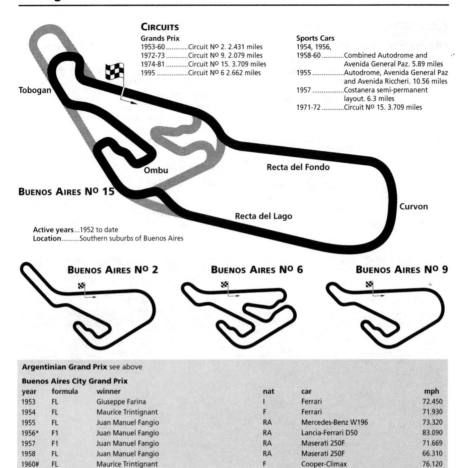

CIRCUITS

Grands Prix
1953-60 ....Circuit Nº 2. 2.431 miles
1972-73 ....Circuit Nº 9. 2.079 miles
1974-81 ....Circuit Nº 15. 3.709 miles
1995 ....Circuit Nº 6 2.662 miles

Sports Cars
1954, 1956,
1958-60 ....Combined Autodrome and
Avenida General Paz. 5.89 miles
1955 ....Autodrome, Avenida General Paz
and Avenida Riccheri. 10.56 miles
1957 ....Costanera semi-permanent
layout. 6.3 miles
1971-72 ....Circuit Nº 15. 3.709 miles

Tobogan

Ombu

Recta del Fondo

BUENOS AIRES Nº 15

Curvon

Recta del Lago

Active years...1952 to date
Location.........Southern suburbs of Buenos Aires

BUENOS AIRES Nº 2

BUENOS AIRES Nº 6

BUENOS AIRES Nº 9

Argentinian Grand Prix see above

Buenos Aires City Grand Prix

year	formula	winner	nat	car	mph
1953	FL	Giuseppe Farina	I	Ferrari	72.450
1954	FL	Maurice Trintignant	F	Ferrari	71.930
1955	FL	Juan Manuel Fangio	RA	Mercedes-Benz W196	73.320
1956*	F1	Juan Manuel Fangio	RA	Lancia-Ferrari D50	83.090
1957	F1	Juan Manuel Fangio	RA	Maserati 250F	71.669
1958	FL	Juan Manuel Fangio	RA	Maserati 250F	66.310
1960#	FL	Maurice Trintignant	F	Cooper-Climax	76.120

At Buenos Aires except *at Mendoza and #at Cordoba

Buenos Aires 1000 kms/World Sports Car race

year	formula	winner	nat	car	mph
1954	SC W	Giuseppe Farina/Umberto Maglioli	I	Ferrari 375MM	93.221

AUSTRALIA

MAJOR CHAMPIONSHIPS

Australian Touring Car Championship

year	driver	nat	car
1960*	David McKay	AUS	Jaguar 3.4
1961*	Bill Pitt	AUS	Jaguar 3.4
1962*	Bob Jane	AUS	Jaguar 3.8
1963*	Bob Jane	AUS	Jaguar 3.8
1964*	Ian Geoghegan	AUS	Ford Cortina GT
1965*	Norm Beechey	AUS	Ford Mustang
1966*	Ian Geoghegan	AUS	Ford Mustang
1967*	Ian Geoghegan	AUS	Ford Mustang
1968*	Ian Geoghegan	AUS	Ford Mustang
1969	Ian Geoghegan	AUS	Ford Mustang
1970	Norm Beechey	AUS	Holden Monaro
1971	Bob Jane	AUS	Chevrolet Camaro
1972	Bob Jane	AUS	Chevrolet Camaro
1973	Allan Moffat	AUS	Ford Falcon
1974	Peter Brock	AUS	Holden Torana XU1
1975	Colin Bond	AUS	Holden Torana L34

year	driver	nat	car
1976	Allan Moffat	AUS	Ford Falcon
1977	Allan Moffat	AUS	Ford Falcon
1978	Peter Brock	AUS	Holden Torana A9X
1979	Rob Morris	AUS	Holden Torana A9X
1980	Peter Brock	AUS	Holden Commodore
1981	Dick Johnson	AUS	Ford Falcon
1982	Dick Johnson	AUS	Ford Falcon
1983	Allan Moffat	AUS	Mazda RX-7
1984	Dick Johnson	AUS	Ford Falcon
1985	Jim Richards	NZ	BMW 635 CSi
1986	Robbie Francevic	AUS	Volvo 240T
1987	Jim Richards	NZ	BMW M3
1988	Dick Johnson	AUS	Ford Sierra RS500
1989	Dick Johnson	AUS	Ford Sierra RS500
1990	Jim Richards	NZ	Nissan Skyline GT-R
1991	Jim Richards	NZ	Nissan Skyline GT-R
1992	Mark Skaife	AUS	Nissan Skyline GT-R
1993	Glenn Seton	AUS	Ford Falcon EP
1994	Mark Skaife	AUS	Holden Commodore VP

*championship decided by a one-off race

Australian Manufacturers Championship for 2-litre Touring Cars

year	driver	nat	car
1994	Tony Longhurst	AUS	BMW 318i

Australian Gold Star Championship

year	driver	nat	car
1957	Lex Davison	AUS	Ferrari 625
1958	Stan Jones	AUS	Maserati 250F
1959	Len Lukey	AUS	Cooper T45-Climax
1960	Alex Mildren	AUS	Cooper T51-Maserati
1961	Bill Patterson	AUS	Cooper T51-Climax
1962	Bib Stillwell	AUS	Cooper T55-Climax
1963	Bib Stillwell	AUS	Brabham-Climax
1964	Bib Stillwell	AUS	Brabham-Climax
1965	Bib Stillwell	AUS	Brabham-Climax
1966	Spencer Martin	AUS	Brabham-Climax
1967	Spencer Martin	AUS	Brabham BT11-Climax
1968	Kevin Bartlett	AUS	Brabham BT23D-Alfa Romeo
1969	Kevin Bartlett	AUS	Mildren-Alfa Romeo
1970	Leo Geoghegan	AUS	Lotus 59B-Waggott
1971	Max Stewart	AUS	Mildren-Waggott
1972	Frank Matich	AUS	Matich A50-Repco
1973	John McCormack	AUS	Elfin MR5-Repco

year	driver	nat	car
1974	Max Stewart	AUS	Lola T330-Chevrolet
1975	John McCormack	AUS	Elfin MR6-Chevrolet
1976	John Leffler	AUS	Lola T400-Chevrolet
1977	John McCormack	AUS	McLaren M23-Chevrolet
1978	Graham McRae	AUS	McRae GM3-Chevrolet
1979	Johnnie Walker	AUS	Lola T332-Chevrolet
1980	Alfredo Costanzo	AUS	Lola T430-Chevrolet
1981	Alfredo Costanzo	AUS	McLaren M26-Ford
1982	Alfredo Costanzo	AUS	Tiga FA81-Ford
1983	Alfredo Costanzo	AUS	Tiga FA81-Ford
1984	John Bowe	AUS	Ralt RT4-Ford
1985	John Bowe	AUS	Ralt RT4-Ford
1986	G Watson	AUS	Ralt RT4-Ford
1987*	David Brabham	AUS	Ralt RT30-Ford
1988	Rohan Onslow	AUS	Cheetah Mk8-Ford
1989	Rohan Onslow	AUS	Ralt RT20-Holden
1990	Simon Kane	AUS	Ralt RT21-Holden
1991	Mark Skaife	AUS	SPA 003-Holden
1992	Mark Skaife	AUS	SPA 003-Holden
1993	Mark Skaife	AUS	Lola T91/50-Holden
1994	Paul Stokell	AUS	Reynard 91D-Holden

*Championship decided by a one-off race which supported the Australian GP. Rules: Formula Libre 1957-63, Tasman 1964-69, F5000 1970-81, Formula Pacific 1982-88, Formula Brabham (called Formula Holden in 1989) 1989 to date

MAJOR INTERNATIONAL RACES

AUSTRALIAN GRAND PRIX

year	formula	circuit	winner	nat	car	mph
1928	(h)	Phillip Island	Arthur Waite	GB	Austin 7	58.500
1929	(h)	Phillip Island	Arthur Terdich	AUS	Bugatti T37A	62.202
1930	(h)	Phillip Island	Bill Thompson	AUS	Bugatti T37A	65.000
1931	(h)	Phillip Island	Carl Junker	AUS	Bugatti T39	69.152
1932	(h)	Phillip Island	Bill Thompson	AUS	Bugatti T37A	75.476
1933	(h)	Phillip Island	Bill Thompson	AUS	Riley 9 "Brooklands"	63.940
1934	(h)	Phillip Island	Bob Lea-Wright	AUS	Singer Nine Le Mans	62.914
1935	(h)	Phillip Island	Les Murphy	AUS	MG P-type	66.259
1937	(h)	Victor Harbour	Les Murphy	AUS	MG P-type	68.352
1938	(h)	Bathurst	Peter Whitehead	GB	ERA B-type	55.744
1939	(h)	Lobethal	Allan Tomlinson	AUS	MG TA	79.421
1947	(h)	Bathurst	Bill Murray	AUS	MG TC	59.589
1948	(h)	Point Cook	Frank Pratt	AUS	BMW 328 "Touring"	64.432
1949	FL	Leyburn	John Crouch	AUS	Delahaye 135	82.526
1950	FL	Nuriootpa	Doug Whiteford	AUS	Ford Special	105.144
1951	FL	Narrogin	Warwick Pratley	AUS	G Reed Special-Ford	63.839
1952	FL	Bathurst	Doug Whiteford	AUS	Lago-Talbot T26C	75.042
1953	FL	Albert Park	Doug Whiteford	AUS	Lago-Talbot T26C	82.854
1954	FL	Southport	Lex Davison	AUS	HWM-Jaguar	88.123
1955	FL	Port Wakefield	Jack Brabham	AUS	Cooper T40-Bristol	71.939
1956	FL	Albert Park	Stirling Moss	GB	Maserati 250F	95.996
1957	FL	Caversham	Lex Davison/Bill Patterson	AUS	Ferrari 625	74.286
1958	FL	Bathurst	Lex Davison	AUS	Ferrari 625	81.764
1959	FL	Longford	Stan Jones	AUS	Maserati 250F	188.206
1960	FL	Lowood	Alec Mildren	AUS	Cooper T51-Maserati	94.481
1961	FL	Mallala	Lex Davison	AUS	Cooper T51-Climax	70.773
1962	FL	Caversham	Bruce McLaren	NZ	Cooper T62-Climax	90.425
1963	FL	Warwick Farm	Jack Brabham	AUS	Brabham BT4-Climax	79.341
1964	2.5 l	Sandown Park	Jack Brabham	AUS	Brabham BT7A-Climax	96.809
1965	2.5 l	Longford	Bruce McLaren	NZ	Cooper T79-Climax	114.740
1966	2.5 l	Lakeside	Graham Hill	GB	BRM P261	94.838
1967	2.5 l	Warwick Farm	Jackie Stewart	GB	BRM P261	87.677
1968	2.5 l	Sandown Park	Jim Clark	GB	Lotus 49T-Ford	101.572
1969	2.5 l	Lakeside	Chris Amon	NZ	Ferrari 246	100.144
1970	F5000	Warwick Farm	Frank Matich	AUS	McLaren M10B-Holden	94.001
1971	F5000	Warwick Farm	Frank Matich	AUS	Matich A50-Holden/Repco	93.234
1972	F5000	Sandown Park	Graham McRae	NZ	McRae GM1-Chevrolet	109.447
1973	F5000	Sandown Park	Graham McRae	NZ	McRae GM2-Chevrolet	103.922
1974	F5000	Oran Park	Max Stewart	AUS	Lola T330-Chevrolet	86.285
1975	F5000	Surfers' Paradise	Max Stewart	AUS	Lola T400-Chevrolet	89.124
1976	F5000	Sandown Park	John Goss	AUS	Matich A53-Holden/Repco	111.723
1977	F5000	Oran Park	Warwick Brown	AUS	Lola T430-Chevrolet	86.029

year	formula	circuit	winner	nat	car	mph
1978	F5000	Sandown Park	Graham McRae	NZ	McRae GM3-Chevrolet	107.505
1979	F5000	Wanneroo Park	John Walker	AUS	Lola T332-Chevrolet	95.839
1980	F1/F5000	Calder	Alan Jones	AUS	Williams FW07-Ford	94.569
1981	Pacific	Calder	Roberto Moreno	BR	Ralt RT4-Ford	88.687
1982	Pacific	Calder	Alain Prost	F	Ralt RT4-Ford	89.139
1983	Pacific	Calder	Roberto Moreno	BR	Ralt RT4-Ford	88.992
1984	Pacific	Calder	Roberto Moreno	BR	Ralt RT4-Ford	84.678
1985	F1 W	Adelaide	Keke Rosberg	SF	Williams FW10-Honda	95.689
1986	F1 W	Adelaide	Alain Prost	F	McLaren MP4/2C-TAG Porsche	100.991
1987	F1 W	Adelaide	Gerhard Berger	A	Ferrari F187	102.246
1988	F1 W	Adelaide	Alain Prost	F	McLaren MP4/4-Honda	101.967
1989	F1 W	Adelaide	Thierry Boutsen	B	Williams FW13-Renault	81.947
1990	F1 W	Adelaide	Nelson Piquet	BR	Benetton B190-Ford	103.938
1991	F1 W	Adelaide	Ayrton Senna	BR	McLaren MP4/6-Honda	80.201
1992	F1 W	Adelaide	Gerhard Berger	A	McLaren MP4/7A-Honda	106.689
1993	F1 W	Adelaide	Ayrton Senna	BR	McLaren MP4/8-Ford	107.530
1994	F1 W	Adelaide	Nigel Mansell	GB	Williams FW16B-Renault	105.754

CIRCUITS AND OTHER RACES

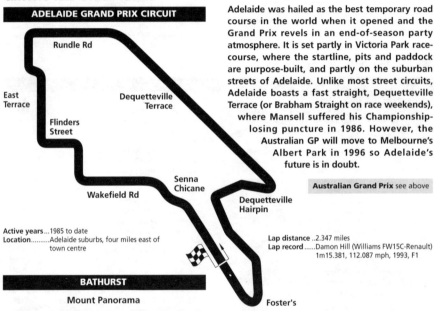

ADELAIDE GRAND PRIX CIRCUIT

Rundle Rd

East Terrace

Dequetteville Terrace

Flinders Street

Senna Chicane

Wakefield Rd

Dequetteville Hairpin

Active years...1985 to date
Location..........Adelaide suburbs, four miles east of town centre

Foster's

Adelaide was hailed as the best temporary road course in the world when it opened and the Grand Prix revels in an end-of-season party atmosphere. It is set partly in Victoria Park racecourse, where the startline, pits and paddock are purpose-built, and partly on the suburban streets of Adelaide. Unlike most street circuits, Adelaide boasts a fast straight, Dequetteville Terrace (or Brabham Straight on race weekends), where Mansell suffered his Championship-losing puncture in 1986. However, the Australian GP will move to Melbourne's Albert Park in 1996 so Adelaide's future is in doubt.

Australian Grand Prix see above

Lap distance ..2.347 miles
Lap record ......Damon Hill (Williams FW15C-Renault)
1m15.381, 112.087 mph, 1993, F1

BATHURST

Mount Panorama

The arrival of the Armstrong 500 from Phillip Island in 1963 established Bathurst as one of the most picturesque and demanding road courses in the world. With sheer drops, the daunting Skyline section and mile-long Conrod Straight, Mount Panorama is a true challenge. The Armstrong developed into Bathurst's annual touring car classic, known simply in Australia as "The Great Race". Traditionally a battle between

Australian Holdens and Fords, the race has attracted strong European participation which culminated in its inclusion in the one-off World Touring Car Championship. A chicane (Caltex Chase) was introduced to slow cars on the Conrod Straight but it is now taken flat-out and its dangers were highlighted by the death of Don Watson during practice for the 1994 race.

Australian Grand Prix see above

Bathurst 1000						
year	formula	winner	nat	car	mph
1963	TC	Harry Firth/Bob Jane	AUS	Ford Cortina GT	64.689
1964	TC	Bob Jane/George Reynolds	AUS	Ford Cortina GT	n/a
1965	TC	Barry Seton/Midge Bosworth	AUS	Ford Cortina GT500	69.204
1966	TC	Rauno Aaltonen/Bob Holden	SF/AUS	Morris Cooper S	70.049
1967	TC	Harry Firth/Fred Gibson	AUS	Ford Falcon XR GT	72.808
1968	TC	Bruce McPhee/Barry Mulholland	AUS	Holden Monaro GTS 327	74.793

BATHURST

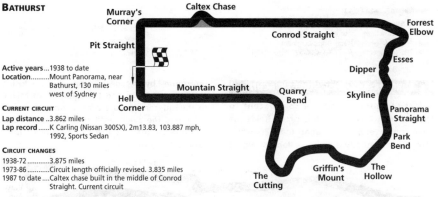

Murray's Corner
Caltex Chase
Forrest Elbow
Conrod Straight
Pit Straight
Dipper
Esses
Mountain Straight
Quarry Bend
Skyline
Hell Corner
Panorama Straight
Park Bend
Griffin's Mount
The Hollow
The Cutting

Active years...1938 to date
Location.........Mount Panorama, near Bathurst, 130 miles west of Sydney

CURRENT CIRCUIT
Lap distance ..3.862 miles
Lap record......K Carling (Nissan 300SX), 2m13.83, 103.887 mph, 1992, Sports Sedan

CIRCUIT CHANGES
1938-72 ....3.875 miles
1973-86 ....Circuit length officially revised. 3.835 miles
1987 to date ....Caltex chase built in the middle of Conrod Straight. Current circuit

year	formula	winner	nat	car	mph
1969	TC	Colin Bond/Tony Roberts	AUS	Holden Monaro GTS 350	77.023
1970	TC	Allan Moffat	AUS	Ford Falcon XW GTHO	76.755
1971	TC	Allan Moffat	AUS	Ford Falcon XY GTHO	81.728
1972	TC	Peter Brock	AUS	Holden Torana LJ XU1	83.521
1973	TC	Allan Moffat/Ian Geoghegan	AUS	Ford Falcon XA GT	85.220
1974	TC	John Goss/Kevin Bartlett	AUS	Ford Falcon XA GT	79.510
1975	TC	Peter Brock/Brian Sampson	AUS	Holden Torana L34	87.186
1976	TC	Bob Morris/John Fitzpatrick	AUS/GB	Holden Torana L34	87.796
1977	TC	Allan Moffat/Jacky Ickx	AUS/B	Ford Falcon XC	89.486
1978	TC	Peter Brock/Jim Richards	AUS/NZ	Holden Torana A9X	92.403
1979	TC	Peter Brock/Jim Richards	AUS/NZ	Holden Torana A9X	94.175
1980	TC	Peter Brock/Jim Richards	AUS/NZ	Holden Commodore VC	91.955
1981	TC	Dick Johnson/John French	AUS	Ford Falcon XD	93.957
1982	TC	Peter Brock/Larry Perkins	AUS	Holden Commodore VH	95.666
1983	TC	Peter Brock/Larry Perkins/John Harvey	AUS	Holden Commodore VH	96.535
1984	TC	Peter Brock/Larry Perkins	AUS	Holden Commodore VK	97.872
1985	TC	John Goss/Armin Hahne	AUS/D	Jaguar XJ-S	93.415
1986	TC	Allan Grice/Graeme Bailey	AUS	Holden Commodore VK	96.024
1987	TC	Peter Brock/David Parsons/Peter McLeod	AUS	Holden Commodore VL	86.935
1988	TC	Tony Longhurst/Tomas Mezera	AUS	Ford Sierra RS500 Cosworth	88.369
1989	TC	Dick Johnson/John Bowe	AUS	Ford Sierra RS500 Cosworth	95.441
1990	TC	Allan Grice/Win Percy	AUS/GB	Holden Commodore	n/a
1991	TC	Jim Richards/Mark Skaife	NZ/AUS	Nissan Skyline GT-R	98.371
1992	TC	Jim Richards/Mark Skaife	NZ/AUS	Nissan Skyline GT-R	n/a
1993	TC	Larry Perkins/Gregg Hansford	AUS	Holden Commodore	95.877
1994	TC	Dick Johnson/John Bowe	AUS	Ford Falcon EB	88.037

SANDOWN PARK

Sandown Park shares its facilities with a horse-racing venue as Aintree used to in England. Formerly a mainstay of the Tasman Cup, the infield section was added in 1984 to comply with FIA circuit length regulations and a round of the World Sports Car Championship was held here. The exercise was repeated four years later but at present Sandown is purely being used for national events.

Active years...1962 to date
Location.........Springvale, 16 miles south-east of Melbourne

CURRENT CIRCUIT
Lap distance ..2.410 miles
Lap record......Jean-Louis Schlesser (Sauber C9/88-Mercedes-Benz), 1m33.58, 92.712 mph, 1988, Group C Sports Cars

CIRCUIT CHANGES
1962-83 ....Current national circuit. 1.929 miles
1984 ....2.425 miles
1985 to date ....Current circuit

Australian Grand Prix see above

World Sports Car race

year	formula	winner		nat	car	mph
1984	SC W	Stefan Bellof/Derek Bell		D/GB	Porsche 956	82.912
1988	SC W	Jean-Louis Schlesser/Jochen Mass		F/D	Sauber C9/88-Mercedes-Benz	89.698

SURFERS' PARADISE STREET CIRCUIT

A fast temporary road course adjacent to Queensland's Gold Coast, this circuit holds the once-controversial Australian Indycar Grand Prix. It is essentially a series of long straights interrupted by chicanes. Despite the race losing money every year and the addition of Miami to the Indycar calendar a new contract should safeguard the event until at least 1998. A permanent circuit outside the city once held Tasman Cup races.

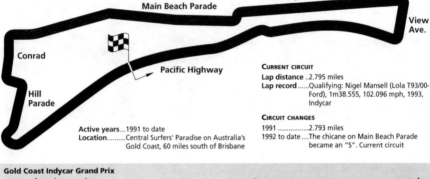

The Esplanade
Main Beach Parade
View Ave.
Conrad
Pacific Highway
Hill Parade

CURRENT CIRCUIT
Lap distance ..2.795 miles
Lap record ......Qualifying: Nigel Mansell (Lola T93/00-Ford), 1m38.555, 102.096 mph, 1993, Indycar

CIRCUIT CHANGES
1991 ....2.793 miles
1992 to date ....The chicane on Main Beach Parade became an "S". Current circuit

Active years...1991 to date
Location..........Central Surfers' Paradise on Australia's Gold Coast, 60 miles south of Brisbane

Gold Coast Indycar Grand Prix

year	formula	winner		nat	car	mph
1991	Indycar	John Andretti		USA	Lola T91/00-Chevrolet	81.953
1992	Indycar	Emerson Fittipaldi		BR	Penske PC21-Chevrolet	77.561
1993	Indycar	Nigel Mansell		GB	Lola T93/00-Ford	97.284
1994	Indycar	Michael Andretti		USA	Reynard 94I-Ford	80.994

AUSTRIA

MAJOR INTERNATIONAL RACES

AUSTRIAN GRAND PRIX

year	formula	circuit	winner	nat	car	mph
1963	F1	Zeltweg	Jack Brabham	AUS	Brabham BT3-Climax	96.350
1964	F1 W	Zeltweg	Lorenzo Bandini	I	Ferrari Dino 156	99.161
1965	SC	Zeltweg	Jochen Rindt	A	Ferrari 250LM	97.130
1966	SC	Zeltweg	Gerhard Mitter/Hans Herrmann	D	Porsche 906 Carrera 6	99.680
1967	SC	Zeltweg	Paul Hawkins	AUS	Ford GT40	95.290
1968	SC W	Zeltweg	Jo Siffert	CH	Porsche 908/8	106.831
1969	SC W	Österreichring	Jo Siffert/Kurt Ahrens Jr	CH/D	Porsche 917	115.769
1970	F1 W	Österreichring	Jacky Ickx	B	Ferrari 312B	129.269
1971	F1 W	Österreichring	Jo Siffert	CH	BRM P160	131.645
1972	F1 W	Österreichring	Emerson Fittipaldi	BR	Lotus 72D-Ford	133.298
1973	F1 W	Österreichring	Ronnie Peterson	S	Lotus 72D-Ford	133.995
1974	F1 W	Österreichring	Carlos Reutemann	RA	Brabham BT44-Ford	134.097
1975	F1 W	Österreichring	Vittorio Brambilla	I	March 751-Ford	110.295
1976	F1 W	Österreichring	John Watson	GB	Penske PC4-Ford	132.000
1977	F1 W	Österreichring	Alan Jones	AUS	Shadow DN8A-Ford	122.972
1978	F1 W	Österreichring	Ronnie Peterson	S	Lotus 79-Ford	118.016
1979	F1 W	Österreichring	Alan Jones	AUS	Williams FW07-Ford	136.501
1980	F1 W	Österreichring	Jean-Pierre Jabouille	F	Renault RE20	138.671
1981	F1 W	Österreichring	Jacques Laffite	F	Ligier JS17-Matra	134.013
1982	F1 W	Österreichring	Elio de Angelis	I	Lotus 91-Ford	138.064
1983	F1 W	Österreichring	Alain Prost	F	Renault RE40	138.866
1984	F1 W	Österreichring	Niki Lauda	A	McLaren MP4/2-TAG Porsche	139.108
1985	F1 W	Österreichring	Alain Prost	F	McLaren MP4/2B-TAG Porsche	143.612
1986	F1 W	Österreichring	Alain Prost	F	McLaren MP4/2C-TAG Porsche	141.554
1987	F1 W	Österreichring	Nigel Mansell	GB	Williams FW11B-Honda	146.277

CIRCUITS AND OTHER RACES

ÖSTERREICHRING

The Österreichring was built in 1969, but it seems to be from the age before bland facilities were normal. Set in the mountains above the unpopular Zeltweg airfield it replaced, the new circuit is a magnificent collection of fast corners and steep elevation change. The Bosch Kurve, 180 degrees and no run-off, is awesome. A chicane was built at the first corner following Mark Donohue's fatal accident in 1975, but that is the only slow corner. The Österreichring also had a reputation of providing the surprise result of the season;

Vittorio Brambilla, John Watson, Alan Jones and Elio de Angelis all scored their first Grand Prix victory here. However, when the 1987 Grand Prix was stopped twice by startline accidents the Österreichring was removed from the Grand Prix calendar.

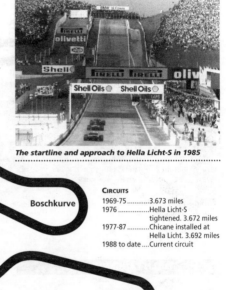

The startline and approach to Hella Licht-S in 1985

CURRENT CIRCUIT
Lap distance ..3.636 miles
Lap record...Nigel Mansell (Williams FW11B-Honda), 1m28.318, 150.493 mph, 1987, F1 (remains the official lap record despite minor changes having been made to the circuit since 1987)

Dr. Tiroch Kurve

Boschkurve

Schikane

CIRCUITS
1969-75 ....3.673 miles
1976 ....Hella Licht-S tightened. 3.672 miles
1977-87 ....Chicane installed at Hella Licht. 3.692 miles
1988 to date ....Current circuit

Rindt Kurve

Active years...1969 to date
Location.........45 miles north-west of Graz, 125 miles south-east of Salzburg

Hella Licht-S

Austrian Grand Prix see above

Jochen Rindt Trophy

year	formula	winner	nat	car	mph
1972	F2 E	Emerson Fittipaldi	BR	Lotus 69-Ford	126.161

European Formula Three race

year	formula	winner	nat	car	mph
1977	F3 E	Anders Olofsson	S	Ralt RT1-Toyota	106.234
1978	F3 E	Anders Olofsson	S	Ralt RT1-Toyota	113.861
1979	F3 E	Alain Prost	F	Martini MK27-Renault	116.432
1980	F3 E	Michele Alboreto	I	March 803-Alfa Romeo	116.658
1981	F3 E	Mauro Baldi	I	March 813-Alfa Romeo	119.129
1982	F3 E	Emanuele Pirro	I	Euroracing 101-Alfa Romeo	118.335
1983	F3 E	Tommy Byrne	IRL	Ralt RT3/83-Toyota	119.329
1984	F3 E	Gerhard Berger	A	Ralt RT3/84-Alfa Romeo	120.560

International Formula 3000 race

year	formula	winner	nat	car	mph
1985	F3000 INT	Ivan Capelli	I	March 85B-Cosworth	127.322
1986	F3000 INT	Ivan Capelli	I	March 86B-Cosworth	128.107

World Sports Car race (also see Austrian GP)

year	formula	winner	nat	car	mph
1970	SC W	Jo Siffert/Brian Redman	CH/GB	Porsche 917	121.608
1971	SC W	Pedro Rodriguez/Richard Attwood	MEX/GB	Porsche 917K	123.063
1972	SC W	Jacky Ickx/Brian Redman	B/GB	Ferrari 312P	125.396
1973	SC W	Henri Pescarolo/Gérard Larrousse	F	Matra-Simca MS670	129.652
1974	SC W	Henri Pescarolo/Gérard Larrousse	F	Matra-Simca MS670C	128.595
1975	SC W	Henri Pescarolo/Derek Bell	F/GB	Alfa Romeo T33TT/12	105.652
1976	SC W	Dieter Quester/Gunnar Nilsson	A/S	BMW 3.0 CSL	114.388

SALZBURGRING

The home of the Austrian motorcycle Grand Prix, the Salzburgring nestles in a beautiful valley above the Austrian city. Two fast sections are joined by slow turns at each end, although these straights were broken up by a chicane in 1976. Formula Two and European Touring Cars visited regularly in the seventies but it is now little used for international categories.

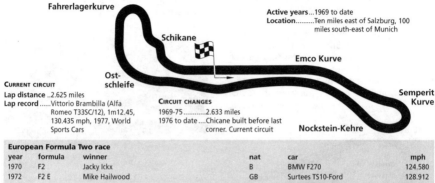

Active years...1969 to date
Location.........Ten miles east of Salzburg, 100 miles south-east of Munich

CURRENT CIRCUIT
Lap distance ..2.625 miles
Lap record ......Vittorio Brambilla (Alfa Romeo T33SC/12), 1m12.45, 130.435 mph, 1977, World Sports Cars

CIRCUIT CHANGES
1969-75 ....2.633 miles
1976 to date ....Chicane built before last corner. Current circuit

European Formula Two race

year	formula	winner	nat	car	mph
1970	F2	Jacky Ickx	B	BMW F270	124.580
1972	F2 E	Mike Hailwood	GB	Surtees TS10-Ford	128.912
1973	F2 E	Vittorio Brambilla	I	March 732-BMW	132.117
1974	F2 E	Jacques Laffite	F	March 742-BMW	130.454
1975	F2 E	Jean-Pierre Jabouille	F	Elf 2J-BMW	130.874
1976	F2 E	Michel Leclère	F	Elf 2J-Renault	122.596

World Sports Car race

year	formula	winner	nat	car	mph
1976	SC WSC	Jochen Mass	D	Porsche 936	125.163
1977	SC WSC	Vittorio Brambilla	I	Alfa Romeo T33SC/12	126.557
1978	SC E	Reinhold Jöst	D	Porsche 908/3 Spyder	119.096

TULLN-LANGENLEBARN

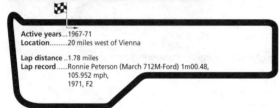

Active years...1967-71
Location.........20 miles west of Vienna

Lap distance ..1.78 miles
Lap record ......Ronnie Peterson (March 712M-Ford) 1m00.48, 105.952 mph, 1971, F2

An operational airfield a mile from the River Danube which held a European F2 race for the first five years of the championship. Facilities were rudimentary, straw bales marking the course. Local hero Jochen Rindt obliged the crowds by winning the first three races.

Flugplatzrennen/European Formula Two race

year	formula	winner	nat	car	mph
1967	F2 E	Jochen Rindt	A	Brabham BT23-Ford	97.552
1968	F2 E	Jochen Rindt	A	Brabham BT23C-Ford	99.137
1969	F2 E	Jochen Rindt	A	Lotus 59B-Ford	101.899
1970	F2 E	Jacky Ickx	B	BMW F270	101.351
1971	F2 E	Ronnie Peterson	S	March 712M-Ford	88.434

ZELTWEG

Another temporary airfield circuit which proved extremely unpopular when in 1964 it held the first World Championship Grand Prix in Austria. The bumpy concrete surface caused a high rate of attrition but Lorenzo Bandini survived to record his only victory. The Austrian GP switched to Sports Cars before Zeltweg was replaced by the new Österreichring in 1969.

Active years...1958-69
Location.........70 kms north-west of Graz, 200 kms south-east of Salzburg
Lap distance ..1.988 miles
Lap record ......Dan Gurney (Brabham BT7-Climax) 1m10.56, 101.429 mph, 1964, F1

Austrian Grand Prix see above

BELGIUM

MAJOR CHAMPIONSHIPS

Belgian Touring Car Championship

year	class	driver	nat
1972	Group 1	Chris Tuerlinx	B
	Group 2	Claude Bourgoignie	B
1973	Group 1	PY Bertinchamps	B
	Group 2	Claude Bourgoignie	B
1976	Overall	Alain Semoulin	B
1977	Overall	Albert Vanierschot	B
1978	Overall	Claude Bourgoignie/	
		Albert Vanierschot	B
1979	Overall	Jean-Michel Martin	B
	Class 1	F de Caluwe	B
	Class 2	Jean-Michel Martin	B
1980	Overall	Jean-Michel Martin	B
	Class 1	P Ferminée	B
	Class 2	M de Mol	B
	Class 3	Jean-Michel Martin	B
1981	Overall	Pierre Dieudonne	B
	Class 1	JL Heco	B
	Class 2	Pierre Dieudonne	B
	Class 3	Alain Semoulin	B
1982	Group A	Alain Semoulin	B
	Class 1	B Carlier	B
	Class 2	Raijmond van Hove	B
	Class 3	Alain Semoulin	B
1983	Overall	Huweler	B
	over 2500 cc	Eddy Joosen	B
	2500 cc	du Bois	B
	1600 cc	Huweler	B
1984	Group N overall	Michel de Deyne	B
	over 2500 cc	Michel de Deyne	B
	2500 cc	Michel Maillien	B
	2000 cc	Roger Rutten	B
	1600 cc	D de Sterck	B

year	class	driver	nat
	1300 cc	C Corthals	B
1985	Group N overall	Alain Semoulin	B
	over 2500 cc	Guy Neve	B
	2500 cc	Alain Semoulin	B
	2000 cc	Albert Vanierschot	B
	1600 cc	Dominique Holvoet	B
	1300 cc	Thierry van Dalen	B
1986	Group N overall	Jean-Michel Martin	B
	Class 1	Verreydt	B
	Class 2	P Menage	B
	Class 3	Albert Vanierschot	B
	Class 4	Jean-Michel Martin	B
1987	Group N overall	Alain Semoulin	B
	over 2500 cc	Alain Semoulin	B
	2500 cc	Jean-Michel Martin	B
	1600 cc	Pascal Tillekaerts	B
	1300 cc	Alain Plasch	B
1988	Division 1	Alain Semoulin	B
	Div 2 over 3000 cc	Guy van Mol	B
	2000 cc	Eric Bachelart	B
	1600 cc	Pascal Tillekaerts	B
	1300 cc	E van Esch	B
1989	Division 1	Jean-Michel Martin	B
	Division 2	Pascal Tillikaerts	B
1990	Division 1	Jean-Michel Martin	B
	Division 2	Wolfgang Haugg	B
1991	Division 1	Philippe Verellen	B
	Division 2	Pascal Witmeur	B
1992	Division 1	Pierre-Alain Thibaut	B
	Division 2	P Menage/Michel Delcourt	B
1993	FIA Class 2	Philippe Verellen	B
	Div 2 over 2000 cc	Pierre-Alain Thibaut	B
	Div 2 2000 cc	Pascal Witmeur	B
1994	FIA Class 2	Thierry Tassin	B
	Procar 2000 cc	Michel Luxen/Michel Plennevaux	B
	Procar 1600 cc	Sébastien Ugeux	B

MAJOR INTERNATIONAL RACES

BELGIAN GRAND PRIX

year	formula	circuit	winner	nat	car	mph
1925	GP	Spa-Francorchamps	Antonio Ascari	I	Alfa Romeo P2	74.859
1930	GP	Spa-Francorchamps	Louis Chiron	MC	Bugatti T35C	71.834
1931	GP	Spa-Francorchamps	"W Williams"/Caberto Conelli	GB/I	Bugatti T51	81.277
1933	GP	Spa-Francorchamps	Tazio Nuvolari	I	Maserati 8CM	88.956
1934	GP	Spa-Francorchamps	René Dreyfus	F	Bugatti T59	87.414
1935	GP	Spa-Francorchamps	Rudolf Caracciola	D	Mercedes-Benz W25B	98.441
1937	GP	Spa-Francorchamps	Rudolf Hasse	D	Auto Union C	104.426
1939	GP	Spa-Francorchamps	Hermann Lang	D	Mercedes-Benz W163	92.250
1947	F1	Spa-Francorchamps	Jean-Pierre Wimille	F	Alfa Romeo 158	95.860
1949	F1	Spa-Francorchamps	Louis Rosier	F	Lago-Talbot T26C	97.422
1950	F1 W	Spa-Francorchamps	Juan Manuel Fangio	RA	Alfa Romeo 158	110.046
1951	F1 W	Spa-Francorchamps	Giuseppe Farina	I	Alfa Romeo 159	114.326
1952	F2 W	Spa-Francorchamps	Alberto Ascari	I	Ferrari 500	103.127
1953	F2 W	Spa-Francorchamps	Alberto Ascari	I	Ferrari 500	112.470
1954	F1 W	Spa-Francorchamps	Juan Manuel Fangio	RA	Maserati 250F	115.064
1955	F1 W	Spa-Francorchamps	Juan Manuel Fangio	RA	Mercedes-Benz W196	118.833
1956	F1 W	Spa-Francorchamps	Peter Collins	GB	Lancia-Ferrari D50	118.445
1958	F1 W	Spa-Francorchamps	Tony Brooks	GB	Vanwall VW5	129.920
1960	F1 W	Spa-Francorchamps	Jack Brabham	AUS	Cooper T53-Climax	133.622
1961	F1 W	Spa-Francorchamps	Phil Hill	USA	Ferrari Dino 156	128.144
1962	F1 W	Spa-Francorchamps	Jim Clark	GB	Lotus 25-Climax	131.891
1963	F1 W	Spa-Francorchamps	Jim Clark	GB	Lotus 25-Climax	113.815
1964	F1 W	Spa-Francorchamps	Jim Clark	GB	Lotus 25-Climax	132.790
1965	F1 W	Spa-Francorchamps	Jim Clark	GB	Lotus 33-Climax	117.155
1966	F1 W	Spa-Francorchamps	John Surtees	GB	Ferrari 312	113.930
1967	F1 W	Spa-Francorchamps	Dan Gurney	USA	Eagle AAR104-Weslake	145.982
1968	F1 W	Spa-Francorchamps	Bruce McLaren	NZ	McLaren M7A-Ford	147.133
1970	F1 W	Spa-Francorchamps	Pedro Rodriguez	MEX	BRM P153	149.936
1972	F1 W	Nivelles	Emerson Fittipaldi	BR	Lotus 72D-Ford	113.353
1973	F1 W	Zolder	Jackie Stewart	GB	Tyrrell 006-Ford	107.728

year	formula	circuit	winner	nat	car	mph
1974	F1 W	Nivelles	Emerson Fittipaldi	BR	McLaren M23-Ford	113.102
1975	F1 W	Zolder	Niki Lauda	A	Ferrari 312T	107.042
1976	F1 W	Zolder	Niki Lauda	A	Ferrari 312T2	108.095
1977	F1 W	Zolder	Gunnar Nilsson	S	Lotus 78-Ford	96.630
1978	F1 W	Zolder	Mario Andretti	USA	Lotus 79-Ford	111.364
1979	F1 W	Zolder	Jody Scheckter	ZA	Ferrari 312T4	111.225
1980	F1 W	Zolder	Didier Pironi	F	Ligier JS11/15-Ford	115.812
1981	F1 W	Zolder	Carlos Reutemann	RA	Williams FW07C-Ford	112.111
1982	F1 W	Zolder	John Watson	GB	McLaren MP4/1B-Ford	116.213
1983	F1 W	Spa-Francorchamps	Alain Prost	F	Renault RE40	119.136
1984	F1 W	Zolder	Michele Alboreto	I	Ferrari 126C4	115.209
1985	F1 W	Spa-Francorchamps	Ayrton Senna	BR	Lotus 97T-Renault	118.096
1986	F1 W	Spa-Francorchamps	Nigel Mansell	GB	Williams FW11-Honda	126.470
1987	F1 W	Spa-Francorchamps	Alain Prost	F	McLaren MP4/3-TAG Porsche	127.794
1988	F1 W	Spa-Francorchamps	Ayrton Senna	BR	McLaren MP4/4-Honda	126.407
1989	F1 W	Spa-Francorchamps	Ayrton Senna	BR	McLaren MP4/5-Honda	112.818
1990	F1 W	Spa-Francorchamps	Ayrton Senna	BR	McLaren MP4/5B-Honda	131.553
1991	F1 W	Spa-Francorchamps	Ayrton Senna	BR	McLaren MP4/6-Honda	130.405
1992	F1 W	Spa-Francorchamps	Michael Schumacher	D	Benetton B192-Ford	118.360
1993	F1 W	Spa-Francorchamps	Damon Hill	GB	Williams FW15C-Renault	134.662
1994	F1 W	Spa-Francorchamps	Damon Hill	GB	Williams FW16B-Renault	129.344

CIRCUITS AND OTHER RACES

BASTOGNE

The Circuit des Ardennes was the first major race held on a closed course (rather than city-to-city events) making it the forerunner of today's racing. It also began a tradition of racing in the area which continues today at Spa-Francorchamps. The race was suggested by Pierre de Crawhez who won the second event. The 1904 race, on an extended circuit, produced the closest finish: Heath defeating Teste by just one minute.

Ardennes Circuit

year	formula	winner	nat	car	mph
1902	GP	Charles Jarrott	GB	Panhard 70	54.459
1903	GP	Pierre de Crawhez	F	Panhard 70	54.696
1904	GP	George Heath	USA	Panhard 70	56.405
1905	GP	Victor Hémery	F	Darracq	61.483
1906	GP	Arthur Duray	F	Lorraine-Dietrich	66.351
1907	Kaiserpreis	Lord Brabazon of Tara	GB	Minerva	60.067
	GP	Pierre de Caters	B	Mercedes	57.739

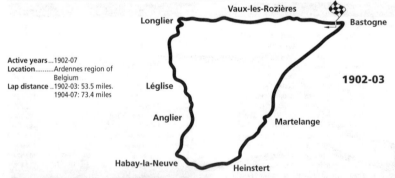

Active years...1902-07
Location..........Ardennes region of
Belgium
Lap distance ..1902-03: 53.5 miles.
1904-07: 73.4 miles

1902-03

CHIMAY

Home of the Grand Prix des Frontières, the race title reflecting Chimay's proximity to the French border. The fast temporary road course to the north of the town became outdated and dangerous during the 1960s and it was not used for racing after 1972.

Grand Prix des Frontières

year	formula	winner	nat	car	mph
1926	Cyc	Roger Pierard	B	Salmson GS	61.602
1927	Cyc	Guy d'Havrincourt	F	Salmson GP	61.045
1928	V	Yves Giraud-Cabantous	F	Salmson GS	67.176
1929	GP	Goffredo Zehender	I	Alfa Romeo 6C-1750	68.578
1930	750 cc	Marcel Rouleau	B	Amilcar CE	52.976
	SC	Willy Longueville	B	Bugatti T37A	69.119
	GP	Georges de Marotte	B	Salmson GP	68.261

Grand Prix des Frontières

year	formula	winner	nat	car	mph
1931	FL	Arthur Legat	B	Bugatti T37A	70.840
1932	GP	Arthur Legat	B	Bugatti T37A	72.972
1933	GP	Willy Longueville	B	Bugatti T35B	75.479
1934	GP	Willy Longueville	B	Bugatti T35B	73.266
1935	GP	Rudolf Steinweg	D	Bugatti T51A	78.269
1936	SC	Eddie Hertzberger	NL	MG K3 Magnette	74.699
1937	2000 cc	Eddie Hertzberger	NL	MG K3 Magnette	76.523
	2000 cc SC	Ernst Henne	D	BMW 328	73.774
	FL	Hans Ruesch	CH	Alfa Romeo 8C-35	81.340
1938	2000 cc	Ralph Roese	D	BMW 328	72.912
	FL	Maurice Trintignant	F	Bugatti T51	80.190
1939	SC	Ralph Roese	D	BMW 328	77.063
	GP	Maurice Trintignant	F	Bugatti T51	80.370
1946	FL	Leslie Brooke	GB	ERA B-type	75.000
1947	FL	"B Bira"	SM	Maserati 4CL	82.130
	SC	Yves Giraud-Cabantous	F	Delahaye 135S	78.940
1948	1100 cc SC	Raymond de Sauge	F	Cisitalia 508C-Fiat	68.026
	2000 cc SC	Raymond de Sauge	F	Cisitalia 508C-Fiat	72.323
	SC	Guy Mairesse	F	Delahaye 135S	79.400
1949	F1	Guy Mairesse	F	Lago-Talbot T26C	86.420
	F2	Emile Cornet	B	Veritas RS	78.120
1950	F2	Johnny Claes	B	HWM 50-Alta	84.845
1951	F2	Johnny Claes	B	Simca-Gordini 11	82.450
1952	F2	Paul Frère	B	HWM 51/52-Alta	90.236
1953	F2	Maurice Trintignant	F	Gordini 16	94.251
1954	F1	"B Bira"	SM	Maserati 250F	98.539
1955	SC	Benoit Musy	CH	Maserati A6GCS	94.970
1956	SC	Benoit Musy	CH	Maserati 300S	102.820
1957	SC	Franco Bordoni	I	Maserati 200S	99.440
1958	SC	Brian Naylor	GB	JBW-Maserati	93.430
1959	SC	Mike Taylor	GB	Lotus 15-Climax	105.560
1960	F2	Jackie Lewis	GB	Cooper T45-Climax	117.102
1961	FJ	John Love	RSR	Cooper-BMC	n/a
1962	FJ	José Rosinski	F	Cooper-Ford	102.870
1963	FJ	Jacques Maglia	F	Lotus-Ford	110.400
1965	F3	John Cardwell	GB	Brabham-Ford	110.605
1966	F3	Martin Davies	AUS	Brabham BT10-Ford	111.390
1967	F3	Peter Westbury	GB	Brabham BT21-Ford	111.990
1969	F3	Jean Blanc	CH	Tecno 69-Ford	113.434
1970	F3	David Purley	GB	Brabham BT28-Ford	113.670
1971	F3	David Purley	GB	Brabham BT28-Ford	n/a
1972	F3	David Purley	GB	Ensign F371-Ford	122.311

CHIMAY

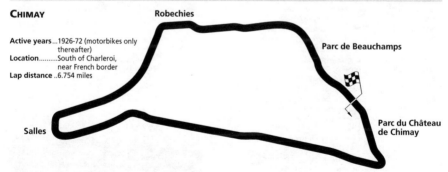

Robechies

Active years ...1926-72 (motorbikes only thereafter)
Location ....South of Charleroi, near French border
Lap distance ..6.754 miles

Parc de Beauchamps

Parc du Château de Chimay

Salles

NIVELLES-BAULERS

A safe but bland circuit built near Brussels. When Spa fell from favour in the early 1970s Nivelles held the Belgian GP twice, won both times by Emerson Fittipaldi. However, the teams hated it and the championship did not return again. Nivelles went bankrupt and was sold in October 1977, closing soon after.

Belgian Grand Prix see above

European Formula Two race

year	formula	winner	nat	car	mph
1973	F2 E	Jean-Pierre Jarier	F	March 732-BMW	110.197

NIVELLES-BAULERS

Active years...1971-78
Location.........20 miles south of Brussels
Lap distance ..2.314 miles
Lap record......Denny Hulme (McLaren M23-Ford) 1m11.31,
116.820 mph, 1974, F1

SPA-FRANCORCHAMPS

When the shortened Spa-Francorchamps Circuit opened for the 1979 24-hour race, there were worries that it would be a shadow of its former self. However, the new section had been built in character with the original and it is now the finest road course visited by the Grand Prix circus. The old course, from the start at La Source through Eau Rouge and up the hill to Les Combes remains. A new link road was built across the valley to rejoin the old circuit on the blast back to La Source. Previously the course, which had been designed by Jules de Thier using narrow public roads, continued through

Andrea de Cesaris leads from the start of the 1983 Belgian Grand Prix at Spa

Malmédy, onto the Masta straight, passing between the houses at the fearsome Masta Kink, to a hairpin at Stavelot before the equally fast return leg to complete the lap. Eau Rouge was considered by many to be the most demanding corner in Grand Prix racing until a chicane was built in 1994. The weather has always been a major factor, often raining at one section but dry at another. Allied to questions regarding its safety this led to the closure of the old circuit in the early 1970s.

Belgian Grand Prix see above

Spa 24 hours

year	formula	winner	nat	car	mph
1924	TC	Henri Springuel/Becquet	F	Bignan	48.700
1925	TC	André Lagache/René Leonard	F	Chenard-Walcker	56.670
1926	TC	André Boillot/Louis Rigal	F	Peugeot	59.500
1927	TC	Robert Sénéchal/Nicolas Caerels	F/B	Excelsior	57.120
1928	TC	Boris Ivanowski/Attilio Marinoni	F/I	Alfa Romeo	63.800
1929	TC	Robert Benoist/Attilio Marinoni	F/I	Alfa Romeo	63.020
1930	TC	Attilio Marinoni/Pietro Ghersi	I	Alfa Romeo	68.500
1931	TC	Prince Dimitri Djordjadze/Goffredo Zehender	RUS/I	Mercedes-Benz	65.800
1932	TC	Antonio Brivio/Eugenio Siena	I	Alfa Romeo	72.600
1933	TC	Louis Chiron/Luigi Chinetti	MC/I	Alfa Romeo	72.660
1934*	TC	Jean Desvignes/Norbert Mahe	F	Bugatti	72.460
1936	TC	Francesco Severi/Raymond Sommer	I/F	Alfa Romeo	77.670
1938	TC	Carlo Pintacuda/Francesco Severi	I	Alfa Romeo	77.570
1948	SC	St John Horsfall/Leslie Johnson	GB	Aston Martin	72.070
1949	SC	Luigi Chinetti/Jean Lucas	I/F	Ferrari	78.700
1953	SC W	Giuseppe Farina/Mike Hawthorn	I/GB	Ferrari 340MM	95.052
1964	TC	Robert Crevits/Gustave Gosselin	B	Mercedes-Benz 300SE	102.440
1965	TC	Pascal Ickx/Gérard Langlois van Ophem	B	BMW 1800TISA	98.710
1966	TC	Jacky Ickx/Hubert Hahne	B/D	BMW 2000TI	104.710
1967	TC	Jean-Pierre Gaban/"Pedro"	B	Porsche 911	104.920
1968	TC	Erwin Kremer/Willi Kauhsen/Helmut Kelleners	D	Porsche 911	103.680
1969	TC	Guy Chasseuil/Claude Ballot-Lena	F	Porsche 911	110.610
1970	TC	Gunther Huber/Helmut Kelleners	A/D	BMW 2800CS	110.010
1971	TC	Dieter Glemser/Alex Soler-Roig	D/E	Ford Capri RS	113.521
1972	TC	Jochen Mass/Hans-Joachim Stuck	D	Ford Capri RS2600	116.467
1973	TC	Toine Hezemans/Dieter Quester	NL/A	BMW 3.0 CSL	114.516
1974	TC	Jean Xhenceval/Alain Peltier/Pierre Dieudonne	B	BMW 3.0 CSL	102.376
1975	TC	Pierre Dieudonne/Jean Xhenceval/Hughes de Fierlandt	B	BMW 3.0 CSL	110.018
1976	TC	Jean-Marie Detrin/Nino Demuth/"Chavan"	F/LUX/B	BMW 3.0 CSL	105.840
1977	TC	Eddy Joosen/Jean-Claude Andruet	B/F	BMW 530i	105.730
1978	TC	Gordon Spice/Teddy Pilette	GB/B	Ford Capri	111.732
1979	TC	Jean-Michel Martin/Philippe Martin	B	Ford Capri	79.846
1980	TC	Jean-Michel Martin/Philippe Martin	B	Ford Capri	76.437
1981	TC W+	Pierre Dieudonne/Tom Walkinshaw	B/GB	Mazda RX-7	82.308
1982	TC	Hans Heyer/Armin Hahne/Eddy Joosen	D/D/B	BMW 528i	81.270
1983	TC	Thierry Tassin/Hans Heyer/Armin Hahne	B/D/D	BMW 635 CSi	86.293
1984	TC	Tom Walkinshaw/Hans Heyer/Win Percy	GB/D/GB	Jaguar XJ-S	81.456

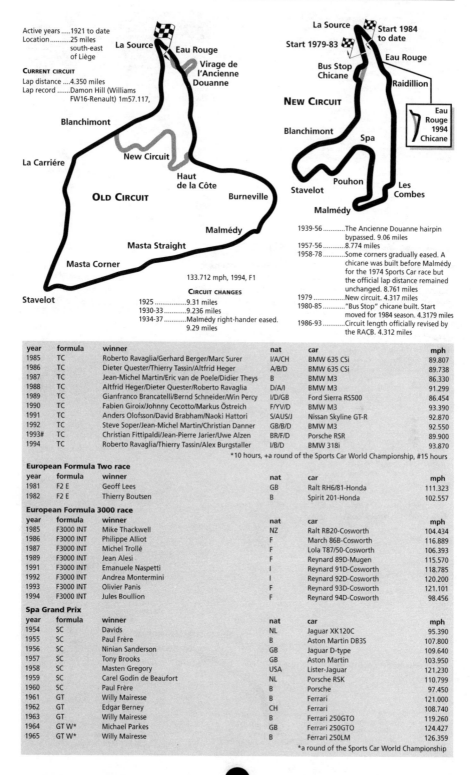

Active years .....1921 to date
Location ....25 miles
south-east
of Liège

CURRENT CIRCUIT
Lap distance ....4.350 miles
Lap record ....Damon Hill (Williams FW16-Renault) 1m57.117,

La Source
Eau Rouge
Virage de l'Ancienne Douanne

Blanchimont

La Carriére
New Circuit
Haut de la Côte
Burneville

OLD CIRCUIT

Malmédy

Masta Straight

Masta Corner

Stavelot

133.712 mph, 1994, F1

CIRCUIT CHANGES
1925 ....9.31 miles
1930-33 ....9.236 miles
1934-37 ....Malmédy right-hander eased. 9.29 miles

La Source
Start 1979-83
Start 1984 to date
Eau Rouge
Bus Stop Chicane
Raidillion

NEW CIRCUIT

Eau Rouge 1994 Chicane

Blanchimont
Spa

Pouhon
Les Combes
Stavelot

Malmédy

1939-56 ....The Ancienne Douanne hairpin bypassed. 9.06 miles
1957-56 ....8.774 miles
1958-78 ....Some corners gradually eased. A chicane was built before Malmédy for the 1974 Sports Car race but the official lap distance remained unchanged. 8.761 miles
1979 ....New circuit. 4.317 miles
1980-85 ...."Bus Stop" chicane built. Start moved for 1984 season. 4.3179 miles
1986-93 ....Circuit length officially revised by the RACB. 4.312 miles

year	formula	winner	nat	car	mph
1985	TC	Roberto Ravaglia/Gerhard Berger/Marc Surer	I/A/CH	BMW 635 CSi	89.807
1986	TC	Dieter Quester/Thierry Tassin/Altfrid Heger	A/B/D	BMW 635 CSi	89.738
1987	TC	Jean-Michel Martin/Eric van de Poele/Didier Theys	B	BMW M3	86.330
1988	TC	Altfrid Heger/Dieter Quester/Roberto Ravaglia	D/A/I	BMW M3	91.299
1989	TC	Gianfranco Brancatelli/Bernd Schneider/Win Percy	I/D/GB	Ford Sierra RS500	86.454
1990	TC	Fabien Giroix/Johnny Cecotto/Markus Östreich	F/YV/D	BMW M3	93.390
1991	TC	Anders Olofsson/David Brabham/Naoki Hattori	S/AUS/J	Nissan Skyline GT-R	92.870
1992	TC	Steve Soper/Jean-Michel Martin/Christian Danner	GB/B/D	BMW M3	92.550
1993#	TC	Christian Fittipaldi/Jean-Pierre Jarier/Uwe Alzen	BR/F/D	Porsche RSR	89.900
1994	TC	Roberto Ravaglia/Thierry Tassin/Alex Burgstaller	I/B/D	BMW 318i	93.870

*10 hours, +a round of the Sports Car World Championship, #15 hours

European Formula Two race

year	formula	winner	nat	car	mph
1981	F2 E	Geoff Lees	GB	Ralt RH6/81-Honda	111.323
1982	F2 E	Thierry Boutsen	B	Spirit 201-Honda	102.557

European Formula 3000 race

year	formula	winner	nat	car	mph
1985	F3000 INT	Mike Thackwell	NZ	Ralt RB20-Cosworth	104.434
1986	F3000 INT	Philippe Alliot	F	March 86B-Cosworth	116.889
1987	F3000 INT	Michel Trollé	F	Lola T87/50-Cosworth	106.393
1989	F3000 INT	Jean Alesi	F	Reynard 89D-Mugen	115.570
1991	F3000 INT	Emanuele Naspetti	I	Reynard 91D-Cosworth	118.785
1992	F3000 INT	Andrea Montermini	I	Reynard 92D-Cosworth	120.200
1993	F3000 INT	Olivier Panis	F	Reynard 93D-Cosworth	121.101
1994	F3000 INT	Jules Boullion	F	Reynard 94D-Cosworth	98.456

Spa Grand Prix

year	formula	winner	nat	car	mph
1954	SC	Davids	NL	Jaguar XK120C	95.390
1955	SC	Paul Frère	B	Aston Martin DB3S	107.800
1956	SC	Ninian Sanderson	GB	Jaguar D-type	109.640
1957	SC	Tony Brooks	GB	Aston Martin	103.950
1958	SC	Masten Gregory	USA	Lister-Jaguar	121.230
1959	SC	Carel Godin de Beaufort	NL	Porsche RSK	110.799
1960	SC	Paul Frère	B	Porsche	97.450
1961	GT	Willy Mairesse	B	Ferrari	121.000
1962	GT	Edgar Berney	CH	Ferrari	108.740
1963	GT	Willy Mairesse	B	Ferrari 250GTO	119.260
1964	GT W*	Michael Parkes	GB	Ferrari 250GTO	124.427
1965	GT W*	Willy Mairesse	B	Ferrari 250LM	126.359

*a round of the Sports Car World Championship

World Sports Car race/Spa 1000 kms

year	formula	winner	nat	car	mph
1966	SC W	Michael Parkes/Ludovico Scarfiotti	GB/I	Ferrari 330P3	131.693
1967	SC W	Jacky Ickx/Dick Thompson	B/USA	Mirage Mk1-Ford	120.481
1968	SC W	Jacky Ickx/Brian Redman	B/GB	Ford GT40	120.516
1969	SC W	Jo Siffert/Brian Redman	CH/GB	Porsche 908/8	141.196
1970	SC W	Jo Siffert/Brian Redman	CH/GB	Porsche 917	149.409
1971	SC W	Pedro Rodriguez/Jackie Oliver	MEX/GB	Porsche 917K	154.759
1972	SC W	Brian Redman/Arturo Merzario	GB/I	Ferrari 312P	145.042
1973	SC W	Derek Bell/Mike Hailwood	GB	Mirage M6-Ford	151.885
1974	SC W	Jacky Ickx/Jean-Pierre Jarier	B/F	Matra-Simca MS670C	147.950
1975	SC W	Henri Pescarolo/Derek Bell	F/GB	Alfa Romeo T33TT/12	133.324
1982	SC W	Jacky Ickx/Jochen Mass	B/D	Porsche 956	102.244
1983	SC W	Jacky Ickx/Jochen Mass	B/D	Porsche 956	108.274
1984	SC W	Stefan Bellof/Derek Bell	D/GB	Porsche 956	105.599
1985	SC W	Bob Wollek/Mauro Baldi/Riccardo Patrese	F/I/I	Lancia LC2	105.220
1986	SC W	Thierry Boutsen/Frank Jelinski	B/D	Porsche 962	111.833
1987	SC W	Martin Brundle/Johnny Dumfries/Raul Boesel	GB/GB/BR	Jaguar XJR-8	101.974
1988	SC W	Mauro Baldi/Stefan Johansson	I/S	Sauber C9/88-Mercedes-Benz	101.607
1989	SC W	Mauro Baldi/Kenneth Acheson	I/GB	Sauber C9/88-Mercedes-Benz	113.706
1990	SC W	Jochen Mass/Karl Wendlinger	D/A	Mercedes-Benz C11	111.165

ZOLDER

Zolder is the circuit at which Gilles Villeneuve died and is famous for little else. A memorial stands above the pits to commemorate the revered French-Canadian. Even before 1982 it was an unloved venue - rough, hard on brakes and littered with chicanes. In 1986, Zolder was renovated with another chicane at the point where Villeneuve had crashed, but international motorsport had already turned its back on Zolder. The highlight has recently been the early-season German Touring Car and F3 meeting.

Belgian Grand Prix see above

European Formula Three race

year	formula	winner	nat	car	mph
1977	F3 E	Piercarlo Ghinzani	I	March 773-Toyota	93.748
1978	F3 E	Teo Fabi	I	March 783-Toyota	78.357
1979	F3 E	Alain Prost	F	Martini MK27-Renault	98.906
1980	F3 E	Thierry Boutsen	B	Martini MK31-Toyota	95.201
	F3 E	Philippe Streiff	F	Martini MK31-Toyota	100.839
1981	F3 E	Mauro Baldi	I	March 813-Alfa Romeo	102.901
1982	F3 E	Oscar Larrauri	RA	Euroracing 101-Alfa Romeo	101.655
1983	F3 E	Emanuele Pirro	I	Ralt RT3/83-Alfa Romeo	102.348
1984	F3 E	John Nielsen	DK	Ralt RT3/84-Volkswagen	102.885

European Formula Two race

year	formula	winner	nat	car	mph
1975	F2 E	Michel Leclère	F	March 752-BMW	104.784
1980	F2 E	Huub Rothengatter	NL	Toleman TG280-Hart	107.725
1983	F2 E	Jonathan Palmer	GB	Ralt RH6/83-Honda	110.399

International Formula 3000 race

year	formula	winner	nat	car	mph
1988	F3000 INT	Olivier Grouillard	F	Lola T88/50-Cosworth	104.234

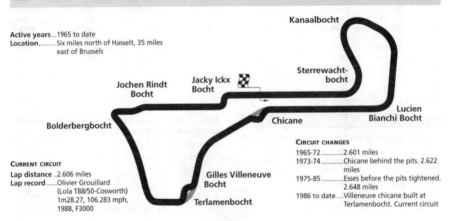

Active years...1965 to date
Location.........Six miles north of Hasselt, 35 miles east of Brussels

Kanaalbocht

Sterrewacht-bocht

Jochen Rindt Bocht

Jacky Ickx Bocht

Lucien Bianchi Bocht

Bolderbergbocht

Chicane

CURRENT CIRCUIT
Lap distance ..2.606 miles
Lap record ......Olivier Grouillard
(Lola T88/50-Cosworth)
1m28.27, 106.283 mph,
1988, F3000

Gilles Villeneuve Bocht

Terlamenbocht

CIRCUIT CHANGES
1965-72 ....2.601 miles
1973-74 ....Chicane behind the pits. 2.622 miles
1975-85 ....Esses before the pits tightened. 2.648 miles
1986 to date ....Villeneuve chicane built at Terlamenbocht. Current circuit

BRAZIL

MAJOR CHAMPIONSHIPS

Torneio Formula Two Championship

Brazil's equivalent to the Argentinian Temporada

year	driver	nat	car
1971	Emerson Fittipaldi	BR	Lotus 69-Ford
1972	Emerson Fittipaldi	BR	Lotus 69-Ford

Brazilian Formula Three Championship

Run concurrently with the Sud-Am F3 Championship until 1993

year	driver	nat	car
1989	Christian Fittipaldi	BR	Reynard 883-Alfa Romeo
1990	Osvaldo Negri Jr	BR	Ralt RT32-Volkswagen
1991	Marcos Gueiros	BR	Ralt RT33-Mugen
1992	Marcos Gueiros	BR	Ralt RT33-Mugen
1993	Fernando Croceri	RA	Ralt RT33-Mugen
1994	Cristiano da Matta	BR	Dallara 394-Mugen

Brazilian Touring Car Championship

year	driver	nat	car
1988	Andreas Mattheis	BR	Volkswagen Passat 1.6 turbo
1989	Gunnar Volmer/		
	Antonio da Matta	BR	Volkswagen Passat 1.6
1990	Andreas Mattheis/		
	Ricardo Cosac	BR	Volkswagen Passat 1.6
1991	Paulo Gomes/		
	Claudio Girotto	BR	Volkswagen Passat Voyage 1.6

1992	Andreas Mattheis/		
	Paulo Judice	BR	Ford Escort 1.6
1993	Andreas Mattheis/		
	Paulo Judice	BR	Ford Escort 1.8
1994	Egon Herzfield/		
	Vicente Daudt	BR	Ford Escort 1.8

Brazilian Stock Car Championship

year	driver	nat	car
1979	Paulo Gomes	BR	Chevrolet Opala
1980	Ingo Hoffman	BR	Chevrolet Opala
1981	Affonso Giaffone Jr	BR	Chevrolet Opala
1982	"Alencar Jr"	BR	Chevrolet Opala
1983	Paulo Gomes	BR	Chevrolet Opala
1984	Paulo Gomes	BR	Chevrolet Opala
1985	Ingo Hoffman	BR	Chevrolet Opala
1986	Marcos Gracia	BR	Chevrolet Opala
1987	José "Zeca"		
	Giaffone	BR	Chevrolet Opala
1988	Fabio Sotto Mayor	BR	Chevrolet Opala
1989	Ingo Hoffman	BR	Chevrolet Opala
1990	Ingo Hoffman	BR	Chevrolet Opala
1991	Ingo Hoffman/		
	Angelo Giombelli	BR	Chevrolet Opala
1992	Ingo Hoffman/		
	Angelo Giombelli	BR	Chevrolet Opala
1993	Ingo Hoffman/		
	Angelo Giombelli	BR	Chevrolet Opala
1994	Ingo Hoffman	BR	Chevrolet Opala

MAJOR INTERNATIONAL RACES

BRAZILIAN GRAND PRIX

year	formula	circuit	winner	nat	car	mph
1972	F1	Interlagos	Carlos Reutemann	RA	Brabham BT34-Ford	112.882
1973	F1 W	Interlagos	Emerson Fittipaldi	BR	Lotus 72D-Ford	114.219
1974	F1 W	Interlagos	Emerson Fittipaldi	BR	McLaren M23-Ford	112.226
1975	F1 W	Interlagos	Carlos Pace	BR	Brabham BT44B-Ford	113.390
1976	F1 W	Interlagos	Niki Lauda	A	Ferrari 312T	112.751
1977	F1 W	Interlagos	Carlos Reutemann	RA	Ferrari 312T2	112.913
1978	F1 W	Rio de Janeiro	Carlos Reutemann	RA	Ferrari 312T2	107.423
1979	F1 W	Interlagos	Jacques Laffite	F	Ligier JS11-Ford	118.514
1980	F1 W	Interlagos	René Arnoux	F	Renault RE20	117.406
1981	F1 W	Rio de Janeiro	Carlos Reutemann	RA	Williams FW07C-Ford	96.589
1982	F1 W	Rio de Janeiro	Alain Prost	F	Renault RE30B	113.018
1983	F1 W	Rio de Janeiro	Nelson Piquet	BR	Brabham BT52-BMW	108.944
1984	F1 W	Rio de Janeiro	Alain Prost	F	McLaren MP4/2-TAG Porsche	111.540
1985	F1 W	Rio de Janeiro	Alain Prost	F	McLaren MP4/2B-TAG Porsche	112.793
1986	F1 W	Rio de Janeiro	Nelson Piquet	BR	Williams FW11-Honda	114.937
1987	F1 W	Rio de Janeiro	Alain Prost	F	McLaren MP4/3-TAG Porsche	114.696
1988	F1 W	Rio de Janeiro	Alain Prost	F	McLaren MP4/4-Honda	117.086
1989	F1 W	Rio de Janeiro	Nigel Mansell	GB	Ferrari 640	115.592
1990	F1 W	Interlagos	Alain Prost	F	Ferrari 641	117.577
1991	F1 W	Interlagos	Ayrton Senna	BR	McLaren MP4/6-Honda	116.246
1992	F1 W	Interlagos	Nigel Mansell	GB	Williams FW14B-Renault	118.172
1993	F1 W	Interlagos	Ayrton Senna	BR	McLaren MP4/8-Ford	102.883
1994	F1 W	Interlagos	Michael Schumacher	D	Benetton B194-Ford	127.694

CIRCUITS AND OTHER RACES

BRASILIA

A modern racing facility built at a reputed cost of $3.5 million and opened in 1974. The inaugural non-championship Presidenta Medici GP attracted a crowd of 85,000 but sadly this was the only international race to have been held here.

Presidenta Medici Grand Prix

year	formula	winner	nat	car	mph
1974	F1	Emerson Fittipaldi	BR	McLaren M23-Ford	108.348

Racing Around the World

BRASILIA

Curva Scavone

Curva Le Guezec

Juncão

Curve Fittipaldi

Ferradu Ra

Retão Julio Delamare

Entrada Do Miolo

Active years...1974 to date
Location.........Brasilia
Lap distance ..3.402 miles
Lap record.....Emerson Fittipaldi (McLaren M23-
Ford), 1m51.62, 109.722 mph,
1974, F1

Curve
Do Moco

INTERLAGOS

AUTODROMO JOSÉ CARLOS PACE

Interlagos was a magnificent facility in its original form, the first corner as testing as any in
Grand Prix racing. The track followed a tortuous
course, winding back on itself in a natural bowl
in the smog-filled suburbs of Sao Paulo. When

The 1991 Brazilian Grand Prix at the refurbished Interlagos

the circuit regained the Brazilian Grand Prix in
1990, it was on a reduced but still demanding
configuration. The new Senna "S" had replaced
the first corner and two more link roads reduced
the length to 2.687 miles. The circuit is now
named after Carlos Pace who scored his only
Grand Prix win here in 1975. This was Senna
country, and when he spun out of the 1994 race
the disappointed crowd filed home.

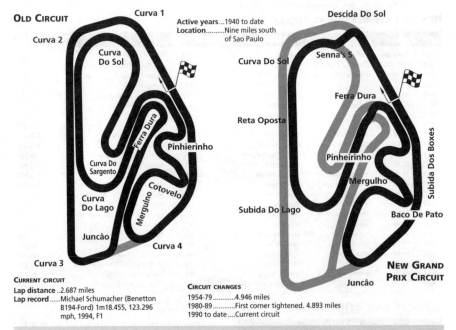

OLD CIRCUIT

Curva 1

Curva 2

Curva Do Sol

Ferra Dura

Pinhierinho

Curva Do Sargento

Cotovelo

Curva Do Lago

Mergulho

Juncão

Curva 4

Curva 3

CURRENT CIRCUIT
Lap distance ..2.687 miles
Lap record.....Michael Schumacher (Benetton
B194-Ford) 1m18.455, 123.296
mph, 1994, F1

Active years...1940 to date
Location.........Nine miles south
of Sao Paulo

Descida Do Sol

Senna's S

Curva Do Sol

Ferra Dura

Reta Oposta

Pinheirinho

Mergulho

Subida Do Lago

Subida Dos Boxes

Baco De Pato

NEW GRAND PRIX CIRCUIT

Juncão

CIRCUIT CHANGES
1954-79 ....4.946 miles
1980-89 ....First corner tightened. 4.893 miles
1990 to date ....Current circuit

Brazilian Grand Prix see above

Torneio Formula Two races

year	formula	winner	nat	car	mph
1971	F2	Emerson Fittipaldi	BR	Lotus 69-Ford	108.100
	F2	Emerson Fittipaldi	BR	Lotus 69-Ford	105.934
1972	F2	Emerson Fittipaldi	BR	Lotus 69-Ford	109.729
	F2	Carlos Pace	BR	Surtees TS15-Ford	111.274
	F2	Mike Hailwood	GB	Surtees TS10-Ford	110.684

RIO DE JANEIRO

AUTODROMO NELSON PIQUET, JACAREPAGUA
Built on a reclaimed marsh, Rio's Jacarepagua circuit is as uninspiring as Interlagos is demanding. It is flat, with constant radius corners and a long back straight. Races were

Active years...1978 to date
Location..........20 miles west of Rio de
Janeiro
Lap distance ..3.126 miles
Lap record......Gerhard Berger (Ferrari
F187) 1m32.943,
121.081 mph,
1988, F1

normally run in stifling heat and humidity. However, Alain Prost must have enjoyed it, winning half of the ten Brazilian Grands Prix held here before the race returned to Interlagos.

Brazilian Grand Prix see above

CANADA

MAJOR CHAMPIONSHIPS

Can-Am Challenge	Formula Atlantic
see page 340–41	see United States

MAJOR INTERNATIONAL RACES

CANADIAN GRAND PRIX

year	formula	circuit	winner	nat	car	mph
1961	SC	Mosport Park	Pete Ryan	CDN	Lotus 19-Climax	88.380
1962	SC	Mosport Park	Masten Gregory	USA	Lotus 19-Climax	88.520
1963	SC	Mosport Park	Pedro Rodriguez	MEX	Ferrari 250P	91.550
1964	SC	Mosport Park	Pedro Rodriguez	MEX	Ferrari 330P	94.360
1965	SC	Mosport Park	Jim Hall	USA	Chaparral 2B-Chevrolet	93.780
1966	Can-Am	Mosport Park	Mark Donohue	USA	Lola T70-Chevrolet	101.870
1967	F1 W	Mosport Park	Jack Brabham	AUS	Brabham BT24-Repco	82.647
1968	F1 W	St Jovite	Denny Hulme	NZ	McLaren M7A-Ford	97.223
1969	F1 W	Mosport Park	Jacky Ickx	B	Brabham BT26-Ford	111.185
1970	F1 W	St Jovite	Jacky Ickx	B	Ferrari 312B	101.269
1971	F1 W	Mosport Park	Jackie Stewart	GB	Tyrrell 003-Ford	81.956
1972	F1 W	Mosport Park	Jackie Stewart	GB	Tyrrell 005-Ford	114.282
1973	F1 W	Mosport Park	Peter Revson	USA	McLaren M23-Ford	99.130
1974	F1 W	Mosport Park	Emerson Fittipaldi	BR	McLaren M23-Ford	117.520
1976	F1 W	Mosport Park	James Hunt	GB	McLaren M23-Ford	117.843
1977	F1 W	Mosport Park	Jody Scheckter	ZA	Wolf WR1-Ford	118.032
1978	F1 W	Montreal	Gilles Villeneuve	CDN	Ferrari 312T3	99.671
1979	F1 W	Montreal	Alan Jones	AUS	Williams FW07-Ford	105.577
1980	F1 W	Montreal	Alan Jones	AUS	Williams FW07B-Ford	107.794
1981	F1 W	Montreal	Jacques Laffite	F	Ligier JS17-Matra	85.301
1982	F1 W	Montreal	Nelson Piquet	BR	Brabham BT50-BMW	107.895
1983	F1 W	Montreal	René Arnoux	F	Ferrari 126C2B	106.035
1984	F1 W	Montreal	Nelson Piquet	BR	Brabham BT53-BMW	108.162
1985	F1 W	Montreal	Michele Alboreto	I	Ferrari 156/85	108.535
1986	F1 W	Montreal	Nigel Mansell	GB	Williams FW11-Honda	110.734
1988	F1 W	Montreal	Ayrton Senna	BR	McLaren MP4/4-Honda	113.192
1989	F1 W	Montreal	Thierry Boutsen	B	Williams FW12C-Renault	93.030
1990	F1 W	Montreal	Ayrton Senna	BR	McLaren MP4/5B-Honda	111.304
1991	F1 W	Montreal	Nelson Piquet	BR	Benetton B191-Ford	115.291
1992	F1 W	Montreal	Gerhard Berger	A	McLaren MP4/7A-Honda	117.332
1993	F1 W	Montreal	Alain Prost	F	Williams FW15C-Renault	117.867
1994	F1 W	Montreal	Michael Schumacher	D	Benetton B194-Ford	109.509

CIRCUITS AND OTHER RACES

MONTREAL

CIRCUIT GILLES VILLENEUVE
With young Québecois Gilles Villeneuve rapidly becoming a major star in 1978 and concerns for

the safety of Mosport Park being expressed, a new circuit in Montreal was prepared in record time to hold the Canadian GP. It was on the man-made Ile de Notre Dame in the middle of the St Lawrence Seaway. Villeneuve provided the perfect start by winning his first Grand Prix in the inaugural race. When Villeneuve was killed in 1982, the circuit was renamed in his honour. Sadly, that year's race was also a tragic affair: Ricardo Paletti was killed in a horrific startline accident. Montreal's attempt to diversify and hold a Sports Car race in 1990 was marred when Jesus Pareja's Brun Porsche crashed, thankfully without injury.

Canadian Grand Prix see above

World Sports Car race

year	formula	winner	nat	car	mph
1990	SC W	Mauro Baldi/Jean-Louis Schlesser	I/F	Mercedes-Benz C11	95.363

MONTREAL

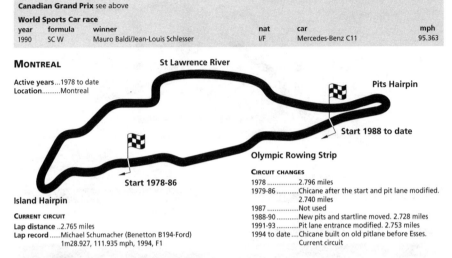

St Lawrence River

Active years...1978 to date
Location..........Montreal

Pits Hairpin

Start 1988 to date

Olympic Rowing Strip

CIRCUIT CHANGES
1978 ....2.796 miles
1979-86 ....Chicane after the start and pit lane modified.
2.740 miles
1987 ....Not used
1988-90 ....New pits and startline moved. 2.728 miles
1991-93 ....Pit lane entrance modified. 2.753 miles
1994 to date ....Chicane built on old pitlane before Esses.
Current circuit

Start 1978-86

Island Hairpin

CURRENT CIRCUIT
Lap distance ..2.765 miles
Lap record ......Michael Schumacher (Benetton B194-Ford)
1m28.927, 111.935 mph, 1994, F1

MOSPORT PARK

A beautiful and sweeping circuit, Mosport Park held the first international race in Canada when Stirling Moss won the 1961 Player's 200. It was always renowned as a drivers' circuit although changeable weather marred many a meeting. In the late 1970s the circuit's safety facilities were questioned and Mosport lost the Canadian GP to Montreal. Sports Cars also left Mosport after Manfred Winkelhock was killed in 1985.

Canadian Grand Prix see above

Player's 200/Can-Am race

year	formula	winner	nat	car	mph
1961	SC	Stirling Moss	GB	Lotus	86.740
1962	SC	Masten Gregory	USA	Lotus	90.270
1963	SC	Chuck Daigh	USA	Lotus 19-Climax	90.930
1964	SC	Bruce McLaren	NZ	Cooper-Oldsmobile	92.510
1965	SC	John Surtees	GB	Lola T70-Chevrolet	96.515
1966	Can-Am	Bruce McLaren	NZ	McLaren Elva-Oldsmobile	n/a
1967	Can-Am	Denny Hulme	NZ	McLaren M6A-Chevrolet	105.926
1969	Can-Am	Bruce McLaren	NZ	McLaren M8B-Chevrolet	105.901
1970	Can-Am	Dan Gurney	USA	McLaren M8D-Chevrolet	110.214
1971	Can-Am	Denny Hulme	NZ	McLaren M8F-Chevrolet	109.330
1972	Can-Am	Denny Hulme	NZ	McLaren M20-Chevrolet	110.660
1973	Can-Am	Charlie Kemp	USA	Porsche 917/10	108.645
1974	Can-Am	Jackie Oliver	GB	Shadow DN4A-Chevrolet	111.990
1976	SC W	Jackie Oliver	GB	Shadow DN4A-Chevrolet	111.393
1977	Can-Am	Patrick Tambay	F	Lola T333CS-Chevrolet	111.819
1978	Can-Am	Alan Jones	AUS	Lola T333CS-Chevrolet	115.374
1979	Can-Am	Jacky Ickx	B	Lola T333CS-Chevrolet	113.673
1980	Can-Am	Patrick Tambay	F	Lola T530-Chevrolet	115.145
1981	Can-Am	Teo Fabi	I	March 817-Chevrolet	115.526
	Can-Am	Teo Fabi	I	March 817-Chevrolet	117.279
1982	Can-Am	Al Unser Jr	USA	Frissbee GR3-Chevrolet	110.350
	Can-Am	Al Unser Jr	USA	Frissbee GR3-Chevrolet	116.658
1983	Can-Am	Jacques Villeneuve	CDN	Frissbee GR3-Chevrolet	111.780
1983	Can-Am	Jim Crawford	GB	Ensign RK180B-Ford	116.310
1984	Can-Am	Michael Roe	IRL	VDS 002-Chevrolet	95.740
	Can-Am	Michael Roe	IRL	VDS 002-Chevrolet	113.750
1985	Can-Am	Horst Kroll	USA	Frissbee-Chevrolet	n/a
	Can-Am	Rick Miaskiewicz	USA	Frissbee-Chevrolet	n/a
1986	Can-Am	Horst Kroll	USA	Frissbee KR3-Chevrolet	n/a
	Can-Am	Paul Tracy	CDN	Frissbee KR3-Chevrolet	n/a

MOSPORT PARK

Active years...1961 to date
Location..........60 miles east of Toronto
Lap distance ..2.459 miles
Lap record ......Hans-Joachim Stuck
(Porsche 962) 1m09.775,
126.871 mph, 1985,
Group C Sports Cars

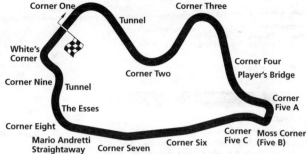

Corner One
Tunnel
Corner Three
White's Corner
Corner Four
Player's Bridge
Corner Two
Corner Nine
Tunnel
Corner Five A
The Esses
Corner Eight
Mario Andretti Straightaway
Corner Seven
Corner Six
Corner Five C
Moss Corner (Five B)

Indycar race

year	formula	winner	nat	car	mph
1967	Indycar	Bobby Unser	USA	Eagle 67-Ford	99.609
	Indycar	Bobby Unser	USA	Eagle 67-Ford	n/a
1968	Indycar	Dan Gurney	USA	Eagle 68-Ford/Weslake	103.993
	Indycar	Dan Gurney	USA	Eagle 68-Ford/Weslake	106.784
1977	Indycar	AJ Foyt Jr	USA	Coyote-Foyt/Ford	90.723
1978	Indycar	Danny Ongais	USA	Parnelli VPJ6B-Cosworth	87.164

World Sports Car race

year	formula	winner	nat	car	mph
1976	SC WSC	Jackie Oliver	GB	Shadow DN4A-Chevrolet	111.393
1977	SC W	Peter Gregg/Bob Wollek	USA/F	Porsche 934	99.630
1980	SC W	John Fitzpatrick/Brian Redman	GB	Porsche 935-K3	100.354
1981	SC W	Rolf Stommelen/Harald Grohs	D	Porsche 935	93.665
1984	SC W	Jacky Ickx/Jochen Mass	B/D	Porsche 956	103.489
1985	SC W	Derek Bell/Hans-Joachim Stuck	GB/D	Porsche 962	104.941

SANAIR SUPERSPEEDWAY

A strange short tri-oval which briefly held a round of the Indycar World Series at the behest of the Molson brewery. Rick Mears crashed during the inaugural 1984 race, severely crushing his legs. Although the circuit was smooth it was far too tight for Indycars. Sanair slipped from the Indycar calendar when Molson switched their sponsorship to a new race in Toronto.

Active years...1984-86
Location..........St Pie, eastern
suburbs of
Montreal
Lap distance ..0.826 miles
Lap record ......Qualifying:
Rick Mears
(Penske PC15-
Chevrolet),
20.074s,
148.132 mph,
1986, Indycar

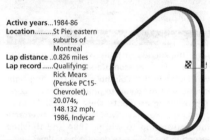

Indycar race

year	formula	winner	nat	car	mph
1984	Indycar	Danny Sullivan	USA	Lola T800-Cosworth	111.707
1985	Indycar	Johnny Rutherford	USA	March 85C-Cosworth	89.996
1986	Indycar	Bobby Rahal	USA	March 86C-Cosworth	103.157

ST JOVITE

Like Mosport Park with which it shared the Canadian GP, St Jovite was a picturesque, undulating road course. The highlight was Namerow Corner which cars entered steeply uphill and exited downhill. However, the circuit was narrow and bumpy and when the drivers complained after the 1970 Grand Prix the race did not return.

Active years...1964-70, 1975 to date
Location..........Lake Moore, 90 miles
from Montreal

CURRENT CIRCUIT
Lap distance ..2.650 miles

Lap record ......Clay Regazzoni (Ferrari 312B) 1m32.2,
103.471 mph, 1970, F1

CIRCUIT CHANGES
1964-65 ....1.5 miles
1966 to date ....Extended. Current circuit

Racing Around the World

Canadian Grand Prix see above

Indycar race

year	formula	winner	nat	car	mph
1967	Indycar	Mario Andretti	USA	Brawner/Hawk-Ford	87.151
	Indycar	Mario Andretti	USA	Brawner/Hawk-Ford	92.401
1968	Indycar	Mario Andretti	USA	Brawner/Hawk-Ford	96.492
	Indycar	Mario Andretti	USA	Brawner/Hawk-Ford	90.022

TORONTO

EXHIBITION PLACE

Run under the impressive gateway landmark, Toronto is a fast circuit that now rivals Long Beach as North America's best street race. Laid out in the grounds of the Canadian National Exhibition, it is a cross between a street circuit and a demanding road course - combining the best of both types of venue. Michael Andretti scored his fourth Toronto victory in the 1994 race.

Active years...1986 to date
Location.........12 miles west of central Toronto

Lap distance ..1.780 miles
Lap record ......Qualifying: Robby Gordon
(Lola T94/00-Ford), 58.154s,
110.191 mph, 1994, Indycar

Molson Indy Toronto

year	formula	winner	nat	car	mph
1986	Indycar	Bobby Rahal	USA	March 86C-Cosworth	87.414
1987	Indycar	Emerson Fittipaldi	BR	March 87C-Chevrolet	95.991
1988	Indycar	Al Unser Jr	USA	March 88C-Chevrolet	91.994
1989	Indycar	Michael Andretti	USA	Lola T89/00-Chevrolet	90.901
1990	Indycar	Al Unser Jr	USA	Lola T90/00-Chevrolet	74.127
1991	Indycar	Michael Andretti	USA	Lola T91/00-Chevrolet	99.143
1992	Indycar	Michael Andretti	USA	Lola T92/00-Ford	97.898
1993	Indycar	Paul Tracy	CDN	Penske PC22-Chevrolet	96.510
1994	Indycar	Michael Andretti	USA	Reynard 94I-Ford	96.673

VANCOUVER

After the success of Molson's Toronto race, the brewing giant sponsored a second street race in Vancouver, British Columbia. The resulting tight nine-turn circuit seems to promote contact racing and resulting accidents. Only Michael Andretti and Al Unser Jr have won here. Unser overcame food poisoning to win in 1994 and finished second in the 1992 race despite his Galmer being launched into the air after crashing with Emerson Fittipaldi early in the race. The track has not been popular with the drivers who have complained about the lack of passing opportunities.

Active years...1990 to date
Location.........Pacific Place by
Vancouver's
waterfront

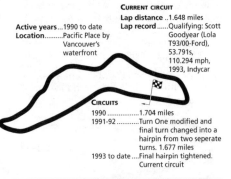

CURRENT CIRCUIT
Lap distance ..1.648 miles
Lap record ......Qualifying: Scott
Goodyear (Lola
T93/00-Ford),
53.791s,
110.294 mph,
1993, Indycar

CIRCUITS
1990 ....1.704 miles
1991-92 ....Turn One modified and
final turn changed into a
hairpin from two seperate
turns. 1.677 miles
1993 to date ....Final hairpin tightened.
Current circuit

Molson Indy Vancouver

year	formula	winner	nat	car	mph
1990	Indycar	Al Unser Jr	USA	Lola T90/00-Chevrolet	77.345
1991	Indycar	Michael Andretti	USA	Lola T91/00-Chevrolet	93.888
1992	Indycar	Michael Andretti	USA	Lola T92/00-Ford	98.796
1993	Indycar	Al Unser Jr	USA	Lola T93/00-Chevrolet	91.794
1994	Indycar	Al Unser Jr	USA	Penske PC23-Ilmor	88.896

CURACAO

CIRCUITS AND RACES

WILLEMSTAD

A bumpy street circuit around downtown Willemstad that was used for the sole Curacao Grand Prix, a non-championship Formula 3000 race in 1985. When the organizers, who had commissioned the Sports Car Club of America to run the event, realized that there was no possibility of a full Grand Prix the exercise was not repeated.

Curacao Grand Prix

year	formula	winner	nat	car	mph
1985	F3000	John Nielsen	DK	Ralt RB20-Cosworth	75.64

WILLEMSTAD CIRCUIT

Active years...1985
Location.........Willemstad, Curacao
Lap distance ..2.206 miles
Lap record ......John Nielsen (Ralt RB20-
              Cosworth), 1m44.725, 75.833 mph,
              1985, F3000

CZECH REPUBLIC

MAJOR INTERNATIONAL RACES

CZECH GRAND PRIX						
year	formula	circuit	winner	nat	car	mph
1930	GP	Brno	Hermann zu Leiningen/			
			Heinrich-Joachim von Morgen	D	Bugatti T35B	62.781
1931	GP	Brno	Louis Chiron	MC	Bugatti T51	73.262
1932	GP	Brno	Louis Chiron	MC	Bugatti T51	66.564
1933	GP	Brno	Louis Chiron	MC	Alfa Romeo Tipo-B "P3"	63.611
1934	GP	Brno	Hans Stuck	D	Auto Union A	79.118
1935	GP	Brno	Bernd Rosemeyer	D	Auto Union B	82.396
1937	GP	Brno	Rudolf Caracciola	D	Mercedes-Benz W125	86.041
1949	F1	Brno	Peter Whitehead	GB	Ferrari 125	78.680
1950	F1	Brno	Vaclav Hovorka	CS	Maserati	n/a

Known as Masaryk GP 1930-37

CIRCUITS AND OTHER RACES

BRNO

Until 1986 Brno was a daunting road circuit with echoes of a previous era, still visited by the European Touring Car Championship. A new motorsport complex was built in 1987 in an attempt to lure modern Grand Prix racing to the Czech Republic. Like the new Nürburgring it was rather bland in comparison to the old circuit. The original venue was 18 miles of dusty, narrow roads south-west of the town and was the longest circuit used at the time. Bernd Rosemeyer scored his first Grand Prix win here in 1935 but Hitler's occupation of Czechoslovakia ended racing in 1937. A reduced 11-mile circuit (omitting the challenging Östrovacice section), opened in 1949 and 200,000 spectators saw Peter Whitehead's victory in the Czech GP that year. Local, Vaclav Hovorka, driving a Maserati, won in 1950 but racing did not return until 1962 when a Formula Junior race was held. The old pits and barriers still exist to provide a reminder of the past.

Active years...Road course: 1930-86.
              Automotodrom: 1987 to date
Location.........Nine miles north-west of Brno,
              80 miles north-west of Bratislava

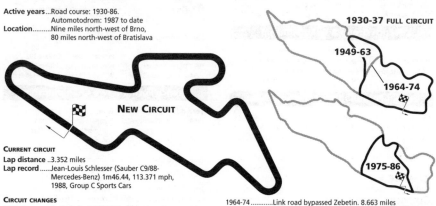

1930-37 FULL CIRCUIT

1949-63

1964-74

NEW CIRCUIT

1975-86

CURRENT CIRCUIT
Lap distance ..3.352 miles
Lap record ......Jean-Louis Schlesser (Sauber C9/88-
              Mercedes-Benz) 1m46.44, 113.371 mph,
              1988, Group C Sports Cars

CIRCUIT CHANGES
1930-37 ....Anti-clockwise. 18.109 miles
1949-63 ....Connecting road from Zebetin to Popuvky built.
              Direction of racing now clockwise. 11.061 miles
1964-74 ....Link road bypassed Zebetin. 8.663 miles
1975-86 ....Another new road linked the start to Kohoutovice.
              6.789 miles
1987 to date ....New Automotodrom built. Current circuit

Masaryk and Czech Grand Prix see above					
World Sports Car race					
year	formula	winner	nat	car	mph
1988	SC W	Jean-Louis Schlesser/Jochen Mass	F/D	Sauber C9/88-Mercedes-Benz	106.373

EUROPEAN GP

A courtesy title awarded annually by the FIA to Europe's World Championship races in rotation. The honour of being the European Grand Prix was of little importance until 1983. Since then the race has been a Grand Prix in its own right, staged five times when other races have been cancelled.

EUROPEAN GRAND PRIX

year	formula	circuit	winner	nat	car	mph
1983	F1 W	Brands Hatch	Nelson Piquet	BR	Brabham BT52B-BMW	123.165
1984	F1 W	Nürburgring	Alain Prost	F	McLaren MP4/2-TAG Porsche	119.138
1985	F1 W	Brands Hatch	Nigel Mansell	GB	Williams FW10-Honda	126.507
1993	F1 W	Donington Park	Ayrton Senna	BR	McLaren MP4/8-Ford	102.910
1994	F1 W	Jerez	Michael Schumacher	D	Benetton B194-Ford	113.387

FRANCE

MAJOR CHAMPIONSHIPS

French Supertourism Championship

year	driver	nat	team	car
1976	Jean-Pierre Beltoise	F	-	BMW 3.0 CSI
1977	Jean-Pierre Beltoise	F	-	BMW 530 IUS
1978	Lucien Guitteny	F	-	Ford Capri RS
1979	Dany Snobeck	F	Snobeck Racing	Ford Capri RS
1980	Dany Snobeck	F	Snobeck Racing	Ford Escort RS2000
1981	Jean-Pierre Malcher	F	Garage du Bac	BMW 320i
1982	René Metge	F	Tom Walkinshaw Racing	Rover 3500
1983	Alain Cudini	F	Snobeck Racing	Alfa Romeo GTV6
1984	Dany Snobeck	F	Snobeck Racing	Alfa Romeo GTV6
1985	Jean-Louis Schlesser	F	Marlboro	Rover Vitesse
1986	Xavier Lapeyre	F	ROC Compétition	Audi 200 Quattro
1987	Erik Comas	F	Sonica	Renault 5 Maxi-Turbo
1988	Jean Ragnotti	F	Sonica	Renault 21 turbo 4 x 4
1989	Jean-Pierre Malcher	F	Pelras Compétition	BMW M3
1990	Jean-Pierre Malcher	F	Pelras Compétition	BMW M3
1991	Xavier Lapeyre	F	ROC Compétition	Audi 80 Quattro
1992	Marc Sourd	F	ROC Compétition	Audi 80 Quattro
1993	Frank Biela	D	ROC Compétition	Audi 80 Quattro
1994	Laurent Aiello	F	Peugeot Sport	Peugeot 405 Mi16

French Group A Championship

year	driver	nat	team	car
1987	Fabien Giroix	F	Garage du Bac	BMW M3
1988	Jean-Pierre Malcher	F	Pelras Compétition	BMW M3

French Formula Three Championship

year	driver	nat	team	car
1964	Henry Grandsire	F	Henry Grandsire	Alpine T64-Renault
1965	Jean-Pierre Beltoise	F	Matra Sports	Matra MS5-Ford
1966	Johnny Servoz-Gavin	F	Matra Sports	Matra MS5-Ford
1967	Henri Pescarolo	F	Matra Sports	Matra MS5-Ford
1968	François Cevert	F	Volant Shell	Tecno 68-Ford
1969	François Mazet	F	Volant Shell	Tecno 69-Ford/ Lotus 59-Ford
1970	Jean-Pierre Jaussaud	F	Tecno Racing Cars	Tecno 69-Ford/ Martini MW5-Ford
1971	Patrick Depailler	F	Automobiles Alpine	Alpine A360-Renault
1972	Michel Leclère	F	Automobiles Alpine	Alpine A364-Renault
1973	Jacques Laffite	F	Automobiles Martini	Martini MK12-Ford
1974-77	NO SERIES			

year	driver	nat	team	car
1978	Alain Prost	F	Automobiles Martini	Martini MK21B-Renault
	Jean-Louis Schlesser	F	Jean-Louis Schlesser	Chevron B38-Toyota
1979	Alain Prost	F	Automobiles Martini	Martini MK27-Renault
1980	Alain Ferté	F	Automobiles Martini	Martini MK27/31-Renault
1981	Philippe Streiff	F	Ecurie Motul Nogaro	Martini MK34-Alfa Romeo
1982	Pierre Petit	F	Dave Price Racing	Ralt RT3-Toyota/ Ralt RT3-Volkswagen
1983	Michel Ferté	F	ORECA	Martini MK39-Alfa Romeo
1984	Olivier Grouillard	F	ORECA	Martini MK42-Alfa Romeo
1985	Pierre-Henri Raphanel	F	ORECA	Martini MK45-Alfa Romeo
1986	Yannick Dalmas	F	ORECA	Martini MK49-Volkswagen
1987	Jean Alesi	F	ORECA	Martini MK49/52-Alfa Romeo/ Dallara 387-Alfa Romeo
1988	Erik Comas	F	ORECA	Dallara 388-Alfa Romeo
1989	Jean-Marc Gounon	F	ORECA	Reynard 893-Alfa Romeo
1990	Eric Hélary	F	Formula Project	Reynard 903-Mugen/ Ralt RT34-Mugen
1991	Christophe Bouchut	F	Graff Racing	Ralt RT33-Volkswagen
1992	Franck Lagorce	F	Promatecme	Dallara 392-Opel
1993	Didier Cottaz	F	Formula Project	Dallara 393-Fiat
1994	Jean-Philippe Belloc	F	Winfield Racing	Dallara 394-Fiat

French Formula Two Championship

year	driver	nat	team	car
1964	Jack Brabham	AUS	Brabham Racing Organisation	Brabham BT10-Ford
1965*	Jim Clark	GB	Ron Harris Team Lotus	Lotus 35-Ford
1966	Jack Brabham	AUS	Brabham Racing Organisation	Brabham BT18-Honda/Brabham BT21-Honda
1967	Jochen Rindt	A	Winkelmann Racing	Brabham BT23-Ford
1968	Jackie Stewart	GB	Matra International	Matra MS7-Ford

*Officially a team championship but Clark scored all his team's points

French Formula Renault Championship

year	driver	nat	car
1968	Jean Max	F	Grac MT5-Renault
1969	Denis Dayan	F	Grac MT5-Renault

1970	François Lacarrau	F	Martini MK4-Renault
1971	Michel Leclère	F	Alpine-Renault
1972	Jacques Laffite	F	Martini MK8-Renault
1973-74	NO FRENCH SERIES		
1975	Christian Debias	F	Martini MK15R-Renault
1976	Alain Prost	F	Martini MK17-Renault
1977	Joel Gouhier	F	Martini MK20-Renault
1978	Philippe Alliot	F	Martini MK24-Renault
1979	Alain Ferté	F	Martini MK26-Renault
1980	Denis Morin	F	Martini MK30-Renault
1981	Philippe Renault	F	Martini MK33-Renault
1982	Gilles Lempereur	F	Martini MK36-Renault
1983	Jean-Pierre Hoursourigaray	F	Martini MK38-Renault
1984	Yannick Dalmas	F	Martini MK41-Renault
1985	Eric Bernard	F	Martini MK44-Renault
1986	Erik Comas	F	Martini MK48-Renault
1987	Claude Degremont	F	Martini MK51-Renault
1988	Ludovic Faure	F	Martini MK54-Renault
1989	Olivier Panis	F	Martini MK57-Renault
1990	Emmanuel Collard	F	Martini MK59-Renault
1991	Olivier Couvreur	F	Alpa FR91-Renault
1992	Jean-Philippe Belloc	F	Martini MK63-Renault
1993	David Dussau	F	Martini MK65-Renault
1994	Stéphane Sarrazin	F	Martini MK65-Renault

European Formula Renault Championship

year	driver	nat	car
1972	Alain Cudini	F	Alpine-Renault
1973	René Arnoux	F	Martini MK11-Renault
1974	Didier Pironi	F	Martini MK14-Renault
1975	René Arnoux	F	Martini MK15-Renault
1976	Didier Pironi	F	Martini MK18-Renault
1977	Alain Prost	F	Martini MK20-Renault
1978-92	NO SERIES		

1993	Olivier Couvreur	F	Alpa FR93-Renault
1994	James Matthews	GB	Van Diemen FR94-Renault

Peugeot 905 Spyder Cup

Introduced to promote Peugeot with an open-cockpit 905 shape mandatory and chassis design open to choice; Martini and WR are the leading constructors.

year	driver	nat	car
1992	Eric Hélary	F	Martini-Peugeot
1993	Eric Hélary	F	Martini-Peugeot
1994	William David	F	Martini-Peugeot

The 1956 French Grand Prix at Reims with Olivier Gendebien leading Francesco Godia-Sales

MAJOR INTERNATIONAL RACES

FRENCH GRAND PRIX

year	formula	circuit	winner	nat	car	mph
1906	GP	Le Mans	Ferenc Szisz	H	Renault AK	62.887
1907	GP	Dieppe	Felice Nazzaro	I	Fiat	70.604
1908	GP	Dieppe	Christian Lautenschlager	D	Mercedes	69.045
1912	GP	Dieppe	Georges Boillot	F	Peugeot L76	68.502
1913	GP	Amiens	Georges Boillot	F	Peugeot EX3	72.141
1914	GP	Lyon	Christian Lautenschlager	D	Mercedes GP	65.504
1921	GP	Le Mans	Jimmy Murphy	USA	Duesenberg	78.105
1922	GP	Strasbourg	Felice Nazzaro	I	Fiat 804	79.198
1923	GP	Tours	Henry Segrave	GB	Sunbeam	75.325
1924	GP	Lyon	Giuseppe Campari	I	Alfa Romeo P2	70.957
1925	GP	Montlhéry	Robert Benoist/Albert Divo	F	Delage 2LCV	69.726
1926	GP	Miramas	Jules Goux	F	Bugatti T39A	66.882
1927	GP	Montlhéry	Robert Benoist	F	Delage 15S8	78.299
1928	SC (h)	St Gaudens	"W Williams"	GB	Bugatti T35C	65.639
1929	GP	Le Mans	"W Williams"	GB	Bugatti T35B	82.557
1930	FL	Pau	Philippe Étancelin	F	Bugatti T35C	90.566
1931	GP	Montlhéry	Achille Varzi/Louis Chiron	I/MC	Bugatti T51	78.447
1932	GP	Reims	Tazio Nuvolari	I	Alfa Romeo Tipo-B "P3"	89.350
1933	GP	Montlhéry	Giuseppe Campari	I	Maserati 8C-3000	81.487
1934	GP	Montlhéry	Louis Chiron	MC	Alfa Romeo Tipo-B "P3"	85.023
1935	GP	Montlhéry	Rudolf Caracciola	D	Mercedes-Benz W25B	77.377
1936	SC	Montlhéry	Jean-Pierre Wimille/Raymond Sommer	F	Bugatti T57G	77.849
1937	SC	Montlhéry	Louis Chiron	MC	Talbot T150C	82.444
1938	GP	Reims	Manfred von Brauchitsch	D	Mercedes-Benz W154	100.990
1939	GP	Reims	Hermann Müller	D	Auto Union D	105.239
1947	F1	Lyon	Louis Chiron	MC	Lago-Talbot	77.389
1948	F1	Reims	Jean-Pierre Wimille	F	Alfa Romeo 158	102.951
1949	SC	St Gaudens	Charles Pozzi	F	Delahaye	88.137
1950	F1 W	Reims	Juan Manuel Fangio	RA	Alfa Romeo 158	104.829
1951	F1 W	Reims	Luigi Fagioli/Juan Manuel Fangio	I/RA	Alfa Romeo 159	110.962
1952	F2 W	Rouen-les-Essarts	Alberto Ascari	I	Ferrari 500	80.281

year	formula	circuit	winner	nat	car	mph
1953	F2 W	Reims	Mike Hawthorn	GB	Ferrari 500	113.646
1954	F1 W	Reims	Juan Manuel Fangio	RA	Mercedes-Benz W196	116.613
1956	F1 W	Reims	Peter Collins	GB	Lancia-Ferrari D50	122.964
1957	F1 W	Rouen-les-Essarts	Juan Manuel Fangio	RA	Maserati 250F	100.016
1958	F1 W	Reims	Mike Hawthorn	GB	Ferrari Dino 246	126.148
1959	F1 W	Reims	Tony Brooks	GB	Ferrari Dino 246	128.136
1960	F1 W	Reims	Jack Brabham	AUS	Cooper T53-Climax	132.530
1961	F1 W	Reims	Giancarlo Baghetti	I	Ferrari Dino 156	120.510
1962	F1 W	Rouen-les-Essarts	Dan Gurney	USA	Porsche 804	103.225
1963	F1 W	Reims	Jim Clark	GB	Lotus 25-Climax	126.005
1964	F1 W	Rouen-les-Essarts	Dan Gurney	USA	Brabham BT7-Climax	108.766
1965	F1 W	Clermont-Ferrand	Jim Clark	GB	Lotus 25-Climax	89.216
1966	F1 W	Reims	Jack Brabham	AUS	Brabham BT19-Repco	137.655
1967	F1 W	Le Mans-Bugatti	Jack Brabham	AUS	Brabham BT24-Repco	98.912
1968	F1 W	Rouen-les-Essarts	Jacky Ickx	B	Ferrari 312	100.452
1969	F1 W	Clermont-Ferrand	Jackie Stewart	GB	Matra MS80-Ford	97.709
1970	F1 W	Clermont-Ferrand	Jochen Rindt	A	Lotus 72-Ford	98.417
1971	F1 W	Paul Ricard	Jackie Stewart	GB	Tyrrell 003-Ford	111.655
1972	F1 W	Clermont-Ferrand	Jackie Stewart	GB	Tyrrell 003-Ford	101.563
1973	F1 W	Paul Ricard	Ronnie Peterson	S	Lotus 72D-Ford	115.112
1974	F1 W	Dijon-Prenois	Ronnie Peterson	S	Lotus 72E-Ford	119.770
1975	F1 W	Paul Ricard	Niki Lauda	A	Ferrari 312T	116.598
1976	F1 W	Paul Ricard	James Hunt	GB	McLaren M23-Ford	115.833
1977	F1 W	Dijon-Prenois	Mario Andretti	USA	Lotus 78-Ford	113.705
1978	F1 W	Paul Ricard	Mario Andretti	USA	Lotus 79-Ford	118.306
1979	F1 W	Dijon-Prenois	Jean-Pierre Jabouille	F	Renault RE10	118.867
1980	F1 W	Paul Ricard	Alan Jones	AUS	Williams FW07B-Ford	126.143
1981	F1 W	Dijon-Prenois	Alain Prost	F	Renault RE30	118.294
1982	F1 W	Paul Ricard	René Arnoux	F	Renault RE30B	125.023
1983	F1 W	Paul Ricard	Alain Prost	F	Renault RE40	124.124
1984	F1 W	Dijon-Prenois	Niki Lauda	A	McLaren MP4/2-TAG Porsche	122.711
1985	F1 W	Paul Ricard	Nelson Piquet	BR	Brabham BT54-BMW	125.092
1986	F1 W	Paul Ricard	Nigel Mansell	GB	Williams FW11-Honda	116.842
1987	F1 W	Paul Ricard	Nigel Mansell	GB	Williams FW11B-Honda	117.152
1988	F1 W	Paul Ricard	Alain Prost	F	McLaren MP4/4-Honda	116.482
1989	F1 W	Paul Ricard	Alain Prost	F	McLaren MP4/5-Honda	115.455
1990	F1 W	Paul Ricard	Alain Prost	F	Ferrari 641/2	121.626
1991	F1 W	Magny-Cours	Nigel Mansell	GB	Williams FW14-Renault	116.992
1992	F1 W	Magny-Cours	Nigel Mansell	GB	Williams FW14B-Renault	111.409
1993	F1 W	Magny-Cours	Alain Prost	F	Williams FW15C-Renault	115.726
1994	F1 W	Magny-Cours	Michael Schumacher	D	Benetton B194-Ford	115.717

Officially known as Grand Prix de l'Automobile Club de France until 1967

ACF PARIS RACES

The ACF retrospectively awarded the GP de l'ACF title to these Paris city-to-city races of 1895-1903

year	formula	circuit	winner	nat	car	mph
1895	-	Paris-Bordeaux-Paris	Emile Levassor	F	Panhard	15.000
1896	-	Paris-Marseille-Paris	Mayade	F	Panhard	15.690
1898	-	Paris-Amsterdam-Paris	Fernand Charron	F	Panhard	26.880
1899	-	Tour de France	René de Knyff	F	Panhard	30.180
1900	-	Paris-Toulouse-Paris	Alfred Levegh	F	Mors	40.180
1901	-	Paris-Berlin	Henri Fournier	F	Mors	44.180
1902	-	Paris-Vienna	Marcel Renault	F	Renault	38.960
1903	-	Paris-Madrid*	Fernand Gabriel	F	Mors	65.240

*stopped at Bordeaux

GRAND PRIX DE FRANCE

Prior to 1968 various races carried the title Grand Prix de France, organized by clubs which wanted to rival the GP de l'ACF. However, apart from the 1949 race (which was a true F1 Grand Prix while the ACF event was for Sports Cars) the GP de France was always of secondary importance. The Grand Prix de France title was also used to describe a series of F2 races in 1952.

year	formula	circuit	winner	nat	car	mph
1911	FL	Le Mans	Victor Hémery	F	Fiat	56.710
1912	3 litre	Le Mans	Paul Zuccarelli	I	Lion-Peugeot	64.870
1913	GP	Le Mans	Paul Bablot	F	Delage Y	77.339
1934	GP	Montlhéry	Benoit Falchetto	F	Maserati	86.930
1935	GP	Montlhéry	Raymond Sommer	F	Alfa Romeo	90.320
1949	F1	Reims	Louis Chiron	MC	Lago-Talbot T26C	99.951

France

CIRCUITS AND OTHER RACES

ALBI

Racing started near Albi on the tree-lined Circuit des Planques by the River Tarn in 1933. Unusually, the pits and startline were on the shortest of straights, before the road twisted through St Antoine, dipping and climbing to St Juery. The cars then slowed for an extreme hairpin before negotiating a railway level crossing and a hump leading to two flat and fast legs which completed the lap. Shortened in 1951, it

was closed on safety grounds in 1955 following the Le Mans disaster. The Grand Prix d'Albi resumed in 1959 at the Aerodrome. On the western outskirts of town, it was flat and featureless in comparison with the previous circuit. First events were for Formula Junior and its replacement, F3. There were some rumours of holding the French GP in 1970 but having briefly been a F2 race, the circuit now holds French Supertourism and F3 Championship races.

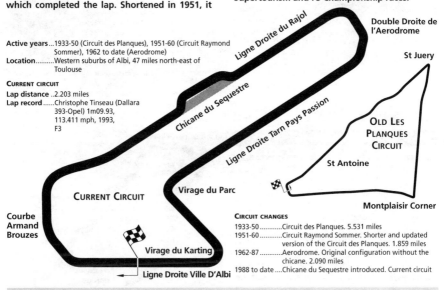

Active years...1933-50 (Circuit des Planques), 1951-60 (Circuit Raymond Sommer), 1962 to date (Aerodrome)
Location.........Western suburbs of Albi, 47 miles north-east of Toulouse

CURRENT CIRCUIT
Lap distance ..2.203 miles
Lap record ......Christophe Tinseau (Dallara 393-Opel) 1m09.93, 113.411 mph, 1993, F3

CIRCUIT CHANGES
1933-50 ....Circuit des Planques. 5.531 miles
1951-60 ....Circuit Raymond Sommer. Shorter and updated version of the Circuit des Planques. 1.859 miles
1962-87 ....Aerodrome. Original configuration without the chicane. 2.090 miles
1988 to date ....Chicane du Sequestre introduced. Current circuit

Albi Grand Prix					
year	formula	winner	nat	car	mph
1933	V	Pierre Veyron	F	Bugatti T51A	79.517
1934	V	Pierre Veyron	F	Bugatti T51A	80.138
1935	V	Pierre Veyron	F	Bugatti T51A	85.774
1936	V	"B Bira"	SM	ERA B-type	92.069
1937	V	Raymond Mays/Humphrey Cook	GB	ERA C-type	90.422
1938	V	Luigi Villoresi	I	Maserati 6CM	90.165
1939	V	Johnnie Wakefield	GB	Maserati 4CL	93.912
1946	F1	Tazio Nuvolari	I	Maserati 4CL	91.737
1947	F1	Louis Rosier	F	Lago-Talbot T26C	88.607
1948	F1	Luigi Villoresi	I	Maserati 4CLT/48	99.882
1949	F1	Juan Manuel Fangio	RA	Maserati 4CLT/48	98.420
1950	F1	Louis Rosier	F	Lago-Talbot T26C	99.725
1951	F1	Maurice Trintignant	F	Simca-Gordini 15	101.299
1952	F1	Louis Rosier	F	Ferrari 375	101.972
1953	F1	Louis Rosier	F	Ferrari 375	105.514
1954	SC	Roberto Mieres	RA	DB	66.333
1955	F1	André Simon	F	Maserati 250F	81.690
1959	FJ	Colin Davis	GB	Taraschi	78.577
1960	FJ	Henry Taylor	GB	Cooper-BMC	80.395
1962	FJ	Peter Arundell	GB	Lotus 22-Ford	93.820
1963	FJ	Peter Arundell	GB	Lotus 27-Ford	96.500
1964	F2	Jack Brabham	AUS	Brabham BT10-Ford	95.716
1965	F2	Jim Clark	GB	Lotus 35-Ford	99.986
1966	F2	Jack Brabham	AUS	Brabham BT21-Honda	100.607
1967	F2	Jackie Stewart	GB	Matra MS7-Ford	109.178
1968	F2	Henri Pescarolo	F	Matra MS7-Ford	109.677
1969	F2	Graham Hill	GB	Lotus 59B-Ford	108.982
1970	F3	Jean-Pierre Jarier	F	Tecno 70-Ford	88.178
1971	F2 E	Emerson Fittipaldi	BR	Lotus 69-Ford	102.843

year	formula	winner	nat	car	mph
1972	F2 E	Jean-Pierre Jaussaud	F	Brabham BT38-Ford	105.902
1973	F2 E	Vittorio Brambilla	I	March 732-BMW	108.059
1974	Renault	Marc Sourd	F	Martini MK14-Renault	100.519
1975	Renault	René Arnoux	F	Martini MK15-Renault	107.498
1976	Renault	Didier Pironi	F	Martini MK18-Renault	107.007
1977	Renault	Alain Prost	F	Martini MK20-Renault	106.567
1978	Renault	Philippe Alliot	F	Martini MK20-Renault	102.533
1979	F3	Alain Prost	F	Martini MK27-Renault	110.353
1980*	F3	Philippe Streiff	F	Martini MK31-Toyota	90.309
1981	F3	Philippe Alliot	F	Martini MK34-Alfa Romeo	111.004
1982	F3	François Hesnault	F	Ralt RT3-Alfa Romeo	112.134
1983	F3	François Hesnault	F	Ralt RT3-Volkswagen	112.389
1984	F3	Cathy Müller	F	Ralt RT3-Alfa Romeo	112.309
1985	F3	Paul Belmondo	F	Reynard 853-Volkswagen	109.650
1986	F3	Jean Alesi	F	Dallara 386-Alfa Romeo	111.363
1987	TC	Xavier Lapeyre	F	Audi 200 Quattro	104.428
1988	F3	Eric Chéli	F	Dallara 388-Alfa Romeo	108.173
1989	F3	Eric Hélary	F	Reynard 893-Alfa Romeo	108.642
1990	F3	Ludovic Faure	F	Dallara 390-Volkswagen	108.847
1991	F3	Olivier Panis	F	Ralt RT35-Alfa Romeo	110.439
1992	F3	Stéphane Gregoire	F	Dallara 392-Alfa Romeo	111.268
1993	F3	Christophe Tinseau	F	Dallara 393-Opel	113.113
1994	F3	Christophe Tinseau	F	Dallara 394-Opel	110.897

At Albi except *at Nogaro

CLERMONT-FERRAND

CIRCUIT LOUIS ROSIER/CIRCUIT DE MONTAGNE D'AUVERGNE/CHARADE

The Automobile Club de France had designed a 30-mile permanent road course at Puy de Dôme near Clermont-Ferrand in 1908. Although the project was stillborn, a Grand Prix circuit was to open in the beautiful surroundings of Clermont-Ferrand 50 years later. The Circuit Louis Rosier, now known as Charade, held the French GP on four occasions. It twists and undulates around two extinct volcanos with no real straight, apart from at the start. The old venue closed in 1988, replaced by a shortened circuit on the site.

French Grand Prix see above

Carrefour de Gravenoire
La Carrière
Puy de Gravenoire
Carrefour de Champeaux
Le Belvedere
Thedes (Village)
Puy de Charade
Charade (Village)
Virage Rosier

Active years...1958-88
Location..........Three miles west of Clermont-Ferrand, 95 miles from Nevers, 110 miles west of Lyon, 115 miles east of Limoges

CURRENT CIRCUIT
Lap distance ..2.4 miles
Lap record ......n/a

CIRCUIT CHANGES
1958-88 ....Grand Prix circuit. 5.005 miles
1989 to date ....Current circuit

CROIX-EN-TERNOIS

A tight, twisting circuit which now hosts a round of the French F3 Championship. Sometimes used by F1 teams for testing prior to Monaco due to the succession of slow corners.

Active years...1973 to date
Location..........20 miles west of Arras
Lap distance ..1.18 miles
Lap record ......Michel Trollé (Martini MK49-Volkswagen), 51.00s, 83.294 mph, 1986, F3

European Formula Three race

year	formula	winner	nat	car	mph
1976	F3 E	Conny Andersson	S	March 763-Toyota	76.756
1977	F3 E	Derek Daly	IRL	Chevron B38-Toyota	77.363
1981	F3 E	Mauro Baldi	I	March 813-Alfa Romeo	77.980
1983	F3 E	Pierluigi Martini	I	Ralt RT3/83-Alfa Romeo	79.694

France

DIJON-PRENOIS

The third circuit to have been used in the area when it opened in 1972. Although picturesque and demanding in parts, it was always too short. Despite being extended in 1976 Dijon eventually lost the Grand Prix to Circuit Paul Ricard. Many of the races it did hold were memorable - providing first Grand Prix victories for Jabouille and Renault (1979), Prost (1981) and Rosberg (1982 Swiss GP) but it will always be remembered as the scene of the greatest modern day duel, as René Arnoux

and Gilles Villeneuve battled for second place in the 1979 French GP, repeatedly swapping positions in the closing laps, banging wheels on and off the road – irresponsible to some, exhilarating to most.

Active years...1972 to date
Location..........Ten miles north of Dijon, 185 miles east of Paris

CURRENT CIRCUIT
Lap distance ..2.361 miles
Lap record   Jean-Louis Schlesser (Sauber C11-Mercedes-Benz) 1m08.973, 123.231 mph, 1990, Group C Sports Cars

CIRCUIT CHANGES
1972-76 ....2.044 miles
1977 to date ....Current circuit

French Grand Prix see above

Swiss Grand Prix (also see Switzerland)

year	formula	winner	nat	car	mph
1975	F1	Clay Regazzoni	CH	Ferrari 312T	79.867
1982	F1 W	Keke Rosberg	SF	Williams FW08-Ford	122.272

International Formula 3000 race

year	formula	winner	nat	car	mph
1985	F3000 INT	Christian Danner	D	March 85B-Cosworth	113.079
1988	F3000 INT	Martin Donnelly	GB	Reynard 88D-Cosworth	117.776
1989	F3000 INT	Erik Comas	F	Lola T89/50-Mugen	117.470

European Formula Three race

year	formula	winner	nat	car	mph
1978	F3 E	Teo Fabi	I	March 783-Toyota	103.986

World Sports Car race

year	formula	winner	nat	car	mph
1973	SC W	Henri Pescarolo/Gérard Larrousse	F	Matra-Simca MS670	114.350
1975	SC W	Arturo Merzario/Jacques Laffite	I/F	Alfa Romeo T33TT/12	112.333
1976	SC W	Jacky Ickx/Jochen Mass	B/D	Porsche 935	105.607
	SC WSC	Jacky Ickx/Jochen Mass	B/D	Porsche 936	115.499
1977	SC WSC	Arturo Merzario/Jean-Pierre Jarier	I/F	Alfa Romeo T33SC/12	102.570
1978	SC W	Bob Wollek/Henri Pescarolo	F	Porsche 935	99.367
1979	SC W	Reinhold Jöst/Volkert Merl/Mario Ketterer	D/D/CH	Porsche 908/4	100.327
1980	SC W	Henri Pescarolo/Jürgen Barth	F/D	Porsche 935	96.009
1989	SC W	Bob Wollek/Frank Jelinski	F/D	Porsche 962	110.805
1990	SC W	Jean-Louis Schlesser/Mauro Baldi	F/I	Mercedes-Benz C11	113.107

International GT race

year	formula	winner	nat	car	mph
1994	GT	Michel Ferté/Michel Neugarten	F/B	Venturi 600LM	96.211

LA CHATRE

A regular venue for the European F3 Championship during the 1980s. It is a short part-temporary/part-permanent circuit which lacks pits, and the paddock is in the town square a mile away! Only 18 cars are permitted to start.

Active years...1961 to date
Location..........180 miles south of Paris
Lap distance ..1.445 miles
Lap record ......Ivan Capelli (Martini MK42-Alfa Romeo), 1m03.34, 82. 128 mph, 1984, F3

European Formula Three race					
year	formula	winner	nat	car	mph
1980	F3	Michele Alboreto	I	March 803-Alfa Romeo	79.525
1981	F3	Philippe Alliot	F	Martini MK34-Alfa Romeo	80.550
1982	F3	Philippe Alliot	F	Martini MK37-Alfa Romeo	81.150
1983	F3	Roberto Ravaglia	I	Ralt RT3/83-Toyota	80.154
1984	F3	Ivan Capelli	I	Martini MK42-Alfa Romeo	81.067

LE MANS

24 HEURES DU MANS

The Le Mans 24-hours vies with the Monaco Grand Prix and Indianapolis 500 for the title of the world's most famous race. It is also one of the last remaining old-fashioned road courses, using public roads which are normally open to general traffic. The current circuit was first used for the 1921 French GP although the originally loose roads were soon layed with tarmac. The 1955 24-hour race was marred by the worst disaster in motor racing history - the Mercedes of "Pierre Levegh" crashed into the crowd opposite the pits killing the driver and more than 80 spectators. The recriminations were felt throughout the world, with racing suspended in France as safety was investigated and the Swiss authorities placing a ban on motor racing which stills remains in force. The organizers have had continual battles with the FIA in recent years but while Sports Car racing has all but died, the 24 heures du Mans continues with a mix of GT and old Sports Cars.

French Grand Prix see above

Grand Prix de France see above

Le Mans 24 hours see page 251

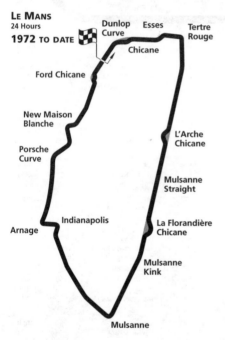

LE MANS
24 Hours
1972 TO DATE

Dunlop Curve — Esses — Tertre Rouge — Chicane — Ford Chicane — New Maison Blanche — Porsche Curve — Arnage — Indianapolis — L'Arche Chicane — Mulsanne Straight — La Florandière Chicane — Mulsanne Kink — Mulsanne

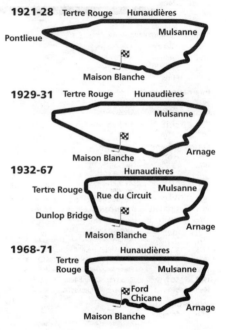

1921-28 Tertre Rouge — Hunaudières — Pontlieue — Mulsanne — Maison Blanche

1929-31 Tertre Rouge — Hunaudières — Mulsanne — Maison Blanche — Arnage

1932-67 Hunaudières — Tertre Rouge — Rue du Circuit — Mulsanne — Dunlop Bridge — Maison Blanche — Arnage

1968-71 Hunaudières — Tertre Rouge — Mulsanne — Ford Chicane — Maison Blanche — Arnage

Active years...1921 to date
Location..........Three miles south of Le Mans,
130 miles south-west of Paris

CURRENT CIRCUIT

Lap distance ..8.451 miles
Lap record ......Eddie Irvine (Toyota TS010) 3m27.295,
146.765 mph, 1993, Group C Sports Cars

CIRCUIT CHANGES

1921-28 ....Original circuit, western hairpin at Pontlieue.
10.726 miles
1929-31 ....Western end of circuit shortened with the "Rue du
Circuit" link road for safety reasons. 10.153 miles
1932-55 ....The current track from the pits straight to Tertre
Rouge was built. Dunlop bridge installed after the
first corner. 8.378 miles
1956-67 ....Following the 1955 disaster the pits straight
was widened and the Dunlop Corner eased.
8.365 miles
1968-71 ....Ford chicane built before the start. 8.369 miles
1972-78 ....Old Maison Blanche bypass in a new circuit layout
from Arnage to the Ford chicane. 8.476 miles
1979-85 ....Tertre Rouge tightened to accommodate new
ring-road built around Le Mans. 8.467 miles
1986 ....Roundabout built at Mulsanne necessitated a new
corner. 8.406 miles
1987-89 ....Chicane built at Dunlop Corner. 8.410 miles
1990 ....Two chicanes built on the Mulsanne straight.
8.450 miles
1991 to date ....Arnage and Indianapolis modified. Current circuit

LE MANS

Bugatti Circuit

Designed by Charles Deutsch, who divided his time between being chief engineer for the French Department of Bridges and Roads and being a partner of DB racing car constructors. It incorporates the main straight from the Circuit des 24 heures with a tight section behind the pits. Although the Bugatti circuit held the 1967 French GP, it was not regularly used until 1987, when the track held a round of the FIA Formula 3000 series.

Les "S" du Garage Bleu

Chemin Aux Boeups

Virage du Musée

Dunlop Curve

Virage du Garage Vert

Virage de la Chapelle

Active years...1965 to date

Current Circuit
Lap distance ..2.753 miles
Lap record .....Christian Fittipaldi
(Reynard 91D-Mugen)
1m30.65, 109.331 mph,
1991, F3000

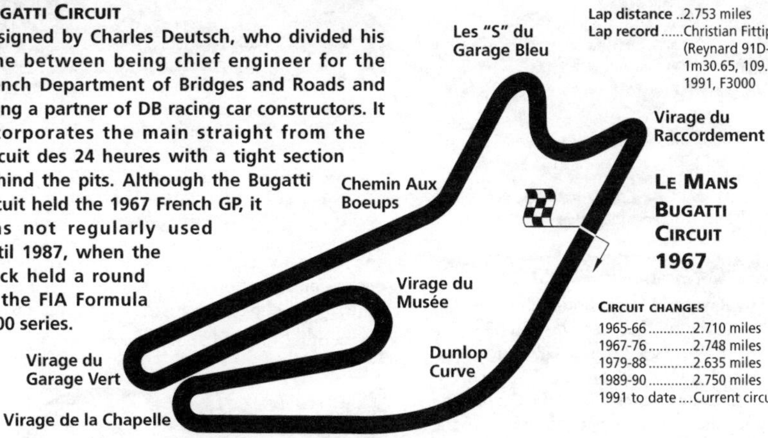

Virage du Raccordement

Le Mans Bugatti Circuit 1967

Circuit changes
1965-66 ....2.710 miles
1967-76 ....2.748 miles
1979-88 ....2.635 miles
1989-90 ....2.750 miles
1991 to date ....Current circuit

French Grand Prix see above

International Formula 3000 race

year	formula	winner	nat	car	mph
1986	F3000 INT	Emanuele Pirro	I	March 86B-Cosworth	105.240
1987	F3000 INT	Luis Perez Sala	E	Lola T87/50-Cosworth	102.044
1988	F3000 INT	Olivier Grouillard	F	Lola T88/50-Cosworth	102.842
1989	F3000 INT	Erik Comas	F	Lola T89/50-Mugen	104.718
1990	F3000 INT	Erik Comas	F	Lola T90/50-Mugen	103.565
1991	F3000 INT	Antonio Tamburini	I	Reynard 91D-Mugen	88.316

MAGNY-COURS

The Circuit Jean Behra - as it was formerly known - was a second-division, slightly run-down circuit best known as home of the Martini-racing car constructor, when political pressure began to be exercised on its behalf in the 1980s. President Mitterand, so long a supporter of French racing in general and the Ligier team in particular, supported moves for the French GP to be held in the Nevers region. A major redevelopment of Magny-Cours was completed in time for the race to be held in 1991, Ligier having already moved into the new industrial park. After the fast open layout of Circuit Paul Ricard, Magny-Cours suffers by comparison.

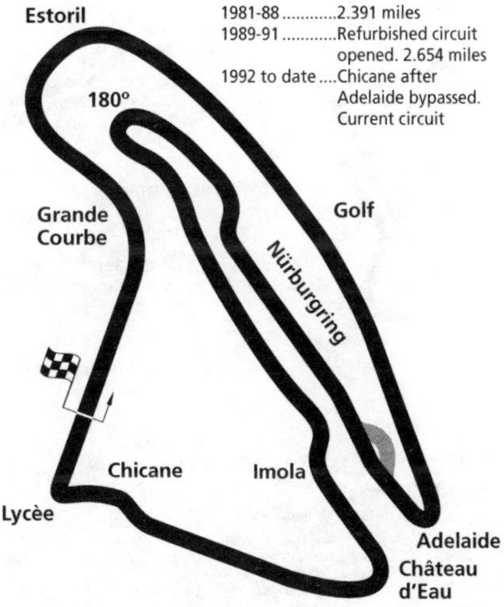

Active years...1961 to date
Location..........Seven miles south of Nevers, 155 miles south of Paris

Current circuit
Lap distance ..2.641 miles
Lap record ......Nigel Mansell (Williams FW14B-Renault)
1m17.070, 123.363 mph, 1992, F1

Circuit changes
1961-70 ....1.24 miles
1971-80 ....Extended. 2.361 miles
1981-88 ....2.391 miles
1989-91 ....Refurbished circuit opened. 2.654 miles
1992 to date ....Chicane after Adelaide bypassed. Current circuit

Estoril

180°

Grande Courbe

Golf

Nürburgring

Chicane

Imola

Lycée

Adelaide Château d'Eau

French Grand Prix see above

Non-Championship Formula Two race

year	formula	winner	nat	car	mph
1975	F2	Jean-Pierre Jabouille	F	Elf 2J-BMW	102.947

International Formula 3000 race

year	formula	winner	nat	car	mph
1992	F3000 INT	Jean-Marc Gounon	F	Lola T92/50-Cosworth	109.172
1993	F3000 INT	Franck Lagorce	F	Reynard 93D-Cosworth	96.293
1994	F3000 INT	Jules Boullion	F	Reynard 94D-Cosworth	107.600

European Formula Three race

year	formula	winner	nat	car	mph
1978	F3 E	Jan Lammers	NL	Ralt RT1-Toyota	98.401
1979	F3 E	Alain Prost	F	Martini MK27-Renault	98.542
1980	F3 E	Thierry Boutsen	B	Martini MK31-Toyota	98.781
1981	F3 E	Philippe Alliot	F	Martini MK34-Alfa Romeo	101.259
1982	F3 E	Alain Ferté	F	Martini MK37-Alfa Romeo	101.525
1983	F3 E	John Nielsen	DK	Ralt RT3/83-Volkswagen	97.829
1984	F3 E	Ivan Capelli	I	Martini MK42-Alfa Romeo	102.472

World Sports Car race

year	formula	winner	nat	car	mph
1991	SC W	Yannick Dalmas/Keke Rosberg	F/SF	Peugeot 905B	106.064
1992	SC W	Philippe Alliot/Mauro Baldi	F/I	Peugeot 905B	113.787

MONTLHÉRY

Designed by Raymond Jamin and built in 1924 as a banked oval, the road course was completed in time to hold the 1925 French GP. Tragically, Antonio Ascari was killed during that race but Montlhéry became France's leading Grand Prix circuit before the war. Against the debut of the much vaunted Mercedes-Benz and Auto Union teams in the 1934 race, Louis Chiron scored an unexpectedly convincing victory for Alfa Romeo. It proved to be unrepresentative of the era and, rather than suffer inevitable German wins, the organizers turned to Sports Cars for the Grands Prix of 1936 and 1937. It was not a popular move and for the 1938 Grand Prix Montlhéry lost the race to Reims, never to regain it. After the war Montlhéry introduced the Paris 1000 kms Sports Car race, but an accident in 1964 left two drivers and three officials dead. The circuit fell into decline and temporarily closed in 1973. After a lengthy absence from international motor racing, Montlhéry revived the Paris 1000 kms in 1994 as part of the new International GT series.

CURRENT CIRCUIT

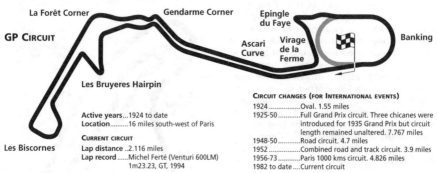

GP CIRCUIT

Active years...1924 to date
Location..........16 miles south-west of Paris

CURRENT CIRCUIT
Lap distance ..2.116 miles
Lap record ......Michel Ferté (Venturi 600LM)
1m23.23, GT, 1994

CIRCUIT CHANGES (FOR INTERNATIONAL EVENTS)
1924 ....Oval. 1.55 miles
1925-50 ....Full Grand Prix circuit. Three chicanes were introduced for 1935 Grand Prix but circuit length remained unaltered. 7.767 miles
1948-50 ....Road circuit. 4.7 miles
1952 ....Combined road and track circuit. 3.9 miles
1956-73 ....Paris 1000 kms circuit. 4.826 miles
1982 to date ....Current circuit

French Grand Prix see above

Paris 1000 kms

year	formula	winner	nat	car	mph
1956	SC	Jean Behra/Louis Rosier	F	Maserati 300S	93.357
1960	GT	Olivier Gendebien/Lucien Bianchi	B	Ferrari 250GT	91.441
1961	GT	Ricardo Rodriguez/Pedro Rodriguez	MEX	Ferrari 250GT	95.448
1962	GT	Ricardo Rodriguez/Pedro Rodriguez	MEX	Ferrari 250GTO	98.015
1964	SC W	Graham Hill/Jo Bonnier	GB/S	Ferrari 330P	96.500
1966	SC	Michael Parkes/David Piper	GB	Ferrari 250LM	95.880
1967	SC	Jacky Ickx/Paul Hawkins	B/AUS	Mirage Mk1-Ford	85.217
1968	SC	Hans Herrmann/Rolf Stommelen	D	Porsche 908	100.242
1969	SC	Jean-Pierre Beltoise/Henri Pescarolo	F	Matra MS650	105.454
1970	SC	Jack Brabham/François Cevert	AUS/F	Matra-Simca MS660	106.729
1971	SC	Derek Bell/Gijs van Lennep	GB/NL	Porsche 917	99.000
1972*	SC	Gérard Larrousse/Jean-Pierre Beltoise	F	Lola T282-Ford	102.645
1994	GT	Henri Pescarolo/Jean-Claude Basso	F	Venturi 600LM	81.710

At Montlhéry except at *Rouen-les-Essarts

NOGARO

CIRCUIT PAUL ARMAGNAC

Set on the northern edge of Nogaro, a small sleepy town south of Bordeaux, the Circuit Paul Armagnac is a combination of a tight complex around the pits (which formed the original circuit) and two long straights, one of which runs parallel to an airfield runway. In recent years the Grand Prix de Nogaro has been a round of the FIA Formula 3000 Championship, but in 1994 this was cancelled and replaced by Formula Renault.

Double Courbe de Caupenne (built 1989)

Courbe de l'Aviation

Virage de la Ferme

Ligne Doite de l'Aerodrome

Courbe Roger Dubos

Le S du Lac

Courbe Henri Oreiller

Epingle de l'Ecole

Double Courbe Claude Storez

Active years...1962 to date
Location..........40 miles north-west of Pau, 75 miles west of Toulouse, 90 miles south-east of Bordeaux

CURRENT CIRCUIT
Lap distance ..2.259 miles
Lap record ......Jules Boullion (Reynard 93D-Cosworth) 1m20.25, 101.339 mph, 1993, F3000

CIRCUIT CHANGES
1962-72 ....1.118 miles
1973-88 ....Extended. 1.939 miles
1989 to date ....Modifications to east end of circuit. Current circuit

Nogaro Grand Prix

year	formula	winner	nat	car	mph
1960	FJ	Basini	F	Raineri	52.512
1961	FJ	John Love	RSR	Cooper	58.416
1962	FJ	Jo Schlesser	F	Brabham-Ford	61.722
1963	FJ	Jean Vinatier	F	Lotus-Ford	59.261
1964	F3	Pierre Ryser	CH	Cooper-Ford	57.959
1965	F3	Trevor Blokdyk	ZA	Brabham-Ford	67.176
1966	F3	Jean-Pierre Jaussaud	F	Matra MS5-Ford	66.200
1967	F3	Henri Pescarolo	F	Matra MS5-Ford	66.068
1968	F3	François Cevert	F	Tecno 68-Ford	68.814
1969	F3	François Mazet	F	Tecno 69-Ford	69.019
1970	F3	Jean-Pierre Jaussaud	F	Martini MW5-Ford	71.040
1971	F3	Jean-Pierre Jabouille	F	Alpine-Ford	73.462
1972	SC	Jean-Pierre Beltoise	F	Chevron	73.461
1973	SC	Gérard Larrousse	F	Lola-BMW	83.887
1974	F2	Patrick Tambay	F	Elf 2/A367-BMW	92.672
1975	F2 E	Patrick Tambay	F	March 752-BMW	93.666
1976	F2 E	Patrick Tambay	F	Martini MK19-Renault	94.273
1977	F2 E	René Arnoux	F	Martini MK22-Renault	93.695
1978	F2 E	Bruno Giacomelli	I	March 782-BMW	95.476
1979	F1/F2	Emilio de Villota	E	Lotus 78-Ford	95.663
1980	F3	Philippe Streiff	F	Martini MK31-Toyota	90.309
1981	F3	Philippe Streiff	F	Martini MK34-Alfa Romeo	90.743
1982	F3 E	James Weaver	GB	Ralt RT3/82-Toyota	91.950
1983	F3 E	Pierluigi Martini	I	Ralt RT3/83-Alfa Romeo	91.849
1984	F3 E	John Nielsen	DK	Ralt RT3/84-Volkswagen	94.408
1985	TC E	Tom Walkinshaw/Win Percy	GB	Rover Vitesse	78.868
1986	TC E	Roberto Ravaglia/Gerhard Berger	I/A	BMW 635 CSi	81.481
1987	TC E	Fabien Giroix/Jean-Pierre Jaussaud	F	BMW M3	81.278
1988	TC E	Klaus Ludwig/Klaus Niedzwiedz	D	Ford Sierra RS500	83.094
1989	TC	Jean Ragnotti/Jean-Louis Bousquet	F	Renault 21 turbo	82.218
1990	F3000 INT	Eric van de Poele	B	Reynard 90D-Cosworth	92.647
1991	F3000 INT	Christian Fittipaldi	BR	Reynard 91D-Mugen	100.149
1992	F3000 INT	Luca Badoer	I	Reynard 92D-Cosworth	99.841
1993	F3000 INT	Franck Lagorce	F	Reynard 93D-Cosworth	99.737
1994	Renault	Stéphane Sarrazin	F	Martini MK65-Renault	86.686

PAU

The 1901 GP de Pau is the first recorded instance of an event having the title Grand Prix. The French GP was held on a ten-mile circuit outside the picturesque Pyrenees town in 1930, but three years later, in the February snow, a circuit in the city was introduced for the second Grand Prix de Pau. It has been used, almost uninterrupted and without alteration, ever since. After the Station hairpin, overlooked by a steep hill which acts as a spectator bank, the road climbs to the narrow Pont Oscar. Another hairpin, almost too tight for modern F3000 cars, follows and leads to the challenging Parc Beaumont section before the track winds its way back to the startline to complete the lap.

The 1957 Pau Grand Prix

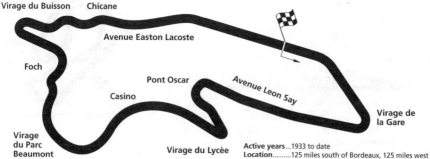

Virage du Buisson   Chicane

Avenue Easton Lacoste

Foch

Pont Oscar   Avenue Leon Say

Casino

Virage de la Gare

Virage du Parc Beaumont   Virage du Lycèe

Active years...1933 to date
Location..........125 miles south of Bordeaux, 125 miles west of Toulouse
Lap distance ..1.715 miles
Lap record ......Emanuele Naspetti (Reynard 92D-Cosworth) 1m09.82, 88.428 mph, 1992, F3000

French Grand Prix see above

Pau Grand Prix

year	formula	winner	nat	car	mph
1901	FL	Maurice Farman	F	Panhard 24CV	46.986
1933	GP	Marcel Lehoux	DZ	Bugatti T51	47.280
1935	GP	Tazio Nuvolari	I	Alfa Romeo Tipo-B "P3"	51.993
1936	GP	Philippe Étancelin	F	Maserati V8RI	50.829
1937	SC	Jean-Pierre Wimille	F	Bugatti T59S	51.051
1938	GP	René Dreyfus	F	Delahaye 145	54.449
1939	GP	Hermann Lang	D	Mercedes-Benz W163	54.903
1947	F1	Nello Pagani	I	Maserati 4CL	51.798
1948	F1	Nello Pagani	I	Maserati 4CL	53.015
1949	F1	Juan Manuel Fangio	RA	Maserati 4CLT/48	52.598
1950	F1	Juan Manuel Fangio	RA	Maserati 4CLT/48	58.245
1951	F1	Luigi Villoresi	I	Ferrari 375	57.264
1952	F2	Alberto Ascari	I	Ferrari 500	56.595
1953	F2	Alberto Ascari	I	Ferrari 500	60.597
1954	F1	Jean Behra	F	Gordini 16	62.299
1955	F1	Jean Behra	F	Maserati 250F	62.138
1957	F1	Jean Behra	F	Maserati 250F	62.804
1958	F2	Maurice Trintignant	F	Cooper T43-Climax	59.359
1959	F2	Maurice Trintignant	F	Cooper T51-Climax	57.336
1960	F2	Jack Brabham	AUS	Cooper T45-Climax	63.929
1961	F1	Jim Clark	GB	Lotus 18-Climax	63.517
1962	F1	Maurice Trintignant	F	Lotus 18/21-Climax	64.477
1963	F1	Jim Clark	GB	Lotus 25-Climax	61.619
1964	F2	Jim Clark	GB	Lotus 32-Ford	n/a
1965	F2	Jim Clark	GB	Lotus 35-Ford	57.390
1966	F2	Jack Brabham	AUS	Brabham BT18-Honda	68.420
1967	F2	Jochen Rindt	A	Brabham BT23-Ford	75.085
1968	F2	Jackie Stewart	GB	Matra MS7-Ford	74.928

year	formula	winner	nat	car	mph
1969	F2	Jochen Rindt	A	Lotus 59B-Ford	76.497
1970	F2	Jochen Rindt	A	Lotus 69-Ford	n/a
1971	F2	Reine Wisell	S	Lotus 69-Ford	77.125
1972	F2 E	Peter Gethin	GB	Chevron B20-Ford	76.889
1973	F2 E	François Cevert	F	Elf 2/A367-Ford	79.302
1974	F2 E	Patrick Depailler	F	March 742-BMW	67.367
1975	F2 E	Jacques Laffite	F	Martini MK16-BMW	81.491
1976	F2 E	René Arnoux	F	Martini MK19-Renault	81.478
1977	F2 E	René Arnoux	F	Martini MK22-Renault	81.083
1978	F2 E	Bruno Giacomelli	I	March 782-BMW	80.602
1979	F2 E	Eddie Cheever	USA	Osella FA2/79-BMW	65.601
1980	F2 E	Richard Dallest	F	AGS JH17-BMW	79.861
1981	F2 E	Geoff Lees	GB	Ralt RH6/81-Honda	80.570
1982	F2 E	Johnny Cecotto	YV	March 822-BMW	82.546
1983	F2 E	Jo Gartner	A	Spirit 201-BMW	71.329
1984	F2 E	Mike Thackwell	NZ	Ralt RH6/84-Honda	83.778
1985	F3000 INT	Christian Danner	D	March 85B-Cosworth	81.886
1986	F3000 INT	Mike Thackwell	NZ	Ralt RT20-Honda	82.276
1987	F3000 INT	Yannick Dalmas	F	March 87B-Cosworth	82.099
1988	F3000 INT	Roberto Moreno	BR	Reynard 88D-Cosworth	83.218
1989	F3000 INT	Jean Alesi	F	Reynard 89D-Mugen	83.371
1990	F3000 INT	Eric van de Poele	B	Reynard 90D-Cosworth	84.212
1991	F3000 INT	Jean-Marc Gounon	F	Ralt RT23-Cosworth	85.630
1992	F3000 INT	Emanuele Naspetti	I	Reynard 92D-Cosworth	86.502
1993	F3000 INT	Pedro Lamy	P	Reynard 92D-Cosworth	86.219
1994	F3000 INT	Gil de Ferran	BR	Reynard 94D-Judd	85.295

PAUL RICARD

A flat and dusty modern circuit at Le Castellet in southern France, built on a grand scale with great facilities thanks to finance from pastis tycoon Paul Ricard. The mile-long Mistral straight dominates the full circuit and is followed by the dauntingly fast Signes corner. Heralded as very safe, the Grand Prix stopped using the full circuit after Elio de Angelis was killed while testing in 1986. Political pressure in France led to the Grand Prix moving to Magny-Cours in 1991.

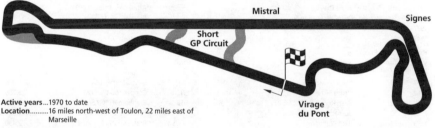

Active years...1970 to date
Location..........16 miles north-west of Toulon, 22 miles east of Marseille

GRAND PRIX CIRCUITS

Full circuit
Active years...Used for Grands Prix from 1970-85. Reintroduced for 1994 International GT race
Lap distance ..3.610 miles
Lap record ......Keke Rosberg (Williams FW10-Honda) 1m39.914, 130.072 mph, 1985, F1

Short circuit
Active years...Used for Grands Prix from 1986-90
Lap distance ..2.369 miles
Lap record ......Nigel Mansell (Ferrari 642) 1m04.402, 132.425 mph, 1990, F1

French Grand Prix see above

European Formula Three race

year	formula	winner	nat	car	mph
1977	F3 E	Beppe Gabbiani	I	Chevron B38-Toyota	91.573
1985*	F3 E	Alex Caffi	I	Dallara 385-Alfa Romeo	93.629
					*European F3 Cup

World Sports Car race

year	formula	winner	nat	car	mph
1974	SC W	Jean-Pierre Beltoise/Jean-Pierre Jarier	F	Matra-Simca MS670C	112.200
1977	SC WSC	Arturo Merzario/Jean-Pierre Jarier	I/F	Alfa Romeo T33SC/12	89.801

International GT race

year	formula	winner	nat	car	mph
1994	GT	Bob Wollek/Jean-Pierre Jarier/Jesus Pareja	F/F/E	Porsche 911 turbo SLM	n/a

REIMS

Reims was a spectacular, triangular road course using public roads on which frequent slipstreaming battles decided its races. It was also fast and the quest for speed led the organizers to cut down trees and demolish houses in order to ease the corners. New sections of permanent circuit were built and the old, decaying pits can still be seen. Run by the flamboyant Raymond "Toto" Roche for the AC de Champagne, it was the dominant French circuit during the 1960s, but financial and political problems forced Reims to close in 1970.

Active years...1925-70
Location.........West of Reims at the villages of Thillois and Gueux

CIRCUIT CHANGES
1925-51 ....Reims-Gueux. 4.865 miles
1952 ....4.472 miles. Gueux village bypassed by linking the finishing straight (D27) with the Virage de la Hovette
1953-70 ....Link road extended to join the Soissons-Reims public road at the new Virage de Muizon. 5.187 miles

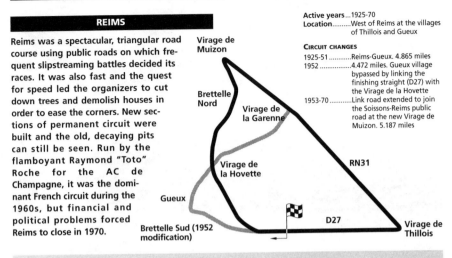

French Grand Prix see above

Grand Prix de France see above

Marne Grand Prix

year	formula	winner	nat	car	mph
1925	FL	Pierre Clause	F	Bignan	63.611
1926	FL	François Lescot	F	Bugatti T35	68.451
1927	FL	Philippe Étancelin	F	Bugatti T35B	70.603
1928	GP	Louis Chiron	MC	Bugatti T35B	80.580
1929	GP	Philippe Étancelin	F	Bugatti T35C	83.607
1930	GP	René Dreyfus	F	Bugatti T35B	85.967
1931	GP	Marcel Lehoux	DZ	Bugatti T51	86.909
1933	GP	Philippe Étancelin	F	Alfa Romeo 8C "Monza"	88.180
1934	GP	Louis Chiron	MC	Alfa Romeo Tipo-B "P3"	79.257
1935	GP	René Dreyfus	F	Alfa Romeo Tipo-B "P3"	82.552
1936	SC	Jean-Pierre Wimille	F	Bugatti	87.140
1937	SC	Jean-Pierre Wimille	F	Bugatti	90.120
1947	F1	Christian Kautz	CH	Maserati 4CL	95.800

Reims Grand Prix

year	formula	winner	nat	car	mph
1952	F2	Jean Behra	F	Gordini 16	105.837
1957	F1	Luigi Musso	I	Lancia-Ferrari D50	124.046
1962	F1	Bruce McLaren	NZ	Cooper T60-Climax	126.290
1964	F2	Alan Rees	GB	Brabham BT10-Ford	118.990
1965	F2	Jochen Rindt	A	Brabham BT16-Ford	121.920
1966	F2	Jack Brabham	AUS	Brabham BT18-Honda	122.430
1967	F2	Jochen Rindt	A	Brabham BT23-Ford	134.065
1968	F2	Jackie Stewart	GB	Matra MS7-Ford	129.167
1969	F2	François Cevert	F	Tecno 69-Ford	136.514

Reims 12 hours

year	formula	winner	nat	car	mph
1953	SC	Peter Whitehead/Stirling Moss	GB	Jaguar	105.520
1954	SC	Peter Whitehead/Ken Wharton	GB	Jaguar	104.540
1956	SC	Duncan Hamilton/Ivor Bueb	GB	Jaguar	111.010
1957	GT	Paul Frère/Olivier Gendebien	B	Ferrari	104.020
1958	GT	Paul Frère/Olivier Gendebien	B	Ferrari	106.050
1964	SC W	Graham Hill/Jo Bonnier	GB/S	Ferrari 250LM	126.649
1965	SC W	Pedro Rodriguez/Jean Guichet	MEX/F	Ferrari 365P2	122.759
1967	SC	Jo Schlesser/Guy Ligier	F	Ford GT40 Mk2	127.294

ROUEN-LES-ESSARTS

Set in attractive woodland, Rouen-les-Essarts was one of Europe's finest circuits. Opened by the AC de Normand in 1950, Rouen was modernized in 1952 with new pits, grandstand and wider track. The run down to the cobbled Nouveau Monde hairpin was breathtaking, but sadly very dangerous and a chicane was built to slow the cars in 1973. The return uphill required a strong engine. Rouen has also had its fair share of tragedy: Jo Schlesser was killed during the 1968 French GP, two died in an F3 race in 1970 and Gerry Birrell perished during the 1973 F2 race.

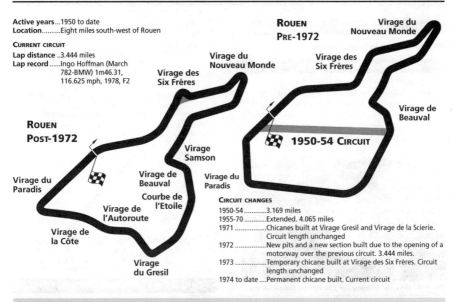

Active years...1950 to date
Location.........Eight miles south-west of Rouen

CURRENT CIRCUIT
Lap distance ..3.444 miles
Lap record ......Ingo Hoffman (March
782-BMW) 1m46.31,
116.625 mph, 1978, F2

ROUEN PRE-1972

Virage du Nouveau Monde
Virage des Six Frères
Virage des Six Frères
Virage du Nouveau Monde
Virage de Beauval

ROUEN POST-1972

1950-54 CIRCUIT

Virage Samson
Virage du Paradis
Virage de Beauval
Virage du Paradis
Courbe de l'Etoile
Virage du Paradis
Virage de l'Autoroute
Virage de la Côte
Virage du Gresil

CIRCUIT CHANGES
1950-54 ....3.169 miles
1955-70 ....Extended. 4.065 miles
1971 ....Chicanes built at Virage Gresil and Virage de la Scierie. Circuit length unchanged
1972 ....New pits and a new section built due to the opening of a motorway over the previous circuit. 3.444 miles.
1973 ....Temporary chicane built at Virage des Six Frères. Circuit length unchanged
1974 to date ....Permanent chicane built. Current circuit

French Grand Prix see above

Paris 1000 kms see Montlhéry

Rouen-les-Essarts Grand Prix

year	formula	winner	nat	car	mph
1951	F2	Giannino Marzotto	I	Ferrari 166/F2	75.315
1952*	F2 W	Alberto Ascari	I	Ferrari 500	80.281
1953	F1	Giuseppe Farina	I	Ferrari 500	84.446
1954	F1	Maurice Trintignant	F	Ferrari 625	81.892
1956	SC	Eugenio Castellotti	I	Ferrari	103.380
1957*	F1 W	Juan Manuel Fangio	RA	Maserati 250F	100.016
1958	SC	Jean Behra	F	Porsche	89.520
1959	F2	Stirling Moss	GB	Cooper T45-Borgward	96.899
1960	SC	Jack Fairman	GB	Aston Martin	88.350
1961	SC	Lucky Casner	USA	Maserati	92.250
1962*	F1 W	Dan Gurney	USA	Porsche 804	103.225
1963	FJ	Paul Hawkins	AUS	Brabham-Ford	98.980
1964*	F1 W	Dan Gurney	USA	Brabham BT7-Climax	108.766
1965	F2	Jim Clark	GB	Lotus 35-Ford	103.400
1966	F2	Denny Hulme	NZ	Brabham BT18-Honda	105.290
1967	F2	Jochen Rindt	A	Brabham BT23-Ford	116.760
1968*	F1 W	Jacky Ickx	B	Ferrari 312	100.452
1969	F3	Jean-Pierre Jaussaud	F	Tecno 69-Ford	102.878
1970	F2 E	Jo Siffert	CH	BMW F270	118.617
1971	F2 E	Ronnie Peterson	S	March 712M-Ford	109.657
1972	F2 E	Emerson Fittipaldi	BR	Lotus 69-Ford	114.096
1973	F2 E	Jean-Pierre Jarier	F	March 732-BMW	110.022
1974	F2	Hans-Joachim Stuck	D	March 742-BMW	96.699
1975	F2 E	Michel Leclère	F	March 752-BMW	112.445
1976	F2 E	Maurizio Flammini	I	March 762-BMW	112.196
1977	F2 E	Eddie Cheever	USA	Ralt RT1-BMW	114.460
1978	F2 E	Bruno Giacomelli	I	March 782-BMW	114.265
1980	F3	Alain Ferté	F	Martini MK27-Renault	102.520
1982	F3	Pierre Petit	F	Ralt RT3/82-Volkswagen	104.400
1983	F3	Michel Ferté	F	Martini MK39-Alfa Romeo	105.810
1984	F3	Frederic Delavallade	F	Martini MK42-Alfa Romeo	106.560
1985	F3	Yannick Dalmas	F	Martini MK45-Alfa Romeo	95.570
1986	F3	Frederic Delavallade	F	Ralt RT30-Volkswagen	108.150
1987	F3	Jean Alesi	F	Dallara 387-Alfa Romeo	104.220
1988	F3	Eric Cheli	F	Dallara 388-Alfa Romeo	108.990
1989	F3	Jean-Marc Gounon	F	Reynard 893-Alfa Romeo	109.210
1990	F3	Eric Hélary	F	Reynard 903-Mugen	108.860
1991	F3	Christophe Bouchut	F	Ralt RT33-Volkswagen	105.203
1992	F3	Stéphane Gregoire	F	Dallara 392-Alfa Romeo	109.585
1993	F3	Guillaume Gomez	F	Dallara 393-Fiat	110.513

*French Grand Prix

GERMANY

MAJOR CHAMPIONSHIPS

German Touring Car Championship

year	driver	nat	team	car
1984	Volker Strycek	D	Gubin	BMW 635 CSi
1985	Per Stureson	S	IPS	Volvo 240 turbo
1986	Kurt Thiim	DK	Nickel	Rover Vitesse 3.5
1987	Eric van de Poele	B	Zakspeed Racing	BMW M3
1988	Klaus Ludwig	D	Grab	Ford Sierra RS500
1989	Roberto Ravaglia	I	Schnitzer	BMW M3

The 1993 German Touring Car champion, Nicola Larini

year	driver	nat	team	car
1990	Hans-Joachim Stuck	D	Schmidt Motor Sport	Audi V8 Quattro
1991	Frank Biela	D	Audi Zentrum Reutlingen	Audi V8 Quattro
1992	Klaus Ludwig	D	AMG Motorenbau	Mercedes-Benz 190E Evo2
1993	Nicola Larini	I	Alfa Corse	Alfa Romeo 155 V6 Ti
1994	Klaus Ludwig	D	AMG Motorenbau	Mercedes-Benz C Class

ONS/ADAC Touring Car Cup

A series new to 1994 based on the FIA Class 2 (2-litre) rules

year	driver	nat	team	car
1994	Johnny Cecotto	YV	Team Warthofer	BMW 318i

German Formula Three Championship (including Formula Junior)

year	driver	nat	team	car
1950	Toni Krauzer	D	Toni Krauzer	Cooper-JAP
1951	Walter Kornossa	D	Walter Kornossa	Scampolo-BMW
1952	Hellmut Deutz	D	Hellmut Deutz	Scampolo-DKW/ Norton
1953	Adolf Lang	D	Adolf Lang	Cooper-JAP
1960*	Gerhard Mitter	D	Gerhard Mitter	Mitter-DKW
1961*	Kurt Ahrens Jr	D	Kurt Ahrens Jr	Cooper-Ford
1963*	Kurt Ahrens Jr	D	Kurt Ahrens Jr	Cooper-Ford
1975	Ernst Maring	D	Jagermeister Maco Racing	Maco 375-Ford/ Maco 375-Toyota
1976	Bertram Schäfer	D	Valvoline Deutschland	Ralt RT1-BMW/ Ralt RT1-Toyota
1977	Peter Scharmann	A	Team Warsteiner Eurorace	Toj F302-BMW/ Toj F302-Toyota
1978	Bertram Schäfer	D	Klaus Zimmermann Racing	Ralt RT1-BMW/ Ralt RT1-Toyota
1979	Michael Korten	D	Klaus Zimmermann Racing	March 793-Toyota
1980	Frank Jelinski	D	Bertram Schäfer Racing	Ralt RT3/ 80-Toyota
1981	Frank Jelinski	D	Bertram Schäfer Racing	Ralt RT3/ 81-Toyota
1982	John Nielsen	DK	Volkswagen Motorsport	Ralt RT3/ 82-Volkswagen
1983	Franz Konrad	A	Scuderia Teutonia	Anson SA4-Toyota/ Anson SA4- Alfa Romeo
1984	Kurt Thiim	DK	Malte Bongers Racing	Ralt RT3- Alfa Romeo
1985	Volker Weidler	D	Josef Kaufmann Racing	Martini MK45- Volkswagen
1986	Kris Nissen	DK	Volkswagen Motorsport	Ralt RT30- Volkswagen
1987	Bernd Schneider	D	Schubel Rennsport	Dallara 387- Volkswagen
1988	Joachim Winkelhock	D	WTS Racing	Reynard 883- Volkswagen
1989	Karl Wendlinger	A	Helmut Marko	Ralt RT33- Alfa Romeo
1990	Michael Schumacher	D	WTS Racing	Reynard 903- Volkswagen
1991	Tom Kristensen	DK	Volkswagen Motorsport	Ralt RT35- Volkswagen
1992	Pedro Lamy	P	WTS Racing	Reynard 923-Opel
1993	Jos Verstappen	NL	WTS Racing	Dallara 393-Opel
1994	Jorg Müller	D	RSM Marko	Dallara 394-Fiat

*Formula Junior. 1960, 1961 and 1963 were unofficial championships

Polifac Formula Three Championship

year	driver	nat	team	car
1974	Giorgio Francia	I	Scuderia Mirabella MM	March 743- Toyota

East German Formula Three Championship

year	driver	nat	car
1950	Richard Weiser	DDR	Weiser-BMW
1951	Daniel Zimmermann	DDR	Zimmermann
1952	Willy Lehmann	DDR	Lehmann-BMW
1953	Willy Lehmann	DDR	Lehmann-BMW/ Scampolo-BMW
1954	Willy Lehmann	DDR	Scampolo-BMW
1955	Willy Lehmann	DDR	Scampolo-BMW
1956	Willy Lehmann	DDR	Scampolo-BMW

German Racing Championship

Originally introduced for Group 2-4 Touring Cars, the Deutsche Rennsportmeisterschaft switched to Group 5 Sports Cars in 1977 (briefly threatening to overshadow the World title). 1985 was a poor final year before it was replaced by the Group C-based Supercup.

year	driver	nat	team	car
1973	Dieter Glemser	D	Zakspeed Racing	Ford Escort
1974	Dieter Glemser	D	Zakspeed Racing	Ford Escort
1975	Hans Heyer	D	Zakspeed Racing	Ford Escort
1976	Hans Heyer	D	Zakspeed Racing	Ford Escort
1977	Rolf Stommelen	D	Georg Loos	Porsche 935
1978	Harald Ertl	A	Schnitzer	BMW 320i turbo
1979	Klaus Ludwig	D	Porsche Kremer Racing	Porsche 935-K3
1980	Hans Heyer	A	Lancia Corse	Lancia Beta Monte Carlo
1981	Klaus Ludwig	D	Zakspeed Racing	Ford Capri
1982	Bob Wollek	F	Jöst Racing	Porsche 936C
1983	Bob Wollek	F	Jöst Racing	Porsche 956
1984	Stefan Bellof	D	Brun Motorsport	Porsche 956B
1985	Jochen Mass	D	Jöst Racing	Porsche 956
1986	Hans-Joachim Stuck	D	Porsche System Engineering	Porsche 962
1987	Hans-Joachim Stuck	D	Porsche System Engineering	Porsche 962
1988	Jean-Louis Schlesser	F	Team Sauber Mercedes	Sauber C9/ 88-Mercedes-Benz
1989	Bob Wollek	F	Jöst Racing	Porsche 962

ADAC GT Cup

year	driver	nat	car
1993	Johnny Cecotto	YV	BMW M3 GTR
1994	Ralf Kelleners	D	Porsche 911 RSR

Interserie

Inaugurated in 1970 as Europe's answer to Can-Am, Interserie has remained a mainly German affair

year	driver	nat	car
1970	Jurgen Neuhaus	D	Porsche 910
1971	Leo Kinnunen	SF	Porsche 917S
1972	Leo Kinnunen	SF	Porsche 917/10
1973	Leo Kinnunen	SF	Porsche 917/10K turbo
1974	Herbert Müller	CH	Porsche 917/20K turbo/ Porsche 917/30 turbo
1975	Herbert Müller	CH	Porsche 917/20K/ Porsche 908/3 Spyder
1976	Herbert Müller	CH	Sauber C5-BMW
1977	Helmut Bross	D	Lola T298-BMW
1978	Reinhold Jöst	D	Porsche 908/3 turbo
1979	Kurt Lotterschmid	D	Toj C205-BMW
1980	Kurt Lotterschmid	D	Toj C205-BMW
1981	Roland Binder	D	Lola T297-BMW
1982	Roland Binder	D	Lola T297-BMW
1983	Walter Lechner	A	March-Ford
1984	Klaus Niedzwiedz	D	Ford Zakspeed C1/8
1985	Roland Binder	D	Persy-BMW Can-Am
1986	"John Winter"	D	Porsche 956
1987	Walter Lechner	A	Porsche 962
1988	Jochen Dauer	D	Porsche 962
1989	Walter Lechner	A	Porsche 962
1990	Bernd Schneider	D	Porsche 962-K6
1991	Bernd Schneider	D	Porsche 962
1992	Manuel Reuter	D	Kremer K7-Porsche
1993	Giovanni Lavaggi	I	Kremer K7-Porsche
1994	Johan Rajamaki	S	Footwork-Judd

MAJOR INTERNATIONAL RACES

GERMAN GRAND PRIX

year	formula	circuit	winner	nat	car	mph
1926	SC	Avus	Rudolf Caracciola	D	Mercedes	83.719
1927	SC	Nürburgring	Otto Merz	D	Mercedes-Benz S	63.313
1928	SC	Nürburgring	Rudolf Caracciola/Christian Werner	D	Mercedes-Benz SS	64.429
1929	SC	Nürburgring	Louis Chiron	MC	Bugatti T35C	66.297
1931	GP	Nürburgring	Rudolf Caracciola	D	Mercedes-Benz SSKL	67.227
1932	GP	Nürburgring	Rudolf Caracciola	D	Alfa Romeo Tipo-B "P3"	73.946
1934	GP	Nürburgring	Hans Stuck	D	Auto Union A	76.353
1935	GP	Nürburgring	Tazio Nuvolari	I	Alfa Romeo Tipo-B "P3"	75.384
1936	GP	Nürburgring	Bernd Rosemeyer	D	Auto Union C	81.783
1937	GP	Nürburgring	Rudolf Caracciola	D	Mercedes-Benz W125	82.745
1938	GP	Nürburgring	Dick Seaman	GB	Mercedes-Benz W154	80.685
1939	GP	Nürburgring	Rudolf Caracciola	D	Mercedes-Benz W163	75.194
1950	F2	Nürburgring	Alberto Ascari	I	Ferrari 166/F2	77.710
1951	F1 W	Nürburgring	Alberto Ascari	I	Ferrari 375	83.723
1952	F2 W	Nürburgring	Alberto Ascari	I	Ferrari 500	82.162
1953	F2 W	Nürburgring	Giuseppe Farina	I	Ferrari 500	83.876
1954	F1 W	Nürburgring	Juan Manuel Fangio	RA	Mercedes-Benz W196	82.832
1956	F1 W	Nürburgring	Juan Manuel Fangio	RA	Lancia-Ferrari D50	85.496
1957	F1 W	Nürburgring	Juan Manuel Fangio	RA	Maserati 250F	88.780
1958	F1 W	Nürburgring	Tony Brooks	GB	Vanwall VW4	90.268
1959	F1 W	Avus	Tony Brooks	GB	Ferrari Dino 246	143.331
1960	F2	Nürburgring	Jo Bonnier	S	Porsche 718	80.232
1961	F1 W	Nürburgring	Stirling Moss	GB	Lotus 18/21-Climax	92.255
1962	F1 W	Nürburgring	Graham Hill	GB	BRM P57	80.314
1963	F1 W	Nürburgring	John Surtees	GB	Ferrari Dino 156	95.785
1964	F1 W	Nürburgring	John Surtees	GB	Ferrari 158	96.535
1965	F1 W	Nürburgring	Jim Clark	GB	Lotus 33-Climax	99.710
1966	F1 W	Nürburgring	Jack Brabham	AUS	Brabham BT19-Repco	86.707
1967	F1 W	Nürburgring	Denny Hulme	NZ	Brabham BT24-Repco	101.408
1968	F1 W	Nürburgring	Jackie Stewart	GB	Matra MS10-Ford	85.714
1969	F1 W	Nürburgring	Jacky Ickx	B	Brabham BT26-Ford	108.428
1970	F1 W	Hockenheim	Jochen Rindt	A	Lotus 72-Ford	124.082
1971	F1 W	Nürburgring	Jackie Stewart	GB	Tyrrell 003-Ford	114.451
1972	F1 W	Nürburgring	Jacky Ickx	B	Ferrari 312B2	116.616
1973	F1 W	Nürburgring	Jackie Stewart	GB	Tyrrell 006-Ford	116.793
1974	F1 W	Nürburgring	Clay Regazzoni	CH	Ferrari 312B3	117.330
1975	F1 W	Nürburgring	Carlos Reutemann	RA	Brabham BT44B-Ford	117.734
1976	F1 W	Nürburgring	James Hunt	GB	McLaren M23-Ford	117.182
1977	F1 W	Hockenheim	Niki Lauda	A	Ferrari 312T2	129.589
1978	F1 W	Hockenheim	Mario Andretti	USA	Lotus 79-Ford	129.425
1979	F1 W	Hockenheim	Alan Jones	AUS	Williams FW07-Ford	134.309
1980	F1 W	Hockenheim	Jacques Laffite	F	Ligier JS11/15-Ford	137.252
1981	F1 W	Hockenheim	Nelson Piquet	BR	Brabham BT49C-Ford	132.570
1982	F1 W	Hockenheim	Patrick Tambay	F	Ferrari 126C2	130.448
1983	F1 W	Hockenheim	René Arnoux	F	Ferrari 126C3	130.819
1984	F1 W	Hockenheim	Alain Prost	F	McLaren MP4/2-TAG Porsche	131.613
1985	F1 W	Nürburgring	Michele Alboreto	I	Ferrari 156/85	118.762
1986	F1 W	Hockenheim	Nelson Piquet	BR	Williams FW11-Honda	135.751
1987	F1 W	Hockenheim	Nelson Piquet	BR	Williams FW11B-Honda	136.951
1988	F1 W	Hockenheim	Ayrton Senna	BR	McLaren MP4/4-Honda	120.021

year	formula	circuit	winner	nat	car	mph
1989	F1 W	Hockenheim	Ayrton Senna	BR	McLaren MP4/5-Honda	139.543
1990	F1 W	Hockenheim	Ayrton Senna	BR	McLaren MP4/5B-Honda	141.270
1991	F1 W	Hockenheim	Nigel Mansell	GB	Williams FW14-Renault	143.565
1992	F1 W	Hockenheim	Nigel Mansell	GB	Williams FW14B-Renault	145.909
1993	F1 W	Hockenheim	Alain Prost	F	Williams FW15C-Renault	145.327
1994	F1 W	Hockenheim	Gerhard Berger	A	Ferrari 412T1B	137.906

GERMAN GRAND PRIX FORMULA TWO CLASS

year	formula	circuit	winner	nat	car	mph
1931	Cyc	Nürburgring	Dudley Froy	GB	Riley 9	58.030
1932	V	Nürburgring	Henri Tauber	D	Alfa Romeo 6C-1500	66.360
1957	F2	Nürburgring	Edgar Barth	DDR	Porsche 550RS	82.418
1958	F2	Nürburgring	Bruce McLaren	NZ	Cooper T45-Climax	86.332
1966	F2	Nürburgring	Jean-Pierre Beltoise	F	Matra MS5-Ford	80.055
1967	F2	Nürburgring	Jackie Oliver	GB	Lotus 48-Cosworth	96.683
1969	F2	Nürburgring	Henri Pescarolo	F	Matra MS7-Cosworth	100.915

CIRCUITS AND OTHER RACES

AVUS

The start of the 1937 Avusrennen won by Hermann Lang

Built in the Grunewald district of Berlin, the circuit design for Avus was simple: two straights joined by a slightly banked corner at Charlottenburg and a hairpin six miles south at Nikolasse. From 1937 until it was dismantled in 1967, the 43-degree banked North Curve (or "Wall of Death") boosted average lap speeds to over 170 mph. At the end of the war the southern end ran into the Soviet zone, so a new South Curve was built, cutting the circuit in half. The German GP has been held twice at Avus, Caracciola's private Mercedes winning the inaugural event in 1926 and Brooks succeeding in 1959. Both were tragic affairs: in 1926 Adolf Rosenberger crashed into a scoring hut killing the three occupants and Jean Behra died in a Sports Car race supporting the 1959 event. Avus, further-reduced in length, now hosts German Touring Car, F3 and 2-litre races.

Südkurve

New Südkurve

Nordkurve

Avus
1921-67

Active years...1921 to date
Location..........South-western suburbs of Berlin

CURRENT CIRCUIT
Lap distance ..1.640 miles
Lap record ......Stefano Modena (Alfa Romeo 155 V6 TI), 53.44s, 110.479 mph, 1994, German Touring Cars

CIRCUIT CHANGES
1921-36 ....12.16 miles
1937-39 ....North curve banking built. 11.98 miles
1951-67 ....New South Curve built as half the circuit was in Soviet held territory. 5.157 miles
1968-88 ....North Curve banking dismantled. 5.039 miles
1989-91 ....3.032 miles
1992 to date ....Current circuit

German Grand Prix see above

Avusrennen

year	formula	winner	nat	car	mph
1931	FL	Rudolf Caracciola	D	Mercedes-Benz SSKL	115.047
1932	FL	Manfred von Brauchitsch	D	Mercedes-Benz SSKL	120.431
1933	FL	Achille Varzi	I	Bugatti T54	128.140
1934	FL	Guy Moll	DZ	Alfa Romeo Tipo-B "P3"	127.182
1935	FL	Luigi Fagioli	I	Mercedes-Benz W25B	148.232
1937	FL	Hermann Lang	D	Mercedes-Benz W125 streamlined	162.063
1951	F2	Paul Greifzu	DDR	BMW Eigenbau	112.582
1952	F2	Rudolf Fischer	CH	Ferrari 500	115.922
1953	F2	Jacques Swaters	B	Ferrari 500	118.907
1954	SC	Richard von Frankenberg	D	Porsche	120.200
1962	GT	Edgar Berney	CH	Ferrari	126.450
1963	GT	Peter Nöcker	D	Jaguar	131.050
1966	SC	Udo Schutz	D	Porsche Carrera 6	142.795
1967	SC	Günther Klass	D	Porsche Carrera 6	n/a

year	formula	winner	nat	car	mph
1976	F3	Conny Andersson	S	March 763-Toyota	n/a
1978	SC	Toine Hezemans	D	Porsche 935	n/a
1980	Procar	Manfred Schurti	FL	BMW M1	132.310
1983	SC	Bob Wollek	F	Porsche 956	144.480
	F3	Rudi Seher	D	Anson SA3-Toyota	117.350
1984	TC	Olaf Manthey	D	Rover Vitesse	113.014
1985	TC	Klaus Niedzwiedz	D	Ford Sierra XR4Ti	117.207
1986	TC	Volker Weidler	D	Mercedes-Benz 190E	116.960
1987	TC	Frank Biela	D	Ford Sierra XR4Ti	119.697
1988*	TC	Johnny Cecotto	YV	Mercedes-Benz 190E	122.115
	TC	Johnny Cecotto	YV	Mercedes-Benz 190E	122.488
1989*	TC	Roberto Ravaglia	I	BMW M3	111.155
	TC	Klaus Niedzwiedz	D	Ford Sierra Cosworth	111.102
1990*	TC	Hans-Joachim Stuck	D	Audi V8 Quattro	112.593
	TC	Hans-Joachim Stuck	D	Audi V8 Quattro	114.165
1991*	TC	Hans-Joachim Stuck	D	Audi V8 Quattro	118.305
	TC	Frank Biela	D	Audi V8 Quattro	118.429
1992*	TC	Steve Soper	GB	BMW M3	101.713
	TC	Bernd Schneider	D	Mercedes-Benz 190E	102.363
1993*	TC	Roland Asch	D	Mercedes-Benz 190E	94.821
	TC	Roland Asch	D	Mercedes-Benz 190E	102.387
1994*	TC	Stefano Modena	I	Alfa Romeo 155 V6 Ti	97.153
	TC	Stefano Modena	I	Alfa Romeo 155 V6 Ti	96.935

*From 1988 German Touring Car races had two heats with no aggregate winner. Note: other race details: n/a

HOCKENHEIM

On 7 April 1968, in an accident which has yet to be fully explained, Jim Clark died during the Formula Two Deutschland Trophäe at Hockenheim. The circuit has held the German GP since 1977 but it is still Clark's death for which it is best known. The circuit stretched from the edge of Hockenheim town to the Ostkurve but, when the Autobahn that now provides unrivalled access was built in 1966 the circuit was redesigned by John Hugenholtz and reduced in length. Hockenheim first held the Grand Prix in 1970 while the Nürburgring was being modernized. Chicanes were built on the two main straights for that race, and after Patrick Depailler died in testing in 1980, a third chicane was installed at the previously demanding Ostkurve. In the wet, Hockenheim has appalling visibility, a contributing factor to the accident which ended Didier Pironi's career in 1982.

Hockenheim in 1988: the German Grand Prix

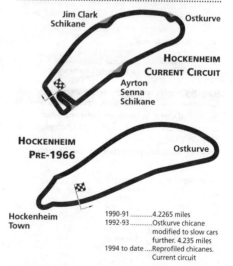

Active years...1939 to date
Location..........15 miles south-west of Heidelberg, 55 miles south
of Frankfurt

CURRENT CIRCUIT
Lap distance ..4.220 miles
Lap record ......David Coulthard (Williams FW16-Renault),
1m46.211, 143.036 mph, 1994, F1

CIRCUIT CHANGES
1929-65 ....4.78 miles
1966-70 ....Modified circuit due to building of an autobahn.
4.206 miles
1970-81 ....Chicanes inserted on the two main straights, first
used 1970 German GP. 4.219 miles
1982-89 ....First chicane reconstructed and Ostkurve installed.
4.2236 miles

1990-91 ....4.2265 miles
1992-93 ....Ostkurve chicane
modified to slow cars
further. 4.235 miles
1994 to date ....Reprofiled chicanes.
Current circuit

German Grand Prix see above

Jim Clark Trophy

year	formula	winner	nat	car	mph
1969	F2 E	Jean-Pierre Beltoise	F	Matra MS7-Ford	123.615
1970	F2 E	Clay Regazzoni	CH	Tecno 70-Ford	123.070
1971	F2 E	François Cevert	F	Tecno 71-Ford	116.168
1972	F2 E	Jean-Pierre Jaussaud	F	Brabham BT38-Ford	118.562

year	formula	winner	nat	car	mph
1973	F2 E	Jean-Pierre Jarier	F	March 732-BMW	122.809
1974	F2 E	Hans-Joachim Stuck	D	March 742-BMW	124.060
1975	F2 E	Gérard Larrousse	F	Elf 2/A367-BMW	122.047
1976	F2 E	Hans-Joachim Stuck	D	March 762-BMW	123.845
1977	F2 E	Jochen Mass	D	March 772P-BMW	124.485
1978	F2 E	Bruno Giacomelli	I	March 782-BMW	125.993
1979	F2 E	Keke Rosberg	SF	March 792-BMW	125.859
1980	F2 E	Teo Fabi	I	March 802-BMW	125.448
1981	F2 E	Stefan Johansson	S	Toleman T850-Hart	125.591
1982	F2 E	Stefan Bellof	D	Maurer MM82-BMW	120.565
1983	F2 E	Jonathan Palmer	GB	Ralt RH6/83-Honda	121.795
1984	F2 E	Roberto Moreno	BR	Ralt RH6/84-Honda	123.163

Jochen Rindt Trophy

year	formula	winner	nat	car	mph
1971	F1	Jacky Ickx	B	Ferrari 312B	126.218
1972	F2 E	Emerson Fittipaldi	BR	Lotus 69-Ford	103.107
1973	F2 E	Jochen Mass	D	Surtees TS15-Ford	122.966
1974	F2 E	Jean-Pierre Jabouille	F	Elf 2/A367-BMW	123.514
1975	F2 E	Jacques Laffite	F	Martini MK16-BMW	122.211

Other European Formula Two races

year	formula	winner	nat	car	mph
1967	F2 E	Frank Gardner	AUS	Brabham BT23-Ford	122.366
1968	F2 E	Jean-Pierre Beltoise	F	Matra MS7-Ford	117.612
	F2 E	Tino Brambilla	I	Ferrari Dino 166	123.240
1970	F2 E	Dieter Quester	A	BMW F270	115.348
1972	F2 E	Tim Schenken	AUS	Brabham BT38-Ford	120.224
1974	F2 E	Patrick Depailler	F	March 742-BMW	121.352
1976	F2 E	Hans-Joachim Stuck	D	March 762-BMW	124.301
	F2 E	Jean-Pierre Jabouille	F	Elf 2J-Renault	122.663
1978	F2 E	Bruno Giacomelli	I	March 782-BMW	125.809
1979	F2 E	Stephen South	GB	March 792-BMW	125.096
1980	F2 E	Teo Fabi	I	March 802-BMW	127.239
1982	F2 E	Corrado Fabi	I	March 822-BMW	120.537
1984	F2 E	Pascal Fabre	F	March 842-BMW	121.958

International Formula 3000 race

year	formula	winner	nat	car	mph
1990	F3000 INT	Eddie Irvine	GB	Reynard 90D-Mugen	126.277
1991	F3000 INT	Emanuele Naspetti	I	Reynard 91D-Cosworth	128.311
1992	F3000 INT	Luca Badoer	I	Reynard 92D-Cosworth	130.630
1993	F3000 INT	Olivier Panis	F	Reynard 93D-Cosworth	129.473
1994	F3000 INT	Franck Lagorce	F	Reynard 94D-Cosworth	126.770

World Sports Car race

year	formula	winner	nat	car	mph
1977	SC W	Bob Wollek/John Fitzpatrick	F/GB	Porsche 935	116.023
1985	SC W	Derek Bell/Hans-Joachim Stuck	GB/D	Porsche 956C	115.328

KASSEL-CALDEN

An airfield circuit in Northern Germany which used to host a round of the European F3 Championship. As that championship was abandoned, Kassel-Calden reverted to promoting national events.

Active years...1976 to date
Location..........75 miles south of Hannover
Lap distance ..1.609 miles
Lap record......Oscar Larrauri (Euroracing 101-Alfa Romeo)
1m04.87, 89.293 mph, 1982, F3

European Formula Three race

year	formula	winner	nat	car	mph
1976	F3 E	Riccardo Patrese	I	Chevron B34-Toyota	n/a
1977	F3 E	Nelson Piquet	BR	Ralt RT1-Toyota	101.603
1978	F3 E	Anders Olofsson	S	Ralt RT1-Toyota	102.505
1979	F3 E	Michael Korten	D	March 793-Toyota	101.264
1980	F3 E	Michele Alboreto	I	March 803B-Alfa Romeo	104.960
1982	F3 E	Emanuele Pirro	I	Euroracing 101-Alfa Romeo	87.381

NORISRING

One of the first German circuits used after the war, the Norisring is a simple circuit on the grounds of Hitler's Nuremberg Nazi rallies of the 1930s. The track passes either side of the imposing concrete grandstands which hold 40,000 spectators. The Norisring takes its name from the ancient word Nürnberg (Noris) to avoid confusion with the more famous Nürburgring. A 200-mile race with healthy prize money has been held since 1967. Originally a round of the German Sports Car Championship, it is now part of the Touring Car series.

NORISRING

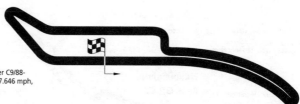

Active years...1947 to date
Location..........105 miles north of Munich, 150 miles south-east of Frankfurt
Lap distance ..1.429 miles
Lap record ......Jean-Louis Schlesser (Sauber C9/88-Mercedes-Benz) 47.79s, 107.646 mph, 1988, Group C Sports Cars

Norisring 200 miles

year	formula	winner	nat	car	mph
1967	SC	Frank Gardner	AUS	Lola T70 Mk2-Chevrolet	n/a
1968	SC	David Piper	GB	Ferrari P4	106.146
1969	SC	Brian Redman	GB	Lola T70 Mk3B-Chevrolet	110.990
1970	SC	Jürgen Neuhaus	D	Porsche 917	111.300
1971	SC	Chris Craft	GB	McLaren M8E-Chevrolet	114.291
1972	SC	Leo Kinnunen	SF	Porsche 917/10T	94.936
1973	SC	Leo Kinnunen	SF	Porsche 917/10T	93.231
1974	SC	Hans-Joachim Stuck	D	BMW 3.0 CSL	88.560
1975	SC	Toine Hezemans	NL	Porsche Carrera RSR	89.144
1976	SC	Bob Wollek	F	Porsche 934	89.338
1977	SC	Manfred Schurti	FL	Porsche 935	n/a
1978	SC	Bob Wollek	F	Porsche 935	95.496
1979	SC	Rolf Stommelen	D	Porsche 935	n/a
1980	SC	John Fitzpatrick	GB	Porsche 935	86.290
1981	SC	Bob Wollek	F	Porsche 935-K4	93.200
1982	SC	Jochen Mass	D	Porsche 956	94.850
1983	SC	Stefan Bellof	D	Porsche 956	n/a
1984	SC	Manfred Winkelhock	D	Porsche 956B	100.990
1985	SC	Klaus Ludwig	D	Porsche 956B	102.440
1986	SC W	Klaus Ludwig	D	Porsche 956	101.087
1987	SC W	Mauro Baldi/Jonathan Palmer	I/GB	Porsche 962GTi	101.831
1988	SC	Jean-Louis Schlesser	F	Sauber C9/88-Mercedes-Benz	102.610
1989	SC	Frank Jeliski	D	Porsche 962	100.040
1990*	TC	Hans-Joachim Stuck	D	Audi V8 Quattro	87.562
	TC	Roberto Ravaglia	I	BMW M3	91.117
1991*	TC	Kurt Thiim	DK	Mercedes-Benz 190E	93.632
	TC	Hans-Joachim Stuck	D	Audi V8 Quattro	93.440
1992*	TC	Joachim Winkelhock	D	BMW M3	94.219
	TC	Steve Soper	GB	BMW M3	94.453
1993*	TC	Nicola Larini	I	Alfa Romeo 155 V6 TI	94.514
	TC	Nicola Larini	I	Alfa Romeo 155 V6 TI	95.170
1994*	TC	Nicola Larini	I	Alfa Romeo 155 V6 TI	96.590
	TC	Kris Nissen	DK	Alfa Romeo 155 V6 TI	96.770

*From 1988 German Touring Car races had two heats with no aggregate winner

European Formula Two race

year	formula	winner	nat	car	mph
1973	F2 E	Tim Schenken	AUS	Motul M1-Ford	100.429

NÜRBURGRING

The greatest road racing circuit in the world. 14 miles and 176 corners, the old 'Ring was a never-ending succession of evocative turns and changing gradient. After the start, which is dominated by a castle overlooking Nürburg village, the cars race out into the mountains, to Flugplatz (where they leave the ground), Adenau Bridge, Karussel, Wippermann, Pflanzgarten, Tiergarten and so on. The organizers tried to keep the 'Ring up to date, resurfacing in 1957 and completely rebuilding large parts in 1970. But following Niki Lauda's near-fatal accident in 1976 the CSI ruled that the Nordschleife was no longer safe for F1. Government investment helped build a modern Grand Prix track at the old start/finish area. However, the result was an uninspiring "designed-by-computer" venue which suffers in comparison with the original. The old pits were replaced with a new complex and a modern hotel now overlooks the startline. For enthusiasts, the old circuit, or Nordschleife, is thankfully still used for Touring Cars.

Approaching the Flugplatz on the old Nürburgring

Active years ...1926 to date
Location ....40 miles west of Koblenz, 44 miles south of Bonn

CURRENT CIRCUIT (NEW GRAND PRIX CIRCUIT)
Lap distance ..2.822 miles
Lap record ......Teo Fabi (Jaguar XJR-14) 1m21.533, 124.603 mph,
1991, Group C Sports Cars

NORDSCHLEIFE/
GRAND PRIX CIRCUIT CHANGES
1927-66 ....14.167 miles
1967-82 ....Circuit
resurfaced,
some bumps
eased in 1970.
14.189 miles
1983 ....Shortened
while new circuit was being built. 12.944 miles
1984 to date ....Nordschleife and new Grand Prix circuit combined. 15.43 miles
1984 to date ....New Grand Prix Circuit

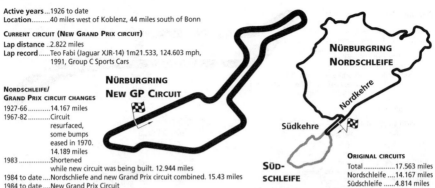

ORIGINAL CIRCUITS
Total ....17.563 miles
Nordschleife ....14.167 miles
Südschleife ......4.814 miles

German Grand Prix see above

European Grand Prix see above

Eifelrennen

year	formula	winner	nat	car	mph
1927	SC	Rudolf Caracciola	D	Mercedes-Benz S	59.960
1928	SC	Otto Spandel	D	Steyr	54.490
1929	SC	W Bartsch	D	Amilcar	45.130
1930	GP	Heinrich-Joachim von Morgen	D	Bugatti T35B	67.233
1931	GP	Rudolf Caracciola	D	Mercedes-Benz SSK	67.649
1932	GP	Rudolf Caracciola	D	Alfa Romeo 8C "Monza"	70.681
1933	GP	Tazio Nuvolari	I	Alfa Romeo 8C "Monza"	70.450
1934	GP	Manfred von Brauchitsch	D	Mercedes-Benz W25A	76.070
1935	GP	Rudolf Caracciola	D	Mercedes-Benz W25B	73.027
1936	GP	Bernd Rosemeyer	D	Auto Union C	72.846
1937	GP	Bernd Rosemeyer	D	Auto Union C	83.183
1939	GP	Hermann Lang	D	Mercedes-Benz W163	84.201
1949	SC	Karl Kling	D	Veritas	69.960
1950	F2	Fritz Riess	D	AFM 3-BMW	73.685
1951	F2	Paul Pietsch	D	Veritas Meteor	71.463
1952	F2	Rudolf Fischer	CH	Ferrari 500	77.303
1953	F2	Emanuel de Graffenried	CH	Maserati A6GCM	70.388
1954	SC	Günther Bechem	D	Borgward	73.360
1955	SC	Juan Manuel Fangio	RA	Mercedes-Benz	81.080
1956	GT	W Shock	D	Mercedes-Benz	76.080
1957	GT	Heine Walter	CH	Porsche	75.280
1958	GT	Wolfgang Seidel	D	Ferrari	74.630
1959	FJ	Wolfgang von Trips	D	Stanguellini-Fiat	77.670
1960	FJ	Dennis Taylor	GB	Lola Mk2-Ford	70.030
1961	FJ	Jo Siffert	CH	Lotus 20-Ford	75.250
1962	FJ	Peter Warr	GB	Lotus 22-Ford	85.560
1963	FJ	Gerhard Mitter	D	Lotus-DKW	77.550
1964	F2	Jim Clark	GB	Lotus 32-Ford	91.100
1965	F2	Paul Hawkins	AUS	Alexis Mk6-Ford	79.390
1966	F2	Jochen Rindt	A	Brabham BT18-Ford	78.700
1967	F2 E	Jochen Rindt	A	Brabham BT23-Ford	90.476
1968	F2	Chris Irwin	GB	Lola T100-Ford	101.783
1969	F2 E	Jackie Stewart	GB	Matra MS7-Ford	104.237
1970	F2	Jochen Rindt	A	Lotus 69-Ford	101.348
1971	F2 E	François Cevert	F	Tecno 71-Ford	105.994
1972	F2	Jochen Mass	D	March 722-Ford	106.298
1973	F2 E	Reine Wisell	S	GRD 273-Ford	93.163
1975	F2 E	Jacques Laffite	F	Martini MK16-BMW	112.015
1976	F2	Freddy Kottulinsky	S	Ralt RT1-BMW	110.550
1977	F2 E	Jochen Mass	D	March 772P-BMW	114.899
1978	F2 E	Alex Ribeiro	BR	March 782-Hart	115.098
1979	F2 E	Marc Surer	CH	March 792-BMW	105.279
1980	F2 E	Teo Fabi	I	March 802-BMW	112.443
1981	F2 E	Thierry Boutsen	B	March 812-BMW	117.738
1982	F2 E	Thierry Boutsen	B	Spirit 201-Honda	117.836
1983	F2 E	Beppe Gabbiani	I	March 832-BMW	118.926
1985	F3000 INT	CANCELLED - SNOW			
1986	TC	Volker Weidler	D	Mercedes-Benz 190E	88.093
1987	TC	Manuel Reuter	D	Ford Sierra XR4Ti	89.553
1988*	TC	Kurt Thiim	DK	BMW M3	91.229
	TC	Dany Snobeck	F	Mercedes-Benz 190E	91.554
1989*	TC	Steve Soper	GB	BMW M3	88.094
	TC	Steve Soper	GB	BMW M3	88.528
1990*	TC	Steve Soper	GB	BMW M3	93.914
	TC	Steve Soper	GB	BMW M3	94.314

year	formula	winner	nat	car	mph
1991*	TC	Klaus Ludwig	D	Mercedes-Benz 190E	97.298
	TC	Klaus Ludwig	D	Mercedes-Benz 190E	97.300
1992*	TC	Frank Biela	D	Audi V8 Quattro	88.903
	TC	Roland Asch	D	Mercedes-Benz 190E	97.708
1993*	TC	Nicola Larini	I	Alfa Romeo 155 V6 TI	98.724
	TC	Klaus Ludwig	D	Mercedes-Benz 190E	98.701
1994*	TC	Klaus Ludwig	D	Mercedes-Benz C Class	89.510
	TC	Nicola Larini	I	Alfa Romeo 155 V6 TI	88.370

*From 1988 German Touring Car races had two heats with no aggregate winner.

International F3000 race

year	formula	winner	nat	car	mph
1985*	F3000 INT	CANCELLED - SNOW			
1992	F3000 INT	Luca Badoer	I	Reynard 92D-Cosworth	115.142
1993	F3000 INT	Olivier Panis	F	Reynard 93D-Cosworth	113.945

*Eifelrennen

World Sports Car race

year	formula	winner	nat	car	mph
1953	SC W	Alberto Ascari/Giuseppe Farina	I	Ferrari 340MM	74.692
1956	SC W	Stirling Moss/Jean Behra/Harry Schell/Piero Taruffi	GB/F/USA/I	Maserati 300S	80.621
1957	SC W	Tony Brooks/Noel Cunningham-Reid	GB	Aston Martin DBR1/300	82.447
1958	SC W	Stirling Moss/Jack Brabham	GB/AUS	Aston Martin DBR1/300	84.322
1959	SC W	Stirling Moss/Jack Fairman	GB	Aston Martin DBR1/300	82.508
1960	SC W	Stirling Moss/Dan Gurney	GB/USA	Maserati T61	82.805
1961	SC W	Masten Gregory/Lucky Casner	USA	Maserati T61	79.297
1962	SC W	Olivier Gendebien/Phil Hill	B/USA	Ferrari Dino 246SP	82.661
1963	SC W	John Surtees/Willy Mairesse	GB/B	Ferrari 250P	82.689
1964	SC W	Ludovico Scarfiotti/Nino Vaccarella	I	Ferrari 275P	87.293
1965	SC W	John Surtees/Ludovico Scarfiotti	GB/I	Ferrari 275P2	90.539
1966	SC W	Phil Hill/Jo Bonnier	USA/S	Chaparral 2D-Chevrolet	89.306
1967	SC W	Udo Schutz/Joe Buzzetta	D/USA	Porsche 910/6	90.434
1968	SC W	Jo Siffert/Vic Elford	CH/GB	Porsche 908/8	95.048
1969	SC W	Jo Siffert/Brian Redman	CH/GB	Porsche 908/8	100.957
1970	SC W	Vic Elford/Kurt Ahrens Jr	GB/D	Porsche 908/3	102.528
1971	SC W	Vic Elford/Gérard Larrousse	GB/F	Porsche 908/3	106.471
1972	SC W	Ronnie Peterson/Tim Schenken	S/AUS	Ferrari 312P	103.572
1973	SC W	Jacky Ickx/Brian Redman	B/GB	Ferrari 312P	111.190
1974	SC W	Jean-Pierre Beltoise/Jean-Pierre Jarier	F	Matra-Simca MS670C	113.557
1975	SC W	Arturo Merzario/Jacques Laffite	I/F	Alfa Romeo T33TT/12	109.775
1976	SC W	Dieter Quester/Albrecht Krebs	A/D	BMW 3.0 CSL	100.448
1977	SC W	Toine Hezemans/Tim Schenken/Rolf Stommelen	NL/AUS/D	Porsche 935	104.486
1978	SC W	Klaus Ludwig/Hans Heyer/Toine Hezemans	D/D/NL	Porsche 935	105.288
1979	SC W	Manfred Schurti/John Fitzpatrick/Bob Wollek	FL/GB/F	Porsche 935	104.755
1980	SC W	Rolf Stommelen/Jürgen Barth	D	Porsche 908/3	106.341
1981	SC W	Hans-Joachim Stuck/Nelson Piquet	D/BR	BMW M1	105.758
1982	SC W	Riccardo Patrese/Michele Alboreto/Teo Fabi	I	Lancia LC1	105.762
1983	SC W	Jochen Mass/Jacky Ickx	D/B	Porsche 956	104.637
1984	SC W	Stefan Bellof/Derek Bell	D/GB	Porsche 956	97.163
1986	SC W	Mike Thackwell/Henri Pescarolo	NZ/F	Sauber C8-Mercedes-Benz	92.080
1987	SC W	Eddie Cheever/Raul Boesel	USA/BR	Jaguar XJR-8	105.145
1988	SC W	Jean-Louis Schlesser/Jochen Mass	F/D	Sauber C9/88-Mercedes-Benz	95.929
1989	SC W	Jean-Louis Schlesser/Jochen Mass	F/D	Sauber C9/88-Mercedes-Benz	107.316
1990	SC W	Mauro Baldi/Jean-Louis Schlesser	I/F	Mercedes-Benz C11	112.692
1991	SC W	David Brabham/Derek Warwick	AUS/GB	Jaguar XJR-14	111.950

300 km Sports Car race

year	formula	winner	nat	car	mph
1976	SC WSC	Reinhold Jöst	D	Porsche 908/3	89.818
1978	SC E	Giorgio Francia	I	Osella PA6-BMW	107.684

Nürburgring 24 hours

year	formula	winner	nat	car	mph
1970	TC	Hans-Joachim Stuck/Clemens Schickentanz	D	BMW 2002TI	n/a
1971	TC	Prince von Hohenzollern/Gerhold Pankl	D/A	BMW 2002TI Alpina	73.324
1972	TC	Helmut Kelleners/Gerhold Pankl	D/A	BMW Alpina	n/a
1973	TC	Niki Lauda/Hans-Peter Joisten	A/D	BMW CSL Alpina	n/a
1976	TC	KN Quirin/H Hechler/F Müller	D	Porsche Carrera	n/a
1977	TC	F Müller/H Hechler	D	Porsche Carrera	n/a
1978	TC	F Müller/H Hechler/F Geschwendtner	D	Porsche Carrera	n/a
1979	TC	H Kummle/K Mauer/Winni Vogt	D	Ford Escort	n/a
1980	TC	D Selzer/W Wolf/M Schneider	D	Ford Escort RS	n/a
1981	TC	H Doring/D Gartmann/F Müller	D	Ford Capri	n/a
1982	TC	D Gartmann/Klaus Ludwig/Klaus Niedzwiedz	D	Ford Capri	n/a
1984	TC	A Felder/FJ Bohling/Peter Oberndorfer	D	BMW 635	n/a
1985	TC	A Felder/J Hamelmann/R Walterscheid-Müller	D	BMW 635	n/a
1986	TC	Markus Östreich/Otto Rensing/Winni Vogt	D	BMW 325i	83.330
1987	TC	Klaus Ludwig/Klaus Niedzwiedz/Steve Soper	D/D/GB	Ford Sierra Cosworth	n/a
1988	TC	Edgar Dören/Gerhard Holup/Peter Faubel	D	Porsche Carrera	n/a
1989	TC	Emanuele Pirro/Roberto Ravaglia/Fabien Giroix	I/I/F	BMW M3	94.216
1990	TC	Altfrid Heger/Joachim Winkelhock/Frank Schmickler	D	BMW M3	n/a

year	formula	winner	nat	car	mph
1991	TC	Kris Nissen/Joachim Winkelhock/Armin Hahne	DK/D/D	BMW M3	n/a
1992	TC	Johnny Cecotto/Christian Danner/Marc Duez/ Jean-Michel Martin	YV/D/B/B	BMW M3	63.830
1993	TC	Antonio de Azevedo/Franz Konrad/ Oernulf Wirdheim/Frank Katthofer	BR/A/S/D	Porsche Carrera	84.280
1994	TC	Fred Rostberg/Frank Katthofer/Karl-Heinz Wlazik	D	BMW M3	77.591

European Formula Three race

year	formula	winner	nat	car	mph
1975	F3 E	Freddy Kottulinsky	S	Modus M1-BMW	104.260
1976	F3 E	Conny Andersson	S	March 753-Toyota	101.282
1977	F3 E	Piercarlo Ghinzani	I	March 773-Toyota	88.897
1978	F3 E	Anders Olofsson	S	Ralt RT1-Toyota	106.484
	F3 E	Patrick Gaillard	F	Chevron B43-Toyota	107.655
1980	F3 E	Thierry Boutsen	B	Martini MK31-Toyota	105.972
1981	F3 E	Oscar Larrauri	RA	March 813-Toyota	94.370
1982	F3 E	Oscar Larrauri	RA	Euroracing 101-Alfa Romeo	98.467
1984	F3 E	Johnny Dumfries	GB	Ralt RT3/83-Volkswagen	103.697
1987*	F3 E	Roland Ratzenberger	A	Ralt RT31-Volkswagen	87.972
	F3 E	Victor Rosso	RA	Ralt RT31-Volkswagen	98.496
1988#	F3 E	Joachim Winkelhock	D	Reynard 883-Volkswagen	86.239

*EFDA Euroseries races. #European F3 Cup

SOLITUDE

A narrow temporary circuit set in the wooded countryside near Stuttgart which briefly held an important non-championship F1 race. Used mainly for motorcycles, a car Grand Prix was run sporadically. The Mercedes-Benz Grand Prix team occasionally used the circuit for testing in the 1930s, especially prior to races at the Nürburgring which the Solitude circuit resembled. When the circuit closed in 1965 the Solitude GP was revived on two occasions at Hockenheim.

Glemseck Corner

Active years...1922-65
Location.........Near Stuttgart
Lap distance ..7.1 miles
Lap record ......Jim Clark (Lotus 25-Climax) 3m49.1, 111.567 mph, 1963, F1

Solitude Grand Prix

year	formula	winner	nat	car	mph
1925	FL	Otto Merz	D	Mercedes	58.470
1926	FL	Otto Merz	D	Mercedes	57.290
1927	FL	August Momberger	D	Bugatti	63.070
1950	F2	Karl Kling	D	Veritas	80.840
1956	SC	Hans Herrmann	D	Porsche	92.020
1959	FJ	Michel May	CH	Stangellini-Fiat	85.940
1960	F2	Wolfgang von Trips	D	Ferrari Dino 156	102.190
1961	F1	Innes Ireland	GB	Lotus 21-Climax	105.202
1962	F1	Dan Gurney	USA	Porsche 804	100.677
1963	F1	Jack Brabham	AUS	Brabham BT3-Climax	106.213
1964	F1	Jim Clark	GB	Lotus 33-Climax	91.435
1965	F2	Chris Amon	NZ	Lola T60-Ford	104.080
1968*	SC	David Piper	GB	Ferrari P3/4	126.266
1969*	SC	Hans Herrmann	D	Lola T70 Mk3B-Chevrolet	128.950

*held at Hockenheim

TAUNUS

Venue for the Kaiserpreis, a one-off event organized for modified 8-litre touring cars to rival the French GP. The huge entry (92 cars) necessitated qualifying heats but the event was not repeated. The circuit used part of the 1904 Gordon Bennett Trophy circuit.

Active years...1907
Location.........Open roads from Homburg to Weilburg
Lap distance ..75 miles
Lap record ......Vincenzo Lancia (Fiat), 1h21m55.6, 54.927 mph, 1907, Kaiserpreis class

Esch
Reichen-bach
Königstein
Glashütten
Neuveilnau
Emmerhausen
Eiserhausen
Saalburg
Lützendorf
Homburg
Usingen
Weilburg
Wehrheim
Gravenweisbach
Einhausen

Kaiserpreis

year	formula	winner	nat	car	mph
1907	Kaiserpreis	Felice Nazzaro	I	Fiat	52.489

GREAT BRITAIN

MAJOR CHAMPIONSHIPS

British Touring Car Championship

year	series sponsor	driver	nat	team	car
1958		Jack Sears	GB	Jack Sears	Austin A105 Westminster
1959		Jeff Uren	GB	Jeff Uren	Ford Zephyr
1960		Doc Shepherd	GB	Don Moore	Austin A40
1961		John Whitmore	GB	Cooper Car Company	Mini Cooper
1962		John Love	RSR	Vita	Mini Cooper
1963		Jack Sears	GB	Wilment	Ford Galaxie/Lotus Cortina
1964		Jim Clark	GB	Team Lotus	Lotus Cortina
1965		Roy Pierpoint	GB	Roy Pierpoint	Ford Mustang
1966		John Fitzpatrick	GB	Broadspeed	Ford Anglia
1967		Frank Gardner	AUS	Alan Mann Racing	Ford Falcon
1968		Frank Gardner	AUS	Alan Mann Racing	Ford Escort/Ford Cortina
1969		Alec Poole	GB	Equipe Arden	Mini Cooper S
1970		Bill McGovern	GB	George Bevan	Sunbeam Imp
1971		Bill McGovern	GB	George Bevan	Sunbeam Imp
1972	Wiggins Teape	Bill McGovern	GB	George Bevan	Sunbeam Imp
1973		Frank Gardner	AUS	SCA European Road Services	Chevrolet Camaro
1974	Castrol	Bernard Unett	GB	Chrysler Dealer Team	Hillman Avenger
1975	Southern Organs	Andy Rouse	GB	Broadspeed	Triumph Dolomite Sprint
1976	Keith Prowse	Bernard Unett	GB	Chrysler Dealer Team	Chrysler Avenger GT
1977	Tricentrol	Bernard Unett	GB	Chrysler Dealer Team	Chrysler Avenger GT
1978	Tricentrol	Richard Longman	GB	Richard Longman	Mini 1275GT
1979	Tricentrol	Richard Longman	GB	Richard Longman	Mini 1275GT
1980	Tricentrol	Win Percy	GB	Tom Walkinshaw Racing	Mazda RX7
1981	Tricentrol	Win Percy	GB	Tom Walkinshaw Racing	Mazda RX7
1982	Tricentrol	Win Percy	GB	Toyota GB	Toyota Corolla
1983	Trimoco	Andy Rouse	GB	Andy Rouse Engineering	Alfa Romeo GTV6
1984	Trimoco	Andy Rouse	GB	Andy Rouse Engineering	Rover Vitesse
1985	Trimoco	Andy Rouse	GB	Andy Rouse Engineering	Ford Sierra 2.3 turbo
1986		Chris Hodgetts	GB	Toyota GB	Toyota Celica GT
1987	Dunlop	Chris Hodgetts	GB	Toyota GB	Toyota Corolla GT
1988	Dunlop	Frank Sytner	GB	Prodrive	BMW M3
1989	Esso	John Cleland	GB	Dave Cook/Vauxhall Dealer Sport	Vauxhall Astra GTE 16v
1990	Esso	Robb Gravett	GB	Trakstar	Ford Sierra RS500
1991	Esso	Will Hoy	GB	Vic Lee Motorsport	BMW M3
1992	Esso	Tim Harvey	GB	Vic Lee Motorsport	BMW 318is
1993	Auto Trader	Joachim Winkelhock	D	Schnitzer	BMW 318i
1994	Auto Trader	Gabriele Tarquini	I	Alfa Corse	Alfa Romeo 155 TS

British Formula Three Championship (including Formula Junior)

year	series sponsor	driver	nat	team	car
1951	Autosport	Eric Brandon	GB	Ecurie Richmond	Cooper T15-Norton
1952	Autosport	Don Parker	GB	Don Parker	Kieft C52-Norton
1953	Autosport	Don Parker	GB	Don Parker	Kieft C53-Norton
1954	BRSCC National	Les Leston	GB	Les Leston	Cooper T31-Norton
1955	BRSCC National	Jim Russell	GB	Cooper Car Company	Cooper T37-Norton
1956	BRSCC National	Jim Russell	GB	Cooper Car Company	Cooper T42-Norton
1957	BRSCC National	Jim Russell	GB	Cooper Car Company	Cooper T43-Norton
1958	BRSCC National	Trevor Taylor	GB	Trevor Taylor	Cooper T43-Norton
1959	BRSCC National*	Don Parker	GB	Don Parker	Cooper T43-Norton
1960	BRSCC National*	Jack Pitcher	GB	Jack Pitcher	-
	John Davy*	Jim Clark	GB	Team Lotus	Lotus 18-Ford
	Motor Racing*	Jim Clark/Trevor Taylor (tied)	GB	Team Lotus	Lotus 18-Ford
1961	BRSCC National*	Mike Ledbrook	GB	Mike Ledbrook	-
	John Davy*	Bill Moss	GB	Chequered Flag Racing	Gemini Mk3A-Ford/Lotus 18-Ford
	Motor Racing*	Trevor Taylor	GB	Team Lotus	Lotus 20-Ford
1962	John Davy*	John Flemming	GB	John Flemming	-
1963	Express & Star*	Peter Arundell	GB	Ron Harris Team Lotus	Lotus 27-Ford
1964	Express & Star	Jackie Stewart	GB	Tyrrell Racing	Cooper T72-BMC
	BRSCC	Rod Banting	GB	Rod Banting	Lotus 31-BMC
1965	BRSCC	Tony Dean	GB	Tony Dean	Lotus-Ford
1966	Les Leston	Harry Stiller	GB	Motor Racing Stables	Brabham BT16-Ford/Brabham BT18-Ford
1967	Les Leston	Harry Stiller	GB	Motor Racing Stables	Brabham BT18-Ford/Brabham BT21-Ford
1968	Lombank	Tim Schenken	AUS	Sports Motors	Chevron B9-Ford/Titan Mk3-Ford/ Brabham BT21X-Ford
1969	Lombank	Emerson Fittipaldi	BR	Jim Russell Racing	Lotus 59-Ford

Racing Around the World

year	series sponsor	driver	nat	team	car
1970	Forward Trust	Carlos Pace	BR	Jim Russell Racing	Lotus 59-Ford
	Lombank	Dave Walker	AUS	Team Lotus	Lotus 59-Ford
	Shell	Tony Trimmer	GB	Race Cars International	Lotus 59-Ford/Brabham BT28-Ford
1971	Lombank	Roger Williamson	GB	Wheatcroft Racing	March 713M-Ford
	Shell/Motor Sport	Dave Walker	AUS	Team Lotus	Lotus 69-Ford
1972	Forward Trust	Roger Williamson	GB	Wheatcroft Racing	GRD 372-Ford/March 723-Ford
	Lombard	Rikky von Opel	FL	Team Ensign	Ensign F372-Ford
	Shell/Motor Sport	Roger Williamson	GB	Wheatcroft Racing	GRD 372-Ford/March 723-Ford
1973	Forward Trust	Ian Taylor	GB	Chris Andrews	March 733-Ford
	Lombard	Tony Brise	GB	Team Kent Messanger	GRD 372-Ford/GRD 373-Ford/ March 733-Ford
	John Player	Tony Brise	GB	Team Kent Messanger	GRD 373-Ford/March 733-Ford
1974	Forward Trust	Brian Henton	GB	March Engineering	March 743-Ford/March 743-Toyota
	Lombard	Brian Henton	GB	March Engineering	March 743-Ford/March 743-Toyota
1975	BP	Gunnar Nilsson	S	March Engineering	March 753-Toyota
1976	ShellSport	Bruno Giacomelli	I	March Engineering	March 763-Toyota
	BP	Rupert Keegan	GB	British Air Ferries	March 743-Toyota/Chevron B34-Toyota
1977	Vandervell	Stephen South	GB	Team BP	March 763-Toyota/March 773-Toyota
	BP	Derek Daly	IRL	Derek McMahon Racing	Chevron B38-Toyota
1978	Vandervell	Derek Warwick	GB	Warwick Trailers	Ralt RT1-Toyota
	BP	Nelson Piquet	BR	Greg Siddle	Ralt RT1-Toyota
1979	Vandervell	Chico Serra	BR	Project 4 Racing	March 793-Toyota
1980	Vandervell	Stefan Johansson	S	Project 4 Racing	March 803-Toyota/March 803B-Toyota/ Ralt RT3-Toyota
1981	Marlboro	Jonathan Palmer	GB	West Surrey Racing	Ralt RT3/81-Toyota
1982	Marlboro	Tommy Byrne	IRL	Murray Taylor Racing	Ralt RT3/82-Toyota
1983	Marlboro	Ayrton Senna	BR	West Surrey Racing	Ralt RT3/83-Toyota
1984	Marlboro	Johnny Dumfries	GB	Dave Price Racing	Ralt RT3/83-Volkswagen
1985	Marlboro	Mauricio Gugelmin	BR	West Surrey Racing	Ralt RT30-Volkswagen
1986	Lucas	Andy Wallace	GB	Madgwick Motorsport	Reynard 863-Volkswagen
1987	Lucas	Johnny Herbert	GB	Eddie Jordan Racing	Reynard 873-Volkswagen
1988	Lucas	JJ Lehto	SF	Pacific Racing	Reynard 883-TOM's Toyota
1989	Lucas	David Brabham	AUS	Bowman Racing	Ralt RT33-Volkswagen
1990		Mika Häkkinen	SF	West Surrey Racing	Ralt RT34-Mugen
1991		Rubens Barrichello	BR	West Surrey Racing	Ralt RT35-Mugen
1992		Gil de Ferran	BR	Paul Stewart Racing	Reynard 923-Mugen
1993		Kelvin Burt	GB	Paul Stewart Racing	Reynard 933-Mugen/Dallara 393-Mugen
1994		Jan Magnussen	DK	Paul Stewart Racing	Dallara 394-Mugen

*Formula Junior

British Formula One Championship

year	series sponsor	driver	nat	team	car
1969	VAT 69	Jackie Stewart	GB	Matra International	Matra MS80-Ford
1977	ShellSport Group 8	Tony Trimmer	GB	Melchester Racing	Surtees TS19-Ford
1978	Aurora AFX	Tony Trimmer	GB	Melchester Racing	McLaren M23-Ford/McLaren M25-Ford
1979	Aurora AFX	Rupert Keegan	GB	Charles Clowes Racing	Arrows A1-Ford
1980	Aurora AFX	Emilio de Villota	E	RAM Racing	Williams FW07-Ford/Williams FW07B-Ford
1982		Jim Crawford	GB	AMCO Racing	Ensign N180B-Ford

British Formula Two Championship

year	series sponsor	driver	nat	team	car
1957	Autocar	Tony Marsh	GB	Tony Marsh	Cooper T43-Climax
1958	Autocar	Jack Brabham	AUS	Cooper Car Company	Cooper T45-Climax
1959	Autocar	Stirling Moss	GB	RRC Walker Racing Team	Cooper T43-Borgward
1960	Autocar	Jackie Lewis	GB	H&L Motors/Alan Brown	Cooper T45-Climax
1964	Autocar	Mike Spence	GB	Ron Harris Team Lotus	Lotus 32-Ford
1965	Autocar	Jim Clark	GB	Ron Harris Team Lotus	Lotus 35-Ford
1966	Autocar	Jack Brabham	AUS	Brabham Racing Organization	Brabham BT18-Honda/Brabham BT21-Honda
1967	Autocar	Alan Rees	GB	Winkelmann Racing	Brabham BT23-Ford
	British	Jochen Rindt	A	Winkelmann Racing	Brabham BT23-Ford
1972	John Player	Niki Lauda	A	March Engineering	March 722-Ford

British Formula 3000 Championship (renamed Formula Two in 1992)

year	series sponsor	driver	nat	team	car
1989		Gary Brabham	AUS	Bromley Motorsport	Reynard 88D-Cosworth
1990		Pedro Chaves	P	Mansell Madgwick	Reynard 90D-Cosworth
1991		Paul Warwick*	GB	Mansell Madgwick	Reynard 90D-Cosworth
1992	Halfords	Yvan Müller	F	Omegaland	Reynard 91D-Cosworth
1993	Halfords	Philippe Adams	B	Madgwick International/ Argo Racing	Reynard 92D-Cosworth/ Reynard 91D-Cosworth
1994	Venson Group	José Luis di Palma	RA	Madgwick International	Reynard 92D-Cosworth

*Warwick won the championship posthumously, having died in an accident at Oulton Park

British Formula 5000 Championship

year	series sponsor	driver	nat	car
1969	Guards	Peter Gethin	GB	McLaren M10A-Chevrolet
1970	Guards	Peter Gethin	GB	McLaren M10B-Chevrolet
1971	Rothmans	Frank Gardner	AUS	Lola T192-Chevrolet/ Lola T300-Chevrolet
1972	Rothmans	Gijs van Lennep	NL	Surtees TS11-Chevrolet
1973	Rothmans	Teddy Pilette	B	Chevron B24-Chevrolet
1974	Rothmans	Bob Evans	GB	Lola T332-Chevrolet
1975	ShellSport	Teddy Pilette	B	Lola T400-Chevrolet
1976	ShellSport	David Purley	GB	Chevron B30-Ford

Became British Group 8 Championship, see British Formula One Championship

British Formula Atlantic Championship

year	series sponsor	driver	nat	car
1971	Yellow Pages	Vern Schuppan	AUS	Palliser WDB4-Ford
1972	Yellow Pages	Bill Gubelmann	USA	March 72B-Ford
1973	Yellow Pages	Colin Vandervell	GB	March 73B-Ford
	BP	John Nicholson	NZ	Lyncar 005-Ford
1974	John Player	John Nicholson	NZ	Lyncar 005-Ford
	Southern Organs	Jim Crawford	GB	March 73B-Ford/ March 74B-Ford

1975	John Player	Tony Brise	GB	Modus M1-Ford
	Southern Organs	Ted Wentz	USA	Lola T360-Ford
1976	Indylantic	Ted Wentz	USA	Lola T460-Ford
1977-78	NO SERIES			
1979	Hitachi	Ray Mallock	GB	Ralt RT1-Ford/ Ralt RT4-Ford
1980	Hitachi	David Leslie	GB	Ralt RT4-Ford
1981		Ray Mallock	GB	Ralt RT4-Ford
1982		Alo Lawler	IRL	Ralt RT4-Ford
1983		Alo Lawler	IRL	Ralt RT4-Ford

The 1986 British Grand Prix, the last to be held at Brands Hatch

MAJOR INTERNATIONAL RACES

BRITISH GRAND PRIX

year	formula	circuit	winner	nat	car	mph
1926*	GP	Brooklands	Robert Sénéchal/Louis Wagner	F	Delage 15S8	71.661
1927*	GP	Brooklands	Robert Benoist	F	Delage 15S8	85.586
1935#	GP	Donington Park	Richard Shuttleworth	GB	Alfa Romeo Tipo-B "P3"	63.928
1936#	GP	Donington Park	Hans Ruesch/Dick Seaman	CH/GB	Alfa Romeo Tipo-C "8C-35"	69.187
1937#	GP	Donington Park	Bernd Rosemeyer	D	Auto Union C	82.856
1938#	GP	Donington Park	Tazio Nuvolari	I	Auto Union D	80.486
1948	F1	Silverstone	Luigi Villoresi	I	Maserati 4CLT/48	72.270
1949	F1	Silverstone	Emanuel de Graffenried	CH	Maserati 4CLT/48	77.307
1950	F1 W	Silverstone	Giuseppe Farina	I	Alfa Romeo 158	90.950
1951	F1 W	Silverstone	José Froilan Gonzalez	RA	Ferrari 375	96.107
1952	F2 W	Silverstone	Alberto Ascari	I	Ferrari 500	90.921
1953	F2 W	Silverstone	Alberto Ascari	I	Ferrari 500	92.975
1954	F1 W	Silverstone	José Froilan Gonzalez	RA	Ferrari 625 (555)	89.687
1955	F1 W	Aintree	Stirling Moss	GB	Mercedes-Benz W196	86.468
1956	F1 W	Silverstone	Juan Manuel Fangio	RA	Lancia-Ferrari D50	98.661
1957	F1 W	Aintree	Tony Brooks/Stirling Moss	GB	Vanwall VW4	86.803
1958	F1 W	Silverstone	Peter Collins	GB	Ferrari Dino 246	102.049
1959	F1 W	Aintree	Jack Brabham	AUS	Cooper T51-Climax	89.884
1960	F1 W	Silverstone	Jack Brabham	AUS	Cooper T53-Climax	108.695
1961	F1 W	Aintree	Wolfgang von Trips	D	Ferrari Dino 156	83.907
1962	F1 W	Aintree	Jim Clark	GB	Lotus 25-Climax	92.247
1963	F1 W	Silverstone	Jim Clark	GB	Lotus 25-Climax	107.341
1964	F1 W	Brands Hatch	Jim Clark	GB	Lotus 25-Climax	94.141
1965	F1 W	Silverstone	Jim Clark	GB	Lotus 33-Climax	112.017
1966	F1 W	Brands Hatch	Jack Brabham	AUS	Brabham BT19-Repco	95.479
1967	F1 W	Silverstone	Jim Clark	GB	Lotus 49-Ford	117.642
1968	F1 W	Brands Hatch	Jo Siffert	CH	Lotus 49B-Ford	104.831
1969	F1 W	Silverstone	Jackie Stewart	GB	Matra MS80-Ford	127.254
1970	F1 W	Brands Hatch	Jochen Rindt	A	Lotus 72-Ford	108.687
1971	F1 W	Silverstone	Jackie Stewart	GB	Tyrrell 003-Ford	130.480
1972	F1 W	Brands Hatch	Emerson Fittipaldi	BR	Lotus 72D-Ford	112.058
1973	F1 W	Silverstone	Peter Revson	USA	McLaren M23-Ford	131.752
1974	F1 W	Brands Hatch	Jody Scheckter	ZA	Tyrrell 007-Ford	115.735
1975	F1 W	Silverstone	Emerson Fittipaldi	BR	McLaren M23-Ford	120.019
1976	F1 W	Brands Hatch	Niki Lauda	A	Ferrari 312T2	114.236
1977	F1 W	Silverstone	James Hunt	GB	McLaren M26-Ford	130.357
1978	F1 W	Brands Hatch	Carlos Reutemann	RA	Ferrari 312T3	116.607
1979	F1 W	Silverstone	Clay Regazzoni	CH	Williams FW07-Ford	138.799
1980	F1 W	Brands Hatch	Alan Jones	AUS	Williams FW07B-Ford	125.690
1981	F1 W	Silverstone	John Watson	GB	McLaren MP4/1-Ford	137.638
1982	F1 W	Brands Hatch	Niki Lauda	A	McLaren MP4/1B-Ford	124.713
1983	F1 W	Silverstone	Alain Prost	F	Renault RE40	139.218

year	formula	circuit	winner	nat	car	mph
1984	F1 W	Brands Hatch	Niki Lauda	A	McLaren MP4/2-TAG Porsche	124.436
1985	F1 W	Silverstone	Alain Prost	F	McLaren MP4/2B-TAG Porsche	146.274
1986	F1 W	Brands Hatch	Nigel Mansell	GB	Williams FW11-Honda	129.756
1987	F1 W	Silverstone	Nigel Mansell	GB	Williams FW11B-Honda	146.208
1988	F1 W	Silverstone	Ayrton Senna	BR	McLaren MP4/4-Honda	124.142
1989	F1 W	Silverstone	Alain Prost	F	McLaren MP4/5-Honda	143.645
1990	F1 W	Silverstone	Alain Prost	F	Ferrari 641/2	145.204
1991	F1 W	Silverstone	Nigel Mansell	GB	Williams FW14-Renault	131.227
1992	F1 W	Silverstone	Nigel Mansell	GB	Williams FW14B-Renault	134.098
1993	F1 W	Silverstone	Alain Prost	F	Williams FW15C-Renault	134.223
1994	F1 W	Silverstone	Damon Hill	GB	Williams FW16-Renault	128.314

*also known as English GP. #Donington GP

TOURIST TROPHY

year	formula	circuit	winner	nat	car	mph
1905	TC	Isle of Man	John Napier	GB	Arrol-Johnston	33.960
1906	TC	Isle of Man	Charles Rolls	GB	Rolls-Royce 20hp	39.400
1907	TC	Isle of Man	Ernest Courtis	GB	Rover 20hp	28.800
1908	FL	Isle of Man	W Watson	GB	Napier-Hutton	50.300
1914	FL	Isle of Man	Kenelm Lee Guinness	GB	Sunbeam	56.440
1922	FL	Isle of Man	Jean Chassagne	F	Sunbeam	55.782
1928	SC (h)	Ards	Kaye Don	GB	Lea-Francis	64.060
1929	SC (h)	Ards	Rudolf Caracciola	D	Mercedes-Benz SS	72.820
1930	SC (h)	Ards	Tazio Nuvolari	I	Alfa Romeo 6C	70.880
1931	SC (h)	Ards	Norman Black	GB	MG Midget C-type	67.900
1932	SC (h)	Ards	CR Whitcroft	GB	Riley 9	74.230
1933	SC (h)	Ards	Tazio Nuvolari	I	MG Magnette K3	78.650
1934	SC (h)	Ards	Charles Dodson	GB	MG Magnette NE	74.650
1935	SC (h)	Ards	Fred Dixon	GB	Riley 1.5	76.900
1936	SC (h)	Ards	Fred Dixon/Charles Dodson	GB	Riley 1.5	78.010
1937	SC (h)	Donington Park	Gianfranco Comotti	I	Talbot-Darracq	68.700
1938	SC (h)	Donington Park	Louis Gérard	F	Delage	67.610
1950	SC (h)	Dundrod	Stirling Moss	GB	Jaguar XK120	75.150
1951	SC (h)	Dundrod	Stirling Moss	GB	Jaguar XK120C	83.550
1953	SC (h) W	Dundrod	Peter Collins/Pat Griffith	GB	Aston Martin DB3S	81.710
1954*	SC (h) W	Dundrod	Paul Armagnac/Gérard Laureau	F	DB-Panhard	68.750
1955	SC W	Dundrod	Stirling Moss/John Fitch	USA	Mercedes-Benz 300SLR	88.323
1958	SC W	Goodwood	Stirling Moss/Tony Brooks	GB	Aston Martin DBR1/300	88.328
1959	SC W	Goodwood	Carroll Shelby/Jack Fairman/	USA/GB/		
			Stirling Moss	GB	Aston Martin DBR1/300	89.406
1960	GT	Goodwood	Stirling Moss	GB	Ferrari 250GT	85.580
1961	GT	Goodwood	Stirling Moss	GB	Ferrari 250GT	86.620
1962	GT	Goodwood	Innes Ireland	GB	Ferrari 250GTO	94.050
1963	GT	Goodwood	Graham Hill	GB	Ferrari 250GTO	95.140
1964	SC/GT W	Goodwood	Graham Hill	GB	Ferrari 330P	97.132
1965	SC/GT W	Oulton Park	Denny Hulme	NZ	Brabham BT8-Climax	94.069
1966	SC	Oulton Park	Denny Hulme	NZ	Lola T70 Mk2-Chevrolet	95.170
1967	TC	Oulton Park	Andrea de Adamich	I	Alfa Romeo Giulia GTA	80.650
1968	SC	Oulton Park	Denny Hulme	NZ	Lola T70 Mk3-Chevrolet	99.060
1969	SC	Oulton Park	Trevor Taylor	GB	Lola T70 Mk3B-Chevrolet	96.800
1970	TC	Silverstone	Brian Muir	AUS	Chevrolet Camaro Z28	99.940
1972	TC	Silverstone	Jochen Mass/Dieter Glemser	D	Ford Capri RS2600	106.530
1973	TC	Silverstone	Derek Bell/Harald Ertl	GB/A	BMW 3.0 CSL	108.783
1974	TC	Silverstone	Stuart Graham	GB	Chevrolet Camaro Z28	96.710
1975	TC	Silverstone	Stuart Graham	GB	Chevrolet Camaro Z28	97.710
1976	TC	Silverstone	Jean Xhenceval/Pierre Dieudonné/			
			Hughes de Fierlandt	B	BMW 3.0 CSL	101.361
1977	TC	Silverstone	Dieter Quester/Tom Walkinshaw	A/GB	BMW 3.0 CSL	105.496
1978	TC	Silverstone	Raijmond van Hove/Eddy Joosen	B	BMW 3.0 CSL	102.084
1979	TC	Silverstone	Martino Finotto/Carlo Facetti	I	BMW 3.0 CSL	103.980
1980	TC	Silverstone	Umberto Grano/Harald Neger/			
			Heribert Werginz	I/A/A	BMW 635 CSi	102.190
1981	TC	Silverstone	Tom Walkinshaw/Chuck Nicholson	GB	Mazda RX7	103.130
1982	TC	Silverstone	Tom Walkinshaw/Chuck Nicholson	GB	Jaguar XJ-S	100.490
1983	TC	Silverstone	René Metge/Steve Soper	F/GB	Rover Vitesse	99.317
1984	TC	Silverstone	Helmut Kelleners/			
			Gianfranco Brancatelli	D/I	BMW 635 CSi	92.980
1985	TC	Silverstone	Tom Walkinshaw/Win Percy	GB	Rover Vitesse	103.880
1986	TC	Silverstone	Denny Hulme/Jeff Allam	NZ/GB	Rover Vitesse	103.457
1987	TC	Silverstone	Enzo Calderari/Fabio Mancini	CH/I	BMW M3	100.847
1988	TC	Silverstone	Andy Rouse/Alain Ferté	GB/F	Ford Sierra RS500	103.935
1994#	TC W	Donington Park	Paul Radisich	NZ	Ford Mondeo Ghia	89.400

*World Championship points awarded for overall result which was won by Mike Hawthorn/Maurice Trintignant (Ferrari 750). #The Tourist Trophy was awarded to the winner of the 1994 FIA Touring Car World Cup

BRITISH EMPIRE TROPHY

year	formula	circuit	winner	nat	car	mph
1932	FL	Brooklands	John Cobb	GB	Delage V12/LSR	126.360
1933	FL	Brooklands	Stanislav Czaykowski	PL	Bugatti T54	123.554
1934	FL (h)	Brooklands	George Eyson	GB	MG Magnette K3	80.010
1935	FL (h)	Brooklands	Fred Dixon	GB	Riley 6	75.470
1936	FL (h)	Donington	Dick Seaman	GB	Maserati 8CM	66.300
1937	FL (h)	Donington	Raymond Mays	GB	ERA C-type	62.960
1938	FL (h)	Donington	Charles Dodson	GB	Austin	69.620
1939	FL (h)	Donington	Tony Rolt	GB	ERA B-type	75.910
1947	F1	Douglas	Bob Gerard	GB	ERA B-type	68.020
1948	F1	Douglas	Geoffrey Ansell	GB	ERA B-type	67.710
1949	F1	Douglas	Bob Gerard	GB	ERA B-type	71.060
1950	F1	Douglas	Bob Gerard	GB	ERA B-type	70.050
1951	SC (h)	Douglas	Stirling Moss	GB	Frazer-Nash LM	67.270
1952	SC (h)	Douglas	Pat Griffith	GB	Lester-MG	64.200
1953	SC (h)	Douglas	Reg Parnell	GB	Aston Martin DB3S	73.960
1954	SC (h)	Oulton Park	Alan Brown	GB	Cooper T22-Bristol	70.560
1955	SC (h)	Oulton Park	Archie Scott-Brown	GB	Lister-Bristol	73.520
1956	SC (h)	Oulton Park	Stirling Moss	GB	Cooper T39-Climax	83.720
1957	SC	Oulton Park	Archie Scott-Brown	GB	Lister-Jaguar	84.210
1958	SC	Oulton Park	Stirling Moss	GB	Aston Martin DBR2/390	87.450
1959	F2	Oulton Park	Jim Russell	GB	Cooper T45-Climax	76.932
1960	FJ	Silverstone	Henry Taylor	GB	Lotus 18-Ford	80.780
1961	IC	Silverstone	Stirling Moss	GB	Cooper T53-Climax	104.580
1970	F3	Oulton Park	Bev Bond	GB	Lotus 59A-Ford	96.580
1971	F3	Oulton Park	Dave Walker	AUS	Lotus 69-Ford	96.730
1972	Hist	Silverstone	Willie Green	GB	Maserati T61	*
1973	Hist	Silverstone	Neil Corner	GB	Maserati 250F/Aston Martin DNR4/300	*
1974	Hist	Silverstone	John Harper	GB	Lister-Jaguar	*
1977	Hist	Donington Park	Neil Corner	GB	BRM P25	84.080
1978	Hist	Donington Park	Neil Corner	GB	BRM P25	82.530
1990	SC W	Silverstone	Martin Brundle/Alain Ferté	GB/F	Jaguar XJR-11	128.830
1991	SC W	Silverstone	Derek Warwick/Teo Fabi	GB/I	Jaguar XJR-14	122.037
1992	SC W	Silverstone	Derek Warwick/Yannick Dalmas	GB/F	Peugeot 905B	122.651

*Historic Racing and Sports Car championship held at Silverstone

CIRCUITS AND OTHER RACES

AINTREE

Aintree was a flat and largely featureless circuit built outside the Grand National racecourse, scene of Britain's greatest horse race. Its corners were slow and unchallenging, with the exception of the difficult Melling Crossing. However, spectator facilities were unrivalled and within a year of opening, Aintree held the British GP. Aintree hosted that race on five occasions before the International circuit was closed in 1964. Stirling Moss starred here, winning the 200-mile race four times, memorably scoring his first Grand Prix success in 1955, and two years later sharing Vanwall's first Championship victory with Tony Brooks. After 1964 the short circuit remained, but Aintree's fame is once more restricted to horse racing.

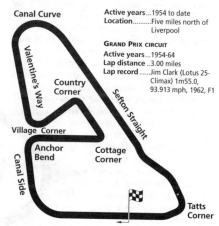

Active years...1954 to date
Location..........Five miles north of Liverpool

GRAND PRIX CIRCUIT
Active years...1954-64
Lap distance ..3.00 miles
Lap record ......Jim Clark (Lotus 25-Climax) 1m55.0, 93.913 mph, 1962, F1

Canal Curve
Valentine's Way
Country Corner
Sefton Straight
Village Corner
Anchor Bend
Cottage Corner
Canal Side
Tatts Corner

British Grand Prix see above

Aintree 200

year	formula	winner	nat	car	mph
1954	FL	Stirling Moss	GB	Maserati 250F	85.435
1956	F1	Stirling Moss	GB	Maserati 250F	84.273
1958	F1/F2	Stirling Moss	GB	Cooper T45-Climax	85.664
1959	F1/F2	Jean Behra	F	Ferrari Dino 246	88.763
1960	F2	Stirling Moss	GB	Porsche 718	88.410
1961	F1	Jack Brabham	AUS	Cooper T55-Climax	78.066
1962	F1	Jim Clark	GB	Lotus 24-Climax	92.653
1963	F1	Graham Hill	GB	BRM P57	94.392
1964	F1	Jack Brabham	AUS	Brabham BT7-Climax	93.457

BIRMINGHAM

Britain's first street race took 15 years to plan, but lasted just five. Racing had been banned on the open roads of mainland Britain until the Birmingham Road Race Bill was passed by Parliament in 1985. A round of the FIA Formula 3000 series was secured and the event was notable for noise, accidents, unglamorous surroundings and sometimes chaotic race schedules. The circuit was quick with average speeds of over 100 mph in the dry. The dual carriageway to and from Halfords Corner, a roundabout-turned-hairpin with a pronounced bump on entry, was the quickest part of the track. The pits were by the start in the forecourt of Bristol Street Motors and the paddock in a multi-storey car park! The first Birmingham Super Prix was marred by torrential rain. A year later Stefano Modena won conclusively although the star was Roberto Moreno who finished second after starting from the back of the grid. Plans to lengthen the circuit in 1991 to comply with FIA demands were shelved as the much publicized event slipped quietly from the racing calendar.

Pershore Street
Bristol Street
Sherlock Street
Belgrave Middleway
Peter Barwell Hill
Halfords Corner

Active years...1986-90
Location..........Birmingham city centre
Lap distance ..2.470 miles
Lap record ......Roberto Moreno (Ralt RT21-Honda) 1m22.91, 107.249 mph, 1987, F3000

Birmingham Super Prix

year	formula	winner	nat	car	mph
1986	F3000 INT	Luis Perez Sala	E	Ralt RT20-Cosworth	59.872
1987	F3000 INT	Stefano Modena	I	March 87B-Cosworth	105.353
1988	F3000 INT	Roberto Moreno	BR	Reynard 88D-Cosworth	105.630
1989	F3000 INT	Jean Alesi	F	Reynard 89D-Mugen	105.243
1990	F3000 INT	Eric van de Poele	B	Reynard 90D-Cosworth	105.291

BRANDS HATCH

Brands Hatch was the home of 500 cc F3 racing when it opened for cars on 16 April 1950. By 1964 it had become a full Grand Prix circuit, Jim Clark scoring a convincing home win. It then alternated with Silverstone, holding 14 Grands Prix (British and two European) before Silverstone won an exclusive contract to stage the British GP from 1987. The Indy circuit offers some of the best viewing possible and the Grand Prix circuit is one of the most demanding in the world with Paddock Hill Bend a truly great corner. Short run-off areas have raised the question of safety, illustrated by the horrific accidents during the 1988 Formula 3000 meeting in which Johnny Herbert and Michel Trollé were severely injured.

Derek Minter Straight
Westfield Bend
Hawthorn Bend
Dingle Dell
Hawthorn Hill
Pilgrims Drop
Druids
Dingle Dell Corner
Hailwood Hill
Stirlings Bend
Graham Hill
Paddock Hill Bend
Graham Hill Bend
Cooper Straight
Clearways
McLaren
Brabham Straight
Surtees
Clark Curve

Active years...1950 to date
Location..........Near Farningham, 20 miles south-east of London

CURRENT GRAND PRIX CIRCUIT

Lap distance ..2.6002 miles
Lap record ......Emanuele Naspetti (Reynard 91D-Cosworth), 1m13.86, 126.736 mph, 1991, F3000

GRAND PRIX CIRCUIT CHANGES

1950-53 ....Original Indy circuit. 1 mile
1954-59 ....Track widened, Druids Hill Bend added, direction of racing now reversed to clockwise. 1.24 miles
1960-75 ....Grand Prix circuit opened. 2.65 miles
1976-87 ....Paddock Hill Bend and Bottom Straight modified. 2.6136 miles
1988 to date ....Current circuit

British Grand Prix see above

European Grand Prix see above

Race of Champions

year	formula	winner	nat	car	mph
1965	F1	Mike Spence	GB	Lotus 33-Climax	96.583
1967	F1	Dan Gurney	USA	Eagle AAR102-Weslake	98.589
1968	F1	Bruce McLaren	NZ	McLaren M7A-Ford	100.773
1969	F1	Jackie Stewart	GB	Matra MS80-Ford	108.646
1970	F1	Jackie Stewart	GB	March 701-Ford	109.108
1971	F1	Clay Regazzoni	CH	Ferrari 312B2	108.041
1972	F1/F5000	Emerson Fittipaldi	BR	Lotus 72D-Ford	112.215
1973	F1/F5000	Peter Gethin	GB	Chevron B24-Chevrolet	110.837
1974	F1/F5000	Jacky Ickx	B	Lotus 72D-Ford	99.958
1975	F1/F5000	Tom Pryce	GB	Shadow DN5A-Ford	113.792
1976	F1	James Hunt	GB	McLaren M23-Ford	108.111
1977	F1	James Hunt	GB	McLaren M23-Ford	116.363
1979	F1	Gilles Villeneuve	CDN	Ferrari 312T3	117.718
1983	F1	Keke Rosberg	SF	Williams FW08C-Ford	117.787

Rothmans World Championship Victory Race

year	formula	winner	nat	car	mph
1971	F1/F5000	Peter Gethin	GB	BRM P160	111.822

John Player Challenge Trophy

year	formula	winner	nat	car	mph
1972	F1/F5000	Jean-Pierre Beltoise	F	BRM P180	106.360

Rothmans £50,000

year	formula	winner	nat	car	mph
1972	Various	Emerson Fittipaldi	BR	Lotus 72D-Ford	109.836

European Formula Two race

year	formula	winner	nat	car	mph
1967	F2 E	Jochen Rindt	A	Brabham BT23-Ford	101.376
1984	F2 E	Philippe Streiff	F	AGS JH19C-BMW	106.524

International Formula 3000 race

year	formula	winner	nat	car	mph
1987	F3000 INT	Julian Bailey	GB	Lola T87/50-Cosworth	119.270
1988	F3000 INT	Martin Donnelly	GB	Reynard 88D-Cosworth	120.813
1989	F3000 INT	Martin Donnelly	GB	Reynard 89D-Mugen	120.662
1990	F3000 INT	Allan McNish	GB	Lola T90/50-Mugen	108.277
1991	F3000 INT	Emanuele Naspetti	I	Reynard 91D-Cosworth	123.905

Daily Mail Indy Trophy

year	formula	winner	nat	car	mph
1978	Indycar	Rick Mears	USA	Penske PC6-Cosworth	95.789

World Sports Car race

year	formula	winner	nat	car	mph
1967	SC W	Mike Spence/Phil Hill	GB/USA	Chaparral 2F-Chevrolet	93.080
1968	SC W	Jacky Ickx/Brian Redman	B/GB	Ford GT40	95.959
1969	SC W	Jo Siffert/Brian Redman	CH/GB	Porsche 908/8	100.219
1970	SC W	Pedro Rodriguez/Leo Kinnunen	MEX/SF	Porsche 917	92.147
1971	SC W	Andrea de Adamich/Henri Pescarolo	I/F	Alfa Romeo T33/3	97.169
1972	SC W	Jacky Ickx/Mario Andretti	B/USA	Ferrari 312P	105.118
1974	SC W	Jean-Pierre Beltoise/Jean-Pierre Jarier	F	Matra-Simca MS670C	107.510
1977	SC W	Jacky Ickx/Jochen Mass	B/D	Porsche 935	98.181
1979	SC W	Reinhold Jöst/Volkert Merl	D	Porsche 908/4	100.605
1980	SC W	Riccardo Patrese/Walter Rohrl	I/D	Lancia Beta Monte Carlo	99.383
1981	SC W	Guy Edwards/Emilio de Villota	GB/E	Lola T600-Ford	99.917
1982	SC W	Jacky Ickx/Derek Bell	B/GB	Porsche 956	98.763
1983	SC E	Derek Warwick/John Fitzpatrick	GB	Porsche 956	100.771
1984	SC W	Jonathan Palmer/Jan Lammers	GB/NL	Porsche 956	109.202
1985	SC W	Derek Bell/Hans-Joachim Stuck	GB/D	Porsche 962	111.598
1986	SC W	Bob Wollek/Mauro Baldi	F/I	Porsche 956GTi	104.621
1987	SC W	Raul Boesel/John Nielsen	BR/DK	Jaguar XJR-8	111.807
1988	SC W	John Nielsen/Martin Brundle/Andy Wallace	DK/GB/GB	Jaguar XJR-9	112.311
1989	SC W	Mauro Baldi/Kenneth Acheson	I/GB	Sauber C9/88-Mercedes-Benz	111.003

Cellnet Super Prix

year	formula	winner	nat	car	mph
1986	F3	Andy Wallace	GB	Reynard 863-Volkswagen	92.489
1987	F3	Johnny Herbert	GB	Reynard 873-Volkswagen	90.416
1988	F3	Gary Brabham	AUS	Ralt RT32-Volkswagen	87.400
1989	F3	Mika Häkkinen	SF	Ralt RT33-Mugen	98.316

BROOKLANDS

Brooklands became Europe's first permanent circuit when it opened on 17 July 1907 (the Milwaukee Mile had first held a race in 1903). As Grand Prix racing began to capture the imagination on the continent, Brooklands held Britain's first such race in 1926 and repeated it in 1927. With the starting straight, test hill and liberal use of straw bales various circuit layouts were possible. A permanent Grand Prix circuit named after Sir Malcolm Campbell was introduced in 1937, although by then Donington Park was already playing host to the continental teams. High speed and society atmosphere were central to the Brooklands folklore. The fastest ever lap recorded on the outer circuit was 143 mph when Brooklands closed for World War Two, never to reopen. Part of the Members banking remains, overlooking the clubhouse which is now a museum.

British Grand Prix see above

British Empire Trophy see above

CRYSTAL PALACE

Originally, Crystal Palace was a twisting road course but when it reopened after the war the RAC ruled that the sinuous infield was too tight and so it was bypassed, making it essentially an

Active years...1907-39
Location..........Weybridge, 20 miles south of London

BANKED OUTER CIRCUIT
Active years...1907-39
Lap distance ..2.767 miles
Lap record......John Cobb (Napier-Railton) 1m09.44, 143.451 mph

MOUNTAIN CIRCUIT
Lap distance ..1.17 miles
Lap record......Raymond Mays (ERA) 84.31 mph, 1936

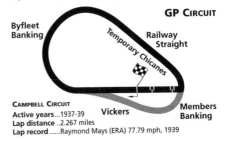

CAMPBELL CIRCUIT
Active years...1937-39
Lap distance ..2.267 miles
Lap record......Raymond Mays (ERA) 77.79 mph, 1939

GRAND PRIX CIRCUIT
Active years...1926-27
Lap distance ..2.616 miles
Lap record......Henry Segrave (Talbot 700), 1m49.5, 80.006 mph, 1926, GP

oval with kinks. The Palace could only hold a limited number of races a year due to the proximity of houses and eventually noise objectors and growing safety concerns forced the Greater London Council to close it on 23 September 1972.

Active years...1937-72
Location..........Anerley Hill, Sydenham, South London

CIRCUIT CHANGES
1937-39............2.00 miles
1953-72............Infield section bypassed by new link road from Park to Stadium Curve. 1.39 miles

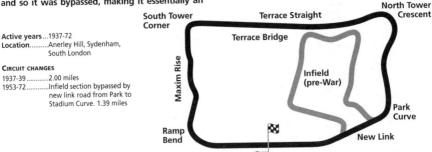

European Formula Two races

year	formula	winner	nat	car	mph
1967	F2	Jacky Ickx	B	Matra MS5-Ford	93.420
1968	F2 E	Jochen Rindt	A	Brabham BT23C-Ford	93.692
1970	F2	Jackie Stewart	GB	Brabham BT30-Ford	99.440
1971	F2 E	Emerson Fittipaldi	BR	Lotus 69-Ford	99.168
1972	F2 E	Jody Scheckter	ZA	McLaren M21-Ford	100.385

DONINGTON PARK

Donington Park began as a motorcycle circuit in 1931 under the guidance of Fred Craner. Car racing followed two years later and in 1935 a Grand Prix was held. It was an expanded club race at first but in 1937 the all-conquering German teams entered with Rosemeyer scoring the last win of his meteoric career. Despite the Munich crisis, both Auto Union and Mercedes-Benz returned in 1938. Auto Union won again this time with Nuvolari behind the wheel. Like Brooklands in the south, Donington did not reopen immediately after the war. However the land was bought in 1971 by Tom Wheatcroft who successfully reopened the venue six years later. He also built a museum to house the largest collection of single-seater racing cars in the world. Since 1977 Donington has held European Touring Cars, Formulae Two, 3000 and Three, the Motorcycle Grand Prix and, in 1993, a full F1 World Championship Grand Prix. Wheatcroft's lifelong dream was realized when Ayrton Senna won the wet European GP.

DONINGTON
1977 TO DATE

Craner Curves — Old Hairpin — Starkey's Bridge — Mclean's Corner — Redgate — Goddard Corner — Wheatcroft Straight — Coppice Corner — Melbourne Hairpin — The Esses — Starkey's Straight

Active years...1931-39, 1977 to date
Location..........Eight miles south of Derby, 35 miles north-east of Birmingham

CURRENT CIRCUIT
Lap distance ..2.500 miles
Lap record ......Ayrton Senna (McLaren MP4/8-Ford) 1m18.029, 115.342 mph, 1993, F1 (set on a lap through the pitlane)

CIRCUIT CHANGES
1931-33 ....2.19 miles
1934-36 ....Track extended to Starkey's Hairpin. 2.55 miles
1937-39 ....Old Melbourne Corner added. 3.125 miles
1977-95 ....New circuit built on sight of pre-war venue. 1.9573 miles
1985 to date ....New Melbourne Hairpin opened. Current circuit

Dunlop Bridge — Melbourne Corner — **DONINGTON 1931-39** — Mclean's Corner — Redgate Corner — Starkey's Corner — Coppice Corner

European Grand Prix see above

British Empire Trophy see above

Donington Grand Prix

year	formula	winner	nat	car	mph
1935	GP	Richard Shuttleworth	GB	Alfa Romeo Tipo-B "P3"	63.928
1936	GP	Hans Ruesch/Dick Seaman	CH/GB	Alfa Romeo Tipo-C "8C-35"	69.187
1937	GP	Bernd Rosemeyer	D	Auto Union C	82.856
1938	GP	Tazio Nuvolari	I	Auto Union D	80.486

European Formula Two race

year	formula	winner	nat	car	mph
1977	F2 E	Bruno Giacomelli	I	March 782/772P-BMW	105.039
1978	F2 E	Keke Rosberg	SF	Chevron B42-Hart	104.555
1979	F2 E	Derek Daly	IRL	March 792-BMW	106.188
1981	F2 E	Geoff Lees	GB	Ralt RH6/81-Honda	106.998
1982	F2 E	Corrado Fabi	I	March 822-BMW	108.593
1983	F2 E	Jonathan Palmer	GB	Ralt RH6/83-Honda	107.249
1984	F2 E	Roberto Moreno	BR	Ralt RH6/84-Honda	107.404

International Formula 3000 race

year	formula	winner	nat	car	mph
1985	F3000 INT	Christian Danner	D	March 85B-Cosworth	101.185
1987	F3000 INT	Luis Perez Sala	E	Lola T87/50-Cosworth	103.772
1990	F3000 INT	Erik Comas	F	Lola T90/50-Mugen	103.798
1993	F3000 INT	Olivier Beretta	MC	Reynard 93D-Cosworth	109.48

European Formula Three race

year	formula	winner	nat	car	mph
1977	F3 E	Brett Riley	NZ	March 773-Toyota	98.142
1978	F3 E	Derek Warwick	GB	Ralt RT1-Toyota	99.330
1979	F3 E	Brett Riley	NZ	March 783/793-Triumph	80.856
1981	F3 E	Mike White	ZA	March 813-Alfa Romeo	100.797
1982	F3 E	James Weaver	GB	Ralt RT3/81-Toyota	100.903
1983	F3 E	Martin Brundle	GB	Ralt RT3/83-Toyota	93.242
1984	F3 E	Johnny Dumfries	GB	Ralt RT3/83-Volkswagen	85.842

World Sports Car race

year	formula	winner	nat	car	mph
1989	SC W	Jochen Mass/Jean-Louis Schlesser	D/F	Sauber C9/88-Mercedes-Benz	101.210
1990	SC W	Jean-Louis Schlesser/Mauro Baldi	F/I	Mercedes-Benz C11	103.638
1992	SC W	Mauro Baldi/Philippe Alliot	I/F	Peugeot 905B	107.719

DUNDROD

The finest and most demanding British circuit of the 1950s, Dundrod was a natural road course which had everything from a tight hairpin to numerous fast corners. However, the earth banks which lined the circuit allowed no room for error and made it dangerous. The Ulster Automobile Club who promoted meetings always suffered from a lack of finance and often from bad weather. Dundrod closed after three drivers lost their lives during the 1955 Tourist Trophy.

The 1953 Ulster Trophy race at Dundrod

DUNDROD

Active years...1950-55
Location.........Nine miles north-west of Belfast, Northern Ireland

Lap distance ..7.416 miles
Lap record ......Mike Hawthorn (Jaguar D-type), 4m42, 94.672 mph, 1955, Sports Cars

Quarterland Corner
Ireland's Corner
Wheeler's Corner
Cochranstown Corner
Tornagrough Corner
Quarry Corner
Leathamstown Corner

Tourist Trophy see above

Ulster Trophy

year	formula	winner	nat	car	mph
1950	F1	Peter Whitehead	GB	Ferrari 125	84.326
1951	F1	Giuseppe Farina	I	Alfa Romeo 159	91.456
1952	F1	Piero Taruffi	I	Ferrari 375	81.432
1953	F2	Mike Hawthorn	GB	Ferrari 500	86.488
1955	FL	Desmond Titterington	GB	Jaguar D-type	89.860

GOODWOOD

In 1946, Australian Tony Gaze suggested to the Duke of Richmond and Gordon that the Westhampnett airfield near Chichester, from which Gaze had flown his Hurricane during the war, would be ideal for motor racing. Two years later Goodwood Motor Circuit opened for its first race, replacing Brooklands as the home of the BARC. With some of the Surrey circuit's atmosphere, Goodwood was more like a road course than an airfield venue and the traditional Easter Monday meeting was an annual highlight. However, the Duke closed the circuit in 1966 due to safety concerns, although it continued to be used for testing. Unfortunately, it will be remembered as the place where Stirling Moss ended his career in an accident in 1962, and where Bruce McLaren lost his life when testing in June 1970. Bertrand Fabi, a future Grand Prix star from Canada, was also killed while testing for the coming Formula Three season in 1987. Testing is now limited but the popular Festival of Speed historic hill climb is held in the grounds of nearby Goodwood House.

Lavant Straight
Woodcote Corner
Lavant Corner
Paddock Bend
St Mary's Corner
Fordwater
Madgwick Corner

Active years...1948-66
Location..........Two miles north of Chichester, 30 miles west of Brighton, 60 miles south of London
Lap record ......Jackie Stewart (BRM P261) and Jim Clark (Lotus 33-Climax) 1m20.4, 107.463 mph, 1965, F1 (with chicane)

CIRCUIT CHANGES

1948-51 ....2.38 miles
1952-66 ....Chicane inserted at Paddock on 14 April 1952. 2.40 miles

Tourist Trophy see above

Glover Trophy

year	formula	winner	nat	car	mph
1953	FL	Ken Wharton	GB	BRM P15	90.470
1954	FL	Ken Wharton	GB	BRM P15	86.400
1955	F1	Roy Salvadori	GB	Maserati 250F	89.247
1956	F1	Stirling Moss	GB	Maserati 250F	94.349
1957	F1	Stuart Lewis-Evans	GB	Connaught B-Alta	90.655
1958	F1	Mike Hawthorn	GB	Ferrari Dino 246	94.885
1959	F1	Stirling Moss	GB	Cooper T51-Climax	90.314
1960	F1	Innes Ireland	GB	Lotus 18-Climax	100.387
1961	F1	John Surtees	GB	Cooper T53-Climax	95.747
1962	F1	Graham Hill	GB	BRM P57	102.648
1963	F1	Innes Ireland	GB	Lotus 24-BRM	102.439

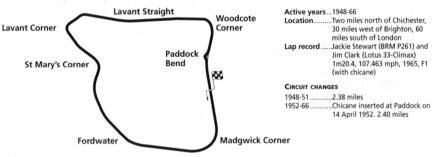

Other Formula One races

year	formula	winner	nat	car	mph
1949	F1	Reg Parnell	GB	Maserati 4CLT/48	86.430
	F1	Reg Parnell	GB	Maserati 4CLT/48	82.890
1950	F1	Reg Parnell	GB	Maserati 4CLT/48	77.609
	F1	Reg Parnell	GB	BRM P15	81.704
1951	F1	"B Bira"	SM	Maserati 4CLT/48	86.838
	F1	Giuseppe Farina	I	Alfa Romeo 159	95.115
1952	F1	José Froilan Gonzalez	RA	Ferrari 375	88.238
1954	F1	Reg Parnell	GB	Ferrari 625	88.758
	F1	Reg Parnell	GB	Ferrari 625	87.591
	F1	Stirling Moss	GB	Maserati 250F	91.489
1962	F1	Bruce McLaren	NZ	Cooper T55-Climax	99.050
1964	F1	Jim Clark	GB	Lotus 25-Climax	104.909
1965	F1	Jim Clark	GB	Lotus 25-Climax	105.067

BARC Nine hours

year	formula	winner	nat	car	mph
1952	SC	Peter Collins/Pat Griffith	GB	Aston Martin DB3	75.420
1953	SC	Reg Parnell/Eric Thompson	GB	Aston Martin DB3S	78.940
1955	SC	Peter Walker/Dennis Poore	GB	Aston Martin DB3S	82.240

MALLORY PARK

A club circuit built around a lake on the site of a former grass-track and opened in 1956. Mallory Park has suffered from the proximity of Donington, its future being threatened during the 1980s. The major race to have been held here was the 2000 Guineas, a non-championship F1 race in 1962 which attracted the likes of Clark, Hill, Brabham and eventual winner John Surtees. The European F2 Championship opened at Mallory in 1972 and 1973 but the track was too short to hold international events in the modern era.

Active years...1956 to date
Location..........Near Hinckley, eight miles south-west of Leicester
Lap distance ..1.35 miles
Lap record ......Ricardo Zunino (Arrows A1B-Ford), 40.06s, 121.319 mph, 1979, F1

Gerard's Bend — Kirkby Straight — Stebbe Straight — Lake Esses — Devil's Elbow — Shaw's

International 2000 Guineas

year	formula	winner	nat	car	mph
1962	F1	John Surtees	GB	Lola Mk4-Climax	93.375

European Formula Two race

year	formula	winner	nat	car	mph
1972	F2 E	Dave Morgan	GB	Brabham BT35-Ford	108.657
1973	F2 E	Jean-Pierre Jarier	F	March 732-BMW	112.245

OULTON PARK

Oulton Park is one of Britain's most challenging circuits, although it is too narrow to be considered for more international events. The traditional Gold Cup meeting started in 1954, a year after the circuit had opened. The event, once a major non-championship F1 race, suffered during the 1980s with no suitable category to promote, but it is now a round of the British Touring Car Championship. Initially Oulton was approximately square, although within a year it was extended to a hairpin next to the lake. Various alterations to this section followed until it was bypassed in 1975. The hairpin was reopened in 1989 but further modifications were necessary following Paul Warwick's fatal accident at the fast Knickerbrook corner in 1991.

Active years...1953 to date
Location..........Near Tarporley, ten miles south of Chester, 35 miles south-east of Liverpool

Deer Leap — Old Hall Corner — Lodge Corner — Island Bend — The Avenue — Lakeside — Shell Oils Corner — Foulstons — Hill Top — Cascades — Water Tower — Druids — Clay Hill — Knickerbrook

CURRENT CIRCUIT
Lap distance ..2.776 miles
Lap record ......n/a

CIRCUIT CHANGES
1953 ....1.504 miles
April 1954 ....Extended to lower lake. 2.23 miles
Aug 1954-75 .....Esso bend added to extension. 2.761 miles
1975-82 ....Link road from Cascades to Knickerbrook built, long circuit retained for motorcycle races. 1.654 miles
1989-91 ....Lakeside loop reopened. 2.769 miles
1992 to date ....Chicane at Knickerbrook. Current circuit

Tourist Trophy see above

British Empire Trophy see above

International Gold Cup

year	formula	winner	nat	car	mph
1954	F1	Stirling Moss	GB	Maserati 250F	83.468
1955	F1	Stirling Moss	GB	Maserati 250F	85.941
1956	F2/SC	Roy Salvadori	GB	Cooper T41-Climax	83.843
1957	F2	Jack Brabham	AUS	Cooper T43-Climax	84.963
1958	SC	Roy Salvadori	GB	Lotus 15-Climax	84.990
1959	F1	Stirling Moss	GB	Cooper T51-Climax	96.294
1960	F1	Stirling Moss	GB	Lotus 18-Climax	93.858
1961	F1	Stirling Moss	GB	Ferguson P99-Climax	88.828
1962	F1	Jim Clark	GB	Lotus 25-Climax	97.702
1963	F1	Jim Clark	GB	Lotus 25-Climax	98.337
1964	F2	Jack Brabham	AUS	Brabham BT10-Ford	95.500
1965	F2	John Surtees	GB	Lola T60-Ford	96.400
1966	F1	Jack Brabham	AUS	Brabham BT19-Repco	100.041
1967	F1/F2	Jack Brabham	AUS	Brabham BT24-Repco	106.319
1968	F1	Jackie Stewart	GB	Matra MS10-Ford	109.256
1969	F1/F5000	Jacky Ickx	B	Brabham BT26A-Ford	109.570
1970	F1/F5000	John Surtees	GB	Surtees TS7-Ford	110.803
1971	F1/F5000	John Surtees	GB	Surtees TS9-Ford	114.955
1972	F1/F5000	Denny Hulme	NZ	McLaren M19A-Ford	115.725
1973	F5000	Peter Gethin	GB	Chevron B24-Chevrolet	114.443
1974	F5000	Ian Ashley	GB	Lola T330-Chevrolet	114.639
1975	F5000	David Purley	GB	Chevron B30-Ford	93.055
1976	F1/F5000	Guy Edwards	GB	Brabham BT42/44B-Ford	105.603
1977	G8	Derek Bell	GB	Penske PC3-Ford	103.953
1978	F1/F2	Tony Trimmer	GB	McLaren M25-Ford	106.381
1979	F1/F2	David Kennedy	IRL	Wolf WR4-Ford	106.627
1980	F1/F2	Guy Edwards	GB	Arrows A1-Ford	107.796
1981	Hist	John Surtees	GB	Maserati 250F	67.200
1982	F1	Tony Trimmer	GB	Fittipaldi F8-Ford	104.283
1983	Thunder	Richard Budge/Vin Malkie	GB	Chevron B19-Ford	91.900
1984	Thunder	Peter Lovett/Ian Taylor	GB	Lola T594C-Mazda	101.490
1985	Thunder	Tim Lee Davey/Neil Crang	GB/AUS	Tiga GC84-Ford	103.020
1986	Thunder	John Foulston/John Brindley	GB	Lola T530-Chevrolet	103.510
1987	Thunder	John Foulston/John Brindley	GB	Lola T530-Chevrolet	103.950
1988	F3	Gary Brabham	AUS	Ralt RT32-Volkswagen	108.990
1989	F3000	Paulo Carcasci	BR	Reynard 88D-Cosworth	105.537
1990	F3000	Richard Dean	GB	Reynard 90D-Mugen	122.290
1991	F3000	Paul Warwick*	GB	Reynard 90D-Cosworth	121.995
1992	F3000	Yvan Müller	F	Reynard 91D-Cosworth	107.144
1993	TC	Joachim Winkelhock	D	BMW 318i	93.620
1994	TC	Joachim Winkelhock	D	BMW 318i	94.600

*Race stopped when Warwick suffered a fatal accident while leading, he was awarded victory posthumously

Oulton Park International Trophy

year	formula	winner	nat	car	mph
1971	F1	Pedro Rodriguez	MEX	BRM P160	115.128

Spring Trophy

year	formula	winner	nat	car	mph
1967	F1	Jack Brabham	AUS	Brabham BT20-Repco	104.944

SILVERSTONE

A bleak wartime airfield but within three years of peace, Silverstone was the new home of the British GP. Two years later, in the presence of King George VI, it held the first round of the new World Championship when Giuseppe Farina led an Alfa Romeo clean sweep of the top three positions. The circuit remained an unbroken succession of quick corners until Jody Scheckter triggered a seven-car pile-up at Woodcote in 1973; a chicane was built there for the next British GP. It was replaced by a series of corners prior to more permanent renovations being made in 1991. When JJ Lehto and Pedro Lamy crashed during testing in 1994 further alterations were made to improve safety still further. Having alternated the Grand Prix, first with Aintree and then Brands Hatch, Silverstone now holds the race exclusively.

British Grand Prix see above

Tourist Trophy see above

British Empire Trophy see above

International Trophy

year	formula	winner	nat	car	mph
1949	F1	Alberto Ascari	I	Ferrari 125	89.580
1950	F1	Giuseppe Farina	I	Alfa Romeo 158	90.157
1951*	F1	Reg Parnell	GB	Ferrari 375	61.899

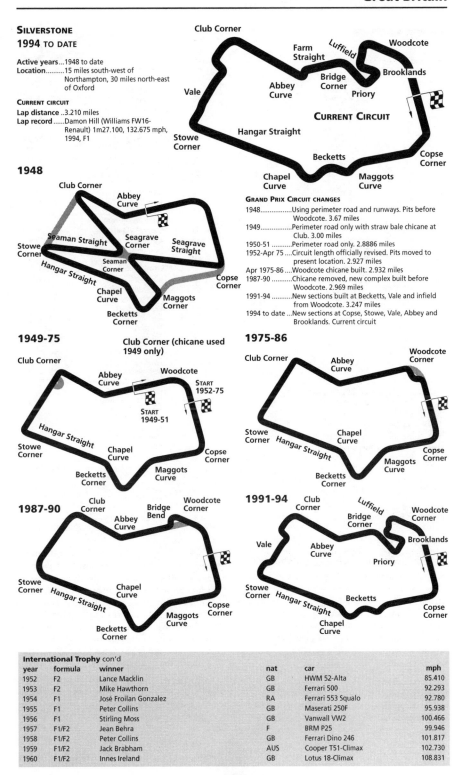

SILVERSTONE
1994 TO DATE

Active years...1948 to date
Location..........15 miles south-west of
Northampton, 30 miles north-east
of Oxford

CURRENT CIRCUIT
Lap distance ..3.210 miles
Lap record ......Damon Hill (Williams FW16-
Renault) 1m27.100, 132.675 mph,
1994, F1

1948

CURRENT CIRCUIT

Club Corner
Farm Straight — Luffield — Woodcote
Bridge Corner — Brooklands
Abbey Curve — Priory
Vale
Hangar Straight
Stowe Corner
Becketts
Copse Corner
Chapel Curve — Maggots Curve

Diagram 1948 labels
Club Corner
Abbey Curve
Seaman Straight — Seagrave Corner — Seagrave Straight
Stowe Corner
Hangar Straight
Seaman Corner
Chapel Curve
Becketts Corner
Maggots Corner
Copse Corner

GRAND PRIX CIRCUIT CHANGES
1948.................Using perimeter road and runways. Pits before
Woodcote. 3.67 miles
1949.................Perimeter road only with straw bale chicane at
Club. 3.00 miles
1950-51 ....Perimeter road only. 2.8886 miles
1952-Apr 75 ....Circuit length officially revised. Pits moved to
present location. 2.927 miles
Apr 1975-86 ....Woodcote chicane built. 2.932 miles
1987-90 ....Chicane removed, new complex built before
Woodcote. 2.969 miles
1991-94 ....New sections built at Becketts, Vale and infield
from Woodcote. 3.247 miles
1994 to date ...New sections at Copse, Stowe, Vale, Abbey and
Brooklands. Current circuit

1949-75

Club Corner (chicane used 1949 only)

Club Corner
Abbey Curve — Woodcote
START 1952-75
START 1949-51
Hangar Straight
Stowe Corner
Chapel Curve
Copse Corner
Becketts Corner
Maggots Curve

1975-86

Club Corner
Abbey Curve
Woodcote Corner
Stowe Corner
Hangar Straight
Chapel Curve
Copse Corner
Maggots Curve
Becketts Corner

1987-90

Club Corner
Abbey Curve
Bridge Bend
Woodcote Corner
Stowe Corner
Hangar Straight
Chapel Curve
Copse Corner
Maggots Curve
Becketts Corner

1991-94

Club Corner — Luffield
Bridge Corner
Woodcote Corner
Vale
Abbey Curve
Brooklands
Priory
Stowe Corner
Hangar Straight
Becketts
Copse Corner
Chapel Curve

International Trophy con'd					
year	formula	winner	nat	car	mph
1952	F2	Lance Macklin	GB	HWM 52-Alta	85.410
1953	F2	Mike Hawthorn	GB	Ferrari 500	92.293
1954	F1	José Froilan Gonzalez	RA	Ferrari 553 Squalo	92.780
1955	F1	Peter Collins	GB	Maserati 250F	95.938
1956	F1	Stirling Moss	GB	Vanwall VW2	100.466
1957	F1/F2	Jean Behra	F	BRM P25	99.946
1958	F1/F2	Peter Collins	GB	Ferrari Dino 246	101.817
1959	F1/F2	Jack Brabham	AUS	Cooper T51-Climax	102.730
1960	F1/F2	Innes Ireland	GB	Lotus 18-Climax	108.831

International Trophy con'd

year	formula	winner	nat	car	mph
1961	IC	Stirling Moss	GB	Cooper T53-Climax	87.040
1962	F1	Graham Hill	GB	BRM P57	99.730
1963	F1	Jim Clark	GB	Lotus 25-Climax	108.125
1964	F1	Jack Brabham	AUS	Brabham BT7-Climax	110.355
1965	F1	Jackie Stewart	GB	BRM P261	111.664
1966	F1	Jack Brabham	AUS	Brabham BT19-Repco	116.063
1967	F1	Michael Parkes	GB	Ferrari 312	114.650
1968	F1	Denny Hulme	NZ	McLaren M7A-Ford	122.176
1969	F1	Jack Brabham	AUS	Brabham BT26A-Ford	107.002
1970	F1/F5000	Chris Amon	NZ	March 701-Ford	124.186
1971	F1/F5000	Graham Hill	GB	Brabham BT34-Ford	128.527
1972	F1/F5000	Emerson Fittipaldi	BR	Lotus 72D-Ford	131.806
1973	F1/F5000	Jackie Stewart	GB	Tyrrell 006-Ford	132.827
1974	F1/F5000	James Hunt	GB	Hesketh 308-Ford	133.577
1975	F1	Niki Lauda	A	Ferrari 312T	134.335
1976	F1	James Hunt	GB	McLaren M23-Ford	132.579
1977	F2 E	René Arnoux	F	Martini MK22-Renault	125.736
1978	F1	Keke Rosberg	SF	Theodore TR1-Ford	96.637
1979	F2 E	Eddie Cheever	USA	Osella FA2/79-BMW	114.033
1980	F1/F2	Eliseo Salazar	RCH	Williams FW07-Ford	133.887
1981	F2 E	Mike Thackwell	NZ	Ralt RH6/81-Honda	115.246
1982	F2 E	Stefan Bellof	D	Maurer MM82-BMW	115.066
1983	F2 E	Beppe Gabbiani	I	March 832-BMW	120.683
1984	F2 E	Mike Thackwell	NZ	Ralt RH6/84-Honda	135.393
1985	F3000 INT	Mike Thackwell	NZ	Ralt RB20-Cosworth	114.363
1986	F3000 INT	Pascal Fabre	F	Lola T86/50-Cosworth	118.711
1987	F3000 INT	Mauricio Gugelmin	BR	Ralt RT21-Honda	130.989
1988	F3000 INT	Roberto Moreno	BR	Reynard 88D-Cosworth	132.273
1989	F3000 INT	Thomas Danielsson	S	Reynard 89D-Cosworth	131.523
1990	F3000 INT	Allan McNish	GB	Lola T90/50-Mugen	134.293
1992	F3000 INT	Jordi Gene	E	Reynard 92D-Mugen	121.439
1993	F3000 INT	Gil de Ferran	BR	Reynard 93D-Cosworth	119.465
1994	F3000 INT	Franck Lagorce	F	Reynard 94D-Cosworth	119.509

*race abandoned due to heavy rain after seven laps

Other European Formula Two races

year	formula	winner	nat	car	mph
1967	F2 E	Jochen Rindt	A	Brabham BT23-Ford	116.659
1975	F2 E	Michel Leclère	F	March 752-BMW	123.726
1980	F2 E	Derek Warwick	GB	Toleman TG280-Hart	130.597

European Formula Three race

year	formula	winner	nat	car	mph
1980	F3 E	Mike White	ZA	March 803B-Toyota	119.763
1981	F3 E	Roberto Moreno	BR	Ralt RT3/81-Toyota	122.634
1982	F3 E	Emanuele Pirro	I	Euroracing 101-Alfa Romeo	121.741
1983	F3 E	Martin Brundle	GB	Ralt RT3/83-Toyota	122.400
1984	F3 E	Johnny Dumfries	GB	Ralt RT3/83-Volkswagen	124.430
1987*	F3 E	Steve Kempton	GB	Reynard 873-Alfa Romeo	117.541

*European F3 Cup

Daily Express Indy Silverstone

year	formula	winner	nat	car	mph
1978	Indycar	AJ Foyt Jr	USA	Coyote-Foyt/Ford	104.361

World Sports Car race

year	formula	winner	nat	car	mph
1976	SC W	John Fitzpatrick/Tom Walkinshaw	GB	BMW 3.0 CSL	106.041
1977	SC W	Jacky Ickx/Jochen Mass	B/D	Porsche 935	112.393
1978	SC W	Jacky Ickx/Jochen Mass	B/D	Porsche 935	114.837
1979	SC W	John Fitzpatrick/Bob Wollek/Hans Heyer	GB/F/D	Porsche 935	111.416
1980	SC W	Alain de Cadenet/Desiré Wilson	GB/ZA	De Cadenet LM-Ford	114.348
1981	SC W	Dieter Schornstein/Harald Grohs/Walter Rohrl	D	Porsche 935	100.177
1982	SC W	Riccardo Patrese/Michele Alboreto	I	Lancia LC1	117.196
1983	SC W	Derek Bell/Stefan Bellof	GB/D	Porsche 956	123.202
1984	SC W	Jacky Ickx/Jochen Mass	B/D	Porsche 956	122.137
1985	SC W	Jacky Ickx/Jochen Mass	D/B	Porsche 962	126.831
1986	SC W	Derek Warwick/Eddie Cheever	GB/USA	Jaguar XJR-6	129.083
1987	SC W	Eddie Cheever/Raul Boesel	USA/BR	Jaguar XJR-8	123.421
1988	SC W	Eddie Cheever/Martin Brundle	USA/GB	Jaguar XJR-9	128.639
1990*	SC W	Martin Brundle/Alain Ferté	GB/F	Jaguar XJR-11	128.830
1991*	SC W	Derek Warwick/Teo Fabi	GB/I	Jaguar XJR-14	122.037
1992*	SC W	Derek Warwick/Yannick Dalmas	GB/F	Peugeot 905B	122.651

*British Empire Trophy - also see above

SNETTERTON

Another former World War Two airfield turned racing circuit. Snetterton is essentially a national venue, its highlight in recent years has been the Willhire 24-hour race for production saloon cars. However, it was the venue for the first round of the new European Formula Two Championship in 1967.

CURRENT CIRCUIT

Lap distance ..1.952 miles
Lap record ......Gareth Rees (Reynard 93D-Cosworth) 59.970s, 117.179 mph, 1994, F3000

CIRCUIT CHANGES

1951-64 ....2.71 miles
1965-73 ....Russell Bend introduction before the pits. Official lap distance remained 2.71 miles
1974-89 ....New short circuit opened. 1.917 miles
1990 ....Russell Bend reprofiled. 1.949 miles
1991 to date ....Current circuit

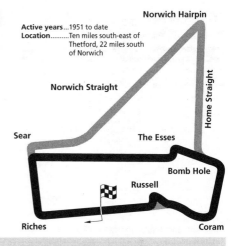

Active years...1951 to date
Location.........Ten miles south-east of Thetford, 22 miles south of Norwich

Guards 100 European Formula Two race					
year	formula	winner	nat	car	mph
1967	F2 E	Jochen Rindt	A	Brabham BT23-Ford	108.987

THRUXTON

Orginially a motorcycle circuit which also held a few car meetings in 1953 and 1954. When Goodwood closed in 1966, Thruxton was chosen as the new home of the BARC and reopened for cars on 17 March 1968. The highlight of the circuit's racing calendar was the Easter Monday F2 race which was named in honour of three-time race winner Jochen Rindt after his death at Monza in 1970. Rising costs of the new Formula 3000 killed the meeting after the 1985 race. The trophy was presented again for a historic F2 race as part of Thruxton's 25th anniversary celebrations in 1993.

Active years...1950-65 (motorbikes plus a few car meetings), 1968 to date
Location.........Five miles west of Andover, Hampshire

CURRENT CIRCUIT

Lap distance ..2.356 miles
Lap record ......Dave Coyne (Reynard 90D-Cosworth) 1m03.66, 133.233 mph, 1991, F3000

CIRCUIT CHANGES

1952 ....1.89 miles
1953-65 ....Using runways. 2.757 miles
1968 to date ....Used perimeter road. Current circuit

European Formula Two race (prior to Jochen Rindt Trophy)					
year	formula	winner	nat	car	mph
1968	F2 E	Jochen Rindt	A	Brabham BT23C-Ford	109.424
1969	F2 E	Jochen Rindt	A	Lotus 59B-Ford	112.649
1970	F2 E	Jochen Rindt	A	Lotus 69-Ford	112.729
Jochen Rindt Trophy					
year	formula	winner	nat	car	mph
1971	F2 E	Graham Hill	GB	Brabham BT36-Ford	112.901
1972	F2 E	Ronnie Peterson	S	March 722-Ford	117.169
1973	F2 E	Henri Pescarolo	F	Motul M1-Ford	114.449
1975	F2 E	Jacques Laffite	F	Martini MK16-BMW	115.980
1976	F2 E	Maurizio Flammini	I	March 762-BMW	116.287
1977	F2 E	Brian Henton	GB	Boxer PR276-Hart	117.817
1978	F2 E	Bruno Giacomelli	I	March 782-BMW	117.392
1979	F2 E	Rad Dougall	ZA	March 782-Hart	121.156
1980	F2 E	Brian Henton	GB	Toleman TG280-Hart	121.148
1981	F2 E	Roberto Guerrero	USA	Maurer MM81-BMW	121.405
1982	F2 E	Johnny Cecotto	YV	March 822-BMW	121.823
1983	F2 E	Beppe Gabbiani	I	March 832-BMW	121.669
1984	F2 E	Mike Thackwell	NZ	Ralt RH6/84-Honda	123.026
1985	F3000 INT	Emanuele Pirro	I	March 85B-Cosworth	117.413
1993	Hist F2	Marc Surer	CH	March 792-BMW	112.220

HOLLAND

MAJOR CHAMPIONSHIPS

Dutch Production Car Championship

A new Group N series which gradually took over from Holland's previous Group A touring car series

year	class	driver	nat
1986	3000 cc	Hans Hugenholtz	NL
	2000 cc	Geerlof Stan	NL
	Non-turbo	Arie Ruitenbeck	NL
1987	3000 cc	Frank Eglem	NL
	2000 cc	J Bodt	NL
	1600 cc	N van't Hoff	NL
1988	over 2500 cc	Klaas Visser	NL
	2500 cc	Paul Fauchey	NL
	1600 cc	Evert Bolderhey	NL
1989	over 2500 cc	P Fontijn	NL
	2500 cc	P Dam	NL
	1600 cc	R Nobels	NL
	1300 cc	Egbert Top	NL
1990	over 2000 cc	Cor Euser	NL
	2000 cc	P van Splunteren	NL
	1300 cc	Roger Ciapponi	NL
1991	over 2000 cc	Hans van de Beek	NL
	2000 cc	Patrick Huisman	NL
	1300 cc	Roger Ciapponi	NL
1992	over 2000 cc	Tom Langeberg	NL
	2000 cc	Tom Coronel	NL
	1400 cc	Egbert Top	NL
1993	over 2000 cc	Peter Kox	NL
	2000 cc	Cor Euser	NL
	1400 cc	Toon van der Haterd	NL
1994	over 2000 cc	Cor Euser	NL
	2000 cc	Donald Molenaar	NL
	1400 cc	Toon van der Haterd	NL

MAJOR INTERNATIONAL RACES

DUTCH GRAND PRIX

year	formula	circuit	winner	nat	car	mph
1950	F1	Zandvoort	Louis Rosier	F	Lago-Talbot T26C-DA	76.616
1951	F1	Zandvoort	Louis Rosier	F	Lago-Talbot T26C-DA	78.445
1952	F2 W	Zandvoort	Alberto Ascari	I	Ferrari 500	81.089
1953	F2 W	Zandvoort	Alberto Ascari	I	Ferrari 500	81.033
1955	F1 W	Zandvoort	Juan Manuel Fangio	RA	Mercedes-Benz W196	89.623
1958	F1 W	Zandvoort	Stirling Moss	GB	Vanwall VW10	93.915
1959	F1 W	Zandvoort	Jo Bonnier	S	BRM P25 (59)	93.446
1960	F1 W	Zandvoort	Jack Brabham	AUS	Cooper T53-Climax	96.254
1961	F1 W	Zandvoort	Wolfgang von Trips	D	Ferrari Dino 156	96.190
1962	F1 W	Zandvoort	Graham Hill	GB	BRM P57	95.425
1963	F1 W	Zandvoort	Jim Clark	GB	Lotus 25-Climax	97.522
1964	F1 W	Zandvoort	Jim Clark	GB	Lotus 25-Climax	98.001
1965	F1 W	Zandvoort	Jim Clark	GB	Lotus 33-Climax	100.851
1966	F1 W	Zandvoort	Jack Brabham	AUS	Brabham BT19-Repco	100.091
1967	F1 W	Zandvoort	Jim Clark	GB	Lotus 49-Ford	104.392
1968	F1 W	Zandvoort	Jackie Stewart	GB	Matra MS10-Ford	84.645
1969	F1 W	Zandvoort	Jackie Stewart	GB	Matra MS80-Ford	111.025
1970	F1 W	Zandvoort	Jochen Rindt	A	Lotus 72-Ford	112.930
1971	F1 W	Zandvoort	Jacky Ickx	B	Ferrari 312B2	94.047
1973	F1 W	Zandvoort	Jackie Stewart	GB	Tyrrell 006-Ford	114.349
1974	F1 W	Zandvoort	Niki Lauda	A	Ferrari 312B3	114.722
1975	F1 W	Zandvoort	James Hunt	GB	Hesketh 308-Ford	110.484
1976	F1 W	Zandvoort	James Hunt	GB	McLaren M23-Ford	112.684
1977	F1 W	Zandvoort	Niki Lauda	A	Ferrari 312T2	116.120
1978	F1 W	Zandvoort	Mario Andretti	USA	Lotus 79-Ford	116.918
1979	F1 W	Zandvoort	Alan Jones	AUS	Williams FW07-Ford	116.619
1980	F1 W	Zandvoort	Nelson Piquet	BR	Brabham BT49-Ford	116.190
1981	F1 W	Zandvoort	Alain Prost	F	Renault RE30	113.709
1982	F1 W	Zandvoort	Didier Pironi	F	Ferrari 126C2	116.399
1983	F1 W	Zandvoort	René Arnoux	F	Ferrari 126C3	115.639
1984	F1 W	Zandvoort	Alain Prost	F	McLaren MP4/2-TAG Porsche	115.604
1985	F1 W	Zandvoort	Niki Lauda	A	McLaren MP4/2B-TAG Porsche	119.977

CIRCUITS AND OTHER RACES

ZANDVOORT

Holland's only racing circuit, Zandvoort was a regular Grand Prix circuit until 1985. It was designed by John Hugenholtz using the communications roads that had been left by the departing German army after World War Two. The combination of a fast final corner into the long pits straight before the famous 180-degree Tarzan corner produced plenty of overtaking and great racing. Zandvoort struggled after the end of the Dutch GP, going bankrupt and being taken over by the town council in 1988. Dutch noise pollution laws have forced the circuit to be altered, a man-made sand dune had to be built between the town and a new, shorter circuit in 1989 which is now used. The major event is now the F3 Marlboro Masters which rivals the Monaco F3 GP as the most prestigious race for that category in Europe.

Active years ...1948 to date
Location ....Northern suburbs of
Zandvoort, eight miles
west of Haarlem, 15 miles
west of Amsterdam

CURRENT CIRCUIT

Lap distance ..1.565 miles
Lap record ......Kelvin Burt (Reynard 923-
Mugen) 1m01.043,
92.296 mph, 1992, F3

**ZANDVOORT
OLD GRAND PRIX CIRCUIT**

**ZANDVOORT
NEW CIRCUIT**

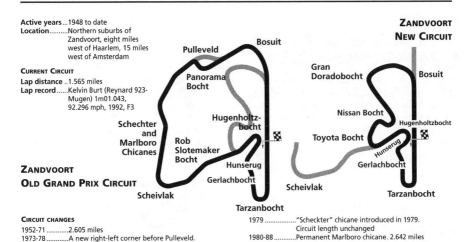

CIRCUIT CHANGES

1952-71 ....2.605 miles
1973-78 ....A new right-left corner before Pulleveld.
2.626 miles

1979 ...."Scheckter" chicane introduced in 1979.
Circuit length unchanged
1980-88 ....Permanent Marlboro chicane. 2.642 miles
1989 to date ....New shorter circuit opened. Current circuit

Dutch Grand Prix see above

Zandvoort Grand Prix

year	formula	winner	nat	car	mph
1948	FL	"B Bira"	SM	Maserati 4CL	73.250
1949	F1	Luigi Villoresi	I	Ferrari 125	77.120

European Formula Two race

year	formula	winner	nat	car	mph
1967	F2 E	Jacky Ickx	B	Matra MS5-Ford	104.852
1968	F2 E	Jean-Pierre Beltoise	F	Matra MS7-Ford	105.794
1979	F2 E	Eddie Cheever	USA	Osella FA2/79-BMW	113.139
1980	F2 E	Richard Dallest	F	AGS JH17-BMW	93.993

International Formula 3000 race

year	formula	winner	nat	car	mph
1985	F3000 INT	Christian Danner	D	March 85B-Cosworth	101.026

European Formula Three race

year	formula	winner	nat	car	mph
1976	F3 E	Riccardo Patrese	I	Chevron B34-Toyota	102.642
1977	F3 E	Anders Olofsson	S	Ralt RT1-Toyota	103.263
1978	F3 E	Jan Lammers	NL	Ralt RT1-Toyota	104.335
1979	F3 E	Alain Prost	F	Martini MK27-Renault	104.428
1980	F3 E	Mauro Baldi	I	Martini MK31-Toyota	100.396
1981	F3 E	Mauro Baldi	I	March 813-Alfa Romeo	102.672
1982	F3 E	Oscar Larrauri	RA	Euroracing 101-Alfa Romeo	102.130
1983	F3 E	John Nielsen	DK	Ralt RT3/83-Volkswagen	101.668

Marlboro Masters of Formula Three

year	formula	winner	nat	car	mph
1991	F3	David Coulthard	GB	Ralt RT35-Mugen	88.182
1992	F3	Pedro Lamy	P	Reynard 923-Opel	90.145
1993	F3	Jos Verstappen	NL	Dallara 393-Opel	90.900
1994	F3	Gareth Rees	GB	Dallara 394-Mugen	77.212

HUNGARY

MAJOR INTERNATIONAL RACES

HUNGARIAN GRAND PRIX					
year	formula	circuit	winner	nat	car	mph
1936	GP	Budapest	Tazio Nuvolari	I	Alfa Romeo Tipo-C "8C-35"	69.373
1986	F1 W	Hungaroring	Nelson Piquet	BR	Williams FW11-Honda	94.320
1987	F1 W	Hungaroring	Nelson Piquet	BR	Williams FW11B-Honda	95.211
1988	F1 W	Hungaroring	Ayrton Senna	BR	McLaren MP4/4-Honda	96.554
1989	F1 W	Hungaroring	Nigel Mansell	GB	Ferrari 640	103.908
1990	F1 W	Hungaroring	Thierry Boutsen	B	Williams FW13B-Renault	104.035
1991	F1 W	Hungaroring	Ayrton Senna	BR	McLaren MP4/6-Honda	104.318
1992	F1 W	Hungaroring	Ayrton Senna	BR	McLaren MP4/7A-Honda	107.157
1993	F1 W	Hungaroring	Damon Hill	GB	Williams FW15C-Renault	105.831
1994	F1 W	Hungaroring	Michael Schumacher	D	Benetton B194-Ford	105.444

CIRCUITS

HUNGARORING

The first circuit to hold a Grand Prix behind the Iron Curtain, the Hungaroring attracted an estimated crowd of 200,000 for that first race. Unfortunately it has precious few overtaking opportunities as it is designed more like a street circuit than a purpose-built facility. This makes Nigel Mansell's 1989 victory from 12th on the grid all the more impressive.

Hungarian Grand Prix see above

CURRENT CIRCUIT
Lap distance ..2.466 miles
Lap record .....Nigel Mansell (Williams FW14B-Renault)
1m18.308, 113.368 mph, 1992, F1

HUNGARORING

Active years...1986 to date
Location..........12 miles east of Budapest

Deviation 1986-88

CIRCUIT CHANGES
1986-88............2.494 miles
1989 to date ....Original diversion bypassed by straight. Current circuit

NEPLIGET PARK

BUDAPEST
The first Hungarian GP was held in Budapest's Nepliget Park in 1936 when Tazio Nuvolari held off the all-conquering German teams in his underpowered Alfa Romeo. Racing returned to Hungary in the early 1960s at Ferhegy airfield before Formula Three and European Touring Cars returned to Nepliget Park on a modified circuit.

Hungarian Grand Prix see above

NEPLIGET PARK POST-WAR CIRCUIT

Active years...1936-72
Location..........Nepliget Park, central Budapest

NEPLIGET PARK 1936 GP CIRCUIT

CIRCUITS
1936 ....3.10 miles
1945-72 ....3.29 miles

ITALY

MAJOR CHAMPIONSHIPS

Italian Superturismo Championship

year	driver	nat	team	car
1987	Michele di Gioia	I	Michele di Gioia	BMW M3
1988	Gianfranco Brancatelli	I	Jolly Club	Alfa Romeo 75 turbo
1989	Johnny Cecotto	YV	Schnitzer	BMW M3
1990	Roberto Ravaglia	I	Schnitzer	BMW M3
1991	Roberto Ravaglia	I	CiBiEmme Engineering	BMW M3
1992	Nicola Larini	I	Alfa Corse	Alfa Romeo 155 GTA
1993	Roberto Ravaglia	I	CiBiEmme Engineering	BMW 318i
1994	Emanuele Pirro	I	Audi Sport Italia	Audi 80 Quattro

The 1921 Targa Florio, with Max Sailor pictured

Italian Formula Three Championship

year	driver	nat	team	car
1964	"Geki" Russo	I	"Geki" Russo	de Sanctis-Ford
1965	Andrea de Adamich	I	Andrea de Adamich	Lola T53-Ford/Brabham-Ford
1966	Tino Brambilla	I	Scuderia Madunina	Brabham BT15-Ford
1968	Franco Bernabei	I	Franco Bernabei	Tecno 68-Ford
1969	Gianluigi Picchi	I	Tecno Racing Team	Tecno 69-Ford
1970	Giovanni Salvati	I	Giovanni Salvati	Tecno 70-Ford
1971	Giancarlo Naddeo	I	Giancarlo Naddeo	Tecno 69-Ford
1972	Vittorio Brambilla	I	Team Brambilla	Birel 72-Alfa Romeo/Brabham BT35-Ford
1973	Carlo Giorgio	I	Jolly Club/Trivellato Racing	Ensign LNF3-Ford/March 733-Ford
1974	Alberto Colombo	I	Scuderia del Lario	GRD 374-Ford/March 743-Toyota
1975	Luciano Pavesi	I	Scuderia ala d'Oro	Brabham BT41-Toyota/March 753-Toyota
1976	Riccardo Patrese	I	Trivellato Racing	Chevron B34-Toyota
1977	Elio de Angelis	I	Trivellato Racing	Chevron B38-Toyota/Ralt RT1-Toyota
1978	Siegfried Stohr	I	Trivellato Racing	Chevron B43-Toyota
1979	Piercarlo Ghinzani	I	Euroracing	March 793-Alfa Romeo
1980	Guido Pardini	I	Ferdinando Ravarotto	Dallara 380-Toyota
1981	Eddy Bianchi	I	Pioneer Team del Porto	Martini MK34-Toyota/Martini MK34-Alfa Romeo
1982	Enzo Coloni	I	Enzo Coloni Racing	March 813-Alfa Romeo/Ralt RT3-Alfa Romeo
1983	Ivan Capelli	I	Enzo Coloni Racing	Ralt RT3-Alfa Romeo
1984	Alessandro Santin	I	Enzo Coloni Racing	Ralt RT3-Alfa Romeo
1985	Franco Forini	CH	Forti Corse	Dallara 385-Volkswagen
1986	Nicola Larini	I	Enzo Coloni Racing	Dallara 386-Alfa Romeo
1987	Enrico Bertaggia	I	Forti Corse	Dallara 387-Alfa Romeo
1988	Emanuele Naspetti	I	Forti Corse	Dallara 388-Alfa Romeo
1989	Gianni Morbidelli	I	Forti Corse	Dallara 389-Alfa Romeo
1990	Roberto Colciago	I	Prema Racing	Reynard 903-Alfa Romeo
1991	Giambattista Busi	I	Piemme Motors	Dallara 391-Volkswagen
1992	Massimiliano Angelelli	I	RC Motorsport	Dallara 392-Opel
1993	Christian Pescatori	I	Supercars	Dallara 393-Fiat
1994	Giancarlo Fisichella	I	RC Motorsport	Dallara 394-Opel

Italian Prototype Championship

An open cockpit sports car series introduced in 1988 using 2.5-litre 6-cylinder Alfa Romeo engines.

year	driver	nat	car
1988	Stefano Sanesi	I	Lucchini SN88-Alfa Romeo
1989	Stefano Sanesi	I	Lucchini SN89-Alfa Romeo
1990	Stefano Sanesi	I	Lucchini SP90-Alfa Romeo
1991	Giorgio Francia	I	Osella PA16-Alfa Romeo
1992	Fabio Mancini	I	Osella PA16-Alfa Romeo
1993	Ermanno Martinello	I	Lucchini P3-Alfa Romeo
1994	Ermanno Martinello	I	Lucchini P3-Alfa Romeo

Italian Super Car GT Championship

year	driver	nat	car
1992	Rosario Parasiliti	I	Ferrari F40
1993	Marco Brand	I	Ferrari F40
1994	Vittorio Colombo	I	Ferrari F40

MAJOR INTERNATIONAL RACES

ITALIAN GRAND PRIX

year	formula	circuit	winner	nat	car	mph
1921	GP	Brescia	Jules Goux	F	Ballot 3L	89.937
1922	GP	Monza	Pietro Bordino	I	Fiat 804	86.905
1923	GP	Monza	Carlo Salamano	I	Fiat 805	91.037
1924	GP	Monza	Antonio Ascari	I	Alfa Romeo P2	98.738
1925	GP	Monza	Gastone Brilli-Peri	I	Alfa Romeo P2	94.823
1926	GP	Monza	"Sabipa"	F	Bugatti T39A	85.880
1927	GP	Monza	Robert Benoist	F	Delage 15S8	108.072
1928	GP	Monza	Louis Chiron	MC	Bugatti T35C	99.361
1931	FL	Monza	Giuseppe Campari/Tazio Nuvolari	I	Alfa Romeo 8C "Monza"	96.317
1932	FL	Monza	Tazio Nuvolari/Giuseppe Campari	I	Alfa Romeo Tipo-B "P3"	103.152
1933	FL	Monza	Luigi Fagioli	I	Alfa Romeo Tipo-B "P3"	108.584
1934	GP	Monza	Rudolf Caracciola/Luigi Fagioli	D/I	Mercedes-Benz W25A	65.513
1935	GP	Monza	Hans Stuck	D	Auto Union B	85.949
1936	GP	Monza	Bernd Rosemeyer	D	Auto Union C	83.532
1937	GP	Livorno	Rudolf Caracciola	D	Mercedes-Benz W125	78.954
1938	GP	Monza	Tazio Nuvolari	I	Auto Union D	96.870
1947	F1	Milan	Carlo Felice Trossi	I	Alfa Romeo 158	70.346
1948	F1	Turin	Jean-Pierre Wimille	F	Alfa Romeo 158	70.317
1949	F1	Monza	Alberto Ascari	I	Ferrari 125	105.046
1950	F1 W	Monza	Giuseppe Farina	I	Alfa Romeo 159	109.709
1951	F1 W	Monza	Alberto Ascari	I	Ferrari 375	115.533
1952	F2 W	Monza	Alberto Ascari	I	Ferrari 500	110.049

year	formula	circuit	winner	nat	car	mph
1953	F2 W	Monza	Juan Manuel Fangio	RA	Maserati A6SSG	110.694
1954	F1 W	Monza	Juan Manuel Fangio	RA	Mercedes-Benz W196	111.992
1955	F1 W	Monza	Juan Manuel Fangio	RA	Mercedes-Benz W196	128.494
1956	F1 W	Monza	Stirling Moss	GB	Maserati 250F	129.733
1957	F1 W	Monza	Stirling Moss	GB	Vanwall VW5	120.279
1958	F1 W	Monza	Tony Brooks	GB	Vanwall VW5	121.220
1959	F1 W	Monza	Stirling Moss	GB	Cooper T51-Climax	124.388
1960	F1 W	Monza	Phil Hill	USA	Ferrari Dino 246	132.063
1961	F1 W	Monza	Phil Hill	USA	Ferrari Dino 156	130.107
1962	F1 W	Monza	Graham Hill	GB	BRM P57	123.620
1963	F1 W	Monza	Jim Clark	GB	Lotus 25-Climax	127.743
1964	F1 W	Monza	John Surtees	GB	Ferrari 158	127.779
1965	F1 W	Monza	Jackie Stewart	GB	BRM P261	130.468
1966	F1 W	Monza	Ludovico Scarfiotti	I	Ferrari 312	135.928
1967	F1 W	Monza	John Surtees	GB	Honda RA300	140.509
1968	F1 W	Monza	Denny Hulme	NZ	McLaren M7A-Ford	145.420
1969	F1 W	Monza	Jackie Stewart	GB	Matra MS80-Ford	146.972
1970	F1 W	Monza	Clay Regazzoni	CH	Ferrari 312B	147.081
1971	F1 W	Monza	Peter Gethin	GB	BRM P160	150.759
1972	F1 W	Monza	Emerson Fittipaldi	BR	Lotus 72D-Ford	131.599
1973	F1 W	Monza	Ronnie Peterson	S	Lotus 72D-Ford	132.616
1974	F1 W	Monza	Ronnie Peterson	S	Lotus 72E-Ford	135.117
1975	F1 W	Monza	Clay Regazzoni	CH	Ferrari 312T	135.498
1976	F1 W	Monza	Ronnie Peterson	S	March 761-Ford	124.117
1977	F1 W	Monza	Mario Andretti	USA	Lotus 78-Ford	128.010
1978	F1 W	Monza	Niki Lauda	A	Brabham BT46-Alfa Romeo	128.949
1979	F1 W	Monza	Jody Scheckter	ZA	Ferrari 312T4	131.844
1980	F1 W	Imola	Nelson Piquet	BR	Brabham BT49-Ford	114.906
1981	F1 W	Monza	Alain Prost	F	Renault RE30	129.893
1982	F1 W	Monza	René Arnoux	F	Renault RE30B	136.411
1983	F1 W	Monza	Nelson Piquet	BR	Brabham BT52B-BMW	135.177
1984	F1 W	Monza	Niki Lauda	A	McLaren MP4/2-TAG Porsche	137.019
1985	F1 W	Monza	Alain Prost	F	McLaren MP4/2B-TAG Porsche	141.400
1986	F1 W	Monza	Nelson Piquet	BR	Williams FW11-Honda	141.903
1987	F1 W	Monza	Nelson Piquet	BR	Williams FW11B-Honda	144.551
1988	F1 W	Monza	Gerhard Berger	A	Ferrari F187/88C	141.998
1989	F1 W	Monza	Alain Prost	F	McLaren MP4/5-Honda	144.230
1990	F1 W	Monza	Ayrton Senna	BR	McLaren MP4/5B-Honda	146.995
1991	F1 W	Monza	Nigel Mansell	GB	Williams FW14-Renault	147.107
1992	F1 W	Monza	Ayrton Senna	BR	McLaren MP4/7A-Honda	146.448
1993	F1 W	Monza	Damon Hill	GB	Williams FW15C-Renault	148.595
1994	F1 W	Monza	Damon Hill	GB	Williams FW16B-Renault	147.702

MILLE MIGLIA

year	formula	circuit	winner	nat	car	mph
1927	SC	Brescia-Rome-Brescia	Ferdinando Minoia/Giuseppe Morandi	I	OM	48.270
1928	SC	Brescia-Rome-Brescia	Giuseppe Campari/Giulio Ramponi	I	Alfa Romeo 1500S	52.580
1929	SC	Brescia-Rome-Brescia	Giuseppe Campari/Giulio Ramponi	I	Alfa Romeo 1750S	56.050
1930	SC	Brescia-Rome-Brescia	Tazio Nuvolari/Giovanni-Battista Guidotti	I	Alfa Romeo 1750S	62.780
1931	SC	Brescia-Rome-Brescia	Rudolf Caracciola/Wilhelm Sebastian	D	Mercedes-Benz SSKL	63.210
1932	SC	Brescia-Rome-Brescia	Baconin Borzacchini/Amedeo Bignami	I	Alfa Romeo 8C "Monza"	68.670
1933	SC	Brescia-Rome-Brescia	Tazio Nuvolari/Decimo Compagnoni	I	Alfa Romeo 8C "Monza"	67.850
1934	SC	Brescia-Rome-Brescia	Achille Varzi/Amedeo Bignami	I	Alfa Romeo 8C "Monza"	71.440
1935	SC	Brescia-Rome-Brescia	Carlo Pintacuda/Alessandro della Stufa	I	Alfa Romeo Tipo-B "P3"	71.720
1936	SC	Brescia-Rome-Brescia	Antonio Brivio/Carlo Ongaro	I	Alfa Romeo 2900A	76.010
1937	SC	Brescia-Rome-Brescia	Carlo Pintacuda/Paride Mambelli	I	Alfa Romeo 2900A	71.710
1938	SC	Brescia-Rome-Brescia	Clemente Biondetti/Aldo Stefani	I	Alfa Romeo 2900A	84.610
1940	SC	Brescia	Huschke von Hanstein/Walter Baumer	D	BMW 328	104.200
1947	SC	Brescia-Rome-Brescia	Clemente Biondetti/Emilio Romano	I	Alfa Romeo 2900B	70.140
1948	SC	Brescia-Rome-Brescia	Clemente Biondetti/Giuseppe Navone	I	Ferrari 166S	75.453
1949	SC	Brescia-Rome-Brescia	Clemente Biondetti/Ettore Salani	I	Ferrari 166MM	82.109
1950	SC	Brescia-Rome-Brescia	Giannino Marzotto/Marco Crosara	I	Ferrari 195S	77.000
1951	SC	Brescia-Rome-Brescia	Luigi Villoresi/P Cassani	I	Ferrari	76.130
1952	SC	Brescia-Rome-Brescia	Giovanni Bracco/Alfonso Rolfo	I	Ferrari 225S	80.360
1953	SC W	Brescia-Rome-Brescia	Giannino Marzotto/Marco Crosara	I	Ferrari 340MM	88.967
1954	SC W	Brescia-Rome-Brescia	Alberto Ascari	I	Lancia D24	87.267
1955	SC W	Brescia-Rome-Brescia	Stirling Moss/Denis Jenkinson	GB	Mercedes-Benz 300SLR	98.519
1956	SC W	Brescia-Rome-Brescia	Eugenio Castellotti	I	Ferrari 290MM	85.891
1957	SC W	Brescia-Rome-Brescia	Piero Taruffi	I	Ferrari 315S	95.383
1958	Reg	Brescia	Luigi Taramazzo/Gerino Gerini	I	Ferrari	Regularity test
1959	Reg	Brescia	Carlo Abate/Gianni Balzarini	I	Ferrari	Regularity test
1961	Reg	Brescia	Gunnar Andersson/Carl Lohmander	S	Ferrari 250GT	Regularity test

TARGA FLORIO

year	formula	circuit	winner	nat	car	mph
1906	TC	Madonie	Alessandro Cagno	I	Itala	29.031
1907	GP	Madonie	Felice Nazzaro	I	Fiat 60HP	33.450
1908	GP	Madonie	Vincenzo Trucco	I	Isotta-Fraschini	35.457
1909	GP	Madonie	Francesco Ciuppa	I	SPA	33.972
1910	GP	Madonie	Tullio Cariolato	I	Franco	29.380
1911	GP	Madonie	Ernesto Ceirano	I	SCAT	29.081
1912	FL	Madonie	Cyril Snipe/Pedrini	GB/I	SCAT	27.620
1913	FL	Madonie	Felice Nazzaro	I	Nazzaro	33.780
1914	FL	Madonie	Ernesto Ceirano	I	SCAT	36.080
1919	FL	Madonie	André Boillot	F	Peugeot EX5	34.194
1920	FL	Madonie	Guido Meregalli	I	Nazzaro GP	31.743
1921	FL	Madonie	Giulio Masetti	I	Fiat 451	36.187
1922	FL	Madonie	Giulio Masetti	I	Mercedes GP/14	39.204
1923	FL	Madonie	Ugo Sivocci	I	Alfa Romeo RLTF	36.772
1924	FL	Madonie	Christian Werner	D	Mercedes PP	41.023
1925	FL	Madonie	Meo Costantini	F	Bugatti T35	44.497
1926	FL	Madonie	Meo Costantini	F	Bugatti T35T	45.679
1927	FL	Madonie	Emilio Materassi	I	Bugatti T35C	44.159
1928	GP	Madonie	Albert Divo	F	Bugatti T35B	45.659
1929	GP	Madonie	Albert Divo	F	Bugatti T35C	46.210
1930	GP	Madonie	Achille Varzi	I	Alfa Romeo P2	48.481
1931	GP	Madonie	Tazio Nuvolari	I	Alfa Romeo 8C "Monza"	41.065
1932	GP	Madonie	Tazio Nuvolari	I	Alfa Romeo 8C "Monza"	49.272
1933	GP	Madonie	Antonio Brivio	I	Alfa Romeo 8C "Monza"	47.558
1934	GP	Madonie	Achille Varzi	I	Alfa Romeo Tipo-B "P3"	43.013
1935	GP	Madonie	Antonio Brivio	I	Alfa Romeo Tipo-B "P3"	49.181
1936	SC	Madonie	Costantino Magistri	I	Lancia	41.690
1937	V	Palermo	Guilio Severi	I	Maserati 6CM	66.920
1938	V	Palermo	Giovanni Rocco	I	Maserati 6CM	71.020
1939	V	Palermo	Luigi Villoresi	I	Maserati 6CM	84.780
1940	V	Palermo	Luigi Villoresi	I	Maserati 4CL	88.718
1948	SC	Madonie	Clemente Biondetti/Igor Troubetskoy	I	Ferrari	55.008
1949	SC	Madonie	Clemente Biondetti/Aldo Benedetti	I	Ferrari	50.639
1950	SC	Madonie	Mario Bornigia/Giancarlo Bornigia	I	Alfa Romeo	53.870
1951	SC	Madonie	Franco Cortese	I	Frazer-Nash	45.570
1952	SC	Madonie	Felice Bonetto	I	Lancia	49.700
1953	SC	Madonie	Umberto Maglioli	I	Lancia	50.100
1954	SC	Madonie	Piero Taruffi	I	Lancia	55.850
1955	SC W	Madonie	Stirling Moss/Peter Collins	GB	Mercedes-Benz 300SLR	59.833
1956	SC	Madonie	Umberto Maglioli/Huschke von Hanstein	I/D	Porsche	56.370
1957	Reg	Madonie	Fabio Colonna	I	Fiat	Regularity test
1958	SC W	Madonie	Luigi Musso/Olivier Gendebien	I/B	Ferrari 250TR	58.907
1959	SC W	Madonie	Edgar Barth/Wolfgang Seidel	DDR/D	Porsche 718 RSK	56.737
1960	SC W	Madonie	Jo Bonnier/Hans Herrmann/Graham Hill	S/D/GB	Porsche RS60	59.239
1961	SC W	Madonie	Wolfgang von Trips/Olivier Gendebien	D/B	Ferrari Dino 246SP	64.271
1962	SC W	Madonie	Willy Mairesse/Ricardo Rodriguez/Olivier Gendebien	B/MEX/B	Ferrari Dino 246SP	63.468
1963	SC W	Madonie	Jo Bonnier/Carlo Abate	S/I	Porsche RS62	64.566
1964	SC W	Madonie	Antonio Pucci/Colin Davis	I/GB	Porsche 904GTS	62.297
1965	SC W	Madonie	Nino Vaccarella/Lorenzo Bandini	I	Ferrari 275P2	63.730
1966	SC W	Madonie	Willy Mairesse/Herbert Müller	B/CH	Porsche 906 Carrera 6	61.492
1967	SC W	Madonie	Paul Hawkins/Rolf Stommelen	AUS/D	Porsche 910/8	67.613
1968	SC W	Madonie	Vic Elford/Umberto Maglioli	GB/I	Porsche 907/8	69.042
1969	SC W	Madonie	Gerhard Mitter/Udo Schutz	D	Porsche 908/8	72.991
1970	SC W	Madonie	Jo Siffert/Brian Redman	CH/GB	Porsche 908/3	74.659
1971	SC W	Madonie	Nino Vaccarella/Toine Hezemans	I/NL	Alfa Romeo T33/3	74.608
1972	SC W	Madonie	Arturo Merzario/Sandro Munari	I	Ferrari 312P	76.142
1973	SC W	Madonie	Gijs van Lennep/Herbert Müller	NL/CH	Porsche 911 Carrera RSR	71.266
1974	SC	Madonie	Gérard Larrousse/Ballestrieri	F/I	Lancia Stratos	n/a
1975	SC	Madonie	Nino Vaccarella/Arturo Merzario	I	Alfa Romeo	n/a
1976	SC	Madonie	"Amphicar"/Armando Floridia	I	Osella	n/a
1977	SC	Madonie	Raffaele Restivo/"Apache"	I	Chevron	n/a

CIRCUITS AND OTHER RACES

ENNA-PERGUSA

A high-speed slipstreaming circuit built around Lake Pergusa in an arid and stifling bowl on the island of Sicily. On a good lap, the drivers would only really brake for the first corner of the original circuit, but since the 1970s it has been interrupted by three chicanes, the first of which is almost certain to cause a shunt on the opening lap. The Mediterranean GP began as a non-championship F1 race in 1962, and two years later Jo Siffert upset the form-book to win the first of successive victories, narrowly beating Jim Clark on both occasions. The Mediterranean GP is now a permanent fixture on the Formula 3000 calendar.

ENNA-PERGUSA

Active years...1961 to date
Location..........Sicily

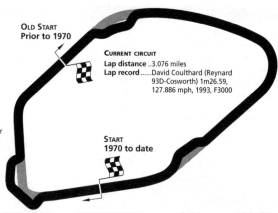

OLD START
Prior to 1970

CURRENT CIRCUIT
Lap distance ..3.076 miles
Lap record ......David Coulthard (Reynard
93D-Cosworth) 1m26.59,
127.886 mph, 1993, F3000

START
1970 to date

CIRCUIT CHANGES

1961-69 ....Original circuit, no chicanes. 2.983
miles
1970 ....Chicane inserted immediately after
the original start, pits moved onto
other side of circuit. 3.010 miles
1971-75 ....Second chicane built. 3.011 miles
1975 to date ....Chicane built at first corner, used
for 1975 F2 race (but not Sports
Cars). Current circuit

Mediterranean Grand Prix

year	formula	winner	nat	car	mph
1962	F1	Lorenzo Bandini	I	Ferrari 156	128.892
1963	F1	John Surtees	GB	Ferrari 156	137.653
1964	F1	Jo Siffert	CH	Brabham BT11-BRM	137.698
1965	F1	Jo Siffert	CH	Brabham BT11-BRM	139.308
1966	F3	Jonathan Williams	GB	de Santis-Ford	n/a
1967	F2 E	Jackie Stewart	GB	Matra MS7-Ford	142.727
1968	F2 E	Jochen Rindt	A	Brabham BT23C-Ford	142.780
1969	F2 E	Piers Courage	GB	Brabham BT30-Ford	142.327
1970	F2 E	Clay Regazzoni	CH	Tecno 70-Ford	127.157
1972	F2 E	Henri Pescarolo	F	Brabham BT38-Ford	123.819
1973	F2 E	Jean-Pierre Jarier	F	March 732-BMW	129.207
1974	F2 E	Hans-Joachim Stuck	D	March 742-BMW	128.231
1975	F2 E	Jacques Laffite	F	Martini MK16-BMW	110.767
1976	F2 E	René Arnoux	F	Martini MK19-Renault	115.092
1977	F2 E	Keke Rosberg	SF	Chevron B40-Hart	114.991
1978	F2 E	Bruno Giacomelli	I	March 782-BMW	118.062
1979	F2 E	Eje Elgh	S	March 792-BMW	116.895
1980	F2 E	Siegfried Stohr	I	Toleman TG280-Hart	117.532
1981	F2 E	Thierry Boutsen	B	March 812-BMW	118.369
1982	F2 E	Thierry Boutsen	B	Spirit 201-Honda	119.725
1983	F2 E	Jonathan Palmer	GB	Ralt RH6/83-Honda	118.327
1984	F2 E	Mike Thackwell	NZ	Ralt RH6/84-Honda	120.505
1985	F3000 INT	Mike Thackwell	NZ	Ralt RB20-Cosworth	119.103
1986	F3000 INT	Luis Perez Sala	E	Ralt RT20-Cosworth	119.627
1987	F3000 INT	Roberto Moreno	BR	Ralt RT21-Honda	119.797
1988	F3000 INT	Pierluigi Martini	I	March 88B-Judd	121.198
1989	F3000 INT	Andrea Chiesa	CH	Reynard 89D-Cosworth	122.187
1990	F3000 INT	Gianni Morbidelli	I	Lola T90/50-Cosworth	119.815
1991	F3000 INT	Emanuele Naspetti	I	Reynard 91D-Cosworth	123.926
1992	F3000 INT	Luca Badoer	I	Reynard 92D-Cosworth	126.521
1993	F3000 INT	David Coulthard	GB	Reynard 93D-Cosworth	126.946
1994	F3000 INT	Gil de Ferran	BR	Reynard 94D-Judd	131.153

European Formula Three race

year	formula	winner	nat	car	mph
1976	F3 E	Riccardo Patrese	I	Chevron B34-Toyota	101.092
1977	F3 E	Oscar Pedersoli	I	Ralt RT1-Toyota	107.930
1978	F3 E	Michael Bleekemolen	NL	Chevron B43-Toyota	109.640
1979	F3 E	Piercarlo Ghinzani	I	March 793-Alfa Romeo	105.790
1982	F3 E	Oscar Larrauri	RA	Euroracing 101-Alfa Romeo	111.011
1984	F3 E	Ivan Capelli	I	Martini MK42-Alfa Romeo	112.675

World Sports Car race

year	formula	winner	nat	car	mph
1975	SC W	Arturo Merzario/Jochen Mass	I/D	Alfa Romeo T33TT/12	122.440
1976	SC WSC	Jochen Mass/Rolf Stommelen	D	Porsche 936	105.869
1977	SC WSC	Arturo Merzario	I	Alfa Romeo T33SC/12	103.878
1978	SC E	Giorgio Francia/"Gimax"	I	Osella PA6-BMW	105.687
1979	SC W	Lella Lombardi/Enrico Grimaldi	I	Osella PA7-BMW	98.908
1981	SC W	Guy Edwards/Emilio de Villota	GB/E	Lola T600-Ford	103.310

IMOLA

AUTODROMO ENZO E DINO FERRARI

Before the tragic 1994 race, Imola was a highlight of the early part of the Grand Prix season. The deaths of Ayrton Senna and Roland Ratzenberger reawakened safety concerns, particularly regarding the ultra-quick Tamburello where Berger and Piquet, to name but two, had already crashed heavily. Set in the undulating Castellaccio Park outside Imola, it is a fast succession of demanding corners broken up by three chicanes. It did not reach the forefront of international motor racing until it was refurbished in the early 1970s. The year after Ronnie Peterson was killed at Monza, Imola held a non-championship F1 race and with the authorities looking for an alternative to Monza, Imola was chosen to hold the 1980 Italian GP. However, Monza was back in favour a year later and Imola was awarded the San Marino GP - a title of convenience referring to the principality 50 miles away. Major revisions, including chicanes at Tamburello and Villeneuve, have been made for 1995.

Active years...1954 to date
Location.........Outskirts of Imola, 20 miles south-west of Bologna

1994 CIRCUIT
Lap distance ..3.132 miles
Lap record ......Damon Hill (Williams FW16-Renault) 1m24.335, 133.696 mph, 1994, F1

CIRCUIT CHANGES
1954-73 ....3.118 miles
September 1973 ....Varianta Bassa built. 3.183 miles
1974-80 ....Variante Alta added. 3.144 miles
1981-94 ....Chicane built at Acqua Minerale

Italian Grand Prix see above

San Marino Grand Prix (also see Misano)

year	formula	winner	nat	car	mph
1981	F1 W	Nelson Piquet	BR	Brabham BT49C-Ford	101.214
1982	F1 W	Didier Pironi	F	Ferrari 126C2	116.662
1983	F1 W	Patrick Tambay	F	Ferrari 126C2B	115.201
1984	F1 W	Alain Prost	F	McLaren MP4/2-TAG Porsche	116.366
1985	F1 W	Elio de Angelis	I	Lotus 97T-Renault	119.189
1986	F1 W	Alain Prost	F	McLaren MP4/2C-TAG Porsche	121.929
1987	F1 W	Nigel Mansell	GB	Williams FW11B-Honda	121.303
1988	F1 W	Ayrton Senna	BR	McLaren MP4/4-Honda	121.647
1989	F1 W	Ayrton Senna	BR	McLaren MP4/5-Honda	125.490
1990	F1 W	Riccardo Patrese	I	Williams FW13B-Renault	126.073
1991	F1 W	Ayrton Senna	BR	McLaren MP4/6-Honda	120.353
1992	F1 W	Nigel Mansell	GB	Williams FW14B-Renault	127.142
1993	F1 W	Alain Prost	F	Williams FW15C-Renault	122.810
1994	F1 W	Michael Schumacher	D	Benetton B194-Ford	123.188

Imola Grand Prix

year	formula	winner	nat	car	mph
1954	-	Umberto Maglioli	I	Ferrari	87.053
1955	SC	Cesare Perdisa	I	Maserati	87.861
1956	SC	Eugenio Castellotti	I	OSCA	87.562
1963	F1	Jim Clark	GB	Lotus 25-Climax	99.380

Dino Ferrari Grand Prix

year	formula	winner	nat	car	mph
1979	F1	Niki Lauda	A	Brabham BT48-Alfa Romeo	118.026

European Formula Three race

year	formula	winner	nat	car	mph
1977	F3 E	Piercarlo Ghinzani	I	March 773-Toyota	101.789
1978	F3 E	Patrick Gaillard	F	Chevron B43-Toyota	103.190
1981	F3 E	Mauro Baldi	I	March 813-Alfa Romeo	101.749
1983	F3 E	Pierluigi Martini	I	Ralt RT3/83-Alfa Romeo	103.857
1986*	F3 E	Stefano Modena	I	Reynard 863-Alfa Romeo	85.602

*European F3 Cup

European Formula Two race

year	formula	winner	nat	car	mph
1970	F2 E	Clay Regazzoni	CH	Tecno 70-Ford	115.331
1971	F2	Carlos Pace	BR	March 712M-Ford	115.040
1972	F2 E	John Surtees	GB	Surtees TS10-Ford	118.866

International Formula 3000 race

year	formula	winner	nat	car	mph
1986	F3000 INT	Pierluigi Martini	I	Ralt RT20-Cosworth	111.365
1987	F3000 INT	Stefano Modena	I	March 87B-Cosworth	113.507

World Sports Car race

year	formula	winner	nat	car	mph
1974	SC W	Henri Pescarolo/Gérard Larrousse	F	Matra-Simca MS670C	99.975
1976	SC WSC	Jacky Ickx/Jochen Mass	B/D	Porsche 936	104.820
1977	SC WSC	Vittorio Brambilla	I	Alfa Romeo T33SC/12	105.121
1983	SC	Teo Fabi/Hans Heyer	I/D	Lancia LC2/83	99.639
1984	SC W	Stefan Bellof/Hans-Joachim Stuck	D	Porsche 956B	105.359

MISANO

AUTODROMO SANTAMONICA

Just inland from Rimini, the Autodromo Santamonica is a flat, anti-clockwise circuit which was a regular for Formula Two until that series ended. Closer to San Marino than Imola, it held an F3 San Marino GP before Imola's World Championship event started. Misano now hosts national Touring Car and Formula Three rounds.

MISANO

Active years...1972 to date
Location..........12 miles south of Rimini
Lap distance ..2.167 miles
Lap record ......Roberto Moreno (Ralt RH6/84-Honda) 1m08.50, 1984, F2

Adriatic Grand Prix/European Formula Two race

year	formula	winner	nat	car	mph
1973	F2	Wilson Fittipaldi	BR	Brabham BT40-Ford	102.021
1975	F2	Maurizio Flammini	I	March 742-BMW	94.675
1976	F2	Hans-Joachim Stuck	D	March 762-BMW	104.742
1977	F2 E	Lamberto Leoni	I	Chevron B40-Ferrari	105.784
1978	F2 E	Bruno Giacomelli	I	March 782-BMW	105.777
1979	F2 E	Brian Henton	GB	Ralt RT2-Hart	104.738
1980	F2 E	Andrea de Cesaris	I	March 802-BMW	107.371
1981	F2 E	Michele Alboreto	I	Minardi FLY281-BMW	108.256
1982	F2 E	Corrado Fabi	I	March 822-BMW	99.480
1983	F2 E	Jonathan Palmer	GB	Ralt RH6/83-Honda	108.305
1984	F2 E	Mike Thackwell	NZ	Ralt RH6/84-Honda	110.474

European Formula Three race

year	formula	winner	nat	car	mph
1980	F3 E	Mauro Baldi	I	Martini MK31-Toyota	100.742
1981	F3 E	Mauro Baldi	I	March 813-Alfa Romeo	87.162
1983	F3 E	Tommy Byrne	IRL	Ralt RT3/83-Toyota	101.984
1989*	F3 E	Gianni Morbidelli	I	Dallara 389-Alfa Romeo	104.265

*European F3 Cup

San Marino Formula Three Grand Prix (also see Imola)

year	formula	winner	nat	car	mph
1978	F3	Teo Fabi	I	March 783-Toyota	100.920
1979	F3	Michele Alboreto	I	March 793-Toyota	96.650

World Sports Car race

year	formula	winner	nat	car	mph
1978	SC W	Bob Wollek/Henri Pescarolo	F	Porsche 935	94.018

MONZA

Set in a park in Monza just north of Milan, the Autodromo Nazionale offered a fast, slip-streaming road course (now interrupted with chicanes) and a bumpy banked oval which has long since been disused. Opened on 28 August 1922, Monza has a special atmosphere and probably the most passionate fans in the world.

There have been some great races, Peter Gethin's 1971 Italian GP win was not only the quickest Grand Prix of all time but also the closest. Similar slipstreaming classics resulted in groups of cars finishing as one in 1967 and 1969. But Monza has had more tragedy than most: from Emilio Materassi and 27 spectators in 1928 to Ronnie Peterson in 1978 the list is a long and depressing one.

Monza

Active years...1922 to date
Location.........Ten miles north west of Milan

CURRENT CIRCUIT
Lap distance ..3.625 miles
Lap record ......Damon Hill (Williams FW16-Renault) 1m25.930, 151.868 mph, 1994, F1

CIRCUIT CHANGES
1922-33 ....6.214 miles
1934 ....2.69 miles
1935-36 ....4.32 miles
1938 ....4.35 miles
1950-54 ....3.915 miles
1955-56, 1960-61 ....6.2137 miles

1957-59, 1962-71....3.573 miles
1972-73 ....3.588 miles
1974-75 ....3.592 miles
1976 ....Used for the World Sports Car race early in year. 3.585 miles
1976-94 ....Chicanes installed after start and before Lesmo One. 3.6039 miles
1994 to date ....Second Lesmo tightened, Curva Grande reprofiled. Current circuit

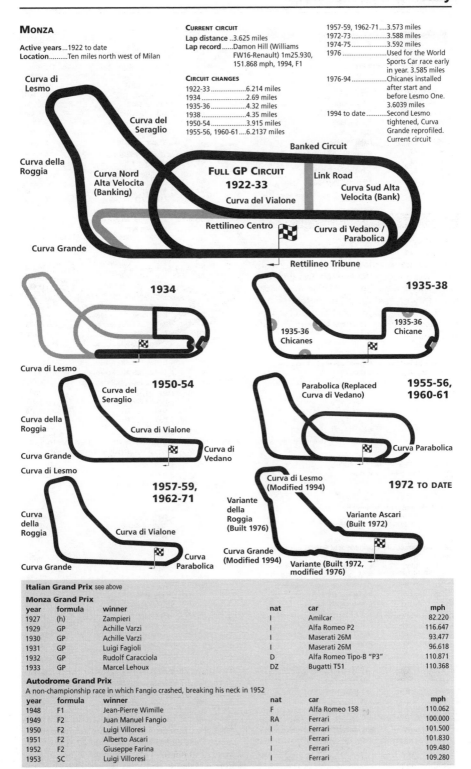

Italian Grand Prix see above

Monza Grand Prix

year	formula	winner	nat	car	mph
1927	(h)	Zampieri	I	Amilcar	82.220
1929	GP	Achille Varzi	I	Alfa Romeo P2	116.647
1930	GP	Achille Varzi	I	Maserati 26M	93.477
1931	GP	Luigi Fagioli	I	Maserati 26M	96.618
1932	GP	Rudolf Caracciola	D	Alfa Romeo Tipo-B "P3"	110.871
1933	GP	Marcel Lehoux	DZ	Bugatti T51	110.368

Autodrome Grand Prix

A non-championship race in which Fangio crashed, breaking his neck in 1952

year	formula	winner	nat	car	mph
1948	F1	Jean-Pierre Wimille	F	Alfa Romeo 158	110.062
1949	F2	Juan Manuel Fangio	RA	Ferrari	100.000
1950	F2	Luigi Villoresi	I	Ferrari	101.500
1951	F2	Alberto Ascari	I	Ferrari	101.830
1952	F2	Giuseppe Farina	I	Ferrari	109.480
1953	SC	Luigi Villoresi	I	Ferrari	109.280

Monza Grand Prix Formula Two race

year	formula	winner	nat	car	mph
1980	F2	Derek Warwick	GB	Toleman TG280B-Hart	123.967

Monza Lottery Grand Prix

year	formula	winner	nat	car	mph
1959	GT	Alfonso Thiele	USA	Ferrari 250GT	97.840
1960	FJ	Colin Davis	GB	OSCA-Fiat	104.660
1961	FJ	Tony Maggs	ZA	Cooper-BMC	106.300
1962	FJ	Peter Arundell	GB	Lotus 22-Ford	113.460
1963	FJ	Jacques Maglia	F	Lotus 27-Ford	113.750
1964	F3	Geki Russo	I	de Sanctis-Ford	99.696
1965	F3	Picko Troberg	S	Brabham-Ford	114.200
1966	F3	Jonathan Williams	GB	de Sanctis-Ford	114.280
1967	F3	Jonathan Williams	GB	de Sanctis-Ford	88.968
1968	F2	Jonathan Williams	GB	Brabham BT23C-Ford	130.078
1969	F2	Robin Widdows	GB	Brabham BT23C-Ford	133.869
1970	F5000	Mike Walker	GB	McLaren M10B-Chevrolet	140.343
1971	F2	Dieter Quester	A	March 712M-BMW	135.550
1972	F2	Graham Hill	GB	Brabham BT38-Ford	137.181
1973	F2 E	Roger Williamson	GB	March 732-BMW	124.110
1974	F3	Alessandro Pesenti-Rossi	I	GRD 374-Ford	113.760
1975	F3 E	Larry Perkins	AUS	Ralt RT1-Ford	116.799
1976	F3 E	Riccardo Patrese	I	Chevron B34-Toyota	112.524
1977	F3 E	Elio de Angelis	I	Ralt RT1-Toyota	113.476
1978	F3 E	Jan Lammers	NL	Ralt RT1-Toyota	94.510
1979	F3 E	Mike Thackwell	NZ	March 793-Toyota	114.082
1980	F3 E	Michele Alboreto	I	March 803-Alfa Romeo	113.443
1981	F3	Eddy Bianchi	I	Martini MK34-Alfa Romeo	97.213
1982	F3 E	Oscar Larrauri	RA	Euroracing 101-Alfa Romeo	115.625
1983	F3 E	John Nielsen	DK	Ralt RT3/83-Volkswagen	116.290
1984	F3 E	Gerhard Berger	A	Ralt RT3/84-Alfa Romeo	115.723
1985	F3	Franco Forini	CH	Dallara 385-Volkswagen	117.080
1986	F3	Nicola Larini	I	Dallara 386-Alfa Romeo	115.740
1987	F3	Enrico Bertaggia	I	Dallara 387-Alfa Romeo	116.280
1988	F3	Rinaldo Capello	I	Dallara 388-Alfa Romeo	116.170
1989	F3	Gianni Morbidelli	I	Dallara 389-Alfa Romeo	118.270
1990	F3	Mauro Martini	I	Dallara 390-Alfa Romeo	116.880
1991	F3	Luca Badoer	I	Dallara 391-Alfa Romeo	120.821
1992	F3	Vincenzo Sospiri	I	Dallara 392-Mugen	119.057
1993	F3	Giancarlo Fisichella	I	Dallara 393-Fiat	119.018
1994*	F3	Luca Rangoni	I	Dallara 393-Fiat	119.850
	F3	Luca Riccitelli	I	Dallara 393-Fiat	120.170

1980 race was originally to be a British F1 Championship event but not enough entries were received.
*Run as two heats without an aggregate winner

Race of Two Worlds/Monza 500

year	formula	winner	nat	car	mph
1957	Indycar	Jimmy Bryan	USA	Kuzma-Offenhauser	160.060
1958	Indycar	Jim Rathmann	USA	Watson-Offenhauser	166.720

International Formula 3000 race

year	formula	winner	nat	car	mph
1988	F3000 INT	Roberto Moreno	BR	Reynard 88D-Cosworth	129.717
1990	F3000 INT	Erik Comas	F	Lola T90/50-Mugen	132.902

Filippo Caracciolo Trophy/World Sports Car race

year	formula	winner	nat	car	mph
1965	SC W	Michael Parkes/Jean Guichet	GB/F	Ferrari 275P2	125.897
1966	SC W	John Surtees/Michael Parkes	GB	Ferrari 330P3	102.089
1967	SC W	Chris Amon/Lorenzo Bandini	NZ/I	Ferrari 330P4	121.158
1968	SC W	Paul Hawkins/David Hobbs	AUS/GB	Ford GT40	117.219
1969	SC W	Jo Siffert/Brian Redman	CH/GB	Porsche 908/8	126.945
1970	SC W	Pedro Rodriguez/Leo Kinnunen	MEX/SF	Porsche 917	144.566
1971	SC W	Pedro Rodriguez/Jackie Oliver	MEX/GB	Porsche 917K	147.387
1972	SC W	Jacky Ickx/Clay Regazzoni	B/CH	Ferrari 312P	105.944
1973	SC W	Jacky Ickx/Brian Redman	B/GB	Ferrari 312P	150.671
1974	SC W	Arturo Merzario/Mario Andretti	I/USA	Alfa Romeo T33TT/12	130.896
1975	SC W	Arturo Merzario/Jacques Laffite	I/F	Alfa Romeo T33TT/12	132.341
1976	SC WSC	Jacky Ickx/Jochen Mass	B/D	Porsche 936	136.610
1977	SC WSC	Vittorio Brambilla	I	Alfa Romeo T33SC/12	114.803
1978	SC E	Reinhold Jöst	D	Porsche 908/3	106.865
1980	SC W	Alain de Cadenet/Desiré Wilson	GB/ZA	De Cadenet LM-Ford	109.570
1981	SC W	Edgar Dören/Jurgen Lässig/Gerhard Holup	D	Porsche 935	94.989
1982	SC W	Henri Pescarolo/Giorgio Francia/Jean Rondeau	F/I/F	Rondeau M382C-Ford	112.023
1983	SC W	Bob Wollek/Thierry Boutsen	F/B	Porsche 956	119.855
1984	SC W	Derek Bell/Stefan Bellof	GB/D	Porsche 956	122.146
1985	SC W	Manfred Winkelhock/Marc Surer	D/CH	Porsche 962	121.951
1986	SC W	Hans-Joachim Stuck/Derek Bell	D/GB	Porsche 962	125.357

year	formula	winner	nat	car	mph
1987	SC W	Jan Lammers/John Watson	NL/GB	Jaguar XJR-8	123.085
1988	SC W	Martin Brundle/Eddie Cheever	GB/USA	Jaguar XJR-9	128.012
1990	SC W	Mauro Baldi/Jean-Louis Schlesser	I/F	Mercedes-Benz C11	130.816
1991	SC W	Martin Brundle/Derek Warwick	GB	Jaguar XJR-14	129.003
1992	SC W	Geoff Lees/Hitoshi Ogawa	GB/J	Toyota TS010	137.607

CIRCUIT OF MUGELLO

Mugello had a long racing history before the modern racing facility was opened. The Circuit of Mugello used some of the same roads as the Mille Miglia including the famed Futa Pass. A mixture of slow and fast sections, of surfaces and gradient change. Surprisingly safe, although Günther Klass was killed in 1967.

MUGELLO OLD CIRCUIT

Active years...1920-69
Lap distance ..41.135 miles

Firenzuola
San Piero
Santa Lucia

Mugello Circuit

year	formula	winner	nat	car	mph
1920	FL	Giuseppe Campari	I	Alfa Romeo 40/60	37.621
1921	FL	Giuseppe Campari	I	Alfa Romeo 40/60	38.696
1922	FL	Alfieri Maserati	I	Isotta-Fraschini	41.750
1923	FL	Gastone Brilli-Peri	I	Steyr VI Klausen	41.423
1924	FL	Giuseppe Morandi	I	OM 665	40.627
1925	FL	Emilio Materassi	I	Itala Special 4.7	43.259
1926#	FL	Emilio Materassi	I	Itala Special 4.7	73.013
1928	GP	Emilio Materassi	I	Talbot T700	43.968
1929	GP	Gastone Brilli-Peri	I	Talbot T700	44.525
1955*	SC	Umberto Maglioli	I	Ferrari	66.650
1964	GT	Gianni Bulgari	I	Porsche 904	65.650
1965	GT	Antonio Nicodemi/Mario Casoni	I	Ferrari 250LM	66.020
1966	SC	Gerhard Koch/Jochen Neerpasch	D	Porsche 906 Carrera 6	66.717
1967	SC	Gerhard Mitter/Udo Schutz	D	Porsche 910/8	76.241
1968	SC	Lucien Bianchi/Nino Vaccarella/Nanni Galli	B/I/I	Alfa Romeo T33	75.154
1969	SC	Arturo Merzario	I	Abarth 2000	77.647

*officially known as Targa Mugello. On the Circuit of Mugello except #at Cascine

MUGELLO

AUTODROMO MUGELLO
A spectacular F1-standard facility set in a valley near Barberino di Mugello in the Tuscan hills.

Mugello is underused and with Monza and Imola already holding Grands Prix its chances are limited. Jean Alesi was injured here in 1994 while testing for Ferrari which had bought the circuit in 1988.

MUGELLO NEW CIRCUIT

Active years...1974 to date
Location..........14 miles north of Florence, 80 miles north-east of Pisa
Lap distance ..3.259 miles
Lap record......Alessandro Zanardi (Reynard 91D-Mugen) 1m38.367, 119.272 mph, 1991, F3000

European Formula Two race

year	formula	winner	nat	car	mph
1974	F2 E	Patrick Depailler	F	March 742-BMW	105.386
1975	F2 E	Maurizio Flammini	I	March 742-BMW	103.530
1976	F2 E	Jean-Pierre Jabouille	F	Elf 2J-Renault	105.790
1977	F2 E	Bruno Giacomelli	I	March 772P-BMW	107.203
1978	F2 E	Derek Daly	IRL	Chevron B42-Hart	108.545
1979	F2 E	Brian Henton	GB	Ralt RT2-Hart	108.375
1980	F2 E	Brian Henton	GB	Toleman TG280B-Hart	108.955
1981	F2 E	Corrado Fabi	I	March 812-BMW	108.994
1982	F2 E	Corrado Fabi	I	March 822-BMW	110.169
1983	F2 E	Jonathan Palmer	GB	Ralt RH6/83-Honda	109.542
1984	F2 E	Mike Thackwell	NZ	Ralt RH6/84-Honda	111.512

International Formula 3000 race

year	formula	winner		nat	car	mph
1986	F3000 INT	Pierluigi Martini		I	Ralt RT20-Cosworth	104.940
1991	F3000 INT	Alessandro Zanardi		I	Reynard 91D-Mugen	117.684

European Formula Three race

year	formula	winner		nat	car	mph
1980	F3 E	Corrado Fabi		I	March 803-Alfa Romeo	101.170
1981	F3 E	Emanuele Pirro		I	Martini MK34-Toyota	102.792
1982	F3 E	Oscar Larrauri		RA	Euroracing 101-Alfa Romeo	102.980
1984	F3 E	Ivan Capelli		I	Martini MK42-Alfa Romeo	104.569

World Sports Car race

year	formula	winner		nat	car	mph
1975	SC W	Gérard Larrousse/Jean-Pierre Jabouille		F	Alpine A442-Renault	101.993
1976	SC W	Jacky Ickx/Jochen Mass		B/D	Porsche 935	94.277
1977	SC W	Rolf Stommelen/Manfred Schurti		D/FL	Porsche 935	87.399
1978	SC W	Toine Hezemans/John Fitzpatrick/Hans Heyer		NL/GB/D	Porsche 935	95.116
1979	SC W	John Fitzpatrick/Manfred Schurti/Bob Wollek		GB/FL/F	Porsche 935	85.450
1980	SC W	Riccardo Patrese/Eddie Cheever		I/USA	Lancia Beta Monte Carlo	95.840
1981	SC W	Lella Lombardi/Giorgio Francia		I	Osella PA9-BMW	96.031
1982	SC W	Michele Alboreto/Piercarlo Ghinzani		I	Lancia LC1	98.630
1983	SC	Bob Wollek/Stefan Johansson		F/S	Porsche 956	101.571
1985	SC W	Jacky Ickx/Jochen Mass		B/D	Porsche 956C	103.239

PESCARA

A magnificent road course which was the longest circuit to hold a World Championship Formula One race. Pescara featured two four-mile straights, with the opening eight miles of the lap climbing and twisting through the villages inland from Pescara. The road came complete with level crossings and barely guarded corners. Cancellation of races in 1957 elevated the Pescara GP to World Championship status, the race won by Moss for Vanwall. The circuit and its facilities had changed little in the 40 years since Enzo Ferrari won the inaugural event when it closed in the early 1960s.

Lap distance ..16.032 miles
Lap record ......Stirling Moss
(Vanwall VW5) 9m44.6,
98.726 mph,
1957, F1

Active years...1924-61
Location.........The Abruzzi
region on Italy's
Adriatic coast

Pescara

The 1950 Coppa Acerbo at Pescara showing Luigi Fagioli, who finished third

Coppa Acerbo/Pescara Grand Prix

year	formula	winner		nat	car	mph
1924	FL	Enzo Ferrari		I	Alfa Romeo RL	65.055
1925	FL	Guido Ginaldi		I	Alfa Romeo RL	58.073
1926	FL	Luigi Spinozzi		I	Bugatti T35	63.007
1927	FL	Giuseppe Campari		I	Alfa Romeo P2	64.961
1928	GP	Giuseppe Campari		I	Alfa Romeo P2	68.453
1930	GP	Achille Varzi		I	Maserati 26M	75.604
1931	GP	Giuseppe Campari		I	Alfa Romeo Tipo-A	81.912
1932	GP	Tazio Nuvolari		I	Alfa Romeo Tipo-B "P3"	87.148
1933	GP	Luigi Fagioli		I	Alfa Romeo Tipo-B "P3"	88.601
1934	GP	Luigi Fagioli		I	Mercedes-Benz W25A	80.513
1935	GP	Achille Varzi		I	Auto Union B	85.979
1936	GP	Bernd Rosemeyer		D	Auto Union C	86.483
1937	GP	Bernd Rosemeyer		D	Auto Union C	87.621
1938	GP	Rudolf Caracciola		D	Mercedes-Benz W154	83.754
1939	V	Clemente Biondetti		I	Alfa Romeo 158	83.310
1947	SC	Vincenzo Auricchio		I	Stanguellini-Fiat	72.190
1948	SC	Alberto Ascari/Giovanni Bracco		I	Maserati	83.260
1949	SC	Franco Rol		I	Alfa Romeo	75.200
1950	F1	Juan Manuel Fangio		RA	Alfa Romeo 158	84.168
1951	F1	José Froilan Gonzalez		RA	Ferrari 375	85.506

year	formula	winner	nat	car	mph
1952	SC	Giovanni Bracco/Paolo Marzotto	I	Ferrari	79.730
1953	SC	Mike Hawthorn/Umberto Maglioli	GB/I	Ferrari	79.830
1954	F1	Luigi Musso	I	Maserati 250F	87.493
1956	SC	Robert Manzon	F	Gordini	82.880
1957	F1 W	Stirling Moss	GB	Vanwall VW5	96.525
1960	FJ	Denny Hulme	NZ	Cooper-BMC	84.110
1961*	SC W	Lorenzo Bandini/Giorgio Scarlatti	I	Ferrari 250TR	88.176

*Pescara 4 hours. Known as Coppa Acerbo before World War Two

VALLELUNGA

Vallelunga has been the home of the Rome GP since 1963. Originally it was a tiny oval but the circuit was extended by a loop through a newly blasted cutting in 1967 and further modernized in 1971. Vallelunga has been in dispute with the FIA since the introduction of Formula 3000 and the Rome GP has not been held since 1991. It was scheduled for use in 1994 but was cancelled mid-season.

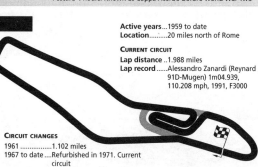

Active years...1959 to date
Location.........20 miles north of Rome

CURRENT CIRCUIT
Lap distance ..1.988 miles
Lap record......Alessandro Zanardi (Reynard 91D-Mugen) 1m04.939, 110.208 mph, 1991, F3000

CIRCUIT CHANGES
1961 ....1.102 miles
1967 to date ....Refurbished in 1971. Current circuit

Rome Grand Prix

year	formula	winner	nat	car	mph
1925*	FL	Carlo Masetti	I	Bugatti T35	60.594
1926#	FL	Aymo Maggi	I	Bugatti T35	61.648
1927	FL	Tazio Nuvolari	I	Bugatti T35	68.840
1928~	GP	Louis Chiron	MC	Bugatti T35C	78.274
1929~	GP	Achille Varzi	I	Alfa Romeo P2	79.402
1930~	GP	Luigi Arcangeli	I	Maserati 26M	83.135
1931^	GP	Ernesto Maserati	I	Maserati V4	91.393
1932^	GP	Luigi Fagioli	I	Maserati V5	95.203
1947>	F1	Franco Cortese	I	Ferrari 125	54.990
1949>	F2	Luigi Villoresi	I	Ferrari 166/F2	62.550
1950>	F2	Alberto Ascari	I	Ferrari 166/F2	62.320
1951>	F2	Mario Raffaeli	I	Ferrari 166/F2	61.200
1954+	F1	Onofre Marimón	RA	Maserati 250F	106.198
1956+	SC	Jean Behra	F	Maserati 300S	103.170
1963	F1	Bob Anderson	RSR	Lola Mk4-Climax	77.874
1964	F2	Jo Schlesser	F	Brabham BT10-Ford	n/a
1965	F2	Richard Attwood	GB	Lola T60-Ford	81.790
1966	F3	Tino Brambilla	I	Brabham BT16-Ford	79.930
1967	F2 E	Jacky Ickx	B	Matra MS7-Ford	88.945
1968	F2 E	Tino Brambilla	I	Ferrari Dino 166	92.604
1969	F2 E	Johnny Servoz-Gavin	F	Matra MS7-Ford	92.894
1971	F2 E	Ronnie Peterson	S	March 712M-Ford	97.330
1973	F2 E	Jacques Coulon	F	March 732-BMW	98.617
1974	F2 E	Patrick Depailler	F	March 742-BMW	100.829
1975	F2 E	Vittorio Brambilla	I	March 752-BMW	96.925
1976	F2 E	Jean-Pierre Jabouille	F	Elf 2J-Renault	99.334
1977	F2 E	Bruno Giacomelli	I	March 772P-BMW	100.748
1978	F2 E	Derek Daly	IRL	Chevron B42-Hart	100.426
1979	F2 E	Marc Surer	CH	March 792-BMW	101.241
1980	F2 E	Brian Henton	GB	Toleman TG280-Hart	102.103
1981	F2 E	Eje Elgh	S	Maurer MM81-BMW	101.990
1982	F2 E	Corrado Fabi	I	March 822-BMW	102.343
1983	F2 E	Beppe Gabbiani	I	March 832-BMW	103.385
1984	F2 E	Mike Thackwell	NZ	Ralt RH6/84-Honda	102.029
1985	F3000 INT	Emanuele Pirro	I	March 85B-Cosworth	103.036
1986	F3000 INT	Ivan Capelli	I	March 86B-Cosworth	102.601
1987	F3000 INT	Stefano Modena	I	March 87B-Cosworth	103.791
1988	F3000 INT	Gregor Foitek	CH	Lola T88/50-Cosworth	101.782
1989	F3000 INT	Fabrizio Giovanardi	I	Leyton March 89B-Judd	104.541
1991	F3000 INT	Alessandro Zanardi	I	Reynard 91D-Mugen	108.295

At Vallelunga except at *Monte Mario, #Valle Guila, Parioli, ~Tre Fontana, ^Littorio, >Terme di Caracalla, +Castel Fusano

Madunina Grand Prix

year	formula	winner	nat	car	mph
1971	F2 E	Mike Beuttler	GB	March 712M-Ford	97.136

Coppa Italia

year	formula	winner	nat	car	mph
1961	F1	Giancarlo Baghetti	I	Porsche 718	65.145

Italian Republic Grand Prix

year	formula	winner	nat	car	mph
1972	F1	Emerson Fittipaldi	BR	Lotus 72D-Ford	97.839

European Formula Three race

year	formula	winner	nat	car	mph
1976	F3 E	Gianfranco Brancatelli	I	March 763-Toyota	93.691
1977	F3 E	Oscar Pedersoli	I	Ralt RT1-Toyota	94.230
1978	F3 E	Teo Fabi	I	March 783-Toyota	95.659
1979	F3 E	Piercarlo Ghinzani	I	March 793-Alfa Romeo	95.095
1981	F3 E	Mauro Baldi	I	March 813-Alfa Romeo	n/a
1983	F3 E	Emanuele Pirro	I	Ralt RT3/83-Alfa Romeo	96.920

World Sports Car race

year	formula	winner	nat	car	mph
1973	SC W	Henri Pescarolo/Gérard Larrousse/François Cevert	F	Matra-Simca MS670	96.087
1976	SC W	Jacky Ickx/Jochen Mass	B/D	Porsche 935	89.129
1977	SC WSC	Vittorio Brambilla	I	Alfa Romeo T33SC/12	95.402
	SC W	Luigi Moreschi/"Dino"	I	Porsche 935	82.475
1978	SC	Reinhold Jöst/Mario Casoni	D/I	Porsche 908/3	92.568
	SC W	Bob Wollek/Henri Pescarolo	F	Porsche 935	88.219
1979	SC W	Lella Lombardi/Giorgio Francia	I	Osella PA7-BMW	87.742
1980	SC W	Giorgio Francia/Roberto Marazzi	I	Osella PA8-BMW	89.487

JAPAN

MAJOR CHAMPIONSHIPS

All-Japan Formula 3000 Championship (formerly Formula 2000 and Formula Two)

year	driver	nat	team	car
1973	Motoharu Kurosawa	J	Heroes Racing	March 722-BMW
1974	Noritake Takahara	J	Takahara Racing	March 742-BMW
1975	Kazuyoshi Hoshino	J	Heroes Racing	March 742-BMW
1976	Noritake Takahara	J	Takahara Racing	Nova 512-BMW
1977	Kazuyoshi Hoshino	J	Heroes Racing	Nova 512B-BMW/Nova 532P-BMW
1978	Kazuyoshi Hoshino	J	Heroes Racing	Nova 532-BMW/Nova 522-BMW
1979	Keiji Matsumoto	J	Le Mans Company	March 782-BMW/March 792-BMW
1980	Masahiro Hasemi	J	Nova Engineering	March 802-BMW
1981	Satoru Nakajima	J	I&I	Ralt RH6/80-Honda/March 812-Honda
1982	Satoru Nakajima	J	Team Ikuzawa	March 812-Honda/March 822-Honda
1983	Geoff Lees	GB	Team Ikuzawa	Spirit 201-Honda/March 832-Honda
1984	Satoru Nakajima	J	Heroes Racing	March 842-Honda
1985	Satoru Nakajima	J	Heroes Racing	March 85J-Honda
1986	Satoru Nakajima	J	Heroes Racing	March 86J-Honda
1987	Kazuyoshi Hoshino	J	Leyton House	March 87B-Honda/Lola T87/50-Honda
1988	Aguri Suzuki	J	Footwork Formula	Mooncraft 030-Yamaha/March 87B-Yamaha/Reynard 88D-Yamaha
1989	Hitoshi Ogawa	J	Stella International	Lola T88/50-Mugen/Lola T89/50-Mugen
1990	Kazuyoshi Hoshino	J	Heroes Racing	Lola T90/50-Mugen
1991	Ukyo Katayama	J	Heroes Racing	Lola T91/50-Cosworth/Lola T90/50-Cosworth
1992	Mauro Martini	I	Nova Engineering	Lola T92/50-Mugen
1993	Kazuyoshi Hoshino	J	Hoshino Racing Team	Lola T92/50-Cosworth
1994	Marco Apicella	I	Dome	Dome MF104-Mugen

Formula 2000 1973-77, Formula Two 1978-86, Formula 3000 1987 to date

All-Japan Sports-Prototype Championship

year	driver	nat	team	car
1983	Vern Schuppan/Naohiro Hujita	AUS/J	Trust Racing	Porsche 956
1984	Naoki Nagasaka/Keiichi Suzuki	J	Auto Beaurex	Lotec M1C-BMW
1985	Kunimitsu Takahashi/Kenji Takahashi	J	Alpha Racing Team	Porsche 962
1986	Kunimitsu Takahashi/Kenji Takahashi	J	Alpha Racing Team	Porsche 962
1987	Kunimitsu Takahashi/Kenneth Acheson	J/GB	Alpha Racing Team	Porsche 962
1988	Stanley Dickens/Hideki Okada	S/J	From A Racing	Porsche 962
1989	Kunimitsu Takahashi/Stanley Dickens	J/S	Alpha Racing Team	Porsche 962
1990	Masahiro Hasemi/Anders Olofsson	J/S	NISMO	Nissan R90CP
1991	Kazuyoshi Hoshino/Toshio Suzuki	J	NISMO	Nissan R91CP
1992	Kazuyoshi Hoshino/Toshio Suzuki	J	NISMO	Nissan R92CP

Championship officially decided by the driver who leads the greatest distance in the winning car - both drivers are included, the first of which was official champion

All-Japan GT Championship

year	driver	nat	car
1993	Masahiko Kageyama	J	Nissan Skyline GT-R
1994	Masahiko Kageyama	J	Nissan Skyline GT-R

All-Japan Touring Car Championship

year	driver	nat	team	car
1985	Naoki Nagasaka/ Kazuo Mogi	J	Auto Beaurex	BMW 635CSi
1986	Aguri Suzuki/ Takao Wada	J	NISMO	Nissan Skyline RS
1987	Naoki Nagasaka	J	Object T	Ford Sierra RS/ Ford Sierra RS500
1988	Hisashi Yokoshima	J	Object T	Ford Sierra RS500
1989	Masahiro Hasemi/ Anders Olofsson	J/S	Hasemi Motorsport	Nissan Skyline
1990	Kazuyoshi Hoshino/ Toshio Suzuki	J	NISMO	Nissan Skyline GT-R
1991	Masahiro Hasemi/ Anders Olofsson	J/S	Hasemi Motorsport	Nissan Skyline GT-R
1992	Hideo Fukuyama/ Masahiro Hasemi	J	NISMO	Nissan Skyline GT-R
1993	Masahiko Kageyama	J	Hoshino Racing	Nissan Skyline GT-R
1994	Masanori Sekiya	J	TOM's	Toyota Corona

Championship officially decided by the driver who leads the greatest distance in the winning car - where appropriate both drivers are included, the first of which was official champion

All-Japan Formula Three Championship

year	driver	nat	team	car
1979	Toshio Suzuki	J	Heroes Racing	Ralt RT1-Toyota
1980	Shuroko Sasaki	J	Shuroko Sasaki	March 793/ 803-Toyota

1981	Osami Nakako	J	Hayashi Racing	Hayashi 320-Toyota
1982	Kengo Nakamoto	J	Hayashi Racing	Ralt RT3-Toyota
1983	Yoshimasa Fujiwara	J	Umeda Racing	Ralt RT3-Toyota
1984	Shuji Hyoudo	J	Hayashi Racing	Hayashi 322-Toyota
1985	Kouji Sato	J	Le Garage Cox	Ralt RT30-Volkswagen
1986	Akio Morimoto	J	Le Mans Company	Ralt RT30-Toyota
1987	Ross Cheever	USA	Funaki Racing Team	Reynard 873-Toyota
1988	Akihiko Nakaya	J	Le Garage Cox	Ralt RT32-Mugen
1989	Masahiko Kageyama	J	Leyton House	Ralt RT33-Mugen
1990	Naoki Hattori	J	Le Garage Cox	Ralt RT34-Mugen
1991	Paulo Carcasci	BR	TOM's	TOM's 031F-TOM's Toyota
1992	Anthony Reid	GB	Tomei Sport	Ralt RT35-Mugen
1993	Tom Kristensen	DK	TOM's	TOM's 033F-TOM's Toyota
1994	Michael Krumm	D	TOM's	TOM's 034F-TOM's Toyota

Geoff Lees, the 1983 Japanese Formula 3000 champion

MAJOR INTERNATIONAL RACES

JAPANESE GRAND PRIX

year	formula	circuit	winner	nat	car	mph
1976	F1 W	Fuji	Mario Andretti	USA	Lotus 77-Ford	114.111
1977	F1 W	Fuji	James Hunt	GB	McLaren M26-Ford	129.167
1987	F1 W	Suzuka	Gerhard Berger	A	Ferrari F187	119.842
1988	F1 W	Suzuka	Ayrton Senna	BR	McLaren MP4/4-Honda	119.241
1989	F1 W	Suzuka	Alessandro Nannini	I	Benetton B189-Ford	121.744
1990	F1 W	Suzuka	Nelson Piquet	BR	Benetton B190-Ford	122.375
1991	F1 W	Suzuka	Gerhard Berger	A	McLaren MP4/6-Honda	125.609
1992	F1 W	Suzuka	Riccardo Patrese	I	Williams FW14B-Renault	124.286
1993	F1 W	Suzuka	Ayrton Senna	BR	McLaren MP4/8-Ford	115.248
1994	F1 W	Suzuka	Damon Hill	GB	Williams FW16B-Renault	94.250

CIRCUITS AND OTHER RACES

AUTOPOLIS

NIPPON AUTOPOLIS
An ultra-modern facility built with no expense spared to attract Grand Prix racing to a remote mountain region of Kyushu, Japan's southern island. Nippon Autopolis made it as far as a provisional F1 calendar but bankruptcy dented hopes of holding the Asian GP.

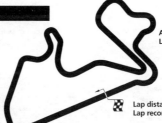

Active years...1992 to date
Location..........19 miles north-east of Kumamoto, 50 miles south-east of Fukuoka

Lap distance ..2.904 miles
Lap record ......Teo Fabi (Jaguar XJR14) 1m27.188, 119.907 mph, 1991, Group C Sports Cars

World Sports Car race					
year	formula	winner	nat	car	mph
1991	SC W	Michael Schumacher/Karl Wendlinger	D/A	Mercedes-Benz C291	110.525

FUJI

The original plan for Fuji was as an American-style 2.5-mile superspeedway with road course and 30-degree banking set in the shadow of Mount Fuji. However, the money ran out before both ends of banking could be built leaving a six-km road course with a fearsomely banked curve at one end. In 1974, the organizers changed the direction to clockwise and a new downhill right first corner bypassed the banking. For two years Fuji held a round of the F1 World Championship, James Hunt struggling through the rain to win the 1976 World Championship. A year later, Gilles Villeneuve's Ferrari somersaulted into a prohibited area killing a marshal and a spectator - the Grand Prix did not return.

Chicane

Banking

Active years...1965 to date
Location..........40 miles north-west of Yokohama, 62 miles west of Tokyo

CURRENT CIRCUIT
Lap distance ..2.777 miles
Lap record ......Kazuyoshi Hoshino (Nissan R92CP) 1m14.088, 134.937 mph, 1992, Group C Sports Cars

CIRCUIT CHANGES
1965-73 ....Original circuit with banking at one end. 3.728 miles
1972-82 ....Banking bypassed. 2.709 miles
1983 ....2.7067 miles
1984-86 ....2.7404 miles
1986-92 ....Chicane inserted at last corner. 2.759 miles
1993 to date ....Second chicane built. Current circuit

Japanese Grand Prix see above

Euro-Macau-Fuji Formula Three Challenge

year	formula	driver	nat	car	mph
1990	F3	Michael Schumacher	D	Reynard 903-Volkswagen	95.810
1991	F3	Jordi Gene	E	Ralt RT35-Mugen	110.859
1992	F3	Roberto Colciago	I	Dallara 392-Opel	110.155
1993	F3	Tom Kristensen	DK	TOM's 033F-Toyota	111.320

World Sports Car race

year	formula	driver	nat	car	mph
1982	SC W	Jacky Ickx/Jochen Mass	B/D	Porsche 956	115.567
1983	SC W	Derek Bell/Stefan Bellof	GB/D	Porsche 956	122.988
1984	SC W	Stefan Bellof/John Watson	D/GB	Porsche 956	112.603
1985	SC W	Kazuyoshi Hoshino	J	March 85G-Nissan	84.125
1986	SC W	Paolo Barilla/Piercarlo Ghinzani	I	Porsche 956	112.803
1987	SC W	Jan Lammers/John Watson	NL/GB	Jaguar XJR-8	109.478
1988	SC W	Martin Brundle/Eddie Cheever	GB/USA	Jaguar XJR-9	113.755

SUZUKA

Designed by John Hugenholtz as a test circuit for Honda, Suzuka is unusual in that it is a figure-of-eight, and it is set in an amusement park. Setting for the Japanese Grand Prix since 1987, it has been the scene of championship showdowns between Senna and Prost in 1989 and 1990 when the bitter rivals collided.

Active years...1962 to date
Location..........50 miles south-west of Nagoya, 93 miles west of Osaka

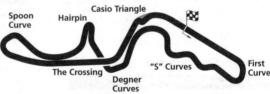

Spoon Curve

Hairpin

Casio Triangle

The Crossing

Degner Curves

"S" Curves

First Curve

CURRENT CIRCUIT
Lap distance ..3.641 miles
Lap record ......Nigel Mansell (Williams FW14B-Renault) 1m40.646, 1992, F1

CIRCUIT CHANGES
1962-82 ....3.731 miles
1983-86 ....Chicane inserted before the start. 3.694 miles
1987 to date ....Circuit refurbished. Current circuit

Japanese Grand Prix see above

World Sports Car race

year	formula	winner	nat	car	mph
1989	SC W	Jean-Louis Schlesser/Mauro Baldi	F/I	Sauber C9/88-Mercedes-Benz	106.015
1990	SC W	Jean-Louis Schlesser/Mauro Baldi	F/I	Sauber C9/88-Mercedes-Benz	109.392
1991	SC W	Mauro Baldi/Philippe Alliot	I/F	Peugeot 905	111.468
1992	SC W	Derek Warwick/Yannick Dalmas	GB/F	Peugeot 905B	113.147

International GT 1000 kms race

year	formula	winner	nat	car	mph
1994	SC/GT	Jean-Pierre Jarier/Bob Wollek/Jesus Pareja	F/F/E	Porsche 911 RSR	91.950

TI AIDA

AIDA

Designed as an exclusive club where Japan's elite could drive Grand Prix cars, Tanaka International (TI) held the inaugural Pacific GP in 1994. Although the circuit is inaccessible the race was a success, with nearly 100,000 spectators on race day. The track itself is tight and narrow but the race has been included once again on the Grand Prix calendar for 1995.

Attwood Curve

Moss "S"

Williams Corner

Hairpin Corner

Hobbs Corner

Mike Knight Corner

Revolver Corner

Piper Corner

First Corner

Redman Corner

Last Corner

Active years...1992 to date
Location..........Aida village, near Kobe
Lap distance ..2.314 miles
Lap record .....Michael Schumacher (Benetton B194-Ford), 1m14.023, 112.538 mph, 1994, F1

Pacific Grand Prix

year	formula	winner	nat	car	mph
1994	F1 W	Michael Schumacher	D	Benetton B194-Ford	108.685

LIBYA

CIRCUITS AND RACES

MELLAHA

Mellaha was an ultra-fast blast around a salt lake which developed into one of the classic venues of the 1930s. It had started in 1925 on a relatively slow Tripoli circuit but the introduction of a lottery made it one of the richest races in the world. The first Mellaha race, held in 1933, produced perhaps the most well-known example of race-fixing. The top drivers conspired with a lottery ticket holder to ensure that Achille Varzi won the race, the prize money being shared. Unhappy with the German domination of Grand Prix racing the Italian organizers switched to the Alfa- and Maserati-dominated voiturette category for the 1939 race. Mercedes-Benz responded by building two W165 voiturettes in absolute secrecy and finishing first and second!

The 1939 Tripoli Grand Prix at Mellaha with Hermann Lang's Mercedes leading from team-mate Rudi Caracciola

Mellaha Lake

Active years...1933-40
Location..........Between Tripoli and Tagiura
Lap distance ..8.165 miles
Lap record ......Hans Stuck (Auto Union C) 3m25.73, 142.877 mph, 1937, GP

Tripoli Grand Prix

year	formula	winner	nat	car	mph
1925*	FL	Renato Balestrero	I	OM 665	58.718
1926*	FL	François Eysserman	F	Bugatti T35	68.092
1927*	FL	Emilio Materassi	I	Bugatti T35C	82.071
1928*	GP	Tazio Nuvolari	I	Bugatti T35C	77.982
1929*	GP	Gastone Brilli-Peri	I	Talbot T700	83.243
1930*	GP	Baconin Borzacchini	I	Maserati V4	91.063
1933	GP	Achille Varzi	I	Bugatti T51	105.086
1934	GP	Achille Varzi	I	Alfa Romeo Tipo-B "P3"	116.024
1935	GP	Rudolf Caracciola	D	Mercedes-Benz W25B	123.406
1936	GP	Achille Varzi	I	Auto Union C	129.412
1937	GP	Hermann Lang	D	Mercedes-Benz W125	132.440
1938	GP	Hermann Lang	D	Mercedes-Benz W154	127.840
1939	V	Hermann Lang	D	Mercedes-Benz W165	123.291
1940	V	Giuseppe Farina	I	Alfa Romeo 158	128.611

At Mellaha except *at Tripoli

MACAU

CIRCUITS AND RACES

GUIA CIRCUIT, MACAU

The annual Macau Grand Prix in November has replaced the Monaco GP support race as the most important Formula Three race of the year. Ever since Ayrton Senna won the first F3 race it has been the unofficial World Cup for the category, pitching the best European and Japanese based runners against "stars" stepping down from F1 and F3000. As the Macau landscape has changed, the circuit has remained remarkably unaffected. Statue Corner at the start of the lap is a tight right-hander that has often been the seen of a pile-up. It follows a fast main stretch (which used to pass between the sea and a reservoir) and leads onto the twisting, narrow return leg.

Active years ... 1954 to date
Location .... 45 miles south-east of Hong Kong
Lap distance .. 3.801 miles
Lap record ...... Rickard Rydell (TOM's 033F-Toyota) 2m17.40, 99.589 mph, 1993, F3

Macau Grand Prix

year	formula	winner	nat	car	mph
1954	SC	Eddie Carvalho	HK	Triumph TR2	47.802
1955	SC	Robert Ritchie	HK	Austin Healey 100	58.002
1956	SC	Doug Steane	HK	Mercedes-Benz 190SL	54.147
1957	SC	Arthur Pateman	GB	Mercedes-Benz 300SL	59.605
1958	SC	Chan Lye Choon	SGP	Aston Martin DB3S	61.921
1959	SC	Ron Hardwick	HK	Jaguar XKSS	58.882
1960	SC	Martin Redfern	HK	Jaguar XKSS	65.973
1961	FL	Peter Heath	GB	Lotus 15-Climax	65.270
1962	FL	Arensio Laurel	PI	Lotus 22-Ford	66.178
1963	FL	Arensio Laurel	PI	Lotus 22-Ford	68.000
1964	FL	Albert Poon	HK	Lotus 23-Ford	70.629
1965	FL	John MacDonald	HK	Lotus 18-Ford	67.183
1966	FL	Mauro Bianchi	B	Alpine T66-Renault	71.126
1967	FL	Tony Maw	MAL	Lotus 20B-Ford	65.645
1968	FL	Jan Bussell	SGP	Brabham BT23C-Ford	72.697
1969	FL	Kevin Bartlett	AUS	Mildren-Waggott	83.781
1970	FL	Dieter Quester	A	BMW F270	81.424
1971	FL	Jan Bussell	SGP	McLaren M4C	73.684
1972	FL	John MacDonald	HK	Brabham BT36	85.420
1973	FL	John MacDonald	HK	Brabham BT40	86.400
1974	Pacific	Vern Schuppan	AUS	March 72B-Ford	81.693
1975	Pacific	John MacDonald	HK	Ralt RT1-Ford	86.948
1976	Pacific	Vern Schuppan	AUS	Ralt RT1-Ford	92.228
1977	Pacific	Riccardo Patrese	I	Chevron B40-Ford	91.004
1978	Pacific	Riccardo Patrese	I	Chevron B42-Ford	93.368
1979	Pacific	Geoff Lees	GB	Ralt RT1-Ford	95.083
1980	Pacific	Geoff Lees	GB	Ralt RT1-Ford	95.557
1981	Pacific	Bob Earl	USA	Hayashi 220P-Toyota	93.578
1982	Pacific	Roberto Moreno	BR	Ralt RT4-Ford	92.902
1983	F3	Ayrton Senna	BR	Ralt RT3/83-Toyota	95.579
1984	F3	John Nielsen	DK	Ralt RT3/84-Volkswagen	94.446
1985	F3	Mauricio Gugelmin	BR	Ralt RT30-Volkswagen	94.320
1986	F3	Andy Wallace	GB	Reynard 863-Volkswagen	94.328
1987	F3	Martin Donnelly	GB	Ralt RT31-TOM's Toyota	93.922
1988	F3	Enrico Bertaggia	I	Dallara 388-Alfa Romeo	94.726
1989	F3	David Brabham	AUS	Ralt RT33-Volkswagen	96.617
1990	F3	Michael Schumacher	D	Reynard 903-Volkswagen	95.765
1991	F3	David Coulthard	GB	Ralt RT35-Mugen	96.572
1992	F3	Rickard Rydell	S	TOM's 032F-TOM's Toyota	96.498
1993	F3	Jorg Müller	D	Dallara 393-Fiat	97.770
1994	F3	Sasha Maassen	D	Dallara 394-Opel	93.208

Guia Race

year	formula	winner	nat	car	mph
1972	TC	John MacDonald	HK	Austin Cooper	63.196
1973	TC	Peter Chow	HK	Toyota Celica	64.388
1974	TC	Nobuhide Tachi	J	Toyota Celica	71.936
1975	TC	Nobuhide Tachi	J	Toyota Celica	74.941

year	formula	winner	nat	car	mph
1976	TC	Herb Adamczyk	HK	Porsche 911 Carrera RS	75.520
1977	TC	Peter Chow	HK	Toyota Celica	76.650
1978	TC	Peter Chow	HK	Toyota Celica	80.207
1979	TC	Herb Adamczyk	HK	Porsche 911 Carrera RSR	83.319
1980	TC	Hans-Joachim Stuck	D	BMW 320i Turbo	84.233
1981	TC	Manfred Winkelhock	D	BMW 320i Turbo	85.547
1982	TC	Helmet Greiner	HK	Porsche 911 Carrera RSR	83.447
1983	TC	Hans-Joachim Stuck	D	BMW 635 CSi	79.695
1984	TC	Tom Walkinshaw	GB	Jaguar XJ-S	85.662
1985	TC	Gianfranco Brancatelli	I	Volvo 240T	83.400
1986	TC	Johnny Cecotto	YV	Volvo 240T	83.239
1987	TC	Roberto Ravaglia	I	BMW M3	78.397
1988	TC	Altfrid Heger	D	BMW M3	83.369
1989	TC	Tim Harvey	GB	Ford Sierra RS500 Cosworth	84.200
1990	TC	Masahiro Hasemi	J	Nissan Skyline GT-R	85.982
1991	TC	Emanuele Pirro	I	BMW M3	88.561
1992	TC	Emanuele Pirro	I	BMW M3	89.319
1993	TC	Charles Kwan	HK	BMW M3	86.930
1994	TC	Joachim Winkelhock	D	BMW 318i	81.759

MALAYSIA

CIRCUITS AND RACES

SHAH ALAM

Active years...1968 to date
Location..........13 miles north-west of Kuala Lumpar

Originally known as Batu Tiga, and sometimes referred to as Selangor in deference to the palace overlooking the circuit. The Selangor 800 Sports Car race is the only World Championship race to have been held in Malaysia. It was run in the heat of the start of the monsoon season! Only 3000 spectators paid to watch and so the exercise was not repeated. The circuit was closed in 1977 after an accident claimed the lives of six children. After improvements costing a reported £100,000 Shah Alam was reopened with better protection for spectators.

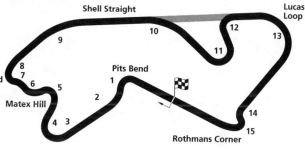

CURRENT CIRCUIT
Lap distance ..2.295 miles
Lap record......Jochen Mass (Porsche 962) 1m24.52, 97.752 mph, 1985, Group C Sports Car

CIRCUIT CHANGES
1968-84 ....2.1 miles
1985 to date ....Current circuit

Selangor World Sports Car race					
year	formula	winner	nat	car	mph
1985	SC W	Jochen Mass/Jacky Ickx	D/B	Porsche 962	89.988

MEXICO

MAJOR CHAMPIONSHIPS

Mexican Formula Two Championship

New championship using Formula Atlantic chassis and 2.2-litre Chrysler engines which replaced Formula K

year	driver	nat	car
1990	Enrique Contreras	MEX	March-Chrysler
1991	Carlos Guerrero	MEX	March-Chrysler
1992	Carlos Guerrero	MEX	March-Chrysler
1993	Allen Berg	CDN	Ralt RT40-Chrysler
1994	Fernando Plata	MEX	Ralt RT40-Chrysler

Marlboro Cup Formula K Championship

year	driver	nat	car
1984	Enrique Contreras	MEX	Enco-Chrysler
1985	Gilberto Jimenez	MEX	CDD Lider-Chrysler
1986	Gilberto Jimenez	MEX	CDD Lider-Chrsyler
1987	Gerardo Martinez	MEX	Martiga R1FH87-Chrysler
1988	Oscar Manautou	MEX	Martiga R1FH88-Chrysler
1989	Gerardo Martinez	MEX	Martiga R1FH89-Chrysler

International Formula Three Championship
(also known as Pan-American Formula Three Championship)

Inaugurated in 1990 with only Reynard 903s allowed. The Reynard 933 became the standard chassis from 1993

year	driver	nat	car
1990	Carlos Guerrero	MEX	Reynard 903-Alfa Romeo
1991	Adrian Fernandez	MEX	Reynard 903-Alfa Romeo
1992	Cesar Tiberio Jimenez	MEX	Reynard 903-Alfa Romeo
1993	Carlos Guerrero	MEX	Reynard 903-Alfa Romeo/ Reynard 933-Alfa Romeo
1994	Carlos Guerrero	MEX	Reynard 933-Alfa Romeo

Major International Races

MEXICAN GRAND PRIX

year	formula	circuit	winner	nat	car	mph
1962	F1	Mexico City	Jim Clark/Trevor Taylor	GB	Lotus 25-Climax	90.314
1963	F1 W	Mexico City	Jim Clark	GB	Lotus 25-Climax	93.305
1964	F1 W	Mexico City	Dan Gurney	USA	Brabham BT7-Climax	93.326
1965	F1 W	Mexico City	Richie Ginther	USA	Honda RA272	94.272
1966	F1 W	Mexico City	John Surtees	GB	Cooper T81-Maserati	95.722
1967	F1 W	Mexico City	Jim Clark	GB	Lotus 49-Ford	101.418
1968	F1 W	Mexico City	Graham Hill	GB	Lotus 49B-Ford	103.804
1969	F1 W	Mexico City	Denny Hulme	NZ	McLaren M7A-Ford	106.156
1970	F1 W	Mexico City	Jacky Ickx	B	Ferrari 312B	106.786
1986	F1 W	Mexico City	Gerhard Berger	A	Benetton B186-BMW	120.111
1987	F1 W	Mexico City	Nigel Mansell	GB	Williams FW11B-Honda	120.176
1988	F1 W	Mexico City	Alain Prost	F	McLaren MP4/4-Honda	122.343
1989	F1 W	Mexico City	Ayrton Senna	BR	McLaren MP4/5-Honda	119.263
1990	F1 W	Mexico City	Alain Prost	F	Ferrari 641/2	122.819
1991	F1 W	Mexico City	Riccardo Patrese	I	Williams FW14-Renault	122.877
1992	F1 W	Mexico City	Nigel Mansell	GB	Williams FW14B-Renault	123.759

CARRERA PANAMERICANA

year	formula	winner	nat	car	mph
1950	Production	Hershal McGriff/Ray Elliot	USA	Oldsmobile	77.430
1951	SC	Piero Taruffi/Luigi Chinetti	I	Ferrari Vignale	88.070
1952	SC	Karl Kling/Hans Klenk	D	Mercedes-Benz	102.590
1953	SC W	Juan Manuel Fangio/Bronzoni	RA/I	Lancia Sport V6	105.150
1954	SC W	Umberto Maglioli	I	Ferrari 375 Plus	107.930

Circuits and other Races

MEXICO CITY

Autodromo Hermanos Rodriguez

6000 ft above sea level, Mexico's Grand Prix circuit has a chequered history of tragedy and drama. The first Mexican GP was marred by the death in practice of local hero Ricardo Rodriguez, and Grand Prix racing abandoned Mexico after the 1970 race when the notorious crowd control degenerated into chaos. John Surtees clinched a dramatic last lap World Championship victory here in 1964. The final corner is a fearsome 180-degree lightly-banked turn, although it was modified after Senna crashed there in 1991.

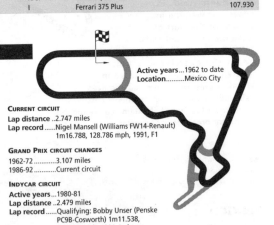

Active years...1962 to date
Location..........Mexico City

Current circuit
Lap distance ..2.747 miles
Lap record ......Nigel Mansell (Williams FW14-Renault) 1m16.788, 128.786 mph, 1991, F1

Grand Prix circuit changes
1962-72 ....3.107 miles
1986-92 ....Current circuit

Indycar circuit
Active years ...1980-81
Lap distance ..2.479 miles
Lap record ......Qualifying: Bobby Unser (Penske PC9B-Cosworth) 1m11.538, 124.751 mph, 1981, Indycar

Mexican Grand Prix see above

Indycar race

year	formula	winner	nat	car	mph
1980	Indycar	Rick Mears	USA	Penske PC9-Cosworth	116.329
1981	Indycar	Rick Mears	USA	Penske PC9B-Cosworth	103.487

World Sports Car race

year	formula	winner	nat	car	mph
1989	SC W	Jean-Louis Schlesser/Jochen Mass	F/D	Sauber C9/88-Mercedes-Benz	104.877
1990	SC W	Jochen Mass/Michael Schumacher	D	Mercedes-Benz C11	107.000
1991	SC W	Keke Rosberg/Yannick Dalmas	SF/F	Peugeot 905B	108.093

MONACO

CIRCUITS AND RACES

MONTE CARLO

Monte Carlo is the original round-the-houses race, an anachronism now perhaps, with Grand Prix cars barely able to overtake, but it remains the glamour event in Formula One. The idea of cigarette manufacturer, Antony Nogues, the first race was won by the enigmatic "W Williams" in 1929. Much of the course for the "race of a thousand corners" remains the same, although a chicane has been added at Ste Devote, a swimming pool section was built on reclaimed land, Loews Hotel built over the tunnel and the road now continues to a hairpin at La Rascasse. Two men have crashed into the harbour, Ascari in 1955 and Hawkins ten years later while both Fagioli (1952) and Bandini (1967) were killed here.

Portier corner during the 1958 Monaco Grand Prix

Active years...1929 to date
Location..........Central Monte Carlo, 11 miles east of Nice

CURRENT CIRCUIT
Lap distance ..2.068 miles
Lap record ......Michael Schumacher (Benetton B194-Ford)
1m21.076, 1994, 91.825 mph, F1

CIRCUIT CHANGES
1929-50 ....1.976 miles
1955-72 ....1.954 miles
1973-75 ....New tunnel built under Loews Hotel, swimming pool section built and La Rascasse added. 2.037 miles
1976-85 ....Ste Devote and La Rascasse altered. 2.058 miles
1986 to date ....New chicane built. Current circuit

Monaco Grand Prix

year	formula	winner	nat	car	mph
1929	GP	"W Williams"	GB	Bugatti T35B	50.198
1930	GP	René Dreyfus	F	Bugatti T35B	53.637
1931	GP	Louis Chiron	MC	Bugatti T51	54.099
1932	GP	Tazio Nuvolari	I	Alfa Romeo 8C "Monza"	55.814
1933	GP	Achille Varzi	I	Bugatti T51	57.048
1934	GP	Guy Moll	DZ	Alfa Romeo Tipo-B "P3"	56.051
1935	GP	Luigi Fagioli	I	Mercedes-Benz W25B	58.166
1936	GP	Rudolf Caracciola	D	Mercedes-Benz W25C	51.696
1937	GP	Manfred von Brauchitsch	D	Mercedes-Benz W125	63.266
1948	F1	Giuseppe Farina	I	Maserati 4CLT	59.744
1950	F1 W	Juan Manuel Fangio	RA	Alfa Romeo 158	61.331
1952	SC	Vittorio Marzotto	I	Ferrari 225MM	58.200
1955	F1 W	Maurice Trintignant	F	Ferrari 625	65.805
1956	F1 W	Stirling Moss	GB	Maserati 250F	64.936
1957	F1 W	Juan Manuel Fangio	RA	Maserati 250F	64.718
1958	F1 W	Maurice Trintignant	F	Cooper T45-Climax	67.979
1959	F1 W	Jack Brabham	AUS	Cooper T51-Climax	66.669
1960	F1 W	Stirling Moss	GB	Lotus 18-Climax	67.473
1961	F1 W	Stirling Moss	GB	Lotus 18-Climax	70.697
1962	F1 W	Bruce McLaren	NZ	Cooper T60-Climax	70.417
1963	F1 W	Graham Hill	GB	BRM P57	72.447
1964	F1 W	Graham Hill	GB	BRM P261	72.673
1965	F1 W	Graham Hill	GB	BRM P261	74.363
1966	F1 W	Jackie Stewart	GB	BRM P261	76.539
1967	F1 W	Denny Hulme	NZ	Brabham BT20-Repco	75.848
1968	F1 W	Graham Hill	GB	Lotus 49B-Ford	77.811

Racing Around the World

year	formula	winner	nat	car	mph
1969	F1 W	Graham Hill	GB	Lotus 49B-Ford	80.171
1970	F1 W	Jochen Rindt	A	Lotus 49C-Ford	81.836
1971	F1 W	Jackie Stewart	GB	Tyrrell 003-Ford	83.478
1972	F1 W	Jean-Pierre Beltoise	F	BRM P160B	63.842
1973	F1 W	Jackie Stewart	GB	Tyrrell 006-Ford	80.969
1974	F1 W	Ronnie Peterson	S	Lotus 72E-Ford	80.747
1975	F1 W	Niki Lauda	A	Ferrari 312T	75.534
1976	F1 W	Niki Lauda	A	Ferrari 312T2	80.357
1977	F1 W	Jody Scheckter	ZA	Wolf WR1-Ford	79.611
1978	F1 W	Patrick Depailler	F	Tyrrell 008-Ford	80.360
1979	F1 W	Jody Scheckter	ZA	Ferrari 312T4	81.339
1980	F1 W	Carlos Reutemann	RA	Williams FW07B-Ford	81.200
1981	F1 W	Gilles Villeneuve	CDN	Ferrari 126CK	82.040
1982	F1 W	Riccardo Patrese	I	Brabham BT49D-Ford	82.185
1983	F1 W	Keke Rosberg	SF	Williams FW08C-Ford	80.460
1984	F1 W	Alain Prost	F	McLaren MP4/2-TAG Porsche	62.620
1985	F1 W	Alain Prost	F	McLaren MP4/2B-TAG Porsche	86.020
1986	F1 W	Alain Prost	F	McLaren MP4/2C-TAG Porsche	83.661
1987	F1 W	Ayrton Senna	BR	Lotus 99T-Honda	82.088
1988	F1 W	Alain Prost	F	McLaren MP4/4-Honda	82.519
1989	F1 W	Ayrton Senna	BR	McLaren MP4/5-Honda	84.137
1990	F1 W	Ayrton Senna	BR	McLaren MP4/5B-Honda	85.813
1991	F1 W	Ayrton Senna	BR	McLaren MP4/6-Honda	85.619
1992	F1 W	Ayrton Senna	BR	McLaren MP4/7A-Honda	87.200
1993	F1 W	Ayrton Senna	BR	McLaren MP4/8-Ford	86.272
1994	F1 W	Michael Schumacher	D	Benetton B194-Ford	88.046

Rainier Cup

year	formula	winner	nat	car	mph
1936	V	"B Bira"	SM	ERA B-type	52.990
1937	SC	Laury Schell	F	Delahaye 145	51.320

Prix de Monte Carlo

year	formula	winner	nat	car	mph
1950	F3	Stirling Moss	GB	Cooper-JAP	55.680
1952	SC	Robert Manzon	F	Gordini	57.120

Monaco Formula Three Grand Prix

year	formula	winner	nat	car	mph
1959	FJ	Michel May	CH	Stanguellini-Fiat	60.620
1960	FJ	Henry Taylor	GB	Cooper T52-BMC	64.660
1961	FJ	Peter Arundell	GB	Lotus 20-Ford	64.810
1962	FJ	Peter Arundell	GB	Lotus 22-Ford	67.460
1963	FJ	Richard Attwood	GB	Lola Mk5A-Ford	69.280
1964	F3	Jackie Stewart	GB	Cooper T72-BMC	65.940
1965	F3	Peter Revson	USA	Lotus 35-Ford	67.039
1966	F3	Jean-Pierre Beltoise	F	Matra MS5-Ford	70.600
1967	F3	Henri Pescarolo	F	Matra MS5-Ford	70.938
1968	F3	Jean-Pierre Jaussaud	F	Tecno 68-Ford	71.576
1969	F3	Ronnie Peterson	S	Tecno 69-Ford	74.719
1970	F3	Tony Trimmer	GB	Brabham BT28-Ford	74.030
1971	F3	Dave Walker	AUS	Lotus 69-Ford	71.650
1972	F3	Patrick Depailler	F	Alpine A367-Renault	60.926
1973	F3	Jacques Laffite	F	Martini MK12-Ford	74.446
1974	F3	Tom Pryce	GB	March 743-Ford	76.097
1975	F3	Renzo Zorzi	I	GRD 374-Lancia	75.515
1976	F3	Bruno Giacomelli	I	March 763-Toyota	74.841
1977	F3	Didier Pironi	F	Martini MK21-Toyota	74.451
1978	F3	Elio de Angelis	I	Chevron B38-Toyota	74.974
1979	F3	Alain Prost	F	Martini MK27-Renault	75.718
1980	F3	Mauro Baldi	I	Martini MK31-Toyota	74.707
1981	F3	Alain Ferté	F	Martini MK34-Alfa Romeo	77.246
1982	F3	Alain Ferté	F	Martini MK37-Alfa Romeo	77.483
1983	F3	Michel Ferté	F	Martini MK39-Alfa Romeo	77.353
1984	F3	Ivan Capelli	I	Martini MK42-Alfa Romeo	77.351
1985	F3	Pierre-Henri Raphanel	F	Martini MK45-Alfa Romeo	77.090
1986	F3	Yannick Dalmas	F	Martini MK49-Volkswagen	75.921
1987	F3	Didier Artzet	F	Ralt RT30-Volkswagen	75.313
1988	F3	Enrico Bertaggia	I	Dallara 388-Alfa Romeo	73.304
1989	F3	Antonio Tamburini	I	Reynard 893-Alfa Romeo	74.668
1990	F3	Laurent Aiello	F	Dallara 390-Volkswagen	57.470
1991	F3	Jorg Müller	D	Reynard 913-Volkswagen	75.449
1992	F3	Marco Werner	D	Ralt RT36-Opel	75.554
1993	F3	Gianantonio Pacchioni	I	Dallara 393-Fiat	76.352
1994	F3	Giancarlo Fisichella	I	Dallara 394-Opel	76.156

MOROCCO

MAJOR INTERNATIONAL RACES

MOROCCAN GRAND PRIX						
year	formula	circuit	winner	nat	car	mph
1925	TC	Casablanca	de Vaugelas	-	Delage	59.220
1926	TC	Casablanca	E Meyer	-	Bugatti	63.750
1927	TC	Casablanca	G Rost	-	Georges Irat	77.050
1928	TC	Casablanca	E Meyer	-	Bugatti	91.780
1930	SC(h)	Casablanca	C Benitah	-	Amilcar	69.800
1934	GP	Anfa	Louis Chiron	MC	Alfa Romeo Tipo-B "P3"	81.094
1957	F1	Ain Diab	Jean Behra	F	Maserati 250F	112.652
1958	F1 W	Ain Diab	Stirling Moss	GB	Vanwall VW5	116.227

MOROCCAN GRAND PRIX FORMULA TWO CLASS						
year	formula	circuit	winner	nat	car	mph
1958	F2	Ain Diab	Jack Brabham	AUS	Cooper T45-Climax	105.057

CIRCUITS AND OTHER RACES

AIN DIAB

CASABLANCA

As a French colony, it is not surprising that there had been a Moroccan GP before World War Two. The event returned in 1957 on a new circuit near Casablanca, when racing in Europe was threatened by the Suez crisis. In six weeks, with the blessing of King Mohammed V, the Royal Automobile Club of Morocco designed a course using the public roads of Casablanca's Ain-Diab suburb, the desert road towards Azemmour and the coast road through the Sidi Abderhaman forest. The first race was a non-championship affair, but the 1958 Moroccan GP was the venue for the championship showdown between Mike Hawthorn and Stirling Moss.

Moroccan Grand Prix see above

Active years...1957-58
Lap distance ..4.724 miles
Lap record ......Stirling Moss (Vanwall VW5)
2m22.5, 119.343 mph, 1958, F1

NEW ZEALAND

MAJOR CHAMPIONSHIPS

New Zealand International Championship

year	formula	driver	nat	car
1976	2.0 l/F5000	Ken Smith	NZ	Lola T332-Chevrolet
1977	Pacific	Keke Rosberg	SF	Chevron B34-Ford
1978	Pacific	Keke Rosberg	SF	Chevron B39-Ford
1979	Pacific	Teo Fabi	I	March 78/79B-Ford
1980	Pacific	Dave McMillan	NZ	Ralt RT1-Ford
1981	Pacific	Dave Oxton	NZ	Ralt RT4-Ford
1982	Pacific	Roberto Moreno	BR	Ralt RT4-Ford
1983	Pacific	Allen Berg	CDN	Ralt RT4-Ford
1984	Pacific	Ken Smith	NZ	Ralt RT4-Ford
1985	Pacific	Ross Cheever	USA	Ralt RT4-Ford
1986	Pacific	Jeff MacPherson	USA	Ralt RT4-Ford
1987	Pacific	Mike Thackwell	NZ	Ralt RT4-Ford
1988	Pacific	Paul Radisich	NZ	Ralt RT4-Ford
1989	Pacific	Dean Hall	USA	Swift DB4-Ford
1990	Pacific	Ken Smith	NZ	Swift DB4-Ford
1991	Pacific	Craig Baird	NZ	Swift DB4-Toyota
1992	Pacific	Craig Baird	NZ	Reynard 92H-Toyota
1993	Pacific/			
	Brabham	Craig Baird	NZ	Reynard 92H-Toyota
1994	Brabham	Paul Stokell	AUS	Reynard 90D-Holden

New Zealand Gold Star Championship

Replaced by the International Championship as New Zealand's premier championship. Pacific and F5000 eligible in 1977, until enough Formula Pacific cars were available, F5000 cars were allowed to compete in 1977 under a handicap system. Although Ken Smith won every race he still lost the series to Dave McMillan on calculation of this system!

year	driver	nat	car
1957	Ross Jensen	NZ	Ferrari 750 Monza/Austin-Healey
1958	Ross Jensen	NZ	Maserati 250F
1959	Bruce McLaren	NZ	Cooper T45-Climax
1960	Syd Jensen	NZ	Cooper T45-Climax
1961	Denny Hulme	NZ	Cooper T51-Climax
1962	Pat Hoare	NZ	Ferrari 256
1963	Angus Hyslop	NZ	Cooper T45-Climax
1964	Jim Palmer	NZ	Cooper T45-Climax
1965	Jim Palmer	NZ	Brabham BT7A-Climax
1966	Jim Palmer	NZ	Lotus 32B-Climax
1967	Roly Levis	NZ	Brabham BT18-Ford
1968	Jim Palmer	NZ	McLaren M4A-Cosworth

year	driver	nat	car
1969	Roly Levis	NZ	Brabham BT23-Cosworth
1970	Graham McRae	NZ	Begg FM2-Chevrolet/
			McLaren M10A-Chevrolet
1971	Graeme Lawrence	NZ	Ferrari Dino 246T/
			Brabham BT29-Cosworth
1972	David Oxton	NZ	Begg FM4-Chevrolet

year	driver	nat	car
1973	David Oxton	NZ	Begg FM5-Chevrolet
1974	David Oxton	NZ	Begg FM5-Chevrolet
1975	Graeme		
	Lawrence	NZ	Lola T332-Chevrolet
1976	Ken Smith	NZ	Lola T332-Chevrolet
1977	Dave McMillan	NZ	Ralt RT1-Ford

MAJOR INTERNATIONAL RACES

NEW ZEALAND GRAND PRIX

year	formula	circuit	winner	nat	car	mph
1950	FL	Ohakea	John McMillan	NZ	Jackson-Ford	63.809
1951	FL	Ohakea	George Smith	NZ	GeeCeeEss-Mercury	66.403
1954	FL	Ardmore	Stan Jones	AUS	Maybach Mk1	72.500
1955	FL	Ardmore	"B Bira"	SM	Maserati 250F	78.750
1956	FL	Ardmore	Stirling Moss	GB	Maserati 250F	78.900
1957	FL	Ardmore	Reg Parnell	GB	Ferrari 555	76.940
1958	FL	Ardmore	Jack Brabham	AUS	Cooper T43-Climax	79.360
1959	FL	Ardmore	Stirling Moss	GB	Cooper T45-Climax	82.800
1960	FL	Ardmore	Jack Brabham	AUS	Cooper T51-Climax	86.600
1961	FL	Ardmore	Jack Brabham	AUS	Cooper T53-Climax	87.800
1962	FL	Ardmore	Stirling Moss	GB	Lotus 21-Climax	72.300
1963	FL	Pukekohe	John Surtees	GB	Lola Mk4-Climax	85.410
1964	FL	Pukekohe	Bruce McLaren	NZ	Cooper T70-Climax	87.846
1965	FL	Pukekohe	Graham Hill	GB	Brabham BT11A-Climax	89.512
1966	2.5 l	Pukekohe	Graham Hill	GB	BRM P261	83.010
1967	2.5 l	Pukekohe	Jackie Stewart	GB	BRM P261	100.971
1968	2.5 l	Pukekohe	Chris Amon	NZ	Ferrari 246T	102.638
1969	2.5 l	Pukekohe	Chris Amon	NZ	Ferrari 246T	105.139
1970	F5000	Pukekohe	Frank Matich	AUS	McLaren M10A-Chevrolet	103.810
1971	F5000	Pukekohe	Neil Allen	AUS	McLaren M10B-Chevrolet	107.883
1972	F5000	Pukekohe	Frank Gardner	AUS	Lola T300-Chevrolet	106.329
1973	F5000	Pukekohe	John McCormack	AUS	Elfin MR5-Holden/Repco	89.960
1974*	F5000	Wigram	John McCormack	AUS	Elfin MR5-Holden/Repco	114.419
1975	F5000	Pukekohe	Warwick Brown	AUS	Lola T332-Chevrolet	87.137
1976	F5000	Pukekohe	Ken Smith	NZ	Lola T332-Chevrolet	98.688
1977	Pacific	Pukekohe	Keke Rosberg	SF	Chevron B34-Ford	94.010
1978	Pacific	Pukekohe	Keke Rosberg	SF	Chevron B39-Ford	97.111
1979	Pacific	Pukekohe	Teo Fabi	I	March 78/79B-Ford	n/a
1980	Pacific	Pukekohe	Steve Millen	NZ	Ralt RT1-Ford	98.920
1981	Pacific	Pukekohe	Dave McMillan	NZ	Ralt RT1-Ford	104.600
1982	Pacific	Pukekohe	Roberto Moreno	BR	Ralt RT4-Ford	107.184
1983	Pacific	Pukekohe	David Oxton	NZ	Ralt RT4-Ford	107.005
1984#	Pacific	Pukekohe	Davy Jones	USA	Ralt RT4-Ford	100.080
1984#	Pacific	Pukekohe	Ross Cheever	USA	Ralt RT4-Ford	91.530
1986	Pacific	Pukekohe	Ross Cheever	USA	Ralt RT4-Ford	n/a
1987	Pacific	Pukekohe	Davy Jones	USA	Ralt RT4-Ford	107.190
1988	Pacific	Pukekohe	Paul Radisich	NZ	Ralt RT4-Ford	n/a
1989	Pacific	Pukekohe	Dean Hall	USA	Swift DB4-Ford	106.213
1990	Pacific	Pukekohe	Ken Smith	NZ	Swift DB4-Ford	106.390
1991	Pacific	Pukekohe	Craig Baird	NZ	Swift DB4-Toyota	106.470
1992	Pacific	Manfeild	Craig Baird	NZ	Reynard 92H-Toyota	106.836
1993	Pacific	Manfeild	Craig Baird	NZ	Reynard 92H-Toyota	104.420
1994	Brabham	Manfeild	Greg Murphy	NZ	Reynard 90D-Holden	n/a

*Run concurrently with the Lady Wigram Trophy. #Two races in 1984, first in January, second in December. 1952-53, 1985 no race

CIRCUITS AND OTHER RACES

PUKEKOHE

The home of the New Zealand GP until 1991 when it moved to Manfeild, Pukekohe is a flat circuit built around a racecourse. The hairpin which follows the long back straight is the trickiest point on the circuit, while spectator banks give excellent viewing near the startline. The long circuit is little used.

New Zealand Grand Prix see above

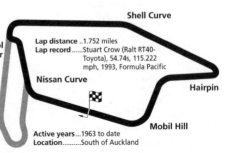

Shell Curve

Castrol Corner

Lap distance ..1.752 miles
Lap record ......Stuart Crow (Ralt RT40-Toyota), 54.74s, 115.222 mph, 1993, Formula Pacific

Nissan Curve

Hairpin

Mobil Hill

Active years...1963 to date
Location..........South of Auckland

WELLINGTON

The Wellington touring car race is now ten years old, and has now replaced the Grand Prix as New Zealand's top international race. The temporary street circuit is lined by concrete and armco barriers and allows little room for error.

Active years...1985 to date
Location..........Wellington harbour

CURRENT CIRCUIT
Lap distance ..1.988 miles
Lap record ......Pierre Dieudonné
(Ford Sierra RS500),
1m31.24, 78.439 mph,
1987, Group A Touring
Cars (on old circuit)

CIRCUIT CHANGES
1985-88 ....2.006 miles
1989 to date ....Current circuit

Touring Car race

year	formula	winner	nat	car	mph
1985	TC	Michel Delcourt/Robbie Francevic	B/AUS	Volvo 240 turbo	n/a
1986	TC	Peter Brock/Allan Moffat	AUS	Holden Commodore	67.560
1987	TC	Peter Brock/Allan Moffat	AUS	Holden Commodore	70.550
1988	TC	Emanuele Pirro/Roberto Ravaglia	I	BMW M3	75.748
1989	TC	Emanuele Pirro/Roberto Ravaglia	I	BMW M3	70.426
1990	TC	Emanuele Pirro/Johnny Cecotto	I/YV	BMW M3	78.780
1991	TC	Emanuele Pirro/Joachim Winkelhock	I/D	BMW M3	71.750
1992	TC	Tony Longhurst/Paul Morris	AUS	BMW M3	n/a
1993	TC	Owen Evans/Bruno Eichmann	NZ/CH	Porsche 911	66.790
1994	TC*	Joachim Winkelhock	D	BMW 318i	70.860
	TC	Tim Harvey	GB	BMW 318i	70.770

*Two heats, no overall winner

WIGRAM

An operational Airforce base which has hosted the Lady Wigram Trophy since 1949. Refurbishment meant that the race was held at nearby Ruapuna Park in 1990 and 1991.

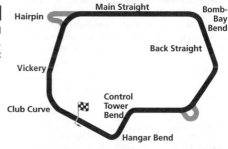

Active years...1949 to date
Location..........Near Christchurch
Lap distance ..2.2 miles
Lap record ......Graham McRae (McRae GM2-Chevrolet), 1m07.65, 117.074 mph, 1975, F5000

New Zealand Grand Prix see above

Lady Wigram Trophy

year	formula	winner	nat	car	mph
1949	FL	Marrie Proctor	NZ	Riley	66.165
1950	FL	Hec Green	NZ	RA-Wolseley	69.791
1951	FL	Les Moore	NZ	Alfa Romeo Tipo-B "P3"	68.033
1952	FL	Les Moore	NZ	Alfa Romeo Tipo-B "P3"	76.787
1953	FL	Ron Roycroft	NZ	Alfa Romeo Tipo-B "P3"	77.568
1954	FL	Peter Whitehead	GB	Ferrari 125	85.800
1956	FL	Peter Whitehead	GB	Ferrari 500	78.900
1957	FL	Peter Whitehead	GB	Ferrari 555	81.170
1958	FL	Archie Scott-Brown	GB	Lister 57/1-Jaguar	83.930
1959	FL	Ron Flockhart	GB	BRM P25	85.040
1960	FL	Jack Brabham	AUS	Cooper T51-Climax	89.460
1961	FL	Jack Brabham	AUS	Cooper T53-Climax	78.250
1962	FL	Stirling Moss	GB	Lotus 21-Climax	93.270
1963	FL	Bruce McLaren	NZ	Cooper T62-Climax	93.820
1964	FL	Bruce McLaren	NZ	Cooper T70-Climax	94.130
1965	FL	Jim Clark	GB	Lotus 32B-Climax	95.159
1966	2.5 l	Jackie Stewart	GB	BRM P261	95.269
1967	2.5 l	Jim Clark	GB	Lotus 33-Climax	97.046
1968	2.5 l	Jim Clark	GB	Lotus 49T-Ford	102.602
1969	2.5 l	Jochen Rindt	A	Lotus 49B-Ford	103.102
1970	F5000	Frank Matich	AUS	McLaren M10A-Chevrolet	101.363
1971	F5000	Graham McRae	NZ	McLaren M10B-Chevrolet	104.937
1972	F5000	Graham McRae	NZ	McRae GM1-Chevrolet	112.920

year	formula	winner	nat	car	mph
1973	F5000	Graham McRae	NZ	McRae GM1-Chevrolet	114.274
1974*	F5000	John McCormack	AUS	Elfin MR5-Holden/Repco	114.419
1975	F5000	Graham McRae	NZ	McRae GM2-Chevrolet	115.021
1976	F5000	Ken Smith	NZ	Lola T332-Chevrolet	111.918
1977	Pacific	Tom Gloy	USA	Tui BH2-Ford	109.440
1978	Pacific	Larry Perkins	AUS	Ralt RT1-Ford	110.306
1979	Pacific	Dave McMillan	NZ	Ralt RT1-Ford	n/a
1980	Pacific	Dave McMillan	NZ	Ralt RT1-Ford	109.250
1981	Pacific	David Oxton	NZ	Ralt RT4-Ford	106.300
1982	Pacific	Roberto Moreno	BR	Ralt RT4-Ford	106.890
1983	Pacific	Allen Berg	CDN	Ralt RT4-Ford	106.198
1984+	Pacific	Davy Jones	USA	Ralt RT4-Ford	107.477
1984+	Pacific	Ross Cheever	USA	Ralt RT4-Ford	105.817
1986	Pacific	Jeff MacPherson	USA	Ralt RT4-Ford	109.860
1987	Pacific	Paul Radisich	NZ	Ralt RT4-Ford	108.182
1988	Pacific	Dean Hall	USA	Swift DB4-Ford	n/a
1989	Pacific	Hiro Matsushita	J	Swift DB4-Ford	108.780
1990#	Pacific	Craig Baird	NZ	Swift DB4-Ford	86.970
1991#	Pacific	Ken Smith	NZ	Swift DB4-Ford	90.308
1992	Pacific	Craig Baird	NZ	Reynard 92H-Toyota	97.510
1993	Pacific	Craig Baird	NZ	Reynard 92H-Toyota	115.500
1994	Brabham	Paul Stokell	AUS	Reynard 90D-Holden	n/a

*Run concurrently with New Zealand GP. +Two races in 1984, first in January, second in December. At Wigram except #at Ruapana

POLAND

CIRCUITS AND RACES

LWOW

Poland's only international race was organized on the narrow and dangerous streets of Lwow by the Malopolski Klub Automobilowy. The many sharp corners caused frequent accidents and kept average speeds down to 50 mph.

Active years...1930-33
Location..........Central Lwow on the Russian border

Lap distance ..1.865 miles
Lap record ......Rudolf Caracciola (Alfa Romeo 8C "Monza")
2m02.8, 54.674 mph, 1932, Grand Prix

Lwow Grand Prix

year	formula	winner	nat	car	mph
1930	FL	Henryk Liefeld	PL	Austro-Daimler	50.530
1931	GP	Hans Stuck	D	Mercedes-Benz SSK	48.308
1932	GP	Rudolf Caracciola	D	Alfa Romeo 8C "Monza"	53.221
1933	GP	Eugen Bjornstad	N	Alfa Romeo 8C "Monza"	51.123

PORTUGAL

MAJOR CHAMPIONSHIPS

Portuguese Touring Car Championship		
year driver	nat	car
1992 Hernani Castro Lopo	P	Honda Civic VTi
1993 Ni Amorim	P	Opel Astra GSi
1994 Pedro Faria	P	Toyota Carina

MAJOR INTERNATIONAL RACES

PORTUGUESE GRAND PRIX						
year	formula	circuit	winner	nat	car	mph
1951	SC	Oporto	Casimiro de Oliveira	P	Ferrari	78.210
1952	SC	Oporto	Eugenio Castellotti	I	Ferrari	85.710
1953	SC	Oporto	N Pinto Nogueira	P	Ferrari	85.380
1954	SC	Monsanto	José Froilan Gonzalez	RA	Ferrari	82.770
1955	SC	Oporto	Jean Behra	F	Maserati 300S	91.650
1957	SC	Monsanto	Juan Manuel Fangio	RA	Maserati	86.890
1958	F1 W	Oporto	Stirling Moss	GB	Vanwall VW10	105.041
1959	F1 W	Monsanto	Stirling Moss	GB	Cooper T51-Climax	95.310

year	formula	circuit	winner	nat	car	mph
1960	F1 W	Oporto	Jack Brabham	AUS	Cooper T53-Climax	109.279
1965	F3	Cascais	Rod Banting	GB	Cooper-Ford	n/a
1966	F3	Cascais	Jürg Dubler	CH	Brabham-Ford	n/a
1967	F3	Montes Claros	Carlos Gaspar	P	Brabham BT21-Ford	n/a
1968	SC	Montes Claros	Carlos Gaspar	P	Ford GT40	n/a
1969	SC	Montes Claros	Manuel Pinto	P	Porsche Carrera 6	n/a
1984	F1 W	Estoril	Alain Prost	F	McLaren MP4/2-TAG Porsche	112.184
1985	F1 W	Estoril	Ayrton Senna	BR	Lotus 97T-Renault	90.200
1986	F1 W	Estoril	Nigel Mansell	GB	Williams FW11-Honda	116.598
1987	F1 W	Estoril	Alain Prost	F	McLaren MP4/3-TAG Porsche	116.959
1988	F1 W	Estoril	Alain Prost	F	McLaren MP4/4-Honda	116.219
1989	F1 W	Estoril	Gerhard Berger	A	Ferrari 640	118.943
1990	F1 W	Estoril	Nigel Mansell	GB	Ferrari 641/2	120.377
1991	F1 W	Estoril	Riccardo Patrese	I	Williams FW14-Renault	120.315
1992	F1 W	Estoril	Nigel Mansell	GB	Williams FW14B-Renault	121.493
1993	F1 W	Estoril	Michael Schumacher	D	Benetton B193B-Ford	124.119
1994	F1 W	Estoril	Damon Hill	GB	Williams FW16B-Renault	114.069

Note: other race details: n/a

CIRCUITS AND OTHER RACES

ESTORIL

The need for a replacement race for the final Grand Prix of 1984 gave Estoril the opportunity to join the World Championship and it has remained ever since. Estoril first held a race on 18 June 1972 but fell into disrepair in the late 1970s. At the time it had the dubious reputation of cancelling events at short notice. The 1984 GP saw the closest ever finish to the Championship – Niki Lauda edging out McLaren team-mate Alain Prost by half a point in the series. Ayrton Senna scored his first Grand Prix win here a year later, a masterly performance in atrocious conditions. Prost had an eventful race here in 1993 securing his fourth world crown and announcing his retirement within 24 hours. A new hairpin was built for the 1994 Grand Prix to slow cars at Turn Nine. The climate has made Estoril a popular winter testing venue for the F1 teams but facilities are limited.

Active years...1972 to date
Location.........Four miles north of Estoril, 20 miles west of Lisbon

CURRENT CIRCUIT
Lap distance ..2.709 miles
Lap record ......David Coulthard (Williams FW16B-Renault) 1m22.446, 118.289 mph, 1994, F1

CIRCUIT CHANGES
1972-93 ....2.703 miles
1994 to date ....A new hairpin was constructed at Turn Nine. Current circuit

Portuguese Grand Prix see above

European Formula Two race

year	formula	winner	nat	car	mph
1973	F2	Jean-Pierre Jarier	F	March 732-BMW	99.748
1975	F2 E	Jacques Laffite	F	Martini MK16-BMW	85.271
1976	F2 E	René Arnoux	F	Martini MK19-Renault	100.947
1977	F2 E	Didier Pironi	F	Martini MK22-Renault	102.015

International Formula 3000 race

year	formula	winner	nat	car	mph
1985	F3000 INT	John Nielsen	DK	Ralt RB20-Cosworth	104.790
1994	F3000 INT	Jules Boullion	F	Reynard 94D-Cosworth	104.879

World Sports Car race

year	formula	winner	nat	car	mph
1977	SC WSC	Arturo Merzario	I	Alfa Romeo T33SC/12	95.625

MONSANTO

Scene of the Portuguese Sports Car GP in the early 1950s, Monsanto also held an F1 World Championship event in 1959. Set in a park in the hills north of Lisbon, the main straight was part of the road to Estoril.

MONSANTO 1959

Active years...1953-59
Location.........North of Lisbon

Lap distance ..3.5 miles (1954-57); 3.38 miles (1959)
Lap record ......Stirling Moss (Cooper T51-Climax) 2m05.07, 97.290 mph, 1959, F1

Portuguese Grand Prix see above

OPORTO

Like Monsanto, a temporary circuit which hosted a Sports Car race in the early 1950s before being included in the F1 World Championship. The round-the-houses circuit consisting of a mixture of fast and slow corners, tramlines and cobbles and passed a fish-drying factory at the conclusion of the lap. Safety concerns forced the circuit to close.

Portuguese Grand Prix see above

Active years...1950-60
Location..........North of Portugal
at the mouth of the
River Douro

Rua par da Fonleda

Estrada

Estrada da Circunvalacoa

Lap distance ..4.65 miles (1950-54); 4.603 miles (1958-60)
Lap record......John Surtees (Lotus 18-Climax) 2m27.53, 112.322 mph, 1960, F1

Avenida da Boavista

Esplanada do Rio de Janeiro

Avenida da Antunes Gumaraes

VILA REAL

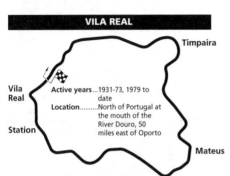

Timpaira

Vila Real

Active years...1931-73, 1979 to date
Location..........North of Portugal at the mouth of the River Douro, 50 miles east of Oporto

Station

Mateus

A classic Portuguese road race for Sports Cars until the 1974 race was cancelled due to political upheaval in Portugal, the circuit losing its international licence. A street circuit in its most raw state, the road is lined by lampposts, walls and houses, and passes over bridges and a level crossing. Since the circuit reopened in 1979 only national touring car events have been held.

Lap distance ..4.303 miles
Lap record......Carlos Gaspar (Lola T292-Ford) 2m19.92, 110.712 mph, 1973, Sports Car

Vila Real International Sports Car race

year	formula	winner	nat	car	mph
1931	SC	Gaspar Sameiro	P	Ford	n/a
1932	SC	Vasco Sameiro	P	Invicta	n/a
1933	SC	Vasco Sameiro	P	Alfa Romeo	n/a
1934	SC	Antonio Heredia	P	Bugatti	n/a
1936	SC	Vasco Sameiro	P	Alfa Romeo	n/a
1937	SC	Vasco Sameiro	P	Alfa Romeo	n/a
1938	SC	Vasco Sameiro	P	Alfa Romeo	n/a
1949	SC	José Cabral	P	Allard	58.800
1950	SC	Piero Carini	I	OSCA	n/a
1951	SC	Giovanni Bracco	I	Ferrari	66.650
1952	SC	Casimiro de Oliveira	P	Ferrari	n/a
1958	SC	Stirling Moss	GB	Maserati	84.730
1967	SC	Mike de Udy	ZA	Lola T70 Mk3-Chevrolet	n/a
1968	SC	Mike de Udy	ZA	Lola T70 Mk3-Chevrolet	99.842
1969	SC	Chris Craft/David Piper	GB	Porsche 908	98.670
1970	SC	Teddy Pilette/Gustav Gosselin	B	Lola T70 Mk3B-Chevrolet	95.053
1971	SC	Jorge de Bagration	E	Porsche 908	102.040
1972	SC	Claude Swietlick	CH	Lola T290-Ford	101.233
1973	SC	Carlos Gaspar	P	Lola T292-Ford	107.603

ROMANIA

CIRCUITS AND RACES

BUCHAREST

Limited fields have entered Romania's only international races to date. Hans Ruesch, a competent journeyman at best, defeated local driver Jean Calcianu by nearly quarter of an hour in the opening race!

Active years...1937-39
Location..........Central Bucharest
Lap distance ..2.299 miles
Lap record......Hans Ruesch (Alfa Romeo Tipo-C "8C-35"), 2m06, 65.686 mph, 1937, Formula Libre

Bucharest Grand Prix

year	formula	winner	nat	car	mph
1937	FL	Hans Ruesch	CH	Alfa Romeo Tipo-C "8C-35"	65.600
1939	FL	Hans Stuck	D	Auto Union D	n/a

SOUTH AFRICA

MAJOR CHAMPIONSHIPS

South African Drivers' Championship

year	driver	nat	car
1953	Doug Duff	ZA	Riley
1954	Bill Jennings	ZA	Riley
1955	Frank Brodie	ZA	MG
1956	Bill Jennings	ZA	Riley
1957	Bill Jennings	ZA	Riley
1958	Ian Fraser-Jones	ZA	Porsche RS
1959	Ian Fraser-Jones	ZA	Porsche RS
1960	Syd van der Vyver	ZA	Cooper-Alfa Romeo
1961	Syd van der Vyver	ZA	Lotus 18-Alfa Romeo
1962	Ernest Pieterse	ZA	Heron-Alfa Romeo/
			Lotus 20-Climax
1963	Neville Lederle	ZA	Lotus 20-Climax
1964	John Love	RSR	Cooper T55-Climax
1965	John Love	RSR	Cooper T55-Climax
1966	John Love	RSR	Cooper T79-Climax
1967	John Love	RSR	Cooper T79-Climax/
			Brabham BT20-Repco
1968	John Love	RSR	Brabham BT20-Repco/
			Lotus 49-Ford
1969	John Love	RSR	Lotus 49B-Ford
1970	Dave Charlton	ZA	Lotus 49C-Ford
1971	Dave Charlton	ZA	Lotus 49C-Ford
1972	Dave Charlton	ZA	Lotus 72D-Ford
1973	Dave Charlton	ZA	Lotus 72D-Ford
1974	Dave Charlton	ZA	McLaren M23-Ford
1975	Dave Charlton	ZA	McLaren M23-Ford
1976	Ian Scheckter	ZA	March 76B-Ford
1977	Ian Scheckter	ZA	March 77B-Ford
1978	Ian Scheckter	ZA	March 78B-Ford
1979	Ian Scheckter	ZA	March 79B-Mazda
1980	Tony Martin	ZA	Chevron B31-Mazda
1981	Bernard Tilanus	ZA	March 77B-Mazda/
			March 792-Mazda
1982	Graham Duxbury	ZA	March 822-Mazda
1983	Ian Scheckter	ZA	March 832-Mazda
1984	Ian Scheckter	ZA	March 832-Mazda
1985	Trevor van Rooyen	ZA	Maurer MM83-Mazda
1986	Wayne Taylor	ZA	Ralt RT4-Mazda
1990	Anthony Taylor	ZA	DAW Mk1-Volkswagen
1991	Mike Briggs	ZA	Swift-Volkswagen
1992	Shaun van der Linde	ZA	Swift-Volkswagen
1993	Duncan Vos	ZA	Swift-Volkswagen
1994	Marco dos Santos	ZA	Swift-Volkswagen

Formula One 1962-75, Formula Atlantic 1976-86, no series 1987-89, Formula GTi (not counted as official championship) 1990 to date

South African Touring Car Championship

year	driver	nat	car
1992	Deon Joubert	ZA	BMW 535i
1993	Mike Briggs	ZA	Opel Astra GSi
1994	Shaun van der Linde	ZA	BMW 318i

MAJOR INTERNATIONAL RACES

SOUTH AFRICAN GRAND PRIX

year	formula	circuit	winner	nat	car	mph
1934	(h)	East London	Whitney Straight	USA	Maserati 8CM	95.680
1936	(h)	East London	Mario Massacurati	I	Bugatti T35B	87.430
1937	(h)	East London	Pat Fairfield	ZA	ERA A-type	89.170
1938	(h)	East London	Buller Meyer	ZA	Riley	86.530
1939	V	East London	Luigi Villoresi	I	Maserati 4CM	99.670
1960*	FL	East London	Paul Frère	B	Cooper T45-Climax	84.880
1960#	FL	East London	Stirling Moss	GB	Porsche 718	89.240
1961	F1	East London	Jim Clark	GB	Lotus 21-Climax	92.200
1962	F1 W	East London	Graham Hill	GB	BRM P57	93.594
1963	F1 W	East London	Jim Clark	GB	Lotus 25-Climax	95.116
1965	F1 W	East London	Jim Clark	GB	Lotus 33-Climax	98.004
1966	F1	East London	Mike Spence	GB	Lotus 33-Climax	97.750
1967	F1 W	Kyalami	Pedro Rodriguez	MEX	Cooper T81-Maserati	97.095
1968	F1 W	Kyalami	Jim Clark	GB	Lotus 49-Ford	107.422
1969	F1 W	Kyalami	Jackie Stewart	GB	Matra MS10-Ford	110.617
1970	F1 W	Kyalami	Jack Brabham	AUS	Brabham BT33-Ford	111.703
1971	F1 W	Kyalami	Mario Andretti	USA	Ferrari 312B	112.341
1972	F1 W	Kyalami	Denny Hulme	NZ	McLaren M19A-Ford	114.224
1973	F1 W	Kyalami	Jackie Stewart	GB	Tyrrell 006-Ford	117.140
1974	F1 W	Kyalami	Carlos Reutemann	RA	Brabham BT44-Ford	116.222
1975	F1 W	Kyalami	Jody Scheckter	ZA	Tyrrell 007-Ford	115.548
1976	F1 W	Kyalami	Niki Lauda	A	Ferrari 312T	116.649
1977	F1 W	Kyalami	Niki Lauda	A	Ferrari 312T2	116.589
1978	F1 W	Kyalami	Ronnie Peterson	S	Lotus 78-Ford	116.699
1979	F1 W	Kyalami	Gilles Villeneuve	CDN	Ferrari 312T4	117.192
1980	F1 W	Kyalami	René Arnoux	F	Renault RE20	123.189
1981	F1	Kyalami	Carlos Reutemann	RA	Williams FW07B-Ford	112.306
1982	F1 W	Kyalami	Alain Prost	F	Renault RE30B	127.860
1983	F1 W	Kyalami	Riccardo Patrese	I	Brabham BT52B-BMW	126.096
1984	F1 W	Kyalami	Niki Lauda	A	McLaren MP4/2-TAG Porsche	128.369
1985	F1 W	Kyalami	Nigel Mansell	GB	Williams FW10-Honda	129.835
1992	F1 W	Kyalami	Nigel Mansell	GB	Williams FW14B-Renault	118.230
1993	F1 W	Kyalami	Alain Prost	F	Williams FW15C-Renault	115.840

*run 1 January, #run 27 December

CIRCUITS AND OTHER RACES

EAST LONDON

Built using part of the 1936-39 Prince George circuit, a new Grand Prix circuit was opened at East London in July 1959. It held the South African GP until the rise of Kyalami proved irresistible, and the race moved.

South African Grand Prix see above

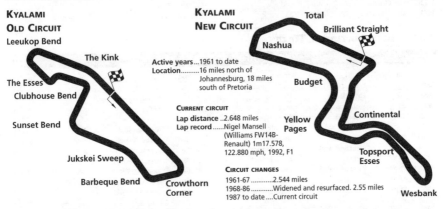

Potters Pass Curve

Main Straight

Rifle Bend

Active years...1959 to date
Location..........East London, adjacent to the Indian Ocean

Cox's Corner

The Esses

Cocobana Corner

Beacon Bend

The Sweep

Butts Bend

Beach Straight

Back Straight

Lap distance ..2.436 miles
Lap record .....Jack Brabham (Brabham BT19-Repco) 1m25.2, 102.929 mph, 1966, F1

KYALAMI

Originally a superb circuit with a long main straight cresting the brow of a hill opposite the pits before descending to the demanding first corner at Crowthorne, Kyalami first staged the South African GP in 1967 and has been its home ever since. Curiously, while links with South Africa were severed by other sports, the Grand Prix remained until the 1985 race was boy-cotted by some teams. The race returned in 1992 as apartheid was ending, but on a revised circuit. Kyalami had been completely rebuilt using part of the existing track, with improved facilities but without the splendour of the old circuit. Overtaking is near-impossible so racing has proved to be processional, placing even greater importance on qualifying. Continual financial and political problems are a constant threat to the future of Kyalami.

KYALAMI
OLD CIRCUIT

Leeukop Bend

The Kink

The Esses

Clubhouse Bend

Sunset Bend

Jukskei Sweep

Barbeque Bend

Crowthorn Corner

KYALAMI
NEW CIRCUIT

Total

Brilliant Straight

Nashua

Active years...1961 to date
Location..........16 miles north of Johannesburg, 18 miles south of Pretoria

Budget

CURRENT CIRCUIT
Lap distance ..2.648 miles
Lap record ......Nigel Mansell (Williams FW14B-Renault) 1m17.578, 122.880 mph, 1992, F1

Yellow Pages

Continental

Topsport Esses

CIRCUIT CHANGES
1961-67 ....2.544 miles
1968-86 ....Widened and resurfaced. 2.55 miles
1987 to date ....Current circuit

Wesbank

South African Grand Prix see above

Rand Nine hours

year	formula	winner	nat	car	mph
1958*	SC	Ian Fraser-Jones/Tony Fergusson	ZA	Porsche Speedster	62.330
1959*	SC	Hugh Carrington/Chris Fergusson	ZA	Dart-Climax	63.670
1960*	SC	John Love/Dawie Gous	RSR/ZA	Porsche RS Spyder	68.340
1961*	SC	Dawie Gous/John Love	ZA/RSR	Porsche RS Spyder	74.740
1962	SC	David Piper/Bruce Johnstone	GB/ZA	Ferrari GTB	76.840
1963	GT	David Piper/Tony Maggs	GB/ZA	Ferrari GTO	82.760
1964	SC	David Piper/Tony Maggs	GB/ZA	Ferrari 250LM	84.885
1965	SC	David Piper/Richard Attwood	GB	Ferrari 365P2	85.661
1966	SC	David Piper/Richard Attwood	GB	Ferrari 365 P2/3	82.260
1967	SC	Jacky Ickx/Brian Redman	B/GB	Mirage-Ford	96.900
1968	SC	Jacky Ickx/David Hobbs	B/GB	Mirage-Ford	88.900
1969	SC	David Piper/Richard Attwood	GB	Porsche 917	92.366
1970	SC	Jacky Ickx/Ignazio Giunti	B/I	Ferrari 512S	104.833
1971	SC	Clay Regazzoni/Brian Redman	CH/GB	Ferrari 312P	100.580
1972	SC	Arturo Merzario/Clay Regazzoni	I/CH	Ferrari 312P	103.275
1973	SC	Reinhold Jöst/Herbert Müller	D/CH	Porsche 908/3	102.007
1974#	SC W	Henri Pescarolo/Gérard Larrousse	F	Matra-Simca MS670C	99.875

At Kyalami except *at Grand Central, Johannesburg. #reduced to a six hour race due to the oil crisis

Kyalami 1000 kms/World Sports Car race

year	formula	winner	nat	car	mph
1975	SC/GT	Hans Heyer/Paul Hennige/Jochen Mass	D/ZA/D	Ford Escort RS	n/a
1976	SC	Gunnar Nilsson/Jody Scheckter/Harald Grohs	S/ZA/D	BMW 3.0 CSL	93.150
1977	SC	Hans Heyer/Jody Scheckter	D/ZA	Ford Escort RS	98.154
1978	SC	Brian Cooke/Phil Adams	ZA	Datsun 140Z	n/a
1979	SC	Helmut Kelleners/Eddie Keizan	D/ZA	BMW M1	n/a
1981	SC	Jochen Mass/Reinhold Jöst	D	Porsche 908	103.240
1982	SC	Jacky Ickx/Jochen Mass	B/D	Porsche 956	107.307
1983	SC W	Derek Bell/Stefan Bellof	GB/D	Porsche 956	108.490
1984	SC W	Riccardo Patrese/Alessandro Nannini	I	Lancia LC2	110.374
1986	SC	Piercarlo Ghinzani	I	Porsche 956	120.660
1987	SC	Jochen Mass	D	Porsche 962	115.250

SPAIN

Spanish Touring Car Championship

Adopted FIA Class 2 rules in 1994

year	driver	nat	car
1992	Carlos Palau	E	Ford Sierra Cosworth
1993	Luis Perez Sala	E	Nissan Skyline GT-R
1994	Adrian Campos	E	Alfa Romeo 155TS

MAJOR INTERNATIONAL RACES

SPANISH GRAND PRIX

year	formula	circuit	winner	nat	car	mph
1913	TC	Guadarrama	Carlo de Salamanca	E	Rolls-Royce	54.000
1923	GP	Sitges	Albert Divo	F	Sunbeam	96.962
1926	FL	Lasarte	Meo Costantini	F	Bugatti T35	78.829
1927	GP	Lasarte	Robert Benoist	F	Delage 15S8	82.524
1928	SC (h)	Lasarte	Louis Chiron	MC	Bugatti	68.456
1929	GP	Lasarte	Louis Chiron	MC	Bugatti T35B	74.124
1930	GP	Lasarte	Achille Varzi	I	Maserati 26M	88.990
1933	GP	Lasarte	Louis Chiron	MC	Alfa Romeo Tipo-B "P3"	85.954
1934	GP	Lasarte	Luigi Fagioli	I	Mercedes-Benz W25A	99.413
1935	GP	Lasarte	Rudolf Caracciola	D	Mercedes-Benz W25B	104.491
1951	F1 W	Pedralbes	Juan Manuel Fangio	RA	Alfa Romeo 159	98.771
1954	F1 W	Pedralbes	Mike Hawthorn	GB	Ferrari 553 Squalo	97.452
1967	F1/F2	Jarama	Jim Clark	GB	Lotus 49-Ford	83.595
1968	F1 W	Jarama	Graham Hill	GB	Lotus 49-Ford	84.407
1969	F1 W	Montjuich Park	Jackie Stewart	GB	Matra MS80-Ford	92.893
1970	F1 W	Jarama	Jackie Stewart	GB	March 701-Ford	87.220
1971	F1 W	Montjuich Park	Jackie Stewart	GB	Tyrrell 003-Ford	97.174
1972	F1 W	Jarama	Emerson Fittipaldi	BR	Lotus 72D-Ford	92.355
1973	F1 W	Montjuich Park	Emerson Fittipaldi	BR	Lotus 72D-Ford	97.843
1974	F1 W	Jarama	Niki Lauda	A	Ferrari 312B3	88.484
1975	F1 W	Montjuich Park	Jochen Mass	D	McLaren M23-Ford	95.529
1976	F1 W	Jarama	James Hunt	GB	McLaren M23-Ford	93.016
1977	F1 W	Jarama	Mario Andretti	USA	Lotus 78-Ford	92.537
1978	F1 W	Jarama	Mario Andretti	USA	Lotus 79-Ford	93.524
1979	F1 W	Jarama	Patrick Depailler	F	Ligier JS11-Ford	95.963
1980	F1	Jarama	Alan Jones	AUS	Williams FW07B-Ford	98.358
1981	F1 W	Jarama	Gilles Villeneuve	CDN	Ferrari 126CK	95.267
1986	F1 W	Jerez	Ayrton Senna	BR	Lotus 98T-Renault	104.069
1987	F1 W	Jerez	Nigel Mansell	GB	Williams FW11B-Honda	103.673
1988	F1 W	Jerez	Alain Prost	F	McLaren MP4/4-Honda	104.131
1989	F1 W	Jerez	Ayrton Senna	BR	McLaren MP4/5-Honda	106.485
1990	F1 W	Jerez	Alain Prost	F	Ferrari 641/2	106.268
1991	F1 W	Catalunya	Nigel Mansell	GB	Williams FW14-Renault	116.563
1992	F1 W	Catalunya	Nigel Mansell	GB	Williams FW14B-Renault	99.019
1993	F1 W	Catalunya	Alain Prost	F	Williams FW15C-Renault	124.418
1994	F1 W	Catalunya	Damon Hill	GB	Williams FW16-Renault	119.533

PENYA RHIN GRAND PRIX

year	formula	circuit	winner	nat	car	mph
1921	V	Villafranca	Pierre de Vizcaya	E	Bugatti T22	53.136
1922	V	Villafranca	Kenelm Lee Guinness	GB	Talbot-Darracq 56	65.251
1923	V	Villafranca	Albert Divo	F	Talbot T70	67.503
1933	GP	Montjuich Park	Juan Zanelli	RCH	Alfa Romeo 8C "Monza"	59.098

year	formula	circuit	winner	nat	car	mph
1934	GP	Montjuich Park	Achille Varzi	I	Alfa Romeo Tipo-B "P3"	64.633
1935	GP	Montjuich Park	Luigi Fagioli	I	Mercedes-Benz W25B	66.997
1936	GP	Montjuich Park	Tazio Nuvolari	I	Alfa Romeo Tipo-C "8C-35"	69.297
1946	GP	Pedralbes	G Pelassa	E	Maserati	80.250
1948	F1	Pedralbes	Luigi Villoresi	I	Maserati	89.440
1950	F1	Montjuich Park	Alberto Ascari	I	Ferrari 375	56.409

CIRCUITS AND OTHER RACES

ALBACETE

A narrow and twisting modern circuit on the flat countryside outside the quiet Spanish town of Albacete. When the International Formula 3000 championship visited in 1992, a small crowd saw a dull race with overtaking near-impossible.

Location..........2.5 miles east of Albacete, 100 miles north-west of Alicante

Active years...1991 to date

Lap distance ..2.236 miles
Lap record......Andrea Montermini (Reynard 92D-Cosworth) 1m21.94, 98.238 mph, 1992, F3000

International Formula 3000 race

year	formula	winner	nat	car	mph
1992	F3000 INT	Andrea Montermini	I	Reynard 92D-Cosworth	94.873

CATALUNYA

BARCELONA

The Circuito de Catalunya at Montmelo is Barcelona's fourth Grand Prix circuit following Villafranca, Pedralbes and Montjuich Park. Built at great expense the circuit won the Spanish Grand Prix in the backlash surrounding Martin Donnelly's near-fatal accident at Jerez. The 1991 race featured Ayrton Senna and Nigel Mansell wheel-to-wheel the length of the long main straight as they battled over the World Championship. A temporary tyre chicane was installed for the 1994 race at the Nissan corner as Formula One struggled to overcome its self doubt and safety concerns.

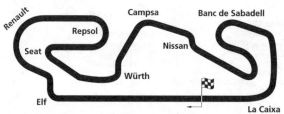

Active years...1991 to date
Location..........22 miles north of Barcelona
Lap distance ..2.9497 miles (lap distance unchanged by 1994 chicane)
Lap record......Without 1994 chicane: Michael Schumacher (Benetton B193B-Ford) 1m20.989, 131.116 mph, 1993, F1
With temporary chicane: Michael Schumacher (Benetton B194-Ford) 1m25.155, 124.701 mph, 1994, F1

Spanish Grand Prix see above

International Formula 3000 race

year	formula	winner	nat	car	mph
1992	F3000 INT	Andrea Montermini	I	Reynard 92D-Judd	113.836
1994	F3000 INT	Massimiliano Papis	I	Reynard 94D-Judd	110.462

JARAMA

John Hugenholtz, the creator of both Zandvoort and Suzuka, was hired by the Real Automovil Club de Espana to design a new circuit at Jarama on the site of one of the fiercest Spanish Civil War battles. Like Zandvoort, the new circuit has a long main straight leading into the first corner, but the track behind the pits is tight and slow. In 1981 Gilles Villeneuve, whose turbocharged Ferrari was all power and no handling, held off a train of four cars to record his most unlikely, and last, victory. Since its last Grand Prix, Jarama has been extended and international racing returned in 1994 with a round of the new GT series.

CURRENT CIRCUIT
Lap distance ..2.392 miles
Lap record......Anders Olofsson (Ferrari F40) 1m37.506, 88.315 mph, 1994, GT

Active years...1967 to date
Location..........18 miles north of Madrid

Ascari
Rampa
Pegaso
Portago
Monza
Farina
Bugatti
Varzi
Le Mans
Fangio
Tunel
Nuvolari

CIRCUIT CHANGES
1967-90 ....2.1154 miles
1991 to date ....Extended. Current circuit

Spanish Grand Prix see above

Madrid Grand Prix

year	formula	winner	nat	car	mph
1967	F2 E	Jim Clark	GB	Lotus 48-Ford	81.661
1968	F2 E	Jean-Pierre Beltoise	F	Matra MS7-Ford	84.464
1969	F1/F5000	Keith Holland	GB	Lola T142-Chevrolet	79.956
1971	F2 E	Emerson Fittipaldi	BR	Lotus 69-Ford	84.885

Other European Formula Two races

year	formula	winner	nat	car	mph
1969	F2 E	Jackie Stewart	GB	Matra MS7-Ford	84.983
1983	F2 E	Mike Thackwell	NZ	Ralt RH6/83-Honda	92.857

International Formula 3000 race

year	formula	winner	nat	car	mph
1986	F3000 INT	Pierluigi Martini	I	Ralt RT20-Cosworth	n/a*
1987	F3000 INT	Yannick Dalmas	F	March 87B-Cosworth	92.884

*time not published

European Formula Three race

year	formula	winner	nat	car	mph
1977	F3 E	Nelson Piquet	BR	Ralt RT1-Toyota	85.291
1978	F3 E	Alain Prost	F	Martini MK21B-Renault	86.456
1979	F3 E	Alain Prost	F	Martini MK27-Renault	86.280
1980	F3 E	Mauro Baldi	I	Martini MK31-Toyota	88.399
1981	F3 E	Alain Ferté	F	Martini MK34-Alfa Romeo	89.297
1982	F3 E	James Weaver	GB	Ralt RT3/82-Toyota	89.057
1983	F3 E	Pierluigi Martini	I	Ralt RT3/83-Alfa Romeo	89.404
1984	F3 E	Johnny Dumfries	GB	Ralt RT3/83-Volkswagen	90.527

World Sports Car race

year	formula	winner	nat	car	mph
1987	SC W	Jan Lammers/John Watson	NL/GB	Jaguar XJR-8	92.269
1988	SC W	Eddie Cheever/Martin Brundle	USA/GB	Jaguar XJR-9	92.180
1989	SC W	Jochen Mass/Jean-Louis Schlesser	D/F	Sauber C9/88-Mercedes-Benz	89.239

International GT race

year	formula	winner	nat	car	mph
1994	GT	Jesus Pareja/Jean-Pierre Jarier/Dominique Dupuy	E/F/F	Porsche 911 turbo SLM	83.144

JEREZ

Built near the sherry town of Jerez de la Frontera to host the 1986 Spanish Grand Prix, Jerez is a slow circuit with excellent facilities. However, it proved to be too far from the major cities to attract more than a sprinkling of spectators. The most demanding section was behind the paddock with two fast right-handers and little run-off area. It was here that Martin Donnelly crashed in qualifying for the 1990 race, prompting the Grand Prix circus to move to the new Catalunya circuit near Barcelona. For the 1994 European GP a new chicane was built at the point where Donnelly had crashed.

Active years...1986 to date
Location..........Six miles north-west of Jerez, 60 miles south of Seville

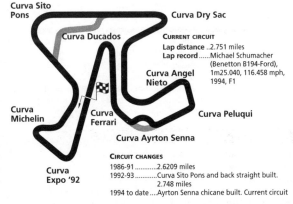

CURRENT CIRCUIT
Lap distance ..2.751 miles
Lap record ......Michael Schumacher (Benetton B194-Ford), 1m25.040, 116.458 mph, 1994, F1

CIRCUIT CHANGES
1986-91 ....2.6209 miles
1992-93 ....Curva Sito Pons and back straight built. 2.748 miles
1994 to date ....Ayrton Senna chicane built. Current circuit

Spanish Grand Prix see above

European Grand Prix see above

International Formula 3000 race

year	formula	winner	nat	car	mph
1988	F3000 INT	Johnny Herbert	GB	Reynard 88D-Cosworth	95.572
1989	F3000 INT	Eric Bernard	F	Lola T89/50-Mugen	96.186
1990	F3000 INT	Erik Comas	F	Lola T90/50-Mugen	96.627
1991	F3000 INT	Christian Fittipaldi	BR	Reynard 91D-Mugen	96.448

World Sports Car race

year	formula	winner	nat	car	mph
1986	SC W	Oscar Larrauri/Jesus Pareja	RA/E	Porsche 962	91.508
1987	SC W	Eddie Cheever/Raul Boesel	USA/BR	Jaguar XJR-8	91.847
1988	SC W	Jean-Louis Schlesser/Mauro Baldi/Jochen Mass	F/I/D	Sauber C9/88-Mercedes-Benz	93.941

LASARTE

In the tradition of Nürburgring, Spa and Brno, Lasarte was a long demanding pre-war road course which was the home of Grand Prix racing in Spain from its opening in 1923 until 1935. Also known as San Sebastian, the northern port close to Lasarte, it was run anti-clock-wise.

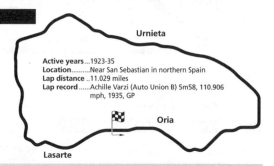

Urnieta

Active years...1923-35
Location..........Near San Sebastian in northern Spain
Lap distance ..11.029 miles
Lap record......Achille Varzi (Auto Union B) 5m58, 110.906 mph, 1935, GP

Oria

Lasarte

Spanish Grand Prix see above

European Grand Prix see above

San Sebastian Grand Prix

year	formula	winner	nat	car	mph
1923	GP	Albert Guyot	F	Rolland Pilain	57.851
1924	GP	Henry Segrave	GB	Sunbeam	64.101
1925	GP	Albert Divo/André Morel	F	Delage 2LCV	76.720
1926*	GP	Jules Goux	F	Bugatti T39A	70.530
1927	FL	Emilio Materassi	I	Bugatti T35C	80.663
1928	GP	Louis Chiron	MC	Bugatti T35C	82.588

*European Grand Prix

MONTJUICH PARK

BARCELONA

When the Penya Rhin Grand Prix was revived for Grand Prix cars in 1933 it took place in Barcelona's undulating Montjuich Park. After the war it was out of use until Jarama was built outside Madrid in 1966 when it was hastily recommissioned so Barcelona could share the Grand Prix. The circuit remained essentially unaltered until the tragic 1975 Grand Prix when Rolf Stommelen, leading a race for the first time, crashed into the crowd killing four spectators.

Active years...1933-75
Location..........Montjuich Park in central Barcelona, near Plaza de Espana

La Pergola
Tribuna Viraje
Pueblo Espanol
Tribuna Riug y Taulet
San Jordi
Tribuna Tecnica
Palico Agricultura
Tribuna Teatro Griego
Tunel de la Fuxarda

Lap distance ..2.355 miles
Estadio
Lap record......Ronnie Peterson (Lotus 72E-Ford) 1m23.8, 101.169 mph, 1973, F1

Spanish Grand Prix see above

Penya Rhin Grand Prix see above

Barcelona Grand Prix/European Formula Two race

year	formula	winner	nat	car	mph
1966	F2	Jack Brabham	AUS	Brabham BT18-Honda	65.820
1967	F2	Jim Clark	GB	Lotus 48-Ford	88.350
1968	F2	Jackie Stewart	GB	Matra MS7-Ford	89.716
1970	F2 E	Derek Bell	GB	Brabham BT30-Ford	93.333
1974	F2 E	Hans-Joachim Stuck	D	March 742-BMW	96.837

PEDRALBES

An unusually fast "round-the-houses" circuit with wide straights and fast, open corners. Pedralbes held the final Grand Prix of 1951 when a poor tyre choice by Ferrari handed

Fangio his first championship victory. The race returned three years later with Mike Hawthorn scoring his second GP victory.

Spanish Grand Prix see above

Active years...1946-55
Location.........Western suburbs of Barcelona

Avenida de la Victoria

Paseo de Manuel Girona

Carretera de Cornella a Fogas de Tordera

PEDRABLES 1951-55

Avenida del Generalisimo Franco

Calle de Numancia

CIRCUIT CHANGES

1946-50 ....2.774 miles
1951 ....3.925 miles. Lap record: Juan Manuel Fangio (Alfa Romeo 159) 2m16.93, 1951, F1
1954-55 ....3.936 miles. Lap record: Alberto Ascari (Lancia D50) 2m20.4, 1954, F1

SWEDEN

MAJOR CHAMPIONSHIPS

Nordic Formula Three Championship

year	driver	nat	car
1992	Peter Aslund	S	Ralt RT35-Volkswagen
1993	Magnus Wallinder	S	Ralt RT35-Volkswagen/ Reynard 913-Mugen
1994	Magnus Wallinder	S	Reynard 913-Mugen

Swedish Formula Three Championship (including Formula Junior)

year	driver	nat	car
1961*	Yngve Rosqvist	S	Lotus 18-Ford
1962*	Yngve Rosqvist	S	Cooper-Ford
1963*	Gunnar Karlsson	S	Lola-Ford
1964	Sven Mattsson	S	Lotus-Ford
1965	Picko Troberg	S	Brabham-Ford
1966	Fredy Kottulinsky	S	Lotus 35-Ford
1967	Reine Wisell	S	Brabham-Ford
1968	Ronnie Peterson	S	Tecno 68-Ford
1969	Ronnie Peterson	S	Tecno 69-Ford
1970	Torsten Palm	S	Brabham BT28-Ford
1971	Torsten Palm	S	Brabham BT28-Ford/ Brabham BT35-Ford
1972	Conny Andersson	S	Brabham-Ford
1973	Hakan Dahlqvist	S	Merlyn 22-Ford
1974	Conny Andersson	S	March 743-Toyota
1975	Conny Ljungfeldt	S	March 743-Toyota
1976	Conny Ljungfeldt	S	Viking TH1A-Toyota
1977	Anders Olofsson	S	Ralt RT1-Toyota
1978	Anders Olofsson	S	Ralt RT1-Toyota
1979	Slim Borgudd	S	Ralt RT1-Toyota
1980	Thorbjorn Carlsson	S	Ralt RT1-Toyota
1981	Bengt Tragardh	S	March 803B-Toyota
1983	Leo Andersson	S	Ralt RT3-Toyota
1984	Leif Lindstrom	S	Ralt RT3-Toyota
1985	Thomas Danielsson	S	Reynard 853-SAAB/ Reynard 853-Volkswagen
1986	Niclas Schonstrom	S	Reynard 863-Volkswagen
1987	Mikael Johansson	S	Ralt RT31-Alfa Romeo
1988	Mikael Johansson	S	Ralt RT31-Alfa Romeo
1989	Jan Nilsson	S	Reynard 883-Volkswagen
1990	Niclas Jonsson	S	Reynard 903-Mugen
1991	Niclas Jonsson	S	Reynard 903-Mugen
1992	Peter Aslund	S	Ralt RT35-Volkswagen
1993	Magnus Wallinder	S	Ralt RT35-Volkswagen/ Reynard 913-Mugen
1994	Magnus Wallinder	S	Reynard 913-Mugen

*Formula Junior

Nordic Touring Car Championship

Has replaced the Swedish series as the region's leading Touring Car Championship. Run to FIA Class 2 rules in 1993 although no Class 2 cars competed that year!

year	driver	nat	car
1992	Kris Nissen	DK	BMW M3
1993	Peggan Andersson	S	BMW M3
1994	Slim Borgudd	S	Mazda Xedos 6

Swedish Touring Car Championship

year	class	driver	nat
1959	1600 cc	Gunnar Andersson	S
	1300 cc	Karl-Rune Eriksson	S
	1000 cc	Erik Carlsson	S
1960	1600 cc	Tom Trana	S
	1150 cc	Sigurd Isacson	S
	850 cc	Erik Carlsson	S
1961	1600 cc	Tom Trana	S
	1150 cc	Sigurd Isacson	S
	850 cc	Gosta Karlsson	S
	700 cc	Lennart Gillmo	S
1962	1600 cc	"Gunnar Christin"	S
	1150 cc	Tom Trana	S
	850 cc	Erik Berger	S
1963	3000 cc	Bo Ljungfeldt	S
	1300 cc	Jan-Erik Andreasson	S
	850 cc	Gosta Karlsson	S
1964	over 1300 cc	Bo Ljungfeldt	S
	1300 cc	Borje Osterberg	S
	850 cc	Sigvard Johansson	S
1965	over 1300 cc	Svante Vorrsjo	S
	1300 cc	Picko Troberg	S
	850 cc	Gosta Karlsson	S
1966	over 1600 cc	Bo Ljungfeldt	S
	1600 cc	Erik Berger	S
	1000 cc	Leif Englund	S
1967	over 1600 cc	Boo Brasta	S
	1600 cc	Svante Vorrsjo	S
	1000 cc	Leif Englund	S
1968	over 1600 cc	Bjorn Rothstein	S
	1600 cc	Erik Berger	S
	1000 cc	Olof Wijk	S
1969	over 1600 cc	Bengt Ekberg	S
	1600 cc	Bo Ljungfeldt/Erik Berger	S
	1000 cc	Gosta Pettersson	S
1970	2000 cc	Bengt Ekberg	S
	1000 cc	Gosta Pettersson	S
1971	over 1600 cc	Bo Ljungfeldt	S
	1600 cc	Bengt Odelfors	S
	1300 cc	Johnny Green	S
1972	over 3000 cc	Bengt Ekberg	S
	3000 cc	Bo Emanuelsson	S
	1600 cc	Bengt Odelfors	S
	1300 cc	Bjorn Steenberg	S
1973	over 1300 cc	Boo Brasta	S
	1300 cc	Bjorn Steenberg	S
1974	over 2000 cc	Bengt Ekberg	S
	2000 cc	Carl Piper	S
	1300 cc	Bengt Odelfors	S
	1150 cc	Lennart Persson	S

year	class	driver	nat	year	class	driver	nat
1975	Group 1	Bo Emanuelsson	S	1980	1600 cc	Thomas Lindstrom	S
	over 2000 cc	Rune Tobiasson	S	1981	2500 cc	Erik Noyer	DK
	2000 cc	Carl Piper	S		1600 cc	Thomas Lindstrom	S
	1150 cc	Bengt Odelfors	S	1982	1600 cc	Thomas Lindstrom	S
1976	Special	Bo Emanuelsson	S	1984		Anders Dahlgren	S
	1150 cc	Bengt Odelfors	S	1985		Anders Berggren	S
1977	Special	Bo Emanuelsson	S	1986		Stig Gruen	S
	Standard	Thomas Lindstrom	S	1987		Peggan Andersson	S
1978	Special	Leif Nilsson	S	1988		Lennart Bohlin	S
	Standard	Sven Edlund	S	1989		Peggan Andersson	S
1979	Special	Jan Lundgardh	S	1990		Stig Blomqvist	S
	Standard	Sven Edlund	S	1991		Peggan Andersson	S
1980	2500 cc	Ulf Larsson	S	1992		Peggan Andersson	S

MAJOR INTERNATIONAL RACES

SWEDISH GRAND PRIX

year	formula	circuit	winner	nat	car	mph
1955	SC	Kristianstad	Juan Manuel Fangio	RA	Mercedes-Benz	99.720
1956	SC W	Kristianstad	Maurice Trintignant/Phil Hill	F/USA	Ferrari 290MM	94.692
1957	SC W	Kristianstad	Jean Behra/Stirling Moss	F/GB	Maserati 450S	97.889
1973	F1 W	Anderstorp	Denny Hulme	NZ	McLaren M23-Ford	102.645
1974	F1 W	Anderstorp	Jody Scheckter	ZA	Tyrrell 007-Ford	101.125
1975	F1 W	Anderstorp	Niki Lauda	A	Ferrari 312T	100.462
1976	F1 W	Anderstorp	Jody Scheckter	ZA	Tyrrell P34-Ford	100.912
1977	F1 W	Anderstorp	Jacques Laffite	F	Ligier JS7-Matra	100.884
1978	F1 W	Anderstorp	Niki Lauda	A	Brabham BT46B-Alfa Romeo	104.158

CIRCUITS AND OTHER RACES

ANDERSTORP

SCANDINAVIAN RACEWAY

Built on a marsh in the expanse of central Sweden, Anderstorp came to prominence in the early 1970s, years of boom for Swedish motorsport inspired by the success of Ronnie Peterson. But for a deflating tyre in the closing laps of the 1973 Swedish GP, Peterson would have given the locals the result they wanted, but he was never to triumph in his home race. The long backstretch (which is also a runway) and the slightly banked corners made Anderstorp a set-up compromise and often produced surprising results. The six-wheel Tyrrell and the infamous Brabham "fan-car" scored their only Grand Prix wins here, and Jacques Laffite scored his and Ligier's first victory in 1977. When both Peterson and his heir-apparent, Gunnar Nilsson, died during 1978, the Swedish Grand Prix was lost, and although the European Touring Car Championship visited during the next decade Anderstorp is now little more than a run-down club circuit.

Active years...1968 to date
Location.........Four miles east of Gislaved, 100 miles south-east of Gothenburg

CURRENT CIRCUIT
Lap distance ..2.505 miles
Lap record ......Niki Lauda (Brabham BT46B-Alfa Romeo) 1m24.836, 106.299 mph, 1978, F1

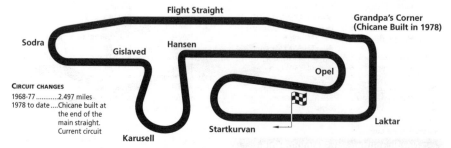

CIRCUIT CHANGES
1968-77 ....2.497 miles
1978 to date ....Chicane built at the end of the main straight. Current circuit

Swedish Grand Prix see above						
European Formula Three race						
year	formula	winner		nat	car	mph
1975	F3 E	Conny Andersson		S	March 753-Toyota	92.390

KARLSKOGA

Karlskoga was Ronnie Peterson's home circuit. It is a flat succession of straights and hairpins which provides good viewing. The 1970 Kannonloppet was marred by an accident in which five spectators were killed forcing the circuit to close for two years.

Active years...1955 to date
Location..........44 miles east of Karland, 155 miles west of Stockholm

Velodron Bend

Trossen Curve

Esses

Paddock Curve

Hairpin

Stirling Moss leads Sweden's own Joakim Bonnier on his way to victory in the 1960 Kannonloppet at Karlskoga

Lap distance ..1.864 miles
Lap record......Patrick Depailler (March 742-BMW) 1m12.1, 93.071 mph, 1974, F2

Kannonloppet

year	formula	winner	nat	car	mph
1955	SC	G Carlsson	S	Ferrari	n/a
1956	SC	G Carlsson	S	Ferrari	n/a
1957	SC	Peter Ashdown	GB	Lotus	n/a
1958	SC	Stirling Moss	GB	Maserati	n/a
1959	SC	Stirling Moss	GB	Cooper	67.700
1960	SC	Stirling Moss	GB	Lotus	67.870
1961	F1	Stirling Moss	GB	Lotus 18/21-Climax	72.498
1962	F1	Masten Gregory	USA	Lotus 24-BRM	78.292
1963	F1	Jim Clark	GB	Lotus 25-Climax	69.417
1964	F2	Jack Brabham	AUS	Brabham-Ford	76.294
1965	F2	Jack Brabham	AUS	Brabham-Ford	78.484
1966	F2	Jack Brabham	AUS	Brabham BT21-Honda	76.320
1967	F2	Jackie Stewart	GB	Matra MS7-Ford	86.010
1968	SC	David Piper	GB	Ferrari P4	n/a
1969	F3	Ronnie Peterson	S	Tecno 69-Ford	82.166
1970	SC	Chris Craft	GB	McLaren M8C-Ford	83.660
1973	F2 E	Jean-Pierre Jarier	F	March 732-BMW	90.620
1974	F2 E	Ronnie Peterson	S	March 742-BMW	91.621
1977	F3	Anders Olofsson	S	Ralt RT1-Toyota	85.830
1978	F3 E	Jan Lammers	NL	Ralt RT1-Toyota	86.959
1981	F3	Thorbjorn Carlsson	S	Ralt RT3-Toyota	n/a
1982	F3	Thorbjorn Carlsson	S	Ralt RT3-Volkswagen	n/a
1983	F3	Mats Karlsson	S	TMS 833-Toyota	n/a
1985	F3	Joackim Lindstrom	S	Ralt RT30-Volkswagen	86.379

Note: Incomplete list of results

KINNEKULLE

Set in a spectacular valley, Kinnekulle held a round of the European F2 Championship in 1973. The circuit was built in an old quarry on the edge of Lake Vanern.

Active years...1969 to date
Location..........20 miles south-west of Linkoping

Lap distance ..1.286 miles
Lap record ......Niclas Jonsson (Reynard 903-Mugen) 47.41s, 97.651 mph, 1993, F3

Swedish Gold Cup

year	formula	winner	nat	car	mph
1971	F2	Ronnie Peterson	S	March 712M-Ford	92.581
1973	F2 E	Jochen Mass	D	Surtees TS15-Ford	91.651

European Formula Three race

year	formula	winner	nat	car	mph
1979	F3 E	Richard Dallest	F	Martini MK27-Toyota	88.822

KNUTSTORP

A short circuit which for a time was Sweden's only international venue, regularly holding European Formula Three races.

CIRCUIT CHANGES
1970-79 ....1.367 miles
1980 to date ....Current circuit

Active years...1970 to date
Location.........45 miles north of Malmo

CURRENT CIRCUIT
Lap distance ..1.292 miles
Lap record ......Niclas Jonsson (Reynard 903-Mugen) 55.854s,
83.274 mph, 1990, F3

European Formula Three race

year	formula	winner	nat	car	mph
1976	F3 E	Conny Andersson	S	March 763-Toyota	78.517
1977	F3 E	Anders Olofsson	S	Ralt RT1-Toyota	79.956
1978	F3 E	Anders Olofsson	S	Ralt RT1-Toyota	79.498
1979	F3 E	Alain Prost	F	Martini MK27-Renault	80.125
1980	F3 E	Corrado Fabi	I	March 803-Alfa Romeo	77.576
1981	F3 E	Mauro Baldi	I	March 813-Alfa Romeo	80.037
1982	F3 E	Oscar Larrauri	RA	Euroracing 101-Alfa Romeo	80.131
1983	F3 E	John Nielsen	DK	Ralt RT3/83-Volkswagen	80.671
1984	F3 E	Claudio Langes	I	Ralt RT3/84-Toyota	80.082
1987*	F3 E	Peter Zakowski	D	Ralt RT31-Volkswagen	75.322
	F3 E	Dave Coyne	GB	Reynard 873-Volkswagen	68.916

*EFDA Euroseries F3 race

KRISTIANSTAD

Closed public roads through the villages near Kristianstad. It held the first three Swedish Grands Prix as Sports Car races.

Swedish Grand Prix see above

Active years...1955-57
Location..........Near Kristianstad, 390 miles from Stockholm

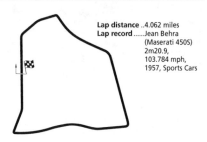

Lap distance ..4.062 miles
Lap record ......Jean Behra
(Maserati 450S)
2m20.9,
103.784 mph,
1957, Sports Cars

MANTORP PARK

CURRENT CIRCUIT
Lap distance ..1.942 miles
Lap record ......Johnny Cecotto
(March 812-
BMW) 1m11.69,
97.520 mph,
1981, F2

CIRCUIT CHANGES
1969-80 ....Circuit No3.
2.543 miles
1981 to date ....Circuit No2.
Current circuit

Rome
Paris Bend
Chicane
Start Turn
New Bend
The Strip
Sand Trap

**MANTORP PARK
CIRCUIT Nº2**

Mantorp Park was built with finance from BP Sweden with three configurations and a drag strip. The European Formula Two Championship visited from 1971 (when Peterson won) until 1973, and again in 1981 and 1982. New Swedish star, Stefan Johansson scored a popular victory in the penultimate race. Mantorp Park has now returned to being a national venue.

Active years...1969 to date
Location..........Ten miles west of Linkoping

European Formula Two race

year	formula	winner	nat	car	mph
1970	F2	François Cevert	F	Tecno 70-Ford	103.515
1971	F2 E	Ronnie Peterson	S	March 712M-Ford	103.506
1972	F2 E	Mike Hailwood	GB	Surtees TS10-Ford	103.784
1973	F2 E	Jean-Pierre Jarier	F	March 732-BMW	107.616
1981	F2 E	Stefan Johansson	S	Toleman TG280B-Hart	94.499
1982	F2 E	Johnny Cecotto	YV	March 822-BMW	96.514

European Formula Three race

year	formula	winner	nat	car	mph
1976	F3 E	Gianfranco Brancatelli	I	March 763-Toyota	101.219

SWITZERLAND

MAJOR CHAMPIONSHIPS

Swiss Formula Three Championship

With motor racing banned in Switzerland their F3 championship is a collection of hill climbs and races held in Italy, France and Germany. It is the least competitive series in Europe.

year	driver	nat	car
1979	Beat Blatter	CH	Lola-Toyota
1980	Jakob Bordoli	CH	Ralt RT1-Toyota
1981	Marcel Wettstein	CH	Ralt RT1-Toyota
1982	Jo Zeller	CH	Ralt RT3-Toyota
1985	Jakob Bordoli	CH	Ralt RT3-Toyota
1986	Gregor Foitek	CH	Dallara 386-Volkswagen
1989	Jacques Isler	CH	Dallara 388-Alfa Romeo
1990	Jo Zeller	CH	Ralt RT34-Alfa Romeo
1991	Jo Zeller	CH	Ralt RT34-Alfa Romeo
1992	Jo Zeller	CH	Ralt RT35-Alfa Romeo
1993	Rudi Schurter	CH	Dallara 393-Opel
1994	Rudi Schurter	CH	Dallara 394-Opel

MAJOR INTERNATIONAL RACES

SWISS GRAND PRIX						
year	formula	circuit	winner	nat	car	mph
1934	GP	Bremgarten	Hans Stuck	D	Auto Union A	87.176
1935	GP	Bremgarten	Rudolf Caracciola	D	Mercedes-Benz W25B	89.964
1936	GP	Bremgarten	Bernd Rosemeyer	D	Auto Union C	100.519
1937	GP	Bremgarten	Rudolf Caracciola	D	Mercedes-Benz W125	98.594
1938	GP	Bremgarten	Rudolf Caracciola	D	Mercedes-Benz W154	89.213
1939	GP	Bremgarten	Hermann Lang	D	Mercedes-Benz W163	96.036
1947	F1	Bremgarten	Jean-Pierre Wimille	F	Alfa Romeo 158	95.632
1948	F1	Bremgarten	Carlo Felice Trossi	I	Alfa Romeo 158	91.020
1949	F1	Bremgarten	Alberto Ascari	I	Ferrari 125	90.927
1950	F1 W	Bremgarten	Giuseppe Farina	I	Alfa Romeo 158	92.766
1951	F1 W	Bremgarten	Juan Manuel Fangio	RA	Alfa Romeo 159	89.140
1952	F2 W	Bremgarten	Piero Taruffi	I	Ferrari 500	92.586
1953	F2 W	Bremgarten	Alberto Ascari	I	Ferrari 500	97.171
1954	F1 W	Bremgarten	Juan Manuel Fangio	RA	Mercedes-Benz W196	99.211
1975	F1	Dijon-Prenois (F)	Clay Regazzoni	CH	Ferrari 312T	79.867
1982	F1 W	Dijon-Prenois (F)	Keke Rosberg	SF	Williams FW08-Ford	122.272

CIRCUITS AND RACES

BREMGARTEN

Set in forests between the north-western outskirts of Bern and the River Wohlensee, Bremgarten was a succession of quick corners without a straight worthy of the name. It had the reputation of being dangerous, and the trees overhanging the circuit made it particularly hazardous in the wet. Bremgarten asked for a special combination of skill and bravery and only the best were quick. Opened in 1931 for motorbikes, the first Swiss GP for cars was held in 1934, continuing until motor racing was banned in Switzerland in the aftermath of the Le Mans disaster of 1955. There were a number of serious accidents, and Bremgarten has had more than its share of fatalities, from Hugh Hamilton in the first Swiss Grand Prix to Achille Varzi and Christian Kautz in the 1948 event.

Swiss Grand Prix see above

Wohlenstrasse

Glasbrunnen

Eyematt Corner

Lap record ......Juan Manuel Fangio (Mercedes-Benz W196) 2m39.7, 101.981 mph, 1955, F1

Eicholz

Forsthaus Corner

Active years...1931-54
Location.........North-west suburbs of Bern
Lap distance ..4.524 miles

Bethlehem

UNITED STATES OF AMERICA

MAJOR CHAMPIONSHIPS

NASCAR Winston Cup

year driver	nat	team	car
1949 Red Byron	USA	Parks Novelty	Oldsmobile
1950 Bill Rexford	USA	Julian Buesink	Oldsmobile
1951 Herb Thomas	USA	Thomas/	Plymouth/
		Sandford Motors/	Oldsmobile/
		Fabulous	Hudson
1952 Tim Flock	USA	Ted Chester	Hudson
1953 Herb Thomas	USA	Fabulous	Hudson
1954 Lee Petty	USA	Petty Engineering	Dodge/Chrysler
1955 Tim Flock	USA	Mercury	
		Outboards/	Chrysler/
		Westmoreland	Chevrolet
1956 Buck Baker	USA	Satcher Motors/	Ford/Chrsyler/
		Kiekhaefer	Dodge
1957 Buck Baker	USA	Hugh Babb/	
		Buck Baker	Chevrolet
1958 Lee Petty	USA	Petty Engineering	Oldsmobile
1959 Lee Petty	USA	Petty Engineering	Oldsmobile/
			Plymouth
1960 Rex White	USA	Piedmont/Friendly	Ford/Chevrolet
1961 Ned Jarrett	USA	Courtesy/	
		BG Holloway	Ford/Chevrolet
1962 Joe Weatherly	USA	Bud Moore	Pontiac
1963 Joe Weatherly	USA	Bud Moore*	Pontiac/Chrysler/
			Plymouth/
			Dodge/Mercury
1964 Richard Petty	USA	Petty Engineering	Plymouth
1965 Ned Jarrett	USA	Bondy Long	Ford
1966 David Pearson	USA	Cotton Owens	Dodge
1967 Richard Petty	USA	Petty Enterprises	Plymouth
1968 David Pearson	USA	Holman-Moody	Ford
1969 David Pearson	USA	Holman-Moody	Ford
1970 Bobby Isaac	USA	K&K Insurance	Dodge
1971 Richard Petty	USA	Petty Enterprises	Plymouth
1972 Richard Petty	USA	Petty Enterprises	Plymouth/Dodge
1973 Benny Parsons	USA	LG de Witt	Chevrolet
1974 Richard Petty	USA	Petty Enterprises	Dodge
1975 Richard Petty	USA	Petty Enterprises	Dodge
1976 Cale Yarborough	USA	Junior Johnson	Chevrolet
1977 Cale Yarborough	USA	Junior Johnson	Chevrolet
1978 Cale Yarborough	USA	Junior Johnson	Oldsmobile
1979 Richard Petty	USA	Petty Enterprises	Chevrolet
1980 Dale Earnhardt	USA	Osterlund Racing	Chevrolet
1981 Darrell Waltrip	USA	Junior Johnson	Buick
1982 Darrell Waltrip	USA	Junior Johnson	Buick
1983 Bobby Allison	USA	Di Gard Racing	Buick
1984 Terry Labonte	USA	Billy Hagan	Chevrolet
1985 Darrell Waltrip	USA	Junior Johnson	Chevrolet
1986 Dale Earnhardt	USA	Richard Childress Racing	Chevrolet
1987 Dale Earnhardt	USA	Richard Childress Racing	Chevrolet
1988 Bill Elliott	USA	Elliott Brothers	Ford
1989 Rusty Wallace	USA	Raymond Beadle	Pontiac
1990 Dale Earnhardt	USA	Richard Childress Racing	Chevrolet
1991 Dale Earnhardt	USA	Richard Childress Racing	Chevrolet
1992 Alan Kulwicki	USA	Alan Kulwicki	Ford
1993 Dale Earnhardt	USA	Richard Childress Racing	Chevrolet
1994 Dale Earnhardt	USA	Richard Childress Racing	Chevrolet

*Weatherly drove the majority of the 1963 season for Bud Moore in a Pontiac and then a Mercury. However, Moore did not enter all of the races and Weatherly also drove Pontiacs for Fred Harb, Pete Stewart, Cliff Stewart, Worth McMillion, a Chrysler for Major Melton, a Plymouth for Petty Engineering and a Dodge for Wade Younts!

IMSA GT Championship

GTP (including World Sports Cars)

year driver	nat	car
1971 Peter Gregg/		
Hurley Haywood	USA	Porsche 914/6
1972 Hurley Haywood	USA	Porsche 911S
1973 Peter Gregg	USA	Porsche Carrera
1974 Peter Gregg	USA	Porsche Carrera
1975 Peter Gregg	USA	Porsche Carrera
1976 Al Holbert	USA	Porsche Carrera/Chevrolet Monza GT
1977 Al Holbert	USA	Chevrolet Monza GT
1978 Peter Gregg	USA	Porsche 935
1979 Peter Gregg	USA	Porsche 935
1980 John Fitzpatrick	GB	Porsche 935
1981 Brian Redman	GB	Porsche 935/Lola T600-Chevrolet
1982 John Paul Jr	USA	Lola T600-Chevrolet/Porsche 935
1983 Al Holbert	USA	March 83G-Porsche/
		March 83G-Chevrolet/Porsche 935
1984 Randy Lanier	USA	March 83G-Chevrolet/
		March 84G-Chevrolet
1985 Al Holbert	USA	Porsche 962
1986 Al Holbert	USA	Porsche 962
1987 Chip Robinson	USA	Porsche 962
1988 Geoff Brabham	AUS	Nissan GTP ZX-T
1989 Geoff Brabham	AUS	Nissan GTP ZX-T
1990 Geoff Brabham	AUS	Nissan GTP ZX-T/Nissan NPT-90
1991 Geoff Brabham	AUS	Nissan R90C/Nissan NPT-90/
		Nissan NPT-91
1992 Juan Manuel Fangio II	RA	Eagle Mk3-Toyota
1993 Juan Manuel Fangio II	RA	Eagle Mk3-Toyota
1994*Wayne Taylor	ZA	Kudzu-Mazda

*World Sports Cars

IMSA Lights

year	driver	nat	car
1985	Jim Downing	USA	Argo JM16B-Mazda
1986	Jim Downing	USA	Argo JM19-Mazda
1987	Jim Downing	USA	Argo JM19B-Mazda
1988	Tom Hessert	USA	Tiga GT286-Buick/Tiga GT286-Chevrolet/Tiga GT288-Buick
1989	Scott Schubot	USA	Spice SE88P-Buick
1990	Tomas Lopez	MEX	Spice SE90P-Buick
1991	Parker Johnstone	USA	Spice SE90P-Acura
1992	Parker Johnstone	USA	Spice SE91P-Acura
1993	Parker Johnstone	USA	Spice SE92P-Acura

Other IMSA Categories

	GTO		GTU		GTS	
year driver		nat	driver	nat	driver	nat
1971 Dave Heinz		USA	-		-	
1972 Phil Currin		USA	Hurley Haywood	USA	-	
1973 -			Bob Bergstrom	USA	-	
1974 -			Walt Maas	USA	-	
1975 -			Bob Sharp	USA	-	
1976 -			Brad Frisselle	USA	-	
1977 -			Walt Maas	USA	-	
1978 Dave Cowart		USA	Dave White	USA	-	
1979 Howard Meister		USA	Don Devendorf	USA	-	
1980 Luis Mendez		USA	Walt Bohren	USA	-	
1981 Dave Cowart		USA	Lee Mueller	USA	-	
1982 Don Devendorf		USA	Jim Downing	USA	-	
1983 Wayne Baker		USA	Roger Mandeville	USA	-	

GTO		GTU		GTS	
year driver	nat	driver	nat	driver	nat
1984 Roger Mandeville	USA	Jack Baldwin	USA	-	
1985 John Jones	CDN	Jack Baldwin	USA	-	
1986 Scott Pruett	USA	Tom Kendall	USA	-	
1987 Chris Cord	USA	Tom Kendall	USA	-	
1988 Scott Pruett	USA	Tom Kendall	USA	-	
1989 Pete Halsmer	USA	Bob Leitzinger	USA	-	
1990 Dorsey Schroeder	USA	Lance Stewart	USA	-	
1991 Pete Halsmer	USA	John Fergus	USA	-	
1992 Irv Hoerr	USA	David Loring	USA	Steve Millen	NZ
1993 Charles Morgan	USA	Butch Leitzinger	USA	Tom Kendall	USA
1994 Joe Pezza	USA	Jim Pace	USA	Steve Millen	NZ

Indy Lights

year	series sponsor	driver	nat	car
1986*		Fabrizio Barbazza	I	Wildcat 86A-Buick
1987*		Didier Theys	B	Wildcat 86A-Buick
1988*	HFC	Jon Beekhuis	USA	Wildcat 86A-Buick
1989*	HFC	Mike Groff	USA	Wildcat 86A-Buick
1990*	HFC	Paul Tracy	CDN	Wildcat 86A-Buick
1991	Firestone	Eric Bachelart	B	Wildcat 86A-Buick
1992	Firestone	Robbie Buhl	USA	Wildcat 86A-Buick
1993	Firestone	Bryan Herta	USA	Lola T93/20-Buick
1994	Firestone	Steve Robertson	GB	Lola T93/20-Buick

*known as American Racing Series

IMSA Barber-SAAB Pro-Series

year	driver	nat	car
1986	Willy Lewis	USA	Mondiale Barber-SAAB
1987	Ken Murillo	USA	Mondiale Barber-SAAB
1988	Bruce Feldman	USA	Mondiale Barber-SAAB
1989	Robbie Buhl	USA	Mondiale Barber-SAAB
1990	Rob Wilson	NZ	Mondiale Barber-SAAB
1991	Bryan Herta	USA	Mondiale Barber-SAAB
1992	Robert Amren	S	Mondiale Barber-SAAB
1993	Kenny Brack	S	Mondiale Barber-SAAB
1994	Diego Guzman	CO	Mondiale Barber-SAAB

International Race of Champions (IROC)

year	driver	nat	car
1974	Mark Donohue	USA	Porsche Carrera
1975	Bobby Unser	USA	Chevrolet Camaro
1976	AJ Foyt Jr	USA	Chevrolet Camaro
1977	AJ Foyt Jr	USA	Chevrolet Camaro
1978	Al Unser	USA	Chevrolet Camaro
1979	Mario Andretti	USA	Chevrolet Camaro
1980	Bobby Allison	USA	Chevrolet Camaro
1984	Cale Yarborough	USA	Chevrolet Camaro
1985	Harry Gant	USA	Chevrolet Camaro
1986	Al Unser Jr	USA	Chevrolet Camaro
1987	Geoff Bodine	USA	Chevrolet Camaro
1988	Al Unser Jr	USA	Chevrolet Camaro
1989	Terry Labonte	USA	Chevrolet Camaro
1990	Dale Earnhardt	USA	Dodge Daytona
1991	Rusty Wallace	USA	Dodge Daytona
1992	Ricky Rudd	USA	Dodge Daytona
1993	Davey Allison*	USA	Dodge Daytona
1994	Mark Martin	USA	Dodge Avenger

*Allison won the series posthumously, having been killed in a helicopter accident. Terry Labonte replaced him for the final race.

North American Formula 5000 Championship

year	driver	nat	car
1967*	Gus Hutchison	USA	Lotus 41-Chevrolet
1968*	Lou Sell	USA	Eagle-Chevrolet

year	driver	nat	car
1969*	Tony Adamowicz	USA	Eagle-Chevrolet
1970*	John Cannon	CDN	McLaren M10B-Chevrolet
1971*	David Hobbs	GB	McLaren M10B-Chevrolet
1972	Graham McRae	NZ	McRae GM1-Chevrolet
1973	Jody Scheckter	ZA	Trojan T101-Chevrolet/ Lola T330-Chevrolet
1974	Brian Redman	GB	Lola T332-Chevrolet
1975	Brian Redman	GB	Lola T332-Chevrolet/ Lola T400-Chevrolet
1976	Brian Redman	GB	Lola T332C-Chevrolet

*known as Formula A

North American Toyota Atlantic Championship (formerly Formula Atlantic)

year	division	driver	nat	car
1974		Bill Brack	CDN	Lotus 69-Ford
1975		Bill Brack	CDN	Chevron B29-Ford
1976		Gilles Villeneuve	CDN	March 76B-Ford
1977		Gilles Villeneuve	CDN	March 77B-Ford
1978		Howdy Holmes	USA	March 78B-Ford
1979		Tom Gloy	USA	Ralt RT1-Ford
1980		Jacques Villeneuve	CDN	March 80A-Ford
1981		Jacques Villeneuve	CDN	March 81A-Ford
1982		Dave McMillen	NZ	Ralt RT4-Ford
1983		Michael Andretti	USA	Ralt RT4-Ford
1984		Dan Marvin	USA	Ralt RT4-Ford
1985	Eastern	Michael Angus	USA	Ralt RT4-Ford
	Western	Jeff Wood	USA	Ralt RT4-Ford
1986	Eastern	Scott Goodyear	CDN	Ralt RT4-Ford
	Western	Ted Prappas	USA	Ralt RT4-Ford
1987	Eastern	Calvin Fish	GB	Ralt RT4-Ford
	Western	Johnny O'Connell	USA	Ralt RT4-Ford
1988	Eastern	Steve Shelton	USA	Swift DB4-Ford
	Western	Dean Hall	USA	Swift DB4-Ford
1989	Eastern	Jacko Cunningham	USA	Swift DB4-Ford
	Western	Hiro Matsushita	J	Swift DB4-Ford/ Swift DB4-Toyota
1990	Eastern	Brian Till	USA	Swift DB4-Toyota
	Western	Mark Dismore	USA	Swift DB4-Toyota
1991		Jovy Marcelo	RP	Swift DB4-Toyota
1992		Chris Smith	USA	Swift DB4-Toyota
1993		David Empringham	CDN	Ralt RT40-Toyota
1994		David Empringham	CDN	Ralt RT41-Toyota

SCCA Super Vee Championship

year	driver	nat	car
1971	Bill Scott	USA	Royale-Volkswagen
1972	Bill Scott	USA	Royale-Volkswagen
1973	Bertil Roos	S	Tui BH3-Volkswagen
1974	Elliott Forbes-Robinson	USA	Lola T320-Volkswagen
1975	Eddie Miller	USA	Lola T324-Volkswagen
1976	Tom Bagley	USA	Zink Z11-Volkswagen
1977	Bob Lazier	USA	Lola T324-Volkswagen
1978	Bill Alsup	USA	Argo JM2-Volkswagen
1979	Geoff Brabham	AUS	Ralt RT1-Volkswagen
1980	Peter Kuhn	USA	Ralt RT1-Volkswagen/ Ralt RT5-Volkswagen
1981	Al Unser Jr	USA	Ralt RT5-Volkswagen
1982	Michael Andretti	USA	Ralt RT5-Volkswagen
1983	Ed Pimm	USA	Ralt RT5-Volkswagen/ Anson SA4-Volkswagen
1984	Arie Luyendyk	NL	Ralt RT5-Volkswagen
1985	Ken Johnson	USA	Ralt RT5-Volkswagen
1986	Didier Theys	B	Martini MK47-Volkswagen/ Martini MK50-Volkswagen
1987	Scott Atchison	USA	Ralt RT5-Volkswagen
1988	Ken Murillo	USA	Ralt RT5-Volkswagen
1989	Mark Smith	USA	Ralt RT5-Volkswagen
1990	Stuart Crow	USA	Ralt RT5-Volkswagen

Trans-Am Championship

		DRIVERS' CHAMPIONSHIP			MANUFACTURERS' CHAMPIONSHIP
year	class	driver	nat	car	constructor
1966		Horst Kwech/Gaston Andrey	AUS/CH	Alfa Romeo GTA	Ford
1967		Jerry Titus	USA	Ford Mustang	Ford
1968		Mark Donohue	USA	Chevrolet Camaro	Chevrolet
1969		Mark Donohue	USA	Chevrolet Camaro	Chevrolet
1970		Parnelli Jones	USA	Ford Mustang	Ford
1971		Mark Donohue	USA	Ford Javelin	American Motors
1972		George Follmer	USA	Ford Javelin	American Motors
1973		Peter Gregg	USA	Porsche 911 Carrera RS	Chevrolet
1974		Peter Gregg	USA	Porsche 911 Carrera RS	Porsche
1975		John Greenwood	USA	Chevrolet Corvette	Chevrolet
1976	Overall	George Follmer	USA	Porsche 934 turbo	Porsche
	Class 1	George Follmer	USA	Porsche 934 turbo	-
	Class 2	Jocko Maggiacomo	USA	Ford Javelin	-
1977	Class 1	Bob Tullius	USA	Jaguar XJS	Porsche
	Class 2	Ludwig Heimrath	CDN	Porsche 934	Porsche
1978	Class 1	Bob Tullius	USA	Jaguar XJS	Jaguar
	Class 2	Greg Pickett	USA	Chevrolet Corvette	Chevrolet
1979	Class 1	Gene Bothello	USA	Chevrolet Corvette	Chevrolet
	Class 2	John Paul	USA	Porsche 935	Porsche
1980		John Bauer	USA	Porsche 911SC	Chevrolet
1981		Eppie Wietzes	CDN	Chevrolet Corvette	Chevrolet
1982		Elliott Forbes-Robinson	USA	Pontiac Trans-Am	Pontiac
1983		David Hobbs	GB	Chevrolet Camaro	Chevrolet
1984		Tom Gloy	USA	Ford Capri RS	Lincoln Mercury
1985		Wally Dallenbach Jr	USA	Ford Capri RS	Lincoln Mercury
1986		Wally Dallenbach Jr	USA	Chevrolet Camaro	Lincoln Mercury-Merkur
1987		Scott Pruett	USA	Mercury Merkur XR4Ti	Lincoln Mercury-Merkur
1988		Hurley Haywood	USA	Audi Quattro 200	Audi
1989		Dorsey Schroeder	USA	Ford Mustang	Ford
1990		Tom Kendall	USA	Chevrolet Beretta	Chevrolet
1991		Scott Sharp	USA	Chevrolet Corvette	Chevrolet
1992		Jack Baldwin	USA	Chevrolet Camaro Z28	Chevrolet
1993		Scott Sharp	USA	Chevrolet Camaro Z28	Chevrolet
1994		Scott Pruett	USA	Chevrolet Camaro Z28	Chevrolet

MAJOR INTERNATIONAL RACES

AMERICAN GRAND PRIZE

year	formula	circuit	winner	nat	car	mph
1908	GP	Savannah	Louis Wagner	F	Fiat	65.111
1910	GP	Savannah	David Bruce-Brown	USA	Benz	70.554
1911	Indycar	Savannah	David Bruce-Brown	USA	Fiat S74	74.458
1912	GP	Milwaukee	Caleb Bragg	USA	Fiat S74	68.396
1914	Indycar	Santa Monica	Eddie Pullen	USA	Mercer	77.324
1915	Indycar	San Francisco	Dario Resta	I	Peugeot EX3	56.000
1916	Indycar	Santa Monica	Howdy Wilcox/Johnny Aitken	USA	Peugeot EX5	85.723

UNITED STATES GRAND PRIX (also see Detroit and Dallas)

year	formula	circuit	winner	nat	car	mph
1958	SC	Riverside	Chuck Daigh	USA	Scarab	88.800
1959	F1 W	Sebring	Bruce McLaren	NZ	Cooper T45-Climax	98.827
1960	F1 W	Riverside	Stirling Moss	GB	Lotus 18-Climax	98.996
1961	F1 W	Watkins Glen	Innes Ireland	GB	Lotus 21-Climax	105.410
1962	F1 W	Watkins Glen	Jim Clark	GB	Lotus 25-Climax	110.835
1963	F1 W	Watkins Glen	Graham Hill	GB	BRM P57	111.288
1964	F1 W	Watkins Glen	Graham Hill	GB	BRM P261	113.515
1965	F1 W	Watkins Glen	Graham Hill	GB	BRM P261	110.312
1966	F1 W	Watkins Glen	Jim Clark	GB	Lotus 43-BRM	117.438
1967	F1 W	Watkins Glen	Jim Clark	GB	Lotus 49-Ford	123.584
1968	F1 W	Watkins Glen	Jackie Stewart	GB	Matra MS10-Ford	127.604
1969	F1 W	Watkins Glen	Jochen Rindt	A	Lotus 49B-Ford	129.108
1970	F1 W	Watkins Glen	Emerson Fittipaldi	BR	Lotus 72-Ford	129.549
1971	F1 W	Watkins Glen	François Cevert	F	Tyrrell 002-Ford	115.096
1972	F1 W	Watkins Glen	Jackie Stewart	GB	Tyrrell 005-Ford	117.483
1973	F1 W	Watkins Glen	Ronnie Peterson	S	Lotus 72D-Ford	118.055
1974	F1 W	Watkins Glen	Carlos Reutemann	RA	Brabham BT44-Ford	119.120
1975	F1 W	Watkins Glen	Niki Lauda	A	Ferrari 312T	116.098
1976	F1 W	Watkins Glen	James Hunt	GB	McLaren M23-Ford	116.427
1977	F1 W	Watkins Glen	James Hunt	GB	McLaren M26-Ford	100.978

year	formula	circuit	winner	nat	car	mph
1978	F1 W	Watkins Glen	Carlos Reutemann	RA	Ferrari 312T3	118.581
1979	F1 W	Watkins Glen	Gilles Villeneuve	CDN	Ferrari 312T4	106.456
1980	F1 W	Watkins Glen	Alan Jones	AUS	Williams FW07B-Ford	126.369
1989	F1 W	Phoenix	Alain Prost	F	McLaren MP4/5-Honda	87.370
1990	F1 W	Phoenix	Ayrton Senna	BR	McLaren MP4/5B-Honda	90.586
1991	F1 W	Phoenix	Ayrton Senna	BR	McLaren MP4/6-Honda	93.018

VANDERBILT CUP

year	formula	circuit	driver	nat	car	mph
1904	GP	Long Island	George Heath	USA	Panhard 70	52.223
1905	GP	Long Island	Victor Hémery	F	Darracq 80hp	61.492
1906	GP	Long Island	Louis Wagner	F	Darracq 120hp	61.434
1908	GP	Long Island	George Robertson	USA	Locomobile	64.380
1909	Indycar	Long Island	Harry Grant	USA	Alco	62.796
1910	Indycar	Long Island	Harry Grant	USA	Alco	65.181
1911	Indycar	Savannah	Ralph Mulford	USA	Lozier	74.076
1912	Indycar	Milwaukee	Ralph de Palma	USA	Mercedes	68.980
1914	Indycar	Santa Monica	Ralph de Palma	USA	Mercedes	75.500
1915	Indycar	San Francisco	Dario Resta	I	Peugeot EX3	66.400
1916	Indycar	Santa Monica	Dario Resta	I	Peugeot	87.155
1936*	Indycar	Roosevelt Raceway	Tazio Nuvolari	I	Alfa Romeo 12C-36	65.503
1937*	Indycar	Roosevelt Raceway	Bernd Rosemeyer	D	Auto Union C	82.234

WK Vanderbilt Cup except *George Vanderbilt Cup

MARLBORO CHALLENGE

year	formula	circuit	driver	nat	car	mph
1987	Indycar	Tamiami Park	Bobby Rahal	USA	Lola T87/00-Cosworth	108.782
1988	Indycar	Tamiami Park	Michael Andretti	USA	Lola T88/00-Cosworth	91.989
1989	Indycar	Laguna Seca	Al Unser Jr	USA	Lola T89/00-Chevrolet	105.580
1990	Indycar	Nazareth	Rick Mears	USA	Penske PC19-Chevrolet	153.484
1991	Indycar	Laguna Seca	Michael Andretti	USA	Lola T91/00-Chevrolet	105.455
1992	Indycar	Nazareth	Emerson Fittipaldi	BR	Penske PC21-Chevrolet	156.127

CIRCUITS AND OTHER RACES

ATLANTA INTERNATIONAL RACEWAY

Built in 1959 just outside Georgia's state capital, Atlanta is a high-banked (24-degree) super- speedway with the best viewing on the current NASCAR calendar. Although Indycars visited in the 1960s and late 1970s, Winston Cup races in March and the season finale in November are now the highlights of Atlanta's year.

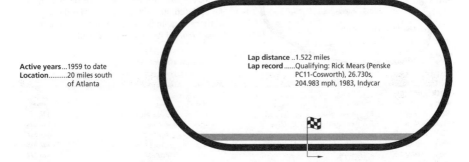

Active years...1959 to date
Location..........20 miles south of Atlanta

Lap distance ..1.522 miles
Lap record ......Qualifying: Rick Mears (Penske PC11-Cosworth), 26.730s, 204.983 mph, 1983, Indycar

Indycar race						
year	formula	winner		nat	car	mph
1965	Indycar	Johnny Rutherford		USA	Watson-Ford	143.807
1966	Indycar	Mario Andretti		USA	Brawner/Brabham-Ford	141.362
1978	Indycar	Rick Mears		USA	Penske PC6-Cosworth	143.286
1979	Indycar	Rick Mears		USA	Penske PC7-Cosworth	182.094
	Indycar	Johnny Rutherford		USA	McLaren M24B-Cosworth	157.758
	Indycar	Johnny Rutherford		USA	McLaren M24B-Cosworth	163.976
1981	Indycar	Rick Mears		USA	Penske PC9B-Cosworth	147.224
	Indycar	Rick Mears		USA	Penske PC9B-Cosworth	167.196
1982	Indycar	Rick Mears		USA	Penske PC10-Cosworth	164.750
1983	Indycar	Gordon Johncock		USA	Wildcat Mk9C-Cosworth	146.133

CAESARS PALACE

LAS VEGAS

Nowhere reflects the madness that afflicted Formula One in the United States during the 1980s as well as Caesars Palace Hotel and Casino in Las Vegas. Over two miles of racing circuit bordered by concrete barriers twisting through the car park – no visual landmarks and no atmosphere, just the new show in town. The organizers employed Long Beach promoter, Chris Pook, and used taxi drivers to bed in the new tarmac. The general reaction was that it was better than expected but Formula One lasted just two years. During this time Caesars Palace staged the final race of the championship and Nelson Piquet (1981) and Keke Rosberg (1982) claimed their first World Championship crowns here. The event switched to Indycars for the following season on a modified oval layout. Turns 1, 6 and 10 were combined to bypass the infield hairpins but Indycars soon moved on.

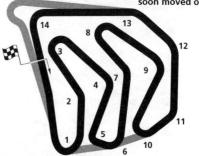

Active years...1981-84
Location..........The car park of Caesars Palace Hotel in central Las Vegas

GRAND PRIX CIRCUIT (1981-82)
Lap distance ..2.268 miles
Lap record......Michele Alboreto (Tyrrell 011-Ford), 1m19.639, 102.523 mph, 1982, F1

INDYCAR CIRCUIT (1983-84)
Lap distance ..1.125 miles
Lap record......Qualifying: Danny Sullivan (Lola T800-Cosworth), 39.952s, 101.372 mph, 1984, Indycar

Las Vegas Grand Prix

year	formula	winner	nat	car	mph
1981	F1 W	Alan Jones	AUS	Williams FW07C-Ford	97.992
1982	F1 W	Michele Alboreto	I	Tyrrell 011-Ford	100.110
1983	Indycar	Mario Andretti	USA	Lola T700-Cosworth	87.192
1984	Indycar	Tom Sneva	USA	March 84C-Cosworth	93.702

CHARLOTTE

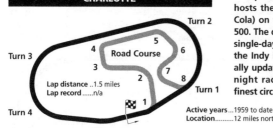

Turn 2

Turn 3

5
4
3
Road Course
6
7
2
8
Turn 1

Lap distance ..1.5 miles
Lap record......n/a

1

Turn 4

A superb high-banked superspeedway which hosts the World 600 (now sponsored by Coca-Cola) on the same weekend as the Indianapolis 500. The crowd for that race is the second largest single-day sporting attendance, beaten only by the Indy itself. The facilities have been continually updated, including new floodlights to allow night racing, making Charlotte arguably the finest circuit of its type in the World.

Active years...1959 to date
Location..........12 miles north of Charlotte, North Carolina

Coca Cola/World 600

year	formula	winner	nat	car	mph
1960	NASCAR	Joe Lee Johnson	USA	Chevrolet	107.735
1961	NASCAR	David Pearson	USA	Pontiac	111.633
1962	NASCAR	Nelson Stacey	USA	Ford	125.552
1963	NASCAR	Fred Lorenzen	USA	Ford	132.418
1964	NASCAR	Jim Paschal	USA	Plymouth	125.772
1965	NASCAR	Fred Lorenzen	USA	Ford	121.772
1966	NASCAR	Marvin Panch	USA	Plymouth	135.042
1967	NASCAR	Jim Paschal	USA	Plymouth	135.832
1968	NASCAR	Buddy Baker	USA	Dodge	104.207
1969	NASCAR	Lee Roy Yarborough	USA	Mercury	134.361
1970	NASCAR	Donnie Allison	USA	Ford	129.680
1971	NASCAR	Bobby Allison	USA	Mercury	140.442
1972	NASCAR	Buddy Baker	USA	Dodge	142.255
1973	NASCAR	Buddy Baker	USA	Dodge	134.890
1974	NASCAR	David Pearson	USA	Mercury	135.720
1975	NASCAR	Richard Petty	USA	Dodge	145.327
1976	NASCAR	David Pearson	USA	Mercury	137.352
1977	NASCAR	Richard Petty	USA	Dodge	137.676
1978	NASCAR	Darrell Waltrip	USA	Chevrolet	138.355

year	formula	winner	nat	car	mph
1979	NASCAR	Darrell Waltrip	USA	Chevrolet	136.674
1980	NASCAR	Benny Parsons	USA	Chevrolet	119.265
1981	NASCAR	Bobby Allison	USA	Buick	129.326
1982	NASCAR	Neil Bonnett	USA	Ford	130.058
1983	NASCAR	Neil Bonnett	USA	Chevrolet	140.707
1984	NASCAR	Bobby Allison	USA	Buick	129.233
1985	NASCAR	Darrell Waltrip	USA	Chevrolet	141.807
1986	NASCAR	Dale Earnhardt	USA	Chevrolet	140.406
1987	NASCAR	Kyle Petty	USA	Ford	131.483
1988	NASCAR	Darrell Waltrip	USA	Chevrolet	124.460
1989	NASCAR	Darrell Waltrip	USA	Chevrolet	144.077
1990	NASCAR	Rusty Wallace	USA	Pontiac	137.650
1991	NASCAR	Davey Allison	USA	Ford	138.951
1992	NASCAR	Dale Earnhardt	USA	Chevrolet	132.980
1993	NASCAR	Dale Earnhardt	USA	Chevrolet	145.504
1994	NASCAR	Jeff Gordon	USA	Chevrolet	139.450

CLEVELAND

BURKE LAKEFRONT AIRPORT

Indycars have visited the still-operational Burke Lakefront Airport in Cleveland on the shores of Lake Erie since 1982. Although an unattractive venue and unpopular with the drivers; the wide, bumpy runways allow numerous lines to be taken into the corners, surprisingly good racing and plenty of overtaking. Spectators can see almost all of this flat venue from the grandstands.

Active years...1982 to date
Location..........Burke Lakefront Airport, near Cleveland

1982-89

CURRENT CIRCUIT
Lap distance ..2.369 miles
Lap record ......Qualifying: Paul Tracy (Penske PC22-Chevrolet), 59.168s, 144.139 mph, 1993, Indycar

CIRCUIT CHANGES
1982-89 ....2.485 miles
1990 to date ....First corner bypassed. Current circuit

Cleveland Grand Prix

year	formula	winner	nat	car	mph
1982	Indycar	Bobby Rahal	USA	March 82C-Cosworth	101.438
1983	Indycar	Al Unser	USA	Penske PC11-Cosworth	108.421
1984	Indycar	Danny Sullivan	USA	Lola T800-Cosworth	118.974
1985	Indycar	Al Unser Jr	USA	Lola T900-Cosworth	124.331
1986	Indycar	Danny Sullivan	USA	March 86C-Cosworth	127.362
1987	Indycar	Emerson Fittipaldi	BR	March 87C-Chevrolet	128.703
1988	Indycar	Mario Andretti	USA	Lola T88/00-Chevrolet	124.546
1989	Indycar	Emerson Fittipaldi	BR	Penske PC18-Chevrolet	128.330
1990	Indycar	Danny Sullivan	USA	Penske PC19-Chevrolet	112.483
1991	Indycar	Michael Andretti	USA	Lola T91/00-Chevrolet	117.530
1992	Indycar	Emerson Fittipaldi	BR	Penske PC21-Chevrolet	133.292
1993	Indycar	Paul Tracy	CDN	Penske PC22-Chevrolet	127.913
1994	Indycar	Al Unser Jr	USA	Penske PC23-Ilmor	138.026

DAYTONA

The self-styled "World Center of Racing", Daytona Beach is the spiritual home of NASCAR, and is now headquarters to the organization. The season-opening Daytona 500 has been NASCAR's most prestigious event since the speedway opened in 1959. The first event could only be decided by a photo-finish three days after the event (Lee Petty's Oldsmobile declared the winner) and NASCAR's traditions of close racing continue today. In 1961 the road course using the infield road course and the banking was used for the Continental, a Sports Car race which developed into the 24-hour race in 1966. The dirt required to make the imposing 31-degree banking created the 44-acre Lake Lloyd in the infield.

Active years...1959 to date
Location..........Four miles from Atlantic Ocean in Daytona Beach, Florida, 45 miles north-east of Orlando, 90 miles south-east of Jacksonville

OVAL CIRCUIT
Active years...1959 to date
Lap distance ..2.5 miles
Lap record ......Qualifying: Bill Elliott (Ford Thunderbird) 42.783s, 210.364 mph, 1987, NASCAR

ROAD COURSE
Active years.........................1961 to date
Current lap distance ....3.560 miles
Lap record ......Qualifying: PJ Jones (Eagle Mk3-Toyota) 1m33.875, 136.521 mph, 1993, IMSA GTP

ROAD COURSE CIRCUIT CHANGES
1966-74 — 3.810 miles
1975-83 — Chicane inserted by Lake Lloyd. 3.840 miles
1984 — 3.870 miles
1985 to date — Current circuit

Daytona 24 hours

year	formula	winner	nat	car	mph
1966	SC W	Ken Miles/Lloyd Ruby	USA	Ford GT40 Mk2	107.388
1967	SC W	Lorenzo Bandini/Chris Amon	I/NZ	Ferrari 330P4	105.681
1968	SC W	Vic Elford/Jochen Neerpasch/Rolf Stommelen/Jo Siffert/Hans Herrmann	GB/D/D/CH/D	Porsche 907/8	106.697
1969	SC W	Mark Donohue/Chuck Parsons	USA	Lola T70 Mk3B-Chevrolet	99.267
1970	SC W	Pedro Rodriguez/Leo Kinnunen	MEX/SF	Porsche 917	114.866
1971	SC W	Pedro Rodriguez/Jackie Oliver	MEX/GB	Porsche 917K	109.203
1972*	SC W	Jacky Ickx/Mario Andretti	B/USA	Ferrari 312P	122.643
1973	SC W	Peter Gregg/Hurley Haywood	USA	Porsche 911 Carrera RS	106.274
1975	SC W	Peter Gregg/Hurley Haywood	USA	Porsche 911 Carrera RS	109.440
1976	SC	Peter Gregg/Brian Redman/John Fitzpatrick	USA/GB/GB	BMW 3.0 CSL	104.042
1977	SC W	John Graves/Hurley Haywood/Dave Helmick	USA	Porsche 911 Carrera RSR	108.801
1978	SC W	Rolf Stommelen/Toine Hezemans/Peter Gregg	D/NL/USA	Porsche 935	108.743
1979	SC W	Danny Ongais/Hurley Haywood/Ted Field	USA	Porsche 935	109.409
1980	SC W	Rolf Stommelen/Reinhold Jöst/Volkert Merl	D	Porsche 935	114.303
1981	SC W	Bob Garretson/Bobby Rahal/Brian Redman	USA/USA/GB	Porsche 935	113.153
1982	SC	John Paul/John Paul Jr/Rolf Stommelen	USA/USA/D	Porsche 935	114.794
1983	SC	Preston Henn/Bob Wollek/Claude Ballot-Lena/AJ Foyt Jr	USA/F/F/USA	Porsche 935	98.781
1984	SC	Sarel van der Merwe/Tony Martin/Graham Duxbury	ZA	March 83G-Porsche	103.119
1985	SC	AJ Foyt Jr/Bob Wollek/Al Unser/Thierry Boutsen	USA/F/USA/B	Porsche 962	104.162
1986	SC	Al Holbert/Derek Bell/Al Unser Jr	USA/GB/USA	Porsche 962	105.484
1987	SC	Chip Robinson/Derek Bell/Al Unser Jr/Al Holbert	USA/GB/USA/USA	Porsche 962	111.599
1988	SC	Martin Brundle/John Nielsen/Raul Boesel/Jan Lammers	GB/DK/BR/NL	Jaguar XJR-9	107.943
1989	SC	John Andretti/Derek Bell/Bob Wollek	USA/GB/F	Porsche 962	92.009
1990	SC	Davy Jones/Jan Lammers/Andy Wallace	USA/NL/GB	Jaguar XJR-12	112.857
1991	SC	"John Winter"/Frank Jelinski/Henri Pescarolo/Hurley Haywood/Bob Wollek	D/D/F/USA/F	Porsche 962	106.633
1992	SC	Masahiro Hasemi/Kazuyoshi Hoshino/Toshio Suzuki	J	Nissan R91CP	112.897
1993	SC	PJ Jones/Mark Dismore/Rocky Moran	USA	Eagle Mk3-Toyota	103.504
1994	SC	Scott Pruett/Paul Gentilozzi/Butch Leitzinger/Steve Millen	USA/USA/USA/NZ	Nissan 300ZX	104.800

*Six hour race

Other World Sports Car races

year	formula	winner	nat	car	mph
1964	SC W	Phil Hill/Pedro Rodriguez	USA/MEX	Ferrari 250GTO	98.303
1965	SC W	Ken Miles/Lloyd Ruby	USA	Ford GT40	100.050
1981	SC W	Roger Manderville/Amos Johnson	USA	Mazda RX-3	97.146

Daytona 500

year	formula	winner	nat	car	mph
1959	NASCAR	Lee Petty	USA	Oldsmobile	135.521
1960	NASCAR	Junior Johnson	USA	Chevrolet	124.740
1961	NASCAR	Marvin Panch	USA	Pontiac	149.601
1962	NASCAR	"Fireball" Roberts	USA	Pontiac	152.529
1963	NASCAR	Tiny Lund	USA	Ford	151.566
1964	NASCAR	Richard Petty	USA	Plymouth	154.334
1965	NASCAR	Fred Lorenzen	USA	Ford	141.539
1966	NASCAR	Richard Petty	USA	Plymouth	160.627
1967	NASCAR	Mario Andretti	USA	Ford	146.926
1968	NASCAR	Cale Yarborough	USA	Mercury	143.251
1969	NASCAR	Lee Roy Yarborough	USA	Ford	157.950
1970	NASCAR	Pete Hamilton	USA	Plymouth	149.601
1971	NASCAR	Richard Petty	USA	Plymouth	144.462
1972	NASCAR	AJ Foyt Jr	USA	Mercury	161.551
1973	NASCAR	Richard Petty	USA	Dodge	157.205
1974	NASCAR	Richard Petty	USA	Dodge	140.894
1975	NASCAR	Benny Parsons	USA	Chevrolet	153.649
1976	NASCAR	David Pearson	USA	Mercury	152.181
1977	NASCAR	Cale Yarborough	USA	Chevrolet	153.218
1978	NASCAR	Bobby Allison	USA	Ford	159.730
1979	NASCAR	Richard Petty	USA	Oldsmobile	143.977
1980	NASCAR	Buddy Baker	USA	Oldsmobile	177.602
1981	NASCAR	Richard Petty	USA	Buick	169.651
1982	NASCAR	Bobby Allison	USA	Buick	153.991
1983	NASCAR	Cale Yarborough	USA	Pontiac	155.979
1984	NASCAR	Cale Yarborough	USA	Chevrolet	150.994
1985	NASCAR	Bill Elliott	USA	Ford	172.265
1986	NASCAR	Geoff Bodine	USA	Chevrolet	148.124
1987	NASCAR	Bill Elliott	USA	Ford	176.263
1988	NASCAR	Bobby Allison	USA	Buick	137.531
1989	NASCAR	Darrell Waltrip	USA	Chevrolet	148.466
1990	NASCAR	Derrike Cope	USA	Chevrolet	165.761
1991	NASCAR	Ernie Irvan	USA	Chevrolet	148.148
1992	NASCAR	Davey Allison	USA	Ford	160.256

year	formula	winner		nat	car		mph
1993	NASCAR	Dale Jarrett		USA	Chevrolet		154.972
1994	NASCAR	Sterling Marlin		USA	Chevrolet		156.930
Indycar race							
year	formula	winner		nat	car		mph
1959	Indycar	Jim Rathmann		USA	Watson-Offenhauser		170.261

DENVER

A tight street circuit used twice by the Indycar circus, both races won by Al Unser Jr. The high altitude of Denver, Colorado posed particular problems for the teams, particularly for cooling and brakes. Unusually, the pits were on a corner.

Active years...1990-91
Location..........Central Denver
Lap distance ..1.900 miles

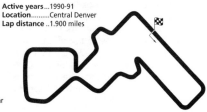

Lap record ......Qualifying: Michael Andretti (Lola T91/00-Chevrolet), 1m25.896, 79.631 mph, 1991, Indycar

Indycar race							
year	formula	winner		nat	car		mph
1990	CART	Al Unser Jr		USA	Lola T90/00-Chevrolet		71.243
1991	CART	Al Unser Jr		USA	Lola T91/00-Chevrolet		68.141

DETROIT

12 10 9 8
14 11
13
Turn 5 Bypassed 1983 7
6
15 5
Tunnel 16 4
17 19 3
18 20 2
1

Active years...1982-91
Location..........Central Detroit

CITY CENTRE STREET CIRCUIT

An unloved and bumpy street circuit which was replaced as the venue for the Detroit Grand Prix in 1992 by Belle Isle. Ayrton Senna was the acknowledged master when the race was a Formula 1 event but in 1989 the organisers switched to Indycars.

Lap distance ..2.493 miles (1982); 2.500 miles (1983-91)
Lap record ......Ayrton Senna (Lotus 99T-Honda) 1m40.464, 89.584 mph, 1987, F1

DETROIT

BELLE ISLE

The start of Indycar racing's road course season, Belle Isle has been the scene of the Detroit Grand Prix since it moved from the downtown circuit in 1992. A 14-turn temporary road course in parkland on an island across from Detroit, the capital of America's motor industry.

Active years...1992 to date
Location..........Belle Isle, in Detroit River
Lap distance ..2.100 miles

Lap record ......Qualifying: Nigel Mansell (Lola T94/00-Ford), 1m09.582, 108.649 mph, 1994, Indycar

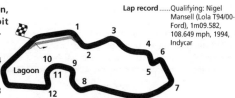

Detroit Grand Prix							
year	formula	winner		nat	car		mph
1982	F1 W	John Watson		GB	McLaren MP4/1B-Ford		78.140
1983	F1 W	Michele Alboreto		I	Tyrrell 011-Ford		81.158
1984	F1 W	Nelson Piquet		BR	Brabham BT53-BMW		81.679
1985	F1 W	Keke Rosberg		SF	Williams FW10-Honda		81.702
1986	F1 W	Ayrton Senna		BR	Lotus 98T-Renault		84.971
1987	F1 W	Ayrton Senna		BR	Lotus 99T-Honda		85.697
1988	F1 W	Ayrton Senna		BR	McLaren MP4/4-Honda		82.221
1989	Indycar	Emerson Fittipaldi		BR	Penske PC18-Chevrolet		76.112
1990	Indycar	Michael Andretti		USA	Lola T90/00-Chevrolet		84.902
1991	Indycar	Emerson Fittipaldi		BR	Penske PC20-Chevrolet		78.824
1992*	Indycar	Bobby Rahal		USA	Lola T92/00-Chevrolet		81.989
1993*	Indycar	Danny Sullivan		USA	Lola T93/00-Chevrolet		83.116
1994*	Indycar	Paul Tracy		CDN	Penske PC23-Ilmor		86.245

At Detroit city center except *Belle Isle

Racing Around the World

ELKHART LAKE

ROAD AMERICA

A 5.3-mile road course around Elkhart Lake was used between 1950-53 but when racing was outlawed on public roads in Wisconsin local businessmen built the new Road America circuit in the hills two miles east of the lake. It is the most picturesque and challenging road course in the United States, but suffers from changeable weather. It has provided some of Indycars surprise results, Hector Rebaque winning the inaugural event and Jacques Villeneuve (Gilles's brother) triumphing four years later. His nephew, Jacques junior, convincingly scored his first Indycar victory in 1994.

Active years...1955 to date
Location..........1.5 miles south-east of Elkhart Lake, 50 miles
north of Milwaukee

Lap distance ..4.000 miles
Lap record......Qualifying: Paul Tracy (Penske PC23-Ilmor),
1m45.416, 136.602 mph, 1994, Indycar

Road America Indycar race

year	formula	winner	nat	car	mph
1982	Indycar	Hector Rebaque	MEX	March 82C-Cosworth	109.156
1983	Indycar	Mario Andretti	USA	Lola T700-Cosworth	99.410
1984	Indycar	Mario Andretti	USA	Lola T800-Cosworth	116.347
1985	Indycar	Jacques Villeneuve	CDN	March 85C-Cosworth	114.066
1986	Indycar	Emerson Fittipaldi	BR	March 86C-Cosworth	81.833
1987	Indycar	Mario Andretti	USA	Lola T87/00-Chevrolet	120.155
1988	Indycar	Emerson Fittipaldi	BR	Lola T87/00-Chevrolet	122.215
1989	Indycar	Danny Sullivan	USA	Penske PC18-Chevrolet	122.803
1990	Indycar	Michael Andretti	USA	Lola T90/00-Chevrolet	106.192
1991	Indycar	Michael Andretti	USA	Lola T91/00-Chevrolet	126.205
1992	Indycar	Emerson Fittipaldi	BR	Penske PC21-Chevrolet	110.656
1993	Indycar	Paul Tracy	CDN	Penske PC22-Chevrolet	118.408
1994	Indycar	Jacques Villeneuve (Jr)	CDN	Reynard 94I-Ford	114.634

Road America World Sports Car race

year	formula	winner	nat	car	mph
1981	SC W	Rolf Stommelen/Harald Grohs	D	Porsche 935	105.415

FAIR PARK

DALLAS

A one-off event held in 100-degree heat in July 1984. The track surface disintegrated as the meeting progressed but against the odds the Grand Prix was an exciting affair with Keke Rosberg eventually scoring his only win of the year. Nigel Mansell had qualified on pole but ended the race in a state of collapse after trying to push his broken Lotus across the finish line. It was also memorable as the only race in which Osella scored points.

Lap distance ..2.424 miles
Lap record......Niki Lauda (McLaren MP4/2-
TAG Porsche) 1m45.353,
82.830 mph, 1984, F1

Active years...1984 (used once)
Location..........Central Dallas

Dallas Grand Prix

year	formula	winner	nat	car	mph
1984	F1 W	Keke Rosberg	SF	Williams FW09-Honda	80.283

INDIANAPOLIS MOTOR SPEEDWAY

The Indianapolis 500, the world's greatest race watched by the world's largest one-day sporting crowd. Like the Le Mans 24 hours, Indy is bigger than the series of which it is a part. The Indianapolis 500 was the only race held at the speedway since 1916 until the NASCAR Brickyard 400 in 1994. Today, as ever, the Indianapolis Motor Speedway remains at the heart of Indycar racing and its politics, with circuit president, Tony

George, threatening a breakaway championship. Speedway owner Carl Fisher decided to use bricks to pave the circuit earning the nickname, the Brickyard. Indianapolis has always attracted overseas interest, Frenchman Jules Goux won the third race with help of a bottle or two of fine champagne, Jim Clark and Graham Hill both won in the 1960s while Holland's Arie Luyendyk scored his first Indycar win here. They say that there are two types of Indianapolis drivers - those who have hit the wall, and those who are going to hit the wall.

INDIANAPOLIS

Active years...1909 to date
Location..........Six miles east of central Indianapolis
Lap distance ..2.5 miles
Lap record ......Race: Michael Andretti (Lola T90/00-Ford) 39.218s,
229.488 mph, 1990, Indycars
Qualifying: Roberto Guerrero (Lola T92/00-Buick)
38.690s, 232.619 mph, 1992, Indycars

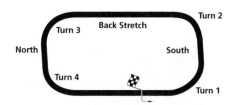

Indianapolis 500 see page 308

Other Indycar races

year	formula	winner	nat	car	mph
1909	Indycar	Bob Burman	USA	Buick	53.772
	Indycar	Louis Strang	USA	Buick	64.739
	Indycar	Leigh Lynch	USA	Jackson	57.983
1910	Indycar	Tom Kincaid	USA	National	71.669
	Indycar	Ray Harroun	USA	Marmon	72.058
	Indycar	Ray Harroun	USA	Marmon	70.551
	Indycar	Bob Burman	USA	Marquette-Buick	74.447
	Indycar	Joe Dawson	USA	Marmon	73.468
	Indycar	Eddie Hearne	USA	Benz	75.030
	Indycar	Howdy Wilcox	USA	National	72.238
	Indycar	Eddie Hearne	USA	Benz	78.851
	Indycar	Johnny Aitken	USA	National	71.466
1916	Indycar	Johnny Aitken	USA	Peugeot	89.440

Brickyard 400

year	formula	winner	nat	car	mph
1994	NASCAR	Jeff Gordon	USA	Chevrolet Lumina	131.932

LAGUNA SECA

Laguna Seca is built in the mountains of California's Monterey peninsula at the US Army base of Fort Ord. Laguna is great for spectators and a true challenge for drivers, with its striking elevation change and the aptly named Corkscrew – the plunging left-right esses at the top of the course. In 1988 a new section was opened across the infield lake after Turn 1, now a downhill hairpin. Both IMSA and Indycars have been regular visitors here with Bobby Rahal almost unbeatable early in his Indycar career.

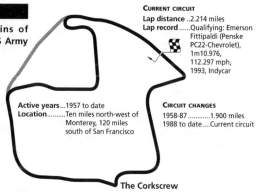

CURRENT CIRCUIT
Lap distance ..2.214 miles
Lap record ......Qualifying: Emerson Fittipaldi (Penske PC22-Chevrolet), 1m10.976, 112.297 mph, 1993, Indycar

Active years...1957 to date
Location..........Ten miles north-west of Monterey, 120 miles south of San Francisco

CIRCUIT CHANGES
1958-87 ....1.900 miles
1988 to date ....Current circuit

The Corkscrew

Monterey Grand Prix

year	formula	winner	nat	car	mph
1964	SC	Roger Penske	USA	Chaparral-Chevrolet	93.850
1965	SC	Walt Hansgen	USA	Lola T70-Chevrolet	97.310
1966	Can-Am	Phil Hill	USA	Chaparral 2E-Chevrolet	98.040
1967	Can-Am	Bruce McLaren	NZ	McLaren M6A-Chevrolet	101.613
1968	Can-Am	John Cannon	CDN	McLaren M1B-Oldsmobile	85.600
1969	Can-Am	Bruce McLaren	NZ	McLaren M8B-Chevrolet	105.830
1970	Can-Am	Denny Hulme	NZ	McLaren M8D-Chevrolet	106.071
1971	Can-Am	Peter Revson	USA	McLaren M8F-Chevrolet	109.210
1972	Can-Am	George Follmer	USA	Porsche 917/10	108.794
1973	F5000	Jody Scheckter	ZA	Trojan T101-Chevrolet	111.620
1974	F5000	Brian Redman	GB	Lola T332-Chevrolet	112.418
1975	F5000	Mario Andretti	USA	Lola T332-Chevrolet	114.167
1976	SC	Jim Busby	USA	Porsche 911 Carrera RSR	93.961
1977	SC	David Hobbs	GB	BMW 320i turbo	98.533
1978	Can-Am	Al Holbert	USA	Lola T333CS-Chevrolet	112.595
1979	Can-Am	Bobby Rahal	USA	Prophet/Lola-Chevrolet	113.211
1980	Can-Am	Al Unser	USA	Frissbee GR3-Chevrolet	108.728
1981	Can-Am	Teo Fabi	I	March 817-Chevrolet	115.895
1982	Can-Am	Al Unser Jr	USA	Frissbee GR3-Chevrolet	114.151
1983	Indycar	Teo Fabi	I	March 83C-Cosworth	106.943

year	formula	winner	nat	car	mph
1984	Indycar	Bobby Rahal	USA	March 84C-Cosworth	119.105
1985	Indycar	Bobby Rahal	USA	March 85C-Cosworth	112.923
1986	Indycar	Bobby Rahal	USA	March 86C-Cosworth	119.693
1987	Indycar	Bobby Rahal	USA	Lola T87/00-Cosworth	118.879
1988	Indycar	Danny Sullivan	USA	Penske PC17-Chevrolet	94.090
1989	Indycar	Rick Mears	USA	Penske PC18-Chevrolet	94.174
1990	Indycar	Danny Sullivan	USA	Penske PC19-Chevrolet	103.556
1991	Indycar	Michael Andretti	USA	Lola T91/00-Chevrolet	103.604
1992	Indycar	Michael Andretti	USA	Lola T92/00-Ford	99.996
1993	Indycar	Paul Tracy	CDN	Penske PC22-Chevrolet	106.303
1994	Indycar	Paul Tracy	CDN	Penske PC23-Ilmor	92.978

LONG BEACH

Long Beach has been transformed from being down-at-heel and seedy to being a thriving modern town since the race started in 1975. After a trial race for Formula 5000, race promoter Chris Pook attracted the F1 World Championship to the United States Grand Prix West (a cumbersome title which soon changed). Clay Regazzoni walked away with that race but was grievously injured four years later. Since the race switched to Indycars as F1 became more expensive it has been dominated by the Andretti family (Mario had already won in a Formula 1 car) and Al Unser Jr whose five wins include four consecutive victories. City redevelopment has gradually shortened the course, so that it is now essentially two parallel straights joined by twisting "Mickey Mouse" sections at each end. Long Beach remains a crowd-puller and the popularity of Grand Prix racing in North America began to fade when the race was lost to Indycars.

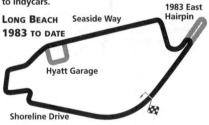

LONG BEACH 1983 TO DATE — Seaside Way, 1983 East Hairpin, Hyatt Garage, Shoreline Drive

LONG BEACH 1975-81 — Shoreline Drive, Pine Avenue, Finish, Start, Linden Avenue, Ocean Boulevard

LONG BEACH 1982 — Finish, Ocean Boulevard, Shoreline Drive, Start

Active years...1975 to date
Location..........Central Long Beach

CURRENT CIRCUIT
Lap distance ..1.590 miles
Lap record ......Qualifying: Paul Tracy (Penske PC23-Ilmor), 52.708s, 108.598 mph, 1994, Indycar

CIRCUIT CHANGES
1975-81 ....2.020 miles
1982 ....West hairpin bypassed and a kink introduced on Shoreline Drive at Linden. 2.130 miles
1983 ....Old start straight no longer used, Seaside Way used, east hairpin shortened, start moved to Shoreline. 2.035 miles
1984-91 ....East hairpin moved away from Ocean. 1.670 miles
1992 to date ....Hyatt Garage bypassed. Current circuit

Long Beach Grand Prix					
year	formula	winner	nat	car	mph
1975	F5000	Brian Redman	GB	Lola T332-Chevrolet	86.324
1976	F1 W	Clay Regazzoni	CH	Ferrari 312T	85.572
1977	F1 W	Mario Andretti	USA	Lotus 78-Ford	86.889
1978	F1 W	Carlos Reutemann	RA	Ferrari 312T3	87.096
1979	F1 W	Gilles Villeneuve	CDN	Ferrari 312T4	88.356
1980	F1 W	Nelson Piquet	BR	Brabham BT49-Ford	88.448
1981	F1 W	Alan Jones	AUS	Williams FW07C-Ford	88.144
1982	F1 W	Niki Lauda	A	McLaren MP4/1B-Ford	81.479
1983	F1 W	John Watson	GB	McLaren MP4/1C-Ford	80.625
1984	Indycar	Mario Andretti	USA	Lola T800-Cosworth	82.894
1985	Indycar	Mario Andretti	USA	Lola T900-Cosworth	87.694
1986	Indycar	Michael Andretti	USA	March 86C-Cosworth	80.965
1987	Indycar	Mario Andretti	USA	Lola T87/00-Chevrolet	85.333
1988	Indycar	Al Unser Jr	USA	March 88C-Chevrolet	83.655
1989	Indycar	Al Unser Jr	USA	Lola T89/00-Chevrolet	85.503
1990	Indycar	Al Unser Jr	USA	Lola T90/00-Chevrolet	84.227
1991	Indycar	Al Unser Jr	USA	Lola T91/00-Chevrolet	81.195

year	formula	winner	nat	car	mph
1992	Indycar	Danny Sullivan	USA	Galmer G92-Chevrolet	91.945
1993	Indycar	Paul Tracy	CDN	Penske PC22-Chevrolet	93.089
1994	Indycar	Al Unser Jr	USA	Penske PC23-Ilmor	99.283

MEADOWLANDS

During the 1980s Formula One and then Indycars searched for a venue in New York City, suggestions ranging from Central Park to Flushing Meadow; the temporary circuit in the grounds of the Meadowlands Sports Arena was an unsatisfactory compromise. Despite being close to downtown Manhattan the race never attracted a worthwhile crowd and the circuit was unpopular with almost everybody. A change to a "modified" oval failed to save the race from disappearing from the calendar in 1992.

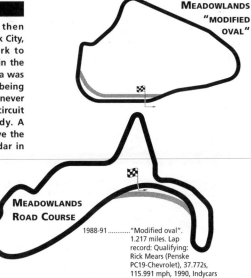

MEADOWLANDS "MODIFIED OVAL"

MEADOWLANDS ROAD COURSE

Active years...1984-91
Location..........Meadowlands Sports Arena, East Rutherford, New Jersey

CIRCUIT CHANGES

1984-87 ....Road Course. 1.682 miles. Lap record: Qualifying: Michael Andretti, 1m00.535, 100.028 mph, (March 86C-Cosworth), 1986, Indycar

1988-91 ...."Modified oval". 1.217 miles. Lap record: Qualifying: Rick Mears (Penske PC19-Chevrolet), 37.772s, 115.991 mph, 1990, Indycars

Indycar race

year	formula	winner	nat	car	mph
1984	Indycar	Mario Andretti	USA	Lola T800-Cosworth	80.742
1985	Indycar	Al Unser Jr	USA	Lola T900-Cosworth	90.167
1986	Indycar	Danny Sullivan	USA	March 86C-Cosworth	92.340
1987	Indycar	Bobby Rahal	USA	Lola T87/00-Cosworth	86.032
1988	Indycar	Al Unser Jr	USA	March 88C-Chevrolet	99.352
1989	Indycar	Bobby Rahal	USA	Lola T89/00-Cosworth DFS	81.863
1990	Indycar	Michael Andretti	USA	Lola T90/00-Chevrolet	97.291
1991	Indycar	Bobby Rahal	USA	Lola T91/00-Chevrolet	95.551

MIAMI

GP CIRCUIT

Active years...1983 to date
Location..........Downtown Miami
Lap distance ..1.873 miles
Lap record .....Davy Jones (Jaguar XJR-14) 1m05.402, 103.098 mph, 1992, SC Sports Cars

Biscayne Blvd

*Direction Changing for 1995 Race

GRAND PRIX CIRCUIT

The Miami Grand Prix was traditionally a highlight of the IMSA GTP Championship but the circuit has switched to Indycars since an interim Trans-Am race in 1994. For the 1995 race, the circuit direction is reversed to clockwise to eliminate the bottleneck at what was Turn 1. Promoter Ralph Sanchez plans a long-term move to a purpose built oval/road course complex currently being planned for the neighbouring Homestead district.

Miami Grand Prix

year	formula	winner	nat	car	mph
1983	IMSA SC	Al Holbert	USA	March 83G-Chevrolet	55.417
1984	IMSA SC	Brian Redman/Doc Bundy	GB/USA	Jaguar XJR-5	72.623
1985	IMSA SC	Al Holbert/Derek Bell	USA/GB	Porsche 962	68.342
1986	IMSA SC	Bob Wollek/Paolo Barilla	F/I	Porsche 962	79.309
1987	IMSA SC	Geoff Brabham/Elliott Forbes-Robinson	AUS/USA	Nissan GTP ZX-T	82.927
1988	IMSA SC	Price Cobb/James Weaver	USA/GB	Porsche 962	77.203
1989	IMSA SC	Geoff Brabham/Chip Robinson	AUS/USA	Nissan GTP ZX-T	81.358
1990	IMSA SC	Geoff Brabham/Chip Robinson/Bob Earl	AUS/USA/USA	Nissan GTP ZX-T	82.426
1991	IMSA SC	Raul Boesel	BR	Jaguar XJR-10	84.470
1992	IMSA SC	Geoff Brabham	AUS	Nissan NPT92	92.040
1993	IMSA SC	Juan Manuel Fangio II	RA	Eagle Mk3-Toyota	88.632
1994	Trans-Am	Tom Kendall	USA	Ford Mustang	68.760

Racing Around the World

MIAMI

TAMIAMI PARK

The previous attempt to establish Indycars in Miami was on a temporary road course laid out in the suburban Tamiami Park. It had neither the character nor the attendance of the spring IMSA race downtown and floundered after four years. The 1988 Marlboro Challenge, however, was a titanic duel between Al Unser Jr and eventual winner Michael Andretti, ending on the penultimate lap when Unser crashed while trying to repass Andretti on the damp track.

Active years...1985-88
Location..........Suburbs of Miami
Lap distance ..1.784 miles
Lap record......Qualifying: Danny Sullivan (Penske PC17-Chevrolet), 55.062s, 116.639 mph, 1988, Indycar

Marlboro Challenge see above

Miami Indycar race

year	formula	winner	nat	car	mph
1985	Indycar	Danny Sullivan	USA	March 85C-Cosworth	95.915
1986	Indycar	Al Unser Jr	USA	Lola T86/00-Cosworth	106.322
1987	Indycar	Michael Andretti	USA	March 87C-Cosworth	94.873
1988	Indycar	Al Unser Jr	USA	March 88C-Chevrolet	101.471

MICHIGAN INTERNATIONAL SPEEDWAY

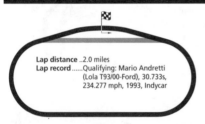

Lap distance ..2.0 miles
Lap record......Qualifying: Mario Andretti (Lola T93/00-Ford), 30.733s, 234.277 mph, 1993, Indycar

Active years...1968 to date
Location..........Irish Hills, Michigan, 45 miles south-east of Ann Arbor, 65 miles west of Detroit

Michigan International Speedway holds the only 500-mile Indycar race other than Indianapolis itself. The track surface is rough despite being resurfaced in 1986, and MIS has a reputation for breaking cars and being dangerous. Quicker than Indy due to the high banking (18 degrees), spectators can see the whole circuit from the grandstands. Designed by Charlie Moneypenny, who was also responsible for Daytona, and now owned by Roger Penske. A 3.31-mile Grand Prix course was used for two years until MIS concentrated on staging oval events. Stirling Moss was the Director of Road Racing when MIS opened.

Michigan 500

year	formula	winner	nat	car	mph
1981	Indycar	Pancho Carter	USA	Penske PC7-Cosworth	132.890
1982	Indycar	Gordon Johncock	USA	Wildcat Mk8B-Cosworth	153.925
1983	Indycar	John Paul Jr	USA	Penske PC10-Cosworth	134.862
1984	Indycar	Mario Andretti	USA	Lola T800-Cosworth	133.482
1985	Indycar	Emerson Fittipaldi	BR	March 85C-Cosworth	128.220
1986	Indycar	Johnny Rutherford	USA	March 86C-Cosworth	137.140
1987	Indycar	Michael Andretti	USA	March 87C-Cosworth	171.493
1988	Indycar	Danny Sullivan	USA	Penske PC17-Chevrolet	180.654
1989	Indycar	Michael Andretti	USA	Lola T89/00-Chevrolet	160.210
1990	Indycar	Al Unser Jr	USA	Lola T90/00-Chevrolet	189.727
1991	Indycar	Rick Mears	USA	Penske PC20-Chevrolet	167.230
1992	Indycar	Scott Goodyear	CDN	Lola T92/00-Chevrolet	177.625
1993	Indycar	Nigel Mansell	GB	Lola T93/00-Ford	188.203
1994	Indycar	Scott Goodyear	CDN	Lola T94/00-Ford	159.800

Other Indycar races

year	formula	winner	nat	car	mph
1968	Indycar	Ronnie Bucknum	USA	Eagle 68-Drake/Offenhauser	161.812
1970	Indycar	Gary Bettenhausen	USA	Gerhardt-Drake/Offenhauser	140.625
1971	Indycar	Mark Donohue	USA	McLaren M16A-Drake/Offenhauser	146.074
1972	Indycar	Joe Leonard	USA	Parnelli-Offenhauser	139.316
1973	Indycar	Roger McCluskey	USA	McLaren M16B-Offenhauser	161.146
	Indycar	Bill Vukovich Jr	USA	Eagle 73-Offenhauser	134.026
	Indycar	Johnny Rutherford	USA	McLaren M16C-Offenhauser	157.243
1974	Indycar	Bobby Unser	USA	Eagle 74-Offenhauser	141.717
	Indycar	Al Unser	USA	Eagle 74-Offenhauser	142.141
1975	Indycar	AJ Foyt Jr	USA	Coyote-Foyt/Ford	158.907
	Indycar	Tom Sneva	USA	McLaren M16C-Offenhauser	176.160
1976	Indycar	Gordon Johncock	USA	Wildcat-DGS/Offenhauser	165.033
	Indycar	AJ Foyt Jr	USA	Coyote-Foyt/Ford	164.068

year	formula	winner	nat	car	mph
1977	Indycar	Danny Ongais	USA	Parnelli VPJ6B-Cosworth	149.152
	Indycar	Gordon Johncock	USA	Wildcat-DGS/Offenhauser	175.250
1978	Indycar	Johnny Rutherford	USA	McLaren M24B-Cosworth	159.941
	Indycar	Danny Ongais	USA	Parnelli VPJ6B-Cosworth	146.246
1979	Indycar	Bobby Unser	USA	Penske PC7-Cosworth	n/a
	Indycar	Gordon Johncock	USA	Penske PC6-Cosworth	170.976
	Indycar	Bobby Unser	USA	Penske PC7-Cosworth	155.342
1980	Indycar	Johnny Rutherford	USA	Chaparral 2K-Cosworth	148.515
	Indycar	Mario Andretti	USA	Penske PC9-Cosworth	167.494
1981	Indycar	Rick Mears	USA	Penske PC9B-Cosworth	125.957
1982	Indycar	Bobby Rahal	USA	March 82C-Cosworth	140.515
1983	Indycar	Rick Mears	USA	Penske PC10B-Cosworth	182.325
1984	Indycar	Mario Andretti	USA	Lola T800-Cosworth	168.523
1985	Indycar	Bobby Rahal	USA	March 85C-Cosworth	163.657
1986	Indycar	Bobby Rahal	USA	March 86C-Cosworth	181.701

MID-OHIO

Active years...1962 to date
Location..........50 miles north-east of Columbus, 80 miles south-west of Cleveland

The Mid-Ohio Sports Car Course is a pristine and demanding road course set in undulating countryside near Lexington, Ohio. It suffers from being too narrow but has been a regular autumn Indycar race since it was bought by the late Jim Trueman (owner of the championship-winning Truesports team) in the early 1980s. Teo Fabi scored Porsche's only Indycar win here in 1989.

Carousel
Chute
Jump
Esses
1
Chicane
Keyhole
Speed Trap

CURRENT CIRCUIT
Lap distance ..2.250 miles
Lap record ......Qualifying: Al Unser Jr (Penske PC23-Ilmor), 1m07.773, 119.517 mph, 1994, Indycar

CIRCUIT CHANGES
1962-89 ....2.400 miles
1990 to date ....Current circuit

Indycar race

year	formula	winner	nat	car	mph
1980	Indycar	Johnny Rutherford	USA	Chaparral 2K-Cosworth	86.601
1983	Indycar	Teo Fabi	I	March 83C-Cosworth	99.297
1984	Indycar	Mario Andretti	USA	Lola T800-Cosworth	100.939
1985	Indycar	Bobby Rahal	USA	March 85C-Cosworth	107.628
1986	Indycar	Bobby Rahal	USA	March 86C-Cosworth	103.998
1987	Indycar	Roberto Guerrero	USA	March 87C-Cosworth	108.021
1988	Indycar	Emerson Fittipaldi	BR	Lola T87/00-Chevrolet	90.062
1989	Indycar	Teo Fabi	I	March 89P-Porsche	105.395
1990	Indycar	Michael Andretti	USA	Lola T90/00-Chevrolet	86.160
1991	Indycar	Michael Andretti	USA	Lola T91/00-Chevrolet	100.265
1992	Indycar	Emerson Fittipaldi	BR	Penske PC21-Chevrolet	107.864
1993	Indycar	Emerson Fittipaldi	BR	Penske PC22-Chevrolet	102.704
1994	Indycar	Al Unser Jr	USA	Penske PC23-Ilmor	109.079

MILWAUKEE

Active years...1903 to date
Lap distance ..1.0 mile

WISCONSIN STATE FAIR PARK

The oldest permanent racing circuit in the world, its first race on 11 September 1903 was four years before Brooklands opened. Set in the heart of America's brewery town, the Wisconsin State Fair Park is a lightly-banked (9-degrees), bumpy short oval. It now traditionally holds its race the week after Indy. Paved following the August 1953 event. Both Jim Clark (1963) and Nigel Mansell (1993) scored their first oval wins here.

Lap record ......Qualifying: Raul Boesel (Lola T93/00-Ford), 21.719s, 165.755 mph, 1993, Indycar

Indycar races

year	formula	winner	nat	car	mph
1912	Indycar	Ralph de Palma	USA	Mercedes	68.962
	Indycar	Bill Endicott	USA	Mason	55.699
	Indycar	Mortimer Roberts	USA	Mason	58.799

year	formula	winner	nat	car	mph
1939	Indycar	Babe Stapp	USA	Stevens-Miller	83.663
1941	Indycar	Rex Mays	USA	Stevens-Winfield	82.248
1946	Indycar	Rex Mays	USA	Stevens-Winfield	84.814
1947	Indycar	Bill Holland	USA	Wetteroth-Offenhauser	87.280
	Indycar	Charles van Acker	USA	Stevens-Offenhauser	85.960
	Indycar	Ted Horn	USA	Horn-Offenhauser	84.336
1948	Indycar	Emil Andres	USA	Kurtis-Offenhauser	85.320
	Indycar	Johnny Mantz	USA	Kurtis-Offenhauser	85.327
	Indycar	Myron Fohr	USA	Marchese-Offenhauser	86.734
	Indycar	Tony Bettenhausen	USA	Marchese-Offenhauser	86.734
1949	Indycar	Myron Fohr	USA	Marchese-Offenhauser	83.615
	Indycar	Johnnie Parsons	USA	Kurtis-Offenhauser	85.817
1950	Indycar	Tony Bettenhausen	USA	Wetteroth-Offenhauser	85.027
	Indycar	Walt Faulkner	USA	Kurtis KK2000-Offenhauser	87.315
1951	Indycar	Tony Bettenhausen	USA	Kurtis-Offenhauser	90.041
	Indycar	Walt Faulkner	USA	Kuzma-Offenhauser	91.342
1952	Indycar	Mike Nazaruk	USA	Kurtis-Offenhauser	92.255
	Indycar	Chuck Stevenson	USA	Kurtis KK4000-Offenhauser	81.392
1953	Indycar	Jack McGrath	USA	Kurtis KK4000-Offenhauser	93.634
	Indycar	Chuck Stevenson	USA	Kuzma-Offenhauser	89.580
1954	Indycar	Chuck Stevenson	USA	Kuzma-Offenhauser	97.527
	Indycar	Manuel Ayulo	USA	Kuzma-Offenhauser	96.261
1955	Indycar	Johnny Thomson	USA	Kuzma-Offenhauser	98.844
	Indycar	Pat Flaherty	USA	Kurtis KK500B-Offenhauser	95.033
1956	Indycar	Pat Flaherty	USA	Watson-Offenhauser	98.847
	Indycar	Jimmy Bryan	USA	Kuzma-Offenhauser	92.733
1957	Indycar	Rodger Ward	USA	Lesovsky-Offenhauser	97.789
	Indycar	Jim Rathmann	USA	Epperly-Offenhauser	98.134
1958	Indycar	Art Bisch	USA	Kuzma-Offenhauser	94.013
	Indycar	Rodger Ward	USA	Lesovsky-Offenhauser	97.809
1959	Indycar	Johnny Thomson	USA	Lesovsky-Offenhauser	98.609
	Indycar	Rodger Ward	USA	Watson-Offenhauser	96.317
1960	Indycar	Rodger Ward	USA	Watson-Offenhauser	99.465
	Indycar	Len Sutton	USA	Watson-Offenhauser	100.131
1961	Indycar	Rodger Ward	USA	Watson-Offenhauser	103.860
	Indycar	Lloyd Ruby	USA	Watson-Offenhauser	101.638
1962	Indycar	AJ Foyt Jr	USA	Watson Trevis-Offenhauser	100.860
	Indycar	Rodger Ward	USA	Watson-Offenhauser	100.015
1963	Indycar	Rodger Ward	USA	Watson-Offenhauser	100.585
	Indycar	Jim Clark	GB	Lotus 29-Ford	104.452
1964	Indycar	AJ Foyt Jr	USA	Watson-Offenhauser	100.346
	Indycar	Parnelli Jones	USA	Lotus 34-Ford	104.751
1965	Indycar	Parnelli Jones	USA	Kuzma/Lotus 34-Offenhauser	101.747
	Indycar	Joe Leonard	USA	Hallibrand-Ford	97.277
	Indycar	Gordon Johncock	USA	Gerhardt-Offenhauser	100.453
1966	Indycar	Mario Andretti	USA	Brawner/Brabham-Ford	95.655
	Indycar	Mario Andretti	USA	Brawner/Brabham-Ford	104.060
1967	Indycar	Gordon Johncock	USA	Gerhardt-Ford	98.643
	Indycar	Mario Andretti	USA	Brawner/Hawk-Ford	105.386
1968	Indycar	Lloyd Ruby	USA	Mongoose-Drake/Offenhauser	100.739
	Indycar	Lloyd Ruby	USA	Mongoose-Drake/Offenhauser	108.735
1969	Indycar	Art Pollard	USA	Gerhardt-Drake/Offenhauser	112.156
	Indycar	Al Unser	USA	Lola T152-Ford	106.758
1970	Indycar	Joe Leonard	USA	Colt 70-Ford	108.299
	Indycar	Al Unser	USA	Colt 70-Ford	114.304
1971	Indycar	Al Unser	USA	Colt 71-Ford	114.912
	Indycar	Bobby Unser	USA	Eagle 71-Drake/Offenhauser	109.384
1972	Indycar	Bobby Unser	USA	Eagle 72-Offenhauser	109.131
	Indycar	Joe Leonard	USA	Parnelli-Offenhauser	111.652
1973	Indycar	Bobby Unser	USA	Eagle 73-Offenhauser	113.957
	Indycar	Wally Dallenbach	USA	Eagle 73-Offenhauser	108.320
1974	Indycar	Johnny Rutherford	USA	McLaren M16C/D-Offenhauser	110.226
	Indycar	Gordon Johncock	USA	Eagle 74-Offenhauser	118.752
1975	Indycar	AJ Foyt Jr	USA	Coyote-Foyt/Ford	114.042
	Indycar	Mike Mosley	USA	Eagle 75-Offenhauser	114.393
1976	Indycar	Mike Mosley	USA	Eagle 76-Offenhauser	121.557
	Indycar	Al Unser	USA	Parnelli VPJ6B-Cosworth	121.907
1977	Indycar	Johnny Rutherford	USA	McLaren M24-Cosworth	92.962
	Indycar	Johnny Rutherford	USA	McLaren M24-Cosworth	103.798
1978	Indycar	Rick Mears	USA	Penske PC6-Cosworth	120.677
	Indycar	Danny Ongais	USA	Parnelli VPJ6B-Cosworth	108.385
1979	Indycar	AJ Foyt Jr	USA	Parnelli VPJ6C-Cosworth	108.955
	Indycar	Roger McCluskey	USA	Lola T500B-Cosworth	117.135

year	formula	winner	nat	car	mph
1980	Indycar	Bobby Unser	USA	Penske PC9-Cosworth	112.773
	Indycar	Johnny Rutherford	USA	Chaparral 2K-Cosworth	105.063
1981	Indycar	Mike Mosley	USA	Eagle 81-Chevrolet	113.839
	Indycar	Tom Sneva	USA	March 81C-Cosworth	118.013
1982	Indycar	Gordon Johncock	USA	Wildcat Mk8B-Cosworth	126.978
	Indycar	Tom Sneva	USA	March 82C-Cosworth	109.132
1983	Indycar	Tom Sneva	USA	March 83C-Cosworth	116.104
1984	Indycar	Tom Sneva	USA	March 84C-Cosworth	118.030
1985	Indycar	Mario Andretti	USA	Lola T900-Cosworth	124.162
1986	Indycar	Michael Andretti	USA	March 86C-Cosworth	116.788
1987	Indycar	Michael Andretti	USA	March 87C-Cosworth	111.853
1988	Indycar	Rick Mears	USA	Penske PC17-Chevrolet	122.819
1989	Indycar	Rick Mears	USA	Penske PC18-Chevrolet	130.160
1990	Indycar	Al Unser Jr	USA	Lola T90/00-Chevrolet	133.670
1991	Indycar	Michael Andretti	USA	Lola T91/00-Chevrolet	134.557
1992	Indycar	Michael Andretti	USA	Lola T92/00-Ford	138.031
1993	Indycar	Nigel Mansell	GB	Lola T93/00-Ford	110.970
1994	Indycar	Al Unser Jr	USA	Penske PC23-Ilmor	118.804

NAZARETH

PENNSYLVANIA INTERNATIONAL RACEWAY

Roger Penske bought the site of a previous 1.125-mile dirt track (where two Indycar races had been held in the 1960s), paved it and reopened the shortened venue in 1987. It was fitting that Michael Andretti should win that race in his family's home town. It is an odd tri-oval with some elevation change. Although officially a one-mile oval, Nazareth is in fact 0.94 miles long, resulting in fast official speeds. As the final oval of the year, and the penultimate Indycar World Series event of the year, Nazareth has often decided the championship.

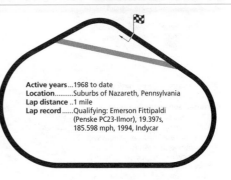

Active years...1968 to date
Location..........Suburbs of Nazareth, Pennsylvania
Lap distance ..1 mile
Lap record ......Qualifying: Emerson Fittipaldi
(Penske PC23-Ilmor), 19.397s,
185.598 mph, 1994, Indycar

Marlboro Challenge see above

Indycar race

year	formula	winner	nat	car	mph
1968	Indycar	Al Unser	USA	Ward-Offenhauser	99.558
1969	Indycar	Mario Andretti	USA	Kuzma-Offenhauser	105.851
1987	Indycar	Michael Andretti	USA	March 87C-Cosworth	128.971
1988	Indycar	Danny Sullivan	USA	Penske PC17-Chevrolet	148.526
1989	Indycar	Emerson Fittipaldi	BR	Penske PC18-Chevrolet	134.759
1990	Indycar	Emerson Fittipaldi	BR	Penske PC19-Chevrolet	112.700
1991	Indycar	Arie Luyendyk	NL	Lola T91/00-Chevrolet	131.310
1992	Indycar	Bobby Rahal	USA	Lola T92/00-Chevrolet	128.848
1993	Indycar	Nigel Mansell	GB	Lola T93/00-Ford	158.686
1994	Indycar	Paul Tracy	CDN	Penske PC23-Ilmor	131.141

NEW HAMPSHIRE INTERNATIONAL SPEEDWAY

After a succession of new temporary street circuits to join the Indycar Championship, the short oval at Loudon, New Hampshire is a refreshing addition to the series. While Milwaukee is run-down, New Hampshire is modern, with excellent spectator facilities and viewing. Just over a mile long with 12-degree banking, the 1993 event saw Nigel Mansell win a mighty contest with Paul Tracy by under half a second.

Active years...1992 to date
Location..........Loudon, New Hampshire

Lap distance ..1.058 miles
Lap record ......Emerson Fittipaldi (Penske PC23-Ilmor) 21.753s, 175.093 mph, 1994, Indycar

New England 200 Indycar race

year	formula	winner	nat	car	mph
1992	Indycar	Bobby Rahal	USA	Lola T92/00-Chevrolet	133.621
1993	Indycar	Nigel Mansell	GB	Lola T93/00-Ford	130.148
1994	Indycar	Al Unser Jr	USA	Penske PC23-Ilmor	122.635

Racing Around the World

ONTARIO MOTOR SPEEDWAY

Built at a reported cost of US$25.5m close to Los Angeles, it is ironic that Ontario Motor Speedway should close due to lack of finance. The inaugural event on 6 September 1970 was the F1 versus F5000 Questor Grand Prix on the road course. A full F1 World Championship race was scheduled in 1972 but it was cancelled. Thereafter, racing was concentrated on the Superspeedway. Its turns were quicker than Indy and were banked at nine degrees. It held the California 500 as part of the Indycar National Championship and a capacity 180,000 crowd watched the first full 500-mile Indycar race to be held outside Indiana.

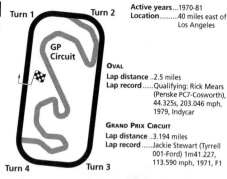

Active years...1970-81
Location..........40 miles east of Los Angeles

OVAL
Lap distance ..2.5 miles
Lap record ......Qualifying: Rick Mears (Penske PC7-Cosworth), 44.325s, 203.046 mph, 1979, Indycar

GRAND PRIX CIRCUIT
Lap distance ..3.194 miles
Lap record ......Jackie Stewart (Tyrrell 001-Ford) 1m41.227, 113.590 mph, 1971, F1

California 500

year	formula	winner	nat	car	mph
1970	Indycar	Jim McElreath	USA	Coyote-Ford	160.106
1971	Indycar	Joe Leonard	USA	Colt 71-Ford	152.355
1972	Indycar	Roger McCluskey	USA	McLaren M16B-Offenhauser	148.995
1973	Indycar	Wally Dallenbach	USA	Eagle 73-Offenhauser	157.660
1974	Indycar	Bobby Unser	USA	Eagle 74-Offenhauser	157.017
1975	Indycar	AJ Foyt Jr	USA	Coyote-Foyt/Ford	154.344
1976	Indycar	Bobby Unser	USA	Eagle 76-Offenhauser	143.246
1977	Indycar	Al Unser	USA	Parnelli VPJ6B-Cosworth	152.074
1978	Indycar	Al Unser	USA	Lola T500-Cosworth	145.158
1979	Indycar	Bobby Unser	USA	Penske PC7-Cosworth	146.795
1980	Indycar	Bobby Unser	USA	Penske PC9-Cosworth	156.372

California 500 qualifying races

year	formula	winner	nat	car	mph
1973	Indycar	Wally Dallenbach	USA	Eagle 73-Offenhauser	179.919
	Indycar	Johnny Rutherford	USA	McLaren M16C-Offenhauser	164.162
1974	Indycar	AJ Foyt Jr	USA	Coyote-Foyt/Ford	176.873
	Indycar	Johnny Rutherford	USA	McLaren M16C/D-Offenhauser	172.673
1975	Indycar	AJ Foyt Jr	USA	Coyote-Foyt/Ford	177.085
	Indycar	Wally Dallenbach	USA	Eagle 75-Offenhauser	150.305

Other Indycar races

year	formula	winner	nat	car	mph
1977	Indycar	AJ Foyt Jr	USA	Coyote-Foyt/Ford	154.073
1978	Indycar	Danny Ongais	USA	Parnelli VPJ6B-Cosworth	162.810
1979	Indycar	AJ Foyt Jr	USA	Parnelli VPJ6C-Cosworth	154.279
1980	Indycar	Johnny Rutherford	USA	Chaparral 2K-Cosworth	162.016

Questor Grand Prix

year	formula	winner	nat	car	mph
1971	F1/F5000	Mario Andretti	USA	Ferrari 312B	54.849

PHOENIX INTERNATIONAL RACEWAY

PIR is not a place for the faint-hearted, witness Mansell's accident in practice for the 1993 race. Traditionally, it is the first oval of the Indycar season and venue for much of the Championship's pre-season testing. Banked at 11 degrees in turns 1 and 2, and 9 degrees in 3, Phoenix has an awkward dogleg on the back stretch. Drivers are flat-out except for touching the brakes entering Turn 1. Laps are now under 20 seconds so lapping traffic is guaranteed throughout the race. Racing had been held at the Arizona State Fairgrounds dirt oval since 1910 prior to PIR opening in 1964.

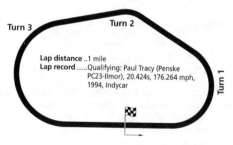

Active years...1964 to date
Location..........South-west outskirts of Phoenix

Lap distance ..1 mile
Lap record ......Qualifying: Paul Tracy (Penske PC23-Ilmor), 20.424s, 176.264 mph, 1994, Indycar

Indycar race

year	formula	winner	nat	car	mph
1915*	Indycar	Earl Cooper	USA	Stutz	64.390
1950*	Indycar	Jimmy Davies	USA	Ewing-Offenhauser	78.020

year	formula	winner	nat	car	mph
1951*	Indycar	Johnnie Parsons	USA	Kurtis KK4000-Offenhauser	84.626
1952*	Indycar	Johnnie Parsons	USA	Kurtis KK4000-Offenhauser	85.878
1953*	Indycar	Tony Bettenhausen	USA	Kurtis-Offenhauser	83.916
1954*	Indycar	Jimmy Bryan	USA	Kuzma-Offenhauser	84.524
1955*	Indycar	Jimmy Bryan	USA	Kuzma-Offenhauser	83.862
1956*	Indycar	George Amick	USA	Lesovsky-Offenhauser	91.826
1957*	Indycar	Jimmy Bryan	USA	Kuzma-Offenhauser	86.001
1958*	Indycar	Jud Larson	USA	Lesovsky-Offenhauser	92.738
1959*	Indycar	Tony Bettenhausen	USA	Kuzma-Offenhauser	88.458
1960*	Indycar	AJ Foyt Jr	USA	Meskowski-Offenhauser	89.078
1961*	Indycar	Parnelli Jones	USA	Kuzma-Offenhauser	n/a
1962*	Indycar	Bobby Marshman	USA	Meskowski-Offenhauser	92.122
1963*	Indycar	Rodger Ward	USA	Watson-Offenhauser	85.026
1964	Indycar	AJ Foyt Jr	USA	Watson-Offenhauser	107.536
	Indycar	Lloyd Ruby	USA	Halibrand-Offenhauser	107.736
1965	Indycar	Don Branson	USA	Watson-Offenhauser	106.456
	Indycar	AJ Foyt Jr	USA	Bignotti/Lotus 34-Ford	99.986
1966	Indycar	Jim McElreath	USA	Brabham-Ford	98.819
	Indycar	Mario Andretti	USA	Brawner/Brabham-Ford	104.686
1967	Indycar	Lloyd Ruby	USA	Mongoose-Drake/Offenhauser	86.295
	Indycar	Mario Andretti	USA	Brawner/Hawk-Ford	109.872
1968	Indycar	Bobby Unser	USA	Eagle 68-Drake/Offenhauser	100.938
	Indycar	Gary Bettenhausen	USA	Gerhardt-Drake/Offenhauser	104.972
1969	Indycar	George Follmer	USA	Gilbert-Chevrolet	109.866
	Indycar	Al Unser	USA	Lola T152-Ford	110.109
1970	Indycar	Al Unser	USA	Colt 70-Ford	n/a
	Indycar	Swede Savage	USA	Eagle 70-Ford	116.807
1971	Indycar	Al Unser	USA	Colt 71-Ford	111.565
	Indycar	AJ Foyt Jr	USA	Coyote-Ford	110.701
1972	Indycar	Bobby Unser	USA	Eagle 72-Offenhauser	102.825
	Indycar	Bobby Unser	USA	Eagle 72-Offenhauser	127.618
1973	Indycar	Gordon Johncock	USA	Eagle 73-Offenhauser	115.015
1974	Indycar	Mike Mosley	USA	Eagle 74-Offenhauser	116.681
	Indycar	Gordon Johncock	USA	Eagle 74-Offenhauser	124.202
1975	Indycar	Johnny Rutherford	USA	McLaren M16D-Offenhauser	110.971
	Indycar	AJ Foyt Jr	USA	Coyote-Foyt/Ford	111.055
1976	Indycar	Bobby Unser	USA	Eagle 76-Offenhauser	107.918
	Indycar	Al Unser	USA	Parnelli VPJ6B-Cosworth	107.695
1977	Indycar	Johnny Rutherford	USA	McLaren M24-Cosworth	111.395
	Indycar	Gordon Johncock	USA	Wildcat-DGS/Offenhauser	108.596
1978	Indycar	Gordon Johncock	USA	Wildcat-DGS/Offenhauser	116.757
	Indycar	Johnny Rutherford	USA	McLaren M24B-Cosworth	120.974
1979	Indycar	Gordon Johncock	USA	Penske PC6-Cosworth	119.389
	Indycar	Al Unser	USA	Chaparral 2K-Cosworth	123.203
1980	Indycar	Tom Sneva	USA	Phoenix-Cosworth	99.926
1981	Indycar	Johnny Rutherford	USA	Chaparral 2K-Cosworth	116.681
	Indycar	Tom Sneva	USA	March 81C-Cosworth	112.266
1982	Indycar	Rick Mears	USA	Penske PC10-Cosworth	118.727
	Indycar	Tom Sneva	USA	March 82C-Cosworth	110.997
1983	Indycar	Teo Fabi	I	March 83C-Cosworth	126.671
1984	Indycar	Tom Sneva	USA	March 84C-Cosworth	120.551
	Indycar	Bobby Rahal	USA	March 84C-Cosworth	98.048
1985	Indycar	Al Unser	USA	March 85C-Cosworth	120.644
1986	Indycar	Kevin Cogan	USA	March 86C-Cosworth	120.346
	Indycar	Michael Andretti	USA	March 86C-Cosworth	134.676
1987	Indycar	Roberto Guerrero	USA	March 87C-Cosworth	138.020
1988	Indycar	Mario Andretti	USA	Lola T88/00-Chevrolet	121.993
1989	Indycar	Rick Mears	USA	Penske PC18-Chevrolet	126.112
1990	Indycar	Rick Mears	USA	Penske PC19-Chevrolet	126.291
1991	Indycar	Arie Luyendyk	NL	Lola T91/00-Chevrolet	129.988
1992	Indycar	Bobby Rahal	USA	Lola T92/00-Chevrolet	130.526
1993	Indycar	Mario Andretti	USA	Lola T93/00-Ford	123.847
1994	Indycar	Emerson Fittipaldi	BR	Penske PC23-Ilmor	107.437

At Phoenix International Raceway except *at Arizona State Fairgrounds

Racing Around the World

PHOENIX GRAND PRIX CIRCUIT

The last of the North American temporary street circuits to hold the F1 United States Grand Prix. The inaugural race was held in the mid-summer desert heat before switching to the Spring.

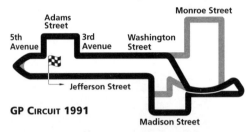

GP CIRCUIT 1991

Grand Prix racing, however, was never a hit in Phoenix and when a local ostrich race drew a bigger crowd, the event was cancelled!

United States Grand Prix see above

Active years...1989-91
Location.........Central Phoenix

INAUGURAL GRAND PRIX CIRCUIT (1989-90)
Lap distance ..2.360 miles
Lap record ......Gerhard Berger (McLaren MP4/5B-Honda), 1m31.050, 93.312 mph, 1990, F1

FINAL GRAND PRIX CIRCUIT (1991)
Lap distance ..2.312 miles
Lap record ......Ayrton Senna (McLaren-Honda) 1m21.434, 102.208 mph, 1991, F1

POCONO

Set deep in the Pennsylvania countryside, Pocono is unique among America's superspeedways. Like Daytona, it is a tri-oval but all three corners are different, the banking on Turns 1, 2 and 3 being 14, 8 and 6 degrees respectively. Pocono regularly held Indycars for two decades but it suffered from being too bumpy and the series moved elsewhere. The possibility of the Indy Racing League, a breakaway championship proposed by the Speedway President Tony George, has reawakened talk of Indycars at Pocono.

GP CIRCUIT 1992

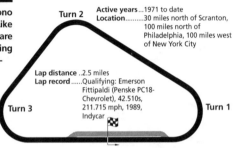

Active years...1971 to date
Location.........30 miles north of Scranton, 100 miles north of Philadelphia, 100 miles west of New York City

Lap distance ..2.5 miles
Lap record ......Qualifying: Emerson Fittipaldi (Penske PC18-Chevrolet), 42.510s, 211.715 mph, 1989, Indycar

year	formula	winner	nat	car	mph
Pocono 500 Indycar race					
1971	Indycar	Mark Donohue	USA	McLaren M16A-Drake/Offenhauser	138.650
1972	Indycar	Joe Leonard	USA	Parnelli-Offenhauser	154.781
1973	Indycar	AJ Foyt Jr	USA	Coyote-Foyt/Ford	144.948
1974	Indycar	Johnny Rutherford	USA	McLaren M16C/D-Offenhauser	156.701
1975	Indycar	AJ Foyt Jr	USA	Coyote-Foyt/Ford	140.712
1976	Indycar	Al Unser	USA	Parnelli VPJ6B-Cosworth	143.622
1977	Indycar	Tom Sneva	USA	McLaren M24-Cosworth	152.131
1978	Indycar	Al Unser	USA	Lola T500-Cosworth	142.261
1979	Indycar	AJ Foyt Jr	USA	Parnelli VPJ6C-Cosworth	134.995
1980	Indycar	Bobby Unser	USA	Penske PC9-Cosworth	151.454
1981	Indycar	AJ Foyt Jr	USA	March 81C-Cosworth	137.196
1982	Indycar	Rick Mears	USA	Penske PC10-Cosworth	145.879
1983	Indycar	Teo Fabi	I	March 83C-Cosworth	134.852
1984	Indycar	Danny Sullivan	USA	Lola T800-Cosworth	137.303
1985	Indycar	Rick Mears	USA	March 85C-Cosworth	151.676
1986	Indycar	Mario Andretti	USA	Lola T86/00-Cosworth	152.107
1987	Indycar	Rick Mears	USA	March 86C-Chevrolet	156.373
1988	Indycar	Bobby Rahal	USA	Lola T88/00-Judd	133.713
1989	Indycar	Danny Sullivan	USA	Penske PC18-Chevrolet	170.720

PORTLAND

For ten years this has been Indycars visit to America's Pacific north-west region. The Festival Curves are a difficult combination of surfaces - tarmac and concrete. The race forms part of Portland's town festival, attracting many locals, but few visitors due to Portland's inaccessibility. The 1986 event witnessed the closest finish to an Indycar race since 1923, Mario Andretti celebrating Father's Day by edging out his son Michael by just 0.07 seconds!

Active years...1984 to date
Location.........West Delta Park, near Portland
Lap distance ..1.950 miles
Lap record ......Qualifying: Al Unser Jr (Penske PC23-Ilmor), 1m00.071, 116.862 mph, 1994, Indycar

CIRCUIT CHANGES
1984-90 ....1.915 miles
1991 ....1.922 miles
1992 to date ....Current circuit

Indycar race

year	formula	winner	nat	car	mph
1984	Indycar	Al Unser Jr	USA	March 84C-Cosworth	105.478
1985	Indycar	Mario Andretti	USA	Lola T900-Cosworth	107.083
1986	Indycar	Mario Andretti	USA	Lola T86/00-Cosworth	107.760
1987	Indycar	Bobby Rahal	USA	Lola T87/00-Cosworth	108.591
1988	Indycar	Danny Sullivan	USA	Penske PC17-Chevrolet	101.881
1989	Indycar	Emerson Fittipaldi	BR	Penske PC18-Chevrolet	103.605
1990	Indycar	Michael Andretti	USA	Lola T90/00-Chevrolet	110.269
1991	Indycar	Michael Andretti	USA	Lola T91/00-Chevrolet	115.208
1992	Indycar	Michael Andretti	USA	Lola T92/00-Ford	105.219
1993	Indycar	Emerson Fittipaldi	BR	Penske PC22-Chevrolet	96.312
1994	Indycar	Al Unser Jr	USA	Penske PC23-Ilmor	108.371

RIVERSIDE

Set in the desert near the San Bernadino mountains, Riverside succumbed to the urban sprawl of Los Angeles and closed in 1988. It held the first US GP, a Sports Car race in 1958 and hosted the event again (a full World Championship Grand Prix) two years later. The three layouts were challenging, the uphill esses particularly demanding. Dan Gurney normally excelled here, winning the early season NASCAR race five times and the Indycar event twice.

The 1960 United States Grand Prix at Riverside

LONG SPORTS CAR
3.25 MILES

STOCK CAR
2.62 MILES

SHORT SPORTS CAR
2.547 MILES

Active years...1957-88
Location.........East of Los Angeles

United States Grand Prix see above

Indycar race

year	formula	winner	nat	car	mph
1967	Indycar	Dan Gurney	USA	Eagle 67-Ford/Weslake	107.995
1968	Indycar	Dan Gurney	USA	Eagle 68-Ford/Weslake	112.548
1969	Indycar	Mario Andretti	USA	Brawner/Hawk-Ford	107.786
1981	Indycar	Rick Mears	USA	Penske PC9B-Cosworth	113.176
1982	Indycar	Rick Mears	USA	Penske PC10-Cosworth	111.783
1983	Indycar	Bobby Rahal	USA	March 83C-Cosworth	111.956

World Sports Car race

year	formula	winner	nat	car	mph
1981	SC W	John Fitzpatrick/Jim Busby	USA	Porsche 935-K3	107.563

SEBRING

Racing began on the concrete runways of Sebring in 1950 and two years later the first of the now traditional 12-hour races was held. The first World Championship United States GP was held here in 1959 although that was the only time Grand Prix racing has visited. The abrasive surface was improved with some tarmac in 1987.

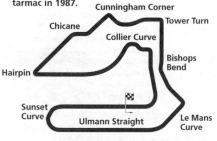

SEBRING INTERNATIONAL RACEWAY
CURRENT CIRCUIT

Active years...1950 to date
Location.........90 miles from Tampa and Orlando

The start of the 1957 Sebring 12 hours with the Maserati of Stirling Moss leading

Racing Around the World

CURRENT CIRCUIT

Lap distance ..3.700 miles
Lap record ......Qualifying: Juan Manuel Fangio II
(Eagle Mk3-Toyota), 1m46.135,
125.501 mph, 1993, IMSA Sports
Cars
Race: Geoff Brabham (Nissan
NPT90), 1m49.616, 121.515 mph,
1992, IMSA Sports Cars

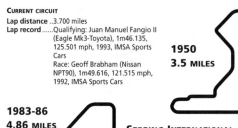

1950
3.5 MILES

1952-82
5.2 MILES

1983-86
4.86 MILES

SEBRING INTERNATIONAL
RACEWAY

1987-90
4.11 MILES

CIRCUIT CHANGES

1950-51	............3.5 miles
1952-82	............5.2 miles
1983	................4.85 miles
1984-86	...........4.86 miles
1987-90	...........4.11 miles
1991 to date	....Current circuit

United States Grand Prix see above

Sebring 12 hours

year	formula	winner	nat	car	mph
1952	SC	Harry Gray/Larry Kulok	USA	Frazer-Nash	62.830
1953	SC W	John Fitch/Phil Walters	USA	Cunningham C4R-Chrysler	74.961
1954	SC W	Stirling Moss/Bill Lloyd	GB/USA	OSCA MT4	72.370
1955	SC W	Mike Hawthorn/Phil Walters	GB/USA	Jaguar D-type	78.860
1956	SC W	Juan Manuel Fangio/Eugenio Castellotti	RA/I	Ferrari 860 Monza	84.067
1957	SC W	Juan Manuel Fangio/Jean Behra	RA/F	Maserati 450S	85.360
1958	SC W	Peter Collins/Phil Hill	GB/USA	Ferrari 250TR	86.667
1959	SC W	Dan Gurney/Chuck Daigh/Phil Hill/Olivier Gendebien	USA/USA/USA/B	Ferrari 250TR	81.467
1960	SC W	Olivier Gendebien/Hans Herrmann	B/D	Porsche 718 RSK	84.928
1961	SC W	Phil Hill/Olivier Gendebien	USA/B	Ferrari 250TR	90.700
1962	SC W	Jo Bonnier/Lucien Bianchi	S/B	Ferrari 250TR	89.142
1963	SC W	John Surtees/Ludovico Scarfiotti	GB/I	Ferrari 250P	90.390
1964	SC W	Michael Parkes/Umberto Maglioli	GB/I	Ferrari 275P	92.363
1965	SC W	Jim Hall/Hap Sharp	USA	Chaparral 2D-Chevrolet	84.720
1966	SC W	Lloyd Ruby/Ken Miles	USA	Ford GTX1	98.626
1967	SC W	Mario Andretti/Bruce McLaren	USA/NZ	Ford GT40 Mk4	102.901
1968	SC W	Hans Herrmann/Jo Siffert	D/CH	Porsche 907/8	102.512
1969	SC W	Jacky Ickx/Jackie Oliver	B/GB	Ford GT40	103.363
1970	SC W	Ignazio Giunti/Nino Vaccarella/Mario Andretti	I/I/USA	Ferrari 512S	107.290
1971	SC W	Vic Elford/Gérard Larrousse	GB/F	Porsche 917K	112.501
1972	SC W	Jacky Ickx/Mario Andretti	B/USA	Ferrari 312P	111.511
1973	SC	Peter Gregg/Hurley Haywood/Dave Helmick	USA	Porsche Carrera	97.854
1975	SC	Brian Redman/Allan Moffat/Sam Posey/Hans-Joachim Stuck	GB/AUS/USA/D	BMW 3.0 CSL	102.640
1976	SC	Al Holbert/Michael Keyser	USA	Porsche 911 Carrera RSR	99.667
1977	SC	George Dyer/Brad Frisselle	USA	Porsche 911 Carrera RSR	101.322
1978	SC	Brian Redman/Charles Mendez/Bob Garretson	GB/USA/USA	Porsche 935	103.978
1979	SC	Bob Akin/Rob McFarlin/Roy Woods	USA	Porsche 935	103.466
1980	SC	Dick Barbour/John Fitzpatrick	USA/GB	Porsche 935	109.520
1981	SC W	Bruce Leven/Hurley Haywood/Al Holbert	USA	Porsche 935	106.044
1982	SC	John Paul/John Paul Jr	USA	Porsche 935	105.401
1983	SC	Wayne Baker/Jim Mullen/Kees Nierop	USA/USA/CDN	Porsche 934	91.273
1984	SC	Maurizio de Narvaez/Hans Heyer/Stefan Johansson	CO/D/S	Porsche 935	106.364
1985	SC	Bob Wollek/AJ Foyt Jr	F/USA	Porsche 962	113.787
1986	SC	Bob Akin/Hans-Joachim Stuck/Jo Gartner	USA/D/A	Porsche 962	115.852
1987	SC	Jochen Mass/Bobby Rahal	D/USA	Porsche 962	101.859
1988	SC	Klaus Ludwig/Hans-Joachim Stuck	D	Porsche 962	108.782
1989	SC	Geoff Brabham/Chip Robinson/Arie Luyendyk	AUS/USA/NL	Nissan GTP ZX-T	112.742
1990	SC	Derek Daly/Bob Earl	IRL/USA	Nissan GTP ZX-T	102.993
1991	SC	Geoff Brabham/Derek Daly/Gary Brabham	AUS/IRL/AUS	Nissan NPT90	91.626
1992	SC	Juan Manuel Fangio II/Andy Wallace	RA/GB	Eagle Mk3-Toyota	110.724
1993	SC	Juan Manuel Fangio II/Andy Wallace	RA/GB	Eagle Mk3-Toyota	70.699
1994	SC	Steve Millen/Johnny O'Connell/John Morton	NZ/USA/USA	Nissan 300ZX	100.634

United States of America

TRENTON

NEW JERSEY STATE FAIRGROUNDS
Built immediately after World War Two on the site of a 0.5-mile dirt oval (which had been used in 1914), the New Jersey State Fairgrounds was a mainstay of Indycar racing until 1979. Paved for its second race in 1957, it was a lightly banked oval. It was always well-attended and

traditionally held two races, one in the spring and one in the autumn.

TRENTON

Active years...1946-79
Location.........Trenton, New Jersey

CIRCUITS
1946-56 ....Dirt. 1 mile
1957-68 ....Paved. 1 mile
1969-79 ....Extended. 1.5 miles

Indycar race

year	formula	winner	nat	car	mph
1949	Indycar	Myron Fohr	USA	Marchese-Offenhauser	75.765
1957	Indycar	Pat O'Connor	USA	Kuzma-Offenhauser	100.279
1958	Indycar	Len Sutton	USA	Kuzma-Offenhauser	95.527
	Indycar	Rodger Ward	USA	Lesovsky-Offenhauser	99.368
1959	Indycar	Tony Bettenhausen	USA	Kuzma-Offenhauser	91.161
	Indycar	Eddie Sachs	USA	Meskowski-Offenhauser	97.398
1960	Indycar	Rodger Ward	USA	Watson-Offenhauser	95.486
	Indycar	Eddie Sachs	USA	Kuzma-Offenhauser	99.223
1961	Indycar	Eddie Sachs	USA	Kuzma-Offenhauser	98.680
	Indycar	Eddie Sachs	USA	Kuzma-Offenhauser	101.013
1962	Indycar	AJ Foyt Jr	USA	Meskowski-Offenhauser	101.102
	Indycar	Rodger Ward	USA	Watson-Offenhauser	100.977
	Indycar	Don Branson	USA	Watson-Offenhauser	102.529
1963	Indycar	AJ Foyt Jr	USA	Meskowski-Offenhauser	102.492
	Indycar	AJ Foyt Jr	USA	Watson Trevis-Offenhauser	100.403
	Indycar	AJ Foyt Jr	USA	Watson Trevis-Offenhauser	101.358
1964	Indycar	AJ Foyt Jr	USA	Watson-Offenhauser	104.530
	Indycar	AJ Foyt Jr	USA	Watson-Offenhauser	105.590
	Indycar	Parnelli Jones	USA	Lotus 34-Ford	96.415
1965	Indycar	Jim McElreath	USA	Brabham-Offenhauser	97.186
	Indycar	AJ Foyt Jr	USA	Bignotti/Lotus 34-Ford	98.361
	Indycar	AJ Foyt Jr	USA	Bignotti/Lotus 34-Ford	99.953
1966	Indycar	Rodger Ward	USA	Lola T90-Drake/Offenhauser	99.905
	Indycar	Mario Andretti	USA	Brawner/Brabham-Ford	105.127
1967	Indycar	Mario Andretti	USA	Brawner/Hawk-Ford	109.838
	Indycar	AJ Foyt Jr	USA	Coyote-Ford	92.223
1968	Indycar	Bobby Unser	USA	Eagle 68-Drake/Offenhauser	103.397
	Indycar	Mario Andretti	USA	Brawner-Drake/Offenhauser	104.543
1969	Indycar	Mario Andretti	USA	Brawner/Hawk-Ford	139.591
	Indycar	Mario Andretti	USA	Brawner-Ford	134.382
1970	Indycar	Lloyd Ruby	USA	Mongoose-Drake/Offenhauser	135.967
	Indycar	Al Unser	USA	Colt 70-Ford	137.639
1971	Indycar	Mike Mosley	USA	Eagle 71-Ford	132.562
	Indycar	Bobby Unser	USA	Eagle 71-Drake/Offenhauser	140.778
1972	Indycar	Gary Bettenhausen	USA	McLaren M16B-Offenhauser	145.642
	Indycar	Bobby Unser	USA	Eagle 72-Offenhauser	143.880
1973	Indycar	AJ Foyt Jr	USA	Coyote-Foyt/Ford	138.359
	Indycar	Mario Andretti	USA	Parnelli-Offenhauser	149.626
	Indycar	Gordon Johncock	USA	Eagle 73-Offenhauser	135.025
1974	Indycar	Bobby Unser	USA	Eagle 74-Offenhauser	128.708
	Indycar	AJ Foyt Jr	USA	Coyote-Foyt/Ford	135.372
	Indycar	Bobby Unser	USA	Eagle 74-Offenhauser	156.069
1975	Indycar	AJ Foyt Jr	USA	Coyote-Foyt/Ford	154.646
	Indycar	Gordon Johncock	USA	Wildcat-Offenhauser	123.511
1976	Indycar	Johnny Rutherford	USA	McLaren M16E-Offenhauser	147.499
	Indycar	Gordon Johncock	USA	Wildcat-DGS/Offenhauser	135.929
1977	Indycar	Wally Dallenbach	USA	Wildcat-DGS/Offenhauser	151.288
1978	Indycar	Gordon Johncock	USA	Wildcat-DGS/Offenhauser	130.988
	Indycar	Mario Andretti	USA	Penske PC6-Cosworth	120.080
1979	Indycar	Bobby Unser	USA	Penske PC7-Cosworth	121.003
	Indycar	Bobby Unser	USA	Penske PC7-Cosworth	147.915
	Indycar	Rick Mears	USA	Penske PC7-Cosworth	129.808

WATKINS GLEN

The current Bill Milliken-designed circuit is the third circuit to have been used in this area of New York State. The first, founded by Cameron Argetsinger, was 6.6 miles long and opened on 2 October 1948. Fatal accidents in two successive years forced its closure; a transitional 4.6 mile road course in the hills was used from 1953 until the permanent venue on the hilltop near Watkins Glen village was opened in 1956. The Glen was home of Grand Prix racing in the United States from 1961 but it fell into disrepair when the US GP moved to the unsatisfactory street circuits of Detroit and Phoenix. Under new management it was refurbished and is thriving once more as a NASCAR venue. The annual Budweiser at the Glen is now arguably the biggest road race in America.

Active years...1956 to date
Location.........Five miles south of Lake Seneca, 260 miles north-west of New York City

GP CIRCUIT 1971
TO DATE

New Chicane

The 90

Loop

Chute

CURRENT GRAND PRIX CIRCUIT
Lap distance ..3.377 miles
Lap record ......Alan Jones (Williams FW07B-Ford)
  1m34.068, 129.238 mph, 1980, F1

GP CIRCUIT 1956-70

Fast Bend

Back Straight

Loop Chute
Loop Chicane

Esses

Front Straight

Esses

Loop

The 90

(NASCAR)

CIRCUIT CHANGES
1956-70 ....2.35 miles
1971 ....Widened, new straight before "The 90". Used for 1971 Sports Car race. 2.43 miles
1971-74 ....Grand Prix extension opened. 3.377 miles
1975 to date ....New Chicane inserted. Current circuit

United States Grand Prix see above

Indycar race

year	formula	winner	nat	car	mph
1979	Indycar	Bobby Unser	USA	Penske PC7-Cosworth	121.012
1980	Indycar	Bobby Unser	USA	Penske PC9-Cosworth	99.500
1981	Indycar	Rick Mears	USA	Penske PC9B-Cosworth	108.273

World Sports Car race

year	formula	winner	nat	car	mph
1968	SC W	Jacky Ickx/Lucien Bianchi	B	Ford GT40	111.873
1969	SC W	Jo Siffert/Brian Redman	CH/GB	Porsche 908/8	113.607
1970	SC W	Pedro Rodriguez/Leo Kinnunen	MEX/SF	Porsche 917	120.368
1971	SC W	Andrea de Adamich/Ronnie Peterson	I/S	Alfa Romeo T33/3	112.864
1972	SC W	Jacky Ickx/Mario Andretti	B/USA	Ferrari 312P	109.392
1973	SC W	Henri Pescarolo/Gérard Larrousse	F	Matra-Simca MS670	111.895
1974	SC W	Jean-Pierre Beltoise/Jean-Pierre Jarier	F	Matra-Simca MS670C	108.157
1975	SC W	Henri Pescarolo/Derek Bell	F/GB	Alfa Romeo T33TT/12	85.220
1976	SC W	Rolf Stommelen/Manfred Schurti	D/FL	Porsche 935	97.804
1977	SC W	Jacky Ickx/Jochen Mass	B/D	Porsche 935	96.847
1978	SC W	Toine Hezemans/John Fitzpatrick/Peter Gregg	NL/GB/USA	Porsche 935	81.738
1979	SC W	Don Whittington/Klaus Ludwig/Bill Whittington	USA/D/USA	Porsche 935	98.449
1980	SC W	Riccardo Patrese/Hans Heyer	I/D	Lancia Beta Monte Carlo	77.747
1981	SC W	Riccardo Patrese/Michele Alboreto	I	Lancia Beta Monte Carlo	92.240

Budweiser at the Glen NASCAR race

year	formula	winner	nat	car	mph
1986	NASCAR	Tim Richmond	USA	Chevrolet	90.463
1987	NASCAR	Rusty Wallace	USA	Pontiac	90.682
1988	NASCAR	Ricky Rudd	USA	Buick	74.096
1989	NASCAR	Rusty Wallace	USA	Pontiac	87.242
1990	NASCAR	Ricky Rudd	USA	Chevrolet	97.452
1991	NASCAR	Ernie Irvan	USA	Chevrolet	98.977
1992	NASCAR	Kyle Petty	USA	Pontiac	85.827
1993	NASCAR	Mark Martin	USA	Ford	84.771
1994	NASCAR	Mark Martin	USA	Ford	84.771

VENEZUELA

MAJOR INTERNATIONAL RACES

VENEZUELAN GRAND PRIX						
year	formula	circuit	winner	nat	car	mph
1955	SC	Caracas	Juan Manuel Fangio	RA	Maserati 300S	81.710
1956	SC	Caracas	Stirling Moss	GB	Maserati 300S	84.250
1957	SC W	Caracas	Peter Collins/Phil Hill	GB/USA	Ferrari 412	95.864

CIRCUITS

CARACAS

An international Sports Car race had been held at Caracas for two years before the event gained World Championship status in 1957. *Autosport* described the course as "very tricky", indeed the drivers' association protested to the FIA that it was too dangerous to hold such an event. It did proceed as planned, with one serious accident, but the event was not repeated.

Venezuelan Grand Prix see above

CARACAS

Active years...1955-57
Location..........Central Caracas
Lap distance ..6.2 miles
Lap record......Stirling Moss (Maserati 300S), 3m38.0,
   102.385 mph, 1957, Sports Cars

YUGOSLAVIA

MAJOR INTERNATIONAL RACES

YUGOSLAVIAN GRAND PRIX					
year	formula	winner	nat	car	mph
1939	GP	Tazio Nuvolari	I	Auto Union D	81.201

CIRCUITS AND RACES

KALEMAGDAN PARK

BELGRADE

On the day that England declared war on Germany the only Yugoslavian Grand Prix was held on a cobbled street circuit in Belgrade. The circuit was uninspiring, only five cars started, and somewhat events elsewhere overshadowed the race!

Yugoslavian Grand Prix see above

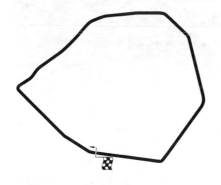

Manfred von Brauchitsch leads Hermann Lang in the Yugoslav Grand Prix in 1939

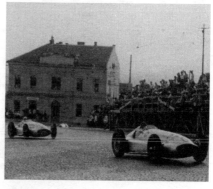

BELGRADE

Active years...1939 (used once)
Location..........Kalemagdan Park, central Belgrade
Lap distance ..1.734 miles
Lap record......Hermann Müller (Auto Union D), 1m14.0,
   84.357 mph, 1939, GP

Jim Clark and Colin Chapman, winners at Spa in 1964

The following pages are an index of international racing drivers who have achieved any of the following:

- Raced in World Championship Grands Prix, or attempted to qualify for an event.
- Won a pre-1950 Grand Prix or a World Sports Car, Indycar, Tasman Cup or European F3 Championship race.
- Finished in the top six of an F2 or F3000 Championship race.
- Won an important international event such as a non-championship national Grand Prix, the Daytona 24 hours or Sebring 12 hours, World/Coca-Cola 600 or Daytona 500 NASCAR events, Bathurst, Spa 24 hours or Tourist Trophy.
- Won a national championship of F3 or higher, or a national Touring Car Championship overall (class wins not recorded).

Every care has been taken to publish dates of birth and, where applicable, death but on occasion it has proved impossible to find the information.

Note: Number in brackets is occasion, on which a driver did not start/qualify for a Grand Prix

A ....

RAUNO AALTONEN
SF. Born: 17.1.1938, Turku
Major race wins: 1966 Bathurst

CARLO ABATE
I. Born: 10.7.1932, Turin
World Sports Car Championship. Race wins: 1963 Targa Florio
Other major race wins: 1959 Mille Miglia

GEORGE ABECASSIS
GB. Born: 21.3.1913, Chertsey. Died: 18.12.1991,Ibstone, Buckinghamshire
World Championship Grand Prix Record

years	starts	wins	2nd	3rd	4th	5th	6th	PP	FL	points
1951-52	2	-	-	-	-	-	-	-	-	-

Best result: no finishes. **Best qualifying:** 10th

JOHANN ABT
D
1970 European Touring Car 1000 cc Champion

KENNETH ACHESON
GB. Born: 27.11.1957, Cookstown
1987 Japanese Sports Car Champion (with Kunimitsu Takahashi)
World Championship Grand Prix Record

years	starts	wins	2nd	3rd	4th	5th	6th	PP	FL	points
1983; 1985	3(7)	-	-	-	-	-	-	-	-	-

Best result: 12th. **Best qualifying:** 23rd

	wins	2nd	3rd	4th	5th	6th	PP	FL	points
European F2 Ch	-	2	1	1	1	2	-	1	23

Championships: 1981 15th, 1982 7th, 1983 10th
World Sports Car Championship. Race wins: 1989 Brands Hatch, Spa

CHARLES VAN ACKER
USA
Indycar Championship. Race wins: 1947 Milwaukee Race 2

ANDREA DE ADAMICH
I. Born: 13.10.1941, Trieste
1966 and 1967 European Touring Car 1600 cc Class Champion, 1968 Temporada F2 Champion; 1965 Italian F3 Champion
World Championship Grand Prix Record

years	starts	wins	2nd	3rd	4th	5th	6th	PP	FL	points
1968; 1970-73	30(6)	-	-	2	-	-	-	-	-	6

Best Championship: 1973 15th. **Best qualifying:** 7th

	wins	2nd	3rd	4th	5th	6th	PP	FL	points
European F2 Ch	-	1	-	1	-	-	-	-	10

Championships: 1968 10th, 1972 19th
World Sports Car Championship. Race wins: 1971 Brands Hatch, Watkins Glen
Other major race wins: 1967 Tourist Trophy

TONY ADAMOWICZ
USA. Born: 2.5.1941, Torrance, California
1969 North American F5000 (Formula A) Champion

PHILIPPE ADAMS
B. Born: 19.11.1969, Mouscron
1993 British F2 Champion
World Championship Grand Prix Record

year	starts	wins	2nd	3rd	4th	5th	6th	PP	FL	points
1994	2	-	-	-	-	-	-	-	-	-

Best result: 16th. **Best qualifying:** 25th

WALT ADER
USA. Born: 15.12.1913,Califon, New Jersey. Died: 25.11.1982
Indycar Championship. Race wins: 1947 Atlanta

KURT ADOLFF
D. Born: 5.11.1921, Stuttgart
World Championship Grand Prix Record

year	starts	wins	2nd	3rd	4th	5th	6th	PP	FL	points
1953	1	-	-	-	-	-	-	-	-	-

Best result: no finishes. **Best qualifying:** 27th

FRED AGABASHIAN
USA. Born: 21.8.1913, Modesto, California. Died: 13.10.1989, Alamo, California
Indycar Championship. Race wins: 1949 Sacramento

KURT AHRENS JR
D. Born: 19.4.1940, Braunschweig
1961 and 1963 German F3 Champion
World Championship Grand Prix Record

years	starts	wins	2nd	3rd	4th	5th	6th	PP	FL	points
1966-69	4	-	-	-	-	-	-	-	-	-

Best result: 12th. **Best qualifying:** 17th

	wins	2nd	3rd	4th	5th	6th	PP	FL	points
European F2 Ch	-	-	1	2	1	-	-	-	19

Championships: 1968 6th, 1969 9th
World Sports Car Championship. Race wins: 1969 Austrian GP, 1970 Nürburgring

LAURENT AIELLO
F. Born: 23.5.1969, Montrouge
1994 French Supertourism Champion

	wins	2nd	3rd	4th	5th	6th	PP	FL	points
Int F3000 Ch	-	-	1	-	1	1	1	-	7

Championships: 1991 15th, 1992 13th
Major race wins: 1990 Monaco F3 GP

JOHNNY AITKEN
USA. Born: n/a. Died: 8.12.1918, influenza
Pre-1950 Grands Prix. Race wins: 1916 American GP
Indycar Championship. Race wins: 1910 Atlanta Race 4, Indianapolis Race 9, 1916 Cincinnati, Indianapolis Race 2, Sheepshead Race 2, Sheepshead Race 3, American GP

BOB AKIN
USA. Born: 6.3.1936
Major race wins: 1979 and 1986 Sebring 12 hrs

MICHELE ALBORETO
I. Born: 23.12.1956, Milan
1980 European F3 Champion

Michele Alboreto
....

World Championship Grand Prix Record

years	starts	wins	2nd	3rd	4th	5th	6th	PP	FL	points
1981-94	194(21)	5	9	9	10	8	6	2	5	186.5

Drivers A–Z

Best Championship: 1985 2nd. **Race wins:** 1982 Las Vegas GP, 1983 Detroit GP, 1984 Belgian GP, 1985 Canadian GP, German GP. **Best qualifying:** 1st.

European F2 Ch	wins	2nd	3rd	4th	5th	6th	PP	FL	points
	1	-	1	-	-	-	1	1	13

Championships: 1981 15th, 1982 7th, 1983 10th. **Race wins:** 1981 Misano

World Sports Car Championship. Race wins: 1981 Watkins Glen, 1982 Silverstone, Nürburgring, Mugello

European F3 Championship. Race wins: 1980 Österreichring, La Châtre, Monza, Kassel-Calden

JEAN ALESI
F. Born: 11.6.1964, Avignon

1989 FIA F3000 Champion; 1987 French F3 Champion

World Championship Grand Prix Record

years	starts	wins	2nd	3rd	4th	5th	6th	PP	FL	points
1989-94	85(1)	-	4	9	9	5	3	1	1	100

Best Championship: 1994 5th **Best result:** 2nd. **Best qualifying:** 1st

Int F3000 Ch	wins	2nd	3rd	4th	5th	6th	PP	FL	points
	3	2	-	1	3	2	2	1	50

Championships: 1988 10th, 1989 1st. **Race wins:** 1989 Pau GP, Birmingham, Spa

JEFF ALLAM
GB. Born: 19.12.1954, Epsom

Major race wins: 1986 Tourist Trophy

NIEL ALLEN
AUS

Tasman Cup. Race wins: 1970 Sandown Park, 1971 New Zealand GP, Teretonga

TOM ALLEY
USA. Born: n/a. Died: 1953

Jean Alesi
....

Indycar Championship. Race wins: 1914 Minneapolis, 1917 Chicago Race 4

PHILIPPE ALLIOT
F. Born: 27.7.1954, Voves

1978 French Formula Renault Champion

World Championship Grand Prix Record

years	starts	wins	2nd	3rd	4th	5th	6th	PP	FL	points
1984-90; 1993-94	109(7)	-	-	-	1	5	-	-	7

Best Championship: 1982 7th. **Best qualifying:** 5th

European F2 Ch	wins	2nd	3rd	4th	5th	6th	PP	FL	points
	-	-	-	2	-	1	1		4

Championships: 1983 12th

Int F3000 Ch	wins	2nd	3rd	4th	5th	6th	PP	FL	points
	1	-	-	-	1	1	-		10

Championships: 1985 16th, 1986 9th. **Race wins:** 1986 Spa

World Sports Car Championship. Race wins: 1991 Suzuka, 1992 Donington, Magny-Cours

European F3 Championship. Race wins: 1981 Magny-Cours, La Châtre, 1982 La Châtre

BOBBY ALLISON
USA. Born: 3.12.1937, Miami, Florida. Father of Davey, brother of Donnie

1983 NASCAR Champion

Major race wins: 1971, 1981 and 1984 World 600, 1978, 1982 and 1988 Daytona 500

CLIFF ALLISON
GB. Born: 8.2.1932, Brough, Westmorland

World Championship Grand Prix Record

years	starts	wins	2nd	3rd	4th	5th	6th	PP	FL	points
1958-61	16(2)	-	1	-	1	2	2	-	-	11

Best Championship: 1960 12th. **Best qualifying:** 5th

World Sports Car Championship. Race wins: 1960 Buenos Aires

DAVEY ALLISON
USA. Born: 25.2.1961, Hollywood, Florida. Died: 13.7.1993, Talladega, helicopter accident. Son of Bobby

1993 IROC Champion

Major race wins: 1991 World 600, 1992 Daytona 500

DONNIE ALLISON
USA. Born: 7.9.1939, Miami, Florida. Brother of Bobby

Major race wins: 1970 World 600

UWE ALZEN
D. Born: 18.8.1967

Major race wins: 1993 Spa 24 hrs

GIOVANNA AMATI
I. Born: 20.7.1962, Rome

World Championship Grand Prix Record

year	starts	wins	2nd	3rd	4th	5th	6th	PP	FL	points
1992	-(3)	-	-	-	-	-	-	-	-	

Best qualifying: 30th

GEORGE AMICK
USA. Born: 24.10.1924, Vernonia, Oregon. Died: 9.4.1959, Daytona

Indycar Championship. Race wins: 1956 Langhorne, Phoenix, 1957 Atlanta

CHRIS AMON
NZ. Born: 20.7.1943, Bulls

1969 Tasman Champion

World Championship Grand Prix Record

years	starts	wins	2nd	3rd	4th	5th	6th	PP	FL	points
1963-76	96(12)	-	3	8	4	7	7	5	3	83

Best Championship: 1967 4th. **Best qualifying:** 1st

European F2 Ch	wins	2nd	3rd	4th	5th	6th	PP	FL	points
	-	-	-	-	1	-	-		

World Sports Car Championship. Race wins: 1966 Le Mans 24 hrs, 1967 Monza, Daytona 24 hrs

Tasman Cup. Race wins: 1968 New Zealand GP, Levin, 1969 New Zealand GP, Levin, Australian GP, Sandown Park, 1975 Teretonga

Other major race wins: 1970 International Trophy, 1971 Argentinian GP

NI AMORIM
P

1993 Portuguese Touring Car Champion

"AMPHICAR"
I

Major race wins: 1976 Targa Florio

BOB ANDERSON
GB/RSR. Born: 19.5.1931, Hendon. Died: 14.8.1967, Silverstone, testing

World Championship Grand Prix Record

years	starts	wins	2nd	3rd	4th	5th	6th	PP	FL	points
1963-67	25(4)	-	-	1	-	1	2	-	-	8

Best Championship: 1964 11th. **Best qualifying:** 7th

GIL ANDERSON
USA

Indycar Championship. Race wins: 1913 Elgin Race 2, 1915 Elgin Race 2, Sheepshead Race 1

CONNY ANDERSSON
S. Born: 28.12.1939, Stockholm

1972 and 1974 Swedish F3 Champion

World Championship Grand Prix Record

years	starts	wins	2nd	3rd	4th	5th	6th	PP	FL	points
1976-77	1(4)	-	-	-	-	-	-	-	-	

Best result: no finishes. **Best qualifying:** 26th

European F3 Championship. Race wins: 1975 Anderstorp, 1976 Nürburgring, Avusrennen, Croix-en-Ternois, Knutstorp

GUNNAR ANDERSSON
S. Born: 1927, Ragard

Major race wins: 1961 Mille Miglia

LEO ANDERSSON
S

1983 Swedish F3 Champion

PER-GUNNAR "PEGGAN" ANDERSSON

S. Born: 15.8.1957, Falkenberg

1993 Nordic Touring Car Champion; 1987, 1989, 1991 and 1992 Swedish Touring Car Champion

EMIL ANDRES

Born: 22.7.1911, Chicago

Indycar Championship. Race wins: 1948 Milwaukee Race 1

JOHN ANDRETTI

USA. Born: 12.3.1963, Bethlehem, Pennsylvania. Nephew of Mario, cousin of Michael and Jeff

Indycar Championship. Race wins: 1991 Surfers Paradise

Other major race wins: 1989 Daytona 24 hrs

MARIO ANDRETTI

USA (emigrated from Italy in 1955). Born: 28.2.1940, Montona, Trieste (I). Father of Michael and Jeff, uncle of John

1978 World Champion; 1965, 1966, 1969 and 1984 Indycar Champion; 1979 IROC Champion

Mario Andretti

World Championship Grand Prix Record

years	starts	wins	2nd	3rd	4th	5th	6th	PP	FL	points
1968-72; 1974-82	128	(3)	12	2	5	7	7	5	18	10	180

Race wins: 1971 South African GP, 1976 Japanese GP, 1977 Long Beach GP, Spanish GP, French GP, Italian GP, 1978 Argentinian GP, Belgian GP, Spanish GP, French GP, German GP, Dutch GP. **Best qualifying:** 1st

World Sports Car Championship. Race wins: 1967 Sebring 12 hrs, 1970 Sebring 12 hrs, 1972 Daytona, Sebring 12 hrs, Brands Hatch, Watkins Glen, 1974 Monza

Indycar Championship. Race wins: 1965 Indianapolis Raceway Park, 1966 Milwaukee Race 1, Langhorne Race 1, Atlanta, Indianapolis Raceway Park, Milwaukee Race 2, Indiana State Fairgrounds, Trenton Race 2, Phoenix Race 2, 1967 Trenton Race 1, Indianapolis Raceway Park, Langhorne Race 2, St Jovite Race 1, St Jovite Race 2, Milwaukee Race 2, Indiana State Fairgrounds, Phoenix Race 2, 1968 St Jovite Race 1, St Jovite Race 2, Du Quoin, Trenton Race 2, 1969 Hanford, Indianapolis 500, Pikes Peak, Nazareth, Trenton Race 1, Springfield, Trenton Race 2, Seattle Race 1, Riverside, 1970 Castle Rock, 1973 Trenton Race 2, 1978 Trenton, 1980 Michigan, 1983 Elkhart Lake, Las Vegas GP, 1984 Long Beach GP, Meadowlands, Michigan 500, Elkhart Lake, Mid-Ohio, Michigan, 1985 Long Beach GP, Milwaukee, Portland, 1986 Portland, Pocono 500, 1987 Long Beach GP, Elkhart Lake, 1988 Phoenix, Cleveland, 1993 Phoenix

Other major race wins: 1967 Daytona 500

MICHAEL ANDRETTI

USA. Born: 5.10.1962, Bethlehem, Pennsylvania. Son of Mario

1991 Indycar Champion; 1983 North American Formula Atlantic Champion; 1982 SCCA Super Vee Champion

World Championship Grand Prix Record

year	starts	wins	2nd	3rd	4th	5th	6th	PP	FL	points
1993	13	-	-	1	-	1	1	-	-	7

Best Championship: 1993 11th. **Best qualifying:** 5th

Indycar Championship. Race wins: 1986 Long Beach GP, Milwaukee, Phoenix, 1987 Milwaukee, Michigan 500, Nazareth, Miami, 1989 Toronto, Michigan 500, 1990 Detroit GP, Portland, Meadowlands, Mid-Ohio, Elkhart Lake, 1991 Milwaukee, Portland, Cleveland, Toronto, Vancouver, Mid-Ohio, Elkhart Lake, Monterey GP (Laguna Seca), 1992 Portland, Milwaukee, Toronto, Vancouver, Monterey GP (Laguna Seca), 1994 Surfers Paradise, Toronto

Other major race wins: 1988 and 1991 Marlboro Challenge

KEITH ANDREWS

USA. Born: 15.6.1920, Denver. Died: 15.5.1957, Indianapolis, practice

Indycar Championship. Race wins: 1954 Pikes Peak

GASTON ANDREY

CH. Born: 8.8.1926

1966 Trans-Am Champion (with Horst Kwech)

JEAN-CLAUDE ANDRUET

F. Born: 13.8.1940

Major race wins: 1977 Spa 24 hrs

MASSIMILIANO "MAX" ANGELELLI

I. Born: 15.12.1966

1992 Italian F3 Champion

ELIO DE ANGELIS

I. Born: 26.3.1958, Rome. Died: 15.5.1986, Marseille hospital following a testing accident at Paul Ricard

1977 Italian F3 Champion

World Championship Grand Prix Record

years	starts	wins	2nd	3rd	4th	5th	6th	PP	FL	points
1979-86	108	2	2	5	11	17	6	3	-	122

Best Championship: 1984 3rd. **Race wins:** 1982 Austrian GP, 1985 San Marino GP. **Best qualifying:** 1st

	wins	2nd	3rd	4th	5th	6th	PP	FL	points
European F2 Ch	-	-	1	-	-	-	-	-	4

Championships: 1978 14th

European F3 Championship. Race wins: 1977 Monza Lottery GP

Other major race wins: 1977 Monaco F3 GP

MICHAEL ANGUS

USA

1985 North American (Eastern) Formula Atlantic Champion

"APACHE"

I

Major race wins: 1977 Targa Florio

MARCO APICELLA

I. Born: 7.10.1965, Bologna

1994 Japanese F3000 Champion

World Championship Grand Prix Record

year	starts	wins	2nd	3rd	4th	5th	6th	PP	FL	points
1993	1	-	-	-	-	-	-	-	-	-

Best result: no finishes. **Best qualifying:** 23rd

	wins	2nd	3rd	4th	5th	6th	PP	FL	points
Int F3000 Ch	-	7	3	3	4	1	2	7	71

Championships: 1987 19th, 1988 11th, 1989 4th, 1990 5th, 1991 5th

PAUL ARMAGNAC

F

Major race wins: 1954 Tourist Trophy

BILLY ARNOLD

USA. Born: 1906. Died: 10.11.1976

1930 Indycar Champion

Indycar Championship. Race wins: 1930 Indianapolis 500, Altoona Race 1, Altoona Race 2

CHARLES ARNOLD

USA

Indycar Championship. Race wins: 1909 Portland Race 2

RENÉ ARNOUX

F. Born: 4.7.1948, Pontcharra, near Grenoble

1977 European F2 Champion

René Arnoux

World Championship Grand Prix Record

years	starts	wins	2nd	3rd	4th	5th	6th	PP	FL	points
1978-89	149(15)	7	9	6	7	8	5	18	12	181

Best Championship: 1983 3rd. **Race wins:** 1980 Brazilian GP, South African GP, 1982 French GP, Italian GP, 1983 Canadian GP, German GP, Dutch GP. **Best qualifying:** 1st

	wins	2nd	3rd	4th	5th	6th	PP	FL	points
European F2 Ch	6	5	1	1	1	1	2	6	104

Championships: 1976 2nd, 1977 1st. **Race wins:** 1976 Pau GP, Mediterranean GP (Enna), Estoril, 1977 International Trophy (Silverstone), Pau GP, Nogaro GP

DIDIER ARTZET

F. Born: 10.2.1963, Nice

	wins	2nd	3rd	4th	5th	6th	PP	FL	points
Int F3000 Ch	-	-	1	-	-	-	-	-	4

Championships: 1990 15th

Major race wins: 1987 Monaco F3 GP

PETER ARUNDELL

GB. Born: 8.11.1933, Ilford

1963 British F3 (Formula Junior) Champion

World Championship Grand Prix Record

years	starts	wins	2nd	3rd	4th	5th	6th	PP	FL	points
1963-64; 1966	11	-	-	2	1	-	1	-	-	12

Best Championship: 1964 8th. **Best qualifying:** 4th

Major race wins: 1961 and 1962 Monaco FJ GP

ALBERTO ASCARI

I. Born: 13.7.1918, Milan. Died: 26.5.1955, Monza, testing. Son of Antonio

1952 and 1953 World Champion

World Championship Grand Prix Record

years	starts	wins	2nd	3rd	4th	5th	6th	PP	FL	points
1950-55	31	13	4	-	2	1	1	14	14	141.64

Race wins: 1951 German GP, Italian GP, 1952 Belgian GP, French GP, British GP, German GP, Dutch GP, Italian GP, 1953 Argentinian GP, Dutch GP, Belgian GP, British GP, Swiss GP. **Best qualifying:** 1st

Pre-1950 Grands Prix. Race wins: 1949 Swiss GP, Italian GP

World Sports Car Championship. Race wins: 1953 Nürburgring, 1954 Mille Miglia

Other major race wins: 1949 International Trophy, 1950 German GP

Alberto Ascari

ANTONIO ASCARI

I. Born: 15.9.1888, Moratica di Bonferraro, Sorga. Died: 26.7.1925, Montlhery, French GP. Father of Alberto

Pre-1950 Grands Prix. Race wins: 1924 Italian GP, 1925 Belgian GP

PETER ASHDOWN

GB. Born: 16.10.1934, Danbury, Essex

World Championship Grand Prix Record

year	starts	wins	2nd	3rd	4th	5th	6th	PP	FL	points
1959	1	-	-	-	-	-	-	-	-	-

Best result: 12th. **Best qualifying:** 23rd

IAN ASHLEY

GB. Born: 26.10.1947, Wuppertal (D)

World Championship Grand Prix Record

years	starts	wins	2nd	3rd	4th	5th	6th	PP	FL	points
1974-77	4	-	-	-	-	-	-	-	-	-

Best result: 17th. **Best qualifying:** 20th

GERRY ASHMORE

GB. Born: 25.7.1936

World Championship Grand Prix Record

years	starts	wins	2nd	3rd	4th	5th	6th	PP	FL	points
1961-62	3	-	-	-	-	-	-	-	-	-

Best result: 16th. **Best qualifying:** 24th

PETER ASLUND

S. Born: 22.11.1967, Karlstad

1992 Nordic F3 Champion; 1992 Swedish F3 Champion

BILL ASTON

GB. Born: 29.3.1900, Stafford. Died: 4.3.1974, Lingfield

World Championship Grand Prix Record

year	starts	wins	2nd	3rd	4th	5th	6th	PP	FL	points
1952	1	-	-	-	-	-	-	-	-	-

Best result: no finishes. **Best qualifying:** 30th

DICK ATKINS

USA

Indycar Championship. Race wins: 1966 Sacramento

RICHARD ATTWOOD

GB. Born: 4.4.1940, Wolverhampton

World Championship Grand Prix Record

years	starts	wins	2nd	3rd	4th	5th	6th	PP	FL	points
1964-65; 1967-69	17	-	1	-	1	-	2	-	1	11

Best Championship: 1968 13th. **Best qualifying:** 6th

	wins	2nd	3rd	4th	5th	6th	PP	FL	points
European F2 Ch	-	-	1	-	-	-	1	4

Best Championship: 1968 12th

World Sports Car Championship. Race wins: 1970 Le Mans 24 hrs, 1971 Österreichring

Tasman Cup. Race wins: 1966 Levin

Other major race wins: 1963 Monaco FJ GP

MANUEL AYULO

USA. Born: 20.10.1921, Los Angeles. Died: 16.5.1955, Indianapolis, practice

Indycar Championship. Race wins: 1954 Darlington, Milwaukee Race 2

Richard Attwood

B

ERIC BACHELART

B. Born: 28.2.1961, Brussels

1991 Indy Lights Champion

LUCA BADOER

I. Born: 25.1.1971, Montebelluna, Treviso

1992 International F3000 Champion

World Championship Grand Prix Record

year	starts	wins	2nd	3rd	4th	5th	6th	PP	FL	points
1993	12(2)	-	-	-	-	-	-	-	-	-

Best result: 7th. **Best qualifying:** 21st

	wins	2nd	3rd	4th	5th	6th	PP	FL	points
Int F3000 Ch	4	1	-	-	1	2	5	3	46

Championship: 1992 1st. **Race wins:** 1992 Mediterranean GP (Enna), Hockenheim, Nürburgring, Nogaro GP

GIANCARLO BAGHETTI

I. Born: 25.12.1934, Milan

1966 European Touring Car 1000 cc Class Champion

World Championship Grand Prix Record

years	starts	wins	2nd	3rd	4th	5th	6th	PP	FL	points
1961–67	21	1	-	-	1	1	-	1	14

Best championship: 1961 9th. **Race wins:** 1961 French GP. **Best qualifying:** 6th

JORGE DE BAGRATION
E

	wins	2nd	3rd	4th	5th	6th	PP	FL	points
European F2 Ch	-	-	-	-	-	1	-	-	2

Championship: 1968 17th

GRAEME BAILEY
AUS

Major race wins: 1986 Bathurst

JULIAN BAILEY
GB. Born: 9.10.1961, Cobham

World Championship Grand Prix Record

years	starts	wins	2nd	3rd	4th	5th	6th	PP	FL	points
1988; 1991	7(13)	-	-	-	-	-	1	-	-	1

Best championship: 1991 18th. Best qualifying: 21st

	wins	2nd	3rd	4th	5th	6th	PP	FL	points
Int F3000 Ch	1	-	-	1	-	1	-	-	13

Championship: 1987 7th. Race wins: 1987 Brands Hatch

CRAIG BAIRD
NZ. Born: 22.7.1970

1991, 1992 and 1993 New Zealand International Champion

BUCK BAKER
USA. Born: 4.3.1919, Hartville

1956 and 1957 NASCAR Champion

BUDDY BAKER
USA. Born: 25.1.1941, Florence, South Carolina

Major race wins: 1968, 1972 and 1973 World 600, 1980 Daytona 500

WAYNE BAKER
USA. Born: 18.12.1941

Major race wins: 1983 Sebring 12 hrs

MAURO BALDI
I. Born: 31.1.1954, Reggio Emilia

1990 World Sports Car Champion (with Jean-Louis Schlesser); 1981 European F3 Champion

World Championship Grand Prix Record   *Mauro Baldi*

years	starts	wins	2nd	3rd	4th	5th	6th	PP	FL	points
1982–85	36(5)	-	-	-	1	3	-	-	5

Best championship: 1983 16th. Best qualifying: 7th

World Sports Car Championship. Race wins: 1985 Spa, 1986 Brands Hatch, 1987 Norisring 200 miles, 1988 Jerez, Spa, 1989 Suzuka, Brands Hatch, Spa, 1990 Suzuka, Monza, Dijon, Nürburgring, Donington, Montréal, 1991 Suzuka, 1992 Donington, Magny-Cours

European F3 Championship. Race wins: 1980 Zandvoort, Misano, Jarama, 1981 Vallelunga, Österreichring, Zolder, Zandvoort, Croix-en-Ternois, Misano, Knutstorp, Imola

Other major race wins: 1980 Monaco F3 GP, 1994 Le Mans 24 hrs

JACK BALDWIN
USA. Born: 31.5.1948

1992 Trans-Am Champion

RENATO BALESTRERO
I. Born: 1898. Died: 1948

Major race wins: 1925 Tripoli GP

BOBBY BALL
USA. Born: 26.8.1925, Phoenix. Died: 27.2.1954, Phoenix from injuries inflicted at the Carrel Speedway on 4.1.1953

Indycar Championship. Race wins: 1952 San José

FULVIO MARIA BALLABIO
I. Born: 8.10.1954, Milan

	wins	2nd	3rd	4th	5th	6th	PP	FL	points
European F2 Ch	-	-	-	-	1	1	-	-	3

Championship: 1983 17th

BALLESTRIERI
I

Major race wins: 1974 Targa Florio

CLAUDE BALLOT-LENA
F. Born: 4.8.1936, Paris

Major race wins: 1969 Spa 24 hrs, 1983 Daytona 24 hrs

MARCEL BALSA
F. Born: 9.1.1901, St Frion. Died: 11.8.1984

World Championship Grand Prix Record

year	starts	wins	2nd	3rd	4th	5th	6th	PP	FL	points
1952	1	-	-	-	-	-	-	-	-	-

Best result: no finishes. Best qualifying: no time set

GIANNI BALZARINI
I

Major race wins: 1959 Mille Miglia

LORENZO BANDINI
I. Born: 21.12.1935, Barce (LT). Died: 10.5.1967, Monaco GP

World Championship Grand Prix Record

years	starts	wins	2nd	3rd	4th	5th	6th	PP	FL	points
1961–67	42	1	2	5	2	4	3	1	2	58

Best championship: 1964 4th. Best qualifying: 1st. Race wins: 1964 Austrian GP

World Sports Car Championship. Race wins: 1961 Pescara, 1963 Le Mans 24 hrs, 1965 Targa Florio, 1967 Monza, Daytona 24 hrs

HENRY BANKS
USA. Born: 14.6.1913, London (GB)

1950 Indycar Champion

Indycar Championship. Race wins: 1950 Detroit

WARWICK BANKS
GB. Born: 12.7.1939

1964 European Touring Car Champion

ROD BANTING
GB. Born: 31.5.1941

1964 BRSCC British F3 Champion

FABRIZIO BARBAZZA
I. Born: 2.4.1963, Monza

1986 American Racing Series Champion

World Championship Grand Prix Record

years	starts	wins	2nd	3rd	4th	5th	6th	PP	FL	points
1991; 1993	8(12)	-	-	-	-	-	2	-	-	2

Best championship: 1993 17th. Best qualifying: 20th

	wins	2nd	3rd	4th	5th	6th	PP	FL	points
Int F3000 Ch	-	-	-	1	-	-	-	-	3

Championship: 1990 16th

JOHN BARBER
GB

World Championship Grand Prix Record

year	starts	wins	2nd	3rd	4th	5th	6th	PP	FL	points
1953	1	-	-	-	-	-	-	-	-	-

Best result: 8th. Best qualifying: 16th

SKIP BARBER
USA. Born: 16.11.1936, Carlisle, Pennsylvania

World Championship Grand Prix Record

years	starts	wins	2nd	3rd	4th	5th	6th	PP	FL	points
1971–72	5(1)	-	-	-	-	-	-	-	-	-

Best result: 16th. Best qualifying: 20th

DICK BARBOUR
USA

Major race wins: 1980 Sebring 12 hrs

PATRICK BARDINON
F

	wins	2nd	3rd	4th	5th	6th	PP	FL	points
European F2 Ch	-	-	-	-	-	-	-	-	1

Championship: 1977 20th

PAOLO BARILLA
I. Born: 20.4.1961, Milan

World Championship Grand Prix Record

years	starts	wins	2nd	3rd	4th	5th	6th	PP	FL	points
1989–90	9(6)	-	-	-	-	-	-	-	-	-

Best result: 11th. Best qualifying: 14th

	wins	2nd	3rd	4th	5th	6th	PP	FL	points
Int F3000 Ch	-	-	1	-	-	-	-	-	3

Championship: 1988 17th

World Sports Car Championship. Race wins: 1985 Le Mans 24 hrs, 1986 Fuji

WOOLF BARNATO

GB. Born: 1895. Died: 27.7.1948, medical operation

Major Sports Car races. Race wins: 1928, 1929 and 1930 Le Mans 24 hrs

RUBENS BARRICHELLO

BR. Born: 23.5.1972, Sao Paulo

1991 British F3 Champion; 1990 GM-Lotus Euroseries Champion

World Championship Grand Prix Record

years	starts	wins	2nd	3rd	4th	5th	6th	PP	FL	points
1993–94	31(1)	-	-	1	5	1	-	1	-	21

Best championship: 1994 6th. Best qualifying: 1st

	wins	2nd	3rd	4th	5th	6th	PP	FL	points
Int F3000 Ch	-	2	2	-	2	3	-	2	27

Championship: 1992 3rd

MICHAEL BARTELS

D. Born: 8.3.1968, Plettenberg

World Championship Grand Prix Record

year	starts	wins	2nd	3rd	4th	5th	6th	PP	FL	points
1991	-(4)	-	-	-	-	-	-	-	-	-

Best qualifying: 28th

	wins	2nd	3rd	4th	5th	6th	PP	FL	points
Int F3000 Ch	-	3	2	1	-	1	-	1	30

Championships: 1990 22nd, 1992 4th, 1993 11th

EDGAR BARTH

DDR. Born: 26.11.1917, Herold-Erzegeberge. Died: 20.5.1965, Ludwigsburg

World Championship Grand Prix Record

years	starts	wins	2nd	3rd	4th	5th	6th	PP	FL	points
1953; 1957–58; 1960; 1964	5	-	-	-	-	-	-	-	-	-

Best result: 7th. Best qualifying: 12th

World Sports Car Championship. Race wins: 1959 Targa Florio

Other major race wins: 1957 German GP F2 Class

JÜRGEN BARTH

D. Born: 10.12.1947, Thoum

World Sports Car Championship. Race wins: 1977 Le Mans 24 hrs, 1980 Nürburgring, Dijon

KEVIN BARTLETT

AUS. Born: 25.5.1940

1968 and 1969 Australian Gold Star Champion

Tasman Cup. Race wins: 1970 Warwick Farm, 1972 Teretonga

Other major race wins: 1969 Macau GP. 1974 Bathurst

GIORGIO BASSI

I. Born: 20.1.1934, Milan

World Championship Grand Prix Record

year	starts	wins	2nd	3rd	4th	5th	6th	PP	FL	points
1965	1	-	-	-	-	-	-	-	-	-

Best result: no finishes. Best qualifying: 22nd

NORMAN BATTEN

USA. Born: n/a. Died: 12.11.1928, lost at sea aboard the SS Vestris

Indycar Championship. Race wins: 1925 Indianapolis 500, 1926 Atlantic City Race 3

ERWIN BAUER

D. Born: 17.7.1912. Died: 2.6.1958, Nürburgring 1000 kms

World Championship Grand Prix Record

year	starts	wins	2nd	3rd	4th	5th	6th	PP	FL	points
1953	1	-	-	-	-	-	-	-	-	-

Best result: no finishes. Best qualifying: 33rd

JOHN BAUER

USA. Born: 14.9.1949

1980 Trans-Am Champion

WALTER BAUMER

D. Born: n/a. Died: World War Two

Major race wins: 1940 Mille Miglia

ASTRUBEL BAYARDO

BR

World Championship Grand Prix Record

year	starts	wins	2nd	3rd	4th	5th	6th	PP	FL	points
1959	-(1)	-	-	-	-	-	-	-	-	-

Best qualifying: no time set

ELIE BAYOL

F. Born: 28.2.1914, Marseille

World Championship Grand Prix Record

years	starts	wins	2nd	3rd	4th	5th	6th	PP	FL	points
1952–56	7(1)	-	-	-	-	1	1	-	-	2

Best championship: 1954 18th. Best qualifying: 10th

CAREL GODIN DE BEAUFORT

NL. Born: 10.4.1934, Maarsbergen. Died: 3.8.1964, Nürburgring, German GP practice

World Championship Grand Prix Record

years	starts	wins	2nd	3rd	4th	5th	6th	PP	FL	points
1957–64	28(3)	-	-	-	-	-	4	-	-	4

Best championship: 1963 14th. Best qualifying: 8th

DON BEAUMAN

GB. Born: 26.7.1928. Died: 9.7.1955, Wicklow, Northern Ireland, Leinster Trophy race

World Championship Grand Prix Record

year	starts	wins	2nd	3rd	4th	5th	6th	PP	FL	points
1954	1	-	-	-	-	-	-	-	-	-

Best result: 11th. Best qualifying: 17th

GÜNTHER BECHEM

D. Born: 21.12.1921. Died: 1980

World Championship Grand Prix Record

year	starts	wins	2nd	3rd	4th	5th	6th	PP	FL	points
1953	1	-	-	-	-	-	-	-	-	-

Best result: no finishes. Best qualifying: 30th

BECQUET

F

Major race wins: 1924 Spa 24 hrs

NORM BEECHEY

AUS

1970 Australian Touring Car Champion

JON BEEKHUIS

USA. Born: 31.3.1960, Zurich (CH)

1988 American Racing Series Champion

JEAN BEHRA

F. Born: 16.2.1921, Nice. Died: 1.8.1959, Avus, Sports Car race

World Championship Grand Prix Record

years	starts	wins	2nd	3rd	4th	5th	6th	PP	FL	points
1952–59	52(1)	-	2	7	2	4	6	-	1	51.14

Best championship: 1956 4th. Best qualifying: 2nd

World Sports Car Championship. Race wins: 1956 Nürburgring, 1957 Sebring 12 hrs, Swedish GP

Other major race wins: International Trophy (Silverstone)

DEREK BELL

GB. Born: 31.10.1941, Pinner

1985 (with Hans-Joachim Stuck) and 1986 World Sports Car Champion

World Championship Grand Prix Record

years	starts	wins	2nd	3rd	4th	5th	6th	PP	FL	points
1968–72, 1974	9(7)	-	-	-	-	-	1	-	-	1

Best championship: 1970 22nd. Best qualifying: 8th

	wins	2nd	3rd	4th	5th	6th	PP	FL	points
European F2 Ch	1	-	7	4	2	2	2	2	83

Championships: 1968 4th, 1969 5th, 1970 2nd, 1971 13th, 1973 8th. **Race wins:** 1970 Montjuich Park

World Sports Car Championship. Race wins: 1971 Buenos Aires, 1973 Spa, 1975 Spa, Le Mans 24 hrs, Österreichring, Watkins Glen, 1981 Le Mans 24 hrs, 1982 Le Mans 24 hrs, Brands Hatch, 1983 Silverstone, Fuji, Kyalami, 1984 Monza, Nürburgring, Spa, Sandown Park, 1985 Hockenheim, Mosport Park, Brands Hatch, 1986 Monza, Le Mans 24 hrs, 1987 Le Mans 24 hrs

Other major race wins: 1973 Tourist Trophy, 1987, 1986 and 1989 Daytona 24 hrs

Derek Bell

JEAN-PHILIPPE BELLOC

F. Born: 24.4.1970

1994 French F3 Champion

STEFAN BELLOF

D. Born: 20.11.1957, Giessen. Died: 1.9.1985, Spa 1000 kms

1984 World Sports Car Champion; 1984 German Racing Champion

World Championship Grand Prix Record

years	starts	wins	2nd	3rd	4th	5th	6th	PP	FL	points
1984–85	20(1)	-	-	-	1	-	1	-	-	4

Best championship: 1985 15th. **Best qualifying:** 16th

	wins	2nd	3rd	4th	5th	6th	PP	FL	points
European F2 Ch	2	2	1	1	2	1	2	6	42

Championships: 1982 4th, 1983 9th. **Race wins:** 1982 International Trophy (Silverstone), Jim Clark Trophy (Hockenheim)

World Sports Car Championship. Race wins: 1983 Silverstone, Fuji, Kyalami, 1984 Monza, Nürburgring, Spa, Imola, Fuji, Sandown Park

PAUL BELMONDO

F. Born: 23.4.1963, Paris

World Championship Grand Prix Record

years	starts	wins	2nd	3rd	4th	5th	6th	PP	FL	points
1992; 1994	7(20)	-	-	-	-	-	-	-	-	-

Best result: 9th. **Best qualifying:** 17th

	wins	2nd	3rd	4th	5th	6th	PP	FL	points
Int F3000 Ch	-	-	-	1	1	-	-	3

Championships: 1987 18th, 1990 22nd

TOM BELSO

DK. Born: 27.8.1942, Copenhagen

World Championship Grand Prix Record

years	starts	wins	2nd	3rd	4th	5th	6th	PP	FL	points
1973–74	2(3)	-	-	-	-	-	-	-	-	-

Best result: 8th. **Best qualifying:** 21st

	wins	2nd	3rd	4th	5th	6th	PP	FL	points
European F2 Ch	-	-	1	1	-	-	-	5

Championship: 1972 17th

JEAN-PIERRE BELTOISE

F. Born: 26.4.1937, Paris

1968 European F2 Champion; 1967 Temporada F3 Champion; 1965 French F3 Champion; 1976 and 1977 French Supertourism Champion

World Championship Grand Prix Record

years	starts	wins	2nd	3rd	4th	5th	6th	PP	FL	points
1966–74	86(2)	1	3	4	3	10	5	-	4	77

Best championship: 1970 9th. **Race wins:** 1972 Monaco GP. **Best qualifying:** 2nd

	wins	2nd	3rd	4th	5th	6th	PP	FL	points
European F2 Ch	4	5	4	3	-	1	7	5	75

Championships: 1967 3rd, 1968 1st. **Race wins:** 1968 Hockenheim, Jarama, Zandvoort, 1969 Hockenheim

World Sports Car Championship. Race wins: 1974 Nürburgring, Watkins Glen, Paul Ricard, Brands Hatch

Other major race wins: 1966 Monaco F3 GP, German GP F2 Class, 1970 Buenos Aires Sports Car race

ALDO BENEDETTI

I

Major race wins: 1949 Targa Florio

Jean-Pierre Beltoise

JOHN DUDLEY BENJAFIELD

GB. Born: 6.8.1887, North London. Died: n/a

Major Sports Car races. Race wins: 1927 Le Mans 24 hrs

ROBERT BENOIST

F. Born: ?.3.1895, Auffargis. Died: 12.9.1944, Buchenwald Prisoner of War camp, executed

Pre-1950 Grands Prix. Race wins: 1925 French GP, 1927 French GP, Spanish GP, Italian GP, British GP

Major Sports Car races. Race wins: 1937 Le Mans 24 hrs

Other major race wins: 1929 Spa 24 hrs

OLIVIER BERETTA

MC. Born: 23.11.1969, Monte Carlo

World Championship Grand Prix Record

year	starts	wins	2nd	3rd	4th	5th	6th	PP	FL	points
1994	9(1)	-	-	-	-	-	-	-	-	-

Best result: 7th. **Best qualifying:** 17th

	wins	2nd	3rd	4th	5th	6th	PP	FL	points
Int F3000 Ch	1	-	3	1	-	1	-	20

Championship: 1993 6th. **Race wins:** 1993 Donington

ALLEN BERG

CDN. Born: 1.8.1961, Calgary

1983 New Zealand International Champion; 1993 Mexican F2 Champion

World Championship Grand Prix Record

year	starts	wins	2nd	3rd	4th	5th	6th	PP	FL	points
1986	9	-	-	-	-	-	-	-	-	-

Best result: 12th. **Best qualifying:** 25th

ERWIN BERGDOLL

USA

Indycar Championship. Race wins: 1911 Philadelphia Race 1

GEORGES BERGER

B. Born: 14.9.1918, Brussels. Died: 23.8.1967, Nürburgring

World Championship Grand Prix Record

years	starts	wins	2nd	3rd	4th	5th	6th	PP	FL	points
1953–54	2	-	-	-	-	-	-	-	-	-

Best result: no finishes. **Best qualifying:** 20th

GERHARD BERGER

A. Born: 27.8.1959, Wörgl

World Championship Grand Prix Record

years	starts	wins	2nd	3rd	4th	5th	6th	PP	FL	points
1984–94	163	9	15	14	18	8	8	10	16	306

Best championship: 1988, 1990, 1994 3rd. **Race wins:** 1986 Mexican GP, 1987 Japanese GP, Australian GP, 1988 Italian GP, 1989 Portuguese GP, 1991 Japanese GP, 1992 Canadian GP, Australian GP, 1994 German GP. **Best qualifying:** 1st

European F3 Championship. Race wins: 1984 Österreichring, Monza

Other major race wins: 1985 Spa 24 hrs

ANDERS BERGGREN

S

1985 Swedish Touring Car Champion

FRANCO BERNABEI

I. Born: 1940, Rome

1968 Italian F3 Champion

	wins	2nd	3rd	4th	5th	6th	PP	FL	points
European F2 Ch	-	-	-	1	-	-	-	2

Championship: 1969 15th

ERIC BERNARD

F. Born: 24.8.1964, Istres

World Championship Grand Prix Record

years	starts	wins	2nd	3rd	4th	5th	6th	PP	FL	points
1989–91; 1994	45(2)	-	-	1	1	3	-	-	10

Best championship: 1990 13th. **Best qualifying:** 8th

	wins	2nd	3rd	4th	5th	6th	PP	FL	points
Int F3000 Ch	1	2	1	4	-	1	3	3	88

Championships: 1988 8th, 1989 3rd. **Race wins:** 1989 Jerez

ENRICO BERTAGGIA

I. Born: 19.6.1964, Noale

1987 Italian F3 Champion

World Championship Grand Prix Record

years	starts	wins	2nd	3rd	4th	5th	6th	PP	FL	points
1989; 1992	-(8)	-	-	-	-	-	-	-	-	-

Best qualifying: 37th

		wins	2nd	3rd	4th	5th	6th	PP	FL	points
Int F3000 Ch		-	-	-	1	-	-	-	-	2

Championship: 1993 17th

Major race wins: 1988 Monaco F3 GP, Macau GP

GARY BETTENHAUSEN

USA. Born: 18.11.1941, Tinsley Park, Chicago. Son of Tony Sr, brother of Tony Jr

Indycar Championship. Race wins: 1968 Phoenix Race 2, 1970 Michigan, 1972 Trenton Race 1, 1973 Texas

TONY BETTENHAUSEN SR

USA. Born: 12.9.1916, Tinsley Park, Chicago. Died: 12.5.1961, Indianapolis 500, practice. Father of Gary and Tony Jr

1951 and 1958 Indycar Champion

Indycar Championship. Race wins: 1946 Goshen, 1947 Goshen, Springfield, 1948 Milwaukee Race 3, 1949 Du Quoin, Detroit, 1950 Milwaukee Race 1, Springfield Race 2, Bay Meadows, 1951 Milwaukee Race 1, Langhorne, Springfield Race 1, Du Quoin Race 1, Du Quoin Race 2, Syracuse, Denver, San José, 1953 Syracuse, Phoenix, 1956 Syracuse, 1959 Trenton Race 1, Phoenix

MIKE BEUTTLER

GB. Born: 13.4.1940, Cairo (ET). Died: 29.12.1988, San Francisco (USA)

World Championship Grand Prix Record

years	starts	wins	2nd	3rd	4th	5th	6th	PP	FL	points
1971–73	28(1)	-	-	-	-	-	-	-	-	-

Best result: 7th. Best qualifying: 11th

	wins	2nd	3rd	4th	5th	6th	PP	FL	points
European F2 Ch	1	1	1	4	-	-	-	1	39

Championships: 1971 7th, 1972 9th, 1973 7th. Race wins: 1971 Vallelunga

LUCIEN BIANCHI

B. Born: 10.11.1934, Milan (I). Died: 30.3.1969, Le Mans, testing. Brother of Mauro

World Championship Grand Prix Record

years	starts	wins	2nd	3rd	4th	5th	6th	PP	FL	points
1959–63; 1965; 1968	17(2)	-	-	1	-	-	2	-	-	6

Best championship: 1968 17th. Best qualifying: 12th

World Sports Car Championship. Race wins: 1962 Sebring 12 hrs, 1968 Watkins Glen, Le Mans 24 hrs

MAURO BIANCHI

B. Brother of Lucien

Major race wins: 1966 Macau GP

GINO BIANCO

BR

World Championship Grand Prix Record

year	starts	wins	2nd	3rd	4th	5th	6th	PP	FL	points
1952	4	-	-	-	-	-	-	-	-	-

Best result: 18th. Best qualifying: 12th

FRANK BIELA

D. Born: 2.8.1964, Neuss

1991 German Touring Car Champion; 1993 French Supertourism Champion

CHARLES BIGELOW

USA

Indycar Championship. Race wins: 1911 Oakland Race 1

AMEDEO BIGNAMI

I

Major race wins: 1932 and 1934 Mille Miglia

ROLF BILAND

CH

		wins	2nd	3rd	4th	5th	6th	PP	FL	points
European F2 Ch		-	-	-	-	1	-	-	-	1

Championship: 1983 20th

HANS BINDER

A. Born: 12.6.1948, Zell-am-Ziller

World Championship Grand Prix Record

years	starts	wins	2nd	3rd	4th	5th	6th	PP	FL	points
1976–78	13(2)	-	-	-	-	-	-	-	-	-

Best result: 8th. Best qualifying: 18th

	wins	2nd	3rd	4th	5th	6th	PP	FL	points
European F2 Ch	-	1	-	4	1	-	-	-	21

Championships: 1975 13th, 1976 7th

ROLAND BINDER

D

	wins	2nd	3rd	4th	5th	6th	PP	FL	points
European F2 Ch	-	-	-	1	-	1	-	-	5

Championship: 1973 19th

CLEMENTE BIONDETTI

I. Born: 18.10.1898, Budduro, Sardinia. Died: 24.2.1955, Florence

World Championship Grand Prix Record

year	starts	wins	2nd	3rd	4th	5th	6th	PP	FL	points
1950	1	-	-	-	-	-	-	-	-	-

Best result: no finishes. Best qualifying: 25th

Major race wins: 1938, 1947, 1948 and 1949 Mille Miglia, 1948 and 1949 Targa Florio

"B BIRA"

SM. Born: 15.7.1914, Bangkok. Died: 23.12.1985, London (GB). Real name: Prince Birabongse Bhanuban of Siam (now Thailand)

World Championship Grand Prix Record

years	starts	wins	2nd	3rd	4th	5th	6th	PP	FL	points
1950–54	19	-	-	-	2	1	1	-	-	8

Best championship: 1950 8th. Best qualifying: 5th.

PABLO BIRGER

RA. Born: 6.1.1924, Buenos Aires. Died: 9.3.1966, Buenos Aires

World Championship Grand Prix Record

years	starts	wins	2nd	3rd	4th	5th	6th	PP	FL	points
1953; 1955	2	-	-	-	-	-	-	-	-	-

Best result: no finishes. Best qualifying: 9th

HENRY "TIM" BIRKIN

GB. Born: 1896, Nottingham. Died: 22.6.1933, London, after burning his arm at the Tripoli GP

Major Sports Car races. Race wins: 1929 and 1931 Le Mans 24 hrs

GERRY BIRRELL

GB. Born: 30.7.1944, Glasgow. Died: 23.6.1973, Rouen

	wins	2nd	3rd	4th	5th	6th	PP	FL	points
European F2 Ch	-	-	-	1	1	3	-	-	11

Championships: 1971 11th, 1973 21st

ART BISCH

USA. Born: 10.11.1926, Mesa, Arizona. Died: 6.7.1958, Atlanta

Indycar Championship. Race wins: 1958 Milwaukee Race 1

NORMAN BLACK

GB

Major race wins: 1931 Tourist Trophy

HARRY BLANCHARD

USA. Born: n/a. Died: 31.1.1960, Buenos Aires

World Championship Grand Prix Record

year	starts	wins	2nd	3rd	4th	5th	6th	PP	FL	points
1959	1	-	-	-	-	-	-	-	-	-

Best result: 7th. Best qualifying: 16th

BEAT BLATTER

CH

Major race wins: 1979 Swiss F3 Champion

MICHAEL BLEEKEMOLEN

NL. Born: 2.10.1949, Amsterdam

World Championship Grand Prix Record

years	starts	wins	2nd	3rd	4th	5th	6th	PP	FL	points
1977–78	1(4)	-	-	-	-	-	-	-	-	-

Best result: no finishes. Best qualifying: 25th
European F3 Championship. Race wins: 1978 Enna

ROBERT BLOCH
F
Major Sports Car races. Race wins: 1926 Le Mans 24 hrs

TREVOR BLOKDYK
ZA. Born: 30.11.1935, Krugersdorp. Died: 1995

World Championship Grand Prix Record

years	starts	wins	2nd	3rd	4th	5th	6th	PP	FL	points
1963; 1965	1(1)	-	-	-	-	-	-	-	-	-

Best result: 12th. Best qualifying: 19th

STIG BLOMQVIST
S. Born: 29.7.1946, Lindesberg
1990 Swedish Touring Car Champion

MARK BLUNDELL
GB. Born: 8.4.1966, Barnet

World Championship Grand Prix Record

years	starts	wins	2nd	3rd	4th	5th	6th	PP	FL	points
1991; 1993–94	46(2)	-	-	3	-	3	1	-	-	19

Best championship: 1993 10th. Best qualifying: 4th

	wins	2nd	3rd	4th	5th	6th	PP	FL	points
Int F3000 Ch	-	3	2	-	2	4	-	1	31

Championships: 1987 14th, 1988 6th, 1989 11th
World Sports Car Championship. Race wins: 1992 Le Mans 24 hrs

GEOFF BODINE
USA. Born: 18.4.1949, Elmira, New York State
Major race wins: 1986 Daytona 500

RAUL BOESEL
BR. Born: 4.12.1957, Curitiba
1987 World Sports Car Champion

World Championship Grand Prix Record

years	starts	wins	2nd	3rd	4th	5th	6th	PP	FL	points
1982–83	23(7)	-	-	-	-	-	-	-	-	-

Best result: 7th. Best qualifying: 17th
World Sports Car Championship. Race wins: 1987 Jerez, Silverstone, Brands Hatch, Nürburgring, Spa
Other major race wins: 1988 Daytona 24 hrs

ANDRÉ BOILLOT
F. Born: 1891. Died: 1932. Brother of Georges
Major race wins: 1919 Targa Florio, 1926 Spa 24 hrs

GEORGES BOILLOT
F. Born: 1885. Died: 21.4.1916, Verdun, shot down while fighting for the French Air Service. Brother of André
Pre-1950 Grands Prix. Race wins: 1912 and 1913 French GP

COLIN BOND
AUS. Born: 15.8.1941
1975 Australian Touring Car Champion
Major race wins: 1969 Bathurst

BOB BONDURANT
USA. Born: 27.4.1933, Evanston, Illinois

World Championship Grand Prix Record

years	starts	wins	2nd	3rd	4th	5th	6th	PP	FL	points
1965–66	9	-	-	-	1	-	-	-	-	3

Best championship: 1966 14th. Best qualifying: 11th

FELICE BONETTO
I. Born: 9.6.1903, Manerbio, Brescia. Died: 21.11.1953, Silao, Carrera Panamericana

World Championship Grand Prix Record

years	starts	wins	2nd	3rd	4th	5th	6th	PP	FL	points
1950–53	15(2)	-	-	2	3	3	1	-	-	17.5

Best championship: 1951 8th. Best qualifying: 2nd
Major race wins: 1952 Targa Florio

NEIL BONNETT
USA. Born: 30.7.1946. Died: 11.2.1994, Daytona
Major race wins: 1982 and 1983 World 600

JO BONNIER
S. Born: 31.1.1930, Stockholm. Died: 11.6.1972, Le Mans 24 hrs

World Championship Grand Prix Record

years	starts	wins	2nd	3rd	4th	5th	6th	PP	FL	points
1956–71	104(4)	1	-	-	1	10	8	1	-	39

Best championship: 1959 8th. Race wins: 1959 Dutch GP. Best qualifying: 1st
World Sports Car Championship. Race wins: 1960 Targa Florio, 1962 Sebring 12 hrs, 1963 Targa Florio, 1966 Nürburgring
Other major race wins: 1960 German GP

ROBERTO BONOMI
RA. Born: 30.9.1919, Buenos Aires

World Championship Grand Prix Record

year	starts	wins	2nd	3rd	4th	5th	6th	PP	FL	points
1960	1	-	-	-	-	-	-	-	-	-

Best result: 11th. Best qualifying: 17th

PIETRO BORDINO
I. Born: 22.11.1887, Turin. Died: 16.4.1928, Alessandria, in practice
Pre-1950 Grands Prix. Race wins: 1922 Italian GP
Indycar Championship. Race wins: 1922 Beverly Hills Race 2, Cotati Race 1

JAKOB BORDOLI
CH
1980 and 1985 Swiss F3 Champion

TOMMY "SLIM" BORGUDD
S. Born: 25.11.1946, Borgholm
1994 Nordic Touring Car Champion; 1979 Swedish F3 Champion

World Championship Grand Prix Record

years	starts	wins	2nd	3rd	4th	5th	6th	PP	FL	points
1981–82	10(5)	-	-	-	-	-	1	-	-	1

Best championship: 1981 18th. Best qualifying: 20th

GIANCARLO BORNIGIA
I
Major race wins: 1950 Targa Florio

MARIO BORNIGIA
I
Major race wins: 1950 Targa Florio

BACONIN BORZACCHINI
I. Born: 28.9.1898, Terni. Died: 10.9.1933, Monza GP
Major race wins: 1930 Tripoli GP, 1932 Mille Miglia

MIDGE BOSWORTH
AUS
Major race wins: 1965 Bathurst

LUKI BOTHA
ZA. Born: 16.1.1930

World Championship Grand Prix Record

year	starts	wins	2nd	3rd	4th	5th	6th	PP	FL	points
1967	1	-	-	-	-	-	-	-	-	-

Best result: no finishes. Best qualifying: 17th

GENE BOTHELLO
USA
1979 Trans-Am Champion

CHRISTOPHE BOUCHUT
F. Born: 24.9.1966, Voirons
1991 French F3 Champion
Major Sports Car races. Race wins: 1993 Le Mans 24 hrs

JEAN-CHRISTOPHE "JULES" BOULLION
F. Born: 6.2.1971
1994 International F3000 Champion

	wins	2nd	3rd	4th	5th	6th	PP	FL	points
Int F3000 Ch	3	3	-	1	-	-	-	2	48

Drivers A–Z

Championships: 1993 8th, 1994 1st. **Race wins:** 1994 Spa, Estoril, Magny-Cours

CLAUDE BOURGOIGNIE
B
1978 Belgian Touring Car Champion

	wins	2nd	3rd	4th	5th	6th	PP	FL	points
European F2 Ch	-	1	1	1	-	1	-	-	16

Championship: 1975 7th

THIERRY BOUTSEN
B. Born: 13.7.1957, Brussels

World Championship Grand Prix Record

years	starts	wins	2nd	3rd	4th	5th	6th	PP	FL	points
1983–93	163(1)	3	2	10	8	11	7	1	1	132

Best championship: 1988 4th. **Race wins:** 1989 Canadian GP, Australian GP, 1990 Hungarian GP. **Best qualifying:** 1st

	wins	2nd	3rd	4th	5th	6th	PP	FL	points
European F2 Ch	5	4	2	3	-	2	8	2	88

Championships: 1981 2nd, 1982 3rd. **Race wins:** 1981 Eifelrennen (Nürburgring), Mediterranean GP (Enna), 1982 Eifelrennen (Nürburgring), Spa, Mediterranean GP (Enna)

World Sports Car Championship. Race wins: 1983 Monza, 1986 Spa

European F3 Championship. Race wins: 1980 Nürburgring, Zolder, Magny-Cours

Other major race wins: 1985 Daytona 24 hrs

JOHN BOWE
AUS. Born: 16.4.1954
1984 and 1985 Australian Gold Star Champion
Major race wins: 1989 and 1994 Bathurst

JOE BOYER
USA. Born: 1890, Detroit. Died: 2.9.1924, Altoona, Pennsylvania, from injuries inflicted in the previous day's Indycar race
Indycar Championship. Race wins: 1919 Uniontown Race 7, Cincinnati, 1924 Indianapolis 500

LORD BRABAZON OF TARA
GB. Born: 8.2.1884, Kent. Died: 17.5.1964, Chertsey
Major race wins: 1907 Ardennes Circuit (Kaiserpreis class)

DAVID BRABHAM
AUS. Born: 5.9.1965, Wimbledon (GB). Son of Jack, brother of Geoff and Gary
1989 British F3 Champion; 1987 Australian Gold Star Champion

World Championship Grand Prix Record

years	starts	wins	2nd	3rd	4th	5th	6th	PP	FL	points
1990; 1994	24(6)	-	-	-	-	-	-	-	-	-

Best result: 10th. **Best qualifying:** 21st
World Sports Car Championship. Race wins: 1991 Nürburgring
Other major race wins: 1989 Macau GP, 1991 Spa 24 hrs

GARY BRABHAM
AUS. Born: 29.3.1961, Wimbledon (GB). Son of Jack, brother of Geoff and David
1989 British F3000 Champion

World Championship Grand Prix Record

year	starts	wins	2nd	3rd	4th	5th	6th	PP	FL	points
1990	-(2)	-	-	-	-	-	-	-	-	-

Best qualifying: 34th

	wins	2nd	3rd	4th	5th	6th	PP	FL	points
Int F3000 Ch	-	-	2	-	1	-	-	-	10

Championships: 1989 17th, 1990 11th
Major race wins: 1991 Sebring 12 hrs

GEOFF BRABHAM
AUS. Born: 20.3.1952, Sydney. Son of Jack, brother of Gary and David
1988, 1989, 1990 and 1991 IMSA GT Champion; 1981 Can-Am Champion; 1979 SCCA Super Vee Champion
Major Sports Car Races. Race wins: 1989 and 1991 Sebring 12 hrs, 1993 Le Mans 24 hrs

JACK BRABHAM
AUS. Born: 2.4.1926, Hurstville, Sydney. Father of Geoff, Gary and David

Jack Brabham (right) – the first man to win the World Championship in a car bearing his own name

1959, 1960 and 1966 World Champion; 1958 and 1966 British F2 Champion; 1964 and 1966 French F2 Champion

World Championship Grand Prix Record

years	starts	wins	2nd	3rd	4th	5th	6th	PP	FL	points
1955–70	126(2)	14	10	7	13	5	7	13	12	261

Race wins: 1959 Monaco GP, British GP, 1960 Dutch GP, Belgian GP, French GP, British GP, Portuguese GP, 1966 French GP, British GP, Dutch GP, German GP, 1967 French GP, Canadian GP, 1970 South African GP. **Best qualifying:** 1st

	wins	2nd	3rd	4th	5th	6th	PP	FL	points
European F2 Ch	-	2	-	1	-	1	-	-	-

World Sports Car Championship. Race wins: 1958 Nürburgring
Tasman Cup. Race wins: 1964 Australian GP, 1967 Longford
Other race wins: 1955 Australian GP, 1958 Moroccan GP F2 Class, 1959 International Trophy (Silverstone), 1963 Australian GP, Austrian GP, 1964 International Trophy (Silverstone), 1966 International Trophy (Silverstone), 1969 International Trophy (Silverstone)

GIOVANNI BRACCO
I. Born: 6.6.1908, Biella. Died: 6.8.1968
Major race wins: 1952 Mille Miglia

BILL BRACK
CDN. Born: 26.12.1935, Toronto
1973, 1974 and 1975 North American Formula Atlantic Champion

World Championship Grand Prix Record

year	starts	wins	2nd	3rd	4th	5th	6th	PP	FL	points
1968–69; 1972	3	-	-	-	-	-	-	-	-	-

Best result: no finishes. **Best qualifying:** 18th

KENNY BRÄCK
S. Born: 21.3.1966

	wins	2nd	3rd	4th	5th	6th	PP	FL	points
Int F3000 Ch	-	-	1	-	-	1	-	-	5

Championship: 1994 11th

CALEB BRAGG
USA
Pre-1950 Grands Prix. Race wins: 1912 American GP

ERNESTO "TINO" BRAMBILLA
I. Born: 31.1.1934, Monza. Brother of Vittorio
1966 Italian F3 Champion

World Championship Grand Prix Record

years	starts	wins	2nd	3rd	4th	5th	6th	PP	FL	points
1963; 1969	-(2)	-	-	-	-	-	-	-	-	-

Best qualifying: 15th

	wins	2nd	3rd	4th	5th	6th	PP	FL	points
European F2 Ch	2	-	1	-	-	4	1	2	38

Championships: 1968 2nd, 1969 7th, 1972 19th. **Race wins:** 1968 Hockenheim, Rome GP (Vallelunga)

VITTORIO BRAMBILLA
I. Born: 11.11.1937, Monza. Brother of Tino
1972 Italian F3 Champion

478

World Championship Grand Prix Record

years	starts	wins	2nd	3rd	4th	5th	6th	PP	FL	points
1974–80	74(5)	1	-	-	1	2	5	1	1	15.5

Best championship: 1975 11th. **Race wins:** 1975 Austrian GP. **Best qualifying:** 1st

	wins	2nd	3rd	4th	5th	6th	PP	FL	points
European F2 Ch	3	2	1	1	2	2	2	1	58

Championships: 1970 13th, 1971 18th, 1973 4th, 1975 13th. **Race wins:** 1973 Salzburgring, Albi GP, 1975 Rome GP (Vallelunga)
World Sports Car Championship. Race wins: 1977 Monza, Vallelunga, Imola, Salzburgring

ANTONIO BRANCA
CH. Born: 15.9.1916. Died: 10.5.1985, Sierre

World Championship Grand Prix Record

years	starts	wins	2nd	3rd	4th	5th	6th	PP	FL	points
1950–51	3	-	-	-	-	-	-	-	-	-

Best result: 10th. **Best qualifying:** 13th

GIANFRANCO BRANCATELLI
I. Born: 18.1.1950, Turin

1985 European Touring Car Champion (shared with Thomas Lindstrom); 1988 Italian Touring Car Champion

World Championship Grand Prix Record

year	starts	wins	2nd	3rd	4th	5th	6th	PP	FL	points
1979	-(3)	-	-	-	-	-	-	-	-	-

Best qualifying: 25th

	wins	2nd	3rd	4th	5th	6th	PP	FL	points
European F2 Ch	-	-	-	1	-	-	-	-	3

Championship: 1977 17th
European F3 Championship. Race wins: 1976 Mantorp Park, Vallelunga
Other major race wins: 1984 Tourist Trophy, 1989 Spa 24 hrs

ERIC BRANDON
GB. Born: 18.7.1920, London. Died: 8.8.1982

1951 British F3 Champion

World Championship Grand Prix Record

years	starts	wins	2nd	3rd	4th	5th	6th	PP	FL	points
1952; 1954	5	-	-	-	-	-	-	-	-	-

Best result: 8th. **Best qualifying:** 12th

DON BRANSON
USA. Born: 6.6.1920, Rantoul, Illinois. Died: 12.11.1966, Ascot, California

Indycar Championship. Race wins: 1962 Langhorne Race 2, Trenton Race 3, 1965 Phoenix Race 1, Du Quoin, Sacramento, 1966 Springfield

MANFRED VON BRAUCHITSCH
D. Born: 15.8.1905, Hamburg

Pre-1950 Grands Prix. Race wins: 1937 Monaco GP, 1938 French GP

TOMMY BRIDGER
GB. Born: 24.6.1934, Welwyn. Died: 30.7.1991, Aboyne, Aberdeenshire

World Championship Grand Prix Record

year	starts	wins	2nd	3rd	4th	5th	6th	PP	FL	points
1958	1	-	-	-	-	-	-	-	-	-

Best result: no finishes. **Best qualifying:** no time set

MIKE BRIGGS
ZA

1993 South African Touring Car Champion; 1991 South African Drivers' Champion

GASTONE BRILLI-PERI
I. Born: 24.3.1893, Montevarchi, Florence. Died: 22.3.1930, Tripoli GP practice

Pre-1950 Grands Prix. Race wins: 1925 Italian GP
Other major race wins: 1929 Tripoli GP

TONY BRISE
GB. Born: 28.3.1952, Dartford. Died: 29.11.1975, London, aircraft accident with Graham Hill Racing

1973 Lombard and John Player British F3 Champion

World Championship Grand Prix Record

year	starts	wins	2nd	3rd	4th	5th	6th	PP	FL	points
1975	10	-	-	-	-	-	1	-	-	1

Championship: 19th. **Best qualifying:** 6th

CHRIS BRISTOW
GB. Born: 2.12.1937, London. Died: 19.6.1960, Spa, Belgian GP

World Championship Grand Prix Record

years	starts	wins	2nd	3rd	4th	5th	6th	PP	FL	points
1959–60	4	-	-	-	-	-	-	-	-	-

Best result: 10th. **Best qualifying:** 4th

ANTONIO BRIVIO
I. Born: 27.12.1905, Biella. Died: 1995

Major race wins: 1932 Spa 24 hrs, 1933 and 1935 Targa Florio, 1936 Mille Miglia

PETER BROCK
AUS. Born: 17.8.1945

1974, 1978 and 1980 Australian Touring Car Champion

Major race wins: 1972, 1975, 1978, 1979, 1980, 1982, 1983, 1984 and 1987 Bathurst

FRANK BRODIE
ZA

1955 South African Drivers' Champion

PETER BROEKER
CDN. Born: 15.5.1929

Peter Brock

World Championship Grand Prix Record

year	starts	wins	2nd	3rd	4th	5th	6th	PP	FL	points
1963	1	-	-	-	-	-	-	-	-	-

Best result: 7th. **Best qualifying:** 21st

TONY BROOKS
GB. Born: 25.2.1932, Dukinfield

World Championship Grand Prix Record

years	starts	wins	2nd	3rd	4th	5th	6th	PP	FL	points
1956–61	38(3)	6	2	2	1	3	-	3	3	75

Best championship: 1959 2nd. **Race wins:** 1957 British GP (with Moss), 1958 Belgian GP, German GP, Italian GP, 1959 French GP, German GP. **Best qualifying:** 1st
World Sports Car Championship. Race wins: 1957 Nürburgring, 1958 Tourist Trophy

ALAN BROWN
GB. Born: 20.11.1919, Malton, Yorkshire

World Championship Grand Prix Record

years	starts	wins	2nd	3rd	4th	5th	6th	PP	FL	points
1952–54	8(1)	-	-	-	-	1	1	-	-	2

Best championship: 1952 16th. **Best qualifying:** 9th

WALT BROWN
USA. Born: 30.12.1911, Springfield, New York. Died: 29.7.1951, Williams Grove

Indycar Championship. Race wins: 1948 Langhorne

WARWICK BROWN
AUS. Born: 24.12.1949, Sydney

1975 Tasman Champion

World Championship Grand Prix Record

year	starts	wins	2nd	3rd	4th	5th	6th	PP	FL	points
1976	1	-	-	-	-	-	-	-	-	-

Best result: 14th. **Best qualifying:** 23rd
Tasman Cup. Race wins: 1974 Adelaide, 1975 New Zealand GP, Oran Park
Other major race wins: 1977 Australian GP

DAVID BRUCE-BROWN
USA. Born: 1890. Died: 1.10.1912, Milwaukee, American GP practice

Pre-1950 Grands Prix. Race wins: 1910 American GP, 1911 American GP (counted for the revised AAA Indycar Championship)
Indycar Championship. Race wins: see above

ADOLF BRUDES
D. Born: 15.10.1899. Died: 5.11.1986

World Championship Grand Prix Record

year	starts	wins	2nd	3rd	4th	5th	6th	PP	FL	points
1952	1	-	-	-	-	-	-	-	-	-

Best result: no finishes. Best qualifying: no time set

MARTIN BRUNDLE
GB. Born: 1.6.1959, King's Lynn
1988 World Sports Car Champion

World Championship Grand Prix Record

years	starts	wins	2nd	3rd	4th	5th	6th	PP	FL	points
1984–94	131(7)	-	2	6	6	11	7	-	-	83

Best championship: 1992 6th. Best qualifying: 3rd

World Sports Car Championship. Race
wins: 1987 Spa, 1988 Jarama, Monza,
Silverstone, Brands Hatch, Fuji, 1990
Silverstone, Le Mans 24 hrs, 1991 Monza
European F3 Championship. Race
wins: 1983 Silverstone, Donington Park
Other major race wins: 1988 Daytona 24
hrs

JIMMY BRYAN
USA. Born: 28.1.1927, Phoenix, Arizona.
Died: 19.6.1960, Langhorne, Pennsylvania
1954, 1956 and 1957 Indycar Champion

Martin Brundle
....

Indycar Championship. Race wins:
1953 Sacramento, 1954 Langhorne, Indiana State Fairgrounds,
Sacramento, Phoenix, Las Vegas, 1955 Langhorne, Springfield, Du
Quoin, Indiana State Fairgrounds, Sacramento, Phoenix, 1956
Springfield, Milwaukee Race 2, Du Quoin, Indiana State
Fairgrounds, 1957 Detroit, Phoenix, 1958 Indianapolis 500

CLEMAR BUCCI
RA. Born: 4.9.1920, Santa Fé

World Championship Grand Prix Record

years	starts	wins	2nd	3rd	4th	5th	6th	PP	FL	points
1954–55	5	-	-	-	-	-	-	-	-	-

Best result: no finishes. Best qualifying: 10th

RONNIE BUCKNUM
USA. Born: 5.4.1936, Alhambra, California. Died: 22.4.1992,
California, diabetes complications

World Championship Grand Prix Record

years	starts	wins	2nd	3rd	4th	5th	6th	PP	FL	points
1964–66	11	-	-	-	1	-	-	-	-	2

Best championship: 1965 14th. Best qualifying: 6th
Indycar Championship. Race wins: 1968 Michigan

IVOR BUEB
GB. Born: 6.6.1923, London. Died: 1.8.1959, Clermont-Ferrand,
Auvergne F2 Race

World Championship Grand Prix Record

years	starts	wins	2nd	3rd	4th	5th	6th	PP	FL	points
1957–59	5(1)	-	-	-	-	-	-	-	-	-

Best result: 8th. Best qualifying: 16th
World Sports Car Championship. Race wins: 1955 and 1957 Le
Mans 24 hrs

LUIS-PEREIRA BUENO
BR

World Championship Grand Prix Record

year	starts	wins	2nd	3rd	4th	5th	6th	PP	FL	points
1973	1	-	-	-	-	-	-	-	-	-

Best result: 12th. Best qualifying: 20th

GIUSEPPE BUGATTI
I. Born: 1.3.1965, Brescia

	wins	2nd	3rd	4th	5th	6th	PP	FL	points
Int F3000 Ch	-	-	1	-	2	-	-	-	8

Championship: 1991 11th, 1992 16th

ROBBIE BUHL
USA. Born: 2.9.1965, Detroit
1992 Indy Lights Champion

DAVE BUICK
USA

Indycar Championship. Race wins: 1910 Elgin Race 1

IAN BURGESS
GB. Born: 6.7.1930, London

World Championship Grand Prix Record

years	starts	wins	2nd	3rd	4th	5th	6th	PP	FL	points
1958–63	16(4)	-	-	-	-	-	1	-	-	-

Best qualifying: 13th.

ALEX BURGSTALLER
D

Major race wins: 1994 Spa 24 hrs

BOB BURMAN
USA. Born: 23.4.1884, Imlay City, Michigan. Died: 8.4.1916,
Corona, California

Indycar Championship. Race wins: 1909 Indianapolis Race 1,
Lowell Race 1, 1910 Indianapolis Race 4, 1914 Kalamazoo, 1915
Oklahoma City, Burlington

KELVIN BURT
GB. Born: 7.9.1967, Birmingham
1993 British F3 Champion

JIM BUSBY
USA. Born: 14.6.1942

World Sports Car Championship. Race wins: 1981 Riverside

JAN BUSSELL
SGP

Major race wins: 1968 and 1971 Macau GP

ROBERTO BUSSINELLO
I. Born: 4.10.1927, Pistoia

World Championship Grand Prix Record

years	starts	wins	2nd	3rd	4th	5th	6th	PP	FL	points
1961; 1965	2(1)	-	-	-	-	-	-	-	-	-

Best result: 13th. Best qualifying: 21st

JOE BUZZETTA
USA. Born: 1937, Brooklyn, New York

World Sports Car Championship. Race wins: 1967
Nürburgring

TOMMY BYRNE
IRL. Born: 6.5.1958, Drogheda
1982 British F3 Champion

World Championship Grand Prix Record

year	starts	wins	2nd	3rd	4th	5th	6th	PP	FL	points
1982	2(3)	-	-	-	-	-	-	-	-	-

Best result: no finishes. Best qualifying: 26th
European F3 Championship. Race wins: 1983 Österreichring,
Misano

RED BYRON
USA. Born: 3.12.1915, Boulder, Colorado. Died: 11.11.1960,
Chicago
1949 NASCAR Champion

C ···

GIULIO CABIANCA
I. Born: 19.2.1923, Verona. Died: 15.6.1961, Modena, testing

World Championship Grand Prix Record

years	starts	wins	2nd	3rd	4th	5th	6th	PP	FL	points
1958–60	3(1)	-	-	-	1	-	-	-	-	3

Best championship: 1960 19th. Best qualifying: 4th

MARIO ARAUJO DE CABRAL
P. Born: 15.1.1934

World Championship Grand Prix Record

years	starts	wins	2nd	3rd	4th	5th	6th	PP	FL	points
1959–60; 1963–64	4(1)	-	-	-	-	-	-	-	-	-

Best result: 10th. Best qualifying: 14th

PHIL CADE
USA. Born: 12.7.1916, Charles City, Iowa

World Championship Grand Prix Record

year	starts	wins	2nd	3rd	4th	5th	6th	PP	FL	points
1959	-(1)	-	-	-	-	-	-	-	-	-

Best qualifying: 18th

ALAIN DE CADENET
GB. Born: 27.11.1945

World Sports Car Championship. Race wins: 1980 Monza, Silverstone

NICOLAS CAERELS
B

Major race wins: 1927 Spa 24 hrs

ALEX CAFFI
I. Born: 18.3.1964, Rovato
1985 European F3 Cup winner

World Championship Grand Prix Record

years	starts	wins	2nd	3rd	4th	5th	6th	PP	FL	points
1986–92	56(21)	-	-	-	1	1	1	-	-	6

Best championship: 1989 16th. Best qualifying: 3rd
Major race wins: 1985 European F3 Cup

ALESSANDRO CAGNO
I. Born: 2.5.1883, Turin. Died: 23.12.1971

Major race wins: 1906 Targa Florio

ENZO CALDERARI
CH. Born: 18.04.1952, Bienne

Major race wins: 1987 Tourist Trophy

GIUSEPPE CAMPARI
I. Born: 8.6.1892, Fanfullo, Lodi, near Milan. Died: 10.9.1933, Monza GP

Pre-1950 Grands Prix. Race wins: 1924 French GP, 1931 Italian GP, 1933 French GP

Other major race wins: 1928 and 1929 Mille Miglia

JOHN CAMPBELL-JONES
GB. Born: 21.1.1930, Epsom

World Championship Grand Prix Record

years	starts	wins	2nd	3rd	4th	5th	6th	PP	FL	points
1962–63	2	-	-	-	-	-	-	-	-	-

Best result: 11th. Best qualifying: 19th

ADRIAN CAMPOS
E. Born: 17.6.1960, Valencia
1994 Spanish Touring Car Champion

World Championship Grand Prix Record

years	starts	wins	2nd	3rd	4th	5th	6th	PP	FL	points
1987–88	17(4)	-	-	-	-	-	-	-	-	-

Best result: 14th. Best qualifying: 16th

MARCOS CAMPOS
BR
1994 Formula Opel Euroseries Champion

JOHN CANNON
CDN. Born: 21.6.1937, London (GB)
1970 North American Formula A (F5000) Champion

World Championship Grand Prix Record

year	starts	wins	2nd	3rd	4th	5th	6th	PP	FL	points
1971	1	-	-	-	-	-	-	-	-	-

Best result: 14th. Best qualifying: 26th

	wins	2nd	3rd	4th	5th	6th	PP	FL	points
European F2 Ch	-	-	1	-	-	-	-	-	4

Championship: 1971 16th

WILLIAM "SHORTY" CANTLON
USA. Born: n/a. Died: 30.5.1947, Indianapolis 500

Indycar Championship. Race wins: 1930 Akron, 1931 Altoona Race 3, Altoona Race 4, 1934 Syracuse

HEITEL CANTONI
U

World Championship Grand Prix Record

year	starts	wins	2nd	3rd	4th	5th	6th	PP	FL	points
1952	3	-	-	-	-	-	-	-	-	-

Best result: 11th. Best qualifying: 23rd

IVAN CAPELLI
I. Born: 24.5.1963, Milan
1986 International F3000 Champion; 1984 European F3 Champion; 1983 Italian F3 Champion

World Championship Grand Prix Record

years	starts	wins	2nd	3rd	4th	5th	6th	PP	FL	points
1985–93	93(5)	-	2	1	1	4	4	-	-	31

Best championship: 1988 7th. Best qualifying: 3rd

	wins	2nd	3rd	4th	5th	6th	PP	FL	points
Int F3000 Ch	3	1	3	2	-	-	3	2	51

Championships: 1985 7th, 1986 1st. Race wins: 1985 Österreichring, 1986 Rome GP (Vallelunga), Österreichring
European F3 Championship. Race wins: 1984 Magny-Cours, La Châtre, Enna, Mugello
Other major race wins: 1984 Monaco F3 GP

RUDOLF CARACCIOLA
D. Born: 30.1.1901, Remagen. Died: 28.9.1959, Lugano (CH)
1935, 1937 and 1938 Grand Prix European Champion

Rudolf Caracciola

Pre-1950 Grands Prix. Race wins: 1926 German GP, 1928 German GP, 1931 German GP, 1932 German GP, 1934 Italian GP, 1935 French GP, Belgian GP, Swiss GP, Spanish GP, 1936 Monaco GP, 1937 German GP, Swiss GP, Italian GP, Masaryk GP, 1938 Swiss GP, 1939 German GP

Other major race wins: 1929 Tourist Trophy, 1931 Mille Miglia, 1935 Tripoli GP

PAULO CARCASCI
BR. Born: 7.1.1964
1991 Japanese F3 Champion

BOB CAREY
USA. Born: 24.9.1905, Anderson, Indiana. Died: 16.4.1933, Ascot
1932 Indycar Champion

Indycar Championship. Race wins: 1932 Detroit Race 1, Syracuse

PIERO CARINI
I. Born: 6.3.1921, Sondrio. Died: 30.5.1957, 6 heures de Forez, St Etienne (F)

World Championship Grand Prix Record

years	starts	wins	2nd	3rd	4th	5th	6th	PP	FL	points
1952–53	3	-	-	-	-	-	-	-	-	-

Best result: no finishes. Best qualifying: 19th

TULLIO CARIOLATO
I

Major race wins: 1910 Targa Florio

WILLIE CARLSON
USA. Born: n/a. Died: 4.7.1915, Tacoma, Washington

Indycar Championship. Race wins: 1913 San Diego Race 2

THORBJORN CARLSSON
S
1980 Swedish F3 Champion

Drivers A–Z

DUANE "PANCHO" CARTER JR
USA. Born: 11.6.1950, Racine, Wisconsin. Son of Duane Sr
Indycar Championship. Race wins: 1981 Michigan 500

EDDIE CARVALHO
HK
Major race wins: 1954 Macau GP

LLOYD "LUCKY" CASNER
USA. Born: 1916. Died: 10.4.1965, Le Mans
World Sports Car Championship. Race wins: 1961 Nürburgring

P CASSANI
I
Major race wins: 1951 Mille Miglia

ROBERTO DEL CASTELLO
I

	wins	2nd	3rd	4th	5th	6th	PP	FL	points
European F2 Ch	-	-	1	1	-	1	-	-	8

Championships: 1982 16th, 1983 12th, 1984 15th

EUGENIO CASTELLOTTI
I. Born: 10.10.1930, Milan. Died: 14.3.1957, Modena, testing
World Championship Grand Prix Record

years	starts	wins	2nd	3rd	4th	5th	6th	PP	FL	points
1955–57	14	-	2	1	1	1	1	1	-	19.5

Best championship: 1955 3rd. Best qualifying: 1st
World Sports Car Championship. Race wins: 1956 Sebring 12 hrs, Mille Miglia, 1957 Buenos Aires

HERNANI CASTRO LOPO
P
1992 Portuguese Touring Car Champion

PIERRE DE CATERS
B. Born: 1875. Died: 1944
Major race wins: 1907 Ardennes Circuit (GP Class)

ROBERT LA CAZE
MA. Born: 26.2.1917, Paris (F)
World Championship Grand Prix Record

year	starts	wins	2nd	3rd	4th	5th	6th	PP	FL	points
1958	1	-	-	-	-	-	-	-	-	-

Best result: no finishes. Best qualifying: no time set

JOHNNY CECOTTO
YV. Born: 25.1.1956, Caracas
1989 Italian Touring Car Champion; 1994 German 2-litre Touring Car Cup winner
World Championship Grand Prix Record

years	starts	wins	2nd	3rd	4th	5th	6th	PP	FL	points
1983–84	18(5)	-	-	-	-	-	1	-	-	1

Best championship: 1983 19th. Best qualifying: 1st

	wins	2nd	3rd	4th	5th	6th	PP	FL	points
European F2 Ch	3	3	3	1	-	4	-	2	64

Championships: 1981 12th, 1982, 2nd. **Race wins:** 1982 Jochen Rindt Trophy (Thruxton), Pau GP, Mantorp Park
Other major race wins: 1990 Spa 24 hrs

ERNESTO CEIRANO
I
Major race wins: 1911 and 1914 Targa Florio

ANDREA DE CESARIS
I. Born: 31.5.1959, Rome
World Championship Grand Prix Record

years	starts	wins	2nd	3rd	4th	5th	6th	PP	FL	points
1980–94	208(6)	-	2	3	7	4	6	1	1	59

Best championship: 1983 8th. Best qualifying: 1st

	wins	2nd	3rd	4th	5th	6th	PP	FL	points
European F2 Ch	1	2	1	-	1	2	1	-	29

Championships: 1979 21st, 1980 5th. **Race wins:** 1980 Misano

FRANÇOIS CEVERT
F. Born: 25.2.1944, Paris. Died: 6.10.1973, Watkins Glen, US GP practice
1968 French F3 Champion

DUANE "PANCHO" CARTER JR
[continued]

World Championship Grand Prix Record

years	starts	wins	2nd	3rd	4th	5th	6th	PP	FL	points
1969–73	47(1)	1	10	2	2	2	2	-	2	89

Best championship: 1971 3rd. **Race wins:** 1971 United States GP. Best qualifying: 2nd
World Sports Car Championship. Race wins: 1973 Vallelunga

	wins	2nd	3rd	4th	5th	6th	PP	FL	points
European F2 Ch	3	1	2	1	2	1	-	3	52

Championships: 1969 3rd, 1970 6th, 1971 5th. **Race wins:** 1971 Jim Clark Trophy, Eifelrennen (Nürburgring), 1973 Pau GP

EUGÈNE CHABOUD
F. Born: 12.4.1907, Lyon. Died: 28.12.1983, Montfermeil
World Championship Grand Prix Record

years	starts	wins	2nd	3rd	4th	5th	6th	PP	FL	points
1950–51	3	-	-	-	-	1	-	-	-	1

Best championship: 1950 20th. Best qualifying: 10th
Major Sports Car races. Race wins: 1938 Le Mans 24 hrs

ALAIN DE CHAGNY
B
World Championship Grand Prix Record

year	starts	wins	2nd	3rd	4th	5th	6th	PP	FL	points
1959	-(1)	-	-	-	-	-	-	-	-	-

Best qualifying: 20th

JAY CHAMBERLAIN
USA
World Championship Grand Prix Record

year	starts	wins	2nd	3rd	4th	5th	6th	PP	FL	points
1962	1(2)	-	-	-	-	-	-	-	-	-

Best result: 15th. Best qualifying: 20th

CHAN LYE CHOON
SGP
Major race wins: 1958 Macau GP

COLIN CHAPMAN
GB. Born: 19.5.1928, Richmond, Surrey. Died: 16.12.1982, Norfolk
World Championship Grand Prix Record

year	starts	wins	2nd	3rd	4th	5th	6th	PP	FL	points
1956	-(1)	-	-	-	-	-	-	-	-	-

Best qualifying: 5th (qualifying time set by Harry Schell)

DAVE CHARLTON
ZA. Born: 27.10.1936, Redcar, Yorkshire (GB)
1970, 1971, 1972, 1973, 1974 and 1975 South African Drivers' Champion
World Championship Grand Prix Record

years	starts	wins	2nd	3rd	4th	5th	6th	PP	FL	points
1965; 1967–68; 1970–75	11(3)	-	-	-	-	-	-	-	-	-

Best result: 12th. Best qualifying: 8th

FERNAND CHARRON
F. Born: 1866. Died: 13.8.1928
Pre-1950 Grands Prix. Race wins: 1900 Gordon Bennett Trophy

JEAN CHASSAGNE
F
Major race wins: 1922 Tourist Trophy

GUY CHASSEUIL
F
Major race wins: 1969 Spa 24 hrs

"PIERRE CHAUVET"
A. Born: 21.7.1943. Also raced as Fritz Glatz and Umberto Calvo

	wins	2nd	3rd	4th	5th	6th	PP	FL	points
European F2 Ch	-	-	-	-	1	-	-	1

Championship: 1984 15th

"CHAVAN"
B
Major race wins: 1976 Spa 24 hrs

PEDRO CHAVES
P. Born: 27.2.1965, Oporto
1990 British F3000 Champion

World Championship Grand Prix Record

year	starts	wins	2nd	3rd	4th	5th	6th	PP	FL	points
1991	-(14)	-	-	-	-	-	-	-	-	-

Best qualifying: 32nd

		wins	2nd	3rd	4th	5th	6th	PP	FL	points
Int F3000 Ch		-	-	1	-	-	-	-	-	3

Championship: 1990 16th

EDDIE CHEEVER

USA. Born: 10.1.1958, Phoenix, Arizona. Brother of Ross

World Championship Grand Prix Record

years	starts	wins	2nd	3rd	4th	5th	6th	PP	FL	points
1978; 1980–88	132(11)	-	2	7	5	4	7	-	-	70

Best championship: 1983 6th. **Best qualifying:** 2nd

World Sports Car Championship. Race wins: 1980 Mugello, 1986 Silverstone, 1987 Jerez, Silverstone, Nürburgring, 1988 Jarama, Monza, Silverstone, Fuji

		wins	2nd	3rd	4th	5th	6th	PP	FL	points
European F2 Ch		4	5	4	2	5	2	2	4	106

Championship: 1976 9th, 1977 2nd, 1978 4th, 1979 4th.
Race wins: 1977 Rouen GP, 1979 International Trophy (Silverstone), Pau GP, Zandvoort

ROSS CHEEVER

USA. Born: 12.4.1964, Rome (I). Brother of Eddie

1985 New Zealand International Champion; 1987 Japanese F3 Champion

GASTON CHEVROLET

USA. Born: 1892, France. Died: 26.11.1920, Beverly Hills

1920 Indycar Champion

Indycar Championship. Race wins: 1919 Sheepshead Race 4, Uniontown Race 7, Sheepshead Race 5, 1920 Indianapolis 500

LOUIS CHEVROLET

USA. Born: 1878, La Chaux de Fonds (CH). Died: 6.6.1941

Indycar Championship. Race wins: 1909 Crown Point Race 2, Lowell Race 3, Riverhead Race 4, 1917 Cincinnati, Chicago Race 3, Sheepshead Bay, Ascot Race 2, 1918 Uniontown Race 4, Uniontown Race 6, 1919 Tacoma

ANDREA CHIESA

CH. Born: 6.5.1964, Milan (I)

World Championship Grand Prix Record

year	starts	wins	2nd	3rd	4th	5th	6th	PP	FL	points
1992	3(7)	-	-	-	-	-	-	-	-	-

Best result: no finishes. **Best qualifying:** 20th

		wins	2nd	3rd	4th	5th	6th	PP	FL	points
Int F3000 Ch		1	3	-	-	3	1	-	-	34

Championships: 1988 20th, 1989 6th, 1990 7th. **Race wins:** 1989 Mediterranean GP (Enna)

ETTORE CHIMERI

YV. Born: 1924. Died: 27.2.1960, Cuban Sports Car GP

World Championship Grand Prix Record

year	starts	wins	2nd	3rd	4th	5th	6th	PP	FL	points
1960	1	-	-	-	-	-	-	-	-	-

Best result: no finishes. **Best qualifying:** 21st

LUIGI CHINETTI

I (emigrated to USA). Born: 17.7.1906, Milan. Died: 17.8.1994

Major Sports Car races. Race wins: 1932, 1934 and 1949 Le Mans 24 hrs
Other major race wins: 1933 and 1949 Spa 24 hrs

LOUIS CHIRON

MC. Born: 3.8.1899, Monte Carlo. Died: 22.6.1979, Monte Carlo

World Championship Grand Prix Record

years	starts	wins	2nd	3rd	4th	5th	6th	PP	FL	points
1950–51; 1953; 1955–56	15(3)	-	-	1	-	-	2	-	-	4

Best championship: 1950 9th. **Best qualifying:** 8th

Pre-1950 Grands Prix. Race wins: 1928 San Sebastian GP, Spanish GP, 1928 Italian GP, 1929 German GP, Spanish GP, 1930 Belgian GP, 1931 Monaco GP, French GP, Masaryk GP, 1932 Masaryk GP, 1933 Masaryk GP, Spanish GP, 1934 French GP, 1937 French GP, 1947 French GP, 1949 GP de France

Other major race wins: 1933 Spa 24 hrs, 1934 Moroccan GP

SANDRO CINOTTI

I

		wins	2nd	3rd	4th	5th	6th	PP	FL	points
European F2 Ch		-	-	-	1	-	-	-	-	2

Championship: 1975 25th

FRANCESCO CIUPPA

I

Major race wins: 1909 Targa Florio

JOHNNY CLAES

B. Born: 11.8.1916, Fulham (GB). Died: 3.2.1956, Brussels, tuberculosis

World Championship Grand Prix Record

years	starts	wins	2nd	3rd	4th	5th	6th	PP	FL	points
1950–53; 1955	23(2)	-	-	-	-	-	-	-	-	-

Best result: 7th. **Best qualifying:** 10th.

JIM CLARK

GB. Born: 4.3.1936, Kilmany, Fife. Died: 7.4.1968, Hockenheim, F2 race

1963 and 1965 World Champion; 1965, 1967 and 1968 Tasman Champion; 1964 British Touring Car Champion; 1965 British F2 Champion; 1965 French F2 Champion; 1960 Motor Racing (tied with Trevor Taylor) and Brands Hatch British F3 (Formula Junior) Champion

Jim Clark

World Championship Grand Prix Record

years	starts	wins	2nd	3rd	4th	5th	6th	PP	FL	points
1960–68	72(1)	25	1	6	4	3	1	33	28	274

Race wins: 1962 Belgian GP, British GP, United States GP, 1963 Belgian GP, Dutch GP, French GP, British GP, Italian GP, Mexican GP, South African GP, 1964 Dutch GP, Belgian GP, British GP, 1965 South African GP, Belgian GP, French GP, British GP, German GP, 1966 United States GP, 1967 Dutch GP, British GP, United States GP, Mexican GP, 1968 South African GP.
Best qualifying: 1st.

		wins	2nd	3rd	4th	5th	6th	PP	FL	points
European F2 Ch		1	-	-	-	-	-	1	2	-

Race wins: 1967 Jarama

Indycar Championship. Race wins: 1963 Milwaukee Race 2, 1965 Indianapolis 500

Tasman Cup. Race wins: 1966 Warwick Farm, 1967 Levin, Lady Wigram Trophy, Teretonga, Lakeside, Sandown Park, 1968 Lady Wigram Trophy, Surfers' Paradise, Warwick Farm, Australian GP

Other major race wins: 1961 South African GP, 1962 Mexican GP, 1963 International Trophy (Siverstone), 1967 Spanish GP

JOHN CLELAND

GB. Born: 15.7.1952, Wishaw, Scotland

1989 British Touring Car Champion

FRANK CLEMENT

GB. Born: 1886. Died: ?.2.1970

Major Sports Car races. Race wins: 1924 Le Mans 24 hrs

EMMANUEL CLÉRICO

F. Born: 30.12.1969, Paris

		wins	2nd	3rd	4th	5th	6th	PP	FL	points
Int F3000 Ch		-	-	-	-	-	-	1	1	-

PRICE COBB

USA. Born: 10.12.1954, Dallas

World Sports Car Championship. Race wins: 1990 Le Mans 24 hrs

KEVIN COGAN

USA. Born: 31.3.1956, Culver City, California

World Championship Grand Prix Record

years	starts	wins	2nd	3rd	4th	5th	6th	PP	FL	points
1980–81	-(2)	-	-	-	-	-	-	-	-	-

Best qualifying: 25th

Indycar Championship. Race wins: 1986 Phoenix

EMMANUEL COLLARD

F. Born: 3.4.1971, Paris

	wins	2nd	3rd	4th	5th	6th	PP	FL	points
Int F3000 Ch	-	-	2	3	-	-	1	-	17

Championships: 1992 8th, 1993 11th

PETER COLLINS

GB. Born: 8.11.1931, Kidderminster. Died: 3.8.1958, Nürburgring, German GP

World Championship Grand Prix Record

years	starts	wins	2nd	3rd	4th	5th	6th	PP	FL	points
1952–58	32(3)	3	3	3	1	1	2	-	-	47

Best championship: 1956 3rd. **Race wins:** 1956 Belgian GP, French GP, 1958 British GP. **Best qualifying:** 2nd

World Sports Car Championship. Race wins: 1953 Tourist Trophy, 1955 Targa Florio, 1957 Venezuelan GP, 1958 Buenos Aires, Sebring 12 hrs

Other major race wins: 1955 and 1958 International Trophy (Silverstone)

BERNARD COLLOMB

F. Born: 7.10.1930

Peter Collins

World Championship Grand Prix Record

years	starts	wins	2nd	3rd	4th	5th	6th	PP	FL	points
1961–64	4(2)	-	-	-	-	-	-	-	-	-

Best result: 10th. **Best qualifying:** 17th

ALBERTO COLOMBO

I. Born: 23.2.1946, Varedo, Liano

1974 Italian F3 Champion

World Championship Grand Prix Record

year	starts	wins	2nd	3rd	4th	5th	6th	PP	FL	points
1978	-(3)	-	-	-	-	-	-	-	-	-

Best qualifying: 28th

	wins	2nd	3rd	4th	5th	6th	PP	FL	points
European F2 Ch	-	-	3	5	5	9	-	1	48

Championships: 1975 26th, 1976 17th, 1977 7th, 1978 8th, 1979 13th, 1980 10th

ENZO COLONI

I. Born: 17.10.1946

1982 Italian F3 Champion

FABIO COLONNA

I

Major race wins: 1957 Targa Florio

ERIK COMAS

F. Born: 28.9.1963, Romans

1990 FIA F3000 Champion; 1987 French Supertourism Champion; 1988 French F3 Champion

World Championship Grand Prix Record

years	starts	wins	2nd	3rd	4th	5th	6th	PP	FL	points
1991–94	59(4)	-	-	-	-	1	5	-	-	7

Best championship: 1992 11th. **Best qualifying:** 7th

	wins	2nd	3rd	4th	5th	6th	PP	FL	points
Int F3000 Ch	6	4	1	2	1	-	5	4	90

Championships: 1989 2nd, 1990 1st. **Race wins:** 1989 Le Mans, Dijon, 1990 Donington, Jerez, Monza, Le Mans

FRED COMER

USA. Born: n/a. Died: 12.10.1928

Indycar Championship. Race wins: 1926 Atlantic City Race 4

GIANFRANCO COMOTTI

I. Born: 24.7.1906, Brescia. Died: 10.5.1963, Bergamo

World Championship Grand Prix Record

years	starts	wins	2nd	3rd	4th	5th	6th	PP	FL	points
1950; 1952	2	-	-	-	-	-	-	-	-	-

Best result: 12th. **Best qualifying:** 18th

Major race wins: 1937 Tourist Trophy

DECIMO COMPAGNONI

I

Major race wins: 1933 Mille Miglia

CABERTO CONELLI

I

Pre-1950 Grands Prix. Race wins: 1931 Belgian GP

GEORGE CONNOR

USA. Born: 16.8 1908, San Bernardino, California

Indycar Championship. Race wins: 1946 Atlanta

GEORGE CONSTANTINE

USA. Born: 22.2.1918

World Championship Grand Prix Record

year	starts	wins	2nd	3rd	4th	5th	6th	PP	FL	points
1959	1	-	-	-	-	-	-	-	-	-

Best result: no finishes. **Best qualifying:** 15th

ENRIQUE CONTRERAS

MEX. Born: 21.5.1962

1984 Mexican Formula K Champion; 1990 Mexican F2 Champion

EARL COOPER

USA. Born: 1886. Died: 23.10.1965

1913, 1915 and 1917 Indycar Champion

Indycar Championship. Race wins: 1912 Tacoma Race 2, 1913 Tacoma Race 1, Tacoma Race 2, Santa Monica, Corona Race 1, Corona Race 2, 1914 Tacoma Race 2, 1915 San Diego, Elgin Race 1, Minneapolis, Phoenix, San Francisco Race 2, 1917 Ascot, Chicago Race 1, Minneapolis Race 1, Tacoma, 1921 Fresno Race 2, 1924 Fresno, 1925 Charlotte Race 1, 1926 Salem Race 2, Charlotte Race 2

DERRIKE COPE

USA. Born: 3.11.1958, San Diego, California

Major race wins: 1990 Daytona 500

JOHN CORDTS

CDN. Born: 23.7.1935

World Championship Grand Prix Record

year	starts	wins	2nd	3rd	4th	5th	6th	PP	FL	points
1969	1	-	-	-	-	-	-	-	-	-

Best result: no finishes. **Best qualifying:** 19th

FRANCO CORTESE

I. Born: 1903, Oggebbio

Major race wins: 1951 Targa Florio

ENZO CORTI

I

	wins	2nd	3rd	4th	5th	6th	PP	FL	points
European F2 Ch	-	-	-	-	-	-	-	-	2

Championship: 1969 15th

LORA "LL" CORUM

Born: 1895. Died: 1949

Indycar Championship. Race wins: 1924 Indianapolis 500

MEO COSTANTINI

F. Born: 1889, Vittorio Veneto. Died: 1940, Milan (I)

Pre-1950 Grands Prix. Race wins: 1926 Spanish GP

Other major race wins: 1925 and 1926 Targa Florio

ALFREDO COSTANZO

AUS. Born: 3.1.1943

1980, 1981, 1982 and 1983 Australian Gold Star Champion

DIDIER COTTAZ

F. Born: 23.5.1967, Bourgoin

1993 French F3 Champion

	wins	2nd	3rd	4th	5th	6th	PP	FL	points
Int F3000 Ch	-	1	1	-	1	1	-	-	13

Championship: 1994 5th

JACQUES COULON

F. Born: 15.1.1942

	wins	2nd	3rd	4th	5th	6th	PP	FL	points
European F2 Ch	1	-	3	3	1	1	-	1	38

Championships: 1973 5th, 1974 13th. **Race wins:** 1973 Rome GP (Vallelunga)

DAVID COULTHARD

GB. Born: 27.3.1971, Twynholm

World Championship Grand Prix Record

year	starts	wins	2nd	3rd	4th	5th	6th	PP	FL	points
1994	8	-	1	-	1	2	1	-	2	14

Best championship: 1994 8th. **Best qualifying:** 3rd

	wins	2nd	3rd	4th	5th	6th	PP	FL	points
Int F3000 Ch	1	3	3	1	-	-	-	3	42

Championships: 1992 9th, 1993 7th, 1994 9th. **Race wins:** 1993 Mediterranean GP (Enna)

Other major race wins: 1991 Marlboro Masters of F3, Macau GP

PIERS COURAGE
GB. Born: 27.5.1942, Colchester. Died: 21.6.1970, Zandvoort, Dutch GP

World Championship Grand Prix Record

years	starts	wins	2nd	3rd	4th	5th	6th	PP	FL	points
1966–70	28(2)	-	2	-	1	2	1	-	-	20

Best championship: 1968 19th. **Best qualifying:** 4th

	wins	2nd	3rd	4th	5th	6th	PP	FL	points
European F2 Ch	1	2	4	-	1	-	1	-	37

Championships: 1967 4th, 1968 6th. **Race wins:** 1969 Mediterranean GP (Enna)

Tasman Cup. Race wins: 1968 Longford, 1969 Teretonga

GÉRARD DE COURCELLES
F

Major Sports Car races. Race wins: 1925 Le Mans 24 hrs

ERNEST COURTIS
GB

Major race wins: 1907 Tourist Trophy

HOWARD COVEY
USA

Indycar Championship. Race wins: 1909 Portland Race 1

DAVE COYNE
GB. Born: 31.3.1958

1987 EFDA F3 Euroseries Champion

Major race wins: 1987 Knutstorp EFDA F3

CHRIS CRAFT
GB. Born: 17.11.1939, Porthleven, Cornwall

World Championship Grand Prix Record

year	starts	wins	2nd	3rd	4th	5th	6th	PP	FL	points
1971	1(1)	-	-	-	-	-	-	-	-	-

Best result: no finishes. **Best qualifying:** 25th

JIM CRAWFORD
GB. Born: 13.2.1948, Dunfermline

1982 British F1 Champion

World Championship Grand Prix Record

year	starts	wins	2nd	3rd	4th	5th	6th	PP	FL	points
1975	2	-	-	-	-	-	-	-	-	-

Best result: 13th. **Best qualifying:** 25th

	wins	2nd	3rd	4th	5th	6th	PP	FL	points
European F2 Ch	-	-	-	1	-	1	-	-	4

Championship: 1981 16th

PIERRE DE CRAWHEZ
F

Major race wins: 1903 Ardennes Circuit

ALBERTO CRESPO
RA. Born: n/a. Died: 1991

World Championship Grand Prix Record

year	starts	wins	2nd	3rd	4th	5th	6th	PP	FL	points
1952	-(1)	-	-	-	-	-	-	-	-	-

Best qualifying: 26th

ANTONIO CREUS
E

World Championship Grand Prix Record

year	starts	wins	2nd	3rd	4th	5th	6th	PP	FL	points
1960	1	-	-	-	-	-	-	-	-	-

Best result: no finishes. **Best qualifying:** 22nd

ROBERT CREVITS
B

Major race wins: 1964 Spa 24 hrs

CHARLES CRICHTON-STUART
GB. Born: 10.3.1939, London

1966 Temporada F3 Champion

PATRICK CRINELLI
I. Born: 5.8.1971

1993 GM-Lotus Euroseries Champion

FERNANDO CROCERI
RA. Born: 6.1.1960

1993 Sud-Am F3 Champion; 1993 Brazilian F3 Champion

TONY CROOK
GB. Born: 16.2.1920, Manchester

World Championship Grand Prix Record

years	starts	wins	2nd	3rd	4th	5th	6th	PP	FL	points
1952–53	2	-	-	-	-	-	-	-	-	-

Best result: 21st. **Best qualifying:** 25th

MARCO CROSARA
I

World Sports Car Championship. Race wins: 1953 Mille Miglia

Other major race wins: 1950 Mille Miglia

GEOFFREY CROSSLEY
GB. Born: 11.5.1921, Baslow, Derbyshire

World Championship Grand Prix Record

year	starts	wins	2nd	3rd	4th	5th	6th	PP	FL	points
1950	2	-	-	-	-	-	-	-	-	-

Best result: 9th. **Best qualifying:** 12th

JOHN CROUCH
AUS

Major race wins: 1949 Australian GP

STUART CROW
USA. Born: 21.8.1959

1990 SCCA Super Vee Champion

ALAIN CUDINI
F. Born: 19.4.1946

1983 French Supertourism Champion

	wins	2nd	3rd	4th	5th	6th	PP	FL	points
European F2 Ch	-	-	-	-	-	1	-	-	-

Championship: 1974 16th

BILL CUMMINGS
USA. Born: 1914. Died: 8.2.1939

1934 Indycar Champion

Indycar Championship. Race wins: 1930 Langhorne, Syracuse, 1932 Oakland, 1933 Detroit, Syracuse, 1934 Indianapolis 500

JACKO CUNNINGHAM
USA

1989 North American (Eastern) Formula Atlantic Champion

NOËL CUNNINGHAM-REID
GB

World Sports Car Championship. Race wins: 1957 Nürburgring

D

GUIDO DACCO
I. Born: 10.9.1942, Limiate

	wins	2nd	3rd	4th	5th	6th	PP	FL	points
European F2 Ch	-	-	-	1	1	1	-	-	6

Championships: 1983 12th, 1984 13th

	wins	2nd	3rd	4th	5th	6th	PP	FL	points
Int F3000 Ch	-	-	-	-	2	2	-	-	6

Championship: 1985 13th

ANDERS DAHLGREN
S

1984 Swedish Touring Car Champion

HAKAN DAHLQVIST
S

1973 Swedish F3 Champion

	wins	2nd	3rd	4th	5th	6th	PP	FL	points
European F2 Ch	-	-	-	1	-	-	-	-	3

Championship: 1973 26th

CHUCK DAIGH

USA. Born: 29.11.1923, Long Beach, California

World Championship Grand Prix Record

year	starts	wins	2nd	3rd	4th	5th	6th	PP	FL	points
1960	3(3)	-	-	-	-	-	-	-	-	-

Best result: 10th. Best qualifying: 16th

World Sports Car Championship. Race wins: 1959 Sebring 12 hrs

PATRICK DAL BO

F

	wins	2nd	3rd	4th	5th	6th	PP	FL	points
European F2 Ch	-	-	-	1	-	-	-	-	7

Championships: 1969 19th, 1972 15th

WALLY DALLENBACH

USA. Born: 12.12.1936. Father of Wally Jr

Indycar Championship. Race wins: 1973 Milwaukee, California 500 Qualifying Race 1, California 500, 1975 California 500 Qualifying Race 2, 1977 Trenton

WALLY DALLENBACH JR

USA. Born: 23.5.1963, New Brunswick, New Jersey. Son of Wally Sr

1985 and 1986 Trans-Am Champion

RICHARD DALLEST

F. Born: 15.2.1951

	wins	2nd	3rd	4th	5th	6th	PP	FL	points
European F2 Ch	2	-	-	1	3	1	2	-	28

Championships: 1980 6th, 1981 16th, 1982 17th. **Race wins:** 1980 Pau GP, Zandvoort

	wins	2nd	3rd	4th	5th	6th	PP	FL	points
Int F3000 Ch	-	-	-	1	-	-	-	-	3

Championship: 1986 17th

European F3 Championship. Race wins: 1979 Kinnekulle

YANNICK DALMAS

F. Born: 28.7.1961, Le Beausset, Toulon

1992 World Sports Car Champion (with Derek Warwick); 1986 French F3 Champion

World Championship Grand Prix Record

years	starts	wins	2nd	3rd	4th	5th	6th	PP	FL	points
1987–90; 1994	23(27)	-	-	-	-	-	1*	-	-	-

Best qualifying: 15th. *Dalmas was not eligible for points as the car was not entered in the championship (1987).

	wins	2nd	3rd	4th	5th	6th	PP	FL	points
Int F3000 Ch	2	-	-	1	-	1	3		20

Championship: 1987 5th. **Race wins:** 1987 Pau GP, Jarama

World Sports Car Championship. Race wins: 1991 Magny-Cours, Mexico City, 1992 Silverstone, Le Mans 24 hrs, Suzuka

Other major race wins: 1986 Monaco F3 GP, 1994 Le Mans 24 hrs

DEREK DALY

IRL. Born: 11.3.1953, Dublin

1977 BP British F3 Champion

World Championship Grand Prix Record

years	starts	wins	2nd	3rd	4th	5th	6th	PP	FL	points
1978–82	49(15)	-	-	-	2	3	3	-	-	15

Best championship: 1980 10th. Best qualifying: 7th

	wins	2nd	3rd	4th	5th	6th	PP	FL	points
European F2 Ch	3	4	2	-	1	1	-	5	62

Championships: 1977 18th, 1978 3rd, 1979 3rd. **Race wins:** 1978 Mugello, Rome GP (Vallelunga), 1979 Donington Park

European F3 Championship. Race wins: 1977 Croix-en-Ternois

Other major race wins: 1990 and 1991 Sebring 12 hrs

THOMAS DANIELSSON

S. Born: 4.12.1964, Kungsbacha

1985 Swedish F3 Champion

	wins	2nd	3rd	4th	5th	6th	PP	FL	points
Int F3000 Ch	1	-	1	-	-	1	-	-	14

Championship: 1989 7th. **Race wins:** 1989 International Trophy (Silverstone)

CHRISTIAN DANNER

D. Born: 4.4.1958, Munich

1985 International F3000 Champion

World Championship Grand Prix Record

years	starts	wins	2nd	3rd	4th	5th	6th	PP	FL	points
1985–87; 1989	36(11)	-	-	-	1	-	1	1	-	4

Best championship: 1986 18th. Best qualifying: 16th

	wins	2nd	3rd	4th	5th	6th	PP	FL	points
European F2 Ch	-	2	5	4	3	3	2	2	53

Championships: 1981 18th, 1982 13th, 1983 5th, 1984 5th

	wins	2nd	3rd	4th	5th	6th	PP	FL	points
Int F3000 Ch	4	-	3	1	-	1	2	4	52

Championship: 1985 1st. **Race wins:** 1985 Pau GP, Dijon, Zandvoort, Donington Park

Other major race wins: 1992 Spa 24 hrs

JORGE DAPONTE

RA. Born: 5.6.1923, Buenos Aires. Died: ?.3.1963

World Championship Grand Prix Record

year	starts	wins	2nd	3rd	4th	5th	6th	PP	FL	points
1954	2	-	-	-	-	-	-	-	-	-

Best result: 11th. Best qualifying: 17th

JOCHEN DAUER

D. Born: 10.1.1952, Nuremberg

	wins	2nd	3rd	4th	5th	6th	PP	FL	points
European F2 Ch	-	-	-	1	-	-	-	-	2

Championship: 1980 15th

JIMMY DAVIES

USA. Born: 18.8.1929, Glendale, California. Died: 11.6.1966, Chicago

Indycar Championship. Race wins: 1949 Del Mar, 1950 Phoenix, 1954 Springfield

COLIN DAVIS

GB. Born: 29.7.1932, London. Son of Sammy Davis

World Championship Grand Prix Record

year	starts	wins	2nd	3rd	4th	5th	6th	PP	FL	points
1959	2	-	-	-	-	-	-	-	-	-

Best result: 11th. Best qualifying: 17th

World Sports Car Championship. Race wins: 1964 Targa Florio

FLOYD DAVIS

USA. Born: Illinois. Died: 31.5.1977

Indycar Championship. Race wins: 1941 Indianapolis 500

SAMMY DAVIS

GB. Born: 9.1.1887, London. Died: 9.1.1981. Father of Colin Davis

Major Sports Cars races. Race wins: 1927 Le Mans 24 hrs

LEX DAVISON

AUS. Born: n/a. Died: 14.2.1965, Sandown Park, Australian GP practice

1957 Australian Gold Star Champion

Major race wins: 1954, 1957, 1958 and 1961 Australian GP

JOE DAWSON

USA. Born: 1889, Indianapolis. Died: 18.6.1946

Indycar Championship. Race wins: 1910 Indianapolis Race 5, 1912 Indianapolis 500

RICHARD DEAN

GB. Born: 7.10.1965. Son of Tony

	wins	2nd	3rd	4th	5th	6th	PP	FL	points
Int F3000 Ch	-	-	-	1	-	-	-		2

Championship: 1990 19th

TONY DEAN

GB. Born: 1932. Father of Richard

1965 British F3 Champion

JEAN-DENIS DELETRAZ

CH. Born: 1.10.1963, Geneva

World Championship Grand Prix Record

years	starts	wins	2nd	3rd	4th	5th	6th	PP	FL	points
1994	1	-	-	-	-	-	-	-	-	-

Best result: no finishes. Best qualifying: 25th

	wins	2nd	3rd	4th	5th	6th	PP	FL	points
Int F3000 Ch	-	-	2	-	-	-	-	-	8

Championship: 1988 13th

NINO DEMUTH
LUX
Major race wins: 1976 Spa 24 hrs

PATRICK DEPAILLER
F. Born: 9.8.1944, Clermont-Ferrand. Died: 1.8.1980, Hockenheim, testing
1974 European F2 Champion; 1971 French F3 Champion

World Championship Grand Prix Record

years	starts	wins	2nd	3rd	4th	5th	6th	PP	FL	points
1972; 1974-80	95	2	10	7	6	6	5	1	4	141

Best championship: 1976 4th. Race wins: 1978 Monaco GP, 1979 Spanish GP. Best qualifying: 1st

	wins	2nd	3rd	4th	5th	6th	PP	FL	points
European F2 Ch	4	9	2	2	1	1	7	8	119

Championships: 1972 3rd, 1973 3rd, 1974 1st. Race wins: 1974 Pau GP, Mugello, Hockenheim, Rome GP (Vallelunga)
Other major race wins: 1972 Monaco F3 GP

JEAN DESVIGNES
F
Major race wins: 1934 Spa 24 hrs

JEAN-MARIE DETRIN
B
Major race wins: 1976 Spa 24 hrs

WILLI DEUTSCH
D

	wins	2nd	3rd	4th	5th	6th	PP	FL	points
European F2 Ch	-	-	-	1	-	-	-	-	4

Championship: 1976 12th

HELMUT DEUTZ
D
1952 German F3 Champion

MICHEL DE DEYNE
B
1984 Belgian Touring Car Champion

STANLEY DICKENS
S. Born: 7.5.1952, Farila
1988 (with Hideki Okada) and 1989 (with Kunimitsu Takahashi) Japanese Sports Car Champion
World Sports Car Championship. Race wins: 1989 Le Mans 24 hrs

PIERRE DIEUDONNÉ
B. Born: 24.3.1947, Brussels
1976 European Touring Car Champion (shared with Jean Xhenceval); 1981 Belgian Touring Car Champion
World Sports Car Championship. Race wins: 1981 Spa 24 hrs
Other major race wins: 1974 and 1975 Spa 24 hrs, 1976 Tourist Trophy

BERT DINGLEY
USA. Born: n/a. Died: 7.4.1966
Indycar Championship. Race wins: 1909 Portland Race 3, Santa Monica Race 2, 1911 Oakland Race 3

SPARTICO DINI
I. Born: 1943, Greve, near Florence
1969 European Touring Car 1600 cc Class Champion

PEDRO DINIZ
BR. Born: 22.5.1970, Sao Paulo

	wins	2nd	3rd	4th	5th	6th	PP	FL	points
Int F3000 Ch	-	-	-	1	-	-	-	-	3

Championship: 1994 12th

"DINO"
I
World Sports Car Championship. Race wins: 1977 Vallelunga

DUKE DINSMORE
USA. Born: 10.4.1913, Williamstown. Died: 12.10.1985, Daytona Beach
Indycar Championship. Race wins: 1950 Sacramento

LOU DISBROW
USA
Indycar Championship. Race wins: 1911 Jacksonville, Philadelphia Race 3, 1913 Galveston Race 1, Galveston Race 3

MARK DISMORE
USA
1990 North American (Western Division) Toyota Atlantic Champion
Major race wins: 1993 Daytona 24 hrs

ALBERT DIVO
F. Born: 1895, Paris. Died: ?.11.1966, Paris
Pre-1950 Grands Prix. Race wins: 1923 Spanish GP, 1925 French GP, San Sebastian GP
Other major race wins: 1928 and 1929 Targa Florio

FRED DIXON
GB. Born: 1892, Yorkshire. Died: 1956
Major race wins: 1935 and 1936 Tourist Trophy

PRINCE DIMITRI DJORDJADZE
RUS
Major race wins: 1931 Spa 24 hrs

FRANK DOCHNAL
USA

World Championship Grand Prix Record

year	starts	wins	2nd	3rd	4th	5th	6th	PP	FL	points
1963	-(1)	-	-	-	-	-	-	-	-	-

Best qualifying: no time set

CHARLES DODSON
GB
Major race wins: 1934 and 1936 Tourist Trophy

JOSÉ DOLHEM
F. Born: 26.4.1944, Paris. Died: 16.4.1988, light plane accident near St Etienne

World Championship Grand Prix Record

year	starts	wins	2nd	3rd	4th	5th	6th	PP	FL	points
1974	1(2)	-	-	-	-	-	-	-	-	-

Best result: no finishes. Best qualifying: 26th

	wins	2nd	3rd	4th	5th	6th	PP	FL	points
European F2 Ch	-	-	1	-	-	-	1	6

Championships: 1972 27th, 1974 14th

KAYE DON
GB. Born: n/a. Died: 1981
Major race wins: 1928 Tourist Trophy

MARTIN DONNELLY
GB. Born: 26.3.1964, Belfast

World Championship Grand Prix Record

years	starts	wins	2nd	3rd	4th	5th	6th	PP	FL	points
1989–90	13(2)	-	-	-	-	-	-	-	-	-

Best result: 7th. Best qualifying: 11th

	wins	2nd	3rd	4th	5th	6th	PP	FL	points
Int F3000 Ch	3	2	1	-	-	-	2	3	43

Championships: 1988 3rd, 1989 8th. Race wins: 1988 Brands Hatch, Dijon, 1989 Brands Hatch
Other major race wins: 1987 Macau GP

MARK DONOHUE
USA. Born: 18.3.1937, Summit, New Jersey. Died: 19.8.1975, Graz hospital following an accident at the Austrian GP
1973 Can-Am Champion; 1974 IROC Champion; 1968, 1969 and 1971 Trans-Am Champion

World Championship Grand Prix Record

years	starts	wins	2nd	3rd	4th	5th	6th	PP	FL	points
1971; 1974–75	14(2)	-	-	1	-	2	-	-	-	8

Best championship: 1975 15th. Best qualifying: 8th

World Sports Car Championship. Race wins: 1969 Daytona 24 hrs
Indycar Championship. Race wins: 1971 Pocono 500, Michigan, 1972 Indianapolis 500
Other major race wins: 1966 Canadian GP

EDGAR DÖREN
D. Born: 6.10.1942, Wuppertal
World Sports Car Championship. Race wins: 1981 Monza

RAD DOUGALL
ZA. Born: 7.9.1951

	wins	2nd	3rd	4th	5th	6th	PP	FL	points
European F2 Ch	1	1	1	-	1	3	1	-	24

Championships: 1978 13th, 1979 5th. **Race wins:** 1979 Jochen Rindt Trophy (Thruxton)

KEN DOWNING
GB. Born: 5.12.1917, Chesterton, Staffordshire
World Championship Grand Prix Record

year	starts	wins	2nd	3rd	4th	5th	6th	PP	FL	points
1952	2	-	-	-	-	-	-	-	-	-

Best result: 9th. **Best qualifying:** 5th.

BOB DRAKE
USA. Born: 14.12.1924. Died: 18.4.1990
World Championship Grand Prix Record

year	starts	wins	2nd	3rd	4th	5th	6th	PP	FL	points
1960	1	-	-	-	-	-	-	-	-	-

Best result: 13th. **Best qualifying:** 22nd

RENÉ DREYFUS
F. Born: 1905, Nice. Died: 16.8.1993, New York
Pre-1950 Grands Prix. Race wins: 1930 Monaco GP, 1934 Belgian GP

PADDY DRIVER
ZA. Born: 13.5.1934, Johannesburg
World Championship Grand Prix Record

years	starts	wins	2nd	3rd	4th	5th	6th	PP	FL	points
1963; 1974	1(1)	-	-	-	-	-	-	-	-	-

Best result: no finishes. **Best qualifying:** 21st

PIERO DROGO
YV. Born: 8.8.1926, Vignale Monferrato. Died: 28.4.1973, Bologna
World Championship Grand Prix Record

year	starts	wins	2nd	3rd	4th	5th	6th	PP	FL	points
1960	1	-	-	-	-	-	-	-	-	-

Best result: 8th. **Best qualifying:** 15th

BERNARD DE DRYVER
B. Born: 19.9.1952, Brussels
World Championship Grand Prix Record

year	starts	wins	2nd	3rd	4th	5th	6th	PP	FL	points
1977	-(1)	-	-	-	-	-	-	-	-	-

Best qualifying: 31st

	wins	2nd	3rd	4th	5th	6th	PP	FL	points
European F2 Ch	-	-	-	-	1	2	-	-	4

Championships: 1975 22nd, 1977 20th

DOUG DUFF
ZA
1953 South African Drivers' Champion

JOHN DUFF
GB
Major Sports Car races. Race wins: 1924 Le Mans 24 hrs

JOHNNY DUMFRIES
GB. Born: 26.4.1958, Rothesay
1984 British F3 Champion
World Championship Grand Prix Record

year	starts	wins	2nd	3rd	4th	5th	6th	PP	FL	points
1986	15(1)	-	-	-	1	1	-	-	3

Best championship: 1986 13th. **Best qualifying:** 8th

	wins	2nd	3rd	4th	5th	6th	PP	FL	points
Int F3000 Ch	-	-	-	-	1	-	-	1

Championship: 1985 16th

World Sports Car Championship. Race wins: 1987 Spa, 1988 Le Mans 24 hrs
European F3 Championship. Race wins: 1984 Donington Park, Silverstone, Nürburgring, Jarama

CLIFF DURANT
USA
Indycar Championship. Race wins: 1918 Tacoma Race 1, Tacoma Race 2, 1919 Santa Monica

ARTHUR DURAY
F. Born: 1881, New York. Died: 1954
Major race wins: 1906 Ardennes Circuit

"LEON DURAY"
USA. Born: n/a. Died: ?.5.1956. Real name: George Stewart
Indycar Championship. Race wins: 1926 Salem Race 4, Charlotte Race 9, 1927 Culver City, 1928 Salem Race 1

PIERO DUSIO
I. Born: 13.10.1899, Scurzolengo d'Asti. Died: 7.11.1975, Buenos Aires
World Championship Grand Prix Record

year	starts	wins	2nd	3rd	4th	5th	6th	PP	FL	points
1952	-(1)	-	-	-	-	-	-	-	-	-

Best qualifying: no time set

GRAHAM DUXBURY
ZA
1982 South African Drivers' Champion
Major race wins: 1984 Daytona 24 hrs

GEORGE DYER
USA
Major race wins: 1977 Sebring 12 hrs

E

BOB EARL
USA. Born: 13.1.1950, Great Bend, Kansas
Major race wins: 1981 Macau GP, 1990 Sebring 12 hrs

DALE EARNHARDT
USA. Born: 29.4.1951, Kannapolis, North Carolina
1980, 1986, 1987, 1990, 1991, 1993 and 1994 NASCAR Champion; 1990 IROC Champion
Major race wins: 1986, 1992 and 1993 World 600

Dale Earnhardt

GEORGE EATON
CDN. Born: 12.11.1945, Toronto
World Championship Grand Prix Record

years	starts	wins	2nd	3rd	4th	5th	6th	PP	FL	points
1969–71	11(2)	-	-	-	-	-	-	-	-	-

Best result: 10th. **Best qualifying:** 9th

BERNIE ECCLESTONE
GB. Born: 28.10.1931, St Peters, Suffolk
World Championship Grand Prix Record

year	starts	wins	2nd	3rd	4th	5th	6th	PP	FL	points
1958	-(1)	-	-	-	-	-	-	-	-	-

Best qualifying: 21st

SELWYN EDGE
GB. Born: 1868, Sydney (AUS). Died: 1940
Pre-1950 Grands Prix. Race wins: 1902 Gordon Bennett Trophy

GUY EDWARDS
GB. Born: 30.12.1942, Liverpool
World Championship Grand Prix Record

years	starts	wins	2nd	3rd	4th	5th	6th	PP	FL	points
1974; 1976–77	11(5)	-	-	-	-	-	-	-	-	-

Best result: 7th. **Best qualifying:** 14th
World Sports Car Championship. Race wins: 1981 Enna, Brands Hatch

Vic Elford

GB. Born: 10.6.1935, Peckham

World Championship Grand Prix Record

years	starts	wins	2nd	3rd	4th	5th	6th	PP	FL	points
1968–69; 1971	13	-	-	-	1	2	1	-	-	8

Best championship: 1969 13th. **Best qualifying:** 5th

	wins	2nd	3rd	4th	5th	6th	PP	FL	points
European F2 Ch	-	-	-	1	-	-	-	-	3

Championship: 1972 24th

World Sports Car Championship. Race wins: 1968 Daytona 24 hrs, Targa Florio, Nürburgring, 1970 Nürburgring, 1971 Sebring 12 hrs, Nürburgring

Eje Elgh

S. Born: 15.6.1953, Karlskoga

	wins	2nd	3rd	4th	5th	6th	PP	FL	points
European F2 Ch	2	2	2	2	3	3	1	-	53

Championships: 1978 11th, 1979 9th, 1981 4th. **Race wins:** 1979 Mediterranean GP (Enna), 1981 Rome GP (Vallelunga)

Bill Elliott

USA. Born: 8.10.1955, Cumming, Georgia
1988 NASCAR Champion

Major race wins: 1985 and 1987 Daytona 500

Frank Elliott

USA

Indycar Championship. Race wins:
1917 Uniontown Race 2, 1922 Beverly
Hills Race 5, Cotati Race 3, Cotati Race 4,
1925 Culver City Race 2

Vic Elford

Paul Emery

GB. Born: 12.11.1916, Chiswick. Died: 3.2.1993, Epsom

World Championship Grand Prix Record

years	starts	wins	2nd	3rd	4th	5th	6th	PP	FL	points
1956; 1958	1(1)	-	-	-	-	-	-	-	-	-

Best result: no finishes. **Best qualifying:** 23rd

David Empringham

CDN
1993 and 1994 North American Toyota Atlantic Champion

Bill Endicott

USA

Indycar Championship. Race wins: 1910 Atlanta Race 2, Long Island Race 1, 1912 Milwaukee Race 2

Paul England

AUS. Born: 28.3.1929

World Championship Grand Prix Record

year	starts	wins	2nd	3rd	4th	5th	6th	PP	FL	points
1957	1	-	-	-	-	-	-	-	-	-

Best result: no finishes. **Best qualifying:** no time set

Harald Ertl

A. Born: 31.8.1948, Mannheim (D). Died: 7.4.1982, aircraft accident near Giessen (D)
1978 German Racing Champion

World Championship Grand Prix Record

years	starts	wins	2nd	3rd	4th	5th	6th	PP	FL	points
1975–78; 1980	19(9)	-	-	-	-	-	-	-	-	-

Best result: 7th. **Best qualifying:** 17th

	wins	2nd	3rd	4th	5th	6th	PP	FL	points
European F2 Ch	-	-	1	-	-	1	-	-	6

Championships: 1975 19th, 1976 15th

Major race wins: 1973 Tourist Trophy

Nasif Estefano

RA. Born: 18.11.1932, Concepcion-Tucuman. Died: 21.10.1973. Possibly called Estefano Nasif

World Championship Grand Prix Record

years	starts	wins	2nd	3rd	4th	5th	6th	PP	FL	points
1960; 1962–63	1(2)	-	-	-	-	-	-	-	-	-

Best result: 14th. **Best qualifying:** 20th

Philippe Étancelin

F. Born: 28.12.1896, Rouen. Died: 13.10.1981, Neuilly-sur-Seine

World Championship Grand Prix Record

years	starts	wins	2nd	3rd	4th	5th	6th	PP	FL	points
1950-52	12	-	-	-	-	2	-	-	-	3

Best championship: 1950 13th. **Best qualifying:** 4th.

Pre-1950 Grands Prix. Race wins: 1930 French GP

Major Sports Car races. Race wins: 1934 Le Mans 24 hrs

Cor Euser

NL. Born: 25.4.1957, Haarlem

	wins	2nd	3rd	4th	5th	6th	PP	FL	points
Int F3000 Ch	-	-	-	1	-	-	-	-	2

Championship: 1988 19th

Bob Evans

GB. Born: 11.6.1947, Newent, Gloucestershire
1974 British F5000 Champion

World Championship Grand Prix Record

years	starts	wins	2nd	3rd	4th	5th	6th	PP	FL	points
1975–76	10(2)	-	-	-	-	-	-	-	-	-

Best result: 9th. **Best qualifying:** 20th

Gary Evans

GB. Born: 21.10.1960

	wins	2nd	3rd	4th	5th	6th	PP	FL	points
Int F3000 Ch	-	-	-	1	1	-	-	-	2.5

Championship: 1987 21st, 1989 17th

Wim Eyckmans

B

	wins	2nd	3rd	4th	5th	6th	PP	FL	points
Int F3000 Ch	-	-	-	-	1	-	-	-	1

Championship: 1994 17th

François Eysserman

F

Major race wins: 1926 Tripoli GP

F

Corrado Fabi

I. Born: 12.4.1961, Milan. Brother of Teo
1982 European F2 Champion

World Championship Grand Prix Record

years	starts	wins	2nd	3rd	4th	5th	6th	PP	FL	points
1983–84	12(6)	-	-	-	-	-	-	-	-	-

Best result: 7th. **Best qualifying:** 11th

	wins	2nd	3rd	4th	5th	6th	PP	FL	points
European F2 Ch	6	2	3	2	1	-	4	5	86

Championships: 1981 4th, 1982 1st. **Race wins:** 1982 Mugello, Rome GP (Vallelunga), Hockenheim, Donington Park, Misano

European F3 Championship. Race wins: 1980 Mugello, Knutstorp

Teo Fabi

I. Born: 9.3.1955, Milan. Brother of Corrado
1991 World Sports Car Champion; 1979 New Zealand International Champion

World Championship Grand Prix Record

years	starts	wins	2nd	3rd	4th	5th	6th	PP	FL	points
1982; 1984–87	64(7)	-	-	2	2	4	1	3	2	23

Best championship: 1987 9th. **Best qualifying:** 1st

	wins	2nd	3rd	4th	5th	6th	PP	FL	points
European F2 Ch	3	1	2	3	-	1	2	2	51

Championships: 1979 10th, 1980 3rd. **Race wins:** 1980 Jim Clark Trophy (Hockenheim), Eifelrennen (Nürburgring), Hockenheim

World Sports Car Championship. Race wins: 1982 Nürburgring, 1991 Silverstone

Indycar Championship. Race wins: 1983 Pocono 500, Mid-Ohio, Monterey GP (Laguna Seca), Phoenix, 1989 Mid-Ohio

European F3 Championship. Race wins: 1978 Zolder, Dijon, Vallelunga

Other major race wins: 1983 Imola 1000 kms

PASCAL FABRE

F. Born: 1.1.1960, Lyon

World Championship Grand Prix Record

year	starts	wins	2nd	3rd	4th	5th	6th	PP	FL	points
1987	11(3)	-	-	-	-	-	-	-	-	-

Best result: 9th. Best qualifying: 22nd

	wins	2nd	3rd	4th	5th	6th	PP	FL	points
European F2 Ch	1	-	1	-	2	1	-	-	18

Championships: 1982 15th, 1984 8th. Race wins: 1984 Hockenheim

	wins	2nd	3rd	4th	5th	6th	PP	FL	points
Int F3000 Ch	1	1	1	-	1	-	1	1	15.5

Championship: 1986 7th. Race wins: 1986 International Trophy (Silverstone)

CARLO FACETTI

I. Born: 26.6.1935, Cormano, Milan

1979 European Touring Car Champion (shared with Martino Finotto)

World Championship Grand Prix Record

year	starts	wins	2nd	3rd	4th	5th	6th	PP	FL	points
1974	-(1)	-	-	-	-	-	-	-	-	-

Best qualifying: 27th

Major race wins: 1979 Tourist Trophy

LUIGI FAGIOLI

I. Born: 9.6.1898, Osimo, Ancona. Died: 20.6.1952, Monaco Sports Car GP practice

World Championship Grand Prix Record

years	starts	wins	2nd	3rd	4th	5th	6th	PP	FL	points
1950–51	7	1	4	1	-	-	-	-	-	32

Best championship: 1950 3rd. Race wins: 1951 French GP (with Fangio). Best qualifying: 2nd

Pre-1950 Grands Prix. Race wins: 1933 Italian GP, 1934 Italian GP, Spanish GP, 1935 Monaco GP

JACK FAIRMAN

GB. Born: 15.3.1913, Smallfield, Surrey

World Championship Grand Prix Record

years	starts	wins	2nd	3rd	4th	5th	6th	PP	FL	points
1953; 1955–61	12(1)	-	-	-	1	1	-	-	-	5

Best championship: 1956 10th. Best qualifying: 11th

World Sports Car Championship. Race wins: 1959 Nürburgring, Tourist Trophy

JUAN MANUEL FANGIO

RA. Born: 24.6.1911, Balcarce, near Buenos Aires

1951, 1954, 1955, 1956 and 1957 World Champion

World Championship Grand Prix Record

years	starts	wins	2nd	3rd	4th	5th	6th	PP	FL	points
1950–51; 1953–58	51	24	10	1	6	-	-	29	23	278.64

Race wins: 1950 Monaco GP, Belgian GP, French GP, 1951 Swiss GP, French GP (with Fagioli), Spanish GP, 1953 Italian GP, 1954 Argentinian GP, Belgian GP, French GP, German GP, Swiss GP, Italian GP, 1955 Argentinian GP, Belgian GP, Dutch GP, Italian GP, 1956 Argentinian GP (with Musso), British GP, German GP, 1957 Argentinian GP, Monaco GP, French GP, German GP. **Best qualifying:** 1st

World Sports Car Championship. Race wins: 1953 Carrera Panamericana, 1956 Sebring 12 hrs, 1957 Sebring 12 hrs

Juan Manuel Fangio

JUAN MANUEL FANGIO II

RA. Born: 19.9.1956, Balcarce, near Buenos Aires. Nephew of Juan Manuel sr

1992 and 1993 IMSA GT Champion

	wins	2nd	3rd	4th	5th	6th	PP	FL	points
Int F3000 Ch	-	-	-	-	-	1	-	-	1

Championship: 1985 16th

Major race wins: 1992 and 1993 Sebring 12 hrs

PEDRO FARIA

P

1994 Portuguese Touring Car Champion

GIUSEPPE FARINA

I. Born: 30.10.1906, Turin. Died: 30.6.1966, Chambéry (F), road accident

1950 World Champion

World Championship Grand Prix Record

years	starts	wins	2nd	3rd	4th	5th	6th	PP	FL	points
1950–55	33(1)	5	9	6	3	2	1	5	5	127.33

Race wins: 1950 British GP, Swiss GP, Italian GP, 1951 Belgian GP, 1953 German GP. Best qualifying: 1st

Pre-1950 Grands Prix. Race wins: 1948 Monaco GP

World Sports Car Championship. Race wins: 1953 Spa 24 hrs, Nürburgring, 1954 Buenos Aires

Other major race wins: 1940 Tripoli GP, 1950 International Trophy (Silverstone)

MAURICE FARMAN

F. Born: 1868. Died: n/a

Major race wins: 1901 Pau GP

Giuseppe Farina

WALT FAULKNER

USA. Born: 16.2.1920. Died: 22.4.1956

Indycar Championship. Race wins: 1950 Milwaukee Race 2, 1951 Darlington, Milwaukee Race 2

PHILIPPE FAVRE

CH. Born: 11.12.1961, Geneva

	wins	2nd	3rd	4th	5th	6th	PP	FL	points
Int F3000 Ch	-	1	-	-	-	1	1	6

Championship: 1989 13th

HARLAN FENGLER

USA. Born: n/a. Died: 1.4.1981

Indycar Championship. Race wins: 1923 Kansas City Race 2, 1924 Beverly Hills

WILLIAM FERGUSON

ZA

World Championship Grand Prix Record

year	starts	wins	2nd	3rd	4th	5th	6th	PP	FL	points
1972	-(1)	-	-	-	-	-	-	-	-	-

Best qualifying: 27th

WE FERGUSON

USA

Indycar Championship. Race wins: 1913 Galveston Race 2

ADRIAN FERNANDEZ

MEX. Born: 20.4.1965, Mexico City

1991 Mexican F3 Champion

GIL DE FERRAN

BR. Born: 11.11.1967, Paris (F)

1992 British F3 Champion

	wins	2nd	3rd	4th	5th	6th	PP	FL	points
Int F3000 Ch	3	2	2	-	1	-	2	1	49

Championships: 1993 4th, 1994 3rd. Race wins: 1993 International Trophy (Silverstone), 1994 Pau GP, Mediterranean GP (Enna)

ENZO FERRARI

I. Born: 18.2.1898, Modena. Died: 14.8.1988, Modena

Major race wins: 1924 Coppa Acerbo

ALAIN FERTÉ

F. Born: 8.10.1955, Falaise. Brother of Michel

1980 French F3 Champion

	wins	2nd	3rd	4th	5th	6th	PP	FL	points
European F2 Ch	-	-	-	-	3	-	-	-	6

Championships: 1983 12th, 1984 13th

	wins	2nd	3rd	4th	5th	6th	PP	FL	points
Int F3000 Ch	-	1	1	1	1	2	-	-	17

Championships: 1985 9th, 1986 13th, 1989 16th

World Sports Car Championship. Race wins: 1990 Silverstone

European F3 Championship. Race wins: 1981 Jarama, 1982 Magny-Cours
Other major race wins: 1981 and 1982 Monaco F3 GP, 1988 Tourist Trophy

MICHEL FERTÉ
F. Born: 8.12.1958, Falaise. Brother of Alain
1983 French F3 Champion

	wins	2nd	3rd	4th	5th	6th	PP	FL	points
European F2 Ch	-	2	3	1	1	1	1	-	30

Championships: 1983 20th, 1984 3rd

Int F3000 Ch	-	3	6	1	1	2	2	2	47

Championships: 1985 5th, 1986 5th, 1987 14th, 1988 20th
Other major race wins: 1983 Monaco F3 GP

IRA FETTERMAN
USA
Indycar Championship. Race wins: 1919 Uniontown Race 4, 1921 Uniontown Race 2

TED FIELD
USA
World Sports Car Championship. Race wins: 1979 Daytona 24 hrs

HUGHES DE FIERLANDT
B
Major race wins: 1975 Spa 24 hrs, 1976 Tourist Trophy

MARIA TERESA DE FILIPPIS
I. Born: 11.11.1926

World Championship Grand Prix Record

years	starts	wins	2nd	3rd	4th	5th	6th	PP	FL	points
1958–59	3(2)	-	-	-	-	-	-	-	-	-

Best result: 10th. Best qualifying: 15th

MARTINO FINOTTO
I. Born: 11.11.1933
1979 European Touring Car Champion (shared with Carlo Facetti)
Major race wins: 1979 Tourist Trophy

BOB FINNEY
USA
Indycar Championship. Race wins: 1955 Pikes Peak

HARRY FIRTH
AUS
Major race wins: 1963 and 1967 Bathurst

LUDWIG FISCHER
D

World Championship Grand Prix Record

year	starts	wins	2nd	3rd	4th	5th	6th	PP	FL	points
1952	-(1)	-	-	-	-	-	-	-	-	-

Best qualifying: no time set

RUDOLF FISCHER
CH. Born: 19.4.1912, Zurich. Died: 30.12.1976

World Championship Grand Prix Record

years	starts	wins	2nd	3rd	4th	5th	6th	PP	FL	points
1951–52	7(1)	-	1	1	-	-	1	-	-	10

Best championship: 1952 4th. Best qualifying: 5th

CALVIN FISH
GB. Born: 22.7.1961, Norwich
1987 North American (Eastern Division) Formula Atlantic Champion

MIKE FISHER
USA

World Championship Grand Prix Record

year	starts	wins	2nd	3rd	4th	5th	6th	PP	FL	points
1967	2	-	-	-	-	-	-	-	-	-

Best result: 11th. Best qualifying: 18th

GIANCARLO FISICHELLA
I. Born: 15.2.1973, Rome
1994 Italian F3 Champion

Major race wins: 1994 Monaco F3 GP

JOHN FITCH
USA. Born: 4.8.1917, Indianapolis

World Championship Grand Prix Record

years	starts	wins	2nd	3rd	4th	5th	6th	PP	FL	points
1953; 1955	2	-	-	-	-	-	-	-	-	-

Best result: 9th. Best qualifying: 20th
World Sports Car Championship. Race wins: 1953 Sebring 12 hrs, 1955 Tourist Trophy

CHRISTIAN FITTIPALDI
BR. Born: 18.1.1971. Son of Wilson, nephew of Emerson
1991 International F3000 Champion; 1990 Sud-Am F3 Champion; 1989 Brazilian F3 Champion

World Championship Grand Prix Record

years	starts	wins	2nd	3rd	4th	5th	6th	PP	FL	points
1992–94	40(3)	-	-	3	1	1	-	-	12

Best championship: 1993 13th. Best qualifying: 6th

	wins	2nd	3rd	4th	5th	6th	PP	FL	points
Int F3000 Ch	2	3	2	1	-	-	4	1	47

Championship: 1991 1st. Race wins: 1991 Jerez, Nogaro GP
Other major race wins: 1993 Spa 24 hrs

EMERSON FITTIPALDI
BR. Born: 12.12.1946, Sao Paulo. Brother of Wilson, uncle of Christian
1972 and 1974 World Champion; 1989 Indycar Champion; 1971 and 1972 Brazilian F2 Torneio; 1969 British F3 Champion

World Championship Grand Prix Record

years	starts	wins	2nd	3rd	4th	5th	6th	PP	FL	points
1970–80	144(5)	14	13	8	9	5	8	6	6	281

Race wins: 1970 United States GP, 1972 Spanish GP, Belgian GP, British GP, Austrian GP, 1973 Argentinian GP, Brazilian GP, Spanish GP, 1974 Brazilian GP, Belgian GP, Canadian GP, 1975 Argentinian GP, British GP. Best qualifying: 1st

	wins	2nd	3rd	4th	5th	6th	PP	FL	points
European F2 Ch	6	2	2	-	2	-	5	5	25

Championship: 1970 3rd. Race wins: 1971 Jarama, Crystal Palace, Albi GP, 1972 Jochen Rindt Trophy (Hockenheim), Rouen GP, Jochen Rindt Trophy (Österreichring)

Indycar Championship. Race wins: 1985 Michigan 500, 1986 Elkhart Lake, 1987 Cleveland, Toronto, 1988 Mid-Ohio, Elkhart Lake, 1989 Indianapolis 500, Detroit GP, Portland, Cleveland, Nazareth, 1990 Nazareth, 1991 Detroit GP, 1992 Surfers' Paradise, Cleveland, Elkhart Lake, Mid-Ohio, 1993 Indianapolis 500, Portland, Mid-Ohio, 1994 Phoenix

Emerson Fittipaldi

Other major race wins: 1972 Race of Champions, Italian Republic GP (Vallelunga), Rothmans £50,000, 1974 Presidenta Medici GP (Brasilia), 1992 Marlboro Challenge

WILSON FITTIPALDI
BR. Born: 25.12.1943, Sao Paolo. Father of Christian, brother of Emerson

World Championship Grand Prix Record

years	starts	wins	2nd	3rd	4th	5th	6th	PP	FL	points
1972–73; 1975	35(3)	-	-	-	-	1	1	-	-	3

Best championship: 1973 15th. Best qualifying: 9th

	wins	2nd	3rd	4th	5th	6th	PP	FL	points
European F2 Ch	-	-	-	5	2	2	-	-	32

Championships: 1971 6th, 1972 12th, 1973 13th
Major race wins: 1973 Misano non-championship F2

THEO FITZAU
D. Born: n/a. Died: 18.3.1982

World Championship Grand Prix Record

year	starts	wins	2nd	3rd	4th	5th	6th	PP	FL	points
1953	1	-	-	-	-	-	-	-	-	-

Best result: no finishes. Best qualifying: 21st

JOHN FITZPATRICK
GB. Born: 9.6.1943, Birmingham
1980 IMSA GT Champion; 1966 British Touring Car Champion

World Sports Car Championship. Race wins: 1976 Silverstone, 1977 Hockenheim, 1978 Mugello, Watkins Glen, 1979 Mugello, Silverstone, Nürburgring, 1980 Mosport Park, 1981 Riverside
Other major race wins: 1976 Daytona 24 hrs, Bathurst, 1980 Sebring 12 hrs, 1983 Brands Hatch 1000 kms

PAT FLAHERTY
USA. Born: 6.1.1926, Glendale, California
Indycar Championship. Race wins: 1955 Milwaukee Race 2, 1956 Indianapolis 500, 1956 Milwaukee Race 1

MAURIZIO FLAMMINI
I. Born: 1949

	wins	2nd	3rd	4th	5th	6th	PP	FL	points
European F2 Ch	3	1	4	-	1	2	2	1	54

Championships: 1974 16th, 1975 6th, 1976 6th, 1979 16th. **Race wins:** 1975 Mugello, 1976 Jochen Rindt Trophy (Thruxton), Rouen GP
Other major race wins: 1975 Misano non-championship F2

JACK FLEMING
USA
Indycar Championship. Race wins: 1909 San Leandro

JOHN FLEMMING
GB
1962 British F3 (Formula Junior) Champion

JAN FLINTERMAN
NL. Born: 2.10.1919
World Championship Grand Prix Record

year	starts	wins	2nd	3rd	4th	5th	6th	PP	FL	points
1952	1	-	-	-	-	-	-	-	-	-

Best result: 9th. **Best qualifying:** 15th

TIM FLOCK
USA. Born: 5.11.1924, Fort Payne, Alabama
1952 and 1955 NASCAR Champion

RON FLOCKHART
GB. Born: 16.6.1923, Edinburgh. Died: 12.4.1962, aircraft accident
World Championship Grand Prix Record

years	starts	wins	2nd	3rd	4th	5th	6th	PP	FL	points
1954; 1956–60	13(2)	-	-	1	-	-	2	-	-	5

Best championship: 1956 11th. **Best qualifying:** 8th
World Sports Car Championship. Race wins: 1956 and 1957 Le Mans 24 hrs

ARMANDO FLORIDIA
I
Major race wins: 1976 Targa Florio

MYRON FOHR
USA. Born: 1913
Indycar Championship. Race wins: 1948 Milwaukee Race 3, Springfield, 1949 Milwaukee Race 1, Trenton

GREGOR FOITEK
CH. Born: 27.3.1965, Zurich
1986 Swiss F3 Champion
World Championship Grand Prix Record

years	starts	wins	2nd	3rd	4th	5th	6th	PP	FL	points
1989–90	7(15)	-	-	-	-	-	-	-	-	-

Best result: 7th. **Best qualifying:** 20th

	wins	2nd	3rd	4th	5th	6th	PP	FL	points
Int F3000 Ch	1	-	2	-	-	1	-	-	15

Championship: 1988 7th. **Race wins:** 1988 Rome GP (Vallelunga)

GEORGE FOLLMER
USA. Born: 27.1.1934, Phoenix
1972 Can-Am Champion; 1972 and 1976 (overall and class 1) Trans-Am Champion
World Championship Grand Prix Record

year	starts	wins	2nd	3rd	4th	5th	6th	PP	FL	points
1973	12(1)	-	-	1	-	-	1	-	-	5

Best championship: 1973 13th. **Best qualifying:** 11th
Indycar Championship. Race wins: 1969 Phoenix Race 1

LUIS FONTES
GB. Born: 1914. Died: World War II, killed in action while serving with the RAF
Major Sports Car races. Race wins: 1935 Le Mans 24 hrs

ELLIOTT FORBES-ROBINSON
USA. Born: 31.10.1943, San Francisco
1982 Trans-Am Champion; 1974 SCCA Super Vee Champion

FRANCO FORINI
CH. Born: 22.9.1958
1985 Italian F3 Champion
World Championship Grand Prix Record

year	starts	wins	2nd	3rd	4th	5th	6th	PP	FL	points
1987	2(1)	-	-	-	-	-	-	-	-	-

Best result: no finishes. **Best qualifying:** 26th

	wins	2nd	3rd	4th	5th	6th	PP	FL	points
Int F3000 Ch	-	-	-	-	-	1	-	-	1

Championship: 1986 21st

PHILIP FOTHERINGHAM-PARKER
GB. Born: 22.9.1907. Died: 15.10.1981
World Championship Grand Prix Record

year	starts	wins	2nd	3rd	4th	5th	6th	PP	FL	points
1951	1	-	-	-	-	-	-	-	-	-

Best result: no finishes. **Best qualifying:** 16th

ANTHONY JOSEPH "AJ" FOYT JR
USA. Born: 16.1.1935, Houston, Texas
1960, 1961, 1963, 1964, 1967, 1975 and 1979 (USAC) Indycar Champion
World Sports Car Championship. Race wins: 1967 Le Mans 24 hrs
Indycar Championship. Race wins: 1960 Du Quoin, Indiana State Fairgrounds, Sacramento, Phoenix, 1961 Indianapolis 500, Langhorne, Du Quoin, Indiana State Fairgrounds, 1962 Trenton Race 1, Milwaukee Race 1, Langhorne Race 1, Sacramento, 1963 Trenton Race 1, Langhorne, Trenton Race 2, Du Quoin, Trenton Race 3, 1964 Phoenix Race 1, Trenton Race 1, Indianapolis 500, Milwaukee Race 1, Langhorne, Trenton Race 2, Springfield, Du Quoin, Indiana State Fairgrounds, Sacramento, 1965 Trenton Race 2, Springfield, Indiana State Fairgrounds, Trenton Race 3, Phoenix Race 2, 1967 Indianapolis 500, Springfield, Du Quoin, Trenton Race 2, Sacramento, 1968 Castle Rock, Indiana State Fairgrounds, Sacramento, Hanford Race 2, 1969 Indiana State Fairgrounds, 1971 Phoenix Race 2, 1973 Trenton Race 1, Pocono 500, 1974 California 500 Qualifying Race 1, Trenton Race 2, 1975 California 500 Qualifying Race 1, California 500, Trenton, Milwaukee, Pocono 500, Michigan, Phoenix, 1976 Texas, Michigan, 1977 Ontario, Indianapolis 500, Mosport Park, 1978 Texas, Silverstone, 1979 Texas, Milwaukee, Pocono 500, Texas
Other major race wins: 1972 Daytona 500, 1981 Pocono 500 (non-championship USAC Indycar race), 1983 Daytona 24 hrs, 1985 Daytona 24 hrs, Sebring 12 hrs

AJ Foyt Jr

FRED FRAME
USA. Born: 1895. Died: 25.4.1962
Indycar Championship. Race wins: 1932 Indianapolis 500

ROBBIE FRANCEVIC
AUS
1986 Australian Touring Car Champion

GIORGIO FRANCIA
I. Born: 8.11.1947, San Giorgio di Piano, Bologna
World Championship Grand Prix Record

years	starts	wins	2nd	3rd	4th	5th	6th	PP	FL	points
1977; 1981	-(2)	-	-	-	-	-	-	-	-	-

Best qualifying: 30th
World Sports Car Championship. Race wins: 1979 Vallelunga, 1980 Vallelunga, 1981 Mugello, 1982 Monza

	wins	2nd	3rd	4th	5th	6th	PP	FL	points
European F2 Ch	-	-	2	4	1	-	1	17

Championships: 1975 7th, 1976 17th

CLAUDIO FRANCISCI
I

	wins	2nd	3rd	4th	5th	6th	PP	FL	points
European F2 Ch	-	-	-	1	-	-	-		4

Championship: 1972 19th

IAN FRASER-JONES
ZA

1958 and 1959 South African Drivers' Champion

JOHN FRENCH
AUS

Major race wins: 1981 Bathurst

HEINZ-HARALD FRENTZEN
D. Born: 3.5.1967, Munich

World Championship Grand Prix Record

year	starts	wins	2nd	3rd	4th	5th	6th	PP	FL	points
1994	15(1)	-	-	-	1	1	2	-	-	7

Best championship: 1994 13th. Best qualifying: 3rd

	wins	2nd	3rd	4th	5th	6th	PP	FL	points
Int F3000 Ch	-	-	-	-	3	2	-	-	8

Championships: 1990 16th, 1991 14th

FRANCK FRÉON
F. Born: 16.3.1962, Paris

	wins	2nd	3rd	4th	5th	6th	PP	FL	points
Int F3000 Ch	-	-	-	1	-	-	-	-	2

Championship: 1990 19th

PAUL FRÈRE
B. Born: 30.1.1917, Le Havre (F)

World Championship Grand Prix Record

years	starts	wins	2nd	3rd	4th	5th	6th	PP	FL	points
1952–56	11	-	1	-	1	1	-	-	11

Best championship: 1956 7th. Best qualifying: 6th

World Sports Car Championship. Race wins: 1960 Le Mans 24 hrs

LEONEL FRIEDRICH
BR. Born: 17.12.1948

1987 Sud-Am F3 Champion

BRAD FRISSELLE
USA

Major race wins: 1977 Sebring 12 hrs

JOE FRY
GB. Born: n/a. Died: 29.7.1950, Blandford

World Championship Grand Prix Record

year	starts	wins	2nd	3rd	4th	5th	6th	PP	FL	points
1950	1	-	-	-	-	-	-	-	-

Best result: 10th. Best qualifying: 20th

YOSHIMASA FUJIWARA
J

1983 Japanese F3 Champion

HIDEO FUKUYAMA
J. Born: 13.8.1955, Owase

1992 Japanese Touring Car Champion (with Masahiro Hasemi)

NESTOR GABRIEL FURLAN
RA. Born: 13.10.1964

1989 Sud-Am F3 Champion

	wins	2nd	3rd	4th	5th	6th	PP	FL	points
Int F3000 Ch	-	-	-	-	1	-	-	-	1

Championship: 1991 19th

HIROSHI FUSHIDA
J

World Championship Grand Prix Record

year	starts	wins	2nd	3rd	4th	5th	6th	PP	FL	points
1975	-(2)	-	-	-	-	-	-	-	-

Best qualifying: 25th

G ···

JEAN-PIERRE GABAN
B

Major race wins: 1967 Spa 24 hrs

GIUSEPPE "BEPPE" GABBIANI
I. Born: 2.1.1957, Piacenza

World Championship Grand Prix Record

years	starts	wins	2nd	3rd	4th	5th	6th	PP	FL	points
1978; 1981	3(14)	-	-	-	-	-	-	-	-

Best result: no finishes. Best qualifying: 20th

	wins	2nd	3rd	4th	5th	6th	PP	FL	points
European F2 Ch	4	3	4	4	2	1	2		87

Championships: 1978 19th, 1979 5th, 1980 16th, 1982 5th, 1983 3rd. Race wins: 1983 International Trophy (Silverstone), Jochen Rindt Trophy (Thruxton), Eifelrennen (Nürburgring), Rome GP (Vallelunga)

European F3 Championship. Race wins: 1977 Paul Ricard

PHILIPPE GACHE
F. Born: 31.5.1962, Avignon

	wins	2nd	3rd	4th	5th	6th	PP	FL	points
Int F3000 Ch	-	-	-	-	1	-	-	1	2

Championship: 1991 16th

BERTRAND GACHOT
B/F (dual nationality). Born: 22.12.1962, Luxembourg

World Championship Grand Prix Record

years	starts	wins	2nd	3rd	4th	5th	6th	PP	FL	points
1989–92; 1994	36(37)	-	-	-	1	3	-	1	5

Best championship: 1991 12th. Best qualifying: 10th

World Sports Car Championship. Race wins: 1991 Le Mans 24 hrs

	wins	2nd	3rd	4th	5th	6th	PP	FL	points
Int F3000 Ch	-	2	-	2	1	1	1	-	21

Best championship: 1988 5th

PATRICK GAILLARD
F. Born: 12.2.1952, Paris

World Championship Grand Prix Record

year	starts	wins	2nd	3rd	4th	5th	6th	PP	FL	points
1979	2(3)	-	-	-	-	-	-	-	-

Best result: 13th. Best qualifying: 23rd

	wins	2nd	3rd	4th	5th	6th	PP	FL	points
European F2 Ch	-	-	-	1	1	-	-	-	5

Championship: 1979 15th

European F3 Championship. Race wins: 1978 Imola, Nürburgring

DIVINA GALICA
GB. Born: 13.8.1946, Malmesbury, Wiltshire

World Championship Grand Prix Record

years	starts	wins	2nd	3rd	4th	5th	6th	PP	FL	points
1976; 1978	-(3)	-	-	-	-	-	-	-	-

Best qualifying: 27th

GIOVANNI "NANNI" GALLI
I. Born: 2.10.1940, Bologna

World Championship Grand Prix Record

years	starts	wins	2nd	3rd	4th	5th	6th	PP	FL	points
1970–73	17(3)	-	-	-	-	-	-	-	-

Best result: 9th. Best qualifying: 15th

	wins	2nd	3rd	4th	5th	6th	PP	FL	points
European F2 Ch	-	-	-	-	-	1	-	-	8

Championship: 1969 7th

OSCAR GALVEZ
RA. Born: 17.8.1913, Buenos Aires. Died: 16.12.1989, Buenos Aires

World Championship Grand Prix Record

year	starts	wins	2nd	3rd	4th	5th	6th	PP	FL	points
1953	1	-	-	-	-	1	-	-	2

Best championship: 1953 13th. Best qualifying: 9th

FRED GAMBLE
USA. Born: 17.3.1932, Pittsburgh, Pennsylvania

World Championship Grand Prix Record

year	starts	wins	2nd	3rd	4th	5th	6th	PP	FL	points
1960	1	-	-	-	-	-	-	-	-	-

Best result: 10th. Best qualifying: 14th

HOWDEN GANLEY
NZ. Born: 24.12.1941, Hamilton

World Championship Grand Prix Record

years	starts	wins	2nd	3rd	4th	5th	6th	PP	FL	points
1971–74	35(6)	-	-	2	1	2	-	-	10

Best championship: 1972 12th. Best qualifying: 4th

HARRY GANT
USA. Born: 10.1.1940, Taylorsville, North Carolina
1985 IROC Champion

FRANK GARDNER
AUS. Born: 1.10.1931, Sydney
1967, 1968 and 1973 British Touring Car Champion; 1971 British F5000 Champion

World Championship Grand Prix Record

years	starts	wins	2nd	3rd	4th	5th	6th	PP	FL	points
1964–65, 1968	8(1)	-	-	-	-	-	-	-	-

Best result: 8th. Best qualifying: 11th

	wins	2nd	3rd	4th	5th	6th	PP	FL	points
European F2 Ch	1	-	1	2	1	1	-	-	33

Championship: 1967 2nd. Race wins: 1967 Hockenheim

Tasman Cup. Race wins: 1971 Warwick Farm, 1972 New Zealand GP

BOB GARRETSON
USA
1981 World Sports Car Champion

World Sports Car Championship. Race wins: 1981 Daytona 24 hrs

Other major race wins: 1978 Sebring 12 hrs

JO GARTNER
A. Born: 24.1.1954, Vienna. Died: 1.6.1986, Le Mans 24 hrs

World Championship Grand Prix Record

year	starts	wins	2nd	3rd	4th	5th	6th	PP	FL	points
1984	8	-	-	-	-	1*	-	-	-

* Not entered in World Championship so no points awarded.
Best qualifying: 22nd

	wins	2nd	3rd	4th	5th	6th	PP	FL	points
European F2 Ch	1	-	-	1	1	2	-	-	16

Championships: 1981 19th, 1982 17th, 1983 6th. Race wins: 1983 Pau GP

Other major race wins: 1986 Sebring 12 hrs

PETER GAYDON
GB. Born: 6.5.1941

	wins	2nd	3rd	4th	5th	6th	PP	FL	points
European F2 Ch	-	-	-	-	-	-	-	-	1

Championship: 1970 18th

TONY GAZE
AUS. Born: 3.2.1920, Melbourne

World Championship Grand Prix Record

year	starts	wins	2nd	3rd	4th	5th	6th	PP	FL	points
1952	3(1)	-	-	-	-	-	-	-	-

Best result: 15th. Best qualifying: 16th

FRANK GELNAW
USA

Indycar Championship. Race wins: 1910 Long Island Race 2

OLIVIER GENDEBIEN
B. Born: 12.1.1924, Brussels

World Championship Grand Prix Record

years	starts	wins	2nd	3rd	4th	5th	6th	PP	FL	points
1956; 1958–61	14(1)	-	1	1	2	1	2	-	-	18

Best championship: 1960 6th. Best qualifying: 3rd

World Sports Car Championship. Race wins: 1958 Targa Florio, Le Mans 24 hrs, 1959 Sebring 12 hrs, 1960 Sebring 12 hrs, Le Mans 24 hrs, 1961 Sebring 12 hrs, Targa Florio, Le Mans 24 hrs, 1962 Targa Florio, Nürburgring, Le Mans 24 hrs

JORDI GENE
E. Born: 5.12.1970, Barcelona

	wins	2nd	3rd	4th	5th	6th	PP	FL	points
Int F3000 Ch	1	1	1	1	1	-	1	-	24

Championships: 1992 5th, 1994 12th. Race wins: 1992 International Trophy (Silverstone)

PAUL GENTILOZZI
USA. Born: 6.2.1950

Major race wins: 1994 Daytona 24 hrs

IAN GEOGHEGAN
AUS
1964, 1966, 1967, 1968 and 1969 Australian Touring Car Champion; 1970 Australian Gold Star Champion

Major race wins: 1973 Bathurst

ELMER GEORGE
USA. Born: 15.7.1928, Hockerville, Oklahoma. Died: 30.5.1976, Terre Haute, Indiana

Indycar Championship. Race wins: 1957 Syracuse

BOB GERARD
GB. Born: 19.1.1914, Leicester. Died: 26.1.1990, South Croxton, Leicestershire

World Championship Grand Prix Record

years	starts	wins	2nd	3rd	4th	5th	6th	PP	FL	points
1950–51; 1953–54;										
1956–57	8	-	-	-	-	-	3	-	-	-

Best qualifying: 10th

LOUIS GÉRARD
F

Major race wins: 1938 Tourist Trophy

GERINO GERINI
I. Born: 10.8.1928, Rome

World Championship Grand Prix Record

years	starts	wins	2nd	3rd	4th	5th	6th	PP	FL	points
1956; 1958	6(1)	-	-	-	1	-	-	-	-	1.5

Best championship: 1956 25th. Best qualifying: 15th.

Major race wins: 1958 Mille Miglia

PETER GETHIN
GB. Born: 21.2.1940, Ewell
1974 Tasman Champion; 1969 and 1970 British F5000 Champion

World Championship Grand Prix Record

years	starts	wins	2nd	3rd	4th	5th	6th	PP	FL	points
1970–74	30(1)	1	-	-	-	-	2	-	-	11

Best championship: 1971 9th. Race wins: 1971 Italian GP.
Best qualifying: 5th

	wins	2nd	3rd	4th	5th	6th	PP	FL	points
European F2 Ch	1	1	1	-	1	-	2	3	22

Championships: 1968 12th, 1972 9th, 1973 13th. Race wins: 1972 Pau GP

Tasman Cup. Race wins: 1974 Pukekohe, Sandown Park

Other major race wins: 1971 World Championship Victory Race, 1973 Race of Champions

PIETRO GHERSI
I. Born: 1899. Died: 1972

Major race wins: 1930 Spa 24 hrs

PIERCARLO GHINZANI
I. Born: 16.1.1952, Riviera d'Adda, Bergamo
1977 European F3 Champion; 1979 Italian F3 Champion

World Championship Grand Prix Record

years	starts	wins	2nd	3rd	4th	5th	6th	PP	FL	points
1981; 1983–89	76(35)	-	-	-	-	1	-	-	-	2

Best championship: 1984 19th. Best qualifying: 13th

World Sports Car Championship. Race wins: 1982 Mugello, 1986 Fuji

	wins	2nd	3rd	4th	5th	6th	PP	FL	points
European F2 Ch	-	-	1	-	-	-	-	-	3

Best championship: 1978 16th

European F3 Championship. Race wins: 1977 Nürburgring, Zolder, Imola, 1979 Vallelunga, Enna

JUAN CARLOS GIACCHINO
RA. Born: 7.12.1958
1988 Sud-Am F3 Champion

BRUNO GIACOMELLI
I. Born: 10.9.1952, Borgo Pancarale, Brescia
1978 European F2 Champion; 1976 ShellSport British F3 Champion

World Championship Grand Prix Record

years	starts	wins	2nd	3rd	4th	5th	6th	PP	FL	points
1977–83; 1990	69(14)	-	-	1	1	3	1	1	-	14

Best championship: 1981 15th. **Best qualifying:** 1st

	wins	2nd	3rd	4th	5th	6th	PP	FL	points
European F2 Ch	11	1	1	1	-	1	11	9	114

Championships: 1977 4th, 1978 1st. **Race wins:** 1977 Rome GP (Vallelunga), Mugello, Donington Park, 1978 Jochen Rindt Trophy (Thruxton), Jim Clark Trophy (Hockenheim), Pau GP, Rouen GP, Nogaro GP, Mediterranean GP (Enna), Misano, Hockenheim

Other major race wins: 1976 Monaco F3 GP

"GIANFRANCO"
I. Real name: Gianfranco Trombetti

	wins	2nd	3rd	4th	5th	6th	PP	FL	points
European F2 Ch	-	-	1	-	-	1	-	-	5

Championships: 1975 19th, 1977 20th

DICK GIBSON
GB. Born: 16.4.1918, Bourne

World Championship Grand Prix Record

years	starts	wins	2nd	3rd	4th	5th	6th	PP	FL	points
1957–58	2	-	-	-	-	-	-	-	-	-

Best result: no finishes. **Best qualifying:** no time set

FRED GIBSON
AUS

Major race wins: 1967 Bathurst

ANDREA GILARDI
I

	wins	2nd	3rd	4th	5th	6th	PP	FL	points
Int F3000 Ch	-	-	-	-	2	-	-	-	2

Championship: 1993 17th

ANDREW GILBERT-SCOTT
GB. Born: 11.6.1958, Cookham Dene

	wins	2nd	3rd	4th	5th	6th	PP	FL	points
Int F3000 Ch	-	-	1	-	-	-	-	-	4

Championship: 1989 15th

"GIMAX"
I. Born: 14.4.1967. Real name: Carlo Franchi

World Championship Grand Prix Record

year	starts	wins	2nd	3rd	4th	5th	6th	PP	FL	points
1978	-(1)	-	-	-	-	-	-	-	-	-

Best qualifying: 28th

RICHIE GINTHER
USA. Born: 5.8.1930, Hollywood. Died: 20.9.1989

World Championship Grand Prix Record

years	starts	wins	2nd	3rd	4th	5th	6th	PP	FL	points
1960–67	52(1)	1	8	5	6	4	4	-	3	107

Best championship: 1963 2nd. **Race wins:** 1965 Mexican GP. **Best qualifying:** 2nd

MICHELE DI GIOIA
I
1987 Italian Touring Car Champion

CARLO GIORGIO
I
1973 Italian F3 Champion

	wins	2nd	3rd	4th	5th	6th	PP	FL	points
European F2 Ch	-	-	1	-	-	-	-	-	3

Championship: 1975 22nd

FABRIZIO GIOVANARDI
I. Born: 14.12.1966, Sassuolo

LÉONCE GIRARDOT
F. Born: 1864. Died: 1922
Pre-1950 Grands Prix. **Race wins:** 1901 Gordon Bennett Trophy

YVES GIRAUD-CABANTOUS
F. Born: 8.10.1903, St Gaudens. Died: 31.3.1973

World Championship Grand Prix Record

years	starts	wins	2nd	3rd	4th	5th	6th	PP	FL	points
1950–53	13	-	-	-	1	1	-	-	-	5

Best championship: 1950 13th. **Best qualifying:** 5th

FABIEN GIROIX
F. Born: 17.9.1960, St Maur
1987 French Touring Car Champion (Group A)

	wins	2nd	3rd	4th	5th	6th	PP	FL	points
Int F3000 Ch	-	-	-	1	-	-	-	-	3

Championship: 1988 17th

Major race wins: 1990 Spa 24 hrs

IGNAZIO GIUNTI
I. Born: 30.8.1941, Rome. Died: 10.1.1971, Buenos Aires 1000 kms

World Championship Grand Prix Record

year	starts	wins	2nd	3rd	4th	5th	6th	PP	FL	points
1970	4	-	-	-	1	-	-	-	-	3

Best championship: 1970 17th. **Best qualifying:** 5th
World Sports Car Championship. Race wins: 1970 Sebring 12 hrs

JIMMY GLEASON
USA. Born: n/a. Died: 12.9.1931, Syracuse
Indycar Championship. Race wins: 1931 Altoona Race 2

DIETER GLEMSER
D
1971 European Touring Car over 2000 cc Class Champion; 1973 and 1974 German Racing Champion
Major race wins: 1971 Spa 24 hrs, 1972 Tourist Trophy

HELMUT GLÖCKLER
D

World Championship Grand Prix Record

year	starts	wins	2nd	3rd	4th	5th	6th	PP	FL	points
1953	-(1)	-	-	-	-	-	-	-	-	-

Best qualifying: no time set

TOM GLOY
USA. Born: 11.6.1947
1984 Trans-Am Champion; 1979 North American Formula Atlantic Champion

FRANCESCO "CHICO" GODIA-SALES
E. Born: 21.3.1921, Barcelona. Died: 28.11.1990, Barcelona

World Championship Grand Prix Record

years	starts	wins	2nd	3rd	4th	5th	6th	PP	FL	points
1951; 1954; 1956–58	13(1)	-	-	-	2	-	1	-	-	6

Best championship: 1956 7th. **Best qualifying:** 9th

CHRISTIAN GOETHALS
B. Born: 4.8.1928

World Championship Grand Prix Record

year	starts	wins	2nd	3rd	4th	5th	6th	PP	FL	points
1958	1	-	-	-	-	-	-	-	-	-

Best result: no finishes. **Best qualifying:** no time set

GUILLAUME GOMEZ
F. Born: 25.7.1969, Orléans

	wins	2nd	3rd	4th	5th	6th	PP	FL	points
Int F3000 Ch	-	-	2	1	-	1	1	-	12

Championship: 1994 7th

JOSÉ FROILAN GONZALEZ
RA. Born: 5.10.1922, Arrecifes, Buenos Aires

	wins	2nd	3rd	4th	5th	6th	PP	FL	points
Int F3000 Ch	1	1	-	1	2	3	-	-	25

Championships: 1989 10th, 1990 10th, 1991 11th. **Race wins:** 1989 Rome GP (Vallelunga)

World Championship Grand Prix Record

years	starts	wins	2nd	3rd	4th	5th	6th	PP	FL	points
1950–57; 1960	26	2	7	6	2	1	-	3	6	77.64

Best championship: 1954 2nd . **Race wins:** 1951 British GP, 1954 British GP. **Best qualifying:** 1st.
World Sports Car Championship. Race wins: 1954 Le Mans 24 hrs
Other major race wins: 1954 International Trophy (Silverstone)

OSCAR GONZALEZ
U

World Championship Grand Prix Record

year	starts	wins	2nd	3rd	4th	5th	6th	PP	FL	points
1956	1	-	-	-	-	1	-	-	-	

Best qualifying: no time set

SCOTT GOODYEAR
CDN. Born: 20.12.1959, Toronto
1986 North American (Eastern Division) Formula Atlantic Champion
Indycar Championship. Race wins: 1992 and 1994 Michigan 500

MARC GOOSSENS
B. Born: 30.11.1969

	wins	2nd	3rd	4th	5th	6th	PP	FL	points
Int F3000 Ch	-	-	-	1	1	-	-	3

Championship: 1994 12th

ALDO GORDINI
F. Born: 20.5.1921, Bologna (I)

World Championship Grand Prix Record

year	starts	wins	2nd	3rd	4th	5th	6th	PP	FL	points
1951	1	-	-	-	-	-	-	-	-	-

Best result: no finishes. **Best qualifying:** 17th

JEFF GORDON
USA. Born: 4.8.1971, Vallejo, California
Major race wins: 1994 World 600, Brickyard 400 (Indianapolis)

JOHN GOSS
AUS
Tasman Cup. Race wins: 1975 Sandown Park
Other major race wins: 1974 Bathurst, 1976 Australian GP, 1985 Bathurst

GUSTAVE "TAF" GOSSELIN
B
Major race wins: 1964 Spa 24 hrs

MIKE GOTH
USA

	wins	2nd	3rd	4th	5th	6th	PP	FL	points
European F2 Ch	-	-	-	-	1	-	-	2

Championship: 1970 16th

HORACE GOULD
GB. Born: 20.9.1921, Southmead. Died: 4.11.1968, Southmead

World Championship Grand Prix Record

years	starts	wins	2nd	3rd	4th	5th	6th	PP	FL	points
1954–58; 1960	14(3)	-	-	-	1	-	-	-	-	2

Best championship: 1956 19th. **Best qualifying:** 10th.

JEAN-MARC GOUNON
F. Born: 1.1.1963, Aubenas
1989 French F3 Champion

World Championship Grand Prix Record

years	starts	wins	2nd	3rd	4th	5th	6th	PP	FL	points
1993–94	9	-	-	-	-	-	-	-	-	-

Best result: 9th. **Best qualifying:** 22nd

	wins	2nd	3rd	4th	5th	6th	PP	FL	points
Int F3000 Ch	2	1	1	3	1	4	-	1	43

Championships: 1990 9th, 1991 6th, 1992 6th. **Race wins:** 1991 Pau GP, 1992 Magny-Cours

JULES GOUX
F. Born: 1878. Died: 1965, France
Pre-1950 Grands Prix. Race wins: 1921 Italian GP, 1926 French GP, European GP

Indycar Championship. Race wins: 1913 Indianapolis 500
Other major race wins: 1912 Sarthe Cup

EMANUEL DE GRAFFENRIED
CH. Born: 18.5.1914, Paris (F)

World Championship Grand Prix Record

years	starts	wins	2nd	3rd	4th	5th	6th	PP	FL	points
1950–56	22(2)	-	-	-	1	3	4	-	-	9

Best championship: 1953 8th. **Best qualifying:** 5th.
Pre-1950 Grands Prix. Race wins: 1949 British GP

STUART GRAHAM
GB
Major race wins: 1974 and 1975 Tourist Trophy

HENRY GRANDSIRE
F
1964 French F3 Champion

UMBERTO GRANO
I
1978, 1981 and 1982 European Touring Car Champion (shared with Helmut Kelleners in 1981 and 1982)
Major race wins: 1980 Tourist Trophy

HARRY GRANT
USA. Born: n/a. Died: ?.10.1915, Sheepshead Bay, New York
Indycar Championship. Race wins: 1909 and 1910 Vanderbilt Cup

JOHN GRAVES
USA
World Sports Car Championship. Race wins: 1977 Daytona 24 hrs

ROBB GRAVETT
GB. Born: 2.5.1956, London
1990 British Touring Car Champion

HARRY GRAY
US
Major race wins: 1952 Sebring 12 hrs

KEITH GREENE
GB. Born: 5.1.1938, London

World Championship Grand Prix Record

years	starts	wins	2nd	3rd	4th	5th	6th	PP	FL	points
1959–62	3(2)	-	-	-	-	-	-	-	-	-

Best result: 15th. **Best qualifying:** 19th

JOHN GREENWOOD
USA
1975 Trans-Am Champion

PETER GREGG
USA. Born: 4.5.1940, New York. Died: 15.12.1980, Jacksonville, suicide
1971, 1973, 1974, 1975, 1978 and 1979 IMSA GT Champion (1971 shared with Hurley Haywood); 1973 and 1974 Trans-Am Champion
World Sports Car Championship. Race wins: 1973 Daytona 24 hrs, 1975 Daytona 24 hrs, 1977 Mosport Park, 1978 Daytona 24 hrs, Watkins Glen
Other major race wins: 1973 Sebring 12 hrs, 1976 Daytona 24 hrs

MASTEN GREGORY
USA. Born: 29.2.1932, Kansas City. Died: 8.11.1985, Porto Ercole, Rome (I)

World Championship Grand Prix Record

years	starts	wins	2nd	3rd	4th	5th	6th	PP	FL	points
1957–63; 1965	38(5)	-	1	2	3	2	-	-	21

Best championship: 1957 6th. **Best qualifying:** 3rd
World Sports Car Championship. Race wins: 1957 Buenos Aires, 1961 Nürburgring, 1965 Le Mans 24 hrs
Other major race wins: 1962 Canadian GP

ALLAN GRICE
AUS. Born: 21.10.1942
Major race wins: 1986 and 1990 Bathurst

PAT GRIFFITH
GB. Born: 1924. Died: 28.1.1980
World Sports Car Championship. Race wins: 1953 Tourist Trophy

GEORGES GRIGNARD
F. Born: 25.7.1905, Paris. Died: 7.12.1977
World Championship Grand Prix Record

year	starts	wins	2nd	3rd	4th	5th	6th	PP	FL	points
1951	1	-	-	-	-	-	-	-	-	-

Best result: no finishes. **Best qualifying:** 16th

BOBBY GRIM
USA. Born: 4.9.1924, Coal City, Indiana
Indycar Championship. Race wins: 1960 Syracuse

ENRICO GRIMALDI
I
World Sports Car Championship. Race wins: 1979 Florio Cup

MIKE GROFF
USA. Born: 16.11.1961, Van Nuys, California
1989 American Racing Series Champion

HARALD GROHS
D. Born: 28.1.1944, Essen
World Sports Car Championship. Race wins: 1981 Silverstone, Mosport Park, Elkhart Lake

OLIVIER GROUILLARD
F. Born: 2.9.1958, Toulouse
1984 French F3 Champion
World Championship Grand Prix Record

year	starts	wins	2nd	3rd	4th	5th	6th	PP	FL	points
1989–92	41(21)	-	-	-	-	-	1	-	1	1

Best championship: 1989 26th. **Best qualifying:** 8th

	wins	2nd	3rd	4th	5th	6th	PP	FL	points
Int F3000 Ch	2	1	2	4	1	3	3	2	49

Championships: 1985 12th, 1986 13th, 1987 17th, 1988 2nd. **Race wins:** 1988 Le Mans, Zolder

STIG GRUEN
S
1986 Swedish Touring Car Champion

BRIAN GUBBY
GB. Born: 17.4.1934, Epsom
World Championship Grand Prix Record

year	starts	wins	2nd	3rd	4th	5th	6th	PP	FL	points
1965	-(1)	-	-	-	-	-	-	-	-	-

Best qualifying: 24th

BILL GUBELMANN
USA

	wins	2nd	3rd	4th	5th	6th	PP	FL	points
European F2 Ch	-	-	-	1	1	-	-	6

Championship: 1973 13th

MARCOS GUEIROS
BR. Born: 11.5.1970
1992 Sud-Am F3 Champion; 1991 and 1992 Brazilian F3 Champion

ANDRÉ GUELFI
F. Born: 6.5.1919
World Championship Grand Prix Record

year	starts	wins	2nd	3rd	4th	5th	6th	PP	FL	points
1958	1	-	-	-	-	-	-	-	-	-

Best result: no finishes. **Best qualifying:** no time set

MIGUEL ANGEL GUERRA
RA. Born: 31.8.1953, Buenos Aires
World Championship Grand Prix Record

year	starts	wins	2nd	3rd	4th	5th	6th	PP	FL	points
1981	1(3)	-	-	-	-	-	-	-	-	-

Best result: no finishes. **Best qualifying:** 22nd

	wins	2nd	3rd	4th	5th	6th	PP	FL	points
European F2 Ch	-	-	1	2	3	2	-	-	18

Championships: 1979 8th, 1980 9th

CARLOS GUERRERO
MEX. Born: 20.11.1957
1991 and 1992 Mexican F2 Champion; 1990, 1993 and 1994 Mexican F3 Champion

ROBERTO GUERRERO
USA (emigrated from Colombia). Born: 16.11.1958, Medellin (CO)
World Championship Grand Prix Record

years	starts	wins	2nd	3rd	4th	5th	6th	PP	FL	points
1982–83	21(8)	-	-	-	-	-	-	-	-	-

Best result: 8th. **Best qualifying:** 11th

	wins	2nd	3rd	4th	5th	6th	PP	FL	points
European F2 Ch	1	-	-	2	-	1	-	-	16

Championship: 1981 7th. **Race wins:** 1981 Jochen Rindt Trophy (Thruxton)

Indycar Championship. Race wins: 1987 Phoenix, Mid-Ohio

MAURICIO GUGELMIN
BR. Born: 20.4.1963, Joinville
1985 British F3 Champion
World Championship Grand Prix Record

years	starts	wins	2nd	3rd	4th	5th	6th	PP	FL	points
1988–92	74(6)	-	-	1	1	1	1	-	1	10

Best championship: 1988 13th. **Best qualifying:** 5th

	wins	2nd	3rd	4th	5th	6th	PP	FL	points
Int F3000 Ch	1	2	2	1	-	1	2	-	33

Championships: 1986 13th, 1987 4th. **Race wins:** 1987 International Trophy (Silverstone)
Other major race wins: 1985 Macau GP

JEAN GUICHET
F. Born: 1927, Marseille
World Sports Car Championship. Race wins: 1964 Le Mans 24 hrs, 1965 Monza, Reims

GIOVANNI-BATTISTA GUIDOTTI
I. Born: 1904, Bellagio
Major race wins: 1930 Mille Miglia

KENELM LEE GUINNESS
see "Lee Guinness"

LUCIEN GUITTENY
F. Born: 17.6.1944
1978 French Supertourism Champion

STEN GUNNARSSON
S

	wins	2nd	3rd	4th	5th	6th	PP	FL	points
European F2 Ch	-	-	1	-	-	-	-	5

Championship: 1973 19th

DAN GURNEY
USA. Born: 13.4.1931, Port Jefferson, New Jersey
World Championship Grand Prix Record

years	starts	wins	2nd	3rd	4th	5th	6th	PP	FL	points
1959–68; 1970	86(1)	4	8	7	2	5	5	3	6	133

Best championship: 1961 3rd. **Race wins:** 1962 French GP, 1964 French GP, Mexican GP, 1967 Belgian GP. **Best qualifying:** 1st
World Sports Car Championship. Race wins: 1959 Sebring 12 hrs, 1960 Nürburgring, 1967 Le Mans 24 hrs
Indycar Championship. Race wins: 1967 Riverside, 1968 Mosport Park Race 1, Mosport Park Race 2, Riverside, 1969 Indianapolis Raceway Park Race 1, Brainerd Race 2, 1970 Sears Point
Other major race wins: 1967 Race of Champions (Brands Hatch)

MALCOLM GUTHRIE
GB

	wins	2nd	3rd	4th	5th	6th	PP	FL	points
European F2 Ch	-	-	-	-	-	-	-	2

Championship: 1969 15th

ALBERT GUYOT
F. Born: date n/a, Orleans. Died: 1933
Major race wins: 1923 San Sebastian GP

H

ARMIN HAHNE
D. Born: 10.9.1955, Moers
Major race wins: 1982 and 1983 Spa 24 hrs, 1985 Bathurst

HUBERT HAHNE
D. Born: 28.3.1935, Moers
1966 European Touring Car over 1600 cc Class Champion

World Championship Grand Prix Record

years	starts	wins	2nd	3rd	4th	5th	6th	PP	FL	points
1966–70	3(2)	-	-	-	-	-	-	-	-	-

Best result: 10th. Best qualifying: 14th

		wins	2nd	3rd	4th	5th	6th	PP	FL	points
European F2 Ch		-	1	-	3	1	-	-	-	38

Championships: 1967 12th, 1969 2nd, 1970 13th
Major race wins: 1966 Spa 24 hrs

MIKE HAILWOOD
GB. Born: 2.4.1940, Great Milton, Oxfordshire. Died: 23.3.1981, road accident near Birmingham
1972 European F2 Champion

World Championship Grand Prix Record

years	starts	wins	2nd	3rd	4th	5th	6th	PP	FL	points
1963–65; 1971–74	50	-	1	1	5	1	2	-	1	29

Best championship: 1972 8th. Best qualifying: 4th
World Sports Car Championship. Race wins: 1973 Spa

		wins	2nd	3rd	4th	5th	6th	PP	FL	points
European F2 Ch	2	5	-	-	2	-	1	2		55

Championship: 1972 1st. Race wins: 1972 Mantorp Park, Salzburgring

MIKA HÄKKINEN
SF. Born: 28.9.1968, Helsinki
1990 British F3 Champion; 1988 GM-Lotus Euroseries Champion

World Championship Grand Prix Record

years	starts	wins	2nd	3rd	4th	5th	6th	PP	FL	points
1991–94	48(2)	-	1	6	2	2	3	-	-	43

Best championship: 1994 4th. Best qualifying: 2nd
Major race wins: 1989 Cellnet Super Prix

BRUCE HALFORD
GB. Born: 18.5.1931, Hampton-in-Arden, Warwickshire

World Championship Grand Prix Record

years	starts	wins	2nd	3rd	4th	5th	6th	PP	FL	points
1956–57; 1959–60	8(1)	-	-	-	-	-	-	-	-	-

Best result: 8th. Best qualifying: 11th

DEAN HALL
USA. Born: 11.11.1957, Palo Alto, California
1988 North American (Western Division) Formula Atlantic Champion; 1989 New Zealand International Champion

JIM HALL
USA. Born: 23.7.1935, Abilene, Texas

World Championship Grand Prix Record

years	starts	wins	2nd	3rd	4th	5th	6th	PP	FL	points
1960–63	11(1)	-	-	-	1	1	-	-	3

Best championship: 1963 12th. Best qualifying: 12th
World Sports Car Championship. Race wins: 1965 Sebring 12 hrs
Other major race wins: 1965 Canadian GP

DUNCAN HAMILTON
GB. Born: 30.4.1920, Cork (IRL). Died: 13.5.1994, Sherborne, Dorset

World Championship Grand Prix Record

years	starts	wins	2nd	3rd	4th	5th	6th	PP	FL	points
1951–53	5	-	-	-	-	-	-	-	-	-

Best result: 7th. Best qualifying: 10th
World Sports Car Championship. Race wins: 1953 Le Mans 24 hrs

PETE HAMILTON
USA
Major race wins: 1970 Daytona 500

GEORGE HAMMOND
USA
Indycar Championship. Race wins: 1952 Pikes Peak

DAVID HAMPSHIRE
GB. Born: 29.12.1917, Mickleover, Derbyshire. Died: 25.8.1990, Newton Solney, Derbyshire

World Championship Grand Prix Record

year	starts	wins	2nd	3rd	4th	5th	6th	PP	FL	points
1950	2	-	-	-	-	-	-	-	-	-

Best result: 9th. Best qualifying: 16th

JOHN HANDLEY
GB
1968 European Touring Car 1000 cc Class Champion

SAM HANKS
USA. Born: 13.7.1914, Columbus. Died: 27.6.1994
1953 Indycar Champion
Indycar Championship. Race wins: 1953 Springfield Race 2, Du Quoin, 1954 Du Quoin, 1957 Indianapolis 500

MEL HANSEN
USA. Born: n/a. Died: 5.6.1963
Indycar Championship. Race wins: 1948 Atlanta, 1949 Springfield Race 1

GREGG HANSFORD
AUS. Born n/a. Died: 5.3.1995, Phillip Island
Major race wins: 1993 Bathurst

WALT HANSGEN
USA. Born: 28.10.1919, Westfield, New Jersey. Died: 7.4.1966, Orléans (F) following an accident at Le Mans

World Championship Grand Prix Record

years	starts	wins	2nd	3rd	4th	5th	6th	PP	FL	points
1961; 1964	2	-	-	-	-	1	-	-	-	2

Best championship: 1964 16th. Best qualifying: 14th

HARRIS HANSHUE
USA
Indycar Championship. Race wins: 1909 Santa Monica Race 1

HUSCHKE VON HANSTEIN
D. Born: 3.1.1911, Halle
Major race wins: 1940 Mille Miglia, 1956 Targa Florio

RON HARDWICK
HK
Major race wins: 1959 Macau GP

MIKE HARRIS
RSR. Born: 25.5.1939, Mufulira, Zambia

World Championship Grand Prix Record

year	starts	wins	2nd	3rd	4th	5th	6th	PP	FL	points
1962	1	-	-	-	-	-	-	-	-	-

Best result: no finishes. Best qualifying: 15th

CUTH HARRISON
GB. Born: 6.7.1906, Sheffield. Died: 22.1.1981, Sheffield

World Championship Grand Prix Record

year	starts	wins	2nd	3rd	4th	5th	6th	PP	FL	points
1950	3	-	-	-	-	-	-	-	-	-

Best result: 7th. Best qualifying: 13th

RAY HARROUN
USA. Born: 12.1.1879, Spartanburg, Pennsylvania. Died: 19.1.1968, Anderson, Indiana
1910 Indycar Champion
Indycar Championship. Race wins: 1910 Atlanta Race 1, Indianapolis Race 2, Indianapolis Race 3, 1911 Indianapolis 500

BRIAN HART
GB. Born: 7.9.1936, Enfield

World Championship Grand Prix Record

year	starts	wins	2nd	3rd	4th	5th	6th	PP	FL	points
1967	1	-	-	-	-	-	-	-	-	-

Best result: no finishes. **Best qualifying:** no time set

	wins	2nd	3rd	4th	5th	6th	PP	FL	points
European F2 Ch	-	1	-	-	2	-	1		13

Championships: 1967 10th, 1968 12th, 1971 20th

HARRY HARTZ
USA. Born: 1896. Died: 26.9.1974
1926 Indycar Champion

Indycar Championship. Race wins: 1922 San Carlos, 1923 Fresno Race 2, 1926 Atlantic City Race 1, Atlantic City Race 2, Atlantic City Race 5, Salem Race 5, Charlotte Race 8

JOHN HARVEY
AUS
Major race wins: 1983 Bathurst

TIM HARVEY
GB. Born: 20.11.1961, Farnborough
1992 British Touring Car Champion
Major race wins: 1989 Guia Race

MASAHIRO HASEMI
J. Born: 13.11.1945, Tokyo
1980 Japanese F2 Champion; 1990 Japanese Sports Car Champion (with Anders Olofsson); 1989, 1991 and 1992 Japanese Touring Car Champion (1989 and 1991 with Anders Olofsson and 1992 with Hideo Fukuyama)

World Championship Grand Prix Record

year	starts	wins	2nd	3rd	4th	5th	6th	PP	FL	points
1976	1	-	-	-	-	-	-	-	1	-

Best result: 11th. **Best qualifying:** 10th
Major race wins: 1992 Daytona 24 hrs

RUDOLF HASSE
D. Born: 30.5.1906, Sassonia. Died: 1942
Pre-1950 Grands Prix. Race wins: 1937 Belgian GP

NAOKI HATTORI
J. Born: 13.6.1966, Yokkaichi
1990 Japanese F3 Champion

World Championship Grand Prix Record

year	starts	wins	2nd	3rd	4th	5th	6th	PP	FL	points
1991	-(2)	-	-	-	-	-	-	-	-	-

Best qualifying: 31st
Major race wins: 1991 Spa 24 hrs

PAUL HAWKINS
AUS. Born: 12.10.1937, Melbourne. Died: 26.5.1969, Oulton Park, Tourist Trophy practice

World Championship Grand Prix Record

year	starts	wins	2nd	3rd	4th	5th	6th	PP	FL	points
1965	3	-	-	-	-	-	-	-	-	-

Best result: 9th. **Best qualifying:** 14th
World Sports Car Championship. Race wins: 1967 Targa Florio, 1968 Monza
Other major race wins: 1967 Austrian GP

MIKE HAWTHORN
GB. Born: 10.4.1929, Mexborough, Yorkshire. Died: 22.1.1959, Guildford
1958 World Champion

World Championship Grand Prix Record

years	starts	wins	2nd	3rd	4th	5th	6th	PP	FL	points
1952–58	45(2)	3	9	6	7	2	3	4	6	127.64

Race wins: 1953 French GP, 1954 Spanish GP, 1958 French GP.
Best qualifying: 1st
World Sports Car Championship. Race wins: 1953 Spa 24 hrs, 1954 Tourist Trophy overall, 1955 Sebring 12 hrs, Le Mans 24 hrs
Other major race wins: 1953 International Trophy (Silverstone)

BOY HAYJE
NL. Born: 3.5.1949, Amsterdam

World Championship Grand Prix Record

years	starts	wins	2nd	3rd	4th	5th	6th	PP	FL	points
1976–77	3(4)	-	-	-	-	-	-	-	-	-

Best result: 15th. **Best qualifying:** 21st

HURLEY HAYWOOD
USA. Born: 4.5.1948, Chicago
1971 and 1972 IMSA GT Champion (1971 shared with Peter Gregg); 1988 Trans-Am Champion

World Sports Car Championship. Race wins: 1973 Daytona 24 hrs, 1975 Daytona 24 hrs, 1977 Daytona 24 hrs, 1977 Le Mans 24 hrs, 1979 Daytona 24 hrs, 1981 Sebring 12 hrs, 1983 Le Mans 24 hrs

Other major race wins: 1973 Sebring 12 hrs, 1979 and 1991 Daytona 24 hrs, 1994 Le Mans 24 hrs

EDDIE HEARNE
USA. Born: n/a. Died: 9.2.1955
1923 Indycar Champion

Indycar Championship. Race wins: 1910 Indianapolis Race 6, Indianapolis Race 8, 1911 Cincinnati Race 2, 1917 Uniontown Race 3, Ascot Race 3, 1918 Uniontown Race 3, Tacoma Race 3, 1921 Cotati Race 1, Beverly Hills Race 11, 1923 Kansas City Race 1, Altoona

GEORGE HEATH
USA. Born: Long Island, New York
Major race wins: 1904 Ardennes Circuit, WK Vanderbilt Cup

PETER HEATH
GB
Major race wins: 1961 Macau GP

WILLI HEEKS
D. Born: 13.2.1922, Moorlage

World Championship Grand Prix Record

years	starts	wins	2nd	3rd	4th	5th	6th	PP	FL	points
1952–53	2	-	-	-	-	-	-	-	-	-

Best result: no finishes. **Best qualifying:** 18th

ALTFRID HEGER
D. Born: 24.1.1958, Essen
Major race wins: 1986 and 1988 Spa 24 hrs

LUDWIG HEIMRATH
CDN. Father of Ludwig Jr
1977 Trans-Am Class 2 Champion

ERIC HÉLARY
F. Born: 10.8.1966, Paris
1990 French F3 Champion

	wins	2nd	3rd	4th	5th	6th	PP	FL	points
Int F3000 Ch	-	-	1	1	1	-	-	-	9

Championship: 1991 8th
Major race wins: 1993 Le Mans 24 hrs

THEO HELFRICH
D. Born: 13.5.1913, Frankfurt-am-Main. Died: 29.4.1978

World Championship Grand Prix Record

years	starts	wins	2nd	3rd	4th	5th	6th	PP	FL	points
1952–54	3	-	-	-	-	-	-	-	-	-

Best result: 12th. **Best qualifying:** 21st

DAVE HELMICK
USA
World Sports Car Championship. Race wins: 1977 Daytona 24 hrs
Other major race wins: 1973 Sebring 12 hrs

VICTOR HÉMERY
F. Born: 1876, Brest. Died: 9.9.1950, suicide
Major race wins: 1905 Ardennes Circuit, WK Vanderbilt Cup

PETE HENDERSON
USA
Indycar Championship. Race wins: 1917 Chicago Race 6

PRESTON HENN
USA
Major race wins: 1983 Daytona 24 hrs

BRIAN HENTON

GB. Born: 19.9.1946, Derby
1980 European F2 Champion; 1974 Forward Trust and Lombard British F3 Champion

World Championship Grand Prix Record

years	starts	wins	2nd	3rd	4th	5th	6th	PP	FL	points
1975; 1977;										
1981–82	19(18)	-	-	-	-	-	-	1	-	

Best result: 7th. Best qualifying: 11th

	wins	2nd	3rd	4th	5th	6th	PP	FL	points
European F2 Ch	6	6	4	2	3	2	8	12	123

Championships: 1974 22nd, 1975 10th, 1977 10th, 1978 16th, 1979 2nd, 1980 1st. **Race wins:** 1977 Jochen Rindt Trophy (Thruxton), 1979 Mugello, Misano, 1980 Jochen Rindt Trophy (Thruxton), Rome GP (Vallelunga), Mugello

JOHNNY HERBERT

GB. Born: 25.6.1964, Brentwood
1987 British F3 Champion

World Championship Grand Prix Record

years	starts	wins	2nd	3rd	4th	5th	6th	PP	FL	points
1989–94	63(3)	-	-	-	4	2	2	-	-	18

Best championship: 1993 9th. Best qualifying: 4th

	wins	2nd	3rd	4th	5th	6th	PP	FL	points
Int F3000 Ch	1	-	1	-	-	2	1		13

Championship: 1988 8th. **Race wins:** 1988 Jerez

World Sports Car Championship. Race wins: 1991 Le Mans 24 hrs
Other major race wins: 1987 Cellnet Super Prix

DON HERR

USA
Indycar Championship. Race wins: 1911 Elgin Race 2, 1912 Indianapolis 500

HARVEY HERRICK

USA
Indycar Championship. Race wins: 1911 Bakersfield, Santa Monica Race 4

HANS HERRMANN

D. Born: 23.2.1928, Stuttgart

World Championship Grand Prix Record

years	starts	wins	2nd	3rd	4th	5th	6th	PP	FL	points
1953–55; 1957–61;										
1966; 1969	18(2)	-	-	1	2	-	1	-	1	10

Best championship: 1954 6th. Best qualifying: 4th.
World Sports Car Championship. Race wins: 1960 Sebring 12 hrs, Targa Florio, 1968 Daytona 24 hrs, Sebring 12 hrs, 1970 Le Mans 24 hrs

Other major race wins: 1966 Austrian GP

BRYAN HERTA

USA. Born: 23.5.1970
1993 Indy Lights Champion

FRANÇOIS HESNAULT

F. Born: 30.12.1956, Neuilly-sur-Seine

World Championship Grand Prix Record

years	starts	wins	2nd	3rd	4th	5th	6th	PP	FL	points
1984–85	19(2)	-	-	-	-	-	-	-	-	-

Best result: 7th. Best qualifying: 13th

HANS HEYER

D. Born: 16.3.1943, Mönchengladbach
1974 European Touring Car Champion; 1975, 1976 and 1980 German Racing Champion

World Championship Grand Prix Record

year	starts	wins	2nd	3rd	4th	5th	6th	PP	FL	points
1977	1									

Best result: no finishes. Best qualifying: 27th.

	wins	2nd	3rd	4th	5th	6th	PP	FL	points
European F2 Ch	-	-	-	-	-	-	-	-	1

Championship: 1976 17th
World Sports Car Championship. Race wins: 1978 Mugello, Nürburgring, 1979 Silverstone, 1980 Watkins Glen
Other major race wins: 1982 Spa 24 hrs, 1983 Spa 24 hrs, Imola 1000 kms, 1984 Sebring 12 hrs, Spa 24 hrs

TOINE HEZEMANS

NL. Born: 14.4.1943, Eindhoven
1970 European Touring Car over 1600 cc Class Champion; 1971 European Touring Car 2000 cc Class Champion; 1973 European Touring Car Champion

World Sports Car Championship. Race wins: 1971 Targa Florio, 1977 Nürburgring, 1978 Daytona 24 hrs, Mugello, Nürburgring, Watkins Glen

Other major race wins: 1973 Spa 24 hrs, 1978 Daytona 24 hrs

BENNETT HILL

USA. Born: n/a. Died: 1977
Indycar Championship. Race wins: 1922 Fresno Race 2, 1923 Beverly Hills Race 2, 1924 Culver City, 1926 Culver City, Fresno Race 1, Salem Race 3

DAMON HILL

GB. Born: 17.9.1960, Hampstead. Son of Graham

Damon Hill

World Championship Grand Prix Record

years	starts	wins	2nd	3rd	4th	5th	6th	PP	FL	points
1992–94	34(6)	9	9	3	1	-	1	4	10	160

Best championship: 1994 2nd. **Race wins:** 1993 Hungarian GP, Belgian GP, Italian GP, 1994 Spanish GP, British GP, Belgian GP, Italian GP, Portuguese GP, Japanese GP. Best qualifying: 1st

	wins	2nd	3rd	4th	5th	6th	PP	FL	points
Int F3000 Ch	-	1	1	2	-	1	3	2	17

Championships: 1990 13th, 1991 7th

GEORGE HILL

USA
Indycar Championship. Race wins: 1913 San Diego Race 1

GRAHAM HILL

GB. Born: 15.2.1929, Hampstead. Died: 29.11.1975, Elstree, aircraft accident. Father of Damon
1962 and 1968 World Champion

World Championship Grand Prix Record

years	starts	wins	2nd	3rd	4th	5th	6th	PP	FL	points
1958–75	176(3)	14	15	7	9	7	9	13	10	289

Race wins: 1962 Dutch GP, German GP, Italian GP, South African GP, 1963 Monaco GP, United States GP, 1964 Monaco GP, United States GP, 1965 Monaco GP, United States GP, 1968 Spanish GP, Monaco GP, Mexican GP, 1969 Monaco GP. Best qualifying: 1st

	wins	2nd	3rd	4th	5th	6th	PP	FL	points
European F2 Ch	1	2	1	2	1	4	2	1	3	-

Race wins: 1971 Jochen Rindt Trophy (Thruxton)

World Sports Car Championship. Race wins: 1972 Le Mans 24 hrs

Indycar Championship. Race wins: 1966 Indianapolis 500

Tasman Cup. Race wins: 1966 New Zealand GP, Australian GP

Other race wins: 1962 and 1971 International Trophy (Silverstone), 1963 and 1964 Tourist Trophy

Graham Hill

PHIL HILL

USA. Born: 20.4.1927, Miami, Florida
1961 World Champion

World Championship Grand Prix Record

years	starts	wins	2nd	3rd	4th	5th	6th	PP	FL	points
1958–64; 1966	48(3)	3	5	8	2	-	3	6	6	98

Race wins: 1960 Italian GP, 1961 Belgian GP, Italian GP. Best qualifying: 1st

World Sports Car Championship. Race wins: 1956 Swedish GP, 1957 Venezuelan GP, 1958 Buenos Aires, Sebring 12 hrs, Le Mans 24 hrs, 1959 Sebring 12 hrs, 1960 Buenos Aires, 1961 Sebring 12 hrs, Le Mans 24 hrs, 1962 Nürburgring, Le Mans 24 hrs, 1966 Nürburgring, 1967 Brands Hatch

Phil Hill

John Hindmarsh
GB
Major Sports Car races. Race wins: 1935 Le Mans 24 hrs

Peter Hirt
CH. Born: 30.3.1910

World Championship Grand Prix Record

years	starts	wins	2nd	3rd	4th	5th	6th	PP	FL	points
1951–53	5	-	-	-	-	-	-	-	-	-

Best result: 7th. **Best qualifying:** 16th

David Hobbs
GB. Born: 9.6.1939, Leamington Spa
1971 North American Formula A (F5000) Champion; 1983 Trans-Am Champion

World Championship Grand Prix Record

year	starts	wins	2nd	3rd	4th	5th	6th	PP	FL	points
1967–68; 1971; 1974	7	-	-	-	-	-	-	-	-	-

Best result: 7th. **Best qualifying:** 12th

	wins	2nd	3rd	4th	5th	6th	PP	FL	points
European F2 Ch	-	-	-	1	-	-	-	-	2

Championship: 1968 17th
World Sports Car Championship. Race wins: 1968 Monza
Tasman Cup. Race wins: 1972 Adelaide

Chris Hodgetts
GB. Born: 6.12.1950, Tanworth-in-Arden, Worcestershire
1986 and 1987 British Touring Car Champion

Ingo Hoffman
BR. Born: 18.2.1953, Sao Paulo

World Championship Grand Prix Record

years	starts	wins	2nd	3rd	4th	5th	6th	PP	FL	points
1976–77	3(3)	-	-	-	-	-	-	-	-	-

Best result: 7th. **Best qualifying:** 19th

	wins	2nd	3rd	4th	5th	6th	PP	FL	points
European F2 Ch	-	-	3	4	3	2	-	2	34

Championships: 1976 14th, 1977 7th, 1978 6th
Major race wins: 1978 Buenos Aires F2

Al Holbert
USA. Born: 11.11.1946, Pennsylvania. Died: 30.9.1988, Columbus, Ohio, aircraft accident
1976, 1977, 1983, 1985 and 1986 IMSA GT Champion
World Sports Car Championship. Race wins: 1976 Sebring 12 hrs, 1983 Le Mans 24 hrs, 1986 Le Mans 24 hrs, 1987 Le Mans 24 hrs
Other major race wins: 1976 Sebring 12 hrs, 1986 and 1987 Daytona 24 hrs

Bob Holden
AUS
Major race wins: 1966 Bathurst

Bill Holland
USA. Born: 18.12.1907, Philadelphia. Died: 20.5.1984, Tuscon
Indycar Championship. Race wins: 1947 Milwaukee Race 1, Langhorne, 1949 Indianapolis 500

Keith Holland
GB
Major race wins: 1969 Madrid GP (Jarama)

Howdy Holmes
USA. Born: 14.12.1947, Ann Arbor, Michigan
1978 North American Formula Atlantic Champion

Gerhard Holup
D
World Sports Car Championship. Race wins: 1981 Monza

Ted Horn
USA. Born: 27.2.1910, Cincinnati. Died: 10.10.1948, Du Quoin
1946, 1947 and 1948 Indycar Champion
Indycar Championship. Race wins: 1947 Bainbridge, Milwaukee Race 3, Dallas, 1948 Dallas, Springfield

St John Horsfall
GB. Born: n/a. Died: 1949, Silverstone, International Trophy
Major race wins: 1948 Spa 24 hrs

Kazuyoshi Hoshino
J. Born: 1.7.1947, Tokyo
1975 and 1977 Japanese F2000 Champion; 1978 Japanese F2 Champion; 1987, 1990 and 1993 Japanese F3000 Champion; 1991 and 1992 Japanese Sports Car Champion (with Toshio Suzuki); 1990 Japanese Touring Car Champion (with Toshio Suzuki)

World Championship Grand Prix Record

years	starts	wins	2nd	3rd	4th	5th	6th	PP	FL	points
1976–77	2	-	-	-	-	-	-	-	-	-

Best result: 11th. **Best qualifying:** 11th

	wins	2nd	3rd	4th	5th	6th	PP	FL	points
European F2 Ch	-	-	-	1	-	-	-	-	3

Championship: 1983 16th
World Sports Car Championship. Race wins: 1985 Fuji
Other major race wins: 1992 Daytona 24 hrs

Markus Hotz
CH

	wins	2nd	3rd	4th	5th	6th	PP	FL	points
European F2 Ch	-	-	-	-	-	1	-	-	1

Championship: 1976 17th

Raijmond van Hove
B
Major race wins: 1978 Tourist Trophy

Earl Howe
GB. Born: 1884. Died: ?.7.1964
Major Sports Car races. Race wins: 1931 Le Mans 24 hrs

Will Hoy
GB. Born: 2.4.1953, Royston
1991 British Touring Car Champion

Günther Huber
A
Major race wins: 1970 Spa 24 hrs

Hughie Hughes
USA. Born: n/a. Died: 2.12.1916, Uniontown, Pennsylvania
Indycar Championship. Race wins: 1911 Elgin Race 1, Philadelphia Race 4, 1912 Elgin Race 1, 1914 Tacoma Race 1

Naohiro Hujita
J
1983 Japanese Sports Car Champion (with Vern Schuppan)

Denis "Denny" Hulme
NZ. Born: 18.6.1936, Te Puke. Died: 4.10.1992, Bathurst, heart attack
1967 World Champion; 1968 and 1970 Can-Am Champion

Denny Hulme

World Championship Grand Prix Record

years	starts	wins	2nd	3rd	4th	5th	6th	PP	FL	points
1965–74	112	8	9	16	11	8	9	1	9	248

Race wins: 1967 Monaco GP, German GP, 1968 Italian GP, Canadian GP, 1969 Mexican GP, 1972 South African GP, 1973 Swedish GP, 1974 Argentinian GP. **Best qualifying:** 1st

	wins	2nd	3rd	4th	5th	6th	PP	FL	points
European F2 Ch	-	-	-	1	-	-	-	-	-

World Sports Car Championship. Race wins: 1965 Tourist Trophy (car ineligible for championship points)
Other major race wins: 1968 International Trophy (Silverstone), 1966 and 1986 Tourist Trophy

James Hunt
GB. Born: 29.8.1947, Belmont, Surrey. Died: 15.6.1993, Wimbledon, heart attack
1976 World Champion

World Championship Grand Prix Record

years	starts	wins	2nd	3rd	4th	5th	6th	PP	FL	points
1973–79	92(1)	10	6	7	7	2	3	14	8	179

Race wins: 1975 Dutch GP, 1976 Spanish GP, French GP, German GP, Dutch GP, Canadian GP, United States GP, 1977 British GP, United States GP, Japanese GP. **Best qualifying:** 1st

	wins	2nd	3rd	4th	5th	6th	PP	FL	points
European F2 Ch	-	-	-	1	-	-	-	-	5

Championship: 1972 17th

Other major race wins: 1974 and 1976 International Trophy (Silverstone), 1976 and 1977 Race of Champions

JIM HURTUBISE
USA. Born: 5.12.1932, North Tonawanda, New York. Died: 6.1.1989, Port Arthur, Texas, heart attack

Indycar Championship. Race wins: 1959 Sacramento, 1960 Langhorne, 1961 Springfield, 1962 Springfield

James Hunt

GUS HUTCHISON
USA. Born: 26.4.1937, Atlanta, Georgia
1967 North American Formula A (F5000) Champion

World Championship Grand Prix Record

year	starts	wins	2nd	3rd	4th	5th	6th	PP	FL	points
1970	1	-	-	-	-	-	-	-	-	-

Best result: no finishes. **Best qualifying:** 22nd

HUWELER
B
1983 Belgian Touring Car Champion

SHUJI HYOUDO
J
1984 Japanese F3 Champion

MARIO HYTTEN
CH. Born: 20.4.1957

	wins	2nd	3rd	4th	5th	6th	PP	FL	points
Int F3000 Ch	-	1	-	-	1	-	-	-	8

Championship: 1985 10th

I

JOSÉ MARIA IBANEZ
RA. Born: 1.2.1921
World Sports Car Championship. Race wins: 1955 Buenos Aires

JACKY ICKX
B. Born: 1.1.1945, Brussels
1982 and 1983 World Sports Car Champion; 1967 European F2 Champion; 1965 European Touring Car over 1600 cc Class Champion; 1979 Can-Am Champion

World Championship Grand Prix Record

years	starts	wins	2nd	3rd	4th	5th	6th	PP	FL	points
1966–79	116(6)	8	7	10	4	7	4	13	14	181

Best championship: 1970 2nd. **Race wins:** 1968 French GP, 1969 German GP, Canadian GP, 1970 Austrian GP, Canadian GP, Mexican GP, 1971 Dutch GP, 1972 German GP. **Best qualifying:** 1st

	wins	2nd	3rd	4th	5th	6th	PP	FL	points
European F2 Ch	3	1	2	1	2	2	3	4	45

Championship: 1967 1st. **Race wins:** 1967 Zandvoort, Rome GP (Vallelunga), 1970 Tulln

World Sports Car Championship. Race wins: 1967 Spa, 1968 Brands Hatch, Spa, Watkins Glen, 1969 Sebring 12 hrs, Le Mans 24 hrs, 1972 Daytona, Sebring 12 hrs, Brands Hatch, Monza, Österreichring, Watkins Glen, 1973 Monza, Nürburgring, 1974 Spa, 1975 Le Mans 24 hrs, 1976 Mugello, Vallelunga, Monza, Imola, Le Mans 24 hrs, Dijon, 1977 Silverstone, Le Mans 24 hrs, Watkins Glen, Brands Hatch, 1978 Silverstone, 1981 Le Mans 24 hrs, 1982 Le Mans 24 hrs, Spa, Fuji, Brands Hatch, 1983 Nürburgring, Spa, 1984 Silverstone, Mosport Park, 1985 Mugello, Silverstone, Selangor

Other major race wins: 1966 Spa 24 hrs, 1971 Jochen Rindt Trophy (Hockenheim), 1974 Race of Champions, 1977 Bathurst

PASCAL ICKX
B
Major race wins: 1965 Spa 24 hrs

JESUS IGLESIAS
RA. Born: 22.2.1922, Pergamino

World Championship Grand Prix Record

year	starts	wins	2nd	3rd	4th	5th	6th	PP	FL	points
1955	1	-	-	-	-	-	-	-	-	-

Best result: no finishes. **Best qualifying:** 17th

TETSU IKUZAWA
J

	wins	2nd	3rd	4th	5th	6th	PP	FL	points
European F2 Ch	-	1	-	-	-	-	-	-	9

Championship: 1970 6th

TAKI INOUE
J. Born: 5.9.1963, Kobe

World Championship Grand Prix Record

year	starts	wins	2nd	3rd	4th	5th	6th	PP	FL	points
1994	1	-	-	-	-	-	-	-	-	-

Best result: no finishes. **Best qualifying:** 26th

INNES IRELAND
GB. Born: 12.6.1930, Kirkcudbright, Scotland. Died: 22.10.1993, Reading, cancer

World Championship Grand Prix Record

years	starts	wins	2nd	3rd	4th	5th	6th	PP	FL	points
1959–66	50(3)	1	2	1	4	4	2	-	1	47

Best championship: 1960 4th. **Race wins:** 1961 United States GP. **Best qualifying:** 2nd

Other major race wins: 1960 International Trophy (Silverstone), 1962 Tourist Trophy

ERNIE IRVAN
USA. Born: 13.1.1959, Modesto, California
Major race wins: 1991 Daytona 500

Innes Ireland

EDDIE IRVINE
GB. Born: 10.11.1965, Conlig, Northern Ireland

World Championship Grand Prix Record

years	starts	wins	2nd	3rd	4th	5th	6th	PP	FL	points
1993–94	14(1)	-	-	-	1	1	2	-	-	7

Best championship: 1994 14th. **Best qualifying:** 4th

	wins	2nd	3rd	4th	5th	6th	PP	FL	points
Int F3000 Ch	1	1	3	3	-	2	1	-	38

Championships: 1989 9th, 1990 3rd. **Race wins:** 1990 Hockenheim

CHRIS IRWIN
GB. Born: 27.6.1942, London

World Championship Grand Prix Record

years	starts	wins	2nd	3rd	4th	5th	6th	PP	FL	points
1966–67	10	-	-	-	-	1	-	-	-	2

Best championship: 1967 16th. **Best qualifying:** 9th

	wins	2nd	3rd	4th	5th	6th	PP	FL	points
European F2 Ch	-	1	-	-	1	-	1	-	16

Championships: 1967 6th, 1968 22nd

BOBBY ISAAC
USA. Born: 1.8.1934
1970 NASCAR Champion

JACQUES ISLER
CH. Born: 14.8.1956, Zurich
1989 Swiss F3 Champion

BORIS IVANOWSKI
F
Major race wins: 1928 Spa 24 hrs

J

JEAN-PIERRE JABOUILLE
F. Born: 1.10.1942, Paris
1976 European F2 Champion

World Championship Grand Prix Record

years	starts	wins	2nd	3rd	4th	5th	6th	PP	FL	points
1974–75; 1977–81	49(7)	2	-	-	1	-	-	6	-	21

Best championship: 1980 8th. Race wins: 1979 French GP, 1980 Austrian GP. Best qualifying: 1st

		wins	2nd	3rd	4th	5th	6th	PP	FL	points
European F2 Ch	5	4	4	2	1	5	6	109

Championships: 1970 16th, 1972 14th, 1973 26th, 1974 4th, 1975 5th, 1976 1st. Race wins: 1974 Jochen Rindt Trophy (Hockenheim), 1975 Salzburgring, 1976 Rome GP (Vallelunga), Mugello, Hockenheim

World Sports Car Championship. Race wins: 1975 Mugello

JOHN JAMES
GB. Born: 10.5.1914, Packwood, Warwickshire

World Championship Grand Prix Record

year	starts	wins	2nd	3rd	4th	5th	6th	PP	FL	points
1951	1	-	-	-	-	-	-	-	-	-

Best result: no finishes. Best qualifying: 17th

BOB JANE
AUS

1962, 1963, 1971 and 1972 Australian Touring Car Champion

Major race wins: 1963 and 1964 Bathurst

JEAN-PIERRE JARIER
F. Born: 10.7.1946, Charenton-le-Pont

1973 European F2 Champion

World Championship Grand Prix Record

years	starts	wins	2nd	3rd	4th	5th	6th	PP	FL	points
1971; 1973–83	133(10)	-	-	3	2	6	3	3	3	31.5

Best championship: 1979 10th. Best qualifying: 1st

		wins	2nd	3rd	4th	5th	6th	PP	FL	points
European F2 Ch	7	2	3	1	-	-	5	3	88

Championships: 1971 8th, 1973 1st. Race wins: 1973 Mallory Park, Jim Clark Trophy, Nivelles, Rouen GP, Mantorp Park, Karlskoga, Mediterranean GP (Enna)

World Sports Car Championship. Race wins: 1974 Spa, Nürburgring, Watkins Glen, Paul Ricard, Brands Hatch, 1977 Dijon, Paul Ricard

Other major race wins: 1993 Spa 24 hrs

DALE JARRETT
USA. Born: 26.11.1956, Newton, North Carolina. Son of Ned

Major race wins: 1993 Daytona 500

NED JARRETT
USA. Born: 10.12.1932, Newton, North Carolina. Father of Dale

1961 and 1965 NASCAR Champion

CHARLES JARROTT
GB. Born: 1877. Died: 1944

Major race wins: 1902 Ardennes Circuit

JEAN-PIERRE JAUSSAUD
F. Born: 3.6.1937

1970 French F3 Champion

		wins	2nd	3rd	4th	5th	6th	PP	FL	points
European F2 Ch	2	1	1	4	1	6	2	2	62

Championships: 1967 17th, 1968 17th, 1971 9th, 1972 2nd, 1973 13th, 1975 17th, 1976 17th. Race wins: 1972 Jim Clark Trophy, Albi GP

World Sports Car Championship. Race wins: 1978 and 1980 Le Mans 24 hrs

Other major race wins: 1968 Monaco F3 GP

FRANK JELINSKI
D. Born: 23.5.1958, Hannover

1980 and 1981 German F3 Champion

		wins	2nd	3rd	4th	5th	6th	PP	FL	points
European F2 Ch	-	-	-	1	2	1	-	-	8

Championships: 1982 12th, 1983 20th

World Sports Car Championship. Race wins: 1986 Spa, 1989 Dijon

Other major race wins: 1991 Daytona 24 hrs

CAMILLE JENATZY
B. Born: 4.11.1868, Brussels. Died: 7.10.1913, shot accidently during wild boar hunt

Pre-1950 Grands Prix. Race wins: 1903 Gordon Bennett Trophy

JOHN JENKINS
USA

Indycar Championship. Race wins: 1911 Cincinnati Race 1

DENIS JENKINSON
GB. Born: 11.12.1920, London

World Sports Car Championship. Race wins: 1955 Mille Miglia

BILL JENNINGS
ZA

1954, 1956 and 1957 South African Drivers' Champion

CESAR TIBERIO JIMENEZ
MEX. Born: 4.7.1969

1992 Mexican F3 Champion

GILBERTO JIMENEZ
MEX

1985 and 1986 Mexican Formula K Champion

GEORGE JOERMANN
USA

Indycar Championship. Race wins: 1912 Santa Monica Race 1

MIKAEL "MICKE" JOHANSSON
S. Born: 13.5.1962

1987 and 1988 Swedish F3 Champion

STEFAN JOHANSSON
S. Born: 8.9.1956, Vaxjo

1980 British F3 Champion

World Championship Grand Prix Record

years	starts	wins	2nd	3rd	4th	5th	6th	PP	FL	points
1980; 1983–91	79(24)	-	4	8	7	4	3	-	-	88

Best championship: 1986 5th. Best qualifying: 2nd

		wins	2nd	3rd	4th	5th	6th	PP	FL	points
European F2 Ch	2	1	1	4	-	2	5	-	42

Championships: 1981 3rd, 1982 8th. Race wins: 1981 Jim Clark Trophy (Hockenheim), Mantorp Park

World Sports Car Championship. Race wins: 1988 Spa

Other major race wins: 1983 Mugello 1000 kms, 1984 Sebring 12 hrs

GORDON JOHNCOCK
USA. Born: 5.8.1936, Hastings, Michigan

1976 Indycar Champion

Indycar Championship. Race wins: 1965 Milwaukee Race 3, 1967 Milwaukee Race 1, Hanford, 1968 Hanford Race 1, Langhorne Race 1, 1969 Castle Rock, Brainerd Race 1, 1973 Indianapolis 500, Phoenix, 1974 Milwaukee Race 2, 1974 Phoenix, 1975 Trenton, 1976 Michigan, Trenton, 1977 Michigan, Phoenix, 1978 Phoenix, Trenton, 1979 Phoenix, Michigan Race 1, 1982 Indianapolis 500, Milwaukee, Michigan 500, 1983 Atlanta

AMOS JOHNSON
USA. Born: 9.4.1941

World Sports Car Championship. Race wins: 1981 Daytona

DICK JOHNSON
AUS. Born: 26.4.1945

1981, 1982, 1984, 1988 and 1989 Australian Touring Car Champion

Major race wins: 1981, 1989 and 1994 Bathurst

JOE LEE JOHNSON
USA. Born: 9.11.1929, Cowpens, South Carolina

Major race wins: 1960 World 600

JUNIOR JOHNSON
USA. Born: 28.6.1931

Major race wins: 1960 Daytona 500

KEN JOHNSON
USA. Born: 28.11.1962

1985 SCCA Super Vee Champion

LESLIE JOHNSON
GB. Born: 1911. Died: 8.6.1959, Withington, Gloucestershire

World Championship Grand Prix Record

year	starts	wins	2nd	3rd	4th	5th	6th	PP	FL	points
1950	1	-	-	-	-	-	-	-	-	-

Best result: no finishes. **Best qualifying:** 12th
Major race wins: 1948 Spa 24 hrs

VAN JOHNSON
USA
Indycar Championship. Race wins: 1959 Langhorne

BRUCE JOHNSTONE
ZA. Born: 30.1.1937, Durban

World Championship Grand Prix Record

year	starts	wins	2nd	3rd	4th	5th	6th	PP	FL	points
1962	1	-	-	-	-	-	-	-	-	-

Best result: 9th. **Best qualifying:** no time set

ALAN JONES
AUS. Born: 2.11.1946, Melbourne. Son of Stan
1980 World Champion; 1978 Can-Am Champion

World Championship Grand Prix Record

years	starts	wins	2nd	3rd	4th	5th	6th	PP	FL	points
1975–81; 1983; 1985–86	116(1)	12	7	5	8	5	2	6	13	206

Race wins: 1977 Austrian GP, 1979 German GP, Austrian GP, Dutch GP, Canadian GP, 1980 Argentinian GP, French GP, British GP, Canadian GP, United States GP, 1981 Long Beach GP, Las Vegas GP. **Best qualifying:** 1st
Other major race wins: 1980 Spanish GP, Australian GP

DAVY JONES
USA. Born: 1.6.1964, Chicago
Major race wins: 1990 Daytona 24 hrs

Alan Jones

JOHN JONES
CDN. Born: 19.10.1965, Thunder Bay, Ontario

	wins	2nd	3rd	4th	5th	6th	PP	FL	points
Int F3000 Ch	-	1	1	1	1	1	-	-	16

Championships: 1986 21st, 1987 11th, 1990 12th

PARNELLI JONES
USA. Born: 12.8.1933, Texarkana, Arkansas. Father of PJ
Indycar Championship. Race wins: 1961 Phoenix, 1962 Indiana State Fairgrounds, 1963 Indianapolis 500, 1964 Milwaukee Race 2, Trenton Race 3, 1965 Milwaukee Race 1

PJ JONES
USA. Born: 23.4.1969. Son of Parnelli
Major race wins: 1993 Daytona 24 hrs

STAN JONES
AUS. Father of Alan
1958 Australian Gold Star Champion
Major race wins: 1959 Australian GP

TOM JONES
CDN

World Championship Grand Prix Record

year	starts	wins	2nd	3rd	4th	5th	6th	PP	FL	points
1967	-(1)	-	-	-	-	-	-	-	-	-

Best qualifying: 19th

NICLAS JONSSON
S. Born: 4.8.1967
1990 and 1991 Swedish F3 Champion

EDDY JOOSEN
B
Major race wins: 1977 and 1982 Spa 24 hrs, 1978 Tourist Trophy

REINHOLD JÖST
D. Born: 24.4.1937, Absteinach
World Sports Car Championship. Race wins: 1976 Nürburgring 300 km, 1979 Dijon, Brands Hatch, 1980 Daytona 24 hrs

DEON JOUBERT
ZA
1992 South African Touring Car Champion

JUAN JOVER
E

World Championship Grand Prix Record

year	starts	wins	2nd	3rd	4th	5th	6th	PP	FL	points
1951	-(1)	-	-	-	-	-	-	-	-	-

Best qualifying: 18th

CARL JUNKER
AUS
Major race wins: 1931 Australian GP

K

MASAHIKO KAGEYAMA
J. Born: 8.8.1963
1993 Japanese Touring Car Champion; 1993 and 1994 Japanese GT Champion; 1989 Japanese F3 Champion

TOMAS KAISER
S. Born: 2.11.1956

	wins	2nd	3rd	4th	5th	6th	PP	FL	points
European F2 Ch	-	-	-	4	-	-	-	-	3
Int F3000 Ch	-	-	-	2	1	-	-	-	7

Championship: 1984 11th
Championships: 1985 14th, 1986 13th

SIMON KANE
AUS
1990 Australian Gold Star Champion

OSWALD KARCH
D. Born: 6.3.1917, Ludwigshafen

World Championship Grand Prix Record

year	starts	wins	2nd	3rd	4th	5th	6th	PP	FL	points
1953	1	-	-	-	-	-	-	-	-	-

Best result: no finishes. **Best qualifying:** 34th

GUNNAR KARLSSON
S
1963 Swedish Formula Junior Champion

UKYO KATAYAMA
J. Born: 29.5.1963, Tokyo
1991 Japanese F3000 Champion

World Championship Grand Prix Record

year	starts	wins	2nd	3rd	4th	5th	6th	PP	FL	points
1992–94	46(2)	-	-	-	-	2	1	-	-	5

Best championship: 1994 17th. **Best qualifying:** 5th

WILLI KAUHSEN
D
1967 European Touring Car 1000 cc Class Champion
Major race wins: 1968 Spa 24 hrs

KEN KAVANAGH
AUS

World Championship Grand Prix Record

year	starts	wins	2nd	3rd	4th	5th	6th	PP	FL	points
1958	-(2)	-	-	-	-	-	-	-	-	-

Best qualifying: 19th

HIROSHI KAZATO
J. Born: 13.3.1949

	wins	2nd	3rd	4th	5th	6th	PP	FL	points
European F2 Ch	-	-	-	2	1	-	-	-	7

Championships: 1972 24th, 1973 21st

RAY KEECH
USA. Born: 1898. Died: 15.6.1929, Altoona, Pennsylvania, racing
Indycar Championship. Race wins: 1928 Detroit, Salem Race 2, Syracuse, 1929 Indianapolis 500

RUPERT KEEGAN
GB. Born: 26.2.1955, London
1979 British F1 Champion; 1976 BP British F3 Champion

World Championship Grand Prix Record

years	starts	wins	2nd	3rd	4th	5th	6th	PP	FL	points
1977–78; 1980;										
1982	25(12)	-	-	-	-	-	-	-	-	-

Best result: 7th. Best qualifying: 13th

BRUCE KEENE
USA

Indycar Championship. Race wins: 1911 Santa Monica Race 1

EDDIE KEIZAN
ZA. Born: 12.9.1944, Johannesburg

World Championship Grand Prix Record

years	starts	wins	2nd	3rd	4th	5th	6th	PP	FL	points
1973–75	3	-	-	-	-	-	-	-	-	-

Best result: 13th. Best qualifying: 22nd

HELMUT KELLENERS
D. Born: 29.12.1938

1980, 1981 and 1982 European Touring Car Champion (shared with Sigi Muller Jr in 1980 and Umberto Grano in 1981 and 1982)
Major race wins: 1968 and 1970 Spa 24 hrs, 1984 Tourist Trophy

JOE KELLY
IRL. Born: 13.3.1913

World Championship Grand Prix Record

years	starts	wins	2nd	3rd	4th	5th	6th	PP	FL	points
1950–51	2	-	-	-	-	-	-	-	-	-

Best result: no finishes. Best qualifying: 18th

STEVE KEMPTON
GB. Born: 8.2.1960, Nottingham

1987 European F3 Cup winner

TOM KENDALL
USA. Born: 17.10.1966

1990 Trans-Am Champion

DAVID KENNEDY
IRL. Born: 15.1.1953, Sligo

World Championship Grand Prix Record

year	starts	wins	2nd	3rd	4th	5th	6th	PP	FL	points
1980	-(7)	-	-	-	-	-	-	-	-	-

Best result: no starts. Best qualifying: 25th

LORIS KESSEL
CH. Born: 1.4.1950, Lugano

World Championship Grand Prix Record

years	starts	wins	2nd	3rd	4th	5th	6th	PP	FL	points
1976–77	3(4)	-	-	-	-	-	-	-	-	-

Best result: 12th. Best qualifying: 23rd

	wins	2nd	3rd	4th	5th	6th	PP	FL	points
European F2 Ch	-	-	-	2	-	-	-	-	7

Championship: 1975 16th

BRUCE KESSLER
USA

World Championship Grand Prix Record

year	starts	wins	2nd	3rd	4th	5th	6th	PP	FL	points
1958	-(1)	-	-	-	-	-	-	-	-	-

Best qualifying: 21st

MARIO KETTERER
CH

World Sports Car Championship. Race wins: 1979 Dijon

MICHAEL KEYSER
USA

Major race wins: 1976 Sebring 12 hrs

GLEN KIDSTON
GB

Major Sports Car races. Race wins: 1930 Le Mans 24 hrs

TOM KINCAID
USA

Indycar Championship. Race wins: 1910 Atlanta Race 4, Indianapolis Race 1

LEO KINNUNEN
SF. Born: 5.8.1943, Tampere

World Championship Grand Prix Record

year	starts	wins	2nd	3rd	4th	5th	6th	PP	FL	points
1974	1(5)	-	-	-	-	-	-	-	-	-

Best result: no finishes. Best qualifying: 26th

HANS KLENK
D. Born: 18.10.1919, Kunzelsan

World Championship Grand Prix Record

year	starts	wins	2nd	3rd	4th	5th	6th	PP	FL	points
1952	1	-	-	-	-	-	-	-	-	-

Best result: no finishes. Best qualifying: no time set

PIET DE KLERK
ZA. Born: 16.3.1936, Pilgram's Rest

World Championship Grand Prix Record

year	starts	wins	2nd	3rd	4th	5th	6th	PP	FL	points
1963; 1965;										
1969–70	4	-	-	-	-	-	-	-	-	-

Best result: 10th. Best qualifying: 16th

KARL KLING
D. Born: 16.9.1910, Giessen

World Championship Grand Prix Record

years	starts	wins	2nd	3rd	4th	5th	6th	PP	FL	points
1954–55	11	-	1	1	2	1	-	-	1	17

Best championship: 1954 5th. Best qualifying: 2nd

ERNST KLODWIG
DDR. Born: 23.5.1903. Died: 15.4.1973

World Championship Grand Prix Record

years	starts	wins	2nd	3rd	4th	5th	6th	PP	FL	points
1952–53	2	-	-	-	-	-	-	-	-	-

Best result: 15th. Best qualifying: 32nd

WILLIAM KNIPPER
USA

Indycar Championship. Race wins: 1909 Lowell Race 2

HELMUTH KOINIGG
A. Born: 3.11.1948, Vienna. Died: 6.10.1974, Watkins Glen, United States GP

World Championship Grand Prix Record

year	starts	wins	2nd	3rd	4th	5th	6th	PP	FL	points
1974	2(1)	-	-	-	-	-	-	-	-	-

Best result: 10th. Best qualifying: 22nd

FRANZ KONRAD
A. Born: 8.6.1951, Graz

1983 German F3 Champion

WALTER KORNOSSA
D

1951 German F3 Champion

MICHAEL KORTEN
D

1979 German F3 Champion
European F3 Championship. Race wins: 1979 Kassel-Calden

FREDDY KOTTULINSKY
S

1966 Swedish F3 Champion

	wins	2nd	3rd	4th	5th	6th	PP	FL	points
European F2 Ch	-	-	-	-	-	-	-	-	1

Championship: 1976 17th
European F3 Championship. Race wins: 1975 Nürburgring

PETER KOX
NL. Born: 23.2.1964

1989 GM-Lotus Euroseries Champion

MIKKO KOZAROWITSKY
SF. Born: 17.5.1948, Helsinki

World Championship Grand Prix Record

year	starts	wins	2nd	3rd	4th	5th	6th	PP	FL	points
1977	-(2)	-	-	-	-	-	-	-	-	-

Best qualifying: 31st

WILLI KRAKAU
D

World Championship Grand Prix Record

year	starts	wins	2nd	3rd	4th	5th	6th	PP	FL	points
1952	-(1)	-	-	-	-	-	-	-	-	-

Best qualifying: no time set

RUDOLF KRAUSE
DDR. Born: 30.3.1907. Died: 11.4.1987

World Championship Grand Prix Record

years	starts	wins	2nd	3rd	4th	5th	6th	PP	FL	points
1952–53	2	-	-	-	-	-	-	-	-	-

Best result: 14th. Best qualifying: 26th

TONI KRAUZER
D

1950 German F3 Champion

ALBRECHT KREBS
D

World Sports Car Championship. Race wins: 1976 Nürburgring

ERWIN KREMER
D. Born: 26.6.1937

Major race wins: 1968 Spa 24 hrs

TOM KRISTENSEN
DK. Born: 7.7.1967

1991 German F3 Champion; 1993 Japanese F3 Champion

HORST KROLL
USA

1986 Can-Am Champion

MICHAEL KRUMM
D. Born: 19.3.1970

1994 Japanese F3 Champion

PETER KUHN
USA

1980 SCCA Super Vee Champion

KURT KUHNKE
D

World Championship Grand Prix Record

year	starts	wins	2nd	3rd	4th	5th	6th	PP	FL	points
1963	-(1)	-	-	-	-	-	-	-	-	-

Best qualifying: 26th

LARRY KULOK
USA

Major race wins: 1952 Sebring 12 hrs

ALAN KULWICKI
USA. Born: 14.12.1954, Greenfield, Wisconsin. Died: 1.4.1993, Tennessee, aircraft accident

1992 NASCAR Champion

MOTOHARU KUROSAWA
J. Born: 1942

1973 Japanese F2000 Champion

MASAMI KUWASHIMA
J. Born: 14.9.1950

World Championship Grand Prix Record

year	starts	wins	2nd	3rd	4th	5th	6th	PP	FL	points
1976	-(1)	-	-	-	-	-	-	-	-	-

Best qualifying: 26th

	wins	2nd	3rd	4th	5th	6th	PP	FL	points
European F2 Ch	-	-	1	-	-	-	-	-	4

Championship: 1974 14th

HORST KWECH
AUS

1966 Trans-Am Champion (with Gaston Andrey)

L ···

TERRY LABONTE
USA. Born: 16.11.1956, Corpus Christi, Texas

1984 NASCAR Champion; 1989 IROC Champion

JACQUES LAFFITE
F. Born: 21.11.1943, Magny-Cours

1975 European F2 Champion; 1973 French F3 Champion

World Championship Grand Prix Record

years	starts	wins	2nd	3rd	4th	5th	6th	PP	FL	points
1974–86	176(4)	6	10	16	7	9	11	7	6	228

Best championship: 1981 4th. **Race wins:** 1977 Swedish GP, 1979 Argentinian GP, Brazilian GP, 1980 German GP, 1981 Austrian GP, Canadian GP. Best qualifying: 1st.

	wins	2nd	3rd	4th	5th	6th	PP	FL	points
European F2 Ch	7	5	2	-	-	7	6	91	

Championships: 1974 3rd, 1975 1st. **Race wins:** 1974 Salzburgring, 1975 Estoril, Jochen Rindt Trophy (Thruxton), Eifelrennen, Pau GP, Jochen Rindt Trophy (Hockenheim), Mediterranean GP (Enna)

World Sports Car Championship. Race wins: 1975 Dijon, Monza, Nürburgring

Other major race wins: 1973 Monaco F3 GP

ANDRÉ LAGACHE
F

Major Sports Car races. Race wins: 1923 Le Mans 24 hrs, 1925 Spa 24 hrs

FRANCK LAGORCE
F. Born: 1.9.1968, L'Hay-les-Roses

1992 French F3 Champion

World Championship Grand Prix Record

year	starts	wins	2nd	3rd	4th	5th	6th	PP	FL	points
1994	2	-	-	-	-	-	-	-	-	-

Best result: 11th. Best qualifying: 20th

	wins	2nd	3rd	4th	5th	6th	PP	FL	points
Int F3000 Ch	4	2	-	1	2	-	5	4	55

Championships: 1993 4th, 1994 2nd. **Race wins:** 1993 Magny-Cours, Nogaro GP, 1994 International Trophy(Silverstone), Hockenheim

CHRIS LAMBERT
GB

	wins	2nd	3rd	4th	5th	6th	PP	FL	points
European F2 Ch	-	-	1	-	-	-	-	-	3

Championships: 1968 15th

JAN LAMMERS
NL. Born: 2.6.1956, Zandvoort

1978 European F3 Champion

World Championship Grand Prix Record

years	starts	wins	2nd	3rd	4th	5th	6th	PP	FL	points
1979–82; 1992	23(18)	-	-	-	-	-	-	-	-	-

Best result: 9th. Best qualifying: 4th

	wins	2nd	3rd	4th	5th	6th	PP	FL	points
Int F3000 Ch	-	-	1	-	-	-	-	-	3

Championship: 1993 15th

World Sports Car Championship. Race wins: 1984 Brands Hatch, 1987 Jarama, Monza, Fuji, 1988 Le Mans 24 hrs

European F3 Championship. Race wins: 1978 Zandvoort, Monza Lottery GP, Magny-Cours, Karlskoga

Other major race wins: 1988 and 1990 Daytona 24 hrs

ROBS LAMPLOUGH
GB. Born: 4.6.1940, Gloucester

	wins	2nd	3rd	4th	5th	6th	PP	FL	points
European F2 Ch	-	-	-	-	-	-	-	-	1

Championship: 1967 17th

PEDRO LAMY
P. Born: 20.3.1972, Aldeia Galega

1992 German F3 Champion; 1991 GM-Lotus Euroseries Champion

World Championship Grand Prix Record

years	starts	wins	2nd	3rd	4th	5th	6th	PP	FL	points
1993–94	8	-	-	-	-	-	-	-	-	-

Best result: 8th. Best qualifying: 18th

	wins	2nd	3rd	4th	5th	6th	PP	FL	points
Int F3000 Ch	1	2	1	2	-	-	2	2	31

Championship: 1993 2nd. **Race wins:** 1993 Pau GP

Other major race wins: 1992 Marlboro Masters of F3

VINCENZO LANCIA

I. Born: 24.8.1881, Fobello di Valsesia. Died: 15.2.1937, Turin

Major race wins: 1904 Coppa Florio

FRANCESCO "CHICO" LANDI

BR. Born: 14.6.1907. Died: 7.6.1989, Sao Paulo

World Championship Grand Prix Record

years	starts	wins	2nd	3rd	4th	5th	6th	PP	FL	points
1951–53; 1956	6	-	-	-	1	-	-	-	-	1.5

Best championship: 1956 25th. **Best qualifying:** 11th

ADOLF LANG

D

1953 German F3 Champion

HERMANN LANG

D. Born: 6.4.1909, Bad Cannstatt. Died: 19.10.1987, Bad Cannstatt

1939 Grand Prix European Champion (see page 195)

World Championship Grand Prix Record

Hermann Lang

years	starts	wins	2nd	3rd	4th	5th	6th	PP	FL	points
1953–54	2	-	-	-	1	-	-	-	-	2

Best championship: 1953 13th. **Best qualifying:** 11th

Pre-1950 Grands Prix. Race wins: 1939 Belgian GP, Swiss GP

Major Sports Car races. Race wins: 1952 Le Mans 24 hrs

Other major race wins: 1937, 1938 and 1939 Tripoli GP

CLAUDIO LANGES

I. Born: 20.7.1960, Brescia

World Championship Grand Prix Record

year	starts	wins	2nd	3rd	4th	5th	6th	PP	FL	points
1990	-(14)	-	-	-	-	-	-	-	-	-

Best qualifying: 32nd

	wins	2nd	3rd	4th	5th	6th	PP	FL	points
Int F3000 Ch	-	1	-	1	2	2	-	-	15

Championships: 1986 17th, 1988 15th, 1989 12th

European F3 Championship. Race wins: 1984 Knutstorp

GÉRARD LANGLOIS VAN OPHEM

B

Major race wins: 1965 Spa 24 hrs

RANDY LANIER

USA. Born: 22.9.1954

1984 IMSA GT Champion

XAVIER LAPEYRE

F. Born: 13.4.1942

1986 and 1991 French Supertourism Champion

NICOLA LARINI

I. Born: 19.3.1964, Lido di Camaiore

1992 Italian Touring Car Champion; 1993 German Touring Car Champion; 1986 Italian F3 Champion

World Championship Grand Prix Record

years	starts	wins	2nd	3rd	4th	5th	6th	PP	FL	points
1987–92; 1994	44(26)	-	1	-	-	-	-	-	-	6

Best championship: 1994 14th. **Best qualifying:** 6th

OSCAR LARRAURI

RA. Born: 19.8.1954, Rosario

1982 European F3 Champion

World Championship Grand Prix Record

years	starts	wins	2nd	3rd	4th	5th	6th	PP	FL	points
1988–89	7(14)	-	-	-	-	-	-	-	-	-

Best result: 13th. **Best qualifying:** 18th

World Sports Car Championship. Race wins: 1986 Jerez

European F3 Championship. Race wins: 1981 Nürburgring, 1982 Mugello, Nürburgring, Zolder, Zandvoort, Monza, Enna, Knutstorp

GÉRARD LARROUSSE

F. Born: 23.5.1940, Lyon

World Championship Grand Prix Record

year	starts	wins	2nd	3rd	4th	5th	6th	PP	FL	points
1974	1(1)	-	-	-	-	-	-	-	-	-

Best result: no finishes. **Best qualifying:** 28th

	wins	2nd	3rd	4th	5th	6th	PP	FL	points
European F2 Ch	1	2	-	1	-	1	-	1	26

Championship: 1975 4th. **Race wins:** 1975 Jim Clark Trophy (Hockenheim)

World Sports Car Championship. Race wins: 1971 Sebring 12 hrs, Nürburgring, 1973 Vallelunga, Dijon, Le Mans 24 hrs, Österreichring, Watkins Glen, 1974 Imola, Le Mans 24 hrs, Österreichring, Kyalami, 1975 Mugello

Other major race wins: 1974 Targa Florio

JUD LARSON

USA. Born: 21.1.1923, Grand Prairie, Missouri. Died: 11.6.1966, Reading, Pennsylvania

Indycar Championship. Race wins: 1956 Sacramento, 1957 Du Quoin, Indiana State Fairgrounds, 1958 Atlanta, Phoenix

JÜRGEN LÄSSIG

D. Born: 25.2.1943, Tuttlingen

World Sports Car Championship. Race wins: 1981 Monza

NIKI LAUDA

A. Born: 22.2.1949, Vienna

1975, 1977 and 1984 World Champion; 1972 British F2 Champion

World Championship Grand Prix Record

years	starts	wins	2nd	3rd	4th	5th	6th	PP	FL	points
1971–79; 1982–85	171(6)	25	20	9	7	7	5	24	24	420.5

Race wins: 1974 Spanish GP, Dutch GP, 1975 Monaco GP, Belgian GP, Swedish GP, French GP, United States GP, 1976 Brazilian GP, South African GP, Belgian GP, Monaco GP, British GP, 1977 South African GP, German GP, Dutch GP, 1978 Swedish GP, Italian GP, 1982 Long Beach GP, British GP, 1984 South African GP, French GP, British GP, Austrian GP, Italian GP, 1985 Dutch GP. **Best qualifying:** 1st

	wins	2nd	3rd	4th	5th	6th	PP	FL	points
European F2 Ch	-	1	2	1	-	2	2	-	33

Championships: 1971 10th, 1972 5th

Other major race wins: 1975 International Trophy (Silverstone), 1979 Dino Ferrari GP (Imola)

GÉRARD LAUREAU

F

Major race wins: 1954 Tourist Trophy

ARENSIO "DODGIE" LAUREL

PI. Born: n/a. Died: 19.11.1967, Macau GP

Major race wins: 1962 and 1963 Macau GP

ROGER LAURENT

B. Born: 21.2.1913, Liège

Niki Lauda

World Championship Grand Prix Record

year	starts	wins	2nd	3rd	4th	5th	6th	PP	FL	points
1952	2	-	-	-	-	1	-	-	-	-

Best qualifying: 20th

CHRISTIAN LAUTENSCHLAGER

D. Born: 13.4.1877, Magstadt. Died: 1954

Pre-1950 Grands Prix. Race wins: 1908 and 1914 French GP

CHRIS LAWRENCE

GB. Born: 27.7.1933

World Championship Grand Prix Record

year	starts	wins	2nd	3rd	4th	5th	6th	PP	FL	points
1966	2	-	-	-	-	-	-	-	-	-

Best result: 11th. **Best qualifying:** 18th

GRAEME LAWRENCE

NZ

1970 Tasman Champion

Tasman Cup. Race wins: 1970 Levin, 1975 Levin, Adelaide

Bob Lazier
USA. Born: 22.12.1938. Father of Buddy
1977 SCCA Super Vee Champion

Bob Lea-Wright
AUS
Major race wins: 1934 Australian GP

Nicolas Leboissetier
F. Born: 5.6.1971

	wins	2nd	3rd	4th	5th	6th	PP	FL	points
Int F3000 Ch	-	-	-	1	-	-	-	-	3

Championship: 1993 15th

Michel Leclère
F. Born: 18.3.1946, Paris
1972 French F3 Champion

World Championship Grand Prix Record

years	starts	wins	2nd	3rd	4th	5th	6th	PP	FL	points
1975–76	7(1)	-	-	-	-	-	-	-	-	-

Best result: 10th. **Best qualifying:** 18th.

	wins	2nd	3rd	4th	5th	6th	PP	FL	points
European F2 Ch	4	3	2	2	3	1	5	3	81

Championships: 1974 6th, 1975 2nd, 1976 4th. **Race wins:** 1975 Rouen GP, Silverstone, Zolder, 1976 Salzburgring

Mike Ledbrook
GB
1961 BRSCC British F3 (Formula Junior) Champion

Neville Lederle
ZA. Born: 25.9.1938, Theunissen
1963 South African Drivers Champion

World Championship Grand Prix Record

years	starts	wins	2nd	3rd	4th	5th	6th	PP	FL	points
1962; 1965	1(1)	-	-	-	-	-	1	-	-	1

Best championship: 1962 18th. **Best qualifying:** 10th

Kenelm Lee Guinness
GB. Born: n/a. Died: 1937
Major race wins: 1914 Tourist Trophy

Geoff Lees
GB. Born: 1.5.1951, Atherstone
1981 European F2 Champion; 1983 Japanese F2 Champion

World Championship Grand Prix Record

years	starts	wins	2nd	3rd	4th	5th	6th	PP	FL	points
1978–80; 1982	5(7)	-	-	-	-	-	-	-	-	-

Best result: 7th. **Best qualifying:** 16th

	wins	2nd	3rd	4th	5th	6th	PP	FL	points
European F2 Ch	3	3	-	1	3	1	1	5	55

Championship: 1978 14th, 1981 1st. **Race wins:** 1981 Pau GP, Spa, Donington Park

World Sports Car Championship. Race wins: 1992 Monza
Other major race wins: 1979 and 1980 Macau GP

John Leffler
AUS
1976 Australian Gold Star Champion

Arthur Legat
B. Born: 1.11.1898, Haine St Paul. Died: 23.2.1960, Haine St Pierre

World Championship Grand Prix Record

years	starts	wins	2nd	3rd	4th	5th	6th	PP	FL	points
1952–53	2	-	-	-	-	-	-	-	-	-

Best result: 13th. **Best qualifying:** 19th

JJ Lehto
SF. Born: 31.1.1966, Espoo. Real name: Jyrki Jarvilehto
1988 British F3 Champion

World Championship Grand Prix Record

years	starts	wins	2nd	3rd	4th	5th	6th	PP	FL	points
1989–94	62(8)	-	-	1	1	1	1	-	-	10

Best championship: 1991 12th. **Best qualifying:** 4th

	wins	2nd	3rd	4th	5th	6th	PP	FL	points
Int F3000 Ch	-	-	1	1	1	-	-	6

Championship: 1989 13th

Hermann zu Leiningen
D. Born: 1901
Pre-1950 Grands Prix. Race wins: 1930 Masaryk GP

Butch Leitzinger
USA
Major race wins: 1994 Daytona 24 hrs

Gijs van Lennep
NL. Born: 16.3.1942, Bloemendaal
1972 British F5000 Champion

World Championship Grand Prix Record

years	starts	wins	2nd	3rd	4th	5th	6th	PP	FL	points
1971; 1973–75	8(2)	-	-	-	-	-	2	-	-	2

Best championship: 1973, 1975 19th. **Best qualifying:** 20th.
World Sports Car Championship. Race wins: 1971 Le Mans 24 hrs, 1973 Targa Florio, 1976 Le Mans 24 hrs

Joe Leonard
USA. Born: 4.8.1934, San Diego, California
1971 and 1972 Indycar Champion

Indycar Championship. Race wins: 1965 Milwaukee Race 2, 1970 Milwaukee Race 1, 1971 California 500, 1972 Michigan, Pocono 500, Milwaukee Race 2

René Leonard
F
Major Sports Car races. Race wins: 1923 Le Mans 24 hrs, 1925 Spa 24 hrs

Lamberto Leoni
I. Born: 24.5.1953, Argenta

World Championship Grand Prix Record

years	starts	wins	2nd	3rd	4th	5th	6th	PP	FL	points
1977–78	1(4)	-	-	-	-	-	-	-	-	-

Best result: no finishes. **Best qualifying:** 17th

	wins	2nd	3rd	4th	5th	6th	PP	FL	points
European F2 Ch	1	-	1	-	1	1	-	14

Championships: 1975 19th, 1977 11th, 1983 20th. **Race wins:** 1977 Misano

	wins	2nd	3rd	4th	5th	6th	PP	FL	points
Int F3000 Ch	-	-	2	3	1	1	-	1	20

Championships: 1985 10th, 1987 8th

John Lepp
GB

	wins	2nd	3rd	4th	5th	6th	PP	FL	points
European F2 Ch	-	-	-	1	-	-	-	3

Championship: 1973 26th

Frank Lescault
USA
Indycar Championship. Race wins: 1909 Riverhead Race 2

Les Leston
GB. Born: 16.12.1920, Nottingham
1954 British F3 Champion

World Championship Grand Prix Record

years	starts	wins	2nd	3rd	4th	5th	6th	PP	FL	points
1956–57	2(1)	-	-	-	-	-	-	-	-	-

Best result: no finishes. **Best qualifying:** 12th

"Pierre Levegh"
F. Born: 22.12.1905, Paris. Died: 11.6.1955, Le Mans 24 hrs. Real name: Pierre Bouillon

World Championship Grand Prix Record

years	starts	wins	2nd	3rd	4th	5th	6th	PP	FL	points
1950–51	6	-	-	-	-	-	-	-	-	-

Best result: 7th. **Best qualifying:** 9th

Bruce Leven
USA. Born: 27.9.1945
World Sports Car Championship. Race wins: 1981 Sebring 12 hrs

Dave Lewis
USA. Born: n/a. Died: 13.5.1928, Los Angeles
Indycar Championship. Race wins: 1919 Uniontown Race 3, 1926 Altoona Race 1, Charlotte Race 3, Charlotte Race 7, 1927 Atlantic City

Jackie Lewis

GB. Born: 1.11.1936, Stroud, Gloucestershire
1960 British F2 Champion

World Championship Grand Prix Record

years	starts	wins	2nd	3rd	4th	5th	6th	PP	FL	points
1961–62	9(1)	-	-	-	1	-	-	-	-	3

Best championship: 1961 13th. Best qualifying: 13th

Stuart Lewis-Evans

GB. Born: 20.4.1930, Beckenham. Died: 25.10.1958, East
Grinstead, following an accident at the Moroccan GP

World Championship Grand Prix Record

years	starts	wins	2nd	3rd	4th	5th	6th	PP	FL	points
1957–58	14	-	-	2	2	1	-	2	-	16

Best championship: 1958 9th. Best qualifying: 1st

Fredy Lienhard

CH

	wins	2nd	3rd	4th	5th	6th	PP	FL	points
European F2 Ch	-	-	-	-	1	-	-	-	1

Championship: 1983 20th

Guy Ligier

F. Born: 12.7.1930, Vichy

World Championship Grand Prix Record

years	starts	wins	2nd	3rd	4th	5th	6th	PP	FL	points
1966–67	12(1)	-	-	-	-	-	1	-	-	1

Best championship: 1967 19th. Best qualifying: 11th

Shaun van der Linde

ZA
1994 South African Touring Car Champion; 1992 South African
Drivers Champion

Werner Lindermann

D

	wins	2nd	3rd	4th	5th	6th	PP	FL	points
European F2 Ch	-	-	-	-	-	-	-	-	2

Championship: 1969 15th

Leif Lindstrom

S
1984 Swedish F3 Champion

Thomas Lindstrom

S
1985 European Touring Car Champion (shared with Gianfranco
Brancatelli)

Roberto Lippi

I. Born: 17.10.1926, Rome

World Championship Grand Prix Record

year	starts	wins	2nd	3rd	4th	5th	6th	PP	FL	points
1961	1(2)	-	-	-	-	-	-	-	-	-

Best result: no finishes. Best qualifying: 28th

Al Livingstone

USA

Indycar Championship. Race wins: 1910 Elgin Race 2

Conny Ljungfeldt

S
1975 and 1976 Swedish F3 Champion

Bill Lloyd

USA. Born: 12.7.1923, New York

World Sports Car Championship. Race wins: 1954 Sebring 12 hrs

Frank Lockhart

USA. Born: 1903, Dayton, Ohio. Died: 25.4.1928, Daytona Beach,
Florida

Indycar Championship. Race wins: 1926 Indianapolis 500,
Charlotte Race 4, Charlotte Race 5, Altoona Race 2, Fresno Race 2,
Charlotte Race 6, 1927 Altoona Race 2, Charlotte Race 1, Salem
Race 2, Salem Race 3

Dries van der Lof

NL. Born: 23.8.1919, Emmen. Died: 24.5.1990, Enschede

World Championship Grand Prix Record

year	starts	wins	2nd	3rd	4th	5th	6th	PP	FL	points
1952	1	-	-	-	-	-	-	-	-	-

Best result: no finishes. Best qualifying: 14th

Carl Lohmander

S

Major race wins: 1961 Mille Miglia

Lella Lombardi

I. Born: 26.3.1943, Frugarolo, Alessandria. Died: 3.3.1992, Milan,
cancer

World Championship Grand Prix Record

years	starts	wins	2nd	3rd	4th	5th	6th	PP	FL	points
1974–76	12(5)	-	-	-	-	-	1	-	-	.5

Best championship: 1975 21st. Best qualifying: 22nd

World Sports Car Championship. Race wins: 1979 Florio Cup,
Vallelunga, 1981 Mugello

Tony Longhurst

AUS. Born: 1.10.1957, Sydney
1994 Australian 2-litre Touring Car Champion

Major race wins: 1988 Bathurst

Richard Longman

GB
1978 and 1979 British Touring Car Champion

Ernst Loof

D. Born: 4.7.1907, Neindorf. Died: 3.3.1956, Bonn, brain tumour

World Championship Grand Prix Record

year	starts	wins	2nd	3rd	4th	5th	6th	PP	FL	points
1953	1	-	-	-	-	-	-	-	-	-

Best result: no finishes. Best qualifying: 31st

Fred Lorenzen

USA. Born: 30.12.1934, Elmhurst, Illinois

Major race wins: 1963 and 1965 World 600, 1965 Daytona 500

Henri Louveau

F. Born: 25.1.1910. Died: 7.1.1991

World Championship Grand Prix Record

years	starts	wins	2nd	3rd	4th	5th	6th	PP	FL	points
1950–51	2	-	-	-	-	-	-	-	-	-

Best result: no finishes. Best qualifying: 11th

John Love

RSR. Born: 7.12.1924, Bulawayo
1962 British Touring Car Champion; 1964, 1965, 1966, 1967, 1968
and 1969 South African Drivers' Champion

World Championship Grand Prix Record

years	starts	wins	2nd	3rd	4th	5th	6th	PP	FL	points
1962–65; 1967–72	9(1)	-	1	-	-	-	-	-	-	6

Best championship: 1967 11th. Best qualifying: 5th

Pete Lovely

USA. Born: 11.4.1926, Livingston

World Championship Grand Prix Record

year	starts	wins	2nd	3rd	4th	5th	6th	PP	FL	points
1959–60; 1969–71	7(4)	-	-	-	-	-	-	-	-	-

Best result: 7th. Best qualifying: 16th

Roger Loyer

F. Born: 5.8.1907. Died: 24.3.1988

World Championship Grand Prix Record

year	starts	wins	2nd	3rd	4th	5th	6th	PP	FL	points
1954	1	-	-	-	-	-	-	-	-	-

Best result: no finishes. Best qualifying: 15th

Jean Lucas

F. Born: 25.4.1917, Le Mans

World Championship Grand Prix Record

year	starts	wins	2nd	3rd	4th	5th	6th	PP	FL	points
1955	1	-	-	-	-	-	-	-	-	-

Best result: no finishes. Best qualifying: 22nd

Major race wins: 1949 Spa 24 hrs

JEAN LUCIENBONNET

F

World Championship Grand Prix Record

year	starts	wins	2nd	3rd	4th	5th	6th	PP	FL	points
1959	-(1)	-	-	-	-	-	-	-	-	-

Best qualifying: 23rd

KLAUS LUDWIG

D. Born: 5.10.1949, Roisdorf

1988, 1992 and 1994 German Touring Car Champion; 1979 and 1980 German Racing Champion

	wins	2nd	3rd	4th	5th	6th	PP	FL	points
European F2 Ch	-	-	-	-	1	-	-	-	4

Championship: 1976 12th

World Sports Car Championship. Race wins: 1978 Nürburgring, 1979 Le Mans 24 hrs, Watkins Glen, 1984 Le Mans 24 hrs, 1985 Le Mans 24 hrs, 1986 Norisring 200 miles

Other major race wins: 1988 Sebring 12 hrs

LEN LUKEY

AUS

1959 Australian Gold Star Champion

TINY LUND

USA

Major race wins: 1963 Daytona 500

BRETT LUNGER

USA. Born: 14.11.1945, Wilmington, Delaware

World Championship Grand Prix Record

years	starts	wins	2nd	3rd	4th	5th	6th	PP	FL	points
1975–78	34(9)	-	-	-	-	-	-	-	-	-

Best result: 7th. **Best qualifying:** 13th

	wins	2nd	3rd	4th	5th	6th	PP	FL	points
European F2 Ch	-	-	-	1	-	-	-	-	4

Championships: 1972 24th, 1973 31st

ARIE LUYENDYK

NL. Born: 21.9.1953, Sommelsdyk

1984 SCCA Super Vee Champion

Indycar Championship. Race wins: 1990 Indianapolis 500, 1991 Phoenix, Nazareth

Other major race wins: 1989 Sebring 12 hrs

LEIGH LYNCH

USA

Indycar Championship. Race wins: 1909 Indianapolis Race 3

HERB LYTLE

USA

Indycar Championship. Race wins: 1910 Atlanta Race 3

M ···

SASHA MAASSEN

D. Born: 28.9.1969, Aachen

Major race wins: 1994 Macau GP

JOHN MacDONALD

HK. Born: 1936, Worcester (GB)

Major race wins: 1965, 1972, 1973 and 1975 Macau GP

MIKE MacDOWEL

GB. Born: 13.9.1932, Great Yarmouth

World Championship Grand Prix Record

year	starts	wins	2nd	3rd	4th	5th	6th	PP	FL	points
1957	1	-	-	-	-	-	-	-	-	-

Best result: 7th. **Best qualifying:** 15th

HERBERT MacKAY-FRASER

USA. Born: 23.6.1927. Died: 14.7.1957, Reims, F2 race

World Championship Grand Prix Record

year	starts	wins	2nd	3rd	4th	5th	6th	PP	FL	points
1957	1	-	-	-	-	-	-	-	-	-

Best result: no finishes. **Best qualifying:** 12th

LANCE MACKLIN

GB. Born: 2.9.1919, London

World Championship Grand Prix Record

years	starts	wins	2nd	3rd	4th	5th	6th	PP	FL	points
1952–55	13(2)	-	-	-	-	-	-	-	-	-

Best result: 8th. **Best qualifying:** 9th

Major race wins: 1952 International Trophy (Silverstone)

JEFF MacPHERSON

USA. Born: 9.6.1956, Santa Ana, California

1986 New Zealand International Champion

DAMIEN MAGEE

GB. Born: 17.11.1945, Belfast

World Championship Grand Prix Record

years	starts	wins	2nd	3rd	4th	5th	6th	PP	FL	points
1975–76	1(1)	-	-	-	-	-	-	-	-	-

Best result: 14th. **Best qualifying:** 22nd

JOCKO MAGGIACOMO

USA

1976 Trans-Am Class 2 Champion

TONY MAGGS

ZA. Born: 9.2.1937, Pretoria

World Championship Grand Prix Record

years	starts	wins	2nd	3rd	4th	5th	6th	PP	FL	points
1961–65	25(2)	-	2	1	1	2	3	-	-	26

Best championship: 1963 8th. **Best qualifying:** 4th

CONSTANTINO MAGISTRI

I

Major race wins: 1936 Targa Florio

UMBERTO MAGLIOLI

I. Born: 5.6.1928, Biella

World Championship Grand Prix Record

years	starts	wins	2nd	3rd	4th	5th	6th	PP	FL	points
1953–57	10	-	-	2	-	-	1	-	-	3.33

Best championship: 1954 18th. **Best qualifying:** 7th.

World Sports Car Championship. Race wins: 1954 Buenos Aires, Carrera Panamericana, 1964 Sebring 12 hrs, 1968 Targa Florio

Other major race wins: 1953 and 1956 Targa Florio

JAN MAGNUSSON

DK. Born: 4.7.1973

1994 British F3 Champion

NORBERT MAHE

F

Major race wins: 1934 Spa 24 hrs

GUY MAIRESSE

F. Born: 10.8.1910, La Capelle, L'Aisne. Died: 24.4.1954, Montlhéry, Paris Cup practice

World Championship Grand Prix Record

years	starts	wins	2nd	3rd	4th	5th	6th	PP	FL	points
1950–51	3	-	-	-	-	-	-	-	-	-

Best result: 9th. **Best qualifying:** 11th

WILLY MAIRESSE

B. Born: 1.10.1928, Momignies. Died: 2.9.1969, Ostend, suicide

World Championship Grand Prix Record

years	starts	wins	2nd	3rd	4th	5th	6th	PP	FL	points
1960-63	12	-	-	-	1	1	-	-	-	7

Best championship: 1962 14th. **Best qualifying:** 3rd.

World Sports Car Championship. Race wins: 1962 Targa Florio, 1963 Nürburgring, 1966 Targa Florio

JEAN-PIERRE MALCHER

F. Born: 19.2.1950

1981, 1989 and 1990 French Supertourism Champion; 1988 French Touring Car Champion

GUILLERMO MALDONALDO

RA. Born: 29.10.1952

1983, 1984 and 1985, 1986 Codasur F2 Champion

RAY MALLOCK
GB. Born: 12.4.1951

	wins	2nd	3rd	4th	5th	6th	PP	FL	points
European F2 Ch	-	1	-	-	1	-	-		7

Championships: 1975 26th, 1977 12th

PARIDE MAMBELLI
I

Major race wins: 1937 Mille Miglia

OSCAR MANAUTOU
MEX. Born: 9.9.1956
1988 Mexican Formula K Champion

FABIO MANCINI
I

Major race wins: 1987 Tourist Trophy

ROGER MANDERVILLE
USA. Born: 22.9.1941
World Sports Car Championship. Race wins: 1981 Daytona

NIGEL MANSELL
GB. Born: 8.8.1953, Upton-on-Severn
1992 World Champion; 1993 Indycar Champion

Nigel Mansell

World Championship Grand Prix Record

years	starts	wins	2nd	3rd	4th	5th	6th	PP	FL	points
1980–92; 1994	185(4)	31	17	11	8	6	9	32	29	482

Race wins: 1985 European GP, South African GP, 1986 Belgian GP, Canadian GP, French GP, British GP, Portuguese GP, 1987 San Marino GP, French GP, British GP, Austrian GP, Spanish GP, Mexican GP, 1989 Brazilian GP, Hungarian GP, 1990 Portuguese GP, 1991 French GP, British GP, German GP, Italian GP, Spanish GP, 1992 South African GP, Mexican GP, Brazilian GP, Spanish GP, San Marino GP, French GP, British GP, German GP, Portuguese GP, 1994 Australian GP. Best qualifying: 1st

	wins	2nd	3rd	4th	5th	6th	PP	FL	points
European F2 Ch	-	1	-	-	1	-	-		8

Championship: 1980 12th

Indycar Championship. Race wins: 1993 Surfers Paradise, Milwaukee, Michigan 500, New Hampshire, Nazareth

ENRIQUE MANSILLA
RA

	wins	2nd	3rd	4th	5th	6th	PP	FL	points
European F2 Ch	-	-	-	-	2	-	-		2

Championship: 1983 19th

GAUDENZIO MANTOVA
I

	wins	2nd	3rd	4th	5th	6th	PP	FL	points
European F2 Ch	-	-	-	-	2	-	-		4

Championship: 1977 14th

SERGIO MANTOVANI
I. Born: 22.5.1929, Milan

World Championship Grand Prix Record

years	starts	wins	2nd	3rd	4th	5th	6th	PP	FL	points
1953–55	7(1)	-	-	-	-	2	-	-		4

Best championship: 1954 15th. Best qualifying: 9th

JOHNNY MANTZ
USA. Born: 18.9.1918, Hebron, Indiana. Died: 25.10.1972
Indycar Championship. Race wins: 1948 Milwaukee Race 2

ROBERT MANZON
F. Born: 12.4.1917, Marseille

World Championship Grand Prix Record

years	starts	wins	2nd	3rd	4th	5th	6th	PP	FL	points
1950–56	28(1)	-	-	2	2	1	-	-		16

Best championship: 1952 6th. Best qualifying: 3rd.

ROBERTO MARAZZI
I

	wins	2nd	3rd	4th	5th	6th	PP	FL	points
European F2 Ch	-	-	-	2	-	-		6

Championships: 1976 10th, 1978 20th

World Sports Car Championship. Race wins: 1980 Vallelunga

JOVY MARCELO
RP. Born: 21.7.1965. Died: 15.5.1992, Indianapolis, practice
1991 North American Toyota Atlantic Champion

ONOFRE MARIMÓN
RA. Born: 19.12.1923, Buenos Aires. Died: 31.7.1954, Nürburgring, German GP practice

World Championship Grand Prix Record

years	starts	wins	2nd	3rd	4th	5th	6th	PP	FL	points
1951; 1953–54	11(1)	-	-	2	-	-		1	8.14

Best championship: 1953 11th. Best qualifying: 4th

ERNST MARING
D
1975 German F3 Champion

HELMUT MARKO
A. Born: 27.4.1943, Graz

World Championship Grand Prix Record

years	starts	wins	2nd	3rd	4th	5th	6th	PP	FL	points
1971–72	9(1)	-	-	-	-	-	-	-		-

Best result: 8th. Best qualifying: 6th

	wins	2nd	3rd	4th	5th	6th	PP	FL	points
European F2 Ch	-	-	-	-	-	-	-		1

Championship: 1971 20th

World Sports Car Championship. Race wins: 1971 Le Mans 24 hrs

STERLING MARLIN
USA. Born: 30.6.1957, Franklin, Tennessee
Major race wins: 1994 Daytona 500

TARSO MARQUES
BR

	wins	2nd	3rd	4th	5th	6th	PP	FL	points
Int F3000 Ch	-	-	-	1	-	-		1	3

Championship: 1994 12th

LESLIE MARR
GB. Born: 14.8.1922, Durham

World Championship Grand Prix Record

years	starts	wins	2nd	3rd	4th	5th	6th	PP	FL	points
1954–55	2	-	-	-	-	-	-		-

Best result: 13th. Best qualifying: 19th

TONY MARSH
GB. Born: 20.7.1931, Stourbridge, Gloucestershire
1957 British F2 Champion

World Championship Grand Prix Record

years	starts	wins	2nd	3rd	4th	5th	6th	PP	FL	points
1957–58; 1961	4(1)	-	-	-	-	-	-		-

Best result: 15th. Best qualifying: 20th

BOBBY MARSHMAN
USA. Born: 1936, Hatfield, Pennsylvania. Died: 3.12.1964, Phoenix, testing
Indycar Championship. Race wins: 1962 Phoenix

EUGÈNE MARTIN
F. Born: 24.3.1915, Suresnes

World Championship Grand Prix Record

year	starts	wins	2nd	3rd	4th	5th	6th	PP	FL	points
1950	2	-	-	-	-	-	-		-

Best result: no finishes. Best qualifying: 7th

JEAN-MICHEL MARTIN
B. Born: 19.6.1953
1979, 1980, 1986, 1989 and 1990 Belgian Touring Car Champion
Major race wins: 1979, 1980, 1987 and 1992 Spa 24 hrs

MARK MARTIN
USA. Born: 9.1.1959, Batesville, Arkansas
1994 IROC Champion

PHILIPPE MARTIN
B

Major race wins: 1979 and 1980 Spa 24 hrs

SPENCER MARTIN

AUS

1966 and 1967 Australian Gold Star Champion

TONY MARTIN

ZA

1980 South African Drivers' Champion

Major race wins: 1984 Daytona 24 hrs

GERARDO MARTINEZ

MEX. Born: 10.10.1947

1987 and 1989 Mexican Formula K Champion

GIANCARLO MARTINI

I. Born: 16.8.1947, Lavezzola. Uncle of Pierluigi

	wins	2nd	3rd	4th	5th	6th	PP	FL	points
European F2 Ch	-	-	2	-	4	3	-	-	22

Championships: 1974 16th, 1975 15th, 1976 7th

MAURO MARTINI

I. Born: 17.5.1964

1992 Japanese F3000 Champion

PIERLUIGI MARTINI

I. Born: 23.4.1961, Lugo di Romagna, Bologna. Nephew of Giancarlo

1983 European F3 Champion

World Championship Grand Prix Record

year	starts	wins	2nd	3rd	4th	5th	6th	PP	FL	points
1984–85;										
1988–94	110(5)	-	-	-	2	4	4	-	-	18

Best championship: 1991 11th. **Best qualifying:** 2nd

	wins	2nd	3rd	4th	5th	6th	PP	FL	points
European F2 Ch	-	1	-	-	-	-	-	-	6

Championship: 1983 10th

	wins	2nd	3rd	4th	5th	6th	PP	FL	points
Int F3000 Ch	4	4	2	-	1	-	2	2	67

Championships: 1986 2nd, 1987 11th, 1988 4th. **Race wins:** 1986 Imola, Mugello, Jarama, 1988 Mediterranean GP (Enna). **European F3 Championship. Race wins:** 1983 Nogaro, Jarama, Imola, Croix-en-Ternois

DAN MARVIN

USA. Born: 13.8.1952

1984 North American Formula Atlantic Champion

GIANNINO MARZOTTO

I

World Sports Car Championship. Race wins: 1953 Mille Miglia

Other major race wins: 1950 Mille Miglia

VITTORIO MARZOTTO

I

Major race wins: 1952 Monaco GP

GIULIO MASETTI

I. Born: 1895, Florence. Died: 25.4.1926, Madonie Circuit, Targa Florio

Major race wins: 1921 and 1922 Targa Florio

JOCHEN MASS

D. Born: 30.9.1946, Munich

1972 European Touring Car Champion; 1985 German Racing Champion

World Championship Grand Prix Record

years	starts	wins	2nd	3rd	4th	5th	6th	PP	FL	points
1973–80; 1982	105(9)	1	1	6	7	4	9	-	2	71

Best championship: 1977 6th. **Race wins:** 1975 Spanish GP. **Best qualifying:** 4th

	wins	2nd	3rd	4th	5th	6th	PP	FL	points
European F2 Ch	4	3	1	-	2	3	4		43

Championships: 1972 28th, 1973 2nd. **Race wins:** 1973 Swedish Gold Cup (Kinnekulle), Jochen Rindt Trophy (Hockenheim), 1977 Jim Clark Trophy (Hockenheim), Eifelrennen (Nürburgring)

World Sports Car Championship. Race wins: 1975 Florio Cup, 1976 Mugello, Vallelunga, Monza, Imola, Florio Cup, Dijon, Salzburgring, 1977 Silverstone, Watkins Glen, Brands Hatch, 1978 Silverstone, 1982 Spa, Fuji, 1983 Nürburgring, Spa, 1984

Silverstone, Mosport Park, 1985 Mugello, Silverstone, Selangor, 1988 Jerez, Brno, Nürburgring, Sandown Park, 1989 Le Mans 24 hrs, Jarama, Nürburgring, Donington, Mexico City, 1990 Spa, Mexico City

Other major race wins: 1972 Tourist Trophy, Spa 24 hrs, 1987 Sebring 12 hrs

EMILIO MATERASSI

I. Born: 1889, Florence. Died: 9.9.1928, Monza, Italian GP

Major race wins: 1927 Tripoli GP, Targa Florio, San Sebastian GP

FRANK MATICH

AUS. Born: 1935, Sydney

1972 Australian Gold Star Champion

Tasman Cup. Race wins: 1970 New Zealand GP, Lady Wigram Trophy, 1971 Surfers' Paradise, 1972 Warwick Farm, 1973 Surfers' Paradise

Other major race wins: 1970 and 1971 Australian GP

JOE MATSON

USA

Indycar Championship. Race wins: 1909 Crown Point Race 1

KEIJI MATSUMOTO

J. Born: 26.12.1949, Kyoto

1979 Japanese F2 Champion

HIRO MATSUSHITA

J. Born: 14.3.1961, Kobe

1989 North American (Western Division) Formula Atlantic Champion

SVEN MATTSSON

S

1964 Swedish F3 Champion

TONY MAW

MAL

Major race wins: 1967 Macau GP

JEAN MAX

F. Born: 27.7.1947, Marseille

World Championship Grand Prix Record

year	starts	wins	2nd	3rd	4th	5th	6th	PP	FL	points
1971	1	-	-	-	-	-	-	-	-	-

Best result: no finishes. **Best qualifying:** 23rd

MICHEL MAY

CH. Born: 18.8.1934, Stuttgart (D)

World Championship Grand Prix Record

year	starts	wins	2nd	3rd	4th	5th	6th	PP	FL	points
1961	2(1)	-	-	-	-	-	-	-	-	-

Best result: 11th. **Best qualifying:** 14th

Major race wins: 1959 Monaco Formula Junior GP

TIMMY MAYER

USA. Born: 22.2.1938, Dalton, Pennsylvania. Died: 28.2.1964, Longford (AUS). Brother of Teddy

World Championship Grand Prix Record

year	starts	wins	2nd	3rd	4th	5th	6th	PP	FL	points
1962	1	-	-	-	-	-	-	-	-	-

Best result: no finishes. **Best qualifying:** 12th

REX MAYS

USA. Born: 1913. Died: 6.11.1949, Del Mar, California

1940 and 1941 Indycar Champion

Indycar Championship. Race wins: 1936 Goshen, 1940 Springfield, Syracuse, 1941 Milwaukee, Syracuse, 1946 Langhorne, Indiana State Fairgrounds, Milwaukee

FRANÇOIS MAZET

F. Born: 26.2.1943, Paris

1969 French F3 Champion

World Championship Grand Prix Record

year	starts	wins	2nd	3rd	4th	5th	6th	PP	FL	points
1971	1	-	-	-	-	-	-	-	-	-

Best result: 13th. **Best qualifying:** 24th

KENNETH McALPINE

GB. Born: 21.9.1920, Chobham

World Championship Grand Prix Record

years	starts	wins	2nd	3rd	4th	5th	6th	PP	FL	points
1952–53; 1955	7	-	-	-	-	-	-	-	-	

Best result: 13th. Best qualifying: 13th

PERRY McCARTHY

GB. Born: 3.3.1962, London

World Championship Grand Prix Record

year	starts	wins	2nd	3rd	4th	5th	6th	PP	FL	points
1992	-(10)	-	-	-	-	-	-	-	-	-

Best qualifying: 29th

ROGER McCLUSKEY

USA. Born: 24.8.1930, Texas. Died: 29.8.1993, Indianapolis

1973 Indycar Champion

Indycar Championship. Race wins: 1966 Langhorne Race 2, 1968 Springfield, 1972 California 500, 1973 Michigan, 1979 Milwaukee

DAVE McCONNELL

CDN

	wins	2nd	3rd	4th	5th	6th	PP	FL	points
European F2 Ch	-	-	1	-	-	-	-	-	6

Championship: 1973 13th

JOHN McCORMACK

AUS

1973, 1975 and 1977 Australian Gold Star Champion

Tasman Cup. Race wins: 1973 New Zealand GP, Adelaide, 1974 New Zealand GP

ROBERT McDONOUGH

USA. Born: n/a. Died: 10.12.1945

Indycar Championship. Race wins: 1925 Altoona Race 2, Laurel Race 2

JIM McELREATH

USA. Born: 18.2.1928, Arlington, Texas

Indycar Championship. Race wins: 1965 Trenton Race 1, Langhorne Race 1, Langhorne Race 2, 1966 Phoenix Race 1, 1970 California 500

ROB McFARLIN

USA

Major race wins: 1979 Sebring 12 hrs

BILL McGOVERN

GB

1970, 1971 and 1972 British Touring Car Champion

JACK McGRATH

USA. Born: 8.10.1919, Los Angeles. Died: 6.11.1955, Phoenix

Indycar Championship. Race wins: 1950 Langhorne, Syracuse, 1952 Syracuse, 1953 Milwaukee Race 1

BRIAN McGUIRE

AUS. Born: 13.12.1945, Melbourne. Died: 29.8.1977, Brands Hatch

World Championship Grand Prix Record

year	starts	wins	2nd	3rd	4th	5th	6th	PP	FL	points
1977	-(1)	-	-	-	-	-	-	-	-	-

Best qualifying: 35th

DAVE McKAY

AUS

1960 Australian Touring Car Champion

BRUCE McLAREN

NZ. Born: 30.8.1937, Auckland. Died: 2.6.1970, Goodwood, testing

1967 and 1969 Can-Am Champion; 1964 Tasman Champion

World Championship Grand Prix Record

years	starts	wins	2nd	3rd	4th	5th	6th	PP	FL	points
1958–70	100(4)	4	11	12	7	11	5	-	3	196.5

Best championship: 1960 2nd. **Race wins:** 1959 United States GP, 1960 Argentinian GP, 1962 Monaco GP, 1968 Belgian GP. Best qualifying: 2nd

	wins	2nd	3rd	4th	5th	6th	PP	FL	points
European F2 Ch	-	-	1	1	1	-	-	-	

World Sports Car Championship. Race wins: 1966 Le Mans 24 hrs, 1967 Sebring 12 hrs

Tasman Cup. Race wins: 1965 Australian GP, 1968 Teretonga

Other major race wins: 1958 German GP F2 Class, 1962 Australian GP, 1968 Race of Champions

PETER McLEOD

AUS

Major race wins: 1987 Bathurst

DAVE McMILLEN

NZ. Born: 5.5.1944

1980 New Zealand International Champion; 1982 North American Formula Atlantic Champion

EATON McMILLIAN

USA

Indycar Championship. Race wins: 1909 Denver

ALLAN McNISH

GB. Born: 29.12.1969, Dumfries

	wins	2nd	3rd	4th	5th	6th	PP	FL	points
Int F3000 Ch	2	1	1	-	3	2	1	1	36

Championships: 1990 4th, 1991 16th, 1992 11th. **Race wins:** 1990 International Trophy (Silverstone), Brands Hatch

BRUCE McPHEE

AUS

Major race wins: 1968 Bathurst

GRAHAM McRAE

NZ. Born: 5.3.1940, Wellington

1971, 1972 and 1973 Tasman Champion; 1972 North American F5000 Champion; 1978 Australian Gold Star Champion

World Championship Grand Prix Record

year	starts	wins	2nd	3rd	4th	5th	6th	PP	FL	points
1973	1	-	-	-	-	-	-	-	-	-

Best result: no finishes. Best qualifying: 28th

Tasman Cup. Race wins: 1970 Teretonga, Surfers' Paradise, 1971 Levin, Lady Wigram Trophy, Sandown Park, 1972 Levin, Lady Wigram Trophy, Surfers' Paradise, Australian GP, 1973 Levin, Lady Wigram Trophy, Sandown Park, 1975 Lady Wigram Trophy

Other major race wins: 1972, 1973 and 1978 Australian GP

RICK MEARS

USA. Born: 3.12.1951, Wichita, Kansas

1979 (CART), 1981 and 1982 Indycar Champion

Indycar Championship. Race wins: 1978 Milwaukee, Atlanta, Brands Hatch, 1979 Indianapolis 500, Trenton Race 3, Atlanta, 1980 Mexico City, 1981 Atlanta Race 1, Atlanta Race 2, Riverside, Michigan, Watkins Glen, Mexico City, 1982 Phoenix, Atlanta, Pocono 500, Riverside, 1983 Michigan, 1984 Indianapolis 500, 1985 Pocono 500, 1987 Pocono 500, 1988 Indianapolis 500, Milwaukee, 1989 Phoenix, Milwaukee, Monterey GP (Laguna Seca), 1990 Phoenix, 1991 Indianapolis 500, Michigan 500

Other major race wins: 1990 Marlboro Challenge

CHARLES MENDEZ

USA

Major race wins: 1978 Sebring 12 hrs

CARLOS MENDITÉGUY

RA. Born: 10.8.1915, Buenos Aires. Died: 28.4.1973

World Championship Grand Prix Record

years	starts	wins	2nd	3rd	4th	5th	6th	PP	FL	points
1953–58; 1960	10(1)	-	-	1	1	1	-	-		9

Best championship: 1957 14th. Best qualifying: 6th

World Sports Car Championship. Race wins: 1956 Buenos Aires

ALAIN MENU

CH. Born: 9.8.1963, Geneva

	wins	2nd	3rd	4th	5th	6th	PP	FL	points
Int F3000 Ch	-	-	-	-	-	2	-	-	2

Championship: 1991 16th

GUIDO MEREGALLI

I. Born: 1894. Died: 1959

Major race wins: 1920 Targa Florio

HARRY MERKEL

D

World Championship Grand Prix Record

year	starts	wins	2nd	3rd	4th	5th	6th	PP	FL	points
1952	-(1)	-	-	-	-	-	-	-	-	-

Best qualifying: no time set

VOLKERT MERL

D

World Sports Car Championship. Race wins: 1979 Dijon, Brands Hatch, 1980 Daytona 24 hrs

SAREL VAN DER MERWE

ZA. Born: 5.12.1946, Port Elizabeth

Major race wins: 1984 Daytona 24 hrs

CHARLES MERZ

USA. Born: n/a. Died: 8.7.1952

Indycar Championship. Race wins: 1911 Oakland Race 2, Santa Monica Race 2, 1912 Elgin Race 2

OTTO MERZ

D. Born: 1889, Cannstadt. Died: 19.5.1933, Avusrennen

Pre-1950 Grands Prix. Race wins: 1927 German GP

ARTURO MERZARIO

I. Born: 11.3.1943, Civenna, near Como

World Championship Grand Prix Record

years	starts	wins	2nd	3rd	4th	5th	6th	PP	FL	points
1972–79	57(29)	-	-	3	-	2	-	-	11

Best championship: 1973 12th. **Best qualifying:** 3rd

	wins	2nd	3rd	4th	5th	6th	PP	FL	points
European F2 Ch	-	-	-	1	1	-	-	-

World Sports Car Championship. Race wins: 1972 Spa, Targa Florio, 1974 Monza, 1975 Dijon, Monza, Florio Cup, Nürburgring, 1977 Dijon, Florio Cup, Estoril, Paul Ricard

Other major race wins: 1975 Targa Florio

RENÉ METGE

F. Born: 23.10.1941, Montrouge

1982 French Supertourism Champion

Major race wins: 1983 Tourist Trophy

LOUIS MEYER

USA. Born: 1904

1928, 1929 and 1933 Indycar Champion

Indycar Championship. Race wins: 1928 Indianapolis 500, Altoona, 1929 Altoona Race 1, Altoona Race 2, 1931 Detroit, 1933 Indianapolis 500, 1935 Altoona, 1936 Indianapolis 500

TOMAS MEZERA

AUS (emigrated from Czechoslovakia). Born: 5.11.1958

Major race wins: 1988 Bathurst

RICK MIASKIEWICZ

USA. Born: 22.3.1953

1985 Can-Am Champion

ROBERTO MIERES

RA. Born: 3.12.1924, Mar de Plata

World Championship Grand Prix Record

years	starts	wins	2nd	3rd	4th	5th	6th	PP	FL	points
1953–55	17	-	-	-	3	2	2	-	1	13

Best championship: 1955 8th, 7 pts. **Best qualifying:** 6th.

FRANÇOIS MIGAULT

F. Born: 4.12.1944, Le Mans

World Championship Grand Prix Record

year	starts	wins	2nd	3rd	4th	5th	6th	PP	FL	points
1972; 1974–75	13(3)	-	-	-	-	-	-	-	-	-

Best result: 14th. **Best qualifying:** 14th

	wins	2nd	3rd	4th	5th	6th	PP	FL	points
European F2 Ch	-	-	1	1	1	-	-	8

Championships: 1971 11th, 1976 17th

ALEC MILDREN

AUS

1960 Australian Gold Star Champion

Major race wins: 1960 Australian GP

JOHN MILES

GB. Born: 14.6.1943, Islington

World Championship Grand Prix Record

years	starts	wins	2nd	3rd	4th	5th	6th	PP	FL	points
1969–70	12(3)	-	-	-	-	1	-	-	2

Best championship: 1970 19th. **Best qualifying:** 7th

	wins	2nd	3rd	4th	5th	6th	PP	FL	points
European F2 Ch	-	-	1	-	-	-	-	4

Championship: 1969 11th

KEN MILES

USA. Born: 1.11.1918, Sutton Coldfield (GB). Died: 17.8.1966, Riverside

World Sports Car Championship. Race wins: 1965 Daytona, 1966 Daytona 24 hrs, Sebring 12 hrs

ANDRÉ MILHOUX

B. Born: 9.12.1928, Bressoux

World Championship Grand Prix Record

year	starts	wins	2nd	3rd	4th	5th	6th	PP	FL	points
1956	1	-	-	-	-	-	-	-	-	-

Best result: no finishes. **Best qualifying:** no time set

STEVE MILLEN

NZ. Born: 17.2.1953

Major race wins: 1994 Daytona 24 hrs, Sebring 12 hrs

EDDIE MILLER

USA

1975 SCCA Super Vee Champion

TOMMY MILTON

USA. Born: 1893, St Paul, Minnesota. Died: 11.7.1962

1920 (by AAA revisions – see page 320) and 1921 Indycar Champion

Indycar Championship. Race wins: 1917 Providence Race 2, Providence Race 3, 1918 Uniontown Race 1, 1919 Uniontown Race 1, Sheepshead Race 1, Uniontown Race 2, Uniontown Race 6, Elgin, 1920 Beverly Hills Race 4, Uniontown Race 1, Tacoma, Uniontown Race 2, 1921 Beverly Hills Race 4, Indianapolis 500, Tacoma, 1922 Beverly Hills Race 1, Beverly Hills Race 3, Beverly Hills Race 6, Kansas City, 1923 Indianapolis 500, 1924 Charlotte, 1925 Culver City Race 1, Charlotte Race 2

FERDINANDO MINOIA

I. Born: 2.6.1884, Milan. Died: 28.6.1940

Major race wins: 1927 Mille Miglia

GERHARD MITTER

D. Born: 30.8.1935, Schonlinde, Sudetenland. Died: 1.8.1969, Nürburgring, German GP practice

1960 German F3 Champion

World Championship Grand Prix Record

years	starts	wins	2nd	3rd	4th	5th	6th	PP	FL	points
1963–67; 1969	5(2)	-	-	-	1	-	-	-	3

Best championship: 1963 12th. **Best qualifying:** 12th

	wins	2nd	3rd	4th	5th	6th	PP	FL	points
European F2 Ch	-	-	-	-	-	-	-	2

Championship: 1967 15th

World Sports Car Championship. Race wins: 1969 Targa Florio

Other major race wins: 1966 Austrian GP

STEFANO MODENA

I. Born: 12.5.1963, San Prospero

1987 FIA F3000 Champion; 1986 European F3 Cup winner

World Championship Grand Prix Record

years	starts	wins	2nd	3rd	4th	5th	6th	PP	FL	points
1987–92	70(11)	-	1	1	1	1	2	-	-	17

Best championship: 1991 8th. **Best qualifying:** 2nd

	wins	2nd	3rd	4th	5th	6th	PP	FL	points
Int F3000 Ch	3	1	-	2	-	2	-	1	41

Championship: 1987 1st. **Race wins:** 1987 Rome GP (Vallelunga), Birmingham, Imola

Other major race wins: 1986 European F3 Cup

ALLAN MOFFAT
AUS (emigrated from Canada)
1973, 1976, 1977 and 1983 Australian Touring Car Champion
Major race wins: 1970, 1971, 1973 and 1977 Bathurst, 1975 Sebring 12 hrs

KAZUO MOGI
J. Born: 2.2.1953
1985 Japanese Touring Car Champion (with Naoki Nagasaka)

GUY MOLL
DZ. Born: 1910. Died: 15.8.1934, Pescara, Coppa Acerbo
Pre-1950 Grands Prix. Race wins: 1934 Monaco GP

ANDREA MONTERMINI
I. Born: 30.5.1964, Sassuolo

World Championship Grand Prix Record

year	starts	wins	2nd	3rd	4th	5th	6th	PP	FL	points
1994	-(1)	-	-	-	-	-	-	-	-	-

Best qualifying: 27th

	wins	2nd	3rd	4th	5th	6th	PP	FL	points
Int F3000 Ch	3	1	4	2	-	-	5	4	55

Championships: 1990 8th, 1991 10th, 1992 2nd. **Race wins:** 1992 Barcelona, Spa, Albacete

Other major race wins: 1992 Buenos Aires F3000

ROBIN MONTGOMERIE-CHARRINGTON
USA. Born: 22.6.1915, London (GB)

World Championship Grand Prix Record

year	starts	wins	2nd	3rd	4th	5th	6th	PP	FL	points
1952	1	-	-	-	-	-	-	-	-	-

Best result: no finishes. **Best qualifying:** 15th

LOU MOORE
USA. Born: 12.9.1904, Hinton, Oklahoma. Died: 25.3.1956
Indycar Championship. Race wins: 1931 Altoona Race 1, Syracuse

ROCKY MORAN
USA. Born: 3.2.1950, Pasadena, California
Major race wins: 1993 Daytona 24 hrs

GIUSEPPE MORANDI
I. Born: 1894. Died: 1.11.1977
Major race wins: 1927 Mille Miglia

GIANNI MORBIDELLI
I. Born: 13.1.1968, Pesaro
1989 European F3 Cup winner; 1989 Italian F3 Champion

World Championship Grand Prix Record

year	starts	wins	2nd	3rd	4th	5th	6th	PP	FL	points
1990–92; 1994	50(2)	-	-	-	-	1	2	-	-	3.5

Best championship: 1994 22nd. **Best qualifying:** 6th

	wins	2nd	3rd	4th	5th	6th	PP	FL	points
Int F3000 Ch	1	-	2	1	-	1	-	-	20

Championship: 1990 7th. **Race wins:** 1990 Mediterranean GP (Enna)

ANDRÉ MOREL
F
Pre-1950 Grands Prix. Race wins: 1925 San Sebastian GP

ROBERTO MORENO
BR. Born: 11.2.1959, Rio de Janeiro
1988 FIA F3000 Champion; 1982 New Zealand International Champion

World Championship Grand Prix Record

years	starts	wins	2nd	3rd	4th	5th	6th	PP	FL	points
1982; 1987; 1989–92	25(34)	-	1	-	2	1	1	-	1	15

Best championship: 1991 10th. **Best qualifying:** 5th

	wins	2nd	3rd	4th	5th	6th	PP	FL	points
European F2 Ch	2	3	2	-	-	-	3	2	44

Championship: 1982 2nd. **Race wins:** 1984 Jim Clark Trophy (Hockenheim), Donington Park

	wins	2nd	3rd	4th	5th	6th	PP	FL	points
Int F3000 Ch	5	1	3	2	4	1	7	4	76

Championships: 1985 14th, 1987 3rd, 1988 1st. **Race wins:** 1987 Mediterranean GP (Enna), 1988 Pau GP, International Trophy (Silverstone), Monza, Birmingham

European F3 Championship. Race wins: 1981 Silverstone

Other major race wins: 1982 Macau GP, 1981, 1983 and 1984 Australian GP

LUIGI MORESCHI
I
World Sports Car Championship. Race wins: 1977 Vallelunga

DAVE MORGAN
GB. Born: 7.8.1944, Shepton Mallet, Somerset

World Championship Grand Prix Record

year	starts	wins	2nd	3rd	4th	5th	6th	PP	FL	points
1975	1	-	-	-	-	-	-	-	-	-

Best result: no finishes. **Best qualifying:** 23rd

	wins	2nd	3rd	4th	5th	6th	PP	FL	points
European F2 Ch	1	-	1	3	1	1	-	-	31

Championships: 1972 6th, 1973 12th. **Race wins:** 1972 Mallory Park

HEINRICH-JOACHIM VON MORGEN
D. Born: n/a. Died: 28.5.1932, Nürburgring, Eifelrennen practice
Pre-1950 Grands Prix. Race wins: 1930 Masaryk GP

AKIO MORIMOTO
J. Born: 24.9.1960, Hyogo
1986 Japanese F3 Champion

BOB MORRIS
AUS. Born: 4.10.1948
1979 Australian Touring Car Champion
Major race wins: 1976 Bathurst

JOHN MORTON
USA. Born: 17.2.1942
Major race wins: 1994 Sebring 12 hrs

SILVIO MOSER
CH. Born: 24.4.1941, Zurich. Died: 26.5.1974, Monza 1000 kms
1964 Temporada F2 Champion

World Championship Grand Prix Record

years	starts	wins	2nd	3rd	4th	5th	6th	PP	FL	points
1966–71	12(8)	-	-	-	-	1	1	-	-	3

Best championship: 1969 16th. **Best qualifying:** 13th

	wins	2nd	3rd	4th	5th	6th	PP	FL	points
European F2 Ch	-	-	-	1	-	1	-	-	7

Championships: 1968 15th, 1971 18th, 1973 29th

MIKE MOSLEY
USA. Born: 13.12.1944. Died: 3.3.1984
Indycar Championship. Race wins: 1971 Trenton Race 1, 1974 Phoenix, 1975 Milwaukee, 1976 Milwaukee, 1981 Milwaukee 150

BILL MOSS
GB
1961 John Davy British F3 (Formula Junior) Champion

World Championship Grand Prix Record

year	starts	wins	2nd	3rd	4th	5th	6th	PP	FL	points
1959	-(1)	-	-	-	-	-	-	-	-	-

Best qualifying: no time set

STIRLING MOSS
GB. Born: 17.9.1929, West Kensington
1959 British F2 Champion

World Championship Grand Prix Record

year	starts	wins	2nd	3rd	4th	5th	6th	PP	FL	points
1951–61	66(1)	16	5	3	3	2	1	16	19	186.64

Race wins: 1955 British GP, 1956 Monaco GP, Italian GP, 1957 British GP (with Brooks), Pescara GP, Italian GP, 1958 Argentinian GP, Dutch GP, Portuguese GP, Moroccan GP, 1959 Portuguese GP, Italian GP, 1960 Monaco GP, United States GP, 1961 Monaco GP, German GP. **Best qualifying:** 1st

World Sports Car Championship. Race wins: 1954 Sebring 12 hrs, 1955 Mille Miglia, Tourist Trophy, Targa Florio, 1956 Buenos Aires, Nürburgring, 1957 Swedish GP, 1958 Nürburgring, Tourist Trophy, 1959 Nürburgring, Tourist Trophy, 1960 Nürburgring

Other major race wins: 1950, 1951, 1955, 1958, 1959, 1960 and 1961 Tourist Trophy, 1956 and 1961 International Trophy (Silverstone), Australian GP

Stirling Moss
....

BRIAN MUIR
AUS. Born: n/a. Died: 11.9.1983

Major race wins: 1970 Tourist Trophy

RALPH MULFORD
USA. Born: 1885. Died: 23.10.1974

1911 and 1918 Indycar Champion

Indycar Championship. Race wins: 1910 Elgin Race 3, 1911 Philadelphia Race 2, Vanderbilt Cup, 1912 Brighton Beach, 1913 Columbus, 1914 Galveston Race 1, Galveston Race 2, Galveston Race 3, Galesburg, 1915 Des Moines, 1917 Omaha, Providence Race 1, Chicago Race 5, 1918 Uniontown Race 2, Uniontown Race 5, Uniontown Race 7, 1919 Sheepshead Race 2

BARRY MULHOLLAND
AUS

Major race wins: 1968 Bathurst

JIM MULLEN
USA

Major race wins: 1983 Sebring 12 hrs

HERBERT MÜLLER
CH. Born: 11.5.1940, Reinach. Died: 24.5.1981, Nürburgring

World Sports Car Championship. Race wins: 1966 Targa Florio, 1973 Targa Florio

HERMANN MÜLLER
D. Born: 1909. Died: 30.12.1975, Ingolstadt

1939 European Grand Prix Champion (see page 195)

Pre-1950 Grands Prix. Race wins: 1939 French GP

JORG MÜLLER
D. Born: 3.9.1969

Major race wins: 1991 Monaco F3 GP, 1993 Macau GP

SIEGFRIED "SIGI" MÜLLER
D. Father of Sigi Müller Jr

1975 European Touring Car Champion (shared with Alain Peltier)

SIEGFRIED "SIGI" MÜLLER JR
D. Son of Sigi Müller

1980 European Touring Car Champion (shared with Helmut Kelleners)

YVAN MÜLLER
F. Born: 16.8.1968

1992 British F2 Champion

	wins	2nd	3rd	4th	5th	6th	PP	FL	points
Int F3000 Ch Championship: 1993 17th	-	-	-	1	-	-	-	-	2

SANDRO MUNARI
I. Born: 27.3.1940, Cavarzere, Venice

World Sports Car Championship. Race wins: 1972 Targa Florio

GINO MUNARON
I. Born: 2.4.1928, Turin

World Championship Grand Prix Record

year	starts	wins	2nd	3rd	4th	5th	6th	PP	FL	points
1960	4	-	-	-	-	-	-	-	-	-

Best result: 13th. Best qualifying: 8th

KEN MURILLO
USA

1988 SCCA Super Vee Champion

GREG MURPHY
NZ

Major race wins: 1994 New Zealand GP

JIMMY MURPHY
USA. Born: 1894, San Francisco. Died: 15.9.1924, Syracuse

1922 and 1924 Indycar Champion

Pre-1950 Grands Prix. Race wins: 1921 French GP

Indycar Championship. Race wins: 1920 Beverly Hills Race 1, Beverly Hills Race 3, Fresno, 1921 Beverly Hills Race 3, Beverly Hills Race 9, Beverly Hills Race 10, San Carlos, 1922 Beverly Hills Race 4, Fresno Race 1, Cotati Race 2, Indianapolis 500, Uniontown, Tacoma, Beverly Hills Race 7, 1923 Beverly Hills Race 1, Fresno Race 1, 1924 Altoona Race 1, Kansas City, Altoona Race 2

LES MURPHY
AUS

Major race wins: 1935 and 1937 Australian GP

BILL MURRAY
AUS

Major race wins: 1947 Australian GP

DAVID MURRAY
GB. Born: 28.12.1909, Edinburgh. Died: 5.4.1973, Las Palmas, Canary Islands (E)

World Championship Grand Prix Record

years	starts	wins	2nd	3rd	4th	5th	6th	PP	FL	points
1950–52	4(1)	-	-	-	-	-	-	-	-	-

Best result: no finishes. Best qualifying: 15th

LUIGI MUSSO
I. Born: 29.7.1924, Rome. Died: 6.7.1958, Reims, French GP

World Championship Grand Prix Record

years	starts	wins	2nd	3rd	4th	5th	6th	PP	FL	points
1953–58	24(1)	1	5	1	1	1	-	-	1	44

Best championship: 1957 3rd. Race wins: 1956 Argentinian GP (with Fangio). Best qualifying: 2nd

World Sports Car Championship. Race wins: 1957 Buenos Aires, 1958 Targa Florio

N
....

BERND NACKE
D. Born: 21.12.1921. Died: 1980

World Championship Grand Prix Record

year	starts	wins	2nd	3rd	4th	5th	6th	PP	FL	points
1952	1	-	-	-	-	-	-	-	-	-

Best result: no finishes. Best qualifying: no time set

GIANCARLO NADDEO
I

1971 Italian F3 Champion

NAOKI NAGASAKA
J. Born: 24.4.1953

1984 Japanese Sports Car Champion; 1985 (with Kazuo Mogi) and 1987 Japanese Touring Car Champion

SATORU NAKAJIMA
J. Born: 23.2.1953, Okazaki

1981, 1982, 1984, 1985 and 1986 Japanese F2 Champion

World Championship Grand Prix Record

years	starts	wins	2nd	3rd	4th	5th	6th	PP	FL	points
1987–91	74(6)	-	-	-	2	2	6	-	1	16

Best championship: 1987 11th. Best qualifying: 6th

	wins	2nd	3rd	4th	5th	6th	PP	FL	points
European F2 Ch Championship: 1982 13th	-	1	-	-	-	-	-	-	6
Int F3000 Ch Championship: 1986 10th	-	-	-	1	2	-	-	-	7

OSAMI NAKAKO
J. Born: 20.8.1954

1981 Japanese F3 Champion

KENGO NAKAMOTO
J
1982 Japanese F3 Champion

AKIHIKO NAKAYA
J. Born: 3.11.1957
1988 Japanese F3 Champion

ALESSANDRO NANNINI
I. Born: 7.7.1959, Siena

World Championship Grand Prix Record

years	starts	wins	2nd	3rd	4th	5th	6th	PP	FL	points
1986–90	76(2)	1	2	6	4	2	4	-	2	65

Best championship: 1989 6th. Race wins: 1989 Japanese GP.
Best qualifying: 3rd

		wins	2nd	3rd	4th	5th	6th	PP	FL	points
European F2 Ch	-	2	1	2	3	-	2	1		28

Championship: 1982 10th, 1983 7th, 1984 9th
World Sports Car Championship. Race wins: 1984 Kyalami

JOHN NAPIER
GB
Major race wins: 1905 Tourist Trophy

MAURIZIO DE NARVAEZ
CO. Born: 18.5.1941
Major race wins: 1984 Sebring 12 hrs

ESTEFANO NASIF
see 'Nasif Estefano'

EMANUELE NASPETTI
I. Born: 24.2.1968, Ancona
1988 Italian F3 Champion

World Championship Grand Prix Record

years	starts	wins	2nd	3rd	4th	5th	6th	PP	FL	points
1992–93	6	-	-	-	-	-	-	-	-	-

Best result: 11th. Best qualifying: 21st

		wins	2nd	3rd	4th	5th	6th	PP	FL	points
Int F3000 Ch	5	1	-	1	1	3	2	4		59

Championships: 1989 17th, 1990 22nd, 1991 3rd, 1992 6th. **Race wins:** 1991 Mediterranean GP (Enna), Hockenheim, Brands Hatch, Spa, 1992 Pau GP

MASSIMO NATILI
I. Born: 28.7.1935, Ronciglione, Viterbo

World Championship Grand Prix Record

year	starts	wins	2nd	3rd	4th	5th	6th	PP	FL	points
1961	1	-	-	-	-	-	-	-	-	-

Best result: no finishes. Best qualifying: 28th

GIUSEPPE NAVONE
I
Major race wins: 1948 Mille Miglia

BRIAN NAYLOR
GB. Born: 24.3.1923, Salford. Died: 8.8.1989, Marbella (E)

World Championship Grand Prix Record

years	starts	wins	2nd	3rd	4th	5th	6th	PP	FL	points
1957–61	7(1)	-	-	-	-	-	-	-	-	-

Best result: 13th. Best qualifying: 7th

MIKE NAZARUK
USA. Born: 2.10.1921, Newark, New Jersey. Died: 1.5.1955, Langhorne
Indycar Championship. Race wins: 1952 Milwaukee Race 1

FELICE NAZZARO
I. Born: 1880, Turin. Died: 21.3.1940, Turin
Pre-1950 Grands Prix. Race wins: 1907 French GP, 1922 French GP
Other major race wins: 1907 and 1913 Targa Florio, 1907 Kaiserpreis

PIERO NECCHI
I

		wins	2nd	3rd	4th	5th	6th	PP	FL	points
European F2 Ch	-	1	3	1	1	-	-	1		23

Championships: 1978 6th, 1981 11th

TIFF NEEDELL
GB. Born: 29.10.1951, Havant

World Championship Grand Prix Record

year	starts	wins	2nd	3rd	4th	5th	6th	PP	FL	points
1980	1(1)	-	-	-	-	-	-	-	-	-

Best result: no finishes. Best qualifying: 23rd

JOCHEN NEERPASCH
D. Born: 1939, Krefeld
World Sports Car Championship. Race wins: 1968 Daytona 24 hrs

HARALD NEGER
A
Major race wins: 1980 Tourist Trophy

OSVALDO NEGRI JR
BR. Born: 29.5.1964
1990 Brazilian F3 Champion

JAC NELLEMAN
DK

World Championship Grand Prix Record

year	starts	wins	2nd	3rd	4th	5th	6th	PP	FL	points
1976	-(1)	-	-	-	-	-	-	-	-	-

Best qualifying: 27th

AFFONSO GIAFFONE NETO
BR
1991 Sud-Am F3 Champion

PATRICK NEVE
B. Born: 13.10.1949, Brussels

World Championship Grand Prix Record

years	starts	wins	2nd	3rd	4th	5th	6th	PP	FL	points
1976–77	10(3)	-	-	-	-	-	-	-	-	-

Best result: 7th. Best qualifying: 19th

		wins	2nd	3rd	4th	5th	6th	PP	FL	points
European F2 Ch	-	-	1	-	-	-	-	1		4

Championships: 1977 14th

CHUCK NICHOLSON
GB
Major race wins: 1981 and 1982 Tourist Trophy

JOHN NICHOLSON
NZ. Born: 6.10.1941, Auckland

World Championship Grand Prix Record

years	starts	wins	2nd	3rd	4th	5th	6th	PP	FL	points
1974–75	1(1)	-	-	-	-	-	-	-	-	-

Best result: 17th. Best qualifying: 26th

HELMUT NIEDERMAYR
D. Born: 29.11.1915. Died: 3.4.1985

World Championship Grand Prix Record

year	starts	wins	2nd	3rd	4th	5th	6th	PP	FL	points
1952	1	-	-	-	-	-	-	-	-	-

Best result: no finishes. Best qualifying: no time set

JOHN NIELSEN
DK. Born: 7.2.1956, Varde
1982 German F3 Champion

		wins	2nd	3rd	4th	5th	6th	PP	FL	points
Int F3000 Ch	1	5	2	1	1	3	2	1		51

Championships: 1985 4th, 1986 6th. **Race wins:** 1985 Estoril
World Sports Car Championship. Race wins: 1987 Brands Hatch, 1988 Brands Hatch, 1990 Le Mans 24 hrs
European F3 Championship. Race wins: 1983 Magny-Cours, Monza, Zandvoort, Knutstorp, 1984 Zolder, Nogaro
Other major race wins: 1984 Macau GP, 1985 Curacao GP, 1988 Daytona 24 hrs

BRAUSCH NIEMANN
ZA. Born: 7.1.1939, Durban

World Championship Grand Prix Record

years	starts	wins	2nd	3rd	4th	5th	6th	PP	FL	points
1963; 1965	1(1)	-	-	-	-	-	-	-	-	-

Best result: 14th. Best qualifying: 15th

KEES NIEROP
CDN. Born: 16.3.1958
Major race wins: 1983 Sebring 12 hrs

JOE NIKRENT
USA
Indycar Championship. Race wins:
1909 Los Angeles-Phoenix

LOUIS NIKRENT
USA
Indycar Championship. Race wins:
1911 Santa Monica Race 3

GUNNAR NILSSON
S. Born: 20.11.1948, Helsingborg. Died: 20.10.1978, Charring Cross Hospital, London, cancer
1975 British F3 Champion

World Championship Grand Prix Record

years	starts	wins	2nd	3rd	4th	5th	6th	PP	FL	points
1976–77	31(1)	1	-	3	1	3	1	-	1	31

Best championship: 1977 8th. **Race wins:** 1977 Belgian GP. **Best qualifying:** 3rd

	wins	2nd	3rd	4th	5th	6th	PP	FL	points
European F2 Ch	-	-	1	-	-	-	-	-	6

Championship: 1973 13th
World Sports Car Championship. Race wins: 1976 Österreichring

JAN NILSSON
S
1989 Swedish F3 Champion

KRIS NISSEN
DK. Born: 20.7.1960, Arnum
1992 Nordic Touring Car Champion; 1986 German F3 Champion

PETER NÖCKER
D
1963 European Touring Car Champion

HIDEKI NODA
J. Born: 7.3.1969, Osaka

World Championship Grand Prix Record

year	starts	wins	2nd	3rd	4th	5th	6th	PP	FL	points
1994	3	-	-	-	-	-	-	-	-	-

Best result: no finishes. **Best qualifying:** 23rd

	wins	2nd	3rd	4th	5th	6th	PP	FL	points
Int F3000 Ch	-	-	1	-	1	-	-	-	6

Championship: 1994 9th

RODNEY NUCKEY
GB. Born: 26.6.1929, London

World Championship Grand Prix Record

year	starts	wins	2nd	3rd	4th	5th	6th	PP	FL	points
1953	1	-	-	-	-	-	-	-	-	-

Best result: 11th. **Best qualifying:** 20th

TAZIO NUVOLARI
I. Born: 16.11.1892, Casteldario, near Mantua. Died: 11.8.1953, Mantua
Pre-1950 Grands Prix. Race wins: 1931 Italian GP, 1932 Monaco GP, Italian GP, French GP, 1933 Belgian GP, 1935 German GP, 1936 Hungarian GP, 1938 Italian GP, Donington GP, 1939 Yugoslavian GP
Major Sports Car races. Race wins: 1933 Le Mans 24 hrs
Indycar Championship. Race wins: 1936 Vanderbilt Cup
Other major race wins: 1928 Tripoli GP, 1930 and 1933 Tourist Trophy, 1930 and 1933 Mille Miglia, 1931 and 1932 Targa Florio

O

ROBERT O'BRIEN
USA

World Championship Grand Prix Record

year	starts	wins	2nd	3rd	4th	5th	6th	PP	FL	points
1952	1	-	-	-	-	-	-	-	-	-

Best result: 14th. **Best qualifying:** 22nd

Gunnar Nilsson
....

JOHNNY O'CONNELL
USA. Born: 24.7.1962
1987 North American (Western Division) Formula Atlantic Champion
Major race wins: 1994 Sebring 12 hrs

PAT O'CONNOR
USA. Born: 9.10.1928, North Vernon, Indiana. Died: 30.5.1958, Indianapolis
Indycar Championship. Race wins: 1956 Darlington, 1957 Trenton

EDDIE O'DONNELL
USA. Died: 25.11.1920, Beverley Hills, racing
Indycar Championship. Race wins: 1915 Glendale, Ascot, Galesburg

ERIC OFFENSTADT
F

	wins	2nd	3rd	4th	5th	6th	PP	FL	points
European F2 Ch	-	-	-	1	-	-	-	2

Championship: 1968 17th

HITOSHI OGAWA
J. Born: 15.2.1956, Tokyo. Died: 24.5.1992, Suzuka F3000 race
1989 Japanese F3000 Champion
World Sports Car Championship. Race wins: 1992 Monza

HIDEKI OKADA
J. Born: 28.11.1958, Tokyo
1988 Japanese Sports Car Champion (with Stanley Dickens)

BARNEY OLDFIELD
USA. Born: 3.6.1878, Monticello, Toledo, Ohio. Died: 4.10.1946
Indycar Championship. Race wins: 1915 Venice, Tucson

JACKIE OLIVER
GB. Born: 14.8.1942, Chaswell Heath, Romford
1974 Can-Am Champion

World Championship Grand Prix Record

years	starts	wins	2nd	3rd	4th	5th	6th	PP	FL	points
1967–73; 1977	50(2)	-	-	2	-	2	1	-	1	13

Best championship: 1968 13th. **Best qualifying:** 2nd

	wins	2nd	3rd	4th	5th	6th	PP	FL	points
European F2 Ch	-	-	-	3	1	1	-	-	17

Championships: 1967 14th, 1968 5th
World Sports Car Championship. Race wins: 1969 Sebring 12 hrs, Le Mans 24 hrs, 1971 Daytona 24 hrs, Monza, Spa, 1976 Mosport Park
Other major race wins: 1967 German GP F2 Class

ANDERS OLOFSSON
S. Born: 31.3.1952
1990 Japanese Sports Car Champion (with Masahiro Hasemi); 1989 and 1991 Japanese Touring Car Champion (with Masahiro Hasemi); 1977 and 1978 Swedish F3 Champion
European F3 Championship. Race wins: 1977 Zandvoort, Österreichring, Knutstorp, 1978 Nürburgring, Österreichring, Knutstorp, Kassel-Calden
Other major race wins: 1991 Spa 24 hrs

DANNY ONGAIS
USA. Born: 21.5.1942, Hawaii

World Championship Grand Prix Record

years	starts	wins	2nd	3rd	4th	5th	6th	PP	FL	points
1977–78	4(2)	-	-	-	-	-	-	-	-	-

Best result: 7th. **Best qualifying:** 21st
World Sports Car Championship. Race wins: 1979 Daytona 24 hrs
Indycar Championship. Race wins: 1977 Michigan, 1978 Ontario, Texas, Mosport Park, Milwaukee, Michigan

CARLO ONGARO
I
Major race wins: 1936 Mille Miglia

ROHAN ONSLOW
AUS
1988 and 1989 Australian Gold Star Champion

RIKKY VON OPEL
FL. Born: 14.10.1947, New York (USA)
1972 Lombard British F3 Champion

World Championship Grand Prix Record

years	starts	wins	2nd	3rd	4th	5th	6th	PP	FL	points
1973–74	10(4)	-	-	-	-	-	-	-	-	-

Best result: 9th. Best qualifying: 14th

KARL OPPITZHAUSER
A

World Championship Grand Prix Record

year	starts	wins	2nd	3rd	4th	5th	6th	PP	FL	points
1976	-(1)	-	-	-	-	-	-	-	-	-

Best qualifying: not allowed to practice

FRITZ D'OREY
BR. Born: 25.3.1938. Died: 1961

World Championship Grand Prix Record

year	starts	wins	2nd	3rd	4th	5th	6th	PP	FL	points
1959	3	-	-	-	-	-	-	-	-	-

Best result: 10th. Best qualifying: 17th

MARKUS ÖSTREICH
D. Born: 3.7.1963, Fulda
Major race wins: 1990 Spa 24 hrs

ARTHUR OWEN
GB. Born: 23.3.1915, London

World Championship Grand Prix Record

year	starts	wins	2nd	3rd	4th	5th	6th	PP	FL	points
1960	1	-	-	-	-	-	-	-	-	-

Best result: no finishes. Best qualifying: 11th

DAVE OXTON
NZ
1981 New Zealand International Champion

P

GIANANTONIO PACCHIONI
I. Born: 23.12.1969
Major race wins: 1993 Monaco F3 GP

CARLOS PACE
BR. Born: 6.10.1944, Sao Paulo. Died: 18.3.1977, Mairipora, aircraft accident
1970 Forward Trust British F3 Champion

World Championship Grand Prix Record

years	starts	wins	2nd	3rd	4th	5th	6th	PP	FL	points
1972–77	72(1)	1	3	2	5	3	2	1	5	58

Best championship: 1975 6th. Race wins: 1975 Brazilian GP.
Best qualifying: 1st

	wins	2nd	3rd	4th	5th	6th	PP	FL	points
European F2 Ch	-	1	-	1	-	-	1	1	7

Championships: 1971 20th, 1972 15th

JIM PACKARD
USA
Indycar Championship. Race wins: 1960 Springfield

NELLO PAGANI
I. Born: 11.10.1911, Milan

World Championship Grand Prix Record

year	starts	wins	2nd	3rd	4th	5th	6th	PP	FL	points
1950	1	-	-	-	-	-	-	-	-	-

Best result: 7th. Best qualifying: 15th

CARLOS PALAU
E
1992 Spanish Touring Car Champion

RICARDO PALETTI
I. Born: 16.5.1958, Milan. Died: 13.6.1982, Montréal, Canadian GP

World Championship Grand Prix Record

year	starts	wins	2nd	3rd	4th	5th	6th	PP	FL	points
1982	2(6)	-	-	-	-	-	-	-	-	-

Best result: no finishes. Best qualifying: 13th

	wins	2nd	3rd	4th	5th	6th	PP	FL	points
European F2 Ch	-	2	-	-	-	1	-	1	13

Championship: 1981 8th

TORSTEN PALM
S. Born: 23.7.1947, Kristinehamn
1970 and 1971 Swedish F3 Champion

World Championship Grand Prix Record

year	starts	wins	2nd	3rd	4th	5th	6th	PP	FL	points
1975	1(1)	-	-	-	-	-	-	-	-	-

Best result: 10th. Best qualifying: 21st

	wins	2nd	3rd	4th	5th	6th	PP	FL	points
European F2 Ch	-	-	1	-	-	1	-	1	6

Championships: 1973 21st, 1974 16th

JOSÉ LUIS DI PALMA
RA. Born: 31.3.1966
1994 British F2 Champion

RALPH DE PALMA
USA. Born: 1883, Troia, Foggia (I). Died: 31.3.1956
1912 and 1914 Indycar Champion

Indycar Championship. Race wins: 1909 Riverhead Race 1, 1912 Santa Monica Race 2, Elgin Race 3, Elgin Race 4, Milwaukee Race 1, 1913 Elgin Race 1, 1914 Santa Monica Race 1, Elgin Race 1, Elgin Race 2, 1915 Indianapolis 500, Kalamazoo, 1916 Des Moines, Minneapolis, 1917 Chicago Race 2, 1918 Chicago Race 1, Chicago Race 2, Sheepshead Race 1, Sheepshead Race 2, Sheepshead Race 3, 1919 Sheepshead Race 3, 1920 Elgin, 1921 Beverly Hills Race 1, Beverly Hills Race 5, Beverly Hills Race 6

JONATHAN PALMER
GB. Born: 7.11.1956, London
1983 European F2 Champion; 1981 British F3 Champion

World Championship Grand Prix Record

years	starts	wins	2nd	3rd	4th	5th	6th	PP	FL	points
1983–89	83(5)	-	-	-	1	4	3	-	1	14

Best championship: 1987 11th. Best qualifying: 9th

	wins	2nd	3rd	4th	5th	6th	PP	FL	points
European F2 Ch	6	1	4	1	2	2	5	3	85

Championships: 1982 9th, 1983 1st. Race wins: 1983 Jim Clark Trophy (Hockenheim), Donington Park, Misano, Mediterranean GP (Enna), Zolder, Mugello

World Sports Car Championship. Race wins: 1984 Brands Hatch, 1987 Norisring 200 miles

"PAM"
I
1969 European Touring Car 1000 cc Class Champion

MARVIN PANCH
USA
Major race wins: 1961 Daytona 500; 1966 World 600

OLIVIER PANIS
F. Born: 2.9.1966, Lyon
1993 International F3000 Champion

World Championship Grand Prix Record

year	starts	wins	2nd	3rd	4th	5th	6th	PP	FL	points
1994	16	-	1	-	-	1	1	-	-	9

Best championship: 1994 11th. Best qualifying: 6th

	wins	2nd	3rd	4th	5th	6th	PP	FL	points
Int F3000 Ch	3	1	2	-	-	1	-	2	42

Championships: 1992 10th, 1993 1st. Race wins: 1993 Hockenheim, Nürburgring, Spa

JEAN-PIERRE PAOLI
F. Born: 3.5.1940

	wins	2nd	3rd	4th	5th	6th	PP	FL	points
European F2 Ch	-	1	-	-	-	-	2	-	6

Championship: 1974 11th

PETER DE PAOLO
USA. Born: 1898. Died: 26.11.1980
1925 and 1927 Indycar Champion

Indycar Championship. Race wins: 1925 Fresno, Indianapolis

500, Altoona Race 1, Laurel Race 1, Salem, 1926 Miami, Salem Race 1, 1927 Altoona Race 1, Salem Race 1, Charlotte Race 2

MASSIMILIANO PAPIS
I. Born: 3.10.1969

	wins	2nd	3rd	4th	5th	6th	PP	FL	points
Int F3000 Ch	1	-	-	2	1	2	1	-	19

Championships: 1993 10th, 1994 13th. **Race wins:** 1994 Barcelona

GUIDO PARDINI
I

1980 Italian F3 Champion

JESUS PAREJA
E. Born: 6.3.1955, Madrid

World Sports Car Championship. Race wins: 1986 Jerez

DON PARKER
GB. Born: 11.11.1908, Ramsgate

1952, 1953 and 1959 (Formula Junior) British F3 Champion

MICHAEL PARKES
GB. Born: 24.9.1931, Richmond. Died: 28.8.1977, road accident near Turin (I)

World Championship Grand Prix Record

year	starts	wins	2nd	3rd	4th	5th	6th	PP	FL	points
1959; 1966–67	6(1)	-	2	-	-	1	-	1	-	14

Best championship: 1966 8th. **Best qualifying:** 1st

World Sports Car Championship. Race wins: 1964 Sebring 12 hrs, 1965 Monza, 1966 Monza, Spa

Other major race wins: 1967 International Trophy (Silverstone)

REG PARNELL
GB. Born: 2.7.1911, Derby. Died: 7.1.1964, Derby, after a medical operation

World Championship Grand Prix Record

years	starts	wins	2nd	3rd	4th	5th	6th	PP	FL	points
1950–52; 1954	6(1)	-	-	1	1	-	-	-	9

Best championship: 1950 9th. **Best qualifying:** 4th

Major race wins: 1951 International Trophy (Silverstone)

TIM PARNELL
GB. Born: 25.6.1932, Derby

World Championship Grand Prix Record

years	starts	wins	2nd	3rd	4th	5th	6th	PP	FL	points
1959; 1961; 1963	2(2)	-	-	-	-	-	-	-	-	-

Best result: 10th. **Best qualifying:** 25th

BENNY PARSONS
USA

1973 NASCAR Champion

Major race wins: 1975 Daytona 500, 1980 World 600

CHUCK PARSONS
USA. Born: 6.2.1924, Bruin, Kentucky

World Sports Car Championship. Race wins: 1969 Daytona 24 hrs

DAVID PARSONS
AUS

Major race wins: 1987 Bathurst

JOHNNIE PARSONS
USA. Born: 4.7.1918, Los Angeles. Died: 8.9.1984, Van Nuys, California. Father of Johnny Jr

1949 Indycar Champion

Indycar Championship. Race wins: 1948 Du Quoin, 1949 Dallas, Milwaukee Race 2, Syracuse, Springfield Race 2, Langhorne, 1950 Indianapolis 500, Darlington, 1951 Phoenix, Bay Meadows, 1952 Phoenix

JIM PASCHAL
USA. Born: 12.5.1926, High Point, North Carolina

Major race wins: 1964 and 1967 World 600

ARTHUR PATEMAN
GB

Major race wins: 1957 Macau GP

RICCARDO PATRESE
I. Born: 17.4.1954, Padua

1976 European F3 Champion; 1976 Italian F3 Champion

World Championship Grand Prix Record

years	starts	wins	2nd	3rd	4th	5th	6th	PP	FL	points
1977–93	256(1)	6	17	14	8	15	13	8	15	281

Best championship: 1992 2nd. **Race wins:** 1982 Monaco GP, 1983 South African GP, 1990 San Marino GP, 1991 Mexican GP, Portuguese GP, 1992 Japanese GP. **Best qualifying:** 1st

	wins	2nd	3rd	4th	5th	6th	PP	FL	points
European F2 Ch	-	3	2	-	1	2	2	2	32

Championship: 1977 4th

World Sports Car Championship. Race wins: 1980 Brands Hatch, Mugello, Watkins Glen, 1981 Watkins Glen, 1982 Silverstone, Nürburgring, 1984 Kyalami, 1985 Spa

European F3 Championship. Race wins: 1976 Zandvoort, Enna, Monza Lottery GP, Kassel-Calden

Other major race wins: 1977 and 1978 Macau GP

CYRUS PATSCHKE
USA

Indycar Championship. Race wins: 1911 Indianapolis 500 (with Ray Harroun)

BILL PATTERSON
AUS

1961 Australian Gold Star Champion

Major race wins: 1957 Australian GP

JOHN PAUL
USA. Father of John Jr

1979 Trans-Am Class 2 Champion

Major race wins: 1982 Daytona 24 hrs, Sebring 12 hrs

JOHN PAUL JR
USA. Born: 19.2.1960, Muncie, Indiana. Son of John Sr

1982 IMSA GT Champion

Indycar Championship. Race wins: 1983 Michigan 500

Other major race wins: 1982 Daytona 24 hrs, Sebring 12 hrs

LUCIANO PAVESI
I

1975 Italian F3 Champion

	wins	2nd	3rd	4th	5th	6th	PP	FL	points
European F2 Ch	-	-	-	-	-	1	-	-	1

Championship: 1977 20th

DAVID PEARSON
USA. Born: 22.12.1934, Woodruff, South Carolina

1966, 1968 and 1969 NASCAR Champion

Major race wins: 1961, 1974 and 1976 World 600, 1976 Daytona 500

AL PEASE
CDN. Born: 15.10.1921

World Championship Grand Prix Record

years	starts	wins	2nd	3rd	4th	5th	6th	PP	FL	points
1967–69	2(1)	-	-	-	-	-	-	-	-	-

Best result: no finishes. **Best qualifying:** 16th

David Pearson

OSCAR PEDERSOLI
I. Born: 3.4.1951

	wins	2nd	3rd	4th	5th	6th	PP	FL	points
European F2 Ch	-	-	-	-	1	2	-	-	4

Championships: 1979 21st, 1980 14th

European F3 Championship. Race wins: 1977 Enna, Vallelunga

"PEDRO"
B

Major race wins: 1967 Spa 24 hrs

PEDRINI
I

Major race wins: 1912 Targa Florio

ALAIN PELTIER
B
1975 European Touring Car Champion (shared with Sigi Muller)
Major race wins: 1974 Spa 24 hrs

ROGER PENSKE
USA. Born: 20.2.1937, Shaker Heights, Ohio

World Championship Grand Prix Record

years	starts	wins	2nd	3rd	4th	5th	6th	PP	FL	points
1961–62	2	-	-	-	-	-	-	-	-	-

Best result: 8th. Best qualifying: 13th

WIN PERCY
GB. Born: 28.9.1943, Tolpuddle, Dorset
1980, 1981 and 1982 British Touring Car Champion
Major race wins: 1984 and 1989 Spa 24 hrs, 1985 Tourist Trophy, 1990 Bathurst

CESARE PERDISA
I. Born: 21.10.1932, Bologna

World Championship Grand Prix Record

years	starts	wins	2nd	3rd	4th	5th	6th	PP	FL	points
1955–57	7(1)	-	-	2	-	1	1	-	-	5

Best championship: 1956 15th. Best qualifying: 6th
World Sports Car Championship. Race wins: 1957 Buenos Aires

LARRY PERKINS
AUS. Born: 18.3.1950, Murrayville. Brother of Terry
1975 European F3 Champion

World Championship Grand Prix Record

years	starts	wins	2nd	3rd	4th	5th	6th	PP	FL	points
1974; 1976–77	11(4)	-	-	-	-	-	-	-	-	-

Best result: 8th. Best qualifying: 13th
European F3 Championship. Race wins: 1975 Monza Lottery GP
Other major race wins: 1982, 1983, 1984 and 1993 Bathurst

TERRY PERKINS
AUS. Brother of Larry
European F3 Championship. Race wins: 1975 Danish GP

XAVIER PERROT
CH. Born: 1.2.1932, Zurich

World Championship Grand Prix Record

year	starts	wins	2nd	3rd	4th	5th	6th	PP	FL	points
1969	1	-	-	-	-	-	-	-	-	-

Best result: no finishes. Best qualifying: no time set

	wins	2nd	3rd	4th	5th	6th	PP	FL	points
European F2 Ch	-	-	-	1	1	1	-	-	11

Championships: 1969 13th, 1972 13th

HENRI PESCAROLO
F. Born: 25.9.1942, Montfermeil, Ile de France
1967 French F3 Champion

World Championship Grand Prix Record

years	starts	wins	2nd	3rd	4th	5th	6th	PP	FL	points
1968–76	57(8)	-	-	1	1	3	-	1	12

Best championship: 1970 12th. Best qualifying: 5th

	wins	2nd	3rd	4th	5th	6th	PP	FL	points
European F2 Ch	2	4	2	3	3	-	3	1	50

Championships: 1968 2nd, 1969 4th, 1970 10th. Race wins: 1972 Mediterranean GP (Enna), 1973 Jochen Rindt Trophy (Thruxton)
World Sports Car Championship. Race wins: 1971 Brands Hatch, 1972 Le Mans 24 hrs, 1973 Vallelunga, Dijon, Le Mans 24 hrs, Österreichring, Kyalami, 1975 Spa, Österreichring, Watkins Glen, 1978 Dijon, Misano, Vallelunga, 1980 Dijon, 1982 Monza, 1984 Le Mans 24 hrs, 1986 Nürburgring
Other major race wins: 1967 Monaco F3 GP, 1969 German GP F2 Class, 1970 Buenos Aires 1000 kms, 1991 Daytona 24 hrs

CHRISTIAN PESCATORI
I. Born: 1.12.1971, Brescia
1993 Italian F3 Champion

	wins	2nd	3rd	4th	5th	6th	PP	FL	points
Int F3000 Ch	-	-	-	-	1	-	1	-	1

Championship: 1994 17th

ALESSANDRO PESENTI-ROSSI
I. Born: 31.8.1942, Bergamo

World Championship Grand Prix Record

year	starts	wins	2nd	3rd	4th	5th	6th	PP	FL	points
1976	3(1)	-	-	-	-	-	-	-	-	-

Best result: 11th. Best qualifying: 21st

	wins	2nd	3rd	4th	5th	6th	PP	FL	points
European F2 Ch	-	1	-	5	2	2	-	1	30

Championships: 1974 16th, 1975 9th, 1976 15th, 1977 9th

JOSEF PETERS
D. Born: 16.9.1914, Dusseldorf

World Championship Grand Prix Record

year	starts	wins	2nd	3rd	4th	5th	6th	PP	FL	points
1952	1	-	-	-	-	-	-	-	-	-

Best result: no finishes. Best qualifying: no time set

RONNIE PETERSON
S. Born: 14.2.1944, Orebro. Died: 11.9.1978, Milan, following Italian GP accident
1971 European F2 Champion; 1968 and 1969 Swedish F3 Champion

World Championship Grand Prix Record

years	starts	wins	2nd	3rd	4th	5th	6th	PP	FL	points
1970–78	123	10	10	6	5	7	4	14	9	206

Best championship: 1978 2nd. Race wins: 1973 French GP, Austrian GP, Italian GP, United States GP, 1974 Monaco GP, French GP, Italian GP, 1976 Italian GP, 1978 South African GP, Austrian GP. Best qualifying: 1st

	wins	2nd	3rd	4th	5th	6th	PP	FL	points
European F2 Ch	6	1	4	1	2	2	9	7	68

Championships: 1970 4th, 1971 1st. Race wins: 1971 Rouen GP, Mantorp Park, Tulln, Rome GP (Vallelunga), 1972 Jochen Rindt Trophy (Thruxton), 1974 Karlskoga
World Sports Car Championship. Race wins: 1971 Watkins Glen, 1972 Buenos Aires, Nürburgring
Other major race wins: 1969 Monaco F3 GP

KELLY PETILLO
USA. Born: 1902, Huntington Park, California. Died: 30.6.1970
1935 Indycar Champion
Indycar Championship. Race wins: 1934 Los Angeles, 1935 Indianapolis 500, St Paul, Langhorne

PIERRE PETIT
F. Born: 27.9.1957
1982 French F3 Champion

	wins	2nd	3rd	4th	5th	6th	PP	FL	points
European F2 Ch	-	-	1	1	1	-	-	-	10

Championship: 1984 9th

KYLE PETTY
USA. Born: 2.6.1960, Randlemann, North Carolina. Son of Richard
Major race wins: 1987 World 600

LEE PETTY
USA. Born: 14.3.1914, Randleman, North Carolina. Father of Richard
1954, 1958 and 1959 NASCAR Champion

RICHARD PETTY
USA. Born: 2.7.1937, Level Cross, North Carolina. Father of Kyle
1964, 1967, 1971, 1972, 1974, 1975 and 1979 NASCAR Champion
Major race wins: 1973, 1979 and 1981 Daytona 500

Richard Petty

ALFREDO PIAN
RA

World Championship Grand Prix Record

year	starts	wins	2nd	3rd	4th	5th	6th	PP	FL	points
1950	-(1)	-	-	-	-	-	-	-	-	-

Best qualifying: no time set

PAOLO DELLE PIANE
I. Born: 1.5.1964, Bologna

	wins	2nd	3rd	4th	5th	6th	PP	FL	points
Int F3000 Ch	-	-	-	-	1	-	-	-	2

Championship: 1993 17th

FRANÇOIS PICARD
F. Born: 26.4.1921, Villefranche-sur-Saone

World Championship Grand Prix Record

year	starts	wins	2nd	3rd	4th	5th	6th	PP	FL	points
1958	1	-	-	-	-	-	-	-	-	-

Best result: no finishes. Best qualifying: no time set

GIANLUIGI PICCHI
I

1971 European Touring Car 1300 cc Class Champion; 1969 Italian F3 Champion

GREG PICKETT
USA

1978 Trans-Am Class 2 Champion

ROY PIERPOINT
GB

1965 British Touring Car Champion

ERNEST PIETERSE
ZA. Born: 4.7.1938, Parons-Bellville

1962 South African Drivers Champion

World Championship Grand Prix Record

years	starts	wins	2nd	3rd	4th	5th	6th	PP	FL	points
1962–63; 1965	2(1)	-	-	-	-	-	-	-	-	-

Best result: 10th. Best qualifying: 12th

PAUL PIETSCH
D. Born: 20.6.1911, Neustandt

World Championship Grand Prix Record

years	starts	wins	2nd	3rd	4th	5th	6th	PP	FL	points
1950–52	3	-	-	-	-	-	-	-	-	-

Best result: no finishes. Best qualifying: 7th

ANDRÉ PILETTE
B. Born: 6.10.1918, Paris (F). Died: 27.12.1993. Father of Teddy, son of Theodore

World Championship Grand Prix Record

years	starts	wins	2nd	3rd	4th	5th	6th	PP	FL	points
1951; 1953–54; 1956; 1961; 1963–64	9(5)	-	-	-	-	1	3	-	-	2

Best championship: 1954 18th. Best qualifying: 8th

TEDDY PILETTE
B. Born: 26.7.1942, Brussels. Son of André

1973 and 1975 British F5000 Champion

World Championship Grand Prix Record

years	starts	wins	2nd	3rd	4th	5th	6th	PP	FL	points
1974; 1977	1(3)	-	-	-	-	-	-	-	-	-

Best result: 17th. Best qualifying: 27th

Tasman Cup. Race wins: 1974 Surfers' Paradise

Other major race wins: 1978 Spa 24 hrs

ED PIMM
USA. Born: 3.5.1956

1983 SCCA Super Vee Champion

CARLO MARIA PINTACUDA
I. Born: n/a. Died: 1972, Milan

Major race wins: 1935 and 1937 Mille Miglia, 1938 Spa 24 hrs

LUIGI PIOTTI
I. Born: 27.10.1913. Died: 19.4.1971

World Championship Grand Prix Record

year	starts	wins	2nd	3rd	4th	5th	6th	PP	FL	points
1955–58	6(3)	-	-	-	-	-	1	-	-	-

Best qualifying: 12th.

DAVID PIPER
GB. Born: 2.12.1930, Edgware

World Championship Grand Prix Record

year	starts	wins	2nd	3rd	4th	5th	6th	PP	FL	points
1959–60	2(1)	-	-	-	-	-	-	-	-	-

Best result: 12th. Best qualifying: 21st

NELSON PIQUET
BR. Born: 17.8.1952, Rio de Janeiro

1981, 1983 and 1987 World Champion; 1978 BP British F3 Champion

World Championship Grand Prix Record

years	starts	wins	2nd	3rd	4th	5th	6th	PP	FL	points
1978–91	204(3)	23	20	17	18	15	7	24	23	485.5

Race wins: 1980 Long Beach GP, Dutch GP, Italian GP, 1981 Argentinian GP, San Marino GP, German GP, 1982 Canadian GP, 1983 Brazilian GP, Italian GP, European GP, 1984 Canadian GP, Detroit GP, 1985 French GP, 1986 Brazilian GP, German GP, Hungarian GP, Italian GP, 1987 German GP, Hungarian GP, Italian GP, 1990 Japanese GP, Australian GP, 1991 Canadian GP. Best qualifying: 1st

World Sports Car Championship. Race wins: 1981 Nürburgring

European F3 Championship. Race wins: 1977 Kassel-Calden, Jarama

Nelson Piquet

RENATO PIROCCHI
I. Born: 26.3.1933, Notaresco, Teramo

World Championship Grand Prix Record

year	starts	wins	2nd	3rd	4th	5th	6th	PP	FL	points
1961	1	-	-	-	-	-	-	-	-	-

Best result: 12th. Best qualifying: 29th

DIDIER PIRONI
F. Born: 26.3.1952, Villecresnes, Paris. Died: 23.8.1987, Isle of Wight (GB), powerboat accident

World Championship Grand Prix Record

year	starts	wins	2nd	3rd	4th	5th	6th	PP	FL	points
1978–82	70(2)	3	3	7	3	6	7	4	5	101

Best championship: 1982 2nd. Race wins: 1980 Belgian GP, 1982 San Marino GP, Dutch GP. Best qualifying: 1st

	wins	2nd	3rd	4th	5th	6th	PP	FL	points
European F2 Ch	1	2	2	2	-	1	1	38

Championship: 1977 3rd. Race wins: 1977 Estoril

World Sports Car Championship. Race wins: 1978 Le Mans 24 hrs

Other major race wins: 1977 Monaco F3 GP

EMANUELE PIRRO
I. Born: 12.1.1962, Rome

1994 Italian Touring Car Champion

World Championship Grand Prix Record

years	starts	wins	2nd	3rd	4th	5th	6th	PP	FL	points
1989–91	37(3)	-	-	-	-	1	1	-	-	3

Best championship: 1991 18th. Best qualifying: 7th

	wins	2nd	3rd	4th	5th	6th	PP	FL	points
European F2 Ch	-	1	-	3	-	3	-	-	18

Championship: 1984 6th

Int F3000 Ch	3	5	1	2	1	1	4	3	67

Championships: 1985 3rd, 1986 3rd. Race wins: 1985 Jochen Rindt Trophy (Thruxton), Rome GP (Vallelunga), 1986 Le Mans

European F3 Championship. Race wins: 1981 Mugello, 1982 Österreichring, Silverstone, Kassel-Calden, 1983 Vallelunga, Zolder

JACK PITCHER
GB

1960 BRSCC British F3 (Formula Junior) Champion

BILL PITT
AUS

1961 Australian Touring Car Champion

ERIC VAN DE POELE
B. Born: 30.9.1961, Verviers

1987 German Touring Car Champion

World Championship Grand Prix Record

year	starts	wins	2nd	3rd	4th	5th	6th	PP	FL	points
1991–92	5(24)	-	-	-	-	-	-	-	-	-

Best result: 9th. Best qualifying: 15th

	wins	2nd	3rd	4th	5th	6th	PP	FL	points
Int F3000 Ch	3	1	1	2	2	2	-	-	49

Championships: 1989 5th, 1990 2nd. **Race wins:** 1990 Pau GP, Birmingham, Nogaro GP

Other major race wins: 1987 Spa 24 hrs

JÉROME POLICAND
CH. Born: 1.10.1964, Geneva

	wins	2nd	3rd	4th	5th	6th	PP	FL	points
Int F3000 Ch	-	-	1	-	1	1	-	-	5

Championships: 1992 17th, 1993 11th, 1994 16th

ART POLLARD
USA. Born: 5.5.1927. Died: 12.5.1973, Indianapolis 500, practice

Indycar Championship. Race wins: 1969 Milwaukee Race 1, Dover Downs

JACQUES POLLET
F. Born: 2.7.1932

World Championship Grand Prix Record

years	starts	wins	2nd	3rd	4th	5th	6th	PP	FL	points
1954–55	5	-	-	-	-	-	-	-	-	-

Best result: 7th. **Best qualifying:** 12th

JOHN POLLOCK
GB

	wins	2nd	3rd	4th	5th	6th	PP	FL	points
European F2 Ch	-	-	-	-	-	1	-	-	1

Championship: 1969 19th

BEN PON
NL. Born: 9.12.1936, Leiden

World Championship Grand Prix Record

year	starts	wins	2nd	3rd	4th	5th	6th	PP	FL	points
1962	1	-	-	-	-	-	-	-	-	-

Best result: no finishes. **Best qualifying:** 18th

ALEC POOLE
GB

1969 British Touring Car Champion

ALBERT POON
HK

Major race wins: 1964 Macau GP

DENNIS POORE
GB. Born: 19.8.1916, London. Died: 12.2.1987, London

World Championship Grand Prix Record

year	starts	wins	2nd	3rd	4th	5th	6th	PP	FL	points
1952	2	-	-	-	1	-	-	-	-	3

Best championship: 1952 13th. **Best qualifying:** 8th

ALFONSO DE PORTAGO
E. Born: 11.10.1928, London (GB). Died: 12.5.1957, Mille Miglia

World Championship Grand Prix Record

years	starts	wins	2nd	3rd	4th	5th	6th	PP	FL	points
1956–57	5	-	1	-	-	1	-	-	-	4

Best championship: 1956 15th. **Best qualifying:** 9th

SAM POSEY
USA. Born: 26.5.1944, New York

World Championship Grand Prix Record

years	starts	wins	2nd	3rd	4th	5th	6th	PP	FL	points
1971–72	2	-	-	-	-	-	-	-	-	-

Best result: 12th. **Best qualifying:** 18th

Major race wins: 1975 Sebring 12 hrs

CHARLES POZZI
F. Born: 27.8.1909, Paris

World Championship Grand Prix Record

year	starts	wins	2nd	3rd	4th	5th	6th	PP	FL	points
1950	1	-	-	-	-	1	-	-	-	-

Best qualifying: 16th

Pre-1950 Grands Prix. Race wins: 1949 French GP

TED PRAPPAS
USA. Born: 14.11.1955, Santa Monica, California

1986 North American (Western Division) Formula Atlantic Champion

WARWICK PRATLEY
AUS

Major race wins: 1951 Australian GP

FRANK PRATT
AUS

Major race wins: 1948 Australian GP

JACKIE PRETORIUS
ZA. Born: 22.11.1934, Potchefstroom

World Championship Grand Prix Record

years	starts	wins	2nd	3rd	4th	5th	6th	PP	FL	points
1965; 1968; 1971; 1973	3(1)	-	-	-	-	-	-	-	-	-

Best result: no finishes. **Best qualifying:** 20th

ERNESTO PRINOTH
I

World Championship Grand Prix Record

year	starts	wins	2nd	3rd	4th	5th	6th	PP	FL	points
1962	-(1)	-	-	-	-	-	-	-	-	-

Best qualifying: 27th

DAVID PROPHET
GB. Born: 9.10.1937, Hong Kong. Died: 29.3.1981, Silverstone

World Championship Grand Prix Record

year	starts	wins	2nd	3rd	4th	5th	6th	PP	FL	points
1963; 1965	2	-	-	-	-	-	-	-	-	-

Best result: 14th. **Best qualifying:** 14th

ALAIN PROST
F. Born: 24.2.1955, St Chamond

1985, 1986, 1989 and 1993 World Champion; 1979 European F3 Champion; 1978 (with Jean-Louis Schlesser) and 1979 French F3 Champion

World Championship Grand Prix Record

years	starts	wins	2nd	3rd	4th	5th	6th	PP	FL	points
1980–91; 1993	199(3)	51	35	20	10	5	7	33	41	798.5

Race wins: 1981 French GP, Dutch GP, Italian GP, 1982 South African GP, Brazilian GP, 1983 French GP, Belgian GP, British GP, Austrian GP, 1984 Brazilian GP, San Marino GP, Monaco GP, German GP, Dutch GP, European GP, Portuguese GP, 1985 Brazilian GP, Monaco GP, British GP, Austrian GP, Italian GP, 1986 San Marino GP, Monaco GP, Austrian GP, Australian GP, 1987 Brazilian GP, Belgian GP, Portuguese GP, 1988 Brazilian GP, Monaco GP, Mexican GP, French GP, Portuguese GP, Spanish GP, Australian GP, 1989 United States GP, French GP, British GP, Italian GP, 1990 Brazilian GP, Mexican GP, French GP, British GP, Spanish GP, 1993 South African GP, San Marino GP, Spanish GP, Canadian GP, French GP, British GP, German GP.
Best qualifying: 1st

Alain Prost

European F3 Championship. Race wins: 1978 Jarama, 1979 Österreichring, Zolder, Magny-Cours, Zandvoort, Knutstorp, Jarama

Other major race wins: 1979 Monaco F3 GP, 1982 Australian GP

STÉPHANE PROULX
CDN. Born: 12.12.1965, Quebec. Died: 21.11.1993, Ste Adele, Quebec,

	wins	2nd	3rd	4th	5th	6th	PP	FL	points
Int F3000 Ch	-	-	-	-	1	-	-	1	2

Championship: 1989 17th

SCOTT PRUETT
USA. Born: 24.3.1960, Sacramento, California

1987 and 1994 Trans-Am Champion

Major race wins: 1994 Daytona 24 hrs

TOM PRYCE
GB. Born: 11.6.1949, Ruthin, Denbighshire. Died: 5.3.1977, Kyalami, South African GP

World Championship Grand Prix Record

years	starts	wins	2nd	3rd	4th	5th	6th	PP	FL	points
1974–77	42	-	-	2	3	-	4	1	-	19

Drivers A–Z

Best championship: 1975 10th. **Best qualifying:** 1st

	wins	2nd	3rd	4th	5th	6th	PP	FL	points
European F2 Ch	-	1	1	1	2	-	1	1	20

Championships: 1973 10th, 1974 9th
Major race wins: 1974 Monaco F3 GP, 1975 Race of Champions

ANTONIO PUCCI
I. Born: 1923, Palermo
World Sports Car Championship. Race wins: 1964 Targa Florio

EDDIE PULLEN
USA
Pre-1950 Grands Prix. Race wins: 1914 American GP
Indycar Championship. Race wins: 1912 Tacoma Race 1, 1914 American GP, Corona, 1915 Tacoma Race 2, 1921 Beverly Hills Race 7

DAVID PURLEY
GB. Born: 26.1.1945, Bognor Regis. Died: 2.7.1985, Bognor Regis, aircraft accident
1976 British F5000 Champion
World Championship Grand Prix Record

years	starts	wins	2nd	3rd	4th	5th	6th	PP	FL	points
1973–74; 1977	7(4)	-	-	-	-	-	-	-	-	-

Best result: 9th. **Best qualifying:** 16th

	wins	2nd	3rd	4th	5th	6th	PP	FL	points
European F2 Ch	-	2	1	-	-	-	-	-	17

Championships: 1972 19th, 1974 5th

CLIVE PUZEY
ZA
World Championship Grand Prix Record

year	starts	wins	2nd	3rd	4th	5th	6th	PP	FL	points
1965	-(1)	-	-	-	-	-	-	-	-	-

Best qualifying: no time set

Q

DIETER QUESTER
A. Born: 30.5.1939, Vienna
1968 and 1969 European Touring Car over 1600 cc Class Champion; 1977 and 1983 European Touring Car Champion
World Championship Grand Prix Record

years	starts	wins	2nd	3rd	4th	5th	6th	PP	FL	points
1969; 1974	1(1)	-	-	-	-	-	-	-	-	-

Best result: 9th. **Best qualifying:** 25th

	wins	2nd	3rd	4th	5th	6th	PP	FL	points
European F2 Ch	1	4	1	-	1	-	-	3	45

Championships: 1970 4th, 1971 3rd. **Race wins:** 1970 Hockenheim
World Sports Car Championship. Race wins: 1976 Nürburgring, Österreichring
Other major race wins: 1970 Macau GP, 1973 Spa 24 hrs, 1977 Tourist Trophy, 1986 Spa 24 hrs, 1988 Spa 24 hrs

R

IAN RABY
GB. Born: 22.9.1921, London. Died: 7.11.1967, London after an accident in the Zandvoort F2 race
World Championship Grand Prix Record

years	starts	wins	2nd	3rd	4th	5th	6th	PP	FL	points
1963–65	3(4)	-	-	-	-	-	-	-	-	-

Best result: 11th. **Best qualifying:** 17th

	wins	2nd	3rd	4th	5th	6th	PP	FL	points
European F2 Ch	-	-	-	1	-	-	-	7

1967 12th

PAUL RADISICH
NZ. Born: 9.10.1962, Auckland
1993 and 1994 Touring Car World Cup winner; 1988 New Zealand International Champion

JEAN RAGNOTTI
F. Born: 29.8.1945, Carpentras
1988 French Supertourism Champion

BOBBY RAHAL
USA. Born: 10.1.1953, Medina, Ohio
1986, 1987 and 1992 Indycar Champion
World Championship Grand Prix Record

year	starts	wins	2nd	3rd	4th	5th	6th	PP	FL	points
1978	2	-	-	-	-	-	-	-	-	-

Best result: 12th. **Best qualifying:** 20th

	wins	2nd	3rd	4th	5th	6th	PP	FL	points
European F2 Ch	-	-	2	1	2	-	-	10

Championship: 1979 11th
World Sports Car Championship. Race wins: 1981 Daytona 24 hrs
Indycar Championship. Race wins: 1982 Cleveland, Michigan, 1983 Riverside, 1984 Phoenix, Monterey GP (Laguna Seca), 1985 Mid-Ohio, Michigan, Monterey GP (Laguna Seca), 1986 Indianapolis 500, Toronto, Mid-Ohio, Sanair, Michigan, Monterey GP (Laguna Seca), 1987 Portland, Meadowlands, Monterey GP (Laguna Seca), 1988 Pocono 500, 1989 Meadowlands, 1991 Meadowlands, 1992 Phoenix, Detroit GP, New Hampshire, Nazareth

Bobby Rahal

Other major race wins: 1987 Sebring 12 hrs, Marlboro Challenge

GIULIO RAMPONI
I
Major race wins: 1928 and 1929 Mille Miglia

PIERRE-HENRI RAPHANEL
F. Born: 27.5.1961, Algiers (DZ)
1985 French F3 Champion
World Championship Grand Prix Record

years	starts	wins	2nd	3rd	4th	5th	6th	PP	FL	points
1988–89	1(16)	-	-	-	-	-	-	-	-	-

Best result: no finishes. **Best qualifying:** 18th

	wins	2nd	3rd	4th	5th	6th	PP	FL	points
Int F3000 Ch	-	-	3	1	3	1	-	20

Championships: 1986 12th, 1987 13th, 1988 13th
Major race wins: 1985 Monaco F3 GP

JIM RATHMANN
USA. Born: 16.7.1928, Valparaiso, Indiana
World Championship Grand Prix Record. Race wins: 1960 Indianapolis 500
Indycar Championship. Race wins: 1957 Milwaukee Race 2, 1959 Daytona, 1960 Indianapolis 500

ROLAND RATZENBERGER
A. Born: 4.7.1962, Salzburg. Died: 30.4.1994, Imola, San Marino GP qualifying

Dieter Quester

World Championship Grand Prix Record

year	starts	wins	2nd	3rd	4th	5th	6th	PP	FL	points
1994	1(2)	-	-	-	-	-	-	-	-	-

Best result: 11th. **Best qualifying:** 26th
Major race wins: 1987 Nürburgring EFDA F3

ROBERTO RAVAGLIA
I. Born: 26.5.1957, Mestre
1987 World Touring Car Champion; 1986 and 1988 European Touring Car Champion; 1989 German Touring Car Champion; 1990, 1991 and 1993 Italian Touring Car Champion
European F3 Championship. Race wins: 1983 La Châtre
Other major race wins: 1985, 1988 and 1994 Spa 24 hrs

HECTOR REBAQUE
MEX. Born: 5.2.1956, Mexico City
World Championship Grand Prix Record

years	starts	wins	2nd	3rd	4th	5th	6th	PP	FL	points
1977–81	41(17)	-	-	-	3	1	2	-	-	13

Best championship: 1981 11th. **Best qualifying:** 6th

	wins	2nd	3rd	4th	5th	6th	PP	FL	points
European F2 Ch	-	-	-	1	-	-	-	-	3

Championship: 1975 22nd

Indycar Championship. Race wins: 1982 Elkhart Lake

MARTIN REDFERN
HK

Major race wins: 1960 Macau GP

BRIAN REDMAN
GB. Born: 9.3.1937, Burnley

1981 IMSA GT Champion; 1974, 1975 and 1976 North American F5000 Champion

World Championship Grand Prix Record

years	starts	wins	2nd	3rd	4th	5th	6th	PP	FL	points
1967–68; 1970–74	12(4)	-	-	1	-	2	-	-	-	8

Best championship: 1972 12th. Best qualifying: 10th

	wins	2nd	3rd	4th	5th	6th	PP	FL	points
European F2 Ch	-	1	-	1	-	1	-	-	18

Championships: 1967 9th, 1968 9th

World Sports Car Championship. Race wins: 1968 Brands Hatch, Spa, 1969 Brands Hatch, Monza, Spa, Nürburgring, Watkins Glen, 1970 Targa Florio, Spa, Österreichring, 1972 Spa, Österreichring, 1973 Monza, Nürburgring, 1980 Mosport Park, 1981 Daytona 24 hrs

Other major race wins: 1975 Long Beach GP, 1976 Daytona 24 hrs, 1978 and 1975 Sebring 12 hrs

Brian Redman

ALAN REES
GB. Born: 12.1.1938, Newport, Monmouthshire

1967 Autocar British F2 Champion

World Championship Grand Prix Record

years	starts	wins	2nd	3rd	4th	5th	6th	PP	FL	points
1966–67	3	-	-	-	-	-	-	-	-	-

Best result: 9th. Best qualifying: 15th

	wins	2nd	3rd	4th	5th	6th	PP	FL	points
European F2 Ch	-	1	1	-	1	1	-	-	24

Championships: 1967 5th, 1968 22nd

GARETH REES
GB. Born: 12.3.1969

1992 GM-Lotus Euroseries Champion

Major race wins: 1994 Marlboro Masters of F3

GIANCLAUDIO "CLAY" REGAZZONI
CH. Born: 5.9.1939, Lugano

1970 European F2 Champion

World Championship Grand Prix Record

years	starts	wins	2nd	3rd	4th	5th	6th	PP	FL	points
1970–80	132(4)	5	13	10	8	9	7	5	15	212

Best championship: 1974 2nd. Race wins: 1970 Italian GP, 1974 German GP, 1975 Italian GP, 1976 Long Beach GP, 1979 British GP. Best qualifying: 1st

	wins	2nd	3rd	4th	5th	6th	PP	FL	points
European F2 Ch	3	2	1	2	1	4	1		62

Championships: 1968 6th, 1969 10th, 1970 1st. Race wins: 1970 Hockenheim, Mediterranean GP (Enna), Imola

World Sports Car Championship. Race wins: 1972 Monza

Other major race wins: 1971 Race of Champions, 1975 Swiss GP

ANTHONY REID
GB. Born: 21.6.1959

1992 Japanese F3 Champion

TOMMY REID
IRL

	wins	2nd	3rd	4th	5th	6th	PP	FL	points
European F2 Ch	-	-	-	-	-	-	-	-	1

Championship: 1970 18th

DARIO RESTA
I. Born: 1884, Milan. Died: 3.9.1924, Brooklands (GB)

1916 Indycar Champion

Pre-1950 Grands Prix. Race wins: 1915 American GP

Indycar Championship. Race wins: 1915 San Francisco Race 1, Chicago Race 1, Chicago Race 2, Sheepshead Race 2, American GP, 1916 Indianapolis 500, Chicago Race 1, Omaha, Chicago Race 2, Vanderbilt Cup

RAFFAELE RESTIVO
I

Major race wins: 1977 Targa Florio

CARLOS REUTEMANN
RA. Born: 12.4.1942, Santa Fé

World Championship Grand Prix Record

years	starts	wins	2nd	3rd	4th	5th	6th	PP	FL	points
1972–82	146	12	13	20	11	3	7	6	5	310

Best championship: 1981 2nd. Race wins: 1974 South African GP, Austrian GP, United States GP, 1975 German GP, 1977 Brazilian GP, 1978 Brazilian GP, Long Beach GP, British GP, United States GP, 1980 Monaco GP, 1981 Brazilian GP, Belgian GP. Best qualifying: 1st

	wins	2nd	3rd	4th	5th	6th	PP	FL	points
European F2 Ch	-	1	9	-	2	3	2	1	67

Championship: 1970 13th, 1971 2nd, 1972 4th

Other major race wins: 1972 Brazilian GP, 1981 South African GP

MANUEL REUTER
D. Born: 6.12.1961, Mainz

World Sports Car Championship. Race wins: 1989 Le Mans 24 hrs

LANCE REVENTLOW
USA. Born: 24.2.1936, London (GB). Died: 24.7.1972, Colorado, aircraft accident

World Championship Grand Prix Record

year	starts	wins	2nd	3rd	4th	5th	6th	PP	FL	points
1960	1(3)	-	-	-	-	-	-	-	-	-

Best result: no finishes. Best qualifying: 16th

PETER REVSON
USA. Born: 27.2.1939, New York. Died: 22.3.1974, Kyalami, testing

1971 Can-Am Champion

World Championship Grand Prix Record

years	starts	wins	2nd	3rd	4th	5th	6th	PP	FL	points
1964; 1971–74	30(2)	2	2	4	3	3	-	1	-	61

Best championship: 1973 5th, 38 pts. Race wins: 1973 British GP, Canadian GP. Best qualifying: 1st

Indycar Championship. Race wins: 1969 Indianapolis Raceway Park Race 2

Other major race wins: 1965 Monaco F3 GP

BILL REXFORD
USA

1950 NASCAR Champion

GEORGE REYNOLDS
AUS

Major race wins: 1964 Bathurst

JOHN RHODES
GB. Born: 18.8.1927, Wolverhampton

1968 European Touring Car 1600 cc Class Champion

World Championship Grand Prix Record

year	starts	wins	2nd	3rd	4th	5th	6th	PP	FL	points
1965	1	-	-	-	-	-	-	-	-	-

Best result: no finishes. Best qualifying: 21st

ALEX RIBEIRO
BR. Born: 7.11.1948, Belo Horizonte

World Championship Grand Prix Record

years	starts	wins	2nd	3rd	4th	5th	6th	PP	FL	points
1976–77; 1979	10(10)	-	-	-	-	-	-	-	-	-

Best result: 8th. Best qualifying: 17th

	wins	2nd	3rd	4th	5th	6th	PP	FL	points
European F2 Ch	1	2	3	1	2	2	1		46

Championships: 1976 5th, 1977 14th, 1978 8th

JIM RICHARDS
NZ. Born: 2.9.1947

1985, 1987, 1990 and 1991 Australian Touring Car Champion

Major race wins: 1978, 1979, 1980, 1991 and 1992 Bathurst

KEN RICHARDSON
GB

World Championship Grand Prix Record

year	starts	wins	2nd	3rd	4th	5th	6th	PP	FL	points
1951		-(1)	-	-	-	-	-	-	-	-

Best qualifying: 10th

EDDIE RICKENBACHER
USA. Born: 8.10.1890. Died: 23.7.1973, Zurich (CH)

Indycar Championship. Race wins: 1914 Sioux City, 1915 Sioux City, Omaha, Providence, 1916 Sheepshead Race 1, Tacoma, Ascot

KURT RIEDER
A

	wins	2nd	3rd	4th	5th	6th	PP	FL	points
European F2 Ch		-	-	-	-	-	-	-	1

Championship: 1973 31st

FRITZ RIESS
D. Born: 11.7.1922, Nuremburg

World Championship Grand Prix Record

year	starts	wins	2nd	3rd	4th	5th	6th	PP	FL	points
1952			1							

Best result: 7th. Best qualifying: no time set

Major Sports Car races. Race wins: 1952 Le Mans 24 hrs

LOUIS RIGAL
F

Major race wins: 1926 Spa 24 hrs

BRETT RILEY
NZ. Born: 30.7.1953

European F3 Championship. Race wins: 1977 Donington Park, 1979 Donington Park

JOCHEN RINDT
A. Born: 18.4.1942, Mainz (D). Died: 5.9.1970, Monza, Italian GP practice
1970 World Champion; 1967 British F2 Champion; 1967 French F2 Champion

Jochen Rindt

World Championship Grand Prix Record

years	starts	wins	2nd	3rd	4th	5th	6th	PP	FL	points
1964–70	60(2)	6	3	4	6	1	1	10	3	109

Race wins: 1969 United States GP, 1970 Monaco GP, Dutch GP, French GP, British GP, German GP. **Best qualifying:** 1st

	wins	2nd	3rd	4th	5th	6th	PP	FL	points
European F2 Ch	12	1	-	-	-	-	8	11	-

Race wins: 1967 Snetterton, Silverstone, Nürburgring, Brands Hatch, 1968 Thruxton, Crystal Palace, Tulln, Mediterranean GP (Enna), 1969 Thruxton, Tulln, 1970 Thruxton

World Sports Car Championship. Race wins: 1965 Le Mans 24 hrs

Tasman Cup. Race wins: 1969 Lady Wigram Trophy, Warwick Farm

Other major race wins: 1965 Austrian GP

JOHN RISELEY-PRICHARD
GB. Born: 17.1.1924, Hereford

World Championship Grand Prix Record

year	starts	wins	2nd	3rd	4th	5th	6th	PP	FL	points
1954	1	-	-	-	-	-	-	-	-	-

Best result: no finishes. Best qualifying: 21st

ROBERT RITCHIE
HK

Major race wins: 1955 Macau GP

GIOVANNI DE RIU
I

World Championship Grand Prix Record

year	starts	wins	2nd	3rd	4th	5th	6th	PP	FL	points
1954		-(1)	-	-	-	-	-	-	-	-

Best qualifying: 21st

RICHARD ROBARTS
GB. Born: 22.9.1944, Steeple, Essex

World Championship Grand Prix Record

year	starts	wins	2nd	3rd	4th	5th	6th	PP	FL	points
1974	3(1)	-	-	-	-	-	-	-	-	-

Best result: 15th. Best qualifying: 22nd

"FIREBALL" ROBERTS
USA. Born: 20.1.1931, Daytona Beach. Died: 24.5.1964

Major race wins: 1962 Daytona 500

FLOYD ROBERTS
USA. Born: 1901. Died: 30.5.1939, Indianapolis
1938 Indycar Champion

Indycar Championship. Race wins: 1938 Indianapolis 500

MORTIMER ROBERTS
USA

Indycar Championship. Race wins: 1912 Milwaukee Race 3

TONY ROBERTS
AUS

Major race wins: 1969 Bathurst

BRIAN ROBERTSON
CDN
1972 North American Formula Atlantic Champion

GEORGE ROBERTSON
USA. Born: 1884, New York. Died: 3.7.1955
1909 Indycar Champion

Indycar Championship. Race wins: 1909 Lowell Race 4, Philadelphia

STEVE ROBERTSON
GB. Born: 4.7.1965, London
1994 Indy Lights Champion

BRIAN ROBINSON
GB

	wins	2nd	3rd	4th	5th	6th	PP	FL	points
European F2 Ch		-	-	-	-	1	-	1	1

Championship: 1981 19th

CHIP ROBINSON
USA. Born: 29.3.1954
1987 IMSA GT Champion

Major race wins: 1987 Daytona 24 hrs

PHILIP ROBINSON
GB

	wins	2nd	3rd	4th	5th	6th	PP	FL	points
European F2 Ch		-	-	-	-	-	-	-	2

Championship: 1967 15th

GEORGE ROBSON
USA. Born: n/a. Died: 2.9.1946, Atlanta

Indycar Championship. Race wins: 1946 Indianapolis 500

GIOVANNI ROCCO
I

Major race wins: 1938 Targa Florio

ALBERTO RODRIGUEZ LARRETA
RA. Born: 14.1.1934, Buenos Aires. Died: 11.3.1977

World Championship Grand Prix Record

year	starts	wins	2nd	3rd	4th	5th	6th	PP	FL	points
1960		1	-	-	-	-	-	-	-	-

Best result: 9th. Best qualifying: 15th

PEDRO RODRIGUEZ
MEX. Born: 18.1.1940, Mexico City. Died: 11.7.1971, Norisring Sports Car race. Brother of Ricardo

World Championship Grand Prix Record

years	starts	wins	2nd	3rd	4th	5th	6th	PP	FL	points
1963–71	55	2	3	2	4	4	7	-	1	71

Best championship: 1968 6th, 18 pts. **Race wins:** 1967 South African GP, 1970 Belgian GP. **Best qualifying:** 2nd

World Sports Car Championship. Race wins: 1965 Reims, 1968 Le Mans 24 hrs, 1970 Daytona 24 hrs, Brands Hatch, Monza, Watkins Glen, 1971 Daytona 24 hrs, Monza, Spa, Österreichring

Other major race wins: 1963 and 1964 Canadian GP

RICARDO RODRIGUEZ

MEX. Born: 14.2.1942, Mexico City. Died: 2.11.1962, Mexico City, Mexican GP practice. Brother of Pedro

World Championship Grand Prix Record

years	starts	wins	2nd	3rd	4th	5th	6th	PP	FL	points
1961–62	5(1)	-	-	-	1	-	1	-	-	4

Best championship: 1962 12th. **Best qualifying:** 2nd

World Sports Car Championship. Race wins: 1962 Targa Florio

MICHAEL ROE

IRL. Born: 8.8.1955

1984 Can-Am Champion

AL ROGERS

USA

Indycar Championship. Race wins: 1948, 1949, 1950 and 1951 Pikes Peak

WALTER ROHRL

D. Born: 7.3.1947, Regensburg

World Sports Car Championship. Race wins: 1980 Brands Hatch, 1981 Silverstone

FRANCO ROL

I. Born: 5.6.1908. Died: 18.6.1977

World Championship Grand Prix Record

years	starts	wins	2nd	3rd	4th	5th	6th	PP	FL	points
1950–52	5	-	-	-	-	-	-	-	-	-

Best result: 9th. **Best qualifying:** 7th

ALFONSO ROLFO

I

Major race wins: 1952 Mille Miglia

ALAN ROLLINSON

GB. Born: 15.5.1943, Walsall

World Championship Grand Prix Record

year	starts	wins	2nd	3rd	4th	5th	6th	PP	FL	points
1965	-(1)	-	-	-	-	-	-	-	-	-

Best qualifying: 23rd

	wins	2nd	3rd	4th	5th	6th	PP	FL	points
European F2 Ch	-	-	-	-	1	-	-	5

Championship: 1967 17th, 1969 11th

Tasman Cup. Race wins: 1973 Teretonga

CHARLES ROLLS

GB

Major race wins: 1906 Tourist Trophy

TONY ROLT

GB. Born: 16.10.1918, Bordon, Hampshire

World Championship Grand Prix Record

years	starts	wins	2nd	3rd	4th	5th	6th	PP	FL	points
1950; 1953; 1955	3	-	-	-	-	-	-	-	-	-

Best result: no finishes. **Best qualifying:** 10th

World Sports Car Championship. Race wins: 1953 Le Mans 24 hrs

EMILIO ROMANO

I

Major race wins: 1947 Mille Miglia

JEAN RONDEAU

F

World Sports Car Championship. Race wins: 1980 Le Mans 24 hr

BERTIL ROOS

S. Born: 12.10.1943, Gothenburg

1973 SCCA Super Vee Champion

World Championship Grand Prix Record

year	starts	wins	2nd	3rd	4th	5th	6th	PP	FL	points
1974	1	-	-	-	-	-	-	-	-	-

Best result: no finishes. **Best qualifying:** 23rd

	wins	2nd	3rd	4th	5th	6th	PP	FL	points
European F2 Ch	-	-	-	-	1	-	-	2

Championships: 1973 31st, 1974 22nd

BASIL VAN ROOYEN

ZA. Born: 19.4.1938, Johannesburg

World Championship Grand Prix Record

years	starts	wins	2nd	3rd	4th	5th	6th	PP	FL	points
1968–69	2	-	-	-	-	-	-	-	-	-

Best result: no finishes. **Best qualifying:** 9th

TREVOR VAN ROOYEN

ZA

1985 South African Drivers' Champion

KEJIO "KEKE" ROSBERG

SF. Born: 6.12.1948, Stockholm (S)

1982 World Champion; 1977 and 1978 New Zealand International Champion

World Championship Grand Prix Record

years	starts	wins	2nd	3rd	4th	5th	6th	PP	FL	points
1978–86	114(14)	5	8	4	11	9	1	5	3	159.5

Race wins: 1982 Swiss GP, 1983 Monaco GP, 1984 Dallas GP, 1985 Detroit GP, Australian GP. **Best qualifying:** 1st

	wins	2nd	3rd	4th	5th	6th	PP	FL	points
European F2 Ch	3	2	1	2	1	-	2	1	55

Championships: 1976 10th, 1977 6th, 1978 5th, 1979 12th.
Race wins: 1977 Mediterranean GP (Enna), 1978 Donington Park, 1979 Jim Clark Trophy (Hockenheim)

World Sports Car Championship. Race wins: 1991 Magny-Cours, Mexico City

Other major race wins: 1978 International Trophy (Silverstone), 1983 Race of Champions

MAURI ROSE

USA. Born: 26.5.1906, Columbus, Ohio. Died: 1.1.1981, Michigan

1936 Indycar Champion

Indycar Championship. Race wins: 1932 Detroit Race 2, 1936 Syracuse, 1939 Syracuse, 1941 Indianapolis 500, 1947 Indianapolis 500, 1948 Indianapolis 500

BERND ROSEMEYER

D. Born: 14.10.1909, Lingen. Died: 28.1.1938, Frankfurt-Darmstadt autobahn, record attempt

1936 Grand Prix European Champion

Pre-1950 Grands Prix. Race wins: 1935 Masaryk GP, 1936 German GP, Swiss GP, Italian GP, 1937 Donington GP

Indycar Championship. Race wins: 1937 Vanderbilt Cup

JEAN-LOUIS ROSIER

F. Son of Louis

Major Sports Car races. Race wins: 1950 Le Mans 24 hrs

LOUIS ROSIER

F. Born: 5.11.1905, Chapdes Beaufort. Died: 29.10.1956, Neuilly-sur-Seine, three weeks after an accident during the Salon de Paris Cup at Montlhéry. Father of Jean-Louis

World Championship Grand Prix Record

years	starts	wins	2nd	3rd	4th	5th	6th	PP	FL	points
1950–56	38(1)	-	-	2	2	2	2	-	-	18

Best championship: 1950 4th. **Best qualifying:** 6th

Pre-1950 Grands Prix. Race wins: 1949 Belgian GP

Major Sports Car races. Race wins: 1950 Le Mans 24 hrs

Other major race wins: 1950 and 1951 Dutch GP

YNGVE ROSQVIST

S

1961 and 1962 Swedish Formula Junior Champion

CARLO ROSSI

I

	wins	2nd	3rd	4th	5th	6th	PP	FL	points
European F2 Ch	-	-	1	1	1	-	-	6

Championship: 1981 13th

ANDRÉ ROSSIGNOL

F

Major Sports Car races. Race wins: 1925 and 1926 Le Mans 24 hrs

VICTOR ROSSO

RA

Major race wins: 1987 Nürburgring EFDA F3

HUUB ROTHENGATTER
NL. Born: 8.10.1954, Bussum

World Championship Grand Prix Record

years	starts	wins	2nd	3rd	4th	5th	6th	PP	FL	points
1984–86	25(5)	-	-	-	-	-	-	-	-	-

Best result: 7th. **Best qualifying:** 21st

	wins	2nd	3rd	4th	5th	6th	PP	FL	points
European F2 Ch	1	1	-	2	3	3	-	-	30

Championships: 1979 18th, 1980 7th, 1981 13th. **Race wins:** 1980 Zolder

ANDY ROUSE
GB. Born: 2.12.1947, Dymock, Gloucestershire
1975, 1983, 1984 and 1985 British Touring Car Champion
Major race wins: 1988 Tourist Trophy

HANS ROYER

	wins	2nd	3rd	4th	5th	6th	PP	FL	points
European F2 Ch	-	-	-	-	-	1	-	-	1

Championship: 1977 20th

BERNARD RUBIN
GB
Major Sports Car races. Race wins: 1928 Le Mans 24 hrs

LLOYD RUBY
USA. Born: 12.1.1928, Wichita Falls, Texas

World Championship Grand Prix Record

year	starts	wins	2nd	3rd	4th	5th	6th	PP	FL	points
1961	1	-	-	-	-	-	-	-	-	-

Best result: no finishes. **Best qualifying:** 19th

World Sports Car Championship. Race wins: 1965 Daytona, 1966 Daytona 24 hrs, Sebring 12 hrs

Indycar Championship. Race wins: 1961 Milwaukee Race 2, 1964 Phoenix Race 2, 1967 Phoenix Race 1, Langhorne Race 1, 1968 Milwaukee Race 1, Milwaukee Race 2, 1970 Trenton Race 1

GROVER RUCKSTELL
USA
Indycar Championship. Race wins: 1915 Tacoma Race 1

JEAN-CLAUDE RUDAZ
CH

World Championship Grand Prix Record

year	starts	wins	2nd	3rd	4th	5th	6th	PP	FL	points
1964	-(1)	-	-	-	-	-	-	-	-	-

Best qualifying: 20th

RICKY RUDD
USA. Born: 12.9.1956, Chesapeake, Virginia
1992 IROC Champion

CARLOS RUESCH
RA. Born: 20.10.1943

	wins	2nd	3rd	4th	5th	6th	PP	FL	points
European F2 Ch	-	-	1	1	1	1	-	-	14

Championship: 1971 17th, 1972 11th

HANS RUESCH
CH. Born: Zurich
Pre-1950 Grands Prix. Race wins: 1936 Donington GP

JIM RUSSELL
GB
1955, 1956 and 1957 British F3 Champion

GIACOMO "GEKI" RUSSO
I. Born: 23.10.1937, Milan. Died: 18.6.1967, Caserta
1964 Italian F3 Champion

World Championship Grand Prix Record

years	starts	wins	2nd	3rd	4th	5th	6th	PP	FL	points
1964–66	2(1)	-	-	-	-	-	-	-	-	-

Best result: 9th. **Best qualifying:** 20th

PAUL RUSSO
USA. Born: 10.4.1914, Kenosha, Wisconsin. Died: 15.2.1976, Daytona Beach

Indycar Championship. Race wins: 1950 Springfield Race 1, 1951 Detroit

JOHNNY RUTHERFORD
USA. Born: 12.3.1938, Coffeyville, Kansas
1980 Indycar Champion
Indycar Championship. Race wins: 1965 Atlanta, 1973 California 500 Qualifying Race 2, Michigan Race 2, 1974 California 500 Qualifying Race 2, Indianapolis 500, Milwaukee Race 1, Pocono 500, 1975 Phoenix, 1976 Trenton, Indianapolis 500, Texas, 1977 Phoenix, Milwaukee, Texas, Milwaukee, 1978 Michigan, Phoenix, 1979 Atlanta Race 1, Atlanta Race 2, 1980 Ontario, Indianapolis 500, Mid-Ohio, Michigan, Milwaukee, 1981 Phoenix, 1985 Sanair, 1986 Michigan 500

Johnny Rutherford

TROY RUTTMAN
USA. Born: 11.3.1930, Mooreland, Oklahoma

World Championship Grand Prix Record

year	starts	wins	2nd	3rd	4th	5th	6th	PP	FL	points
1958	1(1)	-	-	-	-	-	-	-	-	-

Best result: 10th. **Best qualifying:** 18th

Indycar Championship. Race wins: 1952 Indianapolis 500, Raleigh

PETER RYAN
CDN. Born: 10.6.1942. Died: 2.7.1962, Paris (F)

World Championship Grand Prix Record

year	starts	wins	2nd	3rd	4th	5th	6th	PP	FL	points
1961	1	-	-	-	-	-	-	-	-	-

Best result: 9th. **Best qualifying:** 13th
Major race wins: 1961 Canadian GP

RICKARD RYDELL
S. Born: 22.9.1967
Major race wins: 1992 Macau GP

S

"SABIPA"
F. Born: 1890
Pre-1950 Grands Prix. Race wins: 1926 Italian GP

EDDIE SACHS
USA. Born: 28.5.1927, Bethlehem, Pennsylvania. Died: 30.5.1964, Indianapolis
Indycar Championship. Race wins: 1956 Atlanta, 1958 Langhorne, Indiana State Fairgrounds, 1959 Syracuse, Trenton Race 2, 1960 Trenton Race 2, 1961 Trenton Race 1, Trenton Race 2

ENRIQUE SAENZ VALIENTE
RA
World Sports Car Championship. Race wins: 1955 Buenos Aires

BORIS "BOB" SAID
USA. Born: 5.5.1932, New York

World Championship Grand Prix Record

year	starts	wins	2nd	3rd	4th	5th	6th	PP	FL	points
1959	1	-	-	-	-	-	-	-	-	-

Best result: no finishes. **Best qualifying:** 13th

LUIS PEREZ SALA
E. Born: 15.5.1959, Barcelona
1993 Spanish Touring Car Champion

World Championship Grand Prix Record

years	starts	wins	2nd	3rd	4th	5th	6th	PP	FL	points
1988–89	26(6)	-	-	-	-	-	1	-	-	1

Best championship: 1989 26th. **Best qualifying:** 9th

	wins	2nd	3rd	4th	5th	6th	PP	FL	points
Int F3000 Ch	4	1	1	2	5	-	2	1	57.5

Championships: 1986 4th, 1987 2nd. **Race wins:** 1986 Mediterranean GP (Enna), Birmingham, 1987 Donington Park, Le Mans

CARLO SALAMANO
I. Born: n/a. Died: 19.1.1969
Pre-1950 Grands Prix. Race wins: 1923 Italian GP

ETTORE SALANI
I
Major race wins: 1949 Mille Miglia

ELISEO SALAZAR
RCH. Born: 14.11.1954, Santiago
World Championship Grand Prix Record

years	starts	wins	2nd	3rd	4th	5th	6th	PP	FL	points
1981–83	24(13)	-	-	-	-	1	1	-	-	3

Best championship: 1981 18th. **Best qualifying:** 12th

	wins	2nd	3rd	4th	5th	6th	PP	FL	points
Int F3000 Ch	-	-	-	1	-	-	-	1	1.5

Championship: 1986 19th
Major race wins: 1980 International Trophy (Silverstone)

BOB SALISBURY
GB

	wins	2nd	3rd	4th	5th	6th	PP	FL	points
European F2 Ch	-	-	-	-	-	-	-	-	1

Championship: 1973 31st

MIKA SALO
SF. Born: 25.9.1967, Helsinki
World Championship Grand Prix Record

year	starts	wins	2nd	3rd	4th	5th	6th	PP	FL	points
1994	2	-	-	-	-	-	-	-	-	-

Best result: 10th. **Best qualifying:** 22nd

ROY SALVADORI
GB. Born: 12.5.1922, Dovercourt, Essex
World Championship Grand Prix Record

years	starts	wins	2nd	3rd	4th	5th	6th	PP	FL	points
1952–62	47(3)	-	1	1	1	2	5	-	-	19

Best championship: 1958 4th. **Best qualifying:** 2nd
World Sports Car Championship. Race wins: 1959 Le Mans 24 hrs

GIOVANNI SALVATI
I
1970 Italian F3 Champion

BRIAN SAMPSON
AUS
Major race wins: 1975 Bathurst

NINIAN SANDERSON
GB. Born: 14.5.1925. Died: 1.10.1985, Glasgow, cancer
World Sports Car Championship. Race wins: 1956 Le Mans 24 hrs

CONSALVO SANESI
I. Born: 28.3.1911, Terranuova Bracciolini
World Championship Grand Prix Record

years	starts	wins	2nd	3rd	4th	5th	6th	PP	FL	points
1950–51	5	-	-	-	1	-	1	-	-	3

Best championship: 1951 12th. **Best qualifying:** 4th

ALESSANDRO SANTIN
I
1984 Italian F3 Champion

	wins	2nd	3rd	4th	5th	6th	PP	FL	points
Int F3000 Ch	-	-	-	-	2	-	-		1.5

Championship: 1986 19th

ROSCOE SARLES
USA. Born: n/a. Died: 17.9.1922, Kansas City
Indycar Championship. Race wins: 1919 Ascot, Uniontown Race 5, 1920 Beverly Hills Race 5, 1921 Beverly Hills Race 2, Uniontown Race 1, Cotati Race 2

SHUROKO SASAKI
J
1980 Japanese F3 Champion

KOUJI SATO
J
1985 Japanese F3 Champion

DAVID "SWEDE" SAVAGE
USA. Born: 26.8.1946. Died: 2.7.1973, Indianapolis, after accident on 30.5.1973
Indycar Championship. Race wins: 1970 Phoenix Race 2

LUDOVICO SCARFIOTTI
I. Born: 18.10.1933, Turin. Died: 8.6.1968, Rossfeld, hill climb
World Championship Grand Prix Record

years	starts	wins	2nd	3rd	4th	5th	6th	PP	FL	points
1963–68	10(2)	1	-	-	2	-	2	-	1	17

Best championship: 1966 10th. **Race wins:** 1966 Italian GP. **Best qualifying:** 2nd
World Sports Car Championship. Race wins: 1963 Sebring 12 hrs, Le Mans 24 hrs, 1964 Nürburgring, 1965 Nürburgring, 1966 Spa

GIORGIO SCARLATTI
I. Born: 2.10.1921, Rome
World Championship Grand Prix Record

year	starts	wins	2nd	3rd	4th	5th	6th	PP	FL	points
1956–61	12(3)	-	-	-	-	1	1	-	-	1

Best championship: 1957 20th. **Best qualifying:** 5th
World Sports Car Championship. Race wins: 1961 Pescara

BERTRAM SCHÄFER
D
1976 and 1978 German F3 Champion

PETER SCHARMANN
A
1977 German F3 Champion

IAN SCHECKTER
ZA. Born: 22.8.1947, East London, near Durban. Brother of Jody
1976, 1977, 1978, 1979, 1983 and 1984 South African Drivers' Champion
World Championship Grand Prix Record

years	starts	wins	2nd	3rd	4th	5th	6th	PP	FL	points
1974–77	18(2)	-	-	-	-	-	-	-	-	-

Best result: 10th. **Best qualifying:** 16th

JODY SCHECKTER
ZA. Born: 29.1.1950, East London, near Durban. Brother of Ian
1979 World Champion; 1973 North American F5000 Champion
World Championship Grand Prix Record

years	starts	wins	2nd	3rd	4th	5th	6th	PP	FL	points
1972–80	112(1)	10	14	9	9	7	4	3	5	255

Race wins: 1974 Swedish GP, British GP, 1975 South African GP, 1976 Swedish GP, 1977 Argentinian GP, Monaco GP, Canadian GP, 1979 Belgian GP, Monaco GP, Italian GP. **Best qualifying:** 1st

	wins	2nd	3rd	4th	5th	6th	PP	FL	points
European F2 Ch	1	-	-	1	-	1	-	1	15

Championship: 1972 8th. **Race wins:** 1972 Crystal Palace

HARRY SCHELL
USA. Born: 29.6.1921, Paris (F). Died: 13.5.1960, Silverstone, testing
World Championship Grand Prix Record

years	starts	wins	2nd	3rd	4th	5th	6th	PP	FL	points
1950–60	56	-	1	1	3	7	4	-	-	32

Best championship: 1958 5th. **Best qualifying:** 2nd
World Sports Car Championship. Race wins: 1956 Nürburgring

TIM SCHENKEN
AUS. Born: 26.9.1943, Sydney
1968 British F3 Champion
World Championship Grand Prix Record

years	starts	wins	2nd	3rd	4th	5th	6th	PP	FL	points
1970–74	34(2)	-	-	1	-	1	1	-	-	7

Best championship: 1971 14th. **Best qualifying:** 5th

	wins	2nd	3rd	4th	5th	6th	PP	FL	points
European F2 Ch	2	4	3	2	3	4	-	4	33

Drivers A–Z

Championships: 1970 12th, 1971 4th. Race wins: 1972 Hockenheim, 1973 Norisring
World Sports Car Championship. Race wins: 1972 Buenos Aires, Nürburgring, 1977 Nürburgring

ALBERT SCHERRER
CH. Born: 28.2.1908. Died: 5.7.1986

World Championship Grand Prix Record

year	starts	wins	2nd	3rd	4th	5th	6th	PP	FL	points
1953	1	-	-	-	-	-	-	-	-	-

Best result: 8th. Best qualifying: 18th

DOMENICO "MIMMO" SCHIATTARELLA
I. Born: 17.11.1967, Milan

World Championship Grand Prix Record

year	starts	wins	2nd	3rd	4th	5th	6th	PP	FL	points
1994	2	-	-	-	-	-	-	-	-	-

Best result: 19th. Best qualifying: 26th

HEINZ SCHILLER
CH. Born: 25.1.1930, Frauenfeld

World Championship Grand Prix Record

year	starts	wins	2nd	3rd	4th	5th	6th	PP	FL	points
1962	1	-	-	-	-	-	-	-	-	-

Best result: no finishes. Best qualifying: 20th

BILL SCHINDLER
USA. Born: 6.3.1909, Middletown, New York. Died: 20.9.1952, Allentown, Pennsylvania

Indycar Championship. Race wins: 1952 Springfield

JEAN-LOUIS SCHLESSER
F. Born: 12.9.1948, Nancy. Nephew of Jo
1989 and 1990 (with Mauro Baldi) World Sports Car Champion; 1985 French Supertourism Champion; 1978 French F3 Champion (with Alain Prost); 1988 German Racing Champion

World Championship Grand Prix Record

years	starts	wins	2nd	3rd	4th	5th	6th	PP	FL	points
1983; 1988	1(1)	-	-	-	-	-	-	-	-	-

Best result: 11th. Best qualifying: 22nd
World Sports Car Championship. Race wins: 1988 Jerez, Brno, Nürburgring, Sandown Park, 1989 Suzuka, Jarama, Nürburgring, Donington Park, Mexico City, 1990 Suzuka, Monza, Dijon, Nürburgring, Donington Park, Montréal

JO SCHLESSER
F. Born: 18.5.1928, Madagascar. Died: 7.7.1968, Rouen, French GP. Uncle of Jean-Louis

World Championship Grand Prix Record

years	starts	wins	2nd	3rd	4th	5th	6th	PP	FL	points
1966–68	3	-	-	-	-	-	-	-	-	-

Best result: no finishes. Best qualifying: 17th

	wins	2nd	3rd	4th	5th	6th	PP	FL	points
European F2 Ch	-	-	1	1	1	-	-	18

Championships: 1967 8th, 1968 11th

FREDY SCHNARWILER
CH

	wins	2nd	3rd	4th	5th	6th	PP	FL	points
European F2 Ch	-	-	-	-	1	-	-	1

Championships: 1980 16th

BERND SCHNEIDER
D. Born: 20.7.1964, Saarbrucken
1987 German F3 Champion

World Championship Grand Prix Record

years	starts	wins	2nd	3rd	4th	5th	6th	PP	FL	points
1988–90	9(25)	-	-	-	-	-	-	-	-	-

Best result: 12th. Best qualifying: 15th
Other major race wins: 1989 Spa 24 hrs

LOUIS SCHNEIDER
USA. Born: 1899, California. Died: 27.9.1942
1931 Indycar Champion

Indycar Championship. Race wins: 1931 Indianapolis 500

RUDOLF SCHOELLER
CH. Born: 27.4.1902. Died: 7.3.1978

World Championship Grand Prix Record

year	starts	wins	2nd	3rd	4th	5th	6th	PP	FL	points
1952	1	-	-	-	-	-	-	-	-	-

Best result: no finishes. Best qualifying: no time set

NICLAS SCHONSTROM
S
1986 Swedish F3 Champion

DIETER SCHORNSTEIN
D. Born: 28.6.1940, Aachen
World Sports Car Championship. Race wins: 1981 Silverstone

DORSEY SCHROEDER
USA. Born: 25.9.1952
1989 Trans-Am Champion

ROB SCHROEDER
USA. Born: 11.5.1926

World Championship Grand Prix Record

year	starts	wins	2nd	3rd	4th	5th	6th	PP	FL	points
1962	1	-	-	-	-	-	-	-	-	-

Best result: 10th. Best qualifying: 17th

MICHAEL SCHUMACHER
D. Born: 3.1.1969, Hurth-Hermuhlheim
1994 World Champion; 1990 German F3 Champion

World Championship Grand Prix Record

years	starts	wins	2nd	3rd	4th	5th	6th	PP	FL	points
1991–94	52	10	10	7	3	1	2	6	15	201

Race wins: 1992 Belgian GP, 1993 Portuguese GP, 1994 Brazilian GP, Pacific GP, San Marino GP, Monaco GP, Canadian GP, French GP, Hungarian GP, European GP. Best qualifying: 1st
World Sports Car Championship. Race wins: 1990 Mexico City, 1991 Autopolis
Other major race wins: 1990 Macau GP

VERN SCHUPPAN
AUS. Born: 19.3.1943, Boolero
1983 Japanese Sports Car Champion (with Naohiro Hujita)

Michael Schumacher

World Championship Grand Prix Record

years	starts	wins	2nd	3rd	4th	5th	6th	PP	FL	points
1972; 1974–75; 1977	9(4)	-	-	-	-	-	-	-	-	-

Best result: 7th. Best qualifying: 14th
World Sports Car Championship. Race wins: 1983 Le Mans 24 hrs
Other major race wins: 1974 and 1976 Macau GP

RUDI SCHURTER
CH
1993 and 1994 Swiss F3 Champion

MANFRED SCHURTI
FL
World Sports Car Championship. Race wins: 1976 Watkins Glen, 1977 Mugello, 1979 Mugello, Nürburgring

UDO SCHÜTZ
D. Born: 1936
World Sports Car Championship. Race wins: 1967 Nürburgring, 1969 Targa Florio

ADOLFO SCHWELM CRUZ
RA. Born: 28.6.1923, Buenos Aires

World Championship Grand Prix Record

year	starts	wins	2nd	3rd	4th	5th	6th	PP	FL	points
1953	1	-	-	-	-	-	-	-	-	-

Best result: no finishes. Best qualifying: 13th

BILL SCOTT
USA. Born: 10.10.1948
1971 and 1972 SCCA Super Vee Champion

DAVE SCOTT
GB. Born: 14.5.1962, Petersfield

	wins	2nd	3rd	4th	5th	6th	PP	FL	points
European F2 Ch	-	-	-	1	1	1	-		3

Championship: 1983 17th

RICHARD SCOTT
GB. Born: 8.11.1946, Aberdeen

	wins	2nd	3rd	4th	5th	6th	PP	FL	points
European F2 Ch	-	-	-	-	-	-	-		2

Championship: 1973 29th

ARCHIE SCOTT-BROWN
GB. Born: 13.5.1927, Paisley. Died: 18.5.1958, Spa

World Championship Grand Prix Record

year	starts	wins	2nd	3rd	4th	5th	6th	PP	FL	points
1956	1	-	-	-	-	-	-	-	-	-

Best result: no finishes. Best qualifying: 10th

PIERO SCOTTI
I. Born: 11.11.1909, Florence. Died: 14.2.1976

World Championship Grand Prix Record

year	starts	wins	2nd	3rd	4th	5th	6th	PP	FL	points
1956	1	-	-	-	-	-	-	-	-	-

Best result: no finishes. Best qualifying: 12th

DICK SEAMAN
GB. Born: 4.2.1913, Sussex. Died: 25.6.1939, Spa, Belgian GP

Pre-1950 Grands Prix. Race wins: 1936 Donington GP, 1938 German GP

JACK SEARS
GB. Born: 16.2.1930, Northampton. Father of David
1958 and 1963 British Touring Car Champion

WILHELM SEBASTIAN
D

Major race wins: 1931 Mille Miglia

ARTHUR SEE
USA

Indycar Championship. Race wins: 1909 Riverhead Race 5

HENRY SEGRAVE
GB. Born: 22.9.1896, Baltimore (USA). Died: 13.6.1930, Lake Windermere, record attempt

Pre-1950 Grands Prix. Race wins: 1923 French GP, 1924 San Sebastian GP

WOLFGANG SEIDEL
D. Born: 4.7.1926. Died: 1.3.1987

World Championship Grand Prix Record

years	starts	wins	2nd	3rd	4th	5th	6th	PP	FL	points
1953; 1958; 1960–62	10(2)	-	-	-	-	-	-	-	-	-

Best result: 9th. Best qualifying: 13th

World Sports Car Championship. Race wins: 1959 Targa Florio

GÜNTHER SEIFERT
D

World Championship Grand Prix Record

year	starts	wins	2nd	3rd	4th	5th	6th	PP	FL	points
1962	-(1)	-	-	-	-	-	-	-	-	-

Best qualifying: 30th

MASANORI SEKIYA
J. Born: 27.11.1949
1994 Japanese Touring Car Champion

LOU SELL
USA
1968 North American Formula A (F5000) Champion

LORD SELSDON
GB

Major Sports Car races. Race wins: 1949 Le Mans 24 hrs

ALAIN SEMOULIN
B
1976, 1982, 1985, 1987 and 1988 Belgian Touring Car Champion

ROBERT SÉNÉCHAL
F. Born: 1892. Died: n/a

Pre-1950 Grands Prix. Race wins: 1926 British GP

Other major race wins: 1927 Spa 24 hrs

AYRTON SENNA
BR. Born: 21.3.1960, Sao Paulo. Died: 1.5.1994, Bologna Hospital, following an accident during the San Marino GP at Imola
1988, 1990 and 1991 World Champion; 1983 British F3 Champion

World Championship Grand Prix Record

years	starts	wins	2nd	3rd	4th	5th	6th	PP	FL	points
1984–94	161(1)	41	23	16	7	6	3	65	19	614

Race wins: 1985 Portuguese GP, Belgian GP, 1986 Spanish GP, Detroit GP, 1987 Monaco GP, Detroit GP, 1988 San Marino GP, Canadian GP, Detroit GP, British GP, German GP, Hungarian GP, Belgian GP, Japanese GP, 1989 San Marino GP, Monaco GP, Mexican GP, German GP, Belgian GP, Spanish GP, 1990 United States GP, Monaco GP, Canadian GP, German GP, Belgian GP, Italian GP, 1991 United States GP, Brazilian GP, San Marino GP, Monaco GP, Hungarian GP, Belgian GP, Australian GP, 1992 Monaco GP, Hungarian GP, Italian GP, 1993 Brazilian GP, European GP, Monaco GP, Japanese GP, Australian GP.

Best qualifying: 1st

Other major race wins: 1983 Macau GP

Ayrton Senna

DORINO SERAFINI
I. Born: 22.7.1909, Pesaro

World Championship Grand Prix Record

year	starts	wins	2nd	3rd	4th	5th	6th	PP	FL	points
1950	1	-	1	-	-	-	-	-	-	3

Best championship: 1950 13th. Best qualifying: 6th

GABRIELE SERBLIN
I

	wins	2nd	3rd	4th	5th	6th	PP	FL	points
European F2 Ch	-	-	3	1	2	-	-	-	21

Championships: 1973 31st, 1975 10th

FRANCESCO "CHICO" SERRA
BR. Born: 3.2.1957, Sao Paulo
1979 British F3 Champion

World Championship Grand Prix Record

years	starts	wins	2nd	3rd	4th	5th	6th	PP	FL	points
1981–83	18(15)	-	-	-	-	-	1	-	-	1

Best championship: 1982 26th. Best qualifying: 15th

	wins	2nd	3rd	4th	5th	6th	PP	FL	points
European F2 Ch	-	-	3	-	-	-	-		9

Championship: 1980 10th

DOUG SERRURIER
ZA. Born: 9.12.1920, Germiston

World Championship Grand Prix Record

years	starts	wins	2nd	3rd	4th	5th	6th	PP	FL	points
1962–63; 1965	2(1)	-	-	-	-	-	-	-	-	-

Best result: 11th. Best qualifying: 14th

GEORGES "JOHNNY" SERVOZ-GAVIN
F. Born: 18.1.1942, Grenoble
1969 European F2 Champion; 1966 French F3 Champion

World Championship Grand Prix Record

years	starts	wins	2nd	3rd	4th	5th	6th	PP	FL	points
1967–70	12(1)	-	1	-	-	1	1	-	-	9

Best championship: 1968 13th. Best qualifying: 2nd

	wins	2nd	3rd	4th	5th	6th	PP	FL	points
European F2 Ch	1	1	1	1	3	2	1	1	55

Championships: 1967 6th, 1969 1st. Race wins: 1969 Rome GP (Vallelunga)

Drivers A–Z

BARRY SETON
AUS. Father of Glenn
Major race wins: 1965 Bathurst

GLENN SETON
AUS. Born: 5.5.1965. Son of Barry
1993 Australian Touring Car Champion

TONY SETTEMBER
USA. Born: 1930

World Championship Grand Prix Record

years	starts	wins	2nd	3rd	4th	5th	6th	PP	FL	points
1962–63	6(1)	-	-	-	-	-	-	-	-	-

Best result: 8th. Best qualifying: 18th

FRANCESCO SEVERI
I
Major race wins: 1936 and 1938 Spa 24 hrs

GIULIO SEVERI
I
Major race wins: 1937 Targa Florio

PHIL "RED" SHAFER
USA
Indycar Championship. Race wins: 1924 Syracuse

JAMES "HAP" SHARP
USA. Born: 1.1.1928, Midland, Texas. Died: ?.5.1993

World Championship Grand Prix Record

years	starts	wins	2nd	3rd	4th	5th	6th	PP	FL	points
1961–64	6	-	-	-	-	-	-	-	-	-

Best result: 7th. Best qualifying: 15th
World Sports Car Championship. Race wins: 1965 Sebring 12 hrs

SCOTT SHARP
USA. Born: 14.2.1968
1991 and 1993 Trans-Am Champion

WILLIAM SHARP
USA
Indycar Championship. Race wins: 1909 Riverhead Race 3

WILBUR SHAW
USA. Born: 13.10.1902, Shelbyville. Died: 30.10.1954, Decatur, Indiana, aircraft accident
1937 and 1939 Indycar Champion
Indycar Championship. Race wins: 1929 Toledo, Cleveland, Syracuse, 1930 Detroit, Bridgeville, 1937 Indianapolis 500, 1939 Indianapolis 500, 1940 Indianapolis 500

BRIAN SHAWE-TAYLOR
GB. Born: 29.1.1915, Dublin (IRL)

World Championship Grand Prix Record

years	starts	wins	2nd	3rd	4th	5th	6th	PP	FL	points
1950–51	2	-	-	-	-	-	-	-	-	-

Best result: 8th. Best qualifying: 12th

CARROLL SHELBY
USA. Born: 11.1.1923, Leesburg, Texas

World Championship Grand Prix Record

years	starts	wins	2nd	3rd	4th	5th	6th	PP	FL	points
1958–59	8	-	-	-	-	1*	-	-	-	-

Best qualifying: 6th. *Shared drive, no points awarded
World Sports Car Championship. Race wins: 1959 Le Mans 24 hrs, Tourist Trophy

TONY SHELLY
NZ. Born: 2.2.1937, Wellington

World Championship Grand Prix Record

year	starts	wins	2nd	3rd	4th	5th	6th	PP	FL	points
1962	1(2)	-	-	-	-	-	-	-	-	-

Best result: no finishes. Best qualifying: 18th

STEVE SHELTON
USA. Born: 16.5.1949
1988 North American (Eastern Division) Formula Atlantic Champion

DOC SHEPHERD
GB
1960 British Touring Car Champion

RICHARD SHUTTLEWORTH
GB. Born: n/a. Died: 1940, killed in action
Pre-1950 Grands Prix. Race wins: 1935 Donington GP

EUGENIO SIENA
I. Born: n/a. Died: 15.5.1938, Tripoli GP
Major race wins: 1932 Spa 24 hrs

JO SIFFERT
CH. Born: 7.7.1936, Friburg. Died: 24.10.1971, Brands Hatch, Rothmans F1 Victory race

World Championship Grand Prix Record

years	starts	wins	2nd	3rd	4th	5th	6th	PP	FL	points
1962–71	96(4)	2	2	2	7	2	5	2	4	68

Best championship: 1971 4th. Race wins: 1968 British GP, 1971 Austrian GP. Best qualifying: 1st

	wins	2nd	3rd	4th	5th	6th	PP	FL	points
European F2 Ch	1	1	1	-	-	-	1	-	-

Race wins: 1970 Rouen
World Sports Car Championship. Race wins: 1968 Daytona 24 hrs, Sebring 12 hrs, Nürburgring, Austrian GP, 1969 Brands Hatch, Monza, Spa, Nürburgring, Watkins Glen, Austrian GP, 1970 Targa Florio, Spa, Österreichring, 1971 Buenos Aires

HERMANOS DA SILVA RAMOS
F/BR (dual nationality). Born: 7.12.1925, Paris

World Championship Grand Prix Record

years	starts	wins	2nd	3rd	4th	5th	6th	PP	FL	points
1955–56	7	-	-	-	-	1	-	-	-	2

Best championship: 1956 19th. Best qualifying: 14th

ANDRÉ SIMON
F. Born: 5.1.1920, Paris

World Championship Grand Prix Record

years	starts	wins	2nd	3rd	4th	5th	6th	PP	FL	points
1951–52; 1955–57	11(1)	-	-	-	-	2	-	-	-	-

Best qualifying: 4th
Major race wins: 1955 Albi GP

FABRIZIO DE SIMONE
I. Born: 30.3.1971

	wins	2nd	3rd	4th	5th	6th	PP	FL	points
Int F3000 Ch	-	1	-	-	1	-	-	7

Championship: 1994 8th

GIAMPIERO SIMONI
I. Born: 12.9.1969

	wins	2nd	3rd	4th	5th	6th	PP	FL	points
Int F3000 Ch	-	-	-	-	2	-	-	2

Championships: 1992 17th, 1993 21st

UGO SIVOCCI
I. Born: 1885, Milan. Died: 8.9.1923, Monza, Italian GP practice
Major race wins: 1923 Targa Florio

MARK SKAIFE
AUS. Born: 4.4.1966
1992 and 1994 Australian Touring Car Champion; 1991, 1992 and 1993 Australian Gold Star Champion
Major race wins: 1991 and 1992 Bathurst

CHRIS SMITH
USA. Born: 4.9.1966
1992 North American Toyota Atlantic Champion

KEN SMITH
NZ
1976, 1984 and 1990 New Zealand International Champion

MARK SMITH
USA. Born: 10.4.1967
1989 SCCA Super Vee Champion

TOM SNEVA

USA. Born: 1.6.1948, Spokane, Washington

1977 and 1978 Indycar Champion

Indycar Championship. Race wins: 1975 Michigan, 1977 Texas, Pocono 500, 1980 Phoenix, 1981 Milwaukee, Phoenix, 1982 Milwaukee, Phoenix, 1983 Indianapolis 500, Milwaukee, 1984 Phoenix, Milwaukee, Las Vegas GP

Tom Sneva

CYRIL SNIPE

GB

Major race wins: 1912 Targa Florio

DANY SNOBECK

F. Born: 2.5.1946

1979, 1980 and 1984 French Supertourism Champion

JIMMY SNYDER

USA. Born: n/a. Died: 29.6.1939, Cohokia, Illinois

Indycar Championship. Race wins: 1938 Syracuse

MOISES SOLANA

MEX. Born: 1936. Died: 27.7.1969, Valle de Bravo hill climb

World Championship Grand Prix Record

years	starts	wins	2nd	3rd	4th	5th	6th	PP	FL	points
1963–68	8	-	-	-	-	-	-	-	-	-

Best result: 10th. Best qualifying: 7th

ALEX SOLER-ROIG

E. Born: 29.10.1932, Barcelona

World Championship Grand Prix Record

years	starts	wins	2nd	3rd	4th	5th	6th	PP	FL	points
1970–72	6(4)	-	-	-	-	-	-	-	-	-

Best result: no finishes. **Best qualifying:** 17th

Major race wins: 1971 Spa 24 hrs

RAYMOND SOMMER

F. Born: 31.8.1906, Paris. Died: 10.9.1950, Cadours, Haute Garonne GP

World Championship Grand Prix Record

year	starts	wins	2nd	3rd	4th	5th	6th	PP	FL	points
1950	5	-	-	-	1	-	-	-	-	3

Best championship: 1950 13th. Best qualifying: 5th.

Pre-1950 Grands Prix. Race wins: 1936 French GP

Major Sports Car races. Race wins: 1932 and 1933 Le Mans 24 hrs, 1936 Spa 24 hrs

STEVE SOPER

GB. Born: 27.9.1951, Harrow

Major race wins: 1983 Tourist Trophy, 1992 Spa 24 hrs

VINCENZO SOSPIRI

I. Born: 7.10.1966, Sorli

	wins	2nd	3rd	4th	5th	6th	PP	FL	points
Int F3000 Ch	-	4	2	3	3	2	-	1	49

Championships: 1991 8th, 1993 7th, 1994 4th

GEORGE SOUDERS

USA. Born: 1903. Died: 26.7.1976

Indycar Championship. Race wins: 1927 Indianapolis 500

MARC SOURD

F. Born: 27.4.1946

1992 French Supertourism Champion

STEPHEN SOUTH

GB. Born: 19.2.1952, Harrow

1977 Vandervell British F3 Champion

World Championship Grand Prix Record

year	starts	wins	2nd	3rd	4th	5th	6th	PP	FL	points
1980	-(1)	-	-	-	-	-	-	-	-	-

Best qualifying: 27th

	wins	2nd	3rd	4th	5th	6th	PP	FL	points
European F2 Ch	1	-	2	1	1	-	2	2	22

Championships: 1978 16th, 1979 5th. **Race wins:** 1979 Hockenheim

"MIKE SPARKEN"

USA. Born: 16.6.1930, Neuilly-sur-Seine (F). Real name: Michel Poberejsky

World Championship Grand Prix Record

year	starts	wins	2nd	3rd	4th	5th	6th	PP	FL	points
1955	1	-	-	-	-	-	-	-	-	-

Best result: 7th. Best qualifying: 23rd

MIKE SPENCE

GB. Born: 30.12.1936, Croydon. Died: 7.5.1968, Indianapolis 500 practice

1964 British F2 Champion

World Championship Grand Prix Record

years	starts	wins	2nd	3rd	4th	5th	6th	PP	FL	points
1963–68	36(1)	-	-	1	3	6	2	-	-	27

Best championship: 1965 8th. Best qualifying: 4th

World Sports Car Championship. Race wins: 1967 Brands Hatch

Other major race wins: 1965 Race of Champions, 1966 South African GP

RUSSELL SPENCE

GB. Born: 3.1.1960

		wins	2nd	3rd	4th	5th	6th	PP	FL	points
Int F3000 Ch		-	1	1	-	-	1	-	-	10.5

Championships: 1986 23rd, 1987 10th

GORDON SPICE

GB. Born: 18.4.1940, London

Major race wins: 1978 Spa 24 hrs

HENRI SPRINGUEL

F

Major race wins: 1924 Spa 24 hrs

ALAN STACEY

GB. Born: 29.8.1933, Broomfield, Essex. Died: 19.6.1960, Spa, Belgian GP

World Championship Grand Prix Record

years	starts	wins	2nd	3rd	4th	5th	6th	PP	FL	points
1958–60	7	-	-	-	-	-	-	-	-	-

Best result: 8th. Best qualifying: 8th

NELSON STACEY

USA

Major race wins: 1962 World 600

EGBERT "BABE" STAPP

USA. Born: n/a. Died: 17.9.1980

Indycar Championship. Race wins: 1927 Charlotte Race 3, 1939 Milwaukee

GAETANO STARRABBA

I. Born: 3.12.1932, Palermo

World Championship Grand Prix Record

year	starts	wins	2nd	3rd	4th	5th	6th	PP	FL	points
1961	1	-	-	-	-	-	-	-	-	-

Best result: no finishes. Best qualifying: 30th

DOUG STEANE

HK

Major race wins: 1956 Macau GP

ALDO STEFANI

I

Major race wins: 1938 Mille Miglia

CHUCK STEVENSON

USA. Born: 15.10.1919, Sidney, Montana

1952 Indycar Champion

Indycar Championship. Race wins: 1952 Milwaukee Race 2, Du Quoin, 1953 Milwaukee Race 2, 1954 Milwaukee Race 1

IAN STEWART

GB. Born: 15.7.1929, Edinburgh

World Championship Grand Prix Record

year	starts	wins	2nd	3rd	4th	5th	6th	PP	FL	points
1953	1	-	-	-	-	-	-	-	-	-

Best result: no finishes. Best qualifying: 20th

JACKIE STEWART

GB. Born: 11.6.1939, Milton, Dumbartonshire. Brother of Jimmy, father of Paul

1969, 1971 and 1973 World Champion; 1966 Tasman Champion; 1969 British F1 Champion; 1968 French F2 Champion; 1964 Express & Star British F3 Champion

World Championship Grand Prix Record

years	starts	wins	2nd	3rd	4th	5th	6th	PP	FL	points
1965–73	99(1)	27	11	5	6	5	3	17	15	360

Race wins: 1965 Italian GP, 1966 Monaco GP, 1968 Dutch GP, German GP, United States GP, 1969 South African GP, Spanish GP, Dutch GP, French GP, British GP, Italian GP, 1970 Spanish GP, 1971 Spanish GP, Monaco GP, French GP, British GP, German GP, Canadian GP, 1972 Argentinian GP, French GP, Canadian GP, United States GP, 1973 South African GP, Belgian GP, Monaco GP, Dutch GP, German GP. **Best qualifying:** 1st

	wins	2nd	3rd	4th	5th	6th	PP	FL	points
European F2 Ch	3	5	-	-	1	-	2	3	-

Race wins: 1967 Mediterranean GP (Enna), 1969 Nürburgring, Jarama

Tasman Cup. Race wins: 1966 Lady Wigram Trophy, Teretonga, Sandown Park, Longford, 1967 New Zealand GP, Australian GP

Other major race wins: 1964 Monaco F3 GP, 1965 International Trophy (Silverstone), 1969 Race of Champions, 1970 Race of Champions 1973 International Trophy (Silverstone)

JIMMY STEWART

GB. Born: 6.3.1931, Bowling, Dunbartonshire. Brother of Jackie

World Championship Grand Prix Record

year	starts	wins	2nd	3rd	4th	5th	6th	PP	FL	points
1953	1	-	-	-	-	-	-	-	-	-

Best result: no finishes. **Best qualifying:** 15th

MAX STEWART

AUS

1971 and 1974 Australian Gold Star Champion

Tasman Cup. Race wins: 1974 Teretonga, Oran Park

Other major race wins: 1974 and 1975 Australian GP

PAUL STEWART

GB. Born: 29.10.1965, Geneva (CH). Son of Jackie

	wins	2nd	3rd	4th	5th	6th	PP	FL	points
Int F3000 Ch	-	-	1	1	2	2	-	-	13

Championships: 1992 13th, 1993 9th

HARRY STILLER

GB

1966 and 1967 British F3 Champion

BIB STILLWELL

AUS

1962, 1963, 1964 and 1965 Australian Gold Star Champion

SIEGFRIED STOHR

I. Born: 10.10.1952, Rimini

1978 Italian F3 Champion

World Championship Grand Prix Record

year	starts	wins	2nd	3rd	4th	5th	6th	PP	FL	points
1981	9(4)	-	-	-	-	-	-	-	-	-

Best result: 7th. **Best qualifying:** 13th

	wins	2nd	3rd	4th	5th	6th	PP	FL	points
European F2 Ch	1	3	2	2	2	1	1	-	46

Championships: 1979 8th, 1980 4th. **Race wins:** 1980 Mediterranean GP (Enna)

PAUL STOKELL

AUS

1994 New Zealand International Champion; 1994 Australian Gold Star Champion

ROLF STOMMELEN

D. Born: 11.7.1943, Siegen. Died: 24.4.1983, Riverside 6 hrs

1977 German Racing Champion

World Championship Grand Prix Record

years	starts	wins	2nd	3rd	4th	5th	6th	PP	FL	points
1969–76; 1978	54(9)	-	-	1	-	4	2	-	-	14

Best championship: 1970 11th. **Best qualifying:** 7th

	wins	2nd	3rd	4th	5th	6th	PP	FL	points
European F2 Ch	-	-	-	-	1	2	-	-	-

World Sports Car Championship. Race wins: 1967 Targa Florio, 1968 Daytona 24 hrs, 1976 Florio Cup, Watkins Glen, 1977 Mugello, Nürburgring, 1978 Daytona 24 hrs, 1980 Daytona 24 hrs, Nürburgring, 1981 Mosport Park, Elkhart Lake

Other major race wins: 1982 Daytona 24 hrs

LOUIS STRANG

USA. Born: n/a. Died: 20.7.1911

Indycar Championship. Race wins: 1909 Indianapolis Race 2

PHILIPPE STREIFF

F. Born: 26.6.1955, Grenoble

1981 French F3 Champion

World Championship Grand Prix Record

years	starts	wins	2nd	3rd	4th	5th	6th	PP	FL	points
1984–88	53(1)	-	-	1	1	1	2	-	-	11

Best championship: 1986 13th. **Best qualifying:** 5th

	wins	2nd	3rd	4th	5th	6th	PP	FL	points
European F2 Ch	1	5	4	3	5	-	-	-	74

Championships: 1982 6th, 1983 4th, 1984 4th. **Race wins:** 1984 Brands Hatch

		wins	2nd	3rd	4th	5th	6th	PP	FL	points
Int F3000 Ch		-	-	1	-	4	-	-	-	12

Championships: 1985 8th

European F3 Championship. Race wins: 1980 Zolder

VOLKER STRYCEK

D

1984 German Touring Car Champion

HARTWELL "STUBBY" STUBBLEFIELD

USA. Born: n/a. Died: 21.5.1935, Indianapolis 500, practice

Indycar Championship. Race wins: 1932 Roby

HANS STUCK

D. Born: 27.12.1900, Varsavia (A). Died: 9.2.1978, Grainau. Father of Hans-Joachim

World Championship Grand Prix Record

years	starts	wins	2nd	3rd	4th	5th	6th	PP	FL	points
1952–53	3(1)	-	-	-	-	-	-	-	-	-

Best result: 14th. **Best qualifying:** 14th

Pre-1950 Grands Prix. Race wins: 1934 German GP, Swiss GP, Masaryk GP, 1935 Italian GP

HANS-JOACHIM STUCK

D. Born: 1.1.1951, Grainau. Son of Hans

1985 World Sports Car Champion (with Derek Bell); 1990 German Touring Car Champion; 1986 and 1987 German Racing Champion

World Championship Grand Prix Record

years	starts	wins	2nd	3rd	4th	5th	6th	PP	FL	points
1974–79	74(7)	-	-	2	3	5	2	-	-	29

Best championship: 1977 11th. **Best qualifying:** 2nd

	wins	2nd	3rd	4th	5th	6th	PP	FL	points
European F2 Ch	5	3	1	-	-	7	5		43

Championship: 1974 2nd. **Race wins:** 1974 Montjuich Park, Jim Clark Trophy (Hockenheim), Mediterranean GP (Enna), 1976 Jim Clark Trophy (Hockenheim), Hockenheim

World Sports Car Championship. Race wins: 1981 Nürburgring, 1984 Imola, 1985 Hockenheim, Mosport Park, Brands Hatch, 1986 Monza, Le Mans 24 hrs, 1987 Le Mans 24 hrs

Other major race wins: 1972 Spa 24 hrs, 1974 Rouen GP (non-championship), 1975 Sebring 12 hrs, 1986 Sebring 12 hrs, 1988 Sebring 12 hrs

OTTO STUPPACHER

A

World Championship Grand Prix Record

year	starts	wins	2nd	3rd	4th	5th	6th	PP	FL	points
1976	-(4)	-	-	-	-	-	-	-	-	-

Best qualifying: 26th

PER STURESON

S. Born: 22.3.1948

1985 German Touring Car Champion

Danny Sullivan
USA. Born: 9.3.1950, Louisville, Kentucky
1988 Indycar Champion

World Championship Grand Prix Record

year	starts	wins	2nd	3rd	4th	5th	6th	PP	FL	points
1983	15	-	-	-	-	1	-	-	-	2

Best championship: 1983 17th. Best qualifying: 9th

	wins	2nd	3rd	4th	5th	6th	PP	FL	points
European F2 Ch	-	-	-	1	-	-	-	-	2

Championship: 1977 18th

Indycar Championship. Race wins: 1984 Cleveland, Pocono 500, Sanair, 1985 Indianapolis 500, Miami, 1986 Meadowlands, Cleveland, 1988 Portland, Michigan 500, Nazareth, Monterey GP (Laguna Seca), 1989 Pocono 500, Elkhart Lake, 1990 Cleveland, Monterey GP (Laguna Seca), 1992 Long Beach GP, 1993 Detroit GP

Marc Surer
CH. Born: 18.9.1951, Aresdorf
1979 European F2 Champion

World Championship Grand Prix Record

years	starts	wins	2nd	3rd	4th	5th	6th	PP	FL	points
1979–86	81(7)	-	-	-	2	2	7	-	1	17

Best championship: 1985 13th. Best qualifying: 5th

	wins	2nd	3rd	4th	5th	6th	PP	FL	points
European F2 Ch	2	7	6	2	2	-	3	3	94

Championships: 1977 13th, 1978 2nd, 1979 1st. **Race wins:** 1979 Eifelrennen (Nürburgring), Rome GP (Vallelunga)

World Sports Car Championship. Race wins: 1985 Monza

Other major race wins: 1985 Spa 24 hrs

John Surtees
GB. Born: 11.2.1934, Tatsfield
1964 World Champion; 1966 Can-Am Champion

John Surtees

World Championship Grand Prix Record

years	starts	wins	2nd	3rd	4th	5th	6th	PP	FL	points
1960–72	111(2)	6	10	8	5	8	3	8	11	180

Race wins: 1963 German GP, 1964 German GP, Italian GP, 1966 Belgian GP, Mexican GP, 1967 Italian GP. **Best qualifying:** 1st

	wins	2nd	3rd	4th	5th	6th	PP	FL	points
European F2 Ch	1	1	1	-	-	-	2	-	-

Race wins: 1972 Imola

World Sports Car Championship. Race wins: 1963 Sebring 12 hrs, Nürburgring, 1965 Nürburgring, 1966 Monza

Andy Sutcliffe
GB. Born: 9.5.1947, Mildenhall, Suffolk

World Championship Grand Prix Record

year	starts	wins	2nd	3rd	4th	5th	6th	PP	FL	points
1977	-(1)	-	-	-	-	-	-	-	-	-

Best qualifying: 32nd

	wins	2nd	3rd	4th	5th	6th	PP	FL	points
European F2 Ch	-	-	1	-	1	1	-	-	7

Championship: 1974 10th

Len Sutton
USA. Born: 9.8.1925, Portland, Oregon

Indycar Championship. Race wins: 1958 Trenton Race 1, 1959 Springfield, 1960 Milwaukee Race 2

Aguri Suzuki
J. Born: 8.9.1960, Tokyo
1988 Japanese F3000 Champion; 1986 Japanese Touring Car Champion (with Takao Wada)

World Championship Grand Prix Record

years	starts	wins	2nd	3rd	4th	5th	6th	PP	FL	points
1988–94	59(23)	-	-	1	-	3	-	-	7

Best championship: 1990 10th. Best qualifying: 6th

Keiichi Suzuki
J. Born: 21.3.1949
1984 Japanese Sports Car Champion

Toshio Suzuki
J. Born: 10.3.1955, Saitama
1990 Japanese Touring Car Champion (with Kazuyoshi Hoshino); 1979 Japanese F3 Champion

World Championship Grand Prix Record

year	starts	wins	2nd	3rd	4th	5th	6th	PP	FL	points
1993	2	-	-	-	-	-	-	-	-	-

Best result: 12th. Best qualifying: 23rd

Major race wins: 1992 Daytona 24 hrs

Ed Swart
NL
1965 European Touring Car 1000 cc Class Champion

Jacques Swaters
B. Born: 30.10.1926, Brussels

World Championship Grand Prix Record

years	starts	wins	2nd	3rd	4th	5th	6th	PP	FL	points
1951; 1953–54	7(1)	-	-	-	-	-	-	-	-	-

Best result: 7th. Best qualifying: 13th

Major race wins: 1953 Avusrennen

Bob Sweikert
USA. Born: 20.5.1926, Los Angeles. Died: 17.6.1956, Salem, Indiana
1955 Indycar Champion

Indycar Championship. Race wins: 1953 Indiana State Fairgrounds, 1954 Syracuse, 1955 Indianapolis 500, Syracuse

Frank Sytner
GB. Born: 29.6.1944, Liverpool
1988 British Touring Car Champion

Ferenc Szisz
H. Born: 1873. Died: ?.6.1970, Tiszaszentimre
Pre-1950 Grands Prix. Race wins: 1906 French GP

T

Noritake Takahara
J. Born: 6.6.1951, Tokyo
1974 and 1976 Japanese F2000 Champion

World Championship Grand Prix Record

year	starts	wins	2nd	3rd	4th	5th	6th	PP	FL	points
1976–77	2	-	-	-	-	-	-	-	-	-

Best result: 9th. Best qualifying: 19th

Kenji Takahashi
J. Born: 18.5.1946. No relation to Kunimitsu
1985 and 1986 Japanese Sports Car Champion (with Kunimitsu Takahashi)

Kunimitsu Takahashi
J. Born: 29.1.1940, Tokyo. No relation to Kenji
1985, 1986 (both with Kenji Takahashi), 1987 (with Kenneth Acheson) and 1989 (with Stanley Dickens) Japanese Sports Car Champion

World Championship Grand Prix Record

year	starts	wins	2nd	3rd	4th	5th	6th	PP	FL	points
1977	1	-	-	-	-	-	-	-	-	-

Best result: 9th. Best qualifying: 22nd

PATRICK TAMBAY
F. Born: 25.6.1949, Paris
1977 and 1980 Can-Am Champion

World Championship Grand Prix Record

years	starts	wins	2nd	3rd	4th	5th	6th	PP	FL	points
1977–79;										
1981–86	114(10)	2	4	5	6	8	7	5	2	103

Best championship: 1983 4th. Race wins: 1982 German GP, 1983 San Marino GP. Best qualifying: 1st

	wins	2nd	3rd	4th	5th	6th	PP	FL	points
European F2 Ch	2	5	5	4	1	1	6	1	86

Championships: 1974 7th, 1975 2nd, 1976 3rd. Race wins: 1975 and 1976 Nogaro GP
Other major race wins: 1974 Nogaro GP (non-championship)

ANTONIO TAMBURINI
I. Born: 15.9.1966, Arezza

	wins	2nd	3rd	4th	5th	6th	PP	FL	points
Int F3000 Ch	1	-	1	4	1	1	-	1	28

Championships: 1990 13th, 1991 4th.
Race wins: 1991 Le Mans
Other major race wins: 1989 Monaco F3 GP

LUIGI TARAMAZZO
I

Major race wins: 1958 Mille Miglia

GABRIELE TARQUINI
I. Born: 2.3.1962, Guilianova Lido
1994 British Touring Car Champion

Patrick Tambay

World Championship Grand Prix Record

years	starts	wins	2nd	3rd	4th	5th	6th	PP	FL	points
1987–92	37(40)	-	-	-	-	-	1	-	-	1

Best championship: 1989 26th. Best qualifying: 11th

	wins	2nd	3rd	4th	5th	6th	PP	FL	points
Int F3000 Ch	-	1	3	3	3	-	-	1	33

Championships: 1985 6th, 1986 10th, 1987 8th

PIERO TARUFFI
I. Born: 12.10.1906, Albano Laziale, Rome. Died: 12.1.1988, Rome

World Championship Grand Prix Record

years	starts	wins	2nd	3rd	4th	5th	6th	PP	FL	points
1950–52; 1954–56	18	1	3	1	2	2	1	-	1	41

Best championship: 1952 3rd. Race wins: 1952 Swiss GP. Best qualifying: 2nd
World Sports Car Championship. Race wins: 1956 Nürburgring, 1957 Mille Miglia
Other major race wins: 1954 Targa Florio

THIERRY TASSIN
B. Born: 11.1.1959
1994 Belgian Touring Car Champion

	wins	2nd	3rd	4th	5th	6th	PP	FL	points
European F2 Ch	-	1	-	5	3	3	1	-	30

Championships: 1982 17th, 1983 7th, 1984 6th

	wins	2nd	3rd	4th	5th	6th	PP	FL	points
Int F3000 Ch	-	-	-	-	-	1	-	1	1

Championship: 1985 16th
Major race wins: 1983, 1986 and 1994 Spa 24 hrs

ANTHONY TAYLOR
ZA
1990 South African Drivers' Champion

HENRY TAYLOR
GB. Born: 16.12.1932, Shefford, Bedfordshire

World Championship Grand Prix Record

years	starts	wins	2nd	3rd	4th	5th	6th	PP	FL	points
1959–61	8(2)	-	-	-	1	-	-	-	-	3

Best championship: 1960 19th. Best qualifying: 13th
Major race wins: 1960 Monaco Formula Junior GP

IAN TAYLOR
GB. Born: 28.1.1947. Died: 7.6.1992, Spa-Francorchamps
1973 Forward Trust British F3 Champion

JOHN TAYLOR
GB. Born: 23.3.1933, Leicester. Died: 6.9.1966, Koblenz Hospital after an accident at the German GP a month earlier

World Championship Grand Prix Record

years	starts	wins	2nd	3rd	4th	5th	6th	PP	FL	points
1964; 1966	5	-	-	-	-	1	-	-	1

Best championship: 1966 17th. Best qualifying: 16th

MIKE TAYLOR
GB. Born: 24.4.1934, London

World Championship Grand Prix Record

years	starts	wins	2nd	3rd	4th	5th	6th	PP	FL	points
1959–60	1(1)	-	-	-	-	-	-	-	-

Best result: no finishes. Best qualifying: 19th

TREVOR TAYLOR
GB. Born: 26.12.1936, Sheffield
1958 British F3 Champion; 1960 (tied with Jim Clark) and 1961 Motor Racing British Formula Junior (F3) Champion

World Championship Grand Prix Record

years	starts	wins	2nd	3rd	4th	5th	6th	PP	FL	points
1959; 1961–64;										
1966	27(2)	-	1	-	-	-	2	-	-	8

Best championship: 1962 10th. Best qualifying: 3rd
Major race wins: 1962 Mexican GP, 1969 Tourist Trophy

WAYNE TAYLOR
ZA/GB. Born: 14.7.1960, East London (ZA)
1994 IMSA World Sports Car Champion; 1986 South African Drivers' Champion

WILLIAM TAYLOR
USA

Indycar Championship. Race wins: 1917 Uniontown Race 1

ARTHUR TERDICH
AUS

Major race wins: 1929 Australian GP

MAX DE TERRA
CH. Born: 6.10.1918. Died: 29.12.1982

World Championship Grand Prix Record

years	starts	wins	2nd	3rd	4th	5th	6th	PP	FL	points
1952–53	2	-	-	-	-	-	-	-	-

Best result: 9th. Best qualifying: 19th

ANDRÉ TESTUT
MC

World Championship Grand Prix Record

years	starts	wins	2nd	3rd	4th	5th	6th	PP	FL	points
1958–59	-(2)	-	-	-	-	-	-	-	-

Best qualifying: 24th

TEDDY TETZLAFF
USA. Born: n/a. Died: 1929, California

Indycar Championship. Race wins: 1912 Santa Monica Race 3, Tacoma Race 3, Tacoma Race 4

MIKE THACKWELL
NZ. Born: 30.3.1961, Auckland
1984 European F2 Champion; 1987 New Zealand International Champion

World Championship Grand Prix Record

years	starts	wins	2nd	3rd	4th	5th	6th	PP	FL	points
1980; 1984	2(3)	-	-	-	-	-	-	-	-

Best result: no finishes. Best qualifying: 24th

	wins	2nd	3rd	4th	5th	6th	PP	FL	points
European F2 Ch	9	6	8	3	2	2	9	15	164

Championships: 1980 8th, 1981 6th, 1982 10th, 1983 2nd, 1984 1st. Race wins: 1981 International Trophy, 1983 Jarama, 1984 International Trophy, Jochen Rindt Trophy (Thruxton), Rome GP (Vallelunga), Mugello, Pau GP, Misano, Mediterranean GP (Enna)

	wins	2nd	3rd	4th	5th	6th	PP	FL	points
Int F3000 Ch	4	3	-	1	-	-	5	4	55.5

Championships: 1985 2nd, 1986 8th. Race wins: 1985 International Trophy, Spa, Mediterranean GP (Enna), 1986 Pau GP
World Sports Car Championship. Race wins: 1986 Nürburgring
European F3 Championship. Race wins: 1979 Monza Lottery GP

LÉON THÉRY
F. Born: 1878. Died: 1909, tuberculosis
Pre-1950 Grands Prix. Race wins: 1904 and 1905 Gordon Bennett Trophy
Other major race wins: 1904 and 1905 Gordon Bennett French Trial

DIDIER THEYS
B. Born: 19.10.1956, Nivelles
1987 American Racing Series Champion; 1986 SCCA Super Vee Champion

	wins	2nd	3rd	4th	5th	6th	PP	FL	points
European F2 Ch	-	-	-	-	-	3	-	-	3

Championship: 1984 11th
Major race wins: 1987 Spa 24 hrs

PIERRE-ALAIN THIBAUT
B
1992 Belgian Touring Car Champion

ALFONSO THIELE
USA. Born: 1922
World Championship Grand Prix Record

year	starts	wins	2nd	3rd	4th	5th	6th	PP	FL	points
1960	1	-	-	-	-	-	-	-	-	-

Best result: no finishes. Best qualifying: 9th

KURT THIIM
DK. Born: 3.8.1958, Vojens
1986 German Touring Car Champion; 1984 German F3 Champion

HERB THOMAS
USA. Born: 4.6.1923, Harnett County, North Carolina
1951 and 1953 NASCAR Champion

JOE THOMAS
USA. Born: n/a. Died: 28.12.1965
Indycar Championship. Race wins: 1921 Beverly Hills Race 8, Fresno Race 1

RENÉ THOMAS
F. Born: 7.3.1886, Perigueux. Died: 22.9.1975
Indycar Championship. Race wins: 1914 Indianapolis 500

BILL THOMPSON
AUS
Major race wins: 1930, 1932 and 1933 Australian GP

DICK THOMPSON
USA
World Sports Car Championship. Race wins: 1967 Spa

ERIC THOMPSON
GB. Born: 4.11.1919, Surbiton
World Championship Grand Prix Record

year	starts	wins	2nd	3rd	4th	5th	6th	PP	FL	points
1952	1	-	-	-	1	-	-	-	-	2

Best championship: 1952 16th. Best qualifying: 9th

STEVE THOMPSON
GB
Tasman Cup. Race wins: 1973 Warwick Farm

JOHNNY THOMSON
USA. Born: 9.4.1922. Died: 24.9.1960, Allentown, Pennsylvania
Indycar Championship. Race wins: 1955 Milwaukee Race 1, 1957 Langhorne, 1958 Springfield, Du Quoin, Syracuse, Sacramento, 1959 Milwaukee Race 1

LESLIE THORNE
GB. Born: 23.6.1916, Greenock. Died: 13.7.1993, Troon, Ayrshire
World Championship Grand Prix Record

year	starts	wins	2nd	3rd	4th	5th	6th	PP	FL	points
1954	1	-	-	-	-	-	-	-	-	-

Best result: 14th. Best qualifying: 23rd

BERNARD TILANUS
ZA
1981 South African Drivers' Champion

BRIAN TILL
USA. Born: 26.3.1960, Houston, Texas
1990 North American (Eastern Division) Toyota Atlantic Champion

BUD TINGELSTAD
USA. Born: 4.4.1928, Frazee, Minnesota. Died: 30.7.1981, Indianapolis
Indycar Championship. Race wins: 1966 Du Quoin

SAM TINGLE
RSR. Born: 24.8.1921, Manchester (GB)
World Championship Grand Prix Record

years	starts	wins	2nd	3rd	4th	5th	6th	PP	FL	points
1963; 1965;										
1967–69	5	-	-	-	-	-	-	-	-	-

Best result: 8th. Best qualifying: 14th

DESMOND TITTERINGTON
GB. Born: 1.5.1928, Cultra, County Down
World Championship Grand Prix Record

year	starts	wins	2nd	3rd	4th	5th	6th	PP	FL	points
1956	1	-	-	-	-	-	-	-	-	-

Best result: no finishes. Best qualifying: 11th

JERRY TITUS
USA. Born: n/a. Died: ?.8.1970
1967 Trans-Am Champion

ALESSANDRO DE TOMASO
RA. Born: 10.7.1928, Buenos Aires
World Championship Grand Prix Record

years	starts	wins	2nd	3rd	4th	5th	6th	PP	FL	points
1957; 1959	2	-	-	-	-	-	-	-	-	-

Best result: 9th. Best qualifying: 12th

ALLAN TOMLINSON
AUS
Major race wins: 1939 Australian GP

CHARLES DE TORNACO
B. Born: 7.6.1927, Brussels. Died: 18.9.1953, Modena GP practice
World Championship Grand Prix Record

years	starts	wins	2nd	3rd	4th	5th	6th	PP	FL	points
1952–53	2(2)	-	-	-	-	-	-	-	-	-

Best result: 7th. Best qualifying: 13th

PAUL TRACY
CDN. Born: 17.12.1968, Toronto
1990 American Racing Series Champion
Indycar Championship. Race wins: 1993 Long Beach GP, Cleveland, Toronto, Elkhart Lake, Monterey GP (Laguna Seca), 1994 Detroit, Nazareth, Monterey GP (Laguna Seca)

BENGT TRAGARDH
S
1981 Swedish F3 Champion

JUAN TRAVERSO
RA

	wins	2nd	3rd	4th	5th	6th	PP	FL	points
European F2 Ch	-	-	-	1	-	-	-	-	3

Championship: 1979 18th

JEAN TRÉMOULET
F. Born: n/a. Died: World War II, motorcycle accident while on a mission for the French resistance
Major Sports Car races. Race wins: 1938 Le Mans 24 hrs

TONY TRIMMER
GB. Born: 24.1.1943, West Kingsdown
1977 (Group 8) and 1978 British F1 Champion; 1970 Shell British F3 Champion

World Championship Grand Prix Record

years	starts	wins	2nd	3rd	4th	5th	6th	PP	FL	points
1975–78	-(7)	-	-	-	-	-	-	-	-	-

Best qualifying: 26th

Major race wins: 1970 Monaco F3 GP

MAURICE TRINTIGNANT

F. Born: 30.10.1917, Ste Cecile-les-Vignes. Three brothers also raced (including Louis who died at Peronne in 1933)

World Championship Grand Prix Record

year	starts	wins	2nd	3rd	4th	5th	6th	PP	FL	points
1950–64	82(2)	2	3	5	4	8	3	-	1	72.33

Best championship: 1954 4th. Race wins: 1955 Monaco GP, 1958 Monaco GP. Best qualifying: 3rd

World Sports Car Championship. Race wins: 1954 Le Mans 24 hrs, Tourist Trophy overall, 1956 Swedish GP

WOLFGANG VON TRIPS

D. Born: 4.5.1928, Horrem, Cologne. Died: 10.9.1961, Monza, Italian GP

World Championship Grand Prix Record

years	starts	wins	2nd	3rd	4th	5th	6th	PP	FL	points
1956–61	27(2)	2	2	2	3	4	3	1	-	56

Best championship: 1961 2nd. Race wins: 1961 Dutch GP, British GP. Best qualifying: 1st

World Sports Car Championship. Race wins: 1961 Targa Florio

ALBERTO TRIVERO

I

Major race wins: 1925 Tripoli GP Race 1

PICKO TROBERG

SF

1965 Swedish F3 Champion

MICHEL TROLLÉ

F. Born: 23.6.1959

	wins	2nd	3rd	4th	5th	6th	PP	FL	points
Int F3000 Ch	1	1	3	-	1	1	-	2	25.5

Championships: 1987 6th, 1988 11th. Race wins: 1987 Spa

CARLO FELICE TROSSI

I. Born: 1908, Biella. Died: 9.5.1949, Milan, cancer

Pre-1950 Grands Prix. Race wins: 1947 Italian GP, 1948 Swiss GP

IGOR TROUBETSKOY

I

Major race wins: 1948 Targa Florio

VINCENZO TRUCCO

I

Major race wins: 1908 Targa Florio

CARLO TRUCI

I

1970 European Touring Car 1600 cc Class Champion

DUILIO TRUFFO

I

	wins	2nd	3rd	4th	5th	6th	PP	FL	points
European F2 Ch	-	-	-	4	3	1	1		12

Championships: 1974 16th, 1975 10th

BOB TULLIUS

USA. Born: 7.12.1936, Rochester, New York State

1977 and 1978 Trans-Am Class 1 Champion

GUY TUNMER

ZA. Born: 1.12.1948, Ficksburg

World Championship Grand Prix Record

year	starts	wins	2nd	3rd	4th	5th	6th	PP	FL	points
1975	1	-	-	-	-	-	-	-	-	-

Best result: 11th. Best qualifying: 25th

COSIMO TURIZIO

I

	wins	2nd	3rd	4th	5th	6th	PP	FL	points
European F2 Ch	-	-	-	-	1	-	-		1

Championship: 1974 22nd

U

TONI ULMEN

D. Born: 25.1.1906, Dusseldorf. Died: 4.11.1976, Dusseldorf

World Championship Grand Prix Record

year	starts	wins	2nd	3rd	4th	5th	6th	PP	FL	points
1952	2	-	-	-	-	-	-	-	-	-

Best result: no finishes. Best qualifying: 16th

BERNARD UNETT

GB

1974, 1976 and 1977 British Touring Car Champion

AL UNSER

USA. Born: 29.5.1939, Albuquerque, New Mexico. Brother of Bobby, father of Al Jr

1970, 1983 and 1985 Indycar Champion; 1978 IROC Champion

Indycar Championship. Race wins: 1965 Pikes Peak, 1968 Nazareth, Indianapolis Raceway Park Race 1, Indianapolis Raceway Park Race 2, Langhorne Race 2, Langhorne Race 3, 1969 Milwaukee Race 2, Du Quoin, Sacramento, Seattle Race 2, Phoenix Race 2, 1970 Phoenix Race 1, Indianapolis 500, Indianapolis Raceway Park, Springfield, Milwaukee Race 2, Du Quoin, Indiana State Fairgrounds, Sedalia, Trenton Race 2, Sacramento, 1971 Rafaela Race 1, Rafaela Race 2, Phoenix Race 1, Indianapolis 500, Milwaukee Race 1, 1973 Texas, 1974 Michigan, 1976 Pocono 500, Milwaukee, Phoenix, 1977 California 500, 1978 Indianapolis 500, Pocono 500, California 500, 1979 Phoenix, 1983 Cleveland, 1985 Phoenix, 1987 Indianapolis 500

Other major race wins: 1985 Daytona 24 hrs

AL UNSER JR

USA. Born: 19.4.1962, Albuquerque, New Mexico. Son of Al Sr

1990 and 1994 Indycar Champion; 1982 Can-Am Champion; 1986 and 1988 IROC Champion; 1981 SCCA Super Vee Champion

Indycar Championship. Race wins: 1984 Portland, 1985 Meadowlands, Cleveland, 1986 Miami, 1988 Long Beach GP, Toronto, Meadowlands, 1988 Miami, 1989 Long Beach GP, 1990 Long Beach GP, Milwaukee, Toronto, Michigan 500, Denver, Vancouver, 1991 Long Beach GP, Denver, 1992 Indianapolis 500, 1993 Vancouver, 1994 Long Beach GP, Indianapolis 500, Milwaukee, Portland, Cleveland, Mid-Ohio, New Hampshire, Vancouver

Other major race wins: 1986 and 1987 Daytona 24 hrs, 1989 Marlboro Challenge

Al Unser Jr

BOBBY UNSER

USA. Born: 20.2.1934. Brother of Al Sr

1968 and 1974 Indycar Champion; 1975 IROC Champion

World Championship Grand Prix Record

year	starts	wins	2nd	3rd	4th	5th	6th	PP	FL	points
1968	1(1)	-	-	-	-	-	-	-	-	-

Best result: no finishes. Best qualifying: 19th

Indycar Championship. Race wins: 1966 Pikes Peak, 1967 Mosport Park Race 1, Mosport Park Race 2, 1968 Stardust, Phoenix Race 1, Trenton Race 1, Indianapolis 500, Pikes Peak, 1969 Langhorne, 1970 Langhorne, 1971 Milwaukee Race 2, Trenton Race 2, 1972 Phoenix Race 1, Milwaukee Race 1, Trenton Race 2, Phoenix Race 2, 1973 Milwaukee, 1974 California 500, Trenton, Michigan, Trenton Race 3, 1975 Indianapolis 500, 1976 Phoenix, California 500, 1979 Trenton Race 1, Trenton Race 2, Michigan Race 2, Watkins Glen, California 500, Michigan, 1980 Milwaukee, Pocono 500, Watkins Glen, California 500, 1981 Indianapolis 500

LOUIS UNSER

USA. Uncle of Al Unser Sr and Bobby Unser

Indycar Championship. Race wins: 1947 and 1953 Pikes Peak

JEFF UREN

GB

1959 British Touring Car Champion

ALBERTO URIA
U

World Championship Grand Prix Record

years	starts	wins	2nd	3rd	4th	5th	6th	PP	FL	points
1955–56	2	-	-	-	-	-	1	-	-	-

Best result: 6th. Best qualifying: 21st

V ···

NINO VACCARELLA
I. Born: 4.3.1933, Palermo

World Championship Grand Prix Record

years	starts	wins	2nd	3rd	4th	5th	6th	PP	FL	points
1961–62; 1965	4(1)	-	-	-	-	-	-	-	-	-

Best result: 9th. Best qualifying: 14th

World Sports Car Championship. Race wins: 1964 Nürburgring, Le Mans 24 hrs, 1965 Targa Florio, 1970 Sebring 12 hrs, 1971 Targa Florio

Other major race wins: 1975 Targa Florio

IRA VAIL
USA. Born: 1894, Brooklyn. Died: 21.4.1979

Indycar Championship. Race wins: 1917 Minneapolis Race 2

COLIN VANDERVELL
GB

	wins	2nd	3rd	4th	5th	6th	PP	FL	points
European F2 Ch	-	1	-	-	1	1	-	-	12

Championship: 1973 9th

WES VANDERVOORT
USA

Indycar Championship. Race wins: 1967 Pikes Peak

ALBERT VANIERSCHOT
B

1977 and 1978 Belgian Touring Car Champion

ACHILLE VARZI
I. Born: 8.8.1904, Galliante, near Milan. Died: 30.6.1948, Bremgarten, Swiss GP practice

Pre-1950 Grands Prix. Race wins: 1929 Monza GP, 1930 Monza GP, Spanish GP, 1931 French GP, 1933 Monaco GP

Other major race wins: 1930 Targa Florio, 1933 Tripoli GP, 1934 Tripoli GP, Targa Florio, 1936 Tripoli GP

JOS VERSTAPPEN
NL. Born: 4.3.1972, Montfort (F)

1993 German F3 Champion

World Championship Grand Prix Record

year	starts	wins	2nd	3rd	4th	5th	6th	PP	FL	points
1994	10	-	-	2	-	1	-	-	-	10

Best championship: 1994 10th. Best qualifying: 6th

Major race wins: 1993 Marlboro Masters of F3

PIERRE VEYRON
F. Born: 1903, Lozere. Died: 3.10.1970, Cap d'Eze

Major Sports Car races. Race wins: 1939 Le Mans 24 hrs

GILLES VILLENEUVE
CDN. Born: 18.1.1950, Chambly, Quebec. Died: 8.5.1982, Leuvern Hospital, following accident during practice for Belgian GP at Zolder. Brother of Jacques, father of Jacques Jr

1976 and 1977 North American Formula Atlantic Champion

World Championship Grand Prix Record

Gilles Villeneuve

years	starts	wins	2nd	3rd	4th	5th	6th	PP	FL	points
1977–82	67(1)	6	5	2	2	3	3	2	8	107

Best championship: 1979 2nd. Race wins: 1978 Canadian GP, 1979 South African GP, Long Beach GP, United States GP, 1981 Monaco GP, Spanish GP. Best qualifying: 1st

Other major race wins: 1979 Race of Champions

JACQUES VILLENEUVE SR
CDN. Born: 4.11.1955, Chambly, Quebec. Brother of Gilles, uncle of Jacques Jr

1983 Can-Am Champion; 1980 and 1981 North American Formula Atlantic Champion

World Championship Grand Prix Record

years	starts	wins	2nd	3rd	4th	5th	6th	PP	FL	points
1981; 1983	-(3)	-	-	-	-	-	-	-	-	-

Best qualifying: 27th

Indycar Championship. Race wins: 1985 Elkhart Lake

JACQUES VILLENEUVE JR
CDN. Born: 9.4.1971. Son of Gilles, nephew of Jacques Sr

Indycar Championship. Race wins: 1994 Elkhart Lake

LUIGI VILLORESI
I. Born: 16.5.1909, Milan

Luigi Villoresi
···

World Championship Grand Prix Record

years	starts	wins	2nd	3rd	4th	5th	6th	PP	FL	points
1950–56	31(3)	-	2	6	2	3	4	-	1	49

Best championship: 1951 5th, 18 pts. Best qualifying: 2nd.

Pre-1950 Grands Prix. Race wins: 1948 British GP

Other major race wins: 1939 and 1940 Targa Florio, 1951 Mille Miglia

EMILIO DE VILLOTA
E. Born: 26.7.1946, Madrid

1980 British F1 Champion

World Championship Grand Prix Record

years	starts	wins	2nd	3rd	4th	5th	6th	PP	FL	points
1976–78; 1981–82	2(13)	-	-	-	-	-	-	-	-	-

Best result: 13th. Best qualifying: 23rd

World Sports Car Championship. Race wins: 1981 Enna, Brands Hatch

ALFONSO GARCIA DE VINUESA
E. Born: 30.12.1960

	wins	2nd	3rd	4th	5th	6th	PP	FL	points
Int F3000 Ch	-	-	-	-	-	1	-	-	1

Championship: 1987 19th

WINNI VOGT
D

1987 European Touring Car Champion

OTTORINO VOLONTERIO
CH. Born: 7.12.1917, Orselina

World Championship Grand Prix Record

years	starts	wins	2nd	3rd	4th	5th	6th	PP	FL	points
1954; 1956–57	3	-	-	-	-	-	-	-	-	-

Best result: 11th. Best qualifying: 20th

JOSEPH VONLANTHEN
CH. Born: 31.5.1942, St Ursen

World Championship Grand Prix Record

year	starts	wins	2nd	3rd	4th	5th	6th	PP	FL	points
1975	1	-	-	-	-	-	-	-	-	-

Best result: no finishes. Best qualifying: 29th

	wins	2nd	3rd	4th	5th	6th	PP	FL	points
European F2 Ch	-	1	1	-	-	-	-	-	10

Championships: 1973 21st, 1975 17th

EARL DE VORE

USA. Born: n/a. Died: 12.11.1928, lost at sea with the SS Vestris

Indycar Championship. Race wins: 1926 Charlotte Race 1

DUNCAN VOS

ZA

1993 South African Drivers' Champion

BILL VUKOVICH

USA. Born: 13.12.1918, Alameda, California. Died: 30.5.1955, Indianapolis 500. Father of Bill Jr

Indycar Championship. Race wins: 1952 Detroit, Denver, 1953 Indianapolis 500, 1954 Indianapolis 500

BILL VUKOVICH JR

USA. Born: 29.3.1944. Son of Bill Sr, father of Bill III

Indycar Championship. Race wins: 1973 Michigan Race 1

SYD VAN DER VYVER

ZA

1960 and 1961 South African Drivers' Champion

W

FRED WACKER

USA. Born: 10.7.1918, Chicago

World Championship Grand Prix Record

years	starts	wins	2nd	3rd	4th	5th	6th	PP	FL	points
1953–54	3(2)	-	-	-	-	-	1	-	-	-

Best result: 6th. Best qualifying: 15th

TAKAO WADA

J. Born: 24.6.1953

1986 Japanese Touring Car Champion (with Aguri Suzuki)

LOUIS WAGNER

F. Born: ?.2.1882, Pre-Saint-Gervais. Died: 1960

Pre-1950 Grands Prix. Race wins: 1908 American GP, 1926 British GP

Other major race wins: 1906 WK Vanderbilt Cup

ARTHUR WAITE

GB

Major race wins: 1928 Australian GP

ALISTAIR WALKER

GB

	wins	2nd	3rd	4th	5th	6th	PP	FL	points
European F2 Ch	-	-	-	-	1	-	-	-	6

Championships: 1970 11th, 1971 20th

DAVE WALKER

AUS. Born: 10.6.1941, Sydney

1970 (Lombank) and 1971 (Shell) British F3 Champion

World Championship Grand Prix Record

years	starts	wins	2nd	3rd	4th	5th	6th	PP	FL	points
1971–72	11	-	-	-	-	-	-	-	-	-

Best result: 9th. Best qualifying: 12th

Major race wins: 1971 Monaco F3 GP

JOHNNIE WALKER

AUS

1979 Australian Gold Star Champion

Tasman Cup. Race wins: 1974 Levin, 1975 Surfers' Paradise

Other major race wins: 1979 Australian GP

PETER WALKER

GB. Born: 7.10.1912, Huby, Leeds. Died: 1.3.1984, Worcester

World Championship Grand Prix Record

years	starts	wins	2nd	3rd	4th	5th	6th	PP	FL	points
1950–51; 1955	4	-	-	-	-	-	-	-	-	-

Best result: 7th. Best qualifying: 10th

Major Sports Car races. Race wins: 1951 Le Mans 24 hrs

TOM WALKINSHAW

GB. Born: 14.8.1946, Mauldslie, Scotland

1984 European Touring Car Champion

World Sports Car Championship. Race wins: 1976 Silverstone, 1981 Spa 24 hrs

Other major race wins: 1984 Spa 24 hrs, 1977, 1981, 1982 and 1985 Tourist Trophy

ANDY WALLACE

GB. Born: 19.2.1961, Oxford

1986 British F3 Champion

	wins	2nd	3rd	4th	5th	6th	PP	FL	points
Int F3000 Ch	-	-	-	1	1	1	-	-	4.5

Championship: 1987 16th

World Sports Car Championship. Race wins: 1988 Le Mans 24 hrs, Brands Hatch

Other major race wins: 1986 Cellnet Super Prix, Macau GP, 1990 Daytona 24 hrs, 1992 and 1993 Sebring 12 hrs

RUSTY WALLACE

USA. Born: 14.8.1956, St Louis

1989 NASCAR Champion; 1991 IROC Champion

Major race wins: 1990 World 600

LEE WALLARD

USA. Born: 7.9.1910, Schenectady, New York. Died: 28.11.1963, St Petersburg, Florida

Indycar Championship. Race wins: 1948 Du Quoin, 1951 Indianapolis 500

MAGNUS WALLINDER

S

1993 and 1994 Nordic F3 Champion; 1993 and 1994 Swedish F3 Champion

HEINI WALTER

CH. Born: 28.7.1927, Ruti

World Championship Grand Prix Record

year	starts	wins	2nd	3rd	4th	5th	6th	PP	FL	points
1962	1	-	-	-	-	-	-	-	-	-

Best result: 14th. Best qualifying: 14th

PHIL WALTERS

USA

World Sports Car Championship. Race wins: 1953 and 1955 Sebring 12 hrs

DARRELL WALTRIP

USA. Born: 5.2.1947, Owensboro, Kentucky

1981, 1982 and 1985 NASCAR Champion

Major race wins: 1978, 1979, 1985, 1988 and 1989 World 600; 1989 Daytona 500

RODGER WARD

USA. Born: 10.1.1921, Beloit, Kansas

1959 and 1962 Indycar Champion

World Championship Grand Prix Record

years	starts	wins	2nd	3rd	4th	5th	6th	PP	FL	points
1959; 1963	2	-	-	-	-	-	-	-	-	-

Best result: no finishes. Best qualifying: 17th

Indycar Championship. Race wins: 1953 Springfield Race 1, Detroit, 1957 Milwaukee Race 1, Springfield, Sacramento, 1958 Milwaukee Race 2, Trenton Race 2, 1959 Indianapolis 500, Milwaukee Race 2, Du Quoin, Indiana State Fairgrounds, 1960 Trenton Race 1, Milwaukee Race 1, 1961 Milwaukee Race 1, Syracuse, Sacramento, 1962 Indianapolis 500, Trenton Race 2, Milwaukee Race 2, Syracuse, 1963 Milwaukee Race 1, Springfield, Indiana State Fairgrounds, Sacramento, Phoenix, 1966 Trenton Race 1

DEREK WARWICK

GB. Born: 27.8.1954, Alresford. Brother of Paul

1992 World Sports Car Champion (with Yannick Dalmas); 1978 Vandervell British F3 Champion

World Championship Grand Prix Record

years	starts	wins	2nd	3rd	4th	5th	6th	PP	FL	points
1981–90; 1993	146(16)	-	2	2	8	9	9	-	2	71

Best championship: 1984 7th. Best qualifying: 3rd

European F2 Ch	wins	2nd	3rd	4th	5th	6th	PP	FL	points
	1	3	3	1	1	-	4	1	44

Championships: 1979 20th, 1980 2nd. **Race wins:** 1980 Silverstone

World Sports Car Championship. Race wins: 1986 Silverstone, 1991 Monza, Silverstone, Nürburgring, 1992 Silverstone, Le Mans 24 hrs, Suzuka

European F3 Championship. Race wins: 1978 Donington Park

Other major race wins: 1980 Monza GP F2 race, 1983 Brands Hatch 1000 km

PAUL WARWICK

GB. Born: 29.1.1969. Died: 21.7.1991, Oulton Park Gold Cup. Brother of Derek

1991 British F3000 Champion

G WATSON

AUS

1986 Australian Gold Star Champion

JOHN WATSON

GB. Born: 4.5.1946, Belfast

John Watson

World Championship Grand Prix Record

years	starts	wins	2nd	3rd	4th	5th	6th	PP	FL	points
1973–83; 1985	152(2)	5	6	9	9	7	11	2	5	169

Best championship: 1982 2nd. **Race wins:** 1976 Austrian GP, 1981 British GP, 1982 Belgian GP, Detroit GP, 1983 Long Beach GP. **Best qualifying:** 1st

European F2 Ch	wins	2nd	3rd	4th	5th	6th	PP	FL	points
	-	1	1	-	3	1	-	-	19

Championships: 1971 14th, 1972 19th, 1973 21st, 1974 11th

World Sports Car Championship. Race wins: 1984 Fuji, 1987 Jarama, Monza, Fuji

W WATSON

GB

Major race wins: 1908 Tourist Trophy

JOE WEATHERLY

USA

1962 and 1963 NASCAR Champion

JAMES WEAVER

GB. Born: 4.3.1955, London

European F3 Championship. Race wins: 1982 Donington Park, Nogaro, Jarama

VOLKER WEIDLER

D. Born: 18.3.1962, Heidelberg

1985 German F3 Champion

World Championship Grand Prix Record

year	starts	wins	2nd	3rd	4th	5th	6th	PP	FL	points
1989	-(10)	-	-	-	-	-	-	-	-	-

Best qualifying: 30th

Int F3000 Ch	wins	2nd	3rd	4th	5th	6th	PP	FL	points
	-	-	1	-	2	-	-	-	5

Championship: 1988 15th

World Sports Car Championship. Race wins: 1991 Le Mans 24 hrs

KARL WENDLINGER

A. Born: 20.12.1968, Kufstein

1989 German F3 Champion

World Championship Grand Prix Record

years	starts	wins	2nd	3rd	4th	5th	6th	PP	FL	points
1991–94	35(1)	-	-	-	3	1	3	-	-	14

Best championship: 1993 11th. **Best qualifying:** 5th

Int F3000 Ch	wins	2nd	3rd	4th	5th	6th	PP	FL	points
	-	-	1	-	2	-	-	-	8

Championships: 1990 19th, 1991 11th

World Sports Car Championship. Race wins: 1990 Spa, 1991 Autopolis

KARL VON WENDT

D

1967 European Touring Car over 1600 cc Class Champion

HERIBERT WERGINZ

A

Major race wins: 1980 Tourist Trophy

CHRISTIAN WERNER

D. Born: 19.5.1892, Stuttgart. Died: 17.6.1932, Bad Cannstatt

Pre-1950 Grands Prix. Race wins: 1928 German GP

Other major race wins: 1924 Targa Florio

MARCO WERNER

D. Born: 27.4.1966

Major race wins: 1992 Monaco F3 GP

PETER WESTBURY

GB. Born: 26.5.1938, London

World Championship Grand Prix Record

years	starts	wins	2nd	3rd	4th	5th	6th	PP	FL	points
1969–70	1(1)	-	-	-	-	-	-	-	-	-

Best result: no finishes. **Best qualifying:** 25th

European F2 Ch	wins	2nd	3rd	4th	5th	6th	PP	FL	points
	-	1	-	2	-	-	-	-	23

Championships: 1969 5th, 1970 9th, 1971 14th

MARCEL WETTSTEIN

CH

1981 Swiss F3 Champion

KEN WHARTON

GB. Born: 21.3.1916, Smethwick. Died: 12.1.1957, Ardmore (NZ)

World Championship Grand Prix Record

years	starts	wins	2nd	3rd	4th	5th	6th	PP	FL	points
1952–55	15(1)	-	-	-	1	-	1	-	-	3

Best championship: 1952 13th. **Best qualifying:** 7th

CR WHITCROFT

GB

Major race wins: 1932 Tourist Trophy

MIKE WHITE

ZA. Born: 2.7.1954

European F3 Championship. Race wins: 1980 Silverstone, 1981 Donington Park

REX WHITE

USA

1960 NASCAR Champion

TED WHITEAWAY

GB. Born: 1.11.1928, Feltham

World Championship Grand Prix Record

year	starts	wins	2nd	3rd	4th	5th	6th	PP	FL	points
1955	-(1)	-	-	-	-	-	-	-	-	-

Best qualifying: 22nd

DOUG WHITEFORD

AUS

Major race wins: 1950, 1952 and 1953 Australian GP

GRAHAM WHITEHEAD

GB. Born: 15.4.1922, Harrogate. Died: 15.1.1981, Basildon, Berkshire. Half-brother of Peter

World Championship Grand Prix Record

year	starts	wins	2nd	3rd	4th	5th	6th	PP	FL	points
1952	1	-	-	-	-	-	-	-	-	-

Best result: 12th. **Best qualifying:** 12th

PETER WHITEHEAD

GB. Born: 12.11.1914, Menston, Yorkshire. Died: 21.9.1958, Tour de France Automobile. Half-brother of Graham

World Championship Grand Prix Record

year	starts	wins	2nd	3rd	4th	5th	6th	PP	FL	points
1950	10(2)	-	-	1	-	-	-	-	-	4

Best championship: 1950 9th. **Best qualifying:** 8th

Pre-1950 Grands Prix. Race wins: 1949 Czech GP

Major Sports Car races. Race wins: 1951 Le Mans 24 hrs

Other major race wins: 1938 Australian GP

BILL WHITEHOUSE

GB. Born: 1.4.1909, London. Died: 14.7.1957, Reims, F2 race

World Championship Grand Prix Record

year	starts	wins	2nd	3rd	4th	5th	6th	PP	FL	points
1954	1	-	-	-	-	-	-	-	-	-

Best result: no finishes. **Best qualifying:** 19th

SIR JOHN WHITMORE

GB. Born: 16.10.1937

1965 European Touring Car 1600 cc Class Champion; 1961 British Touring Car Champion

BILL WHITTINGTON

USA. Born: 11.9.1949. Brother of Don and Dale

World Sports Car Championship. Race wins: 1979 Le Mans 24 hrs, Watkins Glen

DON WHITTINGTON

USA. Born: 23.1.1946. Brother of Bill and Dale

World Sports Car Championship. Race wins: 1979 Le Mans 24 hrs, Watkins Glen

ROBIN WIDDOWS

GB. Born: 27.5.1942, Witney

World Championship Grand Prix Record

year	starts	wins	2nd	3rd	4th	5th	6th	PP	FL	points
1968	1	-	-	-	-	-	-	-	-	-

Best result: no finishes. **Best qualifying:** 18th

	wins	2nd	3rd	4th	5th	6th	PP	FL	points
European F2 Ch	-	-	3	1	1	-	-	21

Championships: 1967 10th, 1968 22nd, 1969 13th, 1970 6th

EPPIE WIETZES

CDN. Born: 28.5.1938

1981 Trans-Am Champion

World Championship Grand Prix Record

years	starts	wins	2nd	3rd	4th	5th	6th	PP	FL	points
1967; 1974	2	-	-	-	-	-	-	-	-	-

Best result: no finishes. **Best qualifying:** 17th

HOWDY WILCOX

USA. Born: 1889, Indianapolis. Died: 23.9.1923, Altoona, Pennsylvania. No relation of Howdy II

1919 Indycar Champion

Pre-1950 Grands Prix. Race wins: 1916 American GP

Indycar Championship. Race wins: 1910 Indianapolis Race 7, 1916 American GP, 1919 Indianapolis 500, 1923 Indianapolis 500

MIKE WILDS

GB. Born: 7.1.1946, Chiswick

World Championship Grand Prix Record

years	starts	wins	2nd	3rd	4th	5th	6th	PP	FL	points
1974–76	3(5)	-	-	-	-	-	-	-	-	-

Best result: no finishes. **Best qualifying:** 22nd

CHRIS WILLIAMS

	wins	2nd	3rd	4th	5th	6th	PP	FL	points
European F2 Ch	-	-	-	-	1	-	-	2

Championships: 1968 17th

JONATHAN WILLIAMS

GB. Born: 26.10.1942, Cairo (ET)

World Championship Grand Prix Record

year	starts	wins	2nd	3rd	4th	5th	6th	PP	FL	points
1967	1	-	-	-	-	-	-	-	-	-

Best result: 8th. **Best qualifying:** 16th

"W WILLIAMS"

GB. Born: 1903, Montrouge, near Paris. Died: 1943, Paris, shot by Gestapo having been arrested on 2.8.1943. Real name: William Grover-Williams

Pre-1950 Grands Prix. Race wins: 1928 French GP, 1929 Monaco GP, French GP, 1931 Belgian GP

ROGER WILLIAMSON

GB. Born: 2.2.1948, Leicester. Died: 29.7.1973, Zandvoort, Dutch GP

1971 (Lombank) and 1972 (Forward Trust and Shell) British F3 Champion

World Championship Grand Prix Record

year	starts	wins	2nd	3rd	4th	5th	6th	PP	FL	points
1973	2	-	-	-	-	-	-	-	-	-

Best result: no finishes. **Best qualifying:** 18th

	wins	2nd	3rd	4th	5th	6th	PP	FL	points
European F2 Ch	1	-	-	-	-	1	1	11

Championships: 1973 10th. **Race wins:** 1973 Monza Lottery GP

DESIRÉ WILSON

ZA. Born: 26.11.1953, Johannesburg

World Championship Grand Prix Record

year	starts	wins	2nd	3rd	4th	5th	6th	PP	FL	points
1980	-(1)	-	-	-	-	-	-	-	-

Best qualifying: 27th

World Sports Car Championship. Race wins: 1980 Monza, Silverstone

Other major race wins: 1980 Brands Hatch British F1 race (first woman to win an F1 race)

VIC WILSON

GB. Born: 14.4.1931, Kingston-upon-Hull

World Championship Grand Prix Record

years	starts	wins	2nd	3rd	4th	5th	6th	PP	FL	points
1960; 1966	1(1)	-	-	-	-	-	-	-	-	-

Best result: no finishes. **Best qualifying:** 16th

JEAN-PIERRE WIMILLE

F. Born: 1908, Paris. Died: 28.1.1949, Buenos Aires GP practice

Pre-1950 Grands Prix. Race wins: 1936 French GP, 1947 Swiss GP, Belgian GP, 1948 French GP, Italian GP

Major Sports Car races. Race wins: 1937 and 1939 Le Mans 24 hrs

Other major race wins: 1948 Monza GP

JOHN WINGFIELD

GB

	wins	2nd	3rd	4th	5th	6th	PP	FL	points
European F2 Ch	-	-	-	-	1	-	-	1

Championship: 1972 28th

JOACHIM WINKELHOCK

D. Born: 24.10.1960, Waiblingen. Brother of Manfred

1988 European F3 Cup winner; 1988 German F3 Champion; 1993 British Touring Car Champion; 1994 Asia-Pacific Touring Car Champion

World Championship Grand Prix Record

year	starts	wins	2nd	3rd	4th	5th	6th	PP	FL	points
1989	-(7)	-	-	-	-	-	-	-	-	-

Best qualifying: 35th

Major race wins: 1988 European F3 Cup

MANFRED WINKELHOCK

D. Born: 6.10.1951, Waiblingen. Died: 12.8.1985, Mosport Park 1000 kms. Brother of Joachim

World Championship Grand Prix Record

year	starts	wins	2nd	3rd	4th	5th	6th	PP	FL	points
1980; 1982–85	47(9)	-	-	-	-	1	-	-	-	2

Best championship: 1982 22nd. **Best qualifying:** 5th

	wins	2nd	3rd	4th	5th	6th	PP	FL	points
European F2 Ch	-	1	4	1	3	-	1	1	31

Championships: 1978 8th, 1979 16th, 1980 13th, 1981 10th

World Sports Car Championship. Race wins: 1985 Monza

BILL WINN

USA. Born: n/a. Died: 20.8.1938, Springfield, Illinois

Indycar Championship. Race wins: 1934 Springfield, 1935 Springfield, Syracuse, 1937 Syracuse

"JOHN WINTER"

D. Born: 2.8.1949, Bremen. Real name: Louis Krages

World Sports Car Championship. Race wins: 1985 Le Mans 24 hrs

Other major race wins: 1991 Daytona 24 hrs

REINE WISELL
S. Born: 30.9.1941, Motala
1967 Swedish F3 Champion

World Championship Grand Prix Record

years	starts	wins	2nd	3rd	4th	5th	6th	PP	FL	points
1970–74	22(1)	-	-	1	2	1	1	-	-	13

Best championship: 1971 9th. **Best qualifying:** 6th

	wins	2nd	3rd	4th	5th	6th	PP	FL	points
European F2 Ch	1	-	-	-	-	1	-	-	-

Race wins: 1973 Eifelrennen (Nürburgring)

SPENCER WISHART
USA. Born: n/a. Died: 22.8.1914, Elgin, Illinois
Indycar Championship. Race wins: 1912 Columbus

BOB WOLLEK
F. Born: 4.11.1943, Strasbourg
1983 European Sports Car Champion; 1982, 1983 and 1989 German Racing Champion

	wins	2nd	3rd	4th	5th	6th	PP	FL	points
European F2 Ch	-	2	2	-	3	3	-	-	41

Championships: 1971 20th, 1972 7th, 1973 6th

World Sports Car Championship. Race wins: 1977 Mosport Park, Hockenheim, 1978 Dijon, Misano, Vallelunga, 1979 Mugello, Silverstone, Nürburgring, 1983 Monza, 1985 Spa, 1986 Brands Hatch, 1989 Dijon

Other major race wins: 1983 Mugello 1000 kms, 1983, 1985, 1989 and 1991 Daytona 24 hrs, 1985 Sebring 12 hrs

JEFF WOOD
USA. Born: 20.1.1957, Wichita, Kansas
1985 North American Formula (Western Division) Atlantic Champion

CLIFF WOODBURY
USA. Born: n/a. Died: 13.11.1984
Indycar Championship. Race wins: 1928 Salem Race 3, 1929 Detroit

ROY WOODS
USA
Major race wins: 1979 Sebring 12 hrs

ROELOF WUNDERINK
NL. Born: 12.12.1948, Eindhoven

World Championship Grand Prix Record

year	starts	wins	2nd	3rd	4th	5th	6th	PP	FL	points
1975	3(3)	-	-	-	-	-	-	-	-	-

Best result: no finishes. **Best qualifying:** 19th

X

JEAN XHENCEVAL
B
1976 European Touring Car Champion (shared with Pierre Dieudonné)
Major race wins: 1974 and 1975 Spa 24 hrs, 1976 Tourist Trophy

Y

CALE YARBOROUGH
USA. Born: 27.3.1939, Timmonsville
1976, 1977 and 1978 NASCAR Champion; 1984 IROC Champion
Major race wins: 1968, 1977, 1983 and 1984 Daytona 500

LEE ROY YARBOROUGH
USA. Born: 17.9.1938, Jacksonville, Florida. Died: 7.12.1984
Major race wins: 1969 Daytona 500, World 600

HISASHI YOKOSHIMA
J. Born: 28.12.1957, Ibaragi
1988 Japanese Touring Car Champion

Z

PETER ZAKOWSKI
D. Born: 13.5.1966
Major race wins: 1987 Knutstorp EFDA F3

ALESSANDRO ZAMPEDRI
I. Born: 3.10.1969, Brescia

	wins	2nd	3rd	4th	5th	6th	PP	FL	points
Int F3000 Ch	-	-	1	-	2	-	-	-	8

Championships: 1992 12th, 1993 11th

ALESSANDRO ZANARDI
I. Born: 23.10.1966, Bologna
1990 European F3 Cup winner

World Championship Grand Prix Record

year	starts	wins	2nd	3rd	4th	5th	6th	PP	FL	points
1991–94	25(3)	-	-	-	-	-	1	-	-	1

Best championship: 1993 20th. **Best qualifying:** 13th

	wins	2nd	3rd	4th	5th	6th	PP	FL	points
Int F3000 Ch	2	4	-	-	-	-	3	3	42

Championship: 1991 2nd. **Race wins:** 1991 Rome GP (Vallelunga), Mugello

EMILIO ZAPICO
E

World Championship Grand Prix Record

year	starts	wins	2nd	3rd	4th	5th	6th	PP	FL	points
1976	-(1)	-	-	-	-	-	-	-	-	-

Best qualifying: 27th

GOFFREDO ZEHENDER
I. Born: 1901, Reggio Calabria. Died: 7.1.1958
Major race wins: 1931 Spa 24 hrs

JO ZELLER
CH
1982, 1990, 1991 and 1992 Swiss F3 Champion

LEN ZENGEL
USA
Indycar Championship. Race wins: 1911 Elgin Race 3

VITTORIO ZOBOLI
I. Born: 24.6.1968, Bologna

	wins	2nd	3rd	4th	5th	6th	PP	FL	points
Int F3000 Ch	-	-	1	-	-	-	-	-	3

Championship: 1992 13th

RENZO ZORZI
I. Born: 12.12.1946, Turin

World Championship Grand Prix Record

years	starts	wins	2nd	3rd	4th	5th	6th	PP	FL	points
1975–77	7	-	-	-	-	1	-	-	1

Best championship: 1977 19th. **Best qualifying:** 17th
European F3 Championship. Race wins: 1975 Monaco F3 GP

RICARDO ZUNINO
RA. Born: 13.4.1949, Buenos Aires

World Championship Grand Prix Record

years	starts	wins	2nd	3rd	4th	5th	6th	PP	FL	points
1979–81	10(1)	-	-	-	-	-	-	-	-	-

Best result: 7th. **Best qualifying:** 9th

	wins	2nd	3rd	4th	5th	6th	PP	FL	points
European F2 Ch	-	-	-	-	3	2	-	-	9

European Championships: 1977 20th, 1978 11th

SELECTED BIBLIOGRAPHY

MAGAZINES AND ANNUALS

Auto Action (Australia)

Autocourse (Hazleton, Richmond, UK)

Auto Hebdo (France)

Autosport (Haymarket, Teddington, UK)

Autosprint (Italy)

Autosport Yearbook and Directory (Haymarket, Teddington, UK)

Motoring News (Standard House, London)

On Track (USA)

Touring Car Year (Nott Organisation, Dorking, UK)

MEDIA GUIDES

British Touring Car Series Guide (Q Editions, Caterham)

Deutsche Tourenwagen-Meisterschaft Media Guide (ITR, Leipheim, Germany)

FIA Yearbook of Automobile Sport (FIA, Paris)

Formula 3000 Championship Guide (Q Editions, Caterham/Charles Stewart & Co Ltd, London)

IMSA Yearbook (RJ Reynolds, Winston-Salem, USA/IMSA, Tampa, USA)

Indycar Media Guide (CART/IndyCar, Bloomfield Hills, Michigan, USA)

NASCAR Yearbook and Press Guide (NASCAR, Daytona Beach, USA/UMI Publications, Charlotte, USA)

USAC Yearbook (USAC, Indianapolis, USA)

24 heures du Mans Informations Presse (ACO, Le Mans, France)

World Sportscar Championship Guides (Q Editions, Caterham)

BOOKS

American Automobile Racing Albert R Bochroch (Patrick Stevens, Cambridge, 1974)

L'Année Formule 3 1992 Alain Pernot, Eric Briquet and Jean-Michel Desnoues (Autopresse/Jean-Pierre Taillandier, Boulogne, 1992)

Australia's Greatest Motor Race 1960 to1989 Bill Tuckey and David Greenhalgh (Chevron, Hornsby, Australia, 1989)

Australian Touring Car Championship – 30 Fabulous Years Graham Howard and Stewart Wilson (Chevron, Hornsby, Australia, 1989)

A-Z of Formula Racing Cars David Hodges (Bay View, Bideford, Devon, 1990)

The Complete History of Grand Prix Motor Racing Adriano Cimarosti (Motor Racing Publications, Croydon, 1990)

Cooper Cars Doug Nye (Osprey, London 1987)

Dictionaire des Pilotes de Formula 1 Dominique Pascal (Editions Dominique Pascal, Septeuil, France, 1990)

The Encyclopedia of Motor Racing Anthony Pritchard and Keith Davey (Robert Hale & Co, London, 1969)

The Encyclopedia of Motor Sport edited by GN Georgano (Ebury Press and Michael Joseph, London, 1971)

Endurance Racing 1982-91 Ian Briggs (Osprey, London, 1992)

Fabulous Fifties – American Championship Racing Dick Wallen (Dick Wallen Productions, Escondido, California, 1993)

Ferrari Sixth Edition Hans Tanner and Doug Nye (Foulis/Haynes, Sparkford, l984)

The Formula 1 Record Book 1961-65 John Thompson with Duncan Rabagliati and Paul Sheldon (Leslie Frewin, London, 1974)

Formula 1 Register F3 Fact Books Paul Sheldon with Duncan Rabagliati and Yves de la Gorce (St Leonards Press, Shipley, West Yorkshire, 1991-92)

Formule Renault Christian Courtel (Editions Acla, Paris, 1981)

Francorchamps 1922-47 and1948-60 Jean-Paul Delsaux (Delsaux, Jauchelette, Belgium, 1986)

The French Grand Prix David Hodges (Temple, London, 1967)

The German Grand Prix Cyril Posthumus (Temple, London, 1966)

The Golden Era of New Zealand Motor Racing Graham Vercoe (Reed, Auckland, New Zealand, 1993)

The Gordon Bennett Races Lord Montagu (Cassell, London, 1965)

Gran Premio d'Italia Paolo Montagna (Autodromo Nazionale, Monza, Italy, 1982)

Gran Premio di Tripoli Alberto Redaelli (Luigi Reverdito Editore, Italy, 1989)

Grand Prix!, volumes 1-3 Mike Lang (Haynes, Sparkford, 1981, 1982 and 1983 respectively)

La Grand Prix des Frontières à Chimay André Biaumet (Biamet, Morlanwelz, Belgium, 1986)

Grand Prix Racing Facts and Figures 1894-1963 George Monkhouse and Roland King-Farlow (Foulis, London, 1950 - this edition 1964)

The Guinness Complete Grand Prix Who's Who Steve Small (Guinness, Enfield, 1994)

Gurney's Eagles Karl Ludvigsen (Motorbooks International, Osceola, Wisconsin, USA, 1992)

The History of English Racing Automobiles Limited David Weguelin (White Mouse Editions, London, 1980)

The History of the Grand Prix Car 1945-65 and 1966-91 Doug Nye (Hazleton, Richmond, Surrey, 1993 and 1992 respectively)

The Illustrated History of the Indianapolis 500 Jack C Fox (Carl Hungness, Speedway, Indiana, USA, 1967 - this edition 1984)

Lotus – All The Cars Anthony Pritchard (Aston Publications Ltd, Bourne End, Buckinghamshire, 1990 - this edition 1992)

March – The Grand Prix and Indy Cars Alan Henry (Hazleton, Richmond, Surrey, 1989)

Maserati - A History Anthony Pritchard (David and Charles, Newton Abbot, Devon, 1976)

Mercedes-Benz Grand Prix Racing 1934-1955 George C Monkhouse (White Mouse Editions, London, 1983)

The Monaco Grand Prix David Hodges (Temple, London, 1964)

Monza 1922-72 (SIAS, Milan, 1972)

Motor Racing – The Records by Ian Morrison (Guinness, Enfield, 1987)

The Official 50-race History of the Australian Grand Prix (R and T, Sydney, Australia, 1986)

Power and Glory, volume 1 - William Court (MacDonald, London, 1966)

The Racing Fifteen-Hundreds David Venables (Transport Bookman, London, 1984)

Racing the Silver Arrows Chris Nixon (Osprey, London, 1986)

A Record of Grand Prix and Voiturette Racing, volumes 1-8 Paul Sheldon with Duncan Rabagliati (St Leonards Press, Shipley, West Yorkshire, 1987-94)

The United States Grand Prix Doug Nye (Batsford, London, 1978)

24 heures du Mans, volumes 1 and 2 Christian Moity and Jean-Marc Teissedre (JP Barthelemy, Le Mans, 1992)

The World Atlas of Motor Racing Joe Saward (Hamlyn, London, 1989)